Who's Who In California

**Biographical Reference Works
Published By
The Who's Who Historical Society**

Who's Who In California

Who's Who In California Business and Finance

Who's Who In North American Dining and Lodging

Who's Who In Los Angeles County

The Twenty-Third Edition
1994

Published by
The Who's Who Historical Society
1928 - 1994

TWENTY-THIRD EDITION
Edna L. Barrett
Executive Director and Editor

International Standard Book Number ISBN 1-880142-02-3
Library of Congress Catalog Card Number 56-1715
International Standard Serial Number 0511-8948

PRINTED IN THE UNITED STATES OF AMERICA

Contents

Dedication

Lives of great men all remind us
We can make our lives sublime.
And, departing, leave behind us
Footprints on the sands of time.

- Henry Wadsworth Longfellow

There is a tide in the affairs of men,
Which, taken at the flood,
Leads on to fortune.

- William Shakespeare

Destiny is not a matter of chance,
It is a matter of choice;
It is not a thing to be waited for,
It is a thing to be achieved.

- William Jennings Bryant

Honorary Board of Directors

Abbreviations

AA Associate in Arts
AAAS American Association for the Advancement of Science
A.and M. Agricultural and Mechanical
AARP American Association of Retired Persons
AAU Amateur Athletic Union
AAUP American Association of University Professors
AAUW American Association of University Women
AB Arts, Bachelor of
ABA American Bar Association
ABC American Broadcasting Company
acad. academy, academic
accred. accredited, accreditation
achiev. achievement
ACLU American Civil Liberties Union
A.C.P. American College of Physicians
A.C.S. American College of Surgeons
ADA American Dental Association
adj. adjunct, adjutant
adj.gen. adjutant general
adm. admiral
adminstr. administrator
adminstrn. administration
adminstrv. administrative
adv. advisor, advanced
advt. advertising
advy. advisory
AEC Atomic Energy Commission
aero. aeronautical, aeronautic
AFB Air Force Base
AFL-CIO American Federation of Labor and Congress of Industrial Organizations
AFTRA American Federation TV and Radio Artists
agri., agric. agriculture, agricultural
agt. agent
agy. agency
AIA American Institute of Architects
AIEE American Institute of Electrical Engineers
AIM American Institute of Management
ALA American Library Association
Ala. Alabama
Am., Amer. American, America
AM Arts, Master of
AMA American Medical Association

A.M.E. African Methodist Episcopal
Amtrak National Railroad Passenger Corporation
anat. anatomical, anatomy
ANTA American National Theatre and Academy
anthropol. anthropological
AP Associated Press
APC A Professional Corporation
APO Army Post Office
appt. appointment, appointed
arb. arbitrator, arbitration
ARC American Red Cross
archeol. archeological
arch. architecture
archtl. architectural
Ariz. Arizona
Ark. Arkansas
arty. artillery
ASCAP American Society of Composers, Authors and Publishers
ASCE American Society of Civil Engineers
ASME American Society of Mechanical Engineers
assn. association
assoc. associate, associated
asst. assistant
ASTM American Society for Testing and Materials
astron. astronomical
AT&T American Telephone & Telegraph Company
atty. attorney
AUS Army of the United States
aux. auxiliary
AVMA American Veterinary Medical Association

B. Bachelor
b. born
BA Bachelor of Arts
BAgr Bachelor of Agriculture
BBA Bachelor of Business Administration
BBC British Broadcasting Corporation
B.C. British Columbia
BCE Bachelor of Civil Engineering
Bch. Beach
BCL Bachelor of Civil Law
BCS Bachelor of Commercial Science

BD Bachelor of Divinity
bd. board
Bdo. Bernardino
BEdn Bachelor of Education
BEE Bachelor of Electrical Engineering
BFA Bachelor of Fine Arts
biblio. bibliographical
biog. biography
biol. biological
BJ Bachelor of Journalism
BL Bachelor of Letters
bldg. building
BLS Bachelor of Library Science
bn. battalion
bot. botanical
BPE Bachelor of Physical Education
br. branch
BRE Bachelor of Religious Education
brig.gen. brigadier general
Brit. British, Britannica
BS Bachelor of Science
BSA Boy Scouts of America
BTh Bachelor of Theology
bur. bureau
bus. business

CAA Civil Aeronautics Administration
CAB Civil Aeronautics Board
Calif. California
Cal Poly California Polytechnic State University
Cal Tech California Institute of Technology
Can. Canada
cand. candidate
CAP Civil Air Patrol
capt. captain
Cath. Catholic
cav. cavalry
CBC Canadian Broadcasting Company
CBI China, Burma, India Theatre of Operations
CBS Columbia Broadcasting System
CC Country Club
CE, C.E. Civil Engineer, Corps of Engineers
CEO Chief Executive Officer
cert. certificate, certified, certification
CFO Chief Financial Officer
ch. church
ChD Doctor of Chemistry
chem. chemical, chemistry
ChFC Chartered Financial Consultant
Chgo. Chicago
chmn. chairman
chpt. chapter
CIA Central Intelligence Agency
CIC Counter Intelligence Corps
Cleve. Cleveland
clin. clinical

clk. clerk
CLU Chartered Life Underwriter
CMA California Medical Association
cmdr., cdr. commander
Co. Company, County
C. of C. Chamber of Commerce
col. colonel
coll. college
Colo. Colorado
com. committee
comd. commanded
comdg. commanding
comdr. commander
comdt. commandant
comm. community, communication
commd. commissioned
comml. commercial
commn. commission
commr. commissioner
comms. communications
conf. conference
Cong. Congress
congl. congressional
Conn. Connecticut
cons. consultant, consulting
consol. consolidated
constl. constitutional
constn. constitution
constrn. construction
contbd. contributed
contbg. contributing
contbr. contributor
contr. contractor
conv. convention
C.O.O. Chief Operating Officer
coop., co-op cooperative
coord. coordinator, coordinating
CORE Congress of Racial Equality
corp. corporation
corr. correspondent, corresponding
C.P.A., CPA Certified Public Accountant
C.P.C.U. Chartered Property and Casualty Underwriter
CPH Certificate of Public Health
cpl. corporal
CPR Cardio-Pulmonary Resuscitation
cred. credential/s, credentiales
ct. court
ctr. center
C.Z. Canal Zone

d., dau. daughter
DAgr Doctor of Agriculture
DAR Daughters of the American Revolution
DAV Disabled American Veterans
DC Doctor of Chiropractic
D.C., DC District of Columbia

DCL Doctor of Civil Law
DCS Doctor of Commercial Science
DD Doctor of Divinity
DDS Doctor of Dental Surgery
dec. deceased
def. defense
Del. Delaware
del. delegate, delegation
DEng Doctor of Engineering
dep. deputy
dept. department
desc. descendant
devel. development, developed
DFA Doctor of Fine Arts
DFC Distinguished Flying Cross
DHL Doctor of Hebrew Literature
dipl. diploma
dir. director
dist. district
distbg. distributing
distbn. distribution
distbr. distributor
disting. distinguished
div. division, divinity, divorced
DLitt Doctor of Literature
DMD Doctor of Medical Dentistry
DMS Doctor of Medical Science
DO Doctor of Osteopathy
DOD, DoD Department of Defense
D.P. Data Processing
DRE Doctor of Religious Education
DS, DSc Doctor of Science
D.S.C. Distinguished Service Cross
D.S.M. Distinguished Service Medal
DST Doctor of Sacred Theology
DTM Doctor of Tropical Medicine
DVM Doctor of Veterinary Medicine
DVS Doctor of Veterinary Surgery

E. East
ea. eastern
ecol. ecological
econ. economics, economical
ED Doctor of Engineering
ed. editor, edited
EdB Bachelor of Education
EdD Doctor of Education
edit. edition
EdM Master of Education
edn. education
ednl. educational
EDP Electronic Data Processing
EE, E.E. Electrical Engineer
EEO Equal Employment Opportunity
E.Ger. German Democratic Republic
elec. electrical
elem. elementary

EM Engineer of Mines
empl. employee
ency. encyclopedia
Eng. England, English
engr. engineer
engring. engineering
entomol. entomological
environ. environmental
EOP Equal Opportunity Program
EPA Environmental Protection Agency
epidemiol. epidemiological
ERA Equal Rights Amendment
ESL English as a Second Language
ETO European Theatre of Operations
exam. examination, examining
exec. executive
exhib., exhbn. exhibit, exhibitor, exhibition
expo. exposition
exptl. experimental
FAA Federal Aviation Administration
FBI Federal Bureau of Investigation
FCC Federal Communication Commission
FDA Food and Drug Administration
FDIC Federal Deposit Insurance Corporation
fed. federal
fedn. federation
fgn. foreign
FHA Federal Housing Administration
fin. financial, finance
Fla. Florida
Flr Floor
fmr. former
found. foundation
FPC Federal Power Commission
FPO Fleet Post Office
frat. fraternity, fraternal
FRS Federal Reserve System
Ft. Fort
f.t. full time
FTC Federal Trade Commission

Ga. Georgia
GAO General Accounting Office
gastroent. gastroenterological
GATT General Agreement of Tariff and Trades
GCM Good Conduct Medal
gen. general
geneal. genealogical
geog. geographical, geographic
geol. geological
geophys. geophysical
gerontol. gerontological
gov. governor
govt. government
govtl. governmental
grad. graduate
GSA General Services Administration

Gt. Great
gynecol. gynecological

hd. head, head of
hdqrs., hq. headquarters
HEW Department of Health, Education and Welfare
HHD Doctor of Humanities
hist. historical, historic, history
HM Master of Humanics
HOA Home Owners Association
hon. honorary, honorable
Ho. of Dels. House of Delegates
Ho. of Reps. House of Representatives
hort. horticultural
hosp. hospital
H.S. High School
HUD Department of Housing and Urban Development
Hwy. Highway

Ia. Iowa
IBM International Business Machines Corporation
ICC Interstate Commerce Commission
ICU Intensive Care Unit
Ida. Idaho
IEEE Institute of Electrical & Electronics Engineers
IGY International Geophysical Year
Ill. Illinois
illus. illustrated
ILO International Labor Organization
IMF International Monetary Fund
Inc. Incorporated
incl. include, including
Ind. Indiana
indep. independent
Indpls. Indianapolis
indsl. industrial
inf. infantry
info. information
ins. insurance
insp. inspector
inst. institute
instl. institutional
instr. instructor
internat. international
intro. introduction
IRS Internal Revenue Service
ITT International Telephone & Telegraph   Corp.

JAG Judge Advocate General
Jaycees Junior Chamber of Commerce
JD Juris Doctor
j.g. junior grade
jour. journal

jr. junior
jt. joint
jud. judicial

Kans. Kansas
K.C. Knights of Columbus
K.T. Knight Templar
Ky. Kentucky

L.A. Los Angeles
lab. laboratory
L.A.C.C. Los Angeles City College
lang. language
laryngol. laryngological
L.D.S. Latter Day Saints
lectr. lecturer
legis. legislation, legislative
LHD Doctor of Humane Letters
L.I. Long Island
lib. library
lic. license, licensed
lit. literature
LittB Bachelor of Letters
LittD Doctor of Letters
LLB Bachelor of Laws
LLD Doctor of Laws
LLM Master of Laws
Ln Lane
lt. lieutenant
Ltd. Limited
LWV League of Women Voters

m. married
M. Master
MA Master of Arts
mag. magazine
MAgr Master of Agriculture
maj. major
Mass. Massachusetts
math. mathematics, mathematical
MBA Master of Business Administration
M.C. Medical Corps
mcht. merchant
mcpl. municipal
MCS Master of Commercial Science
MD Doctor of Medicine
Md. Maryland
mdse. merchandise
mdsg. merchandising
ME, M.E. Mechanical Engineer
Me. Maine
mech. mechanical
med. medical
MEE Master of Electrical Engineering
mem. member
Meml., Mem. Memorial
met. metropolitan

metall. metallurgical
meterol. meteorological
Mex. Mexico
MF Master of Forestry
MFA Master of Fine Arts
mfg. manufacturing
mfr. manufacturer
mgmt. management
mgr. manager
M.I. Military Intelligence
Mich. Michigan
mil. military
Minn. Minnesota
MIS Management Information Systems
Miss. Mississippi
mktg. marketing
MLS Master of Library Science
M.L.S. Multiple Listing Service (real estate)
mng. managing
Mo. Missouri
Mont. Montana
M.P. Member of Parliament
MPH Master of Public Health
MPhil Master of Philosophy
Mpls. Minneapolis
MRE Master of Religious Education
MS, MSc Master of Science
MST Master of Sacred Theology
MSW Master of Social Work
Mt. Mount
MTS member technical staff
mus. museum
MusB Bachelor of Music
MusD Doctor of Music
MusM Master of Music
mycol. mycological

N. North
NAACP National Association for Advancement of Colored People
N.Am. North America
NAM National Association of Manufacturers
NAREB National Association of Real Estate Boards
NASA National Aeronautics and Space Administration
NASD National Association of Securities Dealers
nat. national, naturalized
NATO North Atlantic Treaty Organization
NBC National Broadcasting Corporation
N.C., N.Caro. North Carolina
NCCJ National Conference of Christians and Jews
N.D., N.Dak. North Dakota
NE Northeast
NEA National Education Association

Nebr. Nebraska
neurol. neurological
Nev. Nevada
NG National Guard
N.H. New Hampshire
NHL National Hockey League
NIH National Institutes of Health
NIMH National Institute of Mental Health
N.J. New Jersey
NLRB National Labor Relations Board
N.M., N.Mex. New Mexico
No. Northern
NORAD North American Air Defense
NOW National Organization for Women
NRC National Research Council
nse. nurse
NSF National Science Foundation
nsg. nursing
num. numerous
numis. numismatic/s
NW Northwest
NY, N.Y. New York
NYC, N.Y.C. New York City
N.Z. New Zealand

OAS Organization of American States
ob-gyn obstetrics-gynecology
obstet. obstetrical
OD Doctor of Optometry
OEEC Organization of European Economic Cooperation
OEO Office of Economic Opportunity
O.E.S. Order of Eastern Star
ofcl. official
ofcr. officer
Oh. Ohio
Okla. Oklahoma
OMD Doctor of Oriental Medicine
ophthal. ophthalmological
opr. operator
ops. operations
orch. orchestra
Ore., Oreg. Oregon
orgn. organization
orgzr. organizer
OSHA Occupational Safety and Health Administration
OSS Office of Strategic Services
osteo. osteopathic
otol. otological
otolaryn. otolaryngology

Pa., Penn. Pennsylvania
PC, P.C. Professional Corporation
paleontol. paleontological
Pasa. Pasadena
path. pathology, pathological

PEN Poets, Playwrights, Editors, Essayists and Novelists
P.E.O. women's organization
pfc private first class
pgm. program
pgmg. programming
pgmr. programmer
PHA Public Housing Administration
pharm. pharmacy, pharmaceutical
PharmD Doctor of Pharmacy
PharmM Master of Pharmacy
PhB Bachelor of Philosophy
PhD Doctor of Philosophy
Phila. Philadelphia
philos. philosophical
photog. photography, photographer, photographic
phys. physical, physician
physiol. physiological, physiology
Pitts. Pittsburgh
Pkwy, Pky Parkway
plnr. planner
POB, PO Box Post Office Box
Poly. polytechnic, polytechnical
P.R. Puerto Rico, Public Relations
prep. preparatory
pres. president
Presbyn. Presbyterian
presdl. presidential
prin. principal
proc. proceedings, processing (data)
prod. produced, producer (theatrical)
prodn. production
prof. professor
profl. professional
prog. program
prop. proprietor
Prot. Protestant
pro tem pro tempore
PRSA Public Relations Society of America
PSRO Professional Services Review Organization
psychiat. psychiatric
psychol. psychological, psychology
p.t. part-time
PTA Parent-Teachers Association
ptnr. partner
pub. publisher, publishing, published
publ. publication
publs. publications
pvt. private

radiol. radiological
RCA Radio Corporation of America
Rd Road
R&D Research & Development
R.E. Real Estate

re regarding, relevant to
rec. recreation
ref. reference
reg. region, regional, registered
regt. regiment
rehab. rehabilitation, rehabilitate
rels. relations
rep. representative
Res., res. Residence, Reserve, research
ret. retired
rev. review, revised
rhinol. rhinological
R.I. Rhode Island
RN, R.N. Registered Nurse
ROTC Reserve Officers Training Corps
R.R. Railroad
RV recreational vehicle

s. son
S. South
SAC Strategic Air Command
Sacto. Sacramento
SAG Screen Actors Guild
SALT Strategic Arms Limitation Talks
S.Am. South America
SAR Sons of the American Revolution
savs. savings
S&L Savings & Loan
SB Bachelor of Science
S.B. Santa Barbara
SBA Small Business Administration
S.C., S.Caro. South Carolina
ScB Bachelor of Science
ScD Doctor of Science
sch. school
sci. science scientific
SCLC Southern Christian Leadership Conference
S.Dak. South Dakota
S.D. San Diego
SE Southeast
sec. secondary
secty., sec. secretary
SEC Securities and Exchange Commission
sect. section
S.F. San Francisco
seismol. seismological
sem. seminary
s.g. senior grade
sgt. sergeant
S.J. Society of Jesus (Jesuit)
so. southern
soc. society
sociol. sociological
sor. sorority
spkr. speaker
spl. special

splst. specialist
splty. specialty
St. State, Saint, Street
sta. station
stats. statistics
STB Bachelor of Sacred Theology
STD Doctor of Sacred Theology
Ste Suite
subcom. subcommittee
subs. subsidiary
supr. supervisor
supt. superintendent
supvy. supervisory
surg. surgical, surgery
svc. service
svs. services
SW Southwest
sys. system

tchg. teaching
tchr. teacher
tech. technical, technology, technological, technologist
techn. technicial
Tel. & Tel. Telephone & Telegraph
temp. temporary
Tenn. Tennessee
Tex., Tx. Texas
ThD Doctor of Theology
theol. theology, theological
tng. training
transf. transferred
transl. translator, translation
transp. transportation
treas. treasurer
TV, t.v. television

UAW United Auto Workers
UC University of California
UCLA University of California at Los Angeles
U.K. United Kingdom
UN United Nations
UNESCO United Nations Educational, Scientific and Cultural Organization
UNICEF United Nations International Children's Emergency Fund
univ. university
UPI United Press International
urol. urological
US, U.S. United States
USA United States of America, U.S. Army
USAAF United States Army Air Force
USAF United States Air Fore
USAFR United States Air Force Reserve
USAR United States Army Reserve
USC University of Southern California

USCG United States Coast Guard
USCGR United States Coast Guard Reserve
USDA United States Department of Agriculture
USIA United States Information Agency
USMC United States Marine Corps
USMCR United States Marine Corps Reserve
USN United States Navy
USNR United States Naval Reserve
USO United Service Organizations
USPHS United States Public Health Service
USPS United States Postal Service
U.S.S. United States Ship
USSR Union of Soviet Socialist Republics

VA Veterans Administration
Va. Virginia
vet. veteran
VFW Veterans of Foreign Wars
v.p. vice president
vis. visiting
VISTA Volunteers in Service to America
vocat. vocational
vol. volunteer
vs. versus
Vt. Vermont

W. West
WAC Women's Army Corps
Wash. Washington
WAVES Women's Reserve, U.S. Naval Reserve
W.D.C. Washington D.C.
west., we. western
WHO World Health Organization
W.I. West Indies
Wis. Wisconsin
W.Va. West Virginia
Wyo. Wyoming

x-c cross-country

YMCA Young Men's Christian Association
YMHA Young Men's Hebrew Association
YWCA Young Women's Christian Association
yr. year
YR Young Republicans organization

zool. zoological
-, to date

Guide to Biographies

The biographical profiles in **Who's Who In California** are arranged alphabetically according to the surname of the biographee. Where identical surnames occur, the first name is used. If both surname and first given name are identical, the second given name is used to arrange the profiles alphabetically.

In the case of compound hyphenated surnames, the profiles are arranged according to the first member of the compound.

Some biographees delete part of their full name in ordinary usage. In those instances parentheses are used to indicate that portion of the name which is deleted. For example, SMITH, J(OHN) indicates that the usual form of the name is J. Smith.

Each biographical profile is composed of the following data, offered in chronological order as a convenient guide:

1. Name
2. Occupation
3. Birthdate and Place
4. Parents
5. Marriage
6. Children
7. Education
8. Career
9. Career Related Activities

10. Awards and Honors
11. Memberships
12. Creative Works
13. Military Service
14. Political Affiliation
15. Religious Affiliation
16. Recreation/Hobbies
17. Residence Address
18. Office Address

Who's Who in California

AARON, ROY HENRY, entertainment company executive, lawyer; b. Apr. 8, 1929, Los Angeles; s. Samuel Arthur and Natalie (Krakauer) A.; m. Theresa Gesas, Dec. 20, 1953; children: Jill; edn: BA Univ. Calif., Berkeley 1951; LLB Univ. Southern Calif. 1956; admitted Calif. bar 1957. Career: counsel Pacht, Ross, Warne, Bernhard & Sears, Inc. Los Angeles 1957-79; sr. v.p. gen. counsel Plitt Theatres, Inc. and Plitt Theatre Holdings, Inc., LA 1978-80, pres., c.o.o. 1980-85; pres. Plitt Entertainment Group, Inc., LA 1985-90; pres. c.e.o. Showscan Corp., LA 1985-; lectr. Calif. Continuing Edn. of Bar; lectr. continuing legal edn. Loyola Univ. Law Sch., LA; mem: ABA, Calif. Bar Assn., Fellow Am. Bar Found. (life), LA Co. Bar Assn. (trustee 1977-83, v.p. 1979-80, pres. 1982-83), Beverly Hills Bar Assn., Women Lawyers LA, editorial bd. USC Law Rev. 1954-56, Motion Picture Pioneers (bd. dir.), Am. Judicial Soc., Vista Del Mar Child Care Svc. (1968-80, trustee, exec. com.), Reiss-Davis Child Study Ctr. 1977-80, United Crusade Campaigns (v.p. lawyers div.); civic: Jewish Fedn. Council Greater LA (bd. dir.), Rape Treatment Ctr. Santa Monica Hosp. (adv. bd.), UCLA Performing Arts; Order of Coif. Ofc: Showscan Corp 1801 Century Park E #1225 Los Angeles 90067

AASAND, KAREN LEA, international financial consultant; b. Jan. 11, 1955, Oakland; d. Ian Marshall and Joyce (Croze) Watson; m. Henry Aasand, Dec. 20, 1980; edn: BS fin., Golden Gate Univ. 1982. Career: account exec. Equitec Leasing Co., Oakland 1983-84; fin. planner AIS Fin. Services 1984-86; prin., owner Aasand Fin. Planning 1986-; tchr. Contra Costa Coll., San Pablo 1986-; honors: Golden Gate Univ. scholar 1980, outstanding acad. achievement Wall St. Jour. 1979, biog. listing Who's Who in West; mem: Internat. Assn. Fin. Planners, Consortium, Adventure Unlimited (chmn. bd. 1983-86), YMCA; Republican; Christian Scientist; rec: swimming, skiing, water skiing. Ofc: Aasand Financial Services 519 17th St Ste 700 Oakland 94612-1503

ABBATE, GERALDINE-VITTORIA, international business cross-cultural consultant and trainer; b. Mar. 27, 1952, Chgo.; d. Calogero Charles and Geraldine (Desborough) Abbate; m. Mahmoud Maghsoudi, Sept. 9, 1978; edn: BA, Univ. of Ill., Chgo. 1973; MA, N.E. Illinois Univ., 1975; tchg. credentials in English lang. and lit., Ill., Calif. Career: Western Regional Dir. ELS Educational Services Inc. 1974-79; founder/owner InterCultural Consultants, Internat.-USA, San Francisco 1979-; cons. and trainer in internat. business and inter-cultural skills development for internat. bus. execs.; honors: Phi Delta Kappa, 1973-74, official rep. ESL Language Centers, 1979-, listed Who's Who Am. Women, Who's Who Notable Italian-Americans, Community Leaders of Am.; mem: Internat. Consultants Found., Internat. Communication Assn., San Francisco C. of C. Women's Internat. Bus. Alliance, Calif. C.of C., Am. Soc. for Tng. & Devel., Nat. Assn. Women Business Owners, Women Entrepreneurs, Bay Area Profl. Women & Network, Soc. for Intercultural Edn., Tng. & Research, civic: Amnesty Internat., No. Calif. Consultative Grp. on Am. and World Affairs, World Affairs Council; rec: folk dancing, flute, writing, photog. Ofc: InterCultural Consultants International-USA, 278 Post St Ste 405 San Francisco 94108

ABBOTT, RUSSELL JOSEPH, computer science educator; b. Mar. 1, 1942, Bklyn.; s. Samuel and Lillian (Ginsberg) A.; m. Gail Ann Whitley, May 6, 1981; children: Michael b. 1981, Julian b. 1985, Danielle b. 1987; edn: BA, Columbia Univ., 1962; MA, Harvard Univ., 1963; PhD, USC, 1973. Career: prof. computer sci. CSU Los Angeles, 1987-; author: Software Development (1986), various jour. articles. Ofc: Dept. Math. and C.S., CSULA, 5151 State University Dr L.A. 90032

ABDEL-AZIZ, SABRY MOHAMED, certified public accountant; b. May 8, 1934, Alexandria, Egypt, nat. 1974; s. Mohamed Abdel Aziz; m. Azima Hamad, Aug. 29, 1957; children: Samar and Sahar (twins) b. 1960; edn: BA, Alexandria Univ., 1955, dipl. in taxation, 1962; MBA, NY Univ. Grad. Sch. of Bus., 1973; C.P.A., Calif. Career: Russell & Co., Alexandria, Egypt 1952-55; Alex. Ins. Co., 1956-60; acctg. mgr. Rakta Pulp & Paper, 1960-70; credit analyst M.H.T. Co., NY, NY 1970-74; chief internal auditor/v.p. ABN Bank, Los Angeles 1974-88; cons. Crescent Accounting (CPA) 1988-; mem: Am. Inst. CPAs, Calif. Soc. CPAs, Egyptian Accts. and Auditors; civic: Islamic Ctr. of So. Calif., Islamic Soc. of Orange Co., Egyptian Am. Orgn.; Republican; Moslem; rec: travel. Res: 19132 E Gold Ln Walnut 91789 Ofc: 2127 E Ball Rd Anaheim 92806

ABDUL-JABBAR, KAREEM (ALCINDOR, LEWIS FERDINAND), former professional basketball player; b. NYC, Apr. 16, 1947; s. Ferdinand Lewis and Cora Alcindor; m. Habiba (Janice Brown), 1971 (div. 1973); children: Habiba, Kareem, Sultana, Amir; edn: BA, UCLA 1969. Career: basketball player Milw. Bucks 1969-75; Los Angeles Lakers 1975-89; honors: NBA all-time leading scorer 1984, Maurice Podoloff Cup, Most Valuable Player NBA (1971, 72, 74, 76, 77, 80), NBA All-Star Team (1970-87, 89), NBA 35th Anniv. All-Time Team 1980, NBA Playoff MVP (1971, 85), Rookie of the yr. 1970, NCAA Tournament Outstanding Player 1967, 68, 69; author (with P. Knobler) Giant Steps: An Autobiography of Kareem Abdul-Jabbar (1983), Kareem (with M. McCarthy, 1990); num. television appearances incl. episodes: Mannix, Diff'rent Strokes, The Man from Atlantis, Tales from the Darkside, Pryor's Place, The After School Spl.; movies: Fletch 1985, Airplane 1980, The Fish that Saved Pittsburg 1979; Muslim. Ofc: c/o L.A. Lakers The Forum PO Box10 Inglewood 90306

ABE, GREGORY, microbiologist, educator; b. Nov. 25, 1954, Los Angeles; s. Mabel (Tsumori) Abe; edn: AA, L.A. Valley Coll., 1978; PharmD, USC, 1988; BS, CSU Los Angeles, 1990, MBA, 1992. Career: virologist CSU Los Angeles, 1988-90, assoc. prof., 1990-; rec: tennis, golf, fishing. Res: 10404 Fairgrove Ave Tujunga 91042 Ofc: CSULA, 5151 State University Dr Los Angeles 90032

ABEL, TIMOTHY, lawyer; b. Dec. 30, 1929, Williams; s. Allen Raymond and Consuelo (Benham) A.; m. Louise, June 14, 1953; children: Elizabeth Ellen b. 1958, John Allen b. 1961, Robert William b. 1962; edn: AA, UC Berkeley 1953; JD, UC Hastings Coll. of Law 1957; lic. Real Estate Broker, Calif. Career: law practice, Hayward 33+ yrs., currently: senior ptr. law firm Abel & Abel, also pres. Hayward Properties, pres. West California Properties; mem: So. Alameda Co. Bar Assn. (pres.), Alameda Co. Bar Assn. (dir.); mil: sgt. UMSC 1950-52; (2) Pres. Unit Citation, (4) Battle Stars, Korean Campaign; Republican; Methodist; rec: skiing, tennis, golf. Res: 300 Sheridan Ave. Piedmont 94611 Ofc: Abel & Abel, 1331 B St Ste 3 Hayward 94541

ABELES, JUDITH, lawyer and loan broker; b. Nov. 28, 1937, New York; d. Jack and Minnie (Rubin) Abeles; edn: BA philosophy, Bklyn. Coll. 1958; JD, Western State Univ. Coll. Law, San Diego 1978; LL.M, Univ. Exeter, England 1980; diploma Private Internat. Law, Hague Acad. Internat. Law, Netherlands 1980; Europa Inst., Amsterdam 1981-82. Career: legal intern Council of Europe, Strasbourg, France 1982-83; sole practice, San Diego 1983-84; staff atty. ACLU, San Diego 1984; sole practice, San Diego 1984-; instr. Nat. Univ. Sch. Law 1985-; Univ. Redlands 1986-87; dir. Utility Consumers Action Network 1987-; Able-Disabled Advocates 1987-; honors: U.S. Congress Citizen of Month 1988, Vols. in Parole Outstanding Atty. of Year 1989; mem: Citizens Equal Opportunity Commn., City Watchdog Com. (chair 1985-), Vol. Lawyers Program, Legal Aid Soc.; Gallon Club; Nat. Women's Political Caucus; newsletter pub. 1980-81, articles in profl. jour. 1977, 78; rec: gardening. Res: 3318 Arthur Ave San Diego 92116

ABERNETHY, ROBERT JOHN, real estate developer; b. Feb. 28, 1940, Indianapolis, Ind.; s. George Lawrence and Helen Sarah (McLandress) A.; edn: BA, Johns Hopkins Univ. 1962; MBA, Harvard Univ. 1968; cert. real estate, UCLA 1974; cert constrn. 1974. Career: asst. to deputy campaign mgr. Humphrey for Pres., Wash. D.C. 1968; asst. to chief scientist Phoenix missile program Hughes Aircraft Co., Los Angeles 1968-69, asst. program mgr., Iroquois Night Fighter and Night Tracker, Culver City 1969-71, asst. to controller, space and comm. group, El Segundo 1971-72, controller tech. div. 1972-74; pres. Am. Standard Devel. Co., Los Angeles 1974-; dir: Storage Equities, Glendale 1980-, Marathon Nat. Bank, L.A. 1982-, L.A. BanCorp. 1982-89, Self Serv. Stg. Assn., San Francisco 1978-83, L.A. Met. Water Dist. 1989-; honors: Alpha Lambda; civic: So. Calif. Planning Congress, Parker Found., L.A. City Planning Commn., 1984-88, L.A. Econ. Devel. Council (v.chmn. 1988-), Ctr. for Study of Democratic Instns. (v.chmn. 1985-), L.A. Theatre Ctr.; mil: lt. USNR 1962-66; rec: sailing, skiing. Res: 5800 W Century Blvd Los Angeles 90009-0855 Ofc: American Standard Development Co. 5221 W 102nd St Los Angeles 90045

ABPLANALP, DELLOY ORVAL, holistic health company owner; b. Nov. 28, 1931, Salt Lake City; s. Orval Ross and Elva Bernice (Hatch) A.; m. Kathleen Thurman, 1959; children: Denise b. 1960, David b. 1962, Matthew b. 1969; grandchildren: Elena, Elizabeth, Daniel, James, Johnny, and Justin; edn: BS, Brigham Young Univ., 1959; elementary, secondary teaching credentials. Career: mission service Church of Jesus Christ of Latter Day Saints, 1951-53; school tchr. 1959-61, 1988-89; acctg. & payroll clk., L.A. City Fire Dept. and Dept. Water & Power, 1961-74; tchr. holistic health, 1974-, mgr., dir. five herb cos.; sales mgr. Los Angeles Herald Examiner, 1983-88; awards: Million Dollar Club, Amtec Ind. (4), sales and leadership awards Natures Sunshine Products, and Enrich Corp.; mem: Delta Phi 1955-59, Nat. Health Fedn. 1970-, L.D.S. Sociables 1965-70; publs: Holistic Health Booklet (1977), Dial An Herb Wheel (1976); mil: pfc Army Signal Corps; Democrat. (county chmn. 1959); L.D.S. Ch. (elder, tchr.); rec: youth coach, referee AYSO Soccer and Little League Baseball. Ofc: Holistic Health Integrated, 4917 N Baldwin Ave Temple City 91780

ABRAHAM, ALBERT DAVID, retired railroad official, translator; b. Feb. 15, 1924, Baghdad, Iraq; naturalized U.S. citizen, Dec. 13, 1972; s. David and Mariam (Shawootha) A.; m. Lily, Jan. 12, 1958, (div. Dec. 1978); children: Peter b. 1962, Paul b. 1965; edn: BA, English (honors), San Francisco St. Univ.,

1975; BA in Law, Blackstone, Chgo. 1976; master gardener Univ. Calif. Coop. Ext., 1985. Career: translator and interpreter (Eng., Arabic, Syriac) U.S. and Brit. Armed Forces, Basrah, Iraq 1942-45; translator Basrah Petroleum Co., Iraq 1947-54; chief translator Brit. Bank of the M.E., Baghdad 1958-67; claims investigator So. Pacific Transp. Co., San Francisco 1967-86, ret.; horticultural gardening cons. The Home Depot, San Leandro 1988-92; vol. horticultural cons. Alameda County; awards: military commendn. Hq. Persia & Iraq Command 1942-45, outstanding civic service San Leandro C.of C. 1989, Optimist Internat. Honour Roll 1989; clubs: Moose (Castro Valley), Optimist (San Leandro, pres. 1988-89); Democrat; Christian; rec: dancing, horticulture, writing. Res: 1090 Hyde St San Leandro 94577

ABRAM, ALICE WILSON, account manager, Telephone Systems Division; b. Oct. 4, 1945, Glendale; d. Mack Lloyd and Jessie Lee (Andrues) Wilson; m. Wil C. Abram, June 8, 1974. Career: telephone svs. analyst Los Angeles County, 1980-85, supvg. analyst 1985-88, communications analyst 1988-, L.A. County voice mail mgr., respons. for pgm. devel, consulting, mktg. system with 10,000+ users, 1985-; currently acct. mgr. Telephone Sys. Div., respons. for all voice comm. in L.A. Co.; telecom auditing, frequent speaker re Telecom; awards: employee of mo. L.A. Co., 1987; mem. Telecommun. Assn. (nominating com. 1982-, So. Calif. chapt. mem. of yr. 1987); pres. Food Pantry-LAX (non-profit food source, feeds 35,000/yr.) mem. L.A. Ladies Book Club; Democrat; rec: aerobics, travel, gourmet cooking. Ofc: County of Los Angeles 1100 N Eastern Ave Los Angeles 90063

ABSHIRE, LYNN THOMAS, computer scientist, executive; b. June 10, 1944, Twin Falls, Ida.; s. Joyce (Jack) and Viola M. (Bittner) Abshire; children: Mark b. 1968, Timothy b. 1971, Matthew b. 1979; edn: AS, Ore. Tech. Inst. 1967. Career: sr. tech., process control programmer Union Carbide Corp., S.D. 1969-70; d.p. mgr. Solitron Devices Inc. 1970-74; sr. res. and devel. programmer Gen. Automation Inc., Anaheim 1974-75; corp. d.p. mgr. VTN Corp., Irvine 1975-83; tech. support mgr. DMA Comm. 1983; customer service mgr. Studio Software, Costa Mesa 1983-85; currently computer systems mgr. Greiner Engring., Santa Ana; computer cons. 1986-; v.p. Profl. Cons. Group Inc. 1986-; mil: E-5 USN 1961-65; Republican; Prot.; rec: computers, electronics, music. Res: 27861 Perales Mission Viejo 92692 Ofc: Greiner Engineering, 1261 E Dyer Rd Santa Ana 92705

ACUNA, DEANNE ROBERTA, private investigator; b. Mar. 17, 1939, Long Beach; d. Dean Robert Gardner and Roberta Lillian (Ross); m. George Getz; children: David b. 1960, Kimberly b. 1965; edn: AA, Long Beach City Coll. 1972; Lic. pvt. investigator (AQ009787). Career: investigator law firm Perona-Langer LaTorraca, Beck, 1979-89; Santoni & Laski Investigations, Tustin 1990-91; owner, prin. pvt. investigation firm, Acuna and Associates, 1991-; owner Reality Realty Co., Long Beach 1976-79, real estate developer, consultant 1984-; awards: acad. scholarships 1970-72; mem: Calif. Assn. of Licensed Investigators, Women in Constrn., Long Beach Com. 300, Attys. Legal Services Referral Network (dir.), Hispanic Amnesty Persons (translator and counselor), Long Beach Civic Light Opera Womens Guild; Democrat; avocation: tchr. wholistic health concepts. Res: 2462 Monogram Ave Long Beach 90815

ADAIR, DIANNA LYNN, software engineer, planning commissioner; b. Jan. 23, 1950, Woodbury, N.J.; d. Marion Ezelle and Opal Jeanette (Keller) Braden; m. Vernon H. Adair, July 30, 1973; edn: BS, Utah State Univ., 1972; postgrad. studies Stanford Univ. 1983-86; MBA, Pepperdine Univ., 1991. Career: gymnastics coach Fla. Sch. for Deaf and Blind, St. Augustine 1972-76; sr. software engr. Unisys Corp., Santa Clara 1982-89; c.e.o. Volpar Inc., 1984-; bd. dir. El Camino Hosp., Mountain View 1990-; mem: IEEE; civic bds: Sunnyvale Planning Commn. 1988-, Sunnyvale Voting Div. (elections inspr. 1986-87), Sunnyvale Sch. Dist. Edn. Found. 1988-, Emergency Response Team (capt.), Women in the Arts- Nat. Museum (nat. mus. council 1988-), Smithsonian Instn. (Fellow); clubs: Toastmasters (pres. 1983, area gov. 1983-84, ATM 1985), Decathlon, Churchill; editor book: Parts by Application (1985). Res: 399 E Maude Ave Sunnyvale 94086 Ofc: Volpar, Inc. 941 Laurelwood Rd Santa Clara 95054-2717

ADAMS, JACK, screenwriter, producer, director, educator; b. Sept. 15, 1952, Lakehurst, N.J.; s. John Carey and Dorothy Jeanne (Conover) A.; m. Shirley Janulewicz, June 28, 1975; children: Carey Miller, Chanine Angelina, Mikael Walter, Jozef Conover; edn: MusB in music edn., Univ. Dela., 1974. Career: pres. Koala Studio, Valencia 1977-; v.p. devel. Unifilms Inc., North Hollywood 1984-; co-founder ScripTip, 1990; instr. film, TV writing and script analysis: Coll. of the Canyons, Valencia 1988-; L.A. City Coll. 1989-; EveryWoman's Village, Van Nuys, Info. Exchange, L.A., Learning Tree Univ., Chatsworth, Info. Network, S.Pasadena, 1990-; Univ. Wis., Madison, USIA, W.D.C., Moorpark Coll., Oxnard Coll., Northwestern Univ., Classes Unlimited, S.Pasadena, Glendale Comm. Coll., 1991-; founding mem. bd. dirs., ofcr. L.A. Filmmakers Workshop, 1989-91; founder, Santa Clarita Scriptwriters' Workshop; mem. Larry Wilson Devel. Workshop, Paramount Studios; mem. Storyboard Devel. Group, Paramount Studios, 1989-, Le Group; pres. Entertainment Writers' Workshop, 1990; pres. NBC Writers' Workshop; mem.

KNX Speakers Bur. (CBS Radio) 1989-; mem. Independent Feature Project West; composer (film) EAT, 1980 (Filmex award 1981, best short film award Cinemagic mag. 1981); writer, co-creator sitcom pilot LOLA, Universal Studios, 1991; writer, developer sitcom pilot FAT FARM; writer, prod., dir. sitcom pilot BOX #22; line prod. sitcom pilot, ZEBRA, and IT'S NOT MY FAULT; mem: Am. Film Inst. (alumni assn. writers workshop), Scriptwriters' Network (bd. advrs.), Film Artists Network, Independent Writers So. Calif. Scriptwriters' Caucus, Assn. Information Systems Profls. (bd. 1983), Freelance Screenwriters' Forum (founding bd., TV editor, F.S.F. Newsletter 1990-, columnist Screenwrite Now mag. 1991-), Comedy Writers Co-op (founding ABC), Wis. Screenwriters Forum (cons., advr. 1989-91); active YMCA Indian Guides/Indian Princesses and Trailblazers pgms. (chief Apache Tribe 1990); rec: tennis, still photog., music. Res/Ofc: 22931 Sycamore Creek Dr Santa Clarita 91354-2050 Ph:805/297-2000

ADAMS, ROY W., JR., lawyer; b. May 8, 1950, Delano; s. Roy W. and Helen Lucille (Todd) A.; m. Lucy Boyd, July 14, 1973; children: Whitney b. 1985, Trevor b. 1985; edn: BSEE, UC Berkeley 1972; JD, UCLA 1980; admitted St. Bar Calif. 1980. Career: res. engr. Lawrence Livermore Labs., Livermore 1972-77; atty., assoc. Brobeck Phleger & Harrison, San Francisco 1980-82; ptnr. Thelen Marrin Johnson & Bridges 1982-; pres., dir. Calif. Symphony, Orinda 1987-89; mem: Assn. for Corp. Growth, Am. Bar Assn., Bar Assn. San Francisco; articles and proceeding paper pub. (1987); rec: music, theatre, dance. Ofc: Thelen Marrin et al 2 Embarcadero Center Ste 2200 San Francisco 94111

ADAMSON, MARY ANNE, utilities research analyst; b. June 25, 1954, Berkeley; d. A. Frank and Frances I. (Key) A.; m. Richard John Harrington, Sept. 20, 1974; edn: BA (highest honors) geography & gt. distinction in gen. scholarship, UC Berkeley, 1975, MA, 1976, postgrad. (cand. PhD) 1978. Career: scientist Lawrence Livermore Nat. Lab., Livermore 1978-83, cons. 1983-86; systems engr. ESL (Electromagnetic Systems Lab.), Sunnyvale 1986-90; res. analyst PG&E, San Francisco 1990-; awards: Phi Beta Kappa 1975, citation for outstanding undergrad. accomplishment dept. geography UC Berkeley 1975; mem: Assn. of Am. Geographers (1975-, Life), UC Alumnae Assn. (1975-, Life), Commonwealth Club S.F., Toastmasters Internat. Blue Monday Club S.F. (edn. v.p. 1991), Nat. Speleol. Soc. Diablo Grotto Chpt. (exec. bd., editor 1982-86), Mountain Medicine Inst. Oakland (asst. chief engr. 1983-). Ofc: PG&E, 201 Mission St Ste PI802A San Francisco 94105

ADEN, GARY D., healthcare executive, administrator; b. June 30, 1942, Beatrice, Nebr.; s. Fred P. and Evelyn M. (Whiteside) Aden; m. Carol Dumpert, June 25, 1966; children: Marcie b. 1970, Jeremy b. 1974; edn: BA, Univ. Nebr., 1964, JD, 1966; MS, Univ. Pittsburgh, 1968; Career: asst. adminstr. Albert Einstein Coll. of Medicine, Bronx, NY, 1968-72; dir. health economics American Hosp. Assn., Chgo., 1972-75; sr. v.p. Pennsylvania Hosp., Phila., 1975-85; exec. v.p. and c.o.o. American Healthcare Systems, San Diego, 1985-; bd. dirs: Health Industry Bus. Com., Phoenix, Az. (bd. govs. 1990-), Health Insights, Baton Rouge, La. (bd. chmn. 1984-86), Hosp. Assn. of Pa., Harrisburg, Pa. (chmn. Com. on Finance 1982-83), Delaware Valley Hosp. Council, Phila., Pa. (bd. chmn. 1979-80); mem: Am. Coll. of Healthcare Execs. (Fellow, 1981-), Nebr. State Bar Assn. 1966-, N.Y. Bar Assn. 1970-; civic: Comprehensive Health Center, San Diego (bd. 1989-); publs: articles in Modern Hospital (1968), Hospital Financial Management (1974), Hospitals (1976, 77, 79, 81); Republican; First Christian Ch.; rec: golf, bicycling, squash, running. Res: 8450 Cliffridge Ln La Jolla 92037 Ofc: American Healthcare Systems 12730 High Bluff Dr Ste 300 San Diego 92130

ADKINS, THOMAS JAY, manufacturing company financial executive; b. Sept. 12, 1953, Compton; s. Eugene L. and Faye Ilene (Kindy) A.; m. Marilee Kay Jennings, July 15, 1972; children: Benjamin b. 1973, Timothy b. 1976, Mark b. 1982, Stephen b. 1986; edn: AA, El Camino Coll. 1983; BS magna cum laude, USC 1986. Career: sr. acct. Martin Marietta Aluminum, Torrance 1980-84; fin. adminstr. Internat. Light Metals 1984-87; dir. fin. Magna Mill Products, South Gate 1987-88; controller Internat. Light Metals, Torrance 1988-; chmn. supervisory com. Martin Maretta Fed. Credit Union; honors: Alpha Gamma Sigma; mem: Nat. Assn. Accts., Controllers Council; Christian. Res: 2627 W 175th St Torrance 90504 Ofc: International Light Metals Corp. 19200 S Western Ave Torrance 90509

ADLER, ALLAN WILBUR, silversmith; b. May 8, 1916, Mazula, Mont.; s. August M. and Daisey B. (Fox) A.; m. Rebecca Blanchard, Mar. 24, 1938; children: Linda Diane (Mrs. Wm. Hughes), b. 1942; Cindy Alice (Mrs. Scott Larson), b. 1952. Career: pres. Allan Adler, Inc. 1940-, bd. chmn. 1981-; designed and made the pins worn by the first seven Am. Astronauts; designed the silver flatware and holloware for the Calif. Gov.'s Mansion for Gov. Edmund Brown; designed the American Film Inst. Award 1972; designed the Famous Stevenshoe shoe campaign button; designed original Pres. Eisenhower Golf Trophy for Bob Hope Desert Classic tournament.; awards: Calif. Living Treasure 1984, Good Design Award, Mus. of Modern Art 1956, Scissors Award for Design, Calif. Fashion Grp. 1949; honored by The Smithsonian Instn. (1982) documenting 40 years of Am. Silversmithing and Allan Adler's Contbn. to

Design; mem. Los Angeles County Mus. of Art, Newport Harbor Yacht Club; Presbyterian; rec: yachting, fishing. Res: 3263 Oakdell Rd Studio City 91604 Ofc: Allan Adler, Inc. 13080 Montague St Pacoima 91331

ADLER, ERWIN ELLERY, lawyer; b. July 22, 1944, Flint, Mich.; s. Ben and Helen M. (Schwartz) A.; m. Stephanie Ruskin, June 8, 1967; children: Lauren M. b. 1974, Michael B. b. 1977, Jonathan S. b. 1981; edn: BA, Univ. of Mich., 1963, JD, Harvard Law Sch., 1966, LL.M, Univ. of Mich. Law Sch., 1967. Career: assoc. Pillsbury Madison & Sutro law firm, 1967-73; assoc., partner law firm Lawler, Felix & Hall, 1973-82; ptnr. law firm Rogers & Wells, 1982-84; ptnr. law firm Richards, Watson & Gershon, Los Angeles 1985-; bd. dirs. Hollywood Opera Assocs. 1975-76; bd. dirs. Childrens Scholarships Inc. 1978-79; v.chmn. Appellate Advocacy Com. American Bar Assn.; honors: Phi Beta Kappa, Phi Kappa Phi; mem. Am. Bar Assn. 1967-, Calif. Bar Assn. 1967-, LA Athletic Club; Jewish; rec: photog., jogging. Res: 872 Norman Pl Los Angeles 90049 Ofc: Richards, Watson & Gershon, 333 So Hope St 38th Flr Los Angeles 90071

AFABLE, CARLOS BOSA, mortgage banker; b. Dec. 15, 1943, Masbate, Phil., nat. 1976; s. Eleno T. and Tita B. (Bosa) A.; m. Aurora, Sept. 16, 1967; 1 son, Carl, b. 1974; edn: BS, ChE, Univ. of Santo Tomas, Manila, Phil. 1967; Profl. Chem. Engr., Phil. Inst. of Chem. Engring., 1967; Graduate Realtors Inst. (GRI) 1991; profl. courses L.A. City Coll. 1971-72, CSU Northridge 1979-81. Career: asst. instr. Chem. Dept., Tech. Inst. of Phil. 1967-68; lead foreman Coco Chemicals (Phil.) Inc., 1968-69; supr. Chemical Industries of the Phil., Rizal 1969-70; shift supr. Wacker Chemicals, Los Angeles 1972-77; staff scientist Hughes Research Labs, Malibu 1977-89; mortgage banker CBA Certified Funding, Beverly Hills, 1991-; mem: Am. Assn. of Crystal Growth, AAAS, UST Alumni Assn. of So. Calif., Thomasian Engrs. Club (L.A.); profl. publs. in field; Republican; R.Cath.; rec: chess, computers. Res: 1107 S Plymouth Blvd Los Angeles 90017 Ofc: CBA Certified Funding, 2417 Beverly Blvd Ste 204 Los Angeles 90057

AGAMALIAN, JOHN KARL, disposal company president; b. Nov. 28, 1958, Los Angeles; s. George and Elizabeth Adele (Farris) A.; edn: BS, USC, 1981. Career: mktg. rep. Burroughs Corp., Dallas, Tx. 1981-82; pres. and c.e.o. A-Trojan Disposal, Los Angeles 1982-; owner: Bay Co. Mortgage, So Cal Sweeping, JBA Construction; mem. USC Associates, L.A. C.of C., GLASMA. Res: 57 San Miguel Pasadena 91105 Ofc: A-Trojan Disposal Co Inc 5600 Alhambra Ave Los Angeles 90032

AGUIRRE, JOHN, architect; b. June 29, 1924, Los Angeles; s. John and Mary (Jurado) A.; m. Marilyn Cummings, 1952; edn: BS, Harvard Univ. 1949; diplome Univ. de Paris 1950. Career: prin. Aguirre Associates, Inc., Idyllwild; mem: Am. Inst. Architects; mil: US Navy 1943-46; Catholic. Ofc: Aguirre Associates, Inc. Idyllwild 92349

AHDAN, PAUL S., marketing & sales company president; b. Apr. 20, 1942, Punjab, nat. U.S.A. 1964; s. G.S. and K.K. Ahdan; m. Jennie K., Mar. 26, 1965; 1 child, Ranbir; edn: AMIEX (MBA) Reg. St. Polytech Inst. of Export, London 1971; BSME, Heald's Engring., S.F. 1975; MBA (Calif.) 1992. Career: asst. import-export mgr. Singer Bus. Machines, San Leandro, Calif. 1968-74; gen. traffic mgr. Commodore Bus. Machines, Palo Alto 1974-75; contracts mgr. Granger Assocs., Menlo Park 1975-77; internat. mktg. mgr. Fairchild Camera & Instrument Corp., Mt. View 1977-83; internat. sales & mktg. mgr. Boschert Inc., Sunnyvale 1983-84; v.p. sales & mktg. PAD S.A., Paris, Fr., 1985-87; internat. sales & mktg. ops. mgr. Alcatel N.V., Info. Systems Div., 1987-88; dir. internat. sales PEGI, San Carlos 1988-89; pres. Rantronics Internat. Ltd., Los Altos 1989-, also pres. Rancor Internat. Ltd., W.Ger. 1990-; Sikh; rec: sports, stamps, coins, travel.

AHRENS, ERICK K.F., computer software executive; b. Feb. 22, 1949, Detroit, Mich.; s. Herman F. Ahrens and Evelyn V. (Metcalf) Finch; m. Dorothy A. Swiercz, June 22, 1972; edn: AA in math., Coll. of San Mateo, 1975; BS in engring., UC Berkeley, 1980; MBA, San Francisco St. Univ., 1987. Career: computer pgmr. Victor Comptometer, S.San Francisco 1975; res. and devel. engr. Earl and Wright, San Francisco 1976-83; v.p. Molecular Design Ltd., San Leandro 1984-; honors: Alpha Gamma Sigma 1975; mem: Assn. for Computing Machinery 1979-, IEEE Computer Soc. 1988-, Am. Chem. Soc. 1985-; clubs: Marin Sail and Power Squadron, Novato (past comdr.), Corinthian Yacht, Tiburon (Flag secty.); publs: tech. papers; mil: machinist mate USN 1969-73; rec: sailing. Res: PO Box 20984 Castro Valley 94546 Ofc: MDL, 2132 Farallon Dr San Leandro 94577

AIJIAN, PAUL MISAK, minister, psychotherapist; b. Sept. 20, 1917, Detroit, Mich.; s. Misak Michael and Mabel Maude (Schuyler) A.; m. Arlys Ehlers, Dec. 19, 1950; children: Rachael b. 1952, Phillip b. 1954, David b. 1956, Rebecca b. 1958, Stephen b. 1962; edn: BA, UCLA, 1940; tchg. credential 1941; BD, San Francisco Theol. Sem., 1944, STM, 1946; PhD, USC, 1947. Career: pastor Hollenbeck Presbyterian Ch., Los Angeles 1947-49; pastoral asst. Wilshire Presbyterian Ch. 1950-54; head English dept. Biola Univ. 1949-54; faculty Talbot Theological Seminary 1951-53; pastor St. John's Presbyterian Ch., Long Beach 1955-63; faculty philosphy Univ. Mississippi, Oxford 1963-64; head. dept. philosophy North Central Coll., Naperville, Ill. 1965-66; pastor First Presbyterian Ch., North Hollywood 1966-80; dir. grad. study Am. Inst. Family Rels., Los Angeles 1980-83; dir. Am. Family Counseling Services, Woodland Hills 1983-85; sr. counselor The Healing Tree, Burbank 1985-88; adj. prof. U.S. Internat. Univ., San Diego 1985-88; honors: Phi Epsilon Theta, Phi Xi Phi, man of year No. Hollywood Community Adult Sch. 1981; mem: Kiwanis (pres. 1974-75), Long Beach Mental Health (pres. 1961-62); Democrat; Prot. Res: 29924 Violet Hills Dr Canyon Country 91351 Ofc: The Healing Tree 905 S Lake Ave Ste 201 Burbank 91502

AILSHIE, ROGER ALLEN, auditor; b. Sept. 27, 1962, Hutchinson, Kans.; s. Roger Howard and Jeanette Ray (McCall) A.; edn: BS acctg., Baker Univ., 1987. Career: staff acct. Lindburg & Vogel, Hutchinson, Kans. 1987-88; senior auditor D.C.A.A., Mountain View, Calif. 1989-; recipient profl. award for superior accomplishment DCAA (1989); mem: Assn. of Govt. Accts., Zeta Chi frat. (pres. 1987), Sunshine Club Mtn. View (pres. 1990-91); Methodist; rec: basketball, raquetball, softball. Res: 1276 C St Hayward 94541 Ofc: DCAA, 321 Castro St Mountain View 94041

AIRES, RAMON HESS, consultant and technical advisor to management, ret. engineering executive; b. March 15, 1927, Lancaster, Pa.; s. Ray G. and Anna (Hess) A.; m. Jane Elizabeth Hawk, Sept. 6, 1952; children: Victoria b. 1953, David b. 1954, Mark b. 1957, Lisa b. 1959, Timothy b. 1962; edn: BEE, Cornell Univ. 1950; MSEE, Univ. Pa. Phila. 1959; reg. profl. engr. in control systems engr., 1978-. Career: engr. Philco, Phila., Pa. 1950-54; mgr., engr. RCA Defense Electronic Products, Camden, Princeton and Sommerville, N.J., 1954-65; chief engr. RCA Avionic Systems, Van Nuys, Calif. 1965-81; Sperry Avionics 1981-82; v.p. ops.and engring. Teloc Inc. 1982-86; v.p. and tech. adv. to the pres. Datatape Inc. (a Kodak Co.), Pasadena 1986-93; advy. bd. CSU Northridge 1974-92; awards: RCA Corp. David Sarnoff Tech. Achievement award (1978); mem: IEEE (sr.), Inst. Advancement Engring. (fellow), Masons; 10 patents (1952-86); mil: USN 1945-46; Presbyterian; rec: model trains, railroading, cars, music, pipe organs, computers, stock market. Res: 16653 Pineridge Dr Granada Hills 91344-1849

AKER, "DEE" DIANNE LEE, cross-cultural psychologist/anthropologist, educator, university president; b. July 5, 1941, Kankakee, Ill.; d. Herald W. Stockton and Marjorie (Martin) Walley; m. William Bryson Smith, July 15, 1989; edn: BS biol./sociol., Southwest Mo. St. Univ., 1963; MA internat. affairs, Ohio Univ., 1973; PhD humanistic psych./cultural anthropology, The Union Inst., Cinti. 1977. Career: vol. Peace Corps Colombia, S.A. 1963-64; resrch. asst. N.J. Neuro-Psychiat. Inst., Princeton 1965-67; soc. wkr. L.A. County Dept. Soc. Svs., 1968-72; vol. Kibbutz and archaeol. site, Israel 1968; coord. supr. Frontier Dist. Mental Health Ctr., Washington County, Oh. 1974-75; ldr. in residence Esalen Inst., Big Sur 1975-79; cons. prin., U.S., Canada, Europe, Israel, Africa, 1975-80; East-West Vis. Scientist Exchange, Poland, 1979; faculty U.S. Internat. Univ., San Diego 1978-79, faculty USIU-Africa, Nairobi, Kenya 1979-84, univ. dean 80-82, dir. 82-84, asst. v.p. USIU, San Diego 1984-87, dir. USIU Orange County Graduate Center, Irvine 1985-90; dean academic affairs Univ. for Humanistic Studies, 1991-93, pres. 1993-; prod./host weekly TV interview show "Women" KUSI-TV, San Diego 1985-91, Emmy Award nominee: "Women - The Uganda Women's Effort to Save the Orphan" 1990; cons./pres. Daker Cross-Cultural Prodns., 1986-91; prod./dir. video documentaries: Uganda: An African Phoenix 1987, Women of Gulfito 1988, Women Leaders of Uganda: A Quiet Revolution in Africa 1990; correspondent Women's Times (monthly. column) 1992-; numerous profl. papers and presentations; awards: Honors throughout academic career, Nat. Phys. Edn. Hon. Soc., Alpha Kappa Delta 1961-63, Who's Who Am. Colls. and Univs. 1963, Ohio Univ. grad. asst. 1972-3, Who's Who in Kenya 1982-84, lifetime achiev. Saddleback Comm. Coll. 1986, Philanthropy Award for profl. achiev. Nat. Soc. Fundraising Execs. L.A. 1987, career achiev. Rancho Santiago Coll. 1988, `Wonderwoman 1990' Award for Edn. San Diego Women's Directory and Small Bus. Assn. 1990; mem. The Woman's Found./O.C. (advy. bd. 1986-), OEF/Women in Bus. for Women in Econ. Devel. 1986-90, San Diego Human Rels. Comm. Media Task Force 1987-92, Carl Rogers Inst. for Peace La Jolla (founding bd., staff 1986-90), Am. Women in Radio and TV (1990-, advy. bd. 1991-), Nat. Acad. TV Arts and Scis. 1989-, Assn. for Women in Devel. 1987-, World Trade Ctr. Inst./O.C., World Trade Ctr. Assn. O.C. 1985-86, Ctr. for Studies of the Person, La Jolla (fellow), The Union Inst. San Diego Ctr. (advy. bd. 1991-); rec: Asian art, photography, adventure travel. Res: 3340 del Sol Blvd #194 San Diego 92154 Ofc: University for Humanistic Studies 2002 Jimmy Durante Blvd Del Mar 92014

ALAIMO, TERRY ELLEN, artist; b. June 12, 1942, Rochester, N.Y.; d. Bernard and Mildred Michlin; m. S. Richard Alaimo, Jr., June 18, 1961 (div. 1979); children: Samuel b. 1966, Deborah b. 1969; edn: Rochester Inst. of Tech. Sch. of Art & Design 1961; cert. Am. Inst. Paralegal Studies 1983-84. Career: art dir. Monroe Litho Inc., Rochester, N.Y. 1961-66; fine arts Terry Alaimo Studio 1969-82; fine artist, Rockport, Mass. 1982-84; mediator Crime & Justice Found. Essex Co. Cts., Boston and Gloucester, Mass. 1982-84; paralegal Ross & Watson, Gloucester, Mass. 1984; Swartz & Swartz, Boston, Mass. 1983; fine artist, illustrator Terry Alaimo Studio, Laguna Beach 1984-; art dir. Empringham, Bradley & Ho (EBH Publications) 1992; cons. TRW-Redi Property Data, Calif. 1993; exhibits: poetry and visual arts, The Smithsonian, 1976; Miniature Painters, Sculptors & Engravers Soc., Wash. D.C. Art Club, 1975; Mus. of Duncans, Paris and N.Y.C., 1979; one woman shows Washington Art Expo. 1976, 78, 79, 80; awards: Miniature Art Soc. Fla. semi-abstract 1977, Chautaqua (N.Y.) Inst. Award Exh. of American Art 1977, Staudenmaier award Rochester Art Club 1978, 81, Laguna Art Mus. All Calif. Show small-scale 1986; mem: Am. Arbitration Assn., Printing Industries of Am., North Shore Art Assn.; publs: illustrator, Homeowners Guide to Re-roofing, Montage Pub., Jose Cuervo Internat. 1991; OC Ad News Illustration Issue 1991; Calif. Art Review 1989; Unitarian; rec: bicycling, golf, travel. Ofc: Terry Alaimo Studio 2233 Martin St Irvine 92715

ALANIZ, MIGUEL JOSE CASTANEDA, city librarian; b. Oct. 21, 1944, Los Angeles; s. Francisco Martinez and Amalia (Castaneda) A.; m. Mercedes, June 7, 1980; edn: AA edn., Chabot Coll. 1972; BS child/human devel., CSU Hayward 1974; MLS, CSU Fullerton 1975; MPA, CSU San Bernardino, 1988; Calif. Comm. Coll. Tchg. credential. Career: Spanish Services librarian, Alameda Co. 1975-77; branch lib. mgr. San Jose Public Library 1977-78, Santa Ana Public Library 1978-79; coord. Young Adult/ Outreach Svcs., San Bernardino Co. Library 1979-82, div. chief of tech. processing, 1982-84; city librarian City of Azusa 1984-; awards: grad. res. fellow in library sci., CSUF 1974-75; mem: Am. Library Assn., Calif. Library Assn., Reforma (Nat. Assn. Hispanic Librarians), cofounder Bibliotecas Para La Gente (orgn. providing lib. svcs. in Spanish lang.); mil: E5 AUS 1965-71; rec: collect exotic autos, rare books, unusual pets. Ofc: City of Azusa Library 729 N Dalton Ave Azusa 91702

ALARID, WILLIAM MORRIS, engineer, publisher; b. July 4, 1936, Santa Fe, N.M.; s. Jack Justice and Retha (Daniel) A.; m. Elsie Kathleen Sutherland, Nov. 20, 1965; children: Christine b. 1970, David b. 1973; edn: BSAE, Ind. Inst. Tech. 1957. Career: engr. Northwest Airlines, St. Paul, Minn. 1957-58; mgr. Aerojet Gen., Sacto. 1958-65; project engr. Aerospace Corp., Vandenberg AFB 1965-; pres. Puma Publishing, Santa Maria 1986-; awards: Pub. Library Assn. best of best 1989, Toastmasters Internat. 1st place humorous speech 1971, Aerojet Gen. engring. excellence 1956; mem: Am. Mensa Ltd., Publishers Mktg. Assn., Assn. Research & Enlightenment, COSMEP, Internat. Assn. Indep. Publishers, Sertoma Internat. (membership chmn. 1966-71), Toastmasters Internat. (v.p. 1968-72), BSA (chmn. 1984-88), Explorer Post (chmn. 1988-), Alpha Gamma Epsilon (v.p. 1955-56); author: Free Help from Uncle Sam 1988, Money Sources for Small Business 1991; editor ESP newsletter 1980; Republican; R.Cath.; rec: skiing, hiking, writing. Res: 1670 Coral Dr Santa Maria 93454

ALBERT, LOUIS E(UGENE), JR., educator; b. Sept. 19, 1945, Portland, Me.; s. Louis Eugene, Sr. and Mary Rita (Joyce) A.; m. Marty Jean Pugsley, July 1, 1972 (div. 1981), remarried July 1, 1990; edn: AA, Los Angeles Pierce Coll., 1969; BA, health sci., health edn., phys. edn., CSU Northridge, 1971; MPH (candidate) pub. health, CSUN, 1987-; Calif. Comm. Colls. instr. credentials, 1974-. Career: coll. prof. LA Valley Coll., Van Nuys; supr. grad. pub. health (MPH) student tchr./field training program, CSU Northridge, 1978-; organizer L.A. Comm. Coll. Dist. series 'Wellness: Employee Workshop' presented LA Valley Coll., Fall 1982, LA City Coll. and LACC Dist. Office, Spring 1985; program dir. Health Fair Expo '90, LA Valley Coll, 4/90; organizer, dir. num. coll. and comm. forums re contemporary health issues, agencies and human services, Vietnam Veterans; awards: LA Valley Coll. Pres.'s Commendn. for service to the coll. (1990), LAVC Academic Senate distinguished service award 1990; mil: cpl. USMC 1963-66, decorated Purple Heart, Combat Action Rib., Presdl. Unit cits. w/rib. and bronze star, GCM, Nat. Def. Svc., Vietnam Svc. w/2 bronze stars, Repub. Vietnam meritorious unit citations (2) w/rib. bar and palm, Repub. Vietnam campaign medal; mem. Disabled Am. Vet. (life), 1st Marine Div. Assn. (life); R.Cath.; rec: outdoors, skiing, camping. Ofc: Los Angeles Valley College, 5800 Fulton Ave Van Nuys 91401

ALBERT, RONALD PETER, lawyer; b. Sept. 10, 1956, Utica, N.Y.; s. Raymond J. and Monica (Fischer) A.; edn: AB econs. (magna cum laude), UC Davis, 1979; JD, UC Berkeley, 1983; admitted bar: Calif.; lic. Calif. R.E. Broker. Career: acct. Davidson, Dreyer & Hopkins, San Francisco, 1979-80; atty. Law Offices of Ronald P. Albert, San Diego, 1983-87; prof. of law Syracuse Univ., Utica, N.Y., 1987-88; atty. law firm Griffinger Levinson Freed & Heinemann, San Francisco, 1988-; pro bono vol. Tax-Aid, S.F., 1989-, Volunteer Lawyers Service Progam, S.F., 1990-; honors: Moot Ct. Bd. and California Law Rev., UC Berkeley 1982-83; mem: Am. Bar Assn. (1983-, sect. taxation 1988-), State Bar Calif. 1983-, New York State Bar 1984-, Bar Assn. San Francisco 1988-; mem. Kts. of Col. Ofc: Griffinger Levinson Freed & Heinemann, One Market Plaza Ste 2400 San Francisco 94105

ALDRICH, DAVID LAWRENCE, public relations executive; b. Feb. 21, 1948, Lakehurst N.A.S., NJ; s. Clarence Edward and Sarah Stiles (Andrews) A., Jr., LCDR, USN (ret.); m. Benita Massler, Mar. 17, 1974; edn: Ocean Co. Coll., NJ 1967-8, Sophia Univ., Tokyo 1970-1, BA, CSU Dominguez Hills 1976.

Career: reporter/columnist Ocean Co. Daily Observer, NJ 1967-68; asst. public information, City of Carson, Ca. 1974-77; pub. rels. mgr./adminstv. asst. Calif. Federal Svgs, Los Angeles 1977-78; v.p./group supr. Hill & Knowlton, L.A. 1978-81; v.p./mgr. W. Div., Ayer Public Relations, N. W. Ayer, L.A. (bd. Western Region) 1981-84; pres. Aldrich & Assoc., Inc. Public Relations Counsel, 1984-; mem. bd. dirs., chmn. mktg. advy. bd. Drum Corps Internat.; mil: USAF 1968-72. Democrat; rec: travel, drum & bugle corps competitions. Res: 25 15th Pl #704 Long Beach 90802 Ofc: Aldrich & Assoc., Inc. 110 Pine Ave Ste 510 Long Beach 90802

ALDRICH, MICHAEL RAY, educator, librarian, historian; b. Feb. 7, 1942, Vermillion, S.D.; s. Ray J. and Lucile W. (Hamm) A.; m. Michelle Cauble, Dec. 26, 1977; edn: AB, Princeton, 1964; MA, Univ. So. Dak., 1965; PhD, St. Univ. N.Y., Buffalo 1970. Career: Fulbright tutor Govt. Arts and Commerce Coll., Indore, Madhya Pradesh, India 1965-66; founder Lemar Internat., 1966-71; faculty Sch. Critical Studies, Calif. Inst. Arts, Valencia 1970-72; workshop leader Esalen Inst., San Francisco 1972; co-director AMORPHIA, Inc. (non-profit nat. marijuana res. gp.), Mill Valley 1969-74; curator Fitz Hugh Ludlow Memorial Library, San Francisco 1974-; program coord. Youth Environment Study, AIDS Outreach Tng. Ctr., S.F. 1989-90; program coord. Calif. AIDS Intervention Tng. Ctr., 1990-; freelance writer, photographer, lectr., expert witness, cons. on drug research (splst. in drug laws, hist. & literature) colls., confs., publishers, service groups; author: The Dope Chronicles 1850-1950 (1979),Coricancha, The Golden Enclosure 1983; co-author: High Times Ency. of Recreational Drugs 1978, Fiscal Costs of Calif. Marijuana Law Enforcement 1986, Methods of Estimating Needle Users at Risk for AIDS 1989; editor drug edn. books, ed. Marijuana Rev. 1968-74, Ludlow Library Newsletter 1974-, mem. editorial rev. bd. Jour. Psychoactive Drugs (1981-, editor Marijuana theme issue 1987), contbr. Cocaine Handbook 1981, contbg. ed. High Times 1979-86, research photogr. Life mag. 1984; mem. advy. bd. Nat. Orgn. for Reform of Marijuana Laws 1976-; mem. Princeton Univ. Working Group on Future Drug Policy 1990-; past mem. bd. dirs. Calif. Marijuana Initiative 1971-74, Ethnopharmacology Soc. 1976-84; NIDA grantee for AIDS research 1987-88. Ofc: Ludlow Library, POB 640346 San Francisco 94164

ALEKSICH, STEVEN, engineer; b. Apr. 7, 1920, Peoria, Ill.; s. Zivan and Matilda (Boda) A.; edn: BSME, Bradley Univ. 1955; Reg. Profl. Engr., Calif. Career: airframe design engr./ standards engr., North Am. Aviation Inc., Downey 1955-60; mem. tech. staff Apollo/Saturn, Rockwell Corp. 1960-68; components engr. Lockheed Aircraft, Burbank 1968-70; components engr. Litton Systems, Inc. Van Nuys/ Woodland Hills 1970-73; mem. tech. staff, project engr. Space Shuttle, Rockwell Internat., Downey 1974-75; standards engr. Kirk Mayer Inc. (job shop) TRW, Redondo Beach 1975-76; senior prodn. design engr. Northrop Corp., Hawthorne 1976-87; sr. engr./scientist McDonnell Douglas Corp., Long Beach 1988-90; mem. US Marine Raider Assn. (v.p. bd. dirs.); mil: cpl. USMC 1942-45; Eastern Orthodox; rec: design, make and play tamburas (stringed musical instruments of Serbian origin similar to mandolins and guitars). Res: 8227 Arrington Ave Pico Rivera 90660

ALEN, RUPERT O., structural engineer; b. June 8, 1915, Kingsburg; s. Olaf and Julia Adelina (Nystrom) A.; m. Virginia Sandell (div. 1967); children: Helen b. 1942, James b. 1944; m. Eleanor Simon (div. 1981); son, Erich b. 1969; edn: BS, UC Berkeley 1937; MS, 1939. Career: sr. engring. aide Caltrans, Eureka 1937-38; jr. engr. Corps of Engrs., Los Angeles 1939-42; Concrete Ship Constrn., National City 1942-43; materials testing engr. Lockheed Aircraft, Burbank 1943-46; structural engr. Hillman & Nowell, Los Angeles; K. Bardizbanian, Beverly Hills 1947-50; St. Div. of Arch., Sacto. 1950-53; Earl Taylor Architects 1954-56; LeRoy F. Green Assoc. 1956-76; City of Oxnard 1976-83; R.O. Alen Cons. Engrs. 1983-; mem: Toastmasters (club pres. 1969, 72, 90), Calif. Farm Bureau (chapt. pres. 1964); author: History of My Family 1988; mil: seaman 1c. USN 1945-46; Republican; American Presbyterian; rec: photog., commodity trading, travel. Res: 1301 Glenwood Dr Oxnard 93030 Ofc: 995 W 7th St Oxnard 93030

ALEREZA, TAGHI, engineering and economics research company president; b. Aug. 24, 1943, Meshed, Iran, nat. 1979; s. Hossain and Zahra (Attaran) A.; m. Lillie Mojan, Sept. 2, 1986; children: Alexander, Nicholas; edn: BME, Auburn Univ., Ala. 1969; MSME, and PhD, George Washington Univ., 1972, 1977; reg. profl. engr. Career: design engr. Hydrasearch, Inc. Annapolis, Md. 1969-72; program mgr. Hiltman Assocs., Inc., Columbia, Md. 1972-79; pres. ADM Associates, Inc., Sacramento, Calif. 1979-; honors: Pi Tau Sigma 1968; mem. Internat. Building Performance Simulation Assn. (bd. dirs. 1988-), Am. Soc. Htg., Refr. & Air Condtg. Engrs. (subcom. chmn. 1985-); publs: 30+ tech. papers. Res: 5105 N Ravina Ln Fair Oaks 95628 Ofc: ADM Associates, Inc. 3299 Ramos Circle Sacramento 95827

ALEXANDER, GEORGE JONATHON, law professor, author; b. Mar. 8, 1931; married, 2 children; edn: AB (cum laude, Naval Scholar), Coll. of Univ. of Pa., 1953; JD (cum laude, Law Board Scholar), Univ. of Pa. Sch. of Law, 1959; LLM and JSD (Sterling Fellow), Yale Law Sch., 1965, 1969; admitted bar: Calif., Ill., N.Y., Supreme Ct. of U.S. and var. Fed. Cts. Career: instr. in law and Bigelow tchg. fellow Univ. Chgo. Law Sch. 1959-60; prof. of law, assoc. dean (2 yrs.) Syracuse Univ. Coll. of Law 1960-70; prof. of law Santa Clara Univ. Sch. of Law 1970-, dean of law 1970-85, dir. Inst. Internat. and Comparative Law 1986-; vis. scholar Stanford Law Sch. (1985-86, 92); pvt. law practice in antitrust, trade secrets and other trade regulations, civil liberties, problems of aging and invol. commitment; judge pro tem Santa Clara Co. Municipal Ct. 1979-; cons. on ednl. pgms., panelist Comptroller General's Resrch. and Edn. Adv. Panel (R.E.A.P.), 1977-; frequent lectr. univs. and bar assn. and med. assn. confs.; awards: Order of Coif 1968, Justinian Hon. Soc. 1970, Am. Inst. for Pub. Service finalist Nat. Jefferson Award for Gt. Pub. Service Benefiting Disadvantaged 1984, Edwin J. Owens Lawyer of Yr. Award 1985; mem: Soc. of Am. Law Tchrs. (bd. govs. 1974-, exec. com. 1975-80, pres. 1980-82), Nat. Senior Citizens Law Ctr. (bd. govs. 1983-90, exec. com. 1983-89, pres. 1986-89), Am. Bar Assn. (chair com. on legal problems of the aged 1969-83, chair subcom. on discrimination 1979-83), Assn. of Am. Law Schs. Sect. on Aging and the Law (founding mem., exec. com. 1985-, chair 1989-90), Calif. Bar Assn. (CEB advy. com. 1970-85, com. on law sch. edn. 1970-85, exec. com. sect. on legal svs. and chair com. on legal problems of aging 1976-79), N.Y. Civil Liberties Union (bd. 1962-70, v.ch. 1964-69), Specialized Suport Svs. (bd. 1984-87), Internat. Assn. for Adv. Tchg. and Resrch. in Intellectual Property 1982-, Internat. Assn. Constnl. Law 1983-, Internat. Fedn. of Aero. & Astro./ Internat. Inst. of Space Law (Life 1968-), Assn. of the U.S. (dir. and mem. 1970-83), Internat. Inst. of Human Rights 1984-, Internat. Commn. for Human Rights, London (hon. mem. advy. com. 1972-), Am. Assn. for Abolition of Involuntary Mental Hospitalization (co-founder, bd. ch. 1970-79); mil: ofcr. USN 1953-56, Reserve 1956-64; author book chapters in numerous law books, 11+ law books 1960-, incl. Honesty and Competition: False Advtg. Law and Policy Under FTC Adminstrn. (Syracuse Press, 1967, transl. into Mandarin 1987), Writing a Living Will: Using a Durable Power-of-Atty. (Praeger Press 1988); Internat. Perspectives on Aging (Nijhof Press 1992, editor), The Right to Be Responsible (unpub.). Res: 11600 Summit Wood Los Altos Hills 94022

ALEXANDER, HENRY ALAN, university vice president and dean, philosopher; b. Aug. 24, 1953, Berkeley; s. Ernest and Frances Evelyn (Conolley) A.; m. Shelley Tornheim, Aug. 24, 1975; children: Aliza b. 1979, Yonina b. 1982, Yehuda b. 1985; edn: AB philosophy (summa cum laude, highest dept. hons., Phi Beta Kappa) UCLA, 1976; BA, and B.Lit rabbinics, Univ. of Judaism, 1977; Rabbi, MA Judaic studies, Jewish Theol. Sem. of Am., 1982; EdS evaluation studies, Stanford Univ., 1982, PhD edn. and humanities 1985. Career: tchg. asst. Stanford Univ. 1979-80, also res. asst. San Jose Tchr. Corps Proj.; preceptor in edn., dir. of leadership devel. Jewish Theol. Sem. of Am., 1980-82; instr., asst. prof., asso. prof. of philosophy and edn. Univ. of Judaism, 1983-, dean, 1990-, and v.p. of academic affairs 1992-, also adminstr., bd. dirs. Lee Coll. (undergrad. sch.) 1984-89, dean 1989-; vis. lectr. UCLA Sch. of Edn., 1989-, Hebrew Univ. of Jerusalem 1982-83; author num. book chpts., essays and jour. articles; Jewish, Conservative. Ofc: University of Judaism 15600 Mulholland Dr Los Angeles 90077

ALEXANDER, JOHN DAVID, college president emeritus; b. Oct. 18, 1932, Springfield, Tenn.; m. Catharine Coleman, 1956; children: Kitty, John, Julia; edn: BS, Southwestern at Memphis, 1953; postgrad., Louisville Presbyterian Theol. Sem. 1953-54; PhD, Oxford Univ. 1957. Career: instr., asst. prof., assoc. prof. Old Testament, San Francisco Theol. Sem. 1957-65; pres. Southwestern at Memphis 1965-69; pres. Pomona Coll., Claremont 1969-91, president emeritus and Trustees Professor, 1991-; Am. Sec. Rhodes Scholarship Trust 1981-; bd. dirs., Am. Council on Edn. 1981-; Nat. Commn. on Acad. Tenure 1971-72, Panel of Gen. Profl. Edn. of the Physician, Assn. Am. Med. Colls. 1982-85; trustee, Tchrs. Ins. and Annuity Assn. 1970-; Woodrow Wilson Nat. Fellowship Found. 1978-, Webb Sch., Claremont 1970-72; dir. Great Western Fin. Corp. 1973-, British Inst. 1979-, Comm. Supported TV So. Calif., KCET, Inc. 1979-; bd. of overseers Huntington Library, Gardens and Art Gal., 1991-; trustee Seaver Inst., 1992-; bd. dirs., Louisville Presbyterian Theol. Sem. 1966-69; honors: Rhodes Scholar, Christ Ch. Coll., Oxford Univ. 1954; Hon. degrees: LLD, USC 1970, Occidental Coll. 1970, Centre Coll. of Kentucky 1971, LHD, Loyola Marymount Univ. 1984, LittD, Rhodes Coll. 1984; mem: Assn. Am. Colls. (commn. on liberal lng. 1967-69, chmn. commn. on instl. affairs 1970-73); So. Assn. Colls. and Schs. (exec. council of commn. on colls. 1969); Am. Council on Edn. (dir. 1981-); Am. Oriental Soc.; Soc. Bible Lit.; Soc. for Religion in Higher Edn.; Los Angeles C.of C. (dir. 1972-73); Phi Beta Kappa; Phi Beta Kappa Alumni So. Calif. (pres. Alpha Assn. 1974-76); Omicron Delta Kappa; Bohemian (San Francisco); Century Assn., NYC; Zamorano. Ofc: Pomona College, 333 College Way, Claremont 91711

ALEXANDER, KENNETH SIDNEY, mathematics educator; b. Mar. 3, 1958, Seattle; s. Stuart Murray and Elspeth (Dautoff) A.; m. Crystal Czarnecki, Aug. 21, 1982; children: Glenn b. 1992; edn: BS, Univ. Wash., 1979; PhD, M.I.T. 1982. Career: mem. Mathematical Scis. Resrch. Inst., Berkeley 1982-83; acting asst. prof. Univ. Wash., 1983-86; asst. prof. Univ. So. Calif., L.A. 1986-90, assoc. prof. 1990-; awards: Phi Beta Kappa 1979, Univ. Wash. Pres.'s Medal 1979; mem: Am. Math. Soc. 1988-, Inst. of Math. Stats. (fellow 1991); book

editor: Spatial Stochastic Processes (1991), contbr. numerous articles in profl. jours. 1982-; rec: flutist, photog. Ofc: Dept. Math. DRB 155 Univ. of So. Calif., Los Angeles 90089-1113

ALLAN, ROBERT MOFFAT, JR., executive, educator; b. Dec. 8, 1920, Detroit; s. Robert M. and Jane (Christman) A.; m. Harriet Spicer, Nov. 28, 1942; children: Robert M., III, Scott, David, Marilee; edn: BS, Stanford Univ., 1941; Stanford Grad. Sch., 1941-42; MS, UCLA, 1943; Loyola Law Sch., 1947-50. Career: economist res. dept. Security First Nat. Bank 1942; exec. Marine Insurance 1946-53; asst. to pres. Zinsco Elec. Prods. 1953-55, v.p., dir. 1956-59; asst. to pres. The Times-Mirror Corp., Los Angeles 1959-60, corporate v.p. 1961-64; pres., dir. Cyprus Mines Corp. 1964-67; pres. Litton Internat. 1967-69; pres. US Naval Postgraduate Sch. Found., prof. internat. mgmt., 1969-85; bd. dirs. US Naval Acad.; bd. trustees Monterey Inst. Fgn. Studies (senior fellow 1976), Pomona Grad. Sch., Claremont Grad. Sch., Boys Republic, Del Monte Forest Homeowners; awards: Helms Athletic Found. award (1947, 49), outstanding businessman of yr., L.A., Nat. Assn. Accts. 1966, Sailing Hall of Fame 1969, US Coast Guard Merit award, Medal for Heroism 1990, US Navy meritorious service award 1976; mem: Merchants and Mfrs. Assn. (bd.), Intercollegiate Yachting Assn., Phi Gamma Delta, Phi Delta Phi; mil: capt. US AAF, 1942-46, WWII; clubs: Newport Harbor Yacht (commodore 1962), Trans-Pacific Yacht, Carmel Valley Country. Res: 7026 Valley Greens Cir #11 Carmel 93923

ALLARD, JOHN BRERETON, II, chief of staff California State Legislature; b. Mar. 12, 1957, Turlock; s. John Brereton and Betty LaRue (Brown) A.; m. Lisa Ann Duvall, Aug. 23, 1986; edn: BA political sci. and history, CSU Sacramento 1984, Pi Sigma Alpha. Career: state field coordinator Carol Hallett for Lt. Gov. 1982; adminstrv. asst. Huckaby Marsh & Rodriguez Inc., Sacto. 1984-85; campaign coordinator All Santa Cruz Coalition 1985; legislative aide Calif. State Legislature 1985-86; campaign coordinator Tim Leslie for Assembly 1986-90, Tim Leslie for Senate 1991-; chief of staff Calif. State Legislature 1986-; awards: Outstanding Young Men of Am. (1985), Who's Who Among Am. H.S. Students (1974, 75); mem: Roseville C.of C. (v.p. 1991-, dir. 1989-, City Council/C.of C. Task Force, edn., exec. dir. search, fin., gov. rels., special events coms.), Roseville Community Health Found. (sec. 1991-, dir. 1989-, Comm. Partnerships, Hosp. Replacement Proj., nominating, public relations, special events coms.), South Placer Transportation Management Assn. (dir. 1991-, Gov. Rels. Com.), Am. Political Sci. Assn., CSU Alumni Assn., Comstock Club; Calif. Republican Party State Central Com.; Presbyterian; rec: camping, skiing (snow, water), gardening, photography. Address: Roseville 95747

ALLEN, DAVID HARLOW, logistician, educator; b. May 26, 1930, Lynn, Mass.; s. Donald H. Allen and Miriam Ellsworth (Harlow) Wilson; m. Roberta Arlene Miller, July 15, 1952; children: Donald b. 1954, Richard b. 1956, William b. 1958; edn: BGS in business, Univ. Omaha, 1967; MBA, NM Highlands Univ., 1978; Certified Profl. Logistician, Cert. Cost Estimator/Analyst. Career: served to lt. col. US Air Force 1948-78: team dir. of mat. Air Force Insp. & Safety Ctr., Norton AFB, Ca. 1969-72; asst. dep. comdr. for maint., squadron comdr. SAC Bomb Wing, Dyess AFB, Tx. 1972-74; dep. dir. of logistics AF Test & Evaluation Ctr., Kirtland AFB, NM 1974-78, ret., decorated merit. svc., bronze star, commendn. medals; systems analyst, project engr., ARINC Research, Santa Ana 1978-84; dep. program mgr. logistics & logistics project mgr. Northrop Corp., Newbury Park, CA 1984-91; indep. consultant, Thousand Oaks, Ca. 1991-; sr. lectr. West Coast Univ. Coll. of Bus. and Mgmt., L.A. 1988-, mem. acquisition & contract mgmt. curricula com. 1991-, Faculty Senate 1992-, past asst. dean WCU/ Ventura Co. Ctr., 1988-91; mem: Soc. Logistics Engrs. (1975-, chpt. chmn. 1988-90, com. chmn. So. Calif. Logistics Workshop and Conf. 1988-), Engrs. Week Com. Ventura -Santa Barbara Ctys. 1990, Configuration & Data Mgmt. Assn. 1989-, Soc. Cost Estimating & Anal. 1988-, Am. Mgmt. Assn. 1982-, Am. Security Council (nat. advy. bd. 1983-), Phi Kappa Phi 1978-; pub. articles in field (1954, 67, 75, 76); Republican; Prot.; rec: swimming, racquetball, golf, bowling. Res: 428 Moondance St Thousand Oaks 91360

ALLEN, JEFFREY MICHAEL, lawyer; b. Dec. 13, 1948, Chgo.; s. Albert A. and Miriam F. (Feldman) A.; m. Anne Marie Guaraglia, Aug. 9, 1975; children: Jason b. 1978, Sara b. 1980; edn: BA with great distinction, UC Berkeley, 1970, JD, Boalt Hall Law Sch., 1973; admitted bar: Calif. (1973), U.S. Supreme Ct., U.S. Ct. Appeals (9th cir.), U.S. Dist. Cts. (No., Cent., So., E. dists. Calif.); lic. real estate broker 1975. Career: ptnr. Graves, Allen, Cornelius & Celestre (and predecessor firms), Oakland 1973-; lectr. St. Mary's Coll., Moraga 1975-; spkr. numerous cont. legal edn. pgms. for Am. Bar Assn.; dir: various computer consulting corps., dir. var. real estate and related service corps.; judge pro tem Oakland Municipal Ct.; arbitrator Am. Arbitration Assn., Alameda County Superior Ct. Panel of Arbitrators; honors: Calif. Scholarship Fedn. (life), Varsity Forensics Team (state & nat. speech tournaments, 1st pl. USF invitational tournament 1965), Nat. Forensic League Student Senate (pres. 1966), recipient of Ford Grant Funds through the Ctr. for the Study of Law and Society 1965-66, Phi Beta Kappa 1970, Calif. State Scholar, Univ. Calif. Alumni Scholar 1966-69, staff/project editor Calif. Law Review 1971-73, staff Ecology Law Quarterly 1971-72; mem: Am. Bar Assn. (chair real prop. com., gen. practice sect. 1987-, v.chair 1985-87 & 92, program bd. 1991-93, advocacy coord. 1993-), State Bar of Calif., Alameda Co. Bar Assn., Am. Trial Lawyers Assn., Calif. Trial Lawyers Assn.; civic: Rotary (chmn. coms.), Commonwealth Club of Calif., Oakland C.of C., Family Service of the East Bay (pres. 1989-, 1st v.p. 1988-89, dir. 1987-), PTA/Oakland (sch. pres. 1986-88, treas. 84-86), mem. various advy. coms. Oakland Public Schs., Oakland Metropolitan Forum 1987-, Oakland Strategic Planning Com. 1988-89; contbr. articles on computers and litigators in var. law jours.; Democrat; rec: soccer coach (nat. "C" lic.) and USSF lic. referee: Bay Oaks Soccer Club (commr. 1988-), CNRA Dist. 4 Referee Administr. 1993-, Jack London Youth Soccer League (dir. 1988-), Calif. Youth Soccer Assn.- Dist. 4 (asst. dist. commr. 1990-93, mem. bd. dirs. 1990-, referee coord. 1993-), CYSA Dist. 4 Competitive League (pres. & mem. bd. dirs. 1990-93), secty., bd. dirs. CYSA 1993-;soccer, skiing, computers, family activities. Ofc: Graves Allen Cornelius & Celestre, 2101 Webster St Ste 1600 Oakland 94612

ALLEN, LINDA JEAN, licensed acupuncturist; b. May 26, 1952, San Francisco; d. Sol Cecil and Sarah Doris (Herring) Allen; edn: BA in social sci., Univ. of Tex., Austin 1974, MA in foreign lang. edn., 1978; M.T.O.M., Emperor's Coll. of Trad. Chinese Medicine, Santa Monica 1989; H.M.D., PhD, College of Homeopathy, Marina del Rey 1993; lic. acupuncturist State of Calif. Dept. of Consumer Affairs 1989; bd. certified naturopathic physician. Career: assoc. acupuncturist Bodymind Systems Med. Ctr., Santa Monica 1989-92; acupuncturist, self-employed, L.A. 1993-;guest speaker, Chinese med. & herbalism, KIEV 870 AM Radio; honors: Dean's List Emperor's Coll. of Trad. Chinese Medicine 1989; mem. Calif. Acupuncture Assn. 1989-, Nat. Commn. for Cert. of Acupuncturists (Diplomate in Acupuncture cert. #6250) 1990-, Am. Assn. of Acupuncture & Oriental Medicine 1991-, Calif. State Homeopathic Med. Soc. 1993-, Am. Naturopathic Med. Assn.; rec: traveling, gardening.

ALLEN, MELANIE, clinical and forensic psychologist, educator, writer, consultant; b. Dec. 8, 1939, Mpls.; d. Samuel David and Francis Marilyn (Fagen) Finkelstein; edn: Univ. of Minn. 1956-58; BA cinema, w/honors, UCLA, 1961; The Sorbonne-Paris, 1963-64; BA psych., CSU Northridge, 1969; PhD psych., USC, 1974. Career: prodn. asst. Ency. Britannica Films 1961-62; Fulbright Fellowship to Inst. de Filmologie, The Sorbonne, 1963-64 and appt. Bd. of Ed., Rives (Revue des echanges univs.); story dept. hd. and film writer for prod. Norman Lear, Tandem Prodns.,Columbia Pictures 1965-67; grad. tchg. fellowship USC 1969-72; NIMH fellowship/intern in clin. psych. 1972-73, HEW Maternal and Child Care postdoc. fellowship 1973-74, consulting psychologist 1974-79, Children's Hosp. of L.A.; instr. psych. and humanities divs. Art Center Coll. of Design 1973-77; guest lectr. Calif. Inst. of the Arts 1975-76; prof. psych. Antioch Coll./West 1973-79; pvt. practice clin. psychology specializing in family systems, pediatric and forensic psychology, therapy for members of entertainment industry, Sherman Oaks and Westlake Village, 1974-; asst. prof. CSU Northridge 1974-81; technical and creative cons. to film industry; lectr. various univs., hosps., schools, pub. agencies; mem. bd. of eds. Jour. of Humanistic Psychol. 1980-89; dir. grad. tng. pgm in psychol. Ryokan Coll. 1983-87; numerous guest appearances on radio and TV; author: Primary: An Intro. to Humanistic Psychology, w/ Charlotte Buhler (1972), Make em Laugh w/ Wm. Fry (1975), Old Macdonald Had a Farm: The American Dream on Trial (filmplay & book, in progress), 100+ short stories, poems and articles; honors: Chimes (acad. hon.), Tau Beta Sigma, Sigma Alpha Iota (music), Psi Chi (psych. frat.), Delmar Ickes Award CSU Northridge 1969, recogn. for theoretical achievements in psychology, invited guest Intl. Invitational Cong. on Humanistic Psychology (Amsterdam 1970, Wurzburg, Ger. 1971), Nat. Endowment for Humanities Conf. (Tucson 1975), 1st Internat. Cong. on Humour and Laughter (Wales 1976); rec: music, photography, videography, travel, criminology. Res: Sherman Oaks 91403-4215 Offices: Sherman Oaks and Westlake Village 91362

ALLEN, MICHAEL B., lawyer; b. Oct. 17, 1949, Columbus, Oh.; edn: BSME, Univ. of Pittsburgh, 1972; JD, San Mateo Law Sch., 1978; admitted bar: Calif. 1978, and U.S. Dist. Ct. no. dist. Calif. Career: in-house counsel Fluor Corp., 1978-80; ptnr. law firm Himmelheber & Allen, 1980-85; pres. of law corp., Burlingame 1985-92, Redwood City 1992-, special emphasis on real estate, constitution. matters, ins., bus. and bankruptcy; mem: Am. Bar Assn., San Mateo Co. Bar Assn., Lawyers Club of San Francisco, Assn. of Gen. Contrs. Ofc: 10 Twin Dolphin Dr Ste R-500 Redwood City 94065

ALLER, SONIA KONIALIAN, speech/language pathology supervisor; b. Sept. 10, 1944, Aleppo, Syria; nat. U.S. citizen 1976; d. Assadour Konialian and Yeghisapet Bezdikian; m. Wayne Kendall Aller, April 8, 1969; edn: BA, Beirut Coll. for Women (Lebanon) 1966; PhD, Indiana Univ. 1978; instr. Baakline High Sch., Lebanon 1966-67; asst. instr psychology Indiana Univ., Bloomington, Ind. 1969-74; research assoc. Center for Behavioral Research Am. Univ. of Beirut, Lebanon 1974-75; dept. chair, asst. prof. psychology St. Mary of the Woods Coll., Ind. 1982-83; speech pathologist II, USC Medical Ctr. 1983-87, acting chief speech pathology sect. 1987; supvr. speech/lang. pathology Children's Hosp. of Los Angeles 1987-; acting dir. of training in comm. disorders, Univ. of So. Calif. Affiliated Program; v.p. Learning Unltd., Studio City 1983-; grants: Ford Foundation grant, 1974-75, Nat. Sci. Foundation grant,

1979-81, Nat. Endowment for the Humanities grant, 1982; mem: Am. Speech Language & Hearing Assn., Calif. Speech & Hearing Assn., Assn. for Women in Sci., Calif. Neuropsychological Soc., Computer Users in Speech & Hearing, Sigma Xi; co-author book chapt. (pub. 1979); rec: swimming, classical music. Res: 17745 Stagg St Reseda 91335 Ofc: Childrens Hospital of Los Angeles 4650 Sunset Blvd Los Angeles 90027

ALLISON, LAIRD BURL, professor emeritus of management; b. Nov. 7, 1917, Saint Marys, W. Va.; s. Joseph Alexander and Opal Marie (Robinson) A.; m. Katherine Hunt, Nov. 25, 1943; 1 son, William, b. 1945; m. 2d. Genevieve Elmore, Feb. 1, 1957; edn: BS in personnel and indsl. rels., magna cum laude, USC 1956; MBA, UCLA 1958. Career: lectr., asst./assoc./ prof. of mgmt., CSU Los Angeles 1956-83, asst. dean undergrad. studies, Sch. of Business and Econ. 1971-73, and assoc. dean ops., 1973-83; prof. emeritus of mgmt., CSULA; vis. asst. prof. of mgmt. CSU Fullerton, summer 1970; collaborated in devel. of new degree program, BS Mgmt. Sci., CSULA 1963; honors: Phi Kappa Phi, Beta Gamma Sigma, Omicron Delta Epsilon, Phi Eta Sigma, Ford Found. Faculty Fellow (1960); mem: Acad. of Mgmt., Alpha Kappa Psi Profl. Bus. Frat., Am. Assn. of Individual Investors, The Am. Acad. of Polit. and Social Sci., The Inst. of Mgmt. Scis. (TIMS), Western Econ. Assn. Internat., World Future Soc., Am. Assn. Retired Persons, Faculty Emeriti Assn. CSULA (v.p. programs 1986-87, v.p. adminstrn. 1987-88, pres. 1988-89, exec. com. 1990-91, treas. 1991-93), Calif. State Univ. Assn. of Emeriti Profs., Ret. Public Employees Assn. of Calif. (chpt. pres. 1990-92), U.S. Naval Inst., The Navy League of U.S., American Legion, USS Astoria Assn; mil: chief interior communications electrician, USN, 1936-51, decorated Am. Def., Am. Theatre, Asia-Pacific Theatre, WWII Victory, Good Conduct, battles: Coral Sea, Midway, Guadalcanal, Savo.; survivor of sinking of USS Astoria (CA 34) in Battle of Savo. Rec: history, travel, photog., hiking. Res: 2176 E Bellbrook St Covina 91724

ALMQUIST, HERMAN JAMES, biochemist, co-discoverer vitamin K; b. March 3, 1903, Helena, Mont.; s. Harry and Marie (Ericson) A.; m. Viola Dorothy Pimentel, Oct. 7, 1935; children: Alan b. 1944, Eric b. 1947; edn: BS, Mont. St. Univ. 1925; PhD, UC Berkeley 1932. Career: instr., asst. prof., assoc. prof. UC Berkeley 1932-44; dir. res. F.E. Booth Co., San Francisco 1944-48; dir. res., v.p. The Grange Co., Modesto 1948-68; dir. Annual Reviews Inc., Palo Alto 1942-70; researcher in field of nutrition, co-discoverer Vitamin K, and its isolation, identification and synthesis; author numerous book chapters, 185+ sci. articles; honors: Sigma Xi, Phi Kappa Phi, Mont. St. Univ. Hon. D.Sc. 1952, Borden Co. award 1939, St. of Calif. Legislature Citation 1967; mem: Am. Inst. Nutrition (fellow), Poultry Science Assn. (fellow), AAAS (fellow), Masons, Alpha Chi Sigma; mil: 1st lt. Mont. Nat. Guard 1927-30; Republican; rec: woodworking, philately. Res: 5231 Mississippi Bar Dr Orangevale 95662

ALOIA, ROLAND C., scientist, educator; b. Dec. 21, 1943, Newark, N.J.; s. Roland S. and Edna (Mahan) A.; m. Kathryn A. Platt, June 15, 1974; edn: BS, St. Marys Coll. 1965; PhD, UC Riverside 1970; postdoctoral, City of Hope 1975. Career: research biologist UC Riverside 1975-76; asst. prof. Loma Linda Univ. Sch. of Medicine 1976-79, assoc. prof. 1979-89, prof. anesthesia 1989-; res. chemist J.L. Pettis Vets. Hosp. 1979-; pres. Cancer Hibernation Res. Found., San Bernardino 1988-; Loma Linda Vets. Assn. for Research & Edn. 1988-; awards: UC Riverside NIH predoctoral scholarship 1969-70, Calif. Heart Assn. postdoctoral fellowship 1971-74, Outstanding Service 1983-85; mem: Sigma Xi, AAAS, Am. Oil Chemists Soc., N.Y. Acad. Sci., Am. Soc. for Cell Biology, Calif. Heart Assn. (v.p. 1983-85, pres. 1980-81, 1984-86, v.p. 1979-80, 1982-84); ed. Membrane Fluidity in Biology, vols. 1 & 2 (1983), vols. 3 & 4 (1985 w/J.M. Boggs), sr. series ed. Advances in Membrane Fluidity, vols. 1-3 (1988), vol. 4 (1990); rec: flying, jogging, marksmanship. Ofc: Anesthesia Service Pettis VA Hospital 11201 Benton St Loma Linda 92357

ALONZO, GREGORY, professional speaker and sales trainer; b. Apr. 9, 1954, San Bernardino; s. Rudy and Remi (Vicente) A.; m. Joanne Beth Reitz, June 18, 1992; edn: BA in internat. relations, Pitzer Coll., Claremont 1980. Career: sales mgr. CBS Advertising, Santa Barbara 1980-87; v.p. sales PacTel, Irvine 1987-90; profl. speaker Success Unlimited, Brea 1990-; mem: Profl. Speakers Network (Orange County chapt. pres. 1992-93), Nat. Speakers Assn., Toastmasters Internat. (speakers bur. chair 1991-92, TM of Yr. Orange Co. 1991-92), Speaker of the Year 1992; author tape series "Attitude Selling" (1991), "Paths to Power" (1992), pub. articles, profl. speakers network tapes "Unlimited Success" (1993); mil: E5, sgt. USMC 1972-76; Democrat; R.Cath.; rec: collecting art. Ofc: R. Gregory Alonzo Unlimited 101 W Central Ave Ste B111 Brea 92621

AL-QAZZAR, AYAD, educator; b. Aug. 23, 1941, Baghdad, Iraq, U.S. citizen; s. Ali and Sharafa (Ahmad) Al-Q.; 1 child, Mayad b. 1964; edn: BA, Univ. Baghdad, 1963; BA, UC Berkeley, 1966, PhD, 1969. Career: asst. prof. CSU Sacramento, 1969-75, assoc. prof. 1975-81, prof. 1981-; vis. prof. Univ. Calif. Berkeley 1970-, Qatar Univ., Doha-Qatar, 1981; awards: Univ. of Calif. Award, UCB (1966-68), Meritorious award CSU Sacto. 1986; mem: AAUG, World Affairs Council, Mensa, ASA, Comstock Club; author: Women in the Middle East (1979), The Arab World (1978), The Arab American Community (1978),

The Arabs World Note Book (1989); Indep.; Islam; rec: tennis, walking, swimming. Res: 3501 Dutch Way Carmichael CA 95608 Ofc: California State Univ., 6000 J St Sacramento CA 95819

ALTER, GERALD L., business executive; b. Aug. 24, 1910, Rensselaer, Ind.; s. Leslie and Lettie (Willis) A.; m. Margaret A. Davis, Sept. 15, 1939; children: Judith Ann (dec.), John Edward; edn: Business Coll. 1927-28. Career: clk. and office mgr., 1929-35; bldg. contractor, 1936-45; real estate broker and insurance agt., 1946-; pres. Alter Realty & Ins., Leads, Inc., investments, Alter Ins. Agcy., Inc., REMCO Real Estate Mgmt. Co., Alter Devel. Co.; pres. Developers & Builders; mem: Torrance-Lomita-Carson Board Realtors (pres. 1978, v.p. 1980-81), Calif. Assn. Realtors (dir. 1978-81), Nat. Assn. Realtors, Torrance C.of C. (past dir.), Am. Legion, OX-5 (pioneer airmen org.), Rotary; civic: Torrance Police Reserves (1946-62), City of Torrance Planning Commn. (commr. 1966-82, chmn. 1982-83), Torrance Water Commn. (1984-92, chmn. 87-88), Harbor Area United Way (past bd.). Res: 1337 Engracia Ave Torrance 90501 Ofc: 2305 Torrance Blvd Torrance 90501

ALTSHILLER, ARTHUR LEONARD, physics teacher; b. Aug. 12, 1942, N.Y.C.; s. Samuel Martin and Betty Rose (Lepson) A.; m. Gloria Silvern, Nov. 25, 1970 (div. 1975); m. Carol Heiser, Aug. 16, 1980; edn: BS physics, Univ. Okla., 1963; MS physics, CSU Northridge, 1971. Career: electronics engr. Garrett Corp., Torrance 1963-64, Volt Tech. Corp., Phoenix, Az. 1965, Aerojet Gen. Corp., Azusa, Calif. 1966-68, Magnavox Rsch. Labs., Torrance 1968-69; senior engr. Litton Guidance & Control, Canoga Park 1969; physics tchr. Van Nuys High Sch. (L.A. Unified Sch. Dist.), Van Nuys, 1971-; math. instr., eve., Los Angeles Valley Coll., 1986-; awards: Cert. of Honor Westinghouse Science Talent Search 1990, listed Who's Who in Am. Edn. 1992-93, Who's Who Am. Tchrs. 1992-93, Who's Who in West 1992-93; mem: Am. Assn. of Physics Tchrs. (So. Calif. sect. 1971-), Am. Assn. of Sci. 1985-, Nat. Council of Math Tchrs. 1985-, Santa Monica Astronomical Soc. 1991-; So. Calif. region meeting presentations on teaching concepts & demonstrns. in physics edn., AAPT 1971-; Democrat; Jewish; rec: tennis, chess, table tennis, cycling, swimming. Res: 6776 Vickiview Dr West Hills 91307 Ofc: Van Nuys High School 6535 Cedros Ave Van Nuys 91411

AMELIO, GILBERT FRANK, electronics company executive; b. Mar. 1, 1943, N.Y., NY; s. Anthony and Elizabeth (DeAngelis) A.; m. Glenda Charlene; children: Anthony Todd, Tracy Elizabeth, Andrew Ryan; edn: BS, MS, and PhD in Physics, Georgia Inst. Tech., 1965, 1967, 1968. Career: mem. tech. staff Bell Tel. Labs, Murray Hill, N.J. 1968-71; v.p./gen. mgr. Fairchild, Mtn. View, Ca. 1971-83; pres. Semi. Products Div., Rockwell Internat., Newport Beach 1983-88, pres. Comms. Systems Div., 1988-91; pres. and c.e.o. Nat. Semiconductor, Santa Clara 1991-; dir., nat. advy. bd. Georgia Inst. Tech. 1981-87, mem. c.e.o. roundtable UC Irvine 1985-89; recipient Masaru Ibuka Consumer Electronics Award, IEEE (1991); mem: Semiconductor Ind. Assn. (dir. 1983-, chmn. 1993-), IEEE (Fellow, 1974-81); holder 16 patents; Republican; R.Cath. Ofc: National Semiconductor 2900 Semiconductor Dr MS 16-100 Santa Clara 95052-8090

AMORES, PATRICIO ESTUARDO, rehabilitation counselor; b. Mar. 29, 1950, Quito, Ecuador, S.A.; s. Joel and Eulalia (Bravo) Amores; m. Maguadalupe Sanchez, Aug. 16, 1989; 1 dau., Maria Teresa; edn: BA and BS, San Diego State Univ., 1979. Career: adminstrv. analyst City of San Diego, 1980-82; adminstrv. asst. San Diego Community Colls., 1982-83, placement dir. Rutledge Coll., 1982-84; revenue ofcr. IRS, San Diego 1984-86; counselor Bravo Rehabilitation, San Diego 1986-; instr. Basic Edn., S.D. Comm. Coll. 1986-88; mem: Personnel Mgmt. Assn. Aztlan (pres. 1983-84), Organizational Rehab Assn. (pres. 1988-89); Republican; R.Cath.; rec: soccer, TWA-Khow-Do. Res: 4818 54th St San Diego 92115 Ofc: Bravo Rehab PO Box 15824 San Diego 92175

ANAND, SATYA PAUL, clinical chemist/diagnostic company president; b. Sept. 10, 1942, Jammu, India; s. Ladha Ram and Lajwanti (Devi) A.; m. Santosh Rani, May 6, 1947; children: Anu b. 1969, Atul b. 1971, Ajay b. 1973; edn: BS, G.M.Sc. Coll., 1963; MS, Univ. of Jammu, 1965; PhD, Univ. of New Delhi, 1972; post-doc.Univ. of Ga. 1973-74. Career: asst. prof. chem. Govt. Coll. Bhadarwah, 1965-68; assoc. prof. chem. Reg. Engg. Coll., Srinagar, Kashmir 1971-73; asst. prof. CSU Los Angeles 1975-76; res. assoc. Argonne Nat. Lab., Univ. Chgo., Ill. 1974-76; lab. training UC Irvine Med. Ctr., Calif. 1976-78; hosp. cons. L.A. and Orange, 1977-79; tech. Dir. Physicians Reference Lab. Huntington Beach 1979-81; Dir. RIA Referral Lab., La Mirada 1981-83; dir./CEO BioDiagnostic Internat., La Habra, Walnut 1983-; awards: merit scholar G.M.Sc. Coll. Jammu (1961-65, res. fellow Univ. of New Delhi 1968-71, merit UCI Med. Ctr. UC 1976-77, honor cert. BioDiag. Internat. (1985, 87, 89); mem: Am. Assn. Clin. Chem., Am. Chem. Soc., Nat. Geography; inventor, developer Lioui Sera Products 1982-, Lioui Ura Products 1985-87; Vedanta; Spiritualism; rec: yoga, walking, philanthropy, philosophy, ranch animals. Res: 2500 Alamo Hts Dr Diamond Bar 91765 Ofc: Bio Diagnostic International 150 Commerce Way Walnut 91789

ANANIA, PATRICIA ZAJESKI, real estate broker; b. Dec. 17, 1951, Chgo.; d. Daniel Myron and Jessie (Hibma) Zajeski; div.; edn: student, Northwestern Univ. 1970-72, 92-; De Anza Coll. 1977-79; lic. Real Estate Broker. Career: sales rep. Ponderosa Homes, Pleasanton 1978-86; broker/prin. 1986-91, specialist new residential home sales Associates + Anania, Dir. of Sales and Mktg. Mission Peak Development Co., Fremont; awards: Sales and Mktg. Council Sales Achiev. (1979-86, 90-91), SMC MAME Merit Award 1991, Dean's List and Hon. Scholastic Soc. Northwestern Univ. 1971-72; mem: Building Industry Assn., Sales and Mktg. Council, Fremont C.of C. (bd. dir. 1991, govtl. affairs com.); Rosicrucian Order, A.M.O.R.C.; rec: swimming, reading, designing. Address: Fremont 94538

ANARGYROS, NEDRA F. HARRISON, model, entertainer, retired cytologist; b. Dec. 3, 1915, NY, NY; d. Leverette Roland and Florence Martha (Pickard) Harrison; grandmother Florence Willingham Pickard, author, painter; m. Spero Drosos Anargyros, Oct. 21, 1940 (div. 1969); edn: att. pub. schs. Delray Beach, Fla., grad. Tifton (Ga.) H.S., att. Emerson Coll. Boston 1934-36, UC San Francisco 1957. Career: Power's model 1938; original model for The Dragon Lady of Milton Caniff's Terry & the Pirates 1939; posed for Salvador Dali for his painting "Madonna of the Sea;" rode the Quadrille on horseback for first year of the N.Y. World Fair in Wild West & Rodeo; small role in Albert Johnson's The American Jubilee 1939-40; lic. student pilot Tifton, Ga. 1941, grad. pilot tng. pgm. Avenger Field, Sweetwater, Tex. 1942; supr. cytology lab UCSF/San Francisco Gen. Hosp., ret. 1988; mem: Am. Soc. Clin. Pathologists (affil.), Am. Soc. Cytotechnology (affil.), Women Flyers of Am., DAR (nat. 1st v. regent 1970), DAR of S.F./La Puerta de Oro chpt. (regent 1990), Colonial Dames of Am., Huguenot Soc. of Calif., UDC, Phi Mu Gamma, Pres.'s Club of Mercer Univ. (Macon, Ga.), Who's Who of Amer. Women, Who's Who In The West; Republican; Christian Science; rec: travel, scuba (cert. 1972). Res: The Sequoias, 1400 Geary Blvd Studio Apt 5-N San Francisco 94109 and 2503 Clay St San Francisco 94115

ANASTASIOU, MARY M., pediatrician; b. June 11, 1954, England (nat. 1983); d. Thalis M. and Elli (Nicolopoulou) Michaelides; m. Stephen Anastasiou, Jan. 4, 1980; children: Alex b. 1981, Christine b. 1987; edn: MD, Univ. Athens Med. Sch. Greece 1979. Career: intern, resident, chief resident Kaiser Hosp., Oakland 1982-85; pvt. practice pediatrics, Pleasanton 1985-; mem: AMA, ACCMA; Christian; rec: swimming, tennis. Res: 3501 Kamp Dr Pleasanton 94588 Ofc: 5565 W Las Positas Blvd Ste 240 Pleasanton 94588

ANDARMANI, ANDY, food scientist/consultant/lecturer; b. June 1, 1933, Teheran, Iran, came to U.S. 1955, naturalized 1970; s. Sadrollah and Batool (Sarraf) A.; m. Susan Dee Blanton, Nov. 7, 1964; dau. Kristine Aryana b. 1973; edn: BS in agric. (pomology/fruit sci.), Calif. Polytechnic St. Univ., San Luis Obispo 1960, MA agric. edn., 1963. Career: quality control lab. techn. Contadina Foods Inc., San Jose, Calif. (under supvn. of USDA) summers 1960, 62, 63; advisor in agricultural edn. Ministry of Edn., Teheran, Iran 1961; chief chemist Crown By-Products Co., San Jose 1963-66; res., tech. asst. Sunsweet Growers Inc., San Jose 1967-69, chief chemist in chg. res. lab. 1969-74 (devel. new tenderness testing instrument for quality control and new lab. test procedure for estimating juice yield from prunes, 1970, 74, devel. new methods for processing prunes and apricots to better preserve natural quality and extend shelf-life 1971, 72), mgr. product R&D 1974-75; mgr. dried fruit research Diamond/Sunsweet Inc., Stockton (following merger of Sunsweet and Diamond Walnut Growers, Inc., another Calif. grower co-op.) 1975-77; prin. Andy Andarmani Consulting Svs., Cupertino 1978-, cons., lectr. in fruit and beverage technology; mem: Cal Poly Alumni Assn., Inst. of Food Technologists (Nat. and No. Calif. chpt. 1968-), Soc. of Wine Educators (Nat. and No. Calif. chpt. 1990-), The Monterey Wine Festival Monks Club 1987-, Nat. Geographic Soc. (1964-66, 1973-), AARP 1992-, Am. Oil Chemists' Soc. 1964-67, Dried Fruit Assn. of Calif. (sci. advy. com. 1969-77), Calif. Prune Advy. Board (dried fruit and tree nuts industry res. com. 1969-77), Calif. Raisin Advy. Board (stored products coord. com. 1971-73); past mem. Cal Poly S.L.O. clubs: Crop Sci., Internat. Rels., Iranian Students Assn. (founder, v.p. 1959-60), Radio Sta. KATY (panel discussion mem. 1959-60); author: ABC's of Fruit Handling (plant ops. reference guide 1974); contbg. author (first reference book and first coll. text in field) Ency. of Food Tech. (1974), Elements of Food Technology (1977), (AVI Pub. Co., Inc. Westport, Conn.); Democrat; rec: hiking, swimming, photography, travel, classical music, internat. issues re world peace, trade, environment, food supply, human rights, nutrition and health. Ofc: Andy Andarmani Consulting Services, PO Box 148 Cupertino 95015

ANDERBERG, ROY ANTHONY, journalist; b. Mar. 30, 1921, Camden, N.J.; s. Arthur R. and Mary V. (McHugh) A.; m. Louise M. Brooks, Feb. 5, 1953; children: Roy, Mary; edn: AA, Diablo Valley Coll., 1975. Career: enlisted U.S. Navy, 1942, commd. officer, final 1946; waterfront columnist Pacific Daily News, Agana, Guam 1966-67; public relations officer Naval Forces, Mariana Islands, 1967; travel editor Contra Costa Times, Calif. 1968-69; entertainment and restaurant editor Concord Transcript, 1971-75; dining editor Rossmoor News, Walnut Creek, 1977-78; free-lance non-fiction journalist, 1976-; mem: U.S. Power Squadron, DAV, Ret. Officers Assn., American Legion, V.F.W.,

U.S. Submarine Vets. WWII Assn.; clubs: Martinez Yacht, Treasure Island Yacht, Rossmoor Yacht, Toastmasters. Democrat. Res: 1840 Tice Creek Dr #2228, Walnut Creek 94595 Ofc: PO Box 52 Concord 94522

ANDERSON, ANTHONY EDWARD, university librarian; b. Apr. 2, 1952, Pasadena; s. Herbert Raymond and Eugenia Caroline (Moore) A.; edn: AA, Pasadena City Coll., 1972; BA in Eng. lit./theater arts, Occidental Coll., 1974; MSLS, USC Sch. of Library and Information Mgmt., 1977, BA Slavic languages and literatures, USC, 1981. Career: librarian Jet Propulsion Lab., Pasadena 1983-85; librarian Univ. of So. Calif., 1981, 1985-; mem: Am. Lib. Assn., Calif. Acad. and Res. Librarians Assn., Edward Elgar Soc.; civic: Pasa. Sister Cities Com. (gen. chair 1986-), Friends of Pasa. Pub. Libs. (v.p. 1989-), People to People L.A. Co. chpt. (sec. 1986-87), mem. Pasa. Strategic Planning Com. 1984-86; Democrat; Episcopalian; rec: running, swimming, internat. relations, fgn. languages. Res: 1956 Woodlyn Rd Pasadena 91104-3244 Ofc: Von KleinSmid Library, USC, Los Angeles 90089-0182

ANDERSON, BRADFORD WILLIAM, food manufacturing company sales executive; b. Feb. 17, 1956, Redlands; s. B. W. and Helen Louise (Wisel) A.; m. Diane Hutt, Aug. 21, 1981; children: David B.; edn: BS mgmt., Univ. Redlands, 1978; MBA, CSU San Bernardino, 1982. Career: store mgr. Finger's Market, Redlands 1974-79; territory mgr., sr. terr. mgr./tnr. Carnation Co., Fullerton 1980-83, dist. sales coord. 1983-85, nat. mgr. sales planning Carnation Co., L.A. 1985-91, nat. mgr. & sales technology Nestle, Glendale, 1991-; instr. Chaffey Coll., 1985-; awards: Harris Memorial Scholar, Harris' Dept. Store, Redlands 1975, Pat Patterson Mem. Award, Santa Fe Fed. Savings, Redlands 1975, Outstanding Young Men in Am., Jaycees (1984, 87), listed Who's Who in West (1988, 90, 92), Who's Who in World 1992, Men of Achievement 1988, other biog. references; mem: Univ. Redlands Alumni Assn., Alpha Gamma Nu Alumni, CSUSB Alumni Assn., Inland Counties Food Industry Sales Club; civic: L.A. Zoo Support Group, Friends of Santa Ana Zoo, Muchenthaler Theater 1987-, Diamond Bar Ranch Festival, Diamond Bar Improvement Assn., Redlands Jaycees, trustee Diamond Bar Congregational Ch., Diamond Bar Children's Ctr. Parent's Aux.; publ: article in field, 1987; Republican; United Ch. of Christ; rec: skiing, racquetball, travel. Res: 24442 Rosegate Pl Diamond Bar 91765 Ofc: Nestle Food Co. 800 N Brand Blvd Ste 19 Glendale CA 91203

ANDERSON, DAVID ELLIOTT, aerospace engineer; b. Apr. 24, 1964, Portland, Ore.; s. Richard Harold and Barbara Janet (Elliott) A.; edn: BS, M.I.T., Cambridge, Mass., 1986; MS, M.I.T., 1988; career: design techn. KALT Mfg., Portland, Ore., 1981-84; software techn. M.I.T. Athena Project, Cambridge, Mass., 1985; summer intern Douglas Aircraft Co., Long Beach, Calif., 1985; res. asst. M.I.T. Space Systems Lab., Cambridge, Mass., 1985-88; sr. engr./scientist McDonnell Douglas, Huntington Beach, Calif., 1988-; mem., Am. Inst. of Aeronautics & Astronautics Space Automation & Robotics Tech. Com., Wash., D.C., 1990-; awards: Eagle Scout, Boy Scouts of Am., Portland, Ore., 1979; mem: Chi Phi 1982-, Tau Beta Pi 1986-, Sigma Xi 1988-, Sigma Gamma Tau 1986-, Am. Inst. of Aeronautics & Astronautics 1988-, Robotics Soc. of So. Calif.; baritone, Pacific Chorale; author: over 14 publ. profl. papers, 1988-; Episcopal; rec: singing (baritone). Res: 15572 Mayflower Huntington Beach 92647. Ofc: McDonnell Douglas 5301 Bolsa M/C 17-1 Huntington Beach 92647

ANDERSON, EVON LANA, marketer; b. Feb. 12, 1945, Portland, OR; d. Woodrow Wilson and Hazel Dell (McLamore) A.; children: Michelle Anderson, Osceola Carter-Anderson; edn: AA Coll. of Alameda 1975; BS human rel., organizational beh., Univ. San Francisco 1982; MBA mktg, John F. Kennedy Univ. 1987; Career: adminstrv. asst. Peralta Coll. Dist., Oakland 1973-85; tech. asst. Research & Devel. 1985-89; coordinator mktg 1989-; cons. Anderson & Assoc., Oakland 1979-; awards: Nat. Black MBA's, MBA of Year 1989-90 and Com. of Year 1989; appt. Oakland Mayor's Council - OPS 1990-; mem: Nat. Black MBA Assn. (1986-, S.F. chpt. pres. 1991-92, v.p. ops 1990, fund chair 1986-89), Am. Mktg. Assn. 1990-, Oakland C. of C. (bus. com. 1991-); Democrat; Methodist. Ofc: Peralta College District 333 E Eigth St Oakland 94606

ANDERSON, HOLLY GEIS, medical clinic president and c.e.o., educator; b. Oct. 23, 1946, Waukesha, Wis.; d. Henry H. and Hulda S. Geis; m. Richard Kent Anderson, June 6, 1969; edn: BA, Azusa Pacific Univ., 1970. Career: prop. Oak Tree Antiques, San Gabriel 1975-82; founder, pres. Premenstrual Syndrome Treatment Clinic, Inc. Arcadia 1982-; founder, pres. Hormonal Treatment Centers, Inc. (in-hosp. treatment prog.) 1992-; lectr. seminars on womens' illnesses i.e. PMS, post partum depression, hysterectomy, menopause, and the use of natural hormones; radio bdcst. personality "PMS Clinic with Holly Anderson" 1990-; TV guest authority on shows including: Mid Morning L.A., 1988, America, 1985, Tom Snyder Show, 1986, Montel Williams Show, 1992; mem. The Dalton Soc. (research PMS), Nat. Assn. Female Execs.; author: audio cassette, What Every Woman Needs to Know About PMS 1987; audio cassette, PMS Talk 1989; video cassette, The PMS Treatment Program 1989; Republican; rec: write poetry, travel. Ofc: 150 N Santa Anita Ste 755 Arcadia 91006 Tel: 818/447-0679

ANDERSON, IRIS ANITA, educator; b. Aug. 18, 1930, Forks, Wash.; d. James Adolphus and Alma Elizabeth (Haase) Gilbreath; m. Donald Rene Anderson; children: Karen C. b. 1952, Susan A. b. 1953, Gayle L. b. 1957, Brian D. b1959; edn: BA teaching, Univ. Wash. 1969; MA Eng., Seattle Univ. 1972; tchg. cred. English lang. K-12 (1977), Adminstrn. (1978), Comm. Colls. (1978). Career: tchr. Issaquah (Wash.) Sr. High Sch. 1969-77; tchr. Los Angeles Sr. H.S. 1977-79 (also dist. curriculum council chmn., middle sch. plan, edn. assn. curriculum chmn., planned programmed budget proj. chmn., edn. assn. instructional planning chmn. trimester system, accreditation evaluation, advisor Nat. Honor Soc., YMCA-YWCA v.p.); honors: W-Key Activities Scholarship Hon. (Univ. Wash.); mem: Wash. Speech Assn., Nat. Edn. Assn., CRTA, Sigma Kappa, AAUW, Palm Springs Press Women; civic: vol. UCLA Jules Stein Eye Inst., Santa Monica Hosp. Aux. Volunteers (hosp. nutrition vol.), active L.W.V., Nat. Thespians, Desert Beautiful, Palm Springs Panhellenic, Rancho Mirage Republican Women, Bob Hope Cultural Ctr., The Living Desert (Palm Desert), others; clubs: Palm Desert Women's, Rancho Mirage Women's, Indio Women's, CPA Wives, Desert Celebrities, Round Table West; publ: Conservationist's Dilemma (Sea Pen, Marine Sci. Soc. of the Northwest 1975); Republican; Prot. Address: PO Box 6000 Palm Desert 92261

ANDERSON, MARJORIE BETH, marriage and family counselor; b. Oct. 9, 1914, Chgo.; d. Louis Saran and Margaret Zaida (Goodman) Strauss; m. Montague Allen Anderson, Mar. 27, 1938 (div.); children: Kent b. 1944 (dec.), Sherry b. 1945, Craig b. 1948; edn: BA psych., UCLA, 1932-36, 71-72; MA psych., Sierra Univ., 1982; lic. Marriage Family Child Counselor, Calif. 1985. Career: pvt. practice MFCC, Costa Mesa 1985-; volunteer profl. grief-support group ldr. Oasis Senior Citizens Ctr., Corona del Mar, and Irvine Senior Ctr., Irvine; civic: Hoag Hosp. Aux. (original convenor), Orange Co. Panhellenic (founding mem.), Candy Stripers (1 of 3 founders), Nightengales (founding mem.), Children's Theater Guild (charter), Lido Isle Players (charter), Las Almas de Mardan (charter), active in Scouting, sch. room mother & PTA coms., Cotillion chaperone, sponsor Junior Board of Control Lido Isle; Agnostic; rec: photography, travel, crafts, gardening. Ofc: Pat Patton and Associates, 2900 Bristol G104 Costa Mesa 92626

ANDERSON, RAYMOND HARTWELL, JR., engineer; b. Feb. 25, 1932, Staunton, Va.; s. Raymond Hartwell and Virginia Boatwright (Moseley) A.; m. Dana Wilson, Sept. 5, 1959; children: Kathryn, b. 1960, Margaret, b.1962, Susan, b. 1963; edn: BS, ceramic eng.,Va. Polytech. Inst. 1957, BS, metallurg. eng. 1958, MS, metallurg. eng. 1959. Career: metallurgical engr. Gen.Dynamics, Ft. Worth, Tex. 1959-61; senior metallurgical engr. Babcock & Wilcox Co., Lynchburg, Va. 1961-65, Douglas Aircraft Co., Santa Monica, Ca. 1965-67; materials R&D splst. McDonnell Douglas, Santa Monica 1967-71, senior technical splst. McDonnell Douglas, Huntington Bch. 1971-87, senior specialist Space Station Pgm., 1987-; mats., teaching staff Univ. Calif. Irvine, 1991-; asst. prof. metallurgy, Va. Poly. Inst. 1958-59; cons. engr., metallurgy, 1967-68; honors: Tau Beta Pi (earth sci.), Alpha Sigma Mu (metals), Omicron Delta Kappa (leadership), Sigma Gamma Epsilon, Scabbard & Blade (mil.); mem: Am. Soc. for Metals (1957-, tchg. staff 1966-69), Corrosion Soc. 1957-70, Am. Ceramic Soc. 1957-70, Am. Nuclear Soc. 1961-65, Am. Welding Soc. 1991-, De Moly 1952-; BSA Merit Badge Com. 1970. Patentee (2); publs: contbr. sci. jours. Mil: lst lt. AUS Ord.1954-56, Nat. Svc. ribbon.; Republican; Prot. rec: sports cars, philately, gardening, stereo music systems. Res: 1672 Kenneth Dr Santa Ana 92705 Ofc: McDonnell Douglas, 5301 Bolsa Ave Huntington Bch 92647

ANDERSON, RICHARD HAYDEN, physician, psychiatrist; b. Sept. 17, 1921, Hayden, Ariz.; s. Victor Emmanuel and LaVona (McClendon) A.; m. Bernice A. Meacham, Sept. 7, 1944; children: Michael b. 1946, Ronald b. 1950, Brian b. 1951; edn: BA, Univ. Utah 1943; MD, 1945; cert. Am. Bd. Psychiatry & Neurology 1952. Career: resident VA,. Palo Alto 1948-51, chief of psychiatry, Salt Lake City, Utah 1952-55, chief profl. services 1955-57; assoc. supt. Mendocino St. Hosp., Ukiah 1957-59; assoc. supt. Fairview St. Hosp., Costa Mesa 1959-60; pvt. practice, Santa Cruz 1960-92 (ret.); asst. clin. prof. Univ. Utah Med. Sch., Salt Lake City 1952-57; lectr. psychiatry UCSF Med. Sch. 1957-59; program chief Co. Mental Health, Santa Cruz 1960-63; dir. psychiatry Dominican Santa Cruz Hosp. 1969-75; honors: Phi Eta Sigma, Phi Kappa Phi, Phi Beta Kappa, Alpha Omega Alpha; mem: CMA, Am. Psychiatric Soc. (fellow), Santa Cruz Co. Med. Soc.; articles pub. in med. jours 1945-57; mil: capt. AUS Med. Corps 1946-48; rec: golf, photography, travel. Res: 22 Ortalon Ave Santa Cruz 95060

ANDERSON, WARREN E., company president; b. May 22, 1951, Pittsburgh, Pa.; s. Warren E. and Mary Kay (Fletcher) A.; edn: BSME, Univ. Cincinnati 1974; MBA, Santa Clara Univ. 1982; Calif. Coll. Tchg. Credl. 1978; IBM Sys. Sci. Inst. 1980; Certified Data Processor 1981. Career: computer programmer Mitre Corp. Boston 1974-75; mgr. sales & mktg. sys., sr. sys,. analyst Intel Corp., Santa Clara 1975-80; database adminstr. Capital Preservation Fund Palo Alto 1980-82; pres., chmn. Anderson Soft-Teach, San Jose 1982-; honors: Herman Schneider Scholar 1973, Cooper-Bessemer Scholar 1969, Admission w/ Distinction (Univ. Cincinnati 1969), Football Scholar 1969; mem: Inst. for

Certification of Computer Profls., Kiwanis Key Club (pres. 1968-69), Sophos Hon. Soc. 1970-71, Delta Tau Delta (asst. treas. 1971-72); publ: Life Insurance as an Investment (Coop Engrg. Mag. 1969). Ofc: 2680 N First St San Jose 95134

ANDREWS, CANDACE LOU, radio executive; b. Apr. 20, 1957, Larson AFB, Wash.; d. Louis Warren Wilson and Lucie Elizabeth (Halley) A.; edn: BA psychology and BBA mgmt., Univ. Tx., Austin 1979. Career: with GranTree Furniture Rental: sales rep., then asst. sales/ mktg. mgr. in Austin, TX 1979-83, Denver, Colo. 1983-84, sales & mktg. mgr. Inland Empire, CA 1984-86; v.p. development & operations Shepherd Comms., Yucaipa, CA 1993-, ops. mgr.1986-93; mem: Nat. Religious Bdcstrs., Nat. Assn. of Bdcstrs., Christian Mgmt. Assn., Fellowship of Christian Athletes, Longhorn Assocs. (charter mem.), Tx. Exes Alumni Assn. (life), Yucaipa C.of C., Friends of Turkey (vol. 1987-), Awana Commander 1989-91, Faith Bible Ch. (asst. fin. secty 1988-90, fin. secty. 1990-91); Republican; Christian; rec: outdoors, biking. Ofc: Shepherd Communications PO Box 1000 Yucaipa 92399-1000

ANDRIANO-MOORE, RICHARD GRAF, retired naval officer, teacher; b. Petaluma; s. Norvel Moore and Thelma Elizabeth (Cook) Koch-Andriano; desc. from the Grafen von Andriano and Brentano di Tremezzo of Italy and Germany; m. Janice Hironaka, Jan. 10, 1976 (div. Feb. 1990); children: Erika b. 1976, Stephen b. 1978; edn: BA, CSU San Jose 1956; grad. work UC Riverside; MBA, Pepperdine Univ. 1977; cert. Naval War Coll., Newport, R.I. 1980-81, 1981-82; Surface Warfare Ofcr., USN, 1972. Career: sch. tchr. (7th, 8th gr.) Oasis Sch., Thermal, Calif. 1960-63; commnd. ensign USN 1957, 1st lt., gunnery ofcr. USS Jefferson County (LST 1068) 1957-60; personnel and legal ofcr. USS Maury (AGS-16) 1963-65, CO Naval & Marine Corps Reserve Tng. Ctr., Pt. Arthur, TX 1965-68, dept. hd./ops. ofcr. USS Muliphen (LKA-61) 1968-69, asst. Surface & ASW Pgm. ofcr., 1970-72, Surface Pgm. ofcr. 11th Naval Dist. 1972-74, CO Hunters Pt. Naval Reserve Ctr., San Francisco 1974-75, CO Navy and Marine Corps Reserve Ctr., San Bruno 1975-79, dir. adminstrn. Nat. Com. for Employer Support of the Guard and Reserve, Office of Secty. Def., Wash DC 1979-82, comdr. recruiting coord. Region 1, Alameda 1982-84, chief of staff Naval Reserve Readiness Command Region 20, Treasure Is., S.F. 1984-85, ret. Cdr. USN, 8/1/85; decorated Def. Merit. Service 1982, Navy Commendn. (1973, 85), authorized by Sec. of Def. to wear the Office of the Secty. of Def. ID Badge 1980, Command Ashore Insignia 1974, Surface Warfare Insignia 1978, USN Recruiting Badge w/2 gold wreaths (1983, 84), Expt. Pistol Shot 1978; honors: War Service Medal 1974, Silver Good Citizenship Medal 1978, Patriot Medal 1985, Meritorious Service Medal 1987, Bronze Good Citizenship Medal 1993, SAR; Knight, Noble Company of the Rose 1986, distinguished alumni San Jose State Univ. 1991; Guardian at Glasclune Castle 1993; 2d deg. Brown Belt, Kodakan Judo Assn., Tokyo; mem: Navy League of U.S. (hon. dir. San Mateo Co. Council 1975-79), Retired Ofcrs. Assn., Reserve Ofcrs. Assn., Sigma Nu Frat. (chpt. pres. 1955), Nat. Soc. SAR (pres. S.F. chpt. 1976-77, chmn. Nat. DAR Cmte 1979-81, v.p. N. Calif. Soc. SAR 1984-86, pres. Calif. Soc. SAR 1986-7), Mil. Order of Loyal Legion of U.S., Calif. Commandery (Recorder 1976-78, v.comdr. 1978-82, comdr. 1982-88), The Augustan Soc., Gen. Soc. of Mayflower Desc., Gen. Soc. of the War of 1812, Hospitaler Order of St. John of Jerusalem (Companion of Honor 1983, Knight 1991), Naval Order of U.S., Fedn. Des Combattants Allies En Europe; civic: Cultural Soc. of Marin, Webelos Scout Den Leader (1987-89, den leader award 1989), Scoutmaster Troop 18 (1989-92), Scouter's Tng. Award 1989, Scoutmaster Award of Merit 1992, camp dir. Boy Scout Camp Masonite-Navarro 1992-93, dist. Boy Scout exec. Redwood Empire Council RSA; mem. Precinct Bd. (insp. 1987-90); chief ed. Calif. Compatriot 1986-87; Republican; Prot.; rec: travel, Civil War relics, genealogy. Res: 197 Upland Dr Petaluma 94952

ANEMA, DURLYNN CAROL, education consultant, author; b. Dec. 23, 1935, San Diego; d. Durlin L. Flagg and Carolyn L. (Janeck) Owen; m. Charles J. Anema, Jan. 18, 1955 (dec. 1986); children: Charlynn Raimundi b. 1955, Charles Jay Jr. b. 1957, Richard F. b. 1963; edn: BA, CSU Hayward, 1968, MS, 1977; EdD, UOP, 1984; PhD Trinity Theological Seminary 1993. Career: secondary tchr. San Leandro Unified Sch. Dist., 1970-72, Hayward Unified Sch. Dist. 1972-75, vice prin. Hayward USD 1975-77, Lodi USD 1977-80; dir. Lifelong Learning, Univ. of the Pacific, Stockton 1981-84, faculty 1989-; prof. comm. Univ. of the Pacific 1984-89; instr. Nat. Univ., Sacto. 1989-91; edn. consultant statewide 1989-; columnist Stockton Record 1984-89; dir. San Joaquin Authors Symp., Stockton 1985-; awards: Phi Kappa Phi 1984, Susan B. Anthony award San Joaquin Co. Commn. on Women 1989, listed Who's Who Am. Univs. 1982, Who's Who in West 1984-; mem. AAUW, Delta Kappa Gamma, Phi Delta Kappa; civic bds: San Joaquin Co. Childrens Commn. 1986-92, Tierro del Oro Girl Scouts (advy. bd. 1988-); author 7+ books incl. Options (1993), Don't Get Fired (1978, 90), Get Hired (1979, 90), Sharing an Apt. (1981); Christian; rec: biking, hiking, travel. Res/Ofc: 401 Oak Ridge Ct Valley Springs 95252

ANGELE, ALFRED ROBERT, law enforcement union executive director, retired police officer; b. Dec. 9, 1940, NYC; s. Alfred Otto and Alma Margaret (Branda) A.; m. Barbara Ann Chavez, Sept. 30, 1961; children: Cindy b. 1963, Lynda b. 1967; edn: AA, L.A. Valley Coll.; Calif. Comm. Colls. life tchg. cred. in police sci. Career: patrolman Burbank Police Dept., 1963-67, detective 1967-

74, sgt. 1974-78; expert in narcotics and dangerous drugs; dept. self def. instr.; instr. self defense and pub. sector labor relations; car club youth advisor; exec. director Calif. Orgn. Police & Sheriffs, Sacto. 1978- (mem. 1975-, sec. 1976-78); sec.treas. Calif. Police & Sheriffs Found., Sacto. 1990-; mem., ofcr. Internat. Union of Police Assns. (IUPA), AFL-CIO, W.D.C., 1980-92 (dir. 1981-85, internat. sec.treas. 1985-90, sec.treas. emeritus 1990-92); A financial conservative, he is credited with bringing Burbank Police Ofcrs. Assn., Calif. Orgn. of Police & Sheriffs and the IUPA to sound fiscal positions. gov. appt. Commn. on Peace Officer Stds./Tng., Sacto. 1979-84; mem. AFL-CIO Observer Team sent to Nicaragua to monitor presdl. election (2-25-90); mem. Hon. Host Com. of the Nationwide Tour of the Bill of Rights, 1991, rep. Calif. Law Enforcement; awards: Mike Maggiora Memorial humanitarian award 1980, 1st recipient Burbank Jaycees officer of month award 1977, B.P.O.A. dir. of yr. 1972, Burbank Police Dept. profl. esteem award, law enf. editor of yr. I.U.P.A. 1987, commendns./ltrs. of appreciation from Burbank Bar Assn., BPO Elks, C.H.P., Burbank P.D., Houston Police Patrolmans Union, Women Peace Ofcr. Assn. Calif., Gov. of Calif., Gov. of Ala., Calif. Senate & Assembly, L.A. Mayor, Mayor's Drug & Alc. Abuse Com. Burbank, LA Co. D.A. Ofc., Calif. Dept. Corrections, Ret. Pub. Employees Assn. Calif., C.O.P.S.; mem: Calif. Narcotics Ofcrs. Assn. 1969-73, Calif. Narcotics Infor. Network 1972-74, Police Advy. Council for Car Clubs 1967-70, B.P.O.A. (1963-, only pres. to hold 5 consecutive terms 1976-81); contbr. articles in law enforcement jours., guest editorials for USA Today; mil: seaman USNR 1957-58, cpl. E4 USMC 1958-62, comms. instr. 3d Marine Div. Schs. 1960-61; Democrat; R.Cath.; rec: home remodeling, music, veh. restoration. Ofc: 175 E Olive Ave Ste 400 Burbank 91502

ANGELO, HOMER GLENN, educator; b. June 8, 1916, Alameda; s. Alfred Heath and Elizabeth (Glenn) A.; m. Ann Berryhill, Nov. 12, 1943; children: Christiane b. 1947, Alexander b. 1951, Nancy b. 1953; edn: AB, UC Berkeley 1938; JD, 1941; LL.M, Columbia Univ. N.Y. 1947. Career: prof. law UC Davis 1968; prof. Inst. D'Etudes Europennes Univ. Libre de Bruxelles, Brussels 1968; civic: The Family (SF), Bohemian (SF), The Carlton, Flyfishers, Savice (London), Cercle Royal Gaulois (Brussels), Club de la Fondation Universitaire (Brussels); Prot. Res: Sage House Jacks Valley Rd Genoe NV 89411 also: 100 Thorndale Dr Ste 150 San Rafael 94903

ANGUIANO, LUPE, education and employment consultant, entrepreneur; b. Mar. 12, 1929, La Junta, Colo.; d. Jose and Rosario (Gonzales) A.; edn: MA adminstrn. and edn., Antioch Univ. 1978. Career: religious tchr. Our Lady of Victory Missionary Sister, 1949-65; supr. teenage leadership pgm. (15 Teen-Post projects) Los Angeles Fedn. of Neighborhood Ctrs. 1965-66; helped write Bilingual-Bicultural Edn. Act., US Ofc. of Edn., 1967-68; S.W. regl. dir. NAACP Legal Def. and Edn. Fund, 1969; HEW pgm. chief Women's Action, Calif. Region, 1970-73; regl. dir. (S.W. region) for the Spanish Speaking, Nat. Council of Cath. Bishops, 1973-77; founder, pres. and c.e.o. Nat. Women's Employment and Edn. Inc. (NWEE), 1977-91, founder/adminstr. Women's Employment and Edn. Model Pgm. (WEEMP) 1973, also designed a Model Child Care Tng. Pgm., devel. funding for WEE affil. pgms. in San Antonio, Dallas and El Paso, Phoenix, Tacoma, Denver, NYC, Ventura, Calif. and LA, 1980-88; pres. and c.e.o. Lupe Anguiano and Assocs., 1982-; honors: featured in CBS-TV "An American Portrait," in Poster series for Statue of Liberty Centennial (2/85), in book Local Heroes- The Rebirth of Heroism in America (Lexington Books 1987), in CBS-TV "60 Minutes segment "Getting Off Welfare" (11/80), in A Gallery of Women traveling nat. exhib. by Adolph Coors Co. (1985-87), recipient Nat. Leadership Award from Nat. Network of Hispanic Women 1989, Fedn. of Republican Women, Wash DC 1985, Geo. Wash. Medal, Freedom Found. 1985, listed in 100 US Influential Hispanics for the 1980's, Hispanic Bus. Mag. 1983, listed America's New Women Entrepreneurs 1986, recipient Brandeis award Nat. Women's Pol. Caucus 1983, Pres.'s Volunteer Action Award 1983, Vista Award 1980, Woman of the 80s, Ms. Mag. 1980, citation, Texas State House of Reps. 1978; mem. Guadalupe Cultural Arts Ctr./San Antonio, Am. Mgmt. Assn., Am. Soc. of Profl. and Exec. Women, Nat. Assn. Female Execs., Nat. Womens Pol. Caucus (adv. council), Women in Communs., San Antonio Mexican C.of C.; Republican; R.Cath. Res/Ofc: 3727 Country Club Dr #12 Long Beach 90807

ANJARD, RONALD P., administrator; b. July 31, 1935, Chgo.; s. Auguste L. and Florence M. Byrne A.; m. Marie B. Sampler, Jan. 26, 1957; children: John R., Michele M., Michael M., Ronald P., Jr.; edn: BS in Metall. Engring., Carnegie Mellon Univ., 1957; MS/MBA in Indsl. Adminstrn., Purdue Univ., 1968; AS, Indiana Univ., 1973; BS in Bus. Adminstrn., U.S.N.Y., 1978; BA in Humanities, T.A. Edison Coll., 1979; PDE, Univ. of Wis., 1979; PhD in Edn., Calif. Poly. Univ., 1981; PhD in Metall. Engring., Calif. Poly. Univ., 1982; MS-CRM, Webster Univ., 1990; career: div. qual. mgr. AVX/JMI, San Diego, 1981-83; corp. dir. Kaypro Corp., S.D., 1983-85;qual. mgr., CPT, S.D., 1985-89; pres., AIC/ASPT, S.D. 1987-; v.p., Triage Network, S.D., 1989-; SPC coord. & internal cons., Gen. Dynamics ESI, 1989-; adjunct faculty, USC and UCSD; awards: Who's Who in Am. 1975-, Gov. Voluntary Action Commendation 1975,1978, Who's Who in Technology Today 1984-, Jaycees Distinguished Service Award 1970, Am. Soc. Registry 1980-, Who's Who in the World 1978-,

Am. Men and Women of Sci. 1979-, Who's Who in Fin. and Ind. 1988-, Outstanding Ind. Young (Party) State Award 1970, Am. Bus. Reg. 1980-, U.S. Lib. of Cong. Listing of Engring. Authors 1974-, GM Comm. Service Award 1970, Notable Am. 1978-, Internat. Authors 1978-, Am. Edn. Reg. 1980-, Am. Scientific Reg. 1980-; Am. Pub. Who's Who 1988, Dict. of Internat. Biography 1976-, Who's Who in the Semiconductor Industry 1986-, Writer's Who's Who (UK) 1978-, Who's Who in History 1982-, Golden Poet Award, 1988, appointed Sagamore of the Wabash by Gov. of Ind. 1979, Personalities of the West and Midwest 1977-, Who's Who in Religion 1975-, Nat. Soc. Reg. 1977-, Sigma Xi Nat. Sci. Honorary 1973-, Layman of the Year Award 1971; Engr. of Distinction 1973-, Best Poets of 1988, Outstanding Young Men in Am. 1970, Who's Who in Am. Christian Leadership 1989, Am. Hall of Police 1987-, IBA Yearbook (UK) 1979, Biography of the Year 1986, Am. Cultural Arts Reg. 1980-, Howard Cty. Heart Citations 1973-75, Am. Civil Service Reg. 1988-, Am. Poetry Assn. Poet of Merit 1989, Two Thousand Notable Am. 1988, Internat. Dir. of Disting. Leadership 1989; mem: ISHM, ASQC, Deming Users Group, IEEE (exec. com.), ASTM (ed. rev. bd., coms.), IEPS, ACS, AIME., Sigma Xi, Am. Soc. for Metals, Internat. Soc. for the Investigation of Ancient Civilizations, Am. Bar Assn.; civic: councilman, Howard Co., Ind., 1980; township trustee, Clay Twnshp, Ind., 1970-75; Young Rep., state vice chmn, 5th dist. chmn, Ind.; S.D. Republican Central Comm.; chmn-small bus., United Fund; chmn cong. action com., C. of C.; active in many historical soc. and church councils; author: 950+ articles and publs. in 17 countries; mil: capt., Army; rec: history, archeology, anthropology, photography. Ofc: AIL 10942 Montego Dr. Ste A2 San Diego 92124

ANNECHARICO, ARTHUR LESTER, film production company president and executive producer; b. Nov. 13, 1941, NY, NY; s. Arthur Alfred Annecharico and Judy (Campbell) Adamson; m. Elizabeth Martha Shages, May 8, 1967; children: Cynthia, Denton; edn: New Rochelle (NY) H.S., Munich (Ger.) Univ. Career: pres. Sound Art Studios, N.Y.C., 1967-72; producer/director TV and motion pictures, San Diego 1974-79; v.p. devel. Metromedia Producers Orgn., Los Angeles 1979-82; pres. and c.e.o. The Arthur Co., Los Angeles 1983-; freelance director/producer; author screenplays: Run for Blue; Father Forgive Me; Rocky Road; Safe At Home; What A Dummy, The New Dragnet, Adam-12, and The Munster's Today, F.B.I.-The Untold Stories; awards: 2 Emmys for "Run for Blue" 1981, 3 Laurels for TV commercials, NY 1971, Gray Ad award NY Advt. Assn., Film Advy. Board award of excellence, Salvation Army Evangeline Booth award, L.A. 1988, M.A.D.D. recogn. award, L.A. 1988; civic bds: Calif. advy. bd. Salvation Army, fin. advy. bd. St. Monica's Ch.; clubs: Harley Owners Group, Airplane Owners & Pilots Assn.; mil: 1st lt. Army 82d Airborne Div. 1958-60; rec: flying (comml., multi-engine, helicopter, fixed wing pilot), boating, fishing, motorcycles, parachuting. Ofc: The Arthur Company 11835 W. Olympic Blvd Ste 650 Los Angeles 90064

ANSPACH, DENNY SYKES, radiologist; b. Feb. 5, 1934, Chgo.; s. William Earl and Rachel Mae (Sykes) A.; m. Carol Jacobs, June 22, 1958, and May 14, 1988; children: David b. 1962, Carolyn b. 1965; m. Polly Dakin, 1981, div. 1987; edn: AB, Stanford Univ., 1956, MD 1960, postgrad. splty. 1961-64; diagnostic radiologist Am. Bd. Rad., 1965. Career: capt. US Army and chief radiology Kirk Army Hosp., Aberdeen Proving Ground, Md. 1964-66; radiologist Radiolog. Assocs. of Sacramento Inc., Sacto., Ca. 1966-81; Green Mountain Radiology, Montepelier, Vt. 1981-87; indep. contr. radiologist 1987-90; radiologist (breast only) Univ. Calif. Davis Med. Ctr., Sacto. 1990-, Mammographia, Sacto. 1991-; asst. clin. prof. UC Davis 1970-77, 90-, founder Breast Imagery Study Gp. 1991-; awards: merit CalState Resources Agy., Sacto. 1978; mem: Am. Coll. Radiology (fellow 1982, councilor 197-81, 86-88), AMA 1966-, Calif. Radiol. Assn. (1966-); civic: Calif. State Railroad Mus., Sacto. (prin. founder 1964-), mem. Railway & Locomotive Hist. Soc. (Pac. Coast chpt. bd. 1961-81, 87-), Antique & Classic Boat Soc. (bd. 1988-91); clubs: Sutter (bd. 1978-82), Tahoe Yacht (Homewood); Republican; Prot.; rec: all RR subjects, antique boats. Res: 710 Coronado Blvd Sacramento 95864 Ofc: Mammographia, 920 29th St Sacramento 95816

ANTIN, MICHAEL, tax lawyer; b. Nov. 30, 1938, Milwaukee, Wis.; s. David Boris and Pauline (Mayer) A.; m. Evelyne Judith Hirsch, June 19, 1960; children: Stephanie b. 1967, Bryan b. 1970, Randall b. 1974; edn: BS, UCLA 1960; JD, UC Berkeley Boalt Hall 1963; admitted St. Bar Calif. 1964. Career: pres., chmn. of bd. Antin Litz & Gilbert, Los Angeles 1963-91; dir: West Coast Bank, Encino 1979-83, Ventura Co. Nat. Bancorp 1985-, chmn. bd. Conejo Valley Nat. Bank 1983-86; lectr. ABA Pgms. Dallas 1979, HI. 1980, WDC 1982, profl. tax seminars, and Cont. Edn. of the Bar, 1969-; instr. Solomon S. Huebner Sch. of CLU Studies 1977-; author: How to Operate Your Trust or Probate (Layman Pub. Co., 1983), numerous articles on taxation, estate planning, probate law; coauthor med. & dental regulations-Profl. Corporations Act; Fellow Am. Coll. Trust & Estate Counsel, Fellow Am. Coll. Tax Counsel, mem: Am. Bar Assn. (tax sect., profl. service orgns., chmn.), Calif. Bar Assn. (tax, probate and trust law sect.), L.A. Co. Bar Assn. (tax sect.), Beverly Hills Bar Assn., W. Pension Conf., Beverly Hills Estate Planning Council (pres. 1981-82); civic: Harvard Sch. Parents Assn. (dir., treas. 1988-89), Bel Air Knolls Homeowners Assn. (pres. 1975-77), Sherman Oaks Little League (pres. 1983-4, 87-89); club:

Regency; mil: airman USAF 1959-65, Reserve; Democrat; Jewish; rec: x-c skiing, tennis, jogging. Res: 16565 Park Lane Dr Los Angeles 90049 Ofc: Antin & Taylor 1875 Century Park E. Ste 700 Los Angeles 90067 Ph. 310/788-2733

ANTONOVICH, MICHAEL D., county supervisor; b. Aug. 12, 1939, Los Angeles; s. Michael and Francis (McColm) A.; single; edn: BA, CSU Los Angeles 1963, MA, 1967; grad. Pasadena Police Acad., Reserve Officer Sch. 1967; Rio Hondo Reserve Ofcr. Adv. Tng. Sch. 1978; Hoover Inst. and Intercollegiate Studies Inst. Stanford 1968-70; sr. exec. pgm. Harvard Univ. Sch. of Govt. 1984, 87; Air War Coll. 1984. Career: govt.-hist. tchr. L.A. Unified Sch. Dist. 1966-72; instr. Pepperdine Univ. 1980, CSU Los Angeles 1979, 85; mem. bd. trustees L.A. Comm. Coll. Dist. 1969-73;elected Calif. State Assembly 1972-78, Republican Whip 1976-78; L.A. Co. Bd. of Supervisors, 5th Dist., 1980- chmn. 1983, 1987, 1991; mem. Presdl. Fulbright Commn. 1991-93, Presdl. Commn. on Privatization 1987-88, Atty. Gen.'s Advy. Bd. for Missing Children 1987-88, County-wide Crim. Justice Coord. Com. (chmn. 1983, 87), Pres.'s U.S.-Japan Advy. Commn. 1984, Commn. of White House Fellowships Reg. Panel 1981-86, County Suprs. Assn. of Calif. (bd.), S. Coast Air Quality Mgmt. Dist., L.A. Coliseum Commn.; honors: Outstanding Young Men Am., Menachim Begin achiev. medal Bar-Ilan Univ. 1983, alumni of yr., merit award CSULA (1977, 87), John Marshall H.S. disting. alumni 1984, Nisei VFW outstanding American 1985, Topanga C.of C. service 1983, L.A. Co. Deputy Sheriffs Assn. Victims of Violent Crimes Found. award (1981, 83), L.A. Co. Taxpayers Assn. award 1981, Nat. Taxpayers Union award 1984, dedication of Antonovich Canyon Wildlife Way Station 1984, Foster Parents Assn. Caring Award 1987, Didi Hirsch Comm. Mental Health award 1984, Brotherhood Crusade Award appreciation for leadership (1983, 87, 91), United Way Award for outstanding leadership to the comm. (1983, 87, 91), S.F.V. Interfaith Council award 1983, The Valley Shelter Award 1987, Good Scout Award 1987, Calif. Traditional Music Soc. commendn. of support 1991, L.A. Co. Probation Dept. commendn. of support 1991, Al-Impian of the Year 1991, Assn. of Comm. Health Agencies outstanding leadership 1991, The Ministers Fellowship and Focus 90's of S.F.V. outstanding leadership 1991, PTA hon. service 1991, Internat. Footprint Assn. outstanding citizen 1991, Thomas Jefferson Res. Ctr. Responsible Am. Award 1990, Chaplain's Eagles "Brother's Keeper" Award 1990, The Home Visitation Ctr. outstanding & invaluable svc. 1990, Nat. Fedn. of Indian-Americans public ofcl. of year 1989, Estonian League of W.Coast public ofcl. of yr. 1989; civic: Tournament of Roses Com., Glendale Sym. (bd. govs. 1973-), Glendale C.of C. 1975-, Elks, Good Shepherd Lutheran Home for Retarded Children, Native Sons of Golden West, L.A. Zoo Assn., So. Pasa. Police Dept. Reserves, The Philadelphia Soc., Sigma Nu Frat. Ofc: 869 Hall of Administration 500 W Temple St L.A. 90012

APPELBAUM, BRUCE DAVID, physician; b. Apr. 24, 1957, Lincroft, NJ; s. John S. and Shirley B. (Wolfson) A.; edn: BS pharm., Rutgers Univ., 1980; MS pharmacology, Emory Univ., 1983, PhD pharmacology 1985; MD, Med. Coll. of Ga., 1989; dipl. Nat. Bd. Med. Examiners, 1990. Career: research assoc. dept. pharmacology Emory Univ., Atlanta, Ga. 1985, dept. psychiatry Med. Coll. of Ga., Augusta 1989; resident physician dept. psychiatry UC Irvine, 1989-; cons. psychiatrist Avalon Med. Group, Garden Grove 1990-; com. mem. Bd. of Quality Assurance, Sterling Health Ctr., Anaheim 1991-; awards: NIH nat. resrch. service (1982), Eastern Student Res. Forum, Miami, Fla. (1984), Nat. Student Resrch. Forum, Galveston, Tx. (1987), listed Who's Who in West (1992-3); mem: AMA, Am. Psychiat. Assn., Calif. Psychiat. Assn., Orange Co. Psychiat. Soc., Sigma Xi (1985-); publs: 7+ articles in peer jours. (1983, 84, 85, 86); Democrat; Jewish; rec: photography. Ofc: Univ. Calif., Irvine Medical Ctr. 101 City Dr S Orange

APPLEBERRY, WALTER THOMAS, aerospace engineer; b. Mar. 8, 1926, Wilmington, N.C.; s. William Pembrook and Carroll Ernesteen (Shingleton) A.; m. Mae Magdalene Bozeman, Feb. 21, 1953; children: Thomas Kent b. 1957, Robert William b. 1958, Rebecca Jean b. 1958; edn: BSME, CSU Long Beach, 1974. Career: supr. McDonnell Douglas, Long Beach 1965-69; dynamic test supr. Rockwell Intl., Downey 1982-84, crew systems project mgr., 1984-88, advanced engring. sr. staff engr., 1989-; awards: McDonnell Douglas design engr. award 1966, Rockwell Inventor of Yr. nom. 1977, Engr. of Yr. nom., Pi Tau Sigma 1970-; inventor mechanisms (24 patents); 5 pub. articles; Republican; Mormon; rec: music composition, violin, piano, choral. Res: 3440 Val Verde Ave Long Beach 90808 Ofc: Rockwell Intl. Corp. 12214 Lakewood Blvd Downey 90241

APPLETON, JAMES ROBERT, university president; b. Jan. 20, 1937, No. Tonawanda, N.Y.; s. Robert Martin and Emma (Mollnow) A.; m. Carol Koelsch, Aug. 8, 1959; children: Steven J. b. 1960, Jon M. b. 1963, Jennifer b. 1966; edn: AB, Wheaton Coll., 1958; MA, and PhD, Mich. State Univ., 1963, 1965. Career: assoc. dir. and vis. lectr. Mich. State Univ., 1963-65; assoc. dean Oakland Univ., Rochester, Mich. 1965-68; dean student life 1968-69, v.p./assoc. prof. 1969-72; v.p./assoc. prof. USC, L.A. 1972-87; pres. and univ. prof. Univ. of Redlands, 1987-; mem. NCAA Pres.'s Commn., 1992-; trustee S.F. Presbyterian Sem., San Anselmo 1985-; pres., ofcr. Nat. Assn. Student Personnel Adminstrs., 1969-76; awards: Phi Kappa Phi 1981, Fred Turner

Award NASPA 1980, One of 100 Emerging Young Leaders of the Acad., Change & ACE, W.D.C. 1978; mem: Western College Assn. (pres. 1992-), AAUP, Am. Assn. of Higher Edn., Am. Council on Edn., Western Assn. of Schs. and Colls. S.F. (accreditation com. 1976-), Indep. Colls. of So. Calif. (dir.), Inland Action Inc. (dir.), Alpha Tau Omega frat.; clubs: University (LA), Redlands CC; author: Pieces of Eight (1978), guest editor NASPA J. (4/71); num. articles and monographs; mil: 1st lt. AUS 1958-60; Presbyterian; rec: vocal music, sports. Office of the President, Univ. of Redlands, Redlands 92373

APYAN, ROSEANNE LUCILLE, vascular nurse specialist; b. Jan. 25, 1949, Kenosha, Wis.; d. Sarkis and Angel (Hovegimian) A.; edn: RN, Decatur (Ill.) Mem. Hosp. Sch. of Nsg., 1972; BS, Millikin Univ., 1972; Calif. Comm. Colls. instr. cred., 1977; cert. CCRN (1981, 87), BCLS. Career: R.N., St. Joseph's Med. Ctr., Burbank 1972-82, asst. hd. nse. Intensive Care Unit 1978-80, hd. nse. 1980-82; vascular nse. splst. Dr's. Dulawa, Andros, Harris, Oblath and Schneider, Burbank 1982-93; honors: Internat. Woman of Yr. (1991-92), listed Who's Who in West 1992, Who's Who in Am. Women; mem. Soc. for Peripheral Vascular Nsg. (1983-, trustee 1989-93), Am. Assn. Critical Care Nurses 1975-; vol. L.A. Special Olmpics 1990-92, L.A. Marathon 1989; clubs: Single Ski Club of L.A. 1975-, TriNetwork Ski Club 1987-; contbr. 7+ articles in profl. jours.; Republican; Prot.; rec: skiing, tennis, walking, sewing. Res: 330 N Maple St #G Burbank 91505

ARABIAN, ARMAND, state appellate court justice; b. Dec. 12, 1934, NY, NY; s. John and Aghavnie (Yalian) A.; m. Nancy Megurian, Aug. 26, 1962; children: Allison Ann b. 1965, Robert Armand b. 1969; edn: BSBA (disting. military grad.), Boston Univ. Coll. of Bus. Admin., 1956; JD (class pres.), Boston Univ. Sch. of Law, 1961; LLM, USC, 1970; admitted Calif. St. Bar 1962. Career: dep. dist. atty. Los Angeles Co., 1962-63; pvt. practice law, Van Nuys 1963-72; apptd. by Gov. Reagan judge Municipal Ct., 1972-73, judge Superior Ct., L.A. Co., 1973-83; apptd. by Gov. Deukmejian assoc. justice Ct. of Appeal, 1983-; grad. Appellate Judges Sem., Inst. of Judicial Adminstrn., NYU, 1984, grad. Nat. Coll. State Court Judges, Univ. Nev., Reno 1974; honors: Silver Shingle of Boston Univ. Sch. of Law 1981, recogn. Calif. Sexual Assault Investigators Assn. 1978, San Fernando Valley Bar Assn. (1976, 77), Womens' Caucus of Western State Sch. of Law 1973, Senate and Assembly Resolutions, appreciation for 10-year dedicated judicial service- S.F.V. Crim. Cts. Bar Assn., L.A. Bd. of Police Commrs., L.A. Mayor, City Council and Co. Bd. Suprs. 1982, others; mem: Calif. Judges Assn. 1972-, S.F.V. Crim. Cts. Bar Assn. 1965-86, Internat. Footprint Assn. (chapt. founder 1970-), Sigma Phi Epsilon (1952-, dist. gov. 1968-69); mil: 1st lt. Army Inf. 1956-58, grad. Airborne Pathfinder and Jumpmaster Sch.; Republican; Armenian Apostolic. Ofc: Court of Appeal 3580 Wilshire Blvd Los Angeles 90010

ARAKAWA, MITSUAKI, principal development engineer, management and professional, consultant; b. Dec. 6, 1943, Japan; s. Kiyoshi and Suzuko (So) A.; m. Reiko, Oct. 16, 1970; children: Masahiro b. 1971, Kenji b. 1974; edn: BS, Seoul Univ., 1966. Career: engring. mgr. Japan Electron Optics Lab. (JEOL), Tokyo, Japan 1970-77; assoc. devel. engr. UC San Francisco Dept. of Radiology, 1977; product mgr. Bruker Instruments, Billerica, Mass. 1979; prin. devel. engr. and map engr. UCSF, 1979-; cons. mgmt. and profl. engr., prodn. cons. Toshiba America MRI Inc. 1980-; mem: IEEE, Soc. of Magnetic Resonance in Medicine; inventor: 18 patents in MRI field, 4 patents pending; author 40+ tech. publs. in MRI field; rec: literature, classical music, play piano. Res: 1005 Lakeview Dr. Hillsborough 94010 Ofc: UCSF-RIL 400 Grandview Dr. South San Francisco 94080

ARANDA, BENJAMIN, judge; b. Jan. 3, 1940, Brawley; s. Benjamin Aranda and Concepcion (Pesqueira) Calvin; m. Emma Salazar, May 29, 1965; children: Rebecca b. 1966, Maria Cristina b. 1968, Ruth b. 1970, Benjamin IV b. 1971, Andrea b. 1973, Danielle b. 1976, Carlos b. 1976, David b. 1977, Tania b. 1977, Frederick b. 1979, Eric b. 1980; edn: AB, and JD, Loyola Univ., L.A. 1962, 1969; admitted bar: Calif. 1970-79, U.S. Fed. Dist. Cts. (cent. dist. Calif. 1970, e. dist. Calif. 1978), US Ct. Appeals (9th cir. 1971). Career: atty., ptnr. Harris & Aranda, Marina del Rey 1970-79; judge municipal ct. South Bay Judicial Dist., Torrance 1979-; chair Mcpl. Ct. Judges Assn. 1987-88; justice pro tem St. Ct. Appeals, 1986; judge pro tem L.A. Superior Ct. 1987-88; vis. judge Avalon Justice Ct. 1986, 87, 88; appt. L.A. Co. jud. procedures commn. 1987-88, co. crim. justice coord. com. 1987-88, courthouse security task force 1988; honors: Loyola Univ. editor The Dial (pre-legal soc.) and The Cinder (stu. handbook), pres. YR, Pius X Medallion, Confrat. of Christian Doctrine 1975, disting. svc. Calif. Youth Auth. 1976, Alpha Delta Gamma nat. award of merit and man of yr. (1970, 79), Nat. Interfrat. Conf. Ho. of Dels. award of merit 1966, Hon. Ky. Col. 1965), hon. citizen City New Orleans 1963 and Kansas City 1964, commendn. Constl. Rights Found.1978, disting. citizen City of L.A. 1966, resolutions City and Co. of L.A., Santa Monica, Calif. St. Assem. and Senate 1979, White House Honors presented by First Lady Nancy Reagan 1987 and Great Am. Family award 1987, Adoption Family of yr. and Gov.'s proclamation (11/87), nat. judicial medallion Hispanic Nat. Bar Assn. 1988, role model of month Univision TV Network, Miami (1/89), others; mem: Hispanic Nat. Bar Assn. (1st nat. pres. 1978, 1979, 1980), Mex.-Am. Bar Assn. (pres. 1977, trustee

1973-80), ABA (commn. on opps. for minorities 1986-90, host com. 1990), St. Bar Calif. (editl. bd. Calif. Lawyer 1981-84, spkr. Conf. of Bar Presidents 1977, 80), Minority Bar Assn. (co-founder, chair 1977), L.A. Co. Bar Assn. (trustee 1977-79, pres.'s council 1981-82); civic: bd. dirs. Blue Cross of Calif., Woodland Hills 1982-89, bd. chmn. 1986-89; bd. dirs. Blue Cross of So. Calif. 1981-83; pres./chmn. Save Our Calif. Kids, Inc. L.A. 1985-89; bd. dirs. Little Company of Mary Hosp., Torrance 1991-, Centurion Club, benefit hosp. (pres. 1976); mem. Alpha Delta Gamma Frat. (nat. pres. 1963-4, 64-66, 72-74, founding pres. Alpha Delta Gamma Ednl. Found.), Phi Delta Phi, Public Advocates Inc., S.F. (dir. 1979-89), South Bay-Harbour Vol. Bur. (bd. 1984-89, chair nom. com. 1985, 87, 88), South Bay Assn. of Chambers of Commerce (founding dir., legal counsel 1976-79), El Segundo C.of C. (v.p. 1975, dir. 1972-75, 77-79), judges panel of Great Am. Family of the Yr. and Hispanic Am. Family of the Year (1987, 88), Kiwanis (El Segundo past pres. founder Torrance Club), LMU Alumni Assn. (dir., v.p. 89-93), Westside Legal Svs. (dir. 1981-83), AYSO Soccer Torrance (reg. bd. 1979-82); frequent speaker and lectr. profl. confs., author 5 books incl. History of the Hispanic Lawyer (Lawyear Pub., 1988); Republican; R.Cath.; rec: family. Ofc: 825 Maple Ave Torrance 90503

ARANIBAR-ZERPA, ALBERTO, neurologist; b. Nov. 23, 1926, Lima, Peru; s. Nazario Celso and Marina Hortensia (Zerpa) A.; edn: MD, Univ. of San Marcos, Lima 1959; lic. physician-surgeon Calif. 1986. Career: instr. neurology Univ. of San Marcos, 1953-58; neuropathologist Santo Toribio Hosp., Lima, Peru 1955-60; Fulbright scholar Neurological Inst./St. of N.Y., N.Y.C. 1960-61; neurology resident Univ. of Kansas, K.C., Ks. 1961-62; neurology resident 1962-65, neurophysiology fellow 1965-67, EEG fellow 1967-71, Univ. of Minn., Mpls.; research neurologist Univ. of Graz, Austria 1972-81; epileptology fellow Univ. of Utah, Salt Lake City 1983-85; physician neurologist Neurological Group, Los Angeles 1986-; mem: Am. Epilepsy Soc., Western EEG Soc., Am. Acad. of Neurology (clin. assoc. 1962-); editor 4 books: Cerebral Vascular Disease I, II, III (1977, 79, 81), EEG and Clinical Neurophysiology (1980), numerous articles in med. jours. (1956-81); R.Cath.; rec: electronics, computer pgmg. Res: 431 S Burnside Ave #11-E Los Angeles 90036 Ofc: 1818 S Western Ave Ste 304 Los Angeles 90006

ARCADI, JOHN ALBERT, urologist, research professor; b. Oct. 23, 1924, Whittier; s. Antonio and Josephine Louisa (Ramirez) A.; m. Doris M. Bohanan, Apr. 11, 1951; children: Patrick, Michael, Judith, Timothy, Margaret, William, Catherine; edn: Whittier Coll. 1942-44, BS cum laude, Univ. Notre Dame, 1947, MD, Johns Hopkins Med. Sch., 1950. Career: intern, asst. resident, 1950-54, chief resident Brady Urol. Inst., The Johns Hopkins Hosp., 1954-55; urologist solo pvt. practice, Whittier 1955-; asst. prof. urol. Univ. So. Calif. Med. Sch., L.A. 1957-60; resrch. assoc. Whittier Coll., 1957-65, resrch. prof. 1965-; mem. bd. dirs. Presbyterian Hosp., Whittier 1989-92; awards: Franklin Mall, Johns Hopkins 1948, pvt. practice urol. Am. Found. Urologic Disease 1986, 89; mem: Am. Assn. for the Adv. Scis. (fellow 1953), Am. Coll. Surgeons (fellow), Am. Urol. Assn., Am. Assn. Anatomists, Endocrine Soc.; civic: Whittier Hist. Soc. (bd. 1989-92); author 50+ sci. publs. (1948-); Republican; R.Cath. (pastoral coun. 1989-92); rec: photography, stamp & coin collection. Ofc: PO Box 9220, 13113 Hadley St Whittier 90608

ARCADI, VICTORIA CARMELA, chiropractor, educator; b. July 9, 1954, New Brighton, Pa.; d. Victor Larry and Gloria Rose (LaGrotta) Arcadi; edn: BA, UCLA 1977; DC (magna cum laude), Cleveland Chiropractic Coll. 1984; lic. Chiropractor Calif. 1985; Diplomate Nat. Bd. Chiropractic Examiners; Cert. Practitioner Applied Kinesiology. Career: preceptorship, intern 1984-85; prof. Cleveland Chiro. Coll., Los Angeles; pvt. practice 1985-, cons. pre-natal and labor, staff chiropractor Gentle Birth Ctr. Med. Group, Glendale 1987-; mem: Cleveland Chiropractic and UCLA Alumni Assn., Calif. and Am. Chiropractic Assn., Assn. Childbirth At Home Internat.; civic: Women's Referral Svc., U.S. Tennis Assn; innovator new techniques in chiropractic treatment for women in labor and newborns (1985-); rec: tennis, swimming, running. Ofc: 14755 Ventura Blvd Ste 202 Sherman Oaks 91403 Ph: 818/905-5028

ARELLANO, EUGENE WALTER, physician-surgeon; b. Nov. 4, 1927, Los Angeles; s. Frederico and Petrita Beaubien (Abreu) A.; m. Judith Ellen Boam, Oct. 21, 1970; children: Debra b. 1952, Kimberlee b. 1956, Edward b. 1963, Eugene b. 1971, Melinda b. 1972; edn: undergrad. work Stanford Univ., AA, UCLA; DO, Coll. of Osteopathic Physicians & Surgeons, L.A. 1953; MD, UC Irvine 1962; bd. certified, Diplomate Am. Board of Family Practice. Career: solo practice physician-surgeon, Glendale 1953-; lt. col., by congl. appt., USAF Med. Corps, overseas duty 1977; group practice phys. Glendale Adventist Med. Diagnostic Center 1978-80, solo practice in Glendale, 1980-; attdg. staff Glendale Adventist Med. Ctr; Glendale Comm. Hosp. chief of staff 1975, pres. elect 1981-83; secty. bd. dirs. Assoc. Med. Group, Glendale 1979-80; asst. clin. instr. int. medicine, Coll. Osteo. Phys. & Surg. 1955-57; honors: physicians recogn. awards, AMA, CMA; Fellow Am. Acad. of Family Physicians 1978; mem: AMA, CMA, L.A. Co. Med. Assn., Glendale Dist. Med. Assn., UCLA Alumni Assn. (life), Calif. Acad. Family Phys., World Med. Assn., Assn. of Mil. Surgeons of the U.S., Royal Soc. of Medicine, Latin-Am. Advsy. Council, L.A. Dist. Atty. Advsy. Council, Calif. Thoroughbred Breeders Assn., Horsemens

Benevolent Protective Assn.; breed and race throroughbred horses with stakes winners in USA, England, and France (1962-); Republican; R.Cath.; rec: garden, swim, basketball, travel. Res: 605 Meadowgrove Pl La Canada-Flintridge 91011 Ofc: E.W. Arellano, MD, Inc. 609 S Glendale Ave Glendale 91205

AREND, ROBERT LEE, educator; b. Aug. 30, 1944, Bridgman, Mich.; s. Delbert Lee and Dorothy Evelyn (Martin) A.; m. Joanne Prince, June 4, 1977; children: Julie Eve b. 1971, Joshua b. 1979; edn: BA, Moody Bible Inst., 1968; BA, W. Mich. Univ., 1968; MA, Trinity Evangelical Divinity Sch., 1970; MA, Northwestern Univ., 1971; postgrad. Purdue Univ., 1973-76; Calif. Comm. Colls. life instr. cred. Eng., suprvn., humanities, and speech. Career: asst. prof. English, Grace Coll., Winona Lake, Ind. 1971-76; tutor, grad. asst. Purdue Univ. 1974-76; prof. and dept. chair Eng. dept. Christian Heritage Coll., El Cajon, Ca. 1977-90, also publs. advisor 1985-90, ann. judge literature contests 1990-; asst. prof. Eng., San Diego Miramar Coll., 1990-, p.t. faculty Cuyamaca Coll., El Cajon 1982-90, Palomar Comm. Coll., San Marcos 1981-; freelance tutor, writer, 1982-; editl. advy. bd. for new textbooks, Collegiate Press; awards: Outstanding Young Men of Am. 1974, tchg. award and yearbook dedication Christian Heritage Coll. 1990, listed Who's Who in West 1991; mem: Nat. Coun. of Tchrs. of Eng., Modern Language Assn., Shakespeare Assn., Sigma Tau Hon. Soc.; author 3 college textbooks, numerous articles in scholarly jours.; Republican; Baptist; rec: reading, tennis, hiking, writing, jogging. Res: 1838 Somerset Ave Cardiff 92007 Ofc: 10440 Black Mountain Rd San Diego 92126

ARGUE, JOHN C., lawyer; b. Jan. 25, 1932, Glendale; s. J. Clifford and Catherine Emily (Clements) A.; m. Leah Elizabeth Moore, June 29, 1963; children: Eliabeth Anne b. 1967, John Michael b. 1968; edn: AB in commerce, fin., Occidental Coll. 1953; LLB, USC Law Sch. 1956; (Hon.) LLD Occidental Coll. 1987; admitted bar: Calif. 1957. Career: atty., ptnr. Argue & Argue, Los Angeles 1958-59, Flint & MacKay, 1960-72, sr. ptnr. Argue Pearson Harbison & Myers, 1973-; advr. LAACO, Ltd.; dir: Avery Internat. Inc., CAL MAT Inc., TCW/DW Family of Mutual Funds, Rose Hills Memorial Park; trustee: USC, Occidental Coll., Pomona Coll. (v.chmn.); bd. govs. UCLA Med. Sch.; pres. USC Assoc.; dir. L.A. Area C.of C. (chmn. 1989); honors: Sports Headliner of Year, L.A. Press Club 1978, Sparkplug Award as The Man Most Responsible for Bringing the 1984 Olympics to LA, LA Area C.of C. 1979, William May Garland award, So. Calif. Com. for the Olympic Games 1979, Spirit of Los Angeles award, L.A. Hdqtrs. City Assn. 1979, Centennial award 1980 and Hall of Fame 1984, LA Athletic Club, Track Hall of Fame, Occidental Coll. 1980, disting. service, Am. Heart Assn. LA 1982, Merit award, USC Gen. Alumni Assn. 1984, Disting. Eagle Scout Award, BSA 1984, Outstanding Citizen PRISMS award, Pub. Rels. Soc. Am. 1985, Calif. Ptnrship Award 1985, The Emmett Award, 100 Club 1985, Brotherhood Award Los Angeles YMCA 1987, BSA's Vincent T. Lombardi Award 1985, Bill Of Rights Freedom Award 1986, Downtown Leadership Award 1987, Man of the Year 1988 by L.A.P.D., Salerni Collegian (hon.), Scapa Praetor (hon.); mem: Town Hall (pres. 1985), Chancery Club (pres. 1985), SCCOG (pres. 1972-), LAOOC (founding chmn.), So. Calif. Golf Assn. (pres. 1980), Republican Assocs., Am. Heart Assn. (dir., pres. 1981-2), Central City Assn., World Affairs Council, LA Hdqtrs. City Assn.; clubs: California (pres. 1983-84), Oakmont Country (pres. 1972), Flint Cyn. Tennis, Riviera RCC, LA Athletic, LA Country, Rotary (LA), The Newcomen Soc., 100 Club of LA, Lincoln, Twilight; mil: staff, Comdr.-in-Chief, US Army Europe, Heidelberg, Ger. 1957-58; Republican; Prot.; rec: golf, tennis, skiing. Res: 1314 Descanso Dr La Canada 91011 Ofc: Argue Pearson, 801 South Flower St Los Angeles 90017

ARNDT, ROLF DIETER, radiologist, educator; b. Dec. 14, 1941, W. Germany; nat. 1957; s. Ernst and Lieselotte A.; m. Peggy Sue Sander, June 24, 1966 (div. 1988); children: Ava b. 1969, Lisa b. 1972; edn: BA, Occidental Coll. 1964; MD, UCLA Sch. Medicine 1968; cert. Am. Coll. Radiology 1974. Career: asst. prof. radiology UCLA Med. Center, Los Angeles 1974-75; staff radiologist St. John's Hosp. Health Center, Santa Monica 1975-; assoc. clin. prof. radiology UCLA Med. Center 1985-, assoc. clin. prof. 1974-; honors: Phi Beta Kappa; mem: Am. Coll. Radiology, L.A. Co. Med. Soc., L.A. Co. Med. Assn., Calif. Radiological Soc.; author: Clin. Arthrography, 1981, 85; translator: Mammography, 1977; num. articles pub. in med. jours. 1968-88; mil: lt. comdr. USN 1970-72; Protestant; rec: sailing. Ofc: St. John's Hospital Health Center Dept. Radiology 1328 22nd St Santa Monica 90404

ARNOLD, FRANK JOSEPH, consultant; b. July 24, 1929, Los Angeles; s. Francis Joseph and Bina Agnes (Cavanaugh) A.; m. Matea Rivera; son, Norman b. 1964; grad. Cathedral H.S., L.A. 1947. Career: peace and civil rights activist, San Francisco 1963-66; community organizer, San Jose 1967-75; exec. bd. Central Labor Council, Santa Clara County 1976-82, chair edn. com. 1979-81; founding mem. Southwest Labor Studies Conf., 1975-; workshop mgr. Rehab. Mental Health, San Jose 1980-81; business mgr. Catholic Charities, Vocational Learning & Treatment Ctr. (sheltered workshop for adults with emotional disabilities), Santa Clara County, 1981-92, ret.; appt. exec. bd. Mid-Peninsula Conversion Project, Mt. View 1978, labor studies advy. com. San Jose City Coll. 1978-79, exec. bd. Economic & Social Opportunities (ESO) City of San Jose 1979-80; recipient outstanding service award Cath. Charities S.C. Co.

1986; publs: numerous articles on labor issues (hist. & current), papers presented at univ. confs. in U.S. and Mexico, author payroll computer pgm. `Timecard' (1986). Res/Ofc: 3293 Aramis Dr San Jose 95127

ARO, GLENN SCOTT, environmental and safety executive; b. Jan. 18, 1948, Balt.; s. Raymond Charles, Sr. and Elizabeth Virginia (Coppage) A.; mMarlene Rose Lefler, Jan. 8, 1972 (div. 1987); children: Vincent b. 1974, Marlena b. 1976; edn: BS in M.E., G.M. Inst., 1972; MBA fin. acctg., Wayne State Univ., 1980; reg. environmental assessor Calif., EPA, 1990. Career: staff engr. Gen. Motors, Balt., Detroit, and Van Nuys, Ca. 1972-84; sr. engr. New United Motor (GM-Toyota), Fremont, Ca. 1984-86; div. mgr. env. & maint. FMC Corp., San Jose 1986-89; cons. exec. sales Gaia Systems, Menlo Park 1990-92; mgr. Hughes Environmental Systems, Manhattan Beach 1992-; corp. mgr. env. & safety Ampex Corp., Redwood City 1990-; instr. env. compliance mgmt. Foothill Coll. 1992; lectr. Taiwan EPA and Taiwan Ind. Tech. Res. Inst., 1989; honors: judgeship Invest In Am., Mtn. View 1988; mem. Peninsula Indsl. & Bus. Assn. (dir., past v.p.), Calif. Bus. Roundtable (Toxics Awareness Proj. panel 1989-), Environ. Working Gp. (tech. com. 1986-88); author: Developing a Nat. Environmental Policy in a Global Mkt. (1989); Republican; R.Cath.; rec: running, reading, movies. Res: 2836 Palos Verdes Dr West Palos Verdes Estates 90274

ARONI, SAMUEL, professor emeritus of architecture and urban design; b. May 26, 1927, Kishinew, Romania, naturalized US citizen 1972; s. David Aharoni and Haia (Apoteker) Zalmanovici-A.; m. Malca Corenfeld, Nov. 11, 1956; children: Ruth b. 1958, Miriam b. 1959; edn: BCE (hons.) Univ. of Melbourne, Australia 1955; MS, UC Berkeley, 1965, PhD, 1966; chartered engr., Austr. Career: cons. in field of structures and concrete mats., Australia; lectr. Univ. Melbourne 1955-63; tchg. fellow UC Berkeley 1963-66; assoc. prof. San Francisco State Coll. 1966-67; res. engr. Am. Cement Corp., Riverside 1967-70; prof. Grad. Sch. Arch. and Urban Planning, UCLA 1970-91, actg. dean 1974-75, 83-85, emeritus prof. 1991-, dir. Spl. Acad. Cooperative Projects, Internat. Studies & Overseas Pgms., UCLA 1991-; mem. editl. advy. bd. Architl. Sci. Rev. (Australia) 1971-, Internat. Jour. for Devel. Technology 1984-; mem. bd. govs. Ben Gurion Univ. of Negev 1983-, bd. Architl. Res. Centrs. Consortium, Inc. (1982-93, exec. bd. 1983-86, 89-, v.p. 1985-86), US Geol. Survey earthquake cas. gp. 1989-, NSF Engring. Directorate MSME advy. com. 1985-90, NSF pgm. applied sci. and res. appl. (ASRA) panel of reviewers 1979-; awards: Austr. Town Pl. Inst. prize 1955, Hon. Founder Award Ben-Gurion Univ. of Negev 1984, J. James R. Croes gold medal ASCE 1981; mem: ASCE 1965-, Am. Concrete Inst. 1958-, Sigma Xi 1967-, Earthquake Engring. Res. Inst. 1980-, ASTM, Instn. of Engrs. (Austr.); Jewish; rec: chess. Res: 24249 Martha St Woodland Hills 91367

ARONSON, JONATHAN DAVID, educator; b. Oct. 28, 1949, St. Louis, Mo.; s. Adam and Judith (Spector) A.; m. Joan Abrahamson, May 28, 1984; children: Adam b. 1987, Zachary b. 1989; edn: AB, Harvard, 1971; MA, Stanford Univ., 1975, PhD, 1977. Career: res. fellow CFIA, Harvard, 1975-76; internat. economist US Trade Reps. Ofc., W.D.C. 1982-83; asst. prof. internat. rels., USC, 1977-82, assoc. prof., 1982-88, prof. 1988-, prof. Annenberg Sch. USC, 1988; author: Money and Power (1977), coauthor: Trade Talks (1985), When Countries Talk (1988), Mng. the World Econ. (1993) Res: 10575 Fontenelle Way Los Angeles 90077-1901 Ofc: Sch. Intl. Relations, USC, L.A. 90089-0043 Ph 310/740-2129

ARREDONDO, FREDERICK JOSEPH,computer technology recruiting company president; b. San Antonio, Tx.; s. Ephraim Alfonso and Margaret S. (Rios) A.; m. Mary Sue Bradford, Jan. 31, 1970; children: Anthony b. 1970, Russell b. 1973; edn: BS chemistry, Univ. Tx. Austin 1963; MBA, CSU Sacto. 1974; reg. rep. (1987). Career: instr. CSU, Sacto. 1973-74; sales rep. IBM Corp., San Francisco 1974-78; Digital Equipment Corp., Santa Clara 1978-80; cons. Coopers & Lybrand, San Francisco 1981-82, 82-85; cons. Alexander Grant 1982; MIS mgr. City and County of San Francisco 1985-89; pres. No. Calif. Search, Redwood City 1989-; honors: outstanding student CSUS 1974, Beta Gamma Sigma; mem: IEEE, BSA (cubmaster 1977-83); mil: lt. comdr. USN 1963-70, commendation medal 1969; Democrat; Presbyterian; rec: golf, skiing, jogging, violin. Ofc: Northern California Search 333 Twin Dolphin Dr Ste 145 Redwood City

ARROW, KENNETH J., economist, professor emeritus; b. Aug. 23, 1921, NY, NY; s. Harry I. and Lillian (Greenberg) A.; m. Selma Schweitzer, Aug. 31, 1947; children: David, b. 1962; Andrew, b. 1965; edn: B.Sc. soc. sci., The City Coll. 1940; MA, Columbia Univ. 1941; PhD, 1951. Career: res. assoc. Cowles Commn. for Research in Economics, Chgo., Ill. 1947-49; asst. prof. economics Univ. of Chgo. 1948-49; acting asst., assoc. and prof. of economics, statistics and ops. res., Stanford Univ., Stanford, CA 1959-68; prof. economics, James Bryan Conant Univ. prof., Harvard Univ., Cambridge, Ma 1968-79; Joan Kenney prof. of economics, prof. of ops. res., Stanford Univ., Stanford, Ca. 1979-91, prof. emeritus 1991-; pres. Soc. for Social Choice and Welfare, 1992-; pres. Internat. Economic Assn. 1983-86; pres. Internat. Soc. for Inventory Res. 1983-88; dir: Varian Assocs., Inc., Fireman's Fund; honors: John Bates Clark Medal, Am. Economic Assn. 1957, Nobel Prize in Economic Sci. 1972, Order of the Rising Sun 2d class Govt. of Japan; mem: Econometric Soc. (fellow, pres. 1958), Am. Econ. Assn. (distng. fellow, pres. 1972), Inst. of Mgmt. Scis. (pres. 1962), Nat. Acad. of Scis., Am. Philosophical Soc., Am. Acad. of Arts and Scis., Finnish Acad. of Scis., British Acad.; author: Social Choice and Individual Values (1951, 2d edit. 1963), Essays in the Theory of Risk-Bearing (1971), Limits of Organization (1974); Collected Papers, 1983-85; Studies in the Mathematical Theory of Inventory and Prodn.; Studies in Linear and Nonlinear Programming; A Time Series Analysis of Interindustry Demands; Pub. Investment, the Rate of Return and Optimal Fiscal Policy; Studies in Resource Allocation Processes; Social Choice and Multicriterion Decision-Making; mil: capt. U.S. Army Air Corps 1942-46; Democrat; Jewish; rec: bicycling, music. Res: 580 Constanzo St Stanford 94305 Ofc: Dept Economics Stanford Univ. Stanford 94305

ARSHAM, GARY, medical educator; b. 1941, Cleveland, Oh.; s. Sanford Ronald and Florence A.; m. Diana Silver, 1971; edn: AB cum laude Harvard Univ., 1963; MD, Case-Western Reserve, 1967; PhD, Univ. Ill., 1971. Career: fellow in med. edn. Univ. Ill., Chgo. 1968-71; asst., assoc. dean curriculum devel., asst. prof. medicine and health scis. comm. State Univ. N.Y., 1971-72; assoc. prof., prof. health professions edn. Univ. of Pacific, San Francisco 1972-79; chmn. Coun. on Edn. Pacific Med. Ctr., S.F. 1976-81; v.p. Arsham Consultants Inc., S.F. 1981-; adminstr. Pacific Vision Found., 1977-84, dir. edn., 1983-; nat. advy. bd. John Muir Hosp. Med. Film Fest. 1981-; task force on interdisciplinary edn. Nat. Jt. Practice Commn. 1973-74; bd. dirs. US-China Ednl. Inst. 1980-, secty. 1986-88; coauthor: Diabetes: A Guide to Living Well (1989, 2nd ed. 1992), chief editor Family Medicine Reports, S.F. (1983); mem: Am. Coll. Physicians (fellow), Am. Ednl. Resrch. Assocs., Assn. Am. Med. Colls., Assn. Study Med. Edn., Assn. Hosp. Med. Edn. (exec. com. 1980-84, sec-treas. 1982-84), Am. Diabetes Assn. (bd. S.F. chpt. 1984-, No. Calif. affil. 1986-87, Calif. affil. 1987-, pres. S.F. chpt. 1990-91, v.p. Calif. affil. 1992-93), Am. Assn. Diabetes Educators (assoc. editor 1985-92), Calif. Med. Assn., S.F. Med. Soc., Am. Assn. Individual Investors (bd. S.F. chpt. 1984-88), Harvard Club S.F. (bd. 1981-, pres. 1984-86), Lane Med. Soc. (Sommelier 1985-), Tech. Security Analysts Assn. Ofc: PO Box 15608 San Francisco 94115

ARSURA, EDWARD LOUIS, physician, educator; b. June 28, 1950, N.Y., NY; s. Louis and Edith (Cagnoni) A.; m. Donna J. Ross, Sept. 3, 1983; children: Alexandra b. 1986, Edward b. 1989; edn: BS, St. John's Univ., NY 1972; MD, Univ. Bologna, Italy 1978. Career: internal med. intern and resident Maimonides Med. Ctr., Bklyn. 1979-, asst. physician 1981-82, med. cons. 1981-82, asst. dir. medicine and med. edn. 1983-84, assoc. attdg. phys. dept. medicine 1984-86, assoc. dir. medicine and med. edn. 1984-86, attdg. phys., medicine 1986-90, dir. gen. Int. Med. & Gerontology 1986-88; attdg. phys., medicine St. Vincent's Hosp., NY 1988-90, chief Residency Tng. 1988-89; attdg. phys., chmn. dept. medicine, Kern Med. Ctr., Bakersfield, Ca. 1989-; assoc. clin. prof. medicine UC Los Angeles 1989-; awards: Maimonides Med. Ctr. resident of yr. 1979, chief res. 1982-83, tchr. of yr. (1984, 85, 86, 87); mem: Am. Fedn. of Clin. Res. 1983-, Assn. of Program Dirs. of Int. Med. 1983-, Am. Heart Assn. 1983-, Soc. of Gen. Int. Medicine 1983-, Am. Coll. of Physicians 1984-, Myasthenia Gravis Found. 1988-, Kern Co. Med. Soc. 1990-, Calif. Med. Assn. 1990-, Kern Co. Unit Am. Calif. Soc. (bd. 1990-); publs: 30+ jour. articles, 19 abstracts, 13 presentations (1981-). Res: 7713 Calle Los Batiquitos Bakersfield 93309 Ofc: Kern Medical Ctr. 1830 Flower St Bakersfield 93305

ARTHUR, BRENDA KAY, financial consultant, insurance broker; b. May 28, 1951, Charleston, W.Va.; d. Earl W. and Martena (Miller) Arthur; edn: BA sociology, W. Va. Univ., 1972; EdM in social agencies counseling, Univ. of Dayton, 1975; CLU 1993; ChFC and RHU studies in progress. Career: agent New York Life Ins. Co., Long Beach 1981-85, co-chair NY Life Ins. Co. Womens Network So. Pacific Region 1983-85; reg. rep. New York Life Securities Corp., Long Beach 1983-85; fin. cons. CIGNA Securities, CIGNA Ind. Fin. Services, Irvine 1985-87; fin. cons./planner Financial Services Unlimited, Inc. Newport Beach 1987-88; reg. rep. Southmark Securities Corp., 1987-88; MKA Financial Services Inc., 1988-90; reg. rep. Corp. Benefit Svcs. 1988-90; BKA Consulting, 1990-; reg. rep. Sun Am. Securities 1992-; awards: recipient company and industry profl. awards 1981-, New Orgn. Leader CIGNA Individual Fin. Services Co. feature story in nat. mo. mag. Approach Mag. 1986, Outstanding Young Women Am. 1984, disting. West Virginian awarded by Gov. W.Va. 1986, life bd. govs. Am. Biographical Inst. 1988, listed World Who's Who of Women 1988, Who's Who of Am. Women (1989-90, 92), Who's Who in Profl. & Exec. Women (1987, 88, 89), 2000 Notable Am. Women, Internat. Register of Profiles 1988-89, Internat. Hall of Leaders 1988-89, Who's Who In Am. 1994; mem: Internat. Assn. for Fin. Planning, Nat. Assn. Life Underwriters/Long Beach Chpt., Am. Soc. CLU/ChFC, PACE participant, qualifyer; Charitable Giving Council Orange County (charter), Orange County Employee Benefit Council; Assn. Health Insurance Agents; civic: Zonta Internat. Irvine/Saddleback Valley chpt. (v.p., bd. 1986-88, 91-92), Adam Walsh Child Resource Ctr./affil. of Nat. Ctr. for Missing and Exploited Children (advy. bd., exec. bd.); rec: travel, biking, tennis. Res: 1737 N Oak Knoll Dr Anaheim 92807 Mail: PO Box 18353 Anaheim 92817-8353

ARTINGSTALL, THOMAS, electrical and mechanical engineer; b. Oct. 28, 1920, Chgo.; s. Wm. Thomas and Louise Mary (Hanson) A.; m. Laura Ann Swanson, June 23, 1946 (div. 1955); m. Arloah Darlene Norelius, June 25, 1965; edn: BME, Ill. Inst. Tech., 1944; grad. studies USC, 1956; Reg. Profl. Engr., Calif., Ill. Career: designer Solar Capacitor Co., Los Angeles 1945-48; chief designer, developer Kollsman Instrument, 1948-55; mem. radar/antenna/transmitter devel. staff Autonetics, Anaheim 1956-70; tech. res. staff Los Angeles Aircraft, 1970-71, engring. splst. Rockwell Internat., Downey 1977-78; chief engr. Space Div. So. Calif., Yorba Linda, 1980-93; cons. engr. Pace-Arrow, Pomona 1970-78; engring., devel. and res., Swanson Electronics, Arcadia 1965-70; patents in field; mem. ASME, Nat. Mgmt. Assn., Profl. Engrs. Assn.; civic: ad hoc city incorporation com. 1966, archtl. com. 1968, parks & rec. dept. 1975 City of Yorba Linda; club: Langlauflers Ski; Democrat; R.Cath.; rec photography, skiing, camping, fishing. Res: 19622 Larkridge Dr Yorba Linda 92686-6423

ASAMI, SHINTA, terminal operating company executive; b. Jan. 21, 1925, Japan; s. Wasuke and Mitsu A.; m. Toshiko Hori, Nov. 8, 1953; children: Keiko b. 1954, Takashi b. 1957, Tohru John b. 1960; edn: Tokyo Univ. of Mercantile Marine, 5 yrs. Career: ship ofcr. and capt. "K" Line, 1945-1961; New York Port Captain 1961-63; gen. mgr. Port Harbor Div. 1970-72; pres. Internat. Transportation Service, Long Beach, Ca. 1972-90, chmn. bd. 1990-; pres. Huskey Terminal & Stevedoring Co. Inc., Tacoma, Wa. 1983-90; pres. TransBay Container Terminal, Oakland, Ca. 1986-90; dir. Kaiser Internat. Inc., L.A. 1986-90; chmn. bd. and c.e.o. Rail-Bridge Terminal (N.J.) Corp., Elizabeth, N.J. 1987-90; bd. dir. and v.p. Japanese C.of C. So. Calif.; pres. Saitama Kenjin Kai of So. Calif.; v.p. Kenjinkai Kyogikai; exec. bd. Boy Scouts of Am., Long Beach Area Council 1991-; clubs: Indian Wells CC, PGA West CC, Los Coyotes CC; rec: golf. Res: 5651 Burlingame Ave Buena Park 90621 Ofc: 1281 Pier J Ave Long Beach 90802

ASHCROFT, RICHARD THOMAS, computer peripheral company executive; b. Nov. 9, 1934, Utica, N.Y.; s. Edwin William and Ann Catherine (Bogan) A.; m. Beverly Rita Trimm, July 6, 1957; children: Mark b. 1958, Catherine b. 1959, Thomas b. 1960, Pamela b. 1964; edn: BEE, Clarkson Univ., 1956; grad. work in bus. adminstrn. Univ. Rochester 1963-64. Career: instrument engr. E.I. du Pont, Niagara Falls 1956-57, power engr. 1957-60; engr. Gen. Dynamics/ Electronics, Rochester, NY 1960-61, product mgr. 1962-64, mktg. mgr. 1964-68; v.p. mktg. Aydin Energy Systems, Palo Alto 1968-75; v.p. Internat. Stanford Technology Corp., Sunnyvale 1975-78; pres. and c.e.o. Internat. Imaging Systems, Milpitas 1979-; honors: distinguished alumni Clarkson Univ. 1991; mem. Electronics Assn. of Calif. (dir. 1984-87), Am. Electronics Assn. (dir. 1989-92), United Way Santa Clara Co. (electronics div. vol. 1984-), Family Service Assn., Santa Clara Co.(dir. 1992-); mil: capt. US Army Signal Corps 1957, 61-62. Ofc: International Imaging Systems 1500 Buckeye Dr Milpitas 95035

ASHE, JOHN H., neuroscientist, educator; b. Mar. 27, 1944, Phila.; s. John H. Ashe, Sr. and Gloria (Jones) Faison; div.; 1 child John Miles b. 1981; edn: AA, San Bdo. Valley Coll., 1970; BA in psych. (physiol.), highest honors, UC Riverside, 1972; PhD biol. scis. (UC Regents grad. fellow), UC Irvine, 1977; postdoc. res. tng., 1977-80: UCSF Med. Sch. Dept. Physiology, NIH postdoc. fellow in neurophysiology 1977-78, NIMH interdisciplinary res. postdoc. fellow 1979. Career: tchg. asst. UC Irvine 1973-77; asst. res. physiologist UCSF Med. Sch. 1979-80; asst. prof. UC Riverside 1980-84, assoc. prof. 1984-90, prof. 1990-, mem. grad. pgm. biomed. scis. 1987-, grad. pgm. neurosci. 1989-; mem. UC Ctr. for Neurobiology of Learning and Memory, UC Irvine, 1984-; mem: AAAS, Am. Soc. for Cell Biology, Am. Physiol. Soc., Soc. for Neurosci., Internat. Brain Resrch. Orgn./World Fedn. of Neuroscientsts, NY Acad. Scis.; rec: jazz. Ofc: Depts. Neuroscience and Psychology 075 Univ. Calif., Riverside 92521

ASHLEY, SHARON ANITA, pediatric anesthesiologist; b. Dec. 28, 1948, Goulds, Fla.; d. John Henry Ashley and Johnnie Mae (Everett) Mitchell; children: Cecili b. 1974, Nicole b. 1979, Erika b. 1986; edn: BA, Lincoln Univ., 1970; post baccalaureate certif. Pomona Coll., Claremont, 1971; MD, Hahnemann Univ., 1976. Career: physician-pediatric anesthesiologist specialist Martin L. King, Jr. Hosp., Los Angeles 1976-; honors: Nat. Merit finalist 1966, King Drew Med. Center Outstanding Tchr. of Yr., dept. anesth. 1988-89 and Outstanding Faculty of Year 1990-91, listed Who's Who in Am.; mem: AMA, CMA, Nat. Med. Assn., Am. Soc. Anesthesiology, Calif. Soc. Anesth. (alt. del. 1991), L.A. Co. Med. Assn., Alpha Kappa Alpha Sor.; pub. article in Jour. of Student Nat. Med. Assn. (1974), pub. article Anesthesia Analgesia (1993); Democrat; Baptist; rec: sailing, reading. Res: 1555 5th St Manhattan Beach 90266

ATKINSON, DOROTHY GILLIS, scholarly association executive; b. Aug. 5, 1929, Malden, Mass.; d. George Edward and Grace Margaret (Campagna) G.; m. Sterling K. Atkinson Jr., June 25, 1950, div. Dec. 1982; children: Kim b. 1955, Paul b. 1958; edn: BA, Barnard Coll., 1951; MA, UC Berkeley, 1953; PhD, Stanford Univ., 1971. Career: asst. prof. Stanford Univ., 1973-83; assoc. prof. UC Berkeley, 1984; exec. dir. Am. Assn. for the Advancement of Slavic Studies, Stanford 1981-; cons. fed. govt. agys., 1983-; awards: Pulitzer scholar, Mellon grantee, Stanford Univ. fellow, grantee Irex, Ford, and Fulbright; mem.

advy. coun. US Dept. State 1984-; mem. Internat. Coun. for Soviet & East European Studies (exec. bd. 1985-), Nat. Coun. of Area Studies Assns. 1986-, Internat. Res. & Exchanges Bd. (exec. bd. 1991-); author: The End of the Russian Land Commune (1983), coeditor: Women in Russia (1976). Ofc: AAASS, Jordan Quad/Acacia Bldg, 125 Panama St Stanford 94305-4130

ATKINSON, SHERIDAN EARLE, lawyer, financial analyst; b. Feb. 14, 1945, Oakland, Calif.; s. Arthur Sheridan and Esther Louise (Johnson) A.; m. Marjorie, Aug. 13, 1966; children: Ian b. 1972; edn: BS, Univ. Calif. 1966; JD, Univ. San Francisco 1969; MBA, Univ. Calif. 1971; postgrad. study, Univ. So. Calif., CSUH, Humboldt State Coll.; admitted Calif. State Bar 1970. Career: prin. Atkinson & Assoc. fin. and mgmt. cons. corp. and bus. valuations San Francisco 1968-; assoc. Charles O. Morgan, Jr., S.F. 1972-76; solo law practice, San Francisco, Bay Area and Roseville, 1976-; mem: Am., Calif. bar assns.; mil: USAR 1970-76; Republican. Res: 1045 Key Route Blvd Albany 94706

ATLAS, DONALD H., physician, ret.; b. Aug. 31, 1913, Chicago, Ill.; s. Herman and Raya (Ginsberg) A.; m. Nora Glassenberg, June 27, 1937; children: Stephen b. 1944, James b. 1949; edn: BS, Northwestern Univ. 1934; BS, 1936; MD, 1938; PhD, 1940; mil: AUS 1942-46; Democrat; rec: music. Res: La Jolla 92037

AUERBACH, BRADFORD CARLTON, lawyer; b. April 17, 1957, Bethesda, Md.; s. Richard Carlton and Rita (Argen) A.; m. Jane Donnan Irwin, April 30, 1988; edn: BA, Hamilton Coll. 1979; JD, Boston Coll. 1982; admitted St. Bar Calif. Career: atty. Peter J. Sullivan, Marina del Rey 1984-89; atty. The Walt Disney Home Video, Burbank 1989-92; v.p. and gen. counsel Philips Interactive Media of America, 1992-; asst. prof. Loyola Univ., Los Angeles 1984; awards: Nat. Mock Trial Championships 1982; mem: Am. Trial Lawyers Assn., Am. Bar Assn., Santa Monica Bar Assn., Beverly Hills Bar Assn., Paladins of Temerity L.A.; article pub. in profl. jour. (1983), west coast correspondent Time Out mag. (London). Res: 1390 S Marengo Ave Pasadena 91106 Ofc: 11111 Santa Monica Blvd L.A. 90025

AULENBACHER, LOUIS WILLIAM, title company executive; b. Dec. 19, 1955, Mexico City, Mex., naturalized U.S. 1962; s. Walter E. and Rosalva Phoebe (Armendariz) A.; edn: AA, Multnomah Bible Sch., Portland 1984; BSBA cand. Univ. of Phoenix, S.F.; R.E. sales lic. Tex. and Calif., cert. R.E. tax appraiser- urban & rural Oreg. 1981. Career: customer service rep. Western Title Co., Portland 1984; mktg. dir. Reliance Title Co., Houston 1984-85; title ofcr. World Title Co., Orange, Calif. 1985-87; title splst. American S&L Assn., Stockton 1987-88; advy. title ofcr. N. American Title, Redwood City 1988-89; Calif. trustee, sale specialist Fidelity National Title, Irvine 1989-90, nat. claims officer, 1990-; recipient Dennis Spearman achiev. award Multnomah Bible Sch. 1983; summer intern Arbutus Youth Pgm., San Andreas, Calif. 1982, group home supr. Youth Progress Assn. Portland, Oreg. 1981-83; mem. Calif. Trustees Assn., World Affairs Council, Nat. Panel of Consumer Arbitrators, U.S. Chess Fedn.; author unpub. book, poetry; Republican (Nat. Com. 1988-, Calif. Assembly 1989-); Prot.; rec: chess, geopolitics, vol. work w. delinquent youth. Res: 3001 Redhill B-5 #108-139 Costa Mesa 92626

AULIK, DAVID JAMES, food industry executive, consultant, business and technology transfer specialist; b. Nov. 17, 1943, Antigo, Wis.; s. Raymond John and Emma (Schweitzer) A.; m. Susan Marie Foster, Aug. 2, 1981; children: Bond Aaron b. 1984, Taylor Jasmin b. 1987, Joshua Raymond b. 1988; edn: BS (athletic scholar), MS, and PhD in food chemistry, Univ. Wis., 1966, 1968, 1971, MBA in mktg./mgt., 1976. Career: mgmt. trainee Pet Inc., Hickory, N.C. 1966-67; research asst. Univ. Wis., 1967-71, postdoctoral fellow 1971-72; exec. asst., interdeptl. coord., mgr. nutrition div., dir. client svs., WARF Institute Inc. (now Hazleton Labs. div. Corning), Madison, Wis., 1972-77; founder/c.e.o. Aulik Consulting Group Inc., 1977-, participant in devel. of 2500+ food products for 200+ client cos.; owner Pogen's Cookies, Compton, 1991-; c.e.o. and v.chmn. bd. ITD Corp., Carpenteria, Ca. 1990-; bd. dir. Henri's Food Products Co., Milw.; food counsel Nutri / System Franchisees (NSF), Janesville, Wis.; founder Freshen's Premium Frozen Yogurt, Atlanta, Ga.; consultant restaurant chains incl. Jack-In-The-Box, Winchell's, Internat. Dairy Queen, Hardee's, Marriott, Quaker Oats, Kraft General Foods, Pizza Hut, Arby's, Internat. House of Pancakes, Denny's, others; mem: Agricultural Research Inst., Am. Assn. of Cereal Chemists, Inst. of Food Technologists, Res. & Devel. Assocs., Sigma Xi; pub. research and tech. articles in field; Republican; rec: music, wine, gardening, football, basketball, running. Ofc: Aulik Consulting Group, Inc. 190 Alviso Dr Camarillo 93010

AUSENBAUM, HELEN EVELYN, psychologist/social worker; b. May 16, 1911, Chgo.; d. Herbert Noel and Mayme Eva (Bircher) Ausenbaum; edn: stu. Univ. of Ill., Urbana 1930-2; AB, UC Berkeley 1938, MSW 1956; postgrad. stu. CSU Hayward 1976-8, JFK Univ., Orinda 1976; lic. clin. social worker (LCSW), diplomate NASW, Calif. cred. school psychologist, 1956-. Career: social worker Alameda Co. Welfare Commn., 1939-42, American Red Cross, San Francisco 1942-43; exec. dir. ARC, Richmond 1943-51; tchr. Richmond Public Schs. 1951-53; sch. social worker/sch. psychologist Oakland Public Schs.

1953-76; program dir. Let's Rap pgm. McChesney Jr. H.S., Oakland 1970-82; currently pgm. dir. Diablo Valley Found. for Aging, Support Service for Elders, Walnut Creek; apptd: Orinda Commn. on Aging (1976-, chair 1978-81), Contra Costa Co. Mental Health Com. on Aging, Lincoln Child Ctr. Oakland (bd. dirs. 1976-87), Contra Costa Co. Advy. Council On Aging (pres. 1985-86), Triple A Council of Calif. 1985-86, Calif. State Coordinating Com. for Mental Health and Older Adults, East Bay Elder Abuse Prevention (Consortium, Advy. Devel. Bd. 1987); awards: Am.Red Cross scholarship 1942-43, appreciation award Richmond Service Clubs, Oakland Principals Club Award 1976, certif. Orinda City Council; mem: Calif. Tchrs Assn., Nat. Assn. of Social Workers (charter), Calif. Assn. of Sch. Social Workers, Am. Soc. on Aging, AAUW; Democrat; Presbyterian; rec: photography, travel, coins & stamps. Res: 1840 Tice Creek Dr Apt 2402 Walnut Creek 94575 Ofc: Orinda Counseling Center 1 Camino Sobrante Ste 21 Orinda 94563

AUTRY, ORVON GENE, singer, actor, broadcasting executive; b. Sept. 29, 1907, Tioga, Tex.; s. Delbert and Elnora (Ozmont) A.; m. Ina Mae Spivey, Apr. 1, 1932 (dec. 1980); m. 2d. Jacqueline Ellam, July 1981; edn: grad., Tioga High Sch. 1925. Career: railroad telegraph operator, Sepulpa, Okla. 1925; first phonograph record of cowboy songs 1929; radio artist Station WLS, Chicago 1930-34; motion picture actor in 93 films, 1934-; starred in 88 musical Western feature pictures, 91 half-hour TV pictures; pres., chmn. bd. Calif. Angels; chmn. bd. Golden West Broadcasters, owner radio stations: KMPC AM/FM Hollywood, KVI-AM and KPLZ-FM, Seattle; mem: Internat. Footprinters; Masons (33 deg.); Shriners; Elks; composer 250+ songs incl. That Silver-Haired Daddy of Mine, 1931, You're the Only Star in My Blue Heaven, 1938, Dust, 1938, Tears On My Pillow, 1941, Be Honest With Me, 1941, Tweedle O'Twill, 1942; Here Comes Santa Claus, 1948; mil: USAAF, 1942-45. Address: c/o Golden West Broadcasters, 5858 W Sunset Blvd (POB 710) Hollywood 90078

AVALOS, PHILIP CHAVEZ, exercise sports specialist, physiologist, strength & conditioning coach; b. Mar. 11, 1954, Orange; s. Emilio Sanchez and Amelia (Chavez) A.; edn: Fullerton Coll. 1975-78, CSU Fullerton 1979; BS, and MS, Univ. Ariz., 1985, 1986; PhD Pacific Western Univ. 1993; strength and conditioning splst. Nat. Strength Coaches Assn. C.S.C.S. 1979. Career: strength & conditioning coach- tennis, soccer, football, basketball, Anaheim H.S., 1980-85, 86-87; football, Tucson (Ariz.) H.S., 1985-86; asst. tnr. soccer, football Orange H.S., 1987-88; tchr. Brea Sch., 1987-88; instr., strength & conditioning coord./asst. football coach Pomona Coll., Claremont 1988-91; asst. football coach Etiwanda High Sch. 1991-92; co-head football coach Bonita High Sch. 1992-93; mem: Am. Assn. of Health Phys. Edn. Recreation and Dance, Nat. Tchrs. Assn., Nat. Coaches Assn., Nat. Strength and Conditioning Coaches Assn., Womens Sports Fitness Assn., Assoc. mem. Scripts Inst. of Oceanography 1992, Am. Runners & Fitness Assn., Nat. Trust of Historic Preservation, assoc. mem. Univ. San Diego, UN-official world record power bench press May 9, 1990 181 lbs. class (686.5 lbs.), record holder 181 lbs. class power bench press Jan. 21, 1987 (555.4 lbs.); mil: radioman 2c USN 1972-75, USNR 1975-79; rec: powerlifting. Res: 525 W 9th St Claremont 91711

AVERBOOK, BERYL DAVID, vascular surgeon; b. Aug. 17, 1920, Superior, Wis.; s. Abraham B. and Clara (Ziechig) A.; m. Gloria Sloane, Apr. 2, 1955; children: Bruce Jeffery b. 1956, Allen Wayne b. 1960; edn: Superior St. Tchrs. Coll. 1938-39; BS, Univ. Wis. 1942, MD, 1945; postgrad. tng. Univ. of Colo. 1948-50; diplomate, special qualifications in gen. vascular surgery, Am. Board of Surgery. Career: intern Akron (Ohio) City Hosp. 1945-46; surgical resident Fort Logan VA Hosp., Denver, Colo. 1948-50; Rochester (NY) Gen. Hosp. 1950-51; Wadsworth VA Hosp., Los Angeles 1951-54; chief surg. serv. Harbor Gen. Hosp., L.A. 1954-61; instr. in surg. Univ. Calif. Med. Ctr., L.A. 1954-58, asst. prof. surg. 1958-61, clin. asst. prof. surg. 1961-65; pvt. practise splst. in tumor and vascular surg., Torrance 1961-; Fellow A.C.S., mem. Soc. for Clin. Vascular Surgery, AMA, CMA, L.A. Co. Med. Assn., NY Acad. of Sci., Soc. of Head & Neck Surgeons, Long Beach Surg. Soc., L.A. Acad. of Medicine, Am. Geriatric Soc., UCLA Harbor Collegium (bd. dirs.), Am. Men of Medicine; mil: capt. M.C. AUS. Res: 6519 Springpark Ave Los Angeles 90056 Ofc: Beryl D. Averbook, MD 3640 Lomita Blvd #202 Torrance 90505

AXON, DONALD CARLTON, architect, consultant; b. Feb. 27, 1931, Haddonfield, NJ; s. William Russell, Sr. and Gertrude (Ellis) A.; m. Janice, Mar. 16, 1968; children: Donald b. 1953, James b. 1955, Marianne b. 1957, Darren b. 1958, William b. 1961, (step): Jonathan b. 1948, Elise b. 1956; edn: B.Arch., Pratt Inst. 1954; MS arch., Columbia Univ. 1966; arch. NY 1959, Calif. 1971, Pa. 1963. Career: ptnr. Bailey & Axon AIA Assocs. Long Beach 1960-66; programmer, project mgr. CRS, Houston 1966-69; pgmr./planner Kaiser Permanente Med. Care Group, Los Angeles 1969-75; pgmr./ med. dir. DMJM, L.A. 1975-79; proj. mgr. Lyon Assocs. L.A. 1979-80; pres. DCA/AIA Inc., L.A. 1980-; instr. Building Science Pgm., USC, 1978-82; instr., team leader AHA-UCLA sponsored planning & programming seminar 1975; guest lectr. UCLA Sch. of Arch. 1976, 77, Texas A&M Grad. Sch. Arch. 1977; liaison Kaiser Found. Hosps., UCLA Sch. of Arch. and Urban Planning Hosp. Pgm. 1973; profl. advisor Univ. Texas Dept. Arch. 1968-69; advisor to chmn. Rice Univ. Sch. of Arch. Masters Pgm. in Hosps. 1968-69; profl. dir. Future Archs. of Am.

1965-66; honors: Honor Award (Progressive Architecture Design Awards Pgm. 1955), First Prize (student team proj. 1953), Full Tuition Scholarship (Columbia Univ.), L.A. Beautiful Award (for KFH Norwalk Hosp.), Excellence in Design (Orange Co. chpt. AIA); Fellow AIA (nat. bd. dirs. 1987-89, chmn. com. on Arch. for Health 1980), mem. Los Angeles Chpt. AIA (bd. dirs. 1983-84, pres. 1986), Calif. Council AIA, Archtl. Found. of L.A. (founding mem., pres. 1987-89), Internat. Conf. Bldg. Officials, Forum for Healthcare Planning (dir. 1982-, chmn. regl. pgm. com., v.p. 1991-92), Am. Hosp. Assn., Assn. Western Hosps., Internat. Hosp. Fedn., Fellow Royal Soc. Health, Archtl. Guild (USC), Crestwood Hills Assn. (bd. 1971-83, pres. 1973-75), Brentwood Community Fedn. (bd. 1973-75, 1st v.p. 1974-75); gubnat. appt. bd. mem. Building Safety Bd., Ofc. of Statewide Health Planning & Devel. 1984, Calif. Seismic Safety Commn. Hosp. Act Task Force 1976-77, and Hosp. Act Legislation Task Force 1980. Ofc: Donald C. Axon FAIA 823 Hanley Ave Los Angeles 90049

AZCUE, PEDRO ARTURO, real estate marketing; b. Sept. 12, 1955, Mexico City, Mex.; s. Pedro Paulo Azcue and Lilly (Aderman) Mena; m. Ana Elena Attolini, Dec. 21, 1979; children: Pedro b. 1982, Derrick b. 1984, Axel b. 1987; edn: BS indsl. engring. (hons.), Univ. Iberoamericana, Mexico City, 1977; MBA, Stanford Grad. Sch. of Bus., 1981; reg. industrial engr., Mex. 1977. Career: investments ofcr. Banco de Mexico, Mexico City 1977-79; assoc. La Salle Partners, Chicago, Ill. 1981-84, v.p. La Salle Partners, Dallas, Tx. 1984-92, senior v.p. La Salle Partners, Los Angeles 1992-; speaker Banco de Mexico, Mexico City, 1977, Indsl. Devel. Council, Nashville, Tenn., 1992; honors: best student of Mexico, Instituto Mexicano de Cultura, Mexico City 1977; mem. Calif.-Mexico Project 1989-, US-Mex. C.of C. 1989-; club: Jonathan (L.A.); publs: R.E. articles (1991, 92); mil: Mexico 1976-77; R.Cath.; rec: travel. Res: 24939 Alicante Dr Calabasas 91302 Ofc: LaSalle Partners 355 S Grand Ave Ste 4280 Los Angeles CA 90071

BACHER, ROSALIE WRIDE, retired school administrator, counselor; b. May 25, 1925, Los Angeles; d. Homer Martin and Reine (Rogers) Wride; m. Archie Bacher, Jr., Mar. 30, 1963; edn: AB, Occidental Coll. 1947, MA, 1949; grad. work in counseling, sch. adminstrn., USC, 1949; Calif. life tchg. credentials: elem. and secondary tchg./ adminstrn., pupil personnel. Career: faculty Long Beach Unified Sch. Dist. 1959-89: English, Latin and history tchr. Jordan High Sch. 1949-55, counselor Jordan H.S. 1955-65, Lakewood H.S. 1966; research asst. Sch. Dist. Research Office 1967; v. principal Washington Jr. H.S. 1968, asst. principal Lakewood H.S. 1969, v. principal Jefferson Jr. H.S. 1970-81, v.principal John Marshall Jr. H.S., 1981-87, v. principal Lindbergh Jr. H.S. 1986-87; counselor Millikan H.S. 1988, Hill Jr. H.S. 1988-89, ret. 1989; mem. Vice and Asst. Principals Assn. (chair vocat. Guidance Steering Com., ofcr.); honors: Phi Beta Kappa 1947; mem: Pi Lambda Theta (pres. O.C. chpt.), Delta Kappa Gamma (pres. Delta Psi chpt., st. chair Profl. Affairs), Phi Delta Gamma (USC chpt. pres.), AAUW; MA thesis: A Hist. of the Long Beach oil fields and their influence on the city of L.B.; Republican; Christian Sci.; rec: home, garden, and dog. Res: 265 Rocky Point Rd Palos Verdes Estates 90274

BAERG, RICHARD HENRY, podiatric physician, educator, medical-legal consultant; b. Jan. 19, 1937, Los Angeles; s. Henry Francis and Ruth Elizabeth (Loven) B.; m. Yvonne Marie Estrada, Nov. 23, 1987; children (by previous marriage): Carol b. 1963, William b. 1967, Michael b. 1969, Yvette b. 1970; gr.dau., Brie Ann b. 1991; edn: AA, Reedley Coll., 1956; BS, DPM, and MSc, Calif. Coll. Pod. Med., S.F. 1965, 1968, 1970; MPH, UC Berkeley, 1971; DSc, NYCPM, 1980; LittD, OCPM, 1984; postdoctoral intern Highland Hosp., Oakland 1969; surgical resident Pacific Coast Hosp., S.F. 1970; Inst. for Ednl. Mgmt. Harvard Univ., 1975; lic. podiatric physician Calif. BMQA 1968; bd. cert. Am. Bd. Pod. Orthopedics & Primary Pod. Med., Am. Bd. Pod. Surg., Am. Bd. Pod. Pub. Health. Career: academic dean NY Coll. of Pod. Med., NYC 1971-74; dean and exec. v.p. Calif. Pod. Med. Ctr., San Francisco 1974-78; pres. Ill. Coll. Pod. Med., Chgo. 1978-79; dir. pod. svs. Veterans Affairs, Wash. DC 1979-86; exec. dir. Am. Board of Pod. Orthopedics, Wash. DC 1980-90; v.p./med. dir. Orthopedics Dr. Footcare, Montclair, Calif. 1986-90; asst. prof. Calif. Coll. Pod. Med., S.F. 1970-71, clin. assoc. prof. Stanford Med. Sch. 1974-76, clin. prof. NY Coll. Pod. Med. 1971-74, Calif. Coll. Pod. Med. 1974-78, Univ. of Osteo. Med., Des Moines, Ia. 1984-, Univ. N.C. Sch. of Medicine 1992-; Barry Univ. Sch. of Pod. Med., Fla. 1992-; private practice in Beverly Hills, 1976-78, Montclair, 1987-90, Redlands, 1990-92; appt. by Gov. Deukmejian to St. Dept. Consumer Affairs Bd. of Podiatric Medicine 1989-90; chmn. Pod. Health Sect. A.P.H.A., 1992-94; awards: USPHS fellow 1970-71, nominee Rockerfeller Pub. Svs. Wash. DC 1979, mem. Nat. Academies of Practice, Wash.D.C. (distinguished dr. honoree 1986), Kenison Award Assn. of Pod. Med. Wash. DC 1985; mem: Am. Pod. Med. Assn., Calif. Pod. Med. Assn., Am. Assn. of Colls. of Pod. Med. (pres. 1980), Am. Coll. of Foot & Ankle Surgeons (Fellow), Am. Coll. of Foot Orthopedics (Fellow), Acad. of Ambulatory Foot Surgery (Fellow), Assn. of Mil. Surgeons, Commonwealth Club Calif., Masons; author chapt. on Govt. Health Policy in Textbook of Pub. Health, 27 articles in J. of Am. Pod. Med. Assn.; mil: AUS Med. Corps 1958-66; Republican; Prot.; rec: piano, opera, classical music. Res: 461 E California Blvd Pasadena 91106

BAHAN, JOSEPH ROBERT, doctor of chiropractic; b. July 29, 1963, Lynwood, Calif.; s. Joseph William and Judith Ann (Willenbring) B.; edn: BS and DC, Cleveland Chiropractic Coll., L.A. 1989; lic. DC, State of Calif. 1990. Career: dir. of radiology Ward Chiropractic, Long Beach 1988-, dr. of chiropractic 1990-; owner/DC Bahan Chiropractic Center, Dana Point 1993-; instr. for intact spine-meningeal systems at num. chiro. ctrs. 1989-, So. Calif. Coll. Chiro. 1993; res. on S-M effects on muscular dystrophy Ward Chiro., Long Beach 1991-, Bahan Chiro., Dana Point 1993-; field dr.'s cons. Ward Chiro. and Capperauld Chiro. 1992-; featured guest/interviews on muscular dystrophy, num. radio and T.V. stas. 1992-93, KNBC-TV (Today Show), N.Y. 1993; interview/feature for 5 newspaper and 2 mag. articles 1992-93; mem. Calif. Chiro. Assn. 1993-; author: articles pub. in Chiropractic Economics 1991, The American Chiropractor 1992; Republican; Roman Catholic; rec: jet skiing (asst. tech. inspector for Internat. Jet Sports Boating Assn.), marlin fishing. Res: 8145 Woolburn Dr. Huntington Beach 92646 Ofc: Bahan Chiropractic Center 34207 Coast Hwy Suite 101 Dana Point 92629

BAHARVAR, JAMSHID JIM, physician, internist; b. June 15, 1947, Teheran, Iran; s. Morad and Azize (Haroonian) B.; m. Oct. 1985; edn: grad., Am. Coll. Teheran 1962; Pahlavi Univ. Med. Sch. 1971; lic. phys. NY, Calif. 1979. Career: intern Jewish Meml. Hosp. NY 1975-76; resident Long Island Jewish Med. Ctr. NY 1976-77; fellowship geriatric med. Jewish Inst. for Geriatric Care 1976-77; fellowship nuclear med. L.I. Jewish Hosp.1977-78; phys. pvt. practice Santa Monica 1978-; instr., cons. var. hosps.; on staff 10 hosps. in LA area; mem: World Med. Assn., Am. Geriatric Soc., Am. Coll. Phys., Am. Soc. Internal Med.; publs: articles in med. jours.; mil: med. ofcr. Iran Army 1972-73; Jewish; rec: sports, music, piano, dancing, sailing. Ofc: 2001 Santa Monica Blvd Ste 1050 Santa Monica 90404

BAILEY, ALEX STUART, engineering manager; b. June 23, 1952, San Diego; s. Robert Earwood and Marcelle Adalyn (Groff) B.; m. Terri Anne Marsh, May 31, 1986; children: Kyle b. 1988, Corinne b. 1990; edn: AA, Canada Coll., 1972; BA, UC Berkeley, 1974; MBA, Santa Clara Univ., 1982. Career: satellite ops. engr. Lockheed Missiles & Space Co., Sunnyvale 1974-78, mgmt. devel. program 1978-80, senior res. engr. 1980-82; staff engr. ultrasystems def. & space 1982-85; program mgr. 1985-88; engrg. mgr. GTE Government Systems, Mtn. View 1988-; honors: Calif. Scholarship Fedn. 1970, Outstanding Young Men of Am. 1989, listed Who's Who in West 1992; mem. Smithsonian Instn. (assoc. 1975-), US Fencing Assn., Bay Area Mil. Miniature Soc.; rec: European medieval history, medieval arms & armor, antiques, fencing, softball. Res: 1634 Juanita Ave San Jose 95125 Ofc: GTE Government Systems PO Box 7188 Mountain View 94039

BAILEY, K. DALE, psychologist; b. May 10, 1936, Belvedere, So.Carolina; s. Samuel K. and Emma M. (Thompson) B.; m. Gwendolyn McKeithen, 1964 (div. 1972); children: Brenda Susan b. 1967, Phillip Oliver b. 1969; m. Phyllis Kay Bekemeyer, June 23, 1984; edn: BA, Coll. of Wooster, Ohio 1958; STB, Harvard Div. Sch., 1961; ThD, Sch. of Theol. at Claremont 1967; cert. Manchester, Oxford, England 1960. Career: minister of counseling, First Methodist Ch., Pasadena 1963-64; priv. practice Albany 1964-93; cons. Pasadena Council of Churches 1966-69, S.F. General Hosp. 1974-75; Valencia St. Med. Clinic, S.F. 1974-84, Am. Internat. Assurance Co., Singapore 1978-79; mem: Am. Psychological Assn., Alameda Co. Psychological Assn.; Presbyterian; rec: remodeling, landscaping. Res: 1250 Washington Ave Albany 94706

BAILEY, MICHAEL JOHN, computer scientist; b. Oct. 16, 1953, Phila.; s. Theodore W. and Anne (Pomeroy) B.; edn: BSME, Purdue Univ., 1975, MSME, 1976, PhD, 1979; Calif. lic. EIT. Career: tech. staff Sandia Nat. Labs, Albuquerque 1979-81; asst., assoc. prof. Purdue Univ., 1981-85; dir. adv. devel. Megatek, San Diego 1985-89; mgr. of sci. visualization San Diego Supercomputer Ctr., San Diego 1989-; assoc. adj. prof. UC San Diego, 1989-; cons. in field; recipient Ralph Teeter Award SAE 1983; mem. Assn. Computing Machinery 1979-, ACM Siggraph (dir. 1986-90, conf. co-ch. 1991), Nat. Computer Graphics Assn. 1980-, Am. Soc. Mech. Engrs. 1976-. Ofc: SDSC, PO Box 85608 San Diego 92186

BAILEY, TRACEY LEIGH, acupuncturist, herbalist; b. Jan. 14, 1960, Torrance, Calif.; d. Barry C. and Susanne Mae (LeVan) B.; m. Gary Eugene Beck, Sept. 22, 1991; children: Carter b. 1992; edn: El Camino Coll., Lawndale, Calif., 1978-80, 1982-83; Coll. of the Virgin Islands, St. Thomas, 1980-81; Calif. Acupuncture Coll., L.A., 1984-86; MS, O.M.D., SAMRA Univ., L.A., 1986-88; adv. study in Oriental medicine, Zhejiang Univ., Hangzhou, China P.R.C., 1990; lic. acupuncturist, Doctor of Oriental Medicine, Calif.; Career: staff acupuncturist, Turnaround Drug Treatment Ctr., L.A., 1987; acupuncturist/herbalist, Adv. Sports Care and Chiropractic Clinic, Redondo Beach, 1989-90; doctor of Oriental medicine, clinic dir., Ocean Side Acupuncture, Manhattan Beach, 1991-; tchr., South Bay Adult Sch., Manhattan Beach, 1990-; tchr./lectr., UC Long Beach, 1990-; lectr., Redondo Beach Sr. Citizens, 1990-; mem. Calif. Acupuncture Assn., 1987-, Am. Assn. of Acupuncture & Oriental Medicine, 1992-, Manhattan Beach C. of C.; editor: book, Dermatology-Chinese Medicine, 1990; rec: Koshiki karate. Ofc: Ocean Side Acupuncture 1104 Highland Ave Suite 1 Manhattan Beach 90266

BAIRD, RAND JAMES, chiropractor; b. Mar. 29, 1948, Chgo.; s. Arch Emery and Harriet Mary (Kowalski) B.; edn: BS in med. record adminstrn., Univ. Ill., Chgo. 1970; BA in psych., Univ. Ill., Urbana 1972; MPH, Univ. Ill. Med. Sch., 1975; DC, Cleveland Chiropractic Coll., 1982; lic. DC, Calif. 1982. Career: assoc. dir. med. records Michael Reese Hosp., Chgo. 1970-71; asst. dir. med. records Cook County Hosp., Chgo. 1971-74; asst. adminstr./dir. med. records Rush-Presbyn.-St. Luke's Med. Ctr., Chgo. 1974-77; dir. med. records Cedars-Sinai Med. Ctr., Beverly Hills 1978-79; pvt. solo practice of chiropractic, Torrance 1982-; bd. trustees Cleveland Chirop. Coll. Bd. of Trustees, 1989-; cons. various hosps., nursing homes, coll. clinics; instr., post-grad. faculty Thornton Comm. Coll., South Holland, Ill. 1975-77, Pierce Comm. Coll. 1978-82, Pasadena Coll. of Chirop. 1985, 86, Palmer Coll. of Chirop.-West 1986, Cleveland Chirop. Coll. of Kansas City 1985, 89, Logan Coll. of Chirop., St. Louis, Mo. 1987, Western States Chirop., Portland, Oreg. 1983, 1985-; med. staff Pacific Hosp., Long Beach 1988-; assoc. prof. L. A. Chiropractic Coll., 1985-; negotiator, rep. ACA, ICA, CCE, CCA and the Canadian Chirop. Assn. in negotiations with APHA, 1979-; mem: Internat. Chiropractors Assn. (seminar speaker 1987, 88, hosp. privileges com. 1985-, Disting. Fellow 1985, ICA merit award 1984), Internat. Coll. Chiropractors Inc. (Fellow 1987), Am. Chiropractic Assn. (pub. health com. 1987-, merit service award 1984), Calif. Chirop. Assn. (seminar speaker 1985, hosp. privileges com. 1985-, Disting. service award 1989-90), Los Angeles S.W. Chirop. Soc. (disting. service award 1983-84, 84-85, 89-90), L.A. Co. Chiro. Soc. (disting. service award 1989-90, Botterman Memorial award 1985-86), Am. Mensa, Am. Pub. Health Assn. (radiol. health sect., chirop. forum, Council Govs.), Am. Med. Record Assn., Council on Chirop. Edn. (chmn. pub. health panel 1984-), Delta Omega 1985-, NY Acad. Scis. 1985-; publs: 40+ articles in 10 different profl. jours., numerous seminars; Republican; R.Cath.; rec: ice hockey player, writing, bicycling, travel. Ofc: Chiropractic Health Center 3750 Sepulveda Blvd Torrance 90505-2513

BAKER, CAMERON, lawyer; b. Dec. 24, 1937, Chgo.; s. D. Cameron and Marion (Fitzpatrick) B.; m. Katharine Solari, Sept. 2, 1961; children: Cameron b. 1963, Ann b. 1964, John b. 1967; edn: Univ. of Notre Dame 1954-57; AB, Stanford Univ. 1958; LLB, UC Berkeley 1961, admitted to practice: Calif. Supreme Ct. 1962, US Dist. Ct. (So. Dist. Calif. 1962, No. Dist. Calif. 1963), US Ct. of Appeals (9th Cir.) 1963. Career: atty., assoc. Adams, Duque and Hazeltine, Los Angeles 1961-62; Pettit & Martin, San Francisco 1962- (exec. com. 1971-82, 1984-88, mng. ptnr. 1972-81, 1984-87); dir.(mem. Audit Com.) Leslie Salt Co., S.F. 1971-78; dir. Lassen Volcanic Nat. Park Found.; elected City Council, Belvedere 1976-80, mayor 1978-79; Union Internationale des Avocats; mem: Am. Bar Assn. (sects. on bus. law, and internat. law and practice), San Francisco Bar Assn. (dir. 1966, 72-73), San Francisco Barristers' Club (pres. 1966), San Francisco Lawyers Com. for Urban Affairs (dir. 1975-83), No. Calif. NAACP Legal Defense Fund (steering com.), Boalt Hall Alumni Assn. (dir. 1982-84), Phi Delta Phi (pres. 1961), Beta Theta Pi; clubs: Bohemian, Tiburon Peninsula. Res: 38 Alcatraz Ave Belvedere 94920 Ofc: Pettit & Martin 101 California St 35th Flr San Francisco 94111

BAKER, D. KENNETH, college president; b. Oct. 2, 1923, Glasgow, Scotland, nat. 1956; s. David Thomas and Edith Rose (Horner) B.; m. Vivian Christian Perry, Sept. 13, 1947; 1 son, Richard R., b. 1955; edn: BSc, McMaster Univ. (Hamilton, Can .) 1946; PhD, Univ. of Penna. 1953. Career: asst., assoc., prof. of physics, Union College, Schenectady, NY 1953-65; mgr. profl. personnel and univ. relations General Electric Resrch. and Devel. Ctr., Schenectady, NY 1965-67; acting pres. St. Lawrence Univ., Canton, NY 1969 (Feb.-Sept.), v.p. and dean, 1967-76; pres. Harvey Mudd Coll., Claremont, Calif. 1976-; cons.: Alco Products, Schenectady, NY 1954-55; Gen. Elec. Co., Schenectady 1956-57; Nat. Sci. Found., W.D.C. 1954-64; Agy. for Internat. Devel., W.D.C. 1962; Ronald Press Co., NYC 1964; advr. Advy. Council Los Angeles Council of Engrs. and Scientists, 1976-78; mem. (chmn. 1982, 83) Advisory Com. Inst. for the Advance. of Engring. 1978-; mem: American Inst. of Physics, Rotary (Claremont), California Club (LA), Newcomen Sunset, Sunset (Pasa.), University Club (Claremont); co-author w/A.T. Goble: Elements of Modern Physics. Res: 495 East Twelfth St Claremont 91711 Ofc: Harvey Mudd College, Kingston Hall, Claremont 91711

BAKER, ELAINE MARGARET, healthfood restaurateur, cookbook author, nutritionist, artist; b. July 25, 1925, Vancouver, B.C. (Am. parentage); d. George McLeod and Olive Margaret (Marsh) Ross; m. James E. Baker, Aug. 25, 1952 (div. 1963); children: Beau b. 1953, Bart b. 1957, Ben b. 1963; edn: BA, and grad. studies, 1943-50: Univ. Wash., Seattle, Art Center Coll. of Design, Pasa., Chouinard Art Inst., L.A., Cal-Art (full scholarship 1949-50). Career: asst. fashion artist Best's Apparel, Seattle 1950-51; fashion layout artist J.W. Robinson, Los Angeles 1951-52; art dir. Coulter's Dept. Store, Los Angeles 1955-57; restaurateur, co-creator, ptnr. Aware Inn (pioneer gourmet health food restaurant), West Hollywood 1958-63, sole prop. 1963-78; creator, co-owner Old World Restaurant (pioneer family-style health food) West Hollywood, Beverly Hills, Westwood, Palm Springs, 1965-67, sold concept 1967; nutritionist/instr. Pritikin Longevity Center, Santa Monica 1980-83; prop. Aware Food Service (catering & food cons. service), Malibu 1984-; awards: million dollar club for selling most U.S. savings bonds USN Supply Depot, Seattle, 1944; best editorial art Pac. Northwest Art Directors Show, 1951; Aware Inn rated Three Star restaurant So. Calif. Rest. Writers Assn., L.A. (1971, 72, 73, 74, 75), rest. critic Paul Wallach's "E" award for Aware Inn (1974); mem. MOCA Art Mus. (charter 1985-), Malibu Community Ctr., 1985-, Gamma Phi Beta Sor.; Democrat; rec: drawing, crafts, int. decor, garden, parapsychology. Ofc: Aware Food Service 30602 Vista Sierra Dr Malibu 90265

BAKER, GEORGE ALLEN, mathematics educator; b. Oct. 31, 1903, Robinson, Ill.; s. Edward Sheridan and Ida (Everingham) B.; m. Grace Elizabeth Cummins, June 12, 1930; children: George Allen Jr., John Cummins; edn: BS, Univ. Ill., 1926, PhD, 1929. Career: res. fellow Columbia Univ., N.Y.C., 1929-30; assoc. statistician USPHS, WDC 1929; prof. math. Shurtleff Coll., Alton, Ill. 1931-34, Miss. Women's Coll., Hattiesburg, 1934-36; statistician Dept. Agri. Bur. Home Econs., Birmingham and Wash. DC, 1936-37; prof. math., stats. UC Davis, 1937-, faculty research lectr. 1955-56; mem: Inst. Math. Stats. (fellow), Biometric Soc. (v.p. 1950), Am. Math. Soc., Math. Assn. Am., Am. Statis. Assn., Econometric Soc., AAAS (fellow), Sigma Xi, Pi Mu Epsilon, Gamma Sigma Delta; author: Statistical Techniques Based on Probabilistic Models (1962), contbr. articles to profl. jours. Res: 507 Eisenhower St Davis 95616 Ofc: Univ. Calif. Dept. Math., Davis 95616

BAKER, GUY EUGENE, insurance agent; b. April 16, 1945, San Bernardino; s. Luther Thomas and Kathlyn B.; m. Colleen Dee Hubbard, July 15, 1967; children: Stacie b. 1969, Todd b. 1971, Andrew b. 1980, Ellen b. 1982; edn: BS econ., Claremont McKenna Coll. 1967; MBA fin., USC 1968; MSFS, Am. Coll. 1984; MSM, 1985; chartered life underwriter, chartered fin. cons., cert. fin. planner, reg. health underwriter. Career: sales Pacific Mutual, Newport Beach 1966-81; pres. Assoc. Ins. Concepts 1977-; coboard Bayly Martin & Fay Compensation Strategies, Costa Mesa 1984-86; mng. ptnr. Baker Thomsen Assoc., Newport Beach 1986-; faculty UC Irvine 1985-; bd: dirs., faculty, speaker Am. Coll., Bryn Mawr 1985; awards: Gen. Agents & Mgrs. Assn. Orange Co. agent of year 1978, Pacific Mutual agent of year 1977, Preston Hotchkiss award 1971; mem: Top of the Table (bd. dirs.), Assn. Advanced Underwriting (bd. dirs.), Million Dollar Round Table (past dir.), Orange Co. Assn. Life Underwriters (past pres.), Am. soc. CLU and CHFC, Internat. Assn. Fin. Planners, Mexico Christian Missions (bd. dirs. 1989-), Mission Viejo CC; articles pub. in profl. jours. 1977-, contbg. ed. Probe (1988-), 250 speeches on sales motivation (1977), author: Bakers Dozen (1989); Republican; Christian; rec: piano, writing, golf. Ofc: Baker Thomsen Associates 4940 Campus Dr Ste 300 Newport Beach 92660

BAKER, L. LILLIAN, artist, writer, historian, lecturer, political activist; b. Dec. 12, 1921, Yonkers, N.Y.; m. Roscoe A. Baker; children: Wanda Georgia, George Riley; edn: El Camino Coll., 1952, UCLA, 1968, 77. Career: continuity writer Sta. WINS, N.Y.C. 1945-46; columnist, freelance writer, reviewer Gardena Valley News, Gardena, Ca. 1964-76; freelance writer, editor, 1971-; lectr. in field, founder/editor Internat. Club for Collectors of Hatpins and Hatpin Holders, monthly newsletter "Points" and annual Pictorial Jour., 1977-, conv. and seminar coordinator 1980-92; dir. Ams. for Hist. Accuracy, 1972, Com. for Equality for All Draftees, 1973; South Bay campaign chair S.I. Hayakawa for US Senate 1976; witness US Commn. Wartime Relocation 1981; witness US Senate Judiciary Com. 1983, US Ho. Reps. appropriations subcom. 4/5/89, Judiciary com. 1986; honors: Freedoms Found. 1971, annual award Conf. Calif. Hist. Socs. 1983, monetary award Hoover Instn. Stanford Univ. 1985, "The Lillian Baker Collection" estab. permanent archives Hoover Instn. Stanford Univ. 1990, Life Fellow Internat. Biographical Assn., Cambridge, Eng., listed Who's Who in World 1991-92, Who's Who in Am. 1993-94, Who's Who American Women 1988-91; mem: Nat. League Am. Pen Women, Nat. Writers Club, Art Students League N.Y. (life), Nat. Historic Soc. (founding), Nat. Trust Historic Preservation (founding); author: Collector's Ency. of Hatpins and Hatpin Holders (1976, 2d edit. 1988, rev. 1993 3rd printing); 100 Years of Collectible Jewelry 1850-1950 (1978, rev. editions 1986, 88, 90); Art Nouveau and Art Deco Jewelry (1980, rev. editions 1985, 88, 91); The Concentration Camp Conspiracy: A Second Pearl Harbor 1981, recipient "Merit Award for Scholarship" from Conf. of Calif. Hist. Socs., 1983; Hatpins and Hatpin Holders: An Illustrated Value Guide (1983, updated 1988, 90); Creative and Collectible Miniatures 1984, Fifty Years of Collectible Fashion Jewelry: 1925-1975 (1986, 3d edit. 1991); Dishonoring America: The Collective Guilt of American Japanese (1988, Webb Research Group); American and Japanese Relocation in WWII: Fact, Fiction and Fallacy (1990, Webb Resrch. Gp.), a 1990 Pulitzer Prize nominee, recipient 1991 "George Washington Honor Medal" in public comms. from Freedoms Found. at Valley Forge; The japanning of America: Redress & Reparations Demands by Japanese-Americans (1991, Webb Resrch. Gp.); 20th Century Fashionable Plastic Jewelry 1992; The Common Doom 1992, pen-name Liliane L. Baker); also articles and poetry; historian for Ex-POWs and American Survivors of Bataan and Corregidor (filed amicus curae brief Case 89-607 JG Penn Fed. Dist. Ct., W.D.C., testing constitutionality of PL100-383, 1988); contbg. author Vol. VII Time-Life Ency. of Collectibles 1979; numerous radio and TV appearances; address: 15237 Chanera Ave Gardena 90249

BAKER, RICHARD W., structural engineer, engineering manager, architectural engineering consultant; b. Aug. 16, 1945, Glendale; s. Elwood V. and Eleanor J. (Vickers) B.; m. Judith K. Fields, July 5, 1969; children: Carrie A., Brian R.; edn: AA, Pasadena City Coll., 1965; BS in architectural engring., Calif. State Polytech. Coll., S.L.O. 1968. Career: naval architect Long Beach Naval Shipyard, 1968-69; stress engr. Lockheed Aero. Systems Co., Burbank 1969-73, 75-87, group engr. 1987-89, project structures engr., 1989-90, deputy chief engr. - F-117A, 1991-; stress engr. Rockwell Internat., Downey, 1974; architectural engineering cons. prin., Cerritos 1972-; mem. AIAA; civic: youth coach City of Cerritos Parks & Rec. Dept. 1982-87, Frontier Little League, Cerritos (mgr. 1985-93); editor Aircraft Stress Analysis 1987; Republican; Methodist. Res: 13518 La Jara St Cerritos 90701 Ofc: Lockheed Adv. Development Co. Dept. 72-02, Bldg 90-4 A-1 PO Box 250 Sunland 91041

BAKST, ABRAHAM ALFRED, engineer, real estate executive, investor, presidential advisor; b. Jan. 12, 1922, Palmer, Mass.; s. Isadore and Minnie (Kaplan) B.; a Manhattan synogogue (now a church) built in 1890 was named after his gr.gr.gr.grandfather Aaron David (orthodox rabbi in Russia); m. Pauline Day (Dep. Atty-Gen. of Hawaii 1948-9) July 10, 1948, div. 1959; 1 dau. Katherine (hd. tchr. Child Care Devel. Ctr., UCI and CSU Long Beach, 1973-6) b. 1949; edn: Bklyn. Coll. 1938-42, Univ. Hawaii 1946-7, Cal Poly 1949-50; AA in real estate, Long Beach City Coll. 1961; Orange Coast Coll. 1978-9; mil. certs., Bellevue/Naval Resrch Lab. 1943-44. Career: radar insp. War Dept., N.J. 1942; petty ofcr. USNR (radio, radar supr. P.T. Boat Squad.), So.Pac. 1942-5; teletype opr. War Dept., Hawaii 1946-7; electronic engr. all Naval and Marine Corps Air Stations, 14th Naval Dist. (H.I.), Pearl Harbor 1947-9, pioneered first VHF radio teletype and terminal network in Navy 1947, asst. proj. engr. VLF radio propagation characteristic test, Pac. area 1948; electronic sci./staff Navy Dept., Inyokern 1950; electronic engr.: Douglas Aircraft, Rockwell Internat., Hughes Aircraft, Hoffman Radio, Varec Indus., 1951-8; supr. Nebeker Realty, Calif. 1958-61; owner/ broker/ investor Bakst Realty Enterprises, Anaheim 1961-; founder/ pub./ed. News Forecasting Newsletter 1958; advisor on news foresight to 8 Am. Presidents and the US Congress (1953-87, 1991-). Honors: capt. (champion) Bklyn. Coll. chess team, H.S. champion chess team, listed in World Almanac-1942 for chess play in coll. tourn. 1941, later was Hawaiian Chess Champion; listed in P.T.Boats Knights of the Sea 1982. Jewish; rec: news analysis, chess. Address: 210 N Brookhurst St Anaheim 92801

BALASH, JEFFREY LINKE, investment banker; b. Nov. 2, 1948, N.Y., NY; s. George Everett and Jeanne Marie (Linke) B.; m. Brenda Sue Coleman, Nov. 22, 1991; edn: BA econs. (summa cum laude), Princeton Univ., 1970; MBA (Baker Scholar) Harvard Bus. Sch., 1974, JD (cum laude), Harvard Law Sch., 1974. Career: asst. to chmn. Louis-Dreyfus Corp., N.Y., NY 1974-76; dir. Avon Products, 1976-79; mng. dir. Lehman Bros. Kuhn Loeb, 1979-85; mng. dir. Drexel Burnham Lambert, Beverly Hills 1985-90; founding ptnr. Anthem Partners, LP, Los Angeles 1991-92; awards: Churchill Scholar English Speaking Union S.F. (1970), Loeb Rhodes Fin. Prize Harvard Bus. Sch. 1973, civic: Joffrey Ballet, L.A. (bd. 1986-89), Harvard Bus. Sch. Alumni Council (1989-92); Republican; R.Cath.; rec: tennis, wt. tng., jazz, wine, film. Res: 9430 Readcrest Dr Beverly Hills 90210

BALCH, GLENN MCCLAIN, JR., clergyman, university administrator; b. Nov. 1, 1937, Shattuck, Okla.; s. Glenn McClain and Marjorie (Daily) B.; m. Diana Gale Seeley, Oct. 15, 1970; children: Bryan, Gayle, Wesley, Johnny; edn: stu., Panhandle State Univ. 1958-60, So. Methodist Univ. 1962-64; BA, S.W. State Univ. Okla. 1962; BD, Phillips Univ. 1965; MA, Chapman Coll. 1973, MA in Edn. 1975, MA in Psych. 1975; PhD, U.S. Internat. Univ. 1978; postgrad., Claremont Grad. Sch. 1968-70, Univ. Okla. 1965-66; ordained minister Methodist Ch. 1962. Career: senior minister First Meth. Ch., Eakly, Okla. 1960-63, First Meth. Ch., Calumet, Okla. 1963-65, Goodrich Memorial Ch., Norman, Okla. 1965-66, First Meth. Ch., Barstow, Calif. 1966-70; asst. dean Chapman Coll., Orange 1970-76; v.p. Pacific Christian Coll., Fullerton 1976-79; pres. Newport Univ., Newport Beach 1979-82; sr. minister Brea United Meth. Ch. 1978-89; pres. and c.e.o. So. Calif. Inst., Brea 1988-; edn. cons. USAF 1974-75; mental health cons. U.S. Army 1969; cons. Hanford Police Dept. 1983-; civic bds: Comm. Advy Bd. Minority Problems 1975, Mayor's rep. to County Dependency Prevention Commn. 1968-69, For Kid's Sake (chmn. bd. 1986-90), Brea Economic Devel. Com.; awards: man of yr. Barstow Jr. C.of C. 1969, Ea. Star religious tng. awards 1963, 1964, Broadhurst fellow 1963-65; mem. Calif. Marriage Therapists Assn., Am. Assn. for Marriage & Family Therapy, Rotary (532 dist. gov. 1987-88, 88-89), Masons, Shriners, Elks. Res: 1016 Steele Dr Brea 92621 Ofc: 401 S Brea Blvd Brea 92621

BALDWIN, LEE EDWARD, import-export executive; b. Aug. 5, 1913, McGregor, Minn.; s. Archie H. and Ella N. (Pearthree) B.; m. Ines Muccioli; children: L. Edward, Joyce Karen; edn: BS in engring., Univ. of Minn., 1937; reg. profl. mech. engr., Calif. (M00207). Career: chief engr. Weston Hydraulics, hydraulic & pneumatic specialists, Burbank 1945-51; chmn. bd. Ratron Internat., Ltd., 1951-, cons. in aircraft servo mechanisms and full engring. in gas purification work for the missile ind.; chmn. bd. Columbine Internat., Ltd. 1982-, builder and importer-exporter of plastic welding equipt.; mem. Nat.

Roofing Contrs. Assn., Industrial Fabrics Assn., Inst. of Environmental Scis.; inventor: several servo-mechanisms patents; rec: gardening, classic autos. Ofc: Ratron International Ltd. 21029 ITASCA Chatsworth 91311

BALDWIN, SHERRIE ELLEN, trade consultant; b. Mar. 4, 1946, Chgo., Ill.; d. Bernard Jacob Taub and Rose Rae Ellenhorn; m. Paul Thomas Baldwin, 1971 (div. 1990); children: Marina b. 1976; edn: BA, Univ. of Ill. 1967; TESOL cert., UC Irvine 1981-82; cert. internat. bus., Am. Grad. Sch. Internat. Mgmt. (Ariz.) 1986; Calif. tchg. credentials. Career: staff ed. Geol. Soc. of Am., Boulder, Colo. 1972-73; assoc. ed. Newport Life Mag., Newport Bch. 1974-76; public rels. coord. Endevco, San Juan Capistrano 1978-81; lectr. UC Irvine 1982-84, Irvine Valley Coll. 1984-87; pgm. coord. Am. Grad. Sch. Internat. Mgmt., Orange Co. 1989-; pres. Baldwin Sai Bei Co., Laguna Hills 1986-; pgm. ch. World Trade Ctr., Santa Ana 1988-89; subject splst. internat. bus., Coastline Comm. Coll. 1989-90, advy. com. internat. bus. cert. 1989-, seminar on China Trade 1990; honors: recipient grad. scholarship Stanley W. Call Foundation, Costa Mesa 1989-90; mem: World Trade Ctr. Assn. of Orange Co. (moderator China Bus. Forum, 1990); International Mktg. Assn., Am. Grad. Sch. of Internat. Mgmt. (alumni assn. 1986-); author numerous articles profl. jours. 1974-77; rec: travel, horticulture, piano music, writing. Address: 25092 Ericson Way Laguna Hills 92653

BALES, TERRY WALLACE, educator; b. Apr. 4, 1945, Upland; s. Bruce Burton and Lois Jean (Ingram) B.; m. Deborah Orr, Dec. 19, 1981; edn: BA, USC 1967, MA, 1969. Career: reporter/ed. United Press Internat. 1966-67, sports corres. UPI 1967-; tchr. Whittier High Sch., 1969-71; prof. Rancho Santiago Coll., Santa Ana 1971-, chmn. telecomms. dept. 1982-; exec. prod. Cable TV News, KYOU-TV, Santa Ana; honors: Phi Beta Kappa 1967, NDEA Title IV Fellow 1969, Nat. Fedn. of Local Cable Programmers 1st Place award (1986, 87, 92), Coll. Media Advisers award 1987, Nat. teaching excellence award Univ. Texas 1989; mem: Sigma Delta Chi, Radio-TV News Directors Assn., Coll. Media Advisers, Hollywood Radio-TV Soc., Acad. of TV Arts and Scis., Nat. Fedn. of Local Cable Programmers, USC Gen. Alumni Assn., Faculty Assn. of Comm. Colls., Rancho Santiago Coll. Speakers Bureau; thesis: Frederick Lewis Allen: Case History of a Contemporary Historian (1969); Democrat; Prot.; rec: collect books, videos of old t.v. shows, Civil War trivia. Res: 11691 Montecito Rd Rossmoor 90720 Ofc: Rancho Santiago College 17th at Bristol Sts Santa Ana 92706

BALESTRERI, THEODORE JEROME, restaurateur/developer; b. June 30, 1940, Bklyn.; s. Vincent Jerome and Viola Georganne (Crispo) B.; m. Velma, May 16, 1971; children: Theodore, II b. 1972; Vincent Frank b. 1977; edn: Monterey Penin. Coll., 1959; grad. Lewis Hotel Mgmt. Sch., W.D.C.; cert. (FMP) Food Mgmt. Profl., 1991. Career: ptnr/owner, founder Sardine Factory restaurant in Cannery Row area of Monterey, 1968- (respons. for redevel. of Cannery Row hist. area; corp. owns 70%), later acquired The Rogue restaurant (on Wharf #2), San Simeon Restaurant (nr Hearst Castle) San Simeon, The Gold Fork in Carmel (fmrly The Butcher Shop); current bd. chmn./pres. (parent co.) Restaurants Central/ Foursome Development; also active in commercial real estate and opr. franchise for Wendy's Internat. (3-county area, N.Calif.); guest lectr. var. state and nat. conventions, univs., bus. and financial instns., restaurant/ hotel seminars and convs.; apptd. commr. Tourism by Gov. Deukmejian, 1988-, Gov. Wilson, 1992-; honors: Gold Plate Award, Am. Acad. of Achievement 1982, Silver & Gold Plate Awards, Internat. Foodservice Mfrs. Assn. 1984, Hon. Dr. of Foodservice, NAFEM 1985, Hon. DBA in hospitality mgmt. Johnson & Wales Univ. 1987, Escoffier Soc. Award Medallion, Restaurant Bus. Mag. Leadership Award 1989, Edn. Found. of NRA Diplomate Award, numerous civic awards; feature cover article w/wife Velma, Money Mag. (11/81); restaurant awards for The Sardine Factory incl. The Ivy Award (Travel/ Holiday Mag., 1971-), Di Rona Award 1993, Nation's Rest. News Hall of Fame, Mobil Travel Guide Award, The Armstrong Gourmet Guide as one of Calif.'s Top 10 Restaurants, one of 50 restaurants in USA to serve at Pres. Reagan's Inauguration 1981, 1985; mem. Nat. Restaurant Assn. (dir., pres. 1985-86), NRA/ACF Culinary Team Found. (chmn. 1992), Edn. Found. of NRA (dir., chmn. 1991-92), Distinguished Restaurants of No. Am. 1993, Calif. Restaurant Assn. (dir., pres. 1983-84), The Culinary Inst. of Am. (dir., corp. mem.), Monterey Peninsula Hotel and Restaurant Assn. (dir., past pres.), No. Calif. Restaurant Assn. (dir., past pres. & founder), Confrerie de la Chaine des Rotisseurs (dir., past chpt. pres.); mil: US Army; R.Cath.; rec: tennis, golf, racquetball. Res: POB 655 Pebble Beach 93953 Ofc: Restaurants Central/ Foursome Development 765 Wave St Monterey 93940

BALLESTEROS, ANTONIO VILLANUEVA, engineer; b. July 24, 1939, La Union, Philippines, nat. 1971; s. Primitivo Estolas and Mauricia Sapitula (Villanueva) B.; m. Victoria, July 18, 1965; children: Evelyn, b. 1966, Antonio Jr., b. 1968, Judith, b. 1971; edn: BS in electrical engring., Mapua Inst. of Tech., 1961, BS in mechanical engring., 1964; mgmt. courses, Wayne State Univ. 1971-73; Reg. Profl. Engr., Mich. 1971, Fla. 1979, Calif. 1982, Colo. 1984, Nev. 1984. Career: supvsg. project engr. Power and Communications Engineering Services, Manila, Phil. 1961-66; electrical engr. Ford Motor Co., 1966-67, Wyandote Chem. Corp., v.p./asst. dir. electrical engring., 1979-82; sr.

electrical engr., office mgr. Cohen & Kanwar Inc., Los Angeles 1982-85; v.p./ chief elect. engr. Pacific International Engineers, L.A. 1985-87; prin. Ballesteros & Assocs., Burbank 1987-; mem: Illuminating Engring. Soc., Assn. of Consulting Electrical Engrs., Nat. Soc. of Profl. Engrs., Nat. Fire Protection Assn., Calif. Soc. of Profl. Engrs.; lodge: Loyal Order of Moose (Glendale #641); clubs: Broken Tee Golf, De Bell Golf; R.Cath.; rec: golf, running. Res: 719 E. Bethany Rd Burbank 91504 Ofc: Ballesteros & Associates, 359 E Magnolia Blvd Ste A Burbank 91502-1132

BALLINGER, CHARLES EDWIN, educator, association executive; b. June 3, 1935, West Mansfield, Oh.; s. William Edwin and Mildred Arlene (Jester) B.; m. Venita Dee Riggs, Dec. 24, 1937; edn: BA, De Pauw Univ., 1957; MA, Ohio State Univ., 1958, PhD, 1971. Career: sch. tchr., Ohio, 1958-62; lab. sch. instr. Ohio State Univ., Columbus 1962-64; asst. supt. of schs. N. Canton City Schs., Ohio 1964-67; cons. Franklin County Schs., Ohio 1967-70; cons. Ohio Dept. of Edn., 1970-71; curriculum coordinator San Diego County Schs., San Diego, Ca. 1971-; exec. dir. Nat. Assn. for Year-Round Education, San Diego 1980-; mem: Assn. for Supvn. and Curriculum Devel. 1964-, Am. Education Research Assn. 1967-, Phi Delta Kappa 1967-; author: Year-Round School 1987; Republican; United Methodist. Ofc: Nat. Assn. for Year-Round Education, 6401 Linda Vista Rd San Diego 92111

BANGASSER, RONALD P., physician; b. Jan. 25, 1950, Freeport, Ill.; s. Paul Francis and Florence (Ihm) B.; m. Susan, June 19, 1971; children: Debra b. 1978, Sandra b. 1981; edn: BA, Northwestern Univ. 1971; MD, Chgo. Medical, 1975. Career: hyperbaric oxygen research St. Lukes Presbyn. Hosp., Milw., 1975; navy diving med. officers tng., through Undersea Med. Soc., 1977; family practice residency, UCLA, 1978; pvt. practice physician Valley Family Medical Group, Yucaipa 1977-; med. dir./bd. dir. Redlands Med. Group 1986-; pres. Sea To Sea Scuba Dive Shop, Inc. 1978-90; pres. Smart Center, sports medicine clinic 1987-90; med. staff Redlands Community Hosp. (hosp. bd. dirs. 1988-, chmn. continuous quality improvement com. 1992-, chief of staff 1990-92, exec. com. 1981-92, sec.treas. 1986-88, chmn. credentials com. 1987-89, chmn. hosp. util. rev. com. 1984-87, dir hyperbaric med. dept. 1989-, past chmn. F.P. Dept.); team phys. San Bernardino Valley Coll. 1977-, diving med. safety ofcr. CSU Long Beach 1982-, instr. nurse practitioner UCSD 1980-82, Family Practice staff instr. UCLA 1979; team phys. San Bernardino Spirit profl. baseball team 1987-; dir. Just For You Volunteers (bd. pres. 1986-87); awards: Tiny Campora Award (1984), Sir Turtle Tourism Award Cayman (1984); mem: AMA (del. 1992-, alt. del. 1989-91, AMA HMSS com. REF Com. B, AMA HMSS com. on ops.), CMA (del. 1989-, alt. del. 1985-89, CMA HMSS vice chmn. 1991-, del. 1987-), San Bernardino County Med. Soc. (dir. 1977-78, 1980-, sec. 1988-89, v.p. 1989-90, pres. 1991-92), CALPAC (bd. dir. 1990-), Found. for Med. Care (med. dir. 1984-89, chmn. cent. practice & review com. 1986-, bd. 1984-, pres. 1986-88), United Foundations for Med. Care (bd. 1987-, pres. 1991-92), Nat. Assn. Underwater Instrs. (diving instr. 1975-, reg. mgr. 1977-85, speaker annual Internat. Conf. on Underwater Edn. 8 yrs. 1976-86, conf. dir. So. Calif. Conf. on Underwater Edn. 1980-81, conf. dir. NAUI Dives Cayman 1984, instr. underwater photog.); R.Cath.; rec: scuba diving. Res: 12724 Valley View Redlands 92373 Ofc: Valley Family Medical Group 11985 Fourth St Ste 100 Yucaipa 92399

BANGHAM, ROBERT ARTHUR, certified orthotist; b. Sept. 12, 1942, San Antonio, Tex.; s. Robert Dave and Marguerite Catherine (Wyckoff) B.; edn: orthotics and prosthetics and med. related courses Northwestern Univ., 1965, 71, 76, N.Y. Univ., 1969, Washtenaw Comm. Coll., 1971, Boston Childrens Hosp., 1979, Marshall Hale Mem. Hosp., 1980, Orthomedics Inc., Brea, Calif. 1981, Flex-Foot Inc., S.F., 1988, Nat. Orthotic Labs., Winter Haven, Fla. 1990; cont. edn. Am. Acad. of Orthotists and Prosthetists 1981-: Cert. Am. Bd. Orthotics (C.O. #821) 1971; VA B.K. Prosthetics Approved 1976-. Career: orthotist John R. Reets, C.O., Ann Arbor, Mich. 1960-65; orthotics supr. Dreher-Jouett Inc., Chgo. 1965-68; cert. orthotist, lectr. & clinician Univ. Mich. Med. Ctr., Ann Arbor 1968-75; pvt. practice, 1970-75; mgr., practitioner and clinician Wright & Filippis Inc., Alpena, Mich. 1975-78; Hittenbergers Inc., Oakland and Concord, Calif. 1978-90; western reg. mktg. mgr. Nat. Orthotic Labs., 1990;owner, founder, pres. and c.e.o. Mobile Orthotic & Prosthetic Assocs., Antioch, Calif. 1990-, patient care offices: Antioch, Concord, Fairfield, Oakland, and Sacramento; mem. VA Prosthetics and Orthotics Workshop Team (R&D) 1989-, author basic course "Intro. to Orthotics" taught in 100+ Acute and Extended Care Facilities 1982-, guest lectr. Tech. Sch. of Orthopedics, San Jose 1989-, lectr. profl. meetings and cont. edn. courses nat.; lic. Foster Parent and Home, Contra Costa Co., 1984-; advy. com. foster care edn. pgm. Diablo Valley Comm. Coll. 1989-92; advy. com. on ind. living svs. pgm. Los Medanos Comm. Coll., 1992; mem., past pres. 1989-90 Calif. Coalition of Allied Health Professions, appt. AB 1327 Advy. Com. (re staffing in Allied Health Professions) to Calif. Health & Welfare Agy. dept. hlth. planning & devel., 1990-92; mem: Am. Orthotic and Prosthetic Assn., Am. Acad. of Orthotists and Prosthetists (nat. bd. dirs. 1989-91, nat. sci. pgm. chmn. 1989-91, chmn. SIG/Spinal Orthotics Soc. 1991-93 and secty. SIG/Lower Extremity Orthotics Soc. 1992-93, N. Calif. Chpt. bd. dirs., rep. to Calif. Coalition of Allied Health Prof., AAOP liaison rep. to Am. Back Soc., past pres.), Internat. Soc. Orthotists

and Prosthetists, Am. Acad. of Neurol. & Orthopedic Surgeons (Fellow, hd. dept. orthotics 1992), Am. Back Soc. (Fellow, inter-profl. rels. com., spinal orthotics workshop presentor 1991, v.ch. com. on orthotics), Inc. Council of Growing Businesses; civic: Yosemite Assn., State Foster Parents Assn., Internat. Platform Assn.; publs: articles in profl. jours. (3), numerous papers presented (1970s-); Jehovah's Witness minister; rec: reading, gardening, travel, computers. Ofc: Mobile Orthotic & Prosthetic Associates, PO Box 3016, 3705 Sunset Ln Ste B Antioch 94531-3016

BANGS, ROBERT LOUIS, real estate appraiser, acquisition agent; b. Oct. 26, 1920, Puyallup, Wash.; s. Arthur Edward and Sadie (Sieff) B.; m. Vera Elizabeth Link, July 5, 1946 (div. 1961); m. 2d. Patricia Bertha Campbell, Oct. 9, 1986; 1 dau., Katherine Lee b. 1950; edn: BA, Univ. Wash. Seattle 1943; Willamette Univ. Career: right of way agt. CalTrans, Fresno 1947-59; real estate appraiser Chas Mitchell Co., San Jose 1959-60; acquisition agt. Pingry & Casalina, San Jose 1960-61; St. Calif. Real Estate div., Sacto. 1961-85; ret.; econ. study pub. (1949); mil: 1st lt. AUS 1943-46, Bronze Star and Combat Infantry Badge 1945; Democrat; Prot.; rec: fishing, hunting. Res: 14700 Carlos Cir Rancho Murieta 95683

BANKER, NANCY, healthcare company executive; b. Nov. 27, 1944, Washington, DC.; d. Max P. and Lillian (Steinkohl) Sirmay; m. Richard Banker, Sept. 10, 1969; 1 son, Sam b. 1975; edn: BA, Mills Coll. 1967; MA, San Francisco St. Univ. 1970. Career: tchr. Diablo Valley Coll., Pleasanton 1971-73; cons., Oakland 1972-74; program mgr. Far West Lab. 1974-77; dir. adminstrn. Med Am./Calif. Emergency Physicians Med. Group, Oakland 1982-86, v.p. adminstrn. 1986-89; pres. Entremed 1988-; v.p. Levison Associates, Inc. 1993-; faculty Golden Gate Univ. 1988-, St. Mary's Coll. 1990-, Calif. Coll. of Podiatric Medicine 1990-; ptnr. Hermes Fund Ltd., Oakland 1982-; fellow, Inst. Ednl. Leadership; mem: Healthcare Execs. of No. Calif. (pres.-elect), Career Resources Development Ctr. (bd. dirs. 1989-), The Physician Relations Group, Oakland/Piedmont JCC (pres. 1982, 84); author: articles pub. in profl. jours.; rec: bicycling, ice skating. Address: Oakland 94602

BANKS, GLADYS LUNELL, nurse; b. Oct. 1, 1941, Washington, Ga.; d. John W. and Magnolia (Martin) Huff; m. Howard Banks, Apr. 21, 1961; children: Sandra b. 1961, Howard Jr. b. 1963, Janet b. 1965; edn: AA, L.A. Southwest Coll., 1978; lic. Voc. Nse., 1978. Career: nse. Navy Reg. Med. Ctr. Hosp., Long Beach 1978-79; VA Hosp., Long Beach 1979-83; Las Flores Convalescent Hosp., Gardena 1985-; awards: medal of merit and Presdl. Task Force, White House, Wash. DC 1984; civic: Challengers Boys & Girls Club, L.A. 1971-75; Republican (Pres. Inner Cir., US Senatl. Club); Pentecostal, Acad. Cathedral Ch. Choir, Inglewood 1977-, Women of Faith 1983-; rec: sewing and designing, reading. Res: 1532 W 111th Pl Los Angeles 90047

BAO, JOSEPH YUE-SE, orthopaedist, microsurgery pioneer, educator; b. Feb. 20, 1937, Shanghai, China, naturalized U.S. citizen 1989; s. George Zheng-En and Margaret Zhi-De (Wang) B.; m. Delia Way, Mar. 30, 1963; children: Alice b. 1964, Angela b. 1968; edn: MD, Shanghai First Med. Coll., China 1958. Career: orthopaedist Shanghai 6th People's Hosp., Shanghai 1958-78, orthopaedist in charge 1978-79, v.chief orthopaedist 1979-84; research assoc. Orthopaedic Hosp./Univ. So. Calif., Los Angeles, 1985-90, coord. microvascular svs. 1989-91; vis. clinical assoc. prof. Univ. So. Calif. 1986-89, clin. assoc. prof. dept. orthopaedics, 1989-, attdg. physician L.A. County-USC Med. Ctr., Los Angeles, 1986, 1990-; consulting specialist orthopaedics and reconstrv. surgery Rancho Los Amigos Med. Ctr., Downey 1986; mem: Internat. Microsurg. Soc. 1984-, Am. Soc. for Reconstrv. Microsurgery 1989-, Orthopaedic Research Soc. 1992-; author, coauthor publs. in med. jours., books on microsurgery, orthopaedic surgery 1963-, incl. Hand Replantation (1963, world's 1st reported replantation), rat toe replantation 1990 and transplantation 1993. Res: 17436 Terry Lyn Ln Cerritos 90701 Ofc: Dept. Orthopaedics LAC-USC Medical Ctr. 2025 Zonal Ave COH 3900 Los Angeles 90033

BARAD, JILL ELIKANN, toy company president; b. May 23, 1951, NY, NY; d. Lawrence Stanley and Corinne (Schuman) Elikann; m. Thomas Barad, Jan. 28, 1979; children: Alexander b. 1979, Justin b. 1982; edn: BA English & psychology, Queens Coll. 1973. Career: product mgr. mktg. Coty Cosmetics, NY, NY 1976-78; product mgr. mktg. Mattel Toys, Inc. Los Angeles 1981-82, dir. mktg. 1982-83, v.p. mktg. 1983-85, sr. v.p. mktg. 1985-86, exec. v.p. product design 1986-88, exec. v.p. mktg. & product devel. 1988-90, pres. 1990-; dir: Bandai/Mattel, Tokyo 1987-, Arco Toys H.K.; honors: Business Week mag. list of Fifty Women to Watch (6/87); civic: Rainbow Guild/Amie Karen Cancer Fund L.A. (charter), American Film Inst., L.A. Co. Mus.; rec: film, wt. lifting. Ofc: Mattel Toys, Inc. 5150 Rosecrans Ave Hawthorne 90250

BARASH, ANTHONY H., lawyer; b. Mar. 18, 1943, Galesburg, Ill.; s. Burrel B. and Rosalyne J. (Silver) B.; m. Jean Anderson, May 17, 1965; children: Elizabeth b. 1965, Christopher b. 1969, Katherine b. 1970, Andrew b. 1970; edn: AB cum laude, Harvard Coll., 1965; JD, Univ. Chgo., 1968; admitted bar: Calif. 1969. Career: atty., assoc. Irell & Manella, Los Angeles 1968-71; assoc.

Cox, Castle & Nicholson, 1971-74, ptnr. 1975-80; ptnr. Barash & Hill, 1980-84, Wildman, Harrold, Allen, Dixon, Barash & Hill, 1984-87, Barash & Hill, 1988-93; ptnr. Seyfarth, Shaw, Fairweather & Geraldson 1993-; bd. dir: Deauville Restaurants Inc. 1981-; trustee Pitzer Coll. 1981-, v.chmn. 1984-; bd. dir. St. Matthew's Parish Sch., Pacific Palisades 1975-78; trustee Windward Sch., 1985-86; mem: ABA (taxation, bus. law, real property sects.), Am. Bar Found. (Fellow), Calif. Bar Assn. (real property, bus. law and taxation sects., del. 1973-75, 76-93), L.A. County Bar Assn. (co-chmn. spl. com. prepaid legal ins. 1969-72, real property, bus. and corp. law sects., pro bono coun., trustee 1989-90), Beverly Hills Bar Assn. (bd. govs.1979-81, 88-93, pres. 1992-93), Beverly Hills Bar Assn. Found. (bd. dirs. 1981-93, pres. 1983-86); Public Counsel (bd. dirs. 1980-87, pres. 1986-87, chmn. Capital Campaign 1989-93);clubs: Regency (L.A.), Harvard of So. Calif. Res: 825 Amalfi Dr Pacific Palisades 90272 Ofc: Seyfarth, Shaw, Fairweather & Geraldson 2029 Century Park E Ste 3300 Los Angeles 90067 Ph: 310/277-7200

BARATTA, MARIO ANTHONY, civil engineer; b. Oct. 17, 1942, San Salvador, El Salvador; nat. US cit. 1961; s. Mario Augusto and Maria (Rivera) B.; m. Barbara Smith, June 13, 1964; children: Anthony Paul b. 1966, Lisa Marie b. 1969; edn: BCE, Santa Clara Univ. 1964, MBA 1983; MSCE (structures) Stanford Univ. 1971; cert. Nat. Security Mgmt., Indsl. Coll. Armed Forces 1975; Reg. Civil Engr. Calif., Hawaii, Canal Zone. Career: mil. civil engr., cdr. US Navy 1961-84: ofcr. in chg. constrn., Yokosuka, Japan 1964-67, Canal Zone 1967-69; pub. works dept. Marine Corps Air Station, El Toro, Calif. 1971-73; nuclear weapons effects ofcr. Offutt AFB, Nebr. 1973-76; ofcr. in chg. of constrn. and prodn. engring. ofcr. Naval Shipyard, Pearl Harbor, Hawaii 1976-78; asst. acquisition ofcr. Pacific Div. Naval Facilities Engring. Cmd. 1978-80; pub. works/ ofcr. in chg. constrn. Moffett Field Naval Air Sta. 1980-83; dir. Facilities Systems Office, Port Hueneme 1983-84, ret. 1984, decorated Bronze Star w/Combat V, Jt. Service, Nat. Def. Service, Vietnam Service w/4 Stars, Rep. Vietnam Meritorious Unit Cit., Cross of Gallantry w/Palm; dir. constrn. services County of Santa Clara, 1984-86; v.p. Ruth & Going Inc. 1986-87; v.p. A-N West Inc./gen. mgr. San Jose br. 1987-; chmn. San Jose St. Univ. Industry Advy. Bd.; awards: energy conservation award Pearl Harbor Naval Shipyard 1978, commendn. Comdr. Naval Forces Southern Command 1969, Tau Beta Pi, J.H. Brunier Award ASCE/ S.F. 1989, Dean of Engineering SJSU comm. service award 1991, APWA meritorious service award 1991, APWA nat. merit. service award 1992, various appreciation awards for coaching soccer teams; mem: ASCE (chair nat. com. on equal opportunity pgms.), ASCE/ San Jose br. (pres. 1991-92), SAME, NSPE, APWA (pres. South Bay Area chpt. 1992), CSPE, Silicon Valley Engring. Council (pres. 1990), ACELSCO (scholarship com. chair), Commonwealth Club (S.F.), CELSOC, Toastmasters Internat. (pres. Pearl Harbor Club 1978), Engineer's Club San Jose, U.S. Navy League (pres. Santa Clara Valley Council 1989, pres.'s plaque award); past pres. soccer clubs in Hawaii 1976-80 and Nebr. 1975-76; pub. article in Military Engineer (1974); rec: jogging, bowling, computers. Res: 3127 Rasmus Cir San Jose 95148 Ofc: A-N West Inc., 2635 N First St Ste 208 San Jose 95134

BARAZONE, MOUNQUE, holistic health practioner, massage & sports therapist, marketing executive, inventor, geosynthetic consultant, lecturer; b. Dec. 9, 1948, Cleveland, Ohio; s. Abraham and Helen (Leverstein) B.; m. Colleen S., July 12, 1993; edn: Cleveland State Univ. 1967-71; Mueller Coll. of Holistic Studies 1991-93. Career: floor supr. May Co. 1965-67; mgr., trainee F.W. Woolworth, 1967-69; mgr. Chagrin Valley "66", Moreland Hills, Ohio 1969-73; v.p. Data Information Services Corp., Chgo. 1973-78; adminstrv. asst. to the pres., W.J. Lazynski Inc. Contrs., Milwaukee 1978-80; founder/ pres./ bd. chmn. Earth Fabrics Inc., 1980-86; pres. Geotextile Apparatus and Consulting Co. (equip. mfr.) 1980-; v.p./dir. A.C.F. West Inc., Richmond, Va. 1986-89; comptroller, v.p./dir. Construction Computer Software Corp., 1989-; pres. BodyEngineering 1991-; therapist Team Dennis Conner - Stars & Stripes America's Cup Defense Boat, 1991-92; asst. instr. Mueller Coll. 1992-; faculty ASCE Cont. Edn. course on geosynthetics; past dir. Data Info. Service Corp.; dir. Lake Calif. POA; lectr. Stanford Univ., ASCE stu. chapt. CSUF 1985, ASCE, So. Calif. 1987, US Forest Svc. 1984, 85, 86, 87; lectr. 1988-: Co. of Santa Barbara, Nev. Dept. Transp. (2), Caltrans, Calif. Geotech. Engrs. Assn. No. & So. sects., City of L.A. (5t 1989), L.A.Co. Pub. Works Dept. (5t 1988, 5t 1990), ASCE Kern br. 1991, Nat. Pavement Conv. 1993; internat. lectures 1989-Denmark (2), Sweden, Norway, Germany, Netherlands (2); awards: appreciation Geotech. Engr. Assn. 1989, tech. merit Los Angeles City Dept. Public Works 1989, tech. excellence So. Calif. Public Works Assn. 1989, lead sales distbr. Crown Zellerbach 1982, 83, 84, 85, mktg. excellence Exxon Chem. 1985, lead we. sales div. Amoco Fabrics & Fibers Co. 1986, 87, 88, 89 and top salesman distbr. 1987; mem. Assoc. Gen. Contrs. Am. (disaster assist. com.), Indsl. Fabrics Assn. Internat., Soc. Am. Mil. Engrs., Nat. Fedn. of the Blind. (Pres.'s Club), Greenpeace, PETA, Internat. Kempo Karate Assn., Am. Massage Therapy Assn., Calif. Massage Therapy Assn.; inventor: machinery to install paving fabrics on hwys. (6 US patents #4555073, 1985, continuation #4,669,330, 10/13/87), universal mounting brackets and mech. folding system (Pat. #4,705,229 11/10/87), Dual PVC Stretching mechanism for paving fabric (pat. #4,742,970 1987), material handling equip.: a fabric roll puller (pat. pend), braking mechanism for rotatable core support for a fabric roll (Pat. #4,657,199, 1987), multi-shafted adjustable roll mover (pat. pend.), device for supporting a roll of material to a vehicle (Pat. #4,664,332 1987); copyrighted Constrn. Bid Mgmt. computer system; pub. tech jours. articles and papers in geosynthetic fields, massage and sports; ednl. video in geosynthetic field; Messianic Jewish, Rel. Sci.; rec: sailing, snorkel, karate, computers, flower gardening. Res: PO Box 6769 San Diego 92166-0769

BARBER, LAURAINE MARGARET, county executive; b. Sept. 14, 1930, Los Angeles; d. Fred Paul and Laura May (Sigafoose) Leonard; m. Robert Ellis Barber, Jan. 30, 1954; children: Paul Kevin, b. 1958, Cheryll Cecille, b. 1960, Michelle Louise, b. 1962; edn: AA, Glendale City Coll. 1951; BA edn., CSU Long Beach 1955. Career: tchr., Pre-School and Child Care, Glendale 1948-49, Baldwin park 1949-59; jr. high sch. tchr. Brethren Schs., 1955-72; dir. Pre-Sch., 1974-76; executive director Fedn. of Community Coordinating Councils, Los Angeles Co., 1978-, pres. 1978-85, re-elected pres. 1991-93, consultant to 80 councils re coordination of human services in L.A. County, community networking cons. to bus. corps., govt. agys. and civic orgns.; mem. L.A. Co. Commn. on Alcoholism, Narcotics And Dangerous Drugs; honors: Hannah Sullivan award, Kenyon Scudder award; mem. Calif. Assn. of Alc. & Drug Pgm. Execs.; civic: Film Advy. Bd., The Way Out Ministries, Long Beach Health Advy. Com. (chmn.), So. Calif. Coalition Chemical People II (vol. coord.), L.A. Federal Exec. Bd. (v.chair U.S. Constn. Bicentennial Com.), Asian Svs. Coalition, Fedn. of Filipino-Amer. Assns Inc. (secty.), Calif. Youth Auth. Regional Citizens Com., Charles Drew Headstart Policy Council & Steering Com. (past), South Bay-Long Beach Svs. Area Advy. Com. (co-chair), Asian Advy. Com., Palos Verdes Substance Abuse Com., Long Beach Drug Suppression Com., past ldr. Campfire Girls, Boy Scouts; author (book) You, Me, We; (record) It's Time for the We in America; devel. the community volunteer campaign theme: California Gold Rush; rec: travel, people; Republican; Prot. Res: 3109 Lees Ave Long Beach 90808 Ofc: F.C.C.C. 1945 Long Beach Blvd Long Beach 90806

BARBER, THEODORE FRANCIS, aircraft mechanic; b. Jan. 29, 1931, Port Jervis, NY; s. Theodore and Frances Mary (Gross) B.; m. Beverly Ann Horton, Mar. 15, 1961 (div. Dec. 1965); 1 child, Theodore Francis Barber, Jr.; edn: student, Arlington Sch. Flight & Engring., Tillamook, Oreg., 1951-52; Jet Engine Specialist Sch., Chanute AFB, Rantou, Ill., 1952; lic. comml. eel fisherman State of Pa., 1964; career: carpenter, Erie R.R., Port Jervis, NY, 1947-49; laborer, Erie R.R., Port Jervis, NY, 1950; mail handler, Erie R.R., Jersey City, 1950-51; locomotive fireman Erie R.R., Port Jervis, 1951-59, locomotive engr., 1959-66; miniature golf course owner/operator, Matamoras, Pa., 1963-65; lipstick moulder, Kohmar Labs., Port Jervis, NY, 1966; interior installer Douglas Aircraft Co., Long Beach, Calif., 1966-67; field and svc. aircraft mechanic, Douglas and McDonnell Douglas Aircraft Co., Long Beach, 1967-; structure assembly mechanic Northrop Corp., Anaheim, Calif., 1969-70; exptl. flight test mechanic McDonnell Douglas Aircraft Co., Long Beach, 1971, 77; co-owner C&B Sabot Fiberglass Boat Mfrs., 1976; mech. test technician Space Shuttle Arrowhead Products, Los Alamitos, Calif., 1976077; B-1 bomber tool maker No. Am. Rockwell, El Segundo, Calif., 1977; realtor, Real Estate Store, Fullerton, Calif., 1976-79; metal fitter, toolmaker, F-18, Northrop, Hawthorn, Calif., 1978-79; toolmaker, Satellite & Space Shuttle Div., No. Am. Rockwell, Seal Beach, Calif., 1984; walnut orchard grower, C&B Orchard, Fresno, Calif., 1982-83; mem: Am. Legion, Moose, Gold Wing Road Riders; mil: USAF, 1951-55; rec: motorcycling, classic auto restoration, gourmet cooking. Res: 499 Creighton Rd Orange Park FL 32073

BARBERS, RICHARD GEORGE, academic physician, administrator; b. Jan. 12, 1949, Calasiao, Philippines, nat. US cit. 1975; s. Jesus Victor and Mary (Fernandez) B.; edn: BS, Loyola Coll. 1971, MD, Georgetown Univ. 1975; bd. cert. Internal Medicine, Pulmonary Disease, Allergy & Immunology. Career: intern Internal Medicine, USC-Los Angeles Co. Med. Ctr., 1975-76; resident, Int. Medicine, UCLA-Cedars Sinai Med. Ctr. 1976-78, postdoc. fellowship UCLA Med. Ctr. in Clin. Immunol. & Allergy, 1979-81, in Pulmonary Disease, 1981-82; asst. prof. medicine USC Sch. of Medicine/assoc. dir., dir. UCLA Asthma and Immunologic Lung Disease Ctr., 1982-87; asst. prof. medicine Univ. Mass. Med. Sch., 1987-90; dir. Univ. Mass. Aerosolized Pentamidine Pgm. 1987-90; assoc. prof. med. USC Sch. of Med. 1990-, dir. USC Bronchoscopy Service 1991-, medical dir. USC Lung Transplant Pgm. 1992-; honors: Tri Beta; Fellow Am. Coll. of Physicians, Fellow Am. Coll. of Chest Physicians, Fellow Am. Coll. of Allergy and Immunology, Fellow Am. Acad. of Allergy and Immunology, mem. Am. Thoracic Soc., Am. Fedn. of Clin. Research, Internat. Heart and Lung Transplant Soc.; publs: numerous research papers and articles in med. journals; Independent-Democrat; R.Cath.; rec: sailing, bridge, marathon runner. Ofc: Univ. of So. Calif. School of Medicine Div. Pulmonary and Critical Care Medicine, GNH 11-900, 2025 Zonal Ave Los Angeles 90033

BARKER, GRACE KATHRYN, marriage and family counselor; b. June 16, Toms River, N.J.; d. Atwood Reynel and Eleanor Steinman (Magee) Applegate; son, Gregory; edn: AA, El Camino Coll., 1968; BA, CSU Long Beach, 1972; MA, Azusa-Pac. Univ., Calif. Family Study Ctr., 1977; certifs. in addictions counseling

(CAARD) 1973, soc. services, 1974, adult tchg. cred., 1978, UCLA; lic. Marriage Family Child Counselor (M13716) Calif. Career: adminstrv. splst., Secty. special proj. of the Air Force, 1961-70; secty. to Dir. Engring., Internat. Pgm., USAF Space & Missile Sys. Org., 1971-74; staff counselor Drug Abuse Ctr., Ft. MacArthur, 1974-75; MFCC intern Clare Found. (alco.) 1976, and Harbor View House (comm. mental health), 1976-79; MFCC therapist pvt. practice, Torrance 1979-; originator and instr. course: Healthful Living; honors: Outstanding performance award USAF 1972-73; fmr. mem: Am. Red Cross (jr.), Am. Womens' Vol. Service, PTA (secty., hist., com. chair 1955-61), Calif. Student Soc. Welfare Assn. (state v.p. 1970-71); mem: Calif. Assn. Marriage, Family Therapists 1981-, Alumni Univ. Patrons CSULB 1986-, Azusa-Pac. Univ. 1977-, Calif. Family Study Ctr. 1981-, Soc. Work Aux. CSULB 1980-; civic: charter mem. Republican Presidential Task Force 1981-, Senatorial Club 1983-, Advy. Com. Cong. R. Dornan (1976, Dornan in '88), Gr. LA Zoo Assn. (charter 1967-), RRRC (charter 1987-), Women in the Arts (charter 1986-), L.A. Cty. Art Mus. Charter II 1987-, Natural Hist. Mus. 1983-, Nature Conservancy 1983-, Statue of Liberty Ellis Is. Found. 1984-, Friends of the Observatory 1986-, Nat. Trust for Historic Preservation 1987, Nat. Parks Conserv. Assn. 1988-, Earthwatch 1988, Mono Lake Com. 1988-, The Wilderness Soc. 1987-; Am. Film Inst. 1988-; Clubs: Balboa Ski Club 1986-, Snowfliers Ski Club 1987-; Episcopalian; rec: tennis, dancing, travel, skiing. Res: 25819 Skylark Dr Torrance 90505

BARKER, GREG ALLEN, architect; b. Sept. 25, 1955, Minneapolis, Minn.; s. James Henry and Bonita Jean (Jacobson) B.; m. Jennifer Carol Allen, July 11, 1981; 1 dau., Jenna b. 1988; edn: BS, Calif. Polytech. St. Univ. 1978; M.Arch., Univ. Ill. 1983. Career: job captain Paul R. McAllister Architect, San Jose 1979-81; survey coordinator Hawley Stowers Architect 1981; instr., researcher Univ. Ill., Champaign 1983-84; intern architect Wallace Holm Architects, Monterey 1984-85; David Goldstein Architect, Solvang 1985-86; project mgr., v.p. Jay Farbstein & Assoc., San Luis Obispo 1986-; instr. aikido Cuesta Coll. 1987-; awards: Sch. Architecture Univ. Ill. Edward C. Earl prize 1983, Am. Collegiate Sch. Architecture Research 1983, Univ. Ill. Undergrad. Instruction 1984, Amoco Corp. award 1985; mem: Am. Inst. Architects, Environ. Design Research Assn.; author: thesis pub. 1983; Democrat; Zen; rec: Aikido. Res: 120 Cerro Romauldo Ave San Luis Obispo 93401 Ofc: 1411 Marsh St Suite 204 San Luis Obispo 93401

BARKER, HAROLD N., police chief; b. Aug. 4, 1937, Ventura; s. Wm. Perry and Evelyn Inez (Beckwith) B.; children: Russell b. 1961, Terri b. 1963; edn: AA, Ventura Coll., 1966; BS, CSU Los Angeles, 1969; MPA, USC, 1972; grad. Command Coll. 1987, FBI Acad., session 86. Career: police capt. Santa Paula Police Dept., 1957-74; asst. sheriff San Mateo County Sheriff, Redwood City 1974-83; chief of police San Francisco Internat. Airport, 1979-80; dir. security Shorenstein Co., San Francisco 1983-84; chief of police City of Folsom, 1984-; instr. Ventura Coll. 1968-72, La Verne Coll. 1969-72; awards: J. Edgar Hoover medal F.B.I., Wash. DC 1969, chair of year Calif. Peace Officers, Sacto. 1978, volunteer of year Folsom C.of C. 1986, chief of year Folsom P.D. 1987; civic: Rotary (pres. 1972), Shriners (provost marshal 1987-90), Elks, Folsom C.of C. (pres. 1993); mil: Col. State Mil. Reserve Army Nat. Guard; Prot.; rec: hunting, golf. Res: 2661 Larsen Dr Camino 95709 Ofc: Folsom Police, 46 Natoma St Folsom 95630

BARKOVICH, BARBARA ROSE, consultant; b. Dec. 18, 1950, Tokyo, Japan; d. Anthony and Mildred (Donner) B.; edn: BA, UCSD 1972; MS, St. Univ. N.Y. 1974; PhD, UC Berkeley 1987. Career: asst. energy policy analyst NSF, Wash. D.C. 1974-75; research splsts. Calif. Pub. Utilities Commn., San Francisco 1975-78, dir. policy and planning 1978-83; asst. v.p. First Interstate Bancorp, Los Angeles 1983-84, v.p. 1984-85; cons. 1985-87; ptnr. Barkovich & Yap, Emeryville, Calif. 1987-; dir. Women Energy Associates, San Francisco 1985-; dir. Freewheelers Assn. Inc. 1989-93; dir. Pacific Energy and Resources Center, 1991-; dir. Philharmonia Baroque Orchestra 1993-; apptd. energy engring. bd. Nat. Research Council, 1990-; awards: Fed. Energy Adminstrn. energy conservation award, 1976; mem: Audubon Canyon Ranch (docent); author Regulatory Interventionism in Utility Industry, 1989; rec: opera, chamber music, bird watching. Address: San Rafael 94901

BARNARD, THELMA WILENE, nurse; b. July 27, 1927, Brinkley, Ark.; d. Owen Cecil and Lela Martha (Forbess) Young; m. Wm. Robert Wright, Sept. 13, 1942 (dec. July 3, 1968); children: Brendia Faye b. 1943, David Earl b. 1945, Elvin Rex b. 1947; m. Earl C. Barnard, June 16, 1973 (dec. Nov. 4, 1990); 1 stepson, Russell Earl Barnard b. 1958; edn: dipl. Wayne (Ill.) Sch. of Nursing Hosp., 1946; nsg. lic. Calif., Contra Costa Coll., 1954; operating rm. nurse tng. Contra Costa Co. Hosp. Tng. Pgm., 1956-60; nat. cert. OR Technician, 1973. Career: nse. Kaiser/Permanente, Richmond, Calif. 1952-54; opr. rm. nse. Contra Costa County, Martinez 1954-69; prop. Rex's Restaurant, Pleasant Hill 1969-72; opr. rm. nse. Martinez Comm. Hosp., Martinez 1972-74; Mt. Diablo Hosp., Concord 1979-87; lectr. nutrition Joy Health Services, Martinez 1978-; owner, Shaklee distbr. (nutritional products); vol. nse. Civil Defense Contra Costa Co. 1954-81; honors: tchr. of year Assemblies of God, Richmond 1960; civic: Campfire Girls, Richmond (co-ldr. 1957-62), Scouts of Am., San Pablo (ldr. 1953-54), Womens Council, Richmond 1954-69, Assembly's Missionettes

(coord., ldr. 1962-68), Christian Pentecostal Ladies Assn. 1984-; Republican; Ch. of God; rec: volunteer work w/youth and elderly, needlework, gardening, genealogy. Res: 1148 Heavenly Dr Martinez 94553

BARNARD-WALTON, JO ELLEN, surgeon; b. Dec. 24, 1941, Los Angeles; d. Marion Cecil and Cleo Pauline (Fenderson) B.; m. Lewis Richard Walton, Dec. 19, 1971; children: Lewis Richard Walton, Jr. b. 1981; edn: BA, La Sierra Coll. 1962; MD, Loma Linda Univ. 1966; bd. cert. Am. Bd. of Surgery. Career: surgical res. Loma Linda Univ. White Meml. Hosp. 1972; intern Riverside Gen. Hosp. 1967. Career: surgeon Niles Surgical and Med. Group, Bakersfield 1973-; staff San Joaquin Comm. Hosp. (exec. com. 1985-); honors: alumna of yr. Southwestern Adventist Coll. 1988, Personalities of the West & Mid West, Outstanding Young Women of Am.; mem: AMA, Calif. Med. Assn., Kern Co. Med. Assn., Loma Linda Univ. Womens Auxiliary (pres. 1974-75), Bakersfield Adventist Acad. School Board (chair 1985-86); author: How To Live Six Extra Years (Woodbridge, 1981); Seventh Day Adventist; rec: Arabian horses, travel, music, swimming, health lectures. Res: 2701 Rio Vista Bakersfield 93306 Ofc: Niles Surgical and Medical Group 2121 Nile St Bakersfield 93305

BARNES, WILLIE R., lawyer; b. Dec. 9, 1931, Dallas, Tex.; s. Jasper M. and Mary L.(Roberts) B.; m. Barbara Bailey Barnes, Aug. 17, 1985; children: Michael b. 1954, Sandra b. 1957, Traci b. 1962, Wendi b. 1970, Brandi b. 1979; edn: BA, UC Los Angeles, 1953, JD, UCLA Law Sch, 1959. Career: staff atty. Calif. Dept. of Corporations, Los Angeles 1960-79, suprvg. corporations counsel 1968-70, asst. commnr. 1970-75, corporations commnr. 1975-79; pvt. practise atty., ptnr./chmn. corp. & securities dept. law firm Manatt, Phelps, Rothenberg & Phillips, Los Angeles 1979-88; ptnr. Wyman Bautzer Kuchel & Silbert, 1989-91; ptnr. Katten Muchin Zavis & Weitzman, 1991-92; ptnr. Musick, Peeler & Garrett 1992-; dir., Public Counsel; mem. Calif. St. Senate Commn. on Corporate Governance; arbitrator Am. Arbitration Assn.; advy. bd. Inst. for Corporate Counsel; honors: UCLA Law Sch. Alumnus of the Year (1976), pres.'s award Black Businessmen Assn. L.A. (1978); mem: Calif. State Bar Assn. (Bus. Sect., v.p. exec. com. corporations com. 1983-86, com. on corp. governance & take-overs), L.A. County Bar Assn. (exec. com. bus. & corp. sect.), Beverly Hills Bar Assn. (exec. com. corps. & comml. sect.), Am. Bar Assn. (bus. law sect., mem. fed. regulation of securities, state regulation of securities, franchise and commodities coms.), Midwest Securities Commnrs. Assn. (pres. 1978-79), North Am. Securities Adminstrs. Assn. (1st v.p. 1978-79), UCLA Law Alumni Assn. (v.p. 1973, dir., gen. counsel 1982-86), Inst. of Certified Fin. Planners (chmn. leveraged real estate task force 1985-86); recipient Resolution of Commendn. Calif. Senate 1979, and Calif. Assembly 1979; co-mng. editor Calif. Bus. Law Reporter 1982-83; mil: pfc US Army 1954-56; Indep. Commn. to Rev. L.A. Police Dept.; rec: sports, photog. Ofc: Musick, Peeler & Garrett, One Wilshire Blvd Ste 2100 Los Angeles 90017

BARRETT, REGINALD HAUGHTON, wildlife biologist, educator; b. June 11, 1942, San Francisco; s. Paul Hutchison, Sr. and Mary Lambert (Hodgkin) B.; m. Katharine Lawrence Ditmars, July 15, 1967; children: Wade Lawrence b. 1984, Heather Elizabeth b. 1987; edn: BS game mgmt., Humboldt State Univ., 1965; MS wildlife mgmt., Univ. Mich., 1966; PhD zoology, UC Berkeley, 1971; cert. wildlife biologist 1980. Career: staff res. UC Berkeley, 1970-71; res. scientist C.S.I.R.O., Canberra, Australia 1972-75; prof. of wildlife mgmt. UC Berkeley, and dir. Sagehen Creek Field Sta., Dept. of Environmental Sci. Policy and Mgmt. 1976-; awards: Rho Sigma 1962, Chi Sigma Epsilon 1963, Xi Sigma Pi 1964, Who's Who Among Am. Univs. and Colls. 1964, undergrad. scholar Nat. Wildlife Fedn. 1964, Sigma Xi undergrad. res. award 1965, Bruce R. Dodd Award 1966, Phi Kappa Phi 1966, Union Found. Wildlife Res. Grant 1968-70, NSF grad. fellow 1965-70, Sigma Xi 1971, profl. achiev. Humboldt St. Univ. Alumni 1986, R.F. Dasmann profl. of yr. Wildlife Soc. we. sect. 1989; mem: The Wildlife Soc., Soc. for Range Mgmt., Soc. of Am. Foresters, Am. Soc. of Mammalogists, Ecol. Soc. of Am., Orinda Hist. Soc. (life), Nat. Wildlife Fedn. (life), Nat. Audubon Soc. (life), Sierra Club (life), Austr. Mammal Soc. 1972-, AAAS, Calif. Acad. Scis. (1975-), Pacific NW Natural Hist. Soc., Resource Modeling Assn., others; publs: 70+ profl. papers and jour. articles; Episcopalian; rec: hunting, fishing, hiking, boating, camping, photography. Ofc: Univ. California, 145 Mulford Hall Berkeley 94720

BARRETT, RICHARD HEWINS, oil company executive; b. Dec. 5, 1949, Pittsburgh, Pa.; s. Robert Hewins and Joan Lea (Mantler) B.; m. Virginia Kristine Arentzen, Apr. 14, 1973 (div. Jan. 1992); children: Robert b. 1975, Jeffrey b. 1977, Douglas b. 1980; m. 2d. Evelyn Paige Sexton, June 27, 1992; edn: BS, Penn State Univ., 1971, MBA, 1973; profl. desig. CCM, CDP, Treas. Mgmt. Assn. 1990. Career: senior cons. Gulf Oil Corp., Pittsburgh, Pa. 1982-85; supr. systems support Chevron Corp., San Francisco 19185-86, senior cash mgmt. analyst 1986-87, mgr. banking ops. 1987-90, mgr. receivables acctg. Chevron U.S.A., Concord 1990-91, mgr. bus. serv. Chevron Products Co., S.F. 1991-; adj. prof. Salisbury State Coll., Md. 1975; instr. Golden Gate Univ., S.F. 1987-89; mem. Treasury Mgmt. Assn. 1987-; civic: Moon Area Soccer Assn., Coraopolis, Pa. (treas. 1983-85), Mustang Soccer League, Danville (treas. 1988-91); Republican; Presbyterian (trustee, elder 1981-84); rec: soccer, skiing, pers. computing, woodworking, music. Res: 244 St Christopher Dr Danville 94526

BARRIOS, ALFRED ANGEL, psychologist; b. Oct. 1, 1933, N.Y., N.Y.; s. Arthur and Carmen (Vidal) B.; BS, Caltech, 1955; MA, UCLA, 1964, PhD, 1969. Career: assoc. Dr. William S. Kroger, Inst. of Comprehensive Medicine, Beverly Hills, 1972-74; cons. City of Hope Pain Ctr., 1975; clin. psychologist, dir. Self Programmed Control Center, Culver City 1976-, specialist in stress management: inventor stress control biofeedback cards, pioneer in psychoneuroimmunol. approach to curing cancer, his self-programmed control pgm. introduced in schs. nat.; cons. Govt. Title III pgm. for minority students 1969-72; vis. prof. UCLA undergrad. recruitment & devel. dept. 1971-72; instr. psych. dept. East L.A. Coll. 1970-72; Santa Monica City Coll. 1975; Southwest Coll. 1975-76; honors: doc. diss. "Towards Understanding the Effectiveness of Hypnotherapy" nom. for Creative Talent Award 1969; speaker num. confs. and workshops; Christian; rec: beach volleyball. Res: 11959 Nebraska Ave Los Angeles 90025 Ofc: SPC Center, 11949 Jefferson Blvd Ste 104 Culver City 90230

BARRON, STEPHANIE, museum curator; b. Sept. 24, 1950, N.Y., NY; d. Manuel art, 1980-; advisor Nat. Endowment for the Arts 1984-87; adj. faculty CSU Fullerton 1982-83; awards: John J. McCloy fellow Am. Coun. on Germany, N.Y. 1981, Fed. Rep. of Germany Order of Merit 1/c, Bonn 1984, NEA mus. profls. award 1987; mem: Coll. AA Assn., Am. Assn. of Museums, Internat. Com. on Museums, Com. Internat. Museums of Modern Art; author: German Expressionism 1915-1925 (1988), "Degenerate Art": The Fate of the Avant-Garde in Nazi Germany (1991), (cat.) German Expressionist Sculpture (1983), and coauthor 2 books. Res: 1301 Schuyler Rd Beverly Hills 90210 Ofc: L.A. County Museum of Art 5905 Wilshire Blvd Los Angeles 90036

BARTALINI, MARILYN DARLENE, real estate broker; b. Sept. 1, 1938, Fort Bragg; d. Lyle James Robertson and Hilda Virginia (Lawrence) Roberts; m. Robert Bartalini, Aug. 16, 1958; children: Debora b. 1960, Cynthia b. 1962; edn: Coll. of the Redwoods, Lumbleau R.E. Schs., 1973; Anthony's R.E. Schs., 1973-; Calif. lic. R.E. Broker; desig: Realtor. Career: bookkeeper, teller, bank secty. Coast Nat. Bank, Ft. Bragg 1955-60, 1966-70; supr. teller line and bookkeeping dept. Savings Bank, 1970-73; R.E. sales agt. Spring Realty, 1973-74; Northern Calif. Prop., 1974-77; R.E. broker/owner Blue Pacific Realty, 1977-82; Head Realty, 1982-83; Seaside Real Estate, 1983-85; Century 21 Fort Bragg Realty, 1985-89; Mendo Realty, 1989-; Amway distbr. 1990-, International Networking Assn. 1990-; recipient profl. awards: million dollar producer (1977, 86, 87), $3mil. producer 1979, $2mil. producer (1978, 88), Century 21 R.E. Winners' Circle, highest units sales and listings Mendocino County, Lake County and a portion of Sonoma County 1988; mem: Coastal Mendocino Bd. of Realtors (by laws and long range plng. coms. 1978-79, dir. 1979-82, treas. 85-86, MLS com. 86-88), Calif. Assn. Realtors, Nat. Assn. Realtors, Native Daus. of the Golden West 1967-, Mendocino Coast Hosp. Found., Norman Vincent Peale Positive Thinkers Club, Found. for Christian Living 1980-, AARP, Breakthrough, Intercessor, Internat. Platform Assn.; Democrat; R.Cath.; rec: fine arts, reading, travel, walking. Res: 1184 N Main St No.29 Fort Bragg 95437 Ofc: 650 N Main St Fort Bragg 95437

BARTOLOTTA, VINCENT J., JR., lawyer; b. May 23, 1945, Monongahela, Pa.; s. Helen Kurilko; m. Judith Ann, June 1, 1968; children: Nicolas Andrew b. 1981, Vincent, III b. 1971, Bret Anthony b. 1974, Garrett Michael b. 1979; edn: BA, Univ. Pitts., 1967, JD, 1970; admitted bar: Dist.Col., Pa., Calif. Career: trial lawyer pvt. practice, San Diego; mem. advy. bd. S.D. Sockers Profl. Soccer Team; mem. bd. American Ireland Fund; honors: List of 83 San Diegans to Watch 1983, Am. Lawyer Mag. list of top 20 small law firms in U.S., Best Lawyers in Am. (ann. 1986-93); mem: Am. Bar Assn., Am. Trial Lawyers Assn., Am. Bd. of Trial Advocates, Allegheny Co. Bar Assn., San Diego Co. Bar Assn. (code of conduct com.), San Diego Trial Lawyers Assn. (pres. 1990, Outstanding Trial Lawyer award 1981, 88, 89, 91), San Diego Co. Barristers Club; civic bds: St. Vincent de Paul/Joan Kroc Ctr. for Homeless (dir.), Am. Trauma Soc. (pres. S.D. chpt.), Rancho Santa Fe Youth (chmn. bd. govs., past pres. bd. dirs.), S.D. 1984 Olympic Com.; R.Cath.; rec: golf, soccer. Res: PO Box 2596 Rancho Santa Fe 92067 Ofc: 2550 Fifth Ave Ste 1100 San Diego 92103

BARTON, MARILYN SUE, lawyer; b. Aug. 28, 1932, Granite, Okla.; d. Artie Gene Bowman and Margaret Roberta (Harris) Tucker; children: Bruce Richard b. 1963, Craig Andrew b. 1965; edn: BA, UC Berkeley 1953; JD, 1956; admitted Calif. Supreme Ct. 1957, lic. real estate broker Calif. 1987. Career: assoc. atty. Weberg Dalton Landis & Cardon, Bellflower 1957; ptnr. Weberg & Barton 1957-60; assoc. gen. counsel Rexall Drug & Chemical Co., Los Angeles 1961-63; sole practice, Bellflower 1968-85; panel chair Edn. Appeal Bd., Wash. D.C. 1982-; gen. counsel Modern Development Co., 1989-; mem. L.A. Co. Commn. on Judicial Procedure 1979-81; lectr. real estate law, L.A. Co. 1960-61; judge pro-tem Los Cerritos Municipal Ct., Bellflower 1970-76; awards: Bus. & Profl. Womens Club Woman of Year 1973; mem: Boalt Hall Alumni Assn. Berkeley (dir. 1970-74), Bellflower Unified Sch. Dist. (bd. trustees 1969-76), Girl Scouts of Am. (com. chr. 1973-74), Soroptimists; 3 legal opinions pub. in profl. jours. (1988); Republican (Rep. Central Com.); Ch. of Christ; rec: skiing, scuba diving, sailing. Address: Seal Beach 90740-6500

BASCOM, EARL WESLEY, rodeo cowboy, sculptor-artist, writer; b. June 19, 1906, Vernal, Utah; s. deputy sheriff John W. and Rachel C. (Lybbert) B.; paternal cousin to western artists Frederic S. Remington and Charles M. Russell; m. Nadine Diffey, Dec. 20, 1939; children: Denise, Glen, Doris, John, Dona; edn: BS, Brigham Young Univ., 1940, postgrad. 1965, 66; postgrad. Univ. Calif. 1969; Career: profl. rodeo cowboy, 1918-40; dir. first rodeo, state of Miss. at Columbia, Miss. 1935, 36, 37; pres. Bascom and Wilkerson, 1947-51; owner Two Bar Quarter Circle Ranch 1951-; pres. High Desert Artists, Inc. 1964-65, pres. Bascom Fine Arts 1967-; owner Diamond B Ranch 1975-; art teacher Barstow H.S. and J.F. Kennedy H.S., Barstow, Calif. 1966, 67; pres., co-founder Buckaroo Artists of America 1978—; actor, western movie "The Lawless Rider" 1954; actor in Roy Rogers/Marriott Corp. commercials 1968, 69; art exhibits: Utah Artists, Provo (1971), Cowboy Artists, Temecula 1972, Desert Southwest Artists, Palm Desert and La Jolla (1974), Mormon Fest. of Arts 1975, Cochise Mus., Wilcox, Az. 1976, Frank Tenney Johnson Invitational, Palm Springs 1979, Sun Valley, Idaho 1980, New Orleans 1981, Santa Anita Nat. Horse Show, Arcadia 1982, Cheyenne Frontier Days, Wyo. 1983, Weighorst/Bascom Exh., Alpine, Ca. 1984, Old Time Athletes, S.L.C., Utah 1985, National Salon, Springville, Utah 1986, Golden Boot Awards Exh., Woodland Hills, Ca. 1986, Internat. Art Exh., San Diego 1990, Equestrian Art Fest., Del Mar 1991, Oxford House, Salt Lake City 1992, World Cup Exh., Del Mar, Ca. 1992, Hollywood Park Exh., Cerritos, Ca. 1992, Brigham Young Univ., Provo, Utah 1992, Las Vegas, NV 1993; represented in permanent collections: Frederic S. Remington Art Mus., Gene Autrey Western Heritage Mus., Norwegian-Am. Mus., Danish Immigrant Mus., Denver Art Mus., Santa Barbara Mus. of Art, Whitney Mus. of Am. Art, Dallas Mus. of Fine Arts, Utah Mus. of Fine Arts, Tucson Mus. of Art, BYU Mus. Art, Old West Mus. (Cheyenne), Nat. Cowboy Hall of Fame (Oklahoma City), North Am. Cowboy and Pioneer Mus. (Ft. Worth), Canadian Rodeo Hall of Fame Mus. (Alberta), Univ. of Iowa, Art Mus.; producer first rodeo in Mississippi history at Columbia, Miss. 1935; awards: Reserve-Champion, steer decoration competition, North Am. Championship Calgary Stampede 1933, set arena record, Raymond, Alberta 1933, set world record time in steer decoration, Lethbridge, Alberta 1933, Third Pl. World Standings, Rodeo Assn. of Am. 1933, All-Around Rodeo Championships- Lethbridge Stampede, Lethbridge, Alberta 1934, Raymond Stampede, Raymond, Alberta (1935, 40), Ute Stampede, Nephi, Utah 1935, War Bonnet Roundup, Pocatello, Ida. 1937, Pacific Intl. Livestock Expo. Rodeo, Portland, Ore. 1939, named Stirling Stampede's First Rodeo Clown 1931, Sterling Sunset Soc. 1981, honoree Cardston Stampede Com. 1982, Raymond Stampede Com. 1984, Dinosaur Roundup Rodeo Assn. 1989, San Bdo. Co. Fair Rodeo Com. 1989, inducted Canadian Rodeo Hall of Fame 1984, Utah Sports Hall of Fame 1985, Raymond Sports Hall of Fame 1987, Hon. Parade Marshall-Cardston, Alberta 1982, Raymond, Alberta 1984, Columbia, Miss. 1985, Vernal, UT 1989, outstanding senior citizen award Dept. Gerontology BYU 1987, honoree Nat. Outlaw and Lawman Assn., Reno, Nev. 1990, special recogn. B.Y.U. Emeritus Club 1992; elected fellow, Royal Soc. of Arts, London 1993; Resolutions from Calif. St. Senate, Miss. St. House & Senate, Co. San Bdo., and Cities of Victorville, Calif. and Vernal, Utah; mem: Am. Foundrymens Soc., Western Writers of Am., Profl. Rodeo Cowboys Assn. (hon. life), Canadian Rodeo Cowboys Assn., Cowboys Turtle Assn. (past), Nat. Old Timers Rodeo Assn., Canadian Rodeo Hist. Assn. (founder), Nat. Outlaw and Lawmen Assn. (life), Outlaw Trail Hist. Assn., Nat. Soc. Sons of Utah Pioneers (life), US Mormon Battalion Soc.(life), Western Heritage Soc. (life), Deseret Bus. & Profl. Assn., Interstake Bus. & Profl. Assn., Assn. Latter-Day Media Artists, BYU Emeritus Club; works: designed and made rodeo's 1st hornless bronc saddle (1922), also rodeo's 1st one-hand bareback rigging (1924), designed rodeo chaps (1926), invented rodeo exerciser (1928); bibliography: Who's Who in the West, Who's Who in Am., Who's Who in the World, Who's Who in Am. Art, Who's Who in Western Writers of Am.; Jon Scott (dir.) "Midnight's Last Ride - 1933" KBTV Denver (1983); Dick Dorwald (dir.) "Earl Bascom - An Artist and a Legend" K27-TV, Victorville (1984); "Cowboy Artist - Earl Bascom" KVVT-64 (1989); Michael Amundson (dir.) "Take Willy With You" (1989); author, illustr. "The Hist. of Bareback Bronc Riding" Western Horseman (6/90); illustr. book "Memories I Could Do Without and Other Short Stories" by Lyle Lybbert (1983); Cong. Jerry Lewis (author) "Earl Bascom - An American Hero" US Congl. Record (1985); Republican; Mormon; rec: saddle collection.; Res: Diamond B Ranch 15669 Stoddard Wells Rd Victorville 92392

BASSFORD, FORREST, journalist, livestock industry communications consultant; b. Feb. 2, 1906, Fountain, Okla.; s. Horace Albert and Vilura (McGinnis) B.; m. Marian Louise Horton, Oct. 12, 1929; children: Marilyn Ann b. 1937, Karen Lee (Kaytes) b. 1940, Dale H. b. 1944; edn: BS in animal husbandry, Colorado St. Univ., 1929. Career: county agric. ext. agt. Colo. Extension Service, Julesburg, Colo., 1929; editor Brush (Colo.) News, 1929; field rep. Denver Daily Record Stockman, 1930-34; American Hereford Journal, Kansas City, Mo. 1934-40; editor: The Record Stockman newspaper, Westerner Mag., Denver 1940-47; editor, gen. mgr., exec. editor, publisher Western Livestock Journal, Los Angeles then Denver, 1948-77; founding pub. Charolais Journal, Houston, Tx. 1977-78; sec.treas. then exec. dir. Livestock Publications Council, Denver then Houston, then Encinitas, Calif. 1974-92; awards: Colo. Cattlemen

Assn. life mem., 1962, Am.-Intl. Charolais Assn. merit. svc., 1970, Iowa Beef Improvement Assn. friendship & svc., 1971, Mo. Charolais Breeders Assn. outstanding contbns., 1972, Marketeers livestock marketeer of yr., 1972, Mile Hi CowBelles father of yr., 1973, Nebr. Animal Agriculture Week commendn., 1973, Am. Polled Hereford Assn. spl. recogn., 1974, Am. Gelbvieh Assn. notable contbns., 1974, Beef Improvement Fedn. pioneer, 1976, Calif. Beef Cattle Improvement Assn. commendn., 1976, Colo. St. Univ. Honor Alumnus, 1977, Gamma Sigma Delta disting. svc. to agric., 1977, Colo. Cattle Feeders Assn. top choice, 1977, Am. Soc. of Farm Mgrs. & Rural Appraisers merit. svc. in comms., 1977, Livestock Publs. Council headliner, 1980, Alpha Gamma Rho Jerry Litton Memorial, 1983, Intl. Stockmen's Sch. Honor Guest, 1985, Beef Improvement Fedn. amb., 1989; mem., dir. Western Stock Show Assn., 1940-, San Diego County, Calif. and Nat. Cattlemens Assns., 1978-; author: Century of Endurance, Hist. of Wyoming Hereford Ranch, 1983, thousands of livestock indus. features and reports, 1930-; mil: 1st sgt. Troop E, Wyo. Nat. Guard 1920-25, 2d lt. Field Arty. Reserve 1929-40; Republican; Episcopalian; rec: photog., fishing, writing. Res: 927 Elmview Dr Encinitas 92024

BATEMAN, MARIA NIKI, real estate broker; b. Mar. 3, 1948, Youngstown, Ohio; d. Nicholas George and Sophia N. (Pamfilis) Loijos; children: Michael Nicholas Loijos b. 1969; edn: grad. Ukiah H.S. 1966; bus. mgmt. CSU Sacto. 1966-67, CSU Sonoma 1983-84; Calif. R.E. lic. 1974, R.E. Broker/Notary Public 1986; C.R.S. designation, 1990. Career: former real estate sales staff MacElhenny, Levy & Co. Inc., Merrill Lynch Realty, sales and tng. supr. 1979-83, subdiv. sales mgr. 1980-83; owner/broker Foust & Co., Santa Rosa, 1985-90; broker assoc. Frank Howard Allen, 1990-; dir. Golden Pacific Financial 1984; honors: Virginia Kline Memorial award Board Member of Year, Am. Red Cross 1987, life mem. Million Dollar Club, Sonoma Co. M.L.S. 1976; mem: Sonoma Co. Bd. Realtors (bd. dirs. 1983-84, Ethics instr. 1982-83), Ducks Unlimited (charter mem. Womens Chpt.), Womens Council of Realtors, Am. Red Cross Redwood Empire Chpt. (chair bd. dirs. 1988-90, fin. devel. chair 1987-88), Soroptimists Internat. (recording secty. 1989-); Republican; Eastern Orthodox; rec: tennis, racquetball, ski, photog., sewing. Res: 930 Buckingham Dr Windsor 95492 Ofc: Frank Howard Allen, 2245 Montgomery Dr Santa Rosa 95405

BATES, CRAIG DANA, museum curator; b. Aug. 2, 1952, Oakland; s. Dana Raymond and June (Robinson) B.; m. Jennifer Dawn Bernido, May 12, 1973, div. June 1987; child: Carson b. 1981. Career: park technician Nat. Park Service, Yosemite N.P., 1973-76, Indian cultural splst. 1976-80, asst. curator 1980-82, curator of ethnography 1982-; resrch. assoc. Santa Barbara Mus. Natural Hist. 1983-; cons. Brooklyn Mus. (N.Y.) 1988-89, Oakland Mus. 1991-92; instr. Yosemite Assn., 1977-88, Point Reyes Nat. Hist. Assn., 1978-88; publs: 90+ articles on Native Am. cultures, coauthor 2 books: Legends of the Yosemite Miwok 1981, Tradition and Innovation: A Basket Hist. of the Indian People of the Yosemite-Mono Lake Area 1990; avocation: Native Am material culture. Ofc: National Park Service PO Box 577 Yosemite National Park 95389

BATESOLE, DALE F., clergyman, television host; b. Oct. 1911, Ferguson, Iowa; s. John Floyd and Elsie Rebecca (Campbell) B.; m. Carolyn J. Dewey, Dec. 17, 1987; edn: Grad. Safety Engr., Kansas Univ. Ext. 1943; Ordained Minister, Unity Sch. of Christianity 1959. Career: br. mgr. Western Grocer Co., Marshalltown, Iowa 1930-48; sales rep. Schultz Burch Biscuit Co. 1948-56; minister Unity Christ Ch., St. Louis, Mo. 1958-64; co-founder Forsyth Sch., St. Louis, Mo. 1961; faculty Unity Sch. of Christianity 1960-61; founder, 1st exec. dir. Charles and Myrtle Fillmore Found., Lee's Summit, Mo. 1964-67; sch. bd. trustee Maricopa Co. Sch. Dist. 1970-71; cons. to psychiat. svc. VA Hosp., Phoenix, Ariz. 1971-76; founder Unity Ch. of Sedona, Ariz. 1973; orginator, presenter Psycho-Cybernetics Sems. nationwide 1973; instr. Psycho-Cybernetics, No. Ariz. Univ. Coll. of Bus. Admin. 1975-77; minister Unity of the Desert, Palm Springs 1977-79; prod./dir./host daily TV pgm. "There Is A Way" (fmr. "The Unity Way") 1979-86; pres. Unity Student Minister's Assn.; counselor, tchr., lectr. A.A. 1960-; mem. Assn. of Unity Churches; publs: newspaper articles, columns for Red Rock News, Sedona, Ariz. 1973, 1974, Carefree Enterprise, Carefree, Ariz. 1970-72; Republican; rec. tennis, music, jogging. Res: 909 Sandpiper Palm Desert 92260 Ofc: There Is A Way, 350 Prescott Ave El Cajon 92020

BATTIN, CYNTHIA ANN, electrical engineer; b. Aug. 29, 1957, Tucson, Ariz.; d. Gene and Peggy Ann (Purcell) Price; m. Richard Scott Battin, June 23, 1990; edn: BSEE, San Diego St. Univ., 1986; cert. qual. assur. ASQC 1989, electronics tech. USN 1976. Career: E-5, electronics tech. USN, 1975-81; electronics engr. Alexander Sys. Co., San Diego 1984-86; jr. engr. intern Naval Ocean Sys. Ctr., 1985-86; reliability engr. ARINC Res. Corp., 1987-; recipient athletic awards- mem. volleyball teams in USN, Inter-Service, and SDSU; mem. IEEE, SMTA, ASQC, Toastmasters S.D. (ofcr., TM of Yr. Club 1990, TM of Yr Area 1991, CTM, ATM); Republican; Christian; rec: sports, outdoors, dog. Res: 4881 35th St San Diego 92116-1907 Ofc: ARINC Research 4055 Hancock St San Diego 92110

BAUER, JEROME LEO, JR., chemical engineer; b. Oct. 12, 1938, Pitts.; s. Jerome L. and Anna Mae (Tucker) B.; div.; children: Lori, Trish, Jeff; edn: BSChemE, Univ. dayton, 1960; MSChemE, Pa. State Univ., 1963; postgrad.,

Ohio State Univ., 1969; Reg. profl. engr., Ohio. Career: asst. prof. chem. engring. Univ. Dayton, Ohio 1963-67; mgr. advanced composites dept. Ferro Corp., Cleveland 1967-72; engring. material and process specifications mgr. Lockheed Missiles & Space Co. Inc., Sunnyvale, Calif. 1972-74; design specialist Convair div. Gen. Dynamics, San Diego 1974-76, project devel. engr. 1976-77; dir. research Furane div. M&T Chemicals Inc., Glendale 1980-82; mem. tech. staff Jet Propulsion Lab. Caltech, Pasadena 1977-80, 82-91; The Aerospace Corp., L.A. 1991-; awards: Phi Lambda Upsilon, Delta Sigma Epsilon, Meritorious Achiev. AIChE 1983; mem: Am. Inst. Chem. Engrs. (founder, chmn. Dayton sect. 1964-66, special projects chmn. Cleveland sect. 1968-69), Soc. for Advance. Material Process Engring. (No. Calif. sect. mem. chair 1973-74, San Diego secty. 1974-75, chmn. 1976, Los Angeles sect. chmn. 1977, nat. treas. 1978-82, gen. chmn. 31st internat. symposium exhibition, Las Vegas, Nev. 1986, internat. v.p. 1987-89, internat. pres. 1990), Internat. Electronics Packaging Soc. (Los Angeles chpt. pres. 1982); editor: Materials Sciences for Future (1986); contbr. articles to profl. jours.; St. Luke Episcopal Ch., La Crescenta (sr. warden 1981); Republican. Res: P.O. Box 3298 El Segundo 90245 Ofc: The Aerospace Corp. PO Box 92957 Los Angeles 90009

BAUER, PATRICIA MC COLLUM, college librarian; b. Nov. 29, 1920, Spreckles, Calif.; d. John Edgar and Maude Rae (Smiley) McCollum; m. Francis Harry, Apr. 12, 1945 (div. 1951); edn: BA, UC Berkeley, 1949, MA hist., 1951, MLS, 1959. Career: librarian Stanford Res. Inst., Menlo Park 1959-62; Livermore Rad. Lab., Livermore 1965-66; Head-Royce Sch., Oakland 1966-67; Oakland Pub. Schs., 1967-76; assoc. prof., head librarian Patten Coll., Oakland 1976-; recipient numerous awards in photography; mem: Calif. Native Plant Soc., Audubon Soc., Placer Art League, Fort Ross Interpretive Assn., Nat. Parks & Conserv. Assn., Camping Women, Calif. Acad. of Sci.; publs: article (1951), co. brochures (1960), 2 books in prog.; Democrat; R.Cath.; rec: photog., travel, camping, reading. Res: 40551 Airport Rd Little River 95456

BAUER, STEVEN MICHAEL, cost containment engineer; b. Nov. 8, 1949, Hemet; s. Donald Richard, Sr. and Jeanne Patricia (Lamont) B.; m. Myung-Hee Min, Sept. 10, 1983; children: Claudia Margaret b. 1984, Monica Anne b. 1985; edn: BA, CSU San Bernardino 1971, BS physics, 1984. Career: asst. then assoc. nuclear engr. SCE, Rosemead 1973-88, cost containment engr. 1988-; cons. res. JL Pettis VA Hosp., Loma Linda 1978-79; cons. mtn. planning San Bdo. County 1975-76; awards: volunteer of yr. Am. Red Cross 1990-91, listed Who's Who in Sci. & Engring. 1991, Who's Who in West (1992); civic bds: Am. for Energy Indep. (mem. chair 1991-), Neighborhood Watch Assn. San Bernadino (sec. 1991-92, v.p. 1993-), Sierra Club (chpt. secty. 1991-92), Kts. Col. Fontana (chmn. Pro-life 1984-92), Union of Concerned Scientists (chpt. orgnzr. San Bdo. 1991-), Newport Found. 1991-, Casa Colina Hosp. (fellow 1987-90), St. Labre Indian Sch. 1984-, LA Co. Mus. of Art (1984-), So. Poverty Law Ctr. (1986-91); Democrat (cpgn. wkr., precinct ldr. Re-elect Cong. G.E. Brown); R.Cath.; rec: gardening, writing. Res: 131 W Monroe Ct San Bernardino 92408-4137

BAUMHOFF, WALTER HENRY, headmaster; b. May 27, 1937, N.Y.C.; s. Joseph and Elli (Schillig) B.; edn: BA, Wagner Coll., 1959; MS, Indiana Univ., 1961; postgrad. Harvard Univ., Stanford Univ. Career: asst. dir. scholarship/fin. aid Ind. Univ., Bloomington 1960-61; dean of freshmen St. Lawrence Univ., Canton, NY 1961-65, dean of students 1965-71; faculty dept. psychiat./behav. scis. Stanford Univ., 1973-74; dean of admissions Dominican Coll., San Rafael 1974-78; headmaster The Buckley Sch., Sherman Oaks 1978-; mem. Valley Coun., L.A. Co. Mus. of Natural Hist. 1987, St. James Club; Republican; rec: skiing, sailing. Res: 5000 Ambrose Ave Los Angeles 90027 Ofc: 3900 Stansbury Ave Sherman Oaks 91423

BEASLEY, BRUCE MILLER, sculptor; b. May 20, 1939, Los Angeles; s. Robert Seth and Bernice (Palmer) B.; m. Laurence Leaute, May 21, 1973; children: Julian Bernard, Celia Beranice; edn: Dartmouth Coll., 1957-59; BA, UC Berkeley, 1962. Career: sculptor in metal and plastic, major sculptures commd. by State of Calif. 1967, US Govt. 1976, Oakland Mus. 1976, Miami (Fla.) Internat. Airport 1978, San Francisco Internat. Airport 1981, Stanford Univ. 1982, Fed. Home Loan Bank, S.F. 1992, Cities of Eugene, Oreg. 1974, San Francisco 1976, Salinas 1977, Anchorage, Alaska 1984; awards include Andre Malraux Purchase Award, Biennale de Paris 1961; One- man shows at Everett Ellin Gal., L.A., Kornblee Gal., N.Y.C., Hansen-Fuller Gal., S.F., David Stuart Gal., L.A., Andre Emmerich Gal., N.Y.C., De Young Mus., S.F., Santa Barbara Mus. Art, Fine Arts Gal., San Diego, Sonoma State Univ., Rohnert Park, The Oakland Mus., Fresno Art Mus., John Natsoulas Gal., Davis, Galerie Scheffel, Bad Homburg, Germany; Group shows include Mus. Modern Art, NYC, Guggenheim Mus., NYC, Albright Knox Gal., Buffalo, La Jolla Art Mus., Musee d'Art Modern, Paris, S.F. Mus. Art, Krannert Art Mus. of Univ. Ill., Jewish Mus., NYC, Luxembourg Gardens, Paris, Calif. Palace of Legion of Honor, S.F., De Young Mus., Middleheim (Germany) Sculpture Park, Yorkshire (England) Sculpture Park, Santa Barbara Art Mus., others; represented in permanent collections of Mus. Modern Art, Guggenheim Mus., Musee d'Art Modern, Paris, L.A. County Art Mus., Univ. Art Mus. of UC Berkeley, Oakland Mus., Wichita (Kans.) Art Mus., San Francisco Art Commn., Santa Barbara Art Mus., Dartmouth Coll., others; mem. Nat. Mus. Am. Art, Crocker Art Mus. Res: 322 Lewis St Oakland 94607-1236

BEATY, PAUL RICHARD, biologist; b. June 2, 1946, Ames, Iowa; s. Harold Huxford and Judith Helen (Skromme) B.; m. Sue Ann Weber, Sept. 7, 1968; children: Joel b. 1969, Christopher b. 1973, Michael b. 1978; edn: BS Eastern Illinois Univ., 1969; MS, Univ. Ill., Urbana 1976, PhD, 1979. Career: tchr. Unit 7 Schools, Tolono, Ill. 1969-72; refuge mgr. Illinois Dept. Conservation, Wilmington, Ill. 1972-73; assoc. scientist Illinois Natural History Survey, Urbana, 1974-78, asst. profl. scientist, 1978-79; dir. aquatic res. Coachella Valley Water Dist., Coachella, Calif. 1980-86; pres., prin. Southwest Aquatics, Beaty & Associates, Palm Desert, Calif. 1986-; mem: Calif. Lake Mfg. Soc. (dir. 1986-), Western Aquatic Plant Mgmt. Soc. (mem. 1981-, v.p. 1992-93, pres. 1993-), No. Am. Lake Mgmt. Soc. 1986-, Aquatic Plant Mgmt. Soc. 1981-, Am. Fisheries Soc. 1976-; civic: Riverside Co. Sch. Dist. Org. (1987-, chair 1989-), Optimist (Palm Desert club pres. 1992-93), Palm Desert Palnning Commn. 1993-, Desert Youth Sports Org. (dir.), Palm Desert Youth Sports (dir., League rep.), P.O.N.Y. Baseball (Region Palomino dir.); num. profl. articles and speeches in field; rec: golf, camping, fishing. Ofc: Beaty & Associates PO Box 13212 Palm Desert 92255

BEAUMAN, JOHN GERALD, aerospace group technical director; b. July 28, 1936, NYC; s. Lorenz and Constance; m. Sharon; children: Deborah Ann, Gerald, Brenda, and John Jr.; edn: engring. student SUNY, 1966-70; BSME, Calif. Coast Univ., 1976, MSME, 1983. Career: technical mgr. aircraft systems Fairchild Republic Co., Farmingdale, N.Y., 1965-82, participant in design of the F-105G, F-14, A-10, and Boeing's 767 and 757; technical mgr. flt. control hardware design & devel., tech. mgr. flt. controls integration, tech. mgr. systems integration, Northrop B-2 Div., Pico Rivera, Calif. 1982-88; group tech. dir. for systems and technology integration Parker Bertea Aerospace Group, Parker Hannifin Corp., Irvine 1988-; mem. AIAA, NCOSE; civic: Montefino Homeowners Assn. Diamond Bar (pres. 1982-86, newsletter editor & pub. Montefino Spotlight 82-86); author: Flight Control Iron Birds (1983); Republican; Presbyterian. Res: 824 Candlewood St Brea 92621

BECHTEL, STEPHEN D., JR., industrialist; b. May 10, 1925, Oakland; s. Stephen D. and Laura (Peart) Bechtel; m. Elizabeth Mead Hogan, 1946; children: 3 daughters; edn: civil engr. stu. Univ. of Colo. 1943-44; BS, Purdue Univ. 1946; MBA, Stanford Univ. 1948; Hon. Dr. Engrg., Purdue Univ. 1972; Hon. Dr. of Sci., Univ. of Colo. 1981. Career: employed by Bechtel 1941-, held broad variety of jobs and responsibilities both in the field and San Francisco Home Office; dir. 1951-; v.p. 1952-55; sr. v.p. 195-57; exec. v. p. 1957-60; pres. 1960-73; chmn. 1973-90, chmn. emeritus 1990-; chmn. Sequoia Ventures, Inc., 1980-; bd. dir. Internat. Bus. Machines; mem. Nat. Acad. of Engineering (past chmn.), The Business Council (past chmn.), Conference Bd. (life councillor and past chmn.), The Business Roundtable (policy com.), Labor-Mgmt. Group; 3d of trustees Calif. Inst. of Technology; mem. Internat. Advy. Council, Inst. for Internat. Studies, Stanford Univ.; awards: Hon. Chairman NSPE 1990 Nat. Engineers' Week, French Legion of Honor Officer, Engineering News Record-Constrn. Man of Year 1974, Moles' Award for Outstanding Achiev. in Constrn. 1974, ASCE Civil Engring. Mgmt. award 1979, ASME Centennial award 1982, AAES Chmn.'s award 1982, Herbert Hoover Medal 1980, Washington Award 1985, Am. Jewish Com.'s Inst. of Human Relations award 1987; clubs: The Beavers, Commonwealth of Calif., Augusta Nat. Golf, Bankers (SF), The Blind Brook (NYC), The Mount Royal (Montreal), Pacific Union (SF), Ramada (Houston), SF Golf, SF Tennis, Thunderbird CC (Palm Springs), Vancouver (B.C.), Villa Taverna (SF), The York (Toronto); publs: New Edisons and New Technologies (1979), Calif.'s Contbn. to the Multiplier Effect (1979), The Climate for Innovation (1979), Technology: Found. for America's Future Well Being (1980), others; mil: USMCR 1943-48; Prot.; rec: golf, tennis, hiking, photog. Res: POB 3809 San Francisco 94119 Ofc: 50 Beale St San Francisco 94105

BECK, JOHN CHRISTIAN, physician/academic division director; b. Jan. 4, 1924, Audubon, Iowa; m. Dr. Arlene Fink; edn: BS, McGill Univ., 1944, MD, 1947, MS, 1951, diploma in experimental medicine, 1952; PhD (hon.) Ben Gurion Univ., Tel Aviv 1981; MD lic. Calif. BME, 1978. Career: prof. UC San Francisco, 1978-79; prof. UC Los Angeles, 1979-, dir. Multicampus Div. of Gerontological Medicine and Gerontology, UCLA, 1987-92; dir. Long Term Care National Res. Ctr., L.A. 1988-; dir. Older Americans Independence Ctr., L.A. 1991-; awards: Allan T. Bailey Memorial Award, Am. Coll. Physicians 1985, Bruce Hall Memorial Lecture, Garvan Inst. of Med. Res. Sydney, Australia 1989, Duncan Graham Award The Royal Coll. Physicians and Surgeons, U.K. 1989, Joseph T. Freeman Award Gerontol. Soc. of Am. 1990, Irving S. Wright Award Am. Fedn. on Aging Res. 1991; mem: AAAS, Am. Clin. and Climatol. Assn., Am. Coll. of Physicians, Am. Diabetes Assn., Am. Fedn. for Clin. Research, Am. Geriatric Soc. Ofc: UCLA, 10833 Le Conte Ave 32-144CHS Los Angeles 90024-1687

BECK, THOMAS EDWIN, studio furniture maker; b. Dec. 31, 1946, Stockton; s. Harold Marquis and Verna (Johnson); m. Ellen Marie Hill, June 11, 1973; 1 son, Alexander b. 1982; edn: San Francisco City Coll. 1964-66, UC Berkeley 1966-67, Coll. of the Desert 1984-85, Calif. Poly. State Univ. 1985. Career: journeyman carpenter United Brotherhood of Carpenters & Joiners, Portland, Oreg. 1972-; cabinetmaker apprentice to Drago Dimitri (Yugoslavian

master), Calgary, Can. 1976-79; owner Thomas Beck Fine Furniture, Morongo Valley, Calif. 1981-; cons. San Bdo. Co. Regional Employment; awards: Best of Show Bellevue (Wash.) Art Mus. 1990; conscientious objector Vietnam War; Democrat; rec: technical rockclimbing, bass fishing. Res/Ofc: 52355 Altadena Dr Morongo Valley 92256-9671 Ph: 619/363-6155

BEDRICK, JEFFREY KEITH, artist, muralist; b. Oct. 4, 1960, Providence, R.I.; s. Barry David and Ann Glenda (Rosenberg) B.; edn: pvt. apprenticeship Gage Taylor, artist, Woodacre, 1977-79; filmmaking, San Francisco St. Univ., 1983. Career: fine artist, exh. num. galleries internat. 1978-; muralist and decorative painting num. cos., San Francisco 1981-; prodn. artist/animator Colossal Pictures, S.F. 1982-; freelance illustrator var. corps. internat. 1986-; designer: internat. "Earthquake Emblem" for Red Rose Collection 1992; illustrator book: Weather (1989 Doubleday); mem. US Hang Gliding Assn. 1991-, World Affairs Council, S.F. Soc. of Illustrators; rec: hang gliding, raquetball, billiards, chess. Ofc: Millennium Studios 477 25th Ave Ste 6 San Francisco 94121 Tel: 415/387-9928

BEEBE, JOHN ELIOTT, III, psychiatrist; b. June 24, 1939, Washington, D.C.; s. John Eliott and Patricia (Boden) B.; edn: BA, Harvard Univ. 1961; MD, Univ. Chgo. 1965. Career: psychiatric resident Stanford Hosp., Stanford 1968-71; chief resident Adult Psychiatry Clinic, Stanford Hosp. 1970-71; pvt. practice psychiatry, San Francisco 1971-; asst. prof. psychiatry UCSF Med. Center 1977-; courtesy staff California Pacific Med. Center 1971-; mem: C.G. Jung Inst. S.F., Internat. Assn. Analytical Psychology, No. Calif. Psychiatric Soc., Am. Psychiatric Assn.; author/ed. Psychiatric Treatment, 1975; ed. Jung Inst. Library Jour., 1979-; ed. Money Food Drink Fashion, 1986; ed. Aspects of The Masculine, 1989; co-ed. Jour. of Analytical Psychology (1990-); author Integrity in Depth, 1992; mil: sr. asst. surgeon USPHS; Democrat; rec: songwriting, screenwriting. Ofc: 337 Spruce St San Francisco 94118

BEFU, BEN, professor emeritus; b. Aug. 14, 1927, Los Angeles; s. Juma and Komaki (Shimizu) B.; m. Grayce Yayoi Yano, Aug. 14, 1954; children: MaryLynn b. 1960, AnneMarie b. 1968; edn: BA, UCLA, 1953; MA, UC Berkeley, 1956; PhD, Stanford Univ., 1966. Career: instr. Rafu Daini Gakuen, Los Angeles 1949-53; sp2 US Army 1954-57: linguist, intel. specialist US Army, Tokyo, Japan 1955-57; civilian mil. intel. analyst US DoD, Tokyo 1957-58, linguist, analyst US Govt., Tokyo 1958-60; actg. asst. prof. UCLA, Los Angeles 1964-66, asst. prof. 1966-72, assoc. prof. 1972-91, chmn. Oriental Lang. Dept. 1975-78, prof. emeritus 1991-; vis. asst. prof. Stanford Univ., summer 1965; awards: Commendn. Army Language Sch. Presidio of Monterey 1955, Commendn. 500th Mil Intel Gp Tokyo, Japan 1959, NDFL fellow 1961-64, Instrnl. Improvement award UCLA Academic Senate 1977; mem: Assn. of Asian Studies 1962-, Am. Oriental Soc. 1964-90, Assn. of Teachers of Japanese (1975-, bd. govs. 1983-86), Nat. Scholarly Advy. Council for the Japanese Am. Nat. Museum 1991-; Sierra Club, Nat. Audubon Soc., Nat. Parks and Conserv. Assn.; author: Worldly Mental Calculations (1976), articles "Monumenta Serica" (1968), Critical Survey of Short Fiction" (1987). Res: 1535 10th St Manhattan Beach 90266 Ofc: UCLA, Dept of EALC, 405 Hilgard Ave Los Angeles 90024

BEHRENDT, JOHN THOMAS, lawyer; b. Oct. 26, 1945, Syracuse, Kans.; s. Thomas Franklin and Anna Iola (Carrithers) B.; m., 1967 (div.); children: Todd Thomas, Gretchen Jean; m. 2d Theresa Ann Elmore, Oct. 27, 1985; edn: BA, Sterling Coll.; JD (cum laude), Univ. Minn.; admitted bar: Calif. 1971, Tex. 1973, N.Y. 1984. Career: atty. assoc., then ptnr. Gibson, Dunn & Crutcher, Los Angeles 1970-71, 1974-; mem: Am. Bar Assn., Los Angeles County Bar Assn.; clubs: Jonathan (L.A.), Union League (N.Y.), Tuxedo (Tuxedo Park, N.Y.); mil: capt. JAGC, AUS 1971-74. Ofc: Gibson Dunn & Crutcher, 333 S Grand Ave Los Angeles 90071 also: 200 Park Ave New York NY 10001

BEIERLE, ROBERT THOMAS, scientist, electronics engineer, inventor; b. Nov. 3, 1945, Long Beach; s. William Frank and Dolores (Mounce) B.; m. Sally Jane Benson, Nov. 18, 1982; child: Troy Albert Emery b. 1988; edn: AS, Mt. San Antonio Coll. 1972; BSEE, Calif. St. Polytech. Univ. 1975, grad. stu. 1984. Career: design engr. General Dynamics, Pomona 1975-79; principal designer Hughes Aircraft GEADGE pgm. (German Air-Ground Environ. Def. Sys.), Fullerton 1979-82; sr. mem. tech. staff/ hd. guidance control design gp. ADCAP pgm. Hughes Aircraft 1982-, senior staff engr., tech. supr.; tchg. asst., radar sys. & signal processing, Cal Poly Pomona 1976-77; awards: co-designer guidance & control sys. for Cal Poly Rose Parade Float- recipient Princess award 1974, Cal Poly academic scholar 1975, IEEE Student Chpt. acad. outstanding scholar 1975, Hughes Aircraft Div. zero defects award 1984 also two patent awards 1989 and four div. invention awards; mem: IEEE; Nat. Mgmt. Assn.; mil: sgt. USAF 1963-67, Vietnam, Nat. Defense Svc., GCM; R.Cath.; rec: landscape design, sailing, inventing. Res: 20980 E Gold Run Dr Diamond Bar 91765 Ofc: Hughes Aircraft, Ground Systems Group, Malvern and Gilbert Fullerton 92634

BEILBY, ALVIN LESTER, professor of chemistry; b. Sept. 17, 1932, Watsonville; s. Claud Eldred and Elma Fern (Hockabout) B.; m. Ruby Irene Nelson, June 21, 1958; children: Mark Alfred b. 1959, Lorene Sigrid b. 1961;

edn: BA, San Jose State Univ., 1954; Harvard Univ., 1954-55; PhD, Univ. Wash., Seattle 1958. Career: faculty Pomona Coll., Claremont, Calif. 1958-: chemistry instr. 1958-60, asst. prof. 1960-66, assoc. prof. 1966-72, prof. 1972-, dept. chair 1972-85; vis. scholar Univ. Ill., Champaign-Urbana, 1964-65; guest worker and res. chemist Nat. Bur. of Stds., Gaithersburg, Md. 1971-72; guest wkr. Lockheed Palo Alto Rsch. Lab., Palo Alto 1979-80; guest prof. Uppsala Univ., Sweden 1986-87; awards: Petroleum Res. Fund Faculty Award for adv. scientific study Am. Chem. Soc., Univ. Ill. 1964-65, NSF sci. faculty, profl. devel. award Lockheed Palo Alto Res. Lab. 1979-80; mem: A.C.S. 1956-, Soc. of Sigma Xi 1958-, AAAS 1983-, Assn. of Am. Med. Colls. (1966-76, 81-93), Western Assn. of Advisors for the Health Professions (mem. 1970-76, 81-93, first chair 1970-71); publs: Lab. Manual for Chem.: A Quantitative Approach (coauthor 1969), editor: Modern Classics in Analytical Chem. (vol.I 1970, vol.II 1976); Democrat; United Ch. of Christ (moderator Claremont United Ch. of Christ, Congl. Ch. 1975-77, bd. dirs. So. Calif. Conf. 1983-85, moderator So. Calif. Conf. 1984-85); corporate mem. Congregaional Homes Inc., Pomona 1986-92, Calif. Christian Home, Rosemead (bd. dirs. 1990-, treas. 1993-); rec: English Handbell ringing, travel, color photography. Res: 663 Hood Dr Claremont 91711 Ofc: Pomona College 645 N College Ave Claremont 91711

BELL, CHARLES ARTHUR, warehousing and box fabrication co. president; b. March 16, 1937, Sacramento; s. Samuel and Hilda Bell; m. Jacquelin Marie Clarke, Sept. 30, 1953; children: Renee Y. b. 1966, Courtney C. b. 1988; edn: BA, CSU Sacto. 1973. Career: asst. mgr. Wells Fargo Bank, Sacto. 1962-72; regional v.p. U.S. Dept. of Commerce 1972-75; loan analyst Spanish Speaking Unity Council, Oakland 1975-77; asst. mgr. Calif. Canadian Bank, Palo Alto 1977-79; loan ofcr. U.S. Small Bus. Adminstrn., San Francisco 1979-82; sr. cons. Price Waterhouse, Sacto. 1982-84; pres. Am. Stitching, Fairfield 1984-; pres. Charles Bell & Assoc. 1980-; awards: Calif. St. Senate Select Com. Small Bus. Cert. of Recognition 1984, Anheuser Busch Minority Econ. Devel. 1984, Republican Presdl. Task Force Commn. 1986, No. Calif. Outstanding Black Business 1991; mem: Nat. Beverage Packaging Assn., Brewer & Beverage Packaging Assn.; civic bds: Grant Union H.S. Dist. (by-law com. 1974-76), No. Calif., United Way (Napa/Solana bd. dirs. 1991, co-chair Fairfield/Suisun 1991), Solano County Fair (bd. dirs. 1991); club: Rancho Solano Country (bd. govs. 1989-); mil: E-3 AUS 1960-62; Republican (Presdl. Task Force, Repub. Senatorial Inner Circle); Prot.; rec: fishing, golf, community work. Ofc: American Stitching and Box Inc. POB 2133 Fairfield 94533

BELLANCA, LOUIS CHARLES, lawyer; b. June 26, 1943, Buffalo, NY; s. Russell Michael and Christine Mary (Fasciana) B.; m. Jayne Gardner, Sept. 5, 1970; children: Dayna, b. 1974, Erin, b. 1977; edn: AAS, Erie Comm. Coll. 1962; stu. Pasadena City Coll. 1962-3, Glendale Coll. 1963-4, Valley Coll. 1965-7; JD, LLB, Univ. San Fernando Valley, 1972; admitted bar: Calif. 1972, U.S. Dist. Cts. 1977. Career: optician, Superior Optical Co., Los Angeles 1962-72; pvt law practice, Beverly Hills 1973; staff atty. Mansell & Giddens, Los Angeles 1973-74; atty., assoc. Grancell, Kegel & Tobin, L.A. 1974-75; mng. atty. Levy, Koszdin, Goldschmid & Sroloff, Long Beach and Santa Ana, 1975-78; atty., sec., CFO law firm Towner, Kristjanson, Bellanca & Hill, Santa Ana and Tustin 1978-82, pres. 1980-82; pres. Kristjanson, Bellanca & Hill, 1982-85; pres. Kristjanson, Bellanca, Roselinsky, Gerrick & Hudes, 1985-87; v.p. Baziak & Bellanca, 1988-; Workers' Compensation judge pro tem 1982-, Workers' Compensation Arbitration Panel 1991-; awards: Master of Ophthalmic Optics 1972, Fellow Internat. Acad. of Opticianry 1965, James Bass and Loren Michael Mem. awards Jaycees (1967, 68); mem: Workers Compensation Claims and Def. Counsel Assn. (secty.1978), Long Beach Bar Assn., Calif. Applicant's Attorneys Assn., Orange Co. Bar Assn. (chmn. Workers Compensation Sect. 1990), Lex Romana; civic: Northridge Jaycees (past pres. 1969-70), Sunland-Tujunga Jaycees (v.p. 1967, state dir. 1968); Republican; Christian; rec: boating, bicycling, running. Res: Huntington Beach Ofc: Baziak & Bellanca, 1327 N Broadway St Santa Ana.

BELLEVILLE, PHILIP FREDERICK, lawyer; b. Apr. 24, 1934, Flint, Mich.; s. Frederick Charles and Sarah Adeline (Cottrell) B.; m. Geraldean Bickford, Sept. 2, 1953; children: Stacy, b. 1957; Philip II, b. 1958; Jeffrey, b. 1961; edn: BA, honors in econ. and high distinction, Univ. of Mich. 1956, JD, 1960; admitted to State Bar of Calif. 1961. Career: atty., assoc. Latham & Watkins, L.A., Calif. 1960-68, partner L.A. and Newport Bch. 1968-73, (chmn. Litigation Dept. L.A., Newport Bch., Calif. and Wash. D.C. 1973-80), partner L.A., Orange County, San Diego, Wash. D.C., 1980-, Chgo. 1983-, N.Y.C. 1985-, San Francisco 1990-, London 1990-, Moscow 1992-; awards: James B. Angell Scholar 1955-6, Phi Beta Kappa 1955, Phi Kappa Psi 1955, Order of the Coif 1960; mem. So. Calif. steering com. NAACP Legal Def. Fund Inc. 1979-; advy. bd. San Pedro/Penninsula Hosp. 1980-88; mem: Am. Bar Assn. (Antitrust Law and Crim. Justice sects.), State Bar of Calif. (Antitrust, Trade Reg. Law & Bus. Law sects.), Los Angeles Co. Bar Assn. (Bus. Trial Lawyers sect.), Assn. of Bus. Trial Lawyers; clubs: City (L.A.), Palos Verdes Golf, Jack Kramer Tennis, Rolling Hills Tennis, Caballeros, Portuguese Bend; Republican; Prot.; rec: antiques, classic autos, art and literature. Ofc: Latham & Watkins, 633 W Fifth St Los Angeles 90071-2007

BELLIS, CARROLL J., surgeon; b. May 11, 1908, Shreveport, La.; s. Joseph E. and Rose (Bloome) B.; m. Mildred E., Dec. 26, 1951; children: Joseph, b. 1940, David, b. 1944; edn: BS, 1930, MS, 1932, PhD in physiol., 1934, MD, 1936, PhD in surg., 1941, Univ. of Minn. Career: teaching fellow in Physiol., Univ. of Minn.; Alice Shevlin fellowship in physiology, Univ. of Minn.; instr. in surgery U. of Minn. Medical Sch.; surgical cons. to Surgeon-Gen. US Army; currently: pvt. practice of surgery; staff St. Mary Med. Ctr.; cons. in surg., Long Beach Gen. Hosp.; prof./chmn. Dept. of Surgery, Calif. Coll. of Medicine. Honors: Sigma Xi, AOA, Phi Beta Kappa, recipient Charles Lyman Green Prize in Physiol., Mpls. Surgical Soc. Prize, Miss. Valley Med. Soc. Annual Awd. 1955. Dip. Am. Bd. of Surgery, Fellow Am. Coll. of Surgeons, Fellow Nat. Cancer Inst., Fellow Am. Coll. of Gastroenterol., Fellow Am. Geriatrics Soc., Fellow Internat. Coll. of Surgeons, Fellow of the Sci. Council, Internat. Coll. of Angiology, Fellow Phlebology Soc. of Am., mem. Am. Assn. for Study of Neoplastic Diseases, Am. Assn. of Hist. of Medicine, AAAS, NY Acad. of Scis., Am. Med. Writers Assn., Irish Med. Assn. (hon.), Hollywood Acad. of Medicine, Pan Am. Med. Assn. Author 51+ publs. in field incl. 3 books: Fundamentals of Human Physiology, Critique of Reason, Lectures in Medical Physiology; mil: col. US Army M.C., 1941-5. Res: 3 South Quail Ridge Rd Rolling Hills 90274 Ofc: 1045 Atlantic Ave Ste 1011 Long Beach 90813

BELT, AUDREY E., social worker; b. June 23, 1948, New Orleans; edn: BS, Grambling State Univ., La. 1970; MSW, Univ. Mich., 1972. Career: adult pro-bation ofcr. City and County San Francisco, 1973-74, child welfare worker dept. social svs., 1974-79; research and planning specialist City of Ann Arbor Model Cities Interdisciplinary Agy., Mich.; indep. res. & planning cons.; awards: Grambling State Univ. scholar 1966-70, Univ. Mich. scholar 1971-72, Alpha Kappa Delta Nat. Hon. Soc.; mem: Am. Bar Assn., Nat. Assn. Soc. Workers (edn. task force), Am. Orthopsychiat. Assn., Child Welfare League Am., Am. Humane Soc., Black Am. Polit. Assn. Calif. (legis. com.); Democrat; R.Cath. Res: POB 5319 San Francisco 94101-5319

BELTRAMI, ALBERT PETER, government executive; b. Feb. 26, 1934, Sacto.; s. Battista "Bob" and Anastasia "Annie" B.; m. Patricia J. Kearns, July 28, 1957; children: Katharine Clare b. 1964, Robert Richard b. 1965; edn: AA, Modesto Jr. Coll., AB pol. sci., UC Berkeley, and MA in pub. adminstrn., UC Berkeley. Career: dep. marshal Modesto Municipal Ct., 1954-55; adminstrv. asst. County of San Luis Obispo, S.L.O. 1960-61, asst. adminstrv. ofcr. 1961-65; county adminstrv. ofcr. County of Mendocino, Ukiah 1965-90; cons. local govt. fin. & ops., affil. Pub. Service Skills, Inc. Sacto. 1990-91; CEO County of Stanislaus, Modesto 1991-93; deputy dir. Intergovernmental Affairs, Office of Gov. Wilson, Calif. 1993- advy. com. Golden Gate Univ. Grad. Sch. Pub. Adminstrn. 1975-80; gov. appt. mem. Calif. No. Coast Reg. Water Quality Control Bd. 1972-93, chmn. 1989; atty. gen. appt. mem. Calif. Law Enforce. Telecomms. Advy. Com. 1974-90; dir. Mendocino Devel. Corp., 1987-89; mem: Calif. Assn. Co. Adminstrv. Ofcrs. (sec. 1979-80, v.p. 80-81, pres. 81-82), AM Soc. for Pub. Adminstrn. 1965-, Inter City Mgmt. Assn. 1965-; clubs: Commonwealth of Calif. (SF), Elks (SLO), Lions (Ukiah), Elks (Ukiah); author: California - Golden Gate Report (6/88); mil: cdr. USNR Active 1957-60, 6/84 Ret.; Republican; R.Cath.; rec: chess, gardening. Res: 145 Mendocino Pl Ukiah 95482 Tel: 707/462-6230

BELVILLE, DONALD R., physician; b. Jan. 22, 1924, Fairmont, Minn.; s. Harold R. and Olga Louise (Lindell) B.; m. Ruth, Nov. 23, 1946; children: Mark b. 1954, John b. 1955, Charles b. 1958, Judith b. 1961; edn: USC 1946-49; BA, Univ. of Iowa 1949, MD, 1953; Diplomate Am. Coll. of Radiol. (1961). Career: staff radiol. Long Beach Comm. Hosp. 1961-66, medical director , dept. chief radiology, 1966-89, ret.; trustee Long Beach Comm. Hosp. Found.; mem: ACR, AMA, Calif. Med. Assn., LACMA, Fillmore Condit Club, Freedom Found. Valley Forge; co-developer Angiocor x-ray 1970; mil: capt. AUS Med. Corps 1955-57; Republican; Prot.; rec: photog., travel, golf. Res: 5051 Crescent Dr Anaheim 92807

BENECH, GRANT FRANCIS, real estate co. executive; b. Aug. 21, 1957, San Jose; s. Wallace Edmond and Flora Mae (Infante) B.; edn: AA, Modesto Jr. Coll. 1977, BS, UC Berkeley 1979, MBA (cum laude), 1981; Calif. lic. R.E. Broker 1984; Cert. R.E. Appraiser 1987. Career: chief finl. ofcr., treas., secty. California Capital Exports, Inc., Oakland 1981-84; splst./cons. Bank of Am. Mortgage Banking, Menlo Park 1984-85; pres. Realequity Assocs., Inc., Oakland and San Jose 1985-; pres. Am. Western Financial, Inc., Oakland, Cupertino, San Francisco, 1988-; mem. Calif. Assn. of Residential Lenders (v.p. 1989), World Trade Assn., Commonwealth Club of Calif., Cal Business Alumni; publs: An Analysis of Alternative Mortgage Instruments (Bank Am. 3/81); Republican; Cath.; rec: sports car/racing enthusiast, tennis, golf. Res: 2521 Regent St, 8, Berkeley 94704

BENHAM, PRISCILLA CARLA, college president; b. Jan. 30, 1950, Berkeley, Calif.; d. Carl Thomas and Bebe (Harrison) Patten; m. Donald William Benham, Mar. 30, 1986; children: Charmaine Priscilla b. 1989; edn: BS, Patten Coll., Oakland 1969; BA, Holy Names Coll., Oakland 1970; MA (with honors), Wheaton Coll., Wheaton, Ill. 1972; PhD, Drew Univ., Madison,

N.J. 1976. Career: teaching fellow Drew Univ. 1974-75; prof. Patten College, Oakland 1975-, pres. 1983-; co-pastor Christian Cathedral, Oakland 1964-, choral dir. 1975-; v.p. Christian Evangelical Churches of Am., Oakland 1989-; bd. dirs. Am. Assn. of Presidents of Indep. Colls. & Univs., Malibu 1990-; bd. dirs. Regional Assn. of East Bay Colls. & Univs., Oakland 1991-; editorial bd. Journal of Pentecostal Theology, Cleveland, Tenn. 1991-; listed in: Notable Americans 1979, Personalities of America 1979, Who's Who of Women 1982, Who's Who in Religion 1985, Who's Who in the West 1986, Men and Women of Distinction 1988; mem.: Am. Acad. of Religion/Soc. of Biblical Lit., Bar-Ilan Assn. of the Greater Bay Area 1984-, Assn. of Indep. Colls. & Univs. 1984-, Presidents of Small Indep. Colls. 1991-, Oakland C.of C. 1987-; co-author: Before the Times 1980, The World of the Early Church 1990; Christian Evangelical; rec: skiing. Ofc: Patten College 2433 Coolidge Ave Oakland 94601

BENJAMIN, KARL, painter, professor of art; b. Chgo., 1925; edn: Northwestern Univ. 1943; BA, Univ. of Redlands, 1949; MA, Claremont Grad. Sch., 1960. Career: mil: US Navy 1943-46; painter, 1951-, Loren-Barton Babcock Miller Prof. of Fine Arts/ artist in residence Pomona Coll., also prof. of art Claremont Grad. Sch.; awards: NEA visual art grant, $15,000 (1983, 1986); permanent mus. collections internat.; major exhibits include: Univ. of Redlands, Falk-Raboff Gal., LA 1953, Pasadena Art Mus., LA Art Assn. 1954, Jack Carr Gal. Pasadena, "10th Ann. Newport Harbor Art Exh." Newport Beach 1955, "Art in Architecture" Municipal Art Gal., LA 1956, "Calif. Drawings" Pomona Coll. and UC Riverside Art Depts. and Herschel Chipp, also shown Long Beach Mus. of Art 1957, Occidental Coll. 1958, "4 Abstract Classicists" LA Co. and S.F. Museums; "New Talent" Am. Fedn. of Arts: Wichita Art Mus., Time Inc. NY, Univ. Ala., Howard Univ., others 1959, Esther-Robles Gal. LA (1959, 60, 62, 64), "West Coast Hard Edge" Inst. of Contemp. Arts London, Queen's Coll. Belfast; "Purist Painting" Am. Fedn. of Arts: Andrew Dickson White Art Mus. Ithaca, NY, Walker Art Ctr. Mpls., Speed Mus. Louisville, Mus. of Art Syracuse, N.C. Mus. of Art, Columbus Gal. of Fine Arts Ohio; "LA Co. Mus. of Art Ann. Exh. 1960, Auckland Art Gal. N.Z. (1961, 71), Bolles Gal. S.F., La Jolla Mus. of Art 1961, "50 California Artists" Whitney Mus. N.Y., Walker Art Ctr. Mpls., Albright-Knox Art Gal. Buffalo, Des Moines Art Ctr. Ia.; "Geometric Abstraction in Am." Whitney Mus. NY, Boston Inst. Contemp. Art, others; "The Artist's Environment West Coast" Amon Carter Mus. of We. Art Ft. Worth, Tx., UCLA Art Gals., Oakland Art Mus.; Santa Barbara Mus. Art (1962), "Liturgical Art" Mount St. Mary's Coll. L.A. (1963), "New Accessions, USA" Colo. Springs Fine Arts Ctr. 1964, "The Responsive Eye" Mus. Modern Art N.Y., City Art Mus. St. Louis, Seattle Art Mus., Pasadena Art Mus., Balt. Mus. Art; "Art Across Am." Mead Corp., M. Knoedier & Co. N.Y., Toledo Mus. of Art, Cleve. Inst. Art, Wadsworth Atheneum Hartford, Contemp. Arts Ctr. Cinti., Isaac Delgado Mus. New Orleans, Commercial Mus. Phila., others; "The Colorists 1950-1965" S.F. Mus. Art; "Calif. Artists" Witte Memorial Mus. San Antonio; "Survey of Contemp. Art" Speed Mus. Art Louisville; "Denver Mus. Art Annual" 1965, "S.F. Art Inst. 85th Ann. Exh." S.F. Mus. Art; "Am. Painting" Va. Mus. Fine Arts 1966, "30th Biennial Exh. of Am. Painting" Corcoran Gal. WDC; The White House 1967, Henri Gal. WDC, Santa Barbara Mus. Art 1968, "LA Ann. Art Exh." Municipal Art Gal. 1969, Wm. Sawyer Gal. S.F. 1971, Univ. Redlands 1972, Tortue Gal. Santa Monica (1975, 77, 78, 80), "Painting and Sculpture in Calif.: The Modern Era" S.F. Mus. Art, Nat. Collection of Fine Arts WDC 1976, "35th Biennial Am. Painting" Corcoran Gal.; "4 From Calif." Dorothy Rosenthal Gal. Chgo. 1977, Francine Seders Gal., Seattle (1978, 79, 80, 83, 86), "Art, Inc: Am. Paintings From Corp. Collections" Montgomery Mus. Fine Arts Ala., Corcoran Gal., Indpls. Mus. Art, San Diego Mus. Art; "Los Angeles Abstract Painting" Univ. N.M., UC Riverside 1979, "survey, 1970-1980" Univ. Redlands, "partial retrospective" Cheney-Cowles Mus. Spokane, Wa., Whitman Coll. Sheehan Gal.; "West Coast: Art For the Pres.'s House" S.F. Mus. Art, The V.P.'s House WDC 1980, "Paintings of the 50s" Pepperdine Univ.; Nat. Mus. Am. Art, WDC 1981, Univ. Wash., Stella Polaris Gal. LA 1982, "A Focus on Calif." LA Co. Mus. Art, "20th Century: SF Mus. Modern Art Collection" 1984, "The Calif. Colorists" Shasta Coll., Redding Art Mus., San Jose Inst. Contemp. Art, Palm Springs Mus., Pomona Coll.; "Color Forms" Sec. Pac. Nat. Bank Gal. LA 1985, "Insights" Laguna Art Mus. 1987, A Retrospective Exh. 1955-1987" CSU Northridge; "A Decade of Abstraction" Seattle Ctr. 1989, "Turning the Tide: Early LA Modernists 1920-1956" Laguna Art Mus., Oakland Mus., McNay Art Inst. San Antonio 1990, "Survey of Geometric Abstractions" Marc Richards Gal. Santa Monica; "Ten Year Survey" D.P. Fong Gal. San Jose (one person show) 1991, "Paintings 1955-1990" Snyder Fine Art N.Y. (one-person show) 1992. Res/Studio: 675 W Eighth St Claremont

BENJAMIN, STUART ALLAN, lawyer, film producer, entertainment co. executive; b. Apr. 25, 1946, Los Angeles; s. Gerald T. and Victorine B. (Ritter); m. Alise Humple, 1991; children: Jennifer b. 1977, Matthew b. 1978; edn: BS in fin. (magna cum laude), USC, 1967; JD, Harvard Law Sch., 1970. Career: atty., assoc. Wyman, Bautzer, Christensen, Kuchel & Silbert, Los Angeles 1970-75, ptnr. 1975-88, of counsel 1988-91; pres. and c.o.o. New Visions Inc. and New Visions Pictures (video and film prodn.) 1971-91; pres. Stuart Benjamin Productions, 1991-; exec. prod. feature films: White Nights, LaBamba, Everybody's All American, Billy Galvin, Queens Logic, The Long Walk Home,

Mortal Thoughts, Defenseless; exec. v.p./dir. New Visions Entertainment Corp., 1988-91; dir: Boston Celtics 1976-78, San Diego Clippers 1978-81, New Visions Pictures 1971-; mem.: Am. Bar Assn., Calif. State Bar, Beverly Hills Bar Assn., L.A. Co. Bar Assn.; civic: L.A. County Mus. of Art (sponsor); Democrat; Jewish; rec: tennis, politics, film, literature. Ofc: Stuart Benjamin Productions, 12700 Ventura Blvd Ste 120 Studio City 91604-2469

BENNETT, BRADFORD CARL, somatic educator; b. May 27, 1953, Dayton, Oh.; s. Carl Vernor and Norma June (Linkinhoker) B.; edn: BS, Univ. Wis., Madison 1975; MS, Stanford Univ., 1976, PhD, 1982. Career: staff engr. Acurex Corp., Mtn. View 1983-88; sr. res. scientist MCAT Inst., 1988-93; assoc. Novato Inst. for Somatic Res. & Training, Novato 1990-; dir. Somatic Learning Center 1993-; mem: Trager Inst., Somatics Soc., Assn. for Humanistic Psych., Somatic Community, Am. Inst. Aero. & Astro.; clubs: Cloud Hands West, S.F. (chair 1989-90, 91-92), Tai Chi; pub. articles in Somatics J. (1991, 92); rec: backpacking, basketball. Address: 270 Valley St San Francisco 94131

BENNETT, BRIAN O'LEARY, electric utility regional executive; b. Dec. 5, 1955, Brooklyn, N.Y.; s. Robert Joseph and Barbara Ashton (Michael) B.; edn: BA econ., George Washington Univ. 1982; JD, Southwestern Univ. Sch. of Law 1982. Career: legislative caseworker U.S. Sen. James L. Buckley, W.D.C. 1973-77; legislative asst. Cong. Bob Dornan 1977-78, dist. field rep., L.A. 1978-83; dir. comms. Calif. Dept. Housing & Comm. Devel., Sacto. 1983-84; chief of staff, U.S. Cong. R.K. Dornan, WDC 1985-89, campaign mgr. Dornan in 84, 86, 88, Garden Grove; mem. Calif. Bush for Pres. Organizing Com., L.A. 1986-88, del. Calif. State Republican Party Platform Com., Burbank 1988, del. Republican Nat. Conv. 1988, 92 Calif. del. selection com. 1988, 92; regional affairs mgr. So. Calif. Edison Co., 1989-; honors: Outstanding Young Men of Am.; civic: Orange Co. Pro Life PAC, Calif. Republican Party (state central com.), Orange Co. Forum (bd. dirs.) Orange Co. Public Affairs Assn. (bd. dirs.), World Affairs Council of Orange Co. (bd. dirs.), Orange Co. Urban League (bd. dirs.); contbr. Los Angeles Times; R.Cath.; rec: history, racquetball, travel, movies. Ofc: So. California Edison Co. 1325 S Grand Ave Santa Ana 92705

BENNETT, LAWRENCE ALLEN, psychologist, consultant in criminal justice; b. Jan. 4, 1923, Selma, Calif.; s. Allen Walter and Eva Eleanor (Hall) B.; m. Beth J. Thompson, Aug. 14, 1948; children: Glenn Livingston, Yvonne Irene Solis; edn: BA, Fresno St. Coll., 1949; MA, Claremont Grad. Sch., 1954, PhD, 1968. Career: supvg. psychologist Calif. med. facility Calif. Dept. Corrections, Vacaville 1955-60, departmental supr. clin. psychology, Sacto. 1960-67, chief of res., 1967-76; dir. Ctr. for Study of Crime, Delinquency and Corrections, So. Ill. Univ., Carbondale 1976-79; dir. Office of Program Evaluation, 1979-84; dir. Crime Prevention and Enforcement Div. Nat. Inst. of Justice, W.D.C. 1985-86; dir. Adjudication and Corrections Div. 1987-88; practicing clin. psychologist, also crim. justice consultant, Sacto. 1988-; faculty p.t. UC Davis, UC Berkeley, 1959-76, CSU Sacto. 1988-; appt. bd. Calif. Crime Technol. Res. Found. 1970-75, Calif. State Interdepartmental Coord. Council (1967-76, chmn. 1970); juvenile advy. bd. State of Ill. 1977-79; bd. dirs. Am. Justice Inst., Sacto. (1970-79, 88-, pres. 1991-); commr. Calif. Blue Ribbon Commn. on Inmate Population Mgmt. 1988-90; mem: Acad. of Crim. Justice Scis., Am. Psychol. Assn., Am. Soc. Criminology, Am. Correctional Assn., Evaluation Res. Soc., Assn. for Correctional Res. and Info. Mgmt. (pres. 1989-90); mil: US Army 1942-45, 50-51, decorated bronze star with o.l.c.; publs: coauthor (w/ T.S. Rosenbaum and W.R. McCollough) Counseling in Correctional Environments (1978), contbr. articles to profl. jours.; Unitarian. Res: 1129 Rivara Cir Sacramento 95864 Ofc: 2717 Cottage Way Ste 15 Cottage Center Sacramento 95825

BENNETT, WILLIAM PERRY, real estate lawyer/broker; b. Aug. 28, 1938, Inglewood; s. George William and Lenora (Perry) B.; m. Linda Lee Schneider, Aug. 19, 1961; children: Gregory b. 1962, Mark b. 1966, Carin b. 1968; edn: BA, CSU Long Beach 1961; MA (magna cum laude), Grace Theol. Sem.; JD (magna cum laude), USC Law Sch. 1964. Career: atty., ptnr. Powars Tretheway & Bennett, Long Beach 1964-79; atty., sr. ptnr. William P. Bennett, Seal Beach 1979-90; sr. atty. R.E. Dept., Wise, Wiezorek, Timmons & Wise, Long Beach 1991-; general counsel Campus Crusade for Christ 1991-; R.E. broker/pres. Century 21 Pacific Coast Realty 1979-87, Pacific Coast Properties 1987-; assoc. prof. CSU Long Beach 1965-87; awards: USC Law Sch. law review, 1965, Long Beach C.of C. businessman of year, 1987, Jaycees comm. service, 1973-74, Kiwanis kiwanian of year, 1971; mem: Long Beach Bd. Realtors, Long Beach Bar Assn. (bd. gov. 1970-71, 73-74, 75-76), Long Beach Area March of Dimes (bd. dir. & legal advr. 1973-90, Kiwanis (lt. gov. 1975-76), Long Beach Barristers (pres. 1971), Seal Beach C.of C. (pres. 1985-86, 89-90), CSU Advy. Bd., 1982-87, Am. Arbitration Assn. Panel 1965-. L.A. Co. Arbitration Panel 1989-; mil: 2d. lt. USMCR 1959-65; Republican; Christian; rec: edn. Res: 311 Ocean Ave Seal Beach 90740 Ofc: Pacific Coast Properties PO Box 2460 Seal Beach 90740

BENSON, JAMES BERNARD, clinical hypnotherapist; b. May 8, 1930, Phila.; s. James Bernard and Elizabeth Sloan (Smeaton) B.; m. Hiroko Nakamura, Apr. 14, 1955; edn: BA in police sci., Pacific Coll., Van Nuys 1978. Career: crim. investigator, ssgt. (E-6) US Marine Corps, El Toro 1947-66; delinquent loan ofcr. Bank America, Los Angeles 1966-85; clin. hypnotherapist practice, Anaheim 1985-; awards: LLD (hon.) Nat. Law Enforcement Acad., Fla., Apr. 22, 1968, DD (hon.) Ch. of Gospel Ministry, San Diego, PhD in Hypnotherapy (hon.) St. John's Univ., Springfield, La., Jan. 10, 1988, Fellow in Clin. Hypnotherapy, Am. Assn. Profl. Hypnotherapists, Dec. 15, 1986; mem: Nat. Bd. for Hypnotherapy and Anesthesiology 1982, Nat. Soc. Clin. Hypnotherapists 1988-, Am. Assn. Criminologists 1960-, Internat. Assn. Counselors and Therapists 1991-; editor police poetry anthologies: Devotion in Blue (1973), Lawman's Lament (1974); Republican; Prot.; rec: photography, writing, cooking. Res: 1400 S Sunkist St Sp 199 Anaheim 92806

BENZ, RONALD THOMAS, otolaryngologist; b. April 17, 1942, Milwaukee, Wisc.; s. Herman S. and Beatrice M. (Quinn) B.; m. Rita Kautza, Nov. 27, 1971; children: Michael, b. 1976, Jennifer, b. 1978, Nicholas, b. 1980; edn: BS, Carroll Coll. 1964; MD, Marquette 1968. Career: internship and residency in otolaryngology L.A. Co.-USC Med. Ctr. 1968-69, 1971-75; otolaryngologist pvt. practice 1976-, bd. dirs. Sharp Rees Stealy Med. Group, 1989-; asst. clin. prof. surgery UC San Diego Med. Sch.; pres. San Diego Academy of Otolaryngology; staff Coronado Hosp. (chief of staff 1983), chief otol. dept. Childrens Hosp. 1986-, Mercy Hosp. (v.chief 1984-90); mem: AMA, CMA, San Diego Med. Soc., Am. Coll. Surgeons (fellow 1987), Am. Acad. Otolaryngology (fellow), Head & Neck Soc.; club: Cottilian (pres. 1989-90); mil: lt. USNR (MC) 1969-71; R.Cath.; rec: sports, travel. Ofc: 2001 4th Ave San Diego 92101

BERBERIAN, BERNARD, art director; b. Oct. 26, 1948, Hifa, Palestine, nat. Canadian; s. Nazar and Yevkine (Nalbandian) B.; m. 1978, div. 1986; children: Shaunt b. 1981, Ara b. 1983; edn: BA, Ontario Coll. of Art, Can. 1972. Career: w/advtg. design group Leonard Kurass, San Francisco 1972-74; design Patterson and Hall 1974-78; design Bernard Berberian, Los Angeles 1978-79; owner, pres., chief ed., art dir. UNIARTS Advertising, Glendale 1979-; created Calif. UNIARTS Armenian Directory Yellow Pages, 1980, Pocket Directory Yellow Pages, 1991; rec: music, travel tennis. Res: 1038 Alcalde Way Glendale CA 91207-1124 Ofc: UNIARTS Advertising, Glendale.

BERDON, SONDRA KAY, pharmacist, lecturer; b. Nov. 3, 1953, Paducah, Ky.; d. John and Laura Mae (Weaver) B.; edn: El Paso Comm. Coll., Colo. Spgs. 1971-72; BS pharm. scis., Univ. Ariz. Coll. of Pharmacy, 1976; lic. pharmacist Ariz., Calif. Career: intern Univ. Ariz. Health Scis. Ctr., Tucson 1972-76; pharmacist 3 clinic pharms. in Tucson and Marana, Az. 1976-77; pharmacy mgr. Tempe Store, Fed Mart Inc., Phoenix 1977-78; sr. staff pharmacist Dept. Pharm. Green Hosp. of Scripps Clinic and Res. Found., La Jolla 1978-, course instr. nursing certification pgms. in oncology, gerontology, sleep and drug treatment, pharmaceutical calculations, pain mgmt. and pharmacology, hypertension, and neurology; frequent speaker on drug topics in schs., univs., and various profl. and civic groups; video: "Recommended Handling for Cytotoxic Agents" for Winfield Corp., S.D. (c. 1984); honors: Pharmacist of Yr., San Diego Co. Pharmacists Assn. 1987; mem: Am. Soc. Hosp. Pharmacists, Calif. Soc. Hosp. Pharmacists, S.D. Soc. Hosp. Pharmacists, Am. Pharmaceutical Assn., Calif. Pharmacists Assn., S.D. Co. Pharmacists Assn. (pres. 1990-91, bd. 1987-, chair pub. affairs com. 1987-), Am. Inst. of History of Pharmacy, Am. Cancer Soc./S.D. (bd. 1985-87); rec: doll collector, history of pharmacy collection. Res: 4935 Via Lapiz San Diego 92122 Ofc: Green Hospital, Scripps Clinic 10666 N Torrey Pines Rd La Jolla 92037

BEREND, ROBERT ERNEST, lawyer; b. July 8, 1956, Los Angeles; s. George Charles and Olga (Jozsef) B.; edn: att. UCLA 1973-74, San Francisco St. Univ. 1975, BA in biophysics, UC Berkeley, 1978; JD, Southwestern Univ., 1981; admitted bar: Calif. 1988, US Tax Ct., Calif. Supreme Ct., US Dist. Ct. for Calif.; Calif. lic. Ins. Agt. (life and disability and variable annuity) 1983, R.E. Broker 1985, S.E.C. Reg. Inv. Advisor 1985, Stockbroker NASD lic. Series 7 and 63, 1983-. Career: co-founder and legal researcher Temporary Law Clerks, L.A. 1981-82; acct. exec. Dean Witter Reynolds, 1983-84; broker, asst. to chmn. Central Real Estate, 1985-86; Reg. Inv. Advr. 1985-, stockbroker H.D. Vest, 1988-; atty., assoc. Rucker and Clarkson, 1988-89; Leland Stark, Beverly Hills, 1989; atty./assoc. counsel Calif. Assn. of Realtors, Los Angeles, 1989-; instr. adult edn. 1985-87; frequent lectr. univs. and colls., various assns. and profl. groups; num. media interviews; awards: IRS cert. of appreciation for work in the VITA tax pgm., Southwestern Univ. cert. of disting. service, listed Who's Who in Young Am. Professionals; mem: Social Investment Forum L.A. (co-founder 1986), Beverly Hills Estate Planning Council, Calif. Bar Assn., L.A. Co. Bar Assn. (vol. Landlord/ Tenant Mediation Svs.), MENSA 1985-, Sierra Club 1985-; author: The New Investor's Compass (1989), course curriculum "Financial Planning in Real Estate", 12+ mag. articles re fin. planning, and legal aspects of real estate; rec: scuba, travel, cooking. Ofc: Calif. Assn. of Realtors 525 S Virgil Ave Los Angeles 90020

BERESTYNSKI, ADAM S., architect, urban planner (retired); b. May 5, 1927, Krakow, Poland; s. Adam and Kazimiera B.; m. Magdalena Steinhagen, Oct. 4, 1957; 1 son, Peter b. 1958; edn: MSc in arch. and city planning, Polytechnic Univ., Krakow 1951. Career: mgr. arch. and planning dept. City of Krakow,

Poland 1960-64; arch. and urban designer Royal Afghan Ministry of Pub. Works, Kabul, Afghanistan 1964-66; assoc. planner City of Fremont, Calif. 1969-70; urban designer VTN Consol. Inc., Irvine 1970-76; asst. dir. planning Bein, Frost & Assocs., Newport Beach 1976-81; mgr. planning and devel. control Saudi Arabian Parsons Ltd., Yanbu, S.A. 1982-89; instr. Calif. Comm. Coll., 1977; awards: III gr. award Polish Soc. Architects 1963, 4 philatelic awards 1991-93; mem: AIA (assoc. 1971-), Am. Inst. of Planners (assoc. 1972-), Am. Planning Assn. 1977-, Assn. of Environmental Profls. 1978-, Am. Philatelic Soc. 1989-; publs: articles in profl. jours. 1951-70, contbr. articles to mo. "Kultura" Paris, Fr. (1968-71); mil: Polish Underground Resistance Army (A.K.) 1943-45; Republican; R.Cath.; rec: stamps, mtn. hiking, travel, distance swimming. Res: 2845 Chillon Way Laguna Beach 92651

BERETTA, GIORDANO BRUNO, computer scientist; b. Apr. 14, 1951, Brugg, Switz.; s. Modesto Carlo and Hildegard (Wenger) B.; edn: MS math., Swiss Fed. Inst. Tech., Zurich 1977, PhD in c.s., 1984; dipl. math. ETH Dr. Sc. Tech. ETH, Swiss Govt. (1984). Career: systems rep. Burroughs (Switzerland), Zurich 1977-80; asst. Swiss Fed. Inst. Tech., Zurich 1980-83; cons. Logitech S.A., Apples, Switz. 1984; scientist Xerox PARC, Palo Alto, Calif. 1984-90; senior scientist Canon Information Systems, Palo Alto 1990-; recipient profl. achiev. award Xerox Corporate Resrch. Gp., Palo Alto 1989; mem: Assn. for Computing Machinery, Swiss Math. Soc., Soc. for Imaging Sci. & Tech., IEEE Computer Soc., Internat. Soc. for Optical Engring., Optical Soc. Am., Internat. Soc. Color Council; rec: photography. Res: 1760 Newell Rd Palo Alto 94303 Ofc: Canon Information Systems 4009 Miranda Ave Palo Alto 94304

BERETZ, PAUL B., manufacturing company executive; b. Oct. 15, 1938, Wash. D.C.; s. O. Paul and Marthe (Szabo) B.; m. Jane M., Nov. 9, 1963; children: Charles, Melissa, John, Michele, Claudine; edn: BBA, Univ. Notre Dame, 1960; MBA, Golden Gate Univ. 1974. Career: asst. treas. Crown Zellerbach, San Francisco 1983-86; prin. P.B. Beretz & Co., S.F. 1986-91; sr. treas./mgr., Applied Materials Inc., Santa Clara 1991-; faculty St. Mary's Coll., Moraga 1978-80, Golden Gate Univ., S.F. 1980, UC Berkeley 1990-; mem., past pres. Univ. Notre Dame Bay Area Alumni Org. (1975-, Award of Yr. 1987), nat. bd. dir. Univ. Notre Dame Alumni Assn. 1983-86, mem. Olympic Club San Francisco; author: Managing Commercial Credit 1981, articles in fin. & mgmt. 1980-90; Democrat; R.Cath.; rec: tennis, gardening, hiking. res: Alamo 94507

BERG, DAVID, writer/artist; b. June 12, 1920, Brooklyn, NY; s. Morris Isaac and Bessie (Friedman) B.; m. Vivian Lipman, March 3, 1949; children: Mitchel b. 1952, Nancy b. 1955; edn: Art Students League 1937-38; Cooper Union 1939-41; Iona Coll. 1974; Coll. of New Rochelle 1975. Career: writer/artist Will Eisner The Spirit - Backgrounder; Death Patrol 1940-41; Fawcett 1941-43; Archie 1949-52; Timely 1941-42 and 1949-59; Mad Mag. The Lighter Side of.. 1956-; 15 paperbacks trans. into 12 lang., Mad's Dave Berg Looks at ..USA, ..People, ..Things, ..Our Sick World, ..Modern Thinking, ..Living, Mad's Dave Berg Takes a Loving Look, Mad's Dave Berg Looks Around, Listens, Laughs, Mad's Dave Berg Looks at You, ..The Neighborhood, .. Our Planet, ..Today, Dave Berg's Mad Trash, My Friend GOD, Roger Kaputnic and GOD, Japanese, German, French, English lang. tching. books, 1986; Mad Mag.; creative cons. NBC T.V. 1978; judge Miss Am. Contest; honors: David Berg Day mayoral proclamation Westchester Co. N.Y. (5/7/78), B'nai B'rith Youth Services Award 1978, Chair of Great Cartoonists, UCLA Student Body 1975, ThD (hon.) Reconstruction Rabbinical Coll., Lubavitchor Youth Service Award 1987; mem: Nat. Cartoonists Soc., Internat. Platform Soc., Author's Guild, Writer's Guild; civic: Boy Scouts, Girl Scouts, Little League, PTA, B'nai B'rith, Pioneer Skippers Assn., City of New Rochelle (chmn. of rec.), Thornton-Donovan Sch. (bd. dirs.); mil: staff sgt., chem. warfare tech., sta. chief 20th AF Pacific 1942-46; Army war corr. 1945; Democrat; Hebrew; rec: model building, photog. coin collecting. Res: 14021 Marquesas Way Ste 307C Marina del Rey 90292 Ofc: Mad Magazine 485 Madison Avenue New York 10022

BERGER, CAROLYN EMMA, psychologist; b. Dec. 26, 1944, Springfield, Mass.; d. Henry R. and Olivine V. (Richards) Berger; edn: BA, psych., Univ. Mass., 1966; MA, marriage and family counseling, US Internat. Univ., San Diego 1979, PhD psychology, U.S.I.U., 1984; lic. psychologist Calif. 1987. Career: elementary sch. counselor, 1977; vocational rehabilitation counselor VA Regl. Guidance Ctr., 1978-80; patient care vol. Hospice of the North Coast 1983-84; counselor in substance abuse outpatient clinic, San Diego 1984-87; pvt. practice, 1985-; clinical psychologist Owen Clinic, UCSD Medical Center, 1987-; computer cons. CSU San Diego, 1981-83; instr. Sch. of Bus. and Mgmt., U.S. Internat. Univ., 1978-84; mem: Am. Psychological Assn., Acad. of San Diego Psychologists, Soc. of Psychologists in Addictive Behaviors, Calif. Womens Commn. on Alcoholism; Democrat; Self-Realization Fellowship; rec: dancing, travel, equestrienne, gardening, cultural events. Ofc: 3519 Front St San Diego 92103 also: UCSD Medical Center/Owen Clinic, 225 Dickensen St H681 San Diego 92103-9981

BERGER, JAY VARI, executive recruiter; b. Aug. 31, 1944, San Francisco; s. Jack Vari and Ruth (Wasserman) B.; m. Meta Ahlberg, June 14, 1969; children: Karin b. 1971, John b. 1974; edn: BS, Univ. So. Calif., 1966, MS 1967, PhD

1971; Calif. life secondary tchg. cred. 1967. Career: assoc. dean admissions Univ. So. Calif., L.A. 1969-76, dir. admissions 1976-82, asst. v.p. devel. 1982-86; ptnr. Morris & Berger, Pasadena 1986-; co-owner Berger & Berger Internat. (importer childrens apparel), Pasadena 1976-; awards: firm, Morris & Berger, on Executive Recruiter News list of 50 Leading Exec. Search Firms in No. Am., Jan. 1992; mem. Calif. Exec. Recruiters Assn. 1987-, USC Commerce Associates (nat. bd. 1991-); civic: Rotary Pasadena (dir. 1989-), The Sycamores, Altadena (pres. 1990-), The Chandler Sch., Pasa. (pres. 1988-90), Pasadena Pops (dir. 1989-92), Flintridge Prep. Sch. (bd. 1992-); author (childrens' book) Willie The Worm (1988); rec: golf, travel, reading, writing, fishing. Res: 412 Oaklawn Ave So Pasadena 91030 Ofc: Morris & Berger, 201 S Lake Ave Ste 700 Pasadena 91101

BERGESON, MARIAN C., state senator; b. Aug. 31, 1925, Salt Lake City, Utah; d. Ivan H. and Clara Greenwood (Hunter) Crittenden; m. Garth Bergeson, June 16, 1950; children: Nancy b. 1951, Garth b. 1953, Julie b. 1959, James b. 1961; 4 grandchildren; edn: UCLA; BA, Edn., Brigham Young Univ., Provo, Utah, 1949. Career: sch. bd. mem., Newport City Sch. Dist., Newport Beach, Calif., 1964-65; sch. bd. mem., Newport-Mesa Unified Sch. Dist., Newport Beach, 1965-77; state assemblywoman, Calif. State Legislature, Sacto., 1978-84; state senator, Calif. State Legislature, Sacto., 1984-; Minority Whip, Assembly and Senate; former pres., Calif. Sch. Boards Assn.; Republican Party nominee for Lt. Gov., 1990; chair, Women's Legislative Caucus, 1992; mem. State Allocation Bd; chair, Senate Local Gov. Com.; mem. of committees on Appropriations, Ethics, Health & Human Svs., Industrial Relations, Transp., Defense Base Closures; vice chair, Housing and Urban Affairs; chair, Select Com. on Planning for California's Growth; mem. Select Com. on Infant & Child Care and Devel., Select Com. on Source Reduction and Recycling Market Devel., Subcom. on Bonded Indebtedness and Methods of Financing; hon. advy. bd. mem., Concerned Citizens for Adolescent Pregnancy, Ad Hoc Legislative Tourism Caucus; serves on 3 Nat. Conf. of State Legislature Committees: State-Federal Assembly Com. on Fed. Budget & Taxation, Transp. & Communication Com., and Assembly on the Legislature Com. on State-Local Relations; awards & honors: over 50 awards as Legislator of Year, Senator of Year, Woman of Year, Outstanding Public Ofcl. and others; Disting. Svc. award, Brigham Young Univ., 1980-81; Hon. Doctor of Laws degree, Pepperdine Univ., 1993; listed in Who's Who of Am. Women, 2000 Notable Am. Women, Who's Who in US; mem: advy. bd. Oasis Sr. Citizens Ctr., Radio Station KBIG; bd. of adv., Calif. YMCA Model Legislature/Court; bd. of trustees Mem. Health Svs. of Long Beach, 1990-91; hon. dir., C.E.W.A.E.R., 1989; adv., UCI Grad. Sch. of Management Health Care Management Program Bd., 1992; mem. Bus./Industry Advy. Council, State ROP Assn., 1992; civic: charter mem., Advy. Bd. of Trustees, Bolsa Chica Wetlands; advy. bd., St. Jude Med. Ctr.; charter bd. mem., Maternal Outreach Management System; comm. advy. bd., Jr. League of Orange County; advy. council, Mardan Ctr. of Ednl. Therapy; advy. bd., Laguna Art Museum, Adam Walsh Child Resource Ctr., Program for Women Found., Advanced Resources for Foster Kids, Homeless Task Force Building Industry Assn.; hon. mem. bd. dir., Food Distribution Ctr.; mem: Comm. Devel. Council Bd., Rotary Internat. Newport Beach; author: article pub. in Land & Assembly Devel., 1987; legislation on pre-natal health care for low-income families, lower personal income tax, and improved efficiency of Caltrans; Republican; Mormon; rec: shopping. Ofc: Calif. State Senate 140 Newport Ctr. Dr, #120 Newport Beach 92660

BERGIN, ROBERT WAYNE, manufacturing co. executive; b. Feb. 13, 1954, Van Nuys; s. Fredrick Austin and Aileen E. (Hume) B.; m. Linda Ruth Webb, April 23, 1980; children: Austin b. 1981, Amanda b. 1985; edn: BS mgmt., Pepperdine Univ. 1985. Career: sr. planner Litton Guidance Control, Woodland Hills 1976-78; material control supr. Eaton Test Systems 1978-80; product and materials mgr. Magnetic Tech., Canoga Park 1980-85; v.p. Calif. Soap Co., Los Angeles 1985-; mil: SK-5 USN 1972-76; Republican; R.Cath.; rec: numismatics. Ofc: California Soap Co. 1819 E 25th St Los Angeles 90058

BERGMANN, WALT, teacher; b. May 16, 1943, Dinuba, Calif.; edn: AA, Kings River, Reedley, Calif., 1967; BA, Calif. State Univ., Fresno, Calif., 1969. Career: tchr., Traver Sch., Traver, Calif., 1969-; awards: Outstanding Leader, Fed. Youth Employment Program, 1982, 1992; nominated, Who's Who in Calif. 1984; listed, Who's Who of Amer. Teachers, 1992; mem. Calif. Teachers Assn., NEA, 1969-; author: ednl. res. articles: Reading Ability and Vision, 1981.

BERGO, EDWARD THOMAS, JR., construction executive; b. June 6, 1948, Los Angeles; s. Edward T., Sr. and Mary Agnes (Woods) B.; m. Dolores Anie, Apr. 3, 1971; son, Justin Bryan b. 1978; edn: BA, Stanford Univ., 1971; JD, Univ. Santa Clara, 1975. Career: construction mgr. C. Aparicio Cement Co. Inc., San Jose 1975-; mem: No. Calif. Cement Masons (trustee Pension Fund 1983-), AGC Cement Masons (chmn. negotiation com. 1980-), AGC of Calif. (state dir. 1981-82, dist. chmn. 1982, trustee AGC Employers HealthTrust Fund 1988-); mil: s/sgt. USAF Reserve 1970-76; Republican; rec: water skiing, gardening. Res: PO Box 1311 Soquel 95073 Ofc: 506 Phelan Ave San Jose 95112

BERGSTROM, KARL A., specialty retail store chain president; b. Nov. 29, 1926, Gothenburg, Sweden, nat. 1956; s. Carl A. and Jenny A. (Bjorkman) B.;

m. Conny Riis-Klausen, Nov. 28, 1957; children: Pierre, b. 1959; Vickie, b. 1961; edn: BS, summa cum laude, UC Berkeley 1950. Career: v.consul, Swedish Diplomatic Corps. 1946-50; mgr. Container Corp. of Am., San Francisco 1950-53; US Army Svc. 1953-56; mgr. Continental Can Co., Los Angeles 1956-63; founder/chief exec. Bergstroms Childrens Stores, Inc., Anaheim 1963-; chmn. bd. Stanford Distbg. Corp., Hayward; adv. bd: Nat. Bank of So. Calif., Santa Ana, Olympic Nat. Bank, L.A., Traweek Investment Co., Marina Del Rey; honors: Delta Sigma Pi, profl. bus. frat.; mem. Tustin Toastmasters Club (pres. 1978); mil: sgt. US Army 1953 interpreter in Germany, Norway, Denmark & France 1953-56, staff of Gen. Lucius Clay; Republican; Presbyterian; rec: skiing, art collection, classical music. Res: 1662 La Loma Dr Santa Ana 92705 Ofc: Bergstroms Childrens Stores, 1606 Clementine Anaheim 92802

BERKSON, BILL (WILLIAM CRAIG), poet, critic, teacher; b. Aug. 30, 1939, N.Y., NY; s. Seymour and Eleanor (Lambert) B.; m. Lynn Blacker, July 17, 1975; children: Siobhan b. 1969 (adopted), Moses b. 1976; edn: Lawrenceville (N.J.) Sch. 1955-57, Brown Univ. 1957-59, The New Sch. N.Y.C. 1959-60, Columbia Univ. 1959-60. Career: editorial assoc. Portfolio & Art News Annual, N.Y. 1960-63; assoc. prod. "Art/New York" WNDT-TV, N.Y. 1964-65; instr. The New Sch., 1964-69; guest editor Mus. of Modern Art, N.Y. 1965-69; vis. fellow Yale Univ., New Haven, Ct. 1969-70; ed. and pub. Big Sky press, Bolinas, 1971-78; prof. San Francisco Art Inst., 1984-; active in literary & art fields since 1959, author 11 books and pamphlets of poetry, incl.: Saturday Night: Poems 1960-61 (1961), Enigma Variations (1975), Blue Is the Hero (1976), Lush Life (1983); poetry transl. into Italian, Fr., Ger., Dutch, Romanian and Hungarian; anthologies incl.: The Young Am. Poets, 10 Am. Poets, The Young Am. Writers, The World Anth., An Anth. of New York Poets, Best & Company, On the Mesa, Calafia, One World Poetry, Another World, Poets & Painters, Up Late: Am. Poetry Since 1970, Out of this World; poetry recordings on "Disconnected" (Giorno Poetry Systems), and "The World Record" (St. Marks Poetry Project) and in the Am. Poetry Archive (SFSU); writer revs. and articles, regular contbr. Artnews, 1961-63, Arts, 1964-66, Art in America, 1980-, Artforum, 1985-; num. pub. readings and lectures nat.; awards: Dylan Thomas Award, The New Sch. 1959, Poets Found. grantee 1968, NEA creative writing fellow 1979, Marin Arts Council Award 1987, award for criticism Artspace, S.F. 1990, vis. artist/scholar Am. Acad. in Rome 1991. Res: PO Box 389 Bolinas 94924 Ofc: San Francisco Art Institute 800 Chestnut St San Francisco 94924

BERMAN, ELEANORE, artist; b. Sept. 2, 1928, N.Y., NY; d. Isidor and Elsie (Goldstein) B.; m. Frederick Nicholas, div. 1965; m. 2d. Henri Lazarof, div. 1978; edn: BA, UC Los Angeles, 1950; mem: L.A. Printmaking Soc., Artists Equity Assn. (advy. bd. 1980-84), N.W.S., Nat. Water Color Assn., So. Calif. Women's Caucus for the Arts, Nat. Assn. of Women Artists.

BERMAN, MYLES LEE, lawyer; b. July 11, 1954, Chgo.; s. Jordan and Eunice (Berg) B.; m. Mitra Moghimi, Dec. 19, 1981; children: Elizabeth b. 1983, Calvin b. 1990; edn: BA, Univ. Illinois, Champaign, 1976; JD, Kent Coll. of Law, Chgo., 1979; admitted bar: Ill., 1980, US Dist. Ct. No. Dist. Ill., 1980, Calif., 1987, US Dist Ct. Central Dist. Calif., 1988, US Supreme Ct., 1992. Career: Asst. State's Atty. Cook County, Ill., 1980-82; prin. law offices Myles L. Berman, Chgo., 1982-91, Los Angeles, 1988-; judge pro tem Beverly Hills Municipal Ct., 1990-, Traffic Ct. judge pro tem adminstr., 1991-; judge pro tem Culver Municipal Ct., 1992-; probation monitor State Bar of Calif., 1992; mem: Am. Bar Assn., Los Angeles Co. Bar Assn., Santa Monica Bar Assn., Beverly Hills Bar Assn., Century City Bar Assn. (crim. law sect. chair 1989-; Outstanding Svc. award 1990, 92; Editor-Century City Lawyer; Bd. of Gov. 1991-), Calif. Attys. for Crim. Justice, Nat. Assn. of Crim. Defense Lawyers, Crim. Cts. Bar Assn.; Sinai Temple (L.A.); rec: sports. Ofc: 9200 Sunset Blvd Ste 931 Los Angeles 90069

BERMAN, WALTER ELLIOTT, physician-facial plastic surgeon, educator; b. June 9, 1923, Chgo.; s. Matthew and Sonia B.; m. Dorothy Goldstein; children: Ellen Jessica Flashman b. 1950, Andrew Glen Berman, M.D. b. 1953; edn: BA, Univ. of Ill., Champaign, 1943, BS, and MD, Univ. of Ill., Chgo., 1944, 1946; FACS 1960-. Career: surg. intern Mt. Sinai Hosp., Chgo., 1946-47; flight surgeon US Air Corps, 1947-49; ENT resident Los Angeles Veterans Hosp., 1949-51; resident ENT and facial plastic surgery Manhattan EY & Er, NY, NY, 1951-53; clinical prof. head & neck surgery UCLA Med. Sch., 1965-, dir. of facial plastic surgery; guest lectr. / exchange prof. worldwide (100+) 1965-; awards: Baranquer, Med Cinematographer, WDC 1960, teaching awards Am. Acad. of Oto & Head & Neck Surg., WDC (1975, 1982) and Am. Acad. of Facial Plastic & Reconstrv. Surg., WDC (12+, 1970-90); mem: Am. Acad. Facial Plastic & Reconstrv. Surg. (1965-, pres. 1972), Am. Acad. of Cosmetic Surg. (pres. 1978), Calif. Med. Assn., LA Co. Med. Assn.; civic: Music Ctr. LA (1975-, Founding Patron), Vista Del Mar 1970-, LA Co. Art Mus. 1965-, Page Mus. 1980-; author/editor 2 books: Rhinoplasty (1989), Head & Neck Surgery (1984), 12 chapters in med. books (1970-); mil: capt. USAF 1943-49; Hebrew; rec: jogging, writing, teaching. Ofc: Walter E. Berman, M.D. 9001 Wilshire Blvd Ste 100 Beverly Hills 90211

BERNARD, ALEXANDER, city official; b. Apr. 23, 1952, Los Angeles; s. Louis and Hannah (Bergman) B.; m. Diana LoRee Winstead, Dec. 17, 1976; children: Michael, Andrew; edn: AA (magna cum laude), L.A. Valley Coll., 1976; BS (summa cum laude), CSU Los Angeles, 1989. Career: parking meter collector L.A. City Clerk's Office, 1973-79; police ofcr. Los Angeles Airport Police Div., 1979-; honors: Golden Key (life), Phi Kappa Phi (life); mem: Internat. Police Assn., Calif. Peace Ofcrs. Assn., L.A. County Peace Ofcrs. Assn., L.A. Airport Peace Ofcrs. Assn. (pres. 1981-89, dir. 1992-), Peace Ofcrs. Research Assn. Calif. (state bd. dirs. 1984-85, 88-, chpt. pres. 1982-84, 85-87), Indsl. Relations Research Assn., NRA (life), Calif. Rifle and Pistol Assn. (life); contbr. articles to profl. jours.; Democrat; Assemblies of God. Ofc: LA Airport Police Div. 16461 Sherman Way Van Nuys 91406

BERNARD, EARL FRANCIS, financial executive; b. Jan. 13, 1959, Baldwin Park; s. Albert F. and Rose (Ellis) B.; edn: BA, CSU Fullerton 1982; MSH, CSU Long Beach 1989. Career: asst. hosp. adminstr. fin. USC Med. Center, Los Angeles 1982-86; asst. controller Paracelsus Health Care, Pasadena 1986-87, controller 1987-88, CFO 1988-89, CFO, adminstr. 1989-; awards: NHS 1977-82, Dean's Hon. Roll 1986-89; mem: HFMA, Health Care Execs., AHA, CHAAS, Healthcare Forum, Moose Club, Buena Park C.of C.; rec: white water rafting. Ofc: Paracelsus Healthcare Corp. 6850 Lincoln Ave Buena Park 90620

BERNDLMAIER, KARL C., religious brother, counselor; b. Mar. 23, 1940, New York; s. Karl and Bertha (Kaiser) B.; edn: BA, Iona Coll., New Rochelle 1961; MS edn., Chicago St. Univ. 1970; MA, Univ. San Francisco 1976; MMFC, 1977; lic. marriage family and child counselor (MFFC) Calif. 1980; nationally cert. counselor, school counselor, career counselor; basic & advanced cert. in alcohol and drug abuse counseling (UCSC). Career: tchr. Vancouver Coll., Canada 1961-64; Leo High Sch., Chgo., Ill. 1964-66; counselor, tchr. Brother Rice H.S., Chgo. 1966-69; St. Laurence H.S., Oak Lawn, Ill. 1969-70; Palma H.S., Salinas 1970-80; Brother Rice H.S., Birmingham, Mich. 1980-82; Butte Central H.S., Mont. 1982-86; Brother Rice H.S., Chgo. 1986-87; Palma H.S., Salinas 1987-, guidance dir. 1971-80, 1987-; cons. Monterey Diocese Marriage Tribunal 1978-80; mem: Am. Assn. Marriage and Family Counselors, Knights of Columbus; R. Catholic. Address: 919 Iverson Salinas 93901

BERNFIELD, LYNNE, psychotherapist; b. Mar. 16, 1943, NY City, NY; d. Meyer and Lilian Claire (Pastel) Bernfield; m. 1982; edn: BA, Hofstra Univ., Hempstead, NY, 1964; MA, Azusa Pacific Univ., Azusa, Calif., 1981. Career: founder/dir., Writers and Artists Inst., Calif., 1984-; mem. ASCAP 1970, C.A.M.F.T. 1990; author: When You Can You Will, 1993. Ofc: Writers & Artists Inst. 15250 Ventura Blvd #1111 Sherman Oaks 91403 Tel: 818/760-4146

BERNSTEIN, BURTON M., company executive, lawyer; b. May 13, 1937, New York; s. Robert and Betty (Lieberman) B.; m. Judith Katz, June 23, 1962; children: Dina b. 1966, Mara b. 1968; edn: BA, City Univ. N.Y. 1959; JD, Santa Barbara Coll. of Law 1988. Career: sales man N.Y. Life, Bklyn., N.Y. 1959-62; life underwriter Mutual Life of N.Y., NYC 1962-65; v.p., corp. secty. Sovereign Life Ins. Co. Calif., Santa Barbara 1965-; instr. Santa Barbara Coll. of Law 1989; mem: Internat. Claims Assn., Western Home Office Underwriters Assn., Western Claims Assn., Am. Bar Assn., Santa Barbara Bar Assn.; med. article pub. in profl. jour. (1989); mil: sgt. AUS 1959-65. Ofc: Sovereign Life 30 W Sola St Santa Barbara 91101-93101

BERRY, PHILLIP SAMUEL, lawyer; b. Jan. 30, 1937, Berkeley; s. Samuel Harper Berry and Jean Mobley (Kramer) Jenny; m. Michele Ann Perrault, Jan. 16, 1982; children: David b. 1962, Douglas b. 1964, Dylan b. 1966, Justin b. 1972, Matthew b. 1982; edn: BA, Stanford Univ. 1958; LLD, 1961. Career: atty., assoc. Berry Davis, Oakland 1962-69, ptnr. 1969-76; Berry & Berry 1976-; appt. State Bd. Forestry 1974-86; mem. advy. com. Coll. Natural Resources, UC Berkeley 1990-; honors: Sierra Club John Muir award 1978; mem: Sierra Club (nat. pres. 1969-71, 1991-92, dir. 1968-, v.p. 1971-), Sierra Club Legal Defense (trustee 1971-90), Pub. Advocates Calif. (trustee 1971-86), Nature Conservancy, Am. Farmland Trust, Common Cause, Nat. Cattlemans Assn., Am. Alpine Club; articles pub. in profl. jour. 1961-80; mil: 1st lt. USAR 1961-67; rec: mountaineering. Res: 2979 Rohrer Dr Lafayette 94549 Ofc: 1300 Clay St Oakland 94662

BERTACCHI, GLORIA MARIE, consultant pharmacist, entertainer; b. May 1, 1953, Sacramento; d. Jerome J. and Phyllis M. (Herr) B.; edn: PharmD, Univ. Pacific, 1977. Career: lectr./tnr. and pres. National Medical Seminars Inc., Sacto. 1979-; cons. pharmacist and pres. Tempharmacists, National Medical Staffing Inc., 1979-; actress major feature films including: Raide on Entebbe, The Entertainer, Who Will Love My Children; guest host nat. t.v. and radio shows: Geraldo Rivera Show, Morton Downey, Jr. Show, others; civic: Carmichael Park Board (dir. 1987-88), Lodi Community Crusade vs. Drugs (drug abuse lectr. 1980-), UOP Stockton (street drug lab. anal. 1976-78); author 20+ med. books incl. Drugs of Abuse; Athletes and Drugs; Cocaine: Fact and Fantasy; Aids, Sex & Protection; Diet Secrets for Weight Control; Overview of Antibiotics; Osteoporosis: Prevention & Treatment; Drugs, Sex & Aging; Birth Control Choices; Treatment of Sexually Transmitted Diseases; (novel) Hawaiian

Heat; Ofc: Dr. Gloria M. Bertacchi, National Medical Staffing Inc., PO Box 2699 Roseville 95746 Tel: 916/784-6200

BESTE, IAN ROBERT, librarian; b. Jan. 28, 1960, Crescent City; s. Raymond F. and Pattie L. (Erwin) B.; m. Melissa C. Lathrop, April 5, 1986; edn: BA hist., UC Berkeley 1982; MLIS, 1985. Career: librarian UC Berkeley Center for Study and Law Soc. 1983-85; Brobeck Phleger & Harrison, Los Angeles 1985-88; Bryan Cave McPheetens & McRoberts 1988-; mem: So. Calif. Assn. Law Librarians, Am. Assn. Law Librarians; Democrat; Episcopalian; rec: equestrian sports. Ofc: Bryan Cave McPheetens 333 S Grand Ave Ste 3100 Los Angeles 90071

BETTS, BARBARA LANG, lawyer, rancher; b. Apr. 28, 1926, Anaheim; d. W. Harold and Helen (Thompson) Lang; m. Roby F. Hayes, July 22, 1948 (dec.); children: J. Chauncey, IV, b. 1953, Frederick Prescott, b. 1955, Roby F., b. 1957; m. 2d, Bert A. Betts (fmr. Calif. state treas.), July 11, 1962; children: Bruce Harold b. 1966, (step): Bert Alan b. 1950, Randy W. b. 1952, Sally (Joynt) b. 1949, Terry (Marsteller) b. 1946, Linda (Hansen) b. 1947, Leann (Wilson) b. 1954; edn: BA, magna cum laude, Stanford Univ. 1948; LLB, Calif. Western Univ. (fmr Balboa U.), 1951; admitted to Calif. State Bar 1952, US Dist. Ct., S. and N. Dists. Calif. 1952, US Ct. of Appeals, 9th Circuit 1952, US Supreme Ct. 1978. Career: ptnr. law firm Barbara Lang Hayes & Roby F. Hayes, 1952-60; city atty. City of Carlsbad, 1959-63; pvt. law practice, Oceanside 1952-60, San Diego 1960-, Sacto. 1962-; rancher, 1948-58, 1967-; v.p. W.H. Lang Corp., 1964-70; secty. Internat. Prod. Assn., 1967-72; v.p. Isle & Oceans Marinas Inc., 1970-80; secty. Margaret M. McCabe, M.D., Inc. 1976-88; commnr. Carlsbad Planning Commn. 1959, v.p. San Diego County Plnng. Cong.; dir. North S.D. County chpt. for retarded children 1957-57; honors: Phi Beta Kappa 1948, Calif. Scholarship Fedn. (life), inducted Fullerton Union H.S. Wall of Fame 1986; mem: Am., San Diego Co., Calif. Trial Lawyers bar assns., Am. Judicature Soc., Nat. Inst. Municipal Ofcrs. 1959-63, Stanford Club (Sacto.), Stanford Mothers' Club, US Supreme Ct. Hist. Soc., C.of C. (Oceanside, San Diego), North San Diego Co. Assn., Traveler's Aid (chmn. 1952-54), AAUW, Bus. & Profl. Womens Club 1953-63, Soroptimist Internat. (chapt. pres. Oceanside-San Diego), sec. pub. affairs San Diego - Imperial Counties 1954; pres. Presidents' Council - San Diego & Imperial Counties & Mexico 1958-59), San Diego Hist. Soc., Heritage League 2nd Air Div. USAAF, Fullerton Jr. Assistance League 1956-66, DAR 1956-64 (regent Oceanside chpt. 1960-61); Democrat (State Cent. Com. 1954-62, co-chair 28th C.D. 1960-62, del. Dem. Nat. Conv. 1960); Prot.; rec: fishing, hunting. Res: Betts Ranch, Elverta 95626 and 441 Sandburg Dr Sacramento 95819 Ofc: 8701 E Levee Rd Elverta; and 3119 Howard Ave San Diego 92104

BETTS, BERT A., former state treasurer; b. Aug. 16, 1923, San Diego; s. Bert A., Sr., and Alma (Jorgenson) C.; m. Barbara Lang; children: Terry Lou, Linda Sue, Sara Ellen, Bert Alan, Randy Wayne, John Chauncey, Frederick Prescott, LeAnn, Roby Francis, Bruce Harold; edn: BA, Calif. Western Univ. 1950; grad. Internat. Acctg. Soc.; lic. CPA, Calif. 1950. Career: ptnr. CPA firm, 1950, prin. 1951-59; college tchr., acct.-tax., 1950-58; elected State Treas. of Calif., 1958, re-elected 1962-67 (youngest statewide elected ofcl. and the first state-level exec. ofcr. from San Diego County in this century); cons. prin. Betts Fin., R.E. and Mgmt. Consultants, 1967-77; treas. and c.e.o. Internat. Prodn. Assocs. 1968-72; trustee Fidelity Mortgage Investors, 1970-78; dir. Lifetime Communities Inc., 1978-86; awards: hon. life mem. and award for outstanding leadership in mcpl. fin. Municipal Finance Ofcrs. Assn. of U.S. & Canada and the only state treasurer in U.S. awarded the gold medal and scroll of City of Louisville conferred on the most outstanding fiscal ofcr. in U.S. & Can. 1963, hon. life Beta Alpha Psi, hon. life Alpha Kappa Psi and award for bringing highest profl. stds. to Calif. Treasury ops. 1966; former mem. State Soc. Govt. Accts., Nat. Assn. of State Auditors, Comptrollers and Treasurers; mem: Calif. Municipal Treasurers Assn. (hon. life), Municipal Forum of NY (hon. life), Am. Inst. of CPAs, Nat. Assn. of Accts., Am. Accts. Assn., Calif. Soc. of CPAs (past v.p. S.D. chpt.), AF Assn. (past v-comdr.), Second Air Div. Assn., 8th Air Force Hist. Soc., Liberator Club (sponsor "All American" B-24 Liberator), Friends USAF Mus., Confederate Air Force, Smithsonian Air & Space (charter), Am. Mus. Natural Hist. (charter), VFW, Am. Legion, Intl. Order of Foresters, Lemon Grove Mens Club (past pres.), Lions Club, Masons Sigma Phi Epsilon; civic bds: Lemon Grove Sch. Dist. (past pres. bd. trustees), Girl Scouts San Diego (past fin. com.), Boy Scouts Sacto., mem. citizen advy. coms. various govt. agys., S.D. Cerebral Palsy Found. (past treas.), Sacto. Co. Am. Cancer Soc. (pres. 1967-68); mil: B-24 Bomber Pilot 8th AF USAAF 1941-45, 30 combat missions over Europe WWII, decorated D.F.C., Air Medal w. 4 clusters. Res: Betts' Ranch, 8701 E Levee Rd, Elverta 95626; 441 Sandburg Dr Sacramento 95819

BETTS, KARLENE FRANCES, marketing communications consultant; b. Cincinnati, OH; d. Walter T.R. and Flossie Lou (Jordan) Salyers; children: Kirt b. 1968; edn: BS (honors.) Skidmore Coll. 1978. Career: product mgr. UCI, Santa Clara 1978-80; internat. tech. ed. Advanced Micro Devices, Sunnyvale 1980-82; mktg. comms. mgr. Bank of Am., San Francisco 1982-84; cons., San Jose and the Netherlands 1984-88; mktg. comms. mgr. SEEQ Tech. Inc., San

Jose 1988-89; mktg. comms. mgr. 88open Consortium Ltd., San Jose 1990-; cons. prin. 1989-; instr. NY and Calif. 1968-; awards: scholarships Skidmore Coll. 1976-78, Univ. KY 1963, Thousand Is. Art & Craft Sch. 1970; mem: German Am. C. of C., Columbia Co. Comm. Theater, Jr. C. of C., Valatie PTA, Saratoga Springs PTA, Fair Housing Com. San Jose; 20 articles pub.; Democrat; Prot.; rec: internat. travel, languages, art. Address: Los Gatos 95032

BEVERETT, ANDREW JACKSON, real estate and financial consultant; b. Feb. 21, 1917, Midland City, Ala.; s. Andrew J. and Ella L. (Adams) B.; m. Martha Sophia Landgrebe, May 26, 1951; children: Andrew J. III, James Edmund, Faye A.; edn: BS, Samford Univ. 1940; MBA, Harvard Univ. 1942. Career: exec. pos. in corp. plnng. and mgmt. United Air Lines, Chicago, Ill. 1946-66; senior mktg. & economic cons. Mgmt. & Economics Research Inc., Palo Alto 1966-71; senior economist Stanford Research Inst., Menlo Park 1971-72; pres. Edy's on the Peninsula Stores, Palo Alto 1972-78; real estate broker, fin. and tax counselor, Saratoga 1979-; mem: Phi Kappa Phi, Nat. Assn. of Enrolled Agents, Nat. Assn. of Realtors; mil: lt. USNR 1942-46. Res/Ofc: 6325 Whaley Dr San Jose 95135

BHANDARI, SANJIV, architect; b. Mar. 10, 1959, Chandigarh, India; s. Om Parkash and Krishna (Sabherwal) B.; m. Arti, Mar. 10, 1985; children: Nipun B. b. 1991; edn: B.Arch., Chandigarh Coll. of Arch., 1979; postgrad. dipl. Inst. for Housing Studies, Rotterdam, Holland 1982; reg. arch. Council of Architects, India 1982, reg. arch. Calif. 1992. Career: intern Virender Khanna & Assocs., New Delhi 1977; job captain Planners Group, Chandigarh 1979; architect/project dir. P.C.P. Ltd., Diwaniya, Iraq 1980-84; sr. v.p. Brown/McDaniel Inc., San Francisco 1985-; awards: cash awards, outstanding performance P.C.P. Ltd. (1981, 82), merit scholar Punjab Univ. 1978; Editor's Choice Award for Outstanding Achievement in Poetry, Nat. Lib. of Poetry 1993; listed Who's Who in Interior Design 1992-93; The Internat. Who's Who of Intellectuals 1993; Dictionary of Internat. Biography 1993; full mem. Am. Inst. of Architects (AIA); publ. poem Arcadia Poetry Anthology 1993; publ. poem in "Where Dreams Begin" an Anthology, Nat. Lib. of Poetry 1993; thesis: Evolutionary Housing for Urban Poor 1982; rec: internat. travel, sports, writing poetry. Res: 15 Vartan Ct Walnut Creek 94596 Ofc: Brown/McDaniel, Inc. 650 California St Ste 2205 San Francisco 94108

BIANCHINI, VICTOR E., judge; b. Feb. 21, 1938, San Pedro; s. Henry and Judith B.; children: Hannah b. 1971, Amber b. 1974, Amy b. 1989; edn: BA, San Diego St. Coll. 1960; JD, Univ. of San Diego 1963; admitted Calif. Bar 1964. Career: law clk. to Hon. James M. Carter, U.S. Dist. Ct., 1963-64; magistrate U.S. Dist. Ct. So. Dist. Calif., 1974; U.S. Commr. 1968-69; judge Municipal Ct., El Cajon 1982-; assoc. prof. CSU San Diego 1969-73; Western St. Univ. Sch. of Law 1975; founding dean 1980, prof. Nat. Univ. Sch. of Law, 1978-; faculty Calif. Continuing Judicial Studies Pgm. 1986, Calif. Ctr. for Judicial Edn. and Res., Nat. Judicial Coll., Reno; chmn. bd. vis. Univ. San Diego Sch. of Law 1978; mem: Nat. Council of U.S. Magistrates (chmn. bylaws com.), Nat. Conf. of Spl. Ct. Judges, ABA, Calif. State Bar Assn., San Diego Co. Bar Assn. (bd. dirs. 1978, treas., v.p. 1979-80, chmn. ethics com.), Calif. Agri. Labor Rels. Bd. (adminstrv. law ofcr.); vol. free legal clinic for youth (Ocean Beach 1970, S.D. region 1976-); cert. AAU boxing referee and judge; mil: col. USMCR 1960-, Bronze Star with V, 3 air medals, gen. court-martial judge/dep. insp. gen. U.S. Euro. Command, Stuttgart, Ger.; rec: tennis. Ofc: El Cajon Municipal Court 250 E Main St El Cajon 92020

BIANCO, MICHAEL F., corporate financial consulting firm executive; b. Dec. 27, 1940, West Pittston, Pa.; s. Joseph P. and Mary M. (Compitello) B.; m. Marcia E. Schroeder, Apr. 28, 1968; children: Suzanne b. 1972, Francesca b. 1973, Michael Joseph b. 1981; edn: AB, Wilkes Univ., 1962; MPA, Univ. Mich., 1968; Adv. Mgmt. Coll., Stanford Univ., 1981-84. Career: banking ofcr. Chase Manhattan Bank, N.Y.C., 1968-72; pres. and c.e.o. Loeb Rhoades Securities Corp., 1972-77; mng. dir. Security Pacific Leasing Corp., San Francisco 1977-80, Internat. Bank, W.D.C., 1980-81; with Bank of Calif., S.F., 1981-82; v.p. Barclay's Bank, S.F. 1982-84; v.p., mgr. The Hibernia Bank, S.F. 1984-88; pres. Asia Pacific Capital Corp., San Francisco 1987-91; mng. dir. corporate fin. consulting, Arthur Andersen & Co., S.F. 1991-; speaker Business Week Exec. Programs, N.Y., 1987, The Planning Forum, S.F., 1988; awards: fellow James A. Finnegan Found. 1960-61; mem: Calif. Council in Internat. Trade (bd. dirs., treas. 1987-88), Korean Am. C. of C. (dir. 1992-) Japan Soc. No. Calif., World Trade Assn., Univ. Mich. Alumni Assn., Stanford Univ. Alumni Assn.; civic: S.F. Library Assn. (bd. 1986-88); Pacific Basin Council grad. studies prog., Domincan Coll.; clubs: World Trade (S.F.), Foreign Correspondents (Japan); mil: lt. US Navy 1963-67; R.Cath. Res: 1420 Oak Rim Dr Hillsborough 94010 Ofc: Arthur Andersen & Co. 1 Market Plaza Ste 3500 San Francisco 94105

BICKERSTAFF, DONALD MARQUIS, financial consultant; b. Aug. 13, 1959, Glasgow, Scotland; s. David and Ellen Morrison (Gillieland) B.; m. Mary Beth Greisofe, Sept. 7, 1986; children: Meagan Beth b. 1988, Andrew Marquis b. 1990; edn: BA econ., Kingston Univ. 1981; MA, London Univ. 1983. Career: reg. rep. Prudential, San Diego 1984-89; sr. fin. cons. Prudential Fin. Services,

Larkspur 1988-89; cons. Controlled Negotiation Sales Group, Sonora 1988-; awards: Prudential Pres. Trophy 1988, Pres. Citation (1987, 88, 89); guest spkr. Magic 61 Radio talk show "Money Talk," S.F.; mem: Nat. Assn. Life Underwriters, Million Dollar Round Table, Internat. Assn. of Fin. Planners, Nat. Agency Mgmt. Assn., Child Abuse Prevention (mktg., fundraising con. 1988-), KQED - Children's TV Programming, S.F. (fundraising events); poetry pub. Wide World of Poetry (1986), fin. articles pub. in Marin Indep. Jour. (1988-89); Presbyterian; rec: rugby, soccer, tennis. Ofc: Bickerstaff & Associates, Three E Terrace Ct Belvedere Tiburon 94920-2026

BICKMORE, EDWARD CLIFTON, JR., consulting executive; b. Oct. 12, 1929, Upland; s. Edward C. and Vira Jean (Sechrist) B.; m. Norma Kent, Mar. 17, 1950; children: Kennieth b. 1950, Charles b. 1954, Denise b. 1957; edn: AA, Reedley Coll., 1972; BS acctg., CSU Fresno, 1974, grad. studies, 1975. Career: served to lt. cmdr. US Navy, 1947-70; acct. Kings View Corp., Reedley 1974-75, controller 1975-77; gen. mgr. Orange Cove Irrigation Dist., Orange Cove, Calif. 1977-81; prin. Bickmore Bus. Services, Sacto. 1981-; pres. Bickmore & Assocs. Inc., 1987-; gen. mgr. Calif. Water Agencies Jt. Powers Auth. (JPA), Sacto. 1981-83; administr. Central San Joaquin Risk Mgmt. Auth., 1984-, also Vector Control JPA, 1986-, and Bay Cities Jt. Powers Ins. Auth., 1990-; bd. dirs. Calif. Jt. Powers Ins. Auth. 1985-, bd. dirs./v.p. Local Agy. Workers' Compensation Excess Auth. 1992-; honors: Beta Gamma Sigma, Phi Kappa Phi 1973; mem: Calif. Assn. of Jt. Powers Auth. (bd. 1984-88, state pres. 1986-87, legis. com. 1987-, chmn. 1987-88, accreditation com. 1991-), Public Agency Risk Mgrs. Assn., Public Risk & Ins. Mgrs. Assn., Californians for Compensation Reform (bd. 1990-); Republican; Prot.; rec: stamps, woodworking. Res: 6444 Pretty Girl Ct Citrus Heights 95621 Ofc: Bickmore & Associates, Inc. 6371 Auburn Blvd Citrus Hts 95621

BIGELOW, MARY D. (Mrs. Rudy Burton), photographer, electric firm executive; b. Perry, NY; d. Albert E. and Rebecca Ann (Miller) Davis; m. Richard Harned Bates, 1940 (div. 1947), m. 2d Floyd Burget Bigelow, 1948 (div. 1952); 1 dau. Judith Lynne; m. 3d Rudy Gray Burton, Nov. 17, 1962; edn: Rochester Bus. Inst., Am. Inst. Banking 1938; Woodbury Coll. 1944; UCLA 1945. Career: var. banking pos. 1936-41; advt., oil bus. 1944-50; secty./ treas. Emerald Bay Community Assn. Laguna Beach 1950-52, Tel-I-Clear Sys. Inc. Laguna Beach 1952-54; owner, oper. Bigelow Bus. Svcs. Laguna Beach 1954-; owner Meri-Bee Originals, co-owner, mgr. Burton Electric Laguna Beach 1963-; staff photog. USCG Aux. Dist. 11S and Div. II; Mariners Found. Photographer; asst. bd. dirs. Three Arch Bay Dist. So. Laguna 1957-73; awards: Leading Lady in Business Laguna News-Post 1971, numerous civic and photographic awards; mem: Nat. Soc. Public Accts., Inland Soc. Tax Cons. Inc., Soc. Calif. Accts., Dana Point Power Squadron, Laguna Club for Kids (bd.), World Affairs Council, Laguna Beach C.of C., Mermaids (info chmn. Festival of Arts 1966, 67, 68), Cousteau Soc., Nat. League of Am. Penwomen, Lyric Opera, UC Irvine, Laguna Beach Friends of Library, Joe Thurston Found. (bd. 1957-64), First Nighters, Laguna Playhouse; clubs: Altrusa Internat., West Coast Yacht, Dana Pt. Yacht, Riviera; rec: sailing, power boating, photog., dancing, writing. Address: 697 Catalina St Laguna Beach 92651

BIGGERS, RALPH LEE, JR., structural engineer; b. Dec. 23, 1941, Charlotte, N.C.; s. Ralph Lee and Sara Wilma (Kidd) B.; m. Sally Miller, June 21, 1969; children: Lee Anne b. 1970; Sara b. 1971, Katie b. 1974; edn: BSCE, N.C. St. Univ. 1964; MSCE, San Diego St. Univ. 1973; reg. structural engr. Calif. 1973. Career: staff engr. Whitman Atkinson & Assoc., La Jolla 1969-70; expansion mgr. Scott Meml. Baptist Ch., San Diego 1970-71; staff engr. Inter-City Engrs. 1971-73; exec. v.p. Atkinson Johnson & Spurrier Inc. 1974-, corp. secty., dir. 1980-; prin. R.L. Biggers & Associates, La Mesa 1991-; lectr. civil engring, San Diego St. Univ. 1976, 77, 81; awards: ASCE Outstanding Achievement 1976; mem: ASCE, Structural Engrs. Assn. San Diego (v.p.), Structural Engrs. Assn. Calif., Naval Reserve Assn., Soc. Am. Mil. Engrs., Am. Concrete Inst., Christian Heritage Retirement Center (pres. 1979-82), Christian Unified Schs. El Cajon (v.p. 1983-85), Scott Meml. Baptist Ch. (trustee 1986-89); mil: AUS Civil Engring. Corps 1965-69; capt. USNR 1965-; Republican; Baptist; rec: jogging. Res: 2409 Cerro Sereno El Cajon 92019 Ofc: Atkinson Johnson & Spurrier 4121 Napier St San Diego 92110

BILECKI, RONALD ALLAN, financial planner; b. July 15, 1942, Cincinnati, Ohio; s. Allan Frederick and Ruth Hulda (Parker) B.; m. Judy B., Jan. 25, 1946; children: Sherry b. 1967, Sean b. 1970; edn: chem. major, CSU Los Angeles 1968; Cert. Financial Planner, Coll. for Fin. Planning 1982, Reg. Investment Adviser, SEC 1985, Calif. Dept. Corps. 1986. Career: insurance agt. New York Life Ins., Covina 1973-75, asst. mgr. Los Angeles office 1975-79; indep. fin. plnnr., Rosemead 1979-81; pres. Financial Designs Corp., San Gabriel 1981-; fin. planning cons. So. Calif. Edison Co. and So. Calif. Gas Co.; fin. planning seminars for So. Calif. Edison, City of L.A. and L.A. Dept. Water & Power employees, So. Calif. Gas Co., ABC Inc., Rockwell Intl., Pomona First Federal, LORAL EOS, the FAA, and the IRS; mem. Internat. Assn. for Fin. Plnng. Inc., Registry of Fin. Planning Practioners, Internat. Soc. for Retirement Planning; Republican; Christian; rec: western and square dancing, chess, jogging, hiking. Ofc: Financial Designs Corp. 7220 Rosemead Blvd Ste 206 San Gabriel 91775

BILHEIMER, STEPHEN C., business executive, civic leader; b. Arkadelphia, Ark.; s. Charles Wm. and Edna (Carpenter) B.; m. Jeanne Summerfield, May 5, 1928; children: Mary Flave, b. 1935, Peter, b. 1937; edn: BS, Ore. State Coll. 1927; USC; Dr. Bus. Adm., Woodbury Coll. Career: ptnr. dir. Phelps-Terkel, Inc., Los Angeles 1925-54; pres. Silverwoods Stores, 21 stores, 1964-67, chmn. bd. 1967-; dir. Calif. Federal S&L Assn. 1945-; bd. dirs. Good Samaritan Medical Ctr.; past pres. LA Airport Commn.; bd. dirs. Calif. Mus. Sci & Indus.; pres. Calif. Mus. Found.; past pres. LA Stock Exchange, So. Calif. Visitors Council, Central City Assn.; dir. Downtown Businessmen's Assn. 1954; dir. Better Bus. Bur. 1954-; dir. Bel-Air Bay Club 1954-; pres. LA C.of C. 1962-63, dir. 1963-; pres. All-Year Club So. Calif. 1966-67; past pres. LA Rotary Club No. 5; honors: outstanding alumnus, USC Sch. of Bus. Adm., 1963, General Alumni Assn. Award for outstanding serv., 1968; Man of Year, L.A. Realty Bd., 1969; Humanitarian of Year, Aid-United Givers, 1972; Brotherhood Award, NCCJ, 1972; Bishop's Award of Merit, Episcopal Diocese of L.A., 1972; hon. trustee Repub. Assocs.; mem. Masons, Los Angeles Country Club; Episcopalian; rec: hunting, fishing, golf. Res: 142 S Rockingham Ave, West Los Angeles Ofc: 558 S Broadway Los Angeles 90012

BINEGAR, GWENDOLYN ANN, clinical social work administrator; b. Sept. 23, 1924, Phoenix, Ariz.; d. Glenn Marvin and Mary Lenore (Cartwright) Redington; m. Lewis (Bert) Binegar, Nov. 2, 1951; children: Glen, b. 1952; Birne, b. 1954; William, b. 1957; Alan, b. 1959; edn: BS, Iowa St. Univ. 1948; MSS, Bryn Mawr 1967; LCSW Calif. 1974; Acad. of Cert. Soc. Wkrs. 1969. Career: psychiatric soc. wkr. Child Study Inst., Bryn Mawr Coll. 1967-71; med. soc. wkr. Casa Colina Hosp., Pomona 1973-74; supvg. counselor San Gabriel Valley Regional Ctr., Pomona 1975-79; pgm. mgr. high-risk infant projects at all six L.A. County Regional Ctrs., S.G.V. Regional Ctr. 1979; asst. chief, chief case mgmt. services San Diego Regional Ctr. 1981-, assoc. director 1988-; mem: AAMD, Assn. of Regional Center Agys. (chair, chief counselors), Nat. Assn. Soc. Wkrs., Assn. Chief Counselors, COACH (bd., treas.). Republican. Res: 28809 Lilac Rd Valley Center 92082

BIRD, KENNETH DEAN, public health physician; b. Mar. 20, 1952, Oklahoma City, Okla.; s. Earl Alford and Nancy Louise (Jessup) B.; m. Nettie, July 24, 1980; children: Celeste b. 1978, Kenny b. 1982; edn: BS in biol., highest honors, Univ. Texas (Arlington) 1975; MD, honors, Univ. Texas (Galveston) 1979. Career: pediatric residency, Univ. Texas Med. Branch 1980; stu. US Naval Aerospace Med. Inst. 1981, USNR flight surgeon NAS Lemoore, Calif. 1981-84; cdr. USNR, comdg. ofcr. Naval Reserve Naval Hosp. Lemoore 0190, decorated Navy Achievement, Navy Expedit., Humanitarian medals; pvt. gen. practice medicine, Lemoore 1984-86; public health physician Fresno County Dept. of Health, 1986-, medical dir. Fresno County Detention Facilities, 1988-; honors: Alpha Chi, Alpha Omega Alpha, Mu Delta; mem. Naval Reserve Assn., Assn. of Military Surgeons of the U.S.; pres. Lemoore Union Elem. School Bd.; rec: wt. lifting, jogging, backpacking. Res: PO Box 446 Lemoore 93245 Ofc: Adult Detention Facilities 1225 M St Fresno 93721

BIRD, ROBERT JAMES, electronic engineer; b. Oct. 20, 1939, Chgo.; s. Robert and Sally B.; m. Victoria, Jan. 9, 1971; children: Danny b. 1958, Pamela b. 1960, Tracy b. 1964, Robert b. 1980; edn: ASEE, Naval Electronics Acad., BSEE, Orange Coast Coll. Career: asst. engr. Collins Radio Co., Newport Beach 1962-64; project engr. Fender Musical Instruments, Fullerton 1964-67; chief engr. Altec Lansing, Anaheim 1967-74; dir. engring. E.S.S. Inc., Sacto. 1974-76; pres. AB Systems Design, Folsom 1976-86; pres. AB International Electronics, Roseville 1986-; mem: Audio Engring. Soc. 1968-, Nat. Assn. of Music Merchants 1977-, Nat. Sound & Comms. Assn. 1983-, Roseville C.of C., Altec Mgmt. Assn. (past mem., pres. 1971-72); invention: Multi Level Power Supplies (US Pat. 1974); author 3 books: Journal of A.E.S. (1969), Altec Technical Journal (1972, 1973); mil: ET6 USN 1957-62; Republican; Christian Sci.; rec: sailing, M/C riding, swimming, skiing. Res: 105 Strouse Ct Folsom 95630 Ofc: AB International Electronics, 1830-6 Vernon St Roseville 95678

BISGAARD, EDWARD LAWRENCE, financial executive/CPA; b. July 26, 1946, El Centro; s. Edward Lawrence, Sr. and Gail (Chambers) B.; edn: BS, Calif. State Polytechnic Univ., Pomona 1971. Career: senior acct. Arthur Young & Co., Los Angeles 1971-74; controller King Internat. Corp., Beverly Hills 1975-78; asst. treas. 17 mutual funds managed by Capital Research & Mgmt. Co., Los Angeles 1979-86, v.p. Fund Mgmt. and Operations Divs., Capital Research & Mgmt. Co., L.A. 1982-86; owner/gen. mgr. R & R Tire & Auto Service Centers, El Cajon 1987; chief fin. ofcr. Dunham & Greer, Inc. 1988-89; v.p./treas. Atlas Advisers, Atlas Securities, Atlas Funds, Oakland 1989-; mem: AICPA, Calif. CPA Soc.; Republican. Res: 810 Regency Ct Walnut Creek 94596 Ofc: Atlas Advisers, 1901 Harrison St Oakland 94612

BLACK, EILEEN MARY, teacher; b. Sept. 20, 1944, Bklyn.; d. Marvin Mize and Anne Joan (Salvia) Black; edn: liberal arts studies Grossmont Coll., El Cajon 1964; BA, San Diego State Univ., 1967; grad. work UCSD; NDEA grant Syracuse Univ., 1968; Calif. Std. Elem. Tchg. credential, 1967. Career: teacher Highlands Elem. Sch., Spring Valley 1967-83, Northmont Elem., La Mesa Spring Valley Sch. Dist., 1983-; award: 25 year svc. La Mesa Spring Valley

Sch. Dist. 1992; mem: Calif. Tchrs. Assn. 1967-, Nat. Ednl. Assn. 1967-; Republican; R.Cath.; rec: reading, walking, baseball. Res: 9320 Earl St #15 La Mesa 91942 Ofc: Northmont Elementary, 9405 Gregory St La Mesa 91942

BLACK, NOEL ANTHONY, film and television director; b. Jun 30, 1937, Chgo.; s. Samuel A. and Susan (Quan) B.; m. Sandra Ann MacPhail, Dec. 2, 1968 (div.); children: Marco E. b. 1970, Nicole A. b. 1971; m. 2d Catherine Elizabeth Cownie, June 1, 1988; edn: att. Univ. Chgo. 1954-57; BA in theater arts - motion pictures, UCLA, 1958, MA, 1962. Career: film and tv dir., 1966-; director: Skaterdater UA, 1966 (short subject, his 1st film and Am. film winner of most internat. honors in 1966-67, won Grand Prix, Cannes Film Fest.; Statuette of Saint Finbarr Award, and the Waterford Glass Award for Best Film of Fest. from Cork, Ireland; Silver Medal from Moscow; First Prize from Colombo, and Silver Trophy from Cortina); writer-director: The River Boy, 1967 (his 2nd film and winner Lion of St. Mark Award, Venice Internat. Film Fest., 1st Prize Vancouver Internat. Film Fest.); I'm A Fool, PBS, 1977; The Golden Honeymoon, PBS, 1979; Electric Grandmother, NBC, Highgate Pictures, 1981 (George Foster Peabody Award 1982); Eyes of the Panther, Showtime "Nightmare Classics" 1989; The Hollow Boy, American Playhouse, 1991; Trilogy: The American Boy, ABC-TV (his first t.v. spl., U.S. entry at 8th Intl. Monte Carlo TV Fest., winner Cino del Duca, $2000 cash award); Pretty Poison, 20th Century Fox, 1968 (his first feature film, now a film-noire classic); A Man, A Woman & A Bank, Avco Embassy Pictures, 1980; Mischief, 20th Century Fox, 1985 (screenplay & exec. prod.); mini-series: Deadly Intentions (4 hrs.) ABC, 1985; MOW's: The Other Victim, CBS, 1981; Prime Suspect, CBS, 1981; Happy Endings, CBS, 1982; Quarterback Princess, CBS, 1983; Promises To Keep, CBS, 1985; A Time To Triumph, CBS, 1986; My Two Loves, ABC, 1986; Conspiracy of Love, CBS, 1987; The Town Bully, ABC, 1988; Pilots: The World Beyond (1 hr.) CBS, 1977; Mulligan's Stew (90 min.) NBC, 1977; Doctors Wilde (1 hr.) CBS, 1987; Meet The Munceys (1 hr.), ABC, 1988; Episodic: The Baby Sitters Club, Over My Dead Body, The Twilight Zone, Dolphin Cove, Kojak, Hawaii 5-0, Quincy; adj. asst. prof. N.Y. Univ. Graduate Pgm., Inst. of Film and Television, Tisch Sch. of the Arts, 1992-94; mem: Dirs. Guild Am. 1968-, Writers Guild Am. 1973-, Acad. Motion Picture Arts & Scis. 1969-, Acad. TV Arts & Scis. 1976-. Ofc: Starfish Productions 126 Wadsworth Ave Santa Monica CA 90405

BLACK, PATRICIA E., French educator, university international program director; b. Apr. 25, 1955, Amherst, Ohio; d. William Marion and Virginia Eileen (Davidson) B.; m. Douglas Scott Henderson, Oct. 11, 1980; children: Anna Elene, Camille May; edn: BA (high hons.), Oberlin Coll., 1977; MA French lit., Cornell Univ., 1980; DEA in French and Comparative Lit., Universite de Poitiers, 1982; PhD French lit., Cornell Univ., 1985. Career: prof. d'anglais Maison de la Formation de la Chambre de Commerce de Poitiers, 1982-83; tchg. asst. Cornell Univ. 1978-80, 83-84; lectr. in Fr. Potsdam Coll. of SUNY, 1984-86; asst. prof., assoc. prof. of French, CSU Chico, 1986-, interviewer for CSU Internat. Pgm., 1986-90, coord. of French Sect. 1991-92, mem. Dept. Fgn. Language Personnel Com. 1990-92, named director of CSU Internat. Program in France for 1993-94; awards: Phi Beta Kappa 1976, Cornell 1st yr. grad. fellow 1977, travel grantee 1980, Corson Fr. Prize 1980, Oberlin Coll. Alumni fellow 1980, Univ. de Poitiers fellow 1980, others; mem: Modern Language Assn., Soc. Rencesvals (Am.-Can. Br. sec. treas. 1992-), Soc. Guilhem IX, Am. Council on Quebec Studies. Res: 37 Cameo Dr #1 Chico 95926 Ofc: Calif. State University Dept. Fgn. Languages, Chico 95929-0825 Tel: 916/898-5388

BLACKSTOCK, JAMES FIELDING, lawyer; b. Sept. 19, 1947, Los Angeles; s. James Carne and Justine Fielding (Gibson) B.; m. Kathleen Ann Weigand, Dec. 12, 1969; children: Kristin Marie, James Fielding; edn: BA English, USC, 1969; JD, USC Law Ctr., 1976; admitted bar: Calif. 1976, U.S. Dist. Ct. 1977, U.S. Supreme Ct. 1980. Career: editor Bar Exam Information Book, BRC of Calif., 1974; atty. assoc. Hill, Farrer & Burrill, 1976-80; assoc., then ptnr. Zobrist & Vienna (and predecessor firm) 1980-83; v.p. and gen. counsel Tatum Petroleum Corp., 1983-84; ptnr. Sullivan, Workman & Dee, 1984-91; prin. James F. Blackstock, PLC, 1992-; mem. Am. Bar Assn., Calif. Bar Assn., L.A. Co. Bar Assn., USC Commerce Assocs. (pres. nat. bd. dirs.), USC Gen. Alumni Assn. (bd. govs.), USC Cardinal & Gold, USC Legion Lex (bd. 1988-91), Phi Alpha Delta, Sigma Nu; civic: Pasadena Tournament of Roses Assn., La Salle H.S. Bd. Regents (pres. 1990-93), Calif. Mus. Sci. and Ind. Advy. Bd. (1991), Breakfast Round Table, Somebody Cares for the Homeless Found. Pasa. (founding); club: Saddle & Sirloin (past pres.), Rancheros Visitadores, Pasadena BPOE; mil: lt. USN 1969-73, Navy Achiev. Medal w/star; comdr. USNR (Surface Warfare), c.o. Mobile Inshore Undersea Warfare Unit 105; rec: equestrian, racquetball, tennis, USC Rugby Club. Res: 5316 Palm Dr La Canada 91011 Ofc. Tel: 213/621-7600

BLADON, RICHARD ANTHONY, speech professional, b. March 7, 1943, Leicester, U.K.; s. Leonard Harry and Barbara Irene (Jones) B.; m. Deborah McGerry, July 31, 1992; edn: BA, Univ. of Cambridge, Eng., 1965; MA, Univ. of Cambridge, 1968; MPhil, Univ. of Reading, Eng., 1969; PhD, Univ. of Oxford, Eng., 1985; career: lectr. Univ. of Ghent, Belgium, 1965-67; lectr. linguistics, Univ. Coll., N. Wales, U.K., 1969-80; fellow, Wolfson Coll., Oxford, 1980-90; univ. lectr., phonetics Univ. of Oxford, 1980-88; assessor Univ. of Oxford, 1983-84; chair, computing/tchg. ctr. Univ. of Oxford, 1984-88; bd. of delegates Oxford Univ. Press, 1983-84; curator of Bodleian Lib., Oxford, 1983-84; assoc. prof. UC Santa Barbara 1988, UCLA 1989; res. scientist Infovox A.B., Stockholm, 1986-88; prin. mem. tech. Digital Sound Corp., Santa Barbara, Calif., 1988-92; engring. prog. dir. Digital Sound Corp., 1992-; mem: The Philological Soc., 1969-; mem. of council, The Philological Society, 1982-86; Internat. Phonetic Assn., 1975-; mem. council, journal ed., Internat. Phonetic Assn., 1986-90; Acoustical Soc. Amer., 1975-; author: articles in profl. journals and several patents; rec: words, guitar, the outdoors. Res: 1024 San Diego Rd. Santa Barbara 93103. Ofc: Digital Sound Corp. 6307 Carpinteria Ave. Santa Barbara 93013

BLAETTLER, RICHARD BRUCE, school administrator; b. Sept. 3, 1938, San Francisco; s. Henry Walter and Veronica (Smith) B.; m. Barbara Anne Crevier, June 1, 1968; children: Daniel, Derek and Janelle; edn: AA, City Coll. S.F., 1959; BA, San Francisco State Univ., 1962, MA, 1964; EdD, Univ. of La Verne, 1991; Bay Area Admin. Tng. Ctr. 1992; Supts. Acad. 1993; Calif. gen. secondary tchg. and adminstrn. credentials. Career: tchr. and coach Balboa High Sch., San Francisco 1964; Portola Jr. High Sch., S.F. 1964-65; Arroyo High Sch., San Lorenzo 1966-70; athletic dir. and dept. chair Richmond High Sch., Richmond 1970-83, dean of students 1983-90, 91-, dean of students Richmond Adult Sch. 1990-91; also adult sch. instr. San Lorenzo U.S.D., 1968-80, Albany U.S.D., 1979-85; served to E9, sgt. major US Army Spl. Forces, 1960-, corrective therapist Oakland Veterans Adminstrn. Hosp. 1962-64; awards: grantee Springfield Coll., Mass. 1965, Most popular artist Soc. Western Artists, DeYoung Mus., S.F. 1960; mem. Richmond Assn. Sch. Adminstrs. 1983-, Am. Rabbit Breeders Assn. 1984-, Tolenas Farms HOA (pres. 1981-82), City of Fairfield Vision 2020, Sounding Bd. & Sister City Com. 1992-93, Shriners (v.p. Montezuma Club 1991-92, mem. Ben Ali Temple Pipes & Drums 1988-); publs: jour. articles re athletics 1966-, diss: Alternative to Suspension Programs in Calif. 1991; Republican; Prot.; rec: philately, raising show rabbits, playing bag pipes. Res: 4424 Tolenas Rd Fairfield 94533-6613 Ofc: Richmond High School 1250 23rd St Richmond 94804

BLAGDEN, JULIA WHITNEY, management consultant; b. Nov. 21, 1960, NYC, NY; d. George and Josephine Culter Stearns (Swan) Blagden; edn: H.S. diploma (with distinction), Dana Hall Sch., Wellesley, Mass., 1978; BA, psychology, Vassar Coll., Poughkeepsie, NY, 1982; M. of Internat. Management, The Am. Grad. Sch. of Internat. Management, Glendale, Ariz., 1986; NY State Elem. sch. tchr., NY Bd. of Edn., 1982. Career: trade dir./sr. dir., Tradecard of Boston, Inc., Boston, Mass., 1982-84; Eng. tchr. (through AFS Internat. & Chinese Ministry of Edn.), Hubei Univ., Wuhan, People's Republic of China, 1985; mgr., global sourcing, Pacific Marketing Consultants, So. S.F., Calif., 1987; mgr., internat. trade, ACA Pacific, Inc., S.F., 1988; cons., Barakat & Chamberlin, Inc., Oakland, Calif., 1989-91; assoc., Barakat & Chamberlin, Inc., Oakland, 1991-; pres. & speaker, Toastmasters Internat., Glendale, Ariz., 1985-86; mem./adv., Internat. Trade Assn., S.F., 1986-89; mem. Assn. of Demand-Side Management Professionals, Berkeley, 1992; mem. Am. Management Assn., NYC, NY, 1992; awards: Nan Coyle Citizenship award, Dana Hall Sch., 1978; student graduation speaker, Dana Hall Sch., 1978; Sr. Class Pres., Vassar Coll., 1982; student graduation speaker, Vassar Coll., 1982; mem: The Metropolitan Club of S.F., 1987-92; The Social Register, 1960-; The Ivy Club, 1987-; Thunderbird Alumnae Assn., S.F., 1986-; pres., Vassar Club of S.F., 1987-90; fund-raiser, Multiple Sclerosis Soc., Oakland, 1987-88, 91; vocalist: record (12 women a cappella) In The Mood, 1982; co-author, publ. article, 1992; Republican; Episcopalian; rec: rowing, singing, fund raisers, opera, symphony, and other cultural events; Res: 5115 Manila Ave. Oakland 94618-1019. Ofc: Barakat & Chamberlin, Inc. 1800 Harrison St. 18th Flr. Oakland 94612

BLAINE, DEVON, public relations executive; edn: psych. and hist. studies, UCLA. Career: pres./CEO The Blaine Group Inc., Los Angeles; mem: The Consulting Consortium (co-founder), Nat. Small Bus. United (founding pres. Calif. chapt.), L.A. Venture Assn. (pres. 1989, 93), Assn. of Venture Founders, Nat. Assn. Women Bus. Owners (founding bd., past pres.), CEO Clubs (Boston, Chgo., Dallas, L.A., N.Y., S.F., W.D.C.), L.A. Area C.of C., Entrepreneur Club, United Fedn. of Small Bus., Ctr. for Entrepreneurial Mgmt., L.A. Women's Campaign Fund, Pub. Rels. Soc. Am. (Prism Award - on-going corp. comms. pgm. 1985, 88, hon. mention - fin. p.r., consumer media pgm., single-mkt. pgm., 1984), Publicity Club N.Y., Book Publicists So. Calif., Women in Bus., Women in Show Bus., Women's Nat. Book Assn., Variety Club (Tent 25). Ofc: The Blaine Group, Inc. 7465 Beverly Blvd Los Angeles 90036-2706

BLANCHE, JOE ADVINCULA, aerospace engineer, scientist, R.E. broker, reg. tax preparer; b. Sept. 11, 1954, Santa, Ilocos Sur, Philippines, nat. 1978; s. Emilio Peralta and Conception Advincula (Burgonio) B.; m. Albine Selerio Lansangan, Oct. 10, 1982; children: Emmanuel Joseph b. 1985, Earl Jordan b. 1989; edn: certificate in mil. sci. & gen. edn., Univ. of the Philippines, 1973; BS, math., Adamson Univ., Manila, Philippines, 1976; post grad. work in accounting, Chapman Univ., Orange, Calif., 1978; assoc. in applied sci.-avionics sys-

tems, Comm. Coll. of the Air Force, Maxwell AFB, Ala., 1980; post grad. work in elec. engring., Calif. State Univ., Long Beach, 1982-85; certificate in mgmt., Central Texas Coll., Killeen, Tx., 1990; masters cand. in organizational mgmt., Univ. of Phoenix, 1992-; PhD in mgmt., Pacific We. Univ., L.A., 1993. Career: USAF, March AFB, Calif., avionics systems. splst., 1977-79, avionics systems. supr., 1979-80; tchr., Moreno Valley H.S. (Calif.), 1980-81; McDonnell Douglas Corp., Long Beach, field svc electrical, 1981, assoc. engr/sci., 1981-83, engr./sci., 1983-86; lead engr., aerospace, Sikorsky ACFT-UTC, Stratford, Conn., 1986-87; McDonnell Douglas Corp., Long Beach, engr./sci. splst., 1987-88, sr. engr./sci., 1988-; awards: scholarship, Univ. of Philippines, 1972-73; Humanitarian Svc. Medal, USAF, 1978; USAF Good Conduct Medal, 1979; USAF Nat. Defense Svc. Medal, 1976, 92; USAF Res. Meritorious Svc. Medal, 1984, 88, 92; USAF Armed Forces Res. Medal, 1992; mem: Internat. Soc. of Allied Weight Engrs., 1981-; So. Calif. Profl. Engring. Assn., 1981-; Corona-Norco Bd. of Realtors, CAR, NAR, 1988-; Nat. Notary Assn., 1989-; Am. Inst. of Aeronautics & Astronautics, 1991-;civic: mem., Santanians, USA, Inc., 1983-, bd. of dir., 1983-87; mem., Marinduque Assn. of So. Calif., L.A., 1987-; U.P. Alumni Assn. of So. Calif., L.A., 1990-; FIL-AM Assn. of Corona, 1991-; author: status report on US Presidential Helicopter, 1987; management paper, 1992. Mil: tech. sgt., USAF, 1976-81; Republican; Roman Catholic. Ofc: McDonnell Douglas 3855 Lakewood Blvd. Long Beach 90846

BLANCHETTE, JAMES EDWARD, psychiatrist; b. Aug. 28, 1924, Syracuse, NY; s Joseph Marcel and Margaret Catherine (Vincent) Blanchette; m. Shirley Ruth Brisco, Sept. 1, 1948 (dec. May 4, 1981); edn: BA, Syracuse Univ., NY, 1950; MD, SUNY, Syracuse Coll of Med., 1953; Diplomate Am. Bd. Psychiatry and Neurology. Career: intern St. Vincent's Hosp., NYC 1953-54; res. Patton State Hosp., Calif. 1954-55; Met. State Hosp., Norwalk 1957-59; pvt. practice psychiatry, Redlands 1959-; chief profl. edn. Patton State Hosp., 1960-64; tchg. cons., 1964-; staff San Bernardino Comm. Hosp., St. Bernadine Hosp.; USAAF Band, Wash DC, 1945-47; USAAF Med. Corps, 1953-55; mem: Am. Psychiat. Assn. (life fellow), AMA, CMA, Pan-Am. Med. Assn., San Bernardino Med. Soc., So. Calif. Psychiat. Soc. (pres. Inland chpt. 1963-4, 1983-4), Royal Soc. Health, Am. Med. Soc., Am. Chemical Soc., AAAS, Internat. Platform Assn., Phi Mu Alpha, Arrowhead Allied Arts Council (San Bdo. past pres.), Elks, US Power Squadron, Dist. 13, P/D/C; USCG Aux., Hollywood Yacht club; musician ret. (string bass) fmrly with AF Band (Wash DC), Syracuse Sym., Univ. of Redlands Sym., Loma Linda Univ. Sym., Inland Empire Sym., Riverside Sym.; rec: boating. Res: 972 W Marshall Blvd San Bernardino 92405-2848 Ofc: 26 Cajon St Redlands 92373-5296

BLANKENSHIP, JUANITA CHAPMAN, court administrator; b. Feb. 25, 1935, Miles City, MT; d. Terry S. Chapman and June Brown Shelden; m. Thomas H. Blankenship, June 5, 1956 (div. July 1, 1974); edn: BA, Univ. of Montana 1956; MA, Univ. of Nevada 1970. Career: mgmt. asst. U.S. Atomic Energy Commn., Las Vegas 1962-65; administrative analyst Clark County, Las Vegas 1970-73; staff dir./criminal justice planner SRDAC, Las Vegas 1973-80; asst. dir. juror mgmt. Los Angeles Superior Ct. 1981-88, dir. 1988-92; adminstr. litigation support svs. 1992-; advy. com. USC Criminal Justice Training Ctr. 1977-81; awards: Phi Kappa Phi 1956, Public Admin. of Yr. Las Vegas Chapt. ASPA 1978, SCJA Annual Award, sect. on Crim. Justice Admin./ASPA 1983, named grant honoree EFP, AAUW Covina Br. 1986, comm. svc. award Covina Coordinating Council 1990, J.E.M. achievement award 1992; mem: Am. Soc. for Public Admin.,Nat. Assn. for Court Mgmt., Jury Edn. & Mgmt. Forum, CASCA, L.A. Co. Mgmt. Council, Andalucia Townhomes Assn. (bd. dir.), Am. Assn. of Univ. Women, Covina Branch; contbg. author: Handbook for Court Specialists (1976); Democrat; Protestant; rec: tennis, skiing. Ofc: 320 W Temple St 15th Flr Los Angeles 90012

BLANTON, IVELYN, genealogist, retired cosmetologist; b. Feb. 8, 1936, Binger, Ok.; d. Raymond Avril and Minnie Oneida (Jay) Skelton; m. Robert Acie Blanton, Oct. 17, 1957, Ottawa Co., Ok. (dec. July 27, 1989); children: Gary Lynn b. Oct. 18, 1958, Lori Annette (Mrs. Ken Shumway) b. Dec. 20, 1959, James Aubrey b. Feb. 20, 1961, Brenda Marlene (Mrs. Pat Rafael) b. July 20, 1962; edn: grad. Chowchilla Union H.S. 1955, Esquire Beauty Coll., Neosho, Mo. 1972-3, Glamour Beauty Coll., Merced, Calif. grad. 1974; bus. and spl. courses Merced Jr. Coll. 1976-80. Career: line work F & P Cannery, Merced, Ca. seasonal 1953-55; Tylers Cafe, 1956-57; beautician Dorsmae's Beauty Haven, 1976, Bettys Beauty Shop, 1978-79; awards: Chowchilla Dist. Hist. Soc. 1989, DAR Madera Chpt. 1990, Chowchilla Lioness 1990; civic: Chowchilla Dist. Hist. Soc. (life mem., v.p. 1990-92, historian 1988-92), Nat. Soc. Colonial Dames XVII Century (charter org. mem. 1988-), Capt. James Davis Chap. Ceries, Calif. (registrar), Family Name File & Genealogy (queries Heraldry & Coat of Arms 1988-89), Nat. Soc. DAR (charter org. mem. El Portal de las Sierras Chapt. Madera, Ca. 1985-: chapt. ofcr., registrar 1985-90, corr. sec. 1990-93, chapt. chmn. Nat. Com. Lineage Res. 1985-90, Svc. for Veterans 1987, The Flag of USA 1989, pgm. com., pub. rels. 1992-93, chpt. chair Spl. Chpt. coms.- DAR local scholarship, tel., yearbook, 1992-93; pgm. calendar: Good Citizens Tea, Speaker 1993), Friends of the Library Chowchilla 1990-93, Madera Genealogy Soc. 1988-93, Chowchilla Lioness (2d. yr. dir. 1991, 1 yr. dir. 1992), Annabelle Bertram Clinic Chowchilla (treas. 1990-93), Am. Legion

Aux. Unit 660 Le Grand, Merced Co. (2d v.p. 1991, chaplain 1992, sec. treas. 1993), Civil War Descendants Soc., Athens, A. 1992, Daus. of Union Veteran of Civil War 1861-1865 Mo. Dept. Julia Dent Grant, Tent #16, St. Louis 1992-93, Nat. Soc. U.S. Daus. of 1812 (1992-93), NW Ga. Hist. & Geneal. Soc. Inc. Rome, Ga. 1992-93, Pittsburg Co. Geneal. & Hist. Soc. McAlester, Ok. 1991-92, Coffee Co. Hist. Soc. Manchester, Tn. 1992-93, Bedford Co. Hist. Soc. Shelbyville Tn. 1992-93; works: designer for Plaque on Monument of Chowchilla's Robt. Blvd., Point of Hist. Interest 1990; had Govt. headstone placed on Civil War Vet. John Franklin Skelton's grave, Rome, Ga. (1992); assisted editor on book: Yesterdays of Chowchilla 1987; author: Blanton's & Allied Families (1991); The Bolton Families (1993); assisted author, Minnie O. Skelton by finding and compiling the hist. of John Franklin Skelton & 2nd family for her book: Skelton Families, Then & Now (1991), also her asst. on 8 future fam. histories- Martin, Jay, Ferguson, Mooney, Truax, Reaves, Smith, Williams; Democrat; Prot.; rec: genealogy, travel, amateur photography, sewing. Address: PO Box 173 Chowchilla 93610

BLANTON, JOHN ARTHUR, architect; b. Jan. 1, 1928, Houston; s. Arthur Alva and Caroline Arnold (Jeter) Blanton; m. Marietta Newton, Apr. 10,1954 (dec. Apr. 3, 1976); children: Jill Lewis b. 1958, Lynette Rowe b. 1961, Elena Blanton b. 1965; edn: BS, arch., Rice Univ. 1949. Career: assoc., Richard J. Neutra, F.A.I.A., Los Angeles 1950-64; architect pvt. practice, Manhattan Beach 1964-; instr. UCLA ext. 1967-75; instr. Harbor Coll. 1970-72; contbr. book revs. AIA Journal, 1972-75; appt. chmn. Manhattan Beach Bd. of Zoning Adjustment; Manhattan Beach Planning Commn. 1993; honors: Red Cedar Shingle nat. award AIA 1979, C.of C. awards: (1969, 70, 71, 74, 75, 82); mem: AIA, Soc. Architl. Historians; publs: 15-pg. monograph of completed works pub. L'Architettura, Italian archtl. mag. (5/88), work featured in Architecture in Los Angeles: A Compleat Guide (5), Sunset Mag., L.A. Times Home mag., Bicentennial edition AIA Journal, others; mil: US Signal Corps 1951-53; Ofc: John Blanton, AIA, Manhattan Beach 90266

BLANTON, JOHN BERENSON, dentist, educator; b. Feb. 7, 1955, Altadena; s. John Wilson and Mae Berta (Berenson) B.; m. Natalie Son Tang, Jan. 24, 1987; 1 son, Jehan Hohon Blanton-Tang b. 1990; edn: BS chemistry, UCLA 1976; DDS, USC 1984; reg. dentist Calif. Bd. Dental Examiners 1984. Career: cons. engr. Arcadia Machine & Tool, Arcadia 1976-77; res. engr. UCLA Inst. of Geophysics & Planetary Physics, Los Angeles 1977-80; adj. faculty USC Sch. of Dentistry, 1984-85; pvt. practice dentistry, Culver City 1985-; tchr. progressive orthodontic seminars, Boston, Mass. 1988-91; awards: OKU, USC Sch. Dentistry 1984; mem: ADA, Calif. Dental Assn., Western Dental Assn., Acad. Gen. Dentistry, Culver City C.of C.; inventor: Triaxial Load Frame for high pressure ultrasonic velocity determination (1979); mil: s.sgt. AUS ROTC 1968-70; rec: swimming, bicycling, trap & skeet shooting. Ofc: 10730 W Jefferson Blvd Culver City 90230

BLASDALE, ALLAN WALTER, organist and music director; b. July 5, 1953, Berkeley; s. Herbert Halsey and Jean Bevans (Coolbaugh) B.; edn: BA music, UC Berkeley 1976; Ch. Divinity Sch. Pacific 1978-80; Boalt Hall Sch. Law 1974. Career: minister of music Presbyterian Ch. Oakland 1971-72; N. Congregational Ch. Berkeley 1972-83; Ch. of Advent, San Francisco 1983-87; Ch. of Holy Innocents 1987-88; First Congregational Ch. 1988-91; Pilgrim Congregational Ch., Walnut Creek 1975-; organist, Master of the Choristers, St. Stephen's Ch., Orinda, 1991- tchr. organ and piano pvt. practice 1971-; awards: Am. Guild of Organists Regional Competition 1st place (1975, 76); mem: Am. Guild Organists; music composer for organ, piano and chorus 1971-, concert artist; Democrat; Episcopal; rec: hiking, mountaineering, archaeology. Ofc: 66 Saint Stephen's Dr Orinda 94563 Ph: 415/254-3770

BLATT, BEVERLY FAYE, biologist, consultant; b. Mar. 17, 1944, Pittsburgh, Pa.; d. Simon and Sadie (Skigen) B.; m. Marc Harry Lavietes, Aug. 13, 1966 (div. July 31, 1987); children: Bryan Ross b. 1971, Jonathan David b. 1975; m. 2d David Herman Filipek, Dec. 28, 1987; edn: AB (magna cum laude) Vassar Coll., 1965; PhD, Case-Western Reserve Univ., 1969. Career: asst. prof. pathology N.Y.U. Med. Sch., 1971-80; asst. prof. medicine SUNY Downstate Med. Sch., Bklyn. 1980-84; SUNY Stony Brook Med. Sch. 1984-88; sect. hd. clin. immunol. res. Long Island Jewish Med. Ctr., New Hyde Park, NY 1986-88; cons. BFB Bioconsulting, Alameda, Calif. 1988-; awards: grad. fellow NSF 1967-69, postdoc. fellow Am. Cancer Soc. 1969-70, postdoc. fellow NIH 1970-71, grantee NIH (1971-77, 1981-85), grantee NY Arthritis Found. (1981-87); mem: AAAS, Assn. for Women in Sci., Harvey Soc., NY Acad. Scis., Am. Soc. Cell Biol., Vassar Coll. Class of 1965 (25th reunion gift chair, pres. 1990-95), co-chair organizing com. "Women in Bioscience: Opportunities in the 90's" (Stanford Univ. 1/93); publs: sci. res. reports, revs. (1969-88); Temple Israel, Alameda (bd. 1990-95, v.p. 91-92). Ofc: BFB Consulting 3265 Central Ave Alameda 94501

BLAU, ERIC MARK, physician; b. Sept. 27, 1947, Sacramento; s. Sidney and Beatrice (Brainin) B.; m. Julie Gollin, Jan. 16, 1989; edn: BS, UC Davis 1969; MD, UCSD 1973; cert. Am. Bd. Internal Medicine 1977, F.A.C.P. 1992. Career: staff physician So. Calif. Permanente Med. Group, San Diego 1977-; asst. clin.

prof. comm. medicine UCSD Sch. Medicine 1982-88, assoc. clin. prof. 1988-; profl. photographer, San Diego 1982-; awards: Polaroid Corp. Artist Support grant 1988-93, City San Diego Pub. Arts Advy. Bd. grant 1988; author: Common Heroes, 1989; Stories of Adoption, 1993. Ofc: Kaiser Permanente 7060 Clairemont Mesa San Diego 92111

BLECKSMITH, FRED RODRICK, JR., architect; b. Mar. 23, 1937, San Diego; s. Fred Rodrick and Margaret Luca (Scherring) B.; edn: BS in architectural engring., Calif. Polytech. Univ. 1960. Career: pres. Fred Blecksmith Architect, San Diego 1967-; chmn. Architects Consortium, San Diego 1977-; v. chmn. Park & Recreation Bd. Facilities Com. 1978-; mem. Pub. Review Com., S.D. 1978-; awards: Am. Inst. Architects Outstanding Achievement 1980, Exceptional Achievement 1970; mem: Am. Inst. Architects. Ofc: 1706 5th Ave San Diego 92101

BLEIBERG, LEON WILLIAM, surgical podiatrist, executive; b. June 9, 1932, Bklyn.; s. Paul Pincus and Helen (Epstein) B.; m. Beth Daigle, June 7, 1970; children: Kristina Noel, Kelley Lynn, Kimberly Ann, Paul Joseph; edn: student L.A. City Coll. 1950-51, USC 1951, Case Western Reserve Univ. 1951-53; DSc (honors) and DPM, Temple Univ. 1955; PhD, Univ. Beverly Hills, 1970. Career: rotating intern various hosps., Phila. 1954-55; resident various hosp., Montebello, L.A., Calif. 1956-58, surgical podiatrist So. Calif. Podiatry Group, Westchester, L.A., 1956-75; health care economist, researcher Drs. Home Health Care Services, 1976-; pres. Medica, Totalcare, Cine-Medics Corp., World-Wide Health Care Services; healthcare affiliate Internat. div. CARE/ASIA, 1987; pres. International Health Trust, 1991-92; track coach Westlake High Sch., Westlake Village 1990-; podiatric cons. USC Athletic Dept., Morningside and Inglewood High Schs., Internet Corp., Royal Naval Assn., Long Beach, Calif. Naval Sta.; writer, lectr. in field; producer 3 films: The Gun Hawk 1963, Terrified, and Day of the Nightmare; mem: Philippine Hosp. Assn. (appreciation cert. 1964, trophy award for outstanding svc. 1979), Calif. Podiatry Assn. (hon.), Am. Podiatric Med. Assn. (hon.), Royal Soc. Health (England), Western Foot Surgery Assn., Am. Coll. Foot Surgeons, Am. Coll. Podiatric Sports Medicine, Internat. Coll. Preventive Medicine, Acad. TV Arts and Scis., Masons, Shriners; clubs: Hollywood Comedy, Saints and Sinners, Hall Und Beinbruch Ski, Beach Cities Ski, Orange County Stamp, Las Virgenes Track; mil: USN 1955-56, lt. comdr. med. svs. corps Brit.-Am. Cadet Corps, 1984-; civic: Hon. Sheriff Westchester 1962-64, chmn. Nat. Health Care Reform Com., United We Stand; Republican (Life mem. Rep. Nat. Com., Senatl. Inner Circle 1984-86, medal of merit U.S. Presdl. Task Force). Res: 1675 Berkshire Dr Thousand Oaks 91362

BLESSING-MOORE, JOANN CATHERINE, physician, medical educator; b. Sept. 21, 1946, Tacoma, Wash.; d. Harold R. and Mildred Benson B.; m. Robert Chester Moore, Feb. 1978; child: Ahna Blessing-Moore b. 1981; edn: BA, Syracuse Univ. 1968; MD, Upstate Medical Ctr. (NY) 1972; pediatric intern and res. Stanford Univ. Medical Ctr. 1972-75, Fellow in allergy, pediatric pulmonology 1987. Career: asst. clin. prof., full time, Stanford Univ. Hosp. 1977-84; private practice physician and assoc. clinical prof. part time, Stanford Univ. 1984-; boarded in: pediatrics, allergy-immunology, pediatric pulmonology; FDA advy. com. on allergy pulm. drugs; cons. to various orgns. and companies; honors: NY State Acad. Scholarship, 1968-72, CF Found. Fellowship, 1975-77, listed Who's Who Am. Univ. Coll., 1968; fellow: Am. Acad. Allergy, Am. Acad. Pediatrics, Am. Coll. of Chest Physicians; mem: No. Calif. Allergy Found. (bd.), Am. Thoracic Soc., Am. Lung Assn., Am. Acad. Allergy Imm., Am. Coll. Allergy Imm., San Mateo and Santa Clara Co. Lung Assn. (bd. mem., com. mem.); civic: Medical Explorer Scouts (leader), Presbyterian Church, Profl. Women's Orgn.; author: abstracts, articles, chapts. in 2 text books (allergy, pulmonary); co-editor 2 supplements for major jours., editorial bd. med. jour.; Republican; Presbyterian; rec: sailing, swimming, travel, gardening, cooking, music, horses.

BLISS, EDWIN CROSBY, author, lecturer, consultant; b. Feb. 15, 1923, Salt Lake City, Utah; s. Edwin S. and Naomi (Crosby) B.; m. Mary Elizabeth Miller, Jan. 21, 1956; children: William, Rebecca, Roger, Kevin; edn: BS, Univ. Utah, 1948, MS, 1958. Career: editor Deseret News, S.L.C., Ut. 1948-52; lectr. Univ. of Utah 1952-54; magazine editor Columbus (Ohio) Dispatch, 1954-55; asst. to U.S. Senator, WDC 1955-63; public affairs dir. Nat. Assn. of Mfrs., WDC 1963-77; cons. prin. Edwin C. Bliss Assocs., Kingsburg, Ca. 1977-; lectr. Career Track, Boulder, Colo. 1983-91; mem. Am. Mgmt. Assn., Am. Inst. of Parliamentarians (advy. council 1984-92); author: Doing It Now (1983), Getting Things Done (1991), editor: Standard Guide to Parliamentary Procedure (1989); mil: lt. col. US Army, USAR 1944-74. Res/Ofc: 2220 Carolyn St Kingsburg 93631

BLODGETT, ELSIE GRACE, business owner, retired teacher; b. Aug. 2, 1921, Eldorado Springs, Mo.; d. Charles Ishmal and Naoma Florence (Worthington) Robison; m. Charles Blodgett, Nov. 8, 1940; children: Carolyn Doyel, Charleen Bier, Lyndon, Daryl (dec.); edn: Warrensburg State Tchrs. Coll., 1939-40; BA, Fresno State Coll., 1953. Career: tchr. in Mo., 1940-42, and Calif., 1947-72; owner/mgr. rental units 1965-; exec. dir. San Joaquin County Rental Property Assn., Inc. 1970-81; ptnr. Key West Property Mgmt. 1980-84;

owner Crystal Springs Health World, Stockton 1980-87; editor, News Bulletin; honoree w/husband as Mr. and Mrs. Apartment Owner of San Joaquin County (1977); mem: Stockton BBB (bd.), Nat. Apt. Assn. (state treas. 1977-79), Calif. Retired Tchrs. Assn.; civic: Zonta, PTA, Girl Scouts/Boys Scouts of Am., Stockton Goodwill Inds. (bd.), police svc. volunteer 1993; Republican; Methodist. Address: 2285 W Mendocino Stockton 95204

BLUE, JAMES GUTHRIE, city veterinarian, administrator; b. Oct. 22, 1920, Flora, Ind.; s. Van Calvin and Florence Amanda (Guthrie) B.; edn: ensign US Naval Acad., 1943; Northwestern Univ., 1943; AB, Wabash Coll., 1943; DVM, Ohio State Univ., 1950; AA in labor rels., L.A. Trade Tech., 1989. Career: active duty USN 1943-46, served to lt. comdr. USNR 1946-66; city veterinarian Los Angeles, North Hollywood, consultant in vet. medicine, surgery and dentistry; field veterinarian City of Los Angeles 1985-92, actg. chief veterinarian, 1992-93; res. and projects consultant CSU Northridge, 1981-88; mem., secty. Arizona State Vet. Med. Bd., 1976-82; awards: sr. coll. award Am. Vet.' Med. Assn.; mem: Calif. Vet. Med. Assn. (com. environ. health and ecology, state ethics com., profl. ethics com., wellness com. 1985-92), So. Calif. Vet. Med. Assn. (Council mem., PAC, contg. edn. com.), So. Ariz. VMA, Ariz. VMA, Am. VMA, San Diego VMA, Am. Fedn. of State Co. Muni. Employees (Profl. Med. Services) Local 2006 (secty., negotiator, 1983-93), Reserve Officers Assn. (pres. Tucson chpt. 1960, state pres. ROA Ariz. 1961-62), Am. Legion, Mil. Order of World Wars (comdr. Ariz., 1967-70), US Naval Reserve Assn., Scottish Rites, Shrine, Internat. 20-30 Club (hon. life); publs: Puppy Distemper Problem Series, Pulse (So. Calif. VMA jour.); Democrat; Episcopalian. Res: 6116 Fulton Ave #103 c/o Fulton Chateau Van Nuys 91401 Ofc: City of Los Angeles 13131 Sherman Way North Hollywood 91605

BLUM, ROBERT M., obstetrician, gynecologist; b. Mar. 28, 1939, Jersey City, N.J.; s. Philip and Bertha (Hirsch) B.; m. Carole Lammer, June 13, 1964; children: Susan b. 1966, David b. 1968; edn: BA, Rutgers Univ. 1960; MD, Georgetown Univ. 1964. Career: intern Beth Israel Hosp., Newark, N.J. 1964-65; resident Sinai Hosp., Baltimore, Md. 1965-68; asst. chief Kaiser Permanente, Downey 1971-; assoc. prof. UCLA 1978-; mem: L.A. Co. Ob-Gyn. Soc., Am. Coll. Ob-Gyn.; mil: major AUS 1968-70; rec: skiing, fishing, tennis. Res: 4574 Shasta Circle Cypress 90630 Ofc: Kaiser Permanente 9449 Imperial Hwy Downey 90242

BOARINI, EDWARD JAMES, research and development executive; b. Sept. 26, 1949, Chgo.; s. Edward John and Celeste Mary (Butt) B.; m. Marla Bovar, Apr. 25, 1976; 1 son, David b. 1980; edn: BS biology, Univ. Ill., 1975; MS technology mgmt., Pepperdine Univ., 1991. Career: prin. engr. Travenol Labs., Round Lake, Ill. 1975-80, sect. mgr. 1980-82, program mgr. 1982-85; mgr. med. prods. Baxter Pharmaseal, Valencia, Ca. 1986-89, dir. med. prods. 1989-91, dir. tech. svs. 1991-93; v.p. tech. ops. P.S. Medical, Goleta 1993-; mil: PO2 USN 1970-74; rec: skiing, golf, neon art. Ofc: P.S. Medical 125-B Cremona Dr Goleta 93117

BOBROW, MICHAEL LAWRENCE, architect; b. April 18, 1939, New York; s. Jack and Ruth B.; m. Julia Dessery Thomas, March 24, 1980; children: Elizabeth Pressler b. 1964, Erica b. 1967, David b. 1969; edn: B.Arch., Columbia Univ. 1963. Career: 1st lt. USAF, senior architect Office of the Surgeon Gen., W.D.C., 1963-66; Med. Planning Assn., Malibu 1966-72; dir. arch., chairman and principal for design Bobrow Thomas & Assoc. (BTA), Los Angeles 1972-; board mem. UCLA Sch. Pub. Health 1989-; adj. prof. UCLA Sch. Pub. Health 1992-; founder, Coordinator Program in Healthcare Design & lectr. UCLA Sch. Arch. & Planning 1972-80; recipient Design awards Nat. AIA (1986, 88); CCAIA and CMAN (1991); "Outstanding Architects under 40", Bldg. Design & Constn. Magazine 1978; beautification award Los Angeles Bus. Council (1988 and 1991); chmn. Friends of the Schindler House 1980-; chmn. Arts & Architecture Magazine 1983-85; mem: AIA; articles pub. internationally in profl. jours. 1967. Ofc: Bobrow Thomas & Associates (BTA, Inc.) 1001 Westwood Blvd Los Angeles 90024 and Hong Kong.

BOERSMA, LAWRENCE ALLAN, animal welfare administrator; b. Apr. 24, 1932, London, Ont., Can.; s. Harry Albert and Valerie Kathryn (DeCordova) B.; m. Nancy Noble Jones, Aug. 16, 1952 (div. 1962); children: Juliana b. 1954, Dirk b. 1956; m. June Elaine Schiefer, Nov. 22, 1962; children (by marriage) Kenneth McKim b. 1951, Mark McKim b. 1956; edn: BA, Univ. Nebr., 1953, MS, 1955; PhD, Sussex, Eng., 1972; Cert. Fund Raising Exec. (CFRE), Nat. Soc. FRE, 1988. Career: journalism tchr. Technical High Sch., Omaha, Nebr. 1953-55; dir. pub. relations and journ. chair Adams State Coll., Alamosa, Colo. 1955-59; advt. sales Better Homes and Gardens, N.Y.C. 1959-63; advt. account exec. This Week Mag., N.Y.C. 1963-66; Eastern sales dir., mktg. dir. Ladies' Home Journal, N.Y.C. 1966-75; v.p./assoc. publisher Saturday Evening Post also v.p./pub. Country Gentleman, N.Y.C., 1975; v.p., dir. mktg. and advt. sales Photo World Mag., N.Y.C., 1975-77; advt. mgr. La Jolla Light, Calif. 1977-80; photographer prin. Allan/TAnimal Photographers, 1980-, pres. and c.e.o. The Photographic Inst. Internat., 1982-86; dir. community relations San Diego Humane Soc. and S.P.C.A., 1985-; bd. dirs. Spay/Neuter Action Project, 1991-93; Feral Cat Coalition San Diego (chmn. 1992-93); pres./c.e.o. United Animal

Welfare Found. 1992-; instr., prof. advt. Nat. Soc. of Fund Raising Execs., Alexandria, Va. 1992; author/photog. numerous articles in mags. in U.S., Mexico, Canada, Europe, Japan, Australia, S.Africa, S.Am.; named man of yr. Ladies' Home Jour. 1972; mem: Royal Photographic Soc., Bath, Eng. (Fellow 1985), Profl. Photographers of Calif. (Fellow 1986), Profl. Photographers of Am. (Master of Photography award, Chgo. 1985, Photographic Craftsman award, Chgo. 1986), Nat. Soc. Fund Raising Execs. 1986- (bd. dir. San Diego chpt. 1988-89, treas. 1990-91), Pub. Relations Soc. Am. 1987-, Soc. of Animal Welfare Adminstrs. 1986-, Shriners (pres. Businessmens Club Al Bahr Shrine, S.D. 1988), Scottish Rite, Masons 1967-; Republican; Presbyterian. Res: 3503 Argonne St San Diego 92117 Ofc: San Diego Humane Society and S.P.C.A., 887 Sherman St San Diego 92110

BOGAR, ODIS, JR., orthopaedic technologist; b. July 21, 1951, Los Angeles; s. Odis Jerome and Mary Elizabeth (Sims) B.; m. Cassandra, May 10, 1970 (div. Apr. 1978); m. Jacqueline Ann Willis, June 17, 1989 (div. Feb. 1991); children: Tamara b. 1970, Derrick b. 1978; grad. indut. arts Fremont H.S., Los Angeles 1969; cert. Sr. Orthopaedic Technologist NBCOT (1984); Notary Public (1991). Career: orthopaedic tech. and surgery orderly USC - LAC Med. Ctr., Los Angeles 1969-76; hosp. corps U.S. Navy, Santa Ana 1976-78; orthopaedic orderly Santa Monica Hosp., Santa Monica 1978-79; orthopaedic tech. Glendale Memorial Hosp. 1979-81; sr. traction tech. Orthopaedic Hosp., Los Angeles 1980-85; Kaiser Hosp., Los Angeles 1985-; mem: Nat. Assn. Orthopaedic Technologists 1982-, Nat. Notary Assn. 1991-, ACLU 1985-; mil: U.S. Navy 1976-78; Republican; Baptist.

BOGDAN, CAROLYN LOUETTA, accounting executive; b. Apr. 15, 1941, Wilkes-Barre, Pa.; d. Walter Cecil and Ethna Louetta (Kendig) Carpenter; m. James Bogdan, May 5, 1961; son, Thomas J. b. 1967; edn: spl. courses Am. Inst. of Banking. Career: head bookkeeper Forty Fort State Bank, Forty Fort, Pa. 1959-63; hd. bookkeeper U.S. Nat. Bank, Long Beach, Ca. 1963-65; office mgr. United Parts Exchange, 1976-81; contract adminstr. branch credit co-ordinator Johnson Controls Inc., Rancho Dominguez 1981-; acct./co-owner B.E.R.D. (Bogdan Electronic R&D), Lakewood 1981-; notary pub. Johnson Controls, L.A. 1987-; recipient sav. bond awards from Hire the Handicapped and Yearbook Club, Kingston, Pa. (1958, 59), listed Who's Who of Am. Women 17th edit.; mem. Nat. Notary Assn., Am. Inst. of Profl. Bookkeepers, Nat. Assn. for Female Execs.;; civic: staff ofcr. L.A. Co. Sheriff/ RACES (records keeper 1980-), mem. Tournament of Roses Radio Assn. (pin chr. 1975-); Republican; Prot.; rec: needlework, electronics, designing, amateur radio opr. Res: 3713 Capetown St Lakewood 90712 Ofc: Johnson Controls, Inc. 19118 S Reyes Ave Rancho Dominguez 90221

BOGERT, MARGOT INKSTER, trust company deputy division head; b. Feb. 18, 1953, Dunfermline, Scotland, U.K.; d. John Crisp and Elizabeth Fulton-Spence (Inkster) Yellowley; m. John Bogert, Feb. 1, 1975; children: Caitlin b. 1982, Rachel b. 1986; edn: BA, Edinburg Univ., Scotland; CTFA 1991. Career: chief of staff, sr. v.p. Trust Services of Am., Los Angeles 1975-92; mng. dir. and corp. secty. TSA Capital Mgmt. Inc. 1989-92; dep. div. hd. Sanwa Bank, 1992-; YWCA honoree, recipient Distinguished Profl. Woman award 1987; civic: Pasadena Child Edn. Ctr. (bd.), Townhall of Calif.; clubs: City Club on Bunker Hill, L.A. Athletic, La Canada CC; Presbyterian; rec: aerobics, swim, racquetball. Ofc: Sanwa Bank California, 601 S Figueroa Los Angeles CA 90017

BOGGAN, DANIEL, JR., university administrator, b. Dec. 9, 1945, Albion, Mich.; s. Daniel, Sr. and Ruthie Jean (Crum) B.; m. Jacqueline Beal, Oct. 4, 1977; children: DeVone, Daniel, Dhanthan, Alike; edn: BA, Albion Coll., 1967; MSW, Univ. Mich., Ann Arbor 1968. Career: asst. chief adminstr. San Diego County, 1978-79; county adminstr. Essex County, NJ 1979-82; city mgr. City of Berkeley 1982-86; assoc. vice chancellor UC Berkeley, Mar.-Sept. 1986, actg. v. chancellor 1986-87, vice chancellor 1987-; dir. Clorox Corp., Oakland 1990-; civic bds: NFBPA (nat. pres. 1990-91, Oakland bd. 1985-), NAACP (nat. life), YMCA Berkeley (bd. 1988-90), Berkeley Booster (bd. 1986-90); awards: youth leadership NAACP 1965, outstanding pub. adminstr., chapter svc., and marks of excellence Nat. Forum. Black Pub. Adminstrs. (1975, 86, 87); Democrat; Baptist; rec: basketball, equestrian, reading, writing.

BOGGS, DAVID ALLEN, transit executive; b. Apr. 24, 1943, Glendale; s. L. Wade and Lillian C. (Clarry) B.; m. Peggy, June 29, 1963; children: Debbie b. 1965, Christy b. 1969, Ryan b. 1973; edn: AA, Citrus Coll., 1973; BA, Evergreen State Coll., 1974. Career: asst. cashier/ops. ofcr. Bank of Am., Palm Springs 1963-66; ops. analyst Seattle First National Bank, Seattle 1966-68; supvg. acct. Wash. State Dept. Hwys., Olympia 1968-74; mgr. of admin. Wash. State Ferry System, Seattle 1974-77; finance dir./ asst. to the exec. dir. Seattle Metro, 1977-80; finance dir./asst. exec. dir. Houston Metropolitan Transit Auth., Houston 1980-83; gen. mgr. Reg. Transit Dist., Sacramento 1983-88; gen. mgr. Sacramento Municipal Utility Dist., 1988-90; utility and gen. mgmt. cons., 1990-91; dir. transit ops. Laidlaw Transit Mid-Pacific Region, 1991-; mem: bd. dirs. Foundation Health Corp., Sacto. 1990-, Sacto. Safety Council 1986-, United Way 1986-, Chamber of Commerce 1986-1988, HIS Farm 1986-89; advy. bd. USC/Sacto. Pub. Affairs Ctr. 1986-89; active in Scouting (1950s-),

Golden Empire Council BSA (pres. 1991), editorial bd. Calif. Executive 1987-89; awards: Masters fellowship Fed. Hwy. Adminstrn., Seattle 1977, Silver Beaver BSA, Sacto. 1986; mem. Rotary Club Sacto.; Methodist (fin. chmn., bd. 1988-90); rec: collect military medals, square dance, spl. interest in personal orgn. & time mgmt. Res: 9350 Oak Dr Orangevale 95662 Ofc: Laidlaw Transit Inc. 1001 Galaxy Way Ste 406 Concord 94524

BOHN, ROBERT HERBERT, lawyer; b. Sept. 2, 1935, Austin, Tx.; s. Herbert and Alice (Heinen) B.; m. Gay, June 4, 1957; children: Rebecca b. 1958, Katherine b. 1965, Robert, Jr. b. 1968; edn: BBA, Univ. Texas, 1957, LLB. 1963. Career: tax law editor Commerce Clearing House Inc., San Francisco 1964-65; atty., ptnr. The Boccardo Law Firm, San Jose 1965-87, ptnr. Law Firm of Alexander & Bohn, 1987-91; Bohn, Bennion & Niland, 1992-; judge pro tem Superior Ct. Santa Clara Co.; lectr. Calif. Contg. Edn. of the Bar; arbitrator Am. Arbitration Assn.; Am. Bd. of Trial Advocates; Nat. Board of Trial Advocates; listed Who's Who in Am. Law; mem: Calif. Trial Lawyers Assn., Assn. of Trial Lawyers of Am., Calif. State Bar Assn., Santa Clara Co. Bar Assn., Commonwealth Club, Phi Gamma Delta, Churchill Club, World Forum; mil: capt. USAF 1958-61; First Baptist Ch. of Los Altos. Res: 14124 Pike Rd Saratoga 95070 Ofc: 50 W San Fernando St Ste 1020 San Jose 95113

BOLAND, PAULA L., assemblywoman , State of Calif.; b. Jan. 17, 1940, Oyster Bay, N.Y.; d. Pellegrino and Joannina (Stellaborte) Mazzarelli; m. Henry Wroe, div. 1973; m. Lloyd E. Boland, Jr., Aug. 13, 1976; children: Craig Wroe b. 1958, Maryssa Lamb b. 1959, Lloyd E. Boland III. Career: broker/owner, G.H. Realty Corp., Granada Hills, 1980-90; assemblywoman, 38th A.D., Calif. State Assembly, Granada Hills, 1990-; awards: Comm. & Political Vol. of Year, Calif. Republican Assn., 1979; Citizen of Year, Granada Hills C.of C., 1986; Woman Pioneer of Year, City of L.A., 1989; listed Who's Who in Calif., 1988; fellow mem., S.F. Valley Bd. of Realtors, 1973-; fellow mem., Calif. Assn. of Realtors, 1973-; pres., Granada Hills C.of C., 1979-81; founding dir., Bank of Granada Hills, 1983-93; pres., Granada Hills Comm. Hosp. Found., 1984-88; L.A. County delegate, Calif. Republican Party, 1974-; commr., Consumer Affairs, L.A. County, 1980-84; commr., LAFCO, L.A. County, 1985-90; Republican; Catholic. Ofc: 10727 White Oak Ave. Ste. 124 Granada Hills 91344

BOLDREY, EDWIN EASTLAND, physician, retinal surgeon; b. Dec. 8, 1941, San Francisco; s. Edwin Barkley M.D. and Helen Burns (Eastland) B.; m. Catherine Oliphant, Oct. 20, 1973; children: Jennifer Elizabeth b. 1981, Melissa Jeanne b. 1984; edn: BA w.hons., DePauw Univ. 1963; MD, Northwestern Univ. 1967; lic. physician Bd. Med. Examiners Calif. 1968. Career: intern King Co. Hosp., Seattle, Wash. 1967-68; gen. surgery resident Univ. Minn., Mpls. 1968-69; resident ophthalmology UCSF 1971-74; fellow diseases and surgery of retina and vitreous Wash. Univ., St. Louis, Mo. 1974-75; retinal surgeon Palo Alto Med. Clinic 1975-91, chmn. dept. ophthalmology 1990-91; clinical instr. Stanford Univ. 1975-79, clin. asst. prof. 1979-87, clin. assoc. prof. 1987-; attdg. physician VA Hosp. Palo Alto 1975-76, cons. physician 1976-; awards: UCSF Asbury 1973, Heed Ophthalmic Found. fellowship 1974-75, Honor award Am. Acad. of Ophthalmology 1989; mem: Western Retina Study Club (charter mem.; exec. secty., treas. 1983-), Am. Acad. Ophthalmology, Vitreous Soc. (charter mem.), Retina Soc., Peninsula Eye Soc. (secty., treas. 1985-86, v.p. 1986-87, pres. 1987-88), A.C.S., AMA, CMA, Santa Clara Co. Med. Soc.; 25+ articles pub. in sci. jours. (1966-); mil: lt. cmdr. USNR 1969-71; rec: skiing, hiking. Ofc: 525 South Dr Mountain View 94040

BOLEN, JOHN E., art dealer; b. Aug. 27, 1953, Fort Gordon, Ga.; s. James L., Sr. and Peggy J. (Sandstrom) B.; m. Lynne N. Uyeda, July 25, 1976; children: James b. 1979, Kate b. 1982, Claire b. 1988, Paul b. 1992; edn: BA, UCLA, 1975. Career: pres. Bolen Gallery, Inc. Santa Monica 1978-84; owner, pub. Bolen Publishing, Los Angeles 1981-84; art dealer Bolen Fine Arts, Huntington Beach 1984-. Ofc: Bolen Fine Arts PO Box 5654 Huntington Beach 92615-5654

BOLEN, LYNNE N., art dealer, consultant; b. Feb. 19, 1954, San Diego; d. Leon R. and Maria N. (Ishida) Uyeda; m. John E. Bolen, July 25, 1976; children: James b. 1979, Kate b. 1982, Claire b. 1988, Paul b. 1992; edn: BA, UCLA, 1976. Career: v.p. Bolen Gallery, Inc. Santa Monica 1978-84; owner/pub. Bolen Pub., L.A. 1981-84; mgr. Carrington Garrett, Irvine 1984-88; art dealer Bolen Fine Arts, Huntington Beach 1984-, consultant, 1988-. Ofc: Bolen Fine Arts PO Box 5654 Huntington Beach 92615-5654

BOLTON, DEBORAH LEE, clinical nurse specialist, consultant, nursing school educator; b. May 28, 1951, Oakland; d. Raymond N. Bolton and Shirley Peters; edn: AA, Diablo Valley Jr. Coll. 1971; BS, UC San Francisco 1975; grad. sch. of nursing, UCLA 1981. Career: clinical nurse III, IV, UCLA Medical Ctr. 1975-82; CNS-hematology/oncology Huntington Meml. Hosp., Pasadena 1981-; assoc. clin. prof. UCLA grad. sch. of nursing 1985-; assoc. clin. prof. Calif. State Los Angeles 1989-; cons: Bolton Law, Inc., Walnut Creek 1984-, MedLaw, Inc., L.A. 1986-; v.p. Health Communications Found. 1979-82, cons. 1982-85; mem: Greater L.A. Oncology Nursing Soc. (newsletter ed. 1987-92), Calif. Connections, The Wellness Community (exec. pres. 1988-90, bd. dirs. 1988-93), Am. Cancer Soc. (com. mem. 1987-88); author articles for profl. jours.

BONDOC, NICHOLAS ROMMEL, JR., lawyer; b. June 23, 1938, Pomona; s. Nicholas Rommel and Gladys Sue (Buckner) B.; m. Alberta Young, Dec. 13, 1967; children: Daphne, b. 1961, Patience, b. 1970, Margaret, b. 1972, Nicholas, b. 1976; edn: BA, Stanford Univ. 1960, JD, 1963; admitted to practice 1964. Career: assoc. Melvin Belli, San Francisco 1964-66; assoc. Vincent Hallinan, San Francisco 1966-69; sole practitioner, San Francisco 1969-; spec. criminal law 1973-; mem: Phi Beta Kappa; No. Calif. Criminal Trial Lawyers Assn. (pres. 1978-79); San Francisco Bar Assn. (Judiciary Com. 1982-85); singer: Sally Stanford's Valhalla Inn, Sausalito 1977-82; Democrat; Wesleyan. Res: 509 Canyon Rd., Novato 94947 Ofc: 899 Ellis, San Francisco 94109

BORGES, CARLOS R., professor of mathematics; b. Feb. 17, 1939, Sao Miguel, Azores, naturalized U.S. citizen 1965; s. Jose Jacinto Rego and Maria (Rego) Borges; m. Margaret Freitas, Jan. 30, 1958; children: Mary Lou b. 1960, Carlos b. 1961, Michael b. 1962; edn: BS in math., Humboldt State Coll., Arcata 1960; MS in math., Univ. Wash., Seattle 1962, PhD in math., 1964. Career: asst. prof. Univ. of Nevada, Reno 1964-65; asst. prof. Univ. Calif., Davis 1965-68, assoc. prof. 1968-72, full prof. math. 1972-; awards: Fulbright-Hayes, Univ. Columbia, Portugal 1972; Republican; R.Cath.; rec: tennis. Res: 921 Fordham Dr Davis 95616 Ofc: Dept. Math. Univ. California, Davis 95616

BORGES, DAVID JOSEPH, lawyer; b. May 10, 1955, Tulare; s. Joseph R., Jr. and Rosemary (Rogers) B.; children: David J., Jr. b. 1981, Derek J. b. 1983, Dylan J. b. 1985, Daniel J. b. 1987; edn: BA (magna cum laude), CSU Northridge, 1977; JD (magna cum laude), USC, 1980; admitted bar: Calif. 1980, US Dist. Ct. ea. dist. Calif. 1980, US Supreme Ct. 1986; cert. splst. in family law 1985-. Career: atty., assoc. Stringham, Rogers & Graves, Tulare 1980-83, ptnr. 1983-86; pres. David J. Borges, A Law Corp., Visalia 1985-; honors: Phi Alpha Theta, Pi Gamma Mu, USC Scholar 1977-80; mem: ABA, Calif. Bar Assn., Assn. of Trial Lawyers of Am., Calif. Trial Lawyers Assn., Tulare Co. Bar Assn. (dir. 1982-89), Tulare Co. Trial Lawyers (dir. 1982-90), Kings Co. Bar Assn., Calif. Orgn. of Small Bar Assn., Stockton (dir. 1987-); Republican (life mem. Rep. Nat. Com. 1980-, life mem. Rep. Nat. Lawyers Assn. 1985-); life mem. Shotokan Karate of Am. 1973-. Ofc: David J. Borges, ALC, 3330 W Mineral King Ste H Visalia 93291-5762

BORNEMAN, JOHN PAUL (JAY), pharmaceutical executive, writer; b. Oct. 18, 1958, Darby, Pa.; s. John A., III and Ann E. (Conway) B.; m. Anne Marie Albert, July 18, 1980; children: Elizabeth b. 1983; edn: BS in chem., St. Joseph's Univ. 1980, MS chem. 1983, MBA fin. 1987. Career: v.p. Boiron Borneman, Norwood, Pa. 1980-86; dir. mktg. Standard Homeopathic Co., Los Angeles 1986-88, vice pres. 1988-; bd. dirs. Nat. Ctr. for Homeopathy, W.D.C. 1986-; editor Homeopathic Pharmacopoeia of U.S., W.D.C. 1988-; chmn. Council on Homeopathic Edn., W.D.C. 1988-; columnist Resonance Mag., 1986-; mem. Am. Assn. of Homeopathic Pharmacists (chmn. legal & regulatory affairs 1986-), Am. Chem. Soc., Am. Pharmaceutical Assn., Nat. Assn. of Chain Drug Stores, Sigma Xi.

BOROWSKY, PHILIP, lawyer; b. Oct. 9, 1946, Phila.; s. Joshua and Gertrude (Nicholson) Borowsky; m. Judith Goldwasser, Sept. 5, 1970; children: Miriam, b. 1971, Manuel, b. 1975, Nora, b. 1981; edn: BA, UCLA 1967, JD, Univ. of S.F. Law Sch. 1973. Career: atty. law firm Cartwright, Slobodin, Bokelman, Borowsky, Wartnick, Moore & Harris, Inc., San Francisco 1973-, ptnr. 1978-, pres. 1988-; arbitrator Am. Arbitration Assn., mem. Arbitration Panel S.F. Superior Ct.; adj. faculty Hastings Las Sch. 1981-82; spkr. for Practising Law Inst.; mem. Calif. Trial Lawyers Assn. (legis. com.); McAuliffe Hon. Soc. U.S.F. Law Sch.; contbr. law revs.; publ: co-author, Unjust Dismissal; bd. of Editorial Consultants of Bad Faith Law Update; mil: spec.4th cl. US Army, Army Commendn. Medal; Democrat; Jewish; rec: sports. Ofc: 101 California St 26th Flr San Francisco 94111

BORRELL, JERRY, magazine editor; b. May 23, 1952, El Paso, Tx.; s. Gerald and Harriet B.; edn: BA, Univ. Miami 1976; MS, Catholic Univ. Wash. D.C. 1981. Career: researcher Library of Congress, Wash. D.C. 1976-79; co-editor Electronic Publishing Review, Oxford, England 1979-80; sr. editor Computer Graphics World, San Francisco 1980-81; ed. in chief Digital Design, Boston, Mass. 1981-83; sr. ed. Mini Micro Systems 1983-85; ed. in chief Macworld, San Francisco 1985-92; pres., Sumeria 1992-;mem: IEEE, ACM, Soc. Profl. Journalists. Res: 2000 Broadway #712 San Francisco 94115 Ofc: 501 2d St Ste 600 San Francisco 94107

BOSSEN, DAVID AUGUST, manufacturing company president; b. Jan. 9, 1927, Clinton, Ia.; m. Doris Stephens, Sept. 1, 1950; children: Alison, Amy, Julie, Laura; edn: US Naval Acad., Annapolis 1946-49; BS, M.I.T., 1951. Career: indsl. engr. Alcoa, Davenport, Ia., 1951; v.p./gen. mgr. Industrial Nucleonics, Columbus, Oh., 1951-67; founder, pres. and c.e.o. Measurex Corp., Cupertino, 1968-; mem. bd. dirs. Univ. of Maine Pulp & Paper Found., N.C. State Univ. Pulp & Paper Found., Paper Technology Found. We. Mich. Univ. (v.p.); mem. M.I.T. Corporation Devel. Com.; mem. Santa Clara County Mfg. Group (dir.), Bay Area Council (exec. com.), Japan/Western States Assn. (exec. com.); patentee: several in process control; mil: USMC 1945-46. Ofc: Measurex Corp. One Results Way Cupertino 95014

BOST, THOMAS GLEN, lawyer; b. July 13, 1942, Oklahoma City, Okla.; s. Burl J. and Lorene (Croka) B.; m. Sheila Kay Pettigrew, Aug. 27, 1966; children: Amy b. 1970, Stephen Luke b. 1974, Emily b. 1976, Paul b. 1980; edn: BS (summa cum laude) Abilene Christian Univ., 1964; JD, Vanderbilt Univ. Sch. of Law, 1967. Career: instr. David Lipscomb Coll., Nashville, Tenn. 1967; asst. prof. of law Vanderbilt Univ. Sch. of Law, 1967-68; atty. Latham & Watkins, Los Angeles 1968-; honors: Vanderbilt Univ. Sch. of Law Founder's Medal, Order of the Coif 1967; chmn. bd. of regents Pepperdine Univ., also mem. exec., religious stds. coms., and bd. visitors Sch. of Law; mem: Am. Bar Assn. (tax. sect., chair com. on stds. of tax practice 1988-90); clubs: California (L.A.), The Beach (L.A.); State Bar of Calif., L.A. County Bar Assn. (1968-, taxation sect. 1981-82); publs: articles on taxation in Vanderbilt Law Rev., NYU Inst. on Fed. Taxation, Major Tax Planning (USC), Calif. Lawyer; Republican; Culver-Palms Ch. of Christ; rec: reading, hiking. Ofc: Latham & Watkins, 633 W Fifth St Ste 4000 Los Angeles 90071-2007

BOSTIC, BYRON MICHAEL, electronic manufacturers' representative; b. Oct. 17, 1952, Royal Oak, Mich.; s. Clyde Wm. and Barbara Joanne (Kinshella) B.; m. 2d. Melanie D. Lavell, Mar. 15, 1984; children: Byron, II b. 1975, Vanessa b. 1977; edn: electronic engr. E.I.T., Detroit, Mich. 1974; lic. R.E. agt. Calif. Career: quality control tech. Allen Bradley, Ann Arbor, Mich. 1972-73; computer engr. Litton A.B.S., Long Beach 1974-76; q.c. engr. Rockwell Internat., Newport Beach 1977-79; video engr. J.V.C. Corp., Compton 1979-81; sales engr. Sencore Corp., 1981-82; Stanford Applied Engring., 1982-83; sales mgr. So. Calif., Basic Systems Corp., 1983-85; sales engr. Lambda Power Supplies, 1985-86; owner Dynamic Planning Consultants, So. Calif., 1983-, ptnr. West Coast Reps, Western USA, 1986-; mem. Lancaster C.of C.; realtor assoc. Century 21 LWL Realtors, Granada Hills 1988-89, Century 21 Tabor Realtors, 1989-90; High-Speed Data Transmission - HYBRICON, Real-Time Transfers - C.E.S., Geneva, Switz. 1990; recipient corporate awards for tech. and sales excellence Litton 1974, Rockwell 1977, Sencore 1981, image processing Datacube, Peabody, Mass. 1986, live multiprocessing Ironics, Ithaca, N.Y. 1987; VMEBUS+ Force Computers, Campbell 1990; complete image processing, Imaging Technology 1991; vectorizing code on: 860 Sky Computers, Chelmsford, Mass. 1992; Fiber-optic data distbn. interface Interphase, Dallas, Tx. 1992; multiprocessing VME /SUN /PC /Futurebus- Elma, Fremont 1992; real-time data acquisition interfaces- Acromag, Wixom, Mi. (1992); transducers/ strain gages/ load cells/ and accelerometers, Kyowa/Soltec, San Fernando 1992; Songwriter award, So. Calif. Songwriters Guild 1979, winner Battle of the Bands, Gazarri's, Hollywood 1980; organic fruit tree & vegetable rancher; guitar player/ singer/ songwriter, author song and lyrics: Sweet Southern Gal (1979), Joy of Life (1979), Flying Down the Highway Again (1981), I Just Want to Rock N' Roll (1982); Democrat; rec: pets. Ofc: 441 E Whittier Blvd Ste 3A La Habra 90631 Ph: 310/690-9960 FAX 310/697-6167

BOUCHARD, PAUL EUGENE, artist; b. Sept. 26, 1946, Providence, R.I.; s. Paul Marcel and Anna Thersa (Dullea) B.; m. Ann Marie Jones, Nov. 18, 1971, div. 1976; 1 son, Michael Paul; edn: att. Chouinard Art Inst. 1964, El Camino Coll., Torrance 1976; BFA, CSU Long Beach, 1978. Career: E-3, US Navy, 1967-68; recipient award for contbn. to the arts City of Torrance 1985; art in permanent collections: Grants Pass (OR) Mus. of Art, El Camino Coll., Angeles Gate Cultural Ctr. (San Pedro), Art Mus. (CSULB), Municipal Art Collection (Bev. Hills), Sanctuario de Chimayo (NM), Maturango Mus. (Ridgecrest, CA), Coos Art Mus. (Coos Bay, OR), Constnl. Rights Found. (L.A.), Univ. South Dakota, US Dept. of State Art in Embassies Pgm., Combined Forces Mus. of Art, Milperra, NSW Australia; solo exhibitions include: Tylan Intl. Corp. Ofcs. (Carson), Joslyn Ctr. for Arts (Torrance) 1982; Cassman Group (Torrance), El Camino Coll., 1984; Rogue Coll. (Grants Pass, OR) 1987; Maturango Mus., Richmond (CA) Art Ctr., 1988; Franklin Furnace Mus. (NYC) 1988/9; Chabot Coll., Steve Bush Exh. Room (NYC), 1989; Univ. S.D. 1991, Brand Library Art Gals. (Glendale, CA) 1992; numerous group exh. incl. The Australian Nat. Gallery. Res: 33140 Baldwin Blvd Lake Elsinore 92530 Ph: 714/678-7384

BOURGAIZE, LINDA HARPER, special education administrator; b. May 1, 1947, Tacoma, Wash.; d. Donald William and Helen (Harper) Bourgaize; son, Matthew b. 1977; edn: BA, San Jose St. Univ. 1971; MS, 1973. Career: psychologist Whisman Sch. Dist., Mountain View 1973; psychologist, coordinator, dir. Mount Pleasant Sch. Dist., San Jose 1973-81; dir. San Benito/Santa Cruz Counties Spl. Edn. Local Plan Area (SELPA), Aptos 1981-91; pvt. educational cons. 1991-93; dir. Washington Township SELPA; past chair La Selva Beach Recreation Dist.; appt. Calif. St. Dept. Edn. Spl. Edn. Funding Model Task Force 1986-88; mem. Interagy. Task Force, Assemblyman Sam Farr 1984-90; steering com. Coalition for Adequate Funding for Disabled Children, 1987-; cons. Calif. State Dept. Edn. 1975-; awards: La Selva Beach Recreation Dist. SCOPE (1986); mem: Phi Delta Kappa, Calif. SELPA Adminstrs. (chair 1989-90, legislative/finance chair 1991-), Assn. Calif. Sch. Adminstrs. (chair spl. edn. conf. 1986, 87), Council for Exceptional Children-Calif. Assn. of Sch. Bus. Officials, Am. Assn. Sch. Adminstrs., Assn. Supervision & Curriculum Devel., PEO, League Women Voters; Am. Assn. of Univ. Women; Democrat; rec: needlework, travel, politics. Res: 27 Altivo Ave La Selva Beach 95076

BOWER, KATHLEEN ANN, communications and marketing professional; b. Feb. 10, 1962, Stanford, Calif.; d. E. George and Joan Martine (Sorensen) Bower; edn: BS in bus. adminstrn./mktg., San Jose St. Univ. 1984. Career: editl. splst. Regis McKenna Inc., Palo Alto 1980-82; dir. mktg. InterSight Comms. Inc., Los Gatos 1982-84; account exec. Rudolph Design Inc., Santa Cruz 1985; promotional programs mgr. 3Com Corp., Santa Clara 1986-88; group mktg. comms. mgr. Software Pub. Corp., Santa Clara 1988-92;dir. mktg. commn. Global Village Communications, Inc., Mountain View 1993-; columnist San Jose FILM CLIPS Newsletter, San Jose 1982-84; editor PARTNERS Newsletter, Santa Clara 1986-87; co-founder, CONNECT, The Jour. of Computer Networking 1987; honors: ballet Royal Acad. Dance 1968; mem: Am. Mktg. Assn., Peninsula Women in Advt., Pub. Rels. Soc. Am., San Jose Film Commn., S.F. Film & Video Commn., Profl. Media Network (bd. dirs. 1985-86), Beta Gamma Sigma. Res: 509 26th Ave Santa Cruz 95062 Ofc: Global Village Communications, Inc. 685 E. Middlefield Rd Mountain View 94043

BOWLING, LANCE CHRISTOPHER, recording and publishing executive; b. May 17, 1948, San Pedro; s. Dan Parker and Sylvia Lois (Van Devander) B.; edn: BA polit. sci. and history, Pepperdine Univ., 1966-70, MPA, 1973. Career: owner, founder Cambria Records and Pub., Palos Verdes 1972-; editor: Joseph Wagner: A Retrospective of Composer-Conductor 1900-1974 (1976), Hazards Pavilion, Jour. of Soc. for Preservation of So. California Musical Heritage 1985-; author: Eugene Hemmer: Composer-Pianist (1983); producer 50+ Am. Classical records including works by Charles W. Cadman, Madeleine Dring, Mary Carr Moore, John Crown, Ed Bland, Elinor Remick Warren, Florence Price and Erich Wolfgang Korngold; also produced classical music for radio stations KPFK, KFAC, NPR and APR; mem: ASCAP, Assn. Recorded Sound Collections, Music Library Assn., Sonneck Soc., The Soc. for the Preservation of Film Music (bd. dirs. 1991-); clubs: Variety Arts (L.A.), Musical Arts (Long Beach); civic: United Way L.A. (allocation com. region V 1978-85); rec: collect early Calif. books and ephemera, restore 78-RPM recordings, antique autos. Res: 2625 Colt Rd Rancho Palos Verdes 90274 Ofc: Cambria Records and Pub. PO Box 374 Lomita 90717

BOWMAN, LESLIE GREENE, curator; b. Nov. 9, 1956, Springfield, Ohio; d. Robert H. and Phyllis Jane (Weikart) Greene; m. Bradley Guy Bowman, Oct. 10, 1981, div. Feb. 1991; edn: BA (summa cum laude) art hist., Miami Univ., Oh. 1978; MA, Winterthur Pgm. in Early Am. Culture, Henry Francis du Pont Winterthur Mus. /Univ. Dela., 1980. Career: editl. asst., The Papers of Frederick Law Olmsted, W.D.C. 1979-80; curatorial intern Dela. Art Mus. 1980; curatl. asst. decorative arts L.A. Co. Mus. of Art 1980-81, asst. curator 1981-84, assoc. curator 1984-88, curator and dept. hd. decorative arts, 1989-; adj. prof. Sch. Fine Arts, USC, 1988-, instr. design pgms., UCLA Ext., 1988-; frequent lectr. univs., art symposiums; mem. bd. dirs. UCLA Internat. Student Ctr., Decorative Arts Study Ctr., San Juan Capistrano; awards: Charles F. Montgomery Award of Decorative Arts Soc./ Soc. of Architectural Historians, Florence J. Gould Found. seminar scholar at Fontainebleau (10-89); listed Who's Who in West 1991, Who's Who in Am. Women 1991-92, World Who's Who of Women (11th edit.); exhibitions: "Am. Arts & Crafts: Virtue in Design," 1990 (author exh. catalogue); (co-curator W. Morrison Heckscher, Met. Mus. of Art) "American Rococo, 1750-1775: Elegance in Ornament," 1992 (coauthor w/ M. Heckscher of exh. catalogue); cons. curator "Silver in the Golden State" Oakland Mus., 1986-87; installation curator "'The Art that is Life': The Arts & Crafts Movement in Am., 1875-1920" (org. by Mus. Fine Arts, Boston, expanded for L.A. Co. Mus. of Art), 1987; rec: equestrienne. Ofc: L.A. Co. Museum of Art 5905 Wilshire Blvd Los Angeles 90036

BOWYER, C. STUART, eduator, astrophysicist; b. Aug. 2, 1934, Toledo, Ohio; s. H.D. and Elizabeth (McEuen) B.; m. Jane Anne Baker, Feb. 27, 1957; children: William, Robert, Elizabeth; edn: BA, Miami Univ., OH 1956; PhD, Catholic Univ. of Am., W.D.C. 1965. Career: research physicist Naval Research Lab, W.D.C. 1959-67; prof. Catholic Univ. of Am., 1965-67; prof. Univ. Calif., Berkeley 1967-, dir. Ctr. for Extreme Ultraviolet Astrophysics, UCB 1989-; pres. Berkeley Photonics Inc., Orinda 1986-; cons. NASA 1970-, NSF 1970-, Israel Space Agy. 1989-; awards: Vis. Prof. Sci. Research Council, England 1973, Miller Found. Fellow Univ. Calif. Berkeley 1978, Humbolt Prize Prof., Ger. 1982, Fulbright Prof. 1983, Centre Nat. d'Etudes Spatiales Prof., Fr. 1989, Guggenheim Fellow 1992; mem: Am. Inst. of Aeronautics & Astronautics, Internat. Astronomical Union 1970-, Am. Astronomical Soc. 1965-, Am. Geophysical Union 1965-, Astronomical Soc. of Pacific 1980-, Internat. Acad. Astronautics 1982-; author sev. patents in space instrumentation, 400+ astrophysics/geophysics articles (1965-), editor 2 conf. proceedings. Ofc: Center for Extreme Ultraviolet Astrophysics, Univ. of California, Berkeley 94720

BOXER, BARBARA, U.S. senator; b. Nov. 11, 1940, Brooklyn, N.Y.; d. Ira and Sophie (Silvershein) Levy; m. Stewart Boxer, 1962; children: Doug, Nicole; edn: BA, Brooklyn Coll. 1962. Career: stockbroker, N.Y.C. 1962-65; journalist, assoc. editor Pacific Sun 1972-74; congl. aide to rep. 5th Congl. Dist. San Francisco 1974-76; mem. Marin County Bd. Suprs., San Rafael 1976-82, pres., 1980-81; mem. 98th-102d Congresses from 6th Calif. dist., mem. armed services com., select com. children, youth and families; majority whip at large, co-chair

Mil. Reform Caucus, chair subcom. on govt. activities and transp. of house govt. ops. com. 1990-92; mem. U.S. Senate, Wash. DC 1993-; mem. Bay Area Air Quality Mgmt. Bd., S.F. 1977-82, pres., 1979-81; bd. dirs. Golden Gate Bridge Hwy. and Transport. Dist., S.F. 1978-82; founding mem. Marin Nat. Women's Polit. Caucus, Marin Community Video; pres. Dem. New Mems. Caucus 1983; awards: Open Govt. award Common Cause 1980, Rep. of Yr. award Nat. Multiple Sclerosis Soc. 1990, Margaret Sanger award Planned Parenthood 1990; Jewish. Ofc: 307 Cannon House Office Bldg Washington DC 20515

BOYD, ROBERT GIDDINGS, JR., mental health agency executive; b. March 16, 1940, San Juan, P.R.; s. Robert Giddings and Laura Jean (Stephenson) B.; m. Denise Ann Ryll, Dec. 10, 1978; edn: BA, William and Mary Coll., 1962; George Washington Univ., 1966. Career: budget mgr. Goodbody & Co., N.Y.C. 1968-70; bus. mgr. Westminster Sch., Simsbury, Conn. 1970-76; gen. mgr., ptnr. F&R Enterprises Inc., Scottsdale, Ariz. 1976-78; bus. mgr. Orme Sch., Mayer, Ariz. 1978-81; mng. dir. San Diego Symphony Orch. Assn. 1981-84; v.p. San Diego Center for Children 1985-; mem. Am. Symphony Assn., Am. Mgmt. Assn., Rotary Internat.; mil: 1st lt. AUS 1962-64; Prot.; rec: tennis, swimming, hiking. Ofc: San Diego Center for Children 3002 Armstron St San Diego 92111

BOYKIN, RAYMOND FRANCIS, educator; b. Nov. 18, 1953, Santa Monica; s. Francis Raymond and Doris Elaine (Davis) B.; m. Shelley Lynne Ladd, July 30, 1977; children: Jennifer b. 1979, Whitney b. 1981; edn: BA, CSU Fullerton, 1979; MS, San Diego St. Univ., 1976; PhD, St. Louis Univ., Mo. 1986. Career: research scientist Rockwell Internat., Richland, Wa. 1976-80; mgmt. scientist Monsanto, St. Louis, Mo. 1980-86; prof. CSU Chico 1986-; senior cons. PLG, Inc. Newport Beach 1986-; v.chmn. bd. Makaira Ministries, La Mirada 1991-; awards: "innovator" Monsanto 1982, achiev. TIMS, Balt., Md. 1984, CSU Chico: merit performance 1987, 89, Pres.'s achiev. award 1988, outstanding faculty 1988; mem. Soc. for Risk Analysis (treas. 1989-); author: Test Bank - Production Mgmt. (1989, 92), 20+ pub. articles (1979-); Democrat; Christian; rec: basketball, volleyball, golf. Res: 862 Westmont Dr Chico 95926 Ofc: California State University, Chico 95929

BOYLAN, RICHARD JOHN, psychologist; b. Oct. 15, 1939, Hollywood; s. John Alfred and Rowena Margaret (Devine) B.; m. Charnette Marie Blackburn, Oct. 26, 1968 (div. 1984); m. 2d. Judith Lee Sanders, Nov. 21, 1987; children: Christopher b. 1972, Jennifer b. 1973, Stephanie b. 1975; edn: BA, St. John's Coll. 1961; MS edn., Fordham Univ. 1966; MSW, UC Berkeley 1971; PhD, UC Davis 1984; lic. clin. psychologist 1987. Career: supervising counselor S. Campus Comm. Ministry, Berkeley 1970-71; chief, forensic unit Marin Co. Mental Health Dept., San Rafael 1971-77; dir. Calaveras Co. Mental Health Alcohol/Drug Dept., San Andreas 1977-85; sr. mental health counselor Sacto. Co. Mental Health Center, Sacto. 1986-87; lectr. CSU, Sacto. 1985-; regional dir. U.S. Behavioral Health 1988-89; instr., coordinator Nat. Univ., Sacto. 1985-86; lectr. Sierra Comm. Coll., Rocklin 1986-87; UC Davis 1986; preceptor in psychology UC Davis Sch. Medicine 1987-88; awards: Calif. St. Undergrad. scholarship 1958, Calif. St. Grad. scholarship 1969, Who's Who in West, UC Davis Exptl. Station grant 1983, AARP Davis chpt. scholarship 1984; mem: Am. Psychological Assn., Calif. St. Psychological Assn.., Sacto. Soc. Profl. Psychologists, Angels Camp (pres. bd. edn. 1981-84), Sacramentans for Safe Energy, Natural Resources Defense Council, Marin Mun. Water Dist.; author: articles, documents and conf. papers pub. 1984-88; Democrat; Native Am. Taoist; rec: snorkeling, photography, backpacking. Res: 6724 Trudy Way Sacramento 95831 Ofc: Richard Boylan, PhD 3009 O Street Ste. 3 Sacramento 95816

BRADFORD, DAVID PAUL, state court judicial assistant; b. Mar. 23, 1955, Lynwood; s. William H. Johnson and Barbara O'Leary; edn: AA, Citrus Coll., 1975; BA, UCLA, 1978. Career: residence dep. UC Los Angeles, 1978-85; judicial asst. L.A. Co. Superior Ct., Los Angeles 1988-; pres. Bradford & Assocs., L.A. 1985-; pres. AFSME Local 575, L.A. 1992; awards: Chancellor's marshal UCLA 1978, cert. of recogn. Domestic Violence Council L.A. Co. 1990; mem. NY Acad. Scis.; civic: Citizenship Protection Fund, Santa Monica (1991-); Presbyterian; rec: music, movies, numismatics. Ofc: L.A. Superior Ct. 111 N Hill St D-8 Rm 245 Los Angeles 90012

BRADLEY, DONALD DEWAYNE, real estate investor, developer; b. Apr. 12, 1965, San Bernardino; s. Donald Gene and Bonie Jean (Ladd) B.; m. Lynne Christine Chandler, Aug. 7, 1988; edn: dipl. San Gorgonio H.S., San Bernardino. Career: owner/prin. Bradley Investments, San Bernardino 1984-; Bradley Constrn. & Devel., San Bernardino 1988-; mem: Nat. Assn. Realtors, Calif. Realtors Assn., Building Trades Assn., Calif. Assn. Gen. Contractors & Devel., Calif. Apt. Owners Assn., San Bdo. Bd. Realtors, Elks BPOE 836, San Bdo.; Republican; Baptist; rec: numismatics, restoration antique autos. Res: 3056 Golden Ave San Bernardino 92404

BRADLEY, ELIOT E., manufacturing company executive, van conversion specialist; b. Oct. 10, 1915, Fresno; s. Eliot E. and Emma Louise (Hannig) B.; m. Grace Ann Janzen, Jan. 24, 1948 (div. 1978); children: Patricia b. 1949, Craig b. 1950, Stephen b. 1951, Christine b. 1954; m. Virginia Linise Doern,

Sept. 24, 1978; edn: undergrad. UC Berkeley 1934-35; BS in bus. adm., USC, 1939. Career: credit ofcr. Bradley Finance, Fresno 1939-41; insp. Lockheed Aircraft, Burbank 1941-43; v.p. Morey-Bradley Aircraft Products, Burbank 1952-62; mfr. fiberglass roofs (for vans) Glasscrafters div. Bradley Controls Inc., Van Nuys 1962-, and c.e.o. Van De Camper div., 1962-; fiberglass roofs mfd. provide headroom up to 6'1-1/2', van conversions can include l.r., d.r., bdrm., kitchen, & bath w/shower, spl. conversions incl. outfitting mobile dog-grooming vans, and other mobile bus. vans; mem. Sigma Chi frat., Fresno C.of C., 20/30 Club, Optimists Club Burbank; mil: cpl. USAAF 1943-46, Link Trainer instr. Air - Sea Rescue; Republican; Episcopalian; rec: photog., stock trading. Res: 18900 Kinzie St Northridge 91324 Ofc: Van De Camper Div. Bradley Controls, Inc. 7801 Noble Ave Van Nuys 91405

BRADLEY, KENNETH DANIEL, insurance consultant; b. Feb. 13, 1949, Ft. Clayton, Panama C.Z.; s. William Perry and Dorothy (Gill) B.; m. Millajean Miller, Nov. 21, 1987; 1 son, Ian Perry b. 1992; edn: BS in B.A., Seton Hall Univ., South Orange, N.J. 1971; desig: CPCU. Career: rating analyst N.C.C.I., Lyndhurst, N.J. 1971-73; casualty underwriter Central Mutual Ins. Co., N.Y.C. 1973-75; v.p. American Home Assurance, N.Y.C. and Los Angeles, 1975-87; exec. v.p. Alliance Insurance Group, Burbank 1987-92; insurance cons. 1992-; mem. N.A.P.S.L.O. 1980-; rec: tennis, golf. Res: 4758 D La Villa Marina Marina Del Rey 90292

BRADLEY, THOMAS, former mayor; b. Dec. 29, 1917, Calvert, Tex.; s. Lee Thomas and Crenner (Hawkins) B.; m. Ethel Mae Arnold, May 4, 1941; children: Lorraine, Phyllis; edn: undergrad. UCLA 1937-40, LLB, Southwestern Univ., 1956, LLD, 1980; LLD, Brandeis Univ., Oral Roberts Univ., Pepperdine Univ., Loyola Marymount Univ., Calif. Lutheran Univ., Wilberforce Univ., 1974, Whittier Coll., 1976, Yale Univ., USC, Princeton Univ., 1979, Bus. Nat. Univ. Korea, 1979, Antioch Univ., N.C. Central Univ., 1983; PhD (hon.) Humanity Res. Ctr. Beverly Hills, 1976; admitted bar: Calif. 1956. Career: police ofcr. Los Angeles P.D., 1942-62; law practice, 1956-73; mem. Los Angeles City Council, 1963-73; mayor of Los Angeles, 1973-93; founder, dir. Bank of Fin.; bd. dirs. Nat. Urban Coalition, Nat. League Cities (pres. 1974, nat. bd.), League of Calif. Cities (pres. 1979), So. Calif. Assn. Govts. (pres. 1968-69), Nat. Assn. Regional Councils (pres. 1969-71), U.S. Conf. Mayors (advy. bd., v.ch. transp. com.); mem. Nat. Energy Advy. Council, Nat. Commn. on Productivity and Work Quality; awards: African Methodist Episcopal man of yr. 1974, Dr. Martin L. King, Jr. award 1974, Pub. Ofcl. of yr. Los Angeles Trial Lawyers Assn. 1974, CORO Found. award 1978, award of merit Nat. Council Negro Women 1978, J.F.Kennedy Fellowship award Govt. of N.Z. 1978, internat. humanitarian M.E.D.I.C. 1978, city employee of yr. All City Employees Benefits Serice Assn. 1983, Magnin award 1984; mem: L.A. Urban League, NAACP (Spingarn medal 1985), So. Calif. Conf. on Community Rels., L.A. Conf. Negro Elected Ofcls., UN Assn. Los Angeles (bd.), Kappa Alpha Psi; Democrat (Calif. Dem. Central Com., del. Dem. Nat. Mid-Term Conf. 1974, co-ch. Dem. Nat. Conv. 1976); AME (trustee). Office of Mayor City Hall Los Angeles 90012

BRADLEY, WILLIAM RANDOLPH, state legislator/civil engineer; b. Mar. 2, 1919, Loveland, Colo.; s. Wm. Homer and Irene Elizabeth (McBride) B.; m. Margaret Moose, Mar. 28, 1970; children: Billie Lee, Randy Kay; edn: BSCE, USC 1957; MA in pub. adminstrn., San Jose St. Coll. 1966; reg. civil engr., Calif. Career: asst. city engr./street supt. City of Santa Clara 1959-69; city mgr. City of Coronado 1969-72; city mgr./city engr. City of San Marcos 1972-79; civil engr./pres. Bradley & Assocs., 1979-86; elected Calif. State Assemblyman, 1982-; mem: ASCE (fellow 1984), Am. Soc. of Profl. Engrs. 1985; mil: A3/c USN 1944-46; Republican; Baptist; rec: politics. Res: 2182 Montiel Rd San Marcos 92069 Ofc: Calif. State Assembly State Capitol Sacramento 95814

BRADPIECE, THEODORE GRANT, mutual fund supervisor; b. Aug. 31, 1965, Los Angeles; s. Sidney and Naomi Grena (Silton) B.; edn: AB Freeman Sch. of Bus., Tulane Univ., 1987. Career: owner Bradpiece Advising Los Angeles 1987-; brokers' asst. Prudential-Bache, Beverly Hills 1986-88; acct. exec. Baraban Securities, Los Angeles 1988; mutual fund supr. Associated Planners Group Inc., Los Angeles 1988-; lic. NASD series 7; mem: Sierra Club, Tau Epsilon Phi Frat. (dir. 1987-, Fdn. trustee 1989-, co-chair fin. com. 1992-); Epsilon Kappa Alumni Holding Corp. (v.p. 1987-); Tulane Alumni Admissions Com. 1987-; TEP Found. (trustee 1990-); Young Adult Network (co-chmn. 1991-); Nat. Assn. Securities Dlrs. (Bd. of Arbitrators 1992-); Democrat; Jewish; rec: philately, computers, securities, sports, travel, music. Co-Chmn. Young Adults for Alumni & Friends of United Synagogue Youth. Res: 3207 Ellenda Ave Los Angeles 90034 Ofc: Associated Planners Group, Inc. 1925 Century Park East Ste 1900 Los Angeles 90067

BRAHTZ, JOHN FREDERICK PEEL, engineering, research & development planning consultant; b. Jan. 29, 1918, St. Paul, Minn.; s. John Henry August and Charlotte Beatrice (Peel) B.; m. Lise Vetter Work, May 11, 1991; edn: AB in civil engring., Stanford Univ. 1939, MSME, 1947, PhD applied mechs., 1951; reg. profl. engr. Calif. Career: structural res. engr. Consolidated Vultee Aircraft Corp, San Diego 1939-41; project engr. Northrop Aircraft Co., Hawthorne 1951-

53; assoc. prof. UC Los Angeles 1953-57; v.p. engring J.H. Pomeroy & Co., Inc., San Francisco 1957-59; dir. ops. John F. Brahtz Assoc., L.A. 1959-60; res. dept. mgr. Stanford Res. Inst. 1960-63; sr. lctr. UCLA 1963-70; cons. to White House Commn., Nat. Council on Marine Resources and Engring. 1964-68; staff cons. Navy Engring. Lab., San Diego and Port Hueneme 1963-70; cons. res. prof. Stanford Univ. 1986-, on loan by Stanford to US Navy 1986-89, completed 3-yr. investigation into feasibility of floating bases as alternative to fixed land bases overseas, and author NCEL Tech. Report re Modularized Ocean Basing System circa 2000 (R-928, Naval Civil Engring. Lab., Port Hueneme); honors: military commendation U.S. Navy 1944, elected mem. Honorary Res. Sigma Xi 1950, grad. fellowship Stanford Univ. 1946; fellow, Am. Soc. of Civil Engrs.; mem. Am. Soc. for Engring. Edn.; U.S. patent (navy sponsored) 1971; author books (pub. John Wiley & Sons): Ocean Engineering, 1968, Coastal Zone Management: Multiple Use with Conservation, 1972; ed. book series: Construction Management & Engineering, 1970-88; mil: Comdr. U.S. Navy (Ret.); rec: writing non-fiction. Res./Ofc: John F. Peel Brahtz Associates, Planning and Engineering Consultants, 2740 16th Ave Carmel 93923

BRAITHWAITE, CHARLES HENRY, JR., chemical engineering executive, forensic consultant; b. Dec. 16, 1920, Chgo.; s. Charles H., Sr. and Wilhelmina (Huth) B.; m. Bernice Hyde, Apr. 29, 1949; children: Charles III, Betty Susan; edn: AB chem., UCLA, 1941; BSE in chem. eng., Univ. Mich., 1943; MS chem., Carnegie Inst. of Tech., 1948, DSc organic chem., 1949; reg. cons. engr. Calif. Career: engr., elec. insulation devel., Westinghouse Electric, 1943-46; senior res. chemist in petroleum chemistry Shell Oil Co., 1949-51; div. dir. of res. Chlor-Alkali Div., F.M.C. Corp., 1951-57; dir. R&D Productol Co., 1957-59; founder, pres. Cal Colonial Chemsolve, 1959-87, Subsidiaries & Divs. Jack Sons Products Corp., Lee Potter Co., Nat. Testing Standards (analytical lab.); forensic consulting prin. Braithwaite Consulting, 1988-, cons. W.R. Grace Corp., U.S. Borax Corp., Piezo Products Div., Gulton Inds., Fairchild - Stratos Div., Henkel Corp., Monsanto; patentee 8 U.S. patents issued, sev. pending; contbr. articles in trade jours. Res: 11232 Tigrina Whittier 90603

BRAKENSIEK, JAY CLEMENCE, safety officer, industrial hygienist; b. Apr. 23, 1954, Troy, Mo.; s. Clemence Ernst and Juanita Geraldine (Gaylord) B.; m. Kathleen Lorraine Edmonds, July 25, 1981 (div. Aug. 1991); children: Gregory b. 1983, Matthew b. 1987; edn: BS biology, Northeast Mo. State Univ., 1977, MA biosci. edn./biology, 1981; MS indsl. hygiene, USC, 1991; Associate Safety Profl. (A.S.P.) certification, 1992, Calif. Registered Environmental Assessor, 1992. Career: pulmonary splst. Huntington Memorial Hosp., Pasadena 1979-89; safety ofcr. L.A. County Dept. Pub. Works, Alhambra 1990-; instr. biology Citrus Coll., Glendora 1984-85, life scis. Pasadena City Coll., 1985-88; awards: fellow Nat. Inst. of Occ. Health & Safety 1989-91, Citations, Who's Who Environment Registry 1992, listed Who's Who in the West 1992; mem: Am. Indsl. Hygiene Assn., Am. Conf. of Govt. Indsl. Hygienists, Am. Soc. of Safety Engrs., Pub. Agency Safety Mgmt. Assn., Calif. Safety Ofcrs. Org., USC Inst. of Safety & Systems Mgmt. (Triumvirate), USC Gen. Alumni Assn. NE Mo. State Univ. Alumni Assn.; pub. article in field (1992); Republican; Lutheran; rec: backpacking, photography, skiing, sailing, AYSO soccer. Res: 1618 E South Mayflower Ave Monrovia 91016 Ofc: L.A. County Dept. Public Works, Risk Management, 7th Fl Alhambra 91803

BRANDENBURGH, DONALD CARTER, literary agent; b. July 4, 1931, Stuart, Ia.; s. Wilbur H. and Esther Hadley (Carter) B.; m. Mary Isabelle Moore, June 5, 1953; children: Gregory b. 1955, Curtis b. 1957, Brenda b. 1965; edn: BA, William Penn Coll., Oskaloosa, Ia. 1953; MA, Whittier Coll., 1960; MDiv, Talbot Sch. of Theology, La Mirada 1970; tchg. cert. ESL, UC Riverside Ext., 1991; recorded minister, Iowa Yearly Meeting of Friends, 1956. Career: minister Friends Ch., Paton, Ia. 1955-57; minister of Christian edn. Friends Ch., Garden Grove, Ca. 1959-68; bus. adminstr. Calif. Yearly Meeting of Friends, Whittier 1968-73; exec. dir. Nat. Sunday Sch. Assn., Wheaton, Ill. 1973-74; exec. dir. Evangelical Christian Publishers Assn., La Habra 1974-80; assoc. publisher Homes & Land Mag., La Habra 1981-85; minister of visitation La Habra Hills Presbyterian Ch., 1985-87; prin. Brandenburgh & Associates Literary Agcy., Murrieta 1986-; subs. ESL tchr. UC Ext., Riv. 1991-; awards: Hon. citizen State of Texas, Austin 1978, ann. appreciation award Evangelical Pubs. Assn., Anaheim 1984; Republican; Episcopalian (vestry sec. 1992-). Ofc: 24555 Corte Jaramillo Murrieta 92562

BRANDIS, MURRAY, international cookware and housewares trading co. president; b. Jan. 4, 1919, N.Y.C.; s. Frank and Sadie (Kligman) B.; m. Gertrude, Aug. 27, 1939; children: Linda b. 1943, Larry b. 1947; grad. Amarillo Sr. H.S. 1935. Career: pres. General Trading Corp., 1940-, started bus. purchasing salvage mdse. with $8.00 (sales now in $millions), now purch. cookware and housewares from major mfrs. and sell to major chain stores in U.S. and abroad; cons. appraiser various types of mdse.; invited guest of Pres. Carter to attend function for Premier Deng Chou Peng of China (1979); mem. Non Foods Merchandisers West; Shriners (charter El Bekal Shrine), Eastern Star, Masons; mil: m/sgt. Air Corps Supply 1942-45, Australia, New Guinea, Philippines svc.; rec: antique meissen ceramics, ivories. Res: 1125 Tehachapi Dr Long Beach 90807 Ofc: General Trading Corp 757 E 9th St Los Angeles 90021

BRANNAN, WILLIAM WAYLAND, real estate broker; b. July 13, 1923, San Francisco; s. Wm. Smith and Ramona Cora (Hoag) B.; m. Marian Gimby, Mar. 26, 1951; children: Carol b. 1954, John b. 1955, Ann b. 1957, Thomas b. 1959, James b. 1962, Paul b. 1965, Kathleen b. 1969; edn: AB, Stanford Univ. 1952. Career: life ins. salesman Guardian Life, 1951-55; real estate salesman Timmer Realty, 1955-71, Fox & Carskadon, 1971-76, Frank Howard Allen, 1977-82; self-empl. realtor and appraiser, San Rafael 1982-; condr. workshops on telephone techniques throughout No. Calif., 1978-82; honors: Realtor Assoc. of the Year 1980, Marin Co.; dir. St. Vincent's Sch. for Boys; dir. Marin Co. Bd. of Realtors; mem. Kiwanis Club, Serra Club, Knights of Columbus; chmn. 1st Annual Town Picnic Parade, San Rafael 1980; author book and cassette tapes on tel. techniques (1981), art. in Calif. Real Estate Assn. Mag. (1980); mil: company scout, pfc, 517th Parachute Inf. Regt. 1943-45, Purple Heart, Presdl. Citation; Republican; R.Cath.; rec: handwriting analyst, golf. Res: 304 Mission Ave San Rafael 94901 Ofc: Brannan Associates, 4340 Redwood Hwy Ste 145 San Rafael 94903

BRASWELL, SYLVIA PATRICIA, psychologist/mental health analyst; b. Sept. 26, 1946, Quincy, Fla.; d. Ferris and Lillian A. (Wilson) Goldwire; 1 son, Robert b. 1985; edn: BS, N.C. A&T 1969; MSW, Rutgers Univ. 1974; PhD, U.S. Internat. Univ. San Diego 1989; lic. clin. social worker (1982). Career: social worker Essex Co. Welfare, Newark, N.J. 1969-74; social svcs. splst. Day Care Coordinator Council 1974-76; clin. dir. United Comm. Corp. 1976-79; psychiatric soc. worker L.A. County 1979-89, mental health svc. coordinator L.A. County Dept. Mental Health, 1989-; honors: listed Who's Who Am. Women 1981, recogn. award Central City Community Mental Health Ctr. 1981 and Teen World Group Home 1988; mem: Assn. Black Social Workers, L.A. Leggers Inc., NAACP, Renaissance Runners, Nat. Council of Negro Women (chair ethnic minority task force); Democrat; Baptist. Res: 4091 8th Ave Los Angeles 90008 Ofc: Los Angeles County Dept. Mental Health 2415 W Sixth St Los Angeles 90057

BRAUN, JEROME IRWIN, lawyer; b. Dec. 16, 1929, St. Joseph, Mo.; s. Martin H. and Bess (Donsker) B.; m. Dolores F.; children: Aaron b. 1959, Susan b. 1963, Daniel b. 1967; edn: AB (w/distinc.), Stanford Univ., 1951, LL.B, Stanford Law Sch. 1953; admitted bar: Mo. 1953, Calif. 1953, U.S. Supreme Ct., U.S. Dist. Ct. (no. dist. Calif.), U.S. Ct. Appeals (9th cir.), U.S. Tax Ct., U.S. Ct. of Mil. Appeals. Career: atty., assoc. Long & Levit, San Francisco 1957-58; Law Offices of Jefferson Peyser, 1958-62; founding ptnr. Elke, Farella & Braun (now Farella, Braun & Martel), San Francisco 1962-; law instr. San Francisco Law Sch. 1958-69; speaker State Bar convs. in Calif., Ill., Nev., Mont.; frequent moderator, participant Calif. Contg. Edn. of Bar pgms.; chair Ninth Circuit Sr. Advy. Bd., past chmn. lawyer reps. to Ninth Cir. Judicial Conf.; mem. U.S. Dist. Ct. Civil Justice Reform Act Advy. Com.; mem. Calif. Ct. of Appeal First Dist. Appellate Lawyers' Liaison Com.; honors: Order of the Coif, revising ed. Stanford Law Rev., Lloyd W. Dinkelspiel Outstanding Young Leader, Jewish Welfare Fedn. 1967, honoree Mex.-Am. Legal Defense Fund 1979; mem: Am. Bar Assn., Calif. State Bar Assn. (mem., past chmn. Adminstrn of Justice Com.), Bar Assn. San Francisco, Calif. Academy of Appellate Lawyers (past pres.), Am. Judicature Soc. (past dir.), Am. Coll. of Trial Lawyers, mem. Teaching of Trial and Appellate Advocacy Com., Ninth Cir. Hist. Soc. (pres.), No. Dist. Calif. Hist. Soc. (dir.); civic: Jewish Community Fedn. of S.F., the Peninsula, Marin and Sonoma Counties (past pres.); S.F. United Jewish Comm. Ctrs. (past pres.); contbr. numerous articles to profl. jours.; author Calif. St. Bar bill on comparative negligence and contbn.; mil: lst lt. JAG Corps US Army 1954-57, capt. Active Reserve 1957-64; Democrat; Jewish. Ofc: Farella, Braun & Martel, 235 Montgomery St San Francisco 94104

BRAUN, RICHARD RODMAN, real estate agent; b. Feb. 8, 1951, Boston, Mass.; s. Stanley S. and Claire (Rodman) B.; m. Dixie Denman, June 26, 1976; edn: BA, Hartwick Coll. 1973; Univ. London 1972; Univ. Pa. 1971. Career: account exec. Promotional Planning Service, Boston, Mass. 1973-79; Bernard Hodes Advt. (div. Doyle Dane Bernbach), Los Angeles 1979-85; account supr. Thompson Recruitment Advt. (div. J. Walter Thompson 1985-90; R.E. agt. James R. Gary & Co. Ltd., Real Estate, Woodland Hills 1990-; mem: San Fernando Valley Bd. Realtors; Democrat; Unitarian; rec: photography. Res: 22493 Venido Rd Woodland Hills 91364

BRAY, ABSALOM FRANCIS, JR., lawyer; b. Nov. 24, 1918, San Francisco; s. A.F., Sr. (presiding Justice, Ct. of Appeal) and Leila (Veale) B.; grandson of Sheriff R.R. Veale, Contra Costa Co., 1895-1935; m. Lorraine Paule, June 25, 1949; children: Oliver Whitney b. 1954, Brian Keith, b. 1955, Margot Elizabeth, b. 1957; edn: AB Stanford Univ. 1940; JD, USC Sch of Law 1949. Career: legal dept. Iowa Ord. Plant, Burlington 1940-42; pvt. practice law, 1949-, pres. Bray, Breitwieser, Costanza & Bray, APC, attys. at law; advy. bd. Bank of Am. 1953-65; founder and dir. John Muir Nat. Bank, Martinez, 1983-92; awards: Silver Beaver Award BSA 1988, A.F. Bray Award estab. in his father's honor by Kiwanis Club of Martinez; mem: Vets. of Fgn. Wars (cmdr.), Am. Legion (cmdr.), Contra Costa Co. Devel. Assn. (pres. 1959-60), Contra Costa Council (pres.), Navy League of U.S. (pres. Contra Costa council 1981-83), State Bar of Calif., Contra Costa Co. Bar Assn. (past pres.), Contra Costa Co. Tuberculosis and Pub. Health Assn. (past pres.); civic: Martinez High

Twelve Club (pres. 1987), Contra Costa Co. Hist. Soc., E. Clampus Vitus, Martinez Historical Soc. (pres. 1984), Soc. of Calif. Pioneers, Camp Fire Girls (chmn. nat. bd. dirs. 1959-61, 1969-71 and past chmn. Region V, CA, NV, UT, AZ, HI), Boy Scouts Am. John Muir Dist. (chmn. 1968), John Muir Memorial Assn. (pres. 1989-92), Salvation Army (com.), Martinez PTA (life), Rotary Intl. (past pres.), Masons, Elks; mil: lt. USNR 1942-46, WWII, Navy Commendn., Navy Unit Citation; Republican; Episcopalian (Vestry); rec: photog., ship models, hiking. Res: 600 Flora St Martinez Ofc: Bray, Breitwieser, Costanza & Bray, APC, Ward and Ferry Sts., Martinez 94553

BRAZIER, JOHN RICHARD, lawyer, physician; b. Mar. 11, 1940, Olean, N.Y.; s. John R. and Edith (Martin) B.; m. April Tomaszewski, 1968, div. 1978; children: Mark b. 1970, Jennifer b. 1975; edn: AAS, SUNY, 1960; BS engring. physics, Univ. Colo., Boulder 1963; MD, Univ. Colo. Med. Ctr., Denver 1969; JD, Santa Clara Sch. of Law, 1989. Career: instr. surg. and adj. prof. phys. therapy & rehab., N.Y. Univ. 1975-77; asst. prof. surg., div. thoracic & cardiovascular surg., UCLA Med. Ctr., Los Angeles 1977-78, also asst. chief CV surg. Wadsworth VA Hosp.; pvt. practice thoracic & cardiovascular surg., Los Angeles 1978-84; Newport News, Va. 1984-86; mem: Am. Coll. Surgeons, Am. Coll. Chest Physicians, Am. Bar Assn., Assn. Trial Lawyers of Am.; publs: articles (1972-); Indep.; rec: pvt. pilot. Res: 1401 36th St Sacramento 95816

BREDBERG, DONALD J., real estate advisory firm executive; b. June 26, 1957, Milwaukee, Wis.; s. John Haynes and Carol Jean (Faber) B.; m. Stephanie, Dec. 6, 1987; edn: BBA, Univ. Wis. 1979. Career: assoc. Laventhol & Howarth, Los Angeles 1979-82; mgr. real estate services Peat Marwick 1982-85; mgr. strategic planning The Irvine Co., Newport Beach, 1985-87; ptnr., exec.v.p. PBR Real Estate Fin. Services, Irvine, 1987-89; sr. v.p. Newfield Enterprises Int'l., Los Angeles 1989-; owner Bredberg Realty Advisors, 1990-; lectr. Orange County Volunteer Ctr., Santa Ana 1988-; awards: Univ. Wis. W.S. Kies scholar 1978; mem: Building Industry Assn., Nat. Assn. of Office and Indsl. Parks, Urban Land Inst., L.A. Junior Chamber (v.chmn. mgmt. com.), NARSAD, UC Irvine Athletic Found., Nat. Golf Found., Orange Co. Mental Health Assn. (pres., bd. dirs., treas.); article pub. in profl. jour. (1984), computer software creator (1986), owner, co-editor So. Calif. Growth Monitor (1988-); Republican; Methodist; rec: drawing, piano, tennis. Res: 28 Mountain View Irvine 92715 Ofc: Newfield Enterprises Int'l. 2049 Century Park East Ste 3760 Los Angeles 90071

BRENT, IRA M., psychiatrist; b. Nov. 1, 1944, N.Y., NY; married, 1 dau.; edn: BS, Long Island Univ., 1966; MD, Chicago Med. Sch., 1970; Qualified Med. Examiner, US Dept. of Labor. Career: rotating intern UC Irvine Orance Co. Med. Ctr., 1970-71; resident gen. psychiatry Cedars-Sinai Med. Ctr., L.A. 1973-76; psychoanalytic tng. 1974-80; cons. So. Calif. Counseling Ctr., 1976; staff psychiatrist L.A. Co. Dept. Mental Health 1976-77; staff psychiatrist Calif. Med. Gp. 1977-78; med. dir. L.A. Co. Health Dept. Methadone Maint. Clinic, West Hollywood 1979-89, also clin. dir. Day Treatment Pgm. Gateways Hosp. 1980-81; pvt. practice, L.A., 1976-81, pvt. group practice gen. psychiatry, Long Beach, 1981-84,.pvt. practice Decatur, Ill. 1984-89, Roseville, Ca. 1989-; med. dir. Spl. Care Unit, Hillhaven-Fair Oaks (Ca.) Healthcare Ctr. 1989-, The Ctr. for Med. Wt. Mgmt., Sacto. 1991-; cons. Calif. St. Dept. Soc. Svs., Sacto. 1991-; faculty So. Ill. Univ. Sch. of Med. 1986-89, UC Davis Sch. of Med. 1991-; mem: Am. Assn. of Psychoanalytic Physicians (Fellow), Am. Psychiat. Assn., Placer-Nev. Co. Med. Soc., Cent. Calif. Psychiat. Assn., Sacto-El Dorado Co. Med. Soc., Calif. Med. Assn., Am. Soc. Bariatric Physicians, No. Am. Assn. for Study of Obesity, Am. Coll. of Nutrition; mil: capt., flt. surgeon US Air Force, 1971-73. Ofc: 87 Scripps Dr Ste 214 Sacramento 95825 Tel: 916/567-0111 also: 729 Sunrise Ave Ste 101 Roseville 95661 Tel: 916/784-2656

BRENT, RICHARD S., manufacturing program manager; b. July 30, 1949, Pittsburgh, Pa.; s. Irving J. and Sarah Evelyn (Weiss) B.; m. Sharon I., Aug. 17, 1969; children: Andrew, Sarah, Kirah; edn: BA, Sonoma State Coll., Rohnert Park 1972; tchg. cred., 1973. Career: gen. mgr. Solar Warehouse, El Cajon 1980-82; plant mgr. Jet Air Inc., El Cajon 1982-85; program mgr. Solar Turbines Inc., San Diego 1985-; awards: outstanding vol. of year Combined Health Agys. San Diego (1989), Point of Light, Solar Turbines Inc. (1990-91); mem. Solar Profl. Mgmt. Assn. S.D. (bd. pres. 1989); civic: Combined Health Agencies Drive (exec. bd. 1991, 92), Zool. Soc. San Diego Keeper's Club, United Cerebral Palsy S.D. (v.p. 1984), Nat. Kidney Found. S.D. (chmn. 1990-91), United Way S.D. Loaned Exec. 1986, Combined Health Agy. S.D. (exec. com. 1992); club: Sports Chalet Dive; publs: booklet, Who Says you can't do anything? An ecology primer (1970); rec: scuba, reading, touring, gardening.

BREWER, KARA PRATT, university planned giving executive; b. Oct. 29, 1930, Reno, Nev.; d. Kenneth and Kara (Lucas) Pratt; m. David P. Brewer, Sept. 10, 1949; children: Margaret b. 1950, Martin b. 1951, Kenneth b. 1953, Paul b. 1954, Elena b. 1957, Clare b. 1959, Sam b. 1961, Matthew b. 1965; edn: Smith Coll. 1948-49; BA, Univ. of Pacific 1969; MA, 1972; DA, 1976. Career: asst. ed. Pacific Historian, Univ. of Pacific, Stockton 1971, instr. 1971-75, writer in residence 1976, dir. of alumni and parent programs 1977-90, dir. of planned giving, 1990-; conf. chair CASE Dist. VII 1983, conf. co-chair Dist. VII 1982;

awards: Danforth Found. fellowships 1969-71; mem: Pope John XXIII Found. (bd. mem.), St. Marys Interfaith Dining Room (bd. mem.), Am. Com. for Irish Studies; author: Pioneer or Perish: A History of Univ. of Pacific (1977), contbr. book preface to Pacific: Yesterday & The Day Before That (H.S. Jacoby 1989); Democrat; R.Cath.; rec: reading. Res: 94 W Knoles Way Stockton 95204 Ofc University of Pacific Planned Giving Office Stockton 95211

BREWER, LEO, scientist, educator; b. June 13, 1919, St. Louis, Mo.; s. Abraham and Hanna (Resnik) B.; m. Rose Strugo, Aug. 22, 1945; children: Beth b. 1952, Roger b. 1954, Gail b. 1956; edn: BS, Caltech, 1940; PhD, UC Berkeley, 1943. Career: res. assoc. US Army Manhattan Project, Berkeley 1943-46; principal investigator Lawrence Berkeley Lab. (previously known as Radiation Lab.), Berkeley 1943-, assoc. dir. LBL 1967-75, hd. inorganic mats. res. div. 1961-75; asst. prof. dept. chemistry UC Berkeley 1946-50, assoc. prof. 1950-55, prof. 1955-; awards: Great Western Dow Fellow 1942, Guggenheim Fellow 1950, E.O. Lawrence award AEC 1961, R.S. Williams lectr. M.I.T. 1963, H. Werner lectr. Univ. Kans. 1963, O.M. Smith lectr. Okla. St. Univ. 1964, G.N. Lewis lectr. UCB 1964, Faculty lectr. UCB 1966, Corn Products lectr. Penn. St. Univ. 1970, disting. alumni Caltech 1974, W.D. Harkins lectr. Univ. Chgo. 1974, Oak Ridge Nat. Lab. lectr. 1979, Frontiers in Chemistry lectr. Texas A&M 1981, Eyring lectr. Chemistry, Ariz. St. Univ. 1989, Louis C. Jordy res. scholar lectr. Drew Univ. 1983, Leo Brewer Special Festchrift Modern High Temperature Science 1984, Louis Jacob Bircher lectr. Vanderbilt Univ. 1986, Berkeley Citation UCB 1989, Leo Brewer retirement symposium on high temperature and materials chemistry Lawrence Berkeley Lab. 1989, Berkeley Fellow UCB 1992; mem: Alpha Chi Sigma, AAAS (fellow 1960), Am. Acad. of Art and Scis. 1979, AAUP, Am. Ceramic Soc. (Hon. mem. award 1991), Am. Chem. Soc. (Leo Hendrick Baekeland award N.Jersey Sect. ACS 1953, W.Coover lectr., Ames, Iowa sect. ACS 1967), Am. Physical Soc., Am. Soc. for Metals (fellow 1989), Calif. Acad. of Scis., Calif. Assn. of Chemistry Tchrs., Calif. Botanic Soc., Calif. Native Plant Soc., Calorimetry Conf. (H. Huffman lectr. 1966), Coblentz Soc., Combustion Inst., Electrochemical Soc. (lectr. 1970, Palladium Medalist 1971, Henry B. Linford award for disting. tchg. 1988), Fedn. of Am. Scientists, Internat. Plansee Soc. for Powder Metallurgy, Materials Res. Soc., Metallurgical Soc. of AIME (Wm. Hume-Rothery Award 1983, Extractive Metallurgy Sci. Award 1991), Nat. Acad. of Scis. 1959, Optical Soc. Am., Royal Soc. Chemistry, Soc. of Sigma Xi, Tau Beta Pi; coauthor: Thermodynamics (1961), 170+ sci. publs. Ofc: Dept. Chemistry, University of California, Berkeley 94720

BREWSTER, RUDI MILTON, federal judge; b. May 18, 1932, Sioux Falls, S.D.; s. Charles Edwin and Wilma Therese (Rud) B.; m. Gloria Nanson, June 27, 1954; children: Scot b. 1956, Lauri b. 1958, Julie b. 1960; edn: AB Princeton Univ., 1954; JD, Stanford Law sch., 1960. Career: civil trial lawyer and ptnr. law firm Gray, Cary, Ames & Frye, San Diego 1960-84; judge U.S. Dist. Ct., San Diego 1984-; faculty Calif. State Bar cont. edn. seminars; mem: Am. Bar Assn., San Diego Co. Bar Assn. (v.p. 1981-82, dir. 1969-72, del. state conv. 1965-74, mem: State Bar Com. on Unauthorized Practice of Law 1965-68), Am. Civil Trial Lawyers, Am. Board of Trial Advocates, Am. Inns of Ct. (pres. Louis M. Welsh Chapt. #9), San Diego Rotary Club (pres. 1980-81, bd. 1977-82); mil: USN 1954-81, capt. USNR-Ret. JAG Corps; Republican; Lutheran; rec: skiing, hunting, fishing, gardening. Ofc: U.S. District Court, 940 Front St San Diego 92189

BRIGGS, DONALD CLIFFORD, engineering manager; b. Sept. 19, 1932, Los Angeles; s. Clifford Russell and Mildred Louise Wainscott (Shriner) B.; m. Sonja Louise Schwab, May 11, 1963; children: Robin b. 1956, Tammie b. 1960, Linda b. 1964; edn: BSME, Stanford Univ. 1957; MSME, 1958; engring., 1960; MBA, Univ. Santa Clara 1965; MSEE, 1973. Career: engr. AiResearch, Los Angeles 1959-61; engr. ITEK, Palo Alto 1961-65; mgr. Ford Motor Co. 1965-90; mgr. Loral 1990-; awards: Stanford Univ. William Eckert Prize 1959, Sigma Xi, Tau Beta Pi, Beta Gamma Sigma; mem: AIAA (com., assoc. fellow), Nat. Mgmt. Assn., Masons, Elks, Dodge Car Club (v.p.); author: 50+ tech. papers pub.; 5 patents; mil: USN 1953-55; Republican; Protestant; rec: fishing, antique cars. Res: 2713 Doverton Square Mountain View 94040 Ofc: Space Systems/Loral 3825 Fabian Way Palo Alto 94303

BRIGGS, ROBERT NATHAN, electronics enginer (communications); b. Dec. 22, 1946 Miami Beach, Fla.; s. Donald Hicks and Harriett Martha (Mercer) B.; m. Polly Elizabeth Partridge, Dec. 22, 1970; children: Nathan Michael, Carey Robert, Christopher Alan; edn: BSEE, Northrop Inst. of Tech., Inglewood, Calif., 1974; Univ. of Nev., Las Vegas, Nev., 1978-81. Career: electronic engr., Telcom, Inc., Las Vegas, Nev., 1974-75; sr. optics engr., Holmes and Narver, Las Vegas, 1975-81; dir. of QA, Am. Fiber Optics, Signal Hill, Calif., 1981-83; sr. section head, TRW, Inc., Redondo Beach, Calif., 1983-85; optics R&D engr., TRW, Inc. 1985-86; TDRSS project engr., TRW, Inc. 1986-90; chmn., IEEE Student Chpt., Inglewood, Calif., 1973-74; class pres., Northrop Inst. of Tech., Inglewood, Calif., 1973-74; com. mem., Electronics Industries Assn., Wash., DC, 1978-86; awards: President's award, Northrop Inst. of Tech., 1974; Certificate of Appreciation, Electronics Industries Assn., Wash., DC, 1986; Certificate of Appreciation, NASA, Goddard Space Flight

Ctr., 1989; mem: Optical Soc. of Am., 1976-90; Am. Inst. of Aeronautics & Astronautics, Inc., 1985-90; Boy Scouts of Am., L.A. County: Cub Master 1986-91; Scout Master 1991-92; inventor, Security System for Dept. of Energy, 1975; author: FO Standards & Procedures, Electronics Industries Assn., 1978-86; prin. investigator, spacecraft res. projects: Spacecraft Comm. Tech. 1984, Spacecraft Fiber Optic Local Area Network 1984-88; mil: sgt., USAF, 1967-71; Republican; Episcopal. Res: 6532 Verde Ridge Rd. Rancho Palos Verdes 90274. Ofc: TRW Inc. S&TG One Space Park Redondo Beach 90274

BRILL, JOEL VICTOR, physician, educator; b. Jan. 28, 1956, Phila.; s. Earl Burton and Lois Elaine (Werner) B.; m. Laurie Ann Lissner, May 17, 1980; children: Jacob b. 1989, Zachary b. 1991; edn: AB in biology, UCLA, 1976; MD, Chicago Med. Sch., 1980. Career: resident internal medicine UCLA, Sepulveda 19880-83; fellow gastroenterology USC, L.A. 1983-85; pvt. practice gastroenterology, Ventura 1985-; instr. in medicine USC Med. Sch. 1983-; med. staff Ventura Co. Med. Ctr. (dir. gastroent. svs.), Community Memorial Hosp. Ventura (dir. gastrointestinal lab., v.chmn. dept. medicine 1992, chmn. 1993, CQI/TQM Task Force); mem: Am. Coll. Gastroent. (fellow), Am. Gastroenterol. Assn., Am. Soc. for Gastrointestinal Endoscopy, Am. Soc. Parenteral & Enteral Nutrition, Am. Coll. Physicians; rec: reading, travel, cooking. Res: 32 Cerro Crest Dr Camarillo 93010 Ofc: 168 N Brent St Ste 404 Ventura 93003

BRISBIN, ROBERT EDWARD, management consultant, insurance executive; b. Feb. 13, 1946, Bklyn.; m. Sally Ann Norton; edn: BS in B.A., San Francisco State, 1968; cert. safety exec., World Safety Org. Career: field rep. Index Research, San Mateo 1969-82; mgr. loss control Homeland Ins. Co., San Jose 1982-87; ins. exec. Morris & Garritano, San Luis Obispo 1987-; pres. Robert E. Brisbin & Assocs., San Francisco 1975-; mem. Am. Soc. Safety Engrs. 1982-, World Safety Org. 1984-; author: Loss Control for the Small to Medium Size Business (1990), w/ Carol Grant, Workplace Wellness (1992); composer song: America the Land of Liberty (1986); Republican; rec: scuba, writing, flying, musical performance, photography. Address: PO Box 341 Pismo Beach 93448

BROADBENT, AMALIA SAYO CASTILLO, graphic artist, designer; b. May 28, 1956, Manila, Phil., nat. US cit. 1986; d. Conrado Camilo and Eugenia De Guzman (Sayo) Castillo; m. Barrie Noel Broadbent, Mar. 14, 1981; children: Charles b. 1983, Chandra b. 1985; edn: Maryknoll Coll. 1972-73; Karilagan Finishing Sch. 1973; BFA, advt., Univ. of Santo Tomas 1978; French lang. studies Alliance Francaise, Manila, San Francisco 1979-82; Acad. of Art Coll. 1980. Career: graphic artist-designer/prin. A.C. Broadbent Graphics, S.F.; freelance art dir. Ogilvy & Mather Direct; honors: Dean's List 1977, 3d pl. bronze medal, drawing contest 1974, Univ. of Santo Tomas; mem: Nat. Assn. of Female Execs., Makati Dance Troupe, YMCA, Alliance Francaise; works: freehand drawing 'Daing Na Isda' 1974; R.Cath.; Ofc: A.C. Broadbent Graphics, 407 Jackson St Ste 302 San Francisco 94111

BRODERICK, EDWARD MICHAEL, III, corporate lawyer; b. Nov. 4, 1947, Stamford, Conn.; s. Edward Michael Broderick Jr. (dec.) and Lois Caroline (Brown) Contaras; m. Jeanine Lynn Anglea, Mar. 4, 1989; children: Courtney Elizabeth b. 1990, Ashley Noelle b. 1991; edn: BA, St. Anselm Coll., Manchester, N.H. 1969; JD, St. John's Univ. Sch. of Law, 1973; admitted bar: N.Y., 1974, Conn., 1974. Career: adminstrv. asst. legislative affairs Royal Globe Ins. Cos., NY, NY 1969-73; staff atty. 1974-75; asst. counsel and secty. G.E. Credit Corp./Puritan Ins. Co., Stamford, Conn. 1975-79; asst. gen. counsel ITT Financial Corp., also gen. counsel and secty. ITT Lyndon Ins. Group, St. Louis, Mo. 1979-86; v.p. and gen. counsel CalFarm Ins. Cos., Sacramento, Ca. 1986-; mem. Am. Bar Assn. (mem. coms. 1971-), NY State Bar Assn. 1973-, Conn. Bar Assn. 1973-; civic: St. Louis (Mo.) Squires 1985-86; Republican; R.Cath.; rec: skiing, sailing. Ofc: CalFarm Insurance Cos. 1601 Exposition Blvd Sacramento 95815

BRODSKY, STANLEY JEROME, physics professor; b. Jan. 9, 1940, St. Paul, Minn.; s. Sidney Charles and Esther Rene (Levitt) B.; m. Judith Ellen Preis, June 29, 1986; children: Stephen Andrew, David Jonathan; edn: B.Physics, Univ. Minn., 1961, PhD Physics, 1964. Career: research assoc. Columbia Univ., 1964-66; Stanford Linear Accelerator Ctr. (SLAC), Stanford Univ., 1966-: res. assoc. 1966-68, permanent staff 1968-75, assoc. prof. 1975-76, full prof. 1976-; vis. AVCO Assoc. Prof. Physics Dept. Cornell Univ. 1970, vis. prof. natural scis. Inst. for Adv. Study Princeton 1982, vis. prof. Max Planck Inst. for Nuclear Physics Heidelberg Sept. '87 and Mar.-Sept.'88; mem. sci. and ednl. advy. com. Lawrence Berkeley Lab. Univ. Calif. 1986-; mem. bd. referees and editl. bd. Physical Review (Am. Physical Soc.) 1978-79, 85-86; awards: Sr. Disting. U.S. Scientist Award (Humboldt Award) Alexander von Humboldt Found. 1987-, External Sci. Mem. Max Planck Inst. for Nuclear Physics in Heidelberg (3/89-), assoc. editor Nuclear Physics B (1987-), lectr. Disting. Speaker Colloquium Series, Univ. Minn. (2/89), res. grantee U.S./Israel Binat. Found., Weizmann Inst. 1986-90; apptd. bds: NSF Review Panel for Theoretical Physics (chmn. 1980-81), Weizmann Inst. of Science Forum (exec. bd. 1977-), mem. com. on fundamental constants Nat. Res. Council- Nat. Acad. of Scis. 1972-75; coauthor 4 books: Lectures on Lepton Nucleon Scattering and Quantum Chromodynamics

(1982), Quarks and Nuclear Forces (1982), Nuclear Chromodynamics: Quarks and Gluons in Particles and Nuclei (1986), Perturbative Quantum Chromodynamics (1989). Res: 2339 Branner Dr Menlo Park 94025 Ofc: Bin 81, Stanford Linear Accelerator Center, 2575 Sand Hill Rd Menlo Park 94025

BROGDON, RALPH EWING, JR., judge; b. Aug. 12, 1927, Fresno; s. Ralph E. and Doris Elaine (Nilmeier) B.; m. Carol A. Valleau, Oct. 1, 1989; dau., Aleta Marcelle b. 1979 (adopted 4/91); children by previous marriage: John Arthur b. 1946 (dec.), Joan Marie b. 1951, Dirk Ewing b. 1956, Lisa Mary b. 1959, Gregory Ralph b. 1961; edn: att. Menlo Coll., 1947-48; AA, CSU San Jose 1949; BA econ., Stanford Univ. 1951; Stanford Univ. Sch. of Law 1951-53; JD, Southwestern Univ. Sch. of Law 1956; admitted Calif. State Bar 1959. Career: atty. assoc. w/ Boris S. Woolley, Torrance 1959-60; ptnr./assoc. w/ William N. Willens, Lawndale 1959-64; assoc. w/ Truman R. Adkins, Redondo Bch. 1964-67; assoc. w/ Gerald F. Moriarty, Edward Gorman, Norman Miller, John Holtrichter, John Chevalier, R.B. 1967-73; assoc. w/ Tunney & Carlyle, San Jose 1973-74; atty. pvt. practice, Cupertino 1974-89; judge Municipal Ct., Santa Clara Co., 1989-; honors: CSF, Triad Hon. Soc., Menlo Coll. #1 scholar Freshman Class 1947-48, coll. athletics (baseball, basketball);past mem: Santa Clara Co. Bar Assn. (bd. 1976-78), Sunnyvale-Cupertino Bar Assn. (pres. 1978), Santa Clara Co. Trial Lawyers Assn., South Bay Bar Assn. (pres. 1972, chmn. Annual Golf Tourn. 1962-71, chmn. South Bay Legal Aid Found. 1963-65), ABA, Calif. Trial Lawyer's Assn., L.A. Co. Bar Assn., Criminal Cts. Bar Assn.; civic: Am. Cancer Soc. (featured in ACS video of 3 survivors of cancer of larynx, 1985), frequent speaker var. comm. groups and schs. and support counselor for laryngectomy patients pre/post surgery; mem: Stanford Alumni Assn. (life, dir. Stanford Buck Club 1978-87), Stanford Law Soc. of Santa Clara Co., Phi Alpha Delta legal frat. 1952-, Canyon Lake Property Owners Assn. (bd., past pres.), C.of C., Kiwanis (pres. Redondo Bch. 1964), Canyon Lake Men's Golf Club (charter pres. 1970-71) past leader Cub Scouts, Babe Ruth Baseball League; mil: Yeoman 3/c USN 1945-46; Republican; active precinct wkr., campaigner 1950-89, charter chmn. Stanford Univ. Young Repubs. Club 1949; Prot.; rec: golf. Res: 2683 Cardinal Lane San Jose 95125-4810 Ofc: 200 W Hedding St San Jose 95110

BROKL, STANLEY SCOTT, systems engineer, inventor; b. Apr. 20, 1941, Hutchinson, Minn.; s. Arnold Stanley and Annette (Chidlaw) B.; m. Christina Gutierrez; children: Timothy, b. 1961, James, b. 1963, Diana, b. 1964, Deborah, b. 1966; edn: West Coast Univ. 1969-73; AA, Pasadena City Coll. 1971; BS bus., Univ. of La Verne, 1988; USN Grad. Electronic Tech Sch. Career: jr. engr./tech. var. cos. 1960-69; sr. tech. Jet Propulsion Lab., Pasadena 1969, sr. engring. asst. 1973-77; sr. mem. tech. staff RCA Somerville, NJ 1977-80; sr. engr. JPL, 1980-83, tech. group leader and cognizant engr. for Goldstone Solar System Radar, 1984-88; systems engr. LORAL EOS, 1988-90, project engr. for MAIS, Nov. 1991-; proj. engr., show/ride electronics engring. Walt Disney Imagineering, Glendale, 1990-91, in Euro Disney, France, 8/90-7/91; awards: NASA Group Achievement Award "Series X" (10/85), NASA Monetary Award, tech. brief "A General Monitor and Control Interface To The VAX Unibus" (11/86), recognition for var. inventions, NASA (1972, 74, 77, 80); three monetary awards for Patent Appls., RCA (1977, 78, 79); Patentee: Peripheral Interactive Device with Manual Controls (1973), Jam Resistant TV System (1982), Jam Resistant Receiver (1983), Multiple Synchronous Counters with Ripple Read (1984); mem: IEEE, American Radio Relay League (life, section mgr. L.A. Sect. 1980-84); club: Sierra La Vern CC; mil: ETRSN, USN 1958-60; Democrat; Prot.; rec: amateur radio opr. N2YQ (1955-). Res: 2126 E Iron Club Dr La Verne 91750 Ofc: LORAL EOS, 600 E Bonita Pomona CA 91767

BROOKS, EDWARD HOWARD, college administrator; b. Mar. 2, 1921, Salt Lake City, Utah; s. Charles Campbell Brooks and Margery (Howard) Calvin; m. Courtaney Perren, May 18, 1946; children: Merrilee Brooks Runyan b. 1947, Robin Brooks Pollock b. 1949; edn: BA, Stanford Univ., 1942, MA, 1947, PhD, 1950. Career: adminstr. Stanford Univ. 1949-66, vice provost 1966-71; provost Claremont Colls., 1971-81, v.p. Claremont McKenna Coll., 1981-84, provost Scripps Coll., 1987-89, pres. 1989-90, ret.; bd. dir. Sallie Mae, W.D.C., 1972-78; mem. bd. overseers Hoover Instn., Stanford 1972-78, trustee Webb Schs., Claremont 1979-90, trustee Menlo Coll., Atherton 1985-88; mem. Stanford Associates (bd. govs. 1991-), Inst. of Internat. Edn. -West, S.F. (advy. bd. 1985-); clubs: University (L.A., 1971-), Bohemian (S.F., 1971-); mil: capt. field arty. US Army 1942-45; Republican. Res: 337 8th St Manhattan Beach 90266

BROOKS, GLENN ALLEN, audio engineer, video service company buyer; b. Mar. 23, 1960, Pasadena; s. Robert Allen Brooks and Sarah Eloise (Merritt) Bogenreif; m. Tracy Jo Williams, June 11, 1983; children: Joshua Allen-Ray b. 1984, Ashleigh Nicole b. 1987, Jonathan Lincoln b. 1988; edn: AA, Goldenwest Coll., 1983; BS, San Diego State Univ., 1985; Orange Coast Coll. 1978-79; Coastline Comm. Coll. 1983; lic. foster parent, Orange Co. 1990-, Notary Public, Orange Co. 1988-92. Career: audio engr. KPBS-TV, San Diego 1984-85; Group W Productions, Los Angeles 1985-86; KSCI-TV, L.A. 1986-88; conformist Chace Productions Inc., Hollywood 1988; materials coord. Rank Video Svs. Am., Garden Grove 1989-, also TQM facilitator, 1992-; pres. Brooks Concepts Inc., Huntington Beach 1990-92; owner Moriah Recording, San Diego, 1985,

Small World Prodns., H.B. 1986-90; Republican; Christian; rec: water/snow sports, radio controlled gliding. Res: 5522 Harold Pl Huntington Beach 92647 Ofc: Rank Video Services America, 12691 Pala Dr Garden Grove 92641

BROOKS, SAMUEL HERMAN, insurance brokerage firm president; b. March 3,1935, Windsor, Ont., Can.; nat. 1965; s. Jacob Issac and Rachel (Wainger) B.; m. Mary J. (Born) Salazar; children: by prev. marriage) Deborah b. 1955, Robert b. 1957, Judi b. 1959, (stepchild) Gabriel Melendez b. 1982; 2 grandchildren: Jenna Brooks b. 1985, Chad Brooks b. 1988; edn: grad. Calif. Sch. of Insurance, Pasadena 1958; Life Underwriters Tng. Council 1960; num. underwriting courses; Registered Health Underwriter (RHU), Nat. Assn. of Health Underwriters 1979; Life Underwriters Tng. Council Fellow (LUTCF) 1985. Career: agent, staff mgr. Prudential Ins. Co., Whittier 1956-63; estab. own ins. firm, Samuel H. Brooks & Assoc., Beverly Hills 1964-71; moved bus. to Rowland Hts. 1973-; apptd. Calif. Senate Advy. Commn. on Real Property Ins. 1984-, mem Ins. Advy. Commn. to Sen. Frank Hill, chmn. Ins. Advy. Commn. Assemblyman Paul Horcher 1991-; recipient NALU awards: Nat. Quality (1980, 84), Million Dollar Roundtable (qual. 17 yrs., life 1991), 5 Million Dollar Roundtable (1975, 76), Nat. Sales Achievement (6); mem: Nat. Assn. of Life Underwriters, Nat. Assn. of Health Underwriters, Ind. Ins. Agents & Brokers Assn. (Legislative Council, Calif. 1990), Nat. Assn. of Notaries, We. Assn. Ins. Brokers, Walnut Valley C. of C. (bd. 1990-), Better Bus. Bur., 32nd Deg. Mason Shriner, Acad. of Magical Arts; contr. articles Occidental Life Ins. Co. mag.; Republican; Hebrew Christian; rec: music, travel autos. Res: 18103 E Galatina St Rowland Hts 91748 Ofc: Amalgamated Insurance Brokers Corp. 1750 Sierra Leone Ave Rowland Hts 91748

BROWN, EDMUND G. "PAT", lawyer, former governor of California; b. April 21, 1905, San Francisco; s. Edmund and Ida (Schuckman) B.; m. Bernice Layne, Oct. 30, 1930; children: Cynthia, Barbara, Jerry, Kathleen; edn: Univ. Calif. Ext.; LLB, JD, S.F. Coll. Law, 1927. Career: dist. atty. San Francisco, 1943-50; elected State Atty. Gen., Calif., 1950-58; Gov. of Calif., 1959-67; name ptnr. law firm Ball Hunt Hart Brown & Baerwitz, Los Angeles 1968-91; honorary chair Edmund G. "Pat" Inst. of Public Affairs, CSULA, guest lectr. CSU Los Angeles, 1988-; emeritus trustee Univ. Calif., Berkeley Found.; Democrat; R.Cath.; rec: golf, travel. Ofc: 2040 Avenue of the Stars Los Angeles 90067

BROWN, ELIZABETH LILLIAN, retired physician; b. Aug. 12, 1916, NY, NY; d. Joseph and Dora (Engel) B.; m. William Brown, M.D.; edn: MD, Albany Med. Coll. 1940-41, New York Med. Coll., 1941-43; bd. cert. Am. Bd. Allergy, Am. Bd. Pediatrics, subsplty., pediat. allergy. Career: research physicist NASA, 1937-40; intern pediat. Fordham Hosp. 1944; resident pediatrics Flower & Fifth Avenue Hosp., 1944; fellow Mayo Clinic, Rochester, Minn. 1944-45; resident peds. Greenpoint Hosp., Bklyn. 1949-50; pvt. practice pediatrician 1950-92, and allergy only 1970-, med. staff West Hills Med. Ctr. Canoga Park, Calif., West Park Hosp, Canoga Park Hosp., retired May 8, 1992; Fellow Am. Acad. Pediatrics (FAAP), Fellow Am. Acad. Allergy (FAAA), mem. Nat. Soc. Asthma Care Phys. (treas.), L.A. Allergy Soc., L.A. Pediat. Soc., Am. Allergy Assn; author: Yearbook of Pediatrics, Eczema Vaccinatum, Report of a Recovery; Jewish; rec: fishing, ranching. Address: 23300 Erwin St Woodland Hills 91367

BROWN, GEORGE STEPHEN, physics professor; b. June 28, 1945, Santa Monica; s. Paul Gordon and Frances Ruth (Moore) B.; m. Annaclare von Dalen, Sept. 17, 1966, div. 1979; children: Sonya Elena b. 1972; m. Nohema del Carmen Fernandez, Aug. 8, 1981; edn: BS, Caltech, 1967; MS, Cornell, 1968, PhD, 1973. Career: mem. tech. staff Bell Labs, Murray Hill, N.J. 1973-77; senior res. assoc., Stanford Univ., 1977-82, resrch. prof. 1982-91; prof. of physics UC Santa Cruz, 1991-; Fellow Am. Physical Soc. (1985-); author, ed., Handbook on Synchrotron Radiation Research (1992), 100+ sci. articles (1972-); mem. editorial bd. Rev. Scientific Instr. (1983-86); rec: music performance. Res: 740 Alameda Redwood City 94061 Ofc: University California, Santa Cruz 95064

BROWN, HARDY LYNWOOD, publisher, personnel administrator; b. Dec. 8, 1942, Trenton, N.C.; s. Floyd and Essie B.; m. Cheryl Minter, Jan. 26, 1963; children: Lynn b. 1963, Paulette b. 1967, Hardy b. 1971, Regina b. 1987; edn: BA, Johnston Coll., Redlands 1976; spl. courses, USC, 1977, UCLA, 1976. Career: laborer Kaiser Steel Corp., Fontana, 1961-63; customer svc. rep. So. Calif. Edison Co., Rialto; asst. personnel dir. Kaiser Permanente, Fontana, 1970-, dir. outreach and tng., equal opportunity coordinator, regional EEO dir.; publisher Black Voice News, Riverside, 1980-; awards: Renaissance Family, Nat. Council of Negro Women, Riverside 1986, Kool Achiever Award Brown & Williams, Louisville, Ky. 1989, Lay Citizen of Yr. Phi Delta Kappa, Redlands 1989, Lay Citizen of Yr., Home Neighborly orgn. San Bernardino 1990, Award of Honor Nat. Public Schs., Arlington, Va. 1990; mem: Nat. Newspaper Publishers Assn. 1982-, West Coast Black Pubs. Assn. 1982-; civic: San Bernardino Sch. Board (pres. 1987-89), NAACP 1970-, Thursday Morning Group 1987-, San Bdo. Alternative to Gangs Task Force (chmn. 1990-); Democrat; St. Paul AME Ch. San Bdo. (trustee, Sun. Sch. tchr.); rec: carpentry, wood work. Ofc: Black Voice News, 1583 W Baseline San Bernardino 92411

BROWN, HOWARD CLYDE, agriculture and cattle co. president; b. Jan. 19, 1896, San Francisco; s. s. James M. and Lizzie F. (Haskell) B.; m. Ialene Frances Wright, 1918 (dec. 1945): children: Dean Gordon b. 1920, Howard Stanley b. 1922 (dec.); m. Margaret Clark Neitzel, Aug. 16, 1947; edn: AB Univ. of Calif., Davis 1917. Career: ptnr. Brown & Gamble, Santa Maria 1928-43; ptnr. Sinton & Brown Co., Santa Maria 1934-48, pres. 1948-75; recipient Cattleman Special Honor Award, Calif. Cattle Feeders Assn. (1976); Republican; Protestant. Res: 326 E Camino Colegio Santa Maria 93456

BROWN, J. MOREAU, corporate philanthropies consultant; b. June 1, 1916, Evanston, Ill.; s. Dr. James Moreau and Edna Veronica (Cullen) Brown; children: Christine b. 1942, Moreau Stoddard b. 1944, Pamela Ashton b. 1948, Mallory b. 1952; edn: AB, Dartmouth Coll., 1939; M.Ed., St. Lawrence Univ., 1953. Career: dir. admissions St. Lawrence Univ., 1944-52; asst. dean admissions New York Univ., 1952-54; adminstr. edn. support/supr. ednl. awards and grants, General Electric, also assoc. secty. GE Found., 1954-72; v.p. Council Financial Aid to Edn., N.Y.C. 1972-77; cons./prin., San Francisco 1977-; mem. advy. council Beta Theta Pi 1960-, gen. sec./trustee 1960-63; development dir. Found. Teach. Econ., San Francisco 1980-81; awards: outstanding community service GE Elfun Soc., NY 1966-67, patriot medal, gold good citizenship medal SAR, NY (1968, 69), N.Y. St. American Revolution Bicentennial Commn. 1969-77, Bicentennial Council 13 Original States 1973-77; mem: Montefiore Sr. Ctr. (3 term pres. 1985-92), United Jewish Comm. Centers (bd. 1985-92, exec. com. ex officio), Mason Blue Lodge, Shriner, Scottish Rite, SAR (Empire State pres. 1968-69), Marines Memorial Club, Dartmouth Coll. Club; authored first corporate gift matching program "Corporate Alumnus Program" 1954; avocation: public service. Res: 545 Teresita Blvd San Francisco 94127 Ofc: Montefiore Senior Center 3200 California St San Francisco 94118

BROWN, JAMES EDWARD, biochemist; b. Jan. 9, 1945, Columbus, Ind.; s. Edward Alvin and Shirley L. (Hazelleaf) B.; m. Diane Howe, Aug. 14, 1971 (dec. May 29, 1988); children: Peter b. 1972, Roger b. 1978; edn: BS chem., Iowa St. Univ., 1967; PhD chem., Penn State Univ., 1971. Career: postdoctoral fellow Worcester Found. for Exptl. Biology, Shrewsbury, Mass. 1971-73; res. biochemist UCSD Pathology Dept., La Jolla 1973-82; res. mgr. Hemostasis Systems, Helena Laboratories, Beaumont, Tx. 1982-84; sr. staff scientist Cutter Biological, Berkeley 1984-, seminar com. chmn. 1987-88; recipient science & technology awards Cutter Biol. (1986, 87, 88, 89, 90), Cutter Labs. div. sci. award 1989; mem. ACS, AAAS, Alpha Chi Sigma; inventor: Phospholipid Affinity Purification of Factor VIII:C (pat. 1989); pub. jour. articles, Thrombosis Research (1986), Thrombos Haemostas (1987, 89); Methodist (ch. adminstrv. bd.); rec: tennis, golf. Res: 914 Anita Ct Lafayette 94549 Ofc: Cutter Laboratories, 4th and Parker Sts Berkeley 94701

BROWN, LILLIAN ERIKSEN, nurse administrator; b. Feb. 7, 1921, Seattle; d. Peter Louis and Lena (Lien) Eriksen; m. Wm. W. Brown, Jan. 21, 1942, div. Nov. 1962; children: Patricia Lee b. 1952, Michael b. 1954, Kevin b. 1957; edn: att. UC Berkeley 1939-40, dipl. St. Luke's Hosp. Sch. Nursing, San Francisco 1943; AB, CSU San Francisco, 1952; MPA, USC, 1975. Career: RN, Calif. Pub. health nse. San Francisco Dept. Health, 1946-50; asst. dir. nsg. S.F. General Hosp., 1950-56; dir. nsg. Weimar Med. Ctr., Weimar 1956-62, Orange County Med. Ctr., Orange 1962-76; assoc. dir. hosp. and clinics, dir. nsg., lectr. Univ. Calif. Med. Ctr., Irvine 1976-82; assoc. hosp. adminstr. King Khalid Eye Specialist Hosop., Riyadh, S.A., 1982-86; cons. AMI-Saudi Arabia Ltd., Jeddah, 1986-90; mem. advy. bds. various coll. nursing pgms., Consortium to Enhance Grad. Edn. in Nsg., advy. coun. 1970; Gov. Reagan appt. to Calif. Dept. Rehab. planning proj. com. 1967-69, advy. com. 1970-73; Univ. Calif. Ad Hoc Pres.'s com. on hosp. governance 1981-82; Calif. Hosp. Assn. personnel com. 1978-80, nsg task force 1982; Orange County Health Planning Council com. on emergency med. svs. 1977-78, health promotion task force 1978-79; awards: Lauds and Laurels UCI 1981, Lillian E. Brown award estab. in her honor Calif. Nurses Assn. 1989; mem: Am. Acad. Nurses (fellow), ANA (cert. Nse. Adminstr. Advanced), Orange County Dirs. of Nsg. (chair 1968-69), Nat. League for Nsg., APHA, Am. Orgn. Nse. Execs., Nat. Critical Care Inst. Edn., Calif. Hosp. Assn. (personell com. 1978-80, nsg. task force 1982), Calif. Nurses Assn. (dir. at lg. 1961-65, treas. 1965-69, chair Com. on Stds. of Care 1969-73), Calif. Orgn. for Nse. Execs. (hon.), Calif. Soc. for Nsg. Svc. Adminstr., NOW; mil: capt. (Res.) ANC 1946-52; contbr. articles in profl. jours.; Republican; rec: travel, philately. Res: 1806 Nordic Pl Orange 92665

BROWN, NORMAN HUGH, farrier, silversmith; s. Albert Norman and Mary Helen (Lee) B.; m. Diane Celia Matthews; children: Jody b. 1964, Dennis b. 1965, Robert b. 1967. Career: owner/operator Rusty Brown Hoseshoeing; tchr. equine anatomy and physiol. Riverside City Coll. 1984; mem: Western States Farriers Assn. (pres. 1985-87), Am. Farriers Assn. (bd. mem. 1983-87), Tx. Profl. Farriers Assn., Nev. Profl. Farriers Assn.; articles Am. Farriers Jour. and WSFA Jour.; mil: E-4 USMC 1958-62; Republican; rec: flying. Res: 10414 48th St Mira Loma 91752 Ofc: Rusty Brown Horseshoeing.

BROWN, POLLY SARAH, human factors computer interaction specialist; b. Dec. 30, 1952, Cambridge, Mass.; d. David Randolph and Sally (England)

Brown; edn: BA, Mills Coll., 1976; MA, Univ. Denver, 1982, PhD, 1985. Career: computer pgmr. Argonne Nat. Lab., 1976-77; technical writer ESL, Sunnyvale 1978; instr., res. asst., computer pgmr. Univ. of Denver, Co. 1978-85; human factors scientist IBM Research, Yorktown Heights, NY 1985-87, IBM Corp., San Jose, Ca. 1987-91; human-computer interaction cons., Palo Alto 1992-; awards: Phi Beta Kappa 1976, Bruce McCollum Award for scholastic achiev. in math. and the physical scis. Mills Coll. 1976, IBM profl. awards (1987, 91); mem. Assn. for Computing Machinery (computer-human interaction gp. 1985-), Human Factors Soc. (computers tech. gp. 1985-); civic: Sierra Club, NOW; inventor: Highlighting tool (pat. 1988); jour. articles in ACM Transactions on Office Info. Systems (1987), J. of Personality and Social Psych. (1986), others; Democrat; United Ch. of Christ; rec: swimming, reading, music. Res: 410 Sheridan Ave #444 Palo Alto 94306

BROWN, RONALD STAMPER, builder, engineer; b. Feb. 20, 1943, Los Angeles; s. Louis Danial and Felice (Stamper) B.; children: Deborah Lee b. 1963, Darren C. b. 1966; edn: Mount Carmel H.S., 1961; AA, Los Angeles City Coll., 1965; BS, and MBA, CSU Long Beach, 1969; Sencore Electronics Sch. 1987, 88, 89; postgrad. studies: math., Northrop Inst. of Tech.; architectonics in constrn., USC; geology, oil & water well drilling, astrophysics, astronomy & relativity, UCLA; Univ. Mich. Ext. courses in laser engring., superconductors, fiberoptics, electronics; entomology, Calif. Acad. of Sci.; cosmology, Caltech; organic arch. and struct. engring., Architect Geo. Frank Ligar; infrared detectors & systems applications engring., UC Santa Barbara, 1991-92, Assoc. rsch. UNI elec. ground systems, lighting protection and elec. fault locating. Lic: Electrical Engr.; Bldg., Electrical, Plbg. Htg. A/C, Solar, Roofing, Well Drilling, Struct. Pest Control, Air Frames & Power Plants; FCC commercial gen. radio tel. lic. w. radar endorsement; cert. electronic tech. Career: Romer O'Conner Co. Inc., 1965; builder 1970; Brown Termite 1980; Digital Products 1980; mem: IEEE, Nat. Notary Assn., Astronomical Soc. of Pacific, Planetary Soc., Wrightian Soc. of Organic Architecture, Am. Inst. of Wine & Food, Internat. Soc. for Optical Engring., Am. Radio Relay League, NRA, L.A. Co. Mus. of Art, Opera Club, Anza-Borrego Desert Natural Hist. Assn., Nat. Chevy Truck Assn., Mercedes Benz Club Am.; publs: articles on non linear optics; Republican; R.Cath.; rec: flying, sailing, skiing, scuba, amateur radio (adv. class lic. #KD6IFQ), enology. Res: 6630 Newcastle Ave Reseda 91335

BROWN, THAD, tax official; b. May 5, 1927, Vicksburg, Miss.; s. Jack and Ada (Parker) B.; m. Geri Litzius, Jan. 5, 1979; children: Gwendolyn, Janice, Kenneth; edn: BA, S.F. St. Univ., 1950; MPA, Golden Gate Univ., 1965. Career: staff City and County of San Francisco, 1957-: auditor Assessor 1957-65; admnstrv. asst. Mental Health Dept., 1965-68; admnstrv. analyst Office of Chief Adminstr., 1968-69; tax collector, 1969-; honors: disting. service Black C.of C. San Francisco 1982, vol. of yr. United Way Bay Area 1983, outstanding vol. Cal/Neva Community Action, Sacto. 1986, recogn. Econ. Opportunity Council S.F. 1989, resolutions Calif. St. Assembly, Senate, and San Francisco Board of Suprs. 1989; mem. Alpha Phi Alpha (life), Calif. Acad. of Scis. (life, fellow, bd. 1974-89); civic: Econ. Opp. Council of S.F. (bd. chmn. 1978-), United Way of Bay Area (bd. chmn. 1981-83), NAACP (life), World Affairs Council No. Calif. (bd. 1989), S.F. Fine Arts Mus. (bd. 1989), Nat. Fedn. of Neighborhood Ctrs. (v.p. 1975-76), Lions Intl. S.F.; mil: cpl. USAF 1945-46; Prot.; rec: photog., bicycling. Ofc: City Hall Rm 107 San Francisco 94102

BROWN, WILLIAM EDWIN, construction executive, educator; b. Jan. 11, 1934, Belknap, Ill.; s. Samual Edwin and Sarah Elizabeth (Kean) B.; edn: BS, So. Ill. Univ., 1956, MS, 1957; Univ. of Tenn., 1956-57; PhD, The Ohio State Univ., 1964. Career: grad. instr. So. Ill. Univ., 1955, instr. Univ. Tenn. 1956; asst. prof. engring. graphics The Ohio State Univ., 1957-65, asst. to the dean of engring. 1965-67; prof. and dept. engring. technology chair Trenton State Coll., N.J. 1967-76 (devel. curr. and gained State approval for 4 yr. baccalaureate pgm., MS in mech., electrical, and indsl. engring. technology; appt. N.J. Advy. Bd. on Tech. Edn., also State Engring. Tech. Master Planning Com., 1969-76); regional dir. Pub. Employment Rels. Bd., Sacto., 1976-80; gen. contr., prin. Bear Tavern Assoc., Sacto. 1980-; faculty mech. engring. dept. CSU Sacto. 1986-; franchise seminar dir./bus. mgmt. for Dial One of No. Calif., Sacto. 1985-; mem: NEA, Am. Indsl. Arts Assn., Am. Coun. on Indsl. Arts Tchr. Edn., Am. Soc. Engring. Edn., AAU honors: Phi Delta Kappa, Epsilon Pi Tau, Iota Lambda, Phi Alpha Delta profl.-social frat. (advr. 8 yrs.), Outstanding Tchr. Award 1976; United Methodist. Res: 1110 La Sierra Dr Sacramento 95864 Tel: 916/486-9054

BROWNING, GEORGE HUGHEY, notary, retired real estate broker; b. May 3, 1913, Pensacola, Fla.; s. G.B. and Ella Lee (Horton) B.; m. Leona Rucker, Nov. 21, 1942 (div. 1955); children: Gregory Harris b. 1937, Joyce Rochelle b. 1943; m. Thelma Josephine Brooks, Sept. 3, 1956; edn: att. Knoxville Coll., Tenn.; L.A. Jr. Coll. 1934-35; real estate courses UCLA 1957-58; lic. Notary Public 1957-91. Career: founder, owner, opr. electroplating plant, Los Angeles 1947-57; real estate sales assoc. Local Realty, L.A. 1957-65; real estate broker Geo. H. Browning, L.A. 1963-76, ret.; civic: Men & Women of Tomorrow, NAACP, YMCA; lodge: Masonic Prince Hall (33rd Degree, Past Potentate

Honors 8/18/91); Democrat; Baptist; rec: checkers, dominos, cards. Address: 3812 2nd Ave Los Angeles 90008

BRUCE, JOHN ANTHONY, western artist, art consultant; b. Apr. 8, 1931, Los Angeles; s. Merle VanDyke and Katherine Mary (Butler) B.; m. Barbara Jean Kennedy, May 29, 1967 (div. 1988); children: Marsha Lee, Margaret Lorren, James Cole, Glenn Allen, Mark Corwin, Leslie Ann; edn: BA psychology/art, CSU Los Angeles, 1965. Career: design engr. North Am. Aviation Corp., Downey 1952-57; commercial artist Aerojet Gen. Corp., Sacramento 1957-59; advt. mgr. Flow Equipment Co., Santa Fe Springs 1959-63; art dir. Barnes-Camp Advt., Santa Ana 1963-68; Long Beach Independent Press-Telegram News, 1970-73; freelance art cons. Epcot project Walt Disney Enterprises, 1976-77; recipient numerous art awards including John B. Grayback Award Am. Profl. Artists League 1988, Philip Isinberg Award Knickerbocker Artists 1988, Eagle Feather Award Am. Indian and Cowboy Artists (1988, 1989); represented by Bartfield Gal., N.Y.C., El Prado Gal., Sedona, Ariz., Trails West Gal., Laguna Beach, Calif.; one man shows Ghormley Gal., L.A., 1966, Les Li Art Gal., L.A., 1970, Upstairs Gal., Long Beach, 1973, El Prado Gal., Sedona 1987; group shows Newport Beach Invitational, 1964, Laguna Beach Art Festival, 1962, 63, 64, 64, Butler Inst. American Art, Youngstown, Oh. 1970, Allied Artists, 1988; rep. in permanent collections Smithsonian Inst., W.D.C.; mem. Knickerbocker Artists, Am. Indian and Cowboy Artists; mil: AUS 1949-52, Korea; Republican: Studio: 5394 Tip Top Rd Mariposa 95338

BRUNNER, ROBERT FRANCIS, composer, conductor, arranger, songwriter; b. Jan. 9, 1938, Pasadena; s. Francis Rudolph and Barbara Jeanne (Reese) B.; edn: music performance major UCLA, pvt. studies with: Helen Jane Dixon, Santa Monica, Guy Maier of UCLA, Lionel Taylor of The L.A. Conservatory, Dr. Alfred Sendrey of The Leipzig Opera and The Paris Conservatory, Ina Zan, Hollywood. Career: profl. musician since age 11; teenage star of TV series "It's Great To Be Young" as leader of his own 20-piece dance band (for which he wrote 140+ spl. arrangements); composed his first of 7 successful stage musicals at age 16 in 1954; served to capt. USAF (Calif. Air Nat. Guard) 1956-71: conductor and c.o. 562nd USAF Band, toured 7 we. states, 6-time winner "Best Band in the Land" award; staff composer/condr. Walt Disney Studios, 17+ years; owner Brunner Music Publishing Co., Los Angeles; composer music and theme songs for TV shows and feature films incl. "So Many Ways" for Disney film classic, Amy; songwriter (250+ songs) and arranger for vocalists and instrumental groups as: Lawrence Welk, Ray Anthony, Bobby Darin, Maurice Chevalier, Julie Budd, The Lennon Sisters, Shirley Jones, John Raitt, Rhonda Fleming, Anna Maria Alberghetti, Ella Fitzgerald, Sammy Davis Jr., USAF Singing Sergeants, The Am. Pilgrim Chorus, The Kids of the Kingdom, Disneyland Marching Band, White Eagle, The Vocal Majority, New Mousketeers, and The Salt Lake Mormon Tabernacle Choir (his "Suddenly You're Older" their most requested song); composer patriotic anthem "So Many Voices Sing America's Song" (lyrics by Bruce Belland) featured at 1989 Presdl. Inaugural Gala, and at 50th Ann. Celebration and Ofcl. Dedication of Mt. Rushmore; musical director 300+ studio recording sessions; guest condr. The Hollywood Bowl Easter Sunrise Services, The Dallas Symphony, The Salvation Army Hendon Band (U.K.), All-American Coll. Orch. at Walt Disney World, The Los Angeles Debut Orch., others; awards: first recipient Young Musicians Found. Award for classical composition for symphony orch. at age 23 (1961), Emmy nominee for songwriting, his score for Disney's "Castaway Cowboy" one of ten finalists Academy Awards (1974), So. Calif. Motion Picture Council outstanding achiev. in film scoring, Film Advisory Board award of excellence (3t), Freedoms Found. Geo. Washington Honor Medal, ASCAP awards, DAR award, listed Who's Who in Entertainment, Who's Who in West, Who's Who in Am., Who's Who in World; mem: Dramatists Guild, Acad. Motion Picture Arts & Scis. (exec. com. music br.), Screen Composers Assn. (bd.), Songwriters Guild of Am., Soc. of Composers and Lyricists, ASCAP (west coast advy. bd.), Am. Choral Directors Assn., Screen Actors Guild, AFTRA, AGMA, Am. Fedn. of Musicians; Republican; Ch. of Jesus Christ of Latter-Day Saints; rec: skiing, swimming, tennis, horseback riding, photography. Res: 169 N Bowling Green Way Los Angeles 90049

BRUTON, LAURENCE "BRYAN", advertising, public and international government relations executive; b. Feb. 25, 1947, Altadena; s. L. B. and Mary Jayne (Moore) B.; m. Karen, Feb. 2, 1969; children: Wendi Nicole b. 1977; edn: BS telecomms. mgmt.; Air Univ. 1965-69, East N.M. Univ. 1966-68, Am. River Coll. 1969-70, Mt. San Antonio Coll. 1971-73. Career: public relations, advt. and mktg. strategy cons., internat. relations; ptnr. COM3 Multi-Media Productions 1983-84, sole owner 1984-; gen. ptnr. Green-Bruton & Associates, gen. bus. consulting (local, nat., internat.), offices in Sacto. and San Francisco, Calif., Austin and San Antonio, Tx.; owner COM3 Communications Network, Commercial Powerwash Systems, and GO-SOAP; mem: Retired Ofcr. Assn., Internat. Platform Speakers Assn., . Soc. Am. Engrs., Nat. Guard Assn. Calif. Nat. Guard Assn. of U.S.; comm. bds. (PTA, Softball League); invention: antisyphon device utilized for home and crop applications of insecticides etc.; mil: E3 USAF 1965-69, LTC (Ret.) US Army 1970-91; Republican; Baptist; rec: art, reading, fishing, garden. Res: Rt 2 Box 24-0 Burnet TX 78611 Ofc: Green-Bruton & Associates: 190 Cinnabar Way Hercules CA 94547 tel: 510/245-9114

BRUYERE, DENNIS PAUL, real estate broker, general building contractor, entrepreneur; b. Apr. 7, 1947, Ogdensburg, N.Y.; s. Joseph Paul and Audrey L. (Paulsen) B.; div.; children: Garey b. 1967, Paula b. 1970; edn: AA, Compton Jr. Coll. 1968; CSU Los Angeles, UCLA Ext., 1969-72, Pepperdine Univ., 1973; desig: Grad. Realtors Inst. (GRI) Calif. Assn. Realtors 1976, Cert. Residential Splst. (CRS) Nat. Assn. Realtors 1978, Gold Card Exchangor, Nat. Exch. Counselors 1978; var. Century 21 certs. (CIS inv. splst., CRS res. splst., VIP 301 referral broker). Career: sales person Hallmark Realty 1970, LCOA Investment & Realty Inc. 1971, Verpet Devel. 1972, Viren Realty 1973-75; broker/owner and gen. sales mgr. Century 21 Granada Realty (50+ lic. sales agts. in 2 branch offices), Bellflower 1975-89, current owner Granada Realty with Mgmt. & Maint. depts.; real estate investor, Calif., Tex.; tchr. seminars 1977-80; mem. Calif. Assn. Realtors (CAR), Rancho Los Cerritos Bd. Realtors, Long Beach Bd. Realtors; contbg. author "Residential Real Estate Financing" (CAR, 1978); Republican; rec: surf, swim, travel. Res: Paramount 90723

BRYAN, JOHN RODNEY, consultant; b. Dec. 29, 1953, Berkeley; s. Robert Richard and Eloise (Anderson) Putz; m. Karen Nelson Bryan, Jan. 20, 1990; edn: BA, UC San Diego, 1975; MBA, Rutgers Univ., 1984. Career: project mgr. Brooks Internat. Corp., West Palm Beach, Fla. 1985-88; owner Applied Control, Management & Effectiveness Systems, San Diego, Calif. 1989-; program mgr. Western Productivity Group, Palo Alto 1989-; honors: Beta Gamma Sigma 1985; mem: Inst. of Indsl. Engrs. 1986-, ASPA 1993-; Republican; La Jolla Presbyterian Ch. (elder 1991-); rec: singing (classical), gardening. Res: 5796 Scripps St San Diego 92122-3210

BRYANT, ALAN WILLARD, human resources executive; b. Aug. 17, 1940, Glen Ridge, N.J.; s. Alan Willard and Clara Sherman (Clark) B.; m. Karen Koenig; children: Hilary Ann, Christopher Bowman; edn: AB, Dartmouth Coll., 1962, MBA, 1963; postgrad. St. Mary's Univ. Law, San Antonio 1964-65. Career: with General Electric Co., 1965-93: specialist profl. placement Spacecraft Dept. GE Co., King of Prussia, Pa. 1965-66; foreman, methods analyst Television Dept., Syracuse, N.Y. 1966-67; specialist salaried employment Armament Dept., Springfield, Mass. 1967-68; specialist profl. and salaried compensation Information Systems Equip. Div., Phoenix, Ariz. 1968-70; mgr. personnel relations Nuclear Energy Dept., Wilmington, N.C. 1970-72; mgr. relations practices TV Receiver Products Dept., Portsmouth, Va. 1972-76; mgr. employee and community relations Meter Bus. Dept., Somersworth, N.H. 1976-85; mgr. human resources op. Nuclear Energy, San Jose, Calif. 1985-93, mem. senior staff GE leadership course in positive mgmt., Fairfield, Conn. 1981-93, adj. staff, exec. assessment and devel., 1987-93; v.p. Computer Curriculum Corp. 1993-; speaker Am. Mgmt. Assn. Nat. Conf. 1986, speaker US-Japan Institute 1991; recipient awards for public service Gov. Ariz. (1970), Gov. N.H. (1982-84); mem: Soc. for Human Resource Mgmt., Bay Area Human Resource Execs. Council (pres. 1992-93), No. Calif. Human Resources Council, Dover C.of C. (pres. 1984-85), Rotary (disting. svc. award 1985); civic bds: United Way (pres., campaign chair of Strafford Co., Dover, N.H. 1980-81), Strafford Hospice Care, Somersworth (founding pres. 1982-85), Wentworth Douglass Hosp., Dover (trustee 1982-85); mil: capt. US Army 1963-65; author/subject several pub. articles; Republican. Res: 1285 Poker Flat Place San Jose 95120-1766 Ofc: Computer Curriculum Corp. 1287 Lawrence Station Road Sunnyvale 94089

BRYANT, STEVEN HARRY, design engineer; b. Nov. 28, 1946, Des Moines, Iowa; s. Harry Kenneth and Hannah (Levey) B.; edn: AA engring., Fullerton Coll., 1968; BA hist., CSU Long Beach, 1970. Career: sr. structural design engr., aerospace indus., So. Calif., 1966-88; aerospace engring. contr., 1976-, pres. Hawkeye Enterprises (contract engring.), Cathedral City 1986-; listed Who's Who in West, Who's Who in World, Who's Who in Fin. and Ind., Who's Who of Emerging Leaders Am.; mem. Am. Soc. of Engrs. and Architects S. Pasa., Nat. Writers Club, Nat. Corvette Owners Assn., Calif. Astrology Assn., U.S. Hist. Soc.; civic: Cathedral City Citizens for Progress 1989, World Vision for Africa 1985-, Cystic Fibrosis Found. 1987-, Chino Hills Area #19 (commr. 1979-82), Riverside Raceway Booster's Club 1976-82, Statue of Liberty Ellis Island Found. (charter 1984-); contbr. poetry to American Poetry Anthology (1987); Democrat (sec. San Bdo. Co. Dem. Party 1985); Christian/Jew; rec: dancing, skiing, swimming, poetry. Res: 3540 Autumn Ave Chino 91709 Ofc: 31-200 Landau Blvd Ste 1604 Cathedral City 92234

BUBB, BRIAN DAVID, lawyer; b. June 22, 1962, Baltimore, Md.; s. Donald L., Sr. and Louise Mary (Masimore) B.; edn: BS in bus. admin./fin., Albright Coll., Pa. 1985; JD, Pepperdine Univ. Sch. of Law 1988. Career: partner Howarth & Smith, Los Angeles 1993-; tchg. asst. Pepperdine Univ., Malibu 1987-88; mem: Am. Trial Lawyers Assn., L.A. Co. Bar Assn., Calif. Bar Assn.; Republican. Ofc: Howarth & Smith 700 So Flower St Ste 2908 Los Angeles 90017

BUCCIERI, AGOSTINO ROCCO, educator, building contractor, real estate broker; b. Aug. 15, 1892, Cosenza, Italy, came to USA in 1911, naturalized 1922; s. Salvatore and Rosa (Marsico) B.; m. Julia Mary Settino, Feb. 14, 1920 (dec. 1978); children: Mary Frances b. 1923, Agostino Rocco Jr. b. 1928, Julius Samuel b. 1930, Gloria Jean b. 1934; edn: att. public schs. in Etna and Aspinwall, Pa. 1911-1915; Indiana State Normal Sch. 1916-18, Bethany Coll., W. Va. 1918-20; BA, MA edn., Univ. Pittsburgh, 1923, 1931; dipl. in Italian arts & lit., Inst. InterUniversitaria of Romance Languages, Rome 1936; Calif. lic. gen. contr., R.E. broker, 1948-. Career: student tchr. Bethany Coll., Bethany, W.Va. 1918-20; prof. Washington Jefferson Coll., Washington, Pa. 1923-25; prof. Duquesne Univ., Pittsburgh, Pa. 1929-36, also faculty Pittsburgh Acad., Berlitz; building contr., real estate broker, Pittsburgh, Pa., Los Angeles, and Phoenix, 1936-; rec: violinist, photog., gourmet cook, gentleman farmer. Res: 4410 Haskell Ave Encino 91436

BUCEY, CONSTANCE VIRGINIA RUSSELL, educator; b. Aug. 22, 1936, Miami, Fla.; d. Mose and Lillian (Jones) Russell; m. Henry Lee Bucey, Oct. 21, 1966; edn: BS, Va. State Coll. 1959; grad. work, Univ. Fla. 1961-63, UCLA 1970-71; MA, Pepperdine Univ. 1976. Career: tchr. Lee Elem. Sch., South Miami, Fla. 1959-67; Duff Elem Sch., Rosemead, Calif. 1967-74, 1980-82, reading splst. 1974-80; tchr. Hillcrest Elem. Sch., Monterey Park 1983-; dir. Calif. Tchrs. Fed. Credit Union 1977-79, 1981-83; pres. bd. First Fin. Fed. Credit Union 1979, 80, 83-; mem: Nat. Edn. Assn., Nat. Credit Union Pres., Nat. Credit Union Assn., AAUW (1965-80), BPW (1973-83), Alpha Kappa Alpha Sor., Women Aware (1988-, secty. 1990); Episcopal. Res: 871 Ashiya Rd Montebello 90640

BUCHAN, MARY DIGEL, building contractor; b. Oct. 11, 1937, Lakewood, Ohio; d. Otto August and Doris Lucinda (Smart) Digel; m. Ashleigh F. Buchan, Nov. 18, 1959; children: Ashleigh, Jr. b. 1960, Lucinda b. 1975; edn: BA, Ohio Univ. 1959. Career: engring. asst. Jet Propulsion Lab., Pasadena 1960-61; pres. Apex Plastering Co., El Monte 1979-; dir. pension fund Apex Plastering Co.; honors: Woman of Yr. Sierra Madre Athletic Assn. 1975; civic: Anoakia Sch. Parents Assn. (pres. 1972-4, 80-82), Sierra Madres Civic Club (pres. 1968-69), Sierra Madre Baseball Assn., Sierra Madre Woman's Club, Sierra Madre Comm. Hosp. Aux., GSA Brownie leader, Girls' Softball coach (1969-71, 84-87); Republican; Prot.; rec: graphic artist. Res: 138 E Grandview Sierra Madre 91024 Ofc: Apex Plastering Co. 4526 N Rowland El Monte 91731

BUCHANAN, PEGGY KATHRYN, real estate broker; b. Nov. 1, 1943, Los Angeles; d. Howard Eugene and Geraldine Stowe (Young) Kutepoff; m. Donald Gene Buchanan, June 21, 1963; children: Jeffrey Dwayne b. 1965, Kathryn Anna b. 1969, Ryan Eugene b. 1973; edn: AA, Imperial Valley Coll. 1963; real estate courses Coll. of Redwoods 1979-80. Career: real estate broker ABC Realty (JSK); mem. Calif. Assn. Realtors (regional v.p. 1989, state dir. 1988-89), Humboldt Co. Bd. Realtors (pres., bd. dirs., chair 1988), Humboldt Light Opera Co. (bd. dirs. 1986-89); articles pub. 1988; Republican; Mormon; rec: camping. Ofc: 2828 E St., Eureka 95501

BUCKEL, HARRY J., publisher; b. March 7, 1944, Indpls., Ind.; s. Harry J. and Delia (Spellman) B.; m. Helen McGrady, Dec. 16, 1966; children: Susan, Hailey, Sean, Brendan, Megan; edn: BS, BA, Xavier Univ., 1966. Career: pub. San Francisco Progress 1978-80; pub. Gloucester Times, Woodbury, NJ 1980-81; pub. Journal News, Hamilton 1981-82; pres. Pennysaver, Brea 1982-; v.chmn.Third Class Mail Marketing Assn. 1985-92, chmn. Advertising Mail Marketing Assn.; mem. Balboa Bay Club (Newport Beach); mil: 1st lt., U.S. Army, 1967-69; Irish Cath.; rec: hunting, fishing. Ofc: 2830 Orbiter, Brea 92622

BUDLONG, DUDLEY WEBSTER, engineering executive; b. May 9, 1922, Mount Prospect, Ill.; s. Dudley W. and Louise B. (Schiller) B.; children: Gerald, Steven, Bruce, Roger; m. Gladys M. Lacerda, Dec. 15, 1979; edn: BS, Ill. Inst. Tech., 1948, postgrad., 1951-53; postgrad., USC, 1953-54; reg. profl. engr. Calif., N.J., N.Y., Nev., Va., Fla., Mich., Minn., Ak., Utah. Career: asst. staff engr. Standard Oil Co. of Indiana (now AMOCO), Whiting, 1948-51; plant engr. Argonne Nat. Lab., Ill. 1951-53; senior job engr. Bechtel Corp., Los Angeles 1953-54; chief engr. May Engring. Co., Van Nuys 1954-58; pres., chief engr. Budlong and Assocs., Sherman Oaks 1958-69; exec. v.p. Quinton-Budlong Architects, Engrs. and Planners, L.A. 1969-73; pvt. practice cons. Northridge, 1973; pres. Killian Assocs. West Inc., Northridge 1973-78; v.p. facilities systems group Boyle Engring. Corp., Northridge 1974-81; pres. Dudley W. Budlong Cons., Woodland Hills 1981-86, past pres. and chmn. Budlong & Moore Assocs., 1986-90; pres. and ceo Budlong & Associates, Inc. 1990-; mem. planning cabinet Am. Cons. Engrs. Council U.S., 1970-76, chmn. 1975; mem. engring. profl. advy. council, dean's advy. bd. Sch. of Engring. and Computer Science CSU Northridge, 1976-; honors: Tau Beta Pi, Eta Kappa Nu, Alpha Phi Omega, recipient distinguished achiev. L.A. Council Engrs. and Scientists 1986, distinguished internat. engring. achiev. Calif. Council Industrial and Bus. Assocs. 1986, Fellow Inst. Advancement of Engring.; mem. Am. Inst. Plant Engrs. (cert.), Assn. Energy Engrs. (charter), Consulting Engrs. Assn. Calif. (past bd. dirs. and sec.), Consulting Engrs. and Land Surveyors of Calif. (L.A. chapt. pres. 1993), Calif. Soc. Profl. Engrs. (past pres., state dir.), Consulting Elec. Engrs. So. Calif. (past pres., bd. dirs.), Illuminating Engring. Soc., Mech.-Elec. Engrs. Council Calif. (past state chmn.), Industrial Assn. S.F.V.; mil: 2d lt. USAF 1943-45; Emmanuel Presbyterian Ch., Thousand Oaks (deacon). Ofc: Budlong & Associates, Inc. 28720 Roadside Dr Agoura Hills 91301

BUFFO, JOHN ANTHONY, educator, historian; b. Nov. 29, 1935, Antioch, Calif.; s. Neno Peter and Sarah Joan (Russo-Cacciaroni) B.; edn: AA., Diablo Valley Coll., 1955; AB, San Jose St. Univ., 1957; PhD candidate, Columbia Pacific Univ., 1993; Calif. tchg. and sch. adminstrn. creds. Career: teacher Oakland Unified Sch. Dist., 1959-64; counselor U.S. Army Dependents Schs., Nuremberg, Ger. 1964-65; tchg. asst. Sch. of Edn. UOP, 1978-79; tchr. Pittsburg (Calif.) Unif. Sch. Dist. 1965-68, 77-78, 86-94; sch. adminstr. Central Jr. High Sch., Pittsburg 1967-75, principal 1969-75; instr. Los Medanos Coll., 1986-88; pgm. consultant ESL, Pittsburg Adult Edn. Ctr., 1988; awards: Boys Clubs of Am. man of yr. Pittsburg chpt. 1969, Central Jr. H.S. man of yr. 1972, 75; mem: Tau Delta Phi (hon. scholastic soc.), Phi Alpha Theta (nat. hon. hist. soc.) and Sigma Nu Frat. at San Jose St. Univ., Calif. Tchrs. Assn., Assn. of Calif. Sch. Adminstrs., Nat. Assn. Sec. Sch. Principals, Phi Delta Kappa; civic: Contra Costa County Hist. Soc. (pres. 1989-90), Pioneer Fishermen Com. Pittsburg (pgm. chair 1988-91), Sons of Italy in Am. (chapt. pres. 1989-92, county v.p. 1991-93), Am.-Italian Hist. Assn. (v.p. We. Reg. chpt. 1982-84), Italian-Am. Club of Pittsburg (trustee 1988-92), Pittsburg-Isoladelle Femmine Sister City Com. 1992-94, Pittsburg Hist. Soc. (bd. 1970-94), Arts & Cult. Com. Pittsburg (commr. 1974-75), Boys' Clubs Am. (chapt. pres. 1971-72), Citizens' Football Com. Pittsburg (pres. 1972), Model Cities Pittsburg (commr. 1971); publs: numerous articles on Italian-Am. studies, ethnicity, cultural pluralism, history, sports, book and movie revs.; mil: sgt. Calif. Nat. Guard 1954-62; Democrat; R.Cath.; rec: local history, pedagogy, sports, travel, writing, Italian-Am. studies. Res: 2415 Horizon Ln Apt 123 Antioch 94509 Ofc: Pittsburg Unified School District Pittsburg 94565

BUI, CHUNG THE, physician; b. April 26, 1945, Dalat, Vietnam; nat. 1986; s. Quy The and Lien Thi (Pham) B.; m. Tran Pham, Jan. 16, 1974; children: Hong Chi b. 1975, Huy The b. 1981, Quynh Chau b. 1987; edn: Baccalaureate, Jean Jacques Rousseau Sch. 1963; BS, Saigon Faculty of Sci. 1964; MD, Saigon Vietnam Med. Sch. 1971; reg. physician and surgeon Calif. 1986. Career: residency in radiol. Wadsworth Med. Hosp. Ctr. 1986; med. dir. 2nd infantry med. section, S. Vietnam Armed Forces, Quangtri 1972-73; gen. surgeon, 1st field mil. hosp. 1973-75; chief gynecol. section Khanhhoi Womens' Hosp., Saigon 1977-80; postgrad. tng. diagnostic radiol., Wadsworth Med. Center 1984-86; currently M.D. Med. Clin., Santa Ana; awards: Physician Recognition award Saigon Health Dept. 1973, Valiant Medal of Honor w. Gold Star Vietnam Armed Forces 1973; mem: Vietnamese Med. Assn. 1986, AMA 1986; civic: YMCA (Saigon), Vietnamese Med. Armed Forces Assn.; honor award for MD thesis, Surg. Repair of Carotid Arteries in Mil. Hosp. (Saigon 1972); mil: capt. S. Vietnam Armed Forces 1975; Buddhist; rec: camping, fishing, boating. Res: 9612 Scotstoun Dr Huntington Beach 92646 Ofc: Medical and Dental Clinic 5407 West First St Santa Ana 92703

BUIE, ROBERT FRANK, real estate developer; b. May 29, 1942, Washington DC; s. Paul Douglas and Mary Margaret (Bullock) B.; m. Pamela Nosler, Jan. 2, 1984; children: Tatia b. 1969, Garrett b. 1975, Catherine Nicole b. 1987, Erica Anne b. 1988; edn: BS civil engring., Virginia Tech. 1964; MBA, Harvard Univ. 1971. Career: naval flight ofcr. USN, S.E. Asia 1964-69; var. positions Avco Community Developers 1971-75, v.p. gen. mgr. San Diego Div. Avco 1975-78, exec. v.p. Avco Community Developers 1978-83; pres. The Buie Corp., real estate developer San Diego, Orange, and Riverside counties 1983-; mem: Building Industry Assn. (bd. dirs.), Presidents Council, Marbella Assn. (pres.); clubs: San Diego Yacht, Fairbanks Ranch CC, The Centre; mil: lcdr. USN-R, active duty 1964-69; Republican; Methodist; rec: skiing, boating. Res: PO Box 8365 Rancho Santa Fe 92067 Ofc: The Buie Corp. 16935 W Bernardo Dr San Diego 92127

BUKRY, JOHN DAVID, geologist; b. May 17, 1941, Baltimore; s. Howard Leroy and Irene Evelyn (Davis) Snyder; edn: undergrad., Colo. Sch. of Mines 1959-60; BA, The Johns Hopkins Univ. 1963; Univ. Ill. 1965-66; MA, PhD, Princeton Univ. 1965, 1967. Career: geologist US Army Corps of Engrs., Baltimore 1963; research asst. Mobil Oil Co., Dallas 1965; geologist US Geological Survey, La Jolla 1967-75, geologist in charge 1975-84; geologist US Minerals Mgmt. Service, La Jolla 1984-86; geologist US Geological Survey, Menlo Park 1986-; research assoc. Geol. Research Div. UC San Diego 1970-; cons. Deep Sea Drilling Project, La Jolla 1967-1987; guest lectr. Vetlesen Symposium, Columbia Univ., N.Y. 1968, 3d Internat. Planktonic Conf., Germany 1974, British Petroleum Exploration Sem. on nannofossil biostratigraphy, Houston 1989; shipboard micropaleontologist on D/V Glomar Challenger (5 DSDP Cruises 1968-78); mem. NSF-JOIDES Stratigraphic Correlations Panel 1976-79; ed. Marine Micropaleontology 1976-83, editl. bd. Micropaleontology 1985-90; awards: fellowships at Princeton Univ., Mobil Oil Co. 1965-67, Am. Chem. Soc. 1966-67; elected fellow AAAS 1981, Explorers Club 1979, Geol. Soc. of Am. 1975; mem: Am. Assn. of Petroleum Geologists, European Union of Geosciences, Internat. Nannoplankton Assn., The Oceanography Soc., Paleontol. Research Instn., Sigma Xi; civic: S.D. Shell Club, UCSD Ida and Cecil Green Faculty Club, S.D. Soc. Natural Hist., Hawaiian Malacological Soc., Nat. Sci. Tchrs. Soc., The Nature Conservancy, Zool. Soc. of S.D., Calif. Acad. of Sciences; author two sci. books in field; contbr. identification and definitions for 300 new species of fossil marine phytoplankton used to give geological ages for ocean bottom sediments pub. in sci.

jours.; rec: basketball, photog., shell collector. Ofc: USGS (MS-915), 345 Middlefield Rd Menlo Park 94025

BUKWICH, ANTHONY MICHAEL, county juvenile detention administrator; b. Feb. 13, 1937, Los Angeles; s. Michael and Wilhelmina Maria (Noordman) B.; m. Geraldine Fay Bourland, Sept. 3, 1955; children: Michael A. b. 1956, Tersea A. b. 1959, Stephen J. b. 1963, Kathleen M. b. 1964; edn: BA pub. mgmt., St. Marys Coll. 1978. Career: counselor Orange Co. Juvenile Hall, Orange 1962-69; supt. Solano Co. Juvenile Hall, Fairfield 1969-; mem: Calif. Juvenile Detention Adminstrs. Assn. (st. pres. 1972-73, st. secty., treas. 1976-78), Calif. Assn. Probation Inst. Adminstrs. (st. secty., treas. 1986-88); mil: cpl. USMC 1954-57; Democrat; R.Cath. Res: 3486 Springfield Dr Fairfield 94533 Ofc: Solano County Juvenile Hall 2010 W Texas St Fairfield 94533

BURDICK, ROBERT BENJAMIN, retired telephone company services manager; b. Nov. 28, 1936, St. Petersburg, Fla.; s. George Swain and Laura Francis (Woolley) B.; m. Mary Louise Garcia, Nov. 23, 1967; children: Alexander b. 1964, Wade b. 1964, Steven b. 1968, Brian b. 1969; edn: AA, L.A. City Coll. 1975. Career: engr. asst. Sperry Phoenix Co., Phoenix, Ariz. 1958-60; field service mgr. AT&T, Los Angeles 1969-83, field adminstrn. center mgr. 1983-84, services mgr. 1984-85, mgmt. tech. instr. 1985-86, project mgr. 1986-89, ret.; mem: Project Mgmt. Inst. (1st v.p. 1989-, mem. chair 1988-89), Los Padrinos, Monterey Jr. C.of C.; mil: airman 1c. USAF 1954-58; Republican; Prot.; rec: water sports. Res: 11681 Oak St Apple Valley 92308

BURGESON, NICHOLAS R., health care executive/management consultant; b. July 4, 1943, Portland, Oreg.; s. Randolph Benjamin and Grace Ruth (Nimlos) B.; m. Donna Irene MacGlashen, Oct. 17, 1964; children: Tina Lynn b. 1965, Robert Gene b. 1967; edn: AS nsg. sci., Pacific Union Coll., 1964; BS bus. adm., Golden Gate Univ., 1977; MBA, Univ. Beverly Hills, 1981; RN, Calif., W.D.C.; lic. nursing home adminstr. Calif. Career: staff nse. Napa State Hosp. 1964-66; nsg. coord. Adolescent Pgm., Napa State Hosp., 1968-70, asst. to the med. dir. 1970-71; pgm. adminstr. I, II, Hosp. Svs. Sect. Calif. Dept. of Mental Hygiene, Sacto. 1971-72, Calif. Dept. of Health, 1973-77; adminstr. Metropolitan State Hosp., Norwalk 1977-81; assoc. adminstr., chief ops. Loma Linda Comm. Hosp., Loma Linda 1981-82; pres. NRB & Associates, Sacto. 1982-; mgr. psychiatric hosp. devel. Am. Med. Internat. Inc., Beverly Hills 1983-84; stds. compliance coord. Atascadero State Hosp., 1984-86, then dir. info. resources dept., 1986-90; spl. advisor Hosp. Accreditation, Calif. Dept. of Mental Health, Sacto. 1990-; chmn. Jt. Dept. Mental Hlth. and Corrections Task Force on Correctional Psychiat. Svs., 1987; narrated and appeared in 90-min. NBC-TV White Paper "Cry Help" (1970); recipient commendn. Secty. Calif. Health and Welfare Agy., Sacto. 1979, sustained superior accomplishment award Calif. Dept. Mental Hlth. 1987, leadership and scholarship award National Univ. Bd. Trustees, Sacto. 1987; biographical listings in Who's Who in West (22d), Who's Who in Fin. and Indus. (26th), Dir. of Top Computer Execs., Men of Achiev. (14th); mem: Calif. Assn. of Mgmt. Sciences (secty. 1974-77, pres. 1976-77), Forensic Mental Health Assn. of Calif. (dir. 1988-, pres. 1990-92); contbr. articles in Forensic Forum J. (1988-); mil: chief warrant ofcr., staff nse. US Army Nurse Corps, Walter Reed Army Med. Ctr., W.D.C. (hon. disch.) 1966-68; Republican; Prot. Res: 8788 Bluff Ln Fair Oaks 95628 Ofc: 1600 Ninth St Rm 120 Sacramento 95814 Ph: 916/323-9389

BURGESS, MICHAEL, librarian, author, publisher; b. Feb. 11, 1948, Fukuoka, Kyushu, Japan, came to U.S. 1949; s. Roy Walter and Betty Jane (Kapel) B.; m. Mary Alice Wickizer, Oct. 15, 1976; stepchildren: Richard Albert Rogers, Mary Louise Reynnells; edn: AB (honors), Gonzaga Univ., 1969; MLS, USC, 1970. Career: periodicals librarian CSU San Bernardino, 1970-81, prof. and chief cataloger CSU San Bernardino, 1981-; editor Newcastle Pub. Co., North Hollywood 1971-92, pub. Borgo Press, San Bernardino 1975-; advy. editor Arno Press, N.Y.C., 1975-78; author of 70 books, editor, publisher approx. 1950 books; including: Cumulative Paperback Index 1973, Things to Come 1977, Science Fiction and Fantasy Literature 1979, Tempest in a Teapot 1984, Lords Temporal & Lords Spiritual 1985, Futurevisions 1985, Arms Control, Disarmament, & Military Security Dict. 1989, The Work of Colin Wilson 1989, Reference Guide to Science Fiction, Fantasy, and Horror 1992; editor 15 scholarly series incl. Milford Series: Popular Writers of Today (60 vols.), Science Fiction (63 vols.), Stokvis Studies in Historical Chronology and Thought (10 vols.), editor 6 reprint series, 2 jours.; 135+ pub. articles and revs., 80+ publishers' catalogs, 1 pub. short story, 15 major state documents, designer and prodn. mgr. 100+ pub. volumes; awards: Title II fellow USC 1969-70, $2500 MPPP Award 1987, Lifetime Collectors Award 1993, Pilgrim Award 1993; mem: ACLU, NEA, AAUP, Calif. Tchrs. Assn., Am. Library Assn., Calif. Library Assn., Kent Hist. Soc., Sci. Fiction Writers Am., Horror Writers of Am., Calif. Faculty Assn. (Librarians' Task Force 1987-89, ed. LTF Newsletter 1987-89), Sci. Fiction Research Assn., Blue Earth County (Minn.) Hist. Soc., City of San Bdo. Hist. and Pioneer Soc., Grant County (Ky.) Hist. Soc., Internat. Assn. for the Fantastic in Arts, Nat. Geneal. Soc., Internat. P.E.N., Ky. Hist. Soc., Upper Cumberland Geneal. Assn., World SF. Res: PO Box 2845 San Bernardino 92406 Ofc: Calif. State Univ. Library, 5500 University Pkwy San Bernardino 92407

BURKETT, NANCY SCHALLERT (Mrs. William Andrew Burkett), educator, artist, philanthropist; b. May 11, 1917, Winston-Salem, N.C.; d. Dr. Paul Otto and Grace (Jackson) Schallert; m. Richard Morrison Lofton, Aug. 20, 1938 (dec. 1966); children: Nancy Lofton Faridany, and Melissa Lofton; m. Dr. Dwight W. Morrow, Jr., Nov. 25, 1970 (dec. 1976); m. William Andrew Burkett, June 20, 1992; edn: att. Salem Coll., Winston-Salem, 1934-36; AB in English, Univ. N. Carolina, Chapel Hill 1938; grad. study UC Berkeley; Calif. life tchg. credential 1955. Career: feature writer Winston-Salem Journal and Sentinel, 1938-40; Monterey Herald, and Carmel Pine Cone, 1945-50; tchr. Monterey-Carmel Schs., 1952-73; cons. and lectr. on Textbook Edn., 1961-63; designer of Carmel Bach Festival Heraldic Banners, 1951-91, fest. cons. and artist, 1979-89; dir. Burkett Land Co., 1990-; appt. by Gov. Edmund G. Brown to Calif. Curriculum Commn., 1964-68; appt. Calif. Com. to Create Humanities Framework for Schs., 1969-74; appt. Nat. Commn. U.S.M.E.S., supported by AAAS tp improve tchg. of sci. and math., 1969; civic bds: endowment com. Univ. N.Carolina, Chapel Hill (bd. 1977-89), Carmel Bach Festival (dir. 1977-), Friends of Music, Smithsonian Mus., Met. Mus. of N.Y., The Nat. Trust, Monterey Mus. of Art, Carmel Music Soc., Carmel Art Assn., Garden Club Am., Carmel-by-the-Sea Garden Club (bd.), Casa Abrego Club of Monterey (pres. 1985-86), Mt. Rushmore Hall of Records Commn. (trustee 1988-), Sierra Club, Nat. Audubon Assn., Monterey Co. Symphony Assn., Carmel PTA (bd.); mem. Monterey Tchrs. Assn. (bd.), Monterey Hist. and Art Assn., Stanford Univ. Alumni Assn., Univ. N.C. Alumni Assn., Monterey Inst. Internat. Studies; clubs: Carmel Valley Golf & Country, Rocky Creek, Monterey Peninsula Golf & Country, Beach and Tennis, Pebble Beach; All Saints Episcopal Ch., Carmel (vestry). Res: PO Box 2222 Carmel 93921

BURKETT, WILLIAM ANDREW, banker, business executive, former state superintendent of banks; b. July 1, 1913, Herman, Nebr.; s. William H. and Mary (Dill) B.; 7th generation desc. of Stuffel Burkett, emigre to Pa. from Ger., 1700; desc. Maj. Gen. Edward Dodge and Judge John F. Williams, Calif. pioneers, 1849; m. Juliet Ruth Johnson, Oct. 5, 1940 (dec. Mar. 13, 1976); children: Juliet Ann (Mrs. Rodman L. Hooker, Jr.), Katherine C. (Mrs. Jeffrey H. Congdon), William Cleveland; m. Nancy Schallert Morrow, June 20, 1992; edn: stu. Univ. Nebr. 1931-32, Creighton Univ. Law Sch., 1932-33; LLB, Univ. Omaha, 1936. Career: elected nominee Secty. of State Nebr. (R) 1936; candidate for U.S. Congress, Nebr., 1938; regional chief of enforcements War Prodn. Board, 1941-43, ofcr. in chg. Secret and Confidential Sect., chief prosecutor of subversives, USCG, 12th Naval Dist., WWII; sr. spl. agt. intelligence unit US Treasury Dept. 1945-50; cons. and witness Calif. Crime Commn. and US Senate Kefauver Crime Com., 1950-52; exec. v.p. Calif. Employers Assn. Group, Sacramento 1950-53; dir. Calif. Dept. Employment, 1953-55; Supt. Banks, chmn. Dept. Investments Calif., 1955-59, credited by state legis. com. for discovery and correction of State Unemployment Ins. abuses, and for reorgn. of State Dept. Employment and State Banking Dept.; nominee of Nat. Assn. Supts. of Banks & Am. Bankers Assn. for Presdl. appt. to chair FDIC, Wash. DC; dir. Liquidation Yokohama Specie Bank, also Sumitomo Bank, San Francisco, 1955-59; cons. Western Bancorp, S.F., 1959-61; chmn. bd., pres. Security Nat. Bank Monterey Co., Monterey-Carmel 1961-66; chmn. bd. Burkett Land Co., Monterey, 1966-; cons. United Calif. Bank, L.A. 1966-; chmn. bd. Securities Properties Corp., Monterey 1966-; appt. dir. Calif. Emergency Manpower Commn. 1953-55, chmn. Gov.'s Com. Refugee Relief 1953-55, commr. Calif. Securities Commn. 1955-59; candidate for Gov. of Calif. (D) 1978; witness US Senate Banking Com. 1984, US Congress Banking Com. 1991; nat. chmn. Bank and Savings & Loans League, 1991-; guest spkr. on "Needed Reforms" Wash. Press Club 1986; guest spkr. Am. Bankers Assn. 84th Annual Nat. Conv., Chgo.; mem. Internat. Platform Assn., Am., Calif., Independent Bankers Assns., Nat. Assn. Supts. State Banks (pres. 1958-59), Amvets (dept. comdr. Calif. 1947, nat. v.comdr. 1948), Disabled Am. Veterans (life), American Legion (life), Stanford Univ. Alumni Assn., Soc. Calif. Pioneers; civic: Pine Manor Jr. Coll., Chestnut Hill, Mass. (fin. bd. 1967-), Mt. Rushmore Hall of Records Commn. (nat. co-chr. 1991-, co-chr. bd. trustees/founder 1987-), Mt. Rushmore Nat. Memorial Soc. (life, trustee), Nat. Hist. Found. (bd. chmn.), Monterey Co. Hist. Commn., Monterey Hist. and Art Assn. (life mem.), Monterey Sym. Assn. (bd. dirs.), Monterey Mus. Art (trustee), Bishop Kip Sch., Carmel Valley (trustee), Robert Louis Stevenson Sch., Pebble Beach (advy. bd. 1971-), Smithsonian Assocs., Met. Mus. of Art, Bach Festival Assocs., Nat. Trust Found. 1986, The Royal Oak Found. 1986; clubs: Monterey Peninsula Golf & Country, Beach and Tennis, Stillwater Yacht (Pebble Beach), Carmel Valley Golf and Tennis, Commonwealth of Calif., Rotary (S.F.), Sutter Lawn (Sacto.); author: Mount Rushmore National Memorial's History of America, 1776-1904 (1971); rec: swim, golf. Res: Pebble Beach Ofc: 1548 Viscaino Rd (POB 726) Pebble Beach 93953

BURKETT, WILLIAM CLEVELAND, investment banker and management consultant; b. June 3, 1956, San Mateo; s. William Andrew and Juliet Ruth (Johnson) B.; m. Wynn McClenahan, July 4, 1992; edn: BA (hons.), Stanford Univ. 1978; MBA (honors), Yale Univ. 1983. Career: fin. analyst corp. fin. dept. merger and acquisitions, First Boston Corp., 1978-80, New York; internat. coord. Credit Suisse First Boston Ltd., London, England 1980-81; pres. Security Properties Inc. 1981-; mgmt cons. staff McKinsey & Co., San Francisco 1983-

88; v.p. Mehta Burkett Co. Inc. Investment Bankers 1989-; spl advisor to the Pres., Takata Corp.,Tokyo, Japan 1990-; v.chmn. bd./c.e.o European Components Corp., Belfast, Ireland, 1991-; dir. Burkett Land Co. Inc. 1974-; awards: recogn. for unusual ability and personal initiative Conservation Div. U.S. Geol., Dept. of Interior; mem: Delta Upsilon, Stanford Alumni Assn. (life), Yale Univ. Alumni Assn.; civic: Commonwealth Club, Nat. Hist. Found. (pres. 1984-), Mt. Rushmore Nat. Memorial Soc. (life. 1983), Soc Calif. Pioneers (life 1987), MtRushmore Hall of Records Commn.; clubs: Yale, N.Y. Athletic, Pebble Beach; Episcopalian; rec: ski, sailing, tennis. Res: 1901 Pacific Ave San Francisco 94109 also: PO Box 726 Pebble Beach 93953

BURKETT, WYNN MCCLENAHAN (Mrs. William Cleveland Burkett), financial analyst, consultant; b. July 16, 1959, San Francisco; d. James Brice and Sharon (Rosengreen) McClenahan; m. William Cleveland Burkett, July 4, 1992; edn: BA, Stanford Univ., 1981; MA in mgmt., Yale Univ., 1987. Career: legal asst. Cutler & Pickering, W.D.C., 1981-83; financial analyst Morgan Stanley & Co. Inc., NY, NY, 1983-85; consultant, Exec. Office of the President - Office of Mgmt. & Budget, W.D.C., 1986; assoc. The First Boston Corp., NY, NY, 1987-88, San Francisco, 1988-; dir: Burkett Land Company, Pebble Beach; mem. Kappa Kappa Gamma Soc., Stanford Alumni Assn.; Prot.; rec: tennis, running. Res: 1901 Pacific Ave San Francisco 94109

BURNAM, JACK LEONARD, lawyer; b. Sept. 19, 1924, St. Joseph, Mo.; s. Clark A. and Flossie B. B.; m. Eleanor Jackson, 1947; children: Jack, II b. 1953, Joanne Leslie b. 1956; m. 2d Marilyn Kopmann, 1982; edn: AA, San Francisco City Coll. 1944; BA, Univ. Calif. 1947; LLB, UC Hastings Coll. of Law 1951; LLM, JD, Univ. Lincoln 1952. Career: secty., law clerk to US Judge Michael Roche 1953-55; pvt. law practice spec. in personal injury, criminal, probate and family law, San Francisco 1955-; judge pro tem Municipal Ct., San Francisco, 1985-, Napa, 1989-; mem: ABA, S.F. Bar Assn., Calif. Trial Lawyers Assn., Am. Trial Lawyers Assn.; clubs: Napa Valley CC, Elks; civic: PTA (pres. 1971), BSA (ofcr. 1975), Mt. Retreat Corp. (dir.); publs: book chpts. concerning legal activities for prisoners in Alcatraz (1963, Doubleday), numerous law jour. articles; Democrat; Prot.; rec: swimming, golf. Res: 434 Montecito Blvd Napa 94558 Ofc: One Hallidie Plaza Ste 805 San Francisco 94102 also: Ste 280 Lincoln Square 575 Lincoln Ave Napa 94558

BURNETT, CAROL STEVENS, real estate co. executive; b. Feb. 15, 1939, Portland, Ore.; d. Ellis John and Rachael (Williams) Stevens; m. G. Keith Burnett, Sept. 8, 1962; children: Keith, Jr. b. 1967, Michael b. 1970; edn: BS, Ore. State Univ. 1961; Calif. lic. Real Estate Broker (1978). Career: secty., asst. The Draper Cos., San Francisco 1962-64; adminstrv. asst. Dohemann & Co., San Rafael 1964-67; real estate sales Parker Assocs., Saratoga 1974-76, Saratoga Foothills 1976-78; sales asso. Cornish & Carey Realtors 1978-86, sr. v.p./mgr. Saratoga Office, 1986-; recipient corp. sales achievement awards (1983, 84), leading (highest dollar volume) in Santa Clara Co. (1990, 91); mem: Nat. Assn. Realtors, Calif. Assn. Realtors, San Jose Bd. of Realtors, Los Gatos/Saratoga Bd. of Realtors (dir. 1983, 84; chair Grievance 1985, chair Bd. Orientation & Tng. 1986), FIABCI (Intl. R.E. Fedn.); civic bds: KTEH-TV Ch. 54 (dir. 1991-), Saratoga C.of C. (dir. 1986-), Junior League of San Jose 1974-, S.J./Cleveland Ballet Council 1986, Saratoga Ednl. Found. 1982-84, Saratoga Rotary; club: Brookside Swim & Racket (pres. 1984-86); Republican; Episcopal; rec: tennis, travel. Ofc: Cornish & Carey Realtors 12175 Saratoga/Sunnyvale Rd Saratoga 95070

BURNHAM, JEFFREY ALAN, tile contractor; b. April 24, 1955, Kalamazoo, Mich.; s. Clifford Roger and Phyllis JoAnne (Axe) B.; m. Jong Ja Jun, Sept. 5, 1990; children by previous marriage: Jason b. 1971, Marie b. 1974; edn: All West Constrn. Sch. Career: Little Baer Tile, Running Springs 1975-77; tile setter Sunset Tile Co., Redlands 1977-84, supt. 1984-87, pres. 1987-; mem: Nat. Tile Contractors Assn., Building Industry Assn. Riverside, Allied Constrn. Industry; Republican; rec: fundraising. Ofc: Sunset Tile Inc. 700 New York St Redlands 92374

BURNS, DAVID MICHAEL, physician; b. May 6, 1947, Boston, Mass.; s. John Joseph and Catherine Rose (Riley) B.; edn: BS, Boston Coll. 1968; MBS, Dartmouth Med. Sch. 1970; MD, Harvard Med. Sch. 1972. Career: med. intern and resident Boston City Hosp., Mass. 1972-74; med. ofcr. Nat. Clearinghouse Smoking & Health CDC, Atlanta, Ga. 1974-76; pulmonary fellow Pulmonary Div. UCSD Med. Center 1976-79, faculty, prof. medicine 1979-, med. dir. Resp. Ther. 1980-; cons. Am. Coll. Chest Physicians 1979-; cons. Office on Smoking & Health, Rockville 1979-; mem: ACS, ACCP, ATS, CTS, Smoking & Health Report (edn. bd.), Advy. Group, Advocacy Inst., Comm. Intervention Trial Smoking Cessation-NIH; ed. and sci. ed. Surgeon General's Report 1980-83, 84-87; 2 book chapters. 1980, 85, 89; rec: scuba diving. Res: 1309 Windsor Rd Cardiff 92007 Ofc: University of California Medical Center Pulmonary Div. 225 W Dickinson St San Diego 92103

BURROUGHS, KATE, entomologist; b. Oct. 31, 1953, Hayward; d. Erwin S. and Mary Adele (Henderson) Burroughs; m. David L. Henry, July 12, 1975; 1 son, Michael b. 1985; edn: BS entomology, UC Berkeley, 1975; bd. cert. entomologist E.S.A., 1980. Career: entomologist Calif. Dept. Food & Agr., Sacto. 1975-78; entomologist, cons., Sebastopol, 1978-80; entomologist Harmony Farm Supply, Sebastopol 1980-; mem: Assn. of Applied Insect Ecologists (1976-, past pres.), Am. Soc Enology & Viticulture 1989-, Calif. Certified Organic Farmers 1976-, Com. for Sustainable Agriculture 1980-, USDA Nat. Sustainable Agriculture Advy. Council 1993-; civic: Organic Gardening & Nutrition Club Santa Rosa, Graton Community Club, Sonoma Co. Orchid Soc.; contbg. author: Future Is Abundant (1980), book editor: Controlling Vegetable Pests (1991), num. articles in field; rec: orchidist. Ofc: Harmony Farm Supply, 3244 Hwy 116 No, Sebastopol 95472

BURTON, BERTHA L., prison representative; b. Apr. 19, 1949, Columbia, S.C.; d. Burt T.N., Sr. and Georgie L. (Lott) Burton; edn: BA (cum laude), Johnson C. Smith Univ., Charlotte, N.C. 1971; MSW, Univ. S.C., 1974. Career: tchr. Columbia (S.C.) Public Schs., 1971-72; acting dir. Gaston Memorial Hosp., Gastonia, N.C. 1972; instr. Benedict Coll., Columbia, S.C. 1974-76; addiction coord. Mid-Carolina Council, 1976-78, Columbia; tnr. counselor Urban Mgmt., San Francisco, Ca. 1980-82; sch. cons. Community Human Services Proj., Monterey, Ca. 1981-85; prison rep. Friends Outside, Correctional Tng. Facility (CTF), San Jose, Ca. 1987-; mem. Friends Outside Monterey Co. (bd. 1987-), Family & Corrections Network 1988-, Pan-Hellenic Council Monterey (sec. treas. 1984-85), Seaside Kiwanis (chair 1984-85), Executive Internat. (Col., S.C. pres. 1977-80), Delta Sigma Theta Sor., W.D.C. (v.p. 1970-71); pub. jour. article "Nurturing Today" (1988); Democrat; Rel. Sci.; rec: swimming, jogging, reading, arts & crafts. Ofc: Friends Outside PO Box 686- CTF Soledad 93960-0686

BUSH, ELMER W., corporate president; b. Nov. 26, 1923, Sacramento; s. Charles J. and Alice Ellen (Pitiman) B.; m. Felomena T. Cimaroli, Nov. 26, 1973; children: Michael M. b. 1959; edn: Master Engr. Aircraft, Dallas Aircraft Engring. Coll. 1943; Mastr Engr. Internal Combustion Engines, Chevrolet Motor Div. 1943; Technical Splst. Turbo Superchargers, Honeywell 1944; Splst. Aircraft Hydraulics, Army Air Force Sch. of Hydraulics 1944; Splst. Hydramatic Props. & Controls, Hamilton Standards Propeller Div. 1944; Master Mech. Engr., US Army Air Force 1944. Career: welding insp. Kaiser Shipbldrs., Richmond 1940-42; master aircraft engr. US Army Air Force; founder, pres., chief chemist Pal-Pen Chemical Corp. 1950-; pres., exec. engr. Condensator Inc. 1975-; inventor: dry cleaning chemicals; patent, Pal-Gun, for spotting garments; patent, condensator supplementary carburetor; farm machinery; mil: m/sgt. US Army Air Force 1943-46, (2) Pres. Unit Citations, 9 Battle Stars, European Theatre, WWII; R.Cath.; rec: boating, water skiing, skin diving. Address: 2010 Trimble Way Sacramento 95825

BUSKE, KENNETH EUGENE, consulting engineering company owner; b. June 18, 1942, Rochester, N.Y.; s. Gilbert Eugene and Genevieve June (Strutt) B.; m. Mary Lawler, April 1, 1961 (div. 1982); children: Richard b. 1961, Scott b. 1975, Joan b. 1975; edn: BSEE, Purdue Univ. 1963; MSEE, 1964; MS indsl. adminstrn., 1965; reg. profl. engr. Va. 1973. Career: engr. IBM, Endicott, N.Y. 1965-68; USN, Wash., DC 1968-73; ARINC Research, Annapolis, Md. 1973-74; Trident Engring. 1974-76; engr., owner Buske Engring. 1974-83, Benicia 1983-; mem: Nat. Soc. Profl. Engrs., Nat. Fire Protection Assn., Assn. Testing Materials, IEEE, Sierra Club; rec: sailing, photography, flying. Res: 302 Marina Village Way Benicia 94510 Ofc: Buske Engineering 302 Marina Village Way Benicia 94510

BUSS, DIETRICH GOTTHILF, historian; b. Sept. 20, 1939, Tokyo, Japan; s. Bernhard August and Katharina Martha (Wenzel) B.; m. Miriam Eleanore Epp, July 10, 1943; children: Eric b. 1970, Julie b. 1972, Natalie b. 1974; edn: BA in edn., Biola Univ., 1963; MA soc. sci., CSU Los Angeles, 1965; PhD history, Claremont Grad. Sch., 1976. Career: social studies faculty Culter Acad., L.A. 1965-66; history faculty Biola Univ., La Mirada 1966-; mem. City of La Mirada Hist. Heritage Commn., 1977-, v.chair 1990-; recipient Charles J. Kennedy Award Econ. and Bus. Hist. Soc. 1978; mem: Org. of Am. Historians 1965-, Econ. and Bus. Hist. Soc. 1976-, Conf. of Faith and History 1976-; author: (econ. biography) Henry Villard, contbr. (rel. biog.) Dict. of Christianity in Am. (1991), Blackwell Dict. of Evangelical Biog. (1993), contbr. Encyclopedia USA (1994); Republican; Evangelical Free Ch. of Am.; rec: outdoorsman, naturalist. Ofc: Biola Univ. 13800 Biola Ave La Mirada 90639

BUTLER, DONALD EARNEST, association executive; b. Mar. 2, 1927, Coatesville, Pa.; s. John Minor and Jane B. (Hawthorn) B.; m. Laura Eaton, Aug. 28, 1948; children: Donald E. b. 1952, Jeffrey E. b. 1956; edn: BS, Franklin & Marshall, 1949. Career: mgmt. staff, 19 yrs., then pres./c.e.o. SSP Industries, 12 yrs., ret. 1979; elected pres. and c.e.o. Merchants and Mfrs. Assn. (human resources agy.) 1979-, mem. bd. dirs. 1973-; dir: Calif. Casualty Ins. Cos., Keenan Properties Inc., C.Itoh, Calif. Offset Printers Inc., Master Halco Inc., SFE Technologies; awards: man of yr. Calif. Bus. Edns. 1970, SME pres.'s award, L.A. 1969, best dressed L.A. Bus. Jour. 1985; mem. Nat. Assn. of Mfs. (dir.), L.A. C.of C. (internat. commerce exec. com.), Japan Amer. Soc. (dir.); civic bds: Verdugo Hills Hosp. (advy. bd.), Glendale Sym. Orch. Assn. (dir., past pres.), BSA L.A. (advy. bd.); clubs: Oakmont CC, Jonathan, Rotary (L.A.); mil: aviator USN 1944-47; Republican; rec: golf, sailing. Res: 1710 Ivy Bridge Rd Glendale 91207 Ofc: 1150 S Olive St Ste 2300 Los Angeles 90015

BUTLER, ROLLYN MELVIN, physician, otolaryngology, facial plastic surgery; b. Apr. 22, 1931, Los Angeles; s. Rollyn C. and Margie (Massey) B.; m. Nora Stewart, Jan. 25, 1958; children: William b. 1959, Lynn b. 1961; edn: BA, Stanford Univ. 1953; MD, 1957. Career: resident UCLA 1965; chief, ear nose throat div. Los Angeles Co. Harbor Gen. Hosp., Torrance 1969-70; physician, ent. splst. Valley Ear Nose Throat Med. Group Inc., Pomona-Upland 1966-; asst. clin. prof. UCLA Sch. Medicine 1970-; pres. Stanford Med. Alumni 1988-89; mem: A.C.S. (fellow), Trilogic Soc. (fellow), Los Angeles Co. Med. Assn., CMA, AMA; author: 6 articles pub. in med. jours; mil: lt. USN 1960-62; Republican; Protestant; rec: skiing, scuba diving, tennis. Ofc: Valley Ear Nose and Throat Medical Group Inc. 297 W Artesia Ave Ste A Pomona 91768

BUTTCHEN, TERRY GERARD, company president; b. July 15, 1958, Madison, Wis.; s. Elmer John and Margaret (Falkenstein) B.; edn: BS, Univ. Wis., Platteville, 1980, MS, 1981. Career: sales mgr. Searle Pharmaceuticals, Chgo. 1982-84; sales mgr. Am. Hosp. Supply, Chgo. 1984-86; pres. Titan Consultants, San Francisco 1986-; instr. Dale Carnegie Seminars, St. Louis, Mo. 1984-; awards: Humanitarian, CSU Northridge 1988, Outstanding Young Man of Am., Montgomery, Ala. 1988, listed Who's Who in West 1992, Who's Who Worldwide 1992; mem: Delta Sigma Phi (v.p. 1987-), Univ. Wis., Platteville (v.p. bd. dirs. 1990-), Order of Omega Hon. Frat. 1989-, Alpha Zeta 1978-, Nat. Interfrat. Conf. 1987-; civic: March of Dimes, S.F. (v.chmn., budget & fin. chair 1990-92); author: How To Buy A Business (1990); Republican; R.Cath. Res: 1800 Pacific Ave #705 San Francisco 94109

BUTTS, KAREN LYNN, clinical social worker, psychotherapist; b. Nov. 30, 1956, Reedley; d. George and Viola Frances (Marshall) Long; m. Kevin Butts, Aug. 5, 1979; children: Devon b. 1987, Nolan b. 1989; edn: BA soc. welfare (cum laude), CSU Fresno, 1978, MSW, 1980; Calif. lic. therapist, lic. clin. soc. wkr. (LCS 10968) 1984; Calif. tchg. cred. adult edn., 1988. Career: medical soc. wkr. Kaweah Delta Dist. Hosp., Visalia 1981-87; Fresno Comm. Hosp., Fresno 1987; soc. wkr. Kings View Psychiat. Ctr., Reedley 1987; childbirth educator and perinatal social wkr. pvt. med. practice of A. Peters M.D. (Ob-Gyn), Fresno 1988-93; owner Growing Families, Child Birth Educ. Svcs. 1993-; pvt. practice therapist, 1991-; initiator and facilitator Visalia community support groups: I Can Cope (oncology edn.) 1983-85, SHARE (perinatal loss gp.) 1983-87, Premature (parent gp.) 1985, Source of Support (parent bereavement gp.) 1986-87; cons. Parents of Murdered Children, Fresno-Tulare 1986; mem: Nat. Assn. Soc. Wkrs., Internat. Childbirth Edn. Assn., Nat. Perinatal Assn., Calif. Perinatal Assn., Central Valley Perinatal Soc. Wk. Cluster (past chair), Tulare Co. Victim-Witness Coord. Council 1985-86, Central Valley Continuity of Care Assn. 1984-86. Res: 272 N Ezie Fresno 93727 Ofc: 5150 N Sixth Ste 149 Fresno 93710

BYRNE, CATHERINE BERNADETTE, librarian; b. Jan. 17, 1939, Dublin, Ireland; nat. 1964; d. John Patrick Byrne and Josephine (McGuinness) Callaghan; edn: BA, Coll. of Notre Dame 1965; MA, San Jose St. Univ. 1973. Career: tchr. St. Jeromes Sch., El Cerrito 1967-69; tchr., librarian parochial schs. in England, Africa and Calif. 1969-85; library adminstr. Oakley Unified Sch. Dist. 1989-; mem: Language Arts Com. (chmn. 1971-73), CMLEA, Calif. Library Assn.; author: A Heritage of Love, poetry Meditations (1965-); Democrat; R.Cath.; rec: philately, music, literature. Res: 5346 Grasswood Circle Concord 94521

CADENA, RAY(MOND) M., county government administrative assistant; b. Nov. 24, 1952, San Antonio, Tx.; s. Lenert Lonnie (stepf.) and Maria Concepcion (Mesquite) Hanna; m. Linda Rodriguez, June 28, 1980; children: Raelynn b. 1981, Lucy b. 1983; edn: BA in sociology, UC Riverside, 1978. Career: engring. aide Riverside Co. Flood Control & Water Conservation, 1972-78; social work assoc. Jerry L. Pettis, Memorial Veterans Hosp. Dist., Loma Linda, 1978; mgr. student svs. Inland Empire Job Corps Ctr., San Bdo., 1978-86; counselor Inland Reg. Ctr., Colton 1986; field rep. Calif. St. Assemblyman Jerry Eaves, Rialto, 1986-87; adminstrv. asst. San Bernardino Co. Supr. Robt. L. Hammock, San Bdo., 1987-; mem. Am. Soc. for Pub. Adminstrn. (exec. council 1989-); civic: Five Yr. Housing Com. San Bdo. City Unified Sch. Dist. 1990-, San Bdo. Area C.of C. (chmn. edn. com. 1990-), San Bdo. Community Hosp. Bd. Trustees 1989-, More Attractive Comm. Found. of San Bdo. (bd. 1991-), Kiwanis Downtown San Bdo. 1989-90; mil: sgt. USAF Res. 1971-77; Democrat; R.Cath.; rec: camping, cycling, wt. tng. Ofc: San Bernardino Co. 385 N Arrowhead Ave 5th Flr San Bernardino 92415-0110

CADY, HARLOW GEORGE, leasing company executive; b. Aug. 31, 1910, Norwich, N.Y.; s. George Albert and Lena Mae (Palmer) C.; m. Zelda Fentress, Mar. 11, 1938; ed. pub. schs. Norwich, N.Y. Career: sales rep. Dentists Supply Co. of N.Y., N.Y.C. 1930-36; dept. mgr. Billings Dental Supply Co., Omaha, Neb. 1936-42; supr. mat. control Convair, San Diego 1942-45; sales mgr. Tooth Div. Austenal Labs., N.Y.C. 1946-49; buyer Convair, San Diego 1950-52; founder/ owner La Jolla Office Equip. and Supply Co., La Jolla 1952-64; founder, pres. and c.e.o. La Jolla Leasing Inc., 1960-; pres. La Jolla Credit Assn. 1958-60; honors: Hole-In-One (2t) Stoneridge CC, Green Valley, Calif. 1973 and Lomas Santa Fe CC, San Diego 1977, both achievements inscribed in The Book of GOWF at Golf Place, St. Andrews Fife, Scotland; civic: organized spl. com. that planted 100+ palm trees in La Jolla bus. district, active La Jolla Town Council (chmn. merchants com. 1955-57 v.p. 1958-60), Rotary 1947-52, Kiwanis 1953-63; Republican; Prot.; rec: orchidist. Res: 1563 Virginia Way La Jolla 92037

CAESAR, CAROL ANN, psychologist; b. June 10, 1945, Jacksonville, Fl.; d. David Union and Helen (Casper) Richards; m. Vance Roy Caesar, Apr. 22, 1967; 1 son, Eric b. 1971; edn: BA Univ. Fla.; MA Fla. Atlantic Univ.; PhD Calif. Sch. of Profl. Psychology; lic. clin. psychologist, Calif. Career: counselor Family Guidance Ctr., Long Beach 1980-84; behavioral scientist Long Beach Memorial Med. Ctr., 1987-90; owner/pres. Life Improvement Ctr., Seal Beach 1989-; mem. bds. Long Beach Family Services 1981-87, Am. Cancer Soc. Long Beach 1985-; mem: Calif. Psychol. Assn., Am. Psychol. Assn., Long Beach Psychol. Assn.; clubs: Old Ranch CC, Long Beach Jr. League (sustaining); Indep.; L.D.S. Ch.; rec: walking. Res: 110 Ocean Seal Beach 90740 Ofc: Life Improvement Ctr. 550 Pacific Coast Hwy Ste 203 Seal Beach 90740

CAGAN, LAIRD QUINCY, venture capitalist; b. Apr. 19, 1958, Chgo.; s. Phillip David Cagan and Elizabeth Quincy (Wright) Rose; edn: BSME, Stanford Univ., 1980, MSME, 1980, MBA, 1985. Career: cons. SRI Internat., Menlo Park, 1980-81; product mgr. Assocs. Corp. of North Am., Dallas 1981-83; assoc. Crosspoint Venture Ptnrs., Menlo Park, 1984-85; mergers & acquisitions dept. Goldman Sachs & Co., N.Y.C., 1985-86; v.p. mergers & acquisitions dept. Drexel Burnham Lambert Inc., Beverly Hills, 1986-90; founder, pres. and c.e.o. Cagan Capital, L.A. 1990-; chmn. bd. Kendura Products Inc., Santa Fe Springs 1990-91; chmn. bd. and c.e.o. Jackson Engring. Co., Chatsworth 1990-93; c.f.o. Summit Environmental Corp., Alhambra 1991-92; rec: soccer, tennis, golf, travel. Ofc: Cagan Capital 10751 Wilshire Blvd Ste 1408 Los Angeles 90024 Tel: 310/470-4499

CAGLE, THOMAS M., electronics engineer; b. Apr.26,1927, Chillicothe, TX; s. William Robert and B. Clyde (White) C.; m. Jane E. De Bute, May 16,1964; children: Kent b. 1965, Thomas b. 1967; edn: BS, Univ. of So. Calif., L.A. 1968. Career: engr. N. Am. Rockwell Corp., L.A. 1950-71; engring. cons., Scottsdale, AZ 1971-77; electronics engr. Dept. of Defense, L.A. 1977-; mem: Inglewood Jaycees (pres., dir.), YMCA Inglewood (pres.), Inglewood Youth Counseling Orgn. (pres.), Ch. of Foothills; copyright held for calculator - nuclear weapon (1962), num. papers pub. in tech. jours. 1954-76; mil: U.S. Navy 1945-46. Res: 10461 Greenbrier Rd Santa Ana 92705

CAIN, THOMAS ROBERT, radiologist, educator; b. Sept. 4, 1951, Sullivan, Mo.; s. Noble William and Evelyn (Scott) C.; m. Emily Hamlin, Mar. 7, 1984; children: Geoffrey Noble b. 1986, Amy Elisabeth b. 1987, Natalie Ann b. 1990; edn: AB (honors with distinction, zoology/psychology majors - magna cum laude), UC Berkeley, 1973; MPH, UCLA, 1974; MD (honors), USC, 1978; diplomate Am. Bd. of Radiology, 1983. Career: medical intern Cedars Sinai Med. Ctr., L.A. 1978-79; med. resident radiology, UCLA, 1980-83; staff radiologist and ptnr. Western Roentgenologic Assocs., Canoga Park 1983-; dir. radiology Panorama Community Hosp., Panorama City 1989-92, chmn. credentials com. 1990-92; medical dir. Morthridge Diagnostic Imaging, 1992-; asst. clin. prof. radiology USC Sch. of Medicine, 1990-; awards: Sealbearer Calif. Scholarship Fedn. 1969, Regents Scholar UCB 1969; mem: AMA, Calif. Med. Assn., Calif. Radiol. Soc. (rep. to CMA spl. panel on Medical Staff Issues, Sacto. 1990-), L.A. Radiol. Soc., Am. Coll. of Radiology (ultrasound sect., nuclear medicine sect.), Calif. Radiologic Soc. of N.Am. (counselor for So. Calif. 1988-), L.A. Cty. Med. Assn., Salerni Collegium/Radiol. Soc. of North Am., Am. Coll. of Nuclear Medicine; rec: classical piano, tennis. Ofc: Western Roentgenologic Associates, 8363 Reseda Blvd., #207 Northridge 91324

CAINES, CLARKE ARTHUR, sales executive; b. Jan. 8, 1961, Lompoc; s. Kenneth Leslie Dore and Josephine Audre (Robinson) C.; edn: BA in pub. personnel mgmt., San Diego St. Univ., 1984. Career: mktg. rep. Xerox Corp., San Diego 1984-85; account exec. Slidemakers West, 1985-86; account exec.,br. mgr. Los Angeles, dist. sales mgr. No. Calif. & Nev., Genigraphics Corp. (profl. svs. co.) 1986-; general mgr. Genigraphics Corp. 1989-92; nat. sales mgr. Pacific Telecom, Inc. 1992-; awards: recipient Genigraphics Mgmt. Award, 1989 (increased new bus. volume 20%), Pres.'s Club, 1987, 88, 89, Sales Sprint Award, 1988, 500K Club, 1988, nat. rookie of yr., 1986-7; Xerox Pres.'s Club, Club Elite, mktg. rep of quarter, 1985; honors: Pi Kappa Alpha most outstanding active mem. and 1st Black Pres., 1981, SDSU Assoc. Students Finance Bd., 1982, scholarship and leadership award, 1982; Democrat; rec: fishing, sporting events.

CALANTAS, THOMAS DE LA CRUZ, JR., real estate and mortgage broker; b. Feb. 9, 1948, Philippines, nat. 1987; s. Tomas Calderon, Sr. and Fermina Eslabon (De La Cruz) C.; m. Ruth, Dec. 29, 1974; 1 son, Thomas Jeff b. 1976; edn: BS, biol., Phil. Union Coll. 1970; respiratory therapy, Am. Vocat. Sch. 1974; grad. De Loux Sch. of Cosmetology 1984; tchr. tng. Riverside City Coll. 1987; Calif. lic.: lic. adminstr. handicapped adult care facility 1980, cosmetologist 1984, R.E. lic. 1989 R.E. broker 1991, Notary Pub. 1991. Career: respiratory therapist San Gabriel Comm. Hosp. 1974-75; respiratory therapist La Vina Hosp. 1975-76; respiratory therapist White Memorial Med. Center 1977; owner/mgr. Orange Blossom Motel, San Bernardino 1979; owner/adminstr. Sunset Plaza

Guest Home, Beaumont 1980-86; owner/adminstr. Lolinda Rancho Guest Home (facility for independent living rehabilitated handicapped) 1983-; ABBA Acad. For Hair (hairstyling sch.) 1986; cosmetologist, owner beauty salons: Delta Con Hair Design, San Bernardino 1986—, and Hair Gallery, Riverside 1987-88; real estate agt. Century 21 Home & Investment, 1989-91; broker, owner Ambassadors Realty, San Bdo. 1991-; broker, pres. Renet Financial- Greater California Mortgage Inc., 1992-; awards: student of mo., 1st place Inter-school competition hair show 1984; mem. City of Loma Linda Citizen Patrol (1992); mem: Bd. of Realtors: San Bernardino, Redlands, and Riverside, Nat. Cosmetologist Assn., Loma Linda, Riverside, and Gr. Riverside Hispanic C.of C. (dir., treas. 1988-89); Loma Linda Filipino 7th-Day Adventist Ch. (fund chmn. 1979-81); rec: classical music, singing. Res: 25050 Tulip Ave Loma Linda 92354 Ofc: Ambassadors Realty 24674 Redlands Blvd San Bernardino 92408

CALDERA, LOUIS EDWARD, legislator; b. Apr. 1, 1956, El Paso, Tx.; s. Benjamin Luis and Soledad (Siqueiros) C.; m. Evagren Orlebeke, Nov. 9, 1991; edn: BS, US Mil. Acad., West Point, NY, 1978; JD, Harvard Law Sch., Cambridge, Mass., 1987; MBA, Harvard Bus. Sch., Boston, Mass., 1987. Career: Army ofcr., US Army, 1978-83; assoc., O'Melveny & Myers, L.A., Calif., 1987-89; assoc., Buchalter Nemer Fields & Younger, L.A., 1990; deputy county counsel, County of L.A., 1991-92; Assembly mem., Calif. State Assembly, Sacramento, 1992-; mil: capt., US Army, 1978-83; Democrat; Roman Catholic. Ofc: 304 S. Broadway Ste. 580, Los Angeles 90013

CALDWELL, COURTNEY LYNN, laywer, legal consulting company executive; b. Mar. 5, 1948, W.D.C.; d. Joseph Morton Caldwell and Moselle (Smith) MacCloskey; edn: undergrad. Duke Univ. 1966-68; BA, UC Santa Barbara, 1970, MA, 1975; JD (highest hons.) George Washington Univ., W.D.C. 1982; admitted bar: D.C. 1984, Wash. 1986, Calif. 1989. Career: summer assoc. law firm Arnold & Porter, W.D.C., 1982, law firm Hufstedler, Miller, Carlson & Beardsley, Los Angeles 1982; judicial clerk US Ct. Appeals, Seattle 1982-83; lawyer, assoc. Arnold & Porter, W.D.C. 1983-85, Perkins Coie, Seattle 1985-88; dir. we. ops. and assoc. general counsel MPC Associates, Inc. Irvine, Calif. 1988-91, senior v.p. 1991-; awards: John Ordranaux Award Geo. Washington Univ. 1980, sr. articles editor G.W. Law Rev. 1981-82, listed Who's Who in Am. Law 1989-, of Practicing Attorneys, of Emerging Leaders in Am., of Am. Women 1992, in the West 1992, in U.S. Execs. 1992; publs: law summaries (Martindale-Hubbell, 1986), articles in law revs., texts; rec: fgn. languages. Ofc: MPC Associates, Inc. 4199 Campus Dr Ste 210 Irvine 92715

CALDWELL, JONI, CEO and general manager, retail furniture; b. Aug. 8, 1948, Chgo., Ill.; d. Bruce and Eloise (Ijams) Caldwell; m. David H. Weisbach, Apr. 23, 1988; div. Oct. 7, 1990; edn: diploma, Marquette (Mich.) H.S., 1965-66; BS, home econ., Mich. State Univ., 1966-70; grad. studies, Mich. State Univ., 1970-75; MA, clinical psychol., Lone Mt. Coll., San Francisco, 1978; career: educator, Grand Blanc H.S., Grand Blanc, Mich., 1970-73; educator, Northwestern Mich. Coll., Traverse City, Mich. 1972-78; educator, Mott Comm. Coll., Flint, Mich., 1974-78; educator, Clio H.S., Clio, Mich., 1974-79; work/study, Esalen Inst., Big Sur, 1979-81; parent educator/vol. coord., Family Resource Ctr., Seaside, 1981-82; c.e.o. and gen. mgr., Futons & Such, Monterey, 1982-; awards: Small Business Excellence Award, Monterey C. of C., 1990; Congressional Award, US Congress, 1990; mem: v.p. (past pres.), New Monterey Bus. Assn., charter mem. 1983-; past pres. and v.p., Monterey Church of Religious Sci., 1984-87; past v.p., Pacific Coast Church, 1987-92; bd. of dirs., Monterey YWCA; 1986-88; com. mem., Monterey C. of C., 1985-87; membership com., Profl. Womens Network, 1989-; listed in Who's Who in the West 1992, Who's Who in the World 1993; civic: fundraising for the Buddy Program, YWCA and MCRS, Monterey; author: home econ. article, 1970; Greens; Metaphysian; rec: travel, reading, personal growth, skiing, sailing, white water rafting, kayaking, remodeling houses. Res: 29 Portola Ave. Monterey 93940. Ofc: Futons & Such 484 Lighthouse Ave. Monterey 93940

CALDWELL, WALTER EDWARD, newspaper editor and publisher; b. Dec. 29, 1941, Los Angeles; s. Harold Elmer and Esther Ann (Fuller) C.; m. Donna Edith Davis, June 27, 1964; children: Arnie-Jo; edn: AA, Riverside City Coll., 1968. Career: sales staff Sears Roebuck & Co., Riverside 1963-65; dispatcher Rohr Corp., 1965-67; trainee Aetna Fin., 1967-68; mgr. Aetna Fin., San Bruno 1968-70, Amfac Thrift & Loan, Oakland 1970-74; free lance writer, 1974-76; news dir. Sta. KAVA Radio, Burney 1977-79; editor/pub. Mountain Echo, Fall River Mills 1979-; contbr. Yearbook of Modern Poetry, 1976; announcer Intermountain Fair Parade, McArthur 1983-, Burney Basin Days Parade 1985-92, Big Valley Days Parade, Adin 1988; candidate Shasta County Bd. Supervisors, Dist. 3, 1992; mem. Calif. Newspaper Publishers' Assn.; civic bds: Intermountain United Way, Burney (pres. 1979, chmn. 1978), Am. Red Cross, Redding (disaster relief wkr. 1988-, disaster action team ldr. 1992-), Shasta County Women's Refuge (bd. dirs. 1988-91), Shasta County Econ. Devel. Corp., Redding (1986-87, 89-91, exec. bd. dirs. 1987), Ea. Shasta County Econ. Devel. Corp. (pres. 1987-89), Shasta County Econ. Devel. Task Force (bd. 1985-86), Girl Scouts, San Jose (troop ldr. 1973-76), Burney Fire Protection Dist. (commr. 1987-91, pres. 1991), Mosquito Abatement Dist., Burney (trustee 1978-87, 1989-, pres. 1990), Burney Basin Days Com. (pres. 1985-86, 88-89), Ea. Shasta

County Sheriff's Flying Posse (observer 1988-); mem. Am. Legion, Burney Basin C.of C. (advt. chmn. 1982), Fall River Valley C.of C. (dir. 1990-), Rotary (chmn. bike race 1981-85, pres. 1987), Masons, Intermountain Shrine Club (sec. 1992-), Lions/ Fall River (youth spkr. 1983-88, dist. bulletin chmn. 1989-91, pres. 1992), Moose; mil: cpl. USMC 1959-63; Republican. Res: 20304 Elm St Burney 96013 Ofc: Mountain Echo Hwy 299 Fall River Mills 96028

CALE, CHARLES GRIFFIN, lawyer, international sports executive; b. Aug. 19, 1940, St. Louis, Mo.; s. Julian Dutro and Judith Hadley (Griffin) C.; m. Jessie Leete Rawn, Dec. 30, 1978; children: Whitney Rawn, Walter Griffin, Elizabeth Judith; edn: BA, Principia Coll., 1961; LLB, Stanford Univ., 1964; LLM, USC, 1966; admitted Calif. Bar 1965. Career: law practice, Los Angeles 1965-; ptnr. Adams, Duque & Hazeltine, 1970-81, Morgan, Lewis & Bockius, 1981-90; c.e.o. and co-chmn. bd. World Cup USA 1994, Inc. 1991;dir. World Cup USA 1994, Inc. 1991-; group v.p. sports L.A. Olympic Organizing Com., 1982-84; assoc. counselor U.S. Olympic Com. (USOC), 1985, special asst. to pres. USOC 1985-88, asst. Chef de Mission of the 1988 U.S. Olympic Team, asst. to pres. USOC and dir. Olympic Delegation (Barcelona) 1988; civic bds: Hallum Prevention Child Abuse Fund, L.A. (dir.), St. John's Hosp. and Med. Ctr., Santa Monica (trustee); awards: Gold Medal of Youth and Sports, France (1984); mem. ABA, State Bar of Calif.; clubs: California, Los Angeles CC, The Beach. Ofc: PO Box 688 Pacific Palisades 90272

CALESCIBETTA, C.C., physician; b. Oct. 1, 1932, Auburn, N.Y.; s. Frank and Maria (Bauso) C.; m. Genevieve Atkins, April 1955 (div. 1974); m. Diane M. Bunkers, Aug. 6, 1976; children: Marcus b. 1957, Carlo b. 1959, Gina b. 1968, Chris b. 1977, Cara Mia b. 1980; edn: BA, San Diego St. Univ. 1956; MD, St. Univ. N.Y. 1960; JD, Pacific Coast Univ. 1988; admitted Calif. St. Bar 1989. Career: dir. med. edn. St. Mary Med.Center, Long Beach 1967-74; med. dir. Renal Center 1970-; pres. Renal Disease Network of So. Calif.; clin. prof. medicine UCLA Sch. of Medicine 1984-; bd. dirs. ESRD Network 1985-, med. review bd. 1982-; Western Med. Review, Torrance 1984-; mem: Am. Bar Assn., L.A. Co. Bar Assn., Am. Soc. Nephrology, Nat. Health Lawyers Assn., F.A.C.P., CMA, AMA, Calif. Bar Assn., So. Calif. Kidney Found.; Republican. Res: 5500 El Parque Long Beach 90815 Ofc: St. Mary Medical Center 1050 Linden Ave Long Beach 90801

CALIVA, JEWEL SARMIENTO, choreographer, artist, designer; b. May 1, 1920, Los Angeles; d. Anthony Sarmiento and Emma Elizabeth (Salmon) Hernandez; granddau. of Domingo Faustino Sarmiento, former Pres. of Argentina; m. Myro Caliva, June 29, 1939 (div. 1969); children: Michael Samuel b. 1941, Tamara Malia b. 1944, Toni Ann b. 1958; edn: Reynolds Acad. of Arts; ballet, Michael Fokine Dance Master; Muriel Stuart Pavolva Student; Spanish ballet, Eduardo Cansino 1926-38. Career: danseuse Hollywood Bowl, Hollywood; ballerina Wilshire Ebell, L.A.; spanish ballet Eastern Star; freelance choreographer 1930-38; choreographer Ominskys, Hollywood 1938-40; artist designer Caliva Bros. Inc., Los Angeles 1950-60, ptnr. Caliva Bros. Inc., Granada Hills 1960-66; owner, artist Jewel's Gallery & Studio, Marina Del Rey 1967-89; protege Dance Master M. Fokine; Muriel Stuart; Reynolds Acad. Arts; mem: Cape Fear Found. (hon. bd. 1981-87), L.A. Museum of Art, Venice Hist. Soc., KCET, Friends of Santa Monica Pub. Library, Poets of Venice; author of poetry (1966); Democrat; Mormon; rec: art shows, antique collecting, yachting. Res: 2340 Abbot Kinney Blvd Venice 90291

CALLAHAN, HAROLD PERRY, certified public accountant; b. May 26, 1928, Sebastapol; s. Perry Wm. and Bessie (Norton) C.; m. Lois Ann Peterson, Jan. 2, 1955; children: Kristel b. 1961, Brenda b. 1965; edn: CSU Chico, 1956; att. UCB, 1955, Golden Gate Univ., 1956-57; C.P.A., Calif. 1957. Career: auditor John F. Forbes & Co., San Francisco 1955-59; ptnr. James Tomlison & Co., S.F. 1960-61; prin. Harold P. Callahan CPA, S.F. 1961-; chief fin. ofcr. Decorative Plant Service Co., S.F. 1986-; mem: Calif. Soc. CPAs, Am. Inst. CPAs, Soc. of Calif. Accts., San Francisco Chpt. S.C.A. (pres. 1977-78), Nat. Soc. of Pub. Accts.; club: The Olympic (S.F.); spkr. S.C.A. profl. meetings (1980, 84, 85, 91); mil: pfc AUS 1950-52; Republican; Presbyterian. Res: 780 Pico Ave San Mateo 94403 Ofc: Harold P. Callahan CPA 1355 Market St Ste 321 San Francisco 94103

CALLAHAN, PAT A., community service volunteer; b. June 17, 1952, Baltimore, Md.; d. Joseph Bernard and Leonard Elizabeth (Clark) Callahan; edn: BA, UC Irvine 1976; CSU Long Beach 1977-79. Career: staff research assoc. UCI 1980-88, mgmt. fellow 1988-89, dir. UCI Campaign Operations 1989-90, Annual Giving 1990-92, UCI Corporate Affairs 1992-; co-chair Co. of Orange Elections Com. 1986-; awards: PFLAG 1986, So. Calif. Woman for Understanding 1988, Orange Co. Human Rels. Commn. Comm. Service 1988, Lauds & Laurels Comm. Service 1988, Toastmasters CTM 1988, ECCO Pol. Service 1990; Orange Co. Pride Woman of Year 1992, mem: Toastmasters, UC Irvine Chancellors Com. Status of Lesbians & Gays, AIDS Walk Orange Co., Women's Roundtable Orange Co. (v.p. 1990-93), HRCF Bd. of Governors 1991-, YWCA (fin. com. 1988); Protestant; rec: photography, cooking. Address: Irvine 92717

CALVERT, ANN MARCINE, editor, publisher; b. Jan. 17, 1943, Cheyenne, Wy.; d. Harold McClure Forde and Elizabeth Ann (Farthing); m. John Jolley, Jr., 1965, div. 1989; m. 2d. David W. Calvert, 1991; children: Helen b. 1968, Kendall b. 1971; edn: BA, Univ. Wyoming, 1964. Career: admin. asst. San Diego Mag. 1964-65; admin. asst. Colo. Women's Coll. 1965-66; reporter Desert Dispatch, Barstow 1976-77; bus. devel. First Interstate Bank, San Diego 1980-82; owner RB Network, S.D. 1982-84; owner, editor and pub. Rancho Magazine, San Diego 1984-; mem. civic bds: BECA Hispanic Scholarship Found. 1988-90, Palomar Coll. Found. 1982-90; awards: meritorious service Navy Relief Soc. 1975, 78, San Bernardino Co. Grand Jury 1976; mem. Chamber of Commerce (Rancho Bernardo pres. 1989-90, Poway bd. mem. 1993-, Escondido, Diamond Gateway), Rotary Internat., San Diego Press Club; Presbyterian Ch. USA (San Diego Presbytery moderator 1986); rec: folk singing, skiing, sailing. Ofc: Pomerado Newspaper Group 13247 Poway Rd Poway 92064

CAMENZIND, MARK J., research chemist; b. Nov. 17, 1956, Palo Alto; s. Paul Vincent and Mildred Martha (Glover) C.; m. Dorothy L. Hassler, Apr. 11, 1992; edn: SB, M.I.T., 1978; PhD, UC Berkeley, 1983. Career: postdoctoral fellow Univ. of British Columbia, Vancouver, B.C. 1983-86; research chemist Salutar, Inc. Sunnyvale, Ca. 1986; Balazs Analytical Lab., Sunnyvale 1986-; mem. Am. Chem. Soc. (1978-), ASTM (com. 1988-), SEMI (stds. com. 1990-); publs: tech. papers in chemistry & semiconductor ind. (1981-); rec: x-c skiing, electronics. Ofc: Balazs Lab. 1380 Borregas Ave Sunnyvale 94089

CAMERON, ELSA SUE, curator, art consultant, educator; b. Nov. 19, 1939, San Francisco; d. L. Don and Betty (Jelinsky) C.; m. Michael Lerner, Dec 24, 1979; edn: BA, San Francisco State Univ., 1961, MA, 1965, tchg. credential, 1962. Career: curator Randall Jr. Mus., San Francisco 1963-65, Fine Arts Mus. Downtown Center 1976-80, San Francisco Airport Galleries 1980-; exec. dir. Community Arts, Inc., S.F. 1973-; reporter Council on Museums, N.Y.C., 1973-80; asst. prof. art edn. Univ. So. Calif., L.A. 1982-83; cons. University Art Mus., Berkeley 1980-82, instr. 1981; instr. 101 California Venture, S.F. 1986-; exhibitions curator OM & M/Olympia & York, L.A. 1988-; cons. Art in Public Places, Miami, Fla. 1988; awards: NEA fellow (1973, 77); mem. Western Regional Conf. (v.p. 1974-75), Am. Assn. Museums; publs: (book) The Art Museum as Educator 1977, (exhibit cat.) Airport Cafe 1986; Ofc: San Francisco International Airport Exhibition Box 8097 San Francisco 94128

CAMERON, JOANNA, actress/producer/director; b. Greeley, Colo.; d. Harold and Erna (Borgens) Cameron; edn: Univ. Calif. 1967-68, Pasadena Playhouse 1968. Career: discovered by Walt Disney while special tour guide at Disneyland, motion picture debut in How to Commit Marriage, 1969; actress in The Amazing Spiderman, other feature films; appear in numerous TV commercials, named in Guiness Book of Records as having the most nat. network programmed TV commercials; actress TV network prime time serial shows including Name of the Game, Medical Center, The Bold Ones, Marcus Welby, Columbo, High Risk, Switch; guest star numerous network TV shows incl. Merv Griffin Show, The Survivors, Love American Style, Mission Impossible, The Tonight Show; star weekly TV series The Shazam-I IS Hour, CBS, 1976-78; host/dir. US Navy closed circuit network pgm. for TV equipped ships 1977, 78, 79, 80; dir. commercials, dir. CBS Preview Special; prod./dir. documentary Razor Sharp, 1981; media cons. to Catholic Bishops on Papal Visit of Pope John Paul II, Calif. 1987; mem: Directors Guild Am., Acad. TV Arts and Scis., AFTRA, Screen Actors Guild, Delta Delta Delta; club: L.A. Athletic. Ofc: Cameron Productions PO Box 1011 Pebble Beach CA 93953

CAMERON, JUDITH LYNNE, mentor teacher in space science, hypnotherapist; b. Apr. 29, 1945, Oakland; d. Alfred Joseph and June Estelle (Faul) Moe; m. Richard Irwin Cameron, Dec. 17, 1967; son, Kevin Dale; edn: AA psych., Sacto. City Coll., 1965; BA psych./German, Calif. St. Univ., 1967; MA reading specialization, San Francisco St. Univ., 1972; postgrad., Chapman Coll.; PhD, Am. Inst. Hypnotherapy, 1987; Calif. tchg. cred. Career: tchr. St. Vincent's Catholic Sch., San Jose 1969-70; Fremont Elem. Sch., 1970-72; LeRoy Boys Home, LaVerne 1972-73; Grace Miller Elem. Sch., LaVerne 1973-80, resource specialist 1980-84; resource specialist, dept. chair Bonita High Sch., LaVerne 1984-, H.S. advisor Peer Counseling Pgm. 1987-, mentor tchr. in space sci. Bonita Unified Sch. Dist. 1988-, Teacher-in-Space dist. cons. 1987-; selected as mem. of nat. faculty Challenger Ctr. for Space Edn., 1991-; owner Pioneer Take-out Franchises, Alhambra and San Gabriel, 1979-85; advisor Air Explorers, Edwards Test Pilot Sch., LaVerne 1987-; mem. Civil Air Patrol, Sq. 68, 1988-; vol. advisor Children's Home Soc., Santa Ana 1980-81; mem: Council Exceptional Children, Calif. Assn. Resource Specialists, Calif. Elem. Edn. Assn., NEA, Calif. Tchrs. Assn., Calif. Assn. Marriage and Family Therapists, Planetary Soc., Orange County Astronomers, Com. Sci. Investigation L5 Soc., Challenger Ctr. for Space Edn., Calif. Challenger Ctr. Crew for Space Edn.; clubs: Chinese Shar-Pei Am., Concord, Rare Breed Dog. Res: 3257 La Travesia Dr Fullerton 92635 Ofc: Bonita High School 115 W Allen Ave San Dimas 91773

CAMPBELL, ARTHUR WALDRON, law professor, writer; b. Mar. 29, 1944, Bklyn.; s. Wilburn Camrock and Janet Louise (Jobson) C.; m. Drusilla Newlon, June 7, 1969; children: Wilburn b. 1976, Matthew b. 1979; edn: AB, Harvard Coll., 1966; JD, West Va. Univ. Coll. of Law, 1971; LLM, Georgetown Univ., 1975; admitted bar: W.Va., 1971, Dist. Col., 1971, Calif. 1974. Career: def. atty. Prettyman Fellows, Georgetown Univ., W.D.C. 1971-72; asst. U.S. Atty., U.S. Justice Dept., W.D.C. 1972-73, senior staff atty. Dist. Col. Law Students in Ct. Pgm. 1973-74, chief civil div. 1974-75, dep. dir. 1975-76; adj. law prof. Georgetown, George Washington, Howard, Catholic, Am. Univ., 1973-76; law prof. Calif. Western Sch. of Law, San Diego 1976-; c.e.o. Trudar Prodns., Inc. 1981-; advr. W.Va. Legis. Com. to recodify juv. code 1971-72; honors: First law student to argue case W.Va. Supreme Ct. Appeals 1971, merit award Freese Elem. Sch., San Diego 1987, appreciation San Diego Sch. Dist. 1989; mem: Am. Bar Assn., Nat. Assn. Crim. Def. Lawyers (task force ldr.), Assn. of Am. Law Schs., Pub. Defenders Inc. San Diego (bd. 1979-86), Appellate Defenders Inc. S.D. (bd. 1979-), Fed. Defenders Inc. S.D. (bd. 1979-); mem. bd. San Diego Repertory Theater (1992-); author: Entertainment Law (1992, 3rd ed. 1993), treatise, Law of Sentencing (1978, 2d. edit. 1991); mil: 1st lt. USAF 1968-69; rec: tennis, backpacking, running. Ofc: Calif. Western School of Law, 350 Cedar St San Diego 92101

CAMPBELL, DONALD OTIS, physician; b. March 3, 1936, Loma Linda; s. Otis W. and Delia E. (Nasser) C.; m. Elizabeth Short, June 22, 1963; children: Catherine D. b. 1964, Julie S. b. 1967; edn: Stanford Univ. 1954-57; MD, USC 1961; Diplomate Am. Bd. Quality Assurance and Utilization Rev. Physicians, 1991. Career: intern, surgical res. Santa Fe Coast Lines Hosp., Los Angeles 1961-63; house physician Santa Fe Hosp., Los Angeles 1965-66; individual pvt. practice of medicine, family and gen. practice, 1966-; med. dir. Torrance Hosp. Independent Practice Assn. (THIPA) 1987-; staff Torrance Memorial Med. Center, Torrance 1966-, chief dept. fam. practice 1983 and 1986, med. staff secty. 1987-88, asst. chief staff 1989-90; mem: Am. Acad. of Family Physicians (Fellow 1981), Am. Coll. Med. Quality (Fellow 1991), AMA, Calif. Med. Assn., L.A. Cty. Med. Assn., Am. Acad. of Medical Dirs., Am. Coll. of Physician Execs., Torrance Health Assn. (life), Salerni Collegium, Phi Chi Med. Frat., Palos Verdes Penin. C.of C. 1968-78 (dir. 74-76) Kiwanis 1966-80; mil: capt. Med. Corps USAF 1963-65; rec: cooking, gardening, woodwork, photog., plate collector. Ofc: 927 Deep Valley Dr Rolling Hills Estates 90274

CAMPBELL, DOUGLAS A., securities broker-dealer; b. Jan. 13, 1929, Toronto, Ont.; s. Douglas and Dorothea Owen (Turner) C.; m. Allegra, Dec. 1970 (div. 1974); edn: BA, McGill Univ., 1951; MBA, Harvard Bus. Sch., 1953; PhD, Columbia Univ., 1972. Career: pres. D.A. Campbell Co. Inc., Los Angeles 1960-; mem: AAAS, Am. Electronics Assn., Nat. Assn. of Petroleum Investment Analysts, NASD Dist. 2 (v.chmn. bus. conduct com. 1986, internat. com. 1988); clubs: Marina City (LA), Knickerbock (NY), Racquet & Tennis (NY); publs: Environmental & Economic Implications of Enhanced Oil Recovery Processes - An Overview; The Third Market: A Catalyst for Change in Securities Market; Mexico - A Korea On Our Doorstep; The Internat. Telephone Cos.- An Opportunity for Growth; A North American Common Market: Mexico's Manifest Destiny; Republican; Episcopalian; rec: skiing, travel. Address: 1150 Brooklawn Dr Los Angeles CA 90077

CAMPBELL, GARY J., management consultant; b. Feb. 21, 1944, Hartford City, Ind.; s. Lloyd W. and Charlotte G. (Stover) C.; children: Clark b. 1968, Stephanie b. 1972, Chad b. 1975; m. Kristin A. Menge, Oct. 13, 1989; edn: BSIE, Purdue Univ., 1966; MBA, Washington Univ., 1968. Career: Emerson Electric, St. Louis, Mo. 1966-68; McDonnell Douglas, Santa Monica 1968-70; prin. A.T. Kearney Inc., internat. mgmt. consultants, Chgo., Ill. 1970-76; v.p. First Nat. Bank of Chgo. 1976-78; prin. Booz Allen & Hamilton, Chgo., Ill. 1978-80; v.p. A.T. Kearney Inc., Internat. Mgmt. Cons., Chgo. 1980-84, v.p., ptnr. in charge west coast ops. Los Angeles 1984-; mem: Cert. Mgmt. Cons., Assn. of Mgmt. Cons., Univ. Club of Chgo., Jonathan Club (Los Angeles), Rotary Five, Sports Club of L.A., Riveria Tennis Club, Kappa Sigma Frat.; Republican; Presbyterian; rec: skiing, running, tennis. Res: 7 Sea Colony Dr Santa Monica 90405 Ofc: A.T. Kearney Inc, Biltmore Tower 500 S Grand Ave Los Angeles 90071

CAMPBELL, IAN DAVID, opera company director; b. Dec. 21, 1945, Brisbane, Australia; s. Colin David and May (Irwin) C.; m. Ann Roslin Spira, Sept. 1, 1985; children: Benjamin b. 1987, David b. 1989; edn: BA, Univ. Sydney, 1967; Assoc. Fellow Australian Inst. of Mgmt., 1991. Career: prin. tenor singer Australian Opera, Sydney 1967-74; senior music ofcr. The Australia Council, 1974-76; gen. mgr. State Opera South Australia, Adelaide 1976-82; asst. artistic adminstr. Met. Opera, NY 1982-83; gen. dir. San Diego Opera, 1983-; awards: Peri Award, Opera Guild So. Calif., L.A. 1985, Headliner of Yr. San Diego Press Club 1991; mem. bd. Opera America, W.D.C. 1986-; mem. Australian Inst. of Arts Adminstrn. 1990-, Rotary Intl. S.D.; rec: golf, squash. Ofc: San Diego Opera PO Box 988 San Diego 92112

CAMPBELL, L. ANDREW, mathematician; b. May 9, 1942, Detroit, Mich.; s. Laughlin Austin and Mary Kennerly (Holmes) C.; m. Janet Rhonda Gore, May 28, 1971, div. July 1978; edn: ScB, M.I.T., 1963; Lic. es Sci., Univ. of Paris, Fr.

1964; MA, Princeton Univ., 1967, PhD 1970. Career: asst. prof. UD San Diego, La Jolla 1969-76; mem. tech. staff, engring. splst., resrch. scientist The Aerospace Corp., El Segundo 1978-; mem. AMS (1966-69, 79-), IEEE Computer Soc. 1985-, IEEE Control Soc. 1988-, ACM (1983-, chair L.A. chpt. 1991-92); civic: volunteer reader Recording for the Blind 1967; rec: contract bridge ACBL Life Master. Ofc: The Aerospace Corp. M1-102, PO Box 92957 Los Angeles 90009

CAMPBELL, MICHAEL LEE, computer scientist; b. Nov. 25, 1958, Los Angeles; s. Earl Junior and Lee (Fitch) C.; m. Asya Glozman, July 11, 1981; children: Sasha b. 1988, Alice b. 1991; edn: BS in math., UC Riverside, 1980; MS in c.s., UCLA, 1982, PhD in c.s., 1986. Career: tchg. asst., res. asst. UCLA Sch. Engring. and Applied Sci., 1980-82, lectr.1987-88; mem. tech. staff math, Hughes Aircraft Co., Electro-Optical and Data Systems Gp., 1982-88, staff engr., sr. staff computer scientist Hughes Aircraft Research Labs., 1988-92; engring. spec. The Aerospace Corp., Computer Systems Div. 1992-; awards: Howard Hughes doctoral fellow 1983-86; mem. Sigma Xi (chpt. pres.), IEEE Computer Soc., Assn. for Computing Machinery; author 10+ publs. re parallel computer software, applications, fault tolerance and architecture, patentee (1 granted, 1 pending); Indep.; Jewish; rec: karate, photography, travel. Ofc: The Aerospace Corp. - M1/102 P.O. Box 92957 Los Angeles 90009-2957

CAMPBELL, REA BURNE, insurance brokerage executive; b. Aug. 13, 1954, Niceville, Fla.; d. Charles Burnette Campbell and Phyllis (Burgan) Patty; edn: BSBA, Univ. So. Miss. 1976; C.P.A. Miss. (1984). Career: mgt. trainee Deposit Guaranty National Bank, Jackson, Miss. 1976-77, credit dept. ofcr. 1977-80, asst. v.p. and asst. mgr. commercial loan ops. 1980-81, v.p./mgr. customer profitability analysis, 1981-83; acctg. mgr. Fred S. James of Miss. 1983-85, controller, Phoenix and Tucson, Ariz. 1985-87; v.p., c.f.o. Sedgwick James Consulting Group, San Francisco 1987-90; employee benefits cons. Sedgwick James of CA, Inc. 1990-; mem: Kappa Delta Alumni Assn. (treas. 1991), Calif. Soc. CPAs (bd. dir. S.F. Chpt.,chair State Com. on Members in Industry); civic: Sierra Club, ARC (CPR instr. vol.), Tax-Aid Volunteers (v.p. publicity 1990-92, bd. dir. & chair of vol. development 1992-); rec: ballroom dance, backpacking, tennis, kayaking. Res: 850 Powell #103 San Francisco 94108 Ofc: Sedgwick, 600 Montgomery 9th Flr San Francisco 94111

CAMPBELL, WESLEY GLENN, economist, educator; b. Apr. 29, 1924, Komoka, Ont., Can.; nat. 1953; s. Alfred Edwin and Delia (O'Brien) C.; m. Rita Ricardo, Sept. 15, 1946; children: Barbara Lee (Gray), b. 1954, Diane Rita (Porter), b. 1956, Nancy Elizabeth, b. 1960; edn: BA, Univ. W. Ont. 1944, MA, Harvard Univ. 1946, PhD, 1948. Career: instr. in econ. Harvard Univ. 1948-51; resrch econ. US Chamber of Commerce, Wash. DC 1951-54; resrch dir. Am. Enterprise Inst. for Public Policy Resrch, Wash. DC 1954-60, program adviser 1960-; director Hoover Instn. on War, Revolution and Peace, Stanford 1960-89, counselor 1989-; bd. trustees Ronald Reagan Presdl. Found. 1985-89, chmn. 1985-87; chmn. Pres's Intelligence Oversight Bd. 1981-90, mem. Pres's Fgn. Intelligence Advy. Bd. 1981-90; chmn. Japan-US Friendship Commn. 1983-89; mem. Univ. Calif. Bd. of Regents 1968-, chmn. 1982; NSF Nat. Sci. Bd. 1972-78, 1990-; Presdl. Com. on Sci. and Tech. 1976; Pres's Commn. on White House Fellow 1969-74; chmn. Reagan-Bush Task Force on Edn. 1980, mem. R.-B. Task Force on Fgn. Policy, and on Inflation Policy, 1980; Personnel Advy. Com. to Pres. Reagan 1980-81; bd. dirs. Com. on the Present Danger, 1976-; advy. bd. Ctr. for Strategic and Internat. Studies 1980-; trustee Herbert Hoover Presdl. Lib. Assn. 1964-; mem. Mont Pelerin Soc. (dir. 1980-86), Philadelphia Soc. (pres. 1965-67); clubs: Bohemian, Cosmos, Commonwealth; mil: Canadian Navy 1943-44. Res: 26915 Alejandro Dr Los Altos Hills 94022. Ofc: Hoover Institution, Stanford 94305-6010

CANNING, BRUCE R., doctor of Oriental medicine, acupuncturist, herbalist; b. Sept. 21, 1955, Whittier, Calif.; s. Glenn R. and Vada (Schurtz) C.; edn: diplomate, Emperors Coll., Santa Monica, 1987; diplomate, DaLian Med. Sch., DaLian, China, 1988; diplomate, Acad. of T.C.M., Beijing, China, 1988; doctor of Oriental Medicine, S.A.M.R.A. Univ., L.A., 1988; diplomate acupuncture, N.C.C.A.; lic. acupuncturist, State of Calif. Career: doctor of Oriental medicine, Westwood Ctr. for Acupuncture, Westwood, Calif., 1988; doctor of Oriental medicine, M. M. Van Benschoten & Assoc., Reseda, Calif., 1989-; tchr. of Qi Gong, Emperors Coll., Santa Monica 1988; awards: 5th Degree Black Belt, (Chinese) Kung Fu S.S., L.A. County, 1986; author: doctoral dissertation, Current Traditional Oriental Medicine in China, 1988; rec: Shing Yi Chuan (internal Kung Fu), Qi Gong, Nei Gong, Yoga, meditation. Ofc: M. M. Van Benschoten OMD, M.A., C.A., & Assoc. 19231 Victory Blvd #151 Reseda 91335

CANOVA-DAVIS, ELEANOR, research biochemist; b. Jan. 18, 1938, San Francisco, Calif.; d. Gaudenzio Enzio and Catherine (Bordisso) Canova; m. Kenneth Davis, Feb. 10, 1957; children: Kenneth b. 1958, Jeffrey b. 1960; grandson: Scott b. 1985; edn: BA, S.F. State Univ. 1968; MS, S.F. State Univ. 1971; PhD, UC Med. Ctr., S.F. 1977; career: lab. asst., Frederick Burk Found. for Edn., S.F., Calif. 1969-71; res. and tchg. asst., UC Med. Ctr., S.F. 1972-77; NIH postdoctoral fellow, UC, Berkeley 1977-80; asst. res. biochemist, UC Med. Ctr., S.F. 1980-84; sr. scientist, Liposome Tech., Menlo Park, Calif. 1984-85; sr.

scientist, Genentech, Inc., So. S.F. 1985-; awards: Honors Convocation award, Dept. of Chem., S.F. State Univ. 1966; grad. div. fellowship, UC Med. Ctr., S.F. 1972-73; Earl C. Anthony Trust for Grad. Student Res., UC, S.F. 1975; Chancellor's Patent Fund award, Grad. Div., UC, S.F. 1976; Nat. Res. Service award, NIH, Berkeley 1977-80; mem: Calif. Scholarship Fedn. 1951-, Am. Chemical Soc. 1971-, The Protein Soc. 1988-; civic: Foxridge PTA and Westborough PTA, So. S.F.; Tiny Tots, S.F., St. Patrick's Circle, So. S.F.; author: numerous pub. articles in prof. journals, articles in various symposia; Catholic; rec: reading, sewing, knitting, bridge. Ofc: Genentech, Inc. 460 Point San Bruno Blvd South San Francisco 94080

CAPORASO, FREDRIC, food science and nutrition educator; b. May 28, 1947, Jersey City, N.J.; s. Pat and Florence C.; m. Karen Denise Kuhle, Dec. 5, 1981; children: Robert b. 1968, Michael b. 1972, Daniel b. 1976, Allison b. 1989; edn: BS, Rutgers Univ. 1969, MS, 1972; PhD, Penn. State 1975. Career: asst. prof. food sci. Univ. of Nebraska 1975-78; mgr. food sci. Am. McGaw, Irvine 1978-82; chmn. food sci. & nutrition Chapman Univ. 1982-, dir. food sci. research ctr. Chapman Univ. 1988-; mem: So. Cal. Inst. of Food Technologists (chmn., ch.-elect, pgm. ch.), Inst. of Food Technologists, coord. Food Sci. Administrators, scientific lectr. 1993-96; author 30+ pub. research articles; rec: running. Ofc: Chapman University , Food Science & Nutrition Dept, Orange 92666

CAPPS, ANTHONY T. (CAPOZZOLO), international public relations executive; b. April 19, Pueblo, Colo.; s. Nicolo and Ann (Salomone) Capozzolo; Career: dance dir., choreographer, prod. mot. pic. TV and radio; feat. Profl. Dance Team, Biltmore Bowl, Cocoanut Grove, L.A.; St. Catherine Hotel, Catalina 1939-42; dance dir., prod. NBC, ABC, KCOP-TV, Columbia Pictures, 20th Century Fox and Calif. studios 1940-60; govt. tours, P.R., Cuba, Jamaica, Dominican Rep., Haiti, 1954; prod. "Latin Holiday" t.v. series; exec. dir. activities Lockheed and Vega Aircraft Co., Burbank, L.A., Glendale, Pomona, Pasadena, Bakersfield, and Taft plants; internat. pub. rels. dir: Howard Manor, Palm Springs Key Club, Country Club Hotel, Palm Springs Ranch Club; Desert Sun Newspapers, KDES Radio P.S., Cameron Ctr. and Cameron Enterprises and Oil Co., Burbank radio sta., Murietta Hot Springs Hotel, Health and Beauty Spa P.S.- Coachella Valley; founder, pres., dir. Tony Capps Ents.; frequent t.v. guest re religion & politics, hist. of ballet & opera; founder/chmn. Nat. Artists Art Patrons Soc., St. Martin's Abbey (Lacey, Wash.), founder Capps-Capozzolo Gallery, St. Martin's Abbey & Coll. (Lacey, Wash.) 1988; fundraiser for num. charities: chair/exec. dir. golf and tennis tournaments, benefit dinners for civic ldrs. and elected ofcls., United Fund, City of Hope (3t), Nat. Cystic Fibrosis Fund, P.S. Bob Hope Golf Classic; created advtsg. gimmick for Colgate and Cugat, Coca Cola; estab. Anthony Capps Art Gal., Eisenhower Med. Ctr.; mem. Nat. Football Found. and Hall of Fame (founder/pres. Tri-Co. chpt., founder/ co-ch. Annual Golf Classic), Nat. Artists and Art Patrons Soc./ City of Hope (founder/pres.), Eisenhower Mem. Hosp. Aux (charter), Opera Guild of the Desert, P.S. Pathfinders, Desert Art Ctr. Coachella Valley, P.S. Desert Mus., AFTRA, Smithsonian Instn., Am. Security Council, LA Co. Mus. Art (Patron), Nat. Trust for Hist. Preserv.; publs: Am. Film Inst., The Reporter, Desert Sun P.S., L.A. Daily News; Republican: Life mem. Presdl. Repub. Task Force, US Senatl. Club (Wash. DC), Repub. Senatl. Inner Circle, The Ronald Reagan Presdl. Found. (charter sponsor), Who's Who in the Republican Party (Wash. D.C.); R.Cath. Res: 2715 Junipero Ave Palm Springs 92262

CAREY, STEVENS ANTHONY, lawyer; b. Mar. 30, 1951, Los Angeles; s. Edward Macdonald and Elizabeth (Heckscher) C.; m. Indy Shriner, Mar. 20, 1987; children: Lauren b. 1987, Meagan b. 1989; edn: BA, MA, and JD, UC Berkeley, 1973, 1975, 1978; admitted bar: Calif. 1978, N.Y. 1988. Career: assoc. Lawler, Felix & Hall, Los Angeles 1978-83; invitation to participate on Hastings Law Jour., 1976, Phi Beta Kappa, offered 4-yr. fellowship from UCLA, 1974, 1st place winner at UCLA Shakespeare Festival, 1969; mem: Calif. State Bar Assn., Los Angeles Co. Bar Ass., Am. Bar Assn.; publs: articles, "Profit Participations: Coping with the Limitations Faced by Pension Funds and REITs", 1986, "Shared Appreciation Loans by Tax-Exempt Pension Funds", 1990, contbr. "How to Avoid Assignment and Sublet Tax Trap", 1990, contbg. editor Real Estate Finance Jour., 1986, 1991-93; co-author, article pub. in Workouts & Asset Management, 1993; Republican; Catholic; rec: piano, tennis. Ofc: Pircher, Nichols & Meeks 1999 Avenue of the Stars, 26th Flr Los Angeles 90067

CARFAGNO, EDWARD CHARLES, film production designer; b. Nov. 28, 1907, Los Angeles; s. Salvatore Frank and Frances Mary (Sereno) C.; m. Lois, Dec. 14, 1939; children: Edward Louis, Carol Lois, Linda Louise; edn: MArch, USC, 1933. Career: draftsman MGM Studios, Los Angeles 1933-38, art dir. 1938-79; production designer Malpaiso Productions 1979-, prodn. designer: The Bird 1988; awards: Am. Olympic Fencing Team 1940, State Champion 1930-50, Oscar awards for The Bad and The Beautiful (1952), Julius Caesar (1953), Ben Hur (1959), thirteen Oscar nominations; Republican; R.Cath.; rec: music, art. Res: 3001 Benedict Canyon Beverly Hills 90210 Ofc: Mapaiso Warner Studios.

CARICATO, CHARLES ROBERT, a.k.a. CHUCK CARR, dance studio executive; b. June 28, 1931, Monessen, Pa.; s. Charles Patrick and Anne (Hurrianko) C.; m. Nancy Willis, Nov. 4, 1967 (div. July 1989); children:

Charlene b. 1968, Tiffany b. 1969, Charles b. 1971, Christian b. 1972; m. Yoni Eisnor, Oct. 28, 1989; edn: BA, Penn State, 1953. Career: account exec. Prudential Ins., Monessen, Pa. 1953-54; instr.- counselor Arthur Murray, Los Angeles 1955-60; mgr. Arthur Murray Studio, Glendale 1960-63; franchisee, pres. Arthur Murray, San Diego 1963-, area dir. Arthur Murray Internat., Coral Gables, Fla. 1985-; pres. Gloria Marshall Figure Salons, San Diego 1973-81; awards: industrious franchisee Arthur Murray (Miami 1980), Studio of Year (1989, 90, 91), VIP Honors and Arthur Gold Award 1991; mem. Penn St. Alumni, Alpha Chi Rho Alumni; Republican; R.Cath. (parish council 1984-85); rec: golf, tennis, sports. Ofc: Arthur Murray 3919 4th Ave San Diego 92103

CARINI, MICHAEL JOSEPH, certified public accountant; b. June 7, 1951, San Francisco; s. Fred Joseph and Anna Elizabeth (Lamb) C.; m. Patricia Anne Vince, Oct. 3, 1981; 1 dau., Gina b. 1983; edn: BS, Univ. San Francisco 1973; C.P.A. Calif. 1979. Career: external auditor Hood & Strong, San Francisco 1973-76; acctg. mgr. Cutter Labs., Emeryville, mgr. MIS 1976-84; controller Kinney Wall Coverings, Oakland 1984-86; Crittendon Publishers, Novato 1986-87; New Zealand Milk Products, Petaluma 1987-89, Regan Holding Co., Petaluma 1989-92, Fritzi California, San Francisco 1992-; mem: Am. Inst. CPA, Calif. Soc. CPA; rec: historical autographs and accordionist. Res: 662 Hudis St Rohnert Park 94928 Ofc: Fritzi California 199 First Street San Francisco 94105

CARLETON, JOHN LOWNDES, psychiatrist; b. Dec. 26, 1925, Seattle; s. John Phillip and Lillian (Lowndes) C.; m. Marie Pak, June 12, 1948 (div. 1968); m. Ellen Andree Masthoff, Apr. 14, 1985; children: John b. 1949, Pakie b. 1950, Daniel b. 1952, Kip b. 1986, Talitha b. 1988; edn: BA, Univ. of Louisville, Ky. 1946; MD, Northwestern Univ. Med., Chgo. 1950; cert. in psychiatry Am. Bd. Psych. & Neurology, 1959. Career: intern Swedish Hosp., Seattle, 1949, resident in surgery, 1952, 1954-55; industrial physician Howe Sound Mining Corp., Holden, WA 1950-52; capt. Med. Corps US Army Reserve, 1952-54; resident psychiatry Johns Hopkins Univ. Med. Sch., Balt. 1955-57; asst. psychiatrist Sheppard & Enoch Pratt Hosp., Towson, Md. 1957-58; private practice, Santa Barbara, Calif. 1958-; trustee Masserman Found., Chgo. 1985-; awards: Founders Award Am. Assn. for Soc. Psych., W.D.C. 1984, Silver Camellia award City of Opatija, Yugoslavia 1976, congress hon. medals World Assn. for Soc. Psych.: Israel, Opatija, Yugo., Lisbon, Portugal, Santa Barbara, CA (1972, 76, 78, 79); mem: Am. Psychiatric Assn. (1957-, life fellow), Am. Coll. Psychiatry (Fellow 1973-), Am. Coll. Physicians (Fellow 1973-), World Assn. for Social Psychiatry (3d. hon. pres. 1970-), Am. Assn. for Social Psychiatry (past pres. 1970-, Jour. editor in chief 1980-87), Nuclear Age Peace Found. Santa Barbara; author 25+ sci. publs. (1957-), co-editor 3 books: Man for Man (1973), What is Alcoholism (1976), The Dimensions of Soc. Psych. (1979); Republican; Unitarian; rec: carpentry, gardening, sailing, hiking. Res/Ofc: 310 Malaga Dr Santa Barbara 93108-2129

CARLSON, CHARLES LONG, financial executive, business consultant; b. Jan. 10, 1917, Olean, N.Y.; s. Charles Julius Carlson and Edna Long; m. June Kreamer, Apr. 10, 1948; children: Yvonne, Shaun, Linda, Maria; edn: BS in B.A., Univ. Buffalo, 1938; CPA, Calif. Career: ptnr. Merle Moore & Co., CPAs, Tucson 1954-55; sec.-treas. comptroller Infilco, Tucson 1955-64; comptroller Traveler Boat Div., Stanray Corp., Chgo. and Danville, Ill. 1964-65; comptroller Dorsett Plastics Co., Santa Clara, Calif. 1966; v.p., sec.-treas. Daniel, Mann, Johnson & Mendenhall, Los Angeles 1966-82, bus. cons., sec. 1982-84, asst. sec. 1984-; dir.: subs. of Infilco & DMJM; sec., dir. Infilco (Australia) Ltd., Infilco (Can.) Ltd., Infilco Mexicana; sec. Gale Separator Co. (Tucson), Catalina Constrn. Co. (Tucson); sec.-treas. Beach Ocean Inc., 1985-, Honolulu Condo Inc. 1985-86; bus. mgr. Westwil Ltd. 1986-92, Hampwil Ptnrs. 1986-; asst. treas. Fuller Co., Catasauqua, Pa.; dir. Gen. Steel Co., Ft. Worth 1960-64; instr. St. Bonaventure Univ., Olean 1948; mem. Am. Inst. CPAs; civic: (Olean): Republican county committeeman 1939, Community Chest (cpgn. gen. chmn. 1950), Olean Gen. Hosp. drive (team chmn. 1952); Tucson C.of C. (tax study com. 1960); mil: 2d lt. USAAF 1944-45; Nazarene Ch. Res./Ofc: 4515 Prairie Rd Paso Robles 93446

CARLSON, M. JOEL, real estate broker-developer; b. May 24, 1952, Hollywood; s. Franklin Joel and Evelyn (Knutson) C.; m. Mary, June 26, 1982; edn: BA, Chapman Coll., 1974; Calif. Comm. Colls. life instr. cred., 1982; profl. credits, desig: RECI, Santa Ana Coll., 1979, CREC (cert. R.E. cons.), American Coll. Idpls. 1980, G.R.I., Grad. Realtors Inst. Career: asst. mgr. Walker & Lee Realty, Villa Park 1976-78; branch mgr. Strout Realty, Buena Park 1978-80; owner/broker Carlson Realty, Orange 1980-85; pres. MJC Realty, Newport Beach 1985-; awards: sales agt. of month Walker & Lee (1st mo. in bus.), $1 Million Club, Strout (1979), Multi-Million $ Club, MJC Realty (1986-); mem: Calif. Assn. Realtors (Master Instr. 1984, author CAR course Intro to R.E. Counseling, 1989), Nat. Assn. Realtors, Newport Mesa Bd. Realtors (edn. chair 1983, 88, dir. 1984, 90, 91), Calif. R.E. Educators Assn. (past pres., Desig. R.E. Instr.-DREI 1989), Kiwanis (past pres. Villa Park 1979, Corona del Mar 1984); publs: (workbook w. 8 tapes) The Secrets of Equity Sharing, 1984, (booklet) So... You Wanna ,Make A Deal, 1985; seminar lectr. (w. workbook) On Your Mark, Get $et, Go!, 1986; Republican; Christian; rec: skiing, golf, lecturing. Ofc: MJC Realty, Inc. 471 N Newport Blvd Ste 100 Newport Beach 92663

CARLSON, PAUL EDWIN, television writer, real estate developer; b. June 29, 1944, San Francisco; s. Carl John and Margueritte E. (Kovatch) C.; m. Sharon Hammond, 1963; children: Kim, b. 1964, Davin, b. 1971, Christina, b. 1979; edn: AA, Yosemite Coll. 1964; BA, CSU Long Beach 1971; Cert. Shopping Center Mgr. (CSM) Internat. Council of Shopping Ctrs. Mgmt. Sch. 1981. Career: police ofcr. (vice & narcotics) Modesto Police Dept. 1964-69; owner Universal Prodns., NYC and Modesto, Ca. 1969-73; gen. mgr. City Investing Co., Beverly Hills and NYC 1973-75; v.p. The Koll Co., Newport Beach 1975-79; v.p. Irvine Co., Newport Beach 1979-80; owner Willows Shopping Center, Concord 1980-83; sr. vice pres. Lee Sammis Co. 1983-85; pres. Am. Devel. Co., 1985-87; bd. chmn. The Carlson Co., 1987-; writer 3 screen plays for NBC's Police Story, comedy writer for NBC-TV Tonight Show, Saturday Night Live, and Late Night with David Letterman; special projects comedy writer for British Bdcstg. Co. (BBC), London; pub. Property Managers Handbook; guest lectr. USC, UCLA, Orange Coast Coll.; real estate cons. Bank of Am., Union Bank, Chevron USA, Aetna Life Ins. Co., James Lang Wooten (G.Brit.), Peoples Rep. of China; commr. Calif. State Juvenile Justice Commn.; ops. chmn. Internat. Council of Shopping Ctrs.; mem. Concord Visitors & Conv. Bur. (bd.), Am. Cancer Soc. (bd. Contra Costa Co.), Mt. Diablo Hosp. (pres. bd. trustees), City of Concord Pavillion (v.p., bd.), past chmn. City of Newport Bch. Traffic Commn.; Republican; Prot.; avocation: youth counseling. Res: 140 Jasmine Creek Dr Corona del Mar 92625 Ofc: The Carlson Co. #3 Corporate Plaza Ste 100 Newport Beach 92660

CARLSON, RICHARD WARNER, journalist, government official; b. Feb. 10, 1941, Boston, Mass.; s. W.E. and Ruth Carlson; m. Patricia Caroline Swanson, Feb. 18, 1979; children: Tucker McNear b. 1969, Buckley Peck b. 1971. Career: journalist Los Angeles Times 1962-63; United Press Internat. 1963-65; ABC-TV, San Francisco and Los Angeles 1966-75; freelance writer, stringer Time Magazine, Look, others 1966-70; dir., prod. documentaries NBC-TV, Burbank 1975; anchorman CBS-TV, San Diego 1975-76; sr. v.p., v.p. fin. Great American Fed. Savings Bank 1976-84; dir. pub. liaison U.S. Info. Agency 1985-86, dir. The Voice of Am., Washington DC 1986-; dir: Delmar News Press 1976, Calif. Gen. Mortgage Inc. 1978, San Diego C.of C.; awards: recipient AP tv & radio awards for investigative reporting, news analysis and commentary (6 awards), Golden Mike awards (4), Emmy awards (3), San Diego Press Club awards (2), Geo. Foster Peabody Award for investigative reporting, L.A. Press Club Grand Award, Nat. Headliners Award; apptd. by Pres. Reagan to President's Council on Peace Corps 1982; mem: Jr. League of San Diego (Fin. Advy. Bd.), La Jolla Soccer League (sponsor), Muscular Dystrophy Assn. (dir. San Diego), Actors & Others (pres. L.A. 1972-76), Rosalind Russel Arthritis Found. (dir.), Fund for Animals (dir. N.Y.), San Diego Coalition (chmn.), Sigma Delta Chi; clubs: La Jolla Beach, Thunderbird CC, Mid Ocean, Capitol Hill; Republican (v.p. Bus. & Profl. Club 1978, Senate advy. Commn. 1978); Episcopalian. Res: 7956 Ave Alamar La Jolla 92037; 3051 N St N.W., Washington DC 20007 (summers) Crockett Island, Lake Christopher, Woodstock, ME 04219 Ofc: Voice of America 330 Independence Ave SW Wash DC 20547

CARMAN, ERNEST DAY, lawyer; b. Mpls.; s. Ernest Clarke and Juanita (Howland Day) C.; m. Deborah Daynes; children (by previous m.): Eric C., Christiane M., and Dayna H.; edn: BA, USC; MA, Stanford Univ.; Dr. es Sci. Pol., Univ. Geneva, Switz.; JD, Univ. San Francisco; admitted bar: Calif., U.S. Supreme Ct. Career: law ptnr. E. Day Carman & Associates, Newport Beach, currently; mil: maj. USMC Reserve (ret.). Res: 720 Cliff Dr Laguna Beach 92651 Ofc: E. Day Carman & Associates 567 San Nicholas Dr Ste 207 Newport Beach 92660

CARNIGLIA, STEPHEN CHARLES, author, educator, consultant on materials science; b. Jan. 15, 1922, San Francisco; s. Harold Chester and Muriel Carlotta (Skinner) C.; m. Phebe Davis, June 20, 1947; children: Stephen Davis b. 1950, William Douglas b. 1955; edn: BS, MS, and PhD in chemistry, UC Berkeley, 1943, 45, 54; Calif. std. gen. secondary tchg. cred., 1946. Career: instr., hd. dept. chemistry, Coll. of Marin, Kentfield 1946-51; dept. hd. inorganic chemicals res. & devel. FMC Corp., Newark, Calif. and Princeton, N.J., 1953-56; sect. chief mats. R&D, Atomics Internat. Div., Rocketdyne Div., Rockwell Internat. Corp., Canoga Park 1956-70; dept. mgr. chem. and mats. R&D, Kaiser Aluminum and Chemical Corp., Pleasanton 1970-86; indep. cons., frequent guest lectr. on materials sci., 1986-, W.W. Clyde Prof. of Engring. Univ. of Utah, 1988, lectr. UCLA and UC Davis, 1987-90; adj. prof. of M.S.&E., UC Davis, 1991-; honors: Phi Beta Kappa 1943, Sigma Xi 1945, Ross Coffin Purdy Award Am. Ceramic Soc. 1974, listed Who's Who in the West, Am. Men and Women of Sci.; mem: Fellow Am. Ceramic Soc. (v.p. 1980), Catalysis Soc. 1982-; civic: Marin Co. Jr. C.of C. 1950; 40+ pub. res. papers, 4 patents, 2 books; mil: pvt. US Army Inactive Res. 1942-43; Republican; United Ch. of Christ; rec: sailing, tennis, bicycling. Address: 115 Wilshire Ct Danville 94526

CARNOW, LANCE S., real estate company administrator; b. Dec. 29, 1959, Montebello; m. Stephanie S. Chandler, May 24, 1987; edn: BA (2), UC Santa Barbara, 1982; MS, Dartmouth, 1985; cert. systems professional (CSP); editor

(book) Pascal for Beginning Pascal Students, 1984, contbr. article, Franchise Financing, 1989. Ofc: Real Property Services 1935 Camino Vida Roble Carlsbad 92008-6599

CARON, DAVID DENNIS, lawyer, educator; b. June 28, 1952, Hartford, Conn.; s. Laurier Dennis and Rita Gertrude (Lafond) C.; m. R'Sue Popowich, May 24, 1975; children: Peter, Marina; edn: BS, USCG Acad., 1974; MSc, Univ. Wales, 1980; JD, UC Berkeley, 1983; diploma, Hague Acad. Internat. Law, 1984; Drs, Leiden Univ., 1985, Dr.Jur., 1990; admitted bar Calif. 1983. Career: lt. US Coast Guard, 1974-79; legal asst. Iran-U.S. Claims Tribunal, The Hague, The Netherlands, 1981-83; atty., assoc. Pillsbury, Madison & Sutro, San Francisco, 1986-87; prof. law UC Berkeley, 1987; dir. studies Hague Acad. Internat. Law, The Hague, The Netherlands, 1987; vis. prof. Cornell Law Sch., 1990; awards: Fulbright scholar U.S./U.K. Fulbright Comm., U.K. 1979-80, Environmental Conservation fellowship, Nat. Wildlife Fedn. 1980-81, Deak Prize for Writing Am. Soc. of Internat. Law 1990, Thelen Marrin Prize for writing UC Berkeley 1983, Order of the Coif; mem: UN Assn., Internat. Studies Assn., Am. Soc. Internat. Law, S.F. Commn. on Fgn. Rels.; publs: numerous articles in law jours., editor-in-chief Ecology Law Quarterly 1982-83, ed. Law of the Sea: U.S. Policy Dilemma (1983), Perspectives on U.S. Policy Toward the Law of the Sea (1985), bd. editors Am. Jour. of Internat. Law (1991-95); rec: classical choral works. Res: 5450 Thomas Ave Oakland 94618 Ofc: University of California School of Law Boalt Hall Berkeley 94720

CARPENTER, DONALD BLODGETT, real estate appraiser, educator; b. Aug. 20, 1916, New Haven, Conn.; s. Prof. Fred Donald and Gwendolen (Blodgett) C.; m. Barbara Marvin Adams, June 28, 1941 (dec. Aug. 1978); m. 2d Lee Burker McGough, Dec. 28, 1980 (div. Apr. 1987); children (nee McGough): Edward G. b.1952, John D. b.1957, William V. b.1959, Andrew J. b.1960, Dorothy J. b.1962, James J. b.1964; edn: Ph.B., Univ. VT 1938; Sonoma St. Univ. 1968-69, Mendocino Comm. Coll. 1977, Coll. of the Redwoods 1984-85; Career: reporter Burlington Daily News, VT, 1938-39; guide chair opr. Am. Express Co., NY World's Fair, 1939; underwriter Gen. Exchange Ins. Corp., Newark, NJ 1939-40; asst. ofc. mgr., priorities splst., 1941-42; sales rep., San Francisco 1946-52; field supt. The Travelers Ins. Co., 1952-58; gen. agent Gen. Am. Life Ins. Co., 1958-59; western reg. supr. Provident Life & Accident Ins. Co., 1959-60; brokerage supr. Aetna Life Ins. Co., 1960-61; maintenance cons. J.I. Holcomb Mfg. Co., Mill Valley 1961-68; sales rep. Onox Inc., Mendocino 1965-68; ednl. svs. rep. Marquis Who's Who, Inc., Mill Valley 1963-68; tchr. and coach Mendocino Jr.-Sr. H.S., 1968; real prop. appraiser County of Mendocino, 1968-81; independent R.E. appraiser 1982-88, ret. 1988; dir: Mendocino Coast Land Devel. Corp. 1991-; instr. Coll. of the Redwoods 1985-87; mem. Nat. Retired Tchrs Assn.; awards: scholarship and leadership Kappa Sigma Internat. Frat. 1937-38, Community Sportsman of the Year 1971; mem: Mendocino County Employees Assn. (1968-81, dir. 1981), Kappa Sigma Intl. Frat. (life), Univ. Vt. Catamount Club (charter), Univ. Vt. Alumni Assn./S.F. (founding pres. 1964), Rotary Internat. (club pres. 1975-76, dist. gov. area rep. 1977-8, club historian 1989-, Paul Harris Fellow 1979-, Rotarian of the Years 1969-88); Am. Legion (1945-, Post Comdr. 1972-3, Past Comdrs. of Calif. (life), Mendocino Cardinal Boosters (charter, life, pres. 1971), Ret. Ofcrs. Assn. (life), Reserve Ofcrs. Assn. of U.S. (life, chpt. pres. 1954, 56, state v.p. 1958-61), Marines Memorial Assn., Naval Order of U.S. (life), Naval Reserve Assn. (life), Navy League of U.S. (Life), Am. Diabetes Assn., Mendocino Art Center (sponsor 1965-), Save the Redwoods League, Mendocino Co. Hist. Soc., Mendocino Hist. Research Inc. (docent 1982-88), Mendocino Coast Geneal. Soc. (pres. 1991-93), Mendocino Coast Stamp Club (charter, dir. 1991-92, v.p. 1993); chief editor univ. newspaper, ed. internat. frat. chapter alumni publication, and ed. Univ. Frosh Handbook (Univ. Vt. 1937-38), editor Rotary Club Membership Directory 1971-, editor Univ. Vt. 50th Yr. Class Reunion Handbook 1983-88; mil: lcdr. USNR, active duty WWII 1942-46, Reserve unit comdg. ofcr. 1967-68, ret. 1968, commendations U.S. Sec. of Navy, 1946, and Comdt. 12th Naval Dist., 1968; Republican; Congregational; rec: history, writing, tennis, football, youth work. Res: Box 87, 10801 Gurley Ln Mendocino 95460-0087

CARPENTER-MC MILLAN, SUSAN, media spokesperson/right to life advocate; b. Dec. 5, 1947, Los Angeles; d. Charles Elmore and Emma (Loua) Carpenter; m. Wm. Neal McMillan III, Aug. 12, 1972; children: Cameo b. 1978, Tara b. 1984; edn: attended. USC, 1968-72. Career: owner clothing stores in LeMors and Glendale, 1973-81; media spokesperson Right to Life orgn., Pasadena 1981-, seminar ldr. and lectr. Life Issues, nat. 1985-; dir. Women's Coalition, Huntington Beach 1987-89; honors: named Calif. pro-life person of year New Life Beginnings, Long Beach, 1986; appt. L.A. Commn. on the Status of Women, 1985-; mem: Beverly Law Sch. Partners (pres. 1974-76), Feminists for Life of Am. (nat. bd. 1986-, Calif. chpt. pres. 1986-), Right to Life League of So. Calif., San Marino Women's Club; pub. articles: USA Today, 1986, RTL Speaks, 1984-; Republican; Prot.; rec: int. design. Ofc: 50 N Hill Ave Ste 306 Pasadena 91108

CARRIGAN, JOHN LIONEL, information specialist/library consultant; b. Sept. 9, 1948, Leadville, Colo.; s. Lionel R. and Helen R. (Plake) C.; m. Brenda

L. (div. 1987); children: Jeff b. 1969, Patrick b. 1974; edn: BS, Tx. A&M Univ. 1970; MS, Cal Tech Pasadena 1973; MS, CSU Fullerton 1979. Career: res. tech. City of Hope Nat. Med. Center, Duarte 1973-74, asst. librarian 1974-76, chief librarian 1976, dir. of library services 1977-85, info. splst. 1985-; indep. library consultant 1976-; mem: Med. Library Assn., Special Library Assn., Am. Library Assn., Assn. Coll. & Research Libraries, Am. Soc. Info. Sci., N.Y. Acad. Scis., Montclair Little League (bd. mem.). Res: 4811 Orchard Montclair 91763 Ofc: City of Hope National Medical Center 1500 E Duarte Duarte 91010

CARRILLO, GILBERTO, engineer; b. Sept. 22, 1926, San Diego; s. Manuel C. and Francisca (Ruiz) C.; m. Maria de Lourdes Paez, Jan. 21, 1957; children: Gilbert A., Elizabeth, Evelyn, Fernando, Maria De Lourdes; edn: BS (honors), San Diego State Univ., 1951. Career: materials and process engr. Convair Div. Gen. Dynamics, San Diego 1950-56; Douglas Aircraft Co., El Segundo 1956-60; tech. dir. Turco Products Inc., Mexico City 1960-68; mgr. environmental engring. Rohr Industries, Riverside, Calif. 1969-; mem. Soc. for Advancement of Materials and Process Engring. (gen. chmn. 1st internat. SAMPE symp. & tech. exhibition dedicated to environmental issues 6/91; nat. gen. chmn. internat. symposium & tech. conf. 1988), SAMPE Inland Empire (chapt. chmn. arrangements com. 1972-76, scholarships chmn. 1976-82, gen. chmn. 1982-83, Best Paper award 1983), VFW; patentee, tech. publs. in field; mil: sgt. USAAF 1945-46; Republican; R.Cath. Res: 5535 Montero Dr Riverside 92509 Ofc: Rohr Industries Materials Engineering 8200 Arlington Ave Riverside 92503

CARRILLO, RICHARD, steel company executive; b. Oct. 29, 1938, Tucson, Ariz.; s. Joseph Gil and Esther (Mendoza) C.; m. Georgia Elinore Armenta, May 7, 1960; children: Veronica Ann b. 1961, Richard Gerard b. 1964; edn: Univ. Ariz. 1961-63, Met. Coll., L.A. 1964. Career: traffic mgr., sales desk mgr. M.S.L. Industries, Los Angeles 1964-65; ops. mgr., adminstrv. mgr. Comstock Steel Co., Tucson, Phoenix, 1960-64, 65-69; adminstrv. mgr. Rio Grande Steel, Phoenix 1969-71; tubular products mgr. Ducommun Metals, Los Angeles 1972-74; sales rep., tubular products mgr. Bernard Epps Co., 1974-83; regional sales mgr. Maruichi American Corp., Santa Fe Springs 1983-; mil: ADR3 USN 1956-59; Democrat; R.Cath.; rec: golf, vintage autos, rare plants. Res: Huntington Beach Ofc: Maruichi American Corp. 11529 S Greenstone Ave Santa Fe Springs 90670

CARROLL, JOEL, retired mathematician; b. Apr. 8, 1924, Hallettsville, Tx.; s. Norman and Otealia (Hargrove) C.; m. Anne M. Merriweather, Aug. 20, 1960; children: Joel Anson b. 1961, Bernard Eugene b. 1963, Harlan Patrick b. 1969; edn: BA, Roosevelt Univ., Chgo. 1950; MS, DePaul Univ., Chgo. 1952; career: analytical statistician, U.S. Railroad Retirement Bd., Chgo. 1952-54; asst. mathematician, Argonne Nat. Lab., Lemont, Ill. 1954-55; computing engr., No. Am. Aviation, Inc., L.A. 1955-58; mathematician, Land-Air, Inc., Point Mugu 1958-61; mathematician, General Precision, Inc., Glendale 1961-63; sr. engr., Northrup Corp., Hawthorne 1963-65; computer scientist, Douglas Aircraft, Santa Monica 1965-66; mathematician, Naval Ocean System Ctr., San Diego 1966-88; awards: Superior Accomplishment, Dept. of Navy 1968; Special Achievement, Naval Ocean System Ctr. 1974; mem: A.C.L.U.; Town Hall of Calif.; hon. fellow, Harry S. Truman Lib. Inst.; Am. Mathematic Soc.; Am. Assn. for Advancement of Science; N. Y. Academy of Science; civic: Pi Mu Epsilon; past secr., Kiwanis; S.D. Assoc. United Church of Christ (moderator 1980-81); Congregational Church (past moderator and treasurer); mil: aviation metalsmith 3/c, Navy, 1943-45; Congregationalist; res: 13307 Olive Grove Poway 92064

CARROLL, PAULA MARIE, security company president, civic activist; b. July 17, 1933, Fresno; d. Paul Edward Mikkelsen and Helen Marie (Anderson) Mack; m. Herman S. Carroll, Jr., Apr. 25, 1954. Career: v.p., co-owner Central Valley Alarm Co. Inc., Merced 1963-, pres. 1988-; civic bds: Hospice of Merced and Mariposa Counties 1979, Consumers for Med. Quality Inc., Merced (founder, pres. 1981), Ombudsmen, Merced (chair 1982-85); honors: Celebrating Women award Co. of Merced 1987, Consumers for Med. Quality grantee and the pres.'s award Calif. Trial Lawyers Assn. 1987, woman of distinction Soroptimist Intl. 1986; mem: We. Burglar and Fire Alarm Assn., Soc. Law and Medicine, Hastings Ctr. Inst. of Society, Am. Mgmt. Assn., Josephson Instn. for the Advancement of Ethics, Nat. Assn. Female Execs., Commonwealth Club of Calif., Internat. Platform Assn., AARP (15th Congl. Dist. coordinator AARP/Vote), Am. Biographical Inst. Res. Assn., Beta Sigma Phi; author: Life Wish (1986), Moment To Moment (1992). Res: 3271 Alder Ave Merced 95340 Ofc: Central Valley Alarm Co., Inc. 620 W 14th St Merced 95340

CARTER, LUCIAN C., college administrator; b. Aug. 27, 1940, Beaumont, Tx.; s. Lucian C. and Ruth (McKenzie) C.; edn: BA in math., BS in Chem., Univ. Tx., Austin 1960, BS in physics 1961; MS physics, Cal Tech, 1968. Career: instr. physics CSU Los Angeles, 1967-75; physics instr. L.A. Trade Tech Coll. 1975-81, dept. chair, sci. and math. 1981-86, asst. dean electronics 1986-88; dean acad. affairs L.A. Southwest Coll. 1988-89; sr. dir. personnel L.A. Comm. Coll. Dist. 1989-; awards: L.A. Trade Tech Coll. innovator of year 1986; mem: Am. Assn. Physics Tchrs. (secty. So. Calif. 1973-91), LACCD Adminstrs. Assn. (pres. 1990-91), Madison Heights Neighborhood Assn. (treas.); author software package 1989; Democrat; Baptist. Res: 1033 S Euclid

Pasadena 91106 Ofc: Los Angeles Community College District 770 Wilshire Blvd Los Angeles 90017

CARTER, MICHAEL RAY, artist, singer and composer, poet and author; b. Dec. 2, 1953, Los Angeles; s. Richard Eugene and Sarah Ann (Carter) C.; edn: Cypress Jr. Coll. Career: freelance artist of Wildlife and Western Art,, 1976-; indep. collector and appraiser memorabilia, oak antiques, Americana, San Diego 1965-; pres. M.R. Carter's American Character Co., San Diego 1988; awards: 2d pl. Fort Verde Days Assn. Inc. 1985, art in permanent collection Roy Rogers-Dale Evans Mus. 1986, best of show UNISYS Corp. (1987 and 1990); listed Who's Who in West, 22d and 23d, Who's Who in Am., 46th, Intl. Dir. of Distinguished Leadership, 3d and 4th, Who's Who in World, 10th, Personalities of Am., 5th and 6th, & award for contbn. to preserv. we. music 1990, Who's Who Emerging Leaders in Am., 3d (1990); mem. Gene Autry Western Heritage Mus., L.A. (charter, founding mem. 1988), Buffalo Bill Hist. Ctr., Cody, Wyo. (patron 1985), Buck Jones Western Corral 1, Lompoc (asst. nat. foreman 1989-90), Western Music Assn. Inc. (founding mem. 1988), N.Am. Hunting Club Inc. (charter, founding mem. 1980-), Statue Liberty Ellis Island Found. (patron 1985), Internat. Platform Assn.; served as co-chair pgm., mktg., New Year's Live at Sea World, San Diego (1991), Christian Celebration Prodns.; rec: collector art of Am. West, actors' autographs & movie memorabilia of Western film (esp. Roy Rogers and Sons of the Pioneers), Am. oak antiques, photography. Address: PO Box 27464 San Diego 92198

CARTWRIGHT, CAROL, university adminstrator, educator; b. June 19, 1941, Sioux City, Iowa; d. Carl Anton and Kathryn Marie (Weishapple) Becker; m. G. Phillip Cartwright, June 11, 1966; children: Catherine E. b. 1970, Stephen R. b. 1972, Susan D. b. 1974; edn: BS edn., Univ. Wis. 1962; M.Ed, Univ. Pittsburgh 1965; PhD, 1968. Career: instr. Coll. of Edn., Univ. Park, Pa. 1967-68, asst. prof. 1967-72; assoc. prof. Pa. St. Univ. 1972-79, prof. 1979-88; prof. human devel. dept. UC Davis 1988-; dean U.G. programs, v. provost office of pres. Pa. St. Univ. 1984-88; v.chancellor acad. affairs UC Davis 1988-; cons. Alliance for Undergrad. Edn. 1988-; bd. dirs. Nat. Center Study of Freshman Year 1987-; honors: Who's Who Am. Colls. & Univs., U.S. Office Edn. grad. fellow 1964-66, Outstanding Young Alumni Univ. Wis. 1971, Internat. Who's Who Women, World Who's Who Women, Bryn Mawr Coll. Provost fellowship 1978, Who's Who Am. Women; mem: Am. Council Edn., Nat. Assn. Land Grant Colls. & Univs., Am. Assn. High Edn:, Nat. Assn. Edn. of Young Children, Council Exempt Children, Am. Ednl. Res. Assn., Alliance Undergrad. (co-chair 1986-88), Davis Art Center (bd. mem. 1988-), Davis Sci. Center (bd. mem. 1989-), Child Devel. Council of Center Co. (pres. bd. dirs. 1977-80), Center Co. United Way (bd. dirs. 1984-88); num. books, articles and tech. reports pub.; Democrat; R.Cath.; rec: jogging, travel. Res: 1216 Marina Circle Davis 95616 Ofc: Academic Affairs, Univ. Calif., 525 Mrak Davis 95616

CARTWRIGHT, ROBERT EUGENE, JR., lawyer; b. Jan. 16, 1956, San Francisco; s. Robert Eugene and Dorothy Gudren (Christopherson) C.; m. Lois Ann Fazendin, May 30, 1988; son, Robert E., III b. 1989; edn: BA, Univ. of Puget Sound, Tacoma 1979; JD, Golden Gate Univ., 1982. Career: research coord. editor California Tort Reporter, San Francisco 1980-82; atty., ptnr. Cartwright, Slobodin, Bokelman, Borowsky, Wartnick, Moore & Harris, Inc., San Francisco; mem: Barristers Club S.F. (pres. 1990, jour. chief ed.), Am. Bar Assn. (Tort and Ins. Practice Sect. editl. bd. The Brief 1987-90, v. chmn. proflism com., emerging issues in tort and ins. subcom.), Calif. Bar Assn., Bar Assn. of S.F. (judicial rev. com. 1989, Am. Inn of Ct. 1989), S.F. Trial Lawyers Assn. (dir.), Calif. Trial Lawyers Assn. (bd. govs., bd. of trustees Roscoe Pound Found.), Assn. of Trial Lawyers of Am. (bd. govs.), S.F. Lawyers Club; writer and lectr. on personal injury and tort law; Democrat; rec: outdoor and individual sports, triathalon, marathon, auto racing. Res: 1240 Paloma Ave Burlingame 94010 Ofc: Cartwright, Slobodin, Bokelman, Borowsky, Wartnick, Moore & Harris, Inc. 101 California St Ste 26th Flr San Francisco 94111

CARUSO, JOSEPH MICHAEL, orthodontist/educator; b. Sept. 20, 1946, Los Angeles; s. Thomas Angelo and Letha Mae (Carter) C.; m. Julie Jensen, June 23, 1968; children: Michael b. 1973, Christopher b. 1977; edn: BA biology La Sierra Coll. 1968; DDS, Loma Linda Univ. 1973, MPH 1975, MS orthodontics 1975; Dipl. Am. Bd. of Orthodontics. Career: estab. dental practice in Newhall, 1975-; assoc. with Dr. Ruel W. Bench, Reseda 1976-80; consulting staff Henry Mayo Newhall Memorial Hosp. for TMJ and Orthognathic surg. 1982-; adj. faculty USC, 1976-77; clin. instr. dept. orthodontics Loma Linda Univ. 1977-, dept. orthodontics co-chmn., pgm. dir. 1989-; clin. lectr. profl. seminars in orthodontics, TMJ and practice mgmt. 1979-, lectr. on ceramics, TMJ & orthodontics in U.S., Brazil, Austr., Japan 1988, 89; awards: 3-M Golden Step Award 1988; mem. San Fernando Dental Soc., LLU Orthodontic Alumni Assn. (pres. 1985-6, 86-7); civic: mem. Cleft Palate team Kaiser Hosp. 1978-79, Boys & Girls Club of Santa Clarita Valley 1977, Newhall Rotary (pres. 1982-83, dir. 1978-84), Coll. of the Canyons Found. Bd. 1983, Friends of Hart Park (dir. 1984), YMCA (advy. bd., dir. 1985); research: devel. cold slab at Unitek 1972, cons. design & devel. of Transcend (TM) ceramic bracket for Unitek/3M 1986-, 2+ res. projects annually LLU 1977-; Republican; Seventh-day Adventist; rec: woodcarving, fish, hunt, inventions. Ofc: Joseph M. Caruso, DDS, MS, Corp. 25044-200 Peachland Ave Newhall 91321

CARVER, CHRISTOPHER, neurosurgeon; b. Apr. 23, 1952, New Rochelle, NY; s. Alexander Henry and Millicent Helene (Balcom) C.; m. Mary Warren, Apr. 16, 1982; edn: BS, Yale Univ., 1973; MD, Univ. Fla., 1977. Career: neurosurgeon, Drs. Phillips, Wahl, Carver, Kaczmar, 1983-; Fellow A.C.S., mem. Monterey Acad. of Medicine, Pan-Pacific Surgical Assn., Surfers Med. Assn., Am. Assn. Neurological Surgeons, AMA, Calif. Assoc. Neurol. Surgeons, Congress Neurol. Surgeons, Monterey Co. Med. Soc., Western Neurosurgical Soc.; publs: articles in refereed jours. include Neurosurgery (4/88, 4/90), J. of Neurosurgery (1981), Surfing Medicine (Fall 88); Republican; Episcopalian; rec: surfing, ski, karate, equestrian. Ofc: 220 San Jose St Salinas 93901

CASANAS, DOMINGO IVAN, insurance consultant; b. May 22, 1957, Pinar Del Rio, Cuba, naturalized U.S. cit. 1976; s. Homobono and Josefa (Rodriguez) C.; m. Laura Sanabria, May 2, 1981; children: David b. 1985, Olivia b. 1987, Kristina b. 1989; edn: BSBA, Univ. San Francisco, 1980. Career: walkathon coord. March of Dimes, S.F. 1972-75; sales cons. Moore Business Forms, Pleasant Hill 1980-81; insurance cons. Allstate Ins. Co., Concord 1981-; speaker Western Ins. Information Svs., 1984-; awards: U.S.F. Varsity NCAA Div.1 Soccer Team 1976-80, Gus Donahue award U.S.F. 1980, Am. Legion achiev. award Calaroga Jr. H.S. Hayward 1971, Allstate sales achiev. awards (1981, 84, 85, 86); founder, mem., newsletter editor Success Achievement Club, Pittsburg 1985-; clubs: Toastmasters Intl. (pres. Delta TM Club, Antioch 1990), Am. Intl. Soccer Club (player 1987-); civic: Salesian Missions (sponsor 1982-), East Contra Costa Little League (vol. 1988-), Delta Youth Soccer (coach, referee 1988-), S.F. Olympic Club Soccer (youth coord. 1976-80), coach summer soccer camps in No. Calif., Neighborhood Watch Pgm. 1985-; Republican; R.Cath.; rec: soccer, motivation tnr., reading, dancing, investing in penny stocks. Res: 1110 Jewett Ave Pittsburg 94565 Ofc: 3135 Clayton Rd Ste 203 Concord 94519

CASCIOLA, STEVEN GEORGE, manufacturing company executive; b. Mar. 25, 1948, Detroit, Mich.; s. Guy and Josephine (Tarantino) C.; m. Anne Ryan, June 17, 1989; edn: courses in arch., engring., mktg., Ariz. State Univ., 1966-. Career: nat. sales dir. Alexia Alexander, Los Angeles 1991-; speaker, lectr. SC. Comms., L.A. 1973-, writer, nat. cons., 1986-; mem: F&A Masons of Calif. (worshipful master 1992, Grand Lodge Committeeman, Speakers Panel), Pasadena Scottish Rite (orator 1992), Philosophical Research Soc. (vol. 1982-), Internat. Platform Assn. 1992-; publs. in field; Republican; R.Cath.; rec: history, comparative religion, Am.'s Destiny. Res: 616 S Burnside Los Angeles 90036

CASE, DOUGLAS NELSON, university student services specialist, fraternities and sororities advisor; b. Dec. 20, 1954, Chgo.; s. Ronald Nelson and Anna Jean (Brown) C.; edn: undergrad. Georgia Tech. 1972-73, Ga. State Univ. 1973-75, BBA (summa cum laude) San Jose State Univ., 1976; grad. bus. adminstrn. San Diego State Univ. 1976-78. Career: univ. student svs. specialist, fraternities and sororities advy., San Diego State Univ., 1978-; mem. San Diego Mayor's Advy. Bd. on Gay and Lesbian Issues, 1992-; bd. dirs. Lobby for Individual Freedom and Equality (LIFE) 1987-; bd. dirs. Project Concern Internat., 1972-82, advy. council 1982-; awards: San Diego City Council spl. commendn. 1990, San Diego Mid-City C.of C. college citizen of yr. 1990, S.D. Democratic Club Doug Scott polit. action award 1990, Outstanding Young Men of Am. (1981, 86), Decade Club Award ACLU 1992, Who's Who in West 1992-93; mem: Assn. of Fraternity Advisors (bd. 1980-90, nat. pres. 1991), Nat. Assn. Student Personnel Adminstrs. 1986-, Am. Coll. Personnel Assn., Kappa Sigma Frat. (scholarship com. 1987-), Coll. Area Comm. Coun. San Diego (exec. bd. 1980-90, pres. 1989-90), San Diego Dem. Club (pres. 1991-), ACLU (bd. San Diego affil. 1978-), Calif. State Dem. Central Com. 1991-, Uptown Dem. Club (pres. 1993-); Democrat (del. Dem. Nat. Conv. 1992, San Diego County cent. com. parliamentarian 1987-); avocation: political activism. Res: 5444 Reservoir Dr #D-20 San Diego 92120 Ofc: Housing & Residential Life, San Diego State Univ., San Diego 92182

CASEY, JOHN MICHAEL, orthopedic surgeon; b. June 23, 1940, St. Louis, Mo.; s. John Charles and Hildagarde Mary (Temmeyer) C.; m. Carolynne Cay Chapman, June 12, 1965; children: Timothy M. b. 1966, Bridget K. b. 1968, Kevin M. b. 1969, Anne C. b. 1971; edn: BS, St. Louis Univ. 1961; MD, Univ. Mo. Columbia 1965; cert. Am. Bd. Orthopedic Surgery 1974. Career: served to CDR, USN, 1964-75: intern Oakland 1965-66, student flight surgeon Pensacola 1966-67, flight surgeon Virginia Beach 1967-69, resident orthopedic surgeon San Diego 1969-73, staff orthopedic surgeon Portsmouth, Va. 1973-75; pvt. med. practice orthopedic surgery, San Diego 1975-; cons. Naval Hosp., San Diego 1976-; asst. clin. prof. surgery UC San Diego 1978-; staff Children's Hosp. San Diego, chief staff 1990-91; fellow Am. Acad. Orthopedic Surgeons; mem: ACOS, Western Orthopedic Assn., Irish Am. Orthopaedic Assocs; club: Stardust CC; mil: Capt. M/C. USNR 1976-92 (ret.); Catholic; rec: golf, jogging. Ofc: 8901 Activity Road San Diego 92126

CASHMAN, GEORGIA EDWINA, commercial printing plant executive; b. Jan. 15, 1932, Johnsonburg, Pa.; d. Ralph Wesley and Gladys Malverta (Harrington) McClintock; m. Robert Lynn Cashman, March 22, 1956; children: Karen b. 1956, Lynn b. 1959, Kim b. 1961; edn: BS edn., Lock Haven Univ. 1952. Career: tchr. Brockway High Sch., Pa. 1953-54; Washington Irving Jr.

High Sch., Los Angeles 1954-55; Crozier Jr. High Sch., Inglewood 1955-56; mgr. Laguna Yachts Inc., Anaheim 1974-76; Pacific Envelope Co., 1976-83; CEO Hallmark Litho. Inc. 1983-; dir. Pacific Envelope Co. 1976-; Delta Stag Truck Body 1988-; City Comm. Corp., Orange 1988-; awards: Am. Bus. Womens Assn. Top 10 Woman of Year 1988-89, Woman of Year 1988, Orange Co. Bd. Suprs. resolution 1988, Anaheim City Council comm. service declaration 1988, Anaheim Arts Council patron of arts 1989, Alumni Achiev. Award Lock Haven Univ. 1992, listed Who's Who U.S. Execs.; mem: Orange C.of C., Am. Bus. Womens Assn. (co-chair Happy Hearts chpt.), Assn. Corp. Growth (dir. Orange Co. chpt.), Anaheim Meml. Hosp. Found. (bd. mem., Double II Club), Anaheim Museum (bd. trustees), Anaheim Aux. Fl. Crittenton Service, Anaheim C.of C., Anaheim Arts Council, Anaheim Visitors & Convention Bureau, Printing Industries Assn., Villa Park Womens League. Res: 18482 Park Villa Pl Villa Park 92667 Ofc: Hallmark Litho Inc. 1230 S Sherman St 92805

CASSEL, RUSSELL N(APOLEON), research psychologist; b. Dec. 18, 1911, Harrisburg, Pa.; s. Herman I. and Sallie A. (Hummer) C.; m. Lan Mieu Dam, Oct. 5, 1965; children: Louis b. 1939, Angelica b. 1942, Gary b. 1953, Lynn b. 1955, Gail b. 1955, Sallie b. 1965, Susie b. 1967; edn: pre law Penn State Univ. 1929-32; BS, Millersville State Univ., Pa. 1937; MEd, Penn State Univ., 1939; EdD, USC, 1949; grad. Army Personnel Consultant Sch., Air War Coll.; Dipl. Am. Bd. Profl. Psychology, 1968, Dipl. Biofeedback Soc., 1980, Fellow Rorschach Inst., 1967. Career: sch. psychologist, tchr. Middle Sch., Dauphin, Pa. 1935-40; served to Col. (Ret.) US Air Force, 1941-70, personnel cons., later, chief clin. psychologist in gen. hosp., active duty Fort Ord, Calif. 1941-46, 1951-57, combat decorations; psychologist pvt. practice, Fontana, Calif. 1946-48; asst. prof. San Diego St. Coll., 1949-51; dir. pupil pers. schools, Lompoc, 1957-61; sr. res. scientist Dept. State in Vietnam and Liberia, 1962-67; prof. Univ. Wisc., Milw. 1967-74; ed. and publ. Proj. Innovation, Chula Vista, Calif. 1974-; frequent lectr., workshops, cons. in chem. dependency rehab.; past ed./pub. 3 nat. jours.: Education; Psychology, A Jour. of Human Behavior; Instructors Jour. (AF jour.); author 8 books incl. The School Dropout Odyssey (Psychologists and Educators, Box 513, Chesterfield, MO 63017), 400+ articles in var. profl. jours., 30 psychol. tests sold by half dozen test publishers, num. computer assessment programs for use in health care; recipient num. profl. awards for innovations in Health Delivery Svs., and Chem. Dependency Rehab., and for publications; lodges: Masonic, Scottish Rite, Shrine, High Twelve; Republican; Lutheran; rec: flying light plane, tennis, bridge. Res: 1362 Santa Cruz Ct Chula Vista 91910

CASSIDY, JOHN JOSEPH, engineering executive; b. June 21, 1930, Gebo, Wyo.; s. Valentine Patrick and Elizabeth Johannah (Johnson) C.; m. Alice Willman, March 15, 1953; children: Val Patrick b. 1956, Jon Allan b. 1957, Debra Kay b. 1962; edn: BSCE, Mont. St. Univ. 1952; MSCE, 1960; PhD, Univ. Iowa 1964; reg. profl. engr. Calif. 1975, Montana 1959, Idaho 1988, Washington 1979. Career: design engr. Mont. Water Conservation Bd., Helena 1955-58; instr. Mont. St. Univ., Bozeman 1958-60; res. asst. Univ. Iowa 1960-63; asst. prof. civil engring. faculty Univ. Mo., Columbia 1963-66, assoc. prof. 1966-68, prof. 1968-74, dept. chmn. 1972-74; asst. chief hydraulic engr. Bechtel Inc., S.F. 1974-76, chief hydrologic engr. 1976-79, 1981-85; dir. Wash. St. Water Resources Res. Center, Pullman 1979-81; mgr. engring. hydraulics/hydrol. Bechtel Corp., S.F. 1985-; hydraulic cons. Morrison Knutsen Co. 1980; spl. cons. New Eng. Power Co. 1985-86, World Bank 1990-91; mem. Nat. Research Council Com. on Global Climate Change 1991-; mem. advy. com. civil engring. Calif. Polytech. St. Univ., San Luis Obispo 1985-; awards: Bechtel fellow 1985, Ford Found. fellow 1968-69, Hydraulics Div. (chmn.), Am. Soc. Civil Engrs. (exec. com. 1980-81); Am. Soc. Civil Engrs. (fellow), Am. Geophysical Union, Am. Water Resources Assn., US Com. on Large Dams, Internat. Assn. for Hydraulic Res. (chmn. Com. on Hydraulics for Dams, Internat. Commn. on Large Dams 1987-); civic: Walnut Creek United Meth. Ch.; publ. 50+ tech. papers on hydraulic engring. and hydrol., coauthor textbook on hydrol., textbook on hydraulic engring., book on hydropower engring.; mil: cpl. AUS 1953-55; Republican; Methodist; rec: woodworking. Res: 4400 Capitol Ct Concord 94518 Ofc: Bechtel Corp. 45 Fremont St 45/31 San Francisco 94119

CASTAGNA, JOSEPH VINCENT, JR., business executive, consultant, investor; b. Dec. 4, 1931, Baltimore, Md.; s. Joseph Vincent and Margaret (Bosson) C.; m. Chalya Regas, June 2, 1956; edn: undergrad. John Hopkins Univ. 1950-51; BA, USC, 1953; Exec. Pgm. Grad. Sch. of Mgmt., UC Los Angeles 1972-73; desig: GRI, Grad. Realtors Inst. 1970, CRB, Cert. R.E. Brokerage Exec. 1972, CRS, Cert. R.E. Mktg. Splst. 1979. Career: insurance broker Alexander & Alexander Inc., Los Angeles 1956-61; sales mgr. Vincent Realty, 1961-63; sales mgr. Mt. Olympus 1963-65; gen. mgr. Vincent Realty 1965-66; bd. chmn. Castagna, a Calif. Corp.; pres. Castagna Realty, 1966-, pres. Castagna Insurance 1971-76, pres. Castagna Yachts 1984-, bd. chmn. Escrow Center, Inc.; dir: Lincoln Title Co., Pacifica Encinitas, Ponto Corp.; mem: Nat. Assn. Realtors, Calif. Assn. Realtors (dir. 1975-80), Los Angeles Board Realtors (dir. 1975-80), Rec. Boaters of Calif. (dir 1993-), Nat. Boating Fedn.; clubs: Calif. Yacht, Fourth of July Yacht, Pacific Coast Yachting Assn. (dir. 1980-, Commodore 1989), North Am. Cruiser Assn. (dir. 1980-83) U.S. Coast Guard

Aux. 1974-, Santa Monica Bay Power Fleet (Commodore 1978), So. Calif. Cruiser Assn. (Commodore 1981), SAR Internat. Order of Blue Gavel, Beta Beta Pi; awards: So. Calif. Cruiser Racing Champion 1975, Santa Monica Bay Power Fleet Champion 1979, Nat. Cruiser Racing Co-champion 1981; Republican; R.Cath.; rec: boat racing & cruising, travel, bus. consulting. Ofc: Castagna 5701 Hollywood Blvd Los Angeles 90028

CASTAGNETTO, PERRY MICHAEL, retail sales executive; b. Jan. 22, 1959, San Francisco; s. William Joseph and Patricia Mary (Williams) C.; edn: BA, San Jose St. Univ., 1985; Calif. real estate lic., 1989. Career: asst. mgr. Golfland, San Jose 1978-85; dept. mgr. Orchard Supply Hardware, San Jose 1987-; prop. Castagnetto Enterprises, 1991-; honors: Alumnus of Yr. Kappa Sigma frat. SJSU (1985, 1987); mem. Kappa Sigma Alumni Assn. 1985-; Republican; R.Cath.; rec: woodworking, sculpting, landscaping. Res/Ofc: Castagnetto Enterprises 450 Avenida Arboles San Jose 95123

CASTOR, WILBUR WRIGHT, consultant, lecturer; b. Feb. 3, 1932, Harrison Township, Pa.; s. Wilbur W. and Margaret (Grubbs) C.; m. Donna Ruth Schwartz, Feb. 9, 1963; children: Amy, Julia, Marnie; edn: BA, St. Vincent Coll., 1959; PhD, Calif. Univ. Advanced Studies, 1986-. Career: sales rep. IBM, Pittsburgh and Cleveland, 1959-62; v.p. data processing ops. Honeywell, Waltham, Mass. 1962-80; pres./c.e.o. Aviation Simulation Tech., Lexington, Mass. 1980-82; senior v.p. Xerox Corp., El Segundo, Calif. 1982-89; pres. bd. dirs. Internat. Acad., mem. bd. trustees Information Inst., Santa Barbara; mem. World Future Soc.; clubs: Caballeros (Rolling Hills), Tennis, U.S. Senators; author: (play) Un Certaine Soirire 1958, (musical comedy) Breaking Up 1960; contbr. articles to profl. jours.; mil: capt. USN 1953-58; Republican; rec: flying, scuba, music, writing. Res: 19 Georgeff Rd Rolling Hills 90274

CASTRO, JO ANNE BERGERON, insurance agent; b. Oct. 15, 1961, Oakland; d. Leo Thurlow and Dorothy Ann (Santos) Bergeron; m. Frank Stanley Castro; child: Keith R. b. 1984; edn: grad. Livermore H.S. 1978. Career: office clk. Fremerey & Bergeron Ins. Brokers (estab. 1967, in business for 25 yrs. 1992), Dublin 1977-79, personal lines mgr. 1979-80, ins. solicitor 1980, ptnr., 1982-, commercial lines mgr. 1985-, pres. (F&D Ins. Inc.) 1987-; ins. consultant Dublin C.of C. 1986-; formed music mgmt. co., Ultimate Productions, 1991-, currently featuring: A Hard Rock N Roll Group "Idol Threat", owner/opr. full sound and recording studio in Tracy; ptnr. RKJ Catering, 1987-; awards: Dublin C.of C. pres. award 1987, govt. bus. liaison award 1987, Miss California Teen runner up 1977, Hon. mention for poem "California" pub. 1991 World of Poetry; Multiple Sclerosis diagnosis, 1986; mem: Dublin C.of C. (dir. 1985-90, v.p. 1987-88, 89-90, Dedicated Service Award 1990), Indep. Ins. Agents of Am., Nat. Assn. Female Execs.; participant host family in Am. Culture Concepts Inc., Am./Taiwanese high sch. student exchange pgm. 1992; composer/ arranger radio commercial (1989); R.Cath.; rec: singer, performer, write, compose, arrange music. Ofc: 7998 Amador Valley Blvd Dublin 94568 Tel: 209/836-0509

CASTRO, RODOLFO HADER, county government executive; b. May 31, 1942, Riverside; s. Doroteo G. and Lillian Lucero (Diaz) C.; edn: AA (honors), Riverside City Coll. 1967; BS (honors), Calif.State Poly. Coll. 1970; MBA, Harvard Univ. 1973; stu. city govt., mgmt., & politics, Oxford Univ. (Eng.) 1980; advanced mgmt. studies, Yale Univ. 1986. Career: dep. dir. Economic Opportunity Bd., 1971; asst. dir. LULAC Nat. Edn. Svc Ctrs, 1973-75; exec. dir. L.N.E.S.C., 1975; exec. dir. Community Service Dept., Co. of San Bernardino, 1976-; pres. Rodolfo H. Castro and Assocs. Inc.; gubnat. appt. mem. Calif. State Social Services Advy. Bd. 1985-90, Calif. Dept. Econ. Opportunity Advy. Commn. 1991-94; appt. San Bernardino County Homeless Task Force (chmn. 1989-91), Childrens Policy Council 1986; advy. bds. Crafton Hills Coll. 1985-88, So. Calif. Gas Co. 1985-88, advy. com. U.S. Constn. Bicentennial 36th Congl. Dist. Calif. 1989-91; awards: Energy Conservation Award, DOE (1980), Resolution 305, Calif. Legislature (5/15/81), recognition, US Congressional Record (5/5/81), CalPoly Sch of Bus. Alumnus of Year (1981), Nat. Assn. of Counties achievement award 1984, Alpha Gamma Sigma (life mem. 1967), San Bernardino Salvation Army leadership award 1990, listed Who's Who in Am. Colls. and Univs. 1971, Who's Who Among Latin Americans in Wash. 1976, Who's Who in West 1982-83, Who's Who Among Hispanic Americans 1991-92; mem: Am. Soc. for Pub. Adminstrn., Mex.-Am. Commn. of San Bdo. (dir.), Mex.-Am. Commn. of San Bdo. (bd. 1980-82), Nat. Community Action Agy. Exec. Directors Assn. (dir. 1980-84), San Bernardino Census Task Force 1989-90, Oxford Preservation Trust (life), Wilsonian Club San Bdo. Co., Harvard Bus. Sch. Alumni Assn. (life), Cal Poly Alumni Assn. (life); publ: "500 Volunteers Help Feed Needy," Calif. County (May/June 1989); mil: sgt.E-5, AUS, State Commendn., Good Conduct; Republican, cand. US Congl. 37th Dist. Calif. 1982 (sustaining Calif. RP, Rep. Nat. Com., Calif. Rep. Hispanic Council, Mex.-Am. Polit. Assn.); R.Cath. Res: 250 N.Phillips, Banning 92220 Ofc: Community Services Dept. County of San Bernardino, 686 E Mill St San Bernardino 92415

CAVANNA, CESAR EDMUND, cryogenic engineer; b. Dec. 1, 1932, Modesto; s. Cesar and Emilia (Luchessa) C.; m. Arleen Louise (Lucchesi) C., Oct. 6, 1962; children: Cynthia b. 1963, Catherine b. 1966, Christina b. 1967, Cheryl b. 1969, Collette b. 1972; edn: AA Modesto Jr. Coll. 1953; BSME Univ.

Calif. Berkeley 1956; lic. mechanical engr. Calif. 1977, reg. assoc. engr. Canada 1978. Career: Lox Equipment Co., Livermore, project engr. 1960-69, chief engr. 1969-77, v.p. engring. 1977-86, exec. v.p. 1986-87; cons. engr. Boster Kobayashi Assoc. 1987-; subcom. chmn. Compressed Gas Assn., N.Y.C. 1977-86; mem. Internat. Oxygen Mfg., Chgo. 1975-86; chmn. Cryogenic Soc. of Am. 1973; mem: Soc. Automotive Engrs., St. Michaels Parish Council (fin. chmn. 1981-85); mil: comdr. USNR 1956-78; Republican; R. Cath.; rec: photog., classic automobiles. Res.: 529 Tyler Livermore 94550 Ofc.: Boster, Kobayashi, Berner, Campbell Associates 59 Rickenbacker Circle Livermore 94550

CEDOLINE, ANTHONY JOHN, psychologist, real estate developer, winery executive; b. Sept. 19, 1942, Rochester, N.Y.; s. Peter Ross and Mary Jane (Anthony) C.; m. Clare DeRose, Aug. 16, 1964; children: Maria b. 1967, Antonia b. 1971, Peter b. 1976; edn: BA, San Jose State Univ., 1965, MS, 1968; PhD, Columbia Pacific Univ., 1983; Calif. lic. psychologist; sch. psychologist, sch. administr. credentials; lic. marriage, fam. child counselor (MFCC); lic. real estate broker 1984. Career: counselor Oak Grove Sch. Dist., San Jose 1968; intern 1968, staff sch. psychologist 1969-72, coord. psychol. services 1972-76, asst. dir. pupil svs. 1977-81, dir. pupil services 1981-85; assessment cons. Newark and Campbell Union Sch. Dists., special edn. cons. Modoc County Schs., special programs auditor Calif. State Dept. of Edn., stress/distress cons. Morgan Hill Unified Sch. Dist.; educational psychologist pvt. practice, ptnr. Cypress Center, 1978-84; co-director Biofeedback Inst. of Santa Clara Co., 1976-85; current pvt. practice with wife, Educational Associates, 1985-; ptnr. DeRose-Cedoline-DeRose Ents. (shopping centers); owner/pres. Sound Investments; mng. ptnr. Cardillo Properties, 1984-; owner/ptnr. Cienega Valley Winery (formerly Almaden Vineyards, now renamed) Hollister 1988-, a Nat. Landmark, begun in 1854 as Palmtag Winery, now with 358 acres of vineyard and covered wine cellar of over 4 acres, largest in we. world according to Guiness Book of Records; jt. venture developer under contract Santa Clara County Housing Auth. to build Sr. Citizen Complex, 1988-; instr. UC Santa Cruz, La Verne Coll. ext. courses, guest speaker on ednl. psych., SJSU; frequent lectr. various profl. groups statewide; co-founder, bd. dirs. Lyceum of Santa Clara County (serving gifted students) 1971-; honors: Tau Delta Phi (1963-68), special recogn. Almaden Pre-School, Lyceum of Santa Clara County 1976, Optimist Club, outstanding tchr. in field of Exceptional Edn. 1975, listed Who's Who in the World, Who's Who in the West; mem: Santa Clara County Assn. Sch. Psychologists (bd.), NEA, Calif. Tchrs. Assn., Nat., Calif. Assn. Sch. Psychologists, Council for Exceptional Children, Calif. Assn. for the Gifted, Assn. Calif. Sch. Adminstrs., Calif. Personnel & Guidance Assn., Biofeedback Soc. Am., The Wine Inst.; sustaining mem. San Jose Hist. Soc. and the Children's Museum; author: Parent's Guide to School Readiness 1971, The Effect of Affect 1975, Occupational Distress and Job Burnout 1982; contbr. articles local newspapers; Republican; R.Cath.; rec: antique cars, antiques, coins, fishing. Res: 1183 Nikulina Ct San Jose 95120

CERETTO, WILLIAM J., physician-cardiologist; b. Sept. 19, 1947, Rock Springs, Wyo.; s. Alvin M. and Bobbie Dees (Clayton) C.; m. Marietta Bonello, June 10, 1978 (div. 1992); children: Mario Dante, b. 1982, Gian Marco, b. 1979; edn: BS, Univ. of Wyo. 1969; MD, Univ. of Colo. 1973. Career: med. intern, resident internal med., US Naval Hosp., San Diego 1973-76, fellowship in cardiology 1976-78, staff cardiologist and dir. Coronary Care Unit 1978-80; staff cardiologist Alvarado Hosp. Med. Ctr., San Diego, dir. Echocardiography Lab. 1980-; asst. clin. prof. UC San Diego Dept. of Med. 1980-; Fellow Am. Coll. Cardiology, Fellow Am. Coll. Chest Physicians, Fellow Council of Clin. Cardiol./Am. Heart Assn., Fellow American Coll. Physicians, mem. San Diego County Med. Soc., S.D. Co. Heart Assn. (bd. dirs., spkrs com.); mem. Am., San Diego Soc. of Echocardiography; bd. dirs. The Cardiovascular Technology Found. of Grossmont Coll.; publs: arts. in med. journals; mil: lcdr. USNR 1973-80; Republican; R. Cath.; rec: skiing, jogging, windsurfing, pro football & baseball. Ofc: Cardiology Dept. Alvarado Hospital Medical Ctr. 6655 Alvarado Rd San Diego 92120

CERNY, RICHARD CHARLES, data processing executive; b. April 24, 1943, New York, NY; s. Frank William and Marie Irene Mandt; m. Xenia, May 20, 1984; children: Dennis b. 1985, Michael b. 1986; edn: AA in bus., Manhattan Comm. Coll. 1976, BS in econ., Queens Coll. 1978; att. Golden Gate Univ. 1980-81. Career: prog., analyst Franklin Bank, Long Isl., N.Y. 1968-70; sr. prog., analyst James Talcott, N.Y. 1971-78; project mgr. Shaklee, San Francisco 1979-81; sr. program mgr. U.S. Lensing 1981-86; section mgr. Tymnet, Inc., San Jose 1986-; mil: lt. cpl., U.S. Marine Reserves 1962-67; R.Cath.; rec: skiing, softball, bicycling. Res: 457 Molimo San Francisco 94127 Ofc: 2560 No First St San Jose 95161

CERRITO, ORATIO A., financial advisor; b. Mar. 10, 1911, Cleveland, Ohio; s. Carl and Lillian (Di Vita) C.; m. Rita McCue, Oct. 2, 1931 (div. 1947); children: Lillian b. 1932, Rita-Diane b. 1939; m. 2d. Maria Capri, Dec. 18, 1947; children: Miriam b. 1948, Linda b. 1952, Claudia b. 1960; edn: John Carroll Univ. 1934-36; LLB, Cleveland Law sch. 1940; admitted Ohio State Bar 1941. Career: foreman Chase Brass & Copper Co., Euclid, OH. 1931-41; atty. assoc. Sindell & Sindell, Cleveland 1941-42; law violations investigator US Dept. of

Labor, Cleveland 1942-44; civilian splst./head of price office (fixed prices for occupied Italy), Allied Mil. Govt., Rome 1944-45; Hqtrs. distbn. ofcr. UN Relief & Rehab. Assn., Athens, Greece 1945-46; pres./gen. mgr. U.S. Store Fixture Co., Cleveland 1946-52; acct. exec. Res. Inst. of Am., Cleveland 1952-54, Los Angeles 1954-60; regl. mgr. Marlin Indsl. Div., So. Calif. 1960-81; fin. advisor/mgr. O.A. Cerrito Family Trust, 1981-. Address: 18173 Santa Cecilia Cr Fountain Valley 92708

CHAMBERLIN, EUGENE KEITH, historian, educator; b. Feb. 15, 1916, Gustine; s. Charles Eugene and Anina Marguerite (Williams) C.; m. Margaret Rae Jackson, Sept. 1, 1940; children: Linda (Davies) b. 1941, Thomas Wayne b. 1944, Rebecca (Washburn) b. 1948, Adrienne Colleen (1950-1981), Eric Carl b. 1963; edn: BA in hist., UC Berkeley 1939, MA in Mexican hist. 1940, PhD in Latin Am. hist. 1949; seminar and field work CSU San Diego and Peru (Fulbright Hays grantee) 1982. Career: reader UC Berkeley in Mex. hist., 1938-40, in Calif. hist., 1945-46; misc. work 1940-41; tchr. Spanish and Latin, Lassen Union High Sch. and Jr. Coll., Susanville 1941-43; tchr. hist., Elk Grove Jt.Union H.S. 1943-45; tchg. asst. UC Berkeley 1946-48; instr., asst. prof. hist. Mont. State Univ., Missoula 1948-54; summer instr. Mont. State Coll., Bozeman, 1953; prof. hist. & govt., San Diego City Coll. 1954-78; vis. lectr. Latin Am. hist., S.D. State Coll. 1965-67; UCLA Ext.1964-66, UCSD Ext. 1966-67; TV lectr. on Mexican and SW hist., recent world hist., S.D. Comm. Colls., 1969-77; prof. hist., Miramar Coll., 1978-83; prof. Calif. and Latin Am. hist., S.D. Mesa Coll. 1983-86; cab driver p.t. S.D. Yellow Cab Co., 1955-76, 86; awards: Rockefeller / Huntington Library grantee 1952, outstanding educator San Diego City Coll. 1970, merit award San Diego Cong. of Hist. 1978, Fulbright-Hays grantee in Peru 1982, award for years of dedicated service to local history, San Diego Hist. Soc. 1991, Resolution of Commendn. from Calif. State Hist. Resources Commn. for over 20 years of installing 30 Calif. Registered Historical Landmark Plaques (11/1/91), honoree San Diego Pub. Library Local Authors Exh. for contbns. to literature in 1990 & 1991 (Jan. 91 and Jan. 92), Plaque award from Squibob Chpt. E Clampus Vitus for 30 years of dedication to preserve Calif. history; mem. Phi Alpha Theta (1946-, Mont. St. Univ. chapt. founder, faculty adv. 1949-54), AAUP (1949-, MSU chapt. secty. 1953-54, pres. S.D. City Coll. chpt. 1956-57, Nat. Council 1967-70, pres. Calif. Conf. 1968-70, acting exec. secty. Calif. 1970-72), Am. Hist. Assn. (mem. 1940-, Hon. 50-yr. mem. 1990-, chmn. Beveridge-Dunning Com. 1984, mem. 82-84), The Westerners/ Calafia Corral & San Diego Corral 1973-, San Diego Co. Congress of Hist. (pres. 1976-77, newsletter ed. 1977-78), Pac. Coast Council on Latin Am. Studies 1955-, Cultural Assn. of the Californias 1964-, E Clampus Vitus (mem., chpt. offcs. 1962-, historian 1970-, bd. proctors 1983-89), Transierra Roisterous Alliance of Sr. Humbugs (1975-, bd. 1980-, pres. 1982-83), Mont. Acad. Scis. 1949-54, San Diego Histo. Soc. (1954-65, 88-); civic: tech. advr. Quechan Indian Tribal Council on Yuma Crossing Master Plan Proj. 1989-90, active vol. Food Bank and Ch. Food Distbg. Ctr. 1989-90); publs: 80+ articles and num. book revs. in profl. jours. and separate pamphlets mostly on NW Mex., American SW, Calif. hist., church hist., hist. comparison of Mex. and Peru 1951-; Democrat; Ch. of the Brethren (nat. conf. del. 1986); rec: hist., gardening. Res: 3033 Dale St San Diego 92104

CHAN, DAVID RONALD, certified public accountant, lawyer; b. Aug. 3, 1948, Los Angeles; s. David Yew and Anna May (Wong) C.; m. Mary Anne Chan, June 21, 1980; children: Eric David, b. 1981, Christina Mary, b. 1982; edn: AB econ., UCLA, 1969; MS bus. adm., UCLA, 1970; JD, UCLA Sch. of Law, 1973; admitted bar: Calif., US Ct. of Appeals 9th Cir., US Claims Ct., US Tax Ct. Career: staff acct. Touche Ross & Co., Los Angeles 1970; acct. Oxnard Celery Distbrs. Inc., L.A. 1971-73; tax dept. Kenneth Leventhal & Co., L.A. 1973-, presently dir. in Nat. Tax Office; real estate broker; co-dir. KL Tax Hall of Fame, 1980-; awards: John Forbes Gold Medal, Calif. Soc. CPA 1970, Elijah Watt Sells Cert. AICPA 1970, Newton Becker Award 1970, Phi Beta Kappa, Beta Gamma Sigma, Beta Alpha Psi, others; mem: Chinese Hist. Soc. of So. Calif. (founder, past bd. dir.), N.Y. Chinatown Hist. Project, Chinese for Affirmative Action, Hawaii Chinese Hist. Center, Chinese Hist. Soc. of Am. (appreciation award 1975), L.A. Co. Bar Assn., So. Calif. Chinese Lawyers Assn., Am. Inst. of CPA, Calif. Soc. CPA, Chinese Am. CPA Soc. So. Calif., Legends of Tax (tax profl. social org.), UCLA Alumni Assn. (life), UCLA Bruin Bench, UCLA Coll. of Letters and Scis. Dean's Council, L.A. Bicentennial 200 Speakers Bur., Am. First Day Cover Soc., L.A. Bd. of Realtors (MLS), Asian Business League; publs: numerous articles on taxation, philately, and Chinese-Am. studies incl: The Five Chinatowns of Los Angeles, A Postcard View of Chinatown, The Tragedy and Trauma of the Chinese Exclusion Laws, Chinese-American Heritage: Hist. and Contemporary Perspectives, Structuring the R.E. Syndicate, Pre-Combination First Day Covers, Sale of Property Developed on Leased Land; contbg. author: The Chinese American Experience; restaurant revs. in East West Chinese Am. Jour.; frequent spkr. on Chinese hist. in US: 1st, 2d Nat. Confs. Chinese-Am. Studies, KCBS TV, Calif. Conf. Hist. Socs., Hist. Soc. So. Calif., L.A. City Schs. Project Follow-Through, 2d Asian Pacific Am. Heritage Week Commemoration (keynote), CHSSC; tax presentations: UCLA Grad. Sch. Mgmt. Advy. Com., Drexel Burnham Lambert; Republican (Nat. Com.); rec: philately, post cards, sports memorabilia, Chinese cuisine. Res: 2540 Wild Oak Dr Los Angeles 90068 Ofc: 2049 Century Park East Ste 1700 Los Angeles 90067

CHAN, FLORENCE MAY HARN, librarian; b. Victoria, B.C., Canada; d. Jack Nam and Eva (Lowe) Yipp; children: Jonathan Hoyt, b. 1960, Barry Alan, b. 1963; edn: BA, Univ. of Brit. Col. 1953; MLS, UC Berkeley 1956; MA, CSU San Jose 1976. Career: circulation/reference asst. Victoria Public Library, B.C. 1953-54; cataloger Golden Gate Coll., San Francisco 1956-57; catalog/ref. libn. Coll. of San Mateo, 1957-60; catalog /reference librarian Canada Coll., Redwood City 1968-75, coord. library service 1975-; honors: Phi Kappa Phi; author: Using Library Resources: a skills building worktext (1976, 1986), profl. jour. articles; mem: Am. Lib. Assn., Calif. Lib. Assn., Soc. of Calif. Archivists, Miniature Book Soc., Dorothy L. Sayers Soc.; civic: Asian American Comm. Council of San Mateo Co. (past pres.), Project READ Literacy Council, San Mateo Co. Hist. Assn.; Episcopalian. Ofc: Canada College 4200 Farm Hill Blvd Redwood City 94061-1099

CHAN, YVONNE Y., investment banker; b. Dec. 21, 1955, San Francisco; d. S.P. and B.K. (Ho) Chan; edn: BA econ., USC, 1978; MBA fin., Northrop Univ., 1980. Career: fin. planning analyst Rockwell Internat., L.A. 1981-82; lending ofcr. Bank Am., San Francisco 1982-83; project mgr., asst. corp. treas. First Pacific Group, San Francisco 1983-87; asst. v.p. American Express Bank, 1988; corporate promotions and property investments, Great Western Internat. Inc., 1989-; Republican; Presbyterian; rec: skiing, sailing, water polo. Ofc: 9080 Santa Monica Blvd PO Box 606 Santa Monica 90406

CHANDLER, BRUCE FREDERICK, physician; b. Mar. 26, 1926, Bohemia, Pike Co.,Pa.; s. Frederick Arthur and Minnie Flora (Burkhardt) C.; m. Janice Piper, Aug. 14, 1954; children: Barbara b. 1955, Betty b. 1956, Karen b. 1959, Paul b. 1961, June b. 1965; edn: pre-med. Penn State, 1942-44; MD, Temple Univ. 1948; renal dialysis Harvard, 1953. Career: rotating intern Temple Univ. Hosp., Phila. 1948-49; med. resident Valley Forge Gen. Hosp., Phoenixville, Pa. 1949-50 and Walter Reed Gen. Hosp., WDC 1950-53; batt. surgeon 2d div. arty. Korea 1953-54; chief renal dialysis unit 45th Evac. Hosp., Korea 1954, and Tokyo Army Hosp., Japan 1954-55; chief gen. med. svc. #3 Walter Reed Gen. Hosp., 1955-58; comdg. ofcr. 45th Field Hosp., Vicenza, Italy 1959-62; pulmonary disease fellow Fitzsimons Gen. Hosp., Aurora, Colo. 1962-63, chief pulmonary service, 1963-64; chief pul. svc. Letterman Gen. Hosp., San Francisco 1964-70; internist in pvt. practice, Ridgecrest, Calif. 1970-76; chief med. svc. VA Hosp., Walla Walla, Wash. 1976-77; outpatient physician VA Med. Ctr. Spokane, Wash. 1977-82; med. cons. Social Security Adminstrn., Spokane 1983-87, ret.; asst. clin. prof. of med. UC San Francisco 1964-70; contbr. 33+ articles in med. jours.; lectr. extensively esp. in field of pulmonary diseases, including in 1963-66 on the true incidence, in sarcoidosis, of pleural effusion and pulmonary cavitation, neither of which had previously been known to occur in that disease; 3 TV appearances on medical panels re Malaria, Shock, Tuberculosis; honors: gold medal, outstanding student Temple Univ. Sch. of Med. 1948, achievement award Walter Reed Gen. Hosp. 1955-58, 45th Field Hosp., Vicenza, Italy 1958-62; mem: AMA, Am. Coll. Physicians (fellow, life mem.), Am. Coll. Chest Physicians (fellow, life mem., gov. 1968-70), Am. Thoracic Soc., N.Y. Acad. of Scis., SETAF Med.-Dent. Soc. Vicenza, Italy (pres. 1958-62), Masons 1960-; vol. Boy Scouts Am. (com. chair 1970-76); mil: col. Med. Corps U.S. Army 1948-70, Legion of Merit; Republican; Methodist; rec: photography, fishing, travel, collect Agatha Christie and Jules Verne books. Res: 6496 N Callisch Ave Fresno 93710

CHANDLER, JOHN HERRICK, college president; b. Aug. 7, 1928, San Francisco; s. Ralph William and Gwen Thornton (Herrick) C.; m. Nancy Gordon Phillips, Dec. 10, 1955; children: John, Seth, Will; edn: AB, UCLA 1952; BD (Danforth fellow), Univ. Chgo. 1958, PhD (fellow), 1963. Ordained to ministry Episcopal Ch. 1960. Career: instr. English Dartmouth Coll., 1961-63; asst. prof. UCLA, 1963-64; assoc. prof., dean spl. programs Ohio Univ., 1964-67; v.p. Danforth Found., St. Louis, 1967-71; pres. Salem Coll. and Acad., Winston-Salem, N.C. 1971-76; pres. Scripps Coll., 1976-; trustee Newton Coll. Sacred Heart, 1970-75, Thacher Sch., 1977-86; dir. Clayton (Mo.) Bd. Edn. 1970-71; clubs: University (LA), Bohemian, Twilight. Ofc: Scripps College, Balch Hall, Claremont 91711

CHANDLER, MARK JOSEPH, municipal executive/international business coordinator; b. June 30, 1956, Albuquerque, New Mex.; s. Everett Marston and Arlene Byrdell (Bahr) C.; m. Amy Helene Schwimmer, July 8, 1984; edn: AB, UC Davis 1978; MBA, UC Berkeley 1983; stu. Tokyo Acad., Japan 1983-84. Career: mgr. mkt. develop. PIE Nationwide, Walnut Creek 1980-83; mgr. sales & mktg. US Sprint, Burlingame 1984-87; internat. business coordinator City of San Francisco 1987-; bd. dirs. Design Council of S.F. 1990-; Advy. Council, Ctr. for Internat. Trade CCSF 1991-; honors: outstanding sr. UC Davis 1978, grad. w/honors UC Davis 1978; mem: World Affairs Council, Pacific Rim Communications Forum, Commonwealth Club, Sierra Club, SPUR, Nature Conservancy, Golden Gate Nat. Parks Assn., Shanghai Sister City Com. (S.F.), Taipei Sister City Com. (S.F.); Democrat; rec: baseball, travel, reading, beachcombing, chanty singing. Res: 1557 Noe St San Francisco 94131

CHANDLER, OTIS, communications co. executive; b. Nov. 23, 1927, Los Angeles; s. Norman and Dorothy (Buffum) C.; m. Bettina Whitaker, Aug. 15,

1981; children (by previous marriage): Norman Brant, b. 1952, Harry Brant, b. 1953, Cathleen, b. 1955, Michael Otis, b. 1958, Carolyn, b. 1963; edn: The Cate Sch., Phillips Acad.; BA, Stanford Univ. 1950. Career: var. mgmt. pos., Times Mirror, 1953-: trainee in mech., editorial, circulation, advt. depts. 1953-57; asst. to pres., 1957-58; mktg. mgr. Los Angeles Times, 1959-60, publisher 1960-80; v.p. Newspaper Div. Times Mirror, 1961-65, dir. 1962-; pres. Newspaper and Forest Products, 1965-66; mem. exec. com., bd. dirs. 1966-, bd. chmn./ editor-in-chief, 1981-86, chmn. exec. com. 1986-; dir: Found., Chandis Securities Co., Chandler-Sherman Corp.; dir. Pres.'s Council on Physical Fitness and Sports; dir. World Wildlife Fund-US; honors: Delta Kappa Epsilon (pres. 1950), 4-Yr. Letterman, capt. Track Team 1950 (Stanford Univ.); co-capt. USAF Track Team 1952; hon. LL.D., Colby Coll. 1966; hon. LL.D., Claremont Grad. Sch. 1978; num. journalism awards: USC 1962, Lovejoy 1966, Columbia Univ. 1967, Univ. Mo. Honor Medal 1969, Ohio Univ. Sch of Journ. Carr Van Anda 1973, Univ. of Ks. Allen White 1975, CORO 1978, Nat. Collegiate Athletic Assn. Theo. Roosevelt 1979, Gallagher Report 1980, Univ. Tex. Coll. Comm. DeWitt Carter Reddick 1982; mem: Am. Newspaper Pubs. Assn. (dir. 1968-77; Found. trustee 1969-78), Am. Soc. Newspaper Editors, Inter-Am. Press Assn., Soc. Profl. Journalists, Sigma Delta Chi; clubs: California, Regency, So. Calif. Safari; mil: Navy midshipman 1946-48; lst lt. USAF 1951-53; rec: classic & sports cars, surfing, hunting, weightlifting, track & field. Ofc: Times Mirror, Times Mirror Square Los Angeles 90053

CHANEY, FREDERICK BENNETT, management education company executive; b. Sept. 8, 1936, Boulder, Colo.; s. Marjorie (Elliott) Hendrickson; m. Linda S. Spearman; children: Melanie, Andrew, Kira, Ari; edn: BS in psych., Purdue Univ., 1959, MS in exptl. psych., 1960, PhD in mgmt. psych., 1962. Career: research asst. The Boeing Co., Seattle 1962-63, N.Am. Ops. div. Rockwell Internat. Corp., 1964-68; pres. Continuing Education Corp., 1968-81; pres./CEO successor firm Vedax Sciences Corp. Santa Ana 1981-; instr. managerial psychology USC, 1969-70; adj. prof. mgmt. Pepperdine Univ., 1970-74; cons. Xerox Corp., Collins Radio, Lockheed Corp., State of Calif., 1969-; awards: NSF fellow 1964; author: (with D.H. Harris) Human Factors in Quality Assurance 1969, articles in profl jours. Ofc: Vedax Sciences Corp. 5000 Birch Blvd Ste 6200 Newport Beach 92660

CHANG, CHI-CHI, acupuncturist; b. Nov. 14, 1945, Bejing, China; d. Joseph Tze-Hsuan and Maria Hsu-Ling (Shen) C.; m. Philip Zee-Pee Hsing, Dec. 12, 1971; div. July 1, 1978; children: Marie T. Hsing b. 1973, Caroline Hsing b. 1982; edn: PhD, SAMRA Univ., Los Angeles, 1984; Doctor of Oriental Medicine, SAMRA Univ., L.A., 1984. Career: acupuncturist, Acupuncture Clinic, Millbrae, Calif. 1980, Piedmont, Calif. 1982-90, Walnut Creek, Calif. 1991; acupuncturist, Oriental Acupuncture Clinic, Hacienda Hts., Calif. 1992-; bd. dir./secty. Acupuncture Inst. for Addiction-Free Life, 1992-; res. com. mem. Amer. Inst. of Chinese Medicine, Inc., S.F., 1992; awards: Outstanding Performance and Service award, Acupuncture Medicine Assn. of So. Calif., 1993; honors: Acupuncture Inst. for Addiction-Free Life, Calif., 1993; mem: United Acupuncturists of Calif. 1980, Calif. Certified Acupuncturists Assn. 1991; Acupuncture Medicine Assn. of So. Calif. 1992; mem. La Puente, Calif. C.of C., 1992; author (2 books): Low Back Pain 1984, Acupuncture Treatment of Arthritis 1984. Ofc: Oriental Acupuncture Clinic 243 Sunnyside Ave Piedmont 94611

CHANG, EDWARD I., real estate broker, management consultant; b. Aug. 31, 1948, Taipei, Taiwan; s. Ming Cheng and Ching Ling (Li) C.;m. Lan, Dec. 14, 1977; 1 dau. Caroline, b. 1981; edn: BS, Tankang Univ. 1972; cert., Univ. of Santa Clara 1977; cert., Western Real Estate Sch. 1982, PhD. Century Univ. 1991; gen. contractor, Calif. 1981; R.E. broker, Calif. 1982. Career: mgr. Chang Brothers Co., Palo Alto, 1975-77; pres. Chinese Fast Food Devel. Ctr., L.A., 1978-81; pres. Eastern Group, L.A., 1981-; v.p. Excom, Inc. 1982-; exec. dir. Wok King Chain Commn., Rep. of China 1978; mem: Calif. Chinese Assn. of Construction Profls.; Chinese-Am. R.E. Profls. of So. Calif.; Chinatown Lions Club; publs: Overseas Chinese Restaurant Operation, 7/78; columnist, World Jour., 1978; Catholic; rec: golf, skiing. Res: P.O. Box 80760, San Marino 91118. Ofc: Eastern Group, Inc., 2001 N. Marianna Ave., Los Angeles 90032

CHANG, MING-LIANG, real estate developer, bank director; b. June 29, 1941, Shanghai, China, nat. US cit. 1973; s. Yung-Ching and Yu-hsiang (Shih) C.; m. Rosa Fu, Dec. 31, 1969; children: Lora b. 1972, Lori b. 1977; edn: BS, Cheng-Kung Univ. 1964; MS, City Univ. of N.Y. 1967. Career: civil engr. Tibbetts-Abbetts-McCarthy-Straton 1966-68; asst. project engr. State of Calif. Dept. of Transp. 1969-75; pres. C & R Constrn. Co. 1975-81; pres. O'shuming Ents. Inc., Alhambra 1980-; dir. United National Bank; mem. ASCE, Alhambra C.of C.; rec: sports, bridge, travel. Res: 1872 S Oakgate St Monterey Park 91754 Ofc: O'shuming Enterprises Inc. 215 W Pomona Blvd Ste 202 Monterey Park 91754

CHANG, SYLVIA TAN, administrator, educator; b. Dec. 18, 1940, Bandung, Indonesia, naturalized 1972; d. Philip Harry and Lydia Shui-Yu (Ou) Tan; m. Belden Chang, Aug. 30, 1964; children: Donald Steven b. 1968, Janice May b. 1970; edn: dipl. nursing, Rumah Sakit Advent, Indonesia 1960; BS, Philippine Union Coll., 1962; MS, Loma Linda Univ., 1967; PhD, Columbia Pacific Univ.,

1987. Career: head nurse Rumah Sakit Advent, Indonesia, 1960-61; critical care nse., team ldr., medicine nse., treatment nse., spl. duty nse. White Mem. Med. Ctr., Los Angeles 1963-64; team coord./team ldr. (med. & surgical units) Loma Linda Univ. Med. Ctr., Loma Linda 1964-66; relief hd. nse., team ldr., critical care nse. Pomona Valley Hosp. Med. Ctr., Pomona 1966-67; relief supr. obstets. Loma Linda Univ. Med. Ctr. 1967, evening supr. 1967-69, noc. supr. 1969-79, adminstrv. supr. 1979-, dir. health service La Sierra Univ. 1988-; faculty mentor Columbia Pacific Univ., 1986-, CPR instr. La Sierra Univ. 1988-, First Aid instr. Phil. Union Coll. 1961-63; annual blood drive coord. La Sierra Univ.; site coord. Health Fair Expo, La Sierra Univ.; honors: Sigma Theta Tau, profl. awards for Teaching Excellence, Disting. Adminstrv. Service to Profession, Women of Achievement Award, Disting. Leadership, Outstanding Contbn. to Health Edn.; listed in Who's Who in Sci. & Engring., Who's Who Among Asian Americans, Who's Who in Am. Nursing, Internat. Who's Who of Profl. & Bus. Women, Who's Who of Am. Women, Internat. Dir. of Disting. Leadership, Personalities of Am., Internat. Book of Honor, Internat. Register of Profiles, Internat. Leaders in Achiev., Dir. of Disting. Americans, 5,000 Personalities of World; mem: Am. Assn. Critical-Care Nurses, Am. Coll. Health Assn., Assn. of Seventh-day Adventist Nurses, Pacific Coast Coll. Health Assn., Sigma Theta Tau Intl. Inc., Adventist Student Personnel Assn. Intl., alumni assns. Philippine Union Coll., LLU Grad. Sch., LLU Sch. of Nsg., Col. Pac. Univ.; Republican; Seventh-day Adventist; rec: music (organ, piano), coin, jade carving, shell & stamp collecting. Res: 11466 Richmont Rd Loma Linda 92354 Ofc: La Sierra Univ., Riverside 92515

CHAO, FRANK W., computer analyst; b. May 21, 1951, Oakland; s. Dr. Fu-Chuan and Lydia Lai-Yuk (Chui) C.; edn: AA, El Camino Coll., 1981; BA, UC Los Angeles, 1973; MBA, USC, 1975; lic. Gen. Radio Tel. Opr., FCC (1979). Career: sales research analyst Mattel Inc., Hawthorne 1976-77; alarm techn. Morse Signal Devices of Calif.,, L.A. 1977-79; radio services techn. Northrop Corp., Hawthorne 1979-82, radio services engr., 1982-92, computer equipment design analyst 1992-; mem: Am. Radio Relay League, Internet Soc., Assn. of Banyan Users Internat., IEEE Computer Soc., Nat. Assn. of Bus. and Ednl. Radio, Nat. Assn. of Radio and Telecomm. Engrs., Nat. Wildlife Fedn., Uniforum; rec: personal computers,baking. Ofc: Northrop Corp. 1 Northrop Ave 726/AV Hawthorne 90250

CHAPMAN, MICHAEL WILLIAM, physician, surgeon, medical educator; b. Nov.29, 1937, Newberry, Mich.; m. Elizabeth Casady; children: Mark John, Craig David; edn: AA, Am. River Coll., 1957; BS, UC San Francisco, 1959, MD, 1962; diplomate Am. Bd. Orthopedic Surg. 1969, 83. Career: intern, mixed med.-surg., S.F. Gen. Hosp. 1962-63, resident orthop. surgery UCSF, 1963-67; fellow Royal Nat. Orthopedic Hosp., London 1967-68; served US Army Med. Corps 1968-70; asst. prof. orthopedic surgery UC San Francisco 1971-76, assoc. prof. 1976-79; asst. chief orthop. surgery S.F. Gen. Hosp. 1971-79, actg. chief orthop. surgery 1972-73; chmn. orthop. surgery UC Davis Med. Ctr., Sacto. 1979-, prof. orthop. surg. 1981-; physician U.S. Nat. Olympic Ski Team, 1976-; assoc. editor: Clin. Orthopaedics and Related Research, J. of Orthopedic Trauma, J. of Bone and Joint Surgery; book revs. New England J. of Medicine 1988-; numerous publs. in med. and profl. jours.; awards: Alpha Omega Alpha, AOA guest resident 1967, Fogarty Sr. Internat. Fellow, Switz. 1978-79, outstanding tchg. UCSF 1972, tchr. of yr. UC Davis 1984, annual Gill Memorial Lectr. Phila. Orthopedic Soc. 1988, Most outstanding book in clin. medicine category "Operative Orthopaedics" Assn. Am. Publishers 1989, AMA physician recogn. award 1989-92; Hon. mem. British Orthopaedic Assn., corr. mem. South African Orthopaedic Assn.; mem: Internat. Soc. for Skiing Safety, Assn. for Study of Internal Fixation (A-O Internat.), Am. Acad. Orthopedic Surgeons, Am. Assn. for Surgery of Trauma, Am. Bd. of Orthopedic Surgeons (bd. dirs. 1985-, oral examiner 1981-, exams. com. 1985-), Am. Orthopedic Assn. (pres. 1990-91, bd. dirs. 1985-88, 88-), Am. Coll. Surgeons, Pan-Pac. Surg. Assn., Internat. Soc. for Fracture Repair, Am. Assn. for Surgery of Trauma AMA, Am. Bd. of Med. Splties, Am. Orthopedic Assn., Am. Orthopedic Soc. for Sports Medicine, Am. Trauma Soc., Assn. of Am. Med. Colls., Assn. of Bone and Joint Surgeons, LeRoy C. Abbott Orthopedic Soc., Paul R. Lipscomb Soc., NW Med. Assns., Orthopedic Research Soc., Orthopedic Trauma Assn. (pres. 1985-6), We. Orthopedic Assn., CMA, Calif. Orthopedic Assn., Sacto.-El Dorado Med. Soc., Wilson Interurban Orthopedic Soc., Sierra Club; Republican; Prot.; rec: skiing, mountaineering, scuba, tennis. Ofc: Dept. Orthopedics, Univ. Calif. Davis Medical Ctr. 2230 Stockton Blvd Sacramento 95817

CHARLES, MICHAEL FELTON, orthopedic surgeon; b. Dec. 22, 1949, San Francisco; s. Felton and Iris Josephine (Pete) C.; m. Beverly Roberts, June 12, 1977; edn: BS Simon Fraser Univ. 1972; MMS Rutger's Med. Sch., Piscataway 1975, MD 1977; bd. cert. in orthopedic surgery 1985. Career: resident Martin Luther King Jr. Hosp., Los Angeles 1978-81, chief resident 1981-82, also orthopedic splst. cons. Martin Luther King Jr. Sickel Cell Ctr. 1980-82,; King-Drew Med. Sch. Admissions Com. 1979-82; S. Central Health Found. 1981-82; pvt. practice orthopedics, Berkeley 1982-; med. dir. Golden Gate Fields Race Track 1987-; team physician Mills Coll.; sports med. cons. St. Mary's Coll. H.S., Berkeley and Acalanes H.S., Lafayette; lectr. on athletic injuries; honors: nat. conf. presenter Am. Orthopedic Residents Assn. 17th Annual Conf.,

Washington 1982; intern of yr. Martin Luther King Jr. Hosp./Drew Med. Ctr. 1978; mem: Am. Acad. of Orthopaedic Surgeons (fellow), Am. Orthopaedic Soc. for Sports Med. (assoc.); publs: Metrizamide Computer Tomography in the Post Operative Spine (1982); rec: photog., biking, creative writing. Ofc: 2500 Milvia St Ste 114 Berkeley 94704

CHARNY, ROBERT DAVID, executive; b. Dec. 16, 1953, Los Angeles; s. Frank and Laura (Burstein) C.; m. Paula, May 1, 1976; children: Heather Kathlene b. 1979, Jonathan Robert David b. 1981; edn: Santa Monica Coll. 1971-2, UCLA 1972-75; lic. dental tech. Tx. (1976); Calif. State and NRA cert. firearm tng. instr., Calif. cert. hunter safety instr. Career: Raydent Lab., Los Angeles 1972; dept. hd. Superdent Lab., Westwood 1975; c.e.o. The Pet Shop, Inc. 1978; trustee Pabst Farms Inc., Oconomowoc, Wis. 1980; c.e.o. Paragon Farm West, 1982; c.e.o. Charny, Coyan & Co. Inc., Diamond Springs, Calif. 1984; c.e.o. Charny Co., 1987-; pres. and c.e.o. Frontier Sports Inc., Placerville 1990-93; owner D & R BBS, 1991-; owner DRCSS Systems, 1993-, Glock, Inc. Police Service Div. cert. armorer; El Dorado Co. Sheriff Dept. citizen firearm course instr.; firearms cons. and instr. Frontier Armory, El Dorado Gun Club; listed Am. Biog. Inst. Directory of Distinguished Leadership (1991 Man of Yr.); mem. Encino Town & Country Merchant Assn. (pres. 1980), El Dorado Rod & Gun Club (pistol chmn. 1987-90, dir. 1988-90, pres. 1991-92), NRA (life), CRPA (life), IHMSA (life); rec: internat. handgun metallic silhouette shooting, combat shotgun & handgun shooting, internat. trap shooting. Ofc: 791 N Circle Dr Diamond Springs 95619

CHATZKY, MICHAEL GARY, lawyer; b. June 14, 1943, Denver, Colo.; edn: BS acctg., Univ. Md., 1966; JD, Univ. Md. Sch. of Law, 1969; admitted Calif. Bar 1970, U.S. Dist. Ct. no. dist. Calif., U.S. Tax Ct., U.S. Ct. Appeals 9th Cir., U.S. Supreme Ct. Career: mem. law firm Margolis, Chtazky, Dunnett & Muehlenbeck, APC, Los Gatos, 1970-80; formed Michael Gary Chatzky, ALC, San Jose 1980-, mng. ptnr. San Jose office law firm Chatzky, Fong and Fong, 1985-89; instr. cont. legal edn. and holder num. seminars Internat. Common Law Exchange Soc. (ICLES), Palo Alto; instr. West Valley Coll., Cabrillo Coll.; mem. Santa Clara Co. Bar Assn. (chmn. internat. law sect. 1989, chmn. tax sect. 1987, 88), Legal Aid Soc. Santa Clara Co. (2d v.p. 1990), Asian Law Alliance San Jose (advy. bd.), ACLU (legal co. No. Calif., S.C.V. chapt. bd., v.ch.); mng. ed. internat. comparative tax law rev. section in The Common Law Lawyer (ICLES jour.); author ICLES handbook: Internat. Tax Planning through the use and application of Foreign Trusts; book chpt. "Foreign Trusts" in Internat. Tax Planning (Mator, S.A., 1982); writer and lectr. widely on fgn. trusts, internat. and domestic taxation. Ofc: 762 El Paseo De Saratoga San Jose 95130

CHAVEZ, LONNIE SAMUEL, clergyman, educator, administrator, retired military engineer; b. May 22, 1929, Gunnison, Colo.; s. Alonzo Samuel and Irene Araminta (Fernandez) C.; m. Evelyn Wright, Oct. 11, 1948; children: Teresa b. 1949, Christine b. 1953, Laura b. 1957; edn: undergrad., Grossmont Coll. 1976-77; BS (cum laude), Christian Heritage Coll. 1978; DD, Calif. Baptist Coll.; grad. USMC Combat Engr. Ofcrs. Sch. 1960, Utilities Ofcrs. Sch. 1965; ordained minister Baptist Ch. 1977. Career: prodn. crew Ralston Purina Co. (Oakland) 1949-50, prodn. leadman (Spokane, Wash.) 1953-56; pvt. US Marine Corps 1946-48; sgt. USMC 1950-52; major USMC 1956-75, decorated Navy Commendn. Medal; pastor First Spanish Baptist Ch., El Cajon 1975-78; missionary Home Mission Bd. Southern Baptist Convention of Calif. (SBCC) 1978-80, seminar instr. and dir. Language Missions SBCC 1980-90, dir. of Missions SBCC, 1990-, So. Baptist New Work Fellowship v.p. 1985-87, pres. 1987-88; recipient appreciation certifs., Fgn. Mission Board, and Baptist World Alliance;mem. Christian Heritage Coll. Alumni, V.F.W.; publs: booklet and workbook: A Winning Strategy for Ethnic Ministries (1982, 1984); Republican; Baptist; rec: fishing, carpentry. Res: 7683 N Meridian Ave Fresno 93720 Ofc: Southern Baptist Convention of Calif. 678 East Shaw Ave Fresno 93710

CHEN, CHAO, acupuncturist; b. Jan. 25, 1925, China, came to U.S. 1982, nat. U.S. citizen 1988; s. Chih-Luan and Shih (Chao) C.; m. Kun-Chieh, June 11, 1959; children: Chiao b. 1960, Yu b. 1962, Justine Wei b. 1967; edn: student traditional chinese medicine, Hong Kong, dipl. Overseas Chinese Med. Coll., H.K. 1963; dipl. Chinese Modern Acupuncture Ctr., Taiwan 1970; OMD, PhD, Asian Am. Univ., San Diego 1985; Cert. Acupuncturist Calif. 1985. Career: lectr. National Cheng-Chi Univ., Taiwan 1975-77; prof. Acad. of Chinese Med., Taiwan 1977-78, Overseas Chinese Med. Coll., H.K. 1977-78, Internat. Research Ctr. for Acupunctural Sci., Taiwan 1978-79; chmn. Chinese Acupuncture Com., Taiwan 1979-82; pres. I-Ching Acupuncture Ctr., Alhambra, Calif. 1982-; res. fellow Chinese Acup. Sci. Resrch. Found., Taiwan 1975-; cons. Chinese Acup. Res. Inst., H.K. 1976-, China Medical Coll., Taiwan 1979-; com. chmn. Chinese Medical Hist. Inst., Taiwan 1980-; awards: 1st academic prize Internat. Sem. on Acup. Taiwan 1976, golden cup 1st Internat. Acup. Symp. Korea 1979, best thesis Acup. Sem. of Repub. of China Taiwan 1979, special academic award Yoga Sem. of the World Japan 1980, 1st prize 2d Internat. Acup. Symp. Korea 1981; mem: Acupuncture Medicine Assn. of So. Calif. (bd. chmn., dir., cons. 1988-, honorary pres. 1991-), Am. I-Ching Archaeology Inst. (cons. 1988-); civic: Accord Club Mont. Park (chmn. 1987), Chinese Long Life Assn. L.A. (dir. 1988); author 5 books: I-Ching Acupuncture (1972), Chen's Acupuncture Theory

as Based on I-Ching and Computer (1975), The Balance of I-Ching (1978), Commentary on Midnight & Midday Method & the Turtle (8) Methods (1980), I-Ching & Acupuncture Theory (1982), I-Ching, Bible & Principles (1991); Christian; rec: photography. Res: 917 S Atlantic Blvd Alhambra 91803 Ofc: I-Ching Acupuncture Center 3303 Del Mar Ave Ste A Rosemead 91770

CHEN, CHIH MING, acupuncturist; b. Apr. 18, 1954, Taichung, Taiwan, R.O.C.; s. Tsun Jin and Yu Ying (Jen) C.; m. Jennifer C. Hu, Mar. 28, 1982; children: Michael b. 1983, Diana b. 1989; edn: BA, Christ's Coll., Taipei, Taiwan, R.O.C.; study of Chinese medicine (3 yrs.), China Scientific Acupuncture Sch., Taipei, Taiwan; doctor of Oriental medicine, Asian Am. Acupuncture Univ., San Diego, Calif.; cert. acupuncturist, Lic. #AC 1271, Calif. Med. Bd. 1981. Career: acupuncturist Shen Yuan Clinic, Taichung, Taiwan 1977-79, Chu Tsai-Nan Acupuncture Clinic, Taipei, Taiwan 1979-84, Scientific Acupuncture Med. Ctr., Whittier, Calif. 1985-88, Modern Acupuncture Med. Ctr., San Bernardino 1988-; acupuncture tchr. Modern Acupuncture Res. Ctr., Taipei, Taiwan 1981-84; acupuncture & acupressure tchr., Modern Acupuncture Res. Ctr., San Bernardino 1990-; awards: Certificate of Appreciation, The Lions Club, Taipei, Taiwan 1977; mem: The Acupuncture Assn., R.O.C. 1979-, Acupuncture Medicine Assn. of So. Calif. 1984-; mem: San Bernardino C.of C. 1989; Christian; rec: traveling, reading. Ofc: Modern Acupuncture Medical Center 1614 North D St San Bernardino 92405

CHEN, DAVID Y. C., acupuncturist; b. May 8, 1950, Taipei, Taiwan; nat. U.S. citizen 1985; s. Frank H.Y. and Josephine S.Y. (Chang) C.; m. Christina, Aug. 2, 1977; children: Phillip b. 1978, David, Jr. b. 1984; edn: Dr. of Oriental Medicine, Scientific Acupuncture Med. Ctr., 1970; OMD, Internat. Acupuncture. Univ. and Res. Inst., 1973; field surgeon, Nat. Def. Med. Coll., 1974; cert. acupuncturist, Calif. 1978; Calif. Comm. Coll. instr. cred., 1982-; provider of Cont. Edn. for RNs, LVNs, Physician's Assistants, Dentists and Podiatrists, Calif. 1983, 86. Career: clinic dir. Scientific Acupuncture Med. Ctr., Whittier, 1978-; staff mem. Calif. Inst. for Spinal Injuries and Disorders, Whittier, 1987-; appt. State Bd. of Med. Quality Assurance. 11th Dist. 1989-93; appt. chief examiner Acupuncture Examining Com 1989, chmn. Acupuncture Com. 1990; mem. Acupuncture Com. 1991, chairperson 1992-93; lectr. Rio Hondo Comm. Coll. 1982-, Fullerton Jr. Coll. 1979, Whittier Presbyn. Hosp. 1982, 83, 85, La Mirada Comm. Hosp. 1985, UC Irvine Med. Ctr. 1984; speaker var. civic groups; awards: appreciation award for comm. svc. Rio Hondo Coll. 1982, Kiwanis Club, Whittier 1984; award for dedication, contributions. & achievements in acupuncture, Acupuncture Res. Inst. 1990; mem: A.R.I. Hollywood Presbyn. Hosp., Chinese Medicine and Herb Assn. (res. fellow 1974), Asian Am. Republican Assn.; research herbal and acupuncture pain control; mil: capt. MC Army, hon. discharge. 1976; Republican; Christian; rec: classical music, homing pigeon racing, fishing. Ofc: Scientific Acupuncture Medical Center, Calif. Pain Control Clinic 14632 E. Whittier Blvd Whittier 90605

CHEN, KUO-CHING, acupuncturist; b. Oct. 17, 1924, Hsiaoshan, Chekiang, China; s. Wen-Jui and Shih (Kung) C.; m. Yuan-Yuan, Mar. 4, 1967; children: Ju-Ching b. 1969, Chi-Yu b. 1972; edn: Chinese Literature & Art Coll., China 1942-45; Chih-Chiang Univ., China 1946-47; advanced acupuncture 1-yr. course, Taiwan 1960; A.M.D., PhD in oriental medicine, Asian Am. Acupuncture Med. Univ., USA 1984; cert. acupuncturist, Calif. St. Bd. (1978); cert. acupuncture instr. Calif. Supt. of Public Instr. (1984). Career: acupuncturist prin., Kuo-Ching Chen Acupuncture and Tui-Na Manipulation Clinic, Taipei, Taiwan 1949-83, acupuncture master of 15 apprentices 1964-85; Chen's, K.C. Acupuncture, South Pasadena 1983-; splst. in clin. treatment of neck pain, back pain and infertility; clinic supr. Acupuncture Coll. of Los Angeles Univ. 1985-87; honors: first doctor in Rep. of China to treat Pres. M. Hubert Maga, Rep. of Dahomey with Acupuncture and Tui-Na Manipulation (1963), plaque inscribed "The Doctor that Performs Wonders" from Fernando Sanchez R., Amb. of Costa Rica (1982), Silver medal from Chinese Acupuncture Soc. (1980); mem. Taipei Acupuncture Assn. (gen. adminstr. 1961-67), Chinese Acupuncture Assn. (1960-, chmn. edition & paper-selection com. 1966-68, chmn. promotion com. 1969), Nat. Commn. for Certification of Acupuncturists (1984-85), Acupuncture Medicine Assn. of So. Calif. (1984-, dir. 1985-86, supr. 1987-88); PhD diss: Intro. of Chinese Acupuncture (1983-84); research: clin. diagnosis using reflex points on hands, face, feet, ears, extra points, Tui-Na Manipulation and acupuncture techniques 1962-; Buddhist; rec. gardening, Chinese brush painting. Ofc: Chen's, K.C. Acupuncture, APC, 2130 Huntington Dr Ste 216 South Pasadena 91030

CHIA, HENRY Y. T., international trading company president; b. June 18,1932, Singapore; s. Mark Chia and Agnes Teo; m. Lye Sim Lee; children: Nicholas b. 1962, Michele b. 1966; edn: BA, London Univ. 1958; Dipl., London Sch. Journalism 1958. Career: pres. secty., dir. info., Singapore 1959-62; dir. Leo Burnett, Asia and U.S. 1962-72; owner Henry Chia Assoc. Group of Companies, Asia and Australia 1972-82; owner, pres., CEO, COO Regalis USA Inc. 1983-; awards: creative circle Asia Ad. Congress 1975, Singapore Police civic campaigns 1974-78; mem: San Diego C.of C.; poetry and articles pub. in newspapers and jours.; Republican; R.Cath.; rec: jogging, travel, church work. Ofc: Regalis USA, Inc. 8361 Vickers St Ste 208 San Diego 92111

CHIA, HSIN-PAO, banking executive; b. May 6, 1920, Shanghai, China; s. Yang-Shan and Jui-Hsueh (Chang) C.; m. Beatrice, Oct. 9, 1943; children: Edward and Amy; edn: BA econs., St. John's Univ., Shanghai 1943. Career: gen. mgr. The Central Bank of China 1962-81; pres. Bank of Communications (now Chiao Tung Bank), Taipei, Taiwan 1981-85; chmn. bd. and c.e.o. Bank of Canton of California, San Francisco 1985-; chmn. Pacific Heritage Museum, S.F. 1985; honors: Most Outstanding in govt. services, R.O.C. 1969, Man of Year Chinatown Neighborhood Ctr., S.F. 1987, Resolution, Board of Suprs. S.F. City and County 1987, bd. dir. YMCA 1991-; clubs: World Trade, Bankers, Lake Merced G&C, Olympic G&C; rec: golf (USGA Honor Club). Ofc: Bank of Canton of California, 555 Montgomery St San Francisco 94111

CHICKS, CHARLES HAMPTON, mathematician; b. Nov. 10, 1930, Sandpoint, Ida.; s. Ralph Raymon and Emma Marie (Robbins) C.; m. Barbara Jean Thomson, June 19, 1956; children: Kathryn b. 1957, Steven b. 1960, R. David b. 1968, Vicki b. 1970; edn: BA, Linfield Coll., 1953; MA, Univ. Oregon, Eugene 1956, PhD, 1960; Stanford Univ., 1956-57. Career: mathematician GTE-Sylvania, Mt. View, Calif. 1957-69; ESL Inc., Sunnyvale, 1969-91, ret.; p.t. instr. Univ. of Santa Clara, 1964-86; trustee Linfield Coll., McMinnville, Oreg. 1972-; trustee Am. Bapt. Seminary of West, Berkeley 1982-91, v.p. Am Baptist Churchs of the West, 1992-93; mem.: Am. Math. Soc. 1959-; Republican; Am. Baptist. Res: 925 Kamsack Ct Sunnyvale 94087

CHIN, MARJORIE SCARLETT, corporate controller; b. Mar. 24, 1941, Reno, Nev.; d. Wing Yee and Jessie (Wong) Echavia; m. Manford Jeffrey Chin, Dec. 26, 1969; edn: AA, Contra Costa Coll., 1969; BS, John F. Kennedy Univ., 1988. Career: treas./controller Maya Corp., South San Francisco 1977-78; fin. and personnel coord. Garretson Elmen Dorf Zinov, San Francisco 1978-82; bus. mgr. Cyclotomics Inc., Berkeley 1982-85; controller JTS Leasing Corp., South S.F. 1985-88; controller and office mgr. Barbary Coast Steel Corp., Emeryville 1988-; bd. dirs. Experience Unlimited, Pleasant Hill 1992-; mem: Nat. Assn. Accts. (Oakland chpt. bd. 1984-85), Calif. Fedn. Bus. & Profl. Womens Club (S.F. chpt. sec. 1980-82), AAUW 1988-, Nat. Assn. Female Execs. 1990-, Am. Mgmt. Assn. (recogn. award 1990); civic: Am. Red Cross (vol. 1978), UNICEF (vol. 1980); rec: photog., gym, hiking, nature studies.

CHING, ERIC S.H., insurance company planning analyst; b. Aug. 13, 1951, Honolulu; s. Anthony D.K. and Amy K.C. (Chong) C.; edn: BS in biol. scis., Stanford Univ., 1973, Stanford-in-Germany, 1973; grad. stu. in marine pop. ecology, UCSB, 1973-74; MBA mktg. & org. beh., Stanford Univ. Sch. of Bus., 1977; MS in hlth. svs. adminstrn., Stanford Univ. Sch. of Medicine, 1977. Career: actg. dep. exec. dir. Santa Clara Co. Health Systems Agy., San Jose (short term contract), 1978; program officer Henry J. Kaiser Fam. Found., Menlo Park 1978-84; dir. strategic planning Lifeguard Inc., Milpitas 1984-90, also dir. ops./v.p. strategic planning Foundation Life Ins. Co. (startup co., subs. Lifeguard), Milpitas 1986-90; senior planning analyst Kaiser Found. Health Plan, Oakland 1990-; mem.: Stanford Alumni Assn. (life), Stanford Bus. Sch. Alumni Assn. (life), Stanford Swordsmasters (pres. 1980-89, mem. varsity fencing team Stanford 1972-73); civic vol. United Way S.C.Co. 1985-90, L.A. Olympic Org. Com. 1984. Ofc: Kaiser Foundation Health Plan, Inc. One Kaiser Plaza 25th Fl Oakland 94612

CHINN, ROGER, architect, city official; b. May 22, 1933, Isleton; s. Gee and Bessie (Toy) C.; m. Rachel Han, Feb. 10, 1961; children: Annette b. 1961, Robert b. 1965; edn: AB arch., UC Berkeley 1957. Career: prin. Roger Chinn Architect AIA, San Francisco 1968-72, 1977-; gen. ptnr. Hertzka & Knowles 1972-77; apptd. planning commr. City of Foster City 1972-80, elected City Council Foster City 1980-, mayor 1981, 84, 85, 90, 92; chmn. S.F. Airport Roundtable 1982-; mem: Am. Inst. of Arch.; civic: Foster City Lions (past pres., dist. gov. 1983-84, Lion of Yr. 1970, Melvin Jones Fellow 1987, Helen Keller Fellow 1988), Foster City Chinese Club (past pres.); author: Rehabilitation Plan of Isleton, Ca., 1982; contbr. Foster City Gen. Plan 1974, County Housing Plan 1976; mil: sp4 AUS 1958-60; Republican; Methodist; rec: hunting, fishing. Res: 833 Constitution Dr Foster City 94404 Ofc: 1485 Bayshore Blvd San Francisco 94124

CHLAD, ARNOLD JOSEPH, physician, surgeon; b. Aug. 18, 1914, St. Paul, Minn.; s. Joseph B. and Otilia (Ekhami) C.; m. Helen Marie Murphy, Nov. 17, 1948 (dec. 1985); children: Cheryl b. 1949, Michele b. 1950, Arnold P. b. 1953, Gary b. 1956, Gregory b. 1962; edn: BS summa cum laude, St. Thomas Coll. 1934; MB, Univ. Minn. 1938; MD, 1939. Career: pvt. practice 1946-; honors: Alpha Omega Alpha; retired mem: CMA, AMA, San Diego Co. Med. Assn.; mil: 1st lt. AUS 1939; Catholic; rec: thoroughbred racehorses. Res: 7849 Revelle Dr La Jolla 92037

CHONG, MARY DRUZILLEA, nurse; b. March 8, 1930, Fairview, OK; d. Charles Dewey and Viola Haddie (Ford) Crawford; m. Nyuk Choy Chong, Aug. 24, 1952 (div. 1968); children: Anthony b. 1954, Dorlinda b. 1955; edn: AA El Camino Jr. Coll. 1950; grad. nurse L.A. County Gen. Hosp. Sch. of Nursing 1953; BSN, PhN, CSU Los Angeles 1968. Career: staff nurse USC-L.A. Cty Gen. Hosp. 1957; UCLA-Harbor Gen. Hosp., Torrance 1958-69; hd. nurse Chest Med. Unit 1969-72; instr. Voc. Nurse Program, YWCA Job Corps, L.A.

1972-74; mobile intensive care nurse Victor Valley Hosp., Victorville 1974-79; dir. nursing San Vincente Hosp., L.A. 1980-82; Upjohn Healthcare Svcs., L.A. 1982-85, Bear Valley Comm. Hosp. Home Health Agcy., Big Bear Lake 186-87; asst. dir. of nursing Care West Palm Springs 1987-88; instr. Valley Coll. of Med. & Dental Care Careers, N. Hollywood 1988-90; staff nurse Hi-Desert Continuing Care Ctr., Joshua Tree 1991-92; mem: AAUW, CSULA Alumni Assn., Internat. Platform Assn.; Democrat; Prot.; rec: gardening, crafts. Res: POB 697 Lucerne Valley 92356 Ofc: Hi-Desert Continuing Care Center 6722 White Feather Rd Joshua Tree 92252

CHOU, CHUNG-KWANG, biomedical engineer; b. May 11, 1947, Chung-King, China, naturalized U.S. citizen 1979; s. Chin-Chi and Yu-lien (Shiao) C.; m. Grace Wong, June 9, 1973; children: Jeffrey b. 1974, Angela b. 1979; edn: BSEE, Nat. Taiwan Univ., 1968; MSEE, Washington Univ., 1971; PhD, Univ. Wash., 1975. Career: res. assoc. Univ. Wash., Seattle 1976-77, asst. prof. 1977-81; res. assoc. prof./assoc. dir. 1981-85; res. scientist City of Hope Med. Center, Duarte 1985-, dir. radiation res. 1991-; cons. Los Alamos Lab. 1986-90, Nat. Council Radiation Protection 1978-; mem. NIH spl. study session 1987-; awards: postdoc. fellow NIH 1976-77, 1st Spl. Award of Decade, Internat. Microwave Power Inst. 1981, outstanding paper award Jour. of Microwave Power 1985, Electromagnetic Acad. 1990-; mem: Bioelectromagnetics Soc. (charter, 1979-), Inst. Elect. and Electronics Engring. (Fellow 1989-), IEEE SCC28 1979-, IEEE USA COMAR (subcom. chmn. 1990-), No. Am. Hypothermia Soc. (charter 1984-), Internat. Microwave Power Inst. 1979-, Radiation Res. Soc. 1984-; author: 120+ book chapters and articles in Bioelectromagnetics and Hyperthermia (1973-), Patent on Intracavitary Microwave applicator (1989); assoc. ed. J. of Bioelectromagnetics 1987-, mem.: editl. bd. IEEE Trans. on Microwave Theory and Techniques 1987-; mil: 2d lt. Army Taiwan 1968-69; Republican; Christian; rec: gardening, fishing. Res: 11 E Longden Ave Arcadia 91006 Ofc: City of Hope National Medical Ctr. Duarte 91010

CHOU, YUE-HONG, professor, cartographer; b. Oct. 14, 1952, Taipei, Taiwan, naturalized U.S. citizen 1991; s. Chang-Shong and Chin-Lien (Cheng) C.; m. Grace Liau, Aug. 11, 1978; children: Jason H. b. 1982, Jonathan W. b. 1990; BS, Nat. Taiwan Univ., 1975; MA, Ohio State Univ., 1979, PhD, 1983; Career: asst. prof. Northwestern Univ., Evanston, Ill. 1984-87, Univ. Calif., Riverside 1987-; prin. investigator: US Forest Service, Riv. 1989-, US Dept. of Navy, San Bruno 1990-92, So. Calif. Assn. of Govts., LA 1990, US Marine Corps, Yuma, Az. 1990-92; cons. Air Pollution Ctr., Riv. 1991-92; awards: CBJ and CKF awards: Nat. Taiwan Univ. 1974, 75; Huntington award Ohio State Univ. 1983, Faculty Honor award Northwestern Univ. 1987, res. grantee US Forest Svc. Berkeley 1990; mem: Assn. of Am. Geographers 1979-, Am. Congress on Surveying & Mapping 1987-, Am. Soc. Photogrammetry & Remote Sensing 1988-, Am. Cartographic Assn. 1988-, Urban Reg. Info. Systems Assn. 1989-; publs: articles in Geographical Analysis 1991, Transp. Planning & Tech. 1991, Photo. Engring. & Remote Sensing 1990, Taiwan Tribune 1990; Evangelical Formosan Ch., Cerritos (chmn. 1992-); rec: travel. Ofc: Dept. Earth Scis. Univ. California, Riverside 92521

CHOY, ALLAN KINN, architect; b. Dec. 5, 1920, Canton, China; s. K.C. and Wong (Shee) C.; m. Mary Yee, July 16, 1950; children: Terence b. 1952, Timothy b. 1954, Bryan b. 1960; edn: BArch, USC 1948. Career: chief architect E.L. McCoy, Bakersfield 1948-59; ptnr. Goss/Choy 1959-67; ptnr. Harding/Choy/Gaines 1967-71; county architect Co. of Kern 1971-88; ret.; architect: Co. Services Bldg., Independence; Am. Nat. Bank, Bakersfield; FBI Bldg., Las Vegas, Nev.; Co. Library, Shafter; mem: Am. Arbitration Assn., AIA, Bakersfield E Rotary Club (dir.); mil: s.sgt. USAAF 1943-46; Republican; Congregationalist. Res: 500 Jamaica Way Bakersfield 93309

CHRISTENSEN, DONN WAYNE, insurance executive; b. Apr. 9, 1941, Atlantic City, NJ; s. Donald F. and Dorothy L. C.; m. Sue H. Kim, Feb. 14, 1987; children: Donn Jr. b. 1964, Lisa b. 1965; edn: BS, Univ. Santa Clara 1964. Career: West Coast div. mgr. Ford Motor Co. 1964-65; agt. Conn. Mutual Life Ins. 1965-68; founder, pres. Christensen & Jones Mgt. & Ins. Svcs. Inc. 1969-; bd. dirs. Research Devel. Systems Inc., Duarte Drug Abuse Council, Mid-Valley Mental Health Ctr.; mem. White Mem. Hosp. Instnl. Review Bd. 1975-, and Com. for Animal Care 1987-; honors: LA Gen. Agents and Mgrs. Assn. Man of Year (4 yrs.); mem: Nat. Assn. Life Underwriters, Nat. Assn. Music Mfrs. & Merchants, Am. Soc. Pension Actuaries; civic: Duarte Drug Abuse Council (pres. 1974-75), Foothill Comm. Concert Assn. (pres. 1970-73), Woodlyn Property Owners Assn. (pres. 1972-73), L'Ermitage Found. 1985; rec: tennis, bicycling, travel. Res: 4000 Pulido Ct Calabasas 91302 Ofc: Christensen & Jones Inc. 77 N Oak Knoll Ste 101 Pasadena 91101

CHRISTENSEN, TED, artist; b. Mar. 20, 1911, Vancouver, Wash.; s. Ted and Francine Catherine (Christensen) C.; edn: Art Center Sch., L.A. 1945, Portland (Ore.) Museum Sch., grad. Otis Art Inst., L.A. 1949. Career: free lance artist-painter, printmaker, potter, San Francisco Bay area since 1949; exhibited in museums and galleries, 60+ one man shows nat., represented in permanent collections in USA, Canada, Denmark, Ger., Switz., Turkey, Spain, Chile, China, and Japan; instr. Coll. of Marin, 1952-60; awards: 50+ awards (1941-), listed

Who's Who in Am. Art, Who's Who in West, Internat. Biographical Inst. (England), World Art Diary (Italy); mem. Marin Watercolor Soc., Mendocino Art Ctr.; publs: feature article, America Artists Mag. (1976), Artist Mag., London (1978), included in book: 20 Landscape Artists & How They Work (pub. Watson Guptil, 1977). Studio: 573 Third St E, Sonoma 95476

CHURCH, WILLIAM HOWARD, management consultant, senior emeritus professor of management; b. June 13, 1911, Boise, Idaho; s. Maxfield I. and Lillian (Kingsbury) C.; m. Winifred Davies, March 19, 1940; 1 son, Addison b. 1946; edn: BA, Whittier Coll. 1933; Calif. Secondary Tchg. Cred., USC 1939, MS, pub. admin., 1940, doctoral work, 1949-50. Career: instr. Fullerton J.C. 1939-41; inspector US Dept. of Justice, Immigration and Naturalization Svc., Los Angeles Dist. Ofc. 1941-42; asst. to Calif. Legislative Auditor 1942; prin. analyst Calif. School Costs for Calif. Taxpayers Assn. 1946-47; prin. analyst Organization Control Sect. Office of Chief Asst. Supt. Los Angeles City Schs. 1947; dir., ptnr., prin. cons. Administrative Management Services 1947-; concurrently: 1st city mgr. City of Whittier 1949-51; vis. prof. USC 1951-52; dir. Internat. Mgmt. Edn. Pgm. for World Bank, Univ. of Ankara 1953; cons. Calif. Legislative Analyst on Calif. Hosp. Admin. Costs Efficiency 1953; cons., trustee Santa Monica Med. and Surgical Svs. Corp. 1953-55; cons. to Presdl. Commn. on Intergovtl. Relations and spl. res. advr. Task Force on Nat. Health Policies, Grant-in-Aid Pgms., Med. Edn. and Hosp. Constrn., Wash. DC 1954-55; deputy mgr. engr. Secty. of Navy 1955-56; civilian founder, academic chmn., sr. prof. mgmt. Naval Postgraduate Sch., Monterey 1956-, emeritus sr. prof. mgmt.; dir. AMS Mgmt. Cons.; technology rep. USN, NSF and Public Technology Inc., 4 cities 1979-81; honors: 1st Fulltime Fellow in Govt., USC 1938; Lambda chpt., Phi Sigma Alpha, USC 1950; Navy Commdn. for Navy Mgmt. Rev. and Control Pgm. CNO 1944; former mem: Commonwealth Club (S.F.) and founder Monterey Bay Area Chpt., Soc. for Adv. of Mgmt. (now. Am. Mgmt. Assn.), Soc. for Adv. of Pub. Adminstrn. (founder Monterey Bay Area Chpt.), Del Monte Forest Property Owners Assn. (past pres.), Pebble Beach Sanitary Dist. (founder and dir. 1970-80), Monterey County Grand Jury (18 mos.), Naval Reserve Assn. (life), Reserve Ofrs. Assn. (life), Am. Political Sci. Assn., Western Govtl. Res. Assn., Nat. Security Council, Navy League, Sunrise Rotary of Monterey; founder and 1st bd. dirs. Mont. Peninsula Fed. Credit Union; works: ed., publr. Handbook of Civilian Personnel Mgmt. for Navy and Marine Corps Ofcrs. 1969-78; mil: capt. USNR, ret., Victory, Am. Field Svc.; Republican; Prot.; rec: golf, swimming, travel. Res: 1071 Marcheta Ln. Pebble Beach 93953 Ofc: Naval Postgraduate School, Code 54Cy, Dept. Admin. Scis., Monterey 93940

CISSNA, ROBERT LEE, mortgage banker, lawyer; b. Apr. 17, 1940, Seattle, Wash.; s. Jack Raymond and Evelyn (Barker) C.; edn: AA cum laude, L.A. City Coll.; cert. history, lit. & arch., lang., Univ. of Perugia, Italy 1962-63; BA in hist., Univ. Wash. 1965; Naval Aviation Ofcrs. Sch. 1966; JD, L.A. Coll. of Law 1974; Calif. lic. real estate broker; admitted Calif. State Bar 1980. Career: promo. Seattle World's Fair 1962; ground mgr. Santa Fair themed amusement park, Federal Way, Wash. 1958-65; Navy-Acct. & Arch. Designer 1966-68; promo. mgr. Johnson Wax Co., Montreal World's Fair 1967; acct. Walt Disney Prodns., Capitol Records and Interpace's Franciscan Dinnerware Plant; controller Tariq M. Shamma Assoc.; sec.treas. Canyon Lake (Ca.) Property Owners Assn.; bd. dirs. Lake Elsinore Park & Rec. Dist.; Radio Show host/producer, owner of parade car collection: appear numerous parades, TV and feature films; postcard publr.; prin./ planner water oriented Amusement Parks; mem: Am., Calif., L.A. Co. bar assns., Am. Fedn. of TV & Radio Artists; Laguna Beach & Benedict Cyn. (Beverly Hills) Property Owners Assns., S.W. 8 Prop. Owners Assn. (Federal Way, Wash.); Polit. fiscal conservative, civil libertarian; Presbyterian; rec: sports, photography, collecting world fair lit., genealogy. Address: PO Box 2262 Hollywood 90078

CITRIN, WILLIE, physician; b. Mar. 18, 1947, Amberg, Germany, naturalized U.S. citizen 1962; s. Abe and Dora (Bril) C.; edn: BA, Rutgers Univ., 1968; MD, N.J. Coll. Med., 1972. Career: served to major US Army, Korea, 1975-77; med. staff Parkview Hosp., Riverside, Calif., 1977-; dir. Parkview Clinic 1977-81; chief dept. medicine 1983-86; chief of staff 1986-88; pvt. med. practice, 1981-; mem. Am. Coll. Physicians 1975-, Am. Soc. Internal Med., Calif. Soc. Int. Med., Am. Med. Assn., Calif. Med. Assn., Riv. 1978-. Ofc: W. Citrin MD, Inc. 3975 Jackson St Ste 203 Riverside 92503

CLABAUGH, ELMER EUGENE, JR., lawyer; b. Sept.18, 1927, Anaheim; s. Elmer Eugene and Eleanor Margaret (Heitshusen) Clabaugh; chldren: Christopher Chapman, Matthew Martinson; edn: BBA cum laude, Woodbury Coll. 1951, BA summa cum laude, Claremont McKenna Coll. 1958, JD, Stanford Law Sch. 1961; Career with US State Dept., Jerusalem, and Tel Aviv, 1951-53; Pub. Adminstrn. Service, El Salvador, Ethiopia, and USA, 1952-57; admitted Calif. Bar 1961; deputy dist. atty. Ventura Co., Calif. 1961-62; atty. law firm Hathaway, Clabaugh, Perrett & Webster in Ventura 1962-79; individual practice, 1979-; State Inheritance Tax referee, 1968-78; city atty. City of Thousand Oaks, 1964-69, City of Simi Valley, 1969-71; mem: bd. dirs. San Antonio Water Conservation Dist., Ventura Co. Found. Port-Harbor 1985-, Ventura Co. Maritime Museum 1988-; bd. dirs. Ventura Community Mem. Hosp.; trustee Ojai Unified Sch. Dist. 1974-; mem: Calif. Bar Assn., Am. Arbitration Assn., Phi Alpha Delta; Rep. rec: hunting, tennis, sailing. Res: 241 Highland Dr Channel Islands Harbor 93035 Ofc: 1190 S Victoria Ave Ste 305 Ventura 93003

CLAES, DANIEL JOHN, medical research director; b. Dec. 3, 1931, Glendale; s. John Vernon and Claribel (Fleming) Claes; m. Gayla Blasdel, Jan. 19, 1974; edn: AB magna cum laude, Harvard Univ. 1953; MD cum laude, Harvard Med. Sch. 1957. Career: intern UCLA, 1957-58; Boywer Found. Fellow, resident in medicine, L.A., 1958-61; pvt. practice spec. in diabetes mellitus, Los Angeles 1962-; Am. Eye Bank Found. vice pres. 1978-, dir./med. res. 1980-; awards: Boywer Found. award for excellence in medicine, 1958; mem. Los Angeles Co. Med. Assn.; clubs: Royal Commonwealth (London) Harvard (So. Calif.), Harvard Med. Sch. (So. Calif.); contbr. to profl. literature on computers in med. and on diabetes mellitus. Ofc: Daniel J. Claes, MD, Inc. 15327 Sunset Blvd Ste A236 Pacific Palisades 90272

CLARK, R. BRADBURY, lawyer; b. May 11, 1924, Des Moines, Ia.; s. Rufus Bradbury and Gertrude Martha (Burns) C.; m. Polly King, Sept. 6, 1949; children: Cynthia b. 1954, Rufus B. b. 1956, John A. b. 1961; edn: BA, Harvard Coll., 1946; JD, Harvard Law Sch., 1951; Dipl.L. Oxford Univ., 1952; D.H.L. (hon.) Ch. Divinity Sch. of the Pacific, 1983. Career: atty., assoc. O'Melveny & Myers, L.A. 1952-61, ptnr. 1962-, mem. mgmt. com. 1983-90; chancellor Episcopal Diocese of L.A. 1967-; dir.: So. Calif. Water Co., San Dimas; Brown Internat. Corp., Covina; Automatic Machinery & Electronics Inc., Covina; Automatic Machinery Corp., Covina; The John Tracy Clinic, L.A.; Economic Resources Corp., L.A.; Prot. Episcopal Ch. Diocese of L.A.; awards: Hon. Canon, Diocese of Los Angeles 1981, Phi Beta Kappa, Fulbright grantee 1951-52; mem. Am. Bar Assn. (subcom. on audit letter responses, com. on law and acctg., com. on legal opinions), Calif. Bar Assn. (corporations com. 1976-77, chmn. drafting com. on gen. corp. law 1977-78, chmn. drafting com. on nonprofit corp. law 1980-84, bus. law sect. exec. com. 1977-78, 1984-87, mem. com. on nonprofit corp. law 1991-), L.A. Co. Bar Assn.; clubs: California (L.A.), Harvard (So. Calif.), Alamitos Bay Yacht, Chancery (L.A.); editor: Calif. Corp. Laws (Ballantine & Sterling), contbr. various articles on corp. matters in law jours.; mil: capt. US Army 1943-46, Bronze star w. OLC, Purple Heart w. OLC, other service awards; Republican; Episcopalian; rec: sailing. Res: 615 Alta Vista Cir South Pasadena 91030 Ofc: O'Melveny & Myers, 400 S Hope St Los Angeles 90071

CLARK, RICHARD WARD, food industry executive, consultant; b. Oct. 23, 1938, N.Y., N.Y.; s. Richard Leal and Dorothy Jane (Whittaker) C.; edn: BA (distinction) Univ. Rochester, 1960; MBA fin., Wharton Sch. Univ. Pa., 1962. Career: corp. planning analyst Campbell Soup Co., Camden, N.J. 1965-67; asst. product mgr. General Mills Inc., Mpls. 1967-70; sr. fin. analyst McKesson Corp., San Francisco 1970-71, asst. div. controller 1970-72, division controller 1972-78, gen. mgr. Grocery Prods. Devel. 1978-79, v.p./ controller McKesson Foods Group 1979-84, dir. strategic planning McKesson Corp. 1984-87; v.p. fin. and c.f.o. Provigo Corp. (market wholesale grocery), San Rafael 1987-89; hotel devel. prin. and cons. Napa Valley Assocs., S.A., San Francisco 1990-; bd. dir. Taylor Cuisine Inc., S.F. 1990-; awards: Sherman fellow Univ. Rochester 1960, Beta Gamma Sigma 1962; mem. Fin. Execs. Inst. (1981-); civic: Salvation Army (Rehabilitation Centers), S.F. (advy. bd. dir. 1984-, chmn. 1993-), Services for Seniors Bd., S.F. (dir. 1990-94); club: Bohemian (S.F.); author: Some Factors Affecting Dividend Payout Ratios (1962); recording artist (tape cassette) "I Love a Piano" Quicksilver Records (1990); mil: lt. jg. USNR 1962-64; Republican; Presbyterian; rec: piano, singing, skiing, tennis, jogging. Res: 2201 Sacramento St #401 San Francisco 94115

CLARK, ROGER WILLIAM, lawyer, educator; b. Aug. 29, 1954, Savanah, Ga.; s. Joseph Logan and Norell (Roper) C.; m. Iraida Vargas-Vila, Oct. 16, 1982 (dec. 1988); son, Joseph Roger b. 1986; edn: BS, Fla. St. Univ., Tallahasee 1975; JD, Rutgers Sch. of Law, 1978; admitted bar: Calif. 1983, Fla. 1978. Career: atty., assoc. Blackwell et al, Miami, Fla. 1978-80; ptnr. Engstrom, Lipscomb & Lack, Los Angeles 1983-; instr. bus. law Fla. Internat. Univ., 1979, Univ. of Phoenix, L.A., 1989-; pres. and chmn. The Iraida Found.; honors: Beta Gamma Sigma; mem: Am. Bar Assn., L.A. Co. Bar Assn.; author radio program & newpaper articles: You and the Law (1982-83); mil: USAF Acad., hon. disch. 1973; Democrat; Prot.; rec: scuba diving. Res: 23334 Berdon St Woodland Hills 91367 Ofc: Engstrom Lipscomb & Lack 3250 Wilshire Blvd Ste 2100 Los Angeles 90010

CLARK, STEVEN MARSTON, motion picture producer; b. Aug. 26, 1947, Pasadena; s. Howard Marston and Lucille Francis (Chester) C.; edn: AA, Pasadena City 1967; Long Beach St. Univ. 1968; UC Berkeley 1970; lic. real estate sales Calif. Career: v.p. Nordland Inc. Real Estate Devel., Sprague River, Oreg. 1971; Morro Strand Inc., Los Angeles 1971-79; pres. Clark Productions, Hollywood 1979—; awards: Republican Task Force Medal of Merit 1982; mem: Screen Actors Guild 1964-, Corona del Mar Republican Assembly (dir., ed.); subject of newspaper articles on production of movie Ralph De Palma Story (1987); Republican; rec: collecting photographs. Ofc: Clark Productions POB 3693 Hollywood 90028

CLARKE, ERNEST PARRISH, architect; b. May 1, 1938, Valdosta, Ga.; s. Wm. David, II, and Margaret Emma (Parrish) C.; m. Susan Foreman; children: Ernest b. 1981, David b. 1983, Michael b. 1987; edn: BS, Calif. Baptist Coll., 1984; lic. architect CA 1973, AZ 1980, NV 1980. Career: corp. v.p. Robert Thomas & Assocs., Newport Beach 1973-76; staff architect Marie Callendar Restaurants, Santa Ana 1976-77; pres. E.P. Clarke, AIA, Santa Ana 1977-; mem: Am. Inst. Arch., Nat. Council of Archtl. Registration Bds., Am. Soc. Engrs. & Arch., Nat. Soc. for Hist. Preservation; works: architect Rose Drive Baptist Ch., Yorba Linda 1977, 1st Christian Ch. of Garden Grove 1982, United Ch. of Sun City 1987, Golden Gate Baptist Theol. Sem., So. Calif. Center, Brea 1988, Good Shepherd Lutheran Ch., Sanctuary, Irvine 1989, Canyon Comm. Ch. of the Nazarene, Corona 1990, First Baptist Ch. & Presch., San Jacinto (1991); mil: 43rd Bomb Wing, SAC, USAF 1961-65; rec: skiing, boating, art, ceramics, computers. Ofc: Clarke Architecture, 2818 N Ridgewood St Santa Ana 92701

CLEARLAKE, WILLIAM, computer software engineer, designer, consultant; b. July 27, 1955, Pittsburgh, Pa.; s. Wm., Jr. and Sadie (Jefferson) Ramsey; m. Brenda Allen, June 16, 1984 (div.); edn: stu. Acad. of Art Coll., S.F. 1979-80, Merritt Coll. 1980-82, Laney Coll. 1982-84, CSU Hayward 1985-86. Career: tech. support Diamond Software, Oakland 1980-81; store mgr. Software USA, 1981-82; tutor in math., sci., Project Interface, City of Oakland 1982-85; pres. Clearlake Consulting, 1985-, cons. CSU Turlock, 1987, Highland Hosp., 1987; proj. mgr. Kyocera Unison Inc., Berkeley 1988; sr. quality assurance engr. Harvard Graphics 3.0 pgm., Software Publishing Co., Mtn. View, 1990-91; QA engr. ExperVision, Santa Clara, 1991-; recipient scholarship and service awards Oakland Project Interface 1983-85; mem: Assn. of Black Scientists and Mathematicians (founder Laney Coll. chpt. 1984); clubs: Cal Sailing (novice skipper), The Kappas (life); author/pub. computer pgm. SimpliFile (1985), coauthor computer pgms: Accounting by Design (1987), Kyocera Scanner (1988), CDR Collection (1989); designed Hypermedia Presentation Sequencer "Preseq" (pat. pending) for MS Windows (1989), author EPS and PCX Graphics filters for Microsoft Powerpoint Windows 3.0 ver. (1990); guest curator exhibit: Contbns. of Nine Black Inventors, Oakland Museum (1986); jazz guitarist for Source of Light (1988), prod. album "The New Music (1989); prod. soundtrack music for film "Off White" (1991). Res: 923 Hamilton Ave Milpitas 95035 Ofc: ExperVision 2933 Bunker Hill Ln Ste 202 Santa Clara 95054

CLEVELAND, CARL SERVICE, (JR.), college president; b. Mar. 29, 1918, Webster City, Ia.; s. Dr. Carl S., Sr. and Dr. Ruth R. (Ashworth) C. (both parents Drs. of Chiropractic); grandmother, Dr. Sylvia L. Ashworth, D.C.; m. Mildred S. Allison, D.C., Mar. 28, 1939 (dec. 1979); son, Dr. Carl S. Cleveland III, D.C., pres. Cleveland Chiro. Coll., Kansas City, Mo., b. 1946; edn: BS physiology, Nebr. Univ., 1947; DC, Cleveland Chiro. Coll., K.C., Mo., 1945, postgrad. studies Cleveland Chiro. Coll., K.C.; lic. DC Missouri 1945, Kans. 1947, Calif. 1950. Career: instr., prof., dean and pres. Cleveland Chiropractic Coll., K.C. and L.A., pres. Cleveland Chiropractic Coll., Los Angeles, 1982-; v.p. Parker Res. Found., Dallas; staff lectr., personal relations counselor; speaker nat., internat. lecture tours, appeared on "So You May Know" tv show (5 yrs.); past mem. Mo. State Anatomical Bd.; awards: Hon. mem. Delta Sigma Chi, distinguished res. award Parker Chiro. Res. Found., Man of Year PCRF, The Sci. Award Medallion Palmer Coll. of Chiro. Davenport, Ia., Res. Award World Chiro. Congress, Montreux, Switz. 1970; mem. Internat. Chiro. Assn. (Distinguished Fellow, ICA Chiropractor of Year 1969, mem. bd. of control, pres. cabinet, ednl. comm., res. found.), No. Am. Assn. of Schs. & Colls., Mo. State Assn. (past pres. res. com.), Nu-Med. Soc., Acad. of Mo. Chiropractors, Beta Chi Rho Frat., Sigma Chi Frat., Sigma Chi Psi Frat.; publs: `Pilot Research Program' Science Rev. (Aug. 1965), studies pathology resulting from subluxating the vertebra in the domestic rabbit with a mechanical splint; Unity Soc. of Practical Chritianity (past pres. Unity Temple, Country Club Plaza). Ofc: 590 N Vermont Ave Los Angeles 90004

CLIFFORD, DAVID M., data processing executive; b. Feb. 20, 1957, Los Angeles; s. Roland M. and Marilyn (Zolnay) C.; m. Lori Rubin, May 25, 1980; children: Derek b. 1985, Matthew b. 1990; edn: AS, Mt. San Antonio Coll. 1980. Career: computer lab. asst. Mt. San Antonio, Walnut 1977-79; programmer, analyst Whittier Union H.S. 1979-83, dir. data processing 1984-; awards: Outstanding Young Men of Am. 1979, Who's Who of Jr. Colls. 1978-79; mem: Calif. Ednl. Data Processing Assn., Planes of Fame Museum; rec: skiing, camping. Ofc: Whittier Union High School District 9401 Painter Ave Whittier 90605

CLINE, FRED ALBERT, JR., librarian; b. Oct. 23, 1929, Santa Barbara; s. Fred Albert and Anna Cecelia (Haberl) C.; edn: San Luis Obispo Public Schools; AB, UC Berkeley, 1952, MLS, 1962. Career: bank exec. Bank Am., San Francisco 1954-60; adminstrv. reference librarian California State Library, Sacramento 1962-67; head librarian Asian Art Museum, San Francisco 1967-; mem: Soc. for Asian Art, Metaphysical Alliance S.F. (dir., sec. 1988-90), Tamalpais Conservation Club S.F. (dir., mem. chair 1990-), Sierra Club, Greenpeace, Nature Conservancy, Calif. Oaks Found.; contbr.: Chinese, Korean and Japanese sculpture in the Avery Brundage Collection 1974; Oral History, Bancroft Library, UCB, of Ruth Hill Cooke 1985; Resident of Internat. House, Berkeley, 1950-52; mil: sgt. US Army Med. Corps 1952-54; Democrat; rec: hik-

ing, music, reading. Res: 825 Lincoln Way #304 San Francisco 94122-2323 Ofc: Library, Asian Art Museum of S.F., San Francisco 94118-4598

CLODIUS, ALBERT HOWARD, educator; b. Mar. 26, 1911, Spokane, Wash.; s. William, Sr. and Mary Hebner (Brown) C.; m. Wilma Charlene Parker, June 3, 1961; children: Helen-Lou (Parker) Namikas b. 1951, John Charles Parker b. 1953; edn: BA, East Wash. State Univ., Cheney 1937; grad. studies Univ. Wash., Seattle 1937-40, Stanford Univ. 1940-42; MA in history, The Claremont Grad. Sch., 1948, PhD in history, 1953. Career: actg. instr. Stanford Univ. 1942-43; instr. Claremont-McKenna Coll., Claremont 1946-50; asst. prof. Pepperdine Coll., L.A. 1952-53; instr. Ventura Comm. Coll., 1953-76, ret.; adj. prof. humanities Northrop Univ., L.A. 1977-87, National Univ., L.A. 1987-89 (ret.); awards: Clarence D. Martin scholar Ea. Wash. State Univ. 1936-37, editl. asst. Pacific Northwest Qtrly. U.Wash. 1938-40, John R. & Dora F. Haynes Found. Fellow 1950-57; mem. Plato Soc. (Perpetual Learning and Tchg. Org.) UCLA Ext., 1980-, vol. tchr. English conversation, UCLA Internat. Student Ctr., 1979-; mil: cpl. US Army Air Corps 1943-46; Democrat; Unitarian; rec: classical music, walking, swimming. Res: 4838 Salem Village Pl Culver City 90230

CLOUD, JAMES MERLE, hospital and education administrator, mnemonics educator; b. Feb. 16, 1947, Winston-Salem, N.C.; s. Merle Vail and Jane (Moore) C.; edn: French lang. studies, Univ. of Paris, 1967; BA in comparative lit., Univ. N.C., 1970; MA in edn. adminstrn., Columbia Pacific Univ., 1979, PhD health care adminstrn., 1980; Calif. lic. nursing home adminstrn., 1989, FAA lic. pvt. pilot, 1980. Career: co-founder, mem. bd. dirs., dir. of edn. Wholistic Health & Nutrition Inst. (pioneer in wellness edn.), Mill Valley 1974-79; co-founder, secty. bd. dirs., dir. admissions Columbia Pacific Univ. (devel. it into the largest non-traditional univ. in USA), San Rafael 1978-84; asst. to the pres. Posada Del Sol (unique solar powered senior residence complex), Sausalito 1985-87; co-founder, v.p. Am. Assn. of Active Seniors, 1988-89, editor & pub. Nat. Directory of 250 Active Senior Orgs. and Communications Resources"; acquisition resrch. and administr. convalescent hosps. in Oakland, 1988-90, Ukiah, 1990-91, Berkeley, 1991; founder Inst. of Applied Memory Sciences (mnemonics edn. for adults, seniors, H.S. and coll. students), 1992-; author: Memorobics! Memory Skills For Foreign Language Students; publs: weekly columns in New Penny Pincher, Ukiah 1990-91, editor: Internat. Mounted Police Assn. Newsletter 1989, The Healthscription, 1978, Guide to Personal Wellness (C.P.U. Press), poetry anthologies (1969, 71); photography exh. "Renaissance Faire Faces" featured in Bay Area cafes 1989; rec: aviation, chess, trap shooting, foreign languages, archeology, travel. Res/Ofc: 4286 Redwood Hwy San Rafael 94903 Tel: 415/677-4779

COBB, GEORGE EDWARD, physician-surgeon; b. Aug. 10, 1930, Oklahoma City, Okla.; s. George Thomas and Nell (Norvell) C.; m. Marilyn Idema, Dec. 11, 1954; children: Deborah b. 1956, Sheryl b. 1962, Christopher b. 1965; edn: BS, Univ. Okla., 1951; MD, Harvard, Boston 1955; bd. certified Am. Coll. of Surgeons 1962;. Career: intern and resident, surgery, Johns Hopkins, Md. 1955-58; resident in general surgery, resident surgery USPHS Hosp., San Francisco 1958-62; surgeon pvt. practice, 1962-; staff John Muir Hosp., Walnut Creek 1962-, Merritt Hosp., Oakland 1962-; Providence Mt. Diablo Hosp., Concord 1986-; bd. certified honors: Phi Beta Kappa (1951), Alpha Omega Alpha (1955); mil: lt. comdr. USPHS 1955-62; Presbyterian (deacon); rec: swimming, biking, snow & water skiing. Ofc: 3501 School St Lafayette 95649

COBB, ROY LAMPKIN, professional services company executive; b. Sept. 23, 1934, Oklahoma City, Okla.; s. Roy Lampkin Sr. and Alice (Ellis) C.; m. Shirley Ann Dodson, June 21, 1958; children: Kendra b. 1959, Cary William b. 1962, Paul Alan b. 1967; edn: BS, Univ. Okla., Norman 1972; grad. work in environmental planning, CSU Northridge, 1978. Career: naval aviator, cdr. US Navy, 1955-78, decorated Air Medal (13), Navy Commendn. svc. in Vietnam 1967; engr. General Dynamics, NAS Pt. Mugu, 1978-81; senior engr. Advanced Technology, Camarillo 1981-91; dept. head Computer Services Corp., Pt. Mugu 1991-; indep. computer cons., 1991-; adj. instr. tchg. computer graphics UC Santa Barbara, 1991; cons. RhC Graphics, Camarillo 1990-; awards: service Boy Scouts Am. Ventura County Coun. 1979; mem: Missile Technology Hist. Assn. editor "Launchings" (1989-), Assn. of Naval Aviators 1988-, Navy League 1991-, Town Hall of Calif. (L.A.); club: Las Posas CC (Camarillo); Republican; Methodist; rec: computers, design. Res: 2481 Brookhill Dr Camarillo 93010

COBB, SHIRLEY ANN, public relations professional, public information official; b. Jan. 1, 1936, Oklahoma City, Okla.; d. William Ray and Irene (Fewell) Dodson; m. Roy Lampkin Cobb, June 21, 1958; children: Kendra b. 1959, Cary Wm. b. 1962, Paul Alan b. 1967; edn: BA journ., Univ. Okla., 1958; coursework Univ. Jacksonville, 1962, Univ. Okla., 1972, UCLA, 1976. Career: information specialist Pt. Mugu Naval Air Station, 1975-76; splty. editor- fashion, religion, News Chronicle, Thousand Oaks 1977-81; media services mgr. City of Thousand Oaks, 1983-; appt. Task Force on Telecomms., League of Calif. Cities, 1991-; honors: Phi Beta Kappa 1958, Who's Who Univs. and Colls. 1958, listed Who's Who Am. Women, Who's Who in the West, in the World

1985-; mem: Calif. Assn. Public Information Officials (pres. 1989-90), Pub. Rels. Soc. Am. (com. chair 1989-), Nat. Assn. Telecomms. Officials (speaker nat. confs. 1989-), Pt. Mugu Officers Wives (pres. 1975-76); civic: Town Hall of Calif., Hospice Camarillo (bd. 1986, aux. 1990-91), Ocean View Sch. Dist. Pt. Mugu (trustee 1976-79); contbr. articles to various publs. (1979-); Republican; Methodist. Res: 2481 Brookhill Dr Camarillo 93010 Ofc: City of Thousand Oaks 2510 Hillcrest Dr Thousand Oaks 91320

COBIANCHI, THOMAS THEODORE, marketing executive; b. July 7, 1941, Paterson, N.J.; s. Thomas and Violet Emily (Bazzar) C.; m. Phyllis Linda Asch, Jan. 6, 1964; children: Michael Douglas b. 1964; edn: elec. engr. program Clemson Univ. 1960-62; BS, Monmouth Coll., 1968, MBA 1973; DBA program U.S. Internat. Univ., San Diego 1992; grad. exec. program The Wharton Sch., 1987. Career: various mgmt. pos. Westinghouse Electric, in Norman, Ok., Phila., N.Y.C., Balt., 1968-80, internat. mgr. Bus. Devel. Westinghouse Electric, Pittsburgh, Pa. 1980-82, dir. Mktg. Westinghouse Electric, Arlington, Va. 1982-86; actg. dir., engring. mgr. General Dynamics, San Diego 1986-89; dir. bus. devel. Teledyne-Ryan Aeronautical, San Diego 1989-90; pres. Cobianchi & Assocs., 1990-91; v.p. strategic planning & pgm. devel. S-Cubed Div. Maxwell Labs., San Diego 1991-; past instr. Towson St. Univ., staff Penn State Univ., guest lectr. intl. bus. Monmouth Coll. and Geo. Washington Univ.; mem. bd. Bus. Advy. Council, U.S. Internat. Univ., 1992-; mem: Armed Forces Comms. & Electronics Assn. 1983-, Navy League S.D. 1989-90, Air Force Assn. 1983-84, Assn. of US Army 1989-90, Assn. of Old Crows 1991-, The Princeton Club (W.D.C., San Diego); civic bds: United Way S.D. (sect. chair 1987-), Cath. Charities S.D. (1989); rec: golf, tennis, skiing, hunting, target shooting. Ofc: S-Cubed Div. Maxwell Labs 3020 Callan Rd San Diego 92121

COCHRANE, TIMOTHY DAVID, banker; b. Aug. 24, 1953, Eureka; s. James William and Alice Loree (Stockton) C.; m. Marie A. Mengel, Feb. 1, 1975; children: Jana b. 1976, Laura b. 1978, Dorothy b. 1980, Rebecca b. 1984; edn: Coll. of the Redwoods 1971-73, CSU Humboldt 1973, 81-82, dipl. Pacific Coast Banking Sch., Univ. Wash., Seattle 1985-87. Career: operatios ofcr. Bank of America, Mt. Shasta 1973-77, asst. mgr. B.of A., Citrus Heights 1977-78; a.v.p. ops. Coast Central Cr. Union, Eureka 1978-81; v.p. and chief fin. ofcr. Bank of Loleta, Eureka 1981-88; pres. and c.e.o. Six Rivers Nat. Bank, Eureka 1988-; instr. Coll. of Redwoods 1984-; chmn. bd. Vector Health Pgm., Eureka 1985-; mem. bd. Eureka City Schs. 1988-; awards: Young Credit Union Leader Calif. Credit Union League, Pomona (1980); clubs: Rotary, Ingomar (Eureka); Republican; Episcopalian; rec: music, camping, hiking. Ofc: Six River National Bank 800 W Harris St Eureka 95501

CODDINGTON, IQBAL JWAIDEH, anthropologist; b. Nov. 25, 1935, Baghdad, Iraq, naturalized U.S. citizen 1985; d. Abdul Massih Elias and Jamila (Jwaideh) J.waideh; m. Joseph Mark Coddington, June 20, 1970 (div. 1992); edn: BA English lit., Baghdad Univ., 1955; Dipl. in English ednl. thought and practice, Univ. London, 1961, Assoc. in Comparative Edn., 1962; MSc in edn., Indiana Univ., 1964, MA anthropology, 1970, PhD anthropology, 1980. Career: tchr. high sch., Baghdad 1955-60; adj. asst. prof. Oklahoma Univ., Norman 1981-85; dept. hd. res. & data collection, asst. dir. Arab Gulf States Folklore Ctr., Doha, Qatar 1985-87; asst. prof. De Anza Coll., Cupertino, Calif. 1989; lectr. p.t. Cogswell Coll. 1991, 92; res. assoc. UC Berkeley, 1988-91, vis. scholar 1992; awards: Baghdad Ministry of Edn. govt. scholar 1960-65; mem. Middle East Studies Assn., Assn. M.E. Womens Studies, AAUW (Palo Alto bd.); civic: Neighbors Abroad, Palo Alto (co-chair internat. vis. com.), Palo Alto Cultural Ctr. (vol.); pub. res. articles in jours. (1985, 86, 87); Democrat; R.Cath.; rec: reading. Res: PO Box 60417 Palo Alto 94306

CODY, EVON G., former Kings County supervisor; b. April 11, 1915, Hanford; s. Andrew Milo and Alice May (Card) C.; m. Ida Marie Dooley, June 2, 1935; past mem. County Supervisors Assn. of Calif., chmn. bd. 5 yrs., dir.; mem. Internat. Cody Family Assn. (pres. 1964-69); Y's Men Laton YMCA (past pres., gov. 1946-47); Kiwanis (pres. 1967, lt. gov. 1970); Farm Bureau (local chmn.); Red Cross of Kings Co. (chmn.); Navy League; mem. bd. Burris Park Mus.; church trustee and Sunday Sch. tchr. 40 yrs.; Kings Co. Historical Soc. chmn. 6 yrs.; chmn. North Kings Co. area planning commn.; dedicated twelve million dollar Govt. Center 1977; appt. by Gov. Brown Calif. State Advy. Bd. Employment; state-legislative com. AARP 1984-89; named Hanford C.of C. citizen of year 1986; Statue commemorating services as County Supervisor 1955-82, installed Kings Co. Govt. Ctr. 1982; When retired given a plank "owner plaque" from Lemoore Naval Air Station. Res: 10342 Dover Ave Hanford 93230

COFER, BERT (BERDETTE) HENRY, consultant; b. Apr. 4, 1928, Las Flores, Tehama Co.; s. William Walter and Violet Ellen (Elam) C.; m. Ann McGarva, June 27, 1954 (dec. Feb. 20, 1990); m. Sally Sheperd, June 12, 1993; children: Sandra Cofer-Oberle b. 1960, Ronald b. 1962; edn: AB, Csu Chico, 1950; MA, UC Berkeley, 1960. Career: tchr. Westwood Jr. - Sr. High Sch., Westwood (Lassen Co.), Ca. 1953-54; Alhambra High Sch., Martinez, Ca. 1954-59; prin. Adult and Summer Sch., Hanford High Sch., Hanford, Ca. 1959-60, asst. supt. 1960-67; dean of bus. services West Hills Coll., Coalinga, Ca.

1967-76; vice chancellor Yosemite Community Coll. Dist., Modesto, Ca. 1976-88, v.chancellor emeritus, 1988-; pres. BHC Associates Inc., Modesto 1988-; chmn. Valley Insurance Jt. Powers Agy., Modesto 1986-88; interim chancellor No. Orange County Comm. Coll. Dist., Fullerton, Ca. 1989-90; pres. Coalinga Indsl. Devel. Corp. 1972-74; mayor City of Coalinga 1974-76; pres. Assn. of Chief Bus. Officers, Calif. Comm. Colls., 1981-82; awards: Coalinga C.of C. Outstanding Citizen 1976, Walter Starr Robie Outstanding Bus. Officer Calif. Comm. Colls. Bus. Officials 1988, Foreman Stanislaus Co. Grand Jury 1987-88; mem: Calif. Assn. of Comm. Coll. Adminstrs. (charter, hon. life 1988), Commonwealth Club, Phi Delta Kappa (1956-, pres. King-Tulare chpt. 1962-63), Lions Clubs Intl. (Hanford/Coalinga/Modesto dist. gov. 1965-66), Am. Legion 1987-, Elks 1987-; publs: com. mem. Nat. Assn. of Coll./Univ. Bus. Ofcls. com. to write 4th Ed. of Coll. & Univ. Bus. Admin. 1977-81, author 2 articles and coauthor 3 articles in profl. jours. (1987, 88); mil: 1st lt. USAF 1951-53; Democrat; Prot.; rec: reading, travel, bowling, golf. Res: 291 Leveland Ln #D Modesto 95350-2255

COHEN, ALAN JAY, psychiatrist; b. Aug. 30, 1956, Phila.; s. Harry Wallace and Shirley Vita (Berman) C.; m. Shannon Bowman, June 25, 1989; children: Brendan Harris b. 1990, Hallie Patricia b. 1992; edn: BA in biology (cum laude), Oberlin Coll., 1978; MD, Jefferson Med. Coll., 1982; intern med./psych. Langley Porter Inst., UC San Francisco, 1982-86, resident psychiatry, 1986-87; fellow psychiatry Inst. of PA Hosp., 1986-87. Career: resrch. fellow, clin. instr. psychiatry Univ. Pa. Hosp., 1986-87; asst. clin. prof. psychiatry UC San Francisco, 1987-; attdg. psychiatrist San Francisco Gen. Hosp., UCSF, 1987-90; pvt. practice, 1990-, attdg. physician East Bay Hosp. (chief of staff 1993, dir. clinical research 1993), Brookside Hosp.; mem. S.F. Dept. Pub. Hlth. Div. of Mental Hlth., Substance Abuse, and Forensic Svs. Pharmacy and Therapeutics Com. and Stds. Subcom.; awards: Nat. Merit Commendn., Haverford Sch. 1974, Sigma Xi 1978, Baldwin Keyes Prize in psychiat. 1982, Harrity Resrch. Fund fellow 1986-87, NIH fellow 1979; mem.: No. Calif. Psychiat. Soc., AMA, Am. Psychiat. Assn., Psychiat. Physicians of Pa., Calif. Med. Assn., Alameda Contra Costa Med. Assn., Calif. Psychiatric Assn.; Ofc: Comprehensive Psychiatric Svs., 37 Quail Ct Ste 200 Walnut Creek CA 94596 Tel: 510/944-1733

COHEN, CYNTHIA MARYLYN, lawyer; b. Sept. 5, 1945, Brooklyn, NY.; d. Bernard and Evelyn (Berman) C.; edn: AB Cornell Univ. 1967; JD cum laude N.Y.U. Sch. of Law 1970; admitted bar: NY 1971, Calif. 1980, Federal Cts. NY and Calif., 1972, 80, 81, 86, U.S. Supreme Ct. 1975. Career: atty., assoc. Simpson Thacher & Bartlett, NYC 1970-76; Kaye, Scholer, Fierman, Hays & Handler, NYC 1976-80; atty., shareholder Stutman, Treister & Glatt Profl. Corp., LA 1980-87; atty., ptnr. Hughes Hubbard & Reed, LA 1987-93; atty., ptnr. Morgan, Lewis & Bockius, LA 1993-; student res. advisor N.Y.U. and mem. student-faculty curriculum and clin. prog. coms. 1968-70; honors: Order of the Coif 1970, Founder's Day Cert. 1969, John Norton Pomeroy Scholar 1968-70, Law Rev. 1968, N.Y.U.; Am. Jurisprudence Awards; Cornell Dean's Scholarship 1963-67; NY State Regents Scholarship 1963-70; mem: Am. Bar Assn. (Antitrust, Litigation sects.), Bar Assn. of City of NY (Trade Reg. Com. 1976-79), NY State Bar Assn. (ch. Class Action Com. 1979), Assn. of Bus. Trial Lawyers, L.A. County Bar Assn. (Antitrust, Comml. Law and Bankruptcy Sects.), Calif. Bar Assn. (Antitrust, Bus. Sects.), Financial Lawyers Conf.; Girl Scouts 1954-59; Delta Gamma Sor.; NY chpt. Am. Cancer Soc. (dir. 1977-80); rec: tennis, collector rare books and wine. Res: 4818 Bonvue Ave. Los Angeles 90027 Ofc: Morgan, Lewis & Bockius, 801 S. Grand Ave. 22nd Floor Los Angeles 90017-3189 Tel: 213/612-2500

COHEN, LAWRENCE MARK, mechanical engineer; b. Oct. 17, 1956, New York; s. Robert Irwin and Beverly Eleanor (Greenstein) C.; m. Victoria Goldblatt, Jan. 17, 1988; edn: BS (summa cum laude), SUNY at Buffalo, 1978; MS, MIT, Calif., 1982. Career: tchg. asst. SUNY 1976-78; analytical engr. Pratt & Whitney Aircraft, E. Hartford, Conn. 1978; research asst. MIT 1978-80; mem. tech. staff TRW Space & Technology, Redondo Beach, Calif. 1980-; res. fellow Dept. Mech. Engring. Stanford Univ. 1984-; honors: Pi Tau Sigma, Tau Beta Pi, Cummins Engine Co. Fellow, TRW, Inc. Industrial Fellow; mem: ASME, Havurah; publs: 4+ articles in sci. jours. (1984-); Democrat; Jewish; rec: hiking, opera, bicycling. Res: 1034 Pine St #2 Menlo Park 94025-3425 Ofc: ME Dept. Stanford University Stanford 94305-3032

COHEN, MARLENE ZICHI, clinical nursing researcher; b. June 1, 1951, Brooklyn, NY; m. David M. Cohen, Mar. 5, 1978; edn: BSN, Univ. of Mich., Ann Arbor, 1974 (magna cum laude); MS, Psychiatric-Mental Health Nsg., Univ. of Mich., 1981; PhD, Nsg., Univ. of Mich., 1984. Career: clinical nsg. (various positions), Ann Arbor, Mich., 1974-84; asst. prof., Ea. Mich. Univ., Ypsilanti, Mich., 1984-85; asst. prof., Univ. of Iowa, Iowa City, 1985-90; res. scientist, City of Hope, Duarte, Calif., 1990-92; dir. Office of Nsg. Res., Univ. of So. Calif. Dept. of Nsg. and Norris Comprehensive Cancer Ctr., L.A., 1992-; Sigma Theta Tau, Gamma Chpt.Pres. 1986-90; com. mem, Sigma Theta Tau Internat., Reg. 2 1988-90; collateral reviewer, Sigma Theta Tau Res. Grants Prog.,1989-92; manuscript reviewer: We. Jour. of Nsg. Res. 1985-, Image 1989-, Qualitative Health Res. 1989-, Res. in Nsg. and Health 1990-, Clinical Nsg. Res. 1991-; reviewer, Oncology Nsg. Soc. grant study sect. 1991; faculty mem.,

Oncology Nsg. Soc. and Nat. Cancer Inst. Cancer Nsg. Res. Short Course 1992; mem., Hadassah Nurses Council Internat. Advy. Bd.; awards: Sigma Theta Tau, induction 1973, Shirley C. Titus Grad. Scholarship 1981, 1984, Rackham Grad. Sch. Fellowship 1981-82, Outstanding Young Woman of Am. award 1982, Am. Assn. of Critical Care Nurses Res. award, Nat. Tchg. Inst. 1988; invited consultation, Hebrew Sch. of Nsg. and Hadassah Med. Orgn., Jerusalem, Israel 1992; mem: Am. Nurses Assn. 1974-, Council of Nurse Researchers 1985-, Iowa Acad. of Sciences 1985-90, Iowa Nurses Assn. 1985-90, Mich. Nurses Assn. 1974-85, Calif. Nurses Assn. 1990-, Midwest Alliance in Nsg. 1982-90, N.Am. Nsg. Diagnosis Assn. 1986-, Sigma Theta Tau 1973-, Oncology Nsg. Soc. 1990-, We. Soc. for Res. in Nsg., We. Inst. of Nsg. 1990-, Soc. for Edn and Res. in Psychiatric-Mental Health Nsg. 1991-, Council on Psychiatric and Mental Health Nsg. 1991-; author: numerous articles and abstracts publ. in profl. nsg. and health journals 1982-,over 50 res. papers presented, keynote speaker and lectr. Nsg. Res. Soc. Conferences 1982-. Ofc: University of Southern California, Dept. of Nursing, 106 Leavey Hall, 320 W. 15th St. Los Angeles 90015

COHEN, PATRICIA FELTZ, educator, nursing consultant, author; b. June 7, 1932, Idpls.; d. Walter Frederick and Marie Ziegler Feltz; m. Stanley J. Cohen, Sept. 1, 1966; children: David Walter b. 1968, Susan Marie b. 1969; edn: RN, St. Joseph Infirmary Sch. of Nursing, 1953; BSN, Indiana Univ., 1960; MA nsg. edn., Teachers Coll. Columbia Univ., 1963, MA edn., 1964. Career: Capt. Nurse Corps US Air Force, 1955-58; thinking skills consultant, lead workshops for tchrs. on logic and math.; nursing consultant; currently program mgr. Amer. Cancer Soc., Orange Co. Unit; coauthor 6 books on nsg., Nursing Care Planning Guides; mem. bd. trustees (elem.) Huntington Beach City Sch. Dist. 1987-90; recipient award for outstanding contbn. to edn. Orange County Dept. Edn., honorary & cont. service awards PTA; mem. Orange County Sch. Bd. Assn., West Orange County Consortium for Special Edn., AAUW, H.Bch. Womens Club; Democrat; R.Cath.; rec: computers, genealogy res. Res: 21731 Saluda Circle Huntington Beach 92646

COHEN, RONALD MORTON, physician, surgeon, ophthalmologist; b. July 9, 1947, Los Angeles; s. Eli Bertran and Aimee (Salomon) C.; m. Ricki Ruth Pasternak, June 23, 1968; edn: BS, UCSF 1968; MD, 1971. Career: intern pathology Harbor Gen. Hosp., Torrance 1971-72; resident ophthalmology UCLA/Jules Stein Eye Inst., Los Angeles 1972-75; pvt. practice ophthalmology, La Mirada 1975-89; ret.; attdg. physician VA Hosp., Long Beach 1975-; mem: L.A. Co. Med. Assn., Orange Co. Soc. Ophthalmology, CMA; article pub. in med. jour. 1970; mil: major USAR 1970-82; Democrat; Jewish; rec: aviation, playing piano, computers. Res: PO Box 3541 Anaheim 92803

COHEN, SEYMOUR I., lawyer; b. Apr. 15, 1931, N.Y.C.; s. Fred and Nettie (Sederer) C.; m. Rhoda Goldner, July 22, 1956; children: Cheryl Lynn, Marcy Ann, Lori Beth; edn: BBA (cum laude) City Coll. N.Y., 1951; LLB, Bklyn. Law Sch., 1954, JD, 1967; MBA, N.Y. Univ., 1960; admitted bar: N.Y. 1954, U.S. Tax. Ct. 1954, Calif. 1973, U.S. Dist. Ct. (cen. dist.) Calif. 1973, U.S. Ct. Appeals (9th cir.) 1973, U.S. Supreme Ct. 1976; CPA, Ohio, Calif. Career: staff acct. S.D. Leidesdorf, N.Y.C., 1958-61; mgr., acct. Rockwell, Columbus, Ohio and Los Angeles, 1961-69; mgr. contracts Logicon, L.A. 1970-71; mgr. internal audit Daylin, 1971-72; contr. NYSE Co., 1972-73; atty., pvt. practice personal injury, probate and gen. practice law, Torrance, Calif. 1973-; mem: Am. Inst. CPA, L.A. County Bar Assn. (appellate ct. com. 1979-, svs. com. 1981-82), South Bay Bar Assn. (pres. 1986-87, chair referral svc. 1977-81), Calif. Bar Assn. (client trust fund commr. 1983, 84), Ohio Inst. CPAs, N.Y. Inst. CPAs, Calif. Inst. CPAs, L.A. Trial Lawyers Assn., N.Y. State Bar Assn.; Jewish; Republican. Res: 30691 Via La Cresta Rancho Palos Verdes 90274 Ofc: 18411 Crenshaw Blvd Ste 411 Torrance 90504 Tel: 310/329-6384

COHEN, (STEPHEN) MARSHALL, university dean, professor of philosophy and law; b. Sept. 27, 1929, N.Y.C.; s. Harry and Fanny (Marshall) C.; m. Margaret Dennes, Feb. 15, 1964; children: Matthew, Megan; edn: BA, Dartmouth Coll., 1951; MA, Harvard Univ., 1953, Jr. fellow Soc. of Fellows 1955-58; spl. student Magdalen Coll., Oxford 1953-54, MA (Oxon.) 1977. Career: prof. philosophy and law, dean of humanities Univ. So. Calif., 1983-; asst. prof. of philosophy and of gen. edn. Harvard Univ. 1958-62; asst., assoc. prof. philosophy Univ. of Chgo. 1962-64, 1964-67, actg. chair Coll. Philosophy 1965-66; assoc. prof. philosophy Rockefeller Univ. 1967-70; prof. philosophy Richmond Coll. (now Coll. of Staten Island) also The Grad. Sch. CUNY, 1970-83; vis. prof. UC Berkeley 1971, Harvard Univ. 1972, New Sch. for Social Resrch. 1973-74, Cornell Univ. 1974, Yale Coll. 1975, Barnard Coll. Columbia Univ. 1979-81, US Mil. Acad., West Point, 1982; awards: Fellow A.C.L.S. 1951-52, Harvard Univ. Sheldon Traveling 1953-54, Soc. Fellows 1955-58, Santayana 1962-63, Yale Law Sch. 1964-65, hon. fellow Trumbull Coll. Yale 1968-73, grantee NEH 1975, vis. fellow All Souls Coll., Oxford 1976-77, Guggenheim fellow 1976-77, Rockefeller Found. Humanities fellow 1977, Inst. for Adv. Study, Princeton 1981-82, prin. investigator: Andrew W. Mellon Found. 1981-83, 91-95, NEH Instnl. Challenge Grant 1988-92; lectureships: "The Meaning of Metaphor" Lowell Inst. Lectures, Boston 1957-58, "Aesthetics and Poetics" Christian Gauss Seminars in Criticism, Princeton 1964-65, Phi Beta Kappa vis. scholar 1975-76, N.Y. Coun. for Humanities Lectr. 1982-83;

mem: Am. Philosophical Assn., Soc. for Philosophy and Pub. Affairs, Amintaphil, USC Council of Deans (1983-, exec. com. 84-90), Phi Kappa Phi (exec. com. 1991-, pres. 1992-93); author: 10+ books incl. Film Theory & Criticism (ed. with Gerald Mast Oxford, 1974; 2d. edit. 1979, 3d. edit. 1985, 4th edit. with Leo Braudy, 1992), numerous essays, articles and reviews in scholarly and literary jours.; editor: Philosophy and Public Affairs (Princeton Univ. Press, 1971-). Ofc: Div. Humanities, Univ. So. Calif., Los Angeles 90089-4012

COHN, DANIEL HOWARD, research scientist, educator; b. Aug. 24, 1955, Santa Monica; s. Sidney Lorber and Mynda Ellen (Zimmerman) C.; m. Ludmila Bojman, May 16, 1982; children: Zachary b. 1986, Marissa b. 1988, Rachel b. 1988; edn: BA, UC Santa Barbara, 1977; PhD, UC San Diego, 1983; grad. student Scripps Inst. Oceanography, UCSD, 1977-83, postdoc. fellow Univ. Wash., Seattle 1983-88. Career: resrch. scientist, asst. prof. Cedars-Sinai Med. Ctr., UC Los Angeles, 1988-; awards: Deans list UCSB 1977, Phi Beta Kappa 1977, Outstanding senior in biology UCSB 1977, Martin Kamen Award UCSD 1983, Eckhardt Prize, Scripps Inst. 1983, NIH postdoc. fellow 1985; mem. AAAS 1977-, OI Found. 1988-, Concern Found. L.A. 1988-; author 25+ book chapters and sci. articles (1978-); Democrat; Jewish; rec: fatherhood, golf, volleyball, cooking, wine. Ofc: Medical Genetics, SSB-3, Cedars-Sinai Med. Ctr. 8700 Beverly Blvd Los Angeles 90048

COHN, ROBERT GREER, professor of French literature; b. Sept. 5, 1921, Richmond, Va.; s. Charles Alfred and Susan (Spilberg) C.; m. Dorrit Zucker, 1948 (div. 1963); children: Stephen b. 1949, Richard b. 1955; m. Valentina Catenacci, Oct. 26, 1965; edn: BA Romance languages, Univ. Va., 1943; MA, Yale Univ., 1947, PhD French, 1949. Career: instr. Yale Univ. 1949-50; asst. prof. Swarthmore Coll. 1952-54, Vassar Coll. 1954-59; assoc. prof. Stanford Univ., 1959-62, prof. French literature 1962-92; founding editor, Yale French Studies, 1948-49; awards: Croix de Guerre Fr. Army; France 1946, Guggenheim fellow (1956-57, 1986-87), Nat. Endowment for Humanities fellow (1969-70, 79-80), ACLS (1969-70); mem. advy. bd. Calif. Assn. of Scholars 1992-; author: L'Oeuvre De Mallarme (1951), Toward The Poems of Mallarme (1965), The Poetry of Rimbaud (1973); mil: t/5 US Army 1943-46; rec: gardening, music. Res: 6 Maywood Ln Menlo Park 94025

COLBERT, EARL JAY, orthodontist; b. Nov. 16, 1942, Wash. DC; s. Lawrence L. and Sylvia (Hirsch) C.; m. Sherry Graham, Oct. 18, 1969; children: Laura, b. 1973, Michele, b. 1974; edn: The American Univ. 1961-63; DDS, Georgetown Univ. Dental Sch. 1967; Cert.Orthodontics, Howard Univ. Coll. of Dentistry 1972. Career: dental ofcr. US Navy Dental Corps, MCRD San Diego and actg. dept. hd. USS Kearsarge, 1967-69; gen. dentistry, Wash. DC 1969-70; self-empl. orthodontist, Huntington Beach 1972-; recipient appreciation, Mayor of Huntington Beach; mem: Naval Reserve Assn., Reserve Ofcrs. Assn., Navy League, Am. Assn. of Orthodont., Huntington Beach C.of C., Sister Cities Assn. (bd. dirs.), Rotary (bd. dirs.), Calif. Childrens Services Panel in Orthdontics for Orange, LA Counties, Nat. Fedn. of Independent Bus.; vol: Civil Defense, Multiple Sclerosis, Orange Co. Music Ctr. Guild, OC Performing Arts Guild; PTA; past pres. Boca Orthodontic Study Gp.; invention: orthodontic rotating device; mil: dental ofcr. USNR 1967-69, Capt. USNR Dental Corps 1969-, cmdg. ofcr. Naval Reserve Fleet Hosp. Combat Zone Hdqtrs. Unit, 1985-86, cmdg. ofcr. Naval Reserve Naval Hosp. Camp Pendleton 319, 1989-91, decorated Meritorious Unit Cit., Armed Forces Expeditionary, Expert Rifleman and Expert Pistol medals, Vietnam Svc.; rec: inventions, models. Res: 3696 Montego Dr Huntington Beach 92649 Ofc: Earl J. Colbert DDS, Inc. 5112 Warner Ave Ste 104 Huntington Beach 92649

COLE, RALPH NOBLE, commercial real estate broker; b. Apr. 17, 1924, Long Beach; s. Ralph Gideon Cole and Louise Noble (Carter) C.; m. Susan, Sept. 6, 1946; children: Alan b. 1953, Alice b. 1955, Randall b. 1956, Charles b. 1959; edn: AB, Stanford Univ., 1947, MBA, Stanford Grad. Sch. of Bus., 1949; certificates: Coro Found., S.F. 1947, Command & Gen. Staff Coll. 1969, USA War Coll. 1976; Calif. lic. real estate broker, realtor 1947. Career: economist US Dept. of Labor, San Francisco 1950-52; dist. mgr. Pacific Tel., S.F. and Seattle, 1952-83; commercial real estate broker Grubb & Ellis, San Rafael 1984-; honors: Phi Beta Kappa, Knight, NATO Grand Priory of St. Sebastian SMOTJ; mem: Nat. Assn. Realtors, Marin County Assn. of Realtors, Commonwealth Club of Calif., Assn. of US Army, Reserve Officers Assn., Stanford Grad. Sch. of Bus. Alumni Assn., Phi Gamma Delta Frat. Alumni Assn., SAR; clubs: Elks; mil: Col. AUS 1943-46, 1949-79; Republican; Presbyterian; rec: boating. Res: 3348 Paradise Dr Tiburon 94920 Ofc: Grubb & Ellis, 899 Northgate Dr Ste 210 San Rafael 94903

COLEMAN, BEVERLY ELAINE, nutritionist, acupuncturist, herbalist, wellness educator and publisher; b. Aug. 10, 1936, Pasadena, Calif.; d. Henry Clarence Coleman (dec.) and Delores Willie (Kennedy) C.; edn: A&I Univ., Nashville, Tenn., 1954-55; L.A. City Coll., 1957; BA, Calif. State Univ., L.A., 1961; tchg. cred., Syracuse Univ., NY, 1964; MPH in behavioral sci./health edn., UCLA, 1969; grad. study, Univ. of So. Calif., 1969; postgrad., CSU, L.A., 1969-70; Shaolin Kung Fu (3 yrs.), Tai Chi (1 yr.), Jin Shin Do and Shiatsu (1 yr.)1969-72; Swedish massage lic., L.A., 1970; cert. applied kinesiology instr.,

1972; cert. foot reflexology with Ingram method, 1973; MS in acupuncture and herbology, Emperors Coll., Santa Monica, 1987; lic. acupuncturist, State of Calif., diplomate of acupuncture, Nat. Comm. for Certification, 1988. Career: juvenile counselor, L.A. Probation Dept. 1962-64; tchr., sci./English/phys. fitness, U.S. Peace Corps, Tanzania, E. Africa 1964-66; asst. prof. anthropology & Swahili lang., CSU, L.A. and Pasadena City Coll. 1968-70; freelance writer 1971-; holistic health cons., founder/dir. NACHES, L.A. 1971-; cons., Calif. State Dept. of Edn., U.S.D.A., United Way, L.A. County, L.A. Sch. Dist. 1979-85; health ed. Calif. Eagle Newspaper, LA. 1979, Uraeus Jour. 1984-85; tchr, health scis., LA. Unified Sch. Dist. 1985-90; lic. acupuncturist and herbalist, private practice, L.A. 1988-; prof. of herbology, Emperor's Coll. of Trad. Oriental Medicine, Santa Monica 1991-; awards: under grad. scholarship, A&I Univ.; H.E.W. Grad. Fellowship, UCLA Sch. of Public Health; Danforth Minority Grad. Fellowship; faculty res. grant, CSU, L.A.; mem: Am. Public Health Assn., Internat. Iridologist Assn., Calif. Acupuncture Assn., U.S. and So. Calif. (Sr.) Tennis Assns.; author: The Coleman Wellness Self-Test, 1985; The Safe Use of Herbs-How To Use Common Household Herbs to Help You Stay Well, 1991; numerous publ. articles, radio programs, TV panels on health and wellness; ed., annual newsletter on holistic health; rec: tennis (nationally ranked, U.S. Sr. Women's Tennis). Res/Ofc: 1515 Alvira St., Los Angeles 90035

COLEMAN, PAUL JEROME, JR., physicist, educator; b. Mar. 7, 1932, Evanston, Ill.; s. Paul Jerome and Eunice Cecile (Weissenbergh) C.; m. Doris Ann Fields, Oct. 3, 1964; children: Derrick b. 1968, Craig b. 1971; edn: BSE in physics, BSE in math, Univ. Mich., 1954, MS in physics, Univ. Mich., 1958; PhD in physics, UCLA, 1965. Career: research scientist Ramo-Wooldridge Corp. (now TRW Systems), 1958-60; hd. interplanetary scis. pgm. NASA, Wash. DC 1961-62; research scientist Inst. of Geophysics and Planetary Physics, UCLA, Los Angeles 1963-66, prof. of geophysics and space physics, 1966-; asst. lab. dir./ mgr. Earth and Space Scis. Div./chmn. Inst. of Geophysics and Planetary Physics, Los Alamos Nat. Lab., Los Alamos, N.M. 1981-84; dir. Inst. of Geophysics & Planetary Physics, UCLA 1989-92; bd. dirs: Universal Monitor Corp. 1971-76, Univ. Technology Transfer, Inc. 1984-, Lasertechnics, Inc. 1985-, Fairchild Space & Def. Corp. 1989-, CACI Internat., Inc. 1990-; apptd. bds. public and non-profit orgns.: LLNL and Los Alamos Nat. Lab., UC (sci. advy. com. 1975-81), Calif. Space Inst., UC (steering com. 1979-82), Univ. Space Resrch. Assn. (trustee 1981-, pres. 1981-), Nat. Inst. for Space Commercialization (dir. 1983-86), San Diego Supercomputer Ctr. (steering com. 1984-, chmn. 1986-88), West Coast Univ. (bd. advisors 1986-), External Tanks (Space Shuttle) Corp. (tech. advy. bd. 1986-), American Technology Initiative (bd. trustees 1990-); cons. num. govt., internat. and public agencies (U.S., Ger., Italy, Australia, Euro. Space Agy.), cons. num. indsl. corps. 1963-; honors: Phi Eta Sigma 1950, Tau Beta Pi 1953, exceptional sci. achievement medal for contbns. to exploration of the solar system NASA 1970 and for contbns. to the exploration of the moon 1972, spl. recogn. by NASA for contbns. to the Apollo Pgm. 1979, John S. Guggenheim Memorial Fellow 1975-76, Sr. Fulbright Scholar 1975-76, Internat. Acad. of Astronautics (elected 1975), Presdl. appointee Nat. Commn. on Space 1985-86, appt. Vice Pres.'s Space Policy Advy. Bd. 1991-; mem: AAAS 1959-, Am. Geophysical Union 1959-, Am. Inst. of Aero. and Astro. 1966-, Am. Physical Soc. 1956-, Soc. of Exploration Geophysicists 1975-90, Fulbright Alumni Assn. 1978-; clubs: Cosmos (WDC), Explorers (NY), Bel Air Bay (LA), Eldorado CC (Palm Desert); mil: 1st lt. USAF 1954-56; R. Cath. Res: 1323 Monaco Dr Pacific Palisades 90272 Ofc: UCLA, 405 Hilgard Ave Los Angeles 90024

COLES, CLARENCE WARREN, author, publisher; b. Oct. 13, 1925, Beloit, Wis.; s. Venice Virgil and Corienne Lois (Marsh) C.; m. Joan Darlene Lorton, Jan. 18, 1981; children: Mark, Greg, Julie, Brian, Liz; edn: B.Journ., Univ. Wash., 1959. Career: writer, staff various newspapers, 1945-50, 1959-61; mem. Cmdr. Hect Expedition charting Arctic Ocean, 1953; personnel recruiter Boeing Airplane Co., Seattle 1954-56; editor/writer McDonnell-Douglas, El Segundo, Calif. 1961-70; technical writer Hughes Helicopters, Long Beach 1970-74; author or coauthor 24 books; owner/pub. Seloc Publs., Cucamonga 1974-; mem. Nat. Marine Mfrs. Assn.; mil: pfc USMC 1942-45, 50-51; Democrat; rec: sailing, woodworking, poetry writing. Ofc: 10693 Civic Center Dr Rancho Cucamonga 91730-3804

COLEY, ROBERT BERNARD, software co. executive; b. Aug. 10, 1951, Bethesda, Md.; s. Robert and Anna C.; m. Denise Bolden, July 4, 1976; children: Robert, Jr. b. 1977, Elena b. 1978; edn: AB, Harvard Univ. 1973; JD and MBA, Stanford Univ. 1977. Career: mgmt. cons. McKinsey & Co., N.Y.C. 1976; mgmt. cons. Am. Mgmt. Systems, Inc., Foster City, Ca. 1977-79; adminstrv. mgr. of ISD, ADPAC Corp., San Francisco 1979-80; pres., c.e.o. and c.f.o. Avalanche Prodns. Inc., Palo Alto 1980-83, PRIMS, Inc., Redwood City 1984-86, PSMG, Inc., Palo Alto 1986-; dir: Avalanche 1980-83, PRIMS 1984-86, RBC Acquisition Corp. 1982-, PSMG, Inc. 1986-; honors: Nat. Merit Achievement 1969, Nat. Honor Soc. 1968-69, academic fellowships 1970-77, Harvard Book Club award, Civitan award 1969, Nat. Tech. Assoc. achievement award 1987, listed Who's Who in Fin. and Ind.; mem: Nat. Assn. of Corp. Dirs., Stanford Bus. Sch. Alumni Assn., Kiwanis Internat.; civic: SAY Little League Basketball (commr., coach 1987-), Palo Alto Little League (asst. coach 1986-

90), Palo Alto Bobby Sox League (pres., bd. v.p., chair fundraising com., coach 1988-), St. Elizabeth Seton School Board (chair fin. com. 1984-87), Palo Alto YMCA Bd. Mgrs. (chair 1992, fin. com. chair 1989-91), SAY Basketball League (commr., coach 1989-); recipient hon. mention Phillip Gerry Poetry Contest 1969; TV guest on topic entrepreneurship; Democrat; Baptist; rec: basketball, tennis, travel. Ofc: PSMG, Inc. 2124 Clarke Ave Palo Alto 94303

COLGREN, RICHARD DEAN, flight controls engineer; b. June 13, 1961, Seattle; edn: BSAA, Univ. Wash., 1982; MSEE, Univ. So. Calif., 1987, PhD in EE, 1992. Career: engr. Northrop Corp., Pico Rivera 1982-84; sr. vehicle systems resrch. engr. Lockheed Corp., Burbank 1984-; mem. Am. Inst. Aero. & Astro. (nat. tech. com. 1989-, sect. chair 1989-90, sect. treas. 1991-, ACC Review chmn. 1992, Sr. Mem. 1989, Assoc. Fellow 1991), Inst. Electrical & Electronics Engrs.; assoc. editor Jour. of Theoretical & Computational Graphics, 1988-91; co-author: Progress in Simulation (1992), num. papers, tech. confs. (1987-), article in CSS Mag. (1989); inventor Miniature Jet Engine (pat. 1991). Ofc: Lockheed (LADC) 7575 N San Fernando Rd Burbank 91520-2533

COLLEY, PETER MICHAEL, playwright, screenwriter; b. Jan. 3, 1949, Scarborough, England, naturalized U.S. citizen 1985; s. Thomas and Irene (Firth) C.; m. Ellen Ross Jenkins, Nov. 22, 1983; edn: Royal Grammar Sch. High Wycombe, Eng. 1968 (Victor Laudorum award as top athlete of yr.); BA (hons.) Univ. of Sheffield, 1971; grad. studies Univ. of W. Ont., Nat. Arts Centre, Can. Career: resident playwright Grand Theatre, London, Ont. 1973-76; instr. of playwrighting Theatre Ont. summer courses; resident playwright Actors' Alley Repertory Theatre, Los Angeles 1989-93; pres. Buckingham Internat. Productions; winner of six nat. and 4 regional awards Can.; stageplays: The Saga of Regin, 1971; The Donnellys, 1974 (pub. MacMillans anthology, and Simon & Pierre); musical, You'll Get Used To It, 1975 (Canadian tour 1988, pub. Simon & Pierre); The Huron Tiger, 1978; I'll Be Back Before Midnight, 1979 (sole credit film version titled "Illusions" 1992; most prod. stage thriller in Can., prodns. in 13 countries and 42 states in U.S., Nat. Brit. tour 1988; pub. Samuel French Inc., NY, Baker's Plays, Boston, Samuel French Ltd., (London); Heads, You Lose! 1981; psychological thriller, The Mark of Cain, 1984 (coauthor of film 1985); philosophical thriller, When The Reaper Calls 1990; Beyond Suspicion, 1991 (Petro-Canada Stage One Awards); feature films: The Mark of Cain, 1990; Illusions, 1992; mem.: Writers Guild of Am./West, ACTRA Writers Guild (Can.), Dramatists Guild (NY), Playwrights Union of Canada, Acad. of Canadian Cinema and TV. Ofc: 20929-47 Ventura Blvd Ste 123 Woodland Hills CA 913645

COLLINGS, MICHAEL ROBERT, professor of English, poet; b. Oct. 29, 1947, Rupert, Idaho; s. Ralph Willard and Thella Marie (Hurd) C.; m. Judith Lynn Reeve, Dec. 21, 1973; children: Michael-Brent b. 1974, Erika b. 1975, Ethan b. 1977, Kendra b. 1979; edn: AA, Bakersfield Coll. 1967; BA, Whittier Coll. 1969; MA, UC Riverside 1973, PhD, 1977. Career: instr. of English UCLA 1978-79; assoc., prof. English, Pepperdine Univ. 1979-; poetry editor "Dialogue", Salt Lake City 1983-89; awards: 1st pl. award Calif. Poetry Assn.,1982, finalist Odyssey Poetry Contest, Brigham Young Univ., 1988, nom. Rhysling award Sci. Fiction Poetry Assn., 1981, 82, 86, Recommendation/Nebula award, Sci. Fiction Writers of Am., 1986, 1st pl. award Calif. Fed. of Chaparral Poets, 1982; mem: Sci. Fiction Research Assn., Sci. Fiction Poetry Assn.; author num. books, monographs, short stories, poetry, book reviews and articles pub. profl. jours. Res: 1089 Sheffield Pl Thousand Oaks 91360-5353 Ofc: Humanities Div., Pepperdine Univ. Malibu 90263

COLLINS, CURTIS ALLAN, oceanographer, educator; b. Sept. 16, 1940, Des Moines, Ia.; s. Ralph Charlie and Noma Lovella (Buckley) C.; m. Judith Ann Petersen, Dec. 21, 1962; children: Nathaniel, Hillary; edn: BS, US Merchant Marine Acad., Kings Pt, NY, 1962; MS, Oregon State Univ., 1964, PhD, 1967. Career: Third mate S.S. Inger, 1967-68; research scientist Pacific Ocean Gp., Nanaimo, Brit. Col., 1968-70; ocean engr. Cities Service Oil, Tulsa, Ok. 1970-71; program mgr. Nat. Sci. Found., W.D.C., 1972-87; prof. Naval Postgrad. Sch., Monterey, Ca. 1987-; dir. MBARI, Monterey 1988-; commissioner, Moss Landing Harbor District, 1993-;awards: Am. Geophy. Union Ocean Scis., W.D.C. 1985, NSF meritorious svc. 1987; mem. AGU Ocean Scis. (pres. 1993-94), Oceanographic Soc. (Council 1989-91), Am. Meterol. Soc. 1980-, Oceanographic Soc. of Japan 1967-; mil: capt. USNR 1963-, decorated Armed Forces Reserve Medal 1973, 83, 93, Nat. Def. Svc. 1991; Democrat; Prot. Rds: 24010 Ranchito del Rio Ct Salinas 93908 Ofc: Code OC/CO, Naval Postgraduate School, Monterey 93943

COLLINS, GERALD CHESTER, bank manager; b. July 28, 1946, Los Angeles; s. Chester and Harriet (Hart) C.; m. Midge Bigham, May 31, 1968; children: Julie b. 1975, Bart b. 1977; edn: BA, CSU Northridge 1971. Career: asst. loan dept. head California Federal, head ofc. 1974-76, asst. v.p., loan dept. head, regl. loan mgr., Visalia 1979-85; regional loan mgr. N. Calif., Gibralter Savings 1985-87, senior v.p. residential loans, 1987-88; branch mgr. Wells Fargo Bank, 1989-93; branch mgr. United Valley Bank 1993-; bd. dirs. The King's Strategist, Inc.; past pres. VIAH Inc.; past pres. Energy Com., City of Visalia; past pres. Cal Fed PAC; tchr. Inst. of Fin. Edn. chpt. 208; mem. Rotary, past mem. West Visalia Kiwanis, Visalia United Methodist Ch. Commn. on Edn., Calif. Nevada Conf. of United Methodist Ch. (Ch. Expansion of Bd. of Conf. Life div.), Christian Bus. Mens Com.; devel. Personal Money Mgmt. System used in seminars & counseling statewide; mil: sp5 AUS 1966-69, GCM; Republican; Methodist; rec: tennis. Res: 1313 Chatham St Visalia 93277 Ofc: United Valley Bank 890 W. Lacey Blvd Hanford 93230

COLLINS, ROBERT, financial executive; b. Feb. 16, 1961, Boston, Mass.; s. Robert James and Dorothea Emily (Murphy) C.; m. Cheryl Mabel, Aug. 16, 1986; children: Carolyn b. 1989; edn: BS political sci., UC Berkeley 1983; MBA, Santa Clara Univ. 1987. Career: fin. analyst U.S. Fleet Leasing, San Mateo 1984-87, mgt. treasury ops. 1987-88; CFO Florentine Italian Foods, San Jose 1988-; mem: Menlo Park City Sch. Dist. (bd. mem. 1983-88, pres. 1988). Ofc: Florentine Italian Foods Inc. 1070 Commercial St Ste 107 San Jose 95112

COLLINS, WILLIAM LEROY, telecommunications engineer; b. June 17, 1942, Laurel, Miss.; s. Henry L. and Christene E. (Finnegan) C.; edn: La Salle Univ., 1969; BS computer sci., Univ. Beverly Hills, 1984. Career: sr. computer opr. Arizona Dept. Public Safety, Phoenix, 1975-78, data communications specialist, 1978-79, supr. computer ops., 1981-82; sr. network control specialist Valley Nat. Bank, Phoenix, 1979-81; mgr. data communications Ariz. Lottery, Phoenix 1982-85; mgr. telecommunications Calif. Lottery, Sacramento 1985-; listed Who's Who Worldwide, Who's Who in Am., Who's Who in West, Who's Who in Sci. & Engring., Intl. Leaders in Achiev., Intl. Directory of Disting. Leadership, Am. Biog. Inst. Man of the Year 1991; mem: AT&T T1 User Group, Sacto. Valley Centrex User Group, Telecommunications Assn. (v.p. edn. Sacto. Valley Chpt. 1990-93), Assn. of Data Comms. Users, Data Processing Mgmt. Assn., Am. Mgmt. Assn., Assn. Computing Machinery, Soc. Mfg. Engrs., K.C., Communications Mgrs. Assn. (CMA), Inst. of Electrical Engrs. (IEEE); mil: sgt. USAF 1964-68; R. Cath. Res: 116 Valley Oak Dr Roseville 95678 Ofc: Calif. State Lottery, 600 N 10th St Sacramento 95814

COLOMER DE SACA, NIDIA MARIA, physician, psychiatrist; b. Mar. 16, 1959, Cuba; d. Manuel and Nidia (Hernandez) Colomer; m. Ricardo E. Saca, MD, Mar. 22, 1986; children (twins): Christina b. 1990, Nidia b. 1990; edn: BS, Univ. of So. Calif., L.A. 1980; MD, George Washington Univ., Wash., DC 1985. Career: med. internship, UCLA, Sepulveda, Calif. 1985-86; psychiatric residency, UCLA, Sepulveda 1986-88; child & adolescent psychiatry specialty, UCLA Harbor, Torrance, Calif. 1988-90; mem: Calif. Hispanic Am. Med. Assn.; rec: spending time with twin daughters. Ofc: 12598 Central Ave. Suite #D Chino 91710

COLVIN, IRIS VENITA IOLA, construction/property management executive; b. Apr. 15, 1914, Ashland, Ore.; d. Clarence Victor and Cozensa Delvina (Clark) Atterbury; m. Lloyd Colvin, Aug. 11, 1938; dau., Joy b. 1940; edn: BA, UC Berkeley 1937; cert. Univ. Heidelberg, Germany 1955; FCC Extra Class radio opr. lic.; Calif. lic. gen. contr./real estate broker. Career: staff W. A. Bechtel Corp., bldg. the Alaska Hwy. and CANOL oil line project during WWII; with US Govt. GSA in Japan after WWII; v.p./treas. Drake Builders, Calif. Corp. (constrn. internat.), 1947-; honors: Delta Epsilon; life mem. No. Calif. DX Club (past pres.), life mem. Am. Radio Relay League (fmr. Calif. QSL mgr.), mem. Radio Club of Am.; author: How to make a Million Dollars in the Construction Business (Prentice Hall), Book of the Month Club selection and also Best Seller list; rec: amateur radio opr. (W6QL), art, writing. Address: 5200 Panama Ave Richmond 94804

COLWELL, BUNDY, mortgage banker, ret.; b. Aug. 24, 1912, Ely, Nev.; s. Alfred Bundy and Pearl (O'Brien) C.; m. Anne Jackson, Aug. 28, 1940; children: Stephen Bundy b. 1943, Penelope Anne Dick b. 1947; edn: BS, BA, Coll. of Commerce, USC 1934, JD, Law Sch. 1936; admitted bar Calif.; Career: atty., dir., v.p., gen. counsel Calif. Fed. Savings and Loan Assn.; incorporating dir. Belmont Savings and Loan Assn.; dir. Great Western Savings So. Calif., chmn. bd. CMT Investment Co.; pres./CEO, chmn. of bd. The Colwell Co., Mortgage Bankers, co. sold to Baldwin United Corp. of Cinti. 1980, currently cons.; mem: ABA, L.A. Bar Assn., Nat. Assn. Real Estate Bds., Nat. Inst. Real Estate Brokers, Nat. Home Builders Inst., Alpha Kappa Psi, Phi Alpha Delta, Lambda Alpha, Commerce Assocs., Mortgage Bankers Assn. Am. (bd. govs., reg. v.p., exec. com., chmn. pub. rel. com., FHA and GI svcg. com., attys. com.), Calif. Mortgage Bankers Assn., So. Calif. Mortgage Bankers Assn., Phi Kappa Tau; civic: Legion Lex, Town Hall, L.A. C. of C., Calif. State C. of C., U.S. C. of C., Masons, Shriners, Gen. Alumni Assn. USC, Trojan Club, Jonathan Club, Ch. of Lighted Window (moderator, chmn. bd. trustees, long range planning com., bldg. fin. com.), Calif. Hist. Soc., Western Hist. Assn., Nat. Geographic Soc., Mont. Hist. Soc., The Westerners, L.A. Posse, Audubon Soc., Nat. Wildlife Assn., Am. Forestry Assn., Izaak Walton League Am., Club de Caza y Pesca de Las Cruces, bd. trustees Flintridge Preparatory Sch. for Boys; Comml. Pilot, rated single and multi engine land and single sea, instr., and flight instr., ground sch. instr., rated navigation, meteorol., and civil air regulations; mil: flight inst. U.S. Army Air Corps. Res: 5239 Don Ricardo Dr Carlsbad 92008

COMSTOCK, MARIE ALKIRE, psychotherapist; b. March 3, 1942, Point Pleasant, NJ; d. Nicholas and Lucille (Vitolo) Bilella; m. Robert Alkire, Jan. 10, 1983; children: Tammy Bevins, Angela Shama; edn: BA, UC Riverside 1978; M., Internat. Univ. Los Angeles 1984; Marriage Family and Child Counselor, Calif.; Psychological Asst., Calif. 1986. Career: substance abuse counselor My Family Inc., Riverside 1977-79; asst. adminstr. Children's Human Devel. Ctr., UC Riverside 1974-80; instr. Riverside City Coll. and child devel. EAP, Alcoholic Studies 1979-; woman's pgm. coord., counselor, outreach coord. Riverside County Mental Health, Drug Abuse Control Svcs., Riverside 1980-84; psychological asst., marriage family child counselor, Center for Active Psychology, Riverside 1981-; instr. San Bernardino Valley Coll., San Bernardino 1985-; bd. mem. Riverside Co. Coalition for Alternatives to Domestic Violence; honors: Riverside Co. Mental Health Recogn. Award 1980; Senior Ctr. Award, Corona 1982; mem: UC Riverside Steering & Task Force Commn., Riverside Co. Local Plnng. Commn., Norco/ Corona Emergency Counsel, UC Riverside Adv. Com. for the Psychology Ctr., Bus. & Profl. Women (pres. Riverside chpt. 1976); publs: articles in child abuse, spousal abuse and cross cultural bilingual research; Democrat; R.Cath.; rec: painting, meditation, yoga. Ofc: 7302 Magnolia Ave Riverside 92504

CONGDON, JEFFREY HARTLEY, real estate broker; b. May 17, 1944, Duluth, Minn.; s. Gilford and Marion Congdon; m. Katherine Cleveland Burkett, Mar. 16, 1974; children: Elisabeth Burkett, Chester Adgate, Katherine Cleveland; edn: Woodside Priory Sch., Menlo Coll., BS, UC Santa Barbara. Career: v.p. Grubb & Ellis Co., San Francisco 1972-74; sr. v.p. Cushman & Wakefield Co., San Francisco 1974-; pres., dir. Congdon Orchards, Yakima, Wa. 1991-; dir. Burkett Land Co. 1974-; dir. Urban Land Inst.; mem. bd. trustees Cathedral Sch. for Boys, bd. trustees Woodside Priory Sch., Portola Valley 1990-, bd. dirs. YMCA S.F.; clubs: Bohemian (SF), Menlo CC, California, S.F. Olympic. Ofc: Bank of America Bldg. 555 California St Ste 2700 San Francisco 94104

CONGDON, KATHERINE BURKETT (Mrs. Jeffrey Hartley Congdon), real estate investor, civic leader; b. June 21, 1947, San Mateo; d. William Andrew and Juliet (Johnson) Burkett; m. Jeffrey Hartley Congdon, Mar. 16, 1974; children: Elisabeth Burkett, Chester Adgate, Katherine Cleveland; edn: Pine Manor Jr. Coll., Chestnut Hill, Mass., Univ. Calif. Berkeley, Briar Cliff Coll., Briarcliff, NY; BA, 1970. Career: v.p. and treas. Nat. Hist. Found. 1970-75; exec. sec. Booze Hamilton, Mgmt. Consultants, San Francisco 1972-74; exec. dir. Med. Research Inst., San Francisco 1974-77; bd. dirs. Burkett Land Co. 1968-; civic: San Francisco Jr. League (bd.), St. Luke's Hosp. Jr. Auxiliary (pres.), Pine Manor Alumni Assn., Kappa Alpha Theta (pres.), Med. Research Inst. S.F. (dir.), S.F. Symphony Aux. (pres.), Mt. Rushmore Hall of Records Com. (trustee), D.A.R. (life); club: Town & Country (SF). Address: 3675 Washington St San Francisco 94118

CONKLIN, RONALD LEWIS, real estate co. executive; b. July 26, 1938, Omaha, Nebr.; s. Lewis Roscoe and Irma Virginia Conklin; married; 4 children: Sheryl b. 1961, William b. 1962, Denise b. 1964, Damon b. 1973; edn: BS, San Jose State, 1961, MBA, Golden Gate Univ., 1981; expert appraiser M.B.A.R.E. Career: dept. mgr. Peterson Tractor Co., Redding 1965-68; mgr. Woodren Realty, Castro Valley 1968-75; owner R.L.C. Commercial Real Estate, Castro Valley 1975-78; pres. and c.e.o. Ron L. Conklin Inc., Castro Valley 1978-; instr. Golden Gate Univ. Grad. Sch. of Fin. 1983; dir. Calif. Real Estate Ednl. Inc. 1983; mem: Soc. for Adv. of Mgmt., Bd. Realtors, Blue Key, Elks, Veterans Club; mil: 1st lt. US Air Force 1961-64; Republican; Lutheran; rec: golf, bridge. Ofc: 3726 Castro Valley Blvd Castro Valley 94546

CONLON, JACK MARTIN, real estate executive; b. Oct. 8, 1931, Parsons, Kans.; s. John Thomas and Alice M. Conlon; m. Kathi Bergman, Feb. 29, 1984; children: Lisa b. 1955, Catherine b. 1957, Julia b. 1958 (dec.), Casey b. 1985; edn: BS, Kansas Univ., 1957; USC, 1957-58; Calif. lic. C.P.A. (1960). Career: CPA, Peat Marwick Mitchell, Los Angeles 1957-59, Kansas City 1960-63; pres. Coachella Valley Sav. & Loan, Palm Springs 1963-72; exec. v.p. Sunrise Co., Los Angeles 1972-76, pres. Sunrise Co., Palm Desert 1976-; instr. Am. Sav. & Loan Inst. 1965-66; mem. Tri-County Soc. of Sav. & Loan Controllers (pres. 1966), Palm Springs Conv. & Vis. Bur. (dir., treas. 1967-72), Palm Springs C.of C. (pres. 1971), Phi Kappa Psi Frat., PGA West, Rancho Santa Fe Farms Golf Club; civic: United Way (dir., treas. 1966-67), Coachella Valley Mountains Conservancy (1991-); mil: US Navy; Republican; rec: golf. Ofc: 42-600 Cook St Palm Desert 92260

CONRAD, JOHN WILFRED, ceramic artist, educator; b. Aug. 3, 1935, Cresson, Pa.; s. Wilfred Lee and Elizabeth (Bouch) C.; m. Barbara Jean Daugherty, June 5, 1963; children: William T. b. 1969, Kristin E. b. 1973; edn: BS art edn., Ind. State Univ., 1958; MFA ceramics, Carnegie-Mellon Univ., 1963; PhD ceramic res., Univ. Pittsburgh, 1970. Career: art instr. Penn Hills (Pa.) High Sch., 1959-64; instr. Carnegie-Mellon Univ., 1961-64; prof. of fine arts Mesa Coll., San Diego 1966-, chmn. art dept. 1980-82, 85-88, academic senator 4 terms; consultant: Kennywood Amusement Park, Pitts., float bldr., artist and cons. 1960-63, Am. Cement Corp., Riverside, Ca. 1968-73, Baby Keepsakes, Thousand

Oaks 1990-, KD Corp., Dallas, Tx. 1983-, various local potteries; devel. unique glazes and clay bodies for individual studio ceramists; exh. ceramics and ceramic sculpture 1963-: Three Rivers Fest., Pitts.; Allied Artists, Pitts.; Tiffany Invitational; Small Sculpture, Nat., Cypress Gal.; Sculpture Gal., San Diego; Soup Tureens, Campbell Mus.; one man show Oceans West Gal., Sa Diego; Group Ceramics Exhibits, Seattle; Ceramic Artists of San Diego; Allied Craftsmen, San Diego; mem.: Ceramic Artists S.D. (bd.), Nat. Coun. Edn. Ceramic Arts (bd.), Allied Craftsmen SD.; author: Ceramic Formulas: The Complete Compendium (MacMillan 1973), Contemporary Ceramic Techniques (Prentice Hall 1976), Contemp. Ceramic Formulas (MacMillan 1980), Ceramic Windchimes (Falcon Pub. 1984), Adv. Ceramic Manual (Falcon Pub. 1988), Studio Potters Dict. (Falcon 1989), Cone Six Ceramics (Falcon 1994), contbr. mag. articles; rec: skiing, ocean fishing, scuba. Res: 770 Cole Ranch Rd Encinitas 92024 Ofc: Art Dept. Mesa Coll. Mesa College Dr San Diego 92111

CONROE, MARK GUSTAV, real estate developer b. Jan. 21, 1958, Hartford, Conn.; s. Wallace Weller Conroe and Marie-Anne (Langenskiold) Conroe-Harris; edn: undergrad. US Mil. Acad., West Point 1976-78; BSCE, Stanford Univ., 1980, MSCE, 1981, MBA, 1985; E.I.T. cert., Calif. 1980. Career: staff scientist Energy Resources Co., Walnut Creek 1981-82; prodn. engr. Sohio Petroleum Co., San Francisco 1982-83; cons. McKinsey and Co., Dallas, Tx. 1984; ptnr. Mozart Devel. Co., Palo Alto 1985-; awards: Pepsico Found. fellow 1984, Ctr. for Engrepreneurship Best Service Co. award- $1500 1984-85, grantee The Shidler Group, Stanford 1985; civic: founder Ctr. for Entrepreneurship, E.Palo Alto 1989-, steering com. Bayshore Workers 1991-, Cancer Support & Edn. Ctr. Menlo Park (bd. 1989-), S.F. Child Abuse Council (bd. 1983-85); pub. article in Real Estate Rev. (1985); Christian; rec: tennis, triathlons, travel. Ofc: Mozart Development Co. 435 Tasso St Ste 300 Palo Alto 94301

CONSIDINE, SHARON CULVER, restauranteur; b. June 6, 1942, San Diego; d. Harold Bell Wright and Elaine Lois (Smith) Culver; m. Timothy Malcolm Considine, Aug. 18, 1962; children: Kevin b. 1963, Kenneth b. 1965, Kelly b. 1970; edn: San Diego St. Univ. 1960-63 (treas. Assoc. Women Students). Career: owner/opr. Mexican Village Restaurant, 1973-; owner/agent TNT Travel Agency, 1975-82; real estate agt., 1976-; bd. dirs. Bank of So. Calif., 1983-; awards: Co. of San Diego Merit Certif. for devel. of Las Ayudantes Aux. 1974, Peninsula YMCA Woman of Yr. 1986, service Coronado Rotary 1988, San Diego Restaurateur of Yr. 1990, Mex-Am. Found. "Amiga de Mexico" 1990, listed Who's Who in We. States 1983, Who's Who in World of Internat. Women 1984; mem: San Diego Restaurant Assn. (founding mem., pres. 1981), Calif. Restaurant Assn. (state bd. 1983-), Coronado C.of C. (dir. 1988-, pres. 1990), Coronado Rotary 1990-, SDSU Alumni Assn. (dir. 1980-84), Pi Beta Phi Sor. Alumnae (past pres.); civic bds: USO (ofcr., dir. 1987-), Aztec Athletic Found. (dir., pres. 1981-85), San Diego Super Bowl Com. (rep. 1984-88), Coronado Hosp. Found. (dir. 1984-89), SDSU Pres.'s Council 1984-89, Industry Council for Hotel and Rest. Mgmt. 1985-86, U.S. Internat. Univ. (dir. 1985-86), Mercy Hosp. Aux. (Pink Lady 1964-69), Ladies Aux. for Retarded Children (mem. and pres. 1970-76), Las Ayudantes for teenagers on probation (founder 1973-75), Pt. Loma Cub Scout Ldr. 1974-75, Sunset View Sch. (tchr.'s asst. 1978-79), Pt. Loma Girl Scout Ldr. 1980-82; Republican; R.Cath.; rec: running, skiing, travel. Ofc: Mexican Village Restaurant 120 Orange Ave Coronado 92118

CONSIDINE, TIMOTHY MALCOLM, certified public accountant; b. Nov. 20, 1940, Palo Alto; s. Charles Ray and Thalia Houston (Kelly) C.; m. Sharon Elaine Culver, Aug. 18, 1962; children: Kevin b. 1963, Kenneth b. 1965, Kelly b. 1970; edn: BS, San Diego St. Univ. 1962; C.P.A. Career: staff Considine & Considine, San Diego 1960-62, sr. 1962-64, mgr. 1964-65, ptnr. 1965-; chmn. San Diego Co. Civil Service; awards: San Diego St. Univ. outstanding alumnus; mem: Am. Inst. C.P.A., San Diego Space & Sci. Found. (bd. trustees); articles pub. in profl. jours. (1970-); Republican; R.Cath.; rec: philately, travel. Res: 545 Ocean Blvd Coronado 92118 Ofc: Considine & Considine 1501 5th Ave Ste 400 San Diego 92101

COOK, DONALD FREDERICK, mechanical engineer; b. July 26, 1916, Bisbee, Ariz.; s. Fred C. and Bessie (Lineberger) C.; m. Alice Lindsay, Feb. 22, 1942 (dec. 1972); children: Donna Lindsay Sedgewick, Nancy Lee Case; edn: pre-engring. UCLA, 1935-37, mech. engring., UCB, 1939; BE, USC, 1942; reg. profl. mech. engr. (ME#4553) Calif. Career: mech. engr. Continental Oil Co., Ventura 1939-41; Army Ordinance, L.A. 1941-42; lt.s.g. USNR 1943-46, office staff U.S. Naval Gun Factory, Wash. DC 1943-45, R.O.I.C. (resident officer in charge) naval ordnance Consol. Steel Co., 1945-46; chief engr. Wilson Oil Tool, Ventura 1946-54; mech. R.O.I.C. USN, Point Mugu 1955-60, supply ofcr. navy yards and docks Port Hueneme 1960-63; project engr. US Small Bus. Adminstrn., L.A. 1963-72, ret. civil service 1972; mem. Profl. Engrs. Calif., Petroleum Club (L.A.), Elks, Am. Legion; Democrat; Ch. of God; rec: swimming, R.V.ing. Res: 1150 Chambersburg Rd Fillmore 93015

COOK, LYNETTE RENE, illustrator, educator; b. Jan. 1, 1961, Herrin, Ill.; d. Kenneth Severin Cook and Charlotte Cecelia Cook-Fuller; edn: BS, Miss. Univ. for Women, 1981, BFA, 1982; MFA, Calif. Coll. of Arts & Crafts, Oakland 1984. Career: freelance artist, San Francisco 1983-; artist, photographer

Morrison Planetarium, Calif. Acad. of Scis., S.F. 1984-; art instr. Calif. Acad. of Scis. 1988-, UC (Ext.) Berkeley 1989-; guest lectr. UC Santa Cruz 1989-; fine artist; exhibits incl. Art of the Cosmos, Hayden Planetarium, Am. Mus. of Natural Hist., NY, NY 1992, Guild of Natural Sci. Illustrs. Nat. Exh. Durham, N.C. 1991, Santa Barbara, Ca. 1989, Denver 1988, Mus. of Natural Hist., Smithsonian, W.D.C. 1986, Naturalists: Paintings and Drawings of Life, Reese Bullen Gal., Humboldt State Univ. 1991, Strybing Arboretum 50th Ann. Exh., S.F. 1990, illustr. Notecubes, gift wrapping paper, cards, mugs, posters for various cos., 1990-; awards: Guild of Natural Sci. Illustrs. (GNSI) Traveling Exh., art selected for permanent collection 1985, 89, 1st pl., 2-dimensional category "Bridge Works" art contest commemmorating 50th ann. of Golden Gate Bridge 1987, DESI Award, Graphic Design: USA 1988, juror "Calif. Species: Biol. Art and Illustrn." The Oakland Mus. 1989, listed Outstanding Young Women Am. 1985, American Artists 1989, Who's Who in the West 1991; mem: GNSI (mem. 1980-, exec. bd. 1986-), Internat. Assn. for the Astronomical Arts 1988-; rec: gardening, cooking, hiking. Ofc: Morrison Planetarium, Calif. Academy of Sciences, Golden Gate Park, San Francisco CA 94118

COOMBS, JIM LE, high school educator; b. June 14, 1964, Wheatridge, Colo.; s. Leroy G. Coombs and Johnnie (Lyles) Maschhoff; edn: H.S. diploma, Immanuel Christian H.S., Ridgecrest, Calif., 1982; BS, Cal Poly, Pomona, Calif., 1987; sec. tchg. cred., Cal Poly, Pomona, 1987. Career: custody control ofcr., USN China Lake, Calif., 1982-86; motor devel. clinician, Cal Poly, 1984-87; CIF basketball ofcl., CIF, Pomona, 1984-91; head freshman football coach and jr. varsity baseball coach, San Dimas H.S., San Dimas, Calif., 1985-91; sci. educator, Ramona Middle Sch., La Verne, Calif., 1988-91; sci. educator, Cathedral City H.S., Cathedral City, Calif., 1991-; QUEST educator, Ramona Middle Sch., 1989-91; head baseball coach and varsity asst. football coach, Cathedral City H.S., 1991-; awards: Academic All-Amer., Nat. Honor Soc., 1986-87; Outstanding Young Men of Amer., 1988-89; listed Who's Who in the West, 1991-92; mem: Fellowship of Christian Athletes 1980-, Nat. Tchrs. Assn. 1989-, Calif. Baseball Coaches Assn. 1988-, Amer. Baseball Coach Assn. 1990-; civic: Cathedral City H.S. Booster Club; PTA, Ramona Middle Sch.; Republican; Baptist; rec: gardening, model trains, wildlife. Res: 30592 Ave. Maravilla Cathedral City 92234 Ofc: Cathedral City H.S., 69250 Dinah Shore Ave. Cathedral City 92234

COOMES, GERALDINE SAWYER, youth counselor, teacher; b. Mar. 20, 1935, San Francisco; d. Albert Pierce and Margaret (Bird) Sawyer; m. Joseph E. Coomes, Jr., June 17, 1955, div. 1985; children: Bryan b. 1960, Harlan b. 1961; edn: AA, Santa Rosa Jr. Coll. 1954; AB with honors, Sacramento State Coll., 1960, grad. work 1965; Univ. of La Verne 1981; Inst. of Children's Literature, Conn. 1987-; Calif. std. tchg. cred., gen. K-8 (1960). Career: recreation dir. Co. of Sonoma, Santa Rosa 1954, playground dir. City of Berkeley 1955, clk. Registrar's ofc. UCB 1955-58; substitute tchr. Sacto. Unified Sch. Dist. 1967-69, San Juan U.S.D., Carmichael 1968-71, Elk Grove U.S.D. 1980-84, Sacto. Co. Office Edn. (2 dists.) 1985-89, Yolo Co. (1 dist.) 1986-89; lab. svs. helper Calgene Inc. (plant bio-genetics firm), Davis 1989-91; tchr. aide The Poppy Patch Child Care Ctr., Sacto. 1991-, also youth counselor Royal Gardens Youth Care Home, Sacto. 1992-93; apptd. Sacto. Co. Office of Voter Reg. & Elections (judge 1964-79, supr. election bd. 1980-85); awards: 3d pl./named Miss Personality, Miss Sonoma County camp. 1953; civic: mgr. singing group The Mockingbirds (vol. entertain nsg. homes), vol., co-chair and Easter bunny for Easter Egg Hunt, Calgene Inc., Davis 1991, PTA (pres. Thos. Jefferson Elem. 1967-68); club: College Greens Swim & Racquet; pubs: World of Poetry Anthols. (1983, 84, 85, 86), Golden Poet Award (1985, 86, 87, 92); Democrat; Presbyterian; rec: write stories for children, write song lyrics, feed blue jays. Res: 8322 Citadel Way Sacramento 95826

COPPERMAN, WILLIAM HAROLD, value engineering consultant; b. Dec. 4, 1932 Cleve., Oh.; s. Jack Jason and Ruth (Rollnick) C.; m. Rena June Dorn, Dec. 26, 1954, div. 1978; children: Randy Lee b. 1956, David Marc b. 1962; edn: BS, Duquesne Univ., Pitts., Pa., 1954; MBA, Univ. So. Calif., L.A., 1962; JD, Univ. San Fernando, L.A., 1977; career: corp. mgr. of value engring. Hughes Aircraft, L.A., 1957-89; pres. Cave, Inc., L.A., 1983-; certified value spec. (CVS) Soc. of Am. Value Engrs., 1983; mem. Miles Value Found., 1977-84; exec. v.p. Soc. of Am. Value Engr., 1984-88; dir. certification bd., SAVE, 1986-88; instr. engring. extension, No. Caro. State, 1986-; dir., Miles Value Found. 1988-; awards: Outstanding Achievement, US Army AMC, 1986; Value Engring. Award, Purchasing Mag., 1987; Achievement in VE, US Army (Huntsville, Ala.), 1977-82; mem: Soc. of Am. Value Engrs (SAVE), 1975-; civic: mem, Nat. Rifle Assn., Am. Legion, Disabled Am. Vet.; author: book, Guide to Value Engring., 1986; ed., dod handbook on Value Engring., 1986; author video tape series, Value Engring., 1987; over 30 pub. articles on Value Engring., 1976-; mil: capt. USA, 1954-62; rec: computer programming, tennis, golf. Ofc: P.O. Box 5488 Playa del Rey 90296

CORCOS, HENRI, real estate broker; b. Jan. 15, 1926, Marrakech, Morroco, naturalized 1981; s. Meyer and Henriette Hanina (Calfon) C.; m. Suzanne, Sept. 10, 1959; children: Alan Simon b. 1961, Rachel Edith b. 1967; edn: C.P.A., Academie d/Algiers (French Univ.), 1947; R.E. broker, Anthony Sch., L.A. 1986. Career: treas. secty. Fougerolle Travaux Publios, Casablanca 1947-49; dir.

Ets: Rouge, Norbonne, France 1953-60; sr. mgmt. cons. George S. May Internat., Paris, Fr. 1960-62; mktg. dir. Publinel, Paris 1962-65; cons./dir. Pronuptia, Paris 1966-74; mgmt. cons. prin., Paris & Los Angeles 1975-77; real estate broker assoc. Wagner Jacobson Inc., L.A. 1977-87; broker/pres. Henri Corcos Brokerage, Sherman Oaks 1988-; recipient numerous mgmt. and R.E. sales awards; mem: Comte Nat. Orgn. Francais, Paris 1961-74, San Fernando Valley Bd. of Realtors 1977-; mil: adj. chief Infanterie 1949-51; Republican; Jewish; rec: sports, bus., travel. Res: 5239 Saville Ave Encino 91436 Ofc: Henri Corcos Brokerage, 14219 Dickens St Ste 4 Sherman Oaks 91403

CORMIER, MARK S., poet; b. Nov. 25, 1960, Dover, Del.; s. Rene Victor and Margaret Mary (Moreau) C.; m. Catherine Elizabeth Breitman, May 30, 1992; edn: H.S. diploma, St. John's Prep., Danvers, Mass. 1978; AB, Dartmouth Coll. 1982. Career: reporter, North Shore Weeklies, Danvers, Mass. 1982-83; caller, Pacific Stock Exchange, S.F. 1983-92; mem. Sutter Station Historical Soc., S.F. 1986-; lectr., Toronado Tempest Oratorical Club, S.F. 1988-92; awards: runner-up Time Capsule, Mills Bldg., S.F. 1992; mem. Dartmouth Alumni Assoc. 1982-; Am. Legion, S.F.; poetry moderator, Cafe Babar, S.F. 1986, 88; ed., 2 books: Dr. Irony 1987, 26 Numbers in the Alphabet 1989; author, 2 books: I Hear a Tear,1988, Lilly 1992; Democrat; Catholic; rec: trapshooting, history. Res: 428 Haight St. San Francisco 94114. Ofc: Pacific Stock Exchange, 2nd Flr Options Flr 220 Bush St. San Francisco 94114

CORNWALL, KENT NEELEY, architect; b. Feb. 26, 1954. Salt Lake City; s. J. Shirl and Lenore (Neeley) C.; m. Susan Hodgkinson, June 19, 1979; children: Jason, 1980; Robert, 1982; Kathryn, 1984; Jeffrey, 1986; Rachel, 1989; Sarah, 1992; edn: BA, Calif. Polytechnic Institute, Pomona, 1979; licensed architect, Calif. State Reg. Bd.; career: vice pres., Cornwall Assoc. Inc., Pasadena, 1980-92; pres., Cornwall Assoc. Inc., Pasadena, 1992-; mem: Nat. Trust for Historic Preservation, 1988-; Monrovia Preservation Group, 1987-; leader, Boy Scouts of Am., 1989-; Calif. and Nat. A.I.A., 1979-; Republican; Ch. Jesus Christ Latter-Day Saints; rec: house restorations; skiing; res: Monrovia.

CORRIGAN, ROBERT ANTHONY, university president; b. Apr. 21, 1935, New London, Conn.; s. Anthony John and Rose Mary (Jengo) C.; m. Joyce Mobley, Jan. 12, 1975; children: Kathleen Marie b. 1960, Anthony John b. 1963, Robert Anthony b. 1965, Erika Mobley b. 1968; edn: dipl. Classical High Sch., Springfield, Mass. 1953; AB, Brown Univ., 1957; MA, Univ. Pa., 1959, PhD 1967. Career: researcher Phila. Historical Commn. 1957-59; lectr. Univ. Gothenburg, Sweden 1959-62, Bryn Mawr Coll. 1962-63; instr. Univ. Pa. and vis. lectr. Phila. Mus. Coll. of Art, 1963-64; instr. Univ. Iowa, 1964-66, asst. prof., assoc. prof. of Eng. and Am. Civilization 1966-1973; vis. prof. Am. Studies, Grinnell Coll. 1970; dean Coll. of Arts and Scis./prof. of Eng., Univ. Mo., Kansas City 1973-74; provost for Arts and Humanities and prof. of English, Univ. Md., College Park 1974-79; chancellor and prof. English, Univ. Mass., Boston 1979-88; pres. and prof. English & Humanities, San Francisco State Univ., 1988-; mem. Calif. St. Univ. Educational Equity Advy. Council 1988-92, Asian Pacific Am. Edn. Advy. Gp. 1989-; dir. First Trade Union Savings Bank, FSB, 1986-88; mem. Econ. Devel. Corp., 1989-91, Modern Greek Studies Found., 1989-, Advy. Council Calif. Acad. Scis., 1988-; mem. ednl. advy. com. JFK Library 1979-88, bd. dirs. JFK Library Found. 1983-91, Friends of the JFK Library, 1983-; trustee Boston Coll. High Sch. 1984-90; editl. advy. bd. Yale Univ. Black Periodical Fiction Proj.; awards: Phi Beta Kappa, full tuition scholar Brown Univ. 1953-57, Clarkson Able Collins, Jr. maritime hist. prize 1956, Univ. Pa. Carnegie fellow 1957-59, Pa. Colonial Soc. essay award (1st pl. 1958, 1959), Smith-Mundt vis. prof. 1959-60, Fulbright lectr. 1960-62, Standard Oil Found. of Ind. tchg. excellence 1968, Nat. Endowment for Humanities/Ford Found. grantee 1969, NEH grantee 1970) NEH proj. grantee to develop Afro-Am. Studies Pgm. 1970-71, 71-74, Rockefeller Found. grantee 1972-75, Mo. State grantee for Summer Inst. on the Black Woman in Am. Culture 1974, US State Dept. lectr. in Africa and Asia 1977, comm. svc. award Freedom House 1985, comm. svc. award Action for Boston Comm. Devel. 1986, Wm. Lloyd Garrison Award of Mass. Ednl. Opp. Assn. 1987, named Distinguished Urban Fellow of The Assn. of Urban Univs. 1992-; mem: No. Am. Council Internat. Assn. of Univ. Presidents (steering com. 1981-), Mass. Council of Pub. Presidents and Chancellors (chmn. 1983-84), Assn. of Urban Univs. (chmn. 1988-92), World Affairs Council (dir. Boston 1983-88, dir. Bay Area 1991-94), San Francisco C.of C. (dir. 1989-92); clubs: University, City; numerous pub. lectures, frequent speaker nat. confs. and assn. annual meetings; contbr. numerous articles in literary jours. Ofc: San Francisco State Univ. 1600 Holloway Ave San Francisco 94132

CORTSEN-DIAZ, LENE, accountant, historical preservation activist; b. Jan. 23, 1941, Copenhagen, Denmark; d. Thorvald Cortsen and Gerda (Christophersen) Jansberg; m. Joseph Jimenez Diaz, Aug. 2, 1969 (div. Apr. 1976); son, Rodrigo Ximenez Diaz b. 1971; edn: Mar Vista H.S., San Diego, 1959; eve. sch., Sacto., 1959-60. Career: asst. lab. tech. Pillsbury, Sacto. 1961-63; asst. accts. payable Soule Steel, San Francisco 1963-64, Beckman & Jurgensen, Copenhagen, Dk. 1964-67, Mechanics Tool, 1968-71; acctg. Transbay Security, San Leandro, Calif. 1980-; civic bds: San Leandro Historical Marker Commn. (chair 1989-), Casa Peralta Found. (pres. 1990-92), mem. Nat.

Trust for Historic Preservation, Oakland Heritage Alliance, San Leandro Hist. Soc., Alameda Co. Hist. Soc.; Democrat; Lutheran; rec: Early California history & preservation. Res: 139 Williams St #B San Leandro 94577

CORWIN, JACK B., industrialist; b. July 10, 1951, New York; s. Howard Stanley and Sydelle (Friedman) C.; edn: BS bus. adminstrn., Univ. Md. 1978; MS mgmt., Yale Univ. 1980. Career: assoc. corp. fin. Advest Inc., Hartford, Conn. 1980-82; Drexel Burnham Lambert, N.Y.C. 1982-83; assoc. exec., corp. service E.F. Hutton 1983-84; v.p. PruCapital, Los Angeles 1984-86; pres. Huntington Holdings 1987-; chmn. Bianchi Holdings Inc., Temecula 1987; dir. Fairchild Industrial Products Co., Winston-Salem, N.C. 1989; mem. bd. dirs. Ketchum-Downtown YMCA; clubs: City Club on Bunker Hill, Yale; Neighborhood Ch. Pasadena; rec: classic autos. Res: 1051 Prospect Blvd Pasadena 91103 and 99 Emerald Bay Laguna Beach 92651

CORY, WILLIAM NICHOLAS, investor; b. June 20, 1911, Walsenberg, Colo.; s. Abraham Namen and Melia (Mittry) C.; m. Faye, May 18, 1946; children: William b. 1948, Robert b. 1949, Carol b. 1952; edn: stu. L.A. City Coll. 1930, Glendale City Coll. 1931-33. Career: mgr./opr. Idaho Motor Co. (400 car storage & service facility), Idaho Falls, Ida. 1934-38; owner/opr. Idaho Motor Co. - Oldsmobile Dealership Automotive Sales, Service and Storage, 1938-41; owner/opr. Cory Motor Co. - Oldsmobile, Packard, Cadillac, Automotive Sales and Service, Marshfield, Wis. 1941-51; capital investor, real estate acquisition, devel. & mgmt., 1951-; honors: life mem. The President's Club, Presdtl. Task Force, Presdtl. Found.; civic: sponsor Heritage Found., Inter-Am. Security Council, Peace Through Strength, Nat. Freedom Found.; contbr. Freedom Fighters Nicaraguan and Afghanistan, African Famine Relief, Inter-American Def.; mil: lt. USNR 1943-46; Republican; Episcopalian; club: San Diego CC; rec: golf. Res: Bonita 92002

COSTA, JOHN ANTHONY, family service agency coordinator; b. Oct. 20, 1946, San Francisco; s. Henry Milton and Martha Florence (Seineke) C.; edn: BA, San Francisco St. Univ., 1969; grad. studies George Washington Univ. 1969-73, Univ. of San Francisco 1987-88. Career: analyst internat. rels. Library of Congress Congressional Research Service, Wash. D.C. 1969-82; coordinator Family Service Agency of San Mateo Co., Burlingame 1984-; civic: Internat. Studies Assn. (chpt. sec. W.D.C. 1970-71), Commonwealth Club S.F., World Affairs Council No. Calif., Bentana Park Condominium Reston, Va. (pres., v.p., secty., 1977-81), bd. mem. St. Dunstan Sch. 1991-92. Res: 2250 Shelter Creek Ln San Bruno 94066 Ofc: Family Service Agency 1870 El Camino Real Ste 107 Burlingame 94010

COTTAM, CALVIN, chiropractor, international lecturer and teacher; b. Mar. 28, 1925, Salt Lake City; s. Nephi Livesay Cottam DC (originator of cranial adjusting, craniopathy) and Edwardena (Parry) C.; edn: grad. Chouinard Art Inst. (now Cal Arts) 1949; MA psych., David Seabury Sch. Psychology, 1953; DC, Cleveland Chiro. Coll., 1965; DC lic. Calif., New Zealand. Career: dr. of chiropractic; co-founder, instr. Found. for Living, Problems Anon., Creative Self Research, 1953-64; radio pgm. co-host: Living Today, L.A. 1954-55; dir. Inst. for the Study of Human Resources 1985-; extensive travel w/parents on cranial adjusting tchg. tours U.S. and Canada; internat. conf. World Chiropractic Cong. Switz. 1970; lecture tours incl. Spain 1971, Greece, USSR, Turkey, Yugoslavia, 1972, Japan, Taipei, Hong Kong, Singapore, Thailand, 1972, France, England, Ireland, Scotland, 1973, Scandinavia, England 1974, Australia, N.Z., Fiji, Tahiti, 1975, U.S., Mex., Can., 1976-, Egypt, Israel, 1983, China, 1983, 84 (invited by Chinese govt., mem. first official chiropractic information exchange group to China 1983), Europe, 1984, Brazil, Argentina, Alaska, 1986, Costa Rica, Panama, Colombia, Mex., 1987, U.K., Ireland, 1988, U.S. cities, Vancouver B.C. 1989, Carribbean 1990; mem: Nat. Writers League (nat. pres. 1958), David Seabury Sch of Psychol. Alumni Assn. (pres. 1955-6), Internat. New Thought Alliance (ch. Govt. Affairs 1957), C.of C., Civil Def., Nat. Vocat. Guidance Assn.; Wilshire Center, Country Club Park Assn. (dir., Info. Council); author: Head First for Health (1952, House-Warven); Fun, How To Take a Vacation Every Day; Living Without Strain; Don't Be Afraid of your Mind; Magic of Meditation; w/Bert M. Anderson: How To Write True To Yourself 1960; w/Reid Rasmussen DC (brother by adoption): Craniopathy for You and Others 1975; Cranial/Facial Adjusting/Craniopathy Step-by-step 1985, Technique in Pictures 1987; Illustrated Seminars 1986; co-prod. w/R. Rasmussen DC: 6 one-hr video tapes re cranial technics 1981; publs: Digest of Chirop. Economics 1981, The Smithsonian 1981; mil: s/sgt M.C. US Army WWII, Korea; rec: comparative studies of ancient/current philosophies. Address: 1017 S Arlington Ave Los Angeles 90019

COULTER, GEORGE PROTHRO, lawyer, vintner; b. June 8, 1930, El Dorado, Ark.; s. Edward Herbert and Estella Martha (Prothro) C.; brother of Murray W. Coulter, hd. biol. dept. Texas Tech Univ.; m. Gloria `Corky' Cohn, Dec. 28, 1952; children: Craig R. b. 1953, Christopher b. 1955, Cameron M. b. 1960; edn: AB in polit. sci., UC Los Angeles, 1951; JD, Geo. Washington Univ., 1957; adv. law, USC, 1958. Career: Lt. US Navy 1951-56, decorated Korean Service, K-1 to K-3 clusters, China Service (extended), UN Service; Nat. Security Agy. 1956-57; atty., assoc. Gordon & Weinberg, Los Angeles 1958-63; ptnr. Coulter & Coulter, 1964-78; atty. prin., now of counsel, Coulter,

Vernoff & Pearson, P.C., 1979-; dir. Parade Properties Inc., 1963-87; gen. ptnr. Welsh Hill Orgn. (vineyard and winery), Temecula Valley 1980-; honors: student body pres. Geo. Washington Univ. Law Sch. 1956-57; three-time individual winner Van Vleck Case Club appellate competition; mem: Theta Xi soc. frat., Phi Delta Phi legal frat., Alpha Phi Omega service frat., Scabbard & Blade mil. hon., Conning Tower naval hon., Hon. Soc. of Cymmrodorion, Les Amis Du Vin; author: "Parallel Lines: The Proth(e)ro(e) Genealogies" (1980), contbr. articles in legal jours. and philatelic jours., chapter author and cons. Calif. State Bar CEB books; Democrat; Presbyterian (elder); rec: genealogy, enology, philately, travel. Res: 589 Cocopan Dr Altadena 91001 Ofc: Coulter, Vernoff & Pearson, P.C., 490 S Fair Oaks Ave Pasadena 91105

COUNTRYMAN, CHARLES CASPER, analytical research chemist; b. Oct. 6, 1913, NYC; s. Walter Guy and Clara Elizabeth (Casper) C.; m. Veronica Mae Lenz, Oct. 3, 1953; edn: BS chem., Univ. Mich., 1934, MS chem., 1935. Career: analytical chemist West End Chemical Co., Westend, Calif. 1935-40; res. chemist Truesdail Labs., Los Angeles 1940-45; mng. chemist Wm. T. Thompson Co., 1945-50; analytical res. chemist Dart Industries Inc., 1950-75, ret.; honors: Nat. Honor Soc. (1931), pres. Chemistry - Physics Club (1930-31), biog. listings in Personalities of Am. (5th edit.), 5000 Personalities of World (2d edit.), Men of Achievement (14th edit.), Dict. of Internat. Biography (21st edit.); mem. Boy Scouts Am. (1925-27); mem. Am. Chem. Soc. (1953-); clubs: Pacific R.R. Soc., San Marino (1972-), Magic Castle, Hollywood (1979-); Republican; R.Cath.; rec: photog., model trains, astronomy, dancing, travel. Res: 19404 Shelford Dr Cerritos 90701

COVINGTON, JON SCOTT, international marketing executive/real estate developer; b. Nov. 18, 1950, Mt. Vernon, Ill.; s. Charles J. and Lois Ellen (Combs) C.; m. Linda Degenhardt, 1969; children: Jason, b. 1970; Eric, b. 1974; Travis, b. 1983; edn: BS, So. Ill. Univ. 1972; MBA, 1980. Career: mgmt. cons. Conley- Pihos Mgmt. Co., Milwaukee, Wisc. 1972-73; area sales mgr., Midwest, J.Frank & Son, Inc., L.A. 1973-75; pres./ founder Backdoor Inc., Mt. Vernon, Ill. 1975-76; pres./ founder Sunshine Prodns., Inc., Mt. Vernon, Ill. 1975-79; pres./ co- founder European Bus. Seminars Inc., Los Gatos 1983-1986; mkts. mgr. internat. sales Apple Computer, Cupertino 1980-86; pres. The Holding Co. Ltd., Cupertino 1986-88; exec. staff The Eh Team, Toronto, Ontario, Canada 1985-; Internat. Mktg. Cons., TGF Consultants, Paris France 1986-88; co-founder, U.S. director World Market Strategies Ltd., San Jose and London, Eng., 1987-; honors: Outstanding Svc. Phi Sigma Epsilon 1972, Canuck award Apple Computer Canada 1982, Outstanding Mkt. Proj., Apple Computer 1982, inducted SIU Alumni Hall of Fame 1989; mem: Am. Mktg. Assn., The Commonwealth Club, World Trade Orgn., Porsche Club of Am.; works: The Microcomputer in Industry Training, T.H.E. Journ. 3/82; The Uses of Apple in Training.. Or `Never Trust a Computer You Can't Carry', Soc. for Applied Learning Technology 1983; Republican; Presbyterian; rec: Porsche auto restoration, internat. travel. Res: 10450 Stokes Ave Cupertino 95014 Ofc: World Market Strategies Ltd., 4307 17th St San Francisco 94114

COVINO, JOSEPH, JR., writer; b. Jan. 24, 1954, Phenix City, Ala.; s. Joseph, Sr. and Eleanor Josephine (Bowen) C.; m. Elizabeth Perkins, June 1978 (div. Apr. 1981), 1 son, Michael John Perkins b. 1980; edn: AA, Pensacola (Fla.) Jr. Coll., 1974, AS law enf., 1980; BA crim. justice, Univ. W.Fla., 1976, BA econs., 1979, BA internat. studies, 1981; law enforcement cert. Fla., 1981. Career: social studies tchr. Cardinal Newman High Sch., West Palm Beach, Fla. 1978-79; author: ...And War For All (1983); Lab Animal Abuse (1990); awarded Alexander Wilbourne Weddell Prize, Geo. Washington Univ., D.C. 1975; Democrat; R.Cath.; rec: trumpet, Japanese Shotokan karate. Ofc: New Humanity Press PO Box 215 Berkeley 94701

COWDEN, ROBERT HAPGOOD, educator; b. Nov. 18, 1934, Warren, Pa.; s. Wallace Hapgood and (Sundelof) C.; m. Jacqueline Viviane Mailloux; children: Jonathan b. 1964, Jennifer b. 1965, Marc b. 1967, Adrienne b. 1969; edn: BA, Princeton Univ. 1956; BM, Eastman Univ. 1959; MM, 1960; DMA, 1966. Career: hd. fine arts Wayne St. Univ., Detroit, Mich. 1972-76; chair music dept. Univ. Nebr., Omaha 1974-76; San Jose St. Univ. 1976-82, prof. music 1976-; chair music CSSSA, Sacto. 1987-; awards: Fulbright scholar, 1959-61, Univ. Neb. grad. fellow, 1976, Univ. Mich. NEH fellow, 1985, NEH grant, 1987, 89, San Jose St. Univ. merit. prof., 1987, 88, 90; author: Concert & Opera Singers, Conductors, Instrumental Viruosi: A Bibliography of Biographical Materials, 1985, 87, 89, Opera Companies of the World: Selected Profiles, 1992; Episcopalian; rec: bibliography, gardening, book collecting. Ofc: San Jose State University Music Dept. San Jose 95192

COWLES, R. VERN, information systems executive; b. Feb. 20, 1943, Imperial, Nebr.; s. Arnold Riedler and Minnie Mable (Hatterman) C.; edn: BA, Doane Coll. 1965; MA, Wash. Univ. St. Louis 1968; MA, Sch. Theology Claremont 1989. Career: data systems analyst Registrar Recorder, City of Norwalk, 1975-77, head tally and mgmt. systems 1977-80, head elec. systems 1981-83, chief elec. systems 1984-, AIDS tng. ofcr. 1988; alt. rep. GIS Advy. Body, L.A. 1988-, chair GISAB stds. com. 1988-, chair GISAB tech. group 1988-91, GIS steering com. 1986-88; L.A. County Mgmt. Council 1984-; awards: L.A. County Prod. Com. plaque

1988, 90, certificate 1989, NACO awards 1979, 1989; literary reviewer G.C. Stone Library; articles in profl. jours. 1987-91; mil: lt. USN 1967-72; Republican; Episcopalian (L.A. Diocese coms. human sexuality, viable parishes, group on small parishes, mem. vestry Christ Ch., Ontario 1985-88); rec: reading, gardening. Res: 2251 Hummingbird Pl Pomona 91767-2147 Ofc: Registrar Recorder County Clerk 12400 Imperial Hwy Norwalk 90650

COX, FRANCES NORALLEN, educator; b. Oct. 15, 1919, Goodyear, Ariz.; d. Arthur Clinton and Florence E. (Miller) Plake; m. N. James Cox, Nov. 24, 1948; children: James b. 1950, Douglas b. 1958; edn: BA, Ariz. State Univ. 1941; stu. CSU San Francisco, Santa Clara Univ., Notre Dame Coll., UC Santa Cruz, UC Berkeley, CSU San Jose; tchg. credentials: elementary- life, Ariz. 1941, Ore. 1950, Calif. 1954, resource splst.- Learning Handicapped, Calif. 1972. Career: classroom tchr. Phoenix, Ariz. 1941-49, Fresno (Ca.) City Schs. 1949-50, Fresno Cty. Schs. 1953-56, Portland (Ore.) City Schs. 1960-64, tchr./resource splst. Palo Alto Unified Schs., 1964-87, ret.; devel. curriculum in Kdg. literature and elem. sci., Phoenix 1941-43; lead panel Assn. for Childhood Edn. Conv., Ariz. St. Univ. 1946, lead demonstr. for 2d gr. games Fresno County Schs., Fresno St. Coll. 1954, lead demonstr. for social studies for Portland City Schs., Portland Tchrs. Inst. 1962, master tchr. Fresno St. Coll. 1953, Ore. St. Univ.; biog. listins in Dir. of Disting. Americans (5th), Internat. Directory of Distinguished Leadership 3rd ed. 1991, World Who's Who of Women 1990-93, World Biog. Hall of Fame 1989; mem: Palo Alto Tchrs. Assn. (recipient WHO Award for outstanding svc. 1986), Remedial Reading Tchrs. 1961-73, Resource Splst. Orgn., Nat. Tchrs. Assn., Calif. Tchrs. Assn. (Polit. Action rep.), NEA, Calif. Retired Tchrs Assn. Mid-Penin. Div., Ariz. St. Univ. Valley of the Sun Mortar Board Alumni, tchr. orgns. in Phoenix, Fresno, and Portland, PTA 1941-, Sigma Phi Gamma Internat. Sor. 1941-47, Commonwealth Club Calif., Internat. Platform Assn., Sierra Club; mil: pilot Civil Air Patrol 1941-42, Pilot Wings 1941; Prot.; rec: travel, politics, environment, art. Res: 911 La Mesa Dr Menlo Park 94028 Ofc: Palo Alto Unified Schools 25 Churchill Ave Palo Alto 94306

COZAD, LYMAN HOWARD, city manager; b. May 22, 1914, Painesville, Ohio; s. Wm. Howard and Ethyl (Phelps) C.; m. Arliss Smith, Sept. 6, 1978; children: Bradford b. 1949, Roberta b. 1958, Kimberly b. 1965; edn: BS bus. adminstrn., Ohio St. Univ., 1935, MPA, 1936; postgrad. studies Yale, 1936-37, USC, 1948-57. Career: dir. examinations Los Angeles City Civil Service Commn., 1939-42; personnel officer Nat. Housing Agy., Wash. DC 1942-43; personnel dir. UNRRA, Wash. DC 1944-47; So. Calif. mgr. Louis J. Kroeger & Assocs., Los Angeles 1947-56; city mgr. City of Colton, 1957-64; adminstrv. ofcr. City of Beverly Hills, 1964-66; city mgr. City of Arcadia, 1966-77; So. Calif. mgr. League of Calif. Cities, 1977-84, ranger rider, p.t. 1985-; v.p. and So. Calif. rep. Public Service Skills Inc., Sacto., 1986-; instr. USC, 1941-42, 48-58, UC Riverside, 1961-63, CSU Long Beach, 1974-77; awards: Fletcher Bowron Award, Scapa Praetor USC 1985; mem: Am. Soc. for Pub. Adminstrn. 1939-, Internat. City Mgmt. Assn. 1957-, past mem. City Mgrs. Dept. LCC Sacto. (pres. 1972), So. Calif. Pub. Pers. Assn. L.A. (pres. 1942); Rotarian (dir. Colton 1961-62, Arcadia 1970-71); pub. articles (1941, 46); mil: pvt. US Army Air Corps 1943-44; rec: hiking, gardening. Res: 952 Canyon View Dr La Verne 91750 Ofc: Public Service Skills, Inc. 1400 K St Ste 400 Sacramento 95814

CRAIN, CLAIRE VIRGINIA (YEGGE), civic historian, teacher, reading specialist; b. Oct. 14, 1914, Sedro Wooley, Washington; d. Robt. Martin and Corinne Queen (Stiles) Yegge; m. John G. L. Crain, Dec. 30, 1939 (dec. Jan. 3, 1991; Industrial R.E. Broker and lic. Practitioner ICC, charter commr. Torrance Airport Commn.); children: Lawrence D. b. 1941, Cliff G. b. 1944; edn: BA in English, UC Los Angeles; MA, CSC Long Beach 1969; Calif. lifetime tchg. creds., cert. to counsel, child welfare and social work. Career: tchr./reading splst. Torrance Unified Sch. Dist., Active Reading orgns. 1955-79; mem: Torrance Library Commn. 1956-74, organizer and Hon. Life mem. Torrance Friends of the Library, initiated the library transfer from County library services to City of Torrance Library System (1966), honored by name on plaque in front of all Torrance City Libraries; named citizen of year Torrance Lions Club, Torrance City Council (1980), AAUW award, Hon. Life mem. and recogn. as organizer of both Torrance Hist. Soc. and Museum (1987); Founder Associated Hist. Societies of Ventura Co. (1988); Life mem. Conf. of Calif. Historical Socs. (regional v.p. for Ventura County); mem. Centinela Valley Hist. Soc., Ventura County Hist. Soc. (docent), Olivas Adobe (docent); Republican; Prot. Res: 85 Poinsettia Gardens Dr Ventura CA 93004

CRAMER, EUGENE NORMAN, engineer - nuclear power; b. Apr. 26, 1932, Arkansas City, KS; s. Norman Charles and Hulda Margaret (Maier) C.; m. Donna (Gagliardi) C., May 18, 1957 (dec. 1984); m. 2d. Marlene (Marjenhoff) C., Dec. 29, 1985; children: Lorene b. 1958, Kristine b. 1959, Eileen b. 1964, Carla b. 1965; edn: BS physics Kansas St. Coll. 1955; grad. Oak Ridge Sch. Reactor Tech. 1959; Claremont Grad. Sch. (MA mgmt. 1976; MBA 1984); reg. profl. engr. Calif. Career: engr. Westinghouse Bettis, Pittsburg 1955-57; devel. engr. Oak Ridge Nat. Lab., Oak Ridge, TN 1959-69; engr. advanced energy systems S. Calif. Edison, Los Angeles 1969-88; mgr. nuclear comms. 1988-; cons. U.S. Atomic Energy Commn. 1961-73; sect. ed. Nuclear Soc. Jour. 1964-69;

secty. Task Force Nuclear Safety Res., Electric Res. Council 1969-74; dir. programs Western Forum for Edn. 1982-; bd. dirs. Am. Nuclear Soc. 1978-81; awards: Am. Nuclear Soc. Merit Award 1981; Inst. Advancement of Engrs. (fellow); mem: Health Physics Soc. (secty. 1982); 35 articles pub. in tech. jours. 1957-; mil: 1st. lt. AUS 1957-59; Republican; R. Cath. Res: 2176 Via Teca San Clemente 92673. Ofc: S. Calif. Edison Box 128 San Clemente 92674

CRANE, STEVEN, company executive; b. Jan. 21, 1959, Los Angeles; s. Roger Deppen and Violet (Heard) C.; m. Peggy Anne Gilhooly, Apr. 25, 1987; dau. Allison Nicole b. 1989; edn: grad. Kurt T. Shery H.S., Torrance, Ca. 1976. Career: sales mgr. Mobar Inc., Torrance 1976-78; v.p. internat. mktg. Fluid Control Internat., Marina del Rey 1978-79; pres. and c.e.o. Fluid Control Internat., Torrance 1979-85; pres. and c.e.o. Kaempen USA Inc., Anaheim 1985-91; senior ptnr., chmn. bd. Western Finance Group Inc., Huntington Beach 1991-; dir. Pharmaceutical Venture Fund, Huntington Beach 1992; dir. TransMillennial Resource Corp. 1992-; dir./chmn. TMRC Venture Fund 1992-; dir. Artist Network 1992-; dir. Environmental Restoration, Inc. 1992-; awarded Legion d'Honneur, Am. Savate Fedn., Chgo. 1989; mem. Vanguard Bus. Leaders 1990-, Am. Savate Fedn. (dir. 1988-); pub. papers: Accessing Public Capital 1992, A Guide to Exempt Equity Offerings 1992; Republican; Prot.; rec: photog., savate, basketball, bird hunting. Ofc: Western Finance Group, Inc. 252 Pacific Coast Hwy Hermosa Beach 90254

CRAWFORD, WAYNE HALBURTON, JR., retired naval officer, financial executive; b. Apr. 20, 1927, Covina; s. Wayne H. and Emogene Victoria (Crews) C.; m. Camille Lamar Tribelhorn, May 15, 1948 (dec. Nov. 24, 1990); children: Gary M.; m. Lillian M. Frank, Sept. 1, 1991; edn: BA, USC, 1947, MS, 1978; MS, US Navy PG Sch., 1961. Career: commd. ensign, advanced through ranks to to capt. US Navy, 1947-77: chief naval ops. info. systems div. USN, W.D.C., 1969-72, asst. for automation orgn. joint chiefs of staff, 1972-75, staff, 1975-77, ret.; decorated Meritorious Service Medal 1975; branch mgr. Downey Savings, La Costa 1978-80; v.p., br. mgr. Central Savings, Coronado 1980-87; Coast Savings, Coronado 1987-88; honors: Phi Kappa Tau; mem. Navy League (v.p. 1985-86), TROA/ Coronado (v.p. 1986-87), Optimist (bd. 1985-87), Hammer Club/S.D., Aerospace Internat. Hall of Fame, Poets/ S.D. Res: 82 Port of Spain Rd Coronado 92118

CRIDER, HOYT, health care executive; b. June 5, 1924, Arley, Ala.; s. Lindsey C. and Bessie P. Crider; m. Judie Watkins, Nov. 2, 1951; children: Kim, Marc; edn: stu. Ga. Sch. of Tech., 1942-43; BS, Univ. S.C. 1946; MA, Univ. of Ala. 1949; D. Pub. Adminstrn., USC, 1954. Career: vis. asst. prof. (with USC team in Iran to estab. a mgmt. curriculum) Univ. of Tehran, 1954-56; adminstrv. analyst (orgn. & mgmt. surveys), L.A. Cty. 1956-59; v.p. Watkins and Watkins Constrn. Co., Hanford and Morro Bay, 1959-64; co-owner/adminstr. Kings Convalescent Hosp., Hanford 1964-66; adminstr. Villa Capistrano Convalescent Hosp., Capistrano Beach 1966-68; ptnr. Hunt and Crider, San Diego Conval. Hosp., 1968-70, pres./ceo, Health Care Enterprises Inc. 1970-; mem. Regional Hlth. Plnng. Commn. Kings Cty. 1963-64; Cert. Fellow Am. Coll. of Nursing Home Adminstrs. (mem. 1968-; pres. 1976-7), Calif. Chpt. ACNHA (pres. 1970-72); mem. Calif. Assn. of Health Facilities (past v.p. local chpt.); Gerontological Soc.; adv. com. to Calif. Bd. of Examiners for Nursing Home Adminstrs. 1972-73; mem. Chamber of Commerce (U.S., La Mesa, El Monte, San Clemente), Nat. Right to Work Com., Nat. Conservative PAC, Wang Computer Sys. Users Soc., AAAS, AARP, Kiwanis (past pres. San Clemente); patron South Coast Area Boys and Girls Club, Orange Co. Music Ctr.; mil: commd. ofcr. USNR 1941-54. Res: 2215 Avenida Oliva San Clemente 92673 Ofc: Health Care Enterprises, Inc. 407 N El Camino Real San Clemente 92672

CRILLY, EUGENE RICHARD, engineering consultant; b. Oct. 30, 1923, Phila., Pa.; s. Eugene John and Mary Virginia (Harvey) C.; m. Alice Royal Roth, Feb. 16, 1952; edn: BA, Central H.S. Phila. 1941; Mech. Engr., Stevens Inst. Tech. 1944; MS, 1949, MS, Univ. Pa. 1951; UCLA 1955-58. Career: res. engr. Keasbey & Mattison Co., 1951-54; sr. engr. L.A. div. No. Am. Aviation, 1954-57; process engr. Northrop div., Northrop Corp., 1957-59; project engr., Q.C. mgr. HITCO, Gardena 1959-62; sr. engr. Rocketdyne & Space divs. No. Am. Aviation 1962-66; sr. res. splst. Lockheed Calif. Co. 1966-74; engring. specialist Rockwell Internat., North American Aircraft, 1974-89; engring. cons., 1989-; instr. econ. of engring. Stevens Inst. Tech. 1946-49; honors: Sigma Xi (1984), Award of Merit Soc. Advancement of Material and Process Engring. (1986), Who's Who Engring.; mem: Soc. Advancement of Material and Process Engring. (L.A. chpt. chmn. 1978-79, nat. dir. 1979-86, nat. treas. 1982-85, chmn. symposium and exhib. 1981), Soc. of Mfg. Engrs. (sr. mem.), Assn. Former Intelligence Ofcrs. (treas. San Diego Chpt. 1990-), Naval Intelligence Profls., Am. Soc. Composites, ASM Internat., V.F.W., Naval Reserve Assn., Mil. Order of World Wars, (adj. S.F.V. chpt. 1985-87, 2nd v. cmdr. 1986-87, cmdr. 1987-89, v.cmdr. West, Dept. Central Calif. 1988-89, cmdr. Cajon Valley - San Diego Chpt. 1990-92, Region XIV Adjutant 1990-91 and ROTC chmn. 1989-91, cmdr. Dept. of So. Calif. (1991-93), v. cmdr, reg. XIV (1992-93), Retired Ofcrs. Assn. (treas. Silver Strand Chpt. 1992-), Navy League of US, US Naval Inst., British United Services Club of L.A., Naval Order of the U.S., Sigma Nu; numerous tech. papers re adhesive bonding and advanced composites; mil: apprentice seaman & ensign USNR

1943-46, comdr. (ret.) 1975; Republican; R.Cath.; rec: Am. & W.W.II history. Address: 276 J Ave Coronado 92118-1138

CROFT, FREDERICK WILLIAM, venture capital executive; b. Mar. 30, 1948, Chgo.; s. William Frederick and Raphaelle (Ahles) C.; edn: AB, CSU Los Angeles, 1972; MA, UCLA, 1974. Career: cons. William M. Mercer, Los Angeles, 1984-85; mgr. technical analysis Walter Kaye Corp., Beverly Hills, 1985-86; sr. cons. KPMG Peat Marwick, Los Angeles, 1986-89; mng. ptnr. Pacific Venture Management, La Crescenta, 1989-; mem. bd. dirs. Nat. Cycle League, NY, NY, 1989-90; publs: mag. articles in Analog (1979-80), Galaxy (1979), Westways (1978); rec: archeology, martial arts, writing, music. Ofc: Pacific Venture Management, 2811 Fairmount Ave Ste 200 La Crescenta 91214

CRONK, MILDRED (Mili) SCHIEFELBEIN, special education consultant; b. May 29, 1909, Waverly, Iowa; d. Emil August and Nettie Marie (Berger) Schiefelbein; m. Dale Cronk, July 20, 1930; children: Barbara (Burress), Bruce, Margaret, Michael; edn: att. Wartburg Coll., Waverly 1927, Tampa Univ., Fla. 1944-45, Los Angeles City Coll., 1957; BA in psych., Calif. State Univ., 1960, MA in spl. edn. supervision, 1971. Career: aircraft communicator, weather observer CAA, Fla. and Calif., 1942-49; dir. Parkview Nursery Sch., Los Angeles 1956-57; tchr. trainable mentally retarded Hacienda-La Puente Unified Sch. Dist., 1961-74; cons. special edn. La Mirada, 1975-, ins-service tnr. for tchrs.; mem. coms: Special Olympics SE Los Angeles Co. 1977, Very Special Arts Orange Co. (bd. 1977-), Internat. Very Special Arts Festival 1981, Very Special Arts Calif. (bd. 1986-, treas. 1987); mem: Am. Assn. on Mental Deficiency (bd. reg. II, ed. Newsette 1975-77, chair publicity com. 1977-79, presenter annual confs.), Council for Exceptional Children (state bd., ed. Calif. State Fedn./Council for Exceptional Children J. 1977-80, past pres. San Gabriel Valley chpt.538, mem. at lg. So. Calif. div. Mental Retardation 1976-79, pres. Calif. div. Mental Retardation 1980-81, chair com. on ofcrs.' handbook, nat. council, div. Mental Retardation 1977-78, presenter Nat. Confs., recipient spl. recognition awards 1976, 77, 78, 79, 89), Assn. for Retarded Citizens SELACO (secty. 1980-81), Nat. Soc. Autistic Children, Nat. Retired Tchrs. Assn., Am. Ceramic Soc. (design div.), Psi Chi; civic: Common Cause, Smithsonian Instn., Wilderness Soc.; author: Create With Clay, 1976, Vocational Skills Taught Through Creative Arts, 1978, Attitude Change Toward TMR Students/ Mainstreaming in Reverse, 1978, Career Education for Trainable Mentally Retarded Students — It's For Life!, 1982, others; Democrat; Res: 13116 Clearwood Ave La Mirada 90638

CROSBY, GEORGE HYDE, stockbroker; b. Jan. 19, 1927, Ely, Nevada; s. Kent Miller and Janice (Hyde) C.; m. Nadine Potter, June 16, 1949; children: Janet, b. 1951; Kent, b. 1952; Mary, b. 1956; Marc, b. 1958; edn: BA, Brigham Young Univ. 1948; Univ. of Utah Law Sch. 1948-51; MBA, Golden Gate Coll. 1965; reg. principal, NASD. Career: Bank of Am., Sunnyvale 1952-54; op. ofcr./ asst. mgr. First Western Bank, Sunnyvale, San Francisco, Riverdale 1954-64; asst. mgr. United Calif. Bank, Gustine, Santa Maria 1964-68; mgr./ v.p. Mid-State Bank, Arroyo Grande, Santa Maria 1968-76; sr. v.p.-economist and director Maguire Investments, Inc., Santa Maria 1976-; instr. bus. admin, Allan Hancock Coll., Santa Maria 1967-85; dir. T.T.O.C. 1977-79; chair. Fin. Commn., Santa Barbara Co. Ret. Bd. 1975-84; mem: Santa Maria C.of C. (pres. 1974); Santa Maria Kiwanis Club (pres. 1973-74, lt. gov. div. 29, 1980-81); Boys Club, Santa Maria (pres. 1979-80); Santa Maria Valley Developers; mil: USN 1944-45 Republican; Latter-day Saints; rec: fencing. Res: 4182 Glenview Santa Maria 93455 Ofc: Maguire Investments, Inc. 1862 S Broadway Santa Maria 93454

CROSBY, WILLIAM MARSHALL, lawyer; b. Jan. 26, 1945, Pasadena; s. Joseph Marshall and Margaret Jane (Aldridge) C.; div.; children: Mary Beth b. 1977, Joseph b. 1978; edn: BA, UC Berkeley 1967; JD, Loyola Law Sch. 1970; admitted bar Calif. 1971; Career: dept. dist. atty. County of Riverside 1971; dep. city atty., Anaheim 1972; atty. pvt. practice in Irvine 1973, 1976-, San Francisco 1974-75; in-house counsel Monex Internat. Ltd., Newport Beach 1975-76; law practice, William M. Crosby Law Corp. 1980-91; ptnr. Barnes, Crosby & Fitzgerald, 1991-; lectr., author re wrongful termination of employment, Calif. Contg. Edn. Bar, trial practice articles OCTLA and CTLA jours., OCBA Jour.; awards: Repub. Youth Assocs. award 1980; mem: Am. Bd. of Trial Advocates, Orange County Bar Assn., Am., Calif., Orange County (bd. 1983-) Trial Lawyers assns., ABA, Plaintiff and Employment Lawyers Assn., Calif. Employment Lawyers Assn. (founding mem.), Sigma Nu, Phi Delta Pi, Calif. Alumni Assn.; civic: Exchange Club Irvine (pres. 1980), Irvine C.of C. (chair govtl. affairs 1992), Newport Harbor Area C.of C., Industrial League of Orange Co., Republican Assocs., Lincoln Club Orange Co., Irvine Workforce Com., South Coast Symphony (dir. 1990-92), Pacific Symphony (dir. 1992), Silver Circle Com. Services Commn. Irvine, Eisenhower Scholarship Found. (trustee 1987), High Hopes Neurol. Recovery Group Inc.; Republican (cand. Calif. State Assembly 1976); Prot.; rec: boating, fishing; Ofc: Barnes, Crosby & Fitzgerald, 18200 Von Karman Ave Ste 820 Irvine 92715

CROSS, GLENN LABAN, engineering/construction executive; b. Dec. 28, 1941, Mt. Vernon, Ill.; s. Kenneth Edward and Mildred Irene (Glenn) C.; m. Kim Lien Duong, Aug. 30, 1968; m. 2d. Tran Tu Thach, Dec. 26, 1975; children: Cindy b. 1977, Cristy b. 1983, Crystal b. 1987, Cassandra b. 1992; edn: BS, Calif. Western Univ. 1981; MBA, 1982. Career: med. splst. USA Spl. Forces, Machinato, Okinawa 1962-65; hosp. adminstrn. splst. USAID Dept. State, Wash. D.C. 1966-68; staff astt. to v.p. and gen. mgr. Pacific Architects & Engrs. Inc., Los Angeles 1968-75; contracts adminstr. AVCO Internat. Services div., Cincinnati, Ohio 1975-77; contract adminstrn. supr. Bechtel Hydro & Comml. Facility, San Francisco 1977-85, cons. Bechtel Power Corp. 1985-90; Ralph M. Parsons Co. Los Angeles Metro, Los Angeles 1990-; awards: Wash. Univ. Nat. Merit scholarship 1960; mem: Nat. Contract Mgmt. Assn., Constrn. Mgmt. Assn. of Am., Am. Mgmt. Assn., Am. Arbitration Assn., Assn. MBA Execs., Assn. Human Research System Profls., Internat. Personnel Mgmt. Assn., Human Resource Planning Soc., Nat. Contract Mgmt. Assn., Constrn. Mgmt. Assn. of Am., Order of DeMolay, Republican Party; author Living With a Matrix 1983; mil: AUS Spl. Forces 1962-64; Republican; Christian; rec: swimming. Res: 25935 Faircourt Ln Laguna Hills 92653 Ofc: Ralph M. Parsons Co. 100 W Walnut Pasadena 91124

CROSS, JAMES FRANCIS, workfare program coordinator; b. Oct. 11, 1950, Montebello; s. Marshall Lane and Rose C.; edn: East L.A. Coll. 1968-70; Whittier Coll. 1970-72; grad., So. Calif. Broadcast Workshop 1975. Career: Los Angeles Co. Dept. of Pub. Social Services eligibility worker 1972-76, eligibility supr. 1976-80, data systems analyst 1980, operations analyst 1981-85, workfare project coordinator 1985-87, division chiefs asst. 1987, dep. district dir. 1987-91, Workfare Program coordinator 1991-; program host KBW AM/FM 1976-77; awards: Brotherhood Crusade leadership (1988, 89, 90, 91), United Way silver (1987, 88, 90, 91), Dept. Pub. Social Services productivity and efficiency 1989; mem: Neighborhood Watch, Los Angeles Co. Mgmt. Council, Citizens Allied for Understanding & Social Awareness (co-founder 1970-73), Kerner Commn. Action Group 1970-71, Wilderness Conf. musical group (co-founder w/Joseph Maldonado 1967-73); song writer "Window to Cry From" 1971; R.Cath.; rec: musician, artist, mil. history. Ofc: DPSS General Relief Program Div., Workfare Program Section, 5445 E Whittier Blvd Los Angeles 90022

CROSS, K. PATRICIA, educator; b. Mar. 17, 1926, Normal, Ill.; d. Clarence L. and Katherine (Dague) Cross; edn: BS in math., Ill. State Univ. 1948; MA psychology, Univ. Ill., 1951, PhD social psych., 1958. Career: math. tchr. Harvard Community H.S., Harvard, Ill. 1948-49; resrch. asst. dept. psych. Univ. Ill., Urbana 1949-53, asst. dean of women 1953-59; dean of women Cornell Univ. 1959-60, dean of students 1960-63; dir. coll. and univ. pgms. Educational Testing Service, Princeton, N.J. 1963-66, Berkeley, Calif. 1966-69, sr. resrch. psychologist ETS, Berkeley 1969-76, distinguished resrch. scientist 1976-80; also resrch. educator Ctr. for R&D in Higher Edn., UC Berkeley 1966-77; prof. and chair dept. adminstrn., planning and social policy Harvard Grad. Sch. of Edn., 1980-88; Elizabeth and Edward Conner Prof. of Edn., UC Berkeley 1988-; vis. prof. Univ. Nebr. 1975-76; keynote speaker and del. internat. and confs.; author 6 books, num. monographs and book chapters, jour. articles; book awards: Am. Council on Edn. Borden Medal for Accent on Learning 1976, Sch. and Soc. outstanding bk. in edn. for Beyond the Open Door 1971, Pi Lambda Theta best books award for The Junior Coll. Student 1968, other awards include 1990 Leadership award Am. Assn. Community and Jr. Colls. 1990, disting. lectr. Am. Soc. for Engring. Edn. 1991, Nat. Coun. of Instrnl. Adminstrs. Award 1990, master tchr. Nat. Inst. for Staff and Orgnl. Devel. 1990, Howard R. Bowen Lectr. Claremont Grad. Sch. 1989, nat. person of yr. Nat. Coun. on Comm. Svs. and Cont. Edn. 1988, Adult Educator of Yr. Coalition of Adult Edn. Orgs., W.D.C. 1987, DeGarmo Lectr. Soc. Profs. of Edn. 1987, E.F. Lindquist award Am. Ednl. Resrch. Assn. 1986, Regents Medal of excellence SUNY 1984, fellow Nat. Policy Ctr. on Edn., Leisure and Cont. Opportunities for Older Ams. 1982-, Delta Sigma Epsilon nat. lectr. 1981, disting. alumni Ill. State Univ. 1980, Delbert Clark award for contbns. to adv. adult edn. 1979, Nat. Acad. of Edn. (elected 1975, v.chair 1981-83), Hon. Degrees- Ill. St. Univ., 1970, Grand Valley State Colls., Mich., 1975, Northeastern Univ., 1975, Our Lady of the Lake Univ., Tx. 1977, Hood Coll., Md. 1979, Loyola Univ. Chgo., Ill. 1980, Marymount Manhattan Coll., NY 1982, Coll. of St. Mary, Neb. 1985, DePaul Univ., Chgo. 1985, Thomas Jefferson Univ., Pa. 1987, SUNY, 1988, Open Univ. of Netherlands 1989. Res: 904 Oxford St Berkeley 94707 Ofc: Univ. of Calif. School of Education ED-04, Berkeley 94720 Tel: 510/642-7441

CROSSETT, JERRY WAYNE, computer graphics company executive; b. May 19, 1938, Wellman, Iowa; s. Merle Omer and Marjorie Evelyn (Loeffler) C.; m. Mary Lou Palmer, June 10, 1961; children: Joy Ann b. 1966, Donald Wayne b. 1971; edn: BSME, Iowa State Univ. 1961; MSME, CalTech, 1964; business certificate, UCLA, 1970. Career: engr., scientist Naval Missile Ctr., Pt. Mugu 1961-63; engr. Douglas Aircraft Co., Santa Monica 1964-71; engr., splst. MDAC Tech. Services, Nagoya, Japan 1971-74; engr. McDonnell Douglas, Huntington Bch. 1974-75; owner, mgr. Action International, Fountain Valley 1975-; honor socs.: Phi Eta Sigma, 1958, Pi Tau Sigma, 1960, Tau Beta Pi, 1961; mem: Orange Co. Internat. Mktg. Assn., Am. Defense Preparedness Assn., NRA, So. Calif. Internat. Skeet Assn. (treas. 1987-); patent for sounding rocket staging device, 1962; Republican; Christian; rec: skeet shooting. Res: 18609 Santa Ramona Fountain Valley 92708

CROWLEY, DAVID JOSEPH, public relations professional; b. June 25, 1934, Malden, Mass.; s. David Joseph and Mary Veronica (O'Donnell) C.; m. Carolyn Ann Parker, June 8, 1957; children: Pamela Ann, Jill Elizabeth, Paul David; edn: AA, Boston Univ., 1953, BS Pub. Rels., 1956. Career: reporter, editor Haverhill Jour., Mass. 1958-62; publicist, sr. publicist GE News Bur., Schenectady, N.Y. 1962-67; supr. GE Western News Bur., Los Angeles 1967-69; mgr. GE Info. Systems, Phoenix, Az. 1969-70; assoc. Carl Byoir and Associates Pub. Rels., Phoenix 1970-72; mgr. GE Nuclear Energy, San Jose, Calif. 1972-88; pres. Pacific News Bur., Campbell, Calif. 1988-; ghost writer speeches, position papers; mem: Nat. Assn. Sci. Writers, Peninsula P.R. Roundtable, Los Altos (chmn. 1988-92), Marines Memorial Club, Rotary Club; civic: Rotocare Inc. (med. help for homeless) San Jose (founding mem. 1988-90), San Jose Hist. Mus. (bd. mem.-at-lg. 1992-, chmn. p.r. com. 1989-92); mil: US Army 1956-58; Republican; R.Cath.; rec: skiing, photog., reading. Res: 1111 Casual Way San Jose 95120 Ofc: Pacific News Bureau 880 E Campbell Ave Ste 202 Campbell 95008 Ph: 408/559-7774

CRUMP, GERALD FRANKLIN, lawyer; b. Feb. 16, 1935, Sacramento; s. John Laurin and Ida May (Banta) C.; m. Glenda Roberts Glass, Nov. 21, 1959; children: Sara Elizabeth, b. 1972, Juliane Kathryn, b. 1974, Joseph Stephen, b. 1977; edn: AB, UC Berkeley 1956, JD, 1959; MA, Baylor Univ. 1966. Career: judge advocate USAF 1960-63; deputy county counsel Los Angeles County 1963-73; legislative rep. 1970-73; chief Public Works Div. 1973-84; sr. asst. co. counsel 1984-85; chief asst. co. counsel 1985-; lectr. Pepperdine Univ. 1978, Univ. Calif. 1982; vice pres. San Fernando Valley Girl Scout Council; mem: State Bar of Calif. (delegate, 1984-), Am. Bar Assn., Los Angeles County Bar Assn. (chmn. Govt. Law Sect. 1983-84), Am. Judicature Soc., Am. Acad. of Polit. and Social Sci., Calif. Historical Soc., Reserve Officers Assn., Air Force Assn., Phi Alpha Delta, Delta Sigma Phi; mil: capt. USAF 1960-63, Reserve 1963-, major general, USAFR, 1993; mobilization asst. to the Judge Advocate Gen., decorated Legion of Merit, Meritorious Service w. 2 o.l.c., AF Commendn.; Res: 4020 Camino de la Cumbre, Sherman Oaks 91423; Ofc: Los Angeles County Counsel, 648 Hall of Administration Los Angeles 90012

CRUZ, JIMMY RAMOS, insurance co. president; b. Apr. 28, 1936, barrio Calahan, Cardona, Rizal, Philippines, nat. U.S. citizen 1978; s. Hermogenes Cruz and Marta Himbing (Ramos) C.; m. Amanda Lacambacal Reyes, Jan. 29, 1956; children: Anamarie b. 1957, Maria Teresa b. 1959, Malou b. 1960, Maryrose b. 1962, Mark James b. 1964; edn: BS elem. edn., Manila Western Colls., 1953. Career: life and disability ins. agent Pioneer Life, Los Angeles 1980-81; general agent American Gen. Life & Accident Ins. Co., 1982-83; mktg. ofcr. American Life & Casualty Ins. Co., Cerritos 1984-86; travel exec. City Tours & Travel of Los Angeles, 1982-; gen. agent Occidental Life Ins. Co., 1987-; pres. Mahal Devel. Co., Lawndale 1987-; awards: cert. Career Assistance Plan Seminar, Occidental Liffe 1987, Resolution for illustrious service L.A. County Bd. Suprs. 1985, Lawndale City Council 1982, Calif. State Assembly 1977, outstanding community service Jaycees 1983, Sulo Unlimited Inc. award for Outstanding Filipino Businessman 1977; mem: Life Underwriters Tng. Council, Philippine Alumni Assn. L.A., Insurance Agents Assn.; civic: Filipino American Soc. of L.A. (pres.), Bayanihan Jaycee L.A. (lt. gov.), Calif. Commnrs. Parks & Rec., Filipino Town Movement, Sister City Assn. Lawndale-Cagayan de Oro, Phil. (organizer); Democrat; Prot.; rec: camping, swim, table tennis, track & field. Res: 4215 W 154th St Lawndale 90260 Ofc: Mahal Development Co. PO Box 1075 Lawndale 90260

CRYER, RODGER EARL, school administrator, counselor, educator; b. Apr. 2, 1940, Detroit, Mich.; s. Earl Wilton and Mary Venetia (Miller) C.; m. Bellaflor, June 22, 1986; children: Joseph b. 1970, Noel b. 1978; edn: undergrad., Ohio Wesleyan Univ. 1958-60; AB, San Diego St. Univ. 1965; AM, Stanford Univ. 1974; PhD, Columbia-Pacific Univ. 1985. Career: counselor/tchr. J.W. Fair Intermediate Sch., San Jose; summer sch. tchr. The Foundry Sch. (Juvenile Ct. Sch. pgm.); principal McKinley Neighborhood Sch., 1988-91; principal G.W. Hellyer Sch., 1991-; counseling pvt. practice; adj. prof. CSU San Francisco and CSU San Jose; chmn. San Jose Parks & Recreation Commn. 1989-90; chmn. supvy. com. Commonwealth Central Credit Union 1990-91, v.chmn. 1989-90; chmn. Recycle Grove Task Force 1989-90; co-owner Guided Learning Assocs. 1987-; awards: summer fellow in sociol., Western Interstate Commn. for Higher Edn.; doctoral dissertation grantee Colgate-Palmolive Fund, Stanford Univ.; mem: Calif. Tchrs. Assn. (State Council rep., budget com. 1983-), Parental Stress Hotline and Services of San Jose, Inc. (vol. counselor 1984-85); works: Decision-Making Heuristic; civic: Steering Com. San Jose Beautiful 1993 (chmn. nominating com.), Guadalupe River Park Task Force 1993; Democrat; Unitarian; rec: bicycling, x-c skiing. Res: 3529 Milburn St San Jose 95148 Ofc: POB 21917 San Jose 95151-1917

CSENDES, ERNEST, finance and technical executive; b. Mar. 2, 1926, Satu-Mare, Rumania, nat. US cit. 1955; s. Edward O. and Sidonia (von Littman) C.; m. Catharine Tolnai, Feb. 11, 1953; children: Audrey Carol b. 1959, Robert A. Edward b. 1963; edn: BA, Protestant Coll., Hungary 1944; BS, Univ. of Heidelberg 1948, MS and PhD, 1951. Career: research asst. organic chem., Univ. of Heidelberg 1950-51; research assoc. biochem. Tulane Med. Sch., New Orleans

1951-52, fellow Harvard Univ. Chem. Dept., Cambridge, Mass. 1952-53; research chemist, Organic Chemicals Dept., E.I. Du Pont de Nemours & Co., Wilmington, Del. 1953-56, Elastomer Chems. Dept. 1956-61; dir. R&D, Armour & Co., Agric. Chem. Div., Atlanta, Ga. 1961-63; v.p. corp. devel. Occidental Petroleum Corp., L.A. 1963-64, exec. v.p. Res., Engring. & Devel. 1964-68, exec. v.p./chief op. ofcr. Occidental Res. & Engring. Corp., L.A., London, Moscow, 1963-68; pres./bd. chmn./CEO TRI Group (offshore finance, investment mgmt. & trusteeing), London, Amsterdam, Rome and Bermuda, 1968-84; bd. chmn./CEO Micronic Technologies Inc., Los Angeles 1981-85; mng. ptnr. Inter-Consult, Ltd. (technical, finance & corporate mgmt.), Los Angeles 1984-; res. in the areas of organic & biochemistry, dyestuffs, elastomers and plastics, fertilizers and pesticides, energy raw materials, petrochemicals, clean coal & acid rain, size reduction of solids, corporate finance and Eurodollar securities; honors: Pro Mundi Beneficio gold medal, Brazilian Acad. of Humanities (1976), acclaimed for regional devel. programs related to agric. and natural resources in Europe, No. Africa, USSR, Far East and India; Fellow AAAS, Fellow Am. Inst. of Chemists, Fellow Royal Soc. of Chem., mem. N.Y. Acad. of Sci., Am. Chem. Soc., Am. Inst. of Chem. Engrs., Am. Inst. Aero. & Astro., Sigma Xi, German Chem. Soc., Global Action Economic Inst. (NY), Explorers Club (NY); works: 250+ books, reports, articles in sci. and trade papers and patents; rec: collect 18th Century decorative arts/France, music (violin & chamber music; graduate Music Conservatory). Res: 514 Marquette St Pacific Palisades 90272

CUCITI, LESLIE MARTIN, accountant; b. May 16, 1953, Fort Ord; d. Gene Arnell and Donna Milre (Goebel) Martin; m. Richard B. Cuciti, Aug. 8, 1981; edn: BS microbiol., San Diego St. Univ. 1974; MBA, USC 1985; cert. mgmt. accountant 1985. Career: fin. analyst Gen. Dynamics 1980-81; bus. mgr. Hughes Aircraft Co., Fullerton 1981-90; cost acctg. mgr. Emerson Computer Power, Irvine 1990-92; controller Sigmapower, Inc., Carson 1992; mgr. financial planning & analysis Beckman Instruments, Inc., Carlsbad; honors: Sigma Iota Epsilon, Beta Gamma Sigma, USC Dean's List; mem: Nat. Assn. Accountants, CMA Soc. So. Calif. (pres. 1992), Alpha Gamma Delta; Republican; Protestant; rec: white water rafting, sailing. Ofc: Beckman Instruments, Inc. 2470 Faraday Carlsbad 92008-4836

CULLER, FLOYD LEROY, JR., electric utility R&D executive and consultant; b. Jan. 5, 1923, Washington, D.C.; s. Floyd Leroy (dec.) and Ora L. (Labee) Culler (dec.); m. Della Hopper, July 3, 1946; 1 son, Floyd Leroy, III; edn: BS, chem. engr., Johns Hopkins Univ., Baltimore, MD 1943; engr. Tenn. Eastman, Oak Ridge, Tenn. 1943-47; design engr. Clinton Labs. 1947-48; section chief Oak Ridge Nat. Lab. 1948-53, dir. chem. tech. div. 1953-65, asst. lab. dir. 1965-70, deputy dir. 1970-73, acting dir. 1973-74, deputy dir. 1974-77; pres. Elec. Power Research Inst., Palo Alto 1978-88, pres. emeritus 1988-; dir: Houston Industries, Inc. and Houston Lighting & Power, 1988-89; mem. U.S. Dept. of Energy Research Advy. Bd. 1984-88; mem. IFS fusion oversight com. Lawrence Livermore Lab., DOE; magnetic fusion oversight com., DOE; advy. com. on nuclear facility safety, DOE; advy. council Oak Ridge Nat. Lab.; awards: E.O. Lawrence Award of AEC, 1967, UN Atoms for Peace Award, 1969, Exceptional Svc. award Am. Nuclear Soc., 1980 and Walter Zinn Award, 1988, Fellow Am. Inst. of Chemists, Fellow Am. Inst. of Chem. Engrs., 1981, TN Outstanding Scientist Award, 1988, inducted Nat. Acad. of Engineering, W.D.C., 1974. Res: 1385 Corinne Ln Menlo Park 94025 Ofc: Electric Power Research Institute 3412 Hillview Ave Palo Alto 94304

CULTON, PAUL MELVIN, educator; b. Feb. 12, 1932, Council Bluffs, Iowa; s. Paul Roland and Hallie Ethel Emma (Paschal) C.; edn: AB, Minn. Bible Coll., Minneapolis, Minn., 1955; BS, Univ. of Nebr., Omaha, 1965; MA, CSU-Northridge, Calif., 1970; EdD, Brigham Young Univ., Provo, Utah, 1981. Career: tchr., Iowa Sch. for the Deaf, Council Bluffs, 1956-70; ednl. splst., instr., dir. Disabled Students Program, Golden West Coll., Huntington Beach, Calif., 1970-88; visiting prof. Univ. of Guam, Agana, Guam, 1977; freelance cons., sign language interpreter, So. Calif., 1988-90; counselor, acting assoc. dean for spl. resource ctr., El Camino Coll., Torrance, Calif., 1990-; cons. on deafness and other disabilities, Calif. Comm. Colleges, other univs. and colls., businesses, K-12 schools, Calif, other states and Guam 1970-90; svc. on task force related to edn. of disabled, Calif. Comm. Colls., 1971-87; part-time instr., Golden West Coll., El Camino Coll., Saddleback Coll., Rancho Santiago Coll., Calif.,. other states and Guam, 1971-74, 1980, 88-90; part-time asst. prof., CSU Dominguez Hills, Northridge, Fresno, Calif., 1973, 76, 80, 87-90; co-chair Hearing Impaired Subcom. Task Force on Mental Health for the Disabled, Calif. Conf. of Mental Health Directors; mem. Com. to Establish Qualifications for Tchrs. of Sign Language, Calif.; awards: mem. Nat. Honor Soc. 1950, Nat. Leadership Training Prog. in the Area of Deafness, CSU Northridge 1970; mem. Olympic Honor Chorus US Internat. Olympic Com. L.A. 1984, Disting. Svc. award, Registry of Interpreters for the Deaf, 1989; Fellow, League for Innovation in the Comm. Coll.; mem. journal bd., founding v.p., treas., Calif. Assn. of Postsecondary Educators of the Disabled; chair, postsecondary edn. com., Conf. of Ednl. Administrators Serving the Deaf; founding sec. Dayle McIntosh Ctr. for the Disabled; mem journal bd., standards com., pres. So. Calif. chpt., Registry of Interpreters for the Deaf; mem: Am. Deafness and Rehabilitation Assn., Nat. Assn. of the Deaf, Calif. Court Interpreters Assn.,

Calif. Assn. of Persons with Handicaps; founding second v.p. Greater L.A. Council on Deafness; treas., bd. mem. Gay Men's Chorus of Long Beach; bd. dirs., hotline, Gay & Lesbian Comm. Ctr., Garden Grove; mem: Common Cause, Am. Civil Liberties Union, Americans for Separation of Ch. and State, Nat. Com. for an Effective Congress, Ctr. for Nat. Independence in Politics, Nat. Assn. of Colored People; author: A Vocabulary Guide For Parents of Preschool Deaf Children, 1970; ed., conf. proceedings, 1970, 71; composer, song: Carry The Light, 1985; Democrat; Am. Humanist Assn.; rec: languages, vocal music, politics, community activism. Res: 2567 Plaza Del Amo 203 Torrance 90503 Ofc: El Camino College 16007 Crenshaw Blvd Torrance 90506

CUMMINGS, ALAN COFFMAN, physicist; b. March 20, 1944, Joy, Tx.; s. Kermit Clyde and Beulah Elsie (Crawford) C.; m. Suzette Yeats, Oct. 27, 1973; child: Travis b. 1975; edn: BA (summa cum laude), Rice Univ., 1966; PhD, Caltech 1973. Career: scientist Caltech Univ., Pasadena 1973-79, sr. scientist 1979-81, mem. profl. staff 1981-; awards: Phi Beta Kappa 1965, Sigma Xi 1966, NSF Fellowship 1966, Woodrow Wilson Fellowship 1966, U.S. Churchill Found. Fellow, plus other awards incl. Voyager Project Cert. of Appreciation; mem: Nat. Acad. of Sci. (com. on Solar-Terrestrial Relationships of the Nat. Res. Council), Am. Physical Soc., Am. Geophysical Union, Planetary Soc.; author and co-author 50+ scientific articles; rec: tennis, birdwatching. Res: 531 W Mariposa Ave Sierra Madre 91024 Ofc: Caltech MC 220-47 Pasadena 91125

CUMMINGS, CYNTHIA LOUISE, physician; b. March 11, 1948, Houston, Tx.; d. William Frances and Arlene Josephine (Peter) Cummings; m. Michael A. Boutte, Jan. 30, 1988; edn: BS biol., Univ. Santa Clara, 1971; MD, Emory Univ. Sch. Med., 1982; bd. cert. Am. Bd. Family Practice 1985, 1991. Career: tech. to coordinator adminstr. No. Calif. Transplant Bank 1971-77; cons. Banco de Oidos Ruben Lenero Hosp., Mexico City 1976; intern internal med. Columbia Univ., Mary Imogene Bassett Hosp., Cooperstown, N.Y. 1982-83; resident family practice Goppert Family Care Center Baptist Med. Center 1983-85; family practice San Jose Med. Group, Los Gatos 1985-, chmn. Dept. Family Practice; psychiatry exec. bd. Good Samaritan Hosp. 1986-91; bd. dirs. Planetree Project, San Jose Hosp. 1987-; asst. med. coordinator U.S. Figure Skating Championships 1985; Hepatitis Vaccine Trials, Alaska 1982; awards: So. Calif. Industry Edn. Medal for Sci. 1965, Bausch & Lomb Medal for Sci. and Math. 1966, Rotary Internat. Exchange Student (1968, 69); mem: Am. Acad. Family Practice 1983-, Calif. Acad. Family Practice 1985-, AMA 1979-, Primary Care Sports Med. Network Santa Clara 1985-, Am. Coll. of Sports Med. 1989-; civic: Nat. Geographic Soc., Smithsonian Inst., Wilderness Medical Soc., Hispanic Arts Cultural Council (San Jose), Calif. Council of Youth (edn. chmn. 1967, 69), Alviso Tutorial Project (coordinator 1967, 68); res. in transplant tissues (1971-76), parasitic infections (Mexico 1976); R.Cath.; rec: x-c skiing, travel, handicrafts, languages (Spanish, Norwegian, French, German). Ofc: San Jose Medical Group 14651 S Bascom Ave Ste 110 Los Gatos 95032

CUMMINGS, GREGG ALEX, project civil engineer; b. May 18, 1963, Oakland; s. Garth Ellis and Shirley Elaine (Wolfe) C.; m. Donna Marie Cavalieri; edn: BSCE, UC Berkeley, 1985; MSCE, San Jose St. Univ., 1989; reg. profl. engr. (civil) Calif. Career: staff engr. Metcalf & Eddy, Palo Alto 1986-89; project engr. Dames & Moore, San Francisco 1989-, project mgr. lectr. 1991-; awards: IFC scholar Acacia Frat., Berkeley 1985; mem.: Am. Soc. Civil Engrs. 1983-, Water Pollution Control Fedn. 1989-, Chi Epsilon, Acacia Frat. Berkeley (house mgr. 1984-85, dir., secty. 1991-); Republican; Methodist; rec: reading, gardening, music. Res: 53 Gladys St San Francisco 94110 Ofc: Dames & Moore 221 Main St Ste 600 San Francisco 94105

CUMMINGS, MARILYN LOUISE, tutoring center owner; b. Sept. 20, 1932, Chgo.; d. Blaine and Ruth Louise (Niekamp) C.; div.; edn: grad. Southern Sem. 1952; CSU Long Beach, 1957-61; spl. courses w/Mae Carden 1969. Career: engring. dept. Pac. Tel. Co., Compton 1953-55; music tchr. Music Center Studios, San Pedro 1955-7, founder/co-dir. Musicland Studios (main ofc., S.P.) 1957-64; music tchr./coord., Betty Thomas Music Sch., Torrance 1965-67, others; dist. mgr. Field Ent. Ednl. Corp. 1967-69; tutor/field rep. Wingrock Sch. Inc., Torrance 1969-71; area mgr. Am. Incentive to Read, L.A. 1969; founder/director Marilyn Cummings Tutoring Ctr., San Pedro 1969-; also: sr. area mgr. 1989-, dist. mgr. World Book - Childcraft, 1990-92; advt. rep. Christian Sci Monitor, (1971-73, 76); honors: Southern Seminary Coll. Dean's list 1951, Alumnae secty. 1988-, sales award Field Ent. Educational Corp. 1967; mem: Accordion Fedn. of No. Am. (judge Music Contest 1956-64, 78-), Sweet Adelines (bd. 1982-4), San Pedro C.of C. 1982- (chair Bus. & Edn. Com. 1986-87), Bus. & Profl. Womens Club, Southern Seminary Coll. Alumnae (class secty. 1989-); Accordion Tchrs Guild, Toastmistress, Hermosa Harmony Singers (v.p. 1977-80); Chorale of Sun Lakes 1991-; asst. coordinator for chartering of Leads Club/San Pedro 1986; devel. successful method for teaching reading to illiterate and slow learners 1969; listed Who's Who Profl. and Exec. Women, Two Thousand Notable Am. Women (1st ed., Hall of Fame), Five Thousand Personalities of World; Christian Science (ch. bd. 1973-76, 90, v.p. C.S. Assn. 1987-90). Res: 730 La Quinta Dr Banning 92220 Ofc: Marilyn Cummings Tutoring Center, 312 No Gaffey St Ste 101-2 San Pedro 90731

CUMMINGS, PHILIP NEIL, dentist; b. Oct. 12, 1946, Stockton; s. Robert Neil Cummings; m. Diane Tomlinson, June 4, 1969, div. 1971; m. Linda Carol Reber, Sept. 26, 1973; children: Lisa b. 1981, Kristen b. 1984; edn: BA psychology, UC Davis, 1969; BS biol., CSU Hayward, 1975; DDS, UCLA, 1979, adv. tng. oral surgery, 1979. Career: parole agent Calif. Dept. of Corrections, 1969-73; solo practice gen. family dentistry, 1979-; chief cons. Professional Alpha Systems Inc., 1981-85, devel. computer software pgm. for medical and dental practices (pgms. used widely in Calif. and Ariz. including oral surg. dept. UCLA Sch. of Dent.); indep. research in devel. of diagnostic analysis procedures, 1985-; honors: Deans list CSUH 1973-75, special award for achiev. Dental Found. of Calif. 1978, outstanding achiev. Western Dental Soc. 1979, F. Gene Dixon Student Leadership Award of Calif. Dental Service 1979, outstanding svc. award in recogn. of service as student body pres. UCLA Sch. of Dentistry 1979, Appollonian hon. soc. 1980-86; mem: Am. Dental Assn., Calif. Dental Assn. (Santa Clara chpt. dental care com. 1981-82, chmn. integrated comms. 1983-84); civic: bd. dirs. Berkeley Comm. Hlth. Ctr. 1973-75, advy. bd. San Jose City Coll. 1983-84; contbr. articles in dental jours.; mil: lt. AUS 1966-69; Republican; R.Cath.; rec: golf, travel, res. & devel. Ofc: 1706 Willow St Ste A San Jose 95125

CUMMINGS, ROCKY BLAINE, corporate tax accountant; b. Sept. 11, 1962, Rheinlander, Wis.; s. Bill George and Arlene Ann (Paremski) C.; m. Kathryn A. Loncarich, 1990; edn: BS mgmt./acctg., San Francisco St. Univ., 1986; MS taxation, Golden Gate Univ., 1991. Career: owner Raffles, San Rafael 1984-88 fin. planner IDS/American Exp., San Francisco 1987-88; co-owner Independent Am. Fin. Services Inc., S.F. 1988-90; tax acct. Consol. Freightways Inc., 1990-; dir. E.S.C.C.S., Petaluma 1987-; mem. S.F. C.of C.; rec: golf, scuba. Ofc: Consolidated Freightways, Inc. 175 Linfield Dr Menlo Park 94025

CUMMINS, WILLIAM ROBERT, advertising agency executive; b. Feb. 18, 1948, Des Moines, Iowa; s. Harold William and Atea (Bulf) C.; edn: BBA, Loyola Univ. of Chicago, 1970; MBA, Northwestern Univ. 1975. Career: acct. exec. Market Research Corp. Am., Chgo., Ill. 1972-74; acct. exec. Market Facts, Los Angeles 1974-76; product res. mgr. Hunt Wesson Foods, Fullerton 1976-78; mgr. market planning Toyota USA, Los Angeles 1978-85; senior v.p., dir. research Rubin Postaer 1985-; honors: Who's Who in Am. Colls. & Univs. 1970; mem: Am. Mktg. Assn. (exec.), So. Calif. Research Soc., Ad Club L.A. (bd. dirs., chmn. edn. com.), Sierra Club; rec: backpacking, skiing. Res: 25672 Lupita Dr Valencia 91355 Ofc: Rubin Postaer & Assoc. 1333 Second St Santa Monica 90401

CURNUTTE, JOHN TOLLIVER III, physician, biochemist; b. Sept. 9, 1951, Dixon, Ill.; s. John Tolliver Curnutte, Jr. and Elizabeth Ann (Mueller) C.; m. Karen Diane Northrop, June 21, 1975; children: Jacqueline b. 1978, John IV b. 1980, Margaret b. 1982; edn: AB, Biochem., Harvard Univ. 1973; MD, Harvard Med. Sch. 1979; PhD, biological chem., Harvard Grad. Sch. of Arts & Sciences 1980. Career: asst. prof., Univ. Mich. Med. Sch., Ann Arbor, Mich. 1983-86; asst. mem. (prof.) The Scripps Res. Inst., La Jolla, Calif. 1986-87, assoc. mem. (prof.) 1987-; assoc. dir., Gen. Clinical Res. Ctr., The Scripps Res. Inst. 1989-; awards: Established Investigator, Am. Heart Assn., Dallas, Tex. 1986-91; Outstanding Young Investigator, 1st Internat. Congress on Inflammation, Barcelona, Spain 1990; mem: Am. Soc. for Clinical Investigation 1988, Am. Soc. of Hematology 1983-; editorial bd.: Blood 1989-, Jour. of Immunology 1992-, Jour. of Biological Chem. 1992-; author: 60 res. articles in prof. journals 1973-; Hematology chapters. in 3 textbooks 1985-; Independent; Roman Catholic; rec: mountain climbing, football, piano. Ofc: The Scripps Research Institute, CAL-1, 10666 No. Torrey Pines Rd. La Jolla 92037

CUROTTO, RICKY JOSEPH, lawyer; b. Dec. 22, 1931, Lomita Park; s. Enrico and Nora Marie (Giusso) C.; m. Anne Kathryn Drobac, June 12, 1954 (div. 1970); m. Lynne Therese Ingram, Dec. 31, 1983; children: Dina b. 1960, John b. 1962, Alexis b. 1969; edn: BS cum laude, Univ. San Francisco 1953; JD, Univ. S.F. Sch. Law 1958; admitted St. Bar Calif. 1959. Career: assoc. atty. Peart Baraty & Hassard, San Francisco1958-60; sr. counsel, asst. secty. BHP Minerals International, Inc. (formerly BHP Utah Internat. Inc.), San Francisco 1961-; dir: Garden Hotels Investment Co., Santa Rosa, Fathom Mgmt. Corp., S.F., Newco Trading Corp., S.F.; Broken Hill Proprietary (USA) Inc., S.F., BHP Transport USA Inc., Oakland, BHP Internat. Marine Transport Inc., Oakland, Family Housing & Adult Resources Inc., Belmont; v.p./dir. Shorebird HOA; trustee emeritus Univ. San Francisco; honors: Pi Sigma Alpha, Phi Alpha Delta, Bureau Nat. Affairs award 1958, U.S.F. disting alumni service 1981, Athletic Hall of Fame 1985, Alumnus of Year USF 1989; mem: Am. Arbitration Assn. (nat. panel of arbitrators 1962-), Bar Assn. San Francisco, Am. Bar Assn., Am. Corp. Counsel Assn., Commonwealth Club Calif., Univ. S.F. Alumni Assn.; article pub. in profl. jour. 1975; mil: 1st lt. AUS 1954-56; Republican; R.Cath. Res: 8201 Shorebird Circle Redwood City 94065 Ofc: BHP Utah International Inc. 550 California St Rm 800 San Francisco 94104

CURTIS, THERESE DODGE, corporate secretary; b. May 1, 1935, Niagara Falls, N.Y.; d. Edward Francis and Agnes (Dell) Dodge; m. Charles R. Curtis, July 30, 1967, div. 1979; edn: cert. Katherine Gibbs Sch., NY, NY, 1956. Career: corporate secty. and dir. Topa Equities, Ltd., L.A. 1964-, also corp.

secty. and dir.: Ace Beverage Co., L.A. 1964-, Paradise Beverages, Honolulu 1980-, West Indies Corp., St. Thomas, V.I. 1982-. Ofc: 1800 Ave of the Stars Ste 1400 Los Angeles 90067

CURTIS, WILLIAM CLAUDE, university safety officer; b. May 24, 1947, Oakland; s. Ralph Lester and Mary Louise (Sparkman) C.; m. Donna, Mar. 31, 1975; children: Roger b. 1970; edn: BS, Loma Linda Univ. 1970; FFL (Fed. Firearm Lic.), NASD Series 7 lic., Life & Disability Ins. lic., Calif. R.E. sales agent. Career: plant foreman Loma Linda Univ. Farms, Riverside 1970-71; carpenter Ralph Curtis Co., Susanville 1972; security ofcr. Sierra Security, San Bernardino 1972-73, Calif. Plant Protection, Colton 1973; patrolman LLU, 1973-75, safety ofcr. LLU Med. Center 1975-76, sgt. 1976-; owner Curtis Firearms (firearms & knives); life mem: Nat. Rifle Assn., Calif. Rifle and Pistol Assn., Nat. Knife Assn., Classic Chevy Club Internat., Sierra Club, Nat. Geographic Soc., Nat. Wildlife Fedn., Am. Assn. of Individual Investors; Republican; Seventh Day Adventist; rec: gun collector, outdoorsman, investor. Res: 26329 Cardigan Place (Box 81) Loma Linda 92354

CUSTIS, L. DWIGHT, JR., management information systems executive; b. Jan. 6, 1944, Jonesboro, Ark.; s. L. Dwight and Edith Lucille (Mouton) C.; m. Nancy Virginia Klein, June 29, 1968; children: Courtney b. 1969, Lara b. 1973; edn: BS math., Wheaton Coll. 1966; MS math., No. Ill. Univ. 1973. Career: programmer, analyst Ford Aerospace, Newport Beach 1968-79, supr. S/W engring, 1979-82, mgr. info. and office systems 1982-83, mgr.corporate data center 1983-87, mgr. engring. computer systems 1987-89, mgr. mfg. computer system 1989-90; dir. info. resource mgmt. Loral Aeronutronic 1990-93, v.p. info. resource mgmt. 1993-; pres. Mission Data, Mission Viejo 1980-93; mem: Grace Comm. Ch. (elder 1987-89), Loral Aeronutronic Mgmt. Club, Orange Coast CSL (pres. 1975-76); Republican; Prot.; rec: computer systems, softball, golf. Res: 27512 Cenajo Mission Viejo 92691 Ofc: Loral Aeronutronic. Ford Rd Newport Beach 92658

CUTHBERTSON, JOHN BROWN, mechanical contractor executive; b. June 7, 1929, Glasgow, Scotland; s. William and Beatrice (Brown) C.; m. Anita Straley, July 16, 1983; children: Stephen John b. 1958; edn: Creighton Selective Central, England 1945; Carlisle Tech. Coll. 1947. Career: apprentice steamfitter David Thompson Ltd. 1947-53; mech. supt. R.D. Purdie 1953-55; Canadian Comstock Co., Canada 1956-60; Harry Lee Inc., Burlingame 1961-68; exec. v.p. Thermal Mechanical, Santa Clara 1968-85; pres. 1985-90; mem: Calif. St. Assn. Plbg. Htg. Cooling Contrs. (state dir. 1989-), Greater Bay Area Assn. Plbg. Htg. Cooling Contrs. (dir. 1978-84, secty. 1985, v.p. 1986, pres. 1987-88, treas. 1989); mil: RAF 1947-49; rec: skiing. Address: 575 Fulton Way Danville 94526

CUTINO, BERT PAUL, restauranteur, developer; b. Aug. 7, 1939, Monterey; s. Paul and Rose (Aiello) C.; m. Bella, Nov. 12, 1972; children: Marc b. 1964, Michele b. 1968, Bart b. 1974; edn: grad. Monterey Union H.S., 1957, AA in bus., Monterey Peninsula Coll., 1964; Certified Executive Chef, Am. Culinary Fedn. (ACF) 1983; Dr. of Culinary Arts (hon.), Johnson & Wales Coll., 1988. Career: founder, ptnr./owner Sardine Factory, Monterey 1968- (award winning restaurant: Mobil Travel Guide - 1977-1992; one of 50 restaurants chosen by Pres. Reagan to serve at Presdl. Inauguration in 1981 & 1984; "Taste of America" and Restaurants and Instns. Mag. "Ivy Award"), responsible for re-development of Cannery Row area; corp. owns 70%, ptnr. of Foursome Devel. Co. and active in real estate; v.chmn. and c.e.o. Restaurants Central, 1973-, franchisee Wendy's (5); bd. dirs. Calif. Culinary Acad.; mem. advy. bd. Monterey Peninsula Coll. Culinary Pgm.; initiated bill intro. by Calif. Assembly Sam Farr to fund culinary arts pgms. in Calif. Community Colls.; instrumental in forming the 1st W. Region Culinary Team that participated in 1988 Culinary Olympics, Frankfurt, W.Ger.; honors: distinguished alumni Calif. Assn. of Colls. 1982, honor soc. American Acad. of Chefs 1984, Antonin Careme Medal for highest achiev. in gastronomy and food service 1987, Fellow for Life in Hon. Order of the Golden Toque (past comdr.-dir.), medal of honor Internat. Les Amis d'Escoffier Soc. (past Amb.-at-large for N.Y. chpt.), several gold medals in culinary competition, chef of yr. ACF Monterey Bay Chapter 1983, chef of yr. Calif. Restaurant Assn. 1984, nat. chef of yr. American Culinary Fedn. 1988, honored as "Diplomat" Calif. Culinary Acad. 1992, recipient 1st Soviet-Am. Culinary Exchange Medallion 1988, spl. award resolutions for community service from Calif. St. Senate (presented by Hon. Henry J. Mello) and Calif. St. Assembly, proclamation Mayor of Monterey, spl. honor from U.S. Congress entered into Congl. Record by Hon. Leon Panetta 1988, listed Who's Who Food Service Execs. 1990-92, Am. Biog. Inst. life fellow, internat. medal of honor; mem: Am. Culinary Fedn. (senior v.p. 1985-89, ACF presdl. medl #3 award, nat. chmn. mil. affairs com., protocol chmn. 1992 USA Nat. Culinary Team, bd. dir. ACF Chef and the Child Found.), Calif. Travel Industry Assn. "F. Norman Claek Entrepreneur Award" 1993; mem: Monterey Peninsula Chefs Assn. (1977-, bd. chmn., past pres.); Internat. Bd. of Les Toques Blanches, Paris, France (Mont. chpt. founder); Soc. for American Cuisine (founding mem.), Am. Inst. of Food and Wine, Confrerie de la Chaine des Rotisseurs (v.chancelier-argentier 1979-), Wine Investigation for Novices and Oenophiles, Kts. of the Vine (Master), Guild of Sommeliers (England), Wine Inst., Internat. Assn. of Cooking Profls., Advance. of Food Service Research, Calif. Rest. Assn., Nat. Rest. Assn., Rest. Bus. Research Advy. Panel 1985-; civic: Sheriff's Advy.

Council (charter), Mont. Penin. C.of C. (past v.p.), Monterey Schs. Found. (life hon. mem., founding bd.), Am. Red Cross (recipient Award of Honor 1989), active fundraising events for March of Dimes (Gala co-chair and hd. culinary judge since 1988), other charities; clubs: Pacheco, Beach and Tennis, Spanish Bay; mil: p.o., hosp. corpsman USNR 1961-67. Res: Jack's Peak, Monterey Ofc: Restaurants Central 765 Wave St Monterey 93940

CUTINO, LOUIS VICTOR, lecturer, nutritionist, poetic, oratorical and philosophical essayist; b. Sept. 7, 1920, Passaic, N.J.; s. Salvatore and Mary (Gullo) C.; father, noted poet, philosopher, scholar and biologist (discoverer of the plant kingdom biochemical equivalent of mother's milk in the animal kingdom; social scientist corresp. with Albert Einstein, Helen Keller, Jan Sibelius, Geo. Santayana re world problems and solutions; literary contbr. many mags. in Italy, and quarterly rev. "Personalist" USC Sch. Philosophy; Italian translator of Prometheus Bound by Aeschylus, hon. by world's great academies); nephew of Leopold Cutino (industrialist, blt. world's largest watch material bus.) and Rudolph Cutino M.D. (prof. ophthalmology Johns Hopkins, and chief of services Bklyn. Coll. Hosp.); Louis, a verified child prodigy, at 2 years of age answered questions and gave 20-minute recitations on hist., literature & music in 3 languages (Fr., Eng., Ital.); m. Avery, July 6, 1946; children: Mary Louise b. 1948, Louis K. b. 1949; m. 2d Geneva, May 15, 1971 (dec.); edn: BA, major Sp. and Latin Am. Affairs, USC, 1954. Career: publications secty. to Gen. Buckner US Army, Alaskan Defense Command 1943-44; duty ofcr. USAF/Material Command, San Bernardino 1955-60; personal rep. and talent scout of Grace Mullen (the founder Redlands Bowl) 1955-60; founder `Project Tijuana' cultural crusade to break psychological barrier between the Anglo-Saxon and Latin cultures to benefit border areas of both Mexico and U.S.A., San Diego - Tijuana 1960-: recent push by Pres. Bush to create common markets between Canada, Mexico and the U.S. was first suggested by L.V. Cutino in his widely circulated letter to Pres. Diaz Ordaz, 12/1/65 (copies to Pres. L.B. Johnson, Am. and Mex. diplomats); began leading Am. pioneer discovery visits to `the other Tijuana' 1960-, frequent lectr. bus. and profl. groups on the true Mexican culture and erroneous Am. conceptions, 1962-; awards: listed Am. Biog. Inst., Man of Year Award 1990, Hall of Fame and Gold medal award 1991-, Fellowship 1992; Man of the Year 1993, Hall of Fame 5,000 personalities of the World 1993 (ded. to L.V. Cutino 1993), listed 500 Leaders of the World 1993; author/pub. book: Project Tijuana (1966, 1970), in library archives Hist. of San Diego, San Diego St. Univ. and San Diego Pub. Lib.; book: A Symphony of Thoughts 1989, essays on universal problems & solutions, containing unpub. letters of Helen Keller to Salvatore C., and also Louis' hist. letters to Mrs. Lyndon B. Johnson, Vice Pres. Humphrey, Pres. Diaz Ordaz, Helen Keller and Billy Graham; booklet "The Soul of God," collection of free-verse spiritual poems 1991; recipient appreciation Pres. L.B. Johnson, Mexican Minister Tourism, ed.-in-chief L.A. Times 1966; rec: gardening. Address: P.O. Box 162 Aberdeen, WA 98520

CUTINO, PETER JOHN, sports manager, coach; b. Apr. 3, 1933, Monterey, Calif.; s. Paul and Rose (Aiello) C.; m. Louise Arlene Donato Sept. 5, 1953; children: Paul b. 1955, Peter b. 1961, Anna b. 1962; edn: BS, Cal Poly, San Luis Obispo, 1957; MS, Cal Poly, 1959. Career: tchr/coach, Oxnard H.S., Oxnard, Calif., 1957-63; faculty/coach, UC Berkeley, 1963-91; mgr., Monterey Sports Ctr., Monterey, 1992-; mem., Men's Internat./Olympic Com. for US Water Polo Inc., 1970; pres., Am. Water Polo Coaches Assn., 1974; mem., US Olympic Com. for World Univ. Games, 1980; chmn., Men's Internat./Olympic Com., US Water Polo Fedn., 1989; mem.: Technical Water Polo Com. for the North & South Am. (Pan Am) Games, 1992, Technical Water Polo Com. of Fedn. Internationale de Nation Amateur, 1992-; awards: NCAA Water Polo Coach of the Year, 1974, 75, 83, 88; Master Coach award, Am. Swimming Coaches Assn., 1980; Centennial award, Alumni Assn. of UC Berkeley, 1984; Contribution to Phys. Edn. & Athletics, 100th US Congress, Congressional Record, 1987; James R. Smith award, US Water Polo, Inc., 1988; mem.: Am. Water Polo Coaches Assn. 1965-, US Water Polo, Inc. 1965-; Nat. Recreation & Park Assn. 1991-; bd. of dir., US Water Polo, Inc., 1968-; mem: Rotary Club, Monterey,; Compari, Monterey; co-author: Polo Manual For Coach & Player, 1972; author: chpt., Water Polo, Sports Source , 1972; chpt., The Driver In Water Polo, The Complete Book of Water Polo, 1986; ed., NCAA Water Polo Rules Book, 1968-69, 1986-90; Democrat; Catholic; rec: writing. Res: 4 Zaragoza Views Monterey 93940. Ofc: Monterey Sports Ctr. 301 E. Franklin Monterey 93940

CUTRI, ALBERT ANTHONY, oral and maxillofacial surgeon; b. Sept. 21, 1947, San Diego; s. Joseph Anthony and Vanda (Alibrandi) C.; m. Sharon Marie Heinz, May 17, 1969; children: Albert Michael b. 1974, Nicholas James b. 1981; edn: BS, Villanova Univ. 1969; DDS, USC 1973; MD, Univ. Neb. Omaha 1976; lic. Am. Bd. Oral & Maxillofacial Surgery 1980. Career: resident, 1976-78; pvt. practice 1978-; cons. Cleft Palate Team, Children's Hosp., San Diego 1978-; dept. dentistry San Diego VA Hosp. 1980, 81; dept. plastic surgery binational surgery team, UCSD Med. Ctr. 1980-; chmn. dept. oral surgery and dentistry Sharp Meml. Hosp. 1986-88, 91-93; mem: Am. Assn. Oral & Maxillofacial Surgery, So. Calif. Acad. Oral Pathology, ADA, So. Calif. Soc. Oral Maxillofacial Surgery, Internat. Microsurgical Soc., Internat. Congress Oral Implantologists, Acad. of Osseointegration, St. Augustine H.S. (bd. trustees 1987-), Laguna Art Museum Historical Collections Council (pres. 1992-);

Republican; Catholic; rec: gardening, bicycling, skin diving, collecting artwork, studying history. Ofc: 9855 Erma Dr #100 San Diego 92131

DAGGETT, ROBERT S., lawyer; b. Sept. 16, 1930, La Crosse, Wis.; s. Willard Manning and Vida Naomi (Sherman) Daggett; bro. Willard M. Daggett, Jr., M.D. (heart and vascular surgeon; Harvard Med. Sch. faculty, staff Mass. Gen. Hosp., Boston; Fellow Am. Coll. of Physiol.; lectr, writer on med. subjects); m. Helen Hosler Ackerman, July 20, 1976; children: Ann Daggett McCluskey b. 1962, John Sullivan Daggett b. 1964; edn: AA, Univ. Wis., 1950; AB with honors in polit. sci. and highest honors in journalism, UC Berkeley, 1952, and JD, 1955; admitted bar: Calif. 1955, US Supreme Ct. 1967, various Fed. Cts. Career: ptnr. San Francisco law firm of Brobeck, Phleger & Harrison, 1966-; major commercial litigation esp. antitrust, intellectual prop., securities, product liability and other corp. litigation; adj. prof. Hastings Coll. of Law and mem. advy. bd. Hastings Center for Trial and Appellate Advocacy; instr. Federal Ct. Practice Pgm. and mem. teaching com. No. Dist. Calif.; demonstrator-instr. Nat. Inst. for Trial Advocacy; arbitrator S.F. Superior Ct., and pvt. commercial arb.; evaluator Fed. Early Neutral Evaluation Pgm.; frequent lectr., writer on legal subjects; judge in Nat. Moot Court competition. Winner, Joffre Debate between UC and Stanford, 1952; asst. coach of debate, Univ. Calif., 1954-55. Mem: Am. Law Institute, Bohemian Club (SF), Commercial Club (SF, dir. 1989-, pres. 1993), Commonwealth Club (SF), State Bar of Calif., Am. Bar Assn.(Sects. on Litigation, Antitrust, Judicial Adminstrn.), Bar Assn. of S.F., Am. Judicature Soc., Fed. Bar Assn. (pres. S.F. ch. 1992-), Phi Delta Phi legal frat., Theta Xi frat., Order of the the Golden Bear, Republican Nat. Lawyers Assn.; past mem. Bd. Visitors, UC Santa Cruz: Coll. V.; Fellow, Am. Bar Found.; Coauthor Rev. of Selected Code Legislation, Cal.Cont.Edn.of Bar 1955; participant in legal pgms., seminars; mil: served to lst lt. US Army JAGC, QMC 1956-60; Republican; Prot.; rec: photog., music. Ofc: Brobeck, Phleger & Harrison, One Market Plaza, San Francisco 94105

DALAL, KANU B., biochemist; b. Jan. 1, 1941, Bombay, India; s. Bhaidas P. and Lalita B. D.; m. Mayuri K., Jan. 20, 1968; children: Manish, Jai; edn: BS, Bombay Univ., 1956, BS (Tech), 1959; MS, Seton Hall Univ., 1961; MS, Utah St. Univ., 1963, PhD, 1967. Career: CSIR fellow Univ. Dept. of Tech., Bombay, India 1960-61; NS fellow Utah State Univ., Logan 1963-69; postdoctoral fellow UC San Francisco 1968-73; res. scientist UC Berkeley 1974-76; sr.res. scientist MRI Preb. Med. Center, San Francisco 1977-82; cons. W.R.L., Albany 1983-84; staff scientist L.B.L., Berkeley 1985-; awards: NIH res. fellow 1963-69, fgn. travel grantee Soc. MS Found. (1970), Sigma Xi; mem: Soc. Nuclear Medicine, Internat. Soc. Neurochemists, Am. Chemical Soc., Soc. Food Technologists, Plant Sci. Club (secty., treas.), Internat. Student Assn. (pres.), S.F. Day Care Assn. (secty., pres.); articles pub. in sci. jours. (1963-); Hindu; rec: swimming, tennis, arts. Ofc: L.B.L. 74/157 One Cyclotron Rd Berkeley 94720

DALIS, IRENE, opera singer, opera company founder-executive; b. Oct. 8, 1925, San Jose; d. Peter Nicholas and Mamie R. (Boitano) Dalis; m. George Loinaz, July 16, 1957 (dec. Mar. 10, 1990); 1 dau., Alida Mercedes b. 1959; edn: AB, San Jose State Coll., 1946, MA, Teachers Coll. Columbia Univ., 1947; Hon. MusM, San Jose St. Univ., 1957, Hon. MusD, Univ. Santa Clara, 1987. Career: principal artist Berlin Opera, Ger. 1955-65, Hamburg Statsoper, Ger. 1966-71, San Francisco Opera, 1958-73, Metropolitan Opera, 1957-77; prof. of music San Jose State Univ., 1977-; exec. dir., founder Opera San Jose, San Jose, Calif. 1984-88, gen. and artistic director 1988-92, general director 1992-; awards: distinguished svc. Tchr.'s Coll., Columbia Univ. 1961, 20th Ann. Honor, Met. Opera, NY, Wagner medallion Bayreuth Fest., Bayreuth, Ger. 1963, Presdl. appt. SJSU 1977, medal of achiev. Acad. of Vocal Arts, Phila., Pa. 1988, Phi Kappa Phi 1980-; mem: Beethoven Soc. (advy. bd. 1985-), San Jose Arts Roundtable 1983-, AAUW (1980-), San Jose Opera Guild, Italian-Am. Heritage Found. S.J., Mu Phi Epsilon; Recording: Parsifal (Wagner) 1964; contbg. editor, Book Revs., Opera Quarterly (1983). Ofc: Opera San Jose, 12 South First St Ste 207 San Jose 95113

DALLAM, TIMOTHY MICHAEL, sales director; b. Sept. 14, 1948, Miami Beach, Fla.; s. Richard Ernest and Wilma Jean (Ball) D.; m. Particia Marie Bridleman, Aug. 25, 1973; children: Michele Elizabeth b. 1977, Nicole Victoria b. 1979; edn: BA, San Jose St. Univ. 1970. Career: asst. production mgr. Blommer Chocolate, Union City 1973-75; quality control mgr. Shade Foods Inc., Belmont 1975-77; product mgr. 1977-78; v.p. sales 1978-86; pres. GRP LA Ent. Inc., S.F. 1986-88; dir. indsl. sales Carriage House Foods, San Jose 1988-; mem: Calif. Dairy Industry Assn. (dir., asst. dir. 1988), Ore. Dairy Industry Assn., Inst. Food Technologists, Am. Assn. Candy Technologists, Wash. St. Dairy Council, Nat. Guard Assn.; writer & lectr. on flavoring ice-cream (1982); mil: E-6 U.S. Army Nat. Guard 1971-77; Republican; Am. Baptist; rec: sailing, skiing, camping. Ofc: Carriage House Foods POB 49009 San Jose 95161-9009

DALLARA, KEN BRADLEY, production/plant manager; b. Jan 10, 1963, Mtn. View, Calif.; s. George Peter and Nadine (Vill) D.; m. Julia Brooke Fairchild, Dec. 6, 1987; 1 son, Dominic Anthony b. 1991; edn: BS in indsl. and systems engring., Univ. of So. Calif., 1985; currently att. Univ. of La Verne

Law Coll. (JD candidate). Career: mfg. engr. Apple Computer, Garden Grove 1984-85; indsl. engr. Hughes Aircraft Co., El Segundo 1985-88; pres. Genoa and Assocs. (industrial and systems engring. consulting firm), Hollywood 1988-89; prodn./plant mgr. Raindrip, Simi Valley 1989-; mem: Am. Inst. Industrial Engrs. (v.p., past dir.), Am. Soc. Mech. Engrs., Archemedes Circle (v.p.), USC Engineering Alumni Assn. (bd.); creator software: Client Maintenance System for Non-Profit Orgns. 1988; pub. papers: Effects of Psychogenic Diseases on Sedentary Workers; Inventory Control Through Use of Vertical Integration; club: Cabrillo Beach Yacht; Republican (task force); Christian; rec: golf, sailboat racing ("Earl of Tasmania"). Res: 12352 Laurel Terrace Dr Studio City 91604 Ofc: Raindrip, Inc. 2250 Agate Ct Simi Valley 93065

DALTON, TIMOTHY VINCENT, service company president; b. Jan. 2, 1946, Hackensack, N.J.; s. Thomas James and Pauline (Haxton) D.; m. Cherie Taylor, Sept. 9, 1978; children: Daniel b. 1980, Annette b. 1984; edn: BS, Univ. Pa. 1966; MD, Harvard Med. Sch. 1970. Career: pres. Dalton Med. Group Inc., El Monte 1977-; Dalton Service Industries Corp., Los Angeles 1984-; mil: major Calif. Army Nat. Guard 1971-79; rec: cattle ranching. Ofc: 10414 Vacco St South El Monte 91733

D'AMICO, JOSEPH THOMAS, manufacturing company executive; b. Jan. 16, 1930, New York; s. Stanislao and Mary (Maniscalco) D'A.; m. Lucille Smith, Dec. 30, 1966; edn: BS mgmt., Fordham Univ. 1951. Career: dir. materiel Loral Electronics, Bronx, N.Y. 1954-65; Philco Ford Corp., Phila., Pa. 1965-70; v.p. materiel Varadyne Industries, Santa Monica 1970-76, v.p. internat. sales 1976-80; dir. materiel Superior Industries, Van Nuys 1981-84, v.p. materiel 1984-; mem: Purchasing Mgmt. Assn. L.A., Export Mgmt. Assn. of L.A.; Republican; R.Cath.; rec: sports, music. Res: 521 Muskingum Ave Pacific Palisades 90272 Ofc: Superior Industries Internat. 7800 Woodley Ave Van Nuys 91406

DAMON, ROBERT BRIAN, licensed acupuncturist; b. May 19, 1961, NY, NY; s. Richard and Grace (Giardina) D.; m. Lisette Ursole Cauchon, Sept. 10, 1990; children: Renata b. 1990; edn: MS, Am. Coll. of Trad. Chinese Medicine, S.F., Calif., 1989. Career: food server, various restaurants, NY and S.F., 1978-88; acupuncturist, Madison Health Profls., El Cajon, Calif., 1989-90; prof., Am. Inst. of Oriental Medicine, San Diego, Calif., 1990-; acupuncturist, private practice, Park Blvd. Health Ctr., San Diego, 1990-; subject matter expert, Nat. Credential Clearinghouse, Calif. State Acupuncture Licensing Exam, 1990-92; mem. Calif. Acupuncture Assn., 1990-; mem. Holistic Aids Response Prog., San Diego, 1990-; author: articles publ. in profl. journals, 1990, 1992; rec: organic gardening, Zymurgy. Res: 3370 29th St. San Diego 92104 Ofc: Park Blvd. Health Ctr. 4545 Park Blvd. 101 San Diego 92116

DAMRON, SIDNEY S., engineering manager; b. Dec. 8, 1925, Flagstaff, Az.; s. Sidney S. Damron and Bertha Myrtle (Carver) D. Rodgers; m. Gloria A. Boitano, Feb. 24, 1952; children: Nancy b. 1955, Kathy b. 1958, Patty b. 1961; edn: BS, Arizona St. Univ., Tempe 1950. Career: engr. Amer. Bdcast., San Francisco, 1950-57; Varian Assocs., Palo Alto, 1957-58; staff engr. Ampex Corp., Redwood City, 1958-67, sr. staff engr., 1967-68, mgr. engring., 1968-72; v.p. engring. Echo Science, Mountain View, 1972-76; program mgr. video recording Datatape Inc., Pasadena, 1977-78, div. mgr. engring. 1978-80, chief video engring. 1980-82, mgr. advanced devel. 1984-; dir. engring. Conrac, Covina, 1982-84; mem: IEEE (sr. mem. 1967), SMPTE; inventions: 6 patents and 7+ profl. papers re Rotary Head Magnetic Instrumentation Recording (1958-76); mil: pvt. Army Air Corps 1944-45; Republican; Christian; rec: Spanish language, literature and history. Ofc: Datatape Inc. 360 Sierra Madre Villa Pasadena 91109

DANA, DEANE, county supervisor; b. July 9, 1926, N.Y.C.; s. Deane andDorothy Bartlett (Lawson) D.; m. Doris Agath Weiler, July 14, 1951; children: Deane III b. 1952, Marguerite b. 1953, (twins) Diane and Dorothy b. 1956; 4 grandchildren; edn: ME, Stevens Inst. of Tech., 1951; Reg. Profl. Engr. Calif. Career: dist. mgr. Pacific Tel. Co. 1953-80; elected supr. 4th Dist. Los Angeles Co. Bd. of Suprs., 1980-, re-elected 3d term 1988-, chmn. bd. 2t, mem. Coliseum Commn. (past pres.), LA. Co. Transp. Commn. (chmn. 1986), So. Calif. Reg. Airport Auth. (chmn. 1987-88); honors: Hon. LLD, Pepperdine Univ. 1985, named Most Caring Pub. Ofcl. by Calif. Ctr. for Fam. Survivors of Homicide 1985, Torch of Liberty Govt. of Israel (1986); mem: Calif. Assn. of Compensatory Edn., Navy League U.S., Am. Legion, Elks, Calif. Motion Picture Council, Californians for A Strong Am., Calif. Shore and Beach Preservation, Pepperdine Univ. Assocs., Santa Monica Coll. Assocs., Internat. Footprint Assn., Venice-Marina Rotary Club, Exec. Bd. L.A. Area Council BSA, Town Hall of Calif.; mil: lt. USAF 1945-47, 1951-53; Republican (Rep. Central Com. of Calif.); Episcopalian; rec: golf, tennis, water skiing. Res: Palos Verdes Estates Ofc: County of Los Angeles 500 W Temple St Ste 822 Los Angeles 90012

DANANDEH, SAEED, PhD researcher and civil engineer; b. Aug. 21, 1952, Tehran, Iran; s. Nosrat and Ghodsieh (Ghaysar) D.; m. Oranous, June 11, 1983; 1 son, Andalib b. 1985; edn: BSC (CNAA) w/honors, Univ. of East London 1976; M.Engr., Sheffield Univ. 1977; Reg. Profl. Civil Engr., Calif. Career: structural eng. asst. Computer Engring., NCR Nat. Cash Register, London, UK 1972; struct. eng. asst. S.B. Tietz and Partners, U.K. 1973-76; civil engr. VTN

Consol. Inc., Irvine 1978-80; civil engr. City of Long Beach, 1980-90; spl. essential plan checking engr. P.E., City of Ontario, 1991-; PhD res. into advanced composite materials, Dept. of Mechanical & Process Engring., Univ. of Sheffield, UK, England, 1993-; mem: ASTM, ASCE, Prestressed Concrete Inst., Am. Concrete Inst., Internat. Conf. of Building Ofcls., Struc. Engrs. Assn. of Calif.; research in field of composites and concrete; Bahai World Faith; rec: sports, movies, cars, travel. Res: (Calif.) 42 Carson Irvine 92720; (UK) Fiat 3, Castlewood Court, Castlewood Dr, Fulwood, Sheffield, England, UK S10 4Fh. Ofc: University of Sheffield Dept of Mechanical and Process Engineering, Mappin Street, Sheffield S1-4Dr. England, UK

DANIEL, ERNO S., physician; b. Dec. 15, 1946, Budapest, Hungary; Derivative Citizen 1964; s. Erno and Katinka (Scipiades) D.; m. Martha Peaslee, Aug. 14, 1976; children: Kristina b. 1977, Michael b. 1979, Mary b. 1980, Monica b. 1987; edn: BS chem., Calif. Inst. of Tech. 1968; MS chem., UC San Diego 1970, PhD phys. chem., 1971; MD, UC Los Angeles 1975; cert. Am. Bd. Internal Medicine, 1981, bd. cert. Geriatrics, 1988, cert. in vascular physics and technology by Am. Registry of Diagnostic Medical Sonographers (ARDMS). Career: teaching and res. asst., UC San Diego 1968-71; resident phys. dept. internal medicine UCLA 1975-78; geriatric and vascular med. specialist, dept. internal med. Santa Barbara Medical Foundation Clinic, 1978-, dept. chmn. int. med. 1984-, mem. Res. and Edn. Com.; med. advy. bd. Alzheimer's Assn. Santa Barbara; awards: Conger Prize CalTech 1967, NSF undergrad. res fellow 1968, Calif. St. Univ. grad. fellow 1968, Outstanding Young Men Am. 1983, travel grantee Internat. Res. and Exchanges Bd. N.Y. 1985, recipient Chairman's award S.B.M.F. Clinic 1986; Fellow A.C.P. 1983, mem. Soc. of Vascular Med. & Biol., Soc. of Vascular Tech., CalTech Alumni (life), UCLA Alumni (life); violinist Santa Barbara Sym. Orch. 1961-64; prod./ co-host TV weekly series "Senior Forum" KCOX TV 3, Santa Barbara 1985-86; contbr. articles in other med. and sci. jours.; rec: computers in health care, American Indian hist. and arts. Ofc: Santa Barbara Medical Foundation, 215 Pesetas Ln Santa Barbara 93102

DANIEL, GARY W., motivational consultant; b. June 22, 1948, Wendall, Idaho; s. Milan C. Daniel and Ila F. (Cox) Harkins; m. Jeannie L. Blandford (div.); m. Sandi Kay Modey, July 26, 1974; children: Kelly Jean b. 1970, Marcus Chauncy b. 1981; edn: AA, Boise Bus. Coll., 1969; master hypnosis (M.H.), Hypnosis Tng. Inst., Santa Rosa, Calif. 1990; cert. master practitioner Neuro Linguistic Programming, Denver 1992. Career: sales mgr. KBBK-FM Radio, Boise 1974-79; sales mgr. ABC-TV (KIVI), Boise 1979-83; owner Video Magic Amusement Co., Caldwell, Idaho 1983-85; owner, c.e.o. Victory Media Group, Petaluma, Calif. 1985-, gen. mgr., dir. Victory Artists (recording label), 1987-; dir. Neuro Achievement Ctr. Petaluma 1989-, devel. therapeutic process NeuroImaging (1990); cons./dir. Victory Records, Santa Rosa 1986-; dir. Bay City Records, Santa Rosa 1989-90; mktg. cons. Capital Business Sys., Napa 1986-, Firenze Records, S.F. 1985-89, KWZ Radio (Boise) 1974-80; awards: Idaho State Bdcstrs. Assn. top radio personality 1971, and most humourous t.v. commercial 1975, Boise Ad Club most creative t.v. commercial 1976, Top mktg. award 1977; mem: Internat. Assn. of NLP, ASCAP (publ. mem.), Am. Council of Hypnotist Examiners (profl. mem.), Am. Assn. Councilors & Therapists (profl. mem.), Am. Assn. Behavioral Therapists, Petaluma C.of C., Bus. Assn. of Petaluma (dir.), Execs. Internat. Santa Rosa; prod. (recording) Shelly T 1987; Republican; Christian; rec: music, flying. Ofc: Victoria Media Group 1321 Commerce St Ste P Petaluma 94954

DANIELSON, WALTER G., lawyer, diplomat; b. July 3, 1903, Anaconda, Mont.; s. John and Tekla Christina (Jonsson) D.; m. Beryl Marie Pearce, Aug. 17, 1935; children: Karin Lynn Godfrey, John Howard; edn: LLB, Univ. Mont., 1929, JD (Hon.), 1970; Pepperdine Univ. Diploma of Honor, 1980, Doctor of Laws, 1991; admitted bar Calif. 1929. Career: sole practice, Los Angeles 1986-; former ptnr. Danielson & St. Clair; vice consul for Sweden, Los Angeles, 1937-55, consul 1955-69, consul gen., 1969-76, consul general emeritus, 1976; sec. Los Angeles Consular Corps, 1976-; honors: cmdr. and Knight Royal Order Vasa, cmdr. Royal Order North Star (Sweden), Officers Cross of Hungary, Knight Royal Order St. Olav, Norway, Knight's Cross 1st class Royal Order Dannebrog, Denmark, distinguished service Calif. Lutheran Univ. (2/24/86) first recipient Sven A. Eliason Merit Award (9/16/88), first recipient annual Chmn's. Award Calif. Med. Ctr. Found. (3/28/89), distinguished service Republic of Honduras (3/12/91); mem. Calif. State Bar, Los Angeles Co. Bar Assn.; clubs: California, Vasa Order Am., Swedish (L.A.), Sigma Chi. Res: 68 Fremont Pl Los Angeles 90005 Ofc: 643 S Olive St Ste 600 Los Angeles 90014

DANKANYIN, ROBERT J., business executive; b. Sept. 4, 1934, Sharon, Pa.; s. John and Anna (Kohlesar) D.; m. Dorothy Jean Kuchel, Aug. 9, 1958 (div. June 1975); children: Douglas, David, Dana; m. Georgia C. Oleson, Apr. 2, 1988 (dec. Sept. 5, 1990); edn: BS, Pa. State Univ., 1956; MBA, USC, 1961; M.Engring., UCLA, 1963. Career: with Hughes Aircraft Co., Culver City: mgr. Mobile ICBM Systems engring. dept., pgm. mgr. Surveyor Sci. Payloads, mgr. Space System Labs, 1956-68; Litton Industries, Beverly Hills: assoc. pgm. mgr. for DD-963 Class Ships, pgm. mgr. for LHA Class Ships, v.p. of pgm. mgmt., 1968-73; group exec. Whittaker Corp., Westwood Village, also pres./chmn. bd. Whittaker Community Devel. Corp., Englewood, Colo., Knoxville, Tenn., and Westwood

Village, Calif., 1973-75; Hughes Aircraft Co., Canoga Park: asst. mgr. for U.S. Roland Pgm. 1975-77, asst. div. mgr. Missile Devel. Div. 1977-84, div. mgr. Land Combat Systems Div. 1984-86, group v.p., then v.p., asst. group exec. Missile Systems Gp. 1986-88, v.p. and asst. group exec. Space & Comms. Gp. Hughes Aircraft Co., El Segundo 1988-89, corporate senior v.p. diversification Hughes Aircraft Co., L.A. 1989-92; senior v.p. bus. devel. 1992-, chmn. bd. Light Valve Products Inc., San Diego; chmn. bd. Hughes/Japan Victor Tech., Inc., Calsbad, Calif. 1990-92; dir.: ADPA, W.D.C. 1986-, Hughes Micro Elec. Ltd., Scotland 1984-, Hughes Environmental Systems Inc., Hughes Espana; profl. ski instr., Bear Mtn. 1991-; awards: editor Inter Frat./Sor. Newsletter Penn State Univ. 1955-56, La Vie 1956, outstanding engring. alumni Penn State Univ. 1992, laid the Kell of LHA-1, Litton Ship Building, Pascagoula, Miss. 1971, Penn State Outstanding Engineering Alumnus 1991, Kakka Delta Rho Ordo Honorium 1992; mem.: Hughes Mgmt. Club, Am. Def. Preparedness Assn. (dir.), Indsl. & Profl. Advy. Coun. Coll. of Engring. Penn State Univ. (chmn.); clubs: Marina City (Marina Del Rey), Riviera CC, Aero Club of So. Calif.; rec: skiing, skin diving, sailing, hiking, fishing, golf. Res: One Catamaran St Marina Del Rey 90292 Ofc: Hughes Aircraft Co. PO Box 80028 Los Angeles 90080-0028

DANZIG, FRANK KENNETH, stockbroker; b. Oct. 22, 1915, NYC; s. Jerome J. and Helen W. (Wolf) D.; m. 2d. Twila, Oct. 10, 1969; children: Victoria Jane D. (Nahum) b. 1947, Priscilla D. (Gardiner) b. 1950; edn: sci., Worcester Acad. 1933; BA, Dartmouth Coll. 1937. Career: with Radio Stations WNEW, WHN and WMCA, NY, also CBS, 1937-42; independent radio dir., prod., Hollywood 1946-52; v.p., secy-treas. Ross-Danzig Prodns., Inc. TV Pgmmg. Co., 1952-62; pres., gen. mgr. Imperial Broadcasting System, Inc. 1958-62; secy-treas. Teen-Age Fair, Inc., 1962-70; 1st v.p. Investments, Dean Witter Reynolds, Inc. 1970-91; mem: Pacific Pioneer Broadcasters (dir. 1979-81), Acad. of TV Arts & Scis., Cancer Res. Assocs./USC (dir. 1987-); club: Mountaingate CC; mil: maj. US Army Signal Corps, 1942-46; rec: jazz, photog. Res: 2122 Century Park Ln #117 Los Angeles 90067

DARBY, RAY E., marketing executive; b. Oct. 14, 1931, Albia, Iowa; s. Ray E. and Mildred (Wood) D.; m. Leonora Fuschi, April 10, 1955; children: Ray Alan, John, Jeffrey, Julie; edn: BS, Drake Univ. 1960; MA, 1966. Career: asst. res. dir. Wallaces Farmer, Des Moines, Iowa 1960-64; dir. market res. AMF Western Tool 1964-68; mktg. mgr. Dial Fin. 1968-70; corp. media dir. Gambles Inc., Mpls., Minn. 1970-73; asst. ADV dir. Handyman Corp., San Diego 1973-78; corp. ADV dir. Handy City, Atlanta, Ga. 1978-79; sr. mktg. mgr. Security Pacific Fin., San Diego 1979-; instr. San Diego Univ. 1987-89; mem: San Diego Direct Mktg. Assn. (coordinator edn. com. 1987-89), Jaycees Des Moines (past advisor), Am. Legion; masters thesis pub. (1966); mil: airman 1c. USAF 1951-55; R.Cath.; rec: gardening, hiking. Res: 4954 Via Cinta San Diego 92122 Ofc: Security Pacific 10089 Willow Rd San Diego 92131

DARLING, SCOTT EDWARD, lawyer; b. Dec. 31, 1949, Los Angeles; s. Dick and Marjorie Helen D.; m. Cynthia D. 1970 (div.); m. Deborah L., Aug. 22, 1981; children: Ryan b. 1976, Jacob b. 1978, Smokie b. 1980; edn: BA, Univ. of Redlands 1972; JD, USC 1975; admitted bar: Calif. Career: travel counselor World Travel Inc., Riverside 1968-72, asst. mgr. 1972-76; campaign mgr. Grant Carner for Congress, Riverside 1976; asso., ptnr. law firm Falsetti, Crafts, Pritchard & Darling, Riverside 1978-84; senior ptnr. Darling, Miller & King, Riverside 1984-; pres. Newport Harbor Devel. Co., Inc. 1983-87; grant reviewer U.S. Dept. HUD 1984-88; bd. dirs. Tel-Law, Inc. (nat. public svc. legal info. system) 1978-80; judge protem Riverside Superior Ct. 1980, 87; mem. Atty's panel Calif. Assn. Realtors; honors: Who's Who In Am. Law 1986-, Who's Who in World 1989-, Outstanding Young Men Am. 1979-86, Calif. Scholarship Fedn. (life), charter mem. H.S. Hall of Fame, Eddie D. Smith award Sickle Cell Orgn. 1981; mem: ABA, Calif. Bar Assn., Riverside Co. Bar Assn. (speakers' bur.), Native Sons of Golden West; civic: Survival Ministries (bd. 1986-89), Am. Red Cross (dir. 1982-84), Am. Heart Assn. (dir. Riv. Co.), UCR Citizens Com. 1978-81, Inland Area Sickle Cell Orgn. (dir. 1980-84), World Affairs Council (1978-84, Friends of Mission Inn 1980-82, Lions Club, Hispanic C.of C. (bd. 1978-82), Riv. Jaycees 1976-86; Republican: cand. for Congress 36th Dist. 1982; asst. treas. Calif. State Republican Party 1980-82; Harvest Christian Fellowship. Res: 1805 Elsinore Rd Riverside 92506 Ofc: Darling, Miller & King, 3697 Arlington Ave Riverside 92506

DARMSTAETTER, JAY EUGENE, educator; b. Nov. 30, 1937, Altadena; s. Eugene Jamison and Virginia (Fagans) D.; edn: AA, LA City Coll., 1958, BA, L.A. State Coll., 1960, MA, 1962, postgrad., USC, 1962-1965. Career: tchr. Los Angeles City Schs. 1960-: athletic dir. 1965-83, announcer CIF so. sect. Artesia 1964-85, L.A. Unified Schs. district announcer 1970-, master tchr. 1983-84; apptd. L.A. County commr. Citizens Community Planning Commn., 1988-; recipient Nat. Def. Edn. Assn. award 1968; mem.: NEA 1977-, United Tchrs. L.A., Calif. Tchrs. Assn., Phi Mu Alpha Sinfonia 1958-; rec: music, announcing, reading. Ofc: Wilson High School 4500 Multnomah St Los Angeles 90032

DARWIN, BILL G., company president; b. Sept. 28, 1929, Bonham, Tx.; s. Walter Lee and Georgia Alice (Burns) D.; m. Bonnie May Urness, Sept. 1, 1950; children: William b. 1952, David b. 1956, Stephanie b. 1960; edn: grad.

Poly H.S. Riverside 1947; lic. contractor 1961, lic. realtor Calif. 1979. Career: floor mechanic Smith Grubbs Co., Riverside 1948-61; owner, pres. Darwin Floors Inc., Grand Terrace 1961-; honors: Girl Scouts golden rule 1970, City of Grand Terrace commend. 1979; mem: Grand Terrace C.of C. (pres. elect), Grand Terrace Lions (1st v.p.), Western Floor Covering Assn. (treas. 1978), San Gabriel Floor Covering Assn. (pres. 1977), Inland Empire Floor Covering Assn. (v.p. 1975-76); Republican; Lutheran; rec: travel, golf. Res: 23175 Palm Ave Grand Terrace 92324 Ofc: Darwin Floors POB 483 Colton 92324

DASCENZI, HAZEL MARIE, real estate broker; b. Sept. 6, 1920, Palestine, Tx.; d. Calvin Coolidge and Sarah Ethel (Evans) Click; m. Samuel Chris Dascenzi (div.); children: Sharron Marie (Beamer) b. 1942, Phillip Chris b. 1954; edn: grad. Lone Pine Union H.S., 1938; spl. courses in R.E. law; Cert. Paralegal, grad. So. Calif. Coll. of Bus. and Law, 1989. Career: broker/owner Hazel's Realty, San Juan Capistrano (prior office in Buena Park), 1959-; broker/cons. and v.p. Harbor View Financial Services, Inc., 1989-; honors: business woman of yr. BPW Club, chair Silverado Days award C.of C., outstanding chairmanship award CREA, woman of yr. Jaycees, mem. San Juan C.of C.; charter mem./past pres. Buena Park 1963, Cypress & La Palma Board Realtors, Buena Park C.of C., Women's Div.), Soroptimist Club Intl. B.P., Bus. & Profl. Womens Club B.P.; listed Who's Who in Real Estate; Republican; Sci. of Mind; rec: gardening, travel, dancing. Res: 33726 Calle Miramar San Juan Capistrano 92675 Ofc: Hazel's Realty 33726 Calle Miramar San Juan Capistrano 92675

DASH, HARVEY DWIGHT, artist; b. June 28, 1924, Bklyn.; s. Irving and Ann (Walters) D.; m. Ruth Strom, May 30, 1946 (dec. June 1975); children: Stefanie Marvel b. 1948, Eric b. 1950, Stuart b. 1952; m. Beverly Leonora Fields, June 26, 1976; edn: BFA, BS in edn., Temple Univ., 1948, MFA, 1949. Career: supr. art Pub. Schs. of Boundbrook, N.J. 1949-51; dir. Dash Art Sch., Plainfield, N.J. 1951-54; head dept. art Tenafly High Sch., N.J. 1954-57; dir. creative arts Paramus High Sch., N.J. 1957-67; founder, dir. Lighthouse Sch. of Art, Upper Grandview, N.Y. 1967-81; pres. Lighthouse Galleries Inc., Nyack, N.J. 1967-70; curator Gallery Five, Grandview, N.Y. 1970-80; one man shows Melbourne Gal., N.Y.C., 1960, Aker Gal., N.Y.C.; group shows Penn. Acad., Phila., Fairleigh Dickenson Univ., others; awards: Berley grantee Italy 1964, Paramus Sch. Sys. 1965; mem. Common Cause, People for the Am. Way; mil: sgt. US Army 1942-44; Democrat; rec: landscape designing, philateley, model R.R. Res: 16345 Bassett Ct Ramona 92065

DAUER, DONALD D., loan agent, consultant, investor; b. June 1, 1936, Fresno; s. Andrew and Erma Mae (Zigenman) D.; m. Laverne, Jan. 23, 1971; children: Gina b. 1971, Sarah b. 1977; edn: BS in B.A., CSU Fresno, 1958; postgrad. work Univ. Wash., Seattle 1964; desig: SRA, Soc. of Real Estate Appraisers, 1965. Career: loan officer First Savings & Loan, Fresno, 1961-71, senior v.p. 1971-78, exec. v.p. 1978-81; pres. Uniservice Corp., Fresno 1976-81; prin. Don Dauer Investment, 1981-; pres. and c.o.o.; dir. Riverbend Internat. Corp., Sanger 1985-89; loan agent Equity Lending Group, Fresno 1989-91; loan ofcr. Norwest Mortgage, Fresno 1993-; dir: University Sav. & Loan 1981-92, Riverbend Internat. 1987-91; mem. Soc. of R.E. Appraisers (past pres. Fresno), past mem. Calif. Mortgage Lenders Assn. (past pres. Cent. Calif.), Fresno Bldg. Material Dealers Assn. (past pres.); civic bds: Valley Childrens Hosp. Foundation, Fresno (1984-93, chmn. 1986-90), Valley Childrens Hosp. (bd. trustees 1987-93, chmn. 1990-92), Youth for Christ/USA (nat. trustee 1989-), Cent. Calif. United Cerebral Palsy Assn. (past), City of Fresno Gen. Svs. Retirement Bd. (past chmn.), CSU Fresno Alumni Trust Council (past pres., bd.); mil: s/sgt. Calif. Air Nat. Guard 1958-65; Republican; Prot.; rec: sports. Ofc: Norwest Mortgage 1616 W. Shaw Ste D-7 Fresno 93711

DAUGHADAY, DOUGLAS ROBERT, electronics engineer; b. Mar. 13, 1954, Highland Park, NJ; s. Robert Owings and Mary (Kirkpatrick) D.; m. Ilene D. Eichel, Feb. 14, 1987; son, Brian Douglas b. 1989; edn: BSEE, cum laude, W. Va. Inst. of Tech. 1976; MSEE, USC 1979; engr. in tng., State of W.Va. 1976. Career: tech. staff Hughes Aircraft Co., Culver City 1977-79; senior engr. Litton Guidance and Control Systems, Woodland Hills 1979-80; lab. engr. Airesearch Mfg. Co. of Calif., Torrance 1980-84; mgr. The Aerospace Corp., El Segundo 1984-; awards: Masters fellowship, Hughes Aircraft Co. (1977-9), Eta Kappa Nu (life); mem: Assn. Computing Machinery, IEEE Computer Soc., 2nd vp., Soc. of Am. Magicians Assembly #22, Nat. Assn. of Underwater Instrs. (1982-), USC Gen. Alumni Assn. (life); Democrat; Christian; rec: magic, scuba diving, photog. Res: Los Angeles; Ofc: The Aerospace Corp. 2350 East El Segundo Blvd El Segundo 90245

DAVE, BHALCHANDRA A., consultant food technologist, microbiologist; b. Dec. 10, 1931, Palanpur, India, U.S. citizen; s. Anantray C. and Chandramani (Joshi) D.; m. Vibha Dave, Jan. 29, 1965; children: Nayana b. 1967, Sunil b. 1968; edn: BSc, and MSc, St. Xavier's Coll., Bombay, 1955, 1958; MS, and PhD, Univ. Calif. Davis, 1962, 1968. Career: tchg. asst. St. Xavier's Coll., Bombay, 1955-58; res. asst. Food Sci. Dept., UC Davis, 1959-65, res. microbiologist 1965-70; res. food scientist DECCO Div. Pennwalt Corp., Monrovia, Calif. 1970-78, supr. res. ops. 1978-83, dir. of res. 1984-87, tech. mgr. DECCO U.S.A./Pennwalt, 1987-91, ret.; pvt. consultant, 1991-; awards: Citrus Industry

Pres.'s Award, Fla. State Horticulture Soc. 1980; mem: Inst. of Food Technologists 1960-, Am. Soc. for Microbiology 1959-, Am. Horticulture Soc. 1980-, Fla. State Horticulture Soc. 1977-, Internat. Citriculture Soc. 1980-, Internat. Soc. Horticulture 1980-; inventor, Patents (3+, 2 pending); publs: 35+ tech. articles (1959-); rec: photography, computer, database, tech. writings. Res: 3731 Pico Circle La Verne 91750 Ph: 714/599-3912 Fax: 714/599-8266

DAVENPORT, ROGER LEE, research engineer; b. Oct. 27, 1955, Sacramento; s. Lee Edwin and Ada Fern (Henderson) D.; m. Becky Alice Youtz, Dec. 31, 1977 (div. Apr. 1992); edn: AB in Physics, UC Berkeley 1977; MS in M.E., Univ. Ariz., Tucson 1979. Career: assoc. engr. Solar Energy Resrch. Inst., Golden, Colo. 1979-82, cons. engr. SERI, Darmstadt, Ger. 1982-84; missionary Eastern European Sem., Vienna, Austria 1984-87; staff researcher Sci. Applications Internat. Corp., San Diego, Calif. 1987-; honors: Phi Beta Kappa UCB 1975; mem. Am. Solar Energy Soc. 1988-, Wycliffe Assocs. 1990-; author, contbr. 1 book, tech. reports and papers, sci. jour. articles (1980-); Evangelical Prot.; rec: sailing, surfing, biking, hiking, flying. Res: 19076 W 59th Dr Golden CO 80403 Ofc: 15000 W 6th Sve Ste 202 Golden CO 80401

DAVIDSON, JAMES F., corporate controller, chief accounting officer; b. Jan. 18, 1952, Albuquerque, N.M.; s. Fred James and Sarah Janet D.; m. Donna Marie, Sept. 12, 1970; children: Lori b. 1971, Jeff b. 1972, Jeanie b. 1975, Michael b. 1980, Christina b. 1988; edn: BA psychology, UC Irvine 1974; MBA fin., UCLA 1976; C.P.A. Calif. 1980. Career: C.P.A., audit mgr. Cooper & Lybrand, Los Angeles 1978-89; corp. controller, chief acctg. ofcr. Cert. Grocers of Calif. 1989-; mgr., cons., C.P.A., instr. Coopers & Lybrand 1985-89; awards: Dist. Attys. Office Los Angeles courageous citizen of year 1987; mem: Calif. Soc. C.P.A., Am. Inst. C.P.A., Fin. Execs. Inst., Am. Mgmt. Assn., Retail Fin. Execs., Lions; Republican; R.Cath.; rec: coaching and refereeing wrestling, judo. Ofc: Certified Grocers of California 2601 S Eastern, Los Angeles 90040

DAVIES, EDWARD DAVID, architect; b. Sept. 4, 1911, Madison, Wis.; s. Rev. Howell David and Julia Hosford (Merrell) D.; m. Marjorie Scheflow, Jan. 30, 1936; 1 son, Robert Huntington b. 1936; edn: ME, Ill. Inst. of Tech. 1931; arch., Univ. Ill., Urbana 1931-34; arch. scholarship Cranbrook Acad. of Art, Mich. 1934-35; reg. architect, Calif. (1948), Ariz., Nev.; Calif. Comm. Colls. life tchr. cred. 1966. Career: arch. design/draftsman J. Robt. F. Swanson AIA, Detroit 1936-37; body designer (Buick) Gen. Motors Corp., 1937; power plant engr. Bigelow-Liptak, 1938; arch. Chicago YMCA 1939; arch. layouts new stores, Montgomery-Ward Co. 1940; proj. coord./chief Convair Aircraft (PB4Y, B-32 USN and Army Contracts) San Diego and Fort Worth Plants, WWII 1941-46, created Master Scheduling System and Prodn. Illustration Div. for Aircraft; archl./office designer/dftsman for Richard J. Neutra FAIA, Los Angeles Studio; chief arch. for S. Charles Lee (theatres), mgr. Los Angeles ofc. (indsl./hosp.), 1948-53; pvt. practice, 1954-64: worked with Walt Disney on New Orleans project at Disneyland, 1954; assoc. arch. George V. Russell, Planner UC Riverside Campus and CSC Dominguez Project; spl. projects for Lockheed Corp. and McDonnell-Douglas Corp.; project arch. Calif. Inst. of Tech. (Planetary and Seismology Lab.), Pasadena; arch. 27 Lutheran Chs., Calif.; faculty (Arch., Hist. & Practice) East Los Angeles Coll., 1956-66; mem: AIA, Calif. Council of Archs. (trustee Ins. Trust Fund 1960-63), AIA/Pasa. (pres. 1959), USC (20 Club), Navy League, Nat. Aeronautic Assn., Chi-Beta frat.; civic: Calif. Planning and Conserv. League (founding 1st v.p.), Pasa. Urban Redevel. Commn. (1st v. chmn. 1951-52), Pasa. Study Downtown Area Renewal (1959-60), Pasa. Beautiful Found. (founding pres.), Pasa. C.of C. (sec. 1961-64), Pasa. Citizens Council for Planning (pres. 1962), Pasa. Art Mus., Mus. of Modern Art N.Y., Los Angeles Co. Art Mus.; designed "Chief Illiniwek" logo for Univ. Ill. (1932); Republican; Prot.; rec: gardening, travel (worldwide). Res: 45100 Brest Rd c/o PO Box 1081 Mendocino 95460

DAVIES, JACK L., vintner; b. June 19, 1923, Cinti.; s. John Lloyd and Celia (Davis) D.; m. Jamie Peterman, March 19, 1960; children: William b. 1961, John b. 1964, Hugh b. 1965; edn: Northwestern Univ. 1942-43, Stanford Univ. 1946-48, MBA, Harvard Univ., 1950. Career: v.p. Avalon Mfg. Co., Los Angeles 1950-52; sr. analyst Kaiser Aluminum, Oakland 1952-55; assoc. McKinsey & Co., San Francisco 1955-60; v.p. mktg. Fiberboard Corp., San Francisco 1960-63; v.p. acquisitions Ducommun Inc., Los Angeles 1963-65; pres. Schramsberg Vineyards, Calistoga 1965-; pres. Caves Transmontanas Lda., Vila Flor, Portugal 1989-; dir. and past chmn. Wine Inst., San Francisco 1975-; honors: Cook's Mag. list of Who's Who of Cooking in Am., N.Y. 1985, wine man of year Friends of Jr. Art Mus. Los Angeles 1984, Junipero Serra award Calif. Wine Patrons L.A. 1984; club: Bohemian (SF); contbr. numerous articles to wine publs. internat.; mil: sgt. USAAF 1943-46; Republican; Prot.; rec: archeology, hiking, historic textiles. Address: Schramsberg Rd Calistoga 94515

DAVIS, BRUCE G., company president; b. Sept. 6, 1939, Pittsburgh, Pa.; s. Wm. R. and Dorothy E. Davis; m. Judy Dickerson, June 29, 1969; children: Nicholas b. 1974, Matthew b. 1975; edn: BS, Oreg. St. Univ., 1961. Career: with Davis Material Handling Co. (founded by father 1954), Los Angeles 1961-, purchased co. 1967, incorporated 1976, current pres.; scoutmaster BSA San Marino 1987-, scoutmaster Nat. Jamboree Troop 1989, exec. bd. San Gabriel

Valley Council BSA, scouting awards incl. dist. award of merit 1987, dist. tng. award 1987, wood badge beads 1987, Baden Powell Cup 1986, Eagle Scout, Order of the Arrow 1955; mem. World Affairs Council, Non Cannonical Calabashes/ Sherlock Holmes Soc., Oneonta Club S.Pasa. (pres. 1983-84), San Marino City Club (scouting com.), Mensa (past); Republican; Presbyterian. Ofc: 5000 Valley Blvd Los Angeles 90032-3925

DAVIS, COLEEN COCKERILL, teacher, bed & breakfast owner, consultant; b. Sept. 20, 1930, Pampa, Texas; d. Charles Clifford and Myrtle Edith (Harris) Cockerill; m. Richard Harding Davis, June 22, 1952, (div. 1984); children: David Christopher, Denis Benjamin (dec. 1979); edn: BS, Univ. Oklahoma, 1951; MS, UCLA, 1952; postgrad. studies UCLA, Whittier Coll., USC; Calif. std., sec. tchg. cred. Career: tchr. and dept. chair home econs. Whittier Union High Sch. Dist., 1952-85, substitute tchr., home tchr. 1985-; cons. 1986-; founder, pres., exec. dir. and co-host, America's Bed & Breakfast, Whittier 1983-, co-host Capital C, and Capital H; mem. Calif. Tchrs. Assn., NEA, Internat. Tour Mgmt. Inst.; civic bds: Whittier C.of C. (amb.), Children of Murdered Parents, Whittier (founder 1984), Parents of Murdered Children, Whittier (S.E./Long Beach chapt. leader 1984), Coalition of Organizations and People, Whittier (founder 1984), Whistle Ltd., Whittier (founder 1984), Fred C. Nelles Sch. (citizen advy. bd.); contbr. articles to newspapers; Republican; Episcopalian; rec: volunteer wk. Address: PO Box 9302 Whittier 90608

DAVIS, FAITH MARGARET, clinical social worker; b. Aug. 16, 1939, Detroit, Mich.; d. Robert Wendell and Cecelia Maxine (McGee) D.; div. 1967; children: Mark b. 1960, Mona b. 1963, Kenneth b. 1965; edn: BA, Marygrove Coll. 1959; MSW, San Francisco St. Univ. 1972; LCSW, lic. clin. social wkr. 1981. Career: social wkr. San Diego Welfare Dept., 1962-64; soc. work supr. Alameda Co. Welfare Dept., Oakland 1964-72; psych. soc. wkr. West Oakland Hlth Ctr. 1971-72; child welfare wkr. Alameda Co. Human Resources, Oakland 1972-73; psych. soc. wkr. Alameda Co. Substance Abuse, 1973-77; clin. dir. East Oakland Drug Abuse, 1977-78; cons. for Verbal Exchange Pgm. 1968-70, cons. Pub. Hlth Nurses 1973-77, cons. Oakland Pub. Schs. 1973-83; num. appreciation awards, Oakland Schools; mem: Nat. Assn. Soc. Wkrs., Bay Area Assn. of Black Soc. Wkrs., Counselors West, Marygrove Coll. and SFSU Alumni Assns., Alpha Kappa Alpha Sor., various PTAs, Toler Hts. Citizens Council, World Peace Orgn.; Democrat; Nichren Shoshu Soka Gakkai of Am. Buddhism; rec: dancing, travel. Res: Oakland Ofc: E. Oakland Comm. Mental Hlth Clinic, 10 Eastmont Mall 400, Oakland 94605

DAVIS, GRAY, state controller; b. Dec. 26, 1942, NY, NY; m. Sharon Ryer, Feb. 20, 1983; edn: BA (cum laude) Stanford Univ., 1964; JD, Columbia Univ. Law Sch., 1967. Career: chief of staff to Gov. Jerry Brown, 1974-81, served as chmn. Calif. Counsel on Crim. Justice, initiated statewide Neighborhood Watch Pgm.; elected rep. 43rd dist. Calif. St. Assembly, 1982-84, 1984-86, chmn. Housing and Community Devel. Com. (authored legis. requiring 10 percent of all apts. blt. with tax-exempt bonds be for very low income tenants; estab. stds. for removal of asbestos from pub. schs.); elected state controller, 1986-90, re-elected 11/90, respons. acctg. and disbursement of all state funds, mem. 56+ state boards and commns. including Bd. of Equalization, State Lands Commn., Commn. on State Finance, St. Bd. of Control, various bond fin. coms., chmn. Franchise Tax Bd.; founder/chmn. Calif. Found. for the Protection of Children (non-profit), co-op. with bus. and labor union to publicize photos of missing children, 1985 award for best pub./pvt. partnership in Calif.; mil: served to capt. US Army, Vietnam, Bronze Star (1969); Democrat. Ofc: State Controller 300 Capitol Mall 18th Fl Sacramento 95814; Mail: POB 942850 Sacramento 94250-5872

DAVIS, JOHN WARREN, contracting specialist; b. Feb. 14, 1946, York, Pa.; gr.grandson, W.F. Davis, founder Anchor Serum Co. and St. Joseph (Mo.) Stockyards and mem. Mo. State Legislature; gr.son, Frank A. Davis Sr., lawyer, St. Joseph, Mo.; son, Lillian M. (Billings) and Frank A. Davis Jr., real estate broker; edn: AA in real estate, San Diego City Coll. 1976; BA in pol. sci., Drake Univ. 1968; MS in acquisition & contract mgmt., West Coast Univ. 1987; Calif. lic. real estate broker ; Cert. Profl. Contract Mgr. (CPCM), Nat. Contract Mgmt. Assn. (1985, recert. NCMA -1995), cert. in contract mgmt., AF Inst. Tech. and NCMA 1989; profl. designation in contracting, US Army Logistics Mgmt. Coll. (ALMAC) and NCMA, 1991, panel mem. Nat. Panel of Arbitrators, Am. Arbitration Assn.; num. profl. tng. studies, DOD. Career: enlisted US Army, service in Vietnam, 1968-72; real estate sales and mgmt./student 1972-79; Naval Ocean Systems Center, San Diego 1979-80; contract intern/adminstr. Office of Naval Research, resident rep. Stanford Univ., 1980-84; contract splst. Naval Weapons Sta., Seal Beach Corona site 1984-86, contract splst. jt. service (Navy/AF) assigned to def. meteorological satellite pgm. Navy Space Systems Activity, Los Angeles AFB, 1986-88; procurement analyst Comdr. Naval Air Force Pacific Fleet, 1988-; instr. West Coast Univ. (chmn. curriculum rev. com. for acquisition Coll. of Bus., WCU), instr. San Diego State Univ. Ext. (chmn. curriculum rev. com. for acquisition Coll. of Extended Studies, SDSU; SDSU del. Nat. Acamenic Conf. for Academic Educators 1991, 1992); author of several prof. jour. articles and presenter at prof. acquisition meetings; awarded Royal Order of Trident for Equatorial Crossing; listed state, nat., internat. biographical directories; mem: Am. Mgmt. Assn., Nat. Contract Mgmt. Assn. (Fellow, ednl. chmn., mentor, Pony Express Award 1992, San Diego chpt.), Am. Bar Assn. (Assoc.), Am. Arbitration Assn.; clubs: Volunteers in Politics (treas.), San Diego Athletic, Sons of the Am. Revolution (SAR); mil: E5 US Army 1968-72, Vietnam Campaign (2/60 device) and Vietnam Svc. (2 stars) medals, Army Commendation, medals,; Episcopalian; rec: sailing, swim, travel. Res: PO Box 620657 San Diego 92162 Ofc: COMNAVAIRPAC (41A) NAS North Island San Diego 92135-5100

DAVIS, JOSEPH HAROLD, pediatrician, clinical professor emeritus; b. Mar. 16, 1914, San Francisco; s. Casper and Phoebe (Shipper) D.; m. Carol May Michels, Aug. 4, 1938; children: Leland b. 1941, Nancy b. 1946, Betsy b. 1950; edn: AB, Stanford Univ., 1933, MD, Stanford Univ., 1938; Calif. Lic. A07906, 1938. Career: pediatrician pvt. practice, San Francisco 1940-42; capt. Medical Corps US Army 1942-45; pediatrician Palo Alto Med. Clinic, Palo Alto 1946-; clin. prof. Stanford Univ. Sch. of Med., 1942-, emeritus prof. 1979-; honors: AOA, Stanford Med. Sch. 1937, Distinguished Eagle Scout 1989 and Scouter of Yr. Stanford Area Council BSA, Palo Alto 1989, lifetime service award Senior Coord. Council Palo Alto 1991; mem: AMA, Calif. Med. Assn., Santa Clara Co. Med. Soc. 1946-, Am. Acad. Pediatrics (1942-, Fellow, newsletter editor No. Calif. chpt. 1981-); civic: adv. Med. Explorer Post 63, Stanford Area BSA 1963-; club: University (Palo Alto); contbr. num. sci. articles in med. jours.; Democrat; Jewish; rec: philately. Res: 40 Anderson Way Menlo Park 94025 Ofc: Palo Alto Medical Clinic 300 Homer Palo Alto 94301

DAVIS, OAKLEY, JR., engineer; b. Sept. 20, 1930, Heilwood, Pa.; s. Oakley M. and Emabel (Decker) D.; m. Gloria T. Foresi, Aug. 7, 1957 (dec. 1981); m. Miriam Joy Berwick, Sept. 28, 1985; children: Jan M. b. 1960, Jeffrey E. b. 1962; edn: BSME, Pa. St. Univ. 1960. Career: design engr. Green Engring. Co., Sewickley, Pa. 1955-57; devel. engr. Aerojet Gen. Corp., Azusa 1961-64; v.p., gen. mgr. W.A. Whitney of L.A. 1965-68; v.p. sales Pow-R-Tron Inc., Home, Pa. 1968-69; gen. mgr. Fabri-Quipt Systems Co., Arcadia 1969-; design drafts-man Penna Dept. Hwys., Ind., Pa. 1951-55; shoe sales Brown Boot Shop 1950-51; waiter Hot Shoppes Marriott, Arlington, Va. 1949-50; awards: First Baptist Ch. mem. of year 1985, Hydra Tool top dealer 1973; mem: Am. Baptist Credit Union (bd. mem.), Fabrications Mfrs. Assn., Am. Mgmt. Assn., Civic Light Opera San Gabriel Valley (dir. 1984-87); articles pub. in tech. jours. 1970-75, seminars on metal fabricating methods 1985-; mil: pfc AUS 1952-54; Republican; Baptist; rec: classic and spl. interest vehicles. Ofc: Fabri-Quipt Systems Co. 420 Rolyn Pl Arcadia 91007

DAVIS, RICHARD, aviation insurance executive; b. March 11, 1947, Pittsburg, Calif.; s. Morgan William and Margaret (Jacobs) D.; m. Valerie Jean Hart, March 18, 1967; children: Kellie Susanne b. 1970, Scott Richard b. 1975; edn: BS, CSU 1971. Career: v.p., western regional mgr. Assoc. Aviation Underwriters, Universal City 1971-; mem: Am. Inst. Chartered Property & Casualty Underwriters, Los Angeles Club, West Hills Property Owners Assn. (v.p. 1988, bd. dirs. 1988, 89); Republican; rec: flying, skiing, travel. Ofc: Associates Aviation Underwriters 10 Universal City Plaza Ste 2350 Universal City 91608

DAWES, DAVID FORD, land and development co. president; b. July 29, 1909, Muskogee, Okla.; s. Maurice and Ethel (Ford) D.; m. Dorothy L. Snyder, Jan. 5, 1933; children: David Alan b. 1934, Stuart Edward b. 1936, Mary Lou b. 1943; edn: Okla. Univ. 1927-28; realtor 1945. Career: store mgr., salesman Safeway Stores 1931-37; milk route sales Golden Gate Creamery Long Beach 1938-39; salesman Automobile Club of So. Calif. 1939-42; personnel Northrup Aircraft Hawthorne 1942-45; realtor David Dawes Realty Torrance 1945-68; pres. Western Land & Devel. Co., pres. Am. Self Storage, Hawthorne; mem: Rancho Carlsbad Country Club 1969-, Calif. Assn. of Realtors (Hon. Life), Gardena Bd. Realtors (1956-69, pres. 1957, Realtor of Year 1962, Hon. Life), Carlsbad Bd. Realtors (pres. 1974), Hawthorne Bd. Realtors, Torrance Bd. Realtors, Masons (32 degree, Worshipful Master 1984), Scottish Rite, San Louis Rey Shrine Club (v.p.), Knights Templar, Rotary, Carlsbad Boys Club; secty., v.p. commr. San Diego County Flood Control 1975-80, Carlsbad Municipal Water Dist. Special Citizens Com. 1973-74. Republican; Prot.; rec: swimming, golf. Res: 3428 Don Juan Dr Carlsbad 92008 Ofc: Western Land & Devel. Co. 5200 El Camino Real 92008

DAWSON, CHANDLER ROBERT, physician; b. Aug. 24, 1930, Denver, Colo.; s. Irvin Milo and Helen (Quick) D.; m. Paula Whitlock Schilt, Oct. 2, 1954; children: Seth b. 1955, Ethan b. 1960, Matthew b. 1962; edn: analytical chemistry Princeton Univ., 1952; MD, Yale Univ., 1956; cert. Am. Bd. of Ophthalmology, 1967. Career: intern N.C. Memorial Hosp., Univ. N.C., 1956-57; sr. asst. surgeon Ctrs. for Disease Control, USPHS Epidemiology Br., 1957-60; resident dept. ophthal. UC San Francisco 1960-63; spl. fellow Bland-Sutton Inst. of Pathology, Middlesex Hosp. Med. Sch., London 1963-64; res. fellow Francis I. Proctor Found. UCSF, 1959-63, asst. res. ophthalmologist 1964-66; asst. clin. prof., asst., assoc. prof. ophthalmology UC San Francisco 1963-, prof. ophthal. in residence 1975-85; co-dir. World Health Orgn. res. ctr. trachoma and prev. of blindness, Francis I. Proctor Found., UCSF, 1970-79, dir. 1979-; assoc. dir., 1970-84, dir. Francis I. Proctor Found. for Res. in Ophthal. UCSF, 1984-;

cons. Div. of Indian Health, USPHS, 1965-; cons. in ophthalmology Marine Hosp. (USPHS) S.F. 1979-; cons. Pan Am. Health Orgn. 1966-; cons. WHO 1966-; counsellor Internat. Orgn. against Trachoma 1974-; mem. NIH visual sci. study sect. 1974- (chmn. 1976-78); mem. Am. Acad. Ophthal. (edn. com. 1974-75), AMA (pgm. com. 1974-77), Internat. Agy. for Prevention of Blindness (exec. bd. 1978-), Internat. Eye Found. (med. advy. bd. 1981-), Assn. for Res. in Vision and Ophthalmology, Ophthalmic Soc. of U.K., Electron Microscope Soc. No. Calif., Am. Soc. for Microbiology, AAAS; awards: Knapp Award 1969, AMA ophthal. sect. hon. mention for exhibit "Trachoma - still world's leading cause of preventable blindness" 1976, Medaille d'Or du Trachoma, La Ligue Contre le Trachome 1978, Am. Acad. of Ophthalmology Honor Award 1979 and exhibit prize 1983; author, coauthor 200+ med. jour. articles, books and book chapters. Ofc: Francis I. Proctor Foundation for Research in Ophthalmology UCSF San Francisco 94143-0412

DAWSON-HARRIS, FRANCES EMILY, writer-poet, civic volunteer; b. Augsburg, Germany, Dec. 7, 1952; d. Emmett C. Jr. and B. Louise (Boddie) Dawson; edn: BSN, nursing, Penn State Univ., 1974; R.N., Dist. Col. Career: staff nurse Howard Univ. Med. Ctr., Wash. D.C., 1974-75, charge nurse 1975-77; civic: Disabled Resource Ctr., Lupus Found. Am., Calif. Assn. Physically Handicapped; mem. Walt Whitman Guild, Penn State Univ. Alumni Assn.; pub. poems include: Live for Today, 1986, With You In Mind, 1987, Reflections, 1988; recipient Golden Poetry award 1985, 86, 87, 88, 89, 90, Excellence in Lit. award Pinewood Poetry, 1987, 88, 89, 90, Merit Poet award APA, 1989; Democrat; Baptist. Res: 6477 Atlantic Ave S Ste 308 Long Beach 90805

DEADRICH, PAUL EDDY, lawyer, realtor (ret.); b. Jan. 30, 1925, Lakeport, Ca.; s. John A. and Grace E. (Jackson) D.; m. Connie Washburn; children: Marjanne Robinson b. 1947, Nancy Wolfer b. 1950, Dianne Deadrich-Rogers b. 1952, Bettianne Buck b. 1955, John F. b. 1963, David b. 1968; edn: AA, UC Berkeley 1946; JD, Hastings Coll. of the Law 1949. Career: real estate sales agt., 1947-50; self-empl. attorney, San Leandro 1950-61; atty., realtor, ins. agt. in Twain Harte, 1961-73; law practice in Loomis 1973-75, in Cameron Park 1975-78; missionary at Apostolic Alliance Mission, Gibi, Liberia 1978-82; atty., realtor in San Leandro 1982-92; atty., Santa Clarita, Ca. 1992-; judge Justice Court, Tuolumne 1964-67; dir. Alameda Contra Costa Transit Dist. 1956-61; phys. edn. instr., coach Mother Lode Christian Sch., Tuolumne 1969-73; adminstr., coach, tchr. Loomis Christian Sch. 1974-75; dir. Calif. Conservatory Theatre 1988-91; past pres. Family Counseling Agy. of So. Alameda Co.; named Outstanding young man of year San Leandro Jr. Chamber 1955; mem: So. Alameda Co. Bd. of Realtors, Tuolumne Co. Bd. of Realtors (pres. 1973), So. Alameda Co. Bar Assn., DAV (past comdr. Chap. 67), Veterans Battle of the Bulge, 11th Armored Div. Assn., Am. Legion Post 117 (San Leandro), Sons in Retirement- Seven Hills; clubs: San Leandro Breakfast (pres. 1985-86) So. San Leandro Kiwanis (pres. 1985-86), Full Gospel Business Mens Fellowship Intl. (San Leandro chpt. pres. 1988-91, exec. v.p. 1983-86, dir. 1986-91), Twain Harte Rotary (pres. 1966-67), Broadmoor Mens (pres. 1958), Chabot Lions (pres. 1956-7), Twain Harte Hi-12 (past pres.), Loyal Order of Moose- Oakland, Clowns of Am. Internat.- Golden Gate (#80), East Belt Lodge F&AM No. 391, Cryptic Masons of CA Lodge No.5, Royal Arch Masons Chpt. 2, Kts. Templar of CA Commandery No.3, Old West Ch. 642 Order of Eastern Star; mil: pfc 11th Armored Div. WWII, France and Belgium, 1943-45, Bronze Star, Purple Heart, Combat Inf. Badge; Creation Missions Ch. (missionary in Liberia 1978-82); rec: gardening, fishing, backpacking. Res: 26516 Cockleburr Way Santa Clarita 96516-2337

DEAN, RICHARD MASON, educator, company president; b. Apr. 4, 1951, Pomona; s. Louis Mason and Mary Louise (Fandre) D.; edn: BS bus. mgt., Calif. State Polytech. Univ. 1974, BS econs. 1978, MSBA 1980, MS econs. 1984; Calif. Life Community Coll. tchg. credentials: bus. edn. 1978, bus. and indsl. mgmt. 1979, administrator 1986, economics, office and related technols., computer & related technols., profl. edn. (Life, 1985), clear single subject Bus. Edn. 1979 (life), Supp. Auth. Math. 1990; Lic. Pvt. Pilot 1988. Career: acct. Rowland Unified Sch. Dist., Rowland Hts. 1975-79; work experience coord. Chaffey Joint Union H.S. Dist., Ontario 1979-82; lectr. Mgmt. Human Resources Dept. Cal Poly Univ., Pomona 1982-85; tchr. Arroyo H.S., El Monte Unif. Sch. Dist. 1985-; pres. University Word Processing, Fullerton 1982-; cons. Gentek Corp., La Verne 1984; guest lectr. General Dynamics, Pomona 1984; cons. Houghton Mifflin Pub. Co., Boston 1984-; mem: Nat. Business Educators Assn., Calif. Bus. Educators Assn., Apartment Owners Assn.; sponsor Arroyo H.S. Info. Systems Club; publs: Easy Computations Software (for appls. in mktg., fin., acctg. and stats.), How to Program in B.A.S.I.C., Easy Librarian Software, (all copyrighted 1982); Republican; Congregational; rec: golf, skiing (snow, water), scuba, travel. Ofc: University Word Processing 2733 Pine Creek Circle Fullerton 92635-2936

DEBRIE, CAROL JEAN (PERALTA), nurse; b. Apr. 14, 1955, Encino, Calif.; d. Harold Richard Wallinger and Beverly Jean (Tuckett) DiDonato; m. Jimmy Lee Peralta, Jan. 19, 1974 (div. Feb. 14, 1985); m. Glen Ray DeBrie, June 15, 1991 (div. Apr. 28. 1993); children: Seth James Peralta b. 1976, Shelbi Jean Peralta b. 1978, Aubrie Anna Peralta b. 1981; edn: diploma, AA Stagg H.S.,

Stockton, Calif.; assoc. degree, San Joaquin Delta Coll., Stockton; currently enrolled in BSN prog., CSU, Dominguez Hills; career: staff nurse ICU, SJGH, French Camp, Calif. 1986-90; ADON. LaSalette Conv., Stockton, Calif. 1990; venipuncture RN, Delta Blood Bank, Stockton 1990-91; utilization review coord., Interplan, Stockton 1991; nsg. supr., CarePoint/HSSI, Stockton 1991-93; dir. of home care, Agostini & Assoc., Stockton 1993-; PRN Registry, home visit nurse 1989-91; Certified Birth Educator, Babes; CPR instr., Amer. Heart Assn.; HHA certification, Agostini & Assoc., Stockton, 1993; awards: Volunteer of the Year, Amer. Cancer Soc., Stockton 1989; mem: bd. of dirs. ACS 1987-88; vol., ACS 1987-;vol., ADA 1989-; Republican. Res: 2352 Polk Way Stockton 95207

DE CAMPLI, WILLIAM MICHAEL, physician, cardiovascular surgeon; b. Dec. 7, 1951, Allentown, Pa.; s. William J. and Bernadine Laura (Diehl) DeCampli; m. Kristi Lynn Peterson, M.D., May 27, 1989; edn: BS, MIT 1973, PhD Harvard 1978; MD, Univ. Miami 1982. Career: Chaim Weizman Fellow in theoretical astrophysics, Caltech 1978-80; Carl and Leah McConnell Fellow in cardiovascular physiology, Stanford Medical Center, Stanford 1984-85, chief resident in general surgery 1987-88, Fellow in peripheral vascular surgery 1988-89, Fellow in cardiovascular surgery 1989-92; Diplomate Am. Bd. of Surgery 1989 and Am. Bd. of Thoracic Surgery 1993; pediatric cardiac surgeon Children's Hospital, Oakland, Calif.; cons. Nat. Acad. of Scis., Wash., D.C. 1985-86; mem. NASA Life Scis. Strategic Planning subcom. 1985-88, NASA Space Station Sci. & Applications subcom. 1988-89; mem: Am. Coll. of Surgeons, Am. Coll. of Chest Physicians, N.Y. Acad. of Scis., Sigma Xi Research Soc.; author or coauthor papers in fields of astronomy, astrophysics, cardiovascular physiology, pediatric cardiac surgery; rec: PADI rescue scuba diver, AA cert. parachutist. Ofc:Center for Cardiac Surgery 2500 Milvia Ave Berkeley 94704

DE CHAMBEAU, KENT LEROY, lawyer; b. July 30, 1926, Bishop, Calif.; s. Arthur Aaron and Iris Rae (Byrne) D.; m. Dolly Eileen Mollart, April 25, 1947; children: Richard b. 1948, Michael b. 1950; grandchild, Amber Rae; edn: AA, UCLA 1948, BA 1950, LLB, 1953, JD, 1960. Career: legislative counsel State of Calif. Legislature, Sacramento 1953-84; legislative advocate Calif. Rifle & Pistol Assn. 1984-89, legislative counsel Gun Owners of Calif. 1989-; legal counsel DeChambeau & Assoc., Inc., Sacramento 1985-; legal advocate Goose Hill Gun Club, Ione 1972-91; legislative advocate Sportsmen Com. on Polit. Edn., Richmond 1988-; honors: grad. staff and command school Judge Advocate Corps., U.S. Army 1952, Resolution of Appreciation award, Calif. legislature 1984, Service Appreciation award, Safari Club 1987, 88, leadership award, Boy Scouts of Am. 1959; mem: Nat. Rifle Assn. (life), Calif. Rifle and Pistol Assn. (life), Calif. Bar Assn., Sacto Safari Club (legis. advisor), Goose Hill Gun Club (trustee), Ducks Unltd.; author: numerous articles pub. profl. jours.; mil: lt., U.S. Army infantry, 1944-46, 1948-54; Republican; Prot.; rec: hunting, camping, fishing. Address: 600-36th St Sacramento 95816

DE CIUTIIS, ALFRED C.M., physician, television producer; b. Oct. 16, 1946, N.Y.C.; s. Alfred Ralph and Theresa Elizabeth (Manko) de C. (the deCiutiis family was first ranked among the nobles of Italy in 893 AD, designated princely family and titled Princes of the Holy Roman Empire in 1629); m. Catherine L. Gohn, Aug. 31, 1987; edn: BS (summa cum laude), Fordham Univ., 1967; MD, Columbia Univ., 1971; Dipl. Am. Bd. Int. Medicine (ABIM), Am. Bd. Med. Oncology. Career: intern N.Y. Hosp. Cornell Med. Ctr., NYC 1971-72, resident 1972-74; fellow clin. immunology Memorial Hosp. Sloan Kettering Cancer Ctr. 1974-75, fellow clin. oncology 1975-76, spl. fellow in immunology 1974-76; guest investigator, asst. physician exptl. hematology Rockefeller Univ., 1975-76; med. practice, splst. in med. oncology, Los Angeles 1977-; producer num. med. TV shows; host cable TV shows, 1981-, med. editor Cable Health Network, 1983-, Lifetime Network 1984-; mem. med. advy. com. 1984 Olympics; co-founder Meditrina Med. Ctr., free out-patient surg. ctr., Torrance; syndicated columnist Coast Media News "The Subject is Cancer" 1980s; awards: Phi Beta Kappa, Alpha Omega Alp[ha, Sigma Xi, Mensa, Leukemia Soc. Am. fellow 1974-76, NY State Regents scholar (1963-67, 67-71), AMA Physicians Recogn. (1978-80, 82-85, 86-89, 89-91, 91-94), Proclamation Calif. State Senate Rules Com. 1982; mem. Fgn. Policy Leadership Proj. The Ctr. for Internat. Affairs, Harvard Univ.; mem: Am. Coll. Physicians (Fellow), Internat. Coll. Physicians and Surgeons (Fellow), AMA, Am. Union Physicians and Dentists, Am. Soc. Clin. Oncology, NY Acad. Sci. (life), CMA, LA Co. Med. Assn., Internat. Health Soc., Am. Pub. Health Assn., AAAS, Am. Geriatrics Soc., Chinese Med. Assn., Drug Info. Assn., Am. Soc. Hematology (emeritus mem.), Nat. Geog. Soc., Internat. Platform Assn.; civic: Italian-Am. Med. (founder 1982), Italian-Am. Med. Legal Alliance LA (co-founder 1982-), Italian-Am. Civic Com. L.A. 1983, Italian-Am. Found. (gov. bd. med. coun.), UCLA Chancellor's Assocs., Cath. League for Civil and Rel. Liberty, Nature Conservancy, Nat. Wildlife Fedn., World Affairs Council LA, Am. Coll. Heraldry Confedn. Chivalry, Fondazione Giovanni Agnelli, Smithsonian Instn. (assoc.), Boston Mus. Fine Arts, Met. Mus.; publs: author first clinical comprehensive description of Chronic Fatigue Syndrome as a neuro-immunologic disorder probably caused by a retrovirus with multi-system complications (Audio Digest Internal Med. Vol. 37 #21, 11/90), extensive bibliography, contbr. num. articles to profl. jours.; mil: capt. Med. Corps US Army 1972-74; Republican; R.Cath.; rec: collecting, reading, hunting, fishing, astronomy. Res: 32062 1/2 Lobo Canyon Agoura Hills 91301 Tel: 818/706-3308

DECKER, PHILIP E., lawyer; b. June 17, 1943, Montclair, N.J.; s. Everett N. and Mary E. (Davey) D.; m. Judith S., June 18, 1968; dau., Christina M. b. 1980; edn: AB (honors pgm), Great Distinction), UC Berkeley, 1969; JD, Boalt Hall Sch. of Law UC Berkeley, 1972; admitted Calif. State Bar, U.S. Dist. Ct. (No. Dist. Calif.), U.S. Ct. Appeals (9th Cir.), 1974. Career: atty., San Jose 1974-; judge pro tem Santa Clara County Superior Ct. 1986-; apptd. (first Public Member appointee) Contractor's State License Bd., St. Calif., 1976-80; chmn. Mayor's Task Force on Condominiums, 1976; co-founder Pub. Interest Law Ctr., San Francisco, 1972, and Pub. Interest Res. Ctr., Berkeley, 1971; honors: Phi Beta Kappa; mem: Calif. Trial Lawyers Assn., Santa Clara Co. Bar Assn., Santa Clara Co. Trial Lawyers Assn., Marin Co. Bar Assn., Exec. Council of Homeowners, S.J. (pres. 1977, bd. dirs. and chmn. Legal Resource Panel), Inverness Yacht Club, Sports Car Club Am., I.M.S.A.; author: Moving in California: A Hard Way to Go (P.I.R.C., 1972); lectr. and author - construction law, condominium law, consumer protection law, 1972-; rec: gardening, auto racing. Law Offices of Philip E. Decker, P.C., 60 S Market St Ste 1110 San Jose 95113

DEEDWANIA, PRAKASH C., physician, medical administrator, educator; b. Aug. 28, 1948, Ajmer, India; s. Gokul C. and Paras (Garg) D.; m. Catherine E.; children: Anne, Ravi; edn: pre-med. Univ. of Rajasthan 1963, MD (honors in pharmacol.), 1969; Diplomate in internal med. 1975, pulmonary 1976, and cardiol. 1977, ABIM. Career: rotating intern, postgrad. res. in medicine J.L.N. Med. Coll. Hosp. Center, Ajmer, India 1970-71; med. intern Coney Is. Hosp./Maimonides Med. Ctr., Bklyn. 1971-72; med. res. VA Med. Ctr., Bronx/Mt. Sinai Sch. of Med., N.Y. 1972-73, chief res. 1973-75; cardiol. fellow Univ. of Ill. Abraham Lincoln Sch. of Med., Chgo. 1975-76, sr. res. fellow in cardiology 1976-77; supv. att. phys. St. Joseph's Hosp., N.Y. 1973-75, Weiss Meml. Hosp., Chgo. 1975-77; cons. in cardiology and pulmonary Bd. of Health, Chgo. 1976-77; chief Cardiology, VA Med. Center/Univ. of Va., Salem 1977-78; dir. Non-Invasive Lab VAMC/Univ. of Ill., Chgo. 1978-80, also dir. Electrophysiology and co-dir. Critical Care Unit; chief Dept. Cardiology and dir. Critical Care Unit, VAMC/UCSF Sch. of Med., Fresno, 1980-, clin. prof. medicine UC San Francisco, 1988-; lectr. in var. areas of cardiovascular disorders at hosps. in the UCSF Med. Edn. Pgm. and comm. hosps. (40 lectures 1990); vis. prof., faculty num. internat. med. confs. and seminars; honors: Dean's List, Govt. Coll., Kota, India 1963-64 and J.L.N. Med. Coll. 1968-69, recipient num. res. awards 1973-91; mem: Fellow Am. Coll. of Chest Physicians 1977, Fellow Am. Coll. of Physicians 1978, Fellow Am. Coll. of Cardiol. 1978, Fellow Am. Heart Assn. Clin. Coun. Cardio. 1978, Am. Fedn. of Clin. Res., The N.Y. Acad. of Sci.; num. publs. in med. jours. 1975-; rec: study of cultures, photog., travel, pen pals. Ofc: VA Medical Center 2615 East Clinton Fresno 93703

DEES, RUSSELL LOWE, historian, lawyer; b. Aug. 4, 1955, Burnet, Tx.; s. Matt M. and Joann (Jones) D.; m. Inge Birgitte Gintberg, Dec. 7, 1984; edn: BA, Southwestern Univ. 1976; PhD, Claremont Grad. Sch. 1985; JD, UC Berkeley 1990. Career: history tchr. Harvey Mudd Coll., Claremont 1979-84; Danish translator Univ. of Aarhus, Denmark 1986-88; law clk. Sidley & Austin, Los Angeles 1989-; honors: Alpha Chi, Timken Sturgis fellow 1979, S.K. Yee scholarship 1988, Haynes dissertation fellow 1983, MacNeel Pierce Found. fellow 1982; mem: Am. Hist. Assn., Renaissance Soc. Am., Ecology Law Quarterly; translator Sensation & Knowledge (1990), articles pub. in scholarly jours. 1986-90; Democrat. Res: 1712 Cedar Ave Berkeley 94703

DE FONVILLE, PAUL BLISS, western history museum and library administrator; b. Mar. 3, 1923, Oakland, Calif.; s. Marion Yancy and Charlotte (Bliss) de F.; m. Virginia Harpell, June 17, 1967; edn: Calif. St. Poly. Univ., S.L.O., 1942-44; Michael Chekhov Group, Hollywood, 1947-52. Career: cowboy various ranches Calif., 1926-52; film actor, Hollywood, 1947-; artist, prin., L.A., 1957-73; pres., Alexandria Coeur de Lion, L.A., 1969-80; founder, pres., adminstr., Cowboy Meml. and Lib. (a museum), Caliente, 1980-; instr. outdoor edn. CSU Bakersfield, 1980; mem. Rep. Presdl. Task Force 1984-, Rep. Senatorial. Inner Circle. 1989-, Nat. Com. 1987, Nat. Rep. Congl. Com. 1990, US Senatorial Club 1988-, Calif. Rep. Assembly 1990-, Rep. Senatorial Commn. 1991; awards: Slim Pickens award Calif. State Horsemen, 1980; Marshall Working Western award Rose Parade Pasadena, 1980; County of Kern Recognition, 1984; Proclamation of Mayors of Bakersfield, 1984, 85; Proclamation Gov. of Calif., 1984; Senate Resolution No. 914, 1988; Calif. Legislative Assembly Resolution No. 2681; Presdl. Order of Merit, 1991; Congl. Cert. of Merit, 1992; Rep. Presdl. Legion of Merit, 1992; listed Who's Who in Rep. Party 1990, Who's Who in West 1992, Who's Who in America-Index 1992-93, Who's Who in America 1993-94; mem: Calif. State Horsemen (life), Equestrian Trails Inc. (life), Forty Niners (life), PRO Rodeo Cowboys Assn. Colo. (Gold Card holder #480), Turtles and Rodeo Cowboys Assn. (life); Baptist; rec: Heritage, horses, cowboys, mountain men, Indians. Res/Ofc: 40371 Cowboy Ln Caliente 93518

DE GANAHL, JOAN TURK, psychotherapist; b. June 12, 1930, New York; d. Richard Jason and Marian (Errington) Turk; m. Carl Brice de Ganahl, Aug. 12, 1967 (div. 1978); children: Sherrill b. 1953, Whitney b. 1955; edn: BA, Syracuse Univ. 1951; MA, John F. Kennedy Univ. 1980; UCSF Med. Center 1981; lic. marriage and family therapist. Career: owner J. Turk Antiques, Palm Beach, Fla.

and Little Silver, N.J. 1971-78; pvt. practice psychotherapist, Walnut Creek 1981-; sex therapist Kaiser Permanente Hosp., Walnut Creek 1981-87, intern supr. 1983-84; speaker Kaiser Permanente 1981-, guest spkr. AAUW 1988, Battered Women, Concord 87, 88, workshop leader AAUW, Orinda 1988; exec. com. Affiliate Task Force, Cont. Edn. Com., Walnut Creek Hosp. 1987-; recipient award AAUW Century Club 1988; mem: AASECT, ORTHO, Calif. Assn. Marriage & Family Therapists, Kappa Alpha Theta, Battered Womens Assn.; book reviewer 1987-; Republican; Presbyterian; rec: Skiing, snorkeling, hiking. Ofc: 1479 Ygnacio Valley Rd Ste 205 Walnut Creek 94598

DE GARMO, E. PAUL, emeritus professor of mechanical and industrial engineering; b. Jan. 29, 1907, Lucerne, Mo.; s. Arthur and Editha (Snider) DeG.; m. Mary Elizabeth Turner, Dec. 26, 1934; children: Richard b. 1938, David b. 1942; edn: BS, Univ. Wash., 1930; MS, Calif. Inst. of Tech., 1937; reg. profl. engr., mech., indsl., Calif. (1949, 1967). Career: engr. Converse Co. Inc., Seattle 1930-31; engr. Firestone Tire & Rubber, Los Angeles 1934-37; prof. indsl. engring. and mech. engring., UC Berkeley, 1937-72, emeritus prof. 1972-; indep. cons. engr., Berkeley 1940-85; U.S. AID mission Japan, 1962; guest prof. Korea Advanced Inst. of Sci., 1975; honors: Lincoln Gold Medal Am. Welding Soc. 1948, Phi Beta Kappa, Sigma Xi, Alpha Pi Mu, Fellow Inst. Industrial Engrs. 1966-, mem. ASME, Am. Welding Soc. (life), Am. Soc. for Metals; coauthor 3 texts: Technical Lettering (2 eds 1941, 1943), Engineering Economy (7 eds 1942-), Materials & Processes in Manufacturing (7 eds), contbr. numerous engring. papers; Republican; Prot.; rec: woodworking. Res: 1860 Tice Creek Dr #1302 Walnut Creek 94595

DEHATE, ANNETTE VERA, executive manager; b. March 25, 1954, Bay St. Louis, Miss.; d. Theodore Russell and Lucy Ann (Whitley) DeHate; m. Mark Warren Smith, June 24, 1989; children: Diannah, Nathaniel; edn: Montgomery Adult Sch. 1979; Cuesta Coll. 1987; Inst. Orgn. Mgmt. 1988-89. Career: office mgr. Cleaning Service, Arroyo Grande 1983-87; word processing splst. Computer Cons., Grover City 1987-88; exec. mgr. Grover City C.of C. 1988-; mem. Co. Council of Chambers, San Luis Obispo 1988-; ed., pub. rels. Five Cities Womens Network, Grover City 1989-; awards: Center for Leadership Devel. scholarship 1989; mem: Calif. C.of C., Am. C.of C. Execs., BSA (parent com. 1987-89), Girl Scouts Am.; ed. Bus. News newsletter 1988-89, Inst. Class newsletter 1989, Five Cities Womens Network 1989, monthly newspaper column Chambers Corner 1988-89; rec: gardening, horseback riding, backpacking. Ofc: Grover City Chamber of Commerce POB 165 Grover City 93483-2015

DE JESUS, MIGUEL A., regional marketing director; b. Oct. 1, 1947, NYC; s. Julio and Eva (Ortiz) de J.; m. Victoria Calero, Aug. 29, 1970; children: Vicki b. 1973, Miguel b. 1974, Christopher b. 1980; edn: BS, Long Island Univ., 1970; MBA, National Univ., 1989. Career: with Xerox Corp. 1971-89: sales rep., NYC 1971-72; sales mgr. Ponce, P.R. 1974-76; br. service mgr. San Juan, P.R. 1977-79; product sales mgr. Rochester, N.Y. 1980-82; dist. mgr. sales San Diego, Calif. 1983-87, major account mktg. mgr. 1988-89; dir. mktg. western zone Paychex, Inc. San Diego 1989-; mem. Am. Mktg. Assn., Am. Assn. of Individual Investors; civic: United Way San Diego (exec. campaign vol.), Rancho Bernardo Youth Basketball Assn. (bd. 1988-). Res: 17715 Azucar Way San Diego 92127

DELANEY, MARION PATRICIA, advertising executive; b. May 20, 1952, Hartford, Conn.; d. William Pride Delaney and Marian Patricia (Utley) Murphy; edn: BA, Union Coll., 1973. Career: acct. exec. Foote, Cone & Belding, N.Y.C., 1974-78; senior acct. exec. Dailey & Assocs., Los Angeles 1978-81; prin., Marnie Delaney Public Relations, L.A. 1981-83; acct. supr. BBDO/West, L.A. 1983-85; v.p., mgmt. supr. Grey Advt., L.A., S.F., 1985-89; sr. v.p., group acct. dir. McCann-Erickson, San Francisco 1989-; Democrat; Congregationalist.

DELL, OWEN EUGENE, landscape architect and contractor; b. Nov. 20, 1950, Chicago, Ill.; s. Arthur Joseph and Irene Anna (Williams) D.; edn: Santa Barbara City Coll. 1971-73. Career: owner County Landscape & Supply, Santa Barbara 1972-; instr. Santa Barbara Botanic Gardens 1988-, UC Santa Barbara 1989-90; founder, chmn. Firescape Garden 1983-; awards: Calif. Landscape Contractors Assn. 1st residential landscape 1983, 2d. specialties 1984, 1st hardscape 1986, 1st xeriscape (statewide) 1991; mem: Calif. Landscape Contractors Assn. (pres. 1983-84, bd. dirs. 1981-, profl. review com. 1983-, co-chair state edn. com. 1984-86), South Coast Landscape Water Mgmt. Task Force, Santa Barbara City Coll. Landscape Horticulture Advy. Com.; author: How To Open & Operate a Home-Based Landscaping Business (in press), profl. jour. articles (1988-), non-tech. writings pub. in The Sun, Brussels Sprout (a haiku jour.), others; Democrat; rec: nature, sports, photography, writing/poetry. Ofc: County Landscape & Supply PO Box 30433 Santa Barbara 93130

DELLIQUADRI, PARDO FREDERICK, educator, administrator, ret.; b. Jan. 20, 1915, Pueblo, Colo.; s. Colombo Frederick and Rose Marie (Russo) D.; m. Velma Lee Ingram, Sept. 9, 1939; children: Toni Cheryl b. 1942, Lyn Christine b. 1944, Geri Michele b. 1948; edn: BA cum laude, Univ. Colo. 1938; MSW, Univ. Neb. 1941. Career: child welfare worker Co. Dept. Pub. Welfare, Yakima, Wash. 1941-42; state statistician Wyo. Welfare Dept., Cheyenne, Wyo. 1942;

dir. childrens service Wyo. Dept. Pub. Welfare 1946-48; supt. child welfare Ill. Dept. Pub. Welfare, Springfield, Ill. 1948-50; dir. childrens and youth Wis. Dept. Pub. Welfare, Madison, Wis. 1950-60; dean sch. of social work Columbia Univ., NYC 1960-67; dean social work Univ. Hawaii 1967-68; chief U.S. Childrens Bureau, WDC 1968-70; dean social work Univ. Wis., Milwaukee 1970-72; Univ. Ala., Tuscaloosa 1972-82; awards: Foneme Internat. Child & Youth 1968, Univ. Colo. Norlin 1969, Univ. Neb. Edith Droce Abbott 1940, U.S. St. Dept. UNICEF 1960-68, U.S. Rep. to Childrens Inst., White House Conf. on Children & Youth Merit, HEW Merit 1963-67, CIU AFL Disting. Service 1965, Fulbright 1980-81; mem: Beverly Hills Demo. Club, Social Services St. Advy. Com., Racho Golf Club (exec. com. 1987-88); 400+ articles in profl. jours. (1939-88); mil: lt. USN 1942-46; Democrat; Prot.; rec: golf. Res: 6527 W 6th St Los Angeles 90048

DELLUMS, RONALD V., congressman; b. Nov. 24, 1935, Oakland; m. Leola Roscoe Higgs; 3 children; edn: AA, Oakland City Coll. 1958; BA, San Francisco State Coll. 1960; M.S.W., Univ. of Calif. 1962. Career: psychiatric social worker Calif. Dept. Mental Hygiene 1962-64; program dir. Bayview Comm. Ctr., San Francisco 1964-65; from assoc. dir. to dir. Hunters Point Youth Opportunity Ctr. 1965-66; planning cons. Bay Area Social Planning Council 1966-67; dir. concentrated employment prog. San Francisco Econ. Opportunity Council 1967-68; sr. cons. Social Dynamics Inc. 1968-70; mem. 92d-102d Congresses form 8th Calif. Dist.; chmn. house com. on D.C. 1979-, chmn house armed svs. subcom. on res. and devel. 1989-; lectr. S.F. State Coll., UC Berkeley; mem. U.S. Del. North Atlantic Group; mem. Berkeley City Council 1967-71; author: Defense Sense: The Search For A Rational Military Policy, 1983; mil: USMCR 1954-56; Democrat. Ofc: U.S. House of Representatives 2136 Rayburn House Office Bldg Washington DC 20515

DE LORCA, LUIS, educator/program developer; b. Oct. 18, 1959, Los Angeles; s. Naomi (Rodriguez) Garcia; m. Lori Ann Vanzant, Mar. 23, 1991; edn: AA, Rio Hondo Comm. Coll., Whittier, 1983; BA, Calif. St. Poly Univ., Pomona, 1989. Career: lifeguard Los Angeles City Rec. Dept., 1980-87; high sch. football coach various schs. So. Calif., 1980-; pres. Exclusive Concepts, Los Angeles, 1987-89; pub. rels. dir. Cal Poly Pomona Music Dept. 1987-89; English tchr. Cathedral High Sch., L.A. 1989-90; resource specialist Special Edn., Whittier High Sch., 1990-; founder, director The Learning Advantage Ctr., Whittier 1991-; founder Homework Club, Whittier H.S., 1990-; founder So. Calif. Latino Students Assn., Pomona, 1987-88; civic: Greenpeace, Fair Housing 1983-, Cousteau Soc., Big Brothers of Am. 1979-81, Operation Share 1977-81; Democrat; Unity; rec: scuba, martial arts, coaching, swimming, handball, skiing. Res: 9427 Tarryton St Whittier 90605

DE LUCHI, STEPHEN F., oral and maxillofacial surgeon; b. May 11, 1952, Alameda; s. Frank S. De L.; edn: BS, UC Berkeley 1974; BS, DDS, UCSF 1978; cert. 1978-79, 1979-82. Career: clin. instr. UCSF 1978-85; pvt. practice oral surgery, San Francisco 1982-89; mem: Am. Assn. Oral & Maxillofacial Surgeons (fellow), Guardsmen S.F., Bachelors of S.F.; Republican; Catholic; rec: golf. Ofc: 450 Sutter St Ste 1525 San Francisco 94108

DE MAINE, GARY, investment advisor; b. June 20, 1956, Norwalk, Conn.; s. Joseph A. and Minnie (DeLorenzo) DeM.; m. Camille York, May 1, 1981 (div. 1985); m. Laurie L. Hurst, March 8, 1987; edn: BA bus. adminstrn., National Univ., S.D. 1983; cert. fin. planner Calif. 1987. Career: fin. analyst Coordinated Planning Design Inc., San Diego 1983-86; portfolio mgr. Briarwood Investment Counsel, San Diego 1986-; mem: Internat. Assn. Fin. Planners, Inst. Cert. Fin. Planners, Kiwanis; mil: USN 1980-83; Republican; R.Cath. Res: 17737 Creciente Way San Diego 92127 Ofc: 11828 Bernardo Plaza Ct San Diego 92128

DEMELLO, AGUSTIN EASTWOOD, director of research/science & engineering writer; b. Oct. 15, 1944, New Bedford, Mass.; s. Manuel and Dora (Eastwood) D; 1 child: *Adragon Eastwood b. 1976 (*see Guinness Book of World Records); edn: AA, Santa Monica Coll., Santa Monica, Calif. 1972; BA, UCLA 1974; MSc, M.C. Inst., London, Eng. 1978; ScD, M.C. Inst., London, Eng. 1981. Career: res. scientist, CSR Inst., Moss Landing, Calif. 1984-86; dir. of res., CSR Inst. 1986-; instr., UC Santa Barbara, 1975-78; instr., Condie Coll., Campbell, Calif. 1985; awards: Academic Merit Scholar, UCLA 1972-74; first Am.-born Flamenco guitarist to perform in major solo concerts at NY Town Hall; mem: Am. Inst. of Aeronautics & Astronautics 1977-, Mensa Internat. 1977-, NY Acad. of Sci. 1978-, Amer. Astronautical Soc. 1979-; author: Black Night Poetry, 1960, 2nd ed., 1964; Tengu, 1962; The Four States of Man, 1979; The Metagalactic System, 1979; Early Development of the Scientific Mind, 1981; Theory of Cosmodynamics, 1984; The Origin and Influence of Flamenco Music on the Classics, 1992; recording artist, record album, El Duende Flamenco, 1965; avocation: concert artist, poet, philosopher, martial arts master. Res: 663 S. Bernardo Ave. Sunnyvale 94087. Ofc: CSR Institute P.O. Box 461 Moss Landing 95039

DEMERS, MARY H., business and management consultant, contracts and procurement professional; b. Bemidji, Minn.; 2 children: Tressa A. and Crystal A., twins, b. 1977; edn: Bemidji State Univ., Univ. of Alaska, Univ. of N.Dak., contract mgmt. pgm. UC Irvine, cert. in mgmt. effectiveness USC Grad. Sch. of Bus. Adm. Career: legal paraprofl. law firms: Massee & Leonard, then Kelly & Luce, 1978-81; contract adminstr. ARCO Oil & Gas Co., Dallas, Anchorage, Pasadena, 1981-86; mgr. contracts sect. County of Orange, GSA/Purchasing, Santa Ana 1986-89; mgr. contracts and procurement Transportation Corridor Agys., Costa Mesa 1989-91; mgmt. cons. Contract Consultants 1991-; awards: Atlantic Richfield's Pres.'s Award for exceptional contbn., State Parliamentarian, Minn. Fedn. Women's Clubs, N.D. Woman of Yr. nominee: Outstanding Young Woman of Am.; mem: Am. Bar Assn. (assoc., public contracts sect., Forum on the Constrn. Ind.), Nat. Contract Mgmt. Assn., Constrn. Mgmt. Assn. of Am., We. Council of Constrn. Consumers (pgm. com.), Volunteer Ctr. of Greater Orange Co.; rec: reading, skiing, travel. Address: PO Box 308 East Irvine 92650

DE MET, EDWARD MICHAEL, neurochemist, educator, consultant; b. July 27, 1949, Elmhurst, Ill.; s. Michael Constantine and Elvira Linnea (Franson) DeM.; m. Aleksandra Chicz, Oct. 22, 1983; edn: student Ill. Inst. of Tech., Chgo. 1963-66, AS, Harper Coll., Palatine, Ill. 1969; BS, Univ. Ill., 1971; PhD, Ill. Inst. of Tech. 1976. Career: res. asst. prof. Univ. Chicago, 1976-80; asst. prof. dept. psychiatry UCLA, 1980-83; UC Irvine 1983-87, assoc. prof. 1988-; res. chemist VA Med. Ctr., West L.A., 1980-83, cons. 1983-; cons. VA Med. Ctr. Long Beach 1986-, Spectra Physics Corp. 1982-84, Stuart Pharmaceuticals 1983, Vydak Inc. 1983, IBM Instruments 1984-, Pfizer Pharmaceuticals 1985-, Fairview State Hosp. 1985-, Abbott Lab. 1986-, Kronos Inc. 1986; awards: USPHS Fellow 1976-78; mem: Soc. Neuroscis., Am. Chem. Soc., AAAS, N.Y. Acad. Sci.; rec: backpacking, rock climbing, sailing. Res: 26322 Los Alamitos Ave Laguna Hills 92653 Ofc: UCI Dept. Psychiatry and Human Behavior Irvine 92717

DEMIANEW, SUZANN HENSLEY, medical group chief information officer and partner in medical management company; b. Nov. 9, 1953, Bryan, Tx.; d. Robert Louis (dec. 1990) and Patricia Ann (Badgley) Hensley; m. Paul Demianew; children: Matthew Patrick b. 1979, Catherine Nicole b. 1982; edn: BS, Eastern Wash. Univ., Cheney, Wa. 1975; MBA, CSU Dominguez Hills, 1986; reg. med. technologist Am. Soc. Clin. Path. 1978. Career: med. tech. Harbor-UCLA Med. Ctr., Torrance 1978-79; mgr. and research assoc. Blood Grouping Lab of REI, Torrance 1980-84; fin. cons. Harbor-UCLA Med. Found., Torrance 1985; adminstrv. analyst King-Drew Med. Found., Los Angeles 1985-86; cons. fin. analyst Am. Med. Internat. (AMI) Beverly Hills 1986; chief info. ofcr. Bay Shores Med. Group, Redondo Beach 1986-, also ptnr. and chief info. ofcr. Med. Management Partners, Inc., Long Beach 1991-; mem: Am. Soc. of Clin. Pathologists, Am. Guild of Patient Acct. Mgrs., IDX Western Region Users Group; civic: Polar Bear Club (Cabrillo Beach), South Bay Bromiliad Assocs. Palos Verdes (winner sweepstakes 1982, 83); contbr. articles in profl. jours. (4); Democrat; rec: growing orchids and bromeliads, painting, aerobics, collecting Am. Indian art. Res: 631 Ave B Redondo Beach 90277 Ofc: Bay Shores Medical Group, Inc. 20406 Earl St Torrance 90503

DENGLER, HUGH JAMES, general building contractor; b. Mar. 2, 1931, Detroit, Mich.; s. Joseph Phillip and Marie Emma (Newman) D.; desc. of Geo. P. Drouillard, transl. and guid with Lewis and Clark Expedition (1806); m. Patricia Ann Morey, Feb. 11, 1956; children: Eric b. 1957, Guy b. 1959, Rex b. 1962, Roger b. 1964, Alan and Iris (twins) b. 1966; edn: Sch. of Real Estate Law (Orlando) 1961-62, architl. drafting, Chgo. Tech. Coll. 1958-60, bldg. constrn., Internat. Corresp. Schs. (Pa.) 1955, Accelerated Real Estate Schs. (S.F.) 1978; lic. gen. contr. 1955-; lic. pvt. pilot 1972-; Notary Public, Fla. 1962-66; citizens radio sta. lic. 1969-74, radio tel. opr. 1972-. Career: carpenter, foreman Joseph Phillip Dengler, Builder, Detroit 1947-50, Dunkirk, N.Y. 1951-52; insp. -assembly, Trim A Seal Corp.'s Detroit 1950-51; insp. -Differential Dept., Ford Motor Co., Detroit 1951; ship carpenter US Navy (MSTS 3 Ships) 1952-55; gen. contr. Dengler Constrn. & Supply Co. in Dunkirk and Fredonia, NY, Orlando, Fla., Santa Rosa, Ca., 1955-; ptnr. Trans-Florida Ins. Corp., also Trans-Florida R.E. Corp.; ptnr. Trans-Florida Mortgage & Inv. Co. Inc. 1960-61; gen. contr. Sears, Roebuck & Co., Santa Rosa 1971-85; awards: Boys Town Honorary Citizen 1956, Excellence award Sears, Roebuck & Co. 1974; clarinetist East Detroit Jr. H.S. Band 1943-46, mem: Latin Club 1946, East Detroit H.S.; Fla. Assn. of Realtors 1961-63, Nat. Pilots Assn. 1972-78, Calif. Licensed Contrs. Assn. (gen. contr. lic. #267991 1973-81), Holy Name Soc. 1951-59, Domain of Golden Dragon Lat. 42 Long. 180 (1952), Calif. State Sheriffs Assn. (assoc. mem. 1987-), VFW, The Am. Legion, Calif. Kts. of Col. (4th deg.), Navy League of U.S. (pres. Sonoma County Council 1991-92), Young Mens Inst., Village of Fredonia, N.Y. Nominating Com. 1969, PTA 1971-72, Catholic Profl. & Bus. Breakfast Club 1990-, Toastmaster Intl. 1961, Nat. Rifle Assn. 1957, Am. Bowling Congress (Kts. of Col. League 1959-60, Hugh + 2, 1989-); publs: Family newsletter (genealogy, 1984-), Labor Policy Curriculum (Buffalo Cath. Diocese 1968); mil: damage controlman wood 3/c USN 1952-55, Reserves 1955-60, Korean Svc., UN, Navy Occup. Europe, Nat. Def. Svc., GC medals (actor in USN tng. film St. Albins Naval Hosp. Long Island NY 1952); R.Cath., Holy Spirit Ch. (Advy. Council, Usher Club 1985-, Men's Club); rec: music (clarinetist), skating, flying. Address: Dengler Construction & Supply Co 1277 St Francis Rd Santa Rosa 95409

DENNEHY, DAVID EDWARD, manufacturing company president; b. Nov. 14, 1937, Nyack, N.Y.; s. Jeremiah Thomas and RuFina Mary (McCarten) D.; m. Lillian Mirtana Vitaly, Nov. 20, 1962; children: Kenneth b. 1963, Catherine b. 1966, Michael b. 1979; edn: BA econ., Dartmouth Coll. 1959; MBA, Amos Tuck Univ. 1960. Career: sales mgr. Ford Motor, Dearborn, Mich. and San Jose 1965-71; personnel dir. Spreckels Sugar Co., San Francisco 1971-83, gen. sales mgr. 1983-84, v.p. mktg. 1984-85, v.p. sales and mktg., Pleasanton 1985-87, pres. 1987-; club: Olympic; mil: capt. AUS Intelligence 1960-64; Republican; R.Cath.; rec: tennis, golf, hiking. Ofc: Spreckels Sugar 4256 Hacienda Dr Pleasanton 94566-4065

DENNING, PAUL FRANKLIN, investment banker; b. June 6, 1942, Akron, Ohio; s. William F. and Marcia (LeDoux) D.; m. Margie A., Dec. 21, 1970; children: Kelli b. 1978, David b. 1980, Travis b. 1982, Kathryn b. 1986; edn: BS, BA, Univ. Akron 1965; MPA, Golden Gate Univ. 1971; Stanford Univ. 1986. Career: v.p. Sutro & Co., S.F. 1972-83; ptnr. Montgomery Securites 1984-89; ptnr. Robertson, Stephens, 1989-; trustee, commr. S.F. Retirement 1981-89; trustee Burke Sch. 1985-; dir. U.S. Diabetes Found. 1978-79; Mayors Task Force Pension Reform 1985; chmn. Port C.of C. 1979; com. founding dir. Council Institutional Investors, Wash. D.C. 1985; awards: Univ. Akron Outstanding Mktg. Student 1965, Outstanding Young Men Am. 1979; mem: St. Francis Yacht Club, We. Addition Neighborhood Assn. (pres. 1976-79), S.F. Ballet Assn., S.F. Museum of Modern Art, S.F. Symphony Assn.; booklet pub. on sale of securities (1986), article pub. in profl. jour. (1989); mil: lt. USN 1966-70, Air Medal 1967-70, Vietnamese Flying Cross 1967; Democrat; Presbyterian; rec: sailing, piano, travel. Res: 2165 California St San Francisco 94115 Ofc: Robertson, Stephens, Ste 1 Embarcadero San Francisco 94111

DEOL, SHIVINDER SINGH, physician; b. June 4, 1953, Ahmedgarh, India, nat. USA 1979; s. Col. Tej Bhan Singh and Joginder Kaur (Benepal) Deol; m. Harjit Kaur, Apr. 9, 1977; children: Randeep b. 1980, Vikramjit b. 1982; edn: Premed., DAV Coll., Chandigarh, India 1971; MBBS, Armed Forces Med. Coll., Poona, India 1975; MD, Univ. of Tenn. Center for Health Scis., Memphis 1981; Diplomate Am. Board of Family Practice 1981, 1987; Fellow Am. Acad. of Family Physicians. Career: group practice Manor Medical Group Inc., Bakersfield 1982-83; solo med. practice, 1983-; bd. dirs. Physicians Radiology Group, Bakersfield 1985-88; chief of staff Alliance Comm. Hosp. 1991-; bd. dirs. Bakersfield Meml. Hosp. IPA 1987-, dept. chmn. fam. practice 1985-86, 89-90; v. chief of staff Bakersfield Comm. Hosp. 1985; pres. Kern Acad. of Family Physicians 1988-; mem: Kern Co. Med. Soc., CMA, AMA, Indian Med. Assn., Am. Acad. of Cosmetic Surgery (Assoc. Fellow), Am. Coll. of Internat. Physicians (Fellow), Am. Geriatric Soc., Am. Soc. of Contemporary Med. & Surg. (Fellow), Intl. Soc. of Plastic Anesth. & Reconstrv. Surgery (assoc. fellow), Am. Assn. Physicians from India, Am. Acad. of Home Care Physicians, Nat. Stroke Assn., Am. Liver Found., Am. Acad. Sclerotherapy, Nat. Headache Found., AFMC Alumni Assn. Am. (exec. com.), Rotary Intl. (Paul Harris Fellow); civic: vol. physician to inpatients Salvation Army Rehabilitation Ctr. 1985-87, donor Xray machine to Mexico, Computer to KMC FP residency; Republican; Sikh; rec: comm. affairs, sports. Res: 1205 Calle Extrano Bakersfield 93304 Ofc: Shivinder S. Deol, MD, 4000 Stockdale Hwy Ste D Bakersfield 93309

DE REGT, JOHN STEWART, real estate development executive; b. San Francisco; s. Christian Anthony and Mary Margaret (Stewart) deR.; m. Mal Padgett, March 21, 1981; children: Kenneth, Thomas, James, Lauren, Mary, Jordan, Keith, Stewart; edn: BCE, Univ. Santa Clara, 1950. Career: pres. Carl Holvick Co., Palo Alto 1957-75; v.p. Holvick deRegt Koering, Sunnyvale 1960-75, pres., owner 1975-86; industrial and office park counsel, Urban Land Inst. 1978-; pres., owner Golden Eagle Devel. Co. Inc. 1987-; contbr. feature articles to Corporate Times, Santa Clara; mem. Nat. Assn. Indsl. Office Parks; civic bds: Bellarmine High Sch., San Jose (regent 1977-), Food Bank, San Jose (dir. 1980-), San Mateo County Devel. Assn. 1975-, YMCA 1984-, Santa Clara Univ. Sch. of Bus. (advy. bd. 1984-), The Exec. Com. 1980-; club: Sharon Heights CC (Menlo Park); mil: AUS 1951-53. Res: 1700 Sand Hill Rd #408 Palo Alto 94304 Ofc: PO Box 716 Menlo Park 94026

DERLOSHON, JACK HARVEY, title insurance co. executive; b. Feb. 8, 1929, Kerosha, Wis.; s. Jack A. and Eleanor B. (La Mere) D.; m. Patricia McGrath, Aug. 6, 1955; children: Kathleen b. 1956, John b. 1958, Greg b. 1959, Jeffrey b. 1960, Steven b. 1962, Dennis b. 1964; edn: BBA, Loyola Univ. 1951; Cert. Pub. Acct. Calif. 1955. Career: audit staff Price Waterhouse, Los Angeles 1953-60; acctg. staff, sr. v.p., chief fin. ofcr. First Am. Title Ins. Co. 1960; dir. Calif., Mid Am., Arizona, Wyoming, First Am. Title Ins. Co.; dir. Los Angeles, Hawaii, First Am. Title Co.; dir. Investors Title Co., First Am. Trust Co.; mem: AICPA, Calif. Soc. CPAs, Am. Land Title Assn., Calif. Land Title Ins. Assn.; civic: Am. Diabetes Assn. (chmn. bd. Orange Co. chpt.), Casa Santa Maria, elder housing (pres.); mil: USNR-SN; Republican; R.Cath. (Diocese of Orange lay fin. com., Sisters of St. Joseph of Orange fin. council); rec: golf. Res: 6208 E Shenandoah Ave Orange 91726 Ofc: First Am Title Ins Co 114 E 5th St Santa Ana 92701

DERSHEM, STEPHEN MICHAEL, research chemist; b. Dec. 1, 1954, San Diego; s. William Aaron and Helen Maureen (Ullery) D.; m. Amanda Margaret Smith, Apr. 19, 1980; edn: BS, San Diego State Univ., 1978, MA, 1981; PhD, Mississippi State Univ., 1986. Career: organic chemist Johnson Matthey, Inc. San Diego 1980-83, cons. 1983-84; res. chemist, research mgr. Quantum Materials Inc., San Diego 1986-, cons. 1985-86; awards: life Calif. Scholarship Fedn., Clairemont H.S. 1972, grad. student of yr. chem. dept. Miss. State Univ. 1984; mem. Am. Chem. Soc. (mem. 1981-, mem. at lg. 1990-93, San Diego sect. exec. bd. 1990-93, S.D. newsletter advt. mgr. 1990-92); inventor, 3 U.S. Patents (1990, 2-1991); Republican; Christian; rec: backpacking. Res: 9097 Truman St San Diego 92129 Ofc: Quantum Materials Inc. 9938 Via Pasar San Diego 92126

DESDIER, STEVEN ROSS, accountant; b. Oct. 11, 1952, San Diego; s. Don Desdier and Audree LaVerne Leischner; edn: BA, summa cum laude, U.S. Internat. Univ. 1970; Cert. in Taxation, UC San Diego 1981; Enrolled Agent, IRS; cert. fin. planner (CFP) Coll. for Fin. Planning; accredited tax advisor and accredited business acct. Accreditation Council for Accountancy & Taxation. Career: asst. menswear buyer Miller's West Dept. Store 1970-77; life & disability ins. agent Home Life Ins. Co. 1976-78; acct. San Francisco AIDS Found. 1985-87; reg. rep. Am. Pacific Securities 1982-89; pres. Desdier Inc. dba DESCO 1977-; honors: recogn. for contbns. GSDBA Found. 1985; appt. Advy. Bd. Calif. Senate Select Com. on Small Bus. Enterprises 1986-91; appt. Senate Small Bus. Advy. Bd. 1991-92; mem: Am. Uniform Assn. (treas. 1990-94, steering com. 1989-93), Gr. San Diego Bus. Assn. (pres. 1984-85, treas. 1980-84, bd. 1980-85), Castro Community & Bus. Alliance (treas., bd. 1991-92), Golden Gate Bus. Assn. (v.p. admin. 1985-86, bd. mem.), Nat. Assn. of Bus. Councils (treas. and bd. mem. 1982-84), San Diego Co. Citizen's Scholarship Found. (treas. 1982-84, bd. mem. 1981-84), Calif. Assn. of Indep. Accts. (v.p. 1985-87, pres.-elect 1987-88, pres. 1988-89), Nat. Soc. of Public Accts. (Calif. state dir. 1991-93, chmn. Soc. Rel. Com. 1993-94), Nat. Assn. of Enrolled Agents, Calif. Soc. Of E.A. (Golden Gate Chpt. bd. 1990-92, 2d v.p. 1992-93), Inland Soc. of Tax Cons.; Republican; Lutheran; rec: coins, oriental art.

DESROCHES, DIANE, educator, writer, actress; b. Nov. 17, 1947, Webster, Mass.; d. Victor Joseph and Rose Blouin; m. Roger John DesRoches, Aug. 27, 1966 (div. 1974); son, Bill b. 1970; edn: AA in French (magna cum laude), Mesa Coll., 1976, BA in English (magna cum laude), San Diego St. Univ., 1979, MA in English, 1981; Calif. Comm. Colls. instr. creds. in lang. arts, literature, and ESL, 1981. Career: freelance writer and editor Word Factory, San Diego 1979-; English as a Second Language instr. San Diego Comm. Coll. Dist., 1982-, Coll. of English Language, San Diego 1982-; awards: Gregg Inst. bus. award, 1965, D.B. Williams scholar SDSU, 1979, Calif. State fellow, 1979, Phi Kappa Phi, Psi Chi, Pi Delta Phi; civic: Neighborhood Watch Pgm. #711 S.D. (founder & block capt. 1985-); Democrat; R.Cath.; rec: ice skating, boogie boarding, swimming, horseback riding. Ofc: Word Factory 2029 Cerrissa Ct Ste F San Diego 92154

DETHLEFSEN, ROLF, engineer, scientist; b. Aug. 30, 1934, Niebuell, Germany, naturalized U.S., 1970; s. Andreas Christian and Clara D.; m. Ingrid Baars, July 28, 1961; children: Olaf b. 1961, Stefan b. 1964, Karin b. 1965, Tanja b. 1974; edn: Dipl. Ing., Technical Univ., Braunschweig, Ger. 1961; MS, M.I.T., 1962, ScD, 1965. Career: lab. asst. M.I.T., 1962-65; staff scientist General Dynamics Convair, San Diego 1965-68; assoc. dir. Allis Chalmers, Milw. 1968-72; sr. project mgr. Brown Boveri Electric, Colmar, Pa. 1972-83; prin. engr. Maxwell Labs., San Diego 1983-; pres. Gould Mgmt. Assn., Greensburg, Pa. 1976-77; nat. secty. Electric Launch Assn., 1988-89; awards: NATO fellow M.I.T. (1961-62); mem: IEEE (senior mem. 1966-), AIAA (senior 1990-), VDI (Assn. German Engrs., 1966), Am. Def. Preparedness Assn. 1986-, Am. Radio Relay League 1990-, New York Acad. of Scis. 1992-; civic: Calif. Rare Fruit Growers, German-Am. Socs. (San Diego), Corps Frisia (Braunschweig, Ger.); patentee, 9 US Patents 1971-92; author 30+ tech. papers (1966-). Res: 13476 Samantha Ave San Diego 92129 Ofc: Maxwell Labs 8888 Balboa Ave San Diego 92123

DEUKMEJIAN, GEORGE, former governor of California; b. June 6, 1928, Menands, NY; s. George and Alice (Gairdian) D.; m. Gloria M. Saatjian, Long Beach, Feb. 16, 1957; children: Leslie Ann, b. 1964, George Krikor b. 1966, Andrea Diane, b. 1969; edn: BA, Siena Coll., 1949, JD, St. John's Univ. Sch. of Law, 1952. Career: deputy county counsel, Los Angeles; former ptnr. law firm Riedman, Dalessi, Deukmejian & Woods, Long Beach; elected rep. Calif. State Assembly 1963-67, elected Calif. State Senate 1967-78, senate majority leader 1969-71, senate minority leader 1974-78; elected state atty. gen. 1978-82, elected state gov. 1982-86, re-elected 1986-90; mil: US Army 1953-55; mem. Navy League, Am. Legion, Elks Club; Episcopalian. rec: golf. Ofc: Long Beach

DE VEY, RICHARD E., instructor; b. July 30, 1932, Washington, D.C.; s. Ernest E. and Emily (Holweg) De Vey; m. Kathleen, Apr. 5, 1953; children: Chris b. 1954, Karlyn b. 1957, Michael b. 1958, David b. 1960, Claudia b. 1960, Richard b. 1969, Sheri b. 1970; edn: BA in edn., (honors), Mich. State Univ., 1954, MA in English/edn., 1959; crim. justice law, UCLA, 1979; MPA, USC Sch. Public Adminstrn., 1980, PhD criminology/juvenile law USC 1992. Career: high sch. tchr., English, Whittier Union HSD, 1963-69; probation ofcr. Los

Angeles County Probation Dept., 1969-92; instr. USC 1992-; pres./CEO De Vey Data Inc., Whittier 1985-; volunteer profl: "In Jesus Si Se Puede", E.L.A. store front therapy for juvenile gang members, 1970-79; bd. mem. Project Jade, Juvenile Div. City of South Gate 1989-; Commr. South Gate Commn. For Youth, 1989-; awards: full tuition scholar MSU Bands 1950-59, All University writing awards, poetry and short stories, MSU (1953, 54); mem: USC Alumni Club Pasa. chpt. 1990-, Phi Mu Alpha music frat. 1954-, Univ. Alumni Symphonic Band (1954-, solo clarinet 1988), Pi Sigma Alpha, Lambda Chpt. Poli. Sci. USC 1980-, Circle Squares Social Square Dance Club (pres. 1985-86); Democrat; Charismatic Christian; rec: gun collector, hunting, fishing. Ofc: L.A. Co. Probation, South Gate Police Dept. 8620 California Ave South Gate 90280

DE VITA, JOSEPH STEPHEN, JR., insurance company executive; b. Dec. 1, 1941, Philadelphia, Pa.; s. Joseph Stephen and Yolanda Grace (Di Padova) De V.; m. Joan Theresa Allen; children: Joseph b. 1966, John b. 1969, Deborah b. 1971; edn: BSBA, St. Josephs Univ.; MBA, Drexel Univ.; CPA, Pa. Career: v.p. Fremont Gen. Corp., Santa Monica 1977-86; senior v.p. and CFO Western Employers Ins. Co., Santa Ana 1986-87; exec. v.p. and CFO Great States Ins. Co., Anaheim 1987-; mem: Am. Inst. CPA, Pa. Inst. CPA; mil: USAF 1960-64; Republican. Res: POB 1931 Walnut 91788-1931

DEVOSS, DAVID ARLEN, journalist, news service editor; b. Aug. 4, 1947, Dallas, Tx.; s. Hugh Arlen and Barbara Helen (Cooper) DeV.; m. Elizabeth Ann Rushton, Dec. 29, 1975; children: Thomas Arlen b. 1981, Matthew Richard b. 1988; edn: BA Univ. of Texas, Austin 1968. Career: corresp. Time Magazine, Houston, Montreal, Detroit, Saigon, 1968-80, Time Mag.bureau chief Bangkok, Mexico City, 1981-85; special reporter Los Angeles Times, L.A. 1985-89; editor East-West News Service, L.A. 1990-; corresp. Asia, Inc. Hong Kong, 1991-; awards include: best sport story of 1987 Sporting News, St. Louis (1987), best sports story AP, L.A. (1987), best education reporting Unity Awards in Media, Lincoln Univ., Jefferson City, Mo. (1989); mem. bd. dirs. Inst. for Democracy in Viet Nam (1988-); clubs: Foreign Correspondent (bd. 1978-81, v.p. 1981-83); author: Insight Guide to Thailand (1982), Bordering on Trouble - Resources & Politics of Latin America (1986), Day in the Life of California (1988), Day in the Life of China (1989), Insider's Guide to Indonesia (1993); Episcopalian. Ofc: East-West News Service, 4159 Stansbury Ave Sherman Oaks 91423

DE VOTO, TERENCE ALAN, broadcasting executive; b. Aug. 2, 1946, San Francisco; s. Albert Anthony and Virginia Louise (Kohnke) De V.; m. Christine McKannay, Jan. 24, 1976; children: Tommy b. 1977, Mark b. 1980, Julie b. 1983, Carolyn b. 1985; edn: BBA, Gonzaga Univ. 1968. Career: v.p. trading dept. Birr, Wilson & Co., 1968-74; account exec. KFOG Radio 1974-78, KSFO Radio 1978-81; local sales mgr., nat. sales mgr., gen. sales mgr., gen. mgr. KYUU Radio 1981-88; v.p. Fuller-Jeffrey Bdcstg., gen. mgr. KHTT and KSRO Radio, 1989-91; pres. radio div. Americom, 1991-; civic bds: Marin Assn. Retarded Citizens (bd., pres. 1989-91), Hanna Boys Ctr. (bd. 1991-); clubs: Olympic, Guardsmen; Republican; R.Cath.; rec: sports, music; res: 295 Oak San Anselmo 94960

DE VRIES, SIMEN, manufacturing company executive; b. Oct. 10, 1934, Leeuwarden, Netherlands; s. Lieuwe and Hendrikje (de Haan) DeV.; m. Attje Kunst, March 2, 1958; children: Jacqueline b. 1959, Simon, Jr. b. 1962, Michael b. 1960, Yvonne b. 1965; edn: BS chem., Utrecht Univ. Netherlands 1955; BS arts, Life Bible Coll. 1977; M.Div., Melodyland Sch. of Theology 1975; Th.D, Calif. Grad. Sch. Career: chemist Drewry Photo Color Co., Glendale 1957; Purex Corp., South Gate 1960; Pabst Brewing Co., Los Angeles 1958-60; Mattews Paint Co. 1960-63; chief chemist Presto Chemicals, Sun Valley 1963-74; asst. mgr. Synres Chemical Co., Anaheim 1974-79; owner Simtec 1979-; v.p. Mastervideo, Fullerton 1979-; mem: Calif. Assn. Small Indep. Bus.; inventor prstec polyester crating system (1979), producer Miracles Today tv program (1982-); mil: cpl. USAF 1955-57; Republican; Christian. Res: 1019 N Lincoln Ave Fullerton 92631 Ofc: 1188 N Grove St Bldgs K and L Anaheim 92806

DEWAR, NICHOLAS ALAN RICHARD, public accountant; b. April 5, 1950, London, England; s. Richard Alistair Robert and Monica Joan (Warne) D.; edn: BA, MA, Trinity Coll. Cambridge England 1972; MS, Antioch Univ. 1982; C.P.A. Calif. 1988. Career: asst mgr. J. Henry Schroder Wagg, London, England 1972-76; gen. mgr. World Wildlife Fund, Caracas, Venezuela 1976-78; tax acct. Seifer Murken Levy & Despina, San Francisco 1983-85; Deloitte Haskins & Sells 1985-88; owner Nicholas Dewar CPA 1988-; awards: Fundacion Gran Mariscal de Ayacucho grant 1980; mem: Comm. Bd. Program Inc. (treas., bd. mem. 1988), Elmwood Inst. (peer 1989), Am. Inst. CPA, Calif. Soc. CPA, Briarpatch, Leander Club Henley-on-Thames England; rec: gardening, rowing. Ofc: 317 Noe St San Francisco 94114

DEWEY, DONALD WILLIAM, editor and publisher; b. Sept. 30, 1933, Honolulu; s. Donald Wm. and Theckla Jean (Engeborg) Dewey; m. Sally Ryan, Aug. 7, 1961; children: Michael b. 1962, Wendy b. 1968; edn: Pomona Coll. 1953-55; Career: sales engr. Pascoe Steel Corp., Pomona 1955-56, div. Reynolds Aluminum Co., Los Angeles 1956-58, Switzer Panel Corp., Pasadena 1958-60; sales and gen. mgr. Western Pre-Cast Concrete Corp., Ontario 1960-62;

founder, editor & pub. R/C Modeler Magazine (1963-), Freshwater and Marine Aquarium Mag. (1978-); pres., bd. chmn. RC Modeler Corp., RCM Publications; v.p., co-dir. Project Alert, Inc. 1981-84; author: Radio Control From the Ground Up (1970), Flight Training course (1973), For What It's Worth (vol.1 1973, vol.2 1975), numerous sci. articles; mem: Am. Radio Relay League, Nat. Assn. Radio Amateurs, Acad. Model Aeronautics, Nat. Aeronautic Assn., Oceanic Assn., Internat. Oceanographic Found., Smithsonian Assocs., Internat. Assn. of Aquatic Animal Medicine, Fedn. of Am. Aquarium Socs., Am. Philatelic Soc., Soc. of Philatelic Americans, Am. Topical Assn., APS Writers Unit 30, Am. First Day Cover Soc., United Postal Stationery Soc., Confederate Stamp Alliance, Am. Air Mail Soc., Bureau Issues Assn., Am. Revenue Assn., Canal Zone Study Group, Pitcairn Islands Study Group, Pet Industries Jt. Adv. Council, NY Acad. of Scis., Smithsonian Instn., Sierra Madre Hist. Soc., Friends Sierra Madre Library (life), Internat. Betta Congress, Am. Killifish Assn., Am. Catfish and Loach Assn., N.Am. Native Fishes Assn., Ludwig von Mises Inst., Rutherford Found., The Endowment Found., The Claremont Inst.; mil: HM-3, Hosp. Corps, USNR 1951-53; Republican (nat. com., US Presdl. Trust, US Congl. & Senatl. Clubs, Conservative Caucus, Presdl. Task Force); Lutheran; rec: writing, R/C modeling, am. radio, stamps. Res: 410 W Montecito Ave Sierra Madre 91024 Ofc: R/C Modeler Corp. 144 W Sierra Madre Blvd Sierra Madre 91024

DEWITT, JOHN BELTON, conservation executive; b. Jan. 13, 1937, Oakland; s. Belton and Florence D.; m. Karma Lee Sowers, Sept. 17, 1960; edn: BA in wildlife conservation, Univ. Calif. Berkeley, 1959. Career: Forest Service, El Dorado Nat. Forest, 1955-56; ranger naturalist Nat. Park Service, Yosemite Nat. Park 1957-58, Mt. Rainer Nat. Park 1959, Death Valley Nat. Monument 1960; Land Law examiner, information ofcr. and land appraiser Bur. of Land Mgmt., 1960-64; asst. secty. Save-the-Redwoods League, 1964-71, exec. dir. and secty., 1971-; dir. Nature Conservancy No. Calif. Chapter 1976-77, advy. council Trust for Public Land 1975-78, conservation advr. to Gov. Jerry Brown 1975-82, dir. Tuolumne River Preserv. Trust 1981-85, advisor to U.S. Secty. of Interior (4 adminstrns.) on nat. conserv. policy 1964-1990), advy. council Anza Borrego Desert Com. 1983-; awards: Nat. Conserv. Award, DAR 1982, Golden Bear Award, Calif. State Park & Rec. Commn. 1982, Gulf Oil Conserv. Award 1985, Calif. State Park Rangers Assn. Award 1985; mem: Sierra Club (conserv. com. 1953-63), Am. Forestry Assn., Nat. Parks Assn., Wilderness Soc., Nat. Audubon Soc.; publs: California Redwood Parks & Preserves (1982, reprinted 1985); Prot.; rec: fishing, hiking, historical resrch., gardening. Ofc: Save-the-Redwoods League 114 Sansome St Ste 605 San Francisco 94104

DEY, SAMUEL EUSTACE, JR., psychiatrist; b. Sept. 5, 1958, Guyana, S.A.; s. Samuel Ezekiel and Pauline Elizabeth (Pollydore) D.; m. Andrea Leona Jenkins, Apr. 1, 1986; children: Samuel Everett b. 1988, Brandon b. 1990; edn: BS in chem. (hons.), Loma Linda Univ., 1981; MD, LLU Sch. of Med., 1983; bd. certified ABPN - Psychiatry 1991, Geriatric Psychiatry 1992. Career: resident phys. LLU Med. Ctr. Dept. Psychiatry, Loma Linda 1983-88; staff psychiatrist Patton State Hosp., Patton 1987-89, 1990-; pvt. practice, San Bernardino 1988-92; pvt. practice, Riverside 1988-; staff psychiatrist San Bdo. County Dept. Mental Health 1989-90; mem: AMA, Am. Psychiat. Assn., CMA, San Bdo. Co. Med. Soc., Riv. Co. Med. Soc., Am. Orthopsychiatric Assn., So. Calif. Psychiat. Soc. (Inland Chpt. pres. 1991-92, sec. treas. 1989-90, pres. elect 1990-91), Am. Profl. Practice Assn., Nat. Med. Assn., Black Psychiatrists of Am., Am. Assn. for Geriatric Psychiatry; rec: stamps, sports, travel. Res: PO Box 51059 Riverside 92517 Ofc: PO Box 51030 Riverside 92517

DIAZ, ELISA G., school board official, retired educator, b. Dec. 24, 1918, Metcalf, Ariz.; d. Gilberto and Maria (Reyes-Montelongo) Gonzalez; m. Leno F. Diaz, Sept. 10, 1949; children: Eduardo b. 1950, Katharine Ann b. 1953; edn: BA, Univ. of Redlands, 1963; grad. work San Bdo. State Univ., UC Riverside; Calif. tchg. credentials. Career: escrow mgr. Coast Federal Sav. & Loan Assn., Los Angeles, 1946-49; tchr. San Bernardino City Unified Sch. Dist., 1963-80; elected School Board, San Bernardino City USD, 1981-91; awards: Latina of the Year Congress of United Communities, San Bdo. (1985), Citizen of Achiev. L.W.V., San Bdo. 1988, Mujer Latina Libreria Del Pueblo Inc., San Bdo. 1991; mem. Assn. of Mexican American Educators 1963, L.W.V. 1965-; R.Cath.; avocation: Study of early childhood, work with children. Res: 1804 Mesa Verde Dr San Bernardino 92404

DIAZ, RAUL ZARAGOZA, university administrator; b. Feb. 18, 1953, Visalia; s. Angel and Benita (Zaragoza) D.; m. Ana Maria Leos, Feb. 18, 1977; children: Raul Alejandro b. 1979, Mauricio Inocencio b. 1983; edn: AA, Coll. of Sequoias 1973; BA, UC Santa Cruz 1975; MS, CSU Sacto. 1977. Career: adminstrv. asst. Campesinos Progresistas, Dixon 1976-77; counselor Dinuba H.S. 1977-79; coordinator, RSVP program CSU Fresno 1979-81, dir. CAMP program 1981-88, dir. UMS 1988-, ag. leadship mentor ALD program 1984-, res. assoc. Nat. HEP CAMP Eval. 1985, cons. sch. of ag. 1986; amnesty instr. SER West 1989; awards: MAPA El Concilio Noche de Hechos; mem: Year Round Task Force Fresno Unified Sch. (affirmative action com. 1989), HEP CAMP Nat. Assn. (pres. 1985-86), Citizens Advy. Com. City of Fresno, Raza Advocates for Calif. Higher Edn., El Concilio de Fresno Inc., Chicano Staff Orgn. (pres. 1981), Mex-Am. Political Assn. (v.p. Fresno chpt. 1988), Tri-Co.

Migrant Head Start (bd. pres. 1983, 84); Democrat; Cath. Res: 15874 Mark Rd Madera 93638 Ofc: Calif. State University Fresno 93740-0067

DI BARTOLOMEO, JOSEPH R., physician; b. Aug. 31, 1937, NY, NY; s. Thomas Albert and Antoinette (Dionisio) DiB.; m. Ericka Theckla, Sept. 8, 1962 (div. 1984); children: Phillip b. 1964, David b. 1967, Raymond b. 1977; m. Maxine Gwen Schalk, Aug. 20, 1989; edn: BS, St. John's Univ., Jamaica, NY, 1959; MD, Georgetown Med. Sch., 1963; bd. cert. Nat. Bd. Med. Examiners, 1964, Am. Bd. of Otolaryngology, 1968. Career: rotating intern Waterbury (Conn.) Hosp., 1963-64, resident gen. surg., 1964-65; resident otol. NY Univ. Bellevue Med. Ctr., 1965-68; att. otolaryngologist Cottage Hosp., Santa Barbara, 1968; chmn. dept. otol. St. Francis Hosp., 1968, 1983-85, chief of staff 1986-87; medical dir. The Ear Foundation, Santa Barbara, 1980-; currently cons. Hard of Hearing Pgm. Santa Barbara Sch. Dist., cons. Speech Comms. Research Lab. Inc., ednl. assoc. Ear Internat.; med. dir. hearing sect. Lions Sight and Hearing Conservation Ctr., 1975; resrch. assoc. dept. speech and hearing UCSB, 1969; mem. med. staff UCLA and asst. clin. prof. UCLA Div. Head and Neck Surg., 1976; cons. Wadsworth VA Hosp., 1982; instr. Am. Acad. of Otolaryngology, 1976-84; awards: outstanding tchg. UCLA 1978-79, honor award Am. Acad. Otol.-Head and Neck Surg. 1986, Fellowship awards: Am. Acad. of Ophthal. and Otol. 1969, Am. Acad. of of Facial Plastic and Reconstrv. Surg. 1969, Am. Coll. of Surgeons sect. otol. 1971, The Triological Soc. 1979; mem: AMA, CMA, Canta Barbara Co. Med. Assn., Royal Soc. of Medicine (London), World Med. Assn., Triol. Soc. (sec. we. sect. 1982-86), Dizziness and Balance Disorders Assn. of Am., Pacific Coast OtoOphthalmol. Soc., Internat. Correspondence Soc. of Ophthalmologists and Otolaryngologists, Centurien Club, Am. Hearing and Speech Assn., Pan Am. Soc. of Otolaryngologists and Bronchoesophagologists, SENTAC, Am. Council of Otol., Am. Auditory Soc., Am. Soc. for Laser Medicine and Surgery, Undersea Med. Soc., Am. Neurotology Soc., The Prosper Meniere Soc.; inventions: Nasal therapy for treatment of patulous Eustachian tube, Prosthesis - middle ear ventilation tube obturator (Oto-Med Inc. Products), Argon Laser for otologic surg. (Coherent Lasers, Med. Div.), A Cable Carrying Guide for Accessory Cords on the Operating Microscope; author chapters in med. books, med. jour. articles; mil: s/sgt. US Army 1955-59; Republican; R.Cath.; rec: scuba, skiing. Ofc: 2420 Castillo St Santa Barbara 93105-4346

DICKERSON, WILLIAM ROY, lawyer, lecturer, judge pro tem; b. Feb. 15, 1928, Uniontown, Ky.; s. Benjamin Franklin and Honor Mae (Staples) D.; edn: BA in acctg., Calif. St. Univ., 1952; JD, UCLA, 1958; admitted bar: Calif. 1959. Career: dep. atty., city prosecutor ex-officio, City of Glendale, 1959-62; atty., assoc. James Brewer, Los Angeles 1962-68, LaFollette, Johnson, Schroeter & DeHaas, 1968-73; solo law practice, 1973-; arbitrator L.A. Superior Ct., L.A. Municipal Ct.; judge pro tem L.A. Superior Ct. Appellate Dept., L.A. Municipal Ct., Small Claims Ct., Traffic Ct.; lectr. in field; mem: Am. Bar Assn., Calif. Bar Assn., L.A. County Bar Assn., Fed. Bar Assn., Soc. Calif. Accts., Am. Film Inst., Internat. Platform Assn.; civic: Los Feliz Improvement Assn. (bd. 1986-88), Zoning Commn., Streets and Hwys. Commn. (co-chair). Address: 813 N Doheny Dr Beverly Hills 90210

DICKEY, GARY ALAN, clergyman; b. Jan. 25, 1946, Santa Monica; s. Charles Harry and Audrey Winifred (White) D.; m. Tamara Jean Kimble, Jan. 11, 1976; edn: BA, UC Los Angeles, 1968; MDiv, Fuller Theol. Sem., Pasadena 1972; DMin, Sch. of Theology, Claremont 1974; ordained minister United Methodist Ch. Career: assoc. pastor Magnolia Park United Meth. Ch., Burbank 1974-78; senior pastor St. James United Meth. Ch., Pasadena 1978-90; First United Meth. Ch., Canoga Park 1990-; supvg. pastor Bd. of Higher Edn., Nashville, Tn. 1978-; exec. com. Calif. Pacific Conf. Bd. of Ordained Ministry, 1980-88, mem., chair Pasadena Dist. com. ordained ministry 1978-90; awards: Citizenship award Sons Am. Rev., Pasa. 1990, Polonia Restituta Polish People's Republic 1990, Paul Harris Fellow Altadena Rotary 1986; mem: Sons Am. Rev. (Calif. Soc. chaplain 1988-), Soc. Descendants of Washington's Army Valley Forge, Rotary Intl. (Altadena pres. 1989-90), Order of the Colonial Acorn 1992-, Sons of Colonial Wars (Calif. Soc. chaplain 1990-), Soc. War of 1812 (Calif. Soc. chaplain 1990-, editor 1991-), Soc. Sons of Am. Colonists, Royal Soc. of St. George, London; Vet. Corps of Artillery, New York; Soc. Sons of Union Vet. of Civil War; Republican; rec: genealog. res., photography, travel. Res: 22167 Bryant St West Hills 91304 Ofc: First United Methodist Church 22700 Sherman Way West Hills 91307

DILLARD, RAYMOND MERRILL, management consultant, company president; b. Oct. 15, 1928, Nebraska, Ind.; s. William H. and Charlotte (Bemish) D.; m. Charlene Squires, May 16, 1953; children: Lora b. 1957, Lynn b. 1960, Scott b. 1963; edn: BS, Canterbury, Danville, Ind. 1950; MBA, Butler Univ., Indpls. 1956; exec. pgm. Wabash, Crawfordsville, Ind. 1956-60. Career: indsl. engr. mgr. P.R. Mallory, Idpls. 1953-59; group v.p. Science Management, Basking Ridge, N.J. 1959-84; pres. Western Group, Palo Alto, Calif. 1984-; mem. F&A Masons, AAO Scottish Rite; club: Fremont Hills CC, Los Altos Hills, Calif. (1970-, past pres.); mil: capt. US Army 1950-52; Republican; Methodist; rec: tennis, bridge. Res: 595 Almond Ave Los Altos 94022 Ofc: Western Group 200 Page Mill Rd Ste 150 Palo Alto 94306

DILLON, DON ALLEN, clergyman; b. Sept. 30, 1958, Simmern, Germany; s. Max Corwin and Beatrice Billie (Salter) D.; m. Rebecca Marie Roberts, Sept. 20, 1980; 1 son, Alexander b. 1990; edn: BA Theology, Pacific Coast Baptist Bible Coll., San Dimas, 1988; ordained So. Baptist Conv. 1976. Career: Career director Bible Baptist Ch., Marysville, Calif. 1981-84; associate pastor Calvary Baptist Ch., Bellflower, 1984-89; asst. pastor Calvary Baptist Ch., Hawthorne, 1989-91; pastor First Baptist Ch., Ripon, 1991-; past mem. Nat. Student Preacher, San Dimas (pres. 1987-88); youth-music dir. West L.A. So. Baptist Assn., Manhattan Beach, 1990; awards: Nat. Eagle Scout, BSA, Anchorage, AK (1976); mil: E4, sgt. USAF 1980-84; Republican; rec: sailing, golf. Res: 834 Baker Ripon 95366 Ofc: First Baptist Church 803 Ripona Ripon 95366

DILLON, FRANCIS PATRICK, human resources executive, management consultant; b. March 15, 1937, Long Beach; s. Wallace Myron and Mary Elizabeth (Land) D.; m. Vicki Lee Dillon, Oct. 1980; children: Cary Randolph, Francis Patrick Jr., Randee, Rick; edn: BA, Univ. Va. 1959; MS, Def. Fgn. Affairs Sch. 1962; MBA, Pepperdine Univ. 1976. Career: traffic mgr., mgr. personnel services Pacific Telephone Co., Sacto. and Lakeport 1966-69; asst. mgr. manpower planning and devel. Pan-Am World Airways, NYC 1969-71; mgr. personnel and orgn. devel. Continental Airlines, Los Angeles 1971-74; dir. personnel Farwest Services Inc., Irvine 1974; dir. human resources Bourns Inc., Riverside 1974-80; dir. employee and comm. rels. MSI Data Corp. 1980-83; pres. Pavi Enterprises 1983-; mgmt. cons. 1983-; pres., CEO Personnel Products & Services Inc. 1984-; pres. Meditrans Inc.; bd. dirs. Health Services Maintenance Orgn. Inc., Youth Services Center Inc.; vol. precinct worker; awards: Disting. Service Jaycees 1969, Jack Cates Meml. Vol. of Year Youth Service Center 1977; mem: Assn. Internal Mgmt. Cons., Am. Soc. Personnel Adminstrn., Personnel Indsl. Rels. Assn., Am. Soc. Tng. & Devel., Am. Electronics Assn. (human resources com., chmn. human resources symposium), Mission Viejo Sailing Club, Toastmasters (pres. 1966-67), Have Dirt Will Travel; mil: lt. cdr. USN 1959-66; asst. naval attache Brazil 1963-65; Republican; Episcopalian. Ofc: Pavi Enterprises 27331 Via Amistoso Mission Viejo 92692

DIMMICK, KEVIN C., organizational change consultant; b. Aug. 21, 1953, Redwood City; m. Debra Herring; 1 dau., April Louise; edn: BA in speech comm., San Diego State Univ.; grad. studies in human resources and organizational devel., Univ. of San Francisco. Career: general mgr. All American Janitorial Services and Supply Co., San Diego 1975-78; personnel rep. Varian Assoc., Palo Alto 1978-81; personnel mgr. Arrowhead, Inc., San Rafael 1981-84; dir. of human resources Coherent Auburn Group, Coherent, Inc., Auburn 1984-93; pres. Dimmick & Assocs., Auburn 1993-; frequent speaker & expert on Self-Managed Work Teams; past instr. Sierra Coll., Rocklin; civic: bd. mem. (past chmn.) Sierra Coll. Mgmt. Advy. Bd.; bd. mem. The Workplace Found.; mem: (past pres.) Merchants & Mfrs. Assn. Sacto. Advy. Bd., former crisis intervention counselor Marin Suicide Prevention Ctr.; author: The Legal Aspects of Management 1992. Res: 11175 Rosemary Dr Auburn 95603

DIMORA, ALFRED JOHN, motor car company president, automobile designer and manufacturer; b. July 4, 1956, Rochester, N.Y.; s. James J. and Mary DiM.; edn: grad. Gates-Chili (N.Y.) High Sch., machinist & welding courses, Santa Barbara (Calif.) City Coll. Career: machinist, n.c. set-up Heize & Phillips Inc., Rochester, N.Y. 1974-76; machinist, prototyping and sales Clenet Coachworks, Santa Barbara 1976-77 (estab. by Alain Clenet 1976, prod. only 250 Clenet I cars, DiMora later bought co. 1982); founder, designer Sceptre Motor Car, Goleta, Calif. 1978-79; owner, pres., c.e.o. Golden Glow Inc., Seattle, Wash. 1979-80; founder, pres., designer UniBody Designs, Santa Barbara 1981-82; co-owner, pres. Clenet Coachworks Inc. 1982-88; designer, pres. and c.e.o. DiMora Motor Car Co., Santa Barbara 1988-; awards: Best Car of Show (Sceptre Car) L.A. Auto Show, Los Angeles 1978, Centennial 100th Year of the Gas Powered Automobile, Automotive Hall of Fame, Midland, Mich. 1986, Best Car of Show & Design (Clenet Series IV) New York Auto Show, N.Y.C. 1987; mem. '57 Chev. Club Santa Barbara; DiMora cars, design and mfg. methods are subject of 1,000+ articles nat. and internat. Ofc: DiMora Motor Car Co. 1187 Coast Village Rd Ste 234 Santa Barbara 93108

DINER, DANIEL BRUCE, biomedical engineer; b. Sept. 14, 1947, Kew Gardens, NY; s. Harry Diner and Miriam Greenberg; edn: BA in physics, Johns Hopkins Univ., Baltimore, Md. 1969; MA in creative writing, Johns Hopkins Univ. 1971; MS, computer sci., Calif. Inst. of Tech., Pasadena 1973; PhD in engring. sci., Calif. Inst. of Tech. 1978. Career: asst. prof., neurology, Univ. of Zurich, Switzerland 1979-81; asst. prof., computer sci., NY Inst. of Tech., Old Westbury, NY 1982-85; human vision cognizant engr. for robotics and teleoperation, Jet Propulsion Lab./Calif. Inst. Tech./NASA, Pasadena 1985-; cons. in field, 1983-; co-owner, Fundamental Magic of Hollywood 1991-; awards: NIH Fellow, Calif. Inst. Tech., Pasadena 1974-78; guest researcher, Hoffman-La Roche, Zurich 1979-81; Jet Propulsion Lab./Calif. Inst. Tech./NASA, Pasadena: NASA Summer Faculty Fellow 1985, recipient NASA New Tech. Innovator awards (10) 1986-92, NASA patent filing awards 1988-90, NASA Group Achievement award 1991; listed Who's Who in the West 1991; mem: Robotics Internat./SME (bd. dir. 1988-90, sr. mem. 1983-); magician mem. Magic Castle of Hollywood; co-author of book, Human Engring. in Stereoscopic Viewing

Devices, 1991; contbr. numerous scientific papers to profl. jours.; rec: backpacking, chess, magic, travel. Ofc. JPL/CALTECH/NASA (198-219) 4800 Oakgrove Dr. Pasadena 91109

DING, MAE LON, personnel management consultant; b. May 7, 1954, Norwalk, Calif.; d. Lock Gee and Ruth (Tang) Ding; edn: BA, UCLA, 1976; MBA, USC, 1978; cert. compensation profl. Am. Compensation Assn. 1986. Career: mgmt. intern 20th Century Fox, L.A. 1976-77; cons. Forum Corp., Boston, Mass. 1978; senior cons. Wyatt Co., Boston 1978-81; senior cons. R.A. Smith & Assocs., Laguna Hills 1981-83; compensation mgr. Allergan Pharmaceutical, Irvine 1983-85; pres. Personnel Systems Assocs., Tustin 1985-; instr. CSU Pomona 1988-89, CSU Long Beach 1988-90, Chapman Univ., Orange 1991; instr. Am. Compensation Assn., Scottsdale, Az. 1985-92; mem. Assn. of Professional Consultants (Anaheim chpt. bd. 1989-93), Am. Compensation Assn. 1983-; civic: SHARE, Corona Del Mar (pres. 1991-92); author: Survey Sources (1991, 92, 93), articles in Personnel News (1992), Personnel (1991), J. of Compensation & Benefits (1991), Chapman Univ. Econ. Review (1992); rec: skiing, mtn. biking. Ofc: Personnel Systems Associates, 2282 Aspen St Tustin 92680

DISHION, CATHERINE D., company president; b. Oct. 8, 1949, Los Angeles; d. Robert Earl and Ginny Lucille (Jones) Jacobson; m. Robert A. Derr, June 22, 1968 (div. 1981); children: Shane Edward; m. Donald R. Dishion, Oct. 17, 1986; edn: BA, CalPoly Pomona, 1970. Career: office mgr. Walton Ents., Upland, 1970-74; corp. ops. mgr. Merrill Lynch Realty, Santa Barbara, 1974-82; pres./mgr. Santa Barbara Placement Agency Inc., and its subs. Santa Barbara Temps, Santa Barbara, 1982-, also career counseling 1988-, resume writing 1989-; honors: "Santa Barbara County Pick" for KABL Network 1990; chair: Santa Barbara Personnel Assn. 1981-, South Coast Bus. Network 1984-, Nat. Assn. Small Bus./L.A., S.B. C.of C. (Small Bus. Com. bd. 1989-), Women's Community Ctr. (exec. bd. 1989-), Women's Day Conference (exec. bd. 1990-); club: University (S.B.); Republican; Baptist; rec: int. design. Ofc: Santa Barbara Placement Agency, Inc. 1300 B Santa Barbara St Santa Barbara 93101

DISSTON, MATTHEW PRATT, economist; b. Feb. 25, 1952, Ft. Washington, Pa.; s. William L. and Julia D.; m. Claudia C., March 21, 1954; children: Galen b. 1983, Melissa b. 1986, Alexandra b. 1988; edn: BA, UC Berkeley 1976. Career: analyst Gladstone Assoc., WDC 1977-80; economist Irvine Co., Newport Beach 1980-82; prin. Research Network, Laguna Hills 1982-; lectr. UC Irvine 1986-; mem: Am. Planning Assn., Bldg. Industry Research Council (treas. 1988-89), Nat. Restaurant Assn., Bldg. Industry Assn., Robinson Ranch Homeowners Assn. (pres. 1988-89, bd. mem. 1987-88); articles pub. in profl. jours. (1988-89). Ofc: Research Network Ltd. 23161 Mill Creek Rd Laguna Hills 92653

DIVOLA, JOHN, artist, educator; b. June 6, 1949, Santa Monica; s. John M. and Marion (Foster) D.; edn: BA, CSU Northridge, 1971; MA, UCLA, 1973, MFA, 1974. Career: grad. tchg. asst. art, photography, UCLA, 1972-74; instr. UCLA summer qtr. 1977, Immaculate Heart Coll., L.A. 1975-79, Loyola Marymount Univ., L.A. 1976-80; vis. instr. USC, 1981; vis. artist Claremont Grad. Sch., 1981; vis. lectr. UCLA, 1982-83; instr. art/photography, Calif. Inst. of the Arts, Valencia 1978-88; prof. art dept. UC Riverside, 1988-, art dept. chair 1991-93; awards: NEA photography fellow (1973-74, 76-77, 79-80, 90-91), John Simon Guggenheim Meml. fellow 1986-87, Mellon fellow Calif. Inst. of Arts 1987-88, fellow Ctr. for Ideas in Soc., UCR 1991-92; num. one person exhs. since 1975 incl. Visual Studies Workshop, Rochester, N.Y., Camerawork Gal., Cinti., Ctr. for Creative Photog. Univ. Az., Tucson, Image Gal., Aarhus, Denmark, L.A. Inst. of Contemp. Art, Vision Gal., Boston, Print Galleri, Copenhagen, Blue Sky Gal., Portland, Ore., Camera Obscura, Stockholm, Sweden, Henry Gal. Univ. Wash., Seattle, Madison (Wis.) Art Ctr., Catskill Ctr. Photog., Woodstock, N.Y. Paul Cava Gal., Phila., Lightwork, Syracuse, N.Y., Grapestake Gal., S.F., Robert Freidus Gal., N.Y.C., Photographers Gal., Melbourne, Aust., No. Kentucky Univ., Gal. Del Cavallino, Venice, Italy, Univ. N.M. Art Mus., Albuquerque, Susan Spiritus Gal., Newport Beach, Jones Troyer Gal., W.D.C., Film in the Cities, St. Paul, Minn., L.A. Municipal Gal. Barnsdall Park (retrospective 1974-85), Jayne Baum Gal., N.Y.C., Gallery Min, Tokyo, Japan (catalog, 1987), Photo Interform, Osaka, Japan, Seibu Gal., Tokyo, Richard Green Gal., L.A., Jayne Baum Gal., N.Y.C., Jan Kesner Gal., L.A., Galerie Niki Diana Marquardt, Paris, Fr. (1990), Univ. Art Gal., UCR (1991), Rewdex Contemporary Art Gal., Koyoto, Japan (1992); numerous group exhs., nat., internat., traveling, since 1973; rep. in permanent collections of corporate and public instns. Res: 245 Ruth Ave Venice 90201 Tel: 310/396-0334

DIXON, DEAN OWEN, executive; b. July 25, 1945, Baraboo, Wis.; s. Myer Eldon and Ruby Luvera (Hupenbecker) D.; m. Gail, May 8, 1965; 1 son, Todd b. 1968; edn: Ariz. St. Univ. 1963-65, CSU Long Beach 1965-67; Career: mgr. Factory Sales/ Traffic, Varec Inc., 1967-70; asst. nat. sales mgr. Merit Abrasive Prods. Inc., 1970-78; territory mgr. Sancap Abrasives Inc., 1978-79; v.p. sales & mktg. Jet and Western Abrasives Inc. 1979-91; gen. mgr. Marathon Abrasives/ Sunmight Abrasives 1991-; awards: Rotary Found. Group Study Exchange to New South Wales, Australia 1980; civic: City of Buena Park

Centennial (exec. bd. 1986-87), B.P. Hist. Soc (1974-, trustee 1978-79, v.p. 1979-84, treas. 1992-), Orange County Hist. Commn. 1980-82, O.C. Hist. Soc. 1978-, B.P. C.of C. 1974-80, Silverado Days Com. 1974-88, B.P. Boys Club (com. 1980-87), Am. Found. for Sci. of Creative Intelligence 1973-, Cultural Arts Found. Buena Park (bd., v.p., v.chmn. 1989-), Buena Park Civic Theater artistic review com. 1986-88, SAR, Calif. Soc. SAR, United Scottish Soc., Clan Keith Soc. (USA); coauthor: GSE Report 1980, A Hundred Years of Yesterdays: A Centennial Hist. of the People of Orange County & Their Communitites 1988, Orange Countiana Vol. V 1992; columnist Buena Park Independent Newspaper 1990-; writer/prod. cable-t.v. prodn.: Natural Hist. in No. Orange County 1985; Republican; Methodist; rec: bibliophile. Ofc: Marathon Abrasives/Sunmight Abrasives 12101 Western Ave Garden Grove 92641

DIXON, GAIL S., community leader; b. Jan. 3, 1943, Northampton, Mass.; d. Walter and Mary Jane (Elder) Hargesheimer; m. Dean O. Dixon, May 8, 1965; son, Todd b. 1968; edn: W. Wash. St. Univ., Bellingham 1960-64. Career: reprographics ind., self-empl., 1964-70; v.p. Great Western Sav. & Loan Assn., Beverly Hills 1970-87; reg. rep. Lincoln National Life, Santa Ana 1987-93; Fullerton Chamber of Commerce 1993-; bd. dirs. Humana Hosp., Anaheim 1976-84, Beach Comm. Hosp., Buena Park 1978-85; honors: Cypress Coll. Americana award 1983, Woman of Achiev. Buena Park Mall Assn. 1984, citation U.S. Congl. Record 1978; mem: Calif. Municipal Treasurers Assn. 1986-93, Am. Found. for the Sci. of Creative Intell. 1974-, Assn. of Calif. Water Agys. 1985-93, Public Affairs Com. 1988-93, Calif. Assn. of Sanitation Agys. 1988-93, Buena Park C.of C. (1st woman pres. in 51 yr. hist. 1978-79, dir. 1974-80), Buena Park Noon Lions Club (1st woman mem. 1989-), Silverado Days Com., B.P. 1974-, North Orange County Girls Club, Fullerton (1974-82, v.p. 1977), Buena Park Coord. Council (sec.treas. 1976-84), Boys Club of Buena Park (assoc. bd. 1974-84), Hugh O'Brian Youth Found. So. Calif. (dir. 1989-92), City of Buena Park Vision 2010 Core Com. (1990-92); Republican; Methodist; rec: entertaining. Ofc: Fullerton Chamber of Commerce 219 E. Commonwealth Ave. Fullerton 92632

DJAWAD, SAID T., paralegal; b. Feb. 27, 1969, Kandahr, Afghanistan; s. Prof. Mir. Hussain Shah and Zakia D.; m. Shamim Rahman, Nov. 16, 1986; edn: BA, Kabul Univ., 1987; postgrad. studies Wilhelms Univ., Muenster, Germany 1985; cert. Long Island Univ., 1986. Career: paralegal Lehnardt & Bauman, NY, NY 1987; Dewey, Ballantine, NY, NY 1988; Steefel, Levitt & Weiss, San Francisco 1989-; mem. Council of Fgn. Affairs, Internat. Soc. for Human Rights, Afghanistan Cultural Soc. (dir.); publs: Modern Dictatorship; Dictatorship of Future, Future of Dictatorship; Occupation of Wakhan: Soviet expansion to the South. Res: 4279 Merced Cir Antioch 94509 Ofc: Steefel, Levitt & Weiss One Embarcadero Center San Francisco 95111

DLUGIE, PAUL DAVID, physician; b. June 17, 1940, Chgo.; s. Samuel R. and Ruth (Mesirow) D.; m. Lida Pira, July 23, 1965; edn: AB, Johns Hopkins Univ. 1961; MD, Chgo. Med. Sch. 1965. Career: physician, capt. Med. Corps USAF, 1966-68; physican pvt. practice, 1968-; medical dir. Testing 1-2-3, subs. of E.N. Phillips Co., Woodland Hills 1991-92; dir. Columbia S&L, Beverly Hills (1984-92); mem. bd. dirs.: Indio Community Hosp. 1975-80, bd. chmn. 1978-80, bd. pres. 1980-85; The Lentz Inst., Indio 1984-91; United Stroke Found., L.A. 1985-; advy. bd. the Foundation for Sight, Palm Desert 1989-; recipient service award The Desert Medical Community, Palm Springs & Indio 1986; mem: AMA, Am. Assn. Family Physicians, Calif. Med. Assn., Riverside Co. Med. Soc.; host weekly medical t.v. show: The Medicine Show, KMIR-TV, NBC affil. 1983-. Ofc: Palm Desert Medical Center, 72-840 Hwy 111 Ste 165-D Palm Desert 92260

DOCKSON, ROBERT RAY, savings and loan executive; b. Oct. 6, 1917, Quincy, Ill.; s. Marshal Ray and Letah L. (Edmondson) D.; m. Katheryn Virginia Allison, Mar. 4, 1944; child, Kathy Kimberlee, b. 1948; edn: AB, Springfield Jr. Coll. 1937; BS, Univ. Ill. 1939; MS fgn. service, USC, 1940, PhD 1946. Career: lectr. USC 1940-41, 45-46, prof., head dept. mktg. 1953-59; dean USC Sch. Bus. Adminstrn. and prof. bus. econs. 1959-69; vice chmn bd. Calif. Fed. Savings & Loan Assn., Los Angeles 1969-70; pres. Calif. Fed. Savs. & Loan Assn. 1970-77, chmn. 1977-88, chief exec. ofcr. 1973-83; chmn. CalFed Inc. 1984-88, chief exec. ofcr. 1984-85, also dir.; instr. Rutgers Univ. 1946-47, asst. prof. 1947-48; economist western home ofc. Prudential Ins. Co. 1948-52, Bank of Am., San Francisco 1952-53; econ. cons., 1953-57; bd. dirs. IT Corp., Computer Scis. Corp.; Am. specialist for U.S. Dept. State; mem. Town Hall 1954-, bd. govs. 1963-65, hon. bd. govs. 1965-, pres. 1961-62; trustee John Randolph Haynes and Dora Haynes Found., Com. for Econ. Devel., Calif. Council for Econ. Edn.; chmn bd. Rose Hills Meml. Park Assn. 1990-92; trustee, pres. Orthopedic Hosp.; bd. councilors USC Grad. Sch. Bus. Adminstrn.; bd. regents, chmn. univ. bd. Pepperdine Univ.; chmn. housing task force Calif. Roundtable; chmn. Commn. on the Future of the Calif. Cts. 1991-93; awards: decorated Star of Solidarity Govt. of Italy, Asa V. Call Achievement award, Disting. Comm. Service award Brandeis Univ., Whitney M. Young Jr. award Urban League 1981, Albert Schweitzer Leadership award, Man of Yr. award Nat. Housing Conf. 1981, Industrialist of Yr. award Calif. Mus. Sci. and Industry 1984; mem: Am. Arbitration Assn., Newcomen Soc. N.

Am., Hugh O'Brian Youth Found., Calif. C.of C. (pres. 1980, bd. dirs. 1981-86), L.A. C.of C. (bd. dirs.), Phi Kappa Phi (Diploma of Honor award 1984), Beta Gamma Sigma, Bohemian Club, Calif. Club., L.A. CC, One Hundred Club, Birnam Wood Golf Club, Thunderbird CC; mil: lt. USNR 1942-44. Ofc: California Federal Bank 5700 Wilshire Blvd Ste 530 Los Angeles 90036-3659

DODGE, PETER H., architect; b. July 1, 1929, Pasadena; s. Irving Crow and Edna (Allison) D.; m. Janice Coor-Pender, Aug. 30, 1952; children: Susan b. 1958, Sarah b. 1963; edn: Art Center Sch., L.A. 1947-49; AB arch., UC Berkeley, 1956; reg. arch. 1961, NCARB 1973. Career: architect Joseph Esherick, Architect, San Francisco 1956-63; assoc. Joseph Esherick and Associates 1965-72; prin. Esherick, Homsey Dodge and Davis, 1972-, corp. pres. 1979-85; proj. architect The Cannery, S.F., Graduate Residence Facility UC Davis, 1960-68; project mgr. TWA Passenger Facilities Expansion, S.F. Intl. Airport, Promontory Point Master Plnng., Newport Bch., 1971; prin.-in-chg. Ctr. for Ednl. Devel., 1973; Chimpanzee Res. Facility, UCSB 1974; We. Airlines Passenger Facilities Expansion, S.F. Intl. Airport 1975; Theater Arts Bldg. CSU Sonoma 1976; Ekahi Village (297 condo. units) Maui, HI 1976; Great American Hamburger Place Bldg., Davis 1977; Citizens Utils. Svc. Ctr., Susanville 1983; R.A.B. Motors Mercedes-Benz Showroom, San Rafael, Mills Coll. Life Sci. Bldg., Boarding Area "B" Expansion S.F. Intl. Airport, 1984; Mills Coll. Art Ctr., 1986, Mills Coll. F.W. Olin Library, 1989; Rand Corp. Facilities, Santa Monica 1985-; Golden Gate Univ., S.F. 1985-; U.S. Embassy, La Paz, Bolivia 1989; Walter Stearn Library CSU Bakersfield, 1991; Geary Theater Restoration, S.F. 1982; lectr. dept. arch. UC Berkeley 1964-69, 71, vis. lectr. S.F. Art Inst. 1965; mem: Am. Inst. of Arch. (corp. mem. 1966-, fellow 1980, dir. Calif. Council AIA 1978-80, dir. No. Calif. 1977-78) AIA San Francisco (pres. 1981, nom. com. 1989), Commonwealth Club; publs: chmn. edtl. bd. Architecture California (1986-88), mem. edtl. bd. Landscape 1987-; mil: 1st lt. US Army Corps Engrs. 1956-58. Res: 67 El Camino Real Berkeley 94705 Ofc: Esherick Homsey Dodge and Davis 2789 25th St San Francisco 94110

DODSON, ARLEEN CECILIA, language educator, chorus director; b. Mar. 18, 1953, Alhambra; d. Moses and Olivia Beatrice (Potts) Baca; m. Walter Anthony Dodson, June 24, 1979; children: Robert, Elizabeth; edn: AA, East Los Angeles Coll., 1973; BA in Spanish, CSU Los Angeles, 1978; Calif. Std. life tchg. credential, multiple subjects w/bilingual emphasis. Career: bilingual aide Alhambra High Sch., 1977-78; tchr. 4th gr. St. Anthony's, San Gabriel 1982-84; bilingual tchr., Spanish, 1st & 2d gr. Garvey Sch. Dist., 1984-86; bilingual tchr. 3rd & 4th gr. Hacienda La Puente Unified Sch. Dist., 1986-; Spanish interpreter Fed. Bldg. Immigration Ct., Los Angeles 1977; awards: Outstanding svc. Garvey Sch. Dist. 1986, Calif. Transplant Games-1st pl. softball (San Luis Obispo, 1991), swimming & softball teams (UCLA, 1992), Women of Achiev. YMCA San Gabriel Valley 1992, County of L.A. award of merit, Sandimune Photo/Essay Contest 1991-92; mem: NEA, Calif. Tchrs. Assn., Assn. Curriculum Devel.; Polycystic Kidney Found. of S. Calif. (bd. mem., kidney transplant recipient 2/19/91, del. conv. 6/92 Polycystic Kidney Four); Democrat; R.Cath. (mem. adult choir St. John Vianney); rec: tchg. music, Spanish; res: 15320 Pintura Dr Hacienda Heights 91745; ofc: Hacienda La Puente Unified School District, 15959 Gale Ave Hacienda Heights 91744

DODSON, CHRISTOPHER THOMAS, federal bank regulator; b. Dec. 3, 1964, Champaign, Ill.; s. John Thomas and Aselean Sheila (Davis) D.; m. Dianne Renae Stuve, Aug. 22, 1992; edn.: BS, We. N.M. Univ., Silver City, N.M.. Career: asst. buyer/mgr., Amer. Stores, Anaheim, Calif., 1987-90; fed. bank regulator, FDIC, Pasadena, Calif., 1990-; pres., Student Body We. N.M. Univ., 1985-87; awards: listed Who's Who Among Amer. H.S. Students 1983, Who's Who Among Amer. Coll. Students 1987, Outstanding Young Men of Amer. 1986, 87, Who's Who in the West 1991, 92, Who's Who in Amer. 1992; mem: L.A. Special Olympics 1988-, Pasadena Fair Housing Commn. 1991-, Amer. Heart Assn. 1992-; ex-officio mem. Bd. of Regents, We. N.M. Univ. 1985-87; dir. Associated Students of N.M., all N.M. universities of higher edn. 1985-87; rec: running, collecting football and baseball cards. Res:762 E. Orange Grove # 4 Pasadena 91104 Ofc: FDIC Pasadena.

DOGAN, EDWARD THOMAS, investor; b. March 7, 1950, Long Island, N.Y.; s. Thomas Richard and Crystal Betty (Russell) D.; m. Cheryl Tynn Deboll, July 7, 1976; children: Brian b. 1980, Jeffrey b. 1981, Tina b. 1982; edn: BS, N.Y. Univ. 1971. Career: salesman, sales mgr. Bedford Chem., Gt. Neck, N.Y. 1968; owner Burgerking, Babaylon, N.Y. 1974-76; owner, pres. L.I. Fund. Raising, Forest Hills, N.Y. 1975-78; pres., chmn. bd. Dogan Electric Corp., NYC 1976-; Coastal Real Estate, Port Washington, N.Y. 1976-; Dogan Mfg. Corp., Staten Island, N.Y. 1975-; awards: Am. Lung Assn. Gold Donar 1988, YMCA Lifetime Achievement 1989, Cancer Found. Gold Supporter 1989; mem: Child Find (sponsor), Los Ninos (chapter), Nat. Rd. Runners Club, AAI, Am. Numestros Soc., S. Am. Archealogy Group, European Investors, Los Angeles C.of C., Law Enforcers USA, Lions, Elks, U.S. Russian Exchange (grand awards com. 1988-89), Acad. Motion Picture Arts & Scis., Grammy awards com.; author: Peace Now, 1987; Democrat; R.Cath.; rec: sports, numismatics, art. Address: Dogan Corp. 2816 Sunset Pl Ste 302 Los Angeles 90005

DOKE, MIMI IRENE, wedding consultant/photographer; b. Nov. 15, 1949, Covina; d. Charles Marshall and Suvia (Dominguez) Anderson; m. Martin L. Huggett, Feb. 13, 1966; children: Lisa b. 1966, Amber b. 1970, Melissa b. 1977; m. James Thomas Doke, Dec. 31, 1984; edn: grad. Sierra Vista H.S., Baldwin Park 1967; accredited bridal cons. (first to be granted cert.). Career: co-owner Alaska Roofing Co., Ukiah 1974-82; photographer, co-owner G.M.I. Studios, 1976-78; photographer cons., owner the Darkroom, Sun Valley, Ida. 1979-81, also owner the Coffee Break, 1979-81; wedding cons./photographer, owner The Wedding Specialist, Redwood Valley, Calif., Lake Havasu City, Ariz., 1982-; nat. t.v. wedding cons. CBS News, 1991-92; mem: Internat. Assn. of Bridal Consultants (speaker and state coord. 1982-), Wedding Photographers Internat. (1982-, nat. speaker 1988-, mem. bd. advisors), Profl. Photographers of Am. (speaker statewide 1988-); publs: poems in Today's Best Poetry (1976), articles in photog. jours. (1988, 89), Bridal Fair mag. (1991); Prot. Ofc: The Wedding Specialist, 3351 Javalina Ln Lake Havasu City AZ 86403

DOLAN, MARYANNE MCLORN, antique dealer, educator, author, lecturer; b. July 14, 1924, N.Y.C.; d. Frederick Joseph and Kathryn Cecilia (Carroll) McLorn; m. John Francis Dolan, Oct. 6, 1951; children: John Carroll, James Francis McLorn, William Brennan; edn: BA, San Francisco St. Univ., 1978, M.A., 1981. Career: owner antique shop, Benicia 1970-; tchr. classes and seminars in antiques and collectibles 1969-: UC Berkeley, UC Davis, UC Santa Cruz, Coll. of Marin, Mills Coll., St. Mary's Coll. Moraga, Solano Coll.; tchr. writing Dolan Sch., 1978-; lecture tours nat.; author books: Vintage Clothing 1880-1960 (1983), Collecting Rhinestone Jewelry 1984, Old Lace & Linens 1989, Commonsense Collecting 1991, 300 Years of American Silver Flatware 1992; weekly column: The Collector 1979-89, numerous articles in various periodicals; mem: Antique Appraisal Assn. of Am. Inc., New England Appraisers Assn., Internat. Soc. Appraisers, Calif. Writers Club, The Costume Soc. of Am., Internat. Platform Assn., Questers, Women's Nat. Book Assn., AAUW; Republican; R.Cath. Res: 138 Belle Ave Pleasant Hill 94523 Ofc: 191 West J St Benicia 94510

DOMBROSKE, LEONA JEAN, hospital pharmacist, home health coordinator; b. Dec. 31, 1957, Garden Grove; d. Ray James and Marlene Jean (Madison) Dombroske; m. John Stanley Ross, Aug. 6, 1983 (div. Sept. 1990); edn: AA, Golden West Coll. 1983; Pharm.D, USC 1987; reg. pharmacist Calif. 1987. Career: foods and attraction hostess Disneyland, Anaheim 1976-78; 1979 Disneyland Ambassador to World 1979; pharm. tech. UC Irvine Med. Center, Orange 1977-78; St. Josephs Hosp. 1980-87, pharm. resident 1987-88; preceptor UC San Francisco Sch. of Pharmacy, S.F. 1987-88; drug usage evaluation coord. Kaiser Permanente, Anaheim 1988-90, home health coordinator, 1990-; mem: Calif. Soc. Hosp. Pharmacists, Am. Soc. Hosp. Pharmacists; author Drug Usage Evaluation (1989), speaker Drug Usage Evaluation seminar 1989. Res: 14122 Hereford St Westminster 92683

DOMBROW, RICHARD LYLE, lawyer; b. Mar. 5, 1944, Flagstaff, Ariz.; s. Roman J. and Clementine C. (Casmire) D.; m. Eileen C., Apr. 3, 1976; children: Derian C. b. 1967, Kathleen b. 1983; edn: BS, San Jose St. Univ. 1966; JD, USC 1969; cert. family law specialist (CFLS) Calif. State Bar 1980. Career: dep. dist. atty. Los Angeles Dist. Atty's Office, 1969; pvt. practice law, Orange 1971-75; senior ptnr. Dombrow and McKenna, Orange 1975-79, pvt. practice, Tustin 1979-84, Santa Ana 1984-; planning commnr. City of Tustin 1972-74; honors: Active 20-30 Intl. Member of the Decade (1970s), Falstaff Mgmt. achievement award 1966; mem: Am. Bar Assn., Calif. Bar Assn. (Family Law Splst. Advy. Com. 1989-93), Orange County Bar Assn. (Family Law Sect. pgm. chmn. 1984-85, pres. 1985-86, exec. com. 1987-91), Family Law Bd. of Specialization 1989-93, State Bar Bd. of Specialization 1993-96; civic: Amicus Publico (bd. 1985-89), Active 20-30 Club Intl. (past pres. Santa Ana 1978, dist. gov. 1979-80), World Council of Young Mens Service Clubs (v.chmn. 1981), Helios at Mammoth HOA (pres. 1985-90), Monarch Bay Terrace HOA (pres. 1989-90); Republican; St. Margaret's of Scotland Episcopal Ch., San Juan Capistrano (Bishop's Com. 1989-92, School Bd. Trustees 1990-93); rec: skiing, hunting, fishing, model bldg. Ofc: 444 W 10th St 2nd Fl Santa Ana 92701

DOMBROWER, MARIO, civil engineer; b. June 26, 1941, La Paz, Bolivia; naturalized U.S. citizen 1959; s. William G. Dombrower and Jenny C. (Gotthelf) Feigenblatt; m. Beatriz Horowitz, Oct. 30, 1965; children: Michael b. 1967, Shirley b. 1969; edn: BSE, CSU Los Angeles, 1966; MPA, CSU Dominguez Hills, 1985. Career: student profl. wkr. County of Los Angeles, 1961-65; civil engr. Dept. Pub. Works, City of Los Angeles 1965-; awards: outstanding scholar Mayor of New York 1959, Tau Beta Pi 1966, Pi Alpha Alpha 1985, Pub. Works Supr. of Mo. City of L.A. DPW (1990); mem: Am. Soc. Civil Engrs. 1977-, Engrs. and Architects Assn. (bd. govs. L.A. chapt. 1982-88, 92-); Democrat; rec: numismatics, plate collecting, music, crosswords, walking. Res: 6215 Rustling Oaks Dr Agoura Hills 91301 Ofc: DPW, City of Los Angeles,650 S Spring St Ste 1200 L.A. 90014

DOMINGUEZ, JOHN CHRISTOPHER, systems engineer; b. Oct. 25, 1954, Los Angeles; s. Camilo and Janet Aileen (Lister) D.; m. Maria Eugenia Claveran, June 11, 1977; edn: BS biology, BS computer sci., UC Irvine, 1977;

MS Computer Sci., Calif. State Univ., Fullerton, 1993. Career: systems programmer Burroughs Corp., Mission Viejo, 1977-81; systems engr. Hughes Aircraft Co., Fullerton 1981-; rec: photography, gardening. Res: 24701 Eloisa Dr Mission Viejo 92691 Ofc: Hughes Aircraft Co. MS 604/E132 PO Box 3310 Fullerton 92634

DONALDSON, JOHN RILEY, physicist, emeritus professor; b. Nov. 24, 1925, Dallas, Tx.; s. John Riley and Marguerette Hoover (Atkinson) D.; m. Shirley Jean Brown, June 30, 1951; children: Nancy b. 1955, Dorothy b. 1957, Jack b. 1960, Jane b. 1960; edn: BS, Rice Univ., 1945, MA, 1947; MS, Yale Univ., 1949, PhD, 1951. Career: physicist Calif. Res. & Devel., Livermore, 1950-53; assoc. prof. Univ. Arizona, Tucson 1953-54; physicist U.S. Army, Frederick, Md. 1954-56; prof. of physics CSU Fresno, Ca. 1956-91, chair dept. physics 1983-91, emeritus prof. 1991-, vol. CSUF, 1991-; honors: All-American Discus, Volleyball AAU (1945, 1951); elected mem., chair Fresno County Bd. of Supervisors 1973-80, Fresno; elected mem. of exec. bd. Calif. Supervisors Assn. of Calif., Sacto. 1979, 80; mem: Am. Physical Soc. 1956-, AAAS 1965-, Am. Assn. of.Physics Tchrs. 1956-; mil: SP3 US Army 1954-56; Democrat; United Ch. of Christ (Coll. Comm. Congl. Ch. 1956-, moderator 1960, 61, choir dir., soloist); rec: music, singing. Res: 4559 N DeWitt Fresno 93727 Ofc: Physics Dept. Calif. State Univ., Fresno 93740-0037

DONKER, RICHARD BRUCE, hospitals organization executive, clinical services administrator; b. Sept. 29, 1950, Modesto; s. Luverne Peter and Ruth Bernice (Hoekenga) D.; m. Susan Gail Content, May 3, 1986; children: Elizabeth Anne; edn: BS biol./chem., Calvin Coll., 1972; grad. work physiology, UC Davis, 1973; MA in ednl. adminstrn. (high honors) CSU Stanislaus, 1978; EdD in ednl. adminstrn. (med. edn.), Univ. of the Pacific, 1980; paramedic cert. Modesto Junior Coll., 1974. Career: EMT instr. Modesto Jr. Coll., 1973-77; paramedic & ops. mgr. Modesto-Ceres Ambulance Co., 1972-75; grant coord. Yosemite Jr. Coll. Dist., 1975-77; hosp. educator Memorial Hosps. Assn. of Stanislaus County, 1977-78, emergency svs. supr. 1977-80, adminstr. flt. ops., trauma svs. cons., dir. ground ambulances, 1978-87, dir. "HealthPlus" community edn. pgms. and employee asst. pgms., also coord. urgent care ctrs. (Meml. Hosp. Med. Ctr., Modesto; Meml. Hosp. Ceres; St. Rose Hosp., Hayward; Emanuel Hosp. Med. Ctr., Turlock; Sonora Comm. Hosp.; Dominican Hosp., SantaCruz; 4-hosp. Mercy Health Care System, Sacto.; Stanford Univ. Med. Ctr., Pal Alto; Moses Taylor Hosp., Scranton, Pa.), 1983-87; also dir. "Golden HealthPLUS" pgm. for seniors with Medicare, 1986-87; negotiator for HMO and PPO contracting 1986-87; v.p. bus. strategies Memorial Hosps. Assn., 1987-89, v.p. clinical svs., 1989-92; mng. director Global Business Network, Emeryville, Calif. 1992-; indep. cons. 1979-; pres. Calif. Aeromedical Rescue & Evacuation Inc., opr. Medi-Flight in Modesto and Stockton and Flight Care in Chico, 1985-; exec. dir. MediPLUS Inc., Preferred Provider Org. (4 hosp., 285+ physicians, other health care providers) 1986-92; appt. Stanislaus Co. Dept. Edn. R.O.P. advy. coun. 1980-90, Stanislaus Co. ER Med. Care Com. (1975-77, 88-90), Calif. St. Task force on Air Ambulance Policies 1984-86, Calif. Assn. of Hosps. and Hlth. Systems Trauma/EMS Com. 1987-, NAS Inst. of Medicine Com. on Pediatric ER Med. Svs., WDC 1991-92; del. People-to-People Intl. Citizens Amb. Pgm., PROC 1988; mem: Am. Acad. Med. Adminstrs. (fellow), Phi Delta Kappa 1978-, Commonwealth Club of Calif. 1980-, Calif. Assn. of Air Medical Svs. (founding pres.); composed, recorded sound tracks for 2 children's films: Snail and Friend, The Spell of Bigfoot (distbd. intl.); numerous publs. and profl. presentations in field; rec: pvt. pilot, scuba, sailing, jazz percussionist, classical pianist, travel. Res: 1322 Edgebrook Dr Modesto 95354

DONNER, NEAL ARVID, teacher; b. Aug. 17, 1942, Wernigerode, Germany; s. Otto Richard Donner and Jane Hilton (Esch) Sweeney; m. Carol Anne Linnell, May 4, 1968 (div. Dec. 1981); children: Erich b. 1971, Rebecca b. 1971; edn: BA, Oberlin Coll., 1964; MA, Univ. Mich., 1968; PhD, Univ. Brit. Col., 1976. Career: tchr. Peace Corps, Ethiopia, 1964-66; asst. prof. Univ. Va., Charlottesville 1976-78; scholar in residence Cimarron Zen Ctr., Los Angeles 1978-79; violin tchr., L.A., 1981-; awards: Canadian Ministry of Edn. grad. fellow in Japan 1974, Japanese Ministry of Edn. grad. fellow 1975, Karl Bray Award of Libertarian Party Calif. 1991; mem. Suzuki Music Assn. 1981-, Amnesty Internat., ACLU, Citizens Against Govt. Waste, Zen Ctr. of L.A.; translator books: (Japanese) Entrepreneur & Gentleman (1976), History of Hindu-Buddhist Thought (1977), (Chinese) The Great Calming & Contemplation (1993), (French/German) The Legacy of Pythagoras (1993); Libertarian Party: candidate Calif. State Assembly (1984, 86), outreach dir. L.A. 1991-, Calif. state v.chair 1989, L.A. Westside chair 1984-88; Buddhist; rec: running. Res: 2739 Westgate Ave Los Angeles 90064

DOOLITTLE, DONALD CHASE, management consultant; b. July 12, 1949, Lincoln, Nebr.; s. Glayne D. and Eleanor (Chase) D.; m. Patricia Joan Stines, Sept. 5, 1970; children: Abigail b. 1976, Andrew b. 1979, Greg b. 1981, James b. 1986; edn: BS (Magna Cum Laude), Univ. of Nebr., 1971; MBA (high distinction), Harvard Bus. Sch.; CPA, Nebr. Career: mktg. and fin. 3M Co., St. Paul, Minn., 1971-79; v.p. Bain & Co., San Francisco, 1979-88; dir. APM Inc., 1988-; dir. Heals Health Plan, Oakland, 1990; awards: Dean's list Univ. Nebr.

1971, Phi Mu Alpha, Phi Eta Sigma, Baker Scholar Harvard Bus. Sch. 1979; mem. Harvard Bus. Sch. of No. Calif.; civic: March of Dimes Gr. Bay Area (dir. 1990-); Republican; rec: instrumental music, sports. Ofc: APM, Inc., 1 Bush St Ste 400 San Francisco 94104

DORNBUSCH, SANFORD MAURICE, sociologist; b. June 5, 1926, New York; s. Meyer and Gertrude (Weisel) D.; m. Barbara Anne Farnham, Feb. 28, 1950; children: Jeffrey Neil b. 1953, Steven Samuel b. 1957; edn: BA, Syracuse Univ. 1948; MAUniv. Chgo. 1950; PhD 1952. Career: assoc. prof. sociology Univ. Wash. 1958-59; asst. prof. sociology Harvard Univ., Cambridge, Mass. 1955-58; prof. sociology Stanford Univ., Palo Alto 1959-, prof. edn. 1977-, Reed Hodgson Prof. of Human Biology 1978-, dir. center for study of families children and youth 1987-; awards: Walter J. Gores award Excellence in Tchg. 1984, Who's Who in World; mem. Am. Sociological Assn. (chmn. social psychology sect., sociology of edn. sect., methodology sect.), Pacific Sociological Assn. (pres. 1963-64); co-editor: Soc. for Res. on Adolescence (pres. 1990-92), Feminism Children & New Families, 1988, Tchr. Evaluation Standards Student Effort, 1984. Res: 841 Pine Hill Rd Stanford 94305 Ofc: Stanford University Dept. of Sociology Stanford 94305-2047

DORNETTE, RALPH MEREDITH, church administr.; b. Aug. 31, 1927, Cincinati.; s. Paul August and Lillian (Bauer) D.; m. Betty Jean Pierce, May 11, 1948; 1 dau., Cynthia Anne Orndorff; edn: AB (Valedictorian), Cincinnati Bible Coll., 1948; Cincinnati Bible Sem., 1948-51; Talbot Theol. Sem., La Mirada, Calif. 1967. Career: assoc. prof. Cincinnati Bible Coll., Oh. 1948-51; senior minister Indian Creek Christian Ch., Cynthiana, Ky. 1946-51; First Christian Ch., Muskogee, Ok. 1951-57; founding minister Bellaire Christian Ch., Tulsa, Ok. 1957-59; exec. dir. So. Calif Evangelistic Assn., Torrance, Calif. 1959-62, 68-77; founding minister Eastside Christian Ch., Fullerton 1962-68; c.e.o. Church Devel. Fund., Fullerton (1968-77, 79-); prof. of ministries Cincinnati (Ohio) Bible Sem. 1977-79, bd. dirs. 1973-77; bd. secty. Midwest Christian Coll., Oklahoma City, 1955-62; honoree, Churchman of Yr., Pacific Christian Coll., Fullerton 1973; mem. No. Am. Christian Conv., Cincinati. (v.p. 1972, exec. com. 1963, 70-72, 80-82); So. Calif. Christian Ministers Assn., Fullerton (pres. 1975), Financial Planning Ministry (pres. 1986-), Homeowners Assn. Anaheim (bylaws com. 1979-80, pres. 1980-82, exec. bd. 1983); author: Bible Answers to Popular Questions (1954, Book II, 1961), Walking With Our Wonderful Lord 1955; rec: travel, photography. Res: 1919 Coronet Sp 182 Anaheim 92801 Ofc: Church Development Fund 905 S Euclid St Fullerton 92632

DORR, LAWRENCE D., physician, orthopaedic surgeon; b. April 13, 1941, Storm Lake, Iowa; s. M. Everett and Evelyn (Knoll) D.; m. Marilyn Minard, April 2, 1962; children: Michael b. 1963, Kristina b. 1967, Randy b. 1969; edn: BA, Cornell Coll. 1963; BA, Iowa Med.Sch. 1963; MS, 1965; L.A. Co.- USC Med. Sch. 1967-68. Career: staff physician Rancho Arthritis, Downey 1977-; assoc. clin. prof. UC Irvine 1983-; assoc. Kerlan-Jobe, Inglewood 1983-; awards: USC Outstanding Resident 1975-76; mem: Am. Acad. Orthopaedic Surgeons, Knee (founding mem., pres. 1990), Hip Soc., Assn. of Arthritic Hip and Knee Surgery (founding mem., v.p. 1991); club: Annandale Golf; editor Techniques in Orthopaedics (1985-), founding editor Journal of Arthroplasty (1983-); designer of APR Hip System 1983, and designer of Apollo Knee System (1992); mil: lt. cmdr. USN 1968-71; Republican; Methodist; rec: sports. Ofc: 501 E Hardy Ste 300 Inglewood 90301

DOUGHERTY, BETSEY OLENICK, architect; b. Oct. 25, 1950, Guantanamo Bay, Cuba; d. Everett Jacob and Charlotte (Kristal) Olenick; m. Brian Paul Dougherty, Aug. 25, 1974; children: Gray Brenner b. 1979, Megan Victoria b. 1986; edn: BA Arch., UC Berkeley, 1972, MArch., 1975; reg. architect Calif., 1978. Career: designer, drafter HO&K, San Francisco 1975-76; job capt. Wm. Blurock & Ptnrs., Newport Beach 1976-78; assoc. architect UC Irvine 1978-79; ptnr. Dougherty + Dougherty, Newport Beach 1979-; awards: design awards Design Internat. 1981, AIA Orange Co. (1981-86, 1990), Illuminating Engr. Soc. 1987, Pacific Coast Builders Conf. grand award; Fellow AIA; mem. AIA/Wash. D.C. (nat. bd. 1989-91), AIA/Calif. (state pres. 1988-89), AIA/Orange Co. (pres. 1984), mem. Assn. Women in Arch., Newport Harbor Art Museum; rec: sailing, travel. Ofc: Dougherty + Dougherty, 3 Civic Plaza Ste 230 Newport Beach 92663 also: 10700 Jersey Blvd Ste 300 Rancho Cucamonga 91730

DOUGHERTY, HOWARD WILLIAM, oil and gas producer; b. Jan. 5, 1915, Kansas City, Mo.; s. Frank C. and Elsie (Braecklein) D.; m. Aug. 3, 1940; children: William, Robert, Patrick, Michael, Mary, Peter; m. 2d. Violeta van Ronzelen, Sept. 15, 1984; edn: BS, Stanford Univ. 1938. Career: oil and gas producer, Pasadena 1947-; dir. Los Angeles Turf Club; pres. Pioneer Kettleman Co., Book Cliffs Oil & Gas Co.; pres. Trend Oil Co.; pres. Bret Harte Realty Co.; dir. and v.p. Hollywood Turf Club 1954-80, dir. emeritus 1980-; mem: Conservation Com. Calif., Ind. Petroleum Assn. of Am., API, IPAA, Am. Inst. Mech. Engrs. (past), Beta Theta Pi; civic: San Gabriel Valley Boy Scouts, Los Angeles Boy Scouts, Pres.'s Circle L.A. Co. Mus., Founders L.A. Music Center, So. Calif. Tennis Assn. (dir.), Youth Tennis Found. of So. Calif. (pres.), Loyola Marymount Univ. (former regent), St. Mary's Coll. (past bd. trustees), Villanova

and Woodside Priory (past bd. trustees), Soc. of Calif. Pioneers; clubs: Los Angeles Country, California, Bohemian, Birnan Wood Golf, Valley Hunt. Res: 379 W Bellevue Dr Pasadena 91105 Ofc: 200 S Los Robles Ave Pasadena 91101

DOUGLASS, ENID HART, educator, oral history program director; b. Oct. 23, 1926, Los Angeles; d. Frank Roland and Enid Yandell (Lewis) Hart; m. Malcolm P. Douglass, Aug. 28, 1948; children: Malcolm Paul Jr., John Aubrey, Susan Enid; edn: BA, Pomona Coll., 1948; MA, Claremont Grad. Sch., 1959. Career: research asst. World Book Ency., Palo Alto 1953-54; exec. secty., asst. dir. oral history pgm. Claremont Grad. Sch., 1963-71, dir. oral history pgm., 1971-, history lectr., 1977-; appt. Calif. Heritage Preservation Comn. 1977-85, chair 1983-85; Planning & Research Advy. Council Calif.; mem. Claremont City Council 1978-86, mayor pro tem 1980-82, mayor 1982-86; recipient disting. alumna award Claremont Graduate Sch. 1981J.V. Mink award Southwest Oral Hist. Assn. 1984, award for outstanding svc. to community L.W.V. 1986; founder Claremont Heritage Inc., 1977-80, bd. dirs. 1986-89; bd. dirs. Pilgrim Place, Claremont; founder, bd. dirs. (v.p. 1990, pres. 1990-) Claremont Community Found.; mem. Oral Hist. Assn. (pres. 1979-80), Southwest Oral Hist. Assn. (founding steering com. 1981), Nat. Council Pub. Hist., L.W.V. (bd. 1957-59); Democrat. Res: 1195 Berkeley Ave Claremont 91711 Ofc: Oral History Pgm. Claremont Graduate School 160 E 10th St Claremont 91711-6165

DOVE, DONALD AUGUSTINE, city and regional planner; b. Aug. 7, 1930, Waco, Tx.; s. Sebert Constantine and Amy Delmena (Stern) D.; m. Cecelia Mae White, Feb. 9, 1957; children: Angela b. 1958, Donald b. 1961, Monica b. 1963, Celine b. 1964, Austin b. 1965, Cathlyn b. 1968, Dianna b. 1970, Jennifer b. 1972; edn: BA, CSU Los Angeles, 1951; MPA, USC, 1966; Cert. Planner, Am. Inst. Cert. Planners, 1975. Career: regional planner L.A. County Regional Planning Commn., 1954-59; cons./rep. King Associates, L.A. 1959-60; research analyst Calif. Div. of Highways, L.A. 1960-66, planner, Sacto. 1966-72; br. mgr. planner Calif. Dept. Transp., L.A. 1972-; publisher Better Neighborhoods Newsletter, L.A. 1992-; guest lectr. urban affairs, pop. forecasting, transp., envir. mgmt., Univ. Calif., Calif. St. Univs., 1966-91; planning commr. (chair) City of Lynwood, and previous cities, 1979-; dir. Dove Found., L.A. 1985-; mem. Am. Planning Assn. 1955-, So. Calif. Assn. for Pub. Adminstrn. (dir. L.A. 1983-87), Que-Up Found. 1993-, Kts. Col. 1982-, Kts. of Peter Claver (1959-, fin. sec. 1976-88), L.A. Civic Ctr. Optimist Club (dir., sec. 1973-); author: Preserving the Urban Environment (1975), articles on travel, environ., urban concensus, etc. (1964-81); mil: cpl. US Army 1952-54; R.Cath.; rec: model making, sailing. Res: 11356 Ernestine Ave Lynwood 90262-3711 Ofc: Calif. Dept. Transportation 120 S Spring St Los Angeles 90012

DOW, FREDERICK WARREN, university professor of international management; b. Aug. 2, 1917, Boston; s. Frederick Vincent and Marcia (McMahon) D.; m. Patricia Rathbone, Oct. 2, 1943; edn: BS in chemistry (magna cum laude) Boston Coll. 1940; MS physical chem. (high distinction) Univ. Mass. 1942; AM ednl. psych. Yale Univ. 1949, PhD adminstrn., 1954. Career: sales personnel mgr. Dow Chemical Co., 1951-59; asst. to gen. mgr. of chem. sales, 1959-61; gen. sales mgr., New York, Dow Chemical Internat., 1961-64; mng. dir. Dow Chemical France, 1964-66; gen. mgr. assoc. cos. Latin Am. and Pacific, Dow Chem. Co., 1966-67; pres. Econ. Devel. Corp., Southbend, Ind., A Model Cities Agy., 1970-74; chmn. exec. com. Minority Venture Co. (Univ. Notre Dame) 1973-77; mng. ptnr. KCD & Assocs., Mgmt. Cons., South Bend, Ind. 1967-79; chmn. bd. Kestrel Inc., Mgmt. Consultants, Carlsbad, Calif. 1979-; Dir.: Berkel Inc., Laporte, Ind. 1975-, Rambend Inc., South Bend (also v.p., treas.) 1970-, Arrar Group N.V. internat. holding co. (v.chmn. bd.) 1985-; apptd. cons. Pres. Johnson's McKinney Commn. (to decrease travel gap), 1968; sci. advy. com. Italy Ministry of Tourism, 1973-89; Sr. Fulbright Scholar, lectr. Catholic Univ. of Ecuador, Quito, 1973-74; prof. mktg., Hayes-Healy Prof. Grad. Sch. of Bus. Univ. Notre Dame, 1967-77; prof. bus. adminstrn. U.S. Internat. Univ., San Diego, 1977-81, prof. internat. mgmt. 1981-, dean USIU Sch. of Bus. and Mgmt., 1986-88; mil: major USAAF, 1943-46, command meteorologist 9th Bombardment Cmd., ETO, awarded Bronze star and Air medal 3 o.l.c.; mem. Sigma Xi, Am. Chem. Soc., Soc. de Chemie Industrielle, Union League Club (NY), Travellers Club (Paris); author book: Estrategia de Planeamiento (1974), articles in bus. jours.; Republican; Episcopalian. Res: 5080 Carlsbad Blvd Carlsbad 92008 Ofc: U.S. International Univ., 10455 Pomerado Rd San Diego 92121

DOW, JAMES RICHARD, industrial designer, set designer, art director; b. Mar. 8, 1943, Long Beach, Calif.; s. Frederic Arthur and Marion Laurine (Lemon) D.; m. Susan Claire Petroni, Apr. 10, 1980; children: Jameson Chase, Ian Thomas Scot; edn: BS design, CSU Long Beach, 1967. Career: designer Universal Pictures, Studio City 1969-72; coordinator, designer Columbia Pictures, Hollywood 1973-76; art dir., creative dir. Paramount Pictures, Hollywood 1976-81; show designer Disney Studios, Burbank 1983-84, Walt Disney Imagineering, Burbank 1984; art dir., designer Dow Design, Newport Beach 1980-; film credits include: Silent Running, Close Encounters of the Third Kind, Star Trek: The Motion Picture, Heavenly Kid, Russkies; TV shows: Cosmos (Emmy award 1980), Mork and Mindy, Little House on the Prairie, Greatest American Hero; various TV commercials; mem: Industrial Designers Soc. Am., Acad. TV Arts and Scis., Am. Film Inst., Exhibit Designers and

Producers Assn.; mil: sgt. Nat. Guard 1963-69; rec: sailing, painting, sculpting. Ofc: Dow Design 872 W 18th St Costa Mesa 92627

DOWELL, ROBERT VERNON, entomologist; b. Sept. 13, 1947, San Francisco; s. Robert Leroy and Clare Adel (Smith) D.; m. Linda Kay Wange, March 15, 1974; children: Elizabeth b. 1987; edn: BS, UC Irvine 1969; MS, CSU Hayward 1972; PhD, Ohio St. Univ. 1976. Career: asst. research scientist Univ. Fla., Ft. Lauderdale 1977-80; pest mgmt. splst. Calif. Dept. Food & Agri., Sacto. 1980-83, assoc. econ. ent. 1983-86, sr. econ. entomologist 1986-; cons. Marine World, Vallejo 1988; instr. UC Davis 1985-; bd. dirs. San Francisco Insect Zoo, San Francisco 1985-; awards: Calif. Dept. Food & Agri. superior accomplishment 1985; mem: Calif. Acad. Sci. (fellow), N. Calif. Entomology Club (pres. 1988), Pacific Coast Entomological Soc. (pres. 1990), AAAS, Entomological Soc. Am.; 60 articles pub. in sci. jours. (1974-), ed. Apple Maggot in West (1989); rec: fishing, butterfly collecting. Ofc: California Dept. of Food and Agriculture 1220 N St Sacramento 95814

DOWNES, JOHN R., author, business consultant; b. Nov. 6, 1938, London, Eng.; nat. US cit. 1952; s. John R. and Edna Jane (Palmer) D.; m. Susan, Aug. 25, 1961; children: Geoffrey b. 1962, Jennifer b. 1963, Scott b. 1966, Jill b. 1969, Joshua b. 1975; edn: Whitworth Coll., Spokane 1956-57, CSU Long Beach 1960-61. Career: pres. Downes Scollard & Oliver Advertising Agy., Washington State 1967-70; pres. Dover American Corp., Spokane 1970-73; pres. National Syndications, Inc. 1973-78; pres. Lease One Corp., 1978-83; pres. Performance Concepts, San Luis Obispo, Calif. 1983-; cons. Manufacturers Hanover Bank, N.Y. 1981-; First Penna. Bank, Phila. 1980-82; devel. NonConfrontation Selling sales philosophy and techniques to reduce confrontation between seller and buyer; prod./creator motivation pgms. and sales training pgms.; conducts workshops, seminars, and sales training confs. for business & industry, author: How to be Irresistible Through the Power of Persuasion (1982); Non-Confrontation Selling (1984); Lease One Showroom Leasing (1980); Apple's Glory (1989); The Blackjack List (1989); Criminal Bent (1991); civic: Human Resources Commn. S.L.O. Co., Citizens Transp. Com. City of San Luis Obispo; listed Internat. Who's Who of Intellectuals; Internat. Directory of Disting. Leadership; Republican; Prot.; rec: tournament chess player, piano, golf, public speaking. Res: 3358 Barranca Ct San Luis Obispo 93401 Ofc: Performance Concepts 1308 Broad St Ste 61 San Luis Obispo 93401

DOWNING, JACQY LESLEY HARRISON, registered nurse, surveyor; b. July 17, 1941, Stone, England; nat. 1958; d. J. Norman Standage and Murielle Mercer (Wood) Harrison; m. Dennis Robert Rowe, April 26, 1959 (div. 1969); m. Robert Downing, Nov. 28, 1970; children: Russell b. 1959, Robert b. 1961; edn: AA summa cum laude, Barstow Coll., 1974; ASN (honors), Grossmont Coll., 1978; BSN, Regents Coll., 1984; MBA health care adminstrn., National Univ., 1986. Career: office mgr. So. Calif. Water Co., Barstow 1965-74; sr. nurse aide Barstow Hosp. 1974-75; vocational nurse Kelly & Profl. Nurses Bureau, San Diego 1976-77; emergency room nurse, nursing supr. Valley Med. Ctr., El Cajon 1977-86; nursing supr., quality assurance coord. Inland Valley Reg. Med. Ctr., Wildomar 1986-88; health facilities evaluator nurse Calif. Dept. Health Svs., San Diego 1988-; critical care transp. nurse Schaeffer Amublance, San Diego 1982-86; nursing inservice instr. Valley Med. Ctr., El Cajon 1984-86; Inland Valley Reg. Med. Center Wildomar 1986-88; emergency med. tech. instr. Mt. San Jacinto Jr. Coll. 1987-88; student mem. Am. Coll. Healthcare Execs.; Eastern Star; Republican; Episcopalian; rec: golf, swimming. Res: 10334 Rancho Carmel Dr San Diego 92128 Ofc: State of Calif. Dept. of Health Services 8885 Rio San Diego 92108

DOYLE, MICHAEL CARROLL, manufacturing executive, lawyer; b. Nov. 29, 1942, Miami, Fla.; s. Carroll and Gwendolyn (Breitenstein) D.; children: Michael Britt b. 1965, William Carroll b. 1967; edn: BBA, Univ, of Cincinnati, 1964; JD (magna cum laude), Chase Coll. of Law, 1969; lic. C.P.A.; Ohio 1966; admitted bar: Ohio 1969, Ga. 1969, Wisc. 1971, Calif. 1975. Career: CPA, Alexander Grant & Co., Cinti., 1964-69; Atlanta, 1969-70; mng. ptnr., Milw. 1970-73; house counsel and nat. dir., Chgo. 1973-74; reg. ptnr., Los Angeles; atty./ptnr. Stone & Doyle, Pasadena 1978-; chmn. and c.f.o. Econolite Control Products, Inc. Anaheim 1978-, California Chassis, Inc. 1982-; mem: ABA, Calif. Bar Assn., Calif. Soc. of CPAs, Am. Inst. of CPAs, San Gabriel Valley Estate Planning Council, President's Circle USC; clubs: Jonathan, Annandale Golf, Flintridge Riding, Flint Canyon Tennis; trustee Episcopal Theol. Sch., Claremont; Homemakers of Pasadena; Republican; Episcopalian; rec: tennis. Ofc: Stone & Doyle 111 S Hudson Ave Ste A Pasadena 91101

DOYLE, MICHAEL JAMES, school principal; b. Aug. 24, 1939, Bell, Calif.; s. Joseph Edward and Irma Louise (Smith) D.; m. Mina Katherine Martensen, Feb. 8, 1964; children: Michael II b. 1967, Mary b. 1970, Matthew b. 1974; edn: BA, Whittier Coll., 1961, ME, 1971. Career: tchr. El Rancho Unified Sch. Dist., Pico Rivera 1961-79, jr. high dept. chair 1967-74, actg. principal 1979; tchg. asst. prin. Alta Loma Sch. Dist., 1979-86, summer sch. prin. 1985, elementary sch. principal, Alta Loma, 1986-; organist and choir director various Luth. chs. So. Calif. 1955-86, St. Paul's Lutheran Ch., Pomona 1986-; mem.: Calif. State Rev. Team, Rancho Cucamonga, 1982-83, Calif. Sch. Leadership Acad., San Bdo. 198689; tchg. awards: Outstanding tchr. of yr. Burke Jr. H.S. PTA, Pico Rivera 1973, Honor svc. Jasper Sch. PTA, Alta Loma 1983, cont. svc. Jasper Sch. PTA 1988, employee recogn. Alta Loma Sch. Dist. (1985; mem: So. Calif. Music Clinic (v.p. 1978-81), Assn. Calif. Sch. Adminstrs. 1979-, Assn. of West End Sch. Adminstrs. 1979-, Am. Guild Organists 1961-, Phi Delta Kappa 1980-; civic bds.: Zion Luth. Sch. Bd., Maywood (1962-67, chmn. 1966-67), Downey City Water Board 1977-78, Luth. H.S. Edn. Com. 1988-, Cucamonga Hist. Soc. 1981-; Democrat; Lutheran, Mo. Synod; rec: music. Res: 2085 N Palm Ave Upland 91786 Ofc: Jasper School 6881 Jasper St Alta Loma 91701

DRACHNIK, CATHERINE MELDYN, art therapist; b. June 7, 1924, Kansas City, Mo.; d. Gerald Willis and Edith (Gray) Weston; m. Joseph Brennan Drachnik, Oct. 6, 1946; children: Denise Elaine, Kenneth John; edn: BS, Univ. Md., 1945; MA, CSU Sacramento, 1975; Calif. lic. Marriage, Family & Child Counselor (MFCC), reg. Art Therapist. Career: art therapist Vincent Hall Retirement Home, also Fairfax (McLean, Va.) and Arlington (Va.) Mental Health Day Treatment Ctrs., 1972-73; art therapist Hope for Retarded, San Jose, Calif., also Sequoia Hosp., Redwood City, 1972-73; supvg. tchr. adult edn. Sacto. Soc. Blind, 1975-77; ptnr. Sacramento Div. Mediation Svs., 1981-82; instr. CSU Sacto. 1975-82, Coll. Notre Dame, Belmont 1975-; art therapist, mental health counselor Psych West Counseling Ctr., Carmichael 1975-; instr. Univ. Utah, S.L.C., 1988-; lectr. in field; art exhs., solo and group juried shows, U.S. and internat.; mem: Am. Art Therapy Assn. (pres. 1987-89, hon. life 1991), No. Calif. Art Therapy Assn., Calif. Coalition of Rehab. Therapists, Nat. Art Edn. Assn., Am. Assn. Marriage and Fam. Therapists, Kappa Kappa Gamma Alumnae Assn. (chpt. pres. 1991-92), Alpha Psi Omega, Omicron Nu; Republican; rec: swimming, golf, theater. Res: 4124 American River Dr Sacramento 95864 Ofc: Psych West Counseling Center 6127 Fair Oaks Blvd Carmichael 95608 Tel: 916/486-2284

DRACHNIK, JOSEPH BRENNAN, retired naval officer, lawyer; b. June 11, 1919, Ross, Calif.; s. George and Mary Ann (Brennan) D.; m. Cay Weston, Oct. 6, 1946; children: Denise b. 1952, Kenneth b. 1957; edn: junior cert. UCB, 1939; BSEE, US Naval Acad. 1942; MS Internat. Affairs, George Washington Univ. 1967; JD, McGeorge Sch. of Law UOP 1981; admitted Calif. St. Bar. Career: served to Capt. US Navy 1942-72, participated in invasion of Guadalcanal 8/7/42, served in major campaigns of WWII on destroyers in Pacific, Comd. Fleet Tug, Destroyer Escort, Destroyer; promoted Capt. USN 1962, Chief of Naval Advy. Mission in Vietnam 1961-64, staff, Secty. of Def. McNamara, 1964-66, staff del. to Australia New Zealand-U.S. (ANZUS) Treaty Conf. 1966, and to SEATO Treaty Conf. 1965; Nat. War College 1967; Comdr. Amphibious Task Force, US Sixth Fleet 1968; c/s to Comdr. Amphib. Force, Atlantic Fleet 1969-70, ret. 6/1/72; Exec. Asst. to Calif. Lt. Gov. Ed Reinecke 1973-74; Cabinet Secty. to Gov. Reagan 1974; atty. in pvt. practice 1982-91; mem. Calif. State Bar, U.S. Naval Acad. Alumni Assn., Navy League; mil. decorations: Navy Unit Cit. (1942), Legion of Merit w/combat star (1964), Merit. Svc. (1966), var. cpgn. medals; rec: woodworking, gardening, golf. Res: 4124 American River Dr Sacramento 95864

DRAKE, FRANK D., professor of astronomy and astrophysics; b. May 28, 1930, Chgo.; s. Richard Carvel and Winifred (Thompson) D.; m. Elizabeth Bell, Mar. 7, 1953 (div. 1977); children: Stephen, Richard, Paul; m. Amahl Zekin Shakhashiri, Mar. 4, 1978; children: Nadia, Leila; edn: BA engring. physics (honors), Cornell Univ., 1952; MS and PhD astronomy, Harvard Univ., 1956, 58. Career: electronics ofcr. USN, 1952-56; Agassiz Station Radio Astronomy Project, Harvard Univ. 1956-58; hd. telescope ops. & sci. svs. div. Nat. Radio Astronomy Observatory, Green Bank, W.Va. 1958-63 (discovered the radiation belts of Jupiter, organized 1st search for ETI signals, Project OZMA 1960; devised Drake Equation- an estimate of communicative extraterrestrial civilizations in our galaxy 1961; chief of lunar & planetary scis. Jet Propulsion Lab, 1963-64; prof. astronomy Cornell Univ. 1964-84: dept. chmn. 1969-71, Goldwin Smith Prof. Astronomy 1976-84, dir. Arecibo (P.R.) Observatory 1966-68, first dir. Nat. Astronomy & Ionosphere Ctr. 1970-81 (constructed first interstellar message transmitted via radio waves from our planet to any ETI "Arecibo Message of 1974"); prof. astronomy & astrophysics UC Santa Cruz, 1984-, dean natural scis. div. 1984-88, actg. asso. v. chancellor 1989-90; apptd: SETI Inst. (pres. 1984-), Astronomical Soc. of Pacific (pres. 1988-90), NRC bd. physics and astronomy (chmn.), NSF (astronomy advy. com., Alan T. Waterman Awards com.), Nat. Acad. of Scis. of U.S.A. (1972-, NAS/NRC astronomy survey coms: Whitford, Greenstein and Field coms.); mem: Internat. Astronomical Union (1960-, chmn. U.S. Nat. Com.), Am. Astronomical Soc. (1958-, chmn. AAS Div. Planetary Scis. 1973), AAAS (fellow 1986, nat. v.p. and chmn. sect. astronomy 1973), Am. Acad. Arts and Scis. (fellow), British Interplanetary Soc. (fellow), Explorers Club, Soc. Sigma Xi; author: "Is Anyone Out There?" (with Dava Sobel) Delacorte Press, 1992; 150+ articles and books, lectr. numerous symposia, documentaries and interviews nat. and internat. media. Ofc: Univ. Calif. Observatory, Santa Cruz 95064

DRAKE, HAROLD ALLEN, historian; b. July 24, 1942, Cinti.; s. Morris and Mollie (Cooperstein) D.; m. Kathleen Ann Senica, May 31, 1969; children: Susan Jennifer b. 1972, Katherine Jessica b. 1978; edn: AB journ., USC, 1963;

MA in English hist., Univ. Wis., 1966, MA classics, 1969, PhD ancient hist., 1970. Career: staff reporter UPI, Los Angeles 1962-65; tchg. asst. Univ. Wis., Madison 1965-68; lectr., asst. prof., assoc. prof., prof. history Univ. Calif. Santa Barbara, 1970-, chair dept. history 1987-90; NEH fellow Inst. Advanced Study Princeton, NJ 1976-77; senior fellow Annenberg Resrch. Inst., Phila., Pa. 1991-92; mem. editl. bd. Classical Antiquity, Berkeley 1986-; awards, UCSB: outstanding tchg. Assoc. Students 1973, Plous award Acad. Senate 1976, prof. of year Mortar Board 1986-87; mem: Phi Beta Kappa (pres. Calif. Lambda 1986-88), Phi Alpha Theta (Internat. Coun. 1982-84), Am. Philol. Assn., Am. Hist. Assn., Soc. for Promotion of Roman Studies; author: In Praise of Constantine (1976), coauthor: Eudoxia and the Holy Sepulchre (1980); articles incl. "Eusebius on the True Cross" (1985), "The Genesis of the Vita Constantini" (1988); Democrat; R.Cath. Res: 423 Los Verdes Dr Santa Barbara 93111 Ofc: Dept. History Univ. Calif., Santa Barbara 93106

DREVER, RICHARD ALSTON, JR., consulting architect; b. Feb. 9, 1936, Kearny, N.J.; s. Richard A. and Dorothy L. (Farrer) D.; m. Ellen M. Cornell, Dec. 21, 1957 (div. Oct. 1978); children: Richard A. III, Diana J., Beverly K.; m. Jane L. Cash, June 1, 1981; edn: AB, Columbia Univ., 1957, B.Arch, 1963, M.Arch, 1963; reg. architect, Calif., Alaska, Ariz., Nev., NCARB. Career: intern Frederick Frost & Associates, N,Y.C., 1961, 63; mem. firm Allen-Drever-Lechowski, Architects, San Francisco, 1963-85, pres. 1983-85; cons. architect, prin. 1985-; ofcr., dir. Medos Corp., S.F. 1979-81; mem: AIA, The Hosp. Forum (chmn. architects sect. 1983-84), The Forum for Health Care Planning; civic bds: Tamalpais Community Svs. Dist. Marin Co. 1970-75, Tamalpais Parks & Rec. Commn. 1968-70; mil: lt. USNR 1957-59; contbr. articles in field. Res/Ofc: 314 Vista De Valle Mill Valley 94941 Tel: 415/381-1380

DREW, WALLACE THOMAS, investment counselor; b. Sept. 16, 1917, Wausau, Wis.; s. Walter Stanley and Christine Elizabeth (Noren) D.; m. Katherine House (dec. Jan. 16 1991); children: Wallace T., Jr. b. 1943, Elizabeth (Carlsson) b. 1946, Katherine (Margolin) b. 1951; m. Ursula Henderson M.D., Oct. 3, 1992; edn: BA, Univ. of Wis. 1937. Career: advt. mgr. Bristol Myers Co., N.Y. 1948-54; sr. v.p./acct. supvr. Cunningham & Walsh, N.Y. 1954-59; v.p., dir. Coty Inc., N.Y. 1959-64; v.p. Beech Nut-Lifesavers, N.Y./pres. Lander Co., N.Y. (wholly owned subs.), 1964-68; mng. dir. Revlon Internat., London, Eng. 1968-71; financial cons./ v.p. Smith Barney Harris Upham & Co., Santa Barbara 1971-; honors: City of Santa Barbara distinguished citizen 1984, recognition award ADL, B'nai B'rith, Santa Barbara Man of Year 1986, Santa Barbara News = Press lifetime achievement award fin. 1989; past mem. Drug Chemical & Allied Trades Assn., NYC (pres. 1968, dir. 1961-68); civic bds: Santa Barbara City Coll. Found. (dir. 1990-), Lobero Theatre Found., S.B. (pres. 1978), Work Inc. handicapped workshop, S.B. (pres. 1979), United Boys Clubs of S.B. (pres. 1987-), S.B. Symphony Assn. (exec. v.p. 1980-), S.B. Arts Council (pres. 1983), Santa Barbara City Coll. (trustee 1991-),Tres Condados Girl Scout Council (treas. 1982-86), Nuclear Age Peace Found.,S.B. (v.p., treas. 1983-), S.B. United Way (treas. 1987-), Piney Woods Country Life Sch., Piney Woods, MS (dir. 1992-); club: Santa Barbara, Bascom Hill Soc. (Univ. Wis.); mil: major US Army Corps of Engr. 1941-46, First US Army Hq., Europe and Philippines, decorated Bronze Star, 7 Battle Stars; Republican; Episcopalian (sr. warden All Saints By The Sea 1984); rec: sailing, collect books. Res: 131 La Vereda Rd Santa Barbara 93108 Ofc: Smith Barney Shearson Inc 1014 Santa Barbara St Santa Barbara 93101

DROHOJOWSKA-PHILP, HUNTER, writer/art critic; b. Sept. 5, 1952, Schenectady, NY; d. Richard A. and Carol Gleason; m. David Anthony Philp, Feb. 6, 1993; edn: BFA, Instituto Allende, Mexico 1975. Career: art ed., L.A. Weekly 1979-85; art writer, Herald Examiner, L.A. 1985-87; chair, dept. liberal arts & sciences., Otis Sch. of Art and Design, L.A. 1987-; film critic, The Japan Times, Tokyo; west coast ed., Artnews Magazine 1983-; co-host, story cons., Arts Illustrated TV series, KCET, L.A. 1985-86; architecture ed., L.A. Style 1986; bd. dir., Found. for Adv. Critical Studies, L.A. 1992; mem: Internat. Assn. of Art Critics 1986-, Coll. Art Assn.,1988-; author: numerous pub. articles in Artnews and Architectural Digest and others; pilot for the L.A. Mus. of Contemporary Art radio series, 1983; radio program on photography, 1983; catalog essays for many contemporary artists; regular contbr. of profl. articles to the L.A. Times; book, Tempest In A Teapot: The Ceramic Art of Peter Shire, 1991; book (in progress), Georgia O'Keeffe (pub., Alfred Knopf); Ofc: Otis School of Art & Design 2401 Wilshire Blvd. Los Angeles 90057

DROTT, CHARLES RAY, certified public accountant, certified fraud examiner, business and litigation consultant; b. Dec. 3, 1939, Plaquemine, La.; s. Wm. Martin and Mamie (Anstead) D.; m. June Ring, Oct. 18, 1986; stepson, Ryan; edn: BS acctg., La. State Univ., Baton Rouge 1964; C.P.A., Calif. and La. Career: audit supr. Touche Ross & Co., 1964-70; chief fin. ofcr. A.C.W., Inc., New Orleans 1970-74; senior ptnr. Allen & Drott, New Orleans 1974-78; audit ptnr. Touche Ross & Co., Los Angeles and other cities, 1978-82; owner Charles R. Drott, CPA, CFE, San Francisco 1982-; key expert witness in large Calif. court cases for various law firms, S.F., San Jose, 1984-; instr. CPA courses, 1978-; evaluate other CPAs' work, 1978-, evaluated acctg. programs Univ. of Nebr. 1981; cons., investigator US Dept. Justice, Calif. State Bd. Acctncy., Calif.

Atty. Gen.'s Office, 1989-; appt. Calif. State Bd. Acctncy. tech. review panel 1986-, reporting stds. com. 1989-; honors: Dean's List L.S.U. 1963, Beta Alpha Psi 1963, functional dir. Touche Ross & Co. 1979-82; mem: Am. Inst. CPAs, Calif. Soc. CPAs, Nat. Assn. Cert. Fraud Examiners; civic: Omaha C.of C. 1980-82, New Orleans Symphony (fundraiser 1974-76), Combined Health Agencies Omaha, Nebr. (bd. dirs. 1980-82); coauthor SEC Practice Manual (1981); 2 pub. manuals: Auditing Quality Control (1982), Personnel Counseling (1981); Prot.; rec: water sports, travel, golf. Res: 15 Pensacola Ct Novato 94949 Ofc: Charles R. Drott, CPA, CFE, One Sansome St Ste 2100 San Francisco 94104

DROWN, EUGENE ARDENT, forest management and development professional; b. Apr. 25, 1915, Ellenburg, N.Y.; s. Frank Arthur and Jessie Kate D.; m. Florence Marian Munroe, Mar. 5, 1938; children: Linda Harriett Oneto, Margaret Ruth Lunn; edn: BS, Utah State Univ., 1938; postgrad. Mont. St. Univ. 1939-40; PhD in pub. adminstrn., Univ. Beverly Hills, 1979; reg. profl. engr., profl. land surveyor, profl. forester, Calif. Career: park ranger National Park Service, Yosemite Nat. Park, 1940-47; forest ranger U.S. Forest Service, Calif. Region, 1948-56; forest mgr. and devel. specialist U.S. Bur. of Land Mgmt., Calif. 1956-70; forest engring. cons., 1970-; R&D coord. US Army at UC Davis, 1961-65; advy. bd. Sierra Coll., Rocklin 1962-; awards: nat. service medal Am. Red Cross 1964; mem: Nat. Soc. Profl. Engrs., Soc. Am. Foresters, Am. Inst. Biol. Scientists, Ecol. Soc. Am., Reserve Ofcrs. Assn. U.S., NRA, Internat. Rescue and First Aid Assn., Internat. Platform Assn., Bulldog Sentinels of Superior Calif., Masons, Shriners; civic: Am. Red Cross (instr. 1954), Boy Scouts Am.; mil: US Army 1941-45, decorated Bronze star, Silver star; Methodist. Res: 5624 Bonniemae Way Sacramento 95824

DROZ, HENRY, music distribution company executive; b. Sept. 26, 1926, Detroit, Mich.; s. Joseph and Katie (Zallman) D.; m. June Jacyno, May 31, 1959; 1 dau., Kathy Ann b. 1961; edn: BA, Wayne St. Univ. 1950. Career: branch mgr. Decca Distbg. Co., Detroit, Mich. 1952-54; pres. ARC Distbg. Co., Detroit 1954-63; v.p. Handleman Co., Detroit 1963-72; v.p. Warner Elektra, Atlantic Corp., Burbank, Calif. 1973-77, pres. and c.e.o. 1977-; awards: T.J. Martell Found. humanitarian of year 1989, City of Hope spirit of life 1989; mem: Sigma Alpha Mu, City of Hope (bd. chmn. music chpt. 1980-82, pres. 1978-80, trustee 1979-); mil: T-4 US Army 1945-46; rec: tennis. Res: 12053 Crest Ct Beverly Hills 90210 Ofc: W.E.A. Corp. 111 N Hollywood Way Burbank 91505

DRUCE, MARY EULALIA, financial executive; b. Aug. 20, 1955, Fort Stockton, Tx.; d. Camilo and Eulalia (Nunez) Garcia; m. Robert Lee Druce, Dec. 3, 1977; edn: BBA, Texas Tech Univ., 1977, MBA, Univ. N.Mex., Albuquerque 1982; lic. CPA, Tx. 1984. Career: acct. Texas Tech Univ., Lubbock 1977-80; software devel. engr. Hewlett Packard, Palo Alto, Calif. 1982-84, cost acctg. analyst 1984-85, gen. acctg. mgr. 1985-86, sr. fin. analyst 1987, networks services bus. mgr., 1988-; awards: math & sci. Soc. of Women Engrs. Ft. Stockton, Tx. 1973, dean's list Texas Tech Univ. 1974-77, fellow Washington Campus Pgm., WDC 1981, Beta Sigma Phi (pres. 1979); mem. Texas Soc. CPA 1984-, Data Proc. Mgmt. Assn. (chpt. pgm. dir. 1985-87), World Affairs Council 1991-; civic: advisor Junior Achievement Palo Alto 1983; publs: articles in field (1987-), newsletter ed. Net Gazette (1989). Res: 32801 Oakdale Ct Union City 94587 Ofc: Hewlett Packard 3000 Hanover Palo Alto 94304

DRYSDALE, GEORGE MARSMAN, venture capitalist; b. Sept. 16, 1954, Manila, Philippines; s. George and Anne (Marsman) D.; m. Diane Elizabeth Rogers, Aug. 17, 1991; edn: BS engring., Harvey Mudd Coll., 1976, MBA, Stanford Univ., 1980, JD, 1980; admitted bar: N.Y., Calif. Career: cons. Braxton Associates, Boston 1980; lawyer Davis Polk & Wardwell, N.Y.C., 1981-83; gen. ptnr. Hambrecht & Quist Venture Partners, San Francisco, 1983-87; asst. to Secty. US Dept. Ag., W.D.C., 1987-88; mng. gen. ptnr. Westar Capital, Costa Mesa, Calif. 1988-91; v.chmn. Marsman-Drysdale Group; pres. Drysdale Enterprises, Newport Beach 1991-; dir: H&Q Ventures, Marsman Group Plantations, Skyvision, Pepsi Marketing; Upside Publ.; Phila. Wireless; Internat. Wireless Communications; exec. dir. Nat. Advy. Council Small Bus., W.D.C. 1991; bd. govs. Harvey Mudd Coll.; mem: Western Assn. Venture Capitalists (bd.); clubs: Guardsmen S.F. 1985, Pacific, N.Y. Athletic, Bahia Corinthian Yacht; Republican; Prot. Ofc: Drysdale Enterprises 620 Newport Center Dr Ste 1100 Newport Beach 92660

DUCKOR, JEROME NOAH, financial consultant; b. Dec. 7, 1942, Fort Wayne, Ind.; s. David and Natalie (Liff) D.; edn: AB, Univ. Miami, 1965; MBA, Golden Gate Univ., 1977. Career: account exec. Parke-Davis & Co., Morris Plains, N.J. 1969-83; gen. mgr. Maternal Care Prod., San Francisco 1984-86; pres. & CEO Best Selection, Inc. San Francisco 1986-88; fin. cons. Shearson Lehman Brothers Inc., 1989-91; account exec. Dean Witter Reynolds, Inc., 1991-; cons. Dental Pik, Mill Valley 1981-83, Infotech, Palo Alto 1987-88; recipient sales excellence award Parke Davis Co. 1977; mem. Med. Mktg. Assn. Irvine, S.F. Ad Club, Commonwealth Club Calif., Am. Heart Assn., Am. Sport Inst., The Museum Soc., The Official Registry of Who's Who of Am. Business Leaders; club: Harbor Point, Mill Valley; catalog editor: Mother & Baby Selection 1986-87; rec: tennis, skiing. Res: 450 E Strawberry Dr Mill Valley 94941 Ofc: Dean Witter Reynolds, Inc. PO Box 66 Corte Madera 94976

DUDELSON, ROBERT FRANKLIN, entertainment executive; b. April 19, 1961, New York; s. Stanley Edward and Jean D.; edn: BA, Pace Univ. 1982. Career: western sales New Line Cinema, N.Y.C. 1982-83, gen. sales mgr. 1983-85, v.p. mktg. Inter Pictures Releasing Corp. 1986-87; pres. Artist Entertainment, Los Angeles 1987-88; v.p. Taurus Entertainment Co., Encino 1988-; tchr. USC Cinema & TV Alumni Assn. 1989; mem: Friars Club, Motion Picture Bookers Club, Variety Club. Res: 888 W Knoll Dr West Hollywood 90069 Ofc: Taurus Entertainment Co. 16000 Ventura Blvd Ste 1201 Encino 91436

DUFF, JAMES GEORGE, financial services executive; b. Jan. 27, 1938, Pittsburg, Kans.; s. James G. and Camilla (Vinardi) D.; m. Linda Louise Beeman, June 24, 1961 (div. 1982); m. Beverly L. Pariseau, Nov. 16, 1984; children: Michele b. 1966, Mark b. 1968, Melissa b. 1972; edn: BSBA, Univ. Kans. 1960; MBA, 1961. Career: fin. staff Ford Motor Co., Dearborn, Mich. 1961-72, dir. product price and warranty Ford of Europe, London, England 1972-74, controller Ford div. Ford Motor Co., Dearborn, Mich. 1974-76, controller car ops. 1976-80, exec. v.p. Ford Motor Credit Co. 1980-88; pres. and COO U.S. Leasing Internat., San Francisco 1988-90, pres and CEO, 1990-; bd. dirs. Ford Motor Credit Co., Dearborn, Mich. 1980-; U.S. Leasing Internat., San Francisco 1988-; Airlease Mgmt. Services Inc. 1988-; civic bds: Bay Area Council (dir. 1990-), mem. Univ. Kans. Sch. of Bus. Bd. Advisors, United Found. (chmn. bus. devel. unit 1980-85, chmn. edn. and local govt. unit 1986-88); Republican. Res: 7 Russian Hill Pl San Francisco 94133 Ofc: U.S. Leasing International 733 Front St San Francisco 94111

DUFFEY, PAUL S., research microbiologist, immunologist; b. Nov. 24, 1939, Oakland; s. Norman David and Saphrona Carol (Korkus) D.; m. Marlen Gregory, Jan. 1961 (dec. June 1975); m. Dixie Anita Herrick, June 26, 1988; edn: BA, San Jose St. Univ., 1963; PhD, Univ. Mich., Ann Arbor, 1974. Career: asst. prof. Univ. of Mich. Med. Sch., Ann Arbor, 1974-75; Univ. of Texas Health Sci. Ctr., San Antonio, Tx. 1976-81; res. microbiologist Calif. St. Dept. of Health Svs., Berkeley, 1981-; appt. Gov.'s Task Force on Biotechnology, Sacto. 1985-; mem: Assn. of Immunologists 1978-, N.Y. Acad. of Scis. 1980-, Sigma Xi 1970-; publs: sci. articles (1976-); R.Cath.; rec: computer design, assembly, pgmmg. Res: 166 Miramonte Dr Moraga 94556 Ofc: Dept. of Health Services 2151 Berkeley Way Berkeley 94704

DUFFUS, JAMES E., research plant pathologist; b. Feb. 11, 1929, Detroit, Mich.; s. John and Dorothy J. (Pellow) D.; m. Rachael B. Anderson, May 17, 1952; children: Mark C. b. 1954, John S. b. 1956, Lisa K. b. 1958; edn: BS hons., Mich. St. Univ. 1951; PhD, Univ. Wis. 1955. Career: plant pathologist U.S. Dept. Agri. ARS, Salinas 1955-81; vis. scientist Tasmanian Dept. Agri., Hobart 1980-81; supvy. research plant pathologist, res. leader U.S. Dept. Agri. ARS, Salinas 1982-, location coord. 1989-; assoc. exptl. station UC Davis and UC Berkeley, 1962-; adj. prof. Univ. Ark., Fayetteville, Ark. 1984-; awards: ARS superior svc. USDA 1968, 83, Scientist of Yr. 1982, Am. Soc. Sugar Beet Technologists Merit. Svc. 1985; mem: Am. Phytopathological Soc. (fellow), Am. Soc. Sugar Beet Technologists (editl. bd.), Internat. Soc. Plant Pathology (virus epidemiology com.), Internat. Soc. Horticultural Sci. (chmn. vegetable), Internat. Working Group Legume Viruses, Lutheran Ch. Good Shepherd (congregational pres. 1965); 170+ res. articles pub. in profl. jours., 1955-, ed. Compendium of Beet Diseases & Insects, 1986; Lutheran. Ofc: U.S. Dept. of Agriculture 1636 E Alisal St Salinas 93905

DUHL, LEONARD J., educator, psychiatrist, health planning consultant; b. May 24, 1926, N.Y.C.; s. Louis and Rose (Josefsberg) D.; m. Lisa, June 8, 1980; children: Pamela, Nina, David, Susan, Aurora; edn: AB, Columbia Univ., 1945; MD, Albany Med. Coll., 1948; dipl. Menninger Sch. of Psychiatry, 1954, Wash. Psychoanalytic Inst., 1964. Career: intern Jewish Hosp., Bklyn. 1948-49; resident in psychiatry Winter VA Hosp., 1949-51, 1953-54, also fellow Menninger Found. Sch. Psychiatry 1949-51; sr. asst. surgeon Health Dept. Martinez, Calif. 1951-53; med. director (Ret.) Pub. Health Svc. 1954-72: psychiatrist NIMH, Bethesda, Md. 1954-64, chief Office of Planning NIMH 1964-66, special asst. to Secty. Dept. Housing & Urban Devel., W.D.C. 1966-68; prof. of public health and city planning, UC Berkeley 1968-, prof. psychiatry Univ. Calif. Med. Sch., San Francisco, 1968-; cons. to WHO, UNICEF, State of Calif. Health Dept., Nat. Civic League, Healthy Cities pgms., other agys.; appt. World Hlth. Orgn. Expert Com. on Env. Hlth. in Urban Devel. 1991; mem. bd. dirs: Partners for Democratic Change 1991, Consultation to Religious Personnel 1991-92, Calif. Inst. for Integral Studies 1990, Louis August Jonas Found. 1989-; mem. The Charles F. Menninger Soc.; author: City of Health: Governance of Diversity (1992), Social Entrepreneurship of Change (1990), Health Planning & Social Change (1986), contbr. articles in N.E. J. Med., J. Prevention, Future Choices, Calif. Architecture, B of NY Acad. of Medicine, World Health; rec: photography, sailing. Ofc: Univ. Calif. Sch. of Public Health 410 Warren Hall Berkeley 94720

DULLY, FRANK EDWARD, JR., physician, aviation safety educator; b. Jan. 19, 1932, Hartford, Conn.; s. Frank Edward and Monica Theresa (Cooney) D.; m. Rebecca Sue Akers, Apr. 23, 1982; children: Kathleen, Ann, Margaret, David, Nancy, Tammy; edn: BS, Coll. of Holy Cross, 1954; MD, Georgetown Univ., 1958; MPH, UC Berkeley, 1970; diplomate Am. Bd. Preventive Medicine. Career: intern D.C. Gen. Hosp., Washington, 1958-59; resident Bridgeport (Conn.) Hosp. 1959-60; pvt. med. practice Shelton, Conn. 1960-64; served to capt. US Navy 1964-87: with Destroyer Squadron 14, 1964-65; USN student flt. surgeon 1965-66; senior med. officer USS Hornet 1966-68, Naval Air Sta., Glynco, Ga. 1968-69; aerospace medicine resident USN, Pensacola, Fla. 1970-72; senior med. officer USS Enterprise, 1972-74; dir. tng. Naval Aerospace Med. Inst., Pensacola 1974-77, comdg. officer 1982-85; senior med. officer First Marine Aircraft Wing, 1977-78, Pacific Fleet Naval Air Force, 1978-82; aviation safety instr. US Naval Postgrad. Sch., Monterey, Calif. 1985-87; ret. 1987; decorated Legion of Merit, Air medal o.l.c., Meritorious Svc. medal; co-editor USN Flight Surgeon manual, 1976; assoc. prof. USC Inst. Safety and Systems Mgmt., Los Angeles 1987-90; cons. in aviation medicine USC Inst. Safety & Systems Mgmt. 1990-; writer and lectr. on aviation safety worldwide 1978-; instr. safety Northwest Airlines, Mpls. 1988-91; mem: Am. Coll. Physicians (Fellow), Am. Coll. Preventive Medicine (Fellow), Aerospace Med. Assn. (Fellow), Internat. Acad. Aviation and Space Medicine, US Naval Flt. Surgeons (pres. 1980-83), Internat. Soc. Air Safety Investig., Am.Helicopter Soc., Acad. Model Aeros.; Republican; R.Cath. Res: 8991 Kingfisher Lake Rd Maceo KY 42355-9737

DUNBAR, MICHAEL PATRICK, water district executive; b. July 31, 1949, Chgo.; s. Thomas Patrick and Patricia (Kocourek) D.; m. Cynthia Long, June 6, 1981; children: Erica b. 1982, Ashley b. 1984, Taryn b. 1986; edn: BS in C.E., Univ. Notre Dame, 1972, MS in E.H.E., 1974; reg. profl. engr. Ind., Calif. Career: engr. John Carollo Eng., Fountain Valley, Calif. 1979-84; senior engr. Dan Boyle Eng., Santa Ana 1984-87; gen. mgr. South Coast Water Dist., Laguna Beach 1987-; dir. Aliso Water Mgmt. Agy., 1992-; dir. South Orange County Reclamation Auth., 1992-; civic: YMCA Laguna Niguel (bd. 1990-); Indep.; R.Cath.; rec: golf, reading, cards. Res: 29521 Los Osos Laguna Niguel 92677 Ofc: South Coast Water District PO Box 30205 Laguna Niguel 92607-0205

DUNCAN, ANDREW MALCOLM, mathematician, audio engineer; b. May 17, 1960, London, England (Am. parentage); s. Glen Malcolm and Eleanor Jane (Watson) D.; m. Gabriella Clementine Borsay, Aug. 23, 1986 (div. Oct. 1987); edn: BS engring., Calif. Inst. of Tech., 1983; MA pure math., UC Santa Cruz, 1989. Career: physics tchr. Pasadena Sch. Dist., 1983-84; pgmr. Cerwin-Vega, Arletta, Ca. 1984-86; cons. E-mu Systems, Scotts Valley 1987-89; cons. Cerwin-Vega, Simi Valley 1989-90; recording engr. MAMA Found., Studio City 1990-92; engr. Philips Interactive Media, Los Angeles 1992-; mem.: Audio Engring. Soc. (1983-, exec. com. L.A. chpt. 1990-92, nat. publication award AES, N.Y.C. 1989), Am. Math. Soc. 1987-, Math. Assn of Am. 1992; inventor: Z-board MIDI controller; publs: math. papers 1988, 91; rec: competitive swimming, music, Shakespeare. Res: 641 Las Lomas Ave Pacific Palisades 90272-3355 Ofc: Philips Interactive Media 11050 Santa Monica Blvd Los Angeles 90025-7511

DUNCAN, THOMAS OSLER, botanist, educator; b. Jan. 15, 1948, Cambridge, Ohio; s. George Wendall and Elizabeth (Fuller) D.; m. Luann Cserr, Nov. 26, 1974 (div. 1983); m. Shelley Diane Williams, Nov. 29, 1986; edn: BS, Ohio St. Univ., 1970; MS, and PhD, Univ. Mich., 1975, 1976. Career: asst. prof. UC Berkeley, 1976-82, assoc. prof. 1982-, director Univ. Herbarium 1982-, assoc. curator of seed plants 1982-; mem. Internat. Assn. for Plant Taxonomy, Am. Soc. of Plant Taxonomists, Calif. Botanical Soc.; publs: (software) MorphoSys (1988), 30+ sci. articles (1970-), ed. (book) Cladiotico: Perspectives on the Reconstruction of Evolutionary History; research: Systematics of Ranunculus; application of numeical methods to systematic problems; floristics of alpine regions; rec: travel, music. Ofc: Univ. Herbarium 6701 San Pablo Ave Berkeley 94720

DUNLAP, JACK STUART, fraud investigator; b. Jan. 6, 1930, Mullens, W.Va.; s. James Edward and Mary Katherine (Carpenter) D.; m. H. June Foglesong, Sept. 26, 1952 (div. 1975); children: Katherine b. 1953, James b. 1957, Jack b. 1962; m. Linda Sue Hayes, May 1, 1978; edn: BS in bus. adminstrn., Concord Coll., 1958; computer courses, Saddleback Coll., 1985-90; cert. fraud examiner 1990, E.A., IRS 1980, lic. pvt. investigator 1981, cert. internat. investigator 1992. Career: fireman, engr. Virginian Railway Co., 1947-59; IRS spl. agt. Toledo, Ohio 1959-64, Charleston, W.Va. 1965-67, San Diego (1967-72, 1977-80, ret. 1980), Los Angeles 1972-75, Santa Ana 1975-77; pvt. investigator Dunlap Investigations, El Cajon 1980-83; pres. Intelligence Investigations Inc., San Diego 1983-86; assoc. Breese & Dunlap Assocs., Lakeside 1986-92; fraud investigator, expert witness, enrolled agt., Dunlap Investigations, San Clemente 1984-; recipient superior performance awards IRS (1976, 78); honors: Eagle Scout BSA 1946; mem: Calif. Assn. Lic. Investigators, San Diego Co. Investigators Assn., Nat. Assn. Cert. Fraud Examiners, Coun. Internat. Investigators Inc.; civic: Singing Hills Little League, El Cajon (coach 1968-72), BSA, Mullens, W.Va. (asst. scoutmaster 1949-52); lodge: AF&A Masons 1951-, Royal Arch Masons 1954-; mil: sgt. US Army 1951-53; Democrat; Prot.; rec: numismatics, gardening. Ofc: Dunlap Investigations PO Box 4328 San Clemente 92674-4328

DUNN, CAROL M., educator, university athletic director; b. Dec. 11, 1949, Washington, D.C.; d. John E. and Evelyn (Kelly) Dunn; edn: BS, Frostburg St Univ. 1973; M.Ed, 1976. Career: tchr., coach Glenridge Jr. H.S., Woodlawn, Md. 1973-75; Bishop Walsh H.S., Cumberland, Md. 1975-78; prof., coach, dept. chair Kans. Newman Coll., Wichita, Kans. 1978-81; prof., coach CSU, L.A. 1981-82, assoc. athletic dir. 1982-88, dir. athletics 1988-; mem. Nat. Assn. Collegiate Directors of Athletics; rec: golf, tennis. Res: 5359 Delta St San Gabriel 91776 Ofc: California State University 5151 State University Dr Los Angeles 90032

DUNSON, BETTY WALKER, clinical social worker; b. Mar. 7, 1947, Fairfield, Ala.; d. Elijah James and Verna Rea (Calloway) Walker; m. Leroy H. Dunson, June 17, 1989; edn: BA, Univ. of Ala. 1968; MSW, Atlanta Univ. 1970; Calif. lic. clin. soc. worker (LCSW); Calif. Comm. Colls. counselor, instr. cred. in pub. svcs. and adminstrn. Career: med. soc. wkr. Atlanta Southside Comp. Health Ctr. 1970; dir. soc. svcs. Trenton Neighboorhood Family Health Ctr, Trento, NJ 1970-3; dir. soc. svcs. Trenton Head Start Pgm. 1973-74; cons./ pgm. analysis & job tng. New Era Learning Corp., Greenvale, NY 1972-3; instr./ mgmt. & supvr. Los Angeles Southwest Coll. Evening div. 1976-79; supervising children's social worker Los Angeles Co. Dept. of Children's Services/Adoptions Div., 1974-; social worker, cons. and trainer, pvt. practice; honors: Delta Sigma Kappa; mem: Nat. Assn. Social Wkrs., Alpha Kappa Alpha Sor., Univ. of Ala. Alumni Assn., Top Ladies of Distinction, Inc. (adv. Top Teens of Am., L.A. chpt.); works: initiated techniques for mainstreaming special-needs children into the regular child care sys.; Democrat; Abundant Life Christian Ch. (chmn. bd. dirs.); rec: acting, floral design, arts & crafts. Res: 2425 Hines Dr Los Angeles 90065 Ofc: L.A. Co. Dept. Childrens Services Adoption Div. 695 S Vermont Ave Los Angeles 90005

DUPONT, DAVID JOSEPH, marketing executive; b. Feb. 5, 1958, Rome, N.Y.; s. Roger Euclid and Claire Marie (Tracy) DuP.; m. Debra Olsen, Oct. 18, 1986; 1 dau., Mariel b. 1989; edn: BSME, Cornell Univ. 1980; MBA, Harvard Univ. 1985. Career: field engr. Schlumberger S.A., Congo, Algeria, Tunisia and Nigeria 1980-83; strategic planner FMC Corp., Chgo., Ill. and Santa Clara 1985-88; product mgr. Hewlett Packard, Sunnyvale 1988-; mgmt. cons. Ayers Whitmore & Co., NYC 1984-85; mem. Stanford Bus. Sch. and Harvard Bus. Sch. New Enterprise Forum; civic: Santa Clara Co. Arts Council (dir. 1989-90), Bus. Vol. for Arts (steering com. chmn. 1988-89), Community Impact, Commonwealth Club of Calif.; R.Cath.; rec: skiing, bicycling, backpacking. Res: 1230 Linder Hill Ln San Jose 95120 Ofc: Hewlett Packard 974 E Arques Ave Sunnyvale 94086

DURANCEAU, CHRISTINE MARIE, physician; b. Sept. 25, 1949, Chartres, France; nat. 1960; d. Jacques Louis and Marcelle Marie (Violeau) Duranceau; m. Patrick Abergel, June 1982 (div. 1985); edn: BA, UC Irvine 1971; PhD, 1977; MD, Yale Sch. Medicine 1981. Career: intern Harbor UCLA Med. Center, Torrance 1981-82, resident emergency medicine 1981-84; emergency physician Glendale Adventist Med. Center, Glendale 1984-86; Eisenhower Med. Center, Rancho Mirage 1986-91, base station dir. 1986-91; co-director Eisenhower Immediate Care Centers, Coachella Valley 1991-92; physician Eisenhower Idyllwild Clinic, Idyllwild 1991-; mem: Am. Coll. Emergency Physicians, Am. Heart Assn., Riverside Emergency Services (directors com. 1987-91), Club Francais Du Desert, Yale Alumni Assn., UC Irvine Alumni Assn. Address: Rancho Mirage 92270

DURFLINGER, JEFFREY DUANE, pharmaceutical validation engineer; b. Mar. 15, 1961, Oakland; s. Laurence Duane and Patricia Etta (Cord) D.; m. Kelly Denise Evans, June 24, 1989; 1 dau., Jenna b. 1991; edn: BS, CSU Chico, 1986; MS Golden Gate Univ. 1993; cert. senior indsl. technologist Nat. Assn. Indsl. Tech., 1992. Career: product devel. mgr. Omni Scientific, Martinez 1986-87; process engr. Alza Corp., Palo Alto 1987-89, Vacaville 1989-92, validation engr. 1992-; tchg. asst. Chico St. Univ., 1986; cons. Polytex Consulting, Sacto. 1988-; recipient profl. awards for spl. achievement Alza Corp. (1991, 92); mem. Soc. of Plastics Engrs. 1984-, Soc. Mfg. Engrs. 1990-; Republican; Methodist. Res: 245 Foster Ln Dixon 95620 Ofc: Alza Corp. 700 Eubanks Dr Vacaville 95688

DURHAM, DON D., restauranteur; b. Sept. 3, 1947, Belmont, Iowa; s. Sherman Kenneth and Elenor Levon (Kendal) D.; m. Carmel Columbell, July 25, 1955; children: Rene L., Tamie L., Danielle; ed. pub. schs., Pierce H.S., Colo. Career: farm work on family dairy farm, Pierce, Colo. 1956-62; cook, mgr., reg. supr. Doggie Diner chain rests., San Francisco 1963-71; cook, mgr., gen. mgr., owner Bill's Place rest., S.F. 1972-; honors: rated Best restaurant in category San Francisco Focus guide (1984, 85, 86, 87, 88), Three Stars, Paul Wallach's Guide (1987, 88), achiev. certif. Nat. Restaurant Assn. 1980, commendn. Calif. State Senate 1985; mem: Clement Street Merchants Assn. (pres. 1988, 91, 92), Council of District Merchants, Nat. Restaurant Assn., Golden Gate Restaurant Assn., S.F. Visitors Bur.; civic: Boutiqe de Noel, Paralysis Project, Friends of Quentin Kopp, Friends of Milton Marks; med. disch. AUS; R.Cath.; rec: video tape archiving & cataloging. Bill's Place, 2315 Clement St San Francisco 94121

DURKIN, WILLIAM THOMAS, JR., physician; b. Feb. 5, 1953, Danbury, Conn.; s. William Thomas and Anne Marita (Deakin) D.; edn: grad. La Salle Acad., Providence, R.I.; BS, and MD, Georgetown Univ., 1975, 1980; bd. cert.

Am. Bd. Emergency Medicine, diplomate Am. Coll. Emergency Physicians. Career: intern Georgetown Univ. Med. Center, Wash. D.C. 1980-81; resident Harvard Surgical Service New England Deaconess, Boston, Mass. 1981-83; staff physician Charlton Memorial Hosp., Fall River, Mass. 1983-84; Associated Emergency Physicians Med. Group, San Diego 1987-, emergency physician Community Hosp. of Chula Vista; instr. adv. cardiac life support Am. Heart Assn. 1985-, instr. adv. trauma life support; instr. EMS Tng. Inst., San Diego; instr. USN Sch. of Health Scis., San Diego, 1985-87; asst. research coord. Paradise Valley Hosp. 1989-; appt. San Diego Co. Emergency Care Com. 1991-93; recipient AMA Physicians Recognition awards (1987, 90); Fellow Am. Coll. Emergency Physicians (FACEP); mem: AMA, Mass. Med. Soc., San Diego Emergency Physicians Soc., N.Y. Acad. Scis., S.D. Zool. Soc.; mil: lt. cmdr. USN 1984-87, Letter Commendation 1985; Republican; R.Cath.; rec: sailing, skiing, investing, autos. Address: 8509 J Villa La Jolla Dr La Jolla 92037

DURST, RODRICK KARL, clergyman, seminary administrator; b. Jan. 6, 1954, Bryan, Tx.; s. Kenneth W. Durst and Joe Ann (Sweeney) Carter; m. Kristina Kage Giddens, Oct. 7, 1954; children: Matthew b. 1981, Lindsay b. 1984, Leesa b. 1989; edn: BA, Calif. Baptist Coll., Riverside 1976; MDiv, Golden Gate Baptist Sem., Mill Valley 1978, PhD, 1988. Career: pastor Coddingtown Baptist Ch., Santa Rosa, 1978-84; sr. pastor Castlewood Baptist Ch., Vallejo 1984-91; dir. So. Calif. Campus Golden Gate Baptist Seminary, Brea 1991-. Ofc: S.C.C.-661BTS, 251 S Randolph Ste A Brea 92621

DUTTON, DONALD STEVEN, information systems executive; b. Mar. 10, 1947, Kalispell, Mont.; s. Donald Zedoc and Roberta Estella (Lewis) D.; edn: Grays Harbor JC 1965-6; BBA, summa cum laude, National Univ. 1977, MBA 1980; cert. computer sci., Coleman Coll. 1973; cert. data processing, Inst. for the Cert. of Computer Profls. 1982. Career: asst. data processing supr. Allied Administrators, San Diego 1972-73; computer ops. Rohr Ind., Inc., Chula Vista 1973-77, comp. pgmmr. analyst 1977-79; sr. pgmmr./analyst Foodmaker Inc., S.D. 1979-80, system project leader 1980-81, software apps. mgr. 1981-84; mgr. Systems, Denny's Inc., La Mirada 1984-86; systems splst. County of Los Angeles, Downey 1986-; adj. faculty National Univ. 1980-, UCSD 1983-84; information systems cons. City of Carlsbad 1983-84; profl. seminars, S.D. Regl. Tng. Ctr. 1983-4; mem: D.P. Mgmt. Assn. (bd. dirs. S.D. chpt. 1981-83, com. chmn.), Toastmasters (past pres.); mil: E4 US Navy 1966-70; Christian. Res: 23426 Coso, Mission Viejo 92692 Ofc: CLA-ISD 9150 E. Imperial Hwy Downey 90242

DUVAL, VIRGINIA HENSLEY, psychologist, research professor; b. Nov. 27, 1948, Marion, N.Caro.; d. Fess Vernon and Shirley Lee (Simpson) Hensley; m. Thomas Shelley Duval, Oct. 4, 1975; edn: BA, USC 1971; MA, 1975, PhD, 1979. Career: behavioral scis. cons. Los Angeles Co. Dept. of Mental Health 1980-84, chief info. systems support bureau 1984-90; res. prof. dept. psych. USC, 1990-; awards: Case Western Reserve Univ. Gen. Motors scholarship 1968-70, USC scholar 1970-75, 8 Nat. Assn. Cos. awards 1985-90; mem: Productivity Mgrs. Network, Am. Psychological Assn., Psychologists in Pub. Service, Soc. Psychological Study of Social Issues, Internat. Assn. Social Sci. Info. Service & Tech.; author: Consistency & Cognition (1983), ed. book chpt. in New Directions in Attribution Research (1976), 20+ articles and papers pub. in profl. jours. (1974-). Ofc: Dept. Psychology, Univ. of So. Calif., Los Angeles 90089-1061

DYCK, ANDREW ROY, philologist, educator; b. May 24, 1947, Chicago, Ill.; s. Roy H. and Elizabeth (Beck) D.; m. Janis Mieko Fukuhara, Aug. 20, 1978; edn: BA, Univ. Wis., Madison 1969; PhD, Univ. Chicago, 1975. Career: sessional lectr. Univ. of Alberta, Edmonton, Can. 1975-76; asst. prof. Univ. Minnesota, Mpls. 1977-78; asst. prof., prof. Univ. Calif., Los Angeles 1976-77, 1978-; awards: Alexander von Humboldt-Stiftung fellow, Bonn, Ger. 1980-89, NEH fellow 1991-92, mem. Inst. for Adv. Study, Princeton 1991-92; mem. Am. Philol. Assn., Calif. Classical Assn., Byzantine Studies Conf. (govng. bd. 1989-), Soc. for the Promotion of Byzantine Studies, U.S. Nat. Com. for Byzantine Studies, Mommsen-Gesellschaft; editor (books): Epimerismi Homerici, I (1983), Michael Psellus, Essays on Euripides & George of Pisidia and on Heliodorus & Achilles Tatius (1986). Ofc: Dept. Classcs UCLA 405 Hilgard Ave Los Angeles 90024-1475

DYER, ALLEN CLAYTON, engineering company president; b. Feb. 8, 1923, Long Beach; s. Clinton Cockrell Dyer and Frances Catherine (Hess) Palmer; m. Mary Louise Sutter, Sept. 3, 1946 (div. 1973); m. Kay Ann Crampton, Feb. 14, 1977; children: Gregory C. b. 1947, Lauren L. b. 1949, Douglas C. b. 1950, Glenn C. b. 1956; stepchildren: Randy J. b. 1961, Jeffrey D. b. 1963, Brady A. b. 1965; edn: BSCE, Stanford Univ. 1947; grad. exec. program, UCLA 1959-60; grad. work USC 1950-51; undergrad. work UCLA 1940-42. Career: engr. Key Contractors Inc., Santa Fe Springs 1947-49; asst. to pres., dept. mgr., chief indsl. engr. Baker Hughes, Los Angeles 1950-67; pres. Ramla Corp., Carmel 1968-; cons. Ramla Corp. 1975-77; mem: ASCE, Inst. Indls. Engrs., Calif. Assn. Airport Execs., Stanford Alumni Assn., Stanford Buck Club, UCLA Exec. Program Assn., Quail Club, Carmel Valley Golf & Country Club, Chi Psi (pres. alumni So. Calif. (1959), Monterey Peninsula Stanford Club (pres. 1984, 85, 88, 89); mil: 1st lt. USAF 1943-45; Republican; Prot.; rec: golf, flying. Res: 24800 Lower Trail Carmel 93921 Ofc: POB 2156 Carmel 93923

DYER, CHARLES ARNOLD, lawyer; b. Aug. 29, 1940, Blairstown, Mo.; s. Charles Arnold and Mary Charlotte (West) D.; m. Marilyn Abadie, Dec. 5, 1983; children: Kristine b. 1965, Erin b. 1973, Kathleen b. 1975, Kerry b. 1986; edn: BJ, Univ. Mo. 1962; JD, UC Hastings Coll. of Law 1970; admitted St. Bar Calif. 1971. Career: atty. Cotchett Hutchinson & Dyer, San Mateo 1971-84; Dyer & White, Menlo Park 1984-; awards: Boys Club Am. Man & Boy 1978; mem: Am. Bd. of Trial Advocates, Am. Arbitration Assn. (Arb.), San Mateo County Bar Assn., Santa Clara County Bar Assn., Palo Alto Bar Assn., San Mateo Co. Trial Lawyers Assn. (pres. 1982), Calif. Trial Lawyers Assn. (v.p. 1983), Assn. Am. Trial Lawyers (st. committeeman 1983); mil: capt. USNR 1963-, Navy Commendn. Medal 1967, Merit. Svc. Medal 1990; Democrat; R.Cath. Ofc: Dyer & White 800 Oak Grove Ave Ste 200 Menlo Park 94025

DYNDA, ERNEST FRANCIS, market development consultant; b. June 20, 1934, Chicago, Ill.; s. Stanley John and Alice Clara (Noble) D.; m. Carole A. Gebhard, Dec. 20, 1964; 1 dau., Allison b. 1967; edn: BS bus., Univ. Ill. 1959. Career: mgr., purchaser Thrifty Drug Stores Co., L.A. 1959-63; sales rep. Internat. Harvester 1963-68; dist. sales mgr. AC-Delco, Gen. Motors, La Mirada 1968-88; cons. Kay Automotive Distributor, Van Nuys 1988-; council mem. City of Agoura Hills 1982-87; awards: Daily News L.A. Top 10 Newsmakers (1984); mem: United Orgn. Taxpayers (pres. 1987-), Am. Legion, Delta Sigma Pi, Las Virgenes City Hood Com. (pres. 1979-82), Las Virgenes C.of C. (dir. 1977-81), Las Virgenes Hist. Soc. (past treas. 1982-88), Masons, Shriners; columnist Las Virgenes Independent 1976-80; mil: E-3 AUS 1955-57; Republican; rec: writing, volunteer work. Ofc: United Organization of Taxpayers Inc. POB 1378 Agoura Hills 91376

EARLY, AMES S., health system president; b. April 18, 1937, Allison, Iowa; s. W.C. and F. Eva Early; m. Beryl J.; 1 dau., Barbara C. Berlat; edn: BA, Drake Univ., Des Moines, Iowa, 1958; Masters, Health Admin., State Univ. of Iowa, 1961. Career: admin. resident, admin. asst. Univ. Minnesota Hosp., Minneapolis 1961-67; exec. dir. Mary Francis Skiff Meml. Hosp., Newton, Iowa 1967-68; asst. admin. Mercy Hosp., Miami, Fla. 1968-70; exec. dir. 1970-76; pres. Scripps Meml. Hosp., La Jolla, Calif. 1976-; award: Headliner of Yr. in Healthcare, San Diego Press Club 1987; mem: So. Fla. Hosp. Assn. (pres. 1974-75, bd. 1971-76), Fla. Hosp. Assn. (bd. 1974-76, var. com.'s 1973-76), Fla. Blue Cross Assn. Hosp. Peer Review Panel 1975-76, Comprehensive Health Planning of So. Fla. (bd. 1974-76, var. com's 1970-76), Calif. Assn. of Hosp. and Health Systems (trustee 1984-, fin. com. 1976, exec. com. 1984, legis. com. 1985, hosp. med. staff bylaws com. 1985-86, treas. 1987, chmn. 1989), Nat. Council of Comm. Hosp. (bd. 1974-84, bd. chmn. 1985-), Hosp. Council of San Diego and Imperial Counties (bd. 1978-80, 1983-86, secty. 1979-80, bd. chmn. 1985), The Healthcare Forum (conv. pgm. & mktg. com. 1987-88), Calif. Polit. Action Com. (bd. 1979-85), United Way San Diego (chmn. hosp. div. 1977, chmn. prof. div. 1980), Blue Cross/Hosp. Advy. Com 1982, Voluntary Hosp. of Am. (bd. 1984-, nom. com. 1989), Voluntary Hosp. of Am. West (bd. 1986-, exec. com. 1986-); mem: Am. Coll. of Healthcare Execs., Am. Hosp. Assn., Am. Assn. of Hosp. Planning. Ofc: Scripps Memorial Hospitals 9888 Genesee Ave La Jolla 92037

EASLEY, IVY JEANNETTE, real estate broker; b. July 8, 1930, San Diego; d. Archie Ernest and Thelma (Beatty) E.; m. Norman Robbins, Jan. 29, 1951; 1 dau., Jeannine b. 1952; edn: grad. San Diego H.S., 1948; R.E., Anthony Sch., 1974; lic. R.E. Broker, Calif. 1979, qualified Fed. Ct. appraiser, expert witness. Career: real estate sales and R.E. fee appraiser: single fam. dwelling, multiple unit, shopping ctrs., 1974-, prin. Easley Realtors 1979-85; honors: spokesperson and one of first women to serve a State Dinner, for Pres. Nixon at Del Coronado Hotel 1969; mem: San Diego Board of Realtors (realtor/atty. com., local govtl. com., task force, 1979-85), Calif. Assn. Realtors, Nat. Assn. Realtors; civic: Community Alert San Diego North Park 1974-85, San Diego H.S. Parents Action Council 1967-68, LBJ Polit. Club 1959-61, Royal Order Moose Lodge; Democrat; Prot.; rec: music, art. Address: San Diego.

EAST, JOHN CLIFFORD, electronics executive; b. Jan. 20, 1945, Amarillo, Tx.; s. John Prather and Francis Louise (Holley) E.; m. Pamela Ann Matson, June 16, 1968; children: Erin b. 1977, Amber b. 1980; edn: BSEE, UC Berkeley 1966; MBA, 1968. Career: engr. Fairchild, Mountain View 1968-76; ops. mgr. Raytheon 1977-78; v.p. AMD, Sunnyvale 1979-88; pres., CEO ACTEL 1988-. Ofc: Actel 955 E Arques Sunnyvale 94086

EATON, BARRY DAVID, city planner; b. Dec. 1, 1937, Oakland; s. Joseph Lloyd and Dorothy (Stockton) E.; children: Colleen Ann, Cathleen Anissa; edn: AB, UC Berkeley 1960; postgrad., USC 1960-62. Career: planning asst. City of Los Angeles 1960-62; city planner and planning dir. City of Azusa 1962-64; planning dir., Stanton 1964-66; Thousand Oaks 1966-70; chief planner, Boise-Cascade Bldg. Co., Los Angeles 1970-71; dir. planning VTN Corp., Irvine 1972-74; dir. gen. planning Raub Bein Frost & Assocs., Newport Beach 1974; chief planner Fullerton 1975-; honors: spl. ecology awards from local environ. groups Thousand Oaks 1960, and Escondido 1961; mem: Am. Inst. Certified Planners, Am. Planning Assn., Calif. Planning and Conservation League, Reg. Plan Assn.; civic: So. Calif. Sierra Club, Mensa, Calif. Tomorrow. Res: POB 802 Corona del Mar 92625 Ofc: City Hall Fullerton 92632

EBINER, ROBERT MAURICE, lawyer, b. Sept. 2, 1927, Los Angeles; s. Maurice and Virginia (Grand) E.; m. Paula H. Van Sluyters, June 16, 1951; children: John, Lawrence, Marie, Michael, Christopher, Joseph, Francis, Matthew, Therese, Kathleen, Eileen, Brian, Patricia, Elizabeth, Ann; edn: JD, Loyola Univ., Los Angeles 1953; admitted bar: Calif. 1954, U.S. Dist. Ct. Calif. 1954. Career: solo practice, West Covina 1954-; judge pro tem Los Angeles Superior Ct. 1964-66, 1991-, arbitrator 1978-; judge pro tem Citrus Muni. Ct. 1966-70; mem. disciplinary hearing panel Calif. State Bar, 1968-75; organizer/incorporator Queen of Valley Hosp., 1959, bd. dirs. Hospital Men's Club 1973-76, bd. dirs. Queen of Valley Hosp. Found. 1983-89; founder/incorporator West Covina Hist. Soc. 1982, bd. dirs. 1982-89; bd. dirs. West Covina United Fund 1958-61, organizer Jt. United Funds East San Gabriel Valley, 1962, bd. dirs. 1961-68; bd. dirs. S.G.V. Cath. Social Svcs., 1969-, pres. 1969-72; bd. dirs. Region II Cath. Social Service, 1970-, pres. 1970-74; trustee L.A. Cath. Charities (fmr. Cath. Welfare Bur.) 1978-; charter bd. dirs. N.E. Los Angeles Co. unit Am. Cancer Soc., 1973-78, chmn. by-laws com. 1973-78; mng. meet dir. Greater La Puente Valley Special Olympics 1985-89, mng. meet dir. BishopAmat Relays 1981-93, mem. MSAC Relays Com. 1978-93; awards: L.A. Co. Human Relations Commn. disting. service award 1978, West Covina "Citizen of Year" 1986, S.G.V. Daily Tribune "Father of Year" 1986, Thomas Kiefer Humanitarian Award 1993; mem: ABA, Calif. Bar Assn., L.A. Co. Bar Assn., L.A. Trial Lawyers Assn., Eastern Bar Assn. L.A. Co. (pres. Pomona Valley 1965-66), West Covina C.of C. (pres. 1960), Am. Arbitration Assn.; clubs: K.C., Bishop Amat H.S. Booster (bd. 1973-, pres. 1978-80), Kiwanis (charter West Covina, pres. 1976-77, lt. gov. Div. 35 1980-81, Kiwanian of Yr. 1978, 82, Disting. Lt. Gov. 1980-81, bd. dirs. Cal-Nev-Ha Found. 1986-92); mil: US Army 1945-47, Korea; active Calif. State Democratic Central Com. 1963-68, campaign mgr. for Congressman Ronald B. Cameron 1964; rec: collector memorabilia: historical, Olympic, and political. Res: 2734 Sunset Hill Dr West Covina 91791 Ofc: 1000 E. Garvey Ave. West Covina 91790

EBITZ, DAVID MACKINNON, museum administrator; b. Oct. 5, 1947, Hyannis, Mass.; s. Robert Creeley and Ann (MacKinnon) Kucera; m. Mary Ann Stankiewicz, Jan. 1, 1983; children: Rebecca b. 1984, Cecilia b. 1987; edn: BA, Williams Coll., 1969; AM, Harvard Univ., 1973, PhD, 1979. Career: tchg. fellow Harvard Univ. 1975-78; asst. prof. Univ. Maine, Orono, Me. 1978-84, assoc. prof. 1984-87, interim dir. Univ. Maine Mus. of Art 1986-87; hd. dept. of edn. and acad. affairs J. Paul Getty Mus., Santa Monica 1987-; curator exhibns., author and lectr. on art, art and museum edn.; honors: Phi Beta Kappa 1968; mem: Coll. Art Assn. 1971-, Nat. Art Edn. Assn. 1987-, Am. Assn. of Museums 1986-, Internat. Ctr. of Medieval Art 1973-. Res: 10865 Pickford Way Culver City 90230 Ofc: J. Paul Getty Museum PO Box 2112 Santa Monica 90407-2112

EBSEN, ROGER ROY, marriage and family therapist; b. Jan. 11, 1947, Santa Monica; s. Christopher Frederick and Irene S. (Simson) E.; m. Kathleen Wage, June 26, 1971; edn: BA sociology, CSU Northridge 1979; MA, 1981. Career: researcher, counselor VA Hosp., Brentwood 1979; staff Woodview Calabasas Hosp., Calabasas 1979-82; clin. dir. care unit Glendale Adventist Hosp. 1982-84; staff Valley Counseling Clin., Sherman Oaks 1980-87; pvt. practice therapy, Woodland Hills 1988; Sherman Oaks 1988; mem: Am. Assn. Marriage & Family Therapists, Calif. Assn. Marriage & Family Therapists, Assn. Humanistic Psychology, Am. Counseling Assn., Assn. Transpersonal Psychology, Group Psychotherapy Assn. So. Calif.; mil: sgt. AUS 1966-68; rec: photography, camping, philosophy. Ofc: 14429 Ventura Blvd Ste 114 Sherman Oaks 91423

ECHEVARRIA, SANTIAGO, company president; b. Aug. 23, Madrid, Spain; s. Felix and Blanca (Manzanares) E.; m. Susgan Hortrude; 1 son, Victor b. 1979; edn: BSME, Nat. Polytechnic Inst., Mexico City; Exec. MBA, The Claremont Grad. Sch. Career: reg. mgr. American Optical, So. Calif., 1969-72; div. mgr. The Southland Corp., So. Calif., 1972-80; v.p. overseas devel. Denny's Inc., Orange, 1980-84; pres. and c.e.o. Internat. Food Concepts., Anaheim, 1984-86; pres. and c.e.o. Intermart Inc., Anaheim Hills, 1986-; gubnat. appt. mem. Calif. State Task Force on Calif.- Mexico Relations; frequent lectr. on internat. mgmt., mktg. & franchising; mem: The Claremont Grad. Sch. Alumni Council, The Peter F. Drucker Grad. Mgmt. Ctr. Alumni Assn., World Trade Ctr. Assn., Internat. Mktg. Assn., Rotary Internat. (Anaheim). Ofc: Intermart, Inc. 5360 E Honeywood Ln Anaheim 92807

ECKER, ANTHONY JOSEPH, orthodontist; b. Apr. 9, 1937, Denver, Colo.; s. Anthony Joseph, Sr. and Esther (Rizzi) E.; m. Doris L., June 14, 1958; children: Anthony III b. 1960, John Michel b. 1964, Robert Daniel b. 1969; edn: DDS, Wash. Univ., St. Louis 1961, MS orthodontics, 1966; Diplomate Am. Bd. of Orthodontics. Career: pvt. practice, splst. orthodontics, Camarillo and Oxnard; mem: Am. Assn. Orthodontists, Am. Dental Assn., Pacific Coast Soc. Orthodontists, Coll. of Am. Bd. of Orthodontics; mil: lt. USN 1961-64; R.Cath. Ofc: 450 Rosewood Ave Camarillo 93010

ECKHAUS, LEONARD I., company president; b. Sept. 18, 1942, NYC; s. Sidney A. and Hortense E.; m. Linda Rosenthal, July 11, 1962; children: Lee, b. 1966, Jill, b. 1969; edn: Newburgh Free Acad. 1957-60, Orange Co. Comm. Coll. 1960-62. Career: senior computer opr. IBM Corp., Poughkeepsie, NY 1967-70;

mgr. Eastern Region Data Centers, TRW Inc., NYC 1970-71; network control mgr. TRW Inc., Anaheim, Calif. 1971-73, mgr. operational planning 1973-74; asst. dir. data processing ops. Los Angeles County Supt. of Schools, Downey 1974-81; pres. Data Center Management Services, 1981-; mem. data proc. advy. bd. Nat. Tech. Inst. for the Deaf; recipient D.P. industry recogn. as leader in computer ops. field; mem: Assn. for Computer Ops. Mgmt. (founding pres. 1980), Internat. Congress of Jewish Marriage Encounter (pres. 1980-81), Jewish Marriage Encounter of So. Calif. (bd. dirs. 1979-81); contbr. numerous tech. and mgmt. articles in The Computer Operations Mag., media coverage in Computerworld, Govt. Computing News, Software News, MIS Week, Computerworld Canada, Wall Street Journal's Employment Daily, Software News, Canadian Data Systems; Jewish; rec: reading, music. Res: 2780 N Chauncey Ln Orange 92667 Ofc: Data Center Mgmt Services 742 E Chapman Ave Orange 92666

EDBERG, STEPHEN J., astronomer; b. Nov. 3, 1952, Pasadena; s. Joseph and Sophie (Pasternak) E.; m. Janet Lynn Greenstein, Dec. 23, 1979; children: Aaron b. 1985, Shanna b. 1989, Jordan b. 1990; edn: AB, UC Santa Cruz, 1974; grad. work UC San Diego, 1974-75, UCLA 1975-77, AM, 1976. Career: solar observer CSU Northridge, 1978-79; calibration scientist Jet Propulsion Lab., Pasadena 1979-81, discipline specialist IHW, JPL, 1981-88, investigation scientist CRAF, JPL, 1986-92, sci. coordinator GLL, JPL, 1989-, investigation scientist Cassini, JPL, 1992; freelance speaker, cons. 1978-; exec. dir. Riverside telescope Makers Conf. Inc., Riv. 1992-; chmn. Corp. for Research Amateur Astronomy, S.F. 1990-; awards: profl. award Astronomical Assn. of No. Calif. 1988, G. Bruce Blair Medal Western Amateur Astronomers 1988, Minor Planet 3672 Stevedberg Internat. Astronomica Union, Paris, Fr. 1988, Sigma Xi research grantee 1974, Chancellor's intern fellow UCLA 1975-77; mem. Am. Astronomical Soc. 1975-, Internat. Amateur Profl. Photoelectric Photometry 1982-; author: Int'l Halley Watch Amateur Observers' Manual (1983), coauthor: Observe Comets (1985), Observe Meteors (1986); rec: bicycling. Ofc: Jet Propulsion Laboratory 4800 Oak Grove Dr Pasadena 91109

EDGETT, STEVEN DENNIS, transportation consultant; b. June 3, 1948, Idpls.; s. Robert Neil and Elizabeth Catherine (Hatch) E.; m. Catherine Ann, June 19, 1971; children: Jeffrey b. 1974, Christopher b. 1977; edn: N.M. State Univ. 1965-67, Univ. of Cincinnati, Oh. 1967-68, Grossmont Coll., La Mesa, Calif. 1970-72. Career: lead designer U.S. Elevator Corp., Spring Valley 1970-76; safety engr. State of Calif., San Diego 1976-78; assoc., dept. head Skidmore, Owings & Merrill, San Francisco 1978-86; pres. Edgett Williams Consulting Group Inc., Mill Valley 1986-; advisor ASCE Coun. on Tall Buildings, 1987-; mem. Constrn. Specs. Inst. 1978-; pub. articles in mags. 1985, 92; rec: mtn. biking, computers, reading. Res: 541 Shasta Way Mill Valley 94941 Ofc: Edgett Williams Consulting Group 100 Shoreline Hwy Ste 250 Mill Valley 94941

EDMUNDS, ALAN VAUGHAN, attorney at law; b. July 17, 1948, Akron, Oh.; s. Burt Vaughan and Rita Ansel Edmunds; m. Kelly Edmunds, June 2, 1975 (div.); children: Danielle b. 1976, Trevor b. 1979, Christopher b. 1983; edn: BA, Univ. of Miami, 1970; JD, Western State, San Diego, 1975; MBA candidate, Univ. of Phoenix, San Diego, 1993. Career: atty., Law Office of Alan V. Edmunds, San Diego, 1976-; instr., Southwestern Coll., Chula Vista, Calif., 1973-75; dir. Childrens Council, San Diego, 1990-; dir. San Diego Missionary Pilots 1990-; mem. San Diego Bar Assn. 1977-, San Diego Trial Lawyers Assn. 1977-; civic: Lions Club, San Diego (program dir. 1976-77); rec: flying, tennis, traveling. Ofc: Alan V. Edmunds, Attorney at Law, 304 Hawthorn St., San Diego 92101

EDWARDS, ARDIS LAVONNE QUAM, teacher, writer, church and civic volunteer; b. July 30, 1930, Sioux Falls, S.Dak.; d. Norman Alvin and Dorothy Margaret (Cade) Quam; m. Paul Edwards (airline capt.), Apr. 18, 1953 (dec. Sept. 12, 1988); children: Kevin b. 1954 (dec. 1980), Kendall b. 1956, Erin b. 1958, Sally b. 1959, Kristin b. 1961, Keely b. 1962; 4 grandchildren: David Paul, Tiffany, Nicole and Brittany; edn: tchg. cred. Augustana Lutheran Coll. 1949; provisional tchg. cred., San Jose St. Coll., San Francisco St. Coll. ext. and summer sessions 1953-1957; FAA lic. pvt. pilot (1984). Career: all pos. to mgr. The Cottage (restaurant), Sioux Falls, S.Dak. 1943-50 (became largest restaurant within 5 state area); one-room school tchr., 8 grades, Colman, S.D. 1949-50, Sioux Falls, S.D. 1950-51, tchr. 1st grade Decoto (Calif.) Sch. Dist. 1952-58; recreation dir. City of Albany, 1951-52; mem. Calif. Tchrs. Assn., Nat. Edn. Assn., PTA, Southwest Airways Pilots Wives, Republic Airlines Retired Pilots Sitting Ducks Assn., Northwest Airlines Retired Pilots Assn., Aircraft Owners and Pilots Assn., AARP, Concerned Women for Am., Nat. Assn. Female Execs.; honors: commendn. from March Fong Eu 1954, special service award Girl Scouts Am. 1971, service awards Arthritis Found. (1974, 75), Who's Who in America, Who's Who in the West, World Who's Who of Women, others; civic: Mission Swim Club, Philomathian Literary Soc., Mission San Jose Restoration Com., Mental Health Assn., Cancer Soc., Heart Assn., March of Dimes, School Room Mother (15 yrs) and Team mother (9 yrs), Brownie co-leader; author: Health Instruction Unit, Study Packet for Tchrs. 1954; Republican; Our Savior Lutheran Ch.: charter mem., ch. historian, mem. adminstrv. bd., Christian Concern and Pastoral Call coms., hon. life mem. Altar Guild, co-chair Silver Anniv. Celebration, tchr. Sunday Sch., Bible Sch. and Christian Week Day Sch., mem.

choir, prayer chain, founder/chair O.S.L.C. Blood Bank 1968-, past pres. L.W.M.L., past hospitality chair, Fraternal communicator and education ofcr. for Lutheran Brotherhood; rec: Bible study, grandchildren, flying, history, antiques.

EDWARDS, BRUCE GEORGE, physician, ophthalmologist; b. Apr. 6, 1942, Idaho Springs, Colo.; s. Bruce Norwood and Evelyn Alice (Kohut) E.; edn: BA, Univ. Colo., Boulder 1964; MD, Univ. Colo. Sch. Medicine 1968. Career: intern U.S. Naval Hosp., San Diego 1968-69, med. ofcr. USS Long Beach 1969-70; U.S. Naval Hosp., Taipei, Taiwan 1970-72; resident, ophthalmology U.S. Naval Hosp., Oakland 1973-76; staff ophthalmologist U.S. Naval Hosp., Camp Pendleton 1976-83; chair med. staff U.S. Naval Hosp., Naples, Italy 1983-85; head, ophthalmology U.S. Naval Hosp., Camp Pendleton 1985-; mem: Am. Acad. Ophthalmology (fellow), AMA, Calif. Assn. Ophthalmology, Assn. Mil. Surgeons of U.S., Pan-Am. Assn. Ophthalmologists, Elks, Marines Meml. Club (assoc. marine); mil: capt. USN Med. Corps 1980-, Naval Achievement Medal 1970; Republican; Protestant; rec: piano playing, hiking, swimming. Ofc: U.S. Naval Hospital Camp Pendleton 92055

EDWARDS, DAVID ELBERT, charitable fundraising and organization consultant; b. July 8, 1933, Los Angeles; s. C. Olin and Ruth Adelia (Crego) E.; m. Elisabeth Battin, June 16, 1957; children: Mark b. 1958, Michael b. 1963, Susan b. 1967; edn: BA, Cascade Coll. 1958; M.Div. Asbury Theol. Sem. 1962; ordained United Methodist Ch. 1968. Career: asst. to the pres., Asbury Theol. Sem., Ky. 1961-68; parish pastor United Meth. Churches in Taft, El Cajon, Pomona, 1968-80; cons. D.M. Lawson Assocs., N.Y. 1980-82; exec. dir. Methodist Hosp. Found., Arcadia 1982-83; v.p. Univ. Advancement, Azusa Pacific Univ., 1983-84; pres. Life Span Concepts, Claremont 1984-; assoc. ptnr. The ProSource Group, L.A. 1986-90; prin. Planned Gift Associates, 1990-; trustee Asbury Theol. Sem.; founding bd. Calif. Parks Ministry; cons. in fundraising, human resource assessment, organization structure var. non-profit orgns.; honors: Outstanding Young Men of Am. 1965, Kentucky Col. 1968, hon. D.Div., ATS 1972; mem. Rotary Internat. (dir. Claremont); publs: num. sermons, promotional copy; mil: sgt. AUS 1953-55; Republican; rec: cabinetry, ceramic potting, golf, sailing. Res: 310 Miramar Claremont 91711 Ofc: Planned Gift Associates, 3111 N Tustin Orange 92665

EDWARDS, DAVID LEROY, lawyer; b. Jan. 11, 1946, Bowling Green, Ohio; s. Ray Junior and Doris Lenore (Nutter) E.; m. Ida Wierschem, Sept. 7, 1976; 1 dau., Kathryn b. 1979; edn: BA, Univ. Pacific 1968; MA, UC Riverside 1975; JD, Loyola Law Sch. 1982. Career: tchr. Rialto Unified Sch. Dist., Rialto 1968-75, sch. adminstr. 1975-80; atty. Rosen Wachtell & Gilbert, L.A.1980-83; Carr Kennedy Peterson & Frost, Redding 1983-88; Tocher Boeckman & Edwards 1988-; honors: Loyola Law Sch. Dean's List 1979-82, contbr. Loyola Law Review 1982, listed Who's Who Am. Colls. & Univs., Calif. St. scholar 1964-68, sports ed. Pacific Weekly UOP 1966-67; mem. Shasta Co. Bd. Edn. bd. trustees 1985-. Ofc: Tocher Boeckman & Edwards 1903 Park Marina Dr Redding 96003

EDWARDS, HEATHER RAE, dentist; b. Jan. 7, 1944, Los Angeles; d. Dick and Doris S. Newcom; m. Arnett Jamison, June 10, 1982; edn: BS, USC 1965; DDS, Univ. of the Pacific 1969. Career: pvt. practice, dental hygienist 1965-75; dentist, comm. dental practice with Synanon Church; dentist, pvt. practice 1982-;contbr. Am J. of Public Health. Res: 50300 Hwy 245 Badger 93603

EDWARDS, JAMES RICHARD, lawyer; b. April 14, 1951, Long Beach; s. Nelson James and Dorothy June (Harris) E.; m. Joan Marie Carriveau, Sept. 24, 1988; edn: BS psychology, Colo. St. Univ. 1973; JD, Univ. San Diego Law Sch. 1977. Career: atty. Downtown Legal Center, San Diego 1977-78; Getty Oil Co., Los Angeles 1978-80; gen. counsel, secty. Logicon Inc., Torrance 1980-85; ptnr. Mirasson Nyznyk & Edwards, Redondo Beach 1985-87; v.p., gen. counsel, secty. Gen. Atomics, San Diego 1987-; dir. Sequoya Fuels Corp., Gore, Okla. 1988-; Chembond Corp., Eugene, Oreg. 1979-80; awards: U.S. Parachute Assn. nat. championship team 1977, 79, 80, F.I.A. world skydiving records 1977, 78, 86, 88; mem: State Bar of Calif., Am. Corp. Counsel Assn., San Diego Bar Assn., Am. Bar Assn., U.S. Parachute Assn.; articles pub. 1986; Republican; rec: skydiving, flying, golf. Ofc: General Atomics POB 95608 San Diego 92138

EFRON, THEODORE, wholesale meat packer; b. May 26, 1944, New York; s. Morris and Pearl E.; m. Barbara Goldstein, June 26, 1965; Career: Efron & Son Meat Packers Inc., Brea, currently; awards: Kiwanis man of year 1980; mem: Fullerton Elks Lodge, Orange Co. Chefs Assn., Am. Culinary Federation, Kiwanis (life, pres. 1980-81), Orange Empire Chefs Assn., Fullerton Elks, Yorba Linda Kiwanis (pres. 1981-82), Placentia Elks (treas. 1965-66). Ofc: Efron & Son Meat Packers Inc. 154 Viking Brea 92621

EGAN, EDWARD JOSEPH, JR., adhesives manufacturing co. president; b. Oct. 4, 1943, NY, NY; s. Edward Joseph, Sr. and Ann (Coakley) E.; m. Elizabeth Schwartz, Jan. 17, 1964 (div.); children: Elisabeth b. 1964, Edward, III b. 1966, Kevin b. 1970, Daniel b. 1977; m. Anne Marie Glennon, Oct. 7, 1989; children: Lillian Anne b. 1990; edn: BA, Notre Dame Univ. 1965; MBA, USC 1969. Career: nat. mktg. mgr. American Can Co., Greenwich, Conn. 1970-

73, region mgr. 1973-76, dir. mktg. & sales 1976-77; pres. General Can Co., Los Angeles 1977-82; pres. W.W. Henry Co., Los Angeles 1982-; pres. West Coast Container, Los Angeles 1986-; mem: Can Mfrs. Inst. (bd. dirs., exec. com.), Carpet Mfrs. of the West, Carpet & Rug Inst., Adhesives & Sealants Council, Nat. Assn. of Floor Covering Dist., Am. Tile Mfrs. Inst., Nat. Paint & Coatins Assn., Co. Calif. Paint & Coatings Assn., Los Angeles C.of C., Town Hall of Calif., Who's Who in Am. Bus.; civic bds: Intra-Sci. Research Found. (chmn. & pres. 1982-92), La Canada Little League (coach 1977-), Am. Heart Assn., Nat. Kidney Found., Am. Cancer Res. Found., Sacred Heart High Sch. Advy. Bd. 1978-83, St. Francis H.S. 1979-87, St. Bede Grammar Sch. (treas. 1976-); clubs: Jonathan, Annandale Golf, La Canada-Flintridge Golf, Winged Foot Golf; Republican (pres. La Canada Young Rep. 1968); R. Cath.; Knight of Malta; rec: golf, swim, tennis, theatre arts. Res: 1437 Edgehill Pl Pasadena 91103 Ofc: W.W. Henry Co. 5608 Soto St Huntington Park 90255

EGAN, WILLIAM JOSEPH, III, lawyer; b. Aug. 15, 1947, New Orleans, La.; s. William Joseph, Jr. and Margaret H. (Harrison) E.; m. Renee, Oct. 16, 1982; children: Jason b. 1983, John b. 1986; edn: BS, Louisiana State Univ., 1970; JD, Tulane Univ., 1975; admitted to the bars of Louisiana State 1975, Calif. 1976, Texas 1977, U.S. Patent 1977. Career: assoc. Deutsch, Kerrigan & Stiles, New Orleans, La., 1975-76; patent atty. Exxon Prod. Research Co., Houston, Tex., 1976-77; patent atty. Chevron Research Co., San Francisco, 1977-80; ptnr. Flehr, Hohbach, Test, Albritton & Herbert, S.F., 1980-90; ptnr. Heller, Ehrman, White & McAuliffe, S.F., 1991-; honors: Tau Beta Pi, Eta Kappa Nu, Tulane Moot Ct. Bd., Phi Delta Phi; mem. Am., La., Tex., Calif. and San Francisco Bar Assns., Patent Law Assn. of S.F.; Democrat; R. Cath.; rec: physical training.

EHRSAM, ELDON EDWARD, operations research analyst; b. July 8, 1936, Bern, Kans.; s. Loyd and Elma Elizabeth (Bauman) E.; m. Clara Louise Schwartz, Nov. 20, 1958; children: Elizabeth Sue b. 1959, Jeffrey b. 1961, John b. 1968, Brian b. 1969; edn: BS, Washburn Univ. 1962; MS, USC 1969; cert. (MS equiv.) UC Santa Barbara 1973; Calif. lic. real estate broker. Career: physicist Naval Ordnance Lab, Corona, Ca. 1962-65; electronic engr. AF Western Test Range, Vandenberg AFB, 1965-68, project engr. Space & Missile Test Center, VAFB 1968-73, telemetry sys. mgr. 1973-76, ops. res. analyst 1976-; real estate broker, Danish Village Realty, Solvang 1976-90, ERA Hunter Realty, Santa Ynez/ Lompoc, 1991-; securities rep. Vestcap Sec. Corp., Solvang 1982-89; honors: BSA District Award 1979, listed Who's Who in West, Jane's Who's Who in Aviation & Aerospace; mem: AIAA (Vandenberg chpt. Council 1980-81), Internat. Platform Assn., Nat. Assn. of Realtors, Nat. Assn. Securities Dealers, Sigma Pi Sigma, Masons, Elks; coauthor 4 tech. papers, presented Internat. Telemetry Confs. 1969-75; Republican; United Methodist; rec: racquetball, jogging, camping. Res: 3087 Fairlea Rd Santa Ynez 93460 Ofc: Air Force Western Space & Missile Center, 6595 Test & Evaluation Group, Code TA, Vandenberg AFB 93437

EICHNER, ROBERT MAURICE, life underwriter; b. Mar. 7, 1942, NY, NY; s. Joseph George and Fay (Malinski) E.; m. Cookie Cohen, Aug. 11, 1962; children: Lori b. 1965, Debi b. 1968, Todd b. 1972; edn: BA, Kent State Univ., 1964. Career: detail man Wyeth Laboratories, Los Angeles 1964-68; sales mgr. Certified Labs, Beverly Hills 1968-70; owner Insurance Salvage, North Hollywood 1970-73; salesman Levitz Furniture, Glendale 1973-75; sales rep. mgr. Metropolitan Life, Canoga Park 1975-84; owner Robert M. Eichner Insurance Services, Woodland Hills 1984-; regional dir. The Regan Group, Novato 1984-, dir. Regan Re Ins. 1986-; secty. SGA Council General Services Life, Novato; awards: Court of the Table, MDRT 1987-88; mem. Nat. Assn. Life Underwriters 1976-, Lovin Levelor (pres. 1991, treas. 1985-87), North Valley Jewish Comm. Ctr.; Republican; rec: camping, computers, philately. Res: 6635 Vickiview Dr West Hills 91307 Ofc: Eichner & Neale 22231 Mulholland Hwy Ste 210 Woodland Hills 91364

EISEMANN, KURT, mathematics professor; b. June 22, 1923, Nuremberg, Germany, naturalized U.S. citizen 1953; s. Dr. Lazarus and Lina (Bacharach) E.; m. Marlene K. Cross, June 22, 1969 (div. 1988); children: Jamin Albert b. 1970, Caroline Ruth b. 1974; edn: BA, Yeshiva Univ., NY 1950; MS, M.I.T., 1952; PhD, Harvard Univ., 1962. Career: sr. and res. mathematician Internat. Business Machines Corp., N.Y.C. and Cambridge, Mass., 1952-61; mgr. mathematical res. Sperry Rand Corp., W.D.C., 1961-63; dir. Computer Ctr. and assoc. prof. Catholic Univ. of Am., W.D.C., 1963-66; tech. dir. Computer Usage Devel. Corp., Boston 1966-68; dir. acad. computing svs. and prof. computer scis. Northeastern Univ., 1968-74; dir. computer svs. and prof. math. and computer sci. Univ. of Missouri, Kansas City, Mo. 1974-82; dir. univ. computing ctr. and prof. math. & compter scis. San Diego State Univ., (1982-92, prof. emeritus (ret.) 1992; lectr. Yeshiva Univ. 1953-55, Cath. Univ. of Am. 1962-63; dir. chem. lab. pgms. Children's Science Camps, Pa. 1970-73; awards: Yeshiva Univ. prize for excellence in math., prize for scholarship, ethics & character 1950, M.I.T. scholar 1950-52, commendn. Gov. Indiana; civic bds: Singles Cultural Club, Boston (founder, chmn. 1967-69), Private School Bd. of Edn. Greater Kansas City (mem., chmn. 1977-80), Private Schs. Regional Edn. Coun., Met. K.C. (bd. 1979-81); publs: numerous papers in math. Ofc: Dept. Math. San Diego State Univ., San Diego 92182

EKELUND, JOHN JOSEPH, college president, admiral; b. Jan. 19, 1928, Washington; s. Kenneth Oscar and Marjorie (Buscher) E.; m. Lynn Marie Schumacher, May 3, 1952; children: John, Jr. b. 1953, Christopher b. 1954, Terri b. 1956, Peter b. 1958, Tracy b. 1960, Patricia b. 1962, Kent b. 1967; edn: BS, US Naval Acad. 1949; MS systems analysis, Univ. Rochester 1969. Career: officer U.S. Navy 1945-83, commnd. ensign 1949, advanced through grades to rear adm. 1976, service in Korea and Vietnam; chief staff Naval Forces, Vietnam, 1972-73; cmdr. guided missile cruiser USS Albany, 1973-75; dean Naval War Coll., 1975-76; dep. dir. naval edn. and tng. Office Chief Naval Ops., WDC 1976-77; nat. intelligence officer CIA, 1977-78; cmdr. US South Atlantic Force, 1978-80; supt. Naval Postgrad. Sch., Monterey, Calif. 1980-83; decorated Legion of Merit (1973, 79, 83), Meritorious Service 1972, Presdl. Unit Cit. 1950, Nat. Intelligence Achiev. U.S. Intelligence Community 1978; pres. Calif. Maritime Acad., Vallejo, 1983-; civic: Napa Solano United Way (pres. 1988-), Vallejo Rotary (dir. 1986-), Vallejo C.of C. (dir. 1986-); mem. US Naval Acad. Alumni Assn., US Naval Inst.; works: devel. modern submarine torpedo fire control solution methodology used internat. (1957); Republican; Cath.; rec: golf, reading. Res: 2 Faculty Dr Vallejo 94590 Ofc: California Maritime Academy, P.O. Box 1392, Vallejo 94590

EL AGIZY, MOSTAFA, professor of management; b. Dec. 14, 1927; s. Mohame Nabih and Aziza El Agizy; m. Nabila Ahmed Amer, Apr. 8, 1956; children: Amr b. 1958, Mona b. 1965; edn: BSc, Cairo Univ., 1949; MS, Cornell Univ., 1958; PhD, UC Berkeley, 1965. Career: sr. mathematician Union Oil Co., Ill. 1965-66; sr. res. assoc. Mobil Oil Corp., N.Y., NY 1966-68; mgmt. scientist IBM Corp., 1968-73; sr. adv. Exxon Corp., Florham Park, N.J. 1973-83; adj. prof. Grad. Sch. Bus. Adminstrn. Rutgers Univ., 1967-83; prof., ops. mgmt., Calif. State Polytechnic Univ., Pomona 1983-; p.t. faculty UC Riverside Grad. Sch. of Mgmt., 1984-; UN cons. Egyptian Petroleum Res. Inst., The Electronic Res. Inst., and faculty of engring. Cairo Univ. 1986-87; cons. Douglas Aircraft Co. 1988; awards: Ford Found. Scholar 1962-65, Exxon's Teagle Found. Scholar 1957-58; mem: Inst. of Mgmt. Sci., Operations Res. Soc. of Am., Am. Inst. of Indsl. Engrs., Am. Prodn. and Inventory Control Soc., Am. Mgmt. Assn.; civic: Boys Club of Pomona (bd. 1984-); contbr. articles to profl. jours., nat. and internat. conf. presentations; Republican; Moslem; rec: swimming, tennis, travel. Res: 5400 Deer Run Ct Alta Loma 91701 Ofc: Cal Poly Univ. 3801 W Temple Ave Pomona 91768

ELAINE, KAREN, musician; b. Nov. 6, 1965, San Jose; d. Gaston Ortega and Alice Lee (Ray) Sanders; edn: H.S. grad. Sch. of Creative & Performing Arts, San Diego, 1983; dipl. music, viola performance profl., Curtis Inst., Phila. 1984-87. Career: principal, solo viola New American Chamber Orch., Detroit 1986-87; prin. viola San Diego Sym. Orch., 1987-90, also asst. prin. viola San Diego Chamber Orch., 1987-90; prin. viola Orquesta Sinfonia de Tijuana, B.C., Mexico 1988-; prof. viola San Diego State Univ. 1989-; prof. viola Chanterelle Music Festival, Povidoux, Switz. (summers 1989, 90); asst. prin. viola, soloist Elkhorn Music Festival, Sun Valley, Idaho 1991-; guest lectr., soloist Internat. Viola Cong., Ithaca, NY 1991; guest soloist Am. Youth Sym., L.A. 1992; awards: 1st pl. grand prize Bruno Giuranna Internat. Viola Competition, Brazil 1988, 1st pl. Rio Hondo Young Artists Comp., Whittier, Ca. 1989, Commn. grant (Gordon Kerry's Viola Concerto) Australia Arts Council, Sydney 1991, Commn concert piece by David Baker 1989, Cinnabar Concerto by David Ward- Steinman 1993, 1992 Grammy Music Com. award nominee, N.Y. 1992; mem. Am. Viola Soc. 1988-; recording soloist: Dello Joio, City of London Sinfonia/ Harmonia Mundi 1990, Bartok, Orq. Sinfonia de Paraiba/ Delos 1988, Bloch, London Sym.Orch. /Laurel 1990; contbr. article in J. Am. Viola Soc. (1991, 92); Democrat; rec: karate, body surfing, sci. fi., chamber music. Res: 208 Welling Way San Diego 92114-5947

ELGIN, GITA, clinical psychologist; b. Santiago, Chile, nat. 1987; d. Serafin and Regina (Urizar) Elguin; m. Bart Body, Oct. 21, 1971; 1 child, Dio b. 1986; edn: PsyD (summa cum laude), Univ. of Chile, 1964; PhD, UC Berkeley, 1976; lic. psychologist (PSY 6901). Career: hosp. psychologist, Santiago, Chile 1964-65, clin. and exptl. psychologist Univ. of Chile 1965-68; clin. psych. intern Alameda County Mental Health Svs., 1968-69; res. asst. UCB, also pre-doctl. intern Kaiser Found. Med. Ctr., Oakland 1970-71; post-doctl. intern Contra Costa Co. Mental Hlth. Svs., 1977; co-founder, clin. dir. Holistic Health Assocs., Montclair, Oakland 1979-; writer, lectr. and workshops on holistic health; publs. in profl. jours. and local newspapers; mem: Am. Psychol. Assn., Calif. St. Psychol. Assn./Alameda Co. Chpt., Montclair Health Profls. Assn. (founding pres. 1983-84), Assn. for Holistic Health, UCB Alumni Assn., No. Calif. Soc. for Clin. Hypnosis, Assn. for Cognitive Behavior Therapy, Assn. for Transpersonal Psych., Psychosynthesis Network, Commonwealth Club of Calif.; awards: research fellow Found. for Research on the Nature of Man, Durham, N.C. 1968, res. grantee on psychol. correlates of EEG-alpha, UCB 1973, NIMH res. fellow in biofeedback, UCB 1973-74; Self-Realization Fellowship; rec: writing, windsurfing, swimming, R.E. investments. Ofc: Holistic Health Associates, Montclair Professional Bldg 2080 Mountain Blvd Ste 203 Oakland 94611

ELIOT, MARK STEVEN, public relations executive, graphic designer; b. Oct. 19, 1954, Burbank; s. Gerald and Eileen (Dougherty) E.; m. Ellen Mary

Steinberg, Sept. 20, 1981; 1 dau., Ashley Elizabeth b. 1986; edn: BA, CSU Long Beach 1976.Career: arts and feature writer Orange Coast Mag., Irvine 1977; pub. rels. promotion dir. KWIZ AM & FM Radio, Santa Ana 1977-82; self employed P.R.Graphic Design, Laguna Hills 1982-83; regional media coord. Rogers Cablesystems, Garden Grove 1983-85; comms. splst. Tustin Unified Sch. Dist. 1985-; com. Tustin Tiller Days 1986-; awards: Cable Advt. Mag. advt. and promotion award 1984, Orange Co. Fair art awards 1982-88, Film Festival award 1979, Orange Co. Advt. Fedn. Awards of Excellence 1978; mem: Tustin C.of C. (bd. dirs. 1986-88), Assn. Tustin Sch. Adminstrs., Nat. Sch. Pub. Rels. Assn., So. Calif. Schs. Pub. Rels. Assn., Masons, Rotary Club, Kiwanis, Tustin Hist. Soc., United Way, BSA; mural artist PepperTree Fair 1973, pub., ed. Cobblestone Art Newspaper 1974-76, Blvd. Comm. Newspaper 1976-77; rec: collect buttons, old toys and books, swimming, basketball. Res: 25362 Brussels Ave Mission Viejo 92691 Ofc: Tustin Unified School District 300 South C St Tustin 92680

ELIZONDO, SERGIO D., educator; b. Apr. 29, 1930, El Fuerte, Sin. Mex., nat. U.S. 1955; s. Cristino Santiago Elizondo and Feliciana (Dominguez) Maldonado; m. Sharon Mowrey, June 8, 1958 (div. Mar. 1971); children: Even D. b. 1959, Sean S. b. 1962; edn: BA, Findlay Coll., Ohio 1958; MA, Univ. N.C., Chapel Hill 1961, PhD in Spanish, 1964. Career: asst. prof. Univ. Texas, Austin 1963-68; assoc. prof. CSU San Bernardino, 1968-71; dean of coll. West Washington St. Univ., Bellingham 1971-72; prof. and hd. Spanish dept. New Mexico State Univ., Las Cruces 1972-90, dir. Inst. Chicano Studies, 1975-90; vis. prof. Mex.Am. literature San Diego State Univ., 1990-; vis. prof. Texas A&I Univ., Kingsville, Tx. 1979; awards: Ford Found. fellow Colegio de Mexico 1971, postdoc. grantee N.Mex. st. Univ., Seville, Spain 1973, NEA fellow, W.D.C. 1981, mencion -short story Revista Cultural Plural, Mexico, D.F. 1985, Gold medal literature Univ. Ciudad Juarez, Mexico 1990; mem: Am. Assn. Tchrs. Spanish and Portuguese 1958-, Calif. Faculty Assn., ACLU, Amnesty Internat., Hemlock; author 5 books: Perros (1972), (fiction) Suruma (1990), Muerte En Una Estrella (1984), (short fiction) Rosa, La Flauta (1980), (poems) Libro Para Batos (1977); mil: pfc US Army 1954-56; Indep.; rec: travel, writing. Res: 5040 Comanche Dr #114 La Mesa 91941

ELLICKSON, DEANE LOUIS, insurance brokerage executive; b. Sept. 16, 1934, Chgo.; s. Ray and Madeline G. (Morris) E.; m. Lorraine, May 31, 1955 (div. July 1991); children: Suzanne b. 1958, Sherri b. 1961, Debra b. 1964, Lorne b. 1968, Deanna b. 1971; edn: stu. law LaSalle Univ. 1958-61, spl. courses, U.S. Internat. Univ., Golden Gate Univ., comm. colls.; Calif. lic. Ins. Broker, life & disab. agent 1960. Career: ins. investigator supr. Retail Credit Co., Santa Monica 1958-60; spl. agt. Bankers Life Co. of Iowa, L.A. 1960-62; group ins. rep. Occidental Life Ins. of Calif., L.A. 1962-65; profl. staff cons. Calif. Tchrs. Assn., Burlingame 1965-79, dept. supr. 1967-75; staff cons. and agcy. coord. Ednl. Comm. Ins. Services Inc., San Mateo 1979-; prop. Rancho Pistachio Co. (pistachio orchard devel. co.), Temecula 1981-; dir. First Finl. Credit Union, Glendale 1985-; recipient suggestion award Retail Credit Co. 1958, achievement award, Occidental Life (1962, 64), service awards: City of Huntington Beach, H.B. Rotary, H.B. Neighborhood Watch 1978, Liberty Bell Award, Orange Co. Bar Assn. 1978, La Cresta Prop. Owners Assn. golden telephone award 1984; civic: Arevalos Elem. Sch. Site Council 1968-79, Fountain Valley Dist. Supt.'s Spl. Advis. Com. 1974-77, H.B. Neighborhood Watch (founding com., bd., pres., 1975-78; secured O.C. grant funds for org. 1977), cons. var. Neighborhood Watch groups in So. Calif. 1975-84, H.B. Police Dept. and Civil Def. Aux. (spl. communs. team 1976-78), LaCresta Prop. Owners Assn. (pres. 1982-83); life mem. Calif. Rifle and Pistol Assn., Nat. Rifle Assn.; publs: Pgn. Dinner Menu & Cookbook (1986); mil: sgt.-major US Army Corps of Engrs., Pres. Unit Cit., Korean War, Good Conduct, 1957; Democrat; rec: shooting, avocado ranching, woodworking. Res: 24850 Hancock Ave, I106, Murrieta 92562 Ofc: Rancho Valley Services, Inc. PO Box 909 Murrieta 92564-0909

ELLINGTON, JAMES WILLARD, mechanical engineer; b. May 26, 1927, Richmond, Ind.; s. Oscar Willard and Leola Lenora (Sanderson) E.; m. Sondra Elaine Darnell, Dec. 6, 1952; children: Ronald b. 1953, Roxanna b. 1956; edn: BSME, West Coast Univ., L.A. 1978. Career: designer NATCO, Richmond, Ind. 1954-67; design engr. Burgmaster, Gardena, Calif. 1967-69; senior mfg. engr. Xerox Corp., El Segundo 1969-84, consulting mem. engring. staff Xerox, Monrovia 1984-87; staff engr. Photonic Automation, Santa Ana 1987-88; sr. mech. engr. Optical Radiation, Azusa 1988; senior staff engr. Omnichrome, Chino 1988-; awards: 2d prize nat. design contest Gray & Ductile Iron Founders Soc., Richmond, Ind. 1966, Team Excellence Xerox Corp., Monrovia (1985); mem. Soc. Mfg. Engrs. 1962-, W.C.U. Alumni Assn., L.A. (bd. 1988-); mil: BT2/c US Navy 1951-52; Republican; Baptist; rec: gardening. Res: 6221 Mitchell Ave Riverside 92505

ELLINGTON, MICHAEL THOMAS, financial officer; b. June 21, 1951, Altus, Okla.; s. Alva Thomas and Clara Jeanne (Elliott) E.; edn: BS, Cal Tech SLO 1979. Career: supervising sr. Arthur Young & Co., Los Angeles 1979-82; dir. analysis MCO Resources, Houston, Tx. 1982-84; CFO Pacific Coast Cement, Los Angeles 1984-; dir. Julian Holdings Inc., Long Beach 1986-; mem: AMA, Am. Inst. C.P.A., Calif. Soc. C.P.A., ARC (fund raising com.);

Republican; rec: golf. Ofc: Pacific Coast Cement Corp. 1800 Century PE Ste 830 Los Angeles 90067

ELLIOT, JOHN GREGORY, aerospace engineer; b. Nov. 9, 1948, Dutch East Indies, came to U.S. 1956; s. Frans Jan and Charlotte Clara (Rosel) E.; m. Jennifer Lee Austin, May 7, 1988; edn: AA, Cerritos Coll., 1974; BS, CSU Long Beach, 1978. Career: design engr. Douglas Aircraft Co., Long Beach 1978-82, lead engr. 1983-89, sect. mgr. elec. installations group 1989-; mem. So. Calif. Profl. Engring. Assn., Douglas Aircraft Co. Management Club, Tennis Club, Surf Club; mil: US Navy 1969-73; Republican; Presbyterian. Ofc: Douglas Aircraft Co., MC 2-90, 3855 Lakewood Blvd Long Beach 90846

ELLIOTT, GEORGE EVERETT, corporate executive; b. Feb. 21, 1928, Springfield, Mo.; s. George E. and Pearl May (Turk) E.; m. Polly Dorothy Lawrence, Jan. 13, 1951; children: Janelle b. 1953, Georgia b. 1955, Matthew b. 1958; edn: BA, Drury Coll. 1947. Career: profl. musician Am. Broadcasting Co., San Francisco 1948-53; v.p. Venton Co. 1953-55; exec. v.p. Dorman Co. 1956-; bd. dirs. Plack Inc. 1967-89; mem: Bohemian Club (v.p. 986-87, pres. 1987-89), French Club, St. Francis Yacht Club; Republican; Prot.; rec: golf, boating. Res: 19 Mt Tallac Ct San Rafael 94903 Ofc: Dorman Co. 599 Mission St San Francisco 94105

ELLIOTT, GORDON JEFFERSON, educator; b. Nov. 13, 1928, Aberdeen, Wash.; s. Harry Cecil and Helga May (Kennedy) E.; m. Suzanne Tsugiko Urakawa, Apr. 2, 1957; children: Meiko Ann, Kenneth Gordon, Nancy Lee, Matthew Kennedy; edn: AA, Grays Harbor Coll., 1948; BA, Univ. Wash., 1950; cert. in Russian Army Language Sch., Monterey 1952; MA, Univ., Hawaii, 1968; Calif. Community Colls. lifetime tchg. credential. Career: English prof. Buddhist Univ., Ministry of Cultures, The Asia Found., Phnom Penh, Cambodia 1956-62, also cons. on Buddhist edn. The Asia Found., San Francisco, 1956-62; English instr. Univ. Hawaii, Honolulu 1962-68, also cons. on English edn., Hawaii State Adult Edn. Dept., 1966-68; dir. orientation English Coll. of Petroleum and Minerals, Dhahran, Saudi Arabia 1968-70; asst. prof. English and linguistics, Univ. Guam, Mangilao, 1970-76; tchr., French and English, Medford Mid High Sch., Oreg. 1976-77; instr. English Merced Coll. 1977-; spkr. conf. on English Edn. in Middle East, American Univ., Cairo 1969; vis. prof. English Shandong Tchrs. Univ., Jinan, China 1984-85; coauthor Cambodian/English (textbooks): English Composition 1962, Writing English 1966, (test) Standard English Recognition Test 1976; pub. articles in profl. jours.; mem. editl. advy. bd. Collegiate Press;awards: tchg. fellow Univ. Mich., Ann Arbor 1956, summer seminar stipend Nat. Endowment for the Humanities, UW, Seattle 1976, travel grantee People's Rep. of China, Beijing 1984-85; mem. Merced Coll. Found., Am. Assn. Woodturners, BPOE, NRA, Am. Near East Refugee Aid, Statue of Liberty Centennial Commn. 1983, Heritage Found., Lincoln Inst.; mil: sgt. US Army Security Agy. 1951-55, Japan; Republican (Rep. Presdl. Task Force 1980-86). Res: 680 Dennis Ct Merced 95340 Ofc: Merced College 3600 M St Merced 95340

ELLIOTT, REED OAKLEY, JR., speech/language pathologist; b. Feb. 7, 1947, Altadena; s. Reed O., Sr. and Doris Josephine (Holland) E.; m. Christine Hinds, Sept. 3, 1976; children: Laine Elizabeth b. 1979, Kyle Walker b. 1982; edn: BA psych., Antioch Coll., 1970; MA commun. disorders (summa cum laude), CSU Northridge, 1986. Career: staff State Dept. of Devel. Services, 1970-: Psych. Tech. Pomona 1971-73, Senior Psych. Tech. Camarillo (1973-75, 78-85), Unit Mgr. 1975-78, Tchr. of Communicatively Handicapped, Dept. of Devel. Services, Camarillo 1985-; speech pathologist pvt. practice, Camarillo 1986-89; expert witness, cons. Dist. Atty., Maui, Hawaii 1986; cons. ednl. staff Lanterman Devel. Ctr., Pomona 1988; p.t. faculty Dept. Communicative Disorders CSU Northridge, 1989-; cons. Horrigan Enterprises group homes, Oxnard, 1991-; exec. com. Mental Health Advy. Bd. Ventura County, 1989-92; profl. presentations Soc. of Neurosci. Conv., New Orleans, 1987, The Assn. for Persons with Severe Handicaps, S.F., 1989, Research & Program Devel. Conf., Dept. of Mental Health, S.F. 1990; Supported Living Connection Conf., VCSELPA, Oxnard, 1991; awards: NSF research grantee 1969, Calif. Dept. of Devel. Serv. research grantee (1989, 90, 91), profl. promise award CSUN Sch. of Comm. & Profl. Studies 1990, listed in Men of Achievement (pub. Cambridge, Eng. 1990); cert. mem. Am. Speech, Language & Hearing Assn. 1985-; civic: Am. Youth Soccer Orgn. (coach 1987-), YMCA Youth Basketball (coach 1988); publs: book chapt. Using STRETCH to tch. comm. skills to people with developmental disabilities" in STRETCH, a life skills curriculum 1990 pub. by Calif. Dept. of Devel. Svs.; A Critical Life Skills Vocabulary 1988; contbr. articles to profl. jours.; Republican; rec: backpacking, musical composition, gourmet cooking, youth coaching. Ofc: Camarillo State Hosp. & Developmental Ctr. Box 6022 Regional Project Camarillo 93011

ELLIOTT, THOMAS JOSEPH, educator; b. Jan. 25, 1941, Boston; s. Thomas Joseph and Anne Teresa (Regan) E.; m. Eugenia Marie Coleman, June 18, 1966; 1 dau., Christine b. 1979; edn: AB (cum laude), Boston Coll., 1963, MA, 1967; PhD, Univ. Mich., 1970. Career: tchr. English and Latin, St. Dominic Savio H.S., East Boston, Mass. 1963-67; tchg. fellow Univ. Mich., Ann Arbor 1968-69; asst. prof. to full prof. English, Calif. Polytech. State Univ.,

Pomona 1970-; vis. fellow Univ. Kent, Canterbury, Eng. 1984; awards: fellow Southeastern Inst. of Medieval & Renaissance Lit., Duke Univ. 1976; mem. Modern Language Assn., Irish Am. Cultural Assn., Medieval Acad. of Am., New Chaucer Soc., others; author: A Medieval Bestiary (1971); textbook essay, College English (1980); talks: "Pilgrimage" Chaucer Congress, Eng., 1990, "Education" UC Berkeley, 1992; Democrat; R.Cath. Res: 982 Richmond Dr Claremont 91711-3348 Ofc: Dept. English Calif. State Polytechnic Univ., 3801 W Temple Ave Pomona 91768

ELLIS, EUGENE JOSEPH, cardiologist, professor emeritus medicine; b. Feb. 23, 1919, Rochester, N.Y.; s. Eugene Joseph and Violet (Anderson) E.; m. Ruth Nugent, July 31, 1943; children: Eugene J., Susan Ellis Renwick, Amy Ellis Miller; edn: AB, USC, 1941, MD, 1944; MS medicine, Univ. Minn., 1950; Diplomate Am. Bd. Internal Medicine and Cardiovascular Diseases. Career: intern USC/L.A. Cty. Hosp. 1944, resident 1946; fellowship Mayo Clinic, 1947-51; dir. dept. cardiology St. Vincent's Hosp., Los Angeles 1953-55, Good Samaritan Hosp., 1955-84, ret.; prof. medicine Univ. So. Calif., L.A. 1965-84, prof. emeritus medicine, 1984-; appt. Med. Bd. of Calif., 1984-, bd. pres. 1988; pres. Calif. State Div. of Med. Quality, 1985-89; exec. com. trustees Univ. Redlands, 1976-86; clubs: Los Angeles CC, Pauma Valley CC (dir. 1980-83), Birnam Wood G.C., Montecito; mil: lt. USN 1944-46; contbr. articles to med. jours.; Republican. Res: 450 Eastgate Lane Santa Babara 92108

ELLISON, TERI HALL, public health nutritionist; b. June 24, 1956, Fresno; d. Harold Robert and Patricia Ann (Dettinger) Hall; m. David Lee Ellison, Sept. 9, 1989; edn: BS, San Jose Univ. 1981; MPH, UC Berkeley 1985. Career: nutrition asst. Santa Clara Co. Health Dept., San Jose 1980-81; dietetic tech. O'Connor Hosp. 1981-83; pub. health nutrition con. Calif. Dept. Health Services, Sacto. 1984-86; ed., res. analyst Calif. Health Fedn. 1986-87; perinatal nutritionist Vacaville Comm. Clinic 1987-88; supervising dietitian Sacto. Co. Health Dept. 1988-; mem: Calif. Conf. of Local Health Dept. Nutritionists (pres. 1991-92, sec. 1989-90); honors: Phi Kappa Phi, San Jose St. Univ. Pres. scholar 1981, Yale Book award 1973, Outstanding Young Woman of Am. 1982, UC Berkeley Regents Fellow 1984, Helen R. Stacey award Am. Pub. Health Assn. 1984; civic: Hispanic Democratic Club Sacto. (v.p. 1986-87), Community Resource Project (bd., treas. 1987-90), Los Medicos Voladores; frequent profl. speaker on diabetes & nutrition in the Mexican Am. population; contbr. articles and pamphlets on nutrition (1984-86); Democrat; Prot.; rec: Spanish. Res: 8178 Heather Grove Ct Sacramento 95828 Ofc: Sacramento County Dept. of Health and Human Services 2251 Florin Rd Ste W Sacramento 95822

ELNICK, ALAN LEE, union representative; b. May 25, 1951, New York; s. Samuel and Mary Edith (Gronish) E.; m. Vicki Janice Samuel, Jan. 26, 1980; children: Michelle b. 1985; edn: BA, Bernard M. Baruch Coll. C.U.N.Y., 1974. Career: asst. to trustee Sheet Metal Workers Union, N.Y.C. 1976-79, special rep., San Francisco 1979-81; bus. agent Hosp. & Instnl. Workers Union, Oakland 1981-86; rep. Union of Am. Physicians & Dentists 1986-; chmn. San Lorenzo Unified Sch. Dist. LVN Tng. Program 1984-86; tchr. Los Medanos Adult Edn. Coll., Pittsburg 1983; mem: Am. Acad. Political & Social Sci., Am. Acad. Political Sci., Contra Costa Health Coalition (secty. 1989, dir. 1987-89), Jewish Comm. Rels. Council, San Francisco Labor Council, Alameda Labor Council, Contra Costa Labor Council, Internat. Platform Assn.; Democrat; Jewish; rec: tennis, golf, cooking. Res: 922 Reddington Ct Walnut Creek 94596 Ofc: Union of American Physician and Dentists 1330 Broadway Ste 730 Oakland 94612

EL-WARDANI, SAYED ALY, oceanographer; b. Feb. 26, 1927, Alexandria, Egypt; s. Aly M. and Bahgat (Elba) El-W.; m. Joan Margaret Newman, June 15, 1956 (div. 1973); m. Mary Elizabeth Houston, July 17, 1989; children: Ramsey Walter and Nile Regina b. 1957; Aladdin Sayed b. 1960; edn: BS hons., chem., Univ. Alexandria Egypt and Kings Coll. London 1948; UC Berkeley 1950-51; MS, Scripps Inst. Oceanography 1952; PhD, 1956. Career: instr. faculty of chemistry, Univ. Alexandria, Egypt 1948-49; asst. research prof., sr. oceanographer dept. oceanography, Univ. Wash., Seattle 1956-59; asst. prof. chemistry and environ. scis. San Jose St. Univ. 1959-63; staff scientist Lockheed Ocean Systems, Sunnyvale and San Diego 1963-68; assoc. prof. Calif. Western Univ., S.D. 1966-68; chief scientist, ptrn. Gen. Ocean Sci. & Resources Ins. 1968-74; mgr. internat. programs Lowry & Assoc., San Diego 1974-77; ptnr., environmental cons. Elwardani & Assocs., 1977-87, cons. environmental impacts, waste water mgmt. for So. Calif. and Orange Co. and Middle East countries; ret. 1987; mem: AAAS, Am. Chem. Soc., Am. Geophysical Union, Geochem. Soc., Marine Tech. Soc., Optimists Club; num. tech. and research articles and papers pub. in sci. jours.; Republican; Moselem; rec: tennis, swimming, travel. Address: 1730 Avenida Del Mundo Coronado CA 92118 also: 7248 Red Ledge Dr Paradise Valley AZ 85253

EMAMJOMEH, JAVAD S., computer company president; b. Aug. 20, 1951, Teheran, Iran; s. Abolghasem S. and Hormat (Raesi) E.; m. Azam Mirshojaee, Jan. 20, 1974; children: Tannaz, Ranna, Neda; edn: BS, Univ. So. Louisiana; HND, ITT (Iran). Career: mgr. Epic Computer, Lafayette, La. 1978-82; mgr. Triad Systems, Sunnyvale 1982-84; mgr. Mainstreet Systems, Carlsbad 1984-

86; pres. Computer Power, Ann Arbor, Mich. 1986-87; v.p. Salepoint, Del Mar 1987-88; pres., CEO Computer Profls., Carlsbad 1988-; rec: fishing.

EMERSON, ANN CRADDOCK, real estate broker; b. June 25, 1918, Lynchburg, Va.; d. Charles Granville and Cora (Fields) Craddock; m. Fletcher Burns Emerson, Dec. 21, 1940; children: Elliott, Charles; edn: BA, Randolph Macon Coll. 1939. Career: real estate broker Casey Properties, Houston, Tx. 1975-88; mem. Calif. Alumni Assn. of Ecole Internat., Alpha Omicron Pi; civic: Junior League Orange Co., Sherman Gardens (vol.), SPCA (bd. 1977-88), Bayou Bend Museum of Fine Arts (docent 1965-76); Republican; Presbyterian; rec: gardening, stockmarket. Res: 2391 Via Mariposa #3A Laguna Hills 92653

EMERY, DARA E., plant breeder; b. July 26, 1922, Los Angeles; s. Paul T. and Ruth A. (Hull) Emery; edn: BS, Calif. Polytechnic St. Univ., 1951. Career: tchr. Los Angeles City Schs. 1953-54; horticulturist Santa Barbara Botanic Garden 1955-81, plant breeder 1981-; horticultural advy. com. Jepson Flora of Calif. UC Berkeley 1987-; advy. com. Landscape Horticultural Program, Santa Barbara City Coll. 1979-; awards: Am. Iris Soc. Mitchell award 1977; mem: Santa Barbara Begonia Soc. (past pres.), Am. Begonia Soc., Am. Penstemon Soc. (dir. at large), Am. Rock Garden Soc., Am. Rose Soc., Santa Barbara Rose Soc., Santa Barbara Horticultural Soc., Channel City Club; author: Seed Propogation of Native Calif. Plants, (booklet) Lupinus Canyon Sunset a New Perennial for the Garden, 1977; editor, Wise Garden Ency., 1988; mil: pfc AUS 1942-45; rec: mysticism, model railways. Res: 517 W Junipero St #2 Santa Barbara 93105 Ofc: Santa Barbara Botanic Garden 1212 Mission Canyon Rd Santa Barbara 93105

EMERY, MYRON DELEUW, lawyer, author, lecturer; b. Aug. 12, 1927, Chgo.; s. Charles Eugene and Dora (Guettel) E.; m. Robin Ann Wein, Oct. 22, 1954 (div. 1976); children: Meg Erin b. 1960, Jason DeLewu b. 1962; edn: AB, Stanford Univ., 1952; JD, Univ. of Denver, 1956; admitted bar: Calif., N.Y., Dist. Col. Bar, U.S. Ct. of Internat. Trade, U.S. Supreme Ct. Career: atty. practicing in fields of bus. and communications law, Los Angeles; gen. counsel to Pub. Rels. Soc. of Am., So. Calif. Bdcstrs. Assn., The Advt. Club of Los Angeles, We. States Advt. Agencies Assn. Inc., Am. Advt. Fedn. we. region, Advt. Review Bd. of So. Calif.; faculty UCLA Ext.; former faculty Art Center Coll. of Design, Southwestern Univ., CSU Northridge, UC Santa Barbara, UC Riverside Ext., UC Irvine Ext.; guest lectr. on legal aspects of advt. USC Sch. of Bus. Adminstrn., numerous univs. and assns.; lectr. agy. fin. mgmt. seminars for Advertising Age in various cities U.S.; tchr. seminars the Learning Tree (non-profit instn.), L.A., and mem. interior design advy. bd.; bd. govs. Internat. Comm. Coll. (campuses in Italy, Fr., Austria, Ireland and Denmark); advy. bd. govs. Univ. of Tel Aviv Film and Comms. Sch., Israel; author chapters in books on advt.; contbg. editor and columnist for Designers West; columnist for Adweek, also B/PAA Communicator (Bus./Profl. Advt. Assn.); mem. Nat. Panel Arbs. of Am. Arbitration Assn.; appt. L.A. County Consumer Affairs Commn., exec. com. L.A. Police Crime Prevention Advy. Counsel, commr. Orange Co. Sheriff's Dept., and past commr. of advt. 1984 Olympics Citizens Advy. Commn.; mil: USN 1945-46. Ofc: 2049 Century Park East Ste 2400 Los Angeles 90067

ENEA, SANTO, dental technician; b. June 2, 1954, Pittsburg, Calif.; s. Joseph Paul and Rosa (Geraci) E.; edn: AA, Diablo Valley Coll. 1974; stu. Los Medanos Jr. Coll. 1978-80; desig: Dental Techn. Career: dental techn., lab. mgr. Yosemite Dent. Lab., Pittsburg, 1975-77, owner 1977-81; dental techn./owner Enea Dent. Lab., Pittsburg 1982-; mem. Nat. Assn. Dental Labs. 1978-84; civic: Pittsburg CofC (named Citizen of Year 1985), Sons of Italy, Pittsburg Bus. & Profl. Assn., Nat. Fedn. of Indep. Businessmen, Pittsburg Hist. Soc.; works: Italian-Am. Fishing Boat Monument (1984), Pittsburg Columbus Day Fest./Parade (84, 85, 86), Delta Fest. Fun Run (82, 83, 84, 85, 86); Democrat; R. Cath.; rec: genealogy. Address: Enea Dental Lab 112 Pueblo Dr Pittsburg 94565

ENGEL, ALBERT E., senior systems engineer for future space systems and technology; b. Jan. 24, 1929, Chgo.; s. Otto and Anna Angella (Andrich) E.; children: Ana Betty Turcios; edn: BSEE, Univ. So. Miss. 1957, MSEE, 1959. Career: tech. rep. Philco Corp., Phila. 1958-59; site mgr. RCA, Camden, N.J. 1959-63; engring. mgr. Aerojet Gen. Corp., Azusa 1963-72; pres./bd. chmn. Defense Systems, Inc., Marina Del Rey 1972-80; senior systems engr. TRW-Space & Technology Gp., Redondo Beach 1980-; currently assigned Mission Plans and Devel. Directorate for Future Space Devel. Washington DC 1988-; mem: National Space Club (Washington DC), Am. Astronautical Soc., Am. Inst. Aero & Astro., IEEE; author 3 major books (documents) mission R & D of conceptual satellites 1980-2020 mil. applications; var. classified mil. publs.; Republican; R.Cath. Res: 105 Woodrow St Taft 93268 Ofc: TRW Space & Technology Gp, One Space Park Redondo Beach 90278

ENGLISH, CHRISTOPHER B.M., biotechnology company executive; b. June 12, 1947, Beckenham, Kent, U.K.; s. Clifford William Frederick and Pamela Marguerite (Schrod) E.; m. Sandra E., Feb. 17, 1977; son, Daniel B.M. b. 1979; edn: BA (honors), Durham Univ., U.K., 1968. Career: advt. exec. G.D. Searle & Co., High Wycombe, Bucks., U.K., 1968-69, market res. asst. 1969-70, sales rep. 1970-71, coordinator overseas 1971-72; managing dir. Baird & Tatlock Ltd., Ndola, Rep. of Zambia, 1972-76; Euro. ops. mgr. G.D. Searle & Co., 1976-78; mktg. mgr. Bio-Rad Labs, Richmond, Calif. 1978-81, gen. mgr. 1981-83; dir. clin. cytometry Becton Dickinson, San Jose 1983-85, v.p. ops. 1985-90, v.p./gen. mgr. 1990-; Fellow Chartered Inst. of Mktg. (FCIM) London, U.K. 1987; mem: No. Calif. Cricket Assn. (v.p. 1980, capt. 1982), Marin Cricket Club (capt. 1980-81, 88, chmn. 1982-84), Lions Club 1973-76; rec: cricket, golf, drama, music. Ofc: Becton Dickinson Immunocytometry Systems, 2350 Qume Dr. San Jose 95131-1807

ENGLISH, DONALD MARVIN, loss control representative; b. July 31, 1951, Raleigh, N.C.; s. Marvin Lee and Lois (Woodard) E.; m. Rebecca Pritchard, Sept. 1970 (div. June 1977); edn: AA, Fresno City Coll., 1991; Miami Univ. 1969-70, 73-74; Univ. Cincinnati 1977-78; CSU Fresno 1980-83; Chartered Property & Casualty Underwriter, Soc. of CPCU, 1989. Career: ins. insp. Commercial Svs., Cinti. 1974-78; loss control rep. Ohio Casualty Ins., Fresno 1978-; mem. Am. Soc. Safety Engrs. 1982-, Soc. CPCU 1989-, East Fresno Exchange Club (pres. 1984-85); mil: sp5 US Army Security Agy. 1970-73; rec: travel. Res: 4417 N Teilman Ave Fresno 93705-1053 Ofc: Ohio Casualty 4420 N First St Ste 106 Fresno 93726

ENGORON, EDWARD DAVID, food service consultant, cookbook author and radio show host; b. Feb. 19, 1946, Los Angeles; s. Leo and Claire (Gray) E.; m. Charlene Scott, Oct. 7, 1970 (div. 1982); edn: BArch, USC, 1969, MBA, 1973, PhD, 1974; MA, Cordon Bleu, Paris 1975. Career: art director ABC, Los Angeles 1964-67, Paramount Pictures, 1967-68, Warner Bros. Pictures, 1968-69; mktg. dir. Lawry's Foods Inc., Los Angeles 1969-74; v.p. Warehouse Restaurants, Marina del Rey, 1968-72; pres. Perspectives, The Consulting Group Inc., San Francisco 1974-82, Los Angeles 1986-; pres. China Rose Inc., Dallas 1982-86; exec. v.p. T.G.I. Fridays Inc., Dallas 1986-87; pres., dir. and c.e.o. Guilt Free Goodies Ltd., Vancouver, B.C. 1986-90, Sugarless Co., Los Angeles 1987-90; pres. Sweet Deceit, Inc.; cons. The Southland Corp., Dallas 1982-86, Pizza Hut Inc., Wichita, Kans. 1975-87, Frank L. Carney Ents., Wichita 1982-87; co-host radio show The Food Show, KABC-AM 790; author cookbook: Stolen Secrets 1980; patentee Pasta Cooking Station 1981, microwave controller 1982; mem: Internat. Assn. of Culinary Professionals, Chaine des Rotisseurs, Foodservice Cons. Soc. Internat., Soc. Motion Picture Art Dirs., Food, Wine & Travel Writers Assn., Masons; civic: Los Angeles Parks (bd. govs. 1971-74), Fine Arts Commn., Tiburon (commr. 1974-76); Republican. Ofc: 11030 Santa Monica Blvd Ste 301 Los Angeles 90025

ENIS, BEN M., marketing educator; b. Jan. 5, 1942, Baton Rouge, La.; s. Ben, Sr. and Marjorie (Wood) E.; m. Randy K. Fetty, Sept. 1, 1962 (div. 1975); m. Sharon Lee Coleman, Jan. 8, 1977; 1 son, Ben M., III; edn: BS, MBA, and PhD, Louisiana St. Univ., 1963, 65, 67. Career: sales supr. So. Bell Tel. Co. 1964; tchg. fellow La. St. Univ. 1966; asst., assoc. prof., prof. Univ. of Houston, 1967-78; Howard Prof. Univ. of Mo. at Columbia 1978-82; vis. prof. Univ. Queensland, Brisbane 1982; prof. USC, 1982-; dir: Countrywide Credit Inc., Pasadena 1984-; tng. cons. L.A. Times 1986-; cons. US Bur. of Census, 1975-81; cons. (expert testimony) O'Melveny & Myers, L.A. 1983-85, 1987-89, Lane Powell, Seattle 1989; awards: Humble Oil doctl. fellow 1965-66, Ford Found. doctl. fellow 1966-67, tchg. excellence award Univ. Houston Faculty Senate 1973, list of top 20 Leaders in Marketing Thought, Marketing News (22/21/85), USC Dean's fellowship for tchg. excellence 1987-89, tchr. of yr. MBA Assn. Univ. Mo. 1978-79; mem: Am. Mktg. Assn., Mensa; coauthor: Marketing, 1985, ed. 7th edit. Marketing Classics, 1991, author: The Marketing Audit, 1991, 70+ articles in res. and tech. jours.; Libertarian; Deist; rec: scuba, skiing, swimming. Res: 4097 Robin Hill Rd La Canada 91011 Ofc: Univ. of So. Calif. University Park Los Angeles 90089-1421

ENNIS, C. BRADY, editor; b. Mar. 19, 1954, Alton, Ill.; s. Calvin Franklin and Virginia Jo (Moody) E.; edn: BA journ., Texas Christian Univ., 1978. Career: advt. copywriter Concordia Publishing House, St. Louis, Mo. 1978; display ad rep. Ft. Worth Star-Telegram, 1979; proofreader Deloitte Haskins & Sells, San Francisco 1980-83; assoc. editor ASU Travel Guide, 1983-86, mng. editor, 1986-89; copy editor Unix World Mag., Mountain View 1990; San Francisco General Hosp. 1991-92; Dept of Public Works 1992-; co-founder and publicist Different Spokes Bicycle Club, S.F. 1982-83; awards: Sigma Delta Chi citation best news story of yr. Texas Christian Univ. 1975, gay sports award Gay Sports mag., S.F. 1983; mem. S.F. Advt. Club 1983-89, Am. Advt. Fedn. 1983-89, Soc. Profl. Journalists 1986-89; rec: drawing, cycling. Res: 1086 Post St #209 San Francisco 94109

ENSMINGER, MARK DOUGLAS, chemist; b. Oct. 11, 1955, Escondido; s. Douglas Lloyd and Mary Theresa E.; m. Marsha Lynn Westerhold, Dec. 20, 1980; edn: BA in economics and BS in chemistry, UC Santa Barbara, 1977, AM in chem., Univ. Ill., 1979, PhD chem., 1982. Career: research chemist Chevron Oil Field Research Co., La Habra, Calif. 1982-86; engring. specialist Northrop Aircraft Div., Hawthorne 1987-91, Northrop B-2 Div., Pico Rivra 1991-; instr. 1990 ISFTA, L.A. 1990; cons. Getty Conservation Inst., Marina del Rey 1986-87; mem: Sigma Xi 1983-, Am. Chem. Soc. 1983-, Am. Physical Soc. 1983-,

Optical Soc. of Am. 1983-, Soc. for Applied Spectroscopy 1989-; contbr. articles to profl. jours.; Evangelical Free Ch.; rec: audio engring. Ofc: Northrop B-2 Div. Dept. W691/62 8900 E Washington Blvd Pico Rivera 90660-3737

ENSOR, KAREN JOYCE, college professor; b. Oct. 8, 1946, Oakland; d. William Dean and Charlotte Joan (Jacobs) Isom; m. William Evan Ensor, April 8, 1965 (dec. 1987); children: Karena b. 1974, Jeremy b. 1977; edn: BS, Western Baptist Bible Coll. 1969; BA, Am. Coll. Jerusalem 1970; MA, Am. Inst. Holy Land Studies 1975; MA, Holy Names Coll. 1976; EdD, Univ. San Francisco 1983. Career: social worker Ministry of Social Welfare, Jerusalem, Israel 1970-71; tchr. Acad. of Christian Edn., Oakland 1971-73; prof. Patten Coll. 1974-, chair dept. of profl. studies 1976-87, library club dir. 1975-76, com. chair Patten Coll. Library 1976-87; sch. cons. DeVoss Sch., San Jose 1981; dir. of credential Patten Coll. 1987-; awards: Patten Coll. hon. student 1965, Gold P 1968, Talent Piano 1969, service 1981, Outstanding Young Woman of Am. 1976; mem: Nat. Assn. Christian Edn., Am. Edn. Res. Assn., Assn. Christian Schs. Internat., Religious Edn. Assn., Phi Delta Kappa, Credential Counselors & Analysts of Calif., Christian Cathedral (ministry bd. co-dir.), Youth Coalition (conf. coordinator); publs: diss., thesis, profl. paper presentation (1979); Republican; Prot.; rec: skiing, swimming, crafts. Ofc: Patten College 2433 Coolidge Ave Oakland 94601

EPCAR, RICHARD, actor, writer, director; b. Apr. 29, 1955, Denver; s. George B. and Shirley (Learner) E.; m. Ellyn Jane Stern, Aug. 15, 1982; children: Jonathan b. 1983, Jacqueline b. 1987; edn: BFA in performing arts, Univ. Arizona, Tucson 1978; postgrad., USC, 1980, UCLA, 1981, Am. Film Inst., 1982. Career: pres. Trouble Shooter Productions, L.A. 1986-; actor (films) including Memoirs of an Invisible Man, D.C. Collins, Incident of War, Street Hawk, Escape to Love, Not of This World, (TV series) Cheers, General Hospital, Guns of Paradise, Matlock, Beverly Hills 90210, Who's Boss?, Sonny Spoons, Moonlighting, Highway to Heaven, Amazing Stories, Fast Times, Crazy Like a Fox, Hell Town, Stir Crazy, Santa Barbara, (on stage) Why a Hero, Dracula, An Evening With Lincoln, Real Inspector Hound, Richard II; actor, writer (stageplay) Take My Wife...Please!, 1980; writer, director English adaptation of Academy Award winning film: Cinema Paradiso; awards: Academy Award nominee - Women on the Verge of A Nervous Breakdown, Haldeman Found. scholar Univ. Ariz. 1973-78, named Nat. Best Actor of Year, Nat. Players 1977, CPC Repertory Group 1980, Irene Ryan Soloist award 1978; civic: L.A. Zoo Assn. 1983-91, Natural History Mus., L.A. 1989-91, Earth Save, L.A. 1990, L.A. Mus. Art 1991, host fall festival Sta. KCET-Pub. TV, L.A. 1980, active Am. Cancer Soc. Ofc: Trouble Shooter Prodns. PO Box 5429 North Hollywood 91616-5429

EPPERSON, VIRGIL OTEHL, JR., law enforcement executive; b. Nov. 26, 1946, Pine Bluff, Ark.; s. Virgil Othel Sr. and Lorena (Gipson) E.; edn: AA, Laney Coll., 1968; BA, CSU Hayward, 1970. Career: lt. Oakland Police Dept., 1981-86; chief of police City of Seaside, 1986-; awards: Nat. Academy, FBI, Quantico, VA 1987, Outstanding Law Enforcement Profl. Internat. Police Assn. 1990; mem: Nat. Orgn. of Black Law Enforcement Execs. 1986-, Monterey Co. Chief Law Enforcement Officers Assn. (secty. 1991-92), Calif. Police Chiefs Assn. 1986-, Rotary Internat.; Presbyterian. Res: 1059 Olympic Lane Seaside 93955 Ofc: Seaside Police Dept. 440 Harcourt Ave Seaside 93955

ERICKSON, ARTHUR CHARLES, architect; b. June 14, 1924, Vancouver, B.C., Canada; s. Oscar and Myrtle (Chatterson) E.; edn: Univ. Brit. Col., Vancouver 1942-44; BArch, McGill Univ., 1950; LLD (hon.) Simon Fraser Univ. 1973, Univ. Manitoba 1978, Lethbridge Univ. 1981, D.Eng. (hon.) Nova Scotia Tech. Coll., McGill Univ. 1971, Litt.D. (hon.) Univ. Brit. Col. 1985. Career: asst. prof. Univ. Oregon, Eugene 1955-56; assoc. prof. Univ. Brit. Columbia 1956-63; ptnr. Erickson-Massey Architects, Vancouver, B.C. 1963-72; prin. Arthur Erickson Architects, offices in Vancouver and Toronto, 1972-90, Los Angeles 1981-91; dir: Campus Planning Associates, Toronto; appt. com. on urban devel. Council of Canada, 1971; bd. dirs. Can. Conf. of Arts, 1972; design advy. council Portland Devel. Commn., Can. Council Urban Research; trustee Inst. Research on Pub. Policy; principle works: Canadian Pavilion at Expo '70, Osaka, Japan (1st prize nat. competition Can., best pavilion award Architectural Inst. of Japan), The Law Courts/Robson Square (honor award), Mus. of Anthropology (honor award), Eppich Residence (honor award), Habitat Pavilion (honor award), Sikh Temple (award of merit), Champlain Heights Community Sch. (award of merit); recipient Molson prize Can. Council for Arts 1967, Triangle award Nat. Soc. Interior Design, Royal Bank of Canada award 1971, Gold medal Tau Sigma Delta 1973, residential design award Can. Housing Council 1975, August Perret award Internat. Union of Architects' Congress 1975, Chgo. Architecture award 1984, Gold medal French Acad. Arch. 1984, Pres.'s award Excellence Am. Soc. Landscape Architects 1979, titled Officer and Companion Order of Canada 1973, 1981, McLennan Travelling scholar, Can. Council fellow 1961; subject of Time mag. cover article and New Yorker profile; mem: AIA (hon. Fellow, Pan Pacific citation Hawaiian chpt. 1963, Gold medal 1986), Royal Archtl. Inst. Can. (Fellow 1980, Gold medal 1984), Archtl. Inst. B.C., Ontario Assn. Architects, Royal Can. Acad. Arts (academician), Am. Soc. Iinterior Designers, Order des Architectes du Quebec, Am. Soc. Planning

Officials, Community Planning Assn. Can., Heritage Can., Planning Inst. B.C., Urban Land Inst.; clubs: Vancouver, U.B.C. Faculty, University; mil: served to capt. Can. Intelligence Corps 1945-46. Ofc: Arthur Erickson Architectural Corp. AE Architect Inc., PO Box 48007 Los Angeles 90048

ERICKSON, ERIC DOUGLAS, chemist; b. July 31, 1955, Astoria, Ore.; s. Douglas Leon and Patricia (Tiebes) E.; m. Barbara Marie Davenport, Sept. 3, 1977; children: Ivy b. 1980, Benjamin b. 1983; edn: BS in chem., Oregon State Univ., 1977; cert. indsl. hygiene, San Diego City Coll., 1980; PhD analytical chem., Mich. State Univ., 1989. Career: chemical technician Amtech Labs, San Diego 1977-78, asst. lab. mgr. 1978-80; res. chemist Naval Weapons Ctr., China Lake 1980-92, pollution abatement pgm. mgr. 1983-84; resrch. chemist, environmental R&D coord. Naval Air Warfare Ctr., China Lake 1992-; recipient long term tng. fellowship Naval Weapons Ctr. 1984-85; mem: Am. Chemical Soc. (1977-, Mojave Desert sect. treas. 1990-91), Sigma Xi (1981-, chapt. pres. 1992), Am. Soc. of Mass Spectrometrists 1986-; civic: Cub Scouts Ridgecrest (Webelos ldr. 1990-93), Sci. Explorer (post adv., Ridgecrest 1992-); inventor: Indicator Tubes for the Detection of TNT in Water (pat. 1984); author (24+) book chapters and sci. jour. articles (1982-91); rec: computer pgmg., reading. Res: 406 S Gordon Ridgecrest 93555 Ofc: Naval Air Warfare Ctr Weapons Div. Code C02353 China Lake 93555

ERICKSON, J. GUNNAR, lawyer; b. Dec. 2, 1946, Washington, D.C.; s. John L. and Sarah Lou (Glenn) E.; m. Barbara Keerins, July 5, 1981; children: Kyle b. 1982, Brent b. 1984; edn: BA, Stanford Univ. 1969; JD, Yale Law Sch. 1975; admitted St. Bar Calif. 1975. Career: atty. Fenwick Davis, Palo Alto 1975-79; Armstrong Hirsch & Levine, Los Angeles 1979-; adj. prof. Pepperdine Law Sch., Malibu 1989; co-author Musicians Guide to Copyright, 1983, contbr. How to Make Your Own Record, 1988, Musician's Manual, 1980. Ofc: Armstrong Hirsch & Levine 1888 Century Park E Ste 1888 Los Angeles 90067

ERICKSON, JAMES H., vice chancellor for university relations and development; b. May 18, 1939, Oak Park, Ill.; s. Chester E. and Ethyl M. (Jackson) E.; m. Janet J. Selburg, June 18, 1966; children: Michael James b. 1971, Richard James b. 1974; edn: BS, Bradley Univ., Peoria, Ill. 1961, MA, 1966; EdD, Indiana Univ., 1970. Career: dir. pub. info. Bradley Univ., Peoria, 1963-69, adj. prof. 1969-84, asst. to the pres. and chancellor, 1970-78, dean of student svs., 1978-82, assoc. v.p., 1982-85; dir. news bureau Indiana Univ., Bloomington, 1969-70, mag. editor: Chalkboard; v. chancellor univ. rel. and devel. UC Riverside, Calif. 1985-; dir. Riverside Co. Economic Devel.; cons. Council on Soc. for Advancement of Edn. (IL); dir. Illinois-Iowa Higher Edn. Consortium (IL); fundraising cons. colls. and charitable orgns., IL and CA, 1980-; commencement speaker for high schs., IL, 1970-85; awards: One of Ten Outstanding Young Men, IL 1971, Citizen of Yr. Peoria 1970, Distinguished service Urban League, IL, Pres.'s Cup United War IL 1978, Merger Award for Pub. Svc. IL 1981, Citizen of the Year, Riverside 1993; mem: Greater Riverside Urban League (pres. 1992), Gr. Riverside C.of C. (bd.), Raincross Club, Riv. Philharmonic Assn. (bd.), Coun. for Advancement and Support of Edn., Assn. of Urban Univs. (newsletter editor); author (Master Plan) "Illinois Private College," contbr. articles to edn. jours.; mil: s/sgt. US Army 1961-63; rec: jogging, basketball. Ofc: Univ. Calif. Riverside 900 University Ave Riverside 92521

ERIKSON, GREGORY ROBERT, corporate banking executive; b. Aug. 7, 1964, Chgo., Ill.; s. Robert Victor Erikson and Patricia (McPike) Hewlett; m. Cassie Diane McCollum, Sept. 22, 1991; edn: BBA, Calif. State Poly. Univ., Pomona (emphasis on mktg./fin.), 1986; Claremont Coll., Claremont, Calif. (minor in mil. sci.), 1987. Career: stockbroker Dean Witter Reynolds, Long Beach, Calif. 1987-88; internat. stockbroker Internat. Assets Advy. Corp., Irvine, Calif. 1989-90; asst. v.p./mgr. PFF Funding, Irvine, Calif. 1990; private banker Union Bank, City of Industry, 1990-19; asst. v.p., entertainment industries World Trade Bank, N.A., Beverly Hills, 1991-92; v.p./branch mgr. of corp./private banking Rancho Vista Nat. Bank, Orange, Calif. 1992-; cons. So. Calif., 1986-; awards: ranked #2 in So. Calif. by Dean Witter, Long Beach, Calif. 1988; mem: Calif. Rep. Party 1986-, Nat. Rifle Assn. 1986-, Indsl. League of Orange County 1990-, Orange County C. of C. 1990-, Amer. Marketing Assn. 1986-; civic: Sigma Chi Fraternity, Evanston, Ill., chapter adv. to Loyola Marymount univ. pres. and current alumni, 1986-92; active in Masonic Lodge #419, Upland, Calif.; author: frequent contributor to Bus. Sect. of Long Beach Press Telegram, 1987-91; mil: first lt. (promotable) AUS, armored cavalry br., 1987-; Republican; Lutheran; rec: scuba, skiing, sailing, golf, tennis. Res: 3625-J Bear St., South Coast Metro 92704

ERNST, ELDON GILBERT, seminary dean and professor; b. Jan. 27, 1939, Seattle; s. Kenneth Gilbert and Bydell (Painter) E.; m. Joy Skoglund, June 12, 1959; children: Michael b. 1962, David b. 1963, Peter b. 1968, Samuel b. 1973, Rachel b. 1982; edn: BA, Linfield Coll., 1961, MDiv, Colgate Rochester, 1964; MA and PhD, Yale Univ., 1965, 1968. Career: prof. American Baptist Sem., Berkeley 1967-82; Graduate Theological Union, 1982-90; dean and professor American Baptist Sem. of the West, Berkeley 1990-; ed., Foundations, Rochester, NY 1975-78; cons. Lutheran History Ctr. of the West, Berkeley 1984-; organizer and convenor GTU Archives Council, 1986-89; awarded

Howd Sociology Prize, Linfield Coll. 1961; mem: Am. Hist. Assn. 1988-, Am. Acad. of Religion 1974-, Am. Soc. of Church History 1967-, Calif. Hist. Soc. 1986-; author: Moment of Truth for Protestant America (1974), Without Help Or Hindrance (1977, 1987), Pilgrim Progression (1993), 30+ jour. and encyclopedia articles (1969-); Democrat; Prot.; rec: piano and singing. Res: 1855 San Antonio Ave Berkeley 94707 Ofc: Graduate Theological Union, 2400 Ridge Rd Berkeley 94709

ERSKINE, JOHN MORSE, physician; b. Sept. 10, 1920, San Francisco; s. Morse and Dorothy (Ward) E.; edn: BS, Harvard Univ., 1942; MD, Harvard, Boston 1945; Diplomate Am. Bd. of Surgery, 1953. Career: surgical intern Univ. of Calif. Hosp., San Francisco 1945-46; research fellow Mass. Gen. Hosp., Boston 1948; resident in surgery Peter Bent Brigham Hosp., 1948-53; Georg Gorham Peters Fellow, St. Mary's Hosp., London, England 1952; med. practice specializing in surg., San Francisco 1954-; asst. clin. prof. Stanford Med. Sch., S.F. 1956-59; asst., assoc. clin. prof. UC Med. Sch., San Francisco 1959-; surg. cons. S.F. Veterans Hosp. 1959-73; founder No. Calif. Artery Bank, 1954-58; mem. Irwin Memorial Blood Bank Commn., 1969-74; bd. dirs. Am. Cancer Soc., S.F. 1963-75; mem: S.F. Surgical Soc. (1956-, v.p. 1984), Pacific Coast Surgical Assn. 1968-, Am. Coll. Surgeons 1956-, S.F. Med. Soc. (1954-, bd. 1965-75), Calif. Med. Assn. 1954-; civic: Greenbelt Alliance S.F. (bd. 1984-), Dorothy Erskine Open Space Fund (chmn. advy. coun. 1988-); author chpts. in books, articles in profl. jours. (1950-); mil: capt. US Army 1946-47; Unitarian; rec: mountaineering, tree farming. Res: 233 Chestnut St San Francisco 94133 Ofc: 2340 Clay St San Francisco.

ESPOY, HENRY MARTI, chemist; b. Oct. 22, 1917, San Francisco; s. Angel Sama and Concepcion (Marti) E.; m. Wilma Johnson, July 15, 1945; children: Mark b. 1951, Yale b. 1957; edn: BS, Loyola Univ. 1939; MA, UCLA 1941. Career: research chemist Van Camp St. Food, Triminal Island 1940-49; tech. dir. Barnett Labs, Long Beach 1950-57; ptnr. Terminal Testing Labs., L.A. 1957-69; dir. Daylin Labs. 1969-76; ptnr. Associated Lab., Orange 1976-; dir. DePar Corp. 1976-; mem: Inst. Food Technologists, Am. Chem. Soc., Am. Oil Chemistry Soc., Assn. Official Analytical Chemists, Elks; 4 patents, num. tech. papers pub.; Republican; rec: walking. Ofc: Associated Laboratories 806 N Batavia Orange 92668

ETCHESON, CRAIG CARLYLE, social scientist; b. June 28, 1955, Huntington, N.Y.; s. Kenneth Carlyle and Rosemarie (Dickson) E.; edn: Spoon River Coll. 1973; BA, Univ. Ill. 1977; MA, 1979; PhD, USC 1985. Career: mgr. data processing RPS Electronics, Los Angeles 1979; instr. USC 1980-89; tech. staff Jet Propulsion Lab., Pasadena 1984; database adminstr. Pacific Telesis, Los Angeles 1985-88; mgr. bus. systems Paramount Pictures, Hollywood 1988-; res. assoc. Inst. Transnational Studies, Los Angeles 1980-; cons. Center for Public Internat. Edn. 1982; Vietnam Vets. of Am. 1983; Computer Tng. Splst. 1984; N. Am. Rockwell 1984; ABACUS Programming Corp. 1985; awards: Univ. Ill. Merriam fellowship 1977, USC Hermann fellowship 1978, Harris fellowship 1980, Haynes Found. 1981, Pi Sigma Alpha; mem: Am. Assn. Artificial Intelligence, Internat. Studies Assn., Am. Political Sci. Assn., Acad. Political Sci., Internat. Political Sci. Assn.; author: Arms Race Theory, 1989, Rise & Demise of Democratic Kampuchea, 1984, num. articles in profl. jours., PhD diss. on Strategy and Structure of Behavior, 1985. Ofc: Paramount Pictures 5555 Melrose Ave Balaban 113 Los Angeles 90038

ETTLICH, WILLIAM F., consulting engineer; b. Jan. 7, 1936, Spokane, Wash.; s. Fred E. Ettlich and Dorothy S. (Olney) Nicholls; m. Dianne L. Lawton, Aug. 24, 1958; children: Pamela b. 1970, Daniel b. 1971; edn: BSEE, Ore. St. Univ. 1957; Harvard Bus. Sch. 1973; reg. profl. engr. Ore., Calif., Nev., Ohio and Colo. Career: project engr. CH2M Hill, Corvallis, Ore. 1959-65; pres. Neptune Micro Floc 1965-74; v.p. CWC, Cameron Park 1974-86; CWC HDR Inc. 1986-87; sr.v.p. HDR Engring. 1987-; dir. CWC 1980-85; trustee CWC ESOT 1980-86; sr. mem. IEEE, ISA; v.p. Marshall Hosp. Found.; club: Rotary (pres. 1987-88); U.S. patents held; articles pub. in tech. jours.; mil: capt. AUS 1957-59; Republican; Presbyterian; rec: sports, skiing. Res: 3417 Strolling Hills Rd Cameron Park 95682 Ofc: HDR Engineering, Inc. 4922 Robert J. Mathews Pky El Dorado Hills 95630

EU, MARCH FONG, state official; b. Mar. 29, 1927, Oakdale; d. Yuen and Shiu (Shee) Kong; children: Matthew Kipling, Marchesa Suyin; edn: BS, UC Berkeley, M.Ed, Mills Coll., EdD, Stanford Univ., postgrad. work Columbia Univ., CSC Hayward; Calif. State Teaching Creds., Jr. Coll. Adm.-Supr. Career: div. chmn. Univ. California Medical Ctr., San Francisco; dental hygienist Oakland Public Schs.; div. supr. Alameda County Schs.; lectr. Mills College; mem. (pres. 1961-62) Alameda Co. Bd. of Edn. 1956-66, pres. Alameda County Sch. Bds. Assn. 1965; spl. cons. Calif. State Dept. Edn.; education, legislative cons. Santa Clara Co. Office of Edn., Sausalito Public Schs., others 1962-66; elected rep. to Calif. State Legislature 15th Assem. Dist., 1966-68, 70-72; elected Calif. Secty. of State, 5 terms, 1974-94; apptd. Calif. Chief of Protocol, 1975-83; chair Calif. State World Trade Commn., 1983-; bd. councillors USC Sch. of Dentistry; awards: Eastbay Intercultural Christian Fellows outstanding achiev.intercultural & interracial relations, Hearst Newspapers' Phoebe

Apperson Hearst Bay Area Disting. Bay Area Women of Yr., Sacto. Dist. Dental Soc. honor award, Calif. Chiropractic Assn. legislative merit, appreciation Calif. R.E. Assn., Lamplighter Award for achiev. in crime prevention Oakland R.E. Bd., V.F.W. Nat. Loyalty Day Award, svc. to edn. Alameda Co. Edn. Assn., achiev. L.A. Chinese Drum and Bugle Corps, Outstanding Legislator of 1973 Calif. Assn. of Marriage and Family Counselors, service March of Dimes, Hon. Law Degree We. State Univ. Coll. of Law of San Diego, service to comm. Irish Israeli Italian Soc. of S.F., Disting. Alumni Calif. Community Coll. and Jr. Coll. Assn., Hon. Law Degree Univ. San Diego Sch. of Law, annual award Nat. Notary Assn., Daisy award Calif. Lndscp. Contrs. Assn., Milton Shoong Hall of Fame humanitarian of yr. 1981, citizen of yr. Council for Civic Unity S.F. Bay Area 1982, woman of achiev. in govt. Calif. Asian/Pac. Womens Network 1983, Democrat of Yr. San Mateo Dem. Cent. Com. 1983, C.A.R.E. Award 1985, leadership S.F. Filipino-Am. C.of C. 1985, woman of yr. Democrats United San Bdo. 1986, disting. service Rep. of Honduras 1987, outstanding Asian Am. Byanihan Jaycees of L.A. 1987, achiev. Calif. Dem. Party Black Caucus 1988, Ladies' Home J. list of America's 100 Most Important Women 1988, BSA L.A. Co. Good Scout Award 1989, spl. appreciation Union of Viet. Student Assns. of So. Calif. 1990, comm. leadership Torat-Haijun Hebrew Acad. 1990, spl. appreciation Nat. Assn. Chinese Am. Bankers 1990, Orange Co. Buddhist Assn. 1990; mem: Am. Dental Hygienists Assn. (pres., life), No. Calif. State Dental Hydienists Assn. (life), L.W.V./ Oakland, Delta Kappa Gamma, AAUW (Oakland br. area rep. in edn.), Calif. Tchrs. Assn., Alameda Co. School Bds. Assn. and Calif. Sch. Bds. Assn., Calif. Interagency Council on Family Planning, Calif. B.P.W. (Woman of Achiev. Golden Gate chpt.), Nat. Womens Political Caucus (outstanding woman 1980), Mental Health Assn. of Alameda Co., Navy League (life), Ebell Club (L.A.), Hadassah (life, woman of achiev. L.A. chpt. 1983); hon. mem: L.A. Advt. Women and Am. Advt. Fedn., Chinese Retail Food Mkts. Assn., So. Calif. State Dental Assn., Calif. Agricultural Aircraft Assn., Calif. Landscape Contrs. Assn., Calif. Women for Agriculture, Folsom Hist. Soc., Phi Alpha Delta Law Frat. Intl., Soroptimist; Democrat (del. Nat. Conv. 1968, exec. com. Calif. Dem. Central Com.). Ofc: 1230 J Street Sacramento 95814

EUSTICE, JOSEPH ANDREW, hotel company executive; b. Jan. 21, 1950, Belmont, Wis.; s. Robert Raymond and June May (Speth) E.; m. Annette Jane Mies, Sept. 9, 1989; 1 dau., Tara b. 1963; edn: BA bus. adminstrn., Univ. Wis. 1972. Career: asst. mgr. Ariz. Inn., Tucson 1978-81; gen. mgr. San Marcos Corp., Chandler, Ariz. 1981-84; Marriott Corp., Fremont 1984-86, La Jolla 1986-88, dist. mgr. 1988-; mem. Marriott Bus. Council 1988-; awards: San Diego C.of C. 2% plus 1987; mem: Fremont Philharmonica (bd. dirs. 1984-86), Fremont C.of C. (bd. dirs. 1984-86), Rotary (internat. rels.); Republican. Res: 2821 Camino Del Mar 82 Del Mar 92014 Ofc: Residence Inn by Marriott 8901 Gilman Dr La Jolla 92037

EVANS, JAMES WILLIAM, metallurgical educator; b. Aug. 22, 1943, Dobcross, Yorkshire, England, naturalized U.S. citizen 1976; s. James Hall and Alice Maud (Dransfield) E.; m. Beverley Lynn Connor, July 22, 1967 (div. 1978); m. Sylvia Marian Johnson, Jan. 5, 1985; children: James b. 1971, Hugh Edmund b. 1987, Claire Meredith b. 1989; edn: BSc chemistry, Univ. of London, Eng. 1964; PhD chem. engring., SUNY at Buffalo, 1970. Career: tech. advisor Internat. Computers, Ltd., London, Eng. 1964-65; chemist Cyanamid of Canada, Ltd., Niagara Falls, Ont., Can. 1965-67; engr. Ethyl Corp., Baton Rouge, La. 1970-72; asst. prof. 1972-76, assoc. prof. 1976-80, prof. metallurgy, dept. mats. sci. and mineral engring. UC Berkeley, 1980-, dept. chmn. 1986-90; prin. investigator Mats. and Chem. Scis. Div., Lawrence Berkeley Lab, 1977-; awards: C.C. Furnas Memorial fellow SUNY, Buffalo 1969-70, extractive metallurgy science award of AIME for best paper 1973, 83, Champion H. Mathewson Gold Medal of Metallurgical Soc. of AIME 1984; mem: Am. Inst. Chem. Engrs., The Minerals, Metals and Materials Soc., The Electrochem. Soc., Iron and Steel Inst. of Japan; inventor, patentee (with G. Savaskan) Battery Using a Metal Particle Bed Electrode (1991); author 150+ tech. publs. Ofc: Dept. Materials Science and Mineral Engineering, Univ. of California, Berkeley 94720 Tel: 510/642-3807

EVERDING, ROBERT GEORGE, university dean; b. Apr. 25, 1945, St. Louis, Mo.; s. R. G. and Elizabeth Jane (Lehman) E.; m. Sarah Page Monroe, June 1, 1969; children: Brian b. 1974, Julia b. 1977; edn: BA, Univ. Mo., Columbia 1967; MA, Univ. Minn., 1969; AM, Stanford Univ., 1972, PhD 1976; lifetime secondary edn. credentials, Mo. and Calif., 1967. Career: program dir. humanities Univ. of Houston, Clear Lake, Tx. 1976-84; external reviewer Univ. of Tx., Dallas 1983; artistic director Houston Shaw Festival, Houston 1978-84; dir. Sch. of Art and Architecture, Univ. of Southwestern Louisiana, Lafayette, La. 1984-88; dean Coll. of Visual & Performing Arts, Humboldt State Univ., Arcata, Calif. 1988-91, dean CSU Summer Arts Program 1989-91, course dir. CSU Faculty Arts Exchange 1992-93 prin. investigator Redwood Arts Project, Arcata (1991-, dir. Redwood Arts Proj. 1992-93); mgmt. bd. Center Arts, Arcata 1988-92; honors: Omicron Delta Kappa 1975, Phi Beta Kappa 1976, Phi Kappa Phi 1991, Am. Bus. Women Assn. bus. assoc. of year, Redwood Chpt. 1991, listed Who's Who in West 1992; mem: Bernard Shaw Soc. 1983-, Phi Beta Kappa Soc., Phi Kappa Phi Soc., Stanford Alumni Assn.; civic bds: Humboldt

Arts Council (bd. dirs. 1988-91), City of Arcata Design Review Com. (chair 1988-92), Acadiana Arts Council, Lafayette, La. (bd. 1986-88), Boy Scouts Am. (asst. scoutmaster 1985-8 publs: (play) Kindergarden (1985), articles in nat., internat. jours. (1979-), editor "Arts Review" UH/CLC Arts (1980-84); mil: sp5 US Army 1971-74. Res: 2711 Hilltop Ct Arcata 95521 Ofc: Humboldt State University, Arcata 95521

EWALD, WILLIAM RUDOLPH, development consultant; b. Jan. 10, 1923, Detroit, Mich.; s. William Rudolph and Rhea Elizabeth (Allen) E.; m. Janeth Hackett, 1948 (div. 1969); dau., Annalisa b. 1953; m. Katharina Clark, 1975 (div. 1976); edn: ScB civil eng., Brown Univ., 1943; grad. work Univ. Mich., Ann Arbor; degree cert. Harvard Univ. Career: decision support systems: sole prop. William R. Ewald Development Consultant, WDC, Santa Barbara, (currently) Los Angeles, 1963-, clients include Edison Electric Inst., NASA, EPA, Commerce, Interior, HEW, US Pub. Health Svc., NSF, Conservation Found., Gen. Electric, Exxon, Am. Inst. of Architects, Am. Inst. of Planners, Weyerhaeuser, Ark. Indsl. Devel. Commn., Commonwealth of Puerto Rico, Gov. Nelson R. Rockefeller, Gov. Winthrop Rockefeller, Appalachian Regional Commn., N.Y. State Office Reg. Planning, Baltimore County, Md., Tom's River, N.J., Albuquerque, N.M., Columbus, Ind.; vis. fellow Ctr. for the Study of Democratic Instns., Santa Barbara, 1970; lectr. Univ. Texas Sch. of Arch., 1971; mem. policy bd. Change in Liberal Edn. Project (Carnegie Corp.) 1973-76; awards: James Manning Scholar, Brown Univ. 1943, Lambda Alpha hon. internat. land econs. frat. 1960, citation Ark. Indsl. Devel. Commn., Little Rock, Ark. 1957; spl. design award Southwest Printing & Graphic Arts Assn. 1959; commendn. Housing & Home Finance Agy. 1960; resolution Am. Inst. of Planners (1966, 67); Earth Day principal speaker Sch. of Arch. Univ. of Mich. 1968; spl. design award (film) Mexico Olympics 1968; nat. lectr. Danforth Found. 1970-72; prin. investigator NSF 1973-76; citation Am. Revolution Bicentennial Award 1976; club: Cosmos (W.D.C. 1969-); works: (author/illustrator childrens' book) Neighbor Flap Foot the City Planning Frog (1952), The Arkansas Ency. (4 vol. reference, 1958), Change Challenge Response, 60 Years Development Policy in New York State (1964), Environment For Man, Environment and Change, Environment and Policy (3 vols., commissioned, edited 1967-68), Signals in The Environment (exhibit USPHS, 1967), Street Graphics (book & film, 1971, HUD Spl. Design Award 1972), A Whole New Way To Think (video, 1978), Street Graphics & The Law (coauthor book, 1988), 100 Short Films About the Human Environment (editor book, 1981), contbr. articles in Brown Alumni Monthly (11/69), Information, Perception & Regional Policy (1976), Ekistics (1976), Computer Graphics World (4/82); mil: s/sgt. US Inf. 1943-46; Episcopal; rec: sailing, skiing. Ofc: 1888 Century Park E #1900 Los Angeles 90067

EWELL, A. BEN, JR., lawyer, businessman; b. Sept. 10, 1941, Elyria, Ohio; s. Austin Bert and Mary Rebecca (Thompson) E., Sr.; desc. John Ewell, b. 1734, Scotland, settled in Plymouth Co., Mass. 1751; children: Austin B., III b. 1978, Brice B. b. 1982; edn: BA, Miami Univ. 1963; LLB, JD, UC Hastings Coll. of Law 1966; admitted Calif. State Bar 1966, US Dist. Ct., E. Dist. Calif. 1967, US 9th Circuit Ct. Appeals 1967, US Supreme Ct. 1982. Career: atty., ptnr. law firm McCormick, Barstow, Sheppard, Wayte & Carruth, Fresno 1970-84; pres. A.B. Ewell, Jr., APC, 1984-; ceo Millerton New Town Devel. Co. 1987-; pres. Brighton Crest Country Club 1990-; past general counsel various water dists. and assns.; appt. Task Force on Prosecution, Courts and Law Reform, Calif. Council on Criminal Justice 1971-74, Fresno County Econ. Dev. Corp. 1987-, Fresno County Water Advy. Com., San Joaquin River Flood Control Assn. (chmn. 1984-88), San Joaquin Valley Agri. Water Com. 1979-88, U.S. SBA Nat. Advy. Council (1981-, co-chmn. 1981-82); mem: Am. Bar Assn., Calif. Bar Assn., Fresno County Bar Assn., Sigma Nu Alumni Assn.; civic: Commonwealth Club of Calif., Citizens for Community Enrichment (bd.) Fresno, City-County Hist. Soc., Fresno City-County C.of C., Fresno State Univ. Pres.'s Club and Bulldog Found., St. Agnes Medical Ctr. Found. (advy. council), Univ. Calif. Valley Medical Education Found. (trustee), Rotary Intl., Firelands Hist. Soc., Spirit of '76 Museum and Hist. Soc., Fresno Met. Museum of Art, History & Sci. (trustee 1983-89, sustaining); pub. research: "The Sufferers Lands" (hist. and settlement of Huron and Erie Cos., OH); Republican (State Central Com. 1974-76, State Exec. Fin. Com. 1988-, Fresno Co. Central Com. treas./exec. com. 1971-72, past v.p. Calif. Repub. Assn. of Fresno, chmn. The Lt. Gov.'s Club Fresno Co. 1980, campaign chmn. var. campaigns; Congregational; rec: hist. research, antique books, guitar, jogging. Ofc: 516 W. Shaw Ave., Ste 200 Fresno 93704

FAGIN, DAVID KYLE, mining executive; b. April 4, 1938, Dallas, Tx.; s. Kyle Marshall and Francis (Gaston) F.; m. Margaret Ann Hazlett, Jan. 24, 1959; children: Kyle b. 1959, Scott Edward b. 1966; edn: BS petroleum engring., Univ. Okla. 1960; So. Methodist Univ. 1968; Am. Inst. Banking 1966-67. Career: engr. Bednar Petroleum Cons., Dallas, Tx. 1959-63, ptnr. 1963-65; bank ofcr. First Nat. Bank 1965-68; v.p. oil and gas Rosario Resources, Greenwich, Conn. 1968-75, exec.v.p., COO 1975-78, pres., COO 1978-80, 80-82; chmn., CEO Fagin Exploration Co., Denver, Colo. 1982-86; dir., pres. and COO Homestake Mining Co., San Francisco 1986-; dir: T. Rowe Price mutual funds, Balt., Md. 1987-, Homestake Gold of Australia, Adelaide

1986-; mem: Internat. Lightning Class Assn. (commodore 1980), Am. Inst. Mining Engrs. (chmn. endowments com.), Soc. Mining Engrs., Am. Petroleum Inst., Dallas Geological Soc., Soc. Petroleum Engrs. (pres. 1970); civic: BSA (dir. 1989), San Francisco C.of C. (dir. 1989-), United Way (v.chmn. S.F.); clubs: Pacific Union (S.F.), World Trade (S.F.), Commonwealth (S.F.), Petroleum (Dallas and Denver); Republican; United Methodist (bd. chmn. 1979); rec: fishing. Res: 2382 Ironwood Pl Alamo 94507 Ofc: Homestake Mining Co. 650 California St San Francisco 94108

FAHDEN, NANCY MARIE, county supervisor; b. July 14, 1923, Martinez; d. Antonio and Jennie (Fontana) Cardinalli; m. Wilbur J. Fahden, Oct. 15, 1945; children: Antone b. 1946, Lyall b. 1949; grad. Alhambra H.S., Martinez. Career: registrar Alhambra High Sch., Martinez 1941-45; elected Contra Costa Co. Board of Supervisors, 1977-, first woman elected in 125 yr. hist. of co.; currently mem. bds.: Assn. Bay Area Govts., CC Med. Services Jt. Conf. Com., CCC Mental Health Advy. Bd., LAFCO, CCC Solid Waste Commn.; recipient appreciation awards: VFW 1988, Kiwanis Club Martinez 1988, Peace Officers Assn. 1984, Nutrition Proj. for Elderly 1984, Contra Costa Co. Child Care Council (1987 Kiddie Award), Contra Costa Co. Bd. Suprs. 10-yr. service 1987, John Muir Memorial Assn. conservation award 1986, Contra Costa Dental Soc. 1986, Martinez Boys Club citizen award 1974, woman of yr. Martinez C.of C. 1975, woman of yr. Rodeo C.of C. 1984, J.C. Penney Co. Golden Rule Award 1985, Nat. Women's Polit. Caucus 1985, Rubicon Programs Inc. pub. service award 1985, others; Democrat; Christian; rec: walking, jogging, gardening. Res: 1153 Hillside Dr Martinez 94553 Ofc: Contra Costa Co. 805 Las Jumtas St Martinez 94553

FALCONE, ALFONSO BENJAMIN, physician; b. July 24, Bryn Mawr, Pa.; s. and Elvira (Galluzzo) F.; m. Patricia J. Lalim, Oct. 22; children: Christopher L., Steven B.; edn: AB chem. (distinction), Temple Univ., 1944, MD (hons.), 1947; PhD biochem., Univ. Minn., 1954; Diplomate Am. Bd. Internal Medicine subspecialty bd. endocrinology and metabolism. Career: med. intern Phila. Gen. Hosp. 1947-48, resident int. med., 1948-49; tchg. fellow internal medicine Univ. Hosp., Univ. Minn., 1949-51; asst. clin. prof. med. Univ. Wis., Madison 1956-59, assoc. clin. prof., 1959-63, asst. prof. Inst. Enzyme Research, 1963-66, vis. prof. 1966-67; med. practice splst. in endocrine and metabolic diseases, Fresno, Calif. 1968-; staff Fresno Community Hosp. (chmn. dept. med. 1973), St. Agnes Hosp., Valley Med. Ctr.; awards: NIH postdoctoral fellow 1951-53, NIH res. grantee 1958-68; Fellow ACP; mem. AMA, Am. Soc. Biochemistry and Molecular Biology, Soc. Clin. Res., Am. Fedn. Clin. Res., Am. Chem. Soc., Am. Soc. Internal Medicine, Am. Assn. for Study Liver Disease, Am. Diabetes Assn., AAAS, Calif. Acad. Medicine, Sigma Xi, Phi Lambda Upsilon, Assn. for Acad. Excellence, Univ. Calif. Fresno Com., Fresno Co. Assn. for Univ. Calif. Campus, Archeol. Inst. of Am.; contbr. articles to med. jours., senior corr. Ettor Majorana Ctr. for Sci. Culture, Erice, Italy; mil: US Army 1944-46, lt. comdr. Med. Corps USNR 1954-56. Ofc: 2240 E Illinois Ave Fresno 93701-2191 Tel: 209/486-0666

FALERO, FRANK, economist, educator; b. Dec. 22, 1937, New York; s. Frank Falero and Lydia M. (Camis) Del Castillo; children: Lisa Ann b. 1963, Sara Francine b. 1968; m. Verna Downing, Whittier, Nov. 22, 1990; edn: AA, St. Petersburg Jr. Coll. 1962; BA hons., history, Univ. S. Fla. 1964; MS, Fla. St. Univ. 1965; PhD, 1967; Career: asst. prof. VPI & SU, Blacksburg, Va. 1967-72; Fulbright scholar Univ. del Pacifico, Lima, Peru 1968-69, res.economist Fed. Reserve, Richmond, Va. 1968; prof. economics and finance CSU Bakersfield, 1972-; economist, Springville 1972-; vis. prof. Univ. Colo., Boulder 1976; commentator KERO TV, Bakersfield 1979-; awards: Golden Mike 1985, CAPTRA excellence 1984, APTRA excellence 1986; 30+ articles and 7 monograms pub. (1964-); mil: AUS 1955-58; rec: scuba diving, skiing. Res: POB 950 Springville 93265

FALICOV, LEOPOLDO MAXIMO, physicist, educator; b. June 24, 1933, Buenos Aires, Argentina, naturalized U.S. citizen 1967; s. Isaias Felix and Dora (Samoilovich) F.; m. Marta Alicia Puebla, Aug. 13, 1959; children: Alexis and Ian; edn: Liceniado chemistry, Buenos Aires Univ. 1957; PhD physics Cuyo Univ. Inst. J.A. Balseiro, Argentina 1958; Cambridge Univ.1960; ScD, Cambridge Univ., Eng. 1977. Career: resrch. assoc. dept. physics Inst. Study Metals, Univ. Chicago 1960-61, instr. physics 1961-62, asst. prof., assoc. prof., prof. physics 1962-69; prof. physics UC Berkeley, 1969-, Miller res. prof. 1979-80, chmn. dept. physics 1981-83; cons. internat.; awards: Alfred P. Sloan Found. fellow 1964-68, vis. fellow Fitzwilliam Coll., Cambridge, Eng. 1966, Fulbright fellow 1969, OAS vis. prof. Argentina 1970, Nordita vis. prof. Univ. Copenhagen (1971-72, 87), Fulbright lectr. Spain 1972, Guggenheim fellow 1976-77, vis. fellow Clare Hall, Cambridge, Eng. 1976-77, exchange prof. Univ. Paris (1977, 84); mem: Third World Acad. Scis. (fellow), Nat. Acad. Sci. (U.S. 1983), Royal Danish Acad. Scis. and Letter Academico Correspondiente, Academia Nacional de Ciencias Exactas, Fisicas y Naturales, Argentina 1990; author: Group Theory and Its Physical Applications (1966), La Estructura Electronica de los Solidos (1967); contbr. articles in profl. jours. Res: 90 Avenida Dr Berkeley 94708 Ofc: Univ. Calif. Dept. Physics, Berkeley 94720 Tel: 510/642-5993

FALLON, RICHARD, utility financial executive; b. Aug. 23, 1953, Los Angeles; s. James John and Frances Odelia (Naiseller) F.; m. Pamela Ellen Friedman, June 22, 1975; children: Seric b. 1977, Michele b. 1980; edn: BA, UCLA 1974; MS, Stanford Univ. 1975; PhD, Rand Corp. Inst. 1980. Career: res. assoc. Rand Corp., Santa Monica 1975-80; internat. mgmt. cons. econ. and fin./dir. mgmt. consulting Coopers & Lybrand, W.D.C. 1980-84, San Francisco 1984-87; dir. fin. mgmt. Pacific Telesis Group 1987-88; c.f.o. Pacific Bell Information Services Group, San Ramon 1988-; honors: Phi Beta Kappa, Calif. State Fellow 1975-80; PhD diss: Rule Based modeling as an analysis tool, pub. Rand Corp. (1980); Republican; R.Cath. Address: San Ramon 94583

FALLON, WILLIAM MICHAEL, seafood packing co. executive; b. Dec. 2, 1946, Pittsburgh, Pa.; m. Rebecca Sudimack, June 13, 1970; edn: BS, Carnegie Mellon Univ.; MBA, Iona Coll. N.Y. Career: H.J. Heinz & General Foods, 1968-82; gen. mgr. Star Kist Foods, Long Beach 1982-87, v.p. adminstrn. 1987-88; chief fin. ofcr. Heinz Pet Products 1988-90; v.p. quality and bus. development Starkist 1990-. Ofc: Starkist Seafood 180 E Ocean Blvd Long Beach 90802

FAN, CHRIS, science company president; b. Jan. 5, 1946, Shin Chu, Taiwan; nat. 1980; s. Chin-Li and Shin-Yin (Lin) F.; m. Sylvia, July 21, 1969; 1 son, Felix b. 1975; edn: BS, Nat. Taiwan Univ. 1968; PhD, Purdue Univ. 1973. Career: research assoc. MIT, Cambridge, Mass. 1973-77; sr. devel. chemist Beckman Instruments Inc., Carlsbad 1977-82; pres. Pacific Biotech Inc., San Diego 1982-; awards: Arthur Young & Venture entrepreneur of year 1988; mem: Inst. Am. Entrepreneurs, Am. Assn. Clin. Chemistry, La Jolla Chamber Music Soc.; patent held for diagnostic system (1989); mil: 2d lt. Air Force Taiwan 1968-69; rec: music, tennis. Ofc: Pacific Biotech Inc. 9050 Camino Santa Fe San Diego 92121

FAN, HUNG Y., biologist, cancer research director; b. Oct. 30, 1947, Beijing, China; s. Hsu Yun and Li Nien (Bien) F.; edn: BS, Purdue Univ., 1967; PhD, M.I.T., 1971. Career: postdoc. fellow M.I.T., Cambridge, MA 1971-73; asst. resrch. prof. Salk Inst., San Diego 1973-81; asst. prof. to full prof. biology Univ. Calif. Irvine 1981-, dir. UCI Cancer Research Inst., 1985-; cons. venture capital firms 1989-; mem. grant rev. panels NIH 1979-, Am. Cancer Soc. 1986-90; awards: Woodrow Wilson fellow 1967-68, Helen Hay Whitney fellow 1971-73, AAAS fellow 1992; mem. AAAS 1985-, Am. Soc. Microbiology 1978-, Am. Soc. Virology 1985-, Am. Cancer Soc. (Orange Co. chpt. bd. 1986-90); author: Biology of Aids (1989, 2d edit. 1991), 80+ jour. articles & revs. (1969-), symp. editor: Viruses That Affect the Immune System (1991); Democrat; rec: chamber music. Ofc: Dept. Molecular Biology & Biochemistry Univ. Calif., Irvine 92717

FARGHER, LAWRENCE LE ROY, real estate broker; b. Sept. 16, 1932, Helena, Montana; s. Lawrence Arthur and Maude Cecilia (Lauson) F.; m. Camille Marie Augusta, May 16, 1953; children: Larry Lee (dec.), b. 1954; Leighton Lynn, b. 1956; Lauson Layne, b. 1957; Lindel Lee, b. 1959; Laure Lynne, b. 1962; edn: BS, Univ. Nebr., Omaha 1954; MBA, Univ. Santa Clara, 1965; designations: CRB & CRS, Nat. Assn. of Realtors 1979, GRI & RECI, Calif. Assn. of Realtors. Career: navigator, aircraft performance engr., USAF 1955-8; engr. Boeing Airplane Co., Wichita 1958; engring. writer, Polaris Launcher, Westinghouse, Sunnyvale 1958-62; hd. systems engring. United Technology Ctr., Sunnyvale 1962-71; owner Realcom Assoc. (gen. real estate brokerage), Santa Clara 1969-; real estate instr. (Lifetime Com. Coll. Cred.), West Valley and Mission Colls.; city councilman 1962-71, mayor 1964-5, City of Santa Clara; awards: Realtor of Year, San Jose R.E. Bd. 1982, various civic awards; mem: San Jose Bd. Realtors (pres. 1983, dir. 1984-7), Calif. Assn. of Realtors (dir. 1969-, regl. v.p. 1986), Nat. Assn. of Realtors (dir. 1987-); contbr. articles in Real Estate Today (NAR), and California Real Estate (CAR); mil: 1st Lt. USAF, S.A.C. 1955-8; Republican (State Central Com. 1968-, Reagan del. to nat. conv. 1976, 80, 84); R.Cath.; rec: hunting, fishing. Res: 2831 Fargher Dr Santa Clara 95051 Ofc: Realcom Associates, 830 Kiely Blvd, Kiely Center, Santa Clara 95051

FARHA, JIMMIE LEROY, commercial real estate brokerage president; b. Feb. 12, 1932, Alva, Okla.; s. Henry S. and Saada Elizabeth (Zakoura) F.; m. Patricia A. Connor, Sept. 14, 1957; children: Jimmie, Jr., b. 1958; Catherine, b. 1961; edn: BA, Wichita Univ., 1954; MA, Webster Univ., 1974. Career: comptroller Travis AFB 1975-77; mgr. Ashwill- Burke, Vacaville 1978-82; broker/mgr. Bishop-Hawk, Vacaville 1982-87; owner/pres. Farha Commercial Real Estate, 1987-; appt. Solano County Grand Jury 1988; recipient award for spl. service Calif. Human Devel. Group 1983; mem: No. Solano Co. Bd. of Realtors, Bay Area Brokers Assn., Solano Commercial Brokers Assn., Council of Military Orgns. (chmn. 1982-83), Air Force Assn. (pres. 1989-90, Community Leader of Yr. award 1982); civic: United Way Vacaville (chmn. 1989), Solano Economic Devel. Corp. (dir. 1987-), Private Industry Council Solano Co. (dir. 1983-, chmn. 1985-87), Vacaville C.of C. (pres. 1987-88, dir. 1983-), Ctr. for Employment Training (indsl. rels. advy. bd. 1982-84), Travis Air Mus. (dir. 1989-); clubs: Rotary Internat. (dir. 1982-83, Paul Harris Fellow), Masons (Hiram Award 1988), Shriners; mil: col. USAF 1954-77, decorated Disting. Service, D.F.C., 8 Air medals, 2 USAF Commendns., Vietnam; rec: walking, swimming. Res: 560 Ridgewood Dr Vacaville 95688 Ofc: Farha Commercial Real Estate, 348 Cernon St Vacaville 95688

FARIES, MCINTYRE, judge, ret.; b. Apr. 17, 1896, Wei Hsien, Shantung, China, Am. parents; s. Wm. Reid and Priscilla Ellen (Chittick) F.; desc. of Wm. Faries, emigre from No. Ireland to S. Caro., 1767; m. Margaret Lois Shorten (dec. 1964), Oct. 7, 1922; m. 2d Geraldyne Brewer Bergh (dec. 1980), Dec. 3, 1965; children: Barbara Lois Simpson b. 1925, Marjorie Anne Gaines b. 1929, edn: BA, Occidental Coll. 1920; law stu. USC 1923, JD, Southwestern Univ. of L.A., 1926; admitted Calif. St. Bar, US Dist. Ct. (So. dist. Calif.), US Circuit Ct. (9th cir.), US Supreme Ct. Career: assoc. counsel Automobile Club of So. Calif., 1922-24; dep. public defender L.A. County, 1924-26, dep. county counsel, 1926-27; instr. law Southwestern Univ. 1926-27; pvt. law practice, 1927-53: Faries and Williamson, later Faries, Williamson & Musick; David R. Faries; sr. ptnr. Faries & McDowell, later Faries, Hackett and Hubbard; judge Superior Ct. of Calif. 1953-67: presiding judge (120 judges) 1961-64, Appellate Dept. 1965-67, ret.; sitting by assignment of Judicial Com., 1968-; mem: L.A. Co. Bar Assn., ABA (met. cts. com., Cont. Edn. of Judiciary sem. 1963), Conf. of Calif. Judges (Found. trustee 1965-67), Am. Judicature Soc., Am. Law Inst.; honors: Phi Beta Kappa, Phi Delta Phi, Phi Gamma Delta, Legion Lex USC, hon. mem. Chinese Am. Citizens Alliance (L.A. Lodge), hon. mem. Hwa Pei (N.China) Benevolent Assn. of So. Calif.; civic: Plaza de Los Angeles Inc., non-profit orgn. for preserv. of Olvera St. and L.A. Plaza area (1928-53) and successor orgn., El Pueblo de Los Angeles (exec. com./pres. 1953-68, bd. chmn. 1968-), LA City 184th Birthday Celebration (El Presidente, 1965), Los Amigos del Pueblo non-profit, El Pueblo Park Assn. non-profit corp. (dir.), El Pueblo de Los Angeles St. Hist. Monument Commn. (founder mem., co-chmn. bd. trustees, pres. 1967-69), Calif. Bicentennial Commn. 1969-, L.A. Co. Bicentennial Commn. 1969-, L.A. Pueblo Park Commn. (pres. 1969-72), Calif. St. Park & Rec. Commn. 1968-69, Gov.'s Conf. on Calif.'s Changing Environ. (chmn. Panel on Air 1969); mem. Pasa. Tournament of Roses (patron), L.A. World Affairs Council, Masons, Am. Legion, Calif. Hist. Soc., Hist. Soc. of So. Calif., USC Law Alumni Assn.; past civic bds: Central City Com. (L.A. redev.), Helms Found. (trustee 1950-69), L.A. Presbyn. Hosp. Com., L.A. Memorial Coliseum Commn. (past pres., 1946-53), S.Pasa.-San Marino H.S. Bd. of Edn. (past pres., 1940-49), Occidental Coll. (trustee), OC Alumni Assn. (past pres.), 6th Dist. Agri. Assn. of Calif. (past pres.), Calif. Water Assn. (past pres.); clubs: Lincoln, San Marino City, Oneonta (past pres.); mil: ensign USNRF 1918-19, WWI, active Republican 1936-53: Calif. chmn. Wendell Wilkie for Pres., 1940, Geo. Murphey for U.S. Senator, v. chmn. St. Central Com. (1938), pres. Calif. Repub. Assem., del Repub. Nat. Conv. (1936, 40, 44, 48, 52), exec. com. election campaigns for Gen. Eisenhower 1952, R.M. Nixon (for Cong., Sen., V.P.), T.F. Kuchel (for Sen.), Wm. F. Knowland (for Sen. 1946, state chmn. 1952), Hon. Earl Warren (for gov. 3t). Res: 2954 E Del Mar Blvd Pasadena 91107

FARLEY, BARBARA SUZANNE, lawyer; b. Dec. 13, 1949, Salt Lake City, Ut.; d. Ross Edward and Barbara Ann (Edwards) F.; m. Arthur Hoffman Ferris, Apr. 9, 1982; children: Barbara Whitney b. 1986, Taylor Edwards b. 1988; edn: BA, Mills Coll., 1972; JD, UC Hastings Coll. of Law, 1976; admitted bar: Calif. 1976. Career: extern Calif. Supreme Ct., San Francisco 1975; atty., assoc. Pillsbury, Madison & Sutro, S.F. 1976-78; Bronson, Bronson & McKinnon, S.F. 1978-80; Goldstein & Phillips, S.F. 1980-84; ptnr. Rosen, Wachtell & Gilbert, S.F. 1984-89; of counsel Lempres & Wulfsberg, Oakland 1989-; arbitrator U.S. Dist. Ct., no. dist. Calif., S.F. 1980-, S.F. Superior Ct. 1985-, judge pro tem S.F. Mcpl. Ct. 1982-; settlement panelist S.F. Bar Assn. 1987-; hearing ofcr., probation monitor Calif.; awards: editorial scholar Hastings, mng. editor Hastings Constnl. Law Qtrly. 1975-76; mem: ABA, S.F. Bar Assn., Alameda Bar Assn., Am. Trial Lawyers Assn., S.F. Com. for Better Govt.; pub. article in Cont. Edn. of the Bar 1985; speaker Nat. Business Inst. 1993; avocation: artist. Ofc: Lempres & Wulfsberg 300 Lakeside Dr Ste 2400 Oakland 94612

FARMER, JANENE ELIZABETH, artist, educator; b. Oct. 16, 1946, Albuquerque, NM; d. Charles Watt and Regina M. (Brown) Kruger; edn: BA art, San Diego State Univ., 1969; tchg. credentials, SDSU, 1984, UC San Diego, 1985. Career: freelance artist, San Diego 1970-, environment art: paintings of rare and endangered animals from around the world; instr. UC San Diego, La Jolla (1979-83, 1992-); tchr. Diocese of San Diego, 1984-87, Ramona Unified Sch. Dist., Ramona 1987-; awards: Calif. Arts Council grantee, UC San Diego Resident Artist 1980-81, Coronado Art & Humanities Council 1983, Univ. San Diego grad. fellow 1984; design affil. Am. Soc. Interior Designers 1980-, mem. Calif. Tchrs. Assn. 1987-; Democrat; R.Cath.; rec: the arts, nature, sports. Res: 4435 Nobel Dr Ste 35 San Diego 92122

FARNUM, NICHOLAS ROBERT, statistician, educator, consultant; b. Dec. 19, 1946, Bremerhaven, Ger.; s. Charles Wm. and Doreen Jean (Spencer) F.; edn: BA math. (cum laude), UC Irvine 1969; PhD, 1975. Career: postdoctoral res. fellow Sch. Pub. Health & Hygiene Johns Hopkins Univ., Balt. 1975-76; prof. dept. mgmt. sci., CSU Fullerton, 1976-; sr. statistician Ford Aerospace, Newport Beach 1983-85; cons. Ford Aerospace, McDonnel Douglas, Carter Hawley Hale, 1976-; mem: Am. Statistical Assn., Am. Soc. Quality Control, Ops. Res. Soc. Am.; author: Quantitative Forecasting Methods (Duxbury Press 1989), num. articles pub. in profl. jours. (1976-); rec: jogging, volleyball, music. Ofc: Dept. Mgmt. Sci. California State University Fullerton 92634

FARSADI, NAY, educational institute president; b. Oct. 15, 1946, Tehran, Iran, nat. 1979; d. Mohammad A. and Kobra (Pirouzian) Shirkhani; children: Lisa b. 1968, Laura b. 1974; edn: AA, Citrus Coll., 1968; BSBA, CSU Los Angeles, 1970; C.P.A. Calif. 1972, real estate lic. 1980. Career: U.S. tax mgr. and audit mgr. Price Waterhouse and Price Waterhouse Internat. in Los Angeles, Houston and Iran, 1970-78, lectr. Price Waterhouse seminars on U.S. taxes for Am. citizens employed by lg. U.S. corps. abroad 1973-78; pres. LCP Internat. Inst., Irvine 1978-, dir. 3 divs: English Language Studies, Ednl. Contract Adminstrv. Svcs., and Internat. Educative and Profl. Tng. Inst.; cons. to internat. sponsors in area of language tng., acquisition, orientation, intercultural communication and pgm. mgmt., 1979-; mem: Am. Inst. CPAs, Tchrs. of English to Speakers of Other Languages (TESOL), Nat. Assn. Fgn. Student Advisors (ATESL chair W.Coast Reg. 1987-88, local arrangements com. chair exhibs. NAFSA Nat. Conf. Long Beach 1987), Am. Mideast Ednl. & Tng. Svc. Inc.; publ: U.S. Tax Booklet for U.S. Citizens Abroad, Price Waterhouse (1975-76); Moslem; rec: flying (lic. pvt. pilot), tennis, swimming, jogging, skiing (snow, water). Res: 27521 Lost Trail Laguna Hills 92653 Ofc: LCP International Institute, 930 AT&T Tower, 8001 Irvine Center Dr Irvine 92718

FASSEL, VELMER ARTHUR, physical chemist, professor and science administrator emeritus; b. Apr. 26, 1919; s. Arthur Edward and Alma (Poppitz) F.; m. Mary Alice Katschke, July 25, 1943; edn: BA, S.E. Missouri State Univ., 1941; PhD, Iowa State Univ., 1947. Career: chemist Manhattan Project, Iowa State Univ., Ames 1942-47, mem. faculty Manhattan Project, Iowa State Univ., 1947-, Disting. prof. sci. and humanities, 1986, prof. chemistry, emeritus sr. scientist, 1986-; sect. chief Ames Lab. US Dept. Energy, 1966-69, dep. dir. Ames Lab. Energy and Mineral Resources Research Inst. 1969-84, prin. scientist Ames Lab. 1984-87, ret.; titular mem., secty., chmn. Commn. Spectrochemistry; Methods of Analysis, Internat. Union Pure and Applied Chemistry; awards: Disting. Alumni S.E. Mo. State Univ. 1965, award Spectroscopy Soc. Pitts. 1969, Maurice F. Hasler award 1971, Anachem award 1971, IR-100 award Res. and Devel. Mag. 1986, Iowa Gov.'s Sci. Medal, Iowa State Univ.'s Disting. Achievement Citation 1987, Eastern Analytical Symp. award 1987; mem: AAAS (Fellow), Optical Soc. Am. (Fellow), Soc. for Applied Spectroscopy (Ann. medal 1964, Strock medal 1986), Am. Chem. Soc. (Fisher award 1979, Chem. Instrumentation award 1983, Iowa award 1983, Analytical Chem. Div. award in Spectrochem. Analysis 1988), Japan Soc. Analytical Chemistry (Hon. mem., medal 1981), Assn. Official Analytical Chemists (Harvey Wiley award 1986), Am. Inst. Physics, Sigma Xi; author 10 patents, 212+ sci. rsch. publs. (on analytical atomic emission and absorption spectroscopy, spectroscopic instrumentation, analytical chemistry), coauthor 1 book. Res: 17755 Rosedown Pl San Diego 92128

FATEMAN, RICHARD J., professor of computer science; b. Nov. 4, 1946, N.Y.C.; m. Martha, June 15, 1968; children: Abigail b. 1971, Johanna b. 1974; edn: BS, Union Coll., 1966; PhD applied math., Harvard Univ., 1971. Career: lectr. math. dept. M.I.T., 1971-74; prof. computer sci., electrical engring. and comp. scis. dept. UC Berkeley, 1974-; mem. Sigma Xi, SIAM, Assn. Computing Machinery; publs: 50+ jour. articles. Ofc: EECS Dept. T021 Univ. California, Berkeley 94720

FATERI, FARDAD, university executive, cross-cultural and organizational behavior expert; b. July 12, 1964, Tehran, Iran; s. Mohammad and Farideh (Miri) F.; m. Farnaz Abdollahi, Nov. 17, 1989; edn: BA, UC Irvine, 1985; MA, CSU Fullerton, 1987; PhD, U.S. Internat. Univ., San Diego, 1989. Career: constrn. supt. New World Developers, Hawthorne, Calif. 1984-86; exec. asst. to the CEO, TiGeh Corp., Tehran, 1986-88; adj. prof. U.S.Internat. Univ., 1988-, grad. advisor 1988-89, asst., then dir. USIU Orange County Ctr., Irvine 1989-, actg. dir. USIU L.A. Co. Ctr., Eagle Rock, 1991-; civic bds: City of Irvine Multi-Cultural Task Force 1990-, Hist. and Cultural Found. of Orange Co. (bd. dirs. 1990-), Iranian New Year Task Force (Irvine coordinator 1989-); pub. articles in profl. jours. incl.: Alternatives to Deadly Force (1990), Methods Dealing with Cross-Cultural Concerns (1990), The Politics of Diversity: From the Melting Pot to the Salad Bowl (1992), The Future of Cultural Diversity: A Paradigm Shift (1992); rec: tennis and volleyball, collect bronze sculptures, community svc. Res: 5 Haggerstone Irvine 92715 Ofc: U.S.I.U., 2500 Michelson Dr Bldg 400 Irvine 92715

FATTORINI, HECTOR OSVALDO, researcher, mathematics professor; b. Oct. 28, 1938, Buenos Aires, Argentina, naturalized U.S. citizen 1980; s Osvaldo Franco and Concepcion (Marti Ros) F.; m. Natalia Lubow Karanowycz, Nov. 4, 1961; children: Maria Elena b. 1961, Sonia b. 1962, Susana b. 1965; edn: lic. in math. scis. Univ. de Buenos Aires, 1960; PhD math., New York Univ., 1965. Career: adj. prof. Univ. Buenos Aires, 1965-66; res. asso. Brown Univ., 1966-67; asst. prof. to full prof. Univ. Calif. Los Angeles, 1967-; prof. titular Univ. of Buenos Aires, Argentina 1973-75; editor and referee sev. scientific jours., revs. for Math. Reviews and Zentralblatt fur Mathematik; rev. Nat. Sci. Found. proposals; awards: ann. research grantee NSF 1967-; mem: Union Matematica Argentina 1958-, Circulo Unidad (Buenos Aires, 1962-), Am. Math. Soc. 1962-, Soc. for Indsl. and Applied Math. 1965-; author: The Cauchy Problem (1983), Second Order Linear Differential

Equations in Banach Space (1985), 60+ sci. papers in various jours. incl. Comm. Pure Appl. Math., SIAM Jour. Control Optim., Math Zeitschrift, others; rec: music. Res: 14701 Whitfield Ave Pacific Palisades 90272 Ofc: Dept. Mathematics Univ. California, Los Angeles 90024

FAUCETT, RALPH EUGENE, physician/naval officer; b. July 28, 1916, Milton, Ind.; s. Clark A. and Iva Mabel (Bertsch) F.; m. Elizabeth C. Carpenter, June 1, 1941; edn: BS, Indiana Univ. 1938; AB, Earlham Coll. 1939; MD, Indiana Univ. 1942; med. lic. Ind. 1943, Ill. 1946, Calif. 1947. Career: intern US Navy Hosp., Great Lakes, Ill. 1943-44, resident internal medicine USN Hosp., San Diego 1946-49, Univ. Pa. Postgrad. Sch. Medicine, Phila. 1950; served to rear admiral USN Med. Corps, retired 1974, decorated Legion of Merit w. Gold Star, Presdl. Unit Citation w. 2 gold stars, Unit Comment.; mem: A.C.P. (life), Royal Soc. Medicine (London), N.Y.C. Acad. Medicine, Theta Chi (v.p. 1932-34), Psi Chi; articles pub. in med. jours.; Republican; Lutheran; rec: photography. Res: 2363 Crescent Dr San Diego 92103-1011

FAUL, DAVID CHARLES, logistics systems analyst, educator; b. July 24, 1936, Hastings, Mich.; s. Charles Ludwig and Geneva (McQuarrie) F.; m. Helen Schultz, June 11, 1960; children: James b. 1962, Jeffrey b. 1964, Scott b. 1965; edn: BBA, Univ. Mich., 1958, MBA, 1959; USN War Coll. Naval Commd. & Staff, 1972; Cert. Profl. Logistician (CPL) Soc. of Logistic Engrs. Career: served to comdr. U.S. Navy 1959-81: shipbd. supply ofcr. USS Mahan (DLG-11) San Diego 1960-62, adminstrv. asst. Naval Supply Depot Seattle 1962-64, shipbd. supply ofcr. USS Preble (DLG-15) San Diego 1964-66, fin. mgr. Fleet Mat. Support Office Mechanicsburg, Pa. 1966-69, inventory control ofcr. Naval Supply Depot Guam 1969-71, instr. and student Naval War Coll. Newport, R.I. 1971-74, aviation repairables pgm. mgr. Phila. 1974-77, supply ofcr. Naval Air Sta. Point Mugu, Calif. 1977-80, inventory & fin. mgr. Naval Support Forces Antartica 1980-81, decorated Meritorious Service 1980; sr. project engr. Hughes Aircraft Co., El Segundo 1981-87; program mgr. Automated Scis. Group, Camarillo 1987-88; logistics analyst Science Applications Internat. Corp., Camarillo 1989-92; Technology Applications Inc. 1992-93 ; bus. adminstrn. lectr. and asst. dean COBM, West Coast Univ., 1988-, instr. LaVerne Univ., 1992-; active Boy Scouts Am. (commr. Camarillo Dist. 1984-90, commr. Ventura County Council 1990-92), Silver Beaver Award 1991, Dist. Award of Merit 1987; mem: Nat. Contract Mgmt. Assn., Soc. of Logistic Engrs. (chpt. chmn. 1990-92), Assn. of Naval Aviation, Missile Tech. Hist. Assn. (bd. 1990-), Point Mugu Fed. Credit Union (bd. chmn. 1987-90), Am. Red Cross Ventura Co. (bd. 1990-), Sigma Alpha Epsilon Frat., Toastmasters, Optimist Club (v.p. Oxnard 1981-82); publs: ed. corresp. course Defense Economics & Decision Making 1974; Republican; Methodist. Res: 1310 Lantana Camarillo 93010 Ofc: Veda, Inc. Camarillo 93010

FAUST, G. THOMAS, executive; b. Sept. 22, 1931, Mt. Carmel, Ill.; s. Gilbert Sefton and Helen Esther (Morray) F.; m. Barbara Lee Roberts, May 9, 1956; children: Jonathan Scott b. 1956, Gilbert Sefton b. 1960, David Thomas b. 1963, Nina Marie b. 1964; edn: BA, UCLA 1953; MBA, 1961. Career: account exec. Hixson & Jorgensen, Los Angeles 1956-62; pres., CEO Faust Day Advt., 1962-68; v.p. Foremost McKesson Inc., S.F. 1968-70; founder, COO Intra Leisure Inc., Redondo Beach 1970-72; Pennsylvania Co., NYC 1972-75; co-founder, ptnr. Enterprise Mgmt. Group, LA 1975-85; Holley & Faust, Redondo Beach 1985-88; owner, CEO G. Thomas Faust & Assoc. Inc., Rancho Santa Fe 1988-; dir. Base 8 Inc., San Diego 1989; guest prof. Claremont Coll. 1980-81; faculty USC Bus. Sch., 1972-74; UCLA Sch. Bus. 1964-66; mil: 1st lt. AUS 1953-56; Republican; rec: golf, skiing, oenology. Res: 1347 Camino Teresa Solano Beach 92075 POB 2832 Rancho Santa Fe 92067 Ofc: 5330 Carroll Canyon Rd Ste 200 San Diego 92121-3758

FAWCETT, J. SCOTT, real estate developer; b. Nov. 5, 1937, Pittsburgh, Pa.; s. William Hagen and Mary Jane (Wise) F., Jr.; m. Anne Mitchell, Dec. 30, 1960; children: Holly b. 1961, John (1965-1983); edn: BS, Ohio State Univ. 1959. Career: dist. dealer rep. Shell Oil Co., San Diego 1962-66; dist. real estate rep. Shell Oil, Phoenix 1967-69; region real estate rep. Shell Oil, San Francisco 1970-71; head office land investments rep. Shell Oil, Houston 1972-75; pres./CEO Marinita Devel. Co., Newport Beach 1976-; lectr. in land devel. related fields; mem: Internat. Council of Shopping Centers (ICSC), Inst. of Business Appraisers, Nat. Assn. of Review Appraisers and Mortgage Underwriters, Calif. Lic. Contractors Assn., Building Indus. Assn., Internat. Right of Way Assn., Internat. Inst. of Valuers, Am. Assn. of Certified Appraisers, Urban Land Inst., Nat. Assn. Real Estate Execs. (pres. L.A. chpt. 1975), US C.of C., Town Hall of Calif., Internat. Platform Assn., Toastmasters (pres. Scottsdale, Ariz. Club 1968, pres. Hospitality T. Club, San Diego 1964), Univ. Athletic Club, Ohio State Univ. Alumni Assn., Phi Kappa Tau Alumni Assn.; mil: M.P., US Army, Mil. Dist. of Wash. 1960-61; Republican; R.Cath.; rec: antiques, tennis, ski. Res: 8739 Hudson River Circle Fountain Valley 92708 Ofc: Marinita Development Co. 3835 Birch St Newport Beach 92660

FEARN, DEAN HENRY, mathematics educator; b. June 8, 1943, Portland, Oreg.; s. Clyde Henry Fearn and Sylvia Adele (Dahl) Christensen; m. Gloria June Wilber, Oct. 1, 1966; children: Neal b. 1971, Justin b. 1976; edn: BS,

Univ. Wash., Seattle 1965; MA, Western Wash. Univ., Bellingham 1967; PhD, UC Davis, 1971. Career: tchg. asst. Western Wash. Univ., 1965-66, Univ. Calif. Davis, 1967-71; senior mathematician Aerojet-General, Rancho Cordova, Ca. 1970; prof. CSU Hayward, 1971-; honors: Pi Mu Epsilon 1965; mem: Am. Stat. Assn. (pres. S.F. chapt. 1991-92), Math. Assn. Am. 1980-, Inst. of Math. Stats. 1980-, SPC Apple computer club Fremont (pres. 1992-93); contbr. articles in profl. jours. (1971-); Democrat; Lutheran; rec: computers. Res: 3255 Sunnybrook Ct Hayward 94541 Ofc: Dept. Statistics, Calif. State University, Hayward 94542

FEATHER, LAWRENCE STEVEN, company executive director; b. Jan. 4, 1955, Hackensack, N.J.; s. Leo and Della Bertha (Shupetsky) F.; m. Barbara Lynn Krone, June 26, 1982; edn: BA (cum laude), Boston Coll., 1977, MEd (hons.), 1978; postgrad. U.S. Internat. Univ., San Diego. Career: child welfare specialist Dept. Soc. Svs., Brockton, Mass. 1978-79; sales/purch. Manor Steel Corp., Park Ridge, Ill. 1979-83; personnel adminstr. Kevan Industries, L.A. 1983-84; cons. Mark Miller & Assocs., Van Nuys 1985-87; personnel tng. supr. Walden Environment, Mission Hills 1987-88, district dir. 1988-92; executive dir. Inner Circle Foster Family Agy., Van Nuys 1990-; mem: Am. Psychol. Assn., Soc. for Industrial & Organizational Psychologists, Personnel & Industrial Relations Assn., Calif. State Psychol. Assn.; Jewish; rec: golf, tennis, books, travel. Res: 20737 Roscoe Blvd Ste 201 Canoga Park 91306

FEE, SUSAN K., art consultant, landscape architect; b. March 14, 1956, Sidney, N.Y.; d. John Cary and Rachel Ann (Burbank) Youmans; m. William Edward Fee, Oct. 12, 1980 (div. 1989); edn: BS cum laude, environ. sci., St. Univ. N.Y. 1978; B.Arch. cum laude, 1979. Career: landscape architect Marmon Mok & Green, Houston, Tx. 1980-83; John Blevens Assoc., Fremont 1984-85; gallery dir. Victor Fischer Gallery, Oakland 1985-87; western mgr. Calif. Fine Art Directory, San Francisco 1987; art cons. Editions Ltd. 1988, 1989-; we. mgr. Kraus Sikes Publishers The Guild 1989-; seminar leader Am. Soc. Landscape Architects, Yosemite Valley 1989, Landscape Architect and Specifier News mag. conf., Las Vegas, Nev. 1987; awards: Am. Soc. Landscape Architects Hon. Service 1988, Calif. Fine Arts Directory Hi Sales 1987; mem: Pub. Art Works (bd. dirs. 1989-92), Am. Soc. Landscape Architects, Toastmasters, N. Montrose Civic Assn., Chi Omega; ed. The Guild 1989, landscape architect San Antonio airport 1983; Democrat; rec: clothes designing, flying, travel. Res: 279 Mangels Ave San Francisco 94131

FEICHTMEIR, EDMUND FRANCIS, retired agricultural chemist; b. July 6, 1915, Ainsworth, Iowa; s. Edmund and Emma (Theis) F.; m. Barbara Elizabeth Wright, Jan. 20, 1943; children: Wendi b. 1946, Kurt b. 1949, Janis b. 1952, Kris b. 1956; edn: BA, UC Berkeley 1937; PhD, 1947. Career: agri. chemist Shell Oil, Modesto 1947-50, field devel., NYC 1950-52, mgr. product devel., Denver, Colo. 1953-57, Modesto 1957-72, mgr. consumer product and agri. research Shell Devel. Co. 1972-79; mem: Ripon Council (councilman 1965-72, mayor 1972-89), Lions; mil: lt. USN 1942-46. Res: 408 Linda Ripon 95366

FEILDER, CLIVE LEE, (screen name: LEE MASON), screen producer, writer; b. Jan. 10, 1939, Brentford, England, perm. resident U.S., 1968-; s. Rt. Hon. Arthur Leonard Feilder (14th Earl of Denbigh) and Lady Dorathy Florence (Packer) Hagger; m. Kathlean M. Quillan, Oct. 4, 1972 (dec. 1980); children: Rachel Eden b. 1974; m. Florence Thorsteinson, Sept. 7, 1991; edn: British GCE, Sir Godfrey Kneller Private, London 1953; BA, Kingston Art Coll., London 1957; MA, Univ. St. Thomas, U.S. Virgin Islands, 1966. Career: head instr. Ron Bailey Sch. Broadcasting, San Jose 1975-76; instr. De Anza Coll., San Jose 1985-87; art director Molesworth Films, USA and Hong Kong, 1986, Artistic Films, Sacramento, Calif. 1987, Transbay Pictures, L.A. 1987-, Penny Ante Films, L.A. 1987-; video producer Ancha Audio Video, Chgo. 1989-91; screen writer, self-empl., Santa Cruz 1991-; awards: Best Designer Set (for 1st film) No. Calif. Film Board, S.F. 1987, Best poem Great Poems Am., Sacto. 1991; mem. Free Lance Writers Union 1979-, Writers Guild Am. 1986-; author: (book) How Far to Neptunas, 1976, (t.v. plays) Chicken Little Comedy Hour, 1976, (radio play) High Wire Radio Choir, 1977, (TV series) It's A Wrap, 1991, (book) Box Car of Dreams, 1992; mil: flt. lt. Royal Air Force 1957-62; Unitarian; rec: writing, theater, sailing, travel. Ofc: Edenwood Productions PO Box 67145 Scotts Valley 95067-7145

FEIMAN, THOMAS EDWARD, certified public accountant; b. Dec. 21, 1940, Canton, Ohio; s. Daniel Thaviu and Adrienne (Silver) F.; m. Marilyn Judith Miller, June 26, 1966; children: Sheri b. 1969, Michael b. 1971; edn: BS econ., Univ. Pa. 1962; MBA, Northwestern Univ. 1963; C.P.A. Calif. 1965. Career: staff auditor Arthur Young & Co., Los Angeles 1963-66; field auditor I.R.S. 1966-68; owner Thomas Feiman CPA 1968-69; ptnr. Wideman Feiman & Co. 1969-74; pres., stockholder Wideman Feiman Levy Sapin & Ko 1974-; sr. instr. UCLA 1968-85; honors: Beta Gamma Sigma, Delta Sigma Rho, Pi Gamma Mu, Omicron Chi Epsilon, IRS Cert. of Award 1968; mem: Northwestern Almuni Club So. Calif. (treas., bd. mem.), Northwestern Bus. Club So. Calif. (pres., founder), Temple Israel Hollywood; Republican; Jewish; rec: golf. Ofc: 4221 Wilshire Blvd Ste 430 Los Angeles 90010

FEIN, WILLIAM, ophthamologist/educator; b. Nov. 27, 1933, NY, NY; s. Samuel and Beatrice (Lipschitz) F.; m. Bonnie Fern Aaronson, Dec. 15, 1963; children: Stephanie Paula b. 1968, Adam Irving b. 1969, Gregory Andrew b. 1972; edn: BS, Coll. of the City of N.Y., 1954; MD, UC Irvine Med. Sch., 1962; diplomate Am. Bd. Ophthamology, 1969, Fellow Am. Coll. Surgeons, 1988. Career: resident ophthalmol., L.A. County Gen. Hosp. 1963-66; post res. tng. in ophthalmic plastic surgery, Manhattan Eye and Ear Hosp. 1966-7; instr. ophthalmol. UCI Med. Sch. 1966-9, instr./assoc. clin. prof. ophthalmol. USC Med. Sch. 1969-; chmn. Dept. Ophthalm. Midway Hosp. 1975-9; v.p. California Eye Med. Clinic, Inc. 1969-83; chief of Ophthalm. Clinic Svcs., Cedars Sinai Med. Ctr. 1979-81, chmn. Div. of Ophthalm., 1981-86; dir. Ellis Eye Ctr. 1984-; frequent lectr. on new techniques in ophthalm. plastic surgery, var. hosps. and convs.; Fellow Am. Coll. of Surgeons 1988, Internat. Coll. of Surgeons 1988; mem. Royal Soc. of Medicine, Am. Soc. of Ophthalmol. Plastic and Reconstrv. Surgery, Am. Acad. Ophthalmology, L.A. Soc. of Ophthalmology, AMA, Calif. Med. Assn., L.A. Co. Med. Assn.; author numerous articles in med. books and jours. describing new ophthalmic surgeries; Jewish. Res: 718 N Camden Dr Beverly Hills 90210 Ofc: 415 N Crescent Dr Beverly Hills 90210

FEINSTEIN, DIANNE, U.S. senator; b. San Francisco, June 22, 1933. d. Leon and Betty (Rosenburg) Goldman; m. Bertram Feinstein, Nov. 11, 1962 (dec.); 1 child, Katherine Anne; m. Richard C. Blum, Jan. 20, 1980; edn: BS, Stanford Univ. 1955; LLB (hon.), Golden Gate Univ. 1977; D. Pub. Adminstrn. (hon.), Univ. Manila 1981; D. Pub. Service (hon.), Univ. Santa Clara 1981; JD (hon.), Antioch Univ. 1983, Mills Coll. 1985; LHD (hon.), Univ. San Francisco 1988. Career: fellow Coro Found., San Francisco 1955-56; with Calif. Women's Bd. Terms and Parole 1960-66; mem. Mayor's com. on crime, chmn. advy. com. Adult Detention 1967-69; mem. Bd. of Suprs., San Francisco 1970-79, pres., 1970-72, 74-76, 78; mayor of San Francisco 1979-88; mem. exec. com. U.S. Conf. of Mayors 1983-88; Dem. nominee for Gov. of Calif. 1990; mem. U.S. Senate, Washington, DC 1993-; mem. Nat. Com. on U.S.-China Rels; mem. Bay Area Conservation and Devel. Commn. 1973-78; awards: Woman of Achievement award Bus. and Profl. Women's Clubs San Francisco 1970, Disting. Woman award S.F. Examiner 1970, Coro Found. award 1979, Coro Leadership award 1988, Pres. medal UC S.F. 1988, Scopus award Am. Friends Hebrew Univ. 1981, Brotherhood/Sisterhood award NCCJ 1986, Comdr.'s award U.S. Army 1986, French Legion of Honor 1984, Disting. Civilian award USN 1987, named Number One Mayor All-Pro City Mgmt. Team City and State Mag. 1987; mem: Trilateral Commn., Japan Soc. of No. Calif. (pres. 1988), Inter-Am. Dialogue, Nat. Com. on U.S.-China Rels. Ofc: 909 Montgomery St Ste 400 San Francisco 94133

FEIT, MICHAEL D., physicist; b. Nov. 15, 1942, Easton, Pa.; s. Joel E. and Kathryn T. (Bracken) F.; m. Lorraine R. Mauriel, Dec. 31, 1967; children: Sean M. b. 1971, Kathryn R. b. 1973; edn: BA, Lehigh Univ., 1964; PhD, Rensselaer Polytechnic Inst., 1970. Career: res. assoc. dept. physics Univ. of Illinois, Urbana 1969-72; physicist dept. physics Lawrence Livermore Nat. Lab, Livermore, Calif. 1972-, optical physics group leader 1992; adj. faculty dept. applied sci. Univ. Calif., Davis 1984-; awards: Phi Beta Kappa, Sigma Xi 1964, physics distinguished achiev. LLNL 1990; mem. AAAS 1964-, Am. Physical Soc. (1964-, Fellow 1988), Optical Soc. of Am. (1990-, Fellow 1992); publs: 60+ tech. jour. articles (1964-). Ofc: LLNL, PO Box 808 MS L-296 Livermore 94550

FELDMAN, DANIEL, federal agency administrator; b. Jan. 16, 1917, Pittsburgh, Pa.; s. Jerome Feldman and Jennie (Schott) Solomon; m. Rose Solomon, Aug. 15, 1937 (dec. 1985); m. Sylvia Swartz Dobkin, Aug. 31, 1986; edn: Univ. Pittsburgh 1969. Career: pres. Automatic Catering, Swissvale, Pa. 1946-56; Interstate United, Pittsburgh, Pa. 1956-61; Dynamic Products 1961-76; mgr., adminstr. U.S. Dept. Energy 1976-80; cons. Score, San Diego 1987-89; mem: SCORE (Service Corps of Retired Execs.) Jewish Comm. Center; invention: automatic dispenser (1960); mil: p.o. USN 1944-45; rec: sports, tennis, table tennis. Res: 13391 Heston Pl San Diego 92130

FELDMAN, HARVEY WOLF, social researcher, ethnographer; b. July 1, 1929, Pittsburgh, Pa.; s. Charles and Fannie (Enoch) F.; edn: BA, Univ. Pittsburgh 1953; MSW, Columbia Univ. 1957; PhD, Brandeis Univ. 1970. Career: res. assoc. Brandeis Univ., Waltham, Mass. 1970-72; fellow Drug Abuse Council, Wash. D.C. 1972-74; assoc. prof. St. Louis Univ., Mo. 1974-76; sr. ethnographer PCP Study, San Francisco 1976-78; project dir. URSA Inst. 1979-83; pres., chief of programs Yes Project 1983-; mem: Am. Sociology Assn., Soc. Study of Social Problems, Nat. Assn. Social Workers, Soc. Applied Anthropology (fellow), Am.Pub. Health Assn., We. Mastiff Fanciers, Mastiff Club Am.; ed. Angel Dust (1979); mil: cpl. AUS 1953-55; Democrat; rec: raising Mastiffs. Ofc: Yes Project 1779 Haight St San Francisco 94117

FELDMAN, LOUIS ARNOLD, mathematics professor; b. Nov. 26, 1941, Bay City, Mich.; s. Henry and Rebecca F.; m. Rosetta Sue Croom, Aug. 3, 1975 (div. April 1981); m. Marry Ellen Rhodes, Oct. 7, 1988; edn: dipl. Arthur Hill H.S., Saginaw, Mich. 1959; BS, Univ. Mich., Ann Arbor 1963; MA, UC Berkeley, 1965, PhD mathematics, 1969. Career: asst. prof. math. CSU Stanislaus, Turlock 1968-71, assoc. prof. 1971-76, prof. math., 1976-; awards:

Woodrow Wilson fellow 1963, NSF grad. fellow 1963, Phi Beta Kappa 1963, Phi Kappa Phi 1963; pub. profl. jour. articles; rec: exercise. Ofc: Calif. State Univ. Stanislaus Dept. Math., 801 W Monte Vista Ave Turlock 95380

FELDMAN, RON LYLE, hotel negotiation specialist; b. Apr. 15, 1950, Los Angeles; s. Julian and Sarah (De Norber) F.; m. Linda, June 16, 1973; children: d. Anna b. 1984; edn: BS, CSU Hayward, 1972, MS, 1974; Calif. sch. counselor credential (1974). Career: counselor Livermore Unified Sch. Dist., 1974-75; profl. bridge player American Contract Bridge League, N.Am., 1975-81, member U.S. Bridge Team, World Championships (1982, 1986); hotel negotiation splst. Hotel Connections, Inc. 1981-, appt. v.chmn. exec. com. Assn. of Travel Marketing, 1990; developed worldwide system w. Citicorp providing discounted hotel rooms & payment in the local currency; invented & designed new automated technology to interpret order requests electronically (via sequential routing of computer file transfer & send data for transaction processing to multiple parties) for inventory based corporations, 1991 (patent pending 1993); honors: Congressional recogn. for work with children; mem. Am. Hotel and Motel Assn. 1987-, Meeting Planners Intl. 1991-, Am. Soc. of Assn. Execs. 1986-, Am. Contract Bridge League (nat. conduct and ethics com. and nat. goodwill com. 1977), Assn. of Profl. Bridge Players (pres. 1982-, oldest ACBL accredited group), Found. for Glaucoma Research 1983-; Indep.; Jewish; avocation: bridge. Res: 606 Western Ave Petaluma 94952 Ofc: Hotel Connections, Inc. 6 Petaluma Blvd North Petaluma 94952

FELICITA, JAMES THOMAS, aerospace co. executive; b. May 21, 1947, Syracuse, NY; s. Anthony Nicholas and Ada (Beech) F.; edn: Syracuse Univ. 1965-66; AB, Cornell Univ. 1969; Harvard Univ. 1969; Univ. So. Calif. 1970; Govt. Contract Mgmt., UC Los Angeles 1974-77. Career: motion picture editor/producer Jacques Descent Prodns. Hollywood 1970-71; social welfare examiner Onondaga County Dept. of Social Svcs. Syracuse, NY 1972-73; underwriter Transamerica Corp. L.A. 1974; contract negotiator US Naval Regional Contracting Ofc., Long Beach 1974-80; contract negotiator Hughes Aircraft Co. El Segundo 1980-81, head NASA contracts 1981-83, mgr. major pgm. contracts 1983-; organized aerospace wing of Calif. Mus. of Sci. & Industry L.A. 1983; honors: NY State Regents Scholar 1965-69, Syracuse Univ. Trustee Scholar 1965-66, Cost Savings Commdn. (Pres. Gerald Ford 1976), Cape Canaveral Missile Space Range Pioneer, Sustained Superior Performance Award (USN 3 yrs.); mem: Nat. Space Club, Planetary Soc., Hughes Mgmt. Club, Cornell Alumni Assn. of So. Calif., Nat. Contract Mgmt. Assn.; Republican; Prot.; rec: military & space models, rare books, modern art. Res: 8541 Kelso Dr Huntington Beach 92646 Ofc: 1700 E Imperial Hwy El Segundo 90245

FELT, JAMES WRIGHT, professor of philosophy, Jesuit priest; b. Jan. 4, 1926, Dallas, Tx.; s. Wright Lafayette and Freda Marie (Brown) F.; edn: AB (hons. Classical), and MA in philosophy, Gonzaga Univ., Spokane 1949, 1950; STL theology, Alma Coll., Calif. 1957; MS physics, St. Louis Univ., Mo. 1962, PhD philosophy, 1965. Career: asst. prof. phil. Santa Clara Univ., Santa Clara, Calif. 1965-69, asso. prof. 1970-83, prof. phil. 1984-, dept. philosophy chair (1967-69, 74-80, 82-83), estab. ann. phil. conf. S.C. Univ., founding editor Logos: Philosophic Issues in Christian Perspective (pub. ann. S.C. Univ. 1980-); co-dir. w/Prof. Geo. Lucas of 6 wk. Summer Inst. on Process Metaphysics, S.C. Univ. 1986-; vis. prof. Inst. European Studies, Vienna 1971, Gonzaga Univ. 1976; lectr.univs., confs., symposiums, presentations nat., internat.; recipient Santa Clara Univ. Pres.'s Recognition Award 1984; mem: Am. Philosophical Assn. 1965-, Am. Cath. Philosophical Assn. (1962-, exec. coun. 1977-80, 89-92), Metaphysical Soc. Am. (1964-, exec. coun. 1994-), Jesuit Philosophical Assn. (1962-, nat. pres. 1981-82); author: "Making Sense of Your Freedom" (Ithaca: Cornell Univ. Press 1994); contbr. numerous essays in phil. jours. (1965-); rec: model R.R. Res: Jesuit Residence, Santa Clara Univ., Santa Clara 95053 Ofc: Dept. Philosophy, Santa Clara Univ., Santa Clara 95053

FENTON, DONALD MASON, chemist, new technology development executive; b. May 23, 1929, Los Angeles; s. Charles Youdan and Dorothy Chaplan (Mason) F.; m. Margaret Keehler, April 24, 1953; children: James Michael b. 1957, Douglas Charles b. 1959; edn: BS, UCLA 1952; PhD, 1958. Career: chemist Rohm & Haas Co., Phila., Pa. 1958-61; sr. res. chemist Union Oil Co., Brea 1962-67, res.assoc. 1967-72, sr. res. assn. 1972-82, mgr. planning devel. 1982-85, mgr. new tech. devel. 1985-, cons. (AMSCO div.) 1967-73; chmn. Petroleum Environ. Res. Forum 1986-88; Gordons Research Cong. Hydrocarbon Chem. 1975; dir. Calif. Engring. Found. 1989-; honors: Sigma Xi; mem: Am. Chem. Soc., Am. Inst. Chemists, Alpha Chi Sigma; 1 book chpt. pub., 10 papers pub. in tech.jours., 90 patents held; mil: cpl. AUS 1953-55; rec: photography. Res: 2861 E Alden Pl Anaheim 92806 Ofc: Unocal Science & Technology POB 76 Brea 92621

FERENCE, HELEN MARIE, nursing director; b. Sept. 1, 1946, Youngstown, Ohio; d. Emery and Josephine (Terlecki) Ference; m. William Venill Nick; edn: diploma, nsg., Youngstown Hosp. Assn., Youngstown, Ohio, 1967; BS, Youngstown Univ., 1970; MS, Ohio State Univ., Columbus, 1972; PhD, NY Univ., NYC, 1979. Career: charge nurse ICU, Youngstown Hosp. Assn., 1967-70; instr. Youngstown Univ., 1970; clinician ICU's, Ohio State Univ., Grant

Hosp., Columbus, 1970-80; instr. Ohio State Univ., 1972-79; asst. prof. Ohio State Univ., 1980; cons. VA, Chillicothe, Ohio, 1973-81; cons. Battelle Mem. Inst., Columbus, 1973-81; cons. Arlington Surgery Ctr.; bd. of dir. Arlington Surgery Ctr.; dir. Nsg. Prog., Arlington Surgery Ctr.; dir. res. qualification, Mt. Sinai Hosp., NYC; clinician Adais-Sinai Hosp., L.A.; awards: Maybelle Wright Award, Youngstown Hosp. Assn. 1967; Sigma Theta Tau Achievement award, Indpls. 1985; Nightingale award, Nightingale Soc., Carmel, Calif. 1990; Nightingale Prize, Nightingale Soc., Eng. 1992; mem: Sigma Theta Tau (v.p.1979-85), Nightingale Soc. (dir. 1986-), Spanish Bay, Pebble Beach; author: Notes on Nsg. Sci., 1991. Res: P.O. Box 862 Pebble Beach 93953

FERER, HARVEY S., aviation consultant; b. Dec. 24, 1924, St. Louis, Mo.; s. Sidney Sapot and Hannah (Cooper); stepfather Allen Ferer; children: Aaron b. 1960, Andrew b. 1965, Ana Michelle b. 1968; edn: Univ. Omaha 1942-43, Doane Coll. 1943-44, UCLA 1947-49; IFR Procedures Splst., FAA (1963). Career: air transport plane cmdr. US Navy, lcdr. USNR-ret. 1943-46, 1949-61, decorated Air Medal, Reserve Medal, Good Conduct, 12 campaign ribbons; IFR procedures splst. FAA, N.Y.C., Atlantic City, Oklahoma City, Los Angeles 1963-85, tng. ofcr. various units FAA 1970-85; aviation cons./prin. H. Ferer & Assocs. 1985-; cons. Mexican govt. on new Mexico City Airport 1975, cons. to South Jersey AirWays, Rocky Mtn Airways, SkyWest 1967-81; recipient commendns. control towers of Atlantic City and Phila. (1968, 70), superior performance award FAA 1980; docent/instr. Santa Monica Mus. of Flying; mem. Inst. of Navigation, Wild Goose Assn.; Republican; Jewish; rec: flying, tennis (trophies 1947-70), photog. Address: 14028 Tahiti Wy Ste 413 Marina Del Rey 90292

FERGUS, GARY SCOTT, lawyer; b. Apr. 20, 1954, Racine, Wis.; s. Russell Malcolm and Phyl Rose (Muratore) F.; m. Isabelle Sabina Beekman, Sept. 28, 1985; children: d. Mary Marckwald Beekman F. b. 1988, s. Kirkpatrick Russell Beekman F. b. 1989; edn: JD, Univ. Wis. Sch. of Law, 1971; SB, Stanford Univ., 1976; LLM, N.Y. Univ., 1981; admitted bar: Wis., 1979, Calif., 1990. Career: atty., assoc. Brobeck, Phleger & Harrison, San Francisco 1980-86, ptnr. 1986-, trial atty. first major consolidated asbestos trial in U.S. 1990; lectr. trial advocacy pgm. Stanford Law Sch., 1990, speaker, instr. trial advocacy pgm. Harvard Law Sch., 1991; supvg. instr. Fed. Trial Practice Pgm. & Negotiations Sem., U.S. Dist. Ct. no. dist. Calif., 1992; mem. Am. Bar Assn.; author (software) Nat. Case Mgmt. for Asbestos Litigation; Recognized leader in use of technology for lawyers in law jour. articles Nat. Law Jour. (7/27/87), and California Lawyer (10/87), "High Tech Attorneys Get the Business" Profit Magazine; rec: sailing, racing. Ofc: Brobeck, Phleger & Harrison, One Market Plaza Spear St Tower San Francisco 94105

FERNANDEZ, FERNANDO LAWRENCE, company president; b. Dec. 31, 1938, New York; s. Fernando and Luz Esther (Fortuno) F.; m. Carmen Dorothy Mays, Aug. 26, 1962; children: Lisa Marie b. 1963, Christopher John b. 1965; edn: ME, Stevens Inst. Tech. 1960; MS, 1961; PhD, Cal Tech Pasadena 1969. Career: thermodynamicist Lockheed Missiles, Sunnyvale 1963-65; div. and dept. mgr. Aerospace Corp., El Segundo 1965-72; program mgr. R&D Assoc., Santa Monica 1972-74; v.p. Physical Dynamics, La Jolla 1974-76; pres. Arete Assoc., Sherman Oaks 1976-; cons. to chief of naval ops. USN, Wash. D.C. 1983-; naval studies bd. 1986; DARPA Dept. of Defense 1980-89; rec: bicycling, skiing. Res: 2159 El Amigo Rd Del Mar 92014 Ofc: Arete Associates POB 8050 La Jolla 92038

FERNANDO, MANUEL, clergyman; b. May 14, 1929, Tuticorin, S.India; perm. U.S. resident since 1974; s. Siluvai Pitchai and Lilly (Mel) F.; m. Lilian Grace Samuel, March 8, 1954 (dec. 1986); children: Enoch b. 1954, Allan b. 1956, Loraine b. 1961, John b. 1962, Ron b. 1964, Steve b. 1965, Randy b. 1966; edn: BA econ., St. Xaviers Coll. 1950; BA in Eng. Bible, So. Calif. Coll. 1962. Career: pres. founder Christ for India Inc., Costa Mesa 1963, 1974-; Christ for India Inc., Madras, India 1964; recipient award for 25 yrs. ministry 1987; publisher, editor journal: Healing Hope 1987-88; Christian; rec: photog., cooking. Address: Santa Ana 92703

FERRILL, V. MIKKI, photographer, photojournalist; b. May 12, 1937, Chgo.; d. Edward R. and Gladys Marie (Black) F.; edn: Wilson Jr. Coll., Chgo. 1957-60, Chicago Art Inst., 1960-63. Career: staff photog. assignments: Mexico This Month; photog. asst. to Ted Williams; Astra Photo Service; black and white printer, Chgo.; Let's Save The Children Pub. Co.; Sigma Photo Agency; SCLC; Photo Cell Inc.; Phototechtronics Inc.; current free-lance in b&w color illstrn., ednl. media, filmstrips, textbooks, and documentary journ.; lectr., workshops Malcolm X Coll., guest lectr. Northeastern Univ. Inner City Studies, Chgo.; instr. Cook County Jail, Urban Gateways Artist-In-Residence Pgm., Chgo.; graphic cons.; works appeared in nat. and internat. magazines and newspapers incl. Life, Time, Chicago Tribune, Chicago Defender, Muhammad Speaks, Ebony, Jet, Institutions, Downbeat, What It Is, Chicago Urban League Newsletter, Muzkiki Pub. Co., Matanan Pub. Co., Knees Pub. Co., Mousenik Pub. Co., Design and Environment, The Woodlawn Org., Photo Cell Inc., U.S. Commn. on Civil Rights, U.S. Embassy, Black Photog.'s Annual, Vols. I and II, Standard Oil, Scott Foresman Pub. Co., Noble Advt., Doyle Dane & Bernbach, Mexico This Month, Burda Publs., Chicago Mag., Pamoja Mag., Black Bus. & Profl. Women,

BART, UC Berkeley Alumni House, East Bay Municipal Dist., San Francisco Examiner, Image Mag., Oakland Tribune, Ten 8 Mag.; exhibits: one woman show and group exh. Sheppard Gal., Chgo., South Side Comm. Art Ctr., Chgo., Lincoln Center, NY, Ea. Wash. State Coll., Mus. of Sci. & Ind., Chgo., Evanston (Ill.) Art Ctr., B&W Photog. Exh. U.S.S.R., Black Photog.'s Annual, NY, Mus. of Modern Art, S.F., Onyx Gal. Jazz Photo Exh., NY, William Grant Still Comm. Art Ctr., LA, Kenkiliba House, NY, Cinque Gal., Studio Mus. of Harlem, NY, Camera Works, London; rep. in permanent collections: C.N. Gormann Mus. of UC Davis; The Blues Aesthetic, Traveling Show, Wash. Projects of the Arts, WDC. Mail: PO Box 4060 Berkeley 94704 Ph:415/533-0911

FERRIN, WILLIAM JOSEPH, lawyer, accountant, real estate broker; b. Jan. 29, 1930, Chicago, Ill.; s. John W. and Ruth (McGurren) F.; m. Lucy D. Leuzzi, June 2, 1956; children: Patricia Mary b. 1956, Kathleen Betty b. 1958, William Joseph b. 1960, Colleen Ann b. 1969; edn: BS, Northwestern Univ. 1951; JD, USC 1956. Career: staff acct. Bauman Finney & Co., Chgo., Ill. 1950-51; Haskins & Sells, L.A. 1956-58; dep. gen. controller Capitol Records Inc., Hollywood 1958-62; secty., controller, dir. Kaufman & Broad Inc., L.A. 1962-64; v.p. fin. Harlan Lee Byron Lasky Co., Sherman Oaks 1965-67; sole practice atty. W.J. Ferrin 1967-84, pres. Law Offices of W.J. Ferrin, a PLC, Woodland Hills 1984-; judge pro tem L.A. Municipal Ct. 1978-; arbitrator Am. Arb. Assn., L.A. Superior Ct. 1974-; mem.: Am. Bar Assn., L.A. Co. Bar Assn., Irish Am. Bar Assn., Assn. Bus. Trial Lawyers, Am. Arbitration Assn., Am. Judicature Soc., L.A. World Affairs Council, Legion Lex Phi Alpha Delta, Little League (past pres.); mil: capt. USMC 1951-54; Republican; R.Cath. Ofc: 5959 Topanga Canyon Blvd Ste 160 Woodland Hills 91367

FIELD, KAREN LYNN, accountant; b. March 29, 1950, Fullerton; d. Deane Arnold and Beverly Ann (Logsdon) McGowen; m. Henry Allen Field, Feb. 22, 1969 (dec. 1977); children: James b. 1969, Kenneth b. 1972; edn: BS, San Diego St. Univ. 1982; CPA (1986). Career: staff acct. Deloitt Haskins & Sells, San Diego 1982-84; controller Dorado Growth Industries 1984-86; Sage Tech. 1986-87; v.p. fin. Monitor Products, Oceanside 1987-90; prin. Karen L. Field, CPA, Escondido 1990-; mem: Nat. Assn. Accts.; Democrat; Prot. Res: 10029 Sage Hill Way Escondido 92026 Ofc: Monitor Products 502 Via del Monte Oceanside 92054

FIELDS, NINA S., clinical social worker; b. New York; d. John and Gladys Marshall (Salit) Shepard; m. Maurice Fields, Mar. 23, 1952; children: Abbie b. 1957, Laura b. 1959, Kenneth b. 1961; edn: BA, Roosevelt Univ. 1953; MSSA, Case Western Reserve 1956; PhD, Calif. Inst. Clin. Social Work 1979. Career: pvt. practice, Encino 1960-; cons. editor, NASW Jour. "Social Work"; lectr. UCLA Ext. 1979-, Northridge Hosp. 1980-, Reiss-Davis Seminars, Los Angeles 1980-; honors: Psi Chi; chair, San Fernando Valley Child Guidance Clinic Profl. Advy. Bd. (v.p. bd. trustees); mem: Inst. Clin. Social Workers (trustee), Nat. Assn. Social Workers; author: The Well-seasoned Marriage, 1986; article pub. in profl. jour. 1983. Ofc: 5353 Balboa Blvd Ste 311 Encino 91316

FIELER, JAMES H., advertising executive; b. Nov. 9, 1942, Cincinnati, Ohio; s. Howard William and Evelyn (Lehmkuhl) F.; m. Margaret Mary Pope, June 28, 1969; children: Sean b. 1972, Erin b. 1976; edn: Cincinnati Art Acad. 1961-62; BS advt., Univ. Cincinnati 1968; Marygrove Univ. 1968; Univ. Md. 1971. Career: exec. Ford Motor Co., Dearborn, Mich. 1966-68; account exec. Young & Rubicam, Detroit, Mich. 1968-70, WDC 1970-72, office head, S.F. 1972-79; pres., owner AIM Inc., Foster City 1989-89; chmn. coll. fund review Menlo Sch. & Coll., Atherton 1987-88; basketball coach Notre Dame Elem., Belmont 1984; awards: City of Foster City Design 1977, Chrysler Plymouth Advt. 1976, Dandy Nat. Advt. award 1978; mem: Bay Vista Townhomes (pres. 1976), No. & So. Chrysler Plymouth Dealers (com. 1972-89, adminstrn. 1979-89), Rotary, BSA (chmn. Belmont 1976-77), St. Lukes Fundraiser (co-chmn. 1987), Concours Lyons; author: Autobile Mktg. 1980; Republican; R.Cath.; rec: art, golf, tennis. Res: 308 Pompano Circle Foster City 94404 Ofc: AIM Inc. 101 Lincoln Centre Circle Ste 250 Foster City 94404

FIFE, LORIN MERRILL, III, lawyer; b. Aug. 25, 1953, Los Angeles; s. Lorin M., Jr. and Marian Ruth (Stromwall) F.; m. Linda Suzanne Schein, June 22, 1975; children: Yoni b. 1979, Ari b. 1983; edn: BS, US Naval Acad., 1975; JD, USC, 1983. Career: midshipman, ofcr. US Navy, 1971-78; English tchr. Ulpan Amerikai, Tel Aviv, Israel 1979, data analyst Israel Ministry of Commerce, 1979-80; law clk. Donovan Leisure Newton & Irvine, L.A. 1980-82; atty., assoc. O'Melveny & Myers, L.A. 1983-89; v.p. and general counsel Sun Life Insurance Co. of Am., v.p. and assoc. general counsel SunAmerica (formerly Broad Inc.), L.A. 1989-; mem. Nat. Assn. of Life Cos. Inv. Com., 1990-, mem. Conf. of Ins. Counsel, Calif. 1989-, mem. Assn. Calif. Life Ins. Cos. Exec. Com. 1992-, mem. advy. com. Ins. Commr. John Garamendi Calif., 1990-; awards: USC Law Sch. moot ct. honors, best brief 1982, merit scholar, Legion Lex fellow 1981-83; mem. Calif. State Bar (Insurance Law Com., chmn. investments subcom. 1991-), L.A. County Bar Assn. (intl. law sect. 1987-89), Adat Ari El, North Hollywood (v.p., dir. 1987-); pub. articles in Municipal Fin. Jour. (1985-87), Urban Lawyer.(1986); Jewish; rec: reading, politics, sports. Ofc: SunAmerica Inc. 11601.Wilshire Blvd 12th Fl L.A. 90025-1748

FIMMEL, RICHARD OSCAR, research scientist/spacecraft missions executive; b. Nov. 29, 1924, Somerville, N.J.; s. Gustav Adolf and Olga (Harmel) F.; m. `Judy' Edeltraud Anna Franke, May 15, 1946; children: Richard Roy b. 1950, Sandra Ileen b. 1953; edn: BS in E.E., MS in E.E., Rutgers Univ., 1949, 1954. Career: research assoc. Rutgers Univ., 1949-51; supr. electronic engr. Evans Signal Lab, Neptune, N.J. 1951-56; sect. chief U.S. Army Signal Research & Devel. Lab, Ft. Monmouth, N.J. 1956-60; mgr. computer products dept. Ampex Internat., Redwood City, Ca. 1960-63; Pioneer project sci. chief NASA- Ames Research Ctr., Moffett Field, Ca. 1963-80, Pioneer missions mgr., 1980-; awards: spl. achiev. NASA-Ames Res. Ctr. (1973, 86), exceptional svc. medals NASA (1974, 80), group achiev. NASA, Wash. DC & Moffett Field (6), superior perf. Ames Res. Ctr. 1986; civic: Los Altos Sister Cities Inc. (bd. 1988-); author 4 books: Pioneer Odyssey, Encounter with a Giant, 1974, Pioneer Odyssey, 1977, Pioneer, First to Jupiter, Saturn & Beyond, 1980, Pioneer Venus, 1983, booklet: The Space Pioneers & Where They Are Now, 1987; mil: T5 US Army Air Corps 1943-47; Republican; Presbyterian; rec: piano & organ, photog. Res: 12350 Hilltop Dr Los Altos Hills 94022 Ofc: NASA-Ames Research Center MS244-14 Moffett Field 94035

FINDLEY, GERALD LEE ELMER, banking consultant; b. Oct. 27, 1920, Truman, Ark.; s. Burl Clinton and Gertrude A. (Tolar) F.; m. Myrtle L. Royer, June 11, 1948; children: Melinda Ann, b. 1952; Gary Steven, b. 1954; Pamela Ann, b. 1956; edn: BS, UCLA 1949, MBA, 1950; Public Acct., State of Calif. 1951. Career: mgr. Research Engring. Dept. Union Bank, Los Angeles 1950-4; mgr. Spl. Projs. Dept. Calif. Bank, L.A. 1954-5; West Coast regl. mgr. Cunneen Co., L.A. 1955-6; pres./owner Gerry Findley & Assoc., Temple City 1956-81; pres./owner Gerry Findley Inc., Brea 1981-; editor The Findley Reports, 1965-92; ed. newsletters: California Banking, 1975-92, Directors' Compass, 1979-92; instr. Univ. Calif. Ext. comml. fin. & factoring, 1952-4; mem: USS Maryland Assn.; Pearl Harbor Survivors Assn.; Masons; Shriners; author: Mergers & Acquisitions of California Banks, (4 vols.) 1955-75; Get Richer - Own the Local Bank, 1978; The Buying and Selling of Banks & Bank Holding Cos. 1981; Promises Kept (autobiog., 1986); author: California Banking - In Pursuit of Premier Performances, 1988; mil: Chief Quartermaster (permanent), USN 1939-45, GCM, Bronze star, Am. Defense, Bronze Letter-A, Am. Cmpgn., Asia-Pac. Cpgn., WWII Victory medals; Republican; Methodist; rec: collector miniatures, buttermolds, Early Am. paintings. Address: Gerry Findley, 169 N Morning Glory St Brea 92621

FINE, RICHARD ISAAC, lawyer; b. Jan. 22, 1940, Milwaukee; s. Jack and Frieda F.; m. Maryellen Olman, Nov. 25, 1982; dau. Victoria Elizabeth; edn: BS, Univ. Wis. 1961; JD, Univ. Chgo. 1964; PhD internat. law Univ. London 1967; cert. Hague Acad. Internat. Law, Netherlands 1965, 66; cert. comparative law Internat. Univ. Comparative Sci., Luxembourg 1966; dipl. superiere Faculte Internat. pour l'Enseignment du Droit Compare, Strasbourg, Fr. 1967; admitted bar: IL 1964, DC 1972, Calif. 1973. Career: trial atty. fgn. commerce sect. antitrust div. U.S. Dept. Justice, 1968-72; chief antitrust div. Los Angeles City Atty.'s Office, also spl. counsel gov. efficiency com., 1973-74; prof. internat., comparative and EEC antitrust law Univ. Syracuse (N.Y.) Law Sch. (overseas program), summers 1970-72; pvt. practice Richard I. Fine and Assocs., Los Angeles 1974; mem. antitrust advy. bd. Bur. Nat. Affairs 1981-; chmn. L.A. advy. com. London School of Economics, 1992-; mem. vis. com. Univ. Chicago, 1992-; mem: ABA (chmn. subcom. internat. antitrust and trade regulations, internat. law sect. 1972-77, co-chmn. com. internat. econ. orgn. 1977-79), Am. Soc. Internat. Law (co-chmn. com. corp. membership 1978-83, mem. exec. council 1984-87, budget com. 1992-), Am. Fgn. Law Assn., Internat. Law Assn., Brit. Inst. Internat. and Comparative Law, Calif. Bar Assn. (chmn. antitrust and trade reg. law sect. 1981-84, exec. com. 1981-88), Retinitis Pigmentosa Internat. (bd. dirs. 1985-90), Los Angeles Cty. Bar Assn. (chmn. antitrust sect. 1977-78), IL Bar Assn., Am. Friends London Sch. Econs. (bd. dirs. 1984-, co-chmn. S.Calif. chpt. 1984-), Am. Trial Lawyers Assn., Phi Delta Phi; publs. in legal jours. Address: 10100 Santa Monica Blvd Ste 1000 Los Angeles 90067

FINEFROCK, JAMES ALAN, journalist, editor; b. May 4, 1947, Bellefontaine, Ohio; s. Richard Harvey and Mary Jane (Smith) F.; m. Diane Curtis, Oct. 31, 1981; children: Jessica b. 1982, John b. 1987; edn: AB, Princeton Univ.; fellow Journalists in Europe, Paris, Fr. Career: reporter South San Francisco Enterprise-Journal, 1971; reporter San Francisco Examiner, 1972-82, investigative editor 1987-89, op-ed editor 1989-91, editor of editorial pages 1991-; honors: Silver Gavel award Am. Bar Assn., W.D.C. (1986, 87), Mark Twain award AP 1979, Best story Investigative Reporters and Editors, Columbia, Mo. 1986. Ofc: San Francisco Examiner 110 Fifth St San Francisco 94103

FINGARETTE, HERBERT, philosopher, educator; b. Jan. 20, 1921, New York; m. Leslie Swabacker, Jan. 23, 1945; 1 dau., Ann b. 1947; edn: BA, UCLA 1947; PhD, 1949. Career: instr., prof. UC Santa Barbara 1948-; spl. asst. to pres. UC Berkeley 1971; cons. World Health Orgn. Alcohol & Drug Addiction, Wash. D.C. 1980; vis. fellow Center for Addiction Research 1978; awards: Harvard Univ. William James lectr. in Religion 1971, Stanford Univ. Evans Wetz lectr. 1977, Dartmouth Univ. Gramlich lectr. 1978, Phi Beta Kappa; mem: Am.

Philosophical Assn. Pacific Div. (pres. 1976-77); author 7 books, including: Self in Transformation, 1963, Self-Deception, 1971, Heavy Drinking, 1988; mil: lt. AUS 1943-46. Ofc: Philosophy Dept. Univ. Calif. Santa Barbara 93106

FINK, BARRY EVAN, lawyer; b. Nov. 22, 1938, Bay City, Mich.; s. Louis Russell and Ida Carol (Meyers) F.; m. Arlene, June 24, 1962; children: David b. 1966, Steven b. 1969; edn: BS in commerce, De Paul Univ., 1960; JD (honors), Univ. Chgo. Law Sch., 1963; C.P.A., Ill. 1963) admitted bar: Ill. 1963, Dist. Col. 1968, Calif. 1969, U.S. Supreme Ct., and var. Fed. Cts.; Cert. Specialist in Tax Law. Career: clk. to Hon. Richard B. Austin, U.S. Dist. Ct., No. Dist. Ill., also faculty John Marshall Law Sch., Univ. Chgo., 1964-67; trial atty. Tax Div., U.S. Dept. of Justice, Wash. DC, 1966-69; atty., sr. ptnr. Christensen, White, Miller, Fink & Jacobs, Los Angeles; mem.: Am. Bar Assn., Bar Assns. of Dist. of Col., Ill., Calif., Los Angeles County, and Beverly Hills, Am. Inst. of CPAs; civic: Arrowhead Lake Assn. (pres. 1985-87), advisor L.A. Co. Sheriff's Dept., past mem. Pres. Carter's Tax Advy. Com., active numerous charitable orgs.; lectr. Calif. Continuing Edn. of the Bar (CEB), contbg. author "Advising California Partnerships" CEB (1988), contbg. author "USC Tax Inst. (1987, 89); Res: Pacific Palisades Ofc: Christensen, White, Miller, Fink & Jacobs, 18th Flr 2121 Avenue of the Stars Los Angeles 90067

FINK, HOWARD JOEL, financial services executive; b. Aug. 4, 1944, Los Angeles; s. Irving Isadore and Ruth (Alexander) F.; m. Hanne Brurberg, May 21, 1966; children: Pauline, b. 1966; Lisa, b. 1969; Vikki, b. 1971; edn: bus. acctg. courses, L.A. Valley Coll. 1962-66; CLU Am. Coll. 1981; Chartered Financial Cons. 1985. Career: dist. sales mgr. (13) stores Firestone Tire and Rubber Co., 1966-72; insurance industry, 1973-; pres. PFP Fin. & Ins. Services Inc., 1977-; pres. Fin. Mgmt. Services, Inc. 1989-; Registered Principal NASD 1987; moderator Life Underwriters Tng. Council, 1982; chmn. advy. bd. Security Life of Denver, 1991-94; awards: sales mgr. of the yr., Pacific Mutual (1979); mem.: Million Dollar Round Table (Kt.), Internat. Assn. of Registered Fin. Planners, Estate Counselors Forum in Bev. Hills (pres. 1990-91), S.F.V. Life Underwriters, UCLA Chancellor's Associates, Valley Industry & Commerce Assoc. (VICA); rec: golf, tennis. Res: 24537 Peachland Ave Newhall 91321 Ofc: Financial Management Services, Inc. 17750 Sherman Way Reseda 91335

FINK, STUART HOWARD, certified public accountant; b. Dec. 13, 1948, New York; s. Arthur Milton and Mollie (Wrubel) F.; m. Robin Heather Heacock, Aug. 25, 1984; 1 dau., Laura b. 1987; edn: BA cum laude, acctg., Queens Coll., N.Y. 1970; MBA fin., Univ. Rochester Grad. Sch. Mgmt 1972; MBA taxation, Golden Gate Univ. 1986; C.P.A., N.Y. 1975, Calif. 1979. Career: sr. accountant Brout & Co., N.Y.C. 1972-78; audit review mgr. Grant Thornton, San Francisco 1978-82; acctg. tax mgr. Jones Schiller & Co. 1982-92; self-employed C.P.A. 1992-; Credit Grantors Com., Calif. Soc. CPA 1980-83; awards: Outstanding Young Men Am. 1985, Arista Hon. Soc. 1965, N.Y. Regents scholarship 1965, Dean's List 1968; mem: Am. Inst. CPA, Calif. Soc. CPA, Commonwealth Club, Stonegate Terrace Homeowners Assn. (pres. 1983-84), Jewish Comm. Red. Social Com., San Francisco Fair (vol. 1983, 85), March of Dimes (vol. 1985); Democrat; Jewish; rec: skiing, scuba diving, oil painting. Res: 19715 Michaels Ct Castro Valley 94546

FINKEN, MARJORIE MORISSE, restaurant columnist; b. June 29, 1918, St. Louis, Mo.; d. William J. and Alice (Seidler) Morisse (O'Hern); gr.granddau. of Ferdinand Diehm, 1842-1916, Imperial and Royal Consul of Austria-Hungary in St. Louis, Mo. 1882-1915; grandniece of Albert Diehm, apptd. food admr. two Ill. counties by Pres. Hoover, 1914-18; bro. Richard Diehm Morisse (dec. 1968), aud. of USC, 20 years; m. John W. Finken, Apr. 26, 1940, div. 1957; 1 son Richard Dale, b. 1943; edn: grad. Los Angeles H.S. 1936; stu. dress design Chouinard Inst. of Art 1937-38; art maj., L.A. City Coll. 1938-40. Career: profl. photographer; freelance photog. and rep. Daily Breeze/News Pilot, 1956-, Copley L.A. Newspapers; restaurant ed. 1956-86, columnist: Munchin' with Marge 1956-; Marge to Midnight 1956-84; apptd. Calif. Rec. Commnr., Manhattan City Sch. Adminstr. 1954-60; awards: first Rose & Scroll, Manhattan Bch C.of C., 1954; mem: Phi Epsilon Phi (secty.-treas. L.A. chpt. 1942-3, 44-5), So. Bay Sym. Assn. (pub. chmn. 1954-5), So. Bay Comm. Arts Assn. (pub. chmn. 1954-6), Women of Moose Lodge No. 323 (secty. 1957-9), South Bay Hosp. Aux. (charter secty., dir. 1959-61), Greater L.A. Press Club, Calif. Press Women (bd., L.A. chpt.), Restaurant Writers Assn. (secty. L.A. Co. 1967-70), Calif. Restaurant Writers Assn. (pres. 1977-79), Los Angeles Mus of Art, Altrusa Internat. Inc. (pres. Redondo Beach chpt. 1983-85), Internat. Brotherhood of Kts. of the Vine (1986-) rec: theater, concerts, art. Res: 223 Ave F Redondo Beach 90277 Ofc: Daily Breeze, 5215 Torrance Blvd Torrance 90509

FINLINSON, JERRY CURT, chemical engineer; b. Jan. 23, 1960, Payson, Utah; s. Bryce R. and Edith (Anderson) F.; m. Ann Catherine Juskiewicz, April 20, 1985; children: Camille b. 1987, Kathleen b. 1989; edn: BSChE magna cum laude, Brigham Young Univ. 1985; MSChE, 1988. Career: summer co-op. IBM, Boca Raton, Fla. 1984; Endicott, N.Y. 1985; tchg. asst. Brigham Young Univ., Provo, Utah 1986, combustion res. asst. 1985-87; chem. engr. Naval Weapons Center, China Lake 1987-; honors: BSA Eagle Scout, Tau Beta Pi, Phi Kappa

Phi, Outstanding Young Men Am., Brigham Young Univ. Trustees scholar 1978-83; mem: Am. Inst.Chem. Engrs.; thesis and article pub. in sci. jour., 1987, 88; Republican; Mormon; rec: beekeeping, barbershop singing. Res: 925-A Atkins Ridgecrest 93555

FINN, SARA, public relations firm president; b. Cincinnati, Ohio; d. Paul Vincent and Freda K. Shiels; m. Thomas Finn, Nov. 11, 1952; edn: BA in English, Maryville Coll., 1950. Career: advtg. and pub. relations rep. San Diego Magazine, 1964-71; dir. pub. relations Univ. San Diego, 1971-1987; founder/pres. Sara Finn Public Relations, 1987, pres. Finn/Hannaford, a division of The Hannaford Co., W.D.C. 1991-; honors: Internat. Papal Soc., Equestrian Order of the Holy Sepulchre (Pope John Paul II 1982, elevated to Lady Comdr. with Star, 1988); mem: Public Relations Soc. of Am. (APR, accredited mem.) PRSA Counsellors Acad., San Diego Press Club, Alumnae of the Sacred Heart (nat. pres. 1979-81); civic: City of San Diego Internat. Affairs Com. (bd.), San Diego Historical Soc. (dir.), Partners for Livable Places (pres.), S.D. County Quincentennial Commn., San Diego C.of C., San Diego Mus. of Art; R.Cath./All Hallows Ch. La Jolla Council of Ministries; rec: travel. Res: La Jolla Ofc: Sara Finn, APR, 1010 Turquoise Ste 201 San Diego 92109 Tel:619/488-1144

FIRST, ALAN RICHARD, distribution company account executive; b. Sept. 26, 1966, Prairie du Chien, Wis.; s. Richard Duanne and Linda Marie (Zable) F.; edn: AA, Long Beach City Coll. Career: carpenter Polandna Constrn., Prairie du Chien, Wis. 1985; production Monona Wire, Monona, Iowa 1985-86; sales, mgmt. C.E.W. Lighting, Paramount 1986-88; account exec. Neway Packaging, Long Beach 1988-; awards: Dale Carnegie effective speaking 1989, sales 1988, Neway Packaging rookie of yr. 1989; mem: Bus. World Hall of Fame; Republican; R.Cath.; rec: hiking, camping. Res: 5273 The Toledo Apt A Long Beach 90803

FISCHER, COLETTE BARBARA, municipal business manager; b. Sept. 22, 1947, Chgo.; d. Aloysius Michael and Ruth Mary (Thomas) Fanning; m. Donald Andrew Walker, Jan. 22, 1968 (div. 1974); m. Robert Eugene Fischer, June 5, 1976; 1 dau., Nicole Marie Fischer b. 1973; edn: Vassar Coll. 1964-66; BS in bus., Calif. Coast Univ., L.A. 1987, MBA, 1990, PhD bus. (cand.). Career: owner, opr. The Bounty Restaurant, Santa Barbara 1976-79, Foremost Dairy 1976-82, The Spur Restaurant 1984-87; bus. office supr. Police Dept. Santa Barbara 1984-85, accts. payable payroll supr. City of Santa Barbara, 1984-87, waterfront bus. mgr., 1987-; Republican; R.Cath.; rec: travel, gourmet cooking, skiing, reading, creative writing. Ofc: 321 E Cabrillo Blvd Santa Barbara 93101

FISCHER, CRAIG LELAND, physician; b. Feb. 17, 1937; s. Emil Carl and Ruth Barbara (Minarcik) F.; m. Sandra L., Feb. 17, 1962; children: Emil Lewis b. 1965, Lisa Anne b. 1968; edn: BS in zool./chem., Kansas State Univ. 1958, MD, Kansas Univ. 1962; Diplomate Am. Board of Family Practice, Cert. in anatomical & clinical pathology, Cert. in nuclear medicine; designated FAA Aviation Medical Examiner (1991-). Career: resident in anatomical pathology (USPHS research fellow path.) Kans. Univ. Med. Ctr. 1962-64; research fellow in nuclear medicine Baylor Univ. 1965-66, research fellow in clin. pathology 1967-68; res. med. ofcr. biomed. research br. NASA Manned Spacecraft Center, Houston 1965-68; pathologist/chief Preventive Medicine Div., Clinical Laboratories, NASA Manned Spacecraft Ctr., Houston 1968-71, dir. clin. labs. Abbot & Assocs., 1971; chief clin. pathol. Eisenhower Med. Ctr., Rancho Mirage 1971-73, dir. labs./hd. pathol. dept. 1973-78, dir. oncol. & immunol. labs. 1976-78; family practice phys. and pathologist/co-dir. Valley Clin. Labs., Palm Desert 1978-80; chief Med. Ops. Br. NASA, Johnson Space Ctr., Houston 1980-82; assoc.dir. Immunopathol. & Toxicol., Univ. of Tx., Galveston 1980-82; pathologist/dir. clin. labs. John F. Kennedy Memorial Hosp., Indio 1982-, dir. postgrad. med. edn.; med. dir. V-Tech Corp., Pomona 1983-; pres. Diametrix, Inc., Indio 1985-89; pres. Fischer Associates 1989-; honors: distinguished military cadet Kans. St. Univ. 1967, NASA Manned Spacecraft Ctr. achievement awards (8), Presdl. Medal of Freedom, Apollo 13 Mission Ops. Team (4/70), Skylab Med. Team, NASA Johnson Space Ctr. 1974, Space Shuttle Launch & Landing Ops. Team STS-3, NASA 1982, Dept. of the Air Force award for meritorious civilian service 1990; Fellow Coll. of Am. Pathologists (coms.), Am. Soc. Clin. Pathologists (Council on Spl. Topics 1979), Am. Coll. Nuclear Physicians, Am. Pub. Health Assn.; mem. AMA, Riverside County Med. Assn. (councilor 1983-, pres. 1989-90), Aerospace Med. Assn., Soc. of NASA Flight Surgeons (pres. 1991), AAAS, Calif. Soc. Pathologists, Palm Springs Acad. of Medicine (pres. 1988-89), Explorers Club; publs: articles in sci. and aerospace med. jours., NASA tech. reports; mil: lt. col. USAFR, Dept. of Air Force Sci. Advy. Bd. HQ, USAF, Wash. D.C. (1986), Nat. Acad. of Engring., Nat. Research Council, Nat. Def. Service Medal. Res: 45-800 Cholame Indian Wells 92260 Ofc: 82-013 Dr. Carreon Blvd Ste P Indio 92201

FISCHER, JEANETTE LUCILLE, occupational therapist; b. Nov. 13, 1937, Albert Lea, Minn.; d. Stewart Joseph and Bessie Lucille (Junk) Stockett; m. Richard Fischer, Oct. 22, 1960; children: Richard Arnold b. 1962, Robert Andrew b. 1966; edn: BS occupational therapy, Washington Univ., 1960; MA in health facility mgmt., Webster Coll., 1981; Reg. Occ. Therapist (OTR) 1960.

Career: occupational therapy dept. aide St. Louis (Mo.) State Hosp., 1958-59; dir. psych. occup. therapy Alexian Brothers Hosp., St. Louis, Mo. 1960-61; dir. occup. therapy Americana Healthcare Center, Florissant, Mo. 1975-79; mgmt. cons. Occupational Therapy Consultants, St. Louis 1978-81; chief occup. therapist Physical Medicine and Rehab. Dept., St. Mary's Health Center, 1979-81; dir. occup. therapy Fullerton Care Convalescent Hosp., Fullerton 1981-84; Orange Region coord. Intermountain Health Care, Rehab. Services, Div. Occup. Therapy, Orange 1984-88, regional clinical edn. cons. Therapy Management, (subs. Intermtn. Health Care), 1988-89; OTR prin., co-owner Gerontic Therapy Services, Seal Beach 1989-; mem: Am. Occupational Therapy Assn. (com. of state assn. presidents 1979-81), Occup. Therapy Assn. of Calif. (Gr. Orange Co. chpt. v.p. 1983-84), L.A. Occup. Therapy Director's Forum, Mo. Occup. Therapy Assn. (1960-81, pres. 1980-81, newsletter ed. 1960-62), World Fedn. of Occup. Therapy; civic: Midland Valley Estates Improvement Assn. (dir. 1974-81, pres. 1972-74); publs: 4 profl. papers 1967, 80, 82, 84, speaker and panelist profl. meetings; Lutheran; rec: travel. Ofc: Gerontic Therapy Services, 4217 Elder Ave Seal Beach 90740

FISCHER, JUDITH LYNN, executive recruiter; b. Jan. 4, 1945, Chicago, Ill.; d. Bernard B. and Claire S. (Sanders) Riman; m. Ronald S. Fischer, Aug. 21, 1966; children: Geoffrey b. 1968, Jody b. 1969; edn: BA art edn., No. Ill. Univ. 1966. Career: art tchr. Mt. Prospect Jr. H.S., Ill. 1966-68; sr. acct., dir. VIP Corp., Los Angeles 1977-81; pres. R J Assoc., Woodland Hills 1981-; del. Calif., White House Conf. on Small Bus. 1986; bd. dirs. Jewish Vocational Services, L.A. 1988-; awards: Tarzana C.of C. Woman of Year 1987, Centinela Bus. & Profl. Women Woman of Year 1987, Nat. Assn. Women Bus. Owners Advocate of Year 1988, Women of Enterprise nom. 1989; mem: Nat. Assn. Women Bus. Owners (chair, nat. convention 1983-, nat. v.p. 1983-, chpt. v.p. 1983-); convenor Youth Job Fair, L.A. 1987, 88, Sen. David Roberti Conf. on Small Bus. 1988; articles pub. in bus. jours. 1988, 89. Ofc: R J Associates 2143 21550 Oxnard Ste 660 Woodland Hills 91367

FISCHER, NEIL JEFFREY, mortgage banking executive; b. Jan. 19, 1955, Portsmouth, Va.; s. Samuel and Rosalie (Woolf) F.; m. Denise Louise Rymer, Feb. 3, 1983 (div. 1986); 1 dau., Sarah b. 1984; edn: BS, Univ. Louisville 1978. Career: auditor Commonwealth of Ky., Frankfort 1978-79; Humana Inc., Louisville, Ky. 1979-81; asst. adminstr. Humana Hosp. West Hills, Canoga Park 1981-82; asst. adminstr. Panorama Comm. Hosp., Panorama City 1982-83; Humana Hosp., Phoenix, Ariz. 1983-84; Palmdale Comm. Hosp. 1984-85; pres., treas. Investors Mortgage Service Co., Burbank 1985-88; v.p. fin. Lowell Smith & Evans Inc., Van Nuys 1988-89; v.p. Property Mortgage Co. Inc., Sherman Oaks 1989-; bd. dirs. Investors Mortgage Service Co., Burbank 1987-88; mem: Univ. Louisville Alumni Club So. Calif.; rec: golf, bicycling. Res: 849 Country Club Dr #8 Simi Valley 93065 Ofc: Property Mortgage Co., Inc. 14724 Ventura Blvd Sherman Oaks 91403

FISH, JONATHAN S., corporate financial officer; b. June 6, 1944, Brooklyn, N.Y.; s. James B. F.; m. Wendy W. Weinstein, May 24, 1969; children: Erica A. b. 1973, Warren G. b. 1975; edn: BA, Middlebury Coll. 1966; MBA, Harvard Grad. Sch. of Bus. Adminstrn. 1968. Career: controller, dir. adminstrn. Wickes Homes, 1974-76; asst. to controller Wickes Corp. 1976-77; v.p. adminstrn. Wickes Furniture 1977-78; v.p., treas. Wickes Cos. 1978-82; v.p. fin. United Publishers 1982-88; v.p., treas. Magma Power Co. 1988-90; v.p. fin. Advanced Marketing Services, Inc. 1990-; mil: USN 1968-71; rec: skiing, backpacking, jogging. Ofc: Advanced Marketing Services, Inc. 5880 Oberlin Dr Ste 400 San Diego 92121

FISHEL, HOWARD EDGAR, physician; b. Mar. 3, 1922, Raleigh, N.C.; s. Allen Thurman and Mattie Ann (Eller) F.; edn: BA, Gettysburg Coll. 1945; MD, Temple Univ. Sch. Medicine 1950; dipl. Nat. Bd. Med. Examiners 1951, Am. Bd. Orthopaedic Surgery 1960. Career: intern Los Angeles Co. Gen. Hosp., L.A. 1950-51; gen. surgery resident S.D. Co. Gen. Hosp., S.D. 1952-53, orthopaedic surgery resident 1953-55; children's orthopaedic resident Shriners Hosp., L.A. 1955-56; pvt. practice orthopaedic surgery, Redondo Beach 1956-84; med./legal cons., Carson 1984-91; ret.; cons., tchr. Orthopaedic Hosp., L.A. 1957-70; UCLA/Harbor Med. Center, Carson 1956-70; awards: S. Bay Hosp. Dist. Disting. Pub. Service 1965; mem: AMA, CMA, Western Orthopaedic Assn., Calif. Orthopaedic Assn., L.A. Co. Med. Assn., Am. Acad. Orthopaedic Surgeons (fellow); 6 articles pub. in med. jours. 1954-75; rec: golf, flying, cabinet making. Address: Torrance 90505

FISHER, BRUCE DAVID, teacher, resource specialist, consultant; b. Dec. 24, 1949, Long Beach; s. Oran Wilfred and Irene May (Genero) F.; m. Mindi Beth Evans, Aug. 15, 1976; children: Jenny b. 1982; edn: BA, Humboldt State Univ., 1976, Calif. Std. Elem. tchr. cred., 1976, Learning Handicapped cred., 1977. Career: instructional svs. specialist Blue Lake Elementary Sch., Blue Lake, Calif. 1977-78; resource specialist Fortuna Elem. Sch., Fortuna 1978-82, 3rd Grade tchr. 1982-87, 5th Grade tchr. 1987-92; cons. Learning Mag., Springhouse, Pa. 1991-92; cons. Ctr. for Teaching Resources 1991-92; dir. Whale Celebration, Eureka, 1989-91, co-dir. Redwood Environmental Edn. Fair, 1989-92; awards: Calif. Tchr. of the Year, Calif. State Dept. Edn. 1991,

Nat. Educators Award, Milken Found., L.A. 1991, Profl. best leadership Learning Mag., Pa. 1991, Favorite teacher award ABC-TV, Burbank 1991, Leadership excellence Calif. Assn. of Sci. Specialists, Long Beach 1990; mem: CTA, Calif. Sci. Tchrs. Assn., Calif. Assn. Hlth., Phys. Edn., Rec. & Dance; civic: Sequoia Park Zool. Soc. 1987-, Am. Heart Assn., Spl. Olympics; publs: article in Learning Mag. 1991, coauthor (curriculum): Zoo Edn. 1990, Green Box Environmental Edn. 1989, Family Wellness 1988; Democrat; rec: whale-watching, photog., sports, travel. Res: 4810 14th St Fieldbrook 95521

FISHER, CARL A., Roman Catholic Bishop; b. Nov. 24, 1945, Pascagoula, Miss.; edn: Epiphany Apostolic Coll., Newburgh, N.Y., St. Joseph's Sem., Oblate Coll., American Univ., Wash. D.C., Princeton Univ., N.J.; ordained priest Roman Cath. Ch., 1973. Career: titular bishop of Tlos, aux. bishop of Los Angeles, 1987-, the first African-Am. Catholic Bishop in Western U.S. Ofc: Archdiocese of Los Angeles 3555 St Pancratius Pl Lakewood 90712-1416

FISHER, DELBERT ARTHUR, academic physician; b. Aug. 12, 1928, Placerville; s. Arthur Lloyd and Thelma (Johnson) F.; m. Beverly Carne, Jan. 1951; children: David b. 1956, Mary b. 1958, Thomas b. 1958; edn: BA, UC Berkeley 1950, MD, UC San Francisco 1953; Diplomate Am. Bd. of Pediatrics 1959. Career: pediatric resident UC San Francisco 1953-55; pediatric endocrinology fellow Univ. Oregon Med. Sch. 1957-60; asst. prof., assoc. prof., prof. of pediatrics Univ. Arkansas Med. Sch. 1960-68; prof. pediatrics UCLA Sch. of Medicine 1968-73, prof. peds. and internal medicine 1973-93, emeritus 1993-, chief Pediatric Endocrinology, Harbor-UCLA Med. Ctr., Torrance 1968-75, research prof. developmental & perinatal biology 1975-85, assoc. chmn. Pediatrics, Harbor-UCLA Med. Ctr. 1974-85, prof./chmn. Dept. Pediatrics, 1985-89, dir. Walter P. Martin Research Ctr., 1987-91; pres. Nichols Institute Reference Laboratories, 1991-93; pres. Nichols Adacemic Associates, chief sci. ofcr. 1993-; chief editor J. Clin. Endocrinol. Metab. 1978-83, Pediatric Research 1984-89; subspecialty com. Pediatric Endocrinology, Am. Acad. Ped. 1976-79, Written Exam com. 1977-80; author 6 books: Research in Congenital Hypothyroidism (Plenum Press, London, 1989); w/ F. DeLange, D. Glinoer, Pediatric Thyroidology (Karger AG, Basel, 1985); 100+ book chpts.; 400+ sci. articles; research in developmental biology and endocrinology and clin. endocrinology; awards: Phi Beta Kappa 1964, Alpha Omega Alpha 1985, NIH Research career devel. award 1964-68, Am. Acad. of Ped. Research Award 1982, Inst. Med. Nat. Acad. Sci. 1988; mem: W. Soc. for Ped. Research (pres. 1982-83), The Endocrine Soc. (pres. 1983-84), Am. Acad. Pediatrics 1960, Soc. Pediatric Research (v.p. 1973-74), Am. Pediatric Soc. (pres. 1992-93), Am. Thyroid Assn. (pres. 1988-89), Am. Soc. Clin. Invest., Assn. Am. Physicians, Lawson Wilkins Ped. Endocrine Soc. (pres. 1982-83); mil: capt. USAF Med. Corps 1955-57; Democrat; Prot.; rec: indian art collecting, swimming, jogging. Res: 24581 Santa Clara Ave Dana Point 92629 Ofc: Nichols Institute, 33608 Ortega Hwy San Juan Capistrano 92690 also: Walter Martin Research Center, Harbor UCLA Medical Center, 1124 W Carson St Torrance 90502

FISHER, JOEL M., executive search company president; b. June 24, 1935, Chicago, Ill.; s. Dan and Nell (Kolvin) F.; m. Linda J. Buss, Aug. 29, 1971; children: Sara b. 1973, Matthew b. 1975; edn: BA, USC 1954; MA, LL.B, UC Berkeley 1961, 62; PhD, Claremont Grad. Sch. 1968. Career: assoc. prof. political sci. CSU, Fullerton 1966-68, 71-73; dir. arts and sci., state legislative div. Republican Nat. Com., Wash. D.C. 1968-69; asst. dep. counsel to the Pres., White House 1969-70; dep. asst. secty. of state internat. econ. and social affairs U.S. Dept. of State 1969-71; vis. prof. Loyola Univ. 1972-74; assoc. prof. Southwestern Univ. Sch. of Law 1974-77; assoc. prof., asst. dean Whittier Coll. Sch. of Law 1977-79; assoc., prin., Ziskind, Greene and Assocs., Beverly Hills 1980-83; v.p. Wells Internat., Los Angeles 1983-84; pres. LawSearch Inc., Encino 1984-; awards: Harvard Nobel Found. 1958, Falk Fellow UCB 1962, Danforth Fellow CSUF 1967, Ford Found. nat. com. fellow 1968-69; civic: Cathedral Corp. of Saint Paul (bd.), Reform Club; publs: 50+ articles and monographs in profl. jours., 1961-, co-editor Citizens for X, 1964, coauthor Legislative Process in Calif., 1973; mil: capt. USAR 1954-68; Republican (dir., exec. com. Repub. Assocs. L.A. Co.); Episcopalian (vestry). Res: 4963 Bluebell Ave North Hollywood 91607 Ofc: 16161 Ventura Blvd Ste 448 Encino 91436

FISHER, PHILIP A., investment manager; b. Sept. 8, 1907, San Francisco; s. Arthur Lawrence and Eugenia (Samuels) F.; m. Dorothy Whyte, Aug. 14, 1943; children: Arthur b. 1944, Donald b. 1947, Kenneth b. 1950; edn: AB, Stanford Univ., 1927, Stanford Grad. Sch. of Bus., 1928. Career: founder mgr. Fisher & Co., 1931-; author: Common Stock and Uncommon Profits (1958), Paths to Wealth Through Common Stocks (1960), Conservative Investors Sleep Well (1975); served to capt. US Army Air Corps, 1942-45. Ofc: Fisher & Co., 520 El Camino Real Ste 422 San Mateo 94402

FISHER, SEYMOUR, physician, ret.; b. Apr. 23, 1907, Chicago, Ill.; s. Mandel and Ida Sarah (Burman) F.; m. Gussie W. Wish, May 1, 1938; children: Ruth Ann b. 1941, Judith Sue b. 1944; edn: BA, Univ. Ill. 1928; MD, Northwestern Univ. 1933. Career: pvt. practice, Chgo., Ill. 1935-38; Ill. Sol and Sail Children's Sch., Normal 1938-40; dir. handicap program St. of Ill., Springfield 1940-41; dir., chief of staff VA Hosps., Indianapolis, Phoenix, S.F.

and L.A. 1946-70; cons. Co. of Los Angeles 1970-84; cons. allergy VA Hosp., L.A. 1970-82; mem: Am. Coll. Allergy & Immunology (fellow), A.C.P. (fellow), Am. Coll. Hosp. Adminstrs. (fellow), Assn. Mil. Surgeons (fellow), Am. Acad. Pediatrics (fellow), Masons, Shriners, B'nai B'rith; articles pub. in med. jours 1938-70; mil: col. AUS 1941-46; USAR 1926-64; Democrat; Jewish; rec: lapidary, bridge. Res: 32120 Village 32 Camarillo 93012

FISK, IRWIN WESLEY, government investigator; b. Nov. 20, 1938, Byers, Kans.; s. Walter Roleigh and Mae Pearle (Irwin) F.; m. Susie Walters, Sept. 9, 1973; children: Mark b. 1968, Paul b. 1970; edn: CSU Los Angeles. Career: asst. exec. dir. Stores Protective Assn., Los Angeles 1964-66; investigator Calif. Dept. Corps., 1966-71, sr. investigator 1971-83, chief investigator, So. Calif. Dist., Calif. Dept. Corps., 1983-, mem. Multistate Law Enforcement Task Force on Fraudulent Telemktg. 1987-; frequent guest speaker comm. colls. and univs., and law enforcement classes; featured guest KWHY-TV, 1986, 87, 88; mem: So. Calif. Fraud Investigators Assn. 1968-, Authors Guild, Nat. Rifle Assn., U.S. Chess Fedn., Masons; publs: articles on investment fraud and related topics; Republican; rec: ham radio (KC6QJB), genealogy, photog., chess. Res: 374 Malcolm Dr Pasadena 91105 Ofc: Calif. Dept. of Corporations, 3700 Wilshire Blvd Los Angeles 90010

FITCH, JOHN RICHARD, newspaper executive; b. June 1, 1938, Newark, Ohio; s. John Clyde and Mildred Josephine (Nethers) F.; children: Joanne b. 1959, Troy b. 1962, Victoria b. 1968, Valerie b. 1973, Megan b. 1984; edn: Baylor Univ. 1958-59; Imperial Valley Coll. 1962-86. Career: advt. sales Associated Desert Newspapers, El Centro 1960-64, advt. mgr. 1964-65, bus. mgr. 1965-66, gen. mgr. 1966-69, ed., publisher 1976-78, pres., editl. publisher 1988-, pres., exec. bd. mem.; awards: CNPA best editl. cartoon 1981, 83, 84, 85, best editl. page 1978, 1st comml. service 1967, Kiwanis lt. gov. disting. 1982; mem: Regional Econ. Devel. Inc. (founder), Calif. Newspaper Publishers Assn. (bd. mem., govtl. affairs chair), El Centro C.of C. (past pres.), El Centro Kiwanis (past pres.), Kiwanis Div. 31 (lt. gov. 1981-82); mil: airman 2c. USAF 1956-60; Prot.; rec: horse ranching. Res: 903 W McCabe El Centro 92243 Ofc: Imperial Valley Press 205 N 8th St El Centro 92243

FITZGERALD, JERRY (JOHN MATHIAS), management consultant; b. April 21, 1936, Detroit, Mich.; s. John Middleton and Jessie Lucy (Call) F.; m. Ardra Elizabeth Finney, Dec. 1, 1962; edn: BS, Engring., Mich. State Univ., 1959; MBA, Univ. Santa Clara, 1964; M.Bus. Econs., Claremont Grad. Sch., 1971, PhD, 1972; CDP (Certificate in Data Processing) 1967, CISA (Certified Information Systems Auditor) 1978. Career: industrial engr. Parke Davis, Detroit 1959-61; stock broker McDonnell & Co., Detroit 1961-62; engr. Lockheed Mis. & Space, Sunnyvale 1962-64; systems analyst Friden, Inc., San Leandro 1964-66; systems analyst UCSF Med. Ctr., San Francisco 1966-69; prof. CSU Pomona, Hayward 1969-74; sr. mgmt. cons. SRI Internat., Menlo Park 1974-77; mgmt. cons./prin. J. FitzGerald & Assoc., Redwood City 1977-; mem: EDP Auditors Assn. (1978-, recipient Joseph J. Wasserman Memorial Award N.Y. 1980), Inst. of Internal Auditors 1977-, Info. Systems Security Assn. 1987-; author six books, 40+ articles; mil: priv. U.S. Marine Corps, 1959. Ofc: Jerry FitzGerald & Associates 506 Barkentine Ln Redwood City 94065-1128 Ph: 415/591-5676

FITZGERALD, MARY CATHERINE, psychologist; b. June 20, 1936, Limerick, Ireland; nat. 1953; d. John and May (Nihill) Fitzgerald; edn: BA, Marymount Coll. 1964; M.Ed, Va. St. Univ. 1974; MS edn., USC 1978; PhD, U.S. Internat. Univ. 1982. Career: tchr. Marymount Univ., Quebec, Canada 1955-65; tchr. Corvallis H.S., Studio City 1973-75; Marymount H.S., Westwood 1975-78; family counselor Robert F. Kennedy Hosp., Hawthorne 1988-; asst. prof. Loyola Marymount Univ., L.A. 1982-, dir. drug studies 1982-; exec. v.p. CAADAC 1984-86; regional dir. So. L.A. Region 1986-88; honors: Beta Kappa Chi, SCATE Woman of Year 1988, Psi Chi, U.S. Internat. Univ. Doctoral Soc. 1982, Loyola Marymount Univ. Moderator of Year 1987; mem: PALM (bd. mem.), Calif. Cert. Bd., Nat. Council Sexual Addiction, Calif. Assn. Alcohol Drug Couselors Edn. Program (edn. com. 1984-88), Calif. Women in Higher Edn., Am. Assn. Univ. Profs. (treas. 1986-88); article pub. in profl. jour., dissertation pub. Women Religious Alcoholics, 1982; R.Cath.; rec: cooking. Res: 8505 Gulana Ave #4112 Playa del Rey 90243 Ofc: Loyola Marymount University Loyola Blvd W 80th St Los Angeles 90045

FITZGERALD, WILLIAM BRENDAN, lawyer; b. May 4, 1936, Waterbury, Conn.; s. Wm. Brendan, Sr. and Margaret (Cunning) F.; m. Teresa Vannini, Oct. 12, 1963 (div. 1980); edn: BA, Yale Univ., 1958; JD, Harvard Univ., 1961; admitted bar: Conn. 1961, Calif. 1985. Career: ptnr. Fitzgerald & Fitzgerald, Waterbury, Conn. 1961-72; ptnr. Carmody & Torrance, Waterbury and New Haven, Conn. 1972-85; ptnr. Haight, Dickson, Brown & Bonesteel, Santa Monica 1985-88; ptnr. Dickson, Carlson & Campillo, 1988-; state trial referee Conn. Superior Ct. 1983-85; mem: Am. Coll. of Trial Lawyers (fellow), Nat. Board of Trial Advocacy (diplomate), Am. Board of Trial Advocates, Am. Bar Assn. (v. chmn. trial techniques com. 1988-), Roscoe Pound Found. (fellow), Conn. Trial Lawyers Assn. (pres. 1985, ed. monthly law report `Forum' 1983-85), Rotary Intl. (fellow); contbr. article in law book "The Trial Masters"

(1983); Republican; R.Cath. Res: 979 Bel Air Rd Los Angeles 90077 Ofc: PO Box 2122, 120 Broadway 3rd Fl Santa Monica 90407-2122

FITZSIMMONS, MARY KATHRYN, educational psychologist; b. April 24, 1928, Newport, Ky.; d. Thomas and Pearl Lena (Stricker) Kane; m. Jose Abascal, April 1952; m. 2d. Fred Fitzsimmons, Feb. 1963 (dec.); 1 son, Thomas A. b. 1964; edn: BA, CSU 1966; MA, 1967; lic. ednl. psychologist 1982, lic. marriage family and child counselor 1976, lic. sch. psychologist 1971. Career: sch. psychologist Simi Valley Unified Sch. Dist., Simi Valley 1971-; marriage family and child counselor, Northridge 1985-; ednl. psychologist 1985-; honors: Ventura Co. Assn. Sch. Psychologists Merit. Service 1988, Kappa Delta Pi, Delta Phi Upsilon, Phi Kappa Phi; mem: Delta Kappa Gamma, Mensa; rec: flamenco dancing. Res: POB 3553 Simi Valley 93093

FLAJOLE, HENRY JOSEPH, II, engineer, company president; b. April 8, 1921, Bay City, Mich.; s. Henry Joseph and Kathryn S. (Maus) F.; m. Dorothy E. Watkins (dec. 1972); m. Phyllis Allene Allison; children: Henry J., Mary M., Faith A., Marcie K.; edn: AS, Univ. Mich. 1950; BSME, Tri State Univ. 1953; Univ. Wis.; PhD human devel., Kensington Univ. 1979; lic. profl. engr. Wis. 1966. Career: chief engr. Motorola Spl. Machine Div., Detroit, Mich. 1961-65; Ansul Co., Marinette, Wis. 1965-68; aerospace mktg. Solar (div. I-H), San Diego 1968-83; pres., owner San Diego Hearing 1973-82; Advanced Surface Mounted Devices 1983-89; Flajole Properties 1973-; cons., bd. mem. ASMD Inc. 1989-; awards: Ansul Co. patents 1967; mem: SMTA; patents held for automatic fire extinguishing control, 1967, auto. clock fusing device, 1963; mil: pvt. USAAC 1943-44; Republican; R.Cath.; rec: inventing, gardening. Res: 403 Sea Ridge Dr La Jolla 92037

FLAMM, DANIEL LAWRENCE, chemical engineer, consultant, educator; b. Sept. 14, 1943 San Francisco, Calif.; s. Gerald R. and Esther Lucile (Zwerling) F.; m. Lois Ellen Canter, Oct. 30, 1965; children: Jonathan, Stephen; edn: BS, math., Mass. Inst. of Tech. 1964; MS, chem. engring., Mass. Inst. of Tech. 1966; ScD, chem. engring., Mass. Inst. of Tech. 1970; reg. profl. engr., Tex. Career: asst. prof., Northeastern Univ., Boston 1969-70; sr. design programmer, Foxboro (Mass.) Co. 1970-72; asst. prof., Tex. A&M Univ., College Sta., Tex. 1972-77; disting. mem. tech. staff, AT&T Bell Labs., Murray Hill, N.J.,1977-89; McKay lectr. dept. elec. engring. UC Berkeley 1988-; v.p. for tech., Mattson Technology, Sunnyvale,1991-92; mem., advanced x-ray optics group, Lawrence Livermore Nat. Labs., Livermore 1992-; lectr., cons. in field; chmn, Am. Water Works Assn. Task Force for Standard Methods, Ozone, 1975-85; chmn., Gordon Conf. Plasma Chemistry, 1980; mem. Internat. Union of Pure and Applied Chemistry subcommittee on Plasma Chemistry 1980-87, advy. bd., rev. bd., NSF 1981-83, 88; awards: recipient, Certificate of Recognition, NASA, Moffett Field, Calif. 1978, 79, Thinker award, Tegal Corp., Petaluma, Calif. 1985; mem: Am. Inst. of Chem. Engrs., Am. Vacuum Soc., Am. Radio Relay League, Materials Res. Soc., Internat. Soc. for Optical Engring., Sigma Xi, Pi Lambda Upsilon; author, co-editor: Plasma Materials Interaction Series; co-editor: Plasma Diagnostics Vol. I, Discharge Parameters and Chemistry, 1989, Plasma Diagnostics Vol. II, Surface Analysis and Interactions, 1989, Plasma-Surface Interactions and Processing of Materials, 1990; mem. editorial bd. profl. journals; contbg. ed., Solid State Tech., 1990-; contbg. ed., Microlithography World, 1992-. Res: 476 Green View Dr. Walnut Creek 94596-5459. Ofc: Univ. of Calif. Dept. Elec. Engring. Berkeley 94720

FLANDERS, ALLEN F., architect; b. Mar. 26, 1945, Paynesville, Minn.; s. Harold E. and Beatrice E. (Schultz) F.; m. Linda J. Strudnick; div. Dec. 31, 1983; m. Cathleen A. Pomatto, Sept. 13, 1986; children: Derek b. 1974, Lyndsey b. 1988; edn: Bachelor of Architecture, Univ. of Minn., 1969; lic. architect, State of Calif., 1974. Career: draftsman George Mastney Assoc., Minneapolis, Minn., 1967-69; draftsman Carl Schulz Assoc., S.F., Calif., 1972-74; proj. architect H. E. Bermudez Assoc., S.F., 1974-75; proj. architect Hellmuth, Obata, Kassabaum, S.F., 1975-77; pres. Hope Design Group, San Diego, 1977-; bd. dir. San Diego Assn. 1990-, San Diego C.of C. 1991-; awards: design award, Robert Presley Detention Ctr., AIA, Riverside, Calif., 1986; design award, Bob Wiley Detention Facility, AIA, Visalia, Calif., 1988; mem: AIA 1974-, Am. Correctional Assn. 1980-; civic: Kiwanis Club, San Diego, 1990-; author publ. article, 1991; mil: lt., USN, 1969-72; rec: travel, woodworking. Ofc: Hope Design Group 4520 Executive Dr. Ste. 300 San Diego 92121

FLANTER, JILL SELEVAN, entertainer, television show host; b. July 8, 1950, Miami Beach, Fla.; d. Bernard E. and Phyllis Anita (Gordon) Selevan; m. Neil Flanter, Dec. 30, 1972 (div. 1974); edn: BA, Univ. Tex., 1972. Career: TV host Palm Springs, Calif. 1985-; neurolinguistic programming expert Advanced Community Technologies, Glendale 1986-; mem. Internat. Brotherhood Magicians, SAG, AFTRA; Republican. Ofc: PO Box 46381 Los Angeles 90046

FLEER, JOHN LAWRENCE, lawyer, psychologist; b. Dec. 24, 1951, Council Bluffs, Iowa; s. John Wilhelm and Pearl Marie (Garber) F.; m. Kathleen Daugherty; children: Jason b. 1978, Juna b. 1986, Alex b. 1986, Jake b. 1987; edn: BA, Gustavus Adolphus Coll. 1974; MA, PhD, Univ. of Wyo. 1975, 1979; intern USC, 1977-78; JD, UC Boalt Hall 1981; admitted Calif. Bar 1981.

Career: counselor Central Wyoming Counseling Center, Casper, Wyo. 1977; clin. psych. intern L.A. County Med. Center, Los Angeles 1977-78; co-dir. Center for Psycholog. and Legal Research, Berkeley 1979-81; trial atty. Crosby, Heafey, Roach and May, Oakland 1981-86; trial atty. Bjork, Fleer and Lawrence, 1986-91; Fleer & Daugherty, 1991-; law/mental health cons.; legal counsel Rape Crisis Svc. of Central Contra Costa Co. 1984-; awards: NIMH Fellow 1974-75, Nat. Endowment for Humanities Fellow 1976-77; mem: Am. Bar Assn., Calif. Bar Assn.,Am. Psychology-Law Soc., W. Psychol. Assn.; profl. jour. publs. in fields of mental health law, offender rehab., profl. liability and suicide; rec: musician, writer, pub. Istanbul Diary (1981). Ofc: Fleer & Daugherty, 2831 Telegraph Ave Oakland 94609

FLEISCHER, WAYNE NEAL, financial planner; b. Jan. 9, 1945, Pittsburgh, Penn.; s. Benjamin and Edna Leatrice (Krauss) F.; m. Rosemarie, Sept. 2, 1979; children: Jennifer b. 1980, Jonathan b. 1982; edn: MS in Mgt. and MS Fin. Svs., American Coll., Bryn Mawr, Pa.; Cert. Fin. Planner (CFP), Chartered Fin. Cons. (ChFC), Chartered Life Underwriter (CLU); Calif. lic. Life & Disability Analyst, Accredited Tax Advisor, Reg. Tax Interviewer; Enrolled Agt., IRS. Career: senior v.p. Planned Asset Management, Inc.; instr. fin. plnng. practitioner, IAFP, LUTC; honors: Top Ventura Fin. Plnng.; mem: IAFP, VALU, ICFP, Nat. Soc. of Pub. Accts., Nat. EA Soc., Registry of Fin. Plng. Practitioners; author: articles for industry; Republican; rec: flying. Ofc: Planned Asset Management, Inc. 300 Esplanade Dr Ste 907 Oxnard 93030 Tel: 818/708-6888

FLEMING, RICHARD SCOTT, organization executive; b. Aug. 9, 1947, Oakland, s. William Fleming and Cornelia Burton (Leas) Crowley; m. Eleanor MarieIto, Nov. 21, 1971 (dec. Jan. 3, 1989); children: Cynthia b. 1974, William b. 1978, Kimberly b. 1980, Creed b. 1981;m. Debra Kay Thomson, Feb. 27, 1993; edn: grad. Tennyson H.S., Hayward 1965, att. CSU Hayward 1965-66, Chabot Jr. Coll. 1969-71. Career: deliveryman Allied Meat Service, San Leandro 1970; claims adjuster Calif. State Auto Assn., Hayward 1970-72; life ins. agt. Conn. Mutual, Oakland 1972-83; independent ins. broker, Ceres 1983-84; exec. v.p. Ceres Chamber of Commerce, 1984-85; gen. mgr. Antioch Chamber of Commerce, 1985-90; exec. dir. Livermore Chamber of Commerce, 1990-; recipient numerous Jaycee Awards at dist., state and nat. levels: Calif. Jaycee of Yr. (1981-82, 1983-84), Calif. Jaycee Recruiter of Yr. 1981-82, US Jaycees Hall of Fame (Tulsa, Okla. 1984), outstanding state chaplain US Jaycees 1982-83, Hamilton Award for best v.p. US Jaycees (1983-84); mem: Oakland Magic Circle (pres. 1979-80), Calif. Assn. C.of C. Execs. 1984-, Am. Assn. C.of C. Execs. 1985-, Livermore Rotary 1991-, Masons 1988-, Jaycees 1981-, DAV 1969-, VFW 1969-; mil: cpl. USMC 1966-69, Vietnam Veteran decorated Purple Heart, s/sgt. USMCR 1972-80; Republican (pres. Hayward area YR 1972); Mormon. Res: 479 Stanford Ct Livermore 94550 Ofc: Livermore Chamber of Commerce 2157 First St Livermore 94550

FLETCHER, LOIS LORETTA, real estate broker; b. Sept. 13, 1926, Leflore Co., Okla.; d. Alec L. and Ruth (Cox) Burnett; m. Eugene Fletcher, Nov. 18, 1959; edn: San Diego State 1942-44, Mesa Coll. 1970-72, UC San Diego 1972, City Coll. 1973; desig: GRI, CRS, CRB, CE, Senior Appraiser, Cert. Counselor. Career: asst. librarian National City Public Library 1942, 43; bookkeeper, asst. prop. mgr. Burnett & Horning, National City 1944-55; real estate sales agent, broker, 1955-, broker/owner Fletcher Realty, Smyrna, Ga. 1955-70, San Diego 1970-; real estate exchange splst., author Beginning Exchange Course for R.E. (1977), instr. R.E. exchange courses; awards: 15 plaques for Exchanging, 52 certs. of Merit and Outstanding Service, R.E. Exchangor of the Year, Past Pres.'s Award S.D. Bd. Realtors 1988, B.P.W. Woman of Achievement, Pres.'s Council of Womens Service, Bus. & Profl. Clubs of San Diego 1980, listed Who's Who Creative R.E., Who's Who Repub. Party; mem: NAR, RAP-Realtors Active in Politics (life), NAR Nat. Mktg. Inst., CRS/Certified R.E. Residential Sales Council (So. Calif. Chpt. pres. 1992), Calif. Assn. Realtors (dir. 1978-89, v.chair conv. com. 1988, mem. credentials com. and conv. com. 1990, Living Scholarship estab. in her name 1990, appt. 5-yr. trustee CAR Scholarship Found., state chair Scholarship Trustees 1991), San Diego Bd. Realtors (v.p., exec. com. 1990, dir 1978-, v.p. 1984, 1986, pres. 1987, Past Pres.'s Award recipient), Calif. Womens Council of Realtors (gov. 1983), 99 Club (pres. So. Calif. chpt. 1986), FLI, NCE, WCR, NIREC, NIREA, University Ave Bus. Assn., Paradise Hills- San Diego Planning Com. 1990-91; Republican (life mem. Presdl. Task Force); R.Cath.; rec: oil painting, gourmet cooking, fishing, piano. Ofc: Fletcher Realty 3583 University Ave San Diego 92104

FLINT, ROBERT THOMAS, clinical psychologist; b. Sept. 16, 1935, Los Angeles; s. Thomas and Louise (Jones) F.; m. Winifred Watters, Aug. 29, 1955 (div. 1971); Gayla Kaibel, May 28, 1974 (div. 1990); children: Jerretta Villines b. 1952, Sean b. 1957, Kathleen Deakins b. 1967, Deirdre b. 1969; edn: BA, San Francisco State Coll. 1961, MA, 1963; PhD, Univ. Minn. 1970; lic. psychologist Calif. 1981. Career: res. psychologist Am. Rehab. Found., Mnpls. 1966-68; instr., asst., assoc. prof. Univ. Minn. 1968-77; psychotherapist pvt. practice/v.p. Judson Family Center 1977-80; chief psychol. svcs. Ashby Med. Gp., Berkeley, Calif. 1980-83; staff psychol. Paul S.D. Berg and Assocs., Oakland 1983-85; pres. Robert T. Flint, PhD, Psychologist, Lafayette 1986-; pvt. practice psychotherapy; forensic psychologist, cons. law enforcement agencies; instr. psychol. profl. tng.; awards: spotlight award Minn. Rehab. Assn. 1968, recogn. for contributions to contg. legal edn. Minn. Bar Assn. 1975, recogn. for contributions to law enforcement Internat. Assn. Women Police 1977, Hon. Mem. Juvenile Ofcrs. Assn. 1979; mem: Am. Psychol. Assn., Calif. State Psychol. Assn., Calif. Applicants Attys. Assn. (asso. mem.), Internat. Assn. Chiefs of Police (asso. mem.), Minn. Health Careers Council (founder, pres. 1965), Central Contra Costa Co. Rape Crisis Svc. (secty. bd. dirs. 1982-83); 24+ sci. publs. (1966-86); 12 video and film tng. pgms. for law enforcement; mil: yeoman 2/c USN 1954-58; Democrat; rec: gardening. Ofc: Robert T Flint, PhD, Psychologist, 3732 Mt Diablo Blvd Ste 362 Lafayette 94549

FLOR, LOY LORENZ, chemist, corrosion engineer, consultant; b. Apr. 25, 1919, Luther, Okla.; s. Alfred Charles and Nellie Marguerette (Wilkinson) F.; m. Virginia L. Pace, Oct. 1, 1946; children: Charles b. 1950, Scott b. 1952, Gerald b. 1954, Donna Jeanne b. 1959, Cynthia Gail b. 1960; edn: BA in chem., San Diego State Coll. 1941; Reg. Profl. Engr., Calif. Career: Helix Water Dist., La Mesa 1947-84, supr. corrosion control 1956-84, chief chemist and supr. of water quality 1963-84; indep. cons., 1984-; mem: Am. Chem. Soc. (chmn. San Diego Sect. 1965), Am. Water Works Assn. (chmn. Water Quality Div., Calif. Sect. 1965), Nat. Assn. of Corrosion Engrs. (chmn. W. Region 1970), Masons; mil: 1st lt. U. S. Army Air Force 1941-45; Republican; Presbyterian; rec: travel/camping, hiking, swimming.

FLORENDO, STEPHEN ZABALA, financial executive; b. Dec. 5, 1955, Manila, Phil., nat. 1975; s. Atty. Jesus Q. and Rosalina A. (Zabala) F.; m. Noel P., July 14, 1979; children: Adam b. 1984, Jonathan b. 1988; edn: AA, City Coll. of S.F. 1979; BA, Golden Gate Univ. Sch. Acctg. 1984. Career: jr. acct. California First Bank, San Francisco 1978-79; acctg. mgr. C.W. Fin. & Ins. Co., S.F. 1979-80; cost acct. Raiser Constrn. Co., San Mateo 1980-81; asst. controller, C.W. Fin. & Ins. Co., San Francisco 1981-85, v.p./controller, 1985-87; controller P.E.W./ABC Group, subs. Western Ins. Group, San Francisco 1987-88; c.f.o. C.W. Fin. & Ins. Co. & Insurance Affiliates, 1988-; mem: Filipino-Am. Profl. Assn. of Calif., S.F. Commercial Club; mil: s/sgt. USAFR 1976-81; Democrat; R.Cath.; rec: golf, camping, jogging, travel. Ofc: 456 Montgomery St., Ste 1020 San Francisco 94104

FLORES, ROSA ALBA, real estate executive and attorney; b. Aug. 14, 1958, Marysville, Calif.; d. Antonio Gallardo and Eva (Sierra) Flores; m. Manuel A. Medrano, Oct. 21, 1989; edn: AB, Harvard Radcliffe Coll., 1980; JD, Harvard Law Sch., 1983; MBA, Stanford Grad. Sch. of Bus., 1987; admitted bar: Calif. 1984. Career: atty. law firm Brobeck Phleger & Harrison, Los Angeles 1983-84; v.p. La Salle Partners, Los Angeles 1987-; awarded La Salle Club Award, La Salle Partners, L.A. 1991; mem: Calif. Bar Assn., L.A. Co. Bar Assn., Building Owners & Mgrs. Assn., Century City C.of C. Ofc: LaSalle Partners, 355 S Grand Ave Ste 4280 Los Angeles 90071

FLOREY, JERRY JAY, aerospace co. strategic planning/market analysis engineer/ executive; b. Apr. 3, 1932, Geddes, S.Dak.; s. Henry Clifford Florey and Lizzie M. Rabie; m. Mary E. Richey, Sept. 17, 1955; children: Glenn David, Janet Renee; edn: BS chem. engring., Oregon State Univ., 1955; Cert. in electronics. Career: from res. engr. to engring. supr. Rockwell Internat., Canoga Park 1955-66, senior project engr. Rockwell Internat., Downey 1966-67, engring. mgr., engring. dir., chief engr. Rockwell Internat., Seal Beach 1967-85, dir. advanced systems, res. and techn. 1985-89; sr. staff mgr. strategic planning/mkt. analysis McDonnell Douglas Space Co., Huntington Beach 1989-; awards: NASA cert. appreciation Marshall Space Flight Ctr., Huntsville, Ala. 1972, Skylab achievement award NASA 1973, Astronaut Person achiev. award NASA 1969; mem: AIAA (Fellow), Nat. Mgmt. Assn., Nat. Mktg. Soc. Am.; civic: scoutmaster BSA, Costa Mesa 1970; Republican. Res: 2085 Goldeneye Pl Costa Mesa 92626

FLORSHEIM, WARNER HANNS, biochemist; b. Dec. 11, 1922, Hamburg, Ger., U.S. cit. 1943; s. Adolph and Elizabeth (Kahn) F.; m. Eva Herzberg, Aug. 1, 1952; children: Renee Anne b. 1953, Margaret Joan Smith b. 1956; edn: BA, MA, PhD, UC Los Angeles, 1943, 44, 49. Career: res. assoc. zoology UCLA, Los Angeles 1948-51, asst. res. anatomist UCLA, Long Beach 1951-53; biochemist US Veterans Adminstrn., Long Beach 1953-; asst. clin. prof. biochem. UCLA, Los Angeles 1955-80; assoc. clin. prof. physiol. UC Irvine, 1980-84, clin. prof. radiol. sci., 1984-; vis. res. fellow Oxford Univ., Eng. 1963-64; mem: Am. Thyroid Assn. 1964-, Clin. Ligand Assay Soc. (1963-, v.p. So. Calif. 1964-67); publs: 2 book chapters, 50+ articles in var. sci. jours. re thyroid physiology and neuroendocrinology. Ofc: Lab. Veterans Hospital 5901 E Seventh St Long Beach 90822

FLOYD, JAMES KEMPER, manufacturing company executive; b. July 27, 1933, Columbus, Ohio; s. Edmund James and Rosamono Richmal (Latta) F.; m. Carol M. Svatos, Sept. 2, 1956; children: Deborah b. 1958, Laura b. 1960, Elaine b. 1961, Raymond b. 1962; edn: BS aero. engring., Ohio St. Univ. 1956; MBA, Univ. Louisville 1978. Career: mgr. engring. Am. Air Filter (noises control div.), Louisville, Ky. 1970-78; dir. engring. Greer Hydraulics, Commerce 1978-81; v.p. engring. U.S. Filter Fluid Systems Corp., Whittier 1981-84, v.p.

ops. and engring. 1984-85, v.p., gen. mgr. 1985-88, pres. 1988-; 3 patents held for gas pulsation dampener, vacuum pump silencer and pneumatic accumulator, 1978-81; articles pub. in tech. jours., 1968-78; mil: capt. AUS 1956-64; Republican; Methodist; rec: photography, jogging, woodworking. Res: 5091 Fairway View Dr Yorba Linda 92686 Ofc: U.S. Filter Fluid Systems Corp. 12442 E Putman St Whittier 90602

FLYNN, JOHN ALLEN, lawyer; b. Jan. 12, 1945, Riverside, Ill.; s. Wm. and Marian Rae (Gustafson) F.; children: Judson b. 1972, Erin b. 1972; m. Georgette A. Kaleiki, Dec. 31, 1988; edn: AB, Stanford Univ. 1966; JD, UC Hastings Coll. of Law 1969; admitted to State Bar of Calif. 1970, US Dist. Cts., US Ct. of Appeals Ninth Cir. 1970, US Sup. Ct. 1975. Career: partner Graham & James, Attys., San Francisco 1969-; guest spkr., Practicing Law Inst., `Maritime Personal Injury,' Los Angeles 1980, San Francisco 1982; guest spkr. Lloyd's of London Press, `Maritime Claims,' S.F. 1984; recipient Am. Jurisprudence Award. in Community Property 1969; mem: Am Bar Assn.; Maritime Law Assn. (Practice and Procedure com. 1983-90, Uniformity of Maritime Law com. 1990-); San Francisco Bar Assn. (chmn. Admiralty Com. 1978-); R.Cath.; rec: golf, swimming. Res: 315 Castle Crest Rd Walnut Creek 94595 Ofc: Graham & James, One Maritime Plaza, Ste 300, San Francisco 94111

FOERTMEYER, WILLIAM LOUIS, artist; b. Feb. 6, 1921, San Francisco; s. Wm. Adolphus and Nelle Mae (Stangle) F.; edn: BA (honors), Yale Coll., 1943, grad. study Columbia Univ. 1948-50, Nat. Acad. of Design 1954-55; mem: Alpha Sigma Phi frat., Yale Club of Monterey; mil: pfc Army Enlisted Reserve 1942-44; Republican. Studio: Carmel-By-Sea 93923

FOLLICK, EDWIN DUANE, college dean, chiropractic physician; b. Feb. 4, 1935, Glendale; s. Edwin Fulfford and Esther Agnes (Catherwood) Follick; m. Marilyn Kay Sherk, March 24, 1986; edn: BA, CSU Los Angeles, 1956, MA, 1961; MA, Pepperdine Univ., 1957; MPA, 1977; PhD and DTheol. St. Andrews Theol. Coll., Seminary of the Free Prot. Episcopal Ch. London, 1958; MS in LS, USC, 1963; MEd, 1964; AdvMEd, 1969; LLB, Blackstone Law Sch., 1966, JD, 1967; DC, Cleveland Chiropractic Coll., L.A. 1972; PhD, Acad. Theatina, Pescara 1978; MAOM orgn. mgmt., Antioch Univ., L.A. 1990. Career: teacher/lib. adminstr. Los Angeles City Schs. 1957-68; law librarian Glendale Univ. Coll of Law 1968-69; coll. librarian Cleveland Chiropractic Coll., L.A. 1969-74, prof. jurisprudence, 1975-, dir. edn. and admissions 1974-85, dean student affairs 1976-92, chaplain of the coll. and dean of edn. 1986-; extern prof. St. Andrews (London) 1961; assoc. prof. Newport Univ. 1982; dir. West Valley Chiropractic Health Center, 1972-; honors: Cavaliere Intl. Order Legion of Honor of Immaculata (Italy); Knight of Malta, Order St. John of Jerusalem; Ritter, Der Intl. Legion Friedrich II von Schwaben Teutonische Miliz; Comdr. Chevalier, Byzantine Imperial Order of Constantine the Great; Comdr. Ritter, Order of St. Gereon; Knight, Order of Signum Fidei; mem: Am. Chiro. Assn., Internat. Chiro. Assn., ALA, NEA, Am. Assn. Sch. Librarians, Assn. Coll. and Resrch. Librarians, Am. Assn. Law Librarians, Intl. Platform Assn., Nat. Geographic Soc., Phi Delta Kappa, Sigma Chi Psi, Delta Tau Alpha. mil: chaplain's asst. US Army Air Def. Command 1958-60; Democrat; Episcopalian. Res: 6435 Jumilla Ave Woodland Hills 91367 Ofc: 7022 Owensmouth Ave Canoga Pk 91303 Ofc: 590 N Vermont Av Los Angeles 90004

FOLTZ, ELDON LEROY, professor of neurological surgery; b. Mar. 28, 1919, Ft. Collins, Colo.; s. Leroy Stuart and Emily Louise (Proctor) F.; m. Katherine C. Crosby, Oct. 18, 1943; children: Sally Jean b. 1946, James Stuart b. 1948, Janice Ann b. 1951, Suzanne Ellen b. 1955; edn: BS (magna cum laude), Mich. St. Univ., E. Lansing, 1941; MD, Univ. Mich., Ann Arbor, 1943. Career: intern dept. surg. University Hosp., Ann Arbor, Mich. 1943-44, asst. resident, surgery, 1946-47; Horace H. Rackham Sch. of Grad. Studies, Univ. Mich., neuropathology and neuroanatomy, 1947; neurosurg. resident Dartmouth Med. Sch. and Hitchcock Clinic, Hanover, N.H., 1947-49; Univ. of Louisville, Ky., 1949-50; resrch. assoc. div. neurosurg. Univ. of Washington, 1950-51, instr. 1951-53, asst. prof. 1953-58, assoc. prof. 1958-64, prof. neurological surgery, 1964-69; cons. neurol. surg. VA Hosp., Long Beach, Calif. 1969-; prof. UC Irvine, 1969-, and chmn. div. neurol. surg. 1969-80; prof. emeritus UC Irvine, 1989-; program dir. Neurol. Surgical Resident Tng., UCI, 1970-80, 85-86; dir. of neurosurgical resrch. UCI, 1982-86; awards: NIMH postdoctoral fellow, 1950-51, Markle Scholar in Med. Sci., 1954-59, Alpha Omega Alpha, Prototype instructional materials in the clin. neuroscis. Dept. HEW, CDC, Atlanta, 1972-74, Outstanding Alumnus Award Coll. of Natural Sci. Mich. St. Univ. ,1980, Schulte Research Fellow Schulte Research Inst., 1983-84, Distinguished Prof. Univ. of Calif., 1987; mem: AMA, Am. Assn. Neurol. Surgeons (ped. neurosurg. subsect.), Am. Coll. of Surgeons, Am. Acad. of Neurology, Am. Electroencephalographic Soc., AAAS, We. Neurosurg. Soc. (pres. 1976-77), We. Electroencephalographic Soc., Calif. Assn. of Neurol. Surgeons, CMA, Neurosurgical Soc. Am. (pres. 1979-80), Phi Chi Med. Frat., Am. Acad. of Neurol. Surgeons, Research Soc. Neurol. Surgeons, Assn. of Am. Med. Colls., Soc. of Sigma Xi, Soc. of Neurol. Surgeons, Orange Co. Med. Assn., Soc. of Neurol. Surgeons of O.C. (pres. 1976-77), Internat. Soc. Pediatric Neurosurgeons, Internat. Soc. Psychiatric Surg., Internat. Soc. for Stereoencephalotomy and Functional Neurophysiology; civic: Irvine Cove Comm.

Assn. (coms. chmn. 1982-83), Annual Parents Hydrocephalus Conf., Golden West Coll. (dir. annual all day cont. edn. conf. 1982-90); publs: 120+ articles in peer-reviewed jours. (primary author 58), numerous abstracts, research studies and acad. lectures; mil: lt. MC-USNR 1944-46; Laguna Beach Congregational Ch. (choir 1971-, music com. 1982-, Com. of Elders 1975-77); rec: sailing. Res: 2480 Monaco Dr Laguna Beach 92651 Ofc: UCI Medical Center 101 The City Dr - Rt.81 (Neurosurgery) Orange 92668

FONES, MONTY GARTH, consultant, writer, retired teacher; b. Dec. 5, 1932, Dalhart, Tx.; s. Wilbur Leslie and Bernice Hazel (Wiley) F.; m. Nancy Jeanne Mills, Dec. 23, 1972; edn: BS math, Panhdle A&M 1955; grad. work, UC Berkeley 1960; MA, San Diego St. Univ. 1964. Career: tchr. Redwood H.S., Visalia 1960-61; Newport Mesa Unified Sch. Dist., Newport Beach and Costa Mesa 1961-89; consultant, 1989-; awards: grantee CAEMAT Media Assn., 1974, NMEA Edn. Assn. Beacon Education Award, 1975, Back Bay High Sch. Teacher of Year, 1983, Newport Schs. Found. grantee, 1987-88, 88-89; civic: Rainbow Warriors of Green Peace, Lions (pres. 1973-4); ed. Colonizing a Planet, 1968, author: Model Rocket Guidebook, 1972, editor Metric Guidebook, 4 Editions, 1972-75, author/editor Tech. in Curriculum, 1989; mil: lt.jg USNR 1956-59; Methodist; rec: music, photog., computing. Res: 2201 Tavern Rd Alpine 91901

FONSECA, EMIDIO LOPES, general building contractor; b. Feb. 9, 1933, Portugal, naturalized May 15, 1964; s. Alfredo Lopes and Maria Augusta (de Jesus) da Fonseca; m. Mary, July 27, 1958; children: Anna Maria b. 1962, David b. 1965, Sandra b. 1968; edn: grad. Internat. Trade Sch., Lisbon; spl. courses Naval Tng. Sch., Radio TV Sch., Gen. Contractors Sch., Mechanics Sch.; lic. B-1 gen. building contr., Calif. Career: carpenter trainee Pacheco Constrn. Ltd., Guimaraes, Portugal 1947-52; machinist mate 1/c Portuguese Navy, 1953-58; formica millman Henderson & Assocs., Berkeley 1958-66; gen. contr./prin., Orinda 1966-; projects include hotel restoration of the York, The Lombard, Chancellor, Hyde Park, Richelieu hotels (all in S.F.); prop. Elekai Motel, South Lake Tahoe 1978-87; awards: scholastic honor roll Portuguese Navy, 1957; Portuguese Govt. medal of honor for service to community 1992; Sears, Roebuck, Concord excellence in contracting award, 1978, 79, 80; biog. listings 5,000 Personalities of World, Internat. Who's Who of Intellectuals, ABIRA life fellow, nat. advr., medals of honor (gold, silver, brass); mem: Licensed Contrs. Assn., 1966-; Carpenters Local #180, Vallejo, 1958-; Nat. S. Bus. United, Better Bus. Bur. (Contra Costa, Alameda, Solano Cos.), Elks Club, Our Lady of Fatima Soc. Thornton, Nat. Trust for Hist. Preservation, ASPA/Portuguese Navy Veterans in USA (Calif. pres. 1992-93);Master Bldrs. Assoc.,Internat. Conf. of Blg. Officials, Republican (Nat. Congl. Club, Presdl. Task Force charter mem. & Honor Roll 1981-, Rep. Nat. Com. 1979-); R.Cath.; rec: travel. Res: 52 Orchard Rd Orinda 94563 Ofc: Emidio Fonseca Remodeling and Construction, 52 Orchard Rd Orinda 94563

FOPPIANO, LOUIS J., vinter; b. Nov. 25, 1910, Healdsburg; s. Louis A. and Matilda (Canata) F.; m. Della, Feb. 17, 1947; children: Louis, Rodney, Susan; Career: pres. L. Foppiano Wine Co., Healdsburg; mem: K.C.; Republican; R.Cath.; rec: flying, hunting. Ofc: PO Box 606 Healdsburg 95448

FORBES, JUDITH L., engineering executive; b. Sept. 27, 1942, Fullerton; d. James Franklin and Lois Virginia (Couse) Forbes; m. Thomas Wilkins, June 8, 1961 (div.); m. Edward Resha, Aug. 2, 1967 (div.); children: Laurel b. 1962, James b. 1963, John b. 1967; edn: BA physics, CSU Fullerton 1974; MS engring., 1979; MBA, USC 1983; PhD, Claremont Gra. Exec. Mgmt. Sch. 1987-. Career: engr. Northrop Electromech., Anaheim 1975-79; tech. staff TRW, San Bernardino 1979-80; project engr., mgr. Northrop Electronics, Hawthorne 1980-87; project mgr. Gen. Research, El Segundo 1987-89; prog. mgr. TRW Technar, Irwindale 1989-; v.p. D.C. Caldwell & Co., Monrovia 1987-; asst. prof. CSU Fullerton 1974-75; awards: Orange Co. Engring. Council Engr. of Merit 1985, CSU Fullerton Disting. Alumni 1987; mem: Soc. of Women Engrs. (pres. L.A. 1981-82, nat. v.p. 1983-85), Am. Inst. Aero. & Astro. (pres. Orange Co. 1986-87), Town Hall of Calif.; articles pub. in tech. jours., 1974-76, 77; author column on tech. mgmt., 1982-87, speaker on engring. and mgmt., 1980-; mil: AC3 USN 1960-61; Democrat; rec: piano, flying, theater. Res: 23557 Casa Loma Dr Diamond Bar 91765 Ofc: TRW Technar, 5462 Irwindale Ave Irwindale 91007

FORD, ELIZABETH BLOOMER (MRS. GERALD R. FORD), First Lady during 38th U.S. Presidency; b. Apr. 8, 1918, Chgo.; d. Wm. Stephenson and Hortence (Neahr) Bloomer; m. William Warren, 1942, div. 1947; m. 2d Gerald R. Ford (elected to Congress 2 weeks after wedding), Oct. 15, 1948; children: Michael Gerald, John Gardner, Steven Meigs, Susan Elizabeth; ed. Bennington Sch. Dance, 1936-38; LLD (hon.), Univ. Mich. 1976. Career: dancer Martha Graham Concert Group, NYC 1939-41; model John Powers Agcy., NYC 1939-41; fashion dir. Herpolsheimer's Dept. Store, Grand Rapids, Mich. 1943-48; dance instr. Grand Rapids, 1932-48; raised 4 children, also active in GOP, Episcopal Ch. and family, 1950s-60s; as First Lady focused on the arts, handicapped and women's issues 1974-78, mem. Nat. Commn. on Observance of Internat. Women's Year 1977; ongoing svc. in field of chemical dependency recovery: trustee Eisenhower Med. Ctr., Rancho Mirage, and pres. bd. dirs. Betty Ford Ctr. (chem. dependency recovery unit), 1982-; Betty Ford cancer resrch., screening & prevention ctrs. opened at Cedars Sinai Hosp., L.A. 1978, Columbia Hosp. for Women, W.D.C. 1980, Blodgett Memorial Hosp., Grand Rapids, Mich. 1987; other affils: co-ch. ERA Countdown Campaign 1981-82, advy. com. State of Calif. Chem. Dependency Recovery Hosp., The Lambs, Inc. nat. tng. ctr. for mentally retarded adults, Libertyville, Ill. (hon. bd. dirs.), Center Theatre of the Performing Arts, P.S. (hon. Golden Cir. Patrons), P.S. Desert Mus. (hon. chair bd. trustees), Nsg. Home Advy. Com. (bd. trustees), White House Preserv. Fund (hon. co-chair), Martha Graham Dance Ctr. (trustee), Nat. Arthritis Found. (hon. trustee), Bob Hope Cultural Ctr. (theatre mgmt. com.); honors: hon. Dr. of Laws Univ. Mich. 1976, recipient num. humanitarian and service awards including Women's Div. Anti-Def. League, B'nai Brith 1975, Ladies Home Jour. 1976, ICCJ 1978), Albert Einstein Coll. of Med. 1979, Friends of Hebrew Univ. 1981, Am. Cancer Soc. 1982, Am. Lung Assn. 1983, Nat. Fedn. of Press Women 1983, Susan G. Komen Found. 1983, Abraxas Found. 1983, Calif. Women's Commn. of Alcoholism 1984, YWCA of Nat. Capitol Area 1985, L.A. Girl Scouts Council 1985, L.A. AIDS Project 1985, Nat. Ctr. for Health Edn. 1986, Nat. Council on Alcoholism 1986, Internat. Ctr. for the Disabled 1987, Gateway Rehab. Ctr. 1987, others; publs: autobiography: The Times of My Life (1979), Betty: A Glad Awakening (1987); Address: PO Box 927 Rancho Mirage 92770

FORD, GERALD RUDOLPH, JR., 38th President of the United States, b. July 14, 1913, Omaha; s. Gerald R. and Dorothy (Gardner) F.; m. Elizabeth Bloomer, Oct. 15, 1945; children: Michael Gerald, John G., Steven M., Susan Elizabeth; edn: AB, Univ. Mich. 1935; LLB, Yale Univ. 1941; LLD (hon) Mich. State Univ., Aquinas Coll., Spring Arbor Coll., Albion Coll., Grand Valley State Coll., Belmont Abby Coll., Western Mich. Univ.; admitted to Mich. State Bar, 1941. Career: law practice in Grand Rapids, Mich. 1941-49; assoc. firm Butterfield, Amberg, Law & Buchen, 1946-51, ptnr. Amberg, Law, Buchen & Fallon, 1951-59, Buchen & Ford, after 1960; elected mem. 81st to 93d congresses from 5th Mich. Dist., mem. Appropriations Com., minority leader, 1954-73; apptd. vice president United States of Am., 1973-74, elected US President, 1974-77; dir: Shearson Lehman Bros., Tiger Internat.; honors: distinguished service award, Grand Rapids Jr. C.of C. 1948, one of ten outstanding young men in US, US Jr. C.of C. 1950, Sports Illus. Silver Anniversary All-American 1959, Congl. distinguished service, Am. Polit. Sci. Assn. 1961, George Washington award, Am. Good Govt. Soc. 1966, Gold Medal award Nat. Football Found. 1972; mem. Am., Mich., Grand Rapids bar assns., Delta Kappa Epsilon, Phi Delta Phi, Masons, University Club, Peninsular (Kent Co.) Club; author: A Time To Heal: The Autobiography of Gerald R. Ford (1979), Global Stability (1982); coauthor: Portrait of the Assassin; mil: served to lcdr. USN 1942-46; Republican; Episcopalian. Address: PO Box 927, Rancho Mirage 92270

FORD, JOHN T., JR., teacher; b. Feb. 17, 1953, Rotan, Tx.; s. John T. and Lala Fern (Shipley) F.; m. Betty Jean Crawford, Aug. 21, 1976; children: Casey b. 1980, Craig b. 1983, Kirk b. 1986; edn: BA, Univ. of Redlands, 1974. Career: tchr. Yucaipa Jt. Unified Sch. Dist., 1976-88; creative coordinator (conceptual art) "Whole Sch. Environments" Green Valley H.S. 1980-84; Vacaville Sch. Dist., 1990-; mem.: dist. task force on technology, and on vocat. edn., 1992-; producer TV4U 1992; awards: Golden Bell award Calif. Sch. Board Research Found. 1987, tchr. of year Calif. Continuation Ednl. Assn. Dist. VIII 1987; mem. Calif. Tchrs. Assn. 1979-; Prot.; rec: reading. Ofc: Will C. Wood High School 998 Marshall Rd Vacaville 95687

FOREMAN, JOHN PATRICK, electrical engineer; b. Aug. 16, 1954, Lake Charles, La.; s. John Calvin Foreman and Daisy Mae (Finley) F. Milsted; edn: BSEE, McNeese St. Univ., 1976; reg. profl. engr. Calif., Tx. La., Ore. Career: electrical engr. Flour Corp., Houston, Tx. 1977-83; Jacob Engring. Group 1983-84; Burgess & Niple Inc. 1984-86; project mgmt. Turpin & Rattan Engring. Inc., S.D. 1986-; mem: Nat. Soc. Profl. Engrs., Calif. Soc. Profl. Engrs. (S.D.chpt.), Tx. Soc. Profl.Engrs. (San Jacinto chpt.), La. Engring. Soc., IEEE; rec: skiing. Res: 1110 24th San Diego 92102

FOREST, IRA, developer; b. Feb. 18, 1920, Milwaukee, Wis.; s. Harry and Frances (Pelsinger) F.; m. Joyce Levine, Nov. 23, 1944 (div. 1970); m. Myrna Miller Snyder, Jan. 9, 1982; children: David b. 1948, Michael b. 1955, Adam b. 1960; edn: BS, Stanford Univ. 1942. Career: engr. Standard Oil Calif., Los Angeles 1942-43, 46-47; sales engr. Kelley Petroleum, Long Beach 1947-49; retail owner Discount Stores 1950-60; builder, developer Forest & Co., Los Angeles 1960-; bd. dirs. Am. West Bank 1987-; mem: BSA (commr. 1967-70), Building Industry Assn. L.A. (past pres., bd. dirs.), Internat. Conf. of Shopping Centers, Stanford Univ. Alumni Assn., Mountain Gate Tennis Club, Palm Springs Racquet Club, Marina City Club; report pub. Congressional Record, WDC "Opportunity for U.S. Builders in Middle East", US Dept. Commerce Trade Missions (1967, 78); mil: capt. USAF 1943-46, 4 air medals, Disting. Flying Cross, presdl. citation 1944; Republican; Jewish; rec: tennis, bicycling, walking. Ofc: Forest & Co. 16861 Ventura Blvd Ste 200 Encino 91436

FORESTIER, DANIELLE, master baker; b. Feb. 28, 1943, Ray, Ariz.; d. Earl Francis Ruth and Dorothy Margaret (Steil) Toms; m. Charles H. Schley II, Nov. 10, 1962 (div. 1982); children: Sara b. 1963, Charles III b. 1964; edn: BA in art, Bennington Coll., 1966; desig: Maitre Boulanger (Master Baker) Chambre de Commerce, Paris, France 1977; cert. tchr. Internat. Assn. of Cooking Professionals, W.D.C. 1986. Career: baker Boulangerie Candalot, Paris, France 1974-77; owner, opr. Les Belles Miches, Santa Barbara, Calif. 1977-81; cons. Forestier, Boulanger, Oakland 1982-; cons. Chopin, Paris, Fr. 1986-89, Anheuser-Busch, St. Louis, Mo. 1985, Am. Inst. of Baking, Manhattan, Ks. (1984, 86), General Mills (1991,92), Calif. Apricot Adv. Bd. 1992; awards: "Best bread in Calif." California Mag., L.A. 1980, listed Who's Who in West 1991; mem: Am. Inst. of Wine & Food (founder 1981-), San Francisco Soc. of Food Profls. 1992-, Amicale de Bon Pain 1987-; contbr. articles in Cook's Mag. (1986-87), Am. Inst. Baking (1990); Democrat; rec: ballet, opera, dining, golf. Res: 470 Weldon Ave Oakland 94610 Ofc: D. Forestier, Maitre Boulanger, 470 Weldon Ave Oakland 94610

FORGHANI, BAGHER, virologist; b. Mar. 10, 1936, Bandar-Anzali, Iran; s. Baba and Jahan (Rahimi) F.; m. Nikoo Alavi, June 12, 1969; children: Niki b. 1971, Nikta b. 1975; edn: PhD, Justus Liebig Univ., Giessen, Ger. 1965. Career: postdoctoral fellow Utah State Univ., Logan 1965-67; asst. prof. Nat. Univ. of Iran, Tehran 1967-69; postdoctoral fellow Calif. State Dept. Health Svs., Berkeley, Calif. 1970-72, research specialist, 1972-82, research scientist, 1982-; scientific advy. bd. Varicella-Zoster Virus Research Found., Inc. N.Y. 1991-; mem: Am. Soc. for Microbiology 1969-, Nat. Registry of Microbiologists 1974-; author: 7 chapters in virological books, 45+ original papers in virology in nat. and internat. sci. jours. (1966-); Moslem. Res: 134 Lombardy Ln Orinda 94563

FORMAN, SANFORD, air freight company president; b. Sept. 22 1932, New York; s. Louis and Rose (Fenster) F.; m. Marilyn Resnick, Aug. 29, 1954; children: Suzanne b. 1956, Jody b. 1959; edn: BS, Fairliegh Dickinson Univ. 1960. Career: nat. ops. mgr. W.T. Grant, N.Y.C. 1958-69; gen. traffic mgr. Mattel Inc., Hawthorne 1970-78; v.p. A. Cesana & Assoc., Los Angeles 1979-88; AFSAC 1979-88; pres. Alliance Air Freight 1985-; Alliance Courier Service 1986-; Air Freight Forwarding Co. 1988-; tchr. L.A. Trade Tech. 1971-78; instr. Golden West Coll., Hungtington Beach 1980-; mem: Western Traffic Conf., Toy Mfg. Am., Traffic Mgrs. Conf. of Calif., Jewish War Vets., DAV; mil: sgt. USAF 1951-55; Democrat; Jewish; rec: skiing, tennis, running. Address: PO Box 88549 Los Angeles 90009

FORMAN, TERRI P., marketing/communications consultant; b. Oct. 1, 1954, Wash. D.C.; d. Joseph and Ethel Frances (London) Pincus; m. Max Robert Forman, Aug. 20, 1978; 1 child, Hallie b. 1988; edn: BA, Univ. of Miami, 1975. Career: assoc. devel. dir. Easter Seal Rehabilitation Ctr., Dade County, Fla. 1979-81; assoc. United Way of Dade County, 1981-82; staff exec. United Way, San Francisco, 1983-91; sr. assoc. 1983-87, mgr. advtg. creative services 1987-88, v.p. communications 1988-90, group v.p. advtg. and communications 1990-91; mktg./ communications cons. 1991-; awards: MOBIUS Award 1991, CLIO Awards (1987, 89), `Best in the West' Am. Advt. Fedn. 1983-89; mem: San Francisco Ad Club, Internat. Assn. of Bus. Communicators, Pub. Rels. Soc. Am., World Affairs Council. Ofc: 1513 Golden Gate Ave San Francisco 94115

FORREST, WILLIAM V., executive compensation consultant; b. July 19, 1952, Pocatello, Idaho; s. William and Margaret Alice (Martin) F.; m. Debra Jean Hutchings, Aug. 20, 1976; children: Benjamin b. 1977, Katherine b. 1979, Matthew b. 1983, Karalyn b. 1984; edn: BA, Brigham Young Univ. 1976; MBA, 1979; chartered life underwriter 1983. Career: sr. cons. Life Ins. Mktg. & Research Assn., Farmington, Conn. 1979-83; account exec. Systema Corp., Chgo., Ill. 1983-85; Hewitt Assoc., Santa Ana 1985-86; sr. cons. Alexander Group, Irvine 1986-87; sr.v.p. Clark Bardes Inc., Pasadena 1987-; honors: Conn. Mutual Life presdl. hon. 1988; mem: Nat. Assn. Life Underwriters, Am. Soc. Cert. Life Underwriters, Pasadena Athletic Club, John Wooden Awards; articles pub. in profl. jours., 1981-84; Republican; Mormon; rec: golf, jogging. Res: 425 San Leandro Dr Diamond Bar 91765 Ofc: Clark Bardes Inc. 199 S Los Robles Ave Ste 650 Pasadena 91101

FORTIN, JEFFREY ALLEN, safety and risk management consultant, entrepreneur; b. June 26, 1957, Worcester, Mass.; s. Albert Alfonse and Bette Louise (Arcand) F.; edn: AA, San Bdo. Valley Coll. 1981; AA in journ., (hons.), Am. River Coll. Sacto. 1982; grad. Calif. Mil. Acad. 1988; desig: REA. Career: pres. and c.e.o. J.Fortin & Assocs., Inc., San Jose 1986-92; pres. and c.e.o. National Environmental & Safety Technologies, San Jose 1992-; safety cons./risk mgr. Central Concrete Supply Co. Inc., 1977-; Central Transport, Inc., 1982-; Quikrete of No. Cal, Inc., 1988-; recipient disting. service award Am. River Coll. (1982); mem. Calif. Trucking Assn. (chmn. Santa Clara County (SCC) Unit 1991-92); civic bds: San Bdo. City Police Commn. (1981), Santa Clara Co. Personnel Bd. (chmn. 1988-), SCC Social Services Advy. Commn. (v. chair 1983-90), SCC Justice Advy. Bd. (1986-88), SCC Youth Found. Inc. (founder, chmn. 1987-), Timpany Ctr. Found. (dir 1989-90), Community Kids to Camp Inc. (dir. 1986-88), student advy. com. Calif. Postsec. Edn. Commn. (1980-81); past mem. Calif. Comm. Coll. Student Govt. Assn. (exec. bd. 1981-82); mil: sgt.

USAF 1974-79, AF Reserve (TSG) 1979-82, Calif. Nat. Guard/USAR (2LT) M.P. 1985-89, decorated USAF Commendn. w./oak leaf, Humanitarian, Presdl. unit Cit., USAF Outstanding unit cit., Good Conduct, Longevity; Democrat; rec: philately, racketball, swimming, jogging. Ofc: NEST, PO Box 610966 San Jose 95161-0966

FOSTER, CLYDE THURSTON, gold mine owner-operator; b. Apr. 30, 1911, Ukiah (his birth cert. is No. 59 in Mendocino Co.); s. Raymond Osborne and Grace Lorain (Thurston) F.; married and widowed twice; edn: Santa Rosa Jr. Coll. 1928-29, Macky Sch. of Mines, Univ. of Nev. 1930-31, Stanford Univ. 1943. Career: first underground mining for father at Twin Sisters Mine in Nevada County, 1927, and Sweetwater Mine (acquired 1933); miner (and owner) Sleeping Beauty Mine 1931-52, and Sweetwater Mine, 1931-93; advisor Sweetwater Mine 1993-; also worked as micropaleontologist (w/micro fossils from Artic Slope) USGS, Fairbanks, Alaska 1946; computer US Corps of Engrs., Anchorage 1948; survey party chief AEC, Atomic Test Site Nev. and hydro elec. projects (Merced River, Tuolumne River, American River, Yuba River, Rancho Seco Nuclear Generating Plant), 1951-73; owner/opr. Sweetwater Mine, Mariposa (mining with the machinery, methods & language of the 1930s), 1952-; instr. Stamp Mill Sch. (the only sch. of its kind) Mariposa Hist. Soc., donated considerable gold collection to the Calif. State Mus., Mariposa; mil: tech. sgt. US Army WWII & Korea, 6 yrs Active Duty, 9 decorations. Address: Veterans Home of Calif. PO Box 1200 Yountville 94599-1297

FOSTER, JAMES MARK, television producer; b. April 6, 1947, Los Angeles; s. John (Glen) Leonard and Artiemese M. (Couturier) F.; m. Linda Kay Rhodes, Jan. 10, 1970 (div. 1983); children: Chelsie Lynn b. 1973, Evan James b. 1977; edn: AA, Pasadena City Coll., 1971; BS, USC, 1973. Career: v.p. Pathfinder Equipment, San Gabriel 1973-76; owner Alignment Enterprises, Costa Mesa 1976-80; pres. Gemini Productions, Irvine 1980-, pres. Ski Dazzle, Inc. 1987-, pres. Orange Co. Post Production, 1991-; honors: Beta Gamma Sigma, Houston Internat. T.V. Soc. Gold 1987; mem: Commerce Captains USC, So. Calif. Ski Writers Assn., E. Clampus Vitas; author (tv series) Ski Scene (1988); mil: E-5 sgt. USMC 1967-69; Republican; R.Cath.; rec: skiing. Ofc: 2082 Business Center Dr # 160 Irvine 92715

FOSTER, WILLIAM JAMES, III, gemologist, city official; b. Dec. 9, 1953, Princeton, N.J.; s. William James, Jr. and Frances Alberta (Savidge) F.; m. Lynn Marie McDonald, June 9, 1975; children: Trevor b. 1979, Tracy b. 1982; edn: BA in geology, Carleton Coll., Northfield, Minn. 1976; CDP, Inst. Certification of Computing Profls., 1983. Career: pgmr., information splst. Univ. of Mo., Kansas City 1979-81; staff cons. DST Systems Inc., K.C., Mo. 1982-86; ptnr. Carats and Crystals, Pismo Beach, 1986-; property mgr. Cypress Landing, 1986-; elected city council, Westwood, Kans. 1980-86, mayor 1986, councilman City of Pismo Beach, 1988-92; founder, dir. Facts About Tomorrow's Energy (non-profit, citizens' edn. gp.) 1981-84; mem: Nat. Assn. of Jewelry Appraisers (NJA), Am. Gem Soc. (reg. jeweler), Pismo Beach C.of C. (pres. 1988); Republican; Methodist; rec: trees (dwarf conifers), flying. Res: 241 Elaine Way Pismo Beach 93449 Ofc: Cypress Landing PO Box 1132 Pismo Beach 93448

FOUST, ROSANNE SKIBO, foreign industrial development executive; b. Feb. 28, 1964, Derby, Ct.; d. John Andrew and Claire Frances (Fallon) Skibo; m. Joseph Victor Foust, Jr. Dec. 30, 1989; edn: BA, Stonehill Coll., North Easton, Mass. 1986; UCLA exec. mgmt. prog. 1993. Career: program coord., dir. spl. events, dir. mktg. Internat. Bus. Ctr. of New England Inc., Boston 1986-88; assoc. dir., regional dir., dir. U.S. ops. Alsace (France) Devel. Agy., Los Angeles 1988-; mem: French Am. Chamber, L.A. (v.p. sec. 1993, v.p. mem. 1992, bd. 1990-91), Junior Achiev. Alumni Assn. 1988-, Am. Mgmt. Assn. 1990-, Nat. Assn. Female Execs. 1989-, LA Co. Mus. of Art 1990-; Republican; R.Cath. Ofc: 2029 Century Park East Ste 1115 Los Angeles 90067

FOWLER, MURRAY ELWOOD, professor of veterinary medicine; b. July 17, 1928, Glendale, Wash.; s. Harry Cyrenus and Elizabeth Hannah (Ruegg) F.; m. Audrey Cooley, June 5, 1950; children: Alan b. 1952, Gene b. 1954, Janet b. 1956, Linda b. 1959, Patricia b. 1962; edn: BS, Utah St. Univ. 1952; DVM, Iowa St. Univ. 1955. Career: practitioner pvt. practice, Van Nuys 1955-58; instr., prof. UC Davis 1958-; honors: BSA Silver Beaver 1979, UC Davis Outstanding Tchr. 1968, 74, Iowa St. Univ. Stange Alumni 1989; mem: Am. Bd. Vet. Toxicology, Am. Coll. Vet. Internal Medicine, Am. Coll. Zoological Medicine, AVMA, Am. Assn. Zoological Vets. (pres. 1978), Morris Animal Found. (trustee 1976-), Sacto. Zoo. Soc. (dir. 1968-); editor: Zoo & Wild Animal Medicine, 1978, 86; author: Restraint & Handling of Wild & Domestic Animals, 1978, Med. & Surgery of S. Am. Camelids, 1989, 170+ articles in sci. jours.; mil: USN 1946-48; Mormon; rec: photog., bird watching. Ofc: Univ. of Calif. School of Veterinary Medicine Room 2017 Davis 95616

FOX, SHEILA, advertising agency president; b. Feb. 11, 1947, Los Angeles; d. James Winton and Sheila (Doyle) Schooler; m. Charles S. Fox, Feb. 14, 1970; edn: BA, CSU Northridge 1969. Career: Leo Burnett Co., Los Angeles 1969-74; Boylhart, Lovett & Dean, L.A. 1974-78; Chapman/Warwick Advtg., San Diego 1978-, pres. 1984-; awards: Irish Woman of Yr. Irish Cong. of So. Calif. 1985;

mem: San Diego State Univ. Ad Club (lectr.), Ad Club of S.D. (bd. dirs. 1982-86, lectr.), S.D. Museum of Art, La Jolla Museum of Contemporary Art, S.D. Zoological Soc., Travel & Tourism Research Assn., Am. Film Inst., co-founder S.D. Olympic Host Com 1982-84, San Diego Super Bowl Task Force (vol. 1989-90), S.D. C.of C., S.D. Conventions & Visitors Bur. (mktg. com. 1980-), Irish Cong. of So. Calif. (St. Patrick's Day Parade Com. 1982-85); mem. mktg. com. Old Globe Theatre 1986-89, Muscular Dystrophy Assn. (Jerry Lewis Labor Day telethon vol., Rainbow Auction com.). Ofc: Chapman/Warwick Advertising 2445 Fifth Ave Ste 401 San Diego 92101

FRAHMANN, DENNIS GEORGE, computer manufacturing company executive; b. June 25, 1953, Medford, Wis.; s. George Henry and Aini (Siikarla) F.; edn: BA, Ripon Coll., 1974; MS, Columbia Univ., 1975; postgrad. Univ. Minn., 1979. Career: free lance writer, Mpls., 1975-77, contbg. editor Mpls.-St. Paul Mag., 1976-79; instructional designer Control Data Corp., Mpls. 1977-80; mgr. customer edn. Xerox Corp., Los Angeles 1980-84, mgr. Xerox Systems Inst., Palo Alto 1984-89, mgr. consultant relations Xerox Corp., L.A. 1989-; speaker trade & profl. assns., 1984-; honors: Phi Beta Kappa 1976; mem. Ripon Coll. Alumni Assn. (bd. 1978-80), MECLA 1983-87; civic: Silver Lake Improvement Assn. (dir. 1988-90); numerous pub. articles in field (1975-); Democrat; rec: running, gourmet cooking.

FRAITAG, LEONARD ALAN, mechanical/design engineer; b. Dec. 23, 1961, N.Y.C.; s. David and Lucille Renee (Jay) F.; m. Dorann Elizabeth Meecham, June 28, 1987; children: Shoshana b. 1989, Aaron b. 1992; edn: AA, Grossmont Coll., 1983; BSME, San Diego State Univ., 1987. Career: design engr. Restaurant Concepts, San Diego 1987; mech. engr. Vantage Assocs. Inc., 1988-89; design engr. Mainstream Engineering Co. Inc., 1989; design engr. Sola/Barnes-Hind, 1989-; honors: Pi Tau Sigma 1987-, cash award Vlier Enerpac, Burbank 1990; lodges: Al Bahr Shrine (noble 1989-), Scottish Rite (32nd deg., class pres.), F&AM Blackmer #442 (master); Democrat; rec: camping, computers, sports. Ofc: Sola/Barnes-Hind, 8006 Engineer Rd San Diego 92111

FRANCIS, TIMOTHY DUANE, chiropractor; b. Mar. 1, 1956, Chgo.; s. Joseph Duane and Barbara Jane (Sigwalt) F.; edn: BS biol., Los Angeles Coll. of Chiropractic 1982, DC (magna cum laude), 1984; MS nutrition/biol., Univ. of Bridgeport 1986; bd. qual. as team physician, LACC Postgrad. Sch. 1984-85. Career: pvt. practice chiropractic, 1984-; faculty Univ. of Nev., Reno 1976-80, L.A. Coll. of Chiropractic 1983-85; honors: Phi Kappa Phi (1978; Scholar of Year award 1980), Charles F. Cutts Scholar 1980, Delta Sigma 1982, Nat. Dean's List 1981-84; Republican; R.Cath.; rec: karate, bodybuilding, shooting. Res: PO Box 81961 Las Vegas NV 89180 Ofc: 3750 S Jonas Las Vegas NV 89103

FRANCO, CRAIG ANTHONY, numismatic investment company executive; b. Nov. 30, 1959, Los Angeles; s. Abelardo Fernandez and Joan Marie (Loveland) F.; m. Erin S.; edn: Calif. Polytech. St. Univ. Pomona, 4 yrs., Univ. La Verne, 2 yrs. Career: numismatist Miller-Contursi, Inc. Newport Beach 1982-86; v.p. fin. DNI, Claremont 1986-87; founder, bd. chmn. and c.e.o. Pacific Rarities Inc., Redlands 1988-; cons. T.G.M. Inc., St. Paul, Minn. 1984-86, Am. Telesis, Newport Beach 1985-88; recipient scholarship Univ. La Verne 1982-84; mem: ANA, IAFP, CSNA, NGC, PCGS, NSDR, CABDAP, PNG, ICTA; civic: speaker for Holy Family Adoption Agency, and Saint Anne's Hosp. 1978-, tchr. Elizabeth Anne Seton Ch. and St. Joseph's Ch., Upland 1986-91, youth minister St. Adelaide's Ch. 1991-92, founder/chmn. The Give Back Foundation (non-profit orgn. for underprivileged youth), bd. dirs. Children's Fund 1993-; publs: numerous pub. articles in field, ed. fin. newsletter "Market Report" (1988-), asst. ed. "MarketWise" 1986-87; Republican; R.Cath.; rec: music, art, literature. Address: PO Box 1064 Redlands 92373 Tel: 909/798-6103

FRANKE, RICHARD H., mathematician, educator; b. Apr. 11, 1937, Herndon, Ks.; s. Claude E. and Beulah E. (Tannehill) F.; m. J. Amelia Franklin, July 6, 1963; children: Evan b. 1967, Tanna b. 1970, Hailey b. 1970; edn: BS math. & physics, Ft. Hays State Coll., Ks. 1959; MS math., Univ. of Utah, S.L.C., 1961, PhD math., 1970. Career: research engr. Boeing Co., Wichita, Ks., Huntsville, Ala., New Orleans, La., 1961-64; research scientist Kaman Nuclear, Colorado Springs, Co. 1964-66; prof. Naval Postgraduate Sch., Monterey, Calif. 1970-, chmn. dept. math 1992-; liaison scientist Office of Naval Research, European Ofc., London 1988-89; vis. prof. Univ. of Utah, S.L.C. 1977, Drexel Univ., Phila. 1980-81; awarded 20-Yr. Service pin USN 1990; mem: Soc. for Indsl. & Applied Math. 1973-, Sigma Xi 1972-, Am. Math. Soc. 1970-75, Math. Assn. of Am. 1978-82, Slant 6 Club of Am. 1990-; civic: AFS, Monterey chpt. 1983-88; editor (book) Mathematical Linkages (1981), 30+ profl. jour. articles (1970-); rec: auto mechanics, sailing. Res: 877 Jefferson St Monterey 93940 Ofc: Naval Postgraduate School Dept. Math., Monterey 93943

FRANKLIN, CHARLES PATRICK, ambulance executive; b. Feb. 12, 1949, Los Angeles; s. Charles Arthur and Patricia Loraine (Haney) F.; m. Laurie Barbara Evanson, April 24, 1982; edn: BS mgmt. mktg., Santa Clara Univ. 1971. Career: player Phila. Phillies Baseball Club, Pa. 1971-73; asst. minor league dir. Calif. Angels Baseball, Anaheim 1973-76; unit production mgr.

KTLA T.V., Hollywood 1976-81; group cable gen. mgr. Group W Cable, Simi Valley 1981-87; gen. mgr. Design Gifts Internat., Corona 1987-89; Courtesy Services, San Bernardino 1989-; substitute tchr. Santa Clara Sch. Dist. 1972-73; cons. Dial One AC, Santa Monica 1983; Layman & Marcus Co., Hollywood 1985; awards: WCAC All League Baseball 1970-71; mem: Assn. Profl. Baseball Players, Diamond Bar C.of C.; author: The Young Oak, 1981; Republican; R.Cath.; rec: golf, carpentry. Ofc: Courtesy Services 338 W 7th St San Bernardino 92401

FRANKLIN, SCOTT H., manufacturing company executive; b. Oct. 27, 1954, Inglewood, Calif.; s. Harrison H. and Marjorie June (Johnson) F.; grad. Pacific Palisades H.S., 1972, stu. Santa Monica Coll., 1975-76. Career: auto sales Sun West Volkswagon, Hollywood 1972-76, Bob Smith Volkswagon, 1976; agt. Royal Ins. Agy., Encino 1976; mechanic Union Plastics Corp., North Hollywood 1977-78; rubber div. mgr. Calif. Gasket & Rubber, Gardena 1978-81, quality control mgr. 1981-82, v.p. ops. 1982-84, pres., CEO and chief ops., 1984-; mem: The Los Angeles Rubber Group Inc. 1981-, Am. Chem. Soc. 1984-, Soc. Mfg. Engrs. (sr. mem. 1987-), Am. Soc. for Quality Control 1990-, ASM Internat. 1990-, Instrument Soc. Am. 1992-, Calif. Mfrs. Assn., Precision Metalforming Assn., Calif. C.of C.; developer: mfg. process CALBOND (US reg. TM, 1988), material "Self-Lubricating Flouroelastomer" 1990; publs: tech. paper, Mixing Silicone Rubber (1986), essay, People Make The Difference (1989); Republican (GOP nat. com.); rec: gourmet cooking, computers. Ofc: California Gasket and Rubber Corp. 1601 W 134th St Gardena 90249

FRANKO, ROBERT MATTHEW, finance and real estate executive; b. 1947, Pittsburgh, Pa.; s. Robert M., Sr. and Ursula F.; m. Melanie Anne Hackett, 1980; edn: BS, Univ. Notre Dame, 1969; MBA, Central Mich. Univ., 1978; MIM, Am. Grad. Sch. of Internat. Mgmt. (Thunderbird Sch.), Phoenix, Az. 1979; reg. investment advisor; lic. gen. contractor, Calif. Career: sales rep. Coulter Electronics, Hialeah, Fla. 1974-75; mktg. mgr. Smith Kline Corp., Valley Forge, Pa. 1975-79; pres. Quality First Internat. Co., Phoenix, Az. 1980-84; sr. v.p. Citibank Arizona, Phoenix 1984-86; mng. dir. Docklands Financial Services, Inc. Costa Mesa, Calif. 1986-; c.f.o. Canary Wharf Devel. Co., London, England 1986-87; treas., bd. mem. Costa Mesa Senior Citizens Corp., 1990-; c.e.o. Pacific Point Partners, Costa Mesa 1988-; cons. Morningside Group 1988-; author: Export Import Operations - A Managers Guide (1979); rec: running. Ofc:Pacific Point Partners 650 Town Center #1900 Costa Mesa 92626

FRASER, EARL DONALD, city planning consultant; b. Sept. 9, 1912, Missoula, Mont.; s. William I. and Grace M. (Beeman) F.; m. Elizabeth Argento, May 16, 1942; edn: B.Arch. in city planning, M.I.T., 1937; M. in regional planning, Harvard Grad. Sch. of Design, 1939; desig: A.I.C.P., Am. Planning Assn. Career: city planner State Planning Boards, Ala. and Miss., 1939-41; senior planner Maryland Nat. Capital Park & Plan. Commn., Silver Spring, Md. 1942-43; planning dir. Kalamazoo, Mich., 1946-53; exec. dir. Redevelopment Agy., San Bernardino 1954-55; planning dir. County of Sacramento, 1955-77; city planning cons. prin., Sacto. 1978-; honors: Alpha Phi Omega disting. service award M.I.T. 1936; mem. Am. Inst. Planners 1948-; civic: Internat. Assn. of Torch Clubs (mem., ofcr., bd. various chpts. 1946-), SIRS (Sacto.); works: dir. local, city, county and reg. plans incl.: American River Pkwy. 1962, Sacramento Met. Airport - Natomas Area Plan 1967, Sacramento County Plan 1973; mil: lt. USN 1943-45; Unitarian-Universalist; rec: numismatics. Res: 2237 Ehrborn Way Sacramento 95825

FRASER, GLORIA JILL, composer; b. Oct 11, 1952, Cincinnati; d. David and Gloria Anna (Sgritta) Fraser; m. Gregg Gower Arreguin, Aug. 18, 1989; edn: MusB, E.Caro. Univ., Greenville 1974; MFA, Calif. Inst. of Arts, 1977. Career: composer, prin. dba Broadscore Music, Beverly Hills; original music feature films: Cutting Class, Personal Best, Hardcore, Reckless, Spirit of the Wind, When You Comin' Back Red Ryder; TV: Carlin on Campus, Breaking the Ice, Sesame Street; TV and radio commercials: Apple Computers, Baskin Robbins, California Cooler, Carl's Junior, Esso, Gen. Foods, Mattel, Lexus, Nissan, Mazda, Mexicana Airlines, Nat. Geographic Mag., Nike, Porsche, Safeway, Shell Oil, Yamaha Motorcycles, others; awards: Clio best local campaign "Buffy's Bedtime", "Confessions" 1986, Clio finalist :60 Radio "Grizzly" Great America, 1987; mem: Am. Fedn. of Musicians, ASCAP, Screen Actors Guild; mag. columnist: Music, Computers & Software Mag. 1986-88. Ofc: Broadscore Music POB 2252 Beverly Hills 91405

FRASSINELLI, GUIDO JOSEPH, aerospace long-range planning advisor; b. December 4, 1927, Summit Hill, Penn.; s. Joseph and Maria (Grosso) F.; m. Antoinette Clemente, 1953; children: Lisa b. 1954, Erica b. 1956, Laura b. 1957, Joanne b. 1960, Mark b. 1961; edn: BS, MS aeronautical engring., M.I.T., 1949; MBA, Harvard Bus. Sch., 1956. Career: res. engr. MIT Aeroelastic Lab, 1949-52; project engr. USAF Flight Dynamics Lab, 1952-54; dynamics engr. Raytheon Co., 1956-58; co-founder/v.p. bus. mgmt. AviDyne Research, 1958-64; asst gen. mgr Kaman AviDyne Div., Kaman Corp., Burlington, Mass. 1964-66; plans integration mgr. L.A. Div., Rockwell Internat., 1966-68; asst dir. Strategic Planning, N. Amer. Aircraft Opns., Space Shuttle Cost/Schedule/Technical Reporting Gp., 1972-76; staff asst. to v.p. Shuttle

Integ. and Ops., 1976-78; R & D proj. ldr. 1978-79; chief analyst, strategic planning, space transp. system div., 1980-85; sr. tech. advisor Advanced Engring., Rockwell Internat., 1985-89, project mgr. 1990-; honors: Sigma Xi, Tau Beta Pi, Phi Kappa Theta, NASA Technology Utilization Award 1971, Astronaut Personal Achievement Award 1985; Assoc. Fellow Am Inst. of Aero. & Astro (tech. comm. on econ. 1983, v. chair. fin. L.A. Sect. 1986-87); civic: The Planning Forum, Town Hall of Calif., EDICT (treas. 1971-76); works: Atomic weapons effects on aircraft, Wind shear design criteria on launch vehicles, Space transp. strategic planning software; mil: lt. USAF, 1952-54, ret. lt. col. Reserve 1976; Republican; R.Cath. (founding com. chmn. St. John Fisher Parish Council 1978-85); rec: accordion, photography, reading Res: 29521 Quailwood Dr Rancho Palos Verdes 90274 Ofc: Rockwell International 12214 Lakewood Blvd Downey 90241

FRAYSSINET, DANIEL FERNAND, software company executive; b. June 25, 1956, Rodez, France; s. Leon Privat and Fernande Marie (Foulquier) F.; m. Chantal Luce Hebrard, June 30, 1979 (div. 1988); m. Corinne Yollande Guillaud, March 4, 1989; 1 dau., Jennifer b. 1989; edn: DEUG math., INSA Villeurbanne France 1976; MSME, 1979. Career: research asst. O.N.S.E.R., Bron, France 1977-78; devel. engr. Centech, Glenview, Ill. 1979-82; pres. I.M.S. Inc., Camarillo 1985-; D.P. Technology Corp. 1982-; mem: S.M.E.; author: Adverse Effect of Intertia & Rigidity of Truck Colliding with Lighter Vehicle, 1978; coauthor (software) Arcade, 1979, Esprit, 1984; R.Cath.; rec: flying, windsurfing, jetskiing. Ofc: D.P. Technology 1150 Avenida Acaso Camarillo 93010

FREEDMAN, STANLEY DAVID, physician; b. Oct. 12, 1935, Pittsburgh, Pa.; s. Joseph and Mary (Shelkrot) F.; m. Saralyn Cohen, Aug. 11, 1957; children: Joseph b. 1962, Eric and Douglas b. 1964; edn: AB, Harvard Coll. 1957; MD, N.Y. Univ. 1961. Career: chief div. of infectious diseases York Hosp., York, Pa. 1969-76; Mercy Hosp., San Diego 1976-77; pres. med. staff Green Hosp. of Scripps Clin., La Jolla 1985-87; head div. on-call physicians Scripps Clin. & Research Found. 1980-, dir. grad. med. edn. 1984-, chmn. dept. grad. med. edn. 1992-, head div. infectious diseases 1977-; asst. prof. medicine Univ. Md. Sch. Medicine, Baltimore 1972-76; asst. clin. prof. medicine UCSD, La Jolla 1976, assoc. clin. prof. 1976-87, clin. prof. 1987-; awards: York Hosp. Outstanding Tchr. Medicine 1974-75, Scripps Clin. Med. Group Disting. Service 1984, Scripps Clinic & Research Found. Outstanding Tchr. Medicine 1990-91; mem: Am. Soc. Microbiol., Infectious Diseases Soc. Am. (fellow), A.C.P. (fellow), San Diego Co. Med. Soc., CMA, UCSD Faculty Club; num. articles and textbook chapters pub. in med. jours.; mil: capt. USAF 1963-65; rec: photography, hiking. Res: 5901 Avenida Chamnez La Jolla 92037 Ofc: Scripps Clinic and Research Foundation 10666 N Torrey Pines Rd La Jolla 92031

FREEDOM, NANCY, neurolinguistic programmer, librarian; b. Sept. 16, 1932, Wash. D.C.; d. William Heman and Lillian Blanche (Martin) Clements; m. Gerald P. Brierley, Apr. 9, 1954 (div. 1969); children: Glenn Anthony, Lynn Hope; edn: BS, Univ. Maryland, 1954; MS, Univ. Wis., 1961; cert. behavioral sci., Univ. Mich., 1971; accelerated tchg. cert., cert. neurolinguistic pgmmg.; Calif. tchg. credential. Career: librarian (I) Madison (Wis.) Public Library, 1961-62; reference and circulation librarian Grandview-Arlington Pub. Libr., Worthington Pub. Libr., Columbus, Ohio, 1964-66; medical librarian Ohio State Univ. Med. Sch., Columbus 1966-68; reference librarian Gen. Motors Inst., Flint, Mich. 1969; librarian (III) Detroit Pub. Libr., 1969-76, Stockton (Calif.) San Joaquin County Pub. Libr., 1977-79; yoga tchr. adult schs. and libraries, Detroit, 1970-76, Calif., 1976-; neurolinguistic cons. and tnr. Freedom Workshop, Oakland 1981-; indexer Ronin Press, Berkeley and Allwon Publ., Irvine; librarian Alameda County Pub. Libr., Hayward Libr., Berkeley Pub. Libr., 1988-; librarian City of Alameda Free Libr., 1992; contbr. book revs. to libr. jours.; mem: Progressive Library Workers, Internat. Assn. Neurolinguistic Pgmmg. (Western states rep., bd.), Calif. Libr. Assn., Assn. Profls. Treating Eating Disorders (speaker), Last Monday Club Womens Network, Omicron Nu, Beta Phi Mu; civic: Open Housing Com. Upper Arlington, Ohio 1967, Pledge of Resistance S.F.Bay Area 1984-88, LWV (chapt. bd. 1957), NOW, Hemlock Soc.; Democrat; Soc. of Friends; rec: early jazz collection, oriental philosophy, social justice. Res/Ofc: Freedom Workshop 540 Alcatraz Ave Ste 205 Oakland 94609-1140 Tel: 415/428-1184

FREEMAN, CHARLES LAWRENCE, researcher; b. Aug. 18, 1905, Newton, Mass.; s. Charles Alfred and Grace Edith (Rumery) F.; m. Phyllis Yates, June 29, 1929; children: Nancy b. 1931, Phyllis b. 1934; edn: BS, US Naval Acad., Annapolis, Md. Career: naval officer U.S. Navy, world wide service 1923-57: cruiser duty 1927-29, submarine duty, New London Co. 1929-34, post grad. sch., Annapolis, Md. 1934-36, submarine command, Honolulu 1936-39, instr. submarine sch., New London Co. 1939-41, submarine command, Southwest Pacific 1941-42, staff command 1942-44, staff command, Atlantic Ocean 1944-46, comdg. ofcr. USS Drew, Pacific Fleet 1945-46, comdg. ofcr. USS Williamsburg (Truman's presidential yacht), Atlantic Fleet 1946-48, comdr. naval sta. U.S. Naval Acad. and USS Reina Mercedes, 1948-51; NATO staff, Paris 1951 and Sixth Fleet, Mediterranean and Pentagon service to 1957 (ret.); researcher Rand Corp., Santa Monica 1957-; author var. research papers;

rec: golf. Res: 601 Country Club Ln Coronado 92118 Ofc: The Rand Corporation 1700 Main St Santa Monica

FREEMAN, JOSH, graphic designer; b. Dec. 4, 1949, Santa Monica; s. Joel David Freeman and Jo (Stack) Napoleon; 1 son, Noah; edn: BFA, UCLA 1972. Career: assoc. designer Anthony Goldschmidt Graphic Design Ltd., Los Angeles 1972-73; prin. Josh Freeman Design 1973-75; ptnr., pres. Freeman Blitzer Assoc. 1975-80; Interrobang Inc. 1980-83; pres. Josh Freeman Assoc. 1983-; awards: num. awards incl. Typographers Internat. Assn. Gold 1983, Nat. Assn. Home Builders Project of Year 1987, Sales & Mktg. Council of Bldg. Industry Project of Year 1987, Builder Mag. Project of Year 1987; mem: Am. Inst. Graphic Arts (pres. L.A. chpt. 1989-91), Art Dirs. Club L.A., Mayors Council for Arts 1978-80; coauthor, illustrator The Thing Nobody Could See, 1972. Ofc: Josh Freeman Associates 8019 1/2 Melrose Ave Ste 1 Los Angeles 90046

FREEMAN, LAURENCE JOSEPH, cosmetic company executive; b. Aug. 3, 1937, New York; s. S. Jerry and Anne (Strassberg) F.; m. Judy M. Shaft, Oct. 16, 1960; children: Mark b. 1962, Jill b. 1965; edn: BA, UCLA. Career: dist. sales mgr. Clairol, Los Angeles 1959-61; mfrs. rep. Freeman Sales 1961-74, CEO 1974-; producer, host Freeman Productions t.v. show 1981-83; corp. dir. Westwood One Co. 1986-; awards: Chivas Regals Extrapreneur 1990; mem: SHARE (bus. advy. council), FACTT (founder), Cancer Research Found. L.A., Aces Cancer Tennis Tournament, CIAO; author: Beauty The Secret is Within You, 1989; mil: airman 3c Calif. Nat. Guard 1959-63. Ofc: Freeman Cosmetic Corp. POB 4074 Beverly Hills 90213

FREEMAN, MARTIN, computer research company principal scientist; b. Sept. 26, 1944, Paterson, N.J.; s. Reubin and Minnie (Kahn) F.; m. Barbara Frutiger Cechmanek, Aug. 17, 1975; children: Robert b. 1979, Michael b. 1985; edn: BEE, Rensselaer Polytechnic Inst., 1965; MSEE, Columbia Univ., 1966; PhD, computer sci., Univ. Pa., 1971. Career: assoc. prof. computer sci. American Univ., Washington., 1971-77; vis. prof. Stanford Univ., Palo Alto 1977-78; mem. tech. staff Bell Laboratories, Whippany, N.J. 1978-82; sr. microprocessor architect Signetics, Sunnyvale, Calif. 1982-86; vis. fellow Stanford Univ., 1986-87; principal scientist Philips Res., Palo Alto 1988-; gen. chmn. Internat. Symp. on Archtl. Support, Palo Alto 1987, Workshop on Transaction Machine Arch., Lake Arrowhead 1988, Hot Chips Symp., Stanford 1991; awards: Tau Beta Pi, Eta Kappa Nu, appreciation IEEE Computer Soc., W.D.C. (1987, 1988), Assn. for Computing Mach., N.Y.C. 1987, listed Am. Men & Women in Sci. 1976, Who's Who in Technology Today 1982, Who's Who in the West 1992; Who's Who in Sci. & Tech. 1993; mem: IEEE (1964-, chmn. nat. tech. com. on microprocessors, W.D.C. 1986-88, chmn. nat. stds. com PI285 Scalable Storage Interface 1990-), Assn. for Computing Machinery 1966-, AAAS 1986-, Internat. Platform Assn.; inventor: Memory Mgmt. & Pattern Matching Units (2 patents, 1985, 87); guest editor J. IEEE Transactions on Computers: Archtl. Support for Pgmg. Languages and Operating Systems (1988), num. journal articles (1971-); rec: film, theater. Res: 4189 Donald Dr Palo Alto 94306 Ofc: Philips Research 4005 Miranda Ave Palo Alto 94304

FREEMAN, MYRNA FAYE, government employee benefits manager; b. Oct. 30, 1939, Danville, Ill.; d. Thomas Gene, Sr. and Dorothy Olive (Chodera) Freeman; m. Lonnie Choate, Aug. 16, 1959 (div. 1987); children: Leslie b. 1965, Gregory b. 1967; edn: BA, San Diego St. Univ., 1977, MA, 1987. Career: employee benefits mgr. City of San Diego, 1974-84; asst. risk mgr. San Diego Co. Office of Edn., 1984-; honors: appreciation, COMBO, S.D. 1977, Phi Kappa Phi 1986, listed Who's Who Among San Diego Women 1983, Who's Who of Am. Women 1992; mem. Calif. Assn. of Sch. Bus. Officials (chair risk mgmt. R&D com. 1987-88), Calif. Women in Govt. (S.D. exec. bd. 1983-84), Risk & Ins. Mgmt. Soc. (San Diego chapt. pres. 1988), S.D. Employers Health Cost Coalition (bd. v.chair 1988), S.D. Group Ins. Claims Council (pres. 1987, treas.), Kaiser Consumer Council (1977-84, pres. 1980), Internat. Found. of Employee Benefits, S.D. Workers' Compensation Forum, Pub. Agency Risk Mgmt. Assn., Calif. Assn. Jt. Powers Authorities, Council of Self-Insured Pub. Agencies, Pub. Risk and Ins. Mgmt. Assn., S.D. Co. Affirmative Action Advy. Bd. (1984-85), Sigma Kappa Sor.; publs: Administrative Impact of Implementing Legislation AB: 528 Retiree Health and Dental Coverage (1987), articles in field (1985-92); Republican; Prot.; rec: sports, numismatics, swimming. Res: 4345 Cartulina Rd San Diego 92124-2102 Ofc: San Diego Co. Office of Education, 6401 Linda Vista Rd #405 San Diego 92111-7399

FREISMUTH, THOMAS PATRICK, financial consultant, company president; b. Jan. 8, 1948, Grosse Pointe, Mich.; s. William Thomas and Margaret Ann (McLaughlin) F.; m. Carolyn Kay Petre, Feb. 19, 1954; children: Thomas Patrick II, Joy Hailey, Maxx Skylar; edn: BA, Mich. State Univ. 1970; Certified Life Underwriter (CLU), Chartered Fin. Cons. (ChFC); reg. investment advisor SEC. Career: sales rep. Aetna Life & Casualty Co., Southfield Mich. 1971-75, pres. Financial Advisory Services, subs. Aetna, Southfield, Mich. 1975-86, c.e.o. 1986-; c.e.o. Financial Advisory Services, San Diego, 1986-; dir: Haas Fin., Southfield, Levin Assocs., Southfield; mem: Internat. Assn. Fin. Planners, San Diego Assn. Life Underwriters, Detroit Assn. Life Underwriters, Registered Investment Advisors Assn., Million Dollar Round Table; civic: Am. Kidney

Found., Detroit (treas. 1976), Big Brothers Orgn., Detroit 1978, Am. Cancer Found., Detroit (fund pgm. 1982-), Eagles, Rotary Internat.; contbr. articles in field; Republican; Unity. Ofc: Financial Advisory Services 450 A St Ste 500 San Diego 92101 also: 12555 High Bluff Dr Ste 333 San Diego 92130

FRENCH, GEORGINE LOUISE, guidance counselor; b. May 15, 1934, Lancaster, Pa.; d. Richard Franklin and Elizabeth Georgine (Driesbach) Beacham; m. Barrie J. French, Feb. 4, 1956; children: Joel B., John D., James D., Jeffrey D.; edn: BA, CSU San Bernardino, 1967; MS, No. Ill. Univ., 1973; DD, Am. Ministerial Assn., 1978; cert. guidance counselor Nat. Board Cert. Counselor, 1985; secondary tchr.; cert. coll. counselor. Career: personnel counselor Sages Dept. Store, San Bernardino, 1965-66; asst. bookkeeper Bank Calif., San Bernardino, 1964-65; tchr. Livermore Sch. Dist., 1968-69; guidance counselor Bur. Indian Affairs, Tuba City, Ariz., 1974-80, guidance counselor Sherman Indian H.S., Riverside, Calif., 1980-82; guidance counselor Ft. Douglas Edn. Ctr., U.S. Army, Salt Lake City, 1982-86; USAF guidance counselor Los Angeles Air Force Sta., 1986-87, education services ofcr. Comiso Air Force Base, Italy 1987-88; extension tchr. Navajo Comm. Coll., Yavapai Coll.; personnel counselor USNR, 1976-86; ordained to ministry Am. Ministerial Assn., 1979; mem: Am. Assn. for Counseling and Devel., AARP; mil: USAF 1954-56; Res: 1721 Aviation Blvd #53 Redondo Beach 92078 Ofc: 6592 ABG/DPE, PO Box 92960 Los Angeles 90009-2960

FRENCH, MARIANNE ETHEL, nurse epidemiologist/practitioner, consultant; b. Jan. 10, 1954, Santa Monica; d. Henry Charles and Theodora Axenty Griswold; edn: BS nursing, CSU Long Beach 1978; MS, currently. Career: clin. instr. nursing CSU Long Beach 1982-83; home IV therapy nse. pvt. practice, Long Beach 1985-87; adult nse. practitioner oncology pvt. practice 1984-87; adminstr., nse. mgr. UC Irvine Cancer Center, Orange 1987-89, nse. epidemiologist USC Cancer Res., Los Angeles 1985-, and coordinator Adult Oncology Nurse Practitioner Pgm. 1990-; ednl. cons. UCSD Med. Center 1989-90; nursing cons. and lectr.; breast health facilitator Am. Cancer Soc.; honors: Orange Co. Oncology Nursing Soc. Pres. award 1989, Internat. Assn. Bus. Communicators Bronze Quill Hon. 1985, Sigma Theta Tau 1983, Am. Cancer Soc. Vol. of Year 1988, Edn. Dept. Vol. of Year 1987; mem: Oncology Nursing Soc., Am. Cancer Soc., Calif. Coalition of Nurse Practitioners, Pageant of Masters (vol.); audiovisual productions for healthcare, 1985-, co-inventor home pro infusion pump, 1984, adult oncology nse. practitioner program CSU Long Beach 1989; Republican; Christian; rec: travel, cooking, exercising. Res: 173 Hearthstone Irvine 92714 Ofc: USC School of Medicine Norris Hospital @800, 2025 Zonal Ave Los Angeles 90033

FRESQUEZ, ERNEST CLIFFORD, executive recruiting consultant; b. May 24, 1955, Roswell, N.M.; s. Bonifacio Archuleta and Lucilla (Lucero) F.; m. Jeanette Acosta, July 20, 1985; children: Eric, Marissa; edn: BABA, N.M. Highlands Univ. 1977; John F. Kennedy Univ. 1980-83; Golden Gate Univ. 1983-85. Career: acctg. asst. Chevron USA, Concord 1977-80, assoc. acct. Chevron Internat., San Francisco 1980-81, budget analyst Chevron Overseas 1981-85; mgmt. auditor ADC Ltd. DOE IG, Albuquerque, N.M. 1985-89; exec. recruiter Fresquez & Assoc., Concord 1989-; mentor Puente Project, Berkeley 1989-; Metas Project, El Cerrito 1989; Nat. Soc. Hispanic MBA, S.F. Chpt. treas. 1991-92; awards: Bus. Hons. Club student of month, 1977; nat. vice-chair-bd. Personnel Mgrs. Assn. Aztlan, 1992-93; mem: Contra Costa Hispanic C.of C. (bd.), Alameda Co. Hispanic C.of C.; Democrat; Congregational; rec: backpacking, tennis. Ofc: Fresquez & Associates 405 14th Street Suite 1040 Oakland 94612

FREW, BARRY ALBERT, information services administrator, educator; b. Feb. 10, 1948, Portland, Oreg.; s. Howard Albert and Dorothy Estelle (Marcum) F.; m. Jeanne Lynn, June 29, 1985; children: Arlen b. 1968, Brian b. 1973; edn: AS, Umpqua Comm. Coll. 1968; BS, Miami of Ohio 1976; MS Info. Systems, Naval Postgrad. Sch. Monterey, 1984. Career: dir. environ. dept. Naval Maintenance & Supply Support Office, Norfolk, Va. 1979-82; dir. inventory control dept. Naval Supply Center, Pearl Harbor, Hawaii 1981-82; prof. Naval Postgrad. Sch., Monterey 1984-, dir. and dean 1990, Computer and Information Services, 1989-; gen. ptnr. J&B Cons., Pebble Beach 1982-; award: Meritorious Civilian Service Award 1993; bd. dirs. Monterey Fed. Credit Union 1989-, v.chmn. bd. 1991-93; instr. Learning Tree Internat. seminars, L.A. 1989-91; mem: Spl. Interest Group on CD-ROM Applications & Tech.; thesis advisor 1984-92, researcher optical storage tech. 1986-92, workshop leader Federal Computer Conf. 1991-92, Navy Microcomputer Conf. 1990, 92, leader Profl. Dept. Seminar 1989, keynote speaker Am. Soc. Mil. Comptrollers 1988; mil: LCDR USN 1968-88, Navy Commend. 1982, 84; rec: flying, softball, running. Ofc: J&B Consulting 3080 Larkin Rd Pebble Beach 93953

FRICK, OSCAR LIONEL,physician, educator; b. Mar. 12, 1923, New York; s. Oscar and Elizabeth (Ringger) F.; m. Mary Elizabeth Hubbard, Sept. 2, 1954; edn: AB, Cornell Univ. 1944; MD, Cornell Univ. Sch. Medicine 1946; MMS, Univ. Pa. Grad. Sch. Medicine 1960; PhD, Stanford Univ. Grad. Sch. Medicine 1964; lic. Am. Bd. Pediatrics 1960, Am. Bd. Allergy & Immunology 1978. Career: intern, Babies Hosp., Columbia, N.Y.C. 1946-47; resident Children's

Hosp., Buffalo, N.Y. 1950-51; postdoctoral fellow Univ. McGill-Allergy, Montreal, Canada 1958-59; UCSF 1959-60; Inst. Immunologie, Paris, France 1960-62; Stanford Univ. 1962-64; asst. prof. pediatrics UCSF 1963-67, assoc. prof. 1967-72, prof. 1972-; awards: Georgetown Univ. Von Pirquet, 1974, Am. Acad. Pediatrics Bret Ratner, 1982; mem: Am. Acad. Allergy & Immunology (pres. 1977-78), Internat. Assn. Allergy & Immunology (secty. 1975-94), Coll. Internat. Allergy & Immunology (exec. com. 1988-92), Am. Pediatric Soc., Am. Acad. Pediatrics, Am. Coll. Allergy & Immunology (fellow), Am. Assn. Immunologists, Am. Thoracic Soc., Am. Lung Assn., FDA (advy. com. allergic drugs 1984-88, chmn. 1987-88); author: 100 articles pub. in sci. jours., 1950-; mil: lt., USNR, USN 1947-49; Republican; Protestant; rec: photography, hiking. Res: 370 Parnassus Ave San Francisco 94117 Ofc: University of California 505 Parnassus Dr San Francisco 94143

FRIDLEY, SAUNDRA LYNN, internal audit executive; b. June 14, 1948, Columbus, Ohio; d. Jerry Dean and Esther Eliza (Bluhm) Fridley; edn: BS, Franklin Univ., 1976; MBA, Golden Gate Univ., 1980. Career: accounts receivable supr. Internat. Harvester Inc., Columbus, Ohio, San Leandro, Calif., 1972-80; senior internal auditor Western Union, San Francisco 1980; internal auditor II, County of Santa Clara, San Jose 1980-82; senior internal auditor Tymshare Inc., Cupertino 1982-84, div. contr. 1984; internal audit mgr. VWR Scientific, Brisbane 1984-88, audit dir. 1988-; internal audit mgr. Pacific IBM Employees Fed. Credit Union, 1989-; mem: Inst. Internal Auditors (pres., founder Tri-Valley chpt., Speakers Bur., Internat. Seminar Com.), Nat. Assn. Female Execs.; civic: Friends of the Vineyards; rec: woodworking, gardening, golf. Res: 862 Bellflower St Livermore 94550 Ofc: VWR Scientific 3745 Bayshore Blvd Brisbane 94005

FRIEDBERG, ROBERT DANA, psychologist; b. Oct. 27, 1955, Orange, N.J.; s. Morton David and Rachelle (Derewitz) F.; m. Barbara Ann Fabe, Aug. 22, 1982; 1 dau., Rebecca Jenae b. 1988; edn: BA cum laude, Hiram Coll. 1977; MA, Univ. Dayton 1980; PhD, Calif. Sch. Profl. Psychology 1987. Career: staff psychologist Univ. Dayton, Ohio 1979-80; staff therapist Youth Diversion Project 1980-81; asst. psychologist Childrens Psychiatric Center, Cincinnati, Ohio 1981-83; postdoctoral psychology asst. Center for Cognitive Therapy, Newport Beach 1987-89; staff psychologist Mesa Vista Hosp., San Diego 1989-; adj. faculty Calif. Sch. Profl. Psychology 1988-; San Diego City Coll. 1988-; honors: Pi Gamma Mu, Alpha Soc., Psi Chi; mem: Calif. St. Psychological Assn., Nat. Assn. Edn. Young Children, Am. Psychological Assn.; articles pub. in profl. jours.; Democrat; Jewish; rec: tennis. Res: 4183 Corte de la Siena San Diego 92130 Ofc: Mesa Vista Hospital 7850 Vista Hill Ave San Diego 92123

FRIEDMAN, LOUIS, winery executive, lawyer; b. Sept. 24, 1939, St. Louis, Mo.; s. Abraham and Elinor (Rubin) F.; m. Kennicia Gillett; children: Cary b. 1965, Stacey b. 1968; edn: BS, Ariz. St. Univ. 1960; LL.B, Loyola Univ. 1964; LL.M, N.Y. Univ. 1967. Career: Price Waterhouse & Co., Los Angeles 1961-64, N.Y.C. 1964-73; v.p.; treas. E. & J. Gallo Winery, Modesto 1973-; mem: Calif. Bar Assn., N.Y. Bar Assn., Am. Inst. C.P.A., Calif. Soc. C.P.A., Am. Bar Assn., Stanislaus Co. Bar Assn., Modesto Rotary Club; Jewish. Res: 508 Andover Ln Modesto 95350 Ofc: E. & J. Gallo Winery 600 Yosemite Blvd Modesto 95354

FRIEDMAN, MILTON, economist, author; s. Jeno Saul and Sarah Ethel (Landau) F.; m. Rose Director, June 25, 1938; children: Janet, David; edn: AB, Rutgers Univ. 1932, LLD, 1968; AM, Univ. Chgo. 1933; PhD, Columbia Univ. 1946; hon. degrees: LLD, St. Paul's (Rikkyo) Univ. 1963, Kalamazoo Coll. 1968, Lehigh Univ. 1969, Loyola Univ. 1971, Univ. N.H. 1975, Harvard Univ. 1979, B.Y.U. 1980, Dartmouth 1980, Gonzaga Univ. 1981; ScD, Rochester Univ. 1971, LHD, Rockford Coll. 1969, Roosevelt Univ. 1975, Hebrew Union Coll. L.A. 1981; LittD, Bethany Coll. 1971; PhD (hon.), Hebrew Univ. Jerusalem 1977; DCS, Francisco Marroquin Univ. Guatemala 1978. Career: assoc. economist Nat. Resources Com., W.D.C. 1935-37; res. staff Nat. Bur. Econ. Res., NY, 1937-45, 48-81; vis. prof. econs. Univ. Wis. 1940-41; prin. economist, tax res. div. US Treasury 1941-43; assoc. dir. res., stats. res. group, war res. div. Columbia Univ. 1943-45; assoc. prof. econs. and bus. adminstrn. Univ. Minn. 1945-46; assoc. prof., prof. econs. Univ. Chgo. 1946-48, 1948-62, Paul Snowden Russell Disting. Service Prof. 1962-82, Emeritus, 1983-; Fulbright lectr. Cambridge Univ., 1953-54; vis. Wesley Clair Mitchell Res. prof. econs. Columbia Univ., 1964-65; fellow Ctr. for Advanced Study in Behavioral Sci., 1957-58; mem. Pres.'s Commn. All-Vol. Army, 1969-70, Pres.'s Commn. on White House Fellows, 1971-74, Pres.'s Econ. Policy Advy. Bd. 1981-88; vis. scholar Fed. Reserve Bank, San Francisco, 1977; sr. res. fellow Hoover Instn., Stanford Univ., 1977-; awards: John Bates Clark medal Am. Econ. Assn. 1951, Nobel prize in econs. 1976, Pvt. Ent. Exemplar medal Freedoms Found. 1978, Chicagoan of year Chgo. Press Club 1972, educator of yr. Chgo. Human United Fund 1973, Grand Cordon of the First Class Order of the Sacred Treasure Govt. Japan 1986, Nat. Medal of Sci. U.S. Govt. 1988, Presdl. Medal of Freedom U.S. Govt. 1988; Fellow Inst. Math. Stats., Am. Stats. Assn., Econometric Soc., Jewish Acad. of Arts and Scis., mem. Nat. Acad. Scis., Am. Econ. Assn. (exec. com. 1955-57, pres. 1967), Royal Econ. Soc., Western Econ. Assn. (pres. 1984-5), Am. Philos. Soc., Mont Pelerin Soc. (dir. 1958-61, pres. 1970-2); club:

Quadrangle; author: Taxing to Prevent Inflation (w/ C. Shoup, R.P. Mack) 1943; Income from Independent Professional Practice (w/ S.S. Kuznets) 1946; Sampling Inspection (w/ H.A. Freeman, F. Mosteller, W.A. Wallis) 1948; Essays in Positive Economics, 1953; A Theory of the Consumption Function, 1957; A Program for Monetary Stability, 1960; Price Theory, 1962; (w/ R.D. Friedman) Capitalism and Freedom, 1962, Free To Choose, 1980, Tyranny of the Status Quo, 1984; (w/ A.J. Schwartz) A Monetary History of the U.S., 1967-1960, 1963, The Great Contraction, 1965, Monetary Statistics of the U.S., 1970, Monetary Trends in the U.S. and the U.K., 1982; Inflation: Causes and Consequences, 1963; The Balance of Payments: Free vs. Fixed Exchange Rates (w/ R. Roosa) 1967; Dollars and Deficits, 1968; The Optimum Quantity of Money and Other Essays, 1969; Monetary vs. Fiscal Policy (w/ W.W. Heller) 1968; A Theoretical Framework for Monetary Analysis, 1972; Social Security (w/ W.J. Cohen) 1972; An Economist's Protest, 1972; There Is No Such Thing As A Free Lunch, 1975; Price Theory, 1976; Milton Friedman's Monetary Framework (w/ R.J. Gordon et al) 1974; Bright Promises, Dismal Performance: An Economist's Protest (w/ W.R. Allen) 1983; ed. Studies in the Quantity Theory of Money, 1956; bd. eds. Am. Econ. Rev., 1951-53, Econometrica, 1957-69; advy. bd. Jour. of Money, Credit, and Banking, 1968-; columnist Newsweek mag. 1966-84, contbg. ed. 1972-84; contbr. arts. to profl. jours. Ofc: Hoover Institution Stanford Univ. Stanford 94305-6010

FRIEMAN, EDWARD ALLAN, university administrator, educator; b. Jan. 19, 1926, NY, NY; s. Joseph and Belle (Davidson) F.; m. Ruth Paula Todman, June 19, 1949 (dec. May 6, 1966); m. Joy Fields, Sept. 17, 1967; children: Jonathan, Michael, Joshua, Wendy, Linda Holiner; edn: BS, Columbia Univ., 1946; MS, Polytechnic Inst. of Brooklyn, 1948, PhD, 1952. Career: instr.physics, res. assoc. Polytechnic Inst. Bklyn., 1945-52; head theoretical div. Plasma Physics Lab., Princeton Univ., 1953-64, prof. dept. astrophysical scis. 1961-64, dep. dir. Plasma Physics Lab, 1964-79; dir. of energy research U.S. Dept. of Energy, W.D.C., 1979-81; exec. v.p. Science Applications Internat. Corp., La Jolla 1981-86; adj. prof. physics UC San Diego, 1981-91, dir. Scripps Instn. of Oceanography, and vice chancellor marine scis. UC San Diego, 1986-; apptd: V.Pres.'s Space Advy. Bd. 1992-, White House Sci. Council (v. chmn. 1981-88), President's Com. on the Nat. Medal of Science (chmn. 1992-93), Secty. of Energy Advy. Bd./SEAB 1990-, SEAB Task Force on DOE Nat. Labs. (chmn. 1991-92), Defense Sci. Bd. ASW Task Force (chmn. 1991-92), Jt. Oceanographic Instns. Inc. (1986-, chmn. 1991-), NASA/Earth Observing Sys. engring. rev. advy. com. (chmn. 3/91-), NRC/Ocean Studies Bd. 1987-, editl. bd. J. of Def. Research 1987-91; cons. Jason Div. The Mitre Corp. 1960-; dir: Science Applications Internat. Corp. 1987-, mem. Sci. Advy. Com. General Motors 1987-93, The Charles Stark Draper Lab., Inc. 1989-; awards: NSF senior postdoc. fellow 1964, John Simon Guggenheim fellow 1970, DOE distinguished service medal 1980, Richtmyer Award, Am. Physical Soc. 1984, distinguished alumni Polytechnic Inst. Bklyn. 1984; mem: Nat. Acad. Scis., Am. Philosophical Soc., Am. Physical Soc., Astronomical Soc., AAAS, Sigma Xi; publs: 80+ in statistical mechanics, theoretical plasma physics, magnetohydrodynamics and kinetic theory; mil: ensign USN 1943-46; rec: piano, tennis, literature. Ofc: Scripps Instn. of Oceanography, U.C.S.D. 9500, Gilman Dr La Jolla 92093-0210

FRIES, HERLUF BECK, ranching consultant; b. April 1, 1915, Easton; s. Christian P. and Emma A. (Beck) F.; m. Geraldine Wood, Aug. 14, 1954; children: Donna b. 1940, Doug b. 1942, Jean b. 1967, Benta b. 1969. Career: cons. Fidinam Corp., Luguna, Switz. and Investors of Ger. and Italy 1977-80; farmer, rancher, Oakhurst 1980-83; mem: Calcot Lamo, Fresno Co. Farm Bureau, Calif. Young Farmers (pres. 1948-49); del. representing agriculture Citizen Amb. Program to Russia, Poland, Czech. (1990); honors: Hon. Degree State Farmer 1950; Grand Marshall, Caruthers Dist. Fair, 50 yrs.; rec: tennis, youth. Address: 1860 S Minnewawa Fresno 93727

FRISCH, JOHN HENRY, financial executive; b. March 3, 1932, Joliet, Ill.; s. Henry P. and Helen W. (Riley) F.; m. Karen M. Blitz, Nov. 22, 1956; children: Penni J. b. 1957, Gary J. b. 1959, Wendi J. b. 1960, Kristi K. b. 1963; edn: BS, Lewis Univ. 1954. Career: controller Fairchild Industries, Manhattan Beach 1956-64; dir. fin. planning Planning Research Corp., Los Angeles 1965-74; corp. controller, treas. Holmes & Narver Inc., Orange 1974-80; controller Bethlehem Steel Corp., Los Angeles 1980-81; v.p. corp. controller Becket Group, Santa Monica 1981-84; corp. controller Modern Alloys Inc., Stanton 1985-86; v.p. fin. and adminstrn. E&L Engring. Inc., Long Beach 1986-; chmn. Planning Commn., Manhattan Beach 1972-74; pres. Think Bridge 1984-; prin., founder FGM Assoc. 1984-; mem: Manhattan Beach Badminton Club (past pres.), Nat. Assn. Accts. (past bd. dirs.), Calif. Assn. Realtors, Nat. Assn. Realtors, Elks; mil: lt.j.g. USN 1954-56; Republican; R.Cath.; rec: badminton, bicycling. Res: 920 John St Manhattan Beach 90266

FROEHLICH, CHARLES W., JR., state appellate court justice; b. Dec. 5, 1928, San Jose; s. Charles W., Sr. and Ruth (Eddy) F.; m. Millicent Gene Davis, May 24, 1951; children: Marion b. 1952, Susan (Marvin) b. 1955, Helen (Trevelyan) b. 1957; edn: AB, Stanford Univ., LLD, UC Berkeley. Career: atty. pvt. practice, San Diego 1956-62, 65-72, 82-88; prof. of law UC Berkeley,

1962-65; judge Superior Ct., San Diego 1972-82; justice Ct. of Appeal, State of Calif., San Diego 1988-; honors: Phi Beta Kappa 1951, Order of the Coif 1956; mem. ABA; mil: 1st lt. AUS 1951-53, Bronze star; Republican; Methodist; rec: farming, winemaking. Res: 1444 Windsong Ln San Diego 92026

FRONCZAK, LISA ANNETTE, account representative; b. June 15, 1958, Turlock; d. Thaddeus Francis and Lola Mae (Curtis) Fronczak; edn: BA social sci., CSU Fresno 1982; tchg. credential 1986. Career: travel agent Vintage World Travel, Modesto 1982-83; Edmonson's Travel, Atwater 1983-85; travel cons. Apex Travel, Turlock 1986-88; acct. rep. PacTel Paging, Modesto 1988-; awards: Wm. Howard Taft Univ. Law Sch. scholar 1988-92; mem: Modesto C.of C., Modesto Womens Network; Republican; R.Cath.; rec: travel, skiing. Res: 204 Buena Vista Modesto 95354 Ofc: PacTel Paging, 4231-B McHenry Ave Modesto 95356 Tel: 209/571-9600

FRYXELL, KARL JOSEPH, educator; b. June 12, 1953, Las Cruces, N.M.; s. Paul Arnold and Greta (Albrecht) F.; m. Patty P.Y. Pang, July 19, 1987; edn: BA and BS, Univ. Texas, 1975; PhD, Caltech, 1983. Career: Helen Hay Whitney postdoctoral fellow, Caltech, 1983-86, mem. profl. staff Caltech 1986-88; asst. prof. biology UC Riverside, 1988-; awards: NSF individual grad. fellow Caltech (1977-80), Helen Hay Whitney postdoc. fellow (1983-86), Phi Beta Kappa, Phi Kappa Phi (1974); mem. Genetics Soc. of Am. Ofc: Dept. Biology Univ. Calif., Riverside 92521

FUJIKAWA, EVA, aerospace/automotive company business management; b. May 27, 1958, Santa Monica; d. Osamu Sam and Teruko (Nakamizo) Fujikawa; edn: BA psychology, social sci., Univ. of Pacific 1979; MBA, Loyola Marymount Univ. 1985. Career: program controls splst. Hughes (subs. of GM), El Segundo 1979-88, program controls splst. comml. and automotive products, Culver City 1988-89, Program Controls Supr. Bus. Ops., El Segundo 1989-, Corporate ATEP, 1991; instr. EDSG, El Segundo 1987-88; mem: Los Angeles World Affairs Council, Am. Mgmt. Assn., Nat. Contract Mgmt. Assn., Soc. Tech. Comm., Internat. Tng. in Comm. (secty.), Japanese Am. Nat. Museum (econ. devel. com. 1988-), So. Calif. Am. Nikkei (bd. mem. 1988-), El Segundo C.of C. (indsl. activities com., govt. activities com.); Methodist; rec: French, Japanese, violin. Res: 1633 E Palm Ave #4 El Segundo 90245 Ofc: Hughes Bldg S1 M/S D347, PO Box 92919 Los Angeles 90009

FUKUHARA, HENRY, artist, instructor, consultant; b. Apr. 25, 1913, Los Angeles; s. Ichisuke and Ume (Sakamoto) F.; m. Fujiko Yasutake, Aug. 18, 1938; children: Joyce b. 1941, Grace b. 1943, Rackham b. 1946, Helen b. 1948; edn: grad. Santa Monica High Sch., 1931. Career: nurseryman, landscape contr. Las Palmas Nurseries, Los Angeles 1935-41; wholesale florist Fukuhara Greenhouses, Deer Park, Long Is., N.Y. 1946-87; artist, instr./cons., L.I., N.Y. 1980-87, Santa Monica, Ca. 1987-; instr. watercolor Huntington (N.Y.) Township Art League 1983-87, East Islip (N.Y.) Mus., 1985-86, Oakdale (N.Y.) Arboretum 1984-86, Parrish Art Mus., Westhampton, N.Y. 1981-86, Jacqueline Penney Studio, Cutchogue, N.Y. 1980-84, Palos Verdes (Ca.) Art Center 1988-91, Joslyn Center of the Arts, Torrance, Ca. 1990, Venice H.S. Adult Sch. 1992-93; art in permanent collections: Heckscher Mus. of Art, N.Y., Abilene Mus., Texas, Nassau Comm. Coll., N.Y., S.U.N.Y. Stonybrook, N.Y., Los Angeles County Mus. of Art, Blaine (Mont.) County Mus., Ralston Mus., Sidney, Mont., San Bernardino (Ca.) County Mus., Santa Monica (Ca.) Comm. Coll., Riverside (Ca.) Mus. of Art, Nagano Mus. of Art, Japan, Hiroshima Mus. of Art, Japan; awards: Strathmore Paper Co., Creative Connection, Golden, Mont., purchase award Nassau Comm. Coll., N.Y., numerous other awards; mem. Watercolor Soc. of Ala., Nat. Watercolor Soc., Pittsburgh Watercolor Soc. Res: 1214 Marine St Santa Monica 90405

FUKUMOTO, BRIAN MICHAEL, manufacturing engineer/program manager; b. June 13, 1967, Offutt AFB, Nebr.; s. Malcolm Tatsumi and Lorraine Sachiko (Noguchi) F.; edn: BSME, UC Berkeley, 1989. Career: mfg. engr. Solectron Corp., Milpitas 1991-92, program mgr. 1992-; mem: Amer. Soc. Mech. Engrs. (assoc. 1985-), Calif. Alumni Assn. 1989-, Berkeley Engring. Alumni Soc. 1989-; Republican (sustaining GOP Nat. Com. 1990-); Prot.; rec: tennis, audio/video-phile, sports cards, piano. Res: 1703 Parkview Green Circle San Jose 95131-3222 Ofc: Solectron Corp. 777 Gibraltar Dr Milpitas 95035

FULGHUM, BRICE ELWIN, employee benefits consultant; b. Aug. 27, 1919, Fredonia, Kans.; s. Byron Harmon and Myrtle (Broderick) F.; married; children: Linda Lee Fulghum McDonald; edn: Univ. Kansas City, The American Coll., San Francisco State Coll.; Chartered Life Underwriter (CLU). Career: asst. to sales mgr. Gas Service Co., Kansas City, Mo. 1939-41; sales mgr. Ace Auto Rental & Sales Co., K.C., Mo. 1945-48; asst. mgr. Owl Drug Co., San Francisco, 1948-50; mgr. Pacific Mutual Life Ins. Co., 1950-61; v.p. Gordon H. Edwards Co., 1959-64; v.p. Federated Life Ins. Co. Calif., 1964-66; gen. mgr. Los Angeles Fulghum Agy. Pacific Mut. Life Ins. Co., 1966-71; v.p. Hendrie Bonding & Ins. Corp., Huntington Beach 1976-77; chmn. bd. PGA Ins. Services Inc., Torrance 1976-; cons. Am. Health Profiles Inc., Nashville; sr. fin. cons. Shearson Hayden Stone Inc., Newport Beach 1977-79; cons. Penn Gen. Agys., L.A. and Employee Benefits Consultants, Santa Ana, 1979-80; cons.

Assn. Calif. State Univ. Profs., 1959-, Profl. Sponsoring Fund, 1979-; mem: Am. Soc. C.L.U.s (Golden Key Soc.), Leading Life Ins. Producers No. Calif. (life mem., pres. 1955), S.F. Peninsula Estate Planning Council (charter), L.A.-S.F.V. Estate Planning Councils (life), Orange County Life Underws. Assn. (editorial advy. bd. Western Underwriter); civic: March of Dimes /La Quinta (chmn. 1991), Am. Cancer Soc. (chmn. fundraising), Community Chest, Am. Heart Assn., Opera Pacific (founder), Commonwealth Club, Town Hall of Calif. (charter mem. Charitable Giving Council Orange Co.); clubs: La Quinta CC, El Niguel CC; mil: Q.M.C., U.S. Army 1941-43; contbr. articles to ins. publs. Res: 77-030 Avenida Fernando La Quinta 92253 Ofc: PO Box 1750 La Quinta 92253

FULLERTON, GAIL JACKSON, university president; b. Apr. 29, 1927, Lincoln, Nebr.; d. Earl Warren and Gladys Bernice (Marshall) Jackson; m. Stanley Fullerton, Mar. 27, 1967; 2 children by previous marriage, Gregory and Cynde Putney; edn: AB, Univ. Nebr. 1949, AM, 1950; PhD, Univ. Oreg. 1954. Career: lectr. sociology Drake Univ., Des Moines 1955-57; asst. prof. Fla. State Univ., Tallahassee 1957-60; prof. sociol. San Jose State Univ., 1963-72, dean, 1972-76, exec. vice pres., 1977-78, pres., 1978-; bd. dirs. San Jose Symphony 1979-, Associated Western Univs., Inc. 1981-; bd. govs. NCCJ of Santa Clara Co., 1981-; trustee Nat. Commn. Cooperative Edn., 1982-; awards: Carnegie fellow, 1950-51, Doherty fellow, 1951-52; mem: AAAS, Internat. Sociol. Assn., Am. Sociol. Assn., Western Coll. Assn. (pres. 1982), San Jose C.of C. (dir. 1978-); author: Survival in Marriage (1972, ed. 1977); coauthor: The Adjusted American (1964). Ofc: San Jose State University, Washington Sq San Jose 95192

FULLERTON, STEPHEN BYRON, company executive; b. July 25, 1949, Cranston, R.I.; s. William Henry and Hazel Lorraine (Twomey) F.; m. Jane Moline Moore, Nov. 15, 1975 (div. 1979); m. Victoria Regina Rodriguez, Dec. 16, 1983; 1 dau., Alexandra b. 1975; edn: BA, Brown Univ. 1971; grad. bus. program, Pepperdine Univ. 1984-85, CSU Dominguez Hills 1976-80; Univ. R.I. 1973-75. Career: asst. dir., corp. materials mgmt. Greatwest Hosp. Inc., Santa Ana 1983-86; dir. material mgmt. Long Beach Comm. Hosp., Long Beach 1985-86; v.p. Materials Mgmt. Corp., Santa Monica 1986-87; v.p., owner Materiel Resource Associates Inc., Long Beach 1986-; p.t. instr. CSU, San Bernardino 1986; Rio Hondo Coll., Whittier 1986; mem: CSIA, AAMA; mil: E-1 AUS 1972. Ofc: Materiel Resource Associates, Inc. 110 Pine Ave Ste 600 Long Beach 90802

FULMER, SCOTT GORDON, archaeologist, environmental planner; b. March 30, 1950, Lawton, Okla.; s. Richard Proctor and Evelyn Marie (Westlind) F.; edn: BA, UC Santa Barbara 1975; grad. study San Diego State; cert. hazardous mat. mgmt., UC San Diego, 1990. Career: cons. archaeologist to various companies 1977-82; archaeologist Caltrans, San Diego 1982-83; archaeologist Calif. Dept. of Parks & Recreation, San Diego 1983-84; environ. mgmt. splst., Co. of San Diego 1984-85; environ. analyst, Port of San Diego 1985-89; project manager Recon, San Diego 1990-; juror of comm. design awards (Orchids & Onions) Am. Inst. Architects, 1989; judge of sci. fair Greater San Diego Sci. Fair, 1984-90; mem: Soc. for Calif. Achaeology (pgm. ch. annual meeting 1983), Nat. Assn. of Environ. Profls., Assn. of Environ. Profls. (past ofcr.), Soc. of Profl. Archaeologists, Soc. for Am. Archaeology; author article pub. 1985, co-auth. article pub. 1987; co-auth. monograph BLM Pubs. in History, Anthropology pub. 1981; rec: golf. Ofc: Recon 7460 Mission Valley Rd San Diego 92108

FULTZ, PHILIP NATHANIEL, management analyst; b. Jan. 29, 1943, NY, NY; s. Otis and Sara L. (Gibbs) F.; m. Bessie L. McCoy, Mar. 11, 1972; edn: AA in bus., Coll. of the Desert, 1980; BA and MA in mgmt., Univ. Redlands, 1980, 1982; Calif. Comm. Colls. instr. credential, bus. mgmt. Career: served to capt. US Marine Corps 1964-78; CETA coord. Morongo Unified Sch. Dist., 29 Palms 1978-80; manpower specialist San Bdo. County, Yucca Valley 1980-85; analyst/tech. writer Advanced Technology Inc., 29 Palms 1985-89; MIK, Inc., 1989-91; mgmt. analyst Morale, Welfare & Recreation, USMC, 29 Palms, 1991-; adj. asst. prof. Chapman Univ., 29 Palms 1989-; civic bds: 29 Palms Water Dist. (elected dir. 1991-), Morongo Basin Coalition for Adult Literacy, 29 Palms (founding dir., tutor 1985-), Unity Home Battered Womens Shelter, Joshua Tree (founding dir. 1983-86); Republican; rec: hunting. Ofc: Morale, Welfare & Recreation, Marine Corps Air Ground Combat Ctr. 29 Palms 92278

FUOTI, JAMES CHARLES, insurance agency president; b. Jan. 13, 1951, Reading, Pa.; s. James and June Elizabeth (Witman) F.; m. Susan, June 24, 1972; edn: BS indsl. mgmt., Purdue Univ. 1972; Chartered Property Casualty Underwriter, Am. Inst. PLU 1976; Accred. Advisor Ins., 1983, Assoc. in Risk Mgmt., 1992, Ins. Inst. of Am. Career: with Hartford Ins. 1972-74; surplus lines broker M.J. Hall & Co. Inc. 1974-77; v.p., ins. agent/broker J.P. Burris Ins. 1977-82; Pickett, Rotholz & Murphy 1982-84, Nationwide Ins. 1984-86; pres. Fuoti Insurance Agency Inc., 1986-; instr. San Joaquin Delta Coll. 1975-76, instr. Insurance Edn. Assn. 1981-; Risk Mgmt. Day Panelist, 1983; awards: USN ROTC Scholar 1968, Continuing Profl. Devel. CPCU 1983-, Independent Agents of No. Calif. Insurance Profl. of Year 1984, PGA Senior Gold Rush Pro-Am Winner 1987; mem: Chartered Property Casualty Underwriters (Sacto.

Valley pres. 1983, edn. chmn. 1990); Purdue Alumni Assn., RIMS Chapter; clubs: Comstock, North Ridge CC, Nat. Assn. of Lefthanded Golfers; rec: golf, music. Ofc: POB 1718 Orangevale 95662

FUTCH, ARCHER HAMNER, JR., physicist; b. Mar. 21, 1925, Monroe, N.C.; s. Archer, Sr. and Emma (Covington) F.; m. Patricia Anne West, June 13, 1964; children: Lisa b. 1957, Jacqueline b. 1960, Tina b. 1961; edn: BS, and MS, Univ. of N.C., Chapel Hill, 1949, 1951; PhD, Univ. Maryland, College Park, Md. 1956. Career: physicist Du Pont, Aiken, S.C., 1955-58; Univ. Calif., Lawrence Livermore Nat. Lab., Livermore 1959-91; honors: Phi Beta Kappa 1949, Sigma Xi 1951; civic bds: Livermore Planning Commn. 1968-72, Livermore City Council (1972-76, Mayor 1976), Alameda County Water Dist. 1976-80; author: Excited Energetic Nuclear Particle Prodn. (Pat. 1969), numerous plasma physics papers (1971-); mil: pfc US Army 1944-46; Republican; Methodist.

FUTTERMAN, JOHN ARTHUR HARDT, physicist; b. Apr. 25, 1955, USNB Yokosuka, Japan; s. Perry and Zelda F.; m. Dorothea Hardt, 1978; edn: BA in physics (honors) Swarthmore Coll., 1977; PhD physics, Univ. of Texas, Austin 1981. Career: mem. tech. staff AT&T Bell Labs., Holmdel, N.J. 1981-84, MTS supr. 1984-86; physicist Lawrence Livermore Nat. Lab., Livermore, Ca. 1987-; honors: Sigma Xi 1977; mem. IEEE (sr. mem. 1988), Am. Physical Soc., Committee of Concerned Scientists; coauthor: Scattering from Black Holes (1988), 5+ sci. papers; rec: photography. Ofc: LLNL Code L-95 PO Box 808 Livermore 94550

GABELMAN, JOHN WARREN, consultant geologist; b. May 18, 1921, Manila, P.I.; s. Charles Grover and Cyprienna Louisa (Turcotte) G.; m. Olive Alexander Thompson, Sept. 22, 1945; children: Barbara Grace b. 1952, Joan Lynn b. 1955; edn: Geological Engr., Colo. Sch. of Mines, 1943, Master Geol. Engring., 1948, DSc, 1949; cert. profl. geologist (#1613) Am. Inst. Profl. Geol., 1967, reg. profl. engr. Colo. (#1226), reg. geol. Calif. (#003790). Career: jr. engr./geol. New Jersey Zinc Co., Gilman, Colo. (1943-44, 46); p.t. instr. Colo. Sch. of Mines, Golden 1946-49; geologist Colo. Fuel & Iron Corp., Pueblo, Colo. 1949-52; Am. Smelting & Refining Co., Salt Lake City, 1953-54; dist. geologist US Atomic Energy Commn., Gr. Junction, Colo. 1954-58, geol. adviser, Latin Am. US AEC, Lima, Peru 1958-61, chief resource appraisal US AEC, Wash. D.C., 1961-74, program mgr. Geothermal, US AEC, 1974-75; mgr. exploration res. Utah Internat. Inc., San Francisco 1975-83; consultant, pres. J.W. Gabelman & Assocs., Danville, 1983-; mem: Geol. Soc. Am. (1949-, Fellow), Soc. Economic Geologists (1948-, Fellow), Am. Assn. Petroleum Geol. (1943-, Emeritus mem.), Soc. Mining Engrs. AIME (1941-), Legion of Honor 1993, Assn. of Exploration Geochemists 1985-, Computer-Oriented Geol. Soc. 1990-; author: Migration of Uranium & Thorium (1977), 110+ profl. papers and jour. articles (1947-); mil: aviation electronic tech. mate 3/c USN 1944-46; Republican; R.Cath.; rec: skiing, fishing, hunting, photography. Res/Ofc: 23 Portland Ct Danville 94526

GABRIEL, MICHAEL, hypnotherapist, educator, author; b. Sept. 27, 1927, Brooklyn, NY; s. Benjamin and Martha (Buslow) Waldman; m. Marie Woltjer, May 27, 1989; children: Celina Waldman b. 1961; edn: BA, Brooklyn Coll., Brooklyn, NY 1950; MA, Sierra Univ., Costa Mesa, Calif. 1987; MA, Columbia Univ., NY, NY 1993. Career: eligibility worker, County of Santa Clara, San Jose, Calif. 1970-72; workshop dir., Wellhouse Seminars, San Jose 1973-; hypnotherapist, private practice, San Jose 1973-; instr., West Valley Coll., Saratoga, Calif. 1979-; presenter at nat. conferences; Assn. for Past Life Res. & Therapies, Pre and Peri-Natal Psychology Assn., Am. Bd. of Hypnotherapy. Nat. Guild of Hypnotherapy; bd. mem., Assn. for Past Life Res. & Therapies 1988-; mem. Pre and Peri-Natal Psychology Assn. 1991-; author: jour. article, 1989; book, Voices From The Womb, 1992; rec: gardening. Res: 1102 Camino Pablo San Jose 95125. Ofc: P.O. Box 8030 San Jose 95155

GABRIEL, ROBERT MICHAEL, insurance executive; b. Oct. 8, 1923, Detroit, Mich.; s. Andrew and Nazara (Karam) G.; m. Louise B. Rassey, Dec. 29, 1946; children: Susan (Potter) b. 1948, Robert b. 1950, Sharyl b. 1959; edn: BS and gen. secondary tchg. cred. UCLA, 1948; grad. Midshipman Sch. Columbia Univ.; Career: ptnr. Gabriel's Food Market, Santa Monica 1946-52; tchr. Los Angeles Sch. Dist., 1949-50, Santa Monica Sch. Dist., 1953-54; owner Bob Gabriel Co., Ins. and Real Estate, Santa Monica 1954-; instr. Navy Ofcr. Tng. Pgm. 1953, instr. real estate Santa Monica Coll. 1962-64; honors: Eagle Scout 1938, service award Santa Monica Bd. of Edn. 1974, recipient 1st Boss of Year awarded by S.M. Jaycees, NCCJ Humanitarian Award, citizen of yr. Santa Monica Bd. of Realtors 1985, medallion award Boys Club Am. (1987, community service Santa Monica Kiwanis Club 1987, citizen of yr. Santa Monica Lions Club 1990; mem. Santa Monica Indep. Ins. Agents (pres. 1964), Reg. Producer Advy. Council- Commercial Union Ins. Cos. (chmn.); civic: Santa Monica Conv. & Visitors Bur. (chmn. bd. 1989-90, 91-92), Santa Monica C.of C. (pres. 1981-82), S.M. Boys Club (pres. 1985-87), S.M. Medical Ctr. (chmn. bd. 1990-92, dir. 1977-), S.M. Med. Found. (bd. 1978-), Santa Monica City Council (councilman 1971-73), S.M. Rec. and Parks Commn. (chmn. 1968), S.M. Hist. Soc. (advy. bd. 1991-), Optimist Club, NCCJ (past chmn.); mil: lcdr USNR-R 1942-64, WWII, Korea; Republican; Eastern Orthodox; rec: sports, volunteerism. Ofc: Bob Gabriel Co. 2325 Wilshire Blvd POB 620 Santa Monica 90406

GADBOIS, RICHARD A., JR., federal district judge; b. June 18, 1932, Omaha, Nebr.; s. Richard A., Sr. and Margaret Ann (Donahue) Bartlett; children: Richard, Gregory, Guy, Geoffrey, Thomas; edn: AB, St. John's Coll., Camarillo 1955; JD, Loyola Univ., L.A. 1958; postgrad. law, USC, 1958-60. Career: dep. atty. gen. Calif., Los Angeles, 1958-59; ptnr. Musick, Peeler & Garrett, 1959-68; v.p. Denny's Inc., La Mirada 1968-71; judge Municipal Ct., Los Angeles 1971-72, Superior Ct., 1972-82, U.S. District Ct., 1982-; decorated Kt., Order of Holy Sepulchre by Pope John Paul II; mem. ABA, Calif. State Bar (profl. ethics com. 1965-70), L.A. County Bar Assn. (trustee 1966-67); Republican; R.Cath. Ofc: 176 U.S. Courthouse, 312 N Spring St Los Angeles 90012

GAEDE, CARL DEAN, architect; b. May 31, 1936, Newton, Kans.; s. John E. and Anna Marie (Reiss) G.; m. Dawn Arlene Dube, April 6, 1968; children: Peter b. 1969, Katrina b. 1974; edn: BS arch. engring., Kans. St. Univ. 1960; B.Arch., 1960. Career: project designer A. Quincy Jones, Frederick E. Emmons, L.A. 1962-64; Skidmore Owings & Merrill, San Francisco 1965-68; Daniel Mann Johnson & Mendenhall, L.A. 1969-72; pvt. practice, 1972-; honors: Phi Kappa Phi, Tau Sigma Delta, Kans. St. Univ. outstanding grad. sr. (1960), AIA hon. award (1982); mem: Tournament of Roses, Univ. Club Pasadena, AIA (Calif. Council); mil: SP-4 AUS 1960-62; Republican; Prot.; rec: fishing, hiking, woodworking. Res: 980 Roxbury Dr Pasadena 91104 Ofc: Gaede & Larson 95 N Marengo Ave Ste 103 Pasadena 91101

GAEDE, RICKY LANE, hotel executive; b. June 14, 1957, Olney, Ill.; s. Herman Ray and Sarah Ann (Spray) G.; m. Debbie Jean McCorkle, May 8, 1982; children: Ashley, Seth. Career: banquet mgr. Ramada, Phoenix, Ariz. 1981-82, food and beverage dir., Bloomington, Ill. 1982-83, Tyler, Tx. 1983-85, Phoenix, Ariz. 1985-86, gen. mgr., Taos, N.M. 1986-88, gen. mgr. Ramada Inn, Cypress, Calif. 1988-; honors: Who's Who in H.S. 1975; mem: Cypress C.of C. (secty. 1988-), Ramada Mgmt. Assn. of Calif., Cypress Pops Orchestra (hon. bd. 1988-), Hotel Motel Assn., Long Beach C.of C.; rec: gardening, basketball, sailing. Res: 9451 Julie Beth Cypress 90630 Ofc: Ramada Inn 5865 Katella Ave Cypress 90630

GAHAN, KATHLEEN MASON, educational counselor; b. May 23, 1940, Long Beach; d. Robert Elwyn Fisher and Jean Mason Campbell; m. Keith Victor Gahan, Apr. 21, 1961; children: Carrie, 1962; Christie, 1966; edn: MA, Calif. State Univ., Long Beach, 1966; BA, Calif. Sate Univ., Long Beach, 1962; Calif. General Secondary Cred., 1965; Calif. Admin. Cred., 1978; Calif. Pupil Services Cred., 1979. Career: tchr. Long Beach Unified Sch. District, Long Beach 1963-70; tchr. Porterville Union High Sch. District, Porterville 1970-76, counselor 1976-; coordinator, Gifted and Talented Edn., Porterville 1976-83; adminstr., Adv. Placement Program, Porterville 1979-; proprietor, El Mirador Ranch, Strathmore 1978-; tchr.-organizer, SAT Workshop 1981-83; exec. com., Math-Science Conference, Tulare Cty. 1982-85; coach, Academic Decathlon Team, Porterville 1977-82, 85; advisor, Drop Out Retention Program, Porterville 1986-; adminstr., Counseling for College-able Hispanics, Porterville 1988-90; Counselor, Partnership Academy in Business, Porterville 1990-; tchr., faculty, staff computer workshops 1992-93; awards: 1st place, Museum of Art, Long Beach 1961; champion Tulare Cty. Academic Decathalon Team 1982, 85; 1st and 2nd place, Aca Orange Blossom Festival Art Show, Lindsay 1988; 2nd place, Coll. of Sequoias Art Show, Visalia 1988; commendation Porterville Sch. Gov. Bd.; 20 Year Service Award, Porterville Public Sch. 1990; Who's Who in the West 1992; hon. mention, Orange Blossom Festival Art Show, Lindsay 1992; Who's Who Am. Women 1994; mem: Calif. Teachers Assn. 1963-, Am. Assn. of Univ. Women 1970-, Porterville Educators Assn. 1970-, Am. Assn. of Individual Investors 1984-, Bible Study, 1986-; civic: 4-H Club, Lindsay, proj. leader 1971-79; Tulare Cty. Herb Soc., Visalia, charter mem. 1983-85; author: pub. articles and poems; ed., Mexican Cooking in Am., 1974; ed., Glory Bee, craft patterns 1979-84; Republican; Ch. of Nazarene; rec: painting, gardening, bridge, travel; res: Lindsay; ofc: Porterville High Sch. 465 W. Olive Ave. Porterville 93257

GAIBER, MAXINE D., museum public relations executive; b. May 6, 1949, N.Y.C.; d. Sidney and Junia Estelle (Gruberg) Oliansky; m. Stuart Gaiber, May 11, 1971; children: Scott Cory b. 1979, Samantha Lauren b. 1981; edn: BA art hist. (magna cum laude, Phi Beta Kappa), Brooklyn Coll., 1970; mgmt. devel. pgm. Harvard Inst. in Arts Adminstr., 1976; MA art hist./museology, Univ. Minn., 1972, PhD studies 1978; cont. edn. Mpls. Coll. of Art and Design, 1973-78, Art Ctr. Coll. of Design, 1985, profl. tng. Smithsonian Instn., Univ. Minn., UC Irvine. Career: tchg. asst. Univ. of Minn., 1970-71; instr. Mpls. Inst. of Arts (MIA), 1972-79, dev. arts-in-edn. pgms. 1972- 73, supr. tours & curriculum svs. 1973-79, assoc. chair edn. div. 1977-79; museum edn. cons. Art Inst. of Chgo., 1979-82, instr. Fall 1980; Kellogg Found. pgm. coord. (tng. pgms. for mus. profls.) Field Mus. of Natural History, Chgo. 1982-83; instr. humanities div. Coll. of DuPage, 1981-83; publications dir., then dir. campaigns and funding res. Art Center Coll. of Design, 1983-88, faculty 1986-89; pub. rels. dir. Newport Harbor Art Mus., Newport Beach 1988-; instr. L.A. Co. Mus. of Art, 1985-; exhibitions: Assimilation: Japan, MIA/Univ. Minn. Sch. Arch. 1974, Japanese Art from the Burke Collection, MIA 1977, Art and Technology, MIA 1979; author teacher's guides and discovery units (American Indian Art, 1972,

Native Arts, 1980, Imperial China, 1980, Indians of the Northwest Coast, 1981, Alaska's Coastal Eskimos, 1981), articles in museum and art jours., annual reports, catalogs, newsletters. Ofc: 850 San Clemente Dr Newport Beach 92660

GALANOS, JAMES, designer; b. Sept. 20, 1924, Phila.; s. Gregory D. and Helen (Gorgoliatos) G. Career: with Hattie Carnegie, 1944; asst. to designer Columbia Pictures Corp., Hollywood 1946-47; trainee Robert Piguet, Paris, France 1947-48; founder, designer Galanos Originals, Beverly Hills 1951-; awards: distinguished service in field of fashion Neiman-Marcus 1954, Am. Fashion Critics award Met. Mus. Art, Costume Inst. 1954, Return award 1956, Hall of Fame 1959, creativity award Internat. Achievments Fair 1956, Filene's Young Talent design award, Boston 1958, Cotton Fashion award 1958, Coty Hall of Fame 1959, London Times Internat. Fashion Award 1965, Lifetime achiev. Council Fashion Designers of Am. 1985, Stanley award Fashion Collectors of Dallas Hist. Soc. 1986, Otis-Parsons design achiev. award 1987; retrospective exhibns. Costume Council L.A. County Mus. Art (1974), Fashion Inst. Tech. 1976. Ofc: 2254 S Sepulveda Blvd Los Angeles 90064

GALES, SAMUEL JOEL, army logistics specialist, equal employment opportunity counselor; b. June 14, 1930, Dublin, Miss.; s. James McNary McNeil and Alice Francis (Smith) Broadus-Gales; m. Martha Ann Jackson (div. Jan. 1978); children: Samuel, II (dec. 1985), Martha Diane Bryant, Katherine Roselein, Karlmann Von, Carolyn B., Elizabeth Angelica; edn: BA, Chapman Univ., 1981, MS, 1987; tchr credential 1987. Career: enlisted, served to master/1st sgt. US Army, 1948-76, ret., decorated Air medal; tchr. Monterey Unified Sch. Dist. 1981-82; Dept. of Army civilian empl. Directorate of Logistics, Fort Ord, 1982-, equal employment opportunity counselor (collateral) DoD 1987-93; Ombudsman, Monterey County, long term care program; mem: American Legion (post comdr. 1973-74); clubs: Forty and Eight (chef-degare 1979, 80), Monterey Chess (pres.), Past Commanders' Club Calif. (pres. Outpost #28 1981-82); civic bds: Family Service Agency, Monterey 1979-85, Episcopal Soc. for Ministry on Aging, Carmel 1980-86, Task Force on Aging, Carmel 1983-87; Peer Counselor 1982-84; Republican; Episcopalian (Eucharist minister, vestry man 1982-85, 1991-94). Res: 1617 Lowell St POB 919 Seaside 93955-0919 Ofc: Self-Service Supply Center 2080 Quartermaster Ave Fort Ord 93941

GALIPEAU, STEVEN ARTHUR, psychotherapist; b. Nov. 10, 1948, Summit, N.J.; s. Arthur Harmars and Theresa Louise (Levesque) G.; m. Teresa Louise Shelton (div. 1983); m. Linda Carlotta Holmwood, Apr. 22, 1984; children: Brendan b. 1985, Owen b. 1988; edn: AB, Boston Coll., 1970; MA psychol. counseling, Univ. of Notre Dame, 1972; MDiv, The Church Divinity Sch. of Pacific, Berkeley 1977; lic. Marriage Family, Child Counselor, BBSE, 1975. Career: psychotherapist Family & Children's Center, Mishawaka, Ind. 1972-74; vicar St. Luke's Ch., Fontana 1977-78; assoc. rector St. Edmund's Ch., San Marino 1978-82; psychotherapist pvt. practice, Studio City, 1975-, dir. Coldwater Counseling Ctr., 1983-; lectr. churches, psych. profl. orgs. in So. Calif. 1977-, lectr. C.G. Jung Inst., Los Angeles 1986-; mem: Am. Assn. for Marriage and Family Therapy 1990-91, Calif. Assn. of Marriage and Family Therapists 1987-, C.G. Jung Inst. of L.A. (cand. 1982-), Nat. Assn. for the Advancement of Psychoanalysis 1992-; author: Transforming Body and Soul: Therapeutic Wisdom in the Gospel Healing Stories (1990); Democrat; Episcopalian. Ofc: Steven A. Galipeau, 4419 Coldwater Canyon Ave Ste E Studio City 91604

GALLARDO, ALBERT JOHN, county transportation authority executive; b. Apr. 8, 1927, Oakland; s. Frank Navarro and Emily (Luque) G.; m. Margaret Theresa McAuliffe, Sept. 25, 1954; children: Albert b. 1955, Susan b. 1957, Julie b. 1963; edn: BSCE, UC Berkeley 1950; lic. civil engr. Calif. 1956. Career: transp. engr. Fed. Hwy. Adminstrn., Sacto. 1950-83; project mgr. Bissell & Karn Inc. 1984-86; exec. dir. Alameda Co. Transp. Authority, Oakland 1987-; nat. dir. ASCE, Sacto 1986-88; awards: U.S. Dept. Transp. Silver Medal 1978, Engrs. Council Service to Profession 1987; mem: ASCE (fellow), Am. Pub. Works Assn., S. Bay Engrs. Club; mil: USN 1945-46; Catholic; rec: history. Res: 3814 Moddison Ave Sacramento 95819 Ofc: Alameda County Transportation Authority 1401 Lakeside Dr Ste 1201 Oakland 94612

GALLISON, H(AROLD) BAILEY, youth agency executive; b. Apr. 6, 1924, Orange, N.J.; s. Harold Hobron and Stella Camilla (Holm) G.; m. Janet C. Frazier, June 23, 1951 (div. 1983); m. Sharilyn Leone Lemkuil, Jan. 27, 1984; children: Claudia Jean (M.D.), and Harold Bailey, II; edn: BA, Univ. Mo., 1948. Career: sales mgr. Carll Mercury Dealership, La Jolla 1951-53; exec. dir. La Jolla Town Council, 1953-63; advt. mgr. Security Pacific Bank, San Diego 1963-70; dir. p.r. Mercy Hosp. and Med. Ctr., San Diego 1970-83; commun. rep. Citadel Communications, San Diego 1983-84; exec. dir. Community Campership Council, 1985-; past pres. So. Calif. Bank Advertisers Assn.; past chmn. La Jolla Civic Ctr. Corp.; awards: outstanding alumni Univ. of Mo., 1987, profl. of yr. San Diego Public Rels. Club S.D., 1973, good neighbor award Miramar Naval Air Station S.D., 1957; mem. Nat. Soc. of Fund Raising Execs. (past v.p., charter mem. San Diego Chpt.), Agency Execs. Assn. S.D., Univ. Mo. Alumni Assn. (mem. Nat. Alumni Board 14 yrs.), US Navy League, Am. Legion, San Diego P.R. Club (past pres.), Kiwanis (La Jolla Club past pres., past lt. gov. div. #21 Cal-Nev-Hawaii Dist.); civic bds: Gillispie Sch. and Child Care Assn., La Jolla (pres. bd. dirs.), Woodlands North HOA (pres.), Kentucky Col., United Way Speakers Bureau, San Diego YMCA, San Diego Padres Action Team; (past): Citizens Advy. Council La Jolla H.S. (past chmn.), La Jolla Bronco Boys Baseball League (past pres.), La Jolla Youth Little League (coach 12 yrs.); mil: enlisted USN 1943-46 (incl. overseas duty); Republican; Presbyterian; rec: tennis, spectator sports, walking, theatre. Ofc: Community Campership Council 7510 Clairemont Mesa Blvd Ste 208 San Diego 92111

GALVAN, ANTHONY, III, television producer, educator, researcher; b. June 2, 1946, Ft. Bliss, El Paso, Tx.; s. T.A. and Soledad (Alvidrez) G.; edn: BA photojourn., Colo. St. Univ., 1973; MA mass comms., Univ. of Colo., Boulder 1978. Career: photo-graphic dir. Nat. Center for Atmospheric Research, Boulder, Colo. 1973-78; asst. prof. Bowling Green State Univ., 1978-82; Canadian t.v. sales TV-Ontario, Toronto, Ont. 1983-86; cons. prin., Los Angeles, 1986-87; asst. prof. Syracuse Univ., N.Y. 1988; owner Dos Gatos, Burbank, Calif. 1988-; market researcher Auto Age Mag., Van Nuys 1987; prodn. res. Nippon Television, Japan 1989-91, Telemundo, San Juan, P.R. 1990; nat. communications dir. Mexican Am. Legal Defense & Educ. Fund, L.A. 1992-(proj. MAS coord. Nat. Assn. for Hispanic Elderly); author: (drama) Tell Them Not To Kill Me (1988), Can't You Hear The Dog Barking (1988), Saintly Misstresses (1988), (children's book) How Mouse Became An Eagle (1991); awards: 1st pl. & hon. mention US All Army Photo Comp., Seoul, Korea 1970, 2d pl. Aspen (Colo.) Film Fest. 1977, Pub. Bdcstg. awards: Network of Hispanic Communicators, Dallas 1984, Native Am. Consortium, Lincoln, Neb. 1985; mem: Screen Actors Guild 1986-, Kendo Fedn. of USA 1989-, So. Calif. Kendo Fedn., S.F.V. Kendo Dojo (pres. 1992); mil: 1st lt. US Army Field Arty. 1966-76; R.Cath.; rec: Kendo, scuba, fishing, travel, flying.

GAMBLE, LARRY WARD, radio station owner, marketing consultant, advertising executive; b. Feb. 1, 1943, Postville, Iowa; s. Adrian Ward and Arlene Isadore G.; m. Sylvia Ann, June 12, 1964; children: Robert Lawrence b. 1970, Johannes Sanger b. 1973; edn: AA, Modesto Jr. Coll. 1964; BA, Fresno St. Coll. 1966, MA, CSU Freano, 1968; postgrad. studies Western Mich. Univ., 1973; cert., N.Y. Sch. Design, 1974. Career: asst. prof. theatre arts Kalamazoo Coll. 1969-74; artist-in-residence Western Mich. Univ., 1975; asst. prof. performing arts Coll. Santa Fe, 1974-76; account exec. KMJ-KSEE TV, Ch. 24, 1977-80; dir. mktg. Pappas Teleproductions, 1980-83; pres., owner KAAT-FM Radio, Oakhurst 1982-; pres., owner KTNS-AM Radio, Oakhurst 1988-; pres., creative dir., owner Wilshire West Communications, and Larry Gamble Public Relations, 1985-89; exec. secty., treas. Calif. Sierra Corp. 1980-86, CEO 1988-; awards: Nat. Silver Medal, Am. Advtg. Fedn. 1983, Golden Oaks awards Fresno Advt. Fedn.; mem: Am. Advtg. Fedn. (gov. Dist. XIV Calif./Nev. 1983-84), Fresno Advtg. Fedn., Toastmasters; civic: mem. Clovis Downtown Steering Com. and founding bd. B.O.O.T. (Bus. Org. of Old Town, Clovis); Democrat; Presbyterian; rec: real estate investments, historic renovation, photog. Res: 2179 Rall Ave Clovis 93612 Ofc: Fifth Avenue Profl. Complex, 621 5th Ave Clovis 93612

GAMMEL, EDWARD O., neurological surgeon; b. Aug. 2, 1930, Danville, Ill.; s. Gordon and Dot G.; m. Patricia Martin, Dec. 26, 1955; children: Susan b. 1956, Leslie b. 1960, Edward, Jr. b. 1962; edn: BA, DePaul Univ., 1952; MD, Howard Med. Sch., 1956. Career: med. intern Seaside Mem. Hosp., Long Beach 1956-57; gen. resident Merced County Gen. Hosp., 1957-58; neurological surgery resident Long Beach Vet. Hosp., 1960-64; pvt. practice neurol. surgery, Sacramento 1964-; clin. instr. neurol. surg. UC Davis, 1969-; mem. AMA, CMA, Sacto. Med. Soc., Congress Neurological Surgery; mil: capt. USAF 1958-60; rec: tennis. Ofc: Gammel & Leigh Medical Corp. 3644 Mission Ave Carmichael 95608

GANGWERE, HEATHER HENDRY, teacher., foreign language and English as a second language; b. April 11, 1964, Orange, Calif.; d. James Hendry (dec.) and Phila Margaret (Hurter) Acuff; m. Walt Lewis Gangwere, Nov. 22, 1986; edn: BA, Univ. of Redlands, Redlands, Calif. 1982-86; career: tchr., Leland H.S., San Jose, Calif. 1988-; chair, foreign lang. dept., Leland H.S. 1991-; dir. of student exchange, Pacific Neighbors, San Jose 1991-; awards: listed in Who's Who of Am. Univ. & Colls., Univ. of Redlands 1985-86, Outstanding Young Women of Am. 1987, Who's Who in the West 1989, Who's Who of Am. Tchrs. 1992; mem: Pacific Neighbors/Sister Cities Internat. 1990-; Redlands Admissions Assistance Program 1990-; Crossroads Bible Ch. Ofc: Leland High School 6677 Camden Ave. San Jose 95120

GANIERE, ROBERT C., corporate financial executive; b. Oct. 14, 1936, Cleveland, Ohio; s. Harold Francis and Elizabeth V. (Gregor) G.; m. Mary Ann Henderson, July 16, 1955; children: Mary b. 1956, Susan b. 1958, Elizabeth b. 1965, Christopher b. 1967, James b. 1972, David b. 1973, Catherine b. 1975, Sarah b. 1978, Rachel b. 1980; edn: BBA acctg., Cleveland State Univ., 1964. Career: staff acct. Performed Line Products, Cleveland, O. 1962; Givelber & Givelber, 1963; Haskins & Sells, 1964; staff acct. to mgr. of tax dept. Harris Kerr Forster & Co., Los Angeles 1964-67; c.f.o. Dr. R.F. Beauchamp et al, Newport Beach and Beauchamp Western Group of Cos., 1967-; dir., sec.-treas. Dental Finance, N.B. 1968-; founder, dir., v.p. Independent Indemnity (Calif.

ins. co.), Newport Beach 1973-; pres., dir. Midlands Co., Newport Beach 1981-87, sec.-treas. 1987-; founder., dir., sec.-treas. Founders Leasing Co., N.B. 1982-, Western Dental Services Inc., N.B. 1984-; dir., sec.-treas. Video Leasing Co., Anaheim 1982-; dir. North Am. Video Corp. (NAVCO), Anaheim 1988-; active Boy Scouts, Huntington Beach (coms., asst. scout master, scout master 1979-87); Ch. of Jesus Christ of Latter Day Saints; rec: scouting, camping, snorkling, economic theory. Ofc: 1641 Langley Ave Irvine 92714 also: Western Dental Services Inc. 300 Plaza Alicante Ste 800 Garden Grove 92640

GANS, ROBERT A., investment co. president; b. July 16, 1941, Port Chester, N.Y.; s. Robt. Altha, Jr. and June (Maule) G.; m. Joyce E., June 17, 1978; children: David b. 1969, Hollis b. 1969, Michael b. 1979, Brian b. 1981; edn: Principia Upper Sch., 1959; BA, Stanford Univ. 1963, MBA, 1968; lic. Real Estate Broker; Reg. Prin., NASD; Cert. Property Mgr. (CPM). Career: chief fin. ofcr. Basile Corp., Douglasville, Pa. 1970-73; treas. Index Systems Inc., Cambridge, Mass. 1973-75; fiscal analyst San Diego Co., Calif. 1975-77; pres./dir. Windsor Jewels U.S.A. Inc. 1977-80; chief fin. ofcr./dir. Data Mgmt. Labs. Inc., San Jose 1980-82; CFO Selanar Corp., Santa Clara 1982-83; pres./dir. Gans Investment Corp., Beverly Hills 1983-87; pres./dir. Robt. Gans and Assocs., Julian, Calif. 1987-; mem: Univ. Housing Gp. (pres.), Univ. Legislature, Inst. Real Estate Mgmt., Internat. Assn. Fin. Planners, Los Angeles Bd. Realtors, Apartment Owners Assn. of L.A.; civic: Rotary Intl. 1988-90, YMCA Indian Guides (chief), AYSO Soccer (coach), Toastmasters (pres.), PTA, Back Country Basketball Inc. (pres.), Intermountain Park and Recreation Inc. (exec. v.p.); mil: capt. USMC 1963-66, 3 Purple Hearts, Bronze Star w/Combat V, Vietnam; rec: jogging, backgammon, U.S. hist. Res: Julian 92036 Ofc: Robert Gans and Associates PO Box 520 Julian 92036

GAPOSCHKIN, PETER JOHN ARTHUR, computer programmer-analyst; b. Apr. 5, 1940, Boston; s. Sergei Illarionovich and Cecilia Helena (Payne) G.; edn: Boston Univ. 1957-58, BSc in math, M.I.T., 1961; MA in astronomy, UC Berkeley, 1965, PhD in physics, 1971; Calif. Comm. Coll. instr. credential; 1c radiotelephone lic. with radar endorsement. Career: resrch. asst. Lawrence Berkeley Lab, 1965-70; postal clk. USPS, Oakland 1971-73; civilian employee (GS-9), USN 1973-79; physicist NAVPRO, Sunnyvale 1973-75; computer pgmr. Fleet Numerical Ocean Ctr., Monterey 1975-79; senior analyst Informatics, Palo Alto 1979-80; pgmr. analyst Bur. Mgmt. Info. Systems, San Francisco Pub. Utilities Commn., 1983-; instr. Diablo Valley Coll., Merritt Coll., Canada Coll., Cogswell Coll., San Francisco City Coll., 1980-82; honors: Dean's list M.I.T. 1961; mem: Am. Math. Soc. 1963-, Am. Astronomical Soc. 1965-, Math. Assn. of Am. 1970-, Internat. Tng. in Communication (1986-, club pres), Data Processing Mgmt. Assn., Assn. Computing Machinery, East Bay Area Radio Club, Toastmasters Intl. (ATM Silver 1986); civic: Am. Red Cross Diaster Svs. Com. (Oakland); publs: PhD thesis: Scattering of Gravitational Waves (1971), articles and lectures on various applications or use of spirals to explain human behavior "Yin-Yang Effect" (1990-92); Green Party; Unitarian-Universalist; rec: amateur radio, swimming. Mail: 1442-A Walnut St #371 Berkeley 94709-1496 Res: 1823-1/2 Delaware St Berkeley 94703-1328 Ofc: Bureau Mgmt. Info. Systems, 414 Mason Rm 501 San Francisco 94102-1718

GARCIA, NICOLAS M., business owner; b. Oct. 28, 1937, San Angelo, Tex.; s. Nicolas W. and Dahlia (Ortega) G.; m. Sally Marie Villa, Sept. 29, 1956; children: Pamela Marie b. 1957, Theresa Ann b. 1959, Nicolas M. Jr. b. 1962; edn: AA, Calif. Coll. of Arts & Crafts, 1962; cert. bus. mgmt., American River Coll., 1976. Career: mktg. Bell Distbg. Co., Sacto. 1967-77; ptnr. Spectrum Sales, 1977-78; dir. of tribal devel. Calif. Tribal Chmns. Assn. Sacto. 1978-80, dir. of planning Sacto. Indian Ctr. 1980-81, author funded proposals for Indian Child Welfare 1979, Career Devel. Pgm. 1981; owner/c.e.o. New Dimension Carpet Maint., Sacto. 1981-89; point of sale mktg. specialist Youngs Market Co. Sacto. Div., 1990-; awards: appreciation Sacto. Employment & Tng. Agy. 1986, Private Industry Council Sacto. 1987; civic: Hispanic C.of C. (bd. 1985-87), Mex.-Am. Alcoholism Pgm. (bd. 1983-85), Sacto. Alliance for the Mentally Ill (bd. 1989-); publ: (brochure) Sacto. Indian Center 1981; mil: seaman USCG 1956-60; Republican; Unity; rec: reading, fishing. Res: 6360 Parkcreek Circle Citrus Heights 95621

GARDNER, FREDERICK BOYCE, library director; b. Mar. 12, 1942, Hopkinsville, Ky.; s. Boyce and Alleen Louise (Brown) G.; edn: BA, Univ. Ky., 1964; MA, Ind. Univ., 1966; postgrad. City Univ. N.Y., 1970-71, CSU Northridge, 1973-76, UCLA, 1982-85. Career: head librarian Univ. Ky. Hopkinsville Community Coll., 1966-69; head, reader's svs. Manhattan Community Coll. CUNY, N.Y.C., 1969-71; reference librarian Calif. Inst. Arts, Valencia 1971-74, head public services, 1974-85, dir. computer services, 1984-86, acting dir. 1987, dean 1988-; cons. Total Interlibrary Exchange, Ventura 1984-85, v.p. 1980-81, pres. 1981-82, chmn. tech. task force 1983-88; exec. bd. Calif. Private Academic Libraries 1988-, chmn. exec. bd. 1990; Calif. Library Networking Task Force, 1990-91; mem: Santa Clarita Interlibrary Network (pres. 1989-), Calif. Conf. on Networking (del. 1985), Am. Library Assn., Calif. Library Assn., Performing Arts Libraries Network of Greater Los Angeles (chmn. 1990); mil: capt. USAF 1968-69; rec: music, computer games, hiking, camping. Ofc: Calif. Institute of the Arts, 24700 McBean Pkwy Valencia 91355

GARDNER, NORD ARLING, university relations director, management consultant; b. Aug. 10, 1923, Afton, Wyo.; s. Arling A. and Ruth (Lee) G.; m. Thora Marie Stephen, Mar. 24, 1945; children: Randall Nord, Scott Stephen, Craig Robert, Laurie Lee; 7 grandchildren; edn: BA, Univ. Wyo. 1945; MS, CSU Hayward 1972; MPA, 1975; postgrad. Univ. Chgo., Univ. Mich., UC Berkeley. Career: Commnd. 2d.lt., advanced through grades to lt. col. US Army, 1942-66, ret. 1966, (Army Commendn. medal); personnel analyst Univ. Hosp. UC San Diego 1966-8; coord. manpower devel. UC Berkeley 1968-75; univ. tng. ofcr. San Francisco State Univ. 1975-80, personnel mgr. 1976-80; exec. dir. CRDC Maintenance Tng. Corp. (non-profit), S.F. 1980-85; founder/gen. mgr. Vericlean Janitorial Service, Oakland 1984-86; bus. developer East Bay Asian Local Devel. Corp. 1983-85; pres. Indochinese Community Ent. USA Ltd. 1985-87; v.p./sec. LAO Internat. Comm. Devel. Corp. 1988-90; ptnr. Oi Kit Building Maint. Service 1988-90; ops. mgr. Phimmason's Internat. Import-Export 1988-89; secty. bd. dirs. New Ideas New Imports Inc., 1989-; adminstrv. asst. to chancellor International Pacific Univ., San Ramon 1990; dir. university relations, International Pacific Univ., 1991-; bus. mgmt. and devel. cons. 1987-, family counselor 1988-; pres./dir. Sandor Assocs. Mgmt. Cons., Pleasant Hill 1973-85, 91-; dir. U.S. Devel.-Educational Foundation Group, 1991-; instr. Japanese, psychol. courses, 1977-88; mem. advy. council S.F. Comm. Coll. Dist.; mem: Retired Ofcrs. Assn., Am. Soc. Tng. and Devel., No. Calif. Human Rels. Council, Am. Assn. Univ. Adminstrs., Internat. Personnel Mgrs. Assn., Coll. and Univ. Personnel Assn. (W. Coast rep.), Am. Legion; clubs: Commonwealth of Calif., UCB Faculty, University (SF); listed nat., internat. biographical ref. books; author: To Gather Stones, 1978; Republican. Res: 2995 Bonnie Ln Pleasant Hill 94523-4547

GARDNER, ROBERT ALEXANDER, human resource development consultant; b. Sept. 16, 1944, Berkeley; s. Robert Alexander and Eleanor (Ambrose) G.; m. Alexandra "Sandie" Ross, Mar. 22, 1987; edn: BA, UC Berkeley 1967, MA, CSU Chico 1974, MS, SFSU 1992. Career: placement counselor Sonoma County Office of Edn., Santa Rosa 1975-76; personnel ofcr. Wells Fargo Bank, San Francisco 1977-80; dir. personnel Transam. Airlines, Oakland 1980-84; human resource devel. cons. Gardner Assocs., Oakland 1983-; instr. Armstrong Coll. Bus. and Mgmt. Div., 1978-80, UC Berkeley Ext., 1980-; career counselor (volunteer) Forty Plus of No. Calif., Oakland 1988-; mem: Career Planning and Adult Devel. Network, Calif. Career Development Assn., Am. Assn. for Counseling and Devel., Calif. Assn. for Counseling and Devel., Rotary Internat., UC Alumni Assn.; publs: The National Review Magazine: A Survey from 1955 to 1973 (CSU Chico 1974); Time Management (Telelearning Systems, Inc. S.F., 1983); Achieving Effective Supervision (UCB, 1984, Revised edit. 1989); Managing Personnel Adminstrn. Effectively (UCB, 1986); Career Counseling: Matching Yourself To A Career (UCB, 1987); mil: 1st lt. AUS Intel. 1970-71, Bronze Star, Cross of Gal. w/star cluster, Rep. of Vietnam Service medals; Republican; Congregational; rec: collect and study antique Chinese Snuff Bottles. Res: 42 Aronia Ln Novato 94945 Ofc: Gardner Associates 3873 Piedmont Ave Ste 3 Oakland 94611

GARDNER, WILFORD ROBERT, physicist; b. Oct. 19, 1925, Logan, Utah; s. Robert and Nellie (Barker) G.; m. Marjorie Louise Cole, June 9, 1949; children: Patricia b. 1956, Robert b. 1958, Caroline b. 1960; edn: BS physics, Utah St. Univ. 1949; MS, Iowa St. Univ. 1951; PhD, 1953. Career: physicist U.S. Salinity Lab., Riverside 1953-66; prof. Univ. Wis., Madison 1966-80; prof., chair Univ. Ariz., Tucson 1980-86; dean natural resources UC Berkeley 1987-; mem: Nat. Acad. Scis., Soil Sci. Soc. Am. (pres. 1989-90); author: Soil Physics (1973); mil: AUS Corps Engrs. 1943-46; Mormon. Ofc: Univ. of Calif. 101 Giannini Hall Berkeley 94720

GARFIELD, HOWARD M., lawyer; b. Aug. 16, 1942, N.Y.C.; s. Jack Garfield and Pearl (Levine) Shaw; m. Elizabeth R. Lehmann, Oct. 23, 1978 (div. Dec. 1991); 1 dau. Mackenzie b. 1985; edn: Columbia Univ., 1960-61; AB (gt. distinction and hons. in humanities), Stanford Univ., 1964; JD (cum laude), Harvard Univ., 1968; admitted bar: Calif. 1968. Career: atty., assoc. Pacht, Ross, Warne, Bernhard & Sears, Los Angeles 1968-70; Ambrose & Malat, Beverly Hills, 1970-71; ptnr. law firm Garrett, Garfield & Bourdette, Santa Monica 1971-74; of counsel Goldstein & Phillips, San Francisco 1978-79; atty., assoc. Long & Levit, S.F., 1978-80, ptnr. 1980-, mng. ptnr. 1983-92; adj. prof. Golden Gate Law Sch., 1979; awards: Phi Beta Kappa 1963, Woodrow Wilson fellow 1964, Danforth fellow 1964; mem: State Bar of Calif. 1968-, Internat. Assn. of Defense Counsel 1986-, Defense Research Inst. 1986-, Bar Assn. of S.F. 1980-, Am. Bar Assn. 1986-, Am. Arbitration Assn. (cert. arbitrator 1990-); civic: Mill Valley Parks & Rec. Commn. (commr. 1990-); club: Scott Valley Swim & Tennis (Mill Valley 1980-); coauthor book: Corporate Directors and Officers Liability, Insurance and Risk Mgmt. (1989), numerous articles (1980-); Democrat; Jewish; rec: opera, Italy, travel. Ofc: Long & Levit 101 California St Ste 2300 San Francisco 94111

GARLAND, G(ARFIELD) GARRETT, sales executive; b. Dec. 17, 1945, Lakewood, Oh.; s. Garfield George and Lois Marie (Calavan) G.; edn: BA, Univ. Colorado, Boulder 1974. Career: broker Marcus & Millichap, Newport Beach, Calif. 1982-84; v.p. Pacific Coast Federal, Encino 1984-85; dir. acquisitions

Prudential Investment Fund, L.A. 1985-86; v.p. A.S.I.A., Los Angeles, Tokyo, 1986-89; senior account exec. Lojack Corp., L.A. 1989-; honors: U.S. Ski Team mem. 1966-67; mem: PGA of Am., World Affairs Council 1990-, L.I.F.E. Found., Am. Legion, V.F.W., Nat. Trust for Hist. Preserv.; mil: capt. US Army 1967-71; Methodist; rec: golf, reading, snow skiing; res: 6846 Pacific View Place LA 90068; ofc: Lojack Corp., 9911 Pico Blvd Ste 1000 Los Angeles 90035

GARRETT, RICHARD MARVIN, chemical engineer, executive; b. June 30, 1921, Lakewood, Ohio; s. Harold B. and Lorraine (Robison) G.; m. Bernice Stewart, Aug., 1951 (div. 1978); children: William b. 1953, Diana b. 1955, Sheryl b. 1957, Richard b. 1963; edn: BSChE, Ohio St. Univ. 1943; naval ofcr. indoctrination, Princeton Univ. 1944; Univ. Chgo. Grad. Sch. 1946; MBA, UC Berkeley 1948. Career: chemical engr. Rohm & Haas, Bristol, Pa. 1943-44; sales Taylor Instruments 1948-52; ptnr. Silver Plastic Co., El Segundo 1952-54; Chem Nickel Co., South Gate 1952-53; ptnr., engr. Carbon Wool Corp., Ojai 1953; pres. Margar Co., Manhattan Beach 1954-; pres. L.A. Council of Engring. Soc. 1960; mem: Am. Inst. Chem. Engrs. (chmn. So. Calif. sect. 1962), Am. Cetacean Soc., Steel Structures Painting Council, Internat. Brotherhood of Magicians, Magic Castle; articles pub. in profl. jours., 1964-85; mil: lt.j.g. USNR 1944-46; rec: tennis, bicycling, travel. Res: 424 7th St Manhattan Beach 90266 Ofc: Margar Co. Box 3253 Manhattan Beach 90266

GARRETT, ROBERT STEPHENS, public relations executive; b. July 12, 1937, Bell, Calif.; s. Sammie Jacob and Martha Ethelwynn (Dench) G.; m. Mary Lynn Harris, Sept. 9, 1955 (div. July 1972); children: Lisa, Julie, Kim; m. Camille Ann Priestley, Feb. 15, 1975; children: Lee Ann, Nikki, Grant; grad. Downey High Sch., Downey. Career: machinist, then head shipping dept. Axelson Mfg. Co., Vernon 1955-60; prodn. control planner, methods analyst autonetics div. Rockwell Internat., Downey, Compton and Anaheim, 1960-70; public relations mgr., property mgr., clinic coord., investigator, property researcher and chief adminstr. bd. and care UMEDCO Inc., Long Beach, 1970-77; dir. ops. Regency Mgmt. Service, Anaheim 1977-78; indep. cons. med. pub. rels., 1978-; awards: Paul Harris Fellow Rotary Internat. 1980, Man of Year Garden Grove C.of C. 1992; civic bds: Boys Club Garden Grove (dir. 1978-, pres. 1993, 1st v.p. 1992, 2nd v.p. 1990-91), Girls Club Garden Grove (vol. 1980-, treas. 1983-84, v.p. 1984-86, pres. 1986), City of Garden Grove Traffic Commn. (commr. 1981-, v.chmn. 1988-89, 1992-93, chmn. 1989-90, 93-94); mem. Rotary Internat. (Paramount bd. dirs. 1975-76, Garden Grove bd. dirs. 1978-79, 1993-94, pres. elect 1994-95, v.p. 1992-93), Elks; rec: collect coins, sportscards, non-sports cards & comics, design and build model cars and,planes. Ofc: PO Box 1221 Garden Grove 92642 Tel:714/539-9047

GARRICK, B. JOHN, scientist, executive; b. March 5, 1930, Eureka, Utah; s. Morrison H. and Zelma (Hoffman) G.; m. Amelia Madson, Sept. 18, 1952; children: Robert S. b. 1954, John M. b. 1956, Ann G. b. 1961; edn: BS, Brigham Young Univ. 1952; MS, UCLA 1962; PhD, 1968; reg. profl. engr. 1976. Career: physicist Phillips Petroleum Co. (atomic energy div.) 1952-54; U.S. AEC 1955-57; pres. Holmes & Narver Inc. Nuclear & Systems Scis. Group 1957-75; pres. and c.e.o. PLG, Inc. 1975-, bd. chmn. BOD, Newport Beach 1988-; instr. UCLA, and MIT; awards: US AEC study grantee UCLA 1954-55, US rep. internat. panels in Pakistan and Korea (1962, 71); Am. Nuclear Soc. (ANS) del. to Eastern Bloc Nations for nuclear power technology exchange 1991; mem: Soc. Risk Analysis (nat. pres. 1989-90, founder So. Calif. chpt. 1986), Inst. Advancement of Engring. (Fellow), Am. Nuclear Soc., Black Business Alliance Bd. Advisors, Govs. Earthquake Preparedness Com. 1983; 200+ articles pub. in tech. jours.; rec: hiking, running, art collecting. Ofc: PLG, Inc., 4590 MacArthur Blvd Ste 400 Newport Beach 92660-2027

GARRIO, ROCCO ROBERT, corporate president; b. Jan. 10, 1949, New York City, N.Y.; s. Anthony Joseph Garrio and Julia (Mochinal) Cragnotti; m. Beth Ann Nurmi, 1973 (div. 1980); children: Nicole b. 1979; m.2d. Vanetta Gale Lindsay, July 4, 1981; children: Anthony b. 1982; edn: Bronx Comm. Coll. (N.Y.) 1966-69; El Camino Coll., Torrance 1976-77. Career: group ldr. Revlon Research Ctr., Bronx, N.Y. 1966-71; chemist Azoplate, div. Am. Hoechst, Murray Hill, N.J. 1972-75; tech. sales, Los Angeles 1975-79; tech. sales Richardson, L.A. 1979-80; tech. sales Howson Algrahy, L.A. 1980-81, dist. mgr. 1981-82; branch mgr. Polychrome Corp., L.A. 1982-84; branch mgr. R&P, Inc., L.A. 1984-86; pres. Distribution West, Inc., Fullerton 1986-; awards: top national salesman Azoplate (1977, 78), mgr. highest sales to quota Polychrome (1983); mem. Orange Co. Litho Club, 1988-; Republican; R.Cath.; rec: target shooting, fishing. Ofc: Distribution West 1895 W Commonwealth #E Fullerton 92633

GARRISON, BETTY BERNHARDT, mathematics professor; b. July 1, 1932, Danbury, Ohio; d. Philip Arthur and Reva Esther (Meter) Bernhardt; m. Robert Edward Kvarda, Sept. 28, 1957 (div. 1964); m. John Dresser Garrison, Jan. 17, 1968; 1 son, John Christopher b. 1969; edn: BA, BS in edn., Bowling Green State Univ., 1954; MA, Ohio State Univ., 1956; PhD, Oregon State Univ., 1962. Career: tchg. asst. Ohio State Univ., Columbus 1954-56; instr. Ohio Univ., Athens 1956-57; San Diego State Univ., 1957-59; tchg. asst. Oregon State Univ., Corvallis 1959-60; asst. prof. San Diego State Univ., 1962-66, assoc. prof. 1966-69, prof. mathematics 1969-; reviewer: Mathematical Reviews, Ann Arbor, Mich.

1966-, Zentralblatt fur Mathematik, Berlin, Ger. 1966-; awards: NSF fellow 1960-62; mem. Am. Math. Soc. 1965-, Math. Assn. of Am. 1965-; pub. articles (1981, 90). Ofc: Dept. Math. Scis. San Diego State University, San Diego 92182

GARTNER, HAROLD HENRY, III, lawyer; b. June 23, 1948, Los Angeles; s. Harold H. and Frances Mildred (Evans) G.; m. Denise Young, June 7, 1975; children: Patrick Christopher b. 1977, Matthew Alexander b. 1982; edn: Pasadena City Coll. 1966-67; Geo. Williams Coll. 1967-68; CSU Los Angeles 1968-69; JD, cum laude, Loyola Univ. Sch. of Law 1972. Career: atty., assoc. Hitt, Murray & Caffray, Long Beach 1972; deputy city atty. City of Los Angeles, 1972-73; atty., assoc. Patterson, Ritner, Lockwood, Zanghi & Gartner (and predecessor firm) Los Angeles, Ventura, San Bernardino, and Bakersfield, 1973-79, ptnr. 1979-, mng. ptnr. 1991-; instr. of law Ventura Coll. of Law 1981-; honors: Am. Jurisprudence Award (Trusts & Equity 1971), St. Thomas More Law Honor Soc. (bd. dirs. 1971-72), Law Review; mem: Am., Calif., Ventura Co. bar assns.; Ventura Co. Trial Lawyers Assn., Assn. of So. Calif. Defense Counsel, Nat. Assn. Defense Counsel, Direct Relief Internat. (bd. trustees); club: Pacific Corinthian Yacht; Republican; rec: sailing, scuba diving, skiing. Res: 6900 Via Alba Camarillo 93012 Ofc: Patterson, Ritner, Lockwood, Zanghi & Gartner, 3580 Wilshire Blvd., Suite 900, Los Angeles 90010

GARZOLI, JOHN H., fine art dealer; b. Nov. 23, 1940, San Francisco; s. Henry John and Evelyn Virginia (Dapello) Garzoli (parents 5th generation San Franciscans); m. Elizabeth Cannon, Nov. 25, 1981; children: Joel b. 1966, Josh b. 1971, Scott Bentley b. 1968, Heather Bentley b. 1970, Greg Bentley b. 1970. Career: fine art dealer, splst. American 19th and 20th Century art, San Francisco 1960s-, Fine Arts cons. Calif. State Senate, active in Capitol restoration project and in formation of Capitol Historic Commn. (restoration and art projects in Sacto. and statewide); civic: Oakland Art Mus., San Francisco museums, Calif. Hist. Soc., Am. Conservatory Theatre, S.F. Ballet Assn., S.F. Symphony Assn., S.F. Zoological Soc. (hon. mem.); advisor Smithsonian Instn.; lender, advisor to 100+ nat. touring art exhibits; mil: USMC, ret.; rec: boating, fishing, tennis; ofc: Garzoli Gallery, 930 B Street San Rafael 94901

GATTO, BENNIE, mayor; b. Dec. 3, 1930, French Camp, Calif.; s. Luigi and Jessie (Chio) G.; m. Joyce Dean Brumley, Feb. 8, 1953; children: Karen b. 1954, James b. 1956; edn: Lathrop Elem. 1936-44, Manteca H.S. 1945, Humphreys Bus. Coll., Stockton 1957; Certified Bd. Dirs. for Credit Unions 1971-81; Interaction Mgmt. Pgm. 1985. Career: served to Ships Serviceman 2cl. US Navy abd. USS Essex, Calif., Hawaii, Wash., 1948-56, also served in Korea, Japan, Philippines, Korean War 1950-53; maint. supr. J.R. Simplot Co., Lathrop, Calif. 1956-86; fireman Manteca-Lathrop Fire Dept., 1959-81; elected mayor City of Lathrop; past pres. Oxy Fed. Credit Union, 1971-81; mem: Manteca Metro. Recreation Commn. (pres. 1973-74); awards: boss of year Am. Bus. Women, Manteca 1975, humanitarian award Contel Tel. Co. 1989, hon. life mem. East Union Athletics 1984, 10-yr. appreciation OXY Credit Union 1981, 22 yr. service Manteca-Latrhop Fire Dept. 1981, 30 yr. appreciation J.R. Simplot Co. 1986; mem. Naval Air Transport Svc., V.F.W., Amvets and Disabled Veterans, Lathrop C.of C. (1956-, past pres.), East Union Athletic Booster Club (1970-, pres. 1974-75), Lathrop Firemans Club (pres. 1971), Lathrop Lions Club (pres. 1960); R.Cath.; rec: golf, sports. Res: 15517 Fifth St (PO Box 104) Lathrop 95330 Ofc: City of Lathrop PO Box 1429 Lathrop 95330

GAYNOR, JOSEPH, international business and technology consultant; b. Nov. 15, 1925, N.Y.C.; s. Morris and Rebecca (Schnapper) G.; m. Elaine Bauer, Aug. 19, 1951; children: Barbara Lynne, Martin Scott, Paul David, Andrew Douglas; edn: BChE, Polytechnic Inst. of Brooklyn, 1950; MS ChE, Case Western Reserve Univ., 1952, PhD phys. chem., 1955, grad. bus. adminstrn. courses. Career: mgr. info. mats. & processes, General Electric Co., Res. & Devel. Ctr., 1955-66; v.p./res. bus. equip. gp. and mgr. mats. R&D, Bell and Howell Co. Central Research Labs., 1966-72; mgr. commercial devel. and mem. Pres.'s Office, Horizons Research Inc., 1972-73; pres. Innovative Technology Assocs., 1973-, proposals, and project mgmt. in U.S., Europe and Japan; honors: Phi Lambda Upsilon, Tau Beta Pi, Alpha Chi Sigma, Sigma Xi, recipient IR-100 Awards (2), Plenary lectr. Internat. Photographic Sci. Congress, Moscow 1970, keynote spkr. US Treasury Dept. ann. conf. on security documents; appt. NAS Materials Advy. Bd. currency study com.; tech. advy. bd. Delphax Corp.; mgmt. advy. bd. Chemical Week; chem. engring. product resrch. panel, editl. bd. Photographic Science and Engineering Jour. and Jour. of Applied Photographic Engring.; guest editor Jour. of Imaging Technology 1988-89; sci. advy. bd. Lehigh Press; mem: AAAS (fellow), ACS, SPSE (senior mem., fellow), AIChE (fellow), SID, SPIE, Internat. Photochemistry Soc., Internat. Soc. for Photobiology; author: Patents (40), publs. (35+), papers presented (40+), editor Proceedings, 1st, 3d Intl. Cong. on Advances in Non-Impact Printing Technologies, (book in progress) Electronic Imaging-Technologies and Applications (Marcel Dekker Inc.). Res: 108 La Brea St Oxnard 93035 Ph: 805/984-2979

GEIST, HAROLD, clinical psychologist; b. July 22, 1916, Pittsburgh, Pa.; s. Alexander and Edna (Liebhaber) G.; edn: AB, Cornell Univ., 1936; AM, Columbia Univ., 1937; PhD, Stanford Univ., 1951; Lic. psychologist, Calif.

Career: advisor edn. vocat. Community Cen. Office, Patterson, N.J. 1946-47; pvt. practice psychology VA, 1947-48; chief psychologist Mare Island Naval Hosp., Vallejo, Calif. 1947-48; pvt. practice psychology, Berkeley, 1955-; cons. Pittsburg, Calif. Unified Sch. Dist. 1954-59; cons. Napa State Hosp., Imola 1970-77, sr. clin. psychologist 1971-80; chief editorial cons. Western Psychol. Services 1967-; instr. Walter Reed Hosp., Wash. DC 1942, vis. prof. Univ. Puerto Rico, Rio Piedras 1953-55, lectr. San Francisco St. Univ. 1966-82, adj. prof. Univ. San Francisco 1980-82; mem: Am. Psychol. Assn. (life), AAAS (life), Calif. St. Psychol. Assn. (chmn. div. edn. and tng. 1960-, ed. newsletter), Interam. Soc. Psychology, Internat. Council Psychologists (fellow), Nat. Gerontol. Soc., Phi Sigma Delta; mil: tech5 Army Med. Service Corps 1942-46; author: Etiology of Idiopathic Epilepsy (1962), Psychol. Aspects of Diabetes (1964), Tennis Psychology (1976), Psychol. Aspects of Rheumatoid Arthritis, Bahian Adventure (1985), others; test: Picture Vocat. Interest Test (15 fgn. adaptations), numerous med. jour. articles incl. 7 articles on validation of picture interest inventory, 1 color video tape, 6 audio tapes; rec: tennis. Res: 2255 Hearst Ave Berkeley CA 94709 Ofc: 2380 Ellsworth Berkeley CA 94704

GELBARD, SHANA, acupuncturist; b. Aug. 18, 1958, Oceanside, N.Y.; d. Martin Leonard and Eva Elizabeth (Cook) Schlossberg; children: Dustin Shawn b. 1981, Dana Rachel b. 1982; edn: acupuncturist, Emperor's Coll., Santa Monica 1989; diplomate, acupuncture, nationally bd. certified. Career: dir., chief of acupuncture dept., Tower Acupuncture at the Cedars Sinai Med. Ofc. Bldgs., L.A., Calif.; pres. Acupuncture Soc. of L.A. 1992-93; awards: Woman of Year, Hollywood Appreciation Soc., L.A. 1991; diplomate, Am. Soc. of Acupuncturists 1989-93; diplomate, Nat. Comm. Certification Acupuncturists 1990-93; diplomate, Am. Acad. of Pain 1992-93; mem: Screen Actors Guild, AFTRA; Nat. Bd. of Acupuncture Orthopedists (bd. eligible); Reflexive Sympathetic Dystrophy, Cedars Sinai Med. Towers W. #585 (pres.) 1990-93; author: screenplay, Enter The Angel, 1987; Democrat; Unitarian; rec: snorkeling, water-skiing, adventurer. Ofc: Tower Acupuncture 8635 West 3rd #585 Los Angeles 90048

GELIS, HUSEYIN, purchasing executive; b. Sept. 5, 1959, Istanbul, Turkey; s. Refik and Gueler (Ovat) G.; edn: BS in telecomms., Ennepe-Ruhr, Witten, W.Ger.; BSBA, Univ. of Phoenix, Calif. Career: research & devel. staff Siemens AG, Witten, W. Ger. 1978-80, mfg. staf 81-82, mat. mgmt. 83-85, purchasing agt. 86-87, purchasing mgr. Siemens Corp., Sunnyvale, Calif. 1987-. Ofc: Siemens Corp. 1151 Sonora Ct Sunnyvale 94086

GENO, RICHARD EARL, life insurance agency manager; b. Mar. 20, 1942, Oakland; s. Claude Earl (dec.) and Florence Jacqueline Geno (dec.); children: Jennifer b. 1965, Deborah b. 1967, Kristin b. 1968, Richard II b. 1969, Lauren b. 1976, Jodi b. 1978, Stephanie b. 1980; edn: BS, UC Berkeley, 1964; MS, The American Coll., 1979, CLU 1970, ChFC 1982, CFP 1983. Career: agent College Life Ins. Co. 1964-74; general agent 1974-82; pres. Richard E. Geno & Assoc. Ins. Svcs., Inc., San Jose 1979-82; agency mgr. The Principal Fin. Group 1982-; awards: Jack Richter Memorial Award, Underwriter of Yr. San Jose Life Underws. Assn. 1980, Million Dollar Round Table 1985-, College Life Ins. Co. sales leader (1972, 76, 78) and #1 Agency (1978, 80, 81, 82); mem: Nat. Assn. Life Underws., San Jose Life Underws. Assn. (dir. 1989-, pres. 1991-92), Am. Soc. of CLUs, CLU/San Jose (dir. 1981-88, pres. 1986-87), San Jose Gen. Agents and Mgr. Assn. (dir. 1975-91, pres. 1980-81, 87-88), Leading Life Ins. Producers of No. Calif. (dir. 1978-80, pres. 1979), Peninsula Life Underwriters (dir. 1971-72); Republican; R.Cath.; rec: Little League baseball, tennis, bridge. Res: 21449 Toll Gate Rd Saratoga 95070 Ofc: The Geno Building 1042 W Hedding Ste 200 San Jose 95126

GENTRY, ROBERT WILTON, physician-surgeon; b. April 11, 1916, Springfield, Mo.; s. Charles Burt Gentry and Kathelene Moore; m. Priscilla Moerdyke, June 21, 1942; m. 2d. Marion P. Mulroney, Sept. 25, 1977; children: Perry Charles, Priscilla Jo; edn: BS, Univ. Conn.; Cornell Univ., 1937; MD, Harvard Med. Sch. 1942; MS surgery, Univ. Minn. 1947; cert. Am. Bd. Surgery 1949; vis. com., bd. trustees Harvard Univ. Med. Sch. 1972-78; mem: L.A. Co. Med. Assn., CMA, AMA (advy. com. motion picture & t.v.), A.C.S. (Fellow), Pan Pacific Surgical Assn., Trudeau Soc., Cavalcade of Health & Med. Progress (pres. L.A. 1956), Harvard Univ. Med. Alumni Assn. (dir. 1980-81, chapt. pres. L.A. 1955-57); clubs: Harvard/L.A. (pres. 1975-76), Valley Hunt, University (Pasadena); num. articles pub. in med. jours.; mil: Medical Adminstrv. Corps 1941-44; Republican; Prot.; rec: Tennessee Walking Horses, avocado grower. Address: Sun Valley 91352

GEORGIADES, GABRIEL GEORGE, aerospace engineer, educator; b. Nov. 23, 1956, Amarousion, Greece; s. George Gabriel and Evanthia Spyrou (Ioannou) G.; edn: BA in physics (cum laude), Jacksonville Univ., 1979; B.aero-space engring., Ga. Inst. of Tech., 1979; MS aerospace engring., Pa. State Univ., 1982; lic. E.I.T., Ga. 1979. Career: structural engr. Piper Aircraft Corp., Lockhaven, Pa. 1979-80; prof. aircraft structrue Embry-Riddle Aeronautical Univ., Prescott, Az. 1982-85; prof. aerospace engring. Cal State Polytechnic Univ., Pomona 1985-; cons. Naval Weapons Ctr., China Lake, 1985-, Lockheed Aircraft Svc. Co., Ontario, 1991-, Field Svc. & Maintenance Co., N. Palm

Springs, 1991-, Wyle Labs, El Segundo 1992-; awards: cert. achiev. NATO, Belgium 1974, C.W. Brownfield Meml. Award US Jaycees, Lockhaven, Pa. 1980, Disting. svc. AIAA-ERAU, Prescott, Az. 1985, Disting. svc. SHSE, Pomona 1991, listed Who's Who in the West 1992; mem: Am. Inst. of Aero. & Astro. (1976-, v.ch. edn. AIAA-SGV 1988-), Sigma Gamma Tau 1979-, Aerospace Edn. Assn. 1991-, Aerial Phenomena Research Org. 1976-; civic: Minority Engring. Pgm., Pomona (advisor 1987-), Math. Engring. Sci. Achiev., Claremont (advy. bd. 1988-), Soc. Hispanics in Sci. & Engring., Pomona (faculty advisor 1989-); author: Aerospace Structures Lab Manual (1988); Greek Orthodox; rec: reading, photography, music. Ofc: Aerospace Eng. Dept. Cal Poly Pomona 3801 W Temple Ave Pomona 91768

GERBER, BARRY ELDON, data processing executive, consultant, technical editor; b. May 12, 1942, Los Angeles; s. Harry and Elsie (Lubin) G.; m. Jane Bernette Margo, June 7, 1962; children: Margot, Karl, Georg; edn: BA, UCLA, 1964, MA, 1966, CPil, 1972. Career: prof. CSU Fullerton, 1968-77; dep. dir. Community Cancer Control, Los Angeles 1977-82; research assoc. Neuropsychiatric Inst. UCLA, 1982-83; v.p. info. systems Zenith Ins., Encino 1983-85; adminstrv. dir. Social Sci. Computing UCLA, 1985-; technical editor mag., Network Computing, 1990-; writer, cons. in field; contbg. editor mag. PC Week, 1988-90. Res: Van Nuys Ofc: UCLA Social Sciences Computing 2121 Bunche Hall Los Angeles 90024

GERBRACHT, BOB (ROBERT) THOMAS, portrait artist and teacher; b. June 23, 1924, Erie, Pa.; s. Earl John and Lula Mary (Chapman) G.; m. Delia Marie Paz, Nov. 27, 1952; children: Mark b. 1954, Elizabeth b. 1956, Catherine b. 1967; edn: BFA, Yale Univ., 1951; MFA, USC, 1952. Career: art and art history tchr. Wm. S. Hart Jr.-Sr. High Sch., Newhall 1954-56; artist in stained glass Cummings Studio, San Francisco 1956-58; art tchr. McKinley Jr. High Sch., Redwood City 1958-60; arts & crafts tchr. Castro Jr. High Sch., San Jose 1960-79; portrait painter, teacher, self-employed, San Jose, San Francisco, 1979-; art instr. Coll. of Notre Dame, Belmont 1958-60, Notre Dame Novitiate, Saratoga 1968, San Jose City Coll. 1968-71, West Valley Coll., Saratoga 1976-79, Univ. Calif. Santa Cruz 1979, 80, 81; awards incl. Best of Show- San Jose Art League (1983, 84), Pastel Soc. of West Coast, Sacto. 1988, Soc. of Western Artists, S.F. (1982, 90), Best Portrait, Soc. We. Artists, S.F. 1985, Am. Artist Achievement Award for Tchr. of Pastels 1993; mem: Pastel Soc. of Am. 1978-,Pastel Soc. of West Coast (advisor 1980-), Soc. We. Artists (trustee 1986-), Calif. Pastel Soc. (advisor 1991-), Commonwealth Club of Calif.; commissions: (oil painting portrait) Mr. Austen Warburton, 1991, Rev. Cecil Williams, 1991; articles in Am. Artist Mag. (1981, 85, 92, 93), Today's Art & Graphics 1982, The Art and Antique Collector 1984, U.S. ART 1989, Profile mag. of Am. Portrait Soc. 1984; mil: T5 US Army 1943-46; Glide Ch. S.F. Res: 1301 Blue Oak Ct Pinole 94564

GERINGER, SUSAN D., university professor, b. Dec. 23, 1954, Madera, Calif.; d. Gaston D. and Betty L. (Crane) Ownbey; m. Steven A. Geringer, Aug. 8, 1975; children: Steven b. 1979, Alexandra b. 1986; edn: BA, Calif. State Univ., Sacto., 1976-78; MA, Calif. State Univ., 1980-84; post-grad. work, N.Y. Univ., 1993. Career: retail exec. Macy's, S.F., Calif., 1978-80; div. chairperson Bauder Coll., Sacto., Calif., 1980-81; instr. Am. Riv. Coll., Sacto., 1982-86; prof. Calif. State Univ., Sacto., 1986-92; retail cons. self-employed, Madera, Calif., 1988-; instr. Calif. State Univ., Fresno, 1992-; expert witness, TASA, Mass., 1991-; awards: Outstanding Alumni, Calif. State Univ., Sacto., 1981; tchg. fellowship, N.Y. Univ. NY, NY, 1989; nat. scholarship, Phi Mu Sor., Atlanta, Ga., 1989; scholarship, NCD-CHEA, Sacto., Calif., 1989; membership, Kappa Omicron NU, Nat. Honor Soc., 1989-;mem: Internat. Textile & Apparel Assn. 1983-, Am. Collegiate Retail Assn. 1989-, The Fashion Group Internat. (S.F. chpt.) 1987-, Costume Soc. 1989-, Am. Assn. of Univ. Women, Madera, Calif.; civic bds: LARCS, Sacto., 1984-87; Children's Receiving Home, 1985-87; Legal Auxiliary, Sacto., 1984-91; pres., C.S.U.S. Home Econ. Alumni, Sacto., 1987-89; author: textbook, Fashion: Color, Line & Design, 1986; coauthor, textbook, History of 20th Century Costume, 1993; presenter, prof. confs., 1991-92; rec: skiing, golf, quilting, racquetball. Ofc: P.O. Box 207 Madera 93639

GERTH, DONALD R., university president; b. Dec. 4, 1928, Chgo.; s. George and Madeleine Agnes (Canavan) G.; m. Beverly Jean Hollman, Oct. 15, 1955; children: Annette Schofield, Deborah Hougham; edn: AB liberal arts, Univ. Chgo. 1947, AM polit. sci. 1951, PhD polit. sci. 1963. Career: Govt. Pub. Service, CSU Chico, 1968-70; assoc. v.p. acad. affairs Univ. of Skopie, Yugoslavia 1969-70; prof. political sci., dir. internat. programs CSU Chico, 1964-76, also v.p. acad. affairs 1970-76; univ. pres. and prof. political sci. CSU Dominguez Hills, 1976-84; prof., univ. pres. CSU Sacramento, 1984-; appt. accreditation hearing com. Com. of Bar Examiners Calif.; Commn. of the Californias (del., edn. com.); mem: Internat. Assn. Univ. Presidents (chair N.Am. Council), Calif. State Univs. Adminstrv. Advy. Council (chair), AASCU (bd. dirs.), Advy. Bd. Inst. of Internat. Edn.; civic: Sacto. C.of C. (chair edn. com.), United Way of Gr. Sacto. (bd.), Sacto. Children's Hosp. Found. (bd.), Sacto. Symph. Assn. (bd.), Sacramento Club (bd.), Port of Sacramento (commodore); author, ed.: An Invisible Giant (1971), coauthor monograph: The Learning Society (1969); contbg. ed. Edn. for the Public Service (1970), Papers

on the Ombudsman in Higher Edn. (1979); mil: capt. USAF 1952-56; Democrat; Episcopalian; rec: tennis, skiing, reading. Ofc: California State University 6000 J St Sacramento 95819-6022

GIBSON, GAYNOR ALLISON, contracts consultant, educator, author; b. Aug. 25, 1919, San Francisco; s. Ray Atherton and Alice Eleanor (Koehncke) G.; m. Manuela Gabellini, Oct. 19, 1947, Florence, Italy; children: Cynthia Rae b. 1949, Micaela b. 1954, Gregory b. 1955, Regina b. 1957, Randy 1963-1982; edn: scholarship Golden Gate Jr. Coll., 1936; Cert. Radar Engr., Stanford Univ., 1942-3; Univ. of Md., 1959-60; hon. MA bus. mgmt., UCLA Ext. Div. 1981; Calif. Life Teachers Cred., Jr. Coll. Career: Children's Opera Co. of San Francisco, 1932-35; Children's Theatre of the Air, KPO NBC Gold Network, 1934-36; grocery chain mgr. Keystone Grocers, San Francisco 1935-38; decorator florist Podesta & Baldocchi, S.F. 1938-42; enlisted, served to lt. col. US Army Signal Corps, 1942-63, retired w/ hon. discharge; 11 mil. decorations include Army Commendn., Berlin Airlift, Presdl. Cit., Korean Medal; mil. radar comms. and Italian interpreter 1942-45, contracting ofcr. world-wide 1945-63: govt. contr. US satellites Explorer I and Pioneer I, Redstone Arsenal, ACA 1957 (w/Dr. Werner Von Braun), asst. chief contracts, plans, procedures, and tng. Jet Propulsion Lab. CalTech; contract negotiator/adminstr. "Ranger" Moon Pgm. 1963-67; sr. contracts negotiator/ adminstr. Navy Phoenix F-14/AWG-9 Radar Pgm. Hughes Aircraft Co. 1967-81; cubmaster Boy Scouts, Altadena 1982; dean of instrn., Procurement & Contracts Tng. Schs. & Consultants, Altadena 1981-; instr. Pasadena City Coll. 1962-91, hd. Purch. & Contracting Dept., ret. 1991; master instr. UCLA, curriculum advy. com. UCLA Ext. Div.; instr. CSU Northridge 1980-86; instr. Northrop Univ. 1982-89, dir. and interim dean to estab. profl. Masters degree in Acquisition & Contracts Mgmt. 1982-85; instr Hughes Aircraft Co. all sites 1967-81; teller Bank of Am., 1990; honors: Calif. Scholarship Soc. 1935, Patriot of Yr. Pasadena 1985-86, Citizen's medal SAR 1986, knighted, Polonia Restituta 1990, named Nat. Educator of Year Nat. Contracts Mgmt. Assn. 1982-83 and recipient special profl. awards for svs. NCMA (1988, 89); mem. Nat. Contracts Mgmt. Assn. (fellow 1981, Nat. Speakers Roster), Purch. Mgmt. Assn. L.A., The Retired Officers Assn. (chpt. pres. 1985, ROTC chmn.), Reserve Officers Assn. Ch.42 (v.p. Army), Am. Legion (cmdr. Post 140, 1990-91-92-93), Military Order of World Wars (life, Marshal, Historian, Adjutant staff ROTC Officer Central Dept. Calif. 1988-89), Navy League, Pasadena C.of C., Altadena C.of C. (bd.), former Glendale mil. affairs com., Pasadena Unified Sch. Dist."Adopt- A- School"; author 23 textbooks on purchasing & contract mgmt.; Republican; R.Cath.; rec: fgn. language studies, golf. Ofc: Procurement & Contract Tng Schools & Cons., 411 W Altadena Dr Altadena 91001-1236

GIDDINGS, DAVID WIGHT, company executive; b. Feb. 5, 1954, Lynwood; s.Edwin and Manya (Koshko) G.; edn: CSU Fullerton, 1972-78. Career: pres. D.W. Giddings Co., Inc., Downey 1972-85; dir. Elsinore Aerospace Services, Inc., Downey 1982-90; owner Jet Set Enterprises, Laguna Niguel 1983-; mem: BBB of the Southland, Window Coverings Assn. of America; Nat. Decorating Products Assn.; rec: computers, electronics. Address: Jet Set Enterprises 26 Newcastle Ln Laguna Niguel 92677

GIDDINGS, MANYA KOSHKO, corporate executive, entrepreneur; b. Sept. 21, 1922, Kansas City, Kans.; d. Stefan and Mehelena (Zybko) Koshko; m. Edwin Wight Giddings, July 12, 1948 (dec. Apr. 15, 1980); children: David Wight b. 1954; edn: AA, Cerritos Coll., 1967, BS, CSU Fullerton, 1970. Career: secty. North American Aviation, Kansas City, Kans. 1941-43; TransWorld Airlines, 1943-48; exec. v.p., pres., chmn. bd. and chief exec. ofcr. Elsinore Aerospace Services Inc., Downey 1971-90, sold co. to Air/Lyon; co-owner, v.p. finance M & G Fire Equipment, Inc., Bonner Springs, KS 1992-; honors: finalist Arthur Anderson Inc. magazine Entrepreneur of Yr., L.A. (1988), mag. cover feature Airline Executive Mag., Atlanta, Ga. (1988); Republican; R.Cath.; rec: writing, gardening. Res: 42 South Peak Dr Laguna Niguel 92677-2903

GIDEON-HAWKE, PAMELA LAWRENCE, fine arts gallery owner; b. Aug. 23, 1945, N.Y.C.; d. Lawrence Ian Verry and Lily S. (Stein) Gordon; m. Jarrett Redstone, June 27, 1964; 1 child, Justin Craig Hawke; graduate West Point 1993.. Career: owner Gideon Gallery Ltd., Los Angeles 1975-; named friend of design industry Designers West Mag. 1987; mem. Am. Soc. Interior Designers (publicist), Internat. Soc. Interior Designers (trade liaison 1986-88), Network Exec. Women in Hosp. (exec. v.p. L.A. chpt.), fundraising chairperson Las Vegas chpt.), Internat. Furnishings and Design Assn. (program chair). Ofc: Gideon Gallery Ltd. 8748 Melrose Ave Los Angeles 90069 and 8121 Lake Hills Drive Las Vegas NV

GIFFORD, JERRI JACKLYN, director student financial services; b. Aug. 13, 1946, Grand Island, Nebr.; d. Vernon Henry and Loretta Mae (Loewen) Koenig; m. Gary Donald Gifford, June 25, 1967; children: Shauna b. 1970, Chip b. 1972; edn: diploma, Lodi Acad., Lodi, Calif., 1964; BS, Andrews Univ., Berrien Springs, Mich.; MA, Loma Linda Univ., Riverside, Calif., 1981; career: tchr. SPA, Escondido, Calif. 1975-79; tchr. Hawaiian Mission Ac., Honolulu, Hawaii, 1979-81; tchr. Southwestern Adv. Coll., Keene, N.C., 1981-85; computer broker Strata Marketing, Santa Cruz, Calif., 1986-88; student finance dir.

Pacific Union Coll., Angwin, Calif., 1988-; cons., tchg., Pacific Union Coll.; mem: CASFAA 1988-, WASFAA 1988-, NASFAA 1988-, WACUBO 1991-; Seventh-Day Adventist; rec: reading, travel.

GILBERT, STEVEN EDWARD, professor of music; b. Apr. 20, 1943, Brooklyn, N.Y.; s. Milton and Sylvia Ruth (Meyerson) G.; m. Patricia Jean King, May 28, 1977 (div. Jan. 2, 1994); children: Jonathan b. 1981, Matthew b. 1989; edn: BA, CUNY/Brooklyn Coll., 1964; MM, Yale Univ., 1967, MPhil, 1969, PhD, 1970. Career: asst. to full prof. dept. of music CSU Fresno, 1970-; ptnr. JAJ Properties, Reno, Nev. 1988-; recipient Student Composers Awards, Broadcast Music Inc., N.Y. (1964, 66, 67); mem: College Music Soc. (1971-, Life), Am. Musicol. Soc. 1969-, Soc. for Music Theory 1977-, Sonneck Soc. 1980-, Nat. Assn. of Scholars 1990-, Yale Club of San Joaquin Valley (pres. 1979-82, 85-86), Porsche Club of Am. (local pres. 1985-86); author: The Music of George Gershwin (in progress), coauthor: Intro. to Schenkerian Analysis (1982), contbr. articles in The Musical Quarterly, J. of Music Theory, Perspectives of New Music, Grove's Dictionaries of Music, The World Book Ency., reviews The Fresno Bee; Republican; Jewish; rec: automobiles, stock trading. Res: 544 Circle Dr South, Fresno 93704 Ofc: Dept. Music Calif. State Univ., Fresno 93740-0077

GILE, BARRIE AVERILL, financial planner; b. Dec. 18, 1938, Waltham, Mass.; s. Harold R. and Geraldine (Olmstead) G.; div.; 1 son: Jason B., b. 1961; edn: Bowdoin Coll. 1956-57; BA, Boston Univ. 1961; reg. fin. planner (RFP), Internat. Assn. Reg. Fin. Planners, 1984; certified investment specialist (CIS), 1993. Career: sales mgr. P.F. Collier, Inc., Hartford, Conn., Springfield and Boston, Mass. 1961-65; sales rep. Prudential Ins. Co. of Am., Salem & Gloucester, Mass. 1965-68; sales mgr., sales rep. Mass. Mutual Life Ins. Co., Boston, Los Angeles and Long Beach 1969-93; reg. fin. planner MML Investors Services, Inc., Long Beach 1984-88; Shearwater Securities Corp., Manhattan Beach and Concord, Ca. 1988-89; Portfolio Asset Management, El Paso, Tx. and Manhattan Beach, Ca. 1990-93; cons. Am. Fedn. of Tchrs., ABC Unified Sch. Dist., Cerritos 1981-93; recipient NALU awards: Life and Qualifying mem. Million Dollar Round Table 1982-93, Nat. Sales Achiev. Award 1981-93, Nat. Quality Award 1967-68, 1981-93; mem: Nat. Assn. Life Underwriters, Internat. Assn. Reg. Fin. Planners, Long Beach Life Underwrs. Assn. (bd. dirs.), Sports Connection Athletic Club, Amnesty Internat., Greenpeace, Sierra Club; rec: collect music CDs & records, sports. Res: 661 25th St Manhattan Beach 90266 Ofc: 100 Oceangate Ste 1400 Long Beach 90802

GILES, JEAN HALL, civic activist, retired business executive; b. March 30, 1908, Dallas, Texas; d. Clarence D. and Elizabeth (McIntyre) Overton; m. Alonzo Russell Hall II, Jan. 23, 1923 (dec. Mar. 30, 1928); children: Marjorie Jean Hall, Alonzo Russell Hall III (dec. July 12, 1988); m. 2d Harry Edward Giles, April 24, 1928 (div. 1937); children: Janice Ruth Giles, and (adopted) Marjean Giles; Career: realtor- notary, Los Angeles Co. 1948-61; building contractor, prop. Los Angeles Real Estate Exchange; ptnr. Tech. Contractors Dir. Volunteer Corps., Los Angeles Area War Chest; capt., cdg. ofcr., organizer SW Los Angeles Unit 1942; major, nat. exec. ofcr. 1943-44; Children's Hosp. Benefit 1945-46; coord. Motor Corps., Los Angeles Area War Chest 1944-45; capt. Communications Corp., U.S. hdqtrs.; honors: PhD (hon.) Calif. State Christian Coll., PhD (hon.) Hamilton State Univ. Ariz., listed World Who's Who, World Who's Who Finance & Industry, Who's Who of Am. Women; past mem: Los Angeles and Nat. Realty Bds.; Am. Inst. of Mgmt., Los Angeles C.of C. (Women's Div.), Los Fiesteros de Los Angeles, Nat. Fedn. of Bus. & Profl. Women (Hollywood chpt.), L.A. World Affairs Council, Hist. Soc. of So. Calif., Los Angeles Art Assn.; Assistance League of So. Calif.; Republican; Prot.; rec: golf (scorer, 18 yrs., L.A. Open). Res: 616 Magnolia Long Beach 90802

GILES, WAYMON KEITH, produce company executive; b. Jan. 27, 1963, Vandenburg AFB; s. Waymon Deadrick and Virginia Mae (Slade) G.; m. Laura Kay Lamb, Aug. 15, 1981; children: Candice, Cassandra. Career: warehouser Antelope Valley Produce, Lancaster 1978-79, sales 1979-80, asst. mgr. 1980-84, mgr. 1984-89, jr. v.p. 1989-; awards: PTA, 1981, goodwill amb. Small World Adventure, 1989; lic. foster parent 1991-; Republican; Assemblies of God (named Father of Yr. 1989, comdr. Royal Rangers 1983-86, coord. Missionettes 1986-92, Bible quiz coach and youth sponsor 1992-, elected deacon, ch. bd. First Assembly of God Ch., Lancaster 1993-96); rec: golf. Ofc: 206 W. Nugent Lancaster 93534

GILLIES, PATRICIA ANN, public health biologist; b. Sept. 23, 1929, Berkeley; d. William W. and Barbara A. (Weddle) Myers; m. Robert W. Gillies, Sept. 17, 1948 (div. Dec. 1968); children: Catherine I. Lindsey b. 1949, Coila L. McGowan b. 1960; edn: AB, CSU Fresno, 1954, MA, 1961. Career: tchr. Parlier Unified Sch. Dist., Parlier 1955-56; insp. US Dept. Agriculture, Fresno 1956-58; tchg. asst. CSU Fresno, 1958-59; public health biologist State of Calif., 1959-; dir. Consolidated Mosquito Abatement Dist., 1974-; mem. Calif. Mosquito & Vector Control Assn. (1963-, regional rep. 1992-), Soc. for Vector Ecologists 1972-, Am. Mosquito Control Assn. 1963-; contbr. to profl. jours. incl. Jour. Economics Entomology, Proc. - Am. Mosquito Control Assn., Calif. Mosquito & Vector Control Assn., Utah Mosquito Abatement Assn.; Democrat; Episcopalian. Res: 7060 E Butler Fresno 93727 Ofc: State Health Dept. 5545 E Shields Ave Fresno 93727

GILMAN, NELSON J., university library director; b. Mar. 30, 1938, Los Angeles; s. Louis L. and Alice (Cohen) G.; m. Virginia L. Ford, May 27, 1961; m. 2d. Lelde B. Patvalds, Nov. 23, 1970; children: Justine C. b. 1963, Seth F. b. 1966; edn: BS, USC, 1959, MS, 1960; MLS, UC Berkeley, 1964. Career: tchr. math. dept. Pasadena H.S., 1960-61, Tamalpais H.S., Mill Valley 1962-63; library adminstrv. intern UCLA Lib., 1964-65, asst. to the Univ. Librarian (in chg. lib. bldg. & plnng.) UCLA, 1965-66, asst. to the Biomedical Librarian, UCLA 1966-67, assoc. biomed. librarian UCLA Biomed. Lib., 1967-69, assoc. dir. Pacific S.W. Reg. Medical Lib. Svc. UCLA Biomedical Library 1969-71; dir. L.A. Co./USC Medical Ctr. Libraries, L.A. 1974-79; assoc. dir. Devel. & Demonstration Ctr. in Contg. Edn. for Health Professionals, USC Sch. of Medicine, 1981-, asst. prof. dept. med. edn. USC Sch. of Medicine, 1971-, dir. Norris Medical Library 1971-, dir. Health Sciences Library System 1984-, USC assoc. dean for libraries & dir. of planning for the Teaching Lib. 1989-90, USC interim dir. Central Library System 1990-91; mem: Am. Lib. Assn., Am. Soc. for Info. Sci., Assn. of Acad. Health Scis. Lib. Dirs. (bd. 1980-83), Med. Lib. Assn. (bd. 1977-79), Special Lib. Assn.; publs: assoc. ed. USC Information Systems Res. Program (1984-), 16+ profl. jour. articles; mil: pfc USAR 1961-67; Democrat; Jewish; rec: gardening. Res: 615 22nd St Santa Monica 90402

GILMARTIN, PLATT JAY, chemical company sales executive; b. Oct. 20, 1952, Morristown, N.J.; s. Thomas Joseph and Ethel Louise (Cooper) G.; m. Kathleen Marie Hall, Jan. 25, 1979; children: Courtney Elizabeth b. 1985, Caitlin Marie b. 1989; edn: BS (summa cum laude), Cook Coll., Rutgers Univ., 1974, Rutgers Grad. sch. of Edn. 1983; grad. mgmt. coursework Claremont Grad. Sch., 1985-86; N.J. tchr. credential, sci. K-12 and FFA Vocational Agriculture 1974. Career: served to capt. US Air Force 1974-79, sq. comdr. Wichita Falls, Tx. 1975-76, det. comdr. Ft. Leonard Wood, Mo. 1977-78, tech. instr. 1977-78, commendn. medal 1976, meritorious service 1978; gen. mgr. J.L. Armitage Co., Newark, N.J. 1980-83; ops. mgr. Tnemec Co. Inc., Compton 1984-90; sr. sales rep. Unocal Chemicals, La Mirada 1991; territory mgr. Ashland Chemical Inc., Orange 1992-; honors: Alpha Tau Alpha 1974, Arnold Air Soc. 1974; mem: L.A. Soc. for Coatings Technology (mfg. com. 1984-), So. Calif. Paint & Coatings Assn.; Republican; R.Cath.; rec: reading, running, biking, sailing, swimming, equestrian. Res: 24158 Royale St Moreno Valley CA 92557

GILSDORF, LEROY GUIDO, financial consultant, tax preparer, retired county government official; b. March 13, 1930, Lawrence, Nebr.; s. George Henry and Jeanette Lena (L'Heureux) G.; m. Jennie Joan Hyde, June 11, 1955; children: Jane b. 1956, Gail b. 1963; edn: Univ. Nebr. 1952-54; Hastings Coll. 1955-56; UC Stanislaus 1961-63. Career: delinquent accounts mgr. Merced Co., 1957-58, hosp. office mgr. 1958-62, asst. auditor-controller 1962-75, Merced Co. auditor controller and recorder R&R, 1976-90, ret.; fin. cons., tax preparer, 1990-; treas. MCML Hosp. Found.; awards: Toastmaster of Year (Distr. 33), Disting. Toastmaster 1985, Merced Co. Employee of Yr. 1971, Govt. Fin. Ofcr. Assn. Cert. of Conformance 1985; mem: Co. Recorders Assn. of Calif. (pres. 1980-81), Co. Auditors Assn. of Calif. (pres. 1987), K.C. (past grand knight, past dist. dep.), Toastmasters (past pres., area gov.), Merco Credit Union (past pres.); mem. and past pres. Our Lady of Mercy Sch. Bd.; club: Merced G&C (1st v.p. Seniors); mil: clk. 2/c USN 1948-52; Democrat; R.Cath. (Fresno Dioceses fin. com.); rec: woodworking, philately, golf. Res: 2302 E Lakeside Dr Merced 95340 Ofc: 2302 E Lakeside Dr Merced 95340

GIOVACCHINI, JAMES ANDREW, physician, surgeon; b. Aug. 22, 1919, Del Rey; s. Amerigo and Jane (Mencarini) G.; m. Norma Kathryn Kealy, Sept. 23, 1944; children: James, Thomas, Robert; edn: BS, Univ. Santa Clara 1941; MD, Creighton Med. Sch. 1944. Roman Catholic. Res: 2221 7th St Sanger 93657 Ofc: 621 O St Sanger 93657

GIRAMONTI, ADRIANA AURORA, chef; b. May 24, 1929, Rome, Italy, nat. US cit. 1961; d. Umberto and Clotilde (Pascale) Silvestri; m. Frank Giramonti, July 7, 1960 (div. Oct. 1988); children: Piero b. 1964, Roberto b. 1967; edn: Armando Diaz Coll. (Italy) 1944; shorthand/ typist, Berlitz Sch. 1952. Career: bkpg. helper, cashier First Class Ristorante Roma 1949-53; pvt., personal secty. Dr. Claudi Roma 1953-56; practical nurse, cook Serra Sanitarium Millbrae 1956; rubber pillow making factory 1957-58; waitress Little Joe Restaurant S.F. 1958-77; chief owner, pres. Giramonti Restaurant Inc. dba Giramonti Rest. in Mill Valley and Adriana Rest. in San Rafael; demonstration classes Macy's S.F. 1984-85, La Cordon Rouge Sausalito 1983, Loni Khun Cooking Tour 1983-84, Culinary Carnival 1984-85; chef demo. on CBS-TV "Good Morning Bay Area, 1987, 88, 89; guest master chef demo. for Italian Festival, Fishermans Wharf, S.F. benefit for problem children, 1988; ABC-TV Ch. 7 guest "Star-Athon 89" and United Cerebral Palsy, 1985; honors: Diploma and Medal (Great Chefs of S.F. 1984), Italian Chef of A.M. San Francisco ABC (1983, 84, 85, 86), Gourmet Mag., Pacific Sun of Marin; publs: Great Chefs of S.F. (from the PBS nat. TV series, Avon Books NY 1983); R.Cath.; rec: dressmaking, artist- hand painted ceramic decorative & serving platters. Ofc: Giramonti Restaurant Inc. 999 Anderson Dr San Rafael 94901

GIRGA, BARBARA ANN, psychotherapist/college counselor; b. Oct. 11, 1937, Rayland, Ohio; d. C. Virgil and Marjorie T. (Diehl) Fisher; children: Susan b. 1963, Robert b. 1966; edn: AA, Bakersfield Coll., 1973; BA, CSU Bakersfield, 1978; MA, 1986; CAC, UCSB, Ky. Christian Coll., 1956. Career: supr. CSU Bakerfield 1975-78; editor Bakersfield Chamber of Commerce publs., 1977-79; diet counselor Nutra-Systems 1980-81; mgr. Water Assn. Kern Co. 1976-81; analyst Occidental Petroleum 1981-86; pvt. practice Bakersfield Counseling Group 1987-; clin. therapist Haven Counseling Center 1986-88; Charter Hosp. 1988-; counselor Bakersfield Coll. 1986-; seminar leader 1976-; workshop instr. 1987-; honors: Chi Sigma Iota 1986, Employee of Year 1978, Employee Performance Bonus 1982; mem: CAMFT, AAMFT, AACD, Am. Businesswomen's Assn. (secty. 1977), CAPH (secty. 1977-79); civic: Jr. League Saturday Adventurers (dir. 1978), C.of C.; poems pub. (Opheus 1979) Calvary Bible Ch.; rec: skiing, reading, writing. Res: 2401 San Ramon Ct. Bakerfield 93304 Ofc: 200 New Stine Rd Bakersfield 93309

GIROD, ERWIN ERNEST, physician; b. Oct. 1, 1944, Los Angeles; s. Dudley L. and Rena M. (Hudson) G.; m. Jill Johnson, Dec. 16, 1967; children: Jeffrey b. 1973, Janette b. 1975; edn: BA (honors), CSU Los Angeles, 1966; MD, UC Irvine, 1970; Calif. Coll. Med.; Dipl. Am. Bd. Internal Med. (1973, Recert. 1980). Career: med. intern L.A.Co.-USC Med. Ctr., 1970-71, resident in internal medicine, 1971-73; US Naval Regional Med. Center, San Diego, 1973-75; ward med. ofcr. Med. Intensive Care Unit, adminstr. Acute Care Areas, asst. clin. prof. med. UC San Diego Sch. Med.; asst. prof. med. Loma Linda Univ. Sch. Med. 1978-80; chief gen. med. section 1978-80, asst. chief med. service 1979-80, VA Hosp. Loma Linda; pvt. practice 1981-; med. staff Huntington Mem. Hosp., 1981-, chmn. Internal Med. Clinic 1984-85; St. Luke Med. Ctr., 1982-, chmn. Utilization Rev. Com. 1989-91, chmn. I.P.A. Util. Rev. Com. 1989-, bd. dirs. St. Luke Hosp. Med. Group; asso. Methodist Hosp. of So. Calif., Arcadia, 1986-, staff phys. Chemical Dependency Recovery Ctr.; Community Lecture Series: Meth. Hosp., and St. Luke Med. Ctr., 1987-; Humanitarian service: asst. prof. med. Punjab Univ., India, and co-dir. intensive care unit Christian Med. Coll. and Brown Memorial Hosp., Ludhiana, Punjab, India 1976-77, Overseas Missionary Fellowship, med. advisor to SW Region-U.S.A., 1988-; honors: Ephebian Soc. L.A. 1962-, Math. award 1962, Alpha Gamma Omega Frat. (1964-, Delta Chpt. pres. 1965-66, Alumni sponsor 1966-, Legion of Honor 1989-, Microbiol. award 1966, Phi Kappa Phi Hon. Soc. 1967-, Admiral Stitt Award for physician who contbd. most to med. edn. from the intern classes at Naval Regional Med. Ctr., S.D. (1973-4, 1974-5); biog. listings: Internat. Register of Profiles, Internat. Book of Honor, Dict. Internat. Biography, 5000 Personalities of World, Men of Achiev., Dir. of Disting. Americans, Personalities of Am., Comm. Leaders of Am., 1990; Internat. Who's Who of Intellectuals, Internat. Dir. of Disting. Leadership, 1991; Fellow Am. Coll. Physicians 1980, mem. Calif. Med. Assn., Christian Med.-Dental Soc.; civic: Pasadena Mayor's Prayer Breakfast Com. 1986, 87, Upper Hastings Ranch Assn. (block capt. 1984-), publs. in profl. jours.; mil: lt. cmdr. USNR, active duty 1973-75; Republican; Congregational; rec: swimming, music, roses. res: 1195 Coronet Ave Pasadena 91107; ofc: Hanson Medical Group Inc. 8332 Huntington Dr San Gabriel 91775

GIRSH, FAYE JOAN, psychologist; b. May 5, 1933, Philadelphia, Pa.; d. Jack and Rose (Rosenberg) Girsh; m. Leon I. Goldberg Feb. 2, 1958 (div. 1978); children: Mark b. 1958, Claudia Otee b. 1960; edn: BA, Temple Univ. 1954; MA, Boston Univ. 1955; EdD, Harvard Univ. 1962; lic. clin. and forensic psychologist 1978. Career: research asst. Harvard Univ., Cambridge, Mass. 1956-57; clin. intern Mass. Mental Health, Boston 1957-58; research psychologist NIMH, Bethesda, Md. 1958-61; instr. psychiatry Emory Univ., Atlanta, Ga. 1961-62; psychology faculty Morehouse Coll. 1965-74; vis. prof. Kyoto Inst. Tech., Japan 1972-73; research assoc. Univ. Chgo. 1974-78; assoc. prof. U.S. Internat. Univ., San Diego 1978-79; clin. psychologist Psychiatry and Law Center 1979-81; adj. faculty Calif. Sch. Profl. Psychology 1980-; honors: Psi Chi, Nat. Inst. Drug Abuse grantee 1970; mem: Hemlock Soc. S.D. (pres. 1988-), Nat. Hemlock Soc. (bd. mem.), Acad. S.D. Psychologists, ACLU (So. Calif., S.D.), Nat. Soc. Psychology in Addictions (pres. 1977-79), Harvard Club S.D. (bd. mem. 1980-), Soc. Profls. in Dispute Resol. (bd. mem. 1987-), Am. Psychological Assn.; 40+ articles and chapters pub. in med. and legal jours.; Democrat; Jewish; rec: travel, play reading. Res: 400 Prospect St #5B La Jolla 92037 Ofc: 401 West A St Ste 1200 San Diego 92101

GISS, JUDITH ELAINE KRIENKE (Mrs. Kenneth A. Giss), real estate broker; b. July 7, 1947, Hawthorne, Calif.; d. Oliver Kenneth and Carol Belle (Manikowske) Krienke; m. Kenneth Arnold Giss, Nov. 24, 1967; edn: att. Az. State Univ., Tempe 1965-67; AA, El Camino Coll., Torrance, 1970; MBA, CSU Dominguez Hills, 1977; Calif. lic. R.E. Broker 1967, Appraiser, Property Mgr. Career: real estate broker, appraiser, property mgr. O.K. Krienke Realty, 1967-; ptnr. G & G Consultants, ptnr. G & G Schools, R.E. Sch., 1978-; awards: outstanding Jaycett Manhattan Beach Jaycees 1974; mem: Nat. Assn. Realtors 1967-, Calif. Assn. Realtors 1967-, South Bay Bd. of Realtors 1967-, Nat. Assn. R.E. Appraisers 1987-, Nat. Notary Assn. 1978-91, Manhattan Beach C.of C., Alumni Assn. Ariz. St. Univ. (life), Alumni Assn. CSUDH, Nat. Soc. Colonial Dames of XVII Century (ct, v.p., sec., historian Jared Eliot Chpt.); civic: Soroptimist

Internat., M.B. (1976-, pres. 1977), Sister City Manhattan Beach 1980-, Friends Manhattan Beach Library 1976-, Pioneer 8's of Redondo Beach (1991-), Soc. for Preserv. of Magical Arts/ Magic Castle 1974-, Soc. for Preserv. of Variety Arts 1980-, Girl Scouts Am., Dolphin Jr. Fed. Womens Club 1967-77, Dutch Club Neerlandia Inc. of Westchester 1987-, Commonwealth Club of Torrance 1988-, M.B. Comm. Ch., M.B. Hist. Soc., Western Stars Redondo Bch. 1990-, Britannia Club 1985-, Internat. Platform Assn. 1990-, Beach Cities Symphony (1990-, patron), Friends of Banning Park 1990-, Hist. Soc. of Centinela Valley 1989-; rec: travel, historical homes, comm. svc. Res: 1609 9th St Manhattan Beach 90266 Ofc: 1716 Manhattan Beach Blvd Manhattan Beach 90266

GITLIN, TODD, author, professor of sociology; b. Jan. 6, 1943, N.Y., N.Y.; s. Max Gitlin and Dorothy (Siegel) Renik; edn: BA, Harvard Univ., 1963; MA, Univ. Mich., 1966; PhD, UC Berkeley, 1977. Career: prof. sociology and director mass communications pgm. UC Berkeley, 1978-; author: Busy Being Born (1974), The Whole World Is Watching (1980), Inside Prime Time (1983), The Sixties: Years of Hope, Days of Rage (1987), The Murder of Albert Einstein (1992), editor: Watching Television (1987), coauthor: Uptown: Poor Whites In Chicago (1970).

GITNICK, GARY LEE, physician; b. Mar. 13, 1939, Omaha, Nebr.; s. Nathan Gitnick and Ann (Tretiak) Hahn; m. Cherna Lee Schrager, June 21, 1963; children: Neil b. 1967, Kimberly b. 1969, Jill b. 1971, Tracy b. 1973; edn: BS, Univ. of Chgo., 1960, MD, 1963. Career: intern internal medicine Osler Medical Service, Balt., Md. 1963-64; fellow int. med. Johns Hopkins Hosp., Balt. 1963-64; resident int. med. Mayo Clinic, Rochester 1964-65, resident gastroenterology, 1967-69; project/ med. officer NIH, Bethesda, Md. 1965-67; prof. of medicine UCLA Sch. of Medicine, Los Angeles 1969-, dir. div. gastro res. labs 1979-, med. dir. UCLA Health Care Program 1985-, chief of staff UCLA Medical Ctr., 1990-92; chief div. digestive diseases, UCLA Sch. of Medicine 1993-; awards: J. Arnold Bargan Award 1969, special appreciation United Liver Assn., L.A. 1988, Special Paul Harris Fellow Rotary Intl., L.A. 1988, award of merit Los Angeles Mayor 1990, Rotarian of Yr. Westwood Village Rotary 1991; pres. Fulfillment Fund 1977-; trustee The Harvard-Westlake Sch.; trustee LEARN 1991-; mem: United Liver Assn. (bd. dirs., chair sci. advy. bd. 1982-), Rotary Intl. (1984-); editor 45+ books: Principles & Practice of Gastro (1988), IBD: Diagnosis & Treatment (1991), Diseases of the Liver & Biliary Tract (1991), The Business of Medicine (1991); mil: lt. col. USPHS 1965-68. Res: 17321 Rancho St Encino 91316 Ofc: Gary Gitnick M.D. 924 Westwood Blvd Ste 515 Los Angeles 90024-7018

GITTLEMAN, ARTHUR PAUL, educator; b. Oct. 7, 1941, N.Y., N.Y.; s. Morris and Clara (Konefsky) G.; m. Carole Anne McGee, July 30, 1966 (div. Jan. 1985); m. Charlotte Marie Singleton, June 1, 1986; 1 dau., Amanda b. 1985; edn: BA, UCLA, 1962, MA, 1965, PhD, 1969 Career: asst. prof. math. dept. CSU Long Beach, 1966-70, assoc. prof., 1970-75, prof. 1975-88, dept. chair 1978-83, prof. computer engring., computer sci. dept., 1988-; mem. Assn. for Computing Machinery 1975-, Mathematical Assn. of Am. 1963-, Inst. Electrical and Electronic Engrs. 1990-; author: History of Mathematics 1975; rec: running, piano. Res: 6572 Montoya Circle Huntington Beach 92647 Ofc: Calif. State Univ., Long Beach 90840

GIVANT, PHILIP JOACHIM, educator, real estate investment co. president; b. Dec. 5, 1935, Mannheim, Germany, nat. US cit. 1940; s. Paul and Irmy (Dinse) G.; m. Kathleen Joan Porter, 1960; children: Philip Paul b. 1963, Julie Kathleen b. 1965, Laura Grace b. 1968; edn: BA, CSU San Francisco 1957, MA, 1960. Career: math. prof. San Francisco State Univ. 1958-60, American River Coll. (Sacto.) 1960-; pres. Grove Ents. Real Estate Investment Co. 1961-; mem. Calif. Community Colls. (CCC) Academic Senate (v.p. 1974-77), Am. River Coll. Acad. Senate (pres. 1966-69), State Chancellor's com. on the Academic Calendar 1977-79; awards: spl. commendn. CCC Academic Senate, spl. human rights award for InterCultural Affairs, CCC 1977, human rights award Fair Housing Commn. Sacto. Co. 1985, named Blues Promoter of the Year, Nat. Blues Found., Memphis 1987, recipient 1st critical achievement award Sacramento Music Awards Acad. 1992; mem. CCC Faculty Assn. 1966-, Am. Soc. for Psychical Res. 1965-, Nat. Blues Found. Memphis (nat. advy. com.), Sacto. Blues Soc. (charter 1980-), Lake Tahoe Keys Homeowners Assn., Sea Ranch Homeowners Assn., Klamath River Country Estates Homeowners Assn., NAACP (life); works: founder/pres. & prod. Sacto. Blues Festival Inc. 1976-; prod. weekly music pgm. "Blues with Phil" on Public Radio St. KVMR, Nevada City; prod. musical festival Folsom State Prison 1979-81, Vacaville State Prison 1985; rec: tennis, music, boating. Address: Grove Enterprises 3809 Garfield Ave Carmichael 95608

GLAD, DAIN STURGIS, aerospace engineer; b. Sept. 17, 1932, Santa Monica; s. Alma Emanuel and Maude La Verne (Morby) G.; m. Betty Alexandra Shainoff, Sept. 12, 1954 (dec. 1973); 1 dau. Dana Elizabeth; m. 2d. Carolyn Elizabeth Giffen, June 8, 1979; edn: BS in engring., UCLA, 1954; MS in E.E., USC, 1963; Reg. Profl. Engr., Calif. Career: electronic engr. Clary Corp., San Gabriel 1957-58; engr. Aerojet Electro Systems Co., Azusa, 1958-72; missile systems div. Rockwell Internat., Anaheim 1973-75; Aerojet Electrosystems,

Azusa 1975-84; support systems div. Hughes Aircraft Co., 1984-90; Electro-Optics Ctr., Rockwell Internat. Corp., Anaheim 1990-; mem: IEEE, Calif. Soc. Profl. Engrs., Soc. Information Display; tech. papers in profl. jours. and proc.; mil: lt. j.g. USN 1954-57. Res: 1701 Marengo Ave South Pasadena 91030 Ofc: Rockwell Intl. Corp. 3370 Miraloma Anaheim 92803

GLASER, RUTH BONNIE, psychologist; b. May 11, 1937, Tenafly, N.J.; d. John Henry and Ruth Louise (Ferris) Thompson; m. Donald Glaser, Nov. 28, 1960 (div.); children: Louise b. 1964, William b. 1965; edn: BA, UC Berkeley 1969; MA, 1985; PhD, 1976. Career: pvt. practice psychology, Berkeley 1976-; psychologist UC Berkeley 1976-89; dean of students, S.F. Inst. Psychoanalytic Psychol. and Psychoanalysis, San Francisco 1984-; clin. faculty Children's Hosp., San Francisco 1979-; researcher UC Berkeley Psychology dept. 1988-, instr. 1980; mem: Am. Psychology Assn. Res: 1140 Grizzly Peak Blvd Berkeley 94708 Ofc: 268 Arlington Berkeley 94707

GLASRUD, BRUCE ALDEN, historian; b. Sept. 20, 1940, Plainview, Minn.; s. Leslie E. and Margaret (Rud) G.; m. Evelyn Pearlene Vestal, Oct. 17, 1964; edn: BA, Luther Coll., 1962; MA, Eastern New Mexico Univ., 1963; PhD, Texas Tech. Univ., Lubbock 1969. Career: instr. history Texas Lutheran Coll., Seguin, Tx. 1964-65; asst. prof. CSU Hayward, Calif. 1968-73, assoc. prof. 1973-78, prof. of history 1978-, chair history dept. 1977-81, 84-86, 92-93; trustee Res. Found., CSUH 1977-81, pres. bd. dirs. Faculty Club CSUH 1978-79, sec., exec. com. CSU Academic Senate, Long Beach 1986-87; dir. University Union 1989-91, v.ch. bd. dirs. CSUH Found. 1991-93; awards: best lectr. CSU Hayward (1972), NEH grantee (1981), MPPPA stipend CSUH (1987, 90), profl. res. leave CSUH 1990-91, distinguished service award Luther Coll. 1992, Outstanding Professor of the Year, 1993 CSUH; mem: Texas State Hist. Assn. 1972-, Western History Assn. 1974-, Immigration Hist. Soc. 1988-, Am. Scandinavian Found. 1989-, Calif. Faculty Assn. (1968-, pres. 1985-87); civic: Greenpeace, ACLU, Amnesty Internat., So. Poverty Law Ctr., NAACP; coauthor: Promises to Keep (1972), The Northwest Mosaic (1977), Race Relations in British No. Am. (1981), numerous scholarly jour. articles and book revs.; Democrat; Lutheran; rec: research, writing. Res: 5030 Seaview Ave Castro Valley 94546 Ofc: Calif. State Univ., Hayward 94542

GLEASON, EDWARD D., computer systems designer; b. July 16, 1958, Los Angeles; s. Donald E. and Irene (Ow) G.; edn: BS, CSU Long Beach, 1984; M.P.P.M., Yale Univ., 1988; lic. C.P.A., Calif., 1986. Career: computer pgmr.cons. in Los Angeles, 1979-83; sr. auditor Quesada Navarro & Co., CPAs, Los Angeles, 1984-86; fixed income analyst Chase Investors Mgmt. Corp., NY, NY, 1986-87; computer sys. designer Transvik Inc., NY, NY, 1988-90; mem: Am. Inst. of CPAs, IEEE, Assn. for Computing Machinery; ed., Yale Jour. on Regulation, 1987-88; rec: scuba, marine aquaculture. Res: 4367 W Avenue N-3 Lancaster 93536

GLENN, BELINDA DEANNE, construction engineer; b. June 27, 1963, Garden City, Kans.; d. Everett Lee and Karin Kaye (Coerber) G.; edn: BS in constrn. sci., Kansas State Univ., 1986. Career: surveyor Coleman Indsl. Constrn., Wichita, Kans. 1986-87; field engr. Herzog Contracting Corp., Los Angeles 1987-89, project engr. Herzog Contracting Corp., Long Beach 1989-90, project engr. Herzog Contracting Corp., Sacramento 1990-92; asst. constrn. engr. Sacramento Regional Transit Dist., Sacramento 1992-; honors: listed Who's Who of Am. Women 1991-92, Who's Who in West 1992-93, Who's Who in Sci. & Engring. 1992-93; mem: Nat. Assn. Female Execs. 1989-, Kans. State Univ. Alumni Assn. 1986-. Res: P.O. Box 1038 Gridley 95948-1038 Ofc: Sacramento Regional Transit Dist. 2811 O St Sacramento 95816

GLENN, JOHN WILEY, transit district president; b. Dec. 2, 1927, Puxico, Mo.; s. Charles Thomas and Minnie Elizabeth (Hodge) G.; m. Betty Berry, June 30, 1951; children: John b. 1955, Sharon b. 1962, Karen b. 1966; edn: BS mktg., S.E. Mo. State Univ. 1952. Career: owner, gen. mgr. John Glenn Adjusters & Adminstrs., offices in Los Angeles, Oakland, San Rafael, San Jose, Calif. and Portland, Oreg. 1966-; v.p. S.F. Bay Area Rapid Transit Dist. (BART) 1978, 85, pres. 1981, 88; dir. Royal Nufoam Corp. 1968-77; organizer and dir. Civic Bank of Commerce, in Oakland, Walnut Creek, San Leandro, Concord, Fremont, Rossmoor, 1984-; trustee Holy Family Coll. 1983-86, Ohlone Coll. Found. 1986; honors: S.E. Missouri State Univ. alumni merit award and Hall of Fame (1986, 89); mem: Calif. Assn. Independent Ins. Adjusters (pres. 1979-80), East Bay Adjusters Assn. (pres. 1970), Am. Public Transit Assn. (bd. dirs. 1981-), Central Coast Claims Assn.; Democrat; United Methodist; rec: gardening, photog., travel; res: 36601 Cuenca Ct Fremont 94536; ofc: John Glenn Adjusters & Administrators, 2201 Broadway Ste 308 Oakland 94612

GLOVER, JAMES THOMAS, financial executive; b. Feb. 23, 1950, Petaluma; s. Arthur Raymond and Minnie (Beaver) G.; m. Kathleen Elizabeth Miller, June 17, 1978; children: Makenzie Terrill b. 1979, Matthew Tyson b. 1982; edn: AA, Chaffey Coll. 1971; BS acctg., Calif. Polytechnic St. Univ., Pomona 1974; MBA, Pepperdine Univ. 1982; C.P.A. Calif. 1976. Career: Artco Engring., Cucamonga 1971-74; mgr. Peat Marwick Mitchell, Newport Beach 1974-80; mgr. western region oil and gas acctg. Aminoil USA/R.J. Reynolds Inc., Huntington Beach

1980-83; controller, corp. acctg., Beckman Instruments, Fullerton 1983-86; sr. dir. fin. planning and analysis Allergan Inc., Irvine 1986-89; v.p., controller Beckman Instruments Diagnostic Systems Group, Brea 1989-93; v.p. & controller Beckman Instruments, Inc. 1993-; mem: Fin. Execs. Inst., Am. Inst. C.P.A., Calif. Soc. C.P.A., YMCA (group leader); mil: s.sgt. Calif. Army Nat. Guard 1970-76; Republican; R.Cath.; rec: golf, sailing. Ofc: Beckman Instruments Inc 2500 Harbor Blvd PO Box 3100 Fullerton 92634-3100

GLYNN, JAMES A., writer, professor of sociology; b. Sept. 10, 1941, Brooklyn; s. James A. and Muriel Marie (Lewis) G.; m. Marie Janet Gates, Dec. 17, 1966; 1 son, David b. 1972; edn: AA, Foothill Coll., 1962; BA, San Jose State Univ., 1964, MA, 1966. Career: prof. sociology Bakersfield Coll., Bakersfield 1966-; adj. prof. CSU Bakersfield, 1988-; adj. prof. CSU Fresno 1968-69, Chapman Coll., Orange 1970-71; text reviewer and consulting editor for several book cos.; awards: Innovator of Yr. League for Innovation for Community Colls., St. Louis, Mo. 1989, Pres.'s Award for textbook author Bakersfield Coll. 1989, Innovator of Yr. Textbook Kern Community Coll. Dist. 1992; mem: Calif. Academic Senate (Bakersfield Coll. pres. 1975-77, state del. 1980-90, Calif. Great Teachers Seminar, Santa Barbara 1990), Faculty Assn. for Calif. Comm. Colls. Sacto. (Council 1987-), Am. Sociol. Assn. 1965-, Calif. Sociol. Assn. (pres. 1992-93, treas. 1990-91), Textbook Authors Assn. 1986-, Kern Comm. Coll. Fedn. of Tchrs. (founder 1976); civic: Reading Is Fundamental (vol. 1979-81), Kern Coun. for Civic Unity (sec. 1968-70); author: Understanding Racial and Ethnic Groups (Bakersfield: Fairway House, 1992), Guide to Social Psychology 1991, Hands On: User's Manual for Data Processing 1986, (with Elbert W. Stewart) Intro. to Sociology (McGraw-Hill Book Co., 1985, prev. editions 1971, 75, 79, internat. edition pub. 1986), cont-bg. author: Using Humor to Teach Sociology (Am. Sociol. Assn., 1988), author: Writing Across the Curriculum Using Sociological Concepts (Fairway House, 1983), Studying Sociology 1979, (with Gregory L. Goodwin) New Directions for Community Colleges (S.F., Jossey-Bass, 1977); Democrat. Res: 4512 Panorama Dr Bakersfield 93306 Ofc: Bakersfield College Bakersfield 93305

GOBAR, ALFRED JULIAN, economic consultant, educator; b. July 12, 1932, Lucerne Valley; s. Julian Smith and Hilda (Millbank) G.; m. Sally Ann Randall, June 17, 1957; children: Wendy Lee, Curtis Julian, Joseph Julian; edn: BA in econs., Whittier Coll., 1953, MA in history, 1955; postgrad. Claremont Grad. Sch., 1953-54; PhD in econs., USC, 1963. Career: asst. to the pres. Microdot Inc., Pasadena 1953-57; regional sales mgr. Sutorbilt Corp., Los Angeles 1957-59; market res. assoc. Beckman Instruments Inc., Fullerton 1959-64; senior mktg. cons. Western Mgmt. Consultants Inc., Phoenix, Az. and Los Angeles, 1964-66; ptnr., prin., chmn. bd. Darley/Gobar Assocs. Inc., 1966-73; pres., chmn. bd. Alfred Gobar Assocs. Inc., Brea 1973-91; pres. and chmn. bd. AJGA, Inc. 1991-; asst. prof. finance USC, 1963-64; assoc. prof. bus. CSU Los Angeles, 1963-68, 70-79, assoc. prof. CSU Fullerton, 1968-69; mktg., fin. adviser 1957-; dir. Quaker City Fed. Savings & Loan Assn., Whittier 1992-; bd. trustees Whittier Coll., 1992-; honors: Lambda Alpha (hon. land econs. frat.); mem. Am. Soc. Real Estate Counselors, Urban Land Inst.; public speaker seminars and convs.; pub. articles in field. Res: 1100 W Valencia Mesa Dr Fullerton 92633 Ofc: 721 W Kimberly Ave Placentia 92670

GODAGER, JANE ANN, psychiatric social worker; b. Nov. 29, 1943, Blue River, Wis.; d. Roy and Elmyra Marie (Hood) Godager; edn: BA, Univ. Wis., Madison 1965; MSW, Fla. State Univ., Tallahassee, 1969; Calif. Lic. Clin. Soc. Worker; Acad. Cert. Soc. Worker, NASW; Bd. Cert. Diplomate in soc. work Am. Bd. BCD's. Career: social worker Dept. Corrections, Wis. 1965-71; State Dept. of Mental Health, Calif. 1972-85; Mental Health Dept., Riverside 1985-86; mental health counselor Superior Court, San Bernardino 1986-; mem. advy. bd. Sch. of Soc. Work, CSU San Bernardino; mem: Kappa Kappa Gamma Alumnae, Nat. Assn. of Soc. Workers; rec: reading, travel. Ofc: MHC/ Superior Ct. 700 E Gilbert Bldg, One, San Bernardino 92415-0920

GOFF, THOMAS MICHAEL, real estate consulting firm executive; b. April 30, 1948, Elgin, Ill.; s. Walter Earl, Jr. and Jeanne Marie (Blanchard) G.; m. Gerrianne M. Ringlespaugh, July 28, 1970; 1 dau., Kristen b. 1981; edn: BS, Univ. of Ill. 1974; MBA, Mich. State Univ. 1976. Career: senior prin. Laventhol & Horwath, Los Angeles 1976-90; exec. Robert Charles Lesser & Co., Beverly Hills 1990-; instr. Mich. State Univ. 1974-76; bd. advisors Hotel Sch. at Calif. Polytechnic Univ., Pomona 1991-; mem. bd. dirs: Small Luxury Hotels & Resorts Assn. (treas. 1987-89), L.A. Visitors & Convention Bureau, Calif. Hotel & Motel Assn., San Gabriel Country Club; mil: 1st lt., U.S. Army 1969-72; Republican; rec: golf. Ofc: Robert Charles Lesser & Co. 11111 Santa Monica Blvd Ste 1800 Los Angeles 90025

GOGOLIN, MARILYN TOMPKINS, educational executive; b. Feb. 25, 1946, Pomona; d. Roy Merle and Dorothy (Davidson) Tompkins; m. Robert Elton Gogolin, Mar. 19, 1969; edn: BA, Univ. LaVerne 1967; MA, Univ. Redlands 1968; MS, CSU Fullerton 1976; Univ. Wash. Seattle 1968-69. Career: speech pathologist Casa Colina Hosp. Rehab. Medicine, Pomona 1969-71; diagnostic tchr. L.A. Co. Office Edn., Downey 1971-72, program splst. 1972-74, program mgr. 1974-76, organizational behavior mgmt. cons. 1976-79, dir.

administrative affairs and asst. to supt. 1979-; exec. dir. Co. Sch. Bds. Assn., Los Angeles 1979-; cons. sch. dists. and profl. assns. 1976-; awards: Univ. LaVerne Sarafin 1967, Univ. Wash. Doctoral Fellowship 1968-69, PTA Hon. Service 1985, 86, Outstanding Young Women in Am. 1977, Who's Who in West, Who's Who Am. Women, Who's Who Emerging Leaders; mem: Am. Ednl. Research Assn., Am. Speech & Hearing Assn., Calif. Speech & Hearing Assn., Am. Mgmt. Assn., Kidney Found. of Desert (founding patron), Turtle Rock Glen Homeowners (pres. 1988, v.p. 1987); club: Silver Sands Racquet (pres. 1991); Baptist; rec: travel, tennis. Res: 15 Sweetwater Irvine 92715 Ofc: Los Angeles County Office of Education 9300 E Imperial Hwy Downey 90242

GOINGS, WILLIE, JR., corrosion engineer; b. Aug. 20, 1938, St. Francisville, La.; s. Willie and Mary Lee (Noflin) G.; m. Hattie P., Mar. 10, 1963; children: Monique b. 1967, Fayvette b. 1969; edn: AS, L.A. Trade Tech. 1969, spl. courses CSULA 1975-77; Reg. Profl. Corrosion Engr., Calif. (No. 1003) 1978. Career: sr. fire control opr. Calif. Army Nat. Guard Nike Hercules Air Def. Missile System, Palos Verdes 1965-67; structure assembler Lockheed Corp., Burbank 1967, McDonnell Douglas Corp., Santa Monica 1967-69; electronics techn. Northrop Nortronics Div., Hawthorne 1969-70; communication techn. So. Calif. Edison Co., Rosemead 1971-73, engring. asst. 1973-78, corrosion splst., 1978-; chmn. So. Calif. Cathodic Protection Com. 1981; honors: Alpha Gamma Sigma 1969, appreciation City of Los Angeles 1983; mem: IEEE, Nat. Assn. of Corrosion Engrs., Los Angeles Council of Black Profl. Engrs., Mason (33 deg.); mil: E5 US Army 1960-65, Good Conduct Medal, Army Commendn., Expt. Missileman; Democrat; Christian; rec: interior decor. Res: 15 Flintlock Ln Bell Canyon 91307 Ofc: So California Edison 2244 Walnut Grove Ave Ste 190 Rosemead 91770

GOLD, RUSSELL STUART, psychologist; b. Jan. 7, 1949, Chicago, Ill.; s. Irving Louis and Victoria (Saltzman) G.; m. Andrea, Aug. 1, 1982; children: Celia b. 1983, Seth b. 1988, Kristen b. 1970, Kristopher b. 1974; edn: AB, Univ. Ill. Champaign 1970; MA, Northwestern Univ. 1973; PhD, Calif. Sch. Profl. Psychology 1978; lic. psychologist 1979. Career: pvt. practice psychology, San Diego 1979-; police psychologist San Diego Co. 1985-89, San Diego Police Dept. 1990-; dir. Child Custody & Family Research Ctr. 1988-; adj. supr. Mercy Hosp. 1979-; mem: Acad. San Diego Psychologists (pres., secty. 1979-), Am. Psychological Assn., Calif. St. Psychological Assn.; Jewish. Ofc: 4060 4th Ave Ste 615 San Diego 92103

GOLDBERG, FRED SELLMANN, advertising agency executive; b. Jan. 22, 1941, Chgo.; s. Sydney Norman and Birdie (Cohen) G.; m. Jerrilyn Toby Tager, Apr. 12, 1964; children: Robin b. 1965, Susanne b. 1968; edn: BS, Univ. Vermont, 1962; MBA, New York Univ., 1964. Career: mktg. research mgr. P. Ballantine & Sons, Newark, N.J. 1964-67; senior v.p., mgmt. supr. Young & Rubicam, N.Y.C. 1967-78, senior v.p. and gen. mgr. Young & Rubicam, Los Angeles 1978-82; exec. v.p., gen. mgr. Chiat Day Inc., San Francisco 1982-85, c.o.o. Chiat Day Inc., Los Angeles 1985-87, pres. and c.e.o. Chiat-Day San Francisco and v. chmn. Chiat-Day Advt., Inc., L.A. 1987-90; founder, pres. and c.e.o. Goldberg Moser O'Neill Advertising, San Francisco 1990-; Republican; Jewish; rec: tennis, music, running. Res: 154 Santa Rosa Ave Sausalito 94965-2035 Ofc: Goldberg Moser O'Neill, 77 Maiden Ln San Francisco 94108

GOLDBERG, HERB, psychologist; b. July 14, 1937, Berlin, Germany; s. Jacob and Ella (Nagler) G.; 1 dau., Amy Elisabeth b. 1981; edn: BA cum laude, City Univ. N.Y. 1958; PhD, Adelphi Univ., N.Y. 1963. Career: prof. psychology CSU Los Angeles 1965-; pvt. practice psychotherapy, Westwood 1966-; honors: Phi Beta Kappa; mem: Am. Psychological Assn.; author: w. George Bach, Creative Aggression, 1974; Hazards of Being Male, 1976; w. Robert Lewis, Money Madness, 1978; New Male, 1979; New Male-Female Relationships, 1983; Inner Male, 1987; What Men Really Want, 1991. Ofc: 1100 Glendon Ave #939 Los Angeles 90065

GOLDBERG, MARK ARTHUR, neuropharmacologist; b. Sept. 4, 1934, N.Y., N.Y.; s. Jacob and Bertha (Gruslausky) G.; widower, 1982; 1 son, Jonathan Lee b. 1971. edn: BS, Columbia Univ., 1955; PhD, Univ. Chicago, 1959, MD, 1962. Career: resident neurology N.Y. Neurolog. Inst., 1963-66; asst. prof. neurology Columbia Univ., 1968-71; prof. neurology and pharmacology, UCLA, Los Angeles, 1971-, chair dept. neurology UCLA/Harbor Med. Ctr., Torrance 1977-; mem: Am. Neurol. Assn. (Fellow), Am. Acad. of Neurology (Fellow), Am. Soc. for Neurochemistry, L.A. Soc. for Neurology (pres.); author numerous book chapters and articles on neuropharmacology; mil: capt. US Army 1966-68. Ofc: UCLA/Harbor Medical Center, 1000 W Carson St Torrance 90509

GOLDFARB, I. JAY, accounting firm executive; b. Mar. 8, 1933, N.Y.C.; s. Joseph and Fay Esther (Hirschhorn) G.; m. Arlene Storch, May 8, 1955; children: Meryl Lori, David; edn: BA in econs., Queen's Coll., N.Y. 1955; CPA, N.Y. 1962, Calif. 1972. Career: staff acct. T.D. Davidson & Co., CPAs, N.Y.C. 1957-59; ptnr. Rashba & Pokart, CPAs 1959-65; chief fin. ofcr. Fabrics by Joyce Inc. 1965-66; ptnr. Clarence Rainess & Co. CPAs 1966-71, co-executive ptnr. 1971-75; senior ptnr. Joseph S. Herbert & Co. CPAs, L.A., Calif. 1975-78;

mng. ptnr. Goldfarb, Whitman & Cohen CPAs, L.A. 1978-; dir: Sam & Libby Inc., San Carlos 1992-; awarded "Spirit of Life" City of Hope 1990; mem. Am. Inst. of CPAs 1962-, N.Y. State Soc. of CPAs 1962-, Calif. State Soc. CPAs 1972-; civic: City of Hope Profls. & Fin. Assocs. (pres. 1974-76, dinner chmn. 1977-79), Boys & Girls Club San Fernando Valley/Pacoima (v.p. 1989, treas. 1990), United Jewish Welfare Fund (major gift com. 1987-); mil: 1st lt. USAF 1955-57; Stephen J. Weiss Temple; rec: golf, bridge. Ofc: Goldfarb, Whitman & Cohen, CPAs 12233 W Olympic Blvd Ste 210 Los Angeles 90064

GOLDING, SUSAN, county supervisor; b. Aug. 18, 1945, Muskogee, Okla.; d. Brage and Hinda Fay (Wolf) G.; m. Richard T. Silberman, July 22, 1984; children: Samuel b. 1971, Vanessa b. 1974; edn: Cert. Pratique De Langue Francaise, Univ. of Paris, 1965; BA Govt. & Internat. Relations, Carleton Coll., 1966; MA Romance Philology, Columbia Univ., 1974. Career: assoc. ed. Jour. of Internat. Affairs of Columbia Univ.; PhD tchg. fellow Emory Univ.; coll. instr. San Diego College Dist.; assoc. pub./gen. mgr. The News Press Group, San Diego -1980; elected San Diego City Council, 1981-83; dep. state secty. of bus., transp., housing State of Calif., Sacto. 1983-84; elected County Bd. of Supervisors, Dist. 3, San Diego 1984-, v. ch. 1988, bd. chmn. 1989; founder Internat. Trade Commn. 1985, chair Alcohol & Drug Prevention Task Force 1987-88, chair Earthquake Preparedness Com. Disaster Council 1986-; awards: Disting. Achiev. Award Carleton Coll. 1991, woman of achiev. Soroptomists Internat. S.D. 1988, One of 10 outstanding ofcls. in U.S. Repub. Nat. Com. 1987, Alice Paul Award Nat. Womens Polit. Caucus S.D. 1987, S.D. Woman of Achiev. 1982, One of 10 outstanding young citizens S.D. 1980; mem: Calif. Elected Womens Asn. for Ednl. Res., Sigma Delta Chi, S.D. Conv. & Vis. Bur. (dir. 1985-), Kiwanis Club, Trusteeship Nat. Womens Forum L.A., Navy League of U.S. (S.D. Council 1981-); Republican (State Central Com., chair Local Elected Ofcls. 1987-); rec: languages, theater & arts, scuba. Ofc: Supervisor, San Diego County Board Supervisors 1600 Pacific Hwy Rm 335 San Diego 92101

GOLDSTONE, JERRY, vascular surgeon, educator; b. Nov. 18, 1940, Ontario, Oreg.; s. Ralph and Annette Lee (Rogoway) G.; m. Linda F. Kay, July 7, 1962; children: Adam E. b. 1969, Lara E. b. 1971, Stefan G. b. 1973; edn: Univ. Wash., Seattle 1958-61; BS (by reciprocity) Univ. Oregon, Eugene; MD (cum laude) Univ. Oregon Med. Sch., Portland 1965; lic. Calif. BME 1966. Career: asst. prof. surgery UC San Francisco, 1972-78, assoc. prof. surg. 1978-80; prof. surgery Univ. Ariz., Tucson 1980-84; prof. surgery UC San Francisco, 1984-, medical director Cardiovasc. Special Care Unit 1986-, v.chmn. dept. of surgery and chief div. vascular surgery, 1987-; cons. Letterman Army Med. Ctr., S.F. 1984-, director STAMP Prog. VA Med. Ctr., S.F. 1984-, cons. David Grant USAF Med. Ctr., Travis AFB, 1985-; awards: clin. investigator VA Med. Ctr. S.F. 1973-76, Outstanding Tchr. nom. Sch. of Med. UCSF 1974, Dean's list, Excellence in Tchg., Univ. Ariz., Tucson 1982, Annual Gore lectr. Royal Australian Coll. of Surgeons, Sydney, Aus. 1985, Harvey Lozman Memorial lectr. Beth Israel Med. Ctr., N.Y.C. 1986; mem: Internat. Soc. for Cardiovascular Surgery (secty., mem. exec. council, 1989-), Vascular Surgery Biology Club (sec. treas. 1989-), Soc. for Vascular Surgery (p.r. com. 1990-), Am. Coll. Surgeons (surgical forum com. 1989-), Western Vascular Soc. (founding mem. 1984-); Sierra Club (S.F.); author med. book chapters (1971-), med. jour. articles (1965-), editor book series: Perspectives in Vascular Surgery (1989-); mil: capt. USAR 1966-75; rec: sports, travel, nature. Ofc: UCSF 505 Parnassus Rm M-488 San Francisco 94143-0222

GONZALEZ, CESAR AUGUSTO (aka Gonzalez-T.,Cesar A.), educator, writer; b. Jan. 17, 1931, Los Angeles; s. Jose Andalon and Camerina (Trujillo) G.; m. Bette L. Beattie, Aug. 30, 1969; edn: BA, Gonzaga Univ., 1953, MA, licentiate in philosophy, 1954; MST, licentiate in sacred theology, Univ. Santa Clara, 1961; postgrad., sociology, UCLA, 1962-65. Career: tchr. Instituto Regional Mexico, Chihuahua, Mex. 1954-57; community devel. specialist Centro Laboral Mexico, Mexico D.F., 1965-68; supr. A.B.C. Headstart, East L.A., Calif. 1968-69; employment counselor Operation SER, San Diego 1969-70; prof. and dept. chair Chicano studies, San Diego Mesa Coll., 1970-; founding chair Raza Consortium, 1971-72; cons. Chicano Fedn. of San Diego County Inc., 1987-89; author book of poetry: Unwinding the Silence (1987), editor, contbr. book of lit. criticism: Rudolfo A. Anaya: Focus on Criticism (1990), coeditor: English Grammar and Comp. (1978, 79), contbr. poetry, short fiction and lit. criticism to scholarly journals, mags., newspapers and anthologies; ed., assoc. ed. literary journals, 1976-: Revista Apple, Ariz. State Univ., Tempe 1991, Sequoya, Santa Ana, Calif. (1990-), Fragmentos de Barro, San Diego (1976-); founding bd. dirs. Mex.-Am. Advy. Com. to L.A. Bd. of Edn., 1969; awards: Fulbright-Hays fellow, Peru 1982, NEH fellow, UCSB 1984, comm. svc. award Chicano Fedn. San Diego Inc. 1982, outstanding tchr. San Diego Mesa Coll. 1985, outstanding tchr. and scholar Concilio of Chicano Studies for San Diego, Imperial Valley and Baja, Calif. 1990, tchg. excellence award Nat. Inst. for Staff and Orgn. Devel. 1993; mem: Am. Fedn. of Tchrs. 1970-, Nat. Assn. of Chicano Studies 1988-, La Raza Faculty Assn. 1970-, Centro Cultural de la Raza (1972-, past bd. mem.), Poets and Writers 1990-, Assn. Internacional de Hispanistas 1991-; Democrat; R.Cath.; rec: travel, reading, music. Ofc: Chicano Studies Dept. San Diego Mesa College 7250 Mesa College Dr San Diego 92111 Ph: 619/627-2751

GOODHEAD, BERNARD, physician-surgeon; b. Oct. 20, 1934, Derby, England; nat. 1975; s. Arthur Reginald and Starletta (Goshawk) G.; m. Susan Richards, March 3, 1963 (div. 1977); m. Arlene Johnson, March 19, 1978; children: Deborah b. 1970, Sheryl b. 1971; edn: BS, Birmingham Univ. England 1958; LRCP, MRCS, London, England 1958; MS, McGill Univ. Canada 1968. Career: intern, England 1958-65; resident 1967-69; fellow Long Beach Heart Assn., Harbor Gen. Hosp., Torrance 1965-66; res. fellow Royal Victims Hosp., Montreal, Canada 1966-67; chief resident dept. surgery Bexar Co. Hosp., Univ. Tx. Med.Sch., San Antonio 1969-71; pvt. practice, Houston and San Antonio, Tx. 1971-73; San Diego 1973-; mem: San Diego Med. Soc., CMA, Soc. Gen. Surgeons San Diego, Southwestern Surgical Congress, A.C.P., English Coll. Surgeons, Pan Pacific Surgical Assn., Internat. Coll. Surgeons, Internat. Soc. Surgeons, FRCS, FACS, FICS; 27 articles pub. in sci. jours.; rec: travel. Res: 1395 Park Row La Jolla 92037 Ofc: 6719 Alvarado Rd Ste 200 San Diego 92120

GOODMAN, STEPHEN KENT, composer, conductor, arranger; b. Aug. 12, 1949, Glendale; s. Kent and Naoma (Noble) G.; m. Elizabeth Anne Blankinship, July 4, 1976 (div. 1982); m. Kelly Kay Ebinger, Apr. 30, 1984; edn: USC, 1968, Calif. Inst. of the Arts 1971-72, Grove Sch. of Music, L.A. 1981-82. Career: profl. conducting debut as "World's Youngest Composer /Condr. of Marches" N.Y.C., July 13, 1966; pioneer work in sonic sculpture 1975-83; recording studio and commercial musical cons., condr., composer, arranger Harlequin Studios, Northridge, Calif. 1979-84; musical compositions rep. by various publishers 1973-; newspaper editor, West Coast Rag, 1991-92; writer articles dealing with music & culture, 1982-; honoree, N.Dak. state recognition 1989; mem: ASCAP (elected 1973 for film score "Maxie"), Christian Instrumental Directors Assn. 1992-, Windjammers Internat. 1990), Maple Leaf Club (Grass Valley), Bohemia Ragtime Soc. (Boulder, Co.); Republican; Lutheran; rec: scuba (wreck) diving, spearfishing. Ofc: PO Box 5459 Fresno 93755-5459

GOODMAN, TERENCE JAMES, actor, director, playwright; b. Nov. 29, 1950, Fort Dodge, Iowa; s. Wayne (Connie) Alva and Helen Loretta (O'Connor) G.; m. Catherine Amy Jackson, May 4, 1992; edn. BFA in theatre arts, Ark. State Univ., 1973; MFA theatre arts, Utah State Univ., 1990, profl. tng. with HB Studio NY, NY 1973, Michael Shurtleff, NY, NY 1974, Charles Conrad, L.A. 1976-77. Career: equity actor profl. theatre 1973-: selected roles include: King of Hearts "Alice in Wonderland" Prince Street Players, N.Y. 1973-74, Charlie "Oh, Lady Lady" Off-Broadway 1974, Smokey "Damn Yankees" (revival) Broadway Nat. Tour 1974, Annas "Jesus Christ Superstar" Broadway Nat. Tour 1975, Judas "Godspell" Off-Broadway 1975, Charlie "Queen of the Soaps" Internat. City Theatre, Los Angeles 1990, also numerous stage appearances in stock, semi and non-profl. theater 1971-; feature films include: (star) "Ode to Billy Joe" Warner Bros. 1975, "Who Done It" Dody Dayton Prodns. 1984, (featured) "Ninja III The Domination" Cannon Prodns. 1985, "Ruthless People" Walt Disney 1986, "Camp Beverly Hills" Touchstone 1988; profl. T.V.: guest star "Laverne and Shirley" ABC 1978, "The Brothers Wright" NBC 1978, principle "Newhart" CBS 1983, semi-regular "Young and the Restless" CBS 1984, series regular "Days of Our Lives" NBC 1985-86, guest star "Hill Street Blues" NBC 1986, "Perfect Strangers" ABC 1987, featured "Knots Landing" ABC 1987, "American River" NBC 1989; nat. commercials incl. AT&T, Denny's Restaurants, Volvo, Long John Silver, Kubota Lawn Mowers, Warner Books, Michelob, RC Cola, 1976-; director "A Lovely Sunday for Creve Coeur" 1989 (meritorious achiev. award for direction, ACT/Am. Coll. Theater Fest., 1990) "Broadway Bound" 1990, Utah State Theatre, Logan; author (optioned written works): "The Times of Danny Bailey" (screenplay, 1978, rev. 80, 82, 83, 85, 91), "Lost in the Sky" (play, 1989), "Puppetman" (screenplay, 1984), "A Mother's Love" (play, in progress); R.Cath.; rec: Mark Twain historian, skiing. Res/Ofc: 426 S Venice Blvd Venice 90291

GOODWINE, JAMES K., JR., aviation consultant; b. Mar. 9, 1930, Evanson, Ill.; s. James K. and Janet B. (Dyer) G.; m. Helen L. Murray, June 6, 1959; children: Kathryn b. 1960, Robert b. 1962; edn: BSME, Purdue Univ., 1952, MSME, 1956, PhD, 1960. Career: research asst. Purdue Univ., 1954-57, instr. 1957-58; research engr. Chevron Research Co., Richmond, Calif. 1959-67; staff engr. United Airlines Co., San Francisco 1967-70, mgr. powerplant engring. 1970-79, mgr. new aircraft and operational engring. 1979-82, dir. engine tech. svs. 1982-87, actg. v.p. tech. svs. 1987, mgr. new technology 1987-89; consultant Aviation Mgmt. Systems, Concord, Mass. also Michael Goldfarb Assocs., Wash. D.C., 1989-; recipient Spl. Recognition Award United Airlines, Chgo. 1978; mem.: Soc. Automotive Engrs. (1959-, sect. chair 1976-77), Sigma Xi 1959-; clubs: Commonwealth (S.F.), Early Ford V-8 San Leandro (pres. regional gp. 1981-82); inventor: Detergent Lube Comp. (Pat. #3405065, 1968), Method of Oper. & Lube (Pat. #3426738, 1969); publs: 8+ tech. papers; mil: cpl. US Army 1952-54; Republican; Prot.; rec: early Ford V-8, collector antique toys. Res: 1423 Enchanted Way San Mateo 94402

GORDON, HELEN HEIGHTSMAN, writer, English professor; b. Sept. 7, 1932, Salt Lake City; d. Fred C. and Florence (Hale) H.; m. Norman C. Winn, Aug. 10, 1950 (div. Sept. 1972); children: Bruce b. 1954, Brent b. 1957, Holly b. 1959; m. Clifton B. Gordon, Feb. 17, 1974; edn: BA in English, CSU Sacramento, 1964, MA, 1967; EdD, Nova Univ., Ft. Lauderdale, 1979. Career:

assoc. prof. English, Porterville Coll., 1967-74; prof. English, Bakersfield Coll., 1974-; mem. and contbr. to jour., English Council of Calif. 2-yr. Colls., 1979-, dir. Region V, 1990-92; presenter at confs.: English Council of Calif. 1991, also at Western Coll. Reading & Learning Assn., Calif. Assn. Tchrs. of English, SW Reg. English Tchrs. Conf., Calif. Tchrs. of English as a Second Language, Nat. Assn. of Developmental Educators and Assn. of Calif. Colls. Tutorial & Learning Assistance; awards: honors pgm. Univ. Utah, S.L.C. 1960, 61, outstanding educator Porterville Coll. 1972, 73, Am. Assn. of Women in Comm. and Jr. Colls. nat. leaders conf. 1983, 85 also Service to Women reg. award, Bakersfield 1991, guest mem. editorial bd. Bakersfield Californian 1988, L.W.V. Calif. distinctive feature writing 1990; mem.: NEA (1967-life), Nat. Council of Tchrs. of English 1967-, Am. Assn. of Women in Comm. & Jr. Colls. (1983-, chapt. pres. 1989), Textbook Authors Assn. 1987-, AAUW, L.W.V. Bakersfield (pres. 1981-83, 89-90); author textbooks: From Copying To Creating (1981, 85), Wordforms: I, II (1985, 90), Developing College Writing (1989), Interplay: Sentences In Context (1991), 20+ articles and resrch. reports; Democrat; Unitarian (Fellowship of Kern Co. pres. 1975-77); rec: bowling, tennis, reading, films, discussion groups. Res: 6400 Westlake Dr Bakersfield 93308-6519 Ofc: English Dept. Bakersfield College, 1801 Panorama Dr Bakersfield 93305

GORDON, MARILYN, clinical hypnotherapist, author, teacher; b. Dec. 11, 1940, Chgo.; d. Harold David and Gertrude (Goldman) Goldberg; div., 1 child, Dana b. 1964; edn: BA in English, Univ. Mich., 1962; grad. studies Univ. Calif. Berkeley; counseling psych. JFK Univ., Orinda; cert. clinical hypnotherapist, 1974. Career: sch. tchr., English lang. & lit., Chgo. Bd. of Edn., Ill. 1965-69; tchr. lang. arts, yoga, Evelyn Wood, Marin County, Calif. 1970-89; clin. hypnotherapist, pvt. practice, 1974-, tchr., writer, tnr., consultant; honors: Phi Beta Kappa 1962, Phi Kappa Phi 1962, Pi Lambda Theta 1962; mem. Am. Council of Hypnotist Examiners 1987-, Nat. Guild of Hypnotists 1989-; author: Healing is Remembering Who You Are (1990), Manual for Transformational Healing with Hypnotherapy (1993); contr. author: Journal of Hypnotism (1992, 93); speaker Internat. Hypnotherapy Conf. 1990-93; audio video tapes, radio and tv appearances; rec: yoga, meditation. Ofc: PO Box 10795 Oakland 94610

GORDON, RUTH VIDA, structural engineer; b. Sept. 19, 1926, Seattle; d. Solomon Alexander and Leah (Yoffe) Gordon; m. Michael Herbert Schnapp, Sept. 28, 1949; children: Madeline Ruth b. 1954, Marcia Lea b. 1955, Michael Gordon b. 1957; edn: BS, Stanford Univ., 1948, MS, 1949; Calif. lic. Civil Engr. 1953, Structural Engr. 1959 (first woman). Career: structural designer Isadore Thompson, Consulting Engr., San Francisco 1950-51; K. P. Norrie, Cons. Engr., Spokane, Wash. 1951; Bechtel Corp., San Francisco 1951-53; civil engr. CALTRANS, S.F. 1953-54; struct. designer Russell Fuller, Cons. Engr., S.F. 1954; Western Knapp Engring. Corp., S.F. 1954-55; struct. engring. assoc. struct. safety sect. Calif. State Architect, S.F. 1956-57, senior struct. designer 1957-59 (first woman), senior struct. engr. 1959-76 (first woman), dist. struct. engr. 1976-86 (first woman); pres. Pegasus Engring. Inc., 1984-; appt. Yacht Harbor Advy. Com., S.F. Rec. & Park Dept. 1986-88, advy. com. master plan S.F. Unified Sch. Dist. 1971-72, engr. mem. of advy. panel Calif. Bd. Architl. Examiners examination revision project 1979-81; awards: Margaret Byrne undergrad. scholar 1943-45, Wing and Garland scholar C.E. Stanford Univ. Grad. Sch. (1st woman recipient 1948-49), woman of achiev. Union Sq. BPW (1975, 82), outstanding svc. Soc. Women Engrs. Golden Gate (1979, 84), Calif. Fedn. of BPW Top Hat Award 1978-79, Working Woman Mag. achiev. 1983, Calif. Dept. Gen. Svs. profl. proficiency 1984, Inducted into Calif. Fedn. of Bus. and Profl. Women BPW Hall of Fame in recog. of outstanding achiev. field of sci. 1992; mem: Struct. Engrs. Assn. No. Calif. (first woman mem. 1953, legis. com. chair 1978-79, del. Calif. Legis. Coun. 1978-79, dir. 1984-86), SF Bay Area Engring. Coun. (dir. 1977-79, first woman pres. 1982-83), Nat. Soc. of Women Engrs. (affirmative action coord. 1979-80, Golden Gate sect. pres. 1978-79, nat. conv. v.ch. 1979, affirmative action chair 1979-80, 84-), ASCE, Math/Sci. Network Coun., Assn. for Women in Sci.; clubs: Union Square BPW, Golden Gate Yacht (sail fleet capt. 1987-88, dir. 1991-93), S.F. Yacht (Aux.), Yacht Racing Assn. S.F. Bay (cert. race ofcr.), US Sailing Assn. (judge, race mgmt. com., sr. race ofcr., N. CA & NV race ofcr.); Democrat (S.F. Dem. Women's Forum, dir. 1976-78, 79-81, 82-83, 85-87, 91-92); rec: sailing, knitting, reading, puzzles. Res: 726-23rd Ave San Francisco 94121 Ofc: Pegasus Engineering, Inc. PO Box 210425 San Francisco 94121-0425

GORELICK, ELLEN CATHERINE, artist, art history educator, civic volunteer; b. Jan. 2, 1946, Chicago, Ill.; d. Martin Francis and Doris Harriet (Adams) Heckmann; m. Walter Lee Gorelick, Dec. 19, 1970; edn: AA cum laude, Coll. of Sequoias 1976; BA cum laude, CSU Fresno 1979; MA, 1982; Career: book div. correspondent Time Inc., Chgo., Ill. 1964-68; accounts receivable supr. Tab Products Co., San Francisco 1968-69; exec.secty. Foremost McKesson Inc., San Francisco 1969-71; McCarthy Land Co., Visalia 1972-74; adminstrv. dir. Creative Center for Handicapped 1979-80; curator Tulare Hist. Museum, Tulare 1984-87; adj. faculty Coll. of Sequoias, Visalia 1985-; civic bds: Tulare-Kings Regional Arts Council (pres. 1989-90), Tulare County Art League (pres. 1977-78), Leadership Tulare (CORE com. 1991-, Alumni chair 1992-), Tulare County Univ. Calif. Campus Expansion Task Force, Visalia 1988-91, Tulare City Sch. Dist. Classrooms for Kids Campaign (co-chair 1989), Tulare City

Historical Soc. Long Range Planning Com. 1991-, Tulare County Sym. 1992-, "Taste Treats in Tulare" Fundraiser (co-chair 1991), City of Tulare Community Improvement Com. 1992-; honors: Phi Kappa Phi, Alpha Gamma Sigma, appreciation awards: City of Tulare 1989, Tulare County Bd. Suprs. 1991, Tulare Dist. Hosp. 1991, Tulare Board of Realtors 1990, named Artist of Year Tulare Palette Club 1985, Tulare Co. Regional Arts Council (1988), Outstanding Young Women of Am. 1979; mem: Les Petits Amis (pres. 1988-89), Valley Oak Garden Club, Tulare Co. Womens Symphony League, AAUW, Acorn Garden Club (pres. 1981-82), Lawyers Wives of Tulare Co. (pres. 1979-89), Tulare Palette Club (pres. 1984-85); artist intaglio print, The Dream (Best of Show Tulare Co. Art League 1983); Democrat; R.Cath.; rec: photog., cooking; res: 433 E Chevy Chase Dr Tulare 93274; ofc: College of the Sequoias 915 S Mooney Blvd Visalia 93277

GORELICK, WALTER LEE, judge; b. Mar. 30, 1945, Los Angeles; s. Leon and Dr. Molly C. (Chernow) G.; m. Ellen, Dec. 19, 1970; edn: BA, UC Los Angeles, 1967; JD, Golden Gate Univ., 1970; cert. specialist criminal law (1977). Career: deputy public defender, asst. pub. defender, chief pub. defender Public Defender's Office of Tulare County, Visalia 1971-80; judge Tulare-Pixley Municipal Court, 1980-; faculty Calif. Judicial Coll., 1983; U.S. advisor Asian Legal Research Inst., Japan 1978-80; Drug Abuse Advy. Bd. to Tulare County Board of Suprs. 1978-87; honors: Outstanding Young Men Am. 1981, Who's Who in Am. Law (1st, 2d edits); civic: Greater Tulare C.of C. 1981-, U.S. Constitution Bicentennial Com. of Tulare 1987-88, Tulare Dist. Hosp. Found. (bd. 1987-), Tulare City Historical Soc. (charter 1984-); author/editor 3 books: Preliminary Hearing Courtroom Handbook (1986, 2nd ed. 1993), Summary of Calif. Driving Under the Influence of Alcohol Cases (1992, 4th edit.), Narcotics Law Manual (1988, rev. 1991), numerous articles on criminal law; rec: current events, gardening, collect stamps, rocks, fruit box labels. Res: 433 E Chevy Chase Dr Tulare 93274 Ofc: Tulare-Pixley Municipal Court 425 E Kern Ave Tulare 93274

GORHAM, JAMES D., real estate executive; b. Feb. 21, 1945, N.Y.C.; s. Thomas Joseph and Mary T. (O'Leary) G.; m. Maryann Pinamonti, Feb. 24, 1979; children: Patrick b. 1980, James b. 1984, Kevin b. 1987, Ernest b. 1990; edn: BS, St. Peters Coll. 1967; MBA, CSU Long Beach 1969; lic. real estate broker; internat. cons. VAC Ownership Industry. Career: secondary school tchr. 1970-73; dir. Fallbrook Community Clinic 1977; pres. J.D. Gorham & Assocs. 1978-, project broker/co-dir. Circle J Resort, Park City, Utah 1984, sales mgr. San Clemente Inn 1985, sales mgr., cons. Fairmont Hot Springs Resort, B.C. Canada 1986, sales mgr. Lawrence Welk Resort Villas, Escondido, Calif., 1986-, gen. sales mgr. and project broker Lawrence Welk Resort Villas, 1990-; awards: `The Volunteer Spirit' award St. Francis School, Vista, Ca. 1990, 10 Million Dollar sales award Lawrence Welk Resort Villas 1990, 6-Million Dollar Club 1982, listed Internat. Directory of Disting. Leadership 1988, Five Thousand Personalities of the World 1989; mem. Am. Resort and Residential Devel. Assn.; Peace Corps volunteer, Malaysia 1969; instr. Shoryn Ryu Karate, 4th Degree Black Belt/Yondan, White Crane Karate Studios; Republican; R.Cath. Res: 149 Rudd Rd Vista 92083

GOSSELIN, EDWARD ALBERIC, historian; b. Feb. 12, 1943, Rutland, Vt.; s. Alberic William and Marie Helen (L'Ange) G.; m. Claudia Isabel Hoffer, July 11, 1970; children: Elisabeth b. 1979, David b. 1982; edn: BA, Yale Univ., 1965; MA, Columbia Univ., 1966, PhD, 1973; auditeur Coll. de France, Paris, 1976. Career: lectr. Brooklyn Coll., 1966-68; asst. prof. CSU Long Beach, 1969-73, assoc. prof. 1973-79, prof. 1979-, chair history dept. 1986-; editor The History Teacher, 1986-; awards: Fulbright fellow, Paris, Fr. 1968-69, NEH fellow, CSULB (1973-74, 80-81), NEH fellow, Univ. Chgo. 1977-78; mem: Soc. for History Edn. (exec. mem. 1986-), Societe Internat. de Didactiques de l'Histoire (editl. advy. bd. 1991-), Am. Hist. Assn. 1975-; author: King's Progress to Jerusalem (1976), (book translator) Giordano Bruno's Ash Wednesday Supper, 1584 (1977), numerous jour. articles and revs. (1970-); Democrat; R.Cath.; rec: music -clarinet. Ofc: Dept. History Calif. State Univ., Long Beach 90840-1601

GOTHOLD, STUART E., Los Angeles County superintendent of schools; b. Sept. 20, 1935, Los Angeles; s. Hubert Eugene and Adelaide Louise (Erickson) G.; m. Jane Ruth Soderberg, July 15, 1955; Jon b. 1956, Susan b. 1958, Eric b. 1967, Ruth b. 1970; edn: BA, Whittier Coll. 1956; MA, 1961; Ed.D, USC 1974. Career: tchr. El Rancho Unfied Sch. Dist., Pico Rivera 1956-61, prin. jr. h.s. 1961-66; curriculum cons. Los Angeles Co. Schs., Downey 1966-69; asst. supt. So. Whittier Sch. Dist., Whittier 1969-71, supt. 1971-77; asst. supt., chief deputy Los Angeles Co. Schs., Downey 1977-80, supt. 1980-; adj. prof. Whittier Coll. 1975-; adj. instr. USC, Los Angeles, currently; bd. mem. Nat. Center Fgn. Language, W.D.C. 1987-; advy. bd. mem. Nat. Computer Systems, Des Moines, Iowa 1988; awards: Delta Epsilon lectr. 1984, Whittier Coll. hon. LL.D 1988; mem: Calif. Assn. Co. Supts. (pres.), Delta Epsilon (pres. 1982-83), Am. Assn. Sch. Adminstrs., Assn. Calif. Sch. Adminstrs., Rotary Internat.; author: Decisions: A Health Curriculum (1971), Inquiry, A Way of Tchg. and Way of Learning (1971); Republican; R.Cath.; rec: tennis, hiking, fishing. Res: 10121 Pounds Ave Whittier 90603

GOTZMER, SHIRLEY ELIZABETH, manufacturer's representative, piano teacher; b. Jan 6, 1930, Chgo.; d. Carter Arno and Margaret L. (Schultz) Rehoff; m. John Degenar; m. Bruno Gotzmer, Jan. 19, 1980; children: Lynnette b. 1949, Michele b. 1958, Robert b. 1959, Tamara b. 1963; edn: music major, Carthage Coll., Ill. 1947-49; sociology degree 1972; spl. courses Ohlone Coll., Univ. Calif., CSU Hayward, John F. Kennedy Univ., (pub. adminstrn.) Anthony Sch. R.E., C.L. Williams; lic. insurance agt. 1984. Career: piano teacher own music studio, 1961-; buyer II, Contra Costa Co., 1979-81; founder, owner Gotzmer Enterprises 1981-, mfr.'s rep., devel. software programs; former buyer City of Concord (6 yrs), adminstrv. asst. to chief engr. Alameda Co. Water Dist. (3 yrs), exec. secty. Kaiser Steel and Kaiser Aluminum Chem. Co. (12 yrs); mem: Calif. Assn. Public Purch. Ofcrs. Inc. (secty. 1985-), Nat. Assn. Purch. Mgrs. No. Calif. 1973-79, civic: 700 Club (prayer counseling), Toastmasters, Homeowners Assn.; clubs: Sons of Norway, Flying Club of No. Calif. (emergency task force 1988-91), Benicia Golf Assn., Yacht Club; author technical books, var. manuals, geneology source book, composer and playwright; rec: golf, music, people, study, blues/jazz, travel. Res: 151 Mt Kennedy Dr Martinez 94553 Ofc: Contra Costa County 1220 Morello Ave Ste 101 Martinez 94553

GOUGH, HARRISON GOULD, psychologist, professor emeritus; b. Feb. 25, 1921, Buffalo, Minn.; s. Harry Betzer and Aelfreda (Gould) G.; m. Kathryn Whittier, Jan. 23, 1943; 1 dau. Jane Kathryn b. 1950; edn: BA, summa cum laude, Univ. Minn. 1942, MA, 1947, PhD, 1949. Career: asst. prof. psychol. Univ. Minn. 1948-49; prof. psychol. and res. psychol. UC Berkeley 1949-86, prof. emeritus 1986-, chmn. psychol. dept. 1967-72, dir. Inst. of Personality Assessment and Research 1973-83; cons. clinical psychologist Veterans Adminstrn., 1950-, U.S. Army, 1987-; dir. Consulting Psychologists Press 1956-; appt. Res. Advy. Com. Calif. Dept. of Corrections, 1958-64; Res. advy. com. Calif. Dept. of Mental Hygiene, 1964-69; Gov.'s Advy. Com. on Mental Health 1968-72; Citizen's Advy. Council Calif. Dept. of Mental Health 1969-72; Clin. projects res. review com. NIMH, 1968-72; awards: Social Sci. Res. Council demobilization fellowship 1946-47, Fulbright Res. Fellow (1958-59, 1965-66), Guggenheim Found. Fellow 1965-66, Univ. of Calif. Berkeley Citation 1986, Bruno Klopfer Disting. Contbn. Award, Soc. for Personality Assessment 1987, Phi Beta Kappa; mem: Am. Psychol. Assn. (Fellow), Internat. Assn. for Cross-Cultural Psychology (Fellow), Soc. for Personality Assessment (Fellow), Calif. State Psychol. Assn. (pres. 1961), Commonwealth Club S.F., Soc. of Mayflower Descendants; author: the Adject. Check List, the Calif. Psychological Inv. and other psychol. tests, 200+ res. papers and monographs on topics of psychol. assessment, perception, cognition and psychodiagnostics, editorial affil. 10 American and fgn. psychol. jours.; mil: 1st lt. US Army 1942-46; Protestant. Res: POB 909 Pebble Beach 93953 Ofc: Dept. Psychology Univ. California Berkeley 94720

GOULIAN, MEHRAN, physician, scientist, educator; b. Dec. 31, 1929, Weehawken, NJ; s. Dicran and Shamiram (Mzrakjian) G.; m. Susan Ann Hook, Aug. 5, 1961; children: Eric, b. 1963; Mark, b. 1964; Jonathan, b. 1968; edn: MD, Columbia Univ., Coll. of Phys. & Surgeons, N.Y. 1954; AB, Columbia Coll., N.Y. 1950; career: fellow in medicine (hematology), Yale Univ. of Med., New Haven, CT 1959-60; res. fellow in medicine (hematology), Mass. General Hosp./Harvard Med. Sch., Cambridge, MA 1960, 1962-63; instr. in medicine, Mass. General Hosp./Harvard Med. Sch., Cambridge, MA 1963-65; fellow in biochemistry, Stanford Univ., Stanford 1965-67; assoc. prof. of medicine, Univ. Chicago, Chicago 1967-70; dir. of hem/onc. Univ. Calif. San Diego, La Jolla 1970-78; prof. of medicine, Univ. Calif. San Diego, La Jolla 1970-; editorial bd., Journal of Biological Chemistry 1983-89, 1990-92; awards: Phi Beta Kappa, Columbia Coll., N.Y. 1950; Alpha Omega Alpha, Columbia Univ. Coll. of Phys. & Surgeons, N.Y. 1953; mem: Am. Soc. of Biochem. & Molecular Biology; Am. Soc. for Clinical Investigation; Am. Soc. of Hematology; Assn. of Am. Phys.; author: 75 pub. works; mil: sr. asst. surgeon, USPHS 1955-57; rec: music; photography; res: 8433 Prestwick Dr., La Jolla 92037. Ofc: Univ. of Calif., San Diego, Dept. of Medicine (0613-G), La Jolla 92093-0613

GRABER-PASTRONE, SYLVIA LUJEAN, criminal defense trial lawyer; b. April 14, 1952, Freeman, S.Dak.; d. Arnold Erwin and Ella May (Bell) Graber; edn: BA, Bethel Coll. 1974; JD, Pepperdine Univ. Sch. Law 1977; admitted St. Bar Calif. 1977. Career: dep. pub. defender Riverside Co. Pub. Defenders Ofc. 1977-; mem: Am. Bar Assn., Calif. Attys. for Criminal Justice, Calif. Pub. Defenders Assn., Calif. St. Bar Assn.; Democrat; Mennonite; rec: speed skating, figure skating, swimming. Ofc: Riverside Public Defenders Office 4200 Orange St Riverside 92325

GRADY, DANIEL BERNARD, real estate company president; b. Nov. 25, 1921, Paris, France; s. Walter Anthony and Jeanne (Precieux) G.; m. Rita Catherine Rhoa, Oct. 11, 1947; children: Michael W. b. 1950, John P. b. 1956; edn: BS, MIT, 1942. Career: v.p. Marnel Co., San Diego 1960-64; v.p. General Devel., Boston, Mass. 1964-66; pres. Sanfric, Inc. 1966-70; pres. Monfric, Inc. 1970-; dir. Housing Conference; award: Man of Yr., Housing Conf. 1979; mem: Nat. Assn. Home Builders (Life dir.), San Diego Comm. Coll. Dist. Bd. Trustees (bd. 1973-90, pres. bd. trustees 1986-90), Kiwanis; author var. magazine articles; mil: lt. cdr., U.S. Navy 1942-46; Republican; R.Cath.; rec: fishing, bridge, travel. Res: 6325 Castejon Dr La Jolla 92037 Ofc: Monfric, Inc. 1915 Morena Blvd San Diego 92110

GRAHAM, ROGER JOHN, professor of journalism and photography; b. Feb. 16, Phila.; s. Wm. K. and Peggy E. (Owens) G.; m. Debbie Kenyon, Dec. 28, 1991; children (by previous marriage): John b. 1968, Robb b. 1972; edn: AA, Los Angeles Valley Coll., 1961; BA, Fresno State Coll., 1962; MA, CSU Fresno, 1967; ABD, UCLA, 1976; Credentials: Elem., Secondary, Junior Coll., Counseling, Comm. Coll. Adminstrn. Career: newspaper staff Turlock Jour. 1962; Fresno Guide 1963; tchr. Riverdale Sch. 1964; Raisin City Sch. 1965; tchr., counselor State Prison, Jamestown 1966; tchr. Kirk Sch. 1966; tchr. trainer UCLA Western Center; prof. journalism and photog. Los Angeles Valley Coll. 1968-, dept. chair Journalism, Photography, and Media Arts, 1990-; vis. prof. Calif. Lutheran Coll. 1974, Pepperdine Univ. 1976, Internat. Edn. Prof., Spain, Summer 1990; awards: NEH Scholar 1981, L.A. Mayors outstanding citizen 1974, UCLA extraordinary svc. 1971, outstanding young men Am. 1971, Nat. Dedication Journalism (1972, 76); mem: Calif. Journalism Assn. Comm. Colls. (pres. 1972), Nat. Comm. Coll. Journalism Assn. (pres. 1978), Sigma Delta Xi, Phi Delta Kappa, Pi Lambda Theta; civic: Am. Legion, YMCA, Hayden's Com. on Schs., Democratic Club Pac. Palisades (pres. 1992); author: Observations on the Mass Media 1976, and articles in The Journalist 1971-76; photo illustrator: The San Fernando Valley 1980; mil: USN 1957; Democrat; rec: hiking, photog. Res: 438 E Rustic Rd Santa Monica 90402 Ofc: LA Valley College 5800 Fulton Ave Van Nuys 91401

GRAMMATER, RUDOLF DIMITRI, retired construction executive; b. Nov. 29, 1910, Detroit; s. D.M. and Amelia (Busse) G.; m. Fredricka W. Cook, Aug. 18, 1943; 1 son, Douglas; edn: Pace Coll. 1928-32; LLB, Lincoln Univ., 1937; CPA, Calif.; admitted bar: Calif. 1938. Career: with Bechtel Corp., San Francisco, 1941-73, treas., v.p., 1955-62, v.p., 1962-71, dir. 1960-73, cons., 1973, v.p., dir. subsidiaries, 1955-71; mem.: Am. Inst. CPAs, Calif. Soc. CPAs, ABA, State Bar of Calif.; club: Menlo CC. Res: 50 Mounds Rd Apt 302 San Mateo 94402

GRANLUND, THOMAS ARTHUR, management consultant; b. Mar. 1, 1951, Spokane, Wash.; s. William Arthur and Louise (Urie) G.; m. Jean MacRae Melvin, May 25, 1974 (div. 1991); edn: BA, Wash. State Univ., Pullman 1973, MBA, Gonzaga Univ., Spokane 1982. Career: 1st lt., B-52 navigator US Air Force, Fairchild AFB, Wash. 1973-78; adminstrv. mgr. Lockheed, Burbank, Ca. 1978-91; mgmt. cons., 1991-; honors: listed Who's Who in West (1992); Who's Who in the World mem. Wash. State Univ. Alumni Assn. (1990-); coauthor 2 screenplays: Identities (1988), Flash (1989). Res: 20924 West Ben Ct Santa Clarita 91350

GRANT, DAVID BROWNE, manufacturing co. executive; b. Apr. 21, 1915, Sharonville, Ohio; s. David J. and Catherine Emma (Browne) G.; m. Elizabeth A. Connolly, May 17, 1942; children: Ann b. 1943, Bonnie b. 1944, David b. 1947, Susan b. 1949, Mary b. 1951, James b. 1953, Patricia b. 1958; edn: BA cum laude, Colgate Univ., 1936; LLB, Yale Univ. Sch. of Law, 1939; admitted Mich. State Bar 1939. Career: atty. Law Offices Eddie Bryant/Vandeveer Haggerty, Detroit 1939-41; sales rep., reg. mgr. Mich., Empire Tool Co., Detroit 1941-42; sales rep. Stone Tool Co., LA 1945-47, pres. 1948-52; owner/pres. Tool Electrolizing Co., LA 1947-50; bd. chmn./pres. Electrolizing, Inc. 1950-; honors: Phi Beta Kappa 1936; mem: Am. Soc. Metals, Am. Rocket Soc., Inst. Aero & Astro., Phi Gamma Delta Frat.; clubs: Jonathan, Newport Beach CC, Braemar CC; mil: lt. USN 1944-47; Republican; Catholic (St. Timothy's Lector Soc., W.L.A. 1964-84, Our Lady Queen of Angels Ch. N.B. Ushers' Soc. 1984-); rec: golf, swim. Res: 3 Northampton Ct Newport Beach 92660 Ofc: Electrolizing, Inc. 1947 Hooper Ave Los Angeles 90011

GRANT, LORRAINE DENISE, journalist; b. Oct. 29, 1965, Vallejo, Calif.; d. Charles Edward and Edna Joann (Morris) Grant; edn: diploma, Vallejo Sr. H.S., Vallejo, Calif.; Solano Coll., Suisun, Calif.; BA in journalism, San Jose State Coll., San Jose, Calif. Career: chief managing ed., Buffalo Soldier Newsmagazine, San Jose, 1990-92; ed., Street Lights, San Jose, 1993-; chief managing ed., Exodus Newsmagazine, San Jose, 1993-; comms. chairperson, NAACP, San Jose, 1992-; rec: writing poetry, reading, cooking, shopping.

GRANT, MARJORIE RUTH, certified public accountant; b. Mar. 4, 1950, Jamaica, West Indies, nat. US cit. 1980; d. Dudley C. and Vera E. (Reynolds) Grant; m. George A. Fuller; edn: BSBA, Roosevelt Univ. 1976, MSA, 1978; lic. C.P.A., Ill., Calif. 1983, Fla. 1989. Career: audit sr. Arthur Andersen & Co., Chgo. 1979-83; CPA/audit supr. Oppenheim, Appel, Dixon & Co., Century City 1984-, Friedman Rosenthal Knell & Co., 1984-85, Coopers & Lybrand, 1986-87, ARCO, Los Angeles 1987-91; owner, prin. M.R. Grant, CPA, 1992-; lectr. in acctg., UCLA 1985, Chgo. State Univ. 1978-83; recipient fund raiser and volunteer awards Free Arts For Abused Children (1984, 85, 91); mem. Am. Inst. CPA, Calif. CPA Soc. (Oil & Gas Com.); civic: Free Arts Clinic for Abused Children (exec. bd., pgm. com.), Grace Comm. Ch. (Sunday Sch. tchr.); rec: photog., tennis. Res: PO Box 6822 Beverly Hills 90212

GRASSO, ROBERT P. (BOBBY), professional musician; b. June 9, 1938, Newark; s. Orazio Ralph and Charlotte (Zywicki) G.; m. Yvonne Roberts, Apr. 10, 1959 (div. 1970); children: Gina Lynn; edn: H.S. grad. Hillside, N.J. 1956. Career: drummer Copa Cabana, N.Y.C. 1968-69; road mgr. Jimmie Rodgers, Los Angeles 1969-74, drummer 1969-, mus. dir. 1974-; v.p. Jimmik Prodns., Santa Monica 1974-76; appeared in film: The World Through the Eyes of Children, 1974; Show of the World, 1970; World Tours, 1973, 75, 84; Big Band Galaxy of Stars U.S. Tour 1988; drummer num. recordings, TV shows; mem. Am. Fedn. Musicians 1958-84; mil: USNR 1956-64; Democrat; Baptist; rec: fishing, boating, golf. Res: 9667 Kewen St Arleta 91331

GRATER, MARGARET KAY, educator; b. July 12, 1942, Cedar City, Utah; d. Russell K. and Evelyn P. Grater; edn: BA, CSU Long Beach 1966; MA, CSU Fresno 1972; PhD, Univ. So. Carolina, 1975. Career: tchr. St. Mary's Jr. H.S., Augusta, Ga 1966-67, Adult Edn. Ctr., Camp Darby, Italy 1967, Woodlake H.S., Woodlake, Calif. 1968-69; staff devel. coord. Fresno Unif. Sch. Dist. 1971-73, 1975, instr., coord. Model Schs. Proj., Univ. S. Carolina 1973-75; prin. Norwalk, La Mirada Unif. Sch. Dist. 1975-80; coord. L.A. Co. Ednl. Resource Consortium (LACERC), L.A. Co. Supt. of Schs. Ofc., Downey 1980-84; cons., Mgmt. Devel. Ctr., L.A. Co. Ofc. of Edn. 1984-92; mgmt. cons. Center for District Leadership, 1992-; pres. Grater & Assocs., Leaders in Excellence Cons. Firm 1986-; instr. sch. adminstrn., CSU Fullerton Grad. Sch. 1980-; instr. ext. classes CSU Fresno, Pepperdine Univ., UC Santa Cruz 1968-78; cons. var. states, dists. 1968-; honors: merit awards, Assn. of Calif. Sch. Adminstrs., Norwalk La Mirada Adminstrn. Assn., Am. Red Cross/Europe 10-Year Svc. Award; mem: CSU Fullerton Educ. Adminstrn. Adv. Bd. 1980-, Assn. of Calif. Sch. Adminstrs. (reg. v.p. 1980-82, reg. dir. 82-85, profl. stds. chair 85-) ALA-COSA (charter v.p. pgms. 1982-, pres. 1984, pres. elect 1992), Norwalk La Mirada Adminstrn. Assn. (pres. 1978-79), L.A. C.of C. (Edn. Com. 1980-), Assn. of Supvn. & Curriculum Devel. 1977-, Phi Delta Kappa (CSUF chpt. v.p. mem. 1986-87), CSUF Partnership Acad. 1982-, La Mirada Coord. Council (parliamentarian 1975-80), Dist. PTA 1975-80; co-author Task Force Report to Calif. Commn. for Tchr. Licensing (1981), Tchr. Preservice & Inservice (1982); Presbyterian; rec: tennis, music, art, writing. Res: 918 Magnolia Ave Placentia 92670 Ofc: Los Angeles Supt. o Schools, 9300 Imperial Hwy Downey 90242

GRAY, IONE YOUNG, lawyer, author, lecturer; b. June 15, 1947, Fort Worth, Tx.; d. Earle Francis and Ione Caddie (Young) Gray; edn: BA, Rice Univ., 1968; JD, Columbia Univ., 1971; admitted bar: Ga., Ill., Calif.; lic. R.E. Broker, Calif. 1976. Career: atty. Paul Weiss Rifkind Wharton & Garrison, NYC 1971; Hansell Post Brandon & Dorsey, Atlanta 1973; legal counsel (highest ranking woman) Caterpillar Tractor Co., Peoria, Ill. 1974; division counsel (highest ranking woman) Whittaker Corp., Los Angeles 1975; division counsel (highest ranking woman) The Colwell Co., L.A. 1976; atty. Law Offices of Ione Young Gray, L.A. 1977-; author: Buy Property Without Cash (1980), Foreclosure Purchasing For Profit (1982), Riches in R.E.O. Investing (1986); guest lectr. UCLA Business Sch., 1982-; show host (t.v.) Riches in Real Estate, 1983-, (radio) Profits in Real Estate, 1984-; mem. State Bar Assns. Ga., Ill., Calif., Women in Business (L.A.). Ofc: 2040 Ave of the Stars Ste 400 Los Angeles 90067

GRAY, JAN CHARLES, lawyer, executive; b. June 15, 1947, Des Moines, Iowa; s. Charles Donald and Mary C. Gray; m. Anita Marie Ringwald, June 6, 1987; children: Charles Jan b. Feb. 3, 1990; BA econ., UC Berkeley 1969; JD, Harvard Law Sch. 1972; MBA, Pepperdine Univ. 1986; admitted bar Calif. 1972, lic. R.E. broker 1973. Career: atty., assoc. Halstead, Baker & Sterling, L.A. 1972-75; senior v.p., gen. counsel and secty. Ralphs Grocery Co., L.A. 1975-; real estate broker, L.A. 1973-; owner American Presidents Resorts, opr.: All American Inn: Custer, American Presidents Cabins & Camp, American Presidents Motel, Custer Motel, French Creek Motel, Custer, S.Dak., All American: Glenrock, Glenrock Motel, Glenrock, Wyo., Big Bear Cabins: Lakeside, Big Bear, Calif.; pres. and c.o.o. Mt. Rushmore Bdcstg. Inc., Radio Station KFCR, Custer, S.Dak.; judge pro tem L.A. Municipal Ct. 1977-; instr. bus. UCLA 1976-, MBA pgm. Pepperdine Univ. 1985-; arbitrator, Am. Arb. Assn., 1977-; honors: Phi Beta Kappa, recipient So. Calif. Grocers Assn. award for outstanding contbns. to food industry 1982, Cal-Nev Soft Drink Assn. appreciation award for No on 11 campaign 1983; civic bds: South Bay Univ. Coll. Law, (bd. trustees 1978-79), Southwestern Univ. Sch. of Law (bd. vis. 1983-), L.A. County Pvt. Industry Council (1982-, exec. com. 1984-, chmn. econ. devel. task force 1986-, chair mktg. com. 1991-), M.L.K. Jr. Gen. Hosp. Auth. 1984-, Aviation Commn. (1986-92, chair 1990-91), L.A. Crime Prevention Advy. Council 1986-, Angelus Plaza Advy. Bd. 1983-85, RecyCAL of So. Calif. (bd. dirs. 1983-90), Santa Monica Hosp. (bd. trustees 1986-91; advy. bd. 1991-); mem. L.A. Co. Democratic Central Com. 1980-90, del. Dem. Nat. Conv. 1980; mem: ABA, Calif. Bar Assn. (exec. com. 1976-81), L.A. Co. Bar Assn. (bd. trustees 1991-, exec. com. Corp Law Depts. Sect. 1975-76, 79-, chair 1989-90, exec. com. Barristers Sect. 1974-75, 79-81), San Fernando Valley Bar Assn. (chmn. Real Prop. Sect. 1975-77), L.A. Pub. Affairs Officers Assn., L.A. World Affairs Council, Calif. Retailers Assn. (supermarket com. 1977-), Food Mktg. Inst. (govt. relations com., govt affairs council, 1977-), So. Calif. Business Assn. (chair 1991-, bd. 1981-, exec. com. 1982-, sec. 1986-), Town Hall Calif., Univ.

Calif. Alumni Assn., Ephebian Soc.; clubs: L.A. Athletic, Harvard of So. Calif.; contbg. author: Life or Death: Who Controls? (Springer Pub. 1976); legal jour. articles; mil: USAR; R.Cath.; rec: tennis, travel. Res: PO Box 407 Beverly Hills 90213 Ofc: Ralphs Grocery Co. PO Box 54143 Los Angeles 90054

GRAY, ROBERT M., professor of electrical engineering; b. Nov. 1, 1943, San Diego; s. Augustine Heard and Elizabeth Dubois (Jordan) G.; m. Arlene Francis Ericson; children: Timothy b. 1965, Lori b. 1967; edn: BS, MS, Mass. Inst. Tech., 1966; PhD, USC, 1969. Career: prof. elec. engring. Stanford Univ., 1969-, dir. Information Systems Laboratory 1981-87; awards: 1976 paper prize IEEE Info. Theory Gp. 1976, 1983 ASSP Sr. Award IEEE ASSP Soc. 1984, IEEE Centennial Medal 1984; Fellow Inst. of Electrical & Electronics Engrs. (1980, mem. 1969-), IEEE Info. Theory Gp. (bd. govs. 1974-80, 84-87, editor in chief IEEE Transactions in Info. Theory 1980-83, co-chair IEEE Internat. Symp. on Information Theory, Sa Antonio, Tx. 1993), Inst. of Math. Statistics (1974-, fellow 1992-), AAAS 1972-, Classification Soc. of N.Am. 1989-, Am. Math. Soc. 1990-; civic: La Honda Fire Brigade (fireman 1970-80, pres. 71-72); coauthor: Random Processes (1986), Vector Quantization & Signal Compression (1992), author: Probability, Random Processes, and Ergodic Properties (1988), Source Coding Theory (1990), Entropy and Info. Theory (1990), 80+ tech. articles; rec: hiking, guilded age history. Ofc: E.E. Dept. Stanford Univ. 127 Durand Stanford 94305-4055

GREEN, CECIL NEIL, state legislator; b. Sept. 13, 1924, Riverside; s. James V. and Hearthia B. (Musgrove) G.; m. Mary Ellen, Jan. 10, 1945 (dec.); m. 2d. Mary D., Apr. 29, 1961; dau. Janyce Smith; edn: courses Long Beach St. Coll. Career: carpenter, constrn. contractor, 1941-50; bus. owner Sport Muffler Shops, Norwalk 1952-75; apptd. commr. Norwalk Planning Commn., 1971-74; planning & zoning splst. Fotomat Corp. Western States, 1976-83; planning/zoning cons. City of Norwalk 1983-87; elected Norwalk City Council 1974-87 (mayor 1976-77, 81-82, 84-85), elected Calif. State Senate, 1987-; former coms: L.A. Co. Narcotics & Dangerous Drugs Commn. (v. chmn.), Calif. Contract Cities Assn. (L.A.Co. pres. 1979), Jt. Powers Ins. Auth. (L.A. Co. pres. 1986-87); honors: mayor of yr. WeTIP Calif. 1976, El Gran Matador, Calif. Contract Cities Assn.; mem: Masons, Scottish Rites, Eastern Star, Shriners, League of United Latin Am. Citizens, Rotary (Paul Harris Fellow), BPOE (Bellflower Exalted Ruler 1961-62), VFW (life), Am. Legion, Moose; mil: chief pharm. mate USN 1942-45, 50-52, WWII, Korea; Democrat; Methodist; rec: fishing, hunting, camping, flying (lic. multi-engine, land & sea, instrument, comml. & flt. instr.). Ofc: State Capitol Rm 2054 Sacramento 95814

GREEN, HILTON A., motion picture producer; b. Mar. 3, 1929, Hollywood; s. Alfred E. and Vivian (Reed) G.; m. Helen Harker, June 6, 1952; children: Wendolyn b. 1954, Bradley b. 1958, Pamela b. 1960; edn: BS, USC, 1952. Career: executive v.p. Universal City Studios, 1968-82; producer H & H Green Productions, Pasadena 1982-; recipient USC Merit Award, L.A. 1982; mem. USC Bd. trustees 1990-; mem. Gen. Alumni Assn. USC (pres. 1991-92); club: Annandale Golf (Pasadena); mil: cpl. US Army 1952-54; Republican; R.Cath.; rec: golf, tennis. Res: 3625 Locksley Dr Pasadena 91107

GREENBERG, MYRON SILVER, lawyer; b. Oct. 17, 1945, Los Angeles; s. Earl W. and Geri (Silver) G.; m. Shlomit Gross, Aug. 23, 1985; children: David b. 1972, Amy b. 1975, Sophie b. 1989, Benjamin b. 1992; edn: BS in bus. adm., UCLA 1967, JD, 1970; admitted Calif. State Bar 1971; CPA, Calif. 1972; certified tax splst., Calif. Bd. Legal Spec. 1977; admitted to US Dist. Ct. (Central) Calif. 1971, US Tax Ct. 1978. Career: staff acct. Touche Ross & Co., Los Angeles 1970-71; assoc. Kaplan, Livingston, Goodwin, Berkowitz & Selvin, Beverly Hills 1971-74; ptnr. Dinkelspiel, Pelavin, Steefel & Levitt, S.F. 1975-80; ptnr. Steefel, Levitt & Weiss, S.F. 1981-82; atty. prin., Larkspur 1982-; profl. lectr. Golden Gate Univ.; lectr. UC Berkeley Ext. 1989-, advy. bd. Certificate Pgm. in Personal Financial Planning, UCB Ext. 1991-; planning com. Real Estate Tax Inst., Calif. Cont. Edn. of the Bar (CEB); honors: bd. editors UCLA Law Review; mem: ABA, Calif. Bar Assn., Marin County Bar Assn., Am. Inst. CPAs; civic: Am. Heart Assn. (bd. dirs., pres. Marin County chpt. 1983-90), Am. Technion Soc. (bd. dirs. No. Calif. chpt.), Larkspur C.of C. (bd. dirs.), San Anselmo Planning Commn. 1976-77, Marin Opera (bd. dirs. 1989-90); author: California Attorney's Guide to Professional Corporations,1977, 1979; Democrat; Jewish. Ofc: Myron S. Greenberg, APC, 700 Larkspur Landing Circle Ste 205 Larkspur 94939

GREENHALL, CHARLES AUGUST, mathematician; b. May 5, 1939, N.Y.C.; s. A Frank and Miriam (Housman) G.; edn: BA, Pomona Coll., 1961; PhD, Caltech, 1966. Career: research assoc. Jet Propulsion Lab., Pasadena 1966-68; asst. prof. Univ. So. Calif., 1968-73; consultant, contr. Jet Propulsion Lab., 1973-77, mem. tech. staff, 1977-; awards: NASA monetary award 1990; mem. Am. Math. Soc., Math. Assn. of Am., Soc. for Indsl. and Applied Math., Inst. of Electrical and Electronic Engrs.; inventor: Frequency Stability Measurement (pat. 1989); Republican; Res: 1836 Hanscom Dr South Pasadena 91030 Ofc: Jet Propulsion Laboratory, 298-100, 4800 Oak Grove Dr Pasadena 91109

GREENSPAN, BERNARD, professor of mathematics emeritus; b. Dec. 19, 1914, N.Y., N.Y.; s. Harry and Yetta (Siegel) G.; m. Beatrice Meltzer, Aug. 26, 1939; children: Valerie b. 1942, Ellen b. 1949; edn: BS (cum laude), Brooklyn Coll., Brooklyn, NY 1935; MA, Brooklyn Coll. 1936; postgrad. work, Columbia Univ. 1936-38; UC Berkeley 1958-59, Rensselaer Poly. 1960; PhD, Rutgers Univ., New Brunswick, N.J. 1958. Career: instr. math., Brooklyn Coll. 1935-44; instr. math., Polytechnic Inst., Brooklyn, NY 1943-44; instr. math., Drew Univ., Madison, N.J. 1944-47, asst. prof. math. 1947-58, assoc. prof. math. 1958-59, prof. math. 1959-81 (chmn. 1959-75), prof. Emeritus 1981-; lectr. & cons., Bell Telephone Labs., Whippany, N.J. 1953-58; dir. Inservice Math. Inst., NSF, Drew Univ. 1961-75; dir. Math. Summer Inst., NSF, Drew Univ. 1962-74; reader (table leader 1972), Advanced Placement Exams, Ednl. Testing Svc., Princeton, N.J. 1966-72; vis. prof., Univ. of Santa Clara 1961; vis. prof., Rutgers Univ. 1971; awards: medalist, math., Brooklyn Coll., Brooklyn, NY 1935, 36; NSF Fellowship, UC Berkeley 1958-59; mem: Sigma Xi, Pi Mu Epsilon, Sigma Phi; mem: Am. Math. Soc. 1961-; Math. Assn. of Am. (past chmn N.J. Section) 1961-; Am. Assn. of Univ. Professors 1947-81; Math. Teachers of N.J. 1947-81; Math. Assn. of Am., No. Calif. Section 1981-; author: mimeographed notes in the Theory of Equations, 1947; article in profl. jour., 1959; over 12 book reviews; Independent; rec: bridge, chess. Res: 9164 Tangerine St. San Ramon 94583

GREER, EDWARD FRANK, physician, surgeon; b. July 28, 1922, Vandalia, Ill.; s. Frank and Lila (Mabry) G.; m. Mary Ilene Jacques, Mar. 10, 1947; children: Cynthia b. 1948, Jackie b. 1949, Elaine b. 1951, Susan b. 1953 (dec.), Jonathan b. 1955, Timothy b. 1957, Edward b. 1959, Patricia b. 1961; edn: BS, Northwestern Univ. 1943; MB , 1946; MD, 1947; lic. physician and surgeon Calif. 1950. Career: physician, surgeon, Vandalia, Ill. 1947-49; Edward Greer Hosp., Robinson, Ill. 1949-57; gen. surgical resident Hahnermann Hosp., Phila. Pa. 1957-59; Abington Meml. Hosp., Abington, Pa. 1959-61; physician, surgeon Palo Alto Stanford Med. Center, Stanford 1961-63; preceptorship gen. surgery Meml. Hosp., Pawtucket, R.I. 1963-64; pres. Los Angeles Co. Med. Assn., surgical sect. 1975; mem: Duarte Rotary; author: Christmas carol pub. 1984; article pub. Medical Hypotheses 1990; mil: 1st lt. AUS 1943-47; Christian; rec: golf, horticulture. Res: 840 Mackey Way Fallbrook

GREGO, PETER, professor of theatre arts, director; b. May 29, 1949, Pittsburgh, Pa.; s. William Joseph, Sr. and Veronica Margaret (Zamulovich) G.; m. Barbara Cavalier, May 1977 (div. Aug. 1991); edn: BFA, Carnegie Mellon Univ., 1972, MFA, 1973. Career: instr. Penn State Univ., New Kensington, Pa. 1973-76; instr., coord. acting pgm. Florida Sch. of Arts, Palatka, Fla. 1976-78; prof. CSU Bakersfield, 1978-84, CSU Northridge, 1984-; director: International City Theatre, Los Angeles 1988-92, Laguna Playhouse 1991, Producers Club, NY, NY 1991, Santa Paula (Calif.) Theatre 1990; awards: Drama-Logue Award, L.A. 1990, best play Arrow Rock Lyceum Theatre, Arrow Rock, Mo. 1991; mem.: Soc. of Stage Dirs. & Choreographers 1988-, Dramatists Guild 1991-; author (play): From Dust Thou Art (1983). Res: 5018 Cartwright Ave North Hollywood 91601

GREGORY, CALVIN LUTHER, insurance agent, educator, counselor; b. Jan. 11, 1942, Bronx, NY; s. Jacob and Ruth (Cherchian) G.; m. Rachel Anna Carver, Feb. 14, 1970, div. 1977; 2 daus: Debby Lynn, Trixy Sue; m. 2d. Carla Deaver, June 30, 1979; edn: AA, L.A. City Coll.; BA, CSU Los Angeles 1964; M.Div., Fuller Theol. Sem. 1968; M.Re.Edn., Southwestern Sem. 1969; D.D., Otay Mesa Coll. San Diego 1982; PhD in religion, Universal Life Ch., Inc. 1982; Ordained minister Am. Baptist Conv. L.A. 1970; real estate lic., Calif. 1969; Notary Public, Calif. 1969. Career: USAF Chaplain, Edwards AFB 1970; pastor First Baptist Ch., Boron, CA 1971; ins. agent Prudential Life Ins. Co., Ventura 1972; mgr. Prudential Ins. Co., Thousand Oaks 1973; casualty ins. agent Allstate Ins. Co., Thousand Oaks 1974; pres. Ins. Agcy. Placement Svc., Thousand Oaks 1975-; counselor Wilshire Presbyterian Ch., Los Angeles, fmr. hd. youth minister, 1974; tchr. polit. sci. Maranatha High Sch., Rosemead; investor/owner apt. bldgs. and real property 1974-; profl. awards: WLRT and Pres.'s citation Prudential 1972, Top-20 sales Southwestern Co. 1967; mem. Forensic Club CSULA 1963, Apartment Assn. L.A. 1975-; Republican; rec: travel, video tapes, jogging. Res: 3307 Big Cloud Circle Thousand Oaks 91360 Ofc: Insurance Agency Placement Service, POB 4407 Thousand Oaks 91359

GRIFFIN, DEBRA KATHLEEN, senior systems analyst; b. Feb. 25, 1954, Corona; d. Laurence Ronald and Mary Louise (Buckley) Seaward; m. William Kirk Griffin, Mar. 24, 1973; 1 son Jason Ryan b. 1978; edn: AA in bus. (4.0, honors), Diablo Valley Coll., 1990; BS in info. sys. mgmt. (3.86 g.p.a., dean's list), Univ. San Francisco, 1991; Carnegie Mellon Univ. Adv. Technology Inst. (4.0), 1993. Career: staff clk. Pacific Telephone, Los Angeles, 1973-76, service rep., 1976-80, business office mgr. 1980-83; planner Pacific Bell, San Ramon, 1983-86, assoc. systems analyst 1986-88, senior systems analyst 1988-, cons. tchr. 1991-; awards: Pacific Bell-Ebbon's Eagle 1982, Quality Circle 1986-89, Quality Excellence Award 1989; civic: Pacific Choral Co. (exec.v.p. 1990-), Crescenta Valley Alumni Chorale (pres. 1979-83), Canyon Creek Little League San Ramon (chief scorekeeper 1984-91); author/prod. musical show script: America -A Family Musical, 1991; performances (voice & dance): Circle Star Theater (San Carlos), Oakland Coliseum, Candlestick Park (S.F.), Oakland

Paramount Theater, Blackhawk Plaza, Disneyland; Republican; Prot.; rec: music - voice/piano, baseball. Ofc: Pacific Bell 2600 Camino Ramon MC 3E700B San Ramon 94583

GRIFFIN, JAMES CLYDE, trucker, political activist; b. Oct. 1, 1937, Tenn.; s. Dewey Sampson and Osa Nelson (Akers) G.; div.; 3 daus.; Career: with Milne Truck Lines, Inc. Whittier, 28 years, now employee Consolidated Freightway, Mira Loma; records 3,200,000+ miles of accident free driving; awards: Truck Driving Roadeos: Heavy-Semi: Calif. State Roadeo 1st Place (1981, 83, 89), L.A. Area Roadeo 1st Place (1978, 79, 81, 82, 83, 89); Calif. Trucking Assn. driver of mo. (7/81, 8/83), KLAC Radio trucker of week (4/74), appreciation Norwalk Sr. Citizens Ctr.; nominated Hiway Goodwill Amb. Road Team Am. Trucking Assn. 1987, "Hiway Heroes" Goodyear Tire & Rubber Co. 1988, Citizen of Yr. Norwalk (6t nominee 1975-80); recipient nat. t.v. publicity as a spokesman for Indep. truckers during fuel shortage of 1973; listed Who's Who in West 1985, Personalities of Am. 1985, Internat. Who's Who of Intellectuals (9th ed.), Almanac -Information Please (1990, 91, 92), others; civic: Norwalk Citizens Action Council (3-term chmn. 6 yrs.), Assem. Bruce Young Advy. Panel (past), Calif. Dept. Motor Vehicles Advy. Panel 1976-80; mem: Norwalk C.of C., Jurupa C.of C., Moose, Elks, Norwalk Rod & Gun Club, Nat. Rifle Assn; American Indep. Party: elected state chmn. 1993-94, st. exec. com., past chmn. cent. com., candidate for Congress 33rd C.D. 1974, cand. for US Senate 1980, cand. for gov. Calif. 1982, cand. for lt. gov. Calif. 1986, nat. cand. for US Pres. 1988; rec: golf, politics, truck roadeos. Res: 5069 Bain St Mira Loma 91752

GRIFFIN, JAMES RAY, aerospace systems engineer; b. Mar. 30, 1943, Vancouver, Wash.; s. William and Esther (Joy) G.; m. Deanna Turek, No 23, 1962; children: Scott b. 1963 (dec. 1984), JoAnn b. 1968, Paul b. 1974, Ellen b. 1979; edn: AA, Riverside City Coll., 1975; BS in E.E., CSU-Long Beach, 1990. Career: tech. Rockwell Internat., Anaheim 1962-69; assoc. test engr. Calif. Computer Products, Anaheim 1969-77; R & D tech. McDonnell Douglas Corp., Long Beach 1977-, electrical engr., data acquisition systems engring. for flt. test aircraft (MD11), 1988-;Democrat; rec: travel, music, camping. Res: 1142 Azalea Circle Corona 91720 Ofc: McDonnell Douglas Corp. 3855 Lakewood Blvd Long Beach 90846

GRIFFIN, MERV E(DWARD), television performer/producer, executive; b. July 6, 1925, San Mateo; s. Merv E., Sr. and Rita Elizabeth (Robinson) G.; m. Julann Elizabeth Wright, May 18, 1958, div. 1976; children: Anthony b. 1959. Career: performer Merv Griffin Show radio sta. KFRC, San Francisco 1945-48; vocalist Freddy Martin's Orch., 1948-52; contract player, star So This is Love, Warner Bros., 1953-55; TV master of ceremonies Game Shows 1958-62, Merv Griffin Show, NBC-TV, 1962-63, Westinghouse Bdcstg. Co., 1965-69, CBS-TV, 1969-72, Metro Media Prodns., syndicated TV, 1972-86; CEO Merv Griffin Ents. (unit of Coca-Cola): prod. Jeopardy!, Wheel of Fortune, Dance Fever; owner 4 radio stas. 1965-, Teleview Racing Patrol Inc., Miami, Fla.; honors: 10 Emmy awards, Medal of Paris; mem. Bohemian Club (SF).

GRIFFITH, J. GORDON, real estate executive; b. Dec. 16, 1934, Council Bluffs, Iowa; s. Frank L. and Geneva (Seitz) G.; children: Stephen J. b. 1950, Jessica Geneva b. 1979; edn: BS, Iowa State Univ., 1956. Career: pres. Centurion Real Estate and Investment Corp., Costa Mesa 1973-; dir. Bio-Trends Internat., Sacto. 1983-; mem.: Building INd. Assn. 1988-; mil: 2d lt. USAF 1954-55; Republican; Prot.; rec: golf, skiing. Ofc: Centurion R.E. & Investment Corp. 575 Anton Blvd 3d Fl Costa Mesa 92626

GRIFFITH, JOHN CHADWICK, JR., lawyer; b. Bern, Switz.; s. John Chadwick and Jane Ann (Berg) G.; edn: BA, Boston Univ., 1980; JD, Univ. Va., 1985, MA, 1990; admitted bar: Ariz. 1986, Calif. 1988. Career: atty., assoc. Winston & Strawn, Phoenix, Az. 1985-88; Graham & James, Los Angeles 1988-; honors: editor Va. Jour. Internat. Law (1984-85), Pi Sigma Alpha, Psi Chi, Phi Theta Kappa; mem: ABA, Ariz. State Bar Assn., Calif. State Bar Assn. Ofc: Graham & James 801 S Figueroa Ste 1400 Los Angeles 90017

GRIMES, RITA CHARLOTTE, publisher; b. May 29, 1923, San Francisco; d. Francesco Vincenzo and Charlotte (Philipsborn) Forzano; m. Philip Stanford Grimes, Dec. 26, 1947; children: Christine Marie b. 1952, Sandra Louise b. 1954; edn: grad., Riverside Bus. Coll. 1941; student, UCLA 1944-45; UC Berkeley 1946-47; Schaefer Sch. of Design, San Francisco 1947. mgr. personal/fin. affairs for retired naval ofcr., 1978; exec. dir. The Occidental Pub. Co., 1978; coord. The American Lives Endowment, 1980; exec. secty. for dir. Health Orgn. Bus. Systems, 1981; cons. Linwood Realty and Fin. Services, 1982; owner/dir. Medical Records Pub. Co., Stanford 1983-, founder/dir. Portola Valley Community Center, publish, design and edit Portola Valley Sch. Dist. newspaper; awards: for "Action in Education" Nat. Sch. Boards Assn., Calif. Gubnatl. Proclamation dedicating October as "Talk About Prescription Month" 1990 on behalf of the Nat. Council on Patient Information and Edn. 1990; mem: Internat. Union for Health Edn. (del. XIII World Conf. on Health Edn., Houston, Tex. 1988, Certified participant Inter-Am. Symp. on Health Edn., Rio De Janiero 1990, Nat. Council on Patient Info. and Edn. (S.F. Health Dept. rep. to Calif. Medication Edn. Coalition & Seniors Regional Pgm., Sacto. 1988); active

P.V. PTA (dir.), No. Calif. Kidney Found. (dir.), Palo Alto Acad. of Art (dir.), KRON-TV Viewer Advy. Council 1985-, TV panelist on prescription drugs KCRA-Sacto. 1988; publs: The Medical and Dental Record Book (listed in Directory of Prescription Drug Info. & Edn. Pgms. & Resources of the Nat. Council on Patient Infor. & Edn., also a permanent item in NCPIE's Food & Drug Adminstrn. Inventory of Resources); research: Cinabar in Calif., mineral water domestic and fgn., alcohol and drug rehab.; Democrat; R.Cath.; rec: edn., travel, horses, design. Res: 1301 Crossgates Ln Almaden Valley San Jose 95120 Ofc: Medical Records Publishing Co. PO Box 8545 Stanford 94309-8545

GRIMM, LUCIEEN CHARLOTTE, fashion designer; b. Apr. 28, 1921, Berlin, Ger.; nat. USA 1962; d. Fritz George and Marie Charlotte (Mietz) Henschel; edn: attended Victoria Oberlyzeum (Berlin) 1931-36, stu. Coll. Fashion Design (Ger.) 1936-69. Career: fashion designer, Germany, 1940-52; fashion designer of Antiguelaces, bridal gowns, dresses, Los Angeles 1952-, business owner, Lucieen, L.A.; honors: listed as Fashion Designer of Berlin, 1952; mem. Art Guild (Berlin); Prot. Res: 752 S Wilton Place Apt 1 Los Angeles 90005 Ofc: Lucieen, 225 N Larchmont Blvd Los Angeles 90004

GRISSOM, LEE ALAN, association executive; b. Sept. 7, 1942, Pensacola, Fla.; s. Levi Aaron and Virginia Sue (Olinger) G.; m. Sharon Kay Hasty, May 14, 1966; children: David, Jonathan, Matthew, Andrew; edn: BA pub. adminstrn., San Diego St. Univ. 1965; MA city planning, 1971. Career: sr. res. assoc. Western Behavioral Scis. Inst., La Jolla 1965-73; mgr. planning div. Greater San Diego C.of C., 1973-74, gen. mgr. 1974-75, pres. and chief ops. ofcr. 1975-; mem. bd. dirs. Econ. Devel. Corp. San Diego 1976; bd. trustees Cal State Univ. 1984-90; awards: SDSU Alumnus of Yr. 1987, Jaycees Outstanding Young Man, San Diego 1976, Calif. 1977, U.S. 1978; club: San Diego Rotary; contbr. 50+ articles and research papers (1965-73); mil: USAR; Republican; rec: jogging. Ofc: 402 W Broadway Ste 1000 San Diego 92101

GROFER, TED (EDWARD JOSEPH), marketing executive, publisher; b. Sept. 20, 1934, Cinti.; s. Edward Joseph and Margaret Mary (McGinley) G.; m. Mary Janet Procissi, Aug. 18, 1962; children: Catherine Mary, Laura Marie, Daniel McGinley; edn: BA, Univ. Cincinnati, 1957; MA, Univ. Iowa, 1959; computer mgmt., National Univ., San Diego 1987. Career: asst. dir. pub. relations Champion Paper, Hamilton, Oh. 1959-61; mktg. dir. The Jam Handy Org., Detroit, Mich. 1961-69; dir. of promo. & res. The Detroit News,1969-74; v.p and publ. The Desert Sun, Palm Springs 1974-80; pres. Ted Grofer Associates, 1980-88; publisher Desert Community Newspapers, Palm Desert 1981-85; gen. ptnr. The Graphic Arts Ctr., Cathedral City 1985-; pres. TGA Publishing, Palm Springs 1989-; exec. director Palm Springs Main Street org., 1990-92, Palm Springs NOW, 1990-92; Downtown Bus. Improvement Dist. P.S., 1990-92; v.p. marketing The Inland Empire Bus. Journal 1993-; exec. com. Catholic Charities of Diocese San Bernardino 1991-; mem. Calif. Main Street 1990-; clubs: Rotary P.S. (Sun-Up, editor 1987-89, social chair 1990-92), The Springs (Rancho Mirage), The Palm Springs (P.S.), Pi Kappa Alpha Frat., Memphis, Tenn. (nat. v.p. 1982-86); publs: res. newspaper mkt. analysis (1980-89), mktg. presentation "The Palm Springs ADI" (1992); Republican; R.Cath. (parish coun. 1988-); rec: rv-ing, dancing, computers. Res: 584 Fern Canyon Palm Springs 92264 Ofc: Palm Springs Main Street 123 N Palm Canyon (193) Palm Springs 92262

GROLLMAN, JULIUS HARRY, JR., cardiovascular and interventional radiologist; b. Nov. 26, 1934, Los Angeles; s. Julius Harry and Alice Carolyn (Greenlee) G.; m. Alexa, March 20, 1959; children: Carolyn b. 1960, David b. 1962, Elizabeth b. 1965; edn: BA, Occidental Coll. L.A.; MD, UCLA; cert. Am. Bd. Radiology 1965; Career: chief cardiovascular radiology Walter Reed Army Hosp., Wash. D.C. 1965-67; to prof. Dept. Radiological Sci., UCLA Sch. of Medicine, 1967-78; chief cardiovascular radiology Little Company of Mary Hosp., Torrance 1978-; cons. VA Hosp. L.A. 1967-; Walter Reed Army Inst. Pathology, Wash. D.C. 1965-67; clin. prof. radiology UCLA 1978-; mem: Am. Coll. Radiology (fellow), We. Angiography Soc. (pres. 1977), N. Am. Soc. Cardiac Imaging (pres. 1991-92), Soc. Cardiac Angiography (fellow), Soc. Cardiovascular and Interventional Radiology (fellow), RSNA, AMA, ARRS, STR, LARS, CRS; civic: Los Angeles Mandolin Orch.; author 6 med. book chapters, 90+ research papers 1964-; mil: capt. USAR 1965-67 Army Commendn. medal; Republican; Presbyterian; rec: music, sailing, hunting; res: 448 27th St Manhattan Beach 90266; ofc: Little Company of Mary Hospital, 4101 Torrance Blvd Torrance 90503

GRONSKE, MYRTLE J., shopping center owner; b. Jan. 27, 1927, Sedro Wooley, Wash.; d. Ole P. and Anna (Howen) Gronske. Career: bookkeeper Sanford Nash, Tacoma, Wash. 1946-48; Grendahls Acctg. Services, 1948-50; hd. acctg. dept. Forrester Realty & Mortgage Co., 1950-68; owner Oakwood Motor Lodge, and The Flame Restaurant, Tacoma 1968-76; owner The Chinowth House Restaurant, Visalia 1978-, also Crepe Myrtle Cottages, 1985-, 1/2 owner Mineral King Plaza Shopping Center, Visalia 1984-, 1/2 owner in redevel. proj. The Old Bakery Plaza 1988-; honors: rec'd City of Visalia Beautification awards for The Chinowth House (1985, 1986, 1990) and The Mineral King Plaza Shopping Center (1986, 1990); Republican; Prot. Res: 700 S Linwood Ave Visalia 93277 Ofc: The Chinowth House 505 S Chinowth Rd Visalia 93277

GROSSER, MORTON, consultant, author; b. Dec. 25, 1931, Phila.; s. Albert Jay and Esther (Mendelstein) G.; m. Janet Zachs, June 28, 1953; son, Adam b. 1961; edn: BS, M.I.T., 1953, MS, 1954; PhD, Stanford Univ., 1961; reg. rep., fin. prin. NASD 1985; Career: design engr. Clevite Transistor, Waltham, Mass. 1955-57; dir. of publication Boeing Corp., Seattle 1964-65; mng. dir. L.H. Alton & Co., San Francisco 1984-87; mgmt. and technology cons./ prin., Menlo Park 1966-83, 87-; dir: L.H. Alton & Co. 1984-87, I-Flow Corp., Torrance 1985-87; awards: Coats & Clark Fellow, M.I.T. 1954, Ford Found. fellow Stanford Univ.1960, NIH postdoctoral fellow UCLA Med. Ctr. 1961-62, Stegner Creative Writing fellow Stanford 1963-64, Commonwealth Club Medal for Literary Excellence 1991; mem: Am. Inst. Aero. & Astro., Am. Soc. Mech. Engrs., Assn. for Computing Machinery, Soc. of Automotive Engrs., The Authors Guild, Astronomical Soc. of the Pacific; author 7 books: The Discovery of Neptune 1962, The Hobby Shop 1967, The Snake Horn 1973 novel, Diesel: The Man & The Engine 1978, Gossamer Odyssey (1981), On Gossamer Wings 1982, The Fabulous Fifty 1990 novel; contbr. articles, fiction and poetry in The Atlantic, Harper's, Holidays, Industrial Design, Natural History, The New Yorker, The Sat. Evening Post, Stanford Mag., Technology Rev., The Whole Earth Catalog, The Writer 1964-; jour. articles in Artibus Asiae, Isis, J. of Asian Studies, Artificial Organs, J. of the Astronomical Soc. of The Pacific, J. of the Franklin Inst., J. of Rehabilitation Research and Devel., Proc. of the Plastic Surg. Research Coun. Restorative Neurology & Neuroscience 1963-; ed. tech. jour. Boeing Sci. Labs. Rev. 1964-65; patentee (3), co-inventor Microelectronic Axon Processor (pat. 1986); Presbyterian; rec: tennis, wt. tng., model bldg; ofc: MG Consulting, 1016 Lemon St Menlo Park 94025

GROSSMAN, REGINA VALDEZ, computer systems analyst, psychotherapist; b. Apr. 29, 1946, Oakland; d. Robert K. and Louisa (Valdez) Mitchell; m. Dr. Stephen Grossman, July 26, 1972; edn: MSW, UC Berkeley 1971; Postmasters cert. in Comm. Mental Health, 1973; MPH, 1973; JD, UCLA Sch. of Law 1980; MCS in computer sci., Univ. San Francisco, 1989; Lic. Clin. Soc. Wkr. (LCSW) Calif. 1974. Career: soc. wkr. staff Children's Hosp. of Oakland 1973-74; Stanford Univ. Med. Ctr. 1974-76; dir. soc. work Kaiser Hosp., South S.F. 1981-83; computer pgmr. Control Data Corp. 1985; computer systems analyst Lockheed 1985-87; software designer Tandem Computers 1987; cons. to legal profession re psycho-social aspects of family law; pvt. practice 1983-; past adminstrv. research for Judge C. Reynoso (fmr Calif. Supreme Ct. Justice); UCLA judicial extern in Marin Co. Superior Ct.; honors: Upsilon Pi Epsilon (comp. sc. hon. soc.), Calif. State Fellow (1964); mem. Profl. Connections for Women (Palo Alto); rec: computers, photography, sports. Res: POB 7315 Menlo Park 94026-7315

GRUEN, CLAUDE, urban economist; b. Aug. 17, 1931, Bonn; came to U.S., 1938; s. Walter and Elsbet (Bronne) G.; m. Nina Jaffe, Sept. 11, 1960; children: Les, Dale, Adam, Joshua, Aaron; edn: BBA, Univ. Cincinnati, 1954, MA, 1962, PhD in econs., 1964. Career: faculty Xavier Univ., Cinti. 1963-64, Univ. Calif., Berkeley 1964-70; economist Arthur D. Little Inc., San Francisco 1964-70; pres., prin. economist Gruen Gruen & Associates, 1970-, cons. municipal and county govts., pub. and pvt. agencies, and commercial developers; mkt., investment and fiscal analysis for major downtown devel. projects in Dayton and Cleveland, Ohio, Scottsdale, Ariz., Medford and Portland, Oreg., Calif. cities of Santa Maria, Chula Vista, Mountain View, Palo Alto, and Pleasanton; frequent testimony on housing and zoning policy, expert witness on real estate litigation in Municipal and Superior Cts. and in No. Dist. Fed. Ct.; condr. fiscal impact studies for many Calif. cities; mem: Real Estate and Urban Economics Assn., Lambda Alpha Hon. We. Regional Sci. Assocs., Urban Land Inst. (urban devel. and mixed-use coun.); contbg. editor The Instnl. Real Estate Letter; contbr. articles in profl. jours. Ofc: 564 Howard St San Francisco 94105-3002 Tel: 415/433-7598

GRUENWALD, OSKAR, research institute executive, consultant; b. Oct. 5, 1941, Yugoslavia, came to U.S., 1961; s. Oskar and Vera (Wolf) G.; edn: AA, Pasadena City Coll., 1964; BA, UC Berkeley, 1966; MA, Claremont Grad. Sch., 1967, PhD, 1972; Calif. life std. tchg. credential. Career: internat. economist U.S. Treasury Dept., W.D.C., 1967-68; vis. res. assoc. Univ. Erlangen, Nurnberg, Germany 1971-72; lectr. Pepperdine Univ., Malibu, Calif. 1972-73, Santa Monica Coll. 1973-76; independent res., writer, Santa Monica, 1976-83; founder and pres. Inst. for Interdisciplinary Research, 1983-; guest lectr. internat., 1976-; research assoc. Ctr. for Russian and East European Studies, Univ. Ill., Champaign, Urbana, summers 1976, 79; cons. Inst. for Advanced Philosophic Research, Boulder, Colo. 1977-, Com. to Aid Democratic Dissidents in Yugoslavia, W.D.C., 1980-; pub. research, Syndicated, Montclair, Calif. 1982-, Freedom House Exchange, N.Y.C., 1985-; awards: NEH Summer Seminar on Political Cultures, Univ. Calif. 1989, Ludwig Vogelstein Found. grantee 1976-77; mem. Am. Polit. Sci. Assn., Am. Philos. Assn., Am. Assn. for Advancement Slavic Studies (cons. Slavic Rev. 1986-), Am. Sci. Affiliation, Inst. for Study Internat. Problems (bd. 1988-), Internat. Christian Studies Assn. (founder, pres. 1983-, editor newsletter 1983-), Delta Tau Kappa; author: The Yugoslav Search for Man (1983); co-editor: Human Rights in Yugoslavia (1986); founder, editor J. Interdisciplinary Studies: Internat. J. Interdisciplinary and Interfaith Dialogue (1989-). Ofc: Inst. Interdisciplinary Research, 2828 3d St Ste 11 Santa Monica 90405 Tel: 310/396-0517

GRUNER, RICHARD STEVEN, professor of law; March 10, 1953, Frankfort, Germany; s. George F. and Irene L. (Obermiller) G.; m. Marie Helen Beall, July 29, 1978; children: Helen Irene b. 1985, Elizabeth Diane b. 1987; edn: BS, Caltech (Pasadena) 1975; JD, USC Law Center 1978; LLM, Columbia Law Sch. (New York) 1982. Career: staff attorney IBM Corp., New York, N.Y. 1978-83; prof. of law Whittier Coll. Sch. of Law, Los Angeles 1983-; mem: New York Bar, Calif. Bar; author articles on expert computer systems in law, 1983-, articles on corp. crime and sentencing, 1985-. Ofc: Whittier College School of Law 5353 W Third St Los Angeles 90020

GRZANKA, LEONARD G., writer; b. Dec. 11, 1947, Ludlow, Mass.; s. Stanley Simon and Claire (Rozkuszka) G.; m. Jannette Donnenwirth, Sept. 3, 1982 (div. 1987); edn: BA, Univ. of Mass. 1972; MA, Harvard Univ., 1974. Career: sales promotion writer Tymshare Transaction Svs., Fremont 1981-82; acct. exec. Strayton Corp., Santa Clara 1981-82; mng. ed. Portable Computer Mag., San Francisco 1982-84; currently No. Calif. Bureau Chief Digital News; columnist California Farmer Mag., S.F. 1984-87, VAR Mag. (W. Coast edit.) and PC Companion Mag., Camden Communications, 1985-87; prin. Grzanka Associates, San Francisco 1984-; lectr. Golden Gate Univ. 1985-87; contbg. ed. Silicon Valley Mag. 1982-85; honors: Phi Beta Kappa 1972, Phi Kappa Phi 1972, Danforth Fellow 1972-74, Japan-US Friendship Commn. Literary Translation Award 1982; mem: Harvard Club of S.F., Press Club S.F. (admissions com.), Calif. Hist. Soc., Ivy Club of No. Calif.; author Neither Heaven Nor Hell (1978); ed. Master Pieces of Contemporary Japanese Crafts, (1977); contbr. Manajo: The Chinese Preface in Kokinshu: A Collection of Poems Ancient & Modern (Princeton 1984); mil: sgt. USAF Pararescue, Sr. Jumpmaster, Vietnam Svc.; Democrat; R.Cath.; rec: writing. Res: 1324 Jackson Apt 5 San Francisco 94109

GUENTHER, ROBERT STANLEY, II, private investment manager; b. Sept. 29, 1950, Orange, Calif.; s. Robert Stanley G. and Fanny (Neuman) Shaw; edn: BA in psych. and sociol., Univ. Calif. Santa Barbara, 1975. Career: investor, Templeton, Calif. 1971-; lodge: Moose, Santa Margarita 1986-; rec: collecting; res: 7245 El Pomar Dr Templeton 93465

GUESS, KENNETH SCOTT, pharmacist; b. Dec. 4, 1959, Glendale; s. Kenneth Ray and Karlyne M. (Dore) G.; m. Misdee, Aug. 8, 1981; children: 1 dau. Elizabeth; edn: Pharm.D, Univ. Pacific; reg. pharmacist Calif. 1983. Career: staff pharmacist, pharm. mgr. Sav-On Drugs, Northridge 1983-90; staff pharmacist Humana Hosp., West Hills 1990-92; clin. pharmacy coordinator Marian Med. Ctr. 1992-; honors: Who's Who Among Am. H.S. Students 1976-78; mem: Pacific Pharmacy Assocs., Alpha Phi Omega, Alpha Alpha Xi, Pharm. Historical Soc., CSHP; Baptist; rec: photography, fly fishing and fly tying. Ofc: Marian Medical Center 1400 E Church St Santa Maria 93454

GUILFORD, ANDREW JOHN, lawyer; b. Nov. 28, 1950, Santa Monica; s. Howard Owens and Elsie Jennette (Hargreaves) G.; m. Loreen Gogain, Dec. 22, 1973; children: Colleen Catherine b. 1979, Amanda Joy b. 1981; edn: AB, summa cum laude, UC Los Angeles 1972, JD, 1975; admitted Calif. St. Bar 1975. Career: atty., assoc. Sheppard, Mullin, Richter & Hampton, Los Angeles and Newport Beach, 1975-, ptnr. 1983-; lectr. Calif. Cont. Edn. of Bar 1978-, The Rutter Group 1983-, Hastings Ctr. for Advocacy, S.F. 1988; Superior Ct. judge pro tem and arbitrator 1983-; awards: fellow Am. Coll. of Trial Lawyers, fellow Am. Bar Assn., winner Poverty Law Ctr. Outstanding Service Award 1991, co-winner State Bar President's Pro Bono Service Award, UC Regents Scholar 1968, UCLA Alumni Assn. Scholar 1968, Phi Beta Kappa 1972, Pi Gamma Mu; mem: Am. Bar Assn., Assn. of Bus. Trial Lawyers, Federal Bar Assn., Calif. Bar Assn. (chmn. delegation to st. conv. 1986, 87), Orange Co. Bar Assn. (chmn. Bus. Litigation Sect. 1983, bd. dirs. 1985-87, ofcr. 1988-90, pres. 1991, chmn. Law and Motion Com. 1982, chmn. Standing Com. for Trial Court Delay Reduction 1987-, Public Law Center (bd. 1990-), Constnl. Rights Found. (bd. 1990), UCLA Law Alumni Assn. (bd. 1992-), Baroque Music Festival (bd. 1992-), Phi Beta Kappa Alumni Assn. (ofcr. 1978-84), Amicus Publico, Center 500, Sigma Pi; publs: UCLA Law Rev. 1975, Calif. CEB; Republican; Episcopal (subdeacon, warden, del. 1976-); rec: theater, photog., sports, poetry, garden. Res: 23 Via Terracaleta Coto De Caza 92679 Ofc: Sheppard, Mullin, Richter & Hampton, 4695 MacArthur Ct 7th Flr Newport Beach 92660

GUNER, OSMAN FATIH, physical-organic chemist; b. Feb. 25, 1956, Manisa, Turkey; s. Ahmet Tarik and Ayse Nurcan (Guneysu) G.; m. Nazli Rukiye Erbay, Apr. 23, 1982; children: Kurt b. 1987, Sibel b. 1990; edn: BS chemistry, Middle East Tech. Univ., Ankara, Turkey 1979, MS organic chem., 1981; PhD phys. org. chem., Va. Commonwealth Univ., Richmond, Va. 1986. Career: postdoctoral fellow Univ. Alabama, Birmingham 1987-89; sr. applications scientist Molecular Design Ltd., San Leandro 1989-93, sr. scientist 1993-; mem: Am. Inst. of Chemists (Fellow), Am. Chem. Soc. 1985-, Calif. Acad. of Scis. 1989-, US Chess Fedn.; lodge: Strict Observance (Richmond, Va.); referee Jour. of Organic Chemistry; contbr. articles in J. Am. Chem. Soc., Org. Chem., J. Chem. Inf. Computer Sci. (1987-); rec: chess, volleyball. Ofc: Molecular Design Ltd. 2132 Farallon Dr San Leandro 94577

GUPTA, DINESH CHANDRA, manufacturing co. executive; b. June 25, 1937, Meerut, India, nat. 1985; s. Faqir Chand and Manorma (Jain) G.; m. Vijay Rastogi, Dec.23, 1963; 1 child, Anju b. 1970; edn: BS, Meerut (India) Coll., 1955, MS in math., 1957; BSEE, Indian Inst. of Sci.,Bangalore, India 1960; MSEE, Carnegie-Mellon Univ., 1961. Career: research asst. Carnegie Inst. of Tech., Pittsburgh, Pa. 1960-61; mem. tech. staff Texas Instruments Inc., Dallas 1961-65; senior engr. GTE Labs. Inc., Bayside, N.Y. 1965-72; mng. dir. Superior Electronic Systems Ltd., Bombay, India 1972-77; senior engr. Unitrode Corp., Watertown, Mass. 1977-79; ops. mgr. Siliconix, Inc. Santa Clara 1979-90; dir. of technology SEH America, Inc., San Jose 1990-; chmn. biennial Internat. Symposium on Semiconductor Processing; advy. editor Solid State Technology; mem. Am. Soc. Testing & Materials (fellow, v.chmn. Com. F-1, Profl. Award of Merit 1986), IEEE (senior), The Electrochemical Soc.; 4 Patents; contbr. 30+ tech. publs., editor 4 books: Silicon Processing, Semiconductor Processing, Emerging Semiconductor Technology, Semiconductor Fabrication: Technology & Metrology; rec: bridge, tennis. Res: 3103 N.E. 115th Circle Vancouver WA 98686-3948 Ofc: SEH America, Inc. 1737 N First St San Jose 95112

GUPTA, VINEET KUMAR, jeweler; b. Oct. 11, 1967, Calcutta, India, nat. U.S. 1970; s. Vinay Kumar and Shibani (Roychowdhury) G.; m. Sangeeta Agarwal, Apr. 26, 1992; edn: BA, Cal Poly, Pomona, 1981. Career: c.e.o. BG Internat. Gems Inc., Los Angeles 1988-; author (collection of poems) The Book of Ishq (1991); rec: automobiles. Res: 2359 S Bluehaven Dr Rowland Heights 91748

GURASH, JOHN THOMAS, manufacturing and insurance company executive; b. Nov. 25, 1910, Oakland; s. Nicholas and Katherine (Restovic) G.; m. Katherine M. Mills, Feb. 4, 1934; 1 son, John Nicholas b. 1939; edn: law, Loyola Univ., L.A. 1936-39. Career: underwriting mgr. Am. Surety Co. of New York, 1930-44; v.p. and dir. Pacific Employers Ins. Co., 1944-53; pres. and organizer, dir. Meritplan Ins. Co. (1st co. to offer direct bill ins. through indep. agents), also exec. v.p. Teachers Ins. Underwriters, 1953-59; v.p. Insurance Co. of North America, 1966-70, dir. 1965-80; exec. v.p. INA Corp., 1968-69, pres. 1969-74, chmn. bd. and CEO 1969-75, chmn. exec. com. 1975-77, dir. 1968-82; dir. Household Finance Corp., 1974-81; chmn. bd. Household Internat. Inc., 1982-83, chmn. exec. com. 1983-84, dir. 1981-84; CEO Purex Industries Inc., 1984-86, chmn. bd. 1984-89, dir. 1974-89; chmn. bd. and dir: CertainTeed Corp. 1978-92, Horace Mann Educators Corp. 1989-, Saint-Gobain Corp. 1991-92 (chmn. emeritus 1992-); dir. Pic 'N' Save Corp., 1984-90, Norton Co., 1990-92; awards: Gold Medal Netherlands Soc., Phila. 1971, Am. Jewish Com. 1971, John Wanamaker 1972, NCCJ nat. human relations award 1973, Sourin award Cath. Philopatrian Literary Inst. 1973, Chevalier French Legion of Honor 1975; mem.: Weingart Found. L.A. (dir.), Pa. Soc., Newcomen Soc. N. Am., Kts. of Malta; clubs: California, Pine Valley GC, Los Angeles CC, Annandale GC, 100, The Valley Hunt; author (book) The Report of the Archdiocesan Advy. Com. on Fin. Crisis of Cath. Schs. in Phila. and Surrounding Counties (1972); rec: golf, reading. Res: 456 S Orange Grove Blvd Pasadena 91105 Ofc: 1000 Wilshire Blvd Ste 610 Los Angeles 90017

GUTIERREZ, OLGA, psychiatrist, consultant, educator; b. Dec. 29, 1929, Buenos Aires, Argentina; d. Gabriel and Soledad (Garcia Bueno) G.; granddau. of Jose San Roman, Dean of Sch. of Medicine, Spain; widow; 1 son, Luis Eduardo, b. 1961; edn: PhD in biochem., Univ. Buenos Aires, 1954; Immunologist, Inst. Pasteur, Paris 1959; MD, Univ. of Buenos Aires, 1967; Dipl. Am. Bd. Psychiatry and Neurology (1987), Dipl. Am. Bd. Child and Adolescent Psychiatry (1989). Career: ednl. asst. Univ. Buenos Aires, 1953-58; res. fellow, Inst. Pasteur, Paris, 1958-60; ednl. chief and research assoc. Univ. Buenos Aires, 1960-70; resrch. fellow Superior Council of Biol. Resrch, Madrid, Spain 1970-71; res. fellow, Reproductive Biol., OB-Gyn, USC, 1971-74; pvt. practice of medicine in Buenos Aires, 1975-77; adult psychiatrist L.A. Co./USC Med. Ctr., 1978, child and adolescent psychiatrist, L.A. Co./USC Med. Ctr., 1982, forensic psychiatrist Dept. Psychiatry, Inst. of Psychiat., Law and Behavioral Scis., USC, 1985; currently staff psychiatrist L.A. Co. Dept. of Mental Health, and staff child and adolescent psychiatrist USC-LAC Child Guidance Clinic; consultant; Awards: Univ. of Buenos Aires Golden Medal 1952, Faculty of Medicine Award 1954, Acad. of Med. Award 1966, Junior Chamber Award 1966, AMA Award 1988; mem: Soc. of Chem. of Uruguay (corres. mem.), Acad. of Pharm. and Biochem. (Arg.), Microbiol. and Immunol. Assn., AMA, Biochem. Assn., Salerni Coll. USC, Am. Acad. of Child and Adolescent Psychiatry; publs: numerous sci. articles rel. to medicine; guest appearances on t.v. and radio re psychiatric issues; rec: sports, swimming, sailing, tennis, music, cinema, theatre, travel. Res: 101 California Ave Apt 507 Santa Monica 90403 Ofc: 746 W Adams Blvd Los Angeles 90007

GUTIERREZ LEE, RICARDO, finance executive; b. Mar. 5, 1924, La Habana, Cuba; s. Dr. Ricardo and Carmen Terry Gutierrez Lee; m. Dr. Lilliam Maldonado, Aug. 25, 1949; children: Dr. Ricardo b. 1951, Alina b. 1953; edn: AA, Academia Baldor, Cuba; certified public acct. Univ. of Havana (cum laude); acctg. courses, UCLA Ext. and CSU Fullerton; real estate lic. (Calif.). Career: credit and collection mgr. U.S. Rubber Co., Cuba 1945-52; asst. con-

troller Ford Motor Co., Cuba 1952-53; general mgr. (family bus.) Tropical Agriculture, Cuba 1963-60; sr. auditor Ernst & Ernst, Colombia 1961-63; sr. auditor Fritz L. Krauth CPA, Garden Grove 1963-68; general mgr. Santa Ana Med. Group, Santa Ana 1968-70; sr. auditor Tosh & Brown Acctcy. Corp., Irvine 1970-74; controller to fin. dir. to v.p. of fin. Komfort Industries, Inc., Riverside 1974-; Republican; R.Cath.; rec: swimming, flying. Res: 19112 Homestead Ln Huntington Beach 92646

GYEMANT, ROBERT ERNEST, lawyer; b. Jan. 17, 1944, Managua, Nicaragua, naturalized 1954; s. Emery and Magda (Von Rechnitz) G.; children: Robert, Jr. b. 1971, Anne Elizabeth b. 1972; m. Sally Bartch Libhart, 1992; edn: AB, UCLA, 1965; JD, Boalt Hall UCB, 1968; C.P.A., Calif. 1968; admitted bar: Calif. 1969, N.Y. 1981; cert. criminal splst. State Bar Calif. Career: lawyer, assoc. Orrick Herrington Rowley & Sutcliffe, San Francisco 1968-70; ptnr. Skornia Rosenblum & Gyemant, 1970-74; prin. R.E. Gyemant, APC, 1974-; prin. Niesar, Cecchini & Gyemant, 1987-89; of counsel to Sullivan, Roche & Johnson 1989-90; prin. Kaye & Gyemant, San Francisco and Pasadena, 1992-; appt. Hon. Vice-Consul Republic of Costa Rica, 1980-; mem: Am. Inst. CPAs, Calif. Soc. CPAs, San Francisco Bar Assn. (ethics com. 1987-), Calif. Trial Lawyers Assn., State Bar of Calif., Assn. of Defense Counsel, N.Y. State Bar, St. Thomas More Soc.; trustee Fr. Am. Bilingual Sch. 1976-79; clubs: N.Y. Athletic, Racquet & Tennis (N.Y.); contbr. Calif. Law Rev. (1968); Republican (alt. del. Rep. Nat. Conv. 1992); Episcopalian. Ofc: Kaye & Gyemant: 333 Pine St 2d Fl San Francisco 94104; 360 W Colorado Blvd 2d Fl Pasadena 91117

HACKBARTH, DOROTHY ALICE, educational consultant; b. Apr. 21, 1921, Naperville, Ill.; d. Walter Dewey and Nellie Louise (Staffeldt) Eichelberger; m. Charles Alfred Hackbarth, Oct. 24, 1942; children: Christofer Lee b. 1944, Cathleen b. 1948, Timothy Scott b. 1952; edn: BA, UC Berkeley, 1964, gen. sec. lifetime tchg. credential, 1965. Career: secty. Lucien Lelong, Chicago 1942-43; telephone opr. Hinsdale (Ill.) Bell Tel. Co., 1943-44; dress designer, self-empl., 1947-55; tchr. Oakland (Calif.) Unified Sch. Dist., 1965-66, tchr. Berkeley Unified Sch. Dist. 1966-78, chair fgn. lang. dept. 1969-74; pres. UNA/USA, A1. Chapter, Oakland 1969-72; chair Nor Cal Coun. 1971-73; pres., founder and CEO Unesco Assn./USA, Inc. Oakland 1971-, UNA/USA Newsletter editor 1972-; awards: fellow Unesco, Paris, France 1971, Berkeleyans for Acad. Excellence tchg. award 1977, Calif. PTA cont. edn. scholar UC Berkeley 1977; mem: Cal Alumni Assn. (1964-, life), Berkeley /Oakland /Piedmont Alumni Club 1991; pub. articles: Patramoine Mondial (1979), Philosophy of Edn.: Teaching Values (1988); Indep.; rec: fgn. lang. study, problem-solving, all kinds of mental exercise, travel, people. Res/Ofc: Unesco Assn./USA, Inc. 5815 Lawton Ave Oakland 94618-1510

HADDAD, WISAM BOULOS, surgeon; b. Mar. 4, 1954, Amman, Jordan, nat. USA 1985; s. Boulos Somail and Taman M. (Hawatmeh) H.; m. Rozanne, June 12, 1977; children: Angie b. 1980, Laila b. 1982, Laura b. 1985; edn: BS, acad. distinction, Andrews Univ. 1976; MD, Loma Linda Univ. 1979; lic. phys. Calif. 1981; bd. cert. Am. Bd. of Surgery 1986. Career: gen. surgical resident Loma Linda Univ., 1980-85; asst. prof. of surgery Loma Linda Univ., 1988-; attdg. surgeon Riverside General Hosp., University Medical Center; instr. in surg. Loma Linda Univ. 1985; honors: Who's Who Among Students in Am. Univs. and Colls. 1975-76, Alpha Omega Alpha, LLU Sch. of Med. Alumni Assn. medal for Distinction in Quest of Excellence 1979, AMA Physicians Recogn. Award 1989; mem: AMA, CMA, Am. Coll. of Surgeons (assoc. fellow); publs: Am. J. of Surgery (1985), Am. J. of Diseases of Children (1982), Univ. Surgeon (1986), papers presented Tri-County Surg. Soc. of So. Calif. Annual Clinic Day (1984, 85, 90); Seventh Day Adventist; rec: gardening, travel, camping, fishing. Res: 16541 Creekside Rd Riverside 92503 Ofc: Riverside General Hospital, 9851 Magnolia Ave Riverside 92503

HAGENBUCH, JOHN JACOB, investment banker; b. May 31, 1951, Park Forest, Ill.; s. David Brown and Jean Iline (Reeves) H.; children: Henry, Hunter, Hilary; edn: AB (magna cum laude), Princeton Univ., 1974; MBA, Stanford Univ., 1978. Career: assoc. Salomon Bros., N.Y.C., 1978-80, v.p., San Francisco, 1980-85; gen. ptnr. Hellman & Friedman, 1985-; bd. dirs. Am. President Cos. Great American Investment & Management Inc., Eagle Industries Inc., StoryFirst Communications Inc.; trustee Town Sch. for Boys; mem.: bd. govs. San Francisco Symphony; clubs: Burlingame CC, Pacific-Union, California Tennis, Villa Taverna. Ofc: Hellman & Friedman 1 Maritime Plaza Ste 1200 San Francisco 94111 Ph: 415/788-5111

HAHN, ELLIOTT JULIUS, lawyer; b. Dec. 9, 1949, San Francisco; s. Leo Wolf and Sherry Marion (Portnoy) H.; m. Toby Rose Mallen, Feb. 14, 1988; children: Kara b. 1985, Brittany b. 1989, Michael b. 1990; edn: BA (cum laude), Univ. Penn., 1971; JD, Univ. Penn. Law Sch., 1974; LLM, Columbia Univ. Sch. of Law, 1980; admitted bar: Calif., N.J., D.C., U.S. Supreme Ct. Career: law clk. Los Angeles County Superior Ct., 1975-76; corp. lawyer ARCO, L.A. 1976-79; assoc. prof. of law Calif. Western Sch. of Law, San Diego 1980-85; atty., assoc. Morgan, Lewis & Bockius, L.A. 1985-87; Milbank, Tweed, Hadley & McCloy, 1987; Whitman & Ransom, 1987-89, ptnr. 1989-; adj. prof. Pepperdine Law

Sch., 1987-, Southwestern Univ. Sch. of Law, 1987-; dir: AMS Blue Waves Inc., 1990-; ATF Charters, Inc., 1991-; listed Who's Who in Am. Law (1985, 86), Who's Who in West; mem: Calif. State Bar Assn. (exec. com. internat. law sect. 1991-, v. chmn. 1992-93), L.A. Co. Bar Assn. (chmn. Pacific Rim com. 1991-92, exec. com. internat. law sect. 1987-), Univ. Penn. Alumni Club of So. Calif. (bd. 1989-); author: Japanese Business Law and the Legal System (1984), articles Calif. Lawyer mag., Bus. Law News, law revs. (1982, 83, 84); Jewish; rec: golf, Lladro collector, baseball memorabilia. Ofc: Whitman & Ransom 633 W Fifth St Ste 2100 Los Angeles 90071

HAHN, ERWIN LOUIS, professor of physics emeritus; b. June 9, 1921, Sharon, Pa.; s. Israel and Mary (Weiss) H.; m. Marian Ethel Failing, Apr. 8, 1944 (dec. Sept. 28, 1978); children: David b. 1945, Deborah b. 1949, Katherine b. 1955; m. Natalie Woodford Thompson, Apr. 12, 1980; stepchildren: Welles b. 1958, Elisabeth b. 1960; edn: BS, Juniata Coll., Huntingdon, Pa. 1943; MS, Univ. Ill., 1948, PhD, 1949. Career: asst. in physics Purdue Univ., 1943-44; resrch. assoc. Univ. of Ill., 1950; instr. Stanford Univ. 1950-52, Nat. Research Council fellow at Stanford 1950-51, cons. Office of Naval Res. 1950-52; assoc. Columbia Univ., and res. physicist IBM Watson Scientific Computing Lab., 1952-55; cons. US AEC, 1955-; asst., assoc., prof. dept. physics Univ. Calif., Berkeley 1955-91: assoc. res. prof. Miller Inst. for Basic Research UCB, 1958-59, res. prof. (1966-67, 1985-86), prof. emeritus 1991-; awards: NRC fellow Stanford Univ. 1950-51, Guggenheim Fellow Oxford Univ., Eng. (1961-66 1969-70), Canadian Research Coun. traveling lectr. series 1964, Hon. D.Sc. Juniata Coll. 1966, Buckley Prize in solid state physics Am. Physical Soc. 1971, 1971 Prize of Intl. Soc. of Magnetic Resonance, Fgn. mem: Royal Instn. of G.B. 1971, Hon. D.Sc. Purdue Univ. 1975, Alexander von Humboldt Award of German Fed. Govt. at Max-Planck Inst., Heidelberg 1976-77, Japanese Phys. Soc. traveling lectr. series 1977, 66th Ann. Faculty Resrch. Lectrship UCB 1979, fgn. assoc. mem. Slovenian Acad. Scis. 1981, hon. mem. Brasenose Coll., Oxford, Eng. 1982; co-winner Wolf Found. Prize in Physics 1983-84, Calif. Inventors Hall of Fame 1984; Dept. Energy Award for sustained res. on NMR with DC Squids (1986); vis. Eastman Prof. Balliol Coll., Cherwell-Simon Lectr., Oxford 1988-89; citation UC Berkeley 1991; fgn. assoc. French Acad. Scis. 1992; co-recipient Comstock Prize, U.S. Nat Acad. of Sci. 1993; apptd. spl. cons. USN 1959, advy. panel to Nat. Bur. Stds. Radio Std. Div. 1961-64, NAS/NRC com. on basic resrch., advr. to US Army Res. Office, Durham 1967-69; mem. Am. Physical Soc. (Fellow, exec. com. div. solid state physics 1967-69), Sigma Xi, Am. Acad. Arts and Scis. (Fellow), Nat. Acad. Scis.; coauthor: Nuclear Quadrupole Resonance Spectroscopy (1958) with T.P. Das; mil: tech. mate US Naval Reserve, WWII, 1944-46; rec: violin, chamber music. Res: 69 Stevenson Ave Berkeley 94708 Ofc: Physics Dept Univ. Calif., Berkeley 94720

HAILE, LAWRENCE BARCLAY, lawyer; b. Feb. 19, 1938, Atlanta, Ga.; m. Ann Springer McCauley, Mar. 28, 1984; children: Gretchen, Eric, Scott; edn: BA in econs., Univ. Texas, 1958, LLB, 1961; admitted bar: Tex. 1961, Calif. 1962, U.S. Supreme Ct. Career: law clk. to fed. judge Joseph M. Ingraham, Houston 1961-62; pvt. practice law San Francisco 1962-67, Los Angeles 1967-, ptnr. Simon, Buckner & Haile, Marina Del Rey 1984-90; prin. Federman, Gridley, Gradwohl, Flaherty & Haile, Los Angeles 1991-; instr UCLA Civil Trial Clinics 1974, 76; lectr. Calif. Cont. Edn. of Bar 1973-74, 80-; nat. panel arbitrators Am. Arb. Assn. 1965-; honors: assoc. editor Texas Law Rev., 1960-61, Phi Delta Phi, Delta Sigma Rho; mem: Calif. Bar Assn., Texas Bar Assn., Internat. Assn. Property Ins. Counsel (founding, pres. 1980), Am. Soc. for Testing and Mats., London World Trade Centre Assn.; club: Marine (London). Ofc: 2029 Century Park East Ste 3110 Los Angeles 90067

HAINING, JEANE MARIE, psychologist; b. May 2, 1952, Camden, N.J.; d. Lester Edward and Adina (Rahn) Haining; edn: BA, CSU Northridge, 1975, MS, 1982; MA, Pepperdine Univ., 1979; PhD, Calif. Sch. Profl. Psych., 1985; Calif. lic. ednl. psych. (1982), lic. psychologist (1987). Career: subs. recreation therapist New Horizons Sch. for Mentally Retarded, Sepulveda 1976-79; sch. psychologist Rialto Unified Sch. Dist., 1979-82; clin. psych. intern Fuller Psychol. Ctr., Pasadena 1984-85; clin. psychologist and intermittent actg. chief psychol. svs. Terminal Island Fed. Prison, 1985-86; community mental health psychologist Sybil Brand Inst., forensic outpatient unit L.A. Co. Dept. Mental Health, 1987-89, also inservice tng. for L.A. Co. Sheriff's Dept.; clinical psychologist Calif. Dept. of Corrections, Parole Outpt. Clinic, 1990-; examiner, ednl. psych., Calif. Bd. Beh. Sci. Examiners, Sacto. 1985; mem. U.S. Dist. Ct., Cent. Dist. of Calif., Psychiatric Panel 1989-, Juvenile Dependency Ct. 730 Evidence Code Experts Panel 1992, Superior Ct. Psychiatric-Psychol. Panel: Juvenile 1992, Superior Ct. Psychiatric-Psychol. Panel: Adult; recipient award outstanding achiev. W. Psych. Conf. for Undergrad. Research, Santa Clara (1974); mem. L.A. Psych. Assn., Forensic Mental Health Assn. Calif.; PhD diss: Schizophrenic Patients decision-making process in regard to medication treatment compliance (1985); Democrat; Lutheran; rec: skiing (capt. CSU Northridge/ So. Calif. Intercollegiate Ski Race Assn. 1975, women's team won 2d pl. overall, and placed within top ten in Individual Womens Championship Races), skating, tennis, racquetball, rock climbing, piano.

HAISCH, BERNHARD MICHAEL, astronomer; b. Aug. 23, 1949, Stuttgart-Bad Canstatt, Germany; s. Friedrich Wilhelm and Gertrud Paula (Dammbacher) H.; m. Pamela S. Eakins, July 29, 1977 (div. 1986); children: Katherine Stuart, Christopher Taylor; m. Marsha A. Sims, Aug. 23, 1986; edn: St. Meinrad Coll., Ind. 1967-68; BS in astrophysics (w/high distinction), Indiana Univ., 1971; PhD astronomy, Univ. Wis., Madison 1975. Career: res. assoc. Jt. Inst. Lab. Astrophysics, Univ. Colo., 1975-77, 78-79; vis. scientist The Astronomical Inst., Utrecht, The Netherlands 1977-78; res. scientist Lockheed Palo Alto Research Lab., 1979-83, staff scientist 1983-;dep. dir. Ctr. for EUV Astrophysics, Univ. Calif. Berkeley 1992-; vis. fellow Max-Planck Institut fur Extraterr. Physik, Garching, Germany 1991-93; guest investigator programs: Internat. Ultraviolet Explorer, Einstein Obs., ROSAT Obs., 1980-; managing ed. Jour. of Sci. Exploration 1988-; assoc. ed. Astrophysical Jour. 1993-; mem: NASA rev. coms.; mem: Internat. Astronomical Union (chmn. Colloquium No. 104: Solar and Stellar Flares, Stanford Univ. 1988), Am. Astronomical Soc., Royal Astron. Soc. (fellow), Am. Inst. Aero. and Astro., European Astron. Soc., Phi Beta Kappa, Sigma Xi, Phi Kappa Phi, Commonwealth Club of Calif.; invention: Anchor Bolt Extractor (US Pat. No. 4,941,252); publs: 70+ papers in sci. jours., (book) Solar and Stellar Flares, with Rodono (Kluwer Acad. Press, 1989), editorial bd.: Solar Physics (1992-95); fgn. languages: speak German, read Dutch, French, Latin; rec: Tae Kwon Do, internat. folk dance, downhill skiing, songwriting. Ofc: Lockheed Palo Alto Research Lab. Div. 91-30, 3251 Hanover St Bldg 252 Palo Alto 94304 Tel: 415/424-3268

HAISLEY, FAY BEVERLEY, academic dean; b. Feb. 20, 1933, Sydney, Australia; came to U.S., 1971; d. Reginald Charles and Edna Irene (Kidd) Sambrook; m. Ian George Haisley, May 11, 1963, div. 1973; edn: BA, Univ. Papua, New Guinea, Port Moresby 1970; MEd (honors) Univ. Oregon, 1971, PhD, 1973; cert. elementary tchr., spl. edn., Oreg., New South Wales, Australia. Career: tchr., principal Dept. Edn., Australia 1952-70; prin., lectr. Dept. Edn., Port Moresby, Papua, New Guiinea 1969-70; lectr. early childhood UC Santa Barbara, 1973-75; asst. prof., assoc. prof. learning disabilities and elem. edn. Univ. Oreg., Eugene 1975-80, assoc. dean, tchr. edn., 1981-84; dean Sch. of Edn. Univ. of Pacific, Stockton 1984-, dir. dean's grant 1977-83; commr. Calif. Commn. on Tchr. Credentialling, 1985-87; dir. spl. project Am. Nepalese Edn. Found., Eugene, Oreg. 1982-84; dir. doctoral dept. edn. program Univ. Guam, 1983-84; dir. Far West Educational Labs 1986-; Bd. of Examiners NCATE, 1989-; awards: grantee U.S. Office Edn. 1979-82, Nat. Inst. Edn. 1981, Oregon State Dept. Edn. 1978; mem: Phi Delta Kappa, Am. Ednl. Research Assn., Assn. Tchr. Educators, Am. Assn. Colls. Tchr. Edn., Calif. Assn. Tchr. Educators (pres. 1988-89), Calif. Assn. for Colls. of Tchr. Edn. (pres. 1991-93); contbr. articles to profl. jours.; Anglican. Ofc: Univ. of the Pacific Sch. Edn. Pacific Ave Stockton 95211

HAKIM, HOSNY F., civil engineer, structural design; b. March 1, 1946, El Maragha, Egypt, nat. US cit. 1983; s. Fawzy H. and Thoria (Ghali) H.; m. Soad, July 20, 1975; children: Marian Grace b. 1981, Rose Mary b. 1982; edn: BS, Univ. of Alexandria 1968; MS, Univ. of Toronto 1977; Reg. Profl. Engr., Wash. 1984, Calif. 1985; gen. engring. contractor, Calif. 1985. Career: research asst. Univ. of Toronto, Canada 1975-77; designer office of Jame Ruderman, NYC 1977-79; engr. Geiger Berger Assn., NY 1978-79; design engr. Ebasco Svcs. Inc., NY 1979-81, Wash. 1981-84; pres. Pacific H H Developers, Inc., Glendale 1984-88; prin. Hakim Engring. Svcs., Torrance 1988-; tchg. asst. Univ. of Toronto 1975-77; tchg. asst. Univ. of Alexandria, Egypt 1968-75; awards: fellowship Univ. of Toronto 1975-76, scholarship Univ. of Alexandria 1963-68; mem. Am. Soc. Civil Engrs., Am. Concrete Inst.; publs: Automated Design of Rigid Steel Frames, Canadian Soc. of Civil Engrs., Conf. Montreal 1977; Christian. Ofc: Hakim Engineering Services, 22907 Marjorie Ave Torrance 90505

HALL, DAVID STANLEY, consultant in aviation safety; b. Jan. 12, 1935, Oak Park, Ill.; s. Clifford Francis and Alice Elizabeth (Brandenburger) H.; m. Arlene Denzler, June 7, 1957 (div. 1983); children: Sheridan b. 1958, D. Michael b. 1960, Tina b. 1964; m. LaNette Vinson, July 21, 1983 (div. 1991); m. Roseann Hannon, PhD, July 31, 1992; edn: BSEE, Ill. Inst. of Tech., 1957, MS in sys. mgmt., USC, 1972; Calif. reg. profl. engr., safety. Career: Lt., naval aviator USN, 1957-62; flight test engr. Lockheed-Calif. Co., Burbank 1962-66; sr. flt. test engr. Garrett/ AiResearch Mfg. Co. of Ariz., 1967-69; cons. in mishap investigation and prevention, 1969-; f.t. faculty Univ. So. Calif. Inst. of Aerospace Safety and Mgmt., 1969-72, guest lectr. in aviation safety USC 1972-73; lectr. and faculty assoc. Ariz. State Univ., 1973-86; product safety splst. Garrett/AiResearch Mfg. Co. of Ariz., 1973-78, supr. engring. flt. test 1976-77; dir. res. Crash Research Inst., Robertson Research Inc., 1979-83; faculty Internat. Ctr. for Safety Edn., Tempe, Az. 1981-, and Internat. Ctr. for Aviation Safety, San Diego, 1986-; mem: Tau Beta Pi, Mensa, Am. Inst. Aero. and Astro., System Safety Soc., Soc. of Automotive Engrs., Internat. Soc. of Air Safety Investigators (past pres. Los Angeles chpt., gen. chmn. 2d, 16th internat. sems., past chmn. bd. of awards); publs. in field. Res: 2111 Lido Circle Stockton 95207 Tel: 209/474-7421

HALL, HUGH A., home furnishings industry leader, civic volunteer; b. Sept. 23, 1926, Durham, N.C.; s. Hugh A. and Grace Mildred (Hartz) H.; m. V. Elaine Hakala (dec. Jan. 23, 1989); children: Stephen L. and Linda Eileen; m. Bonnie Oglesby, Oct. 1990; children by marriage, nee Oglesby: Jeffrey, Terri Lynn (Mrs. Hartman), Karen Michele (Mrs. Dunn), Charles Stanley. Career: owner, ptnr. automotive and indsl. parts & supply cos. in San Diego County, 1950s; pres. Highway Devel. Assn. San Diego Co., 1960s, com. chmn. Try San Diego Co. First, co-chair S.D. Citizens for Better Bus Service, chmn. S.D. Stadium campaign (C.of C.), celebration dir. year-long 200th Anniversary San Diego; exec. dir. U.S. Bicentennial, 1970s; owner, pres. San Diego Rattan, 1974-90; pres. Morena Home Furnishings Dist.; mem., pres. San Diego Co. Home Furnishings Assn.; awards: outstanding svc. U.S. Govt., Calif. Gov.'s nominee for outstanding citizenship 1967, nat. award Outstanding Retailer of Year; mem. San Diego C.of C. (past v.p., dir., Chmn. of Year Award-3), Mission Valley YMCA (bd. 1980-), San Diego Zool. Soc., Nat. Historic Preservation Trust, Scripps Inst. of Oceanography Assocs.; club: Stardust CC; mil: USN 1944-46; rec: swimming, golf, music. Res: 6047 Cirrus St San Diego 92110

HALL, RICHARD DENNIS, freelance writer; b. Apr. 12, 1935, Troy, N.Y.; s. Dennis John and Clara Eleanor (Hanson) H.; m. Joyce Ann Huntington, June 7, 1957; children: Brian Huntington b. 1959, Roger Hanson b. 1961; edn: BS, Boston Univ., 1957. Career: gen. assignment reporter Worcester (Mass.) Telegram and Evening Gazette, 1957-60; city hall reporter and columnist Springfield (Mass.) Union, 1960-65; reporter Fresno (Calif.) Bee, 1965-77, agriculture and water reporter 1977-79, Washington corr. McClatchy Newspapers, W.D.C., 1979-83, agribus. writer Fresno Bee, Fresno 1983-91; freelance writer, agribus. and internat. trade, Hanford, Calif. 1991-; awards: invited guest Agribus. Sem., Taiwan, 1983, Ninth Ann. Conf. European and Am. Journalists, Maastricht, Netherlands, 1985; mem: Western Hist. Club Garden of the Sun Corral 1987-, Nature Conservancy 1984-; author: Fresno County in the 20th Century (1987), Hanford Hometown America (1991); mil: sp3c Army N.G. 1957-63; rec: bird watching, baking bread. Res/Ofc: 1978 Mulberry Dr Hanford 93230

HALLADAY, KAREN SUE, educator, real estate broker, financial planner; b. July 26, 1943, Stockton; d. Dr. Louis, Jr. and Eleanor Sue (Sandberg) Jaques Keene; m. Wayne Halladay, Feb. 4, 1967; edn: BA, 1965 and MA, 1967, highest honors, CSU San Jose; postgrad. work in ednl. psych. and community mental health, UC Berkeley 1970-76; Calif. Std. Elem. tchg. cred., Calif. Comm. Colls. instr., counselor creds.; Calif. lic. R.E. broker; reg. rep. NASD, Cert. Fin. Planner, life/disability ins. agent, 1984-90; Cert. Residential Splst., NAR 1988-. Career: elementary sch. tchr. Lompoc Unified Sch. District, 1967-70; instr. Alan Han Jr. Coll., Santa Maria 1968-70; coll. instr./ supr. student teachers, St. Marys Coll., Moraga 1974-76; R.E. agent, Walnut Creek 1977-81; realtor/prin. Halladay & Assocs., Concord 1982-83; fin. planner 1984-90; broker Security Pacific Real Estate, Walnut Creek; account exec. WZW Financial Services; Southmark Financial Svcs. 1984-86; Pvt. Securities Network, Skaife, 1989-90; mem: Am. Arbitration Assn. (arb.), Nat. Assn. Realtors, Calif. Assn. Realtors (state dir. 1987-, MLS com. 1987-, MLS dist. chair 89-90, MLS com. state v.chair 1991, Profl. Stds. com. 1991-, v.chair 1992, computer com. 1989, PAC 1990), Contra Costa Bd. of Realtors (first woman MLS pres. 1988, v.p. & c.f.o. 1989-90, bylaws com. chair 1989-90, pres. MLS 1991, pres. 1993, profl. stds. panel 1981-84, 88, chair ethics com. 1985, mediator 1987, chair Realtor/title co. relations com., dir. MLS 1986, instr. 1989), Conflict Resolution Panel Contra Costa (bd. 1987), Alamo Improvement Assn. (zoning com. 1989), Structural Com. East Bay Regional Data (chair 1991); Democrat; Episcopalian; rec: scuba, kite flying, swimming, bread baking. Res: 2365 Hagen Oaks Dr Alamo 94507 Ofc: Security Pacific Real Estate, 587 Ygnacio Valley Rd Walnut Creek 94596

HALLER, HOWARD EDWARD, real estate developer, entertainment company executive; b. March 30, 1947, Baltimore, Md.; s. Howard Earl and Clemence Anne (Young) H.; m. Terri Lynne Koster, June 20, 1969; children: Jennifer b. 1970, Justin b. 1973, Jason b. 1979; edn: USC 1968-75; BA, CSU Northridge 1970; MA mgmt., Univ. Redlands; lic. real estate broker Calif., lic. gen. contractor Calif., lic. commercial pilot. Career: reg. mgr. U.S. Leasing Corp., Los Angeles 1973-78; Chemical Bank of N.Y., Santa Monica 1976-77; v.p. Patagonia Corp., Phoenix, Ariz. 1977; pres. and c.e.o. Haller Koster & Haller Corp., Woodland Hills 1977-90; sr. v.p., c.o.o. IFC Capital Corp., Beverly Hills 1977-88; sr. v.p., reg. gen. mgr. United Artists Entertainment, Woodland Hills 1988-91; pres. and c.e.o. Rebel Productions, Hollywood 1991-; prof. CSU Northridge 1980-; Pierce Coll., Woodland Hills 1987-; dir. Rebel Productions, Hollywood 1968-; Ed Haller & Sons Constrn., Woodland Hills 1968-; awards: BSA varsity scout coach of year (1987, 88); mem: AFTRA, Writers Guild of Am. (West), Nat. Realtors Assn., Urban Planning Inst., Builders Ind. Assn., Motion Picture Pioneers, Nat. Eagle Scouts Assn. (life), CSU Northridge Trust Fund (trustee, v.p., past pres.), USC Cinema TV Alumni Assn. (life), CSU Northridge Alumni Assn. (dir., past pres., v.p.), Am. Legion, BSA, AYSO Soccer; screenwriter: TV screenplay, Paper Chase: Real World 101 (1978), feature films, White Lies (1987), Debt of Honor (1991); mil: capt. USAF 1968-70; Republican. Ofc: 23271 Ventura Blvd Woodland Hills 91364

HALLETT, DEAN CHARLES, entertainment company executive; b. June 9, 1958, Encino; s. William Charles and Sally (Lane) H.; m. Kelli Lynn Frisinger, July 2, 1983; children: Drew b. 1989, Makenzie b. 1991; edn: BBA (cum laude), USC, 1980; CPA, Calif. Bd. Acctncy. Career: sr. audit mgr. Ernst & Whinney, Los Angeles 1980-88, exchange visitor Ernst & Whinney, London, Eng. 1986-87, campus recruiting coord., USC, 1985-88; group controller Anthony Industries, Inc. 1988-90; mgr. corp. mgmt. audit Walt Disney Co., Burbank 1990-91, dir. of fin. Buena Vista Pictures Mktg. (div. Walt Disney Studios), 1991-; Republican; rec: skiing, golf. Ofc: Walt Disney Co. 500 S Buena Vista St Burbank 91521-1427

HALLINAN, VIVIAN MOORE, peace activist; b. Oct. 21, 1910, San Francisco; d. Edward Frances and Katherine Rose (Lagomarsino) Moore; m. Vincent Hallinan, Sept. 23, 1932; children: Patrick b. 1934, Terence b. 1936, Michael b. 1939, Matthew b. 1940, Conn b. 1942, Daniel b. 1948; edn: stu. UC Berkeley 3 yrs. Career: investor, apartment mgmt. bus., San Francisco 1933-, bought downtown apartment bldgs. in need of renovation and furnishing, active apt. mgmt. until 1984, semi-ret.; honors: recogn. U.S. Peace Council 1957, outstanding woman of yr. Sun Reporter 1964, outstanding older women in S.F. Older Women League 1983, recogn. for peace activities and work in civil rights Cong. Barbara Boxer and Cong. Ronald Dellums 1984, Gray Panthers 1985, Central Amer. Refugee 1985, M.L. King, Jr. Humanitarian Award 1987, Fifth Annual Age & Youth Award 1988, honoree Nicaraguan Govt. 1988, Veterans Abraham Lincoln Brigade 1989, Eleanor Roosevelt Humanitarian Award of Democratic Womens Forum 1990; civic: chair Comm. Chest Fund Drive, Ross 1947, chair Red Cross Home Nsg. Pgm., Marin Co. 1947, West coast chair `Women for Wallace' for U.S. Pres. Progressive Party ticket 1948, campaigned nat. for Vincent Hallinan for U.S. Pres. Progressive Party ticket 1952, active in Civil Rights Movement w/ Coretta and Martin Luther King, Jr. 1960s, nat. organizer the `Jeannette Rankin Brigade' to protest Vietnam War 1967, mem. del. to meet with peace negotiating teams in Paris rep. U.S., N. Vietnam, and Viet Cong 1968, organized El Salvador's Childrens Relief Pgm. 1983, founded/dir. Project Nat. Interest, orgn. vs. mil. intervention in Central Am. 1984, mem. Womens Internat. League for Peace and Freedom (S.F. pres. 1974-78, 1981-84), Womens Political Caucus, Womens Democrat Club; apptd. San Francisco Human Rights Commn., 1990; publs: book on apt. house ops. (1939), My Wild Irish Rogues (Doubleday, 1952), num. political pamphlets; Democrat; rec: contemporary politics and social injustice. Res: 1080 Chestnut San Francisco 94109 Ofc: Bally Hallinan, Downtown Apartments 535 Geary St Ste 914 San Francisco 94102

HALLORAN, JAMES VINCENT, III, consultant; b. May 12, 1942, Greenwich, Conn.; s. Dr. James Vincent and Rita Lucy (Keator) H.; m. Barbara Sharon Case, Sept. 7, 1974; edn: BME, Catholic Univ. of Am., 1964; MBA, Univ. Chicago, 1973. Career: mktg. rep. Rockwell Internat. Corp., El Segundo 1973-76, bus. area mgr. 1976-80, mgr. of bus. analysis 1980-84; dir. of mktg. H. Silver and Assocs. Inc., Los Angeles 1984-90; program mgr. Technology Training Corp., Torrance 1990-91; prin. Business Information & Analysis, Redondo Beach 1991-; mem: Am. Inst. Aero. and Astro. 1991-, The Planning Forum 1991-, Torrance Area C.of C. 1991-; civic: Redondo Beach Housing Advy. Appeals Bd. 1985-89, Citizens Advy. Bd. for South Bay Union H.S. Dist. 1983; mil: capt. USAF 1964-68, master team chief award SAC, Grand Forks AFB, N.D. 1966; Libertarian; rec: cycling, photography, body surfing. Res/Ofc: Business Information & Analysis, 612 S Gertruda Ave Redondo Beach 90277

HALLUIN, ALBERT PRICE, lawyer; b. Nov. 8, 1939, Wash. D.C.; s. William Ord and Martha (Blundon) H.; children: Marcus A. b. 1964, Russell P. b. 1968; edn: AA, Montgomery Jr. Coll. 1961; BA, La. St. Univ. 1964; JD, Univ. Baltimore 1969; admitted bar: Md. 1970, N.Y. 1985, Calif. 1991, U.S. Patent and Trademark Office 1969, US Supreme Ct. 1976, US Ct. Appeal Fed. Cir. 1982, US Dist. Ct. No. Dist. Calif. 1986. Career: patent examiner US Patent and Trademark Office, Arlington, Va. 1965-69; assoc. atty. Jones, Tullar & Cooper 1969-71; sr. patent atty. CPC Internat. Inc., Englewood Cliffs, NJ 1971-76; counsel Exxon Res. and Engring. Co., Florham Park 1976-83; v.p., chief intellectual property counsel Cetus Corp., Emeryville 1983-90; partner Fliesler, Dubb, Meyer & Lovejoy, San Francisco 1990-92; partner Limbach & Limbach, San Francisco 1992-; mem: Am Intellectual Property Law Assn. (chmn. chem. practice com 1981-83, secty. 1984-85, bd. dir. 1985-88, chmn. biotechnology com. 1990-), N.J. Patent Law Assn. (treas. 1982-83), Am. Bar Assn., Licensing Exec. Soc.; civic: BSA (chmn. troop com., asst. scoutmaster 1977-83); author: U.S. patentee: 7 in catalysis, 1 in biotechnology; songwriter Uncertain (1959), publ. articles: 1990 European Harvard Mouse (Biotechnology Law Report 1990), Patent Battles May Give Way To Cross-Licensing in the 90's (Bioworld 1991), Practice After Amgen and Scripps: The New Biotechnology Practice (Biotechnology Law Report 1991), Enforcement of Biotechnology Patent Rights (W. Coast Biotechnology Patent Conf. Workbook 1/91), Scope of Biotechnology Patent Rights (Chemistry and the Law 8/91), Courts Might Be Locking Up Cures (San Francisco Examiner 2/12/92), The Cure Has A Disease (Am. Chem. Soc. 1992), Protecting Your Biotechnology Inventions (Chemtech 3/93); Republican; Episcopalian; rec: music, backpacking. Ofc: Limbach and Limbach, 2001 Ferry Bldg San Francisco 94111-4262 Tel. 415/433-4150 Fax 415/433-8716

HALSETH, JAMES A., university adminstrator; b. Aug. 19, 1940, Pine City, Minn.; s. Allwyn Yvone and Esther Clarice (Raymond) Halseth; m. Mary Elizabeth Rossi, June 10, 1965; edn: Luther Coll., Decorah, Ia. 1958-59; BA, Concordia Coll., Moorhead, Minn. 1962; MA, Ea. N.M. Univ. 1963; PhD, Texas Tech Univ. 1973. Career: tchg. fellow, Ea. N. Mex. Univ., history, 1962-63, political science, 1963; tchg. asst., history, Texas Tech Univ. 1963-65; instr. of history, San Antonio Coll. 1965-66; instr. of hist., Pacific Lutheran Univ. 1966-68; part-time instr. of hist., Texas Tech Univ. 1968-69; asst. prof. of hist., Moorhead State Univ., Minn. 1971; asst. prof. of hist., Pacific Lutheran Univ. 1970-75, assoc. prof. of hist. 1975-80, prof. of hist. 1980-81; prof. of hist., Texas Lutheran Coll. 1981-86; prof. of hist., Calif. Lutheran Univ. 1986-; chairman, div. of social sciences, Pacific Lutheran Univ., Tacoma, Wash. 1975-81; v.p. for academic affairs and dean, Texas Lutheran Univ. 1981-86; CEO, Texas Lutheran Univ. 1983; v.p. for academic affairs and dean, Calif. Lutheran Univ. 1986-; provost, Calif. Lutheran Univ. 1990-; program devel. for Title I Agency, Olympia, Wash., Tacoma Comm. Coll., Bellevue Comm. Coll., and Pierce County Library System 1971-81; grantsmanship workshop, Bethany Coll. Devel. Office 1984; Mid-Tex. Consortium for Internat. Edn. and Programs 1984-85; bd. mem., Luth. Inst. for Religious Studies Program, Amer. Luth. Ch., Luth. Ch. in Amer. 1983-85; advy. mem., Seguin Ret. Sr. Vol. Program 1981-85; program devel., Guadalupe Valley Comm. Hosp., Warm Springs Rehab. Hosp., McKenna Mem. Hosp. 1983-85; awards: Pi Gamma Mu (Nat. Social Sci. Hon. Soc.) 1962; Silver Key (Univ. Honors Assoc.), Ea. N.M. Univ. 1963; Univ. Fellowship Award, Tx. Tech Univ. 1968; fellowship award, Nat. Seminar for Hist. Adminstrs., Williamsburg, Va. 1965; Faculty Fellowship Award, Amer. Luth. Ch. 1968; mem: Amer. Scandinavian Found. 1986-90, Amer. Assn. of Univ. Professors, Orgn. of Amer. Historians, We. Hist. Assn., We. Social Sci. Assn., Growth Policy Assn. of Pierce Co., Wash., So. Hist. Assn., Pacific NW Hist. Assn., Nat. Trust for Hist. Preservation, Nat. Mgmt. Assistance Assn., Nat. Luth. Deans Conf., Am. Assn. of State and Local Hist., Luth. Edn. Conf. of N. Am., So. Calif. Consortium of Academic Deans, Assn. of Luth. Faculties, Indep. Colls. and Univs. of Tx., Comm. Leaders Club, Thousand Oaks, Special Collections in NW Hist., Pacific Luth. Univ. Lib. (dir., 1972-80), Luth. Inst. for Theol. Studies (bd. mem. 1982-86), Tx. Luth. Coll. (devel. bd. 1981-86, bd. of regents advy. mem. 1981-86), Calif. Luth. Univ.(bd. of regents advy. mem.); coauthor: The Northwest Mosaic: Minority Conflicts in Pacific Northwest History, 1977; numerous scholarly jour. articles and book revs. Res: 1190 Monte Sereno Drive, Thousand Oaks 91360 Ofc: California Lutheran University, 60 W. Olsen Road, Thousand Oaks 91360-2787

HALSTEAD, LESTER MARK, educational psychologist, administrator; b. June 15, 1927, San Pedro; s. Levi L. and Luty June (Newcomer H.; m. Eleanor Grace, Sept. 25, 1949; children: Lester Mark, Jr. b. 1950, Michael Lee b. 1951, Edward Frank b. 1953, Richard Paul b. 1954, Thomas Alexander b. 1955; edn: BS in psych., Brigham Young Univ., Provo, Utah, 1960; MS in clin. psych., Univ. Utah, S.L.C., 1963; PhD in Edn., USC, 1976; lic. Ednl. Psychologist, Calif., 1980. Career: lic. engr. US Merchant Marines, South Pacific, 1944-46; croupier Tropicana Hotel, Las Vegas, Nev., 1957-60; chief psychologist Clark County Juvenile Ct., Las Vegas, 1963-70; sch. psychologist Clark County Sch. Dist., 1963-66; adminstrv. psychologist Baldwin Park Sch. Dist., Calif., 1970-; instr. Parent Guidance, 1975-85; asst. prof. Inst. Counseling/Guidance, Pepperdine Univ., 1977-83; dir. Parent Support Group, Baldwin Park 1975-89, Huntington Beach 1976-89; dir. Perceptual Res. Ctr., Las Vegas, 1957-60; awards: Delta Epsilon 1976-; Internat. Sch. Psychologists Assn. disting. lectr.: Univ. South Hampton, Eng. 1983, Interlaken, Switz. 1987, Europe 1985-87; mem: EDCAL, 1970-; BPOSA, 1970-; Baldwin Park Boys Club Sponsor, 1989-; author: A Tri-Dimensional Theory of Personality, 1980; A Diversified Treatment Model, 1988; Republican (Presdl. Task Force 1987-); LDS Ch.; rec: golf, sailing, skiing, hunting, fishing, research. Res: 5642 Kern Dr. Huntington Beach 92649 Ofc: 4600 Bogart St. Baldwin Park 91706

HALVERSON, ODA SIGRID, licensed acupuncturist; b. Oct. 28, 1937, Hamburg, Germany; nat. U.S. 1966; d. Walter and Leokadya R. (Zaworski) Parian; m. David R. Halverson, Sept. 14, 1968 (div. 1984); children: Leif b. 1973; edn: BA CSU Dominguez, L.A. 1980, MA, CSU 1982; PhD of Chinese Medicine, Internat. Coll., L.A. 1984; MS, SAMRA Univ., L.A. 1987; lic. med. acupuncture, Med. Bd. of Calif.; diplomate in acupuncture, NCCA. Career: secty. Im & Export, Hamburg, Germany 1955-59, L.A. 1961-66; exec. secty. Ducommun, L.A. 1966-68; herbologist, self-employed, L.A. 1980-88; lic. acupuncturist, pvt. practice, Torrance 1988-; lectr. Med. Orgn., Germany 1984; tchr. Dept. of Aging, L.A. 1990-; mem: Oriental Healing Arts Inst. 1976-, Calif. Acupuncture Assn. 1988-; creator of course in biology of cancer, Am. Cancer Soc., L.A. 1981; author: pub. article, Coronary Heart Disease 1984; interested in Buddhism; rec: reading, nature walks, discussion groups. Ofc: Oda S. Halverson PhD LAc, 3655 Lomita Blvd #412 Torrance 90505

HALVERSTADT, JONATHAN SCOTT, actor and seminar leader; b. Oct. 21, 1952, Fresno; s. Lee W. and Dorothy (Weller) H.; m. Paula Anna Saenz, June 20, 1992 (div.); m. 2d. Pamela D. Adams, Dec. 31, 1989; edn: BA, Fresno Pacific Coll. 1977; MS in Counseling, Calif. State Univ., Fresno 1993; Career: owner, Jonathan Scott Productions, Fresno 1978-; owner, Dreikurs Relationship Ctr.,

Fresno,1988-91; exec. editor, Am Magazine, Fresno,1989; announcer, KMJ/KNAX, Fresno 1980-82; announcer, KFIG-FM, Fresno 1979-80; workshop & seminar leader, 1984-;freelance copy writer, 1980-; musical performer & guest speaker US and Scandinavia, 1970-77; ski inst., Sierra Summit 1982-87; asst. inst., Small World Presch. 1974-75; author: Today, Tyndale House Pub., 1974; Communication By Candlelight, Family Life Today, Gospel Light Pub., 1975; Tears Of Your Heart, So Many Songs About Jesus, Gospel Pub. House, 1979; recorded compositions: Mush, orig. music by Jonathan M. Scott, 1977; Tears Of Your Heart, So Many Songs About Jesus, Melody Records, 1977; She Told Me, Valley Grown, KYNO Records, 1978; Help Me Lord, This Is Love, Gabriel Records, 1979; syndicated radio prods: Serve It With Love; Tax Tips with Jack Vance; With Wine and You; Fitness Finesse; tv perf: played Barry Parker on General Hospital, 1985; numerous app. Days Of Our Lives, Young And The Restless, and Capitol, 1983-1987; host, Central Calif. Easter Seal Soc. Telethon; nat. and reg. commercials: Reebok, Toyota, General Foods, NBC-TV, CBS-TV, Norwest Banks, We Are Sportswear, GMC Trucks, plus numerous industrial voice over and on-camera exp.; radio exp: morning news anchor/talk show host, KMJ; on-air pers., KNAX/Fresno, KFIG/Fresno, KFYE/Fresno, KBIF/Fresno, KOAD/Lemoore; mem: nat. bd. dir., Am. Fed. of TV and Radio Artists 1986-1992; v.p. and chmn nominations and publicity, Easter Seal Soc. of Central Calif.; pres. Hidden Gardens Cond. Assn.; Nat. Assn. of Rehab. Prof.; Prof. Ski Inst. Assn.; Screen Actors Guild; Am. Fed. of Musicians; Internat. Brotherhood of Elect. Workers; Methodist; rec: bicycling, backpacking, gourmet cooking, ski-iing, scuba diving. Ofc: Jonathan Scott & Assoc., P.O. Box 16172 Fresno 93755

HAMBRICK, HAROLD E., public relations executive; b. Feb. 17, 1943, New Orleans, La.; s. Harold E. and Mary Ellen (Clark) H.; children: Jefferey, Tyra; edn: BS, Pepperdine Univ., 1976; grad. cert. public relations, UCLA, 1988. Career: office mgr. Watts Health Found., Los Angeles 1967-68; acctg., office mgr. New Communicators Inc., Hollywood 1968-69; sr. acct. Watts Health Found., 1969-75; exec. dir. Western Assn. of Comm. Health Center, 1975-83; v.p. corp. communications Watts Health Found., 1983-; pres. Watts Credit Union 1987-, pres. Black Health Leadership Council, Inc. 1982-, pres. Calif. Black Health Network 1989-91; honors: Assemblyman Curtis Tucker Sr. Health & Human Service Award 1990, Outstanding Young Men of Am. 1978, Danforth Found. `I Dare You' Honor Roll 1961; mem. Gr. Los Angeles Press Club; AME; rec: model ships, photog., videography. Address: Los Angeles

HAMERSLOUGH, WALTER SCOTT, university professor; b. Dec. 15, 1935, Needles, Calif.; s. Walter Kenneth and Frances (Brown) H.; m. V. Darlene Berdan, Dec. 17. 1961; children: K. Scott b. 1963, Rhonda b. 1965; edn: AA, L.A. City Coll., 1955; BS, La Sierra Coll., Riverside, Calif., 1958; MA, Univ. of Redlands, Redlands, Calif., 1964; EdD, Univ. of Oregon, Eugene, 1971. Career: 7-8th grade tchr. Fairview Elem., San Bernardino, Calif., 1959-61; H.S. tchr. Loma Linda Acad., Loma Linda, Calif., 1961-64; prof. La Sierra Univ., Riverside, Calif., 1964-; prof. and chair, dept. of health & phys. edn. La Sierra Univ., 1973-;cons. YMCA, 1970; lectr. Azusa Pacific Coll., 1973; bd. mem./v.p. Alvord Pony League, Riverside, 1976-77; exec. dir. SDA-HPERA, Riverside, 1986-; awards: listed in Who's Who in Calif. 1982, 84, Who's Who in the West,1983-86, Who's Who in Religion 1985; recipient, Zapara Tchg. Award, Gen. Conf., SDA, Wash., DC 1989, Alumnus of the Year, La Sierra Univ. 1990; mem: Am. Alliance for HPERD 1963-; res. chair, v.p., state rep., Calif. Assn. for HPERD, 1963-; bd. mem. We. Coll. PE Soc. 1963-;mem: Phi Epsilon Kappa Frat. 1970, Am. Coll. of Sports Medicine 1980; pres., exec. dir. SDA-HPERA 1983-; civic: SDA Ch., Riverside, Calif.: SS sponsor 1972-79, SS coord. 1981-83, superintendent 1972-88, elder 1972-; sch. bd. mem. La Sierra Acad., Riverside, Calif.; co-author, book, Swim for Child with Impairments, 1977; contbg. author, book, Study Guide/Happiness Homemade, 1975; 2 pub. articles on sch. sports competition; Republican; Seventh-Day Adventist; rec: gardening, reading, tennis, golf. Res: 5133 Harcourt Circle Riverside 92505. Ofc: La Sierra Univ. Riverside 92515

HAMILL, RICHARD DAVID, medical products company executive; b. Jan. 5, 1939, Visalia; s. Edward Charles and Elizabeth (Scheidt) H.; m. Mary Lucinda Kilbourne, Aug. 26, 1961; children: Lucinda b. 1963, Pamela b. 1965, Edward b. 1967, Stephanie b. 1971; edn: BS, Univ. Utah 1960; PhD, 1965; reg. pharmacist Calif., Utah. Career: res. pharmacist Miles Labs., Elkhart, Ind. 1965-66; asst. to sr.v.p. res. and devel. Baxter Labs., Deerfield, Ill. 1966-68, dir. res. adminstrn. 1968-70, dir. quality control Hyland div., Costa Mesa 1970-74, dir. product assurance, Deerfield, Ill. 1974-76; dir. corp. compliance G.D. Searle & Co., Skokie, Ill. 1976-79; pres. Hamill Assoc., Northbrook, Ill. 1979-83; pres., CEO Hycor Biomed. Inc., Garden Grove 1983-; Republican; Christian; rec: pvt. pilot. Res: 22686 Ledana Mission Viejo 92691 Ofc: Hycor Biomedical Inc. 7272 Chapman Garden Grove 92641

HAMM, WILLIAM GILES, banking executive; b. Dec. 29, 1942, W.D.C.; s. John Edwin and Letty Belle (Wills) H.; m. Kathleen Ann Kelley, Sept. 5, 1970; children: Giles b. 1975; edn: AB (magna cum laude) Dartmouth Coll., 1964; MA econs., Univ. Mich., 1966, PhD econs., 1969. Career: budget examiner Bur. of the Budget, W.D.C. 1969-72, chief HUD Br. Ofc. of Mgmt. & Budget, 1972-76, dep. assoc. director 1976-77; legislative analyst Cali Legislature,

Sacramento 1977-86; v.p. World Savings, Oakland 1986-91; sr. v.p. Federal Home Loan Bank of San Francisco, 1991-92, exec. v.p. and c.o.o. 1992-; awards: Colby Govt. Prize, Dartmouth 1964, Phi Beta Kappa 1964, Wm. A Jump Award for exemplary svc. US Govt. 1972; mem: Am. Economics Assn. 1964-, Nat. Acad. of Pub. Adminstrn. (fellow 1983-), Council for Excellence in Govt. (prin. 1986-), Western Legislative Fiscal Officers (pres. 1984-85), Deans Advy. Coun. UC Davis (1983-); mem. bd. vis. Inst. for Policy Studies, Duke Univ. (1986-90); rec: skiing, hiking, bridge, cooking, pers. computers, gardening. Res: 858 Mountain View Dr Lafayette 94549-4214 Ofc: FHL Bank-S.F. 600 California St San Francisco 94108

HAMMER, JOSEPH KEITH, company executive; b. Dec. 4, 1953, Los Angeles; s. Morris Keith and Marjory Carol H.; m. Ada Kathleen Haas, Sept. 6, 1980; children: Joseph, Jr. b. 1982, John Henry b. 1986; edn: AA, Long Beach City Coll., 1974; BS, CSU Los Angeles, 1977; career: non-profit orgn. exec. Long Beach Area Council BSA, 1977-78; dispatcher Long Beach Police Dept., 1978-79; agt. N.Y. Life Ins. Co., Los Angeles 1979-81; v.p. American Typewriter Inc., Westminster 1981-88; coordinator Edgemont Sales 1988-92; ops. mgr. Arrowhead Business Machines, 1992-; mem: So. Calif. Office Machine Dealers Assn. (treas. 1986-88, newsletter ed. 1988-), Downtown Long Beach Assocs. (dir. 1984-87), Long Beach C.of C., Westminster C.of C., Nat. Rifle Assn. (life), All States Masonic Lodge (Past Master, newsletter ed. 1985-86), L.B. Scottish Rite (32 deg.), L.B. Lions (sec. 1984-86), Westminster Lions (pres. 1988-89), Los Alamitos Rotary (dir. 1991-92); Eagle Scout, var. pos. in scouting L.B. & Westminster; contbr. articles in trade jours.; Republican; Christian; rec: trophy hunter, knifemaker.

HAMMERBACK, JOHN CLARK, professor of communication; b. Oct. 6, 1938, San Francisco; s. William Joseph and Susan (Rigik) H.; m. Jean Melton, Aug. 29, 1965; children: Kristen b. 1969, Karen b. 1972; edn: BA, San Francisco St. Coll., 1962; MA, Univ. Oklahoma, 1965; PhD, Indiana Univ., 1970. Career: tchg. asst. Univ. Oklahoma, Norman 1963-65, Indiana Univ., Bloomington 1965-68; prof. comm. CSU Hayward, Calif. 1968-, asst. v.p. CSUH 1989-91; assoc. editor Western Jour. of Communication 1979-81, 84-86, 90-92; dir. Hayward Conf. in Rhetorical Criticism, 1988-; Faculty Affirmative Action ofcr. CSUH 1987-89; mem. bd. dirs. Community Counseling and Edn. Ctr., Fremont 1989-; awards: outstanding lectr. CSUH 1971, exceptional merit CSUH 1984, listed Dir. of Am. Scholars, Who's Who in the West; mem: Western Communication Assn. (1968-, pres. 1983-84), Speech Communication Assn. (1963-, chair pub. address div. 1993), Rhetoric Soc. of Am. 1985-, Calif. Speech Communication Assn. 1975-, Execs. Club WS (pres. 1991-92); coauthor: In Search of Justice (1987), War of Words (1985), author 20+ articles and chapters in books (1971-), 7 book revs. (1967-), 20+ conv. papers (1969-); mil: A2c USN Reserve 1962-68; Prot.; rec: tennis. Res: 203 Fisalia Ct Fremont 94539 Ofc: Speech Comm. Dept. Calif. State Univ., Hayward 94542

HAMMOND, CHARLES EDGAR, data processing executive; b. Dec. 24, 1943, Kellogg, Ida.; s. Charles Wm. and Irene Elizabeth (Hoffman) H.; m. Jennifer Giard, Aug. 12, 1967; children: Christa b. 1973, Robert b. 1976; edn: BBA, Wash. St. Univ. 1967; MBA, Golden Gate Univ. 1973. Career: pgmr./analyst Boeing Airplane Co., Seattle 1967-68; pgmr./analyst Chevron Corp., San Francisco 1969-, div. mgr. Computer Applications Dept., Chevron Information Technology Co., San Ramon 1986-; recipient award of merit Calif. Dept. Rehab. 1981; mem. advy. com. Computer Sci. Re-entry Pgm., UCB 1983-; mem. Alumni Beta Theta Pi Frat., Crow Canyon Ctry Club; rec: Little League Baseball, outdoor activities. Ofc: Chevron Information Technology Co. PO Box 5031 San Ramon 94583

HAMMOND, LOUISE MARIE, photographer; b. July 16, 1934, Oakland (3d gen. Californian); d. Amiel John and Louise Agnes (Grewe) Figrouid; m. 1957-1982; edn: cert. in ornithology Cornell Univ., 1980. Career: photographer prin. Hammond Photography, Oakland 1968-: credits include American Forests, Ariz. Highways, Givaudanian, Horticulture, Westways, Wildlife, and other magazines, Flying Spur Yosemite Calendars (14+ yrs.), postcards, photograph in 1990 Yosemite Renaissance V Centennial Art Competition, B/W salon prints in num. pvt. collections; sales brochure designer Forum Travel, and tour leader in Kenya, Tanzania and Seychelles; acct. Lybrand, Ross Bros. & Montgomery, Oakland 1970-72; bus. mgr. and telethon co-ord. Easter Seal Soc., 1972-78; property and leasing mgr. Broadway Webster Med. Bldg., Summit Med. Bldg., 1978-89; awards: Who's Who In Photography, Nikon Award of Excellence 1983, runner-up Wildlife Photographer of Yr. London; bd. trustees Western Aerospace Mus. 1982-89, secty.-treas. 1982-85, treas. 1985-87; mem: Internat. Freelance Photographers Orgn., Calif. Alumni Assn., Epiphyllum Soc. of Am., Orchid Soc. of Am., Oakland Art Assn., numerous conserv. orgns.; 2 books in progress: culture of epiphytic plants, and photo study of Southwest Canyonlands; Republican; Roman Catholic; rec: hiking, snorkeling, gardening, oil and pastel artist, travel. Address: PO Box 11332 Oakland 94611

HAMMOND, R. PHILIP, research scientist, engineer; b. May 28, 1916, Creston, Iowa; s. Robert Hugh and Helen (Williams) H.; m. C. Vivienne Fox (dec. 1987); edn: BS chem. engring., Univ. So. Calif.; PhD physical chem.,

Univ. Chgo.; reg. profl. engr. Calif., Ill. Career: chief chemist Lindsey Chem. Co., West Chgo, Ill.; group leader Los Alamos Sci. Lab., Los Alamos; program dir. Oak Ridge Nat. Lab., Oak Ridge, Tenn.; sr. scientist R&D Assoc., Marina del Rey; adj. prof. engring. UCLA; design team leader Large Desalination Project, Met. Water Dist. of So. Calif.; cons. engr., Santa Monica; mem U.S. delegation to Internat. Conf. on Peaceful Uses of Atomic Energy 1955, 60, 65; U.S. del. to USSR Desalination Exchange 1964; U.S. study team Mexico Desalination Project; U.S. del. to Internat. Atomic Energy Agency; honors: Sigma Xi; mem: Am. Nuclear Soc.; 100 papers pub. in tech. jours., 25 patents; mil: USCG Aux.; Prot.; rec: sailing, cabinet making, painting. Ofc: POB 1735 Santa Monica 90406

HANCOCK, EMILY STONE, psychologist; b. Nov. 18, 1945, Syracuse, N.Y.; d. Theodore McLennan and Eleanor Sackett (Stone) H.; m. Philip Yenawine, Aug. 28, 1965 (div. 1970); 1 son, Tad; edn: BA, Syracuse Univ. 1971; MSW, Boston Univ., 1974; EdD, Harvard Univ., 1981; Lic. Clinical Social Worker (LCSW), Mass., Calif. Career: clin. social worker Children's Hosp., Boston 1974-77; pvt. practice Mass., Calif., 1976-; co-founder, therapist Divorce Resource Ctr., Cambridge 1976-78; tchg. fellow Harvard 1978-79; counselor Alameda Co. Superior Ct., Oakland 1982-; screening coord. dept. pediatrics, UC San Francisco, 1982-85; faculty Ctr. for Psychological Studies, Albany 1982-; chair Askwith Symp. and Colloquia, Cambridge 1979, editor Harvard Ednl. Rev. 1979-81, fellow HEW 1972-74, fellow Danforth Found. 1978-80, fellow NIMH 1981-82; awards: grantee Radcliffe Coll. (1978, 80), Woodrow Wilson Found. 1980, Phi Beta Kappa, Phi Kappa Phi; mem: Am. Psychol. Assn., Acad. Cert. Soc. Workers; author: The Girl Within (1989), articles in profl. jours.; rec: music. Res/Ofc: 1230 Glen Ave Berkeley 94708-1841 Ph: 510/540-5510

HAND, TERRY LEE, plastic surgeon; b. Oct. 31, 1942, Sunburry, Pa.; s. Leon Russell and Izora (Yeager) H.; m. Lisa, July 10, 1982; children: Tiffany b. 1966, Sara b. 1968, Brianna b. 1986, Christina b. 1987; edn: BA, Susquehanna Univ. 1964; MS, Univ. of Mo. 1966; MD, Temple Univ. Sch. of Med. 1970; UC Davis Sch. of Med. 1976-81; Diplomate Am. Bd. of Plastic and Reconstruction Surgery. Career: pvt. practice plastic surgery; asst. clin. prof. plastic surgery UC Davis; clin. attending plastic surgery V.A. Hosp., Martinez; awards: Babcock Surgical Soc. award 1970; mem: CMA, MMS, AMA, ASPRS; rec: art, ski. Res: 32 Estates Ct San Rafael 94901 Ofc: Terry L Hand MD 750 Las Gallinas #219 San Rafael 94903

HANDEL, JAMES ARTHUR, auto dealership chief financial executive; b. March 30, 1947, Sterling, Ill.; s. Lester Eugene and Grace Irene (Kendell) H.; m. Marjorie Kay Dexter, July 8, 1972; children: James II b. 1977, Kimberly b. 1980; edn: BS, No. Ill. Univ. 1972; Sauk Valley Coll. 1974-75; computer tng. Houston Tx. 1984-85. Career: bus. mgr. Harrison Chevrolet Cadillac, Dixon, Ill. 1974-78; Bun Austin Chevrolet, Sterling, Ill. 1978-79; Jack Winters Enterprises, Highland, Ind. 1979-83; Valley Motor Center, Van Nuys 1983-85; controller Downtown L.A. Motors, Los Angeles 1985-; awards: diamond club Mazda 1981, performance excellence Chevrolet 1975-79; mem. bd. dirs. Workman's Ins.; civic: Church Council POP, Northridge 1987-88, Simi Valley Football League 1985-86, AAL Northridge 1987-89; Republican; Lutheran; rec: bicycling, running, golf. Res: 15338 E Benwood Dr Moorpark 93021

HANEY, FREDERICK MARION, venture capitalist; b. Mar. 5, 1941, Columbus, Ohio; s. George Edward and Margaret Ann (Marion) H.; m. Barbara Breig, June 8, 1963; children: Karen b. 1967, Bradford b. 1969; edn: BA, Ohio Wesleyan Univ. 1963; MS math., Colo. St. Univ. 1965; PhD, Carnegie-Mellon, 1968. Career: product devel. mgr. Scientific Data Systems, El Segundo 1968-70; strategy mgr. Xerox Corp., El Segundo 1970-75; mgr. Computer Scis. Corp., El Segundo 1975-77; mgr. strategic plnng. Xerox Corp. 1977-80; strategic planning/gen. mgmt. TRW, Redondo Beach 1980-83; venture capital mgr. 3i Ventures, Newport Beach 1983-91; pres. Venture Management, 1992-; dir: IC Sensors, Milpitas 1988-, Evernet Inc., L.A. 1989-92, Adaptive Solutions Inc., Portland 1991-, FRS Inc., Sacramento 1985-; Silicon Power Corp., Long Beach 1985-92; chmn. of bd. dirs. Pepgen, Inc., Huntington Beach 1993-; co-founder Technology Bank, Torrance; honors: Omicron Delta Kappa 1963, Balfour Award, Sigma Chi 1963; appt. bds: USC Entrepreneurial Program (advy. bd. 1987-), UCI Accelerate Program (dir. 1991-), Ohio Wesleyan Univ. (Assoc. 1984-); mem: Nat. Assn. of Venture Capitalists, We. Assn. of Venture Capitalists, Orange County Venture Capital Assn., So. Calif. Technical Execs. Network; civic: Project Mexico, Rolling Hills, Ca. 1977-, Palos Verdes Estates Coastline Com. (chair 1974-75); clubs: P.V. Golf, P.V. Tennis; publs: 7+ tech. articles 1968-73; Republican; Presbyterian; rec: golf, tennis, sportfishing. Res: 3433 Paseo Del Campo Palos Verdes Estates 90274

HANKINS, HESTERLY G., III, computer systems scientist, educator; b. Sept. 5, 1950, Sallisaw, Okla.; s. Hesterly G., II and Ruth Faye (Jackson) H.; edn: attended Ventura Coll. 1970, Antelope Valley Coll. 1977, La Verne Univ. 1987; BA in sociology, UC Santa Barbara, 1972, Scholars Program, UCSB (1970); MBA mgmt. info. sys., UCLA, 1974; postgrad. telecomms., Golden Gate Univ., 1985-86; Calif. Comm. Colls. tchr., college supr., chief adminstr. creds. Career:

applications pgmr. Xerox Corp., Marina del Rey 1979-80; computer pgmr. engring. div. Naval Base, Port Hueneme, 1981-84; spl. asst. ceo NAS Moffet Field 1984-85; computer analyst Pacific Missile Test Ctr., Point Mugu 1985-88; MIS specialist Defense Contract Administrv. Svs. Reg., El Segundo 1988-; instr. Ventura Coll., Golden Gate Univ., Chapman Coll., De Anza Coll., National Univ., CORE; SCAS National Univ. faculty; adj. lectr. West Coast Univ. 1987; awards: 20th Century Onyx Scholar 1968, UCSB Dean's List 1971, Alpha Kappa Psi (life, sec. 1973-74), Outstanding Young Men of Am., Montgomery, Ala. Jaycees 1980, SMART beneficial suggestion awards-NSWS-ES 1984, suggestion awards PMTC (Pt. Hueneme 1988, and Pt. Mugu), Arthur Young nominee for Entrepreneur of Year 1987, Pt. Hueneme, outstanding perf. award Weapons Support Directorate CAMAIR, PMTC, Pt. Mugu 1988, Spl. Act Award Def. Contract Adminstrn. Svs. Reg. 1989, profl. appreciation letters (3), listed Who's Who in the World 1993, Who's Who in the West 1993 (21st, 23rd & 24th edns.), Who's Who in Calif. 1993, Internat. Leaders in Achiev. (1st edn.) 1988, Men of Achievement, Am. Men & Women of Sci., Who's Who in Finance & Industry; mem: Assn. for Computing Machinery 1974, Grad. Students of Mgmt. Alumni 1974, IEEE Computer Soc., Fed. Mgrs. Assn., Intergovtl. Council on Technology of Information Processing, Internat. Platform Assn./Am. Lyceum Assn., Nat. Assn. Accts., Calif. Assn. Accts.; civic: City of Oxnard Comm. Relations Bd. 1984, YWCA Benefit Rodeo Assn. (vol. 1975-76), ANRC Blood Donor Campaign 1973, Combined Fed Campaign (Key Person 1978, honors); mem: Palm Springs Tennis Club (P.S.), El Dorado Ranch Estates (San Felipe); author: Campus Computer 1988, Satellites & Teleconference Network Planning, Quotations 1992, ; mem. U.S. Presdl. Task Force (Medal of Merit 1990); United Methodist (parish & ch. rels. 1987-88); rec: chess, reading. Res: 3700 S Sepulveda Blvd West Los Angeles 90034-6851 Ofc: 9920 La Cienega Blvd Inglewood 9030i

HANNON, TIMOTHY PATRICK, lawyer; b. Nov. 29, 1948, Culver City; s. Justin Aloysius and Ann Elizabeth (Ford) H.; m. Patricia Ann, May 1, 1976; children: Sean Patrick b. 1978, James Patrick b. 1980; edn: Wien Univ., Vienna, 1968-69; BA, JD (cum laude), Santa Clara Univ., 1970; Naval War Coll. 1988; admitted bar: Calif. (1974). Career: atty., assoc. Alvan Fisher, Banning 1975; atty., ptnr. Moerdyke & Hannon, Palo Alto 1975-84; atty. Atwood, Hurst, Knox & Anderson, San Jose 1984-86; sole practice atty., Campbell 1986-; instr. Lincoln Univ., San Jose 1988-, De Anza Jr. Coll. 1987-, San Jose St. Univ. 1983-86, UC Santa Cruz 1981; awards; Calif. scholarship 1966-70, Santa Clara Univ. Law Sch. scholar 1971-74, U.S. Govt. Jr. Fulbright 1968-69; mem. Santa Clara Univ. Law Alumni (bd. 1979-, pres. 1984-86), Santa Clara Univ. Nat. Alumni, Nat. Alumni Exec. Com., Menlo Park Housing Commn., Kiwanis San Jose (bd. dirs. 1991-93), Kiwanis Palo Alto (bd. dirs. 1977-79), Naval Reserve Assn.; 2 articles pub. in profl. jours. 1979, 81; mil: comdr. USNR 1978-, sp6 Army/Calif. Nat. Guard 1970-76, Navy Achievement Medal 1986; Republican; R.Cath.; rec: sailing, trains. Res: 806 Buckwood Ct San Jose 95120 Ofc: 1901 S Bascom Ave Ste 1440 Campbell 95008

HANOWELL, ERNEST GODDIN, physician-internist; b. Jan. 31, 1920, Newport News, Va.; s. George Frederick and Ruby Augustine (Goddin) H.; m. Para Jean Hall, June 10, 1945; children: Ernest D., Deborah J. Hanowell Orick, Leland H., Dee P. Hanowell Martinmaas, Robert G.; edn: AB, George Wash. Univ., 1945, MD, 1948; postgrad. Nat. Heart Inst. 1959-61, Tufts Univ. 1960-61, Johns Hopkins 1961-62; diplomate Am. Bd. Internal Medicine. Career: intern, USPHS Hosp., Norfolk, Va. 1948-49; resident internal medicine USPHS Hosp., Seattle 1952-55; chief medicine USPHS Hosp., Ft. Worth 1955-57; dep. chief medicine USPHS Hosp., Boston 1957-59; cons. chest disease Phila. Gen. Hosp. 1960-61; clin. asst. Tufts Med. Sch., and lectr. medicine Hahnemann Med. Coll. 1960-61; asst. prof. Univ. Md. Med. Sch. 1961-64; instr. Univ. Tenn. Med. Sch. 1964-65; chief medicine USPHS Hosp., Memphis 1964-65, Monterey County Gen. Hosp. 1969-70; attdg. staff Cardiac Clinic, Stanford Univ. Med. Sch. 1967-69; med. staff Kaiser Permanente Med. Group, Sacramento 1971-87, ret.; asst. clin. prof. Sch. Med., UC Davis 1973-81; Fellow ACP, Fellow Am. Coll. Chest Diseases, mem. AMA, TB and Health Assn., Crocker Art Mus. Assn., Phi Chi, Salinas School Board (1967-69), Am. Heart Assn. (bd. dirs.); clubs: Commonwealth (S.F.), Comstock (Sacto.); mil: U.S. Army 1943-46. Res: 1158 Racquet Club Dr Auburn 95603

HANSEN, ARLEN J., educator, author; b. Oct. 24, 1936, Rolfe, Iowa; s. Carl E. and Lorene (Kipfer) H.; m. D. Lynn, Aug. 16, 1959; children: Laura b. 1960, Kip b. 1961, James b. 1963; edn: BS, math., Iowa State, 1958; MA English, Univ. Iowa, 1962, PhD English, 1969. Career: lectr. Bradley Univ., Peoria, Ill. 1962-66; prof. of English, Univ. of the Pacific, 1969-, chair English Dept. 1988-91; Fulbright Prof. Univ. of Vienna 1980-81, Aachen, Germany 1985-86; awards: tchg. res. fellow Univ. Iowa 1966-69, grantee Am. Coun. of Learned Socs. 1976, Deutscher Akademischer Austauschdienst 1974, Rockefeller Summer Grant (Am. Film Inst., 1977), Faye and Alex Spanos outstanding tchr. award 1984, NEH travel 1987, UOP outstanding res. 1989, UOP distinguished faculty 1990; appt. advy. screening com. Fulbright Coun. Internat. Exchange of Scholars 1989-, bd. Calif. Coun. for the Humanities 1987-, editl. bd. The Californians: A Mag. of Calif. History 1982-; mem.: Author's Guild, Modern Language Assn., Nat. Council of Tchrs. of English, Conf. on Coll. Composition

and Comm., Am. Literature Assn. Assn. of Depts. of English; author: Expatriate Paris: A Cultural and Literary Guide to Paris of the 1920s (1990, Arcade/Little Brown, ppbk. 1991), book chapters, essays and articles; Democrat. Res: 7819 Rosewood Dr Stockton 95207 Ofc: Dept. English Univ. of the Pacific Stockton.

HANSEN, CHRISTINE M., pharmacist; b. Dec. 26, 1954, Inglewood; d. Dr. Oluf Steffen (M.D.) and Betty Jane (Henderson) Hansen; edn: Golden West Jr. Coll. 1972-75, PharmD, USC, 1979. Career: pharmacy intern Long Beach VA Hosp., Long Beach, summer 1978; clin. pharmacist Cottage Hosp., Santa Barbara, 1979-87, also instr. nsg. edn. in pharmacology at hosp. and coord. of the Drug of the Week pgm. to keep nurses current; instr. public awareness in poison information; mem. Am. Pharmaceutical Assn., Cymbidian Soc. Orange Co., Huntington Harbour Art Assn.; creative: performing classical pianist retirement homes 1975-; fashion modeling and film work, La Belle Agy. and John Robert Powers; watercolor painter, local exhibits; rec: swimming, singing, piano, humor. Res: 238 Reef Ct Santa Barbara 93109

HANSEN, DON CURTIS, envelope manufacturing executive; b. March 13, 1929, Marinette, Wis.; s. Curtis Albert and Dagmar Anne H.; m. Joan Crant, Nov. 9, 1973; edn: bus. admin., Carroll Coll. 1952. Career: purchasing agent Prescott/ Sterling, Menominee, Mich. 1954-62; mfrs. rep. Don C. Hansen Assoc., Phoenix, Ariz. 1962-63; salesmgr. Karolton Envelope Co., San Francisco 1964-72; pres., owner San Francisco Envelope, San Francisco 1972-79; owner Curtis Swann Cards, San Francisco 1977-79; pres., owner Don C. Hansen Inc. dba The Envelope Co., San Francisco 1979-; mem: Printing Industries of No. Calif. (dir. 1980-), Envelope Printing Specialists Assn. NY, NY (pres. 1983-84, dir. 1983-), S.F. Litho & Craftsmans Club, Printing Industries of No. Calif., Envelope Mfrs. Assn. Am., Masons, Ahmed Shrine; clubs: Wing Point CC (Bainbridge Island, Wn.) Harbor Point Tennis, S.F. Tennis (bd. govs. 1988-91); mil: pfc US Army 1952-54; Republican; rec: golf, tennis, skiing, bridge; ofc: The Envelope Co. 2857 Cypress St Oakland 94608-4011

HANSON, L(LOYD) THAXTON, state justice, ret.; b. Aug. 24, 1920, Bloomington, Ill.; s. Emory Earl (LLB, Hon. LLD) and Zae Edna (Thaxton) H.; m. Evelynne Rasmussen; edn: grad. U.S.M.A. Prep Sch., Ft. Sheridan, Ill. 1940; BS, Univ. Ill. Coll. Engring., 1947; JD, Univ. Mich. Sch. of Law, Ann Arbor 1950, grad. Calif. Coll. of Trial Judges, 1968; grad. Nat. Coll. of St. Trial Judges, Univ Nev., at Reno, 1970, grad. course 1972; admitted Calif. St. Bar 1954. Career: atty., assoc. McBain & Morgan, Los Angeles 1954-59; sr. ptnr. Schell & Delamer, 1959-68, spec. trial lawyer of civil litigation, defense, in Superior Cts.; appt. by Gov. Reagan judge Superior Ct., Van Nuys 1968-72, appt. Justice Ct. of Appeal, 1973, elected 1974, and re-elected 12 yr. term 1978-92, ret.; honors: High Sch. R.O.T.C. comdr. The Ligget Rifles precision drill platoon and outstanding cadet all 4 yrs., Univ. Ill.- Lambda Chi Alpha frat. (pres.), Inter-Frat. Council (v.p.), R.O.T.C. grad. Cavalry Tng. Pgm., requested and received Presdl. appt. as 2d lt. 6th U.S. Cavalry Regt. WWII (1942-46), Delta Theta Phi law frat., Hon. LLD Pepperdine Sch. of Law (1974), recipient plaque S.F.V. Crim. Bar Assn. (1973), honor certs. for speech and articles Freedoms Found. at Valley Forge (1973, 74), Resolutions Calif. Assembly and Senate (1976), commendn. Californians Against Crime (1983), commendn. and spl. recogn. in Congl. Record of the U.S. (6/26/72), citations from L.A. City Council, L.A. Co. Bd. Suprs., Assn. of U.S. Army, Internat. Coll. of Armed Forces, other govt. agys.; mem: Calif. Judges Assn., Am. Bar Assn., Am Judicature Soc., Am. Bd. Trial Advocates (past exec., past chmn. publs. com.), L.A. County Bar Assn., Am. Arbitration Assn. (AAA), Am. Soc. of Writers of Legal Subjects (SCRIBES); civic: Americanism Ednl. League/Freedom Ctr. Knotts Berry Farm (exec. com., chmn., trustee, Law and Order man of yr. award 1973), Bill of Rights Commemoration Com. (1982-83), S.F.V. Bus. & Profl. Assn. (charter mem., chmn. 1967-69, Free Enterprise of Yr. award 1976), Univ. Ill. Alumni Assn., Univ. Mich. Alumni Assn.; keynote speaker re Calif.'s Sys. of Justice numerous profl. and civic groups; frequent speaker various orgns. on law subjects, court reforms, patriotism, strong nat. defense; mil: col. Armor, AUS, ret., 6 yrs. Active duty WWII and Korean Conflict, Reserve duty staff Command and Gen. Staff Coll., and dir. higher edn. So. Calif. USAR Sch., Ft. McArthur, San Pedro; Presbyterian; Republican (St. Central Com., cred. com., alt. del. nat. conv. 1964). Ofc: Private Judge, Civil Dispute Resolution, Superior Court Building, 600 S Commonwealth Ave Ste 1200 Los Angeles 90005

HARDCASTLE, ROBERT TAYLOR, management and insolvency consultant; b. Jan. 28, 1952, San Francisco; s. Robt. Leon and Marjorie Pearl (Bryson) H.; m. Karen C. Welch, June 23, 1990; children: Heather b. 1976, Barrett b. 1979, Greysen b. 1983; edn: AA, Bakersfield Coll. 1972; BS, CSU Bakersfield 1974; MBA, Claremont Grad. Sch., 1984. Career: constrn. ind. exec. 1976-85; owner Bottom Line Management Technologies Co., Bakersfield 1986-, also Atlanta 1991-; mem: Am. Mgmt. Assn., Nat. Fire Protection Assn., Am. Fire Sprinkler Assn., Kern Co. Builders Exchange, Kern Co. Contractors Assn. (founding dir.), Cal-State Bakersfield Alumni Assn.; developer: Finally a computer bus. program; contbr. articles various mags. and industry publs.; Republican (Co. Central Com.); R.Cath.; rec: skiing, baseball. Ofc: 4909 Stockdale Hwy Ste 355 Bakersfield 93309-2637

HARDIE, GEORGE GRAHAM, gaming club executive; b. Aug. 19, 1933, Cleveland, Ohio; s. Wm. M., Jr. and Helen (Graham) H.; m. Paula Daniel (div.); children: George, Jr. b. 1967, Jennifer b. 1970; ed. pub. schs. N.Y. and Mass. Career: sales dept. of family candy bus., Hardie Bros., Pittsburgh, Pa.; various mgmt. pos., then owner direct sales agys.; purchased first standardbred horse, 1963, driving, tng. and racing harness horses, 1963-; cons. expert on gaming and racing issues, cons. greyhound racing proposal for State of Hawaii; founder pub. relations and advt. agy. (spec. in initiative qualification and campaign mgmt.) 1973, agy. merged with Profile Inc., 1978-, owner/mgr. Hardie Group, Inc. involved in bus. devel. and acquisitions, gaming cons. and evaluations; owner Emerald Ranch, Inc., thoroughbred horse farm, 1989-; owner/mgr. Profile Communications, Inc. 1990-; owner/mgr Nut Kettle, Inc., gourmet treats and gifts, 1990-; mng. ptnr./gen. ptnr. Bicycle Club Casino (world's largest card casino), Bell Gardens 1981-; recipient Resolutions of commendn. for community service U.S. Cong. Matthew G. Martinez, L.A. Co. Supr. Ed Edelman, Calif. St. Sen. Art Torres, L.A. Dist. Atty. Ira Reiner, and Calif. St. Assemblywoman Gloria Molina; mem: Calif. Harness Drivers Guild (3t pres.), Western Standardbred Assn. (dir.), Golden State Greyhound Assn. (organizer, pres. 1973); civic: elected City Council Cathedral City (mayor 1988-90, mayor pro-tem 1990-91), active Bell Gardens C.of C. (pres. 1986); works: placed initiative to legalize greyhound betting on Calif. 1976 statewide ballot (defeated), won case Hardie vs. Eu in Calif. State Supreme Ct. which established the right to circulate initiatives in Calif. without fin. restrictions 1976, was campaign mgr. for Bell Gardens card club issue (passed 1980). Ofc: Bell Gardens Bicycle Club, 7301 Eastern Ave Bell Gardens 90201

HARDING, CYRIL RICHARD BENNETT, civil engineer; b. Nov. 3, 1906, Torquay, Devon, England; s. Alfred Sidney Cowell and Florence Adeline Augusta (Hall) Harding; emigrated to Lynn, Mass. 1912 with parents, nat. US cit. 1920; m. Ruth Dorothea Jensen, Dec. 7, 1929; children: Richard Bennett, Robert Hall; m. 2d. Joanna Savage, Jan. 1, 1947; children: Joanna Candice, George Thomas; edn: BSCE, M.I.T. 1930. Career: chief engr. Lynn Park Dept. 1930-41 (designed and blt. the largest H.S. stadium in USA 25000 seats; also a cantilevered-roof grandstand for the Lynn baseball club, then a Boston Red Sox farm club; both designs pub. in Christian Sci. Monitor, var. trade publs., local and Boston newspapers); tech. cons., asst. dir. of engring. Stran Steel Div., Great Lakes Steel Corp., Detroit, Mich.; designed Quonset Huts for USN, patented expansion system enabled std. parts to build huge warehouses throughout S.Pac. during WWII; designed the light-wt. steel floats used in USN system for floating dry-docks, floating piers and wharfs, floating bridges; tech. asst. loaned to English Ministry for Reconstrn. 1945, 1941-48; mgr. middle east ops. Johnston Pump Co. of Los Angeles, HQ Athens, Greece 1949-50; design engr., sr. design engr. Wing Group, N. Am. Aviation 1950-60; pres. Peerless Investment Co. (real estate investments), Hollywood 1957-; honors: bow oar, 8-oared crew 1923-25, Nat. Jr. Championship, Poughkeepsie 1925, MIT swim team 1926, MIT rifle team 1927, MIT Drama Club 1928-29, Silver Ski Award, Sun Valley 1941, cert. scuba diver 1953; mem: Soc. of Am. Mil. Engrs. (awarded life mem. 1942), US/LA Power Squadron (cmdr. 1969), MIT Alumni Assn. So. Calif., Hollywood Yacht Club. Address: 7454 Hillside Ave Los Angeles 90046

HARDING, JOANNA SAVAGE (Savich), Olympic athlete, fencing school founder, real estate broker; b. Apr. 30, Detroit, Mich.; d. George Thomas and Gizella D'Aguillar (Vojner) Savich; m. Bela de Tuscan, May 9, 1931; m. 2d. Cyril R.B. Harding, Jan. 1, 1947; children: Joanna Candice and George Thomas Harding; edn: Detroit Sch. of Arts and Crafts 1926-29, Rhode Is. Sch. of Design 1929-30, pvt. stu. portrait painting w/John Hubbard Rich; Santelli Sch. of Fencing 1932-36. Career: co-founder Salle de Tuscan Sch. of Fencing and Club (world's largest Salle d'armes), Detroit 1930-43; US Nat. Champion Women's Foil 1936 and capt. US Womens Olympic Fencing Team (voted Most Beautiful Olympian, Olympic Games Berlin) 1936; fencing tchr. Wayne Univ. and the Cranbrook Sch., Bloomfield Hills, Mich. 1934-36; choreographer and performer in a fencing ballet for full-year run at the Palladium, London 1938-39; World Profl. Champion Women's Foil 1939; fencing exhibs. in prin. cities Europe and Balkan countries 1939-40 (on last convoy lv. France during German invasion WWII); entertainer featured act, fencing and dancing, Broadway musicals incl. Keep Off the Grass, others, NYC 1941-43; USO Sports Unit entertainer Armed Forces in Pacific 1944-45; fencing tchr. 20th Century-Fox Studios, Agnes Moorhead Sch. of Drama, movie double for stars in fencing scenes 1957-62; real estate broker, Hollywood 1945-, dba Peerless Investment Co. 1957-, incorporated, v.p. 1975-; mem. 1984 Olympic Speakers Bureau; first female fencer to wear trousers, subject of Paul Gallico column in the N.Y. News headlined "Pants is for Guys" w/3-col. cartoon; cited in Ency. Britannica (1941 supplement), and Black's Hist. of Aviation as the first person to lift off ground in a heavier-than-air machine using only her own power; first woman cmdr. LA Power Squadron 1988-89. Address: 7454 Hillside Ave Los Angeles 90046

HARDT, JAMES V., research psychologist; b. Feb. 10, 1945, Red Wing, Minn.; s. Dr. Victor Henry and Rosella Margaret (Dille) H.; edn: BS physics, Carnegie Inst. of Tech., 1967; MS psychology, Carnegie-Mellon Univ., 1969, PhD psychology/ psychophysiology, 1974; postdoctoral UC San Francisco - Langley Porter Neuropsychiatric Inst., 1974-77. Career: computer pgmmr.

Computer Center, Carnegie Inst. of Tech., 1965, 66; systems analyst, instr. psychology, Carnegie-Mellon Univ., 1968-71; pre-doc. fellow UCSF Langley Porter Neuropsychiatric Inst., 1971-72, res. assoc. 1973-74, NIMH postdoc. fellow w/Dr. Joe Kamiya, 1976-77: pgmmr. EEG Systems Lab. Langley Porter Inst. 1974-76, res. assoc. on alpha EEG feedback 1976-77, asst. adj. prof. med. psychology Langley Porter Inst., 1979-90; asst. res. psychologist UCSF Brain Wave Group/Human Devel., 1977-79, asst. adj. prof. med. psychology and dir. UCSF Brain Wave Group 1979-90; co-founder, bd. dir., v.p. res. & devel. MindCenter Corp., Palo Alto, 1984-; awards: NIMH Fellow 1976-77, NIMH investigator, grantee "Anxiety & Aging: Intervention with EEG Alpha Feedback 1979-82, Maco Stewart Scholarship and Research Fund 1979-83, Fetzer Found.: Long Term Tng. in EEG Feedback 1976-88, John E. Wertin Fund 1981, Joseph H. Akerman Fund 1981; mem: AAAS, Am. Psychol. Assn., Assn. for Applied Psychophysiology and Biofeedback, Biofeedback Soc. Calif., Soc. for Psychophysiol. Res.; publs: res. papers, num. profl. jour. articles in field; Democrat; Lutheran; hobby: classic cars of the '60s (mem. Pontiac Oakland Club). Res: 1052 Rhode Island St San Francisco 94107 Ofc: MindCenter Corp. 2445 Faber Pl Palo Alto 94303

HARDY, CHARLES EXTER, III, clergyman; b. Dec. 22, 1960, Atlanta, Ga.; s. Charles Exter, Jr. and Loretta (Westmoreland) H.; m. Claudia Gail Barton, Jan. 11, 1986; children: Lauren Nicole b. 1989, "Chase" Charles Exter, IV b. 1991; edn: BS in agric., Univ. Tenn., Knoxville 1982; MDiv, Golden Gate Baptist Theol. Sem., Mill Valley 1987; ordained minister First Baptist Ch., Winters, Calif., 1987. Career: youth minister Rollingwood Baptist Ch., San Pablo, Calif. 1983-84; minister to the deaf El Camino Baptist Ch., Sacto. 1984; asst. youth pastor Narwee Baptist Ch., Australia 1985; asst. pastor First Baptist Ch., El Sobrante, Calif. 1986-87; pastor First Baptist Ch., Winters 1987-90, First Southern Baptist Ch., Davis 1991-; seminar ldr. So. Baptist, Ga., Calif., Ida., 1982-, mem. mission team to Indonesia 1986, Jamaica 1988, Ecuador 1990; led mission team Argentina 1992; mem. nominating com. Sacto. Baptist Assn., 1991-; mem. Winters Ministerial Assn. (pres. 1989-90); listed Outstanding Young Men of Am. (ann., 1984-90), Who's Who in West 1991; author (drama): Cheap Show (1990); rec: photography. Res: 2650 Belmont Dr Davis 95616 Ofc: First Southern Baptist Church, 770 Pole Line Rd Davis 95616

HARKINS, CRAIG, consultant, public speaker; b. May 1, 1936, Boston; s. Edwin Craig and Shirley Nadine (Pike) H.; div.; children: Daniel b. 1962, Sean b. 1964, Lance b. 1968; edn: BA, Colby Coll., 1958; MA English, N.Y. Univ., 1959; dipl. in comm. arts, Columbia Univ., 1963; PhD comm., Rensselaer Polytechnic Inst., 1978. Career: reporter photographer St. Petersburg (Fla.) Evening Independent 1960-61; communication mgr. IBM, San Jose 1961-82; cons. prin./v.p. Hamlin Harkins Ltd. (full-service consulting firm), San Jose 1982-; lectr., pub. speaker rep. by The Speakers Guild, Sandwich, Mass.; adj. faculty Univ. S.F., 1984-, Evergreen Valley Coll., 1982-84, instr. Rensselaer Polytech. Inst., 1976-78; awards: Sigma Tau Chi 1980, Cindy award for IBM tng. film "Little Things" Info. Film Prod. Assn., L.A. 1975, Golden Eagle Council on Int. Ex., NY, NY 1975, 5 performance awards IBM; mem.: Internat. Comm. Assn. 1965-, IEEE Profl. Comm. Soc. (adminstrv. com. 1972-, nat. secty. 1973-76, TR-80, editl. bd. IEEE Spectrum 1974-75), Profl. and Tech. Cons. Assn., Peninsula Mktg. Assn.; civic: United Way Santa Clara Co. (chmn. mkt. res. com.); coauthor with Daniel L. Plung: A Guide for Writing Better Technical Papers (John Wiley & Sons 1982); founder/ed. The Campaigner, a Marine Corps newspaper (rated best in USMCR 1963); prod. or co-prod. 7 award-winning IBM films; mil: cpl. USMCR 1961-66; Democrat; R.Cath.; rec: poetry, swimming. Res: 1301 Mariposa Ave San Jose 95126 Ofc: Hamlin Harkins, Ltd. 1611 The Alameda San Jose 95126-2202

HARLEY, ROBISON DOOLING, JR., lawyer; b. July 6, 1946, Ancon (C.Z.) Panama; s. Robison Dooling and Loyde Hazel (Gouchenauer) H.; m. Suzanne P. Bendel, Aug. 8, 1975; children: Arianne Erin b. 1980, Lauren Loyde b. 1982; edn: BA, Brown Univ. 1968; JD, Temple Univ. 1971; LLM in crim. law, Univ. of San Diego 1984; cert. crim. law splst. Calif. St. Bar (1981, recert. 1986, 91), cert. crim. trial advocate Nat. Bd. Trial Advocates (1982, recert. 1987, 92); admitted bar: New Jersey, Pa., Dist. of Columbia, Calif., U.S. Supreme Ct., U.S. Ct. of Mil. Appeals, U.S. Circuit Ct. Appeals (3d., 9th Cir.), U.S. Dist. Cts. N.J., Pa. (E. Dist.), Calif. (Cent., So. Dists.). Career: judge advocate (trial counsel, def. counsel, mil. judge, asst. staff judge adv.) USMC, 1971-75; asst. agency dir. Safeco Title Ins. Co., Panorama City 1975-77; crim. defense atty. and ptnr. law firm of Cohen, Stokke & Davis, Santa Ana 1977-85; ptnr. Harley & McDermott, Santa Ana 1985-; instr. Orange Co. Coll. of Trial Advocacy, Orange Co. Bar Assn., Univ. Calif. paralegal pgm.; instr. trial advocacy tng. pgms. for fed. govt., USN, USAF, USCG, USMC; judge pro tem Superior and Muni. Cts., Orange Co.; mem: Am., Calif., Pa., N.J. and D.C. bar assns., Calif. Attys. for Crim. Justice, Calif. Pub. Defenders Assn., Nat. Assn. of Crim. Def. Lawyers, Orange Co. Bar Assn. (Judiciary Com., Adminstrn. of Justice Com., Criminal Law Sect.), O.C. Trial Lawyers Assn., Assn. of Trial Lawyers of Am., Calif. Trial Lawyers; bd. dirs. Legal Aid Soc. of O.C.; reported cases: People v. Orduno (1978), Andrus v. municipal ct. (1983), People v. Henderson (1985), People v. Marsh (1985), People v. Brown (1989), People v. Bas (1987), People v. Eilers (1991), People v. Autry (1991), People v. Gentry (1991); mil: lt.col. USMC(R), asst. regl. defense counsel USMC, recipient 3 congratulations cert. from Marine Corps Commandant and commend. from the Comdg. Gen.; Republican; Prot.; rec: sports, phys. fitness. Res: 12 Bayberry Way Irvine 92715 Ofc: Harley & McDermott, Attys. 825 N Ross St Santa Ana 92701

HARRINGTON, HANNAH KARAJIAN, prof.; b. Dec. 25, 1958, Berkeley, Calif.; d. Samuel Levon and Constance Maggie (Moore) Karajian; m. William James Harrington, June 20, 1981; edn: BA, Biblical studies, Patten College, Oakland, Calif., 1978; B. Music, S.F. Conservatory of Music, 1982; MA, Near Eastern studies, UC Berkeley, 1985; PhD, Near Eastern studies, UC Berkeley, 1992; Career: instr. of Modern Hebrew, Patten Acad., Oakland 1978-; instr. of Old Testament & Hebrew, Patten Coll., Oakland 1983-89; Modern Hebrew grad. student instr., UC Berkeley 1986-91; asst. prof. of Old Testament & Hebrew, Patten Coll. 1989-; instr. of post-Biblical Hebrew texts, UC Berkeley 1993; adjunct prof. of Old Testament, Fuller Theological Sem. 1993-; chair, Biblical Studies Div., Patten College 1989-; awards: scholarship, Patten Coll. 1974; Nat. Endowment for Humanities grants, Brown Univ. 1988, Brandeis Univ.,1993; listed Who's Who in the Humanities 1992, Who's Who in Religion 1992-93; mem: Soc. of Biblical Lit.; steering com., Soc. of Biblical Lit., History & Lit. of Early Rabbinic Judaism Section; cellist, Modesto Symphony, Modesto, Calif. 1981-; author: Impurity Systems of Qumran and the Rabbis: Biblical Foundations, 1993; Democrat; Christian Evangelical. Res: 2479 Coolidge Ave. Oakland 94601. Ofc: Patten College 2433 Coolidge Ave. Oakland 94601

HARRIS, CYNTHIA VIOLA, educator; b. Aug. 18, 1948, San Francisco; d. Gilbert and Mary Lee Harris; edn: BA and MA, San Francisco State Univ.; EdD, Nova Univ. Career: tchr. Oakland Public Schs. 1971-80, sch. principal 1980-86, staff devel. and mentor tchr. pgm. coordinator 1986-91, coordinator recruitment, employee support & marketing 1991-; cons. CSU Hayward 1987-88, Kids on Job 1988; honors: "Just Say No" award Within You, Oakland 1988, Networker award Capwell's, Oakland 1985; mem. Assn. Calif. Sch. Adminstrs. (mem. chair 1986-89), Phi Delta Kappa; commr. Self Esteem Alameda Co., 1988; mem. Marcus Foster, Oakland (com. 1983-88); author 3 manuals: Peer Tutoring Expansion, 1985; Self-Esteem For You & Your Students, 1987; Parents as Partners, 1988; Democrat; Pentecostal; rec: fitness, public speaking, travel. Ofc: Oakland Public Schools 1025 Second Ave St Rm 320 Oakland 94804

HARRIS, DAVID JACK, artist; b. Jan. 6, 1948, San Mateo; s. Jack McAllister and Audrey (Fegley) H.; edn: att. San Francisco Art Inst. 1960-66; BA in art (cum laude), San Francisco State Univ., 1971, MA art, 1976; sec. tchg. cred., 1972. Career: art gallery director Galerie De Tours, San Francisco, 1971-72; substitute tchr. high schs. San Francisco, Sequoia, San Mateo, 1973-80; art instr. Chabot Comm. Coll., 1976-81; pres. and owner David Harris Associates, Belmont, Calif., commercial & residential interiors 1978-82, freelance fine artist 1982-; founder, art director and ptnr. Fine Art Publishing, Belmont 1988-; v.p. Coastal Arts League Museum, Half Moon Bay; work in permanent collections Stanford Univ., Cannell and Chaffin (L.A.), Caesar's Palace (Las Vegas), Internat. Red Cross, Litton Inds., Verilink, Foothill Bank (Los Altos), Chartered Bank of London (S.F.), N.Central Wash. Mus., Sheraton Grande (L.A.), Old England Inn (Victoria, B.C.), others; exhibitions: 30+ group and solo exh. 1970-85, one-man shows: Eva Cohon Gal. Chgo. 1986, 88, 90, North Central Washington Mus., Wenatchee 1987, Metro Contemporary Gal., San Mateo 1989, A Gallery, Palm Desert 1989, Five Feet Gal., Laguna Beach 1989, Souder Gal., Burlingame 1990, Robert Wright Gal., Escondido 1990, Coastal Art Mus., Half Moon Bay 1991, The Cannery, S.F. 1991, Maturango Mus., Ridgecrest 1992; publs: Art in Am., Palm Springs Life, Artist Mag., West Art, Confluence Mag., Kiosk, Signature Mag., Southwest Art, Antiques and Fine Art, Artweek, Valley Mag. (1989), San Mateo Times, Wenatchee Times. Ofc: 427 Casa Del Mar Half Moon Bay 94019 Tel: 415/593-4796

HARRIS, GODFREY, consultant, international travel association executive director; b. June 11, 1937, London, England, came to U.S. 1939, naturalized 1945; s. Alfred and Victoria H.; m. Linda Berkowitz, Dec. 21, 1958 (div. 1982); children: Gregrey, Kennith, Mark; edn: BA (gt. distinction) Stanford Univ., 1958; MA (disting. mil. grad.) UCLA, 1960. Career: lectr. Rutgers Univ. 1960-61; Foreign Service ofcr. U.S. State Dept., W.D.C., Bonn, Ger., London, 1962-65, mgmt. analyst Office Mgmt. and Budget, W.D.C., 1965-67; spl. asst. to pres. IOS Devel. Co., Geneva 1967-68; pres. Harris/Ragan Mgmt. Group, Los Angeles 1968-; founder, editor Almanac of World Leaders, 1957-62, Consultants Directory, 1975-76; exec. dir. Soc. of Internat. Travel Reps., 1992-; former west coast rep. Panamanian Export Promo. and Investment Devel. Ctr.; mem: Am. Acad. Consultants (fellow), Assn. Mgmt. Consultants, Stanford Univ. Alumni Assn., London Chamber of Commerce & Industry (mem. secty.), L.A. World Affairs Council, Town Hall Calif., mem. advy. com. on gifted Santa Monica Unified Sch. Dist. (chair 1978-79); author: Panama's Position (1973), The Panamanian Perspective (1987, Fgn. Policy Assn. of Panama), The Ultimate Black Book (1988, The Americas Group), Invasion (1990), The Fascination of Ivory (1991), Talk Is Cheap (1991), Mapping Russia & Its Neighbors (1993), Power Buying (1993); other books and monographs. Ofc: 9200 Sunset Blvd Los Angeles 90069

HARRIS, MICHAEL DAVID, journalist; b. Feb. 11, 1950, Phila., Pa.; s. Morton Louis and Jane (Kirby) H.; edn: BA, Temple Univ., Phila., Pa. 1973; Calif. State, L.A., 1976-79. Career: reporter/ed., Progress Newspapers, Alhambra, Calif. 1977-78; reporter/ed., City News Svc., L.A. 1978-81; reporter/ed., UPI, L.A. 1981-90; ed., KFWB-AM, L.A. 1985-; reporter, L.A. Daily Jour., L.A. 1991-; listed in Who's Who in the West, 1992; author: screenplay, Special Circumstances, 1992; rec: reading, writing, physical fitness, music. Ofc: Daily Journal Corp. 915 E. First St. L.A. 90012

HARRIS, STEPHEN L., humanities professor, author; b. Feb. 5, 1937, Aberdeen, Wash.; s. Glenn E. and Ruby O. (Bell) H.; m. 1965-1985, 2 sons, Geoffrey Edwin b. 1971, Jason Marc b. 1973; edn: BA, Univ. Puget Sound, 1959; MA, Cornell Univ., 1961, PhD, 1964. Career: asst. prof. Wash. State Univ., Pullman 1964-65; asst. prof. Calif. State Univ., Sacramento 1965-70, assoc. prof. 1970-74, prof. humanities 1974-, and dept. chair 1972-76, 1992-; author: Classical Mythology: Images and Insights (1993), Agents of Chaos (1990), Understanding the Bible, 3d. ed. (1992), The New Testament: A Student's Intro. (1988), Fire Mountains of the West (1988), Fire and Ice: The Cascade Volcanoes (1976), Touchstones: Classic Readings in the Humanities (1990); writer, columnist American West (mag.) 1983-89, reviewer Nevada Historical Quarterly 1989-, Oregon Historical Quarterly 1991-, contbr. Columbia Mag., Tacoma, Wash. 1989-; awards: Crown-Zellerbach, Univ. Puget Sound 1957-59, Woodrow Wilson fellow Cornell Univ. 1960-61, Annual Faculty Research Award CSUS 1981-82; Fellow Westar Inst.-Jesus Sem. 1986-, mem: Volcanological Assn. of Sacto. 1988-; rec: mountain climbing in Cascade Range. Ofc: Humanities Dept. Calif. State Univ., Sacramento 95819-6083

HART, FRANK JAMES, systems engineer, technical writer consultant; b. May 8, 1947, San Francisco; s. Frank Hjalmer and Naomi June (Hockett) H.; m. June Ellen Peters, Apr. 28, 1973; children: Bret b. 1981, Katy b. 1989; edn: AS in E.T., Mission Coll., Santa Clara 1980; BSE in comp. sci., San Jose State Univ., 1985. Career: field service engr. Wang Labs., San Mateo 1972-74; applications engr. Signetics, Sunnyvale 1974-86; senior applications engr. Fairchild Semiconductor, Palo Alto 1986-87, systems engr. Intergraph APD, Palo Alto 1987-; cons. tech. writer, Santa Clara, 1990-; mem.: Soc. for Technical Communication 1990-; inventor: Infrared Tracking Device (pat. pending), Interactive Display Devices (pat. 1990); pub. articles on RISC Processors, Interface Techniques (1988, 89, 90, 92); rec: gardening, beer brewing, fishing. Ofc: Intergraph APD 2400 Geng Rd Bldg 4 Palo Alto 94303

HARUDA, FRED DAVID, neurologist; b. Mar. 16, 1950, N.Y.C.; s. Joseph Stanley and Iva Fern (Lindstrom) H.; m. Alexandra S. Francis, PhD, May 28, 1983; children: Ashleigh b. 1985; edn: BA in biology (cum laude) Whitman Coll., 1972; MD, MS path., Univ. of Chgo., Pritzker Sch. of Med., 1976; bd. cert. pediatrics Am. Bd. Peds. 1984, neurology, child neurology Am. Bd. Psychiatry and Neuro. 1986, EEG, Am. Bd. of EEG and Neurophysiology 1988. Career: pediatric intern, resident Johns Hopkins Hosp., Balt. 1976-78; child and adult neurology fellow Columbia Univ. Coll. of Physicians and Surgeons, 1978-81; physician, owner Fred Haruda MD, Salinas, 1981-89, Central Coast Neurological Associates, Salinas, 1989-; clin. instr. UC San Francisco Sch. of Med., 1981-86, asst. clin. prof. 1986-; attdg. physician Salinas Valley Meml. Hosp., Salinas 1981-, cons. San Andreas Regional Ctr., Salinas 1981-, Calif. Children's Svs. Sacto. 1981-, cons. neurologist Natividad Med. Ctr., Salinas 1981-, Mee Meml. Hosp., King City 1988-; med. advy. bd. Monterey Bay Multiple Sclerosis Soc., 1981-; awards: Phi Beta Kappa 1972, Sigma Xi (assoc. 1975, mem. 1991-), summer res. award March of Dimes 1975, Physician's recogn. award AMA, Chgo. (1983, 90); examiner child neurology Am. Bd. Psychiatry and Neurol., Evanston, Ill. 1980; mem: AMA, CMA, Monterey Co. Med. Assn. 1981-, Am. Acad. of Peds. (fellow), Am. Acad. Neurology (EEG, 1981-), Am. Electroencephalographic Soc., Am. Epilepsy Soc., Child Neurol. Soc., Internat. Child Neurol. Soc., Am. Acad. of Clin. Neurophysiology, Am. Med. EEG Soc.; civic: Boy Scouts Am. (district chmn.), Eagle Scout, Salinas; Elks Lodge (614); author 3 chapters in med. texts, numerous profl. jour. articles and sci. presentations; Indep.; Christian; rec: writing, golf, skiing, fishing.

HARVEY, ELAINE LOUISE, artist; b. Mar. 1, 1936, Riverside; d. Edgar Arthur and Emma Lou (Shull) Siervogel; m. Stuart Herbert Harvey, June 16, 1957; children: Kathleen b. 1959, Laurel b. 1961, Mark b. 1964; edn: BA, San Diego State Univ., 1957, Calif. Gen. Std. elem. tchg. credential, 1957. Career: elem. tchr. Cajon Valley Schs., El Cajon 1957-58; watermedia artist, 1975-; art lectr. and demonstrator, art groups in various cities, 1982-, tchr. art seminars 1985-; instr. art Athenaeum Sch. of Music & Arts, 1990-; juror art shows 1985-; trustee San Diego Mus. of Art, 1986; exhibition dir. Nat. Watercolor Soc., Calif. 1988; awards incl. silver San Diego Watercolor Soc. 1986, First Jurors Award S.D. Watercolor Soc. internat. exh., Calif. 1986, Winsor Newton Award Midwest Watercolor Soc., Wis. 1985, Creative Connections award Rocky Mountain Nat. Exh., Colo. 1986, Martha T. McKinnon Memorial Am. Watercolor Soc. 1985, Arjomari/Arches/Rives award Watercolor West, Calif. 1990; mem: Allied Artists of Am. 1989-, Nat. Watercolor Soc. (1986-, dir. 1986, 87, juror 1988), Rocky Mtn. Nat. Watermedia Soc. 1986-, Watercolor West (1985-, dir. 1986-87), West Coast Watercolor Soc. (1988-, pres. 1992-),

San Diego Watercolor Soc. (pres. 1980-81), S.D. Mus. of Art Artists Guild (pres. 1986, dir.); publs: cover picture & article, The Artists Mag. (1987), contbr. paintings & text (book) The New Spirit of Watercolor (1989), (book) Splash (1991), Splash II (1993), Watermedia Techniques for Releasing the Creative Spirit (1992), editor (book) Palate to Palette (1987); Methodist; rec: choral director. Res/Studio: 1602 Sunburst Dr El Cajon 92021

HARVEY, JAMES GERALD, ednl. cons., b. July 15, 1934, California, Mo.; s. William Walter and Exie Marie (Lindley) H; edn. BA, Amherst Coll., 1956; MA., Harvard Univ., 1958; MEdn., Harvard, Univ., 1962. Career: asst. to the dean, Grad. Sch. of Edn. Harvard Univ. 1962-66; dir. of admissions and fin. aid, Grad. Sch. of Edn. Harvard Univ. 1966-69; dir. of counseling, UC, Irvine, 1970-72; ednl. cons., Ednl. Counseling, Los Angeles, Calif., 1972-; honors: Mayo-Smith Fellow in Coll. Admissions, Amherst Coll. 1956-57; Amherst Meml. Fellow , Harvard Univ. 1957-58; UCLA Adminstrv. Fellow 1969-70; mem.: Amer. Ednl. Res. Assn., Nat. Council for Measurement in Edn., Amer. Counseling Assn.; author: ednl. materials, HARVOCAB Vocabulary Program, 1985-; mil: first lt., USAF 1958-61. Res: 1845 Glendon Ave., Los Angeles 90025 Ofc: Educational Counseling, 1845 Glendon Ave., Los Angeles 90025

HARVEY, MARC SEAN, lawyer, consultant; b. May 4, 1960, NY, NY; s. M. Eugene and Coleen (Jones) H.; edn: BA (high hons., Dean's list), So. Illinois Univ., 1980; JD (top 10%), Southwestern Univ., 1983; MBA (pending), Loyola Marymount Univ.; admitted bar: Calif. 1984, Mo. 1985, US Tax Ct. 1985, US Supreme Ct. 1988. Career: counsel US Small Bus. Adminstrn., Los Angeles 1982-83; counsel enforcement div. U.S. SEC, Los Angeles 1983-84; counsel State Farm Ins. Co., L.A. 1984-85; counsel 20th Century Ins. Co., Woodland Hills 1985-86; sole law practice, Encino 1986-; judge pro tem Culver Municipal Ct., 1991-; awards: 1st pl. essay Vets. Fgn. Wars, Collinsville, Ill. 1976, acad. scholar So. Ill. Univ. 1979-80, Nat. Hon. Soc. 1975-77; mem: Am. Bar Assn., L.A. Co. Bar Assn., SAG, AFTRA; Republican: charter/trustee Presdl. Task Force 1981-, Nat. Senatl Com. 1983-, Victory Fund spons. 1984-, Senatl. Inner Circle 1988-, Congl. Leadership Council 1987-; rec: history, travel, art collector. Law Offices of Marc S. Harvey, 16530 Ventura Blvd Penthouse Ste Encino 91436

HARVEY, PAUL W., electronics consultant; b. Aug. 12, 1957; edn: BSEE, M.I.T., 1979. Career: integrated circuit design engr. Harris Semiconductor, Melbourne, Fla. 1979-81; senior IC design engr. Advanced Micro Devices, Sunnyvale, Calif. 1981-85; senior cons. Logical Consulting, Palo Alto 1985-86; owner Integrated Circuit Design Consulting, Santa Clara 1986-, cons. clients incl. Synopsys, Intel, Fujitsu Micro, Gazelle Micro, Watkins Johnson, Kaiser Electronics, Raynet, Logical Svs., Kodak Berkeley Research, Nara; mem. IEEE, Profl. and Tech. Consultants Assn.; co-inventor 22V10 PAL output (pat. no. 4717912). Ofc: Integrated Circuit Design Consulting, 1556 Halford Ave Ste 310 Santa Clara 95051

HARWICH, MATHEW VIVIAL, insurance agent, musician; b. June 12, 1919, Redlands; s. Joseph and Minnie Faye (Vivial) H.; m. Mary Marlene de la Cueva, Nov. 3, 1946; children: Gregory b. 1947, David b. 1955, Mark b. 1965; edn: L.A. City Coll.; Lumbleau Sch. of Real Estate; Anthony Sch. of Ins. Career: agent Allstate Ins. Co., Pomona 1955-; trombonist with the Glentones, Glendora 1979-; ins. and real estate broker Harmark Ins., Hollywood 1945-55; awards: Allstate Ins. Co. honor ring, disting. service; mem: Pomona Concert Band, Ontario Chaffey Band Disabled Am. Vet.; mil: sgt. AUS 1941-45, 1950-52, Purple Heart 1943, Inf. Combat Badge; Republican; R.Cath.; rec: music, model building. Res: 1714 N Vallejo Way Upland 91786 Ofc: Allstate Insurance Co. 504 W Baseline Ste C Glendora 91740

HARWOOD, WARREN PETER, municipal official; b. Sept. 20, 1939, N.Y.C.; s. Daniel and Frances (Sunasky) H.; m. Johanna A., Feb. 13, 1965 (div. 1978); m. Cheryl Socher, Jan. 29, 1986; children: David b. 1971, Allison b. 1986, Daniel b. 1988; edn: BS in bus. adminstrn., UCLA, 1961; MPA USC, 1964; Calif. Comm. Colls. lifetime tchg. credential, 1967. Career: adminstrv. asst. City of Los Angeles, 1961-62; asst. city adminstr. City of South El Monte, 1962-63; city mgr. City of San Jacinto, 1963-65; mgr. Palmdale Chamber of Commerce, 1965-67, Lancaster Chamber of Commerce, 1967-72; lectr. Antelope Valley Coll., Lancaster 1967-72; dep. L.A. Co. Bd. Suprs., 1972-78; alt. dir. South Coast Air Quality Dist., L.A. 1977-78, v.chmn. L.A. Co. Housing Auth. 1977-78; projects coordinator Co. of Los Angeles, 1978-; elected dir. Central & West Basin Water Replenishment Dist., L.A. Co. 1980-83; elected councilman City of Long Beach, 1982-; v. mayor Long Beach 1987-88; awards: youngest city mgr. in Calif., San Jacinto Lions Club (1963), newsmaker of year Antelope Valley Press Club 1972, disting. service Antelope Valley Jaycees 1973, Democrat of yr. 57th A.D. Dem. Central Com. Long Beach 1987; mem: Independent Cities Assn. (pres. 1990-91); civic: Univ. Coop. Housing Assn. L.A. (pres. 1959-61); clubs: Lions, San Jacinto 1964-65, Jaycees, Palmdale 1966-67, Toastmasters, Lancaster 1968-71, Rotary, Lancaster 1969-72; mil: Airman USNR 1961-68; Democrat (Dem. Party Cent. Com. 1982-92); Jewish; rec: salt water fishing. Ofc: City of Long Beach 333 W Ocean Blvd 14th Fl Long Beach 90802

HARZ, KARL JOSEPH, financial co. executive; b. July 10,1 950, Paterson, N.J.; s. Karl Oscar and Vera Marie (Gennaro) H.; m. Marilyn Lee Kindred, Mar. 3, 1974; children: Alexa Marie, Tiffany Ann, Kristopher Joseph; edn: BS, Fairleigh Dickinson Univ., 1972, MBA, 1974; lic. Real Estate broker Tex., Calif.; State of Calif. Public Notary. Career: regional dir., life and disability agt. Lincoln Nat. Life Ins. Co., Los Angeles 1974-76; registered rep. Nat. Plan Coordinators, Inc., Long Beach 1976-77; pension cons., fin. planner Mutual Benefit Life Ins. Co., 1977-78; founder, incorporator, chmn. and c.e.o. Transitional Housing Inc., 1989-; broker Alternative Funding Sources, 1982-; incorporator, pres. Loanlink Corp., 1983-; dir. Province Service Corp. Realtor; recipient cert. of achievement AAU 1972; mem: Nat. Assn. Realtors, Nat. Notary Assn., Palos Verdes Bd. Realtors; clubs: N.Y. Athletic (life), Los Angeles Athletic (profl.). Res: 701 Via Horcada Palos Verdes Estates 90274 Ofc: 322 Vista Del Mar Redondo Beach 90277

HASAN, WAGAR, computer scientist; b. Apr. 1, 1963, Jalaun, India; s. Amir and Fatima (Ali) H.; m. Shirin, June 25, 1990; edn: BS, Computer Sci., IIT, Kanpur, India, 1984; MS, Computer Sci., Stanford Univ., Stanford, Calif., 1988. Career: M.T.S., Hewlett Packard Labs., Palo Alto, Calif., 1988-; mem: ACM, 1989-; author: numerous publ. tech. articles on the design and implementation of database languages. Ofc: Hewlett Packard 1501 Page Mill Rd. 3U Palo Alto 94304-0969

HASKELL, ERIC TODD, educator, museum director; b. Oct. 2, 1950, Marysville, Calif.; s. Coburn and Joanne Dale (Taverner) H.; m. Danielle Floquet, July 7, 1973; children: Olivia Hanna b. 1975, Jean-Christophe b. 1978; edn: Baccalaureate (Lettres) Univ. of Paris, Fr. 1971; BA (cum laude) Pomona Coll., Claremont 1973; MA, UC Irvine, 1975, PhD, 1979. Career: tchg. asst. in French, UC Irvine, 1974-77, tchg. assoc. humanities, 1977-78; lectr. in French, Scripps Coll., Claremont 1978, asst. prof. of French, 1979-85, assoc. prof. French and humanities, 1985-, chair French dept. 1985-90, dir. Clark Humanities Mus., 1984-; curator The Fleming Lecture Series, 1988-90; curator 6 exhs. The Huntington Gallery; co-curator Personal Edens: The Gardens and Film Sets of Florence Yoch (1992); internat. lectr. 100+, various univs. and art museums incl. L.A. Co. Mus. of Art, Stanford, Duke, Harvard, Univ. Calif., Univs. of Amsterdam, Zurich, Paris and Tunis; awards: research and exhibition grantee Mellon Found. 1981, list of nat. lectrs. Garden Club of Am., NY, NY 1991; mem: Decorative Arts Study Ctr. (Curatorial Bd. 1987-), Assn. for Interdisciplinary 19th Century Studies (treas. 1986-88), Philol. Assn. of Pacific Coast (Literature and the Other Arts presiding ofcr. 1983, 87), Claremont Heritage (bd. 1989-90), Rancho Los Alamitos (dir. 1992-), Banning Residence Mus. Found. (dir. 1992-), Modern Language Assn. of Am., Internat. Assn. for Word and Image Studies, Interdisciplinary 19th Century Studies, 19th Century French Studies, Assn. des Vieilles Maison Francaises; publs: (exh. cat.) Transcending Mimesis: The French Illustrated Book (1982), scholarly articles on Baudelaire, Flaubert, Nerval, Rimbaud and Huysmans and French garden history (1970-). Ofc: Scripps College, 1030 Columbia St Claremont 91711-3948

HASTINGS, DIANA M., lawyer; b. Aug. 18, 1956, Stockton; d. Walter Andrew and Jane Frances (Goldsberry) Hastings; m. Robert Charles Temple; edn: BA, Univ. Oreg. 1979; MBA, George Washington Univ. 1981; JD, Cornell Law Sch. 1986; admitted bar: N.Y., Calif., U.S. Dist. Ct. no. dist. Calif., U.S. Ct. Appeals 9th cir. Career: economist U.S. Dept. of Commerce, W.D.C. 1980; fin. analyst Econ. Consulting Services 1980-83; atty., assoc. Milbank, Tweed, Hadley & McCloy, N.Y.C., 1986-88; Pillsbury, Madison & Sutro, San Francisco, 1988-90; Orrick, Herrington & Sutcliffe, S.F., 1990-; mem: Bar Assn. of San Francisco, St. Bar Calif., Am. Bar Assn. (com. on creditors' rights in decedents' estates). Ofc: Orrick, Herrington & Sutcliffe, 400 Sansome St San Francisco 94111

HASTINGS, ROBERT PUSEY, lawyer; b. May 23, 1910, Los Angeles; s. Hill (M.D.) and Mary Garvin (Brown) H.; m. Susan S. Schriber, July 9, 1938 (dec.);children: Susan Hastings Mallory; edn: BA, Yale Univ. 1929; LL.B, Harvard Law Sch. 1933; State Bar Calif. 1936. Career: counsel Motion Picture div. Office Coord. Inter-Am. Affairs 1942-43; ptnr. firm Paul, Hastings, Janofsky & Walker 1946-81, counsel, 1981-; chmn. Calif. campaign USO 1956-57; pres., chmn. bd. LA Civic Light Opera Assn., 1959-65, trustee 1939-79; trustee Calif. Light Opera Assn. 1979; secty., trustee Music Center Operating Co. 1961-65; trustee Harvey Mudd Coll. Sci. and Engring. 1956-, v.chmn. bd. 1956-80; chmn. Thacher Sch. 1965-70, trustee 1938-73; trustee Friends of Claremont Colls. 1970-, pres. 1973-75; trustee Friends Huntington Library and Art Gallery; bd. overseers Huntington Library and Art Gallery; trustee Winston Churchill Found. U.S., Miss Porter's Sch. 1969-73; mem: LA Co. Bar Assns., So. Calif. Harvard Law Sch. Assn. (trustee, chmn. 1967-69), Delta Kappa Epsilon; Republican; Episcopalian (vestryman 1968-69, 72-73); civic clubs: Chancery (L.A.), California (L.A.), Valley Hunt, Sunset (L.A.) (past secty., pres. 1970-71), Zamorano (literary), Lincoln (L.A.), Brit. United Svs. (L.A.), Grolier (N.Y.C.); mil: lt. USNR, 1943-45, decorated Bronze Star w/clasp, Pacific Theater ribbon w/3 clasps, Philippine Liberation w/1 clasp, Am. theater ribbon; Hon. Order British Empire; Republican; Episcopalian; rec: book collecting. Ofc: Paul, Hastings, Janofsky & Walker 555 So Flower St Los Angeles 90071

HATAI, THOMAS HENRY, marketing executive; b. Dec. 27, 1937, Tokyo; came to U.S., 1951; s. Isamu Herbert and Kiyoko (Kume) H.; m. Geraldine (div. 1978); 1 son, Dickson Y. b. Jan. 19, 1970; edn: BS, Woodbury Coll., 1965; supr. internat. dept. Union Bank, Los Angeles 1964-66; sales rep. United Airlines, Los Angeles 1966-69; v.p. far east Travel Systems Internat., Oakbrook, Ill. 1969-75; pres. Hatai Internat., Los Angeles 1975-78; pres., c.e.o. Pace Mktg. Inc., La Habra, Calif., 1978-; pres. D.B.H. Global Ltd., 1983-; dir.: Taiyo Estate Devel. Inc., Taiyo Holding (USA) Inc., dir./secty. Taiyo Leasing USA Inc.; v. chmn. and c.e.o. Yamano Cosmetics Inc. 1991-; pres. Yamano Products, Inc. d.b.a (AVEC) 1992-; mem. United Internat. Club (bd. dirs. 1969 Japan), US Chamber of Commerce; illustrator: The Marty Story 1954, The St. Meinrad Story 1954; Republican; Res: 8544 Buena Tierra Pl Buena Park 90621 Ofc: D.B.H. Global Ltd. 1251-C S Beach Blvd La Habra 90631

HATCH, EDWARD IRVING, gemologist, investor; b. Apr. 25, 1929, Nashville, Tenn.; s. Rufus James and Marion Louise (Jennings) H.; m. Irene Tanaka, Dec. 6, 1955; edn: AA, San Diego Mesa Coll. 1974; AB, CSU San Diego 1976; cert. gemologist Gemol. Inst. Am. 1969. Career: served to ATCS, US Navy 1947-72, ret., decorated Air medal, merit. unit commendn. 4 bronze stars, Korean Service; jewelry industry investor and rental co. prop., 1972-; recipient recogn. award for saving trees in Tecolote Canyon, City Councilman Bruce Henderson 1989, Victory '88 disting. vol. svc. Calif. Repub. Party 1989, vol. svc. award City Councilwoman Judy McCarty; mem: San Diego Co. Apartment Assn. (Owner Operator Council 1990-91); civic: Japanese Am. Cosmopolitan Assn. (pres. Br. One 1955-56), Phi Kappa Phi 1976, Privately Owned Canyons and Environs Com. (founding bd., chmn. 1985-88), Tecolote Canyon Rim Owners Protective Assn. (sec. 1986), S.D. Sato Matsutoyo-Kai Koen-Kai (treas. 1986-88), Tecolote Canyon Citizens' Advy. Com. appt. by Councilman Bruce Henderson 1989-, Nat. Model Railroad Assn. 1991, Fleet Reserve Assn. (Branch 312 v.p. 1992-93, pres. 1993-94); invention: coaxial R.F. Relay and Power Switch Tester, used by USN for electronic maint. 1955-56; Republican (del. S.D. Co. Repub. Party Conv. 1988, precinct chair 78th A.D. 1988-89); R.Cath.; rec: mountaineering, garden, gemological test equip. design, computer pgmmg, model railroad design and construction. Res: 4442 Bertha St San Diego 92117-3803

HATCH, ROBERT FRED, executive; b. Aug. 27, 1934, Chicago; s. Lester Warren and Mabel Dorothy Christina (Fulton) H.; m. Sandra Karen Thunander, Dec. 24, 1964; children: Hilary Joy b. 1969, Holly Christina b. 1972, Heather Daisy b. 1975; edn: BA, Valparaiso Univ., 1958; JD, Northwestern Univ. Sch. of Law, Chgo. 1960. Career: atty. law firm Tenney Sherman Bentley & Guthrie, Chgo. 1960-66; stockbroker White Weld & Co. Inc., Chgo. and Los Angeles, 1966-70; real estate devel., George Elkins & Co., Beverly Hills 1970-72; Donald Bren & Co., Sherman Oaks 1973; owner Robert F. Hatch Inc., L.A. 1973-77; v.p. and dir. real estate mgmt. George Elkins & Co., Beverly Hills 1978-79; pres. Filtration Systems Inc., Hawthorne 1979-80; ptnr. Cambrian Energy Systems, Los Angeles 1980-; elected State Senator 19th dist. Ill., Chgo. 1962-66, elected Republican Party committee, 19th ward chmn., Chgo. 1964-66, del. Republican Nat. Conv., Kansas City, Kans. 1976; appt. Pres. Reagan's Commn. on Housing, W.D.C. 1982; club: Riviera Tennis (1986-); mil: sp3c US Army 1954-55; Republican; Presbyterian; rec: genealogy, history, travel, tennis. Res: 125 N Layton Dr Los Angeles 90049 Ofc: Cambrian Energy Systems 3420 Ocean Park Blvd Ste 2020 Santa Monica 90405

HATCHER, KELSEY WALLACE, real estate broker; b. Dec. 8, 1913, Woodland; s. Earle Kelsey and Venus Virginia (Bullivant) H.; m. Elizabeth Ann Duffy, Mar. 21, 1970; children: Nancy b. 1940, John b. 1942, William b. 1948; 4 stepdaus.: Joann Hawk, Shelly Hawk Larson, Mary Margaret Simonson, Duffy Traynham Donnelly; 13 grandchildren and 2 gt.grandchildren; Calif. lic. R.E. Broker 1970. Career: self employed farmer, Woodland, Calif. 1932-68; sales/repairs Amos Metz Rentals, Woodland 1968-70; mgr. Victor Welding Supplies 1970-73; broker/owner Hatcher Real Estate, 1973-; also farming; past or current mem: Yolo Zamora Water Dist. (pres.), Marys Cemetery Dist. (dir.), Yolo County Farm Bur., Farmers Rice Coop., Associated Farmers, Beet Growers Assn., Tomato Growers Assn., Farm Labor Assn., Nat. Assn. of Realtors, Masons, Elks, Lions; Republican; Episcopalian; rec: travel, hunting, fishing, sports. Res: 103 Casa Linda Dr Woodland 95695 Ofc: Hatcher Real Estate, 612 Main, Woodland 95695

HAUCK, DENNIS WILLIAM, magazine editor, software systems engineer, mathematics consultant; b. Apr. 8, 1945, Hammond, Ind.; s. Floyd Wm. and Wilma (Frey) H.; edn: BS, Indiana Univ., 1969; postgrad., Univ. Innsbruck, Austria, 1970; PhD in math., Univ. Vienna, 1973. Career: systems analyst Trans Am. Corp., East Chicago, Ind. 1973-75; research supr. U.S. Gypsum Co., 1975-79; elec. engr. Howmet Turbine, Reno, Nev. 1979-80; engring. mgr. EPCO, 1980-81; project engr. Campbell Soup Co., Sacto. 1981-83; process mgr. Odenberg Inc., 1983-; freelance writer, 1972-; cons. math. GSW Inc., Phoenix 1977-; editor Jour. of Ufology, 1975-77, Mufon Jour., 1976-, four mags. 1976-78; appeared in film documentary Gold of the Gods, 1978; speaker Internat. Conf. on UFO's, Acapulco, Mex. 1978; mem: AAAS, Instrument Engrs. Soc., Inst. Transpersonal Psychology, Green Peace. Res: 5550 Franklin Blvd Apt 101 Sacramento 95820

HAUSMAN, ARTHUR HERBERT, corporate board director; b. Nov. 24, 1923, Chicago, Ill.; s. Samuel Louis and Sarah Elin H.; m. Helen Mandelowitz, May 19, 1946; children: Susan (dec.), Kenneth b. 1954, Catherine b. 1959; edn: BSEE, Univ. Tx. 1944; MS, Harvard Univ. 1948; reg. profl. engr. D.C. (1988). Career: electronics engr. Engring. Research Assn., St. Paul, Minn. 1946-47; supr., electronics scientist U.S. Govt., Wash. D.C. 1948-60; v.p., dir. of research Ampex, Redwood City 1960-63, v.p. ops. 1963-65, group v.p. 1965-67, exec. v.p. 1967-71, pres., CEO 1971-81, pres., CEO, chmn. bd. 1981-83, chmn. 1983-88; awards: U.S. Govt. Dept. of Defense merit. civilian service (1960); mem: IEEE, Pres. Export Council (export adminstrn. subcom. chmn. 1985-89), MIT Dept. Math Visiting Com., Cosmos Club, Commonwealth Club; articles pub. in tech. jours. (1949-54), patentee in field (1950-55), moderator NATO Conf. 1975; mil: lt.j.g. USNR 1944-50; Republican; rec: amateur radio. Address: Atherton 94027

HAVARD, JOHN FRANCIS, mining consultant; b. Mar. 15, 1909, Helena, Mont.; s. Francis Thompson and Margaret Eliza (Raleigh) H.; m. Faith Hartley, Aug. 19, 1943 (dec. May 11, 1991); children: David b. 1944, Edith Ann b. 1946, John b. 1949, Patrick b. 1953; edn: Montana Sch. of Mines, Butte 1929-32; PhB in geology. Univ. Wis., Madison 1934, PhM and BS in mining engring., 1935, Engr. of Mines, 1943; reg. geologist, engr. various states. Career: engr., works mgr., chief engr. mines U.S. Gypsum Co., Chgo. 1935-52; v.p. Fibreboard Corp., San Francisco 1953-62; v.p. Kaiser Engineers, Oakland 1963-74, senior v.p. 1975-79; indep. cons., Nevada City, Calif. 1980-; appt. U.S. Nat. Com. on Geology, W.D.C., 1975-79; awards: Hardinge Award AIME, NY, NY 1982, distinguished service Univ. Wis. 1986; mem.: Soc. for Mining Metallurgy and Exploration (1935-, past pres., Distinguished Mem., Littleton, Co. 1977), AIME (1935-, past dir., Hon. Mem., N.Y.C. 1984), AAAS (1965-, Fellow), Soc. of Economic Geologists 1948-; numerous pub. tech. papers; Republican; Episcopalian; rec: reading. Res: 181552 Augustine Rd Nevada City 95959

HAVENS, CARL BRADFORD, research scientist, ret.; b. May 30, 1918, Hope, Mich.; s. Boyd L. and Mary Ada (Gransden) H.; m. Grace Jeannette Cummins; children: David b. 1939, Sandra b. 1944, Paul b. 1946; edn: BSCE, Internat. Coll. 1943; Univ. Mich. 1944-45; Mich. St. Univ. 1946-47. Career: group leader Dow Chemical Co., Midland, Mich. 1949-57, production supr., Bay City, Mich. 1957-58, res. mgr., Cleveland, Ohio 1958-64, Findlay, Ohio 1964-66, Fresno 1966-76, research scientist, Granville, Ohio 1976-86; awards: Dow award 1981, Hall of Fame 1982; mem: Am. Chem. Soc., Soc. Plastics Engrs.; 155 U.S. and fgn. patents held (1942-88), 5 papers pub. in sci. jours.; Republican; Presbyterian; rec: skiing, skating, surfing. Address: Fresno 93710

HAWKES, GLENN ROGERS, psychology educator; b. Apr. 29, 1919, Preston, Idaho; s. William and Rae (Rogers) H.; m. Yvonne Merrill, Dec. 18, 1941; children: Kristen, William Ray, Gregory Merrill, Laura; edn: BS in psychology, Utah State Univ., 1946, MS psych., 1947; PhD psych., Cornell Univ., 1950. Career: asst., assoc., full prof. child devel. and psychology Iowa State Univ., Ames 1950-66, chmn. dept. child devel., 1954-66; research psychologist, prof. human devel. Univ. Calif., Davis 1966-89, assoc. dean applied economics and behavioral scis. 1966-83, prof. emeritus 1990-, academic coord. Hubert Humphrey Fellowship Program, 1990-, prof. behavioral scis. dept. family practice Sch. Medicine, chmn. teaching div. 1970-72, chmn. dept. applied behavioral scis. 1982-86; vis. scholar Univ. Hawaii 1972-73, Univ. London 1970, 80, 86; bd. dirs. Creative Playthings Inc. 1962-66; awards: research grantee pvt. foundations and govt. bodies, Iowa State Univ. Faculty Citation 1965, Outstanding Service cit. Iowa Soc. Crippled Children and Adults 1965, cit. Dept. Child Devel. 1980, Coll. Agrl. and Environmental Scis. 1983, named Hon. Lt. Gov. Oklahoma 1966; author: w/Pease, Behavior and Development from 5 to 12 (1962), w/ Frost, The Disadvantaged Child: Issues and Innovations (1966, 2d edit. 1970), w/ Schultz and Baird, Lifestyles and Consumer Behavior of Older Americans (1979), w/ Nicola and Fish, Young Marrieds: The Dual Career Approach (1984), contbr. numerous articles in profl. jours.; mil: US Army 1941-45. Res: 1114 Purdue Dr Davis 95616-1736 Ofc: University California Dept. Applied Beh. Scis. Internat. House 10 College Park Davis 95616

HAWKINS, MARGARET ALLEN, real estate broker, interior designer; b. Oct. 8, 1920, El Centro; d. Paul Verne and Clementine Celeste (Hopking) Allen; m. Charles John Hawkins, Nov. 29, 1941; children: Charles John b. 1944, Johanna b. 1948; edn: B.Edn., UCLA 1942. Career: tchr. Los Angeles City Schs. 1942-43, 1946-47; Minneapolis Schs. 1955-60; interior decorator 1960-66; Theo. Hofstatter & Co., N.Y. 1966-73; Margaret Hawkins, Inc. 1973-76; real estate agent Rand & Stewart, Rancho Santa Fe 1978-79; real estate agent and broker Rancho Santa Fe Properties 1979-80; broker, mng. dir. Fairbanks Ranch 1980-84; pres. RSF Properties 1979; mem: Calif. Assn. Realtors, Am. Soc. Interior Designers, UCLA Alumni Assn., Jr. League, Kappa Alpha Theta, Del Mar Garden Club, Fairbanks Ranch Country; Republican; Protestant; rec: oil painting. Res: 121 Spinnaker Ct Del Mar 92014

HAWTHORNE, DONALD BRUCE, healthcare industry executive; b. Dec. 31, 1955, Los Angeles; s. Donald Claire and Elene Ruth (Roussey) H.; m. Dianne M. Ritter, Oct. 7, 1989; edn: BS, Harvey Mudd Coll. 1977; MBA,

Stanford Univ. 1981. Career: financial plnnr. Westinghouse Electric Corp., Sunnyvale 1978-79; summer intern Morgan Guaranty Trust Co., NY, NY 1980; summer cons. Arabian-Am. Oil Co., Dhahran, Saudi Arabia 1981; sr. finl. analyst treasury dept. Atlantic Richfield Co., Los Angeles 1981-83; sr. finl. analyst corp. plnng. Syntex Corp, Palo Alto 1983-84, finl. plnng. mgr., controller Syntex Corp. Ophthalmics Div., Phoenix, Ariz. 1984-85; mgr. fin. and adminstrn. Genelabs Inc., Redwood City 1985-87, dir. fin. 1987-89, chief fin. ofcr. 1989-90; v.p. fin. and adminstrn. and c.f.o. Oclassen Pharmaceuticals Inc., San Rafael 1990; v.p. fin. and c.f.o. Biocircuits Corp., Sunnyvale 1991-; honors: Calif. State Scholar 1973-77, ARCS (Achievement Rewards for Coll. Scientists) scholar 1976-77, Dean's List distinction, Harvey Mudd Coll. Student Body Pres. 1976-77, Pi Sigma Alpha 1977, scholarship awards Stanford Bus. Sch. 1979-81, Who's Who Among Students in Am. Univs. and Colls. 1976-77, Who's Who in the West 1990; mem: Harvey Mudd Coll. Alumni Assn. (bd. govs. 1981-1987, bd. govs. treas. 1982-3, v.p. 1983-4, pres. 1984-6), Stanford Bus. Sch. Alumni Assn., Assn. of Bioscience Financial Ofcrs.(No. Calif. Bd. 1991-, co-chmn. Nat. Conf. 1992, chmn. Nat. Conf. 1993); bd. trustees Harvey Mudd Coll. 1986-89; Republican (Calif. Rep. Assembly Peninsula chpt. bd. 1987-88, treas. 1988, 11th Senate Dist. dir. 1988-89); R.Cath. Res: 260 Windsor Dr San Carlos 94070 Ofc: Biocircuits Corporation, 1324 Chesapeake Terrace Sunnyvale 94089

HAXTON, RONALD SCOTT, physician, pediatrician; b. Mar. 15, 1942, Los Angeles; s. Alexander Scott and Jacqueline (Adams) H.; m. Betty Jane Glenn, Aug. 7, 1971; edn: BA, Whittier Coll. 1963; MD, Univ. Calif. 1967. Career: intern USC Med. Center, Los Angeles 1967-68; resident, pediatrics UC Irvine 1970-72; pediatrician pvt. practice, Mission Viejo 1972-; mil: lt. USN 1968-70; Independent; rec: gardening, reading. Res: 24461 Zandra Mission Viejo 92691 Ofc: 27800 Medical Center Rd Ste 204 Mission Viejo 92691

HAYES, CLAUDE QUINTEN CHRISTOPHER, science and technology consultant, executive; b. Nov. 15, 1945, N.Y.C.; s. Claude and Celestine (Stanley) H.; edn: BA chemistry and geol. scis., Columbia Univ., 1971, MBA pgm. internat. bus. 1972-73; New York Law Sch. 1973-75; patent law rev. Practicing Law Inst., 1975; JD, Western State Law Sch., 1978; Calif. Comm. Colls. life instr. in chemistry, geophysics, phys. geography, earth sci., phys. sci., geology, law, bus. and law 1976, C.C.C. life supr. cert. 1979. Career: tech. writer Burroughs Corp., San Diego 1978-79; senior systems analyst Gen. Dynamics Convair, 1979-80, advanced mfg. technologist, senior engr. 1980-81; scientist consultant 1979-; govt. contr., cons. USN, 1982, U.S. DoD, 1986-, contr. to DNA, NOSC, DARPA, SDIO, USAF, and US Army, 1988-; faculty San Diego Community Coll. Dist. 1976-82, 85-90; instr. phys. scis. National Univ., San Diego 1980-81; instr. bus. law, earth scis. Miramar Coll., 1978-82 (studentbody Tchr. of Yr. 1982); recipient N.Y.C. citizenship award for sci. activity 1959; patents: Composite Fabric Endothermic Electronic Component Cooling (1984), 3 patents at Gen. Dynamics (1981), patents pending re Aggregate Suspended Particle Electric Charge Collector (1990, 91); mem.: AAAS, Am. Inst. Aero. & Astro. (senior mem.), N.Y. Acad. Scis., Am. Chem. Soc.; R.Cath.; rec: travel, boating, music, films, technology, people. Res/Ofc: 3737 Third Ave #308 San Diego 92103 Tel:619/299-2267

HAYES, GREGORY MICHAEL, school teacher/coach; b. Dec. 28, 1954, Queens, N.Y.; s. John Aloysius, III, and Patricia Marie (Kennedy) H.; m. Jan Marie McGlothlin, Aug. 4, 1990; 1 dau., Megan Kimberly b. June 9, 1992; edn: BA in history, UCLA, 1977, MEd, 1980. Career: grad. asst. men's basketball coach UCLA 1977-79, asst. women's basketball coach UCLA, 1979-81; subs. tchr. Placentia Unified Sch. Dist., 1981-82; tchr./coach Wm. S. Hart Sch. Dist., Santa Clarita 1982-; Canyon High Sch. asst. track coach 1982-89, varsity boys basketball coach 1982-, varsity girls softball coach 1991-, Staying Alive advisor 1988-, substance abuse chair 1986-90; basketball coach Athletes In Action - USA, summers 1978-85; nat. shot doctor Shot Doctor Basketball, USA, Raleigh, N.C. 1986-; NCAA Volleyball line judge 1987-90; awards: Canyon High Sch. most inspirational tchr., coach of yr. 1986, 1987, listed Outstanding Young Men of Am. 1989, listed Who's Who in the West 1991, "All-Star Coach" Daily News Bernie Milligan All-Star Softball Game, Northridge, Calif. 1991; mem. So. Calif. Interscholastic Basketball Coaches Assn. (pres. 1990-92), Fellowship of Christian Athletes (mem., camp coach 1981-), Calif. Tchrs. Assn. 1988-, Canyon Theatre Guild (mem., actor 1988-); civic: L.A. Olympic Sports Fest. (vol. summer 1991), Grace Baptist Ch. Orchestra, Newhall 1991-; pub. articles in SCIBCA Coaches Notebook (1989, 91); Christian; rec: acting, trumpet, sports, reading, bicycling, family activities. Ofc: Canyon High School 19300 W Nadal St Canyon Country 91351

HAYNES, EDITH MAE, college administrator; b. Jan. 23, 1934, Marshfield, Mo.; d. Marion Manning and Delphia Bernice (Richerson) McGaughey; m. Clifford Elmer Gantner, June 12, 1949 (div. 1960); children: Deborah b. 1950, Patti b. 1953, Barbi b. 1956, Clifford b. 1958; edn: D.C., Cleveland Chiropractic Coll., Kansas City, Mo.; lic. D.C., Calif., 1983. Career: purch. agent, Kansas City, Mo.; secty. Cleveland Chiropractic Coll., K.C., Mo., transferred to Los Angeles, 1977-, as gen. office, subsequently dir. admissions, dir. postgrad. edn., dir. of devel./alumni affairs, administrv. asst. to the president; mem: Internat. Chiropractors Assn., Am. Chiropractic Assn., Calif. Chiropractic Assn., Am.

Public Health Assn., Nat. Assn. of Fund Raising Executives, Nat. Notary Assn., Sigma Chi Psi, Delta Tau Alpha; rec: reading, travel. Res: PO Box 9217 Glendale 91226-9217 Ofc: Cleveland Chiropractic College, 590 N Vermont Ave Los Angeles 90004

HAYWARD, FREDRIC MARK, men's rights activist, association executive; b. July 10, 1946, N.Y.C.; s. Irving Michael and Mildred (Feingold) H.; m. Ingeborg Beck, Aug. 18, 1971 (div. Aug. 1974); children: Kil R. b. 1981; edn: BA, Brandeis Univ., 1967; MA, Fletcher Sch. of Law & Diplomacy, 1968, MALD, 1969. Career: sales JNSIII, Paris, France 1965; satellite research TRW Systems, Redondo Beach 1966; diplomatic svc. US State Dept., Bangkok, Thailand 1968; tchr. Concord Pub. Sch., Concord, Mass. 1969-77; exec. director Men's Rights, Inc., Somerville, Mass. 1977-; writer and lectr., Sacramento, Calif. 1977-: articles in newspapers, mags. and jours., and 3 anthologies: Male/Female Roles 1983, Men Freeing Men 1985, To Be A Man 1991; numerous lectures and workshops various univs., groups and confs., frequent guest appearances on local, nat. and fgn. t.v. and radio shows; contbg. writer Spectator, Berkeley 1988-, contbg. editor Liberator, Forest Lake, Minn. 1988-89; mem. advy. bd. Ctr. for Men's Studies, Berkeley 1988-; bd. dirs. Men Internat., Mpls. 1982-86, Nat. Congress for Men., W.D.C. 1981-90; awards: fellow Fletcher Sch. of Law & Diplomacy 1967-69, vis. lectr. Tufts Univ. 1979, fellow Warren Farrell Found., Leucadia, Calif. 1989; mem: Nat. Congress for Men and Children (1981-, bd. 1981-90), Sacramento Valley Men's Council 1992-, AFTRA 1979-; Jewish; rec: guitar, tennis. Ofc: Mr. Inc., PO Box 163180 Sacramento 95816

HEADDING, SALLY (LILLIAN SUSAN), author; b. Jan. 1, 1944, Milw.; d. David Morton and Mary Davis (Berry) Coleman; m. James K. Hill (div. 1976); children: Amy Denise; m. John Murray Headding (div. 1987); edn: BA sociology (GPA 4.0) Univ. Nev., 1975; MA urban affairs, Univ. of Pacific, 1976. Career: served in US Women's Army Corps, spl. assignment to G-2 USAPIC, hon. disch. 1963; asst. buyer/jr. exec. tng. pgm. Gimbels, Milw. 1964-65; new store set-up/ops. mgr. Frandisco Corp. of N.Y., 1966-67; store mgr., actg. reg. mgr. Anita Shops (clothing chain), Los Angeles 1968-69; store mgr., buyer Clothes Closet, (clothing chain), Sunnyvale 1970; human resources devel. Tehachapi State Prison Early Out Parole Pgm., St. Calif., 1971; orgn. co-founder and bd. Community Action Against Rape, Las Vegas, NV 1972-75; owner/opr. Lillian Headding Interiors (commercial medical design), Pittsburg, Calif. 1977-88; mfrs. sales rep. JG West, San Francisco 1989-91; appt. family svs. advy. com. Contra Costa Co. Bd. of Suprs., 1986, numerous city commns., 1976-86; works with police depts. as clairvoyent; recipient commendns. Nevada State Gov., Las Vegas Metro P.D., N.Las Vegas P.D. (1973-74); mem. Calif. Writer's Club (Walnut Creek chpt. pres 1987-88), Philippine, Hawaiian, and Am. Black Belter's Assn. (life 1973); author, as Sally Davis (novels) Willows End (1988), When Gods Fall (1992), short stories and poetry; Democrat; Jewish. Res: 5333 Park Highlands Blvd #33 Concord 94521

HEADLEE, ROLLAND DOCKERAY, bank founder, business consultant; b. Aug. 27, 1916, Los Angeles; s. Jesse William and Cleora (Dockeray) H.; desc. Thomas Wright, English emigrant to Mass. 1634; stu. UCLA; m. Alzora Burgett, May 13, 1939; children: Linda Ann (Pohl), b. 1946. Career: asst. mgr. Finance Assocs. 1946-59; fin. & bus. cons. R.D. Headlee & Assocs. 1959-; acct. exec. and cons. Walter E. Heller & Co. 1962-65; exec. v.p. Genrus Engring. Corp. 1965-67; exec. dir. Town Hall of California, 1967-1987; cons. 1987-; dir.: Am. Internat. Bank, Mfrs. Assocs., Starfire Engring. Co., (past) Genuss Engring., Jolie Cosmetics; nat. radio pgm. moderator Town Hall on the Air; guest lectr. USC Sch. Engring. 1977, 78; tchr. Comparative Religions 1954-69; honored by formal resolutions US Senate 92d & 95th Sessions, US Cong. 91st Session, Calif. State Assembly (1971, 76), City of Los Angeles 1971; mem: Town Hall (life), Detroit Econ. Club, Mensa Internat., L.A. World Affairs Council, L.A. Stock Exch. Club, US Power Squadron, US Coast Guard Aux. (flotilla cmdr.), Commonwealth Club, Newcomen Soc., Com. on Foreign Relations (advy. bd. L.A.), BSA, Oceanic Soc.; editor 11 anthologies re 20+ subjects; guest writer various trade publs.; mil: served to 1st lt. Adj. Gen. Dept. AUS 1943-46, lt.(jg) USCGR post-WWII; Republican; Methodist (adult supt., v.chmn. bd.); rec: skiing, gem/mineral collector, sailing, equestrian. Res: 8064 El Manor Ave Los Angeles 90045 Ofc: Town Hall, R.D. Headlee Associates 523 W Sixth St Ste 232 Los Angeles 90014

HEALEY, WILLIAM JOHN, III, financial executive; b. Aug. 19, 1940, Boston, Mass.; s. William John and Ava Maria (deCordova) H.; edn: private schooling Ridley Coll., St. Catharines, Ont., Can. 1947-56; BA, MA, Oxford Univ. Eng. 1961. Career: exec. v.p. Citicorp, formerly First National City Bank, N.Y.C. 1961-67; c.e.o. Ascarib Ltd., San Francisco 1976-; v.p. Barclays Bank Internat., Durban, South Africa 1968-70; sr. v.p. Johns Manville Corp. N.Y.C. 1970-72; awards: Gov. Gen. Sir Vincent Massay Pub. Speaking award (1954, 56); civic: Republican Club, Royal Historical Assn. (sr. mem.), Hanover Polo Club (Jamaica, B.W.I., chief judge), Royal Yacht Squadron (Cowes, Isle of Wight, Eng.), Royal Debating Soc. (London, Eng., chief moderator); Republican; R.Cath.; rec: travel, polo, ballooning, sailing. Ofc: Ascarib Ltd. PO Box 424764 San Francisco 94142-4764

HEARST, RANDOLPH APPERSON, publishing co. executive; b. Dec. 2, 1915, NYC; s. William Randolph and Millicent (Willson) H.; m. Catherine Campbell, Jan. 12, 1938, div. 1982; children: Catherine; Virginia; Patricia; Anne; Victoria; m. 2d. Maria C. Scruggs, May 2, 1982, div. 1986; m. Veronica deUribe, July 5, 1987; edn: student, Harvard 1933-34. Career: asst. to ed. Atlanta Georgian 1939-40; asst. to pub. San Francisco Call-Bulletin 1940-44, exec. ed. 1947-49, pub. 1950-53; pres./ dir./ CEO Hearst Consol. Publs., Inc. and Hearst Publ. Co. Inc. 1961-64; chmn. exec. com. The Hearst Corp. 1965-73, chmn. bd. 1973-, dir. 1965-, pres. San Francisco Examiner 1972-; trustee Hearst Found.; clubs: Piedmont Driving (Atlanta), Burlingame CC, Pacific Union; mil: capt. USAAF Air Transport Command 1943-45; Cath. Ofc: 110 5th St San Francisco 94103, and 959 Eighth Ave New York City 10019

HEARST, ROSALIE MAY WYNN, philanthropist/foundation executive; b. Mar. 7, Oklahoma City, Okla.; d. Mathis O. and Audell Bertha (Clary) Wynn; m. George Randolph Hearst, Sr. July 16, 1958; edn: Okla. City Coll., UCLA. Career: Hearst representative U.S. Senate Youth Program; pres. George Randolph Hearst Memorial Found. for Diabetic Edn.; pres. Rosalie Hearst Ednl. Found.; bd. mem. Elvirita Lewis Found.; life mem: Eisenhower Med. Ctr., Pathfinders, Tiempo de Los Ninos, Desert Hosp. Aux., Desert Press Club, College of the Desert Aux., Internat. Orphans; board mem: Pathfinder's Ranch Boys Club; former bd. mem: Friends of Cultural Ctr. of Coll. of the Desert, Joslin Diabetes Found., nat. Assistance League of the Desert, Children's Village USA, Opera Guild, Braille Aux. of the Desert, Warner Guidance Ctr. for Emotionally Disturbed Children, Palm Springs Opera Guild; trustee emeritus: The Bob Hope Cultural Ctr.; coordinator Officers Wives Volunteer Services Dibble Gen. Hosp., Palo Alto; coord. Am. Womens Vol. Services Sawtelle Hosp. L.A.; created Rosalie and George Hearst Fellowship in Ophthalmology UC Berkeley; honors include George and Rosalie Hearst named Man & Woman of Yr. City of Hope 1971, lifetime achiev. in comm. svc. Palm Springs Womens Press Club 1987, distinguished woman Northwood Inst. 1988. Res: 550 Camino del Sur Palm Springs 92262

HEATH, DONALD WAYNE, estate planning specialist; b. June 2, 1942, Wendover, Utah; s. Earl Charles and Violet (Susich) H.; m. Barbara Lyn Beesley, Aug. 11, 1963 (div. Nov. 2, 1979); m. 2d. Laurie Jean Lichter Feb. 28, 1981; children: Jeffery b. 1965, Christian b. 1968, Jill b. 1970, Michele b. 1983, Adam b. 1988, Jason b. 1990; edn: BA, bus. adminstrn., Univ. of Nevada, Reno, 1964; CLU, Am. Coll., Pa., 1972; ChFC, Am. Coll., Pa., 1984; LUTCF, Wash. DC, 1988. Career: adjunct prof., Univ. of Nevada 1974-80; commr. of ins., State of Nevada 1979-81; sales mgr., NY Life Ins. Co. 1981-83; field v.p., Integrated Resources 1983-84; securities wholesaler, Angeles Corp. 1984-85; v.p., sales, Ins. Office of Am., Inc. 1985; instr., Univ. of the Pacific 1986-87; instr., San Joaquin Delta Coll. 1987-88; reg. v.p., Capstone Fin. Svc., Inc. 1987-88; reg. marketing dir., Ameritas Variable Life Ins. Co. 1988-91; pres., CEO, Heath Fin. Dynamics Corp. 1985-93; estate & bus. ins. splst., Merrill Lynch, San Diego 1992-; awards: listed Who's Who Among Students in Am. Universities & Colleges 1964, Who's Who in Outstanding Young Men of Am., Jaycees 1972, Who's Who in the West 1991; mem: area gov./club pres., Toastmasters Internat., Reno 1970-77; pres., Univ. of Nevada Alumni Assn. 1976, 1983-86; mem, Rotary Internat. 1977-88; comm. chmn., Greater Reno C.of C. 1977-78; comm. chmn., Calif. Assn. of Life Underwriters 1987-88; mem: Nat. Assn. of Ins. Commrs., Passe Club, Million Dollar Round Table, Am. Soc. of CLU & ChFC, Internat. Assn. for Fin. Planning, Nat. Assn. of Life Underwriters, Nat. Assn. of Securities Dealers. Mil: capt., US Army 1965-70; rec: fishing, camping. Ofc: Merrill Lynch 2400 Imperial Bank Tower 701 B St. San Diego 92101

HECK, OTTO LUDWIG, manufacturing co. executive; b. Aug. 10, 1920, Germany, nat. US cit. 1943; s. Ludwig and Hedwig Clementine (Schirmer) H.; m. Barbara, May 31, 1942; 1 dau. Susanne b. 1947. Career: mgr. customer svc. Angelus Sanitary Can Machine Co., 1960-, v.p. Customer Svc. 1969-, v.p. ops. 1978-, exec. v.p./secty. 1980-, pres./chief ops. 1983-87, chmn./CEO 1987-; dir. Angelus Sanitary Can Machine Co., Angelus Export Co., dir./pres. Angelus Corp. Internat., dir./sec.treas. Henry L. Guenther Found.; mem: Food Industries Internat. Trade Council (dir.), Nat. Assn. of Mfrs., Food Processing Mach. & Suppliers Assn., Old Guard Soc. (FPM & SA), The Presidents Assn., Master Brewers Assn. of Am., U.S. Brewers Assn. (Beer Inst.), The Packaging Inst. of USA, Fgn. Trade Assn. of So. Calif.; mem: U.S. C.of C., Calif. C.of C., Vernon C.of C., 552 Club of Hoag Hosp., Masons, Balboa Bay Club; mil: T5 US Army Engrs. 1943-46, decorated Presdl. Citation, Am. Theatre rib., ETO rib. w/clusters, Victory rib., Expert Rifleman, Good Conduct medal; Republican; Prot.; rec: golf, stamp collection; ofc: Angelus Sanitary Can Machine Co 4900 Pacific Blvd Los Angeles 90058

HEDGE, THOMAS LYLE, physician; b. Sept. 15, 1950, Radford, Va.; s. Thomas Lyle and Mary Frances (Askew) H.; m. Cyd Annette Canavan, Oct. 1, 1978; children: Erin b. 1981, Eric b. 1985, Emily b. 1987, Evan b. 1989; edn: Univ. of Hawaii 1968-71; BA, UC Riverside 1972; MD, USC Sch. Medicine 1976; lic. Am. Bd. Physical Medicine & Rehab. (1981). Career: intern L.A. County-USC Med. Center, Los Angeles 1976-77, resident 1977-80; asst. dir. Center for Rehab. Northridge Hosp. Med. Center 1980-82, assoc. dir. 1985-88,

med. dir. 1988-; lectr. CSU Northridge 1983-; prof. USC Sch. Medicine, Los Angeles 1983-; mem: Am. Congress Rehab., Am. Acad. Physical Medicine, A.C.P., Calif. Med. Assn., Los Angeles City Advy. Council on Disabled; Democrat; Congregational. Ofc: Northridge Hospital Medical Center 18300 Roscoe Blvd Northridge 91328

HEIECK, PAUL JAY, wholesale distributing executive; b. Aug. 6, 1937, San Francisco; s. Erwin N. and Ann C. (Retchless) H.; m. Kathleen Pawela, Oct. 14, 1967; children: Valerie, Yvonne, Elizabeth, Krista, Justin; edn: Golden Gate Coll., 1958. Career: sales rep. Heieck & Moran, San Francisco 1958-63, sec. treas. 1963-69, Heieck Supply, Inc. 1969-76, pres. Heieck Supply, Inc. 1976-90; pres. P.J.H. Investments Inc., 1983-; reg. mgr. Hajoca Corp., 1989-; dir., 1st v.p. San Francisco Board of Trade 1978-82; mem: Am. Supply Assn. (dir. 1984-, v.p. 1987-91, pres. 1992), Western Suppliers Assn. (pres. 1981-83, dir. 1981-85); civic: San Francisco Boys Club (dir. 1972-), Rotary, San Mateo County Mounted Posse; clubs: Sharon Heights Country, Olympic; mil: AUS 1955-57; Republican; Episcopalian. Ofc: P.J.H. Investments, Inc. PO Box 620604 Woodside 94062

HEINER, DOUGLAS CRAGUN, physician, educator; b. July 27, 1925, Salt Lake City, Utah; s. Spencer and Eva Lillian (Cragun) H.; m. Joy Luana Wiest, Jan. 8, 1946; children: Susan b. 1948, Craig b. 1949, Joseph b. 1951, Marianne b. 1954, James b. 1956, David b. 1958, Andrew b. 1960, Carolee b. 1963, Pauli b. 1964; edn: BS, Idaho State Univ., 1945; MD, Univ. Pa. Sch. of Medicine, Phila. 1950; PhD, McGill Univ., Montreal 1969. Career: medic, 1st lt. US Army, Korea 1951-53; tchg. asst. in peds. Harvard Med. Sch., Boston 1954-55; res. fellow, cardio. Child. Med. Ctr., Boston 1955-56; instr., asst. prof. pediatrics Univ. Arkansas Med. Sch., Little Rock 1956-60, actg. head dept. peds. 1957-58; asst., assoc. prof. Univ. of Utah Sch. Med., S.L.C., 1960-66; prof. of pediatrics UCLA Med. Sch., 1969-, dir. Third Year Peds., 1987-92, and chief div. of immunology and allergy, Harbor-UCLA Med. Ctr., Torrance 1969-; awards: 1st prize resident's res. New England Ped. Soc., Boston 1955, outstanding tchr. citation, Student Yearbook dedication, Little Rock, Ark. 1958, outstanding res. award Western Soc. for Ped. Research 1961, NIH spl. research fellow, Montreal 1966-69, Fogarty Internat. Fellow, Univ. of Bern, Switz. 1978-79, Idaho State Univ. distinguished alumnus 1987; mem: Am. Acad. of Allergy and Immunology (fellow), Am. Acad. of Peds. (fellow), Am. Coll. of Allergists (fellow), AAAS, Am. Assn. of Immunologists,, Am. Fedn. for Clin. Research, Soc. for Ped. Research, We. Soc. for Ped. Research; civic: Boy Scouts Am. 1976-81; author: Allergy to Milk (1980), 45 chapters in med. books, 131+ articles, 8 reviews (1955-); Republican; Ch. of Jesus Christ of Latter-Day Saints, Rancho P.V. (High Council 1983-87, High Priests Gp. ldr 1987-); rec: tennis, gardening, fishing. Res: 29158 Oceanridge Dr Rancho Palos Verdes 90274 Ofc: Harbor-UCLA Medical Ctr 1000 W Carson J-4 Torrance 90509

HEINRICH, MILTON ROLLIN, biochemist; b. Nov. 25, 1919, Linton, N.Dak.; s. Fred and Emma (Becker) H.; m. Ramona G. Cavanagh, May 31, 1966; edn: AB, Univ. S.Dak., Vermillion 1941; MS, Univ. of Iowa, 1942, PhD, 1944. Career: NIH postdoc. fellow Univ. Pa., Phila. 1947-49; research assoc. Amherst Coll., 1949-57; NIH senior postdoc. fellow UC Berkeley, 1958-60; asst. prof. biochemistry Univ. So. Calif., Los Angeles 1960-63; branch chief, project scientist NASA, Ames Research Ctr., Moffett Field, 1963-85; cons. Lockheed Missiles & Space, Sunnyvale 1985-; pres. Zerog Corp., Los Altos Hills 1985-91; honors: Phi Beta Kappa, Sigma Xi, Phi Lambda Upsilon, Cosmos Group award NASA 1981, 1984, Space Station Group award NASA 1984, Fellow Explorers Club (NY); mem.: Am. Soc. Biochem. & Molecular Biology 1958-, Am. Chemical Soc. 1942-, Am. Soc. Gravitational & Space Biology 1987-; author numerous book chapters and research papers; editor: Extreme Environments (1976), co-editor: Cosmos 1129 Mission, Plants & Radiation (1981), Cosmos 1129 Mission, Rat Expts. (1981); mil: ltjg USNR 1944-47; rec: travel, photography. Res: 27200 Deer Springs Way Los Altos Hills 94022

HEINZE, RUTH-INGE, educator, researcher, author; b. Nov. 4, 1919, Berlin, Germany, naturalized U.S. citizen 1962; d. Otto Albert and Louise Auguste (Preschel) Heinze; edn: BA, UC Berkeley, 1969, MA, 1971, PhD, 1974. Career: lectr. Mills Coll., Oakland 1974; res. assoc. UC Berkeley, 1974-; staff research asst. Univ. Calif., San Francisco 1975; res. fellow Inst. of Southeast Asian Studies, Singapore 1978; prof. Calif. Inst. of Integral Studies, S.F. 1984-; prof. Saybrook Inst., S.F. 1985-; producer Universal Dialogue, Berkeley 1979-; nat. dir. Independent Scholars of Asia, 1981-; dir. Oakland Asian Cultural Ctr., 1987-; awards: grantee UCB 1969-73, travel grantee Am. Inst. of Indian Studies, W.D.C. (1975, 78), Fulbright-Hays res. grantee, Singapore 1978-79; mem: Assn. for Asian Studies 1974-, Internat. Assn. for the Study of Traditional Asian Medicine 1988-; author: Shamans of the 20th Century (1991), Trance & Healing in SEA Today 1988, Tham Khwan-How to Contain the Essence of Life (1982), editor (book) Proceedings of the Internat. Conf. on the Study of Shamanism & Alt. Modes of Healing, 1984-91; rec: use of sound in healing, acupuncture, Chinese herbal medicine, Reiki. Res: 2321 Russell St #3A Berkeley 94705

HEISER, MICHAEL JAY, advertising agency executive; b. Mar. 10, 1954, Los Angeles; s. Charles E. and Elaine A. (Cole) H.; m. Linda Jean Udell, Nov. 10, 1990; children (nee Pile): Todd b. 1984, Scott b. 1986; edn: BS, CSU Long Beach, 1976; MBA, Univ. So. Calif., 1977. Career: account exec. McCann-Erickson Inc., Los Angeles 1977-79; Ogilvy Mather Inc. 1979; account supr. Dailey & Assocs. Inc. 1979-84; v.p. Poindexter/Osaki/Nissman 1984-86; exec. v.p. Fujii, Heiser & Assocs., Westlake Village 1986-; lectr. CSU Northridge 1989-, Calif. Lutheran Univ., Thousand Oaks 1989-; mem. Advertising Club L.A. 1977-, Cardinal & Gold 1991-, Aircraft Owners & Pilots Assn. 1988-, Nat. Rifle Assn. (life); civic: Simi Valley Aquatics Club (treas. 1991-), Boy Scouts (den leader Simi Valley 1991-), Optimist Club Westlake Village (v.p. 1990-91); Republican; United Methodist; rec: flying, shooting, swimming, youth activities. Ofc: Fujii, Heiser & Associates, 5716 Corsa Ave Ste 200 Westlake Village 91362

HELFOND, WENDY WORRALL, reporter, graphic designer; b. Sept. 11, 1963, Davenport, Ia.; d. Gerald Charles and Joan Margaret (Kraus) Worrall; m. Randy George Helfond, July 11, 1987; children: Katie Jo b. 1989; edn: BA in bdcst. journalism, USC, 1985; cert., Inst. of Children's Literature, Redding Ridge, Ct. 1992. Career: senior employee communications rep. The Walt Disney Co., Burbank 1985-89; editorial asst., reporter, feature writer The Bernardo News (weekly), Rancho Bernardo, Calif. 1991-; awards: employee of mo. Disney Univ., The Walt Disney Co. (3t), listed Who's Who of Young Am. Women 1985, Who's Who in West 1992; mem. USC General Alumni Assn., Town & Gown Jrs., L.A. (1992-, editor 92-), Trojan Junior Aux., L.A. (1985-, editor 1987-89, pres. 1990-91, parliamentarian 1991-), RB Chorale, Rancho Bernardo (1991-, 2d v.p. publicity 1992-), Disneyland Alumni Assn. (1985-), Athletes & Entertainers for Kids (1986-90); R.Cath.; rec: needlepoint, reading, movies. Res: 11456 Palito Court San Diego 92127 Ofc: The Bernardo News, 11717 Bernardo Plaza Ct Ste 120 San Diego 92128

HELSPER, JAMES THOMAS, surgeon, medical researcher, educator; b. Mar. 29, 1924, Mpls.; s. Salvius John and Gretchen Louise (Gleissner) H.; m. 2d. Carolyn Harrison, Dec. 26, 1975; children: James Thomas, Jr. b. 1955, Richard Scott b. 1957, Paige Carla b. 1961, Brian Harrison b. 1981; edn: BS, St. Vincent Coll., Latrobe, Pa. 1945; MD, Jefferson Med. Coll. 1947; grad. stu. Univ. of Penn. 1949-50. Career: med. intern Medical Ctr., Jersey City 1947-48, internal medicine resident 1948-49; surgery resident US Naval Hosp. Portsmouth, Va. 1951-52, Queens Hosp. N.Y.C. 1952-53, Memorial Ctr. for Cancer N.Y.C. 1953-57; former asst. clin. prof. surgery, Loma Linda Univ. Sch. of Medicine; assoc. clin. prof. tumor surgery, USC Sch. of Medicine, Los Angeles; attdg. surgeon L.A. County/USC Med. Ctr., chief surgical svc. service Huntington Memorial Hosp. 1962-, Kenneth Norris Jr. Cancer Hosp.; cons. clinical pgm. Pasadena Found. for Med. Research 1960-81; bd. dirs. Pasadena Found. for Med. Research 1960-, Huntington Med. Research Insts. 1982-; mem: Am. Cancer Soc. (bd. dirs. Calif. div. 1967-, pres. L.A. County Unit 1970-71), AMA, Calif. Med. Assn. (cancer com.), L.A. Co. Med. Soc. (com. on cancer), Pasadena Med. Soc., L.A. Surgical Soc., Am. Soc. Clin. Oncology, Soc. Surgical Oncology, Soc. Head & Neck Surgeons (pres. 1988-89), Am. Radium Soc., Am. Coll. Surgeons, Pan-Pacific Surgical Assn., World Med. Assn., WHO, AAAS, Flying Physicians Assn.; mem. internat. sci. advy. com. UICC; research: devel. Stoma Button (named for author) for laryngectomy patients; contbr. numerous articals in med. jours., article in Aero mag. (9/77); mil: capt. USNR-Ret. 1984, Active (1943-45, 1950-52); Republican; R.Cath.; rec: flying, photography. Res: 580 Arbor St Pasadena 91105 Ofc: 50 Bellefontaine St Pasadena 91105

HEM, JOHN DAVID, research chemist; b. May 14, 1916, Starkweather, N.Dak.; s. Hans Neilius and Josephine Augusta (Larsen) H.; m. Ruth Evans, Mar. 11, 1945 (dec. May 1987); children: John D. b. 1948, Michael b. 1949; edn: undergrad. Minot St. Univ. 1932-36, N.Dak. State Univ. 1937-38, Iowa State Univ. 1938; BS chemistry, George Washington Univ., W.D.C. 1940; Career: chemist Water Resources Div., US Geological Survey, 1940-; analytical chemist in Safford, Az. (1940-42, 43-45), Roswell, N.M. 1942-43, Albuquerque 1945-47, dist. chemist in Albuquerque 1948-53, res. chemist in Denver, Colo. 1953-63, in Menlo Park, Calif. 1963-; instr. in-house tng. facility USGS, Denver 1970-80, research advisor Water Research Com., USGS, Menlo Park (1974-79, 84-); awards: US Interior Dept. meritorious service, distinguished service (1976, 80), Nat. Water Well Assn. science award 1986, O.E. Meinzer award Geologic Soc. Am., Boulder 1990, Special award Internat. Assn. of Geochem. & Cosmochem. 1992; mem: Am. Chemical Soc. (50-yr. mem.), Am. Geophysical Union 1945-, Geochemical Soc.(1951-, Am. Water Works Assn. 1952-, Soc. for Geochemistry and Health 1975-; author: Study & Interpretation of Natural Water Chemistry (1959, 2d ed. 1970, 3d ed. 1985), 100+ book chapters and articles on water chemistry 1945-; Democrat; Lutheran (coun. mem., chmn. Holy Shepherd Luth., Lakewood, Colo. 1957-60, coun. Grace Luth. Ch., Palo Alto, Ca. 1975-77; rec: singing choral music. Res: 3349 Saint Michael Ct Palo Alto 94306 Ofc: USGS 345 Middlefield MS427 Menlo Park 94025

HEMMINGS, PETER WILLIAM, opera company executive; b. Apr. 10, 1934, London, England; s. William and Rosalind Alice Mary (Jones) H.; m. Jane Frances Kearnes, May 19, 1962; children: William b. 1965, Lucy b. 1966, Emma b. 1969, Rupert b. 1970, Sophie b. 1973; edn: undergrad. Mill Hill Sch.,

London 1947-52; MA, classics, Gonville and Caius Coll., Cambridge, 1957. Career: clk. Harold Holt Ltd., London 1957-59; first general mgr. New Opera Company, Sadler's Wells Theatre, London, 1957-65, personal asst. to gen. mgr. then repertory and planning mgr. Sadlers Wells Opera, 1959-65; gen. adminstr. Scottish Opera, Glasgow 1962-77, spearhd. reopening Glasgow's Theatre Royal 1975; gen. mgr. Australian Opera, Sydney 1977-79; mng. director London Symphony Orch., London 1980-84; gen. director Los Angeles Music Center Opera, L.A. 1984-; gen. cons. Compton Verney Opera Project, Eng. 1988-; bd. mem. Sadlers Wells Assn., W.D.C. 1988, Royal Acad. of Music, London 1981-, Opera America, W.D.C. 1989-; v.p. Opera America 1993-; honors: pres. Univ. Opera Group, Cambridge 1956-57, Hon. LL.D., Strathclyde Univ., Glasgow 1978, Fellow Royal Scottish Acad. of Music, Glasgow 1978, Hon. Fellow Royal Acad. of Music, London 1992; club: Garrick (London); works: bdcstr. Digital Planet, Calif. (1992); mil: lt. Royal Signals, 1952-54; Anglican. Res: 775 S Madison Ave Pasadena 91106 Ofc: Los Angeles Music Center Opera, 135 N Grand Ave Los Angeles 90012

HENDERSON, CARL GREGORY, chiropractor; b. Feb. 21, 1947; s. Robert Milton and Vella Rose Henderson; children: Michael b. 1967, Jeanna b. 1970, Jennifer b. 1975; edn: DC, Los Angeles Coll. of Chiro. 1979; ND, DO, Anglo-Am. Inst.; bd. certified thermographer 1987. Career: past employee Kaiser Gypsum Co.; self- defense instr.; current dir. chiropractic/owner Fallbrook Chiropractic Ctr.; owner On-Guard Tng. Inst.; creator self defense sys. for women; lectr. worldwide on chiropractic, self defense and Boy Scouts; author/ pub. Deseret Alphabet Primer (1972); writer/ prod. movie, Women Be Aware (1982); awards: Grand Champion, USFE Karate Championships, Europe 1968, various presdl. sports awards, Black Belt in Nippon Kenpo - Expanded Self-/ Defense; mem. Am. Chiro. Council on Mental Health (past pres.), Council of Diagnostic Imaging, Thermographic Soc. of Calif. (Fellow); civic: Phon-A-Thon organizer, La Paz Clinic/Orphanage, Boy Scouts of Am. (asst. dist. commr., chmn. 1989, dist. chmn. 1990-91), BSA awards include Order of Arrow- Vigil, Silver Beaver 1988, organizer, Scouters Key, Scouters Tng., Den Ldrs. Tng., Arrowhead, and Merit awards; Village Rotary Club (pres. 1985, Paul Harris Fellow 1986, internat. dir. 1989), Polio Plus, Mesoamerica Res. Found. (archaeology); mil: USAR 3 yrs.; USCG capt. lic. and sail aux. 1986; Adv. amateur radio opr. lic. 1989, radio licensed technician; author video: Forever Living Aloe Vera. Ofc: Fallbrook Chiropractic Center, 113 S Vine St Fallbrook 92028

HENDERSON, ROBBE LYNN, educator, psychometrician; b. Nov. 19, 1946, Chgo.; d. Robert Ogden Henderson, Edward (stepf.) and Irene Delores (Parks) Foster; edn: BA, We. Mich. Univ., 1969; MEd, Univ. Ill, Urbana 1972, PhD, 1982. Career: Spanish tchr. H.S. Chgo. (Ill.) Bd. of Edn., 1969-71, Bilingual tchr., 1971-73; reg. supr. Ill. Ofc. of Edn., Chgo., 1973-80; dir. of research Garfield Park Mental Health, Chgo., 1980-81; dir. curriculum devel. City Colleges Chgo., 1981-82; asst., assoc. prof. Western Ill. Univ., Macomb 1982-86; vis. prof. Univ. Calif. Riverside, 1986-87; adj. prof. Univ. of San Diego, 1987-88; assoc. prof. CSU Dominguez Hills, Carson, Calif. 1988-92, full tenured prof. 1992- (coord. ed. adm. prog 1993-); cons. to West Indies Edn., Jamaica, W.I., 1970; liaison to Ministry of Edn., Toronto, Can. 1974; cons. Dillingham Assoc., 1974-86; cons. U.S. Dept. of Labor, assigned to Spain, N.Africa, Canary Is., 1979-80; cons. U.S. Dept. Edn., 1976-; evaluator Rockford (Ill.) Sch. Dist., 1975-; awards: Spelling Bee champion Chicago Daily News 1956, singer Morris Sachs TV Amateur, Chgo. 1958, legislative scholar State of Ill. 1960, Sweetheart Alpha Sphinxmen Champaign 1964, Sweetheart Kappa Scrollers Champaign 1965, v.p. Assn. Women Students WMU 1967-69, Homecoming Queen Court WMU 1968, Who's Who Am. Colls. & Univs. 1969, Minority Grad. Fellow Univ. Ill., Urbana 1970-72, outstanding svc. Crete-Monee Sch., Ill. 1974, regl. supt.'s award Kankakee (Ill.) Schs. 1975, Minority Fellow Univ. Ill. 1978-80, Phi Delta Kappa 1978, Order of Omega WIU-Students 1983, Edn. Profl. Leadership Fellows, W.D.C. 1984, outstanding tchr. WIU Student Body 1984, outstanding black faculty WIU -APHIA 1986, IMAGES Award Profl. 1987, tchg. award City Colls. San Diego (summer 87, 88), AA res. grantee CSUDH 1988-92, Academic Senate CSU Dominguez Hills (v.p. 1990-92, parliamentarian 92-94), Lyle E. Gibson Distinguished Tchr. of Year 1992-93; mem: AERA, NABE, TESOL, ASCD, CAPEA; publs: translator (Children's Sci. series) "Now You Know" Ency. Brit. (1972), jour. article NABE (1986). Ofc: Calif. State Univ. Dominguez Hills HFA B-104 School of Education Carson 90747

HENDRICKSON, THOMAS ROY, architect; b. Sept. 29, 1951, Seattle, Wash.; s. Laurie John and Rose Josephine (Helina) H.; m. Lana Shull, Jan. 12, 1973; children: Aaron b. 1973, Charity b. 1975, Melody b. 1976; edn: BA environmental design, Univ. Wash. 1973; reg. arch. Wash., Calif. 1984. Career: designer Olympic Assoc. Seattle & Richland, Wash. (nuclear projects incl. fusion reactor planning) 1978-82; project arch. Ehrlich-Rominger Archs. Los Altos (hi-tech micro-electronics projects in Calif. NY, Mass.) 1982-86; project arch. George Miers & Assocs. (Novato City Hall, Park Place rental condominiums), San Francisco 1986-87; prodn. mgr. McLellan & Copenhagen, Cupertino, Calif. & Seattle, Wash. (Fred Hutchinson Cancer Resrch. Ctr., University Science Facilities, Lifescan, Biotechnology Projects), 1987-; honors: Seattle

Times Open House 1981; mem: Am. Inst. Archs. (contg. edn. com. 1985), Bay Vista Town Homes Assn. (dir., v.p.); Solar Master Conserver Wash. State 1981; worked on US Solar Demonstration Project 1976; Christian; rec: internat. travel, skiing. Res: 142 Shooting Star Isle Foster City 94404 Ofc: McLellan & Copenhagen, 10051 Pasadena Ave Cupertino 95014

HENEBRY, JOHN PAUL, JR., private investigator; b. Feb. 1, 1964, Los Angeles s. John P. and La Verne M. (Phillips) H.; m. Holly Schaefer; edn: MS bus. entrepreneurship (cum laude, Phi Kappa Psi), USC. Career: v.p. mktg. Pacific Inspections, Inc. (insurance inspections and investigations) Los Angeles; pres. Commercial Concepts Inc. (comml. prodn. co.); mem. World Assn. of Detectives; mem. So. Calif. Underwriters Assn.; clubs: L.A. Athletic, Hollywood Magic Castle (life), Blue Goose Calif. Pond; Republican; R.Cath. Res: 26700 Indian Peak Rd Rancho Palos Verdes 90274 Ofc: Pacific Inspections, Inc. 1212 N Vermont Ave Los Angeles 90029

HENNESSY, JOHN FRANCIS, III, consulting engineer; b. Nov. 27, 1955, New York, N.Y.; s. John Francis, Jr., and Barbara (McDonnell) H.; edn: AB, Kenyon Coll., 1977; BS, Rensselaer Poly. Inst., 1978; MS, M.I.T., 1988. Career: project engineer Syska & Hennessy, New York 1979-83, San Francisco 1983-86, v.p., L.A. 1986-89, chmn. and CEO, N.Y. 1989-; civic bds: Time Square Subway Improvement Corp. (chmn. 1989-), N.Y. Building Cong. (chmn. 1992-), USO New York (1989-), Salvation Army N.Y. (1989-); honors: Sloan fellow M.I.T. (1987); mem: Am. Soc. Refrig. Heating Air Cond. Eng. (ASHRAE), ASME, Nat. Soc. of Prof. Engrs.; R.Cath.; rec: golf, tennis, skiing. Res: 400 East 71st St New York, NY 10021 Ofc: Syska & Hennessy 11 West 42nd St New York NY 10036

HENSEL, JEFFREY, geologist; b. Nov. 15, 1962, Detroit; s. Manfred Karl and Liane Bertha (Frueck) H.; m. Kimberly Ann Habel, Sept. 6, 1986; children: Rachael b. 1990; edn: BS geology, Wayne State Univ., 1984; MS environmental studies, CSU Fullerton, 1992; reg. geologist Calif. and Wy., reg. environmental assessor Cal-EPA, 1990. Career: geologist GMC Associates, Inc. Northville, Mich. 1985-86; BCL Associates, Inc. Huntington Beach 1986-89; Radian Corp., Irvine 1989-; awards: indsl. arts, State of Mich. 1980; mem: Nat. Water Well Assn. 1989-, Ducks Unlimited 1981-; publs: tech. abstracts (1982, 83, 84, 92); Republican; R.Cath.; rec: softball. Ofc: Radian Corp. 7 Corporate Park Ste 240 Irvine 92714

HEPLER, MARTIN EUGENE, management analyst/consultant; b. Oct. 4, 1949, Lancaster, Pa.; s. James Painter and Janet Marie (Hess) H.; m. Rose Ann Baldo, Apr. 14, 1990; edn: AA, Miramar Coll. 1977; BS, San Diego St. Univ., 1980, MPA, 1983; grad. indsl. engring. tech. Career: prodn. mgr. Cerebronic Inc., San Diego 1973-74; aircraft engine tech. Naval Air Rework Facility, San Diego 1974-80, indsl. engring. tech. 1980-83, pgm. coord. 1983-85, internal cons. 1985-86, Total Quality Mgr. 1986-90, TQM dir. General Dynamic Space Systems Div., 1990-91; total quality mgr. NAS Miramar; mgmt. cons./pres. Brenman Assocs., San Diego 1984-, instr. UCSD 1991-; bd. dirs. Clairemont Friendship, S.D. 1978-80; honors: Phi Alpha Alpha 1983, Meritorious Civilian Service Award 1993; mem: Deming Users Group (pres. 1984-), Western Criminology Soc. (life), Internat. Assn. of Quality Circles (S.D. chpt. dir.), V.F.W. (life), Nat. Riflemans Assn.; civic: Zoo Soc. S.D. 1979-, Heart Assn. (instr. 1976-); publ: Internat. Assn. of Quality Circle Transactions 1984; mil: USNR-R AFCM (AW) 1968-; Democrat; R.Cath.; rec: scuba, waterski, run. Ofc: Brenman Assocs. Consultants International 14560 Vintage Dr San Diego 92129

HERMAN, MICHAEL ALAN, musician, music educator, entertainment executive; b. Jan. 11, 1945, Davenport, Iowa; s. William Watt and Leona Lillian (Markovitch) H.; m. Willitte Hisami Ishii, Nov. 23, 1980; edn: Univ. Iowa, 1963-67. Career: bdcstr. host WSUI Radio/TV, Univ. of Iowa, Iowa City, 1964-65; freelance musician, folk and blues, nat. 1965-; guitar tchr., Oakland, Calif. 1973-; owner, entertainment coord., producer Redwood Music, Oakland 1973-92, Topaz Productions, 1992-; entertainment chmn. Mill Valley Fall Arts Fest., Mill Valley 1980-; entertainment coord. San Francisco Folk Music Club, S.F. 1980-85; educator "Blues in the Schools" program 1986-; entertainment cons. Mississippi Valley Blues Soc., Davenport, Ia. 1989-; awards: scholarship Am. Conservatory Theatre, S.F. 1970, cert. merit Nat. Traditional Country Music Found., Council Bluffs, Ia. 1986-88, hon. mention Am. Song Fest., L.A. 1986; mem: Mississippi Valley Blues Soc. 1988-, Quad Cities Friends of the Heritage Arts 1989-, Freedom Song Network (musician, orgnzr., arranger 1986-); civic vol. Helping Hands Proj., S.F. 1990-; publs: musician, songwriter, arranger, prod. (audio cassette albums): Everyday Living (1989), Cow-Cow Boogie (1992), Blues Alive! (1992); songwriter (songs): Rock Island (1975), Truckstop Blues (1986), Phantom of the Jukebox (1987), Rocket to Chicago (1989), Man Or Mouse (1989), New Crossroads (1989), Abuser's Test (1990), Blues for Satchell Paige (1990), Black Drawers (1990), Hero's Blues (1991), Give Me A Granma Every Time (1991); composer (video soundtrack): How Not To Get Elected (1990), Christmas In April (1991); arranger musical score, performer (play) Smokin' (1990); Democrat; rec: fishing, rock hounding, collect guitars, walking, reading. Res: 3416 Coolidge Ave Oakland 94602-3202 Ofc: Topaz Productions PO Box 2725 Oakland 94602

HERNANDEZ, JO FARB, museum director; b. Nov. 20, 1952, Chgo.; d. Leonard and Leanora (Kohn) Farb; m. Sam Hernandez, Sept. 5, 1976; 1 dau., Larissa Anne b. 1988; edn: BA polit. sci./French, Univ. Wis., 1974; MA in folklore, UCLA, 1975; cert. museum mgmt. UC Berkeley, 1981. Career: registr. Mus. of Cultural History, L.A. 1974-75; Rockefeller fellow Dallas Mus. of Fine Art, Dallas, Tx. 1976-77; asst. dir. Triton Mus. of Art, Santa Clara, Calif. 1977, dir. 1978-85; dir. Monterey Peninsula Mus. of Art, 1985-; lectr. various museums and univs. internat., 1975-; grants panelist U.S.I.A., W.D.C. 1992, Calif. Arts Council, Sacto. 1983-86, 88-90, 92; museum assessment surveyor Am. Assn. of Museums, W.D.C. 1990-; exec. com. Western Museums Conf. (1989-91, pgm. chair L.A., 1990); awards: Golden eagle C.I.N.E., W.D.C. 1992, Ralph C. Altman Award Mus. of Cultural History UCLA 1975, special exhibitions NEA, W.D.C. 1984-, gen. op. support, conservation awards Inst. of Mus. Svs., W.D.C. 1985, 86, 91, 92; mem.: Calif. Assn. of Museums (v.p. 1985-91, pres. 1991-), Artable 1986-, Am. Assn. of Museums 1977-; author: The Day of The Dead: Tradition & Change in Contemporary Mexico (1979), Mexican Indian Dance Masks (1982), Three from the Northern Island: Contemporary Sculpture from Kokkaido (1984), Crime & Punishment: Reflections of Violence in Contemporary Art (1984); coauthor: New Furnishings (1985), From Old Times to New Times (1989); intro., editor 16 books including Colors & Impressions: E. Charlton Fortune (1989), The Expressive Sculpture of Alvin Light (1990), The Quiet Eye: Pottery of Shoji Hamada & Bernard Leach (1990), Alan Shepp: The Language of Stone (1991). Ofc: Monterey Peninsula Museum of Art, 559 Pacific St Monterey 93940

HERRICK, ALBERT WILLIAM, investor, ret.; b. Mar. 4, 1906, Liecester, Eng., nat. US cit. 1930; s. Thomas and Harriet Ada (Smith) H.; m. Marian, Apr. 28, 1960; edn: Pasadena City Coll. 1940-48. Career: chemist's asst. Colonial Dames Cosmetics 1924-26; mgr. North East Svc. 1926-30; owner, mgr. H&H Automotive Los Angeles 1930-69, H&H Hardware 1940-69; rancher Tulare County 1969-80; real estate investor 1975-90; honors: Merit Award (Texaco 1965); mem: Rotary, Masons (master mason 50 yrs., Golden Veteran Pin 1986), Kiwanis, Exeter Meml. Hosp. Assn.; trustee First Presbyterian Ch. of Exeter 1972-75; inventor several mechanical devices; Republican; Baptist; rec: travel, woodworking. Res: 2193 W Visalia Rd Exeter 93221

HERRON, SANDRA WHITACRE, psychotherapist, speech pathologist; b. July 1, 1935, Calumet, Mich.; d. Ahti John and Inga Aurora Minerva (Savela) Jaaskelainen; m. James Herron, Oct. 30, 1982; children: Lisa b. 1956, Lance b. 1958, Leslee b. 1961; edn: BA, Whittier Coll. 1956; MA, CSU Fullerton 1969; MA, Sierra Univ. Santa Monica 1984; PhD, Sierra Univ., 1989. Career: psychotherapist New Hope Counseling Svcs., Tustin 1984-, and Crystal Cathedral Counseling Ctr., Garden Grove; fmr speech therapist Magnolia Sch. Dist., Anaheim 1970-91; speaker at seminars 1982-; honors: La Mirada Bus. & Profl. Womens Assn. Outstanding Women of Year (1971); mem: CTA, NEA, CSHA, CAMFT, CAPS; article pub. in profl. jour. (1986); rec: photog. Ofc: New Hope Counseling Center, 17821 E. 17th St. Ste. 190, Tustin 92680 and Crystal Cathedral Counseling Center, 12141 Lewis, Garden Grove 92640 Ph: 714/971-4000

HERSHBERGER, JOHN DOUGLAS, lawyer; b. Jan. 12, 1958, Inglewood, Calif.; s. John Howard and Mary Catherine (Berkstresser) H.; m. Kristine M. Lind, Dec. 30, 1983; dau. Laura Marie b. 1986; edn: BA in hist. (summa cum laude), UCLA, 1979; JD (cum laude), Georgetown Univ. Sch. of Law, 1983; admitted bar: Calif. 1984, U.S. Supreme Ct. Career: clerkship to Hon. Wm. P. Gray, U.S. District Ct., cent. dist. Calif., 1983-84; atty. law firm McKittrick, Jackson, et al, Newport Beach 1984-86; Baker & McKenzie, San Diego 1986-90; Hershberger & Pilsecker, San Diego 1990-; honors: Phi Beta Kappa; mem: Am. Bar Assn. (litigation sect.), Calif. St. Bar, L.A. Co. Bar Assn., Orange Co. Bar Assn., San Diego Co. Bar Assn.; Republican; Cath.; rec: computer technologies. Res: 14479 Rutledge Sq San Diego 92128 Ofc: Hershberger & Pilsecker 550 West "C" St Ste 1850 San Diego 92101

HERST, DOUGLAS JULIAN, lighting company executive; b. June 21, 1943, San Francisco; s. Samuel Bernard and Claire (Beer) H.; m. Carolen Landis, March 20, 1966; children: Chad b. 1973; edn: BS, UC Berkeley 1965. Career: sales Peerless Electric, Berkeley 1965-69, sales mgr. 1969-72, v.p. 1972-74; pres. Peerless Lighting 1974-, dir. 1970-; awards: Govs. award Calif. New Product Competition, 1985; mem: Indsl. Employers & Distributors Assn. (dir. 1985-), Young Pres. Orgn., Illumination Engring. Soc. (pres. Golden Gate chp. 1977-78); club: Concordia Argonaut; article pub. in tech. jour., patents held in lighting, 1981-; rec: running, bicycling, swimming. Ofc: Peerless Lighting POB 2556 Berkeley 94702

HERTWECK, E. ROMAYNE, educator; b. July 24, 1928, Springfield, Mo.; s. Garnett P. and Gladys (Chowning) H.; m. Alma Louise Street, Dec. 16, 1955, 1 son: William Scott, b. 1970; edn: BA, Augustana Coll. 1962; MA, Pepperdine Coll. 1963; EdD, Ariz. State Univ. 1966; PhD, US Internat. Univ. 1978. Career: night ed. Rock Island Argus Newspaper, Ill. 1961-62; grad. tchg. asst. Pepperdine Coll., Los Angeles 1963; counselor, VA, Ariz. State Univ., Tempe, Ariz. 1964; assoc. dir. conciliation ct. Miracopa Co. Superior Ct., Phoenix, Ariz.

1965; instr. Phoenix Coll. 1966; prof. psychol. Mira Costa Coll., Oceanside, Calif. 1967-, dept. chmn. Psychol. Counseling 1973-75, Behavioral Sci. 1976-82, 87-88, 90-91, mem. Academic Senate Council 1968-70, 1985-87, 89-91; prof. psych. World Campus Afloat, S.S. Ryndam, spring 1970; p.t. instr. edn. dept. Univ. of San Diego 1968-69; instr. Chapman Coll. Residence Ctr., Camp Pendleton 1969-78; p.t. lectr. dept. of bus. adminstrn. San Diego State Univ. 1980-84; Sch. of Human Behavior US Internat. Univ. 1984-89; pres. El Camino Preschools, Inc., Oceanside 1985-; bd. dirs. Christian Counseling Ctr., Oceanside (1970-82); civic bds: City of Oceanside Child Care Task Force, 1991-, Oceanside Community Relations Commn., 1991-; Oceanside California Healthy Cities Project 1993-; mem: Am. Psychol. Assn., We. Psychol. Assn., North San Diego Co. Psychol. Assn., Am. Personnel & Guidance Assn., Phi Delta Kappa, Kappa Delta Pi, Psi Chi, Kiwanis, Carlsbad Club, Republican; Prot.; rec: travel, golf, photog. Res: 2024 Oceanview Rd Oceanside Ofc: Mira Costa College, Oceanside.

HERWIG, KARL R., physician, medical educator; b. Nov. 12, 1935, Philadelphia, Pa.; s. Louis and Elizabeth Francis (Myers) H.; m. Barbara Kay Bosscher, Oct. 26, 1963; children: Susan Elizabeth b. 1964, K. Robert b. 1966; edn: BS, Ursinus Coll. 1957; MD, Jefferson Med. Coll. 1961; cert. Am. Bd. Urology 1971. Career: intern, resident Univ. Mich., Ann Arbor 1961-67; staff urologist N.N.M.C., Bethesda, Md. 1967-69; faculty Univ. Mich., Ann Arbor 1969-73; head div. urology Scripps Clinic, La Jolla 1977-; clin. assoc. prof. UCSD 1977-; assoc. prof. Univ. Mich. 1969-77; honors: Alpha Omega Alpha; mem: A.C.S., Am. Urological Assn., Central Surgical, Am. Assn. Endocrine Surgery, AMA, Rotary Del Mar; 42 articles pub. in med. jours. (1966-), 5 book chpts. pub. (1966-); mil: cmdr. USNR 1967-69; Republican; Presbyterian; rec: golf, gardening. Res: Box 2076 Rancho Santa Fe 92067 Ofc: Scripps Clinic 10666 N Torrey Pines La Jolla 92037

HESTER, DOUGLAS A., financial executive; b. Oct. 31, 1951; m. Clarice A. Strebig RN; children: Jonathan b. 1981, Jameson b. 1983, Jacqueline b. 1987; edn: AB, UCLA, 1974; MBA, USC, 1977, MSBA, 1981; CPA, Calif., 1981. Career: summer intern Ernst & Ernst, L.A. 1976; staff acct. Touche Ross & Co., 1977-79; loan ofcr. First Interstate Mortgage Co., San Diego 1983-84, asst. v.p. 1985-87, v.p. 1987-89; v.p./office mgr. Northland Fin. Co., San Diego 1989-92; pres. Scripps Realty Advisors 1992-; grad. tchg. asst. in acctg. USC, 1974-76, instr. 1976-77, lectr. 1977-83, asst. dean Sch. of Acctg., USC, 1979-83, substitute lectr. USC's CMA Review Pgm., faculty adv. for Beta Alpha Psi and Acctg. Soc., guest lectr. numerous acctg. and fin. courses; cons. Financial Appraisals Inc., L.A. 1981, Weyerhaeuser Mortgage 1993, Wells Fargo 1993; awards: coll. scholarship Wedbush Noble Cook Inc., Beta Alpha Psi (1975, pres. Iota chpt. 1976), Fellowship Org. for Res. & Knowledge Award 1977, Beta Gamma Sigma 1977, top grad. in class USC Grad. Sch. Bus. Adminstrn. (1977, 81), USC Acctg. Dept. Chairman's Award 1978, founder Acctg. Soc. USC 1979, Alpha Kappa Psi hon. faculty mem. 1982; mem: Am. Inst. CPAs, Calif. Soc. CPAs, Am. Finance Assn., Building Ind. Assn., Mortgage Bankers Assn. Calif., San Diego Mortgage Bankers Assns., USC Gen. Alumni Assn., USC MBA Alumni, The Accounting Circle USC (bd., pres. 1977, sec. 79-82), Commerce Assocs. USC, UCLA Gen. Alumni Assn., Loyola Marymount Alumni Assn., Alpha Delta Gamma; publs: contbr. Meigs and Mosich Financial Acctg. textbook series, jour. articles and papers in field. Res: 10274 Rue Cannes San Diego 92131 Tel:619/578-2303

HETZEL, MELVYN LEE, banking automation executive; b. July 29, 1939, Los Angeles; s. Myron Walton and Edith Kirstine (Coats) H.; m. Maureen Curtin, Aug. 10, 1968; children: Kirsten b. 1975, Ryle b. 1976; edn: BA, Stanford Univ. 1961; MPA, George Washington Univ. 1964. Career: mgr. I.R.S., San Francisco 1970-71; Bank of America 1971-92; CFO, St. Vincent de Paul Society 1992-; curriculum cons. Univ. San Francisco 1984-86; tchr. U.S. Dept. of Agri. Coll., Wash. D.C. 1967-70; awards: U.S. Presdl. citation (1967), Bank of Am. exceptional performance (1984, 85, 88, 89); St. Vincent de Paul Soc. (treas., dir.), CASE Users Group (secty., dir. 1989), Am. Soc. Pub. Adminstrn. (ed. 1966-69), S.F. Press Club, Young Republicans; author: Project Management Process, 1990; Systems Devel. Process, 1982; numerous profl. papers on automation, 1984-89. Res: 65 Shore View Terrace San Francisco 94121

HEUSCHELE, WERNER PAUL, veterinary virology, research director; b. Aug. 28, 1929, Ludwigsburg, Germany, naturalized U.S., 1951; s. Karl August and Margarete Anna (Wagner) H.; m. 4th, Carolyn Rene Bredeson, Jan. 1, 1983; children: Eric b. 1954, Mark b. 1960, Jennifer b. 1960; edn: undergrad. San Diego State, 1947-50, BA zoology (hons.) UC Davis, 1952, DVM, 1956; tng. res. vet. pathology Armed Forces Inst. of Path., W.D.C., 1965-66; PhD in vet. sci., med. microbiology, virology, Univ. Wis., 1969. Career: veterinarian, mgr. Zoo Hosp. and Labs., San Diego Zoo, 1956-61; res. veterinarian Plum Island Animal Dis. Lab., ARS, USDA, N.Y., 1961-70; assoc. prof. microbiology Coll. Vet. Med. Kansas State Univ., Manhattan 1970-71; hd. virology Jensen-Salsbery Labs., Div. Richardson-Merrill Inc., Kansas City, Ks. 1971-76; assoc. prof. dept. vet. preventive medicine Ohio State Univ., Columbus 1976-78, prof. 1978-81, chmn. dept. grad. com. 1979-81; hd. microbiology /virology, res. dept. San Diego Zoo, Calif. 1981-86, dir. res. Ctr. for Reprodn. Endangered Species, 1986-

; awards: Phi Zeta (1956, chapt. pres. 81-82), Hutchinson Scholar UC Davis 1956, cons. animal hlth. Smithsonian Inst. 1967-68, San Diego Jaycee's Outstanding Young Men 1960, res. assoc. UC Davis Sch. Vet. Med. 1960, rev. panel AVMA Colloquium Purdue Univ. 1971, Sigma Xi 1979, F.K. Ramsey Lectr. Iowa State Univ. 1991, UC Davis Sch. Vet. Med. Alumni Achiev. Award 1991; trustee Columbus (OH) Zoo Assn. (trustee of yr. 1978); tech. and sci. cons. various corps., nat. and fgn. govts.; mem: N.A.S., NRC, Com. Bovine TB Eradication, Panel on Animal Hlth. & Vet. Med., Bd. of Agric., Am. Assn. of Zoo Veterinarians (founding, charter mem., chmn. 1958-59, sec. treas. 1960-61, com. ch. 1982-85), San Diego Biomed. Res. Inst. (v.p. 1959-60, bd. 59-61), Wildlife Disease Assn. (coun. 1981-84, v.p. 85-87), Am. Vet. Med. Assn., Conf. of Res. Workers in Animal Diseases, US Animal Hlth. Assn. (coms.), Am. Assn. Vet. Lab. Diagnosticians, Am. Coll. Vet. Microbiologists (bd. govs. 1984-87), Am. Assn. Wildlife Vets., Am. Assn. of Zool. Parks and Aquariums (animal hlth. com.), Intl. Union for Conserv. of Nature/Vet. Specialist Gp. (species survival commn.), Nature Conservancy, World Wildlife Fund, Nat. Wildlife Fedn., Kiwanis Intl./Balboa Pk. (pres. 1989-90); author 17+ med. books and book chapts., 126+ sci. jour. articles and abstracts; Democrat; rec: music, painting. Ofc: San Diego Zoo, CRES, PO Box 551 San Diego 92112-0551

HEYCK, THEODORE DALY, lawyer; b. Apr. 17, 1941, Houston, Tx.; s. Theodore Richard and Gertrude Paine (Daly) H.; edn: AB, Brown Univ. 1963; LLB, Georgetown Univ. Law Center 1963-65, 71-72; N.Y. Law Sch. 1979; MFA, Drama Centre, London 1967; admitted bar: New York, Calif., U.S. Supreme Ct., U.S. Ct. Appeal (9th cir., 2d cir.), Fed. Dist. Cts. N.Y. (No. dist., So. dist., East dist., West dist.) and Calif. (So. dist., Cent. dist.). Career: self-empl. entertainment industry, 1967-79; paralegal Dist. Atty. Kings Co., Bklyn. 1975-79, asst. dist. atty. 1979-85; dep. city atty. City of Los Angeles, 1985-; mem: Screen Actors Guild, Actors Equity Assn., Nat. Acad. TV Arts & Scis., ABA, Brooklyn Bar Assn., Los Angeles Co. Bar Assn., Am. Trial Lawyers Assn., N.Y. Trial Lawyers Assn., Federal Bar Council; listed Who's Who in Am. Law, Who's Who in Am., Who's Who in West, Who's Who in World; Res: 2106 Live Oak Dr East, Los Angeles 90068 Ofc: City Attorney 200 N Main St 17th Flr Los Angeles 90012

HEYMAN, IRA MICHAEL, university chancellor; b. May 30, 1930, NYC; s. Harold Albert and Judith (Sobel) H.; m. Therese Thau, Dec. 17, 1950; children: Stephen Thomas b. 1961, James Nathaniel b. 1963; edn: AB govt. Dartmouth Coll. 1951; JD, Yale Law Sch. 1956; admitted bar: NY 1956, Calif. 1961. Career: legislative asst. Sen. Irving M. Ives, WDC 1950-51; atty., assoc. Carter, Ledyard and Milburn, NYC 1956-57; law clerk Chief Judge Charles E. Clark, Ct. of Appeals (2d Circuit) New Haven, CT 1957-58; chief law clerk Chief Justice Earl Warren, US Supreme Ct.1958-59; acctg. assoc. prof. law, UC Berkeley, 1959-61, prof. of law 1961-, vice chancellor 1974-80, chancellor UC Berkeley, 1980-; vis. prof. Yale Law Sch. 1963-64, Stanford Law Sch. 1971-72; trustee Dartmouth Coll., 1982-; dir. PG&E, S.F. 1985-; govt. planning and zoning cons. Virgin Islands 1975-76, Am. Samoa 1973-74, County of Kauai, HI 1972-73, Tahoe Reg. Plng. Agy. 1970-75, S.F. Bay Conserv. and Devel. Commn. 1968-70; appt. U.S. Commn. on Civil Rights (sec. Calif. advy. com. 1962-67), City of Berkeley Human Rels. & Welfare Commn. (chmn. 1966-68); honors: review ed. Yale Law Jour. 1956, LLD (hon) Univ. Pacific 1981, LHD (hon) Hebrew Union Coll. 1984, Chevalier de la Legion d'Honneur, France 1985, LLD (hon) Univ. Maryland 1986; mem: Nat. Collegiate Athletic Assn. (div. I subcom. chmn. NCAA Presidents Commn. 1986-88), Nat. Assn. State Univs. and Land-Grant Colls. (exec. com. chair 1986, subcom. audit & fin. 1987-, com. on legal affairs 1988-), Am. Council on Edn. (bd. 1984-85); num. jour. articles, papers and legal documents in areas of civil rights, constnl. law, land plng., metro. govt., housing, environmental law and mgmt., affirmative action; mil: 1st lt. USMC 1951-53, capt. USMCR 1953-58; Democrat; rec: tennis, opera. Office of the Chancellor Univ. of Calif. Berkeley 94720

HIBBEN, JOSEPH WEST, investment banker; b. May 31, 1909, Lakewood, Ohio; s. Fred Martin and Lucy Calvert (West) H.; m. Ingrid Bridget Haut, Feb. 17, 1980; children: Barry Joseph, Bonnie Elizabeth; edn: BA, Princeton Univ. 1931; MBA, Harvard Univ. 1933. Career: ptnr. Kidder Peabody & Co., N.Y.C. 1938-72; pres. Exec. Club, Chicago., Ill. 1965-68; mayor Glenview, Ill. 1967-70; pres. San Diego Comm. Found. 1980-83; dir. La Jolla Museum 1972-; pres. San Diego Museum of Art 1986-90, 1992-93; dir.: Thomas Industries, Louisville, Ky. 1956-89, Parker Hannifin Inc., Cleveland. 1972-84, North Carolina Natural Gas, Fayetteville, N.C. 1959-81, Fin. Fedn., L.A. 1959-79; awards: Distinguished La Jollan award Rotary and San Diego Community Foundation 1987, 1991 Leonardo da Vinci Award for extraordinary leadership to the arts in Calif., Calif. Confedn. of the Arts (11/91); mem. Com. of 100 (dir.), San Diego Opera (fin. v.p., trustee); clubs: University (S.D.), Monterey CC, La Jolla CC, La Jolla Beach & Tennis, Union League Club; Republican; Presbyterian; rec: flying, golf. Res: 7247 Encilia Dr La Jolla 92037 Ofc: 1205 Prospect St Ste 500 La Jolla 92037

HICKERSON, GLENN LINDSEY, aircraft leasing company marketing executive; b. Aug. 22, 1937, Burbank; s. Ralph Millard and Sarah (Lindsey) H.; m. Jane Fortune, Feb. 24, 1973; edn: BA, Claremont McKenna Coll., 1959; MBA, NYU

Stern Grad. Sch. Bus. Adminstrn., 1960. Career: exec. asst. Douglas Aircraft Co., Santa Monica 1962-63, sec. treas. Douglas Fin. Corp., 1964-67; exec. asst. to pres. Universal Airlines, Detroit, Mich. 1967-68, v.p./treas. 1969-72; group v.p. Marriott Corp., W.D.C. 1972-76; v.p. sales Lockheed Calif. Co., Burbank 1976-83; v.p. mktg. Douglas Aircraft Co., Long Beach 1983-89; mng. dir. GPA Asia Pacific Inc., Los Angeles 1989-90; exec. v.p. mktg. GATX Air, San Francisco 1990-; award: H.B. Earhart Found. fellow 1961; mem.: bd. govs. Keck Ctr. for Internat. Strategic Studies, 1988-; club: Wing's NY, 1969-; mil: ltjg USCG Res. 1960-62; Republican; Methodist; rec: sailing. Res: 2562 Green St San Francisco 94123 Ofc: GATX Div. 4 Embarcadero Ctr Ste 2200 San Francisco 94111

HICKEY, MICHAEL JOHN, manufacturing and distribution co. president; b. June 19, 1948, San Gabriel; s. Francis Joseph, Jr. and Marian Ann (McCain) H.; m. Katherine Margaret Saltzer, July 22, 1972; children: Erin and Erika (twins) b. 1976; edn: mech. engring., Cal Poly Pomona 1968; mgmt. devel., Cal Tech, 1974; AA, Orange Coast Coll., 1976. Career: owner/opr. M.J.H. Mfg., Arcadia 1962-82; owner/opr. Marine Ecological Systems (marine research and comml. fishing vessel), Costa Mesa 1975-80; prod. M.E.S. Film Prodn. Co., Costa Mesa 1976-82; pres. and c.e.o. Newport Fastener Co. Inc., Anaheim 1982-; ptnr. M&M Mfg. Co., Riverside, 1988-; ptnr. Newport Architectural Products, Newport Beach, 1988-; guest instr. Const. Apprentice Pgm., So. Calif. 1974-80; dir. A.C.S. Edn. Pgm., Orange Co. 1977-79; guest spkr. Roofing Contr. Assn. So. Calif. 1970-, Am. Cetacean Soc., Orange Co. 1975-80; awards: Disneyland (sponsored) community service award Anaheim 1979, leadership Am. Cetacean Soc. O.C. 1979, Orange Co. Fair best film - non-theatrical 1979 and best profl. film 1980; mem: Nat. Roofing Conrtrs. Assn., We. States Roofing Contrs. Assn., Anaheim C.of C., Constrn. Specifiers Inst.; civic: Whalewatch edn. pgm. Newport Beach (founding dir. 1977-79), Am. Cetacean Soc. (O.C. dir. 1976-79), La Habra Comm. Theatre (actor, dir. 1988-91), Gr. L.A. Childrens' Theatre Long Beach/ Orange Co., Irvine Civic Light Opera (staff 1990-), Stagelight Family Prodns. (staff 1991-); publs: scripts, tech. manuals, contbr. articles to trade jours., travel mags. (1978-); 16mm films: Six Days At La Paz (prod./dir.) 1979, Clay Tile - The Jewel of Roofing (writer/dir. 1980); stage plays: Dracula (prod. 1989), Best Christmas Pageant Ever (prod. 1989), Annie (actor 1987), Sound of Music (actor 1988), stage mgr.- Peter Pan (1989), Music Man (1989), Mary Poppins (1990), Oliver (1991); Democrat; R.Cath.; rec: theatre arts, film, boating, big game fishing. Res: 27 Sycamore Creek Irvine 92715-3428 Ofc: Newport Fastener Co., Inc. 1300 E Gene Autry Way Anaheim 92805

HICKMAN, DAVID FRANCIS, food distribution company marketing executive; b. July 26, 1947, Flint, Mich.; s. Clarence Joseph and Rejeania Emeline (Nickerson) H.; m. Laura Elizabeth Agness, Jan. 27, 1971; edn: BS, Purdue Univ., 1970; MA, Indiana No. Univ., 1978. Career: dept. Armour & Co., Balt. 1970-72, dist. sales mgr., Nashua, N.H. 1972-74, region sales mgr. Pittsburgh, Pa. 1974-75; nat. sales mgr. La Choy Food Products, Archibold, Oh. 1975-85; mktg. mgr. Hunt-Wesson, Inc., Fullerton, Calif. 1985-; recipient internat. sales and mktg. award Beatrice Foods Co., Chgo. 1985; Republican; Congregationalist; rec: computers, travel, reading. Res: 2970 Malaga Circle Diamond Bar 91765 Ofc: Hunt-Wesson, Inc. 1645 W Valencia Dr Ste 653 Fullerton 92633-3899

HIGGINS, K. MILTON, clergyman, church foundation executive; b. Dec. 31, 1936, Kosse, Tx.; s. Leland Alonza and Ida Florine (Ray) H.; m. Jarrene S. Pearce, Feb. 1, 1958; children: Kathrine E. Cruise b. 1959, K. Milton, Jr. b. 1960, Janneth G. Russell b. 1964; edn: BA, Baylor Univ., 1959; BDiv, Golden Gate Baptist Sem., 1962, DMin, 1973; ordained to ministry So. Baptist Ch., 1959. Career: music dir. East Waco Bapt. Chapel, Waco, Tx. 1955-57; music, youth dir. Bosqueville Bapt. Ch. 1957-59; First Bapt. Ch., Gilroy, Calif. 1959-60; pastor First Bapt. Ch., Hilmar, Calif. 1960-62; Hillsdale Blvd. Bapt. Ch., Sacramento 1962-69; First Southern Bapt. Ch., San Mateo 1969-77; First Southern Bapt. Ch., Seaside 1977-79; Richland Bapt. Ch., Richland, Wash. 1979-84; director Calif. Plan of Ch. Finance, Fresno 1984-, exec. v.p. Calif. Baptist Found., 1984-, 1st v.p. Calif. Southern Baptist Convention 1973-74, bd. mem. Golden Gate Baptist theol. Seminary, Mill Valley; bd. mem. various com. Southern Baptist Convention and Calif. Southern Baptist Convention; listed Outstanding Young Men Am. 1971, Who's Who in West 1975-, Who's Who in Religion 1980-, Who's Who in Am. 1984-, Who's Who in Finance 1989-; mem. Assn. of Bapt. Found. Execs. 1984-; contbr. articles in ch. jours. 1975-, "Tieing Up Loose Ends of Life" 1992; Republican; rec: golf, gardening, fishing, hunting. Res: 945 W Alamos Fresno 93705 Ofc: Calif. Baptist Foundation 680 E Shaw Ave Fresno 93710

HILDEBRAND, FRANCES L., computer technologies executive, civic leader; b. Sept. 30, 1943, San Francisco; d. Daniel and Matilda (Wellington) Hildebrand; edn: Barnard Coll.; BS, UC Berkeley 1966; adv. profl. seminars Stanford, MIT. Career: staff Standards/Disaster Recovery, San Francisco 1977; dist. mgr. Buena Park Computer Ctr., Buena Park 1978-80; hardware, asset mgmt., site planning, Pacific Bell, San Francisco 1980-85, dist. mgr. Future Technologies Architecture, Pacific Bell 1986-88, staff dir. Systems Technology Dist., 1988-89, dir. hardware, asset mgmt., operational support, 1989-; advy. com. JFK Univ. graduate pgm. in data proc. 1985, instr., data proc., UCB Ext.

1984; honors: Phi Beta Kappa 1966; civic: Ctr. for Elderly, Suicide Prevention and Grief Related Services, Commonwealth Club, World Affairs Coun., Grand Prix Assn. (past patron), Nob Hill Assn., Gramercy Towers (v.p.); rec: writing, swim, current events. Res: 1177 California St #722 San Francisco 94108 Ofc: Pacific Bell, 2600 Camino Ramon Ste 1E104 San Ramon.

HILGER, FREDERICK LEE, JR., lawyer, financial and real estate executive; b. Feb. 17, 1946, Dallas; s. Frederick Lee Sr. and Maryann Taylor (Ayers) H.; m. Terri Lynn Wilson, May 13, 1984 (div. 1990); children: Matthew Charles, Kristen Leigh; edn: BA, Univ. of the Pacific, 1967; JD, UC Berkeley, 1970; admitted bar: Calif. 1971. Career: sr. tax acct. Touche Ross and Co., San Francisco 1971-73; atty. F.L. Hilger Profl. Corp., Eureka 1973-75; mng. ptnr. Moses Lake Farms, Wash. 1975-78; sr. cons. Sites and Co. Inc., Seattle 1978-79; v.p. ops. mgmt. U.S. Cruises Inc., Seattle 1980-83; pres. and c.f.o. First Nat. Bank, Chico, Calif. 1984-86; pres. and c.e.o. FreeHill Corp., San Marcos 1986-; awards: Outstanding banker Am. Bankers Assn., First Nat. Bank (1984, 1985); mem: Am. Bar Assn., Calif. Bar Assn., San Diego County Bar Assn.; clubs: Olympic (S.F.), Shadowridge Golf; Republican; Presbyterian. Ofc: Freehill Corp. PO Box 1808 San Marcos 92079-1808

HILL, ALAN T., consulting engineer, real estate developer; b. June 5, 1938, Sacto.; m. Bev, June 15, 1963; 4 children; edn: AA, Shasta Jr. Coll.; BSCE, Univ. of Nev., Reno; reg. civil engr. Calif., Ore., Alaska, Nev.; reg. land surveyor Calif., Alaska; lic. real estate broker, and contr. Calif. Career: v.p./div. mgr. CH2M Hill, Redding 1961-82, and in Anchorage, AK 1975-78; cons. engr. Hill Enterprises, Redding 1982-; organizer, dir. North Valley Bank; mem: Am. Soc. of Civil Engrs., Private Indus. Council Redding (pres. 1985-87), Gr. Redding C.of C. (dir. 1982-86), Rotary Internat. (past pres.), Elks; Republican; Prot.; rec: flying, hunting, fishing, skiing. Ofc: Hill Enterprises PO Box 492260 Redding 96049

HILL, LORIE ELIZABETH, psychotherapist; b. Oct. 21, 1946, Buffalo, NY; d. Graham and Elizabeth Helen (Salm) H.; edn: Univ. of Manchester, Eng. 1966-67; BA, Grinnell Coll. 1968; MA, Univ. Wis. 1970; MA, CSU Sonoma 1974; PhD, Wright Inst. 1980. Career: English instr. Univ. of Mo. 1970-71; adminstr./supr. Antioch- West & Ctr. for Independent Living, San Francisco & Berkeley 1975-77; dir. of tng. Ctr. for Edn. & Mental Health, S.F. 1977-80; exec. dir. 1980-81; instr. MA pgm. in psychol. John F. Kennedy Univ., Orinda 1985; psychotherapist, pvt. practice, Berkeley and Oakland, 1981-; speaker on cross-cultural psychology; civic: Psychotherapists for Soc. Responsibility (founding mem.), Nat. Abortion Rights Action League, Nat. Orgn. Women, Big Brothers & Big Sisters of the East Bay (psychologist 1986-88), City of Oakland Youth Skills Devel. Pgm. (vol. instr.); Rainbow Coalition for Jesse Jackson's Pres. Campaign, Ron Dellums Reelection Com., Mental Health Profls. Against Racism (founding mem.); campaign to elect Keith Carson Alameda Cty. Supr., appointed Social Action Chair Alameda Cty. Psychol. Assn., co-chair Cultural Diversity for Calif. Psychol. Assn.; rec: sports, travel. Res: 3028 Brookdale Ave Oakland 94602 Ofc: 2955 Shattuck Ave Berkeley 94705

HILL, LOWELL STANLEY, designer, business owner; b. Feb. 5, 1934, Fort Sheridan, Ill.; s. Jack and Velma Opal (Borton) H.; m. Barbara Matilde Suarez, Nov. 9, 1957; children: Lowell b. 1958, Velma b. 1959, Barbara b. 1961, Sandra b. 1962, Stanley b. 1964; edn: Univ. of Mo. 1953-56; Chaffey Coll. 1959; AA, Mt. San Antonio Coll. 1962, tchrs. creds. 1967. Career: illustrator US Army, Ft. Leonard Wood, Mo. 1953-56; mgr. Stout Sign Co., Long Beach 1957-58; lead man Circuit Bd. Div. Gen. Dynamics, Pomona 1959-63; tech. advr./ store mgr. E.W. Dorn Co., Gardena 1963-70; tchr. Los Angeles Trade Tech. Coll., L.A. 1966-68; owner/ designer/ cons. Lowell S. Hill Enterprises, Ontario 1970-; guest spkr.: Cal Poly Univ., Pomona; Mt. San Antonio Coll., Walnut; Foundation Sch., Montebello; moderator and featured spkr. Screen Printing Internat. Convention, L.A. 1984; guest technical trainee Zurich Bolting Mfg. Co., Switz. 1975; honors: hon. chief Nez Perce Nation (1970); mem: Screen Printing Internat., Nat. Small Bus. Assn., Calif. Assn. Indep. Bus., U.S. C.of C., Rancho Cucamonga C.of C.; civic: L.A. Trade Tech. Coll. trade advy com., Am. Indian Week (v.p 1968-), Boy Scouts of Am. (ldr. 1972-75); research: European methods as applied to design, mfg. of screen printing rel. prods.; original designs of metal frames; first to import the Swiss Harlacher screen stretcher to U.S., 1980; mil: sgt. E-5 AUS 1953-56, Army Champion Pistol Team 1955; Republican; R.Cath.; rec: target shooting, hunting, archery. Res: 775 W 24th St Upland 91786 Ofc: Lowell S. Hill Enterprises, 8555 Red Oak St Rancho Cucamonga 91729

HILLS, ALAN LEE, commercial banker; b. May 3, 1954, Corning, N.Y.; s. Donald Marvin and Velma Jane (Weir) H.; m. Stephanie Lynn Miller, Dec. 15, 1984; 1 son, Zachary b. 1988; edn: BA acctg., Univ. South Fla., 1974; MBA fin., Univ. Pa. Wharton Sch., 1977; cert. in mgmt. acctg. with distinction, Nat. Assn. Accts., 1975; CPA, Fla. 1976. Career: asst. treas. The Bank of New York, N.Y.C., 1977-79; asst. v.p. E.F. Hutton & Co., N.Y.C., 1979-81; v.p. Prudential-Bache Securities Inc., N.Y.C. 1981-84; mng. dir. First Interstate Bank, San Francisco 1984-90; mng. dir. Cogeneration Finance Inc., Mill Valley 1990-91; v.p. Sumitomo Bank Ltd., Los Angeles 1992-; honors: Beta Gamma Sigma 1973, Shell Oil Co. Found. scholar 1976; mem. No. Calif. Cogeneration Assn.,

S.F. (treas., bd. dirs. 1986-92), Commonwealth Club 1986-91, Los Angeles Power Producers Assn. (dir. 1992-); contbg. author: Creative Financing of Cogeneration and Energy Facilities (1981); rec: tennis, sailing, cooking. Ofc: The Sumitomo Bank, Limited 611 West 6th St Ste 3700 Los Angeles 90017

HILTON, WILLIAM BARRON, hotel executive; b. Oct. 23, 1927, Dallas, Tx.; s. Conrad Nicholson and Mary Barron H.; m. Marilyn June Hawley, Chgo., June 20, 1947; children: William Barron, Jr., b. 1948, Hawley Anne, b. 1949, Stephen Michael, b. 1950, David Alan, b. 1952, Sharon Constance, b. 1953, Richard Howard, b. 1955, Daniel Kevin, b. 1962, Ronald Jeffrey, b. 1963. Career: founder, gen. ptnr. Vita-Pakt Citrus Products Co., 1946; v.p./ dir. Hilton Hotels Corp., 1954-66, pres./CEO, chmn./ pres./ c.e.o. 1979-; pres. San Diego Chargers Ltd., 1961-66; pres. Am. Football League, 1965; dir. Mfrs. Hanover Trust Co. 1970-, dir. Conrad N. Hilton Found.; trustee City of Hope; honors: Hon. Dr. of Humane Letters, Univ. of Houston 1986, Hotel Man of Year, Penn State Univ. 1969; mem: LA World Affairs Council, Chevalier Confrerie de la Chaine des Rotisseurs, Magistral Knights Sovereign Mil. Order of Malta, Pres. Council of EAA Fedn.; clubs: Bel Air CC, Los Angeles CC, Morningside CC, Thunderbird CC, Bel-Air Bay; mil: photog. mate USN, 1946; rec: soaring, flying, photog., hunting & fishing. Res: 1060 Brooklawn Dr Holmby Hills 90024 Ofc: Hilton Hotels Corp. 9336 Civic Center Dr Beverly Hills 90210

HINCKLEY, GREGORY KEITH, financial executive; b. Oct. 3, 1946, San Francisco; s. Homer Clair and Josephine F. (Gerrick) H.; m. Mary Chomenko, Feb. 14, 1987; children: Blake b. 1987, Allison b. 1989; edn: BA physics, Claremont McKenna Coll., 1968; MS physics, UC San Diego, 1970; MBA, Harvard Univ., 1972; CPA, Ill., 1977. Career: 2d v.p. Continental Bank, Chgo. 1972-78; dir. finance Itel Corp., San Francisco 1978-79; group controller Raychem Corp., Menlo Park 1979-83; v.p. fin. Bio-Rad Laboratories, Hercules 1983-88; sr.v.p. fin. Crowley Maritime Corp., Oakland 1988-91; v.p. fin. VLSI Technology Inc., San Jose 1992-; dir: Escagenetics Corp., San Bruno 1983-90, dir. Advanced Molecular Systems, Vallejo 1989-; awards: Woods Hole Oceanographic Inst. fellow 1967, Fulbright scholar Nottingham Univ., England 1968-69; mem: Am. Inst. CPAs 1977-, Financial Execs. Inst., Am. Diabetes Assn. No. Calif. (dir. 1985-87). Res: 26201 Catherine Ct Los Altos Hills 94022

HIRSCHMAN, HENRY, eye surgeon; b. June 1, 1931, NY, NY; s. Jerome and Rebecca (Stein) H.; m. Jane Rodgers (artist); children: Jason b. 1960, David b. 1961, Harry b. 1963, Micah b. 1964; edn: undergrad. Seton Hall Univ. 1949-50, Mich. State Univ. 1954-55; MD, Univ. of Mich. 1959. Career: medical dir. Long Beach Eye Inst. (prior: Hirschman Eye Surg. Ctr.), Long Beach; pioneered the use of introcular lenses in cataract surgery, gave first courses in USA on Lens Implant; cons. Intermedics; editor Ocular Surgery News; coauthor (first U.S. textbook on lens implants) Pseudophokos; mem./co-founder Am. Intra Ocular Implant Soc. (chmn. sci. advy. bd.); awards: Binkhorst Medal lecturer 1979; mem. Sierra Club (25-yr. life); rec: photog., skiing, fishing, tennis. Res: 5800 Bayshore Walk Long Beach 90803 Ofc: Long Beach Eye Institute 4100 Long Beach Blvd Long Beach 90807

HITCHCOCK, VERNON THOMAS, lawyer; b. Feb. 21, 1919, Selma, Ind.; s. Lucian Elmer and Loda Alice (King) H.; m. Betty K. Orr, May 24, 1949; children: Brenda, b. 1950; Linda, b. 1953; Nancy, b. 1955; Debra, b. 1957; Randolph, b. 1960; edn: BS, agric., Purdue Univ. 1940; JD, Stanford Univ. 1953; admitted Calif. Bar, U.S. Supreme Ct. Career: naval aviator, USNR, US & Pacific 1941-45; airline pilot Southwest Airways, S.F. 1946; airline pilot TWA, Kansas City, Mo. & San Francisco, Calif. 1947-51; atty. at law., pvt. practice, Healdsburg 1954-55; dep. Atty. Gen., State of Calif., Sacto. 1956; dep. County Counsel, Sonoma County, Santa Rosa 1957-65; exec. dir. Libyan Aviation Co., Tripoli, Libya 1966-67; Legal Counsel Sonoma Co. Schs., Santa Rosa 1967-82; pvt. practice, law 1982-83; ptnr., farm mgr. GHJ Farms 1975-86; originator of Freedom Under Law pgm. for tchg. jr. and sr. high sch. students about Am. law; mem: Reserve Ofcrs. Assn., US; Commonwealth Club, Calif.; Naval Order of US; US Naval Inst.; Quiet Birdmen; Ind. Order of Odd Fellows; Am. Security Council; Alpha Zeta, Purdue chpt.; Indiana 4-H Club; author novel: The Airline to Infinity; mil: comdr. USNR 1941-69; Republican; Episcopalian; rec: trumpet (mem. Las Gallinas Valley Sanitary Dist. Non-Marching Band, Terra Linda), ham radio operator, KB6UOJ. Address: 3411 Sidney Square Santa Rosa 95405

HOANG, TUE NGOC, pharmacist; b. Aug. 21, 1932, Thua Thien, Vietnam; s. Hoang, Duong N. and Huynh, Ly T.; m. Vinh Nguyen, Nov. 21, 1969; children: Tommy Thong b. 1972, John Bao b. 1973, Paul Viet b. 1974, Cecilia Minh Tri b. 1977, Trien H. b. 1979, Thang H. b. 1981, Hong Phuc H. b. 1983, Joseph Loc b. 1988; edn: BS pharm. Faculty of Pharmacy, Saigon 1959; AA qual. assur. Coastline & Orange Coast Colls., 1986; EE cert., FPGEC, 1987; Reg. Pharmacist, Calif., Nev. 1988. Career: resident pharmacist Ministry of Health Saigon 1960-62; lab. mgr. and preceptor of intern pharmacists, Saigon 1961-63; capt., pharmacist Medical Corps (RVNAF) Vietnam 1963-67, comdr. med. depot Pleiku 1965; dir. Ministry Youth & Sports, Saigon 1966-67; dir. Community Pharmacy, Cholon, Viet. 1968-75; self-empl. farmer, van driver, 1976-80; quality control, tech. cons. Minh Khai and Binh Minh Fac., Cholon

1979-81; escaped from Vietnam 9/82, came to USA 9/83; chmn./dir. Nguoi Viet Inc., Westminster, (1987-88,1992-94); dir./owner Orange Pharmacy, 1989-; honors: Ancien Interne des Hopitaux, Ministry of Health Saigon 1963, youth medal Ministry of Youth 1972, outstanding service award Fairview State Hosp., Costa Mesa 1988; mem: Phuc Hung Alumni Assn. (sec. gen. 1985-), Vietnamese Am. Pharmacists Assn., Calif. Pharm. Assn., Am. Pharm. Assn.; civic: mem. DHRRA (dev. hum. resources) Bangkok 1974-, past mem. (Saigon): Sch. for Soc. Services, Du Ca Viet Nam, Saigon Students Assn., 1965 Summer Youth Pgm.; publs: articles in Nguoi Viet 1985-; R.Cath.; rec: computers, phys. fitness. Res: 16243 San Jacinto Fountain Valley 92708

HOARE, TYLER JAMES, sculptor, printmaker; b. June 5, 1940, Joplin, Mo.; s. Melvin James and Dorotha (Beadle) H.; m. Kathy Joyce Quinn, Mar. 9, 1963; dau., Janet Elane Orr b. 1964; edn: stu., sculpture, Univ. Colo. 1959, Sculpture Ctr., N.Y.C. 1960-61, Calif. Coll. Arts and Crafts 1966; BFA, Univ. Kansas, 1963. Career: sculptor and printmaker, Berkeley, 1965-; instr. UC Berkeley, Ext. 1973, 74; guest lectr. art depts. various univs. and colls., 1972-; exhibits internat. incl. San Francisco Mus. of Art, Cinti. Art Mus., Oakland Mus., Library of Congress, L.A. Co. Mus. Art, Pratt Graphics Center, N.Y., Pasadena Art Mus.; in permanent public collections: USIA, SUNY, Oakland Mus.; one man shows, 1964-, incl. UC Berkeley, Derby Gal., Berkeley, Lucien Labaud Gal., S.F. 1966, Free Univ. of Berkeley Gal., Frederic Hobb's S.F. Art Ctr. 1967, Green Gal., S.F. 1968, St. Mary's Coll. Art Gal., Moraga 1969, John Bolles Gal., S.F. (1969, 71, 74), Univ. Lancaster (Eng.), Camberwell Sch. Art, London, England 1971, SUNY, Albany, Atherton Gal., Menlo Park, Ca. 1972, Chabot Coll. Art Gal., Hayward, Stanford Univ., Richmond (Ca.) Art Ctr. 1973, CSU Hayward, Olive Hyde Art Ctr., Fremont 1974, Daly City Civic Ctr., San Mateo Arts Coun., County of San Mateo Hall of Justice 1975, Purdue Univ. Gallery 1 (1976), Spiva Art Ctr. Mo. So. State Coll. 1977, Manner of Speaking, S.F., Stuart Gal., Berkeley 1978, Studio 718, S.F. "Xerox Art 1970-1980" (1980), Geotrope Gal., Berkeley 1981, Studio Nine, Benicia, Marin Co. Civic Ctr., San Rafael 1982, Solano Comm. Coll. Art Gal. 1983, Oakland Art Assn. Gal. 1986, 1975 to 1993 Sculpture on the S.F. Bay, Six WWI Airplanes and Six Ships on the Bay 1988, Coastal Art League Mus., Half Moon Bay 1989, subject videos and films, local and nat. radio and TV shows incl. Bill Moyers PBS "Creativity"; awards incl. Hon. Master Painting, Acad. Italia and dipl. of merit Univ. Delle Arti (Italy), Age of Enlightenment, T.M. Berkeley World Plan Ctr., 4th Ann. Bay Area Graphics competition DeAnza Coll., "Focuserie" Nat. Photog. Exh., Eire, Pa., 32nd Ann. San Francisco Art Fest.; mem: Richmond Art Ctr., L.A. Print Soc., Nat. Soc. Lit. and the Arts, Metal Arts Guild (S.F.), Oakland Mus. Assn., S.F. Art Inst., S.F. Mus. Art, Ctr. for the Visual Arts, Pro Arts (Oakland). Res: 30 Menlo Pl Berkeley 94707

HOBDY, FRANCES LEAP (RADER), real estate broker; b. Mar. 1, 1920, Fresno; d. Edward Gerald and Emma (Tittle) L.; m. Robert J. Rader, Jan. 19, 1943 (dec.); m. Morris M. Hobdy, May 27, 1972 (dec.); children: Robert Rader, Jr. b. 1944, Judith Rader b. 1948; edn: Coll. of William & Mary 1968-69; AA, Palomar Coll. 1976; BA, Newport Univ. 1979; desig: GRI (Graduate Realtors Inst.), Calif. Assn. of Realtors; CRS (Cert Residential Splst.), CRB (Cert RE Brokerage), Nat. Assn. of Realtors. Career: legal secty. Hatchett & Ford, Hampton, Va. 1961-67; realtor assoc. Denny Realty, Escondido 1973-75; broker assoc. Mark, Realtors, Escondido 1975-78; owner/broker Hobdy, Realtors, Escondido 1978-; dir. Fowble & Assocs., San Diego 1974-; trustee BORPAC, 1986-90; honors: resolution Calif. State Legislature 1983, appreciation Fifth Supervisorial Dist. 1983, Escondido Bd. of Realtors Realtor of Yr. 1986 and Special Appreciation Award- Mediator (1985, 89, 90), listed Who's Who in Fin. & Ind., Who's Who of Am. Women, Who's Who in Real Estate in Am., Book of Honor, Grand Amb. of Achiev. Intl., Directory of Distinguished Americans; mem: Escondido Bd. of Realtors (past pres., dir., mediator 1985-), Calif. Assn. of Realtors, Nat. Assn. Realtors, Nat. Mktg. Inst.; civic: Escondido C.of C., Zool. Soc. of San Diego, Smithsonian Assocs., San Diego Opera, Golden Wives Club, Meadowlark CC; Republican; Prot.; rec: exercise, computer. Ofc: Hobby Realtors 10142 Lake Meadow Ln Escondido 92026

HOCH, SALLIE O'NEIL, biologist; b. Feb. 15, 1941, Mineola, N.Y.; d. Thomas F. and Mary (Robinson) O'Neil; m. James A. Hoch, May 17, 1969; children: James A., Jr. b. 1970, Patrick E. b. 1973; edn: St. Mary's Coll., Notre Dame, 1958-60; BS (magna cum laude) St. Bonaventure Univ., Olean, N.Y., 1964; MS, and PhD, Univ. Ill., Urbana, 1966, 1969. Career: postdoctoral fellow Scripps Clinic and Research Found., La Jolla, Calif. 1969-71, asst., assoc. 1971-77, asst. member 1978-83; principal scientist The Agouron Inst., La Jolla 1983-; and senior scientist Agouron Pharmaceuticals Inc., 1984-; mem. Arthritis Found. Research Com. 1989-90; mem. NIH Special Review Coms. 1981, 90, 93; ad hoc grant reviewer NIH, NSF, Lupus Found. of Am.; awards: NIH predoctoral fellow, 1966-68, Am. Cancer Soc. postdoctoral fellow, 1969-71, NIH research career devel. award, 1975-80, research grantee NIH, NSF, Lupus Found. of Am., 1971-; mem: Am. Coll. of Rheumatology, Am. Soc. for Cell Biology, Am. Soc. for Microbiology, Am. Soc. for Biochem. and Molecular Biology, Soc. of Sigma Xi; publs: 60+ research publs., 1968-, current ad hoc reviewer 11 sci. jours.; R.Cath. Res: 1054 Havenhurst Dr La Jolla 92037 Ofc: The Agouron Institute 505 Coast Blvd S La Jolla 92037

HODDER, CLIFFORD ERNEST, JR., educator, ret.; b. July 17, 1923, Waterford, NY; s. Clifford Ernest and Anne Neilson (Gillespie) H.; edn: BA, UC Berkeley, 1949, MA, 1950, gen. secondary cred., 1954; Calif. Comm. Colls. instr. cred., Calif. 1954. Career: tchr. Santa Rosa High Sch., 1955-68; instr. Santa Rosa Jr. Coll., 1968-90, dir. community involvement pgm., 1972-90, ret.; mem. Am. Oriental Soc., Calif. Tchrs. Assn., Nat. Edn. Assn.; mil: cpl. Army Air Corps 1942-46; Democrat; Episcopalian. Res: 4724 Hidden Oaks Rd Santa Rosa 95405 Ofc: Santa Rosa Junior College 1501 Mendocino Ave Santa Rosa 95401

HODES, ABRAM, pediatrician; b. Mar. 2, 1922; s. Samuel and Rachel (Gross) H.; m. Mildred Rose Berzosky, June 22, 1947; children: Alan b. 1949, Jay b. 1951; edn: BS, Penn. State Coll., 1942 (Phi Beta Kappa 1942); BM, Northwestern Univ. Med. Sch., 1945, MD, 1946; bd. cert. Am. Bd. Peds. 1951, diplomate Am. Acad. Pediatrics 1958. Career: sch. pub. health physician San Bernardino County Health Dept., 1950; pvt. practice peds., San Bernardino 1950-89, pediatric staff San Bernardino County Hosp. 1950-87; honoree, named Staff Doctor of Yr. San Bernardino Community Hosp. 1989; mem: San Bdo. County Med. Soc. 1950-, Calif. Med. Assn. (ret.), AMA (ret.), L.A. Pediatric Soc., Hinterland Pediatric Soc., B'nai B'rith (USA chmn. 1990-93, San Bdo. pres. 1991-93), Elks, Optimist (life), Jewish War Veterans; mil: 1st lt. US Army; Republican; Jewish; rec: violin, medical book collector. Res: 604 E Avery St San Bernardino 92404

HODGIN, DAVID T., recreational parks management executive; b. June 8, 1932; s. David Reid and Elva Timberlake (Twamley) H.; m. Claire Evelyn Arnold, July 19, 1953; children: David Arnold, Kathryn Anne, Elizabeth Claire, Amanda Claudia; edn: Wesleyan Univ. 1950-51, BA econ., UC Santa Barbara, 1954; BFT internat. mgmt., Am. Grad. Sch. for Internat. Mgmt., Phoenix 1961; N.Y. Univ. Grad. Sch. of Bus. 1963-65; Cert. Park Opr. (CPO). Career: asst. to v.p. International Paul Hardeman, Inc. Stanton, Calif. 1961; dir. adminstrn. Paul Hardeman S.A., Buenos Aires, Arg. 1962-63; office svs. supr. Owens Corning Fiberglas Corp., NY, NY 1964-65; v.p. adminstrn. Fibraglas S.A., Bogota, Col. 1965-67; bus. analyst Owens Corning Fiberglas Corp., Toledo, Oh. 1967-68; pres. Daire Assocs., Walnut Creek, Calif. 1968-78; pres. Am. Powerwash Corp., Concord 1969-78; v.p./gen. mgr. Sunset Recreation Inc., Menlo Park 1973-77; sr. cons. Leisure Mgmt. Consultants Inc., Concord 1975-77; pres. Pathfinder Cos., Scotts Valley 1977-89, chmn. bd. 1989-; pres. American Holiday Resorts Inc., 1983-; chmn./ceo Calif. Microelectronic Systems Inc. 1989-91; dir: Evergreen Holding Co. Ltd. 1986-, Conifer Reinsurance Ltd. 1987-; mem: Calif. Travel Parks Assn. (pres. 1974-75), Nat. Campground Owners Assn. (v.p. 1976-78, pres. 1978-80); advisor Small Bus. Edn. Pgm. Cabrillo Coll. 1984-89; appt. Calif. Senate and Assembly Select Com. on Small Business, Sacto. 1982-, U.S. Small Bus. Adminstrn. Advy. Council, San Francisco (dist. chmn. 1983-87), Calif. State Conf. on Small Bus., Sacto. (pres. 1986-88); active Calif. Small Bus. Assn., Sacto. (pres. 1988-), Nat. Small Bus. United, Wash. D.C. (trustee 1989-); mil: 1st lt. US Army, Civil Affairs and Mil. Govt., Active 1954-56. Ofc: #2 Blue Hill Scotts Valley 95066-3638

HOFFMAN, MARVIN, computer professional resource co. president; b. July 27, 1933, Wauwatosa, Wis.; s. Sam and Anna (Cohen) H.; m. F. Evelyn Lazar, Sept. 28, 1955; children: Loren b. 1959, Darryl b. 1960; edn: BA math., CSU Northridge 1962; postgrad. wk., CSU and UCLA; Life Tchg. Credential Bus. Data Processing. Career: systems supr. North Am. Rockwell 1961-66; dir. 6000 Software Devel., Control Data Corp. 1966-69; dir. software devel. Ampex Corp. 1969-72; mgr. software devel. F&M Systems Co. 1972-73; dir. R&D Div. Computer Machinery Corp. 1973-76; founder/pres./bd. chmn. XXCAL, Inc. (multi-branch data processing consulting and human resource co.), Los Angeles 1976-; dir: RIMTECH, Rainbow Technology; instr., and mem. advy. com. L.A. City Coll.; bd. mem., pres. L.A. City Coll. Found.; honors: Alpha Gamma Sigma 1958; mem: West LA C.of C., So/Cal/Ten; mil: AG2 USN 1952-56, Korean, Far East Campaign, Good Conduct; Democrat; Jewish; rec: skiing, fishing, jogging. Res: 2423 S Beverly Dr Los Angeles 90034 Ofc: XXCAL, Inc. 11500 Olympic Blvd Ste 459 Los Angeles 90064

HOFFMAN, MICHAEL JEROME, humanities educator, writer; b. Mar. 13, 1939, Phila.; s. Nathan P. and Sara (Perlman) H.; m. Margaret Boegeman, Dec. 27, 1988; children: Cynthia, Matthew; edn: BA, Univ. Pa., 1959, MA, 1960, PhD, 1963. Career: instr. Washington Coll., Chestertown, Md. 1962-64; asst. prof. Univ. Pa., Phila., 1964-67; asst. prof. and prof. UC Davis, 1967-, asst. vice chancellor acad. affairs, 1976-83, chmn. English dept. 1984-89, coordinator of writing programs, 1991-; dir. Humanities Inst., Davis 1987-91; chair jt. projects steering com. Univ. Calif./Calif. State Univs., 1976-87; chair advy. bd. Calif. Acad. Partnership Pgm., 1985-87; dir. Calif. Humanities Project, 1985-91; author: The Development of Abstractionism in the Writings of Gertrude Stein (1965), The Buddy System (1971), The Subversive Vision (1972), Gertrude Stein (1976), Critical Essays on Gertrude Stein (1986), Essentials of the Theory of Fiction (1988), Critical Essays on America Modernism (1992); mem. Modern Language Assn.; mil: USAR 1957-61, Nat. Defense Edn. Act fellow US Govt., 1959-62; Democrat; Jewish; rec: tennis. Res: 4417 San Marino Dr Davis 95616-5012 Ofc: Univ. Calif. Dept. English, Davis 95616 Tel: 916/752-2268

HOFFMAN, PAUL RODERIC, bank executive; b. Oct. 18, 1941, Columbus, Ohio; s. George Martin and Hazel Marie (Hazelett) H.; m. Cheryl, Apr. 7, 1969; edn. grad. Marion Harding H.S., Marion, Ohio 1959. Career: served to major US Marine Corps 1959-84: supply officer 1st FSR, MCB Camp Pendleton 1969-75, supply analyst 1975-76; supply officer Camp Garcia, Vieques, P.R. 1976-77; logistics officer 9th Marine Corps, Shawnee, Ks. 1977-80; contracting officer 29 Palms 1980-84, decorated Navy Achiev. (USMC Combat V 1971, USMC 1977), Navy Commendn. (USMC 1984); asst. v.p. First Community Bank (Bank of Yucca Valley), Yucca Valley 1985-; awards: military mgr. of year Fed. Mgrs. ASSC 29 Palms 1984, Yucca Valley C.of C. Citizen of Year 1986, Yucca Valley Hon. Mayor 1986-87, Business of Yr. Mgr. 1991, Hon. Judge, 29 Palms 1991, Freedom Found. Honor certificate and Honor Medal (1966, 1984), People Helping People award United Way 1992; civic: 29 Palms C.of C. (pres. 1992-93), Joshua Tree Rotary (pres. 1992-93), Tri Valley Little League (pres. 1984-91), Youth Action Com. (chmn. 1987-), Save our Park Com. (chmn. 1988-), United Way Y.V. 1986-87, Joshua Tree C.of C. (treas. 1988-89), Elk Lodge 2314 (Citizen of Yr. 1988-89), Municipal Advy. Yucca Valley 1984-, treas. Old Schoolhouse Project 1991-; rec: youth baseball. Res: 58242 Delano Trail Yucca Valley 92284 Ofc: First Community Bank 7272 Joshua Ln Yucca Valley 92284

HOFFMANN, JON ARNOLD, professor of aeronautical engineering; b. Jan. 13, 1942, Wausau, Wis.; s. Arnold D. and Rita J. (Haas) H.; m. Carol Rae Frye, Sept. 21, 1973; edn: BSME, Univ. Wis., Madison 1964, MSME, 1966; reg. profl. engr. Calif. 1989. Career: prof. aeronautical engring., Calif. State Polytechnic State Univ., San Luis Obispo 1968-; grantee NSF 1970, NASA (prin. investigator, NASA, Edwards AFB 1981-83, Moffett Field 1979-86, 1987, 87-89); recipient merit. performance and profl. promise awards Cal Poly 1985, 86; mem.: ASME 1986-; publs: 5+ articles in sci. jours. of AIAA, ASME, NASA. Ofc: Cal Poly Dept. Aero. Engr., San Luis Obispo 93407

HOFFMEISTER, GERHART, educator; b. Dec. 17, 1936, Giessen, Germany; s. Johannes Emil and Inge (Johannsen) H.; m. Margaret von Poletika, May 28, 1966 (div. Dec. 1988); 1 son, George A. b. 1967; edn: Bacc., Univ. of Bonn, W.Ger., 1963; Teachers Tng. Coll., Cologne, 1966; PhD, Univ. Maryland, 1970. Career: sch. tchr., Cologne, Germany 1964-66; instr. Univ. Maryland, College Park, Md. 1966-70; asst. prof. Univ. Wisconsin, Milw. 1970-74; assoc. prof. Wayne State Univ., Detroit, Mich. 1974-75; assoc. prof. Univ. Calif. Santa Barbara, 1975-79, full prof. of German & comparative literature, 1979-; awards: DAAD stipend German Acad. Exchange Service of Bonn (1962-63, London), grantee Am. Philosophical Soc., Phila. 1974; mem.: Am. Assn. of Tchrs. of German 1970-, Modern Language Assn. Am. 1970-, Goethe Soc. N.Am 1980-, Pacific Coast Philol. Assn. 1976-; coauthor: Germany 2000 Years vol. III (1986), book editor: Goethe in Italy (1988), French Revolution (1989), European Romanticism (1991); rec: swimming, tennis. Res: 117 Calle Alamo Santa Barbara 93105 Ofc: Univ. Calif., Santa Barbara 93106

HOFFNER, CARLETON CROSBY, JR., engineering/management consultant; b. Apr. 23, 1931, Wash DC; s. Carleton Crosby and Josephine Marie (Huber) H.; m. (Mary) Constance Read, June 5, 1953; children: Carol (Walsh) b. 1954, Heidi (Wheatley) b. 1956, Eric Karl b. 1959; edn: Univ. of Va. 1948-49; BS w. distinction, US Naval Acad., Annapolis 1953; BCE, Rensselaer Polytechnic Inst. 1957; MBA, Stanford Univ. 1974; Reg. Profl. Engr., Hawaii 1966. Career: served to Cmdr. US Navy (Ret.) 1949-66: destroyer USS Stickell (DDR-888) in Far East, S.Africa and So. Am., exec. ofcr. submarine chaser USS Tooele (PC-572) at Newport, R.I., qualified for command at sea; pub. works ofcr. on Guam 2 yrs.; instr. contract admin. Civil Engr. Corps Officers Sch., Port Hueneme, Calif. 1960-61; hd. design dept. Navy Facilities, Pearl Harbor, Hawaii 1961-62, constrn. mgmt. engr. Navy Constrn., Pearl Harbor 1962-64, maint. mgmt. engr. Pacific Facilities, Pearl Harbor 1964-66; mil. constrn. prog. Naval Air HQ, Wash DC 1966-68; hd. Pacific Constrn. Br., Navy Facilities HQ, Wash DC 1968-70; dir. Maint. Div., Navy Facilities, San Bruno, Calif.1970-76; dir. Utilities Div., San Bruno 1976-87; mgmt. consultant Univ. Calif., Lawrence Livermore Nat. Lab. and others, 1988-; utilities commr. City of Palo Alto 1991-; honors: Navy Superior Civilian Svc Medal 1987, Engr. of the Year 1986, Stanford-Sloan exec. fellow, Stanford Univ. Grad. Sch. of Bus. 1973, Who's Who Among Students in Am. Univs. 1952-53, Tau Beta Pi, Chi Epsilon; mem. Soc. Am. Mil. Engrs.; clubs: Army-Navy CC (Arlington, Va.), Univ. (Palo Alto); election ofcl. Santa Clara County; works: winner 12+ ice skating championships incl. Nat. Senior Dance and Nat. Junior Pairs titles, mem. U.S.Figure Skating Team, 3d place World Pairs, Paris 1949, capt. US Naval Acad. Varsity Tennis Team 1953; Republican; rec: antique collector, lectr. Address: 4121 Old Trace Rd Palo Alto 94306-3728

HOKAJ, RICHARD RAE, data communications co. executive; b. Oct. 6, 1944, Pittsburgh, Pa.; s. Ignatius P. and Alfreda (Paulson) H.; m. Christine Denise Gaca, July 8, 1967; children: Brigitte Lea b. 1969, Heidi Holly b. 1972, Heather Joy b. 1974; edn: BA math., Washington & Jefferson, 1966; Dipl. Comp.Sci., Edinburgh Univ., Scotland, 1967. Career: staff supr. AT&T, Phila., Pa. and WDC, 1970-73; mgr. GEISCO, Cleveland, Rockville, Md., London, Amsterdam, 1973-81; dir., customer supt. American Satellite Co., Rockville, Md., 1981; v.p./quality assurance and customer supt. United Info. Svc., also v.p./ops UniNet, Kansas City, Mo., 1982-86; indep. cons., 1986-87; v.p. network services Infonet, El Segundo, Calif., 1987-; awards: Disting. military grad. Washington & Jefferson 1966, Rotary Found. fellow Edinburgh Univ. 1966-67, Infonet Pres.'s Club 1989 and Outstanding performance award 1989-90; Delta Tau Delta frat. (treas. 1964-65); civic: Am. Diabetes Assn., Juvenile Diabetes Found. (treas. 1984-87); club: North Ranch CC (Westlake Village); mil: capt. US Army 1967-70, Bronze star Qui Nhon, Vietnam 1970; Republican; R.Cath.; rec: golf, bridge. Res: 3300 Blue Ridge Ct Westlake Village 91362 Ofc: 2100 E Grand Ave El Segundo 90245

HOKANSON, CARL GUSTAF, multinational corporation executive; b. Mar. 9, 1937, Los Angeles; s. Carl Gustaf and Blanche M. H.; m. Mercedes Lasarte (internationally known artist) June 14, 1969; children:, Christer G.; edn: BA in math., Brown Univ., 1959; MBA with distinction, Harvard, 1970 (Student Body Pres.). Career: v.p. mktg. C.G. Hokanson Co. Inc., Los Angeles and Santa Ana, 1960-66; v.p. mktg. and contracts Transp. Support Div., Lear Siegler, Inc. 1966-68; with Lear Siegler Corporate HQ 1970-77 as: v.p. admin., systems & services (military) group 1970-71; v.p. adminstrn., climate control & housing group 1971-73; corp. workout dir. 1973-75; v.p. fin./cfo and dir. S.W. Properties, Inc., 1974-75; pres./ceo LSI Internat., 1975-77; owner Hokanair GmbH & Co., Ger. 1971-84; pres. Carl G. Hokanson & Assoc., Inc. 1978-; pres./ceo/dir. Volpar Aircraft Corp. 1985-87; pres./coo Gibraltar Financial Corp. 1990-91; Boards: C.G. Hokanson Co. Inc. 1963-66; Valley Community Hosp. 1972-73; Olympic Internat. Inc. 1973-74; Erma Maschinen and Waffen Fabrik, GmbH (Ger.) 1973-77; Central de Industria, S.A. (Mex.) 1975-77; No-Sag, S.A., Venezuela and Farfisa Sp.A.(Italy), 1974-77; Arbitrator Am. Arb. Assn.; Life mem. Air Force Assn.; Town Hall of Calif.; Bel Air Country Club. Ofc: 16021 Woodvale Rd Encino CA 91436

HOLDER, GEORGE H., co. executive; b. June 24, 1936, Lafayette, Ind.; s. George A. and Carolyn J. (Switzer) H.; m. Suzanne L. Lamb, Nov. 27, 1976; edn: BS in ag., Purdue Univ., 1957. Career: asst. advt. mgr. Nat. Livestock Producer mag., Chgo. 1960-63; sales rep., advt. mgr., sales mgr. product mgr., mktg. mgr., country mgr. for Thailand, all with Elanco Products Co. div. Eli Lilly and Co., 1963-80; v.p. mktg. Syntex Agribusiness, 1980-83, v.p./gen. mgr. Syntex Agribusiness USA 1984-85, pres. 1985-, and v.p. Syntex Corp.; chmn. bd. dirs. Animal Health Inst.; mem. bd. Calif. 4-H Found.; mil: 1st lt. US Army Arty. 1957-59, Korean Service. Address: Palo Alto 94304

HOLLAND, ELIZABETH, artist; b. July 23, 1913, Detroit; d. Edward Morton Holland and Elsie (Nicols) Brady; m. George Edgar Naylon, Jr., July 20, 1934 (div. 1939); m. 2d, Gene Winans McDaniel, Dec. 29, 1940 (div. 1968); children: Gene Ross b. 1945, Lauralyn b. 1947; edn: student Grand Central Sch. Art, 1930-31, Sarah Lawrence Coll., 1932-33, Ecoles d'arts Americaines, Fountainebleau, France 1932-33. Career: artist, painter, 1929-; tchr. landscape in oils, acrylics and color theory Marin Art and Garden Center, Ross, Calif. 1968-, teach 3 classes weekly in own studio in Bolinas; tchr. Napa Valley Art Assn. 1967-, Tiburon Peninsula Club 1977, summer classes St. Mary's Art Ctr., Virginia City, Nev.; currently profl. group instr. in a new encaustic technique, 1989; showed new technique in preview exh. St. Paul's Gallery, Virginia City, Nev. 1990; one-man shows Casa de Manana, La Jolla 1941, Nevada Art Gal., Reno 1965, St. Mary's Art Gal., Virginia City, Nev. 1966-68, Depot Gal., Yountville 1968, Torrance Gal., San Anselmo 1969, Kaiser Found. 1974; group shows include Oakland Anns, Marin Soc. Artists Shows, Soc. Western Artists Shows, Winblad Gal. S.F., Town and Country Gal., Palo Alto, Gold Hill Gal., Round Hill Mall, Zephyr Cove, Nev., St. Mary's Art Gal., Virginia City, Nev., Rosicrucian Gal., San Jose, Brandy Buck Gal.; represented in permanent collection Artists Studio, Bolinas; producer, dir. Emigrant Trail Show, Nev. and Calif., 1973-74;Bolinas "Stagecoach Barn Annual" 1993; Mainly Marin: Larkspur 1993; awards include Purchase award St. Mary's in Mountains 1968, awards Nevada Heritage Shows; mem: Marin Soc. Artists (juror), Soc. Western Artists (juror), Napa Valley Artists Assn.; Republican; Episcopalian. Res: Box 147-190 Horseshoe Hill Road Bolinas 94924

HOLLENBECK, ALVIN SCOTT, real estate brokerage president, ret.; b. Feb. 7, 1906, San Diego; s. William Fitzpatrick and Mary Otie (Young) H.; m. Grace Granger, Dec. 29, 1945 (dec. Feb. 28, 1989); children: Louise b. 1929, Lois b. 1930, Alvin b. 1932, William b. 1940, Jo-Ann b. 1942; 19 grandchildren, 18 great grandchildren; edn: H.S. grad. 1966, att. Southwestern Coll. 2 yrs., GRI cand. Grad. Real Estate Inst. 1976; lic. R.E. broker, Calif. 1974. Career: chief electrician's mate US Navy 1924-48, 1950-52 (Ret.), decorated Good Conduct, Wartime Service, 26 yrs. active duty; electrician journeyman US Civil Service (1948-50, 1952-70) 20 yr. ret.; real estate sales agt. 1971-74, realtor, owner Hollenbeck Realty, Chula Vista 1974-90; mem: USN Fleet Reserve, Am. Legion, Nat. Assn. Retired Fed. Employees; Republican; Christian Sci.; rec: television, sports, politics. Res: Ocean Bluff Mobile Home Park 3340 Del Sol Blvd Unit 86 San Diego 92154-3455

HOLZER, THOMAS LEQUEAR, geologist; b. June 26, 1944, Lafayette, Ind.; s. Oswald Alois and Ruth Alice (Lequear) H.; m. Mary Elizabeth Burbach, June 13, 1968; children: Holly b. 1970, Elizabeth b. 1972; edn: BSE (cum laude),

Princeton Univ., 1965; MS, Stanford Univ., 1966, PhD, 1970. Career: asst. prof. geology Univ. Conn., Storrs, Ct. 1970-75; adj. environmentalist Griswold & Fuss, Manchester Ct. 1973-75; geologist US Geol. Survey, Menlo Park, Calif. 1975-82, 1984-89, branch chief 1989-, asst. dir. for research USGS, Reston, Va. 1982-84; recipient USGS awards for superior service 1980, public svc. 1991; mem.: Geol. Soc. Am. (1967-, Fellow), Am. Geophysical Union 1968-, Nat. Water Well Assn. 1973-, AAAS 1968-, Sigma Xi 1965-; Foothills Tennis & Swim Club Palo Alto (pres. 1988-89); publs: numerous sci. articles (1970-), book editor, Man-induced Land Subsidence (1984); Republican; Presbyterian; rec: tennis. Res: PO Box 851 Palo Alto 94302 Ofc: US Geological Survey 345 Middlefield Rd MS977 Menlo Park 94025

HOMESTEAD, SUSAN EICHELBAUM, clinical social worker, psychotherapist; b. Sept. 20, 1937, Bklyn., N.Y.; d. Cy Simon and Katherine (Haas) Eichelbaum; m. Robert B. Randall, May 1956; m. 2d George G. Zanetti, Dec. 13, 1962; m. 3d Ronald E. Homestead, Jan. 16, 1973; 1 son, Bruce D. Randall b. Mar. 1957; edn: BA, Univ. of Miami, Fla. 1960; MSW, Tulane Univ., 1967; Lic. Clin. Soc. Wkr. (LCSW) Va., Ca.; ACSW, Acad. Cert. Social Wkrs., 1971; B.C.D., Nat. Assn. Soc. Wkrs. Career: pvt. practice, cons. Richmond, Va., 1971-, also Santa Clara, Ca. 1973-75, 86-88; psychotherapist, cons. Family and Children's Svs., Richmond, Va. 1981-, Richmond Pain Clinic, 1983-84; cons. Health Internat. Va., P.C., Lynchburg, Va. 1984-86; Santa Clara (Ca.) Dept. Soc. Svs., Children's Svs. Bur., 1973-75 and 1986-89; LCSW, cons., 1971-: Childrens' Hosp. at Stanford, Palo Alto, Ca. 1968-70; Franklin Street Psychotherapy & Edn. Ctr., Santa Clara, Loma Prieta Reg. Ctr. 1970-72; chief clin. soc. wkr. Med. Coll. Va., Va. Commonwealth Univ., 1974-79; co-dir. asthma pgm. Va. Lung Assn., Richmond, Va. 1975-79; field supt. 1980 Census; mem: Va. Soc. Clin. Social Work Inc. (charter, secty. 1975-78), NASW (1960s-), Soc. for Psychoanalytic Psychotherapy, Am. Acad. Psychotherapists, Internat. Soc. for Study of Multiple Personality and Dissociation, Am. Assn. Psychiatric Svs. for Children; civic vol.: Peninsula Children's Ctr. Palo Alto, Morgan Ctr. Nursery, Council for Comm. Action Planning Santa Clara Co., Comm. Assn. for Retarded Palo Alto, Am. Cancer Soc. Va. Div. (ad hoc steering com.), Epilepsy Found., Am. Heart Assn., Central Va. Guild for Infant Survival, others; Jewish. Res: PO Box 185 Los Altos CA 94023 (415) 964-2399 also: 9405 River Rd Richmond VA 23229 (804) 740-1100

HONANYAN, (ART) ARDAVAZT, financial executive; b. June 19, 1944, Istanbul, Turkey, naturalized 1963; s. Arthur and Alice Maryam (Muradyan) H.; m. Karen Luise Kruger, Aug. 16, 1986; edn: BA, George Washington Univ., 1967; grad. study Univ. of Oregon, 1967-68; MBA, New York Univ., 1973; cert. mgmt. acct. (CMA) and mem. Inst. of Mgmt. Accts. Career: mgr. corp. planning The Continental Corp., NY, NY 1978-80, asst. secty. 1980-83; v.p. fin. CPI - Pension Services, Irvine, Calif. 1983-89, c.f.o. CPI Group Inc. 1988-90, v.p. and c.f.o. Calif. Central Trust Bank Corp. (CalTrust), Irvine, 1990-; mil: QM3c USNR 1968-70; Republican; Armenian Apostolic. Res: PO Box 9343 Fountain Valley 92728 Ofc: CalTrust 15253 Blake Pky Irvine 92718-2502 Ph:714/380-2318

HONG, SU-DON, company president; b. June 23, 1941, Taiwan, R.O.C., nat. 1985; s. Tien-Shern and Tze (Lee) H.; m. Grace Wang, Jan. 30, 1971; children: Emily b. 1975, Jennifer b. 1976; edn: BS, Nt. Taiwan Univ., 1966; MS, Univ. of Waterloo, Ont., Can. 1970; PhD polymer sci., Univ. of Mass., Amherst 1975. Career: res. assoc. Univ. Calif., Berkeley 1976-77; sr. scientist Jet Propulsion Lab., Pasadena 1977-78, technical group ldr. 1978-85; pres. Sida Corp., Monterey Park 1985-; cons. JPL, 1986; recipient 6 achiev. awards NASA, Wash. D.C. (1978, 79, 80, 81, 82, 83); mem: Sigma Xi, Am. Physical Soc., Am. Chemical Soc.; inventions: Broad Band Optical Radiation Dector (1981), Double Beam Optical Method and apparatus for measuring thermal diffusion (1981); pub. sci. articles (1972-86); Democrat; rec: music, bridge. Res: 10551 E Danbury St Temple City 91780 Ofc: Sida Corporation 1055 Corporate Center Dr Ste 510 Monterey 91754

HOOD, JOHN TYRE, electrical engineer; b. Sept. 26, 1912, Oakland; s. John and Minnie Clarice (Newman) H.; m. Muriel Martina Hinz, Aug. 1, 1935; children: Thomas b. 1940, James b. 1943, David b. 1945; edn: BS in E.E., Univ. Calif. Berkeley, 1934; reg. profl. engr. (E007145) Calif. Career: engr., exec. GE Co., 1934-77: test engr., indsl. control engr., motors engr. GE, Schenectady, NY 1934-39; util./indsl. equip. engr. GE, Portland, Oreg. 1940-45, mgr. 1946-49; Tacoma area mgr., Tacoma, Wash. 1950-59; elec. util. mgr. GE, Seattle 1960-61; indsl. computer engr. GE, San Francisco 1962-63, Transit & RR Dist. mgr., S.F. 1964-68; Transit & RR Regional mgr., 1969-77; asst. to pres. Catenary Transp. Systems, Los Angeles 1978-79; honors: Charles A. Coffin Award, GE, Portland, Oreg. 1948; mem. IEEE (1940-, life mem., past chmn.), Profl. Engrs. of Oregon (pres. 1949), Tacoma Engrs. Club (pres. 1959), Alpha Sigma Phi Frat. (past pres.), Burlingame University Club (past pres.), Calif. Alumni of the Peninsula, AARP; civic: Citizens Advy. Com. San Mateo Co. Transit Dist. (1980-92, chmn. 1983), past dir. and pres. Toastmasters Unit Tacoma C.of C. 1955-59; works: for lumber sawmills, developed electrified log-carriage drives that replaced steam shotguns for superior performance, also same for plywood lathes peeling logs, 1947 thru 1958; from 1964-77, increased GE diesel locomotive market share from 5 percent to 45 percent; Republican; Presbyterian; rec: computers, electronics, advy. S.M. Co. Transit Dist. 1980-92. Res: 105 Denise Dr. Hillsborough 94010

HOOKER, JULIET BURKETT (MRS. RODMAN LENT HOOKER, JR.), educator, civic leader; b. May 21, 1943, Oakland; d. William Andrew and Juliet (Johnson) Burkett; m. Rodman Lent Hooker, Jr., Aug. 16, 1963; children: Peter Burkett, Juliet Morse, Rodman Lent III; edn: undergrad. Mills Coll., BA edn., USC, 1965. Career: bd. dirs. Security Nat. Bank of Monterey County, 1961-65; sec. treas. Nat. Hist. Found. 1966-70; bd. dirs. Burkett Land Co., 1966-; Grubb & Ellis Co., Real Estate Investments, 1977-85; civic bds: Seattle Jr. League Sustainers (pres.), Am. Conservatory (dir.), Northwest Horticulture Soc. (dir.), Mills Coll. Alumni Bd., Children's Hosp. Devel. Bd. Seattle (pres.), active PTA Crystal Springs Sch., Garden Club Am., D.A.R. (life); clubs: Seattle Tennis, Burlingame Country (Hillsborough), Beach (Pebble Beach) also: PO Box 726 Pebble Beach 93953

HOOKER, RODMAN LENT, JR., banker; b. Mar. 14, 1940, Hillsborough, Calif.; s. Rodman Lent and Nancy (Morse) H.; m. Juliet Ann Burkett, Aug. 16, 1963; children: Peter Burkett, Juliana Morse, Rodman Lent III; edn: grad. Cate Sch., att. Menlo Coll., BS, USC, 1965. Career: investment banker, San Francisco 1960-70; trust ofcr. Seattle First Nat. Bank, Seattle 1970-76; sr. v.p. Crocker Nat. Bank, San Francisco 1977-85; sr. v.p. First Interstate Bank, Seattle 1985-; bd. trustees Mills Hosp., past pres. Nat. Hist. Found. 1971; clubs: Pacific Union (SF), Burlingame Country, Seattle Tennis; rec: tennis, golf, skiing. Res: 546 W Santa Inez Hillsborough also: PO Box 726 Pebble Beach 93953

HOPE, GERRI DANETTE, telecommunications officer.; b. Feb. 28, 1956, McClellan AFB (Sacto.) Calif.; d. Albert Gerald and Beulah Rae (Bane) Hope; edn: assoc. of sci., Sierra Coll., Rocklin, Calif. 1977; misc. other credits, Okla. State Univ. 1977-79, Sacto. State Univ. 1980; career: instructional asst. II, San Juan Sch. Dist., Carmichael, Calif. 1979-82; telecomms. supr., Delta Dental Svc., San Francisco 1982-85; telecomms. coord., Farmers Savings, Davis, Calif. 1985-87; telecomms. ofcr., Sacto. Savings Bank, Sacto., Calif. 1987-; partner, Exec. Protocol Svs.; awards: Outstanding Service Award, Sacto. Savings 1990, 1991; advy. panel, Telcom Div., Golden Gate Univ., Sacto. 1992; mem: asst. v.p., TCA (Telecomms. Assn.) 1990-92, v.p. 1993; Am. Philatelic Soc. 1991; Sacto. Philatelic Assn. 1991; Errors, Freaks & Oddities Philatelic Collectors 1991; Nat. Assn. of Female Executives 1992. Republican; Born Again Christian, non-denominational; rec: computers, ceramic Christmas ornaments, reading, cats, animal behavior, philately, Christian Ministry, lectr. in telecomms, toll fraud prevention and awareness. Ofc: Sacramento Savings Bank P.O. Box 661595 Sacramento 95866-1595

HOPKINS, CECILIA ANN, college administrator; b. Feb. 17, 1922, Havre, Mont.; d. Kost L. and Mary (Manaras) Sofos; m. Henry E. Hopkins, Sept. 7, 1944; edn: BS, Mont. State Coll. 1944; MS, San Francisco St. Coll. 1958, 2d. MA, 1967; PhD, Calif. Western Univ. 1977. Career: business tchr. Havre H.S., 1942-44; secty. George P. Gorham Real Estate, 1944-45; escrow secty. Fox & Carskadon Realtors, 1945-50; escrow ofcr. Calif. Pacific Title Ins. Co. 1950-57; bus. tchr. Westmoor H.S., 1957-58; instr. Coll. of San Mateo, 1958-, chair Real Estate Dept. 1963-76, dir. Div. of Business 1976-86, post-retirement dir. real estate dept. 1986-91; cons. Calif. State Dept. Real Estate, Sacto.; chair Calif. Comm. Colls. (CCC) Advy. Commn. 1971-72, mem. advy. coms.: CCC Chancellor 1976-, CCC Real Estate Edn. Endowment Fund 1977, proj. dir. Career Awareness Consortium Com. 1976-; dir. emeritus No. REEA; appt. Calif. State Dept. of R.E. Commnrs. Advy. Com. for Edn. and Res. 1983-; awards: RECI (Real Estate Cert. Inst.) Award, REEA Nat. Award emeritus 1993, Calif. Assn. of Realtors 1982; RECI Geo. Thuss Award 1982, 86; CBEA (Calif. Bus. Education) Commendn. for devel. real estate curriculum and devotion to bus. edn. 1978; Soroptimist Intl. (San Mateo - Burlingame) Woman of Achievement 1979; mem: Delta Pi Epsilon (nat. historian 1967-68, nat. sec. 1968-69), Real Estate Tchrs. Assn. (Calif. state pres. 1964-65, hon. dir. 1965-, Hon. dir. emeritus N. REEA), San Francisco State Coll. Counseling and Guidance Alumni Assn., Calif. Bus. Tchrs. Assn., Alpha Gamma Delta, Theta Alpha Delta, Phi Lambda Theta, AAUW; coauthor: Calif. Real Estate Principles (John Wiley & Sons 1980); rec: travel, antiques, hiking. Res: 504 Colgate Way San Mateo 94402 Ofc: College of San Mateo 1700 W Hilldale Blvd San Mateo 94402

HORNER, LELAND JOHN, city manager; b. March 18, 1933, Pasadena; s. Clealand Archie Shell and Olga Ida (Hokenson) H.; m. Dorothy Jean Cannon, Feb. 1, 1959; children: Cyndi b. 1961, Scott b. 1963, Amy b. 1966, David b. 1968; edn: BA, San Jose St. Univ.; MPA, USC. Career: asst. adminstv. ofcr. City of Gardena 1962-69; asst. city mgr. City of Ventura 1969-73; city adminstr. City of Millbrae 1973-78; city mgr. City of Livermore 1978-; mem: Livermore Rotary Club, Livermore C.of C., Our Saviors Lutheran Ch. (bd. elders 1987-), El Camino Kiwanis (pres. 1968), Alameda City Mgmt. Assn. (chmn. 1983-84); mil: USN 1952-56. Ofc: City of Livermore 1052 S Livermore Ave Livermore 94550

HOROWITZ, BEN, medical center executive; b. Mar. 19, 1914, N.Y.C.; s. Saul and Sonia (Meringoff) H.; m. Beverly Lichtman; 2 children, Zachary b. 1953, Jody b. 1955; edn: BA, Brooklyn Coll., 1940; LLB, St. Lawrence Univ., 1935; New Sch. for Social Research, N.Y., 1942; admitted bar, 1941. Career: director New York Fedn. of Jewish Philanthropies, 1940-45; eastern reg. dir. City of Hope Nat. Medical Ctr., Los Angeles 1945-50, nat. exec. secty. City of Hope, 1950-53, exec. director 1953-85, bd. dir. 1980-, general v.p. 1985-: formulated the role of City of Hope as a pilot ctr. in medicine, science and humanitarianism, and author City of Hope "Torchbearers Creed" 1959; awards: City of Hope nat. awards: Spirit of Life, Gallery of Achiev. (1970, 74), profl. of year Nat. Soc. of Fund Raisers/ So. Calif. 1977, Ben Horowitz Chair in Research estab. at City of Hope 1981, L.A. city street named in his honor 1986; mem: bds. Beckman Research Inst. 1980-, Hope for Hearing Found., UCLA (v.p. 1972-), Forte Found. 1987-92, Leo Baeck Temple (1964-67, 86-89), Church-Temple Corp. for Homeless 1988-, Westwood Property Owners Assn. (bd. 1991-); appt. Calif. Gov.'s Task Force on Flood Relief (1969-74); res: 221 Conway Ave Los Angeles 90024; ofc: City of Hope, 208 West 8th St Los Angeles 90014

HOROWITZ, DAVID CHARLES, consumer correspondent; b. June 30, 1937, NY, NY; s. Max Leo and Dorothy (Lippman) H.; m. Suzanne E. McCambridge, 1973; 2 daus.; edn: BA, hons. journ., Bradley Univ. 1959; MSJ, Northwestern Univ. 1960; CBS Fellow, Columbia Univ. 1962-63. Career: editor-in-chief Tazewell Co. (Ill.) Newspaper, 1956; reporter Peoria (Ill.) Journ. Star, 1957-60; reporter, columnist Lerner Newspapers and Chgo. City News Bureau, 1959-60; newscaster KRNT Radio-TV, Des Moines 1960-62; news writer/ prod. ABC Radio Network, NYC 1963; Far East corr. NBC News, 1963-64; pub. affairs dir. WMCA, NYC 1964-66; corr.-edn. ed., Consumer Ombudsman, KNBC News Action Reporter, L.A. 1966-, spl. features: Consumer Guideline, Of Consumer Interest, Consumer Close/Up; nat. syndicated pgm. David Horowitz Consumer Buyline, Fight Back! with David Horowitz; worldwide Apollo 15 splashdown, 1971; Calif. earthquake 2/9/71; Dem. Conv. 1972; host/exec. prod./dir. of home videotape: The Baby Safe Home (distbd. Embassy-McGraw Hill); synd. columnist Creators Synd. 1989-; Western Internat. Synd. 1989-; synd. TV show Fightback! David Horowitz; host/exec. prod./dir. of home videotape: The Baby Safe Home (Embassy-McGraw Hill); exec. prod. CBS-TV Aftersch. Spl. "Frog Girl: The Jenifer Graham Story" (Genesis Animal Rights Award 1990); exec. prod. feature TV movie "Tears of Joy, Tears of Sorrow" (disting. svc. award, Ill. Bdcstrs. Assn.; 1st place award UPI Bdcstrs. Assn.); author 2 books: Fight Back and Don't Get Ripped Off (1979), The Business of Business (1989); advr. UCLA publs.; pres. Fight Back! Found. for Consumer Edn., 1988-; Consumer Commentator CNBC-TV/FNN, 1990-; synd. Fightback Radio Reports, James Brown Entertainment, 1989-; Fight Back For Your Med. Health, 1991, Vols. 1 thru 4, Dell Books; pres. Medill Sch. of Journalism, So. Calif. Chpt., 1990-; awards: Nat. Radio-TV Daily Award 1963, Emmy for consumer ombudsman KNBC Newsservice, Emmy awards for comsumer reporting (1973, 75, 77, 2 in 1982, 83, 89, 90), resolutions LA City, LA Co., State of Calif. 1979, City of Hope spirit of life award 1979, US Postal Insps. 1981, Vista Del Mar, Jewish Fedn. Council 1981, media award Nat. Soc. of Consumer Affairs Profls. 1982, Calif. State disting. citizen 1982, US Consumer Product Safety Commn. 1982, Calif. Consumer Affairs Assn. 1982, Humane Soc. of the US, LA Press Club, LA Co. Commn. on Alcoholism, Work Tng. Pgm. for Devel. Disabled Young Adults, Golden Mike Award 1986, Excellence in Journalism award of Nat. Assn. for Home Care 1992, many others; frequent TV talk show guest; feature subject in Time Mag. (1/4/82), TV Guide (5/15/82); mem. Child Passenger Safety Assn.; bd. mem: Nat. Bdcst. Edn. Conf., Am. Cancer Soc. Calif. Div., LA Jewish Home for Aged, The Silent Network, The Young Musicians Found. Inc.; advy. bd. S.H.A.R.E., Inc.; patron LA Co. Art Mus.; mem: AFTRA, SAG, W.G.A., BMI, ASCAP, Acad. TV Arts and Scis., Internat. Radio-TV Soc., Radio-TV News Dirs. Assn., Nat. Edn. Writers Assn., The Guardians, Sigma Delta Chi, Phi Delta Kappa, Overseas Press Club of Am., Friars Club; mil: USNR 1954-62. Ofc: NBC-TV 3000 W Alameda Ave Burbank 91523 also: PO Box 49915 Los Angeles 90049

HORTON, MICHAEL LYNN, mortgage banker; b. Oct. 19, 1961, Pasadena, Calif.; s. Jerry Stanley and Mary Louise H.; edn: BA econs., Claremont McKenna Coll. 1983; realtor Calif. 1986. Career: ops. mgr. I.W.S. Pasadena 1977-78; exec. asst. to pres. Harris Constrn. Co. La Verne 1979-80; founder NBB Svcs. 1980; sr. mortgage banker, regional mgr. Sycamore Financial Group, Rancho Cucamonga 1984-87; pres. Boulder Fin. Corp., Rancho Cucamonga 1988-; instr. mortgage finance workshop; honors: life mem. CSF, Outstanding Student of Yr. (Chaffey Comm. Coll. econ. dept. 1980), Calvin G. Justice Meml. Scholar 1980, Doris D. Lepper Meml. Scholar 1981, Outstanding Bus. Student (Chaffey 1981), Dean's List (Chaffey, Claremont Men's Coll.), acad. scholarship (Claremont McKenna 1981), Calif. State Scholar 1981; mem. L.A. World Affairs Coun., West End Executive Assn.; author: A Real Estate Professional's Reference Guide to Mortgage Finance 1985, Money Talks (newsletter); Republican (Calif. Central Com. 1981-91, Pete Wilson nominee to Repub. Senatorial Inner Circle 1985); rec: basketball, racquetball, tennis, water sports. Ofc: Boulder Financial Corp., 9121 Haven Ave Ste 150 Rancho Cucamonga 91730

HORVATH, MATTHEW JOHN, JR., soldier, aviator, engineer, educator; b. Mar. 22, 1922, Campbell, Ohio; s. Matthew John, Sr. and Anna Mary (Miklosko) H.; m. Dorothy Chaney, Dec. 12, 1942; children: Matthew b. 1945, Douglas b. 1951, Darlene b. 1957; grandchildren: Matthew, Steven, Christopher, Sarah; edn: BS electronics, Ariz. St. Univ., 1955; MA secondary sch. adminstrn., CSU Northridge, 1973; MA counseling, Chapman Coll., 1974; PhD human beh., U.S. Internat. Univ. San Diego 1975. Career: enlisted Army Inf. 1939-41, pilot USAF 1941-63, decorated D.F.C., Air Medal w/2 o.l.c., 136th FBW, Korea, 1951-52; sr. flt. test engr. McDonnell Aircraft, St. Louis, Mo. 1963-70; tchr. Rosamond (Calif.) High Sch., 1970-73; high sch. counselor Mojave H.S. (Calif.) 1973-77, adminstr./H.S.-Elem. principal Calif. City 1977-88, cons. counselor Mojave Unified Sch. Dist. 1988-89; sr. liaison engr. Scientific Applications Internat. Corp., 1990-; bus. mem. IEEE (1955-), Am. Legion, PDK Lancaster (pres. 1978-79), Retired Officer Assn. (1975-, chapt. pres. 1991-92), Elks, Moose; civic: vol. elem. sch. counselor; author: Comparative Study of individualized vs. noninvididualized teaching methods in math 1975; Republican; R.Cath.; rec: flying, golf, bridge, walking, traveling. Res: 1152 East Ave J-1 Lancaster 93535

HORWIN, LEONARD, lawyer; b. Jan. 2, 1913, Chgo.; s. Joseph and Jeanette H.; m. Ursula Helene Donig, Oct. 15, 1939; children: Noel S. b. 1940, Leonora Marie b. 1947; edn: BA (honors) UCLA, 1933; LLB (cum laude) Yale Law Sch., 1936; Career: atty., assoc. pioneer law firm Lawler, Felix and Hall, 1936-39; ptnr. (Jack W.) Hardy and Horwin, attys. for L.A. Examiner, Sterling Elec. Motors, others, 1939-42; ptnr. Witkin-Horwin Review Course on Calif. Law, 1939-42; lectr. labor law, USC Law Sch., 1941; counsel Bd. of Econ. Warfare and mem. program adjustment com. and alt. mem. requirements com. War Prodn. Bd., 1942-43; attache U.S. Emb., Madrid, Spain 1943-47; American rep. in Spain, Allied Control Council for Ger., 1945-47; lectr. (in Spanish lang.) on Am. constl. law, Am. Cultural Inst., Madrid, 1945; lectr., fgn. affairs, Town Hall of Calif., other civic groups, 1949; pvt. law practice, 1950-; elected Beverly Hills City Council, 1962, mayor pro tem 1963, mayor 1964, chmn. com. on municipal ct. reorganization League of Calif. Cities, 1963-65; dir. So. Calif. Rapid Transit Dist., 1964-66; com. chmn. Transp. Com. L.A. Goals Council, 1966-70; chmn. Beverly Hills Rent Control Adjustment Com., 1980; publs: numerous articles on legal subjects, ed. Yale Law Jour. 1934-35; awards: Yale Univ. Israel H. Peres Prize for legal writing 1934-35, Yale Univ. Edward D. Robbins Mem. Prize 1935-36; author: Insight and Foresight, 14 vols., Dawn Publications Ltd. 1991; Jewish; rec: community projects, hunting, riding, skiing; res: 434 El Camino Dr Beverly Hills; ofc: 121 S Beverly Dr Beverly Hills 90212

HOSAKA, ROY T., certified public accountant; b. July 20, 1940, Los Angeles; s. Roy S. and Florence (Hattori) H.; m. Leslie C. Morimoto, July 26, 1969; edn: BS, CSU San Diego, 1966; C.P.A., Calif., 1975. Career: auditor State of Calif., San Diego, 1968-70; auditor Touche Ross & Co., San Diego, 1970-72; supr. internal audit California First Bank, San Diego, 1972-73; ptnr. Duane Wheeler & Co., Escondido, 1973-77; pres. Hosaka, Nagel, Goepfert & Co., CPAs, San Diego, 1977-; awards: Certificate of Educational Achievement in Personal Financial Planning, Am. Inst. of Certified Public Accountants; mem: Am. Inst. CPAs, Calif. Soc. CPAs, Scripps Mira Mesa Kiwanis; civic: Salvation Army, Escondido 1976-79, Calif. Ballet, San Diego 1985-88, San Diego Co. Mental Health Advy. Bd. 1983-85; Republican; rec: reading. Res: 10275 Grayfox Dr San Diego 92131 Ofc: Hosaka, Nagel, Goepfert & Co. 1011 Camino Del Rio South #410 San Diego 92108

HOSKINS, DONALD WAKELAND, bank executive; b. June 22, 1960, Columbus, Ohio; s. John Allen and Marilyn (Wakeland) H.; edn: AB, UC Berkeley, 1984; MBA, Univ. Va., 1987; chartered fin. analyst (CFA) 1988. Career: mgmt. trainee Union Bank of Switzerland, New York 1984, project splst. 1985; case writer BAFT Ctr. for Internat. Banking Studies 1986; assoc. Security Pacific Merchant Bank, L.A. 1987-89; asst. v.p. Bank of Yokohama, Ltd., L.A. 1989-; awards: Petipas Scholar Univ. Va. Darden Sch. 1986; mem: Assn. of Investment Mgmt. & Res., L.A. Soc. of Fin. Analysts (bd. govs., chmn. edn. com.), Jonathan Club, L.A. World Affairs Council, Music Center Opera League, and var. alumni assns.; author case studies on Internat. Banking, 1986; Democrat; rec: oenology, travel, languages, opera, triathlons, scuba. Res: 545 S Figueroa St Los Angeles 90071 Ofc: The Bank of Yokohama, Ltd. 777 S Figueroa St Ste 700 Los Angeles 90071

HOTCHNER, BRADLEY ROSS, physician, orthopedic surgeon; b. Aug. 22, 1955, St. Louis, Mos.; s. Selwyn Ross and Beverly June (Novack) H.; m. Cynthia Ann Huckelberry, June 7, 1986; edn: BS (honors), Univ. of Wisc., 1977; MD, St. Louis Univ. 1981, Orthopedic Surg., 1986. Career: intern, general surg. St. Louis Univ., Mo. 1981-82, resident orthopedic surg. 1982-86; fellowship, knee & shoulder, Dr. Robt. Jackson, Toronto, Can. 1990, A-O, Basel, Switz. & West Berlin, W.Ger. 1990, hip & knee joint replacement, Dr. Wayne Pagrosky, Chgo. 1990; staff surg. Palm Springs Med. Ctr. 1986; staff surgeon San Bernardino Co. Hosp. 1987-; asst. clinical prof. orthopedic surgery Loma Linda Univ. 1987-; mem. honor societies: Phi Eta Sigma, Phi Kappa Phi, Phi Beta Kappa. Ofc: San Bernardino Orthopedic Medical Group 780 E Gilbert San Bernardino 92404

HOUSER, JOE JAMES, insurance broker; b. April 17, 1916, Udall, Kansas; s. John Jefferson and Elsie Mae (Effner) H.; m. Sherry Lindberg, July 10, 1978; children: Joe James II b. 1948, Jeffrey Jay b. 1946; edn: var. studies USC, UCLA 1941-46. Career: asst. buyer Bullocks, Los Angeles 1938-41; supvr. North American Aviation, Los Angeles 1941-46; v.p. J.E. Wells Co.Inc., Los Angeles 1946-57; pres., owner Houser Ins. Agency, Los Angeles 1957-; fmr. dir. Insurance Brokers Assn.; recipient service awards: L.A. City and County (1968, 1970), Boys Club of Am. medallion award 1975, Goodwill Industries 1990, LA Elks Lodge (1957, 67, 74), Wilshire C.of C. 1968), Beverly Hills Shrine Club (1964, 67), Elks Roses for the Living 1980, Hyatt House Comm. award 1977; mem. Independent Ins. Agents & Brokers Assn.; life mem: US Navy League, F&AM Masons, L.A. Commandery Knights Templar, L.A. Scottish Rite, Beverly Hills Shrine Club, Al Malaikah Temple of the Shrine, L.A. Elks Lodge (advisor, past pres., past dist. dep. grand exalted ruler), Elks of Los Angeles Found. (gov.); civic: Los Angeles Conservancy, Boys and Girls Club Hollywood (dir.), Boys and Girls Club Am./L.A. Co. Area Council (past chmn.), L.A./ Bombay Sister City Affil. (pres., dir.), Goodwill Inds. So. Calif. (dir.), U.S.O./L.A. Area (past dir.), Wilshire C.of C. (past pres.), Wilshire Rotary Club (past dir.), L.A. Royal Arch Masons, Trojan Shrine CLub, L.A. Philanthropic Found., Am. Film Inst.; Republican Presidential Task Force; Res: 11039 Wrightwood Pl Studio City 91604

HOUSTON, ELIZABETH REECE, educator, administrator; b. June 19, 1935, Birmingham, Ala.; d. Reuben Cleveland and Beulah Elizabeth (Reece) Manasco; edn: BSc, Univ. Texas, Austin 1956; MEdn, Boston Coll., 1969. Career: tchr. Ridgefield (Ct.) Pub. Schs., 1962-63; Northampton (Mass.) Pub. Schs., 1972-73; dir. Jack Douglas Vocat. Ctr., San Jose, Calif. 1974-76; tchr. Santa Clara County Office of Edn., San Jose 1976-80, behavioral specialist 1980-82, staff devel. coordinator 1982-86; instr. CSU San Jose, 1980-86; instr. UC Santa Cruz, 1982-84; director Alternative Schools, Santa Clara Co. Office of Edn., San Jose 1986-; awards: Pres.'s award Soc. of Photo-Optical Engrs. 1979, Sch. Bd. Assn., San Jose 1985, svc. to youth Juvenile Ct. Sch. Adminstrs. of Calif. (1989, 90, 91, 92), Outstanding Educator award Santa Clara Univ. 1992; mem: Juvenile Ct. Sch. Adminstrs. (chair 1986-), Council of Exceptional Children 1976-, Assn. for Supervision and Curriculum Devel. 1982-, Assn. of Calif. Sch. Adminstrs. 1982-; civic: Sudbury (Mass.) Public Health Nurses (dir. 1970-72), Eastfield Ming Quong, Los Gatos (dir. 1978-86); author book chapt., Learning Disabilities (1992), manuals: Behavior Mgmt. for Bus Drivers (1980), Classroom Mgmt. (1983), Synergistic Learning (1986). Res: 12150 Country Squire Ln Saratoga 95070 Ofc: Santa Clara County Office of Education, 100 Skyport Dr Santa Clara 95110

HOUSTON, KENNETH EUGENE, state engineering executive, ret.; b. Sept. 10, 1920, Colby, Kans.; s. Phillip Mathew and Dicy Alice (Braden) H.; div.; children: Phillip Kenneth b. 1949, Tamara Jeanne (Pierson) b. 1950, Robert Kent b. 1953; edn: Fort Hays State Coll. 1938-39, Kans. State Univ. 1940-41, var. engring. courses on corrosion UC Davis, num. spl. tech. courses; Reg. Profl. Engr. (Quality Engr.), Calif. Career: asst. to consulting engr., Aircraft Accessories, Kansas City, Kans. 1941-43; ind. rancher (Angus cattle and small grains), Colby, Kans. 12 years; engring. asst. to chief of Governor Section, also Field Erection Engr., equipt. installed in hydraulic structures, Pelton Water Wheel (San Francisco), B.L.H. (Eddystone, Pa.), 10 yrs.; supvr. E&M Section, insp. equipt. for hydraulic structures, State of Calif. 1965-86 (retd.); cons./instr., control of hydraulic structures, Governor Sch.; club: Elks No. 6; Republican; Baptist; rec: woodworking. Res: 5952 Dolomite Dr Diamond Springs 95619 Ofc: Dept. Water Resources, 1801 Seventh St Sacramento 95802

HOUX, MARY ANNE, businesswoman, county official; b. Kans. City, Mo.; d. Rial Richardson and Geraldine Marie (McHale) Oglevie; m. Phillip Clark Houx, May 12, 1962 (dec.); 1 son, Clark Oglevie b. 1966; edn: BS in edn., Univ. Kans., 1954. Career: sch. tchr. in Mo., Kans., Mich., Calif.; midwest dir. C.A.R.E., Inc., Kansas City, Mo. 1960-63; owner Houx Investments, Chico 1974-; elected Chico Unified bd. of trustees 1977-90 (pres. 1979-81); elected Chico City Council 1990-91; apptd. to Butte County Board of Supervisors, June 1991, elected Nov. 1992 (chair 1993); Calif. Sch. Bds. Assn. (pres. 1987-88); mem. Chico State University Assoc. (pres. 1983-85), Chico State Faculty Wives (pres. 1969-70), Chico C.of C., Commonwealth Club of Calif., Cosmos Club; Republican; R.Cath. Ofc: PO Box 1087 Chico 95927

HOWARD, MURRAY, manufacturing, real estate, property management executive, farmer, rancher; b. July 25, 1914, Los Angeles; s. George A. J. and Mabel (Murray) Howard; edn: BS, UCLA, 1939; C.P.A., Calif. Career: mgr. budget control dept. Lockheed Aircraft 1939-45; pres., chmn. bd. Stanley Foundries, Inc. 1945-59, Howard Machine Products, Inc. 1959-, Murray Howard Realty, Inc. 1959-, Murray Howard Devel., Inc. 1969-, Howard Oceanography, Inc. 1967-, Ranch Sales, Inc. 1968-, Murray Howard Investment Corp. 1961-; owner, gen. mgr. Greenhorn Ranch Co., Greenhorn Creek Guest Ranch, Spring Garden, Calif.; pres., chmn. bd. Murray Howard Cattle Co., Prineville, Oreg.; dir. Airshippers Publ. Corp., La Brea Realty & Devel. Co., Shur-Lok Corp.; apptd. mem. Gov. Calif. Minority Commn.; mem. Nat. Assn. Cost Accts. (dir., v.p.), Nat. Assn. Mfrs. (dir.). Ofc: 1605 W Olympic Blvd Ste 404 Los Angeles 90015

HOWATT, HELEN CLARE, library director; b. Apr. 5, 1927, San Francisco; d. Edward Bell and Helen Margaret (Kenney) H.; edn: BA, Holy Name Coll., 1949; MS in library sci., USC, 1972; joined Order Sisters of the Holy Names, R. Catholic Ch., 1945; cert. advanced studies Inst. Sch. Librarians, Our Lady of the Lake Univ., San Antonio 1966; Calif. (life) tchg. and special services credentials. Career: principal St. Monica Sch., Santa Monica 1957-60, St. Mary Sch., Los Angeles 1960-63; tchr. jr. high sch. St. Augustine Sch., Oakland 1964-69; jr. high math tchr. St. Monica Sch., San Francisco 1969-71, St. Cecilia Sch., San Francisco 1971-77; library dir. Holy Names Coll., Oakland 1977-; awards: NSF grantee (1966), NDEA grantee (1966); mem. Cath. Library Assn. (chair No. Calif. elem. schs. 1971-72), Calif. Library Assn., Am. Library Assn., Assn. Coll. and Research Libraries; publs: contbr. math. curriculum San Francisco Unified Sch. Dist., Cum Notis Variorum (publ. Music Library, UCB), articles in Catholic Library World (1987). Address: Holy Names College Library, 3500 Mountain Blvd Oakland 94619

HOWELL, RICHARD JAMES, aerospace engineer; b. Jan. 9, 1935, San Bernardino; s. Weldon Olin and Barbara May (Mulligan) H.; div.; 1 son, Wesley, b. 1958; edn: AA, Mt. San Antonio Coll. 1965; BS, mech. eng., West Coast Univ. 1974, BS, elec. eng., 1974, 1 yr. postgrad work at Cal Poly, Pomona in mech. eng. 1981; granted life time Secret clearance by US DOD Chief Mil. Tribunal, Wash. DC, 1984. Career: elec. engr. General Dynamics, Pomona 1959-73; elec. engr. USN, Corona 1974-75: uncovered and reported flaws in the USN AN/DSM-75 test equipt. (used to verify flt. worthiness of navy's prin. surface-to-air missile) as reported in NBC-TV documentary 3/75 w. the late Don Harris chief NBC Network News; elec. engr. Metron Corp., Upland 1975-78; sys. analyst Chemsult A.G., Dhahran, Saudi Arabia 1978-79; lead engr./sr. mem. tech. staff TRW Inc. Ballistic Missiles Div., Norton AFB, San Bernardino 1980-, prin. systems design engr. for the Peacekeeper (MX) Missile guidance and control sect., automatic test equipt. for 3d gen. gyroscopes, specific force integration receivers, missile electronic computer assemblies, inertial measurement units and missile guidance and control sets; pres. Howell Eng. Co., Bryn Mawr 1963-; awards: for service asst. football coach, City of Chino Pop Warner Football Assn. 1969; mem. Soc. of Automotive Engrs., IEEE, Am. Soc. Mech. Engrs., The Fibonacci Assn., Assn. of Old Crows, Harley Owners Gp., H.O.G. San Bdo., Am. Motorcyclists Assn., Nat. DeSoto Club, San Bdo. Co. Mus. Assn., Am. Brotherhood Aimed towards Edn., Chrysler Perf. Parts Assn., Calif. Astrology Assn.; donor of ancient Arabian antiquities to San Bdo. Co. Mus., UCLA Dept. of Geology, and Big Bear Valley Hist. Soc.; author: Automotive Engine Piston, Connecting Rod, and Crank Dynamics; Engineering Notes on Piston Displacement Motion, Displacement Motion Velocity, Displacement Motion Acceleration; num. original works on math. & engring.; mil: sgt. USAF 1955-59, GCM, Nat. Defense Svc., AF Longevity Svc.; Republican (state, nat. party, Nat. Fedn. Rep. Women, Nat. Rep. Senatl. Com.); Presbyterian; rec: high performance big block Pontiac wedge, Oldsmobile wedge and Chrysler Corp. Hemi Automotive engineering, theater pipe organ, power lifting, hist. of U.S. steam locomotives. Res: 1125-6B Pine Ave Redlands 92373 Ofc: TRW, Inc., SB2/1052 606 E Mill St San Bernardino 92408

HOYE, WALTER BRISCO, consultant, retired community college district administrator; b. May 19, 1930, Lena, Miss.; s. William H. and LouBertha (Stewart) H.; m. Vida M. Pickens, Aug. 28, 1954; children: Walter B. II, JoAnn M.; edn: BA, Wayne State Univ., 1953. Career: sports, and auto editor Detroit Tribune, 1958-65; sports editor Mich. Chronicle, 1965-68; assoc. dir. pub. relations San Diego Chargers Football Co., 1968-76; media liason NFL, 1972-75; staff ofcr. San Diego Co!l. Dist., 1976-92: community services ofcr. 1976-78, placement ofcr./adminstrv. asst. 1982-83, supr. Placement and Program Support 1983-89, supr. Program Support Services 1989-92, ret.; indep. consultant, 1992-; honors: San Diego County citizen of month 5/79, award of merit United Way 1974; mem: Am. Personnel and Guidance Assn., San Diego Career Guidance Assn., Nat. Mgmt. Assn., Assn. Calif. Community Coll. Adminstrs., Calif. Community Coll. Placement Assn., Internat. Assn. of Auditorium Mgrs.; civic: Am. Red Cross San Diego County (bd.), San Diego Conv. and Tourist Bur., Joint Ctr. Political Studies, San Diego Urban League, Neighborhood Housing Assn., Public Access TV. Res: 6959 Ridge Manor Ave San Diego 92120-3146

HOYT, GEORGE WASHINGTON, newspaper publishing co. president; b. Mar. 26, 1936, Portland, Ore.; s. George W. and Isabell (Murray) H.; m. Joanne, Sept. 1, 1960 (div. 1980); m. Colleen, Apr. 24, 1982; children: Brian Scott b. 1963, Mark b. 1965; edn: BA, Willamette Univ., 1958; MBA, Univ. Oreg., 1963; OPM pgm. Harvard Bus. Sch., 1989. Career: gen. mgr. Times Publications, Beaverton, Oreg. 1963-71; pres./pub. Pioneer Press, Wilmette, Ill. 1971-78; pub./v.p. Washington Star, W.D.C. 1978-81; prodn. dir. Time Inc., N.Y. 1981-85; pres. and c.o.o. Lesher Communications, Inc. Walnut Creek, Calif. 1985-91; pres. San Gabriel Valley Publishing Co., West Covina 1992-; instr. advt., pub. rels. Pacific Univ., Forest Grove, Oreg. 1964-66; mem. Suburban Newspapers of Am. (pres. 1978-79), Calif. Newspaper Publishers Assn. (dir. 1986-88, 1992-); civic bds: San Gabriel Valley Consortium of Commerce & Cities (treas. 1992-93), Contra Costa Taxpayers Assn. (exec. com. 1986-), Contra Costa Co. Exec. Council 1988-, Willamette Univ. (trustee 1989-), United Way Campaign Contra Costa (chmn. 1991-92), Nat. Capital Council

BSA (dir. 1980-81), Cultural Alliance W.D.C. (pres. 1981), Federal City Council W.D.C. (exec. com. 1979-81), Greater W.D.C. Board of Trade (exec. com. 1979-81), Found. for Creative Space W.D.C. (dir. 1980-81); author (newspaper tabloid sect.) Vietnam & Cambodia (1988); mil: E5 sgt. AUS 1958-59; Republican. Res: 216 Lone Hill Rd Glendora 91740 Ofc: San Gabriel Valley Publishing Co. 1210 Azusa Canyon Rd West Covina 91790

HSU, CHIEH SU, engineering professor; b. May 27, 1922, Soochow, Kiangsu, China, naturalized U.S., 1961; s. Chung Yu and Yong Feng (Wu) H.; m. Helen Yung-Feng Tse, Mar. 28, 1953; children: Raymond b. 1954, Katherine b. 1960; edn: grad. Nat. Inst. of Technology, Chungking, China 1945; MS, Stanford Univ., 1948, PhD, 1950. Career: engr. Shanghai Naval Dockyard and Engineering Works, Shanghai, China 1946-47; res. asst. Stanford Univ., Calif. 1948-51; engr. IBM Corp., Poughkeepsie, N.Y. 1951-55; assoc. prof. Univ. of Toledo, Ohio 1955-58; assoc. prof. UC Berkeley, Calif. 1958-64, prof. engring. 1964-, chair div. applied mechanics, 1969-70; tech. editor J. of Applied Mechanics, 1976-82; assoc. ed. 8 profl. journals, 1971-, appt. US Nat. Com. on Theoretical and Applied Mechanics, NAS, 1985-89; sci. advy. bd. Alexander von Humboldt Found., Germany 1985-; awards: Westinghouse Postgrad. fellow Stanford Univ. 1948-50, John Simon Guggenheim fellow, N.Y., N.Y. 1964-65, Miller Rsch. Prof., UC Berkeley 1973-74, centennial award ASME(1980, Alexander von Humboldt Sr. U.S. Scientist Award 1986; mem: ASME (Fellow 1977), Am. Acad. o Mechanics (Fellow 1980), U.S. Nat. Acad. of Engring. (elected mem. 1988), Academia Sinica R.O.C. (elected mem. 1990); author: Cell-to-Cell Mapping (1987), 96+ sci. papers (1951-). Ofc: Dept. Mech. Engring. TM01 Univ. California, Berkeley 94720

HSU, SHU-DEAN, hematologist-oncologist; b. Feb. 21, 1943, Chiba, Japan, came to U.S. 1972; parents: Tetzu and Takako (Koo) Minoyama; m. San-San Hsu, Mar. 3, 1973; children: Deborah Te-Lan, Peter Jie-Te; edn: MD, Taipei Med. Coll., Taiwan 1968; diplomate Am. Bd. Internal Medicine, Am. Bd. Hematology, Am. Bd. Med. Oncology. Career: asst. in medicine Mt. Sinai Sch. Med., N.Y.C., 1975-77; asst. instr. medicine Univ. Texas, Galveston, 1977-78; lectr. Texas A&M Univ., also chief hematology and oncology VA Med. Ctr., Temple, Tx., 1978-80; asst. prof. medicine Univ. Ark., Little Rock, 1980-83; pvt. practice splst. hematology-oncology Visalia Med. Clinic, Visalia, Calif. 1983-; Fellow ACP, mem. N.Y. Acad. Scis., Am. Soc. Clin. Oncology, Am. Soc. Hematology, Calif. Med. Assn., Tulare County Med. Soc.; club: Visalia Racquet. Res: 3500 W Hyde Visalia 93291 Ofc: Visalia Medical Clinic 5400 W Hillsdale Visalia 93291

HU, STEVE SENG-CHIU, research executive/college president; b. Mar. 16, 1922, Yangchou, Kiangsu Province, China; s. Yubin and Shuchang (Lee) H.; m. Lily Li-wan Liu; children: April b. 1962, Yendo b. 1963, Victor b. 1964; edn: BS, Chiao-Tung Univ., Shanghai 1939; MS, Rensselaer Polytech. Inst. 1940; DSc, Mass. Inst. of Tech. 1942. Career: tech dir. Douglas Aircraft's China Aircraft/China Motor Pgms., Calif. & N.J. 1943-48; tech. dir. Kelley Eng. Co., N.Y. & Ariz. 1949-54; sys. engr./meteorology spec. RCA Corp., Ariz. 1955-58; cons. gas dynamics Aerojet Gen. Corp. 1958-59; research scientist Jet Propulsion Lab., Calif. Inst. Tech. 1960-61; tech. dir. Northrop Corp. & Northrop Space Labs., Ala. 1961-72; pres. Univ. of Am. United Research Inst., and Am. Technical Coll., Calif. & Taiwan 1973-; dir. Century Research Inc., Gardena 1973-; nat. dir./exec. v.p. Am. Astronautical Soc., Wash. DC 1963-71; ed. AAS Proceedings of Missiles & Aerospace Vehicle Scis.; prof., part-time, Univ. Ariz. 1957-58, USC 1959-63, 1968-71, Univ. of Ala. 1963-68, Auburn Univ. 1964-66, CSU 1968-71; awards: Salisbury Prize & Sloan Prize, M.I.T. 1942; Merit Cert. & cash award, Commn. of Aeronautical Affairs, Repub. of China 1945; Merit Cert. & cash award for sci. achiev. & dynamic leadership, Northrop/NASA Space Labs. 1966; mem: Am. Astronautical Soc., Inst. of Aeronautics & Astronautics; Nat. Assn. of Tech. Schs.; works: tech. dir. Northrop/NASA Electronic Guidance Sys. for Lunar Landing Vehicle Pgms. 1963-68; author: Theory of Guidance/Control and Optimization of Tactical/Strategic Missiles and Aerospace Vehicles, pub. Univ. of Ala./Century Research Inc. 1969, 73; rec: opera music, dancing, travel. Res: 6491 Saddle Dr. Long Beach 90815 Ofc: Century Research Bldg. 16935 S Vermont Ave Gardena 90247

HUBBARD, CHARLES RONALD, corporate programs executive; b. Feb. 4, 1933, Weaver, Ala.; s. John Duncan and Athy Pauline (Lusk) H.; m. Betty McKleroy, Dec. 29, 1951; 1 son: Charles Ronald II, b. 1957; edn: BSEE, Univ. of Ala. 1960. Career: engr./ mktg. & pgm. mgr. Sperry Corp., Huntsville, Ala., 1960-71; sect. head 1971-74; sr. staff engr. Honeywell, Inc., Clearwater, Fla. 1974-76; mgr. 1976-79; chief engr., Honeywell, Inc., West Covina, Calif. 1979-82, assoc. dir. engring. 1982-84, assoc. dir. Advanced Systems 1984-88, v.p. govt. systems div. Integrated Inference Machines, Anaheim, 1988-91; pres. Synergy Computer Systems, Anaheim 1991-; dir. S&H Office Supplies, Huntsville, Ala. 1972-74; awards: recipient Outstanding Fellow Award, Univ. of Ala. Dept. of Electrical Engring.; mem: IEEE (Govt. Rels. Com.,sect. chmn.); publs: Saturn V/ Apollo and Beyond, Am. Astronautical Soc., 1967; mil: USAF 1953-57; Methodist; rec: jogging, golf. Res: 5460 Willowick Cir Anaheim 92807

HUBER, COLLEEN ADLENE, artist, business owner; b. Mar. 30, 1927, Concordia, Kans.; d. Claude Irvin and Freda Isabel (Trow) Baker; m. Wallace Charles Huber, Oct. 18, 1945 (dec. Oct. 20, 1992); children: Wallace b. 1947, Shawn b. 1948, Devron b. 1951, Candace b. 1953, Melody b. 1955; edn: instr. cert., graphic art, UCLA, 1974-76; BA in art/ communication, CalPoly, Pomona 1983. Career: co-owner/artist Rocket Express Publication, Garden Grove, 1955-58, ad agy. Huber Art & Advt., Garden Grove, 1958-68, Orange 1970-81; sketch artist Walt Disney Prodns., Burbank 1958-59; art director Gray Pub. Corp., Fullerton 1968-76; tchr. graphic art North Orange County Sch. Dist., La Palma 1974-76; magazine publisher: Community Woman (mo.) 1976-79, Objet D'Art (art mag.) 1976-77;.graphic artist, designer Baker Graphics, East San Diego Mag., Rancho San Diego, 1978-88; Shoppers Guide, Upland 1979-81; Bargain Bulletin, Fallbrook 1981-82; Van Zyen Pub., Fallbrook 1982-83; instr. Camp Fire Inc., Orange 1990-91; owner/artist Coco Bien Objet D'Art, Laguna Beach, 1986-; tchr. art fundamentals, City of Lake Elsinore; awards: tchg. awards No. Orange County R.O.P., La Palma 1976-77, Marie Antoinette Viking, Am. Pen Women O.C. 1980, photo journ. 2d pl. state Calif. Press Women 1981, 2d pl. printmaking Upland Art Assn. 1985, 3d pl. printmaking Rancho Cucamonga Fest. 1985, 1st pl. painting Temecula Chamber Wine & Balloon Fest. 1987; mem. Calif. Press Women (O.C. pres. 1986-87), Laguna Niguel Art Assn., Costa Mesa Art Assn., Laguna Beach C.of C. (docent Gallery Night 1988), Anaheim C.of C., Zonta Intl. (Newport Beach v.p. 1990-91); author: Gail (1980); Republican; R.Cath.; rec: dancing. Ofc: Coco Bien Objet D'Art PO Box 5092 Laguna Beach 92651

HUCKABEE, PHYLLIS, gas industry professional; b. Aug. 11, 1963, Andrews, Tx.; d. Tommie Jack and Sylvia (Wingo) H.; edn: BBA in fin., Texas Tech. Univ., Lubbock 1984, MBA, 1986. Career: loan escrow clk. First Federal Savings, Lubbock, Tx. 1984; mgmt. tng. pgm. El Paso (Tx.) Natural Gas, 1986-87, analyst rate dept. 1987-88, specialist, then representative Calif. Affairs, San Francisco, 1988-92; asst. dir. Cambridge Energy Research Associates, Oakland 1992-; mem: Women Energy Assocs. (bd. 1990-), Pacific Coast Gas Assn. 1988-92, Internat. Assn. for Energy Economics (1990-), Berkeley Architectural Heritage Assn.; civic: Performing Arts Workshop, S.F. (bd. 1990-92, advy. bd. 1992-), El Paso Comm. Concerts Assn. (bd. 1988), Business Volunteers for the Arts S.F. 1989, volunteer E. Bay Habitat for Humanity; Democrat; Methodist; rec: photography. Res: 1721 McGee St Berkeley 94703 Ofc: Cambridge Energy Research Associates 1999 Harrison Ste 1440 Oakland 94612

HUDNUT, F. VERNON, aerospace engineer; b. June 25, 1936, Portland, Oreg.; s. Forrest V. and Evelyn May (Lytle) H.; m. Sophie Kwiatkowski, June 16, 1968; children: Steven b. 1970, David b. 1972; edn: BSME, Oregon St. Univ., Corvallis 1958; MS, Univ. Utah, S.L.C., 1965; reg. profl. engr. Calif. (1975-). Career: test engr., project engr. USAF Test Center, Edwards AFB 1958-66; sr. engr. Northrop Corp., Hawthorne 1966-70; cons., Hawthorne 1970-71; gen. engr. Naval Weapons Center, China Lake 1971-78; materials engr., aerospace engr., AFPRO/LMSC, Sunnyvale 1978-87; resident SRM & QA rep., Hubble Space Telescope, NASA/MSFC Resident Office 1987-90; resident assurance mgr., Space Station, NASA/LeRC Resident Office, 1990-; awards: Univ. Utah Tchg. Assistantship 1964-65, Thesis grant 1965; mem: ASME, NSPE, CSPE, ASSE (com. chmn. 1986-88), Masons, Sr. DeMolay (Legion of Honor; Chevalier; PMC; RD; BHK; Advy. Coun. 1960-66; chapt. advr. 1961-62); author Computer Registration (1965), tech. papers pub. (1962-); Republican; Eastern Orthodox Christian; rec: ferroequinology, model railroads. Res: 19971 Lindenbrook Ln Cupertino 95014 Ofc: NASA/LeRC Resident Office POB 3504 Sunnyvale 94088

HUDSON, CHRISTOPHER JOHN, publisher; b. June 8, 1948, Watford, England, came to U.S. 1971; s. Joseph Edward and Gladys Jenny Patricia (Madgwick) H.; m. Lois Jeanne Lyons, June 16, 1979; children: Thomas b. 1959, Ellen b. 1960, Ronald b. 1964, Timothy b. 1966; edn: BA (hons.), Cambridge Univ., 1969, MA (hons.), 1972. Career: promotion mgr. Prentice-Hall Internat., Hemel Hempstead, U.K. 1969-70, area mgr. (U.K., France) 1970-71, mktg. mgr./ dir. mktg./ asst. v.p., Englewood Cliffs, N.J. 1971-76; group internat. dir. ITT Publishing, N.Y., N.Y. 1976-77; pres. Focal Press Inc., N.Y.C., mem. bd. Focal Press Ltd., London, Eng. 1977-82; publisher (journal) Aperture, and v.p. Aperture Found., 1983-86; head of publs. J. Paul Getty Trust, Los Angeles 1986-, pub. J. Paul Getty Museum Jour., 1986-; awards: distinction, merit awards Am. Assn. of Museums (1987, 88), book & journal awards Assn. of Am. Univ. Presses N.Y. (1989, 90, 92),Excellence in Pub. award Assn. of Am. Pubs. 1992, merit award Bookbuilders West, S.F. (1990, 91), publs. award Am. Fedn. of the Arts (1990, 91), we. book award Rounce & Coffin Club (1992,93); mem: Internat. Publishers Assn. 1987-, Internat. Assn. Scholarly Publishers 1988-, US Museums Pub. Group N.Y. (chmn. 1989-),Internat. Assn. of Mus. Publishers Frankfurt, Ger. (steering com. 1989-, chmn 1992-93), Assn. of Am. Publishers N.Y. (trade with Ea. Europe com. 1976-79, intl. fairs com. 1986-88), Hellenic Soc. (London, 1967-), Oxford & Cambridge Club (London), Nat. Heritage Village Kioni, Greece (advy. coun. 1991-); author: Guide to International Book Fairs, 1976; rec: rural preservation projects in Europe & U.S. Ofc: J. Paul Getty Museum 17985 PCH Malibu 90265

HUFF, NORMAN NELSON, computer consultant, educator; b. Apr. 22, 1933, San Diego; s. Cmdr. George Peabody Huff (USN ret.) and Norma Rose (Nelson) Demetz; m. Sharon Kay Lockwood, Sept. 1980; edn: BS chem. engr., Univ. San Diego 1957; Masters Tech. Cert., UCLA 1969-72; MBA, Golden Gate Univ. 1972; cultural doctorate in computer sci., 1987; lic. Profl. Engr. (chem.) Calif. 1958. Career: deep sea salvage ofcr., petroleum engr., CALCO, Venice, Louisiana 1950-51; research chemical/ astrophysics engr. Gen. Dynamics Convair, San Diego 1955-56; entomologist insp. State of Calif. 1956; chem. engr., field surveyor US Gypsum, El Centro 1957-58; USAF 1958-67; pilot, flight test ofcr., fighter pilot, quality control, maint. ofcr., chief of maint., nuclear weapons ofcr., tng. ofcr., pub. relations ofcr.; system programmer, State of Calif.; system programmer Pfizer Inc., Victorville 1972; lectr., dept. chmn. computer sci., pres. Tumbleweed Tech. Inst., Victorville 1967-88; p.t. lectr. Golden Gate Univ. and Chapman Coll., 1972-74; p.t. instr. Inst. des Affaires Internationales, St. Leger, France and World Univ. for Intercultural Studies, Sofia, Bulgaria 1988-; cons. finl. trusts; ednl. critic, trustee, treas. World Univ., Bensom, Ariz. 1989-; honors: Instr. of Year 1968, fellowship 1972 Tumbleweed Tech. Inst., VFW shooting award 1951, athletic awards in swimming, tennis, track, wrestling, shooting, mil. aerial combat 1949-65, Presdl. achievement award, Presdl. medal of merit 1982, 83; mem: Nat. Advy. Bd., Am. Security Council, US Congressional Advy. Bd.; Calif. Bus. Edn. Assn. 1969-73, Inst. of Aero Sci. (pres. 1956-57), Calif. Edn. Computing Consortium (bd., chmn. engring. 1979-86), Internat. Platform Assn., Nat. Rifle Assn., Internat. Biographical Assn. (life patron), Soaring Soc. of Am. (life); author 5 computer sci. texts; contbr. articles in chem., engr. jours. 1957; patent on Fusion Engine Application for Space Travel (Lockheed Aircraft Corp., 1976); mil: USNAR 1950-53, USAFR 1953-57, capt. USAF 1957-67, decorated Air Medal; R.Cath.; rec: viticulture, writing, model bldg., skiing.

HUGHES, CHARLES WILSON, university purchasing executive; b. May 3, 1946, Greenville, Ky.; s. Clifton J. and Christine Vive (Critzer) H.; m. Daniele Kay Martin, Oct. 6, 1973; children: Charles b. 1975, Jennifer b. 1977; edn: BS, Univ. of Tenn., Martin 1967; JD, Univ. Tenn., Knoxville 1971; admitted bar: Tenn. 1971. Career: served to Major US Army (Ret.) 1971-91, meritorious svc. awards 1975, 81, 83, 91: logistics ofcr. Pusan Garrison, Korea 1973-75; chief contract ops. Def. Plant Office, Woodland Hills, Calif. 1976-81; dir. indsl. ops. Wuerzburg MILCOM, Ger. 1981-83; chief ops. Program Mgr. Tank Sys., Warren, Mich. 1983-86; chief contract adminstrn. Def. Contract Adminstrn. Svs., El Segundo, Calif. 1986-90; dir. purchasing CSU Long Beach, 1991-, guest lectr. CSULB 1992; indep. cons. Hughes Assocs., Garden Grove 1989-; awards: merit BSA El Capitan Dist., Garden Grove 1989, silver beaver BSA Orange County 1989, achiev. Junior Achievement, Costa Mesa 1981, achiev. Am. Logistics Assn. Ft. Lee, Va. 1973, 75; mem.: Calif. Assn. Pub. Purchasing Ofcls. 1991-, Nat. Assn. Ednl. Buyers 1991-, Nat. Contract Mgmt. Assn. (1976-, v.p. 1977-78), Marne Assn. 1981-, Retired Ofcrs. Assn. 1991-, Masons (Kts. of Malta), DCAS Computer Users Gp., El Segundo (pres. 1986-88); scoutmaster BSA Troop 147, Garden Grove 1987-92, dist. commr. Orange County 1988-90; publs: articles in trade and profl. jours. (1967-), editor Collection of Poems (1976); Republican; Baptist; rec: stamps and coins, tennis, golf. Res: 10072 Roselee Dr Garden Grove 92640-1826 Ofc: CSU Long Beach 1250 Bellflower Blvd Long Beach 90840-0123

HUGHES, JUDITH MARKHAM, professor of history; b. Feb. 20, 1941, N.Y.C.; d. Sanford H. and Sylvia (Kovner) Markham; m. H. Stuart Hughes, Mar. 26, 1964; 1 son, David; edn: BA (high hons.), Swarthmore Coll., 1962; MA, Harvard Univ., 1963, PhD, 1970. Career: tchg. fellow Harvard Univ. 1965-66, 67-70, asst. prof. social studies, 1970-75; assoc. prof. UC San Diego, 1975-84, prof. history, 1984-; awards: Phi Beta Kappa 1962, Woodrow Wilson fellow 1962-63, Harvard Univ. tuition scholar 1963-64, West European Studies fellow 1972-73, NEH fellow 1974, UC San Diego Acad. Senate grantee 1978, 80, 82, 85, 86, 89, 92; mem.: Am. Hist. Assn., N.Am. Conf. on British Studies, Group for Use of Psychology in History, Assn. Intl. d'Histoire de la Psychanalyse (mem. corr.), We. Assn. of Women Historians (article prize com. 1985); author: To the Maginot Line: The Politics of French Military Preparation in the 1920's (Harvard Univ. Press, 1971), Emotion and High Politics: Personal Relations at the Summit in Late 19th C. Brit. and Ger. (UC Press, 1983), Reshaping the Psychoanalytic Domain: The Work of Melanie Klein, W.R.D. Fairbairn, and D.W. Winnicott (UC Press, 1989), Freud: Mapping an Unconscious Domain (in progress). Res: 8531 Ave de las Ondas La Jolla 92037 Ofc: UCSD Dept. History, 0104, 9500 Gilman Dr La Jolla 92093-0104 Ph: 619/534-1996

HUMPHREY, JO ANN, nurse, educator, administrator, executive; b. July 29, 1937, Missoula, Mont.; d. Henry Albert and Wanda Alene (Anderson) Dray; m. John Francis Humphrey; children: Robb b. 1961, Rand b. 1969; grandchildren: Joshua b. 1991, Dalton b. 1991, Kaitlyn b. 1993; edn: BSN, R.N., Columbia Univ., 1960; MS in nsg. edn., Univ. of Wash., 1969; clin. psychology, U.S. International Univ. Career: faculty, Brigham Young Univ., Provo, Utah; faculty, San Diego St. Univ., dir. nursing, Heartland Comm. Hosp., S.D.; consultant Coordinating Council for Edn. in Health Sciences for San Diego and Imperial Counties; instr. Southwestern Comm. Coll.; founding mem., exec. dir. Assn. for Holistic Health, San Diego; researcher Cassel Psychology Center, Chula Vista and NCRD and Naval Research Center, San Diego; official guest for health care & edn. of govts. of Japan, China, Taiwan, Korea, Philippines, Singapore; current: adminstr. Acad. for Holistic Edn., S.D.; chief exec. ofcr. Custom Box and Packaging Corp., S.D. (founded, 1959); mem. San Diego Co. Self-Esteem Task Force, S.D. Nurses' Assn. (chair by laws comm.), Columbia Univ. Alumni Assn., BYU Alumni Assn., Univ. Wash. Alumni Assn.; listed Who's Who in Calif., 1991, Who's Who in Psychophysiology; publs: Holistic Health... What Is It? and The Holistic Health Practitioner... What Standards Set Him Apart?; Autogenics for Execs: Wellness Attainment with Diagnostic Assessment and Autogenics for Neuro Self Regulation; civic: vol. hostess, S.D. Mormon Temple tours; tchr. S.E. Asian refugees; poll worker; Republican; Ch. of Jesus Christ of Latter-day Saints; rec: modeling, piano, reading, computers. Res: 8263 Camino Del Oro #272 La Jolla 92037 Ofc: Custom Packaging Corp. 4748 Old Cliffs Rd San Diego 92037

HUNTER, JAMES GALBRAITH, JR., lawyer; b. Jan. 6, 1942, Phila.; s. James Galbraith and Emma Margaret (Jehl) H.; m. Pamela Ann (Trott), July 18, 1969 (div.); children: James b. 1973, Catherine b. 1978; m. 2d. Nancy (Scheurwater) H., June 21, 1993; edn: BS in eng. sci., Case Inst. of Tech. 1965; JD, Univ. Chgo. 1967; admitted to Ill. State Bar 1967, Calif. State Bar 1980, US Supreme Ct. 1979, US Cts. of Appeals for the 7th (1967), 4th (1978), 9th (1978), 5th (1982) and Federal 1982 Circuits, US Claims Ct. 1976, US Dist. Cts. Ill. (No., 1967, Central, 1980) and Calif. (So., 1980, Cent., 1980, and No., 1982). Career: atty. ptnr. Hedlund, Hunter & Lynch, Chgo. 1976-82; Latham & Watkins, Hedlund, Hunter & Lynch, 1982-84; ptnr. Latham & Watkins, Los Angeles 1982-, and Chgo. 1984-; mem. ABA, Chgo. Bar Assn., Calif. St. Bar Assn., L.A. Cty. Bar Assn., Metropolitan Club, Chgo. Athletic Assn.; honors: exec. editor Univ. Chgo. Law Rev. 1966-67; mil: lt. USNR 1968-70, Navy Commendn. with combat distg. device, Vietnamese Cross of Gall. with Palm, Vietnam Service, Vietnam Campaign, Nat. Def. Service medals. Ofcs: Latham & Watkins, 633 West Fifth St Los Angeles 90071; 5800 Sears Tower Chicago IL 60606

HUNTER, PAMELA TOMPKINS, public relations counselor; b. Sept. 25, 1948, San Luis Obispo; d. Edgar Logan and Hazel (Herrington) Tompkins; m. Ralph Edward Hunter, Feb. 15, 1979 (div. 1980); edn: Bakersfield Coll.; Coll. of San Mateo; Canada Coll.; UC Berkeley. Career: tchr. Casa de Adobe, San Mateo 1970-73; curriculum planner Napa Coll., Napa 1973-74; editor, writer Scripps League 1974-78; freelance writer, publicist 1976-79; pub. rels., St. Helena and San Francisco 1979-; awards: Assn. Family Physicians writing award; mem: Calif. Farm Bureau, S.F. Food Profls., Les Dames d'Escoffier (v.p. S.F. 1989), Agri. Rels. Council; jour. articles pub.; Democrat. Res: 1969 Yountville Crossroad Yountville 94599 Ofc: Hunter Public Relations 1345 Railroad Ave St Helena 94574

HURLEY, JAMES WILLIAM, financial executive; b. July 4, 1939, St. Cloud, Minn.; s. James Warren and Margaret Caroline (Kapphahn) H.; m. Kathleen Ann Krol, Aug. 26, 1978; children: Rory b. 1982, Jill b. 1984; edn: BS, So. Ill. Univ., 1967; MBA, Northwestern Univ., 1974; C.P.A., Ill. Career: senior auditor Arthur Andersen & Co., Chgo. 1968-72; mgr. taxes Oak Industries Inc., Crystal Lake, Ill. 1972-74; asst. treas. Trans Union Corp., Lincolnshire, Ill. 1974-82; dir. of finance Comdial Technology, Sunnyvale, Calif. 1982-85; dir. fin. reporting DFS Group Ltd., San Francisco 1985-87; consulting prin., Fremont 1987-88; controller KTI Chemicals Inc., Sunnyvale 1988-92; chief financial ofcr. Startech Semiconductor, Inc., Sunnyvale 1993-; mem. Calif. Soc. CPA. Res: 194 Viento Dr Fremont 94536 Ofc: Startech Semiconductor, Inc. 1219 Bordeaux Drive Sunnyvale 94089

HURT, ROBERT GLENN, securities executive, ret.; b. Jan. 31, 1919, Pasadena; s. Dr. Leslie M. (past pres. AVMA) and Effie Mae (McKim) H.; edn: AB, USC, 1940; postgrad. Harvard Bus. Sch. 1941. Career: trainee Calvin Bullock, Ltd., NYC 1946; asst. to west coast head, L.A. 1946-49; northern div. head, 1949-53; resident and sr. v.p. Calvin Bullock, Ltd., San Francisco 1954-87; honors: Order of Ky. Colonels; mem. Alpha Delta Sigma, Phi Kappa Psi, USC Pres. Circle, Am. Legion, Reserve Officers Assn.; clubs: Andreas Canyon, Harvard, City (S.F.), Engineers (S.F.), Commercial (S.F.), Stock Exchange (L.A.); mil: pvt. to col. US Army Infantry 1941-46; comdr. Mil. Order of World Wars; R.Cath. Res: 937 Ashbury St San Francisco 94117

HUSKEY, HARRY DOUGLAS, computer scientist, professor emeritus; b. Jan. 19, 1916, Whittier, N.C.; s. Cornelius and Myrtle (Cunningham) H.; m. Velma E. Roeth, Jan. 2, 1939 (dec. Jan. 1991); children: Carolyn b. 1941, Roxanne b. 1943, Harry Jr. b. 1952, Linda b. 1958; edn: BS, Univ. Idaho, 1937; MA, Ohio State Univ., 1940, PhD, 1943. Career: instr. Univ. of Pa., Phila. 1943-46; temp. principal sci. ofcr. Nat. Phy. Labs, Teddington, Middlesex, England 1947; hd. machine devel. lab. Nat. Bur. Standards, 1948; assoc. dir. Inst. for Numerical Anal., L.A. 1948-54; assoc. dir. computation lab., prof. Wayne Univ., Detroit 1952-53; assoc. prof. UC Berkeley, 1954-58, prof. 1958-67; prof. info. and computer sci. UC Santa Cruz, 1967-86, prof. emeritus 1986-; cons. Bendix Computer Div., L.A. 1954-63; vis. prof. IIT/K, Kampur, UP, India 1963-64, 1972; appt. advy. panel USN, W.D.C. 1968-75, cons. on computers for developing countries UN, 1969-71, project coord. UNESCO, Rangoon, Burma 1980-85; awards: dis-

tinguished alumni Idaho State Univ. 1978, computer pioneer Nat. Computer Conf. 1978, IEEE Computer Soc. 1982, US senior scientist Fulbright-Alexander von Humboldt Found., Mathematisches Institut der Tech. Univ. Munich 1974-75, 25th Ann. medal ENIAC, inducted Univ. Idaho Alumni Hall of Fame, Moscow, Id. 1989; mem: AAAS (Fellow), IEEE Computer Soc. (Fellow, mem. 1950-, editorial bd., chief editor computer group 1965-71, Centennial award 1984), Brit. Computer Soc. (Fellow), Am. Math. Soc., Math. Assn. Am., Assn. Computing Machinery (pres. 1960-62), Am. Fedn. Info. Processing Socs. (governing bd. 1961-63), Sigma Xi; author: Computer Handbook (1960), 70+ research papers (1943-). Res: 656 High St Santa Cruz 95060

HUSKEY, HARRY DOUGLAS, computer scientist, professor emeritus; b. Jan. 19, 1916, Whittier, N.C.; s. Cornelius and Myrtle (Cunningham) H.; m. Velma E. Roeth, Jan. 2, 1939 (dec. Jan. 1991); children: Carolyn b. 1941, Roxanne b. 1943, Harry Jr. b. 1952, Linda b. 1958; edn: BS, Univ. Idaho, 1937; MA, Ohio State Univ., 1940, PhD, 1943. Career: instr. Univ. of Pa., Phila. 1943-46; temp. principal sci. ofcr. Nat. Phy. Labs, Teddington, Middlesex, England 1947; head machine devel. lab. Nat. Bur. Standards, 1948; assoc. dir. Inst. for Numerical Anal., L.A. 1948-54; assoc. dir. computation lab., prof. Wayne Univ., Detroit 1952-53; assoc. prof. UC Berkeley, 1954-58, prof. 1958-67; prof. info. and computer sci. UC Santa Cruz, 1967-86, prof. emeritus 1986-; cons. Bendix Computer Div., L.A. 1954-63; vis. prof. IIT/K, Kampur, UP, India 1963-64, 1972; appt. advy. panel USN, W.D.C. 1968-75; cons. on computers for developing countries UN, 1969-71, project coord. UNESCO, Rangoon, Burma 1980-85; awards: distinguished alumni Idaho State Univ. 1978, computer pioneer Nat. Computer Conf. 1978, IEEE Computer Soc. 1982, US senior scientist Fulbright-Alexander von Humboldt Found., Mathematisches Institut der Tech. Univ. Munich 1974-75, 25th Ann. medal ENIAC, inducted Univ. Idaho Alumni Hall of Fame, Moscow, Id. 1989; mem: AAAS (Fellow), IEEE Computer Soc. (Fellow, mem. 1950-, editorial bd., chief editor computer group 1965-71, Centennial award 1984), Brit. Computer Soc. (Fellow), Am. Math. Soc., Math. Assn. Am., Assn. Computing Machinery (pres. 1960-62), Am. Fedn. Info. Processing Socs. (governing bd. 1961-63), Sigma Xi; author: Computer Handbook (1960), 70+ research papers (1943-). Res: 656 High St Santa Cruz 95060

HUSSAIN, ANJUM, light manufacturing company owner; b. Aug. 12, 1962, Hyderabad, India; nat. 1985; s. Amjad and Syeada (Fatima) H.; edn: BA in management, San Jose, Calif. 1989. Career: quality engr. Karkar Electronics, S.F., Calif. 1983-87; quality engr. Opcom, San Jose 1987-88; quality engr. Lasersonics, San Jose 1988-89; founder/owner, International Computer Systems Printing, Stockton 1990-; chmn Am. Soc. for Quality Control #0604, S.F.; awards: Business of Year award, Mexican-American Chamber of Commerce, Stockton 1993; New Horizon of Year award, American Black Chamber, Stockton 1993; sr. mem. Am. Soc. for Quality Control, 1990-93; mem: Kiwanis 1993-, Greater C.of C. 1993-, Mexican-Am. C.of C. 1993-, African Am. C. of C. 1993-; editor, Health Awareness articles, 1993; publisher, health newsletter on Alcohol and Drug Prevention, 1993; Dawoodi Bohra Society. Res: 3011 Estate Dr Stockton 95209

HUTCHINSON, NANCY ANNE, educator; b. May 3, 1947, Peoria, Ill.; d. E. John and Alvina K. (Zeeck) Richardson; m. Bennett Buckley; children: Amy Ann; edn: BA, Illinois State Univ., 1969; MA, Abilene Christian Univ., 1975. Career: director Call for Help, Abilene, Tx. 1975-78; Methodist Service Ctr., 1978-79; social worker Brentwood Day Care, Austin, Tx. 1979-80; tchr. Cooper High Sch., Abilene, Tx. 1980-90; vis. prof. communication, Pepperdine Univ., Malibu 1990-; honors: Phi Delta Kappa, Delta Kappa Gamma, listed: Who's Who Am. Tchrs. 1992, Who's Who Am. Women 1993, Who's Who in West 1992; mem. AAUW, Junior League Abilene, Tx. 1974-; publs: articles in scholarly jours. (1983, 85); Democrat; Methodist. Res: 24303 Baxter Dr Malibu 90265

HUTCHISON, JOHN WILLIAM, software corporation president; b. Aug. 4, 1938, Long Beach; s. John and Margaret (Marshall) H.; m. Elaine W., Sept. 21, 1964; edn: BSBA, Long Beach St. Univ. 1966; MBA, Pepperdine Univ. 1986. Career: chief data processing City of Long Beach 1960-75; exec. v.p. Tone Software Corp., Anaheim 1975-86, pres. 1986-; awards: CDP; Republican; rec: flying. Res: 1477 Bryant Dr W, Long Beach 90804 Ofc: 1735 S Brookhurst Anaheim 92804

HUYSER, ROBERT ERNEST, executive, retired air force general; b. June 14, 1924, Paonia, Colo.; s. Wm. and Alma Madline (Davis) H.; m. Wanda, Nov. 15, 1942; children: Cheryl b. 1944, Christine b. 1956; edn: courses, Ouachita Baptist Coll. 1944, Modesto Jr. Coll. 1949; AA, So. Miss. Univ. 1955; grad. Air War Coll. 1963; Hon. Dr. of Laws, Univ. of Akron. Career: served to Gen. US Air Force 1943-1981: drafted buck pvt. Army Med. Corps 1943; transferred to Army Air Corps aviation cadet pgm., earned pilot wings and commd. 2d lt. Sept. 1944, command pilot (10,000 hours piloting aircraft from open cockpit to 3 times speed of sound, flew propeller, turbo prop and jet planes: trainers, airlift, fighters, tankers and bombers) combat missions in WWII, Korea and Vietnam; aircraft cmdr. to wing cmdr. S.A.C. 26 yrs., cmdr. 449th Bombardment Wing, Kincheloe AFB, Mich. 1966-68, dir. comand control/dep. chief of staff ops.,

Hqs. SAC, Offutt AFB, Neb. 1968-70, then dir. ops. plans/chief Single Integrated Operational Plans Div., Jt. Strategic Target Plnng. Staff, Hqs. SAC 1970-72; dep. chief of staff, plans and ops. Hqs. USAF, WDC 1972-75; named 4-Star General USAF, 1975 (highest rank in peacetime, 1st draftee to achieve 4-Star Gen. rank USAF); dep. cmdr. in chief U.S. European Command (under Gen. Alexander Haig), Stuttgart-Vaihingen, Ger. 1975-79; cmdr. in chief Military Airlift Command, Scott AFB, Ill. 1979-81, ret. 1981; advisor govts. on nat. defense systems, respons. for US fgn. mil. sales pgms. in 44+ countries in Europe, Middle East and Africa; personal presdl. envoy of Pres. Carter to Iran during final 31 days of the Shah's reign, Jan. 79; decorated Defence Disting. Service Medal (2), Legion of Merit, Bronze Star, Air Medal, Joint Svc. and Army Commendn. medals, AF Commendn. w/2 o.l.c., Presdl. Unit Citation emblem; awards from Republic of Korea and Fed. Republic Ger., 26 ribbons; currently pres./c.e.o. Four Star Ents. Inc., cons. Boeing Co.; Proclamations from 22 State Governors of for dedicated and superior svc. to country on retirement from active duty (7/1/81), letters from US Senators and Congressmen and num. city Mayors; premier Nat. Def. Transp. Assn. DoD award 1981, Silver Beaver award BSA, Geo. Washington honor medal Freedoms Found. Valley Forge 1982, Tennessee Ernie Ford award 1983; mem: No. Calif. Aero Club, Airlift Assn. (bd. chmn.), War Coll. Found. (trustee advy. bd.), Airmans Mem. Found. (bd. dirs.), Rotary, World Affairs Council, A.F. Assn.; mem. advy. bds: San Jose State Univ., San Francisco Univ., Air Univ.; nat. chmn. What's Good with America (patriotism pgm.); BSA Nat. Council (exec. bd.), Santa Clara Co. Scout Council (pres. 1983-84); author: Mission to Tehran (Harper and Row; Andre Deutsch, U.K., Ger., Italy); Republican; Prot.; rec: golf, fishing. Res: 6191 McAbee Rd San Jose 95120

HYNES, WILLIAM MARTIN, II, communications co. executive; b. Sept. 6, 1942, NY, NY; s. Wm. Martin and Norita Maria (Casey) H.; m. Elizabeth Cline, July 3, 1963; m. 2d. Elizabeth J Multer, Dec. 7, 1975; children: Shannon b. 1968, William b. 1978, Brian b. 1980, Casey b. 1983; edn: history major Farleigh Dickinson, 1963. Career: empl. AT&T, New York 1960-65; mgr. telecommunications ABC T.V., N.Y. 1965-78, dir. telecomms. 1978-85; exec. v.p. and c.o.o. Wold Communications, Los Angeles 1985-88; chief ops. ofcr. Stars West, 1988-91; pres. Pacific Syndication, 1991-; instr. New School, N.Y. 1985; awards: Emmy award NATAS 1984; mil: E5 AUS 1966-68; Republican; R.Cath.; rec: running/triathalon. Ofc: Pacific Syndication, 2829 W Burbank Blvd Burbank 91505

IACONO, JAMES MICHAEL, research center director; b. Dec. 11, 1925, Chgo., Ill.; s. Joseph and Angelina (Cutaia) I.; children: Lynn, Joseph, Michael, Rosemary; edn: BS, Loyola Univ., Chgo. 1950; MS, Univ. of Ill. 1952, PhD 1954. Career: chief, Lipid Nutrition Lab Nutrition Inst., ARS, USDA, Beltsville, Md. 1970-75, dep. asst. admin., National Pgm. ARS, USDA, WDC 1975-77, assoc. adminstr. Office of Human Nutrition 1978-82, dir. Western Human Nutrition Res. Ctr., ARS, USDA, San Francisco 1982-; adj. prof. nutrition UCLA 1987-; award: res. career devel. award Nat. Inst. of Health 1964-70; mem: Am. Inst. of Nutr., Am. Soc. of Clinical Nutr., Am. Oil Chemists Soc., Am. Heart Assn. (fellow), Am. Inst. of Chemists (fellow); author 120+ chapters in books, res. & technical papers in fields of nutrition and biochemistry, lipids; mil: served U.S. Army 1944-46. Res: 480-1 Pointe Pacific Dr Daly City 94014 Ofc: Western Human Nutrition Research Center, USDA-ARS POB 29997 San Francisco 94129

IAMELE, RICHARD THOMAS, law librarian; b. Jan. 29, 1942, Newark, N.J.; s. Armando Anthony and Evelyn (Coladonato) I.; m. Marilyn Ann Berutto, Aug. 21, 1965; children: Thomas b. 1966, Ann Marie b. 1968; edn: BA, Loyola Univ., 1963, MSLS, USC, 1967, JD, Southwestern Univ. Sch. of Law, 1976; admitted bar: Calif., 1977. Career: cataloger Univ. So. Calif., L.A. 1967-71; asst. cataloger L.A. County Law Library, 1971-77, asst. reference librarian 1977-78, asst. librarian 1978-80, library director 1980-; mem: Am. Bar Assn. 1980-, Calif. State Bar 1977-, Calif. Library Assn. 1980-, Am. Assn. of Law Libraries 1971-, Coun. of Calif. County Law Librarians 1980-, So. Calif. Assn. of Law Libraries 1971-. Ofc: L.A. Co. Law Library 301 W First St Los Angeles 90012

IBA, SHOZO, physician, radiologist, ret.; b. Nov. 10, 1918, Los Angeles; s. Kennosuke and Sumie (Misumi) I.; m. Margaret; children: Nadine S. b. 1955, Diane A. b. 1956, Lynn E. b. 1957, Mylene M. b. 1958, Wayne S. b. 1959, Elaine M. b. 1961; edn: AB, USC 1940; MS, 1941; MD, Boston Univ. Sch. Med. 1945; cert. Am. Bd. Radiology (1952). Career: intern Mt. Auburn Hosp., Cambridge Hosp., Mass. 1944-45; USPHS, N.Y. St. Hosp., Ray Brook, N.Y. 1946, staff 1947; resident, radiology City Hosp., Cleveland, Ohio 1948-51, asst. radiologist 1952; demonstrator, instr. Western Reserve Med. Sch. 1952; staff L.A. County Harbor Gen. Hosp., 1953-60; staff L.A. Cty. Long Beach General Hos. 1953-61; award: Rotary Club Internat. award; civic: Rotary Club (Huntington Park 1956-71), Civil Defense Com.; Republican; Prot. Address: Shozo Iba MD 27787 Rota Mission Viejo 92692

IBBETSON, GREGORY BRUCE, real estate executive; b. Nov. 7, 1951, Long Beach; s. Edwin Thornton and Harriett Alice (Hudson) I.; m. Trudy, Sept. 11, 1971; children: Gregory b. 1973, Eric b. 1976; edn: AA, Long Beach City Coll.

1976; BA, CSU Dominguez Hills 1978; Lic. Real Estate Broker, Calif. 1981. Career: air traffic controller USAF 1970-73; maintenance crew Union Devel. Co. 1973-74, property mgr. 1974-; dir. Union Devel. Co. 1976; dir., v.p. Dutch Village Bowl 1980-90; secty. Union Devel. of Hawaii Inc. 1985-; honors: Hon. Svc. Award, Bellflower Unif. Sch. Dist. 1984; Realtor of the Year, Rancho Los Cerritos Bd. Realtors 1985; Referee of the Year, AYSO 1982; mem: Calif. Assn. of Realtors (chmn. Pension & Retirement 1986, chmn. Policy Com. 1989), Rancho Los Cerritos Bd. Realtors (treas. 1984, pres. elec. 1985, pres. 1986), Am. Soc. of R.E. Counselors, Bellflower Kiwanis, AYSO (referee), SPMA, Washington Elem. School Site Council (chmn. 1985-86), Bellflower School Site Council (chmn. 1987-89), CSU Dominguez Hills Economic Club (charter pres.), youth coach Image Surf Club/Huntington High Sch. Beach; mil: E-3 USAF, decorated Fgn. Conflict, Marksmanship; Republican; rec: surfing, swimming, skiing. Ofc: Union Development Co. Inc., 16550 Bloomfield Cerritos 90701

ICE, MARIE ANN, educator; b. Jan. 18, 1938, Wiley, Colo.; d. Irvan Oliver and Jennie Elizabeth (Parrish) Ice; edn: BA, Univ. No. Colorado, 1967, MA, 1971; PhD, Univ. Mo., Columbia 1983. Career: instr. Arapahoe Sch. Dist., Littleton, Colo. 1967-70; instr. and supr. Central Missouri State Univ., Warrensburg, Mo. 1973-80; asst. prof. and dir. elem. edn., Marymount Coll., Salina, Kans. 1983-85; assoc. prof. CSU Bakersfield, Calif. 1986-, Reading Pgm. coord. 1986-91; awards: postdoc. tng. in child language pgm. Univ. of Kansas 1985-86; mem. Internat. Reading Assn. 1983-, Nat. Reading Conf. 1986-, Nat. Coun. of Tchrs. of English 1983-, Kern Reading Assn. (treas., v.p. 1990-); publs: articles on Children's Generated Stories (1980-), coauthor CBEST Test Preparation Guide (in press), co-editor (texts) Reading: The Blending of Theory & Practice, I, II (1990, 91); Republican; Lutheran; rec: reading. Res: 3820 Millay Way Bakersfield 93311 Ofc: Calif. State Univ. Bakersfield, 9001 Stockdale Hwy Bakersfield 93311-1099

IERARDI, STEPHEN JOHN, physician; b. July 5, 1960, Honolulu; s. Ernest J. and Roberta (Hackett) I.; m. Erica Ewing, May 28, 1989; children: Daphne Alexandra b. 1991; edn: BA biology (cum laude), Williams Coll., 1982; MD, Univ. Rochester Sch. of Med. & Dentistry, 1986; Diplomate and Fellow Am. Bd. of Family Practice 1989-. Career: resident, chief resident UC Irvine Medical Ctr., Orange (1986-88, 88-89); physician, Saddleback Family Medicine, Laguna Hills 1989-91, ptnr. 1991-; awards: Nat. Merit Scholar 1978, Gannett Publishing scholastic achiev. scholar 1978, UCI Care Awards (1986, 87, 88); mem. Orange County Med. Assn., Calif. Assn. of Family Physicians, Am. Assn. of Family Physicians; rec: surfing, sailing, skiing. Ofc: Saddleback Family Medicine 24953 Paseo de Valencia Ste 3-A Laguna Hills 92653

IKEGAWA, SHIRO, artist; b. July 15, 1933, Tokyo, Japan; came to the U.S., 1956; s. Fujinori and Sumie (Matsuki) I.; div. 1979, 1 child, Jima b. 1967; edn: Tokyo Univ. of Arts; MFA, Otis Art Inst. of L.A., 1961. Career: asst. prof. of art Pasadena City Coll. 1961-67, CSU Los Angeles 1967-76; prof. art Otis Art Inst. of Parsons Sch. of Design, 1979-85, chair printmaking dept.; guest prof. Chouinard Art Sch. 1968-71, Otis Art Inst. 1967, CSU San Francisco 1972, UC Berkeley 1973, Vancouver (B.C.) Sch. of Art 1974, UC Irvine 1974-75, CSU Dominguez Hills 1985; vis. prof. Claremont Grad. Sch. 1987, UC Davis 1989; artist in residence for Detroit Nat. Print Symp., Cranbrook Acad. of Art, Mich. 1980; lectr. univs., colls. and art assns. nat., 1960s-; commissioned works include Two Edition Etchings, L.A. County Mus. of Art (1973), Prints Commn. on Intl. Multiple Exh. in Tokyo, Normura Display Co. Ltd. (1973), 32 Feet Color Etching "Tale of Genji" L.A. Times (1973); awarded num. art prizes 1960-; grantee: Otis Art Inst. Found. 1960, CSULA Found. 1968-72, NEA fellow printmaking 1974, Ford Found. Faculty Enrichment 1977, 1980, NEA fellow for conceptual art and performance art 1981; One-person exhibits incl. Comara Gal., L.A. (1961, 63, 64, 65, 68), Crocker Art Mus., Sacto. (1965), Container Corp. Am., Chgo. (1966), Idaho State Univ., Pocatello, Id. (1966), Santa Barbara Mus. of Art (1966), Beni Gal., Kyoto, Japan (1967), Univ. Idaho, Moscow (1967), Comsky Gal., L.A. (1979), Long Beach Mus. Art (1971), Univ. Colo., Boulder (1972), UC Irvine (1976), Retrospective show Santa Monica High Sch. (1979), Pasadena City Coll. (1979), L.A. Inst. Contemporary Art (1980), Fine Arts Gal., Laguna Beach (1983), CSULA (1983), Shinno Gal., L.A. (1984), No. Ariz. Univ., Flagstaff (1985), Soker-Kaseman Gal., S.F. (1985), Monterey Bay Gal. (1987), So. Oregon Coll., Ashland (1987); participant numerous competitive and invitational annuals and group exhibitions. Res: 323 E Altadena Dr Altadena 91001

ILLING, LILLIAN BAKER, real estate broker; b. April 29, 1922, Bronx, NY; d. William C. and Esther (Berman) Ulrich; m. 1st Frank Baker, Feb. 17, 1945, div. June 17, 1955, 2d. Hans Illing, PhD, April 19, 1962 (dec. Feb. 16, 1987); 1 son, Theodore Lloyd Baker b. 1952; edn: Los Angeles City Coll. 1939-42. Career: indep. insurance agent, 1952-91, and real estate broker, owner Advisory Mortgage Loan Svc., Los Angeles 1962-; Shaklee distbr.; mem. Pacific Beach Toastmasters (adm. v.p. 1989-90); civic: vol. Santa Monica Westside Hotline 1980-91, Crime Prevention splst. 1982-; past mem. Wilhelm Furtwangler Soc. (recording secty. 1978-85); Democrat; Baptist; rec: piano (performed w/ LACC orch. 1941), artist (oil painting). Address: Advisory Mortgage Loan Service, 6112 W 77th St Los Angeles 90045

IMHOFF, MYRTLE MARY ANN, retired educator; b. Oct. 7, 1910, St. Louis, Mo.; d. Clyde C., Sr. and Laura E. (Asmuth) Imhoff; edn: BA, edn. and music, Harris Tchrs. Coll., St. Louis 1931; MA, psych., St. Louis Univ. 1935; PhD, edn. and psych., Washington Univ., St. Louis 1952. Career: estab. and taught Kindergarten, Crystal City, Mo. 1932-34; elem. tchr. St. Louis, Mo. Public Schs., 1934-44; fed. personnel and field rep. Navy Civilian Dept., Civil Service, Wash. DC 1945-46; tchr. Normal Univ., Ill. 1946-47; dir. edn. Brentwood, Mo. Pub. Schs. 1947-48; assoc. prof. Adams State Coll., Alamosa, Colo. 1948-50; lectr. in edn. Wash. Univ. 1952-53; splst. Early Elem. Edn. and generalist Elem. Edn., US Office of Edn., Wash. DC 1958-59, UNESCO curriculum expt./adv. to Ministry of Edn., Thailand 1959-60; prof. edn. CSU Fullerton 1960-68, CSU Los Angeles 1968-, ret.; acad. cons. pvt. sch.; del. regional and nat. ednl. confs., 1960s; Fulbright adv. CSUF 1967-68, advy. bd. World Explorers Pgm. 1965-, adv. Best Books 1971-73, past cons. Coronet Instl. Films, Ednl. Testing Service; awards: Jesse K. Bar hon. fellow, Heerman fellow, McMillan scholar, 1950-52; mem: Kappa Delta Pi, Am. Orthopsychiat. Assn.; past mem. Am. Psychol. Assn., Internat. Council Psychologists, Am. Acad. Pol. and Social Sci., Am. Edn. Res. Assn., Nat. Soc. for Study of Edn., US Com. for Early Childhood Edn., CTA Inst. for Tchg., NEA, Am. Mus. Natural Hist., Day Care and Child Dev. Council Am., World Affairs Council O.C.; author text: Early Elementary Edn., Apppleton Century Croftts 1959, num. reports, articles in ednl. jours.; Republican; Prot.; rec: music, swim. Res: 1824 Arlington, El Cerrito 94530

INGHAM, GEORGE JOSEPH, dentist; b. May 11, 1958, King City; s. George Raymond and Alvira Josephine (Sala) I.; edn: BA summa cum laude, CSU Fresno 1980; DDS, UCSF Sch. Dentistry 1984. Career: pvt. practice gen. dentistry, Greenfield 1985-; honors: Omicron Kappa Upsilon; mem: ADA, Calif. Dental Assn., Monterey Bay Dental Soc., Greenfield Rotary (sec. 1987-89, v.p. 1989-90, pres. 1990-91); rec: wt.lifting, bowling, Spanish language, softball, sports. Ofc: POB 2448 847 Oak Ave Greenfield 93927

INGRAM, JAMES HARLEY, civil engineer; b. May 10, 1932, Turlock; s. Wm. Elbert and Emma Mary Faith (Slonaker) I.; m. Doris Redmond, Feb. 4, 1961 (div. Aug. 1978); 1 son, Gary A. b. 1963, grandson, Ian Alexander b. 1992; m. Theresa Gobert, June 9, 1979; edn· BSME, UC Berkeley, 1959; reg. civil engr., Calif. (1965). Career: mech. engr., Douglas Aircraft Co., Santa Monica 1959-60; Naval Air Station, Alameda 1960-61; jr. engr./asst. hwy. engr. State of Calif. Dept. of Transp., San Francisco 1961-64; CEII/CEIII Co. of Alameda, Oakland and Hayward 1964-68; assoc. engr. City of San Leandro 1968-73; civil engr. Lampman & Assocs., Walnut Creek 1973-74; v.p. Sulser Engrs. & Planners, Hayward/San Leandro 1974-76; engr. City of South S.F., 1976, 1978-79; civil engr. Murray & McCormick, Oakland 1976-78; pub. works dir./city engr. City of San Bruno, 1979-82; city/dist. engr. Foster City/ Estero Mcpl. Improvement Dist., 1982-84; dir. engring./v.p. Tri State Engring. Co., Redwood City 1984-88; civil engr. Reimer Assoc., S.F. 1988-90; pres. Ingram and Assocs., Daly City 1980-; chief engr. and corp. secty. RIMACC, Inc., South S.F., 1990-91; civil engr. Samtrans, 1991-; mem: Am. Soc. Civil Engrs. 1970-, Am. Public Works Assn. (1965-, merit award So. Bay Area 1987, dir. 1988-89, treas. 1990), CSPE/NSPE (1966-70, 1987-); civic: Monte Vista HOA (pres. 1984-87, mgr. 1987-89, 1991- dir. 1989-91); mil: sgt. 1c AUS 1952-56; Republican; Prot.; rec: aircraft, railroading. Res: 184 Monte Vista Ln Daly City 94015 Ofc: Samtrans 1250 San Carlos Ave San Carlos 94070-1306 also: SMCTA Construction Office, DST & Junipero Serra Blvd Daly City 94017-0543

IPPOLITO, ANDREW VICTOR, business executive, diplomat; b. Oct. 13, 1932, New York; s. Agostino and Mary Virgina (Brancaccio) I.; m. M. Jan Zavali, Oct. 30, 1971; six children; edn: BA, Alfred Univ., 1953, grad. studies UCLA 1962-64, Univ. Pa. 1979. Career: dir. corp. devel. EMSCO, Woodland Hills 1964-68; v.p. corp. fin. Cantor, Fitzgerald, Beverly Hills 1968-71, Exec. Securities, Bev. Hills 1971-74; v.p. fin. R.L. Burns Inc., San Bernardino 1974-76, Am. Pacific Internat., Los Angeles 1976-78; chmn. bd./pres. and c.e.o. Discovery Oil Ltd. 1978-; exec. producer film "Grandpapa" (Hemingway) 1984; honors: apptd. hon. consul general of Liberia, L.A. 1984, recipient Alfred Univ. Achievement Award, inducted Hall of Fame -football (1982, 85); mem. L.A. Consular Corps, secty. 1991; trustee Alfred Univ., N.Y., 1983-87, Alfred Univ. Devel. Council 1986-; Pepperdine Univ. Strawberry Music Fest. 1988-; mem. World Affairs Council, Sister Cities Internat., Internat. Visitors Council L.A. (dir. 1992-); mil: 1st lt. AUS 1953-56; Republican; R.Cath.; rec: tennis, skiing, windsurfing. Res: POB 621 Malibu 90265 Ofc: Discovery Oil Ltd. 2049 Century Park E Ste 1930 Los Angeles 90067

IRICK, ROBERT LEE, educational and business executive; b. Aug. 14, 1930, Competition, Mo.; s. Melvin Hollege and Delphia Ruth (Handley) I.; edn: BA, Southwest Mo. State Univ. 1955; cert. Yale Ins. of F.E. Languages, 1951-52; MA, Harvard Univ. 1958, PhD, 1971. Career: v.p., mng. dir. Chinese Materials and Research Aids Service Ctr. Inc., Taipei 1964-74; gen. mgr. Taiwan Enterprises Co. Ltd., Taipei 1970-88; res. dir. Calif. State Internat. Programs, Taipei 1966-91; resident facilitator Friends World Program, Long Island Univ., 1989-; pres. Chinese Materials Center, Hong Kong 1978-88; pres. Chinese Materials Center Publications, San Francisco 1982-; pres. and gen. mgr. Chinese

Materials Center, Taipei 1988-; rep. The Hannaford Co. Inc. 1983-89; v.p. Sen Bin Chemical Industries Corp. 1985-88; v.p. Consul Chemical Industries Corp., 1988-; instr. Yale Univ. 1957; adj. prof., assoc. prof., prof. Nat. Chengchi Univ. 1976-79, Nat. Chengkung Univ. 1974-75, adj. prof. Nat. Taiwan Univ. 1982-83; advisor Chinese Nat. Fedn. of Industries, Nat. Anti-Counterfeiting Com. 1985-89, Intellectual Property Protection Com. 1989-; secty. Advy. Bd. Sino-Am. Comm. Workshop on Cooperation in Scis. and Humanities, Taipei 1965-71; hon. dir. World-Wide Ethical Soc. 1981-; honors: Boys Nation, Lebanon H. Sch. No. 1 grad., Debate Letter (1951), Who's Who Among Students in Am. Colls. and Univs. 1955, Internat. Who's Who in Edn., Men of Achievement, Who's Who in World, Internat. Directory of Scholars & Splsts. in Third World, Who's Who in Library and Info. Services, Directory of Am. Scholars, Internat. Book of Honor; mem: Am. C.of C. (bd. govs., chmn. intellectual prop. & licensing, chmn. APCAC liaison com.), Asia-Pacific Council of Am. Chambers of Commerce (chmn. 1992-, v. chmn. intellectual prop. com. 1990-92), Harvard Club of Taipei (past pres.), Am. Univ. Club Taipei (dir.), Internat. House of Taipei (dir.), Amvets Free China Post 1 (1st v. comdr.), Republicans Abroad/ Taiwan (sr. advisor), Assn. for Asian Studies Inc., Ann Arbor (Com. on East Asian Libraries), Chinese Language Tchrs. Assn., Kappa Alpha Order No. 1, Pres.'s Club Southwest Mo. State Univ. (1950-51), Smithsonian Assocs.; numerous publs. incl. 50th Annual edition SMSU Ozarko; mil: t/sgt. USAF 1951-55, Commendn.; Republican; Seventh-Day Adventist; rec: collect cookbooks. Res: 335 Shields St San Francisco 94132 Ofc: 633 Post St Ste 251 San Francisco 94109

IRVINE, GERALD ANDREW, company president; b. Aug. 10, 1958, Pomona; s. Robert Gerald and Joan (Granberg) I.; m. Bridget, Jan. 9, 1988; children: Andrew b. 1988, (by wife's previous marriage) Elizabeth b. 1983, Johnathan b. 1978; edn: BS econs./mktg. mgmt., Calif. State Polytechnic Univ., Pomona, 1983. Career: city parks pgm. advisor Claremont Parks & Rec., 1974-78; ins. agt. ITT Life, Transamerica Life, Los Angeles, 1978-84; pres. U.S. Rockets, Claremont, 1979-, pub. California Rocketry Publishing, 1979-; program trader Evergreen Financial, 1987-89; adv. Claremont Rocket Soc. 1974-, advr., sect. leader Polaris Sect. 193 Nat. Assn. of Rocketry, Claremont 1974-84, prefect Lucerne Test Range Prefecture #007, TRAI, Claremont 1985-; publs: (tech. report series) Advanced Information Report 3-11 (1980-89), author, ed. Calif. Rocketry Mag. (quarterly 1981-84); Lutheran; rec: rocket and motor design and flights, computer pgmmg., propellant chemistry. Ofc: 4601 Brooks St Ste 7 Montclair 91763

IRWIN, CHARLES EDWIN, JR., physician; b. Dec. 15, 1945, Medford, Mass.; s. Charles Edwin and Molly Esther (Rosenberg) I.; m. Nancie Noen Kester, Apr. 21, 1979; 1 son, Seth Charles b. 1988; edn: BS, Hobart Coll. 1967; BMS, Dartmouth Med. Sch. 1969; MD, UCSF 1971. Career: intern, resident UCSF Med. Center 1971-74, clin. scholar 1974-77, asst. prof. pediatrics 1977-84, assoc. prof. 1984-90, prof. of pediatrics 1990-, dir. div. of adolescent medicine 1980-; vis. prof. Univ. Gothenberg 1988; editorial bd. Jour. Adolescent Health 1980-; editorial bd. Pediatrician 1984-; awards: Soc. Adolescent Medicine Disting. Scholar 1984, Nat. Center Youth Law Disting. Researcher 1988; mem: Soc. Adolescent Medicine (exec. com. 1985-88), Am. Acad. Pediatrics (exec. com., sect. adolescent health 1982-85), Soc. Pediatric Research, Soc. Research Child Devel., Am. Pediatric Soc., Am. Bd. Pediatrics (chair, sub board adolescent medicine); ed. Adolescent Social Behavior & Health 1988; assoc. ed. Pediatrics (Rudolph 1991); Prot.; rec: skiing. Res: 401 Vermont Ave Berkeley 94707 Ofc: University of California Medical Center 400 Parnassus Ave San Francisco 94143

IRWIN, DOROTHY ROBINSON, radio actress, educator, school board official; b. Mar. 8, 1919, Chgo.; d. Richard Irving and Lillian Otilia (Hlavka) Robinson; m. Ralph E. Irwin, Jr. (Lt. Col. USAF-Ret.); children: Richard b. 1955, Phyllis (Muhleman) b. 1957; 3 grandchildren: Matthew and Kristen Irwin, and Fred C. Muhleman; edn: stu. Goodman Theater, Art Inst. of Chgo. 1935-37, Morton Jr. Coll. 1937, USCG Acad. WWII, CSU San Bernardino 1975, piano studies Chgo. Piano Coll. 1927-35. Career: radio bdcstg., nat. network and local Chgo. shows 1937-42, 1945-, acted opposite John Hodiak in "Wings of Destiny," in num. shows with entertainers incl. Bob Hope, Judy Canova, Al Jolson, Jeff Chandler; 1942-45: enlisted apprentice seaman US Navy, WWII, radioman rating, transf. US Coast Guard, commd. lt. (jg), in charge of recruiting and pub. rel. USCG in Ariz., Calif. and N.Mex.; staff asst. adminstr. in Provost Marshal and Comptroller offices var. USAF bases (husband called back to active mil. duty) post-WWII; substitute tchg. in Riverside, Calif. 18+ years, currently tutoring "at risk" students, teach inservice tchg. and workshops for substitute tchrs. (helped prepare substitute book for Alvord Unified Sch. Dist.), mem. AIDS planning com. for Alvord USD; co-chair Riverside Starcapades (student show benefit for the handicapped) 10 yrs., currently judge for show and auditions; elected Alvord USD School Bd. of Edn., Riverside 1984-88, 88-92, bd. clerk 1984, pres. 1985-86, 1989-90; recipient recognition for community service Alvord USD; mem: Riverside Co. Substance Abuse Com. (1985-, secty. 1992-), Riverside C.of C. (edn. com., substance abuse com.), past pres. Cicero Jr. Women's Club 1935, mem. Officers Wives Club Duplicate Bridge Club, Neighborhood Watch; works: ed. music book "Harry Fields at the Piano" (pub. Beverly Hills), poem in anthology A Treasury of Great Poetry, sev. music compositions, writer plays and variety shows for AF and other orgns.; United Methodist (ch. choir); rec: piano, poetry, biographical lit. Res: 11140 Montlake Dr Riverside 92505 Ofc: Alvord Unified School Dist. 10365 Keller Riverside 92505

ISAACS, KRISTINE RAE, travel agency executive; b. Feb. 26, 1947, Los Angeles; d. Murl J. and Pauline R. (Entriken) Wells Thomas; m. David Gordon Isaacs, Oct. 6, 1985; edn: BS cum laude, mgmt., Pepperdine Univ. 1981. Career: bus. analyst Am. Hosp. Supply, Irvine 1979-81, new products mgr. 1981-82; market devel. mgr. Sybron Corp. 1982-83; dir. planning and bus. devel. Ormco, Glendora 1983-84, dir. mktg. 1984-85; v.p. mktg. San Antonio Comm. Hosp., 1986-90; v.p.-West, Physician Computer Network, 1990-91; mem. Women in Bus., Irvine C.of C.; Republican; rec: skiing, travel. Ofc: Uniglobe Advantage Travel 2603 Main St Irvine 92714

ISHII, ROBERT FRANK, real estate development executive; b. Aug. 26, 1956, Albuquerque, N.M.; s. Edward Frank and Rose K. (Matsunami) I.; m. Donna Marie Chun, Aug. 15, 1981; children: Taylor b. 1986, Spenser b. 1989, Chase b. 1991, Larson; edn: BSBA, Univ. Neb. 1982. Career: asst. treas. Centennial Beneficial Corp., Orange 1984-87; exec. v.p., chief operating ofcr. Centennial Group, Inc., Orange 1984-93; asst. dir. Cathedral Mortgage Co., Costa Mesa 1983-84; auditor Avco Corp., Newport Beach 1982-83; branch mgr. Avco Fin. Service, Omaha, Neb. and Council Bluffs, Iowa 1978-82; awards: Pres. Nixon letter of commend. 1974; Christian. Ofc: 22751 Corralejo Mission Viejo 92692-1321

ISHII, ROY T., physician, pediatrician; b. Mar. 29, 1942, Honolulu, Hawaii; s. Cyrus K. and Bessie A. (Tanimoto) I.; m. Gayle F. Fink, Mar. 17, 1973; children: Nichole b. 1979, Andrea b. 1980; edn: BS, Purdue Univ. 1964; MD, UCSF 1968. Career: Lodi Pediatrics, Lodi; mem at large Am. Acad. Pediatrics 1988-89; mem: CMA, AMA; mil: major USAF 1971-73; Republican; Baptist; rec: painting, gardening, fishing, golf. Res: 1224 Midvale Rd Lodi 95240 Ofc: Lodi Pediatrics 900 S Fairmont Ave Ste A Lodi 95240

ISHLER, MICHAEL WILLIAM, structural engineer; b. Dec. 21, 1952, Cleveland; s. William Edward and Elizabeth (Swift) I.; m. Kathleen Ann Abell, Sept. 6, 1975; children: Stephanie Ann, Matthew Scott; edn: BArch, Univ. Cinti., 1977, MS, 1979; SM, M.I.T., 1981. Career: senior engr. Owens Corning Fiberglas, Toledo and Granville, Ohio, 1981-86; assoc. Ove Arup & Ptnrs., London, England 1987-88, L.A., Calif. 1988-93; M.W. Ishler Consulting Structural Engr. 1993-; mem: ASCE (Toledo chpt. sec. treas. 1983-85, Outstanding Engr. 1985), Structural Engrs. So. Calif., Alpha Rho Chi; inventor Double hexagonal mesh air supported fabric roof structure (1985), Parallel compression ring fabric roof structure (1986); Lutheran. Res: 2314 Pearl St Santa Monica 90405

IWASAKI, RONALD SEIJI, insurance claims manager; b. Dec. 10, 1947, Los Angeles; s. Joe Sotowo and Helen Tomiko (Yamaura) I.; m. Elaine Ida Mandel, Jan. 4, 1982; edn: BA in hist., CSU Long Beach, 1970; gen. ins. pgm. Ins. Inst. of Am., 1986; legal principles, Am. Ednl. Inst., 1990; desig: Assoc. in Claims, Ins. Inst. of Am., 1990, Grad. in Claims Adminstrn., Farmers Ins., 1990. Career: mgmt. trainee Goodyear Tire & Rubber Co. 1972, retail sails mgr. Goodyear Service Center, Wilmington 1972-73, store mgr. 1973-76, Goodyear Service Center, Wilmington and Los Angeles; claims trainee, field claims rep., sr. field claims rep. Farmers Ins. Group, Pasadena 1976-80, br. claims supr., cons. instr. 1980-82; br. claims mgr. Farmers Ins. Group, Long Beach 1982-, special claims mgr. 1991-; awards: sales achievement Goodyear Tire & Rubber Co. (1973, 74, 75), recipient profl. awards Farmers Ins. (1985, 86, 88, 90), listed Internat. Directory of Disting. Leadership 1990, Community Leaders of Am. 1991; Republican; rec: reading, music, fishing, dancing. Ofc: Farmers Insurance Group PO Box 4748 Long Beach 90804

JAACKS, JOHN WILLIAM, writer, retired aerospace executive; b. Sept. 3, Chgo., Ill.; s. Oren Ernest and Matilda (Dritlein) J.; m. Marilyn Walker, Sept. 24, 1952; children: John W. II b. 1954, Jeffrey A. b. 1955, Holly W. b. 1956; edn: BS indsl. adminstrn., Univ. Ill. 1949, BS indsl. engrg., 1962; MS bus. adminstrn., Univ. So. Calif. 1971, MA lib. arts, 1983; Reg. Profl. Indsl. Engr. Calif. 1985. Career: navigator/ intercept ofcr. USAF 1952-55, interceptor pilot 1955-60, chief avionics and maintenance Soisterberg, Holland 1962-65, chief pgm. mgmt. Space Systems Div. 1966-67, dir. pgm. control Space Launch Vehicles, Space and Missile Systems Orgn. 1967-73; proj. mgr. Support Systems Div. Hughes Aircraft Co. 1973-90, last pos. as logistics pgm. mgr. of the F/A 18 Program; honors: Chi Gamma Iota 1962, BSA Award of Merit 1971, Silver Beaver 1977; mem: Am. Inst. Indsl. Engrs., Am. Inst. Aero. and Astro., Air Force Assn., USC Alumni Assn., Univ. Ill. Alumni Assn., Boy Scouts of Am.; author (autobiography): Contrails; mil: lt col. USAF 1950-73, Meritorious Service; Republican; Lutheran; rec: sailing, skiing. Res: 3310 Seaclaire Dr Rancho Palos Verdes 90274

JACKS, BRIAN PAUL, physician, psychiatrist; b. May 23, 1943, Regina, Sask., Canada; came to U.S. 1968; s. Dr. Nathan Benjamin and Ida (Nathanson) J.; m. Carole Ann Marks, June 1968 (div. 1973); children: Erica b. 1974; m.

Brooke Ann Foland, Nov. 14, 1976; edn: MD, Univ. Toronto, 1967; Canadian Med. Bds. 1967, Calif. Med. Bds. 1968, Am. Bd. Psychiatry and Neurology, Adult 1974, Child/ Adolescent 76. Career: intern Vancouver (B.C.) Gen. Hosp., 1967-68; resident gen. psychiatry, L.A. County- Univ. So. Calif. Med. Ctr., L.A. 1968-70, child psychiatry, 1970-72, chief resident child psychiatry 1971-72; asst. dir. child/adol. psychiatry outpatient svs. LAC-USC Med. Ctr., 1972-76, ward chief long-term adol. inpatient svs., 1976-79; also faculty USC Sch. of Med. 1972-, assoc. clin. prof. psychiatry USC, 1976-; pvt. practice f.t., 1979-; expert witness Calif. State Bar Assn., 1980-; indep. med. examiner Calif. St. Dept. Indsl. Relations, 1981-, examiner Nat. Bds. in Child/Adol. Psychiatry, 1991-; mem: Am. Acad. Child Psychiatry (Fellow 1979), Am. Psychiatric Assn., Am. Soc. Adol. Psychiatry, So. Calif. Psychiatric Soc. (chmn. com. child/adol. psychiat. 1988), So. Calif. Soc. for Child Psychiatry (com. peer rev. 1985-89, exec. coun., pres. 1982-83), So. Calif. Soc. for Adolescent Psychiatry (exec. coun., pres. 1983-84), USC Psychiatric Alumni in Cont. Edn., Calif. Soc. Indsl. Medicine; lectr. on behavioral modification before numerous groups incl. child and sch. psychologists, student nurses, sch. teachers, sch. and drug counselors, social workers, police and probation ofcrs., students and parents; contbr. chapters in med. books. Ofc: 435 N Bedford Dr, Penthouse W., Beverly Hills 90210-4316

JACKSON, JEWEL A., state youth correctional program manager; b. June 3, 1942, Shreveport, La.; d. Willie Burghardt and Bernice Jewel (Mayberry) Norton; m. Edward James Norman, May 17, 1961 (div. 1968); children: Steven, June Kelly; m. Wilbert Jackson, Apr. 6, 1969; children: Michael, Anthony. Career: with Calif. Youth Authority, 1965-, group supr., San Andreas and Santa Rosa, 1965-67, youth counselor, Ventura 1967-78, senior youth counselor, Stockton 1978-81, treatment team supr, program mgr., Whittier and Ione, 1981-, affirmative action adv. mem., Sacramento 1976-78, equal employment advy. mem., 1978-88; speaker Univ. of Pacific Youth Motivational Project, Stockton, 1985-86; mem: Women in Crim. Justice (No. co-chair 1974-76), Assn. Black Correctional Workers (chpt. v.p. 1979, newsletter editor 1978-80); rec: equestrienne, literature, writing poetry and short stories, designing clothes. Res: PO Box 898 Ione 95640

JACKSON, JOHN HOWARD, physician; b. June 30, 1951, Columbia, Mo.; s. Albert Howard and Jeanette Elizabeth (Hennessee) J.; m. Annette Yangwon Park, June 14, 1975; children: Rebecca b. 1981, Elizabeth b. 1984; edn: BS chemistry, UCLA 1972; MD, George Washington Univ. 1980. Career: intern, resident, internal medicine UCLA 1980-83; pvt. practice, Crescent City Internal Medicine, Crescent City 1983-; med. dir. internal medicine Seaside Hosp. 1984-85, med. dir. cardiopulmonary dept. 1985-90; chief med. staff Sutter Coast Hosp. 1985-87, 1990-92; chmn. profl. review com. Seaside Hosp. 1984-85; honors: Alpha Omega Alpha; mem: A.C.P., Rotary; Republican; Christian; rec: flying, genealogy, archaeology. Res: 800 Bertsch Ave Crescent City 95531 Ofc: Crescent City Internal Medicine 780 E Washington Blvd Ste 202 Crescent City 95531

JACKSON, JOSEPH BRIAN, physician; b. Dec. 23, 1946, Brunswick, Ga.; s. Joseph A. and Maxine (Ross) J.; m. Cathleen Ann Goddard, Feb. 12, 1969 (div. 1981); children: Tracy Rene b. 1972, Brian Eric b. 1975; edn: BS chem., San Diego State Univ., 1969; MD, Loma Linda Univ., 1973. Career: criminalist San Bernardino Sheriffs Crime Lab, San Bdo., 1969-70; intern Santa Clara Valley Med. Ctr., San Jose 1973-74; emergency physician Sharp Cabrillo Hosp., San Diego 1975-82, dep. director emergency svs. 1980-82; medical dir. East County Community Clinic, El Cajon 1982-91; pvt. family practice, San Diego, 1984-88, Ramona, 1991-92; staff physician Logan Heights Family Health Ctr., San Diego 1991-93; chief adult med. Logan Heights Family Health Ctr. 1992-; honors: Nat. Merit Scholar 1964; mem. Am. Coll. of Emergency Physicians 1975-82; rec: art, music. Ofc: 1809 National Ave San Diego 92113

JACKSON ECKSTEIN, VERA ALEENE, manufacturing company executive, television show producer; b. Jan. 20, 1924, Hollywood; d. Frank Murrin and Vera Sophia (Offerman) Jackson; m. Everett Gail Eckstein (div.); children: Candace b. 1947, Frederick b. 1948, Heidi b. 1949, Tiffany b. 1955, Tony b. 1960; edn: grad. L.A. H.S. 1942. Career: owner Aleene's Floral Supply, Temple City 1945-66; Artis Inc., Solvang 1968-; producer, dir. Creative Living, 1988-; awards: PCM Trade Mag. Most Influential Person in Hobby Industry Assn. (1986); mem: Hobby Industry Assn. So. Calif. (pres. bd.dirs.), HIA (bd. dirs.), Art Craft Materials Ins. (bd. dirs. 1988-89), Art Assn. Santa Ynez Valley (pub. chmn. 1985); author: Treasures from Trash (Andiron Press), Super Scrap Craft (New Amer. Library), self pub. 140+ arts and crafts books (Aleene, Inc.), num. tv appearances; rec: gardening. Res: Box 407 Solvang 93463 Ofc: Aleene's, Inc. 85 Industrial Way Buellton 93427

JACOBS, HERBERT HOWARD, investor, executive, developer; b. March 23, 1923, Freeport, N.Y.; s. Murray Lawrence and Anna (Deutsch) J.; m. Blanche Goldman, Jan. 26, 1947; children: Lynne b. 1949, Janis b. 1954, Neil b. 1956, Nancy b. 1958; edn: BSChE, Cornell Univ. 1944; MS engring., Columbia Univ. 1947; PhD, 1955. Career: assoc. Dunlap & Assoc. Inc., N.Y.C. 1949-53, v.p. 1956-62; asst. prof. Columbia Univ., NYC 1953-56; v.p. Hallmark Cards Inc., Kansas City, Mo. 1962-72; pres. April House Inc., Lenexa, Kans. 1972-77; Jacobs Co., La Jolla 1977-; dir. Am. Greetings Corp., Cleveland, Ohio 1982-; cons. Surgeon Gen. U.S., Bethesda, Md. 1956-63; vis. prof. Waseda Univ.,

Tokyo, Japan 1958; mem: Ops. Res. Soc. Am. (fellow, founding mem., awarded Lanchester Prize 1956), Inst. Mgmt. Sci. (founding mem.), Joint Engring. Soc. (accred. com. 1966-72), Midwest Res. Inst. (trustee, exec. com. 1965-72); mil: lt.j.g. USNR 1943-46. Res: 1708 Caminito Ardiente La Jolla 92037

JACOBS, RANDALL BRIAN, lawyer; b. July 8, 1951, N.Y.C.; s. John Jacobs M.D. and Evelyn (Teper) J.; children: Jillian b. 1983; edn: BA, Coll. of Idaho, 1972; JD, Univ. West L.A., 1978; admitted bar: Calif. 1978, W.D.C. 1984, Wisc. 1985; Calif. Comm. Colls. life tchg. credential; NRA cert. firearms instr. Career: private investigator Randy Brian Assocs., Santa Monica 1976-, lawyer B. Randall Jacobs Law Corp., 1978-, real estate broker Morgan Reed & Co., 1978-; reserve dep. sheriff L.A. County 1979-; award: Eagle Scout BSA 1969; mem. Shom Rim Soc., NRA (life); lodges: Mason 32d., John Marshall (B.H.), Shriner, Al Malaikah Temple (L.A.). Ofc: 2309 Ocean Park Blvd Santa Monica 90405-5199

JACOBS, STEPHEN OREL, broadcasting executive; b. Oct. 10, 1941, Lacrosse, Wis.; s. Orel Whitaker and Lucille Marie (Prinsen) J.; m. Jacqueline Lee Andrews, Mar. 30, 1963; children: Kimberly b. 1964, Scott b. 1967, Stephanie b. 1981. Career: account exec. Behan Bdcstg., Lamar, Colo. 1967-69; account exec. Mullins Bdcstg., Denver 1970-71, gen. sales mgr. 1971-72, gen. mgr. 1972-73; gen. mgr. Combined Communications, Phoenix, Az. 1973-75; gen. mgr. Combined Communications/Gannett Inc., San Diego 1975-80; owner/mgr. Behan Bdcstg., Tucson 1980-86; owner/gen. mgr. Par Bdcstg., San Diego 1986-; mem. San Diego Bdcstrs. Assn. (v.p. 1989-); civic: Green Valley Civic Assn., Silver Saddle Assn. (Poway); Republican; Methodist; rec: skiing, building. Res: 16657 Maverick Ln Poway 92064 Ofc: Par Broadcasting 5735 Kearney Villa Rd Ste G San Diego 92123

JACOBSON, ALBERT HERMAN, JR., educator, industrial and systems engineer; b. Oct. 27, 1917, St. Paul, Minn.; s. Albert Herman and Gertrude (Anderson) J.; m. Elaine Virginia Swanson, June 10, 1960; children: Keith b. 1962, Paul b. 1965; edn: BS indsl. eng. (cum laude), Yale Univ. 1939; SM bus. & engring. admin., MIT, 1952; MS applied physics, Univ. Rochester, 1954; PhD mgmt. engring., Stanford Univ. 1976; reg. profl. engr. Calif. Career: personnel asst. Yale Univ., New Haven, Conn. 1939-40; indsl. engr. RCA, Camden, N.J. 1940-43; electronics prodn. ofcr. BUORD, USN 1943-44; res. insp. of naval material Colonial Radio (Sylvania) 1944-45; naval insp. of ordnance Eastman Kodak Co. 1945-46; chief engr./dir. quality control Naval Ordnance Office, Rochester, N.Y. 1946-57; staff engr. Eastman Kodak Co. 1957-59; assoc. dean Coll. Engring. & Arch., Penn State Univ. 1959-61; v.p., gen. mgr. to pres. Knapic Electro-Physics Co., Palo Alto 1961-62; prof. Coll. of Engring. San Jose State Univ. 1962-; co-founder and coord. Cybernetic Systems grad. pgm. 1968-; indep. cons. 1962-; honors: Tau Beta Pi, Sigma Xi, MIT Alfred P. Sloan fellowship in exec. devel. 1951-52, Stanford Univ. NSF fellow 1965-66, Eagle Scout 1931, Scouter's Key & Award of Merit BSA Stanford Council 1976; mem. Am. Soc. Engring. Edn., Inst. Indsl. Engrs., Am. Prodn. & Inventory Control Soc. (bd. 1975-), Masons; civic: YMCA (pres. N.Y. state Young Adults Council 1954-55), Mountain View City Personnel Commn. (chmn. 1968-78), Boy Scouts Am. scoutmaster and mem. Council Stanford Area 1970-83, Campus Lutheran Council San Jose St. Univ. (chmn. 1981-86), mem. Santa Clara Valley Luth. Parish Coun. 1991-; publs: Mil. & Civilian Personnel in Naval Adminstrn. 1952, pub. monograph 1954, R.R. Consolidations & Transp. Policy 1976, editor: Design & Engring. of Prodn. Systems 1984; jour. articles; mil: Lt. Comdr. USNR 1943-46, commendn.; rec: music, photog., swimming, tennis, skiing. Res: 1864 Lime Tree Ln Mountain View CA 94040

JACOBSON, ALLAN STANLEY, computer scientist/astrophysicist; b. June 18, 1932, Chattanooga, Tenn.; s. Max Jacobson and Anne Shavin Lasner; m. Edith Lieberman, 1956 (div. 1981); m. Laura Ann Hilton, Sept. 21, 1986; edn: AB, UCLA 1962; MSc, UC San Diego 1964, PhD, 1968. Career: asst. res. physicist, UC San Diego 1968-69; sr. res. sci. Jet Propulsion Lab, Pasadena 1981-, tech. group supr. JPL High Energy Astrophysics Group 1973-86, asst. sect. mgr. JPL Info Systems div. 1988-; cons: Ashton-Tate Corp., Torrance 1984-88, LNW Res. Corp., Tustin 1980-83; prin. investigator NASA HEAO 3 Gamma-Ray Spectrometer 1970-87; honors: exceptional scientific achievement medal, NASA 1980, Rossi Prize, Am. Astronomical Soc. 1986, Phi Beta Kappa 1962; mem: Am. Astronomical Soc., fellow Am. Physical Soc., IEEE Computer Soc., ACM/Siggraph; author num. articles profl. jours., 1966-; mil: s/sgt. USAF, 1951-54; Democrat; rec: music, singing. Ofc: Jet Propulsion Lab, MS 183-501, 4800 Oak Grove Dr Pasadena 91109

JACOBSON, EDWIN JAMES, physician; b. June 27, 1947, Chgo.; s. Edwin Julius and Rose Josephine (Jirinec) J.; m. Martha, May 29, 1977; children: Emily b. 1986; edn: MD, UCLA, 1976. Career: medical resident UCLA, Los Angeles 1976-79, chief med. res. 1981-82, attdg. physician, assoc. clin. prof. medicine 1982-; honors: Alpha Omega Alpha (1976); author: Clinical Decisions (1987), Il Processo Nella Diagnosc Medica (1992), 22+ articles (1972-). Ofc: 100 UCLA Medical Plaza H690 Los Angeles 90024

JACOBSON, RAYMOND EARL, electronics company executive; b. May 25, 1922, St. Paul, Minn.; s. Albert H. and Gertrude W. (Anderson) J.; m. Margaret

Maxine Meadows, Dec. 22, 1959 (div. 1986); children: Michael David, Karl Raymond, Christopher Eric; edn: BE (high hons.) Yale Univ., 1944; MBA (distinction) Harvard Univ., 1948; BA (Rhodes Scholar) Oxford Univ., 1950, MA, 1954. Career: asst. to gen. mgr. PRD Electronics Inc., Bklyn. 1951-55; sales mgr. Curtiss-Wright Electronics Div., Carlstadt, N.J. 1955-57; dir. mktg. TRW Computers Co., L.A. 1957-60; v.p. ops. Electro-Sci. Investors, Dallas 1960-63; pres. Whitehall Electronics Inc., Dallas 1961-63, dir. 1961-63; chmn. bd. Gen. Electronic Control Inc., Mpls. 1961-63, Staco Inc., Dayton, Ohio 1961-63; pres. Maxson Electronics Corp., Great River, N.Y. 1963-64; pres. Jacobson Assocs., San Jose 1967-; co-founder, pres., chmn. bd., c.e.o. Anderson Jacobson Inc., San Jose 1967-88, also: chmn. Anderson Jacobson, S.A., Paris 1974-88, mng. dir. Anderson Jacobson Ltd., London 1975-85, chmn. Anderson Jacobson Canada Ltd., Toronto 1976-85, chmn. Anderson Jacobson, GmbH, Cologne 1978-83; chmn. CXR Corp., San Jose 1988-; dir: Tamar Electronics Inc., L.A., Rawco Instruments Inc., Dallas 1960-63; lectr. engring. UCLA, 1958-60; mem. underwriting Lloyd's London, 1975-; Eagle Scout 1934, BSA committeeman 1969-81; mem. Sigma Xi, Tau Beta Pi, Am. Assn. Rhodes Scholars, Harvard Racquet; Republican; Lutheran. Res: 1247 Montcourse Lane San Jose 95131-2420 Ofc: CXR Corp. 521 Charcot Ave San Jose 95131-2477

JACOBSON, STEVE EVAN, network television executive; b. May 8, 1955, St. Louis, Mo.; s. Leonard and June Annette (Groff) J.; m. Jane Elizabeth Heal, Sept. 5, 1980; children: Matthew b. 1989, Cameron b. 1990; edn: BA Cinema, Univ. of So. Calif., 1977. Career: producer, writer Walt Disney Prodns., Burbank 1978-79; freelance producer/writer, 1978-80; writer/producer on-air promotion NBC, Burbank 1980-83, mgr. on-air promotion, NBC, Burbank 1983-88; v.p. on-air promotion CBS, L.A., 1988-; awards: bronze Bdcst. Designers Assn., L.A. (1988, 1990), finalist Internat. Film & TV Fest., N.Y. 1988, distinction Promotion Mktg. Assn. of Am., N.Y. 1990, listed Who's Who Among Young Americans 1991, Who's Who in the West 1992; mem. Bdcst. Promotion and Mktg. Execs. 1989-, USC Cinema-TV Alumni Assn. 1982-; exec. producer TV show: Crimetime After Primetime (preview 1991), co-producer, co-writer movie: Junior High School (1978); rec: camping, music, racquetball, baseball. Ofc: CBS, 7800 Beverly Blvd Los Angeles 90036

JACQUES, KENNETH BORDEN, orthopaedic surgeon; b. Dec. 27, 1911, St. Johnsbury, Vt.; s. Frank Bismark and Laura Gertrude (Fessenden) J.; m. Elizabeth Matheson, June 15, 1940; m. 2d. Barbara Johnson Ferguson, Apr. 27, 1984; children: Elizabeth b. 1942, Heather b. 1944; edn: BA, Dartmouth, 1933; MD, CM, McGill Univ., Montreal 1937. Career: asst. residencies, path. Deaconess Hosp., Boston 1937-38, surgery, Montreal Gen. Hosp. 1938-39, med. Royal Victoria Hosp., Montreal 1939-40, neurosurg. Neurological Inst. Montreal 1940; res., surgery, Univ. Alberta Hosp., 1940-41; physician Weyerhauser Timber Co., Longview, Wash. 1941-42; resident, ortho., Orthopaedic Hosp., Los Angeles 1942-43; major Med. Corps US Army Air Corps 1943-46; orthopaedic surgeon private practice, Calif. 1946-; honors: med. staff pres. Hollywood Presbyterian Hosp. 1968-69, honoree McGill Grad. Soc. L.A. 1987 and Orthopaedic Hosp. L.A. 1987; mem: AMA, Calif. Med. Assn., L.A. Co. Med. Soc., Fellow Internat. Coll. Surgeons (So. Calif. sect. pres. 1981-82), Fellow Am. Coll. Surgeons, Am. Acad. Ortho. Surg., McGill Grad. Soc. (pres. 1952, 1990-91, v.p. 1981), Rotary Club; numerous illustrated lectures on orthopaedic surgery posterior lumbar interbody fusion, cerebral palsy, total hip replacement 1947-87; Republican; Prot. Bible Ch. (elder 1954-64); rec: skiing, hiking, bicycling, photog., Bible study. Res: 5759 Valley Oak Dr Los Angeles 90068 Ofc: Jacques Orthopaedic, 5759 Valley Oak Dr Los Angeles 90068

JAKEL, OTTO WILLIAM (Sir Otto W. Jakel), mechanical-electrical engineer, ret.; b. May 20, 1915, Los Angeles; s. Otto Karl and Freda Sofa (Sommers) J.; m. Gwyneth K. Smith, Sept. 21, 1940 (dec. Sept. 30, 1967); children: William K. b. 1942, Margaret K. b. 1945, Gwyneth P. b. 1953; m. Alice M. Moore (Lady Alice), May 17, 1973; edn: BS, Calif. Maritime Acad., 1935; BSE, UC Berkeley, 1941; lic. Unrestricted 3d Mate 1935, reg. profl. mech. engr./elec. engr., Calif. 1945. Career: supr. Underwater Sound Installations on Naval Vessels, Mare Island, N.Y. 1941-46; research engr. U.S. Dept. Agric., Albany, Ca. 1946-48; radio engr. Mare Island Naval Shore Station, 1948-50; senior project engr. Colgate Palmolive Co., Berkeley 1951-78; mem. engring. advy. bd. S.F. City Coll.; instr. Contra Costa Coll.; honors: Tau Beta Pi, Eta Kappa Nu, Kt. Order of St. George awarded by Prince Albert Habsburg-Hohenburg of Austria (June 5, 1990); scoutmaster BSA Troop #104 El Cerrito, skipper El Cerrito Sea Scout Ship #108 BSA 1955-60; mem. US Coast Guard Aux. (life, instr. and past comdr. Flotilla 21), Masons, Shriners (past pres.), Moose; clubs: Pt. San Pablo Yacht (commodore 1975), Sportsmens; Democrat; Episcopalian; rec: boating, garden, camping, dancing, computers, model RR, travel. Res: 7543 Terrace Dr El Cerrito 94530

JAMES, BERT ALAN, architect; b. April 24, 1955, San Fernando; s. Charles Wendel and Elsie (Fred) J.; edn: BA, Calif. Polytechnic Univ. S.L.O., 1978; reg. architect Calif. 1983, cert. project architect NCARB. Career: designer, draftsman Froelich & Kow Architects, Beverly Hills 1978-79; designer, draftsman Howard R. Lanes Assoc., Woodland Hills 1979-80; project mgr. Nash Brown Assoc., Bakersfield 1980-81; project mgr. Roger Grulke Architects, Bakersfield 1981-82; project architect KSA Group Architects, Bakersfield 1982-85; project architect

Milazzo & Assoc., Bakersfield 1985-92; principle Bert A. James Architect 1993-; mem: Am. Inst. Architects (corp. mem., dir. 1992-93), Kern County Officials Assn. (football referee 1983-), Kiwanis Club of Westchester; rec: golf, photog. Res/Ofc: Bert A. James Architect 3612 Sampson Ct Unit C Bakersfield 93309

JANIS, JAY, savings and loan executive; b. Dec. 22, 1932, Los Angeles; s. Ernest and Diana J.; m. Juel Mendelsohn, Sept. 7, 1954; children: Jeffrey b. 1960, Laura b. 1958; edn: AB, Yale Univ. 1954. Career: sr. v.p. Univ. Mass., Boston 1976-77; undersecty. U.S. Dept. H.U.D., Wash., DC. 1977-79; chmn. FHLBB 1979-80; pres. Calif. Fed., Beverly Hills 1981-82; chmn. exec. com. Gibraltar Savings 1984-88, chmn. bd. 1988; dir. Coast Savings 1989-; dir. Mortgage Guarantee Ins. Corp., Milwaukee, Wis. 1970; chmn. bd. Flagship Savings, San Diego 1987-88; dir. FHLBB San Francisco 1985-86; advisor to Gov. of Fla., Miami 1971-74; honors: NAHB Housing Hall of Fame, 1988; mem: Cosmos Club; author: num. articles and papers pub in profl. jours.; Democrat. Ofc: Gibraltar Savings 911 Wilshire Blvd. Beverly Hills 90210

JANKO, RICHARD C. M., classical scholar; b. May 30, 1955, Weston Underwood, England; s. Charles A. and Helen (Murray) J.; m. Michele Ann Hannoosh, May 26, 1984; edn: BA, Trinity Coll. 1976; PhD, 1980. Career: lectr. in Greek Univ. St. Andrews, Scotland 1978-79; research fellow Trinity Coll., Cambridge, England 1979-82; asst. prof. Columbia Univ., N.Y. 1982-84, assoc. prof. 1984-87; prof. UCLA 1987-; awards: Guggenheim Fellow 1986-87, Fellow Nat. Humanities Ctr. 1990; mem: Am. Philological Assn.; author: Homer Hesiod & The Hymns (1982), Aristotle on Comedy (1984), Artistotle Poetics (1987). Res: 714 Barcelona Ave Davis 95616

JANSON, HUGH MICHAEL, audio engineer, composer-pianist; b. May 4, 1936, Tulsa, Okla.; s. Frank K. and Marion (Appleman) J.; m. Toni Rivia Pfeffer, Apr. 12, 1962 (div. 1965); edn: grad. Peddie Sch., 1954; BBA, Univ. Miami, 1958; grad. stu. Westlake Coll. of Music, L.A. 1959-60, Berklee Coll. of Music, Boston 1969-71. Career: R.E. investor, 1963-; pvt. tchr. music theory, 1970-, pres. AAO Music, 1975-; ptnr. Zoo Studios, Los Angeles 1976-79; owner Uncle Morris Sound Services, 1980-; recipient best jazz composition award Lighthouse Coll. Jazz Festival, Hermosa Beach 1960; mem: Internat. Assn. of Jazz Educators, Jazz Heritage Found., Am. Fedn. of Musicians, ASCAP, Audio Engring. Soc.; clubs: Matchmasters, L.A. (treas. 1962-64, mem. of yr. 1962, outstanding mem. 1963), 4-Cylinder Club Am. (founding), U.S. Revolver Assn. (gov. 1963); civic: Project Turnoff, Boston (founding sponsor 1970-71); Republican; Buddhist; rec: radio comms./NSA World Peace Movement. Ofc: c/o Richard M. LeRoy & Co., 1888 Century Park East Ste 815 Los Angeles 90067

JANTZEN, J(OHN) MARC, professor and dean emeritus; b. July 30, 1908, Hillsboro, Kans.; s. John D. and Louise (Janzen) J.; m. Ruth Patton, June 9, 1935; children: John Marc, Myron Patton, Karen Louise; edn: AB, Bethel Coll., Newton, Kans., 1934; AM, Univ. Kans., 1937, PhD, 1940. Career: elementary sch. tchr. Marion County, Kans. 1927-30, Hillsboro, Kans. 1930-31; high sch. tchr. 1934-36; instr. Sch. of Edn. Univ. Kans., 1936-40; asst. prof. Sch. of Edn., Univ. of Pacific, Stockton 1940-42, assoc. prof., 1942-44, prof. 1944-78, prof. emeritus, 1978-, dean. Sch. of Edn., 1944-74, emeritus 1974-, dir. summer sessions, 1940-72; bd. dirs. Educational Travel Inst., 1965-90, ldr. 13 fgn. ednl. seminars; past commn. Commn. for Equal Opportunities in Edn., Calif. Dept. Edn. 1959-69; mem. Nat. Council for Accreditation Tchr. Edn. 1969-72; mem. (past chmn) Calif. Tchrs. Assn. Commn. for Tchr. Edn. 1956-62; honors: Phi Delta Kappa (mem. Internat. Bd. 1966-68), hon. service award Calif. Congress of Parents and Tchrs. 1982, Paul Harris fellow Rotary Found. 1980; mem: Am. Edn. Research Assn. (past pres.) 1954-55 Calif. Edn. Research Assn., Calif. Council for Edn. Tchrs., Calif. Assn. of Colls. For Tchr. Edn. (sec.-treas. 1975-85), Nat. Edn. Assn., Rotary; Methodist. Res: 117 W Euclid Ave Stockton 95204

JAY, DAVID J., computer software engineering consultant; b. Dec. 7, 1925, Gdansk, Poland, nat. 1944; s. Mendel and Gladys Gitta (Zalc) Jakubowicz; m. Shirley Anne Shapiro, Sept. 7, 1947; children: Melvin b. 1948, Evelyn Deborah b. 1950; edn: BS, Wayne State Univ., 1948; MS, Univ. Mich., 1949; grad. work Univ. Cinti. 1951-53, Univ. Mich. 1956-57, M.I.T. 1957; reg. profl. engr. Calif., Mich., Ohio. Career: instr. Univ. Detroit, 1948-51; supr. man-made diamonds, Gen. Electric Co., Detroit 1951-52; asst. to v.p. engring. Ford Motor Co., Dearborn 1956-63; project mgr. Apollo Environmental Control Radiators, N. Am. Rockwell, Downey 1963-68; staff to v.p. corp. planning Aerospace Corp., El Segundo 1968-70; pres. Profl. Bus. Mgmt. Inc., 1970-79; pres.. Jay Consulting Enterprises, Inc., 1979-; mem. Tau Beta Pi (nat. dir. alumni affairs 1972-73, sec.treas. 1972-75, pres. Detroit Alumnus chpt. 1962-63, pres. So. Calif. Alumnus 1963-70), Fellow Inst. for Adv. of Engring., Inst. of Mgmt. Sci. (sect. chmn. 1961-62), Western Greenhouse Vegetable Growers Assn., American Contract Bridge League (life master); club: Long Beach Yacht; works: 3 U.S. patents, 10 tech. papers; mil: ETM 3/c USN 1944-46; Jewish, pres. Temple Beth David; rec: bridge, yachting. Res: 13441 Roane Circle Santa Ana 92705 Ofc: 14771 Plaza Dr Ste F Tustin 92680

JAYARAM, SUSAN ANN POTTER, executive secretary; b. Nov. 23, 1930, Stockton; d. George Leroy and Violet Yvonne (Rushing) Potter; m. M. R.

Jayaram, July 2, 1960; edn: Pasadena Coll., 1951-52, Woodbury Coll., 1960, AA, Long Beach City Coll., 1959. cert. profl. secty. (CPS). Career: secty. to mgr. First Western Bank, Los Angeles 1953-56; secty. to pres. Studio City Bank, 1957-60; secty. to exec. v.p. Union Bank, Los Angeles, 1962-81; secty. to v. chmn. Imperial Bank, Los Angeles 1981-82; personal secty. to Howard B. Keck, chmn. W. M. Keck Found., 1982-; civic: Citizens for Law Enforcement Needs (sec., bd. advisors, 1972-74), L.A./Bombay Sister City Com., DAR (Susan B. Anthony chpt.), Freedoms Found. at Valley Forge (L.A. chpt.), US Navy League (Long Beach Council), League of the Americas (pres. 1988-90); clubs: Los Angeles (dir., secty. 1967-81), The Verdugo, Old Ranch CC; editor: The Los Angeles Club Panorama, 1979-80, California Clarion, 1978-80; Republican. Ofc: H.B. Keck 555 S Flower St Los Angeles 90071

JAYMES, DOROTHY LEE, municipal administrator, union trustee; b. Mar. 10, 1934, New Orleans, La.; d. Hampton Moten and Dr. Beulah Mae (Houston) Jones; div. Herbert Harrison; m. 2d Charles Royal Jaymes, June 1968 (dec. 1985); children: Brenda J. Perkins, Beulah M. Winfield (RN), Mary P.H. Offray, B.J. Harrison (M.Sgt.); edn: Heald Bus. Coll., S.F. 1966-72; Patten Bible Coll., Oakland 1978-80; BS, Univ. San Francisco, 1983; Career: owner, tchr. Clabon Kindergarten, New Orleans 1960-62; owner, whlse. retail furniture & appliance store, New Orleans, LA 1960-65; mgr., supr. municipal handicapped pgm. San Francisco, 1978-90; mgr. and adminstr. dept city planning San Francisco, 1990-92; physical plant mgr., City Planning, San Francisco 1992-; trustee and ofcr. Local 790 SEIU, AFL/CIO, San Francisco 1983-; shop steward/counselor Local 790, (1977-); del. S.F. Labor Counsel 1983-; del. S.F. Organizing Proj. 1983-90; chapter pres. 949 Presidio Muni/PUC, S.F. 1983-90; advy. bd. RTA Transit Auth. Oakland 1982-90; awards: service AMICAE/Zeta Phi Beta, S.F. 1981-82, civic leadership Third Baptist Ch. S.F. 1986, dean's award Patten Bible Coll. 1980, unionist of year Local 790 (1989), leadership Muni Elderly & Handicapped S.F. 1990, achiev. recogn. Univ. S.F. and poster honoree in Civic Ctr. BART Sta. and Train (3 mos. 1983); biog. listings incl. Who's Who Profl. Human Services, Nat. Ref. Inst. 1991, hon. mem., Who's Who Registry Worldwide 1992, Pres Inauguration 1993, chtr. mem., Amer. For Change, presdl. task force 1993, books & awards of Marquis Who's Who Publs., Am. Biog. Inst., Internat. Biog. Ctr.; mem. O.E.S. (worthy matron 1953-60, grand dep. 1959-60, instr. 1967-), Nat. Women League Voters, Commonwealth Club (S.F.), Golden Gate Nat. Park Assn., HERE; Democrat (registrar, nat. fund raiser 1980-); Baptist; rec: sports, fishing, music, movies, dancing, singing. Res: 1665 Golden Gate Ave #12 San Francisco 94115 Ofc: 450 McAllister St 5th Fl., San Francisco 94102

JAYNES, PHIL, safety consultant; b. May 10, 1923, Chicago; s. Philip S. and Katherine (Barrett) J.; m. Amy, Dec. 15, 1948; children: Edith O'Laughlin b. 1949, Phyllis Lappin b. 1952, Wendy Neves b. 1960, Lisa Johnson b. 1962; edn: cert. Yale Univ., 1944; BA, Univ. Chicago, 1948; MA, Loyola Univ., Chgo. 1963; Certified Safety Profl. Career: sr. safety engr. Inland Steel Co., E.Chicago, Ill. 1949-85; safety dir. No. Am. Refractories, Gary, Ind. 1987; pres. Phil Jaynes & Assocs. 1972-; author: training film: Saved by the Belt, 1984, book chapter in Testing Fabrics with Molten Metals (ASTM, 1985), pub. articles in field; appt. to River Commns. by 3 Govs. of Indiana, 1974, 78, 82 (chmn. Little Calumet River Commn. 1973-75); appt. Citizen Ambassador and mem. U.S. Safety & Health Mission to P.R.O.China, 1983; mem. Internat. Exec. Service Corps/ IESC, cons. China, 1985-86, Brazil, 1988; named the Sun Newspaper Man of the Week, Lansing, Ill. 1971; mem: Am. Soc. Safety Engrs., Am. Industrial Hygiene Assn., Sacto. Area Council on Occup. Safety and Health, Nat. Safety Council; mil: 1st lt. USAAF 1942-46; Republican; Unitarian (past pres. Unitarian Universalist Comm. Ch.); rec: bridge, sailing, tennis. Ofc: Phil Jaynes & Associates 7414 Sun Point Ln Sacramento 95828-6219

JEFFERSON-BRAMHALL, RONA LEE, tax preparer, executrix of estates; b. Nov. 26, 1900, Salisbury, Tenn.; d. John Thomas and Margaret Ann (Moore) Tice; m. William Tanner, Feb. 22, 1922; 1 dau. Colette b. 1924; m. Ray Carlton Bramhall, Dec. 24, 1982; edn: Univ. So. Calif. 1937-40; enrolled agent IRS 1978; reg. parliamentarian. Career: clerk Census Bureau Wash. DC 1941; clerk, editor Safety Sun, Corps of Engrs., L.A. 1942-49; USAF clerk, prodn. splst, indsl. splst. contractor plants Hawthorne, Inglewood, Culver City 1950-70; income tax preparer, executrix self-empl. 1960-; listed Internat. Directory of Disting. Leadership, 2000 Notable Am. Women, 5000 Personalities of World, World Who's Who of Women, Internat. Who's Who of Intellectuals, Personalities of Am.; mem: L.A. World Affairs Council, Scripps Clinic and Research Found., Nat. and Calif. Assn. Parliamentarians (state treas.), Internat. Toastmistress Club (all local ofcs., reg. treas.), Order of Eastern Star (So. Coast Assn. pres. 1988, Belles & Bldrs. of So. Calif. pres. 1979, Grand Rep. Ky. 1984-85), Order of White Shrine of Jerusalem (WHP 1989-90), Am. Biog. Inst. Resrch. Assn. (life dep. gov.), Sierra Club, Viennese 200 Club (secty., treas., pres.); Prot.; rec: stamps, dancing, travel. Res: 5537 Littlebow Rd Palos Verdes 90274

JEFFERY, JAMES NELS, state emergency services official; b. May 16, 1944, Torrance; s. Daryl Fredrick and Mildred Evelyn (Sogard) J.; edn: AA, Long Beach City Coll., 1964; CSU Long Beach 1964-65, CSU Sacramento 1979-80. Career: firefighter, capt. Los Angeles Fire Dept., 1965-87; dir. Long Beach Search & Rescue Unit, 1968-; asst. chief fire div. Calif. Office Emergency

Services, Riverside 1987-; rep. Firescope Communications, Riv. 1979-, coauthor Emergency Plans; awards: disting. service Long Beach Jaycees 1977, comm. service Long Beach Fire Dept. 1978, Silver Beaver BSA 1983, commendn. Mayor of Los Angeles 1985; mem: Calif. State Firemens Assn., Nat. Coordinating Council on Emergency Mgmt., So. Calif. Assn. Foresters and Fire Wardens, L.A. Fire Fighters Assn., Lions, Elks; civic: Boy Scouts Am., L.B. (chmn. service com. 1979-81, tng. com. 1982-), L.B. Community Epilepsy Clinic (bd. 1971-72); Republican; Lutheran. Res: 3916 Cerritos Ave Long Beach 90807 Office Emergency Fire Services PO Box 55157 Riverside 92517

JEFFREY, HELENE BARBARA, business owner, civic activist; b. Fresno; d. A. and N. Yeretzian; m. John A. Jeffrey; children: John, Jody; edn: psych., UC Berkeley ext. Career: owner Calif. Equipment & Fixture Co., Oakland 1965-85; govt. installation of refrigeration and air conditioning for U.S. Army, Navy, Air Force; music cons., owner Orinda Music, Orinda 1972-; civic: Pro America, Farm Animal Reform Movement, PETA/People for Ethical Treatment of Animals, In Defense of Animals, Humane Soc. of U.S., Contra Costa County SPCA; Republican (listed in charter issue Republican Party Who's Who 1991, also 1992 edit); mem. Repub. Nat. Com., Geo. Bush Presdl. Task Force life mem. and Honor Roll also Wall of Honor on West wall of courtyard the White House, U.S. Senatorial. Club preferred mem., Repub. Senatorial. Inner Circle, Ronald Reagan Presdl. Found. sustaining sponsor, Library sponsor, nom. Presdl. Round Table 1990, Repub. Legion of Merit 1992, at-lg. del. 1992 Repub. Platform Planning Com. (recipient V.P. commendation 1992); rec: music. Ofc: Orinda 94563

JELLEY, JOSEPH G., real estate chain president; b. Apr. 19, 1937, Blairsville, Pa.; s. Joseph G. and E. (Freidline) J.; m. Patricia A. Tremellen, July 29, 1982; children: Joseph b. 1957, James b. 1959, Joanna b. 1961, John b. 1962; edn: BS, cum laude, Tri-State Univ. 1957; GRI, Calif. 1978; Cert. Residential Splst., Nat. Assn. Realtors 1979; cert. R.E. broker, mgr., N.A.R. 1980. Career: sales mgr. Robert Hall Co., NY 1962-64; mdsg. supt. Sears Roebuck & Co., NY 1964-70; midwest dist. sales mgr. Melville Shoe Co., Foxmoor Div., NY 1971-74; senior reg. v.p. V.E. Howard & Co., Del Mar 1975-76; founder/pres. Western State Pacific Pines Corp., Del Mar 1976-; pres. The Jelley Co., Inc., a real estate chain 1976-; pres. Del Mar Morgage Co. Inc. 1978-; profl. lectr. and cons. in fin., mktg., and mgmt.; recipient numerous awards; mem: Nat. Assn. Realtors, Calif. Assn. Realtors, Internat. Assn. R.E. Appraisers (senior); contbr. numerous articles on fin. and real estate, San Diego Co. newspapers, periodicals; rec: creative design, writing. Res: 13635 Pine Needles Dr, Del Mar 92014 Ofc: The Jelley Co., Inc. 1312 Camino Del Mar Del Mar 92014

JEMISON-SMITH, PEARL, registered nurse, HIV educator and consultant; edn: Ipswich and East Suffolk Hosp., Eng. 1956-58; AA, RN, Fullerton Comm. Coll. 1971; Calif. tchg. credential comm. coll. 1979; BS, Univ. of Phoenix, Az. 1982; certification in Infection Control. Career: staff nurse intensive care unit UCI Medical Ctr., Orange 1971-74, head nurse 1974-77, nurse epidemiologist 1977-88, AIDS coordinator 1988-92; mem: UCI Med. Ctr. committees: infection control 1978-92, standards 1972-89, nursing quality assurance 1985-87, safety 1982-92, tissue/transfusion 1982-87, antibiotic review 1980-88, patient complaint 1986-88, nursing policy and procedure 1980-92, AIDS comm. coordinating council 1987-, MCMG planning com. 1988-89; cons.: Luther Med. Co. 1982-83, Quality Health Mgmt. Systems 1985-90, Fairview State Hosp. 1984, Protec Containers 1986, Visiting Nurses Assn. 1984, Med-Com Systems 1987-; frequent lectr. various orgns. and businesses; honors: Alpha Gamma Sigma Fullerton Coll., 1971, Zonta Woman Award, 1970, Woman of Yr. Fullerton Coll., 1971, Student Nurse of Yr. So. Calif., 1971, Lauds and Laurels, Comm. Service UCI, 1984, The Bishop Daniel Corrigan Award, 1986, Humanitarian award Human Rels. Com., 1987, Humanitarian award Elections Com. of Orange. Co., 1987, Donna Law award, 1988, Disting. Service Award, OCHCA, 1988, YWCA Excellence in Health, 1990; mem: Assn. for Practitioners in Infection Control (num. committees and bd. ofcs. held since 1979), Nat. Critical Care Inst. (nursing edn. cons. 1986-), Nat. Intravenous Therapy Assn. (ed. bd. 1981-88), Trainex Corp. (bd. advisor 1975-76), Intravenous Nurses Soc. (ed. bd. 1988-); civic: ACTION (ch. 1985-93), AIDS Services Foundation (founding bd. mem. 1986-), Orange Co. AIDS Task Force 1985-86, HIV Advy. Com. (Orange Co.), Hospice Orange Co. (bd. chair 1990), Am. Lung Assn. (bd. dirs. for Orange Co., Calif. and Nat. branches, also num. committee positions since 1980), Orange Co. HIV Planning Advy. Council (chair 1992-), Hospice Mem. Found. (chair 1992-); num. articles pub. profl. jours. Res: 11531 Montlake Dr Garden Grove 92641

JENDEN, DONALD J., educator, pharmacologist; b. Sept. 1, 1926, Horsham, Sussex, England; nat. U.S. cit. 1958; s. Wm. Herbert and Kathleen Mary (Harris) J.; m. 1950, 3 children; edn: scholarship, chem. & physics, Westminster Med. Sch., Univ. of London, 1944; BSc in physiology (first class), Kings Coll. London, 1947; MB, BS, distinction in pathology, pharmacology & therapeutics, medicine, surgery & gyn./ob. (Univ. Gold Medal), Westminster Med. Sch., Univ. of London, 1950. Career: awards: NSF sr. postdoctoral fellow/hon. res. assoc. dept. biophysics Univ. Coll., London, 1961-62, Hon. PhD in pharmaceutical chemistry Univ. Uppsala, Sweden, 1980, Fulbright short-term sr. scholar Australia, 1983, Wellcome Vis. Prof. Univ. Alabama, 1984. Career: lectr. in

pharmacology UC Med. Ctr., San Francisco 1950-51, USPHS postdoc. fellow 1951-53, asst. prof. pharmacology 1952-53; asst. prof. UCLA, 1953-56, assoc. prof. 1956-60, prof. pharmacology 1960-, actg. dept. chmn. 1956-57, dept. chmn. pharmacology UCLA Sch. of Med. 1968-89; mem. The Brain Research Inst., UCLA, 1961-, prof. biomathematics UCLA 1967-; lt. Med. Corps USNR, assigned to Naval Med. Res. Inst., Bethesda, Md. 1954-56; cons. govt. agys. NIH, NIMH, Los Alamos Sci. Lab., Nat. Inst. on Aging (chmn. aging rev. com. 1985-87), others; mem. nat. sci. advy. com. Am. Fedn. for Aging Research 1985-; mem: AAAS, Am. Chem. Soc. Div. of Medicinal Chemistry, Am. Coll. Neuropsychopharmacology (Fellow), Am. Physiol. Soc., Am. Soc. for Mass Spectrometry, Am. Soc. for Med. Sch. Pharmacology, Am. Soc. of Neurochemistry, Am. Soc. for Pharmacology & Exptl. Therapeutics, Assn. for Med. Sch. Pharmacology, NY Acad. of Sci., The Physiol. Soc. (London), Soc. for Neurosci., West Coast Coll. of Biol. Psychiatry (charter fellow), We. Pharmacology Soc. (pres. 1970); mem. editl. bds. Alzheimer Disease and Associated Disorders an Intl. J., Life Scis., Neurobiology of Aging, Neuropsychopharmacology, Research Comms. in Chemical Pathology and Pharmacology, Substance and Alcohol Actions/Misuse; contbr. 400+ sci. publs. Res: 3814 Castlerock Rd Malibu 90265

JENKINS, THOMAS M., judge; b. Mar. 7, 1921, Benton, Ill.; s. Thomas M. and Ruby (Lasley) J.; m. Anne Oakhill, July 13, 1944; children: Thomas Mark, III b. 1949, Jo Anne b. 1950, Dirk b. 1954; edn: B.Ed., Chgo. State Univ. 1943; LLD, UC Hastings 1949. Career: atty. Hanson, Bridgett, Marcus & Jenkins, 1950-75; judge Superior Ct., State of Calif., Co. of San Mateo, 1975-90; elected mayor and councilman City of San Carlos, 1962-74; bd. dirs. League of Calif. Cities, 1970-74; mem: Gov.'s Hosp. Advy. Council 1963-67; chmn. bd. Calif. Ctr. for Judicial Edn. 1982-90, Calif. Judicial Council 1972-76, Calif. Judges Assn. (exec. bd. 1979-83), State Bar of Calif. (v.p., bd. govs. 1969-72, chmn. Conf. of Dels. 1967), Am. Bar Assn. (Ho. Dels. 1959-64); civic: Peninsula Comm. Found. (bd. 1985-), Mills-Peninsula Hosp. Senior Care Pgms. (chmn., bd. 1985-90), Friends Svs. for Aging, Phila. (advy. bd. 1984-88), Living at Home Pgm., N.Y. (advy. bd. 1985-89), United Way of Calif. (pres. bd. 1976-77), Am. Assn. of Homes for the Aging (pres. 1966-67, bd. 1962-68), No. Calif. Presbyn. Homes (bd., chmn., 1977-92), S.F. Assn. for Mental Health (bd. 1971-76), Campfire Girls (v.chmn., nat. bd. dirs. 1962-66); Democrat; Prot. Res: 711 Terrace Rd San Carlos 94070 Ofc: Superior Court Hall of Justice Redwood City 94063

JENNINGS, WILLIAM H., city attorney; b. Sept. 14, 1942, St. Joseph, Mo.; s. Harold Thomas and Elaine May (Van Andle) J.; m. Rita Susan Sugar, Nov. 23, 1986; edn: BS (physics), Univ. of Mo. 1964; MA (econ.), USC 1975, JD, 1975; admitted bar: Calif., U.S. Dist. Ct., so., cent., no., ea. dists., U.S. Ct. Appeals, 9th cir. Career: instr. banking law, legal writing, contracts, commercial law and Uniform Comml. Code, USC Law Center and UCLA Ext. 1977-86; high sch. tchr. Fountain Valley H.S. 1967-70; Thomas Jefferson "1776", New York City, N.Y. 1970-71; atty., assoc. Freshman, Marantz, Beverly Hills 1981-86; Rosen, Wachtell, Los Angeles 1986-87; atty., ptnr. Chrystie & Berle, Los Angeles 1988-91; sole practice, Santa Monica 1991-92; city atty., Hollister, Calif. 1992-; city councilman Santa Monica City Council 1979-90: mayor pro tem 1983-86, apptd. Los Angeles Co. Health Systems Planning Commn. 1980-82, League of Calif. Cities environmental quality com. 1984-89 (div. chair L.A. Co. envir. quality com. 1984-86), L.A. County Hazardous Waste Mgmt. Advy. Com. 1987-90; honors: Omicron Delta Kappa, Pi Mu Epsilon; mem: Beverly Hills Co. Bar Assn., L.A. Co. Bar Assn. (com. evaluate profl. stds. 1986-), USC Law Alumni Assn. (bd. 1984-); author: Guaranty Law (Shepards/ McGraw-Hill, 1993); contbr. newspaper mo. column on UCC law in Los Angeles Daily Journal; thesis: "Transfers of Technology by a Multinational Corp. to a Partly Owned Argentine Subsidiary" 1975; num. articles in profl. jours. on banking and government law; Democrat; Methodist; rec: bicycling, camping, Thomas Jefferson. Ofc: 375 Fifth St Hollister 95023

JENSEN, ALICE DAWLEY, antique dealer and lecturer, civic activist; b. Dec. 20, 1912, Leona, Wisc.; d. Dr. John Hewitt and Mabel Carolyn (Brown) Dawley; m. James A. Ross, Jan. 25, 1932 (dec. 1951); children: James A. b. 1936, Richard John b. 1938, Marcia D. b. 1942; m. Fredrick Morris Jr., Dec. 19, 1952 (dec. June 1983); stepson, Frederick Morris b. 1942; m. Ned Ashton Jensen, Aug. 7, 1984; edn: 2 years nurse tng. Waterbury Hosp., Waterbury, Conn. 1929-32. Career: owner Antique Shop, Green, N.Y., 1959-67; Williamsburg, Va., 1966-83; past bd., sec., Four Valley's Antique Dealers Assn., N.Y.S.; active D.A.R. (Regent 1961-63), Rebekah Lodge (Noble Grand 1968-70), American Legion Aux. (v.p. 1982-84, Votive Lady 1979-83), advy. bd. Office of Human Affairs 1979-83); Ch. of Jesus Christ of Latter Day Saints. Res: Upland 91786

JENSEN, DEBORAH ANN, wedding photographer; b. Dec. 21, 1952, Santa Rosa, 4th gen. Californian; d. David Laurens and Barbara Evelyn (Hackler) Jordan; great grandparents migrated west from Ohio by wagon train in 1874 on the Oregon Trail, settled in Calif. 1870s; m. William Hans Jensen II; children: Natalie, Trudie, Erik; edn: AA in bus. & photography, Mesa Jr. Coll., San Diego, 1973; pvt. studies in piano, 1963-77. Career: metal sculptress, works in Hallmark and other gift stores (12+ states) 1973-76; piano tchr. self-empl. 1976-77; videographer, photographer, florist, pianist Wedding Chapel San Diego,

1977-82; freelance wedding photographer, San Diego, Sacramento, and Auburn area, 1977-; profl. keyboard artist for weddings, 1977-82; Weight Watcher's group leader., photographer, videographer, San Diego, 1987-89, staff instr. photography, 1985-; design & mfr. custom wedding frames for photos, 1991-; listed Who's Who of La Jolla 1988-9; mem. Bridal Mart of Am. (assoc. 1990-); Christian Ch. (pianist 1975-91);profl. soft sculpture, mtr. clocks (Sacramento area crafts store 1991-93); rec: piano, walking (long distance), general photog., painting. Res: Rocklin 95677

JENSEN, GERALD RANDOLPH, editor, graphic artist; b. Aug. 12, 1924, Kalispell, Montana; s. Hans Clemen and Mabel E. (Everson) J.; m. Helen Levine, Dec. 11, 1943; children: Marjorie, b. 1955; edn: G.Th., Life Coll. 1945; Litt.D., Internat. Acad. 1970; MA, Union Univ. 1976; PhD, 1978. Career: regional and nat. dir. Youth & Christian Edn., Internat. Ch. Foursquare Gospel, Los Angeles 1946-54; dir. San Francisco area Youth for Christ 1955-60; v.p. Sacred Records, Whittier 1960-63; dir./ed. internat. publications Full Gospel Businessmen's Fellowship 1963-69, 1985-; pres. Triangle Productions, Burbank 1970-79; pres. Claiborne/ Jensen Advtsg. 1980-82; pres. Jerry Jensen & Assocs., Santa Fe Springs 1982-85; bd. dirs.: High Adventure Ministries (Van Nuys), Found. for Airborne Relief (Long Beach), Ambassadors of Aid (Vancouver, B.C., Canada), Friends in the West (Seattle, Wash.), Internat. Bible Inst. (Santa Fe Springs), Outreach Korea (Torrance); publs. dir. World Missionary Assistance Plan; Wings of Healing; Total Health Mag.; Am. Bible Soc.; Revival Fires; The Methodist Hour; Jimmy Snow Evangelistic Assocs., Nashville, Tenn.; awards: design, Dynamic Graphics 1961, Christian Edn. award Internat. Bible Inst. 1980, spl. service award Golden State Univ. 1983; founder/editor Acts Mag., Voice Mag. (Asian, Scandinavian, European and Spanish editions) FGBMFI, 1977-; youth mags.: Vision, Young America, Today's Youth, Campus, View, Charisma Digest; Republican; Prot.; rec: art collection, golf, travel. Res: 5772 Garden Grove Blvd #482 Westminster 92683 Ofc: Full Gospel Business Men's Fellowship Internat. 3150 Bear St Costa Mesa 92626

JENSEN, JOHN PAUL, JR., engineering executive, consultant; b. Feb. 27, 1917, Sioux City, Iowa; s. John Paul and Bertha (Jorgensen) J.; m. Judith Karker, Nov. 1, 1981; edn: Iowa State Univ. 1937-38; Morningside Coll. 1939-40. Career: vol. Royal Canadian Air Force 1940-41; served in U.S. Air Force 1941-45 with 6th Photogrammetry Sq., aerial maps and bomb charts in 35 countries; consulting engr., v.p. Thermodynamics Universal, Inc., (predecessor co., Communications Cons., Inc.), Burlingame; pres. Chloro-Guard Electronics of Ariz.; sales & advtg. dir. Seagrams Distillery, San Francisco; owner John's Back Bay, Lodi 1976-83; indep. cons. 1984-; Sunworks Solar Electronics Inc. 1984; Nat. Micro Systems Inc. 1984; dir. Consumer Credit Union; mem: Lions Internat., Delta Tau Delta , Lodi C. of C. 1977-83, Woodbridge Golf & Country Club; Republican; Worldwide Ch. of God. Address: POB 810 Pine Grove 95665-0810

JENSEN, MARGARET THERESA, rancher, business owner, activist for the homeless; b. Mar. 19, 1939, Princeton, Wis.; d. Joseph and Margaret (Clark) Hoppa; m. Louis Jensen, Oct. 17, 1959; children: Linda b. 1960, Theresa b. 1961, Michael b. 1962; desig: Assoc. in Risk Mgmt. (ARM), Chartered Property Casualty Underwriter (CPCU) Ins. Inst. of Am. (1980, 81). Career: secty. Russell Moccasin Co., Berlin, Wis. 1957-60; distbn. mgr. Milwaukee Journal & Sentinel, Berlin, Wis. 1963-65; secretarial pos., 1962-68; NML broker's asst. The Walker Agy., Berlin, Wis., 1968-76; service rep. Flinn, Gray & Herterich, Palo Alto, Calif. 1976-77; broker's asst. Robert N. Burmeister, Menlo Park 1977-78; underwriter Boring-R-G-V, Redwood City 1978; insurance coord. Lockheed Missiles & Space Co., Sunnyvale 1979-86; employee benefits adminstr. Lockheed Technical Ops. Co., Inc., Sunnyvale 1987-88; owner/mgr. Jensen's Pick & Shovel Ranch, Angels Camp, 1989-; sponsor, activist for the homeless; honors: E.H. Schroeder Memorial Award, Milw. Jour. 1967, appreciation for outstanding leadership in youth devel. Lockheed Mgmt. Assn. 1987, recipient 15 Productivity Improvement awards-multi-mil. $ cost savings, and Lockheed Employee of Month (4t), Personality of Yr. 1991; dep. gov. Am. Biographical Inst. Res. Assn., mem. Am. Biog. Inst. advy. bd., ABI Woman of Yr. 1990, listed World Who's Who of Women, 2000 Notable Am. Women, Dict. Intl. Biography, Intl. Leaders in Achiev., Dict. Intl. Biography, Intl. Dir. Distinguished Leadership, Who's Who Intellectuals, Personalities Am., Comm. Leaders Am., Men & Women of Distinction, mem: Chartered Prop. Cas. Underw. Soc. (sponsor CPCU Candidate devel. No. Calif. 1982-88), Risk Ins. Mgmt. Soc. (dir., chpt. secty. 1979-), Nat. Mgmt. Soc., Am. Quarter Horse Assn., Calif. Farm Bur. Fedn., We. Mining Council, Calaveras Co. C.of C., Tuolumne Co. Visitors Bur., Calif. Hist. Soc., Columbia (Ca.) C.of C., Calif. Travel Parks Assn., Calaveras Lodging & Visitors Assn.; Berlin (Wis.) Alumni Assn., Don Pedro Homeowners Assn. (LaGrange), Peninsula Academies Palo Alto (mentor 1987), Nat. Trust for Hist. Preservation 1993; R.Cath.; rec: designed & blt. energy efficient home, collect antiques, photog., gold prospecting, roller skating, crafts. Res: 4977 Parrots Ferry Rd (POB 1141) Angels Camp 95222

JENSEN, NANCY BLANCHE, minister, artist, poet, civic activist; b. Oct. 14, 1937, Great Falls, Mont.; d. Antone R. (Count Sir Anthony Rudolph Strocki) and Evalyn Pearl (Fuller) Strosky; m. William Melvin Jensen, May 18, 1970; children: Michael J. Pope b. 1958; edn: John C. Fremont H.S., L.A. 1955; Calif.

lic. collector, 1984-. Works: poet; artist in oils and acrylics; poems pub. in poetry anthologies: Our Western World Most Beautiful Poems (1984), Our Worlds Most Beloved Poems (1984), American Anthology (1985-88), Words of Praise, ed. John Frosts (1987), Best Poems of Today (1987), Favorite Poets (1988); chairperson Patriotic T-Shirts (given free to sch. children) for Bear Valley Elem. Sch. and Glen Martin Sch.; awards: named Citizen of Year Citizens Com. for Right to Bear Arms (1989, 91), golden poet Am. Poetry Press, Santa Cruz (1988, 89), Who's Who in Poetry, golden poet, silver poet awards World of Poetry, Sacto. (1986, 87, 88, 89, 90, 91), best new poet Best Poems of Today 1987; correspondent and writer numerous letters 1970- on local and nat. issues to the U.S. Pres. and other elected govt. ofcls.; mem. Am. Legion Aux. (exec. bd., historian, legis. chair 1989-91), V.F.W. Ladies Aux. Post 7379 (1990-), Nat. Mus. of Women in the Arts (charter mem.), Nat. Rifle Assn., Bear Valley Charcol Burners - Black Powder Club 1990-, Bear Valley HOA, Big Bear Hist. Soc., Elks; Republican (Presdl. Order of Merit 1991, listed Repub. Who's Who 1991, mem. U.S. Senatl. Club 1990-, Presdl. Commn. 1992-; Christian; rec: gardening, walking, fishing. Res: POB 1592 Big Bear City 92314

JENSEN, NED ASHTON, pharmaceutical co. sales representative; b. Dec. 30, 1915, Panguitch, Utah; s. Alvin Mahonri and Emily (Steele) J.; m. Helen Blair, Sept. 3, 1938 (dec. Mar. 1983); children: Linda b. 1939, Blaine b. 1941, Hal b. 1947, Nedra b. 1950; m. Alice Dawley, Aug. 7, 1984; edn: grad. Manual Arts H.S., 1935 (pres. Letterman's Soc., Amestedian Club, sec. Assoc. Student Body, mem. Track and Field Team, Cross Country Team); PharmB, Univ. So. Calif., 1939; lic. pharmacist Calif. Career: sales rep. Eli Lilly & Company, 1941-81, rep. in every So. Calif. Terr. except Glendale and Bev. Hills; faculty, lectr. mktg. & transp., USC Sch. of Pharmacy, 1962-65; co-founder (w. late wife Helen) and pres. Spastic Children's Found., 1946-48; honors: So. Calif. Cross Country Track & Field Champion, AAU Champion 1934-35, USC 4-yr. athletic scholarship and 4-yr. Varsity Letterman 1935-39, USC Life Pass, inducted nat. champion Helms Hall of Fame, All Time Great Track Team/ Track and Field Team, All Time Great/ Medley Relay Team (880 leg), Skull and Mortar (pres.), Phi Delta Chi; mem. USC Pharmacy Alumni Assn. (pres. 1945-47, Gen. Alumni bd. USC), QSAD Centurions/USC 1976-80, Toastmasters Intl. (pres. Wilshire Club, area gov., 1945-55), Am. Legion 1955-58; works: 450 Poems, 70 Short Stories, 3 Novels (unpub.), 50 Musical Compositions with Lyrics; wrote music and lyrics for 25 yrs. of the Los Angeles ABCD Musical Ensemble; Ch. of Jesus Christ of Latter Day Saints (Bishop 1962-68). Res: Upland 91786

JENSEN, STEPHEN EDWARD, county official; b. Sept. 15, 1949, San Mateo; s. Philip Albert and Florence (Henderson) J.; m. Kathleen Beatrice Fitzbuck, Sept. 18, 1976; edn: AA, De Anza Coll., 1969; BS, CSU Chico, 1972; Calif. lic. Gen. Bldg. Contr. 1973, R.E. Broker 1981. Career: owner/mgr. Jensen Constrn. Co., Magalia, 1973-84; owner/broker Pines Realty, Magalia, 1981-84; plan check engr. DES Inc., Sacto., 1985-86; dir. Dept. Bldg. & Safety County of Lake, Lakeport 1986-89; chief building insp. County of Marin, San Rafael, 1989-; mem: Co. Bldg. Ofcls. Assn. of Calif. (1st v.p., dir. 1986-, sec. Sacto. Valley chpt. ICBO 1989), Internat. Assn. of Bldg. Ofcls., Calif. Bldg. Ofcls., Internat. Assn. Plbg. & Mech. Ofcls. / IAPMO Walnut (com. chmn. stds., res., 1986-); Republican; rec: fishing, collect antique tools, woodworking. Res: 21453 Shainsky Rd Sonoma 95476 Ofc: Marin County DPW, PO Box 4186 San Rafael 94913

JENSEN, WILLIAM HANS, II, wedding consultant/photographer and videographer, lawn care co. owner, farmer; b. Dec. 17, 1955, on family farm Webster City, Ia.; s. William and Phyliss (hd. dietitian Sharps Mem. Hosp., San Diego, 30 yrs.) J.; m. Deborah Ann Jordan (profl. pianist and wedding photog.); children: Natalie, Trudie, Erik; edn: grad. Madison H.S. 1975, photography courses Consumes City Coll. 1987. Career: salesman motorcycles, 1975-85; wedding cons., photog. and videographer, 1987-, also design & mfr. custom frames for wedding photographs 1991-; 3d generation owner family farm in Iowa, 70-acre corn farm, 1989-; clubs: Coast to Coast, RPI, Thousand Trails; Watchtower Soc.; rec: off-road motorcycling, travel, reading and singing, ministry. Address: 2333 Eagle Ct Rocklin 95677

JENSTAD, NELS LINDEN, music composer, publisher; b. Mar. 15, 1956, Mpls.; s. Donald Linden and Elizabeth Marie (Holmes) J.; edn: music & arts major Contra Costa Coll., 1974-80, Saddleback Coll., 1981-83. Career: performer/composer X-perimental Chorus, Herman LeRouxe PhD, Conductor, El Cerrito, Ca. 1976-79; prodn. mgr. Contra Costa Sym. Assn., Orinda 1977-79; performer, music writer, 1978-; producer, pub. Nels Jenstad Music Publishing, San Juan Capistrano 1988-; music tchr. Metro Sch. of Music, Santa Ana 1990-; awarded Composer in Residence, Musical Arts of Contra Costa County, Richmond 1979; mem. Am. Soc. of Composers Authors and Publishers 1986-, Internat. Platform Assn. 1992-; composer/musician: L.P. sound recording, "Synthesis Ltd." (1985), recording, "World Processor" (1988), concert and audio & video recordings- ensemble: Sincere Fibers (1985-87), Blue Trees (1988), M.A.N. Foundation (1990-92), songwriter guitarist "Crayon Revolution" (1992-93); Indep.; rec: film, video, nature trails. Ofc: Nels Jenstad Music, 31921 Camino Capistrano Ste 9273 San Juan Capistrano 92675

JEUN, BUDDY H., engineer; b. Nov. 6, 1939, China; nat. 1977; s. Wan Ton and Sin Toa (Leung) J.; m. Fung K. Jeun, Dec. 30, 1968; dau., Rebecca W. b. 1990; edn: BSc in math, Univ. Montreal Canada 1965; MS math and statistics, George St. Univ. 1974; PhD in E.E., Univ. Mo., Columbia 1979. Career: res. asst. Georgia St. Univ. 1972-74; tchg. asst. Univ. of Mo., Columbia 1974-79; sr. scientist Lockheed Electronics Co., Houston 1977-80; tech. staff Rockwall Internat. Co. 1980-85; splst. Aerojet Electro Systems Co., Azusa 1985-87; sr. staff engr. Lockheed Aircraft Service Co., Ontario 1987-; awards: NASA group achieve. award, W.D.C. 1981 and NASA public service award, W.D.C. 1982; mem: IEEE, Computer Soc. of Am.; publ: The Design and Implementation of an Improved Multivariate Classification Scheme (Univ. Mo., 1979); rec: tennis, swimming. Res: 21344 Spring St Walnut 91789 Ofc: Lockheed Aircraft Service Co. POB 33 Ontario 91762

JEZYCKI, CHARLES WOJCIECH STANISLAW, management & marketing consultant; b. Sept. 5, 1936, Warsaw, Poland; nat. 1957; s. Karol P. and Wanda Cecylia (Krzyzanowska) J.; m. Helen Marie Flaherty, July 9, 1961 (div. 1986); m. Barbara L. Wascom Oct. 7, 1989; children: Charles b. 1962, Camille b. 1963, Charles David b. 1964, Stefan b. 1967, Craig b. 1968, Patrick b. 1968, Jennifer b. 1971; edn: BS, Univ. S.F. 1956; MBA, S.F. St. Univ. 1980; tchg. credential (1980). Career: personnel rep. St. Compensation Ins., S.F. 1959-65; personnel and. pub. rels. dir. Queen of Valley Hosp., Napa 1965-68, asst. adminstr. 1968-85, v.p. 1985-88; pres. Exec. Mgmt. Consulting Group 1988-; realtor Vintage Properties, 1991-93; v.p. Peninsula Blood Bank, Burlingame 1993-; honors: Calif Soccer Assn. Hall of Fame 1989, League Official of the Year awarded by Soccer Magic, Calif. monthly soccer publ. 1989, Calif. Legislature resolution 1988, Who's Who in West, Outstanding Young Men Am.; mem: Napa Co. Assn. of Realtors, Nat. Assn. of Realtors, Napa C.of C. (pres., bd.), Napa Co. Emergency Med. Care Com. (chmn., bd. mem.), N. Bay Hosp. Conf. (pres., bd. mem.), Leadership Napa Valley (bd., mem. selection com.), Am. Coll. Healthcare Execs., Calif. Soccer Assn. (v.chmn. 1987-91, exec. bd. 1988-), Napa Senior Soccer League (chmn. select com., coaching adminstr., pres., 1981-88), N. Bay Soccer League (pres. 1985-), Edinburgh Academy Academicals, Scotland 1956-, Napa City Civil Service Commn. (chmn. 1969-78), Kiwanis, Napa Ambassadors Club (pres.); 2 articles pub. in med. jours., 1972, 73; articles pub. on soccer Napa Register (1965-) and Soccer Magic (1990-); mil: E-4 AUS 1956-59; Republican; R.Cath.; rec: backpacking, skiing, soccer. Res: 740 Marlin Ave #1 Foster City 94404 Ofc: Peninsula Blood Bank 1791 El Camino Real Burlingame 94010

JIMMINK, GLENDA LEE, mentor teacher, artist; b. Feb. 13, 1935, Lamar, Colo.; d. Harold Dale and Ruth Grace (Ellenberger) Fasnacht; m. Gary Jimmink, Oct. 24, 1964 (div. 1984); son, Erik Gerard; edn: BA, Univ. LaVerne, 1955. Career: tchr. Pomona Unified Sch. Dist., 1955-61; Palo Alto Unified Sch. Dist.; 1961-65, San Rafael Sch. Dist., 1966-, rep. Curriculum Council (1983-87, 89-91), mentor teacher and creator of geography curriculum, 1989-90; pub. World Geography Handbook for Teachers; artist, pub. calendar: Dry Creek Valley 1987, others; mem: Calif. Tchrs. Assn., NEA, San Rafael Tchrs. Assn., Marin County Curriculum Connection; civic: Marin Arts Council San Rafael 1989-, PTA San Rafael 1966-, adv. Black Student Union, Big Bros./Big Sisters (big sis. 1988-93), Sierra Club, Earthwatch, Nature Conservancy; rec: golfing, sailing, horticulture, drawing. Res: 1205 Melville Sq #203 Richmond 94804 Ofc: San Rafael School Dist. 225 Woodland Ave San Rafael 94901

JOECK, NEIL ARCHIBALD, international political analyst; b. Feb. 16, 1950, Montreal, Canada; s. Werner F. and Nancy (Archibald) J.; m. Melinda Erickson, Sept. 16, 1972; children: Morgan b. 1981, Graeme b. 1983; edn: BA, UC Santa Cruz 1973; MA, Carleton Univ. Canada 1976; MA, UCLA 1980; PhD, 1986. Career: vol. Vols. in Asia, Stanford 1970; adminstrv. asst. UC Berkeley 1976-78; lectr., researcher Center for Internat. & Strategic Affairs UCLA 1979-86; res. fellow Inst. on Global Conflict & Cooperation, UCSD, La Jolla 1986-87; internat. political analyst Lawrence Livermore Nat. Lab., Livermore 1987-; cons. War & Peace in Nuclear Age, Boston 1986; tchr. Chinese Acad. of Social Sci., Beijing, China 1987; advisor Nuclear Suppliers Research Project, Monterey Inst. Internat. Studies 1988-89; awards: UCLA Graham fellowship 1984, UCSD IGCC fellowship 1985-87, Bank of Am. Gimbel fellowship 1983; author, ed. Strategic Consequences of Nuclear Proliferation in S. Asia (1986), ed. Arms Control & Internat. Security (1984), monograph Comprehensive Test Ban (1986), articles and editorial pub.; Democrat; rec: travel, 20th century American fiction, detective fiction. Ofc: LLNL L-389 POB 808 Livermore 94550

JOHARI, SHYAM, computer consultant; b. June 30, 1948, Jodhpur, India; s. Mohan L. and Gauri D. (Taparia) J.; m. Kamala Baheti, Nov. 22, 1972; children: Priti, Umesh; edn: BS. Univ. Jodhpur 1965; MS, 1967; MS, Univ. Ill. 1969; PhD, 1975. Career: sr. systems analyst western area devel. center Burroughs Corp., Irvine 1975-77; sr. splst. internat. group, Detroit 1977-80; mktg. splst. 1980-82, asst. to v.p. quality 1982-84; mgr. data comms. fin. systems group 1984-86; sr. cons. Joseph & Cogan Assocs. (subsid. Unisys Corp.), Naperville, Ill. 1986-87; mgr. performance group Tandem Computers Inc., Cupertino 1987-; assoc. editor Performance Evaluation Rev. (ACM Sigmetrics) 1987-; mem: Assn. Computing Machinery, IEEE (computer soc.), Computer Measurement Group; Hindu. Res: 3181 Heritage Valley Dr San Jose 95148 Ofc: Tandem Computer, Inc. 19333 Vallco Pkwy, LOC 252-10 Cupertino 95014

JOHN, WALTER, JR., physicist; b. Feb. 16, 1924, Newkirk, Okla.; s. Walter and Carrie (Hollingsworth) J.; m. Carol Salin, Jan. 22, 1954; children: Kenneth, Laura, Claudia, Leslie; edn: BS, Calif. Inst. Tech. 1950; PhD, UC Berkeley 1955. Career: instr. Univ. of Ill. 1955-58; sr. physicist Lawrence Livermore Nat. Labs., Livermore 1958-71; prof. Calif. State Coll., Turlock 1971-74; res. scientist Calif. Dept. of Health Services, Berkeley 1974-; dir. Am. Assn. for Aerosol Res., WDC 1987-92; ed. bd. Aerosol Sci. Tech. 1988-; ed. bd. Applied Occupational and Environmental Hygiene 1989-; Fellow, Am. Physical Soc.; mem: Am. Conference Gov. Indsl. Hygienists (mem. aerosol sampling procedures com.), Am. Assn. of Physics Tchrs., Sigma Xi, Tau Beta Pi; author 90+ articles in books and profl. jours. on nuclear physics, x-rays, aerosols and air pollution; mil: served U.S. Army, 1943-46. Res: 195 Grover Ln Walnut Creek 94596 Ofc: Calif Dept Health 2151 Berkeley Way Berkeley 94704

JOHNSON, BRUCE, television producer, screenwriter; b. July 7, 1939, Oakland; s. Robert Steele and Edith Kristene (Pederson) J.; m. Kathleen Ross, Nov. 5, 1966; children: Jonathan Alan, Grant Fitzgerald; edn: S.F. City Coll. 1958-60, BA, USC, 1962. Career: producer and head writer television shows: Gomer Pyle 1967-68, Jim Nabors Hour 1969-71, Arnie 1971-72, The Little People 1972-73, The New Temperature's Rising Show 1973-74, Sierra 1974-75, Excuse My French (Canada) 1975-76, Alice 1976-77, Blansky's Beauties 1977, Quark 1977-78, Angie 1978-79, Mork and Mindy 1978-82, Webster 1982-89, The People Next Door 1989, Doghouse 1990-91; Flesh 'N Blood 1991-92; Hangin' with Mr. Cooper 1992-93; numerous movies of the week and pilots for TV; awards: People's Choice best t.v. show award for Mork and Mindy (1979), Photoplay mag. best evening t.v. show (1979), Emmy nomination for best comedy series (1979); mem: Writers Guild Am.-West, Producers Guild Am., Caucus for Prods. Writers and Dirs.; mil: USAF Reserve 1962-68.

JOHNSON, BURELL CARVER, manufacturing and marketing executive, ret.; b. Aug. 10, 1924, Bessemer, Ala.; s. Burell Carver and Bertha Mae (Waldrop) Loveless J.; m. Ada L. (Sherry) Calhoun, Dec. 9, 1944 (div. 1982); children: Gaylen Denise b. 1956, Heide Carol b. 1963; edn: BS, USC 1951. Career: med. sales rep. Chemetron Corp., Nat. Cylinder Gas div., Los Angeles 1951-55, asst. dist. mgr. 1955-58, dist. mgr., San Leandro 1958-67; v.p., gen. mgr. Puritan Bennett Aero Systems Co., El Segundo 1967-90, ret.; mem: Aviation Distbrs., Mfrs. Assn. (past pres.), Nat. Bus. Aircraft Assn., Aircraft Owners & Pilots Assn., City of Palos Verdes Estates (mayor 1978-80, city council 1976-78), Masons (Past Master), Scottish Rite, Shriner; mil: 2d. lt. USMC 1942-46; Republican; Prot.; rec: flying, golf, photog. Res: 32759 Seagate Dr Rancho Palos Verdes 90274 Ofc: Puritan Bennett Aero Systems Co. El Segundo 90245

JOHNSON, DANIEL LEE, SR., state transportation agency administrator; b. July 6, 1936, Yuba City; s. John Clem Johnson and Verginia Nellie (Hammons) Clark; m. Myra Jeanne Vetter, Mar. 13, 1955 (div. 1966); children: Daniel, Jr. b. 1955, John Ora b. 1958 (dec.), Michael b. 1959, Theodore b. 1963; m. Loretta Faye McMullen, Mar. 3, 1968 (div. 1972); m. Carolyn Ann Nelson, Oct. 12, 1974 (div. 1992); grad. Yuba City H.S., 1954, att. Yuba Coll., 1955-71, cert. UC Davis, 1974. Career: sales Standard Oil, Grass Valley 1956-57; freelance artist, 1953-89; draftsman Calif. Div. Highways, Marysville 1956-71; police ofcr. Yuba City Police Dept. 1961-71; graphic artist Caltrans, Marysville 1971-79, sr. delineator 1979-91, adminstr. 1991-; recipient Caltrans 25-Year award, Sacto. 1981, Dist. director award, Marysville 1987, Affirmative Action award 1988, Sustained Superior Accomplishment award, Caltrans, Sacto. 1990, winner First Award in Publicity Competition, Calif./Nev. Moose Assn. Inc. (1980, 89, 90, 91, 92), listed Who's Who in West 1992-93, Who's Who in the West 1993, Dictionary of Internat. Biographies 1993; chmn. Caltrans Disabled Advy. Com. 1981-88; mem: Am. Red Cross, Yuba City (instr. 1974-84), Am. Legion 1988-, E. Clampus Vitus 1972-, Nat. Rifle Assn. (1974-, charter founder 2nd amendment task force 1993, life mem.), Citizens Right to Keep Arms (1986-, Citizen of Yr. 1989, 90, 91, 92), Dist. 3 Quarter Century Club (1981-, dir. 1985-87), Loyal Order of Moose Lodge No.1204 Yuba City (1969-, Moose Call bulletin editor 1971-, First Pl. Internat. Bulletin Award and 2d Pl. Internat. Award for Editl. Excellence, L.O.O.M. (1990, 92), publicity dir. 1977-, gov. 1982-83, Moose of Yr. award 1990-91, Comm. Svc. award Cal/Nev Moose Assn. 1990, nat. Shining Star award nominee 1990-91), Legion of the Moose (1978-, Fellowship degree 1989), mem. 25 Club in Membership -50 Div.; inventor: rubber powered boats, Johnson's Marina Boat Regatta (1981-87); mil: p.o. 3c USN 1953-61; Republican; Methodist; rec: hunting, fishing, boating, radio control modeling. Ofc: Caltrans PO Box 911 Marysville 95901

JOHNSON, DAVID DEAN BRIAN, structural engineer; b. Feb. 7, 1956, North Hollywood; s. Charles Walton and Marcia Miriam (Baile) J.; 4th generation Los Angelonian, great-great grandson of San Fernando Valley pioneers Neils and Ann Wilden Johnson; edn: BS, CSU Northridge 1980; grad. studies, UCLA 1986-; Calif. Reg. Profl. Engr.- civil (#34859, 1982), structural (#3032, 1988). Career: design draftsman Aircraft Component Repair Co., Sun Valley 1977-79; struct. designer/ draftsman John Chan & Assoc., Struct. Engrs., Van

Nuys 1979-80; mgr. Calif. Div., KPFF Consulting Engrs., Santa Monica 1980-90; pres. David D.B. Johnson, Structural Engrs., Santa Monica 1990-; mem: Am. Soc. Civil Engrs., Structural Engring. Assn. of So. Calif., Am. Concrete Inst., Earthquake Engring. Research Inst.; Libertarian; Methodist; rec: golf, running, wine tasting. Res: 120 Pico Blvd #409 Santa Monica 90405

JOHNSON, DOROTHY MYERS, jeweler, accountant, ret.; b. Sept. 27, 1917, Magna, Utah; d. Gilbert Yost and Elizabeth (Kitchen) Myers; m. Harvey Kenneth Johnson, Apr. 7, 1944 (div. 1956); edn: grad. University H.S., Oakland 1935. Career: office staff Brisacher Advertising, San Francisco 1935-42; cost acct. Jones & King, Hayward 1942-43; co-owner Johnson Jewelers, Oakland 1944-56; ptnr. Parker & Johnson Jewelers, Hollister 1947-56; staff acctg. Margaret Axell, P.A., San Rafael 1956-79; honors: biog. listings in Two Thousand Notable Am. Women (2d edit.), The Inner Circle of Women 1990, Internat. Dir. of Disting. Leadership (3d edit.), Hall of Fame, Five Thousand Personalities of World 1991; clubs: Internat. Platform Assn., Eastern Star, White Shrine of Jerusalem, Newcomers Club, var. senior orgns., Paradise; past mem. Bus. & Profl. Women; Republican; Prot.; rec: sci. studies, fin., politics. Res: PO Box 1536 Paradise.

JOHNSON, EINAR WILLIAM, lawyer; b. Apr. 6, 1955, Fontana; s. Carl Wilbur and Judith Priscilla (Orcutt) J.; m. Cynthia, Oct. 9, 1976; children: Brian b. 1977 (dec.), Carl b. 1979, Gregory b. 1980, Christopher b. 1983, Shaun b. 1986, Bradford b. 1989; edn: BA in speech comm., Brigham Young Univ., 1980; JD, J. Reuben Clark Law Sch., Provo, Ut. 1983; admitted Calif. Bar, 1983. Career: asst. debate coach BYU, Provo 1979-80; fin. com. Jed Richardson for Congress, Provo 1980; sales mgr. Ortho Mattress, Orem, Ut. 1979, 81; law clk. Acret & Perrochet, Los Angeles 1982; judicial clerkship U.S. Courts-Hon. A. Sherman Christensen, Salt Lake City 1983-84; litigation atty. law firm Smith & Hilbig, Torrance, 1984-89, litigation ptnr. 1990-; honors: outstanding varsity debater BYU (1974, 80), Am. Jurisprudence awards Bancroft-Whitney 1981, Dean's Cup for top oralist 1982, Am. Inn of Court I, Provo, editor Moot Ct. pgm. J. Reuben Clark Law Sch., and Nat. Moot Ct. Team 1982-83, Nat. Order of Barristers 1983, A.H. Christensen Award for Advocacy 1983; mem: ABA, Calif. State Bar, L.A. Co. Bar Assn., Assn. of Trial Lawyers of Am., Internat. Platform Assn.; publs: law rev. comment (1982), award winning thesis (1983), award winning oratory (1969-80) incl. John Baker's Last Race (1977); Republican (dist. ofcr., state del. Utah Rep. Conv. 1978); Ch. of Jesus Christ of Latter Day Saints (Colorado Mission, Denver 1974-76, Sunday Sch. tchr., L.A. 1986-89, stake high counselor 1989-, Bishop's counselor 1992-93, Elders Quorum Pres. 1993-); rec: photography, guitar, auto restoration, fishing. Res: 211 Via La Soledad Redondo Beach 90277 Ofc: Smith & Hilbig 21515 Hawthorne Blvd Torrance 90503 Tel: 213/540-9111

JOHNSON, (EU)GENE RICHARD, real estate executive; b. July 23, 1930, Tacoma, Wash.; s. Edward Richard and Evelyn L. (Peck) J.; m. LeAnn Noel, June 12, 1954; children: Don b. 1955, Lori b. 1956, Jerry b. 1957, Sheri b. 1961; edn: BA bus. admin., Univ. of Puget Sound, 1956; special courses Univ. Wash., Seattle 1955-56h, UCLA Ext., 1965-75; Cert. Property Mgr. (CPM), IREM (1967). Career: sales acctg. and statistics, Weyerhauser Sales Co., Tacoma, Wash. 1950-56, data proc. supr. Weyerhauser Timber Co., Everett, Wash. 1956-57; adminstrv. auditor, policy issue supr., systems & procedure analyst, supr. systems dept. General America Corp., Seattle 1957-64; property supr./mgr., v.p. William Walters Co., Los Angeles and Long Beach, 1964-77, bd. dirs. 1967-77; founder/pres. G J Property Services Inc., Long Beach 1977-; lectr. UCLA Extension courses 1968-70, Apartment Assn. Calif. 1968-80; awards: gold medal, relay team record 880 yds. H.S. State Track Meet, Wash. State 1948, independent studies Univ. of Puget Sound 1950-54, Varsity Track 1950-54), Sigma Nu pledge class pres. 1950, Melvin Jones Fellow Lions Internat., Long Beach 1987; mem: Inst. of Real Estate Mgmt. 1965-, Building Owners & Mgrs. Assn. 1965-, Long Beach Apt. Assn. 1965-; civic: Downtown Long Beach Assocs. 1965-, Long Beach C.of C. 1977-, Downtown Lions Club L.B. (pres. 1991-92, dir., spl. events chmn. 1985-), L.B. Civic Light Opera (Diamond Terr. 1983-, bd trustees 1990-), St. Mary's Hosp. L.B. (co-ch. Hospice Auction 1988-90), Boys and Girls Club L.B. (bd. dirs. 1990-); mil: ET3 USN 1948-50; Republican; Christian; rec: travel, bowling, theater, sports. Res: 515 Flint Ave Long Beach 90814 Ofc: G J Property Services, Inc. 4201 Long Beach Blvd Ste 306 Long Beach 90807

JOHNSON, FRED IRVING, government health services executive; b. June 5, 1947, Monrovia; s. Floyd Charles and Frances Elizabeth (Shepherd) J.; children: Erik Daniel b. 1976, Heather Leah b. 1978; edn: student, Drury Coll. 1968; AA, Citrus Coll. 1972; BA, CSU Fullerton 1975; MPA, Univ. of San Francisco 1990. Career: credit mgr. Dial Fin. Corp., Los Angeles 1968-69; mgr. electronic systems Instrumentation Div., Kenney Engring. Corp., Monrovia 1970-74; staff acct./auditor Shasta Co., Auditor-Controller's Office 1975-78, mental health adminstr. Dept. Mental Health 1978-79, dep. health svcs. adminstr. Dept. Health Svcs. 1979-82, dept. dir. Health Svcs. Agency 1982, acting dir. 1982-83, dir. 1983-87. hosp. adminstr./controller Shasta Gen. Hosp. 1982-83; director health/med. svcs. Placer County, Health Dept. 1987-; mem. Shasta Co. coms.: Cabinet Advy., Budget Planning, chmn. Staff Advy., secty. Health Svcs. Advy.,

Legislative, Mgmt. Council, Health Ins.; honors: Resolution, Calif. State Senate 1987, merit award Shasta Co. Bd. Suprs. 1986, appreciation, Private Industry Council 1986, Junction Sch. Dist. 1986, Soroptimist Internat. Redding 1985, Shasta Co. Chem. People 1985, Calif. State Advy. Bd. Drug Programs 1984; mem: Calif. Hosp. Assn., County Suprs. Assn. Calif., County Health Care Execs. Assn. (past pres.), Calif. Conf. Local Mental Health Dirs. (exec. bd., var. coms.), Calif. Assn. Co. Alcohol Pgm. Adminstrs., Calif. Assn. Co. Drug. Pgm. Adminstrs., Forensic Assn. Calif., Am. Mgmt. Assn., Healthcare Fin. Mgmt. Assn., Calif. Assn. Pub. Hosps., Shasta Co. Econ. Devel. Task Force, Shasta Co. Inter-Hosp. Advy. Bd., Am. Sch. Bds. Assn., Calif. Sch. Bds. Assn., Shasta Co. Trustee's Assn., Shasta Co. Employee's Fed. Credit Union (credit com.), Placer Health & Welfare Functional Group (chair); civic: S.P.C.A. (v.chair), Rotary (team capt. health svcs.), Palo Cedro Youth Soccer (coach), Cow Creek 4-H Club, Juction Elem. Sch. Dist. (trustee, 3-term pres. 1976-86), IRS Vol. Income Tax Pgm., Lions; mil: E-5 AUS 1965-68, chief personnel splst Batt. Hq.; Republican; Prot.. Res: 1475 Wimbledon Dr Auburn 95603 Ofc: Placer Co. Health Dept. 11484 B Ave Auburn 95603

JOHNSON, JOY L., clinical social worker; b. June 13, 1945, Oakland; d. Bishop La Far Benjamin and Julia (Robinson) J.; son, L. Aaron Smith b. 1979; m. Gabriel B. Donaldson, Jr., 1988; edn: BA sociology, San Francisco St. Univ., 1968, MSW, 1973; Lic. Clin. Social Wkr., 1975. Career: private practice, Oakland 1975-; asst. clin. prof. dept.psychiat. UC Med. Sch., San Francisco 1977-81; clin. social worker Permanente Med. Group, S.F., Richmond, 1981-; awards: NIMH Fellow Mt. Zion Hosp., S.F. 1973-75; mem. Bay Area Black Soc. Wkrs. 1973-; Pentecostal; rec: reading. Ofc: 3215 MacArthur Blvd Oakland 94602

JOHNSON, LEDENE CORDA, quality manager; b. Feb. 19, 1952, San Jose; d. James Guy and Martha Jane (Myers) Corda; m. Charles Glenn Johnson, Nov. 7, 1981; edn: BSBA, Univ. Redlands 1980. Career: receptionist IBM, San Jose 1974-76, secty. 1976-80, mktg. rep. IBM, San Francisco 1980-83, systems engr., Palo Alto 1983-87, mgr. First Line, IBM, S.F. 1987-89, quality mgr. 1990-; mem. Internat. Tng. in Comm., S.F. 1988-90; career counselor Alumnae Resources 1988-93; mem: Woman's Aglow Fellowship (pres. Redwood City Chpt.), Bay Area Profl. Network, Commonwealth Club Calif., Santa Clara Genealogy Soc., Campfire Inc. (bd. 1988-90); Republican; Christian; rec: gardening, golf. Ofc: IBM/ISSC 1510 Page Mill Rd Palo Alto 94304

JOHNSON, LEONIDAS ALEXANDER, optometrist; b. Jan. 16, 1959, Chgo.; s. Rev. Leon and Dolores J.; m. Crystal D. Ellington, June 23, 1990; edn: BA biology, Ill. Wesleyan Univ., 1977-81; BS visual sci., So. Calif. Coll. Optometry, 1983, OD, 1985; stu. Talbot Sch. of Theology, La Mirada 1991-; Calif. reg. optometrist, 1985. Career: optometrist Larry Gotlieb, OD Inc., Redondo Beach 1985-86; James Moses O.D., Inglewood 1986-87; Eyecare USA, Montclair 1987-89, mem. quality assurance com. 1988-89; Pearle Visioncare, Brea 1989-; honors: Optometric recogn. award Pearle Inc. 1990, Outstanding Young Men of Am. 1986, listed The Soc. of Distinguished Am. High Sch. Students 1977, Who's Who in the West (23d); mem. Am. Optometric Assn. 1982-, Calif. Opt. Assn. 1986-, Nat. Optometric Assn. (v.p. So. Calif. chpt. 1993); pub. article in peer rev. jour. (1985); Friendship Baptist Ch., Yorba Linda (trustee 1987-89, deacon 1987-). Res: PO Box 9746 Brea 92622-9746 Ofc: Pearle Visioncare Ste 1046 Brea Mall, Brea 92621

JOHNSON, LISA ANNETTE, dentist; b. Feb. 5, 1956, Montgomery, Ala.; d. Gene Bass and Vera May (Hobdy) J.; edn: BS chem., UC Berkeley 1977; BS dental sci., UC San Francisco 1981, DDS, 1981; Cert. Advanced Cardiac Life Support 1983. Career: dental asst. with x-ray lic. Dr. Sadler, Berkeley, Dr. Johnson, Oakland, and Dr. Brockstein, Montclair 1974-75; tchg. asst. biology Merritt Coll. 1974-75; res. chemist Algea-Hydrogen Project w/Dr. John Beneman, UC Berkeley dept. sanitary engring., Richmond Field Sta., respons. for design and monitoring experiments re buffering and precipitation of nutrients in algae pools, sunlight filtration, enzyme activity and heavy metal content of algae grown on Argon 1975-77; tchg. asst. UC San Francisco Sch. of Dentistry 1977; pub. health dentist Public Health of Alameda Co. 1981; Continuing Edn. Provider, State of Calif.; pvt. dental practice w. emphasis on hosp. dentistry, 1982-; staff Mt. Zion Hosp., S.F., Valley Memorial Hosp. 1982; cons. Saint Rose Hosp. 1983-85; cons. Skilled Nursing Facility, 1983; mem. Acad. for Internat. Med. Studies, Acad. of Gen. Dentistry (nat. sponsor); res. on Oral Pathology in Russia 1988-, pub. by Internat. Medicinal Chemistry Soc. (1990); Address: Lisa Johnson, DDS, 2457 Grove Way Castro Valley 94546

JOHNSON, MARIAN ILENE, educator; b. Oct. 3, 1929, Hawarden, Iowa; d. Henry Richard and Wilhelmina Anna (Schmidt) Stoltenberg; m. Paul Irving Jones, June 14, 1958 (dec. Feb. 26, 1985); m. William Andrew Johnson, Oct. 3, 1991; edn: BA, Univ. LaVerne, 1959; MA, Claremont Grad. Sch., 1962; PhD, Ariz. State Univ., Tempe 1971. Career: elementary sch. tchr. pub. schs. Cherokee, Iowa 1949-52, Sioux City, Ia. 1952-56, Ontario, Calif. 1956-61, Belvedere-Tiburon, Calif. 1962-65, Columbia, Calif. 1965-68; prof. of edn. Calif. State Univ. Chico, 1972-91, also supr. of student tchrs., Center coord. Dept. of Edn.; honors: Phi Delta Kappa 1976-92, Delta Kappa Gamma 1985-92, listed Who's Who- in the World, in Am. Edn., in Am., in the West, of Am. Women; mem. Internat. Reading Assn. 1972-92, AAUW 1985-91; contbr. articles to profl. jours.; travel. Res: 26437 S Lakewood Dr Sun Lakes Az 85248

JOHNSON, PHILIP LESLIE, lawyer; b. Jan. 24, 1939, Beloit, Wis.; s. Philip James and Christabel (Williams) J.; m. Kathleen, May 12, 1979; children: Celeste b. 1984, Nicole b. 1990; edn: AB, Princeton Univ. 1961; JD, USC 1973. Career: pilot US Marine Corps 1961-70; atty., assoc. Tucker & Coddington, 1973-78; ptnr. Engstrom, Lipscomb & Lack, 1978-92; ptnr. Johnson & Nelson, Los Angeles 1992-; lectr. Calif. Cont. Edn. of Bar (CEB) 1990-, speaker So. Methodist Univ. Air Law Symp. 1986, lectr. USC Inst. on Safety & System Mgmt.; mem: Calif. State Bar Assn., LA Co. Bar Assn.; mil: Col.(Ret.) USMC 1961-70, Reserve 1970-92; rec: flying, ski. Res: 5340 Valley View Rd Rancho Palos Verdes 90274 Ofc: Johnson & Nelson, 333 S Grand Ave Ste 1680 Los Angeles 90071

JOHNSON, RICHARD WAYNE, teacher union president, teacher; b. May 21, 1940, Oak Grove, Mo.; s. Luther Lee and Dorothy Nell (Morris) J.; m. Barbara Jean Happel, May 25, 1962; children: Richard Lee b. 1963, Kirk Alexander b. 1968; edn: BS edn., Central Mo. St. Univ. 1962. Career: tchr. L.A. Unified Sch. Dist. 1962-84; mem. United Tchrs. L.A., elected ho. reps. 1970-74, bd. 1974-84, chair W.Area 1978-84, pres. 1984-; awards: ADL Democratic Heritage award 1988; mem: Educators for Social Responsibility, Am. Fedn. Tchrs., Nat. Edn. Assn., Calif. Tchrs. Assn. (state council); contbr. op-ed pages L.A. Times (1987); Democrat; Baptist; rec: scuba diving, writing. Res: 1440 Veteran Ave Los Angeles 90024 Ofc: United Teachers 2511 W 3rd St Los Angeles 90057

JOHNSON, WILLIAM HARRY, international management consultant; b. Oct. 1, 1941, Ridley Park, Pa.; s. Harry Brown and Florence (Round) J.; m. Anna Marie Castellanos, Oct. 19, 1984; edn: BS, Drexel Univ., 1963, MBA, 1967; mfg. methods engr., N.J. Career: mgmt. exec. DuPont Co., Wilmington, Del. 1963-69; bus. analysis mgr. Imperial Chemical Inds., 1970-76; fin. analysis and acquisitions Fluor/Daniel Corp., Irvine, Calif. 1976-78; fin. analysis mgr. Alexander Proudfoot, Chgo. 1978-79; exec. v.p. and c.f.o. Sego Internat., Niagara Falls, Ontario, Can. 1980-82; exec. v.p./gen. mgr. Science Mgmt. Corp., Basking Ridge, N.J. 1982-87; exec. mgr. McDonnell Douglas, Long Beach, Calif. 1987-; dir: Drexel Univ. Alumni Assn. 1991-, Clariton (Pa.) Recycling Assn. Inc. 1990-, Madden Associates, Buffalo Grove, Ill. 1990-, KABB Inc., El Segundo, Ca. 1987-, SEGO Internat., Niagara Falls Ontario, Can. 1980-; Penn Bus. Resources, Santa Ana, Ca. 1982-; awards: MDC extraordinary achiev. McDonnell Douglas 1990, MDC productivity award 1988, chmn.'s productivity award Sci. Mgmt. Corp. 1986, Presdl. Achiev. award Republican Nat. Com., W.D.C. 1988, bd. dirs. outstanding achiev. SEGO Internat. 1981; mem: Inst. of Indsl. Engrs. 1973-, Am. Mgmt. Assn. 1970-, Nat. Productivity Assn. of Canada 1980-, Nat. Assn. of Accts. 1965-, Nat. Petroleum Refinery Assn. 1980-, Am. Mktg. Assn. 1965-, Internat. Productivity Org. 1978-, Dewar's Highlander Clan (Glasgow, Scot.), Lions Club of Kowloon (cent. H.K.), El Segundo (Ca.) Residents Assn.; author: Explosives Distributors (1967), pamphlet: Work Order Guide (1980), articles (1984, 86); Republican (Nat. Com.); Presbyterian; rec: dogs, internat. travel, tennis, swimming, volunteer work. Res: 807 Hillcrest St El Segundo 90245 Ofc: McDonnell Douglas 4060 Lakewood Blvd Long Beach 90801

JOHNSTON, PAMELA MC EVOY, psychologist; b. Mar. 8, 1937, Forest Hills, N.Y.; d. Renny T. and Pamela Shipley (Sweeny) McEvoy; widow of Percy H. "Duke" Johnston; children by previous marriage: Michael B. Anderson, Jeffery A. Thomas, Candy A. Watts, Kenneth L. Anderson; edn: BA, Univ. La Verne, 1978, MS, 1980; PhD, U.S. Internat. Univ., 1982. Career: data processing coord. Ernest Righetti High Sch., Santa Maria 1974-78; instr. psychology, sociology, Allan Hancock Coll., Santa Maria 1977-78; mental health asst. Santa Barbara City Alcoholism Dept., 1977-78; gen. mgr. Professional Suites, San Diego 1978-81; therapist Chula Vista Community Counseling Ctr., San Diego 1978-85, staff pres. 1978; research asst. USIU, 1979-82; research coord. Military Family Research Ctr., San Diego 1981-82; assoc. dir. Acad. Assoc. Psychotherapists, 1982-86; private practice, San Diego 1982-; instr. psychology Mesa Coll., San Diego 1989-90; appt. Delinquency Prevention Commn., 1978; awards: Calif. State scholar 1976-77, State fellow 1979, 80, 81, 82; mem: Am. Psychol. Assn., Am. Assn. Marriage and Family Therapists, Calif. Assn. Marriage and Family Therapists, San Diego County Mental Health Assn. (bd. 1978-80), Rotary Internat. of Rancho Bernardo 1989-, Women's Internat. Ctr. (bd. 1984-), North County InterFaith Council (bd. 1990-92); Republican; R.Cath.; Res: PO Box 1198 Borrego Springs 92004 Tel: 619/767-5224

JOHNSTONE, IAIN MURRAY, statistician, educator, consultant; b. Dec. 10, 1956, Melbourne, Australia; s. Samuel Thomas Murray and Pamela Beatrice (Kriegel) J.; edn: BS hons., Australian Nat. Univ. Canberra 1978; MS, 1979; PhD, Cornell Univ. 1981. Career: asst., assoc. prof. statistics Stanford Univ. 1981-; assoc. prof. biostats. Stanford Univ. Med. Sch. 1989-; prof. statistics and biostatistics, Stanford Univ. Med. Sch. 1992-; assoc. editor Annals of Statistics 1987-91; contbr. articles to profl. jours.; awards: Alfred P. Sloan Research fel-

low, 1988-90, Presdl. Young Investigator NSF, 1985-92; mem: Royal Statistics Soc. (fellow), Inst. Math. Statistics (fellow, program secty.), Am. Statistical Assn., Am. Math. Soc., AAAS. Ofc: Stanford Univ. Dept. Statistics Sequoia Hall Stanford 94305-4065

JOLLEY, DONAL CLARK, artist-painter; b. Oct. 20, 1933, Zion National Park, Utah; s. Donal Jones and Nora (Crawford) J.; m. Virginia Elizabeth Harrison, Nov. 14, 1970; children: Karen b. 1960, Donal b. 1962, Keith b. 1965; edn: BS, Brigham Young Univ., Provo 1959. Career: served to sp4, illustrator, US Army, Germany 1956-57; illustrator Spacetech Lab., Redondo Beach, Calif. 1960-61; illustrator The Aerospace Corp., San Bernardino 1961-71; art instr. San Bdo. Valley Coll., 1973-77; awards: 3rd, Watercolor West, Redlands 1975; Nat. Watercolor Soc. Members cash award, L.A. 1980, 3rd, NWS Members 1992; Am. Indian and Cowboy Artists Assn.- gold medal /watercolor, L.A. 1990, bronze /watercolor 1992; mem. Nat. Watercolor Soc. 1975-, Am. Indian and Cowboy Artists 1990-, Watercolor West 1970-. Res: PO Box 156 Rim Forest 92378

JOLIFF, DAVID EVERETT, chiropractic doctor; b. Aug. 16, 1951, Modesto; s. Walter Washington and Evelyn Vera (Mogensen) J.; m. Suzanne Phillips, Mar. 16, 1973 (div.); children: Amy b. 1974, Todd b. 1977, Amanda b. 1984; edn: AA, Modesto Jr. Coll., 1972; BA, CSU Hayward, 1974; DC, Life Chiropractic Coll., 1983. Career: owner, dir. Jolliff Chiropractic, Modesto 1983-; ext. faculty Life Chiropractic Coll. West, San Lorenzo 1983-; mem. Kale Chiropractic Network, Spartanburg 1986-; awards: clin. excellence Life Chiropractic West, 1983; mem: Calif. Chiropractic Assn. Stanislaus/San Joaquin Soc. (pres. 1988-89), Am. Pub. Health Assn., Intl. Platform Assn., Am. Guild Organists (treas. Stanislaus chpt.), Gateway Rotary (pres.-elect 1991), Modesto C.of C., Modesto Downtown Improvement Assn., Nat. Arbor Day Found., Modesto Jr. Coll. Found. (dir.), Nat. Assn. Watch & Clock Collectors; clubs: Modesto Trade, Commonwealth Club of Calif., Old Fishermans, Lincoln-Continental Owners, Imperial Owners (Sacto.), Cadillac LaSalle, Cadillac Intl.; Republican (Rep. Nat. Com.); Lutheran (choral dir. Emanuel Lutheran Ch., Modesto); rec: collect antique luxury autos, antiques, model R.R. Res: 518-A Needham Ave. Modesto 95354. Ofc: 1218 13th St Modesto 95354

JONES, CHARLIE, television sportscaster; b. Nov. 9, 1930, Ft. Smith, Ark.; s. Ira Fulton and Mary Virginia (Norris) J.; m. Ann, June 16, 1954; children: Chuck b. 1958, Julie b. 1963; edn: undergrad., USC; JD, Univ. of Ark. Law Sch. 1953. Career: sports dir., then station mgr. KFPW, Fort Smith, Ark. 1955-60, dir. t.v. and radio, AFL Dallas Texans 1960, began network bdcstg. with ABC-TV (3 AFL Championship Games) ABC's Wide World of Sports, and sports dir. WFAA-TV, 1960-65; sportscaster NBC-TV, 1965-; play-by-play broadcaster Colorado Rockies TV network 1993-; NBC Host-Announcer for 1986 World Cup Soccer, Mexico City (largest internat. sports event ever); NBC Track and Field announcer 1988 Olympic Games, Seoul, Korea; TV broadcast firsts include: Super Bowl I, first AFL nationally televised game, first NBC SportsWorld, first World Cup Gymnastics, first World Cup Marathon, first World Championships of Track and Field, and first Senior Skins Game; actor (1951-) in over 30 t.v. series incl. Ironside, McMillan, Colombo, The Dick Van Dyke Show, Rich Man - Poor Man, and in 12+ Movies of the Week; motion pictures: Personal Best, Return of the Killer Tomatoes, and Killer Tomatoes Strike Back; hosted t.v. series "Almost Anything Goes" and sports-game show "Pro-Fan;" honors: Emmy award 1973 as writer/prod. and host of documentary "Is Winning The Name of the Game?"; Cine Golden Eagle 1982, bronze medal, N.Y. Film & TV Festival 1982, Freedom Found. Award for PBS series "The American Frontier" (co-prod., co-wrote, co-host w/Merlin Olsen, 1982); Toastmasters Intl. Speech Champion 1956; awarded Headliner of Yr. for outstanding contbns. in field of TV, San Diego Press Club 1986, Univ. of Ark. disting. alumnus 1989; mem. Confrerie Des Chevaliers du Tastevin; mil: 1st lt. USAF 1953-55; Christian; rec: golf. Address: Charlie Jones Associates, Inc. 8080 El Paseo Grande La Jolla 92037

JONES, CLEON BOYD, research engineer; b. Nov. 9, 1961, Norwalk; s. Cleon Earl and Marjorie Helen (McDade) J.; edn: BS in math., Biola Univ., 1983. Career: research librarian Christian Research Inst., San Juan Capistrano 1981-84; flight control engr. Leading Systems Inc., Irvine 1984-90; research engr. Dynamic Research Inc., Torrance 1990-; mem. AIAA; Republican; Res: 12464 Fallcreek Lane Cerritos 90701

JONES, EBON RICHARD, retail food chain executive; b. Aug. 23, 1944, Oak Park, Ill.; s. Ebon Clark and Marilyn B. (Dow) J.; m. Sally Samuelson, Jan. 27, 1968; children: Stephanie Blythe b. 1972, Heather Denise b. 1973; edn: BA (Phi Beta Kappa), Princeton Univ., 1966; MBA, Stanford Univ., 1968. Career: adminstrv. asst. Nat. Air Pollution Control, W.D.C., 1968-70; consultant McKinsey & Co., San Francisco, Paris, 1970-83; exec. v.p. Safeway Inc., Oakland, Calif. 1983-86, group v.p. 1986-88, exec.v.p. 1988-; civic bds: Uniform Code Council (gov. 1984-), Crystal Springs Uplands Sch. (trustee 1986-), San Francisco Zoological Soc. (bd. 1979-, bd. chmn. 1979-85, pres. 1986-90); mil: lt. USPHS 1968-70. Res: 58 Chester Way San Mateo 94402 Ofc: Safeway, Inc. 201 Fourth St Oakland 94660

JONES, KEVIN LANCE, doctor of oriental medicine/acupuncturist; b. Sept. 28, 1948, Santa Monica; s. Francis Byron and Susan Lavergne (Blakely) J.; m. Xiao-Yuan Li, Dec. 14, 1986; edn: BA psych., UC Los Angeles, 1972; Diploma Acupuncture (Valedictorian), Calif. Acupuncture Coll., L.A. 1981; Advanced Dipl. (Keynote speaker and 1st American to graduate with Adv. Dipl.), Beijing Acad. of Traditional Chinese Medicine, Beijing, China 1983; O.M.D., Calif. Acupuncture Coll., 1983; Cert. Acupuncturist, Calif. Career: acupuncturist Professional Acupuncture Group, Cedars-Sinai Med. Towers, Los Angeles 1981-83; acupuncturist Gibbs Inst. of Neuro-Kinesthetics, Hollywood 1982-83; staff acupuncturist Beijing Municipal Hosp. of Traditional Chinese Med., Guang An Men Hosp., Beijing, PRC, 1983; medical-clinical staff San Pedro Peninsula Hosp., Pain Mgmt. Dept., 1983; director Clinic of Dr. Kevin Lance Jones, Westwood 1984-; owner Amerasia Import-Export Co., 1986-, and Amerasia Investment Co., 1987-; instr., assoc. prof. Emperor's Coll. of Traditional Oriental Medicine 1984-, asst. chmn. dept. acupuncture 1989-; instr. Calif. Acup. Coll., Los Angeles 1979-84; editor "The Meridian" for Nat. Acup. Technical Svcs., L.A. 1978-83; honors: appreciation Emperor's Coll. of Traditional Oriental Med. 1986, Calif. Acupuncture Assn. recogn. for outstanding committment to early devel. of C.A.A. 1989, cert. of award Univ. S.F. 1987, special award and merit medal China Acup. Assn., Taipei, Taiwan (1984, 1985), cert. of merit C-Kin Corp. 1985, award of merit as research dir. for C-Kin Project, Noda Shokukin Kogyo, Tokyo, Japan; mem. Calif. Acupuncture Alliance (state sec. 1987, state treas. 1988, chmn. So. Chapt. 1986), C.A.A./Sacto. (appreciation award Acupuncture Day 1987), The Center for Chinese Med.; publs: The Evolution of Oriental Medicine in East Asia (1983), articles on acup. in Advanced Sci. Advy. Jour. (1982), L.A. Weekly (1982), L.A. Times (1979); Eckankar; rec: aviation, photography, Chinese brush painting. Ofc: 1100 Glendon Ave Ste 919 Westwood 90024

JONES, LOUIS WORTH, management analyst, journalist, ret.; b. Jan. 8, 1908, St. Louis, Mo.; s. Ed C. and Vida Pearl (Wrather) J.; m. Pauline Marie Ernest, May 24, 1947; children: David Worth b. 1948, Roger Louis b. 1949, Ethan Ernest b. 1956, Faye b. 1932, Arthur Carlyle b. 1936; edn: Washington Univ. (Honor Soc. scholarship) 1925-27. Career: trainee, adminstrv. ofcr. Farm Security Adminstn., US Dept. Agric., Wash. DC 1934-46; mgmt. analyst War Assets Adminstrn., San Francisco 1946-48; mgmt. analyst US AEC, Los Alamos, N.Mex. 1948-50; mgmt. analyst USN Radiological Defense Lab., S.F. 1950-68; editor and publisher Lou Jones Newsletter, 1959-70; v.p., nonsalaried, The World Univ., Hqtrs. Benson, Ariz.; honors: Nat. Honor Soc., 1925; former mem. Am. Soc. for Pub. Admin., Western Govtl. Research Assn., Nat. Assn. of Intergroup Rels. Ofcls., Internat. Platform Assn.; civic: vol. alt. Civil Def. coord. San Mateo Co. 1957-58; mem. AARP, Mid-Peninsula Council for Civic Unity (pres. 1959-60), Bi-County Commn. on Human Relations, Intergroup Relations Assn. of No. Calif. (founder), Humanist Community of the Peninsula (co-founder); author scripts, Meet Mary Wollstonecraft (c. 1977), Meet Alexander Meiklejohn (c. 1978), lecture "Free Speech: The Great Deception" (c. 1987); Unitarian-Universalist (trustee 1958, mem. of year 1977); rec: music (piano), photog. Res: 511 Verano Ct San Mateo 94402

JONES, MICHAEL OWEN, professor; b. Oct. 11, 1942, Wichita, KS; s. Woodrow Owen and Anne Elizabeth (Blackford) J.; m. Jane Dicker, Aug. 1, 1964; children: David 1967; edn: BA Univ. Kansas, Lawrence, Kans. 1964; MA, Indiana Univ., Bloomington, Ind. 1966; PhD, Indiana Univ. 1970. Career: prof., Univ. Calif., Los Angeles 1968-; dir., Folklore and Mythology Ctr., Univ. Calif., L.A. 1984-91; awards: fellowship, Woodrow Wilson 1968; fellowship, Younger Humanist, UCLA 1971; grant, Nat. Endowment for the Humanities, W.D.C. 1983; fellow, Am. Folklore Soc., W.D.C. 1986; fellow, Soc. for Applied Anthropology 1989; fellow, Folklore Fellows, Finnish Acad. of Sci. and Letters, Helsinki 1990; mem: Am. Folklore Soc. 1968-, Calif. Folklore Soc. 1966-, Soc. for Applied Anthropology 1985-, Acad. of Mgmt. 1986-, Orgn. Development Network 1983-; author: Why Faith Healing?, 1972; The Handmade Object and Its Maker, 1975; Exploring Folk Art, 1987; Craftsman of the Cumberlands, 1988; co-author: People Studying People, 1980; co-editor: Foodways and Eating Habits, 1981; Inside Organizations, 1988; editor: The World of the Kalevala, 1987; Putting Folklore to Use, 1993; rec: collecting and restoring classic cars; ofc: Folklore and Mythology, 1037 G S M- Library Wing University of California Los Angeles 90024-1459

JONES, ROBERT RICHARD, financial/insurance consultant, educator; b. Canton, Oh.; s. Robert Hall and Clara M. (Channell) J.; children: Melinda Lou, Christopher; edn: BA, UC Los Angeles, 1951; cert.: Asian Studies Inst., N.Y.C. 1952-53; MA, New York Univ., 1962; postgrad. Univ. of Pa. Wharton Sch. of Bus., cert.: Fin. Mgmt. and Control, 1974; Chartered Life Underwriter (CLU), American Coll., 1978; Doctorate, Golden Gate Univ., 1991. Career: Western field news reporter, info. ofcr., special events reporter/producer, US Dept. of State, Internat. Information Adminstrn., news corr. United Nations, Voice of America, NYC, 1948-53; Mktg. Div. NY Life Ins. Co., NYC, 1953-66; faculty St. John's Univ. Grad. Sch. Bus., NY, NY, 1960-63; asst. v.p. Gulf Life Ins. Co., Jacksonville, Fla. 1966-68, v.p. sales Mutual Funds 1967, pres. and ceo Fla. Growth Mutual Fund, Jacksonville 1968-69; a.v.p., dir. manpower devel. PALIC, Aetna Variable Annuity Life, Wash. DC and Hartford, Conn., 1969-72;

nat. dir. specialized mktg. Hartford Variable Annuity Life, Hartford Ins. Gp. (subs. ITT), Hartford, Conn. 1972-78, planned & devel. internat. jt. venture with ITT/Brazil, 1975; cons. Robert R. Jones and Assocs., San Francisco, Burlingame 1978-, senior ins. cons. Stanford Research Inst. Int'l (SRI), Fin. Industries Center, Internat. Mgmt. & Econs. Gp., Menlo Park 1982-; research/ expert testimony for ins. litigation, Tech. Advy. Service for Attys. (TASA), 1983-; prof. of bus. Coll. of Notre Dame, Belmont, 1986-; instr. bus. management and insurance, Calif. Comm. Colleges; instr. prelicensing and continuing edn., State of California; honors: Tau Kappa Alpha (speech hon.), Phi Mu Alpha Sinfonia (professional music hon.), Debate and Oratory Champion Wittenberg Univ., State of Ohio Original Oratory award, J.N. Flint, and NBC Radio Scholar, UCLA, Lifetime Theater Award for Outstanding Contbns. to University Theater, UCLA, nat. Award of Excellence, Life Advertisers Assn., AETNA-PALIC $25,000 Corporate Growth Award, ITT Internat. Sales Achiev. Award (1973), Disting. Service Award (1984) and Leadership Award (1985) Internat. Assn. for Fin. Planning S.F.; mem: NYU Alumni Assn. (past NYC pres.), Parents Without Partners (hon. life mem.), UCLA Alumni Assn. NYC (past pres.), Hartford Arts Council (dir.), Meals on Wheels, Hartford, Conn. (vol. com.), Old First Concerts, SF (dir.), Internat. Assn. for Fin. Plng. SF (pres. 1984-85, chmn. 1985-86), Am. Soc. CLU/ChFC (nat. bd. dirs. p.r. com. 1986, Peninsula Chpt. pres. 1986-87), Nat. Assn. Life Underws.; Caminar Mental Health Pgms. San Mateo Co., Calif. (bd. dirs. 1984-86), Safe Rides, San Mateo Co. (adult monitor), vol. mediator San Mateo County Mediation Svc. (1990-), appt. commr. City of Burlingame Senior Commn. (1991-); publs: "Administrative Variables in the California Multi-level Penal System," "Childhood Mental Illness: The Search for Answers to Childhood Autism," num. articles and studies; legal cons. "Materiality of Applicant's Misrepresentation in Application for Life and Health Insurance" pub. in Am. Jurisprudence; mil: USN Comms. Div. 1943-46, decorated Am. Campaign, Victory, Euro. Mideast & African Campaign medals, Armed Forces Network (AFN), 1946-51 (USNR); rec: pvt. pilot, Jaguar XKE. Address: POB 489 Burlingame 94011-0489

JONES, RUSSELL DEAN, real estate developer; b. Aug. 17, 1933, Los Angeles; s. Fred Sylvester and Rose Marie (Mauler) J.; m. Hae Young Lee, Nov. 2, 1986; children (by prior m.): Kellianne Patricia (Jones) Wilder, Katelyn Maura Jones; edn: BBA, Loyola Univ., L.A. 1954, JD, Loyola Law Sch., 1957; admitted bar Calif., lic. real estate broker 1977-. Career: various govt. positions, 1954-64; city adminstr. City of Placentia, 1964-67; asst. dir. Calif. Dept. Housing & Community Devel., Sacramento 1967-68; v.p. Boise Cascade Building Co., L.A. 1968-72; pres. Russell D. Jones Cos., L.A. 1972-81; v.p. hotel devel. Marriott Corp., W.D.C. 1981-90; pres. Russell D. Jones & Assocs., Rancho Palos Verdes 1990-; developer of 20+ hotels, resorts and planned communities; appt. Calif. State subdivision advy. com.1968-71, factory built housing advy. com. 1969-72; honors: Alpha Delta amma (pres. 1956-57), Phi Alpha Delta, Hon. Citizen Republic of Korea; v.p. Building Industry Assn. of Calif. 1971-72; mem. W.G.R.A., Urban Land Inst.; Republican; R.Cath.; rec: gardening, genealogy. Res: 4129 Admirable Dr Rancho Palos Verdes 90274

JORDAN, BARBARA EVELYN, wedding consultant, photographer- still & video, florist, brass sculptor, nurse for the disabled; b. Jan. 9, 1930, Redlands, Calif.; d. Tom and Alma Hackler; m. David Laurens Jordan, Nov. 15, 1947; children: Audrey (artist, rep. galleries in Ga.), David (ldr. disabled communities, initiated transp. for the disabled at SDSU, 1970s), Debbie (pianist, photog.), Becky (R.E. agt.); 8 grandchildren; edn: grad. Lower Lake H.S., photography courses San Diego City Coll., 1980. Career: store mgr. Van de Kamp Bakery, Ventura and San Diego, 1963-69; vol. nurse for disabled, 1966-; brass sculptor and stained glass artist, for FedMart of Calif. chain stores, 1976-79; florist/owner Flower Design Service, San Diego, Sacto., 1976-; awards: 25 yrs. of service for the disabled 1966-91; clubs: Coast to Coast, RPI, Thousand Trails; Watchtower Society; rec: sculpture, travel (Europe, India, SE Asia, China, S.Am., Mexico, Egypt, Israel, Greece). Address: 6008 Sawyer Circle Sacramento 96823

JORDAN, BARBARA SUZANNE, environmental consultant; b. Dec. 14, 1941, Buffalo, N.Y.; d. Joseph Francis and Rita Florence (Martini) Falkner; m. Thomas Vincent Jordan, Apr. 1, 1967 (div. Jan. 1991); children: Shannon b. 1970; edn: BA, DePaul Univ., 1977; MA, Univ. of Phoenix, Az. 1984. Career: program mgr. City of Phoenix, Az. 1978-86; City of San Jose, Ca. 1986-88; project mgr. Brown & Caldwell, Pleasant Hill, Ca. 1989-90; owner Jordan & Company, Concord, CA 1990-; appt. advy. com. on water conservation Calif. Dept. of Water Resource 1986-89; mem. Am. Water Works Assn.: founder, co-chair water conservation com. 1986-, speaker nat. meetings (1987, 89, 91), workshop ldr., moderator, Conserv 90 Presentation, Phoenix, AZ 1990, chmn. jt. strategic planning com. Water Demand Task Force 1984-85; co-chair nat. conf. Nat. Water Resources Assn. 1984; awards: Joey Award San Jose Film & Video Com. 1988, Mercury Award MERFCOMM, Inc. Nat. Media Conf. 1988, Nat. Leadership award Conserv 90, Orlando, Fla. 1990; civic: Museum Com. Los Gatos 1987-89; pub. magazine articles (1988, 90, 91); Democrat; Christian. Res: 1349 Tree Garden Pl Concord 94518-3710 Ofc: Jordan & Company PO Box 5913 Concord 94524

JORDAN, DANNY JOSEPH, certified public accountant; b. Jan. 15, 1948, Detroit, Mich.; s. Homer Augustine and Gertrude Jean (Nuttle) J.; m. Rita Rosina Slagel, Dec. 28, 1973; edn: BS. accounting., Sacto. State Univ. 1971; MBA fin., UC Berkeley 1977; C.P.A. Calif. 1973. Career: sr. auditor Arthur Anderson & Co., San Francisco 1971-73; asst. controller Central Banking System, Oakland 1973-74; controller Pacific Union Assurance Co., S.F. 1974-77, West Coast Life Ins. Co. 1977-78; CFO L.K. Lloyd & Assoc. 1978-80; supr., mgr. Greene Nakahara & Arnold, Oakland 1980-85, ptnr. 1985; owner Dan Jordan CPA, Mill Valley 1985-86; ptnr. Jordan & Decker 1986-; dir. Coast Furniture Co., Oakland 1987-, Calif. No. Consumer Fin. Services 1988-, Ham Enterprises Inc., Richmond 1989-; adminstrv. com. mem. Calif. Soc. CPA's Group Ins. Trust, Redwood City 1980-; awards: Calif. Soc. CPA Top Accounting. Student 1971; mem: Am. Inst. CPA, Calif. Soc. CPA, Nat. Assn. Accountants, Am. Mgmt. Assn.; author: article pub. in profl. jour. 1984, developer computer program 1988; mil: USCGR 1967-72; Republican; rec: tennis. Ofc: Jordan & Decker POB 1755 Mill Valley 94942

JORDAN, DAVID LAURENS, company president, wedding consultant, floral designer, photographer, activist for the disabled; b. May 20, 1929, Alameda; s. Morris Allen and Leona Nadine (Allen) Jordan; m. Barbara Evelyn Hackler, Nov. 15, 1947; children: Audrey, David, Debbie, Becky; edn: grad. Alameda H.S., 1947; photography, San Diego City Coll., 1980. Career: c.e.o. 7Up Bottling Co., Santa Rosa, 1952-58; owner, gen. ptnr. Jordan TV, Santa Rosa, 1958-63; mdsg. mgr. Coca Cola Bottling Co., Ventura, 1963-68; owner, gen. mgr. Discount Photographers & Florists, San Diego, Sacramento, 1976-; owner, dir. RV Accessories Etc., Sacto. 1990-91; minister Watchtower Society, 1954-76; awards: 25 yrs. of service for the disabled 1966-91, Top man of mo. Coca Cola Bottling Ventura 1964), Who's Who of La Jolla 1989; mem. Teamsters 1947-; clubs: Coast to Coast, RPI, Thousand Trails; artist in stained glass, exhibits in stained glass & brass art shows, San Diego (1976-79), Baby Contest Photography Show, S.D. (1976); editor: Jordan-Allen Family History Since Oregon Trail; Allen Family History; Watchtower Society; rec: painting, stained glass, nature photos, domestic & fgn. travel. Address: Discount Photographers & Florists, 6008 Sawyer Circle Sacramento 96823

JORDAN, JAMES HERBERT, marketing executive, writer; b. July 22, 1946, Pittsburg; s. John Frederick and Ruby Loraine (Robinson) J.; m. Teri Bridgman, June 11, 1966; children: Jonni Ann b. 1969, Randi b. 1972; edn: att. San Franciso State Univ. 1964-68, Las Positas Coll., Livermore 1990-91. Career: exec. editor Western Ski Time Mag., San Francisco 1968-71; editor Sunset Mag., Menlo Park 1971-75; mng. editor Home Mag., Palo Alto 1975-76; editor Colorado Mag., Denver 1976; mktg. dir. Multiple Allied Svs., Hayward, Calif. 1977-; prin., writer Jordan/Garvine Advt., Pleasanton 1986-88; prin. Jordan's Village Books, Castro Valley 1980-; author: Exploding the Franchising Myth 1990; contbg. editor to numerous books; editor: Elementary Education Language Primer 1989, Whiplash Mgmt. and Treatment 1991; recipient Calif. Mag. annual magazine award 1975; civic: Citizens Against Redevel. Pleasanton (chmn. 1975), P.A.S.S. Soccer League, Pleasanton (ofcr. 1978); mem. San Francisco Advt. Club, Castro Village Merchants Assn. (bd. 1991-); Republican; Prot.; rec: mosaic designer and builder, mosaic restorations. Res: 7882 Marigold Ct Pleasanton 94588 Ofc: Multiple Allied Services Inc. 3157 Corporate Pl Hayward 94545

JORDAN, R(AYMOND) BRUCE, health services management consultant; b. Mar. 10, 1912, Holland, Mich.; s. Albert Raymond and Aimee (Best) J.; m. Dorothy Caig, June 6, 1942; mbr. BA, CSU Sacramento, 1952; MBA, Stanford Univ. Grad. Sch. of Bus., 1959; lic. pub. acct.; Calif. std. tchg. credential. Career: State Bd. Equalization auditor at Calif. Dept. Employment, 1947-48, mgmt. analyst 1948-52, chief mgmt. analyst hd. office State Bd. Equalization, 1952-59 (originated whole dollar accounting in Calif. State Govt.), chief mgmt. analyst hd. office State Dept. of Mental Hygiene, 1959-63, bus. adminstr. Atascadero State Hosp., 1963-68, Patton State Hosp., San Bernardino 1968-70; recipient Bronze achiev. award Mental Hosp. Service 1963; hosp. mgmt. consultant to 2 hosps. in Victoria, Brit. Col., 1970-72; health services mgmt. cons., Oakland 1972-; cons. govt. Iran, faculty mgmt. tng. Univ. Tehran, 1956; instr. UC Davis, 1963, Cuesta Coll., 1967-68, Monterey campus of Golden Gate Univ., since 1972, adj. prof. 1983-; civic bds: treas. Experience Inc. (distbr. of free vegetables and aid in craft sales, 1973-78), Monterey County Ombudsman pgm. (pres 1976-78), Monterey County Senior Hearing Ctr. (founder, advy. bd. 1977-78); mem. Toastmasters Intl. (ATM), Rotary (past); mil: US Army 1943-46, WWII; author: Management Analysis in Health Services (1982), Supervision -Effective Management (1982), jour. articles in field. Res: 33 Linda Ave Apt 1908 Oakland 94611-4818

JORDAN, THOMAS VINCENT, professor of advertising; b. Aug. 8, 1941, Washington, D.C.; s. Vincent Joseph and Elizabeth Jean (Quinlan) J.; m. Barbara S. Faulkner, Dec. 14, 1941 (div. 1987); children: Shannon Ann b. 1970; edn: AA, San Francisco City Coll. 1968; BA creative writing, San Francisco St. Univ. 1970; MA, 1971. Career: pub. rels. rep. United Airlines, S.F. and Chgo., IL 1968-73; copywriter Leo Burnett Co., Chgo., Ill. 1973-76; mgr. comms., Honeywell Info. Systems, Phoenix, Ariz. 1978-85; adj. prof. advt. Ariz. St. Univ., Tempe 1979-86; assoc. prof. advt. San Jose St. Univ. 1987-; mktg. comm. cons., Phoenix, Ariz. and San Jose 1984-; chmn. Santa Clara Cultural Advy.

Commn. 1991-; awards: United Airlines Pres. award 1973, City of Chgo. Hon. Librarian 1975, Honeywell Info. Systems Merchandiser of Year 1978, Ariz. Alliance of Bus. Commend. 1983, B/PAA Nat. Winner 1989; v.p. univ. relations: Bus. Profl. Advt. Assn. (Internat. Speakers Bureau); mem. Calif. Faculty Assn. (treas.), Mensa (pub. rels. 1978-79), World Future Soc., ACLU; author: Carrion Comfort 1971; newsletter editor: Cargolines 1972-76; profl. jour. articles include: A Guide to Mktg. Comms., Cut Copy vs. Cute Copy, The Plastic Package Paradigm, Radio in 3 Easy Steps, How to Get Press, An Exemplary Internship Program, A Perennially Successful Live Case Proj., The Marketing Comms. Course; mil: airman 1c USAF 1959-63; Libertarian; Humanist; rec: writing, hiking, travel. Res: 1700 Civic Center Dr #602 Santa Clara 95050 Ofc: San Jose State Univ. 1 Washington Sq. San Jose 95192-0055

JORGENSEN, JUDITH ANN, psychiatrist, educator; b. Aug. 31, 1941, Parris Island, S.D.; d. George Emil Jorgensen (dec.) and Margaret Georgia (Jorgensen) Prunk; m. Ronald F. Crown, M.D., July 11, 1970; edn: BA, Stanford Univ., 1963, MD, UCLA, 1968, cert. psychiatry residency, San Diego County Mental Health Services, 1973; bd. certified Psychiatry and Neurology, 1977; diplomate Am. Bd. Sexology. Career: gen. medical physician San Diego Co. Mental Health Services, 1969-70, staff psychiatrist Dept. of Profl. Edn. 1973-76, Children and Adolescent Div. 1973-78; psychiatric cons. San Diego City Coll., 1973-78, 85-86; staff psychiatrist San Diego St. Univ., 1985-87; pvt. practice prin., 1973-; clin. faculty Dept. of Psychiatry UCSD 1976-, asst. clin. prof. of psychiatry 1978-91, assoc. prof. psychiatry 1991-; consulting staff: University Hosp., Southwood Mental Health Ctr., Vista Hill Hosp., past staff Hillside Hosp. 1972-87; honors: CMA cont. edn. cert. 1972-87, AMA Physician's Recognition 1974-94; mem: Calif. Med. Assn., San Diego Co. Med. Soc. (credentials chair 1982-83), Am. Psychiatric Assn., San Diego Soc. of Psychiatric Physicians (mem. chair 1976-78, v.p. 1978-80, fed. legis. rep. 1984-87, fellowship com. 1989-), Am. Soc. for Adolescent Psychiatry, San Diego Soc. for Adolescent Psychiatry (pres. 1981-82), AASECT (cert. sex therapist), Soc. for the Sci. Study of Sex, San Diego Soc. for Sex Therapy and Edn., Am. Med. Womens Assn., Assn. for Women in Sci., NOW, ZLAC Rowing Club; publs: Psychiatric Treatment of Severely Burned Adults, Psychosomatics J. (Nov-Dec 1973), contbr. book chpt. in Current Psychiatric Therapies (ed. Jules Massermann, 1975); rec: skiing, tennis, riding, mosaics; ofc: 470 Nautilus St Ste 211 La Jolla 92037

JOSEPH, JAMES, marine scientist; b. Oct. 28, 1930, Los Angeles; s. Paul B. and Julia (Shaddy) J.; m. Patricia Duffy, Aug. 31, 1958; children: Jerold b. 1961, Michael b. 1964; edn: BS, and MS, Humboldt St. Univ., 1956, 1958; PhD, Univ. of Wash., 1968. Career: asst. scientist in chg. Manta, Ecuador 1958-60; prin. scientist Tuna Commn., 1961-68; dir. Inter-American Tropical Tuna Commn., Scripps Instn. of Oceanography, La Jolla 1969-; dir. Porpoise Res. Found., San Diego; dir. San Diego Oceans Found.; affil. prof. Univ. of Wash.; vis. fellow Ministry of Agri., N.Z. 1975-76; advr. in marine service and fisheries R&D to govts. and nat., internat. orgns.; awards: Nautilus award Marine Technol. Soc., David H. Wallace award Portuguese Hist. Soc., Hon. Dr. L'Universite de Bretagne, Sigma Xi; mem. AIFRB, AAAS; author 2 books, 75+ sci. publs.; mil: s/sgt. AUS Korea 1952-54. Res: 2790 Palomino Circle La Jolla 92037 Ofc: Inter-American Tropical Tuna Commission, c/o Scripps Instn. of Oceanography, La Jolla 92093

JOSEPHSON, DAVID LANE, engineer; b. June 17, 1956, New Haven, Ct.; s. Stanley Davis and Carolyn Virginia (Buck) J.; edn: elect. engring., UC Berkeley, 1975-79. Career: staff engr. KALX-FM Radio, Berkeley 1975-79; systems engr. High Life Helicopters, Puyallup, Wash. 1979-81; systems engr. EG&G Geometrics, Sunnyvale, Calif. 1981-85, dir. China Op., Beijing, China 1985-87, mgr. Military Div., Sunnyvale, Calif. 1987-90; owner Josephson Engineering, San Jose 1990-, mfg. microphones and acoustic equipment, cons. pvt. cos. and govt. agys. nat. and internat., 1980-; mem. Audio Engineering Soc. (1974-, chapt. bd.); num. inventions in field of microphones and acoustics; Democrat; rec: aviation, music, civics. Res: 3729 Corkerhill Way San Jose 95121 Ofc: Josephson Engineering, 2660 John Montgomery Dr Ste 25 San Jose 95148

JOYCE, MARGUERITE PATRICIA, educator; b. Aug. 6, 1945, St. Joseph, Mo.; d. Robert Cephas and Mary Louis (Gorman) Mays; m. Terrance L. Shane, Aug. 13, 1966 (div. Mar. 1970); 1 son, Jeffrey Newson b. 1967; m. Lionel Livingston Joyce, Oct. 23, 1984; edn: BS, Mo. Western State Coll., 1973; EdM, Bowling Green Univ., 1975; EdD, Univ. Nebr., Lincoln, 1978. Career: tchr. Tinley Park (Ill.) H.S., 1973-74, Coffeyville (Kans.) Comm. Coll. 1975-76; asst. prof. Ill. State Univ., Normal, Ill., 1978-81, 82-86; McNeese State Univ., Lake Charles, La. 1986-88; assoc. prof. Nicholls State Univ., Thibodaux, La. 1988-89; Calif. State Univ. L.A., 1989-; cons. in personnel devel. & support staff State Farm Ins., Bloomington, Ill. Summers 1980, 82; awards: grantee Ill. Bd. Higher Edn., Springfield, Ill. 1987, Outstanding Prof., McNeese State Univ., Lake Charles, La. 1987, certificate CBEA, L.A. 1991; mem: Assn. for Bus. Communication 1978-, CBEA (co-editor) 1989-, NBEA 1978-85, Delta Pi Epsilon 1975-, WBEA 1989-; author: 20+ articles re bus. comms., office systems, bus. edn 1978-; textbook, Business Communication - PWS (Kent Pub. Co.); Democrat; Baptist. Ofc: Dept. Office Systems, CSU-LA, 5151 State University Dr Los Angeles 90032

JUBERG, RICHARD KENT, mathematician, professor emeritus; b. May 14, 1929, Cooperstown, N.Dak.; s. Palmer and Hattie Noreen (Nelson) J.; m. Janet Elisabeth Witchell, Mar. 17, 1956 (div. 1984); children: Alison b. 1961, Kevin b. 1963, Hillary b. 1964, Ian b. 1972; m. Sandra Jean Vakerics, July 8, 1989; edn: BS, Univ. Minn., 1952, PhD, 1958. Career: temp. mem. math. studies and res. Courant Inst. of Math. Scis., New York Univ., N.Y.C. 1957-58; instr., asst. prof. Univ. Minn., Mpls. 1958-65; science faculty fellow NSF, Univ. di Pisa, Italy 1965-66; assoc. prof. UC Irvine 1966-72; vis./ assoc. prof. Univ. of Sussex, England 1972-73; prof. UC Irvine, 1974-91, prof. emeritus 1991-; vis. prof. Univ. of Goteborg, Sweden 1981; awards: Tau Beta Pi 1953, temporary mem. Courant Inst. Math. Scis. NYU 1957-58, NSF fellow, Italy 1965-66; mem. Am. Math. Soc. 1958-; contbr. res. articles to profl. jours.; mil: p.o.3c USN 1946-48; Democrat; rec: bird watching; res: 9356-D Mesa Verde Dr Montclair 91763; ofc: Math. Dept. Univ. California, Irvine 92717

JUDD, NORMAN RUSSELL, financial executive; b. Nov. 20, 1948, Wellsville, N.Y.; s. Russell R. and Lois S. (Seitzer) J.; m. Laurie B. Galway, May 3, 1986; child: Brian G. b. 1989; edn: BS in acctg., Northeastern Univ., Boston 1972; cert. CPA, State of Mass., 1985. Career: audit sr. Alexander Grant CPA's, Boston, Mass. 1972-77; audit mgr. Inforex Inc., Burlington, Mass. 1977-79; asst. controller Bay State Gas Co., Canton, Mass. 1979-83; sr. audit mgr. Emhart Corp, Farmington, Conn. 1983-86, dir. of fin. Hardware Group 1986-89; v.p. finance Kwikset Corp., Anaheim 1989-91; v.p. finance Security Hardware Group, Black & Decker, 1991-; mem: AICPA, Mass. Soc. of CPA's, NAA; Republican; Methodist; rec: golf club construction and repair. Ofc: Security Hardward Group Black & Decker 516 E Santa Ana St Anaheim 92803-4250

JUDD, RALPH WAVERLY, writer, lecturer, publisher; b. April 22, 1930, Zillah, Wa.; s. Van Evrie and Theona Ruth (Stanhope) J.; edn: Harvard Coll. 1947-49; BS, US Coast Guard Acad. 1954; MBA, George Washington Univ. 1964; PhD communications, Clayton Univ., 1988. Career: served to cmdr. US Coast Guard 1949-72: airborne ice observer, USCG, Arctic & Antarctic, 1955-57; chief Physics Sect. USCG Acad., New London, Conn. 1962-63; cmdg. ofcr. USCGC Comanche, San Francisco 1964-66, Loran Station, Con Son, Vietnam 1966-67; chief resale systems USCG Hqtrs., W.D.C. 1967-71; cmdg. ofcr. USCGC Rockaway, NY, NY 1971-72, ret.; decorated Command-at-Sea Insignia 1964, CG Unit Commendn. 1966, Combat Action rib. 1966; cross-country coach USCG Acad. 1959-61, writer num. Coast Guard publs. (1960-71), contbr. var. magazines and newspapers, author/pub. (book) Drag Gags, 4 unpub. books on hist. of entertainment (1968-87); awards: cert. of merit Nat. Honor Soc. 1947, Harvard Nat. Scholar 1947, Lifetime Achiev. Golden Academy Award, listed Who's Who in US Writers, Editors & Poets, Internat. Who's Who of Intellectuals; mem: Comedy/Humor Writers Assn., Media Alliance, Nat. Writers Union, Nat. Writers Club, Press Club of S.F., Mensa, ACLU, AARP, S.F. YMCA (PE com.); clubs: Playboy, S.F. Arts Democratic Club; Democrat (Dem. Nat. Com.); Christian; rec: collect special interest movie stills, posters & stage photos, jog, Nautilus, swim. Address: 1330 Bush St Apt. 4H San Francisco 94109

JUDGE, GEORGE GARRETT, professor of econometrics; b. May 2, 1925, Carlisle, Ky.; s. William Everett and Etna (Perkins) J.; m. Sue D., Mar. 17, 1950 (div. Mar. 1976); children: Lisa b. 1953, Laura b. 1956; m. Margaret C., Oct. 8, 1976; edn: BS, Univ. Ky., 1948, MS, Iowa State Univ., 1949, PhD, Iowa State Univ., 1952. Career: asst. prof. Univ. Conn., Storrs 1951-55; prof. Oklahoma State Univ., Stillwater 1955-58; vis. prof. Yale Univ., 1958-59; prof. Univ. Illinois, Urbana 1959-86; prof. UC Berkeley, 1986- mem. Econometric Soc. 1951- Am. Statistical Assn. 1960-; author: Theory and Practice of Econometrics 1980, 85, Introduction to Econometrics 1982, 88, Inference in Econometrics 1978, 86, Spatial Equilibrum 1971; tech. sgt. USAF 1943-45; rec: golf, sailing. Ofc: Univ. California, 207 Giannini Hall Berkeley 94720

JULIEN, RICHARD EDWARD HALE, JR., lawyer; b. July 24, 1939, San Francisco; s. Richard Edward Hale and Sophie (Hill) J.; m. Victoria Ford, Sept. 7, 1963 (div. 1986); children: Sophie b. 1964, Richard b. 1966; edn: BS, MIT 1960; JD, Boalt Hall Sch. Law UC Berkeley 1963; admitted St. Bar Calif. (1964). Career: assoc. atty. Kelso Cotton & Ernst, S.F. 1964-67; sole practitioner, pvt. practice 1967-74; ptnr. Julien & Julien 1974-78; Layman Julien & Lempert 1978-81; pres. Richard Julien Profl. Corp. 1981-; lectr. var. profl. programs; honors: mem. Am. Law Inst., Am. Coll. Tax Counsel, life fellow Am. Bar Found.; mem: Am. Bar Assn., Calif. St. Bar Assn., S.F. Bar Assn.; elected Town Council, Ross 1984-88, mayor 1986-88; mem. Soc. Calif. Pioneers, Phi Delta Theta; clubs: St. Francis Yacht, University; contbr. articles to legal jours.; Republican; R.Cath.; rec: restoration of family ranch. Ofc: 200 Montgomery St., Ste 710 San Francisco 94104

JULIUS, EDWARD HOWARD, college professor; b. May 14, 1952, Boston, Mass.; s. Nathan and Eleanor Frances (Marshall) J.; m. Marion R. Valdez, Aug. 22, 1981; children: Marina b. 1982, Alexandra b. 1986; edn: BA bus. adminstrn., Rutgers Univ. 1974; MS acctg., Univ. Pa. 1975; CPA Ill. 1977. Career: asst. prof. acctg. Chgo. St. Univ., Ill. 1975-77; CSU Northridge 1978-81; asst. prof., assoc. prof., prof. acctg. Calif. Lutheran Univ., Thousand Oaks 1981-; awards: CSU Merit. Performance 1989, CLU Excellence in Tchg. 1988; mem: Am. Inst. CPA,

Ill. C.P.A. Soc., Am. Acctg. Assn., Comm. Leaders Club, Wharton Club So. Calif.; author num. textbook ancillaries, One-A-Day crossword vols. 1-6 (1975-81), articles pub. in profl. jours. (1987, 89); Republican; Jewish; rec: crossword puzzle constructor. Res: 22009 Vincennes St Chatsworth 91311 Ofc: California Lutheran University Dept. of Business 60 Olsen Rd Thousand Oaks 91360

JUNCKER, JUDITH DIANNE, psychotherapist, artist; b. Nov. 18, 1942, Montgomery, Ala.; d. Walter Eugene and Mary Juette (Singleton) Graddy; m. Phillip Bailey, Sept. 9, 1960 (dec.); m. 2d. Rodney Juncker, Aug. 31, 1968; children: Rick b. 1965, Jeff b. 1970; edn: BA, S.F. State Univ., 1968; MA, Am. Acad. Family Studies, 1981; lic. Marriage Family Counselor, lic. Clin. Hypnotherapist, Calif. 1981. Career: NIMH grantee, res. asst. San Francisco St. Univ. 1968-70, Stanford Univ. 1969-70, Harvard Univ. Grad. Sch. of Edn. 1973-77; social work asst. Met. State Hosp., Waltham, Mass. 1971-72; partners' group facilitator Veteran Outreach, San Jose 1979-80; pvt. practice ONTOS, 1981-87, Adult & Child Therapy Ctr. 1987-; cons. various univs. and instns., 1980-; lectr. CSU San Jose 1986-87; adj. faculty Santa Clara Univ.; mem: Am. Assn. of Marriage & Family Therapist, Calif. Assn. Marriage Family Therapist, Assn. for Transpersonal Psychology, Assn. for Humanist Psych., No. Calif. Assn. for Clin. Hypnotherapy; civic: Center for Living with Dying, S.J. (group facilitator 1979-85, outstanding volunteer award 1980, 81, 82, 83), ARIS Project, S.J. (group facilitator 1985-, sem. ldr. for People with AIDS); artist mixed media, works in pvt. collections; Democrat; Prot. Ofc: Adult & Child Therapy Center 1190 S Bascom Ste 216 San Jose 95128

JUNG, CHAI HWAN, life underwriter; b. Jan. 16, 1947, Korea; s. Doo Keun and Mi Ja (Lee) J.; m. Hyon Sook, Apr. 8, 1976; children: Hana Jung b. 1977, James b. 1979; edn: BA, Korea Univ., 1973; grad. Anthony Sch. of Real Estate, 1981; Calif. R.E. broker 1981. Career: mgr. Korea Exchange Bank, 1973-80; dir. Namsan Corp., Korea 1979-81; real estate broker United Business Investment, Los Angeles 1982-84; spl. agent Northwestern Mutual Life Ins. Co., 1982-87; gen. agent Western State Life Ins., 1987-; pres. Joy Toy Co., 1985-; pres. AAlum Internat. Co.; honors: appreciation Korean Consulate General 1986, Korean Ministry of Edn. 1987, Northwestern Mutual Life diamond club 1985, Western State Life 30-30 Club and Elite Club 1987, 88, Nat. Sales achiev. award 1985, 86; mem: Cert. Life Underwriter Assn., Profl. Salesman Assn. USA; civic: Korean School Assn. (pres. 1987, 1988), Korea Univ. Alumni Assn. of So. Calif. (gen. sec. 1986, v.p. 1989, pres. Tae Kwon Do Team), PIOPICO Library Support Team (dir.), Korean Eastern Church School (pres. 1983-90); elder Korean Eastern Presbyn. Ch. 1992; publs: 30+ essays in Korea Times, Korean Street Jour.; Democrat; Christian; rec: travel. Res: 136 Fremont Place W Los Angeles 90005 Ofc: Joy Toy 824 S Wall St Los Angeles 90014 also: AAlum Trading Co. 1110 E 14th St Los Angeles 90021

KABAKOW, HOWARD ARTHUR, investor, housing regulation consultant; b. Oct. 24, 1941, Englewood, N.J.; s. Meyer and Claire K.; m. Lynn Maxa Brody, Aug. 25, 1962 (div. 1970); edn: BS and PhD physics, Caltech, 1962, 1969. Career: research fellow in applied math. Caltech, Pasadena 1969; asst. res. engr. in mechanics & str., UC Los Angeles 1969, actg. asst. prof. 1969-70; asst. prof. math. New York Univ., 1970-71; investor/prin., Los Angeles; dir./pres. HAK Twenty-Eighth St. Corp., L.A. 1985-, HAK Nineteenth St. Corp., Tempe, Ariz. 1989-; awards: Gen. Motors nat. scholar 1958, Hon. Nat. Merit Scholar 1958, 1st pl. leapfrog relay Occidental Coll. 1958, Dean's list Caltech 1958-60, Sigma Xi 1969; mem: AAAS, Apartment Owners Assn. of So. Calif. (dir. legal svcs.), Caltech Alumni Assn. (life), Town Hall of Calif., L.A. World Affairs Council; club: L.A. Athletic; publs: PhD thesis: A Perturbation Proc. for Nonlinear Oscillations (1968, cited in textbooks) and paper (1971), contbr. op-ed. sect. var. periodicals; Republican (Nat. Com. 1984-). Address: PO Box 18410 Encino 91416-8410

KAGEMOTO, HARO, artist; b. Jan. 9, 1952, Tokyo, Japan, naturalized U.S. cit. 1962; s. Herbert Yoshito and Nobuye S. (Furukawa) K.; m. Patricia Mae Jow, Sept. 21, 1991; 1 child, Kenya b. 1982; edn: profl. cert. Sch. of Modern Photography, N.J. 1972; BFA, Univ. Hawaii, 1977; MFA, SUNY, New Paltz, 1979. Career: vis. artist UC Berkeley Ext., San Francisco 1980-83; vis. lectr. San Francisco State Univ., 1983; prodn. mgr. Wonderland Prodns., S.F. 1983-91, director, 1991-; mem. Am. Film Inst. 1987-; author: (poetry collection) Orion's Winter, 1972-75, (short story) Daruma 1976; rec: guitar, reading. Res: 2806 Truman Ave Oakland 94605-4847

KAGEMOTO, PATRICIA JOW, artist/printmaker; b. Feb. 20, 1952, N.Y.C.; d. Tong Fook and Toy Kuen (Lee) Jow; m. Haro Kagemoto, Sept. 21, 1991; edn: Syracuse Univ. Sch. of Art, 1970-71, Hunter Coll., N.Y. 1971-72; BFA, SUNY, New Paltz, 1975. Career: printmaking workshop asst. SUNY at New Paltz, N.Y. 1974-75, printshop asst. 1975; arts and crafts tchr. Neighborhood Service Orgn., Poughkeepsie, N.Y. 1976; printmaking instr. and adminstrv. asst. Communications Village Ltd., Kingston, N.Y. 1977-79, printmaking cons. 1975-84; exhibition auditor N.Y. State Council on the Arts, N.Y.C. 1984-87; gallery asst. Watermark/ Cargo Gallery, Kingston, N.Y. 1988-91; vis. artist N.Y. State Summer Sch. of the Visual Arts, Fredonia, N.Y. 1978; vis. artist SUNY at New Paltz 1983-84; cons. printer The Printmaking Workshop, N.Y.C. 1984; children's printmaking workshop dir. The Woodstock (N.Y.) Library 1989; awards: spl. award in graphics Gallery North, Setauket, N.Y. 1974, America The Beautiful Fund grantee N.Y.C. 1976, 1st and 2d pl. in graphics Catskill Art Soc., Hurleyville, N.Y. 1983, Alumni Printmakers' Invitational SUNY, New Paltz 1984, Ulster County Decentralization grantee N.Y. State Council on the Arts, Woodstock 1989; rec: cats, sewing, gardening. Ofc: Pat Jow Kagemoto 2806 Truman Ave Oakland 94605-4847

KAGIWADA, REYNOLD SHIGERU, engineer; b. July 8, 1938, Los Angeles; s. Harry Yoshifusa and Helen Kinue (Imura) K.; m. Harriet Hatsune Natsuyama, Aug. 19, 1961; children: Julia b. 1968, Conan b. 1969; edn: BS physics, UCLA, 1960, MS physics, 1962, PhD physics, 1966. Career: asst. prof. in residence, UC Los Angeles, 1966-69; asst. prof. USC, 1969-72; engr. TRW, Redondo Beach, 1972-: sect. head, MTS, dept. mgr., sr. scientist 1972-83, lab. mgr. 1984-87, project mgr. 1987-88, MIMIC chief scientist 1988-89, asst. pgm. mgr. 1989-90, advanced technology mgr. 1989-; awards: Gold medal Ramo Technology Award, TRW 1985, ESG Chmn's. award for Innovation 1991, Sigma Pi Sigma 1960-, Sigma Xi 1967-; mem. IEEE (Fellow 1989, pgm. com. 1979-), IEEE Ultrasonic Ferroelectric Freq. Control (sec. treas. 1984-86), IEEE Microwave Theory & Techniques Soc. (v.p. 1991, pres. 1992), Assn. of Old Crows 1980-; author, inventor (9 patents), 44+ publs. and 13 tech. paper presentations; Democrat; Methodist; rec: fishing, biking. Res: 3117 Malcolm Ave Los Angeles 90034 Ofc: TRW, MS M5/1470, One Space Park Redondo Beach 90278

KAHAN, JAMES PAUL, psychologist; b. Oct. 15, 1942, New York; s. Robert Helmen and Janet Rieders (Pressman) K.; m. Edith Jane Lester, Dec. 27, 1970 (div. 1983); m. 2d. Elaine Marie Engman, June 29, 1984; children: Rebecca b. 1978, Emily b. 1988; edn: BA, Reed Coll. 1964; MA, Univ. N.C. Chapel Hill 1966; PhD, 1968; lic. psychologist Calif. 1975. Career: asst. prof., assoc. prof. USC, Dept. Psychology, Los Angeles 1970-80; fellow Netherlands Inst. Advanced Study, Wassenaar, Netherlands 1977-78; vis. prof. Univ. Haifa, Israel 1980-81; sr. scientist RAND Corp., Santa Monica 1981-; prof. RAND Grad. Sch. 1983-; awards: NSF/NATO postdoctoral fellow 1968-69; mem: Am. Psychological Soc. (fellow), Soc. for the Psychological Study of Social Issues (fellow); author: 90+ books and articles pub. in profl. jours. 1965-; rec: folk dancing, folk music, volleyball. Res: Pacific Palisades Ofc: The RAND Corp 1700 Main St Santa Monica 90407-2138

KAHAN, SHELDON JEREMIAH, musician, band leader, singer; b. Mar. 5, 1948, Honolulu; s. Aaron Kahan and Marianne (Royijiczek) Sann; edn: Tel Aviv Univ. 1967-69, Merritt Coll. 1972-74. Career: guitarist The Grim Reapers, Miami Beach, Fla. 1965-66; bassist The Electric Stage, Jerusalem 1969-71; music dir., musician Fanfare, L.A. 1974-75, Jean Paul Vignon & 1st Love, L.A. 1975-76; musician Jenny Jones & Co., L.A. 1976; musician, vocalist Fantasy, L.A. 1977-79; leader, musician, vocalist Fortune, L.A. 1980-83; bassist Johnny Tillotson Show, Nev. 1983; ptnr., musician, vocalist Heartlight, L.A. 1983-84; leader, musician, vocalist The Boogie Bros., L.A. 1984-; spokesperson Moore Oldsmobile & Cadillac, Valencia, Calif. 1987; mem. AFTRA, Am. Fedn. of Musicians; Democrat; Jewish; rec: chess, aerobics, wt. tng., comparative religions. Res: 3915-1/2 Fredonia Dr Los Angeles 90068

KAHAN, WILLIAM M., professor of mathematics and computer science; b. June 5, 1933, Toronto, Ont., Canada; s. Myer and Gertrude (Rosenthal) K.; m. Sheila Kay Strauss, Sept. 1954; children: Ari b. 1962, Simon b. 1964; edn: BA, Univ. Toronto, 1954, MA, 1956, PhD, 1958. Career: lectr. Univ. Toronto, 1954-58, asst. prof., prof. 1960-68; prof. UC Berkeley, 1969-; postdoctoral fellow Cambridge Univ., Eng. 1958-60; vis. assoc. prof. Stanford Univ., 1966; vis. scientist IBM Research, Yorktown Heights, N.Y. 1972-73; cons. IBM, New York, Austin, Tx. 1967, 1984-; cons. Hewlett-Packard, Corvallis, Oreg. 1974-85, Intel, Santa Clara, Ca. 1977-; awards: 1st G.E. Forsythe Award, Assn. for Computing Machinery, N.Y. 1972 and A.M. Turing Award, ACM, N.Y. 1989, Lin. Algebra Paper Award, Soc. for Industrial & Applied Math. 1990; mem: Am. Math. Soc. 1955-, Assn. for Computing Machinery 1961-, Soc. for Indsl. & Appl. Math. 1965-, IEEE Computer Soc. (1989-, com. stds. #754 & 854 for computer arithmetic 1985, 89); co-inventor: Floating-point co-processor INTEL 8087 (1980); publs: num. res. papers on numerical computation (1961-); Jewish; rec: repairing old appliances, autos, etc. Ofc: E.E. & C.S. Dept. Univ. Calif., Evans Hall, Berkeley 94720

KALFAYAN, SARKIS HAGOP, chemist; b. July 2, 1916, Ghaziantep, Cilicia; s. Hagop S. and Eliza (Haleblian) K.; m. Irene Elizabeth Zadourian, April 19, 1954; children: Lawrence b. 1955, Leonard b. 1957, Karen b. 1961; edn: BA, Am. Univ. Beirut Lebanon 1940; MA, 1942; PhD, Case Inst. of Tech. 1950. Career: tchg. asst. Am. Univ. Beirut, Lebanon 1940-42, instr. 1942-47; tchg. asst. Case Inst. Tech., Cleveland, Ohio 1948-50; assoc. prof. chemistry, Mt. St. Mary's Coll., Brentwood 1951-55; postdoctoral research fellow USC, Los Angeles 1955-56; chief chemist Products Research Co. 1956-60; lab. mgr. Chemseal Corp. 1960-61; sr. scientist and group supr. Jet Propulsion Lab., Pasadena 1961-82; awards: Apollo achievement NASA 1969, many recogn. certs.; mem: Am. Chemical Soc., Sigma Xi, N.Y. Acad. Sci., Knights of Vartan (comdr. 1983-85), United Armenian Congregational Ch. (trustee, deacon, mod-

erator 1966-85), Armenian Missionarry Assn. Am. (bd. mem. 1973-76, 85-91), Armenian Evangelical Union (v.moderator 1982-85); contbr. Chemistry in Space, 1972, num. articles pub. in sci. jours., 1961-82, 6 patents in field; Republican; Congregationalist; rec: gardening. Res: 4834 Matley Rd La Canada 91011-1418

KALIFON, DAVID, lawyer, physician; b. Feb. 18, 1946, New York; s. Sam and Rose(Ballon) K.; m. Elizabeth Ann Walker, July 30, 1988; 1 dau., Nicole b. 1973; edn: BA, Rutgers Coll. 1967; MD, Cornell Univ. 1971; JD, UCLA 1988; admitted St. Bar Calif. 1988, Fed. Bar 1989, lic. physician Calif. 1972. Career: emergency physician Valley Presbyterian Hosp., Van Nuys 1975-90; assoc. Hirschtick Chenen, Marina del Rey 1988-; clin. staff UCLA Hosp.; USC-L.A. Co. Gen. Hosp.; honors: Phi Beta Kappa, Alpha Omega Alpha, Henry Rutgers scholar 1966, UCLA Law Review 1986; mem: Am. Coll. Emergency Physicians (fellow), Coll. Legal Medicine (fellow), CMA, Calif. Bar Assn., Am. Bar Assn., Nat. Health Care Lawyers Assn., Calif. Health Care Lawyers Assn., Am. Soc. Legal Medicine; articles pub. in profl. jours. (1989); rec: travel, collecting antique maps. Ofc: Hirschtick Chenen 4720 Lincoln Blvd #200 Marina del Rey 90272

KALM, BERTHA EVELYN, business educator, adventurer; b. Oct. 9, 1914, Calif.; d. Charles and Amanda (Sodergren) Kalm; edn: AA, San Bernardino Jr. Coll., 1933; AB, San Jose State Coll., 1936; gen. secondary tchg. credential, USC, 1939. Career: tchr. Aromas Elem. Sch., Calif. 1936-38; business tchr. Colton High Sch., 1939-40; L.A. City Sch. System, 1942-72: instr. business edn. Manual Arts High Sch. 1944-55, also grade counselor 6+ yrs., instr. bus. edn. Hollywood High Sch. 1963-72, also work experience coord. 7+ yrs.; office work, Los Angeles, 1940-42, 1955-57, US Govt., W.D.C., 1957-58; mem: Calif. Retired Tchrs. Assn. 1973-, Nat. Retired Tchrs. Assn. 1974-, Theta Alpha Delta (bus. tchrs. frat. 1947-); club: Los Angeles Breakfast; Republican; Prot.; avocation: adventure travel: on sabbatical lv. bought & drove auto through Europe (12,000 mi.), then sailed to Greece, Egypt, Jerusalem, Beirut, Paris, and home to L.A. 1952, air and land trips through Central Am., South Am. and Brasilia, Africa, Sicily, Corsica and Portugal 1967-68; res: PO Box 481202 Los Angeles 90048

KALVINSKAS, JOHN JOSEPH, chemical engineer; b. Jan. 14, 1927, Phila.; s. Anthony and Anna (Slezute) K.; m. Louanne Marie Adams, Sept. 3, 1955; 1 child, Adrian b. 1965; edn: BS chem. engring., M.I.T., 1951, MSCE, 1952; PhD chem. engring., Calif. Inst. Tech., 1959. Career: chem. engr. DuPont, Gibbstown, N.J. 1952-55, 59-60; supr., mgr., dir. Rockwell Internat., El Segundo 1960-70; pres. Resource Dynamics Corp., L.A. 1970-74; corporate resrch. dir. Monogram Industries Inc., L.A. 1972; proj. mgr. Holmes & Narver Inc., Anaheim 1974; supr., project mgr., mem. tech. staff Jet Propulsion Lab., Pasadena 1974-; cons. Rockwell Internat., 1972-73, Kinetics Technology Internat., Pasa. 1982-83; awards: Stauffer Found. tchg. fellow CalTech 1957-58, Sigma Xi 1956, 59, Kappa Kappa Sigma 1950, NASA recogn. awards (8) 1975-85; mem: N.Y. Acad. Scis. 1980-, Am. Inst. Chem. Engrs. 1953-, Am. Chem. Soc. 1953-, Town Hall of Calif., MIT Club So. Calif.; inventor, 8 patents chem. engring. appls. 1958-85; coauthor: Nuclear Rocket Propulsion (1962); publs. in field propulsion, energy, env. engring. 1960-87; mil: electronic techn. mate 2/c USN 1944-46; Republican; R.Cath.; rec: jogging. Res: 316 Pasadena Ave #3 South Pasadena 91030 Ofc: JPL, 4800 Oak Grove Dr Pasadena 91109

KAN, HENRY, insurance and financial planning specialist; b. Oct. 10, 1921, China, nat. US cit. 1975; s. Sing-Yuek and Wai-Sing (Li) K.; m. Linda, May 5, 1951; children: Grace b. 1952, John b. 1954; edn: BS, Nat. Sun Yat-Sen and Wu-Han Univ., 1945; MS mech., City Univ. of NY, 1967; MBA, Golden Gate Univ., 1976; Reg. Profl. Engr., Calif. 1972. Career: asst. to v.p., dist. chief engr. Taiwan Sugar Corp., Taiwan 1946-67; adminstrv. mgr. Foremost Dairies Ltd., Taiwan 1967-69; proj. eng. supvr. Bechtel Inc., San Francisco, Petroleum and Nuclear Projects 1969-85; agent and reg. rep. Prudential Ins. Co. of America, 1987-88; pres. Kans Enterprise 1989-; Congo Sugar Refinery Revamping & Op. 1961; Singapore Sugar Refinery Construction Proposal 1965; productivity studies, India & Japan 1965; citations: excellent achiev. and awards, Ministry of Economic Affairs, ROC 1956; Taiwan Sugar Corp., Taiwan 1965, Bechtel Inc., San Francisco 1980; listed: Who's Who in the west 1980, Men of Achievement 1982, Dict. of Internat. Biog. 1982, Personalities of Am. 1985; mem: Am. Soc. Mech. Engrs., Nat. Assn. Life Underws., Calif. Assn. Life Underws., PALU, Internat. House; publs: contb. ed., Taiwan Sugar Hand Book; mil: lt. reserve ofcr. Chinese Army 1941-45; Republican; Christian; rec: philately, gardening, travel, swimming, boating. Res: 40 Moss Wood Ct Danville 94506

KANE, SARAH R., company president; b. Dec. 10, 1918, Eclectic, Ala.; d. Henry Clay and Una Mae (Sanford) Rouse; children: Kimberlin J., II b. 1942, Tracy Peyton b. 1947, Sanford M. b. 1949, Courtney E. b. 1951; edn: Daisy Currie Bus. Coll., 1938, Valley Coll., San Bernardino. Career: exec. secty. Alabama State Bd. of Health, 1938-41; adminstrv. asst. and secty. to chmn. Dept. Orthopaedic Surgery, Wilford Hall Teaching Hosp., San Antonio, Tex. 1958-62; supr. Welcome Wagon Internat., 1966-67; pres. REA Associates, Inc. dba Redlands Employment & Temporary Services, Redlands 1971-; awards: public relations award Calif. Assn. of Personnel Consultants 1978-79, various civic awards- Lions Club, Rotarians, Kiwanis, Soroptimist, 1972-82; mem:

Calif. Assn. of Personnel Consultants. (state dir.), CAPC Inland Empire (chpt. pres. 1978, 81-82), Riverside, San Bernardino and Redlands Chambers of Commerce, Sunrise Rotary Club; anchorperson tv documentary: The Professional Edge on How to Get a Job (1982); Republican; Sci. of Mind (pres. bd. trustees); rec: bridge, sewing, walking. Res: 925 Evergreen Ct (POB 190) Redlands 92373 Ofc: Redlands Employment & Temporary Services, 101 E Redlands Blvd Ste 146 Redlands 92373 Ph: 714/793-3351

KANE, TERENCE MICHAEL, lawyer; b. Nov. 26, 1954, Merced; s. Thomas Jay and Kathryn Ruth (Hassler) K.; m. Judith Ann Keifer, Oct. 5, 1985; edn: BS, Univ. Santa Clara 1975; M.Phil., Oxford Univ. Eng. 1977; JD, USC L.A. 1980; admitted St. Bar Calif. (1980). Career: atty. Overton Lyman & Prince, L.A. 1980-82; clk. Wm. Matthew Byrne U.S. Dist. Ct. Calif. 1982-83; atty. Lapin & Kane, L.A. 1983-84; asst. v.p., counsel So. Calif. Savings, Beverly Hills 1984-85; atty. Dennis Juarez, L.A. 1986-87; Ferrari Alvarez, San Jose 1988-; vol. atty., L.A. 1980-82; panel atty. Rotary Found. fellowship 1975-76; mem: Am. Bar Assn., Santa Clara Co. Bar Assn., Sierra Club; publs: 2 articles in law jours. (1980). Ofc: Ferrari Alvarez Olsen & Ottoboni 333 W Santa Clara Ste 700 San Jose 95113

KANN, MARK E., educator, administrator, author; b. Feb. 24, 1947, Chgo.; s. Sam N. and Ann E. K.; m. Kathy E. Michael, Feb. 13, 1969; children: Simon b. 1973; edn: BA, Univ. Wis., Madison 1968, MA, 1972, PhD, 1975. Career: prof. Univ. So. Calif., L.A. 1975-, assoc. dean 1990-93; v.p. Jefferson Center For Character Educ., Pasadena 1991-; author: On The Man Question (1991), Middle Class Radicalism in Santa Monica (1986), The American Left (1982). Ofc: USC Dept of Political Science University Park Los Angeles 90089-0044

KANZIG, CHRISTOPHER MERRIAM, agriculture industry systems consultant; b. July 23, 1954, Saginaw, Mich.; s. Edward Dudley and Arlene May (Merriam) K.; m. Virginia Shakley, Apr. 12, 1976 (div.); m. Michelle Hagerty, Feb. 11, 1989; children: Mathew b. 1972, Ryan b. 1974, Travis b. 1978, Courtnie b. 1983, Christopher b. 1989; edn: Mt. San Antonio Coll., 2 yrs., computer sci. courses. Career: data processing analyst RKO-KHJ TV/Radio, Los Angeles 1974-77; D.P. consultant IBM/Discovision, Irvine 1977-79; KSI/System Consultants, 1980-; dir: KSI Inc., Internat. Software Systems, Multi Nat. Engineering; author computer system: Growers Accounting (1980-81); awards: appreciation Rialto Jaycees (1984), Blue Banner Growers, Riverside (1986); mem: Western Growers Assn., US Chamber of Commerce; Republican (Nat. Congl. Com. 1980-); R.Cath. Address: 16964 Crestview Ct Victorville 92392

KAO, PHILIP MIN-SHIEN, programmer/analyst; b. Dec. 16, 1963, Los Angeles, Calif.; s. Donald and Jennie (Chen) K.; m. Lori Suzanne Wilson, June 25, 1989; edn: BA, Chemistry, UC San Diego 1985. Career: student engr., Hughes Aircraft Co., Fullerton, Calif. 1983-85; res. asst., Hybritech, Inc., San Diego 1986; res. assoc./technical, SIBIA, La Jolla, 1986-90; analytical chemist, Alliance Pharmaceuticals, S.D. 1990-91; programmer/analyst, Ligand Pharmaceuticals, S.D. 1991-; honors: listed Who's Who in the West 1992-93; mem. Amer. Assn. of Clinical Chemists 1991-, Amer. Chem. Soc. 1981-, AAAS 1990-, Mathematical Assn. of Amer. 1991-; treas. Villarrica Homeowners Assn. 1991-; co-author: presentations, Amer. Chem. Soc., 1988, 89; publ. article in Jour. of Infectious Diseases, 1990; second author, publ. articles in Analytical Biochemistry 1989, Bioconjugate Chemistry 1990. Ofc: Ligand Pharmaceuticals 9393 Towne Centre Dr #100 San Diego 92121

KAPLAN, JOSEPH M., safety council president; b. May 29, 1914, Cleveland, Ohio; s. Edward and Mamie (Krislove) K; m. Henrietta Lurie Kaplan, Mar. 30, 1941; children: Paul Dana, Drew Alan; edn: AB, UCLA 1931-35; masters cert., Harvard, Cambridge, MA 1937-38; instit. of organization mgmt., Univ. of Santa Clara, San Jose 1960-82. Career: dir., So. Calif. War Manpower Conservation Pgm. prior to WWII service; Greater Los Angeles Chapt. Nat. Safety Council, 1939-1979, pres. 1979-; cons. to White House Conf. on Traffic Safety; bd. dirs. March of Dimes; honors: 1st safety exec. designated Chartered Assn. Exec. (CAE), Am. Soc. of Assn. Execs.; recipient Key Award 1974 Outstanding Local Assn. Exec. in the nation; Award of Honor by Assn. of Safety Councils 1973, named Assn. Exec. of Yr. by So. Calif. Soc. of Assn. Execs. 1979; bd. mem. Nat. Safety Council; mem: Am. Soc. of Assn. Exec., Am. Soc. of Safety Engrs., Inst. of Traffic Engrs., Nat. Assn. of Exposition Mgrs., So. Calif. Industrial Safety Soc., Calif. Assn. of Safety Councils, Veterans of Safety Internat. (pres. 1976), Rotary Intl.; mil: US Army during WWII. Ofc: National Safety Council Greater Los Angeles 3450 Wilshire Blvd Ste 700 Los Angeles 90010

KAPLOWITZ, RICHARD ALLEN, academic dean; b. Dec. 12, 1940, Bklyn.; s. Joseph and Sonya (Taub) K.; m. Lisette Feldstein, Dec. 22, 1964 (div. Oct. 1990); children: David, Robert; edn: BA, Bklyn. Coll., 1961; MA, Columbia Univ., 1962; EdD, Harvard Univ., 1970. Career: tchr. schools in New York and France, 1962-67; founding dir. Weekend Coll., C.W. Post Univ., Greenvale, N.Y. 1970-72; dean continuing edn. Merrimack Coll., North Andover, Mass. 1974-80; dir. human resource devel. Raytheon Co., Andover, Mass. 1980-82; pres. Teem Inc., Andover 1982-90; dean New England Inst., Boston 1985-87,

chair grad. div. Notre Dame Coll., Manchester, N.H. 1988-90; v.p. enrollment mgmt. Pacific Grad. Sch. Psychology, Palo Alto, Calif. 1990-; mem. bd. overseers Lawrence Gen. Hosp. 1980-90, Gr. Lawrence Mental Hlth. and Retardation Bd. (pres. 1977-79); mem. Assn. Cont. Higher Edn. (bd. 1979-82); author: Selecting Academic Administrators (1973), Selecting Coll. and Univ. Personnel: The Quest and the Questions (1988); contbr. articles to profl. jours.; Jewish; rec: flying. Res: PO Box 52032 Palo Alto 94303 Ofc: Pacific Graduate School of Psychology 935 E Meadow Palo Alto 94303

KARPILOW, KATHLEEN ANN, association executive, researcher; b. Apr. 30, 1955, Walnut Creek; d. Harry Abraham and Mary Elizabeth Karpilow; m. Steve Sanders, Sept. 13, 1986; edn: AB, UC Davis 1977; PhD, Harvard Univ. 1984. Career: program evaluator Radcliffe Coll., Cambridge, Mass 1981-82; cons. Calif. St. Senate, Sacto. 1982-84; adminstrv. asst. to Mayor City of Sacto. 1985-86; project dir. Calif. St. Senate 1988-89; exec. dir. Calif. Elected Women's Assn. 1988-; honors: Phi Beta Kappa, Downtown Capitol BPW Woman of Year 1988; mem: Coalition of Sacto. Women's Orgns. (pres. 1988-), Sacto. Heritage Inc. (past bd. mem.), Sacto. Women's Campaign (past pres.). Ofc: California Elected Women's Assn. 6000 J Street Sacramento 95819-6100

KARWELIS, DONALD CHARLES, artist; b. Sept. 19, 1934, Rockford, Ill.; s. Charles William and Lucille Ann (Pujdak) K.; 2 sons, Jean b. 1962, Kevin b. 1964; edn: undergrad. Riverside City Coll., 1966-68; BA, UC Irvine, 1968, MFA (summa cum laude), 1971. Career: instr. UC Irvine 1969-71, Riverside City Coll. 1971-72, So. Calif. Art Inst., Laguna Beach 1978-82, Saddleback Coll., Irvine 1979-80; lectr. UC Irvine, 1986-87; One-man shows: Kirk de Gooyer Gal., L.A. 1984, Irvine Fine Arts Ctr. 1986, LJ Gal., Newport Beach 1989, Interior Designer's Inst., Newport Beach 1991, Lithuanian Art Mus., Vilnius 1991; group exhibits: Marilyn Pink Master Prints & Drawings, L.A. 1988, Lithuanian Art Mus., Lithuanian World Ctr. 1990, Irvine Fine Arts Ctr. 1990, Sata Fine Art, Costa Mesa 1991; represented in permanent collections of L.A. County Mus. Art, Newport Harbor Art Mus., Laguna Art Mus., Atlantic Richfield Corp., L.A., Calif. Canadian Bank, L.A.; awards: research grantee Nat. Def. Edn. Act 1970, fellow Nat. Endowment for Arts 1976-77; publ.: Artweek 1987; mil: sgt. USMC 1954-57; Democrat; R.Cath.; rec: cultural anthropology, R.R. ops. Studio: 202-K East Stevens Santa Ana 92707

KASARI, LEONARD SAMUEL, concrete consultant, quality control professional; b. Sept. 22, 1924, Los Angeles; s. Kustaa Adolph and Impi (Sikio) K.; m. Elizabeth P. Keplinger, Aug. 25, 1956; children: Lorraine Carol, Lance Eric; edn: Compton Coll. 1942-43, UCLA 1964-70; reg. Profl. Engr. Calif. Career: gen. constrn. Los Angeles area 1946-61; supr. inspection svc. Osborne Labs., Los Angeles 1961-64; mgr. customer svc. Lightweight Processing, 1965-77; dir. tech. svc. Crestlite Aggregates, San Clemente 1977-78; quality control mgr. Standard Concrete, Santa Ana 1978-92; honors: Hon. Life mem. Calif. PTA 1983, Sam Hobbs Service Award ACI-So. Calif. 1992; mem. Am. Concrete Inst., So. Calif. Structural Engrs. Assn.; civic: Torrance YMCA (bd. mgrs. 1970-, camp dir. High Sierras 1969-81; mil: USN 1943-46; Democrat; Lutheran; res/ofc: 2450 W 233 St Torrance 90501

KASKEL, NEAL T., mergers and acquisitions executive; b. Oct. 6, 1943, Buffalo, N.Y.; s. David and Bertha (Perlmuter) K.; m. Geraldine Slutsky, Apr. 3, 1966; children: Amy b. 1970, Robert b. 1973; edn: BS, DePaul Univ., 1966; MBA, Northwestern Univ., 1972. Career: mktg. resrch. analyst D'Arcy Advt., Chgo. 1966-67; mktg. resrch. supr. Foote, Cone & Belding, Chgo. 1967-72; mgr. mktg. resrch. Armour-Dial, Phoenix, Ariz. 1972-74, Hunt-Wesson, Fullerton, Calif. 1974-79; dir. mktg. svs. FHP, Fountain Valley 1979-81; mktg. mgr. Smith Internat., Irvine 1981-83; v.p. The Geneva Cos., Irvine 1983-; adj. prof. CSU Fullerton, also CSU Long Beach, 1975-90, Univ. of La Verne, 1990-, Univ. of Phoenix, Fountain Valley 1990-; mil: lt. USNR 1966-72; Democrat; Jewish (Jewish Fedn. of Orange Co. bd. 1983-, treas. 91-); rec: tennis, travel. Ofc: The Geneva Cos. 5 Park Plaza Irvine 92714

KASSAR, LYNN M., chief financial officer, secretary/treasurer; b. Feb. 23, 1945, Cleveland, Oh.; d., Clarence T. (dec. 1948) and Mary M. (Jewel) Hughes; m. Denis Filbey, July 4, 1965 (dec.); m. Bruce L. Johnson, Mar. 17, 1971 (widowed Dec. 23, 1978); m. Wayne L. Kassar, Aug. 23, 1980; children: Daniel b. 1966, Charles b. 1971; stepchildren: Anna, Emily b. 1962; edn: AA, De Anza, Cupertino, Calif. 1978; BA, UC Santa Cruz 1987. Career: asst. treas. Citizens Financial Corp., Cleveland, Ohio 1973-76; accounting mgr., Tymshare, Cupertino 1978-80; accounting mgr., Shugart Assoc., Sunnyvale 1980-82; accounting mgr., ESL, Inc., Sunnyvale 1983-85; accounting mgr., Pacific We. Bank, San Jose 1987-90; c.f.o., Traveling Sch., Inc., Santa Cruz 1986-, bd. of trustees 1990-, treas. 1990-; Methodist; rec: reading, spending time with grandchildren. Res: P.O. Box 1491 Aptos 95001. Ofc: Traveling School, Inc. 819-1/2 Pacific Ave. #2 Santa Cruz 95060

KATHOL, ANTHONY LOUIS, real estate development co. financial executive; b. June 12, 1964, San Diego; s. Cletus Louis and Regina Antoinette (Ellrott) K.; m. Kathleen Marie Moore, Jan. 23, 1988; children: Nicole Kathleen b. 1989, Natalie Antoinette b. 1992; edn: BS, Univ. So. Calif., 1986; MBA,

Univ. San Diego, 1988. Career: fin. and budget coord. Atcheson Topeka & Santa Fe Railway, Brea 1988-89; fin. and budget coord. Catellus Devel. Corp., Anaheim 1989-92, mgr. fin. analysis, 1992-; awards: Calif. Building Ind. Assn. fellow, USC 1986, Univ. San Diego fellow econ., mktg. (1987, 88), employee of yr. Catellus Devel. Corp., S.F. 1991; mem. Kts. of Col. (chpt. fin. sec. 1989-90), Future Bus. Leaders of Am. (So. Calif. judge 1991, 92); Republican; R.Cath.; rec: reading, basketball, gardening. Res: 3805 Maxon Ln Chino 91710 Ofc: Catellus Development Corp. 1065 N Pacific Center Dr Ste 200 Anaheim 92806

KATZ, MARTY, producer, motion picture and television production executive, education manager; b. Sept. 2, 1947, Landsburg, Fed. Rep. Germany; m. Campbell Hull, Apr. 29, 1982; edn: UCLA; Univ. Md. Career: dir. film production ABC Circle Films, LA 1971-76; exec. v.p. production Quinn Martin Productions, LA 1976-77; production TV movies 1977-78; production cons., writer, producer Paramount Pictures Corp., Hollywood 1978-80; indep. producer Marty Katz Productions, LA 1980-85; exec. v.p. motion picture and TV productions Walt Disney Studio, Burbank 1985-; supr. production 50+ TV movies that earned 25 Emmy awards; feature producer: Heart Like A Wheel, Lost In America; mil: 1st. lt. US Army, Combat Pictorial Unit director, Vietnam, Bronze star. Ofc: Walt Disney Pictures 500 S. Buena Vista St. Burbank 91521

KATZ, RICHARD DANNY, member, Calif. Legislative Assembly, 39th Dist.; b. Aug. 16, 1950, LA., Calif.; s. Julius and Lillian (Ochacher) K.; m. Gini Barrett, Apr. 12, 1987; edn: BA, Calif. State Univ., San Diego, 1982. Career: graphics artist/printer, self-employed, Sepulveda, Calif.; mem. Calif. Legislative Assembly, 39th Dist., 1980-; chair Assembly Transp. Com., 1985-; mem. Assembly Environmental Safety & Toxic Materials Com.; mem. Assembly Water, Parks & Wildlife Com.; awards: Legislator of the Year: Calif. Assn. of Independent Businesses 1983, The Victims Legal Assistance Council 1987, The Affiliated Committees on Aging 1987, Calif. Assn. of the Physically Handicapped 1987, Nat. Council of Alcoholism & Drug Dependence 1992, League of Calif. Cities 1992; Crimefighter of the Year, Assn. for L.A. Deputy Sheriffs 1992; mem: Advy. Bd Am. Jewish Com., 1980-; bd. dir. Nat. Defenders of Wildlife 1989-93; mem. Valley Industry/Commerce Assn. 1980-, Foothill Police Activity League 1986-; advy. bd. Valley Interfaith Council 1988-; bd. dir. Boys & Girls Club of San Fernando Valley 1985-; author, Calif. legislation: Taxpayers Bill of Rights, Paperwork Reduction Act, Bad Check Law, Regulatory Fairness Act, Computer Education Act of 1983, Children's Poison Prevention Act, legislation to permit market-based water transfers, Proposition 111 (Calif. transp. funding blueprint approved by Calif. voters in June, 1990); Democrat; Jewish; rec: basketball, hiking, horseback riding, country & western music; Ofc: 9140 Van Nuys Blvd. No. 109 Panorama City 91402

KAUFMAN, ALBERT I., lawyer; b. Oct. 2, 1936, N.Y.C.; s. Israel and Pauline (Pardes) K.; m. Ruth Feldman, Jan. 25, 1959; son, Michael b. 1964; edn: AA, L.A. City Coll., 1957; BA, JD, Univ. of San Fernando Valley Coll. of Law, 1964, 66; admitted Calif. bar 1967. Career: asst. hwy. engr. Div. of Hwys., Los Angeles 1956-67; atty. pvt. practice, 1967-; arbitrator Am. Arb. Assn., judge pro tem Los Angeles Superior and Municipal Cts., Family Law mediator, judicial arbitrator L.A. Superior Ct., 1980-; honors: disting. service B'nai Brith Woodland Hills 1969, exceptional svc., comdr.'s commendation Civil Air Patrol Calif. 1977, 86, recogn. Constl. Rights Found. L.A. 1974, 75, 76, 77, 78, hon. tchg. certif. L.A. Unif. Sch. Dist. 1976; mem: ABA, Calif. State Bar, Calif. Trial Lawyers Assn., L.A. Co. Bar Assn., L.A. Trial Lawyers Assn., S.F.V. Bar Assn.; civic: Toastmasters (Woodland Hills pres. 1969), B'nai Brith (Woodland Hills pres. 1971-72); mil: s/sgt. USAF 1959-65, col. Civil Air Patrol 1956-; Republican; Jewish; rec: sailing, flying, motorcycling. Ofc: 17609 Ventura Blvd Ste 201 Encino 91316

KAUFMAN, CARY STEVEN, surgeon; b. Jan. 5, 1948, Los Angeles; s. Carl and Betty K.; m. Leslie; children: Casey b. 1975, Lauren b. 1979, Amanda b. 1983; edn: BS chem., cum laude, UCLA 1969; MD, UCLA Sch. of Med. 1973; Diplomate Am. Bd. Surgery 1981, recert. 1989; MD lic. Wash., Calif., 1975. Career: surg. resident Univ. of Wash. 1973-75, Harbor/UCLA Med. Ctr. 1975-79; gen. and vascular surgeon pvt. practice, Long Beach; asst. surgeon Long Beach Memorial Hosp. 1979-, chief gen./vasc. surg. 1988-90; bd. Memorial Cancer Inst., 1989-94; clin. asst. prof. surg. UCLA 1979-; researcher Nat. Surg. Adjuvant Breast Proj. 1988-; Fellow Am. Coll. of Surgeons, Fellow Internat. Coll. of Surgeons, mem: Long Beach Surgical Soc., Calif. Med. Assn., L.A. Co. Med. Assn., L.A. Surg. Soc., Am. Cancer Soc. Bd. 1984-87, med. advisor Reach for Recovery Pgm. 1981-; contbr. med. journals. Ofc: Cary S. Kaufman MD 701 E 28th St 100 Long Beach 90806

KAUNE, JAMES E., marine engineering executive; b. Mar. 4, 1927, Santa Fe, N.Mex.; s. Henry Eugene and Lucile (Carter) K.; m. Pauline Stamatos, June 24, 1956; children: Bradford Scott, Audrey Lynn, Jason Douglas; edn: BS engring., US Naval Acad., 1950; Naval Engr., naval architecture and marine engring., M.I.T., 1955; BS metallurg. engring., Carnegie Inst. Tech., 1960. Career: commd. ensign US Navy 1950, advanced through grades to capt., 1970, asst. gunnery ofcr. USS Floyd B. Parks 1950-52, project ofcr. USS Gyatt, Boston Naval Shipyard 1955-57, main propulsion ofcr. USS Tarawa 1957-58, asst. planning

ofcr. Her Majesty's Canadian Dockyard, Halifax, Nova Scotia 1960-62, repair ofcr. USS Cadmus 1962-64, fleet maintenence ofcr. Naval Boiler and Turbine Lab., design supt. (responsible all ship repair and modernization design plans) Philadelphia Naval Shipyard, 1964-68, project mgr. USS Midway conversion project, Hunters Point Naval Shipyard, San Francisco 1968-71, material staff ofcr., maintenance mgr. all aircraft carriers in Atlantic Fleet, Norfolk, Va. 1971-74, prodn. ofcr. (responsible all ship and waterfront prodn.) Phila. Naval Shipyard 1974-77, comdg. ofcr. Long Beach (Calif.) Naval Shipyard 1977-80; industrial mgr. Am. Metal Bearing Co., Garden Grove 1979-80; gen. mgr. Todd Shipyards Corp., S.F. Div. 1980-83; v.p. engring. and planning Port Richmond Shipyard Inc., Richmond 1983-84; v.p. engring. and mktg. Service Engineering Co., San Francisco 1984-; mem: Am. Soc. Naval Engrs., US Naval Inst., Am. Soc. Metals, Masons; contbr. articles to profl. jours.; Episcopalian. Res: 403 Camino Sobrante Orinda 94563 Ofc: Service Engineering Corp. Pier 50 San Francisco 94107

KAUR, SWARAJ, biochemist; b. Jan. 30, 1955, Lucknow, U.P., India; d. Kartar Singh and Joginder Kaur; m. Timothy Alan Guetling, July 14, 1991; children: Swaim b. 1992; edn: BS, Lucknow Univ., 1973, MS, 1975, PhD, 1981; MBA, National Univ., San Diego, 1989. Career: jr.and sr. research fellow King George's Med. Coll., Lucknow U.P. India 1978-84; postdoc. res. toxicologist Univ. Calif., Riverside 1984-86; sr. project scientist Alpha Therapeutic Corp., Los Angeles 1986-88, prin. scientist 1988-91, sr. prin. scientist 1992-93, assoc. dir. 1993-; awards: jr. and sr. res. fellowship Council of Scientific & Industrial Res., New Delhi (1976-78, 1978-80), sr. res. fellowship, res. associateship Indian Council of Med. Res., New Delhi (1980-81, 1982-84), postdoc. res. UC Riverside (1984-86); mem. Sigma Xi; publs: jour. articles and presentations sci. meetings; rec: shopping, singing, aerobics, sightseeing. Res: 10395 Vernon Ave Montclair 91763 Ofc: Alpha Therapeutic Corp. 1213 John Reed Ct City of Industry 91746

KAYANI, AMER MAHBOOB, political economist; b. April 21, 1961, Pakistan; nat. 1988; s. Mahboob Ahmed and Khurshid (Khurshid) K.; edn: BA, USC 1985; MPIA, Univ. Pittsburgh 1987. Career: research asst. USC, L.A. 1984-86; cons. U.N., N.Y.C. 1986; res. assoc. Pew Freedom Trust, Pittsburgh, Pa. 1987; evaluator GAO, San Francisco 1988-; cons. City of Oakland 1988; honors: USC Deans Highest Hons. 1984-85, Top 40 grads. 1985, Calif. merit scholarship 1984, Pew Freedom Trust award 1987; mem: Am. Soc. Pub. Adminstrs., World Affairs Council S.F., Am. Political Sci. Assn., Political Risk Anlaysts Assn., Pakistan Student Assn.; work papers pub. on diplomat tng. 1987, case study pub. on Kashmir Conflict 1988; Islam; rec: flying. Res: 939 Lexington Ave #9 El Cerrito 94530 Ofc: GAO 1275 Market St Ste 900 San Francisco 94103

KAYE, RONALD LEE, physician; b. Apr. 15, 1932, Toledo, Ohio; s. Philip and Gertrude (Berman) K.; m. Tobye Fay Davidson, June 19, 1955; children: Brian b. 1957, Todd b. 1959, Douglas b. 1961, Jeffrey b. 1965; edn: BA, and MD, Univ. Mich., Ann Arbor, 1953, 1957. Career: rheumatologist, dir. of medical edn., Palo Alto Medical Clinic, 1963-; honors: Soc. of Sigma Xi (Mayo Clinic, and Stanford), disting. service award Nat. Arthritis Found. 1973; mem: Am. Soc. of Clin. Rheumatology (1973-, past pres.), Am. Med. Assn. (sci. bd. 1963-), Sino-Judaic Inst. (exec. bd. 1973-), U.S. China Ednl. Inst. (exec. bd. 1973-), B'nai Brith; author: Katz's "Textbook of Rheumatology" (1989), 50+ journal articles; mil: capt. USAF 1959-66; Jewish; rec: philately, mineral collection, travel. Res: 2108 Bellview Dr Palo Alto 94301 Ofc: Palo Alto Medical Clinic 300 Homer Ave Palo Alto 94301

KEARNEY, REX THOMAS, JR., lawyer; b. May 9, 1938, Modesto; s. Rex Thomas and Esther Sterling (Weeks) K.; edn: BS, UC Berkeley 1962; LLB, Hastings Coll. of Law 1966; admitted Calif. Bar 1966. Career: deputy dist. atty. Sacramento County, 1967-68; atty., assoc. McDonald & Donahue 1968-74; sr. ptnr. Ingoglia, Marskey & Kearney, Lobner & Bull, Sacto. 1974-; instr. Assn. of Trial Lawyers of Am., Trial Coll. (2 yrs.), Calif. Cont. Edn. of the Bar 1984-; mem: Phi Delta Phi, Am. Bar Assn., Am. Bd. of Trial Advocates (Advocate), Calif. Bar Assn., Sacto. Co. Bar Assn., Def. Res. Inst., No. Calif. Assn. of Def. Counsel; mil: AUS 1957-60; Republican; rec: automobile racing CSRG, tennis. Ofc: Ingoglia, Marskey, Kearney, Lobner & Bull, 3610 American River Dr Ste 140 Sacramento 95864-5900

KEEFFE, SUSAN DEVORE, educator, administrator; b. May 20, 1944, Hastings, Nebr.; d. Richard Geo. and Kathryn DeVore (King) Van Buskirk; m. Philip Lewis Keeffe, Jan. 28, 1966 (div. 1975); children: Darren b. 1970, Kathleen b. 1972; edn: BA in advt., San Jose St. Univ., 1966; MS spl. edn., Dominican Coll., San Rafael 1979; EdD, Univ. San Francisco, 1986. Career: sch. tchr. Richmond Unified Sch. Dist., 1975-, subst. tchr. 1975, Home tchr. 1976, tchr. 3rd/4th gr. 1977, special edn., transitional edn. pgm., 1986-, summer sch. tchg. 1978-88, summer sch. prin. Richmond High Sch. 1985, Castro Elem. 1986, hd. summer sch. principal Richmond Unified Sch. Dist., 1987; p.t. faculty Sch. of Edn., St. Mary's Coll., Moraga 1989-; Program Quality Review reviewer for Contra Costa Co.; honors: nominee and finalist Richmond USD Education Fund teaching excellence award 1991; mem. Seaview Sch. Program Quality Rev. Leadership Team, and v.chair Seaview Sch. School Site Council, 1990-91;

mem. bd. Richmond U.S.D. Comm. Advy. Com. for Special Edn. (past pres., sec. 1983-85); awards: CANHC scholar (1976, 78), CTA scholar 1984, CTIIP grantee (1985, 87), mentor tchr. (1987/88, 89/90, 91/92), State Dept. Edn. exemplary spl. edn. technology pgm. nominee, CANHC educator of yr. 1987, Richmond USD tchr. of yr. 1988; mem. CANHC / ACLD (past pres. West Contra Costa Chpt.), Phi Delta Kappa, Delta Kappa Gamma (past pres.); civic: Chelsea By-The-Bay HOA (pres. 1988-90, bd. v.p. 90-91), Friends of the Red-Tail Hawk (sec. 1989); contbr. 5+ articles in acad. and profl. jours.; Democrat; Unitarian; rec: camping, tropical birds, computers. Ofc: Seaview School, Richmond USD 2000 Southwood Dr San Pablo 94806

KEELER, GEORGE ROBERT, journalism professor; b. May 1, 1954, Pomona; s. Robt. Lee and Lucille Mae (Sarafian) K.; edn: BA, Univ. La Verne, MAT, 1979; PhD, USC, 1990. Career: ed. in chief La Verne Mag. 1976-77; editl. asst. Messenger Mag., Elgin, Ill. 1977-78; assoc. prof. journalism Univ. La Verne 1978-; senior adv. The Thalians Mag., Beverly Hills 1982, 83, writing coach, consultant; awards: Victor DeRose, Paul M. Hinkhouse award Religious Pub. Relations Council 1977, Silver Crown Columbia Univ. 1985, medalist Columbia Scholastic Press Assn. (1982, 83, 85), 7 All-Am. awards Assoc. Collegiate Press (1979-86), Univ. La Verne student svc./humanities scholar 1977, life mem. Calif. Scholastic Fedn.; mem: Sigma Delta Chi, Soc. Profl. Journalists (dir. L.A. chpt. 1986, Mark of Excellence award), L.A. Press Club; civic: Citizens for Environmental Land Protection (founder), Community Assn. for a Responsible Environment (founder), L.A. Co. Marshall Canyon Mounted Assistance (Mountain Bike Unit), Ch. of the Brethren (worship/witness commn. chmn. 1984-86); contbg. writer: History of the Am.-Armenian Internat. Coll.: Promise and Reality (1987); Inquiry Into Who Should Have the Final Authority Over What Is Printed in a Campus Newspaper (1981); numerous profl. jour. articles; rec: white water river kayaking guide, mtn. biking, wedding and magazine photog., trumpet. Res: 381 Baseline Rd Claremont 91711 Ofc: University of La Verne, 1950 Third St La Verne 91750

KEELER, RICHARD LEE, college executive assistant; b. July 19, 1958, Pomona; s. Robert Lee and Lucille Mae (Sarafian) K.; edn: BA, magna cum laude Univ. of La Verne 1980, MA, Univ. of La Verne 1983; MA, Univ. Calif., Berkeley 1989; Career: publicity coordinator Univ. of La Verne, 1980-81; Gen. assignment reporter Claremont Courier newspaper, Claremont 1981-82; assoc. dir. communications, Nat. Energy Research & Info. Inst. (editor, Cogeneration World Mag., Energy Report), Univ. of La Verne, 1983-86, instr. Journalism and Communications, 1985-86; asst. to pres., acting campus dean, Colo. Mtn. Coll., Leadville campus, 1986, Spring Valley Campus 1987; exec. asst. to the Chancellor, Peralta Colls., 1987-; honors: cert. Creativity 1984 Contest, Cogeneration World Mag., listed Who's Who in Am. Colls. and Univs. 1980, Sigma Delta Chi; Republican; Prot. (chmn. Christian Edn.); rec: kayaking. Res: 381 Baseline Rd Claremont 91711

KEENAN, RETHA VORNHOLT, registered nurse, educator, consultant; b. Aug. 15, 1934, Solon, Iowa; d. Charles E. and Helen M. (Konicek) Vornholt; m. Roy V. Keenan, Jan. 5, 1980; 2 sons (nee Iverson): Scott b. 1959, Craig b. 1961; edn: BS in nsg., Univ. of Iowa 1955; MS in nsg. CSU Long Beach 1979; cert. nurse practitioner, mental health, CSULB, 1979; R.N., Calif. Career: mental health cons. Inter-City Home Health Agency, Los Angeles 1979-80; instr. mental health nsg. Los Angeles City Coll. 1980-81, El Camino Coll., Torrance 1981-86, Mt. St. Mary's Coll. 1986, West Los Angeles Coll., Culver City 1981-87; Commencement speaker 1984, 85, 86, 87; awards: NIMH grant for grad. study 1977-78, Phi Kappa Phi 1977, Sigma Theta Tau 1985; mem: Am. Nurses Assn. (Coun. Psychiat. and Mental Health Nsg. 1984-90), Calif. Nurses Assn., AAUW, Delta Zeta Sor., Assistance League of San Pedro, Palos Verdes; major contbg. author: Am. Jour. of Nsg. Question & Answer Book for State Bd. Rev., pub. 1983, rev. 1985, 1987, Nursing Care Planning Guide for Adults, 1987, Nursing Care Planning Guide for Children, 1987, Nursing Care Planning Guide for Psychiatric and Mental Health Nursing, 1988, Critically Ill Adults: Nursing Care Planning Guides, 1988; Republican; Lutheran; rec: travel, writing. Res: 27849 Longhill Dr Rancho Palos Verdes 90274

KEENEY, EDMUND LUDLOW, Scripps Clinic president emeritus; b. Aug. 1908, Shelbyville, Ind.; s. Bayard G. and Ethel (Adams) K.; m. Esther Cox Loney Wight, Mar. 14, 1950; children: Edmund L. Jr., Eleanor (Smith); edn: AB, Ind. Univ. 1930; MD, Johns Hopkins Univ. 1934; diplomate Am. Bd. of Internal Med., subsplty. allergy. Career: intern Johns Hopkins Hosp., 1934-35, med. resident 1935-36, instr. in medicine 1940-48; pvt. medical practice, splst. in allergy, San Diego 1948-55; pres./director Scripps Clinic and Research Found., La Jolla 1955-77, pres. emeritus 1977-; dir. research on fungus infections Ofc. of Sci. Research and Devel., cons. U.S. Navy 1948-64; bd. trustees Univ. San Diego 1974-; honors: Phi Beta Kappa, Alpha Omega Alpha, Beta Theta Pi; mem: AMA (1938-, secty. Sect. on Allergy 1964-65), Fellow Am. Acad. of Allergy (1940-, pres. 1963-64, editl. bd. Journ. of Allergy), Allergy Found. of Amer. (dir.), Am. Soc. for Clin. Investigation 1945-, Fellow Am. Coll. of Phys. 1946-, Western Soc. for Clin. Research 1948-, Western Assn. of Phys. 1955-, Calif. Med. Assn. (sci. bd. dirs.), Rotary, Eldorado Country Club; author: Practical Medical Mycology (Charles C. Thomas, 1955), contbr. num.

articles re allergy, immunology, mycology to profl. jours.; Republican; Presbyterian; rec: golf, fishing, swim; res: 338 Via del Norte La Jolla; ofc: 10666 N Torrey Pines Rd La Jolla 92037

KEESLAR, OREON, author, retired educator and public school administrator; b. Dec. 19, 1907, Orland, Ind.; s. Glenn Leroy and Janette (Gillis) K.; m. Julia May Hackett, Feb. 22, 1936 (dec. Feb. 1988); children: Peter b. 1939, Daniel b. 1944, Mary Judith b. 1947; edn: 2-yr. Normal Dipl., Manchester Coll., 1934; BS edn., Ohio St. Univ., 1938, MA sci. edn. 1939; PhD sci. edn., Univ. of Mich., 1945. Career: 1-room rural tchr. Sand Hill Sch., Angola, Ind. 1929-34, jr. high tchr. Angola Pub. Schs., 1934-37; also scoutmaster and dist. commr. Boy Scouts Am., Anthony Wayne Area Council, 1930-37; university high sch. science tchr. Ohio St. Univ., Columbus 1938-40, Univ. of Mich., Ann Arbor 1940-43; tchr. Plymouth H.S., Plymouth, Mich. 1943-44; Lt. US Naval Reserve 1944-49, ofcr. in chg. rating exams Pensacola Naval Air Base, 1944-46; dir. A-V (audio-visual) edn. and H.S. curriculum coord. Kern County Schs., Bakersfield, Calif. 1946-54; dir. edn. Inyo County Schs., Independence 1954-55; H.S. curriculum coord. Santa Clara County Schs., San Jose 1955-73; instr. A-V, Fresno St. Coll. and UCSB, Ext. courses, 1947-50, on-campus Fresno State, summer 1949; vis. prof. UCLA, 6 summers 1950-55, San Jose St. Coll., summer 1960; active num. tchr. organizations 1954-73, ofcr. and bd. mem. Calif. Sch. Suprs. Assn. (state secty. 1949-50), San Joaquin Valley A-V Assn. Bksfld. (pres. 1947-48), Nat. Science Tchrs. Assn. (chmn. conv. plng. com. Chgo. 1961), past sec.-treas. 8 tchr. orgns. (Math; Sci.; Soc. Studies; Fgn. Languages; HS Librarians; English; Sci. Fair; Jt. Council/Math & Sci.) San Jose, Santa Clara Co., 1954-73; honors: French horn player chosen to rep. the Steuben County Schs. Orch. (NE Ind.) in Dr. Joseph E. Maddy's First National H.S. Orch. (Detroit) made up of 225 of best student musicians nat. 1926; Phi Kappa Phi (1943), Phi Delta Kappa 1937-70, science fair award of honor Calif. Acad. of Sci., San Francisco 1973; civic: Photog. Soc. of Am. 1975-, Gold Rush Chapt. P.S.A. (dir. at lg. 1989-92), Reno Photo Club, Audubon Soc., Nature Conservancy, Wilderness Soc., Sierra Club, others; author: Financial Aids for Higher Education (coauthor, Judy Keeslar Santamaria) (pub. biennially 1963-92, now 800-page book in 15th edit.), series of articles in Science Education J. 1945-50, book chapt. in Film And Education 1948; Democrat; Prot.; rec: photog., cabinetry, bookbinding, fiction writing, travel. Res: 15126 Cavalier Rise Truckee 96161

KEHLER, DOROTHEA FAITH, humanities professor; b. Apr. 21, 1936, N.Y.C.; d. Nathan and Minnie (Coopersmith) Gutwill; widowed; children: Paul Dolid b. 1957, Eve Boyd b. 1959, Jessica Kehler b. 1971, Edward Kehler b. 1973; edn: BA, City Coll. N.Y., 1956; MA, Ohio Univ., 1967, PhD Eng. lit., 1969. Career: instr. MacMurray Coll., Jacksonville, Ill. 1964-65; instr. Ohio Univ., Athens, Oh. 1965-66, teaching fellow 1966-68; lectr. San Diego State Univ., 1969-70, asst., asso. prof. 1970-88, prof. dept. English, 1988-; awards: summer fellow NEH, Harvard Univ. 1983, travel grantee Folger Libr. Inst., W.D.C. 1988, merit. performance and profl. promise SDSU 1988, res., scholarship and creative activity SDSU 1990, English Dept.'s most influential professor tchg. award SDSU 1991; mem: Modern Language Assn. of Am. 1970-, Shakespeare Assn. of Am. 1983-, Internat. Shakespeare Assn. 1984-, Rocky Mountain Modern Language Assn. 1984-, Southeastern Renaissance Conf. 1986-, Philological Assn. of Pacific Coast 1986-, Renaissance Conf. of So. Calif. 1990-; author: Problems in Literary Research (3 revised edits. 1975, 81, 87); editor anthology: In Another Country: Feminist Perspectives on Renaissance Drama (1991); pub. articles in Rocky Mountain Rev., Upstart Crow, Renaissance Papers, other jours.; Democrat; rec: travel, piano, aerobics, theatre, movies. Ofc: English Dept. San Diego State University, San Diego 92182-0295

KEIDSER, JON ERIK, pharmacist; b. Oct. 1, 1961, Torrance, Calif.; s. Karl Erik and Joan Lee (Blackman) K.; edn: H.S. diploma, Judson Sch., Scottsdale, Ariz., 1979; AA, El Camino Coll., Torrance, Calif., 1983; Calif. State Univ., Long Beach, 1984-87; PharmD, USC Sch. of Pharm., L.A., 1990; Pharmacist, State of Calif., 1990. Career: intern pharmacist Maxicare, Torrance, Calif., 1986-90; pharmacist Maxicare, 1990, Rancho Drugs, Rancho Palos Verdes, Calif., 1990-, Valley View Drugs, Whittier, Calif., 1991-, Maxicare, Torrance, Calif., 1992-; chief pharmacist, Maxicare, Hawthorne, Calif., 1993-; clinical pharmacist, preceptor USC Sch. of Pharm., L.A. (pending); awards: Scholarship for Outstanding Students, USC, L.A., 1986; active mem. Phi Delta Chi Frat., 1986-; mem. Am. Pharm. Assn., 1992-93; author/ed.: Maxicare Therapeutic Sub. Letter, 1990; rec: softball, travel.

KEISTER, JEAN CLARE, lawyer; b. Aug. 28, 1931, Warren, Ohio; d. John R. and Anna (Brennan) Keister; child: John b. 1954 (dec. 1975); edn: JD and LLB, Southwestern Sch. of Law, L.A. 1966; admitted bar: Calif. 1967, US Supreme Ct. 1972. Career: atty., solo law practice, Los Angeles, Burbank, Lancaster, 1967-; atty. Bezaire, Bezaire, Bezaire & Bezaire, APC, San Marino 1988-89; legal writer Gilbert Law Summaries, L.A. 1967; instr. Glendale Coll., Glendale 1968; mem. Burbank Bar Assn. (1986-, secr. 1993), Glendale Bar Assn. 1987, Burbank C.of C., Themis Soc. 1989-; write prose and poetry, recipient Golden Poet Award, World of Poetry anthology (1988, 89, 91). Law Offices of Jean Clare Keister, 224 E Olive Ave Ste 219 Burbank 91502

KELLEHER, MATTHEW DENNIS, professor of mechanical engineering; b. Feb. 1, 1939, Flushing, N.Y.; s. James Finbar and Mary Florence (Fitzgerald) K.; m. Jean Esther Jolliffe, May 31, 1969; children: Genevieve b. 1977, Veronica b. 1980; edn: BS engr. sci., Univ. of Notre Dame, 1961, MS in M.E., 1963, PhD in M.E., 1966; reg. profl. engr. Calif. 1973. Career: asst. prof. Univ. of Notre Dame, 1965-66; Ford Found. fellow Dartmouth Coll., 1966-67; assoc. scientist AVCO Res. Lab., Everett, Mass. summer 1967; faculty Naval Postgrad. Sch., Monterey, Calif. 1967-, asst. prof. 1967-72, assoc. prof. 1972-82, prof. mech. engring. 1982-, and dept. chmn. 1992-; cons. Livermore Nat. Lab. 1985-88, Apple Computer Inc., Cupertino 1984; awards: grad. fellow NSF 1963-64, Ford Found. fellow 1966-67, NASA & Am. Soc. for Engr. Edn. fellow 1970, 71, vis. prof. Univ. Notre Dame 1987, senior acad. vis. Oxford Univ., England (1988-89), Sigma Xi 1965-; Fellow ASME 1965-; civic: Lower Carmel Valley advy. com. to Monterey County Planning Commn. 1981-87 (chair 83-86); author chapt. in book: Diffusion of Turbulent Bouyant Jets 1984, 40+ tech. papers 1964-; R.Cath. Res: 25000 Outlook Dr Carmel 93923 Ofc: Naval Postgraduate Sch. Mechanical Engineering Dept., ME/KK, Monterey 93943

KELLER, J. WESLEY, credit union executive; b. Jan. 6, 1958, Jonesboro, Ark.; s. Norman Grady and Norma Lee (Ridgeway) Patrick; m. Patricia Maria Delavan, July 7, 1979; edn: undergrad. Univ. of Miss. 1976-78; BS bus. adm. & mgt., Redlands Univ., 1990. Career: senior collector Rockwell Fed. Credit Union, Downey 1978-79; acct. Lucky Fed. Credit Union, Buena Park 1979-84; pres./CEO Long Beach State Employee Credit Union, 1984-; mem: Calif. Credit Union League (regulatory rev. bd. 1986-87, bd. govs. treas. Long Beach Chpt. 1985), Credit Union Exec. Soc., So. Calif. Credit Union Mgrs. Assn.,bd. dirs. Nat. Assn. State Chartered Credit Unions 1991-, Kiwanis Intl.; Republican; Baptist; rec: photog., skiing, woodworking. Ofc: Long Beach State Employees Credit Union 3840 Long Beach Blvd Long Beach 90807

KELLER, JOHN FRANCIS, management consultant, municipal official; b. Feb. 5, 1925, Mt. Horeb, Wisconsin; s. Francis S. and Elizabeth (Meier) K.; m. Barbara Dawn Mabbott, Feb. 18, 1950; children: Thomas b. 1951, Patricia b. 1952, David b. 1954, Daniel b. 1954, John J. b. 1963; edn: BBA, Univ. of Wisconsin, 1949; MBA, Univ. of Chicago, 1963; SEP, Stanford Univ., 1978; cert. CPA, Wis., Ill. 1959. Career: mgr. acctg. Miller Brewing Co., Milw., 1950-58; controller Maremont corp., Chicago, Ill. 1958-68; v.p. fin. Heublin Inc., St. Paul and San Francisco 1968-80, group v.p. Heublein Wine Group, CEO, 1980-84; pres. ISC Wines of Calif., San Francisco 1983-84; admin. dir. Calif. Wine Mktg. Order 1984-85; mgmt. cons. J.F. Keller & Assoc. 1985-; councilman Hillsborough, Calif. 1982-, mayor Hillsborough 1988-90; asst. prof. CSU Hayward grad. sch. 1979-82; adjunct prof. Golden Gate Univ. grad. sch. of bus. 1983-86; awards: 25-Year award Nat. Assn. Accts., S.F. 1989, distinguished alumni Univ. of Wis. 1990; mem: Calif. Soc. of CPA's 1972-, Wis. Soc. of CPA's 1958-, Serra Club of San Mateo 1987-, Kts. of Col. 1954-, Kts. of Malta 1989-, Kts. of Holy Sepulchre 1990-; mem. (ret.) Nat. Assn. of Accts. 1954-, Financial Execs. Inst. 1972-85; civic bds: Alemany Scholarship Found. (1983-, dir.), Cath. Archdiocese Edn. Development Council 1989-, Seton Med. Ctr. and Seton Health Svs. Found. (bd. dirs. 1988-), Lesley Found. (dir., treas. 1987-), Univ. Wisconsin Found. (exec. com.), Univ. Chicago Found., Justice & Peace Commn. S.F. Cath. Archdiocese (1986-, coord. conf. on Economic Justice - Religion, Business and the Poor, 1989), Specialty Wine Services, Inc. (dir., ofcr.); mil: paratrooper, lt. U.S. Army, 1944-51; Republican; R.Cath. (40th Anniversary com. St. Anthony's Kitchens 1989); rec: golf, charity work, travel. Res: 785 Tournament Dr Hillsborough 94010

KELLER, LYNN ROBIN, educator; b. Oct. 25, 1952, Pasadena; d. Robert Phillips and Colleen Ann (Putnam) K.; m. Dr. Henry Mark McMillan, Oct. 11, 1987; edn: BA, MBA, and PhD, UCLA, 1974, 1976, 1982. Career: asst. prof. UC Irvine Grad. Sch. Mgmt., 1982-89, assoc. prof. 1989-; assoc. pgm. dir. Nat. Science Found., WDC 1989-90, pgm. dir. 1990-91; vis. asst. res. prof. Duke Univ., Durham, N.C. 1987; assoc. editor and contbr. to: Management Science J., Information & Decision Technologies J.; contbr. articles to Risk Analysis, J. of Risk & Uncertainty, Organizational Behavior & Human Decision Processes, other profl. jours.; honors: Beta Gamma Sigma 1976, outstanding grad. UCLA 1982, excellence in tchg. UCI Grad. Sch. of Mgmt. (1982-3, 1985-6); mem: Operations Research Soc. of Am., (council mem. spl. interest group on decision analysis 1986-89), The Inst. of Mgmt. Sci., Alpha Phi Internat. Frat. Inc. (UCLA collegiate pres. and rep. to internat. exec. bd. 1973-4, frat. advisor UCLA 1970s, UCI 1988-9); Ofc: Graduate School Mgmt. Univ. Calif. Irvine 92717

KELLER, SHARON PILLSBURY, speech pathologist, educator; b. Sept. 28, 1935, Los Angeles; d. Edward Gardner and Iris Noriene (Hager) Pillsbury; m Clarence Stanley Keller (dec. 1982); children: Jann Kathleen b. 1956, Jennifer Beth b. 1959, Lauren Elaine b. 1962; edn: AA, Chaffey Comm. Coll. 1971; BA, Univ. La Verne 1978, MS in comm. disorders, 1983; cert. clin. competence sp.-lang. pathologist, ASHA (1983). Career: speech/language pathologist Chino Unified Sch. Dist., Chino 1978-86; Rim of the World Sch. Dist. (pre-K.- 8th gr.), Lake Arrowhead 1986-, also San Bernardino County Pre-Sch. (S.B. 2666) Home Pgm. Mountain Communities, 1988-89; master tchr. for Speech/Language Pathology Interns, Univ. Redlands, 1990-91; cons. Cedu Middle and High Sch.

Running Springs 1991-, cons. Dr. Stanley Kaseno, San Bernardino. 1992-, cons. Assoc. Speech & Hearing Svs. of Chino 1984, trainer Pre-sch. and Parent-child interaction 7 yrs., staff Headstart Chino 3 yrs., Boys Republic High Sch. 1 yr., cons. infant lang. devel./student-parent pgm. Buena Vista Continuation H.S. 3 yrs.; mem: Am. Speech-Lang.-Hearing Assn., Calif. Speech and Hearing Assn., Calif. Tchrs. Assn., Am. Assn. Univ. Women (recording secty.),installed into Delta Kappa Gamma Soc. Internat. Nov. 1992 (charter mem., corr. sec.); civic: anchor Mountain Communities News Falcon Cable TV Ch. 6 (Mondays 6pm), mem. bd. of dirs. Ch. 6 Comm. News and Weather Found., Mtn. Shadow Village HOA (pres.); Republican; Presbyterian (bd. deacons, moderator 1991, English Handbell Choir 1988-92); rec: interior design. Res: PO Box 1745 Crestline 92325 Ofc: Rim of the World Unified School Dist. PO Box 430 Lake Arrowhead 92352

KELLEY, DARSHAN SINGH, nutrition researcher; b. Feb. 5, 1947, Ludhiana, India;nat. 1979; s. Kehar Singh and Ind Kaur (Jassi) K.; m. Daljeet Kaur Janday, Jan. 10, 1979; children: Simranjeet b. 1981, Nirvair b. 1986; edn: BS agri., Punjab Agri. Univ. India 1967; MS hons., biochem., 1969; PhD, biochem., Okla. Univ. 1974. Career: postgrad. fellow Punjab Agri. Univ., Ludhiana, India 1969-70; spl. cons. Okla. Med. Res. Found., Okla. City. 1974-75; research assoc. McArdle Lab. for Cancer Research, Madison, Wis. 1975-80; research asst. prof. W. Va. Univ., Morgantown 1980-83; research chemist, project leader diet and immune status U.S. Dept. Agri., San Francisco 1983-; awards: Punjab Agri. Univ. merit scholarship 1963-69, NIH predoctoral fellowship 1970-74, postdoctoral fellowship 1975-78, RDI research grant 1982-85; mem: Am. Inst. of Nutrition, Am. Soc. Biochem. & Molecular Biology; 28 research articles pub. in sci. jours.; Sikh; rec: fishing, hiking. Ofc: Western Human Nutrition Research Center ARS USDA POB 29997 Presidio of San Francisco 94129

KELLEY, WIN DAVID, emeritus professor, actor, writer; b. Nov. 6, 1923, Pryor, Okla.; s. William O. Kelley and Audrey (Bruce) Woodard; m. Catherine Elizabeth Hann, June 5, 1948; children: Klinda b. 1950, Kasma b. 1951, Kanda b. 1956, Korwin b. 1959; edn: BA cum laude, Pacific Univ. 1950; MEd, Univ. Oreg., 1954; EdD, USC, 1962; also studied at Penn. St. Univ., CSU Long Beach, and CSU Los Angeles. Career: tchr., Prospect, Oreg. 1950-51; tchr., dir. drama and forensics, Coquille, Oreg. 1951-54; Coos Bay, Oreg. 1954-56; prof., dir. drama Compton Coll. 1956-58; prof. (emeritus), dir. drama and forensics Citrus Coll., Glendora 1958-84; vis. prof. USC and Azusa Pacific Univ.; drama columnist Talent Review Mag., N.Y.C.; Coos Bay newspaper; articles pub. Improving Coll. and Univ. Tchg.; freelance writer t.v. and commls.; awards: Portland Civic Theatre Nat. Play awards 1953, Mark Twain Soc. Lit. award 1953, Freedoms Found. George Washington Hon. Medal 1973, DAR Medal of Hon. 1980, biog. listed Leaders in Edn. 4th ed. 1971, Contemporary Authors 1980, Internat. Authors and Writers Who's Who 9th ed. 1982, others; mem: Songwriters Guild of Am., Am. Forensics Assn. (emeritus), Speech Comm. Assn. (emeritus), Actors Equity Assn., Screen Actors Guild, Dramatist Guild, Inland Forensics Assn. (past pres.), Oreg. Speech League (v.p., past pres.), Active Club Internat. (dir. programs 1951-54), Am. Legion (commdr. 1967-68), VFW; author: (play) Waiilatpu: The Place of Rye Grass 1952, (textbook) The Art of Public Address 1962, coauthor Teaching in Community Jr. College 1969, (play) America the Beautiful 1972, Breaking Barriers in Pub. Speaking 1978, (autobiography) The Fades of Memory 1982, The "Elegant" 18th District, Department of California: The First Sixty-Six Years - 1920-1986 (1987), Gertie's Gall: A Collection of Writings By Gertrude Boatright 1991, poetry pub. in Nat. Poetry Anthology 1988 and other anthologies; mil: cpl. US Army Air Corps 1943-45; Republican; Prot.; rec: acting, writing, singing. Res: Carlsbad 92008

KELLOGG, WILLIAM JACKSON, resort manager; b. Sept. 12, 1951, Pasadena; s. William Crowe and Jane Katherine (Jackson) K.; m. Tricia Tenzer, Sept. 23, 1977; children: Tiffany b. 1978, Wendy b. 1981; edn: BA, Dartmouth Coll. 1973. Career: asst. tennis profl. San Marino Tennis Shop, San Marino 1973-74; head tennis profl., gen. mgr. Westlake Tennis & Swim Club, Westlake Village 1974-79; adminstr., La Jolla Beach & Tennis Club, La Jolla 1979-89, pres. 1989-; mem: La Jolla Shores Assn. (dir. 1985-86), Mt. Soledad Meml. Assn. (pres. 1980-), San Diego Dist. Tennis Assn. (pres. 1980-), Tennis Club Mgmt. Assn. So. Calif., So. Calif. Tennis Assn. (exec. dir. 1984-); Republican; Episcopalian; rec: tennis. Ofc: La Jolla Beach & Tennis Club 2000 Sprindrift Dr La Jolla 92037

KELLY, CHARLES EUGENE, II, gastroenterologist; b. Sept. 4, 1958, Salina, Kans.; s. Charles Eugene and Byrdie Inez (Sowell) K.; edn: BA chem., Univ. Kansas, 1980; MD, Univ. Kans. Med. Sch., 1984. Career: intern, resident Univ. Michigan, Ann Arbor 1984-87; fellow Stanford Univ., 1987-92; awards: Dow Chemical scholar, Univ. Kans. 1978, Research fellow Stanford 1988, Nat. Sci. Found. research award Stanford 1989, Eagle Scout 1974, Phi Lambda Upsilon 1980, listed Who's Who Am. H.S. Students 1976, Outstanding Young Men Am. 1986, Who's Who in West 1991; mem: Am. Coll. Physicians (asso. 1990-), Am. Gastroent. Assn. (mem. in tng. 1988-); Baptist; rec: bicycling, jazz, languages, radio controlled cars & planes. Res: 535 Arastradero Apt 313 Palo Alto 94306 Ofc: Mowery Clinic 737 E Crawford Salina KS 67401

KELLY, MICHAEL JOHN, entertainment and production company president; b. Oct. 29, Compton, Calif.; s. Kenneth E. and Beverly Ann (Riley) K.; edn: El

Camino Coll. 1981-83. Career: field supr. The Wackenhut Corp., Los Angeles 1979-80; branch ops. mgr. ABM Security Services 1980-89; pres., gen. mgr. Executive Sound Prodns., Hollywood 1989-, prod. Keep in Touch record album 1989; instr. Rosston Coll. 1989-; freelance writer, contbr.; civic: Hollywood C.of C., Christian Arts & Music Center, Around the Block Club; Democrat; R.Cath.; rec: travel, collect and race autos. Ofc: 6922 Hollywood Blvd Ste 220 Hollywood 90028

KELLY, MICHAEL PATRICK, chiropractor; b. June 10, 1950, Kansas City, Mo.; s. Dean B. and Mary A. Kelly; m. Joyce, Feb. 10, 1978; children: Marsha b. 1973, Megan b. 1983, Aubrey b. 1985; edn: AA, Southwest Mo. State Univ. 1974; DC, Cleveland Chiropractic Coll. 1979; cand. diplomate Chiropractic Bd. of Orthopedic, 1990. Career: intern Pacific Beach Chiropractic Assocs.; dir. Santee Chiropractic Clinic, Santee currently; honors: merit award, Nat. Bd. of Chiropractic Examiners; mem. Acupuncture Soc. of Am., Fellow Internat. Acad. of Clin. Acupuncture, Exchange Club; mil: sgt. US Air Force; Republican; rec: golf. Res: 1187 Rippey St El Cajon 92020 Ofc: Santee Chiropractic Clinic 9317 Mission Gorge Rd Santee 92071

KELLY, RALPH G., consulting company executive; b. Aug. 14, 1919, Chicago, Ill.; s. Walter C. and Virginia A. (Victor) K.; m. Claire E. Moore, 1943 (dec. 1980); m. Patricia H., Feb. 14, 1981; children: Randall Brian b. 1944, Linda Elizabeth b. 1946, Jayme Virginia b. 1951, Scott Harrison b. 1952; edn: BSCE, Purdue Univ., 1938-41, 1946-47; Calif. cert. General Bldg. Contractor; Calif. cert. Real Estate Sales Lic.; cert. priv. pilot. Career: engaged in manufacturing, sales and mgmt. in electrical, garment and construction industries, 1964-85; pres. Shirley & Kelly, Inc., general contractors 1964-85, cons. Shirley & Kelly, Inc. 1985-; lectr. various civic groups; founder Jayme Virginia Kelly Meml. Found. (annual scholarships since 1975); author: book on parenting "Here is One Way — Fun"; Christian. Ofc: Shirley & Kelly, Inc. 3349 Cahuenga Blvd West #3 Los Angeles 90068

KELLY, RANDOLPH O'ROURKE, biologist; b. March 28, 1947, Fresno; s. Robert Milton and Margie May (Muldoon) K.; m. Darlene Curb, 1967 (div. 1971); m. Edith Anne Perry, April 9, 1978; 1 child, Shawn b. 1979; edn: Moss Landing Marine Lab. 1968; BA, Fresno St. Univ. 1970. Career: lab. tech. UC Berkeley, Fresno 1964-70; fish and wildlife seasonal aid Calif. Dept. Fish & Game, Stockton 1970, aquatic biologist, Monterey 1970-77, assoc. marine biologist, Sacto. 1977-81, assoc. fishery biologist, Fresno 1981-; co-chair Nat. Rec. Com. Oceans 1983; mem: Am. Fisheries Soc., World Aquaculture Soc., Nat. Shellfisheries Assn., San Francisco Bay & Estuary Soc.; num. articles in fishery bulletin and profl. jours.; Republican; rec: fishing, hiking, scuba diving. Res: 17333 Livermore Ct Soulsbyville 95372 Ofc: Calif. Dept. of Fish and Game 1234 E Shaw Ave Fresno 93710

KELMAN, BRUCE JERRY, toxicologist, consultant; b. July 1, 1947, Chgo.; s. LeRoy Rayfield and Louise (Rosen) K.; m. Jacqueline Anne Clark, Feb. 5, 1972; children: Aaron Wayne b. 1978, Diantha Renee b. 1982, Coreyanne Louise b. 1983; edn: BS, Univ. Ill., Urbana 1969, MS, 1971, PhD, 1975; D.A.B.T., Am. Bd. of Toxicology, 1980, 85, 90. Career: postdoctoral resrch. assoc. Univ. Tenn., Oak Ridge, 1974-76, asst. prof. and group leader Prenatal Toxicology Gp., 1976-79; mgr. Developmental Toxicology Sect. Battelle Northwest, Richland, Wash. 1980-84, assoc. mgr. Biology and Chemistry Dept. 1984-85, mgr. Internat. Toxicology Office 1986-89, mgr. Biology and Chem. Dept. 1985-89, mgr. New Products Devel. Life Scis. Ctr. Battelle Northwest, 1989-90; mng. scientist, also mgr. Toxicology Dept., Failure Analysis Associates Inc., Menlo Park, Calif. 1990-; adj. prof. N.Mex. State Univ., Las Cruces 1983-; awards: merit award Soc. Exptl. Biology and Medicine, N.W. chpt. 1980, recogn. Molecular Biology Sect., Soc. Toxicology 1989; mem: Soc. Toxicology 1978-, Teratology Soc. 1978-, Soc. for Exptl. Biology and Medicine 1978-, Am. Soc. Exptl. Pharmacology and Therapeutics 1981-, Am. Acad. Veterinary and Comparative Toxicology (Fellow 1985-), Wash. State Biotechnology Assn. (bd. 1989-90); appt. Wash. State Gov.'s Biotechnology Targeted Sector Advy. Com. 1989-90, Seattle Fire Dept. Advy. Council 1988-9); editorial bd. Jour. Trophoblast Research 1983-; co-editor books: Interactions of Biol. Systems with Static and ELF Electric and Magneti Fields 1987, Biol. Effects of Heavy Metals 1990; contbr. 75+ articles to sci. jours. 1975-. Ofc: Failure Analysis Associates, Inc. 149 Commonwealth Dr PO Box 3015 Menlo Park 94025

KELSEY, KATHERINE LOUISE, artist; b. Cleveland, Ohio; d. Adam and Katie (Breckel) McKee; m. Francis Overstreet Kelsey; edn: BS and AM, Columbia Univ., NY; Escuela de Pintura & Escultura, Mexico City; spl. studies Cleveland Sch. of Art, John Huntington Polytechnic.; travelling artist: two Around the World trips, and one Around So. Am. (resulting in num. exhibits of paintings), many trips to Europe and Mexico, month in Alaska; art exhibits in museums and galleries; paintings, sculptures, ceramics, enamels, textile designs, lithographs, and etchings sold in mus. shops and art galleries; recipient 1 Special Award, 2 first prizes, num. Hon. Mentions; business rentals of paintings in Berkeley gallery, Contemporary Arts, now from home/studio; life mem. Cleveland Mus. of Art, mem. YMCA, Humane Soc., Kelsey Kindred; Presbyterian; rec: swimming. Studio: 1753 Lexington Ave El Cerrito 94530

KEMM, THOMAS R., database consultant; b. April 18, 1931, New York; child: Jessica b. 1952; edn: BA, Yale Univ. 1952. Career: project dir. W.R. Simmons & Assoc., N.Y. 1957-63; research dir. McCaffrey & McCall 1963-64; pres. KBK Assoc., Los Angeles 1964-69; v.p. Project 7 Inc., Beverly Hills 1970-71; cons. Nassau Bank & Trust Co., Nassau 1972-73; cons., Nassau, London, Munich and Tel Aviv 1974-80; v.p. Intertech Internat., Taipei 1981-85; cons., N.Y. and L.A., 1986-; speaker and writer on microcomputer database design; mil: lt. AUS 1952-54. Res: 36 Horizon Ave Venice 90291-3641

KENDALL, BRUCE RICHARD, building contractor, real estate broker; b. Feb. 12, 1952, Denver, Colo.; s. Harland Richard and Gerry Lucille (Hastings) K.; m. Kathleen, Jan. 1, 1971; m. 2d. Lisa Hart, Aug. 9, 1987; m. 3d. Michelle Stone, June 26, 1993; children: Jeff b. 1971, Marianne b. 1974; edn: AA, Coll. of Sequoias. Career: supr. Compact Homes, Visalia 1968-74; real estate sales Red Carpet 1974-75; owner Kendall Construction 1975-83, 1988-; owner, ptnr. Visalia Devel. Inc. 1983-88; Mini Mansions Inc. 1985-88; Realty World-Investors 1986-88; owner The House Detective Inc. 1988-; Bruce Kendall & Assoc. 1988-; mem: Sequoia Flying Club; Republican; Presbyterian; rec: flying. Res: 25971 Road 212 Exeter 93221 Ofc: The House Detective and Kendall Construction 25971 Road 212 Exeter 93221

KENNEDY, DONALD PARKER, title insurance company executive; b. Oct. 16, 1918, San Jacinto, Calif.; s. Lewis Rex and Elsie (Parker) K.; m. Dorothy Suppiger, Dec. 20, 1946; children: Parker S. b. 1948, Elizabeth Riney b. 1950, Amy F. b. 1964; edn: BA, Stanford Univ., 1940; LLB, USC Sch. of Law, 1948; admitted bar: Calif. 1949. Career: assoc. counsel Orange Co. Title Co., and successor First American Title Ins. Co., Santa Ana 1948-58, exec. v.p. 1958-63, pres., dir. First American Title Ins. Co., 1963-89, chmn. bd. 1989-, pres., dir. The First American Financial Corp., 1963-; honors: Stanford Univ. Golf Team and NCCA Champion 1939, Nat. Amateur -Pebble Beach, Ca. 1947, inducted Calif. Building Industry Hall of Fame 1989; past pres. and dir. So. Calif. Racing Assn.; mem: Orange Co. Bar Assn., Phi Delta Phi and Zeta Psi frat., Calif. Land Title Assn. (bd. govs., exec. com. 1957-, pres. 1960-61), Am. Land Title Assn. (pres. 1983-84); civic: Chapman Univ. (trustee), USC Presdl. Associates 1990-, UC Riverside Found. (dir. 1990-), Festival of Learning & Performing O.C. (dir.), South Coast Repertory (trustee, dir.), O.C. Bus. Com. for the Arts, Golden Eagle Club of BSA (chmn. 1984), Goodwill Industries (dir. 1986-), past: Santa Ana-Tustin Comm. Chest (pres. 1952), US Savings Bond Pgm. Orange (past chair), Santa Ana Board of Edn. 1953; clubs: Santa Ana CC (pres. 1952), La Quinta CC, Eldorado CC, Lake Arrowhead CC, California, Center, Pacific; mil: lt. M.I. USN 1942-46, PTO, ATO; Republican; Episcopalian; rec: golf. Res: 1628 La Loma Dr Santa Ana 92705 Ofc: First American Title Insurance Co. 114 E Fifth St Santa Ana 92701

KENNEDY, "SARGE" JAMES WILLIAM, JR., special education administrator, consultant; b. Oct. 6, 1940, Santa Rosa; s. James William and Kay Jean (Eaton) K.; m. Lorene Adele Dunaway, May 12, 1962 (div. 1971); children: Sean b. 1962, Erin b. 1964, Mark b. 1966, stepdau. Joy b. 1971; m. Carolyn Judith Nighsonger, Mar. 30, 1972 (div. 1979); m. Patricia Carter Critchlow, Nov. 5, 1988; edn: AA, Napa Coll., 1961; BA, San Francisco State Univ., 1964, MA, 1970. Career: tchr. Napa County Office of Edn. 1968-74, principal 1974-77, SELPA (spl. edn. local plan area) director 1977-83; special edn. compliance cons. DoD Overseas Dependent Schs., Madrid, Spain 1983-84; dir. special programs and svs. Tehama County Dept. Edn., Red Bluff, Calif. 1985-; appt. Wilson Riles Special Edn. Task Force, Calif. 1981-82, Special Edn. Fiscal Task Force, Calif. 1987-89; mem: Calif. Fedn. Council for Exceptional Children (treas. 1990-, jour. editor 1971-77, 81-83), Coun. Exceptional Children (sgt. at arms 1980-91), SFSU Alumni Assn., Phi Delta Kappa; Democrat; rec: history of sports, hist. pop music, Spanish and Portuguese cultures. Ofc: Tehama County Dept. Education PO Box 689 Red Bluff 96080 Ph: 916/527-5811

KENNER, LAUREL, reporter; b. May 18, 1954 Santa Monica, Calif.; d. John Drewson and Mildred May (Bame) Kenner; m. Francisco Urrutia Aguabella, Mar. 20, 1992; edn: BA, fine arts, UCLA, 1977. Career: reporter Newhall Signal, Valencia, Calif., 1984-87, Associated Press, L.A., Calif., 1987, Copley Press, Torrance, Calif., 1988-; awards: Regional award, Aviation/Space Writers Assn., 1989, 91; mem: Soc. of Profl. Journalists 1991-, Investigative Reporters and Editors 1992-; bd. mem. Women at Risk, Santa Monica, 1992-; Christian; rec: piano. Ofc: Copley Los Angeles Newspapers 5215 Torrance Blvd. Torrance 90509

KENOFF, JAY STEWART, lawyer; b. Apr. 29, 1946, Los Angeles; s. Charles Kapp and Martha (Minchenberg) K.; m. Pamela Fran Benyas, Sept. 1, 1979 (div. 1981); m. Luz Elena Chavira, June 9, 1991; edn: BA, UCLA, 1967; JD, Harvard Law Sch., 1970; MS, USC, 1974; admitted bar: Calif. 1971, W.D.C. 1970, U.S. Ct. Appeals (9th cir.) 1974, U.S. Dist. Cts. (so., cent. dists. Calif.) 1974, U.S. Ct. Mil. Appeals 1974. Career: atty., assoc. WymanBautzer Rothman & Kuchel, L.A. 1974-76; Epport & Delevie, Beverly Hills 1976-78; Bushkin Gaims Gaines & Jonas, L.A. 1978-83, ptnr. 1983-86; ptnr. Kenoff & Machtinger, L.A. 1986-; law prof. Northrop Univ. Sch. of Law, L.A. 1980-84; judge pro tem L.A. Municipal Ct. 1984-; W. Dist. Voluntary Settlement Panel L.A. Superior Ct.

1986-; awards: Judge Pro Tem Achievement Award L.A. Mun. Ct. 1986, Freedom Found. Medal, Valley Forge 1973, Phi Beta Kappa 1967; mem: U.S. Naval Inst. 1973-, Naval Reserve Assn. (life), USC Inst. of Sci. & Systems Mgmt. (founding mem., bd. dirs. 1984), UCLA Alumni Assn. (life), USC Alumni Assn. (life), Harvard-Radcliffe Club So. Calif. 1971-; author: Entertainment Industry Contracts: Negotiating & Drafting Guide, vol.1 Motion Pictures, periodic supplements (1986-), contbr. ed. "Entertainment Law & Finance", misc. law jour. articles; mil: cmdr. USNR 1968-91; Democrat; Jewish; rec: tennis, skiing, sailing, motion pictures. Ofc: Kenoff & Machtinger 1999 Avenue of the Stars Ste 1250 Los Angeles 90067

KENYON, DOUGLAS ALAN, risk management & loss control executive; b. Jan. 8, 1953, Binghamton, NY; s. Douglas W. and Edith (Noble) K.; m. Marsha Smith, Mar. 17, 1973; 1 son, Jared b. 1981; edn: cert., Ohlone Coll. 1978; AS, Merrit Coll. 1979; BS, Univ. Redlands 1983; JD, Peninsula Univ., 1990. Career: safety coord., Washington Hosp., Fremont 1975-77; safety & health asst. Stanford Med. Ctr. 1977-78; mgr. safety & environmental health Pacific Med. Ctr. S.F. 1978-83, safety mgr. Browning-Ferris Industries, San Jose, 1983-88, reg. claims mgr. 1988-; instr. safety studies Cogswell Coll., S.F. 1980-83; exec. dir. Instnl. Safety Mgmt. Assocs. 1980-83; recipient Tri-Cities Stamp Out Crime Award 1968; mem: Nat. Safety Council (chmn. reg. 9, Healthcare Sect. 1980-83), Profl. Healthcare Safety Assn. (chmn. exec. bd. 1978-83), Am. Soc. Safety Engrs., No. Calif. Indsl. Safety Soc., Nat. Safety Mgmt. Soc., World Safety Orgn., publs: arts. in var. profl. publs.; mil: E4 USN 1970-74, E5 USAR 1976-82, Presdl. Unit Cit., Good Conduct, Vietnam Svc., Navy Unit Cit., Armed Forces Expeditionary, Vietnam Cross of Gallantry, Vietnam Campaign; Prot.; rec: woodworking, wine tasting. Res: PO Box 225 Moss Landing 95039 Ofc: Browning-Ferris Industries, 150 Almaden Blvd San Jose 95113

KERCHNER, CHARLES TAYLOR, education professor; b. Feb. 18, 1940, Chgo.; s. Charles Wesley and Dorothy Leticia (Taylor); m. Leanne Rose Bauman, Sept. 2, 1962; children: Paige b. 1966, Charles Arthur b. 1968; edn: BS, Univ. Ill., Urbana 1962, MBA, 1964; PhD, Northwestern Univ., 1976. Career: news editor, asst. to gen. mgr. St. Petersburg Times, Fla. 1964-70; assoc. director Illinois Board of Higher Education, Chgo. 1970-72; dir. of funded programs City Colls. of Chicago, 1972; project dir., prof. Northwestern Univ., Evanston, Ill. 1974, 75; prof. edn. and dir. ednl. leadership project The Claremont Grad. Sch., Claremont, Calif. 1976-; cons. num. school dists. and other orgs., 1965-, Rockefeller Found., N.Y. 1990; awards: res. grantee US Dept. of Labor 1990, Carnegie Corp. 1990, Stuart Foundations 1986-90, Nat. Inst. of Edn. 1980; mem. Am. Ednl. Res. Assn. (com. 1976), Bulletin editor: Politics of Edn. Assn. 1980-85; author: The Changing Idea of a Teachers' Union (1988), The Politics of Choice and Excellence (1989), A Union of Professionals (1993); Democrat; Presbyterian; rec: photography. Res: 438 Baughman Ave Claremont 91711 Ofc: The Claremont Graduate School 150 E Tenth St Claremont 91711-6160

KERFOOT, BRANCH PRICE, scientist in electronics; b. May 9, 1925, NY, NY; s. Branch Price and Henrietta McBrayer (Bartlett) K.; m. Carol Saindon, Feb. 13, 1965; children: B. Price, III b. 1967; edn: BE, Yale Univ., 1945; MSE and PhD, Univ. Mich., Ann Arbor, 1947, 1955; JD, Western State Univ., Fullerton 1987; reg. profl. engr. Calif. Career: ensign USNR, Pacific 1945-46, served to lt. cmdr. US Naval Reserve 1942-66; res. engr. Westinghouse Electric, E. Pittsburgh, Pa. 1948; AA engr. Radio Corp. of Am., Moorestown, N.J. 1949-57; prin. engr. Aeronutronic Div. Ford Motor Co., Newport Beach, Calif. 1958-68; prin. scientist McDonnell Douglas, Huntington Beach 1968-90, ret.; tchr. Pasadena City Coll. 1958; advisor Jr. Achievement Calif., 1964, 1979; awards: Sigma Xi 1955, comm. service Ford Motor Co., Newport Beach (1962, 65), prize for patent Inventors Workshop 1990; Life sr. mem. IEEE 1944-, mem. Soc. of the Cincinnati 1950-, Baronial Order of Magna Charta 1992-, Order of the Founders and Patriots of Am. 1993-, Yale Club of Orange Co. 1970-, Classic Car Club Am. 1980-, USNR Assn. (life 1988-), Inventors Forum, Irvine, Calif. (dir. 1990-), Kappa Sigma frat., Newport Harbor Art Mus. (trustee 1973-76); club: Balboa Bay (N.B.); inventor Fluid-Flow Drag Reducers (pat. 1989); pub. tech. articles (1956, 65, 70), editor book: Kerfoot & Related Families Ancestors (1992); Republican; Prot.; rec: classic automobile restoration. Res: 1420 Antigua Way Newport Beach 92660

KERN, WILLIAM HENRY, pathologist; b. Dec. 25, 1927, Nurnberg, Germany, nat. USA 1957; s. Judge Wilhelm and Julie (Maedl) K.; m. Lynn Williams, Aug. 14, 1966; children: Julie Lynn b. 1969, Lisa Catherine b. 1970; edn: Univs. of Erlangen, Vienna and Munich, 1947-52; MD, Univ. of Munich 1952; bd. certified Am. Bd. of Pathology 1958. Career: intern Good Samaritan Hosp. Cincinnati 1952-53, res. in pathology Good Sam Hosp. Cinti and Univ. of Colo. 1953-56; dir. of pathology Hosp. of the Good Samaritan, Los Angeles 1966-91, v.p. bd. of trustees 1975-89, and chmn. medical staff 1972-74, 1987-89; clin. prof. of path. USC Sch. of Medicine 1972-; v.p. bd. dirs. Am. Red Cross, L.A. Chapter 1983-86, and chmn. Blood Op. Com. of L.A. and Orange Counties 1984-86; mem: L.A. Acad. of Medicine (pres. 1980-81), L.A. Soc. of Pathologists (pres. 1968), Am. Soc. of Cytology (pres. 1980-81), Fellow Coll. of Am. Pathologist; clubs: Saddle & Sirloin (pres. 1980), Jonathan, Rancheros

Visitadores (Charro Camp); publs: 120+ sci. papers & book chapters in field of pathology and cancer; mil: capt. M.C. USAR 1956-58; Republican; Prot.; rec: riding, skiing, history, writing. Res: 2321 Chislehurst Dr Los Angeles 90027

KERR, GIB, financial planner; b. Apr. 21, 1927; s. Frances and Gladys (Larmondra) K.; m. Shirley Cochrane, June 15, 1952 (div. 1971); children: Brian, Barry, Randy, Judy, Sandy; edn: grad. Ottawa Tech. H.Sch., Ottawa, Ont., Can. 1945; desig: CFP, ChFC, CLU. Career: lab. asst. Eddy Pulp & Paper, Hull, Quebec, Can. 1946-47; special svs. mgr. Bell Tel. Co., Ottawa 1947-57; owner opr. Spotlight Studios 1957-57; corp. pres. G.K.E. Inc. 1957-70; entertainer, Los Angeles, 1970-77; financial planner, life underwriter, 1977-; lectr. in field; civic: W.L.A. LeTip (pres. 1988-90), LAS-ICFP (bd. 1991-), Beverlywood Mental Health Ctr. (bd. 1989-91); publs: (lectures) Budget for a Lazy Person, 1988, Who's The Boss, 1989; coauthor: Talk and the Secrets of Communication, 1990; tchr., author: Sing-A-Long Guitar (1992); rec: music, philosophy, politics, poetry.

KERTZ, MARSHA HELENE, college professor, certified public accountant; b. May 29, 1946, Palo Alto; d. Joe and Ruth (Lazear) Kertz; edn: BS in acctg., San Jose State Univ. 1976, MBA, 1977; Cert. Pub. Acct. Calif. 1977; Cert. Tax Profl., Am. Inst. of Tax Studies 1993. Career: staff acct. Steven Kroff and Co., Palo Alto 1968-71, 1973-74; controller Rand Teleprocessing Corp., San Francisco 1972; staff acct. Ben F. Priest Acctg. Corp., Mountain View 1974-81; acctg. lectr. San Jose State Univ. 1977-; self employed CPA, audits, tax planning, tax preparation, mgmt. advy. svcs. 1977-; honors: Beta Gamma Sigma 1975, Beta Alpha Psi 1974; mem: Calif. Society of CPAs, Am. Inst. CPAs, Nat. Soc. of Tax Profls., Am. Acctg. Assn.; Democrat; Jewish; rec: play piano. Res: 4544 Strawberry Park Dr San Jose 95129 Ofc: San Jose State Univ. Acctg. - Fin. Dept., San Jose 95192

KETTEMBOROUGH, CLIFFORD RUSSELL, computer scientist; b. June 8, 1953, Pitesti Romania, naturalized U.S. 1989; s. Petre and Constanta (Dascalu) Ionescu; m. Nelia Marie Miller; edn: MS math., Univ. Bucharest, 1976; MS computer sci., West Coast Univ., L.A. 1985, MMIS, 1986; PhD, Pacific Western Univ., 1988; MBA, Univ. of La Verne, 1992; cert. computer programmer. Career: pgmr. Nat. Dept. of Chemistry, Bucharest, Rom. 1976-80; sr. pgmr. analyst Nat. Dept. Metallurgy, Bucharest, Rom. 1980-82; sr. s/w eng. Xerox Corp., El Segundo, Calif. 1983-88; mem. tech. staff NASA/Jet Propulsion Lab., Pasadena 1988-89; task mgr. Rockwell Internat., Canoga Park 1989-91; cons. software engring. tech. 1991-; past pres., sec. Romanian BB Fedn., Bucharest (1978-82); mem. ACM, AMA, MAA, IEEE, AIAA, DECUS; author book (1978), various sci. articles (1980-); mil: major lt. 1978-79; Republican; First United Methodist; rec: sports, travel.

KEWER, RICHARD LEE, educator; b. Dec. 11, 1939, Batavia, N.Y.; s. Joseph John and Helen (Muschinski) Goffard; m. Linda Decker, Jan. 13, 1963, div. 1969; children: Rod b. 1963, Cindy b. 1965; edn: MA, Long Beach State Univ., 1983. Career: pres. Action Management Systems, Newport Beach, Calif. 1981-; educational consultant Long Beach State 1982-; mem. Southern Counties Training Officers Assn., 1985-; author workbooks: Understanding Leadership, 1986, Performance Appraisal, 1987, Management Principles, 1989; mil: E-5, U.S. Navy, 1958-62; Libertarian; rec: volunteer, Special Olympics. Ofc: Action Management Systems Box 9015 Newport Beach 92660

KHANNA, SATISH KUMAR, physicist; b. Dec. 2, 1947, Delhi, India; s. Kishan Chand and Sita Bai (Malhotra) K.; m. Neelam, Dec. 5, 1976; children: Neetu b. 1980, Rohini b. 1983; edn: BS, and MS, Univ. of Delhi, India, 1967, 1969; PhD, Univ. Penn, Phila., 1974. Career: tch. asst., postdoc. Univ. Penn., 1969-76; vis. scientist Univ. de Paris - Sud, Orsay, France 1976; physicist, mem. tech. staff (MTS) Jet Propulsion Lab., Pasadena 1977-84, tech. group supr. 1984-87, asst. section mgr. 1987-89, dep. section mgr. 1989-91, asst. pgm. mgr. 1991-; awards: nat. scholar Univ. Delhi, India 1967-69, fellow Univ. Penn., Phila. 1969-74, Exceptional Service medal NASA 1990; mem. Am. Physical Soc. 1974-, Indian Students Assn. (U.Penn. pres. 1972-74); publs: 50+ tech. papers and 40+ presentations; rec: tennis, travel. Res: 3760 Shadow Grove Rd Pasadena 91107 Ofc: Jet Propulsion Lab 4800 Oak Grove Dr Pasadena 91109

KIBBE, EUGENE VINCENT, photographic artist; b. Mar. 22, 1907, Chgo.; s. Fred and Elsa (Erwig) K.; m. Mary Alice Eger, 1962 (div. 1971); childen: Roger b. 1964, Frances b. 1968; high sch. grad. Strafford, Mo. 1924. Career: news photographer Wide World Photos, Chgo. 1931-38; civilian photographer U.S. War Dept., St. Louis, Mo. 1938-40, 1941-42, chief photog. U.S. War Dept., Alaska Hwy. 1943; H.S. tchr. photography, Springfield, Mo. 1940-41; photog. Olin Industries, East Alton, Ill. 1944-45; legal photographer/prin., San Francisco 1946-48; commercial photog./prin., Fairfax 1948-54; photography instr. Coll. of Marin, Kentfield 1954-75, ret.; artist photographer, photos in museum and private collections, exhibited 373 photographs worldwide 1941-46 (24th ranking photo exhibitor internat.), Am. Annual of Photography list of leading exhibiting photographers 1940s; past bd. dirs. Emeritus Coll. Marin County; Hon. life mem. Royal Photographic Soc. U.K. 1943-, Hon. life mem. Photographic Soc. Am. 1942-,(recipient writing award), mem. Marin Soc. of Artists 1985-; contbr.

numerous articles re the art of photography, J. Photog. Soc. Am. 1945-86; Democrat; Humanist; rec: travel (54+ countries). Res: 1821 Fifth Ave A-112 San Rafael 94901

KIBEL, HARVEY RONALD, real estate developer, business advisor; b. Jun. 15, 1937, NY, NY; s. Ned and Sylvia (Pearlman) K.; m. Isabel Ruth Rogers, June 7, 1959; children: Ellen b. 1964, Paul b. 1967; edn: BSE, Columbia Univ., 1959; MS, USC, 1960; Calif. lic. C.P.A. 1968, R.E. Broker 1970. Career: ptnr. in chg. gen. consulting Peat, Marwick, Mitchell, Los Angeles 1964-71; pres. Open Road, 1971-77; co-founder/pres. Kibel, Jonas, Inc. 1977-84; co-founder/CEO Kibel, Green, Inc., mgrs. of crossroad, conflict & crisis, Los Angeles 1984-; faculty USC, 1960-67; civic bds: UCLA Johnson Cancer Ctr., L.A. (pres. 1990-92), Amer. Cancer Soc. S.F. (chmn. bd. 1970-84), United Way Bd., Boy Scouts Am. Bd. Govs., Chief Execs. Orgn., World Presidents Council, Young Presidents Orgn. (L.A. chmn., Forum pres. 1975-87); awards: best bus. book/top 10 Library Jour. 1982, nat. award of excellence SBIC, W.D.C. 1983, vol. of yr. Amer. Cancer Soc. 1984; mem: Chief Execs. Orgn., World Bus. Council, T. Mgmt. Assn. (bd. 1989); clubs: Regency (L.A.), Riviera CC (L.A.); author: How To Turn Around a Financially Troubled Co. (McGraw-Hill, 1982); rec: tennis, skiing, biking. Ofc: KGI, 2001 Wilshire Blvd Ste 420 Santa Monica 90403

KIDDE, JOHN EDGAR, food processing company executive; b. May 4, 1946, Kansas City, Mo.; s. Gustave Edgar and Mary Sloan (Orear) K.; m. Donna Carolyn Peterson, Aug. 4, 1973; children: Kari b. 1978, Laurie b. 1981, Kellie b. 1984; edn: BA, Stanford Univ., 1968; MBA, Northwestern Univ., 1971. Career: corp. banking ofcr. First Interstate Bank, Los Angeles 1971-73; v.p. ops. Colony Foods Inc., Newport Beach 1973-78; pres. Western Host Food Services, Newport Beach 1978-81; pres., dir. Giuliano's Delicatessen & Bakery, Carson 1981-90; pres., dir., c.e.o. Sona & Hollen Foods, Los Alamitos 1990-; dir. Restaurant Business Mag., NY, NY 1975-78; alumni admissions com. Phillips Acad. 1985-; trustee Harbor Day Sch. 1989-; mem. Stanford Buck Club 1971-, Stanford Club Orange County (pres. 1987-89); club: Balboa Bay 1992-; mil: 1st lt. US Army Reserves 1969-75; Republican; Episcopalian; rec: skiing, scuba, triathlons. Res: 3907 Inlet Isle Dr Corona Del Mar 92625 Ofc: Sona & Hollen Foods, Inc. 3712 Cerritos Ave Los Alamitos 90720

KIDNEY, ROBERT BRIAN, consultant-governmental affairs, former state legislative chief clerk; b. Dec. 15, 1930, San Mateo; s. Robert Henry and Sarah Alina (MacInnis) K./ edn: BA pol. sci., Univ. Mich., Ann Arbor 1960; MA govt., Univ. San Francisco, 1974. Career: asst. clerk of the Assembly, Calif. Legislature, Sacto. 1963-65, asst. chief clerk 1965-88, chief clerk 1988-91, ret.; cons. to The Gualco Group (govt. rels. firm) 1993-; guest lectr. on public affairs UC Davis, Hastings. Coll. Law, State Training Ctr. Sacto., Calif. Journal, others 1974-91; participant symposium on draft rules for the Hungarian Nat. Assembly, Budapest (4/91), seminars- "The Calif. Legislature in Transition" No. Calif. Polit. Sci. Assn., Univ. of Pacific (5/91), "Calif.'s Legislative Process" Assn. of Calif. Ins. Cos., Sacto. (7/91), California Journal, Sacto. (6/92); mem. Sacramento Club, Comstock Club of Sacto., Knights of the Vine, E Clampus Vitus, local cultural orgns.; contbg. author: California's Legislature (biennial revised edits. 1964-86); judicial chapter editor: California Blue Book (1967, 71, 75); co-editor, editor (booklet) Calif. State Assembly (1969-90); mil: USAF 1951-54; R.Cath.; rec: skiing, bicycling, lively arts, entertaining. Res: 317 Hartnell Pl Sacramento 95825-6613

KIEHNE, ANNA M., systems analyst, consultant; b. Dec. 15, 1947, Preston, Minn.; d. Alvin H. and Anna M. (Goldsmith) Kiehne; m. Lyman M. Loveland, June 15, 1991; edn: BA, Winona State Univ., 1969; M.I.B.A., West Coast Univ., 1992; cert. in systems analysis, UCLA, 1984. Career: analyst Home Savings, Irwindale, Ca. 1983-87; Cray Research, Mpls. 1988-89; v.p. Bowest Corp., La Jolla, Ca. 1989-90; cons. Amsys Corp., L.A. 1990-91; indep. cons., San Marcos 1991-; mem. Nat. Assn. Accts. 1982-, Am. Mgmt. Assn. 1990-, Paradox Users Group 1991-; civic: Sister City Internat., Richfield, Minn. 1989, started multifamily recycling project, city pilot project 1990; Democrat; Lutheran; rec: travel, arts & crafts, hiking. Res/Ofc: 1148 Grape St San Marcos 92069

KIELAROWSKI, HENRY EDWARD, marketing executive; b. Dec. 29, 1946, Pittsburgh, Pa.; s. Henry Andrew K. and Evelyn Marie (Kline) Boileau; m. Lynda Blair Powell, Aug. 1971 (div. 1976); children: Amorette, Blair; edn: BA, Duquesne Univ., 1969, MA, 1974, PhD, 1974. Career: pres. Communicators Inc., Pitts. 1974-76; mktg. specialist McGraw-Hill Inc., N.Y.C. 1976-81; mktg. dir. Fidelity S.A., Allison Park, Pa. 1981-86; exec. v.p. ARC Systems Inc., Pitts. 1986-88; v.p. product devel. First Deposit Corp., San Francisco 1988-; mem: Am. Mktg. Assn. (recipient award for Mktg. Excellence 1988), Direct Mktg. Assn.; author: Microcomputer Consulting in the CPA Environment (1987); contbr. articles to profl. jours.; Democrat; rec: fiction writing, music, dance, travel, film. Res: 107 Lyon St San Francisco 94117

KILEY, ROBERT RALPH, political consultant; b. Apr. 21, 1948, Honolulu; s. Kenneth John and Dorothy Irene (Ambrozich) K.; m. Barbara Lynn Weber, Mar. 16, 1985; children: Tiryn b. 1977, Kristin b. 1980; edn: BA psychology, USC, 1975. Career: exec. dir. Republican Party, Orange County, Calif. 1976-79;

v.p. Nason Lundberg & Kiley, Orange 1978-80; owner, pres. Robert Kiley & Assocs., Yorba Linda 1980-; instr. American Campaign Sch., 1990-; advanceman Pres. Ronald Reagan, W.D.C., 1979-88; bd. mem. Board of Psychology, Sacto. 1985-; honors: dean's list USC 1974-75, Outstanding Young Man of Am. 1977-78; mem. USC Alumni Assn. 1975-; Republican. Res: 5028 Vista Montana Yorba Linda 92686 Ofc: Robert Kiley & Associates, 5028 Vista Montana Yorba Linda 92686

KILLEA, LUCY L., California state senator; b. July 31, 1922, San Antonio, Tx.; d. Nelson and Zelime (Pettus) Lytle; m. John F. (Jack) Killea, May 11, 1946; children: Jay b. 1946, Paul b. 1956; edn: BA, Incarnate Word Coll., San Antonio, Tx.; MA, Univ. of S.D.; PhD, UC S.D. Career: analyst M.I. and CIA, 1943-56; mem. S.D. Historical Site Bd., 1969; tchg. and res. asst. UC S.D., 1967-72; lectr. S.D. State Univ., 1976-77; councilwoman S.D. City Council, mem. Metropolitan Transit Devel. Bd. and S.D. County Assn. of Govt., 1978-82; mem., S.D. County Cultural Commn. 1971-78; exec. dir., Fronteras de las Californias 1974-78; commr. S.D. Planning Commn. 1978; deputy mayor City of S.D. 1982; assembly mem. Calif. State Assembly 1982-89; senator Calif. State Senate 1989-; awards: grant, Justice Found., for res. in Spanish lang. manuscripts; Award of Merit, Outstanding Student of Year, Conf. of Calif. Historical Soc., 1966; One of 12 Women of Valor award, Temple Beth Israel, S.D., 1966; res. grant, Mexican and Spanish archival material, UC S.D., 1971; Reg. Planning Award, S.D. Assn. of Planners, 1977; Alumnae of Distinction award, Incarnate Word Coll., 1981; Woman of Year, S.D. Irish Council, 1981; Alice Paul award, Nat. Women's Political Caucus, 1981; Legislative Rookie of Year, Calif. Jour., 1982; Legislator of Year, United Fedn. of Small Bus., 1985; Legislator of Year, Trial Lawyers Assn. and S.D. Bar Assn., 1987; Legislator of Year, Calif. Narcotics Officers Assn., 1988; Media award, Nat. Conf. on Christians and Jews, 1989; Headliner of Year, S.D. Press Club, 1989; Free Speech award, Calif. Common Cause, 1990; Legislator of Year, Vietnam Veterans of S.D. Co. 1991; Special Achievement award, Calif. Resource Recovery Assn., 1991; BPW Hall of Fame, Calif. Fedn. of Bus. and Profl. Women, 1991; Eleventh Person award, Women's Internat. Ctr., Living Legacy Program, 1992; Legislator of Year, Calif. Narcotics Officers Assn., 1992; Legislator of Year, Calif. Women Lawyers Assn., 1993; advy. bd. mem.: UC S.D. Med. Ctr., ElderHelp Comm., Junior League, Girl Scouts; mem: S.D.-Imperial County Council, Bus. and Profl. Women, Calif. Elected Women's Assn. for Edn & Res., Greater S.D. C.of C., Sierra Club, LWV, Historical Societies: Ramona, Alpine, Spring Valley, El Cajon, Lakeside, Mountain Empire, S.D.; author: profl. articles pub. in S.D. Jour. of History, 1966, 1976-77; ed., article pub. in Proceedings, 1976; mil: intelligence ofcr., US Army M.I., CIA 1943-56; Independent; Catholic; rec: running, golf, chamber music. Ofc: 2550 5th Ave. San Diego 92103

KIM, JAE-MAN, professor, Chi-Gong master, acupuncturist, Tui-Na therapist (Chinese masso-therapy); b. Nov. 28, 1958, Seoul, Korea; s. Im-Ok and Yong-Rhea (Shin) Kim; edn: master of Kung-Fu, Choong-Moo Kung-Fu Sch., Seoul, Korea, 1982; cert., gynecology & pediatrics, Royal Univ. of Am., L.A., Calif., 1989; cert., Tui-Na training prog., Calif. Chinese Tui-Na Medical Coll., L.A., 1992; master of Oriental medicine, Royal Univ. of Am., L.A., 1992. Career: Kung-Fu master, Be-Ho & Choong-Moo Kung-Fu Schools, Seoul, Korea, 1982-84; Kung-Fu master, Korean Martial Art Ctr., Yorba Linda, Calif., 1986-87; acupuncturist, C.F Clinic, Monterey Park, Calif., 1989-; prof. of Tui-Na, Royal Univ. of Am., L.A., 1991-; Tui-Na therapist, Royal Univ. of Am. Oriental Med. Ctr., 1993-; prof. of Chi-Gong, Royal Univ. of Am., 1993; awards: Superior Acad. Achievement award 1989, Active Participant award 1991, Cert. Appreciation 1993, Royal Univ. of Am.; mem: Nat. Commn. for the Certification of Acupuncturists 1989, Calif. Acupuncture Com. 1990, Korean Acupuncture and Oriental Medicine Assn. in Calif. 1991; translator: book (from Chinese to Korean), Tui-Na Therapeutics, 1991. Res: 938 S. Ardmore Ave #203 Los Angeles 90006 Ofc: C.F Clinic 934 S. Atlantic Blvd #222 Monterey Park 91754

KIM, KWANG SIK, physician; b. June 9, 1947, Seoul, Korea; s. Tae Jong and Kyung Ja K.; m. Aeran Y., July 30, 1983; children: Melissa Y. b. 1984, Brian Y. b. 1987; edn: BS, Seoul Nat. Univ. 1967; MD, 1971. Career: asst. prof. pediatrics Harbor-UCLA Med. Center 1980-86; assoc. prof. pediatrics Children's Hosp., Los Angeles 1986-91; currently prof. of pediatrics, USC Sch. of Medicine and head, Div. of Infectious Diseases, Children's Hosp. L.A.; awards: Mead Johnson Lab. Outstanding Pediatric Resident 1977, March of Dimes Basic O'Connor grant 1982, Am. Heart Assn. sr. investigator 1983; mem: Am. Soc. Microbiology, Lancefield Soc., Western Soc. Pediatric Res., Am. Pediatric Soc., Pediatric Infectious Diseases Soc., Am. Fedn. for Clinical Res.; author: 67 articles and papers pub. in profl. jours.; mil: flight surgeon Korean Air Force 1971-74. Res: 4808 Asteria St Torrance 90503 Ofc: Children's Hospital of Los Angeles Division of Infectious Diseases 4650 Sunset Blvd Los Angeles 90027

KIMMICH, ROBERT ANDRE, physician, psychiatrist; b. Nov. 2, 1920, Idpls.; s. Dr. John Martin (M.D.) and Renee Marie (Baron) K.; m. Nancy E. Smith, 1945 (div.); children: Robert, John, Nancy; edn: BS, MD, Indiana Univ., 1943, Rockefeller fellow Inst. of Penna. Hosp., Phila. 1944-45. Career: dir. Territorial Hosp., Honolulu, 1951-58; chief psychiatrist Mental Health Dept. San Francisco, 1960-64; dir. Michigan Dept. Mental Health, Lansing, Mi. 1964-68;

chmn. Psychiatric Dept. Childrens' Hosp., San Francisco, 1968-76; asst. prof. Yale Univ. Sch. of Med., 1949-51; assoc. clin. prof. Stanford Univ. Sch. of Med., 1968-82; recipient Distinguished Service Award, No. Calif. Psychiatric Soc., S.F. 1990; Life Fellow Am. Psychiatric Assn. (nat. rep. 1988-), No. Calif. Psychiatric Soc. (pres. elect 1991-93, newsletter editor 1985-), Childrens Hosp. Physicians Assn. (bd. 1985-); mil: capt. Med. Corps AUS 1945-47; rec: sailing, guitar, hiking. Ofc: 341 Spruce San Francisco 94118

KINANE, MICHAEL JOSEPH, lawyer, international trade company president; b. Dec. 28, 1956, Inglewood; s. Arthur David and Rosalee Marie (Peralta) K.; edn: BS in bus., acctg. also BA in sociology, UC Berkeley, 1979, MBA internat. trade, UCB, 1982; JD, Hastings Coll. of Law, 1991; admitted bar: Calif., US Dist. Ct., US Ct. Appeals. Career: sales Thom McAn Shoes, Torrance, 1972-76; research cons. Carnegie Council, Berkeley 1978-79; account exec. Comml. Credit Corp., San Francisco 1979-80; pres. CCE Biotech, Oakland 1983-; Comm. Design 1983-84; Calif. Capital Exports Inc. 1982-; atty., of counsel Law offices of Charles A. Bonner, Sausalito; adj. prof. Nat. Univ., Oakland 1985-86; columnist, The First Edition; jury chair Nat. Ednl. Film Festival; mem: Calif. Trial Lawyers Assn. (bd. dir.), Am. Trial Lawyers Assn., Calif. Bar Assn., Italian Am. Bar Assn.; Fruitvale Merchants Assn. (v.p.), Oakland C.of C., Spanish Speaking Citizens Found. (bd. dir.), Camara de Comercia Mexicana-Americana, Gael Olde Boys Rugby Club, Fruitvale Comm. Devel. Dist. Council (bd. dir.); rec: rugby, skiing, collect childrens' literature. Res: 1844 33rd Ave Oakland 94601 Ofc: California Capital Exports, Inc. 409 13th St 10th Floor Oakland 94612

KING, CLIFTON W., clergyman, managerial development company president; b. June 9, N.C.; s. Samuel Walton Sparks and Annie Elizabeth King; m. Loriene Chase, PhD, May 24, 1974; edn: HDL, ordained minister. Career: minister Santa Anita Ch., Arcadia; Divine Sci. Ch., Beverly Hills; Encino Community Ch., Tarzana 1977-89; St. Pauls Community Ch., Shell Beach, currently; pres. Chase-King Personal Development Ctrs., 1989-, conduct mgmt. seminars for major cos. to increase productivity & assets; pres. Chase/King Managerial Development, Chase/King Prodns. Inc., Chase/King Business Communications; former staff USC Stress Center; mil: US Army Korean War; author: Two-Way Prayer; Happiness Through the Beatitudes; coauthor: The Human Miracle; mem: Internat. Platform Assn., Navy League, Bel Air Council (life), Confrerie de la Chaine des Rotisseurs; clubs: Santa Maria CC, Regency. Res: 375 Palomar Ave Shell Beach 93449

KING, FREDERIC, health services management professional, association executive director; b. May 9, 1937, NYC; s. Benjamin and Jeanne (Fritz) K.; m. Linda Ann Udell, Mar. 17, 1976; children by previous marriage: Coby Allen, Allison Beth, Lisa Robyn, Daniel Seth; edn: BBA cum laude, Bernard M. Baruch Sch. Bus. and Pub. Adminstrn., CUNY, 1958. Career: dir. adminstrn. Albert Einstein Coll. Medicine, Bronx 1970-72; assoc. v.p. health affairs Tulane Med. Ctr., New Orleans 1972-77; dir. fin. Mt. Sinai Med. Ctr., NYC 1977-78; v.p. fin. Cedars-Sinai Med. Ctr., Los Angeles 1978-82; pres. Vascular Diagnostic Services Inc., Woodland Hills 1982-84; exec. dir. South Bay Independent Physicians Med. Group Inc., Torrance 1984-; asso. adj. prof. Tulane Univ. Sch. Pub. Health; asst. prof. Mt. Sinai Med. Ctr.; instr. Pierce Coll., L.A.; listed Who's Who in the West, Who's Who in Soc.; mem: Am. Pub. Health Assn., Healthcare Forum, Am. Hosp. Assn., Calif. Assn. Hosps. and Health Systems, The Presidents Assn.; civic: pres./chmn. bd. dirs. Ohr Eliyahu Academy, dir. Pacific Jewish Ctr.; mil: AUS 1959-62; Republican; Jewish. Res: 1116 Rose Ave Venice 90291 Ofc: 3480 Torrance Blvd Ste 220 Torrance 90503

KING, GEORGE (H.S.H. Prince de Santorini, Count de Florina, Lord of Allington), clergyman, writer, broadcaster; b. Jan. 23, 1919, Wellington, Shropshire, Eng.; s. George and Mary King; m. Dr. Monique Noppe, Jan. 30, 1971; ed. Guisborough Public Sch., Eng., Regent St Polytechnic Inst., London; DD, Bodkin Bible Inst.; PhD in theol. Internat. Theol. Sem.; internat. advy. bd. and ordained minister Internat. Evangelism Crusades Inc.; author 30 pub. books, lectr., tchr. religious bdcstr., producer/dir. num. 16mm docu. films and videotapes, ednl. cassettes; dep. dir. gen. Internat. Biographical Ctr., dep. gov. Am. Biographical Inst. Research Assn.; founder/pres. The Aetherius Soc., (rel., sci., edn. orgn.), met. archbishop The Aetherius Churches; founder, pres., grand master Mystical Order of St. Peter (reg. charity US, reg. UCCI); founder, pres. Coll. of Spiritual Scis., London, Los Angeles; grand master Internat. Chivalric Order Kts. of Justice (reg. charity); hon. lt. grand master The Grand Sovereign Dynastic Hospitaller Order of St. John, Kts. of Malta (reg. UCCI); grand collier The Imperial Sovereign Mil. Orthodox Dynastic Constantinian Order of St. Georges (reg. UCCI); internat. chaplain Am. Fedn. of Police, nat. chaplain Am. Park Rangers Assn., nat. advy. bd. Nat. Chaplains Assn. USA, patron Internat. Acad. of Criminology, nat. advy. bd. Am. Security Council, advy. bd. Intl. Evangelism Crusades Inc. (peace award 1982), granted Letters Patent of Armorial Bearings by Her Majesty's Coll. of Arms, England; mem: Internat. Acad. for Advance. Arts & Scis. (life), Freeman of the City of London, Guild of Freemen City of London (life), Assn. of Freemen of England, Manorial Soc. G.B., Royal Soc. of Health G.B. (affil.), Fellow Royal Soc. of Tropical Medicine and Hygiene G.B., Fellow Royal Commonwealth Soc., The Heraldry Soc. G.B., Royal Nat. Lifeboat Instn. G.B., Hon. Order Ky. Colonels, Nat. Rifle Assn.,

Calif. Rifle and Pistol Club; mil. awards: Grande Croix, l'Etoile de la Paix (France), hon. gen. Polish Armed Forces (in Exile), gold medal for svc. Imperial House of Byzantium, Order of the White Eagle and Order of Virtuti Militari (former) Rep. of Poland (govt. in exile), WWII Def. Medal (U.K.), Battle for Brit. commemorative medal, Cross of Europe, Medal of the Secret Army of Belgium, Cross of Merit w/Swords (Poland), Gen. Wladyslawe Sikorski Centenary Medal; Republican (U.S. Congl. Advy. Bd., life Presdl. Task Force); Address: 6216 Afton Place Hollywood 90028-8205

KING, JAMES ADOLPHUS, real estate broker, ret.; b. May 1, 1911, Guyana, S.A., naturalized 1948; s. Samuel Richard and Grace (Thom) K.; m. Maude, Dec. 8, 1951; children: Patrick b. 1937, Charles b. 1965; m. Marion, May 1, 1979; edn: grad. Jefferson H.S., L.A.; lic. R.E. broker Calif. Career: mgr. convalescent hosp., Los Angeles 1943-50; social svc., L.A. 1950-59; real estate broker/property mgr., L.A. 1959-; awards: hon. life mem. Inglewood Democratic Club 1986; mem. L.A. Real Estate Bd., Kts. of Peter Claver Frat.; Democrat; R.Cath.; rec: baseball, travel. Res: 3532 W 79th St Inglewood 90305

KING, JON LANNING, consulting actury, executive; b. May 8, 1948, Columbus, Nebr.; s. Edward Lanning and Elizabeth Ann (Jaworski) K.; m. Peggy Louise Wright, May 27, 1971 (div. 1988); m. Diana Rae Green, July 29, 1989; edn: BS, Univ. Neb. 1970. Career: systems analyst Transamerica Life, Los Angeles 1972, mgr. direct life product 1973-74; cons. actuary TPF&C 1975-80, prin., cons. actuary 1981-86, v.p., cons. actuary 1986-88; office mgr., cons. actuary Buck Cons. 1986-; mem: Am. Acad. Actuaries, L.A. Actuarial Club (treas. 1982), Western Pension Conf., Pacific States Actuarial Club, Soc. Actuaries, Conf. Actuaries in Pub. Practice; speaker on employee benefits 1979-; rec: golf, bridge, football. Res: 6 Fleet #301 Marina Del Rey 90292 Ofc: Buck Consultants 1801 Century Park E Ste 480 Los Angeles 90067

KINNANE, DENNIS GEORGE, doctor of Oriental medicine, acupuncturist; b. Sept. 28, 1946, Hammond, Ind.; s. George Vincent and Irene Ethel (Smith) K.; edn: BS in pharmacy, Purdue Univ., Lafayette, Ind. 1969; MS in acupuncture, herbology, SAMRA Univ., L.A., Calif. 1987; OMD, SAMRA Univ. 1988; reg. pharmacist; lic. acupuncturist. Career: pharmacist Hook's Drugs, Indianapolis, Ind. 1970-74; Savon Drugs, L.A., Calif. 1975-78; independent pharmacist, L.A. 1978-88; lic. acupuncturist, private practice, Torrance, Calif. 1988-; faculty mem.: SAMRA Univ., L.A. 1988-, So. Bay Adult Sch., Redondo Beach 1989-, Am. Inst. of Oriental Medicine, San Diego 1990-; mem: Calif. Acupuncture Assn. 1990-, Purdue Alumni Assn. 1990-; rec: music, travel, metaphysics. Res: 702 Manhattan Beach Blvd Apt #6 Manhattan Beach 90266 Ofc: Dr. Dennis Kinnane 4015 Pacific Coast Hwy, Ste. 101 Torrance 90505

KINSELL, JEFFREY CLIFT, investment banker; b. Sept. 13, 1951, Santa Barbara; s. Dr. Clift Seybert and Shirlee Grace (Burwash) K.; m. Sherry Anne Majerus, July 4, 1980 (div. 1985); m. Sondra Amy Silvey, May 21, 1987; children: Amy Elizabeth b. 1989, Pamela Suzanne b. 1991; edn: BS biology, Coll. Arts & Sci., Tulane Univ., 1973; MBA in fin., John Anderson Grad. Sch. of Mgmt., UCLA, 1976. Career: asst. v.p. First Boston Corp., N.Y.C., 1976-78, v.p First Boston Corp., San Francisco 1978-88; v.p., western reg. mgr. Paine Webber Capital Markets Inc., S.F. 1988-; honors: Beta Beta Beta, Sigma Alpha Epsilon 1969-73; mem. San Francisco Municipal Bond Club 1978-; Republican; Episcopalian; rec: sailing, travel, photography, scrimshaw. Res: 93 La Espiral Orinda 94563 Ofc: Paine Webber Capital Markets, Inc. 100 California St Ste 1245 San Francisco 94111

KIRBY, ROBERT WILLIAM, real estate broker; b. Nov. 8, 1937, Westwood; s. Oliver William and Nell Vivian (Trickett) K.; edn: BA, Azusa Pac. Univ., 1959; gen. elem. tchg. cred., CSU Stanislaus, 1964; gen. sec. tchg. cred., Univ. of Pacific, 1967; grad. journalism, CSU Fullerton, 1971-74; lic. R.E. broker Calif. 1986. Career: tchr. Lincoln Jr. High Sch., Stockton 1964-68, YMCA Club adv. 1965-68; tchr. Maranatha High Sch., Arcadia 1969-76, baseball coach 1970-76, yearbook /newspaper adv. 1972-76, Key Club adv. 1971-76; real estate agt. Herbert Hawkins Co., Pasadena 1976-82, National Consolidated, Pasadena 1982-86; real estate broker Kirby Properties, Pasadena 1986-; honors: Youth in City Govt., Stockton Unified 1953, pres. Soph. Class, Choir chaplain, editor newspaper Azusa Pacific Univ. (1956-59); mem: Nat. Assn. Realtors, Calif. Assn. Realtors, Pasadena Bd. Realtors, Azusa Pacific Univ. Alumni (bd. dirs. 1972-78, pres. 1976-77, sec. 1974-76), Foothill Apt. Owners Assn.; lodge: Crown City Kiwanis (sec. 1987-88, 91-, bd. 1988-90, v.p. 1988-89); contbr. num. articles to religious, college and club publs., editor: Y.F.C. Jour. "Herald" (1956-57), coll. newspaper "The Interceptor" (1958-59), coll. yearbook "The Sceptor" (1956-57), alumni newsletter "The Collegian" (1974-75); Republican: GOP Nat. Com., Calif. Rep. Party, Citizens Against Govt. Waste, H.A.L.T., Nat. Taxpayer's Union; Congregational; rec: travel, golf, oil painting. Ofc: Kirby Properties 1245 E Walnut Ste 114 Pasadena 91106

KIRCHNER, ERNST KARL, manufacturing company executive; b. June 18, 1937, San Francisco; s. Karl Ewald and Theresa (Muller) K.; m. Ursula Martha Karmann, Sept. 3, 1960; children: Mark Ernst b. 1967, Christl Elaine b. 1968, Steven Thomas b. 1970; edn: BSEE, Stanford Univ., 1959, MSEE, 1960, PhD in

E.E., 1963. Career: tchr. Univ. Arizona, Tucson 1963-65; mem. technical staff Teledyne MEC, Palo Alto 1965-72, project engr. 1972-79, staff engr. 1979-81, mgr. 1981-82, operation mgr. 1982-83, sr. mgr. 1983-84; mgr. engring. Teledyne Microwave, Mountain View 1984-87, dir. engring. 1987-88, v.p. bus. devel. 1988-, v.p. delay device products 1990-; honors: Kappa Kappa Psi 1956, Sigma Xi 1959, Tau Beta Pi 1959; mem: Bd. of Hope Unlimited Internat., IEEE, Am. Physical Soc., Am. Mktg. Assn., Assn. of Old Crows; commr. Town of Atherton 1986-87; patentee; contbr. articles in tech. jours. (1963-); mil: 1st lt. US Army 1963-65, Army Commendn. Medal 1965; Republican; Presbyterian (deacon, elder). Res: 41 Ashfield Rd Atherton 94027 Ofc: Teledyne Microwave 1290 Terra Bella Ave Mountain View 94043

KIRK, CASSIUS LAMB, JR., lawyer, investor; b. June 8, 1929, Bozeman, Mont.; s. Cassius L. and Gertrude V. (McCarthy) K.; edn: AB, pol. sci., Stanford Univ. 1951; JD, UC Berkeley 1954. Career: assoc. law firm of Cooley, Godward, Castro, Huddleson & Tatum, San Francisco 1956-60; staff counsel business affairs, Stanford Univ. 1960-78; chief bus. ofcr., staff counsel, Menlo Sch. and Coll., Menlo Park 1978-81; chmn. bd. Elberli-Kirk Properties, Inc., Menlo Park 1981-; dir: Just Closets Inc., San Rafael, 1987-91; faculty, UC Santa Barbara Wkshop for Coll. Administrs. 1965-73; honors: Order of the Coif, Phi Sigma Alpha, Phi Alpha Delta; mem. Calif. Bar Assn., Stanford Faculty Club; civic: Menlo Towers Assn. (pres. 1978-79, 82-83, 87-88), Palo Alto C.of C. (v.p. for community affairs 1969-70), Allied Arts Guild, City of Menlo Park Advy. Bd.); mil: sp3 US Army, Occ. Ger., GCM; Republican; rec: jogging, travel, opera. Res: 1330 University Dr #52 Menlo Park 94025 Ofc: Eberli-Kirk Properties, Inc. 3551 Haven Ave Unit N Menlo Park 94025

KIRKLAND, BERTHA THERESA, project engineer; b. San Francisco; d. Lawrence and Therese (Kanzler) Schmelzer; m. Thornton Crowns Kirkland, Jr. Dec. 27, 1937, (dec. 1971); children: Kathryn Elizabeth b. 1943, Francis Charles b. 1945. Career: supr. hospital operations, American Potash & Chemical Corp., Trona, 1953-54; office mgr. T.C. Kirkland, Electrical Contractor 1954-58; sec.treas., dir. T.C. Kirkland Inc., San Bernardino 1958-74; electrical estimator/engr. ADD-M Electric, Inc. San Bernardino 1972-82; vice pres. 1974-82; elec. estimator, engr. Corona Industrial Electric, Inc. Corona 1982-83; project engineer Fischbach & Moore, Inc. Los Angeles 1984-91; mem. Arrowhead Country Club; Episcopal. Res: 526 East Sonora St San Bernardino 92404

KITADA, SHINICHI, research biochemist; b. Dec. 9, 1948, Osaka, Japan; came to U.S. 1975; s. Koichi and Asako (Seki) K.; edn: MD, Kyoto Univ., 1973; MS in biol. chem., UCLA, 1977, PhD, 1979. Career: intern Kyoto Univ. Hosp. 1973-74; resident physician Chest Disease Research Inst. 1974-75; res. scholar Lab. Nuclear Medicine and Radiation Biology UCLA 1979-89, asst. res. biochemist Jules Stein Eye Inst. UCLA, 1989-92; research biochemist La Jolla Cancer Research Found., 1992-; awards: Japan Soc. Promotion Sci. fellow 1975-76, Edna Lievre fellow Am. Cancer Soc. 1981-82; mem: Am. Oil Chemists Soc., Sigma Xi, N.Y. Acad. of Scis.; res. papers in field; Presbyterian; rec: swimming, tennis; res: 920 Kline St #301 La Jolla 92037; ofc: La Jolla Cancer Research Foundation 10901 N Torrey Pines Rd La Jolla 92037

KITCHEN, JONATHAN SAVILLE, lawyer; b. June 7, 1948, Lincoln, Eng.; s. Walter Lawrence Michael and Helen Margaret (Hastings) K.; m. Nina Hatvany, 1982; children: Natalie b. 1982, Vanessa b. 1984, Paul b. 1985; edn: stu., Strasbourg Univ., France 1966-67; BA (honors), Durham Univ., Eng. 1970; LLM, Univ. Coll., London 1971; MA, Cambridge Univ., Eng. 1974, PhD, 1976; admitted bar: England & Wales, 1977, Calif., 1978. Career: research fellow Churchill Coll., Cambridge, Eng. 1974-77; teaching fellow, Stanford Law Sch., Palo Alto 1975-76; atty. McCutchen, Doyle, San Francisco 1977-81; ptnr., atty. Baker & McKenzie, San Francisco 1981-; honors: Duke of Edinburgh Scholar, Inner Temple, 1970, Evans Lewis-Thomas Scholar, Sydney Sussex Coll., Cambridge, Eng., 1972-74, Fulbright Scholar in Law to U.S, 1975-76, Bodossaks Fellowship, Churchill Coll., Cambridge, 1974-77; mem: State Bar of Calif., Bar Assn. of San Francisco, Am. Bar Assn., St. Francis Yacht Club; author: 2 books and numerous articles in domestic and foreign law jours.; rec: sailing, skiing. Ofc: Baker & McKenzie, Two Embarcadero Ctr 24th Flr San Francisco 94111-3909

KITCHING, GILBERT EDWARD, obstetrician/gynecologist; b. July 7, 1929, Brooklyn, NY; s. Gilbert James and Kathryn Patricia (Stubbert) K.; m. Joane, Aug. 20, 1955; children: Alfred b. 1951, Gilbert b. 1956, Kenneth b. 1958, Charles b. 1963; edn: BS, Calif. Inst. of Tech. 1952; MD, Univ. of So. Calif. 1956; diplomate Am. Bd. Ob-Gyn. 1967. Career: served to col. US Air Force, 1956-75; med. intern Tripler Army Hosp. Hosp. 1956-58, ob.-gyn. residency 1959-62; wing flt. surgeon Travis AFB 1958-59; chief Ob-Gyn, Clark AFB, Philippines 1962-64, Home AFB, Ida. 1964-65, Vandenberg AFB, Ca. 1965-70, Wiesbaden (W.Ger.) Hosp. 1970-73, Sheppard AFB, Tx. 1973-75, ret. USAF 1975, AF commendn. medal 1970; cmdr. hosps. Chanute AFB 1976-78, and Homestead AFB, Fla. 1978-81; tchr. med. inspection USAF 1981-83, study dir. evaluation of USAF med. services 1982, dep. dir. profl. services USAF Med. Service, 1983-85; staff ob-gyn. Riverside Med. Clinic, Corona, Calif. 1986-88; staff gyn. St. Bernardine Med. Ctr. 1988-; honors: AF meritorious service medal

1976, 78 81, 83, Legion of Merit 1985; Fellow Am. Coll. Obstets. & Gynecol., mem. AMA, CMA, San Bernardino Co. Med. Assn., Soc. of AF Clin. Surgeons; Boy Scouts Am. scoutmaster 1968-71; num. lectures, workshops, and articles in med. and mil. jours.; Republican; R.Cath.; rec: photog., electronics, carpentry. Ofc: 399 E Highland Ave Ste 502 San Bernardino 92404

KITE, DENNIS S., institutional securities sales executive; b. May 10, 1945, Chgo.; s. Allen M. and June T. (Hillman) K.; m. Aleta Lindbeck, Feb. 14, 1982; children: Debra b. 1968, Suzanne b. 1990; edn: BBA, Univ. Wis. 1967; MBA, Univ. Chgo. 1973; desig: Prin., Mcpl. Securities Rulemaking Bd. 1985, Gen. Investment Securities Rep. 1988. Career: trainee, mail clk., teller Nat. City Bank, now Manufacturers Bank, Chgo. 1967-68; adminstrv. asst. Inv. Div. Am. Nat. Bank, Chgo. 1968-70; asst. v.p./reg. mgr. Montgomery Ward Credit Corp., Chgo. 1970-77; account exec. Bank of Am., Bank Investment Sec. Div., Los Angeles 1977-79, v.p./ Houston reg. sales mgr. 1979-82, v.p./reg. sales mgr./dir. BA Asia Ltd., Tokyo, Japan 1982-84, v.p./mgr. retail securities sales So. Calif., Bank of Am. Capital Markets Group, 1984-86, v.p./sr. account exec. 1986-87; instl. sales account exec. Liberty Capital Markets Inc., 1988-; mem: Calif. Municipal Treasurers Assn., Big Ten Club of So. Calif., Univ. Chgo. Grad. Sch. of Bus. Alumni Club, Univ. Wis. Alumni Assn.; civic: Zool. Soc. San Diego, L.A. Art Mus., Sierra Club, Smithsonian, Save the Children (sponsor); contbr. material to Marcia Stigum's book: The Money Markets, Myth Reality & Practice (1978); mil: s/sgt. USAFR 1968-73; Jewish; rec: music, golf, skiing, racquetball. Res: 4 Mondano Laguna Niguel 92677 Ofc: Liberty Capital Markets, Inc. 4 Park Plaza Ste 2000 Irvine 92714

KITTLESON, HAROLD ALVER, electronic mfrs. representative; b. Jan. 9, 1912, Malta, Ill.; s. Elon Edwin and Anna Olena (Hobbet) K.; Great Uncle Ole Kittleson invented and patented barbed wire (1875); m. Ella Hartshorn, Apr. 5, 1941; 1 dau. Betty Ann (York) b. 1942; edn: tchr. cred. Iowa State Tchrs. Coll., Cedar Falls 1932; elec. engrg. Iowa State Coll., Ames 1934-38; cert. Microwave Engring., Cal. Tech., 1941; cert. USN Radar Sch., Phila. 1943; tech. & bus. courses, Lockheed Co., Sperry Electronic Corp. (NY), MIT, UCLA; bus. mgmt. certs., Stanford Univ., 1961-62. Career: wkr. on family farm, Woden, Iowa, -1932; country sch. tchr., Iowa, 1932-34; resrch. asst., E.E., Iowa State Coll, 1936-39; chief elec. engr. American Pubs. supply, Lynn, Mass. 1939-40; hd. electronic test equip. engring. an design, Lockheed Aircraft, No. Hollywood, Ca. 1940-43; coord. engr. AEW Proj., MIT Radiation Lab., Cambridge, Mass. 1944-45; founder/owner/pres. Kittleson Co. (electronic mfrs. rep), Los Angeles 1946-, Continental Components 1955-60; lectr. Lockheed Aircraft 1943; cons. No. Am. Phillips Co. 1957, Gen. Equip. Corp. 1958, Fairchild Recording Equip. Corp. 1960, Airtron 1965; honors: recipient appreciation awards num. profl. and ch. organizations, banquet honoree, named No. 1 Booth Choice (1000 exhibitors) WESCON Show and Conv. 1969; mem: Internat. Platform Assn., Electronic Reps Assn. (pres. 1950), Mfrs. Agents Nat. Assn. (pres. 1955), Precision Measurement Assn. (charter, internat. pres. 1970-72), Meals for Millions Found. (trustee 1975-80); active in charity fundraising; publs: tech. reports, mkt. studies; book on family recollections, 3 vols.; US patent application, 1983; Republican (Election Bd.); Presbyterian (commnr. Gen. Assem.); rec: painting (exhibition of oil paintings, 1992), cosmology, experimental gardening. Res: 20315 Runnymede St Canoga Park 91306

KLASSEN, ALVIN HENRY, mathematics educator, tennis official; b. July 18, 1949, San Bernardino; s. Herman Arthur and Elsie Frieda (Lille) K.; edn: BA, CSU San Bernardino, 1971; MA, San Diego State Univ. 1990; Calif. sec. tchg. cred., 1987; internat. tennis official (Bronze badge) Internat. Tennis Fedn. (ITF), 1992. Career: Supply Corps US Navy, active duty 1975-84; cdg. ofcr. US Navy Reserve, Santa Ana, 1990-, Unit: NR Naval Supply Ctr. San Diego Det. A219; physics instr. and dept. chmn. NROTC Preparatory Sch., USN, San Diego summers 1988-; math. instr. San Diego St. Univ., 1989-; tennis ofcl. U.S. Tennis Assn., White Plains, N.Y. 1985-; awards: Phi Kappa Phi 1987-, Univ. scholar award SDSU 1989, Nat. Def. Service, Navy Achiev. (1991, 92); mem: Naval Reserve Assn. (1984-, San Diego chapt. v.p 1990-, named Jr. Ofcr. of Yr. 1989, Diamond in the Rough award 1990), Math. Assn. of Am. (hon. mem. 1989-), San Diego County Tennis Umpires Assn. (1985-, bd. of dir.), U.S. Tennis Assn. 1985-; civic: judge math div. Greater San Diego Science & Engring. Fair 1988-, San Diego County Blood Bank (Gallon Club 1985-); Ind.; Lutheran; rec: tennis, scuba, skiing, reading. Res: 13119 Bonita Vista #232 Poway 92064-5721

KLEIN, ARNOLD WILLIAM, physician; b. Feb. 27, 1945, Mt. Clemens, Mich.; m. Malvina Kraemer; edn: BA biology (cum laude), Univ. Pa., 1967; MD, Univ. Pa. Sch. of Medicine, 1971; bd. cert. Am. Bd. Dermatology 1977. Career: med. intern Cedars-Sinai Med. Ctr., Los Angeles 1971-72, attdg. physician; dermatology resident Hosp. of Univ. Pa., 1972-73, UCLA Med. Ctr., Los Angeles 1973-75, chief res. dermatology 1975; pvt. practice dermatology, Beverly Hills 1975-; asst. clin. prof. derm. Stanford Univ. 1982-89; assoc. clin. prof. medicine/dermatology UCLA; dir. Am. Found. for AIDS Research; med. advy. bd. Collagen Corp., Lupus Found. of Am., Skin Cancer Found.; editorial bd. Men's Fitness Mag., Shape Mag.; reviewer J. Dermatologic Surgery and Oncology, J. of Sexually Transmitted Diseases, J. of Am. Acad. of Dermatology; Calif. Senate appt. commr. Malpractice Advy. Commn. 1983-88; awards: Phi

Beta Kappa, Sigma Tau Sigma, Delphos, Haney scholar Univ. Pa., Measey scholar Univ. Pa., Phila. Found. fellow, Pub. Health Service post-doc. fellow; media appearances on network t.v., radio and mags.; lectr. and presentations num. med. meetings; author med. textbooks, chapters and articles in profl. jours., 3 ednl. video tapes r Collagen Implantation, 1982, 83, 87. Ofc: 435 N Roxbury Dr Ste 204 Beverly Hills 90210

KLEIN, DAVID, diplomat, foreign service officer, educator and university staff executive; b. Sept. 2, 1919, NY, NY; s. Sam N. Klein and Fannie Helen (Falk) Albam; m. Anne Cochran, Mar. 24, 1953; children: Peter b. 1954, Steven b. 1955, John b. 1956, Barbara b. 1956, Richard b. 1958, Suzanne b. 1958; edn: AB, Bklyn. Coll., 1939; MBA (w. high distinction) Harvard Univ., 1948/1988; MA, Columbia Univ., 1952; PhD cand. Univ. of Md., 1964-65; grad. Nat. War Coll., 1966. Career: ofcr. US Fgn. Service, 1947-75: v.consul Mozambique 1947-49, econ. ofcr. US Emb. Rangoon, Burma 1949-51, 2d secty. US Emb. Moscow 1952-54, pol./econ. ofcr. US Mission, Berlin, Ger. 1955-57, 1st secty. US Emb., Bonn 1957-60, Soviet Desk, US State Dept. 1960-62, senior mem. Nat. Security Council The White House 1962-65, econ., then polit. counselor US Emb. Moscow 1966-68, polit. advr. US Mission Berlin 1968-71, US minister & dep. commandant Berlin, Ger. 1971-74, asst. dir. US Arms Control and Disarmament Agy. 1974-75; exec. dir. John J. McCloy Fund 1975-88; exec. dir. and bd. dirs. American Council on Germany 1975-88; instr., govt., Univ. of Md., 1969-71; asst. to the pres., internat. pgms., Fairleigh Dickinson Univ. 1986-90; vis. prof. Univ. San Diego and UC San Diego 1989-; asst. to pres. internat. pgms. Univ. of Tulsa 1990-; mem: Council on Fgn. Relations (N.Y.), Century Assn. (N.Y.), University Club (N.Y.), Am. Fgn. Service Assn. (W.D.C.); author: The Basmachi, A Study of Soviet Nationalities, 1952, Berlin: From Symbol of Confrontation to Touchstone of Stability (Praeger, 1989); mil: US Army 1941-46, col. USAR (Ret.); Unitarian; rec: tennis, golf, music. Res: 6535 Caminito Kittansett La Jolla 92037

KLEIN, HERBERT GEORGE, newspaper editor; b. Apr. 1, 1918, Los Angeles; s. George and Amy (Cordes) K.; m. Marjorie G. Galbraith, Nov. 1, 1941; children: Joanne L. (Mrs. Robert Mayne), Patricia A. (Mrs. John Root); edn: AB, USC, 1940; Hon. Doctorate, Univ. San Diego, 1989. Career: reporter Alhambra Post-Advocate, 1940-42, news editor, 1946-50; spl. corr. Copley Newspapers, 1946-50, Washington corr., 1950; with San Diego Union, 1950-68: editorial writer 1950-52, editorial page editor 1952-56, associate editor 1956-57, executive editor 1957-58, editor 1959-68; mgr. communications Nixon for President Campaign 1968-69, director communications Executive Branch U.S. Govt., White House, 1969-73; v.p. corp. relations Metromedia, Inc. 1973-77; media cons. 1977-80; editor-in-chief, v.p. Copley Newspapers Inc., San Diego 1980-; mem. Advertising Council, N.Y.; publicity dir. Eisenhower-Nixon campaign in Calif., 1952; asst. press secty. V.P. Nixon campaign, 1956; press secty. Nixon inaugural, 1957, Nixon campaign, 1958; spl. asst., press secty. to Nixon, 1959-61, press secty. Nixon for Gov. campaign, 1962; dir. communications Nixon Presdl. campaign, 1968; awards: Fourth Estate award USC 1947, Alumnus of Yr. USC 1971, Gen. Alumni merit award 1977, spl. service to journalism award 1969, headliner of yr. Greater Los Angeles Press Club 1971, 1st Fourth Estate award of San Diego St. Univ. 1986; civic bds: USC (trustee), Holiday Bowl (chmn.), Clair Burgener Found. of Gr. San Diego Sports Assn. (dir.), Am. Cancer Soc., San Diego (exec. com.), Super Bowl XXII, Olympic Tng. Site Com., San Diego Econ. Devel. Com. (bd.); mem. Am. Soc. Newspaper Editors (past dir.), Calif. Press Assn., Pub. Relations Soc. Am., Gen. Alumni USC (past pres.), Alhambra Jr. C.of C. (past pres.), Greater San Diego C.of C. (exec. com.), Sigma Delta Chi (nat. com. chmn., gen. activities chmn. nat. conv. 1958), Delta Chi, Kiwanis, Rotary (hon.), Commonwealth Club Calif., Bohemian Club, Fairbanks CC; mil: comdr. USNR 1942-46. Res: 5110 Saddlery Sq POB 8935 Rancho Santa Fe 92067

KLEIN, JAMES MIKEL, musician, university professor, orchestra director; b. Aug. 27, 1953, Greenville, S.C.; s. Rubin Harry Klein and Billie Joyce (Mikel) Newton; edn: BMus, Univ. of Texas, Austin 1975, MM, 1977; DMA, Univ. Cincinnati, 1981. Career: tchg. asst. Univ. of Texas, Austin 1975-77, Univ. Cinti. 1977-78; asst. prof. Valparaiso Univ., Ind. 1978-84; assoc. prof. CSU Stanislaus, Turlock, Ca. 1984-; music director Modesto Symphony Youth Orch., 1986-; guest conductor/clinician, worldwide 1984-; adjudicator (music) nat., 1978-; prin. trombone Austin Sym. Orch., Tx. 1973-77, trombone Modesto Sym. Orch., Ca. 1984-; awards: Meritorious Prof. CSU Stanislaus 1988, Outstanding Young Men of Am. 1990, listed Who's Who in Ent., in Entertainment, in the West; mem: Calif. Orch. Directors Assn. (pres. 1990-92), Am. Sym. Orch. League 1984-, Calif. Music Educators Assn. (bd. 1990-94), Am. Fedn. Musicians 1973-; civic: Turlock Arts Fund for Youth (pres. 1986-88), Internat. Friendship Com. City Modesto (subcom. 1989-91), Big Bros./Bis Sisters Modesto (vol.); contbr. articles in various publs., 1978-; rec: backpacking, reading, sailing, racquet sports.

KLEINSMITH, GENE DENNIS, artist, educator; b. Feb. 22, 1942, Madison, Wis.; children: Jon Darin b. 1968, Paul Damon b. 1969, Christin Dana b. 1972; edn: BA in art, Augustana Coll., Sioux Falls, S.D. 1963; grad. work Colo. State Univ., 1966; MFA, Univ. Minn., 1967; MA in art, No. Ariz. Univ., 1969; post-

grad. work Univ. Nev. 1968-71, UC Santa Barbara 1974, No. Ariz. Univ. 1984-85. Career: art instr. high schs. in Brookings, S.D. 1963-64, Ft. Collins, Colo. 1964-65, Needles, Calif. 1967-71; summer instr. Colo. State Univ., Ft. Collins 1966; faculty San Bdo. Valley Coll., eve. div. 1967-71; art dept. chmn., instr. design and painting Victor Valley Coll., 1971-, chmn. artist in residence programs VVC, 1973-; one-man shows: 1981: Apple Valley (Ca.), Yavapai Coll. (Prescott, Az.), Olive Tree Gal. (Ft. Collins, Colo.), No. Ariz. Univ. (Flagstaff), UC Riverside (Ca.), Univ. Minn. (Mankato), Univ. S.D. (Vermillion), 1983: High Desert Symphony (Victor Valley), 1984: Marcia Rodell Gal., L.A. Art of the Olympia, 1990: The Gallery at Victor Valley Coll.; participant numerous invitationals and juried exhibitions; numerous lectures and workshops internat.; presenter Nat. Council on Edn. for Art, Atlanta 1983, Nat. Council on Edn. for the Ceramic Arts, Boston 1984, Keynote speaker 1987; awards: Phi Delta Kappa 1969, Kappa Delta Pi 1969, commendn. Univ. Nev. 1972, Faculty fellow Victor Valley Coll. 1973, Italian Intl. Art Honorarium 1982, French and Greek Art Honorariums 1984, Identite Ceramique, Auxerre, France 1985, Fgn. Artist Abroad, City of Venice, Italy 1989, English and Norweigian grants, London, Bergen, Lillihammer, Oslo 1991, Victor Valley Coll. Educator of Year 1992, San Bdo. County Gold Medal of Excellence in tchg. 1992; mem. Am. Crafts Council, Calif. Art Assn., Calif. Art Council, L.A. County Art Mus., Nat. Council of Art Adminstrs., Nat. Council on Edn. for the Arts, Inst. for Ceramic History, Nat. Council on Edn. for the Ceramic Arts, Optomists Intl., Elks; civic: Christy Joy Nephritis Found. (chmn. 1972); author coll. textbooks: Earth, Fire, Air and Water 1971, Art and Context (1978, 2d edit. 1981, 3d edit. 1986), writer for Humanities TV Series "Search" 1975, articles in art jours. and mags.; rec: travel, swimming. Res: PO Box 9373 Spring Valley Lake Victorville 92392 Ofc: Victor Valley College 18422 Bear Valley Rd Victorville 92392-9699 Ph: 619/245-4271

KLINE, PAMELA IRIS, marketing consultant; b. Aug. 23, 1958, Pittsburgh, Pa.; s. Robert Edward and Rae (Marks) Kline; edn: cert. Univ. of Paris, Fr. 1979; BA, Harvard Coll., 1980; MBA, Harvard Bus. Sch., 1984. Career: mgr. AT&T, Phila. 1980-82; VISA, San Francisco 1983; v.p. Prognostics, Menlo Park 1984-91; dir. Diefenbach Elkins, S.F. 1991-93; principal Regis McKenna, Inc. 1992-; mem. Harvard Fundraising Gp. 1980- (chair Harvard Schs. & Scholarship, San Mateo 1984-), BRAVO 1992-; Republican; rec: scuba, aerobics, swimming, travel, reading. Res: 570 Beale St #416 San Francisco 94105

KLING, JOHN W., (SR.), company executive; b. Dec. 11, 1922, Maysville, Okla.; s. Ernest John and Mary (Cowan) K.; m. Lois Mildred Crownover, Sept. 8, 1944; children: John M., Tim S., Scott E., Mark P. (all 4 sons grad. Montebello High Sch.); in-laws: Marie and Gene Crownover of Llano, Calif., Marie Kearns, Downey, and Marlene Kasparoff, Huntington Beach; edn: grad. Montebello H.S., 1942; classified mil. studies (honors) Univ. Idaho, naval intelligence (Bainbridge Is., Wa.), and Tulane Univ., 1943-44. Career: owner/pres. P.K.B. Produce, Montebello 1945-50; asst. mgr. Safeway Markets, East Los Angeles 1950-60; owner/pres. J&M Fire Extinguisher Co., Montebello 1960-, opr./tnr. Fire Training Schs. for fire depts., city employees, churches, other orgns. 1960-; civic: sponsor local youth, police & fire depts., works with and encourages other cancer patients (11-yr. survivor); awards: Pioneer Business Owner City of Montebello 1991, listed Intl. Book of Hon., Am. Biog. Inst. Man of Yr., Intl. Who's Who of Intellectuals (Cambridge, Eng.), Intl. Biog. Roll of Hon., disting. leadership; mil: M.I. USN 1942-45, decorated 3 Presdl. citations, 52 Presdl. unit citations; Republican; Baptist; rec: building, fishing. Ofc: J&M Fire Extinguisher Co. 623 S Maple Ave Montebello 90640

KLINGE, JOHN EDGAR, investment banker; b. Mar. 1, 1956, Vallejo; s. Andy and Christine Nova (Pasley) K.; edn: BS acctg., summa cum laude, Golden Gate Univ. 1978; MBA, UCLA 1985; C.P.A. Calif. 1980. Career: mgr. Peat Marwick Mitchell & Co., San Francisco 1978-83; assoc. Bank of Am. Capital Markets 1983-85; v.p. investment banking Security Pacific Merchant Bank (now Bank of Am.), Los Angeles 1985-; honors: Beta Gamma Sigma, Golden Gate Acctg. Scholarship; mem: Am. Inst. CPA, UCLA Mgmt. Alumni Assn., Urban Land Inst.; rec: classic cars, golf, water skiing. Res: 1468 N Grand Oaks Ave Pasadena 91104 Ofc: Bank of America 333 S Hope St Ste 1100 Los Angeles 90071

KLINGENSMITH, ARTHUR PAUL, relocation and redevelopment consultant; b. May 23, 1949, Los Angeles; s. Paul A. and Hermine Elinore (Wacek) K.; edn: AA soc. sci., Indian Valley Jr. Coll. 1976; BA indsl. psych., San Francisco State Univ. 1979; MA indsl. psych., Columbia Pacific Univ. 1980; desig: senior right of way cand., Internat. Right of Way Assn. Career: USAF radio ops. instr., Biloxi, Miss. 1968-72, air traffic controller, Novato, Ca. 1972-74; right of way agent Calif. Dept. Transp., San Francisco 1978-85, sr. right of way agent, Sacto. 1985-87; relocation and redevel. cons., statewide Calif., 1984-, founder, v.p. Associated Right of Way Services Inc., 1989-92; tech. cons. computerization of Right of Way process, CalTrans; mem: Am. Arbitration Assn., Internat. Right of Way Assn. (course instr. 1980-), Marin Co. Bd. of Realtors, Nat. Assn. of Housing and Redevel. Officials (NAHRO), Inst. for Noetic Sciences, Am. Presidents Assn.; civic: Kentfield Med. Found. (bd. 1987-89) mil: s/sgt. US Air Force 1968-74, merit service award; Republican; Prot.; rec: auto. restoration, painting, study of Light; res: POB 1050 Novato 94948

KLIVANS, CRAIG LYLE, chiropractor; b. Nov. 20, 1955, Los Angeles; s. Harvey and Marcia Sue (Linker) K.; m. Janet Epstein, Nov. 30, 1985; children: Ross Eric b. 1988, Brett Andrew b. 1990; edn: BA, Hofstra Univ., 1978; BS, Pasadena Chiropractic Coll., 1983, DC 1983; Qualified Med. Examiner, Indep. Disability Evaluator, 1991. Career: assoc. Yerman Chiropractic Group 1983-84; clinician and instr. Pasadena Chiropractic Coll. 1984-85; owner, prin. Klivans Chiropractic Office 1985-; instr. Pasadena Chiropractic 1985-; appt. commr. Calif. State Bd. of Chiropractic Examiners, 1991; honors: Sigma Chi Psi 1983; mem: Am. Chiropractic Assn., Calif. Chiropractic Assn., Internat. Chiropractic Assn., San Fernando Valley Chiropractic Soc. (sec. 1989-90), Encino C.of C.; author, publ: Effects of Low Back Pain on American Business; Republican; Jewish; rec: Skiing, sailing, horseback riding. Ofc: Klivans Chiropractic 16100 Ventura Blvd Ste 9 Encino 91436

KLONER, MARC OWEN, computer software co. president; b. Sept. 23, 1946, Canton, Ohio; s. Simon and Mildred K.; m. Jane, Feb. 15, 1970; child: Megan b. 1983; edn: BE in aero. & astro. engring., Ohio St. Univ. 1968, MS, 1969. Career: assoc. engr. McDonnell Douglas, St. Louis, Mo. 1968; senior engr. Lockheed, Burbank 1969-72; systems analyst NASA Jet Propulsion Lab., La Canada 1972-79; founder/pres. KComp Systems Inc. (computer software co.), Glendale 1979-; rec: tennis. Res: 290 Kempton Rd Glendale 91203 Ofc: KComp Systems Inc 535 N Brand Blvd Ste 601 Glendale 91203

KMET, JOSEPH PAUL, pharmacist; b. Jan. 11, 1942, Chgo.; s. John Norman and Elizabeth Charlotte (Posh) K.; m. Rebecca Patterson, Mar. 29, 1969; edn: BS pharm., Univ. Ariz. 1971; MS nuclear pharmacy, USC 1973; MS computer sci., Corpus Christi St. Univ. 1984; reg. pharm. Calif., Ariz. Career: enlisted USN 1959-63, USNR 1963-75, staff pharmacist Wadsworth VA Hosp., Los Angeles 1973-75, commd. lt. comdr. Med. Service Corps USN 1975-: nuclear pharmacist Naval Regional Med. Center, San Diego 1975-82; asst. chief pharmacist, radiation safety ofcr. Naval Hosp., Corpus Christi, Tx. 1982-85, chief pharmacist 1985, chmn. Mgmt. Info. Sys. Com. 1983-85; hd. Mgmt. Info. Dept., Naval Medical Command, Mid-Atlantic Region, Norfolk, Va. 1985-89; pharmacist ofcr. Naval Hosp., Portsmouth, Va. 1989-90; pharmacist ofcr. Naval Hosp., N.A.S. Lemoore, Calif. 1990-93; pharmacist, Kaaweal Delta Hosp., Visalia, Calif. 1993-; awards: USPHS scholar, 1968-70; mem: Am. Soc. Hosp. Pharmacists 1968-, Soc. of Nuclear Medicine, Calif., So. Calif. Soc. Hosp. Pharmacists 1973-82; contbr. article in J. Nucl. Med., 1979; sci. exhib. Radiol. Soc. N. Am., Chgo. 11/81; mil: lt. cmdr. US Navy 1975-93; Republican; Episcopalian; rec: reading, bicycling, gardening. Ofc: Kaweah Delta Hospital Pharmacy, Visalia

KMET, REBECCA EUGENIA (PATTERSON), community volunteer, pharmacist; b. June 17, 1948, Ellisville, Miss.; d. Eugene Roberts and Ruth Winn (Pettis) Patterson; m. Joseph Kmet, March 29, 1969; edn: BS, Univ. of Ariz. 1971; MBA, National Univ. 1980; reg. pharmacist Calif., Ariz., Tex. Career: pharmacist Defender Star Community Pharmacy, Tucson, Ariz. 1971-72, Santa Monica Bldg. Profl. Pharmacy, Santa Monica 1972-73; US Veteran's Admin., Wadsworth VA Hosp., W. Los Angeles 1974-75; pharmacist Kaiser San Diego Med. Ctr., San Diego 1979-82; participant Current Strategy Forum, Naval War Coll., 1981; profl. continuing edn. instr.; honors: Presdl. achiev. Nat. Congl. Com. 1987, Rho Chi; mem: Marine Corps Historical Found., N.S.D.A.R., Great Bridge Chpt., Navy Historical Found., Wilson Assocs., U.S. English PAC, Kappa Epsilon; mil: Med. Service Corps USN 1975-78; pub. article "Is U.S. Military Power Weakened by Women in the Services?" Amphibious Warfare Rev., Summer 1988; Republican; Episcopalian; rec: reading, art needlework, writing. Res: 985 Murphy Dr Lemoore 93245

KNAPP, J. BURKE, international consultant; b. Jan. 25, 1913, Portland, Ore.; s. Joseph Burke and Cornelia Ann (Pinkham) K.; m. Hilary Eaves, April 5, 1939; m. Iris Hay Edie, Oct. 19, 1976; children: Louis b. 1942, Rosalind b. 1945, Elise b. 1954, Michael b. 1955; edn: AB in econs., Stanford Univ. 1933; BA in politics, philosophy and econs. (Rhodes Scholar), Oxford Univ., 1935, B.Litt, 1936, MA, 1939. Career: asst. to mng. dir. Brown Harriman & Co. Ltd., internat. inv. banking firm, London, Eng. 1936-40; with the Federal Reserve 1940-48, economist Internat. Sect., dir. Internat. Div. and spl. asst. to the Chmn., on leave with State Dept. as econ. adv. in occupied Ger. 1944-45; with U.S. State Dept. 1948-52, economic adv. to 1st U.S. Delegation to NATO in London, Eng. 1 yr., U.S. co-chmn. of Jt. Brazilian-U.S. Econ. Devel. Commn., Rio de Janeiro, Brazil 1 yr.; with the World Bank 1952-78: dir. ops. in Latin Am. 1952-56, v.p. in chg. worldwide lending ops. and chmn. loan com. 1956-72, senior v.p. for ops. and chmn. bd. dirs. in absence of the pres. 1972-78, ret. 1978; cons. to World Bank on policy matters, 1978-81; internat. cons. 1982-: sr. adv. Morgan Grenfell & Co., London, Eng. 1983-; honors: Order of Boyaca, 1980, Stanford Univ. disting. service, 1981, Order of Rising Sun, 1978, Rhodes Scholar Oxford Univ., 1933-36; mem: Wash. Drama Soc. (trustee, pres. 1953-65), Mt. Vernon Coll. (trustee, chmn. exec. com. 1966-72), Stanford Univ. Libraries (vis. com.), Metropolitan Club; Democrat; Prot.; rec: swimming, theatre. Res: 8 Arastradero Rd Portola Valley 94028

KNAUFT, MILFORD ROY, JR., water district director; b. Aug. 26, 1918, St. Paul, Minn.; s. Milford Roy and Marie Camille (Simonet) K.; m. Doris Louise Bovee, Jan. 18, 1946; children: Robert Lee b. 1946, Nancy Louise b. 1949, Sally

Ann b. 1954; edn: UCLA 1936-40. Career: co-owner, gen. mgr. Hollywood Wholesale Paper Corp., Hollywood 1938-61; dist. rep. Congressman Charles Wiggins, Fullerton 1975-79; Cong. Wm. Dannemeyer 1980; exec. dir. World Affairs Council of Orange Co., Santa Ana 1979-88; dir. Yorba Linda Water Dist. 1966-, Metropolitan Water Dist., L.A. 1979-; awards: Golden Bear and Silver Beaver BSA 1979, 81; civic: Orange Co. BSA (past pres.), So. Calif. Coll. Optometry (bd. dirs.), Placentia Comm. Hosp. (bd. dirs.), World Affairs Council Orange Co. (bd. dirs.), Rotary Intl. Yorba Linda (Paul Harris Fellow 1983); mil: lt. US Army Air Corps 1943-46, decorated D.F.C. and Air Medal, 1945; Republican; Presbyterian. Res: 5765 Sunmist Ln Yorba Linda 92686

KNEISEL, CHRISTOPHER DWIGHT, teacher; b. Jan. 31, 1956, Burbank; s. William George and Joyce Rosemary (Fainot) K.; m. Josephine Bernadette Vasari, June 30, 1984; dau., Elizabeth Anna-Maria b. 1991; edn: AA, L.A. Valley Coll. 1977; BA, CSU Los Angeles, 1980, music credential, 1982, grad. studies CSU, 1987, 1991-. Career: instrumental music tchr. Hollenbeck Jr. H.S., L.A. 1982-85; Don Benito, Madison & Linda Vista Elem. Schs., Pasadena 1985-87; tchr. Don Benito Fundamental Sch. 1987-; participant Path to Math., UCLA, 1988-90; mem. Music Educators Nat. Conf. L.A. 1986; honors: Sigma Alpha Phi music scholar 1976, Burbank Womens Chorus music scholar 1974, CSU music scholar, outstanding service award CSULA, CSULA Newman Club (pres. 1981); founding bd. mem. Burbank Chamber Orchestra 1991-; mem: Burbank Chamber Orchestra (cellist), West Los Angeles Symphony (cellist), Phi Alpha Theta history frat., Eta Xi chpt. CSULA 1992-; mem: United Tchrs. of Pasadena (former dir. area 8), Calif. Tchrs. Assn., Nat. Space Soc., Burbank Symphony (cellist), Pasadena Community Orch. (cellist); former mem.: Burbank Symphony Assn., So. Calif. Sch. Band & Orchestra Assn. (mgr. hon. orch. 1983), L.A. Music Tchrs. Assn.; Republican; R.Cath. (usher), mem. Confraternity of the Most Holy Rosary; rec: cello, history, model railroads, hiking, writing. Res: 1920 N Niagara St Burbank 91505 Ofc: Don Benito Fundamental School 3700 Denair St Pasadena 91107

KNIGHT, JESSIE J., JR., association executive; b. Oct. 27, 1950, Springfield, Mo.; s. Jessie J., Sr. and Doris Marie (Hanks) K.; m. B. Camille Williams M.D., Aug. 19, 1978; child: Jessica b. 1980; edn: BA psych., St. Louis Univ., 1973; S.L.U. fellowship Univ. of Madrid, Spain 1972; MBA in mktg., Univ. Wis., Madison 1975; U.S. mem. British-Am. Project for the Successor Generation (lifetime), Johns Hopkins/ Royal Inst. of Internat. Affairs 1990. Career: mktg. mgr. Cervecuria Hondurena, div. Castle & Cooke Foods, San Pedro Sula, Honduras, Central Am. 1975-77; sales plng. mgr. Bumble Bee Seafoods, Castle & Cooke Foods, San Francisco 1974-77; mktg. plng. mgr., group product mgr. Dole Pineapple, Castle & Cooke Foods, S.F. 1979-81; dir. new bus. devel. Castle & Cooke Foods, 1981-83; dir. U.S. and Canadian mktg. Dole Food Co., Castle & Cooke, S.F. 1983-85; v.p. mktg. and corp. ofcr. San Francisco Chronicle, San Francisco Examiner, 1985-92; senior v.p. San Francisco Chamber of Comemrce, 1992-; instr., cons. American Press Inst., Reston, Va. 1988; awards: CLIO awards for ad excellence (1986, 87), Golden Lion, Cannes Film Fest., Fr. 1986, best of show advt. Internat. Newspaper Mktg. Assn., Toronto (1987, 1991), Eleanor Roosevelt Humanitarian Award of UN Assn. 1991; bd. trustees Golden Gate Univ.; bd. Wis. Bus. Alumni, Univ. Wis. Sch. of Bus.; mem. World Affairs Council S.F. (trustee 1986-, v.chmn. exec. com.), Council on Fgn. Rels. (N.Y.), S.F. Com. on Fgn. Affairs, Internat. Visitors Ctr., St. Francis Found., The Asia Found. Ctr. for Asian & Pacific Affairs; clubs: Olympic, The City; Republican (Nat. Com.'s Pres.'s Club); R.Cath.; rec: classical guitar. Ofc: San Francisco Chamber of Commerce 465 California St San Francisco 94104

KNIGHT, VIRGINIA FRANCES, writer, former first lady of California; b. Oct. 12, 1918, Fort Dodge, Iowa; d. Lawrence Frederick and Emma Julia (Miller) Piergue: stepfather: 1923-, E. B. Hershberger, advt. exec. Internat. Harvester Co.; 2 bros: Ralph Gotch Piergue (dec. 1982), Richard B. Hershberger, atty.; mother wrote ofcl. welcome song for 1932 LA Olympic Games; m. C. Lyle Carlson (lt. 15th AF, killed in action WWII 1944), June 28, 1940; m. 2d. Goodwin Jess Knight, Aug. 2, 1954 (Superior Ct. judge 1935-46, lt. gov. Calif. 1946-53, gov. Calif. 1953-59); grad. Los Angeles H.S. 1937. Career: fashion model, Warner Bros. theatres, radio 1937-42; pioneer TV pgms. KHJ, Don Lee Network 1937; Douglas Aircraft 'accomodation sales & emergency procurement/ civic and vets rehabilitation work/ entertainment pgms. for vets. hosps., "Victory House" Pershing Sq./active war bond drives, WWII; assoc. producer, participant TV Tele-Forum and Freedom Forum, 1947-54; First Lady of Calif. 1954-58, ofcl. hostess Nat. Republican Conv., S.F. 1956, planted Virginia Knight Camellia Capitol Park 1958, estab. collection of portraits of Calif. First Ladies for Gov.'s Mansion forseeing it would become a museum; current owner/opr. Elephant-Eagle Gold Mines, Mojave; honors: nat. cit. for sale of war bonds 1941-46, Nat. Viola Queen, Mil. Order of the Purple Heart 1954-55, Dr. in Metaphysics, St. Andrews Ecumen. Coll., London 1955, Hon. Poet Laureate State of Del. 1955, Outstanding Woman of Calif. press award 1956, Ten Best Dressed Women list So. Calif. Fashion Council 1959, fellow (poetry) Am. Inst. of Fine Arts 1969, life mem. Internat. Clover Poetry Assn., Soc. of Literary Designates, Wash DC 1970, Dame Commander, Order of the Crown of Thorns, San Luigi "Disting. Humanitarian" 1977, listed World Who's Who of Women (1989, 90, 91, 92, 93), Ctf. Appreciation, City of Hope Med. Ctr. 1991, Golden State Award 1992,

Comdr. Club "Silver Ldr." D.A.V. 1991-93; mem: Am. Legion Aux. (past pres.), VFW Aux. (hon), Edwin Markham Poetry Soc., Internat. Soc. Poets, Repulican Nat. Com. 1993; civic: founder The Music Center Building Fund Com., Soc. of Arts & Letters (nat. advy. council 1956-58), Ettie Lee Homes for Youth (nat. advy. com.), Stanford Univ. Libraries, Navy League (life mem.); author: The Golden Heritage of Goodwin Knight 1975, series of oral hist. interviews Bancroft Library, UCB 1977-80, mss. Reflections on Life with Goodwin J. Knight; "Virginia Knight California's First Lady, 1954-58," The Bancroft lib. UCB 1987; World of Poetry Golden Globe Award for "A Tribute to the Unknown Soldier" dedicated to Gen. Douglas MacArthur 1988, "Caressing Rain" 1989, "Words" 1989, Who's Who In Poetry 1989; Republican; rec: writing verse, tennis, swim. Res: 540 S Arden Blvd Los Angeles 90020

KNIGHT, WILLIAM J., State Assemblyman; b. Nov. 18, 1929, Noblesville, Ind.; s. William Thomas and Mary Emma (Illyes) K.; m. Gail A. Johnson, Sept. 3, 1983; edn: attended Butler Univ., Ind., Purdue Univ., Ind.; received Commission through Aviation Cadet Program. Career: USAF combat service, 253 missions, So. Vietnam; dir. USAF Fighter Attack Sys. program office, Aeronautical Sys. Div., Wright-Patterson AFB, Ohio; vice comdr. USAF Flight Test Ctr, AF Sys. Command, Edwards AFB; tech. adv. TV show, Call to Glory; councilman City of Palmdale, Calif.; mayor, City of Palmdale; Calif. State Assemblyman, elected 1992; mem. AF Sys. Command Primus Club 1988; chmn. AF Flight Test Hist. Found.; fellow, Soc. of Experimental Test Pilots; assoc. fellow, AM. Inst. of Aeronautics & Astronautics; awards: Allison Jet Trophy Race, Nat. Air Show, Dayton, Oh. 1954; Harmon Internat. Aviator's Trophy, Pres. Lyndon B. Johnson 1968; Octave Chanute Award, Inst. of Aeronautical Sciences; Nat. Aviation Hall of Fame, Dayton, Oh. 1988; Mil. honors: Disting. Flying Cross with two Oak Leaf Clusters; AF Medal with ten Oak Leaf Clusters; Legion of Merit with two Oak Leaf Clusters; mil: col., USAF; Republican; Lutheran. Ofc: State Capitol Sacramento 95814

KNORR, THEODORE HARRY, marketing consultant, editor, publisher; b. March 31, 1935, Toledo, Ohio; s. Harold T. and Eleanor (Worden) K.; m. Donna Lee Glosup, Nov. 6, 1971; children: Susan b. 1958, Sandra b. 1959, Stephen b. 1961, Stewart b. 1964; edn: BA, Univ. of Toledo 1959; grad. studies USC 1964-65, CSU Fullerton 1978, 89; var. courses Orange Coast Coll. 1972-89. Career: printer Kahl Bros., Toledo 1951-57; sr. copywriter Toledo Scale 1957-59; copy contact J.J. Dugan Agy., Mich. 1959-63; advtg. mgr. Avery Label Co., Monrovia, Calif. 1963-65; acct. exec. Barnes Chase Advtg., Santa Ana 1965-69; owner, CASA Advtg., Orange 1970-82; mktg. dir. Ad Com/West Coast, Shrieveport, La. 1982-84; mktg. dir. J.P. Kapp & Assoc., Tustin 1984-86; owner CORE Organization Costa Mesa, 1986-; editor/pub. Today's Old West Traveler, 1989-; awards: honorary life mem. Orange Co. Ad Club, 1979, Linda Blum Award Costa Mesa Civic Playhouse, 1980, 32 various creative awards for advtg. O.C. Ad Club, 1972-82, Nat. Addy award Nat. Ad Fed., 1978, Creative Awards from Western States Advtg. Assn., 1981; mem: Bus./Devel. Assoc. of Orange Co. (pres. 1986-87), O.C. Ad Federation (pres. 1975-77), Comml. Indsl. Devel. Assn.; mem. Costa Mesa Civic Playhouse 1965-; author: bldg. industry articles, 1984; sporting goods msdg. articles, 1986, western non-fict. articles, 1989-91; mil: priv. 1st class, U.S. Army, 1956-57; Independent; rec: dude ranches, western heritage, racquetball, walking. Res: 2614A Columbine Ave Santa Ana 92704 Ofc: Today's Old West Traveler, 2796 Harbor Blvd Ste 410 Costa Mesa 92626

KOBLIN, DONALD DARYL, anesthesiologist, educator; b. Sept. 1, 1949, Chgo.; s. Alvin and Vera K.; edn: BS, UCLA, 1971; PhD, UC Santa Cruz, 1975; MD, Univ. Miami, 1983; residency in anesthesia, Penn State Univ., Hershey, Pa. 1983-86; bd. certified 1987. Career: postdoctoral fellow Caltech, Pasadena 1975-76; research chemist UC San Francisco, 1976-81, asst. prof. 1986-88, assoc. prof. 1988-; honors: Phi Beta Kappa 1971; mem. AMA, ASA, IARS. Ofc: Veterans Administration Hospital, Anesthesiology Service (129), 4150 Clement St San Francisco 94121

KOEHLER, CRAIG CURTIS, chiropractic doctor; b. Sept. 12, 1960 Fresno, Calif.; s. August and Rita Mae (Sherman) Koehler; edn: AA, Fresno Comm. Coll. 1981; DC, L.A. Coll. of Chiropractic 1986, BS 1986; career: internship, Helzer Chiropractic, Bellflower, Calif. 1984-86; internship, L.A. Coll. of Chiropractic, Wittier, Calif. 1986; doctor on staff, Advanced Chiropractic, Huntington Beach, Calif. 1987-88; doctor on staff, Chiropractic Med. Ctr., Westminster, Calif. 1989-91; owner/clinic dir., Koehler Chiropractic, Huntington Beach, Calif. 1992-; instr./cons. Chiropractic Asst. Assoc., Anaheim 1985, L.A. Coll. of Chiropractic 1986, Family Fitness Ctr., Huntington Beach 1987-90, Sports Chalet, Huntington Beach 1988-89; team doctor, Oakland Ballet Co. 1988, Long Beach Ballet Co. 1989; awards: chmn. annual auction, Westminster Chamber, Westminster, Calif. 1990; humorous toastmaster, Toastmasters Internat., Santa Ana 1991; advanced presentation skills, The Cleve. Inst., San Diego 1991; mem: Orange County Chiropractic Assn. 1987-92; Council on Roentgenology 1987; Back School Adminstrn. 1986-87; Calif. Chiropractic Assn. 1988-91; civic: Westminster C. of C. 1990-92; author: publ. articles in Westminster Business Digest 1991; host, prod., writer, t.v. program Focus On Health 1988-91; rec: golf, skiing. Ofc: Koehler Chiropractic 5891 Warner Ave. Huntington Beach 92649

KOENIG, MARIE HARRIET, public relations and fundraising professional; b. Feb. 19, 1919, New Orleans, La.; d. Harold Paul and Sadie Louise (Bole) King; m. Walter William Koenig, June 24, 1956; children: Margaret Marie b. 1957, Susan Patricia b. 1957; edn: La. State Univ. Sch. of Music 1937-39; pre-law Loyola Univ. of S. New Orleans 1942-43; BS history, Univ. LaVerne, 1985. Career: secty. to the state atty. gen. of La., New Orleans 1940-44; contract writer in legal dept. Metro-Goldwyn-Mayer Studios, Culver City 1944-46; legal asst. in law firms, 1946-50; contbns. dept. mgr. of nonprofit group, also sec. asst. treas. of Found. for Soc. Res. (pub. soc. sci. books), and the Found. for Independence, L.A., 1950-56; res. supr. devel. dept. CalTech, Pasadena 1969-70; adv. fin. planning asst. Incentive Res.Corp., L.A. 1970-78; dir. comms., contbns. and pub. rels., IRC, 1978-79; fundraising cons., prin. Res. Cons. Assocs., Pasa. 1979-82; dir. devel. Republican Party of L.A. Co., 1990-92; awards: Proclamation U.S. Hse. of Reps., certs. from Eisenhower-Nixon Nat. Cpgn., Rep. Nat. Com., Calif. State Assembly; mem: Gr. L.A. Press Club, Publicity Club L.A., Women in Comms. Inc., Am. Acad. Pol. and Soc. Scientists; civic: Freedoms Found. at Valley Forge (charter mem. L.A. chapt., coms., mem. Advy. Coun. 21 yrs.), Americans for Free China, Am. Bur. for Med. Aid to (Free) China (chair Altadena unit), Com. to Conserve Chinese Culture (charter, 1st recording sec.), Council Against Communist Aggression (charter), Nat. Trust for Hist. Preserv., Friends of the Nat. Parks at Gettysburg, Town Hall of Calif., L.A. World Affairs Council, Pacific Clinics for abused children (past devel. com.), Pasa. Opera Guild (publicity chair 2t, life Pasa. Area Opera Trust), Masquers Club, Friends of Huntington Library, L.A. Co. Mus. Art, Gene Autry Mus. We. Heritage (charter), Nat. Mus. of Women in the Arts (charter), Pasa. Arts Council (past bd. dirs.), Colonial Williamsburg (Hon. citizen); Republican (active campaigner; Poulson for Mayor L.A., Eisenhower-Nixon, Goldwater for Pres., att. 1964 conv. S.F., mem. Rep. Nat. Com., Nat. Fedn. Rep. Women 1956-, East Pasa. Rep. Women, charter Pasa. Rep. Women Fed., founder Altadena Unit #1 United Republicans of Calif., was mem. YR Club L.A., Bel Air Rep. Women); author: While Treason Flourished Over Us (lecture series), Does the Nat. Council Speak for You?; Prot.; rec: res., history, opera. Res: 205 Madeline Dr Pasadena 91105

KOHNKE, JAMES IRVING, commercial printing co. executive; b. May 31, 1966, San Mateo; s. David John and Loraine (Govier) K.; m. Cathy Sue Lingenfelder; edn: BS bus. adminstrn., fin. and mktg., USC 1988. Career: v.p., treas. Kohnke Printing Co. Inc., San Francisco 1988-; mem: Nat. Assn. Printers & Lithographers (certified graphic arts exec. 1991), Craftsman Club-Litho. Club San Francisco, Alpha Kappa Psi, Olympic Club S.F., San Mateo Elks; Republican; R.Cath.; rec: scuba diving, automobiles, mountain biking, photography. Ofc: Kohnke Printing 375 Fremont St San Francisco 94105

KOKESH, MICHAEL O., corporate lawyer; b. Jan. 27, 1951, Deadwood, S.Dak.; s. Charles Henry and Lyndall Ela Ray (Renfro) K.; m. Sandra Stockton, Sept. 11, 1982; children: Alexandra Jeanne b. 1986, Ashley Bliss b. 1989; edn: BA, BS, Univ. Colo. 1974; JD, UC Hastings Coll. 1979; admitted St. Bar Calif. 1979. Career: bd. mkt. analyst Bank of Am. Capital Markets Group, San Francisco 1974-76; tax cons., internat. tax planning Coopers & Lybrand 1979-82; Tech. Funding Inc. 1978; legal counsel Hassard Bonnington Rogers & Huber 1982-87; ptnr. Hancock, Rothert & Bunshoft, 1987-89; ptnr. Bronson, Bronson & McKinnon, 1989-91; v.p., gen. counsel, corporate secty. and dir. Nat. Reproductive Medical Centers Inc., 1991-; dir: Sundance Minerals Corp.; trustee: Hoppin Found., Culver Education Found., St. Helena Hosp. Found., Pacific Biomedical Res. Inc., Nat. Fertility Inst. Ltd., Pacific Fertility Medical Centers of Calif. Inc.; awards: SAR Leadership Scholar 1969, Phi Alpha Delta, Phi Delta Phi; mem: St. Bar Calif., Bar Assn. San Francisco, Am. Bar Assn.; clubs: Univ. (SF), Metropolitan (SF), St. Francis Yacht (spl. racing mem.); Republican; R.Cath.; rec: sailing, squash, philately. Address: San Francisco 94127

KOKSHANIAN, ARTINE, physician-otolaryngologist; b. Oct. 29, 1936,Aleppo, Syria, naturalized 1981; s. Hagop and Hripsime (Aghayan) K.; m. Billie Jo Olson; children: Ara Arthur b. Feb. 10, 1989, Rita Hripsime b. Mar. 25, 1990, Alex Artin b. Feb. 5, 1992; edn: dipl. Melkonian Edn. Inst., Cyprus 1956; BS, Am. Univ. of Beirut, 1960, MD, 1965; ENT splty. tng. in Baltimore and Toronto; Fellow Am. Coll. of Otolaryngology 1976. Career: residency and fellowship Univ. of Toronto, Can.; chief of otolaryngology Service VA Hosp., Columbia, S.C. 1974-76; pvt. practice physician, ear, nose and throat splst., head and neck surgeon, Glendale, Calif. 1976-; tchg. staff White Memorial Medical Ctr., Los Angeles 1977-; named Teacher of Yr. White Memorial Otolaryngology Found. 1984; mem: Am. Acad. of Otol., L.A. Soc. of Otol., L.A. Co. Med. Assn., Calif. Med. Assn.; Glendale Masonic Lodge; publs: res. papers related to noise and Ototoxic drugs, their effect on human inner ear and hearing; Armenian Apostolic Ch.; rec: music, painting, tennis, skiing. Res: 832 Moorside Dr Glendale 91207 Ofc: Artine Kokshanian M.D. Inc. 1030 S Glendale Ave Ste 506 Glendale 91205

KOLSTOE, GARY MARTIN, computer programmer; b. Oct. 1, 1946, Valley City, N.Dak.; s. Martin Gerhard and Juliana (Jordan) K.; m. Brit Helgesen, Mar. 16, 1968; children: Svein Erik, Anita Yevonne; edn: BA math., Univ. Oregon, Eugene 1969, MA in computer sci., 1973. Career: sr. sys. pgmr. Singer Bus. Mach., San Leandro 1973-76; project mgr. Basic Four Corp., Burlingame 1976-

77; staff pgmr. Memorex, Santa Clara 1977-80; mgr. micro diagnostics Two Pi Corp., Santa Clara 1980-82; mgr. diagnostics Tolerant Transactions, Santa Clara 1982-83; technical staff Cygnet Comms., Santa Clara 1983-84; cons. Telos Consulting, Santa Clara 1984-. Ofc: Telos Consulting, 3333 Bowers Ave Ste 151 Santa Clara 95054

KOLTAI, STEPHEN M., economist, consulting engineer; b. Nov. 5, 1922, Ujpest, Hungary, nat. US cit.; s. Maximilian and Elisabeth (Rado) K.; m. Franciska Gabor, Sept. 14, 1948; children: Eva b. 1951, Susanne b. 1955; edn: M. Engring., Tech. Inst. of Budapest 1948; MBA econs., Univ. of Budapest 1955. Career: engring. cons., var. European countries, 1948-58; economic adviser/secty. Fgn. Diplomatic Service 1958-62; engring. exec. in Switzerland 1963-76; cons. engr./ pres. Pan Business Consulting Corp., Palm Springs 1977-; patentee inventions in computer & printing process; charter mem. Republican Presdl. Task Force; rec: tennis, golf.

KOLTUNOV, SAMSON I., orthopedist-traumatologist; b. Mar. 31, 1923, Zaporozye, USSR; s. Isaak Mark Koltunov and Eugenia Sam. (Zuravitskaya) Koltunova; m. Anna A. Mints MD, Aug. 16, 1947; 1 d., Marinas Levitan b. 1954; edn: H.S. Certif., Zaporozye, USSR, 1940; MD, Medical Institute, Moscow & Lvov, 1948; PhD , Medinstitut, Lvov, 1959; Docent/Assoc. Prof., Medinstitute, Lvov, 1969. Career: Dept. Chief, Traumatology & Orthopedics, State Medical Inst. Training Hosp., Lvov 1948-81, Chief Traumatologist & Orthopedist, City of Lvov 1955-80, Assoc. Prof./Docent, Institut Physical Health, Lvov 1968-78, Med. research, Mobile Cardio-Vascular Service, Inc., L.A. 1982-84, Pres., Functional Health Diagnostic, L.A., 1984-; author: 42 pub. sci. works, 4 in Natl. Lib. of Medicine; mil: maj. Soviet Army Med. Svc.. 1941-45; Republican. Res: 642 West Knoll Dr # 204. Los Angeles 90069 Ofc: Function Health Diagnostic, 642 West Knoll Dr., S-204, Los Angeles 90069

KOMAI, DALE S., multimedia technology publicist, consultant; b. Aug. 19, 1952, Santa Monica; s. Hiroshi and Lillie Y. (Yamato) K.; edn: BS in bus. adm., USC 1974. Career: field examiner Federal Home Loan Bank Board, San Francisco 1974-80; owner/photographer Timely Photo, San Diego 1980-84; business cons. Transcontinental Foods, Inc. Escondido 1983-84; field examiner Federal Home Loan Bank Bd., San Francisco 1984-85, tng. instr. new examiners, field mgr., 1985-88, FHLB S.F. sr. program devel. analyst 1988-89; MIS analyst US Treasury Dept. 1989-91; computer consultant, tnr., 1991-; multimedia trade show coordinator, 1991; honors: bowling trophy USC (1971), Dean's List (1973, 74), merit awards FHLBB 1985, FHLB S.F. 1987, profiled in FHLB's Record Copy newsletter 1988, 2d pl. monologue competition Internat. Platform Assn. Conv. 1990; participant & newsletter staff writer 1988-89, Amer. Dance Friendship Tour to Finland, Soviet Union, 1988; ed. and contbg. writer, IICS Chapter Notes, 1991-; mem: Internat. Interactive Communications Soc., Bay Area Country Dance Soc., Internat. Platform Assn.; Calif. Hist. Soc., Ctr. for Citizen Initiatives; photographer contbr. Jugglers World mag. (1982, 86), San Diego Union newspaper 1982, Access to Learning newspaper (cover 1982), Daily Trojan newspaper 1973; Rel. Sci.; rec: x-c skiing, dancing, singing, computers, fgn. languages. Address: 39120 Argonaut Way #392 Fremont 94538

KOMATSU, S. RICHARD, architect; b. May 5, 1916, San Francisco; s. Denzo and Tome (Fujimoto) K.; m. Chisato Frances Kuwata, Aug. 6, 1943; children: Richard b. 1946, Kathryn Kay b. 1949; edn: BA, UC Berkeley, 1938; cert. in Interior Design, 1939, cert. in Machine Design, 1944, reg. architect, Calif., NCARB, 1951. Career: landscape planner Golden Gate Internat. Exposition, San Francisco, 1938-39; designer, architect Charles F. Strothoff, S.F. 1939-42, 1946-52; asst. project engr. Federal Public Housing Authority, Detroit, Mich. 1943-44; designer Harley, Ellington & Day 1944; architect asso. Donald L. Hardison & Assocs., Richmond, Calif. 1952-57; prin., secty. Hardison & Komatsu Assocs., San Francisco 1957-79; pres., prin. Hardison Komatsu Ivelich & Tucker, S.F. 1979-88, cons. 1988-; architect: 47 water treatment plants and related facilities for East Bay Municipal Utility Dist. 1964-84, 24 water treatment plants and related facilities for Contra Costa Water Dist. 1967-88, main ofc. complex Turlock Irrigation Dist. 1988, pre-design of 6 water reclamation plants, 3 pumping plants and 1 dechlorination facility for the Clean Water Pgm. for Gr. San Diego 1990-92; design advr.: admin., ops. & lab. bldg. Santa Rosa Wastewater Treatment Plant, admin. bldg. Dublin San Ramon Svs. Dis., plant op. ctr. Delta Diablo Sanitation Dist. 1991-92; vis. archtl. advr. Cogswell Coll., S.F. 1981-82; appt. City of El Cerrito design review bd. 1969-78, chmn. 1973-77, planning commn. 1962-75, chmn. 1966-67, var. municipal coms. El Cerrito, and Richmond; numerous design awards incl. AIA award for East Bay Municipal Util. Dist. 1974 and Gov's. Award 1966, Concord City Award 1972, Southeast Water Pollution Control Plant Gold Nugget Award, S.F. 1984, Fairfield-Suisun Waste Water Mgmt. Plant, Cons. Engrs. Assn. of Calif., Fairfield 1978, AIA award for Student Ctr. Complex UC Berkeley 1978, Fellow AIA 1984, Silver Pin achiev. award Nat. Japanese Am. Citizens League, S.F. 1966; invited speaker nat. confs. Nat. Assn. of Home Builders Nat. Conv., Chgo. 1966, Am. Water Works Assn., Newport Beach 1967, S.F. 1970, 72, San Diego 1971, ASCE, Calif./Nev. Water Pollution Control Assn., Lake Tahoe 1972; mem: Am. Inst. of Architects (bd. dirs. 1968-69, chair num. coms.), Am. Water Works Assn., Japanese Am. Citizens League Contra Costa (pres. 1957, dir. 1956-60), Kiwanis

Club S.F. (v.p. 1983, dir. 1984-86), Richmond Art Center (dir. 1956-60), Richmond Ballet Co. (dir. 1956-60); publs: 3 articles on arch. design of water and wastewater fac. 1968, 70, 73; mil: master sergeant U.S. Army, 1944-46; Republican; Presbyterian; rec: watercolor artist, architectural delineator, golf. Res: 1323 Devonshire Dr El Cerrito 94530

KONO, NORM N., insurance executive; b. May 13, 1938, New York; s. Heitaro and Nellie N. (Tanabe) K.; m. Carol A., Nov. 25, 1967; children: Keli Kariko b. 1969, Kevin Shaw b. 1971; edn: BS bus. adminstrn., Roosevelt Univ. 1960. Career: underwriter Bankers Life & Casualty, Chgo., Ill. 1958-60; reinsurance underwriter CNA 1960-68; v.p., dir. Am. Pacific Life & Comml. Bankers Life, Irvine 1968-75; pres. Wespac Life, Tustin 1975-78; sr. v.p. S.C.O.R. Life, Dallas, Tx. 1978-81, Hudson R.E. Life, Sarasota, Fla. 1981-82; pres. Hawaii Underwriters Life Assn., Honolulu 1969-70; mem: Greater Irvine Lions (charter), Hawaii Kai Lions; mil: SP-4 AUS 1962-64; Republican. Res: 1052-C Walnut St Tustin 92680 Ofc: Beech Street Inc. 2 Ada St Irvine 92718

KONSTIN, CONSTANTINE, restaurateur; b. May 21, 1931, Agrinion, Greece; nat. 153; s. Christos and Anastasia (Emirzas) Konstantinidis; m. Sydna Pantoja, Feb. 25, 1955; children: Constantine, Jr. b. 1956, Sydna Christina b. 1959, Ann b. 1961, John b. 1963. Career: restaurateur John's Grill Restaurant, San Francisco 1974-; recipient Key of New Orleans, 1972, Dashiell Hammett Soc. Award, 1978, Proclamation from Sen. Milton Marks, 1981; mem: San Francisco C.of C. 1980-, Dashiell Hammett Soc. (1976-, researcher), Market Street Devel. Proj., S.F. 1980-, AHEPA 1963; fund raiser for San Francisco polit. candidates; Catholic; rec: swimming, golf, fishing. Res: 1306 Portola Dr San Francisco 94127 Ofc: John's Grill, 63 Ellis St San Francisco 94102

KONWIN, THOR W., business executive, real estate developer; b. Aug. 17, 1943, Berwyn, Ill.; s. Frank and Alice S. (Johnson) K.; m. Carol Svitak, Aug. 4, 1967 (div. 1990); 1 son, Christopher b. 1970; edn: AA, Morton Jr. Coll. 1966; BS, Northern Ill. Univ. 1967; MS, Roosevelt Univ. 1971; Career: cost acct. Sunbeam Appliance Co., Chgo. 1968-71, asst. controller 1975-78, controller 1978-81; controller General Molded Products div. Sunbeam Corp., Des Plaines, Ill. 1971-75; c.f.o. Bear Medical Systems Inc., Riverside, Calif. 1981-84 (designed & developed high tech. bldg. for Bear Medical Corp. corp. hq.); structered LBO acquisition from 3M Co., co-founder, cfo, v.p./fin. Bird Products Corp., Palm Springs 1984-; founder, mng. ptnr. TUCKO Rental, Ltd., commercial equip. leasing co., 1985-; co-founder, pres. B&B Ventures Ltd., commercial R.E. devel., 1987-, devel. Fairmont Office Plaza, Riverside; coo BP Holding Inc. 1987-90, acquired W. Stackhouse Assocs. Inc. (laser surgery co.) 1988; exec. v.p. Bird Medical Technologies, 1990-; founder and ceo Equilink Inc. 1990, commercial R.E. devel.; founder and ceo Med One Financial Group 1991, commercial equip. leasing co.; acquired Life Design Systems Inc. (respiratory disposable co.) 1991; designed & devel. high tech. bldg. for Bird Med. Technologies corp. hq., 1991; mil: E-4 US Army 1969-71; rec: buy and sell antiques; res: 68-882 Calle Mula Cathedral City 92234; ofc: Bird Corporation, 3101 E Alejo Rd Palm Springs 92263

KOPLEY, MARGOT B., psychologist; b. Boston, Mass.; d. Edwin S. and Irene J. Kopley; edn: BA, Univ. Rochester 1974; MS, Univ. Miami 1976; MS, Pace Univ. 1982, Psy.D., 1983; lic. psychologist N.Y. 1984, Calif. 1985; cert. sch. psychologist, Calif. 1984, N.Y. 1985. Career: grad. fellowship Mailman Center, Miami, Fla. 1975-76; psychol. intern White Plains Public Schs., 1980-81; psychol. extern Childrens Village, Dobbs Ferry, N.Y. 1981-82; psychol. intern Bergen Pines Co. Hosp., Paramus, N.J. 1982-83; psychologist Ladson Coastal Center, S.C. 1977-78; Putnam Assn. for Retarded Citizens, N.Y. 1979-80; psychologist/clin. dir. Greystone House Inc., Poughkeepsie 1981-84; sch. psychol. Bd. of Cooperative Edn., Valhalla 1983-84; pvt. practice, cons., therapist, Westchester 1980-84; pvt. practice psychologist, North San Diego Co., Calif. 1984-; vol. therapist Parents/ Daughter's/ Son's United, North Coastal Chpt. 1985-87; adj. faculty Nat. Univ., San Diego 1987; recipient appreciation awards San Diego Comm. Child Abuse Council 1986-87, S.D. Dept. Social Svcs. (1985, 86, 87, 88) and North County Assn. Retarded Citizens 1984, listed Nat. Register Health Svc. Providers Psychol.; mem: Am. Bd. of Med. Psychotherapists (Diplomate, Fellow), Am. Psychol. Assn., Nat. Assn. Sch. Psychologists, Calif. State Psychol. Assn. (bd. 1990), San Diego Psychol. Assn. (legis. com. 1988-91, 93, chair 1989-90, women's com. 1988-90), Soc. of Mental Health Profls. (pres. 1985-86), San Diego Com. Child Abuse Coordinating Council (bd., co-chair res. com. 1986-88), North Co. Child Abuse Coalition (case rev. com. 1987-90), Volunteers in Probation Inc. (mem., bd. mem. 1986-87); paper: Eval. of Effects of Residential Placement Upon Psychosocial Competence and Self-Esteem, CASP/NASP 1985, Women: Surviving the Unspoken Tragedies (newsletter, Acad. of S.D. Psychologists 1989); rec: sailing. Ofc: 2003 El Camino Real Ste 202 Oceanside 92054 also: PO Box 230336, 220 Second St Encinitas 92023-0336

KOPP, DAVID JAMES, corporate controller; b. Apr. 19, 1943, San Francisco; s. Alvin J. and Lorraine (Perry) K.; children: Anthony b. 1968, Randall b. 1970; edn: BS, Univ. San Francisco, 1964; MBA, Golden Gate Univ., 1968; C.P.A., Calif. 1968. Career: staff U.S. Gen. Accounting Office, NY, NY 1965-66; ptnr. Pannell, Kerr, Forster & Co., San Francisco 1966-80; fin. and ops. cons. for the hospitality industry/prin. The Kopp Group, 1980-, secty. treas. Internat. Innkeepers Inc., South Laguna 1981-88; secty. treas. Rossi Hotels, 1989-92; U.S. controller Park Inn Internat., San Francisco 1992-; mem. Newcomen Soc. 1970-; club: Olympic (SF); Republican; rec: hunting, fishing, boating. Res: 210 Malcolm Ave Belmont 94002 Ofc: 2 Embarcadero Center Ste 1670 San Francisco 94111 Tel: 415.362-0987 Fax: 415/362-0993

KORDIK, MICHAEL WILLIAM, sales and marketing executive; b. March 30, 1946, Chicago, Ill.; s. George Anton and Mary Aileen (Rinkle) K.; m. Nickcol Karen Peters, Sept. 6, 1968; children: Kimberly b. 1972, Matthew b. 1974, Nathan b. 1981; edn: BS bus. adminstrn., Univ. Ariz. 1968; MBA, Nat. Univ. 1981. Career: ops. mgr. Gen. Electric, Ventura 1969-74, area mgr., San Diego 1975-78, dist. mgr. 1979-80; dir. sales Elgar Corp. 1981-84; cons. Mike Kordik & Assoc., Encinitas 1985-86; controller Agents West Inc., Norwalk 1987-92; pres. Maddox Sales Co., Pico Rivera 1993-; awards: Gen. Electric top 3% mgr. 1980; mem: MACS Users Group (pres. 1991), Nat. Electric Mfg. Rep. Assn., Esperanza H.S. Boosters; author of computer program for sales tracking and order entry 1986; Republican; Fundamentalist; rec: remote control aircraft, computer programming. Res: 19998 Hibiscus Circle Yorba Linda 92686 Ofc: Maddox Sales Co. 7271 Paramount Blvd Pico Rivera 90660

KORF, RICHARD EARL, computer science educator; b. Dec. 7, 1956, Geneva, Switzerland; s. Earl Watkin and Suzanne Michelle (Nacouz) K.; edn: BS E.E. and C.S., M.I.T., 1977; MS, and PhD in computer sci., Carnegie-Mellon Univ., 1980, 1983. Career: asst. prof. computer sci. Columbia Univ., N.Y.C. 1983-85; asst. prof., assoc. prof. computer sci. UCLA, Los Angeles 1985-; awards: NSF Presdl. Young Investigator, W.D.C. 1986, Faculty devel. award IBM 1985; mem. Am. Assn. for Artificial Intelligence 1983-; author: Learning to Solve Problems by Searching for Macro-Operators (1985), 60+ articles in profl. jours. (1977-); Democrat; Presbyterian; rec: mountain climbing. Res: 10470 Colina Way Los Angeles 90077 Ofc: Computer Science Dept. 3532 H Boelter Hall Univ. California, L.A. 90024

KORKIS, KAISER KHAMO, architectural designer, urban planner; b. Apr. 24, 1942, Mosul, Iraq; s. Khamo Matta K. and Warda (Slewa) Yousif; m. Balkis Yousif Gabrail, May 2, 1974; children: Bassam b. 1975, Steve b. 1976, Phillip b. 1985; edn: BSc arch., Univ. of Baghdad, 1968; postgrad. dipl., Polytech. of North London, U.K., 1975; MSc urban design, Heriot-Watt Univ., Edinburgh, 1978; PhD, Strathclyde Univ., Glasgow, 1982. Career: architect Ministry of Housing, Baghdad, 1969-75; Sitto Constrn., Detroit, Mich. 1983-85; Kanther & Woodhouse, Detroit 1985-86; developer Kaiser & Kaiser Constrn., Laguna Hills, Calif. 1988-; R.Cath. Res: 27712 Pinestrap Circle Laguna Hills 92653

KORN, LESTER BERNARD, business executive; b. Jan. 11, 1936, New York; edn: BS hons., UCLA 1959; MBA, 1960; postgrad. Harvard Bus. Sch. 1961. Career: mgmt. cons. Peat Marwick Mitchell & Co., Los Angeles 1961-66,ptnr. 1966-69; chmn., co-founder Korn Ferry Internat. 1969-; U.S. ambassador, U.S. rep. Econ. & Social Council U.N. 1977-88; alt. rep. 42d. and 43rd U.N. Gen. Assembly; bd. dirs: Continental Am. Properties, Leisure Tech., Jospheson Internat. Inc., L.A. Music Center Operating Co., Curb Musifilms, AmBase Corp.; trustee UCLA Found; bd. overseers, bd. visitors, Anderson Grad. Sch. Mgmt. UCLA; mem. advy. council Am. Heart Assn.; spl. advisor, del. UNESCO Inter-gov. Conf. on Edn. for Internat. Understanding Coop., Peace 1983; advy. bd. Women in Film Found. 1983-84; chmn. Commn. on Citizen Participation in Govt., Calif. 1979-82; bd. dirs. John Douglas French Found. for Alzheimers Disease; mem. Republican Nat. Exec. Fin. Com. 1985; Pres. Commn. White House Fellowships; hon. chair 50th Am. Presdl. Inaugural 1985; co-chmn. So. Calif. region NCCJ; trustee Acad. for Advancement Corp. Governance, Fordham Univ. Grad. Sch. Bus. Adminstrn; awards: UCLA Alumni Profl. Achievement 1984; mem: Am. Bus. Conf. (founding mem.), Am. Inst. CPA, Calif. Soc. CPA, Council Am. Ambassadors; clubs: City (Bunker Hill), Hillcrest CC, LA Athletic, Regency, Board Room (NYC); author: The Success Profile (Simon & Schuster 1989). Res: 237 Park Ave New York N.Y. 10017 Ofc: Korn Ferry International 1800 Century Park E Ste 900 L.A. 90067

KORODY, ANTHONY VINCENT, corporate events producer, photographer; b. Mar. 4, 1951, Los Angeles; s. Paul Alexander and Erica K.; m. Jaimie C. Levy, Mar. 13, 1982; 2 children; edn: stu. USC 1970-72. Career: freelance photographer Black Star, Life, Newsweek, 1970; picture editor Daily Trojan, USC, 1971; founder, c.e.o. Fourth Estate Press, L.A. 1971-; photographer, co-founder SYGMA Agence de Press, Paris, 1973-; freelance photographer People, Time, Fortune, Newsweek, 1978-88; co-founder, v.p., dir. Image Stream Inc., L.A. 1978-86; contbg. photographer People Weekly Mag., 1979-87; lectr. Art Center; producer corporate events, clients include Apple Computer, Michelin, Toro, Taco Bell, Computerland; represented in permanent collections Time-Life Bldg., N.Y.C., Ronald Reagan Libr., Sylmar, Calif., ACT Hdqrs.; exhibited in group show 100 Time Mag. Covers, Cochran Gal., W.D.C.; honors: Inc. mag. list of 500 top CEOs 1983, 84, 85; mem. Nat. Press Photographers Assn., Sigma Delta Chi; Republican; R.Cath.; rec: gardening, cooking. Ofc: Fourth Estate Press PO Box 24B63 Los Angeles 90024

KORPMAN, RALPH A., physician, executive, pathologist, researcher, educator; b. Aug. 9, 1952, New York City, N.Y.; s. Ralf and Vera Henriette (Terry) K.; edn: BA, Loma Linda Univ., 1971, MD 1974, intern Loma Linda Univ. Sch. of Medicine, Calif. 1974-75, resident 1975-78, fellow 1978; cert. in exec. mgmt., Claremont Grad. Sch. 1979; diplomate: Am. Bd. of Path., Nat. Bd. of Med. Examiners, Am. Coll. of Phys. Execs. Career: lead systems designer Acad. Records, Loma Linda Univ. 1969-74, systems dir., dept. of path. and lab. med. 1974-; cons., dir. Med. Data Corp., San Bernardino 1976-81; dir. of labs., faculty med. lab., Loma Linda 1979-; asst. prof. Loma Linda Univ. Sch. of Med. 1979-84, assoc. prof. 1984-87, prof. 1987-; dir. KM Corp., Los Angeles 1979-; cons., dir. Creative Ventures Capital Group 1980-; cons., dir. BK Med. Research Found. 1980-; chief scientific adv. to the pres. and bd. chmn. HBO & Co. 1981-83; dir. Med. Devices Corp. 1982-; pres., chmn. Health Data Scis. Corp. 1983-; dir. Pacific Union Coll. Found. 1984-; trustee Pacific Union Coll. 1985-; dir. Burdick Corp. 1986-88; cons. to numerous hosps. and corps. 1977-; lectr. various schools, conferences, orgns.; awards: Entrepreneur of the Year Award, 1992, Sheard-Sanford Award, Am. Soc. Clin. Pathologists, 1975, Harold Hoxie Award, Loma Linda Univ., 1974, Alumni Award, 1974; Alpha Omega Alpha, Sigma Xi; mem: Am. Acad. Med. Dirs., Am. Coll. of Physician Execs. (Distinguished Fellow, chmn. Forum On Med. Informatics), Am. Mgmt. Assn., Am. Med. Assn., Am. Nat. Standards Inst. (ANSI/Healthcare Informatics Standards Planning Panel.), Am. Soc. Clin. Pathologists (Fellow, dir., exhibits advy. com., chmn. govt. rels. com., nominating com.), Am. Soc. Hematology, Assn. for Computing Machinery, Assn. Clin. Scientists (fellow), Calif. Med. Assn., Coll. Am. Pathologists (fellow), Data Processing Mgmt. Assn., Health Industry Mfrs. Assn., IEEE Computer Section, Internat. Health Econ. and Mgmt. Inst., MUMPS User Group (med. informatics com.), NY Acad. Scis., President's Assn., Rand Inst. for Research on interactive Systems, San Bernardino Co. Med. Soc., Young Pres. Orgn.; author "Managing Health Care Costs, Quality, and Technology" book publ. 1986; author 50+ articles, 1984-. Res: POB 6406 San Bernardino 92412 Ofc: Health Data Sciences Corp 268 W Hospitality Ln Ste 300 San Bernardino 92408

KORZELIUS, JOHN MICHAEL, plastic and reconstructive surgeon; b. Dec. 21, 1951, Buffalo, N.Y.; s. Edward Gerald and Teresa (Taaffe) K.; edn: BA biol., SUNY at Buffalo, 1973, MS immunology, 1977, PhD pathology, 1980; MD, Medical Coll. of Wis., 1981. Career: resident surgeon dept. surgery UCLA Sch. of Medicine, Los Angeles 1981-88; awards: NSF res. and tchg. fellow 1975, NIH scientist in tng. fellow 1975-77, N.Y. State predoctoral res. fellow 1977-79 Roswell Park Memorial Inst.; mem: Am. Soc. of Tropical Medicine and Hygiene, Am. Soc. Plastic and Reconstrv. Surg. (affil.), Assn. for Academic Surgery, Assn. of Gnotobiotics, Calif. Med. Assn., Internat. Assn. for Gnotobiology, L.A. Co. Med. Assn., Nat. Council on Internat. Health, N.Y. Acad. of Scis.; author 10+ book chapts., sci. articles on immunology, cancer and reconstrv. surgery; rec: frequent travel as volunteer surgeon in Mexico, SE Asia and Africa. Res: 7861 Woodrow Wilson Dr Los Angeles 90046 Ofc: 2601 W Alameda Ave Ste 314 Burbank 91505

KOSTY, MICHAEL PAUL, physician; b. Sept. 17, 1950, South Bend, Ind.; s. Michael Peter and Irene Wanda (Czajkowski) K.; m. Antonette Christine Leone, May 18, 1980; children: Michael b. 1984, Allison b. 1987; edn: BS engring., UC Berkeley 1972; Cornell Univ. 1973; MA biophysics, UC Berkeley 1975; MD, George Washington Univ. 1979. Career: intern Naval Hosp., San Diego 1979-80; med. ofcr. USS Belleau Wood 1980-81; med. resident Naval Hosp., San Diego 1981-83, fellow 1983-86, staff physician, asst. head div. hematology/oncology 1986-89; asst. clin. prof. UCSD 1986-; currently assoc. dir. edn. & training, Ida M. & Cecil H. Green Cancer Ctr., Scripps Clinic and Research Found., La Jolla; honors: Phi Beta Kappa, Tau Beta Pi; mem: A.C.P., Am. Soc. Clin. Oncology, Am. Soc. Hematology Cancer and Leukemia Group B; articles pub. in med. jours. 1987-93, research 1989-93; mil: commdr. USN 1979-89, active in USNR (commdr. Med. Corps); Democrat; Protestant; rec: amateur radio, woodworking, gardening. Ofc: Ida M. & Cecil H. Green Cancer Center Scripps Clinic and Research Foundation 10666 N. Torrey Pines Rd La Jolla 92037

KOZITZA, GEORGE ANTHONY, college executive; b. June 5, 1941, Mannato, Minn.; s. Andrew Anthony and Mary (Tabet) K.; m. Mary Grace Cedillos, Sept. 1, 1964 (dec. 1976); m. Linda Lee Pepper, Nov. 4, 1978; children: Mary, Michael, Elizabeth, Rebecca; edn: BA, CSU Los Angeles 1961; MA, 1963; Ed.D, USC 1969. Career: asst. supt. Dixon Unified Sch. Dist. 1969-73; asst. supt. bus. Santa Cruz City Sch. 1973-77; bus. mgr. Merced Comm. Coll., Merced 1977-81; asst. supt. bus. Ventura Co. Comm. Coll. Dist. 1981-83; dep. supt. Santa Barbara Co. Sch. 1983-85; v.p. adminstrn. Marin Comm. Coll. Dist., Kentfield 1985-; guest speaker Nat. Assn. Bus. Officials, Atlanta, Ga. 1982; mem: Calif. Assn. Schs. (st. chair fin. com. 1972-74), Assn. Calif. Sch. Adminstrs., Calif. Assn. Sch. Bus., Phi Delta Kappa, Novato Priorities (bd. dirs.), Friends of Indian Valley (founding mem.); publs: Tng. of Maintenance & Ops. Personnel (1969), article in profl. jour. (1973); Democrat; R.Cath. Ofc: Marin Community College District Indian Valley Campus 1800 Ignacio Blvd Novato 94949

KRAFT, ROBERT ARNOLD, physician, ret.; b. Mar. 27, 1924, Seattle, Wash.; s. Vincent Irving and Blanche (Palmer) K.; m. Robby Lee Roberson, June 12, 1949; children: Angela b. 1958, Peter b. 1961, Darius b. 1963; edn: BA, Univ. Wash. 1948, MD, 1954; bd. cert. anatomic & clin. pathology, Am. Bd. Pathology 1962, bd. cert. Am. Bd. Nuclear Medicine 1972; career: family physician practice, Puyallup, Wash. 1955-58; pathologist/nuclear medicine physician Peninsula Hosp., Burlingame 1962-91, dir. Dept. Nuclear Medicine; asst. clin. prof. Pathol. & Nuclear Medicine, UCSF, 1962-; mem. Calif. Radioactive Mats. Mgmt. Forum (state multidisciplinary orgn. for safe low level radioactive waste mgmt.); honors: spl. service award, W. regl. chpts. Soc. of Nuclear Medicine 1986; elected Am. Board of Nuclear Medicine 1990; mem: Soc. Nuclear Medicine (pres. No. Calif. chpt. 1974-75), Am. Coll. of Nuclear Physicians (nat. bd. trustees 1981-84, pres. Calif. chpt. 1978-79, nat. regent 1987-92), South Bay Pathology Soc. (pres. 1968-69); Rotary 1955-58; author book chpt., Nuclear Medicine; mil: capt. USAAF, WWII, lead navigator (30 missions) 8th Air Force; Republican; Methodist; rec: philately, amateur astronomer, orchidist, golf, mining history.

KRAMER, HENRY HERMAN, radiodiagnostic drug consultant; b. Aug. 19, 1930, New York; s. Henry and Anna Marie (Bendhaak) K.; m. Carol Schlamp, Aug. 16, 1959; children: Paul b. 1960, Scott b. 1962, Pamela b. 1966; edn: BA, Columbia Univ. 1952; MA, 1953; PhD, Ind. Univ. 1960. Career: research sci., corp. research and devel. Union Carbide Corp., Tuxedo, N.Y. 1960-65, group leader 1965-67, project mgr. nucleonics research 1967-73, sr. group leader 1973-76, mgr. med. product div. 1976-78; v.p. research and devel. Medi-Physics Inc., Emeryville 1978-89; staff nuclear medicine dept. Johns Hopkins Med. Inst., Baltimore, Md. 1965-66; awards: Union Carbide Corp. IR100 (1969, 75); mem: Am. Coll. Nuclear Physics (fellow), U.S. Council on Energy Awareness (chair radiopharm. com.), Soc. Nuclear Medicine, Am. Chemical Soc., N.Y. Acad. Scis., Am. Nuclear Soc; num. patents and articles pub. in sci. jours.; mil: AUS MC 1953-55; Republican; Lutheran.

KRAMER, KAREN SUE, community and organizational psychologist; b. Sept. 6, 1942, Los Angeles; d. Frank Pacheco Kramer and Velma Eileen (Devlin) Moore; m. Stewart A. Sterling, Dec. 30, 1965 (div. 1974); 1 son, Scott b. 1970; edn: BA, UC Berkeley 1966; MA, U.S. Internat. Univ., S.D. 1977; PhD, Profl. Sch. of Psychology, 1980; lic. marriage famiy and child counselor Calif. 1979. Career: psychometrist UC Berkeley Counseling Center 1966-67; social worker Alameda County 1967-69; probation ofcr. San Diego Co. Probation Dept. 1971-76; clin. and outreach worker Western Inst., San Diego 1976-77; project dir. Womens Resource Center, San Luis Rey 1977-78; advr. USMC Human Resources dept. Camp Pendleton, 1978-80; pvt. practice therapy, Vista 1978-81; prof. human behavior Nat. Univ., San Diego 1979-81; planner San Diego Co. Dept. Health Services 1979-81; social service cons. Calif. Dept. Social Services, 1981-83; affirmative action ofcr. St. Compensation Ins. Fund., San Francisco 1983-87; cons. psychologist Calif. Dept. Mental Health S.F. 1987-89; personnel cons. State Compensation Ins. Fund, 1989-91; reg. property mgr. State Compensation Ins. Fund, 1991-; indep. consulting psychologist for organizational devel., community devel., wellness programing, personal health issues, 1990-; honors: listed Who's Who in Am. Women 1989, Who's Who in Behavioral Scis. 1991; mem. bd. dirs: Network Consulting Services Napa 1989-, Calif. Prevention Network (1989-, editorial advy. bd. 1992-), Calif. Peer Counseling Assn., San Francisco Rehab. Ctr., Chinatown Resource Devel. Ctr., Personnel Mgmt. Assn. Aztlan 1984-87, North County Council Social Concerns (pres. 1977-78); rec: interior design, garden design, travel. Address: 1314 Ordway St Berkeley 94702

KRAMER, LAWRENCE STEPHEN, journalist; b. Apr. 24, 1950, Hackensack, N.J.; s. Abraham and Ann Eve (Glasser) K.; m. Myla F. Lerner, Sept. 3, 1978; children: Matthew b. 1982, Erika b. 1987; edn: BS in journ., pol. sci., Syracuse Univ., 1972; MBA, Harvard Univ., 1974. Career: reporter San Francisco Examiner, S.F. 1974-77; Washington Post, W.D.C. 1977-80; exec. editor The Trenton Times, N.J. 1980-82; asst. mng. editor Washington Post, 1982-86; exec. editor San Francisco Examiner, S.F. 1986-92; pres., dir., exec. editor Data Sport, San Mateo, Calif. 1992-; guest lectr. Harvard Univ. 1980-89; awards: Gerald E. Loeb Award, USC 1977, Nat. Press Club Award, W.D.C. 1979; mem. Soc. Profl. Journalists 1975-, Am. Soc. Newspaper Editors 1980-90 (com. chair 1990); civic: commr. Little League, Tiburon 1992-; Jewish. Res: 8 Auburn Ct Tiburon 94920 Ofc: Data Sport, Inc. 1900 S Norfolk St Ste 160 San Mateo 94403

KRANZ, KATHLEEN NEE, performing musician/pianist; b. May 31, 1951, Fontana; d. Bruce Lester and Margaret Joanne (Nee) Brown; m. Tomas Patten Kranz, July 4, 1978; child: Michael Alexander b. 1988; edn: BA, Fla. State Univ., Tallahassee, 1973, MM, 1977; PhD in music/ theoretical studies, UC San Diego, 1985. Career: musical dir. Actor's Theatre of Louisville, Ky., 1973-74; musical dir. Asolo State Theatre, Sarasota, Fla., 1974-75; faculty, piano, UC San Diego, La Jolla, 1983-87; pvt. tchr. piano, San Diego, 1977-; performer- Sonos, Chamber Music Seattle, Wash. (ea. summer ongoing), Chamber music, San Diego 1978-; master tchr.- Am. Music Scholarship Assn., Batiquitos Festival Del Mar, Calif. 1988, AM Music Scholarship, Cinti., Oh. 1984-86; 20th century music and theory tchr. Suzuki Assn. of Calif., San Diego, 1984-88; pvt. study Aube Tzerko, L.A./Aspen, 1979-88, 91; awards: $500 cash award Fla. Fedn. of Music Clubs 1976, Young Artist in the Schools, Leon County, Fla. 1977, Fulbright Finalist, Fulbright Grant Rotary Club 1977, grad. opportunity fellow UCSD 1981, UCSD Grad. Sch. Alice Hohn fee scholar 1981 and In-candidacy fee grantee (1983, 84); mem: Music Tchrs. Assn. of Calif. (1977-, MTAC high sch. credit chair 1991), Suzuki Assn. of Calif. (sec. 1986-87), College Music Soc. 1985-; publs: (diss.) Structural Functions of Rests in the Piano Works of Franz Schubert (1985); Methodist. Res: San Diego.

KRATOFIL, STEVEN ELLIOTT, dentist; b. Feb. 17, 1959, Inglewood; s. Alexander B. and Lois Roberta (Elliott) K.; m. Elaine Kay Rollos, June 27, 1981; children: Alexander b. 1986, Michael b. 1989; edn: AS, San Bernardino Valley Coll. 1979; BA magna cum laude, USC 1981; DDS, 1985; Praxis Orthodontic Coll., 1987. Career: private practice, Apple Valley 1985-; instr. USC Dental Sch., L.A. 1985-86; team dentist High Desert Mavericks profl. baseball team 1992; cons. dentist, Apple Valley Care Ctr. 1991-;honors: Phi Beta Kappa, Psi Omega, Omicron Kappa Upsilon, USC hons. at entrance 1979, Calif. Scholarship Fedn. 1977; contbr. Dental Sch. Yearbook 1982-85; mem: ADA, Calif. Dental Assn., Tri County Dental Soc., Internat. Assn. for Orthodontics, Rotary Intl.; rec: tennis, golf. Address: Apple Valley 92307

KRAUS, JEFFREY MILES, safety consultant; b. Feb. 3, 1953, Los Angeles; s. Samuel and Naomi (Cholden) K.; m. Joyce, Aug. 18, 1984; edn: BS, CSU Northridge, 1975; desig: cert. safety profl. (CSP), REHS. Career: tech. rep. Fireman's Fund Ins. Co., L.A. 1975-79; sr. loss prevention specialist Great American Ins. Co., L.A. 1979; dir. safety services Bayly, Martin & Fay Inc., ins. brokers, L.A. 1979-86; account exec. Osterloh & Durham Ins. Brokers, Van Nuys 1986-87; senior loss control consultant United Pacific Ins. Co., Redding 1987-89; c.f.o. Four Seasons Pacifica, San Clemente 1986-91; mgr. safety Crawford/FPE, Lafayette 1989-; Republican; Jewish; rec: sports. Ofc: Crawford/FPE PO Box 179 Lafayette 94549-0179

KRAUS, PANSY DAEGLING, gemology consultant, author; b. Sept. 21, 1916, Santa Paula; d. Arthur David and Elsie (Pardee) Daegling; m. Charles Frederick Kraus, Mar. 1, 1941 (div. 1961); edn: AA, San Bernardino Valley Jr. Coll., 1938; edn: Longmeyer's Bus. Coll., 1940; grad. gemologist dipl. Gemmological Assn. Gt. Britain, 1960, Gemological Inst. Am., 1966; career: clk. Convair, San Diego 1943-48; clk. San Diego County Schs. Publs., 1948-57; mgr. Rogers and Boblet Art Craft, San Diego 1958-64; p.t. editorial asst. Lapidary Jour., San Diego 1963-64, assoc. editor 1964-69, ed. 1970-, sr. ed. 1984-85; pvt. practice cons., San Diego 1985-; lectr. local gem and mineral groups, gem & mineral club bulletin editor groups; mem: San Diego Mineral & Gem Soc., Gemol. Soc. San Diego, Gemmol. Assn. Gt. Brit., Epsilon Sigma Alpha; publs: ed., layout dir. Gem Cutting Shop Helps 1964, The Fundamentals of Gemstone Carving 1967, Appalachian Mineral and Gem Trails 1968, Practical Gem Knowledge for the Amateur 1969, Southwest Mineral and Gem Trails 1972, revision ed. Gemcraft (Quick and Leiper, 1977); author Introduction to Lapidary 1987, contbr. articles to Lapidary jour., Keystone Mktg. catalog; ofc: PO Box 600908 San Diego 92160

KRAUS, RICHARD SHOLOM, librarian; b. Nov. 18, 1956, Bklyn.; s. Leonard Henry and Aviva (Rubby) K.; edn: BA, UC Los Angeles, 1978, MLS, 1980. Career: library intern and archival asst. Acad. of Motion Picture Arts & Scis., Beverly Hills 1979-80; lab asst. Instructional Materials Lab. CSU Northridge 1980-83; catalog librarian Cat. Dept. Los Angeles Pub. Library, L.A. 1983-85, serials librarian Acquisitions Dept. 1985-86, adult reference librarian West L.A. reg. branch library 1986-; honors: Phi Beta Kappa 1978, Beta Phi Mu 1980; mem: Am. Library Assn., Special Libraries Assn., Calif. Library Assn., Nat. Librarians Assn.; newsletter editor UCLA/GSLIS Alumni News 1984-87, pub. article in Am. Libraries Jour. (1983); Democrat; rec: baking. Res: 1515 Purdue Ave Apt 5 Los Angeles 90025 Ofc: Los Angeles Public Library, W.L.A. Reg. Br. 11360 Santa Monica Blvd Los Angeles 90025

KRAUTHAMMER, JUERGEN P., physician-surgeon; b. Dec. 19, 1935, Berlin, Germany; s. Simon and Maria Theresa (Karl) S.; m. E. Elizabeth Otero; m. Maureen Laughnan, July 19, 1980; children: William b. 1962, Elizabeth b. 1965; edn: MD, Univ. Buenos Aires Sch. Medicine 1961. Career: clin. research diabetes Joslin Clin. & Baker Clinic Research Lab., Boston, Mass. 1962-63; intern Delaware Co. Memorial Hosp., Drexel Hill, Pa. 1963-64; resident Grad. Hosp. Univ. Pa., Phila. 1964-66; Bryn Mawr Hosp. 1966-69; Henry Ford Hosp., Detroit, Mich. 1969-70; Shadyside Hosp. 1970-71; pvt. practice, Fresno, currently; pres. med. staff Clovis Comm. Hosp., 1984; bd. dirs. Comm. Hosp./St. Agnes Med. Ctr.. Res: 458 E Feather River Dr Fresno 93710 Ofc: 5305 N Fresno Ste 108A Fresno 93710

KRAVETZ, NATHAN, author, educator; b. Feb. 11, 1921, New York, N.Y.; s. Louis Kravetz and Anna Tau; m. Evelyn Cottan, Dec. 10, 1944; children: Deborah Ruth b. 1948, Daniel b. 1951; edn: BEd, UCLA 1941, MA, 1949, EdD 1954; Fellow in Edn., Harvard Univ. 1951-52. Career: teacher, principal Los Angeles Unified Sch. Dist. 1946-64; foreign service ofcr. U.S. Dept. of State,

Lima, Peru 1958-60; prof., chmn. Lehman Coll., New York, N.Y. 1964-76, prof. emeritus of edn. 1979; sr. staff ofcr. UNESCO, Paris, France 1969-72; dir. eval. research Ctr. Urban Edn., New York, N.Y. 1965-69; dean, prof. CSU San Bernardino 1976-91, prof. emeritus of edn 1984; cons.: Ford Foundation, U.S. AID, United Nations Devel. Pgm., UNESCO, Univ. of Lima, Peru.; awards: Sr. Research award, Argentina, Fulbright, 1980, fellowship Harvard Univ., 1951-52; mem: Authors Guild, Authors League of Am., PEN, B'nai B'rith, Jewish Historical Soc. of So. Calif.; author: 8 books, 1954-; editor, Legacy, JHS/SC; editor, the Borgo Press: Studies in Judaica and the Holocaust, 1991-; mil: sgt., U.S. Army Air Corps, 1942-46; Democrat.

KREBS, STEPHEN JEFFREY, professor of viticulture and wine making; b. July 29, 1950, Belvedere, Ill.; s. Leo Gerard and Jean Catherine (Fiedler) K.; m. Julie Lynn, May 6, 1989; edn: BS, plant sci., UC Davis, 1976; MS, horticulture, UC Davis, 1977; PhD, ecology, UC Davis, 1992. Career: student asst. Loan Dept. Peter J. Shields Main Lib., UC Davis, 1970-72, lib. asst. II, 1972-77; tchg. asst. Pomology, UC Davis, 1977; viticulturist and mgr. San Pasqual Vineyards, Escondido, Calif., 1977-79, Mayacamas Vineyards, Napa, Calif., 1980-83; viticultural researcher in Europe and Calif. for book Vines, Grapes and Wine by Jancis Robinson, 1984; viticulturist and mgr. Matanzas Creek Winery, Santa Rosa, Calif., 1984-85, Sunny Slope Ranch, Glen Ellen, Calif., 1986-89; coord. Viticulture and Winery Technology, Napa Valley Coll., 1986-; grower-cooperator Monsanto, pre-registration round-up trials, 1978; wine judge Del Mar Nat. Wine Competition, 1982; instr. Viticulture Dept., Santa Rosa Jr. Coll., 1986-87; viticultural cons. 1978-; curriculum cons. La Comunidad Drop-out Prevention Program; instr. Internat. Wine Acad., S.F., Calif.; awards: Calif. Comm. Coll. Lifetime Credential in Plant Production, Calif. Dept. of Food & Agric. Pest Control Advisor License; scholarship recipient: Wine Spectator, 1989, 90; ASEV, 1989; ASEV Myron Nightingale Scholarship, 1990; profl. mem Am. Soc. for Enology and Viticulture, 1978; mem: Sonoma County Grapegrowers Assn. 1984-89, Sonoma County Vineyard Tech. Group 1984-89, Napa Valley Coll. Environmental Com., Instructional Excellence Com., Napa County Resource Conservation Dist. (advy. com.), Napa County Farm Bureau, Napa Valley Vineyard Tech. Group, Napa Valley Grape Growers Assn.; rec: guitar, auto restoration. Ofc: Viticulture & Winery Technology Napa Valley College Napa 94558

KREITZBERG, FRED CHARLES, construction management co. president and chief executive; b. June 1, 1934, Paterson, N.J.; s. William and Ella (Bohen) K.; m. Barbara, June 9, 1957; children: Kim b. 1959, Caroline b. 1962, Allison b. 1964, Bruce b. 1968, Catherine b. 1969; edn: BS civil engring., Norwich Univ. 1957; Reg. Profl. Engr.: Ala., Alaska, Ark., Az., Calif., Colo., Conn., D.C., Dela., Fla., Ga., Ia., Ida., Ill., Ind., Kans., Ky., Md., Mass., Miss., Mo., Nebr., Nev., N.C., N.H., N.J., N.M., N.Y., Oh., Okla., Oreg., Pa., S.C., S.Dak., Tenn., Tx., Ut., Va., Vt., Wash., Wis., W.V. and Wyo.; Career: asst. supt. Turner Constrn. Co., N.Y.C. 1957; project mgr. for Project Mercury before first astronaut launching, RCA, N.J. 1958-62; schedule and cost mgr. Catalytic Constrn. Co., Pa. 1963-65; cons. Meridien Engring., 1965-68; prin. MDC Systems Corp., 1968-72; owner, dir., pres. and c.e.o. O'Brien-Kreitzberg and Assocs., Inc. (OKA), San Francisco 1972-, constrn. mgmt. major pvt. and govt. projects nat., including S.F. Cable Car rehabilitation, S.F. Airport expansion, Silicon Valley Rail System, L.A. Rail System, world's largest wind tunnel for NASA, Libr. of Congress, Bellevue Hosp., Walter Reed Hosp., John F. Kennedy Internat. Airport Redevel. Pgm., Dallas Area Rapid Transit, New York Schools Pgm., provided emergency scheduling following the Oct. 17, 1989 San Francisco Earthquake; leading nat. authority and expert witness in constrn. mgmt. claims; lectr. Stanford Univ. and UC Berkeley engineering students; awards: Community Fields Amphitheater dedicated in honor of Fred Kreitzberg family by the Marin Comm. Fields Assn. 1987, Disting. Alumnus Norwich Univ., Vt. 1987, Norwich Univ. Kreitzberg Library dedicated 1992, ASCE Construction Mgr. of the Year 1982, Boss of Yr. Nat. Assn. of Women in Constrn. 1987, Engineering News Record Man of Year nominee 1984; mem: ASCE (Fellow 1956), Am. Arbitration Assn., Constrn. Mgmt. Assn. of Am. (founding mem. 1982, bd. dirs.), Soc. of Am. Value Engrs.; civic: Alden Partridge Soc., Norwich Univ. (Bd. dirs.), Comm. Field Assn. (Marin Co. bd. dirs.), Ross Hist. Soc.; works: designed catenary support system for World's largest radio telescope, patent app. by RCA (1960); contbg. author to Critical Path Method Scheduling for Contractor's Mgmt. Handbook (1971); key articles: Repetitive Scheduling (ASCE J. 1984), Cable Car Renovation Project: On Time and On Budget (Proceedings of the Splty. Conf. on Orgn. & Mgmt.), The Constrn. Mgr.-Contractor's Friend or Foe? (Constrn. Consultant, 3 & 4, 87); mil: 1st lt. Corps of Engrs. (Airborne) 1957-58; Cong. Rodef Sholom; rec: running, biking, scuba, tropical fish. Res: 19 Spring Rd Box 1200 Ross 94957 Ofc: O'Brien-Kreitzberg & Associates, Inc. 188 The Embarcadero San Francisco 94105

KREITZER, DAVID MARTIN, artist; b. Oct. 23, 1942, Ord, Nebr.; s. David and Norma (Buls) K.; m. Ana Bueno, June 4, 1973 (div. Feb. 1988); m. Jacalyn Marie Bower, Nov. 25, 1988; children: Anatol b. 1974, Fredricka b. 1989; edn: BS, Concordia Coll., 1965; MA, San Jose State Univ., 1967. Career: faculty San Jose State Univ., 1969-70; Calif. Polytechnic State Univ., San Luis Obispo 1981-91; one-man shows Maxwell Gal., San Francisco 1967-74, Ankrum Gal., Los

Angeles 1970-89; represented by Summa Gal., N.Y.C., 1989-, Stary-Sheets Gal., Irvine, Calif. 1991-; awards: Ciba Geigy Award, Sixth Mobile (Ala.) Annual 1971, Gold medal San Francisco Art Directors Club 1970; publs. include covers (2) Atlantic Monthly 1970, reproduction in book "The Sacred Landscape" 1988, posters (4) Seattle Opera 1981-82; Lutheran. Res: 1442 12th St Los Osos 93402

KREMPEL, RALF HUGO BERNHARD, artist, inventor, author; b. June 5, 1935, Groitzsch, Saxony, Ger.; s. Curt Bernhard and Liesbeth Anna Margarete (Franz) K.; m. Barbara von Eberhardt, Dec. 21, 1967 (div. 1985); 1 son, Karma b. 1983; edn: Wood and Steel Constrn. Coll., Leipzig, Ger. 1949-55. Career: constrn. specialist var. projects world-wide incl. Germany, Congo (Kinshasa), New Guinea, South Pacific; co-owner w/wife San Francisco Private Mint, commemorative medals and bars in silver and platinum 1973-81; artist/prin. San Francisco Painter Magnate 1982-; prop. Stadtgalerie Wiprechtsburg Groitzsch, Saxony, Germany 1991-; paintings exhib: Galerie Salammbo-Atlante, Paris, Fr., invite d'honneur Expo. Artistes Contemporains, le Salon des Nations a Paris (1985); mem: The Museum Soc., S.F. Mus. of Modern Art; invention: Visual Communication System, world-wide message relay, utilizing colors rather than letters in transmission and depiction; 2 USA patents 4/439/160 (1984), 4/552/534 (1985); European patent 0113720 (1988); 3 reg. trademarks; publs: World Intellectual Property Orgn., PCT Gazette (1984), European Patent Bulletin (1984, 1988); rec: art res., photog., writing. Res: 2400 Pacific Ave San Francisco 94115-1275 Ofc: San Francisco Painter Magnate Rincon Ctr San Francisco 94119-3368

KRIENKE, CAROL BELLE MANIKOWSKE, realtor; b. June 19, 1917, Oakland; d. George and Ethel Lucretia (Purdon) Manikowske; m. Oliver Kenneth Krienke, June 4, 1941 (dec. Dec. 24, 1988); children: Diane (Denny) b. 1944, Judith (Giss) b. 1947, Debra (Davalos) b. 1950; edn: stu., Nat. Bus. Tng. Coll., Univ. of Mo.; BS, Univ. of Minn. 1940. Career: youth leadership State of Minn., Congregational Conf., Univ. of Minn. 1940; demonstrator General Foods, Mpls., Minn. 1940-41; war prodn. workers Airesearch Mfg. Co., L.A. 1944; tchr. L.A. City Schs. 1945-49; realtor dba Ethel Purdon, Manhattan Beach 1947-65; buyer Purdon Furniture & Appliances, Manhattan Beach 1949; realtor O.K. Krienke Realty, Manhattan Beach 1965-; honors: hon. life mem. Mira Costa PTA 1964, recipient w. husband the Rose & Scroll Award for outstanding comm. svc. Manhattan Beach C.of C. 1985; mem: Calif. Retired Tchrs. Assn. (life mem. 1988), Torrance-Lomita Board of Realtors, South Bay Board of Realtors (appreciation awards 1974, 1981), Univ. Minn. Alumni Assn. (life),Internat. Platform Assn.; civic: Nat. Soc. New England Women (life), Founders of Hartford, "Poppy Colony", South Bay Council of Girl Scouts USA, Manhattan Beach Coord. Council, Long Beach Area Children's Home Soc. (pres. 1969), Beach Pixies (charter mem., pres. 1967, hon. life mem.), United Way, Beach Cities Sym. (sponsor), DAR (vice regent 1978-79, regent 1992-93), Colonial Dames 17th Century (charter, Jared Eliot chpt., pres. 1979-81), Friends of the Library; Republican; Congregational; rec: travel. Ofc: O.K. Krienke Realty, 1716 Manhattan Beach Blvd Manhattan Beach 90266

KRISSOFF, WILLIAM BRUCE, orthopaedic surgeon; b. Oct. 16, 1946, Grand Rapids, Mich.; s. Abraham and Sylvia (Gittlen) K.; m. Christine McGee, Sept. 16, 1978; children: Nathan Michael b. 1981, Austin Price b. 1983; edn: BA cum laude, Oberlin Coll. 1968; MD Univ. Colo., Denver 1972; S.F. Gen. 1972-73; Univ. Colo., Denver 1973-74; Univ. Calif., Davis 1975-79; dipl. Am. Bd. Orthopaedic Surgery 1980. Career: emergency room physician St. Anthony Hosp., Denver, Colo. 1974-75; pvt. practice orthopaedic surgery, Truckee 1979-; clin. asst. prof. orthopaedics, Univ. Calif. Davis, Sacto. 1981-; chief surgery Tahoe Forest Hosp., Truckee (1987-88, 93); vice chief of staff 1985-86; mem: Am. Acad. Orthopaedic Surgeons, Am. Soc. for Sports Medicine, We. Orthopaedic Assn., CMA, Mountain Area Preservation Soc. (v.p. 1987-88); author: num. articles pub. in med. jours. rec: white water kayaking, skiing, running. Ofc: Mountain Medical Center 10051 Lake St. Truckee 96161

KRIZ, JOSEPH ALOIS, naval officer, educator, writer, business consultant; b. Mar. 16, 1920, Oshkosh, Wisc.; s. Rudy Aloyious and Catherine Ann (Klemmer) K.; m. Doloris Hesser, Aug. 5, 1944; children: Susan Terese (McKechnie),b. 1955, Mary Kay (Cox), b. 1957; edn: Wis. State Univ. 1937-39, BS, US Naval Acad., 1942; MBA, Columbia Univ. 1952; postgrad. stu. GBS Harvard, UC Berkeley. Career: served to Cmdr. Supply Corps, USN, 1942-63; tours as Comptroller/ Supply Dir. of two major Navy air stations; Supply Ofcr. of Aviation Supply Ship during Korean War, prof., four years, US Navy Postgrad. Sch. (estab. 1st grad. bus. sch. in US Mil.); lectr. Univ. of Texas, Arlington, 1 yr.; lectr. UC Berkeley, 2 yrs.; prof./ Small Bus. Coord. Diablo Valley Coll., Pleasant Hill 1965-84, ret.; guest lectr. 1984-; vol. SCORE/ACE pgm. of the Small Bus. Adminstrn. 1970-85; creator/instr. course in Logistics fr Peruvian Naval Acad., Lima, Peru 1949; vol. cons. to Contra Costa County Bd. of Suprs. (new civil svc. personnel code) 1969-71; mem: PROBE study group of the Commn. for Study of Higher Edn. 1972-75; past cons. Allis Chalmers Corp., and Santa Fe Indus.; honors: num. ltrs of commendn., (6) area ribbons from mil. duty WWII, Korean War; Beta Gamma Sigma (bus. hon.), Beta Alpha Psi (acct. hon.), Bus. Tchr. of Year 1973-74 (Diablo Vly Coll), Fellow Found. of Econ. Ed. (1969, 1974); mem: Am. Mgmt. Assn., Soc. for Advanced Mgmt., Western

Mktg. Assn. (bd. govs. 1979-81); author: Your Dynamic World of Business (McGraw Hill 1974), other texts and short arts.; author: (suspense novel) Conch Chowder (1984); Hip Hip Chourre (1991), story of a Korean War Ship; (historical book) "The Devil Mountain" Diablo, in progress; Republican; R.Cath.; rec: bridge, sports. Res: Palma Vista 25 (Box 256) Diablo 94528

KROGH, PETER SUNDEHL, III, family physician, educator; b. Jan. 29, 1953, Chgo.; s. Peter Sundehl Krogh Jr. and Audrey Rose (Kalal) Morgan; m. Cynthia Marie Umano, Mar. 4, 1978; children: Amy b. 1979, Christen b. 1980, Gina b. 1984, Julie b. 1986; edn: BS, USAF Acad., 1975; MD, Rush Med. Coll., 1979; nat. bd. cert. 1980. Career: served to Lt. Col. US Air Force 1975-; family practice resident David Grant USAF Med. Ctr., Travis AFB, Calif. 1979-82; staff family physician Scott USAF Med. Ctr., Scott AFB, Ill. 1982-84; Irsklion USAF Hosp., Crete, Greece 1984-86; David Grant USAF Med. Ctr., Travis AFB, Calif. 1986-, faculty residency pgm. 1986-, dir. family practice residency pgm. 1992-; awarded Fam. Practice tchr. of year David Grant USAF Med. Ctr. 1987-88; mem. Am. Acad. Fam. Physicians 1982-, Uniformed Services Acad. of Fam. Physicians 1982-; Evangelical Christian; rec: outdoors, biking, music. Res: 140 Alturas Ct Vacaville 95688 Ofc: David Grant USAF Med. Ctr./SGHF Travis Air Force Base CA 94535

KRUEGER, KURT A., educator, consultant; b. Jan. 29, 1946, Los Angeles; s. Charles H. and Adlaide M. Krueger; m. Teresa A.; edn: AA, L.A. Valley Coll., 1967; BA, Univ. of Colo. 1969; MS, Mt. St. Mary's Coll. 1972; cert. Siddha Yoga Instr. 1981, USC 1985; Calif. Secondary Teaching Cred. (life) 1972. Career: swim instr., coach Kris Kristenson and Woodland Hills Swim Schools, Van Nuys 1965-70; water polo coach Univ. of Colo. 1968; instr. L.A. Unified Sch. Dist. 1969, 1972-81, 1984-91, Torrance Unified Sch. Dist. 1969-72; faculty Calif. State Univ. L.A. 1980-86; faculty Glendale Coll. 1978-81; founder, dir. Inst. of Sports Psychology, Bombay and Dept. of Practical Sports Psychology, Tarzana 1982-; instr. sports psychology CSU Long Beach 1979, CSU Dominguez Hills 1980, Nat. Inst. of Sports, India 1982, Stockholm Univ. 1983; taught sports psychol. to nat. athletes and coaches of: Am., Argentina, Austr., Great Britain, Finland, India, Japan, New Zealand, Sweden 1978-; instr. Stress Mgmt., Peak Performance, Yoga, Mediation, Winning Ways at L.A.: Valley, Pierce and City Colleges, and Mt. San Antonio, Cerritos, Glendale, Orange Coast, Rio Hondo, Saddleback, Long Beach City, Moorpark and Ventura Colleges, and Calif. State Univ. L.A., U.S. Mil. Acad., St. Xavier's & Somaiya Colleges, Assn. of Sports Medicine (India), IBD Tokyo, GIH-Pedagogic Inst. (Sweden) 1974-; instr. of Stress Mgmt. or Success Systems for: L.A. Unified Sch. Dist. teachers 1978-80, the UN, Calif. State Employees Assn., IBM, Learning Annex, Bozell Advertising Inc, Oxford Univ. Med. Sch., Bajaj Elec. Corp., Young Pres.'s Orgn., Rotary Clubs of Bombay and New Delhi, Delhi Devel. Auth., All India Inst. of Med. Scis.; honors: All-Metropolitan Conf. Water Polo Team (1964, 65), All-American Jr. Coll. Swim Team, Helms Athletic Found. 1966, 4 sch. swimming records Univ. Colo. 1968, sr. Olympic swim championship medals: 4 gold (1979), 3 gold, 3 silver (1980), 2 gold, 1 silver (1981), 2 gold, 1 silver (1984), 2 gold, 1 silver (1985); mem: Internat. Soc. of Sport Psychology, Assn. for Advancement of Applied Sport Psychology (charter), Calif. Parent Teacher Student Assn., Heal the Bay, Sierra Club, Greenpeace; co-cons. on creation of vision-tng. device "AcuVision 2000" for AcuVision Systems Inc, New York, 1986; author 2 books: Japan Hijack (1978), Winning Ways (1994); audio tape: Winning Ways (1988); num. articles in profl. jours. and mags.; rec: skiing, beach volleyball, basketball, hiking, world travel, metaphysics, writing, bicycling. Address: Kurt A. Krueger, Inst. of Sports Psychology, 13120 Bradley Ste 22 Sylmar 91342 Ph. 818/ 377-4012

KUENNING, THOMAS EARL, JR., air force officer, strategic missile center commander; b. Apr. 9, 1945, Paterson, N.J.; s. Thomas Earl and Doris Louise (Heidgerd) K.; m. Shelley Jean Lane, Sept. 23, 1972; children: Kristen b. 1974; edn: BS bus., Miami Univ., Oxford, Oh. 1967; MA bus. adminstrn., Univ. Montana, 1974. Career: served to B.Gen. U.S. Air Force 1967-: missile combat crew mem., instr., evaluator, EWO instr. 341 Strategic Missile Wing, Malmstrom AFB, Mont. 1967-71; plans ofcr. Air Staff Tng. Pgm., HQ AF, Wash. DC 1972-73; chief analysis div. 3901 Strat. Missile Eval. Sq., Vandenberg AFB, Calif. 1973-75; Adv. ICBM Dev. planner, ICBM Regmts., Hq. SAC, Offutt AFB, Nebr. 1976-79; plans ofcr. Directorate of Plans, Wash. DC 1979-82; cmdr. 564 Strat. Missile Sq., Malmstrom AFB, 1982-84, dep. cmdr. 341 Combat Support Gp., Malmstrom AFB, 1984; chief Adv. ICBM Devel. Div., Offutt AFB, Nebr. 1984-87; v.cmdr. 44 Strat. Missile Wing, Ellsworth AFB, S.Dak. 1987-88; cmdr. 351 Strat. Missile Wing, Whiteman AFB, Mo. 1988-90, cmdr. 100th Air Div., Whiteman AFB, 1990-91; cmdr. Strategic Missile Center, Vandenberg AFB, Calif. 1991-; awards: Disting. Graduate Reserve Officer Tng. Course Miami Univ. 1967, Meritorious Svc. medals (3) (1986), Lee R. Williams Trophy, Blanchard Trophy, 351 Strat. Missile Wing, Whiteman AFB 1990, Legion of Merit medal 100 Air Div., Whiteman AFB 1991; life mem. Air Force Assn.; Republican; Lutheran; rec: running, squash, reading.

KUKKONEN, CARL ALLAN, physicist/research director space microelectronics and advanced computing technology; b. Jan. 25, 1945, Duluth, Minn.; s.

Carl Allan and Shirley Minette (Miller) K.; m. Noreen Dorothy Cullen, June 22, 1968; children: Carl b. 1973, Daniel b. 1975; edn: AA, Foothill Coll., 1966; BS in physics UC Davis, 1968; MS and PhD in physics, Cornell Univ., 1970, 1975. Career: research assoc. Purdue Univ., 1975-77; sr. res. scientist Ford Motor Co., Dearborn 1977-79, prin. res. scientist assoc. 1979-80, prin. res. engr. 1980-84; dir. advanced microelectronics pgm. Jet Propulsion Laboratory, Pasadena 1984-87, dir. Ctr. for Space Microelectronics, 1987-, also mgr. Supercomputing Project 1988-, mgr. microelectronics technology pgm. 1988-90, mgr. microelectronics and adv. computing tech., 1990-; awarded NASA Exceptional Achiev. Medal 1992; mem. Am. Physical Soc. 1973-, Nat. Assn. of Watch and Clock Collectors 1970-. Res: 5467 La Forest Dr La Canada 91011 Ofc: JPL M/S 180-604, 4800 Oak Grove Dr Pasadena 91109

KUMLI, RAYMOND PAUL, winery president, information consultant; b. June 6, 1938, San Francisco; s. Wilfred Julius and Nancy Henrietta (Outsen) K.; m. Sherryl Anne Spietz, Oct. 2, 1965; 1 son, Paul b. 1968; edn: BA econ., UC Berkeley 1961. Career: portfolio mgr. Bank of Am., San Francisco 1965-68; municipal splst. L.F. Rothschild & Co. 1968-69; municipal bond dept. mgr. Kidder Peabody & Co. 1969-73; municipal bond splst. First Boston Corp., NYC 1973-76; pres. and c.e.o. McCord Co., San Francisco 1976-89; pres. Goosecross Cellars Inc., a Napa Valley winery; dir. Nat. Pub. Record Research Assn., Tallassee, Fla. 1988-; instr. Coll. of Marin, Kentfield 1989-; club: Olympic; mil: lt. USN 1961-64; Democrat; Episcopalian; rec: golf. Address: POB 846 Ross 94957

KURAISHI, AKARI LUKE, real estate company executive; b. July 29, 1959, Nagano, Japan; came to U.S.A., 1984; s. Atsushi and Kuniko (Tomita) K.; m. Hiromi Lydia Hatae, Oct. 10, 1987; children: Katrina Ayumi b. 1988, Kristin Kasumi b. 1991; edn: BA, Nat. Defense Acad., Yokosuka, Japan 1982; MBA, Univ. of Dallas, Tx. 1986; RIM, Internat. R.E. Inst., 1990. Career: mgr. Gateway Travel & Tours, Dallas 1985-87; portfolio investments Mitsui Real Estate Sales U.S.A. Co., Ltd., Los Angeles 1987-90, mgr. 1990-91, assn. vice pres. 1991-; dir: Alkaly Inc., Orange 1991-, v.p. Santa Ana Corp., Santa Ana 1992-; v.p. Santa Ana Management Corp., Santa Ana 1992-; mem: Internat. R.E. Inst. 1990-, Univ. Dallas Alumni Assn. 1986-, Orange Co. Japanese Am. Assn. 1993-; rec: shooting, music. Res: 2348 E Trenton Ave Orange 92667 Ofc: Mitsui Real Estate Sales U.S.A. Co., Ltd. 601 S Figuroa St Ste 4600 Los Angeles 90017

KURNICK, NATHANIEL B., cancer research physician; b. Nov. 8, 1917, New York; s. Jacob and Celia (Levine) K.; m. Dorothy Manheimer, Oct. 4, 1940 (dec. 1985); m. Sally Anne Kreeger, June 23, 1989; children: John E. Kurnick b. 1942, Katherine b. 1946 (dec. 1965), James T. Kurnick b. 1947; edn: BA, Harvard Univ. 1936; MD, Harvard Med. Sch. 1940; fellow Harvard Med. Sch. 1940-41; intern Mt. Sinai Hosp. 1942, sr. resident, 1946; fellow Rockefeller Inst. 1947; fellow Nobel Inst. 1948-49. Career: asst. prof. medicine Tulane Med. Sch., New Orleans, La. 1949-54; chief hematology service VA Hosp., Long Beach 1954-59; assoc. clin. med. medicine UCLA 1954-64; pvt. practice, Long Beach 1959-83; clin. prof. medicine UC Irvine 1964-; dir. Bixby Lab. Long Beach Comm. Hosp., Long Beach 1982-; cons. VA Hosp. Long Beach 1954-; chmn. cancer act. Long Beach Comm. Hosp. 1968-89, chmn. dept. med. oncology hematology 1982-87; honors: Sigma Xi; mem: Long Beach Soc. Internal Medicine (pres. 1971), A.C.P. (fellow), Internat. Soc. Exptl. Hematology, Am. Soc. Hematology, Western Soc. Clin. Research, Central Soc. Clin. Research, Condit Club, Harvard Club, Garden Grove Union H.S. Dist. (trustee 1960-64); research papers pub. in sci. jours., 1942-; mil: capt. AUS MC 1942-46; Democrat; Jewish; rec: sailing, skiing. Ofc: 1760 Termino Ave Ste G-20 Long Beach 90804

KURTZ-ABBOTT, PAULA J., accounting manager; b. April 20, 1962, Merced; d. Donald G. and Patsy A. (Bradshaw) Kurtz; m. John K. Abbott, Feb. 21, 1987; edn: BA internat. rels., UC Davis 1984; CSU Bakersfield 1985-87. Career: mgmt. trainee Household Fin., Bakersfield 1985; bookkeeper, acct. Barbich Longcrier Hooper & King 1985-87, retirement plan adminstr. 1987-90; accountant Contel 1990-91; acctg. mgr. Pepsi Cola Bottling Co. 1991-; mem: Inst. of Management Accountants, Soc. Prevention Cruelty to Animals; Democrat; rec: home remodelling, bicycling, gardening. Ofc: Pepsi Cola Bottling Co 215 E 21st St Bakersfield 93305

KUWAHARA, STEVEN SADAO, biochemist; b. July 20, 1940, Lahaina, Maui, Hawaii; s. Toshio and Hideko (Sasaki) K.; m. Rene M. Miyajima, June 24, 1972; children: Daniel T. b. 1974, Sara S. b. 1978; edn: BS, Cornell Univ. 1962; MS, Univ. Wisc. 1965, PhD, 1967. Career: research asst. Univ. Wisc. 1962-66; res. assoc. Univ. Wash. Seattle 1966-67; asst. prof. CSU Long Beach 1967-71; asst. res. biol. UC Irvine 1971-73; unit chief Mich. Dept. of Public Health, Lansing 1973-76, sect. chief 1976-82; mgr. test technol. Hyland Therapeutics, L.A. 1982-; adj. res. assoc. Coll. of Human Med., Mich. State Univ. 1980-82; honors: Award of Merit (Long Beach Heart Assn. 1969), Spl. Res. Fellowship (NIH 1971-73); mem: AAAS, Am. Assn. Blood Banks, Am. Chem. Soc., Am. Fedn. Clin. Res., Am. Soc. Microbiology, Soc. for Exptl. Biol. & Med., NY Acad. of Scis., Hemophilia Found. of So. Calif., BSA (scoutmaster); publ: 25 sci. papers, 15 presentations; Buddhist (treas. W. Covina Buddhist Ch.); rec: stamps, gardening. Res: 975 W Amador St Claremont 91711 Ofc: Hyland Therapeutics 1720 Flower Ave Duarte 91010

KUWAYAMA, GEORGE, art museum senior curator; b. Feb. 25, 1925, N.Y.C.; s. Senzo and Kuma K.; m. Lillian Y. Yamashita, Dec. 11, 1961; children: Holly b. 1964, Mark b. 1966, Jeremy b. 1972; edn: BA, Williams Coll., 1948; Inst. of Fine Arts N.Y. Univ.; MA, Univ. Mich., Ann Arbor 1956. Career: Keeper's asst. Cooper Union Museum, N.Y. summer 1954; curator Los Angeles County Mus. of Art, 1959-69, senior curator, 1969-; lectr. Univ. So. Calif., UCLA, CSU Northridge; awards: Charles Freer Scholar, Louise Hackney Fellow, Inter-University Fellow; mem: College Art Assn., Assn. for Asian Studies, Am. Oriental Soc., Internat. House of Japan, China Colloquium; editor and author: Imperial Taste (1989); author: Shippo: The Art of Enameling in Japan (1987), The Quest for Eternity (1987), Japanese Ink Printing (1985); ed. New Perspectives on the Art of Ceramics in China (1992), ed. Ancient Mortuary Traditions of China (1991), ed. Papers on Chinese Funeral Sculptures (1991); mil: pfc Parachute Inf. US Army 1944-46; Indep.; Methodist. Res: 1417 Comstock Ave Los Angeles 90024 Ofc: L.A. County Museum of Art 5905 Wilshire Blvd Los Angeles 90036

KWASKY, ALBERT JOSEPH, naval architecture and marine engineering co. president; b. Nov. 2, 1919, Manistee, Mich.; s. Joseph Albert and Antonia Regenia (Krasniewski) K.; m. Virginia Moore, Aug. 26, 1949; edn: BA, Columbia Coll.; postgrad. electronics engring., 1943-44, Stanford Univ.; electrical engring., 1945, Univ. Calif.; Registered Professional Engr., Calif. 1946. Career: elect. engr. Hurley Marine Works, Oakland 1942-45; elec. engr. Pillsbury & Martignoni, Inc., San Francisco 1946-62, marine engr. 1963-71, marine engr. supvr. 1972-78, mgr. 1979-81, pres. 1982- (only the third pres. of firm founded in 1901, as the first pres. Capt. Albert Pillsbury lived to age 94, and 2d pres. Walter L. Martignoni lived to 101 yrs); editor Electronics Systems Tech. Manual for USS Hancock (CVA-19) and USS Oriskany (CVA-34); mem: US Naval Institute, Navy League of the US, Soc. of Naval Archs. and Marine Engrs.; civic: The Nature Conservancy, Nat. Audubon Soc., Sierra Club, New England Anti-Vivisection Soc.; publs: The Old Lady in Dubuque, The Old Lady in Dubuque's Other Son, The Old Lady in Dubuque's Town, The Old Lady in Dubuque's Neighbors; R.Cath.; rec: tennis, chess, mtn. climbing, bird watching. Res: 2418 Ashby Ave Berkeley 94705 Ofc: Pillsbury & Martignoni, Inc. Pier 1 San Francisco 94111

LABBE, ARMAND JOSEPH, museum anthropologist; b. June 13, 1944, Lawrence, Mass.; s. Armand Henri and Gertrude (Martineau) L.; div.; edn: studies in philosophy, Marist Coll., 1962-63, Russian lang., Indiana Univ., 1963-65, Ger. lang., Univ. Md., West Berlin 1965-67; BA anthropology (cum laude) Univ. Mass., 1969, doctoral pgm. in anthropology 1969-71; MA anthropology, CSU Fullerton, 1986; seminars and workshops UCLA, Smithsonian Instn., Bowers Mus., San Diego Mus. Art; Calif. Comm. Colls. (life) instr. credential anthropology, 1983. Career: Russian language and intelligence analysis US Air Force, W.Berlin, 1965-67; curatorial asst. Bowers Mus., Santa Ana 1978-79, curator anthropology 1979-, chief curator 1986-, director for research and collections 1991-; p.t. faculty Santa Ana Coll., 1981-86, UC Irvine, 1983, 87, 91, CSU Fullerton, 1982-84, 88, UC Irvine 1993; trustee Americas Found. (for purpose of understanding cultures and histories of the Americas), Mass. 1985-; trustee Balboa Art Conservation Ctr., San Diego 1989-, adv. bd. Elan Internat., Newport Beach; author: Man and Cosmos in Prehispanic Mesoamerica 1982, Skywatchers of Ancient California 1983, Ban Chiang: Art and Prehistory of Northeast Thailand 1985, Colombia Before Columbus: The People, Culture and Ceramic Art of Prehispanic Colombia (1986, Spanish edit. 1988), Leigh Wiener: Portraits 1987, Images of Power 1992, co-author Tribute to the Gods: Treasures of the Mueo de Oro 1992; numerous scholarly papers, interviews (t.v. and print media) and lectures; contbg. and sole photographer books and art mags. 1980-; awards: honoree of the Colombian govt. and Colombian Inst. of Anthropology at Museo de Oro, Bogota 1988, Colombian nat. postage stamp inspired by cover of book Colombia Antes de Colon 1989, author-honoree Friends of Library UC Irvine (1987, 1988), inaugural lectr. for Lewis K. Land Memorial Lecture endowed by Friends of Ethnic Art of S.F. at M.H. de Young Mus. 1988, gold 1st pl. award for book entry Ad Club of We. Mass. 1987, recogn. Orange Cty. Bd. Suprs. 1982, Bowers Mus. Found. Bd. Dirs. 1982; mem: AAAS, NY Acad. Scis., Am. Anthropol. Assn. (Fellow), Southwestern Anthropol. Assn., Am. Assn. Museums, We. Museums Conf., Nat. Trust Hist. Preserv., Am. Assn. for State/Local History, Nat. Assn. for Mus. Exh., Am. Mus. Natural History, Smithsonian Instn., San Diego Mus. of Man, Newport Harbor Art Mus., Wilson Ctr. Assocs., Art Asia Mus. (Monterey), Acad. of Polit. Sci., Assn. Corporate Art Curators. Ofc: Bowers Museum 2002 N Main St Santa Ana 92706

LABENSKE, VICTOR KRIS, college professor; b. Dec. 26, 1963, Jonesboro, Ark.; s. George Elbert and Lois (Santo) L.; m. Judith Spaite, June 10, 1989; edn: BA in Music, Point Loma Nazarene Coll., S.D., Calif. 1985; M. of Music, Piano Performance, Univ. of Mo. Conservatory of Music, Kan. City, Mo. 1987; D.M.A. in Piano Performance, Univ. of So. Calif., L.A. 1993. Career: grad. tchg. asst., Univ. of Mo., Kan. City 1985-87; asst. prof. of music, Point Loma Nazarene Coll., S.D., Calif. 1987-; pianist, Opening Ceremonies 1984 Olympics, L.A.; awards: Herb Alpert Music Scholarship, L.A. 1981; first place SAI Composition Competition, Sigma Alpha Iota, Kan. City, Mo. 1986; Academic All-Amer. Scholar, Kan. City 1987; Scholarship, Mu Phi Epsilon, Kan. City

1987; Pi Kappa Lambda Award, L.A. 1993; mem.: Mu Phi Epsilon 1986-, Phi Kappa Phi 1987, Pi Kappa Lambda 1987, ASCAP 1987-; nationally certified mem. Music Teachers Nat. Assn. 1988-; mem. Calif. Profession of Profl. Music Teachers 1988-; v.p., Point Loma Nazarene Coll. Music Alumni Assn. 1991-; handbell choir dir., First Ch. of the Nazarene, S.D. 1987-; creative works: arranger of pub. piano hymn arrangements: Take My Life and Let It Be, 1987; It Is Well With My Soul, 1989; Manger Trilogy, 1990; There Is A Savior, 1990; Church of the Nazarene; rec: gardening. Ofc: Point Loma Nazarene College, 3900 Lomaland Dr. San Diego 92106-2899

LACEY, SUSAN K., county supervisor; b. July 5, 1941, Portland, Ore.; d. Marvin O. and Genevieve Walker; m. Edward Lacey, Mar. 22, 1967; edn: BS law, Univ. Ore. 1963; MS spl. edn., Calif. Lutheran Coll. 1976. Career: staff employment agency, Portland, 2 yrs.; spl. edn. tchr. Santa Paula (Calif.) Sch. Dist., 1967-80; elected co.supr. Dist. I, Ventura Co. Board Suprs., 1980-, reelected 1984-88, bd. chair 1984; mem. Co. Suprs. Assn. of Calif. (CSAC Health & Welfare Com. chair), Nat. Assn. of Counties (human services steering com. subcom. on income maint., NACo work and welfare reform task force), Nat. Criminal Justice Assn. Bd.; honors: life mem. PTA, women of achievement Bus. & Profl. Womens Club 1982, outstanding citizen of yr.Ventura Youth Council 1981, hon. chair Big Sisters/Big Brothers `Bowl for Kids' 1985; mem: Coalition of Labor Union Women, Calif. Assn. of Neurologically Handicapped Children, Phi Delta Kappa, nat. Women Pol. Caucus, Alliance for Mentally Ill of Ventura Co., Ventura Co. Soc. for Autistic Children (bd. dirs.), El Concilio del Condado de Ventura, Oxnard Union H.S. Dist. Interagcy. Council,U.S. Constn. Bicentennial Com. 1987, Ventura C.of C. Speakers Bur., BSA Golden Condor Award Com., Soroptimist Internat., Food Share (bd.), Ventura Co. Legal Guild, Child Passenger Safety Assn. of Ventura Co., Volunteer Caregivers advy. bd., Calif. Women for Agri.; rec: music appreciation. Res: 3700 Dean Dr #802 Ventura 93003 Ofc: County of Ventura 800 S Victoria Ave Ventura 93009

LACHMAN, BRANTON GEORGE, lawyer; b. Nov. 7, 1952, Altadena; s. Richard George and Blanche Marie (Bayless) L.; m. Sally Reid Johnson, Jan. 10, 1981; children: Hannah, Rose; edn: BA music edn., chem., CSU Fullerton, 1975; PharmD, USC Sch. Pharmacy, 1979; JD (summa cum laude, Valedictorian), Western State Univ. Coll. of Law, Fullerton 1992. Career: lic. pharmacist pvt. practice, Riverside 1979-81; hosp. pharmacist Western Med. Ctr., Santa Ana 1981-83; tchr. music Yucaipa High Sch. 1983-84; v.p. Pontil, Inc. Corona 1984-89; clin. asst. prof. pharmacy, adj., USC, 1986-92; clin. pharmacist PHI Health Care Mgmt. Inc., Laguna Hills 1989-90; sci. and music tchr. Centennial High Sch., Corona-Norco Unified Sch. Dist., 1990-92; judicial extern Hon. Edward J. Wallin, 4th Dist. Ct. Appeal, Div. III, 1991; patent litigation extern law firm Christie, Parker & Hale, 1992; civil litigation extern law firm Clayson, Mann, Arend & Yaeger, 1991, joined firm, atty., assoc. 1992-93; atty. assoc. Brunick, Alvarez & Batttersby 1993-; awards: preceptor svc. USC Sch. Pharm 1987, fellow Wm. S. Apple Pharmacy Mgmt. Pgm. 1988, Outstanding Young Men of Am. 1989, editor in chief Western State Univ. Law Rev. (Spring 1991), Honors Moot Ct. semi-finalist best team 1990, outstanding scholastic achiev. West Pub. Co. 1991-92, Am. Jurisprudence Awards, Don Program instr. (torts, property, constnl. law), Who's Who Among Students in Am. Univs. and Colls. 1992, Who's Who in the West 1990, mem. first student group Peter M. Elliott Inn of Ct. mentor pgm. for new attys. (Spring 1992); mem: Am. Pharm. Assn. (nat. chair Home Care sect. 1987), Calif. Pharm. Assn. (founding chair Acad. Home Health Care 1987-90); civic: Corona-Norco USD (science fair judge 1986, 89), Hedrick for Sch. Board (treas. 1988), Corona Peace Watch (founding mem. 1987), Inland Counties Hypertension Coord. Coun. (bd. 1985-90), Corona Fine Arts Com. (pres. 1985), Corona Sr. Citizens Ctr. (med. cons. 1979-89); Republican. Ofc: Brunick, Alvarez & Battersby 1839 Commercenter W. San Bernardino 92412

LACKRITZ, JAMES ROBERT, university educator, administrator; b. Dec. 30, 1950, Columbus, Ohio; s. Irving Ross and Dorothy (Krakoff) L.; m. Karen Marie Kearney, March 23, 1978; children: Kristen b. 1980, Robert b. 1982; edn: BS, Bucknell Univ. 1972; M.Stat., Univ. Fla. 1974; PhD, 1977. Career: tchg. asst., dept. statistics Univ. Fla., Gainesville 1972-77; asst. prof. mgmt. dept. San Diego St. Univ. 1977-81, assoc. prof. 1981-84, prof. 1984-85, prof. IDS dept. 1985-, chair 1986-; founding faculty Inst. Quality & Productivity 1987-; awards: San Diego St. Univ. MPPP 1985, 89, Outstanding Faculty 1987, Am. Statistical Assn. Best Paper 1979; mem: Am. Statistical Assn., Decision Scis. Inst., Balboa Tennis Club (bd. mem. 1980-82, v.p. 1982-84); num. articles pub. in profl. jours., 1977-, author Statistics for Bus., 1990; rec: tennis, skiing. Ofc: San Diego State University IDS Dept. San Diego 92182-0127

LACOURSE, MICHAEL G., college professor; b. Nov. 18, 1958, Manchester, N.H.; s. Gerald R. and June C. (Cullen) L.; edn: BS, Springfield Coll. 1980; MS, Ind. Univ. 1983; PhD, 1989. Career: vis. lectr. Ind. Univ., Bloomington, Ind. 1986-87; lectr. Cal Poly, San Luis Obispo 1987-; cons., 1988-; asst. track and field coach Ind. Univ. 1982-87; honors: Who's Who Among Coll. & Univ., Internat. Youth in Achievement; mem: Research Consortium, Am. Alliance of Health, Physical Edn. & Recreation; articles pub. in profl. jours.; Republican R.Cath.; rec: sports. Res: 1810 Bee Canyon Rd Arroyo Grande 93420 Ofc: Cal Poly 42-209 San Luis Obispo 93407

LACY, SUZANNE, artist, art educator; b. Oct. 21, 1945, Wasco, Calif.; edn: AA in premed. scis. (honors), Bakersfield Coll., 1965; BA zool. scis. (honors), UCSB, 1968; grad. work in psych., Fresno St. Coll., 1971; MFA in soc. design, Calif. Inst. of the Arts, 1973. Career: faculty Fresno St. Coll. 1969-70; Calif. Inst. of Arts 1971-72; UCLA Ext. 1974; S.F. Art Inst. 1975-77; UCSD 1976, 77, 79; Feminist Studio Workshop at the Woman's Bldg., L.A. 1974-79; UC Irvine 1982; Mpls. Coll. of Art and Design 1985-86; Sch. of the Art Inst. of Chgo. 1986; Dayton Hudson disting. vis. artist Carleton Coll. 1987; dean Sch. of Fine Arts, Calif. Coll. of Arts and Crafts 1987-; lectr. series on political art, condr. workshops in univs. nat. 1975-; awards: Calif. St. Scholar 1965-68, 72, CETA grantee 1977, Nat. Endowment of the Arts individual artist fellow 1979, 81, 85, Calif. Arts Council artist in residence 1982, 85, Vesta Award 1982, We. Regional Film fellow 1984, McKnight fellow 1985, Northwest Area fellow 1985, Film in the Cities film fellow 1986, Minn. St. Arts Bd. fellow 1987, Twin Cities Mayor's Award 1988, Calif. Arts Council individual artist fellow 1989, hon. mention S.F. Internat. Film Fest. 1988, Chris Bronze Plaque Columbus Internat. Film Fest. 1988, hon. mention "Crystal Quilt" soundtrack Nat. Fedn. of Comm. Bdcstrs. 1988; mem: Coll. Art Assn., Women's Caucus for Arts (nat. advy. bd. 1979-82), The Woman's Bldg. (bd. dirs. 1974-80); author/pub.: Rape Is (1972), Falling Apart (1976), Three Love Stories (1978), Three Weeks in May (1982), color postcard series: Travels with Mona (1977), contbr. chapters in books, numerous articles in mags. and feminist jours.; works catalogued and reviewed extensively, 1976-, frequent interviews and references in popular press, art and literary jours. Ofc: Calif. College of Arts & Crafts 5212 Broadway Oakland 94618

LAFFER, ARTHUR BETZ, economist; b. Aug. 14, 1940, Youngstown, Ohio; s. William G. and Molly (Betz) L.; m. Traci Hickman, Nov. 7, 1982; children: Tricia b. 1964, Art Jr. b. 1966, Molly b. 1969, Rachael b. 1972, Justin b. 1983, Allison b. 1984; edn: courses, Univ. of Munich, Germany; BA economics, Yale Univ. 1963; MBA, PhD economics, Stanford Univ. 1972. Career: assoc. prof. Bus. Econ., Univ. of Chicago 1970-76; economist, Ofc. of Mgmt. and Budget U.S. Govt. 1970-72; cons. U.S. Secty. Treasury and Secty. Def., 1972-1977; assoc. editorial pages, Wall Street Journal 1972-77; prof. Bus. Econ. USC 1976-84; current: disting. univ. prof. Pepperdine Univ., mem. Pepperdine Bd. of Dirs; founder, chmn. A.B. Laffer Assocs. (econ. research, fin. cons.), Lomita; mem. policy com. and bd. dirs. Am. Council for Capital Formation, WDC; mem. Econ. Policy Adv. Bd. to the President; ed. Marcel Dekker, Inc. series on Econ., Fin. and Bus.; contbtg. ed. Conservative Digest; dir. Gillespie, Laffer, Canto, Inc. (res. firm); honors: two Graham and Dodd awards Fin. Analyst Fed. for articles pub. in Fin. Analysts Jour., disting. svc. award Nat. Assoc. of Investment Clubs, Adam Smith Award 1983, Daniel Webster Award Internat. Platform Assn. 1979; mem: bd. of dirs. Los Angeles Co. Mus. of Natural Hist. (hon. mem.); adv. bd. Taxpayer's Found.; bd. mem. Peninsula Chamber Orch.; adv. bds. SIT Investment Assocs, Inc., Bradford & Marzec, Inc.; bd. mem. Boys Club of Am.; publs: The Financial Analysts Guide to Monetary Policy (1986), The Financial Analysts Guide to Fiscal Policy (1986), Conference on Internatioinal Trade, Foundatiions of Supply-side Economics, International Economics in an Integrated World (1983), Future American Energy Policy (1982), De Fiscus Order Het Mes (1981), L'ellipse ou la Loi des Rendements Fiscaux Decroissants (1981), The Economics of the Tax Revolt: A Reader (1976), Private Short-term Capital Flows, The Phenomenon of Worldwide Inflation (1975); Republican; rec: exotic birds, animals, plants.

LAFLER, DARLYNN JOAN, clinical laboratory scientist; medical technologist; b. July 3, 1961, San Diego; d. David Adam and Carole Joyce (Nicewicz) Lasky; m. Kirk Paul Lafler, July 7, 1984; edn: AS, Grossmont Coll. 1982; BS in microbiol., San Diego St. Univ. 1985; Calif. lic. medical technologist, 1987;cert. clin. lab. scientist, 1987. Career: lab. tech. San Diego Co. Vet., S.D. 1982-85; clin. lab. scientist, med. technologist- Technical Supervisor Sharp Memorial Hospital Laboratory, San Diego 1986-; mem: Am. Soc. Clin. Pathologists, Calif. Assn. for Medical Laboratory Technology, So. Calif. Am. Soc. Microbiology, Nat. Certification Agency for Med. Lab. Personnel Inc., Internat. Platform Assn.; publs: 2 papers (1986, 89); Republican; R.Cath.; rec: tennis, basketball, swimming. Ofc: Sharp Memorial Hospital (Pathology) San Diego 92123

LAFLER, KIRK PAUL, management and computer services executive; b. Feb. 27, 1956, Penn Yan, N.Y.; s. Paul Alton and Eleanor Theresa (Gombar) L.; m. Darlynn Joan, July 7, 1984; edn: BS, Univ. Miami, 1978; MS, 1982; George Washington Univ., 1981. Career: indep. cons., Miami, Fla. 1976-78; jr. programmer analyst Rydacom Inc. 1978-79; systems engr. Electronic Data Systems, W.D.C. 1979-81; programmer analyst Great American Federal, San Diego 1981-82; systems analyst S.D. Gas & Electric 1982-83; sr. systems analyst, engring. prin., 1983-86; pres./CEO Software Intelligence Corp., S.D. 1984-; honors: Electronic Data Systems commendn. 1981, U.S. DOE commendn. 1981, listed in Who's Who in Computer Industry 1989, Who's Who in West 1989-90; mem: Am. Assn. Artificial Intelligence, So. Calif. SAS Users Group (chmn./pres. 1989-), Assn. Computing Machinery, Internat. Platform Assn.; articles pub. in profl. jours. 1981-; Republican; R.Cath.; rec: computers, sailing, scuba diving, marine biology, basketball. Ofc: Software Intelligence Corp. POB 1390 Spring Valley 91979-1390

LAGORIO, IRENE ROSE, artist, writer; b. May 2, 1921, Oakland, Calif.; d. Marcello Natalino and Argentina (Sarmoria) Lagorio (both dec.); edn: AB, UC Berkeley, 1938-41; MA, UC Berkeley, 1942; post-grad. work, Columbia Univ., NY, NY, 1945-46. Career: children's class instr. Calif. Coll. Art, Oakland 1943-44, S.F. Art Inst. 1943; art instr. Napa Jr. Coll., Napa, Calif., 1943-45; supervising tchr. Oakland Public Sch., Oakland, 1945-50; guest lectr.: Holy Names Coll., Oakland, 1971, UC Ext. Div., Berkeley, 1964-66, 1972-73; ednl. curator CPLH Mus., S.F., Calif., 1950; dir. AFGA, 1950-56; pres. Carmel Art Assn., 1972; art critic The Herald, Monterey, Calif., 1974-89; awards: Duncan Vail Award, Calif. W.C. Soc., L.A., 1954; Graphics award, S.F. Mus. of Art, 1955; Am. Color P award, Am. Color Print Soc., Phila. 1960; Chapelbrook Found. Grant, Boston, 1968; Best of Show, Monterey Peninsula Mus. of Art, 1971; numerous others; mem: Pi Lambda Theta Soc. 1942-, Phi Beta Kappa Soc. 1942-, Ars Associated Found., Carmel (v.p. 1950-), Earthquake Engring. Res. Inst., El Cerrito, Calif.; author: book illustrator, Moving to Monterey, 1989; author/illustrator, book, Poetry Shell, 1991; author, book, Art History's Innovators, 1991, Oakland A's in Verse, 1992. Res: P.O. Box 153 Carmel 93921

LAGREEN, ALAN LENNART, public relations executive; b. May 20, 1951, Burbank, Calif.; s. Lennart F. and Mary (Cassara) LaGreen; m. Wendy D. Gilmaker, June 28, 1975; 1 child: Cara b. 1980; edn: BA, Univ. of So. Calif., L.A., 1972. Career: public relations asst. Dames & Moore, L.A., 1972-75; asst. pub. Orange County Illustrated, Newport Beach, 1975; membership mgr. Toastmasters Internat., Santa Ana, 1975-79; dist. adminstrn. mgr. Toastmasters Internat., Santa Ana, 1979-86; meetings coord. Fluor Corp., Irvine, 1986-87; gen. mgr. CCRA, Inc., Santa Ana, 1987-; publicity chmn. Orange County Visual Artists, Garden Grove, Calif., 1990-; mem: Am. Soc. of Assn. Executives (ASAE), 1979-; Reformed Ch. in Am.; rec: photography, model railroads. Res: 120 W. 20th St. Santa Ana 92706

LAM, LUI, physicist, educator; b. Nov. 17, 1944, Lianxian, China; s. Lap-Chung and Lai-Jane (Wong) L.; m. Heung-Mee Lee, July 1, 1972; children: Charlene b. 1977; edn: BS, Univ. Hong Kong, 1965; MS, Univ. Brit. Col., Vancouver 1968; MA, Columbia Univ., NY 1969, PhD, 1973. Career: res.h assoc. CUNY City Coll., N.Y. 1972-75; res. scientist Univ. Instelling Antwerpen, Antwerp, Belgium 1975-76; Univ. Saarlandes, Saarbrucken, Germany 1976-77; assoc. res. prof. Academia Sinica, Inst. of Physics, Beijing, China 1978-83; assoc. prof. Queensborough Comm. Coll., N.Y. 1984-87, and adj. prof. CUNY City Coll., 1985-87; prof. San Jose State Univ., Calif. 1987-; founder, co-editor: Springer Series on Partially Ordered Systems (1987-), Woodward Conf. Series (1988-), Springer-Verlag, N.Y.; planning & steering com. Intl. Liquid Crystal Confs. (1984-90); dir. NATO Advanced Res. Workshop (1990); assoc. ed. Molecular Crystals & Liquid Crystals J. (1981-), editl. mem. Liquid Crystals J. (1986-90); awards: Li Po Kwai scholar Univ. H.K. 1963-65, Eugene Higgin fellow Columbia Univ. 1966-67, Nordita fellow, Denmark 1976, DOE-Assoc. Western Univs. fellow 1989; mem: Am. Physical Soc. 1984-, Intl. Liquid Crystal Soc. (founder, bd. dirs., chair conf. com., 1990-); co-editor 5 books: Wave Phenomena (1988), Nonlinear Structures in Physical Systems (1990), Solitons in Liquid Crystals (1992), Modeling Complex Phenomena (1992), Liquid Crystalline and Mesomorphic Polymers (1993). Ofc: Dept. Physics, San Jose State Univ., San Jose, CA 95192-0106

LAMBERT, THOMAS RICHARD, biologist; b. Dec. 5, 1946, Oakland; s. Harold Wilson and Grace Addison (McHaffie) L.; m. Sally Crenshaw, June 2, 1990; edn: BS, CSU Chico 1969; MS, Humboldt St. Univ. 1973; cert. fishery bilogist (1975). Career: biologist Pacific Gas & scholarship, 1971; mem: Am. Fisheries Soc. (fin. com. chair), Am. Inst. Fishery Research Biologists (dir. 1975-), Conservation Unlimited Alumni Assn. (pres. 1991), Pacific Fishery Biologists, Assn. Power Biologists, Calif. Acad. Sci., Pt. Reyes Bird Observatory, Alexander Lindsay Museum, Nat. Audubon Soc.; articles pub. in profl. jours., 1972-89; rec: scuba diving, birdwatching, travel. Ofc: PG&E 3400 Crow Canyon Rd San Ramon 94583

LAND, JUDY M., educational and environmental products distributor, real estate developer; b. Oct. 6, 1945, Phoenix, Ariz.; d. Sanford K. and Doris Latanne (Hilburn) Land; m. Freddie Rick II; children: Neal McNeil, III b. 1973, Tahnee Land b. 1975; edn: AA, Merritt Coll., 1967; cert. Anthony's Sch. Real Estate, San Diego 1978; MBA, Burklyn Bus. Sch., La Jolla, 1984; lic. R.E. broker/appraiser Calif. 1978, 1985; CREA, Nat. Assn. R.E. Appraisers 1987. Career: v.p. Brehm Communities, San Diego, 1977-78; mgr. investment div. Ayres Real Estate, Encinitas 1978-79; asst. v.p. Summers Properties, La Jolla 1982-85; pres. The Land Co., La Jolla 1979-; cons. Broadmoor Homes, Guttman Constrn. Inc., Alan I. Kay Cos.; awards: Life Spike Club Nat. Assn. of Home Builders/S.D. 1986-90; mem: Nat. Assn. R.E. Appraisers, Nat. Assn. Women Execs., Building Ind. Assn. S.D. (bd. 1985, bd. dirs. Sales & Mktg. Council BIA 1988), Home Builders Council S.D. (pres. 1985, dir. 1982-85); rec: boating, tennis, skiing, swimming. Ofc: Rickland International, 1450 Frazee Rd Ste 714 San Diego 92108 Ph: 619/497-1919, 619/483-1111

LANDERS, VERNETTE, writer, retired school district counselor, civic activist; b. May 3, 1912, Lawton, Okla.; d. Fred and La Verne Trosper; m. Major Paul A.

Lum M.D. (dec. 1955); children: William Tappan; m. 2d. Newlin Landers, May 2, 1959 (dec. Apr. 6, 1990); children: Larry, Marlin; edn: AB (honors), UCLA 1933; MA, 1935; EdD, 1953; tchg. life diploma 1940; gen. pupil personnel svcs. life diploma 1970. Career: tchr. Montebello, Ca. schs., 1935-45, 1948-50, 1951-59; prof. Long Beach City Coll. 1946-47, Los Angeles State Coll. 1950; dean of girls 29 Palms H.S.; dist. counselor Morongo Unified Sch. Dist., 1965-72; coord. Adult Edn. 1965-67; dir. Guidance Project 1967; chg. clk., vol. Landers Post Office, 1962-83; secty. Landers Volunteer Fire Dept. 1972; v.p. Landers Assn. Inc., 1969-71; dir., secty. Desert Ears, emergency radio svc. 1970-73; freelance writer 1944-; recipient silver medal and Dedication pages in biographical ref. books Intl. Biog. Centre 1985, I.B.C. grand amb. of achiev. and life fellow, dep. dir. gen. of the Americas and Intl. Biog. Assn. Honors List of foremost women 20th century for contbns. to research 1987, life fellow and life dep. gov. Am. Biog. Inst. 1986; honors: Intl. Acad. of Poets, London, 1973, hon. degrees Univ. of Arts, Parma, Italy 1982, Leonardo DaVinci Intl. Acad., Rome 1982, World Univ., Tucson 1985; appreciation US Postal Svc. 1984, Morongo Unified. Sch. Dist. 1984, San Gorgonio Girl Scout Council, Certificates of Appreciation 1984-93, life fellow World Literary Acad., Cambridge, Eng. 1985, citizen of yr. Goat Mt. Grange 1987, guest of honor Landers Elementary Sch. groundbreaking ceremony 1989 and Dedication Ceremony LES 1991, Gold Commemorative Medal of Honor Am. Biog. Inst. 1987, Golden Acad. Oscar Award for lifetime achievement, life mem., World Inst. of Achievement 1991, Presdl. Order of Merit from Pres. George Bush 1991, Golden State Award Who's Who Hist. Soc. 1991, One in a Million Award- Internat. Biog. Ctr. 1992, Am. Biog. Inst.-Most Admired Woman of the Decade, Woman of the Yr. 1992; mem: Am., Calif., Personnel and Guidance Assns., Am. Assn. for Counseling & Devel. (25 Yr. mem. pin 1991), NEA, Nat. Assn. Women Deans and Adminstrs., Calif. Tchrs. Assn., I.P.A., Nat. League of Am. Penwomen, Bus. & Profl. Women's Club (pres. Montebello 1940), Toastmistress (pres., Whittier 1957), Soroptimist (29 Palms mem. of year 1967, life 1983, woman of distinc. 1987), Landers Area C.of C. (secty. 1983, presdl. trophy 1986), Friends of Copper Mt. Coll. (bd. 1990-92), Desert Memorial Hosp. Guild (life), Hi Desert Playhouse Guild (life), Hi Desert Nature Museum (life), Homestead Valley Women's Club (life), Phi Beta Kappa, Pi Lambda Theta, Sigma Delta Pi, Alpha Xi Delta Order of the Rose and Order of the Pearl 1989, Pi Delta Phi, Mortar Board, Prytanean Spurs, Morongo Basin Humane Soc. (life 1990); works: Impy 1974, Talkie 1975, Impy's Children 1975, Nineteen O Four 1976, Little Brown Bat 1976, Slo Go 1977, Who and Who Who 1978, Sandy The Coydog 1979, The Kit Fox and the Walking Stick 1980, Poems in New Voices in Amer. Poetry 1974, 75, An Anthol. on World Brotherhood 1975, 81, Rainbow 1984, contbr. "History of Comanche County, Okla." Vol. I 1985, sketch in "The Pen Woman" 1984; rec: wild animals, flying. Res: 632 N Landers Ln Landers 92285

LANDERSMAN, STUART DAVID, military tactical consultant; b. May 26, 1930, Bklyn.; s. Joseph David and Thelma (Domes) L.; m. Martha Britt Morehead, Sept. 2, 1955; children: David b. 1956, Mark b. 1960; edn: BA, Dakota Wesleyan Univ., 1953; MS, Geo. Washington Univ., 1967; Naval War Coll., Newport, R.I., 1967, Nat. War Coll., W.D.C., 1974. Career: capt. US Navy 1953-82, decorated Legion of Merit (1980, 81, 82), Bronze Star w. combat "v" (1979), Navy Commendn. w. combat "v" (1969, 72, 76); scientist Johns Hopkins Univ., Applied Phys. Lab., Laurel, Md. 1982-; Convoy Commodore USN 1983-92, Royal Navy 1984, Canadian Armed Forces 1986; mem. US Naval Inst. 1953-, Surface Navy Assn. 1985-, Nat. Eagle Scout Assn. 1984-; author books on tactics, ship handling, num. articles (1955-); rec: auto repair & restoration, woodworking, historical res. Res: 13220 Cooperage Ct Poway 92064 Ofc: JHU/APL REP (Code 008) COMNAVSURFPAC, NAB Coronado, San Diego 92155

LANDIS, ROSEANN W., psychotherapist; b. Jan. 27, 1932, Detroit, Mich.; d. Wm. A. and Doris R. Wood; m. Donald E. Landis, Nov. 6, 1954; children: Claudia b. 1956, Karla b. 1958, Donald b. 1963, Crane b. 1965; edn: BA in edn., Univ. Mich., Ann Arbor, 1954; MS in marriage, family, child counseling, CSU Dominguez Hills, 1982; lic. MFCC, Calif. Career: tchr. jr. high sch. North Chicago, Ill.; affiliate- hospice, hosp. home health care, Torrance; intern South Bay Ctr. for Counseling, Manhattan Beach, 1981-85; counselor South Bay Senior Services, Hermosa Beach, 1989-90; affiliate St. Peter's Counseling Service, Palos Verdes, 1985-, premarital counseling, Living Proof / Friendly Visitor cons. 1988-; pvt. practice psychotherapist, Rolling Hills Estates, 1985-, numerous lectures, community workshops, and group support groups; mem: Calif. Assn. M.F.C.C. 1985-, Nat. Bd. of Certified Counselors 1988, Anorexia Nervosa Associated Disorders 1985-, Nat. Assn. of Adlerian Psychology 1988-; author (booklet) Growing Through Loss 1990; Democrat; Presbyterian; rec: weaving, reading. Res: 221-B S Francisca Redondo Beach 90277 Ofc:326 Pacific Coast Hwy. #203 Redondo Beach 90277 Tel. 310/318-0071

LANDMAN, MICHAEL DENNIS, physician, head and neck surgeon; b. Dec. 18, 1942, Los Angeles; s. Maurice Seymour and Mary (Silver) L.; m. Erica Mary Ann Berk, Nov. 27, 1971; children: Aaron b. 1973, Shelby b. 1975, Courtney b. 1978, Megan b. 1982; edn: BA w. honors, UCLA 1964; MD w. honors, UCLA Sch. Medicine 1967. Career: intern Harbor Gen. Hosp., Torrance 1967-68; resident gen. surgery UCLA Med. Center, Los Angeles 1968-69, resi-

dent head and neck surgery 1969-72; pvt. practice, Los Angeles 1974-; asst. clin. prof. dept. head & neck surgery, UCLA 1974-; staff Valley Presbyterian Hosp., Van Nuys (staff chief 1985); bd. dirs. Research Study Club, L.A. 1988-; honors: Alpha Omega Alpha, fellow Am. Acad. Otolaryngology, fellow Am. Coll. Surgeons, fellow Am. Acad. Facial Plastic & Reconstructive Surgery, fellow Am. Soc. Head & Neck Surgery; mem: L.A. Soc. Otolaryngology (pres. 1962-63), L.A. Co. Med. Assn., CMA, AMA; contbr. articles to med. jours 1971-; mil: major USAF 1972-74. Ofc: 15243 Vanowen St Ste 203 Van Nuys 91405

LANDMANN, CHERYL ANN, computer systems consultant; b. June 24, 1957, Inglewood; d. Charles Arthur and Arlene Eleanor (Winter) Waters; m. Wayne Landmann, Feb. 20, 1982; children: Angelina b. 1987, Magdalena b. 1989; edn: BS in bus. admin., Univ. Redlands, 1984. Career: data analyst Northrop Corp., Hawthorne 1974-78; bus. pgmr./analyst McDonnell Douglas, St. Louis, Mo. 1978-80; senior bus. pgmr./analyst Northrop Corp., Pico Rivera, Ca. 1980-86; Restaurant Ents., Irvine 1986-88; senior bus. sys. specialist Calcomp Inc., Anaheim 1988; co-owner Maui Express Enterprises, PC consulting, 1989-; sales cons. & mgr. Princess House Inc. (home party sales) 1989-; mem. Nat. Assn. Female Execs.; participating host family AISE fgn. student exchange; Republican; rec: stained glass, needlework. Res: 5960 Via Del Tecolote Yorba Linda 92687

LANEY, MICHAEL L., executive; b. Sept. 10, 1945, Los Angeles: s. Roy and Wanda L.; m. Marti, Dec. 31, 1964; children: Tynna b. 1962, Kristen b. 1968; edn: BS w. honors, CSU Northridge 1967; MBA, UCLA 1969; C.P.A. Calif. 1969. Career: tax splst. Deloitte Haskins & Sells, L.A. 1967-70; asst. prof. acctg. CSU Northridge 1969-71; tax splst., L.A. 1972-75; ptnr. Michael L. Laney, Beverly Hills 1975-80; v.p., controller Ducommun Inc., L.A. 1980-87; sr. v.p., fin. & adminstrn. Monarch Mirror Door Co. Inc., Chatsworth 1987-92; v.p. feature animation div. Walt Disney Co., Glendale 1992-; p.t. instr. CSU Northridge 1970-80; mem: Am. Inst. CPA, Calif. Soc. CPA, Fin. Execs. Inst., Tax Execs. Inst.; rec: golf. Ofc: Walt Disney Company Feature Animation Division 1420 Flower St Glendale 91221-8410

LANG, TZU-WANG, professor of medicine; b. Apr. 15, 1929, Hsiang-Shan Hsien, Chekiang Province, China, nat. US cit. 1977; s. Wang-Chieh and Chun-Hsiang (Chang) L.; grandson of Jing-Bang Lang, the Scholar of the Ching Dynasty (1884-1950); m. Winnie Chi, Apr. 15, 1960; children: Daniel b. 1962, Cathy Mae b. 1972; edn: MB, Nat. Defense Medical Center 1955; MD, Nat. Acad. Bd. in Med. 1955. Career: res. fellow Am. Coll. of Cardiology, 1963-65; prin. investigator Cardiovascular Res., VA Gen. Hosp., Taiwan 1966-68; chief of cardiology, Tri-Service Gen. Hosp., Taiwan 1967-69; sr. res. scientist dept. med. Cedars-Sinai Med. Center, Los Angeles 1969-78; adj. assoc. prof. med. UC Los Angeles 1969-76, assoc. clin. prof. med. UC Los Angeles, 1976-; awards: Gold Medal in sci., Taiwan 1962, Young Investigator award finalist, Am. Coll. Cardiology, Boston 1965; mem: Fellow Am. Coll. Cardiology, Am. Heart Assn., AMA, Calif. Med. Assn.; works:one of the pioneers of synchronized retro-perfusion (SRP) for the treatment of coronary artery disease (Am. Jour. Cardiol. 1976, 78); author over 90 sci. papers and contbr. chapters to 4 textbooks on cardiology; Confucianism. Res: 301 N Elm Dr Beverly Hills 90210. Ofc: 8920 Wilshire Blvd Ste 104 Beverly Hills 90211

LANGENHEIM, JEAN H., professor of biology; b. Sept. 5, 1925, Homer, La.; d. Vergil W. and Jeanette (Smith) Harmon; m. Ralph L. Langenheim, Dec. 21, 1946 (div. 1962); edn: BS, Univ. Tulsa 1946; MS, Univ. Minn. 1949; PhD, 1953. Career: research assoc. UC Berkeley 1954-59; asst. prof. San Francisco Coll. for Women 1957-59; res., tchg. assoc. Univ. Ill., Urbana 1959-62; res. fellow Harvard Univ. Cambridge, Mass. 1962-66; fellow Bunting Inst. 1964-65; asst. prof. UC Santa Cruz 1966-68, assoc. prof. 1968-73, prof. 1973-; awards: Calif. Acad. Sci. fellow 1973, Univ. Tulsa disting. alumni 1979, Australian Nat. Univ. fellow 1980, Radcliffe-Harvard Bunting Inst. annual sci. lectr. 1986, Univ. N.M. Sandia Found. annual lectr. 1987; mem: Assn. Tropical Biology (pres. 1985-86), Ecological Soc. Am. (pres. 1986-87), Internat. Soc. Chemical Ecology (pres. 1986-87), Sierra Club, Am. Assn. Univ. Women, Soc. Prevention of Cruelty to Animals; coauthor Botany: Plant Biology & Its Relation to Human Affairs (1982), 100+ articles in sci. jours. (1955-); Democrat; rec: photog., gardening, travel. Res: 191 Palo Verde Terrace Santa Cruz 95060 Ofc: Dept. Biology University California Santa Cruz 95064

LANGHORST, GARY ARLEN, retired army training specialist; b. June 30, 1928, Portland, Ore.; s. Walter Christian and Elsie Lillian (Miles) L.; m. Helen Ruth Costner (dec. Feb. 26, 1988); 1 son, Richard Arlen b. 1963; edn: Charlotte Coll., 1953-55, BA in hist., Wake Forest Coll., Winston-Salem, N.C. 1956-67; Golden Gate Baptist Theol. Sem. 1957-58. Career: training specialist 351st Civil Affairs Command, US Army Reserve, 1964-88; exec. sec. Lamptey Sports Found., Santa Clara 1988-90; mem. Kiwanis Intl. (Santa Clara 1989-, Milpitas Club 1970-86, pres. 1980-81), Civic Center Club (1986-, pres. 1987-88, sec./treas. 1988-), Div. 12 (lt. gov. 1984-85, area rep. 1985-86, dist. chmn. Support to Spiritual Aims 1986-88, 90-91); mem. North Valley Players of Milpitas (bd.), Calif. Park Ministry (bd. 1986-91); Republican; So. Baptist/Heart of the Valley Baptist Ch. (deacon, tchr. comparative religions, dir. single ministry, dir. senior adults, and minister of music 1989-); rec: church work, music, photography. Res: 1580 Fallen Leaf Dr Milpitas 95035 Ofc: 1397 W Hedding St San Jose 95126

LANSER, HERBERT RAYMOND, financial planner, photographer; b. Dec. 10, 1932, Hollywood; s. Hugo and Anna (Strandlund) L.; m. Evana E. Conway, Apr. 1, 1980 (div.); children: Lynn (dec.), Deborah, Cynthia, Karen, Rick; m. Judy Kay Skousen; children: Zachary, Joshua, Ezekiel; Cert. Fin. Planner (CFP) 1962. Career: prin. Herb Lanser Financial Services, San Mateo 1956-62; Morro Bay 1986-; fin. planner 1962-, cons. various orgns. 1975-, cons. Lanser Vermiculture Svs., Herb Lanser Fin. Svs., Nurnberg, Fed. Republic Germany 1983-85; accomplished photographer, numerous published photos incl. telephone directory and book covers, photog. Internat. Freelance Photog. Orgn. Am. Image, Washington, DC 1991-, model cons. Internat. Freelance Models Orgn., Washington, DC 1992- ; awards: nat. sales leader Prudential Ins. Co., Europe (1985, 87); mem. Nat. Assn. Life Underwriters (S.L.O. Co. chapt. bd. dirs., chmn. pub. service 1989-90, v.p. 1991), Morro Bay C.of C. (bd. dirs., chmn. econ. devel. com. 1990, v.p. 1991, pres. 1992); mil: sgt. US Army 1953-55; author: Profit From Earthworms 1976, articles in profl. jours.; Republican. Ofc: Herb Lanser & Associates PO Box 834 Morro Bay 93443

LANTZ, NORMAN FOSTER, aerospace engineer; b. June 8, 1937, Pekin, Ill.; s. Norman Gough and Lenore Moffett (Elsbury) L.; m. Donnis Ballinger, Sept. 7, 1958 (div. Aug. 1991); children: Katherine b. 1961, Deborah b. 1964, Norman Daniel b. 1967; m. Judith Elaine Peach, Dec. 7, 1991; edn: BSEE, and MSEE, Purdue Univ., 1959, 1961; lic. E.I.T., Ind., 1959. Career: engr. General Electric Co., Phila. 1961-72; senior project engr. The Aerospace Corp., El Segundo 1972-; dir. Internat. Found. for Telemetry, L.A. 1988-; mem. IEEE 1959-, Am. Mgmt. Assn., sr. mem. AIAA 1991-; mil: 2d lt. US Army 1959-67; Republican; South Bay Christian Ch., Redondo Beach (elder, chmn.). Res: 2801 W Sepulveda Blvd #10 Torrance 90505 Ofc: The Aerospace Corp. PO Box 92957 Los Angeles 90009

LAREDO, DAVID CARY, lawyer; b. Feb. 1, 1950, N.Y.C.; s. Joseph A. and Ruth Helen (Mautner) L.; m. Virginia Isabelle Smith, Sept. 23, 1972; children: Christina b. 1980, Josef b. 1984, Michael b. 1987, Matthew b. 1989; edn: BA in English, UCLA, 1972; JD, Southwestern Univ., 1975. Career: served to lt. USNR, 1975-79, staff judge advocate Naval Postgrad. Sch., Monterey; dep. county counsel Monterey County, 1979-81; atty., ptnr. De Lay & Laredo, Pacific Grove 1981-; general counsel Monterey Peninsula Water Mgmt. Dist., 1979-, Pajaro Valley Water Mgmt. Agy., 1986-; instr. Monterey Coll. of Law 1979-82, Monterey Peninsula Coll. 1977-78; dir. Monterey Federal Credit Union (1984-, chmn. bd. 1988-); dir. Children's Services Center (1984-, chmn. bd. 1988-89); mem., v.p. Monterey Penin. Jaycees 1979-84; pub. article: Conducting Effective Meetings (1992), Taking "Charge" of Board Meetings (1992); rec: skiing. Ofc: De Lay & Laredo 606 Forest Ave Pacific Grove 93950

LARGMAN, KENNETH, strategic analyst, strategic defense analysis company executive; b. Apr. 7, 1949, Phila.; s. Franklin Spencer and Roselynd Marjorie (Golden) L.; 1 dau., Jezra b. 1971; edn: State Univ. NY, Old Westbury 1969-70. Career: invented initial version of `Moves and Countermoves Game' to aid U.S. and Soviet political leaders in examination of their options regarding strategic defense and nuclear conflict 1976; c.e.o. World Security Council 1980-; founder Middle East Crisis Center, 1990; devel. computer pgm. to aid govt. leaders in examining Middle East policy options, 1991; developed new theory and system for analysis and testing of policy options, 1992; extensive res. in moves and countermoves in strat. defense; cons. to top US polit. and mil. ofcls.; coauthor computerized game "Interaction of Strategic Defense and Nuclear Conflict: U.S./Soviet Moves and Countermoves," dir., referee and player simulation games in Pentagon, Soviet Emb., and Capitol Hill; mem. World Affairs Council; author: A Method of Discovering Unanticipated Dangers, Problems, and Solutions Related to Defense Policy and Arms Control (1989), numerous books and rsch. papers on strategic defense and prevention of nuclear war; rec: mountaineering, nature, travel, Socratic logic. Ofc: World Security Council, World Trade Ctr San Francisco 94111

LARNER, JULES, physician-surgeon, ret.; b. Oct. 24, 1910, Los Angeles; s. Max and Esther Larner; m. Ruth Genss, Feb. 9, 1955; children: Douglas b. 1950, Jakki b. 1951; edn: MD, Calif. Coll. of Med. 1962; DO, Coll. Osteopathic Physicians & Surgeons. Career: staff physician, founder Sequoia Hosp., Fresno 1942, San Gabriel Valley Hosp., San Gabriel 1948; attending staff Dept. Surgery, L.A. Co. Gen. Hosp., Los Angeles 1953-58; bd. chmn. and pres. Glendora Hosp., Glendora 1960-67; ret.; named Bonds for Israel Man of Year 1968; recipient disting. service awards: San Gabriel Valley Hosp. 1973, Jewish Big Brothers 1975, Jewish Fedn. Council E. Area 1983; mem. San Gabriel Valley Osteopathic Soc. (pres. 1958-59); past mem. Fresno Rotary, Elks, Odd Fellows; mem: Pasadena Bnai Brith, Jewish Fedn. Council United Jewish Fund, Fellow Anti-Defamation League, Del Rey Yacht Club (past bd.); established Larner Educational Trust and Larner Chapel at Temple Shaarei Tikvah, Arcadia; publs: article on San Joaquin Fever; Republican; Jewish; rec: yachting, gardening, golf. Res: 3491 Lombardy Rd Pasadena 91107

LARSEN, CARTER LAWRENCE, vinyardist, investor; b. Feb. 10, 1919, Phila.; s. John Lawrence and Caroline (Miller) L.; m. Carita Martin, June 6, 1952; children: Carter Jr. b. 1955; Martin Scott b. 1953, Brett F.M. b. 1957, Caroline b. 1959; edn: BS, Bucknell Univ., 1940; MBA, Harvard Univ., 1947. Career: banker, investor, vineyardist; pres. Taunton, Inc.; owner/ mgr. Carter Larsen Vineyards; dir: Eastern Oregon Land Co.; Stearns Ranchos; clubs: Pacific Union, Harvard (NYC); mil: Cdr. USNR, WWII, decorated 4 battle stars, Letter of Commendation; Prot. Res: 3621 Washington St San Francisco 94118 also: Alexander Valley, Sonoma County

LARSEN, DONNA K., media consultant, writer; b. Feb. 14, Anniston, Ala.; d. James M. and Lucy Bible; edn: BA, Univ. Alabama, 1970. Career: intern, reporter Anniston (Ala.) Star, 1967-69; feature writer Los Angeles Times, L.A. 1970-75; owner, pres. Larsen Promotions, L.A. 1977-; mem: Hollywood Women's Press Club, Book Publicists So. Calif., L.A. World Affairs Council, Internat. Women's Media Found.; rec: astronomy, astrology, cinema hist., tennis. Ofc: Larsen Promotions 720 S Plymouth Blvd Ste 11 Los Angeles 90005

LARSON, ERIC VICTOR, policy analyst; b. May 29, 1957, Buffalo, N.Y.; s. Ralph William and Marilyn Ruth (Werner) L.; edn: AB polit. sci., Univ. Mich., 1980; policy analysis, RAND Grad. Sch., Santa Monica, PhD cand. Career: statistician Office of Mgmt. & Budget, W.D.C., 1980-82; policy analyst Office of Planning & Evaluation, The White House, 1982-83; policy and systems analyst Nat. Security Council, 1983-88; res. staff mem. Inst. for Defense Analyses, Alexandria, Va. 1988-89; graduate fellow RAND, Santa Monica 1989-, tchg. asst. RAND Grad. Sch., 1990; recipient 2 scholastic distinction honors RAND Grad. Sch. 1991, vis. student to Oxford Univ., St. Antony's Coll., U.K. 1991, Outstanding Young Man of Am. 1986; mem: Operations Research Soc. Am., AAAS, Assn. for Pub. Policy Analysis and Mgmt., Internat. Inst. for the Systems Sciences; mentor Minority Assistance Pgm., RAND (1990, 92); faculty Distinguished Scholars Pgm. Santa Monica High Sch. 1992; First Presbyterian Ch., Santa Monica (trustee, choir); publs: 4+ articles & monographs in field (1991, 92); Presbyterian; rec: music. Ofc: RAND, 1700 Main St Santa Monica 90407

LARSON, FREDERIC RALPH, photojournalist; b. Nov. 16, 1949, Milw.; s. Vern and Evelyn (Suits) L.; m. Jessica Velasquez, Jan. 13, 1980 (div. 1984); m. Vicki Janofsky, April 22, 1988 (div. 1984); m. Vicki Janofsky, Apr. 22, 1988; edn: BA in radio and t.v., San Francisco St Univ. 1975. Career: photographer UPI, San Francisco 1975-79; staff photographer San Francisco Chronicle 1979-; awards: Hiroshima Found. travel pgm. grantee, Japan 1988, finalist Pulitzer Prize S.F. Chronicle 1988, AP Sweepstakes 1988, Nat. Football Hall of Fame best feature football photo 1987, 20+ local awards Bay Area Press Photographers 1979-; mem: Nat. Press Photographers Assn., Calif. Press Photographers Assn., Bay Area Press Photographers Assn.; contbg. photog. (books): Photographer Through our Eyes (1987), Redskins The Team of the Eighties (1988), Super Season SF 49ers (1984), Best of Photojournalist (1985); mil: p.o.3c USNR 1970-76; rec: sports. Ofc: San Francisco Chronicle 901 Mission St San Francisco 94103

LASHER, SUE, elected city official; b. Split, Yugoslavia, came to U.S. 1932; d. Peter and Ida (Purisic) Sorich; 1 son, Eric Lasher. Elected councilwoman City of Santa Clara, 1983-; mem. League of Calif. Cities 1984-, chair Modesto-Santa Clara-Redding Joint Power Agy. 1985-90, mem. Santa Clara County Transp. Commn. 1987-, mem. S.C. Co. Congestion Mgmt. Agy.; mem. Santa Clara Women's League (pres. 1984-86), Soroptimists. Ofc: City of Santa Clara 1500 Warburton Ave Santa Clara 95050

LASITER, JACK BRINKLEY, private investments; b. July 20, 1930, Fort Smith, Ark.; s. Brinkley Cyrus and Ruth Leona (Wear) L.; m. Julia Simmons, June 16, 1957; son, Paul b. 1966; edn: BS, Pepperdine Univ., 1954, MBA, 1975; cert. internal auditor, IIA 1973; career: acct. Aerophysics Devel. Corp., Santa Barbar 1956-57; Kibbee, Peterson & Co., Hollywood 1957-58; Southern Calif. Gas Co., 1958-80, audit support supr. Pacific Lighting Corp., Los Angeles 1980-89, audit support supr. priv. investments 1989-; mem: Inst. Internal Auditors (chmn. scholarship com. L.A. chpt. 1980-81), Town Hall of Calif.; mil: cpl. US Army 1954-56; Republican; Ch. of Christ; rec: book collecting, wood working; res: 1330 N Valley Home Ave La Habra 9063; ofc: 1330 N Valley Home Ave La Habra 90631

LASKA, MARK SROL, dentist; b. Apr. 26, 1945, Pittsburgh, Pa.; s. Sol and Lena Irene (Berman) L.; m. Joan Dunlap, 1973; children: Shawn b. 1963, Sheila b. 1964, Shaye b. 1976; edn: UC Los Angeles 1963-66; DDS, USC Sch. of Dentistry 1970. Career: dentist Group Dental Service, 1970-81, head dentist Group Dental Service, A., 1973-81, dental dir. Group Dental Serv., 1980-81; pvt. practice, Los Angeles 1981-; assoc. with S. Jay Welborn, Pasadena 1981-82; official dentist Los Angeles Clippers Basketball Team (NBA) 1989, 1990; mem. Los Angeles Olympic Citizens Advy. Commn., and L.A. Olympic Medical/ Dental Advy. Commn. 1984; staff dentist Olympic Games, USC Polyclinic 1984; honors: Zeta Beta Tau, Alpha Omega; mem: Acad. of General Dentistry, Am. Acad. of Cosmetic Dentistry, Am. Dental Assn., Calif. Dental Assn., Los

Angeles Dental Soc. (Comm. on Dental Care, 1981-84); civic: Hollywood Los Feliz Jewish Comm. Ctr. (bd. 1979-85, chmn. phys. ed. com. 1981-2), YMCA, Laughlin Park HOA (dir. 1980-, pres. 1981, 84, 86, 87, 89, 90, v.p. 1985, 88, treas. 1983), Los Feliz Improvement Assn. (dir. 1986-87), Los Feliz Mobility Action Com.; Democrat; Jewish; rec: politics, racquetball, running. Res: Los Angeles 90027 Ofc: 3460 Wilshire Blvd Ste 104 Los Angeles 90010

LAST, JEROLD ALAN, professor of medicine and biological chemistry; b. June 5, 1940, N.Y.C.; s. Herbert and Florence L.; m. Elaine Zimelis, June 1, 1975; children: Andrew b. 1968, Matthew b. 1976, Michael b. 1978; edn: BS chemistry, Univ. Wis., 1959, MS biochemistry, Univ. Wis., 1961; PhD biochemistry, Ohio State Univ., 1965; postdoctoral fellow biochemistry, N.Y. Univ. 1966-67. Career: sr. res. scientist Squibb Inst. for Medical Res., New Brunswick, N.J. 1967-69; ed. Proceedings of the NAS, W.D.C., 1970-73; res. assoc. Harvard Univ., Cambridge, Mass. 1973-76; prof. UC Davis, 1976-, dir. UC Systemwide Toxic Substances Res. & Teaching Pgm. 1985-, unit ldr. Respiratory Diseases Unit, Calif. Regional Primate Res. Ctr., Davis 1985-; v. chair Dept. of Internal Med. UC Davis 1985-; mem. editorial bds. various sci. journals, review panels various granting agys.; awards: Frank R. Blood Award Soc. of Toxicology 1979, Joan Oettinger Meml. res. award UC Davis (1979, 1983), Fulbright prof. Montevideo, Uruguay 1983, UCD Sch. of Medicine Faculty res. award 1990, ICI travelling lectr. Soc. of Toxicology 1992, prin. investigator numerous grants in lung biology & toxicology; mem: Am. Soc. Biol. Chemistry and Mol. Biology, Soc. of Toxicology, Am. Thoracic Soc., Calif. Lung Assn.; inventor (3) patents: antimicrobial agents; editor book series: Methods in Molecular Biology, 150+ sci. papers and monographs; rec: referee Am. Youth Soccer Org. Ofc: Univ. California CRPRC, Davis 95616-8542

LATHROP, MITCHELL LEE, lawyer; b. Dec. 15, 1937, Los Angeles; s. Alfred Lee and Barbara Isabella (Mitchell) L.; m. Denice Annette Davis; children: Christin b. 1964, Alexander b. 1967, Timothy b. 1971; edn: BS, US Naval Acad. 1959; JD, USC Law Sch. 1966; admitted bar: Calif., New York, Dist. Col.; cert. civil trial specialist Nat. Bd. Trial Advocacy. Career: dep. county counsel Los Angeles County, 1966-69; atty., assoc., then ptnr. Brill, Hunt, DeBuys & Burby, L.A. 1969-71; ptnr. Macdonald, Halsted & Laybourne, L.A. and San Diego, 1971-80; senior ptnr. Rogers & Wells, S.D., L.A., N.Y., 1980-86; senior ptnr., exec. com. and firm chmn. Adams, Duque and Hazeltine, S.D., L.A., S.F., N.Y.C., 1986-; presiding referee Calif. State Bar Court (1985-87), lectr. in law, Am. Bar Assn., Calif. Judges Assn., Calif. State Bar, Univ. of San Diego, Calif. Western Univ., Practising Law Inst.; mem. bds: Metropolitan Opera Assn., N.Y. (dir.), Met. Opera Nat. Council (v.p., exec. com. chmn., and dir.), San Diego Opera Assn. (v.p. 1985-89, dir.), National Actors Theatre, N.Y. (nat. steering com.); mem: Am., Calif., N.Y., D.C. bar assns., San Diego County Bar Assn. (v.p., dir. 1983-85), Am. Bd. of Trial Advocates, San Diego Co. Bar Found. (dir. 1984-86), Internat. Assn. of Defense Counsel; author: State Hazardous Waste Regulation (Butterworth Legal Pubs., 1991), Environmental Insurance Coverage: State Law and Regulation (Butterworth Legal Pubs., 1991), Insurance Coverage for Environmental Claims (Matthew Bender & Co., 1992); mil: capt. JAGC, USNR, active duty 1959-63, Vietnam Svc.; Republican; R.Cath.; rec: classical music, scuba. Res: 455 Silvergate Ave San Diego 92106-3327 Ofc: Adams, Duque & Hazeltine, 401 West A St 26th Fl San Diego 92101-7910 also: 551 Madison Ave 8th Flr New York NY 10022

LAU, BOBBY WAI-MAN, financial planning executive; b. Dec. 24, 1944, Hong Kong; s. Nelson and Ruby (Choy) L.; edn: BS in math, UC Davis 1969, MA math, 1971; research in math., Calif. Inst. Tech. 1971-72, res. in math and computer sci., UCLA 1972-75. Career: insurance agt. Equitable Life Assurance Soc. of the U.S., Los Angeles 1975-80, dist. mgr. Equitable Financial Cos., 1980-90; pres. Bobby Lau & Assocs. Fin. Services 1976-, Bobby Lau Seminars for Profls. 1979-; chmn. bd. Pension & Benefit Services of America, 1988-; chmn. bd. Success Pension & Insurance Services Corp., 1990-; honors: Hall of Fame, Equitable Fin. Cos. 1986; mem: Internat. Assn. of Fin. Planner, Nat. Assn. of Tax Consultants, Nat. Assn. Life Underwriters; publs. on investments, ins., pensions & tax plnng.; Republican; rec: music, investment. Ofc: 711 West College St Ste 600 Los Angeles 90012

LAU, ELIZABETH KWOK-WAH, social worker; b. Jan. 7, 1940, Hong Kong; nat. 1971; m. Edmond Lau, June 6, 1965; children: Melissa b. 1968, Ernest b. 1971; edn: BA, Brigham Young Univ. 1963; MSW, Univ. Kans. Lawrence 1965. Career: supr. Northeast Comm. Mental Health Center, San Francisco 1969-73; clin. dir. Child Devel. Ctr. 1973-75; program splst. Head Start Program 1975-77; psychiatric social worker V.A. Hosp., Palo Alto 1977-86; med. social worker V.A. Med. Ctr., S.F. 1986-91; social work supr., 1991-; mental health cons. Head Start Program 1970-75; St. Frances Day Home 1971-75; hostess, supr. KTSF TV 1982-; bd. mem. Kai Ming Head Start 1984-; honors: Who's Who Am. Women 1984-85, World Who's Who Women 1988, Federal Employee of Year-Profl. 1990; mem: Nat. Acad. Social Workers, Zion Lutheran Ch. (deaconess 1988-90); author: Innovative Parenting, 1980, How to Love Your Children , 1982, How to Raise a Successful Child, 1984, How to Raise a Bright Child, 1986, How to Understand Your Child, 1987, Everything You Want to Know About Childrearing, 1988, Getting to Know the American,

1990, Best Guidance to Adolescents, 1993; Lutheran; Res: 470 Ortega St San Francisco 94122 Ofc: Veterans Administration Medical Center 4150 Clement St San Francisco 94121

LAUDENSLAGER, WANDA LEE, speech pathologist, real estate broker, contractor; b. July 22, 1929, San Jose; d. Victor Vierra and Florence Lorene (Houck) Silveira; m. Leonard Laudenslager, Apr. 26, 1952; children: Leonard II, b. 1953, Dawn Marie, b. 1954; edn: AA, Coll. of San Mateo 1960; BA, and MA, CSU San Jose 1962, 1965; Calif. std. tchg. cred. 1962, std. supvn., std. designated svs. creds., 1971; Calif. lic. audiometrist, 1962, speech pathologist 1962, R.E. broker 1978, gen. bldg. contr., 1979. Career: speech pathologist, Newark Unif. Sch. Dist. 1962-89, dist. coord. speech, lang. and hearing dept. 1965-83; self-empl. R.E. broker, gen. bldg. contractor; honors: Alpha Gamma Sigma 1960; Phi Kappa Phi; Pi Lambda Theta; Kappa Delta Pi 1962; mem: Am. Speech Lang. & Hearing Assn.; Assn. of Calif. Sch. Adminstrs.; Nat./ Calif. Assns. Realtors; So. Alameda Co. Bd. Realtors; Republican; Presbyterian. Res: 37733 Logan Dr Fremont 94536

LAUER, JEANETTE CAROL, historian, author; b. July 14, 1935, St. Louis, Mo.; d. Clinton Jones and Blanche Aldine (Gideon) Pentecost; m. Robert Harold Lauer, July 14, 1954; children: Jon b. 1955, Julie b. 1957, Jeffrey b. 1961; edn: BS Univ. Mo. St. Louis 1970; MA, Wash. Univ. St. Louis 1972; PhD, 1975. Career: instr., Wash. Univ., St. Louis, Mo. 1972-73; assoc. prof. Comm. Coll. 1974-82; U.S. Internat. Univ., San Diego 1983-; ed. Am. Historical Assn., WDC 1980-88; awards: Univ. Mo. hon. scholarship 1966-69, Woodrow Wilson fellow 1970, Wash. Univ. fellowship 1971-75; mem: Orgn. Am. Historians, Am. Historical Soc.; author: Fashion Power (1981), Spirit & The Flesh (1983), Till Death Do Us Part (1986), Watersheds (1988), num. articles pub. in jours.; Democrat; Presbyterian; rec: jogging, hiking, art. Res: 13949 Davenport San Diego 92129 Ofc: U.S. International University 10455 Pomerado Rd San Diego 92131

LAURENCE, PETER A., city official, real estate broker, investor; b. May 27, 1945, San Francisco; s. A. A. and Beth C. (Caldwell) L.; m. Sheryll M. Horton, July 26, 1970; children: Todd, b. 1966; Alana, b. 1977; Alisa, b. 1978; edn: AA, Diablo Valley Coll. 1969; Calif. lic. real estate sales, 1969, R.E. Broker, 1971; GRI, Grad. Realtors Inst., CAR 1975, Cert. Res. Splst. 1980; Securities 7 Lic., SEC 1983; Career: mgr. American Realty 1969; realtor, ptnr. Better Homes Realty, Walnut Creek 1974-; v.p. Ygnacio Investments Inc. 1982-; pres. Laurence Investments, 1984-; awards: Better Home Realtor of the Year (2t); mem: Clayton Business Assn. (pres. 1989), NAR, Calif. Assn. Realtors (dir. 1980-81), Contra Costa Bd. Realtors (dir. 1978-81, MLS dir. 1989-90), Nat. Assn. Securities Dealers; civic: Clayton City Councilman 1990-, v. mayor Clayton 1992- Special Forces Assn. (pres. Chpt. XXIII), Concord Century Club, VFW Post 1525, Diablo Scholarships, C.of C.; Republican; LDS; rec: golf, skiing, travel. Res: 60 Mt Rushmore Pl Clayton 94517 Ofc: Better Homes Realty, 1511 Treat Blvd Ste 100 Walnut Creek 94598

LAUSEN, P. SANDER, optician; b. Oct. 29, 1934, Aarhus, Denmark, nat. 1973; s. Daniel Severin and Ragnhild (Faurholt) L.; m. Jytte Rasmussen, Jan. 25, 1958 (div. 1984); children: Pia, b. 1960; Rene, b. 1963; edn: BS, Inst. of Tech., Copenhagen, Denmark 1956; M.Ophthalmic Optics 1972; bd. cert. Am. Bd. Opticianry 1967; Fellow Nat. Acad. Opticianry 1967. Career: optician, optometrist Cornelius Knudsen, Aarhus, Denmark 1952-57, C.F. Mc William Ltd., Auckland, NZ 1957-65; dispensing optician/ mgr. Superior Optical Co., Newport Beach 1965-74; mgr. Victor Optical, Laguna Hills 1974-76; prop. Continental Eyewear, Newport Beach 1976-; awards: Man of the Month (2), and Award of Merit Hi-Lite, Superior Optical Co. 1971; mem: Calif. Soc. Ophthalmic Dispensers (bd. dirs. 1971-76), Eastbluff Merchants' Assn. (pres. 1983-84), Newport-Balboa Rotary Club 1977- (sgt. at arms 1983), Newport Beach Tennis Club, Newport Ctr. Toastmasters, Conservative Caucus; research: Aniseikonia and Iseikonic Lenses; Republican; Lutheran; rec: soccer (chief referee Newport-Irvine AYSO 1972-77, bd. dirs. AYSO 1972-77), tennis. Res: 725 Domingo Dr Newport Beach 92660 Ofc: Continental Eyewear "Optique Mobile" 725 Domingo Dr Newport Beach 92660 Tel: 714/640-2020

LAVAL, CLAUDE CONSTANT, III, manufacturing executive; b. May 9, 1935, Fresno; s. Claude Constant Jr. and Marian B. (Kahn) L.; m. Betty Lou Scarbrough, Feb. 1, 1958; children: Melinda, Luann Laval Wiliams; edn: BA, Stanford Univ. 1957. Career: sales mgr. Suppliers Inc., Fresno 1957-60; pres. A-V Electronics Inc. 1960-71; Claude Laval Corp. 1971-; dir. bus. advy. council CSU 1984-; chmn. Parking Authority Fresno 1964-68; mem: Irrigation Assn. (pres. 1983-84), Downtown Assn. Fresno (pres. 1966-68), No. Calif. Dist. Export Council, Water Resource Export Council, Young Pres. Orgn. (chmn. 1983-84), World Bus. Forum (secty., treas. 1985-), Rotary, Sunnyside CC, Fig Garden Swim & Racquet Club, Beta Gamma Sigma. Ofc: Claude Laval Corp. 1911 N Helm St Fresno 93727

LAVELLA, CHERYL ANN, management information systems and materials management executive; b. Sept. 24, 1948, Greensburgh, Pa.; d. Louis J. and Grace M. (Fallovallitta) LaVella; edn: CSU Dominguez Hills 1981; AS, Mt. San Antonio 1982. Career: assembler Filtex, LaVerne 1969-75; stockroom 1975-79;

planner Natter Mfg., Temple City 1979-83; supr. Fairchild Ind. 1983-85; master scheduler Tubing Seal Cap, Azusa 1985-87, system analyst 1987-88; MIS mgr. Pacific Precision Metal 1988-; cons., Claremont 1988-89; pres. Inland ASK User Group, Temple City 1989-; prof. materials program (part-time) UC Riverside 1991-93;awards: Fairchild Ind. achievement, 1985, BPW bus. woman runner-up, 1988, Milt Cook Award of Distinction, 1992, nominated for APICS Outstanding Mem., 1993; mem: Am. Productions & Inventory Control (pres.), APICS (pres. elect 1987-88, v.p. membership 1986-87, v.p. publicity 1981-85), Calif. Literacy (tutor 1987-88), MADD; civic: vol. Riverside Am. Indian Ctr. 1992-93; crisis/suicide counselor Riverside "Helpline" 1992-; rec: classical guitar, antiques, needlecraft. Res: 12399 Balzing Star Ct Rancho Cucamonga 91739 Ofc: Pacific Precision Metals 601 S Vincent Azusa 91702

LAVENTHOL, DAVID A., media company president; b. July 15, 1933, Phila., Pa.; s. Jesse and Clare (Horwald) L.; m. Esther Coons, Mar. 8, 1958; children: Peter b. 1959, Sarah b. 1960; edn: AB, Yale Univ., 1957; MA, Univ. Minn., 1960. Career: reporter, news editor St. Petersburg (Fla.) Times, 1957-62; asst. editor, city editor N.Y. Herald-Tribune, 1963-66; asst. mng. editor Washington Post, 1966-69; exec. editor Newsday, Long Island, NY, 1969, v.p./ed. Newsday (Times Mirror), 1970-78, publisher/CEO 1978-80; group v.p. Times Mirror Co. eastern newspapers gp. 1981-86, sr. v.p. Times Mirror and chmn. Newsday 1986; pres. Times Mirror Co., 1987-; bds: Pulitzer Prize Board 1982-, Internat. Press Inst., London (v. chr. 1985-); Newspaper Advt. Bureau, N.Y. (dir. 1987-), American Press Inst. Reston, Va. (dir. 1988-, chmn. 1988), United Negro Coll. Fund (dir. 1988-), Mus. of Contemporary Art, L.A. (trustee 1989), Calif. Mus. Found. (trustee 1989-), NY City Partnership (dir. 1985-87); awards: (hon.) LittD Dowling Coll., Long Island, NY 1979, (hon.) LLD Hofstra Univ., Long Island, NY 1986; mem. Am. Soc. Newspaper Editors, Am. Newspaper Publishers Assn., Council on Fgn. Rel., Century Club (NY), City Club on Bunker Hill (LA, bd. govs. 1989-); mil: AUS Signal Corps 1953-55. Res: 800 West First St #3202 Los Angeles 90012 Ofc: Times Mirror Co. Times Mirror Sq Los Angeles 90053

LAVERTY, BEN WILLIAM, III, agricultural consultant; b. Oct. 26, 1945, Taft; s. Ben Wm., Jr. and Marilyn Edith (Kruger) L.; children: Ben IV, Bret, Tim, Terra, Tallie; edn: Bakersfield Jr. Coll. 1964-65; BS, Brigham Young Univ. 1967; reg. environmental assessor, Calif.; cert. farm equipt. appraiser, cert. environmental insp. Career: tree crop supr. Belridge Farms, Bakersfield 1968-73; bd. dirs./owner Willow Creek Farms, Oakley, Ida. 1973-80; pres. and c.e.o. Calif. Safety Training Corp., Bakersfield 1980-; mgr./agt. Cal Farm Invest; irrigation cons. Kester Bros. 1978-80, agri. cons. Mobil Oil Corp. 1982-; pres. bd. dirs. Western Kern Resource Conservation Dist. 1982-86; pres. Calif. Resource Conservation Area IX, 1987-88; mem: Calif. Agricultural Prodn. Consultants Assn., Am. Consultants League, Am. Mgmt. Assn.; civic: Boy Scouts Am. Explorer Post Advisor, Bakersfield Coll. Alumni Assn. and Helmet Club (mbr-ship. chmn. 1983-), BYU Cougar Club; publs: agri. economic outlook 1986, Bakersfield Lifestyle mag.; Republican; rec: Masters Track Pgm., woodworking, geneology. Ofc: California Safety Training Corp. 4909 Stockdale Hwy Ste 132 Bakersfield 93309-2637

LAVINE, STEVEN DAVID, college president; b. June 7, 1947, Sparta, Wis.; s. Israel Harry and Harriet Hauda (Rosen) L.; m. Janet M. Sternburg, May 29, 1988; edn: BA, Stanford Univ., 1969; MA, Harvard Univ., 1970, PhD, 1976. Career: tchg. fellow dept. English & Am. lit. Harvard Univ., Cambridge 1971-74; asst. prof. English & Am. lit. Univ. of Mich., Ann Arbor 1974-81, asst. ed. Mich. Quarterly Rev. 1978-81; vis. res. fellow in humanities Rockefeller Found., NY, NY 1981-82, asst., assoc. dir. for arts & humanities, 1983-88; adj. assoc. prof. Grad Sch. of Bus. N.Y. Univ. 1984-85; pres. Calif. Inst. of the Arts, Valencia 1988-; cons. Wexner Found., Columbus, Ohio 1986-87; cons., panelist Nat. Endowment for the Humanities 1981-85; selection panelist INPUT Television Screening Conf., Montreal Canada and Granada, Spain 1985-86; awards: Ford Graduate Prize Fellow, Harvard 1969-74, Charles B. Dexter Travelling Fellow, Harvard 1972, Horace H. Rackham Res.Fellow (18th-c. poetry) and UM Faculty devel. grantee 1978, UM Class of 1923 Award for outstanding tchg. in lit., arts and scis. 1979, UM Faculty recogn. award for disting. res. & tchg. 1980, Mich. Council for the Humanities grant/ organized nat. creative writing conf. 1980; mem: nat. advy. com. Smithsonian Exptl. Gallery, Task Force of Edn. Am. Assn. of Mus., KCRW-FM NPR (bd.), Music Center of LA (operating com.), J.Paul Getty Mus. (vis. com.); co-editor w. Harry Thomas, The Hopwood Anthology: Five Decades of American Poetry (UM Press, 1981), co-editor w/Ivan Karp, Exhibiting Cultures: The Politics and Poetics of Museum Display (Smithsonian Instn. Press 1991), article, Museum News (1989), num. articles in literary revs. and jours., ed. spl. jour. issue Prooftexts (1984). Ofc: Calif. Inst. of the Arts 24600 McBean Pkwy Valencia 91355

LAWRENCE, RONALD LOY, advertising executive; b. Aug. 31, 1944, Alicia, Ark.; s. Elvis James and Rutha Beatrice (Blackshear) L.; m. Pamela Sue Walters, July 23, 1966; children: Melanie b. 1970, Gregory b. 1973, Daryl b. 1975; edn: BSBA, Univ. Nev. 1970. Career: printer, advt. rep. Las Vegas Sun, Las Vegas, Nev. 1963-70; advt. rep., Nev., Tenn., and Calif. 1970-72; advt. dir. Lienett Co., Los Alamitos 1972-75; pres. Lawrence Advertising, Inc., 1975-; v.p., treas. Reed Lawrence Printing, Chino 1985-88; gen. ptnr. Cedarwood

Leasing Co., Fullerton 1985-88; pres. Pinnacle Offset Printing, Hayward and Riverside, 1990-; mem: Alpha Kappa Psi, Noon Lions Club (advt. chmn. 1983-86); pub., editor Golfing News newsletter, 1975-76; mil: E1 AUS 1966; Republican; rec: golf, bowling, fishing. Ofc: Lawrence Advertising, Inc. 2487 E Orangethorpe Ave Fullerton 92631-5304

LAWSON, JAMES LEE, healthcare consultant/R.N.; b. Jan. 7, 1947, Alhambra; s. Charles French and Helen Marie (Gregory) L.; m. Ilene Eleanor Sweeney, Apr. 28, 1973 (div. 1983); m. Marguerite Adams King, Feb. 25, 1984 (div. 1993); children: Charles b. 1976, Sara b. 1980, Zachary b. 1988; edn: grad. advanced and clin. tng. courses USN Hosp. Corps Schs. 1966-74; AA polit. sci., Cypress Coll., 1970; BSBA, Calif. Western Univ., 1976, MBA in healthcare fin. & adminstrn., 1978; ASN, Victor Valley Coll., 1980; JD, Kensington Univ., 1989. Career: US Naval Hosp. Corps 1966-74; hd. nurse, chg. nse. ER Dept., relief supr., La Palma Intercomm. Hosp. and Pioneer Hosp., 1974-76; staff analyst mgmt. engring. svs. San Bernardino County Med. Ctr., 1976-79; dir. nsg. svs. Barstow Comm. Hosp., 1979-80; adminstr. disabled and Vietnam veterans outreach pgm., contr. to Wis. State and grant adminstr. for US Dept. Labor, Vets House Inc. 1980-81; exec. dir. So. Wisconsin Emergency Med. Svs. Council Inc., 1981-83; ER dept. chg. nse. and actg. hd. nse. Westside Dist. Hosp. and Simi Valley Adventist Hosp., paramedic base station hosps., 1983-84; dir. ops. and chief fin. ofcr. The Pasadena Children's Tng. Sch. dba The Sycamores (residential K-12 Spl. Edn. Sch. and psychiat. hosp.), 1984-87; v.p. Kapner, Wolfberg & Assocs. Inc. (nat. healthcare consultancy) 1987-89; pres. James L. Lawson, R.N., APC, Canoga Park 1989-; Republican; Hebrew/Christian; rec: philately. Address: James L. Lawson, R.N., MBA, JD, 136 S. Virgil Ave #241 Los Angeles Ph:213/389-4499

LAWSON, KAY, educator; b. Apr. 21, 1933, Salem, Ore.; d. Arlo C. and Ethel L. (Jones) Davis; m. William Lawson, Apr. 30, 1952; children: Kevin b. 1953, Marta b. 1962; edn: BA, UC Berkeley 1959; MA, 1962; PhD, 1971. Career: prof. political sci. San Francisco St. Univ. 1968-; vis. prof. Rutgers Univ., New Brunswick, N.J. 1982; Columbia Univ., N.Y.C. 1982; Univ. London, England 1987; London Sch. Political Sci. and Economics 1987; Univ. Paris, Nanterre, France 1987; Univ. Paris, Sorbonne 1991-92; Inst. for Study of Politics, Paris 1991-92; mem: Am. Political Sci. Assn. (exec. bd. political organizations and parties: pres. Women's Caucus 1989-90, exec. council 1989-91), Internat. Political Sci. Assn. (gov. Elections and Parties, Com. on Political. Sociology), Nat. and Calif. Com. for Party Renewal (exec. bd. 1980-), Western Political Sci. Assn. (exec. bd. 1978-81), Bay Area Women in Political Sci., World Affairs Council; author: The Human Polity, 1984, 88, 93, The Comparative Study of Political Parties, 1976, Political Parties & Democracy in U.S., 1968; ed.: How Political Parties Work, 1993, When Parties Fail, 1988, Political Parties & Linkage, 1980; Democrat; rec: travel. Res: 389 Gravatt Dr Berkeley 94705 Ofc: Departments of Political Science and International Relations San Francisco State University San Francisco 94132

LAWSON, THOMAS CHENEY, certified fraud examiner, certified international investigator; b. Sept. 21, 1955, Pasadena; s. Wm. McDonald and Joan Bell (Jaffee) L.; m. Carolyn Marie Cox; children: Christopher, Tiffany, Erin, Brittany; edn: CSU Sacto. 1973-77. Career: pres. Tomatron Co., Pasadena 1970-, Tom's Tune Up & Detail, Pasadena 1971-, Tom's Pool Service, Sacto. 1975-, Tom Supply Co., 1975-; mgmt. trainee Permoid Process Co., Los Angeles 1970-75; regional sales cons. Hoover Co., Burlingame 1974-76; mktg. exec. River City Prodns., Sacto. 1977-78; prof. automechanics CSU Sacto. 1973-75; territorial rep. Globe div. Burlington House Furniture Co., 1978; So. Calif. territorial rep. Marge Carson Furniture Inc. 1978-80; pres. Ted L. Gunderson & Assocs., Inc., Westwood 1980-81; pres/c.e.o. Apscreen, Newport Beach 1980-; pres./c.e.o. Creditbase Co., Newport Beach 1982-89; pres. Worldata Corp., Newport Beach 1985-89; shareholder Trademark Enforcement Corp. 1986-93; c.e.o. Carecheck Inc., 1989-; awards: Calif. Rehab. scholar 1974-77; mem. Am. Soc. Indsl. Security (chmn. Orange Co. chpt. 1990), Christian Businessmens' Com., Council of Internat. Investigators, Nat. Pub. Records Research Assn., Personnel & Indsl. Relations Assn. Ofc: 2043 Westcliff Dr Ste 300 Newport Beach 92660

LAWTON, BRIAN MERSHON, dentist; b. July 19, 1950, Seattle, Wash.; s. Raymon Edgar and Rosellen Marie (Layton) L.; m. Rustalyn Elizabeth Bradshaw, June 29, 1985; 1 son. Trevor Mershon b. 1987; edn: UCSD 1968-69; BS biology, Loyola Univ. 1972; DDS, USC 1976. Career: dentist Univ. Lausanne, Switzerland 1976-77; Dr. Hilskieven, Zermatt, Switzerland 1977-78; Sears Dental, Sacto. 1979-80; dentist, pres., owner Granite Bay Dental Brian Lawton DDS Inc., Roseville 1980-; mem: Sunriver Dental Group, Rancho Cordova 1980-; mem: Rotary Internat., Elks, Rancho Cordova C.of C., Roseville C.of C., St. John the Baptist Cath. Ch.; R.Cath.; rec: skiing, fly fishing, water skiing. Res: 7265 Harbor Way Roseville 95661-6505

LAYE, JOHN EDWARD, contingency management consultant; b. May 26, 1933, Santa Monica; s. Theodore Martin Ley and Evelyn Rosalie (Young) Laye; m. Jeanne Tutt Curry, Dec. 23, 1955; children: Linda b. 1961, John Russell b. 1963; edn: AA police sci., L.A. City Coll., 1952; BA polit. sci., USN Postgrad. Sch., Monterey 1967; MS mgmt., USC, 1975; cert., CMC, Inst. Mgmt.

Consultants, 1990. Career: lt. cmdr., aviator US Navy 1951-75, decorated 4x; county govt. exec. Solano Co., Vallejo 1976-81; prin. cons., pres. Applied Protection Systems (contingency plans & tng.), Moraga 1982-; lectr. Emergency Mgmt. Inst., Emmitsburg, Md. 1982-; Univ. Calif. Bus. and Mgmt. extension 1993-; Nat. Council Emergency Mgmt. (1990-, chmn. Bus. & Industry Com. 1992-), curric. advy. com. emergency mgmt. Univ. Calif. Ext. 1992; recipient commendns. Gov's Ofc. of Emergency Svs., Sacto. 1987, Calif. Fire Marshall, Sacto. 1989; mem: Inst. of Mgmt. Consultants (dir. Norcal chpt. 1990-92), USC Triumvirate (dir. 1990-92), Assn. of Contingency Planners 1988-, Orinda Assn. (pres. 1990), Disaster Council (chmn. 1988-92); publs: Calif. Emergency Mgmt. Jour. (1992), num. articles in field, 1978-; Presbyterian; rec: skiing, scuba, running, bicycling. Ofc: Contingency Management Consultants 346 Rheem Blvd Ste 202 Moraga 94556-1541

LAYTON, EDWARD NORMAN, construction executive; b. June 29, 1928, Kellogg, Idaho; s. Ernest Alfred and Ruth Eloise (Thwing) L.;m. Mary Katherine Ketchum, June 29, 1948; children: Norman b. 1950, Cheryl b. 1954, Terri b. 1957, Dennis b. 1958; edn: cert. bus. mgmt., UCLA 1957; lic. General Contractor B1, Calif. 1958. Career: cowboy for Davis Ranch, Ariz. 1944; shop foreman Fiat Metal Products 1948; carpenter 1949-52; carpenter supt. Casnor Constrn. 1952-63, v.p./ part owner 1964-77; founder, past pres. (1978-90), chmn. bd. Ed Layton Construction Co., 1978-; pres. Layton Enterprises Inc.; chmn. bd. Tri-Co. Investment Group Inc., 1976-; dir. Building Industry Assn. So. Calif., 1976-84, v.p. labor 1981-83, chmn. Labor Negotiation Com. 1982-83; mem. bd. trustees: Carpenters Pension Trust for So. Cal., C.I.A.F. Trust Fund for So. Cal., F.C.I.A.F Trust Fund for So. Cal., v.-chmn. F.C.I.A. Trustee Bd.; elected bd. Walnut Valley County Water Dist. 1985-, pres. 1991; commr. Puente Basin Water Agy.; awards: Walnut Valley Citizen of Year 1975, A.I.A. Cabrillo Award for excellence of constrn.- La Mirada City Hall 1970, Pacific Coast Builders Conf. 14 Western States Gold Nugget Award of Merit for excellence of commercial remodel 1981; mem: Building Industry Assn. (rewrote BIA Master Labor Agreement 1980), BIA-Pasadena San Gabriel Valley (Commercial Industrial Council), Nat. Assn. Home Builders, NAHB Spike Club (So. Calif. labor policy dir.), So.Calif. Archeol. Survey Assn.; civic: Men's Club Queen of Valley Hosp., Walnut San Dimas Sheriff Station Booster Club (founding dir.), Citizens Advy. Com. Diamond Bar City General Plan, Citizens Advy. Com. Intercomm. Hosp. Diamond Bar Complex, Walnut Valley C.of C. (bd.), Kiwanis Intl. (Cal-Nev-Ha Found.); club: Via Verde Country; works: first fiberglass domed bldg. for projection and display of stellar films of space flts. 1965; constrn. of 300+ million projects; Republican (Presdl. Task Force); Prot.; rec: amateur archeologist, lapidarist, minerologist. Res: 404 S Lemon Ave Walnut 91789 Ofc: Ed Layton Constrn. Co., Inc., POB 60, Walnut 91789

LAYTON, HARRY CHRISTOPHER, artist, lecturer; b. Nov. 17, 1938, Safford, Ariz.; s. Christopher E. and Eurilda (Welker) L.; m. Karol Barbara Kendall, July 11, 1964 (div. 1989); children: Deborah, Christopher, Joseph, Elisabeth, Faith, Aaron, Gretchen, Benjamin, Justin, Mathew, Peter; edn: LHD, Sussex Coll., Eng. 1969; cert. clin. hypnotherapist. Career: lectr. ancient art, Serra Cath. High Sch., 1963-64, Los Angeles Dept. Parks and Rec., summer 1962, 63, 64; interior decorator Cities of Hawthorne, Lawndale, Compton, Gardena, Torrance, 1960-68; paintings exhibited one-man shows: Nahas Dept. Stores, 1962, 64; group shows: Gt. Western Savs. & Loan, Lawndale 1962, Gardena Adult Sch. 1965, Serra Cath. High Sch. 1963, Salon de Nations Paris 1983; represented in permanent collections: Sussex Coll., Eng., Gardena Masonic Lodge, Culver City-Foshey Masonic Lodge, Gt. Western Savs. & Loan; honors: Alpha Psi Omega, Hon. DD, PhD, St. Matthew Univ., Ohio 1970, Hon. DFA, DSc, London Inst. Applied Research 1972, World of Poetry Golden Poet award (1986, 88, 91) and Silver Poet award 1990, published in World's Best Poems, Internat. Biog. Ctr., Cambridge, Eng., Intl. Order of Merit, apptd. dep. dir. gen. for The Americas 1990, named Intl. Man of Yr. 1991-92; listed Who's Who in West (16-22nd edits.), Who's Who in Fin. and Ind. (25-27th edits.), Who's Who in World (9th-11th edits.); pres. ECHO-SELF Corp., Calif. -Nev. -Dela.; mem: Am. Hypnotherapy Assn., Gardena Valley Art Assn., Centinela Valley Art Assn., Internat. Soc. Artists, Soc. for Early Historic Archaeology, Le Salon Des Nation Paris Geneva, Ctr. Internat. d'Art Contemporain, Am. Councilor's Soc. of Psychological Counselors, Am. Legion, Internat. Platform Assn., Am. Security Council, Masons (32 deg.), Shriners, Knight Templar; Republican. Res: 3658 Centinela Ave Ste 6 Los Angeles 90066 Ofc: Layton Studios Graphic Design, Inc. 12228 Venice Blvd., #514 Los Angeles 90066

LA ZARE, HOWARD TED, engineering executive; b. Oct. 10, 1936, Chicago, Ill.; s. Henry and Jeanne (Sodakoff) La Z.; m. Phyllis F., July 15, 1960; children: Adam b. 1961, Kim b. 1965; edn: BSEE cum laude, West Coast Univ. Sch. of Engring. 1969; BSME magna cum laude, 1970; lic. electrical engr. Calif. 1978. Career: v.p. engring Consolidated Film Industries, Hollywood 1964-84; sr. v.p. engring. Deluxe Labs. Inc. 1984-92; pres. FilmTec International, Chatsworth 1992-; gov. Soc. Motion Picture & TV Engrs., White Plains, N.Y. 1984-85 and 1990-94, editorial v.p. 1985-88, dir. engring. 1984, v.p. motion picture affairs 1982-83, chmn./mem. num. committees 1981-; honors: Academy Awards Class II, 1973, 82; listed Who's Who in U.S. Execs., Who's Who in Calif., Who's Who in Entertainment, Who's Who in Fin. & Ind., Who's Who in Sci. &

Engring., Who's Who Environmental Registry, Standard & Poor's Register for Corporations, Dirs. & Execs., Personalities in Am., Men of Achievement, Internat. Dir. of Disting. Leadership; mem: Soc. Motion Picture & TV Engrs. (fellow), AMPAS 1985-, Am. Soc. Cinematographers, IEEE (sr. mem.), British Kinematograph Sound & TV Engrs.; author: 2 papers pub. in tech. jours., 1972, 75; inventor: shutterless film projector, 1985; Republican: Jewish; rec: chess, tennis, golf. Res: 10825 Fullright Ave Chatsworth 91311 Ofc: FilmTec International 10825 Fullbright Ave Chatsworth 91311

LAZAROVICI, CHRISTIAN EMILIAN, engineering company executive; b. July 2, 1945, Bucharest, Romania; s. Ion Boicu and Ivanca Elena (Gheorghe) L.; m. Felicia, July 16, 1977; child, Alexanru b. 1980; m. Mariana, Mar. 28, 1987; children: Dominique b. 1988, Julian b. 1991; edn: MSEE, Politechnic Inst. of Bucharest, 1968, PhD, 1977. Career: prof. computer sci. dept. Politechnic Inst. of Bucharest, Romania until 1984; sr. electronic engr. TCL Inc., Fremont 1985-87; dir. engring. Westcor Corp., Los Gatos 1987-88, v.p. engring., 1988-91; pres. and c.e.o. Megapower Corp., Campbell 1991-; author 3 tech. books, 20+ articles and tech. reports. Res: 3436 Churin Dr Mountain View CA 94040 Ofc: Megapower Corp., Campbell CA.

LEADEM, JOSEPH ANTHONY, investment advisor; b. Feb. 27, 1926, Trenton, N.J.; s. Edward Anthony and Anna Marie (Tyrrell) L.; m. Joyce Hertog, Feb. 2, 1952; children: Joe b. 1955, Anne b. 1957, John b. 1958, Mary b. 1960, Carol b. 1962, Barbara b. 1967; edn: AB, Central Mich. Univ. 1947; reg. inv. advisor SEC (1972). Career: pres. Joseph A. Leadem Inc., Sacramento; reg. principal Leadem-Bailey & Assocs., Sacto.; pres. Brooklyn Park Property, Inc.; owner Lead-Em Astray Racing Stables, and Lead-Em Astray Farms; civic: Rotary, Sacto. C. of C., Sierra Coll. Found.; mil: USNR; Democrat; R.Cath.; rec: horses, boating, hiking, walking. Res: 5173 Firestone Pl Santa Rosa 95409 also: PO Box 2944 Santa Rosa 95405 Ofc: Joseph A. Leadem, Inc. Ste 107 Bldg B, 7509 Madison Ave Citrus Heights 95610

LEADER, JEFFERY JAMES, educator; b. Oct. 27, 1963, Elmira, N.Y.; s. Dennis Thomas and Jeanne Diane (Smith) L.; m. Margaret Ellen Nieburg, Aug. 26, 1989; son, Derek b. 1990; edn: BS, and BSEE, Syracuse Univ. 1985; ScM, Brown Univ., 1987, PhD, 1989. Career: vis. asst. prof. Harvey Mudd Coll., Claremont 1989-90; asst. prof. math. Naval Postgraduate Sch., Monterey 1990-; honors: Phi Beta Kappa, Tau Beta Pi, Sigma Xi; mem. Am. Math. Soc., Soc. for Indsl. and Appl. Math.; publs: articles in Applied Math. Letters (2, 1991), Rocky Mountain Math. J. (1993); rec: martial arts. Ofc: Naval Postgraduate School, Code MA/LE, Monterey 93943

LEAHY, T. LIAM, business management/turnaround consultant; b. Apr. 15, 1952, Camp Lejuene, N.C.; s. Thomas James and Margaret (Munnelly) L.; m. Shannon Kelly Brooks, Apr. 21, 1990; edn: MA, St. Louis Univ., 1975; spl. tng. Hubbard Coll. of Adminstrn., L.A. 1989. Career: senior consultant Leahy and Assocs., Glendale, Calif. 1982-; pres. Generation Dynamics, N.Y.C. 1985; pres. Journal Graphics, N.Y.C. 1984; mem. Turnaround Mgmt Assn. (bd. 1990-), Am. Council of Execs. (bd. 1992), Consultants Assn. (bd. 1992), U.S. Chamber of Commerce 1985-; numerous articles in gen. and trade periodicals, 1980-; rec: musician, filmmaker. Ofc: Leahy & Associates 19131 Enadia Way Reseda 91335

LEAPHART, ROSE MARIE, customs broker; b. Dec. 21, 1952, Grafton, West Va.; d. George Walter and Gladys Victory (Stockett) Current; m. Timothy Mark Leaphart, July 10, 1976; 1 child, Eric b. 1984; edn: BS, UC Berkeley 1983; lic. customs broker US Dept. Treasury 1980. Career: adminstrv. asst. Mennen Greatbatch, Clarence, N.Y. 1972-76; supr. John V. Carr & Son, Buffalo 1977-79; corp. mgr. Fritz Cos., San Francisco, 1979-88; pres. Leaphart & Associates, 1989-; dir. of internat. svs., The Gap, S.F. 1991-; mem. NAFTZ, NCBFAA, WIT-NC (chapt. organizer 1989, treas. 89-91), SFCBFFA; author 3 texts in field: Basics of Importing, CR19+HTS Study, CHB Exam Prep, 1989; rec: mystery & detection, golf.

LEBAKER, EDWIN HARRISON, III, tax consultant, financial analyst, contracts adminstrator; b. Dec. 23, 1945, Oakland, Calif.; s. Edwin Harrison, Jr. and Clara Francis (Page) LeB.; m. Deborah Kilkenny, July 18, 1981; 1 son: David b. 1982; edn: BS, CSU Hayward 1973; MBA, Golden Gate Univ. 1982. Career: indsl. acct. Varian Assocs., Inc., Palo Alto 1973-77, acctg. mgr. 1977-79; sr. fin. analyst EIMAC, San Carlos 1979-80; cost acctg. mgr. Varian Assocs. 1980-82; bus. mgr., contracts adminstr. ARACOR, Sunnyvale 1982-85, dir. fin. & adminstrn. 1985-89, v.p. finance/adminstrn. 1989-; owner, LeBaker Tax & Financial Cons. Svc. 1980-; mem. Veterans Club (pres. 1973); mil: seaman USN 1966-69, Vietnam Pistol & Rifle Marksmanship; Republican; Prot.; rec: martial arts, jogging, coin collecting. Res: 10582 Esquire Pl Cupertino 95014 Ofc: ARACOR, 425 Lakeside Dr Sunnyvale 94086

LE CLERC, MICHAEL WARD, consultant, mfg. and microcontamination service co. president, expert witness; b. May 29, 1948, Detroit, Mich.; s. Ernest Frederick and Mary Ann (Williams) LeC.; edn: resident agent National Life Ins., Pontiac, Mich. 1971-72; techn. Custom Controls, Warren, Mich. 1972-74; foreman Environator Corp., Columbia, S.C. 1974-75; mgr. Calumet Scientific, Elk

Grove Village, Ill. 1975-77; automatic equip. specialist IBM, San Jose, Calif. 1977-80; mgr. Trilogy Systems, Cupertino 1981-84; pres./bd. chmn. Class-10 Technologies Inc., San Jose 1984-; ptnr. M & J Associates, 1988-91; sr. mem. Inst. of Environmental Scis. 1986-; publs: 6+ tech. articles in trade mags.; mil: s/sgt. USAF 1967-71; rec: fishing, gardening, gourmet cooking. Ofc: Class-10 Technologies, Inc. 1719-D Little Orchard St San Jose 95125

LEDFORD, GARY ALAN, designer, builder, developer; b. Dec. 30, 1946, San Diego; s. Loren Oscar and Madge Francis (Condon) L.; m. Linda Halbert Barker, Jan. 7, 1979; children: Kelly b. 1969, Jeanne b. 1970, Robert b. 1972, Kevin b. 1973; edn: CE, US Army Engrg. Sch. 1967; grad. courses in structures, Univ. of Colo. 1969; sr. housing mktg. specialist, 1990; Calif. lic.: Gen. Engr. Contr., Gen. Bldg. Contr., Hazardous Waste Contr. #328361, Pvt. Patrol Opr. #PPO11098; mem. Spl. Svs. Bur. San Bernardino Co. Sheriff (Badge 5224). Career: platoon ldr., co. comdr., Battalion Civil Engr., US Army Corps of Engrs. (Airborne), Vietnam, 1969; pres. Mastercraft Contractors, Inc., Colorado Springs 1969-73; v.p./ gen. mgr. K.L. Redfern, Inc., Orange, Calif. 1973-75; past pres. Watt Jess Ranch Inc. Current: pres. Mojave Feed & Fuel Corp., chmn. mgmt. com. Watt-Jess/Ledford Ptnrship; pres. LJ&J Investment Corp.; pres. Jess Ranch Security Corp.; gen. ptnr. Ledford/Schaffer-Rogers Ltd., past mng. ptnr. Apple Valley Mall; projects incl. retirement comm., residential devel., shopping ctr., and office park; instr. (Command & Staff), US Army Eng. Sch., Ft. Belvoir, VA 1966 (Nike Missile Support Sys.); awards: 2nd pl. design, Colo. Springs Parade of Homes 1972; mem: Urban Land Inst., Nat. Assn. Home Builders, Nat. Council Sr. Housing, Nat. Rifle Assn. (life), Nat. Plng. Assn., Bldg. Industry Assn., VFW, Internat. Council of Shopping Ctrs., High Desert Constrn. Inds. Assn., Victor Valley Mus. Assn. (life), Victor Valley Cultural Arts Found. (founding), Apple Valley Christian Care Ctrs. (trustee, bd.); works: design, engineering, constrn. projects incl. 26 shopping ctrs., 44 restaurants, 3 Edwards Theatres, 3 schools (L.A. Bd. Edn), Malibu Grand Prix (Pomona), over 100 svc. stations, num. indsl. bldgs., med. facilities, and var. mil. projects; design & devel. contractor computer software (copyrighted 1979), Tuffcore Bldg. Sys. (pat pend. 1981); mil. decorations: Bronze Star (2), Army Commdn. (2), Purple Heart; Republican; Prot.; rec: hunting, equestrian, chess. Res: 14415 Erie, Apple Valley 92307 Ofc: Jess Ranch 11401 Apple Valley Rd Apple Valley 92308

LEDIN, JAMES ALAN, aerospace engineer; b. July 29, 1961, Clinton, Iowa; s. John Ronald and Rosemary Theresa (Dunlavey) L.; m. Lynda Schmidt, Oct. 12, 1991; edn: BS aero. eng., Iowa State Univ., Ames 1983. Career: aerospace engr. Naval Air Warfare Ctr., Pt. Mugu, Ca. 1983-; awards: Nat. Merit Scholar, Ankeny, Ia. 1979, Sigma Gamma Tau 1983-, Tau Beta Pi 1983-; mem. ADI User's Soc. Applied Dynamics Internat., Ann Arbor, Mich. (1984-92, bd. and software librarian 1990-), Mensa 1988-; Libertarian; rec: computer programming, music, photog., reading. Ofc: Naval Air Warfare Ctr Code P03931 Pt Mugu 93042-5000

LEE, CHUNG NAM, Oriental medical doctor; b. Feb. 3, 1942, Pusan, Korea (nat. Aug., 1990); s. Kyungtaek and Sobong (Son) L.; m. Jungja Choi, Feb. 16, 1985; children: Diana b. 1975; edn: BA, Yon Sei Univ., Seoul, Korea, 1965; MSA, OMS of SAMRA, L.A., Calif., 1991; ELD, Golden Gate Sem., LA, Calif., 1991; lic. acupuncturist, MBCAC, 1992. Career: dir., Chun Bo Clinic, L.A., Calif., 1991-; mem. CAA, 1992. Res: 822 1/2 S. Crenshaw Blvd., Los Angeles 90005 Ofc: Chun Bo TCM Clinic 244 S. Western Ave. Los Angeles 90004

LEE, DONNA JEAN, registered nurse; b. Nov. 12, 1931, Huntington Park; d. Louis Frederick and Lena Adelaide (Hinson) Munyon; m. Frank Bernard Lee, July 16, 1949; children: Frank b. 1950, Robert b. 1952, John b. 1954; edn: Bell H.S. grad.; AA in nsg., Fullerton Jr. Coll. 1966; USC Ext. classes Orange Co. Med. Ctr. 1966-71; student 2 wks. abroad Russia Pgm., N.M. Univ., 1982; Calif. lic. RN 1966, AACN/CCRN cert. in intensive care 1972; Career: critical care nursing pos. 1969-85: staff nse. Orange Co. Med. Center, Orange 1966-69, charge nse. relief all intensive care units 1968-69, charge nse. communicable disease unit 1969-71, charge nse. neonatal unit, 5 mos. 1971; staff & charge nse. intensive care units, emergency rm., med.-surgical, maternity, Anaheim Memorial Hosp. 1971-74; agency nse. (staff relief ICU/CCU many hosps. in Orange Co.) Staff Builders, Orange 1974-82; past empl. N.S. International, 1978-89; staff nse. Upjohn HealthCare (now Olsten Healthcare of Orange) 1985-90, also pediatric and geriatric nsg.; currently employed Visiting Nurses Assoc. Support Services (VNASS) of Orange Co. and Olsten Healthcare of Orange Co.(Home Health-Care, Respite and Nat. Certification in IV Therapy), 1990-; plasma pheresis RN, Med. Lab. of Orange, 5 mos. 1978; asst. dir. nurses Skilled Nursing Facility, 1984; listed Who's Who Among Human Service Profls., Who's Who in Am. Nursing; mem: Am. Assn. Critical Care Nurses, Am. Heart Assn., Am. Cancer Soc., Nat. Assn. M.S., Am. Lung Assn., LM,RPTF 1982-, NRA, CIS, NRCC, NRC, NRSC, CRP, Heritage Found., (past) ARC, USDC; Republican (Presdl. Task Force, Presdl. Advy. Com.); Baptist Fundamentalist; rec: travel, aviation, RV-ing, swimming, M.S. res., baking, new friends. Res: 924 S Hampstreet Anaheim 92802

LEE, EDWARD B., financial advisor; b. Sept. 19, 1962, Los Angeles; s. Bok and Suzie L.; edn: BA, and MS, UC San Diego, 1985, 1986. Career: staff research biochemist UC San Diego Cancer Ctr., 1986-88; financial advisor The Equitable, San Diego 1988-92; Asian mktg. mgr. Mutual of New York 1992-; honors: Who's Who Among Young Am Profls. 1988-92, Who's Who in Am. 1992; mem. San Diego Assn. Life Underwriters 1988-, Le Tip Profl. Bus. Networking Orgn. (1988-, pres. 1992); publs: 6+ sci. research papers and abstracts; rec: karate instr. World Tang Soo Do Karate Assn. Ofc: Mutual of New York 6048-A Cornerstone Ct West San Diego 92121 Ph: 619/546-7400

LEE, JAE KU, company president; b. Mar. 20, 1938, Seoul, Korea; s. Chung Hee and Chin Hee (Cho) L.; m. In Pin Kim, May 27, 1964, 1 dau. Elisa b. 1964; edn: BA, Kun Kuk Univ. 1968; MA, 1968. Career: exec. dir. Hwashin Retail & Mfg. Co., 1967; pres. Moolim Bldg. Material Prods. Co., Inc. 1969; pres. and c.e.o. Dai Ocho USA, Inc. 1975-; advr. Spokane C.of C.; pres. Korean American Assn. of San Francisco & Bay Area, mem. Advy. Council on Peaceful Unification Policy to R.O.K. (pres. N.W. dist. USA), Korean Am. Edn. Ctr., Korean Am. Political Assn., Multi Svc. Ctr. for Koreans, San Francisco-Seoul Sister City Commn., No. Calif. Korean Soccer Assn.; mil: R.O.K. Army 1959-61; Republican; Baptist; rec: music, table tennis. Res: 827 W 1st Ave Spokane WA 99204-0401

LEE, JAMES BURDETTE, JR., utilities executive; b. July 7, 1929, McCloud, Calif.; s. James Burdette and Beatrice Allison (Straub) Lee; m. Carolynne Bassett, Sept. 4, 1948; children: Linda Carol b. 1951, Gregory Alan b. 1954. Career: var. pos. with Pacific Gas & Electric Co. 1948-90: quartermaster at Pit 3, then 1st opr.; engring. estimator, Redding 1959-60; dist. representative, Weaverville 1960-64, Anderson 1964-68; area mgr. in Central Valley, Weaverville 1960-73, 77-82, area mgr., Anderson 1973-77; special rep. to Div. Mgr. in Red Bluff, 1982-86; reg. pub. affairs representative, Redding, 1986-90, ret.; appointed dir. 27th Dist. Agricultural Fair, 1992; mem. Pacific Coast Electrical Assn., Pacific Coast Gas Assn., Am. Gas Assn.; civic bds: Inter Counties Chambers of Commerce of No. Calif. (pres. 1980), Gr. Redding C.of C., Trinity County C.of C. (pres. 1981), Anderson C.of C. (pres. 1974), Shasta Dam Area C.of C. (pres. 1970), Red Bluff C.of C., No. Calif. Supervisors' Assn., Sacto. Mother Lode Reg. Assn. of County Suprs., Shasta Cascade Wonderland Assn. (pres. 1977), Shasta County Economic Devel. Assn. (pres. 1976), Shasta Co. Grand Jury, Superior Water Agy., Trinity County United Way (dir. 1979-82, chmn. 81-82), Weaverville Community Service Dist. (elected dir. 1978-82), Weaverville Parks & Rec. Com., Weaverville Lions Club (dir. & past pres. 1960-64, recipient dist. gov.'s spl. recognition award Calif. C.of C.), Shasta Trinity Heart Assn. (chmn. 1970), No. Calif. Planning Council (pres.), Anderson Planning Commn., Anderson Parks & Rec. Com. (chmn. 1967), Weaverville Junior C.of C. (1960-64, pastpres. 1963, disting. service award), Weaverville Little League Assn. (pres. 1963), Anderson Pop Warner Football (dir. 1967-68), Shasta Lake Youth Baseball (pres. 1968-71), Shasta Lake Little League (pres. 1968-71), Shasta Lake Kiwanis (dir. & past pres. 1964-68, chmn. Kiwanis President Council 1968); mem. Rotary, Masonic Lodge, Knights Templar & Royal Arch Masons of Calif., Nor-Cal Shrine Club; Republican; Methodist; rec: philately. Res: 7898 Tucker Ln Redding 96002

LEE, JAMES CHUNG, supermarket owner; b. Sept. 2, 1936, Canton, China; nat. 1952; s. Cambert T. and Kim Yee (Gin) L.; m. Regina, Aug. 16, 1963; children Gregory K. b. 1965, Brenda Soo b. 1971; edn: Golden Gate, 1953; Tech. High, Oakland, 1956; Oakland City Coll., 1957-60. Career: USAR 1960-62; asst. mgr. Eddie's Market, Oakland 1962-64; owner New Food, Oakland 1965-70; owner, Foodland Super, Ukiah 1971-78; owner, Yokayo Super Market 1978-; mil: SP4 AUS 1960-62; rec: tennis. Res: 4510 Lake Ridge Dr Ukiah 95482 Ofc: Yokayo Super Market 731 S State St Ukiah 95482

LEE, JERRY C., university president; b. Nov. 21, 1941; m. Joan Marie Leo; 1 child: Zan Carlton b. 1985; edn: BA, W.Va. Wesleyan Coll. 1963, grad. sch. 1963-64; Sch. of Law, Univ. Baltimore 1967-69; MA, Va. Polytechnic Inst. and State Univ. 1975, EdD, 1977. Career: indsl. rels. adminstr. Gen. Motors Corp., Balt. 1964-65; v.p. adminstrn. Commercial Credit Indsl. Corp., Balt.; v.p., adminstrn. and bus. Gallaudet Univ., WDC 1971-84, pres. 1984-88; pres. National University, San Diego 1988-; lectr. Gallaudet Univ.; lectr. nat. and internat.; honors: 1st honorary doctor of laws degree, Gallaudet Univ. 1986, disting. alumni award Va. Polytechnic Inst. and State Univ. 1985, Eileen Tosney award Am. Assn. of Univ. Admins. 1987, Advancement of Human Rights and Fundamental Freedoms award U.N. Assn. of the USA, One-of-a-kind award from People-To-People 1987, honorary pres., and National Service award Council for Better Speech and Hearing Month 1986, Nat. Assn. of Coll. Auxiliary Svcs. Excellence in Journalism award, Man of Yr. award Alpha Sigma Pi 1984, Gallaudet Coll. Alumni Assn. President's award, Gallaudet Comm. Rels. Award, U.S. Steel Foundation Cost Reduction Incentive award, Nat. Assn. of Coll. and Univ. Bus. Ofcrs., Am. Athletic Assn. of the Deaf award 1987; mem: Am. Assn. of Higher Edn., Am. Assn. of Univ. Admins., Am. Assn. of Univ. Prof., Am. Assn. of School Admins., Am. Mgmt. Assn., Am. Soc. for Personnel Admins., Nat. Assn. of Coll. and Univ. Bus. Ofcrs., Nat. Assn. for Independent Coll. and Univs., Coll. and Univ. Personnel Assn., Soc. for Mgmt. Information Systems; civic: Nat. Collegiate Athletic Assn. Pres.'s Commn., hon. bd. dirs. District of Columbia Spl. Olympics, Sertoma Foundation Nat. Advy. Com. (life mem.), commn. on administration orgn. Rehabilitation International, bd. dirs. People-to-People, bd. dirs. Deafness Res. Foundn., journal advy. bd. Nat. Assn. of College Aux. Services, exec. com. Consortium of Universities of the Wash. Metro. Area, hon. advocacy bd. mem. Nat. Capital Assn. for Coop. Edn., Bureau of Nat. Affairs Personnel Policies Forum; num. articles pub. profl. jours.; rec: tennis. Ofc: National University, 4025 Camino del Rio So, San Diego 92108-4194

LEE, JOHN SUN-CHUNG, certified public accountant; b. Aug. 3, 1955, China; m. Jan-Lih Wang, Apr. 27, 1987; children: Johnson b. 1988, Jennifer b. 1989; edn: BS, CSU Sacramento, 1979, CPA, Calif. (1985); cert. of ednl. achiev. in microcomputer consulting, Calif. Soc. CPAs, 1991. Career: owner John S. Lee, CPA, Monterey Park 1987-; mem. Am. Inst. of CPAs, Calif. Soc. of CPAs; rec: reading. Ofc: John S. Lee, CPA, 2063 S Atlantic Blvd Stes 2J & 2K Monterey Park 91754

LEE, JOHN Y., professor of accounting; b. Nov. 6, 1947, Euisong, Korea, nat. U.S.A. 1986; s. Ta'Ool and Namsu (Lim) L.; m. Jane K., Apr. 6, 1974; children: Patti b. 1975, Hanie b. 1980; edn: BS, Seoul Nat. Univ., 1970; MS, Louisiana St. Univ., 1976, PhD, 1979. Career: asst. prof. SUNY at Buffalo, N.Y., 1978-81; prof. acctg. CSU Los Angeles, 1981-, assoc. dean Sch. of Business 1987-88, chair acctg. dept. 1989-; awards: Rotary Found. fellow 1974-75, Exxon Award for Doctoral Res., La. St. Univ. (1978), Lybrand award Nat. Assn. of Accts. 1990, Outstanding Prof. CSU L.A. 1990, Phi Kappa Phi, Beta Gamma Sigma, Beta Alpha Psi; mem. Am. Acctg. Assn. (dir. mgmt. acctg. sect. 1988-90), Nat. Assn. Accts. (dir. L.A. chpt. 1990-); civic: Carver Found. of ABC Sch. Dist., Cerritos (sec. 1991-); author: Managerial Accounting Changes for the 1990s (1987), (Case book) Tech, Inc. (1989), contbg. author: Understanding Forecasting (1985), Pricing Decisions (1989); Democrat; rec: tennis. Ofc: Calif. State Univ.-L.A., Los Angeles 90032

LEE, JONG MOON, dentist; b. Aug. 4, 1946, Chung Joo, Choong Book, Korea; s. Young Kie and Choon Young (Song) L.; m. Yee, Oct. 6, 1973; children: Joon Y. b. 1974 (USC Dental Sch.), Sung W. b. 1976 (Diamond Bar High Sch.) Sue Y. b. 1981 (Chapparral Jr. High Sch.); edn: grad. Seoul Nat. Univ. Literature and Sci. Sch. 1968; DDS, Seoul Nat. Univ. Sch. Dentistry 1972; DDS, USC Dental Sch. 1979. Career: dentist, capt. Korean Army 1972-75, O.J.T. tng. US Mil. Dental Detach., Seoul 1973-74, secty. of Surgeon Gen., Korean Army HQ 1974-75; postgrad. dental tng. USC 1976-79; dentist/owner Dr. Lee's Dental Office, first office Diamond Bar, 1982-, second office in Ontario; mem: American Dental Assn., Calif. Dental Assn., Korean Dental Assn., USC Korean Dental Alumni Assn. (secty. gen. 1992-93), USC Alumni Assn., Seoul National Univ. Alumni Assn., Kyunggi H.S. Alumni Assn., Diamond Bar C.of C., Korean Am. Fedn. of Eastern Los Angeles (pres. 1992-94); R.Cath.; rec: golf, Aikido instr. Res: 2177 Rocky View Rd Diamond Bar 91765 Dr. Lee's Dental Ofcs: 1108 S Diamond Bar Blvd Diamond Bar 91765 Tel: 909/861-4444 also: 2409-D Vineyard Ave Ontario 91761 Tel: 909/923-9557

LEE, RALPH K., real estate developer; b. Oct. 9, 1951, Salt Lake City; s. Ralph H. and Hattie (Hadlock) L.; m. Jacquelyn Dowdle, Jan. 15, 1974 (div. 1985); children: Ralph Adam b. 1974, Daniel Spencer b. 1976, Linzi b. 1979, Jayme b. 1980, Jordan Duke b. 1982; m. Carol Elaine Redelings, Oct. 24, 1987; st. dau. Annie Rebecca Anderson b. 1978; edn: Cert. urban planning, BS geography, BS polit. sci., Univ. of Utah, 1979; MBA, Univ. of Phoenix, Az. 1987. Career: forward planning dir. PF West Inc., Dallas, Tx., Utah div. 1983-88; forward planning dir. Systems Constrn. Co., Anaheim Hills, 1989-90; proj. mgr. The Orange Coast Group, Seal Beach, Calif. 1990-91; mem. faculty Church Educational Svs., Cypress 1990-, faculty Univ. of Phoenix, Fountain Valley 1991-; dir. special projects Hill Williams Devel. Corp., Anaheim Hills 1991-93; computer pgmr. Stewart Title 1993-; minister L.D.S. Ch., Perth, Australia 1971-72, Adelaide, Austr. 1972-73; designer, cons. R.K. Lee & Assocs., Anaheim Hills 1990-; awards: Eagle Scout 1970, Duty to God Award Mormon Ch. S.L.C. 1971, ranked in top 2% in nation (GATB) Gen. Aptitude Test Battery 1987, Seminary Ch. Ednl. System Award Mormon Ch. Anaheim Hills, Ca. 1991; mem. Nat. Assn. of Home Builders 1991-, Bldg. Industry Assn. of So. Calif. Inc. 1991-; scout master BSA, S.L.C., Ut. 1975-78; composer (new age albums): City Moods (c. 1987), performer, Mac computer synthesizer album: Lucky Dreams (c. 1987); Republican; Ch. of Jesus Christ of Latter-Day Saints; rec: Macintosh computers, music, basketball, reading, racquetball. Res: 530 S Ranch View Cir, 43, Anaheim Hills 92807 Ofc: Stewart Title of Los Angeles 505 N Brand Blvd #1200 Glendale 91203

LEE, ROBERT ERICH, business consultant; b. Dec. 26, 1955, Spokane, Wash.; s. Robert Edward Lee and Edith Frieda (Klasen) Moore; m. Vicky Ann Rowland, Jan. 31, 1981; children: Erich b. 1985, Christopher b. 1988; edn: Vanderbilt Univ. 1973-77; Corpus Christi St. Univ. 1977; Univ. Tx. El Paso 1980. Career: mgr., instr. Neptune Equipment Co., Nashville, Tenn. 1976-77; customer engr. Hewlett Packard, Los Angeles 1977-82, dist. mgr. 1982-85, regional service adminstrn. mgr., North Hollywood 1985-86; dir. MIS Tova Corp., Beverly Hills 1986-87; dir. information technology PrimeSource Inc., Irvine 1987-92; pres. Results from Technology!, Irvine 1992-; listed Who's Who in Fin. & Ind. 1989, Personalities in Am. 1990; mem. Assn. for Computing

Machinery, IEEE, Interex, Town Hall of Calif.; Republican; Prot.; rec: skiing, scuba diving, travel. Res: 1 Shenandoah Irvine 92720 Ofc: Results from Technology! 1 Shenandoah Irvine 92720

LEE, SOON SENG, dermatologist; b. May 1, 1941, Singapore; s. Hwan Chew and Hui Choo (Tan) L.; m. Irene Poh Yeow, Dec. 28, 1968; children: Sandra b. 1970, Kevin b. 1976; edn: MB, BS, Univ. Singapore Faculty of Medicine 1967. Career: resident dermatology Downstate Univ., Bklyn., N.Y. 1971-74; dermatologist Kaiser Permanente, Fontana 1975-77; pvt. practice dermatology, Upland 1978-; clin. asst. prof. USC, L.A. 1980-; Loma Linda Med. Sch. 1982-; mem: Singapore Club, Inland Counties Dermatologic Soc. (secty. 1988, v.p. 1989), Am. Acad. Dermatology (fellow); articles pub. med. jours. 1975-82; rec: fly fishing. Ofc: 639 N 13th Ave Upland 91786

LEE, SUN, research surgeon; b. June 2, 1920, Seoul, Korea; s. Kap T. and Og (Song) L.; m. Jean Hwa, May 7, 1945; children: William b. 1946, Gloria b. 1948, Thomas b. 1959, Marlene b. 1961, Janet b. 1964, Donna b. 1965; edn: MD, Seoul Nat. Univ. Kyung Sung Med. Coll. Career: intern Wheeling Gen. Hosp., W. Va.; resident Ohio Valley Hosp.; res. in gen. surgery St. Francis Hosp., Pittsburgh, Pa.; research fellow Univ. Pittsburgh 1955-57, instr. surgery 1957-61, asst. prof. surgery (res.) Univ. Pitts. 1961; res. assoc. Scripps Cinic Research Found., La Jolla 1964; assoc. prof., prof. surgery/surg. res. UC San Diego 1968-85; dir. San Diego Microsurgical Inst. & Tng. Center, Mercy Hosp., S.D. 1985-; devel. allied microsurgical techniques relating to organ transplatation incl. kidney, liver, pancreas, testis; award: gold medal Internat. Microsurgical Soc. (1978, hon. pres.); founder Internat. Microsurg. Soc. & Internat. Soc. Experi. Microsurg.; mem: Internat. Acad Proctol. (hon. fellow), Am. Soc. Reconstructive Microsurgery, Internat. Soc. Reconstructive Microsurgery; author: Manual of Microsurgery (1985, CRC Press), Experimental Microsurgery (1984, Hallym Coll. Press, 2d edit., Igakushoin Pub.), Color Atlas of Microsurgery (1992, Ishiyaku EuroAmerical Pub.); coauthor sev. books, contbr. 200+ sci. publs.; Republican; Methodist; rec: raise fish, flower garden. Res: 6462 Cardeno Dr La Jolla 92037 Ofc: 311 College Building Mercy Hospital San Diego 92103

LEE, WILLIAM MORRIS, JR., interior designer; b. Nov. 30, 1943, Waco, Tex.; s. Wm. Morris Lee and Lady Ann (Mayfield) Thomason; m. Susan Carroll, Jan. 25, 1964 (div. 1980); children: William III, Robert, Peter; m. Dorothy Lou Ziemke, Feb. 27, 1981; children: Eric, John; edn: BS, Okla. City Univ., 1967. Career: interior designer Nelson's Bartlesville (Okla.) Furniture, 1968-70; Lee & Stham Co., Bartlesville 1970-72; Kashian Bros. Interiors, Wilmette, Ill. 1972-74; Phyllis Morris Originals, Chgo. 1974-75; & E.W. Rost & Son, Janesville, Wis. 1975-80; interior design prin., owner, 1980-, owner Collectibles Outlet, San Jose, Calif. 1986-; mem. Edn. Advy. Bd. Univ. Wis., Madison 1982-85; mem. Am. Soc. Interior Design (bd. 1976-85, treas. 1978-79, admissions chmn. 1979-81), Masons; civic: Janesville C.of C. (bd. 1980-83, treas. 1981, v.p. 1982), Blackhawk Epilepsy Ctr., Janesville (pres. 1978-85); Bibliography: recogn. for Haye residence, House Beautiful Bldg. Guide (1980), Dunn residence, Edgerton Chronicle (1981), Kochell residence, Janesville Gazette (1984). Ofc: 1899 W San Carlos San Jose 95128

LEE, WILSON, engineering manager; b. Aug. 5, 1962, San Mateo; s. Hom Hai and Kam Fung (Wong) L.; m. Magnolia Shell Ho Wong, Sept. 16, 1989; edn: BS in EECS, UC Berkeley, 1984. Career: project mgmt. assoc. Rolm Systems, Santa Clara 1984-85, design engr. 1985-88, mfg. engr. 1988-91, engring. mgr. 1991-; honors: Eta Kappa Nu 1983; pub. articles in California Engineer 1984, 86. Ofc: Rolm Systems 4900 Old Ironsides Dr M/S 302 Santa Clara 95052

LEEUWENBURG, RICHARD PETER, casual shoe company president; b. March 26, 1942, Salt Lake City, Utah; s. Peter M. and Ann (Vermeulen) L.; m. Jann Spence, July 18, 1964; children: Christopher b. 1967, Jay b. 1969; edn: BSIE, Stanford Univ. 1964; MBA, Univ. Chgo. Grad. Sch. Bus. 1967. Career: profl. football player Chicago Bears, Ill. 1965; econ. analyst Continental Oil Co., NYC 1967-69; mgr. ops. consumer packaging div. Boise Cascade, St. Louis, Mo. 1969-87; pres., CEO Van Doren Rubber Co., Orange 1988-. Ofc: Van Doren Rubber Co. 2095 Batavia Orange 92665

LEFF, HARVEY SHERWIN, physicist, educator; b. July 24, 1937, Chicago; s. Jack William and Anne Sharon (Maiman) L.; m. Ellen Janice Wine, Aug. 17, 1958; children: Lisa Michele b. 1962, Robyn Joy b. 1964, Jordan William b. 1969, Jeremy Matthew b. 1969; edn: BS physics, Ill. Inst. of Tech., 1959; MS physics, Northwestern Univ., 1960; PhD physics, Univ. Iowa, 1963. Career: res. assoc. Case Inst. of Technology, 1963-64, asst. to assoc. prof. physics Case Western Reserve Univ., 1964-71; assoc. prof. to prof. physics Chicago State Univ., 1971-79; vis. prof. physics Harvey Mudd Coll. of Sci. & Engring., Claremont, Ca. 1977-78; scientist Oak Ridge Associated Univs., Tenn. 1979-83; prof. physics and dept. chair Calif. State Polytech. Univ., Pomona 1983-; leader in-service workshops (TI-IN Network, Cal Poly U., So. Calif. Edison, Nat. Sci. Tchrs. Assn.) 1985-; state co-coordinator Calif. State Univ. Inst. for Teaching & Learning, Long Beach 1989-; assoc. ed. Am. Jour. of Physics, 1992-95; recipient awards for merit. performance Calif. State Polytech. Univ.,

Pomona (1987, 88, 90); mem: Am. Assn. of Physics Tchrs. (So. Calif. pres. 1991-93), Sigma Xi Sci. Research Soc. (Cal Poly past pres. 1991-92), Calif. Sci. Tchrs. Assn., Am. Physical Soc.; civic: vol. reader Recording for the Blind, Upland; editor (w/A.F. Rex) Maxwell's Demon: Entropy, Information, Computing (1990), author num. articles in profl. jours. (1964-). Res: 538 E Bishop Pl Claremont 91711 Ofc: Calif. State Polytechnic Univ. 3801 W Temple Physics Dept. Pomona 91768

LEFTWICH, JAMES STEPHEN, retail corporate executive; b. Nov. 30, 1956, Stevenage, England; s. James Wright and Del M. (Thompson) L.; m. Carol Anne Petersen, Nov. 7, 1980 (div. Jan. 1982); edn: AA criminal justice, Butte Coll., 1982; BA criminal justice, Southwest Univ., 1992; lic. Hazardous Material Specialist (HMS) 1989, internat. accredited safety auditor 1990. Career: prodn. mgr. Artistic Dyers Inc., El Monte 1976-80; mgr. loss control & risk mgmt. Mervyn's Dept. Store, Hayward 1982-91; dir. risk mgmt. Save Mart Corp., Modesto 1991-; v.p. ops. I.C.S. Corp, Irvine, CA 1993-; dir. Safety Center of Calif., Sacramento 1990-, trustee 1989-90; dir. Bay Area Safety Council, Oakland 1987-88; Reserve Police ofcr., Cotati 1983-85; honors: Class Comdr. 39th Police Acad., Butte County 1982, listed Who's Who in West 1992; mem: Am. Soc. Safety Engrs. 1988-, Nat. Safety Mgmt. Soc., Risk & Ins. Mgmt. Soc., Nat. Fire Protection Assn., Nat. Environmental Tng. Assn. 1989-; co-writer and tech. advisor Safety Tng. videos, 12 1989-91, pub. articles re risk mgmt. 1989-; Republican; R.Cath.; rec: skiing, swimming, biking, hunting.

LEGASPI, CONSUELITO UBAY, accountant; b. Sept. 30, 1942, Manila, Philippines, nat. 1971; s. Jose L. and Patrocinio U. (Ubay) L.; m. Grace Macagba, Oct. 22, 1966; 1 son: Nicholas II, b. 1967; edn: BBA, Univ. of the East 1965; notary pub., Calif. 1974; real estate broker, Calif. 1974; grad. Rio Hondo Police Acad., 1990. Career: asst. payroll mgr. Bullock's, Pasadena 1968; accts. payable supvr., Bethlehem Steel Corp., Los Angeles 1971-82; dept. acct. Los Angeles Times 1982-; realtor/ broker C.U. Legaspi & Assoc., So. Pasadena 1974-; reserve ofcr. Arcadia Police Dept., 1991-; mem: Nat. Assn. of Accountants 1989-, Calif. Reserve Peace Ofcrs. Assn. 1991-, Nat. & Calif. Assns. Realtors, Real Estate Cert. Inst., Calif. Real Estate Edn. Assn., Nat. Notary Assn.; mil: 1st lt. Philippine Army 1963-66, infantryman; R.Cath. Res: 330 Camino Del Sol, So. Pasadena 91030 Ofc: Los Angeles Times, Times Mirror Square, Los Angeles 90053

LEHMAN, ELLEN J., psychologist; b. Feb. 21, 1944, Pittsburgh, Pa.; d. Alan G. and Jane (Anathan) Lehman; m. Charles Kennel; edn: AB, Vassar Coll. 1966; PhD, Cornell Univ. 1975. Career: staff psychologist Marianne Frostig Center for Ednl. Therapy, L.A. 1974-75; contract instr. Calif. Sch. Profl. Psychology 1975-76; instr. Center for Early Edn. 1979-80; pvt. practice, Santa Monica 1975-; supr. Wright Inst., L.A. 1983-; asst. clin. prof. UCLA 1990-; honors: Phi Kappa Phi; mem: Inst. of Contemporary Psychoanalysis 1991-, Am. Psychological Assn., Soc. Research in Child Devel., Vassar Club So. Calif. (admissions chair 1980-84), Topanga Canyon Docents; papers pub. in profl. jours. 1971, 85-. Ofc: 1132 26th St Santa Monica 90403

LEISER, ERIC J., engineer, international sales executive; b. Oct. 13, 1960, NY, NY; s. Werner and Laura (Goldschmidt) L.; m. Cynthia Joy Gordon, May 5, 1991; edn: BS, M.I.T., 1982. Career: engr. Motorola, Phoenix, Az. 1982-85; engr. and sales staff Merck, Germany and Taiwan, 1985-89; mgr. Far Eastern sales and applications Allied-Signal, Milpitas, Calif. 1989-. Res: 5466 Drysdale Dr San Jose 95124 Ofc: Allied-Signal 1090 S Milpitas Blvd Milpitas 95035

LEITMANN, GEORGE, professor of engineering science; b. May 24, 1925, Vienna, Austria, naturalized U.S., 1944; s. Josef and Stella (Fischer) L.; m. Nancy Lloyd, Jan. 28, 1955; children: Josef b. 1957, Elaine b. 1959; edn: BS, Columbia Univ., 1949, MA, 1950; PhD, UC Berkeley, 1956. Career: hd. aeroballistics USN OTS, China Lake, Calif. 1950-57; staff scientist Lockheed Corp., Palo Alto 1957-63; asst., assoc., prof. engring. sci. UC Berkeley 1957-59, 59-63, 63-91, assoc. dean 1980-, prof. emeritus 1991-; instr. USAF Acad., Colo. Springs 1960-65; cons. Martin Co., Denver 1957-65, Aerojet Gen., Sacto. 1960-63, Guggenheim Lab. Princeton, N.J. 1958-60; awards: Pendray Medal, AIAA 1974, Flight Medal, AIAA 1978, Levy Medal, Franklin Inst., Phila. 1982, V. Humboldt Found. Medal, Bonn, Ger. 1991, Berkeley citation UCB 1991, Hon. doctorates Paris, Vienna, Darmstadt; mem: US Nat. Acad. Engring. 1982-, Internat. Acad. Astron. 1978-, fgn. mem. Argentine Acad. Engring. 1987-, AC. Science, Bologna 1978-, AC. Natural Sciences, Russia 1992-; author 11 books in engineering (1962-), 225+ articles in sci. jours. (1956-); 2d. lt. Mil. Intell.; rec: swimming, art collecting, oenology. Ofc: Assoc. Dean Research, College of Engineering, Univ. Calif., Berkeley 94720

LE LIEVRE, ROBERT EARL, physician, child psychiatrist; b. Apr. 10, 1929, Cleveland, Ohio; s. Raymond Earl and Mary Gertrude (Boyd) LeL.; m. Virginia, (div.); son, David F. b. 1955; edn: BA, Amherst Coll. 1951; MD, Case Western Reserve 1957; psychiat., Univ. of Colo. 1963, child psychiat., 1965; lic. M.D., Surgeon, Calif., 1962. Career: chief of childrens services Colo. St. Hosp., 1964-65; chief of comm. services Stone Brandel Center, Chgo. 1968-69; assoc. prof. child psychiatry Univ. Ill. 1970-74, also dir. childrens services Forest Hosp., Des Plains, and sr. cons. Inst. for Juvenile Res., Chgo., 1970-74; asst. prof. psychia-

try UC San Diego 1974-78; current: pvt. practice child and adolescent psychiatry, child psychiatrist East San Diego Co. Mental Health Clinic; chief of staff Rancho Park Hosp., 1991-92, chief dept. psychiatry, 1992-; cons. New Alternative Residential Ctr.; mem: Am. Psychiatric Assn., Am. Acad. of Child and Adol. Psychiatry, Am. Soc. for Adol. Psychiatry, San Diego Soc. for Psychiat. Physician, AMA, San Diego Med. Soc., Calif. Med. Soc.; mil: AUS Chem. Corps 1951-53. Address: 3921 Goldfinch St San Diego 92103

LEMAN, ROBERT ALLAN, engineering executive; b. Nov. 14, 1946, Detroit, Mich.; s. Anthony and Marie V. (Casey) L.;m. Glenda L.; children: Steve b. 1973, Scott b. 1974; edn: BS in chem., CSU Sacto., 1972. Career: ; software engring. mgr. Autek Corp., San Jose 1981-91; diagnostic mgr. Amdahl Corp., Fremont 1991-92; devel. mgr. SEGA of Am., San Carlos 1993-; founder Digital Software Corp., San Jose 1978-; recipient life saving award No. Calif. Transplant Bank, S.F. (1984); civic: Civil Air Patrol, San Jose (emergency service 1984-); mil: airman 2/c USAF; rec: pilot. Res: 3931 Yerba Buena Ave San Jose 95121 Ofc: SEGA of America, San Carlos.

LENNOX, CAROL, computer scientist; b. Dec. 22, 1938, Colorado Springs, Colo.; d. William Orin and Elizabeth (Foster) Lennox; edn: BA, Mills Coll. 1961. Career: systems programmer Control Data Corp., Palo Alto 1963-68; co-founder, mgr. Interactive Systems 1968-70; cons. Polymorphic 1970-71; asst. mgr., interactive Stanford Univ. 1971-75; dir. computing and campus networking Mills Coll., Oakland 1975-; lectr. and co-dir. of Master of Arts grad. program in Interdisciplinary Computer Sci.; cons. EDUCOM, W.D.C., 1982-, trustee 1988-; bd. mem. Microsoft, Redmond, Wash. 1988-; SAC, Corvallis, Ore. 1989-; honors: Who's Who in Computing 1989; mem: Phi Beta Kappa (Zeta chpt. secty.), ACM, AIR, Jr. League (Colorado Springs and Palo Alto); Republican. Res: 400 Irish Ridge Rd Half Moon Bay 94019 Ofc: Mills College 5000 MacArthur Blvd Oakland 94613

LENZO, THOMAS JOHN, training and development consultant; b. Nov. 19, 1949, Waterbury, Conn.; s. John Anthony and Mary Louise (Perezella) L.; edn: BA, Fairfield Univ., 1971; MEd, CSU Los Angeles, 1980. Career: media coordinator Valley Vocat. Ctr., Industry, Calif. 1977-78; librarian Washington Sch., Pasadena 1978-79; tng. specialist Data Electronics, 1979-82; engring. instr. Litton Data Sys., Van Nuys 1982-83; cons. B.P.W. Inc., Costa Mesa 1984-85; cons. pvt. practice, Pasadena 1986-; honors: outstanding student 1979, accomplishment in media 1979, 80, CSU Los Angeles; mem. Soc. for Tech. Communication (sr. mem. 1986-), Am. Soc. for Tng. & Devel. 1978-, Nat. Soc. for Performance Inst. 1982-, Pasadena IBM PC Users Gp. (v.p. 1986-); civic: Towards 2000 Mayoral Commn. Pasadena 1984-85; mil: sgt. E/4 USAF 1972-76, Commendn. medal 1976; R.Cath.; rec: hiking, photography, travel. Res: 2473 Oswego St, 10, Pasadena 91107

LEO, ROBERT JOSEPH, association executive; b. Nov. 24, 1939, Paterson, NJ; s. Dewey J. and Jean (Bianco) L.; m. Margaret Elena Ingafu, Aug. 5, 1962; children: Christopher, Nicholas; edn: BA, Temple Univ. 1960, MA, 1962; PhD, Univ. of Wash. 1968. Career: instr. Monmouth Coll., West Long Branch, NJ 1962-64; spl. asst. to chancellor Dallas Co. Comm. Coll. Dist. 1968-71, dir. spl. svcs. and gov. rels. 1971-76; assoc. exec. dir. League for Innovation in the Community Coll., Los Angeles 1976-80, exec. dir., Dallas 1980-82; exec. dir., Los Angeles Jr. Chamber of Commerce, 1982-; founding pres. Nat. Council Resource Devel., adj. assoc. proj. East Tex. State Univ. 1975-76; chmn. Tex. Health Plnng. Council; honors: distng. service Oak Cliff Jaycees (1973), spl. recogn., Nat. Council Resource Devel. 1981, significant contbn. to fair housing Greater Dallas Housing Opp. Ctr. 1973; civic: Nat. Council Resource Devel., Rotary, Townhall of Calif., Grand People; clubs: L.A. Athletic, Riviera CC; author: articles in field. Res: 4641 Fulton #204 Sherman Oaks 91423 Ofc: Junior Chamber of Commerce, 404 So Bixel St Los Angeles 90017

LEONARD, JAMES HENRY, information systems executive; b. Dec. 25, 1954, Baltimore, Md.; s. Don Jack and Lucille E. (Welter) L.; m. 2d. Cindie Marie Weaver, July 14, 1993; 1 child, Aubrey Nicole b. 1984; edn: BA, Univ. Tx. Austin 1976. Career: computer programmer Austron, Austin, Tx. 1978-80; sr. programmer, analyst Atari, Sunnyvale 1980-83; STC/CRC 1983-84; Genentech, South S.F. 1984-87, mgr. comml. systems 1987-91, assoc. dir. 1991-. Ofc: Genentech 460 Point San Bruno Blvd, South San Francisco 94080

LEONG, CAROL JEAN, electrologist, designer; B. Jan. 9, 1942, Sacramento; d. Walter Richard and Edith (Bond) Bloss; m. Oliver Arthur Fisk III, Apr. 12, 1964 (div. 1973); children: Victoria Kay; edn: BA sociology, San Jose State Univ., 1963; degree, Western Bus. Coll., 1964; cert. profl., Bay Area Coll. Electrolysis, 1978; Calif. reg. clin. and profl. electrologist. Career: profl. model, 1951-64; employment counselor Businessmen's Clearinghouse, Cinti. 1966-67; dir. personnel Kroger Food Corp., Cinti. 1967-68; prop. Carol Leong Electrology, San Mateo, Calif. 1978-, Designs by Carol, 1987-; recipient appreciation San Francisco Lighthouse for the Blind (1981-82, 83); biographical listings in Who's Who in World, Who's Who Am. Women, Who's Who in Fin. and Ind., Who's Who in West, others; mem: Internat. Guild Profl. Electrologists (cont. edn. com.), Profl. Women's Forum 1988-, Nat. Assn. Female Execs., Am.

Electrologists Assn., Electrologists Assn. Calif., Internat. Platform Assn., Chi Omega; civic: Peninsula Humane Soc., San Francisco Zool. Soc., Friends of Filoli; contbr. articles to profl. publs.; Republican; Presbyterian; rec: photog., golf, tennis, ballet, theater. Res: 3339 Glendora Dr San Mateo 94403 Ofc: Carol Leong Electrolysis 36 S El Camino Real Ste 205 San Mateo 94401

LEONG, HENRY YOU, computer engineer; b. Nov. 24, 1957, San Francisco; s. Fong and Helen (Wong) L.; edn: AS, City Coll. San Francisco 1980; San Francisco St. Univ. 1980-82; Control Data Inst. 1983. Career: heart lung tech. Pacific Med. Center, San Francisco 1973-80; asst. mgr. Grand Auto 1980-82; floor mgr. Cassidys Western Outfitters 1982-83; computer engr., mgr. Quotron Systems 1983-89, Phoenix Service Technologies 1989-; asst. volleyball coach City Coll., San Francisco 1976-89; Skyline Coll., San Mateo 1989-; volleyball coach, City Coll., S.F. 1989-91; asst. volleyball coach Chabot Coll., Hayward 1991-92; mem.: Hawaii Sunsetter Volleyball Assn. 1991-, Wei Mo Kung Fu Studio. Address: San Francisco 94122

LEPORIERE, RALPH DENNIS, quality engineer; b. Nov. 8, 1932, Elizabeth, NJ; s. Maximo and Christian Leporiere; m. Judith Louise Crowhurst, Nov. 19, 1960; children: Bonnie Ann, b. 1961; David Anthony, b. 1964; edn: BS, Rutgers Univ. 1954; postgrad. Rutgers Statistics Center 1955-6, 1958-9; Coll. of the Holy Names, Oakland 1965-66; Reg. Profl. Quality Engr., Calif. Career: chemist NY Quinine & Chem. Works, Inc., Newark NJ 1954-55; asst. to chief chemist/qual. control C.D. Smith Pharmaceutical Co., New Brunswick, NJ 1955-56; asst. supvr. qual. control White Labs, Inc., Kenilworth, NJ 1958-60; staff cons. qual. eng. Calif. & Hawaiian Sugar Co., Crockett, Calif. 1960-; chmn./ instr. Qual. Control Dept. Laney Coll., Oakland 1967-87; chmn./ asst. prof. JFK Univ., Martinez 1967-72; instr., mem. advy. com. Annual Stat. Short Course, UC Davis 1969-; mem: Fellow ASQC (S.F. & East Bay Sects.), Soc. of Mfg. Engrs. (senior mem.), Am. Statistical Assn., Am. Chem. Soc., Toastmasters (Vallejo pres. 1965); civic: Am. Canyon Co. Water Dist. (pres. 1973-83, v.p. 1971-73); biog. listings Who's Who in the West, 1970-, Dict. of Internat. Biography, 1984-; mil: Med. Svc. Corps, US Army Environmental Health Labs, Edgewood, MD 1956-58. Res: 618 Kilpatrick St Vallejo 94589 Ofc: Calif. & Hawaiian Sugar Co., 830 Loring Ave Crockett 94525

LEQUESNE, JAMES RICHARD, civil servant, media liaison; b. Mar. 8, 1957, Burbank; s. James Sangster and Lorraine Yvette (Jean) LeQ.; edn: BA, CSU Northridge, 1980. Career: public relations KCSN-FM Radio, Northridge 1976-87; program clerk Veterans Adminstrn., Sepulveda 1984-, media liaison Volunteer Center, San Fernando 1987-; honors: Calif. Scholarship Fedn. (1976), award of merit City of L.A. 1984, Outstanding govt. employee VA USA 1985, 86, 87, 89, 91, Outstanding federal employee 1992, DOVIA award for outstanding volunteerism 1989, 90, 91, Golden State Award 1990, Carnation "Outstanding Volunteer" 1991; civic: L.A. Zoo Assn., Sierra Club, Nat. Public Radio, KCSN (1978-); publs: articles in coll. newspaper 1978, t.v. news reporter 1975-76, ed. Scene mag. 1979-80; Democrat; R.Cath. Res: Northridge 91324

LESCHYN, WADE RICHARD, telecommunications contractor; b. Dec. 13, 1954, Passaic, N.J.; s. Edward C. and Phyllis J.; edn: BA biol., UC Santa Cruz, 1978; Certificate, Environmental Planning, San Francisco St. Univ. Career: technician GTE, San Carlos 1978-79; Pacific Telephone, Palo Alto 1979-84; AT&T, San Mateo 1984-86; Visa, San Mateo 1988-; owner/pres./chief technician WRL Telecom, Redwood City 1986-; founding ptnr. Limitel, Palo Alto 1983-; mem. S.F. Mycological Soc. (pres. 1991-92); Democrat; Unitarian; rec: mushrooming, fishing, gardening. Ofc: WRL Telecom 219 Sequoia Ave Redwood City 94061

LESSARD, ARTHUR GILBERT, meteorologist; b. Apr. 18, 1929, New Bedford, Mass.; s. Arthur P. and Juliette M. (Montminy) L.; m. Maria G. Konrad, Dec. 19, 1960; 1 son, Arthur Jr. b. 1963; m. Crystal A. Ford, Mar. 23, 1985; edn: Eastern N.M. Univ. 1964-66; BS atmospheric sci., Univ. of Hawaii 1971. Career: meteorologist Nat. Weather Service, Wake Island, Pacific 1971-72; Nat. Weather Service Severe Storms Forecast Ctr., Kansas City, Mo. 1972-73; leading forecaster Nat. Weather Service, Topeka, Kans. 1973-74; quality control ofcr. Nat. Weather Service, San Francisco 1974-77; dep. meteorologist in charge Nat. Weather Serv. Los Angeles 1977-79, area mgr./meteorologist in chg. Nat. Weather Serv. Forecast Office, LA 1979-92; dep. dir. National Climate Analysis Ctr., Wash. DC 1992-; govt. liaison to Los Angeles Olympic Organizing Com., 1984 Olympic Games; So. Calif. Nat. Weather Serv. liaison to the Fed. Emergency Mgmt. Agency; mem. Los Angeles Federal Exec. Bd.; Nat. Weather Service Modernization and Associated Restructuring Coordinator for So. Calif.; On US Dept. of Commerce, Nat. Weather Serv. Line Forecasters Honors List 1971, 73; honors: recipient L.A. Co. Bd. Suprs. Award and Scroll for outstanding public service 1989, recogn. by Mayor of Los Angeles for outstanding support to city homeless shelter program (1988, 1992); mem: Am. Meteorol. Soc., Fellow Royal Meteorological Soc., Nat. Weather Assn., Aircraft Owners and Pilots Assn., Nat. Pilots Assn., Nat. Geographic Soc. (contbg. writer NGS publs.), Am. Legion; mil: SMS (E-8) USAF 1951-71, Korean Service, United Nations, Nat. Defense Service medals, USN Merit. Service Commendn. while attached to USN 1966-70; R.Cath.; rec: flying, philately.

Res: 11707 Sunset Blvd Los Angeles 90049. Ofcs: NOAA/National Weather Service, Rm 11102 Federal Bldg 11000 Wilshire Blvd Los Angeles 90024; Climate Analysis Center, NOAA Science Center World Weather Bldg 5200 Auth Road Wash DC 20233

LESSER, HENRY, lawyer; b. Feb. 28, 1947, London, England; s. Bernard Martin and Valerie Joan (Leslie) L.; m. Jane, June 29, 1969; edn: BA (honors), Cambridge Univ. England 1968; MA hons, 1972; LL.M, Harvard Law Sch. 1973. Career: law lectr. Lincoln Coll., Oxford, Eng. 1968-69; barrister, London 1969-70; law lectr. Fitzwilliam Coll., Cambridge 1970-71; atty., assoc. Spear & Hill, N.Y. and London 1973-75; Webster & Sheffield 1976-77; assoc., ptnr. Wachtell Lipton Rosen & Katz, N.Y. 1977-83; ptnr. Gibson Dunn & Crutcher, L.A. 1983-87; ptnr. Fried Frank Harris Shriver & Jacobson 1987-91; ptnr. Irell & Manella, 1991-; honors: Lucas Smith Prize Queens Coll. Cambridge 1966, 67, 68, Squire Law scholar Cambridge Univ. 1968, Harkness fellow Commonwealth Fund of N.Y. 1971, Kennedy scholar Lincolns Inn 1968; mem: Am. Law Inst., Calif. State Bar (vice-chair 1993-94, secty. 1992-93, bus. law sect. exec. com. 1991-92, corporations com. chair 1990-91), L.A. County Bar Assn. (exec. com. bus. law sect.), New York State Bar, Am. Bar Assn., Internat. Bar Assn.; civic: Jonathan Club (L.A.), Harvard Club (N.Y.), Royal Automobile Club (London); num. articles pub. in U.S. and U.K., contbr. 2 legal treatises; rec: long distance running, squash. Res: 1375 Belfast Dr Los Angeles 90069 Ofc: Irell & Manella, 333 S Hope St Ste 3300 L.A. 90071

LESTER, DON KEVIN, orthopaedic surgeon; b. July 21, 1950, Chgo.; s. Donald C. and Bonna E. (Esterson) L.; m. Linda, June 7, 1979; children: Tyler b. 1982, Morgan b. 1986; edn: BA, UC San Diego 1973; MD, UC Irvine Coll. of Med. 1979; bd. certified 1986. Career: orthopaedic intern L.A. Co.-USC Med. Center 1980, grad. orthopaedic residency Penn. State Univ. Hershey Med. Center, Div. Orthopaedic Surgery, 1984; orthopaedic surgeon in pvt. practice, Fresno 1984-; mem. Orthopaedic Res. Soc., Western Med. Assn., Fresno Madera Med. Assn.; contbr. 20 publs. in med. jours., num. presentations nat. profl. meetings (1979-); mil: sgt. USAF Nat. Guard, hon. disch. 1973. Ofc: D. Kevin Lester, MD, Inc. 6085 N First St Fresno 93710

LEUKEL, FRANCIS PARKER, professor of psychology; b. Aug. 29, 1922; s. Walter Anthony and Ruth Brooks (Hostetler) L.; m. Billie Jean Leukel; edn: BS, Univ. of Fla., Gainesville, 1947; MS, Northwestern Univ., Evanston, Ill., 1948; PhD, Univ. of Wash., Seattle, 1955. Career: res. asst., Northwestern Univ., 1947-49; instr., Wash. & Jefferson Coll., Wash., Pa., 1949-50; pre-doctoral fellow, Univ. of Wash., 1950-54; post-doctoral fellow, Univ. of Wash., 1954-55; asst., then full prof., San Diego State Univ., 1956-; fellow, Am. Psychological Soc., 1990-; author: Intro. to Physiol. Psychology, 3 editions, 1968-74; Essentials of Physiol. Psychology, 1972; ed., Issues in Physiol. Psychology, 1974; rec: sailing. Ofc: San Diego State Univ. Psychology Dept. San Diego 92182

LEUNG, CHARLES C., manufacturing company president; b. June 27 1946, Hong Kong; nat. 1981; s. Mo-Fan and Lai-Ping (Tam) L.; m. Jessica Lan Lee; children: Jennifer b. 1975, Cheryl b. 1979, Albert b. 1985; edn: BS, Univ. Hong Kong 1969; MS, Univ. Chgo. 1971; PhD, 1976. Career: sr. scientist Corning Glass Works, Corning, N.Y. 1975-79; sr. staff engr. Motorola, Mesa, Ariz. 1979-81; engring. mgr. Avantek Inc., Newark 1981-88; pres., founder Bipolarics Inc., Los Gatos 1988-; awards: Univ. Chgo. Badminton Champion 1969-74, Univ. Hong Kong 3000 meter record 1969, Commonwealth Scholar British Commonwealth 1969; mem: IEEE, Soc. of Photo-Optical Instrumentation Engrs., Am. Physical Soc., Am. Vacuum Soc., Asian Am. Mfrs. Assn., ASM Internat.; articles pub. in tech. jours. 1972-88, patent held for planaization of wafers 1987, speaker 22d Internat. Field Emission Symp. 1974, Am. Vacuum Soc. Symp. 1975, 76, 36th Physical Electronics Conf. 1975, IEEE Symp. 1985; rec: history, poetry, tennis. Res: 45920 Sentinal Pl Fremont 94539-6942 Ofc: 108 Albright Way Los Gatos 95030

LEUNG, RICHARD JOSEPH, ophthalmologist; b. Oct. 14, 1955, Hackensack, N.J.; s. Bernard and Annamay (Imperiale) L.; edn: BS (high honors), Univ. Md. 1977, MD, 1981; cert. Am. Bd. Ophthalmology 1987. Career: med. intern UC San Diego 1981-82, resident Univ. So. Calif., L.A. 1983-86; fellow Johns Hopkins, Balt. 1981; ophthalmologist California Eye Center, Los Angeles 1986-88; dir. San Diego Eye Center 1988-; clin. instr. UC San Diego 1989-; honors: Phi Eta Sigma 1973, USC Nesburn award 1984; mem: Am. Acad. Ophthalmology (fellow 1988), San Diego Co. Med. Assn., CMA, Nat. Acad. Sports Vision, K.C.; Republican; R.Cath.; rec: photog., computers, skiing. Ofc: San Diego Eye Center 8010 Frost St Ste 600 San Diego 92123

LEVENTER, TERRI, psychologist; b. Sept. 13, New York; d. David and Stella Akrish; m. Seymour E. Leventer, Aug. 20, 1949 (div. 1962); children: David b. 1954, Jerry b. 1956; edn: BA, Hunter Coll. 1944; MA, N.Y. Univ. 1951; EdD, UCLA 1969; lic. Bd. Med. Examiners Psychology 1971. Career: secty., N.Y. and Calif. 1944-52; psychology intern San Fernando Valley Child Guidance, Van Nuys 1968-70; psychologist Northridge Hosp. 1970-78; pvt. practice psychology, Sepulveda 1972-; mem: Am. Psychology Assn., Calif. St. Psychological Assn., S.F.V. Psychological Assn. (pres. 1980), Assn. Child &

Ednl. Psychology, L.A. Co. Psychological Assn., Group Psychotherapy Assn. So Calif. (bd. mem. 1974-), Women's Referral Service; contbr. profl. jour. article; rec: dancing, music. Address: Sepulveda 91343

LEVIN, BARRY RAYMOND, rare book dealer, author; b. June 11, 1946, Phila.; s. Sidney and Bertha (Zwerman) L.; m. Sally Ann Fudge; edn: Santa Monica Coll. 1964-65. Career: production control dispatcher McDonnell Douglas, Santa Monica 1967-69; shot peener Astro Peen Inc., Hawthorn 1969-72; owner Barry R. Levin Science Fiction and Fantasy Literature, Santa Monica 1973-; cons. sci. fiction fantasy and horror films, Hollywood 1976-; firm sponsors annually the Collectors Award for the most collectable author and book of the year in the fields of science fiction, fantasy and horror 1988-; mem: Antiquarian Booksellers Assn. Am., Internat. League of Antiquarian Booksellers, Am. Booksellers Assn., So. Calif. Booksellers Assn., other profl. organizations; co-author: "Book Collectibles By Stephen King: A Price Guide" for The Stephen King Companion, edited by George Beahm 1989; author rare book catalogues: Titles from the Back Room 1981, Great Works & Rarities of Sci. Fiction & Fantasy 1982, One Small Step 1983, others; writer article "The Controversy Over Presentation Copies" AB Bookman's Weekly (8/28/89); profiled in "Pioneering a Sci-Fi Specialty in So. Calif." AB Bookman's Weekly (10/28/91), "Manuscript Collection - An Endangered Species" Publishers Weekly (6/29/92) reprinted The Roundup Quarterly and Sci. Fiction Writers of Am. Bulletin, editorialized by Stanley Schmidt in Analog (2/93); mil: AUS 1965-67, Nat. Defense Service Medal 1966. Ofc: 726 Santa Monica Blvd Ste 201 Santa Monica 90401

LEVINE, SAMUEL EDWARD, engineer; b. Apr. 23, 1930, Los Angeles; s. Isadore Sydney and Rachael (Baron) L.; m. Idele Metz, Dec. 20, 1953 (div. Sept., 1972); m. 2d. Beatrice Alice Bystrom, Mar. 23, 2974; children: Robin b. 1956, Michelle b. 1958, Richard b. 1962, Erik b. 1968; granddau. Alexandra Meyer b. 1991; edn: BS engring, UCLA 1954; MS, 1962; reg. profl. engr. Calif. 1959. Career: engr. Radio Corp. of Am., Camden, N.J. and Los Angeles 1954-61; dir. advanced space comms., tech. staff Aerospace Corp., El Segundo 1961-79; assoc. Levine/Seegel Assocs., Santa Monica 1979-; radar flight test engr. RCA, Palmdale 1955-58; mil. comms. satellite office, D.O.D., Wash., DC 1975, head attack team, Survivability Analysis Group 1977-78; mem: IEEE, Sierra Club, Aircraft Owners & Pilots Assn.; mil: airman 2c. USAFR 1951-52; rec: woodworking, flying, backpacking. Ofc: Levine/Seegel Associates 2601 Ocean Park Blvd Ste 212 Santa Monica 90405

LEVINGSTON, JOHN C.B., company executive; b. Apr. 10, 1929, Pakistan, nat. U.S. citizen 1967; s. Thomas Clarke and Kathleen P. (Farley) L.; m. Elizabeth Baumer, June 6, 1958 (div. 1968); m. Paula Angela Eriksen, Feb. 29, 1980; children: Thomas b. 1981, Alexandra Jane b. 1989; edn: matriculated Harrow, England 1943-47, rec'd mil. commn. Sandhurst, England 1947-49. Career: lt. British Army 1947-52; sales mgr. British-Am. Tobacco, Nairobi, Kenya 1953-55; sales exec. W.L. Mackenzie, Vancouver, Canada 1957-61; pres. Levingston & Assocs., Los Angeles 1978-, chmn. bd. Straightley Films, L.A. 1972-, chmn. and c.e.o. Interactive Telemedia, L.A. 1986-90; mem. Acad. TV Arts & Scis.; lodges: Masonic 1967-, Scottish Rite 1968-, York Rite 1987-, Masonic Press Club 1968-. Ofc: Levingston & Associates PO Box 1951 Beverly Hills 90213

LEVKOFF, GEORGE L., investment banker; b. Oct. 2, 1955, NY, NY; s. Henry L. and Violette (Simon) L.; edn: BS in fin., Lehigh Univ., 1977; MBA fin., Univ. Chgo. 1979; JD, Univ. of Houston, 1985. Career: instnl. bond salesman various firms, Los Angeles 1985-87; v.p. investments National Bank of Long Beach, 1988-90; investment exec. Paine Webber, 1990; Drake Capital Securities Inc., Instnl. Sales/Trading, 1990-. Res: PO Box 5235 Playa Del Rey 90296 Ofc: Drake Capital Securities Inc., 1250 Fourth St 5th Fl Santa Monica 90401 Tel: 310/393-1900 FAX 310/393-3948

LEVY, ALLAN, physician, psychiatrist; b. Oct. 30, 1925, Detroit, Mich.; s. David S. and Ida (Diskin) L. m. Phyllis Kulick, Aug. 6, 1950 (dec. 1973); m. 2d. Maria Cola, Jan. 4, 1975; children: Susan b. 1952, Peter b. 1956; edn: Tufts Coll. 1943-45; MD, Univ. Mich. Ann Arbor 1949. Career: intern Univ. Hosp., Ann Arbor, Mich. 1949-50, resident 1950-53; Agnew St. Hosp., Agnew 1953-54; pvt. practice, San Mateo 1954-70; Peninsula Psychiatric Assn. 1970-; asst. clin. prof. Stanford Univ. 1959-74; councilor N. Calif. Psychiatric Soc., S.F. 1978-79; pres. Peninsula Psychiatric Assn., San Mateo 1970-80; chmn. dept. psychiatry Peninsula Hosp., Burlingame 1970-72; mem: Am. Psychiatric Assn. (life fellow), CMA, San Mateo Co. Med. Assn.; 5 articles pub. in profl. jours. 1954-, book chpt. pub. 1978, paper pub. 1985; mil: lt. USNR 1950-52; Jewish; rec: golf. Res: 50 Mounds Rd #503 San Mateo 94402 Ofc: Peninsula Psychiatric Association 215 N San Mateo Dr Ste 7 San Mateo 94401

LEVY, DAVID STEVEN, college administrator; b. Mar. 9, 1955, Los Angeles; s. Henry and Gloria (Barouh) L.; children: Rachel b. 1986; edn: BA, Occidental Coll., 1977, MA, 1979. Career: student loan ofcr. Bank of Am., Los Angeles 1975-78; financial aid counselor CSU San Bernardino 1978-79, CSU Northridge 1979-80, assoc. dir. fin. aid CSU Dominguez Hills, Carson 1980-82; dir. fin. aid

Occidental Coll., L.A. 1982-88; dir. fin. aid Calif. Inst. of Tech., Pasadena 1988-; cons., instr. The College Board, San Jose 1987-; awards: merit. achiev. Nat. Assn. of Student Financial Aid Adminstrs., Denver 1988, disting. service Western Assn. Stu. Fin. Aid Adminstrs., Long Beach 1990, creative leadership, Pres.'s disting. recogn. awards Calif. Assn. Stu. Fin. Aid Adminstrs., Anaheim (1990, 87); mem. Nat. Assn. SFAA (bd. 1980-), Western Assn. SFAA (ofcr. 1978-), Calif. Assn. SFAA (ofcr. 1978-); publs: consumer info. brochures (3). Res: 41 Northwoods Ln La Crescenta 91214 Ofc: California Institute of Technology MC 12-63 Pasadena 91125

LEVY, JANE, librarian; b. Jan. 31, 1945, Chgo.; d. Robert William and Betty (Amos) Van Brunt; m. Neil Martin Levy, Oct. 19, 1969; children: Ariel, Shoshi, Amos; edn: BA, UC Berkeley, 1967, MLS, 1968. Career: librarian/archivist John Steinbeck Library, Salinas 1970-71; Soc. of California Pioneers, San Francisco 1972-73; librarian Blumenthal Rare Book & Manuscript Library, Magnes Museum, Berkeley 1980-; mem. Soc. of Am. Archivist, Assn. of Jewish Libraries, Latin Am. Jewish Studies Asns., Am. Museum Assn.; coauthor: The Jewish Illustrated Book 1986, 2 pub. articles 1986, 91. Res: 953 Shattuck Berkeley 94707 Ofc: Magnes Museum 2911 Russell Berkeley 94705

LEWIS, CHRISTOPHER HARVEY, executive; b. Mar. 7, 1944, Beloit, Wisc.; s. James Marshall and Miriam Nanette (Galitz) L.; m. Jean Maree Belger, June 7, 1963; children: Christopher b. 1964, Tammy b. 1965, Shawn b. 1968. Career: served to Lt.cdr. US Navy 1963-83; v.p., gen. mgr. Geomarine Inc., San Francisco 1983-84; planning/engring. mgr. Southwest Marine Inc., S.F. 1984-85, corp. dir. of planning/engring. Southwest Marine Inc., San Diego 1985-; mem. Soc. of Naval Architects and Marine Engrs., Am. Soc. Naval Engrs., Port of San Diego Marine Square Club, Propeller Club of U.S. (bd.), Chula Vista C.of C. (bd.), Newcomen Soc., Masons (La Mesa sr. warden 1989-,chmn.), San Diego Co. Masonic Officers' Assn. ; pub. tech. paper (1989); Republican; Lutheran; rec: real estate. Ofc: Southwest Marine Inc. PO Box 13308 San Diego 92170

LEWIS, HILDA PRESENT, educator; b. Mar. 28, 1925, Bridgeport, Ct.; d. Louis David and Yetta (Elstein) Present; children: Daniel b. 1948, David b. 1952, Jonathan b. 1967, Rachel b. 1969; edn: BA, UC Berkeley, 1948, MA, 1956, PhD, 1959. Career: tchr. Richmond Unified Sch. Dist., 1950-52; lectr. Coll. of the Holy Names, Oakland 1957-59; lectr. UC Berkeley, 1958-62; asst. to full prof. and dept. chair San Francisco State Univ., 1962-; vis. prof. Stanford Univ. 1970, 71-72, Leicester Polytechnic, U.K. 1986; researcher in the arts I/D/E/A, L.A. 1973-76; res. assoc. Inst. of Human Devel. UC Berkeley, 1976-78; mem. Nat. Art Edn. Assn. 1964-, editor Art Education 1987-89; mem. U.S. Soc. for Edn. through Art (1978-, v.p. 1983-84), Am. Ednl. Res. Assn. 1962-, Internat. Soc. for Edn. Through Art 1976-; coauthor: Understanding Children's Art For Better Teaching (1973), editor: Art for the Pre-primary Child (1972), Child Art: The Beginnings of Self Affirmation (1966). Res: 17749 Chateau Ct Castro Valley 94552

LEWIS, JASON ALVERT, JR., telecommunications systems technician; b. Aug. 17, 1941, Clarksville, Tex.; s. Jason Allen and Mary (Dinwiddie) L.; edn: Stockton Coll. 1959-60, San Jose Jr. Coll. 1962-63. Career: field engr., telephone technician Pacific Bell, San Francisco, 1983-84; systems technician AT&T, 1984-; patentee in field; biographical listings in Who's Who in West, Who's Who in World, Internat. Who's Who of Intellectuals, Dict. Internat. Biography, Who's Who in Finance and Industry; mem: Internat. Platform Soc., The Planetary Soc.; civic: Cousteau Soc., Astron. Soc. Pacific, S.F. Zool. Soc.; mil: US Army 1964-66; Democrat. Res: 139 Pecks Ln South San Francisco 94080 Ofc: Deputy Governor of American Biographical Institute.

LEWIS, OWEN HARVEY, real estate broker, mortgage loan executive, ret.; b. Mar. 18, 1908, Parnell, Mo.; s. Simeon King and El Dora (Beckwith) L.; m. Opal Mann , Sept. 4, 1927 (author: A Vagabond's Diary, 1987); children: Patricia Ann (Garrison) b. 1935, Glenda Carolyn (Edwards) b. 1939; edn: grad. H.S. Clearmont, Mo., 1925, Mo. Nat. Guard 1921-25; William Jewel Coll., Liberty, Mo. 1926-27. Career: sole owner real estate brokerage and 2nd mortgage loan office, San Dimas and Pomona, 1945-68; ptnr. Lewis-Wheeler Co. (R.E. & investments), Pomona 1968-83; dir. Bank of Industry; elected mayor City of La Verne 1956-60; commr. (chmn. 10 yrs.) L.A. Co. Regional Planning Comn. 1962-80; mem. exec. com., bd. trustees, finance com. Univ. of LaVerne 1976-; honors: citizen of year LaVerne C.of C. 1979; lodges: F&AM Hollenbeck 1930-, Al Malaika Shrine L.A. 1944-, BPOE Pomona 1948-; club: Indian Wells CC; Democrat; Protestant; rec: golf, travel. Res: 900 Bonita Ave LaVerne 91750 also 76955 Robin Dr Indian Wells 92210

LEWIS, RICHARD BOND, advertising agency president; b. April 14, 1925, Atkinson, Nebr.; s. Monte Claire and Lula Pearl (Bond) L.; m. Carol Ann Bigglestone, Nov. 23, 1948; children: Eric b. 1957, Shannon b. 1958, Carrie b. 1961; edn: BA, Art Center Coll. of Design Pasadena 1953; Univ. Ariz. Career: art dir., account exec. Hal Stebbins Inc. advt. agency, Los Angeles 1953-64; account exec. Buxton Advt., Pasadena 1964-65; account mgr. McCann Erickson, Los Angeles 1965-71; pres. Richard Bond Lewis & Assocs., West Covina 1971-; city councilman Covina 1989-; bd. dirs., past pres. Vis. Nurses Assn., commr. West

Covina Personnel Dept.; v.p. West Covina Waste Mgmt. Commn.; presdl. appointee Selective Service Civilian Rev. Bd.; lay leader, del., mem. comms. com. Pacific S.W. Conf., United Methodist Ch. 1979-82; appt. West Covina City Council 1988; awards: Camp Fire Girls spl. svc. 1979, West Covina resolution for svc. 1982, West Covina City Council svc. medal 1988, num. art dir. awards; mem: West Covina C.of C. (com. mem. 1971, 72, 76, pres. 1981-82), West Covina Hist. Soc. (dir.), Kiwanis (pres. 1986-87), Lambda Chi Alpha; mil: staff sgt. AUS 1945-46; Republican. Address: 1112 W Cameron Ave West Covina 91790

LEWIS, ROBERT LEE, III, medical group administrator; b. Sept. 20, 1949, San Francisco; s. Robert, Jr. and Dolores Patricia (Brady) L.; m. Kari B. Hanson, 1989; edn: BS, CSU Fresno 1971, MBA 1978; adv. mgmt., Stanford Univ. 1983. Career: admin. asst. to regional v.p./ops. ofcr. Security Pacific Nat. Bank, Valley Div., 1971-74; service chief Fresno County Health Dept., Rehab. Svcs., 1974-79; adminstrv. dir. Clinical Labs., Stanford Univ. Hosp., 1979-84; pres. Western Div., Internat. Clin. Lab., Dublin 1984-86; adminstr. Good Samaritan Med. Group, a multispecialty group, San Jose/Los Gatos, 1987-90; adminstr. O'Conner Med. Group of Santa Clara Valley, a multisplty. med. gp., 1990-; v.p. Performance Health Care 1986-; adj. faculty MPH Pgm., Coll. of Profl. Studies, Univ. of S.F., 1988-; mem: Am. Group Practice Assn., Healthcare Finance Mgmt. Assn., Coll. Medical Group Adminstrs. (candidate 1992), Pi Omega Pi Frat. (v.p. 1970-71), Stanford Buck Club 1980-; civic: Goodwill Industries (advy. bd. 1977-78), Fresno County Council for Devel. Disabled (ofcr. 1975-79), Mayor's Com. on Hiring the Handicapped 1976-79, Fresno Assn. for the Retarded (dir. 1975-78); publs: Optimizing Productivity: Capital Equipment Acquisition (106 pp., 1985) and ednl. video tape: Tool for Success 1985, pub. Am. Assn. Clin. Chemistry; lectr. profl. confs., 1984-; mem. editl. bd. Syva Monitor 1984; mil: Calif. Army Nat. Guard 1971-76; Res: 108 Durham St Menlo Park 94025 Ofc: O'Conner Medical Group, 105 N Bascom Ave San Jose 95128

LEZA, RICHARD L., venture capitalist; b. April 16, 1947, Laredo, Tx.; s. Gustavo G. and Corina C. (Cordova) L.; m. Cindy G. Rocha, Jan. 6, 1967; children: Richard b. 1968; edn: East L.A. City Coll. 1968; BSCE hons., N.M. St. Univ. 1973; MBA, Stanford Grad. Sch. 1978. Career: sr. engr. Stearns Rogers Inc., Denver, Colo. 1973-74; structural and systems engr. Gen. Atomic Co., San Diego 1974-76; fin. analyst Envirotech Corp., Menlo Park 1977-78; internat. dir. Qume Corp., San Jose 1978-80; chmn. RMC Group Inc., Santa Clara 1981-88; AI Research Corp., Palo Alto 1989-; dir. Floormasters Inc., Azusa 1985-; Bytec S.A. de CV, Mexico City 1985-; AI Research Corp., Palo Alto 1986-; EMS Inc., Oakland 1987-; awards: Hispanic Bus. hon. 1985, Oasis Press outstanding bus. author (1987), N.M.St. Univ. outstanding alumni 1988; mem: Phi Kappa Phi, Stanford Bus. Sch. Alumni Assn., Asia Am. Mfg. Assn.; clubs: NMSU Pres.'s Assn., Stanford (Palo Alto), Elks, Mission Lakes CC, Catholic (Palo Alto); author: Develop Your Bus. Plan (1983, 88), Export Now (1988), newspaper interviews (1984, 88); Republican; R.Cath.; rec: tennis, golf, skiing. Res: 4191 Briarwood Way Palo Alto 94306 Ofc: AI Research Corp. 2003 St Julien Ct Ste 67 Mountain View 94043

LI, MANQUN, acupuncturist; b. Nov. 15, 1965, Shanghai, P.R. China; d. Jianhua Li and Jianlan Duan; m. Jianjun Lu, Oct. 20, 1989; edn: Bachelor's degree, Shanghai Coll. of Traditional Chinese Medicine, Shanghai, P.R. China, 1989; Chinese Med. Doctor, Med. Bd. of China, 1989. Career: Chinese medical doctor Rui Jin Hosp., Shanghai, P.R. China 1989-91; herbalist, Min Tong Herbs, Richmond, Calif. 1992-93; acupuncturist, herbalist, Merry's Acupuncture & Herb Ctr., S.F., Calif. 1993-; Christian. Ofc: Merry's Acupuncture & Herb Center 2087 Union St #3 San Francisco 94123

LIBANOFF, ARTHUR, podiatrist; b. May 17, 1931, Chgo.; s. Leo and Sylvia (Goodman) L.; m. Erliss Ruff, 1955; edn: BS, Univ. of Ill. 1953; DPM, Ill. Coll. of Podiatry 1959. Career: pvt. practice podiatry, La Habra 1960-; residency pgm. and credential com., Podiatric Surg., Beach Comm. Hosp.; honors: Univ. Ill. Dean's List 1949, pres. German Club 1950, pres. Durlacher Honor Soc., Ill. Coll. Podiat. 1955; mil: cpl. US Army 1955-57; Jewish. Ofc: 740 W La Habra Blvd La Habra 90631

LIBBY, RICHARD ALLAN, mathematician; b. Apr. 9, 1958, Pasadena; s. Harold Dean and Ruth Carol (Geerlings) L.; edn: BA Univ. of Calif., San Diego, 1980; MA, 1982; PhD, Univ. of Calif., Santa Cruz 1990; career: res. asst., Stanford Linear Accelerator Ctr., Stanford 1985; tchg. asst., Univ. of Calif., S.D. 1980-82; mathematics instr. 1986-90; res. analyst, Bankers Trust Co. of Calif., San Francisco 1991-92; sr. financial analyst, Bank of America, S.F. 1993-; tutor, mathematics, 1983-; record broker, Glen Canyon Records 1983-84; classical and theater pianist, Santa Cruz Cty. Symphony 1986; deputy court clerk, State Bar of Calif. 1991; awards: assistantship in mathematics, Univ. of Calif., Santa Cruz 1984-90; Who's Who in the West, 1991; mem: Am. Mathematical Soc., Mathematical Assn. of Am., Soc. for Industrial and Applied Mathematics; author: Asymptotics of Determinants and Eigenvalue Distributions for Toeplitz Matrices Associated with Certain Discontinuous Symbols, 1990; Democrat; rec: classical pianist; res: 129 Steiner St. San Francisco 94117-3326. Ofc:Bank of America, Exposure Management #2559, 555 California St. 11th Flr. San Francisco 94104

LIEBIG, PHOEBE STONE, educator, gerontologist; b. Dec. 28, 1933, Cambridge, Mass.; d. Marshall Harvey Stone and Emmy Melita (Portmann) Allen; m. Anthony E. Liebig, June 19, 1954 (div. 1961); child, Steuart b. 1956; edn: Radcliffe Coll., 1951-54; BA, MA, UCLA, 1954-56; postgrad., Info. Sci., UCLA, 1961; PhD, USC, 1983. Career: tchr. Los Angeles Unified Sch. Dist., 1961-70; systems documentation splst. Ancom Systems, Los Angeles, 1970-71; grants adminstr. Univ. So. Calif., LA 1971-83, academic planner, res. prof. and geriatric edn. dir. USC, 1984-86; sr. policy analyst Am. Assn. of Retired Persons, WDC 1986-88; dir. res. pgm., 1988-89, asst. prof. USC, LA 1988-; cons. UCLA Div. of Geriatric Medicine, 1988-; cons. Minority Resource Ctr. on Aging, San Diego, 1989-; mem. bd. Calif. Council of Gerontology & Geriatrics, L.A., 1989-; mem. editorial bds. Jour. of Aging & Social Policy, Boston 1989-, We. Govtl. Researcher, LA 1990-; awards: Hanson Family Asst. Professor USC 1990-1993, grantee Adminstrn. on Aging, WDC 1988-91, AARP Women's Initiative, WDC 1989-90, Haynes Found., LA 1989-90, fellow UCLA/USC Long Term Care Gerontology Ctr., LA 1980, fellow Gerontol. Soc. of Am., WDC 1990; mem: Assn. for Pub. Policy and Mgmt. 1985-, Gerontol. Soc. of Am. (1976-, sect. com. 1979-81), Am. Soc. on Aging (1977-, secty. 1981-83), Am. Soc. for Pub. Adminstrn. 1981-; civic: LA Co. Mus. of Art, Musical Arts Soc., Neo Renaissance Soc. LA (v.p. 1978-83); publs: (monograph) State Teachers' Retirement Systems (1987), num. articles and reports on care and svs. for the elderly (1977-), author and co-editor (book) Calif. Policy Choices for Long-Term Care (1990); Democrat; rec: choral singing, bird watching, gardening, travel. Ofc: Andrus Gerontology Center, Univ. of Southern Calif., Los Angeles 90089-0191

LIENHARD, JAMES BOLAND, electronic data processing consultant; b. Aug. 21, 1958, Glendale; s. Jerome Travers and Patricia Anne (Hanson) L.; m. Melanie Martinez, July 11, 1981 (div. 1987); children: Joshua b. 1983, Joseph b. 1985. Career: systems analyst USC, 1979-80; Sunkist, Sherman Oaks 1980-81; Carte Blanche, L.A. 1981-82; data base adminstr. Litton Data Command, Agoura 1982-83; Lockheed California Co., Burbank 1983-85; pres. JBL Consulting, La Crescenta 1985-88; senior cons. Automated Concepts Inc., Washington, D.C., 1988-92; project cons. Federal Reserve Bank of San Francisco, 1992-. Democrat; R.Cath.; rec: skiing, tennis. Address: PO Box 194342 San Francisco 94119

LIEPMANN, WOLFGANG, physicist; b. July 3, 1914, Berlin, nat. 1945; s. Prof. Dr. Wilhelm L. (M.D.) and Emma (Leser) L.; m. Kate Kaschinsky, June 19, 1939 (div. 1954); m. Dietlind Wegener Goldschmidt, Sept. 27, 1954; children: Till W. b. 1955, Dorian b. 1957; edn: exptl. physics, Univ. of Istanbul 1933-35, Univ. Prague, Czech. 1935, PhD, Univ. of Zurich, Switz. 1938. Career: research fellow Univ. of Zurich 1938-39; res. fellow Calif. Inst. of Tech., Pasadena 1939-45, asst. prof. 1945-46, assoc. prof. 1946-49, prof. 1949-76, Charles Lee Powell Prof. of Fluid Mechanics and Thermodynamics 1976-83, Theodore von Karman Prof. of Aeronautics 1983-85, dir. Graduate Aeronautical Labs. 1972-85, exec. ofcr. for aeronautics 1976-85; mem. res. & tech. advy. com. on basic res. NASA, Wash. DC; awards: physics prize Univ. Zurich 1939, Am. Acad. of Arts and Scis. fellow 1960, Nat. Acad. of Engring. 1965, Ludwig Prandtl Ring - Deutsche Gesellschaft fur Luft - und Raumfahrt (Ger. Soc. for Aero.) 1968, Nat. Acad. of Scis. 1971, Monie A. Ferst award Sigma Xi 1978, Michelson-Morley award 1979, fluid dynamics prize Am. Physical Soc. 1980, fluids engring. award ASME 1984, Indian Acad. of Scis. hon. fellow 1985, Hon. Dr. Engring. Technical Univ. Aachen 1985, Otto Laporte award Am.. Physical Soc. 1985, Nat. Medal of Sci. 1986, Guggenheim medal 1986, Max Planck Inst. fgn. fellow 1988; mem: Am. Inst. Aero. & Astro. (hon. fellow), Am. Physical Soc. (fellow), AAAS (fellow), Sigma Xi, Ger. Soc. for Applied Math. and Mechs.; coauthor: Aerodynamics of a Compressible Fluid (w. A.E. Puckett, 1947), Elements of Gasdynamics (w. A.Roshko, 1957); rec: tennis. Res: 555 Haverstock Rd La Canada-Flintridge 91011 Ofc: Caltech MC 301-46 1201 E California Blvd Pasadena 91125

LIGGINS, GEORGE LAWSON, microbiologist, mfg. co. pres.; b. June 19, 1937, Roanoke, Va.; m. Joyce Preston, Sept. 3, 1966; 1 son, George Lawson b. 1971; edn: BA, Hampton Inst. 1962; MeHarry Med. Coll. 1963; Duke Univ. 1966; MPH, Univ. N.C. 1969; PhD, Univ. Va. 1975; career: med. technologist Vets. Hosp., Hampton, Va. 1964-66; research tech. Univ. N.C. Med. Sch., Chapel Hill 1967-69; postdoctorate Scripps Clinic, La Jolla 1975-76; Salk Inst. 1976-77; research and devel. dir. Baxter Travenol, Round Lake, Ill. 1977-83; pres., COO Internat. Immunology, Murrieta 1983-86; pres., ceo Bacton Assay Systems Inc. 1986-; cons. Beckman Instruments, Brea 1987-88; Baxter Paramz, Irvine 1988-89; awards: NIH HHS fellowship 1975, Am. Cancer Soc. fellowship 1975; mem: Am. Assn. Clin. Chemist, Am.Heart Assn., Am. Soc. Microbiology, Am. Chemical Soc., Am. Soc. Pub. Health; tech. papers abstracts and papers pub. in sci. jours. 1974-; Republican; Methodist; rec: music, sports, tennis; ofc: Bacton Assay Systems, Inc. 772-A North Twin Oaks Valley Rd San Marcos 92069

LIGHTFOOT, WILLIAM HUGH, lawyer (ret.); b. Sept. 3, Minneapolis, Minn.; s. William Homer and Elva Asenith (Albright) L.; m. Trudi; edn: BA, JD, Drake Univ.; LLM (taxation), Golden Gate Univ.; admitted bar: Calif., Tenn., U.S. Supreme Ct. Career: atty. Law Ofcs. Ted L. Mackey, W. Los Angeles

1972; atty. William H. Lightfoot, San Jose 1973-; instr. Landlord-Tenant Law, Cont. Edn. of Bar; mem. Calif. Bar Assn., Commonwealth Club of Calif., Masons, Scottish Rite, Shriners. Am. Legion; mil: 2nd lt., USMC, UN Medal, Korean Svc., Presdl. Unit Citation; Republican; Christian; rec: exercise, politics, social problems. Res: Cambell.

LILLIE, MILDRED L., presiding justice State Court of Appeal; b. Jan. 25, 1915, Ida Grove, Ia.; d. Ottmar A. and Florence E. (Martin) Kluckhohn; m. Cameron L. Lillie, Mar. 18, 1947 (dec. 1959); m. 2d A. V. Falcone, Aug. 27, 1966; edn: AB, UC Berkeley 1935; JD, UC Boalt Hall of Law 1938; hon. degrees: LLD, Western States Univ. Coll. of Law 1966; LLD, Pepperdine Univ. 1979; admitted to practice, State Bar of Calif. 1938, Fed. Ct. 1942, US Supreme Ct. 1961. Career: with the City Atty.'s Ofc., Alameda 1938-39; pvt. law practice Fresno, 1939-42, Los Angeles 1946-47; asst. US Atty., LA 1942-46; judge, Municipal Ct., City of LA 1947-49; judge, Superior Ct., Co. of LA 1949-58; justice Ct.of Appeal, State of Calif. 1958-84, presiding justice, 1984-, assoc. justice pro tem Supreme Ct. of Calif.; adminstrv. presiding justice 2nd Appellate Dist. Ct. of Appeal, 1988-; mem. Calif. Judicial Council 1961-63, 1987-89; bd. trustees Boalt Hall Fund 1986-; bd. vis. Pepperdine Law Sch. 1985-; awards: Cardinal McIntyre award Cath. Press Club LA 1981, LA Times woman of yr. 1952, Muses woman of yr. Mus. of Sci. & Ind. 1980, citation Boalt Hall of Law Alumni Assn. 1985, appellate justice of yr. LA Trial Lawyers Assn. 1986, Humanitarian Award NCCJ 1991; mem: ABA, Fed. Bar Assn., LA Co. Bar Assn., Calif. Judges Assn., Nat. Assn. of Women Judges, Women Lawyers Assn.; civic: LA Area C.of C. (bd. dirs. 1975-82), Town Hall of Calif., Les Dames de Champagne, Pepperdine Univ. Assocs., NCCJ (presiding co-chair 1986-87), L.A. Pops Orch. (bd. 1984-); clubs: Los Angeles Athletic, Ebell (LA), Nat. Bus. Profl. Women, Soroptimist Internat. LA; rec: reading, painting, cooking. Ofc: 300 S Spring St South Tower Los Angeles 90013

LIM, EUSEBIO GAN, otolaryngologist; b. Aug. 14, Manila, Philippines; s. Bien Liong and Bella (Gan) L.; edn: MD, Univ. Santo Tomas, 1952, AA, 1947 Fellow Internat. Acad. of Cosmetic Surgery. Career: otolaryngologist Union Medical Clinic, Huntington Park, Calif.; mem. L.A. Co. Med. Assn.; Fellow Am. Acad. Otol., Am. Acad. Plastic and Reconstrv. Surg., Pan Am. Otorhinolaryngology; mem. Am. Biog. Inst. (resrch. advy. bd.), Intl. Who's Who Intellectuals, and Fellow Intl. Biog. Ctr. Cambridge, Eng.; R.Cath.; rec: photog., car racing. Res: 11730 Sunset Blvd Los Angeles 90049 Ofc: Union Medical Clinic 5421 Pacific Blvd Huntington Park 90255

LIMBAUGH, RONALD HADLEY, historian, educator, administrator; b. Jan. 22, 1938, Emmett, Ida.; s. John Hadley and Evelyn Eloise (Mortimore) L.; m. Marilyn Kay Rice, June 16, 1963; 1 dau. Sally Ann b. 1973; edn: BA, Coll. of Idaho, 1960; MA, Univ. Idaho, 1962, PhD, 1967. Career: history librarian Idaho Historical Soc., Boise 1963-66; instr. Boise Coll., 1964-66; prof. of history Univ. of the Pacific, Stockton, Calif. 1966-, archivist U.O.P. 1968-87, actg. assoc. dean 1975-76, dir. John Muir Center U.O.P., 1989-; dir. Holt-Atherton Ctr., Stockton 1984-87; exec. dir. Conf. of Calif. Hist. Soc., Stockton 1990-; awards: NDEA fellow Univ. Idaho 1960-63, Phi Kappa Phi 1962, Rockwell Hunt Prof. of Calif. Hist. U.O.P. 1989-; mem. Org. Am. Historians 1963-, Western History Assn. 1965-, AAUP 1970-, Phi Kappa Phi (pres. U.O.P. chapt. 1974, 88), Stockton Corral of Westerners (pres. "sheriff" 1978), Jedediah Smith Soc., Stockton (sec. 1989-), Mining Hist. Assn. (1992-, nom. com. 1993-); author: Rocky Mountain Carpetbaggers (1982), numerous articles in hist. jours. (1969-), editor (microform edit.) John Muir Papers (1986), contbg. writer John Muir Newsletter (1981-); mil: pvt. US Army 1955-56; Indep.; Christian Humanist; rec: hiking, golf, birding. Ofc: Univ. of the Pacific 3601 Pacific Ave Stockton 95211

LIN, HUA L., physician-gastroenterologist; b. July 2, 1947, Taiwan, nat. 1984; s. Tsu W. and Yuen (Lu) L.; m. Ching L., May 30, 1976; child: James C. b. 1983; edn: MD, Nat. Taiwan Unvi. Sch. of Med., 7 yrs. Career: intern Beekman Downtown Hosp., N.Y.C. 1974-75, med. resident 1975-76; med. res. Catholic Medical Ctr., Jamaica, N.Y. 1976-77; G.I. fellow Good Samaritan Hosp., Phoenix, Az. 1977-79; gastroenterologist pvt. practice, 1979-, mem. med. staff Mercy Hosp. (also med. dir. GI Lab), Gr. Bakersfield Memorial Hosp. and San Joaquin Hosp., Bakersfield, Calif. 1979-; bd. certified internal medicine ABIM 1978, cert. subsplty. gastroent. 1983; Fellow Am. Coll. Gastroent., mem. Am. Gastroenterol. Assn., Am. Soc. for Gastrointestinal Endoscopy, fellow Am. Coll. Physicians (nat. mem.), Calif. Med. Assn., Kern Co. Med. Soc.; club: Bakersfield Country; Republican; rec: fishing, travel. Ofc: Hua L. Lin MD Inc. 2225 19th St Bakersfield 93301

LIN, JAMES PEICHENG, professor of mathematics; b. Sept. 30, 1949, NY, NY; s. Tung Hua and Susan L.; m. Julie Sano, June 24, 1990; edn: BS, UC Berkeley, PhD, Princeton. Career: asst., asso., prof. math. UC San Diego, 1974-78, 78-81, 81-; vis. prof. Princeton 1978, Hebrew Univ., Jerusalem 1981-82, Neuchatel Univ., Switz. 1984; appt. task force Nat. Res. Council Minority Edn. Bd., 1992-; bd. Asians in Higher Edn., 1987-91; awards: Sloan Found. fellow 1977-78, Phi Beta Kappa, Chancellor's Tchg. Award UCSD 1981, NSF grantee 1974-90; mem. Am. Math. Soc. 1974-; author: Steenrod Squares and

Connectivity in H-Spaces (1990); rec: tennis, fishing, backpacking. Res: 8239 Paseo del Ocaso La Jolla 92037 Ofc: 7157 APM, Univ. Calif. San Diego, La Jolla 92093

LIN, TAO, applications manager; b. Aug. 6, 1958, Shanghai, P.R.O.C.; came to U.S. 1986; s. Zeng-hui Lin and Wei-jing (Wu) Wu; m. Ping Kuo, Aug. 18, 1989; son, Jason b. 1990, dau. Jessie b. 1992; edn: BS, East China Normal Univ., Shanghai, 1982; MS, Tohoku Univ., Sendai, Japan 1985; PhD, Tohoku Univ., 1990. Career: technician Dongfong Electronics Inc., Shanghai 1977-78; research asst. Electronics Research Lab. UC Berkeley, 1986-87, postgrad. researcher 1987-88; application engr. Integrated Device Technology Inc., Santa Clara 1988-90; sr. applications engr. Sierra Semiconductor Corp., San Jose 1990-91; applications mgr. Sierra Semiconductor Corp., San Jose 1991-; mem. IEEE; pub. articles in tech. jours. Res: 3552 Rockett Dr Fremont 94538 Ofc: Sierra Semiconductor Corp. 2075 N Capitol Ave San Jose 95132

LIN, TUNG YEN, civil engineer, educator; b. Nov. 14, 1911, Foochow, China, came to U.S., 1946, nat. 1951; s. Ting Chang and Feng Yi (Kuo) L.; m. Margaret Kao, July 20, 1941; children: Paul b. 1942, Verna b. 1949; edn: BSCE, Chiaotung Univ., Tangshan, China, 1931; MSE, UC Berkeley, 1933; LLD, Chinese Univ., Hong Kong, 1972; Golden Gate Univ. S.F. 1982, Tongji Univ., Shanghai 1987, Chiaotung Univ., Taiwan 1987; reg. profl. engr. (civil, struc.) 35 states incl. Calif. Career: chief bridge engr., chief design engr. Chinese Govt. Railways, 1933-46; asst., assoc. prof., prof. civil engring. UC Berkeley, 1946-76, chmn. div. structural engring., 1960-63, dir. struct. lab., 1960-63; chmn. bd. T.Y. Lin Internat., San Francisco 1953-, hon. chmn. 1988-; pres. Inter-Continental Peace Bridge, Inc. 1968-; cons. to industry, State of Calif., US Dept. of Def.; chmn. World Conf. Prestressed Concrete, 1957, Western Conf. Prestressed Concrete Bldgs., 1960; awards: Freyssinet Medal FIP, London 1974, Berkeley citation 1976, NRC Quarter Century 1977, Institute Honor Award AIA, Wash. DC 1984, Nat. Medal of Science 1986, merit award Am. Consulting Engrs. Council 1987, outstanding alumni of year Univ. Calif. Engring. Alumni Assn. 1984, Hon. Prof. Chiaotung Univ., Tongji Univ., Shanghai Chiaotung Univ. 1982, 84, 85, UC Berkeley Fellow; mem: ASCE (hon., life, Wellington award, Howard medal), Nat. acad. Engring., Academia Sinica, Internat. Fedn. Prestressing (Freyssinet medal), Am. Concrete Inst. (hon.), Prestressed Concrete Inst. (medal of honor); author: Design of Prestressed Concrete Structures (1955, rev. edit., 1963, 3d edit. with N.H. Burns, 1981), Design of Steel Structures (rev. edit., with B. Bresler, Jack Scalzi, 1968), Structural Concepts and Systems (with S.D. Statesbury, 1981, 2d edit. 1988), 100+ profl. papers; Democrat. Res: 8701 Don Carol Dr El Cerrito 94530 Ofc: T.Y.Lin Intl. 315 Bay St San Francisco 94133

LINAWEAVER, WALTER ELLSWORTH, JR., physician, educator; b. Oct 16, 1928, San Pedro; s. Walter Ellsworth (dec. 1989) and Catherine Breathed (Bridges) L.; m. Anne Whitlock, Oct. 5, 1957; children: Catherine b. 1958, Nancy b. 1959, Walter, III b. 1962; edn: BA cum laude, Pomona Coll. Claremont 1952; MD, Univ. Rochester Sch. Med. 1956. Career: intern pediatrics Univ. Rochester Med.Center 1956-57; asst. resident UCLA 1957-58; resident pediatrics Univ. Rochester Med. Ctr. 1958-59; fellow allergy and immunology Univ. Colo. 1959-61, instr. pediatrics Univ. Colo. Sch. Med. 1961; pvt. practice, Riverside 1962-; bd. dirs. Riverside Med. Clin. 1983-89; asst. clin. prof. pediatrics Loma Linda Univ. Sch. Med. 1963-; staff Riverside Comm. Hosp. 1962-; cons. Head Start, River Co. 1965-; honors: Pomona Coll. Athletic Hall of Fame (1979); mem: Am. Acad. Allergy & Immunology (fellow 1965), Am. Acad. Pediatrics (fellow 1962), L.A. Acad. Med. (fellow 1980), Southwestern Pediatric Soc. (fellow 1970), AMA, CMA, River Co. Med. Assn. (1962-); 2 case reports pub. (1960, 76); mil: s.sgt. AUS 1946-48; Republican; Presbyterian; rec: gardening, Am. and Mil. history. Res: 1296 Tiger Tail Dr. Riverside 92506 Ofc: Riverside Medical Clinic 3660 Arlington Ave. Riverside 92506

LINDBERG, DOVIE LOUISE, controller; b. Oct. 18, 1942, Chillicothe, Mo.; d. Basel Jacob and Esther Lucille (Melte) Seifert; m. James Robert Lindberg, Aug. 26, 1966 (div. 1977); edn: AA, Allan Hancock Coll. 1976; BA cum laude, Univ. La Verne 1978. Career: acctg. clk., bookkeeper Rupp Bros. Auto Parts, Chillicothe, Mo. 1960-66; sales clk. J.C. Penney Co., Biloxi, Mich. 1966-67; A/R supr. Broadwater Beach Hotel 1967-68; acctg. clk. Rupp Bros. Auto Parks 1968-69; full charge bookkeeper Llewellyn Co., Ft. Worth, Tx. 1970-71; payroll, A/P supr. Lear Jet Stereo, Tucson, Ariz. 1971-73; acct. Fed. Electric Corp., Vandenberg AFB 1974-79; cost account mgr. Sambos, Carpinteria 1979-80; asst. controller Henningson Durham Richardson, Santa Barbara 1980-81; controller Food Distribution Services, Carpinteria 1981-; awards: Fed. Electric Corp. outstanding employee 1978, Jr. Achievement cons. award 1972; mem: After 5 Club, Goleta Valley C.of C.; Democrat; Baptist; rec: tennis, skiing, dancing. Res: 30 Winchester Canyon Rd Sp #65 Goleta 93117 Ofc: REG Distribution Services 1030 Cindy Ln Carpinteria 93013

LINDGREN, KARIN JOHANNA, lawyer; b. July 18, 1960, Princeton, N.J.; d. William R. and Abigail Hastings (Sangree) Schearer; m. Mark Alden Lindgren; edn: BS in biology, Ursinus Coll. 1982; JD, Southwestern Univ. Sch. of Law, 1985; admitted bar: Pa. 1985-, US Dist. Ct., no., so., ea. and cent.

dists. Calif., 1987-, US Ct. Appeals, 9th cir., 1987-. Career: atty., assoc. Hillsinger & Costanzo, L.A. 1985-89; Sedgwick, Detert, Moran & Arnold, 1989-; mem: Pa. State Bar 1985-, Calif. State Bar 1987-, Wilshire Bar Assn. (pres. 1991-92), ABA (sect. litigation 1985-), L.A. Co. Bar Assn., World Affairs Council L.A., Am. Acad. of Hosp. Attys. of Am. Hosp. Assn. 1988-, Assn. of So. Calif. Defense Counsel 1987-, Am. Assn. Healthcare Risk Mgmt. 1992-; author: Handbook of Medical Liability: A Legal Overview (1988), coauthor: Healthcare Liability Deskbook (1992). Ofc: 3701 Wilshire Blvd 9th Fl Los Angeles 90010-2816

LINDQUIST, MICHAEL LEE, financial services executive; b. Aug. 16, 1953, Augsburg, Germany; s. John D. and Lucille (Casto) L.; m. Lana L. Chism, Apr. 19, 1975; edn: BA in acctg., Central Mo. Univ., 1978. Career: bank examiner Div. Fin., Jefferson City, Mo. 1978-81; job acctg. coord. Farmland Inds., Kansas City, Mo. 1981-83; EDP auditor Broad Inc., Atlanta, Ga. 1983-85, audit mgr. 1985-89, audit director SunAmerica, Inc. (formerly Broad, Inc.), Los Angeles, 1989-; mil: cpl. USMC 1971-73; rec: hang gliding. Ofc: SunAmerica, Inc. 11601 Wilshire Blvd Los Angeles 90025

LINDQUIST, STANLEY E., professor Emeritus, psychologist; b. Nov. 9, 1917, Georgetown, Tx.; s. Elmer H. and Esther Lovina (Nyberg) L.; m. Ingrid Waldren, Aug. 26; children: Douglas b. 1943, Russell b. 1946, Brent b. 1953; edn: BA, Calif. State Univ., Fresno 1940; PhD, Univ. of Chicago 1950; LLD (hon.), Trinity Coll. 1976; career: prof., Trinity Coll., Chgo. 1946-53; res. assoc., Univ. of Chgo. 1949-53; prof., Calif. State Univ., Fresno 1953-89, prof. emeritus 1989-; founder/ pres., Link Care Found., Fresno 1964-, pres. emeritus, 1991-; cons., Liberia, Agape, Monrovia, Liberia 1990-;mem: Am. Psychology Assn. 1950-; pres., ofcr., Am. Sci. Affiliation 1960-; ofcr., pres., Christian Edn. Assn. 1953-; ofcr., pres., Christian Assn. for Psychological Studies 1958-; bd. mem., Pastoral Counseling Inst. 1989-; author: Action Helping Skills, 1975; Reach Out, Become An Encourager, 1983; mil: pfc. US Army Medics, 1943-46; Republican; Evangelical Free Ch.; rec: woodworking, fishing. Res: 5142 N. College Fresno 93704

LINEBERGER, LARRY WATSON, financial executive; b. July 27, 1943, Columbia, S.C.; s. Francis Marion and Margaret (Watson) L.; m., 1961 (div. 1989); children: Barbara Lynn b. 1962, Steven Todd b. 1968; m. Shirley Powers, 1991; edn: BS acctg., Univ. S.C. 1966; exec. program, Carnegie Mellon Univ. 1983; strategic planning, Columbia Univ. 1981; S.C. lic. CPA, 1968. Career: CPA/sr. auditor, S.D. Leidesdorf & Co. (now Ernst & Young), Greenville, S.C. 1966-71; v.p., controller U.S. ops. div. Daniel Internat. 1971-78, v.p., controller, treas. 1978-87; v.p., controller Fluor Corp. and Fluor Daniel, Irvine, Calif. 1987-91, financial cons. 1992-; adj. prof. Univ. South Carolina, Columbia, S.C. 1983-84; honors: USC Beta Alpha Psi acct. of year 1977-78, USC Coll. of Bus. Distinguished Alumnus Award 1987, BSA Silver Beaver 1987; mem: S.Caro. Assn. C.P.A., Am. Inst. C.P.A., Fin. Execs. Inst., Assoc. Gen. Contractors (nat. tax and fiscal affairs com.), Boy Scouts Am. (treas. Greenville BSA 1982-87, Orange County BSA 1989-92), USC Bus. Sch. Profl. Acctg. Advy. Bd. 1984-88, Winthrop Coll. Bus. Sch. Advy. Bd. 1985-87, Greenville YMCA Bd. (treas. 1983-87); Republican; rec: hunting, hiking camping. Res: 2212 Apple Tree Dr Tustin 92680

LINHARDT, MARGARITA AGCAOILI, legal secretary; b. Feb. 25, 1947, Philippines; d. Mariano Edralin and Carmen (Dimaya) Agcaoili; m. Wilbur Linhardt; 1 child: ChristiAnna b. 1977; edn: BS, med. tech., Univ. of Santo Tomas, Manila, Philippines, 1967; postgrad. studies edn., Divine Word Coll., Philippines, 1967; speedwriting, Sch. of Speedwriting, NY, NY, 1973; fin. counselor, Jerical Coll. for Fin. Professionals, Anaheim, Calif., 1982; legal res., The Paralegal Inst., Phoenix, Ariz., 1982. Career: sales, Encyclopedia Britannica, Inc., Makati, Philippines, 1969-70; legal secty. trainee Wellington-Hall Co., L.A., 1975-76; legal secty. Wyman, Bautzer, Rothman, Kuchel & Silbert, L.A., 1979-80; Kindel & Anderson, L.A., 1981-82; fin. counselor Jerical Fin., Anaheim, 1982-83; outside public contact, Royal Reservations, Las Vegas, Nev., 1983, First Am. Travel, Las Vegas, 1984; sales, UBI/SW Bus. Sales, Long Beach, 1985; legal secty. Hufstedler, Miller, Carlson & Beardsley, L.A., 1985-86, McKenna & Cuneo, L.A., 1987, Pryor & Benson, Torrance, Calif., 1988-89; awards: H.S. Salutatorian, Santa Rosa Acad., San Nicolas, Philippines, 1963; current assoc., Am. Mus. of Natural History, Smithsonian; current mem: NAFE, L.A. County Mus. of Natural History, Nat. Trust for Historic Preservation, Nat. Parks & Conservation Assn., World Wildlife Fund, The Cousteau Soc., The Colonial Williamsburg Found.; rec: museums, opera, history, travel. marine & wildlife, films and TV. Res: 1648 West 218th St. #9 Torrance 90501

LINHART, EDDIE G., aerospace manufacturing co. president; b. March 8, 1941, Leachville, Ark.; s. Edward C. and Della I. (Towell) L.; m. Claudia Benninger, May 25, 1962; children: William b. 1968, Bonnie b. 1970; edn: AA, Fullerton Coll. 1970; BA, CSU Long Beach 1975, MA, 1977; Profl. Engr., Calif. 1978. Career: branch mgr. mfg. engring. McDonnell Douglas, Long Beach 1962-79; mgr. mfg. engring. Fairchild Republic, Farmdale, NY 1979-80; v.p. prodn. Avco Aerostructures, Nashville, Tenn. 1980-81; v.p. central mfg. Northrop Aircraft Div., Hawthorne 1981-85; v.p., gen. mgr. Western Gear Corp.,

Industry 1985-87, pres. 1987-88; pres. Precision Aerotech Inc. 1988-90; pres. and c.e.o. Astech/MCI, Inc., 1991-; mem. advy. bd. (chair 1984-88) CSU Los Angeles and CSU Long Beach; honors: Bob Hope award L.A. Council BSA 1985, disting. engrg. achievement S.F.V. Engrs. Council 1986, IAE Fellow 1986, Frank E. Reeves Intl. Interprofl. Memorial award Inst. for Advancement of Engring. 1988, Alumnus of Year CSU-Long Beach 1990, Engr. of Year S.F.V. Engrs. Council 1991; mem: Westec (chmn. advy. bd. 1987), Soc. Mfg. Engrs. (fellow 1989), Soc. Automotive Engrs. (chmn. mfg. activity aerospace sect. 1984-86); civic: exec. bd. BSA L.A. Council; copyrighted thesis: Diffusion Bonding of Metals in Southern California Industries; mil: E-5 USN 1958-62; Republican; Lutheran; rec: golf, fishing, coin collecing. Ofc: 3030 S Redhill Ave Santa Ana 92711

LINKLETTER, ARTHUR GORDON, public speaker, television personality; b. July 17, 1912, Moosejaw, Saskatchewan, Canada; s. Rev. Fulton and Mary (Metzler) L.; m. Lois Foerster, Nov. 28, 1935; children: Jack L. b. 1937, Dawn b. 1939, Sharon b. 1946; edn: BA, San Diego State 1934. Career: announcer KGO, San Diego; TV host People Are Funny (29 yrs.) 1947; House Party, CBS TV daytime, 5 days weekly (30 yrs.) 1946; Talent Scouts, CBS night time, once weekly (2 yrs.) 1958; The Linkletter Show, NBC weekly, night time (2 yrs.) 1970; speaker 100 times yearly; trustee Oil and Gas Exploration, Pepperdine Univ.; mem. 12 bds. of dirs. Springfield Coll., Md.; commr. gen. U.S. Exhibit to Expo '88, Brisbane, Australia, rank of Ambassador; entertainer workers in shipyards No. Calif. during WWII; awards: 9 hon. coll./univ. degrees; disting. svc.: Crusade for Freedom and Mt. Sinai Men's Club and Heart of Gold award 1960; citation disting. svc. Comm. Chests Am., citation meritorious svc. Nat. Council Child Safety, Radio-TV Eds. So. Calif. award outstanding contbn. home entertainment, TV-Radio-Mirror award TV/radio excellence 1949-58, LA City Council/Co. awards work w/youth and fostering good citizenship; svc. awards: Newpaper Boys Am., Nat. Found. Infantile Paralysis, Nat. Nephrosis Found.; Goodwill Award Goodwill Indus. Am., Brotherhood of Children award Foster Parents Plan for War Orphans, Brotherhood award Nat. Conf. of Christians and Jews, Grandfather of Yr. Nat. Father's Day Com. 1962, d'Officier Commandeur Confrerie des Chevaliers du Tastevin 1961, salesman of yr., Houston 1961, Sports award of Yr., Chgo. 1962, House Party nominated for Emmy, best daytime TV pgm. 1962, Man of Yr. City of Hope 1964; civic: Bohemian Club (30 yrs.), YMCA, Foster Parents Plan, World Vision Inst., Toastmasters Supreme, The Masquers, Pres. Council Physical Fitness; BSA, Nat. Heart Fund, chmn. Easter Seals 1961; author: 17 books incl. Kids Say The Darndest Things, 2 yr. best seller list plus 16 other titles; Republican; Prot.; rec: surfing, ski. Res: 1100 Bel Air Rd Los Angeles 90077 Ofc: 8500 Wilshire Blvd Ste 815 Beverly Hills 90211

LINN, ROGER DAVID, lawyer; b. Nov. 7, 1949, Chicago, Ill.; s. Russell Edwin and Ruth Anita (Mueller) L.; m. Debra, June 27, 1981; children: Rachel Erin b. 1983, Tyler Russell b. 1986, Trevor William b. 1990; edn: Florissant Valley Comm. Coll. 1967-68; BS bus. admin., Drake Univ. 1971; JD, Calif. Western Sch. Law 1978; admitted State Bar Calif. 1978. Career: staff atty. U.S. Securities & Exchange Commn., Wash. DC 1978-80, branch chief, Los Angeles 1980-82; corp. counsel Nat. Investment Devel. Corp. 1982-85; ptnr. Van Camp & Johnson, Sacto. 1985-90; Downey Brand Seymour & Rohwer 1990-91; Bartel Eng Miller & Torngren, Sacto. 1991-; instr. UCLA para-legal program 1981-83; mem: Sacto. Co. Bar, Calif. St. Bar (franchise sect.), Calif. Bar Assn., Roseville Rotary, Alpha Kappa Psi, Rotary Internat.; mil: petty ofcr. USN 1971-75, cmdr. USNR, JAGC 1980-; Lutheran; rec: tennis, camping. Ofc: Bartel Eng Miller & Torngren 300 Capitol Mall Ste 1100 Sacramento 95814

LINNELL, MARVIN RICHARD, veterinarian; b. Dec. 10, 1910, Lewis, Wis.; s. Maurice Roy and Anna L. (Combs) L.; m. Mary Williams, June 17, 1941; edn: Oregon St. Coll. 1938-41; UC Davis 1941-42; DVM, Colo. St. Univ. 1944. Career: airplane stunt man 1928-38; timber logger and road construction 1928-29; UC Riverside 1945-47; owner Barstow Veterinary Hosp. 1952-85; ret.; chmn. Citizens Comm. for Better Schools 1952-53; life mem: AVMA, CVMA, OBVMA; mem: Masons, Lions Club; author: The Rattle Snake and Jackrabbit Practice. Res: 36732 Clemens Barstow 92311

LINTON, THOMAS DENSMORE, JR., patent attorney; b. May 2, 1925, Auburn, Ky.; s. Thomas D. and Sally Ruth (Price) L.; m. Sally Diane Kleinhen, Dec. 19, 1953; children: Thomas, III b. 1956, Elizabeth Diane b. 1959, Jennifer Leigh b. 1962, Garwood Price b. 1964; edn: BS, US Naval Acad. 1949; JD, Univ. of Ariz. 1958; cert. patent law, US Patent Office 1960; cert. exec. mgmt., USC, 1966. Career: served to lt. cmdr. US Navy 1943-55, Reserve 1955-, Korean Pres. Unit Cit.; patent counsel Industrial Div. Garrett Corp. 1960-62; patent counsel/general counsel Harvey Aluminum Corp. 1962-66; pvt. patent practice, Los Angeles and Phoenix, Ariz. 1966-; prin. sev. emerging hi-tech. cos.; mem: L.A. Patent Law Assn., State Bar of Ariz. (corp., banking sects.); clubs: Calif. Yacht, L.A. Athletic, Braemar CC, Phoenix CC; Presbyterian; rec: sailing, music, farming. Res: 3404 Colville Place Encino 91436 also: 385 E Coronado Rd Phoenix AZ 85004 Ofc: 16530 Ventura Blvd Ste 600 Encino 91436 also: 234 N Central Ave Ste 722 Phoenix AZ 85004

LIPCHIK, HAROLD, corporate executive; b. Apr. 17, 1928, N.Y.C.; s. Samuel W. and Ida (Gutterman) L. m. Elaine Greenberg, Mar. 23, 1952; children: Alan b. 1953, Debra b. 1956; edn: BSME, Carnegie Mellon Univ., 1948; grad. work in bus. adm. N.Y. Univ., 1948-49. Career: project engr. 1950-54; v.p. AMF Inc., N.Y. 1954-66; v.p. Chromalloy Am. Corp., Clayton, Mo. 1966-71; pres. Water Treatment Corp., City of Industry, Calif. 1968-71; pres., dir. Halco Assocs., Tarzana 1971-; v.p. National Technical Systems, Calabasas 1984-; mem. Assn. for Corporate Growth 1988-; pres. L.A. Hebrew H.S., 1978-84; United Synagogue of Am., L.A. (pres. 1976-78); rec: golf, swimming, fishing. Res: 4429 Trancas Pl Tarzana 91356 Ofc: National Technical Systems 24007 Ventura Blvd Calabasas 91302

LIPPITT, LOUIS, aerospace engineer (ret.); b. Mar. 19, 1924, N.Y., N.Y.; s. Louis Lippitt, Sr. and Susan Davie (Anderson) L.; m. Adele Dorothy Wissmann, June 27, 1948; children: Laurie b. 1951, Craig b. 1953, Bonnie b. 1957, Nancie b. 1961; edn: BS in physics, City Coll. NY 1947; MA in geology, Columbia Univ., NY 1953; PhD in geology, Columbia Univ. 1959; reg. geophysicist, reg. geologist, Calif., 1969. Career: physicist Columbia Univ. 1947-51; physicist N.Y. Univ. 1952-53; geologist/geophysicist Standard Oil Co. Calif. (now Chevron), Oildale, Calif. 1954-58; staff engr. Lockheed Missiles & Space Co., Vandenberg AFB, Calif. 1958-87; part-time instr. Hancock Coll., Santa Maria, Calif. 1969-; part-time instr. Chapman Coll., VAFB, Calif. 1985-86; awards: Honorarium, N.Y. State 1952; fellow (sr.) Geological Soc. of Am. 1954-; mem: Sigma Xi 1954-, Am. Geophysical Union 1958-; civic: project leader 4H, Calif. 1960-77; author: profl. article, 1959. Mil: PFC, US Army 1943-46; Lutheran; rec: sailing, masters swimming. Res: 696 Raymond Ave. Santa Maria 93455-2760

LIPSCOMB, BILLYE RAYE, school administrator; b. Dec. 15, 1934, Calvert, Tx.; d. Hubert Ray and Ruby Lucile (Smitherman) Yount; m. Travis Lipscomb, May 28, 1955; children: Travis, III b. 1957, Camille Yount b. 1963; edn: BA, Baylor Univ., 1956; MA, Sonoma State Univ., 1978; EdD, USC, 1985. Career: classroom teacher Jefferson Co. Schs., Louisville, Ky. 1957-60, and Sanger (Calif.) Unified Sch. Dist. 1962-68; reading splst. Old Adobe Sch. Dist., Petaluma 1970-77, sch. principal 1977-84, dir. curriculum instrn. 1984-85, asst. sch. dist. supt. 1985-92; supt. Old Adobe Sch. Dist. 1992-;summer sch. instr. CSU Fresno 1966, 67; tchr. Instructional T.V. Fresno Co. Schs., 1968; tchr. trng. Sonoma Co. Office of Edn., 1986; mem. bd. Petaluma Ednl. Found. 1984-; awards: federal grantee CSU Fresno 1965, Best dissertation of year USC Sch. of Edn. 1985, nom. Am. Assn. of Sch. Adminstr. Nat. Supt. of Year 1994, listed Who's Who Sch. Dist. Officials 1976-77, Who's Who in American Edn. 1989-90, Who's Who in West 1980-81; speaker Nat. Conf. Women Sch. Execs., New Orleans 1985, Assn. Calif. Sch. Adminstrs., Santa Rosa 1984, Am. Assn. Sch. Adminstrs., Las Vegas 1988, Assn. Calif. Sch. Adminstrs., Long Beach 1988; mem: EDUCARE/support USC Sch. Edn. (pres. 1986-87), Petaluma Boys & Girls Club (bd. 1984-92), Sonoma Co. Assn. Sch. Adminstrs., Petaluma Family Edn. Ctr. (bd. 1980-84), Nat. & Calif. Sch. Public Rels. Assn. 1977-80, Assn. Calif. Sch. Adminstr. (Mentor New Supt.); publ. in ednl. jour. (1986); Democrat; Prot.; rec: history (esp. England under French Regency, and The Antebellum South). Res: 2006 Marylyn Circle Petaluma 94952 Ofc: Old Adobe Union School District, 845 Crinella Dr Petaluma 94952

LIPSHITZ, HOWARD DAVID, biologist; b. Oct. 30, 1955, Durban, S.A., naturalized U.S., 1991; s. Marcus and Annie Zelda (Cohen) L.; m. Susanna Maxwell Lewis, Sept. 13, 1986; children: Sarah Starr b. 1990; edn: BS, Univ. of Natal, S.A. 1975, BSc. (hons) 1976; M.Phil., Yale Univ., 1980, PhD, 1983. Career: postdoctoral fellow Stanford Univ., 1983-86; asst. prof. Calif. Inst. of Tech., Pasadena 1986-92, assoc. prof. 1992-; awards: Damant Science Prize, Univ. of Natal 1975, S.A. National Scholarship Yale Univ. 1978-80, Helen Hay Whitney Found. Fellow, Stanford Univ. 1983-86, Searle Found. scholar Calif. Inst. of Tech. 1988-91; mem. Genetics Soc. of Am. 1979-, AAAS (Fellow), Nat. Sci. Found. (Eukaryotic Genetics Panel 1993-); assoc. ed. "Zygote" 1993-;author book chapters (4, 1981-), jour. articles (17+, 1975-). Ofc: Calif. Inst. of Technology Div. Biology 156-29 Pasadena 91125

LITTLE, PHILIP WAYNE, private investigator, security co. president; b. June 7, 1942, Mercer, Mo.; s. Frank E. and Bertha M. (McConnell) L.; m. 2d. Teri Thompson, Feb. 9, 1991; children: Nicolette Rae b. 1991; children by prev m: Philip Wayne II b. 1963, Wade Alan b. 1964; edn: spl. courses Whitman Tech. Tng. Ctr. 1960, CSU San Jose 1981-82; Calif. lic. Pvt. Investigator 1972. Career: dep. sheriff San Bernardino 1963-70; prin. Phil Little Investigations, San Bernardino 1970-77; owner/pres. West Coast Detectives (120+ agents internat.), No. Hollywood 1977-; num. TV and Radio appearances include 3-hr series on crime prevention Nat. Pub. TV, 700 Club (CBN-TV), 22 Views (KWHY-TV), Midmorning L.A. (KHJ-TV), rel. pgmmg. (KTBN-TV); recipient 220 awards for community involvement, The Prince of Peace award (for work in Middle East) High Adventure Ministries; mem: Nat. Assn. of Chiefs of Police, World Assn. of Detectives, Internat. Police Cong., US Chamber of Commerce; civic: Police Activity League Supporters/ assoc. LAPD (pres.), 1984 Olympics Security Pgm. (cons.), Middle East Relief and Peace Pgm. (cons.), High Adventure Ministries (bd. dirs.), Youth Intervention and Guidance Inc. (bd. dirs.). Ofc: West Coast Detectives 5113 Lankershim No Hollywood 91601

LITTLEFIELD, CHRISTINA BEMKO, lawyer; b. Jan. 26, 1953, Glendale; d. Harold Gregory Bemko and Mary Jane Gillan; m. Douglas Robert Littlefield, May 23, 1974; edn: BA, Mills Coll. 1974; MA, Univ. Md. 1979; JD, UC Davis 1982; admitted bar: Calif. (1983), U.S. Supreme Ct. (1987). Career: pub. affairs ofcr. U.S. Energy Research & Devel. Adminstrn., Oakland 1974-76; coordinator U.S. Energy Info. Center, San Francisco 1976-77; associate atty. in pvt. practice 1983-86; project dir. So. Alameda Domestic Violence Law Project 1986-88; atty. sole practice, Hayward 1986-; honors: writer, ed. UC Davis Law Review (1981, 82); mem: Women Lawyers of Alameda Co. (career chair, bd. 1988-92, del. Calif. State Bar Conv. 1989, 90,91,92), Alameda Co. Bar Assn., Mills Coll. Alumnae Assn. (Oakland br. pres. 1989-90, bd. 89-92); Democrat; Unitarian. Ofc: Littlefield Law Office 22693 Hesperian Blvd Ste 250 Hayward 94541 Ph:510/670-0711

LITZ, CHARLES JOSEPH, JR., aerospace engineer; b. Nov. 5, 1928, Phila.; s. Charles J. Sr. and Marie Anna (Muth) L.; m. Ronalda Clara, Apr. 17, 1971; children: Stacey Ann, Mark Charles; edn: AE, Martin Coll., 1948; BSME, Univ. Dela., 1951; postgrad., Texas Western, 1954-56; MS, La Salle Coll., 1959; M.I.T., Cambridge, MA 1958-62; reg. profl. engr. Career: mech. engr. U.S. Naval Air Devel. Ctr., Johnsville, Pa. 1951-54; mil. service U.S. Army, instr. Army Air Defense Sch., 1954-56; res. assoc., project engr. U.S. Army Advanced Res. Agy., Phila. 1956-60; cons. ballistic missile command for minute man missiles USAF, Phila., 1959-63; elec.-mech. engr. Brown Inst. Minn-Honeywell, Phila. 1956-58; sr. mech. engr. U.S. Army Frankford Arsenal, Phila. 1959-77; sr. design engr. Ford Motor Co., Dearborn, Mich. 1977-81; sr. mfg. engr. Ford Aerospace Co., Newport Beach, Calif. 1981-86; sr. engr. scientist Space Systems Lab., McDonnell-Douglas, Huntington Beach 1986-; recipient award for sci. res. Secty. U.S. Army 1968; mem: ASME; publ. articles: "Simulation Modeling & Testing of a Satellite Despin System" AIAA Flight Simulation Tech. Conf., Boston 1989, "Testing of PAM-S/ULYSSES Despin System" 12th Aerospace Testing Sem., Manhattan Beach 1990, "Unique Utilization of the Design of Experiment Taguchi Methodology and Math Modeling for Cost Effective Pyroshock Testing & Analysis" 14th Aerospace Testing Sem. Manhattan Beach 1993; contbr. num. articles to profl. jours., 11 patents in field; rec: music, reading, fitness, writing, philosophy. Res: 29221 Tieree Laguna Niguel 92677 Ofc: McDonnell Douglas 5301 Bolsa Ave Huntington Beach 92647 Tel: 714/696-2172

LIU, EDWIN H., biochemical ecologist; b. April 11, 1942, Honolulu, Hawaii; s. Edward F. and Margaret (Yuen) L.; m. Jeanne Miyasaka, June 5, 1965 (div. 1983); edn: BA, The Johns Hopkins Univ. 1964; PhD, Mich. St. Univ. 1971. Career: research assoc. Mich. St. Univ., East Lansing, Mich. 1971-73; asst. prof. Univ. S. Caro., Columbia 1973-80; res. prof. Univ. Ga., Aiken, S.C. 1981-85; Newport coord. Calif. Regional Water Quality Control Bd., Riverside 1986-88; regional monitoring coord. EPA, San Francisco 1988-; awards: Am. Soc. Plant Physiologists young scientist 1975, Univ. S.Caro. student govt. (1977, 79); mem: Soc. for Study of Evolution, Ecological Soc. Am., Sigma Xi, Am. Soc. Plant Physiologists, Internat. Wine & Food Soc.; 40 articles pub. in plant biochemistry and ecology jours. Res: 2575 Sir Francis Drake Blvd #40 Fairfax 94930 Ofc: U.S. EPA Region IX 215 Fremont St San Francisco 94105

LIU, JIA-MING, electrical engineering educator; b. July 13, 1953, Taichung, Taiwan, naturalized US 1990; s. Min-chih and Hsin (Lin) L.; m. Vida Hang Chang; children: Janelle b. 1991; edn: BS in electrophysics Nat. Chiao Tung Univ., 1975; SM in applied physics, Harvard Univ., 1979, PhD applied physics, 1982; reg. profl. electrical engr. Taiwan 1977. Career: asst. prof. SUNY at Buffalo, N.Y. 1982-84; sr. mem. tech. staff GTE Labs Inc., Waltham, Mass. 1983-86; assoc. prof. UCLA, Los Angeles 1986-93, prof. UCLA 1993-; cons. JAYCOR, San Diego 1987-, Battelle Inst. 1989-90; awards: Sigma Xi 1984-, Phi Tau Phi 1975-, Patent award GTE Labs Inc. (1986, 87, 88, 89); mem: Optical Soc. of Am. (Fellow 1979-), IEEE Laser and Electro-Optics Soc. (sr. mem. 1982-), Am. Physical Soc. 1980-, Photonics Soc. of Chinese Americans (founding mem. 1988-); author 7 US patents, contbr. articles in profl. jours. Ofc: UCLA 56-147C Eng. IV, E.E. Dept., Los Angeles 90024-159410

LIU, MARGARET, real estate broker, developer, investor; b. Jan. 31, 1941, Chungking, China; d. Tien-Oung and Shin-Yin (Tung) Liu; m. Edward Bauman Collins, Jan. 23, 1982; children: Magdalene, Samuel; edn: BS, UC Berkeley; Montclair St. Univ. 1971-72; Rutgers Univ. 1973. Career: sci. tchr. N.K. Brampton Sch., N.J. 1972-75; pres. Liu Realty Inc., San Francisco, Calif. 1979-, pres. Liu Internat. Mgmt. Inc., S.F. 1984-; dir. National American Bank, S.F. 1984-86, Integrated CMOS System, Sunnyvale 1985-87, Alumnae Resources, S.F. 1988-91, Calif. Pacific Medical Ctr., S.F. 1991-; trustee Grace Cathedral S.F. 1992-; advy. bd. Alumnae Resource S.F. 1991-, and Asian Women Resource Ctr. S.F., 1992-; mem. Development Coun. Family Survival Project S.F. 1992-; v.p. Liu Int'l. Inc., Tex. 1978-85, also v.p. Tex. cos.: Rosemead Inc. 1981-83, Repulse Bay Inc. 1981-89, Preston Oakes Inc. 1981-83, Marinwood Inc. 1981-83, Lebanon Oaks Inc. 1983-85; mem: Nat. Assn. Realtors, Calif. Assn. Realtors; club: St. Francis Yacht Club, S.F.

LLEWELLYN, JOHN FREDERICK, cemetery executive; b. Nov. 16, 1947, Los Angeles; s. Frederick Eaton and Jane Elizabeth (Althouse) L.; d. Sharon b.

1978; m. Linda Garrison, 1989; edn: BA, Univ. Redlands 1970; MBA, USC 1972. Career: foreman Pacific T&T, Orange 1970; underwriter Allstate Ins. Co., Santa Ana 1971-72; asst. to controller Forest Lawn Co., Glendale 1972-73, v.p. 1973-75, exec. v.p. Forest Lawn Memorial-Parks and Mortuaries 1976-88, treas./CFO 1978-83, secty. bd. dirs. 1983-, gen. mgr./c.e.o. 1988-; v.p. Forest Lawn Found. 1978-, trustee 1979-, secty. 1980-, treas./c.f.o. 1978-83; dir. Beneficial Standard Life Ins. Co. 1985-91; mem: Nat. Assn. of Cemeteries (dir. 1977-80), Am. Cemetery Assn. (dir. 1983-91, pres. 1988), Calif. Mortuary Alliance (dir. 1985-), Interment Assn. of Calif. (dir. 1984-, v.p. 1985-, state pres. 1988), Western Cemetery Alliance (dir. 1987-, v.p. 1987-); clubs: Economic Round Table (sec.treas. 1983-85), Newcomen Soc. No. Am., California, Lincoln; civic: Braille Inst. Am. (dir. 1983-), Gr. Los Angeles Visitors & Conv. Bur. (dir. 1981-, v.p. 1985-86, pres. and chmn. 1989-90), Calif. C.of C. (dir. 1991-), M&M Assn. (dir. 1991-), Emphysema Found. of Am. (dir. 1981-82), Glendale Devel. Council (dir. 1984-90, sec. 1986-87), Pershing Square Mgmt. Assn. (dir. 1985-86), Glendale Mem. Hosp. (trustee 1985-91), L.A. Area Council Boy Scouts Am. (dir. 1980-, treas. 1984-85, chmn. Council Advy. Com. on Scouting for Handicapped 1984-86, v. chmn. 1987-93, Commr. 1990-92, chmn. 1992-); publs: Fundamentals of Supervision of Cemetery Managers (3/82), Survey of Interment and Crematory-Columbarium Practices (c 1986), articles in trade mags. and jours. 1975-. Res: 1130 Oakwood Pl Sierra Madre 91024 Ofc: Forest Lawn Memorial-Parks and Mortuaries 1712 S Glendale Ave Glendale 91205

LOCKARD-DIGRE, SUSAN ANNE, educator, consultant; b. Apr. 5, 1942, Youngstown, Ohio; d. Charles William and Anna Gabriella (Choppa) Lockard; m. Erick Loyd Digre, Oct. 21, 1977; children: Colleen b. 1978, Sean b. 1980, Michael b. 1981, Scott b. 1983; edn: BA biol. scis., Coll. of Notre Dame, Belmont, 1964; Calif. State Elementary tchg. credential - Life 1969. Career: educator Sisters of Notre Dame, Saratoga, 1964-68, Our Lady of Angels Sch., Burlingame, Calif. 1968-78, 88-; ednl. cons. (creative approaches for difficult situations) S.S.S. Consultant Services, San Bruno and Pacifica, 1986-; political activist: Dem. Write-In Candidate for Gov. of Calif. 6/90, rec'd local & nat. media coverage; mem. bds: S.F. Archdiocese Pastor Council to Archbishop John Quinn (1986-89, 90-), San Mateo Co. Crisis Pregnancy Ctr. (founding bd., grantwriter 1989-), Concerned Parents and Associates (founder 1989), Burlingame Civic Action Forum 1972-76, Sierra Club Loma Prieta Chpt. (bd. 1972-74); entrepreneur, inventor (math learning game) Math Match-It, several interactive games also practical products for children & adults; author (childrens story) CandyCane&GummyGumDrop (1975); Democrat (Maverick); R.Cath.; rec: writing, problem solving, horse back riding. Res: 780 Edgemar Ave Pacifica 94044

LOEBL, JAMES DAVID, lawyer; b. July 4, 1927, Chgo. Ill.; s. Jerrold and Ruth Diana (Weil) L; m. Joan Dorothy Hirsch, Apr. 8, 1960; children: Jeffrey William b. 1961, Susan Diana Loebl Grasso b. 1962, Ellen Cynthia b. 1965; edn: AB, Princeton Univ. 1948; Grad. Sch., Dept. of Sociology, Univ. of Chgo. 1948-49; JD, Stanford Univ. Sch. of Law 1952. Career: comm. sec. U.S. House of Representatives 1949; deputy atty. gen. Calif. Dept. of Justice 1953-58; travel sec. to Gov. Edmund G. Brown 1959-60; Dept. of Profl. & Vocat. Standards, asst. to dir. 1959-60, deputy dir. 1960, chief deputy dir. 1961, dir. 1961-63; ptnr.: Willard & Loebl 1963-64; Loebl & Bringgold 1964-65; Loebl, Bringggold & Peck 1965-75; Loebl, Bringgold, Peck & Parker 1976-80; Loebl & Parker 1980-81; Loebl, Parker, Murphy & Nelson 1981-87; Loebl, Parker & Nelson 1987-; mem. of bars of Ventura County (pres. 1983), L.A. County, Federal, Calif., Ill., and US Supreme Court; mem., State Bar Adminstrv. Law & Tribunals Comm. 1963-68; dir. Employment Aptitude & Placement Assn. 1970-72; Ventura Co. Superior Ct., judge pro tempore 1972, 74, 85-86; fellow, Am. Bar Found. 1989-; civic: asst. city atty., Ojai, Calif. 1964; bd. dirs. Ventura Co. Forum of the Arts 1965, Ojai Music Festivals 1967-68; v.p. & trustee, Monica Ros Sch., Ojai 1967-74; mem., Ojai City Council 1968-, Ventura Co. Sheriff's Prisoner Classification Comm. 1969-72, Comprehensive Health Svc. Comm. 1970, Sheriff's Civil Svc. Examining Bd., Princeton Sch. Admissions Com.; mayor, City of Ojai 1972-75, 1986-87, 1991-92; exec. comm., Ventura County Assn. of Govt. 1972-75, 1986-87; Ojai representative, So. Calif. Assn. of Govt. 1972-75; Ventura County Reg. Sanitation Dist. 1972-75; Calif. Council on Criminal Justice 1972-75; nominee for Congress, 19th Dist. of Calif. 1974. Mil: lt. comdr., US Coast Guard Res., 1964-74. Res: 715 El Toro Rd Ojai 93023. Ofc: Of Counsel, Muegenburg, Norman & Dowler, 840 County Square Dr., Ventura 93003

LOFGREN, DENNIS CARL, filmmaker; b. May 30, 1947, Duluth, Minn.; s. Carl Oscar and June LaVerne (Johnson) L.; m. Patricia Joyce Tarzian, Feb. 21, 1981 (div. 1984); 1 son, Kristofor b. 1982; m., 2d. Lori Renee Winning, Nov. 16, 1991; edn: BA sci., Gustavus Adolphus Coll. 1970; MS family & child devel., Kansas St. Univ. 1973. Career: pres., owner Auroean Film Co., Mpls., Minn. 1976-77; asst. to pres. Esmerelda Film Co., Los Angeles 1977-78; producer/dir./writer t.v. documentaries and t.v. specials, 1980-; owner/pres. Dennis Lofgren Productions, Santa Monica 1988-; profl. awards include Dupont/Columbia for bdcst. journalism, Christopher for t.v. Specials, ACE award nominations for cable excellence Nat. Acad. of Cable Pgmmg., Best Documentary for t.v. Chgo. Film Fest., Blue rib. American Film Fest., Cine Golden Eagles, Prix Italia (2d) World TV Fest., T.V. Guide year's list `Best We

Saw'; mem: Internat. Documentary Assn., Director's Guild Am., Earth Island Inst., Nat. Wildlife Fedn., Environ. Media Assn.; senior thesis "The Lotus and The Robot, A Report on Traditional Medicine in Modern Taiwan" pub. Minn. Student Proj. for Amity Among Nations 1970; mil: cpl. USMCR 1966-72; rec: tennis, painting. Address: Santa Monica 90403

LOGGINS, JOHN FRANCIS, lawyer; b. Apr. 24, 1941, Monterey Park; s. William F. and Helen A. L.; m. Anette H. Nielsen, Oct. 9, 1965 (div. 1984); children: Peter b. 1966, Paul b. 1968, Christian b. 1971; edn: BA, CSU Los Angeles, 1965; JD, Loyola Univ., 1970; admitted bar Calif., 1972. Career: claims adjuster Allstate Ins., Torrance, 1966-70; negotiator, ptnr. law firm Medearis, Grimm & Loggins, Los Angeles, 1970-77; mng. atty. law offices of Harold V. Sullivan, Inglewood, 1977-80; atty., prin. law offices of John F. Loggins, Long Beach, 1980-; arbitrator L.A. Cty. Superior Ct., 1982-, Am. Arb. Assn., 1980-; lectr. UCLA Paralegal Sch., 1983-, Pepperdine Univ., 1983-; honors: outstanding student govt. ofcr. CSULA, Blue Key nat. hon. frat., Who's Who in Am. Univs. 1965; mem: Calif. Bar Assn. 1972-, L.A. County Bar Assn. 1975-, Calif. Trial Lawyers Assn. 1989-, L.A. Trial Lawyers Assn. 1977-; civic: City of Rancho Palos Verdes Master Plan Com. 1989-90, Amb. L.A. Rams, Anaheim 1990-; book editor: Profile '65 (1965), pub. profl. articles (1978, 81); Republican; R.Cath.; rec: magic. Law Offices of John F. Loggins, 2530 Atlantic Ave #C Long Beach 90806

LOMELI, MARTA, bilingual education teacher; b. Oct. 28, 1952, Tijuana, Mex., naturalized U.S. 1978; d. Jesus Ramirez and Guadalupe (Ascencio) Lomeli; m. Rudolph Benitez Jr., 1978 (div. 1982); children: Pascual b. 1979; m. David Everett Miller, Aug. 16, 1991; edn: BA, San Diego State Univ., 1977; Calif. tchr. credential, 1978. Career: librarian Vista Boy's Club, Vista 1969-70; student recruiter UC San Diego, La Jolla 1970-72; bilingual tchr., 6th grade, National Sch. Dist., National City, 1978-, Nat. Sch. Dist. High Tech. Com. 1993-; advy. coms. prin. and supt., 1986-88; volunteer tutor MECHA, UCSD, 1971-73, St. Vincent de Paul Ctr. for the Homeless, San Diego 1991-; mem. anti-Graffiti patrol, Bell Jr. H.S. 1991-; awards: Mexican Am. Educators scholar, Vista 1970, Black Belt 1st degree in Shaolin Kempo 1992, listed Who's Who Am. Women, Who's Who in West, Who's Who Am. Educators, Who's Who of Emerging Leaders; mem. Nat. Assn. Bilingual Edn, Calif. Assn. Bilingual Edn. 1982-, World Federalist Orgn. 1992-; past pres., co-founder La Raza Club, Vista H.S. 1970; pub. poems (1969, 70, 92); Democrat; rec: drawing cartoons, Karate. Res: 6920 Alsacia St San Diego 92139-2101

LONDON, ROBERT ALAN, holding company executive; b. July 3, 1941, Boston, Mass.; s. Louis Robert and Lucille Rita (Eisenberg) L.; m. Marshalyn Kaufman, Feb. 9, 1964; children: Amy Michelle b. 1966, Lauri Robin b. 1968, Jennifer Lynn b. 1969; edn: BA, Lafayette Coll., 1963; MBA, Columbia Univ., 1965; Temple Law, Phila. 1965-66, Harvard Univ., 1980. Career: asst. v.p. Giant Food Inc., W.D.C., 1966-70; mdse. mgr. Macy's, Newark, N.J. 1970-74; sr. v.p. Glemby, N.Y.C. 1974-86; v.p. Regis, Mpls. 1986-87; chmn. bd. Samson Ent. Inc., Whittier, Calif. 1987-93; adj. prof. Monmouth Coll., 1980-88; pres. Marlaine Consultants, Palos Verdes 1986-; mem. bd. dirs. Schools America, 1987-91, C.A.S.C., 1988-92; Jewish; rec: golf, tennis. Res: 3200 La Rotonda Dr Rancho Palos Verdes 90274

LONG, STEPHEN INGALLS, professor, electrical and computer engineering; b. Jan. 11, 1946 Alameda, Calif.; s. Stanley M. and Mabel C. (Ingalls) L.; m. Molly S. Hammer, Dec. 17, 1966; children: Christopher b. 1971, Betsy b. 1974; edn: BS, UC Berkeley 1967; MS, Cornell Univ., Ithaca, NY 1969; PhD, Cornell Univ. 1974. Career: sr. engr., Varian Assoc., Palo Alto, Calif. 1974-77; mem. of tech. staff, Rockwell, Thousand Oaks, Calif. 1978-81; prof., Univ. of Calif. Santa Barbara 1981-; cons., Jet Propulsion Labs., Pasadena 1990-92, Superconductor Technologies, Inc., Santa Barbara 1991-; awards: Microwave Application award IEEE 1978, Fulbright Scholar 1993; sr. mem. IEEE 1984-; mem. Am. Scientific Affiliation 1989-; author: Gallium Arsenide Digital Integrated Circuit Design, 1990; over 70 profl. jour. articles and conf. papers, 1974-; mil: staff sgt., USAF, 1969-73; Grace Ch. of Santa Barbara; rec: amateur radio, Christian edn., classical guitar. Res: 895 N. Patterson Ave. Santa Barbara 93111. Ofc: Univ. of Calif. ECE Dept. Santa Barbara 93106

LONGA, CELIA LYNN MC GEE, real estate broker; b. March 28, 1942, Los Angeles; d. Lucius Elijah and Louise Elder (Bingham) McGee; m. Victor Longa, Dec. 29, 1959; children: Luz Mary b. 1960, Elizabeth Ann b. 1963, Victor John b. 1965, Angelica Leonora b. 1970; edn: De Anza Coll. 1980; W. Valley Coll. 1981; lic. real estate broker Calif. 1981. Career: secty. Los Angeles Unit Am. Cancer Soc. 1972-73; sales Coldwell Bankers Residential Services; 1977-78; real estate broker, Los Gatos 1981-; interim dir., secty. High Tech. Nat. Bank 1982-83, dir., secty. 1983; mem: Calif. Hist. Center De Anza Coll.; co-author Water in Santa Clara Valley: A History (1981); Republican; rec: writing, historic research. Res: 24777 Miller Hill Rd Los Gatos 95030

LOONEY, CLAUDIA A., academic administrator; b. June 13, 1946, Fullerton; d. Donald F. and Mildred B. (Gage) Schneider; m. James K. Looney, Oct. 8, 1967; 1 son, Christopher K.; edn: BA, CSU Fullerton 1969. Career: youth dir.

YWCA No. Orange Co., Fullerton 1967-70; dist. director Camp Fire Girls, San Francisco 1971-73, asst. exec. director Camp Fire Girls, Los Angeles 1973-77, asst. dir. community resources Childrens Hosp. of Los Angeles, 1977-80; dir. community devel. Orthopaedic Hosp., L.A. 1980-82; sr. v.p. Saddleback Meml. Found./Saddleback Meml. Med. Ctr., Laguna Hills 1982-92; v.p. planning and advancement Calif. Inst. Arts, Santa Clarita 1992-; instr. UC Irvine, Univ. Irvine; mem. steering com. Univ. Irvine; mem. steering com. United Way, L.A. 1984-86; Fellow Assn. Healthcare Philanthropy (nat. chair-elect, chmn. program Nat. End. Conf. 1986, chair-elect, regional dir. 1985-89, fin. com. 1988-, pres., com. chmn. 1987-, Give to Life com. chmn. 1987-91, Orange Co. Fund Raiser of Yr. 1992); mem. Nat. Soc. Fund Raising Execs. Found. (cert., vice chmn. 1985-90, chair-elect 1993), So. Calif. Assn. Hosp. Devel. (past pres., bd. dirs.), Profl. Ptnrs. (chmn. 1986, instr. 1988-), Philanthropic Ednl. Orgn. (past pres.); avocations: swimming, sailing, photography. Ofc: California Institute of the Arts 24700 McBean Pkwy Valencia 91355-9999

LOPER, JAMES L., association executive; b. Sept. 4, 1931, Phoenix, Ariz.; s. John D. and Ellen H. (Leaders) L.; m. Mary Louise Brion, Sept. 1, 1955; children: Elizabeth Serhan b. 1964, James, Jr. b. 1966; edn: BA in journ., Ariz. St. Univ., Tempe 1953; MA in radio & t.v., Univ. Denver, 1957; PhD comm., USC, 1966. Career: Weekend News editor and announcer, p.t. KTAR, NBC Radio, Phoenix and 8-sta. Ariz. Bdcst. System, 1955-56; asst., actg. dir. Bur. of Bdcstg. = Ariz. St. Univ., Tempe 1953-59; asst. prof. and dir. ednl. t.v. CSU Los Angeles, 1960-64; exec. Community Television of So. Calif. (KCET- Ch. 28), Los Angeles 1963-82: v.p. and asst. to pres. 1963-64, dir. ednl. svs. 1964-65, asst. gen. mgr. 1965-66, v.p. and gen. mgr. 1967-71, pres. and gen. mgr. 1971-77, pres. and c.e.o. 1977-82; indep. communications cons., 1982-83; blt. KCET into one of largest public t.v. stations nat., pgmmg. won all major nat. awards incl. Peabody, DuPont, Ohio State, Emmy; founding chmn. Public Broadcasting Service (3 yrs.), spokesman for pub. bdcstg., devel. legislation, appt. to CPB Commn. by Gov. Reagan; founding chmn. Pub. TV Playhouse Inc., N.Y., prod. "American Playhouse" 1980-82; exec. prod. internat. t.v. series "Music in Time" 1982; exec. dir. Acad. of Television Arts and Sciences, and ATAS Foundation (the largest acad. for profls. in t.v. industry with 7000+ mbrs.), orgn. presents annual Primetime Emmy Awards, seminars and forums, pub. EMMY Mag., and supr. ATAS/UCLA Archives a collection of 25,000+ films and tapes of t.v. pgmmg. dating from 1940s), 1984-; adj. prof. USC Sch. of Cinema-TV 1985-; appt. by Gov. Pete Wilson to Calif. Arts Council 1991-; honors: Sigma Delta Chi, Alpha Delta Sigma, Pi Delta Epsilon, Phi Sigma Kappa (Grand Council 1987-90), Alpha Epsilon Rho, disting. alumnus Ariz. St. Univ. 1972, man of yr. Calif. Mus. Sci. and Indus. 1972, Hon. HDL Columbia Coll. 1973, juror rep. U.S. PBS, the Japan Prize Japan Bdcstg. Co., Tokyo 1975, Alumni award of merit USC 1975, gov's award Hollywood chpt. Nat. ATAS 1975, Hon. LLD Pepperdine Univ. 1978, Alumni Hall of Fame Ariz. St. Univ. 1985 and named Centennial Alumnus 1988; exec. bd. Art Center Coll. of Design, Pasa. 1979-; past pres. Assn. of Calif. Pub. TV Stations and W. Ednl. Network; past dir./treas. Hollywood Radio and TV Soc.; mem. Acad. TV Arts & Scis. (former gov., trustee Internat. Council 1979-83, 88-); mem. Mayor's Com. for the Entertainment Indus., L.A. 1989-; mem. Western Fed. Sav. & Loan Assn., L.A. (dir. 1979-93); civic bds: Performing Tree, L.A. (chmn., dir. 1976-87), Permanent Charities Com. of Entertainment Indus. (dir. 1984-), Polytechnic Sch., Pasa. (trustee 1976-82), Town Hall of Calif. (dir. 1981-82), Calif. Civic Light Opera Co. (dir. 1977-, chmn. Musical Theatre Workshop Com.), Pasa. Chamber Orch. (dir. 1983-84), Assocs. of Otis Art Inst. (past pres.), Acad. of Performing and Visual Arts Found. (bd. 1984-89), Salvation Army (advy. bd. 1981-82); author book chapts., contbr. articles in profl. jours., Performing Arts Mag., Passenger Train Jour.; Republican; Presbyterian; rec: R.R. hist. Ofc: Academy of TV Arts and Sciences, 5220 Lankershim Blvd North Hollywood 91601

LOPEZ, FRED ALBERT, III, educator; b. May 30, 1956, San Bernardino; s. Fred Albert Lopez, Jr. and Mary (Moreno) Lopez; div.; 2 children: Celina b. 1981, Sophia b. 1983; edn: BA, CSU San Bernardino, 1979; MA, UC Riverside, 1982, PhD, 1985. Career: adj., asst., assoc. prof. political sci. CSU Bakersfield, 1984-; awards: Nat. Sci. Found. fellow 1980-84, Hispanic Excellence Award (yearly 1977-82), Merit. Performance and Profl. Promise Calif. State Univ. 1989; mem. Pacific Coast Council of Latin Am. Studies (bd. govs. 1991-93); editor jour. Latin American Perspectives (1987-); R.Cath. Res: 3054 Spruce St Bakersfield 93301

LOPEZ, JOHN, JR., infantry officer; b. July 14, 1954, Los Angeles; s. John Soto and Elvira (Jimenez) L.; edn: BA in bus. mgmt., St. Martins Coll., 1983; spl. mil. tng. Army Armor Sch., Fort Knox, 1982, Army Organizational Effectiveness Sch., Fort Ord, 1984, Army Combined Arms Svs. & Staff Sch., Fort Leavenworth, 1986, Defense Language Inst., Presidio of Monterey, 1991; Command & Gen. Staff Coll., Ft. Leavenworth, 1993. Career: major US Army 1975-: platoon ldr. 2d Batt. 39th Inf., 9th Inf. Div., Fort Lewis, Wash. 1978-79, company executive ofcr. 1980, 1st Brigade air ops. ofcr. 1980-82; Div. organizational effectiveness cons. Hq., 2d Inf. Div., Camp Casey, South Korea 1984-85, 2d Brigade co. comdr., 1985-86; recruiting ofcr., San Jose 1986-90; inf. advr. U.S. Military Group, El Salvador 1991-92; corps civil affairs ofcr., HQs., I Corps, Ft. Lewis, Wash. 1992-; decorated Parachute Badge, Expert Inf. Badge,

Merit. Svc. Medal (2), Army Commendation Medal (5), Army Achiev. Medal (2), Joint Service Achiev. Medal, Joint Merit, Unit Award; mem. Assn. of the US Army; civic: Santa Clara Co. Council Boy Scouts 1989, San Jose City C.of C., Civil Air Patrol/ San Gabriel Valley 1969-76, Nat. Rifle Assn., 82nd Airborne Div. Assn., Wash. State Arms Collectors; Republican; Baptist; rec: hiking, hunting, mil. history, marksmanship. Res: 317 S Aspen Ave Azusa 91702

LORD, HAROLD WILBUR, consulting electrical engineer; b. Aug. 20, 1905, Eureka; s. Charles Wilbur and Rossina Camilla (Hansen) L.; m. Doris Shirley Huff, July 25, 1928; children: Joann b. 1929, Alan b. 1932, Nancy b. 1934, Wayne b. 1942; edn: BS in E.E., Calif. Inst. of Tech., 1926; reg. profl. electrical engr., Calif. 1968. Career: electrical engr., res. and devel. electronics engr. Gen. Electric Co., Schenectady, N.Y. 1926-66; consulting elec. engr., 1966-; awards: Coffin Award GE Co. 1933, Inventors Award GE 1966, Centennial Medal IEEE, nat. 1984, Achiev. Award IEEE Magnetics Soc., nat. 1984; mem.: IEEE (Life Fellow, 1967-), AIEE/IEEE (tech. v.p. 1962); inventor, 96 patents (1930-72), tech. publs. J. AIEE/IEEE (8+, 1930-68); mil: 1st lt. Engineer Corps Reserve 1927-31; Republican; Prot.; rec: photography, hi-fi systems. Res: 1565 Golf Course Dr Rohnert Park 94928

LORD, JACK, actor, director, producer, artist, writer; b. Dec. 30, 1930, NYC; s. William Lawrence and Ellen Josephine (O'Brien) Ryan; m. Marie de Narde, Apr. 1, 1952; edn: BFA, N.Y. Univ. 1954. Career: exhibited galleries and museums incl. Corcoran Gallery, Nat. Acad. Design, Whitney Mus., Brooklyn Mus., Lib. of Congress, Biblioteque Nationale, Paris, France; rep. in 37 major mus. permanent collections incl. Met. Mus. of Art, Mus. Modern Art NYC, Fogg Mus., Harvard U., Santa Barbara Mus. Art, Fine Arts Gal. San Diego, Colby Coll. Art Mus., Ga. Mus. Art, Chouinard Art Inst. LA, Calif. Inst. Art, Brit. Mus., others; appearances on Broadway in Traveling Lady (Theatre World award 1959), Cat On A Hot Tin Roof; motion picture performances: Court Martial of Billy Mitchell, Williamsburg - the Story of a Patriot, Tip on a Dead Jockey, God's Little Acre, Man of the West, Hangman, True Story of Lynn Stuart, Walk like a Dragon, Doctor No.; leading roles in TV prodns: Constitution series Omnibus, Playhouse 90, Goodyear Playhouse, Studio One, U.S. Steel; TV film appearances: Have Gun Will Travel (pilot), Untouchables, Naked City Rawhide, Bonanza, Americans, Route 66, Gunsmoke, Stagecoach West, Dr. Kildare, Greatest Show Earth, Combat, Chrysler Theater, 12 O'Clock High, Loner, Laredo, FBI, Invaders, Fugitive, Virginian, Man from Uncle, High Chaparral, Ironside, Twilight Zone, num. others; star series Stoney Burke; prod./star: Hawaii 5-O; creator TV shows: Tramp Ship, Yankee Trader, McAdoo, The Hunter series; writer original screenplay Mellissa 1968; pres. Lord & Lady Ents., Inc. 1968-; honors: St. Gauden's Artist Award 1948, Fame Award 1963, Cowboy Hall of Fame 1963, Am. Legion spl. law enforcement award 1973, City and Co. of Honolulu award for contbn. to tourism 1973, Fed. Exec. Bd. award 1978, Tripler Army Med. Ctr. Citizen of Year 1979, Hawaii Assn. of Bdcstrs. Award 1980, Am. Legion Good Guy award 1981; mem.: Screen Actors Guild, Am. Fedn. of T.V. & Radio Actors, Actors Equity Assn., Am. Guild of Variety Artists, Dirs. Guild of Am.; mil: 2nd ofcr., navigator US Merchant Marines; rec: running, swimming. Ofc: Hawaii Five-O Studios, Ft. Ruger Honolulu HI 96816; c/o J. Wm. Hayes, 132 S Rodeo Dr Beverly Hills 90212

LORENTSON, HOLLY JEAN, hospice administrator/executive; b. Nov. 27, 1956, Minneapolis, Minn.; d. Leslie Arnold and Mary Ann Jean (Anderson) Lorentson; edn: BA nursing, Coll. St. Catherine, 1978; MPH, Univ. Minn., 1986. Career: reg. nse. Abbott N.W. Hosp., Mpls., Minn. 1978-79; intern San Francisco Home Health & Hospice, 1983; acting dir. community nursing svs.Ebenezer Soc., Mpls. 1979-84; patient care coord. San Diego Hospice 1984-85, exec. dir. 1985-88, pres. 1988-; honors: Who's Who Am. Women, Who's Who Fin. & Industry; mem. Nat. Hospice Orgn. (nat. bd. 1991), Calif. State Hospice Assn. (founding v.p.), Calif. Assn. Health Services at Home, CAHSAH, San Diego Downtown Rotary; thesis pub. (1986), contbr. reference text Caresharing (1989); rec: backpacking, travel, sports. Res: 5892 Adelaide Ave San Diego 92115 Ofc: San Diego Hospice 4311 Third Ave San Diego 92103

LO SCHIAVO, JOHN JOSEPH, university chancellor, clergyman; b. Feb. 25, 1925, San Francisco; s. Joseph and Anna (Re) Lo Schiavo; edn: AB, Gonzaga Univ., Spokane 1948, MA, 1949; STL (Licentiate in Sacred Theol.), Alma Coll., Los Gatos 1962; ordained priest (S.J.) Soc. of Jesus, R.Cath. Ch. (1955). Career: v. principal Brophy Coll. Prep, Phoenix, Ariz. 1958-61; instr. Philos. and Theol., Univ. San Francisco, 1950-52, 1956-57, 61-62, dean of students 1962-66, v.p. Student Affairs 1966-68; pres. Bellarmine Coll. Prep., San Jose 1968-75; rector Jesuit Community Univ. San Francisco 1975-77; pres. Univ. San Francisco 1977-91, chancellor, 1991-, univ. bd. trustees 1964-68, 1969-91, bd. chmn. 1970-73; mem. bd. dirs. St. Mary's Hosp. 1990-; trustee Sacred Heart Schs. 1991-; trustee San Francisco Consortium 1977-91; mem. Assn. of Jesuit Colls. and Univs. (dir. 1977-91), Assn. of Independent Calif. Colls. and Univs. (exec. com. 1978-91); honors: Alpha Sigma Nu (life), Nat. Jesuit Honor Soc., NCCJ Inc. (S.F. dir. 1982-); clubs: Olympic, Bohemian, Il Cenacolo; Republican; rec: golf. Address: Univ. of San Francisco, Ignatian Hts San Francisco 94117

LOUCA, ALEXANDRE, systems technology manager; b. June 14, 1944, Cairo, Egypt, nat. 1987; s. Sadek Louca and Yvonne (Assaf) Papouchado; m. Georgette El Sokary, Jan. 30, 1972 (div. Dec. 1987); children: Karine b. 1977, Christine b. 1984; edn: BSc aeronautical engring. Faculty of Polytechnique Cairo Univ., 1969; 3-yr. PhD degree in fluid mechanics, Faculty of Polytechnique, Univ. of Paris VI, Fr.; dipl. computer pgmg. Control Data Inst., Paris, Fr., 1972; courses in computer "C" lang., also Spanish lang. (4.0 g.p.a.), El Camino Coll. 1991; Calif. real estate lic., 1992; fluent in English, Arabic, French. Career: pgmr./analyst Jacques Borel Internat., Paris, Fr. 1974-78; pgmr./analyst California Milling Corp., Los Angeles 1979-80; sr. systems cons. American Savings & Loan, Fullerton 1980-82, d.p. cons., 1982; data systems mgr. First Interstate Services, Los Angeles 1982-85; data systems mgr. Toyota Motor Sales USA, HQ, Torrance 1985-90, planned & installed complete data systems dept. supporting Toyota Motor Credit Corp. (TMCC), systems technology mgr. TMCC, 1990-; awards: Sporting Club (Egypt): champion of Egypt in diving 1968, and in table tennis 1964, champion of English schs. in boxing 1962, drummer Cairo Univ. Orch. 1968, technical achiev. First Interstate Svs. of Calif. 1983, feature article Spotlight - Toyota fitness mag. 1990; rec: dancing, working out, drumming, travel, swimming, flying. Ofc: Toyota Motor Credit Corp. 19001 S. Western Ave. Torrance 90509

LOUGHEED, ARTHUR LAWRENCE, financial/pension services firm principal; b. Aug. 11, 1944, Fresno; s. Evan A. and Irene E. (Westby) L.; m. Nancy L. Sanderson; children: Christopher, b. 1967; Jennifer, b. 1969; Evan, b. 1975; edn: Albion Coll. 1963-64; AA, Orange Coast Coll. 1964; USC Grad. Sch. of Law 1964-65; MS finl. svcs., American Coll., Bryn Mawr 1980, MS mgmt., 1985; desig: ChFC, Chartered Fin. Cons. 1987, CLU, Am. Soc. Chartered Life Underwriters 1973, Chartered Property and Casualty Underwriter, Soc. CPCU 1980, Certified Financial Planner (CFP) 1992. Career: Farmers Ins. Gp., Los Angeles, served Santa Ana, Calif. & Pocatello, Idaho; agent/ Div. Agcy. mgr./ Regional life mgr. Aetna Life & Casualty Ins. Co., Hartford Conn., served Los Angeles 1974-77; mgr. of estate, bus. & pension sales CNA Ins. Cos., Chgo., Ill., served Los Angeles & Chgo. 1977-81; reg. dir. life sales ofcs./ nat. dir. mktg. & sales tng. Berkshire Group 1981-; currently, pres./ gen. agent The Bershire Life Ins. Co., San Diego; lectr. on ins. Glendale Coll., Univ. of Ill., Chgo., De Paul Univ., Chgo., UC San Diego, UC Irvine; reg. instr./ sem. leader Ins. Ednl. Assn. of San Francisco; honors: Alpha Gamma Sigma 1964, Toppers Club Farmers Ins. Group 1965-69, Regionaire Aetna Life & Casualty 1975-; mem. Nat., Calif., San Diego & Glendale/ Burbank Assns. of Life Underwriters, Am. Soc. CLUs; Soc. Chart. Property & Casualty Underwriters, Internat. Assn. of Financial Plnng., Saddleback Kiwanis (Mission Viejo), San Diego C.of C.; mem. curriculum advy. com. fin. planning UC San Diego, 1988-; editor assoc. CALUnderwriter mag. 1976, contbg. ed. California Broker mag. 1987-, contbr. articles on fin. and photog. in var. newspapers and mags.; Republican; Luthern; rec: fishing, history, literature. Res: 4793 Panorama Dr San Diego 92116 Ofc: Berkshire Group, 3545 Camino del Rio S San Diego 92108

LOUIE, MAY CHONG, dentist; b. May 3, 1956, Los Angeles; d. Wing Chong and Cheong Yoe (Lee) Louie; m. Benson T.C. Au, DMD; edn: BS magna cum laude, USC, 1978; DDS, UCLA, 1982; Fellow Acad. Dentistry Internat. 1987. Career: dentist, comm. Monrovia Unified Sch. Dist., Monrovia 1982-85; dentist Wenzlaffs DDS Inc., Hollywood 1982-84; Lehman Med. Dental, Garden Grove 1985-89; Rosenberg DDS Inc., Woodland Hills 1985-89; pvt. practice, La Puente, 1990-; staff dentist Hollywood Presbyterian Med. Center, Los Angeles 1982-89; Nat. Health Fair 1982-84; dentist, presentor Dental Hygiene 1982-86; vol. dentist USC/UCLA Mobile Dental Clinic 1978-82; instr. Joint Ednl. Project 1977-78; dentist Geriatric Dentistry 1982-84; honors: Phi Beta Kappa, USC Dean's List 1974-78, Acad. Dentistry Internat. fellowship 1987, Lehman Med. Outstanding Achievement 1986, Nat. Forensic League Distinc. 1974; mem: Acad. Gen. Dentistry, Acad. Dentistry Internat. (fellow), Am. Assn. Women Dentists, So. Calif. Acad. General Dentistry, Oral Pathology, Apollonians, Acad. Reconstructive & Cosmetic Dentistry, Asian Bus. League, L.A. Women Dentists Soc., Delta Sigma Delta, Alpha Phi Omega, Ephebian Soc.; article and speeches pub. (1974, 1972-74); Christian; rec: music, handicrafts, travel. Address: Arcadia 91006

LOVELL, JEFFREY D., investment banker; b. Apr. 21, 1952, N.Y.C.; s. Lewis Frederick and Pauline (Dailey) L.; m. Elaine Worley, Apr. 26, 1980; children: McKenzie b. 1984, Alexander b. 1987; edn: BS in bus. adm., Univ. Colorado, Boulder 1974; grad. studies internat. relations, Regents Coll., London (w/ Univ. So. Calif.) 1986-87; reg. securities prin. NASD, 1984. Career: financial analyst General Dynamics Corp., San Diego 1974-76; mktg. rep./cons. SEI Corp., Wayne, Pa. 1976-79; regional v.p. SEI Corp., Los Angeles 1980-81, v.p. nat. sales SEI Corp., Wayne, Pa. 1982-83, sr. v.p. SEI Corp., L.A., 1983-85, mng. director SEI Financial Services (U.K.) London, 1985-88; pres., prin., co-founder Putnam Lovell Inc., Manhattan Beach, Calif. 1988-; trustee PIC Pinnacle Inv. Trust (a series mutual fund) Pasadena 1992-; gen. ptnr. Manhattan Investment Ptnrs. (venture capital L.P.), Manhattan Beach 1988-90;gen. ptnr. Highland Capital Advisors L.P. 1992-; dir: Eagle Mgmt. and Trust Co., Houston 1992-; honors: Beta Gamma Sigma 1974; mem. USC Associates 1990-, Univ. Colo. Alumni Assn. 1988-, Manhattan Friends of the Arts 1985-; club: Manhattan CC; pub. articles re internat. investing in trade jours. 1984-86; Republican (Rep. Nat.

Com. 1980-); St. Andrews Presbyterian Ch., Redondo Beach; rec: skiing, tennis. Res: 1 Evergreen Ln Manhattan Beach 90266 Ofc: Putnam Lovell Inc. 317 Rosecrans Ave Manhattan Beach 90266 and 19 Fulton St NY, NY 10038

LOVEN, ANDREW WITHERSPOON, environmental engineering co. executive; b. Jan. 31, 1935, Crossnore, N.C.; s. Andrew Witherspoon Loven and Annie Laura (Crowell) Stewart; m. Elizabeth Joann DeGroot, June 20, 1959; children: Laura Elizabeth, James Edward; edn: BS, Maryville Coll. 1957; PhD, Univ. N. Caro. 1962; reg. profl. engr. Va., Ga., Iowa, Md., N.Caro., S.Caro., D.C., Ohio, Fla. Career: res. assoc. Univ. N. Caro., Chapel Hill 1962-63; sr. res. chemist Westvaco Corp., Charleston, S.Caro. 1963-66, mgr. carbon devel. 1966-71; mgr. engring. concepts Engineering-Science, Inc., McLean, Va. 1971-74; v.p. and reg. mgr. 1974-80, group v.p. 1980-86, Atlanta, Ga.; pres., chmn. bd. and CEO, Pasadena, 1986-; honors: Alpha Gamma Sigma, Sigma Xi, NSF grantee 1958-59; mem: Am. Acad. Environ. Engrs. (membership com. 1985-), Water Pollution Control Fed., Am. Inst. Chem. Engrs., Am. Water Works Assn., Nat. Soc. Profl. Engrs.; club: Willow Springs; contbr. articles to profl. jours.; rec: golf, hiking. Res: 514 Starlight Crest Dr La Canada 91011 Ofc: Engineering-Science, Inc. 75 N Fair Oaks Pasadena 91103

LOW, HARRY W., police commission president, retired appellate presiding justice; b. Mar. 12, 1931, Oakdale; s. Tong and Ying (Gong) L. m. Mayling Jue, Aug. 24, 1952; children: Lawrence b. 1953, Kathleen b. 1957, Allan b. 1962; edn: AA, Modesto Jr. Coll. 1950, AB, UC Berkeley 1952, LLB, 1955. Career: tchg. assoc. Boalt Hall 1955-56; dep. atty. gen. Calif. Dept. of Justice, 1956-66; commnr. Workers' Compensation Appeals Bd. 1966; municipal ct. judge 1966-74, presiding judge 1972-73; superior ct. judge 1974-82, supvg. judge Juvenile Ct. 1981-82; presiding justice Ct. of Appeal, San Francisco 1982-92; pres. S.F. Police Commn., 1992-; speaker, instr. var. judicial seminars and study coms.; faculty Calif. Judges Coll. 1976-83, Nat. Coll. of Judiciary 1977-79, Inst. of Ct. Mgmt. 1976-81; bd. CJER Journal; chmn. ABA Appellate Judges Conf. 1990-91; mem. bd. dirs. Nat. Center for State Cts.; conf. guest lectr. at meetings of Ida., Wash., Ariz., Va., Mich. and Nev. Judiciaries; co-chmn. past confs. on Media and the Law; ed. Courts Commentary 1973-76; chmn. bd. vis. US Mil. Acad., West Point 1981; mem: Calif. Judges Assn. (pres. 1978-79), Calif. Council on Criminal Justice, Edn. Center for Chinese (bd. chmn. 1969-), S.F. City Coll. Found. (pres. 1978-87), Chinese-Am. Citizens Alliance (nat. pres. 1989-93, Grand Bd.), Calif. Jud. Council 1979-81, USF (pres. 1987-88); mem. bd. dirs: Salesian Boys Club, St. Vincent's Home for Boys, Friends of Rec. and Parks, S.F. Zoological Soc., Law in the Free Soc., NCCJ, World Affairs Council, Chinatown Youth Task Force, Mayor's China Gateway Com.; Democrat; rec: gardening, S.F. hist. Res: 104 Turquoise San Francisco 94131 Ofc: Judicial Arbitration and Mediation Services, 111 Pine St San Francisco 94111

LOWERY, WILLIAM DAVID, congressman; b. May 2, 1947, San Diego; s. Thomas Henry and Eve L. (Howard) L.; m. Kathleen Ellen Brown, Sept. 7, 1968; children: Ashley Colleen b. 1978, Alison Elizabeth b. 1981, Thomas Harrington b. 1985; edn: CSU San Diego 1965-69, Calif. Western Sch. of Law 1970. Career: self-empl., 1973-77; with California Group, 1977-79; elected councilman City of San Diego, 1977-80, dep. mayor 1980; U.S. rep. from 41st Dist. Calif., 97th -100th congresses, 1981-; mem. of the Grace Caucus, mem. Republican Study and Republican Policy Coms., Environment and Energy Study Conf., High Tech. Task Force, Congl. Coalition for Soviet Jewry, Congl. Caucus for Ethiopian Jewry, Citizens for the Republic, congl. advy. bd. Future Bus. Leaders of Am.; past chmn. Calif. League of Cities; bd. Calif. Water Found. 1978-79, Council liaison to Unified Port Commn.; mem. Urban League S.D., Navy League; bd. vis. U.S. Mil. Acad.; awards: YMCA Red Triangle, Amigo de Distinction Mexico and Am. Found.; R. Cath. Ofc: 2433 Rayburn House Office Bldg. Washington D.C. 20515

LOWNDES, DAVID ALAN, programmer-analyst; b. Oct. 28, 1947, Schenectady, N.Y.; s. John Henry and Iris Anne (Hepburn) L.; m. Peggy Welco, May 3, 1970; children: Diana b. 1978, Julie b. 1982; edn: AB, UC Berkeley, 1969, grad. study 1972-73. Career: newspaper acct., credit mgr. The Daily Californian, Berkeley 1973-75, bus. mgr., 1975-76; acct. Pacific Union Assurance, San Francisco 1976-77, acctg. mgr. 1977-78; senior acct. Univ. Calif., San Francisco 1978-88, senior pgmr.-analyst, 1988-; mem. Birmingham and Midlands Soc. for Genealogy and Heraldry 1987-, Bay Area Roots Users Goup 1990-, Am. Canadian Geneal. Soc. 1991-, No. NY Am.-Canadian Genealogical Soc. 1992-; rec: genealogy, microcomputing. Ofc: Univ. of California, 250 Executive Park Blvd. Ste 2000 San Francisco 94143

LOZANO, CARLOS, educator; b. Jan. 12, 1913, Zamora, Mexico; nat. 1942; s. Epifanio and Julia (Tejeda) L.; edn: BA, UC Berkeley 1941; PhD, 1962. Career: asst. prof. George Washington Univ., Wash., D.C. 1959-63; assoc. prof. St. Louis Univ., Mo. 1963-64; prof. Univ. Oreg., Eugene 1964-66; prof. and chair dept. of modern languages, St. Marys Coll., Moraga, CA 1966-70; prof. and founding chair, dept. of fgn. languages, CSU Bakersfield 1970-81, NEH chair Comparative Literature, Scranton Univ., 1982, prof. emeritus, spl. asst. to pres., CSU Bakersfield 1984-; honors: AUS Legion of Merit 1949, Govt. of Chile Medalla Militar del Ejercito 1949, UC Berkeley Therese F. Collin travelling fellowship 1955-56, Calif. Fgn. Language Tchrs. Assn. tchr. of year 1973, Calif. St. Senate commend. 1981; mem: Acad. Spanish Language of Americas, Explicacion de Textos Literarios (ed. CSU Sacto.); Hispanic Press CSU (co-founder); Hispanic Excellence Scholarship Fund, CSU Bakersfield; Liaison Com. Bilingual Cultural Com. Univ. Calif. Articulation Conf., Mex. Am. Educators Assn.; author: Elemental Odes of Pablo Neruda (1961); My Horse Gonzalez, transl. of "Caballo de Copas", novel of F. Alegria (1964); with F. Alegria, Novelistas Contemporaneos Hispano-Americanos (1964); Ruben Dario y El Modernismo en Espana (1968); The Other Fire, transl. of "El Otro Fuego" poetry of David Valjalo, Madrid (1989); La Influencia de Ruben Dario en Espana; The Maypole Warriors, transl. of Manana Los Guerreros, novel of F. Alegria (Latin Am. Literary Rev. Press, Pittsburg, Pa. 1992); Rafe and the Sun Arrow, novel (pending 1992/3); 25+ articles in profl. jours.; mil: major AUS 1942-53; Democrat; R.Cath.; rec: poetry and prose, translating. Res: 2807 Elm Bakersfield 93301 Ofc: California State University Office of the President Bakersfield 93301

LU, NANCY CHAO, professor; b. May 29, Sian, China; d. Lun Yuan Chao and Su-mei (Tsang) Lu; m. Chyi Kang Lu, Mar. 19, 1966; children: Richard Hsiang, 1967; edn: BS, Nat. Taiwan Univ., Taipei, 1963; MS, Univ. Wyoming, Laramie, 1965; PhD, Univ. Calif., Berkeley, 1973; registered dietitian, Am. Dietetic Assn., 1988. Career: tchg. asst. Univ. Wyoming, Laramie, 1963-64, Univ. Calif., Berkeley, 1964, 70; tchg. assoc. UC Berkeley, 1978, 1979-80; lectr. San Jose State Univ., 1980-82; assoc. prof. San Jose State Univ., 1982-87 (tenured 1986), prof., 1987-; proj. coordinator NIH Nematode grant, UC Berkeley, 1978-80; awards: Most Outstanding Nutrition & Food Sci. Prof., 1989; Meritorious Performance and Professional Promise Award, San Jose State Univ., 1986; Who's Who In Calif., 1986; Calif. State Univ. Affirmative Action Faculty Devel. Award, 1984, 1985, 1986; Who's Who of Am. Women, 1977; Ellsworth Dougherty Award, 1976; NIH Postdoctoral Fellowship, 1973-75; UC Berkeley Postdoctoral Fellow, 1976-78; mem: Am. Dietetic Assn., Am. Inst. Nutrition, Inst. Food Technologists, Iota Sigma Pi (res. 1977), Sigma Xi, Soc. Experimental Biology and Medicine, Soc. Nematology; author and co-author of numerous publ. articles and res. papers; ofc: Dept. Nutrition & Food Science, San Jose State Univ. San Jose 95192

LUCE, R. DUNCAN, distinguished professor of cognitive science; b. May 16, 1925, Scranton, Pa.; s. Robert Renselear and Ruth Lillian (Downer) L.; m. Gay Gaer, June 1950 (div. 1967); m. Cynthia Newby, Oct., 1967 (div. 1977); m. Carolyn Ann Scheer, Feb. 27, 1988; children: Aurora b. 1972; edn: BS, MIT 1945; PhD, 1950. Career: staff MIT, Cambridge, Mass. 1950-53; asst. prof. Columbia Univ., NYC 1953-57; lectr. Harvard Univ., Cambridge, Mass. 1957-59; prof. Univ. Pa., Phila. 1959-69; vis. prof. Inst. Advanced Study, Princeton, N.J. 1969-72; prof. UC Irvine 1972-75; prof. Harvard Univ. 1976-88, emeritus 1988-; distinguished prof. UC Irvine 1988-; fellow Center Advanced Study in Behavioral Scis., Stanford 1954-55, 66-67, 87-88; awards: Am. Acad. Arts & Scis. fellow 1966, Nat. Acad. Sci. 1972; mem: Soc. Math. Psychology (past pres.), Psychometric Soc. (past pres.), Am. Psychological Soc. (past bd. dirs.), Fedn. of Cognitive, Behavioral and Psychol. Scis. (past pres.); coauthor: Games & Decisions (1957), Foundation of Measurement (1971, 89, 90), author: Individual Choice Behavior (1959), Response Times (1986); mil: ensign USNR 1943-46; rec: art and antiques, gardening. Res: 20 Whitman Ct Irvine 92715 Ofc: Univ. of Calif. Social Science Tower Irvine 92717

LUCE, TERRY JEAN, medical-legal consultant; b. Sept. 21, 1954, La Cross, Wis.; d. Charles Harold and Sharon Gail (Schuttenhelm) Luce, Jr.; edn: AA, East L.A. City Coll. 1975; BS, St. Josephs Coll. 1985; reg. nurse Calif. (1975). Career: nursing supr. Covina Valley Comm. Hosp., 1979-80, pediatric cons. 1980-81; coordinator Utilization Rev. and Quality of Care, Calif. Medical Review Inc., San Francisco 1981-85, medicare contracts adminstr., 1985-87; asst. dir. of nursing St. Francis Heights Hosp., 1987; independent health care consultant, 1987-93; utilization review nse. Health Plan of San Mateo, supplemental case mgr. 1989-92, Health Services asst. mgr. 1992-; listed Who's Who in Nursing 1987, Who's Who in Women of Am. 1978; publ: article in J. of Am. Sociol. March, 1974. Res: 1551 Southgate Ave #117 Daly City 94015 Ofc: Health Plan of San Mateo 1500 Fashion Island Blvd Ste 300 San Mateo 94404

LUDDEN, JEROME A., JR., physician, surgeon; b. July 7, 1911, Pomona; s. Jerome A. and Minnie Alta (Newkirk) L.; m. Ruth Adelaide Arary, June 12, 1937; children: James Robert b. 1939, Elizabeth Ann b. 1942; edn: BA, Pomona Coll. 1933; BS medicine, Univ. So. Dakota Vermillion 1935; MD, Tufts Univ. 1937. Career: physician and surgeon; mem: Santa Cruz Co. Med. Soc. (pres. 1952), Lions (pres. 1948); mil: lt. cmdr. USN 1942-51; rec: jewelry making, woodworking, gardening. Res: Dominican Oaks-C202, 3400 Paul Sweet Road Santa Cruz 95065

LUDWIG, CARL LAWTON, operations/product assurance executive/engineer; b. Nov. 22, 1930, San Francisco; s. Carl Lawton Sr. and Alberta (Cook) L.; m. Patricia Anabo, Dec. 31, 1953; children: Debra Kim b. 1954; Michael Jon b. 1957; edn: student (student body pres.), Los Angeles Pacific Coll.; BSEE, Western State Coll. of Engring. 1958; Reg. Profl. Engr., Calif. Career: gen.

supvr. Ryan Areo Electronic Div., 1962; mgr. mfg., test & quality assurance Litton Ind. Guidance Control, 1970; dir. reliability & quality assurance Amecom, College Park, Md. 1974; dir. quality assurance Litton Ind. Guidance & Control 1985; v.p. product assurance Pacesetter Systems Inc. (a Siemens co.), Sylmar 1985-90; v.p. quality/ops. Litton Applied Technology Div., San Jose 1990-; mem: Am. Soc. Quality Control, Nat. Conf. of Standards Lab., Nat. Security Ind. Assn., Internat. Soc. Hybrid Microelectronics, Highpoint Homeowners Assn. (pres.), Pacific Corinthian Yacht Club, YMCA (Indian Guide dir. 1968), Boy Scouts of Am. (life, Sea Scout); mil: s/sgt. USAF 1950-54; Republican; Prot.; rec: flying, sailing, tennis, artistic hobbies. Res: 1283 Quail Creek Cir San Jose 95120 Ofc: Litton Applied Technology 4747 Hellyer Ave San Jose 95150-7012

LUECKE, MICHAEL CLARE, biotechnology company executive; b. Dec. 28, 1941, Chicago Hts., Ill.; s. Clare Albert and Kathleen Margaret (Cornet) L.; m. Marjorie Ann Johnson, Feb. 20, 1967 (div. 1984); m. Donna Mary Burtch, Nov. 17, 1984; children: Michelle b. 1968, Kimberly b. 1974, Megan & Ryan (twins) b. 1988; edn: BS, Univ of Notre Dame 1963; MBA, Northwestern Univ. 1965. Career: market analyst Xerox Corp., Rochester, N.Y. 1968-70; finl. analyst CIBA-Geigy Ltd., Basel, Switzerland 1970-72, corporate planner, Ardsley, N.Y. 1972-76; dir. corp. strategy SmithKline Corp., Phila. 1976-77, general mgr., Cologne, Germany 1977-79; planning mgr. Texaco, Inc., White Plains, N.Y. 1979-80; dir. new ventures Sterling Drug Inc, New York, N.Y. 1980-83; dir. bus. planning Becton Dickinson, Paramus, N.J. 1983-84; dir. acquisitions Bristol-Myers Prod., New York, N.Y. 1984-87; pres., CEO Clonetics Corp., San Diego 1987-89; pres., CEO Verigen, Inc. San Diego 1989-90; v.p. bus. development ICN Pharmaceuticals, Costa Mesa 1991-; honors: mem. Nat. Honor Soc. 1959, Airborne qualification, U.S. Army 1965, letter of commendation U.S. Army 1965; mem: SO/CAL/Ten, CONNECT, Notre Dame Alumni Club; author article pub. profl. jour. 1972; mil: 1st lt., U.S. Army 1965-68; Republican (YR Club treas. 1961-63); Lutheran; rec: ocean swimming, running, family. Res: 3120 Governor Dr San Diego 92122 Ofc: ICN Pharmaceuticals, Inc. 3300 Hyland Ave Costa Mesa 92626

LUEGGE, WILLARD ARTHUR, chemist; b. Mar. 19, 1931, Oak Park, Ill.; s. Theodore Wilhelm and Irma Minnie (Schoepfer) L.; m. Joanna Carleen Wechter, Sept. 1, 1951; children: Sherylene b. 1952, Lynette b. 1959; edn: BA, Indiana Univ., 1953, grad. work Ind. Univ. Ext., Univ. Louisville, UCLA, 1955-65; Calif. tchg. credential, sec. sci. tchr. 1961. Career: res. chemist Louisville Cement Co., Speed, Ind. 1956-60; quality control chemist Calif. Portland Cement Co., Mojave, Calif. 1960-61; chemistry tchr. Palmdale (Calif.) High Sch., 1961-90, sci. dept. chair 1964-79; res. chemist USAF Rocket Propulsion Lab., Edwards AFB, summers 1966, 67, 68; owner, dir. PM Labs, Lancaster 1968-89; cons. prin extractive metallurgical chemistry, Lancaster 1989-; bd. dir. Bryman Refining Co., Inc. 1992-; awards: Chem. Tchr. of Year, Am. Chemical Soc., W.D.C. 1967, NSF grantee (1963, 64); mem: Western Mining Council 1989-, Western Public Lands Coalition 1992-; inventor assay kit (1970); Presbyterian; rec: travel, reading, mining archaeology, spectator- baseball, basketball, auto racing. Res: 560 E Avenue J-1 Lancaster 93535 Ph: 805/948-1915

LUEVANO, FRED, JR., computer systems executive; b. June 21, 1943, Alamogordo, N.M.; s. Fred Macias and Margaret (Baca) L.; m. Lupe Olmos, July 11, 1964; children: Michael b. 1965, James Paul b. 1971; edn: AA, Fullerton Coll. 1975; BA, Univ. Redlands 1979; MAM, 1985. Career: mgr. computer ops. Hoffman Electronics, El Monte 1971-76; mgr. computer ops. and tech. services, City of Anaheim 1976-79; mgr. data processing Wyle Data Services, Huntington Beach 1979-83; mgr. corp. computing Northrop Corp., Hawthorne 1983-85, mgr. computer ops. Northrop Aircraft 1985-, dir. disaster recovery Northrop Corp. 1983-85, dir. disaster recovery & security 1985-91, mgr. systems mgmt. 1991-; cons. info. systems, La Habra Heights 1971-; city council cand. City of La Habra Heights 1982; mem. bd. dirs. Disaster Recovery Inst., 1990-; speaker Assn. Computer Ops. Mgrs., Chgo., Ill. 1983, San Diego 1988; mem: Am. Mgmt. Assn., Telecomms. Assn., Assn. Computer Ops. Mgrs., Northrop Mgmt. Club, BSA (cub master 1979-84, com. chmn. 1975-79), La Habra Parents for Swimming Inc. (pres. 1986-89), Red Coach Club (pres. 1979-80); article pub. in profl. jour. (1989); mil: E-5 USN 1961-65; Republican; R.Cath.; rec: fishing, basketball, art collecting. Ofc: Northrop Corp. One Northrop Ave M/S 770/31 Hawthorne 90250

LUFRANO, TONY RICHARD, artist, real estate investor; b. Jan. 26, 1929, Chicago, Ill.; s. Anthony and Lena (Ohren) L.; m. Harriet Joanne Gibson; children: Tony b. 1952, Lizabeth b. 1957, Peter b. 1961; edn: cert., Chgo. Art Inst. 1947; BA, Chgo. Acad. Fine Arts 1950. Career: artist Jerry Bryant Stuio, Chgo., Ill. 1949-50; art dir. Montgomery Ward, Oakland 1953-60; pres. Lufrano Assoc., 1960-81; pres. Lufrano Zensen Props., 1970-; Exhibits in art galleries, 1985-; rec: art. Res: 6 Doris Pl Berkeley 94705 Ofc: Lufrano & Associates 6 Doris Pl Berkeley 94705

LUNA, CARMEN E., bank executive; b. Feb. 11, 1959, Los Angeles; d. Roberto C. and Gloria (Encinas) Luna; edn: BA psych., Univ. Redlands, 1981; MPA, USC Sch. of Pub. Adminstrn., 1983. Career: field rep. Assemblywoman

Gloria Molina, 56th A.D., East L.A. 1982-84; legis. rev. coord./mgmt. asst. Dept. Water & Power, Los Angeles 1984-85; budget/adminstrv. analyst Chief Adminstrv. Ofcr. City of L.A., 1985-87; asst. chief of staff Lt. Gov. Leo McCarthy, L.A. Dist. Ofc., 1987-89; cons. New Economics for Women (housing devel. pgm.) 1989; asst. v.p. American Savings Bank Comm. Outreach Dept., 1989-; honors: Univ. Redlands sr. of yr. 1981 and pres. Assoc. Students 1980-81; civic bds: Angeles Girl Scout Council (dir. 1984-, Calif. G.S. Council Legis. Com. 1986-88), CSULA Hispanic Support Network 1988-, Comn. Femenil Mexicana Nacional Inc. (pres. 1987-90, outstanding svc. award), E.L.A. Voter Registration & Voter Proj. (1984, 86, 88, outstanding vol. 1984), Bilingual Found. of the Arts (bd. 1989-), Women's Campaign Fund (bd. 1986-); Democrat; R.Cath. Res: 5418 Percy St Los Angeles 90022

LUNDE, DOLORES BENITEZ, teacher; b. Apr. 12, 1929, Honolulu, Hawaii; d. Frank Molero and Matilda (Francisco) Benitez; m. Nuell Carlton Lunde, July 6, 1957; 1 dau. Laurelle b. 1959; edn: BA, Univ. Oregon, Eugene 1951, grad. work 1951-52, USC, 1953-54, Colo. State Univ. 1957-58, CSU Fullerton 1967-68; Calif. tchg. credentials: gen. secondary life, 1952, language devel. specialist, 1990; career: tchr. Brawley Union High Sch. Dist., Brawley, Calif. 1952-55; Fullerton Union High Sch. Dist. 1955-73; tchr. aide Placentia Unified Sch. Dist. 1983-85; tchr. Fullerton Sch. Dist. 1988, Fullerton Union HSD Alternative and Cont. Edn., 1985-91, Fullerton Union High Sch. Dist. 1989-; innovator in tests, tchg. tools and audio-visual aids 25+ yrs.; presenter regional and state convs. 1986-87; advisor internat. & Spanish clubs, La Habra 1965-72; awards: named gift honoree AAUW Fullerton 1985, tchr. of year Fullerton Union HSD 1989; mem: Nat. Edn. Assn., Calif. Tchrs. Assn., Fullerton Secondary Tchrs. Assn., Tchrs. of English to Speakers of Other Languages, AAUW (life mem., ed. 1979-80, corr. sec. 1981-83, pgm. v.p. 1983-84, vol. tchr. 1974-77); Lutheran (Luth. Soc. Svs. vol. 1981-82); rec: singing, folk dancing, guitar, travel; res: 4872 N Ohio Yorba Linda 92686; ofc: Buena Park High School 8833 Academy Dr Buena Park 90621

LUNDE, GREGORY JAMES, management consultant; b. Feb. 27, 1949, Fargo, ND; s. Palmer James and Freda M. L.; m. Sherryl, Jan. 12, 1986; children: Mark b. 1988, Erik b. 1989; edn: BA, Augsburg Coll., 1971; AM, Univ. S. Dak., 1972; MBA, Claremont Graduate Sch., 1983, MA, 1989; PhD, So. Calif. Inst., 1991; profl. desig: cert. mgmt. cons. (CMC), Inst. of Mgmt. Consultants, NY, 1991. Career: quality control analyst 3M Co., St. Paul, Minn. 1972-76; economic planner ND State Planning Div., Bismarck 1976; planning and mgmt. cons. prin., pres. NOR-CON Devel. Corp., ND, 1976-82; systems coordinator Hughes Aircraft Co., Los Angeles 1984-85; dir. of planning Bank of North Dakota, Bismarck 1986; pres. Poly-Centric Strategies II (exec. & MIS cons.), Los Alamitos 1987-93;pres. Colligated Systems (bus. intelligence, mgmt. cons.), Los Alamitos 1993-; instr., history, Jamestown (N.D.) Coll. 1981; awards: Claremont Grad. Sch. univ. fellow 1981-83, tchg. asst. grant Univ. So. Dak. 1971-72; mem: Assn. of MBA Execs., Inst. of Mgmt. Consultants, Cypress C.of C., Los Alamitos C.of C.; publs: Strategic Management and Planning Systems 1988, Bank of ND Strategic Plan 1986, land use manual Town & Country Pgm. 1980, ND Econ. Dev. Strategy 1979-80; rec: running, hunting, fishing. Res: 12100-131 Montecito Rd Los Alamitos 90720 Ofc: Colligated Systems, 12100-131 Montecito Rd Los Alamitos 90720

LUNDQUIST, WEYMAN IVAN, lawyer; b. July 27, 1930, Worcester, Mass.; s. Hilding Ivan and Florence Cecilia (Westerholm) L.; m. Joan Durrell,Sept. 15, 1956 (div. 1977); m. Kathryn E. Taylor, Dec. 28, 1978; children: Weyman b. 1958, Jettora b. 1963, Erica b. 1963, Kirk b. 1965, Derek b. 1985; edn: BA, Dartmouth Coll. 1952; LL.B, Harvard Law Sch. 1955; admitted bar: Mass. 1955, Ak. 1961, Calif. 1963. Career: atty., assoc. Bowditch & Dewey, Worcester, Mass. 1957-60; asst. atty. Office of U.S. Attorney, Mass., Ak., 1960-62; atty., assoc. Heller Ehrman White & McAuliffe, San Francisco 1963-65; v.p., counsel St. Mutual Life Ins. Co., Worcester, Mass. 1965-67; ptnr. Heller Ehrman White & McAuliffe, San Francisco 1967-; Henry Luce vis. prof. environ. studies Dartmouth Coll., N.H. 1980, 84; trustee Natural Resources Defense Council, N.Y. 1982-; awards: Center for Pub. Resources Significant Achievement 1987; mem: Am. Bar Assn. (litigation sect. founder, past chmn., ABA/Soviet Bar Assn. liaison com.), Am. Coll. Trial Lawyers, Lawyers Alliance Nuclear Arms Control (co-founder S.F. chpt.), Am. Antiquarian Soc., Fgn. Rels. Council, People to People Internat. (U.S. advy. com.), Sierra Club, Calif. Tomorrow (past pres., dir. 1977-82), League to Save Lake Tahoe (dir. 1972-88), Swedish Am. C.of C. (dir. 1978-86, pres., dir. 1982-85); author Promised Land (and Other Courthouses Adventures (1987), num. articles pub. in profl. jours.; mil: pvt. 1c. AUS 1955-57; rec: squash, soccer, skiing, running. Res: 3725 Broderick San Francisco 94123 Ofc: 333 Bush St 33rd Flr San Francisco 94104

LUNDSTROM, MARY FRANCES, art curator; b. June 23, 1948, Hollywood; d. Archibald DeNorville and Ivy Kate (Whitworth) Meyer; m. Eric Arthur Lundstrom, June 26, 1971; children: Tara Carina b. 1979; edn: BA art, San Diego State Univ., 1971; numerous art workshops. Career: draftsman Genge Inds., Ridgecrest 1967-68; draftsman, illustrator Naval Weapons Ctr., China Lake 1969-70; subs. tchr. Albuquerque Pub. Sch., N.M. 1971-72; subs. tchr. Kern County High Sch., China Lake 1972-74; real estate sales Coldwell Banker, Ridgecrest

1974-86; art instr. Cerro Coso Comm. Coll., 1986-91; art curator Maturango Museum, Ridgecrest 1986-; free lance artist, 1970-; grants reviewer Inst. of Mus. Svcs. 1993-; awards: fellowship name grant award AAUW, China Lake 1987; juror mixed media show Lancaster (Calif.) Art Mus., 1990; mem: AAUW (1972-, past pres.), High Desert Council of the Arts 1979-, Arts Council of Kern 1986-, Enamel Guild West 1980-, San Diego Enamel Guild 1980-, Enamelist Soc. 1980-, Calif. Assn. of Museums 1986-, Desert Art League (Ridgecrest); Democrat; Episcopalian; rec: art, swimming, travel. Res: 731 W Howell Ave Ridgecrest 93555 Ofc: Maturango Museum 101 E Las Flores Ridgecrest 93555

LUNGREN, DANIEL EDWARD, lawyer; b. Sept. 22, 1946, Long Beach, Calif.; s. John Charles and Lorain Kathleen (Youngberg) L.; m. Barbara Kolls, Aug. 2, 1969; children: Jeffrey Edward, Kelly Christine, Kathleen Marie; edn: AB (cum Laude), Notre Dame Univ., Ind. 1968; post grad., Univ. of So. Calif. Law Sch. 1968-69; JD, Georgetown Univ., Washington, D.C. 1971; admitted Calif. Bar 1972. Career: staff asst. to Senators George Murphy and William Broc 1969-71; spl. asst. to co-chmn., Republican Nat. Comm. & dir., spl. programs 1971-72; assoc., selected as partner, Ball, Hunt, Hart, Brown & Baerwitz, Long Beach 1971-78; mem. 96-97th Cong. from 34th Calif. Dist., and 98-100th Cong. from 42nd Calif. Dist. 1974-89; partner, Diepenbrock, Wulff, Plant & Hannegan, Sacramento 1989-90; elected Atty. Gen., State of Calif. 1990-; Nat. Comm. Representative from Calif. 1989-; awards: Good Samaritan Award, L.A. Council of Mormon Churches 1976; mem: Calif. State Peace Officers Standards & Training Commn. 1991-, Calif. Judicial Council's Commn. on the Future of the Courts 1991-, Conf. of We. Attorneys Gen. 1991-, Nat. Assn. of Attorneys Gen. 1991-, President's Commn. on Model State Drug Laws 1992-; civic: bd. dir. Long Beach Chpt. Am. Red Cross 1976-88; bd. dir. Long Beach Boys Club 1978-88; author: publ. articles in The Journal of the Inst. for Socioeconomic Studies, 1985 and the San Diego Law Review, 1987; co-author: publ. articles in Loyola Law Review, 1984 and UCLA Law Review, 1992; Republican; Roman Catholic; rec: weight lifting, racquetball, bicycling. Ofc: 1515 K Street, #600, Sacramento 95814

LUO, ANNA S., real estate consultant; b. Mar. 26, 1963; d. George Y. and Amy J. (Fine) L.; m. George C. Tan, Jan. 16, 1985; edn: BA, UC Berkeley, 1984; att. M.I.T. Sch. of Arch. 1988-90, MS in R.E. Devel. and Investment, M.I.T. Ctr. for Real Estate, 1991. Career: design team Rasmussen Ingle Anderson Architects & Engrs., San Francisco 1986-87; designer, coordinator Community Design Collaborative, S.F. 1987-88; real estate cons. The Beacon Co., Devel. Gp., Boston 1989; real estate cons. Mass. Exec. Office for Admin. and Fin., Div. Capital Planning and Ops., Boston 1989; real estate cons. Pacific Union Company, San Francisco 1992-; founder, mgr. Delta Omega, S.F., 1986-88; mgr. real estate properties, San Francisco and Burlingame, 1984-; awards: Nat. Honor Soc., S.F. 1977-81, Who's Who Among Am. H.S. Students 1979-81, Blue Chip Co. Award Jr. Achiev. of the Bay Area 1981, Bank of Am. Award 1981, Calif. State Scholar 1981-85, Emerson Award M.I.T. 1988; mem: SFAIA (steering com. Intern Devel. Pgm. 1986-88), MIT/Harvard R.E. Forum 1990-91, The Urban Land Inst. 1990-; rec: travel, swimming, classical piano. Ofc: 2390 39th Ave Ste 2 San Francisco 94116

LUONG, MINH A., university forensics program director and debate coach; b. Apr. 19, 1964, Neptune, N.J.; s. Tri and Jit Kim (Lim) L.; edn: BA rhetoric, UC Berkeley, 1988; MA in speech & comm. studies, San Francisco St. Univ., 1991. Career: fleet sales mgr. Val Strough Co., Oakland 1984-86; fin. mgr. San Rafael BMW, 1987-88; fleet sales mgr. Doten Honda -Acura -Oldsmobile -GMC Truck, Berkeley 1988-90; instr. pub. speaking, debate coach UC Berkeley 1987-, S.F. State Univ. 1989-, dir. forensics pgm. UCB, 1988-; dir. California Invitational, 1988-; awards: nat. champion Lincoln-Douglas Debate, Cross Examination Debate Assn. 1987, Cameron Pagter Award UCLA Debater of Year 1988, Newcomer award, Collegiate Debate Coach of Yr. 1989; mem: Nat. Forensic League (life), Commonwealth Club Calif., Asian Bus. Assn. (life); Republican; Res: PO Box 5695 Hercules 94547

LUST, PETER, JR., microwave engineer; b. Apr. 21, 1960, Montreal, Que.; Can.; came to U.S. 1975, naturalized 1987; s. Peter Clark and Evelyn (Heymanson) L.; Gloria Ruth Bingle, Apr. 5, 1985; children: Peter Alexander III, Elizabeth Ann, Mathew Eric; edn: stu. Lowry Tech. Tng. Ctr., Comm. Coll. A.F., Albuquerque, US Air Force Acad.; BSEE, Pcific Western Univ., 1990. Career: enlisted USAF, 1979, resigned, 1982; computer meterologist Electro Rent, Burbank 1982-84; microwave engr., program mgr. satellite and space shuttle communications systems Transco Products, Camarillo 1984-90, internat. tech. mktg. mgr. 1990-; prin. Electronic Note Company, Port Hueneme, 1984-; cons. satellite & microwave comms., 1984-; awards: Technology award USAF 1980, Discovery award NASA 1987, Internat. Leaders in Achiev. Cambridge; mem: Assn. Old Crows, Channel Islands Health Club; Republican; rec: computer programming, hiking, swimming, model airplanes. Ofc: Electronic Note Co 300 Esplande Dr #931 Oxnard 93030 Ph. 805/981-3931

LUTZ, JEFFREY CHRISTIAN, aerospace engineer; b. Nov. 25, 1959, La Mesa; s. Jimme Christian L. and Grace Evelyn (Weaver) Durreli; m. Stephanie Pearl Aldrich, Nov. 25, 1979; children: Jeremiah b. 1982, Stephan b. 1985; edn:

BS in aerospace engring., San Diego State Univ., 1989. Career: aircraft assembler Teledyne Ryan Aeronautical, San Diego 1985-86, design engr. 1989-; mem. Mensa 1983-, Calif. Historical Gp. 1982-; mil: sr. airman E4 USAF 1979-81; Green; agnostic; rec: living history- Am. Revolution, US Civil War, WWI, WWII. Ofc: Teledyne Ryan Aeronautical 2701 Harbor Dr Dept 340 San Diego 92701-1085

LYKINS, JAY ARNOLD, religious mission founder, president; b. Feb. 13, 1947, Shattuck, Okla.; s. George Eldridge and Lucy Lee (Croom) L.; m. (Mary) Lynn Turner, Jan. 3, 1970; children: Marilee b. 1974, Amy b. 1974, Jason b. 1977; edn: BA, Covenant Coll., 1973; MBA, Kennedy-Western Univ., 1987, PhD, 1988. Career: owner Environment Control, Nashville, Tenn. 1974-78; bus. adminstr. Youth for Christ, Atlanta, Ga. 1978-81; internat. adminstr. Young Life, Colorado Springs, Colo. 1981-86; founder, pres. Global Reach, Pleasanton, Calif. 1982-; mem: Assn. of MBA Execs., Ctr. for Entrepreneurial Mgmt., Internat. Council for Small Bus., Am. Consultants League; club: Nob Hill CC, Snellville, Ga. (pres. 1980-81); author: Values In the Marketplace (1982), 200+ tng. manuals re bus./Biblical principles (1982-), thesis: Islamic Bus. (1988); mil: E5 USN 1966-68; Republican; Presbyterian; rec: scuba, biking. Res: 7897 Meadowbrook Ct Pleasanton 94588 Ofc: Global Reach PO Box 234 Pleasanton 94566

LYLES, GARY DONALD, safety engineer; b. Jan. 24, 1942, Los Angeles; s. Albert Clayton and Ada Elizabeth (Moore) L.; m. Kathleen Ann Richards, Aug. 15, 1981; edn: BS psychology, Univ. Md., Balt. 1963; BA sociology, Air Univ., USAF, 1967; cert. environ. health & safety law, UCLA, 1991; reg. profl. safety engr. Calif. 1988. Career: v.p. and gen. mgr. Paramount Television, Century City 1972-80; asst. gen. mgr. Greyhound Lines, L.A. 1980-85; safety engr. LA City Dept. Water & Power, LA 1985-; chmn. bd. VSF Inc., LA 1969-78; awards: Commercial commendn. Acad. TV Arts & Scis. 1978; mem: Public Agency Mgmt. Assn. (pres. 1991-), So., Calif. Indsl. Safety Soc. 1988-, Calif. Safety Congress 1985-, Am. Soc. Safety Engrs. 1989-; civic bds: Norco Mounted Police (pub. affairs ofcr. 1992-), bd. dirs. State Coalition Senior Citizens LA 1974-80, ABC School, LA 1970-78, commr. Norco Dept. Parks & Rec. 1978-81, commr. Dept. Urban Redevel. Long Beach 1983-85; club: Shoreline Yacht Club (Long Beach); mil: lt. US Navy 1960-63, Flotilla cmdr. USCG Aux. 1991-; Republican; Prot.; rec: yachting, polo, travel. Res: 5206 Tierra Bonita Dr Whittier 90601 Ofc: L.A. Dept. Water & Power 123 S Figueroa St Rm 300 Los Angeles 90012

LYNCH, JOHN WILLIAM, JR., company chairman; b. April 23, 1927, Detroit, Mich.; s. John William and Shirley Olive (Block) L.; m. Dixie June Kirby, Aug. 20, 1949; children: John b. 1950, Daniel b. 1952, Theodore b. 1954, David b. 1962; edn: AA, Coll. of Sequoias, 1949; Stanford Grad. Sch. Bus. 1953-54; BA, San Jose St. Univ., 1951. Career: exec. Westinghouse, Sunnyvale 1951-54; exec. U.S. Steel, Pittsburg Wks. 1954-67; exec. Whittaker Corp., L.A. 1967-72; Hergenrather & Co. 1972-73; U.S. Postal Service, Wash. D.C. 1973-76; chmn. bd. J. W. Lynch & Associates, Inc., Newport Beach 1978-; pres. Lynch & Co., Orange; chmn. Clarity Capital Corp., Orange 1985-; dir. Mederi Med. Systems Inc., Tustin 1988-93; dir. Trans World Express, Costa Mesa 1985-88; awards: Air Force Assn. Nat. Pres.'s Citation 1990, Nat. Exceptional Service Award 1989, Nat. Medal of Merit 1988, listed Who's Who in the West, Who's Who in California; mem: Calif. Air Force Assn. (pres. 1988-90, chmn. 1990-91), Aircraft Owners & Pilots Assn., Stanford Grad. Sch. Bus. Alumni Assn.; civic: Duell Voc. Inst. Ind. Advy. Council 1961-64, nom. Concord Young Man of the Year 1958, Contr Costa Cty. Taxpayers Assn. 1961-64, United Way (loaned exec. 1961-63), BSA (inst. rep. 1962-66), Concord Personnel Board (chmn. 1963-67), Chatsworth C.of C. (dir. 1967-69), Mt. Vernon, VA Youth Athletic League (dir., baseball, basketball coach 1974-76), Newport Beach C.of C. (dir. 1982-83), E. Clampus Vitus, Rotary Internat. (dir. Newport Beach Sunrise Rotary Club 1990- dir. 1991-, pres. 1992-93), Gen. Curtis E. LeMay Found. (Orange cty. chmn. 1991-93, chmn. LeMay Golf Scholarship Tour. 1993); mem: Columbia Toastmasters (pres. 1958); Holbrook Hgts. Comm. Assn. (dir. 1956-58), Pacific Light Opera Assn. 1956-66, N. Calif. Indsl. Rel. Council (ch. mem. 1963-67), Chatsworth Club 1967-69, Pers. & Indsl. Rel. Assn. 1967-71, Fresno Rotary Club 1977-78, Fresno Exchange club 1977-78, Dick Richards Breakfast Club, Town Hall of Calif. 1967-88, Commonwealth Club of S.F. 1959-75, Nat. Rifle Assn., candidate Calif. State Board of Equalization 1978, nom. Calif. Pub. Utilities Commn. 1978, Air Force Assn., nat. v.p. -Far W. Reg. 1993); mil: USAAC 1944-46; Republican (pres. Concord YR 1958-60); Prot.; rec: flying, golf, hunting. Address: Newport Beach 92660

LYNCH, MARGARET MARY-MAHONEY, hotel executive, financial executive, civic worker, socialite; b. Sept. 8, 1920, San Francisco; d. Jeremiah John (financier and civic leader) and Suzanne (McKeen) Mahoney; m. Joseph David Lynch, June 10, 1945; children: Timothy J. M. b. 1952, Suzanne Marie; edn: dipl. St. Paul's Sch., S.F., 1940; cert. in realty & hotel mgmt., CSU San Francisco, 1967; CPM, Cert. Property Mgr., Calif. Assn. Realtors, 1988. Career: accounts clk. Mahoney Estates Corp., San Francisco;, 1940-45; property mgr. Mahoney Estates Group, 1945-, mng. ptnr./owner, 1950, gen. ptnr./chief fin. ofcr., 1950-62; owner/ptnr./dir. finance Hotel Pierre, 1962-78; majority owner, ptnr. Lynch Corp. Group, 1978-, chief fin. ofcr. 1985-, gen. ptnr. Lynch Realty & Investments Corp.; honors: exec. of yr. Nat. Assn. Female Execs., S.F. 1990, biog. listings in

Who's Who in Am. Women, World's Leading & Most Influential Women, Personalities of U.S. & World, Am.'s 2000 Notable Women, Who's Who World Intellectuals, Register Disting. Intl. Leadership, Intl. Social Register, Am. Biog. Inst. Woman of Year 1991, Intl. Order of Merit award Intl. Biog. Ctr., Cambridge, Eng., Dictionary of Internat. Biogr. (23rd) named 1 of 10 most Prominent Women Leaders; mem: Calif. Hotel & Motel Assn./ S.F. (exec. policy com. 1978), Calif. Assn. Realtors (cons. 1988-92), Calif. Credit / Metro Assn. Sacto. (bd. dirs. 1970-92), NAFE, San Francisco C.of C. (policy coms. 1986-), Bay Area Council (social coms. 1988-), U.S.-China Business Council (fin. com. 1989-); clubs: Palo Alto Womens' (social com. 1973-), San Francisco Womens' (pub. rels. com. 1982-), Villa Taverna (social coms. 1990-); publs: research, essays and jour. articles re hotel & motel mgmt., legal aspects of realty & hotel mgmt., social protocol & entertainment (1986, 90, 91); Republican; R.Cath.; rec: theatre, opera, ballet, gardening. Res: 501 Forest Ave Palo Alto 94301 Ofc: Hotel Pierre Group - Lynch Corp. 540 Jones St Ste 210 San Francisco 94102

LYNCH, TIMOTHY JEREMIAH MAHONEY, lawyer, real estate holding co. executive, civic leader; b. June 10, 1952, San Francisco; s. Joseph D. and Margaret Mary (Mahoney) L.; edn: MS, JD, Golden Gate Univ., 1981; MA, PhD, Univ. S.F., 1983; adv. law degrees Inter-Am. Acad. of Internat. Law, 1988, Harvard Ctr. for Internat. Affairs, 1989; cert. atty.-arb. Am. Arbitration Assn., Calif. St. Bar, Internat. Bar, London Ct. of Arbitration; Harvard Bus. Sch. Adv. Mgmt. Pgm., 1991. Career: pres. Lynch Real Estate Co., San Francisco, 1978-82; CEO and chmn. Lynch Realty & Investment Corp. 1985-; chmn., mng. dir. law firm T. Lynch & Assocs., P.C. 1987-; CEO and chmn. Lynch Holdings Group (leverage buy-outs, acquisitions in banking, petroleum, electronics, auto. ind., agric. land, hotels, properties) 1991-; sr. ptnr., corporate counsel L.A. Ctr. for Internat. Commercial Arbitration and Municipal Securities Rule-Making Bd., W.D.C.; appt. Pres. Bush's Advy. Commn. on Domestic Economic and Social Issues Priorities 1991-; arbitrator: Iran-U.S. Claims Tribunal, The Hague 1989-; advy. bd. J.P. Morgan & Co. 1993-; dir. Morgan Stanley Internat. Finance Group; mem. Arb. Panels Pacific Coast Stock Exchange, NASD; mem. Nat. Assn. Corporate Directors (c.e.o.'s pub. policy conf. mem. 1992-); corp. mem. U.S.- China Bus. Council, W.D.C. 1987-; bd. councillors Fgn. Svc. Inst., U.S. St. Dept., W.D.C. 1988-; chmn. U.S.- Middle East Relations Com., W.D.C. 1989-; chmn. legis. inv. com. Calif. Council for Internat. Trade, 1988-; chmn. Calif. State Commn. on Internat. Edn. & Culture, 1990-91; corp. mem. 1991-; Trilateral Commn., Conference Board, Nat. Assn. of Corp. Dirs., Fin. Execs. Inst., World Bus. Acad., Council on Fgn. Relations, Calif. Council on Internat. Trade (PAC); mem. Special Projects on U.S.-Vietnam Trade/Econ. Normalization Council, Persian Gulf, Ctr. for Internat. Devel. Policy, W.D.C.; awards: Presdl. Order of Merit for outstanding civic leadership and svc. to nation 1991, civic leader of yr. Downtown Assn. S.F. 1986, contbns. to theatre arts S.F. Theatrical Assn. 1989, Am. Law Inst./ABA Special Award for Outstanding Service to Law Profession 1990, Georgetown Univ. Sch. of Fgn. Service ldrship com. and 1 of 5 outstanding bus. ldrs. in Am. 1992, Euro Money Publ. list of Corporate World's Top Lawyers in field of internat. corp. law 1992, listed Intl. Social Register, Who's Who in Am. Law, Who's Who in Am., Who's Who in U.S. Leaders, Who's Who Emerging Leaders of Am., Who's Who in World, Who's Who Internat., London (55th edit., 1991/2), Who's Who Worldwide 1993, Who's Who in Am. Bus., Dictionary of Internat. Biogr. (named 1 of 20 most prominent leaders 1993), Dir. of Litigation Attorneys, Dir. of Corporate Counsel (ABA/ Prentiss-Hall), Dir. of World Arbitrators (Parker Sch., Columbia Sch. of Law), Dir. of Trial Lawyers, Dir. of Trial Judges (ATL), Dir. of Alternative Dispute Resolution Specialists (Soc. Profls. in Dispute Resolution, W.D.C.), Dir. of Am. Bank Attys. (Capron Publs.); recipient Golden State Award for outstanding leadership & civic service to Calif., Award of Honor for exceptional achiev.; elected Am. Acad. of Diplomacy (W.D.C.), Nat. Acad. of Conciliators Award for Contbns. to Commercial Dispute Settlement, Nat. Acad. of Arbitrators Univ. Mich. Bus. Sch., British Inst. of Internat. & Comparative Law (U.K.), Practicing Law Inst. (N.Y., S.F.); mem: Internat. Bar Assn., Am. Trial Lawyers Assn., S.F. Trial Lawyers Assn., Internat. Law Assn., S.F. Realtors Assn., Inter-Am. Bar Assn., Am. Fgn. Law Assn., Am. Soc. of Internat. Law (W.D.C.), W.D.C. Fgn. Law Soc., Soc. of Profls. in Dispute Resolution, Al-Shaybani Soc. of Internat. Law, Westchester-Fairfield Corporate Counsel Assn., Am. Assn. for Advancement of Slavic Studies, Nat. Inst. of Soviet & E.European Studies, Middle East Inst. (W.D.C.), Am. Polit. Sci. Assn., Asia Soc. (NY, NY), Univ. S.F. Alumni Assn., Middle East Studies Assn. (Univ. Ariz.), European Comm. Studies Assn., Latin Am. Studies Assn., Japan Soc. of N.Calif. (S.F.), Internat. Platform Assn.; civic bds: Connacher Gal. of Late Modern Euro. and Am. Art, Wash. D.C. Opera Soc. (trustee), Downtown Assn. of S.F. (chmn. Bay Area Economic Forum), Bay Area Council, S.F. C.of C. Downtown Assn. S.F. (bd.), S.F. Planning & Urban Res. Assn. (chmn. city policy groups 1984), Internat. Vis. Ctr. (advy. bd. 1987-, citizen diplomatic corps), Heritage Found. (elected Pres.'s Club, named Most Influential Conservative Leader in U.S. 1991), Ford Found. - UNESCO Human Rights Edn. Fund (NY, NY), UN Fund for Human Rights & Justice, World Affairs Council of No. Calif., Boys Town of Italy Org. (co-ch. Exec. Dinner com.), Jesuit Seminary Assn. (elected Sr. Fellow, Minister of Scapular: Order of Our Lady of Mount Carmel), Christo del Rey Monastery (elected Inst. of Patristic & Byzantine Studies; installed Ancient Clerics of Pope St. Sylvester III of Rome, Vatican,

Italy for leadership and service to Cath. Community of U.S. and world), Am. Bus Roundtable 1993, Com. for Econmic Devel. (assoc. mem.); clubs: Commercial, Commonwealth, Calif. Yacht, Pebble Beach Tennis, Villa Taverna, Palm Beach Yacht, Saks Fifth Avenue Fashion; numerous publs. in areas of internat. law, trade, and fgn. rels.; Republican (Rep. Senatl. Inner Circle); R.Cath.; rec: music, fine arts, yachting, corp. Learjet. Ofc: Lynch Realty Investment Corp. 540 Jones St Ste 201 San Francisco 94102

LYND, GRANT ALBERT, lawyer; b. Aug. 21, 1949, Los Angeles; s. John Joseph and Janet (Grant) L.; m. Amy Suehiro, May 9, 1985; children: Shenandoah Grant b. 1969, Amy Janet b. 1986; edn: AA police sci., Mt. San Antonio Coll. 1969; BA, CSU Fullerton 1971, MA in hist., 1978, MPA, 1980; JD, Loyola Univ. 1984; Calif. Std. Sec. tchg. cred. 1972; cert. UCLA Ctr. for Labor Res. and Edn., 1973; cert. law enforcement; admitted Calif. St. Bar, US Ct. Appeals (9th cir.), US Dist. Ct. (Cent. dist.). Career: police cadet Covina Police Dept., 1968-70; staff Calif. St. Univ. Police Dept., CSUF, 1970-75; employee rels. rep. (labor grievance and arbitration litigation) Calif. St. Employees' Assn. SEIU-AFL-CIO, 1975-79; dir. acad. rights div. Calif. Faculty Assn., NEA-CTA-CSEA-AAUP, 1979-84; pvt. practice atty., ptnr. Lynd & Suehiro, Westminster 1984-89; Law Offices of Grant A. Lynd, 1989-; varsity wrestling coach Santiago High Sch. 1972-73; law clerk L.A. Co. Superior Ct. 1983; honors: Phi Alpha Theta 1975, Dept. of Justice study grant 1970-71; mem. Am., Calif., Orange Co., Los Angeles Co. bar assns., Calif. Trial Lawyers Assn. Res: 3745 Prestwick Los Angeles Ofc: 14340 Bolsa Chico Rd Ste B Westminster 92683

LYNN, BERT DANIEL, airline executive, ret.; b. Dec. 22, 1916, Cleveland Ohio; s. Abraham and Helen (Bellick) L.; m. June Beckstrand, June 4, 1946; children: Karen b. 1948, Gary b. 1953; edn: BA magna cum laude, Western Reserve Univ. 1938. Career: aviation editor Steel Mag., Cleveland, Oh. 1938-39; exec. asst. to v.p. pub. rels., Douglas Aircraft Co., Santa Monica 1940-47; gen. mgr. Lynn-Western Advt. Agency, Los Angeles 1948-49; dir. advt. and pub. rels. Western Airlines 1950-64, v.p. advt. and sales promotion 1965-82; ret.; p.t. mktg. instr. Brigham Young Univ., Provo, Utah 1982-84, CSU Long Beach 1982-84; mktg. cons., Laguna Niguel 1986-; dir. publicity and promotion Hill Cumorah Pageant, Palmyra, N.Y. 1988-89; honors: Phi Beta Kappa, Western Reserve Univ. Soc. 1938, L.A. Olympic Games Citizens Advy. Commn. 1983-84, Air Force Assn. Airpower award 1951, Adviews Socrates award 1963, 64, 68, 69; mem: Air Force Assn. (western regional v.p. 1950), Calif. Tourism Commn. 1965, Assoc. Latter-Day Media Artists (2d. v.p. 1985), L.A. Better Bus. Bur. (dir. 1955-56), Visitor & Convention Bur. L.A. (chmn. advt. com. 1980-81); mil: major USAF 1944-46, USAFR 1950-53; Republican; Mormon; rec: archaeology. Res: Laguna Niguel 92677

LYON, IRVING, biomedical researcher; b. May 10, 1921, Los Angeles; s. Charles and Bella (Kvitky) L.; m. Harriette Goodman, Oct. 16, 1948; children: David b. 1950, Charles b. 1953, Lawrence b. 1956; edn: AB, UCLA, 1942, MA, 1949; PhD physiol. (mammalian, gen.), UC Berkeley, 1952; grad. studies USC 1947-48. Career: research asst. endocrinol. UCLA, 1941; lab. asst. and tchg. asst., mammal anat. & gen. embryol., USC, 1947-49; res. lab. asst. physiol. dept. UC Berkeley, 1949-52; res. biochem. The Toni Co. Med. Dept., Chgo. 1954-58; asst. prof. biol. chem. and res. assoc. orthopedic surg., Univ. Ill., Chgo. 1958-62; assoc. prof. biochem. dept. The Chicago Med. Sch., Chgo. 1962-67; prof. biol. Bennington (Vt.) Coll., 1967-72; sr. visitor Inst. Biol. Chem., Univ. Copenhagen, Denmark 1972-74; special cons. Calif. State Energy Resources Conservation & Devel., L.A. 1975; indep. cons. environ. health & nutrition, L.A. 1975-89; asst. res. physiologist UCLA Med. Sch., p.t. 1979-81; res. asst. UCLA Med. Sch. and res. biochemist US Veterans Adminstrn., L.A. 1981-89, ret.; awards: Rockefeller Found. Fellow, Harvard Sch. Pub. Health 1952-54, Soc. Sigma Xi (pres. Chgo. Med. Sch. chapt. 1967-68), NSF res. fellow, Urbana, Ill. 1970, NSF grant partaicipant, Amherst, Mass. (1971, 72), vis. investigator Jackson Lab., Bar Harbor, Me. 1971, invited lectures various univs. and res. insts. (1963, 4 in 1968); Fellow Internat. Coll. Appl. Nutr., L.A. 1976-89, Fellow AAAS 1967, mem. Am. Physiol. Soc., N.Y., Acad. Scis.; civic: W.O. Douglas Outdoor Classroom (docent Santa Monica Mtns. 1989-), Audubon Soc. (docent Ballona Wetlands, Playa Del Rey 1991-); co-inventor w/wife Bile Acid Emulsions (pat. 1978); author, contbr. 46+ tech. publs. in field of nutritional biochem. (1952-89), 18 energy resources reports (1975); mil: capt. US Army 1942-46, Indep.; rec: classical music, painting, ceramics, ecol./environ. Res: 708-C Grant St Santa Monica 90405-1221

MA, FAI, professor mechanical engineering; b. Aug. 6, 1954, Canton, China, came to U.S. 1977, naturalized 1988; s. Rui-Qi and Shao-Fen (Luo) M.; edn: BS, Univ. Hong Kong, 1977; MS, PhD, Calif. Inst. Tech., 1981. Career: senior research engr. Weidlinger Assocs., Menlo Park, Calif. 1981-82; research fellow IBM, Yorktown Hts., N.Y. 1982-83; senior engr. Standard Oil Co., Cleveland, Ohio 1983-86; assoc. prof. mech. engring. UC Berkeley, 1986-; vis. scholar Oxford Univ., England 1992, Univ. of Stuttgart, Germany 1993; awards: NSF presdl. young investigator grantee 1987, Humboldt Fellowship of Germany 1992, grantee of various agencies 1987-; mem. ASME; publs: Probabilistic Analysis 1983, Computational Mechanics 1989, contbr. articles to profl. jours. Ofc: Mech. Engrg. Dept. Univ. California Berkeley 94720

MABEE, SANDRA IVONNE, musician, clergy; b. Jan. 13, 1955, Puerto Rico; d. Nelson Custodio Noriega and Norma Ruth Eiseman Lee; m. Carl David Mabee, Aug. 2, 1980; children: Rebecca Lee b. 1985; edn.: MA in music, Calif. State Univ., Hayward 1985; BM in music, S.F. Conservatory of Music 1983; BA in biblical studies, Patten Coll. 1977; pastor, dir. of music ministries, Evangelical Ch. Alliance 1991; career: instr., Patten Coll. 1980-88; chairperson, prof. studies div., Patten Coll. 1986-88; minister of music, El Cerrito Christian Ctr. 1988-91; music inst., Hayward Christian Sch. 1989-91; pastor, dir. music ministries, Trinity Church 1992-93; pastor, Unveiled Ch. Ministries, dir. of Music Ministries 1993-; seminar inst., Landmark Sch. of Ministries 1989-91; music inst., Landmark Acad. 1991; adjudicator, Singspiration 1989; principle tympanist, Women's Philharmonic, S.F. 1980-; concerto soloist, Redwood Symphony, Redwood City 1988; awards: scholarship, S. F. Conservatory of Music 1980-83; Internat. Who's Who in Music 1989, Who's Who in the West 1991; Proclamation for Service to Tchg. 1989; 5000 Personalities of the World 1990; compiled seminar Praise and Worship 1990; Women's Philharmonic recording on Koch, 1992; Protestant. Res.: 2153 Santa Clara #C Alameda 94501

MACALLISTER, DONALD, marketing co. president, city official; b. Nov. 26, 1932, Hollywood, Calif.; s. Donald and Ruth (Waidlich) MacA.; m. Marilyn Jean Simmons, Sept. 25, 1955; children: Denise b. 1956, Gayle b. 1960, Michelle b. 1963; edn: AA, Pasadena City Coll. 1958; CSU Los Angeles, 2-1/2 yrs.; grad. (top 10%), USN Aviation Prep. Sch. and Electronics Sch. 1950. Career: electronics tech. Collins Radio, Burbank 1954-57; engrg. prodn. mgr. C.A. Rypinski Co., Pasadena 1957-59; mgr. planning and sch. Wianco Engrg. Co., Pasadena 1959-60; sales engr. A-F Sales Engrg. Inc., Pasadena 1960-65; ops. mgr. No. Andros Devel. Co., Bahamas 1965-67; reg. & internat. sales mgr. Duncan Electronics, Costa Mesa 1967-69; v.p., A-F Sales Engrg. Inc., Pasadena 1969-83; founder/pres. Seevid Inc., Huntington Beach 1983-; dir. Huntington Nat. Bank 1982-; elected City Council Huntington Bch. 1978-86, 87-92, mayor 1979-80, 82; mem: Public Cable-TV Auth. 1978-86, 87-92, chmn. 1981, commr. Harbors, Beaches & Parks Commn. Orange Co. 1983-86, commr. John Wayne Airport, O.C. 1986-91, dir. Huntington Bch. Conf. & Visitor Bur. 1989-; honors: Outstanding Jaycee Costa Mesa 1968, H.B. High Sch. P.T.A. hon. service award and HBHS Citizen of the Year 1974; mem: Electronics Representatives Assn., Soc. for Information Display, Am Soc. for Indsl. Security; civic: H.B. Chamber of Commerce (dir. 1987-88), Elks, Huntington Valley Boys & Girls Club (dir. 1982-86), BSA (area chmn. 1987-88); bd. trustees H.B. Union High Sch. Dist. (1976-79, pres. 1978-79), H. B. 4th of July Parade & Fireworks (pres. 1987-88), trustee H.B. Int. Surfing Mus. 1993-; mil: aviation electronics tech. 3/c USN 1951; Republican; Prot.; rec: politics, woodworking, photog., computers. Res: 1121 Park St Huntington Beach 92648 Ofc: Seevid Inc., 15178 Transistor Ln Huntington Beach 92649

MAC ALPIN, REX NERE, physician, professor emeritus; b. Apr. 25, 1932, Glendale. s. Frederic and Christine C. (Wright) MacA.; m. Carol Elizabeth White, June 22, 1957; children: Anne b. 1962, David. b. 1964; edn: Harvard Coll. 1949-51; BA, Pomona Coll. 1953; MD, UCSF 1957; cert. Am. Bd. Internal Medicine 1965. Career: intern, resident UCSF 1957-60; prof. medicine, cardiology UCLA 1963-88, prof. emeritus 1988-; 100+ articles pub. in sci. jours. 1954-93; mil: lt. cmdr. USNR 1961-63; rec: tennis. Ofc: University of California Division of Cardiology 10833 Le Conte Ave Los Angeles 90024-1679

MACCAULEY, HUGH BOURNONVILLE, stockbroker, banker; b. March 12, 1922, Mt. Vernon, NY; s. Morris Baker and Alma Orcutt (Gardiner) MacC.; m. Felice Cooper, Dec. 2, 1980; edn: Rutgers Univ. 1939-40; Texas Christian Univ. 1948-50; Omaha Univ. 1957-59. Career: acct. exec. Dean Witter, San Bernardino 1974-79; v.p. Great American Securities, San Bernardino 1980-; chmn. bd. Desert Community Bank, Victorville 1980-; chmn. bd. KIST Corp., Riverside 1982-87; dir., chmn. fin. com. Air Force Village West Inc. 1986-88; chmn. bd. Gen & Mrs. Curtis E. LeMay Found., 1988-; mem: Daedalian Soc., Riverside Rotary (dir.); club: Victoria CC; mil: mem. Essex Troop, 102nd Cavalry N.J. Nat. Guard 1940-42, capt. US Army 1943-48, col. US Air Force 1949-73, decorated Legion of Merit w/o.l.c. Air Medal w/2 o.l.c., Air Force Commdn. w/3 o.l.c.; Republican; Presbyterian; rec: golf, aviation, equestrian. Res: 1630 Monroe St Riverside 92504 Ofc: Great American Securities, Inc. 334 W Third St Ste 201 San Bernardino 92401

MACDONALD, DONALD KEITH, inventor, electronics co. president; b. May 20, 1944, Annapolis, Md.; s. Frank Wadsworth and Henrietta Maria (Scott) MacD.; edn: AA, Foothill Coll.; MD, Harvard, 1975, Psychiatrist, 1980; computer degree, Stanford Univ., 1990. Career: chem. tech. res. US Geol. Survey, Menlo Park 1963-70; inventor/mfr. Puzzlepaper (US patent 1970), 1968-; inventor, owner MacDonald Co., MacDonald Controls and Schematic Control, 1967-; owner High Tech Esoteric HiFi and Video Stores (Century Stereo TM), San Jose; recording engr./prod. Neely Plumb (TM) 1960-, recording studio in Sonora, Calif.; owner MacDonald Play Art Co., Inc., Sonora 1991-; Calendar Prodns., Memphis, Tn. (will print old year and new year calendars w/new or old H.S. or coll. photos by satellites/Lockheed, pat. 1991); sole owner MacDonald Bank (F.R.B.) 1988-; owner MacDonald-Cleworth Publishing, Hollywood 1991-; sales dealer Goya & Martin banjo's & guitars by word pgm. on phone & credit card verbal ESS buying & selling by access codes (AT&T, IBM, APPLE, H.P.), also distbr. (wholesale, retail) Masterpiece Art canvass, signed Fine Art prints; mgr., Isle of Skye Brand Co.; prin., The Good Catalog Co. and Q.V.C.; num. inventions include Puzzlepaper- Puzzlemate TM, Puzzlebook TM (1960), programmable mirrors & power seat (for Ford), Abstract Painting & Woodwork Desk-Table & Lamp (1970), Presidential Phone (1970), Two-Conductor Remote Switching and Transmitting Control System (pat. 1971), Indicator and Shutoff for Cartridge Type Tape Recorders; trademarked inventions include- Playwrite Play FM, PlayToy, Play Art, Play Press, Play Sport, (1986-88), Play Show Mate (1991), product Play BodyLotion by Vidal Sassoon (1991); Proton surgery & res. to de-age (pat. 1991); DI Galog TM recording & playback for hi-fi audio close to C.D. quality on reg. Phillips cassette (pat. 1991, lic. to Warner Comm. & Chrysler Flextronics Baby Car Stereo 1992, lic. to Playboy for Neely Plumb TM Art. & FTD Florists to sell, also GEO, dealers); for IBM: Laser Disc Programmable Record Player, Compact Disc Case, design of case Logic Portable Laser Disc Cases: Variable Rate, Digital TV and Stereo FM Computersound, 35mm Color or Black in White Slide,w/ Osciliscopic Info. circ. print code for music or video multiplexed, playback with no moving parts (IBM, H.P., & Kodak) pat. appls. pending; Right Eye to brain & systems to read as compatible music (sent to Harvard and IBM, 1970), system of typing- by moving fingers on a surface- to a phone or FM holograph of brainwave to satellites for bdcst. FM Radio system (IBM Brainal Computers 1974), Porkie Pine Navy Stero Project (1970); recording by feedback to Hi Fi speakers or secret systems (Neely Plumb TM, 1960s, RCA); DAT Digital Audio Tape & compatible verbal & written patent to produce with aid of main frame computer a video monitor picture of what eyes see as stored human brainal computer memory (lic. to Ford, IBM, H.P., Kodak); Verbal & written digital & analoge fractial stereo & multitrack multiplex code for FM and TV bdcstg. (pat. 1989, lic. McIntosh Labs, RCA, CBS, IBM); publ. original "Play Art" TM "Children's Stickback Puzzlepaper" TM "Puzzlebook" TM "by Neely Plumb" TM DKMD (c. 1989 Puzzart Co.); "Sunset Valley" TM; "New Town" TM; Democrat; Citizens Beyond War (presdl. cand. 1980, 83, 88, 92); R.Cath.; rec: hi-fi, electronics. Ofc: MacDonald Controls 20400 Brook Dr Sonora 95370

MACDONALD, JOHN, county supervisor; b. Oct. 17, 1921, Palisade, Colo.; s. Joseph and Lillian Mae (Shawhan) M.; m. Gloria, Apr. 10, 1949; children: Kirk b. 1955, Erick b. 1957, Michael b. 1960; edn: AA, Oceanside-Carlsbad Jr. Coll., BA and MA, CSU Humboldt, EdD, UCLA. Career: coll. dean of Extended Day Div. Oceanside-Carlsbad Jr. Coll., 1957-61; actg. supt., asst. supt. Oceanside/Carlsbad H.S. Dist., 1961-63; supt./pres. Mira Costa Community Coll. Dist., 1963-82; elected mem., dep. mayor Oceanside City Council, 1982-86; elected supr. 5th dist. San Diego Co. Bd. Suprs., 1987-, mem. CSAC (chmn. growth mgmt. and land use subcom.), LEAD Advy. Com., North S.D. Co. Advy. Council; awards: headliner of yr. S.D. Press Club 1986, man of yr. BECA Found. 1987, Nat. Com. for Employer Support of the Guard and Reserve 1987; civic bds: Mira Costa Theatre Arts Found., Mira Costa Coll. Found. (bd.), Spartan Sports Found., Rotary, BECA Found.; mil: radioman 1/c USN 1942-45; Republican; Episcopal; rec: sports. Res: 1725 Cassidy St Oceanside 92054 Ofc: San Diego County 1600 Pacific Hwy Rm 335 San Diego 92101

MACDONALD, JOHN KENYON, naval officer, business executive, state and county legislator; b. June 15, 1916, Pasadena; s. John Forrest and Lois Helen (Warren) MacD.; m. Helen Louise Sweat, June 14, 1947 (dec. 1958); m. Leslie Bune Hodge, May 30, 1968; children: Stuart b. 1948, Stephen b. 1950, Scott b. 1955; edn: BS bus. USC, 1939. Career: dist. mgr. Witt Ice & Gas Co., 1940-41; fleet sales mgr. James E. Waters Dodge and Plymouth, 1946-51; pres., gen. mgr. Ken MacDonald Chevrolet Inc., Ojai 1955-60; owner "Mr. Transportation" Ventura 1958-62; county supr. Ventura Co. Bd. Supervisors 1961-67, 1977-81, chmn. 1962, 65, 79; state assemblyman Calif. Legislature, Sacto. 1967-76; commr. Area Housing Authority, Ventura Co., Camarillo 1986-89; superior ct. referee Ventura Co. 1964-65; superior ct. receiver 1965; honors: USC Skull & Dagger Soc., L.A. Ephebian Soc.; mem: Ojai Valley Retired Profl. Businessmen (past pres.), Am. Legion (past commdr.), Masons, Scottish Rite, Rotary Internat. (Paul Harris Fellow, Ojai bd. dirs. 1978-79); mil: lt. cmdr. USNR 1941-58, active duty 1941-45, 1951-52; Democrat; Presbyterian; rec: boating, landscaping, geneaology. Address: Ojai 93023

MACH, MARTIN HENRY, chemist; b. Feb. 10, 1940 NY, NY; s. William Leon and Marcia (Cohen) M.; m. Nada L. Mach, June 15, 1965 (div. 1974); 1 child: Alissa L. b. 1973; edn: academic, Bronx H.S. of Sci., NY, NY, 1957; BS, City Coll. of NY, 1961; MA, Clark Univ., Worcester, Mass., 1965; PhD, UC Santa Cruz, 1973. Career: assoc. scientist Polaroid Corp., Cambridge, Mass., 1965-69; mem. tech. staff Aerospace Corp., El Segundo, Calif., 1973-81; chief dept. scientist TRW Systems, Redondo Beach, Calif., 1981-; mem: Sigma Xi, 1977-. Ofc: TRW, Bldg. 01/2030, 1 Space Park Dr., Redondo Beach 90278

MACHADO, MARIO J., television broadcaster, producer; b. Apr. 22, 1935, Shanghai, China; s. Carlos Jacinto M.; edn: British pub. sch., Shanghai (multilingual: Portuguese, 2 Chinese dialects); St. Johns Mil. Acad., L.A.; St. Francis Xavier Coll; Career: with IBM five yrs.; controller nat. company; creator/copub. Soccer Corner (1st Amer. soccer mag.); founder/pres. Specials' Ink, Sports

Inc., Primo and Trident Publs., MJM Communications, ICVC and EMMI Ink; profl. bdcstr. 1967-; Host, nat. syndicated series MEDIX, KRLA Connection, Good Day LA, and Calif. People (KTTV-Metromedia); news reporter/anchorman KNXT (CBS) Los Angeles; co-host Noontime Daily KNXT (CBS); analyst for sporting events, KHJ-TV, L.A., 1967-; commentator L.A. Olympics '84 (ABC-TV net.); voice of soccer for CBS-TV Network, 1968, 76; World Cup Soccer Championships bdcst. Mex. 1970, Ger. 1974, Argentina 1978, Spain 1982 ABC-TV; host, Star Soccer, English PBS netwk.; bdcst. 6 yrs. Football League Cup Final, Wembley, 1977; host, The Best of the World Cup, Spanish Intl. Netwk. Argentinian Soccer/Syn.; host weekly series It Takes All Kinds, KNXT; host for Asian comm., Sunset series; host AMA - Cont. Medical Education; in-flt. narrator, TWA's Executive Report, American Airlines, Western Airlines, Singapore Airlines; narrator indsl. film/video tapes; movie credits incl: Blue Thunder, Scarface, King Kong, Brian's Song, Oh God, St. Elmo's Fire, Robocop I, II & III; guest appearances episodic TV; voice of Virginia Slims Tennis Championships, L.A.; co-prod. w/Doron Kauper, docu. on Irving Stone, docu. on Fire Safety; prod. Internat. Stars in Concert and Una Serata Italiana (for Internat. Student Center, UCLA); prod. World Song Fest. in America, and Golden Gate to Spruce Goose Chase; prod: Bev. Hills St. Patricks Day Parade, 1985, 86; El Grito Parade, 1986; Offc'l Spanish Language of TV Rose Parade, 1987; Pet Parade 1987; Jimmie Awards, AAPAA 1988-89; creator, producer: La Linea De La Salud (KWKW Radio), A Tu Salud (KMEX-TV34), Hispanic World of Fords, Hispanic Family of the Year -Entenmans; awards: Father of the Year Awards, Interceptor Award for best documentary, S.F. 1975, Asian of the Year, L.A. City Asian-Amer. Assn. (1978), 7 Emmys and Emmy nominations 1971-77; civic: fmr. commr. cultural affairs City of L.A., presdl. appt. Child Safety Partnership, dir. Calif. Special Olympics, dir. Sprint UCLA, Internat. Student Ctr. UCLA, dir. Am. Beach Volleyball League, dir. Asian Am. Games, dir. Genesis Internat., hon. dir. Amer. Youth Soccer Orgn., founder S.F.V. youth soccer league; host many benefit tennis tourn.; R.Cath.; rec: record collection, tennis, soccer. Ofc: 1109 N Vermont Los Angeles 90029

MACK, CHARLES DANIEL, III, labor union official; b. Apr. 16, 1942, Oakland; s. Charles Daniel, Jr. and Berna (Ferguson) M.; m. Marlene Helen Fagundes, 1960; children: Tammy b. 1961, Kelly b. 1967, Kerry b. 1970, Shannon b. 1972; edn: BA, San Francisco St. Univ., 1964; labor studies, Univ. Calif. Career: elected bus. agent Teamsters Local No. 70, 1966-72, legislative rep. Teamsters 1970-71, secty.-treas. Local 70, 1972-; past trustee and recording secty. Teamster Jt. Council No. 7, apptd. pres. 1982, elected pres. 1984; apptd. Internat. Brotherhood of Teamsters rep. 1984; elected 2d v.p. Alameda County Cent. Labor Council, 1988; mem. Calif. Teamsters Pub. Affairs Coun. (exec. bd.), Nat. Freight Negotiating Com., We. Conf. of Teamsters Policy Com., trustee We. Conf. Teamsters Pension Trust; past bd. dirs. State Compensation Ins. Fund; civic: New Oakland Com., Peralta Comm. Coll. Advy. Com., past bd. dirs. Children's Hosp. of East Bay; Democrat; R.Cath.; rec: jogging. Ofc: Teamsters' Joint Council No. 7 150 Executive Park Blvd Ste 2900 San Francisco 94134

MACK, J. CURTIS, II; association president; b. Dec. 22, 1944, Los Angeles; s. James C. and Ahli C. (Youngren) M.; m. Tamara J. Kriner, Jan. 23, 1988; 2 sons: James Curtis, III b. 1989, Robert Lee b. 1992; edn: BA cum laude, USC 1967; MPA, 1969; MA, 1976. Career: exec. dir. Citizens for the Republic, Santa Monica 1979-85; asst. secty. oceans and atmosphere, U.S. Dept. of Commerce, Wash. D.C. 1985-88; dir: Brentwood Bank of Calif. 1984-85, 1989-; appt. Pres's. Commn. on White House Fellowships, 1984-85; pres. World Affairs Council, Los Angeles 1988-; mem. Nat. Space Club (gov. 1987-88); mil: lt. col. USAFR 1969-; Episcopalian. Ofc: Los Angeles World Affairs Council 917 Wilshire Blvd Ste 1730 Los Angeles 90017

MACLEOD, KATHLEEN BROMLEY, physician; b. Mar. 25, 1953, Oakland; d. LeRoy Alton Bromley and Bernice Honora Doyle; m. Glen Earl MacLeod, Dec. 22, 1973; edn: salutatorian Miramonte H.S., Orinda; BA in bacteriology (high honors), UC Berkeley, 1975; MD, UCLA Sch. of Med., 1984; bd. cert. Am. Bd. Internal Medicine (ABIM) 1987, Am. Bd. Infectious Diseases 1990. Career: staff resrearch assoc. dept. genetics, UC Berkeley, 1976-77 (discovery of one of gene loci regulating expression of mating type in Saccharomyces cerevisiae pub. J. Genetics (9/79); microbiologist Bur. of Epidemiology, Bacterial Zoonoses Br., Ctrs. for Disease Control, Atlanta, Ga. 1978-80, PHS award for isolating Legionella pneumophila from the environment; NIH resrch. fellow 1981, 82; resident internal med. Wadsworth VA Med. Ctr., Los Angeles 1984-87 (infectious diseases rotations at Harbor-UCLA Med. Ctr., Hosp. for Tropical Diseases, London, and Princess Margaret Hosp. for Infectious Diseases, Hong Kong); fellow Infectious Diseases UC Irvine Sch. of Med., Orange 1987-89; solo practice Infectious Diseases, Long Beach, Los Alamitos, and Lakewood. Tel: 213/432-4357 (ID2-HELP) Res: 6310 Bayshore Walk Long Beach 90803

MACRORIE, LAWRENCE EDWARD, manufacturing executive, technical consultant; b. Aug. 9, 1930, Whittier; s. John James Macrorie and Alberta Emily (Alberta) Van Winkle; m. Constance M. Rowe, March 31, 1951; children: Michael b. 1952, John b. 1954, Chris b. 1958, Kathy b. 1960; edn: AA, Mt. San

Antonio Coll. 1950; BA, Whittier Coll. 1952; grad. work Long Beach St. Coll. 1954. Career: tchr. E. Whittier Sch. Dist., Whittier 1952-55; sales engr. Lederle Labs., Pearl River, N.Y. 1956-57; Central Solvents, Santa Fe Springs 1957-58; sales mgr. Hysol Dexter Corp., Olean, N.Y. 1959-64; pres. Lunar Products Inc., El Monte 1964-91 (sold co. 1991), tech. advisor 1991-; devel. epoxy formulations 1985-, sealants, electrically conductive, electrical insulators, adhesives, coatings, used by Space Shuttle, IT&T Comms.; honors: Whittier Coll. Varsity letterman track & field, football 1950-52, Franklin Soc. 1950-52; mem: Nat. Fedn. Indep. Bus., Mojave C.of C., Kts. of Col. (Council 6705, Mojave, California City); Republican; R.Cath. (Ch. Council 1989-); rec: sports. Res: POB J 31529 Neuralia Cantil 93519

MADDY, DONALD LEE, computer company executive, programming consultant; b. Aug. 27, 1949, Whittier, Calif.; s. Keith Thomas and Colleen Joanne (Barlow) M.; m. Lynne Louise Juhnke, June 29, 1985; children: Crystal Lynne b. 1987, Michael Donald b. 1991; edn: nuclear weapons electronics student, Sandia AFB, N.M. 1970; BS in Computer Sci., Calif. State Univ., Sacto., Calif. 1976; Certificate in Data Processing (CDP) 1982. Career: nuclear weapons electronics splst., US Army, Istanbul, Turkey 1970-71; programmer, Water Resources Control Bd., Div. Water Quality, Sacto. 1974-75; programmer, Calif. State Coll., Bakersfield 1976-78; programmer/analyst, Sierra Pacific Power Co., Reno, Nev. 1979-80; sr. programmer/analyst, State of Idaho Transp. Dept., Boise 1980-81, United Grocers Warehouse, Oakland 1981-84; sr. programming cons., Farmers Savings & Loan, Davis 1984-87, Pacific Gas & Electric, Avila Beach 1987-; mem. Amer. Nuclear Soc. 1987-; co-author: Computer Software Security System for the Plant Information Management System, 1992; mil: splst. fifth class, US Army, 1969-72; Republican; rec: model railroading, downhill and cross-country skiing. Ofc: The Maddy Corporation 1220 16th St. Los Osos 93402-1422

MADORSKY, JULIE G., physician; b. June 17, 1945, Hungary; nat. 1967; d. Imre and Georgina (Fazekas) Geiger; m. Melvin A. Botvin, June 12, 1965 (div. 1977); m. 2d. Arthur G. Madorsky, Sept. 17, 1978; children: Ari b. 1969, Danya b. 1971; edn: Univ. London 1961-65; Univ. Pa. Phila. 1965-66; MD, Med. Coll. Pa. 1969; lic. physician and surgeon Nat. Bd. Med. Examiners 1969. Career: asst. prof. rehab. medicine Temple Univ. Hosp., Phila., Pa. 1973-74; program med. dir. Casa Colina Hosp., Pomona 1974-; clin. assoc. prof. UC Irvine 1974-, UCLA 1979-; clin. prof. Coll. Osteopathic Medicine of Pacific, Pomona 1987-; awards: Calif. Govs. Com. Calif. Physician of Year 1987, Pres.'s Com. Employment of Disabled Persons U.S. Physician of Year 1988; mem: Calif. Soc. Physical Medicine & Rehab. (pres. 1992-), So. Calif. Soc. Physical Medicine & Rehab. (pres. 1987-), AMA, CMA, Am. Acad. Physical Medicine & Rehab., Am. Spinal Injury Assn., Am. Med. Women's Assn., Services Center for Indep. Living (bd. mem. 1986-); rec: art, music psychology. Ofc: 255 E Bonita Ave Pomona 91767

MADSEN, ELMA MERRILL, realtor, notary public, genealogical researcher; b. Nov. 11, 1929, Salt Lake City, Utah; d. Thais Abia (dec. Mar. 24, 1964) and Alice (Sessions) Merrill; m. Von Peter Madsen, July 21, 1953; dau., Shirley Yvonne (Dodson); edn: BS in bacteriology and public health (w/distinction), Wash. State Univ., 1950; grad. work Utah State Univ., 1950-52; cert. med. technologist Am. Soc. Clin. Pathologists 1952-63; Calif. R.E. lic. 1987, lic. Notary Public; GRI, Grad. Realtors Inst. Career: clin. tech./animal researcher Dept. Veterinary Medicine Wash. State Univ., Pullman 1952-53; hd. clin. technologist Richland (Wash.) Diagnostic Lab, 1953-55; prodn. mgr. genealogy dept. Mormon Temple, Oakland, Calif. 1965-85; exec. adminstrv. asst. John Grobe Comml. and Indsl. R.E. Co., Walnut Creek, 1985-86; real estate assoc. Mason McDuffie R.E., Inc., Pleasanton, 1986-88; Homeowners R.E., San Ramon, 1988-89; John M. Grubb R.E., 1989; Blackhawk Realty, 1990; California Visions R.E. Co., San Ramon, 1990-; indep. genealogical research, 1965-80; honors: Sigma Alpha Omicron 1950; mem. Am. Biog. Inst. Res. Advy. Bd. (life fellow); mem.: Contra Costa Co. Bd. Realtors, So. Alameda Co. Bd. Realtors, Calif. Assn. of Realtors, Nat. Assn. of Realtors, Nat. Women's Council of Realtors, Contra Costa Co. Women's Council of Realtors, Nat. Assn. Female Execs., Commonwealth Club Calif.; Republican; Ch. of Jesus Christ of LDS; rec: genealogy research, writing. Res/Ofc: 3085-4 Lakemont Dr San Ramon 94583 Ph: 415/735-3085

MADSEN, GEORGE EVERETTE, civil engineer; b. Mar. 15, 1934, Fresno; s. Edward George and Dorothy L. (Smith) M.; m. Sandra Marie Johannes, July 10, 1960; children: Vivian b. 1961, Cheryl b. 1966; edn: BS civil engring w. honors, Calif. Inst. Tech. Pasadena 1955; MS, 1958; reg. civil (1960) and traffic engr. Calif. Career: jr. asst., asst. sanitary engr./lt. j.g. USPHS, Wash. DC 1955-56, Anchorage, Ak. 1956-57; asst. civil engr. Orange Co. Flood Control Dist., Santa Ana 1958-59; sr. sanitary engr. Co. of San Diego 1959-60; asst. city engr., city engr., pub. works dir. City of Costa Mesa 1960-71; mgr. Costa Mesa Sanitary Dist. 1969-71; sr. v.p. Woodside/Kubota & Assoc., Inc. Santa Ana 1971-88; civil engr. Williamson & Schmid, Irvine 1988-; honors: BSA Eagle Scout 1950, Tau Beta Phi, ASCE Outstanding C.E. student 1955; mem: fellow ASCE (Orange Co. Br. secty., treas., v.p., pres. 1967-70), Am. Pub. Works Assn., Orange Co. Water Assn.; Presbyterian (elder); rec: skiing, volleyball, watching sports. Ofc: Williamson & Schmid 15101 Redhill Ave Tustin 92680

MAESTRONE, FRANK EUSEBIO, diplomat; b. Dec. 20, 1922, Springfield, Mass.; s. John Battista and Margaret Carlotta (Villanova) M.; m. Jo Colwell, 1943; cert., U.S. Naval War Coll. 1962-63. Career: 3d. secty. Am. Legation, Vienna, Austria 1948-49; v.consul U.S. Consulate Gen., Hamburg, Germany 1949-53; consul U.S. Consulate, Salzburg, Austria 1954-56; asst. chief Secretariat, St. Dept., Wash. D.C. 1956-58; italian desk ofcr. St. Dept. 1958-60; consul U.S. Consulate, Khorramshahr, Iran 1960-62; political adviser NATO, Paris, France 1963-65; dep. dir. Western Europe, St. Dept., WDC 1965-68; dep. asst. secty. gen. NATO, Brussels, Belgium 1968-71; counselor of embassy U.S. Embassy, Manila, Philippines 1971-73; advisor to pres. U.S. Naval War Coll., Newport, R.I. 1973-74; minister counselor U.S. Embassy, Cairo, Egypt 1974-76; US Ambassador, Kuwait 1976-79; spl. rep. of pres. and dir. Sinai Peacekeeping Mission, WDC 1980-83; exec. dir. World Affairs Council, San Diego 1984-86, mem. bd. 1986-; resident ambassador U.S. Internat. Univ., San Diego 1986-; mem. Internat. Inst. Strategic Studies, London 1975-; honors: Chevalier du Merite Agricole France 1946; numerous newspaper articles pub. on internat. affairs (1984-); mil: 1st lt. AUS 1943-46; R.Cath.; rec: golf. Res: 2824 Curie Place San Diego 92122 Ofc: 10455 Pomerado Rd San Diego 92131

MAFFINI, MARTHA WAHL LEEMAN, educator, florist; b. Jan. 20, 1939, Hartford, Conn.; d. William F. and Virginia (Yenney) Wahl; m. William L. Maffini, July 8, 1982; children: Harry Leeman b. 1972; Amy Leeman, b. 1974; Cara Maffini, b. 1983, Matthew Maffini b. 1986; edn: BS, Univ. of Vermont 1961; M.Ed., Boston Univ. 1965; postgrad., Clark Sch. for Deaf, Smith Coll. 1967; tchr. credentials, deaf and hard of hearing. Career: tchr. speech dept. Central Inst. for Deaf, St. Louis, Mo. 1965-66; supr. lang. problem classes Horace Mann Sch. for the Deaf, Boston, Mass. 1966-69; tchr. hard of hearing Haman Elem. Sch., Santa Clara, Calif. 1970-75, Wilson Jr. High, 1975-80, tchr. communicatively handicapped Buchser Jr. High, 1980-87, Buchser Middle Sch., 1987-; master tchr. audiology, CSU San Jose 1978-83; ednl. cons. Mass. Eye & Ear, Boston 1967; indep. retail florist, designer and cons., 1987-; awards: HEW Fellow 1964-65, Alpha Delta Pi Scholarship Awd. 1961, Outstanding Young Women in Am. 1972; mem: Am. Speech & Hearing Assn., Alexander Graham Bell Assn. for Deaf, Alpha Delta Pi; civic: Girl and Boy Scouts, YMCA, 4-H, St. Andrew's Sch. Board of Edn., Saratoga 1986-, St. Andrew's Parent-Volunteers, Bellarmine Coll. Preparatory H.S. San Jose Mothers' Guild 1987-, Presentation H.S. Parent Vol. San Jose 1987-; profl. publs. in field; Espiscopal; rec: sewing, floral design, collect Early American Primitives. Res: 65 S Milton Ave Campbell 95008 Ofc: Santa Clara Unified Schools, Lawrence Station Rd Santa Clara 95051

MAGARIAN, STEVEN DAN, county sheriff; b. Oct. 13, 1942, Fresno; s. Dan Steve and Alice (Ekparian) M.; m. Joanne Louise Massicci, June 15, 1985; 1 dau. Erica b. 1987; edn: BS, and MS, CSU Fresno, 1972, 1974; Calif. Comm. Colls. life tchg. cred. 1974. Career: dep. sheriff Fresno County Sheriff's Dept., 1968-72, sheriff's sgt. 1972-76, sheriff's lt. 1976-81, sheriff's capt. 1981-83, asst. sheriff 1983-87, sheriff Fresno County 1987-, chmn. Fresno Co. Identification RAN Bd.; instr. CSU Fresno, State Center Jr. Colls., 1984-; appt. by Gov. Deukmejian to Calif. Council of Crim. Justice 1989; awards: outstanding law enforcement ofcr. Fresno Jaycees 1980, recogn. Calif. Nat. Guard, Sacto. 1987, Am. Heart Assn. Fresno 1988, Central Calif. Blood Bank, Fresno 1989, appreciation U.S. Secret Svc., Sacto. 1989; mem: Calif. St. Sheriffs Assn., Calif. Peace Ofcrs. Assn., FBI National Academy Graduates 1980-, Fresno County Inter Agy. 1986-; civic: Am. Heart Assn. (dir. 1988-); mil: airman USAF 1961; Republican; Prot. Ofc: Fresno County Sheriff's Dept. 2200 Fresno St Fresno 93721

MAGNESI, ALEXIS VERONICA, corporate executive; b. June 12, 1955, Bridgeport, Conn.; d. Alex Vincent and Veronica (Pape) Fucci; m. Nathan L. Magnesi, Jr., Dec. 28, 1985; children: Ashley S. b. 1988, Miles A. b. 1989; edn: major eng./jour., So. Conn. State Coll., 2 yrs., bus./personnel mgmt. major UCLA, 1 yr. Career: personnel/acctg. mgr. Postal Instant Press, Los Angeles 1976-80; v.p. personnel Imperial Internat. Inc., Torrance 1980-85; exec. v.p./co-owner USPS Security Inc., Los Angeles 1985-; owner USPS Patrol Inc., 1989-; civic: Youth Employment Summer Pgm., Torrance (chair 1981); recipient appreciation Private Industry Council, Torrance (1981, 82, 83). Ofc: 1264 San Dimas Canyon Rd San Dimas 91773

MAGNUSON, DONALD RICHARD, motion picture and t.v. screenwriter; b. Apr. 23, 1951, Chgo., Ill.; s. Donald O. and Olive J. (O'Keefe) M.; m. Debra Michelle Ruzek, June 9, 1973; children: Jennifer Jean b. 1974, Erick Richard b. 1976; edn: St. Hugh's, Lyons, Ill. 1965; Downers Grove So. H.S. 1969; N. Ill. Univ., journalism, 1969; Coll. of DuPage, Glen Ellyn, Ill., journalism, 1969-71. Career: asst. tchg. tennis pro - Westside Racquet Club 1970-73; Tennaqua Racquet Club 1972; general agent/broker, Telchen Ins. Agency, Villa Park, Ill. 1973; underwriter, Hanover Ins. Co., Chgo., Ill. 1974-76; special risk underwriter, AIG Group, Chg., Ill. 1976-78; casualty mgr., Sayre & Toso, Inc., Chgo., Ill. 1978-82; mgmt., Mead Reinsurance, Dayton, Oh. 1982-86; casualty mgr., Sayre & Toso, Inc., Orange, Calif.,1986-88; casualty mgr., Montgomery & Collins, Los Angeles 1988; film/t.v. screenwriter, Magnuson Entertainment Group, Yorba Linda 1987-; mem: Ferrari Club of Amer. 1987-91, Porsche Club of Amer. 1986-88; screenwriter: teleplay pilot, Black & White, 1989; eight screenplays: The Taiwan Factor, 1989, Another Autumn, 1989, Reunion, 1990, Harry's Harem, 1991, An Aspen Affair (co-written with Christina Cardan 1992), Dancer, 1993, Best Medicine, 1993, Midnight Internment, 1993; Roman Catholic. Ofc: Magnuson Entertainment Group 19866 Ridge Manor Way Yorba Linda 92686

MAHAFFEY, CANDACE MARIE, political organization executive, editor; b. Feb. 11, 1955, Anderson, S.C.; d. Joe Gentry and Hazel Marie (White) Mahaffey; edn: 4 years in electronics & elec. tech., law studies, Northwestern Calif. Univ. Career: political organizer The Conservative Action Lobby, Los Angeles 1988-, editor political newsletter: The Economic Watch, 1989-; computer tech. 1990-; producer American Radio Network 1990-; mem. The Profl. Electronic Technician Assn. (ETA); Prot.; rec: karate, tennis. Ofc: The Conservative Action Lobby PO Box 931602 Los Angeles 90093

MAHLER, GLENN RICHARD, sales executive; b. Melrose Park, IL, May 25, 1949; s. Glenn Morris and Annette Marie (Goersmeyer) M.; m. Carol Cambell Clinton, Feb. 13, 1972 (div. Mar. 1979); children: Dawn Christine, Glenn Richard, Jr.; edn: Univ. Wis. 1969; BA Graylon Coll. 1972; Am. Mktg. Sch., NYC 1985-90; Career: dist. mgr. to corp. mgr. Towle Silversmiths, Newburyport, MA 1972-80; owner Casa de Porcelana, Sedona, AZ 1980-85; dist. mgr. Lladro USA, Dallas, TX 1985-87; we. sales mgr. Lladro USA, Los Angeles 1987-90; nat. sales mgr. Pia Internat., Los Angeles 1990-; mem: Rep. Inner Circle, Washington Big Bros. Am., Dallas 1988, Masons; mil: sgt. USMC 1966-70, Vietnam, Bronze Star 1968, Purple Heart 1968, Naval Air Medal 1968; Methodist. Res: 22123 Figueroa St #131 Carson 90745

MAHONY, ROGER MICHAEL, archbishop; b. Feb. 27, 1936, Hollywood; s. Victory James and Loretta Marie (Baron) M.; edn: AA, Our Lady of Queen of Angels Sem., 1956; BA, St. John's Sem. Coll., 1958, BST, 1962; MSW, Catholic Univ. Am., 1964; ordained priest Roman Cath. Ch., 1962, ordained bishop, 1975; Career: ast. pastor St. Johyn's Cathedral, Fresno, 1962, 68-73, rector 1973-; residence St. Genevieve's Parish, Fresno 1964-, adminstr., 1964-67, pastor 1967-68; titular bishop of Tamascani, aux. bishop of Fresno 1975-80; chancellor Diocese of Fresno, 1970, vicar gen., 1975-80; bishop Diocese of Stockton, 1980-85; archbishop Diocese of Los Angeles, 1985-; diocesan dir. Cath. Charities and Social Service Fresno, 1964-70, exec. dir. Cath. Welfare Bur., 1964-70; exec. dir. Cath Welfare Bur. Infant of Prague Adoption Svc., 1964-70; chaplain St. Vincent de Paul Soc., Fresno 1964-70; chaplain to Pope Paul VI, 1967; mem. faculty extension div. Fresno State Univ., 1965-67; sec. U.S. Cath. bishops ad hoc com. on farm labor Nat. Conf. Bishops, 1970-75; chmn. com. on pub. welfare and income maintenance Nat. Conf. Cath. Charities, 1969-70; bd. dirs. West Coast Reg. Ofc. Bishops Com. for Spanish-speaking, 1967-70; chmn. Calif. Assn. Cath. Charities Dirs., 1965-69; trustee St. Patrick's Sem., Archdiocese of San Francisco, 1974-75; bd. dirs. Fresno Comm. Workshop, 1965-67; trustee St. Agnes Hosp., Fresno; honors: named Young Man of Yr. Fresno Jr. C.of C. 1967; mem: Urban Coalition of Fresno 1968-72, Fresno Co. Econ. Opportunities Commn. 1964-65, Fresno Co. Alcoholic Rehab. Com. 1966-67, Fresno City Charter Rev. Com. 1968-70, Mexican - Am. Council for Better Housing 1968-72, Fresno Redevel. Agy. 1970-75, Canon Law Soc. Am., Nat. Assn. Social Wkrs. Res: 114 E 2nd St Los Angeles 90012 Ofc: Archdiocese of Los Angeles 1531 N 9th St Los Angeles 90012

MAIBACH, HOWARD, professor; b. July 18, 1929, NY, NY; s. Jack Louis and Sidonia (Fink) M.; m. Siesel W., July 8, 1933; children, Lisa, Ed, Todd; edn: AB, Tulane Univ., New Orleans, La. 1950; MD, Tulane Univ. 1955. Career: prof., dermatology, Univ. of Calif. Med. Sch., S.F. 1961-; mem: SID, AMA, ICDR; author and editior of over forty books since 1965; mil: capt., U. S. Army, 1955-58. Ofc: Univ. of Calif. Medical School, San Francisco 94143

MAIBACH, MICHAEL CHARLES, corporate government affairs executive; b. May 14, 1951, Peoria, Ill.; s. Charles Edward and Annette Claire (Pilon) M.; edn: BA (cum laude), No. Ill. Univ. 1973, MA, 1980; BA (cum laude), CSU Hayward 1983; BS, Am. University, Wash. D.C. 1989; att. AU European Inst., summer 1986, Inst. for Internat. Studies, Tokyo, spring 1985, Universidad Ibero-Americana, Mex. City, summer 1974, Oxford Univ., England, summer 1973. Career: machine shop foreman Caterpillar, Inc. 1976-77, Ill. issues mgr., govt. affairs 1977-79, west coast rep. 1979-82, domestic issues mgr. 1983; dir. govt. affairs, Intel Corp., Santa Clara, Calif. and Wash., D.C. 1983-; govt: mem. Bd. of Zoning Adjustment, Menlo Park 1985, staff intern, Ill. State Senate, Springfield, 1975-76, Illinois Humanities Council 1973-75, Dekalb County Bd., Ill. 1972-75, Gov's Fellow, Ill. Dept. of Local Govt., summers 1970, 71; author numerous essays; Republican. Res: 1047 Noel Drive Menlo Park 94025 Ofc: IOntel Corp RN5-24 PO Box 58119 Santa Clara 95052-8119

MAKSYMOWICZ, JOHN ROBERT, electrical engineer; b. Feb. 3, 1956, Bklyn.; s. Theodore John and Helen Mary (Kisinski) M.; edn: BEE (highest hons.), Pratt Inst., Bklyn, N.Y., 1983. Career: electrical engr. IBM Corp., Poughkeepsie, N.Y. 1983; Grumman Aerospace Corp., Bethpage, N.Y. 1983-87; Plessey Electronics, Totowa, N.J. 1987-89; elec. engr., radar designer, The

Aerospace Corp., L. A., Calif. 1989-; awards: Samuel Brown scholar, Cook-Marsh scholar, Pratt Inst. 1979-83, Tau Beta Pi (coll. chpt. pres. 1981-82), Eta Kappa Nu (coll. chpt. pres. 1981-82), Program Recogn. Award, The Aerospace Corp. 1991, 1992; listed in Who's Who in West 1992-3, Who's Who in World 1993-4; mem: IEEE 1980-, Assn. of Old Crows 1982-, US Space Found. 1992-; profl. papers: Pulse Compression Techniques, 1990; Examination of Cross-Polarization ECM, 1991; Detection of Low Earth Orbit Space Debris by a Ground Based Phased-array Radar, 1992; R.Cath.; rec: running, photography, reading, music.

MALLETT, WILLIAM ROBERT, research chemist, fuels consultant; b. Sept. 12, 1932, Painesville, Ohio; s. Richard Colton and Luella Louise (Dewal M.; m. Masuko Sano, Mar. 18, 1957; children: Daryl b. 1969, Stacie b. 1971; edn: BA, Miami Univ., Oxford, Oh. 1961, MS, 1963; PhD, Rensselaer Polytech., Trot, NY 1966. Career: res. chem. Union Oil Co., Brea, Calif. 1966-68, sr. res. chem. 1968-73; vis. res. scientist Maruzen Oil Co., Satte, Japan 1973-75; res. assoc. Union Oil Co., Brea 1975-84; supr. fuels res. Unocal Corp., Brea 1984-90, staff consultant 1990-92; fuels consultant Fuels Consulting Services, Placentia 1992-; mem. Soc. of Automotive Engrs. 1970-, Am. Chemical Soc. 1961-, Am. Soc. for Testing & Mats. 1979-; invention: Gasoline additive 1971; pub. article Gasoline Analysis 1975; mil: s/sgt USAF 1951-55; rec: personal computers, photography, ham radio, astronomy. Res/Ofc: Fuels Consulting Svs. 1273 Genoa Pl Placentia 92670

MALMSTROM, DOROTHY ELVIRA, private school director; b. April 4, 1945, Guatemala City, Guatemala; d. Carl Olof and Esther (Butler) Malmstrom; edn: AA, Chaffey Coll., 1966; BA sociol. (honors), UC Riverside 1969; MA social sci., Azusa Pacific Univ. 1980; postgrad. work, US Internat. Univ. 1983-86; PhD clin. psychology, The Graduate Sch. of The Union Institute, 1992. Career: research sociologist UC Riverside, 1969-70; adminstrv. coord. Yamaha, Indio, Calif. 1971-73; mktg. exec. Good Stuff Natural Bakery, Los Angeles 1974-81; founder/pres. Health Network Inst. Santa Monica 1981-82; co-founder Advance Financial Services Inc., Santa Monica 1982-87; psychol. intern Professional Consultation Services Inc., Los Angeles, 1988-92; dir. Progress School, Santa Monica 1993-; mem: Am. Psychol. Assn., Calif. State Psychol. Assn., L.A. Co. Psychol. Assn., So. Calif. Soc. of Clin. Hypnosis, Nat. Psychol. Advy. Assn.; rec: music, art, nature, walking, hiking, community. Ofc: Progress School 1305 Pico Blvd Santa Monica 90405 Tel: 310/450-1116

MALONE, MARVIN HERBERT, pharmacologist-toxicologist, editor, educator, researcher; b. Apr. 2, 1930, Fairbury, Nebr.; s. Herbert August Frederick and Elizabeth Florinda (Torrey) M.; m. Shirley Ruth Cane, Dec. 21, 1952; children: Carla Margaret, Gayla Christa; edn: BS in pharmacy, Univ. Nebr., 1951, MS in physiology and pharmacology, 1953; postgrad. Rutgers Univ., 1954-55; PhD in pharmacology and pharm. scis., Univ. Nebr., 1958. Career: student asst. Univ. Nebr., Lincoln, 1951-53, 1956-58; research asst. Squibb Inst. Med. Research, New Brunswick, N.J. 1953-56; asst. prof. Univ. New Mexico, Albuq. 1958-60; assoc. prof. Univ. Connecticut, Storrs 1960-69; prof. pharmacology and toxicology Univ. of the Pacific, Stockton 1969-84, Distinguished Prof. 1984-90, chair dept. physiology and pharmacology 1969-70, 1987-90, emeritus prof. 1990-; publisher Wormwood Books and Magazines, 1991-; prin., consulting svs., Wormwood Associates, 1990-; cons.: U. Wash. Drug Plant Labs. 1960-64, Research Pathology Assoc. 1967-70, Amazon Natural Drug Co. 1967-70, Atlas Chem. Inds. ICI USA Inc. 1968-78, SISA Inst. Research Northeastern U. 1977-82, Task Force on Plants for Fertility Regulation WHO Spl. Pgm. for R&D & Rsch. Tng. in Human Reprodn. 1982-88, gubnat. appt. Calif. St. Med. Therap. and Drug Advy. Commn. 1985-90, Herb Research Found. 1990-, Emprise Inc. 1990-92 author: Bucolics and Cheromanics 1963, Experiments in the Pharmaceutical Biol. Scis. 1973; editorial bds: J. Natural Products: Lloydia 1971-, J. Ethnopharmacology (1978-84, 90-), Internat. Jour. Pharmacognosy 1992-; editor: The Wormwood Review, lit. jour. 1960-, Pacific Info. Service on Street-Drugs 1971-78, Am. J. Pharmaceutical Education 1974-79, Pharmat 1984-87, J. Ethnopharmacology 1985-91; contbr. 235+ articles to profl. jours.; awards: special citation UOP Sch. Pharmacy 1991, UOP Order of Pacific 1991, UOP distinction of merit 1980, outstanding svs. plaque Am. Assn. Colls. of Pharmacy 1980, Mead Johnson Labs. award 1964, grantee: USPHS (1960-63, 68-73), US Army 1962-63, Univ. Conn. Research Found. 1964-68, UOP Research 1970-73; Fellow Am. Found. Pharm. Edn. 1956-58; mem. Am. Inst. Chemists (Fellow), AAAS (Fellow), Am. Soc. Pharmacology and Exptl. Therap., Am. Soc. Pharmacognosy, Sigma Xi, Rho Chi, Phi Lambda Upsilon, Phi Kappa Phi; specialties: screening and assay of natural principles from plants and higher fungi, biometrics, pharmacology of inflammation and antiinflammation, pharmacodynamics of psychotropic and autonomic agents, fertility regulation; rec: book, art and little magazine collecting. Res/Ofc: 722 Bedford Rd Stockton 95204-5214 Tel 209/466-8231

MALONEY, GEORGE W., pharmacist; b. Apr. 4, 1915, Onida, So. Dak.; s. William Henry and Katherine Amelia (Vanderkolk) M.; m. Nona Laura McNamar, June 12, 1938; children: Colleen b. 1947, Erin b. 1949; edn: BS, So. Dak. St. Coll. Univ. 1935. Career: asst. mgr., pharmacist Owl Drug Co., Los Angeles 1939 (pres. Future Owl Mgrs. Club); Zenith Prescription Pharm. Inc.

1956-70, owner 1973-74; mem: Calif. Pharmaceutical Assn.; mil: USNR 1942-45; Republican; Prot.; rec: mortar and pestle collecting. Res: 1710 S 3rd Ave Arcadia 91006

MALONEY, JOHN JOSEPH, business manager; b. Aug. 22, 1935, Brooklyn, N.Y.; s. William Francis and Gertrude Elizabeth (Ryder) M.; m. Mary Gail Heller, Dec. 29, 1956; children: John b. 1957, Tamara b. 1958, Sandra b. 1960, Michael b. 1961; edn: BS, N.Y. St. Maritime Coll. 1956; BS, USN Postgrad. Coll. 1964; MS, 1972; MBA, Pepperdine Univ. 1982. Career: gen. mgr. Oceanroutes Inc., Sunnyvale 1980-; Weather Network Inc., Chico 1985-; mem: Navy League; mil: capt. USN 1956-80; R.Cath.; rec: flying, golf. Address: Saratoga 95070

MALOUF, FREDERICK LEROY, composer, software engineer; b. Oct. 7, 1954, Fort Worth, Tx.; s. LeRoy Gabriel and Antoinette Alice (Antoine) M.; m. Bonnie Elizabeth Johanson, Aug. 21, 1977; children: Eric b. 1986, Vanita b. 1990; edn: MusB, Berklee Coll. of Music, Boston 1979; MusM, Bowling Green State Univ., 1981; ArtsD, Ball State Univ., 1985. Career: tech. support mgr. Quintus Computer Systems, Palo Alto 1985-87; software engr. Sequential Circuits Inc., San Jose 1987; Digideck Inc., Mountain View 1987-88; Apple Computer, Cupertino 1988-92; Kaleida Labs Inc., Mountain View 1992- concert producer Chromatonal Productions, Mountain View 1987-; performer with mus. ensemble Tonus Finalis, concerts nat. and in Europe; compositions: Piano Sonato No. 1 (1979), Avatar (1981), Chromatonal (1985), Sacrifice (1988), Variations on Goodbye Pork Pie Hat (1989), Bali Jam (1991), Imijimi (1992), Miks (1992); awards: Richard Levy composition award Berklee Coll. of Music 1979, Stanford Univ. composer in residence Rockefeller Found. 1984, Arts Internat. travel grantee to festivals Warsaw, Poland 1990, 91; mem. IEEE 1987-, Computer Music Assn. 1987-, ASCAP 1988-; Indep.; rec: camping, hiking, swimming, movies. Res: 379 Palo Alto Ave Mountain View 94041 Ofc: Kaleida Labs, Inc. 1945 Charleston Rd Mountain View 94043

MALTZ, ANDREW HAL, computer company executive; b. Feb. 27, 1960, Mineola, N.Y.; s. Joseph A. and Marilyn (Rothchild) M.; m. Leslie Ann Stewart, May 24, 1987; cchildren: Haley b. 1991; edn: BSEE, SUNY at Buffalo, N.Y. 1982. Career: development engr. Ruxton Ltd., Burbank 1982-85; v.p. engring. Cinedco Inc., Burbank 1985-89; v.p. engring. Ediflex Systems Inc., Glendale 1989-91, v.p. operations & engring., 1991-; awards: Tau Beta Pi 1981, Eta Kappa Nu 1981, Emmy for engring. achiev. Acad. of TV Arts & Scis., Hollywood 1986; mem: Soc. of Motion Picture & TV Engrs. 1982-, Tech. Council Motion Picture & Television Industries; Democrat; rec: wine, skiing, cycling. Res: 15106 Weddington St Sherman Oaks 91411 Ofc: Ediflex Systems Inc. 1225 Grand Central Ave Glendale 91201

MANAHAN, MANNY CELESTINO, accountant; b. Apr. 6, San Miguel, Bulacan, Philippines; edn: BBA acctg., Univ. of the East, Manila, Phil. 1963; MBA mgmt., Golden Gate Univ. 1968, contg. edn. MBA (tax) 1984; CPA Calif. 1983. Career: loan counselor Lomas & Nettleton Co. S.F. 1967-68; acctg./ ofc. mgr. Henry Irving & Assocs. S.F. 1968-73; owner Manny Celestino Manahan CPA firm 1973-; p-t instr. acctg. S.F. Comm. Coll. Dist. 1974-78; appt. by Mayor Art Agnos mem. Citizens Com. on Community Devel., 1988-; mem. bd. dirs. TAX-AID Pgm., chmn. fund raising, 1990-92; honors: disting. svc. Golden Gate Univ. 1983, Man of Yr. Men's Club of St. Anne's of the Sunset S.F. 1982), Phil. Inst. CPAs (PICPA) Presdl. Awardee 1982, PICPA outstanding CPA in comm. svc. & 1st Quarter Award 1983, Most Outstanding PICPAN 1981, Outstanding CPA in Pub. Acctg. and Presdl. Awardee 1989; mem: Am. Inst. CPAs, Calif. Soc. CPAs (S.F. chpt. bd. 1989-92, chmn. mem. & hospitality 1989-92), Am. Acctg. Assn., Calif. Soc. Enrolled Agents, East Bay S.F. Assn. Enrolled Agents (bd. 1983-84, chmn. finance, buget & audit 1983-84), Filipino Accts. Assn. of Calif. (pres. 1974-75), Financial Planning Profl. Practices Adv. Panel, Nat. Assn. Enrolled Agents, Nat. Assn. Self Employed, Nat. Assn. Small Bus., Nat. Soc. Public Accts. (awards com. 1983-84), Soc. Calif. Accts., PICPA USA (pres. 1986, exec. v.p. 1985, presdl. adviser 1987-, sustaining life mem., nat. dir. 1984, co-chmn. 1984 conv.), Golden Gate Univ. Alumni Assn. (council 1976-, chmn. devel. com. 1982-, pres. 1980-82, v.p. 1978-80, treas. 1977-78), Fil-Am Soc. St. Anne's (bd. 1976-, pres. 1981), Men's Club St. Anne's (treas.), Golden Gate Univ. Assocs., Am. Biographical Inst. (bd. advisors), ABI Res. Assn., Citizen's Choice, Commonwealth Club of Calif., Clearinghouse for Volunteer Acctg. Services, K.Q.E.D., Republican Presdl. Task Force, US Repub. Senatorial Club; R.Cath.; rec: bowling, dancing, outing, swimming, travel. Address: 2020 Judah St San Francisco 94122-1531

MANCINI, ROBERT KARL, computer analyst; b. May 13, 1954, Burbank; s. Alfred Robert and Phyllis Elaine (Pflugel) M.; m. Barbara Diane Bacon, Aug. 4, 1979; children: Benjamin b. 1981, Bonnie b. 1983; edn: BA econ., UCLA 1976; cert. biblical studies, Multnomah Sch. of Bible 1981; MBA quantatative methods, Santa Clara Univ. 1987. Career: process clk. Am. Funds Service Co., Los Angeles 1976-77; exec. asst. Sierra Thrift & Loan Co., San Mateo 1977-78; scientific programming splst. Lockheed Missiles & Space, Sunnyvale 1978-90; product mgr. Diversified Software Systems Inc., Morgan Hill 1990-; pres. Mancini Computer Services, San Jose 1985-; computer software instr. Heald Coll., San Jose 1990;

computer cons. Mary Kay Cosmetics, Cupertino 1985-86, Valor Software, San Jose 1987, Century 21, Campbell 1987-92, Major Freight Systems, Milpitas 1989-91; honors: Phi Kappa Sigma, LMSC commendn. 1979, 81; mem. UCLA Alumni, Heritage House; civic: City of Morgan Hill Blue Rib. Budget Com. 1992; Republican; Christian (Hillside Ch. Fin. Council); rec: tennis, photography and video photog., gardening. Res: PO Box 1602 Morgan Hill 95038

MANDEL, MAURICE, II, lawyer; b. Hollywood, Calif.; s. Maurice and Wynne M.; edn: Beverly Hills H.S.; BS, USC Sch. of Bus. Adm., 1971, MS, USC Sch. of Edn., 1972; JD, Western State Univ. Coll. of Law, 1979; Calif. life tchg. cred., elem. edn. and adminstrn.; admitted bar: Calif. 1980, U.S. Dist. Cts. (cent. dist. Calif. 1983, we. dist. Tenn. 1987, dist. Az. 1990, so. dist. Calif. 1991), U.S. Ct. Appeals (9th cir. 1983, Fed. cir. 1988), U.S. Supreme Ct. 1987. Career: elementary sch. tchr. Orange Co. 1972-82; lawyer sole practice, Newport Beach 1982-; Comm. Coll. instr. 1987-; honors: USC honored senior 1971 and rider of Trojan Horse (sch. mascot), Calif. Bar Assn. pro bono service awards 1983-87, US Dist. Ct. pro bono service award 1986, OCBA Award of Merit 1987, FBA Award of Merit 1990, Thwarted Thwart award Newport Harbor C.of C. 1989, Kirov Ballet Tovarich award 1989 and Marinskii Teatp award 1992, Perestroika award Moscow Classical Ballet 1988-89, Skrasivi Nogi award Bolshoi Ballet 1990; mem: Am. Bar Assn., Calif. Bar Assn., Orange Co. Bar Assn. (charter mem., OC Bar Found. trustee 1984-87, chmn. legal edn. for youth com. 1984-87), Federal Bar Assn. (spl. appointee nat. membership com., reg. v.chair membership; Orange Co. Chpt. founding pres., del. Calif. Bar, del. nat. conv.; O.C. chpt. coms.- programs, courthouse, judicial selection, reception, newsletter, crim. indigent def., constnl. bi-centennial, Bill of Rights; awards for Chpt. activity and FBA membership, 1987) Am. Trial Lawyers Assn., Calif. Trial Lawyers Assn., Plaintiff Employee Lawyers Assn., Bar Leaders Coun. Dist. 8, Amicus Publico, Orange Co. Women Lawyers, Calif. Employment Lawyers Assn., Employees Rights Council, USC Alumni, MENSA, American Inns of Ct., U.S. Olympic Com. Assoc., U.S. Ski Team associate 1975-, Smithsonian Instn., Friends Am. Ballet Theatre, Opera Pacific Guild, Friends Joffrey Ballet, Calypso Soc., World Wildlife Fedn., L.A. County Mus. Art, Newport Beach Art Mus., Laguna Beach Art Mus., Beverly Hills H.S. Alumni and Scholarship Com., Center Dance Alliance, U.S. Supreme Ct. Hist. Soc., 9th Jud. Cir. Hist. Soc.; rec: sailing, skiing. Res: PO Box 411 Balboa Island 92662 Ofc: 160 Newport Center Dr Ste 260 Newport Beach 92660

MANDELL, ANDREW JOHN, entertainment company executive; b. Sept. 5, 1956, Syracuse, N.Y.; s. Leon H. and Muriel (Glickhouse) M.; m. Robin Lynn Friedman, Jan. 11, 1986; children: Marc b. 1988; edn: BA econ., Univ. Rochester 1978; MBA, Univ. Mich. 1980. Career: CFO Chesapeake area Pepsi Cola, Baltimore, Md. 1980-89; v.p. fin. Walt Disney Imagineering, Glendale 1989-; mem: Univ. Mich. Alumni Assn.; Jewish; rec: sport. Ofc: Walt Disney Imagineering 1401 Flower St Glendale 91221

MANGNALL, RICHARD CURTIS, civil engineer; b. Aug. 4, 1920, Tonica, Ill.; s. Richard Lyle Mangnall and Grace Ellen (Alleman) Mangnall Smith Gehrman; m. Naomi Ruth Addison Russell, July 23, 1946 (dec. 1984); m. Elva Maxine Freeman Michigan, May 1, 1987; children: Susan b. 1948, Richard b. 1952; edn: BS forestry, Univ. Mich. Ann Arbor 1942; Oreg. St. Univ. Corvallis 1946-47; CSU Stanislaus 1973-74; CSU Fresno 1976-78; reg. civil engr. Calif. 1970. Career: engring. assoc. City of Glendale 1954-70, civil engr. 1970-71; asst. dir. pub. works City of Modesto 1971-74; dir. pub. works City of Tulare 1974-87; supervising engr. Brown & Caldwell, Sacto. 1987-89; owner Richard C. Mangnall, Tulare 1989; asst. instr. Oreg. St. Univ., Corvallis 1946-47; program com. Inst. Transp. & Traffic Engring., Berkeley 1980-86, instr. 1987; com. chmn. Inst. Municipal Engrs., Chgo. 1985-92; cons. civil engr. Richard C. Mangnall 1989; awards: Top 10 Pub. Works Leader 1987, Life mem. 1988, and Swearington Award 1990, Am. Pub. Works Assn., nat. cert. of recognition HUD 1982; mem: Am. Pub. Works Assn. (life), Am. Water Works Assn., Water Environment Fedn., ASCE, Am. Soc. Mil. Engrs., Tulare Host Lions, Tulare Elks, Tulare Farm Equipment Show, Tulare C.of C., Pacific Crest Trail Assn., 4th Marine Division Assn., Marines Memorial Club; publs: 3 pamphlets, article in trade jour. (1982-86); Republican; Congregational; rec: backpacking, skiing, fishing, reading. Res: 939 E Pleasant Dr Tulare 93274

MANINGER, R(ALPH) CARROLL, engineer; b. Dec. 24, 1918, Harper, Kans.; s. Earl Dotterer and Mabel Velma (Haskin) M.; m. Jean Kidder, July 1, 1942; children: Margaret b. 1943, Mary-Carroll b. 1950, Emily b. 1950; edn: BS, Calif. Inst. Tech. 1941. Career: mgr. Gen. Precision Inc., Sunnyvale br. 1957-62; head, elec. engring. res. Lawrence Livermore Nat. Laboratory, 1962-85, consultant 1985-. Res: 146 Roan Dr Danville 94526

MANKOFF, ALBERT WILLIAM, writer, institute president; b. Aug. 24, 1926, Newark, N.J.; s. Albert and Dorothy (Klein) M.; m. Audrey Emery, Mar. 17, 1972; 1 son, Robert M.; stepfather to Alison, Cynthia, and Robert E. Lee; edn: BLS, Univ. Oklahoma, 1967. Career: mgr. organization devel. American Airlines, Tulsa, Okla. 1947-69; dir. human resources Peat, Marwick, Mitchell, Chgo. 1969-72; personnel mgr.-Europe, Digital Equip. Co., Geneva, Switz. 1972; ptnr. Lexicon Consulting, Raleigh, N.C. 1973-80; founder Monterey Inst.

of Mgmt., Monterey, Calif. 1980; total quality mgmt. cons. State of Calif., Sacto. 1980-91; pres. Inst. of Am. Historic Technology, Ojai, Calif. 1987-; bd. dirs. Meditation Groups, Inc., Ojai 1992; lectr., facilitator Meditation Mount, Ojai 1992-; bd. dirs, v.p., Psychosynthesis Internat., Ojai 1993-; past mem. Tulsa Urban League (bd. 1961-69), Oasis The Midwest Ctr. for Human Potential Chgo. (bd. 1970-73), Tulsa Employers Assn. for Merit Employment (founder 1967); author: The Star Gods 1973, Trolley Treasures, 3 vols. (1985, 88, 92), The Glory Days 1989, pub. articles re mgmt., historic streetcars, light rail systems, reincarnation, meditation; mil: Army Air Corps 1943-46; Indep. Res: 1223 Gregory St. Ojai 93023 Ofc: PO Box 494 Ojai 93024

MANLOLO, NELSON MAQUINTO, civil engineer; b. Apr. 24, 1951, Philippines, naturalized 1983; s. Fermin Manaba and Salvacion (Maquino) M.; m. Shirley B., July 8, 1978; children: Lorraine Leigh b. 1979, Joseph John b. 1982; edn: BS in C.E., Mapua Inst. of Tech. 1972; reg. civil engr., Calif. 1983, Philippines 1973. Career: civil engr. Dept. of Public Works and Hwys., Philippines 1972-78; designer/draftsman Housley Assocs., Palm Desert 1978-79; designer Ervin Engring., Palm Springs 1979-80; designer Bonadiman Assocs., San Bernardino 1980-81; civil engr. General Seating Co., San Bdo. 1981-82; civil engr. Hacker Engring., Palm Springs 1982-83; civil engr. J.F. Davidson Assocs., Riverside 1983-89; civil engr. Rick Engring. Co., Riverside 1989-90; civil engr. CalTrans Dist. 8, San Bernardino 1990-; civil engr./prin. NM Engineering, 1983-; mem: ASCE 1983-, Internat. Conf. of Building Officials 1983-, Philippine Assn. of Civil Engrs. 1972-, Assn. of Govt. Civil Engrs. of the Philippines 1972-; Republican; R.Cath.; rec: basketball. Res: 22880 Van Buren St Grand Terrace 92324 Tel: 714/783-3258

MANN, "CHARLIE" C. W., writer; b. Mar. 5, 1944, Pasadena; s. Wm. I. and Clarice (White) M.; m. Phyllis W., Aug. 9, 1969; children: Eric b. 1957; edn: AB, Kenyon Coll., PhD, Univ. of Tenn.; postgrad./hon: London Inst. Applied Res., Ga. Inst. Tech., Chattanooga St. Tech. Inst., Control Data Inst. for Adv. Res. Career: exec. dir. CARTA, Chattanooga, Tenn.; TARC, Louisville, Ky.; v.p. PRC Corp., Los Angeles; chief exec. CMA, Yucca Valley; writer CMA syndicated column "BuzzBytes - The Computer Products Review Column" (circ. 92 newspapers in we. states, 9/89), also CMA syndicated series: "BookBytes - Mini Book Reviews" (circ. 23 newspapers in we. states); writer/reviewer consumer/computer products for numerous periodicals, book length manuals for software cos.; awards: Ford Found. fellow pub. affairs. Mail: PO Box 2079 Yucca Valley 92286-2079

MANN, JEANETTE WILLIAMS, university administrator; b. June 29, 1936, Roach, Mo.; d. Jasper J. and Mayme Byler (Legge) Williams; m. Kenneth Earl Mann; children: Kathryn b. 1960, Stephen b. 1963, Rachel b. 1965; edn: AB, Univ. Mo., 1958, MA, 1963, PhD, 1968. Career: caseworker Dept. Human Welfare, Seattle, Wash. 1960-61; instr. Univ. of Missouri, Columbia 1961-68, postdoctoral fellow 1968-71; asst. prof. No. Ill. Univ., De Kalb 1971-76; dir. Affirmative Action Pgms., CSU Northridge, 1976-; trustee Pasadena Area Comm. Coll. 1983-91; awards: Rockefeller Found. fellow 1973-74, Phi Beta Kappa, woman of yr. Nat. Women's Political Caucus, Pasa. 1984, woman of yr. Pasa. Area Comm. Coll. 1984, biog. listing Who's Who in Am. Women; mem: Calif. Comm. Coll. Trustees (conf. com. 1988-89), Calif. Assn. of Comm. Colls. (res. commn. 1987-90), L.A. Basin Equal Opp. League (chair technical seminar 1988-90), Nat. Assn. of Women Dean, Counselors and Administrators (conf. com. 1988-89), Am. Assn. for Affirm. Action (reg. IX dir. 1982-84); civic: Nat. Women's Polit. Caucus Pasa. (exec. com. 1984-), Bus. & Profl. Women Pasa., YWCA Pasa. (personnel com.); Democrat; Prot. Res: 2195 E Orange Grove Blvd Pasadena 91104

MANN, JOHN KEVIN, management consultant; b. June 22, 1956, Stanford, Calif.; s. John Keith and Virginia (McKinnon) M.; m. Christine Suzanna Downs, Dec. 28, 1984; edn: BS, M.I.T., 1978; MBA, Univ. Chicago, 1983. Career: res. analyst Congressional Budget Office, W.D.C., 1978-79; land planner Sundesigns Architects, Glenwood Springs, Colo. 1979-80; devel. planner Hopi Indian Tribe, Kyakotsmovi, Ariz. 1980-81; field mktg. rep. IBM, Chgo., Balt., 1983-88, mkt. devel. IBM, W.D.C., San Francisco, 1989-91; mgmt. cons. IBM, San Francisco, 1992-; honors: Sullivan award Univ. Chicago 1981; Democrat; Christian; rec: yoga. Ofc: IBM Corporation 425 Market St 32nd Fl San Francisco 94105

MANN, MICHAEL MARTIN, corporate development executive; b. Nov. 28, 1939, N.Y.C.; s. Dr. Herbert and Rosalind (Kaplan) M.; m. Mariel Joy Steinberg, Apr. 25, 1965; edn: BS in E.E., Calif. Inst. of Tech., 1960, MS E.E., 1961; PhD E.E., USC, 1969; Exec. MBA, UCLA, 1984; Calif. lic. R.E. broker; bd. cert. in business appraisal, cert. profl. consultant, cert. mgmt. consultant. Career: exec. v.p. Helionetics Inc., Irvine 1984-85, pres. and c.e.o. 1985-86; ptnr. Mann Kavanaugh Chernove & Associates, Los Angeles 1986-87; sr. cons. Arthur D. Little Inc., L.A. 1987-88; pres. Blue Marble Devel. Group Inc., Palos Verdes Estates 1988-; chmn. and c.e.o. Blue Marble Partners, L.A. 1991-; dir: Datum Inc., Anaheim 1988-, Safeguard Health Ents. Inc. 1988-, Decade Optical Systems, Albuq. 1990-, chmn. bd. Management Technology Inc., L.A. 1990-; dir. Am. Bus. Consultants, Inc. 1993-; appt. Army-Sci. Bd. subgroup chmn. Ballistic Missile Def., W.D.C. 1984-88; awards: Hicks fellow CalTech 1961,

leadership So. Calif. Technology Execs. Network, Newport Beach 1986, patriotic civilian svc. commendn. Sec. of Army, W.D.C. 1988; mem: Presidents Assn. 1991-, Consultants Round Table 1991-, IEEE (sr. mem. 1957-), Am. Mgmt. Assn. 1988-; clubs: Palos Verdes Beach & Athletic (P.V.E.), King Harbor Yacht (Redondo Beach); inventor, 12 patents (1962-86), author two books, 50+ articles (1961-); Republican; rec: sailing. Ofc: Blue Marble Partners 406 Amapola Ave Ste 200 Torrance 90501

MANN-LAMBERT, SANDRA MARIE, information systems security executive; b. Nov. 29, 1946, Los Angeles; d. Carl Albert and Bertha Martha Mann; m. J. Louis Lambert, Nov. 16, 1985; edn: BA, Mount St. Mary's Coll., 1968; MS math., USC, 1972; MBA, Pepperdine Univ., 1979; cert. in data proc. (CDP) Inst. for Certification of Computer Profls., 1980; cert. info. systems auditor (CISA) EDP Auditors Assn., 1979. Career: math. instr. Mount St. Mary's Coll., L.A. 1968-72; L.A. City Coll., 1972-76; office mgr. Ralph Williams Ford, Encino 1968-73; internal auditor The Larwin Group Inc., Beverly Hills 1973-75; sr. EDP auditor Hughes Aircraft Co., Los Angeles 1975-76; v.p. and information security mgr. Security Pacific Corp., L.A. 1976-; domestic and internat. information security cons., 1985-86; chair data security com. Bank Adminstrn. Inst., Rolling Meadows, Ill. 1983-86; mem. L.A. Computer Crime Task Force, 1987-89; computer sci. & techn. bd. Nat. Acad. of Scis., WDC 1989-, mem. X9A3 com. Am. Nat. Stds. Inst., WDC 1986-; mem. Information Systems Security Assn., L.A. (founding pres. 1982-85, dir. 1982-89, award for outstanding contbn. 1989); pub. articles, Auerbach Data Security Management Series (1982, 85, 87); rec: tennis, photog., painting, flying. Ofc: Security Pacific Corp. 333 S Beaudry Ave W21-45 Los Angeles 90017

MANOLIS, PAUL GEORGE, corporate executive, university administrator; b. Feb. 4, 1928, Sacramento; s. George C. and Vasiliki (Kalanjopoulos) M.; m. Elene Angelica Zahas, Mar. 7, 1964; children: Alexandra, George, Dimitri, Damian; edn: BA, UC Berkeley, 1952; MA, Harvard Univ., 1954. Career: exec. sec. U.S. Sen. William F. Knowland, Wash. DC 1954-59; with Oakland Tribune, 1959-77, exec. editor 1965-74, asst. gen. mgr. 1968-72, corp. sec. Tribune Pub. Co. 1965-77; pres. BenePlus of Calif., 1979-; v.p. Hellenic Am. Devel. Corp., 1980-; Development Programs, UC Berkeley, 1983-92; dir. Patriarchal Orthodox Inst. 1992-; dir. Franklin Inc. Co., Tribune Bldg. Co.; appt. commr. Calif. Arts Commn., v. chair 1967-71; mem.: jury Pulitzer Prizes 1972, 73; bd. trustees Patriarch Athenagoras Orthodox Inst. at Grad. Theol. Union, Berkeley, (bd. pres. 1986-), Grad. Theol. Union, Anna Head Sch. Oakland, bd. dirs. Holy Cross Coll., Brookline, Mass., Archdiocesan Council Greek Orthodox Ch.; honors: Sigma Delta Chi, Sigma Alpha Epsilon, decorated Gold Cross, Crusader of Holy Sepulchre, Patriarch of Jerusalem; Gold Cross of Mount Athos Ecumenical Patriarch of Constantinople, Archon of Ecumenical Patriarchate; mem. Am. Soc. Newspaper Editors, Calif. Newspaper Pubs. Assn. (dir.); civic bds: Oakland Mus., Oakland Sym., Western Opera Theatre; chmn. bpu. bd. Orthodox Observer; Republican. Res: 100 Guilford Rd Piedmont 94611 Ofc: Orthodox Institute 2309 Hearst Ave Berkeley 94709

MANSON, DAVID JOSEPH, film producer, director; b. Jan. 6, 1952, N.Y.C.; s. Eddy Lawrence and Margery May (Abramson) M.; m. Arla Mae Nudelman (screenwriter/producer, Arla Sorkin), Apr. 4, 1982; stepdau., Lainie Sorkin b. 1971; edn: att. UC Santa Cruz 1970-71; BA (magna cum laude), UC Irvine, 1974. Career: director, actor and stage mgr. for theaters incl. Mark Taper Forum, the Los Angeles Free Shakespeare Fest., Playwrights Horizons and Manhattan Theater Club; senior v.p. creative affairs Stonehenge Prodns., L.A. 1975-80; pres. and c.e.o. Sarabande Prodns., L.A. 1980-, prod. features for Touchstone Pictures, The Walt Disney Co., Tri-Star and Warner Brothers, TV prodns. for cable and network focus on long-forms- miniseries and movies-for-TV; credits: features: The Cemetery Club, Birdy (Cannes Film Fest. special jury award), Bring On the Night (Grammy Award best longform video); miniseries: A Rumor of War (Writer's Guild Award best miniseries), The Word; TV-movies: Those Secrets, Rising Son, Eye On The Sparrow (Christopher Award), The King Of Love, Sessions, Best Kept Secrets, Night Cries, A Love Affair: The Eleanor and Lou Gehrig Story, The Spell, Louis Armstrong: Chicago Style; series: Against The Law (pilot and six episodes), Gang of Four (pilot), Elysian Fields (pilot); mem. Directors Guild Am., Writers Guild Am.; civic: devel. com. Children Now. Ofc: Sarabande Productions 530 Wilshire Blvd Ste 308 Santa Monica 90401

MAPP, JERRY WALTER, medical foundation president and chief executive; b. Sept. 1, 1945, Columbia, Miss.; s. Jerry M. and Louise E. (Foreman) M.; children: Michael A.; edn: BA in religion, Abilene Christian Univ., 1968; postgrad. in religion, Earlham Coll., 1968-69. Career: minister Texas Ch. of Christ, 1968; US Army Chaplaincy 1969-71, Vietnam, decorated Bronze star; residential treatment social worker Good Samaritan Ctr., adminstrv. asst. in chg. devel. and p.r., 1971-74; devel. assoc. Daniel Freeman Med. Ctr., Inglewood 1974-76; spl. edn. dept. Santa Monica Unified Sch. Dist., 1976-77; assoc. dir. devel. Anaheim Memorial Hosp. Devel. Found., 1977-78; dir. devel. and community relations York Sch., 1978-83; indep. cons. not-for-profit orgns. 1983-; v.p. devel. and exec. director Pacific Presbyterian Med. Ctr. Found., San Francisco 1984-91, pres. and c.e.o. Calif. Pacific Med. Ctr. Found. (merger of PPMC and CH of S.F., 6/91) 1991-; dir. workshops on planned giving, grantsmanship and trusteeship; regional conf. speaker for Calif. Assn. of Independent Schs., Council for Advance. and Support of Edn., Nat. Assn. Hosp. Devel., Nat. Soc. Fund Raising Execs.; cons. numerous orgns. including Festival Theater Calif., Monterey Peninsula Found., Family Service Agy., Ctr. for Attitudinal Healing, Eskaton Monterey Hosp., West Coast Univ., Notre Dame Sch., Merritt Peralta Med. Ctr.; bd. mem. KQED Inc.; past bd. mem. Children's Garden Marin County; former instr., devel. & comm. rels. for non-profits, Hartnell Coll., Monterey Peninsula Coll.; mem: Assn. for Healthcare Philanthropy, Nat. Soc. Fund Raising Execs., Commonwealth Club Calif., Rotary Intl. Ofc: California Pacific Medical Center Foundation PO Box 7999 San Francisco 94120 Tel:415/923-3269

MARCELLA, MARY ALICE, publisher, writer; b. July 23, 1922, Warren, Ohio; d. Anthony and Angela Marie (DeSanti) Marcella; m. Arley James Bailes Nov. 19, 1941 (div. 1974); children: Roger James b. 1942, Faith Orpha Ann b. 1950; 2 grandchildren; m. 2d Jack H. Bell, May 10, 1986 (dec. 1989); edn: CSU Long Beach 1963; Orange Coast Jr. Coll. 1968; Palomar Jr. Coll. 1971; Cuesta Jr. Coll. 1977; pre-std. cert., other courses, Am. Inst. Banking 1956-68. Career: direct sales Watkins Prods. Warren, Ohio 1940; owner, oper. refreshment concession, Lake Milton, Ohio 1941; real estate sales Gordon Ball, Warren, Ohio 1952-53; sampler Trumbull Co.- Coca Cola Co. Warren, Ohio 1953-54; teller, escrow ofcr. Bank of Am., var. So. Calif. branches 1956-68; automobile sales Sam Priestly Lincoln Mercury Dealership, Oceanside 1968; escrow ofcr. Escondido Nat. Bank, Poway 1969-71, US Nat. Bank, LaVerne 1972-74, br. mgr. Marina Fed. Savings & Loan, Avalon 1974-76, Crocker Nat. Bank, Paso Robles 1976-78, Indian Wells 1978-80 (opened 5 new escrow ofcs. for above banks); owner, publr. Marcella Press, Palm Desert 1978-; correspondent writer Daily News, Palm Desert Post, contbr. Carlsbad Journal, 1980-; auto leasing rep. Golden Bear Leasing, Del Mar 1982-; lic. life ins. sales rep.; honors: Eistedford Contest Winner 1939, Nat. Honor Soc., speech contest winner (Crocker Nat. Bank 1974), listed Internat. Who's Who of Intellectuals 1990; mem: Norwalk Bus. & Profl. Women's Club (treas. 1960), Chiche's, Bank of Am. Women's Speech Club, Desertair Toastmasters (charter mem., pres. 1979-82), No. County Toastmasters 1982-, Desert Beautiful (Palm Desert 1979-), Desert Four Repub. Women Federated (1st v.p. 1981-82), La Quinta Historical Soc. (founding pres. 1984-87, life mem.); past mem: Bd. of Realtors, Calif. Escrow Assn., Avalon C.of C., Quota Club (Paso Robles, corr. secty. 1978), Dateland Toastmistress Club (historian 1979); author (book of poems) Rhyme and Thought, (song) Color Fills the World, (song lyrics) Between You and Me, Forty Days & Forty Nights, A Million Paths Within My Mind; rec: golf, travel, sewing. Address: P.O. Box 1057 La Quinta 92253-1057

MARCO, DAVID DUANE, biomedical engineer; b. Feb. 3, 1951, Apollo, Pa.; s. Peter M. and Jean Martha (Merlo) M.; m. Nancy Elizabeth Bierman, Nov. 16, 1985; 1 dau. Phoebe Elizabeth b. 1992; edn: BS in biomed. engring., Rensselaer Polytech. Inst., 1973; cert. special competency in cardiac pacing for non-physicians N.Am. Soc. of Pacing & Electrophysiology 1991. Career: clin. engr. Shock & Trauma Unit Albany (N.Y.) Med. Ctr. 1973-75; jr. research engr. Abcor Inc., Wilmington, Mass. 1975-76; biomed. engr. University Hosp., Boston 1976-77; sales rep. and field clin. engr. ARCO Med. Products, San Francisco 1977-81; field clin. engr. Siemens Pacesetter, Oakland 1981-; mem.: N.Am. Soc. Pacing & Electrophysiology (assoc. 1986-), Shiloh Christian Fellowship Oakland (dist. dir. 1990-); contbr. jour. articles in cardiac pacing, trauma (1973-); Republican; Christian; rec: singing, worship music, photography, computing. Res: 140 Hermosa Ave Oakland 94618 Ofc: Siemens Pacesetter 3470 Mt Diablo Blvd Ste A150 Lafayette 94549-3939

MARCUS, ALON, doctor of Oriental medicine; b. 1957, Tel Aviv, Israel; s. Johseph Marcus, MD and Cilla (Furmanovich) M.; m. Ruth P. Goldenberg, MD, Feb. 4, 1990; children: Sivan b. 1993; edn: gen. study, film, Colombia Coll., Chgo., Ill., 1979; AS, Merritt Coll., Oakland, Calif., 1982; L, AC, Am. Coll. of Chinese Medicine, S.F., Calif., 1983; doctor of Oriental medicine, S.A.M.R.A., L.A., Calif., 1986. Career: preceptor AAA, Dr. M. Lee, 1982-83; resident, Canton Muni Hosp., Canton, China 1985; private practice, Berkeley, Calif., 1984-; doctor, Haight Ashbury Free Clinic, S.F., Calif., 1988; tchg. asst., Basics of Orthopedics, San Ramon Regional Med. Ctr., San Ramon, Calif., 1993-; mem: Calif. Assn. of Acupuncturists 1985-, Am. Assn. of Acupuncturists 1985-, Am. Assn. of Orthopedic Medicine 1992-; author: Acute Abdominal Syndromes, Combined Chinese-Western 1991; publ. article on T.C.M., ortho. medicine treatment of shock pain, 1993. Ofc: 1650 Alcatraz Ave Berkeley 94703

MARGOLIN, FRANCES, psychologist; b. Mar. 17, 1922, Montgomery Co., Pa.; d. Harry and Dorothy (Blanc) Mongin; m. Elias Margolin, Mar. 12, 1944; children: Janice b. 1959, John b. 1965, Carol b. 1966, Paul b. 1967; edn: BA, Temple Univ. 1948; MA, Ohio Univ. 1955; PhD, U.S. Internat. Univ., S.D. 1972; lic. Clin. Psychologist, Marriage and Family Counselor, Calif. 1960; Diplomate, Am. Bd. of Profl. Psychology 1982. Career: clin. psychologist Dayton St. Hosp., Dayton, Ohio 1948-55; San Diego Superior Ct., 1955-74; pvt. practice, La Jolla 1974-; honors: listed Nat. Register of Health Care Providers. Res: 887 La Jolla Rancho Rd La Jolla 92037 Ofc: PO Box 3056 La Jolla 92038

MARHOEFER, GORDON JOSEPH, chartered life underwriter, lawyer; b. Aug. 25, 1932, Detroit, Mich.; s. Edwin Louis and Lucy Cecilia (Cavanaugh) Marhoefer; m. Patricia Black Nutter, 1978; children: George, b. 1956; Clifford, b. 1956; Thomas, b. 1958; Robert, b. 1960; (step) Darci, b. 1969; edn: BA, Loyola Univ., L.A. 1954; CLU, Am. College 1966; JD, Loyola Law Sch. 1972; ChFC, Am. College 1983. Career: Pacific Mutual Life Ins. Co., L.A.: adminstrv. trainee 1955-57, agent (Sherman Oaks) 1957-59, adminstrv. asst. 1959-61, mgr. of conservation 1961-64, mgr. advanced underwriting, 1964-67, dir. estate & bus. planning, 1967-72; life underwriter/atty., Newport Beach 1972-; instr. CLU, instr. Life Mgmt. Assn.; honors: Million Dollar Round Table 1977-92; mem: Newport Beach-Irvine Estate Plng. Council (founding dir., bd. 1982-87, pres. 1986-87), Orange Coast Estate Plng. Council, Planned Giving Round Table of Orange County, Calif. Bar Assn., Orange Co. Bar Assn., Am. Soc. of CLUs, Nat. Assn. Life Underwriters, Mensa; civic: Wellness Community of Orange County (dir. 1992), Newport Theatre Arts Ctr. (dir. 1988-91), Costa Mesa Civic Playhouse, Alano Club of Costa Mesa (v.chmn. 1975-76), Burbank Parochial Baseball League (v.chmn. 1968-71); contbr. articles in profl. jours.; Republican (charter pres. Burbank YR); R.Cath.; rec: drama & musical comedy, camping. Res: 342 Sydney Ln Costa Mesa 92627 Ofc: Massachusetts Mutual Life Ins. Co., 610 Newport Ctr Dr Ste 900 Newport Beach 92663

MARION, MICHAEL WILLIAM, clinical audiologist; b. Sept. 30, 1945, Walla Walla, Wash.; s. Wm. Jennings and Mary Alice (Brennan) M.; m. Laurel, Apr. 16, 1983; edn: BS, Univ. Utah, 1968, MS, 1971; Cert. Clin. Competence, Am. Sp.-Lang.-Hearing Assn. Career: dir. clin. services Univ. Wyo., Laramie 1971-73; dir. audiological services Wyoming Otolaryngology, P.C., Casper, Wy. 1973-82; gen. ptnr. Micromar Hearing Conservationists, Upland, Calif. 1982-83; we. reg. mgr. Danavox, Inc., Fullerton 1983-86; owner/dir. clin. services The Hearing Center, Camarillo 1984-; adj. instr. Univ. Wyo. 1973-79; mem. Wyoming Bd. of Hearing Aid Examiners 1979-82; honors: Phi Kappa Phi 1971, disting. service Wyoming Sp.-Hearing Assn. 1979, Outstanding Young Men Am. (1977, 79, 80); mem: Calif. Sp.-Hearing Assn., Hearing Aid Assn. Calif., Am. Sp.-Lang.-Hearing Assn. (Legis. Council and sub-coms.), Am. Acad. of Audiology, Acad. of Dispensing Audiologists, Wyo. Sp.-Hearing Assn. (pres. 1975-76), Camarillo C.of C.; clubs: Jonathan, Lions (past dir.); publs: British Jour. of Audiology (1974), AMA Archives of Otolaryngology (1974); rec: ski, boating. Ofc: The Hearing Center 5800 Santa Rosa Rd Ste 123 Camarillo 93012

MARKEN, GIDEON ANDREW, III, advertising and public relations executive; b. June 24, 1940, Hampton, Iowa; s. Gideon Andrew, II and Cleone Marie (Riis) M.; m. Jeannine Gay Hill, Dec. 28, 1963; children: Tracy Lynn b. 1967, Gideon A. b. 1969; edn: BS, Iowa State Univ., 1972; MBA, Hamilton Inst., 1975; APR, accredited Pub. Relations Soc. Am. Career: pub. relations mgr. Fairchild Instrumentation, Mountain View 1965-66; dir. pub. relations Barnes-Hind Pharmaceuticals, Sunnyvale 1966-67; v.p and pub. relations dir. Bozell-Jacobs Advt., Palo Alto 1967-77; pres. Marken Communications, Santa Clara 1977-; recipient Bronze Awards PRSA, Peninsula chapt. (1977, 80, 85); mem: Pub. Relations Soc. Am. (chapt. pres. 1972, 75), Am. Med. Writers Assn. (pres. 1967), BPAA 1982-, Am. Mgmt. Assn. 1982-, PMA 1982-; publs: 100+ articles on mgmt., mktg., advt., and PR (1967-); mil: sgt. USAF 1962-65; Republican; Lutheran; rec: scuba, sailing, aerobics. Ofc: Marken Communications 3600 Pruneridge Ave Santa Clara 95051

MARKER, MARC LINTHACUM, lawyer, investor; b. July 19, 1941, Los Angeles; s. Clifford Harry and Voris (Linthacum) M.; m. Sandra Yocom, Aug. 28, 1965; children: Victor b. 1970, Gwendolyn b. 1974; edn: Harvard Sch., AB, UC Riverside 1965; JD, USC 1967. Career: asst. v.p., asst. secty. Security Pacific Nat. Bank, Los Angeles 1970-73; chief counsel Security Pacific Leasing Corp., San Francisco 1973-92, secty. 1980, senior v.p. 1981-92, also pres./secty./counsel Security Pacific Leasing Services Corp. 1977-92; dir: Refiners Petroleum Corp. 1977-81, Voris, Inc. (dir. sec. 1973-86); instr. comml. law Am. Inst. of Banking, 1971-72; lectr. Practicing Law Inst., Am. Assn. of Equip. Lessors, 1976-; mem: Am. Bar Assn., Am. Assn. of Equip. Lessors Lawyers Com. (1977-81); clubs: University (L.A.), Army & Navy; mil: cmdr. USCGR 1966-89; Republican; Lutheran; rec: scuba, mountaineering. Res: 41 Lakeside Dr Corte Madera 94925

MARKEY, MICHAEL LYNN, certified financial planner; b. June 6, 1943, Ft. Wayne, Indiana; s. Arnold Leo and Wanda L. (McGowan) M.; m. Irene Torngren, Mar. 11, 1978; children: Michael Arnold b. 1981, Victoria Ingrid b. 1983; edn: CFP, Coll. for Financial Planning, Denver, Co., 1977; MBA, Santa Clara Univ., 1967; BS, San Jose State Univ., 1966; cert. financial planner; cert. real estate broker (Calif) 1971; ptnr. Markey/Coit Investments 1969-; v.p. First Orinda Corp., Orinda, Calif. 1971-73; pres., founder, CEO Orinda Financial Group, Walnut Creek 1973-; NASD registered prin. w/Finl. Planners Equity Corp. and American Investors Co.; mem: Internat. Assn. for Finl. Planning (past v.p. and past dir. East Bay Chapt.) 1973-, Institute of Cert. Financial Planners; co-chmn. of 1980 Greater Bay Area Finl. Planning Conf. and pgm. chmn. 1984 conf.; chmn. Real Estate Outlook Pgms. 1980, 81; ed. advy. bd. to Digest of Finl. Planning Ideas; mil: USAF Reserves, 1967-73; Independent; rec: golf. Res: 48 Tappan Ln Orinda 94563

MARKHAM, REED B., author, educator; b. Feb. 14, 1957, Alhambra; s. John Frederick and Reeda Margaret (Bjarnson) M.; edn: AA, BA, MA, Brigham Young Univ., Provo 1981, 81, 82; AS, BS, Regents Coll., Albany, N.Y. 1981, 82; MPA, USC, 1983; MA, UCLA, 1989; PhD, CPU, San Rafael 1992; career: prof. Chaffey Coll., 1986-87; prof. communications dept. Calif. State Polytech. Univ., Pomona 1987-; mem. EOP acad. planning com. 1989-; pres. bd. trustees Regents Coll., Albany, N.Y. 1983-86; accreditation commn. NAPNSC, Denver, Co. 1989-92; evaluator Am. Council on Edn., W.D.C. 1991-92; awards: Golden Leaves Cal Poly Pres.'s Office (1988, 89, 90), leadership Bicentennial of U.S. Constn., W.D.C. 1989, C-Span Prof. C-Span Network, W.D.C. 1991, Points of Light award The White House 1991; mem: Pub. Relations Soc. of Am., Nat. Assn. of Scholars (D.C.), Doctorate Assn. of N.Y. Scholars, NSIEE (D.C. devel. com. 1985-86), BYU Alumni Assn. (SDA pres.); civic: Tourn. of Roses Parade Club 1988-90; editorial bds: Education Digest, Speaker and Gavel, Public Relations Rev., Nat. Forensic Jour., Forensic Educator, Clearinghouse for the Contemporary Educator; author: Advances in Public Speaking 1990, Public Opinion: R&R 1990, Power Speaking 1990, Effective Speechwriting 1984; Republican; LDS Ch.; rec: athletics. Res: 8832 19th St, 62, Alta Loma 91701 Ofc: Cal Poly Comm. Dept. 3801 W Temple Ave Pomona 91768

MARKOVICH-TREECE, PATRICIA H., economic & political consultant/artist; b. Oakland, Calif.; d. Patrick Joseph and Helen Emily (Prydz) Markovich; children: Michael Sean Treece b. 1965, Bryan Jeffry Treece b. 1967, Tiffany Helene Treece b. 1970; edn: BA in econ., MS in econ., UC Berkeley; postgrad. (Lilly Found. grantee) Stanford Univ., (NSF grantee) Oreg. Grad. Res. Ctr. Career: with public rels. dept. Pettler Advt., Inc.; private practice political and econ. cons.; aide to majority whip Oreg. House of Reps.; lectr., instr., various Calif. institutions., Chemeketa Coll., Oreg., Portland State Univ., Oreg.; commr. City of Oakland, Calif., 1970-74; chairperson, bd. dirs. Cable Sta. KCOM, Piedmont; coord. City of Piedmont, Calif. Gen. Planning Commn.; mem. Piedmont Civic Assn., Core Advy. Com. City of Oakland, Oakland Mus. Archives of Calif. Artists; mem. Internat. Soc. Philos. Enquiry, Mensa (ofcr. S.F. reg.), Bay Area Artists Assn. (coord., founding mem.), Berkeley Art Ctr. Assn., S.F. Arts Commn. File, Calif. Index for Contemporary Arts, Pro Arts. No. Calif. Public Edn. and Govt. Access Cable TV Com. (founding), Triple Nine Soc.; Democrat; Catholic; rec: home improvement. Res/Ofc: 132 Olive Ave. Piedmont 94611-4430

MARKOWITZ, SAMUEL SOLOMON, professor of chemistry; b. Oct. 31, 1931, Bklyn.; s. Max and Florence Ethel (Goldman) M.; children: Michael b. 1960, Daniel b. 1963, Jonah b. 1965; edn: BS, Rensselaer Poly Inst., 1953; MA, Princeton Univ., 1955, PhD, 1957; thesis res. stu. Brookhaven Nat. Lab, Upton, N.Y. 1955-57. Career: NSF postdoctoral fellow Univ. of Birmingham, England 1957-58; U.S. sr. postdoctoral fellow, vis. prof. Faculte Des Scis. de L'Universite de Paris, Orsay, France 1964-65; vis. prof. Weizmann Inst. of Science, Rehovot, Israel 1973-74; prof. of chemistry (freshman, nuclear, analytical chem.) and faculty sr. scientist Univ. Calif. Berkeley and Lawrence Berkeley Lab., Calif. 1958-; elected Berkeley Board of Edn. 1969-73 (pres. 1971-72); awards: Coll. letters in athletics (6) baseball, basketball, soccer, Mary D'Urso Award for Outstanding public servant in pub. edn., Alameda Co. 1973; mem: Am. Chem. Soc. (1953-, chair Calif. sect. 1991, nat. councilor, bd. dirs. 1989-), Am. Physical Soc. 1955-, AAAS (1957-, Fellow); publs: original sci. research in nuclear and enviornmental chemistry (1953-); Jewish, Cong. Beth Israel, Berkeley (pres., bd. trustees 1960-); rec: sports, athletics. Res: 317 Tideway Dr #8 Alameda 94501 Ofc: Dept Chemistry Univ California Berkeley 94720

MARMANN, SIGRID, executive (principal/president); b. Feb. 8, 1938, Voelklingen/Saarland, Germany; d. Leo and Karoline Anna (Weidenhof) Marmann; edn: BS, accounting, Ind. & Handelskammer, Saarbrueckn, Germany 1956; postgraduate study, Norwood College, London, Eng. 1962; postgrad. study, Golden Gate Univ., S.F., Calif. 1970-85; BA, management, St. Mary's Coll., Moraga, Calif. 1984. Career: controller, MOM, Paris, France 1965-69; bookkeeper, Chrissa Imports, Brisbane, Calif. 1970-78; accounting mgr., Highcity Internat., San Anselmo, Calif. 1978-80; accounting mgr. & systems analyst, Kukje Korean Trading Co., E. Rutherford, N.J. 1980-81; asst. treas., Amer. Mercantile Co., Brisbane, Calif. 1981-84; controller, Provident Credit Union, Burlingame 1984; owner, Datatech EDI Systems, San Rafael 1984-; pres./prin., Datatech EDI Systems & Telepay Express, San Rafael 1989-; qualified installer, Great Plains Software; installer, developer, Computer Assoc. Internat., Islandia, NY; devel. of application software for EDI/EFT and fin. svs. for businesses; awards: Nominee Membership award, Electronic Data Interchange, Va. 1990; mem: ANSI ASC X12 Electronic Data Interchange 1989-; primary founder, No. Calif. EDI Users Group 1990-; author: publ. article on EDI, 1992; rec: traveling, skiing, swimming, sailing, fishing, baking. Res: 30 Newport Way, San Rafael 94901

MARONEY, MARION LESTER, corporation founder; b. Nov. 1, 1904, Memphis, Tenn.; s. Charles Gorman and Jennie (Everton) M.; m. Mary Louise Crouse, April 6, 1934; 1 dau., Mary Lelane b. 1940; Career: founder, CEO Sattex Corp., Vernon 1955-84; ret.; honors: BSA Silver Beaver, Scoutmasters Key; civic: Nat. Taxpayers Foundation, Heritage Found., U.S. English, Citizens Against Govt. Waste, BSA (scoutmaster 1932-37, field exec. 1944-45, scoutmaster); author A Guide to Metal & Plastic Finishing, 1989; Republican; Episcopalian.

MARQUEZ, ALBERT JOHN, bank examiner; b. June 3, 1961, Astoria, Oreg.; s. Domingo Cruz and Socorro Camps (Sungahid) M.; m. Annabelle, May 28, 1988; children: Ashley Marie b. 1989, Anthony John b. 1991; edn: BS kinesiology, UCLA; MBA, San Diego State Univ. Career: acct. Dion G. Dyer, APC, San Diego 1984-87; asst. ops. mgr. Reliance Mgmt. Corp., San Diego 1985-86; bank examiner Calif. State Banking Dept., San Diego 1987-; mem. Soc. of Fin. Examiners, Assn. of MBA Execs.; R.Cath.; rec: tennis, photog., computers. Res: Scripps Ranch San Diego 92131 Ofc: Calif. State Banking Dept. 110 West C St Ste 1810 San Diego 92101

MARQUEZ, EMILIO EUSTAQUIO, clergyman; b. Nov. 2, 1938, Pinar del Rio, Cuba, naturalized U.S. citizen 1974; s. Emiliano Marquez and Berta Maria (Suarez) Izquierdo; edn: grad. Calif. Coll. of Commerce, Long Beach; RScF, Religious Sci., L.A., 1980, DD and PhD, Religious Sci., Long Beach, 1981, MDiv, Oceanside, 1991; lic. Religious Sci. Practitioner, Ch. of Religious Sci., Seal Beach 1981. Career: practitioner Religious Sci., Ramona, Calif. 1979-; minister Religious Sci., El Paso, Tex., 1980; pastor and dean, Long Beach, Calif. 1981-85; tchr., Oceanside, Calif. 1981-; founder, pastor, pres. Independent Ch. of Religious Sci. and dean Religious Sci. Theol. Sem., Ramona, Calif. 1988-; liaison AIDS Wholistics, Ramona 1991-; awards: Hon. PhD Religious Sci., Religious Sci. Theol. Sem., Ramona 1989; author: Religion Edn. ministry degree program 1981, Identity Workshop, Sci. of Mind in Action 1981; originator and promoter of "Religion Day" (2nd Sunday of Aug.) observed to honor all religions, second annual observance honored by City of San Diego Mayoral Proclamation of Religion's Day In San Diego (8/11/91); mil: Cuban Army 1956-59; Democrat; avocation: World's Religions reporter. Res: 1313 Termino Long Beach 90804-3014 Ofc: 716 E Valley Pkwy Ste 121 Escondido 92065 Ph: 619/738-0526

MARRINER, DAVID RICHARD, recreational vehicle and mobile home manufacturing financial executive; b. Aug. 10, 1934, Laguna Beach; s. Richard McFarland and Frances Winifred (Phillips) M.; m. Joan Hooper, 1952; children: Marcia Jean b. 1953, Susan Key b. 1957, Sheryl Ann b. 1967; edn: BA hons., Stanford Univ. 1956; CPA 1958. Career: auditor Arthur Andersen & Co., Los Angeles 1957-67; sr.v.p. fin. Fleetwood Enterprises, Riverside 1968-73; v.p. fin. Golden West M.H., Santa Ana 1973; Moduline Internat., Lacey, Wash. 1975-78; treas. Fleetwood Enterprises, Riverside 1979-; mem: Am. Inst. CPA, Calif. Soc. CPA, Riverside C.of C. (dir.), Keep Riverside Ahead (dir.), Stanford Club of Inland Empire (pres. 1987-88); Republican; Prot.; rec: hunting, fishing, skiing. Res: 6255 Appian Way Riverside 92506 Ofc: Fleetwood Enterprises, Inc. POB 7638 3125 Myers St Riverside 92523

MARROQUIN, PATRICIA, journalist; b. Feb. 1, 1957, West Covina; d. Humberto and Josephine (Aragon) Marroquin; m. Gary Neil Harvick, April 14, 1984; 1 stepson, Robert b. 1974; edn: BS, Cal Poly Pomona 1980; MA, Stanford Univ. 1981. Career: newsroom typist San Gabriel Valley Tribune, West Covina 1974-79; newsletter ed. East San Gabriel Valley Consortium 1979-80; nat. copy desk intern Wall Street Jour., NYC 1980; nat. desk copy ed. San Jose Mercury News, San Jose 1981-86; mng. ed. Micro Market World, Menlo Park 1987; copy ed., news ed., makeup ed. Los Angeles Times, Costa Mesa 1987-; fellow Inst. for Journalism Edn., Mgt. Tng. Ctr., Northwestern Univ., 1990; panel organizer Nat. Assn. of Hispanic Journalists Conf., S.F., 1990 and NYC, 1991; judge Pacific Northwest Soc. Profl. Journalists, Sigma Delta Chi Contest 1989; honors: Press Club So. Calif. "Writes of Spring Award" 1979, Opus Mag. Writer of Year 1978-9, Sigma Delta Chi, Soc. Profl. Journalists Graduate of Year 1980, Dean's List and acad. hons. Cal Poly 1975-80, listed Who's Who Among Am. H.S. Students, Who's Who Among Students in Am. Univs. & Colls., Who's Who Among Hispanic Americans 1990-; mem: Nat. Assn. Hispanic Journalists, Calif. Chicano News Media Assn.; co-founder, ed., writer Perspectiva: The Hispanic Newspaper of Record (1988); rec: writing, photog., jogging. Res: 10189 Oriole Ave Fountain Valley 92708 Ofc: LA Times Editorial Dept. 1375 Sunflower Ave Costa Mesa 92626

MARROW, MARVA JAN, photographer, author; b. Apr. 22, 1948, Denver; d. Sydney and Helen Berniece (Garber) M.; edn: Carnegie-Mellon Univ. 1965-67. Career: singer, songwriter RCA Records, Italy 1972-77, lyricist songs for Italian pop artists incl. Lucio Battisti, Battiato, Premiata Forneria Marconi (PFM), Patty Pravo, 1972-; freelance photographer Italy and U.S., 1976-, corr., photographer Italian TV Guide, Milan 1979-, collaborator, photog. various periodicals in U.S. and Europe, contbr. photos for covers and articles in nat. and internat. mags.; author photobook: Inside the L.A. Artist, 1988; dir. acquisitions RAI-TV, Los Angeles, 1990-91, also producer RAI-TV and Radio 1990-; mng. agent Thomas Angel Productions, L.A. 1991-; represented by Shooting Star Photo Agy., USA, Agenzia Marka, Agenzia Masi, Italy, Uniphoto Press Internat., Japan; mem: Motion Picture Assn. of Am., Fgn. Press Assn.; Democrat; rec: cooking, travel, people, breeding show cats. Studio: Altadena Ofc: Shooting Star Agy PO Box 93368 L.A. 90093

MARSDEN, SULLIVAN SAMUEL, JR., professor of petroleum engineering, b. June 3, 1922, St. Louis, Mo.; s. Sullivan S., Sr. and Irene Margaret (Frick) M.; m. Margaret Coolidge, Sept. 4, 1948; children: Sullivan F. b. 1949, Robert S. b. 1951, Mary V. b. 1953, Anastasia E. b. 1955; edn: BA engrg. chem., Stanford Univ., 1944, PhD physical chem., 1948. Career: phys. chemist Tenn. Eastman Co., Oak Ridge, Tenn., 1945; phys. chemist Stanford Res. Inst., Menlo Park, 1947-50; asst. dir. National Chem. Lab., Poona, India, 1950-53; assoc. prof. pet. engrg. Penn. State Univ., Pa. 1953-57; Stanford Univ., 1957-62, prof. pet. engrg., 1963-; awards: Fulbright Awards- Univ. Tokyo, Japan 1963-64, Gubkin Inst., Moscow, USSR 1978, Oil & Gas Inst., Bucharest, Romania 1978; sr. mem. Soc. Petroleum Engrs. 1953-; publs: 100+ tech. papers and presentations, 3 patents issued; Republican; rec: hiking, skiing, photography, gardening. Res: 868 Lathrop Dr Stanford 94305 Ofc: Petroleum Engineering Dept. Stanford 94305-2220

MARSH, THOMAS ARCHIE, sculptor; b. May 7, 1951; s. Archie Glen and Florence Margaret (Weber) M.; m. Marie Jean Sovey, June 14, 1975 (div. Mar., 1981); edn: BFA, Layton Sch. of Art, Milwaukee, Wis. 1971-74; anatomy study, Med. Coll. of Wis., Milwaukee 1973-74; aesthetics study, Univ. of So. Calif., L.A. 1975-76; MFA, Calif. State Univ., Long Beach 1974-77. Career: instr. of sculpture, Calif. State Univ., Long Beach 1978-79; instr. of sculpture, S.F. State Univ., S.F. 1979-80; instr. of anatomy, Acad. of Art Coll., S.F. 1981-; studio asst., Milton Hebald, Sculptor, Rome, Italy 1977-78; public lectures, Univ. of S.F. 1983, 1984, 1986, 1987; solo exhib., Alliance Francaise, S.F. 1982; solo exhib., Univ. of S.F. 1987; co-curated exhib., The Goddess of Democracy, Bedford Gallery, Reg. Ctr. for the Arts, Walnut Creek 1991; awards: Elizabeth Greenshields Found. Award, Montreal, Can. 1977; public installation of drawings (permanent) Univ. of S.F., Lone Mountain Coll., Rossi Lib. 1985; Outstanding Contribution Award, Svc. Ctr. for Chinese Democracy, S.F.C.A. 1991; Cert. of Appreciation, Marin Philosophical Soc., Tiburon 1992, Chinese Democratic Edn. Found., S.F.C.A. 1992; Outstanding Educator Award, Liberal Arts Dept., Acad. of Art Coll., S.F. 1992; S.C.O.P.E. Award for city beautification (bronze sculpture), Santa Cruz 1992; mem: Found. for Chinese Democracy (bd. dirs. 1990), Acad. of Art Coll., S.F. (bd. dirs. 1992-) sculptor, (public) bronze figure, Calif. State Univ., Long Beach campus 1977; (public) bronze portrait bust, UC Berkeley Minor Hall 1984; (public) bronze relief, 343 Sansome St., S.F. 1990; sculptor & co-designer, (public) bronze reliefs, 235 Pine St., S.F. 1990; (public) bronze monument with figure, West Cliff Dr., Santa Cruz,1991; (public) bronze portrait bust, Richard M. Lucas Ctr., Stanford Univ. Med. Sch. 1992; Libertarian; Lutheran; rec: opera. Ofc: Thomas Marsh Sculpture Studio 2377 San Jose Ave. San Francisco 94112

MARSHALL, JEFFERY RYAN, real estate broker; b. Jan. 28, 1950, Hawthorne; s. Wayne Eugene and Onilee Jane (Violett) M.; m. Elizabeth Ann Oakes, Dec. 19, 1969 (div. 1972); m. Julie Ann Papp, Aug. 10, 1974; children: Ryan b. 1970, Anthony b. 1970, Jennifer b. 1977; edn: Control Data Inst. 1969. Career: sales assoc. First Am. Realty, Mission Viejo 1974-78, sales mgr., c.e.o. First Am. Realty Inc. 1978-; awards: Saddleback Valley Bd. Realtors top sales 1977, top lister 1977, top dollar volume 1977; mem: Nat. Assn. Realtors, Calif. Assn. Realtors, Saddleback Valley Bd. Realtors, Victor Valley Bd. Realtors, Oceanside Bd. Realtors, Saddleback C.of C., Oceanside C.of C., Better Bus. Bureau; articles pub. on achievement and motivation (1975-); Republican; Lutheran. Ofc: First American Realty, Inc. 24501 Marguerite Pkwy #5 Mission Viejo 92692

MARSTON, RICHARD WELDEN, lawyer; b. May 8, 1933, Ithaca, NY; s. Winthrop Simon and Sylva Orabelle (Jones) M.; m. Margaret Scholz, Feb. 20, 1960; children: John b. 1962, Ann b. 1964, Robert b. 1965; edn: BS, UC Berkeley 1955, JD, UC Hastings Coll. of Law 1963; admitted U.S. Supreme Ct. 1971. Career: pvt. practice law, San Jose 1964-68; municipal atty. San Jose, Glendale, Beverly Hills & Burbank 1968-88; atty. private practice, 1988-; mem: Calif. Bar Assn., Los Angeles Co. Bar Assn., Glendale Bar Assn., Kiwanis Glendale (dir. 1987-89, v.p. 89-90), SAR (chancellor 1990-), So. Calif. Genealogical Soc. (dir. 1985-86), F&A Masons Jewel City Lodge No. 368, Royal Canyon Property Owners Assn. (secty. 1992-); mil: capt. USAFR 1971; Republican; R.Cath.; rec: dist. running, backpacking, genealogy. Res: 1224 Imperial Dr Glendale 91207 Ofc: 801 N Brand Blvd Ste 950 Glendale 91203

MART, BRADLEY CURTIS, lawyer, executive; b. Oct. 12, 1957, Los Angeles; s. Donald Sanford and Marbeth Mart (Blank) M.; m. Nicole Hanna, 1988; edn: BS pub. affairs/pub. admin. (honors), USC, 1979; JD, Univ. Santa Clara, 1983; admitted Calif. St. Bar 1983. Career: asst. exec. dir. Bay Planning Coalition, San Francisco 1983-88; atty. pvt. general law practice, 1983-; Chief Ops. Bay World Trading, Ltd. (export-import co.), S.F. 1985-; appt: del. White House Conf. on Small Bus. (1986 chmn. state & regional coms.), advy. bd. Senate Select Com. on Small Bus. Ents. (co-ch.), S.F. Leadership Council 1987, asst. to fgn. policy advisor Sen. Edward Kennedy 1977; awards: outstanding participant Nat. Assn. of Comm. Leadership Orgns. (S.F. class of 1987), Best Appellant Brief from Moot Ct. Competition 1981, Emory Law Scholar 1980, USC Scholar 1977-79; mem: Cousteau Soc., World Affairs Council No. Calif., Environ. Protection Agency's S.F. Bay Nat. Estuary Project

(alt. mgmt. com. 1986-88), Oakland Internat. Airport Advy. com. 1986-88, Assn. of Bay Area Govt.'s Bay Trail Planning Project (alt. advy. com. 1986-88), Toastmasters Internat. 1985-87; publs: articles in Meat Plant Mag. (9/88), Meat & Poultry Mag. (1/88), ArborAge Mag. (8/89); res. pub. by Bay Planning Coalition: Landowner Liability and Public Access (1985), The Saved Bay (1987); contbr. poems var. anthologies; rec: travel, photog., writing, rowing, distance swimming. Ofc: Bay World Trading, Ltd., 5 Third St Suite 1018 San Francisco 94103

MARTELLA, VINCENT NICHOLAS, engineer; b. Sept. 12, 1935, New York City; s. Michael and Anna (D'Andrea) Martella; nephew of Dr. Luigi Martella (1911-1971), distinguished Italian architect, professor and painter; m. Jean Susan Scrivani, June 29, 1963; children: Denise, b. 1967, Paul, b. 1970, JoAnne, b. 1978; edn: BSME, Polytech. Inst. of New York, 1966; MSME, Loyola Univ. of Los Angeles, 1972; grad. Cal Tech engring. mgmt. pgm. 1989; Reg. Profl. Mech. Engr., Calif. 1978. Career: stress analyst, F-5 supersonic fighter and 747 comml. jet, Northrop Corp., Hawthorne 1966-68; stress analyst, mil. and comml. helicopters incl. advanced rotorcraft design, Hughes Helicopters Inc., Culver City 1968-71; stress analyst, B-1 Bomber, Rockwell Internat., Los Angeles Div., El Segundo 1971-72; lead engr., San Onofre nuclear power plant, Bechtel Power Corp., Norwalk 1972-77; prin. engr., oil refineries, gas-oil separation units and nuclear power plants, Brown & Root Braun, Alhambra 1977-85; senior engr., F-20 Tigershark aft fuselage structural analysis and loads test; engring. splst. and lead engr., Adv. Tactical Fighter pgm.; senior lead engr., aircraft structural design and analysis, Northrop Corp., Aircraft Div., Hawthorne 1985-; mem: The New York Acad. of Sciences, The Mathematical Assn. of Am., Northrop Mgmt. Club; civic: tutor in math.; Republican; R.Cath.; rec: historical aircraft, travel, sailing. Res: 5308 Vista Del Mar, Cypress 90630 Ofc: Northrop Corp., Aircraft Div., One Northrop Ave, Hawthorne 90250-3277

MARTENS, THOMAS ALLAN, environmentalist; b. Oct. 24, 1945, Stevens Point, Wis.; s. Armin Henry and Marle (Sobczyk) M.; m. Patrical Ellen McCall; children: Lora, Sara; edn: Univ. Wis. 1970-71; Univ. Wis. Madison 1974; MA, Univ. San Francisco. Career: reporter, ed. Contra Costa Times, Walnut Creek 1976-78; edn. ed. Herald & News, Klamath Falls, Ore. 1978-79; ed. N. Lake Tahoe Bonanza, Incline Village 1979-80; Tahoe World, Tahoe City 1980-83; copy ed. Reno Gazette Jour., Nev. 1983-84; exec. dir. League to Save Lake Tahoe 1984-; awards: Calif. Newspaper Publs. Assn. 15 journalism awards 1977-84; mem: Sierra Club, Tahoe Tallac Assn., Friends of Hope Valley, Planning & Conservation League (bd. mem. 1984-), Tahoe Valley Sch. Advy. Com. (bd. mem. 1985-); co-author Five Easy Turns (1980), 60 articles pub. in national and reg. papers (1984-88); mil: radioman 3d. USN 1966-68; Democrat; rec: running, cross country ski racing. Ofc: Box 10110 South Lake Tahoe 95731

MARTIN, CLYDE VERNE, psychiatrist; b. Apr. 7, 1933, Coffeyville, Kans.; s. Howard Verne and Elfrieda Louise (Moehn) M.; m. Barbara Jean McNeilly, June 24, 1956; children: Kent b. 1959, Kristin b. 1960, Kerry b. 1962, Kyle b. 1965; edn: BA, Univ. Kans. 1955; MD, Univ. Kans. Sch. of Med., 1958; MA, Webster Univ. (Mo.) 1977; JD, Thomas Jefferson Coll. of Law (L.A.) 1985; diplomate in psychiatry Am. Bd. Psychiat. and Neurol. 1982; career: minister, supply pastor and co-dir. rel. edn., Methodist Ch., 1951-58; pvt. practice psychiatry in Kansas City, Mo. 1958-84, founder Mid-Continent Psychiatric Hosp., Olathe, Kans. 1972, pres. bd. dirs. Martin Psychiatric Res. Found. 1976-; public practice, 1986-, surveyor Jt. Commn. for Accreditation of Hosps.; editor Corrective and Social Psychiatry 1970-, clin. prof. psychiat. UCSF Med. Sch. 1985-; awards: Phi Beta Pi, Phi Theta Kappa, Nat. Honor Soc. 1950-51, Danforth Scholar 1951, Am. Legion Oratory Contest Winner 1951, dist. gov. Key Clubs Internat. 1951, pres. Kans. Conf. United Meth. Youth 1951-53, Dean's List 1952-54, bd. dirs. Meth. Youthville, Newton, Kans. 1964-74, Outstanding Young Men Am. 1970, lay men. United Meth. Annual Conf. 1972-80, pres. Kansas Area U.M. Com. on Episcopacy 1976-80, AMA phys. recogn. award 1977-92; apptd. FAA Spl. Com. on Major Aircraft Disasters 1978; Fellow: Am. Psychiatric Assn., Royal Soc. of Health (London), Am. Assn. Mental Health Profls. in Corrections, Am. Assn. of Social Psychiatry, World Assn. Social Psychiatry, Masters and Johnson Inst., and Am. Orthopsychiatric Assn.; mem: AMA, Internat. Assn. Group Psychotherapy, Assn. of USAF Psychiatrists, Assn. Mental Health Adminstrs., Am. Assn. Psychiat. Adminstrs., Am. Pub. Health Assn., Am. Acad. Med. Dirs., Am. Correctional Assn., Am. Acad. Psychiat. and the Law, Am. Assn. Sex Educators, Counselors & Therapists, Soc. for Sci. Study of Sex, Pi Kappa Alpha frat.; civic: Native Sons and Daus. Kans., Kans. St. Hist. Soc., Smithsonian Instn., Am. Iris Soc., Am. Horticultural Assn., Univ. Kans. Alumni Assn.; publs: contbr. 4 books, numerous profl. papers and jour. articles, presentations var. nat. and internat. confs. include 10-year study Confrontation gp. therapy with adolescent delinquents using therapists, closed circuit t.v. instant replay and peer confrontation, Proceedings World Cong. Psychiatry, Vienna 1983; mil: col. USAFR-ret. 1964-86, comdr. Med. Svc. USAF 1970-74; United Methodist (local preacher lic. 1951; rec: pvt. pilot, sailor. Res: 4741 Valley End Ln Green Valley / Suisan 94585. Ofc: Box 3365 Fairfield 94533-0587

MARTIN, DONALD WALTER, writer/publisher; b. Apr. 22, 1934, Grants Pass, Ore.; s. George E. and Irma Ann (Dallas) M.; m. Kathleen Elizabeth Murphy July, 1970 (div. May, 1979); m. Betty Woo Mar. 18, 1985; children: Kimberly Ann b. 1959, Daniel Clayton b. 1975. Career: reporter, asst. sports ed., Blade-Tribune, Oceanside, Calif. 1961-65; Sunday ed., Press-Courier, Oxnard, Calif. 1965-69; managing ed., Argus-Courier, Petaluma, Calif. 1969-70; assoc. ed., Motorland Mag., S.F., Calif. 1970-88; founder, co-owner, Pine Cone Press, Columbia, Calif. 1988-; mem: Internat. Assn. of Indep. Publishers 1991-, Soc. of Am. Travel Writers 1992-, Calif. Press Photographers Assn., Sacramento 1965-70, Kiwanis Club, Petaluma 1969-70; author, travel books: Best of San Francisco, 1986, 90, 94, Best of the Gold Country, 1987, 92, Best of Arizona 1990, 93, Inside San Francisco, 1991, Best of Nevada, 1992; Best of the Wine Country, 1991, Oregon Discovery Guide, 1993, N. Calif. Discovery Guide, 1993, Ultimate Wine Book, 1993; mil: staff sgt., USMC, 1952-61; Green Party; rec: hiking, whitewater kayaking, bicycling, travel. Res: 11362 Yankee Hill Rd. P.O. Box 1494 Columbia 95310. Ofc: Pine Cone Press 11362 Yankee Hill Rd. Columbia 95310

MARTIN, GORDON EUGENE, company president and principal research scientist; b. Aug. 22, 1925, San Diego; s. Carl Amos and Ruth Marie (Fountain) Martin; m. Tricia Jane Totten, June 10, 1949; children: Gloria b. 1950, Theodore b. 1953, Kathryn b. 1956, Susan b. 1957; edn: BS in E.E., UC Berkeley, 1947; MS engring., UCLA, 1951; MA physics, San Diego St. Univ., 1961; PhD in E.E., Univ. Texas, Austin 1966. Career: communications officer US Navy, Pacific Ocean, 1943-45; electrical engr. Convair (Gen. Dyn.), San Diego 1947; res. physicist Navy Electronics Lab., San Diego 1947-52; lt. USNR, asst. ofcr. in chg., USN, Bahamas and Conn., 1952-54; res. physicist Naval Ocean Systems Center, San Diego 1954-80; pres. Martin Analysis, San Diego 1980-; cons. USN, Wash. D.C., 1954-80, mem. Piezoelectric Boards USN, W.D.C., 1960-80; acoustics dept. hd. Systems Exploration, San Diego, 1980-82; awards: Outstanding, Navy Lab. San Diego (1954, 56, 60, 62, others), commendn. letter from Dir. of All Navy Labs, Wash. D.C. 1968, num. commendn. letters USN 1973-; mem: Acoustical Soc. of Am. (1950-, Fellow 1980), Inst. Electronics & Electrical Engrs. (1948-, Senior Mem. 1964), NY Acad. of Scis. 1964-, Sigma Xi 1965-, Sigma Pi Sigma 1960-, Acoustical Soc. (S.D. chpt. pres. 1970); patentee -Sonar, Materials, others (1954-80); author: CAE For Piezoelectric Arrays (originator theory and software, 1954-), Inverse Piezoelectric Parameter Method (theory, paper, software 1964), jour. articles re Piezoelectricity (1954-); Prot. (statistician 1968-82, other offices); rec: old rare books, sci. books, square dancing. Res: 3675 Syracuse Ave San Diego 92122-3322 Ofc: M.A.S.T., Inc. 3675 Syracuse Ave. San Diego 92122-3322

MARTIN, JOSEPH, JR., lawyer; b. May 21, 1915; edn: BA, Yale Univ., 1936, LLB, Yale Law Sch. 1939; mem. State Bars of Calif., NY, and D.C.; career: assoc. Cadwalader, Wickersham & Taft,NY, 1939-41; USN (to Lt. Cmdr.) 1941-46; ptnr. Wallace, Garrison, Norton & Ray, San Francisco 1946-55; ptnr. Allan, Miller, Groezinger, Keesling & Martin, 1955-70; Pettit, Evers & Martin 1973-, (Pettit & Martin); gen. counsel Fed. Trade Commn., Wash DC 1970-71; US Amb., US rep. to Geneva Disamarment Conf., 1971-76. Fellow Am. Bar Found.; mem. Pres's Advy. Com. for Arms Control & Disarmament, 1974-78; pres. S.F. Public Utilities Commn. 1956-60; Republican Nat. Committeeman for Calif. 1960-64; dir. Arms Control Assn. 1977-84; dir. Legal Assistance to the Elderly 1981-87; dir.: Arcata Corp. 1982, Astec Industries, Inc. 1987, Allstar Inns, Inc. 1983; treas. Republican Party of Calif. 1956-58; dir. Patrons of Art & Music, Calif. Palace of Legion of Honor, 1958-70, pres. 1963-68; clubs: Pacific-Union (S.F.), Burlingame CC, Yale (of N.Y.); honors: ofcl. commendn. for outstanding service as gen. counsel, FTC 1973, distinguished honoree US Arms Control & Disarmament Agy. 1973, Lifetime achiev., Legal Assistance to the Elderly 1981; Address: c/o Pettit & Martin, 101 California St 35th Flr San Francisco 94111

MARTIN, MICHAEL LEE, orthotist; b. May 30, 1947, Long Beach; s. Troy Lee and Ruth Elizabeth (Hummer) M.; m. Sharon Lee Johnson, Aug. 23, 1969; children: Tanya Lee; edn: att. Northwestern Univ. 1973; AA, Cerritos Coll. 1976; att. UCLA 1976; Diplomate Am. Bd. Orthotists and Prosthetics. Career: cable splicer Gen. Telephone, Dairy Valley, 1956-66; orthotic technician Johnson's Orthopedic, Santa Ana, 1969-73, orthotist, 1974-, pres. Johnson's Orthopedic, Orange, 1989-; pres. Johnson's Orthopedic Designs, Corona; dir. Nat. Academy of Orthotists & Prosthetists 1993; res. advy. bd. mem. Rancho Los Amigos Hosp., Rehab Engring.; research orthotist Rancho Los Amigos Hosp., Downey, 1973; mem: Am. Acad. Orthotists and Prosthetists (sec., pres. So. Calif. chpt. 1976-79, sec., pres. Region IX 1979-87), Orthotic and Prosthetic Provider Network (pres. Calif. chpt. 1980-), Internat. Soc. of Prosthetists & Orthotists; mil: US Army 1966-68, Vietnam; Republican. Res: 16 Oakmont Coto De Caza 92679 Ofc: Johnson's Orthopedic 1920 E. Katella Ste G Orange 92667

MARTIN, PORT ROBERT, engineering executive; b. Aug. 27, 1944, Norfolk, Va.; s. Port Corbett and Edith (Chandler) M.; m. Sandra Lee Polasik, Aug. 20, 1968 (div. 1977); m. Barbara Jeanne Green, Sept. 1, 1979 (div. 1985); children: Michael b. 1971, Theresa b. 1973; edn: BS engring., US Naval Acad. 1966; MA bus., Univ. N.Colo. 1976. Career: real estate sales Mascot Realty, Bonita 1976-

77; tng. splst. Cubic Corp., San Diego 1977-78; engr., branch head Nav Ocean Systems Cen 1983-; adj. prof. Naval War Coll., Newport, R.I. 1985-; awards: Freedom Found. 1965, Fulbright scholar 1966-67; mem: U.S. Naval Inst., Internat. Assn. Marathoners; author: Jr. Ofcr. Orientation Guide (1983), Chief Petty Ofcr. Orientation (1985); poetry writer (1961-), article pub. (1985); mil: capt. USN 1961-, Burke scholar 1966, 2 commendation medals 1981, 83; Prot.; rec: running, writing. Res: 1661 Azusa Ct Bonita 92002 Ofc: Naval Ocean Systems Center 271 Catalina Blvd San Diego 92152-5000

MARTIN, STANLEY ROLAND, general manager, sales and marketing executive; b. Dec. 25, 1943, Jersey City, N.J.; s. Walter John and Lucille (Guadagno) M.; m. Linda Marie Marson, Oct. 11, 1975; children: Craig b. 1987, David b. 1989; edn: BA, Newark St. Coll. 1969; MA, Univ. Md. 1971. Career: vocational coordinator Anne Arundel Co., Annapolis, Md. 1971-77; regional sales 3M Co., St. Paul, Minn. 1978-87; regional sales mgr. Fica Group, Chgo., Ill. 1987-92; gen. mgr. Hotsy Equipment Co., Anaheim 1992-; sr. arbitrator L.A. Autoline Better Bus. Bureau 1986-; awards: Carnation Co. cert. appreciation 1987, A.K.C.A. Koi person of year 1987; mem: Orange Co. Zen Nippon Airinkai (pres. 1987-88, v.p. 1985-87), OCCCO; mil: E-4 N.J. Nat. Guard 1964-70; rec: deep sea fishing, golf, koi. Res: 2421 N Park Blvd Santa Ana 92706 Ofc: Hotsy Equipment Co. 2520 Woodland Dr Anaheim 92801

MARTIN, TIMOTHY PATRICK, executive search/consulting/executive; b. Feb. 5, 1944, Santa Barbara; s. Dr. Walter Patrick and Kathrine Georgia (Runions) M.; stepmother, Margaret Ann Martin; m. Maria Maingot, Aug. 10, 1963; children: Timothy P. Jr. b. 1966, Kathie b. 1967, Rob b. 1971, Dave b. 1972; m. 2d. Lois Goldberg, Mar. 12, 1988; edn: BSBA, Univ. Ariz., 1966; P.M.D., Harvard Grad. Sch., 1980. Career: acct. Atkinson, Lee, Fannelli & Co., Willow Glen 1966-69; sr. acct. Boise Cascade Corp., Sunnyvale 1969-70, plant controller Boise Cascade, Wallula, Wash. 1970-72, div. controller, Boise 1972-77, div. fin. mgr. Itasca, Ill. 1977-81, dir. of information, Boise 1981-84; sr. v.p. adminstrn. Lucky Stores, Inc. San Leandro, Ca. 1984-89; exec. search/ cons. and c.e.o. The Martin Group, Walnut Creek 1989-; civic: Right Direction Project (pres. 1987-88), Bishop Kelly H.S. Bd. (pres. 1982-84); Republican; R.Cath.; rec: boating, water sports. Res: 328 Saclan Terrace Clayton 94517 Ofc: The Martin Group, 1981 N Broadway Ste 430 Walnut Creek 94596

MARTINEZ, FRANK ROBERT, educator, college administrator; b. Dec. 28, 1921, Los Angeles; s. Frank and Caroline (Bassett) M.; m. Lois Margaret Weber, March 16, 1951; children: Larry b. 1953, Jay b. 1955, Mark b. 1956, Barbara b. 1960; edn: BA, Univ. Redlands, 1947; MA, USC, 1953, EdD, 1963. Career: history prof. Citrus Coll., Glendora 1947-52, dean of students 1952-59, dean of instruction 1959-64; v.p. Cuesta Coll., San Luis Obispo 1964-77, pres. 1977-88; mem. Calif. Council for Pvt. Postsec. and Vocat. Edn., Sacto. 1990-; mem. Chancellor's Advy. Com., Calif. Comm. Colls. 1979-84; chmn. accreditation com. We. Assn. Schs. & Colls. 1978-88; mem. Coll. Opportunity Grants Commn. Calif. 1970-75; awards: Univ. Redlands outstanding alumni 1974, La Fiesta Days San Luis Obispo grand marshall 1980; civic bds: United Way (dir. 1958-91), Civil Service Commn., Rotary (pres. 1960); contbr. articles in field of adult edn. (1963-80); mil: cpl. USMC 1942-46; Presbyterian; rec: bullfighting. Res: 2383 Sunset Dr San Luis Obispo 93401

MARTINEZ, LEONORE, social worker; b. June 26, 1930, Santa Rita, N.M.; d. Maria Rivas Martinez; edn: BA, USC 1963; MSW, San Diego St. Univ. 1968; lic. Nat. Bd. Examiners Clin. Social Work 1987; diplomate Am. Bd. Examiners Clin. Social Work. Career: psychiatric social worker Calif. St. Dept. Mental Hygiene, Bakersfield 1968-73; sch. social worker Santa Barbara City Schs. 1973-75; spur., clin. and case worker services Cath. Charities, Santa Barbara 1975-81, dir. 1981-87, regional dir. 1987-91; pvt. practice psychotherapy, Santa Barbara 1991-; awards: Catholic Charities Recognition of Dedicated Service 1975-91, Cert. of Recognition Santa Barbara City Council 1991 and Santa Barbara Bd. Supervisors, Benemerenti Medal (Medal of Merit) from Pope John Paul II, 1992; mem: Calif. Bd. Behavioral Sci., Soc. Clin. Social Work Fellowship; radio show Sunny Today, 1972; Democrat; Cath.; Res: 324 Cordova Dr Santa Barbara 93109 Ofc: Santa Barbara

MARTINEZ y FERRER, MARCELINO CODILLA, JR., hospital administr.; b. Sept. 28, 1947, San Francisco; s. Marcelino Cerenio Martinez and Jacinta Parrilla (Codilla) Ferrer; edn: BA, DSU Sacto. 1972; BS, Univ. Md. 1986; MPA, CSU Hayward 1989. Career: supr. psychiatry Naval Hosp., Manila, Philippines 1976-78; Naval Hosp., Oakland 1978-84; Naval Hosp., Okinawa, Japan 1984-86; educator coord. Naval Hosp., Oakland 1986-88, credentials coord. 1988-89, exec. secty. to med. staff 1989-; cons. Calif. St. Legislature, Sacto. 1970-73; adminstv. asst. Dept. of Elections 1968-70; dir. Tayo Corp., Manila, Philippines 1970-; honors: Phi Kappa Phi, Pi Sigma Alpha, Psi Chi, Medal of Merit Pres. Reagan 1981, Order of Merit Pres. Bush 1989; mem: Commonwealth Club, Republican Presdl. Leadership Council, Am. Acad. Political & Social Sic., Am. Soc. Political Sci., Woodrow Wilson Center, Am. Legion, Calif. Republican League, Bishop Mus., Phila. Mus.; Republican; R.Cath. Res: 39412 Sundale Dr Fremont 94538-1926 Ofc: Quality Assurance 8750 Mt Blvd Oakland 94627-5000

MASON, DEAN TOWLE, cardiologist; b. Sept. 20, 1932, Berkeley, Calif.; s. Ira Jenckes and Florence Mabel (Towle) M.; m. Maureen O'Brien, June 22, 1957; children: Kathleen, Alison; edn: BA chem., Duke Univ. 1954, MD, 1958; Diplomate Nat. Bd. Med. Examiners, Am. Bd. Internal Med. (cardiovascular diseases). Career: intern, med. resident Johns Hopkins Hosp. 1958-61; clin. assoc. cardiol., senior asst. surgeon USPHS, Nat. Heart Inst., NIH 1961-63, asst. sect. dir. cardiovasc. diagnosis, attg. phys., sr. investigator cardiol. 1963-68; prof. med., physiol., chief cardiovasc. med. UC Davis Med. Sch.-Sacto. Med. Ctr. 1968-82; chief phys. Western Heart Inst. and chmn. dept. cardiovascular med. St. Mary's Med. Ctr. S.F. 1983-; co-chmn. cardiovasc.-renal drugs US Pharmacopeia Com. Revision 1970-75; mem. life scis. com. NASA; med. res. review bd. VA, NIH; vis. prof. num. univs.; cons. in field; mem. Am. Cardiovasc. Splty. Cert. Bd. 1970-78; awards: Phi Beta Kappa, Alpha Omega Alpha, res. award Am. Therapeutic Soc. 1965, outstanding prof. UC Davis Med. Sch. 1972, Theodore and Susan B. Cummings Humanitarian award US State Dept./Am. Coll. Cardiol. (1972, 73, 75, 78), Skylab achiev. NASA 1974, merit World Cong. Vascular Diseases 1976, UC Faculty research award 1978, Recogn. for service to internat. cardiol. Am. Coll. Cardiol. 1978, Tex. Heart Inst. award 1979, disting. alumnus Duke Univ. Med. Sch. 1979, sci. citation Inst. Sci. Info. 1980, World Congress on Coronary Heart Disease award 1984; Fellow: Am. Coll. Cardiol. (pres. 1977-78), Am. Coll. Phys., Am. Heart Assn., Am. Coll. Chest Phys., Royal Soc. Med.; mem: Am. Soc. Clin. Investigation, Am. Physiol. Soc., Am. Soc. Pharmacol. and Exptl. Therapeutics (exptl. ther. award 1973), Am. Fedn. Clin. Res., NY Acad Scis., Am. Assn. Univ. Cardiols., Am. Soc. Clin. Pharmacol. and Therapeutics, We. Assn. Phys., AAUP, Western Soc. Clin. Res. (past pres.), El Macero CC; author: Cardiovascular Management (1974), Congestive Heart Failure (1976), Advances in Heart Disease (Vol. 1 1977, Vol. 2 1978, Vol. 3 1980), Cardiovascular Emergencies (1978), Clinical Methods in Study of Cholesterol Metabolism (1979), Principles of Noninvasive Cardiac Imaging (1980), Clinical Nuclear Cardiology (1981), Myocardial Revascularization (1981), Love Your Heart (1982), Cardiology (yearly 1981-), numerous articles, assoc. editor Clinical Cardiology; ed.-in-chief Am. Heart Jour., mem. editl. bds. sci. jours.; Republican; Methodist. Res: 44725 Country Club Dr El Macero 95618 Ofc: Western Heart Institute, St. Mary's Medical Center 450 Stanyan St San Francisco 94117

MASON, HAROLD FREDERICK, retired research chemist; b. Feb. 15, 1925, Porterville; s. Arthur Charles and Mary (McConchie) M.; m. Marian Elizabeth Caldwell, Jan. 30, 1954; children: Charles b. 1955, Richard b. 1956, Catharine b. 1964; edn: BSChE, Cornell Univ. 1950; PhD, Univ. Wis. 1954. Career: chemical engr. Rohm & Haas, Bristol, Pa. 1950-51; research chemist Chevron Research Co., Richmond 1954-61, res. supr. 1961-67, res. mgr. 1967-86; mem: Am. Chem. Soc., Am. Inst. Chem. Engrs., St. Anselms Episcopal Ch. (sr. warden 1976-77); patents for petroleum processing and catalysis; mil: 2d. lt. USAAF 1943-46; Republican; Episcopalian; rec: photog., astronomy, botany. Res: 553 Monarch Ridge Dr Walnut Creek 94596

MASON, JEFFREY LYNN, lawyer; b. Nov. 1, 1944, Philadelphia, Pa.; s. Herbert Lester and Phyllis Louise (Reader) M.; m. Michele Meyer, Aug. 12, 1967 (div. 1989); m. 2d. Kathryn Eileen Karcher, Aug. 26, 1989; children: Jeffrey b. 1970, Meredith b. 1977, Lauren b. 1991; edn: BA, Stanford Univ. 1966; JD, Stanford Univ. Sch. Law 1969; admitted State Bar Calif. 1970, U.S. Court Mil. Appeals 1970, U.S. Supreme Court 1973. Career: assoc. staff, legal counsel Stanford Univ. 1969-70; assoc. Seltzer Caplan Wilkins & McMahon, San Diego 1974-77, ptnr. 1977-91, v.p. bd. dirs. 1977-91, of counsel 1992-; adj. prof. Univ. San Diego Sch. Law 1979-81; awards: U.S. Jaycees Outstanding Young Man Am. 1977; mem: Am. Bar Assn., San Diego Co. Bar Assn., Francis W. Parker Sch. (bd. dirs. 1978-87, v.p. 1981-82, pres. 1982-85), Sigma Alpha Epsilon; mil: capt. AUS Judge Advocate Gen. Corps 1970-74, USAR 1974-77. Ofc: Seltzer Caplan Wilkins & McMahon 750 B St Ste 2100 San Diego 92101

MASSIER, PAUL FERDINAND, engineer; b. July 22, 1923, Pocatello, Idaho; s. John and Kathryn (Arki) M.; m. Miriam Parks, May 1, 1948 (dec. 1975); children: Marilyn b. 1951, Paulette b. 1953; m. 2d Dorothy Hedlund Wright, Sept. 12, 1978; edn: mech. engrg. cert., Univ. Idaho So. Branch (now Idaho State Univ.) 1943; BSME honors, Univ. Colo. 1948; MSME, M.I.T. 1949. Career: engr. Pan Am. Refining Corp. Texas City, Tex. 1948; design engr. Maytag Co. Newton, Iowa 1949-50; research engr. Boeing Co. Seattle, Wash. 1950-55; sr. res. engr. Jet Propulsion Lab. CalTech Pasadena 1955-58, group supr. 1958-82, exec. asst. 1982-83, task mgr. 1983-86, mem. technical staff 1986-; honors: Sigma Xi, Tau Beta Pi, Pi Tau Sigma, Sigma Tau, Professional Achiev. Award Idaho State Univ. 1991, Life Mem. Svc. Award PTA of Calif. 1970, NASA-Apollo Achievement Award 1969 and Basic Noise Research Award 1980, AIAA Sustained Svc. Award 1980-81, Arcadia Congregational Ch. Layman of Year 1971; mem: Am. Inst. Aero. and Astro. (Assoc. Fellow, mem. coms.), Planetary Soc., Am. Biog. Res. Assn. (life fellow), Internat. Biog.Assn. (fellow), Family Genealogy and Hist.; publs: num. articles in tech. jours.; reviewer 7 tech. jours.; mem. plnng. coms./session chmn. for num. tech. confs.; mil: T/4 US Army 1943-46, Good Conduct, Unit Citn.; Congregational; rec: presentation motion picture travelogs, antiques, collectibles. Res: 1000 N First Ave Arcadia 91006 Ofc: Jet Propulsion Lab. 4800 Oak Grove Dr Pasadena 91109

MATARE, HERBERT FRANZ, physicist; b. Sept. 22, 1912, Aachen, W. Germany, nat. 1967; s. Joseph Peter and Paula (Broicher) M.; m. Ursula Krenzien, Dec. 2, 1939; children: Felicitas b. 1944, Vitus b. 1955; m. Dr. Elisabeth Walbert, 1980; child, Victor b. 1983; edn: BS (Abitur) Realgymnasium Aachen/Univ. Geneva 1933; MS (Dipl.Ing.) in physics, Univ. Aachen 1939; PhD (Dr.Ing.) electronics, Univ. of Berlin 1942; PhD solid state physics, Univ. Paris 1950. Career: head Microwave Lab., Telefunken, Berlin, W.Ger. 1939-45; dir. Semiconductor Lab., Westinghouse, Paris, Fr. 1946-52; founder/pres. Intermetall Inc., Dusseldorf, W.Ger. 1952-56; head Semiconductor R&D, Gen. Tel. & Electronics Co., NY 1956-59; dir. of res. TEKADE, Semiconductor Dept. Nuernberg, W.Ger. 1959-61; hd. Quantum Electronics Dept. The Bendix Corp.Res. Labs., Southfield, Mich. 1961-63; tech. dir./mgr. Lear-Siegler Res. Labs. Santa Monica, Ca. 1963-64; asst. chief engr. Douglas Aircraft Co., Santa Monica 1964-66; sci. adv. Rockwell Internat. Anaheim 1966-69; pres. ISSEC (Internat. Solid State Electronics Consultants) 1970-; asst. prof. Univ. Aachen, W.Ger. 1936-45; prof. Univ. Buenos Aires, 1946-48; vis. prof. UCLA 1968-69; vis. prof. CSUF 1969-70; Life Fellow IEEE, NY 1976-; Conf. chmn. internat. meetings: Electrochemical Soc., Chgo. 1955; New York (1958, 1969); Internat. Solid State Conf., Brussels 1959; cons. for UNIDO (United Nations Indsl. Devel. Organization) to Indian Semicond. Industry, 1978. mem. emeritus NY Acad. of Sci.; hon. mem. Inst. for the Advancement of Man; mem: Am. Physical Soc. (Solid State Div.), Electrochem. Soc., Thin Film Div. Am. Vacuum Soc., AAAS, Materials Res. Soc., IEEE- Lasers and Electro-Optics Soc., Nuclear and Plasma Scis. Soc., Power Engring. Soc.; author 4 books: Microwave Receiver Technology (Oldenbourg 1951), Defect Electronics in Semiconductors (Wiley - Interscience 1971), Conscientious Evolution (Carlton Press 1982), Energy: Facts and Future (CRC Press 1988); contbr. 100+ papers to sci. journals; approx. 60 patents incl. First transistor patents from 1948 (Westinghouse, Paris), Semicondr. diode mixer theory and tech., 1st vacuum growth of silicon monocrystals and patent on levitation (1952), growth and study of bicrystals (1955-60), first low temp. transistor (1958, GTE), devel. optical heterodyning with bicrystals (1963), 1st crystal-to-crystal optical comm. link (1961), unipolar tunnel transistor (1965), LPE for LED's (1975); rec: astronomy, biology. Address: 141 Medio Dr Los Angeles90049 and Flandrische Str.48 5100 Aachen Germany.

MATHES, STEPHEN JOHN, plastic surgeon, medical educator; b. Aug. 17, 1943, New Orleans, La.; s. John Ernest and Norma (Deutsch) M.; m. Jennifer, Nov. 26, 1966; children: David b. 1970, Brian b. 1972, Edward b. 1974; edn: BS, La. State Univ., 1964, MD, 1968. Career: gen. surgery fellow, 1975, plastic surg. fellow, 1977, Emory Univ.; asst. prof. dept. surg., div. plastic surg. Washington Univ., St. Louis, Mo. 1977-78; dir. Hartford Burn Unit, Barns Hosp., St. Louis 1977-78; dir. microvascular serv. Washington Univ. Sch. Med., St. Louis 1977-78; assoc. prof. surg. 1978-83, prof. surg. 1983-84, Div. Plastic Surg., Univ. UC San Francisco; prof. surg. and hd. sect. plastic surg. Univ. Mich., Ann Arbor 1984-85; prof. surg. and hd. plastic & reconstrv. surg. Univ. Calif. Sch. of Medicine, S.F. 1985-, prof. growth and devel., Univ. Calif. Sch. of Dentistry, S.F. 1985-; mem. Ethicon Plastic Surgery Advy. Panel; editorial bds. Jour. of Microsurgery 1984-, Contemporary Surgery 1985-, Perspectives in Plastic Surgery 1987, J. of Plastic and Reconstrv. Surg. 1991-; awards: James Barrett Brown Prize for best paper 1982, AMWA best medical book award 1983, 1st prize Plastic Surg. Ednl. Found., Basic Science (1981, 83, 84, 86), Assoc. vis. prof. 1990 for U.S. sponsored by Plastic Surg. Ednl. Found. 1990; mem: Am. Assn. Plastic Surgeons, Am. Soc. Plastic Surgeons, Am. Coll. of Surgeons, Am. Cleft Palate Assn., Am. Trauma Soc., Calif. Soc. Plastic Surgery, Plastic Surgery Research Council (pres. 1987-88), Soc. Univ. Surgeons, Soc. Head and Neck Surgeons, Soc. Surgery of the Hand, Am. Surgical Assn., Pacific Coast Surg. Assn.; author: Clinical Atlas of Muscle & Musculocutaneous Flaps (C.V. Mosby, 1979), Clinical Applications for Muscle and Musculocutaneous Flaps (C.V. Mosby 1982), Plastic Surgery: Principles and Practice (C.V. Mosby 1990); mil: major Ft. Polk Army Hosp. 1970-72; Republican; Episcopal; rec: tennis, gardening. Res: 30 Trophy Ct Hillsborough 94010 Ofc: Div. of Plastic Surgery Univ. of Calif. Ste 509, 350 Parnassus St San Francisco 94143

MATIN, ABDUL, microbiology educator, consultant; b. May 8, 1941 Delhi, India, nat. 1983; s. Mohammed and Zohra (Begum) Said; m. Mimi Keyhan, June 21, 1968; edn: BS, Univ. Karachi, Pakistan, 1960, MS, 1962; PhD, UCLA, 1969; career: lectr., St. Joseph's Coll., Karachi 1962-64; res. assoc., UCLA 1964-71; sci. officer Univ. Groningen, Kerklaan, The Netherlands 1971-75; from asst. to assoc. prof. microbiology Stanford Univ., Calif. 1975-; cons. Engenics 1982-84, Monsanto 1984-; chmn. Stanford Recombinant DNA panel; lectr. ASM Found.; convener of microbiological workshop and confs.; mem, editorial bd. Jour. of Bacteriology; Ann. Rev. Microbiology, Rev. of NSF and other Grants; awards: Fellow Fulbright Found. 1964, NSF 1981-, Ctr. for Biotech. Res. 1981-85, EPA 1981-84, NIH Coll. Biotech., UN. Tokten 1987; mem: AAAS, AAUP, Am. Soc. for Microbiology (found. lectr. 1991-92), Soc. Gen. Microbiology, Soc. Indsl. Microbiology, No. Soc. Indsl. Microbiology (bd. dirs.), Biophysics Soc.; author: contbr. numerous publs. to sci. jours.; rec: reading, music, walking. Res: 690 Coronado Ave Palo Alto 94305-1039. Ofc: Stanford Univ./Dept. of Microbiology & Immunology Fairchild Sci. Bldg. D317 Stanford 94305-5402

MATOSSIAN, JESSE NERSES, scientist; b. Feb. 3, 1952, Los Angeles; s. Hagop Sarkis and Alice Elizabeth (Barsoomian) M.; edn: BS Physics, USC, 1975; MS and PhD Physics, Stevens Inst. of Tech., 1983; career: Hughes Research Labs., Malibu 1983-, mem. tech. staff Plasma Physics Laboratory 1983-91, sr. mem. tech. staff/senior staff physicist, 1992-; awards: Hughes Res. Labs. "Superior Performance Award" nominee 1985 and recipient 1992, recipient 33 division invention awards Hughes Res. Labs., recipient 6 issued patents; listed Amer. Men and Women of Sci. (17th, 18th ed.); mem: Am. Physical Soc. (life), Am. Inst. Aero. and Astro., IEEE, MRS, ASM, N.Y. Acad. Scis., Sigma Xi, patron mem. L.A. Cty Mus. of Art, sustaining mem:/graphics arts council/L.A. Cty Mus. of Art; reviewer Jour. of Propulsion and Power, IEEE Trans. on Electron Devices; rec: art hist., collector 19th and 20th century European paintings, 16th century engravings, classical music, travel. Ofc: Hughes Research Labs. 3011 Malibu Cyn Rd Malibu 90265

MATSUNAGA, GEOFFREY DEAN, lawyer; b. Sept. 30, 1949, Los Angeles; s. Hideo Arthur and Yuri (Yamazaki) M.; m. Masako Inoue, Aug. 20, 1981; children: Ayako, Hideko, Lisa; edn: BS, USAF Acad., Colo. 1971; MBA, UCLA, 1972; JD, UC Berkeley, 1982; admitted bar: Calif. 1982, N.Y. 1983. Career: atty. Milbank, Tweed, Hadley, & McCloy, N.Y. 1982-84, Tokyo, Japan 1984-87; atty. Sidley & Austin, Tokyo, Japan 1987-88, Los Angeles 1988-91; atty. Sheppard, Mullin, Richter, & Hampton, Los Angeles 1991-; mem: ABA, L.A. County Bar Assn., America Japan Soc., Japan Business Assn. of So. Calif., Japan Am. Soc. of So. Calif.; mil: lt. USN 1972-78. Ofc: Sheppard, Mullin, Richter & Hampton, 333 S Hope St Ste 4800 Los Angeles 90071

MATTESON, BYRON ROGER, city official, business executive; b. Jan. 7, 1937, Hartford, Wis.; s. Floyd B. and Martha (Boettcher) M.; children: Tamara b. 1962, Mark b. 1963; edn: AA, San Bernardino Valley Coll., 1957; CSU San Bernardino, 2 yrs. Career: founder/pres. Allstate Business Forms, Inc. 1974-89, Allstate Instant Printing, 1976-, Bear Tanning Salon, 1986-; co-founder Inland Community Bank, 1990-; co-founder Little Sister Truck Wash, 1991-; elected councilman (mayor pro tem) Grand Terrace City Council, 1984-87, mayor 1987-, mem. League of Calif. Cities (pres. Inland Div. 1989); named Outstanding Jaycee of Year 1969; mem. Bus. Forms Distbrs. Assn. of So. Calif. (pres. 1982); civic: Grand Terrace C.of C., Colton C.of C., San Bernardino C.of C., Trade Club of the Inland Empire (hd. trader 1984), Kiwanis, B&B Square Dancers, Grand Terrace Sch. Advy. Bd. (past pres.), 20-30 Club (past pres.), Jaycees (past pres.), Grand Terrace Lions Club 1988-, Indian Y-Guides (chief), Rolling Start, Inc. (bd.); Republican; Methodist; rec: hunting, swimming. Res: 12175 Michigan St Grand Terrace 92324 Ofc: Allstate Printing, 888 La Cadena Colton 92324

MATTHEWS, JUSTUS, composer, university professor; b. Jan. 13, 1945, Peoria, Ill.; s. Charles Justus and Dorothea (Maurer) M.; m. Barbara Matthews, Aug. 15, 1971; children: David b. 1973, Laura b. 1977; edn: BA, Calif. State Univ., Northridge, 1967; MA, 1968; PhD, SUNY Buffalo, 1971. Career: prof., Calif. State Univ. Long Beach, 1971-; num. awards and honors from Calif. State Univ. Long Beach, various universities and the French Ministry of Culture; creative works: numerous compositions for various vocal and instrumental ensembles, one opera, several electronic music compositions; numerous sound designs for plays. Res: 245 Harvard Lane Seal Beach 90740

MATTHEWS, ROBERT LOUIS, community college president; b. June 2, 1930, Tonganoxie, Kans.; s. Mark Hanna, Sr. and Suzie Jane (Brown) M.; m. Ardelle Marie Dunlap, Aug. 26, 1952; children: Mark b. 1953, Brian b. 1957, Scott b. 1962; edn: BS edn., Emporia State Univ., 1952; MA edn., Columbia Univ., 1955; PhD educational leadership/ human behavior, U.S. Internat. Univ., 1971. Career: tchr. San Diego City Sch. Dist. 1955-64, sch. principal 1965-72, dist. dir. of edn. 1972-84; pres. /ECC and Continuing Edn. Centers, San Diego Community Coll. Dist., 1984-; awards: NDEA fellow U.S. Dept. of Edn., WDC 1965, Corant travel award Australian Council of Churches 1971, Rockefeller fellow Rockefeller Found., NYC 1971-72, humanities fellow N.E.H., WDC 1976; mem. Alpha Phi Alpha Frat., S.D. (1951-, past pres., chmn. M.L.King Parade Com. 1984-); civic bds: Southeast Comm. Theatre (1964-, treas.), S.D. Zoological Soc. (edn. com.), Mus. Natural Hist. 1982-, NAACP, S.D. (life), Urban League, S.D. (1965-, pres., Life mem.); author: Black Studies Academic Achievement and the Self Concept of Black Students (1971); mil: cpl. US Army 1952-54; Democrat; Presbyterian; rec: reading, community service, spectator sports. Res: 4931 Dassco Ct San Diego 92102-3717 Ofc: San Diego Community College 5350 University Ave San Diego 92105

MATTOON, SARA (SALLY) HALSEY, personal and professional educator and consultant; b. July 8, 1947, Bronxville, N.Y.; d. Sir Henry Amasa and Dorothy Ann (Teeter) M.; edn: AAS in edn., Bennett Coll. 1967; BS edn./pre-med. scis., So. Conn. State Univ. 1969; MA edn./humanistic psych., CSU Chico 1976. Career: tchr. San Diego Unified Sch. Dist., 1969-72; tchr. Montgomery Creek Sch. Dist., Round Mountain 1972-73; tchr./dir. Chico Youth Devel. Center Inc., 1973-80, mem. bd. dirs. 1980-, bd. chair 1987-; pres Executive Excellence /Sunrise Communications, San Diego, Ca. and Weston, Conn., 1973-, clients nat., Europe and Middle East, instr. seminars on start-up bus. in colls. and univs. 1979-83, moderator for bus. events, guest lectr. business schs. 1983-,

instr. stress reduction and mem. bd. govs. World Plan Executive Council 1978-; honors: Information and Inspiration award W.P.E.C. (9/85), dean's list So. Conn. St. Univ. 1968-9; mem: MIT Enterprise Forum (org. com. mem. 1985-), San Diego Assn. of Profls. practicing Transcendental Meditation Pgm. (pres. 1985-); ed. various orgn. newsletters; rec: solo backpacker in W. Central Alberta, Canada wilderness, European Pyrenees and Alps, above Arctic Circle in Norway. Ofc: Sunrise Communications 625 Law St San Diego 92109-2433

MAUNDER, ELWOOD ("WOODY") RONDEAU, historian, forest conservationist; b. Apr. 11, 1917, Bottineau, N.Dak.; s. Henry Langham and Florence (Blackmore) M.; m. Margaret Fornell, Sept. 19, 1941 (div. 1971); children: Jean Michele b. 1951, Martha b. 1952, Elizabeth b. 1956; m. Eleanor Arge, Feb. 14, 1973; edn: BA in journ., Univ. Minn., 1939; MA in hist., Washington Univ., St. Louis, Mo. 1947; London Sch. of Econ., 1947-48. Career: reporter Minneapolis Times, 1939-40; feature writer Mpls. Star Journal, 1940-41; served with US Coast Guard Reserve 1941-45, combat corresp. European /Mediterranean area 1944-45; mem. staff US delegation at Conf. of Fgn. Ministers, London, Eng. 1947-48; dir. pub. relations fgn. missions Methodist Nat. Mission Bd., NY, NY 1948-50, Ohio Area Methodist Ch., Columbus 1950-52; chmn. world svc. com. Hennepin Ave. Meth. Ch., Mpls. 1958-61; exec. director Forest History Soc. 1952-78, hq. Mpls./St. Paul 1952-64, New Haven, Conn. 1964-69, Santa Cruz, Calif. 1969-78, senior historian FHS 1978-79, curator Forest Hist. Collection Yale Univ. 1964-69; editor-in-chief J. of Forest History, 1956-76 (and preceding publs. FHS newsletter, estab. 1956, and quarterly, Forest History); mem. planning com. 6th Am. Forestry Congress 1974-75; oral history interviewer, 1953-78; author, coauthor 28+ books and numerous articles on hist. of forestry, numerous articles based on 200+ interviews with pub. and pvt. conservation leaders; 4 of these interviews collected in book: Voices from the South: Recollections of Four Foresters 1977; awards: grantee Weyerhaeuser Found. 1960-62, 72-75, Nat. Endowment for Humanities 1973-75, 75-77, Louis and Maud Hill Family Found. 1960-62, 69, Simpson Found. 1974-75, Nat. Resources Council Am. 1974-75, Edwin W. and Catherine M. Davis Found. 1974-75; mem: Oral History Assn. (a founder, mem. first exec. council, first editor OHA quarterly newsletter), Am. Hist. Assn., Soc. Am. Archivists, Orgn. Am. Historians, Am. Forestry Assn., Soc. Am. Foresters, Commonwealth Club of Calif.; clubs: Tennis (Rio Del Mar), Santa Cruz Lawn Bowling; Democrat; Prot.; rec: gardening, internat. peacemaking. Res: 407 Gay Road Aptos 95003

MAXWELL, RAYMOND ROGER, certified public accountant/computerized tax returns; b. Jan. 7, 1918, Farwell, Tx.; s. Frederick W. and Hazel B. (Rogers) M.; m. Jeanne Hollarn, June 16, 1945 (dec. Dec. 21, 1987); children: Donald R. b. 1946, Bruce E. b. 1951, Sabrina G. b. 1955; edn: EdB, Western Ill. State Teachers Coll., 1941; MBA, Univ. Fla., Gainsville, 1949; UCLA Grad. Sch., 1965-68. Career: asst. to bus. mgr. Western Ill. State Tchrs. Coll., Macomb, Ill. 1939-41; apprentice acct. Chas. H. Lindfors, CPA, Ft. Lauderdale, Fla. 1946-48; grad. asst. Univ. of Fla., Gainesville 1948-49; acct. Frederic Dunn-Rankin & Co., CPA, Miami 1949-51; CPA, staff Charles Costar, CPA, Miami 1951; resident auditor/CPA/prin., Ft. Lauderdale, Fla. 1951-56; supt. of public instrn. Broward Co., 1956-61; staff asst. in fin., North American Aviation, Inc., El Segundo, Calif. 1961-65; research & tchg. asst. UC Los Angeles, 1965-68; acctg. prin. Raymond R. Maxwell, CPA, Whittier 1968-; tax mgr. Great Plains Western Corp.; former dir: ADC Engring., Inc. (Whittier), Data-Computer Supply Co., Inc. (Irvine), Maxmillion, Inc. (Fla.), Polychrome Resources, Inc. (Santa Monica); honors: Pi Omega Pi, Kappa Delta Pi, coll. Bachelor Club, editor coll. Student Directory, listed in Trinker's Florida Lives; mem: Am. Inst. CPAs, Tax Execs. Ins.; mil: aviation cadet to 1st lt. Army Air Corps 1942-46; Republican; Christian Sci. (exec. bd. and First Reader 1990-92). Res: 8202 Sargent Ave Whittier 90605 Ofc: 13217 E Whittier Blvd Unit C Whittier 90602

MAY, LEWIS GLOVER, promotions executive; b. Aug. 29, 1943, NY, NY; s. Arthur Glover and Esther Ruth (Boudo) M.; m. Mary Kathleen McKernan, May 9, 1970; son, Dean Glover b. 1976; edn: BA, St. Lawrence Univ., 1965. Career: research coord., asst. nat. advtg. mgr. House of Seagram, NY, NY 1965-72; we. div. mgr. Schenley Industries, NY, NY 1973-78; v.p./gen. mgr. Robert Landau Assocs., NY, NY 1978-79; pres. May & Associates Inc., Los Angeles 1980-86 (sold firm, became HMG West, to Saatchi and Saatchi Comms. Group), pres. The Howard Marlboro Group West (div. Saatchi, PLC, London), NY, NY 1987-89, bd. dirs. The Howard Marlboro Group, worldwide 1988-89; sr. v.p. Francis, Killingbeck, Bain (FKB, USA) West, 1990; senior v.p. QLM Associates, 1991-; honors: `Angel' Peninsula Edn. Found., P.V. Estates 1989-; civic: Town Hall of Calif. (exec. bd. 1988-), Internat. Platform Assn. 1990-, P.V. Estates Breakfast Club 1984-; mil: USN 1965-67; Republican; Episcopalian; rec: golf, boating, fishing. Res: 1705 Via Boronada Palos Verdes Estates 90274 Ofc: Quintman, Lipsky, Mitchell (QLM) West, 2200 Pacific Coast Hwy Ste 316 Hermosa Beach 90254

MAY, RONALD VARNELLE, county official, archaeologist; b. Oct. 26, 1946, Salt Lake City, Utah; s. Russell and Dorothy (Jensen) M.; m. Dale Ellen Ballou, May 8, 1983; edn: AA, Mesa Coll., 1967; BA, San Diego State Univ., 1970; postgrad. work 1972-75, 85-88, grad. cert. pub. history SDSU, 1988; DOD workshop tng. cert., hist. & archaeol. preserv., 1992. Career: dist. liaison archaeologist Calif. Div. Hwys., San Diego County, 1970-73; supvy. archaeologist SDSU Found., San Diego Co., 1971, 73; indep. archaeol. consultant, 1971-; sr. archaeologist David D. Smith & Assocs., So. Calif., 1972-74; anthropology instr. Mesa Coll., 1976-77; environmental mgmt. splst. County San Diego, 1974-, staff mem. County Historical Site Bd., 1986-90; archaeology advr. City of Oceanside, Certified Local Govt. Pgm., 1991; chmn. bd. dirs. Fort Guijarros Mus. Found., San Diego 1981-; editor quarterly jour.; contbr. res. articles on Spanish fortifications, shore-whaling, Calif. Indian pottery, Asian-Am. hist. archaeology to acad. and hist. jours.; awards: Sigma Xi, merit award Inst. History 1982, conservation grantee San Diego Community Found. 1983, Cabrillo award Inst. of History 1985, comm. service Peninsula C.of C. 1987, Mark Raymond Harrington award for conservation archaeology 1987, Knight's Officer, de la Cruz, Order of Civic Merit by King Juan Carlos for promotion of heritage of Spain in Am. announced by Amb. Pedro Temboury, Consul Gen. of Spain at 186th ann. Fiesta of Battle of San Diego Bay (3/19/89), grantee San Diego Co. comm. enhancement 1987, 88, 89, 90, San Diego Cultural Arts Coun. 1990, Cultural Ministry of Spain 1991, Legacy Program Grant ($95,000) for museum devel. 1993; mem: Soc. Am. Archaeology, Soc. Profl. Archaeologists (cert. rev. com. 1990-91), Assn. Conservation Archaeology (reg. coord.), Soc. Hist. Archaeology (mil., urban archaeology groups), San Diego Co. Archaeol. Soc. (pres. 1980-81), Soc. Calif. Archaeology (v.p., ethics chmn., editor 1977-82, special achiev. award 1983, symp. chair `A Visionary Approach to Curation for the 21st Century' 1991), Archaeol. Resource Mgmt. Soc. (treas. 1980-82), Calif. Council for Promotion of History, Save Our Heritage Orgn. (bd. dirs. 1992-94), San Diego Hist. Soc., Nature Conservancy, Greenpeace, San Diego Maritime Soc., E. Clampus Vitus (Clamper of Yr. 1985), SDSU Anthropol. Soc. (pres. 1969, 72), Coun. on Am. Mil. Past; Republican. Ofc: Planning Dept. County of San Diego 5201 Ruffin Rd Ste 5B San Diego 92123

MAYBAY, DUANE CHARLES, recycling systems equipment dealer executive; b. Oct. 5, 1922, Fort Dodge, Iowa; s. Bert and Flo (Hibbard) Lungren; m. Mary Trible Parrish, Dec. 18, 1947 (div. 1972); children: Tina b. 1949, Karen b. 1955; edn: BA, Univ. Wis. 1948. Career: sales engr. Gates Rubber Co., Denver, Colo. 1948-53; asst. sales and mktg. dir. Minute Maid Corp., N.Y.C. 1953-63; pres. Mountain Foods, Los Angeles 1963-75; pres. Resource Recovery Systems 1975-; dir. Shaw Group, Los Angeles 1980-84; Mapletown USA, Tustin 1984-87; mil: lt. col. USAF 1943-45; Republican; rec: antique collecting. Res: 104 Pergola Irvine 92715 Ofc: Resource Recovery Systems POB 17426 Irvine 92713

MAYBERRY-STEWART, MELODIE IRENE, healthcare co. information systems executive; b. Sept. 4, 1948, Cleveland, Oh.; d. Robert Thomas and Marie Ethel (Martin) Hague; div.; children: George Julian b. 1969; edn: BS, Union Coll., 1970; MA sociol., Univ. Nebr. at Lincoln, 1977; MBA, Pepperdine Univ., 1983; MA mgmt., Claremont Grad. Sch., 1988, doctoral pgm. in exec. mgmt. 1987-. Career: proj. evaluator Lancaster Co. Govt., Lincoln, Nebr. 1971-76; instr. res. methods Union Coll., Lincoln, Nebr. 1976-78; with IBM 1976-88: assoc. systems engr. D.P. Div., Lincoln 1978-80; instr. D.P. Div., Los Angeles 1980-82; market support rep., sys. engring. mgr. Nat. Mktg. Div., Newport Beach 1982-84; mgr. Mktg. and Ops. Ctr., Riverside 1985-86; sys. support, telecomms. mktg. mgr. SW Mktg. Div. Area 12, Costa Mesa 1986-88; v.p. info. systems Community Health Corp., Riverside 1988-; guest lectr. in mktg. Loma Linda Univ., 1985-87; author 2 books in field (1982, 83); Democrat; Seventh-day Adventist; rec: piano, singing, fishing, gardening. Ofc: Community Health Corp. 4445 Magnolia Ave Riverside 92501

MAYER, PATRICIA JAYNE, C.M.A., chief financial officer; b. Apr. 27, 1950, Chgo.; d. Arthur and Ruth J. (Greenberger) Hersh; m. Wm. A. Mayer, Jr. Apr. 30, 1971; edn: BS in acctg., CSU Hayward 1975; passed CPA test 1978; Cert. Management Accountant (CMA) 1992. Career: auditor Elmer Fox, Westheimer CPAs, 1976; supvsg. auditor Alameda County Auditors Office, 1976-78, devel. and wrote new auditing procedures 1976; asst. mgr. Gen. Acctg. Dept., CBS Retail Stores dba Pacific Stereo, 1978-79; controller Oakland Unified Sch. Dist., 1979-84; v.p. finance YMCA of San Francisco 1984-; instr. in-house acctg. seminars; mem. Inst. of Management Accountants, Financial Executives Inst.; civic: Dep. County Registrar of Voters 1971-76, draft counselor Mt. Diablo Peace Ctr. 1971-73; Democrat; rec: Dalmatian dogs. Res: 2395 Lake Meadow Circle Martinez 94553 Ofc: YMCA of San Francisco 44 Montgomery St Ste 770 San Francisco 94104

MAYMAN, EVELYN WINIFRED, physician, ret.; b. Apr. 5, 1900, Sauk Rapids, Minn.; d. Edward W. and Harriet A. (Rockwell) M.; edn: BS, Univ. of Minn. 1924; MD, Univ. of Minn. Med. Sch. 1927. Career: physician pvt. practice, Modesto 1930-71; active staff (chief anesthesiologist 10 yrs.) McPheeter's Hosp. 1930-50, St. Mary's Hosp. 1930-45, Memorial Hosp. 1950-71, Modesto Hosp. 1954-71; cons. physician Stanislaus Co. Hosp.; mem: AMA, Stanislaus Co. Med. Soc., Calif. Med. Assn., Modesto Branch Nat. Penwomen (pres. 1968-70); charter mem. Modesto Branch Internat. Soroptomist Club; Senior Activities Inc. 1977-; Shakespeare Club of Modesto; publs: contbr. J. Pediatrics, 1940; Republican; Episcopalian; rec: watercolor painting, silkscreen painting. Res: 900 Brady Ave Modesto 95350

MAZZA, JEAN MARIE, sales executive; b. Sept. 17, 1947, St. Louis, Mo.; d. Henry E. and Bernice Marie (Juengling) Johns; m. Frank Alexander Mazza, Feb. 14, 1974 (div. 1985); edn: Omaha Univ. 1966-68. Career: customer service rep. Northwestern Bell, Omaha, Neb. 1966-68; adminstrv. asst. JBR Devel., Beverly Hills 1969-72; v.p., co-owner Maverick Fashion, Sylmar 1972-78; sales mgr., co-owner Beck Mktg., Studio City 1978-82; v.p. promo. dir. Arrowhead Jewelry, San Rafael 1982-86; nat. sales mgr. Terragrafics Inc., Brisbane 1986-; sales management training & consulting to small/med. mfgrs. and importers (self-employed) 1991-; rec: skiing, hiking, collecting antiques. Res: 241 El Faisan Ave San Rafael 94903 Ofc: P.O. Box 6846 San Rafael 94903

MAZZOLA, ROBERT A., engineer/project manager; b. Oct. 20, 1948, N.Y., N.Y.; s. Vincent and Mildred (Zollo) M.; m. Christine Anne Petersen, Aug. 1, 1987; children: Elizabeth and Christine (twins by prior m.) b. 1975, Robert Vincent b. 1989; edn: BA, Queens Coll., 1972; BS in radiology, Long Island Univ., 1975; MBA, Univ. Ariz., 1984; cert. radiology technologist, ARRT. Career: imaging tech. Nassau County Med. Ctr., East Meadow, N.Y. 1973-76; radiologic tech. SUNY at Stony Brook, N.Y. 1976-77; radiology mgr. FHP, Long Beach, Calif. 1977-78; project engr. Pacific Bell, L.A. 1978-81; project engr. GTE Cal, Westminster 1981-; indep. project mgr., cons., 1988-; awards: Queens Coll. varsity sports 1966-72, Long Island Univ. deans list 1973-74, Guttman Scholar 1975; Republican; Christian; rec: ice hockey, bass guitarist. Res: 7251 Elk Circle Apt 2 Huntington Beach 92647 Ofc: GTE Cal 6774 Westminster Ave Westminster 92683

MCANIFF, EDWARD JOHN, lawyer, lecturer; b. June 29, 1934, N.Y.C.; s. John Edward and Josephine Rose (Toomey) McA.; m. Jane Reiss, June 11, 1960; children: John b. 1961, Maura b. 1962, Anne b. 1964, Jane b. 1965, Peter b. 1967, Kathleen b. 1970; edn: AB (magna cum laude), Coll. of the Holy Cross, 1956; LLB (cum laude), New York Univ. Sch. of Law, 1961; admitted bar: N.Y. 1961, Calif. 1963, Dist. Col. 1968. Career: clk. Justice Alfred T. Goodwin, Supreme Ct. of Oreg., 1961-62; atty., ptnr. O'Melveny & Myers, Calif. 1962-, on sabbatical instr. Stanford Univ. Law Sch. 1974-75, and fgn. law cons. to Freehill, Hollingdale & Page, Sydney, Australia 1981-82; instr. Boalt Hall Sch. of Law, UC Berkeley, 1982-; frequent lectr. contg. legal edn.; civic bds: Mayfield Sr. Sch., Pasadena (trustee 1977-92, chmn. 1980-81), L.A. Master Chorale Assn. , 1987- (pres. 1992-, bd. 1980-81); mem. Am., Calif. and Los Angeles County Bar Assns., College of Holy Cross Alumni Assn. (past pres. So. Calif.), N.Y.U. Law Sch. Alumni Assn. (past secty.); mil: Capt. USNR 1956-87, career reservist; Republican; R.Cath.; rec: hiking, golf. Res: 3315 San Pasqual Pasadena 91107 Ofc: O'Melveny & Myers, 275 Battery St Ste 1600 San Francisco 94111-3305

MC BEATH, RONALD JAMES, university professor; b. April 15, 1927, Auckland, N.Z.; s. James and Eliza Marion (McLean) McB.; m. Marjorie Nicholson, July 24, 1954; children: Scot b. 1957, Heather b. 1959, Andrew b. 1961, Kathryn b. 1962; edn: B.Ed., Univ. Alberta Canada 1957; MS, USC 1958; PhD, 1961. Career: tchr. London Schs., England 1951-54; Calgary Schs., Canada 1954-57; lectr. USC, Los Angeles 1958-61; sr. lectr. Auckland Tchrs. Coll., N.Z. 1961-67; dir. Instructional Res. Center, Univ. of Hawaii 1967-69; San Jose St. Univ. 1969-; internat. cons. Faculty Devel. 1972-89; honors: Phi Kappa Phi Disting. Achievement 1987; mem: Internat. Council for Ednl. Media, Assn. Ednl. Comms. & Tech. (internat. div.), Calif. Library Media Educator (v.p. 1982), Morrin C.of C. (secty. 1955-56); ed. CMLEA Jour. (1982-86), cons. ed. Tech. Trends, Educ. Technology, Ednl. Media Internat. (1985-89), author, editor textbooks (1964, 72, 73, 90); rec: coaching rugby. Res: 888 Helena Dr Sunnyvale 94087 Ofc: San Jose State University Instructional Resources Center, San Jose 95192-0026

MCCAFFREY, STANLEY E(UGENE), retired university president; b. Feb. 26, 1917, Taft, Calif.; s. Joseph Cormack and Dorothy (Bunyard) McC.; m. Beth Connolley, July 6, 1941 (div. Jan. 1991); children: Stephen (Prof., McGeorge Sch. of Law, Sacto.), Nancy (dec. 1984); m. Sue Richardson Heapes; edn: AB, Univ. Calif., Berkeley 1938; LLD (hon.) Golden Gate Univ. 1972, Pepperdine Univ. 1978, Korea Univ. 1981. Career: adminstr. Univ. Calif., Berkeley, 13 years: coord. veterans affairs 1946, exec. mgr. Calif. Alumni Assn. 1948-56, univ. v.p. 1956-60; pres. San Francisco Bay Area Council 1961-71; pres. Univ. of the Pacific, Stockton 1971-87, ret.- during 16 yr. tenure expanded physical campus, budget ($22 mil. to $70+ mil.), enrollment (to 6,000), estab. new Sch. of Bus. and Pub. Adminstrn., and new Sch. of Internat. Studies; internat. pres. Rotary Internat., Evanston, Ill. 1981-82 (emphasis "World Understanding and Peace Through Rotary"); awards: recipient numerous honors and decorations from heads of state of countries visited (75+) as Pres. Rotary Intl. 1981-82, UCB student body pres., varsity football and baseball, Phi Beta Kappa 1938, Order of Golden Bear, The Berkeley Citation for contbns. to the univ. 1969, named to Berkeley Fellows (100 outstanding UC alumni); past pres. Assn. of Indep. Calif. Colls. (2x), Western Coll. Assn.; former bd. trustees Peralta Junior Coll. (pres.), Golden Gate Univ., Coll. of Holy Names; mil: US Navy 1940-45, WWII, decorated Silver Star and Legion of Merit for gal. in action and exceptionally meritorious svc. in the China Theatre; clubs: The Family (S.F.), Bohemian (S.F.), St. Francis Yacht (S.F.), Moraga CC; Congregationalist. Res: 557 Augusta Dr Moraga 94556

MCCAIN GONG, GLORIA MARGARET, pharmacist; b. Oct. 12, 1953, Yreka; d. Kenneth Wayne and Patricia Ann (Farley) McCain; m. Peter-Poon Gong, Apr. 3, 1976; children: George Wayne b. 1977, Cynthia May b. 1978, Miranda Lin b. 1979; edn: AA, Bakersfield Coll., 1972; CSU San Diego, 1972-73; PharmD, Univ. of Pacific, 1976. Career: asst. chief pharmacist West Hills Hosp., Canoga Park 1976-78; pharmacist/owner Gong's Rexall Drugs, Tehachapi 1978—; mem. AAUW (local publ. dir.); R.Cath.; rec: organic gardening, gourmet cooking club. Res: 800 Anita Dr Tehachapi 93561 Ofc: Gong's Rexall Drugs, 201 S Green St Tehachapi 93561

MCCARTHY, JOHN CHARLES, lawyer; b. Nov. 14, 1923, Chgo., Ill.; s. Thomas James and Margaret Mary (Schollmeyer) McC.; m. Lorraine Donovan, Feb. 5, 1960; children: Michael, b. 1961; Mary, b 1962; Sheila, b. 1964; edn: Miami Univ. 1942-44; BSBA, USC, 1947; JD, UCLA, 1952; Diplomate Am. Bd. of Trial Advocates; admitted bar: Calif. 1953. Career: pvt. law practice, Claremont 1954-63; dir. Peace Corps in Thailand, Bangkok 1963-66; partner law firm Young, Henrie & McCarthy, Pomona 1966-75; pres. law firm John C.McCarthy and Associates, Claremont 1975-; lectr./ writer for var. legal groups (incl. Calif. State Bar, Assn. of Am. Trial Lawyers, law schs., Calif. Trial Lawyers Assn., others); honors: UCLA Law Sch. Alumnus of Year 1973, Trial Lawyer of Yr. Calif. Employment Lawyers Assn. 1989; mem: American Trial Lawyers Assn. (nat. chmn. Environmental Law Sect. 1972-74), Calif. Trial Lawyers Assn. (pres. Inland chpt. 1969); clubs: University (pres. 1969), Bahia Corinthian Yacht (Newport Beach); author: Sucessful Techniques in Handling Bad Faith Cases (book & cassettes, 1973), Recovery of Damages in Bad Faith Cases (5th edit. 1990), Recovery of Damages in Wrongful Discharge Cases (Lawpress Corp., Tiburon 2d edit. 1990), book chapters: "Successful Ins. Bad Faith Trials" in Masters of Trial Practice (Wiley Law Publs., 1988), and "Punitive Damages" in California Torts (Matthew Bender 1985); mil: lt. j.g. USN 1943-46; Democrat; R.Cath.; rec: lecturing, skiing, sailing, golf. Res: 1920 Indian Hill Blvd Claremont 91711 Ofc: 401 Harvard Ave Claremont 91711

MCCARTHY, LEO TARCISIUS, state lieutenant governor; b. Auckland, N.Z., Aug. 15, 1930; came to U.S. 1934, nat. 1942; s. Daniel and Nora Teresa (Roche) McC.; m. Jacqueline Lee Burke, Dec. 17, 1955; children: Sharon, Conna, Adam, Niall; edn: BS, Univ. of San Francisco 1955; JD, San Francisco Law Sch. 1961; admitted Calif. St. Bar 1963. Career: supr. Bd. of Supr., San Francisco 1964-68; assemblyman Calif. State Legislature, Sacramento 1969-82, assembly speaker 1974-80; lt. gov. State of Calif., Sacramento 1983-; Democratic nominee U.S. Senate 1988; chmn. Econ. Devel. Commn. of Calif. 1983-; chmn. State Lands Commn. 1989-; regent Univ. Calif. 1983-; trustee State Coll. and Univ. System, Calif. 1983-; chmn. Task Force on Nursing Home Care, Calif. 1982-; mem. Dem. State Cen. Com. 1969-; awards: Outstanding Legislator Planning & Conservation League of Calif. 1971, Outstanding Legislator in U.S. Nat. Council Sr. Citizens 1972, Torch of Liberty award B'nai B'rith 1976; mil: USAF 1951-52. Ofc: Office of Lieutenant Governor State Capitol Rm 1114 Sacramento 95814

MCCLAIN, GEORGETTE, manufacturing company executive, general engineering contractor; b. May 18, 1927, Ventura; d. George W. and Harriet Josephine (Hanawalt) Floyd; m. James Weston McClain, Sept. 3, 1950; children: David b. 1952, Paul b. 1954, Mark b. 1961; edn: BA, Mills Coll. 1949; grad. Sawyer Bus. Coll. 1975; lic. Gen. Engring. Contr., Calif., Nev. (1985). Career: self-empl. piano tchr., Grass Valley 1950-74; office mgr. Gabe Mendez Inc., Newcastle 1976-79, Livingstons Grading & Paving Co., Newcastle 1979-81; pres. A.C. Dike Co., gen. engring. contrs., 1981-; owner Specialty Paving Equipment Co. (mfr. automatic paving equipment) 1981-; mem. Assn. Engring. Constrn. Employers; Republican; Episcopalian. Ofc: A.C. Dike Co., 2788 Venture Dr Lincoln 95648

MCCLELLAN, CRAIG RENE, lawyer; b. June 28, 1947, Portland, Oreg.; s. Charles Russell and Annette Irene (Benedict) McC.; m. Susan Armistead Nash, June 7, 1975; children: Ryan Alexander, Shannon Lea; edn: BS in econs., Univ. Oregon, 1969; JD (magna cum laude), Calif. Western Sch. of Law, 1976; admitted bar: Calif. 1976, U.S. District Courts Ca. So. 1976, Ea. 1991, No. 1991, Cent. 1992, U.S. Supreme Ct. 1991. Career: compliance specialist Cost of Living Council W.D.C., Price Commn., W.D.C., 1972-73, dir. Oil Policy Subcom., 1973; ptnr. law firm Luce, Forward, Hamilton & Scripps, San Diego 1976-87; prin. McClellan & Assocs., San Diego 1987-; honors: Master, American Inns of Court (1991-), Outstanding trial lawyer award San Diego Trial Lawyers Assn. (1981, 83); mem: Am. Bd. of Trial Advocates, Calif. Bar Assn., San Diego County Bar Assn., Assn. Trial Lawyers Am., Calif. Trial Lawyers Assn. (bd. govs. 1985-87), San Diego Trial Lawyers Assn. (bd. 1983-90), Nat. Forensics League; civic: Calif. Western Law Sch. (bd. trustees 1985-89), Sta. KPBS (chair Annual Fundraising Auction 1984); mil: capt. USMC 1969-72. Ofc: McClellan & Associates, 1144 State St San Diego 92101

MCCLURE, DAVID OWEN, military officer; b. May 31, 1940, Fulton, Ky.; s. Guy Junior and Margaret Ruth (Owen) McC.; m. Marian Ann Lemons, Dec. 24, 1962; edn: BA journ./polit. sci., Univ. Ariz., 1962; disting. grad. AF Reserve Officer Tng. Corps, 1962; grad. Squadron Officer Sch., Air Command and Staff

Coll., Indsl. Coll. of Armed Forces, and Air War Coll.; MBA pgm. Univ. N.Dak. AF Inst. of Tech.; cand. PhD pub. adminstrn. Univ. of LaVerne. Career: commd. ofcr., served to col. US Air Force 1962-92: wing information ofcr. 4128th Strategic Wing, Amarillo AFB, Tx. 1962, redesignated 461st Bombardment Wing (H) 1963; first chief of Pub. Info. Div. Aerospace Res. Labs., Wright-Patterson AFB, Oh. 1964, aide-de-camp to OAR cmdr. in Arlington, Va. 1966-69; dir. of info. 56th Spl. Ops. Wing, Nakhom Phanom Royal Thai AFB, Thailand 1969-70; combat crew Minuteman III, Minot AFB, N.D. 1970-73, chief of Launch Control Facilities Mgmt. Div. 1973; exec. ofcr. to Asst. Chief of Staff for Data Systems, Hq., SAC, 1974-76, adminstrv. asst. to the Chief of Staff, 1976-79; cmdr. 67 SMS, 44 SMW, Ellsworth AFB, S.D. 1979-81; exec. ofcr. 4315 Combat Crew Tng. Sq., Vandenberg AFB, Calif. 1981; dep. cmdr. for ops. 351st Strategic Missile Wing, Whiteman AFB, Mo. 1982-84; dep. cmdr. for ops., then v.cmdr. 91st Strat. Missile Wing, Minot AFB, N.D. 1984-86; cmdr. 487th Tactical Missile Wing, Comiso Air Sta., Sicily, Italy 1986-88; cmdr. 4315th Combat Crew Tng. Squadron, Vandenberg AFB, Calif. 1988-90; cmdr. 4392d Aerospace Support Wing, Vandenberg AFB CA, 1990-92 (largest base in Air Force Space Command; On-Scene cmdr. during missile and space launch ops.; respons. for security, civil engring., transp., logistics, disaster preparedness, human resource mgmt. & devel., family support, morale/ welfare/ rec., billeting/feeding svs., and flightline ops. for base comm. of over 15,000; mem. bd. dirs. Santa Barbara Visiting Nurse Assn.; Delta Chi Frat.; Republican; Lutheran. Res: 625 Aspen Vandenberg AFB 93437 Ofc: 4392 ASW/CC Vandenberg AFB 93437

MCCLURE, HOWE ELLIOTT, wildlife biologist, author; b. Apr. 29, 1910, Chgo.; s. Howe Alexander and Clara (Phillips) McC.; m. Lucy Esther Lou Fairchild, Oct. 1, 1933 (dec.); children: Lucy Jeannette b. 1941, Clara Ann b. 1942; edn: BS, Univ. of Illinois, Urbana 1933, MS, 1936; PhD, Iowa State Univ., 1941. Career: asst. entomologist Univ. Ill., Urbana 1930-33; tree expert Ill. Tree Service Co., Peru, Ill. 1934-37; grad. asst. Iowa State Univ., Ames 1937-41; biologist Nebra. Game Forestation & Parks, Ord, Nebr. 1941-44; biologist USPHS, Bakersfield, Calif. 1946-50; ornithologist Walter Reed Army Inst. of Research, Tokyo, Kuala Lumpur, honors: Silver Beaver BSA, Tokyo 1958, Sigma Xi 1933-; mem: Nat. Audubon Soc. (conserv. chmn. Conejo Soc. 1976-), N.E., E., Inland and Western Birdbanding Socs. 1940-, Malayan Nature Soc. (pres. 1962-63), Defenders of Wildlife (1976-, bd. 1978-89); scoutmaster BSA (1933-58); author: Migration and Survival of the Birds of Asia 1974, Haematozoa in the Birds of Eastern and Southern Asia 1978, Bird Banding 1984, Whistling Wings - The Dove Chronicles (1991); mil: lt (jg) USN 1944-46; rec: bird watching, bird banding, stamps. Res: 69 E Loop Camarillo 93010

MCCONNEL, RICHARD APPLETON, aerospace engineer; b. May 29, 1933, Rochester, Pa.; s. Richard A., Sr. and Dorothy (Merriman) McC.; m. Mary Francis McInnis, Apr. 11, 1966 (div. 1984); children: Amy Ellen b. 1967, Sarah Cathrine b. 1971; edn: Washington and Jefferson Coll., Pa. 1951-53; BS engring. US Naval Acad., Annapolis 1957; MS aero. engring.; naval aviator USN 1959; US Naval Postgrad. Sch., Monterey 1966; prog. mgr. NAVAIRDEVCEN, Warminster, Pa. P3C prgms 1971-75; prog. mgr. PALMISTESTCEN, Pt. Mugu, CA, Range Systems 1979-82. Career: advanced through ranks of ensign to cdr. US Navy 1957-82; engr. Raytheon Electro-Magnetic Systems, Goleta, Calif. 1982-87; sr. engr. SRS Technologies, Camarillo 1987-92; sr. engr. High Technology Solutions, Camarillo 1992-; mem. Assn. Old Crows 1982-; rec: skiing, hiking, camping. Res: 1665 Pierside Ln Camarillo 93010 Ofc: 1317 Del Norte Rd Camarillo 93010

MCCORQUODALE, DANIEL ALFRED, senator, educator; b. Dec. 17,1934, Longville, LA; s. Daniel Alfred and Lalla May (Thornton) M.; m. Jean Adrian Botsford; children: Michael; Sharon; Daniel; edn: BS, San Diego State Univ., 1960; tchg. cred., San Diego State Univ., 1960; career: elem. educator National City, Pasadena, and San Jose sch. systems, 1960-72; city council/mayor, Chula Vista, 1964-68; county supervisor, Santa Clara Co., 1972-82; state senator, 12th senate dist., 1982-; chmn., Senate Natural Resources and Wildlife Com.; mem: Agric. and Water Resources Com.; Budget and Fiscal Review Com.; chmn., Subcom. on Justice, Corrections, Resources, and Agric.; Bus. and Professions; Ins., Claims, and Corporations; Transportation; Constitutional Amendments; Public Employment and Retirement; chmn., Special Com. on Developmental Disabilities and Mental Health; mem: Napa State Hosp. Advy. Bd.; Multiple Sclerosis Soc.; chmn, Area VII Developmental Disabilities Bd.; mem: Marine Corps Lge., Modesto; Am. Legion, San Jose; awards: Legislator of Year: Calif. Planning & Conservation League, Peace Officers Res. Assn., Nat. Org. for Women, Sacto.; Advocate of Year, Calif. Assn. Svs. for Children; Outstanding Legislator, Calif. Council Developmental Disabilities; Calif. Governor's Com. for Employment of Disabled Persons; N. Calif. Psychiatric Soc.; United Cerebral Palsy Assn. of Calif.; Calif. Coalition for Mental Health; Calif. Assn. of Retarded Citizens; Parents Helping Parents; Calif. Assn. of Reg. Ctr. Agencies; civic: Haven Women's Ctr., Calif. Women for Agric., Farm Bureau Fedn., Sr. Opportunity Svc. Prog.; author: pamphlet, The Legislative Process, 1990; report, The Lanterman Developmental Disabilities Services Act, 1992; author, SB 124, creates eight cty. reg. air pollution control dist.; SB 238, equalize sch. dist. funding; SB 1383, developmental disabilities reform; SB 1665, increase penalties for infractions to irrigation facilities; SB 387, park bond; SB 1296 create Mentally Disordered Offender Prog.; SB 1541, protections for victims of domestic violence; SB 1862, stalker legislation; SB 354, programs to keep pregnant and parenting teens in sch.; SB 463, wetlands; SB 1563, retirement sys. for judges, SB 1470, money laundering; SB 1112, est. standards for developmental svs.; SB 960, exempt Special Olympics; SB 2210, training law enforcement; SB 1115, treatment of mentally retarded defendants; SB 1045, reg. ctr. budget reduction; mil: sgt., USMC, 1953-56; Democrat; Protestant. Res: Modesto Ofc: State Senate, State of Calif., State Capitol Rm. 4032 Sacramento 95814

MC COY, JAMES THOMAS, pharmacist; b. Jan. 24, 1955, Waltham, Mass.; s. Robert and Marjorie Elizabeth (Damory) McC; m. Christina Rehngren, Sept. 22, 1984; edn: BS pharm., Northeastern Univ., Boston 1979; reg. pharmacist Mass. 1979. Career: clin. pharmacist New England Meml. Hosp., Stoneham, Mass. 1979-81; pharm. supr. Loma Linda Univ. Med. Center, Loma Linda 1981-89; dir. pharm. Loma Linda Comm. Hosp. 1989-; pres. Performance Enterprises 1992-; pres. James McCoy & Assoc. Pharm. Services, Riverside 1982-; honors: nom. New England Meml. Hosp. hosp. pharmacist of year 1981; mem: Am. Soc. Hosp. Pharmacists, Calif. Soc. Hosp. Pharmacists, Inland Soc. Hosp. Pharmacists, Riverside C.of C.; Republican; rec: woodworking, photography. Ofc: Loma Linda Community Hospital 25333 Barton Rd Loma Linda 92354

MCCRACKEN, SHIRLEY ANN, educational consultant; b. Aug. 15, 1937, Rochester, N.Y.; d. Bernard Anthony Ross and Marian Elizabeth (Taliento) Heimann; m. Paul Arthur McCracken, June 25, 1971; children: Donna b. 1967, Glenn b. 1971; edn: BA in math., Nazareth Coll., Rochester, N.Y. 1959; MS math., Marquette Univ., Milw. 1968; PhD human behavior, La Jolla Univ., 1980. Career: tchr., dept. chair Mt. Carmel High Sch., Auburn, N.Y. 1959-68; training asst. Jewish Vocational Svc., Milw. 1969; rehabilitation counselor Curative Workshop, Milw. 1968-69; tchr. Anaheim Union High Sch., Calif. 1969-72; program dir. San Antonio Church, Anaheim 1987-90; trainer, cons., Anaheim 1990-; tchr. Orange Catechetical Inst., Orange 1989-; awards: scholarship Nazareth Coll. 1954-59, NSF inst. grantee- Marquette Univ. 1963, 64, 66, 67 and Anaheim, Ca. 1990, Annie Accolade women's div. Anaheim C.of C. 1978, Named Gift, EF AAUW- Anaheim 1978, Anaheim Hills 1984, and Calif. State AAUW, Sacto. 1991; civic: Ebell Club Anaheim (1975-, pres.), Anaheim Hills AAUW (1982-, secty.), Anaheim AAUW (1972-, bd.), Anaheim Mus., Anaheim Sister Cities Assn.; author: Creative Leadership (1980), book ed: Planning Model for Leadership, Decision Making, Mgmt. Training (1982); Republican; R.Cath. Res: 6553 Calle Del Norte Anaheim 92807

MCCRARY, BARBARA JO, antique auto dealer, insurance agent; b. Jan. 6, 1934, Quinton, Okla.; d. Ben H. and Nan V. (Murrell) Brackett; m. Bill Johnston (div.); m. 2d. Jerry Lee McCrary, Oct. 19, 1973; children: Julie Johnston Hermosillo b. 1952, Terry Ellen Hauff b. 1954, Vickie Lynn Johnston Benedict b. 1956; 5 grandchildren: (nee Hermosillo) Harley and Jay, (nee Hauff) Barbara Jo, Belinda Jean and David Lee, Jr.; gt. grandchildren: Alexie A. Hauff, David Lee "Troy" Hauff, III (children of David Lee, Jr.) and Jason A. Grissom Jr., Samanttha Grissom (children of Belinda Jean); Calif. lic.: Life & Disability, Fire & Casualty (life), Variable Contract agent; lic. Contractor, P.U.C. lic. (freight of mobile homes), lic. Auto dealer. Career: retail sales clk., Merced 1968-69; auto sales Town & Country Chrysler, Merced 1969; sales Travelon Trailer Co., Modesto 1973; ptnr. Bill's Trailer Sales, Merced 1974-77; prop. McCrary's Mobile Homes, Merced 1977-87, Antique Auto dealership, 1987-, My Body Shop (antique auto restoration), 1988-, investor rental property, almond ranch; full time ins. agent Prudential, 1991-; mem. Merced, Mariposa Horsemans Assn.; Republican; Prot.; rec: dancing, fishing, gardening. Res: 2369 Ashby Rd Merced 95348 Ofc: 1950 N Ashby Rd Merced 95340

MC CRAVEN, EVA STEWART MAPES, mental health center administrator; b. Sept. 26, 1936, Los Angeles; d. Paul Melvin and Wilma Zech (Ziegler) Stewart; m. Carl Clarke McCraven, Mar. 18, 1978; children: David Anthony, Lawrence James, Maria Lynn Mapes; edn: BS (magna cum laude) CSU Northridge, 1974; MS, Cambridge Grad. Sch. Psychology, 1987, postgrad. Career: dir. special projects Pacoima Memorial Hosp. 1969-71, dir. health edn. 1971-74; asst. exec. dir. Hillview Community Mental Health Ctr., Lakeview Terrace, 1974-, developer, mgr. Long-term Residential Program 1986-, program mgr. Crisis Residential Program, past dir. dept. consultation and edn.; dir: N.E. Valley Health Corp. 1970-73, Golden State Comm. Mental Health Ctr. 1970-73; awards: nominee Hourglass award Hiltoppers Aux. of Assistance League of So. Calif. 1985, resolution Calif. St. Senate 1988, commendn. and spl. mayor's plaque L.A. Mayor Tom Bradley 1988, recipient commendations for comm. service City & Co. of L.A., Calif. St. Assembly and Senate, Sunland Tujunga Police Support Council & C.of C. 1989; woman of achiev. Sunland Tujunga BPW 1990; mem: Assn. Mental Health Adminstrs. (fellow), Am. Pub. Health Assn., Women in Health Adminstrn., Health Svs. Adminstrn. Alumni Assn. (former v.p.), Bus. and Profl. Women (v.p.), L.W.V.; civic: S.F.V. Coordinating Council Area Assn. (past pres.), Sunland-Tujunga Coordinating Council (past pres.). Ofc: Hillview Center 11500 Eldridge Ave Lake View Terrace 91342

MCCRONE, ALISTAIR WILLIAM, university president; b. Oct. 7, 1931, Regina, Can., nat. U.S. 1961; s. Hugh MacMillan and Kathleen Maude Tallent (Forth) McC.; m. Judith Saari, May 8, 1958; children: Bruce b. 1960, Craig b. 1962, Mary b. 1963; edn: BA, Univ. Sask. 1953; MS (Shell fellow) Univ. Nebr., 1955; PhD geol., Univ. Kans., 1961. Career: wellsite geologist Brit. Am. Oil Co. 1952-53; field geologist Shell Oil Co. 1954-55, field party chief exploration and mapping 1956-58; instr. New York Univ., 1959-61, asst. prof. 1961-64, assoc. prof. 1964-69, assoc. dean Grad. Sch. Arts and Scis./ prof. of geology 1969-70; academic v.p./prof. geol. Univ. of the Pacific, 1970-74, acting pres. 1971; univ. pres./prof. geol., CSU Humboldt, 1974-; mem. CSU Commn. on Ednl. Telecomm. 1983-85, advy. group Exec. Council CSU System 1980-81; awards: Golden Dozen CSUH 1983, Sigma Xi (NYU chpt. pres. 1967-69), Erasmus Haworth Honors Univ. Kans. 1957, Danforth Found. Assoc. 1964-68; mem: Am. Assn. Univ. Adminstrs. (bd. 1986-), Assn. of Am. Colls. (bd. 1989-), Am. Assn. State Colls. and Univs. (state del. 1977-80), Calif. State Auto Assn. (bd. 1988-), Geol. Soc. Am. (fellow), AAAS (fellow), Calif. Acad. Scis. (fellow), Am. Assn. of Petroleum Geologists, Soc. of Econ. Paleontologists and Mineralogists (nat. del. 1967, 68, 69); clubs: Rotary, Saint Andrews Soc. N.Y. (life), University (S.F.); civic: Redwood Empire Assn. (bd. 1983-88), Presbyn. Hosp. Pacific Med. Ctr. S.F. (trustee 1971-74); rec: golf, skiing. Ofc: Humboldt State University Arcata 95521

MCCURDY, STEPHEN RANKIN, interior landscaping company president; b. April 19, 1960, Belfast, No. Ireland; s. Samuel and Daphne (Rushbrook) McCurdy; m. Janet Faith McFarland, July 3, 1982; children: Timothy b. 1989, James b. 1991; edn: cert. craftsman Oakland College of Horticulture, Hertfordshire, Eng. 1979. Career: grower Buena Park Greenhouses, Encinitas 1979-80; sales rep. Thomas Rochford & Sons, Hertfordshire, Eng. 1980-82; grower, mgr. Calif. Exotique, Los Angeles 1983, general mgr. Carson 1984; owner, prin. British Indoor Gardens dba Landscape Images, L.A. 1984-; pres. British Indoor Gardens, Inc., Lake Forest 1987-; instr. seminar San Diego Plantscape, San Diego 1989; judge Norcal Awards, San Francisco 1989; instr., speaker Assoc. Landscape Contractors of Am. 1993; awards: recipient Best Project award from Interiorscape mag. 1986, 90, PIPA awards: service 1987, 92, installation 1988, 90, 91, 92 design 1989, 91, 92, judges award 1989; Distinction Award Assoc. Landscape Contractors of Am.; mem: Profl. Interior Plantscape Assn. (dir. fin. com.1986-88, dir. ways & means com. 1988-), Associated Landscape Contractors of Am., Bldg. Industry Assn., Sales & Mktg. Council, Foilage for Clean Air Council; rec: stamp collecting. Ofc: Gardens Inc Landscape Images 20742 Linear Ln Lake Forest 92630

MCDANIELS, JOHN LEA, lawyer; b. May 30, 1940, San Francisco; s. John Hale and Vivian Maria (Lea) McD.; edn: BA, Stanford Univ. 1962; JD, San Francisco Law Sch. 1969. Mem: Internat. Bar Assn., State Bar of Calif., Inns of Court Society in Calif, Commonwealth Club, Cercle de l'Union, Commanderie de Bordeaux des Etats-Unis, The Assocs. of the Stanford Univ. Libraries (advy. council), The Friends of the Bancroft Library, The Assocs. of St. Francis Memorial Hosp., Soc. of Mayflower Descendants in the State of Calif. (gov. S.F. Peninsula Colony 1987-89), The Pilgrim John Howland Soc.; mil: sp4/c AUS 1962-64; R.Cath. Res: 1250 Jones St San Francisco 94109 Ofc: 220 Montgomery St #2918 San Francisco 94104

MCDONALD, MARIANNE, classicist; b. Jan. 2, 1937, Chgo.; d. Eugene Francis and Inez (Riddle) McDonald; children: Eugene, Conrad, Bryan, Bridget, Kirstie (dec.), Hiroshi; edn: BA (magna cum laude), Bryn Mawr Coll., 1958; MA, Univ. Chgo., 1960; PhD, UC Irvine, 1975. Career: tchg. asst. classics UC Irvine, 1972-74, instr. Greek, Latin and English, mythology, modern cinema, 1975-79, research Thesaurus Linguae Graecae Project, 1979-; prof. Dept. Theatre, UC San Diego, 1990-; vis. research fellow Sch. of Classics, Univ. of Dublin, Trinity Coll., Eire. 1990; bd. dirs. Centrum, Am. Coll. of Greece 1981-, Scripps Hosp. 1981, Am. Sch. Classical Studies 1986-; bd. overseers UC San Diego 1985-; honors: Ellen Browning Scripps Humanitarian 1975, disting. service UC Irvine 1982, Irvine Medal 1987, 3rd Prize Midwest Poetry Ctr. Contest 1987, philanthropist of yr. NCCJ 1986, woman of yr. AHEPA 1988, Hon. Doctorate Am. Coll. of Greece 1988, Woman of Distinction San Diego Regl. Conf. for Women 1990, Gold medal Soc. for the Internationalization of the Greek Language 1991, Gold medal from Mayor of Athens 1991, Gold medal from Mayor of Piraeus 1991, Hon. Dipl. the Archeol. Assn. of Athens 1991, Axios Woman of Year 1991, Hellenic Univ. Womens Assn. of Greece Hypatia Award 1991, AHEPA Acad. of Achievement Award 1992, UC San Diego Civis Universitatis Award 1993; mem: Am. Philol. Assn., Philol. Assn. Pacific Coast, Am. Classical League, MLA, Am. Comparative Lit. Assn., Modern and Classical Language Assn., AAUP So. Calif., Hellenic Soc., Calif. Fgn. Language Tchrs. Assn., Internat. Platform Assn., Am. Biog. Inst. Nat. Bd. Advisors 1982-, KPBS Producers Club, Hellenic Univ. Club (dir.); author: Terms for Happiness in Euripides 1978, Semilemmatized Concordances to Euripides' Alcestis 1977, Cyclops, Andromache, Medea 1978, Heraclidae, Hippolytus 1979, Hecuba 1982, Hercules Furens (1984), Electra (1985), Ion 1985, Trojan Women 1988, Iphigenia in Taurus 1988, Euripides in Cinema: The Heart Made Visible 1983; translator: The Cost of Kindness and Other Fabulous Tales by Shinichi Hoshi 1986; book chapters in Views of Clytemnestra, Ancient and Modern; Tony Harrison: A Critical Anthology; Ancient Sun, Modern Light: Greek Drama on the Modern Stage 1991; numerous articles in scholarly jours. Res: Box 929 Rancho Santa Fe 92067 Ofc: Dept. of Theatre B-044 Univ. California San Diego La Jolla 92093

MCDOWELL, JENNIFER, publisher, composer; b. May 19, 1936, Albuquerque, NM; d. Willard A. and Margaret (Garrison) McDowell; mother is the author, Margaret F. Garrison; grandfather, Lemuel Addison Garrison, former pres. Central College Pella, Iowa; uncle, Lon Garrison, supt. of Yellowstone Nat. Park 1955-63; m. Milton Loventhal (author, playwright and lyricist), July 2, 1973; edn: BA, UC Berkeley, 1957; MA, CSU San Diego, 1958; MLS, UCB, 1963; PhD, Univ. Oregon, Eugene 1973. Career: high sch. tchr. Abraham Lincoln H.S., San Jose 1960-61; freelance ed., Soviet field, 1961-63; res. asst., sociol., Univ. Oreg. 1964-66; ed./pub. Merlin Papers, San Jose 1969-; ed./pub. Merlin Press, 1973-; res. cons. sociol., San Jose 1973-; music publ. Lipstick and Toy Balloons Pub. Co., San Jose 1978-; res., writer Merlin Res. and Writing Center, 1980-; co-creator musical comedy: Russia's Secret Plot to Take Back Alaska, 1983; coauthor 4 plays performed off-off Broadway in 1986: Betsy and Phyllis, The Estrogen Party To End War, Mack The Knife Your Friendly Dentist, The Oatmeal Party Comes to Order; coauthor play "Betsy Meets the Wackey Iraqi" performed Burgess Theatre, 1991; tchr. writing workshops 1969-73; manuscript reader for Journ. of the Sci. Study of Religion, 1974-; composer 160+ songs, on list of composers for Paramount Pictures, 1981-88; co-prod. radio shows, Sta. KALX, Berkeley 1971-72; awards: AAUW doctoral fellow 1971-73, Calif. Arts Council grantee 1976-77, 3 songs incl. in Survey of Am. Music for Bicentennial Yr. 1976, Am. Song Festival 1976-79, Poetry Orgn. for Women 1979, Bill Casey Mem. Award 1980 listed Directory of Am. Poets and Fiction Writers 1980, composer for Harold C. Crain Award (1980) winning play, Simple Gifts by Nancy Gilsenan; honors: Kappa Kappa Gamma, Sigma Alpha Iota, Phi Beta Kappa, Beta Phi Mu; mem: Soc. for the Sci. Study of Religion, Am. Sociological Assn., Poetry Orgn. for Women, Feminist Writers Guild, Internat. Womens Writing Guild; author: Black Politics (1971, featured at Smithsonian Institute in 1992),Contemporary Women Poets an Anthology 1977, Ronnie Goose Rhymes forGrown-ups 1984; contbr. many articles in Bulletin of Bibliography, Jour.for the Sci. Study of Religion, San Jose Studies; poems, essays, plays innumerous books and mags. incl. Women's World, Women Talking, Women Listening, X a Journal of the Arts, others; Democrat; Prot.; rec: tennis, Calif. native plants, hiking. Ofc: Merlin Press, POB 5602 San Jose 95150

MCELROY, LEO FRANCIS, public relations consultant; b. Oct. 12, 1932, Los Angeles; s. Leo Francis Sr. and Helen Evelyn (Silliman) McE.; m. Dorothy Montgomery, Nov. 3, 1956 (div. 1981); children: James b. 1961, Maureen b. 1964, Michael b. 1967, Kathleen b. 1969; m. Judy Lewis, May 30, 1992; edn: BS in English, Loyola Univ., 1953. Career: broadcast newsman in Ill., Calif., 1954-63; news director KFI, KRLA, KABC Radio, Los Angeles, 1963-72; reporter/host KCET-TV, L.A. 1965-74; political editor KABC-TV, L.A. 1974-81; pres. McElroy Communications, Sacramento/Los Angeles, 1981-; special asst. Lt. Gov. of Calif. 1983-84; lectr. (politics) UC Davis 1983-, lectr. (journalism) Sacto. St. Univ. 1985-, lectr. (media) Chamber of Commerce, Sacto. 1985-; honors: Emmy nominations Acad. TV Arts & Scis. (1967, 68, 70, 74, 79), Golden Mike award Radio-TV News Assn., L.A. 1973, Gabriel award Catholic Archdiocese, L.A. 1972, announcer of year Calif. State Fair, Sacto. 1960, Hon. Resolution Calif. State Assembly, Sacto. 1981, writing award Gr. L.A. Press Club 1981; mem: Am. Assn. Political Consultants, Am. Soc. Composers Authors Publishers, AFTRA, SAG; civic: Mental Health Assn. Sacto. (dir. 1985-), Rescue Alliance Sacto. (dir. 1987-), Volunteers in Victim Asst. Sacto. (dir. 1984); author: (book) Uneasy Partners 1984, (play) To Bury Caesar 1952, author/lyricist: (musicals) Mermaid Tavern 1956, Rocket To Olympus 1960, numerous songs incl. Melanie Goodby 1963, Wanderin' Song 1964; mil: 1st lt. USAF 1954-56; Republican; R.Cath.; rec: tennis, songwriting. Res: 8217 Oakenshaw Way Orangevale 95662 Ofc: McElroy Communications 2410 K St Ste C Sacramento 95816 also: 6363 Wilshire Blvd Ste 129 Los Angeles 90048

MCFARLAND, GARY LYNN, civil engineer; b. May 28, 1947, Wichita, Kans.; s. Duard Edward and Leah Jean (Shiner) McF.; m. Carol, June 22, 1974; children: Joseph b. 1979, Patrick b. 1983, Kevin b. 1984; edn: BE in C.E., Ga. Inst. of Tech. 1970; reg. civil engr. Calif. 1976. Career: field engr. R.S. Delamater & Assocs., Wichita, Kans. 1970-71; jr. engr. Goleta Water Dist., 1974-77; consulting engr. McFarland Engring. Inc., 1977-83; pres. Lawrance, Fisk & McFarland Inc., cons. engrs., 1983-; elected bd. dirs. Goleta Water Dist. (1979, 1983), mem. Cachuma Ops. & Maint. Bd., Santa Barbara Co. 1985-87; mem: ASCE, Am. Water Works Assn., Water Pollution Control Fedn.; mil: 1st lt. AUS 1971-73; Orthodox Christian Ch.; rec: pvt. pilot. Res: 213 Hillview Goleta 93117 Ofc: Lawrance, Fisk & McFarland, Inc. 928 Garden St Santa Barbara 93101

MCFARLAND, JUDITH LINDBERG, nutritional consultant, author; b. Oct. 4, 1933, Los Angeles; d. Walter Harold and Gladys (Melcher) Lindberg; m. Don McFarland, Dec. 18, 1955; children: Gary b. 1957, Dan b. 1958, Laura b. 1964, Douglas b. 1966; edn: BS in nutrition, Pepperdine Univ., 1955. Career: nutritional cons. Lindberg Nutrition, founded 1949-, owner 1979-; co-owner

Nutrition Express; coauthor: Take Charge of Your Health (Harper & Row, 1982); interior decorator, owner Judy's Decorating, Rancho Palos Verdes 1967-89; honors: biog. listed Who's Who Internat. Bus. and Profl. Women; mem: Nat. Nutritional Foods Assn. (bd. dirs. 1989-), Golden West Nat. Foods Assn. Inc. (sec. 1987-), Am. Nutrition Soc. (pres. 1975-78, advisor 1978-87), Am. Assn. of Nutritional Consultants 1985-87, Internat. Women in Leadership; civic: YWCA Y-Wives Inglewood (v.p.) 1962-64, pres. 1964-68, advisor 1968-78); frequent lectr. pub. and private schs., civic orgns., numerous church groups; guest various radio and TV programs including: 700 Club, and various pgms. on Trinity Bdcstg. Network; Republican; Christian. Ofc: Lindberg Nutrition 166 Del Amo Fashion Ctr. Torrance 90503

MCGAULEY, JACQUELYNE SUE, researcher; b. Aug. 23, 1951, Los Angeles; d. Richard Courtney and Marion Lucia (Otto) May; m. Patrick Lawrence, Nov. 27, 1980 (div. May 1984); children: Julie Anna b. 1981, Jonathan Daniel b. 1982. Career: instr. General Telephone Co., Downey 1971-82; researcher Ted L. Gunderson Assocs., Santa Monica 1989-; cons. civil and crim. cases Tulsa, Okla. and Calif., 1985-; cons. numerous newspapers and mags. incl. S.F. Examiner, San Jose Mercury News, Washington Post; cons. Child Help- L.A., Kid Safe - Calif., Help Line Houston, Tx., others; speaker L.A. County Health Dept., UCLA, USC, various groups, interview and talkshow guest numerous radio and TV pgms.; award for outstanding service to children Enough 1986; mem. Affirming Children's Truths/ACT (pres. 1984-), Believe the Children (founding mem., exec. bd. 1985-87), Children's Civil Rights Fund (founding bd.), Coalition of Victims Equal Rights/COVER (founding bd. 1985-88), Nat. Coalition of Childrens Justice 1984-, speaker Fresno Growth Ctr. 1993, Foster Parent Conf. Ventura Co. Public Social Svcs. 1993; co-producer film documentary on satanism and ritual abuse 1990-; Christian; rec: painting, art. Ofc: Ted L. Gunderson & Assocs. 2210 Wilshire Blvd Ste 421 Santa Monica 90403

MCGETTIGAN, CHARLES CARROLL, JR., investment banker; b. March 28, 1945, San Francisco; s. Charles Carroll McGettigan and Molly (Fay) Pedley; m. Katharine Havard King, Nov. 1, 1975 (div. 1981); m. Meriwether Lewis Stovall, Aug. 6, 1983; 1 child, Meriwether Lewis Fay; edn: BA govt., Georgetown Univ. 1966; MBA fin., Wharton Sch., Univ. Pa., 1969. Career: assoc., asst. v.p., v.p. Blyth Eastman Dillon, NYC 1970-75, 1st v.p. 1975-78, sr. v.p., San Francisco 1978-80; sr. v.p. Dillon Read & Co., S.F. 1980-83; gen. ptnr. Woodman Kirkpatrick & Gilbreath, S.F. 1983-84; prin., corp. fin. Hambrecht & Quist, Inc., S.F. 1984-88; mng. dir., founder McGettigan, Wick & Co., Inc. S.F. 1988-; dir: Circadian Inc., San Jose 1980-84, Skouras Pictures Inc., Hollywood 1987-, Sungene Techs. Inc., San Jose 1987-88, Raytel Systems Inc., San Jose 1988-89, Shared Techs. Inc., Hartford, Conn. 1988-; advy. dir. Chesapeake Ventures, Baltimore 1984-; trustee St. Francis Meml. Hosp., S.F. 1980-86; advy. bd. dirs. Leavey Sch. Bus. Adminstrn., Santa Clara Univ. 1984-; with USN, 1966; clubs: Brook, Racquet & Tennis (N.Y.), Pacific Union, Bohemian (S.F.), Burlingame CC (Hillsborough), California (L.A.), Boston (New Orleans), Piping Rock (Locust Valley, N.Y.); mil: USN 1966; Republican; R.Cath. Res: 3375 Clay St San Francisco 94118 Ofc: McGettigan Wick & Co., Inc. 50 Osgood Pl San Francisco 94133

MCGIFFEN, THOMAS GLENN, electrical engineer; b. Apr. 19, 1964, Clarion, Pa.; s. Milton Earl, Sr. and Rose Mary (Scarnato) McG.; edn: BS in E.E. (honors and high distinction), Pa. State Univ., 1987; MS in elect. and computer engring., Univ. Ill., Urbana 1989. Career: co-op. engr. Packard Electric, Warren, Ohio 1985; systems engr. Hughes Aircraft Co., El Segundo, Calif. 1987-; awards: G.E. Foundation fellow 1987-88; honors: Who's Who in the West 1992; pub. res. articles in E.E. (1989); Christian; rec: guitarist. Res: 1031 W 132nd St Gardena 90247 Ofc: Hughes Aircraft Co. PO Box 92919 Los Angeles 90009

MCGLYNN, BETTY HOAG, art historian; b. Apr. 28, 1914, Deer Lodge, Mont.; d. Arthur James and and Elizabeth Tangye (Davey) Lochrie; m. Paul Sterling Hoag, Dec. 28, 1936 (div. 1967); children: Peter Lochrie Hoag, Jane Hoag Brown, Robert Doane Hoag; m. Thomas Arnold McGlynn, July 28, 1973; edn: BA, Stanford Univ., 1936; MA, USC, 1967; Calif. std. tchg. cred., secondary. Career: research dir. So. Calif. Archives of American Art, Los Angeles, 1964-67; Carmel Museum of Art, 1967-69; dir. Triton Museum of Art, Santa Clara, 1970; archivist, librarian San Mateo County Historical Soc. Museum, 1972-74; art instr. Monterey Peninsula Coll., 1970, San Jose City Coll., 1971; art appraiser, City of Carmel, 1967, Monterey, 1981; cons., writer, lectr. in field, 1964-; mem. Butte (Mont.) Arts Chateau, Carmel Art Assn. (hon.), Carmel Heritage Soc., Chinese Hist. Soc., Friends of the Bancroft Library, Monterey County Cultural Council, Monterey History and Art Assn. (art cons.), Monterey Peninsula Museum of Art (acquisitions bd. and steering com. for La Mirada), Robinson Jeffers Tor House Found. (art cons.), Hawaiian Hist. Soc., Nat. Museum of Women in the Arts, The Westerners, P.E.O.; author: The World of Mary DeNeale Morgan 1970; Carmel Art Association: A History 1987; various booklets and museum catalogs; contbg. author: Orchid Art of the Orchid Isle (Malama Arts, Honolulu, 1982); Plein Air Painters of California The North 1986; Hawaiian Island Artists and Friends of the Arts (Malama Arts, Kailua-Kona, 1989); jour. editor, contbr.: La Peninsula 1971-75, Noticias 1983-88; Republican. Address: PO Box 5034 Carmel-by-the-Sea CA 93921

MCGOWEN, GERALD ELLIS, biologist; b. Dec. 27, 1946, Muskegon, Mich.; s. Gerald Edward and Helen Lorraine (Ellis) McG.; edn: AS, Southwestern Coll. 1967; BS, San Diego St. Univ. 1970; MS, 1977; PhD, USC 1987. Career: assoc. environ. splst. Occidental Coll., L.A. 1974-78; asst. research curator Natural Hist. Museum L.A. 1978-; tchg. asst. San Diego State Univ. 1971-73; USC 1981-83; Univ. de Concept., Fld., Sta. Dichato, Chile 1980; lectr. CSU Long Beach 1990; tutor Chicano Supp. Service 1970-72; awards: NOAA sea grantee (1978-81), NSF grantee 1989-92; mem: AAAS, Am. Soc. Ichthyologists & Herpetologists, Sigma Xi (life); 9 research articles pub. in sci. jours. (1978-87), 3 book chpts. pub. (1984); Democrat; Prot.; rec: hiking, bicycling, fishing. Ofc: Natural History Museum of Los Angeles County 900 Exposition Blvd Los Angeles 90007

MCGRAW, JOHN VINCENT, JR., insurance company president; b. Dec. 26, 1930, Kansas City, Mo.; s. John V. and Mary C. (Cunningham) McG.; m. Joan Davey, Sept. 10, 1960; children: John b. 1962, Ann b. 1963, Michael b. 1965; edn: Creighton Univ. 1953. Career: U.S. mgr. Elite Ins. Co., San Francisco 1962-69; pres. Eldorado Ins. Co., Palo Alto 1969-76; McGraw Ins. Co., Menlo Park 1976-; mem: Knights of Malta, Sierra Club, Elks, Optimist Club; mil: 1st lt. AUS 1954-56; Republican; R.Cath. Ofc: McGraw Insurance Service 3601 Haven Ave Menlo Park 94025

MCGUIRE, MICHAEL JOHN, consulting, environmental engineer; b. June 29, 1947, San Antonio, Texas; s. James Brendan and Opal Mary (Brady) McG.; m. Deborah Marrow, June 19, 1971; children: David, Anna; edn: BS Civil Engring., Univ. Pa., 1969; MS, and PhD Environmental Engring., Drexel Univ., 1972, 1977; diplomat Am. Acad. Environmental Engring.; reg. profl. engr. Pa., N.J., Calif. Career: sanitary engr. Philadelphia. Water Dept., 1969-73; research assoc. Drexel Univ., Philadelphia. 1976-77; prin. engr. Brown & Caldwell Consulting Engrs., Pasadena 1977-79; water quality engr. Met. Water Dist. of So. Calif., Los Angeles 1979-84, water quality mgr. 1984-86, dir. water quality 1986-90, asst. general mgr. 1990-92, pres., McGuire Environ. Cons., Inc.; cons. to subcom. on adsorbents, safe drinking water com. Nat. Acad. Scis. 1978-79, cons. mem., Technologies Workgroup, USEPA DBP Reg. Neg. 1992-93; honors: Sigma Xi, Sigma Nu, Sigma Tau, Academic Achiev. Award Am. Water Works Assn. 1978, listed Who's Who in West 1981-; mem: Am. Water Works Assn. (edn. div. chmn. 1982-83, Calif.-Nev. sect., governing bd. 1984-87, 1989-, exec. com. 1989-, chmn. 1991-92, Nat. Dir. 1993-, trustee Research Found. 1983-86), Am. Chem. Soc., ASCE, Internat. Water Supply Assn., Internat. Assn. on Water Quality (1972-, specialist group on taste and odor control 1982-, chmn. organizing 1991 Off-Flavor Symp. 1987-91), Internat. Ozone Assn. (internat. bd. dirs. 1992-); editor: (w/ I.H. Suffet) Activated Carbon Adsorption of Organics from the Aqueous Phase, 2 vols. 1980; Treatment of Water by Granular Activated Carbon 1983; 86 tech. jour. articles on trace contaminant control in the water treatment process; rec: swimming, reading, bicycling. Ofc: McGuire Environ. Cons., Inc., 469 25th St. Santa Monica CA 90402-3103

MCINERNEY, LUCILLE THOMAS, retired public relations executive; b. Mar. 3, 1922, Los Angeles; d. Wm. Leonard and Anita L. (Curtis) Thomas, Sr.; div.; children: Tracey Lucille b. 1953, Thomas Mallory b. 1948; edn: Stanford Univ. 1940-43; Wright-MacMahon Exec. Secty. Sch., Beverly Hills 1945. Career: design service dir. pub. relations Channell & Chaffin (design firm), Los Angeles 1974-85; mem: The Costume Council, Los Angeles Co. Mus. of Art, The Luminaries of Estelle Doheny Eye Found., Assocs. of Junior Philharmonic Com., Nine O'Clock Players, Assistance League, Stanford Womens Club; Republican; Religious Sci.; rec: tennis, music, skiing. Res: 664 Elkins Rd Los Angeles 90049

MC INTYRE, DONALD FRANKLIN, city manager; b. May 12, 1930, Chgo.; s. Daniel Maxwell and Lucy Mae (Stickles) McI.; m. Nancy Todd, Sept. 10, 1955; children: Meribeth b. 1957, Todd b. 1958, Scott b. 1959, Alex b. 1961, Thomas b. 1963; edn: BA, Millikin Univ., 1952; MA, Mich. St. Univ., 1953. Career: adminstrv. asst. dept. pub. works City of Richmond, Calif. 1957-60; town mgr. Town of Los Gatos, 1960-67; city mgr. City of Oak Park, Mich. 1967-70; City of Vallejo, Calif. 1970-73; City of Pasadena, Calif., 1973-; honors: varsity football, Delta Sigma Phi frat., pres. Inter-Frat. Council Millikin Univ. 1950-52, grad. assistantship Mich. St. Univ. 1953, outstanding comm. svc. Los Gatos C.of C. 1963-64, alumni merit Millikin Univ. 1976, Clarence Dykstra award ASPA L.A. chpt. 1987, Fletcher Bowron award USC Pub. Adminstrn. Alumni 1988, tech. leadership Pub. Technology Inc. 1988; mem: Nat. League of Cities, League of Calif. Cities, Am. Soc. for Pub. Adminstrn. Internat. City Mgmt. Assn.; civic: United Way reg. II (asso. chr. pub. svc. 1982, 84), Pasa. YMCA (pres. elect 1985), Univ. Club Pasa. 1973-; contbr. article in Pub. Adminstrn. Rev. (1953); mil: capt. USN (Ret.) 1954-57; Presbyterian (elder). Res: 504 Locke Haven St Pasadena 91105 Ofc: City of Pasadena 100 N Garfield Ave Rm 237 Pasadena 91109

MC INTYRE, GARY WADE, architect/project manager; b. Apr. 20, 1950, Cleveland, Ohio; s. Herbert Alvin and Arie Lavora (Griffin) Mc Intyre; m. Cynthia Singfield, Aug. 5, 1982; children: Marisa b. 1985, Gary W., Jr. b. 1986; edn: B.Arch., Howard Univ., 1974; grad. courses interior design & constrn.,

N.Y. Univ., 1978; Assoc. Arch., AIA. Career: asst. dir. Neighborhood Housing Svc., Newark, N.J. 1977-79; asst. dir. Oakland (Calif.) Neighborhood Housing Services, 1979-80; project mgr. tech. serv. Neighborhood Reinvestment (nat. pgm.), 1980-84, Calif. Dist. supr. 1984-85, pgm. trouble-shooter/actg. dir. (6 mo. assignments) N.H.S. of Birmingham, Ala. 1982, Jamaica, N.Y. 1982, Inglewood, Calif. 1983, Menlo Park, Calif. 1983, Great Falls, Mont. 1984; project mgr. Constrn. Control, Oakland 1985-86; proj. mgr. Ebmud Adminstrn. Bldg., Bovis Internat., Oakland 1986-89; Moscone Ctr. Expansion proj. engr. Turner Constrn. Co./BDI, San Francisco 1989-; speaker nat. confs. Neighborhood Reinvestment 1978-81; awards: A.I.A. archtl. preserv. - proj. arch. for Paul Devrouax/Iowa Condominiums, WDC 1977, svc. Neighborhood Reinvestment, Wash. DC 1983, listed Who's Who in Am. Colls. & Univs., Who's Who Black Americans, Outstanding Young Men Am.; mem. Omega Psi Phi Frat., Am. Inst. Arch. (assoc. 1983-); R. Cath.; rec: photog., equestrian, archtl. renovations. Res: 3670 Lily St Oakland 94619 Ofc: Turner Construction Co. 799 Howard St San Francisco 94103

MCINTYRE, ROBERT MALCOLM, utility co. executive; b. Dec. 18, 1923, Portland, Oreg.; s. Daniel A. and Bessie W. (Earsley) McI.; m. Marilyn Westcott, Aug. 27, 1949; 1 dau. Julie b. 1951; edn: BA, UCLA, 1950; graduate study UCLA, USC, Columbia Univ. Career: mgmt. positions So. Calif. Gas Co., 1952-88: v.p. 1970, senior v.p. 1974, dir. 1975-, pres. 1980-85, bd. chmn./CEO 1985-88; dir. Pacific Lighting Service Co. 1975-81; mem. Pacific Coast Gas Assn. (past dir.), Am. Gas Assn., trustee Inst. of Gas Technology; Regent's Professor UC Irvine Grad. Sch. of Mgmt.; honors: 49er Club award Pac. Coast Gas Assn. (1979), Nat. Hispanic Scholarship Award 1980, Mex. Amer. Legal Def. and Ednl. Fund (MALDEF) Award for outstanding service, corporate responsibility 1981, Pacific Pioneer Award, Jr. Chamber of Commerce Award of Merit, NCCJ Humanitarian Award, L.A. Area C.of C. Medici Award, L.A. chpt. NAACP Roy Wilkins Award, decorated Order of the Rising Sun With Gold Rays and Ribbon from His Imperial Majesty Emperor Hirohito of Japan 1988; civic bds: L.A. Area C.of C. (past chmn.), NCCJ (dir.), US-Mex. C.of C. (dir.), L.A. Co. Academic Decathlon, MALDEF (dir.), Korean Am. Centennial Commn., Calif. Council for Environ. and Econ. Balance (dir.), Calif. Found. on Environ. and Economy (dir.), UCLA Found. (trustee), Town Hall of Calif. (bd. govs., life mem.), Plaza de la Raza Bus. Indus. Advy. Bd. (chmn. 1982), Huntington Library Soc. of Fellows, L.A. Music Ctr. Founders, Newport Harbor Art Mus. Bus. Council, Orange Co. Bus. Com. for the Art (steering com.), L.A. Olympic Citizens Advy. Commn., UCLA GSM Dean's Council, Pepperdine Univ. Assocs., USC Assocs., L.A. United Way (bd.), United Way O.C. (exec. com.), Commn. of the California, Mayor Bradley's Ad Hoc Com. on City Fin., L.A. Orthopaedic Hosp. (trustee, exec. com., Lowman Club), Hoag Memorial Hosp. Found. (pres.); clubs: California, Big Canyon Country, Center, Pacific, 100; Phi Kappa Psi; mil: lt.sg USN 1942-46; Republican; Presbyterian; rec: swimming, fishing, golf. Ofc: So. Calif. Gas Co. 555 W Fifth St Los Angeles 90013-1011

MCINTYRE, ROBERT WHEELER, conservation organization executive; b. Aug. 26, 1936, Chicago, Ill.; s. Henry L. and Winifred (Wheeler) McI.; m. Emily Beardsly Taylor, Oct. 12, 1961 (div. 1985); children: Burley b. 1964, Nancy b. 1965, Oliver b. 1967, Shanna b. 1968, Amanda b. 1971; m. Miriam de Jesus Zarate, June 23, 1990; edn: AB in sociology, Stanford Univ. 1959; MBA, Harvard Univ. 1964. Career: loan analyst Wells Fargo Bank, San Francisco 1964-65; supr. budget analysis Ford Aerospace, Palo Alto 1965-69; controller Allied Life Sciences, San Leandro 1969-70; ptnr. Diplomat Mfg. Co., Palo Alto 1970-71; staff cons. Opportunity Through Ownership, San Francisco 1971-72; gen. mgr. Quality Metal Finishers 1972-73; sr. v.p., c.f.o. The Trust for Public Land 1973-; dir. Environ. Vols., Palo Alto 1980-; advy. bds.: Dorothy Erskine Open Space Fund, San Francisco 1978-; Resource Renewal Inst., Sausalito 1988-; Water Heritage Trust, Sausalito 1988-; Peninsula Open Space Trust, Menlo Park 1978-; Marin Headlands Advy. Com., Sausalito 1978-81; awards: Trust for Pub. Lands Presdl. Citation 1988, Environ. Vols. spl. service 1989; mem: Robert C. Wheeler Found. (dir., treas.), Families Adopting Inter-racially (dir. 1971-74), Palo Alto Jr. Achievement (advisor 1966-67); clubs: Harvard (NY), Harvard (Boston), Pacific Athletic (San Carlos), Sundown Tennis (San Mateo); mil: lt. (jg) USN 1959-62; USNR 1962-64; rec: hiking, backpacking, tennis. Ofc: The Trust for Public Land 116 New Montgomery 4th Floor San Francisco 94105

MCKEAN, KEITH EDWARD, transportation engineer, ret. state transportation executive; b. June 1, 1925, Pierre, S. Dak.; s. Harold Ambrose and Essie Irene (Whisler) McK.; m. Emily, Nov. 6, 1954; children: David b. 1955, Patricia b. 1957, Jill b. 1959, Jacquelyn b. 1964; edn: BCE, USC, 1950; Reg. Civil Engr., Calif. (C10691, 1957). Career: project engr. Calif. Div. of Hwys., Los Angeles 1952-61; senior engr. 1961-67; engring. mgr. Calif. Dept. of Transp., Los Angeles 1967-79; Dist. 7 p ogram mgr. for $2 Billion Dollar I-105 Transitway Program, L.A., 1979-83, dir. Dist. 9, Bishop, 1983-87; organizing dir. new state transp. dist., dir. Dist. 12, Santa Ana, 1987-90; v.p. transportation engring. Robert Bein, William Frost & Associates, 1991-; coauthor, faculty Caltrans Mid-Level Mgmt. Tng., 1986-87; chmn. Caltrans Statewide Mgmt. & Devel. Com., Sacto. 1987; mem. UC Irvine civil engr. advy. com. 1988-90, and chmn. curriculum com. Friends of Civil Engring., UCI, 1991-; mem: Am. Road and Trans. Builders Assn. 1983-90, Am. Public Works Assn. (exec. om. L.A.

sect. 1978-80), Am. Soc. of Civil Engrs. (pres. Desert Area br. 984-85, chmn. L.A. sect. Life Member Com. 1991-93, Soc. for Advancement f Mgmt. (pres. L.A. sect. 1981-83), Santa Ana Rotary Club (dir. 1989-91 Civic Center Optimist Club, L.A. (pres. 1977-78, awards: Outstanding res., Gov.'s award, Outstanding Club, Honor Club, 1978); mil: 1st lt. US Amy 1943-46, 1950-52; Republican; R.Cath.; rec: philately, fishing. Res: 4503 Biola Ave La Mirada 90638 Ofc: Robert Bein, William Frost & ssociates, 14725 Alton Pkwy Irvine 92713-9739

MC KEE, CHRISTOPHER FULTON, astrophysicist; b. Sept. 6, 1942, Washington, D.C.; s. William Fulton and Gertrude Anna (Scheele) McK.; m. Suzanne Marie Peshette, June 20, 1965; children: William b. 1968, Christopher b. 1973, Maria b. 1979; edn: AB, Harvard Univ. 1963; PhD, UC Berkeley 1970. Career: research physicist Lawrence Livermore Lab., Livermore 1969-70; research assoc. CalTech, Pasadena 1970-71; asst. prof. Harvard Univ., Cambridge, Mass. 1971-74; asst. prof., prof. UC Berkeley 1974-, dir. space scis. lab. 1985-; cons. Lawrence Livermore Labs. 1970-; honors: Phi Beta Kappa, CalTech Sherman Fairchild disting. scholar 1982; 50+ research articles pub. in sci. jours. Ofc: Univ. of Calif. Physics Dept. Berkeley 94720

MCKEE, ROGER CURTIS, federal magistrate judge; b. Feb. 11, 1931, Waterloo, Ia.; s. James A. and Leonace (Burrell) McK.; m. Roberta Jeanne Orvis, Sept. 4, 1954; children: Andrea b. 1959, Brian b. 1961, Paul b. 1969; edn: BA, Univ. of N.Iowa, 1955; MA, Univ. Ill., Urbana, 1960; JD, Univ. San Diego, 1968; admitted bar Calif., 1970. Career: telegrapher Ill. Cent. R.R., Iowa Div., 1950-55; tng. asst. No. Ill. Gas, Aurora, Ill., 1958-60; industrial rels. General Dynamics Corp., San Diego, 1960-70; law ptnr. Powell & McKee, San Diego, 1970-83; U.S. magistrate judge U.S. Courts, San Diego, 1983-; instr. in law and bus. National Univ., San Diego, 1972-87; mem: Calif. State Bar 1970-, Navy League of the U.S. 1963-, Naval Reserve Assn. 1968-, Submarine League 1978-; civic: Amateur Radio Club of S.D. 1987-, S.D. Dixieland Jazz Soc. (bd. 1984-), Dolphin Mariners (skipper 1986-88); pub. article in Naval Inst. Proceedings, 1958; mil: capt. (ret.) US Naval Reserve 1948-85, Active duty Pacific- Mideast 1955-58; Republican; Presbyterian; rec: amateur radio (KK6XY), hiking, travel, reading. Ofc: U.S. Court House, 940 Front St San Diego 92189

MCKENNA, THOMAS J., retired acrobatic pilot; b. May 12, 1908, Meadowbrook, Pa.; s. John and Bridget (Cassidy) McK.; grad. Cath. Schs., Berwyn, Pa. 1927; grad. flying sch., Wilmington, Del. 1938; soloed in a Curtis JN-4 airplane known as a Jenny in Camden, NJ 1928; FAA lic. #76267, pvt., comml. & instr. rating, 1938. Career: stunt flyer, barnstormer in a Jenny, 1928-, pilot instr. combat flying to Royal Air Force pilots 1940-42, to US Army Cadets 1942-44, War Eagle Field, Lancaster, Ca.; aerobatic flight instr. Santa Barbara Airport (1976 150 h.p. Citabria), Mercury Air Center 1981-91, (his most famous pupil, the late Frank Tallman whose movies incl. The Great Waldo Pepper, and TV series Baa-Baa Black Sheep); his barnstormer past during the early days of aviation is documented in display at the Goleta/Santa Barbara Air Heritage Museum (est. 1991); subject of articles in numerous publs. incl. Pvt. Pilot, Gen. Aviation News and sev. books.; mem: Quiet Birdmen (QB Exec. Com.), Santa Barbara Pilots Assn., OX5 Pioneers of Am., Santa Barbara Flying Club, S.B. Aero Club Inc., Antelope Valley Aero Museum Inc.; Republican; R.Cath. Res: 1312 Shoreline Dr Santa Barbara 93109 Ofc: Mercury Air Center, Santa Barbara Airport.

MCKEVITT, GERALD L., Jesuit priest and historian; b. July 3, 1939, Longview, Wash.; s. Edward Henry and Evelyn Almeda (Acock) McK.; edn: BA, Univ. San Francisco, 1961; MA, USC, 1964; PhD, UCLA, 1972; BST, Gregorian Univ., Rome 1975, ordained priest S.J., Roman Catholic Ch., 1975. Career: dir. univ. archives Santa Clara Univ., Santa Clara, Calif. 1975-85, chair history dept. 1984-88, univ. historian 1985-, assoc. prof. 1981-93, prof. 1993- rector Jesuit Comm. 1993-; honors: Oscar O. Winther Award, Western Hist. Assn. 1991; mem. bd. trustees Gonzaga Univ., Spokane 1988-; Nat. Seminar on Jesuit Higher Edn. 1990-; author: The University of Santa Clara, A History, 1851-1979 (1979), and numerous scholarly articles on Calif. and Western U.S. history. Ofc: History Dept. Santa Clara Univ., Santa Clara 95053

MCKIM, C. LEE (CHARLES LAMOINE), real estate broker, art dealer, telecommunications consultant; b. Apr. 17, 1949, San Jose; s. Clyde Lamoine and Georgia Rose (Sunseri) McKim; m. Alicia, Mar. 14, 1981; 3 stepchildren (nee Rincones): Lorena b. 1961, Ramiro b. 1962, Alicia b. 1965; edn: BA in econ., Univ. San Francisco, 1981. Career: CEO McKimtex, San Jose 1983-86; realtor/owner McKim Realty, 1980-; art dealer, pres. Riva Internat., 1979-89; honors: Confedn. of Chivalry, Ordre Souverain Et Militaire De La Milice Du Saint Sepulcre (Chevaler Comdr. KCMSJ, MCC, holder of Knight's Cross), list-ed Who's Who Hist. Soc., World Inst. of Achiev., Intl. Who's Who Intellectuals, Men of Achiev. Intl. Biog. Ctr., Am. Biog. Inst. man of yr. award; mem: Nat. Assn. Realtors, Calif. Assn. Realtors, San Jose Bd. Realtors; coauthor: Telecommunications Wiring Systems (Prentice-Hall 1991); mil: E5 USN 1968-74; Republican (Rep. Senatorial Inner Circle senatl. commn.); R.Cath.; rec: art, travel. Res: 5261 Edenvale Ave San Jose 95136 Ofc: McKim Realty 5442 Thornwood Dr Ste 140 San Jose 95123 Tel: 408/227-3000, 363-1111 Fax: 408/227-7425

MCKINNON, MICHAEL D., broadcast executive; b. June 12, 1939, Los Angeles; s. Clinton D. and Lucille (McVey) M.; m. Sandra E., May 22, 1973; children: Gaylynn b. 1961, Donnie b. 1962, Michael Dean b. 1964, Mark b. 1968; edn: Univ. of Redlands, Calif. 1958-60; worked various dept.'s San Diego Sentinel newspaper 1960-63; publisher The La Jolla Light/ Journal 1963-; owner KUSI-TV Ch. 51, San Diego; bd. chmn., pres., owner KIII-TV Ch. 3, Corpus Christi, Tx.; pres., owner KBMT-TV Ch. 12, Beaumont, Port Arthur; gen. ptnr. KBVO-TV Ch. 42, Austin, Tx.; elected Texas State Senate 1972-76; dir. Calif. Bdcstrs. Assn. 1986-; pres. Texas Assn. of Bdcstrs. 1971, dir. 1965-72, mem. Small Market Com. 1972-73; ABC News advy. com. 1979-80; bd. mem., exec. com. Television and Radio Polit. Action Com. 1980-83; honors: Boss of Yr. from Nat. Secty.'s Internat. Assn. 1970, Outstanding Young Man of Yr. from Jr. CofC. 1971, Presidential Citation Holder from Pres. Nixon, recip. Special Citation from Nat. LULAC Council for svc. to Mexican-Americans; statewide and local awards for anti-drug program "Drugs A to Z"; mem: Nat. Assn. Bdcstrs., Bdcsting. Promotion Assn.; Assn. Bdcst. Execs. of Texas; Television Bureau of Advtng.; civic: advy. bd. dirs. First City Bank, Corpus Christi, Tx., chmn./bd. govs. Art Mus. of So. Texas, mem. exec. com. Bd. of Trustees of Redlands Univ., Calif., mem. San Diego Historical Soc., San Diego Mus. of Art (President's Cir.), Rest and Aspiration Soc., San Diego. Res: 311 San Antonio Ave San Diego 92106 Ofc: KUSI-TV, Channel 51 4575 Viewridge Ave San Diego 92111

MC LEAN, BONNIE BUTT, doctor of oriental medicine; b. Mar. 9, 1945, New Orleans; d. Dr. Arthur J. (MD) and Barbara (McCreavy) Butt; m. David Speed McLean; children: Arthur Cameron, Douglas Speed; edn: BSN, Duke Univ., 1967; MA, Pepperdine Univ., 1977; grad. Calif. Acupuncture Coll., Westwood, 1984, OMD, 1986; Calif. lic. Acupuncturist 1985. Career: pvt. prac-tice in Santa Monica and Westlake, 1986-; staff Pine Grove Hosp., Canoga Park, 1989-; staff Woodview Calabasas Hosp., Calabasas, 1990-, cons. 1987-; instr. Bresler Ctr., Santa Monica, 1986, Emperors Coll. Traditional Oriental Medicine, 1990, Body Mind Inst., W.Los Angeles, 1990; honors: Nat. Hon. Soc. Pensacola H.S., Fla. 1963, class pres. Duke Univ. Sch. of Nsg. 1987; coauthor Manual of Chinese Medicine and Massage (1985); Democrat; Taoist; avocation: Taoist yoga and meditation. Res: 19711 Valley View Dr Topanga 90290 Ofc: Natural Health Care Group 2730 Wilshire Blvd Santa Monica

MCLEVIE, JOHN GILWELL, educator; b. Nov. 2, 1929, Masterton, N.Z., naturalized U.S. citizen 1987; s. Edward Mitchell and Gwendoline Mary (Faire) McL.; m. Elaine Marianne Foote, May 7, 1955; children: Anne b. 1960, Karen b. 1962, Lynne b. 1964; edn: BA, Victoria Univ. of Wellington, N.Z. 1955, MA, 1957; PhD, Mich. State Univ., 1970. Career: lectr. Univ. of Hong Kong, H.K. 1963-68; chief of party Calif. Education Team, Brasilia, Brazil 1973-76; prof. of edn. Univ. of Houston, Clear Lake, San Diego State Univ., chair Dept. Secondary Edn. SDSU, 1978-80, 82-84; assoc. dean Univ. Houston, Clear Lake, 1984-89; cons. Calif. Commn. on Teacher Credentialing, Sacramento 1989-; integration analyst San Diego Unified Sch. Dist., 1980-81; honors: Phi Delta Kappa leadership award, San Diego 1980-81 and educator of yr., Clear Lake, Tx. 1987-88; mem: State of Calif. Assn. of Tchr. Educators (pres. 1993-), Calif. Council on the Edn. of Tchrs. (bd. 1991-), Assn. of Tchr. Educators (task force mem. legislation 1992); Episcopalian; rec: tennis, photography. Res: 823 W El Dorado Dr Woodland 95695 Ofc: Calif. Commission on Teacher Credentialing,1812 Ninth St Sacramento 95814-7000

MCLURKIN, THOMAS CORNELIUS, JR., government lawyer; b. July 28, 1954, Los Angeles; s. Thomas Cornelius and Willie Mae (O'Connor) McL.; edn: AB, USC, 1976, MPA, 1980; JD, Univ. LaVerne, S.F.V., 1982; PhD in pub. admin., USC, 1993; admitted Calif. Bar 1984. Career: law clk. City of Los Angeles Dept. Water & Power, 1979-82; judicial extern Fed. Magistrate Hon. Ralph J. Geffen (Ret.), L.A. 1982, Fed. Dist. Ct. Judge Hon. Terry J. Hatter, Jr., L.A. 1983; sr. law clk. L.A. County Dist. Atty., 1983; sr. law clk. City of Los Angeles, 1984, dep. city atty., prosecutor criminal br. 1984-89, dep. city atty., tort liability litigator Dept. Water & Power Div. 1989-; honors: Eagle Scout 1970, Honor Medal for Heroism BSA 1984, Outstanding Young Man in Am. Nat. Jaycees 1984; mem: Am. Bar Assn., Assn. of Am. Trial Attys., L.A. Co. Bar Assn., Am. Soc. for Pub. Adminstrn., Langston Law Assn. L.A., USC Gen. Alumni Assn. (bd. govs., exec. com. 1986-90), USC Black Alumni Assn.- Ebonics (bd. dirs., pres. 1988-89), USC Pres.'s Circle (bd. dirs.), Scapa Praetors/USC Sch. Pub. Admin.; civic: L.A. World Affairs Council, BSA L.A. Area Council (bd. dirs., sustaining mem. 1976-), Hillsides Home for Children Pasadena (bd. dirs.), Smithsonian Assocs., Optimist Internat. Hollywood (char-ter mem.); coauthor w/Donald R. O'Connor (hist. ref. book) Facts in American History (1968, 2d edition 1989); mil: capt. USAR JAGC 1987-, currently chief, legal assistance 311th Corps Support Command at Los Angeles (COSCOM); Republican; Holman United Methodist Ch. (exec. bldg. com.); rec: sailing, ten-nis, world history. Res: Pasadena. Office of the City Attorney Water & Power Div. PO Box 111 Beaudry-1848 Los Angeles 90051

MCMILLAN, HORACE JIM, executive, physician, retired; b. Oct. 30, 1919, Mineola, Tx.; s. Lemon Columbus and Joann Aletha (Zollars) McM.; m. Jessie, Oct. 21, 1942, (div.); children: Yvonne Camille (Sawyer) b. 1943, Michelle Louise b. 1972; edn: BS, Prairie View A&M Coll. 1942; MD, Meharry Medical

Coll. 1950; grad. wk. St. Louis Univ. 1945-46; H.M.O. Cert., UC Los Angeles 1975. Career: prin. Family Medical Center, pres. Physicians Inv. Corp., 1988-92; family practice physician, Santa Barbara, 1952-88, ret. 1988; staff St. Francis Hosp., Santa Barbara Cottage Hosp., and Goleta Valley Comm. Hosp. (founder GVCH 9/17/71, one of 10, mem. bd. dirs. 1967-77; appt. 1st chmn. Santa Barbara Mayor's Advy. Com. on Human Relations 1968, chmn. Community Health Task Force 1973-81; innovator of Urban Renewal & Devel., Community Rels. Commn., and fed. Low-Cost Housing for Santa Barbara, 1960s; founder Franklin Neighborhood Center, 1975; mem: Am., Calif., Santa Barbara County Acad. Family Practice 1982-, Am. Assn. for Clin. Immunology and Allergy 1982-88, NAACP (life); awards: resolutions for comm. service Calif. Legislature Assem., County of Santa Barbara Bd. of Suprs. 1988, Franklin Neighborhood Ctr. 10th anniversary award of appreciation for making the center a reality (9/28/85), Afro-Am. Community Ctr. award "for helping us to realize the dream of Martin Luther King, Jr." (1/25/86), 35 yrs. of outstanding comm. svc. NAACP, Maha*rry Med. Coll. pres.'s award for 25 yrs. svc. to mankind 1950-75, Goleta Valley C.of C. award for helping provide outstanding health resource- Goleta V. Comm. Hosp., Com. for Black Culture appreciation for outstanding svc. to comm., appreciation Community Health Task Force, 1990 Endowment for Youth Com. Community Service Award in spl. recogn. for sustaining svs. as a primary mover in improving the quality of life in health svs., housing, employment & edn. in the Santa Barbara Comm. 1990; recipient Santa Barbara Newspress "Lifetime Achiev. Award" with congratulations from Ho. of Representatives and State Senator from S.B. congl. dist.; mil: chief p.o., chief pharmacist mate USN 1942-46, 1st black pharmacists mate in hist. of US Coast Guard; Democrat; Methodist; rec: travel, sports, reading. Res: 2439 Vista Del Campo Santa Barbara 93101

MCMURTREY, NOBLE CARSON, auto parts wholesale distribution executive; b. Feb. 14, 1919, Stella, Mo.; s. John and Myrtle Jane (Moore) McM; m. Stella Mary Polverari, June 4, 1938; children: Jon b. 1940, Don b. 1942, Gene b. 1943; edn: H.S. grad. Stella, Mo. 1936. Career: delivery up to sales rep. Pioneer Mercantile Co., Bakersfield, Calif. 1937-54; chmn. bd. Auto Parts Wholesale, also Southern Auto Supply, Bakersfield, also Henderson Bros., Sacramento, 1956-; ptnr. 4M Investments, Bakersfield 1973-; mem. Calif. Automotive Wholesalers Assn., Sacto. (dir. 1964-67); dir. Pacific Automotive Show, L.A. 1966, 67; mil: storekeeper 2c USN 1943-46; Republican; Methodist; rec: Arabian horses. Res: 1019 Panorama Dr Bakersfield 93305 Ofc: Southern Auto Supply P.O. Box 2426 Bakersfield 93303

MCNEELEGE, MATTHEW KENNETH, financial consultant, author; b. Sept. 28, 1958, Wash.D.C.; s. Hugh Eugene McNeelege and Mary Patricia (Kosik) Teague; edn: BA in econs., Univ. Chicago, 1979; MSA, DePaul Univ., 1983; CPA cert. Ill. 1983, CFA. Career: sr. investment analyst The Signature Group, Schaumburg, Ill. 1980-85; asst. treas. Bell Savings & Loan, San Mateo, Calif. 1985-87; v.p. First Nationwide Bank, San Francisco 1987-92; senior cons. Baytel Associates, S.F. 1990-; mem. Security Analysts Assn. of S.F. 1985-, Univ. Chgo. Alumni (chmn. schs. com. Penin. chpt. 1991-), University Club (S.F.). Res: 140 Faith Dr San Francisco 94110 Ofc: First Nationwide Bank 135 Main 9th Fl San Francisco 94123

MCNEES, CARYL, professor; b. Nov. 5, 1938, Sewickley, Pa.; d. Floyd Raymond and Ione (Earl) McNees; edn: BA, English, Grove City Coll., Pa., 1960; M. Edn., English, Univ. of Pitts., 1968; EdD, English, Univ. of Va., Charlottesville, 1972; MS in Marriage, Family, Child Therapy, Univ. of La Verne, Calif., 1992. Career: H.S. English tchr., Pa.; prof. of English, Cal Poly, Pomona 1972-; cons., Claremont, Calif. Unified Sch. Dist. 1977-78; awards: Kappa Delta, Univ. of Va. 1971; Lychenos Soc., Univ. of Va. 1972; Golden Key Award, Calif. State Univ., Pomona 1990; Psi Chi Honorary, Univ. of La Verne, Calif. 1991; mem: Nat. Council Tchrs. of English 1970-, Modern Lang. Assn. 1972, Calif. Assn. of Marriage, Family, Child Therapists 1989-, Kappa Delta Edn. Honorary; Am. Assn. of Univ. Women, Pomona; author: various articles pub. in edn. and English jours.; Presbyterian; rec: keyboard, piano, tennis, bridge. Ofc: Calif. State Univ., Temple Ave. Pomona 91768

MCNEIL, MALCOLM STEPHEN, lawyer; b. Jan. 7, 1956, San Francisco; s. Henry Stephen and Adeline Elizabeth (LaVoie) McN.; m. Shahrezad Mabourakh; children: Jennifer b. 1975, Geoffrey b. 1977, Vanessa b. 1984; edn: AA, L.A. City Coll. 1976; BA, Antioch Univ. 1980; JD, Loyola Law Sch. 1983; admitted bar: Calif. 1983, U.S. Fed. Ct. no. dist. 1984, cent. dist. 1991, Ct. of Appeals 9th cir. 1989. Career: sales mgr. Metropolitan Life Ins. Co. 1977-82; law clerk Gilbert, Kelly, Crowley & Jennett 1982-83; atty. law firm Briedenbach, Swainston, Yokaitis & Crispo 1983-84, Law Offices Brian F. Zimmerman 1984; Law Offices Malcolm S. McNeil, Los Angeles 1984-; corporate counsel Dunhill Mfg. Corp., Corporate Capital Resources Inc.; instr. Northrop Univ. 1987-; honors: Sigma Tau Sigma 1975, Dean's List 1982, pres. Rep. Law Forum 1981-83, Phi Alpha Delta; mem. Westchester C.of C., Marina del Rey C.of C., Assn. Internationale Des Jeunes Avocats (exec. com.); publs: legal article on pre-judgment interest (1982); Republican; R.Cath.; rec: Judo, skiing, book collecting. Law Offices of Malcolm S. McNeil, 5777 W Century Blvd Ste 1475 Los Angeles 90045-5631 Tel: 310/216-0747 FAX 310/216-5736

MCNELLEY, DONALD BENAGH, lawyer; b. Jan. 25, 1934, Birmingham, Ala.; s. William Wert and Dorothy (Benagh) McN.; m. Ann Lovelace Stewart, June 18, 1955; children: Carolyn b. 1956, Anne b. 1958, Donald B. b. 1962; edn: BA, Univ. Ala. 1955; JD, USC, 1969; admitted St. Bar Calif. 1970. Career: human factors splst. System Devel. Corp., Santa Monica 1959-69; atty. Equity Funding Corp., Los Angeles 1969-72; atty., exec., gen. counsel Bateman Eichler Hill Richards Inc 1972-87; ptnr. Kindel & Anderson, Los Angeles 1987-91; of counsel Schlecht, Shevlin and Shoenberger, Palm Springs, 1991-; instr. Univ. W.L.A. Sch. Law, Culver City 1970-72; mem: Am. Bar Assn. (fed. reg. of securities com.), LA Co. Bar Assn., Securities Industry Assn. (legal and compliance div.); club: Shadow Mountain Racquet; mil: 1st lt. USAF 1955-58; Republican; Episcopalian. Ofc: Schlecht Shevlin & Shoenberger, 801 E Tahquitz Cyn Way Ste 100 Palm Springs 92262

MCNICHOLS, STEPHEN LUCID ROBERT, JR., lawyer; b. June 5, 1943, Denver; s. Stephen Lucid Robert and Marjorie Roberta (Hart) McN.; children: Justin, Chelsea; edn: Monterey Inst. Fgn. Studies, 1964-65; BA, Pomona Coll., 1965; JD, UC Berkeley, 1968; admitted bar: Colo. 1968, Calif. 1969. Career: dep. dist. atty. San Luis Obispo Couty, 1970-73; assoc. Varni, Fraser, Hartwell & Van Blois, Hayward 1973-76; ptnr. Varni, Fraser, Hartwell, McNichols & Rodgers, Hayward 1976-86; Hallgrimson, McNichols, McCann & Inderbitzen (& predecessor firm, San Ramon), Pleasanton 1987-; mem: ABA (litigation sect.), Calif. Bar Assn. (adminstrn. justice com.), Alameda County Bar Assn. (bd. 1986-88), So. Alameda County Bar Assn. (bd. 1978-80), Assn. Trial Lawyers Am., Calif. Trial Lawyers Assn., Alameda-Contra Costa County Trial Lawyers Assn. (bd. 1977-78), Barristers Assn. (bd. 1974-77); civic: Morro Bay Planning Commn. (1970-72, chmn. 1972), Children's Hosp. Found. (bd. 1980-83); Democrat; rec: skiing, running, golf. Res: 947 Redwood Dr Danville 94526 Ofc: Hallgrimson, McNichols, McCann & Inderbitzen, 5000 Hopyard Rd Ste 400 Pleasanton 94588

MC PHERSON, DAVID LESLIE, SR., municipal fire chief; b. Jan. 14, 1946, Oceanside; s. Wm. W. and Ruby (Dealy) McP.; m. Shirley Mae, Feb. 17, 1968; children: Heather b. 1971, Heidi b. 1979, David, Jr. b. 1980; edn: BA, San Diego St. Univ., 1968; MBA, Harvard Univ., 1988; desig: Exec. Fire Ofcr. (EFO). Career: fuels U.S.F.S., Milford, Calif. 1979-82; fire chief Doyle Fire Dept., Doyle, Calif. 1980-82; Kachina Village Fire Dept., Flagstaff, Az. 1982-86; City of Gridley Fire Dept., Gridley, Calif. 1986-; indep. cons. McPherson & Assoc., Gridley 1980-; tng. cons. State of Ariz., Phoenix 1984-86 (state outstanding trainer award 1986); instr. Nat. Fire Assn., Emittsburg, Md. 1983-; mem: Nat. Fire Protection Assn., Butte County Fire Chief Assn. (sec. treas. 1986-), Calif. Fire Chief Assn., Calif. Firemen Assn.; civic: Rotary Internat., Gridley C.of C., Gridley Downtown 1988-; Democrat; CMA; rec: fishing, travel. Ofc: City of Gridley 685 Kentucky Gridley 95948

MCPHERSON, MICHELE THERESE, sales and marketing executive; b. April 13, 1962, Los Angeles; d. John Leonard and Laurene (Kraft) Renk; m. Robert William McPherson, April 29, 1989; edn: El Camino Coll. 1986-87; Riverside Comm. Coll. 1991-93. Career: ops. mgr. Waterline Waterbed, Gardena 1974-82, ops. and sales mgr. Waterworks Waterbeds, Lawndale 1982-87; v.p. customer rels. Arbek Mfg. Inc., Chino 1987-90, nat. marketing dir. 1990-94; awards: WMA Best of Show for Booth Design & POP Materials, Dale Carnegie Grad. Cert. 1981; Democrat; R.Cath.; rec: interior decorating, needlepoint. Address: 4802 Murrietta St Chino 91710

MC PHERSON, ROLF KENNEDY, clergyman, church official; b. March 23, 1913, Providence, R.I.; s. Harold S. and Aimee Elizabeth (Kennedy) McP.; m. Lorna De Smith, July 21, 1931 (dec.); children: Kay b. 1932, Marleen b. 1937 (dec.); edn: grad. So. Calif. Radio Inst., L.A. 1933; Hon. DD, 1941, Hon. LLD, 1988, L.I.F.E. Bible Coll.; ordained Internat. Ch. of Foursquare Gospel 1940. Career: pres. Internat. Ch. of Foursquare Gospel, Los Angeles 1944-88, pres. emeritus 1988-; pres. LIFE Bible Coll. Inc. 1944-88; mem. Echo Park Evangelistic Assn. (pres. 1944-), Pentecostal Fellowship N. Am. (bd. 1948-88), Nat. Assn. Evangelicals (bd. 1946-88); awards: 1st pl. Missionary Digest Film Festival 1956; editor Foursquare Mag., 1940-43. Ofc: Intl. Church of the Foursquare Gospel 1910 W Sunset Blvd Ste 200 Los Angeles 90026

MCQUILLIN, RICHARD ROSS, management consultant; b. Oct. 15, 1956, Elyria, Ohio; s. Wayne Rupp and Frana Rose (Romp) McQ.; m. Riko Koga, Apr. 7, 1991; edn: BSEE, Ohio State Univ., Columbus 1979; MSEE, USC, 1983; MBA, UC Los Angeles, 1990. Career: senior staff TRW, Inc. Redondo Beach 1979-88; senior cons. Deloitte & Touche, Los Angeles 1990-; awards: TRW fellow 1980-86, UCLA fellow 1989-90; mem: IEEE 1980-, Beta Gamma Sigma (life), USC Alumni Assn. (life), UCLA Alumni Assn. (life), TRW Investment Club Redondo Beach (pres. 1984-87), Patio Creek HOA (treas. 1986-90, pres. 1990-); res: 19028 Entradero Ave Torrance 90503-1360; ofc: Deloitte & Touche 333 S Grand Ave Ste 2800 Los Angeles 90071

MCROBERTS, MICHAEL JOSEPH, freight company executive; b. Nov. 2, 1958, Wash. DC; s. Nelson C. and Peggy Ann (Swift) McR.; edn: BS, So. Ill. Univ., 1980; dipl. Am. Inst. C.P.A., 1985. Career: chief fin. ofcr. Westrux

Internat., La Mirada, Calif. 1984-87; v.p. and gen. mgr., Los Angeles Freightliner, Whittier 1987-; Republican; R.Cath. Res: 6401 E Nohl Ranch Rd Anaheim Hills 92807 Ofc: Los Angeles Freightliner, 2429 S Peck Rd Whittier 90601

MCWATTERS, EDD DAVID, filmmaker and novelist; b. Oct. 27, 1930, Ottawa, Ont., nat. US cit. 1980; s. Vernon Wm. and Irene Elizabeth (Langdon) McW.; m. Betty Josephine Hollingshead, Oct. 14, 1976; children: Jon, Lynn, Cindy, Marc, Celene, Bradley, Janet and Timothy; 10 grandchildren; edn: spl. courses Western Univ., cert. Brooks Inst. of Photog. 1962. Career: formed a comedy tumbling act that toured the province with his scout troop, Hamilton, Ont., worked as a young volunteer in servicemens canteen during WWII, as swim instr. for blind and disabled children; became an exhibition ballroom dancer in his twenties and won audition to appear on the Hit Parade Show on TV; moved to Santa Barbara, Calif. to study motion picture production, 1960, during student yrs. put on film shows for Hillcrest Home for cerebral palsy residents and for children in hospitals, during his sr. yr. at Brooks Inst. of Photography directed TV pilot aired on ABC satellite Sta. KEYT Channel 3; hd. of movie dept. Brooks Inst. of Photography, 1964-65; cameraman, editor in Hollywood 1965-70, director and writer, completed 108 TV shows, 30 documentaries; wrote and produced 15 of his own productions, won 80+ awards: The Highwayman (comedy), Egghead Meets Vampire (spl. effects), Bikini Capers (comedy), MagicBottle (fantasy), Wildest Surfer (humor), The Hungry Kook Goes Bazook (comedy), photography instr. Santa Barbara County Probation program for young court wards (ages 13-17) 1972-77, innovative rehabilitative pgm. later expanded to Lompoc and Santa Maria; founder, dir. The Santa Barbara Motion Picture Inst. 1972-73; 1980-82: produced TV pilots, TV commercials, videotaped for Japanese network; writer, songwriter and author, 1982-: 12 novels, his 1st Western novel in press (1991); book of verse (pub. 1991), contbr. 100+ poems in 78 anthologies; 28+ articles pub. based on his experience in filmmaking ind.; pub. in SAC TV News and Film; 6+ songs sold (1990-); winner 26 internat. film festival awards incl. A silver cup at Cannes with his first comedy and bronze medallion for his last comedy, 78+ literary awards, golden poet award, hon. dep. gov. Am. Biographical Inst. 1988; personal letters from both Pres. and Mrs. Bush in appreciation of article written; mem: Photog. Soc. of Am., Soc. of Amateur Cinematographers (Fellow), Sierra Club, Audubon, San Diego Zoo, Smithsonian, AARP, P.S.A. Soc.; Jehovahs Witness; rec: photography. Ofc: Movin Pitchures Co. 5575 Baltimore Dr #105 La Mesa 91942

MEADOWS, ROBERT A., real estate broker; b. July 22, 1928, Chgo.; s. Jesse Williams and Blanche Alice (Taylor) M.; m. Josephine Del Mastro, June 14, 1962; edn: BA, N.M. Highlands Univ., 1952, MA, 1956; postgrad. Univ. New Mexico 1959-61; CRS (Cert. Residential Specialist), GRI (Grad. Realtors Inst.), CREA (Cert. R.E. Appraiser). Career: tchr. high schools in New Mexico and Calif. 1953-84; real estate broker, Pacifica, Calif. 1984-; honors: Who's Who Among Students 1952, Am. Notarial Award, Nat. Notary Assn. 1987; mem: Nat. Assn. Realtors, Residential Sales Council, Calif. Assn. Realtors, Pacifica-Half Moon Bay Bd. Realtors (dir.), Nat. Assn. R.E. Appraisers, Nat. Notary Assn., Pacifica C.of C.; clubs: Lions, Rotary, Pacifica Spindrift Players (bd. 1988-89), Toastmasters (past pres., area gov. 1990-91), Millbrae Arts Commn. (1977-, chmn. 1987-89); works: prod./dir. 30+ musical comedies and plays SF Bay Area, founded Petaluma Comm. Theater, Capuchino Comm. Theatre, founding dir. Vallejo Music Theatre, actor/dir SF Bay Area and No. Calif. 1962-, indsl. tng. films, movie and TV; mem. S.F. Sym. Chorus, Am. Ballet Theatre Chorus; mil: US Army 1946-48; Republican; rec: prod./dir. comm. theatre, singing, chess. Address: Millbrae 94030

MEANS, JAMES ANDREW, engineering technical advisor; b. Oct. 11, 1937, Heavener, Okla.; s. Edward Andrew and Altha Lorena (Nobles) M.; m. Therese Louise Zimmermann, Feb. 21, 1959; children: James A., Jr. b. 1959, William R. b. 1961, Charles E. b. 1962, Vicky M. b. 1966; edn: BSEE, Univ. Ariz., 1962, MSEE, 1966; PhD in E.E., UC Santa Barbara, 1972; MSCS, Chapman Univ., 1989. Career: electronic engr. Pacific Missile Test Ctr., Pt. Mugu 1962-78; tech. dir. Targets & Ranges Div., NAVAIR, Camarillo 1978-79; tech. dir. Space & Missile Test Org., Vandenberg AFB, 1979-89; senior technical advisor SRI Internat., Menlo Park 1990-; adj. full prof. Chapman Univ., 1983-89; awards: Tau Beta Pi 1962, Sigma Xi 1966, Eta Kappa Nu 1972, outstanding profl. of year Pacific Missile Test Ctr., Pt. Mugu 1972, meritorious svc. Navy, Pt. Mugu 1979, outstanding career Air Force, Vandenberg AFB 1989, Allen R. Matthews, ITEA, Fairfax, Va. 1991; mem.: Internat. Test & Eval. Org. 1980-, Internat. Found. for Telemetering (pres. 1989-); inventor: Solid State Circuit Breaker (pat. 1966), Semiconductor Test Set (pat. 1966); mil: p.o. 1c USN 1955-58; Democrat; Baptist; rec: old cars, model planes, computer. Res: 284 St. Andrews Way Lompoc 93436

MEDINA PUERTA, ANTONIO, research and development scientist; b. Jan. 20, 1956, Almeria, Spain; s. Antonio and Maria Mar (Puerta) M.; m. Mary, Sept. 20, 1989; edn: Ing. Sup., electrical engring., Politecnica Univ., Madrid, Spain 1979; OD, Complutense Univ., Madrid 1979; fellow Christ's Coll, Cambridge Univ., U.K. 1981; MS computer sci., M.I.T., 1982, E.E., M.I.T., 1983; PhD in E.E., Politecnica Univ., 1987. Career: optometrist Centro de Vision Luz, Almeria, Spain 1978-79; electro-optical engr. Philips, Eindhoven, Holland 1979-

80; tchg. asst. Univ. Cambridge, England 1980-81; res. asst. M.I.T., Mass. 1981-83; sci. assoc. Eye Res. Inst. Harvard Medical Sch., Boston 1983-88; task mgr. Jet Propulsion Lab., Pasadena, Calif. 1988-, R&D and devel. of optical and electro-optical systems, mgr. adv. imaging systems for remote sensing; mem: Optical Soc. Am., Internat. Soc. for Photo Instrumentation Engring., IEEE, Acad. Applied Sci., Assn. for Res. in Vision and Opthalmology; inventor, 11 patents (Europe, US, Japan); author 17+ sci. peer rev. publs., 13+ presentations at sci. meetings; R.Cath. Res: PO Box 1002 Pasadena CA 91102 Tel:818/577-2872 Fax:818/578-1257

MEECHAM, WILLIAM CORYELL, engineering educator; b. Detroit; s. William Edward and Mabel Catherine (Wilcox) M.; m. Barbara Jane Brown, Sept. 4, 1948 (dec. 1965); children: Janice Lynn, William James; m. Della Fern Carson, Sept. 11, 1965; edn: BS, Univ. Mich., Ann Arbor, 1958-60; prof. Univ. Minn., Mpls. 1960-67; prof. fluid mechanics and acoustics, UCLA, 1967-; cons. Aerospace Corp., El Segundo 1975-80, Rand Corp., Santa Monica 1964-74, Bolt, Beranek and Newman, Cambridge, Mass. 1968-73, Arete Assocs., Encino 1976-;advisor U.S. Congress com. on pub. works, Congl. Record Report N.J. 1972; mem. Calif. Space and Def. Council, U.S. Congress, 1982-; awards: Sigma Xi, Tau Beta Pi, Mich. Alumni scholar 1942-44, Donovan scholar Univ. Mich. 1944-45, UCLA Senate res. grantee 1968-78, NASA res. grantee 1971-; mem: Acoustical Soc. Am. (fellow, gen. meeting chmn. 1973), AIAA (asso. fellow, aeroacoustics com. 1972-75), Am. Phys. Soc. (fluid dynamics div.), Inst. Noise Control Engring.; coauthor (w. R. Lutomirski): Lasar Systems (1973); mil: US Army 1944-46. Res: 927 Glenhaven Dr Pacific Palisades 90272 Ofc: School of Engineering and Applied Sciences Univ. California, Los Angeles 90024

MEHDIZADEH, PARVIZ, insurance executive; b. Sept. 15, 1934, Tehran, Iran; s. Alexander and Sedigheh (Siavooshy) M.; m. Manijeh Sadri, Sept. 12, 1961; children: Sheida, Peyman, Pejman; edn: BS, Forestry Sch., Tehran 1958; MS, N.C. State Univ., Raleigh, 1963, PhD, 1966. Career: pres. Research Inst. Natural Resources, Tehran 1968-73; assoc. prof. Univ. Tehran, 1973-74; prof. environmental scis. Univ. Tabriz, 1974-76; chmn. resolution com. FAO, Rome 1976-77; chmn. natural resources Central Treaty Orgn., Ankars, Turkey 1977-78; special advisor to sec. Ministry of Agriculture, Tehran 1978-79; cons. Minstry of Sci., Tehran 1972-75, UN Univ., Tokyo 1975-76; dist. mgr. American Family Life Assurance Co., Beverly Hills, Calif. 1981-; v.p. Point Internat. Corp., Inc., L.A. 1986-; author: Flowering Plants of Semi-Arid Regions (1976), Economizing of Water Use in Agriculture (1977); editor Khandamhaych Hafteh, London, Eng. (1979); mem. Life Underwriters Assn. (L.A. chpt. Health Ins. Quality Award 1985, 88); clubs: Beverly Hills CC, Friars (L.A.), Rotary Internat. (pres., founder Rancho Park chpt. 1985-86, chmn Found. Com. dist. 5280, 1992); Republican (U.S. Senatorial Club Wash. D.C., charter mem. Rep. Presdl. Task Force 1984). Ofc: American Family Life Assurance Co. 9301 Wilshire Blvd Ste 508 Beverly Hills 90210

MEHTA, SHAILESH JAYANTILAL, bank executive; b. April 22, 1949, Bombay, India; nat. 1981; s. Jayantilal B. and Manjula (Jhaveri) M.; m. Kalpa S. Doshi, Dec. 19, 1973; children: Sameet b. 1975, Sheetal b. 1976; edn: BSME, Indian Inst. Tech. Bombay 1971; MS ops. research, Case Western Reserve Univ. 1973; PhD, ops. research, computer sci., 1975. Career: sr. operations analyst Ameritrust Corp., Cleveland, Ohio 1973-77, v.p. 1977-82, sr. v.p. bank ops. 1982-85, exec. v.p. 1985-86; exec. v.p.and chief operating ofcr.. First Deposit Corp., San Francisco 1986-88, pres. and chief exec. 1988-; listed Who's Who Worldwide, Who's Who In Am., Who's Who U.S. Execs., Who's Who Am. Banking, Who's Who in Finance and Industry; mem. Am. Bankers Assn. Capital Holding Corp. Operating and Policy Com., The Robert Gordon Sproul Assocs. UC Berkeley; Hindu; rec: tennis, travel. Ofc: First Deposit Corp. 88 Kearny St Ste 1900 San Francisco 94108

MELFA, DENNIS WARREN, communications co. executive; b. July 12, 1947, Miami, Fla.; s. Mike and Catherine (Willis) M.; m. Vickie Larue, May 4, 1978; children: Angela b. 1981; edn: AA hons., Prince Georges Coll.; BSBA hons., Southeastern Univ. Career: dir. WUI, WDC 1969-83, mem. support team NASA 1970-80, advr. White House, 1972-82; dir. RCA, Los Angeles 1983-88; div. mgr. MCI Internat., Gardena 1988-; honors: Phi Theta Kappa, NASA Apollo Support award 1971, Skylab Cert. Appreciation 1974, RCA Mgr. of Year 1984, MCI Internat. Top Mgr. Yr. 1988-89; mem: Am. Mgmt. Assn., White House Press Assn., AFCEA, Telecomms. Assn.; civic: Y-Indian Princesses; mil: USAF 1967-69; Republican; Episcopalian (chancel choir, vestry); rec: golf, charities. Res: 1116 Via Nogales Palos Verdes Estates 90274

MENDAL, GEOFFREY OWEN, software company executive; b. May 25, 1961 Chgo., Ill.; s. William Louis and Sandra Ruth (Sol) M.; edn: BS, Univ. of Mich., Ann Arbor, 1983. Career: software engr., Lockheed Corp., Sunnyvale, Calif. 1984-85; res. assoc. Stanford Univ. 1985-90; exec. v.p., SERC, Mountain View, Calif. 1990-; cons., Stanford Univ. 1985-90; conf. chair, ACM SIG Ada 1991-92; awards: best paper, IEEE Computer Soc., Hollywood, Fla. 1986; mem: ACM 1984-, IEEE 1991-; author, Exploring Ada, Vol. 1 & 2, 1984-91; Republican; Jewish; rec: wine tasting, photography. Res: 20580 Shady Oak Lane Cupertino 95014. Ofc: SERC 2555 Charleston Rd. Mountain View 94043

MENDE, HOWARD SHIGEHARU, mechanical engineer; b. Nov. 19, 1947, Hilo, Ha.; s. Tsutomu and Harue (Kubomitsu) M.; edn: BSME, Univ. of Hawaii, 1969; MSME, USC, 1975; M.I.T. 1978; reg. profl. mech. engr. Calif. 1981. Career: tech. staff I Autonetics Div., Rockwell Internat., Anaheim 1970-71, tech. staff II B-1 Div., Los Angeles 1971-77; devel. engr. AiResearch Mfg. Co. of Calif., Torrance 1977-83; tech. staff IV, North Am. Aircraft Ops., Rockwell Internat., Los Angeles 1984-86; GS-0855-012 DCMAO Santa Ana, Def. Logistics Agency 1987-; lectr. Pacific State Univ. 1974- 75; honors: book acknowledgement in Philosophy and Unified Science by Dr. George R. Talbott 1977; mem: Pi Tau Sigma, Am. Soc. Mech. Engrs., Internat. Platform Assn.; Democrat; Buddhist; rec: gardening. Res: 1946 West 180th Pl Torrance 90504 Ofc: Defense Logistics Agy. DCMAO Santa Ana, PO Box C-12700 Santa Ana 92712

MENKES, DAVID, certified public accountant; b. Aug. 5, 1922, Phila.; s. Morris and Pauline (Friedman) M.; m. Rosalie Saperstone, June 17, 1953; children: Elizabeth b. 1954, Pamela b. 1956, Barbara b. 1957, Robin b. 1959; edn: BS, UCLA 1948; Cert. Pub. Acct. Calif. Career: auditor State of Calif., Los Angeles 1948-53; ptnr. Beaver, Menkes & Co., Bellflower 1953-80, dir./prin. Beaver & Menkes Acctg. Corp. 1980-86, pres. Beaver, Menkes & Hass, 1986-90; secty./dir. Bellflower Nat. Bank 1962-67, dir./v. chmn. Mid Cities Nat. Bank 1983-89, dir. Huntington Nat. Bank 1990-; mem: Am. Inst. CPAs, Calif. Soc. CPAs., Bellflower Kiwanis (Kiwanian of Yr. 1979); mil: T/5 AUS 1942-45; rec: bridge, golf. Ofc: Beaver, Menkes & Hass Accounting Corp. 16739 Bellflower Blvd Bellflower 90706

MENNIE, GARY ROY, medical student; b. May 17, 1961, Santa Monica; s. William and Jeannie (Sword) M.; edn: cert. E.M.T., L.A. Comm. Coll., 1984; BA biol., CSU Northridge, 1990, stu. Ross Univ. Sch. of Medicine, 1991-, tchg. asst. Gross Anatomy Lab 1991-92. Career: phlebotomist CSU Health Center, Northridge 1987-88; emergency room EDS Valley Presbyterian Hosp., Van Nuys 1979-91; instr. Helpline Crisis Intervention 1986-91, listener supr. 1987-91; dir. Suicide Prevention Speakers Bur. 1989-90; lab. asst. Los Angeles Community Coll., Woodland Hills 1983-84; honors: Sigma Xi, CSU Found. grant 1988, freshman class pres. Ross Univ. Sch. of Medicine 1991, mem. student affairs com. 1991, honor roll/dean's list 1991, 92, recipient Disting. Scholar Award 1992; mem. Scripps Inst. Research Soc.; Republican (life mem. Rep. Presdl. Task Force, Nat. Rep. Congl. Com.); pub. sci. research in profl. jour. 1988; Res: 8800 Gothic Ave Sepulveda 91343

MENNING, PATRICIA MAXINE, hospital administrator; b. July 6, 1934, Willows; d. Francis Alexander and mildred Elizabeth (Howard) Landon; m. Richard Blaine, July 30, 1952; children: Norman b. 1953, Angelo b. 1955, Cari b. 1956, Kim b. 1960; edn: P.H.T. Cal Poly S.L.O., 1953. Career: administrator Trinity Hosp., Weaverville; owner/opr. Granny's House (bed & breakfast inn), 1987-; past pharmacist asst. Fall River Mills, dental office mgr. Burney, bus. office mgr., personnel dir. and asst. adminstr. Modoc Med. Ctr., Alturas; honors: employee appreciation Trinity Hosp. 1986, Trinity Co. C.of C. nominee for citizen of yr. 1987; mem. Soroptimists, LDS Young Womens Orgn. (pres. 1984-88); painter primitive oils on misc. media (1982-); Republican; Latter Day Saints. Res: 313 Taylor St Weaverville 96093 Ofc: Trinity Hospital 410 N Taylor St Weaverville 96093

MENSH, IVAN NORMAN, professor emeritus of medical psychology; b. Washington, D.C.; s. Shea Jacob and Rose (Clayman) M.; m. Frances Levitas; edn: AB, Geo. Washington Univ., 1940, AM, 1942; PhD, Northwestern Univ., 1948; dipl. in clin. psych. Am. Bd. Profl. Psychology 1952, lic. psychologist, Calif. 1958. Career: social sci. analyst NIH, USPHS, Health Edn. Research, Bethesda, Md. 1941-43; res. asst. Navy Res.Unit Northwestern Univ. 1946-47, USPHS senior clin. fellow, 1947-48; prof. and head div. med. psych., dept. psychiatry Sch. of Medicine Washington Univ., St. Louis Mo. 1948-58; prof. and head div. medical psychology, dept. psychiatry and biobehavioral scis. UCLA Sch. of Medicine, Los Angeles 1958-, Acad. Senate 1958-90, UC Research Com., Calif. Youth Auth. 1990-; cons. Veterans Adminstrn., Mo. and Calif., 1953-; USPHS Special Resrch. Fellow, Inst. Psychiatry, Univ. of London, 1961-62; liaison scientist Office of Naval Research, London 1969-70; Fellow: Am. Psychol. Assn., Am. Psychol. Soc., Western Psychol. Assn., Calif. Psychol. Assn., N.Y. Acad. Scis., Am. Board of Profl. Psychology, Nat. Register of Health Service Providers in Psychology 1974-; author 3 books, 200+ chapters, jour. articles, and reviews; mil: capt. USNR 1943-. Ofc: Dept. Psychiatry and Biobehavioral Scis. UCLA School of Medicine, L.A. 90024-1759

MERCANT, JON JEFFRY, lawyer; b. Dec. 17, 1950, San Jose; s. Anthony J. and Margie Vivian (Diaz) M.; edn: BA, UC Berkeley 1972; JD, UCLA 1975; admitted St. Bar Calif. (1975). Career: practicing atty., Redondo Beach; adj. prof. El Camino Coll.; exec. bd. Calif. Democrat Party 1986-, Dem. nominee State Assembly 1986, mem. L.A. County Central Com. 1986-90; honors: Phi Beta Kappa 1972), UCB Alumni scholar 1968, Nat. Merit scholar, Outstanding Young Men of Am. 1984; mem. AFM, Local 47; COPE chair Calif. Fedn. of Teachers, Local 1388; civic: Peninsula Symphony Assn. (dir.), South Bay Concern (dir., founder), Coastal Environ. Coalition (dir., founder), Retired Senior Volunteer Program (v.chmn. and legal counsel), Consumer Coalition Calif. (dir.), Redondo Beach C.of C. (bd., sec. treas.), Torrance C.of C., Palos Verdes C.of C., Rotary Intl. (N. Redondo bd.); Democrat; rec: music performance. Res: 210 The Village Redondo Beach 90277 Ofc: 707 Torrance Blvd Ste 220 Redondo Beach 90277

MERCER, RICHARD HAMPTON, JR., data processing executive; b. Aug. 12, 1952, Abingdon, Va.; s. Richard Hampton Mercer (dec.) and Helen Olivia (Hull) Spencer; m. Carole Ann Stevens, Feb. 14, 1976; children: Sarah b. 1976, Glen b. 1978; edn: AA, Coll. of Siskiyous (COS), 1972; BA in speech path., CSU Sacramento, 1977, BA in drama, 1977; MPA, National Univ. 1985. Career: legislative clerk 1973-76, computer opr. Legislative Counsel, Sacramento 1977-79, senior computer opr. 1979-80, computer operations supr. I, II, 1980-84, data proc. mgr., I, II, III, 1984-; honors: Bank of Am. Scholarship Award -humanities COS 1971, outstanding acad. achievement Drama, student leadership award, COS 1972, v.p. and pres. COS Student Body 1971, 72, Boy Scouts Am. awards: Eagle Scout 1964, God and Country award, Lutheran, BSA 1965, Vigil Honor, Order of the Arrow 1969; mem. Calif. State Univ. Alumni Assn., Nat. Univ. Alumni Assn.; civic: Calif. Youth Soccer Assn. (coach, referee 1983-90); Democrat; Lutheran; rec: backpacking, acting. Res: 9043 Camden Lake Way Elk Grove 95624

MERCHANT, ROLAND SAMUEL, SR., hospital administrator; b. Apr. 18, 1929, NY, NY; s. Samuel and Eleta (McLymont) M.; m. Audrey Bartley, June 6, 1970; children: Orelia b. 1971, Roland, Jr. b. 1972, Huey b. 1973; edn: BA, NY Univ. 1957, MA, 1960; MS, Columbia Univ. 1963, MS hosp. adminstrn., 1974. Career: asst. statistician NYC Dept. of Health 1957-60, statistician 1960-63, NY TB & Health Assn. 1963-65; biostatistician, adminstrv. coord. Inst. for Surgical Studies Montefiore Hosp. Bronx, NY 1965-72; resident hosp. adminstrn. Roosevelt Hosp. NY 1973-74; dir. health & hosp. mgmt. NYC Dept. of Health 1974-76; asst. adminstr. West Adams Comm. Hosp. Los Angeles 1976, adminstr. 1976; spl. asst. to assoc v.p. for med. affairs Stanford Univ. Med. Ctr. 1977-82, dir. ofc. of mgmt. and strategic planning Stanford Univ. Hosp. 1982-85, dir. mgmt. planning 1986-90; v.p. for strategic planning Cedars-Sinai Med. Ctr., 1990-; lectr. div. of health adminstrn. Columbia Univ. Sch. of Pub. Health 1975-76; lectr., clin. asst. prof., clin. assoc. prof. Stanford Univ. Med. Sch. dept. of family, community and preventive medicine 1977-88, dept. health research & policy, 1988-90; honors: USPHS Fellow (Columbia Univ. 1962-63); fellow: Am. Pub. Health Assn. 1965, Am. Coll. Healthcare Execs. 1985; mem: Am. Hosp. Assn., Nat. Assn. Health Svcs. Execs., NY Acad. Scis.; author: Tuberculosis in New York City 1964, Tuberculosis Morbidity Resumes Decreasing Trend 1965, articles in med. and adminstrv. jours.; mil: US Army 1951-53; Democrat; Baptist (deacon); rec: bowling, fishing; Res: 27335 Park Vista Rd Agoura Hills 91301; Ofc: Cedars-Sinai Medical Center 8700 Beverly Blvd Los Angeles 90048-1869

MERIAM, JAMES LATHROP, retired professor, textbook author; b. Mar. 25, 1917, Columbia, Mo.; s. Junius Lathrop and Mary (Bone) M.; m. Julia Ellen Powers, Dec. 25, 1940; children: Mary Ellen b. 1943, Melissa b. 1946; edn: B.E., Yale Univ., 1939, M.Eng., 1941, Ph.D., 1942; reg. Mech. Engr., Calif., reg. Profl. Engr., N.C. Career: test engr. Pratt & Whitney Aircraft, E.Hartford, Conn., 1940; engr. General Electric Co., W.Lynn, Mass., 1942; instr. to full prof. Univ. Calif. Berkeley, 1942-63; dean and prof. Sch. of Engring. Duke Univ., Durham, N.C., 1963-72; prof. Calif. Polytechnic State Univ., San Luis Obispo, 1972-80; vis. prof. UC Santa Barbara, 1980-90; awards: Yale Engring. Assn. Award for Advancement of Basic & Applied Sci., NYC 1952, Tau Beta Pi Outstanding Faculty award, UCB 1963, Am. Soc. for Engring. Edn., WDC outstanding service award SE Sect. 1975, ASEE Mechanics Div.`Distinguished Educator' and Service award (1978, 1989); mem: Am. Soc. for Engring. Edn. (1952-, Hon. Life mem. 1982), Am. Soc. Mech. Engrs. (1952-, Fellow 1976, Hon. Life mem. 1980), Am. Soc. for Testing & Mats. (affil. 1985-); author textbooks: Mechanics, Part I Statics, Part II Dynamics (1952, 2d edit. 1959), Statics, Dynamics (1966, 2d edit. 1971), Engr. Mechanics, Vol. 1 Statics, Vol. 2 Dynamics (1978, 2d edit. 1986, 3d edit. 1992); mil: lt.jg. USCG Reserve 1944-45; Republican; Prot.; rec: boat building. Res: 4312 Marina Dr Santa Barbara 93110

MERRIFIELD, DONALD PAUL, priest, university chancellor; b. Nov. 14, 1928, Los Angeles; s. Arthur S. and Elizabeth Marian (Baker) M.; edn: BS (physics) Calif. Inst. of Tech. 1950; MS (physics) Univ. of Notre Dame 1951; Ph.L. (philosophy), St. Louis Univ. 1957; PhD (physics) Mass. Inst. of Tech. 1962; STM (theol.), Univ. of Santa Clara 1966; ordained priest, Society of Jesus. Career: instr. physics Loyola Univ. of L.A. 1961-62; lectr. Univ. of Santa Clara Eng. Sch. 1965; cons. theoretical chem. Jet Propulsion Lab, CalTech, 1962-69; pres. Loyola Univ. of Los Angeles, now. Loyola Marymount Univ., 1969-84, chancellor 1984-; awards: S.T.D., USC 1969, service award CalTech 1971; Soc. of Sigma Xi (sci. hon.); mem. bd. dirs. Santa Marta Hosp. Found., trustee Loyola Marymount Univ., Univ. of San Francisco, and St. Joseph Univ.; rec: sailing, travel. Ofc: Loyola Marymount Univ. Loyola Blvd at W 80th St Los Angeles 90045

MERRILL, STEVEN WILLIAM, pyrotechnic consultant; b. Aug. 6, 1944, Oakland; s. David Howard and Etha Nadine (Wright) M.; edn: B.Chem., CSU Hayward, 1987; MBA cand., CSU San Bernardino, 1989-93; lic. pyrotechnic opr. Calif. 1962-. Career: firework assembler Calif. Display Fireworks, Rialto 1970-71; testing technician Hand Chemical Industries, Ontario, Can. 1972-74; chemist Baron Blakesly/Allied Signal, Newark, Calif. 1988-89; dir. R&D, Astro Pyrotechnics, Rialto 1989-91; pyrotechnic cons. Pyro Spectaculars, Rialto 1991-; dir. Merrill Productions Ordnance, Crestline 1975-; expert witness Superior Ct., San Francisco, 1971, Victorville, 1990-91; awards: Bay Area Sci. Fair 1st prize physics 1960, 2d prize physics 1961, finalist Fannie & John Hearst Engring. Scholarship 1961; mem. Pyrotechnic Guild Internat.(charter) 1960-, Western Pyrotechnics Assn. 1989-, Am. Chem. Soc. (anal. div.) 1987-; Oakland Magic Cir. (sec. 1965-70); Christian; rec: sculpture, writing. Res: PO Box 676-23379 Crestline Rd Crestline 92325 Ofc: Pyro Spectaculars 3196 N Locust Rialto 92377

MERRITT, BRUCE GORDON, lawyer; b. Oct. 4, 1946, Iowa City, Iowa; s. William Olney and Gretchen (Kuever) M.; m. Valerie Sue Jorgensen, Dec. 28, 1969; children: Benjamin b. 1976, Alicia b. 1980; edn: AB, Occidental Coll., 1968; JD, Harvard Law Sch., 1972; admitted bar: Calif. 1973. Career: assoc. Markbys (solicitors), London, Eng. 1972-73; atty. assoc., ptnr. Nossaman, Krueger & Marsh, L.A. 1973-79, 79-81; asst. U.S. Attorney, Cent. Dist., Calif., L.A. 1981-85; ptnr. Hennigan & Mercer, L.A. 1986-88; ptnr. Debevoise & Plimpton, L.A. 1989-; lectr., instr. Atty. Gen.'s Trial Advocacy Inst., W.D.C., 1983, 85, Calif. Inst. of Trial Advocacy Skills, L.A. 1986; bd. dirs. Inner City Law Ctr., L.A. 1991-; Am. Coll. of Trial Lawyers (fellow 1992); mem: Calif. State Bar Assn. (1973-, co-chair fed. practice com. litigation sect. 1990-92), L.A. County Bar Assn. (del. state bar conf. 1984-86, fed. cts. com. 1985-86). Ofc: Debevoise & Plimpton 601 S Figueroa St Ste 3700 Los Angeles 90017

MERTA, PAUL JAMES, political cartoonist, film producer; b. July 16, 1939, Bakersfield; s. Stanley Franklin and Mary Ana (Herman) M.; edn: AA, Bakersfield Jr. Coll. 1962; BS engring., CSU San Jose 1962. Career: cartoonist for coll. and nat. mags. 1959-; civilian elec. engr. USAF missiles, San Bernardino Air Material Area 1962-65, elec. countermeasures engr. 1965-72, program mgr., logistics acquisition, Sacto. Air logistics area 1972-90, ret.; t.v./film prod., owner Merge Films 1965; photog./owner The Photo Poster Factory, Sacto. 1971-; owner La Rosa Blanca Mexican Restaurant, Sacto. 1979-91; ptnr. Kolinski and Merta Hawaiian Estates (housing devel.), Hilo 1981-92; political cartoonist California Journal 1958-59, Sacramento Union 1979, Sacramento Legal Journal 1979; cartoons pub. in nat. mags. and regional periodicals; producer TV show, numerous TV commercials and entertainment shorts; rec: flying, skiing, bridge; Res: 4831 Myrtle Ave #8 Sacramento 95841 Ofc: The Photo Poster Factory 1005 12th St Sacramento 95814

MERTZ, KENNETH ALEXANDER, JR., dentist; b. Nov. 20, 1952, Point Pleasant, N.J.; s. Kenneth Alexander and Christine Skipwith (Todd) M.; m. Susan Jeanne Trepiccione, Aug. 3, 1975; children: Kenneth Alexander III b. 1980; edn: BS biol., Fairleigh Dickinson Univ. 1975; DMD, 1980; MPA, Golden Gate Univ. 1985; MS human physiology, Fairleigh Dickinson Univ. 1987. Career: dental ofcr., clinic dir. Naval Reg. Dental Center, Norfolk, Va. 1980-81; dental ofcr., div. ofcr. USS Nimitz 1981-83; Naval Dental Clinic 1983-85; dental ofcr., clinic dir., dept. head Fleet Marine Force Pacific, Camp Pendleton 1988-89; operative dept. head Naval Dental Clinic, Camp Pendleton,1989-; CPR instr. USN & Bergen Co. Heart Assn. 1977-; emergency med. tech. instr. USS Nimitz 1982-83; article referee, book reviewer AMSUS, AGD, USMC Assn. 1986-; awards: Acad. Gen. Dentistry Mastership & Fellowship (1988, 86), USN Achievement Medal (1981, 83), USMC Assn. Command Gen. Leadership (1988), Golden Gate Univ. Cert. of Accomplishment 1985, Fairleigh Dickinson Univ. Surgeons Award to Sr. Dental Students 1980; mem: ADA, Acad. Gen. Dentistry, Assn. Mil. Surgeons of U.S., U.S. Naval Inst., Renachitos Youth Soccer Assn. (referee 1989-), Masons (master mason 1974-); publs: num. articles and reviews; mil: lt.cdr. USN Dental Corps 1980-; Episcopalian; rec: writing, woodworking, youth leadership. Res: 13485 Sawtooth Rd San Diego 92129 Ofc: Naval Dental Clinic Camp Pendleton 92055-5701

METZER, JOHN EDGAR, hatchery owner; b. March 23, 1956, Corvallis, Ore.; s. Olin Oscar and Lois Jean (Fraser) M.; m. Sharon Kay Green, July 10, 1982; children: Janelle b. 1983, Marc b. 1989; edn: AA (Valedictorian), Hartnell Comm. Coll., 1976; BS animal sci., UC Davis, 1978. Career: owner, mgr. Metzer Farms, Gonzalez 1978-; co. dir. Monterey Co. Farm Bureau, Salinas 1981-; honors: Phi Kappa Phi, Outstanding Grad. in Animal Sci. UC Davis 1978, valedictorian Gonzales H.S. 1974; mem. Hartnell Coll. Found., Hartnell Comm. Coll. Bd. Govs. 1980-; Democrat; R.Cath. Res: 26000 Old Stage Rd Gonzales 93926 Ofc: Metzer Farms 26000 Old Stage Rd Gonzales 93926

METZGER, VERNON ARTHUR, management consultant, professor emeritus; b. Aug. 13, 1918, Baldwin Park; s. Vernon and Nellie Catherine (Ross) M.; m. Beth Wilson, Feb. 19, 1955; children: Susan b. 1948, Linda b. 1957; edn: BS, UC Berkeley 1947; MBA, 1948. Career: prof. mgmt. CSU Long Beach 1949-90,

founding faculty member and prof. emeritus CSULB Sch. of Bus. Adminstrn.; mgmt. cons.; mem. Calif. Fair Polit. Practices Com. 1978-84, Orange Co. Transit Com., Fountain Valley Fire Commn. 1959-60, Yugoslavia Mgmt. Team 1977; awards: Outstanding Citizens (Orange Co. Bd. of Suprs.), Soc. for Advancement of Mgmt. (fellow), Beta Gamma Sigma; mem: Soc. for Advancement Mgmt. (pres. & founder Orange Coast Chpt. 1956, 61, 63, regional dir. 1962-63); civic: Orange Co. Democratic League, Orange Co. Indsl. Relations Research Assn.; original founding faculty mem. CSU Long Beach Sch. Bus. Adminstrn. 1949; mil: lt. USNR 1942-45; Democrat; Methodist; rec: backpacking, fishing, hunting. Address: 1938 Balearic Drive Costa Mesa

MEYE, ROBERT PAUL, retired professor and administrator; b. Apr. 1, 1929, Hubbard, OR; s. Robert Carl and Eva Julia (Pfau) M.; m. Mary Alice Cover, June 18, 1951; children: Douglas 1953; Marianne 1954; John 1957; edn: ThM, Fuller Theol. Sem., Pasadena, 1959; BD, Fuller Theol. Sem., Pasadena, 1957; BA, Stanford, 1951; career: prof., N. Baptist Theol. Sem., Lombard, Ill. 1962-77; dean, 1971-77; prof., Fuller Theol. Sem., Pasadena 1977-; dean, Sch. of Theol., Fuller Theol. Sem. 1977-90; assoc. provost, Fuller Theol. Sem. 1990-92; dean emeritus and prof. emeritus, Fuller Theol. Sem. 1992-; awards: Doctor of Divinity, Eastern Baptist Theol. Sem., Phila. 1990; Fellowship, Assoc. Theol. Sch., Pittsburg 1970-71 and 1975-76; mem: Am. Acad. Religion, Inst. of Biblical Res., Soc. of Biblical Lit., Studiorum Novi Testamentum Societas, Christianity Today Inst., Chgo. Soc. of Biblical Res.; author: Jesus and the Twelve; many publ. articles; mil: lt. (jg), Navy, 1946-54; Republican; Protestant, Am. Baptist Churches; rec: photography; gardening; travel; music; reading. Res: 1170 E. Rubio St. Altadena 91001 Ofc: Fuller Theol. Sem. 135 N. Oakland Ave. Pasadena 91182

MEYER, DEANNA MARIE ARRAS, realtor, entertainment and events executive; b. July 9, 1937, New Britain, Conn.; d. Damiano Francis and Angelina Catherine (Reina) Arras; m. 2d, Richard A. Meyer, July 19, 1986; 2 children by previous marriage (nee Yuhas): John b. 1960, Maryann b. 1962; edn: Syracuse Univ. 1957; Ryder Coll. 1959; Calif. R.E. lic. 1980. Career: ptnr. Fashion Artistry By-Ka-Dee; librarian, media center dir. Chino Unified Sch. Dist. 1973-80; realtor/ptnr. ERA Diversified Realty, Chino 1980-84; adminstrv. asst. San Bernardino County Supr., 4th dist., 1983-86, chair San Bernardino Co. Day Creek Project 1984-85, chair Gov.'s com. Neighborhood Watch, San Bernardino. Co. 1985; exec. dir. Prado Tiro Grand Prix Corp., 1986-88, sec.-treas. Prado Tiro Found.; exec. director Decathlon Championship, American Outdoor Sports Associates Inc., 1989, mem. corp. com. and co-chair opening & closing ceremonies Chino Corporate Challenge, 1990, 91, 92; realtor The Western Group, 1991-; honors: Inland Business "Women of the Yr." finalist 1990, Paul Harris Fellow Rotary 1987, hon. service PTA, listed World Who's Who of Women, 5000 Personalities of World, Am. Biog. Inst.; mem. Inland Empire West Assn. of Realtors (bd. 1991-92, sec. 1992-93, v. pres. 1993-94, Legis. com. 1980-, chair 1989, v. chair 1992, co-chair comm. relations 1980-, chair BORPAC 1991-92), civic: Chino C.of C. (bd. 1983-), Soroptimist Internat. of Chino, Chino Comm. Hosp. Bd. Trustees (chair citizens bd. 1992-93), Chino Family YMCA (pres. bd. mgrs., bd. pres. Capital Camp, chair P.R. com.), Chaffey Coll. Found. (bd. dirs., chair Chino Friends of Chaffey Coll., co-chair Planetarium Com.), OPARC, Chino Hist. Soc., L.A. Co. Mus. of Art (patron); Republican; R.Cath.; rec: golf, travel. Res: 778 Via Montevideo Claremont 91711

MEYER, JANET JONES, emergency physician; b. Apr. 2, 1944, Midland, Tx.; d. Kyle Everett and Ruth Lorraine (Pickett) Jones; m. John Joseph Weger, Mar. 5, 1962 (dec. 1972); children: Erica Ruth b. 1963, Mark Christopher b. 1964; m. Anthony Francis Meyer, Aug. 4, 1973 (div. 1981); edn: BA, Ind. Univ. 1973; MD, Loyola Stritch Sch. of Med. 1976. Career: res. physician Highland Hosp.-Duke Univ., Asheville, N.C. 1976-77; emergency physician Reid Meml. Hosp., Richmond, Ind. 1977-79; Silver Cross Hosp., Joliet, Ill. 1979-80; Chapman Gen. Hosp., Orange, Calif. 1980-87, FHP, Fountain Valley 1987-88, La Habra Comm. Hosp. 1983-; fellow Am. Coll. EM Physicians; mem: Soc. of Orange Co. EM Physicians, DAR; Democrat; Jewish; rec: boating. Ofc: Friendly Hills Medical Group 1251 W Lambert Rd La Habra 90631

MEYERS, ROGER J., telegram company executive; b. Feb. 15, 1955, Kansas City, Mo.; s. Henry Julius and Gloria Ann (Tartaglia) M.; m. Marian Berger, Jan. 2, 1983; 2 children; edn: BFA, New York Univ., 1977. Career: founder and c.e.o. American Telegram Corp., Beverly Hills 1986-; honors: nom. Entrepreneur of Yr. Ernst & Young, L.A. (1991, 92, 93). Res: 270 N Canon Dr, 1167, Beverly HIlls 90212 Ofc: American telegram Corp. 9223 Olympic Blvd Beverly Hills 90212

MEYSENBURG, JOHN HAROLD, electronic engineer; b. Dec. 2, 1934, Primrose, Nebr.; s. Harold Peter and Agnes Gertrude (Puetz) M.; m. Mary Ann Augustine, June 17, 1967; children: Peter b. 1971, Amy b. 1976; edn: Radio Engring. Inst. 1954-55, Ricker Coll. 1958, Pasadena City Coll. 1967-71. Career: tech. rep. field engr. Philco Corp. 1959-61; senior tech. TRW Semiconductors 1961-64; sr. electronic tech. in R & D, Quality Control (Project Apollo Spacecraft), Allen Jones Electronics, 1964-65; sr. electronic tech. TRW System, 1965-67; electronic engr. (test asst.) Jet Propulsion Lab., 1967-: helped develop:

High Power Solid State Microwave Switch 1968, Micromin and NASA Std. Transponder 1969-75, RF Test System 1975, Transmitter for Total Hip Joint Bioteleetry System 1980, Solid State X Band Transmitter 1981, ISPM Down Converter 1980-81, mem. of team to devel. and deliver the NASA Microwave Limb Sounder 1985, co-developer of Cassai Deep Space Transponder 1983-92; honors: mem. of the JPL Flight Team to deliver an X-band Down Converter to the Galileo Spacecraft, Magellan and Cassini Spacecrafts; 1953 Bausch & Lomb Hon. Science Award; co-inventor on a patent for Beam Lead Integrated Circuit Test Fixture 1974; NASA awards for Cassini Spacecraft Transponder and advanced error-correcting code res. & devel.; 3d. place (color slides - subject Lightning), L.A. Photog. Center 1956; Boy Scouts Am. San Gabriel Valley (mem. Eagle Board and asst. Merit Badge Counselor 1988); mil: Airman 2/c 1954-59, GCM; Democrat; R.Cath.; rec: photog., radio expt. Res: 6725 Brentmead Ave Arcadia 91007 Ofc: Jet Propulsion Laboratory 4800 Oak Grove Dr Pasadena 91009

MEYSENBURG, MARY ANN, private school administrator; b. Sept. 16, 1939, Los Angeles; d. Clarence H. and Mildred (McGee) Augustine; m. John Harold Meysenburg, June 17, 1967; children: Peter b. 1971, Amy b. 1976; edn: BA (magna cum laude), USC, 1960; life tchg. cred., UCLA, 1971. Career: escrow ofcr. Union Bank, Los Angeles 1962-64; escrow mgr., v.p. Bank of Downey 1964-66; elem. tchr. St. Bruno's Sch., Whittier 1966-70; elem. tchr. Pasadena Unified 1971-84; elem. tchr. Holy Angels Sch., Arcadia 1985-89; v.principal, tchr. Our Mother of Good Counsel, L.A. 1989-91; consulting tchr. Santa Ana Coll. of Bus. 1964-66; catechist Los Angeles Catholic Archdiocese 1978-, master catechist 1988-; eucharistic minister Our Mother of Good Counsel 1989-; historian Phi Delta Kappa (USC) 1991-92; Foundations rep. Phi Delta Kappa, 1992-93; Writing to Read coordinator 1991-93, treas. 1993-94; principal St. Stephen's Sch., Monterey Park 1993-94; honors: Pius X award L.A. Archdiocese 1979, St. Elizabeth Ann Seton award/St. Anne medal, Cath. Com. for Girl Scouting 1988, 89, Bronze Pelican award Cath. Com. for Boy Scouting 1989, Phi Delta Kappa 1988, Teacher Incentive grantee Milken Family Found. 1989, 92, Phi Beta Kappa 1960, Phi Kappa Phi 1960, Phi Alpha Theta nat. hon. hist. soc. 1960; civic: Boy Scouts of Am. (counsellor 1985-), Legion of Mary (sec. Senatus 1980-85), Cath. Com. for Girl Scouts and Campfire (v.chmn. acad. affairs 1985-); publs: ms. History of the Arms Control Disarmament Orgn. 1976, editor The Message newspaper 1986-88; Democrat; R. Cath.; rec: history, tennis, scouting. Res: 6725 Brentmead Ave Arcadia 91007

MICHEL, KARON RAE, executive recruiter training director; b. Dec. 30, 1946, Macomb, Ill.; d. Harry Dale and Jeanette Elvina (Stoke) Shannon; m. Thomas Edward Michel, Apr. 15, 1967, div. 1978; edn: Patricia Stevens Modeling Sch., Milw. 1965-66, Univ. Wisc., Milw. 1966-69. Career: sales promotion mgr. Computer Book Service, Schamburg, Ill. 1969-72; v.p. mktg. Midwestern Mktg. Assn., Charleston, Ill. 1972-75; nat. trainer/mgr. Management Recruiters Intl., Cleveland, Oh. 1977-86; v.p. ops. R.M.E., Inc. Los Angeles 1986-88; internat. tnr. Jenny Craig Centres, Brisbane and Sydney, Austr., Los Angeles, CA 1988-89; dir. tng. Search West, Inc. Los Angeles 1989-; cons. prin. Power Play, Beverly Hills 1986-88; awards: named Hon. Texas Citizen by Texas Gov. 1979, San Francisco mag. list of 100 Most Outstanding Women S.F. 1982, Alan Newman Memorial Award 1992, listed Who's Who of Am. Women (1985-86), World Who's Who of Women (11th), Two Thousand Notable Am. Women (4th), Intl. Dir. of Disting. Leadership 1991; mem: Nat. Assn. for Female Execs., Century City C.of C. (v.p. spkrs. bur. 1986-87), Calif. Assn. Personnel Consultants (dir. 1981-83), Am. Mgmt. Assn. 1980-84, Toastmasters (founder/sec. Jefferson, IA 1975-77); civic: Calif. Special Olympics (1972-, past vol. Charleston and Chgo., Ill.), Girl Scouts Am. (Ill., Wis., Ia., 1959-78); author 3 books: How To Be an Effective Recruiter 1987, How to Manage Recruiters 1987, 30 Effective Meetings for Recruiters 1986; Republican; Prot.; rec: art, games, travel, photography, whitewater rafting, theatre, symphony, sports. Res: 627 San Nicholas Ct. Laguna Beach 92651 Ofc: 750 The City Dr. #100 Orange 92668

MICKEY, NORMAN LEE, social work supervisor, singles dating organization owner; b. Oct. 2, 1939, Antioch, Calif.; s. James Raymond and Jennie Virginia (Moglie) M.; m. Deanna Rolerson, 1961, div. 1968; child: Cathy, b. 1965; edn: BA, psy., San Jose State Coll. 1964; AA, Diablo Valley Coll. 1959. Career: social wkr. Contra Costa Co. Soc. Svc. Dept., 1964-69, supr. social work Contra Costa Social Services Dept. 1969-; founder/owner/dir. Video Introductions (singles video dating orgn.), Concord 1977-, acquisitions of (singles dating services) "Futures" 1989, "Sunrise" 1989, "Upscale Choices" 1990, "Datebank" 1991, and "Latinos Dating Service" 1992; mem: Contra Costa Co. Central Labor Council (exec bd. 1972-75, del. 1970-72), Social Svc. Union S.E.I.U. Local 535, AFL-CIO (Contra Costa Co. chpt., founding pres. 1967-68); S.E.I.U. Local 302 AFL-CIO (exec. bd. 1965-67); Contra Costa Housing Authority tenant appeal referee 1971-81; Contra Costa Co. Merit Board (sub-com. mem. investigating irregular S.S. Dept. promotional practices 1987-89); author, publisher: Romantic Reminders 1980, A Modern Alternative 1986, Partner Compatibility Questionnaire For Singles 1992; Democrat; rec: car customizing (awards), writing, graphic arts, photog. Res: 420 Brookside Dr Antioch 94509 Ofc: Video Introductions, 1950-D Market St Concord 94520

MIECKE, GARY G., engineer/manager; b. March 22, 1946, Buffalo, N.Y.; s. Erwin A. and Ella (Duell) M.; edn: AA, Los Angeles City Coll. 1972; BA, Cal Poly Pomona 1976; Reg. Profl. Engr., Calif. Career: engr./mgr. Selective Services Corp. 1972-; cons. engr., pres. Ella/Omni & Co., Inc. (predecessor co. Omni Corp.) 1975-; mem. Inst. of Indsl. Engring.; civic: Easter Seal Found./Orange (research, cons.), Kiwanis Club, Republican Inner Circle; mil: sgt. US Army 1967-69; rec: sailing, swimming. Address: Omni CAL, Inc. 3610 W Sixth St Ste 366 Los Angeles 90020

MIHALICK, CHARLES RAUTZE, financial executive; b. June 6, 1945, Ashtabula, Ohio; s. Charles and Mary Jane Nina (Williams) M.; m. Lorelei Ann Lindenmayer, Oct. 31, 1964 (div. 1988); m. Nadine Joan Marcon, Sept. 16, 1989; children: Stephanie b. 1972, Chad b. 1974, Christopher b. 1990; edn: BS, Ohio St. Univ. 1971; MBA, USC 1978; C.P.A. Calif. 1973. Career: auditor Coopers & Lybrand, San Francisco 1971-73; corp. acct. Hughes Aircraft, Los Angeles 1973-78; CFO, dir. Pioneer Aluminum Inc. 1978-85; treas. Bell & Howell / Columbia /Paramount Video, Torrance 1985-88; CFO Contain-a-Way Inc., Irvine 1988-89; CFO Enertech, Brea 1989-; honors: Beta Gamma Sigma, Beta Alpha Psi; mem: Am. Inst. C.P.A., Calif. Soc. C.P.A.; mil: E-5 AUS 1966-69; Republican; Episcopalian; rec: skiing, tennis, wt.lifting. Res: 27441 Betanzos Mission Viejo 92692 Ofc: Enertech 2950 Birch St Brea 92621

MIKALOW, ALFRED ALEXANDER, captain/marine diving consultant; b. Jan. 19, 1921, N.Y.C.; m. Janice Brenner, Aug. 1, 1960; children: Alfred, Alexander, Jon Alfred; student Rutgers Univ., 1940; MS, UC Berkeley, 1948; MA, Rochdale Univ., Can. 1950; lic. Merchant Marine capt., Cert. Marine Insp. Career: Lt. CDR. served with USN, 1941-47, 49-50, decorated Purple Heart, Silver Star; capt. and master res. vessel Coastal Researcher I, owner/dir. Coastal Diving Co., Coastal Sch. Deep Sea Diving, Oakland 1950-, Divers Supply, 1952-; pres. Treasury Recovery Inc., 1972-75; comml. diving 44 years, has trained 8,500+ comml. divers including mil. Green Berets, Navy Units, Coast Guard Strike teams, and fgn. students; designer of diving equipment. and recompression chambers, incl. One-Atmosphere Dive Suit and R.O.V. (Remote Observation Veh.) Unit and Wet Subs.; cons. var. hosps. in treatment of diving disease; marine diving contractor, consultant; active cert. marine insp.; mem. advy. bd. Medic Alert Found., Turlock 1960-; mem: Diver's Assn. of Am. (pres. 1970-74), Calif. Assn. of Marine Surveyors (pres. 1987), Internat. Assn. Profl. Divers, Assn. of Diving Contrs. (charter), Marine Technology Soc., Calif. Assn. Pvt. Edn. (no. Calif. v.p. 1971-72), Authors Guild, Internat. Game Fish Assn., US Navy League, US Submarine Veterans of WWII (Vallejo chapter), US Reserve Ofcrs. Assn., Navy Tailhook Assn., Explorer Club (S.F.), Masons (Master Sequoia Lodge, Oakland), Lions Club; author: Fell's Guide to Sunken Treasure Ships of the World 1972, (w/ H. Rieseberg) The Knight from Maine 1974. Res: 52 Mira Loma Orinda 94563 Ofc: 320 29th Ave Oakland 94601

MIKESELL, MARY JANE, psychotherapist; b. Oct. 29, 1943, Rockledge, Fla.; d. John and Mary Christine (Leighty) Wagner; edn: BA, CSU Northridge 1967; MA, Pacific Oaks Coll. 1980; PhD in psych., California Graduate Inst., 1989; lic. Marriage, Family, Child Counselor (MFCC), Calif. Career: tchr. Los Angeles Unified Sch. Dist., 1966-69; photo lab. dir. Oceanograficos de Honduras, Roatan, Honduras, C.A., 1969-70; supr. Los Angeles Life Insurance Co., 1970-72; customer service rep. Beverly Hills Fed. S&L, Beverly Hills 1972-73; consultant, lectr. 1973-; staff CSUN Counseling Center, Northridge 1974-78; hd. office services Pacific Oaks Coll., Pasadena 1978-79; prodn. supr. Frito-Lay Inc., LA 1979-81; circulation supr. Daily News, Van Nuys 1981-82; educational therapist, MFCC intern Ctr. for Human Development, 1982-89, psychol. intern CGI Counseling Ctr., 1987-88 ; psychol. asst., Calabasas 1989-90; proj. coord. Carlson, Rockey & Assocs., Brentwood 1983-84; mem. press staff Southland Olympic News Bur. 1983-84; press staff ATAS Emmy Awards ceremonies, 1983, staff 7-11 Stores/Bicycling mag. Internat. Grand Prix Cycling Race, 1983, Sub-Center steward, press ops., 1984 Water Polo Venue, Pepperdine Univ.; proj. coord. and sys. splst. student ins. div. William F. Hooper Inc., 1985-87; cons. psychol. benefits pgm. Brentwood Ins. Claims Adminstrs. 1985-87; problems analyst Com Systems, 1987-89; school counselor, therapist Poinsettia Found., 1990-91, Calabasas Acad., 1992; cons. Designer Collection by Pingy, L.A. 1985; mem: Am. Assn. of Counseling & Devel., Internat. Assn. Marriage & Fam. Counselors, Am. Psychol. Assn. (asso.), Nat. Assn. Female Execs., Planetary Soc., Calif. Scholarship Fedn.; works: photog. exhib. Canoga Park Mission Gal. 1966, all photos for the Soo Yin Trade Co. catalog 1977, brochure photos for Miss China Town 1977, Archeology Today (multi-media presentation); Republican; Judeo-Christian; rec: photography, writing, research w. mentally gifted children. Res: 1754 Blackwell Dr Simi Valley 93063-3210 Ofc: Emerald Foundation 5200 Telegraph Rd Ventura 93001

MILCHIKER, MARCIA LESLIE, biologist, community college district elected official; b. Aug. 22, 1946, Cleveland, Oh.; d. Sam and Fran (Kain) Greene; m. Dr. Benjamin Milchiker, Nov. 4, 1973; children: Aaron b. 1975, Daniel b. 1978, David b. 1981; edn: BS, Ohio St. Univ., 1968; MS, Cleveland St. Univ., 1974. Career: res. biologist Southwestern Medical, also v.p. Pacific Medical Mgmt., Lake Forest, Ca. 1983-; elected bd. trustees Saddleback Comm. Coll., Mission Viejo, 1985-, pres. 1990-91; mem: Calif. School Boards Assn. (bd., secty. 1990, Comm. Coll. rep. 1991-), Calif. Comm. Colls. Commn. on Legislation & Fin. 1988-, Calif. Council on Gerontology & Geriatrics (bd. 1987-89), Orange Co. Comm. Coll. Legislative Task Force (founding mem. 1986-87, 87-88); United Way (bd. S.Orange Co. Region Council 1988-, nom. com. ch. 1990); mem. Calif. Elected Women's Assn. for Edn. & Res. (state bd. 1990-, nom. com. 1991, founder & charter pres. O.C. chapt. 1987-89), L.W.V. (L.A. exec. com. Presdl. Primary Debates p.r. com. 1988), Soroptomist, B.P.W. Saddleback Valley (legis. ch. 1986, Woman of Yr. award 1986), Orgn. for Rehabilitation through Tng., Womens Roundtable of O.C. (bd.), AAUW, United Jewish Welfare Fund (local chair 1980), Orangewood Home for Abused Children (La Casa Aux. speakers bur. 1984-86), Madame Mojesca Chpt. O.C. Performing Arts Guild, Childrens Home Soc., Camp Havariim Comm. Ctr. (bd., co-founder 1980-90), Jewish Comm. Ctr. (past bd.). Ofc: BOT, Saddleback Community College 28000 Marguerite Pky Mission Viejo 92692

MILLAR, RICHARD W., JR., lawyer; b. May 11, 1938; s. Richard W. and Catherine (Arms) M.; m. Nancy; children: Richard W. III, Kelly Ann, Adam Edward; edn: student Occidental Coll. 1956-59; JD, Univ. San Francisco 1966; admitted bar Calif. 1967, Supreme Ct. 1971. Career: dep. dist. atty., Los Angeles 1967; atty. Iverson & Hogoboom 1967-72; Eilers, Stewart, Pangman & Millar 1973-75; Millar & Heckman 1975-77; ptnr. Millar, Hodges, Bemis & Mozingo (and predecessor firm), Newport Beach 1979-; lectr. Calif. Contg. Edn. Bar.; judge pro tem Orange Co. Superior Ct.; mem: Am. Bar Assn. (litigation sect., trial practice com., ho. of dels. 1990-), Orange Co. Bar Assn. (real estate sect., chmn. bus. litigation sect. 1981, chmn. judiciary com. 1988-90); civic: Bluffs Homeowners Assn. (pres. 1977-78), Newport Hills. Comm. Assn. (pres. 1972), Los Angeles YMCA Camp Branch (bd. 1970-75); club: Balboa Bay; Republican; Episcopalian. Res: 2546 Crestview Dr Newport Beach 92663 Ofc: Millar, Hodges, Bemis & Mozingo, One Newport Pl Ste 900 Newport Beach 92660

MILLARD, NEAL STEVEN, lawyer; b. June 6, 1947, Dallas; s. Bernard and Adele (Marks) M.; edn: BA (cum laude), UCLA, 1969; JD, Univ. Chgo., 1972; admitted bar: Calif. 1972, N.Y. 1990, US Dist. Ct. cent. dist. Calif. 1973, US Tax Ct. 1973, US Ct. Appeals 9th cir. 1987. Career: atty., assoc. Willis, Butler & Schiefly, Los Angeles 1972-75; ptnr. Morrison & Foerster, Los Angeles 1975-84;ptnr. Jones, Day, Reavis & Pogue, Los Angeles 1984-93;ptnr. White & Case, Los Angeles 1993-; instr. CSC San Bernardino, 1975-76; lectr. Practising Law Inst., N.Y.C., 1983-90, Calif. Cont. Edn. of Bar, 1987-89; honors: Phi Beta Kappa, Pi Gamma Mu, Phi Delta Phi; mem: ABA, NY State Bar Assn., Calif. Bar Assn., L.A. County Bar Assn. (trustee 1985-87), L.A. County Bar Found. (bd. 1991-), Pub. Counsel (bd. 1984-87, 1990-93), Univ. Chgo. Law Alumni Assn./ So. Calif. Chpt. (bd. 1981-); civic bds: L.A. Olympics Citizens Advy. Com. (1982-84), Woodcraft Rangers/ L.A. (bd. 1982-91, pres. 1986-88), Altadena Library Dist. Bd. Trustees (1985-86); club: The Calif. Club, Altadena Town and Country; mil: capt. AUS 1970-72. Ofc: White & Case 633 W. Fifth St Ste 1900 Los Angeles 90071

MILLER, ALFRED LEE, dairyman, rancher, investment broker; b. Feb. 5, 1924, Ontario, Calif.; s. Ora Lee and Ethel Harriet (Pettitt) M.; m. R. Jacqueline Smith, July 25, 1958; 1 child, Terry b. 1959; edn: BS, animal sci., UC Davis 1950; supv. cert., CSU Sacto. 1952-56. Career: owner/mgr. dairy 1950-74, owner/mgr. cattle ranch 1974-; civilian supvr. Electronic Div., Army 1951-59; indep. cons. animal sci., finl. investments; youth advisor 4-H and FFA activities; honors: Dairy of Merit 1964-1974; mem. Calif. State Grange (steward 1978-90), Dairyman Feed and Supply Coop. (bd. dirs. 1962-74), Galt C.of C. (bd. 1990), Calif. Milk Producers (bd. dirs. 1964); res. papers: Economic Cycles and their Relation to Investments (1985), Fifty Year Cycles and Today's Investments (1987); mil: pharm. mate 1/c US Navy 1943-46, Good Conduct, Am. Theater, Mid-East Theater w/4 stars, Far-East Theater w/3 stars; Repub.; Galt Bible Ch.; rec: gardening, equestrian, consulting. Address: 9650 Harvey Road Galt 95632

MILLER, ARNOLD LAWRENCE, educator; b. Nov. 7, 1942, NY, NY s. Julius and Anne (Blumenfield) M.; m. Barbara Jean Freeman, Nov. 12, 1966 children: Matthew b. 1972, Jeremy b. 1975; edn: BA, Alfred Univ., NY 1961; MS, Syracuse Univ. 1964, PhD, 1968. Career: postgrad. res. neuroscientist UC San Diego 1971-73, asst. res. neurosci. 1973-74, asst. prof. 1974-80, assoc. prof. 1980-85, prof. neuroscis. 1985-; dir. grad. studies UC San Diego, 1980-, com. on acad. personnel 1986-88, chemical usage com. 1988-, founder & coord. neurosci. information exchange 1980-; guest lectr. Am. Assn. for the Study of Liver Diseases, Chgo. 1984; awards: res.career develop. award NINDS 1975-80, travel award Monash Univ., Clayton, Victoria, Austr. 1982; mem: Soc. of Neurosci., Am. Soc. for Biological Chemists, Soc. of Complex Carbohydrates, Biochem. Soc., Am. Soc. for Cell Biology, Screen Actors Guild, Am. Federation of Radio & Television Artists, San Dieguito Surf Soccer Club (exec. bd. 1982-86); trustee Temple Solel, Encinitas 1980-83, 1985-88, chmn. Rel. Sch. 1982-84; author: num. scientific articles pub. in prof. jours.; rec: acting, sports. Res: 1364 Ahlrich Ave Encinitas 92024 Ofc: Dept Neurosciences, Univ. Calif. Sch of Medicine M-024, La Jolla 92093

MILLER, CLIFFORD ALBERT, business consultant; b. Aug. 6, 1928, Salt Lake City, Ut.; s. Clifford Elmer and LaVeryl (Jensen) M.; m. Barbara, June 22, 1951; m. 2d. Judith Auten, Sept. 20, 1977; children: Clifford b. 1959, Christin b. 1959, Stephanie b. 1962, Courtney b. 1978; edn: Univ. Utah, S.L.C. 1945-49, UCLA, 1956. Career: pres. Braun & Company, L.A. 1955-82, chmn. 1982-86; exec. v.p..Great Western Fin. Corp., Beverly Hills 1986-91; chmn. The Clifford Group, Inc. 1992-; dir. Shamrock Holdings.Inc., Burbank 1979-; trustee Harvey Mudd Coll., Claremont 1974-, chmn. bd. 1991-; chmn. emeritus Los Angeles Master Chorale 1989-; mem. chmn.'s coun. Music Ctr. Unified Fund Campaign, past ofcr., dir. L.A. Jr. Chamber of Commerce; mem. Pi Kappa Alpha, Skull & Bones, Sigma Delta Chi; clubs: California, L.A. Tennis, Lakes CC (Palm Desert). Ofc: The Clifford Group Inc. 4444 Lakeside Dr Ste 120 Burbank 91505

MILLER, DENNIS NEIL, consultant; b. Sept. 15, 1959, Taft, Calif.; s. Thurman and Valarie (Blanco) M.; edn: BS in physics, UC, Santa Barbara, 1989; MBA, Cal Poly, San Luis Obispo, 1992; MS, Cal Poly, 1992; career: foreman Gen. Am. Insulation, Grover City, Calif., 1978-81; prin., 2730 Bldg. Restoration, Arroyo Grande, Calif., 1981-90; cons. Ad Extremum Cons., Arroyo Grande, 1990-92; cons., Andersen Cons., L.A., 1992-; pres. Soc. of Physics Students, Santa Barbara, 1988-89; lectr. Cal Poly, 1991-92; awards: Most Outstanding MBA Student, Cal Poly, 1992; Calif. State Res. Competition Finalist, 1992; mem: Soc. of Physics Students 1987-, Beta Gamma Sigma 1992-, Sigma Iota Epsilon 1991-; author: tech. article, 1992; Republican; Baptist; rec: skiing, volleyball, mountain biking. Res: 470 Newport Ave. Grover City 93433

MILLER, DONELYN SUE CULVER, marriage and family counselor; b. Jan. 11, 1951, Seattle; d. Robert Shaw Culver and Margaret (McAteer) Chesney; m. Curtis W. Miller, Aug. 25, 1974; children: Chesney b. 1978, Brittany b. 1981, Shawn b. 1983, Katelyn b. 1986; edn: BA psych., Westmont Coll., 1973; MA, Azusa Pacific Univ., San Jose ext., 1982; lic. MFCC, Calif. 1987. Career: live-in counselor Arbutus Youth Assn., San Jose 1973-74, caseworker, home supr., 1974-79, foster home director, 1979-82; director Valley Counseling Center, Dublin 1982-83; MFCC intern Growth Unltd, Pleasanton 1982-86, also cons., and tchr. lay-counselor tng.; faculty Azusa Pacific Univ., San Jose 1982-; clinical svs. director Advent Group Ministries, San Jose 1987-, tchr., lay-counselor tnr. Relational Resources, Scotts Valley 1981-89, mem. bd. 1987-; ldr. seminar: To Trust or Not to Trust, 1987; mem: Calif. Assn. Marriage Fam. Therapists, CAPS; civic: school site coun., and carnival co-chair Ben Lomond 1987-, 1988-, Awana ldr., and curriculum coun. Felton 1985-86, 1988-; pub. research: Emotionality Affects Sch. Performance 1973; Democrat; Christian. Res: Box 477 Brookdale 95007 Ofc: Relational Resources 3060 Valencia Ste 7 Aptos 95003

MILLER, EMERSON WALDO, accountant, financial and management consultant; b. Jan. 27, 1920, Green Island, Jamaica, W.I., nat. 1957; s. Adolphus Eustace and Catherine Sarah (Dixon) M.; m. Olive Claire Ford, Apr. 10, 1945; children: Cheryll b. 1945, Hellena b. 1947, Emerson b. 1949, Oliver (Rhodes Scholar 1978) b. 1953, Donald b. 1957, Selwyn b. 1960; edn: student Univ. of Toronto Ext. 1938-43, UC Berkeley 1950-61; BS, State Univ. of NY, Albany 1976; BA, Charter Oak Coll. 1979; ACI dip., Inst. of Commerce (London, Eng.) 1941; FAE dip., (cf. MBA/ CPA), Intern. Acct. & Exec. Corp. of Can. 1945; FFCS dip., Faculty of Sec. & Admin. (Guilford, Surrey, Eng.) 1945; ACEA dip., Assn. of Cost. & Exec. Accts. (London) 1982. Career: cost acct. Poirier & Mclane Corp., NYC 1941-42; principal Emerson Miller & Co., Intern. Acct., Chartered, Kingston, Jamaica W.I. 1942-49; lectr., acctg. & bus. law, Jamaica Sch. of Commerce, Kingston, Jamaica W.I. 1945-48; Tax Examiner/ Conferee Internal Revenue Svc., S.F. 1963-64, sect. chief 1965-70, branch chief 1970-84; maj. segment fin. mgmt. activities Gen. Svc. Admin., US Govt., S.F., Credit Com. chmn. 1969-81, treas. 1981-; dir. 1982- VARO-SF Fed Credit Union, S.F.; prin. Emerson W. Miller, Tax, Financial, Business & Mgmt. Svcs., Edn. VP, GSA-SF chpt., Internat. Toastmasters Club 1965-68; instr., govt. acctg., GSA-SF 1966-69; mem. Mgmt. Improvement Com., Fed. Exec. Bd. 1973-74; pres. S.F. chpt. Assn. of Govt. Accts. 1973-74; honors: GSA Special Achiev. 1969; mem: Am. Acct. Assn., Nat. Assn. Accts., Assn. of Govt. Accts. (SF chpt. pres. 1973-74), Am. Mgmt. Assn., Fin. Mgmt. Assn., British Inst. of Mgmt., Am. Judicature Assn., NY Acad. of Scis., AAAS, Inst. of Commerce (assoc. 1941), Internat. Accts. & Execs. Corp. of Canada (Fellow 1945), Faculty of Sec. & Admin. (Felow 1945), Assn. of Cost & Exec. Accts., Royal Economic Soc. (Fellow 1962); club: British Social and Athletic; publisher: Classified Buyers Dir. (Jamaica) 1948; rec: gardening, cricket. Res: 505 Coventry Rd Kensington 94707 Ofc: POB 471 Berkeley 94701

MILLER, GARY ALAN, commercial banker; b. July 4, 1943, Tempe, Ariz.; s. Lawrence J. and Marjorie F. M.; m. Bonnie Jean Welch, March 31, 1984; children: Karyn b. 1970, Matthew b. 1972, Christopher b. 1973; edn: BA, MA, Ariz. St. Univ. 1967, MA (honors), American Grad. Sch. of Internat. Mgmt., 1972. Career: resident banker Export Import Bank of U.S., WDC 1974; mktg. ofcr. Bank of Am., L.A. 1975-77, asst. v.p., Chgo., Ill. 1977-79; accts. exec., v.p. Nat. Westminster Bank 1979-83, sr. v.p., Los Angeles 1983-; lectr. Elmhurst Coll., Ill. 1978-83; mem: British Am. C.of C. (pres. 1990-91, chmn. 1991-92, dir. 1986-), N.Am. Council of Brit. Am. Bus. Assns. (pres. 1991-92), L.A. Athletic Club, Bel

Air Presbyterian Ch.; mil: 1st lt. AUS 1968-71, Bronze Star 1970, Army Commend. 1971; Republican; Presbyterian; rec: fly fishing, tennis, opera. Ofc: National Westminster Bank 400 S Hope St Ste 1000 Los Angeles 90071-2891

MILLER, GINNY (VIRGINIA) DERN, physical therapist; b. Mar. 15, Highland Park, Mich.; d. Ernest E. and Ruth (Hilgers) Dern; m. Christopher E. Miller, July 8, 1978, div. Dec. 1990; 1 child, Evan Dern b. 1985; edn: BS, Univ. Mich., Ann Arbor 1977; grad. stu. in health care adminstrn. Univ. of La Verne; reg. physical therapist (RPT) Calif. 1977. Career: staff physical therapist Saint Jude Hosp., Fullerton 1978-81, asst. dir. Pain Mgmt. 1981-84, dir. Pain Mgmt. 1984-86, tng. coord. Back to Basics 1981-86; sr. physical therapist Saint Joseph Hos., Orange 1986-87, Outpatient P.T. mgr., 1987-; awarded Orange County P.T. of Year, O.C./Am. P.T. Assn. 1985; mem. Am. P.T. Assn. (1977-, Calif. del., O.C. rep.); R.Cath.; rec: skiing, skating, sailing. Res: 2335 Paseo Circulo Tustin Ranch 92680 Ofc: Irvine Health Center, Centerstone Plaza 4050 Barranca Pkwy Irvine 92714

MILLER, HARRIET EVELYN, management consultant; b. July 4, 1919, Council, Idaho; d. Colwell and Vera (Crome) Miller; edn: BA in chemistry (magna cum laude) Whitman Coll., 1941; MA polit. sci., Univ. Pa., 1949; DHL (Hon.), Whitman Coll., 1979. Career: res. chemist Atlantic-Richfield, Phila. 1944-50; student personnel administr., assoc. prof. and assoc. dean of students Univ. Montana, Missoula, 1950-56; elected Supt. of Pub. Instrn., State of Montana, 1956-69; mgmt. cons., pres. Harriet Miller Assocs., Helena, Mont. 1969-75; assoc. director Am. Assn. Retired Persons/Nat. Retired Tchrs. Assn., Wash. DC, 1975-76, exec. director 1976-77; mgmt. cons. 1977-; exec. dir. US Occupational Safety and Health Rev. Commn., Wash. DC, 1979-81; pres. HMA, Inc., mgmt. consulting firm, 1984-88; commr. Santa Barbara County Parole Commn. 1981-84; commr. Housing Auth. City of Santa Barbara 1982-87, chair 1984-86; elected Santa Barbara City Council 1987-; awards: disting. libr. svc. Mont. Library Assn., spl. award for leadership and svc. in tng. of firemen Mont. State Fire Chiefs Assn., outstanding svc. to Job Corps Office of Economic Opp., "Morning Star Woman" Hon. mem.: Blackfeet Indian Tribe; mem. bd. overseers Whitman Coll., 1983-; lectr. and author numerous articles, speaker nat. and internat. confs. incl. White House Confs. on Edn., Ednl. Demo. Tour Germany, Internat. Symp. on Housing and Environmental Design, W.D.C., UN Sem. on Financing Housing, Geneva, Internat. Council of Homehelp Svs., Frankfurt, Internat. Conf. on Volunteerism, Vienna, Internat. Fedn. on Aging Conf., Madid; mem: Homes for People, Channel City Women's Forum, Shelter Svs. for Women, Get Oil Out, Humane Soc. U.S., AAUW, Delta Kappa Gamma, Phi Kappa Phi, Psi Chi, Phi Beta Kappa, Gray Panthers; local bds.: Comm. Action Commn. 1987-, United Against Crime 1989-, Heath House for people with AIDS 1989-, Westside Neighborhood Med. Clinic 1981-; Unitarian (past trustee). Address: PO Box 1346 Santa Barbara 93102 Tel: 805/564-5319

MILLER, JERRY, university president; b. June 15, 1931, Salem, Oh.; s. Duber Daniel and Ida Claire (Holdereith) M.; m. Margaret Annette Setter, May 30, 1958; children: Gregory b. 1959, Joy b. 1961, Carol b. 1962, Beth b. 1967, David b. 1971; edn: BA, Harvard Univ., 1953; MDiv, Hamma Sch. of Theol., 1957; DD, Trinity Lutheran Sem., 1981; ordained minister Evangelical Lutheran Ch. in America (ELCA) 1957. Career: instr. Wittenberg Univ., Springfield, Oh. 1955-56; res. assoc., intern Cornell Univ., 1956-57; parish pastor Good Shepherd Ch., Cinti. 1957-62; asst. to pres. Ohio Synod (LCA) Columbus, Oh. 1962-66; senior campus pastor and dir. campus ministry Univ. Wis., Madison 1966-69; reg. dir. Nat. Lutheran Campus Ministry, Madison, Wis. 1969-76, and nat. dir., Chgo., Ill. 1977-81; pres. Calif. Lutheran Univ., Thousand Oaks, Calif. 1981-; bd. dirs. Wittenberg Univ., Augustana Coll.; mem: Council of Indep. Colls., Assoc. Indep. Calif. Colls. & Univs. (exec. com. 1984-), Lutheran Coll. Presidents Council, Luth. Ednl. Conf. of No. Am. 1977-, Am. Assn. of Higher Edn., Council for Advance. & Support of Edn., Harvard Alumni Assn.; honors: man of yr. Salem, Ohio 1974, Siebert Found. fellow for study and travel 1975, listed Who's Who in Midwest, Who's Who in Religion 1975, Who's Who in Am. 1987; mem. civic bds.: T.O. Rotary Club, YMCA, Los Robles Hosp., C.of C., United Way, Am. Red Cross Ventura Co.; rec: skiing, golf, hiking, travel. Ofc: California Lutheran Univ. 60 W Olsen Rd Thousand Oaks 91360

MILLER, JON PHILIP, biomedical research laboratories executive; b. Mar. 30, 1944, Moline, Ill.; s. Clyde Sheldon and Alice Lenora (Taes) M.; m. Shirley Ann Hymes, Aug. 21, 1965; children: Melissa b. 1968, Elizabeth b. 1971; edn: AB, Augustana Coll., Rock Is., Ill. 1966; PhD, St. Louis Univ., Mo. 1970; MBA, Pepperdine Univ., Malibu. 1983. Career: res. assoc., sr. biochemist, hd. molecular pharm. group, hd. mol. pharm. & drug metabolism dept. dir. biology div., ICN Pharmaceuticals Inc., Irvine, Calif. 1970-75; SRI Internat., Menlo Park 1974-92: senior bioorganic chem. 1976-78, hd. medical biochem. pgm. 1978-82, assoc. dir., dir. Biomedical Res. Lab. 1982-86, 1986-89, also dir. Biotech. Dept. 1983-89, assoc. dir. Life Sciences Div. 1990-92; regional dir. Panlabs Inc., Foster City 1992-; Indep.; R.Cath.; rec: history, writing, poetry. Ofc: 101 Lincoln Center Dr 4th Fl Foster City CA 94404

MILLER, PAUL JAMES, coffee company executive; b. Aug. 23, 1939, San Mateo; s. Paul and Rita M.; m. Patricia Ann Deruette, Aug. 22, 1964; children: Mike, Britt, Brian; edn: BSBA (hons.), San Jose State Univ., 1962; MBA mktg., Santa Clara Univ., 1964. Career: with Hill Bros. Coffee Inc. (acquired by Nestle 1989), San Francisco 1964-: advt. mgr., then dir. mktg. 1971-75, pres. 1975-83, chmn. bd. and c.e.o. 1983-89, pres. and c.e.o. 1989-91, pres. and c.e.o. Nestle Beverage Co. 1991-; mem: Am. Mgmt. Assn., Grocery Mfrs. Assn., Am. Better Bus. Bur. San Francisco, Conf. Board, U.S. C.of C., Calif. C.of C.; clubs: World Trade, Olympic. Res: 681 Brewer Dr Hillsborough 94010 Ofc: Nestle-Hills, Inc. 345 Spear St San Francisco 94105

MILLER, PHOEBE AMELIA, computer software marketing consultant; b. Jan. 13, 1948, Evanston, Ill.; d. William Prescott and Elizabeth Helen (Lucker) Miller; edn: BA, honors, Univ. of Wis. 1970; grad. work, Stanford Univ. 1973; MBA work, Golden Gate Univ. 1978; ICP Sales Tng. 1979. Career: optics analyst Coherent Radiation, Palo Alto 1970-72; engr. Bechtel Inc. 1972-77; asst. div. mgr. Rand Info. Systems, San Francisco 1977-79; sr. mktg. rep. Computer Scis. Corp., S.F. 1979-81; sr. mktg. cons., mgr. VAR/ distbr. Cognos Corp., Walnut Creek 1981-86; pres. P.A. Miller & Assocs. Inc., S.F. 1986-; awards: ICP Million Dollar Super Seller 1983, Cognos Sales Honor Roll 1982, 83, 84 and Pres.'s Award 1982, 83, V.P. Achiev. Club, Computer Scis. Corp. 1981, Bechtel Corp. Award of Merit for tech. contbr., listed in Who's Who of Am. Bus. Leaders 1991, World Who's Who of Women 1993, 5,000 Personalities of World; publs: contbr. Nat. Structural Engring. Conf. 1976. Res: PO Box 1027 Boca Raton FL 33429 Ofc: P.A. Miller & Assocs. Inc., 1750 Montgomery St San Francisco 94111

MILLER, ROBERT BARRY, corporate controller; b. July 23, 1942, Bernie, Mo.; s. Truman Jackson and Iris Viola (Felton) M.; m. Karen Sue Cool, Jan. 24, 1963, div. 1969; twin sons: Todd and Troy b. 1965; m. Mary Hope Teegen, May 21, 1971; 2 stepdaus.: Kristen b. 1964, Carrelle b. 1966; edn: BSBA, Univ. of Kansas, 1965; cert. acctg. Internat. Acct. Soc., Chgo. 1967; law courses Washburn Univ., 1971. Career: cost acct. Ohse Meat Products, Topeka, Ks. 1965-69, controller/treas. 1969-72; controller/treas. Falcon Rsch., div. WKR, Denver 1972-84; controller/mgr. fin. United Airlines Svs. Corp., Lakewood, Colo. 1984-88; controller/dir. fin. Whittaker Ordnance, div. WKR, Hollister, Calif. 1989-93; controller/bus. mgr. Whittaker Electronic Resources, div. WKR, Simi Valley, Calif. 1993-; mem: ADPA 1989-), DPMA (chpt. pres., treas. 1967-72), NAA (chpt. pgm. dir. 1971-72), Jaycees Topeka (treas. 1970-71); Republican; Prot.; rec: pers. computers, auto restoration. Res: PO Box 3938 Simi Valley 93093-3938 Ofc: Whittaker Electronic Resources 1955 N Surveyor Ave Simi Valley 93063

MILLER, ROBERT STEVEN, educator; b. Aug. 9, 1963, Van Nuys; s. Frederick Earl and Mary Theresa (Brash) M.; edn: AA, L.A. Valley Coll., 1984; BS bus. adm., CSU Los Angeles, 1987, MA hist., 1990. Career: adj. faculty history dept. CSU Los Angeles, 1990-92, study group leader Educational Opportunity Program; awards: Ledeboer scholar Phi Alpha Theta CSULA 1989, Jake Gimbel scholar CSULA 1990, Mu Kappa Tau mktg. hon. soc. 1987, Phi Alpha Theta hist. hon. soc. 1988; mem. Soc. for Historia of Am. Fgn. Relations 1990-, Pi Sigma Epsilon nat. mktg. frat. 1985-; editor hist. jour.: Perspectives, CSULA Hist. Dept. 1991, contbr. articles (1990, 92), contbr. Glendale Law Rev. (1991); Democrat; R.Cath. Res: 13750 Runnymede St Van Nuys 91405 Ofc: CSULA History Dept. 5151 State University Dr Los Angeles 90032

MILLER, ROSS SHELDON, consulting entomologist; b. June 2, 1919; s. Roy Oscar and Lenore (Glen) M.; m. Ruth Carter, May 6, 1944; children: Ross T. b. 1946, Paula S. b. 1945; edn: BS, UC Berkeley 1941; MS, UC Davis 1946; cert. pest control advisor Calif. Career: tech. service mgr. Cal Spray Chem. Corp., Richmond 1946-47; Turlock 1946-48; dist. mgr. United Chem. Corp., 1948-50; gen. mgr. S.A. Camp Fertilizer & Insecticide Co., Shafter 1950-52; mgr. Sunland Industries, Fresno 1952-57; FMC Corp. A.G. Chem. Group 1957-85; cons. 1985-; honors: Alpha Zeta Honor Soc., Who's Who in West 1972; mem: Am. Entomol. Soc., Registry Profl. Entomol., Calif. Crop Prod. Assn., San Joaquin Entomol. Assn., Stockdale Exchange Club, Toastmasters Internat. (past pres.), Reserve Ofcrs. Assn., Navy League of U.S. (life), Retired Ofcrs. Assn. (past pres., life), Naval Aviation Mus. Found. (life), Exchange Club, UC Alumni Assn. (life), Calif. Aggie Alumni Assn. (life), Elks, Am. Legion; contbr. articles Sugar Beet Bull. 1947-48, Implement Record 1948, Agricultural Chemicals 1965, Ariz.-Calif. Farm Press 1980-82; mil: comdr. USNR 1941-61; Republican; Presbyterian; rec: skin diving, gardening, woodwork. Address: 2830 21st St Bakersfield 93301

MILLER, STANLEY RAY, sound system consultant; b. Oct. 25, 1940, Lincoln, Nebr.; s. Maurice Winston and Blanche Fern (Mosier) M.; div.; children: Cordie Lynne b. 1967, Neil Andrew b. 1971; edn: BA, Kearney State Coll. 1965. Career: cons. engr./audio mixer for sound systems and concerts; founder/pres./c.e.o. Stanal Sound Ltd., 1962-89; founder/c.e.o. Sound Mfg. Inc., 1987-; hd. R&D and mfg. of JBL Concert Series; sound system cons. to MCA Concerts, Inc.; chief live concert mixing engr. for Neil Diamond, 1967-, designed, mfd. and toured large sound systems, worldwide 1964-, for Simon &

Garfunkel, Johnny Cash, Christy Minstrels, Young Americans, Bill Cosby, Mac Davis, Dolly Parton, Pink Floyd, Bob Dylan, John Denver, The Osmond Brothers, Donnie & Marie Osmond, Tom Jones and Englebert Humperdink; dir. sound services L.A. theatres: Greek, Pantages, Wilshire, Henry Fonda, Universal Amphitheatre, and Fidler's Green, Denver; supplied sound system for Papal visit L.A., 9/87; sound system designer and supplier to 1984 Olympics; sound designer audio systems for Republican Nat. Convs. 1984, 88; audio cons. to Tour de Trump Intl. Bicycle Race, 5/90; respons. for functional design of 10+ different models of Yamaha Sound Mixing Consoles and other products for Concert Sound Indus.; lectr. on touring sound systems numerous colls., nat. convs. of Audio Engring. Soc., nat. tng. meetings of Altec Sound Contr.-Dealers, JBL Sound Conf. 1989; awards: Kearney State Coll. outstanding alumni award 1986, nom. by Mix Magazine TEC (Technical Excellence & Creativity) sound reinf. engr. 1993; mem. Audio Engring. Soc. 1958-, Profl. Entertainment Prodn. Soc. (treas.), BPOE Lodge 984; Republican; Lutheran. Res: 3336 Primera Ave Hollywood 90068 Ofc: Sound Manufacturing, Inc. 7351 Fulton Ave N Hollywood 91605

MILLER, THOMAS EUGENE, editor, writer; b. Jan. 4, 1929, Bryan, Tx.; s. Eugene Adam and Ella Lucille (Schroeder) M.; edn: BA, Tx. A&M Univ., 1950; MA, Univ. of Tx., 1956; Univ. of Houston, 1956-58; JD, Univ. of Tx., 1966; admitted Tx. State Bar 1966; UC Berkeley, 1983. Career: res. tech., Univ. of Tx. M. D. Anderson Hosp., Houston 1956-58; claims examiner trainee, Social Security Adminstrn., New Orleans 1963; trademark examiner trainee, Dept. of Commerce, Wash., DC 1966; ed., Bancroft-Whitney, S.F. 1966-92; free lance writer, 1975-; deputy dir. gen., Internat. Biog. Assn. 1986-; awards: Phi Eta Sigma, Univ. of Tx. 1947; Phi Kappa Phi, Tx. A&M Univ. 1950; Psi Chi, Univ. of Tx. 1953; Grand Ambassador of Achievement, Internat. Biog. Assn. 1986; Medal of Honor 1988; Man of the Year, Am. Biog. Inst. 1990; Internat. Man of the Year 1992/93; World Intellectual of 1993; mem: Tx. Bar Assn. 1966-, Am. Bar Assn. 1966-, World Literary Acad. 1986-, Nat. Writers Club 1980-, Nat. Assn. of Legal Editors & Writers 1991-92, Am. Soc. of Legal Writers 1992-, Press Club of S.F. (vice chair 1986), Commonwealth Club S.F., World Affairs Council S.F., Internat. Platform Assn. Wash., DC; author: book publ. under pseudonym, 1984; numerous legal articles, 1966-; ed., numerous legal articles; Democrat; Methodist; rec: travel, walking, theater, music. Res: 101 N. Haswell Dr., Bryan, TX 77803

MILLER, VIRGIL LEE, detective agency owner; b. June 27, 1920, Sedalia, Mo.; s. John Ernest and Mary Leona (Webb) M.; m. Kathlyn Virginia Swope, Nov. 11, 1941 (dec. 1971); m. Mildred Elaine Dotson, Dec. 30, 1972; children: Virginia b. 1937, Beverly b. 1940, Richard b. 1942, Dixie b. 1942, Virgil, Jr. b. 1950; edn: LLB, Amer. Sch. Law, Chgo. 1951; BTH, Fundamental Christian Coll., K.C., Mo. 1958, MTh 1960, DTh 1961; ordained minister So. Baptist Ch.; lic. investigator Calif.; cert. profl. investigator (CPI) Calif. Assn. Lic. Investigators Inc. 1988. Career: firefighter Fed. Civil Service, Sedalia AFB, Mo. 1942-55, fire chief in Kans., Mont., Calif., Guam, 1955-73; pastor Baptist churches in Kans., Mont., Calif., Guam 1957-75; owner/mgr. Reliable Detective Agy., Riverside 1976-; recipient superior performance awards Dept. Air Force (1964-65, 1966-67), outstanding honor grad. Tech. Tng. Ctr. Chanute, Ill. 1968; mem: Internat. Assn. of Fire Chiefs, Calif. Assn. Fire Chiefs, Am. Legion Post 289, Calif. Assn. Lic. Investigators, ION; Oddfellows Riverside Lodge 282 (noble grand 1989-90, Dist. 51 dist. dep. grand master 1991-92); mil: sgt. AUS 1939-42; Democrat; Baptist; rec hunting, fishing. Ofc: V.L. Miller, Investigations, 9391 California Ave Ste 37 Riverside 92503

MILLS, BASIL EUGENE, agri-business executive; b. Jan. 18, 1930, Montevideo, Minn.; s. Charles E. and Mary Clare (Brainard) M.; m. Evangeline C., July 2, 1955; children: David G., James L., Susan Elizabeth, Katherine Anne; edn: S.E. Mo. St. Univ., Cape Girardeau 1948, Univ. Colo., Boulder 1948-51. Career: produce buyer Walter S. Markham, Salinas 1953-55; lettuce salesman Royal Packing Co., Salinas 1955-58; pres. Mills Dist. Co., Salinas 1958-; appt. Calif. Iceberg Lettuce Commn. (commr. 1978-92, chmn. 1986-88); mem. bds.: Western Growers Assn. (dir. 1985-), Grower-Shipper Vegetable Assn. of Central Calif. (dir. 1988-93, chmn. 1991-92); honors: Salinas citizen of year 1989, Salinas bus. excellence award Agribus. Div. 1988; civic: Salinas Rotary Club (pres. 1988-89), Salvation Army (dir.), Community Found. for Monterey County (v. p.), Legal Services for Seniors (Coun. of Advisors), Meals on Wheels of Salinas (advy. bd.), Center for Community Advocacy (bd. dirs.); mil: sgt. AUS 7th Army Hq. Stuttgart, W.Ger. 1951-53; Republican; Episcopalian; rec: golf, reading. Res: 298 Corral De Tierra Rd Salinas 93908 Ofc: Mills Distributing Co. PO Box 3070 Salinas 93912

MIR, CARL J., accountant; b. May 14, 1956, New York; s. Jorge E. and Carmen (Diaz) M.; m. Norma Hallado, Aug. 29, 1981; d. Carissa b. 1982, s. Christopher Andrew b. 1993; edn: BA, USC, 1979. Career: Ralphs Grocery Co., Compton, staff accountant 1984-85, supr. 1985-89, asst. mgr. 1989-; honors: Alpha Mu Gamma, Delta Phi Epsilon, Delta Alpha Psi, listed Who's Who Among Hispanic Americans (1991, 93), 2000 Notable Am. Men (1991), Who's Who In Poetry (1992); mem: USC Alumni Assn. (life), Nat. Assn. Accountants; publs: contbr. World of Poetry (1979, 80, 88), Magill's Survey of Cinema (1980); R.Cath.; rec: photog. Address: Downey 90242

MISCHAK, ROBERT MICHAEL, JR., corporate controller; b. Feb. 17, 1958, Plainfield, N.J.; s. Robert M., Sr. and Doris (Marinelli) M.; m. Melissa Patterson Neofes, Sept. 28, 1991; edn: BSBA, Georgetown Univ., 1980; MS, Golden Gate Univ., 1988. Career: corp. banking ofcr. Lloyds Bank Calif., Oakland 1981-82; controller Los Angeles Raiders, El Segundo 1982-83; John Brooks & Co., San Leandro 1983-85; tax assoc. Suttle D'Aquisto & Rowbotham, San Francisco 1985-89; controller Groupe Andre Perry, Ltd., Orinda 1989-90; Altman & Manley, San Francisco 1990-91; Citron Haligman Bedecarre, San Francisco 1991-; publs: article in Sports & Entertainment Lawyer (1989). Ofc: Citron Haligman Bedecarre, 855 Front St San Francisco 94111

MITCHELL, THOMAS EDWARD, JR., marketing information co. executive, retired military officer; b. Apr. 12, 1946, Sacramento; s. Thomas Edward, Sr. and Violet Mae (Southall) M.; m. Terri K. Vance, Apr. 20, 1968; children: Anthony b. 1969, Brian b. 1972; edn: BBA, 1987, MBA, 1988. Career: enlisted ofcr., served to Maj. U.S. Marine Corps (Ret.) 1966-89, assignments all levels of govt. up to Jt. Chiefs of Staff, UN Command, and the Foreign Service; chief tactics instr. USMC, OCS, Quantico, Va. 1973-74; decorated Battlefield Commn. Viet Nam S.E. Asia 1968, Silver Star Viet Nam 1968, DOD Merit. Service Seoul, Korea 1985, JCS Commendation. Medal UN Cmd. 1984, Navy Commendation. Medal Camp Pendleton 1983; exec. Equifax Marketing Decision Systems, mktg. info. co., Encinitas 1989-; dir: Cal-Pacific Steel Structures, Inc., Hawaii and Calif.; honors: Calif. Jr. Coll. Student Govt. Assn./Sacramento v. p. 1965-66; civic: Toys for Tots, Orange Co. (dir. 1974-77), support youth activities, comm. charities; profl. publs.; Republican; Prot.; avocation: internat. affairs. Res: 3264 Chase Ct Oceanside 92056 Ofc: Equifax Marketing Decision Systems, 5375 Sorrento Mesa Pl. Ste. 400 San Diego 92021

MITROFF, NORMAN S., psychologist; b. Aug. 28, 1942, S.F., Calif.; s. Joseph and Mabel M.; children: David b. 1973, Stephen b. 1975; edn: BA, S.F. State Univ., S.F., Calif. 1966, MS, 1968; PhD., Univ. of Portland, Portland, Ore. 1971. Career: psychologist, private practice, Novato, Calif. 1973-; vocat. psychologist, Dept. of Vocat. Rehab., S.F. 1973-78; police psychologist, Fairfax Police Dept., Fairfax, Calif. 1976-86; instr., S.F. State Univ. 1974-75; awards: Diplomate, Am. Bd. of Profl. Psychologists 1976; Certified Sex Therapist, AASECT 1978; Silver Psi, Calif. State Psychol. Assn., 1980; Qualified Med. Evaluator, DIR, Calif. 1991; mem: (past sec.) Calif. State Psychol. Assn.,1971-; (past Pres.) Marin County Psychol. Assn. 1975-; chair, Calif./We., ABPP 1977-81; pres. CPHP 1984-87; author: profl. jour. article 1973, profl. papers on Workers Comp. 1988, 89, 93; rec: racquetball. Ofc: 1025 Fifth St. Novato 94945

MIXON, DAVID G., corporate finance executive; b. Sept. 18, 1952, Tampa, Fla.; s. David S. Waters and Eve Shaw (remarried G. Mixon); m. Deborah, Sept. 10, 1982; children: Shelley, Kristen; edn: BS, Univ. Santa Clara, 1974; MBA, National Univ., 1988; notary pub. Calif. 1986. Career: branch asst., asst. mgr. Fireside Thrift Co., Newark 1974-76, auditor 1976-79, asst. controller 1979-82, controller 1982-84, asst. treas. 1984-85; v.p./controller First Interstate Financial Services Inc., San Diego 1985-90; exec.v.p. finance & data processing Santel Federal Credit Union, San Diego, 1991-; treas. Executive House Assn., Santa Clara 1981-83; mem: Am. Mgmt. Assn., Nat. Corporate Cash Mgrs. Assn.; Republican; rec: skiing, swimming, tennis, golf. Res: 11052 Pinzon Way Rancho Bernardo 92127 Ofc: 5890 Pacific Center Blvd San Diego 92121

MIZE, ROBERT HERBERT, JR., clergyman (ret.); b. Feb. 4, 1907, Emporia, Kans.; s. Robert Herbert and Margaret Talman (Moore) M.; edn: BA, Univ. of Kans., Lawrence, Kans., 1928; General Theol. Sem., NY, NY, 1929-32; STD, General Theol. Sem., 1960. Career: dir., Gen. Sem. Assoc. Mission, Episcopal Ch., Hays, Kans. 1933-41; vicar, St. Stephen's Episcopal Ch., Wakeeney, Kans. 1941-45; founder, dir., St. Francis Boys Homes, Ellsworth & Salina, Kans. 1945-60; bishop of Namibia, Anglican Ch., Windhock, Namibia 1960-68; asst. bishop in Botswana, Anglican Ch., Gaberone, Botswana 1968-70, 73-76; asst. bishop, Diocese of San Joaquin, Episcopal Ch., Fresno, Calif. 1977-89; pres., Boys Homes Assn. of Am. 1958-59; awards: Phi Beta Kappa, Univ. of Kans. 1928; Disting. Svc. Citation, Univ. of Kans. 1954; subject of book, Father Bob and His Boys, by Emily Gardiner Neal, 1960; Episcopal. Res: 530 W. Floradora Apt. 318 Fresno 93728. Ofc: Diocese of San Joaquin 4159 E. Dakota Fresno 93726

MIZUNO, NOBUKO SHIMOTORI, biochemist; b. Apr. 20, 1916, Oakland; d. Shinichiro and Kii (Niyomura) Shimotori; m. Walter Masami, Mar. 20, 1942 (dec. Aug. 10, 1946); edn: BA, UC Berkeley, 1937, MA, 1939; PhD in biochem., Univ. Minn., 1956. Career: research asst. UC Berkeley, 1939-41; instr. Macalester Coll., St. Paul, Minn. 1943-51; research assoc. Univ. Minn., St. Paul 1956-62, Mpls. 1964-79; research biochemist Veterans Adminstrn. Med. Ctr., Mpls. 1962-79, ret.; awards: NSF fellow 1955-56; mem.: Am. Inst. Nutrition 1963-, Am. Soc. Biochem. Mol. Biology 1974-, Am. Assn. Cancer Res. 1963-79, Soc. Experimental Biology Medicine 1971-79, Iota Sigma Pi (nat. sec., historian 1963-72); author, contbr. 50+ revs. and jour. articles in J. Biol. Chem., Science, Biochem., Biochem. Pharmacol., Cancer Res., Chem.-Biol. Interactions, Cancer Chemo. Reports, Proc. Soc. Exptl. Biol. Med., J. Nutrition, Blood, Nature, others. Res: 3628 Loma Way San Diego 92106

MOBLEY, JONNIEPAT MOORE, theatre instructor; b. Aug. 1, 1932, Detroit, Mich.; d. John Patrick and Charlotte P. (Tillman) Moore; m. Dwight Mobley; 1 dau., Eve; edn: BA, Mount St. Mary's Coll., 1962; MA, CSU Los Angeles, 1964; PhD, USC, 1974. Career: instr. Mount St. Mary's Coll., L.A. 1963-67; prof. West L.A. Coll., 1969-78; prof. theatre arts Cuesta Coll., San Luis Obispo 1985-; dir. of plays: Parish Players, S.L.O., 1982, Mission Prep, S.L.O., 1983, 1985; honors: Outstanding Young Women of Am. 1965; mem.: ALPHA 1985-, PETA 1990-; author: NTC's Dictionary of Theatre and Drama Terms (1992). Ofc: Cuesta College San Luis Obispo 93403

MOBLEY, ROBERT WESLEY, real estate investor, naval aviation electronics trainer, administrator; b. Dec. 5, 1925, Jerome, Idaho; s. Frank Kenneth and Blanche Alice (Wasson) M.; m. Rosalie Naglik, June 3, 1950; children: Mark b. 1951, Diane b. 1952; edn: McDonnell Aircraft Co. schs. on aircraft sys. maintenance. 1964-65; Litton Ind. solid state computer sch. 1979; grad. mil. tng. schs. Navy/Marine Corps F/A-18, Electric/Instrument and Flight. Control Systems, Jan. 1990. Career: field svc. engr., assoc. McDonnell Aircraft Co., St. Louis, Mo. 1964-66; field svc. assoc. engr. AiResearch Mfg. Co., Torrance 1966-71; electronics tech. supr. Dept. of Navy Naval Aviation Engring. Svc. Unit., Phila. 1971-, train mil. technicians in electronic computer & sys. installed in aircraft; lectr. pilots on sys. fundamentals and ops.; founder, prin. RMR Enterprises, real estate investment and discount travel agent, 1991-; honors: num. letters of accomplishment from military commands; mem: South Orange County C.of C., USN Fleet Reserve Assn., Internat. Order of Foresters, Internat. Platform Assn.; works: designed new test bench and wrote test procedures to improve ops. of aircraft computers; mil: E-7 Chief USN 1943-64, gen. medals; Democrat; Lutheran; rec: model trains. Res: 27271 Nubles Mission Viejo 92692 Ofc: Naval Aviation Engineering Service Unit, MCAS El Toro, Santa Ana 92709

MODE, V. ALAN, research executive, inorganic chemist, computer scientist; b. May 25, 1940, Gilroy; s. Vincent Alan and Jewel (Clary) M.; m. Sue A. Oleson, Feb. 14, 1964 (div. 1975); m. Jackie Sue Hill, Dec. 23, 1976; 1 dau., Nicolle A. b. 1969; edn: BA magna cum laude, Whitman Coll. 1962; PhD inorganic chemistry, Univ. Ill. 1965; MBA, Golden Gate Univ. 1980. Career: chemist Lawrence Livermore Nat. Lab., Livermore 1965-69, group leader 1969-72, section leader 1972-80, facility mgr. 1984-85, dep. assoc. dir. 1985-; exec. dir. BC Research Council, Vancouver, Canada 1980-84; BC Sci. Council 1982-84; honors: Outstanding Young Men Am., Alfred P. Sloan nat. scholar 1958-62, Ford tchg. fellow 1960-62, Sigma Xi; mem: Am. Mgmt. Assn.; 50+ articles pub. in profl. jours.; rec: gardening, square dancing. Ofc: LLNL, Box 808/L-580 Livermore 94550

MOEN, JOHN THOMAS, lawyer, educator; b. Feb. 7, 1923, Annapolis, Md.; s. Naval Adm. Arthur Thomas and Florence Serena (McCook) M.; m. Avis Wee, Dec. 12, 1953; children: Ava b. 1956, Mary b. 1958, Julie b. 1960; edn: grad. USN Midshipman Sch., 1944; BA and JD, USC, 1944; LLB, Univ. of Mont., 1952; M.Div., Wartburg Theol. Sem., 1967. Career: asst. to Mr. Knutson, law firm Salisbury & Knutson, Los Angeles 1950-52; sr. ptnr. law firm Peterson & Moen, splst. corp. and trial work, Long Beach and Orange Co., 1953-79; sr. ptnr. Moen, Montgomery & Golden, Fullerton, 1980-91; of counsel Geiger & Weber, Santa Ana Hts., 1991-; law prof. Pacific Coast Law Sch. 1953-55, We. State Law Sch. 1968-72, Simon Greenleaf Sch. of Law 1980-; assoc. pastor St. Marks Lutheran Ch., Hacienda Hts., 1972-, pres. Lutheran Credit Union, 1975-, mem. bd. dirs. Southland Lutheran Home, Norwalk, bd. dirs. Lutheran Lay Renewal; awards: Inter-fraternity Scholar, USC 1943, hon. life mem. 4th Dist. PTA, hon. life mem. Kiwanis Internat.; mem: Visiting Nurses of Long Beach (past dir., legal counsel), Lions Internat., Am. Red Cross (chmn.), United Fund (chmn.), Loyal Knights of the Round Table (pres.), Garden Grove C.of C. (dir.), Civil Defense Pgm. of Garden Grove (chmn.), leader Boy Scouts Am. (v. chmn. Long Beach Area Council, Orange Empire Council chmn. citizens com. to send Scouts to Mexico 1964, and chmn. Las Bolsas Dist., chpt. adv. Order of the Arrow), PTA (advy. bd. 4th Dist.), Orange Co. Lutheran High Sch. Assn. (advy. com.), Phi Sigma Kappa, Delta Theta Phi, Alpha Phi Omega, Legion Lex, Trojan Squires, Inter-frat. Scholarship Com.; mil: lt. comdr. USN 1943-46; Republican; rec: golf, tennis, swim. Res: 3061 Lakeview Circle Fullerton 92635 Ofc: Geiger & Weber, 20301 Acacia St Ste 150 Santa Ana Hts 92707-5459

MOERBEEK, STANLEY LEONARD, lawyer; b. Nov. 12, 1951, Toronto, Canada; nat. 1963; s. John Jacob and Mary Emily (Giroux) M.; m. Carol Annette Mordaunt, April 17, 1982; children: Sarah b. 1985, Noah b. 1987; edn: BA, CSU Fullerton 1974; JD, Loyola Law Sch. 1979; admitted St. Bar Calif. 1980. Career: law clk., atty., assoc. McAlpin Doonan & Seese, Covina 1977-81; atty., assoc. Robert L. Baker, Pasadena 1981-82; Miller Bush & Minnott, Fullerton 1982-83; sole practice, Fullerton 1984-; honors: Governor's Scholar (1970), Phi Kappa Phi, lt. gov. ABA Law Student Div., 9th cir. 1979, Kiwanis Plaque of Appreciation 1983, Orange Co. Superior Ct. Cert. Appreciation 1984-88; mem. Calif. Assn. of Realtors Atty. Referral Panel; mem: Heritage Found., Orange Co. Bar Assn., Orange Co. Superior Ct. Pro Tem Panel; Republican; R.Cath.; rec: gardening, sports. Ofc: 1370 N Brea Blvd Ste 210 Fullerton 92635

MOFFATT, JOYCE ANNE, ballet company executive director; b. Jan. 3, 1936, Grand Rapids, Mich.; d. John Barnard and Ruth Lillian (Pellow) M.; edn: BA in Eng. lit., Univ. Mich., 1957, MA in theater, 1960; HHD (hon.) Sch. Psychology, S.F. 1991. Career: stage mgr., lighting designer Off Broadway; costume, lighting and set designer, stage mgr. Stock; subscription mgr. Phoenix Theatre, NY, NY 1963-65; nat. subscription mgr. Theatre Guild/Am. Theater Soc., NY, NY 1965-67; dir. ticket sales City Center of Music and Drama Inc., NY, NY 1967-73, subscription mgr. NY City Ballet and NY City Opera, asst. house mgr. NY State Theater, Lincoln Ctr.; prodn. mgr., gen. mgr. San Antonio Symphony/Opera, Texas 1973-76; gen. mgr. 55th Street Dance Theater Found. Inc., NY, NY 1976-77; gen. mgr. Ballet Theatre Found. Inc., American Ballet Theatre, NY, NY 1977-81; tour mgr. Jerome Robbins Chamber Dance Co. to P.R.O.China under Cultural Exch. Agreement, June-Oct. 1981; v.p. prodn. Radio City Music Hall, NY, NY 1981-83; dir. ops. Cal Performances (4 facilities) UC Berkeley, Calif. 1984-86; performing arts mgmt. cons., prin. Joyce A. Moffatt, Inc., NY, NY 1983-88; v.p. and gen. mgr. San Francisco Ballet Assn., S.F. 1987-; lectr. Yale Univ. MFA pgm., 1980; artist-in-res. City Coll. CUNY, 1981; appt. on site evaluator Nat. Endowment for the Arts, City S.F. Cultural Task Force 1991, dance panel Calif. Arts Council (3 yrs.), dance panel NY St. Council on Arts (3 yrs.); trustee Am. Guild Musical Artists Pension and Welfare Funds; bd. S.F. Bay Area Dance Coalition; bd. S.F. Conv. and Visitors Bur.; mem: Assn. Theatrical Press Agents and Mgrs., Actors Equity Assn., United Scenic Artists Local 829 (lighting), Internat. Alliance Theatrical State Employees Local B-18. Address: 8 Fountain St San Francisco 94114

MOFFITT, CHARLES TUTHILL, corporate chief financial executive; b. Oct. 21, 1942, Orange, Calif.; s. Robert Lovering and Martha Eleanor (Tuthill) M.; m. Gina Gilbert, May 12, 1979; children: (twins) Emily and Julia, b. 1982, Evan b. 1992; edn: BA, UC Los Angeles 1964; MA, Univ. of Wash., Seattle 1966. Career: fgn. svc. ofcr. US Dept. of State 1967-70; spl. asst. to majority leadership US House of Reps. 1970-73; exec. asst. to Mayor of Los Angeles 1973-75; ofcr. United Calif. Bank 1975-79; exec. v.p. Central L.A. Trading Inc. 1979-81; pvt. cons. 1981-82; pres. ST Internat. Inc. 1983-86, Digital Hydraulics Corp. 1984, pres. Lester/Moffitt Inc. 1986-88; CFO, Olympia Industrial, Azusa 1988-; mem: L.A. Com. on Fgn. Relations., Turnaround Mgt. Assn.

MOHOLY, NOEL FRANCIS, clergyman; b. May 26, 1916, San Francisco; s. John Joseph and Eva Gertrude (Cippa) M.; edn: grad. St. Anthony's Seminary, Santa Barbara; S.T.D., Faculte de Theologie, Universite Laval, Quebec, Can. 1948; joined Franciscan Friars, 1935, ordained priest Roman Catholic Ch., 1941. Career: tchr. fundamental theology Old Mission Santa Barbara, 1942-43, sacred theology 1947-58; tchr. languages St. Anthony's Sem. 1943-44; nat. and internat. authority on Saint Irenaeus, Mariology, Calif. history (esp. Fr. Junipero Serra), occupied num. pulpits, asst. in several Franciscan Retreat Houses, retreat master San Damiano Retreat, Danville 1964-67; adminstr. (in U.S.) Cause of Padre Junipero Serra, 1950-55, vice postulator, 1958-, pres. Fr. Junipero Serra 250th Anniversary Assn. Inc. 1964-; condr. series illustrated lectures on cause of canonization of Padre Junipero Serra in all Franciscan study houses in U.S., summer 1952, also lectr. various clubs of Serra Internat. in U.S., Europe and Far East, on NBC-TV in documentary with Edwin Newman "Padre Serra, Founding Father" (1985), PBS-TV on Firing Line with Wm. F. Buckley "Junipero Serra- Saint or Sinner" (1989), CBS, ABC bdcsts., also conducted own local TV series; dir. Old Spanish Days Ins Santa Barbara Inc., 1948-58; mem. building com. for restoration of the hist. facade and towers of Old Mission Santa Barbara, 1950-54, exec. dir./treas. Old Mission Restoration Project, 1954-58; apptd: Calif. Hist. Landmarks Advy. Com. 1962-71, U.S. Mint Annual Assay Commn. 1964, Calif. Bicentennial Celebration Commn. 1967-70, Calif. Hist. Resources Commn. 1971-76, Serra Bicentennial Commn. (pres. 1983-86); decorated Knight Comdr. Order of Isabella la Catolica (Spain, 1965), hon. citizen Petra de Mallorca 1969, Palma de Mallorca 1976, Cross of Merit Sovereign Mil. Order of Knights of Malta 1989; mem: Mariology Soc. Am., Native Sons Golden West, Associacion de los Amigos de Padre Serra, Kts. Col., Calif. Missions Study Assn.; author: Our Last Chance (1931), Saint Irenaeus the Father of Mariology (1952), The California Mission Story (1975), The First Californian (1976), (w. Don DeNevi) Junipero Serra (1985); producer phonograph records: Songs of the Calif. Missions (1951), Christmas at Mission Santa Barbara (1953), St. Francis Peace Record (1957); producer film: The Founding Father of the West (1976). Res./Ofc: Rev. Noel Francis Moholy, O.F.M., Serra Cause Old Mission Santa Barbara 93105-3611

MOLENKAMP, CHARLES R., atmospheric physicist; b. Aug. 26, 1941, San Francisco; s. Charles and Sophia H. (Lappinga) M.; m. Margaret J. Wattron, Aug. 26, 1967; children: Robin b. 1970, William b. 1974; edn: BS, Calvin Coll., 1963; MS, Univ. Ariz., Tucson 1967, PhD, 1972. Career: physicist Lawrence Livermore Nat. Lab., 1972-; honors: Phi Beta Kappa 1972; mem.: Am. Meteorol. Soc. 1969-, Am. Scientific Affiliation 1980-, Am. Assn. for Aerosol Research 1989-; publs: 17+ jour. articles. Ofc: Lawrence Livermore National Lab. L-262 PO Box 808 Livermore 94550

MOLINA, JOHN CHARLES, lawyer, state economic opportunity program administrator, bilingual and migrant education specialist; b. Feb. 28, 1929, Redlands; s. Frank Saenz and Paula (Mesa) M.; m. Sally Boehm, Aug. 10, 1973 (div. 1981); children: Mark b. 1952, Rene b. 1975; m. Berta Figueroa, Dec. 29, 1990; edn: BA edn. and English, San Diego St. Univ., 1951, MA sch. adminstrn., 1956; PhD, Calif. Western Univ., 1968; JD, Southwestern Univ. Sch. of Law, 1980; Calif. tchg. credentials: Life elem. and sec., Life sch. adminstrn.; admitted bar Calif. 1982. Career: asst. bur. chief Div. Intergroup Relations, St. Dept. Edn., Sacto., 1967-70; asst. secty. Office of Bilingual Edn. and Minority Language Affairs, US Dept. Edn., Wash. DC, 1970-78; asst. dean Sch. of Edn., USC, Los Angeles, 1978-81; nat. dir. Migrant Edn., US Dept. Edn., Wash. DC, 1981; spl. asst. to VP/Dir. of Coop. Edn., CSU Fresno, 1981-83; atty. Law Office Molina and Morgan, Santa Ana, 1983-85; principal, Adult Edn. dir. Coachella Valley Unified Sch. Dist., Thermal, 1985-89; chief dep. dir. Calif. Dept. Economic Opportunity, Sacto., 1989-; developed a televised Bilingual Edn. tchr. training pgm. for L.A. Unified Sch. Dist.; supvd. mgmt. & expansion of Nat. Bilingual Edn. Pgm., and Nat. Migrant Edn. Pgm.; appt. City of La Quinta Comm. Svs. Commn., State of Calif. Accreditation Com., L.A. Cultural Heritage Bd., Texas Tech Jour. of Edn. editl. advy. bd.; awards: leadership Calif. Assn. of Bilingual Edn., contbn. to edn. of children San Jose Unified Sch. Dist., contbn. to edn. San Diego St. Univ., outstanding svc. Texas Edn. Assn., Riverside County Principal of the Year; mem: Assn. of Calif. Sch. Adminstrs., Calif. Bar Assn., Desert Schs. Mgmt. Assn., Calif./Nev. Assn. of Community Action Agys.; publs. in field of linguistics, bilingual edn.; Republican; R.Cath.; rec: tennis, golf. Res: 48-119 Calle Seranas La Quinta 92253 Ofc: Calif. Dept. of Economic Opportunity 700 N 10th St Sacramento 95814

MONTEMAYOR, JOANNE MARIE, registered nurse; b. Sept. 10, 1941, Jerome, Ariz.; d. Karl Nickolas and Anna Linda (Worgt) Wilke; m. Casimiro Lopez Montemayor, Oct. 8, 1978; edn: BS nursing, Univ. Colo. Boulder 1965; MN, Univ. Wash. Seattle 1974; reg. nurse, 1989. Career: nursing coord. Redwood Convalescent Center, Castro Valley 1982-83; service dir. Upjohn Health Care Services, Hayward 1983-84; dir. of nursing Wash. Manor Convalescent, San Leandro 1984-86; case mgr. Vesper Hospice 1988, north team leader 1988-89, patient care coord. 1989—; honors: Who's Who Am. Women, Who's Who Am. Nursing Profls., Who's Who Exec. Women; mem: Nat. Hospice Orgn.; author Western Anthology of Poetry, 1989; mil: lt commdr. USN 1959-79; Democrat; Prot.; rec: music, gardening. Res: 272 Stanton Heights Ct Castro Valley 94546

MONTGOMERY, HOWARD GROMEL, employee benefits company executive, naval reserve officer; b. Jan. 21, 1946, Norfolk, Va.; s. John Archibald and Edna (Gromel) M.; m. Audrey Mae Hibl, Oct. 6, 1973; children: Krista Marie b. 1978, Ashli Lynn b. 1984; edn: BA in polit. sci./internat. rels., UC Berkeley, 1968; reg. health & disability underwriter (RHU) Nat. Assn. Health Underws., 1980; fluent in Fr. and Spanish. Career: pres. and ceo Howard Montgomery Assocs., employee benefit plan sales & consulting, 1971-; dir: World Graphics Inc., Pompano Properties Inc.; columnist "GroupAdvisor" distb. local newspapers and bus. newsletters in Calif.; mem. Nat. Assn. Health Underws., Nat. Assn. Health Underws., Leading Producers Roundtable (life 1978-), Calif. Assn. Life Underws., Peninsula Life Underwrs. Assn. (dir., ofcr. 1978-84, hlth. ins. advr. 1982-84); appt. by Calif. State Assembly to Small Bus. Task Force (chmn.), Small Bus. Reps. Roundtable, Calif. State Conf. on Small Bus. (small bus. advy. com.), 1987-; appt. regional area advy. com. U.S. SBA, 1987-; White House Council on Small Bus., 1978-80; mem: Better Business Bur./ San Mateo County (dir. 1983-, chmn. bd. 1987-89, Lois J. Bell achiev. awards 1987-88, rec'd Calif. St. Legislature Proclamation 1989), Burlingame Kiwanis Club (pres. 1975-76, Disting. Pres. Award 1976), Foster City Bus. Devel. Club (pres. 1979-84), Burlingame Ambassadors Club (pres. 1978, Top Dog Award 1978), Calif. C.of C. (1985-, v.ch. Small Bus. Advy. Com. 1987-), Foster City C.of C. (bd. 1978-81, 83-86, treas. 84-86), UC Alumni Assn. (life), World Affairs Council S.F., Commonwealth Club of Calif., San Mateo County Council Boy Scouts Am. (bd. 1972-76, county chmn. mem. 1974), Burlingame C.of C. (bd. 1973-77), Burl. Bicentenial Com. (co-chair 1975-76), Miss Burlingame Pageant (co-chair 1974), Airport Land Use Commn. San Mateo Co. 1975-77, Regional Plng. Com. S.M. Co. 1975-77, Am. Cancer Soc. (Burl. chmn. 1974), Heart Fund (Burl. chmn. 1973); mil: Capt. USNR 1968-, decorated Meritorious Svc. medal 1987, Navy Commendn. medal (1982, 85, 87, 90), Merit. Unit Commendn., Battle Efficiency "E" USS Wiltsie (DD-716), Nat. Def. medal w/star, Vietnam Svc. medal w/star, Naval Reserve Sea Svc. rib. w/star, Armed Forces Reserve medal w/hourglass, Repub. Vietnam Campaign medal, Navy Expert Rifleman, Navy Expert Pistol Shot; mem. Naval Reserve Assn.: 12th Dist. (pres. 1988-), Polaris Chpt. (pres. 1985-87, awarded Navy Recruiting Command's #1 NRA Chapt. in Nation 1987 and #2 Chapt. 1986, Twice A Citizen Award 1987), dir., coord. Chief of Naval Ops. Presentation & Speakers Pgm. (awarded 4 certs. of merit and 3 top nat. ranking awards) 1985-, coord. Command Excellence Sem. Pgm./TQL Pgm. for NAVRESREDCOM reg. 20, 1991-; mem. Navy League of U.S. (life, dir. S.F. Council 1987-), Surface Navy Assn., Reserve Ofcrs. Assn., US Naval Inst., Naval Order of U.S., Naval Enlisted Reserve Assn., Naval War Coll. Found. (alumni mem. 1982-), Nat. Def. Univ. Found. (grad. mem. 1983-), Navy Memorial Found. (charter 1987-); Republican; Presbyterian. Ofc: 1191 Chess Dr Ste 206 Foster City 94404

MONTGOMERY, LAVERTA STEENE, financial consultant; b. Oct. 27, 1936, Fort Worth, Tx.; d. Iris Eugene and Nannie Laverta (Steene) Whitaker; m. Joseph Montgomery (dec.), Aug. 23, 1953; children: Joie b. 1954, Gil b. 1957, Stacy b. 1958 (dec. 1988), Eric b. 1962; edn: bus., govt. and pub. adminstrn. studies Metropolitan Jr. Coll. 1952-54, El Camino Coll. 1966-75, Pepperdine Univ. 1976-77. Career: acct. USAF 1955-67; dir. redevelopment and housing City of Compton, 1971-75, city mgr. 1983-86, city controller 1976-82; apptd. commr. Calif. State Lottery Commn., Sacramento 1985-90; bd. mem. Fair Housing Council of San Fernando Valley 1988; pres. Laverta Montgomery & Assocs., L.A. 1987-; bd. chair The Artex Inc., L.A. 1988-; mem. League of California Cities revenue & taxation com. 1983-84; chair Calif. Muni. Fin. Officers So. Calif. 1981-82, chair L.A. sect. 1980; exec. bd. Forum for Black Pub. Adminstrn., Wash. DC 1985; awards: Ann Brannon Outstanding Alumni, Ft. Worth, Tx. Indep. Sch. Dist., 1988; pub. service citations Calif. State Assembly, L.A. Co. Bd. Suprs., Compton Comm. Coll., Compton Unified Sch. Dist., and City of Compton, 1985; profl. achievement award Reg. Govt. Fin. Officers Assn. of U.S. & Canada, 1980; civic: 100 Black Women of Los Angeles, 1985-; Nat. Council of Negro Women, 1977-; Republican; Baptist; rec: reading. Ofc: Laverta Montgomery & Associates 2696 W Imperial Hwy Inglewood 90303

MONTGOMERY, MICHAEL BRUCE, lawyer; b. Sept. 12, 1936, Santa Barbara; s. Clair Gruwell Montgomery and Florence Louise (Moran) Quigley; m. Pamela Wood 1959 (dec.); m. 2d. Patricia Ferguson, Aug. 28, 1968 (div.); children: Michael b. 1964, Patrick b. 1965 (dec.), Megan b. 1968; m. 3d. Carmen Montalvan, June 16, 1990; edn: BS, UCLA, 1960; JD, USC, 1963; admitted bar: Calif. 1963, Fla. 1987, Hawaii 1988. Career: atty. Calif. State Div. of Hwys. legal dept., 1963-65; atty., assoc. Martin & Flandrick, San Marino 1965-66; pres. Michael B. Montgomery Law Corp., Pasadena 1966-; special counsel Redevel. Agy. cities of Commerce 1969-82, Santa Fe Springs 1970-82, Duarte 1975-82, Monrovia 1977-82; Redevel. Agy. atty. Monterey Park 1973-81, Irwindale Community 1976-82, Huntington Park 1979-92, Walnut 1980-, South El Monte 1989-92; city atty. City of Bradbury 1977-80; appt. commr. Calif. Fair Political Practices Commn. 1985-89, U.S. rep. Internat. Commn. for the Conserv. of the Atlantic Tunas, Madrid 1985-, mem. Pacific Fishery Mgmt. Council 1991-, various State Senate and Congl. coms., Calif. Gov.'s Infrastructure Review Task Force; frequent lectr. municipal assns.; writer on redevel. law and procedures, pub. fin.; expert witness Superior Ct. and st. legis. coms.; mem: State Bar Assns. of Calif., Fla., Hawaii, Am. Bar Assn. (chair subcom. on housing and comm. devel. 1983-84), L.A. Co. Bar Assn. (mem. condemnation subcom.), Pasadena Bar Assn., Irish Am. Bar Assn., C.of C., Kiwanis Club (past pres.); elected South Pasadena City Council 1970-74, 1980-84, mayor 1980-81, mem. South Pasadena Redevel. Agy. 1970-74, 80-84, chmn. 1982-84, chmn. South Pasadena City Commn. 1969; mil: AUS 1954-57, commd. ofcr. USNR; Republican (state chmn. Calif. Rep. Party 1977-79, dir. Cal-Plan 1970-77, ofcr. state exec. com. 1977-85, 90-); Prot.; rec: sportfishing; mem. Internat. Game Fishing Assn., Hawaiian Billfishing Assn. (com. Internat. Billfishing Tourn.), United Sportfishermen Am. (pres. 1987-92). Ofc: 17200 Crossroads Parkway North City of Industry 91746

MOONEY, BRIAN FARRELL, environmental planner; b. Aug. 27, 1950, Chelsea, Mass.; s. Laurence Patrick and Gertrude Adelaide (Miller) M.; m. Linda Jo Kozub, Feb. 19, 1977; children: Sean b. 1978, Ryan b. 1981, Kyle b. 1984; edn: AA, Orange Coast Coll., 1972; BA, San Diego St. Univ., 1975; grad. studies Univ. of San Diego, 1976-77. Career: research asst. San Diego St. Univ., 1973-75, lectr. 1984-; environmental mgmt. splst. County of San Diego, 1975-77; environmental studies co-ordinator County of San Diego, 1977-79; pres. American Pacific Environmental Consultants, Escondido 1979-82; pres. Mooney-Lettieri & Assocs., San Diego 1982-86; pres. Brian F. Mooney Associates, San Diego 1986-; bd. dirs. Revision Resources Inc., 1991-; awards: APA Outstanding Planning Award 1989, juror AIA Orchids & Onions, San Diego 1982, recogn. award Cultural Heritage Commn. S.D. Co. 1976; mem: Assn. of Environmental Profls. (pres. 1984-85, bd. 1983-84, conf. speaker 1982-), Am. Planning Assn. (conf. speaker 1986-), Urban Land Inst., S.D. Hist. Soc.; pub. article in field (1981); Republican; Episcopalian; rec: soccer, basketball, tennis. Ofc: 9903-B Businesspark Ave San Diego 92123

MOORE, C. BRADLEY, chemistry professor, college dean; b. Dec. 7, 1939, Boston; s. Charles Walden and Dorothy (Lutz) M.; m. Penelope Williamson Percival, Aug. 27, 1960; children: Megan Bradley, Scott Woodward; edn: BA, Harvard Univ., 1960; PhD, UC Berkeley, 1963. Career: asst. prof. chemistry UC Berkeley, 1963-68, assoc. prof. 1968-72, prof. 1972-, chemistry dept. v.chair 1971-75, dept. chmn. 1982-86, dean Coll. of Chemistry, 1988-; vis. prof. Faculte des Scis., Paris 1970, 75, Inst. for Molecular Sci., Okazaki, Japan 1979, Fudan Univ., Shanghai 1979, adv. prof. 1988-, vis. prof. Joint Inst. for Lab. Astrophysics, Univ. Colo. Boulder 1981-82; awards: Alfred P. Sloan Found. fellow 1968, Guggenheim Found. fellow 1969, Coblentz award 1973, E.O. Lawrence award 1986, Lippincott award 1987, 1st Inter-Am. Photochem. Soc. award 1988; mem: Am. Phys. Soc. (Fellow), AAAS (Fellow), Am. Chem. Soc. (past chmn. div. phys. chemistry, Calif. sect. award 1977), Nat. Acad. Scis. (chmn. Com. Undergrad. Sci. Educ.); contbr. articles to profl. jours.; editor:

Chemical and Biochemical Applications of Lasers; rec: cycling. Res: 936 Oxford St Berkeley 94707-2435 Ofc: Dept. Chemistry Univ. Calif. 211 Lewis Hall Berkeley 94720 Tel: 415/642-3453

MOORE, CLIFTON ALBERT, municipal airports executive director; b. Jan. 15, 1922, Jamaica Plain, Mass.; s. George Albert and Lylie (Carveth) M.; m. Betty Jean LeBrick, Aug. 29, 1941; children: Dale b. 1943, Steven b. 1946, Kerry b. 1947; edn: grad. Dedham H.S. 1940. Career: electronic tech. City of Los Angeles 1945-49; bldg. and grounds supt. Culver City Unified Sch. Dist., 1950-58; building adminstr. dept. of airports City of L.A. 1959-63, dep. gen. mgr. dept. of airports 1963-68, exec. dir. 1968-; bd. mem., pres. Culver City Board of Edn. 1961-67; honors: extraordinary svc. award FAA (1975), Wm. J. Cutbirth Memorial award Travel & L.A. Transp. Council 1984, Gen. Jimmy Doolittle award USO 1986, Paul Harris Fellow 1986, pub. svc. award Anti-Defamation League 1986; mem: UCLA Bus. Roundtable for Senior Execs. (a founder), USC Aviation Advy. Bd., Fgn. Trade Assn., L.A. Conv. & Vis. Bureau (dir., ex-oficio 1975), Los Angeles C.of C., Culver City Kiwanis (pres. 1956); co-author: Airport Ops. (John Wiley & Sons 1984); mil: chief electricians mate USN 1940-45; Republican; Prot.; rec: writing. Ofc: Los Angeles Dept of Airports POB 92216 Los Angeles 90009-2216

MOORE, HENRY T., JR., state appellate judge; b. Dec. 28, 1932, El Paso, Tex.; s. Henry Trumbull and Bonnie (Platt) M.; m. Lynda Doughty, Nov. 8, 1963; children: Michael, Kenneth, Laura; edn: BA, USC 1954; LLB, 1957; LLM, Harvard Univ. 1958; Judge of the Superior Ct., Calif. 1984. Career: assoc./ partner, law firm Moore & Trinkaus 1958-62; ptnr. Moore & Moore 1962-76; sole practitioner, Century City & of counsel Ward & Heyler 1976-79; sole practitioner (gen. civil & trial practice), Santa Ana 1979-84; judge Superior Court, Co. of Orange 1984-88, assoc. justice Calif. Ct. of Appeal, 1988-; So. Coast Regl. Coastal Commn. 1979-80; L.A. Superior Ct. Panel of Arbitrators, Orange Co. Superior Ct. Panel of Arbitrators 1979-84; judge pro tem L.A. Municipal Ct. 1979; Orange Co. Tax Reform Com. 1976-77; Citizens Adv. Com. to L.A. City Plnng. Dept. 1971-72, L.A. City Atty. Burt Pines 1973-74; honors: Phi Beta Kappa, Phi Kappa Phi, Order of the Coif; mem: Calif. Judges Assn., State Bar of Calif. (chmn. local adminstv. com. 1972), Beverly Hills, L.A. Co. (chmn. pub. rels. com. 1972-74), Orange Co. Bar Assns., Am., L.A., Orange Co. Trial Lawyers Assns., Assn. of Bus. Trial Lawyers, Internat. Acad. of Law & Sci., Am. Judicature Soc.; civic: Mandeville Cyn. Property Owners Assn. (pres. 1971-73); Republican; Presbyterian. Ofc: Court of Appeal, 925 N Spurgeon Santa Ana 92701

MOORE, JOHN WILLIAM, university president; b. Aug. 1, 1939, Bayonne, N.J.; s. Frederick A. and Marian R. (Faser) M.; m. Nancy Baumann, Aug. 10, 1968; children: Matthew b. 1972, Sarah b. 1974, David b. 1979; edn: BS soc. sci./edn., Rutgers Univ., 1961; MS, counseling & student personnel svs., Indiana Univ., 1963; EdD, Penn. State Univ., 1970. Career: asst. v.p. acad. affairs Univ. of Vermont, Burlington 1973-76, assoc. v.p. acad. affairs, 1976-77; v.p. policy & planning Old Dominion Univ., Norfolk, Va. 1977-78, v.p. ednl. svs. 1978-82, exec. v.p. and prof. edn. 1982-85; pres. CSU Stanislaus, Turlock, Calif. 1985-; trustee Gould Med. Found., Modesto 1988-; awards: Disting. service Old Dominion Univ. Alumni Assn. 1985, community svc. Norfolk Commn. for Edn. 1985, leadership United Way Modesto 1986, service Private Industry Council Modesto 1989, Alumni Fellow Penn State Univ. 1990; mem: Soc. for Coll. and Univ. Planning (nat. pres. 1985-86), Am. Assn. of State Colls. & Univs. (Calif. state rep. 1988-), United Way Stanislaus Co. (pres. 1988-89), Turlock C.of C. (bd. 1988-), Pvt. Industry Council Modesto 1987-, Union Safe Bank Advy. Com. 1988-, Rotary Turlock, Sportsmen of Stanislaus 1985-; Methodist; rec: youth soccer coach. Ofc: CSU Stanislaus 801 W Monte Vista Turlock 95380

MOORE, RONALD CLARK, mechanical designer; b. Dec. 18, 1949, Springfield, Ohio; s. Harry Alva and Virginia Kay (Clark) M.; m. Rebecca Jane Culp, Apr. 17, 1971 (div. 1974); m. Emperatriz Seretti, June 21, 1986; edn: AA laser tech., San Jose City Coll., 1979. Career: systems test/mfg. Coherent Radiation, Palo Alto 1976-78; research tech Stanford Res. Inst., Menlo Park 1978-79; satellite sys. test Santa Barbara Research Ctr., Goleta 1979-80; optical test tech. Omex Inc., Santa Clara 1980-82; senior lab specialist IBM Almaden Research Ctr., San Jose 1982-: inventor Serial EP Printer Cartridge (pat. 1989), 9 other patent disclosures; recipient IBM Research Div. award Almaden Res. Ctr. 1992; mil: E3 USMC 1968-70; Democrat; rec: camping, fishing, backpacking. Res: 912 Chelan Dr Sunnyvale 94087 Ofc: IBM Almaden Research Ctr 650 Harry Rd San Jose 95120

MOORE, THOMAS PRESTON, educator; b. Mar. 22, 1951, New Britain, Conn.; s. James Mendon and Lenna Mary (Maguire) M.; m. Monique Pierrette Fargues, July 2, 1989; edn: att. Univ. of Helsinki, Finland 1968-69; BA, Northeastern Univ., Boston 1974; MS, Stanford Univ., 1975; PhD., Virginia Tech, 1986; Cert. Profl. Logistician, Soc. of Log. Engrs. 1988. Career: lab. tech. Cabot Corp. Res. Lab., Billerica, Mass., 1970; res. asst. Avco-Everett Resrch. Lab., Everett, Mass., 1971; marine engr. trainee Nat. Data Buoy Ctr., Bay St. Louis, Ms., 1972-73; served to Major US Army 1976-80 Active Duty, Res. 1980-: exec. ofcr. HQ Btry., 6/33d Field Arty., Fort Sill, Okla., 1976-77, project

ofcr., Dir. of Evaluation USAFAS, Fort Sill, 1977; instr. Army Logistics Mgmt. College, Fort Lee, Va. 1977-80; tchg. asst. IEOR Dept. Virginia Tech, Blacksburg, Va. 1980-81; res. assoc. VA Ctr. for Coal & Energy Res., 1981-82; res. asst. Mgmt. Systems Lab, Virginia Tech, 1982-83, res. assoc. IEOR Dept. 1983-85; asst. prof. of mgmt. sci. Naval Postgraduate Sch., Monterey, Calif. 1986-; honors: Phi Kappa Phi (1974), Army Top 5% Grad. Sch. Scholar 1974, President's Sabre Northeastern Univ. ROTC 1974, Alpha Pi Mu IE Honor Soc. 1981, fellowship Soc. of Log. Engrs., Huntsville, Al. 1984; mem: Decision Scis. Inst. 1988-, Inst. of Indsl. Engrs. 1980-, Ops. Res. Soc. of Am. 1974-, Mil. Order of World Wars (life 1967-), Bikecentennial (life 1980-), Sierra Club 1977-, N.O.W. 1980-; civic bds: Marina City Planning Commn. 1989-, Marina Water Conservation Task Force (chair 1990-), Monterey Penin. Soccer League (pres. 1987-), SW Va. Soccer Assn., Blacksburg, Va. (founder & pres. 1981-84), Metro DC-Va. Soccer Assn. (v.p. 1982-83, newsletter ed. 1982-84), Am. Heart Assn. (CPR instr. 1978-80); publs: (diss.) Optimal Design, Procurement and Support of Multiple Repairable Equipt. and Log. Systems (1986), contbr. jour. articles to: Transportation Res., Proceedings of the 1985 Fed. Acquisition Res. Symposium, Proceedings of 20th Annual Internat. Logistics Symposium (1985), Supply J. Royal Australian Navy (1990). Ofc: Dept. Admin. Sciences Code AS/Mr, Naval Postgraduate School Monterey CA 93943-5008

MOORE, WILLIAM JAMES, journalist; b. Oct. 7, 1943, Corpus Christi, Tx.; s. Edwin Ruthven and Mary Wilson (Clokey) M.; m. Ann Bancroft, May 2, 1976; son, Matthew b. 1982; edn: BA comm. & polit. sci., Stanford Univ., 1965, MA comm., 1966. Career: reporter Arizona Daily Star, Tucson 1962; editor-in-chief Stanford Daily, Stanford, Ca. 1964; reporter San Francisco Chronicle, 1967-79; news editor Oakland Tribune /East Bay Today, 1979-81; metropolitan editor Sacramento Bee, 1982, Forum editor, McClatchy Newspapers (Sacramento Bee), Sacto. 1982-; press aide/volunteer Robert F. Kennedy Presdl. Campaign, S.F. 1968; awards: Best feature writing in No. Calif., S.F. Press Club (1973, 78), Copley Found. fellow at Stanford Univ. 1965-66, two gold medals for newswriting Hearst Found., NYC 1963; contbg. writer Stanford Review 1965, Rolling Stone Mag. 1975; mil: USCG Reserve 1967-73; rec: skiing, pub. speaking (western storyteller). Ofc: McClatchy Newspapers PO Box 15779 Sacramento 95852

MOORING, IVY MAY, psychologist; b. Dec. 31, 1919, Mansfield, England; d. Samuel and Florrie Ellis (Heath) Ellis; m. John P. Shelton, May 24, 1968; 1 son, Michael Leonard (1947-1979); edn: BA, London Univ., 1940; BA, UC Los Angeles, 1953; PhD, USC, 1959; Calif. lic. psychologist 1959; Calif. tchg. cred.-kindergarten primary, gen. elem., supvn. cred., sch. psychologist cred. Career: primary sch. tchr. in English public sch. system, 1940-42, tchr. pvt. secondary sch., 1942-48; tchr. Topanga (Calif.) Elem. Sch. Dist. 1948-55; dir. res. & guidance Palos Verdes Unified Sch. Dist., 1955-62; pvt. practice psychologist spec. in family therapy and learning disabilities, 1961-; coord spl. edn. services L.A. City Sch. Spl. Edn. Br., 1962-63; project dir. Calif. State Mental Retardation Jt. Agencies Project, 1963-65, dir. Mental Retardation Services Bd. of Los Angeles Co., 1965-70, clin. prof. Ctr. for Tng. in Comm. Psychiatry (contg. edn. pgm. for postgrad. mental health profls.) St. Dept. of Mental Health, 1970-79; dir. Dubnoff Ctr. for Child Devel. and Ednl. Therapy (non-profit clinical sch.) 1975-83; bd. chmn. Internat. Found. for Learning Disabilities (non-profit ednl. orgn.), 1983-; mem. Calif. State Devel. Services Com. 1976- vis. prof. UCLA 1966-76, USC 1963-66, CSU Long Beach 1954-63; cons. num. sch. dists. and fed., state and reg. govt. agencies; res. grantee (9) HEW (Voc. Rehab.) Calif. State Depts. of Edn., Mental Hygiene, and Health; awards: Risely Memorial Award 1936, Delta Kappa Gamma state scholar 1955, appreciation Marianne Frostig Ctr. 1971), Dubnoff Ctr. 1983, Resolutions L.A. Co. Bd. Suprs. 1967, L.A. Mayor 1981, Calif. State Assem. 1981, hon. life mem. PTA; t.v. appearances: series of 13 films (Calif. Cong. Parents & Tchrs.), 26 episodes Teenage Trials w/Jerry Dunphy and Regis Philburn (CBS-TV), num. media interviews; frequent speaker health and edn. confs.; mem: Internat. Council for Exceptional Children, Am. Psychol. Assn., Am. Assn. Mental Deficiency (fellow, chmn. Region 2 1975), Am. Acad. of Mental Retardation, AAAS, Calif. St. Psychol. Assn. (dir. 1982-86), Calif. Assn. for Exptl. and Clin. Hypnosis, So. Calif. Nat. Rehab. Assn. (exec. bd. 1964), L.A. Co. Psychol. Assn., L.A. Co. Guidance Assn. (pres. 1961), Delta Kappa Gamma, Phi Lambda Theta, Delta Epsilon, Educare; num. articles in profl. jours. Republican. Res: 12377 Ridge Circle Los Angeles 90049

MOOSSA, A. R., academic surgeon; b. Oct. 10, 1939, Port-Louis, Mauritius; s. Yacoob and Maude (Rochecoute) M.; m. Denise Willoughby, Dec. 28, 1973; children: Pierre b. 1977, Noel b. 1981, Claude b. 1984, Valentine b. 1987; edn: BS, Univ. of Liverpool 1962, MD, 1965; postgrad. tng. Johns Hopkins Univ. 1972-73, The Univ. of Chgo. 1973-74; FRCS, Royal Coll. of Surgeons of England 1970; FRCS Royal Coll. of Surgeons of Edinburgh 1970; FACS, Fellow Am. Coll. of Surgeons. Career: asst. prof. of surgery Univ. of Chgo. 1974, assoc. prof. of surgery 1975, prof. of surg., dir. Surgical Research, and chief Gen. Surgery Service, vice chmn. Dept. of Surgery, Univ. of Chgo. 1977-83; prof. and chmn. Dept. of Surgery, UC San Diego and surgeon-in-chief UCSD Medical Center, 1983-; awards: Hunterian Prof., Royal Coll. of Surgeons 1977, Litchfield lectr. Univ. of Oxford, Eng. 1978, Praelector in Surgery, Univ. of Dundee, Scotland 1979, Hon. Fellow Brazilian Coll. & Surgeons 1988, Hon. Doctor of

Medicine, Univ. of Liverpool 1990, G.B. Ong vis. prof. Univ. of Hong Kong 1992, Hampson Trust vis. prof. Univ. of Liverpool 1992, hon. mem. Assn. de Chirurgie Francaise 1992, hon. mem. Paraguan Surgical Soc. 1992; mem: Am. Coll. of Surgeons, Am. Surgical Assn., Soc. of Univ. Surgeons, Soc. of Surgical Oncology, Am. Soc. of Clin. Oncology, Soc. for Surgery of the Alimentary Tract, Internat. Hepato-Biliary-Pancreatic Assn. (pres. 1989); club: La Jolla Beach and Tennis, Fairbanks Ranch Country; R.Cath.; rec: travel, soccer. Ofc: Dept. of Surgery, UCSD Medical Center 225 Dickinson St San Diego 92103

MOOZ, WILLIAM ERNST, chemical company president; b. Feb. 28, 1929, Staten Island, NY; s. Harold Adolf and Kathryn (Neuschwander) M.; m. Melodie Ione Linn, Sept. 11, 1982; edn: BS, MIT 1950; reg. profl. engr. Calif. Career: asst. to plant mgr. Titanium Metals Corp., Henderson, Nev. 1950-60; econ. engr. U.S. Borax & Chem., Los Angeles 1960-62; exec. v.p. G.B. Smith Chem. Works, Maple Park, Ill. 1962-63; sr. research staff Rand Corp., Santa Monica 1963-88; pres. Met-L-Chek Co. 1963-, dir. 1963-; NDT Europa BV, Amsterdam, Netherlands 1963-; awards: Earl P.L. Apfelbaum Meml. 1985; mem: Am. Inst. Mining & Metallurgical Engrs., Am. Soc. Nondestructive Testing; 2 patents 1952, 100 reports pub. 1963-, author of 7 books; mil: cpl. AUS 1953-55; rec: whitewater river rafting, hiking. Res: Box 1714 Santa Monica 90406 Ofc: Met-L-Chek Co 1639 Euclid St Santa Monica 90404

MORENA, GITA DOROTHY, psychotherapist; b. Aug. 1, 1947, Los Angeles; d. Kenneth Austin and Ozma (Baum) Mantele; m. David Morena, July 5, 1969 (div. 1981); children: Brian b. 1973, Gregory b. 1977; edn: BS biol., Santa Clara Univ.; MS clin. psychol., San Diego St. Univ.; lic. marriage family and child therapist 1973. Career: program dir. Western Inst., San Diego 1974-76; treatment dir. Windmill House 1976-78; cons. Learning Devel. 1975-78; faculty Nat. Univ. 1978-; pvt. practice, San Diego 1976-; graphic artist Gita's Graphics 1985-; honors: Psi Chi; mem: Calif. Assn. Marriage & Family Therapists, S.D. Art Therapy Assn., Sandplay Therapists of Am.; contbr. interpretation of projective drawings 1984, article pub. in profl. jour. 1974; rec: music, meditation, yoga, metaphysics. Address: 3855 Camino Litoral Ste 222 San Diego 92107

MORGAN, FREDERICK WILLIAM, military officer/public relations executive; b. Oct. 2, 1943, Seattle, Wash.; s. Jacob Jesse and Violet Marie (Nord) M.; m. Victoria Milanda Koren, Feb. 4, 1967; children: Christopher b. 1968, Elizabeth b. 1970, Milan b. 1972; edn: BA bus. adminstrn. (disting. mil. grad.), Univ. Wash., Seattle 1965; MS pub. rels., The American Univ., Wash. DC 1972; grad. Air Command and Staff Coll. 1979, Air War Coll. 1983. Career: served to col. US Air Force 1965-: chief internal info. & comm. rels. AF Special Weapons Ctr., Kirtland AFB, N.Mex. 1965-67; wing information ofcr. 7272nd Flying Tng. Wing, Wheelus AB, Libya 1967-69; info. ofcr. Ofc. of Aerospace Res., Arlington, Va. 1969-70; info. staff ofcr. Secty. of the Air Force Ofc. of Info., The Pentagon, WDC 1970-73; spl. asst. for B-1 information Aeronautical Systems Div. Wright-Patterson AFB, Ohio 1973-77; asst. chief pub. info. div. US Air Forces Europe, Ramstein AB, Ger. 1977-79; chief pub. affairs 86th Tactical Fighter Wing, Ramstein AB, Ger. 1979-81; dir. pub. affairs 3rd Air Force, RAF Mildenhall, Eng. 1981-83; dep. dir. pub. affairs US Air Forces Europe, Ramstein AB, Ger. 1983-86; dir. Air Force Ofc. of Pub. Affairs, West. Reg., Los Angeles, Ca. 1986-; awards: service above self Rotary Internat., Seattle 1961, honor grad. Def. Info. Sch., Idpls. 1966, Outstanding Young Men of Am. 1969, Who's Who in Pub. Rels. 1976, Who's Who in Midwest 1977, Who's Who in West 1990; mem: Pub. Relations Soc. Am. (accredited 1973), Aviation/Space Writers Assn., AF Assn. (life), Retired Ofcrs. Assn., Nat. Rifle Assn., Calif. Rifle & Pistol Assn., Arnold Air Soc. (UW chpt. sec. 1963-64), Nat. Soc. of Scabbard & Blade (UW chapt. sec. 1964-65), Christian Fam. Movement (Va. st. publicity chair 1972-73), Boy Scouts Am., RAF Mildenhall, Eng. (com. chmn. 1982-83); editor mo. mag.: Husky Gyro (1964-65), OAR Spectrum (1969-70), publisher weekly newspaper: Tripoli Trotter (1967-69), Kaiserslautern American (1979-81); R.Cath.; rec: sailing, photog., target shooting. Ofc: AFOPA-WR, 11000 Wilshire Blvd Ste 10114 Los Angeles 90024 Tel: (213) 209-7511

MORGAN, KERMIT JOHNSON, lawyer; b. Feb. 13, 1914, Henderson, Iowa; s. Samuel and Jennie Amelia M.; m. Ortrud Impol, Dec. 9, 1960; children: Georgina b. 1942, Wilson b. 1945; edn: BA, Univ. Iowa 1935; JD, USC 1937; admitted Calif. St. Bar (1937). Career: atty./ptnr. Morgan & Armbrister, Los Angeles 1937-; honors: Alpha Tau Omega, Phi Delta Phi; mem: Am. Board of Trial Advocates (nat. pres. 1973, pres. L.A. Chpt. 1971), Internat. Assn. of Defense Council, Assn. of Defense Trial Attys. (bd. dirs. 1983-86), Am. Bar Assn., Calif. Bar Assn., L.A. County Bar Assn., Wilshire Bar Assn.; Republican; Congregational; rec: golf, fishing. Res: 2108 Stradella Rd Los Angeles 90077 Ofc: Morgan & Armbrister 2951 28th St Santa Monica 90504

MORGAN, KILE, city mayor; b. Mar. 22, 1920, Hancock County, Tenn.; s. George Preston and Geneva Mary (Barnard) M.; m. Donna Wilcox, July 28, 1944; children: Janice b. 1945, Kile, Jr. b. 1946, Robert b. 1950; H.S. grad. Ava, Mo. 1938; Calif. lic. real estate broker 1946. Career: prop. car dealer, 1944-46; real estate builder/devel., 1946-66; elected National City City Council, 1960-66, city mayor 1966-86; Kiwanian; Democrat; Baptist; rec: golf. Res: 1223 J Ave National City 91950

MORGAN, KILE, JR., home builder; b. Aug. 6, 1946, National City; s. Kile and Donna Kay (Wilcox) M.; m. Marron Spencer, Aug. 22, 1969; m. Judy Morgan, Feb. 28, 1981; children: Donna Michelle b. 1968; edn: BSCE, and BS bus., Univ. Colo., 1969; MBA, Univ. Santa Clara, 1973. Career: gen. mgr. Kaiser Aetna, Oakland 1973-76; sr. v.p. Broadmoor Homes, Dublin 1977-80; v.p./gen. mgr. Ponderosa Homes, San Ramon 1983-85, exec. v.p. Ponderosa Homes, Pleasanton 1983-85, owner/pres./CEO, 1985-; mem: Building Industry Assn. (state dir. 1987-88, dir., v.p. BIA/No. Calif. 1986-88, pres. BIA/Walnut Creek 1988), Young Pres. Orgn. 1987-; bd. dirs. YMCA/ Hayward 1988; club: Diablo CC; Democrat; Baptist; rec: golf, skiing. Res: 59 Starmont Ln Danville 94526 Ofc: Ponderosa Industries 6671 Owens Dr Pleasanton 94566

MORGAN, REBECCA QUINN, state senator; b. Dec. 4, 1938, Hanover, N.H.; d. Forrest Arthur and Rachel Josephine (Lewis) Quinn; m. James C. Morgan, June 10, 1960; children: Jeff b. 1962, Mary b. 1964; edn: BS, Cornell Univ., 1960; MBA, Stanford Univ., 1978. Career: tchr. various places, 1961-65; asst. v.p. Bank of Am., Sunnyvale 1978-80; elected Palo Alto Bd. of Edn. 1973-78; elected Santa Clara Co. Bd. Suprs. 1981-84; elected Calif. State Senate, Sacto. 1984-; honors: Santa Clara County Woman of Achiev. 1983, Legislator of Year: Calif. Sch. Boards Assn., Calif. Probation Parole & Correctional Assn. 1987-88, Calif. Abortion Rights Action League, Calif. School Age Consortium 1989), NOW Calif. 1990; mem. Calif. Elected Womens Assn.; civic bds: Calif. Leadership, Sacto. (dir. 1987-), YWCA Palo Alto (advy. bd. 1983-, Palo Alto Adolescent Svs. (advy. bd. 1975-), Stanford Bus. Sch. Pres.'s Council 1990-; Republican; Prot.; rec: tennis, skiing, gardening. Ofc: State Capitol Rm 4090 Sacramento 95814

MORI, ALLEN ANTHONY, university dean; b. Nov. 1, 1947, Hazleton, Pa.; s. Primo Philip and Carmella (DeNoia) M.; m. Barbara Epoca, June 26, 1971; children: Kirsten Lynn; edn: BA, Franklin and Marshall Coll., 1969; MEd, Bloomsburg Univ., 1971; PhD, Univ. Pittsburgh, 1975. Career: Special edn. tchr. White Haven State Sch. and Hosp., White Haven, Pa. 1969-70; Hazleton Area Sch. Dist. 1970-71, Pittsburgh Pub. Schs., 1971-74; supr. student tchrs. Univ. Pittsburgh, 1974-75; prof. special edn. Univ. Nevada, Las Vegas 1975-84; dean Coll. Edn., Marshall Univ., Huntington W.Va. 1984-87; dean Sch. Edn., CSU Los Angeles 1987-; hearing officer pub. law 94-142 Nev. Dept. Edn., Carson City 1978-; appt. Nev. gubnat. com. on mental health and mental retardation 1983-84; cons. Ministry of Edn., Manitoba, Can. 1980-82; honors: Phi Beta Delta, Phi Delta Kappa, Pi Lambda Theta, grantee US Dept. Edn. 1976-91, Nev. Dept. Edn., W.Va. Dept. Edn., Calif. State Univ. Chancellor's Office; mem: Assn. Tchr. Educators, Coun. for Exceptional Children (career devel. exec. com. 1981-83), Nat. Soc. for Study of Edn.; Kiwanis Club; author: Families of Children with Special Needs (1983); coauthor: Teaching the Severely Retarded (1980), Handbook of Preschool, Special Education (1980), Adapted Physical Education (1983), A Vocat. Tng. Continuum for the Mentally and Physically Disabled (1985), Teaching Sec. Students with Mild Learning and Beh. Problems (2nd. ed. 1993); contbr. numerous articles, book revs. and monographs to scholarly jours. Ofc: Calif. State Univ. 5151 State University Dr Los Angeles 90032

MORIARTY, DONALD PETER, II, engineering executive; b. Jan. 26, 1935, Alexandria, La.; s. Donald Peter and Catherine Graham (Stafford) M.; m. Diana Mary Blackburn, Feb. 4, 1984; children by previous marriage: Erin b. 1957, Donald, III b. 1960; edn: BS, La. State Univ., 1957; MA, Fla. Atlantic Univ., 1973; grad. US Army Command & Gen. Staff Coll., Fort Leavenworth, Ks. 1977. Career: served to lt. col. US Army (Artillery) 1957-80: commd. arty. ofcr. 1957-74, ops. ofcr. and dir. of instrn. US Army Advisor Sch., Di An, Viet Nam 1970-71; strategic plans ofcr. 32d Air Defense Command, Darmstadt, Ger. 1975-77; C3I Program. dir. Army Air Defense Ctr., Fort Bliss, Tx. 1977-80; mem. NATO, HQ, Brussels, Belgium Tactical Airpower Com. 1977-79, Tri-Svc Group on Air Def. 1978-80, Air Def. Elect. Equip. Com. 1978-80; decorated Air Medal w/clusters 1967, Cross of Gal. w/Palm 1967, Bronze Star w/cluster 1971, Merit. Svc. Medal w/cluster 1977, Legion of Merit 1980; sr. systems engr. Hughes Aircraft Co., Fullerton 1980-82, mgr. eng. design dept. 1982-84, project mgr. 1984-; mem: Gen. Soc. of Mayflower Descendants, Sons of Am. Rev., Phi Alpha Theta, Armed Forces Comms.-Electronics Assn., Acacia Frat. (chapt. sec. 1956-57), Kiwanis West Palm Beach, Fla. (dir. 1972-73), Episcopal Service Alliance (O.C. dir. 1988-89), Am. Coll. of Genealogists (Fellow 1992), pres. Episcopal Synad of Am. 1993-; author: The US Army Officer As Military Statesman, 1930-1965 (1973), Louisiana Ante Bellum (1992); Republican; Episcopalian; rec: cosmology, genealogy. Res: 626 E Riverview Ave Orange 92665 Ofc: Hughes Aircraft Co., 1901 W Malvern St Fullerton 92634

MORLER, EDWARD EDWIN, international negotiator and management consultant; b. May 7, 1940, Oak Park, Ill.; s. Edwin Edward and Malva Ida (Pospicil) M.; edn: BS, Ill. Inst. Tech. 1962; MBA, Univ. Chgo. 1968; PhD, Univ. Md. 1973. Career: cons. Fry Cons. Inc., Chgo., Ill. 1968-69; dir. adminstrv. services Airline Pilots Assn., Wash. D.C. 1969-71; spl. cons. Dept. of Labor 1972; indep. cons. 1973-76; founder, chmn. Effective Comm. Skills Inc., N.Y.C. 1976-78; founder, chmn. Morler Internat. Inc., Sonoma, Ca. 1978-; honors: BSA Eagle Scout 1957, Book of Honor, Comm. Leaders of Am., Disting. Am.; mem. Bel Aire Navy League; mil: lt. USN 1962-66; rec: artist in oils & watercolors, golf, sailing, tennis, writing. Ofc: 1140 Brockman Dr Sonoma 95476

MORRIS, FRANKLIN LEON, certified public accountant; b. July 24, 1939, Ardmore, Okla.; s. Fitzhugh Lee and Orpha Ithel (Whitfield) M.; m. Shelia Kay Sparks, Jan. 20, 1960 (div. 1967); m. LaVeta Beth McCullar, Oct. 28 1967; children: Debby b. 1957, Terry b. 1960, Faron b. 1960, Michele b. 1969; edn: AA, CerroCoso Comm. Coll. 1978; BS, CSU Bakersfield 1980; C.P.A. Calif. 1982. Career: staff acct. Peter C. Brown, Bakersfield 1979-82; controller Coleman Constrn. Inc. 1982-86; owner Franklin L. Morris C.P.A. 1986-; awards: Wall St. Jour. outstanding achievement in acctg. 1980; mem: Stockdale Evening Lions (pres. 1987-88), Internat. Lions (So. region chmn. 1989-), BPA Chpt. Alumni; mil: E-7 USN 1957-76; Democrat; Baptist. Res: 4212 Tyndall Ave Bakersfield 93313 Ofc: 3100 19th St Ste 20 Bakersfield 93301

MORRIS, JEFFREY LEE, data processing executive; b. Dec. 8, 1959, Anaheim; s. Phillip Elliott and Kathleen Francis (Martin) M.; m. Jackie Lynn Sharp, Feb. 19, 1977; children: Jeffrey Loren, Jennifer Lynn, Jessica Nicole; edn: cert. in law enforcement, Orange County Sheriff's Acad., 1981. Career: computer opr. Global Data Corp., Anaheim, 1977-79; supr. data processing Knott's Berry Farm Inc., Buena Park, 1979-; cons. ops. documentation, 1987-88; awards: Appreciation, community service Assn. Calif. Sch. Adminstrs. 1988; mem: Assn. for Computer Ops. Mgmt., Knott's Berry Farm Mgmt. Club; civic: Orange (Calif.) Police Dept. (Reserve Ofcr. 1981-84), Boy Scouts Am. Anaheim (scoutmaster 1983-88), Orange Citizens Steering Com. for Schs. 1987, Crescent Sch. Anaheim (ednl. and legis. liaison 1988); Republican; Lutheran; Res: 138 N Wade Circle Anaheim 92807 Ofc: Knott's Berry Farms, Inc. 8039 Beach Blvd Buena Park 90620

MORRISON, JAMES IAN, research institute president; b. Dec. 22, 1952, Irvine, Scotland; s. James Morrison and Janet Miller (McCondach) Munro; m. Nora Cadham, Dec. 6, 1980; children: David b. 1984, Caitlin b. 1986; edn: B.Phil., Univ. of Newcastle-upon-Tyne, England 1976; MA, Univ. Edinburgh, 1974; PhD, Univ. Brit. Columbia, Vancouver 1985. Career: instr. British Columbia Inst. of Tech., Vancouver, BC, Can. 1980-85, research assoc. 1980-85; research fellow Inst. for the Future, Menlo Park, Calif. 1985-86, dir. health care research pgm. 1986-, pres. 1990-; mem.: nat. advy. bd. Interim Healthcare, Ft. Lauderdale, Fla. 1992-, mem. corp. advy. bd. Bristol-Myers Squibb, Princeton, N.J. 1992-, Environmental Scanning Com. of United Way of Am. 1990-, UNIS Press Advy. Bd. 1990-; awards: Lind Prize for geography Edinburgh Univ. 1973, SSRC scholar Social Sci. Rsch. Council, Univ. of Newcastle-upon-Tyne 1974-76; coauthor 3 books incl.: System in Crisis: The Case for Health Care Reform (1991), article "Satisfaction with Health Systems in Ten Nations" (1990); rec: golf. Ofc: Institute for the Future 2744 Sand Hill Rd Menlo Park 94025-7020

MORTON, HUGH WESLEY, IV, performing arts producer; b. Dec. 8, 1931, Pasadena; s. Hugh Wesley and Timey De Lacey (Hopper) M.; m. Paula Dozois, Nov. 30, 1951 (dec.); son, Wil Guido b. Aug. 11, 1964; edn: BS, Univ. Mont. Billings 1958; Northwestern Univ. Evanston; Univ. Oreg. 1960. Career: mail boy, prod. office clk. Paramount Pictures 1962-64; tchr. and dir. profl. workshop Desilu Studios 1964-66; asst. to controller, asst. to exec. v.p. t.v. production Columbia Pictures T.V. 1966-75; asst. to pres. Burbank Studios 1975-78; dir. Hollywood Central 1978-82; special events producer, director, studio fac coord. Twentieth Century Fox, 1982-90; owner IV Productions; has worked on 300+ episodes of TV pgms., 60+ feature films, music videos and special events including work with Canadian TV and a Russian Documentary in 1987; vol. tchr., dir. Notre Dame Girls Acad. 1965-82; actor Hollywood First Presbyterian Ch., concerts, light opera and soaps; awards: Warn Fed. C.U. Outstanding Contbn. (1977-81), Dirs. Guild Am. Guest Faculty Contbn., Am. Cancer Soc. cert. merit, Glendale C. of C. cert. appreciation, Drama Tchrs. Assn. So. Calif. Blue Ribbon judge, Delta Psi, Omega, Alpha Psi Omega; mem: IATSE, AFTRA, SAG, Acad. of TV Arts and Scis., Internat. Platform Assn., Glendale C.of C., St. Charles Comm. Fair, St. Charles Choir, Hollywood Presbyterian Ch. (drama guild, cathedral choir), L.A. Music Center, Festival of Arts Laguna Beach, Colony Players; actor in Eagles Mere Playhouse Pa., Ashland Oreg. Shakespeare Festival, poetry pub., concert tour of Europe; Presbyterian; rec: singing, teaching theatre. Address: POB 2517 Toluca Lake 91610-0517

MOSBY, DOROTHEA SUSAN, parks and recreation director; b. May 13, 1948, Sacramento; d. William Laurence and Esther Ida (Lux) M.; edn: AA sociol., Bakersfield Coll., 1969; BS recreation, San Jose State Univ., 1972; MPA pub. adm., CSU Dominguez Hills, 1982; cert. Calif. Bd. Rec./Pks., Sacto. 1972. Career: personnel dept. asst. San Jose Parks & Rec. Dept., San Jose 1972-73, neighborhood ctr. dir. 1973-74; sr. rec. leader Santa Monica Rec. & Parks Dept., Santa Monica 1974-76, rec. supr. 1976-83, business div. hd. 1983-88, bus. adminstr. Santa Monica Cultural & Rec. Services, 1988-91; dir. South Gate Parks & Rec. Dept., South Gate 1991-; appt. bd. Calif. Bd. Rec. & Park Cert., 1990-, CPRS State Scholarship Found., 1992-; mem. pub. sector advy. bd. Loyola Marymount Univ. Cont. Edn., 1991-; honors: Pi Alpha Alpha (life mem. 1982); mem. Calif. Park & Rec. Soc. 1976-, Nat. Rec. & Park Assn. 1983-, South Gate Kiwanis (bd. 1992-), Windsor Sq. Hancock Park Hist. Soc. (chair 1988-90); Democrat; Lutheran (ch. treas. 1984-86); rec: flute, piano, reading, biking, tennis. Res: 9329 Elm Vista Dr #103 Downey 90242 Ofc: Parks & Recreation Dept. 4900 Southern Ave South Gate 90280

MOSES, LIONEL ELLIOTT, rabbi; b. Sept. 4, 1949, Toronto, Canada; s. Joseph Phillip and Molly (Stone) M.; m. Joyce Rappaport, Dec. 20, 1981; children: Zev Gershon b. 1983, Jeremy Samuel b. 1986, Ezra Melekh b. 1990; edn: BS, Univ. Toronto 1970; MA, Univ. of Toronto, 1973; MA, Jewish Theological Seminar of Am. 1976; ordained rabbi Jewish Theological Seminary of Am. 1977. Career: asst. rabbi Westchester Jewish Center, Mamaroneck, N.Y. 1977-81; rabbi Jewish Center of Jackson Heights, N.Y. 1981-87; Mosaic Law Congregation, Sacto. 1987-; mem: Westchester Assn. Hebrew Educators (pres. 1979-81), Commn. on Synagogue Rels. (v.p. 1985-87), Com. on Jewish Laws & Standards, Joint Bet Din of Conservative Movement, Sacto. Jewish Profl. Orgn. (founding chair 1987-89), Sacto. Jewish Fedn. (bd. dirs. 1987-), Rabbanical Assembly, N.Y. Bd. of Rabbis, No. Calif. Bd. Rabbis, Soc. Biblical Literature, Center for Learning & Leadership, Multicultural Living Assn. (v.p., founder 1986-87), Jackson Heights Elmhurst Kehillah (bd. mem. 1981-87); Jewish; rec: scholarly writing. Res: 181 Middleton Way Sacramento 95864 Ofc: Mosaic Law Congregation 2300 Sierra Blvd Sacramento 95825

MOSHER, SALLY EKENBERG, company president; b. July 26, 1934, NY, NY; d. Leslie Joseph and Frances Josephine (McArdle) Ekenberg; m. James Kimberly Mosher (dec. 1982), Aug. 13, 1960; edn: BMus, Manhattanville Coll., 1956; postgrad. Hofstra Univ., 1958-60, USC, 1970-73; JD, USC Sch. of Law, 1981; admitted bar: Calif. 1982; Calif. lic. R.E. Broker 1984. Career: musician: pianist, tchr., critic (newspaper), coach, concert mgr., New York and Los Angeles 1957-74; rep. Occidental Life, Pasadena 1975-78; v.p. James K. Mosher Co. Inc., Pasadena 1961-82, pres. 1982-; pres. Oakhill Enterprises, Pasadena 1984-; assoc. White-Howell Inc., Pasadena 1984-; awards: full tuition honor scholar Manhattanville Coll. 1952-56, spl. election Mu Phi Epsilon 1970, Kappa Gamma Pi, Mu Phi Epsilon, Phi Alpha Delta; mem. Assocs. of CalTech, Athenaeum; mem. Am. Bar Assn., Calif. Bar Assn.; civic bds: Foothill Area Community Svs. (dir. 1990-, treas. 1991-92, vice chair 1992-), Pasadena Arts Council (pres. 1989-92, chair advy. bd. 1992-, ofcr. 1966-68, dir. 1986), Junior League Pasadena (dir. 1966-7), Encounters Concerts (dir. 1966-72), USC Friends of Music (dir. 1973-6), Pasadena Chamber Orch. (pres. 1987-88, dir. 1986), Endowment Advy. Commn. Pasadena (chair R.E. sub-com. 1988-90), Calif. 200 Council for Bicentennial of U.S. Constitution (1987-) Pasadena Hist. Soc. (dir. 1989-91), Calif. Music Theatre (dir. 1988-90), Arroyo Seco Council (dir. 1991-); publs: articles and music reviews 1966-72; Republican; Christian; rec: graphic design. Res: 1260 Rancheros Rd Pasadena 91103 Ofc: 711 E Walnut Ste 407 Pasadena 91101

MOSK, STANLEY, state supreme court justice; b. Sept. 4, 1912, San Antonio, Tex.; s. Paul and Minna (Perl) M.; m. Edna Mitchell, Sept. 27, 1936 (dec); children: Richard Mitchell; m. 2d. Susan Jane Hines, Aug. 27, 1982; edn: stu. Univ. of Tex. 1931; PhD, Univ. of Chicago 1933, stu. Law Sch. 1935, Hague Acad. Internat. Law 1970; LLD, Univ. of the Pacific 1970, Univ. of San Diego 1971, Univ. of Santa Clara 1976; Cal Western Univ. 1984; Southwestern Univ. 1986; admitted State Bar of Calif. 1935. Career: practicing atty., Los Angeles 1935-39; exec. secty. to gov. Calif., 1939-42; judge superior ct. Los Angeles County, 1943-58; pro tem justice Dist. Ct. Appeal, Calif., 1954; state atty. gen., also head state dept. justice, 1959-64; justice Calif. Supreme Ct., 1964-; vis. prof. Santa Clara Univ. 1981-82; mem. Calif. Commn. Jud. Qualifications, Calif. Disaster Council, Colo. River Boundary Commn., Calif. Commn.; Peace Ofcr. Stds., Dist. Securities Commn., Calif. Commn. Ofcl. Reports of Cts., Calif. Reapportionment Commn.; state chmn. Thanks to Scandinavia Fund, 1967-8; chmn. S.F. Internat. Film Festival, 1967; bd. regents Univ. Calif., 1940; pres. Vista Del Mar Child Care Svc., 1954-8; recipient disting. alumnus award Univ. Chgo., 1958; mem: Nat. Assn. Attys. Gen. (exec. bd.), Western Assn. Attys. Gen., pres. 1963), ALA, L.A., Santa Monica, S.F., Korean bar assns., Am. Judicature Soc., Am. Legion, Manuscript Soc., Univ. Chgo. Alumni Assn. (pres. No. Calif. 1966-8), Phi Alpha Delta, Bnai Brith; clubs: Commonwealth (SF), Beverly Hills Tennis, Hillcrest Co. (L.A.); mil: served in US Army WWII; mem. Democratic Nat. Com. 1960-64. Res: 1200 California St San Francisco 94109 Ofc: 303 Second St San Francisco 94107

MOSS, CHARLES NORMAN, physician; b. June 13, 1914, Los Angeles; m. Margaret Louise; children: C. Eric b. 1953, Gail L. b. 1956, Lori Anne b. 1967; edn: AB, Stanford Univ. 1940; MD, Harvard Med. Sch. 1944; MPH, UC Berkeley 1955; Senior Flight Surgeon, USAF 1956; Dr.PH, UC Los Angeles 1970; Aviation Med. Examiner, FAA (1970). Career: surg. intern Peter Bent Brigham Hosp., Boston 1944-45; med. ofcr. US Army 1945-49: female ward, Birmingham Gen. Hosp., Van Nuys, 1945; Battalion surg., Shanghai and Peiping, China 1945 47 (responsible med. care for 2500, supr. 18 personnel); med. ofcr. US Air Force 1949-65: Wing Base surg., Wing Flight urg. and Med. Group comdr. 86th Fighter-Bomber Wing, Germany 1949-52, ed. care 6000, supr. 48 personnel; surg., flight surg., and med. group omdr. San Antonio Air Material Area, Kelly AFB, Tx. 1952-54, med. care or 45,000, supr. 65 personnel; Preventive Med. Div., Communicable Disease fcr., Office of AF Surg. Gen., Wash DC 1955-59, supr. preparation & publ. of num. AF regulations and pamphlets, served on var. boards and coms. incl. Nat. Acad. of Sci., Nat. Research Council, Army-AF Master Menu Bd., US Civil Service Examiners; hosp. comdr. and flight surg. NATO Hdqtrs., AF & Army, Izmir, Turkey 1959, med. care for

10,000, supr. 45 med. personnel; chief Missile Test and Range Support Div., Staff Surgeon's Ofc., Atlantic Missile Range and Cape Canaveral 1959-61, med. care for 18,000, supr. up to 80; safety ofcr. and occupational med., Orlando AFB, Fla. and Lookout Mtn. AF Station, Los Angeles, 1961-64, ret. lt. col. 1965; med. dir. No. Am. Rockwell Corp., L.A. div. 1969-70; physician, Los Angeles Co. 1970-: Occupational Health Svc., Dept. of Personnel 1970-73, chief Med. Adv. Unit L.A. Co. Bd. of Retirement, Community Health Servs. 1973-79, med. cons. Health Facilities div. Dept. Health Servs. 1979-81; recipient Physician's Recogn. Awards, AMA, 1969, 72, 76, 79, 82; team physician Am. Weightlifting Team winner World Championships in Paris (1950), and Milan (1951); mem: Assn. Oldetime Barbell and Strongmen (1984-); Presbyterian; rec: nutrition, wt.lifting, photog. Res: 7714 Cowan Ave Los Angeles 90045

MOYER, CRAIG ALAN, lawyer, educator; b. Oct. 17, 1955, Bethlehem, Pa.; s. Charles Alvin and Doris Mae (Schantz) M.; m. Candace, May 3, 1986; children: Jason b. 1976 (step), Chelsea A. b. 1988; edn: BA, USC, 1977; JD, UCLA, 1980. Career: atty., assoc. Nossaman, Krueger, et al, Los Angeles 1980-83; Finley, Kumble, et al, Beverly Hills 1983-85; ptnr. Demetriou, Del Guercio & Lovejoy, L.A. 1985-, gen. counsel American Independent Refiners Assn., 1985-; author: The Hazard Communication Handbook, A Right to Know Compliance Guide, 1990, The Clean Air Act Handbook, 1991, Clark-Boardman Publ.; instr. regulatory framework UC Los Angeles, Environmental Law, Hazardous Materials Certificate Pgm.; instr. regulatory framework environmental law, UC Santa Barbara; lectr. environmental edn. for Pac. Auto Show; spkr. Hazmat Confs. Long Beach 1986-, instr. Air Researchers Bd. Symposium Sacto. 1985-; honors: Tau Kappa Epsilon pres. 1975-76 and Outstanding Alumnus 1983; mem: Calif. Public Interest Research Group (pres. 1978-80), Am. Bar Assn., Calif. St. Bar, L.A. County Bar Assn. (Environmental Law Sect., chair Legislative Rev. Com., Exec. Com.); contbr. articles in law jours.; Republican; Prot.; rec: bicycling. Ofc: Demetriou, Del Guercio, Springer & Moyer 801 S Grand Ave Ste 1000 Los Angeles 90017

MUHAMMAD, RAQUEL ANNISSA, teacher; b. Sept. 3, 1932, Beggs, Okla.; d. John Lovings and Elnora DuBose Crenshaw; m. Amos Muhammad Sr., Nov. 25, 1951; children: Duane Bradford b. 1952, Sharon Hammons b. 1955, Valerie b. 1969, Shana b. 1972, Sita b. 1973, Amos Jr. b. 1974; edn: BA, BS, San Diego State Univ., 1961; MA, U.S. Internat. Univ., San Diego 1975, PhD, 1980; degree Alliance Francaise, Paris, Fr. 1966; Calif. tchg. credentials, adj. prof. and sec. English instr. 1961-95. Career: edn. analyst IDEP/UNESCO, Dakar, Senegal, W.Africa 1964; site administr. Univ. of Islam #8, San Diego, Calif. 1965-75; coord. Clark County Comm. Coll., Las Vegas, Nev. 1978; edn. cons. Operation Independence, 1979; tng. analyst Northrop Corp., San Diego 1979; sec. English tchr. San Diego Unified Sch. Dist., 1980-; adj. prof. Eng. San Diego Comm. Coll., 1989-91; cons. prin. R. Muhammad Educational Services, San Diego 1980-; reader ETS, Berkeley, San Diego, 1987, 88, 90; chair Univ. Islam #2, Chgo. 1987-88; awards: fellow SDAWP, UCSD 1982, listed Who's Who Am. Women, Who's Who Am., Who's Who in West; mem. Nat. Assn. Female Execs., Nat. Edn. Assn. 1978-, Calif. Tchrs. Assn. 1978-, SDTA (1978-, minority affairs coun. 1980-90), CATE 1978-, CATESOL 1978-88, Assn. Black Educators S.D., Nat. Assn. Female Exec., Nat. Coun. Tchrs. of English, Nat. Assn. Univ. Women; publs: newspapers series "Social Change Through Education" (1979), curric. and tchg. guides (4), translator "Histoire d'/Afrique Occidentale (1982-92); Democrat; Islam; rec: travel. Res: 898 Valencia Pky San Diego 92114

MUIR, WILLIAM KER, JR., political scientist; b. Oct. 30, 1931, Detroit, Mich.; s. William Ker and Florence Taylor (Bodman) M.; m. Paulette Irene Walters, Jan. 16, 1960; children: Kerry b. 1962, Harriet b. 1967; edn: BA, Yale Univ., 1954, JD, Univ. Mich., 1958; PhD, Yale Univ., 1965. Career: instr. law Univ. Mich., Ann Arbor 1958-59; assoc., law, Davis Polk, N.Y.C. 1959-60; instr. polit. sci. Yale Univ., 1960-67; law ptnr. Tyler Cooper, New Haven, Ct. 1964-68; prof. political sci. UC Berkeley 1968-, dept. chmn. 1980-83; cons. Oakland Police Dept. 1969-74, Calif. State Legislature, Sacto. 1975-76; commr. Police Review Commn. Berkeley 1980-83; speechwriter Office of US Vice Pres., W.D.C., 1983-85; awards: Edward S. Corwin Prize, Am. Polit. Sci. Assn., W.D.C. 1967, Distinguished tchg. UCB 1974, Hadley B. Cantril Prize Cantril Found., N.Y.C. 1979; author: Law and Attitude Change (1967, 74), Police: Streetcorner Politicians (1976), Legislature (1983), The Bully Pulpit (1992); mil: 2d lt. US Army 1954; Republican; Presbyterian. Res: 59 Parkside Dr Berkeley 94705 Ofc: Dept. Political Science Univ. Calif Berkeley 94720

MUKAI, ROBERT KENGI, sound and lighting engineer; b. Mar. 19, 1962, Vincenza, Italy, came to U.S., 1963; s. Thomas Mamoru and Mihoko (Sato) M.; m. Nancy Ann Baldwin, June 23, 1984; grad. high sch., Redondo Beach, Calif. Career: asst. auto mechanic, head auto mechanic John's 76 Auto Service, Redondo Beach, 1980-82, 84-87; technician Audio Visual Hdqrs. Corp., Inglewood, 1982-84; sound and lighting engr. Century Plaza Hotel, Century City, 1987-; reg. v.p. Primerica Financial Services, Pasadena, 1984-; cameraman, sound and lighting engr., New Life Cable TV Show, Redondo Beach, 1985-87; Republican. Ofc: 1327 Post Ave Ste F Torrance 90501

MULFORD, RAND PERRY, biomedical company executive; b. Sept. 30, 1943 Denver, Colo.; s. Roger Wayne and Ann Louise (Perry) M.; m. Paula Marie Skelley, Aug. 24, 1987; children: Conrad P. Mulford b. 1982, Jeffrey G. Da Vanon b. 1973, Kelley J. Da Vanon b. 1970; edn: BSE in basic engring. (cum laude, NROTC), Princeton, 1965; MBA (high distinction, Baker Scholar), Harvard Bus. Sch., 1972; USN adv. tng. Nuclear Power Sch., Nuclear Reactor Prototype, Submarine Sch., Inertial Navigation, 1965-67; Career: served to Lt. US Navy 1965-70, abd. nuclear-powered Polaris missile submarine, Flotilla commendn. for communications work, meritorious unit citation; mgmt. cons. McKinsey & Co., Inc., Chgo. 1972-80; v.p. planning & control Occidental Chem. Co., Houston, Tx. 1980-82; founder, pres. Technivest Inc., Houston 1982-84; exec. dir. corp. planning Merck & Co., Inc. Rahway, N.J. 1985-89; v.p. fin. and adminstrn. Advanced Tissue Sciences, La Jolla, Calif. 1989-90; CEO Vector Systems, La Jolla 1990-92; c.o.o. Houghten Pharmaceuticals, San Diego 1992-; dir: L.Karp & Sons Inc., Chgo., Quest Med. Inc., Dallas; Medication Delivery Devices, San Diego; mem.: Internat. Forum of Corporate Directors. Res: 2178 Caminito Del Barco Del Mar 92014 Ofc: Houghten Pharmaceuticals 3550 General Atomics Ct San Diego 92121

MULLAN, JACK W., real estate developer; b. Sept. 17, 1924, Ft. Dodge, Iowa; s. Paul B. and Florence (Zeller) M.; m. Beverly Fortner, Feb. 8, 1951; children: Lori Lee, Jill Ann; edn: BS, USC 1950; postgrad. Univ. J.W. Goethe, Frankfurt, Ger. 1953-54; PhD, San Gabriel Univ. 1970. Career: co-pilot United Airlines 1951-53; mgr. Aero Exploration, Frankfurt, Ger. 1954-55; pres. Mullan R.E. and other real estate devel. cos. 1955-; founding chmn. Orange Co. Econ. Devel. Conf. 1963; bd. dirs. Project 21 Orange Coast Assn., pres. 1986-87; Orange Co. Met. Area Com. 1963; chmn. City Newport Beach Air Traffic Advy. Com. 1967-68; fin. steering com. Orange Co. BSA 1959; trustee So. Calif. Aviation Council pres. 1980-81; pres. 1st Redevel. Agency Orange Co. 1986; mem: Calif. Real Estate Assn., Newport Harbor Bd. Realtors (pres. 1960), Aircraft Owners & Pilots Assn., So. Calif. Aviation Council, Nat. P-38 Assn. (founding dir., chmn. P-38 Monument Com.), Pacific Anglers (pres. 1988), Delta Tau Delta; works: co-developer 1st horizontal condominum devel. in Calif.; mil: capt. US Army Air Force 1942-46, PTO. Res: 1826 Tradewinds Ln Newport Beach 92660 Ofc: 3400 Irvine Newport Beach 92660

MULLER, JEROME KENNETH, art dealer, editor, painter, psychologist; b. July 18, 1934, Amityville, N.Y.; s. Alphons and Helen (Haberl) M.; m. Nora Marie Nestor, Dec. 21, 1974; edn: BS, Marquette Univ., 1961; postgrad. CSU Fullerton, 1985-86; MA, National Univ., San Diego, 1988, Newport Psychoanalytic Inst., 1988-90. Career: commercial and editorial photographer, N.Y.C., 1952-55; mng. editor Country Beautiful mag., Milwaukee 1961-62, Reproductions Review mag., N.Y.C. 1967-68; editor, art dir. Orange County Illustrated, Newport Beach 1962-67, art editor, 1970-79, exec. editor/art dir. 1968-69; owner/CEO Creative Services Advt. Agcy., Newport Beach 1969-79; founder/CEO Museum Graphics, Costa Mesa 1978-; tchr. photography Lindenhurst (NY) High Sch., 1952-54; tchr. comic art UC Irvine, 1979; guest curator 50th Anniversary Exhib. Mickey Mouse 1928-78 at The Bowers Museum, Santa Ana 1978; organized Moving Image Exhbn. Museum of Sci. and Indus., Chgo., Cooper-Hewitt Museum, NYC, William Rockhill Nelson Gal., Kansas City, 1981; collect original works of outstanding Am. cartoonists, exhibited in major museums nat.; One-man shows include Souk Gallery, Newport Beach 1970, Gallery 2, Santa Ana 1972, Cannery Gallery Newport Bch. 1974; author: Rex Brandt 1972; contbr. photographs and articles to mags.; awards include two silver medals 20th Ann. Exhbn. Advt. and Editorial Art in West 1965; mem: Am. Assn. Profl. Hypnotherapists, Am. Psychol. Assn., Newport Harbor Art Mus., Mus. Modern Art (NYC), Met. Mus. Art, Am. Fedn. of Arts, Laguna Beach Mus. Art, Alpha Sigma Nu; clubs: Newport Beach Tennis, Gr. Los Angeles Press; mil: USAF 1956-57. Res: 2438 Bowdoin Pl Costa Mesa 92626 Ofc: PO Box 10743 Costa Mesa 92627

MULLER, THOMAS FRANCIS, restaurateur, musician, broadcaster; b. Nov. 17, 1946, San Jose; s. Francis Paul and Gloria Marie (Santoro) M.; m. Sally Ericksen, July 6, 1968; children: Thor Emil b. 1971, Kacy Lauren b. 1973; m. 2d. Janice Tilford, May 8, 1977; dau. Alexandra Kahili b. 1989; edn: BA in bdcst. comms., San Jose St. Univ., 1968. Career: profl. musician and composer, 1963-68, 1971-76; owner Lou's Village, San Jose's oldest restaurant, 1976-; estab. new AM radio stations, Clear Channel Assocs., 1981-, dir. "Alive After Five" 1986-, chmn. bd. 1988-; estab. "Classics of Rock and Roll" Concert Series, 1987 (voted concert of the yr. with Chuck Berry and New Arrivals); mem. Santa Clara Valley Hotel & Rest. Assn., San Jose C.of C., San Jose Conv. & Vis. Bur. (dir. 1989-, treas. 1992), San Jose Downtown Assn. (exec. com. bd. dirs.); honors: winner Cross Puget Sound Row doubles 1987, co-winner Monterey Crossing, co-share course record (Quad Alexandra, 1990); mem. New England and S.F. Peninsula MG"T" Register; clubs: Santa Cruz Yacht, Santa Cruz Rowing (pres. 1984-89); organizer successful annual SCRC Lobster Row 1984-, instrumental in estab. of Lee Faraola Rowing Facility in S.C.Harbor 1989; songwriter: Take Me Back to Lahaina (released 1988); mil: lt. jg USN 1969-71, Vietnam Service medal; Democrat; Christian; rec: ocean rowing, sailing, mountain biking. Ofc: Lou's Village 1465 W San Carlos St San Jose 95126

MUNITZ, BARRY ALLEN, state university system chief executive; b. July 26, 1941, Bklyn.; s. Raymond J. and Vivian (LeVoff) M.; m. Anne Tomfohrde (former assoc. director Houston Grand Opera), Dec. 15, 1987; edn: BA (magna cum laude), Brooklyn Coll. CUNY, 1963; MA, Princeton Univ., 1965, PhD, 1968; cert. Univ. Leiden, Netherlands 1962. Career: asst. prof. lit. and drama UC Berkeley, 1966-68; staff assoc. Carnegie Commn. on Higher Edn. 1968-70; mem. pres.'s staff, then assoc. provost Univ. Illinois System, 1970-72, acad. v.p. 1972-76; v.p., dean faculties Univ. of Houston, Tx., Central Campus, 1976-77, chancellor 1977-82, chmn. Texas Long Range Planning 1980-82; pres. and c.o.o. Federated Devel. Co., N.Y. 1982-91; v.chmn. MAXXAM Inc., L.A. 1982-91; chmn. and c.e.o. United Financial Group; chancellor and c.e.o. Calif. State Univ. System (20 campuses and 9 off-campus ctrs., 34,000 faculty & staff, 350,000 students, offers approx. 1,500 bachelor's degree pgms., 600 master's pgms., 8 jt. doctoral pgms. in 240 areas), 1991-; prof. English literature, CSU Los Angeles 1991-; cons. in univ. governance; mem. Nat. Acad. of Scis. (task force), Nat. Acad. Engring. spons. Govt.-Univ.-Ind. Res. Roundtable (Univ. Research Ent. task force chmn.); special advisor Radcliffe pres. re governance, Radcliffe-Harvard merger agreement; chmn. Inprint Bd. (fundraising for creative Writing pgm.) Univ. of Houston; founding chmn. (fundraising bd.) Univ. Ariz. Humanities Faculty; chmn. Texas Works Together Inc. (statewide employment mgmt. mentor pgm. for low income families); bd. dirs. Ednl. Mgmt. Network (exec. recruitment co.), Nantucket; dir. Family Health Prgm.; dir. KCET Public TV; dir. Am. Council on Educ.; trustee Hospice Texas Med. Ctr.; trustee St. John's Acad.; awards: Distinguished Alumnus Bklyn. Coll. 1979, Univ. Houston Alumni Pres.'s medal 1981, Woodrow Wilson fellow 1963; mem: Phi Beta Kappa (S.W. Region Bd.), Anti-Defamation League (bd.), C.of C. (chmn. econ. devel. council legislative task force for higher edn.); author: Leadership in Colleges & Universities: Assessment & Search (1977), monographs, articles. Office of the Chancellor Calif. State University, 400 Golden Shore Long Beach 90802-4275

MURAKAMI, RICHARD MICHIO, state official; b. Jan. 29, 1932, Florin; s. Kazuo Harvey and Yomiko (Inouye) M.; edn: BS actg., USC 1959. Career: accountant City of L.A. 1958-59; corporation examiner I and II Calif. State Dept. Corporations, 1959-65, corp. examiner III, 1965-68, supr. corporation examiner 1968-79, chief examiner 1979-86; asst. commr. Div. Fin. Services, 1986-, chmn. bd. dirs. Regulatory Devel. Com.; mem. Nat. Assn. Credit Union Suprs. (chmn. Program Com.); awards: Optimist of Year (Optimist Club Uptown L.A. 1971-72), Optimist of Year (Zone 2 Pacific S.W. Dist. Optimist Internat. 1973-74); mem: Nat. Assn. Credit Union Suprs., Nat. Assn. Consumer Credit Admnstrn.; civic: Optimist Club Uptown L.A. (pres.), Montebello-Bella Vista Optimist Club, L.A.-Nagoya Sister City Affliation, Nisei Week Japanese Festival, Pacific S.W. Dist. Optimist Internat. (past lt. gov.); mil: cpl. AUS 1953-55; Republican; Episcopal; rec: photog., bowling. Ofc: Dept Corporations 3700 Wilshire Blvd Los Angeles 90010

MURANAKA, HIDEO, artist; b. Feb. 4, 1946, Mitaka-shi, Tokyo, Japan; came to U.S.A. 1974; s. Nobukichi and Hisae Muranaka; edn: BFA, Tokyo Nat. Univ. of Fine Arts & Music, 1970, MFA, 1972; research stu., traditional Japanese painting 1972-73; mural painting, Fresco 1973-74; faculty of Fine Arts; "INYU" desig., assn. Art Exhibition of INTEN (assn. of traditional Japanese style painting) 1972. Career: artist, painting, printmaking, traditional calligraphy; art tchr. traditional Japanese style painting; exhibits: Eberhard Faber Art Contest 1974, S.F. Art Fest. (1974-77, 82, 85), Internat. Exh. of Botanical Drawings Hunterdon Art Ctr., N.J. 1977, 100 New Acquisitions Brooklyn (NY) Mus. 1978, Calif. State Fair 1978, Pacific Coast States Collection at Vice President's House W.D.C. (1980, 81), Calif. Palace of Legion of Honor, S.F. (purchase 1980), 3d Alaskan Wildlife Art Exh. Anchorage Hist. and Fine Art Mus. 1982, Coos Art Mus. 17th Nov. Annual 1982, Alabama Works on Paper (touring 1983), IEEE Centennial Art Contest, N.Y. (purchase award 1983), El Paso (Tx.) Mus. of Art "24th nat. Sun Carnival" 1986, 30th Nat. Print Exh. Hunterdon Art Ctr., Clinton, NJ 1986, San Diego Art Inst. 33rd Exh. 1987, "Stockton National '88" Haggin Mus., Stockton, Calif., "Am. Drawing Biennial" Muscarelle Mus. of Art Coll. of William and Mary 1988, "The Electrum XVIII" Holter Mus. of Art, Helena, MT 1989, "Fine Arts Inst. 24th Annual" San Bdo. Co. Mus., Redlands, Calif. 1989, The Expo. Internat. d'Arts Plastiques" Chapelle de la Sorbone, Paris and the Mus. de la Commanderie, Bordeaux, Fr. 1990, numerous others; awards include 1st prize Internat. Art Exh. for Museo Hosio in Palazzo Castel Sant'Elia, Viterbo, Italy 1988, 2d prize Internat. Art Exh. for Museo Hosio, Capranica-Viterbo, Italy 1984, Kasaku Prize Shell Oil Co. (1971), Wesleyan Coll. Intl. Exh. of Prints and Drawings (purchase award 1980), Owensboro Mus. of Fine Art, Ky. Mid-Am. Biennial (purchase award 1982), 20th Dulin Nat. Works on Paper Exh. Knoxville (Tenn.) Mus. of Art (purchase award 1988), YERGEAU-Musee Internat. d'Art (Collection Permanente 1991) Canada; listed Who's Who in Am. Art 1986, Who's Who in Soc. 1986, Printworld Dir. 1988, Men of Achiev. 1988, The N.Y. Art Rev. 1988, The Calif. Art Rev. 1989, World Biog. Hall of Fame 1990, American Artists 1990; mem. Lepidopterists Soc.; publs: City Mag. (5/75), S.F. Chronicle (5/75); Christian; rec: music, butterfly collector. Res: 179 Oak St #W San Francisco 94102

MURDOCH, BROCK GORDON, educator; b. Apr. 25, 1948, Vancouver, B.C., Canada, nat. U.S. 1977; s. Groffe Watson and Joyce Isabelle (Armstrong) M.; m. Judith Ann James, June 22, 1971; children: Shandi b. 1975; edn: BA, CSU Fullerton, 1970; MBA, CSU Long Beach, 1977; PhD, UC Irvine, 1984; C.P.A., Calif. 1974. Career: asst. controller W.R. Grace Properties Inc., Newport Beach 1973-74; acctg. instr. Georgia Southern Coll., Statesboro, Ga. 1977-78; assoc. prof. acctg. Chapman Coll., Orange 1978-85; prof. acctg. CSU Chico, 1985-; awards: CSU Profl. Promise (1985-86, 88-89), CSU Chico Coll. of Bus. outstanding researcher and outstanding faculty member, also Inter-Bus. Student Council outstanding tchr. 1988-89; mem. Am. Acctg. Assn. (1977-); contbr. 7+ articles in refereed jours.; rec: rugby, waterskiing, softball. Ofc: Dept. Acctg. & Mgmt. Sci. Calif. State Univ. Chico 95929-0011

MURDOCK, VERONICA J., television and film producer, executive; b. Apr. 22, 1963, San Gabriel, Calif.; d. Joseph B. and Assunta (Scinocca) Nocero; m. James William Murdock, July 22, 1989 (div. Apr. 1992); edn: BA bdcst. journalism, BA history, USC, 1985. Career: operations mgr. Schulman Video, Hollywood 1985-86; scheduler The Post Group, 1986, mgr. of scheduling 1987-90, post prodn. supr. 1990-91; v.p. prodn. Digital Magic, Santa Monica 1991-; pres., c.e.o. Magic Films 1993-; prodn. coord. exercise video "Aerobicise" (1992); awards: Woman of yr. Women in Show Business, L.A. 1991, Blue ribbon judges panel Acad. of TV Arts and Scis., L.A. 1992; mem: Women in Show Bus. (v.p. ways & means 1986-), Women in Film (mem. at lg. 1991-92), American Film Inst. (mem. at lg. 1986-), Acad. TV Arts and Scis. (prodn. execs. peer group 1992-), USC Alumni (coordinating council); civic: Cystic Fibrosis Soc. 1988-, AIDS Proj. L.A. 1989-, Smithsonian 1988-, Mus. Contemporary Art 1991-, Historical Soc. So. Calif. 1990-; Republican; R.Cath.; rec: singing, dancing, outdoors. Res: 1243 Virginia Ave 10, Glendale 91202

MURPHY, FORREST PATRICK, physician-ophthalmologist; b. Nov. 9, 1950, Kansas City, Mo.; s. George Wm. and Dorothy Mary (Conard) M.; edn: BS, US Naval Acad., 1975; MD, Kansas Univ. Med. Ctr., 1978; Diplomate Am. Bd. Ophthalmology 1986. Career: trauma emergency physician John C. Lincoln Hosp., Phoenix, Az. 1979-81; emergency physician Letterman Hosp., San Francisco 1981-82; resident, ophthalmology, Kansas Univ. Med. Ctr., 1982-85; group ophthalmology practice, San Francisco 1985-87, also resident instr. Pacific Med. Ctr.; pvt. practice/pres. Talmadge Eye Center, San Diego 1987-, ophthalmic cons. ReadiCare Centers, 1987-; mem. O.R. planning Com. Mercy Hosp., and exec. com. Mercy Hosp. Laser Ctr., San Diego; honors: Nat. Honor Soc., H.S. 1968, academic biosci. award US Naval Acad. Annapolis 1972, certif. achievement Letterman Hosp. S.F. 1971, Outstanding Young Men of Am. 1979; Fellow Am. Coll. of Surgeons, Fellow Am. Acad. Ophthalmology; mem: San Diego Co. Med. Soc., CMA, Internat. Assn. Ocular Surgeons, Am. Diabetes Assn., Ophthalmol. Assn. - Research to Prevent Blindness Inc., Am. Soc. Cataract & Refractive Surgeons; mil: midshipman USN 1971-73; Republican; Episcopalian; rec: skiing, piano, arts & music. Ofc: Talmadge Eye Center 4453 Euclid Ave San Diego 92115

MURPHY, FREDERICK CLINTON, lawyer; b. Oct. 25, 1922, Willows; s. Frederick Cox and Emma Elizabeth (Fell) M.; m. Ethel Corinne Holland, Aug. 21, 1948; children: Corinne Lee, Kristine Elizabeth, Frederick Clinton, II; edn: AB in pol. sci., UC Berkeley 1947; Hastings Coll. of Law 1947-50; LLB, McGeorge Coll. Law 1951; admitted to Calif. State Bar 1953; cert. splst. in Worker's Comp. 1973. Career: prin. and tchr. Garden Valley Sch. Dist., 1950-51; investigator, Ind. Indemnity, Sacto. 1951-52; lawyer prin., W. Sacto. 1953-1958; atty. State Compensation Ins. Fund, Sacto. 1958-61; referee Ind. Accident Commn., Eureka 1961-63; lawyer, Hanna & Brophy, Sacto. 1963-71, Twohy & Murphy, 1971-76, lawyer prin., F. Clinton Murphy Inc., Sacto. 1976-89, merged into Greve Clifford Diepenbrock & Paras, 1989, ret. 1990; bd. trustees Washington Unified Sch. Dist. 1956-59; honors: Theta Xi, Phi Phi, Delta Theta Phi; past mem. ABA, Calif. State Bar Assn., Sact. County Bar Assn., Am. Judicature Soc. 1960-81, Calif. Compensation Defense Attys. Assn., Valley Indsl. Claims Assn.; lodge: Mason, Order of Eastern Star; mil: s/sgt. US Army 1942-45, Purple Heart, Bronze Star; Repubublican (Yolo County rep. central com. 1954-61, rep. State Central Com. 1961). Res: 1460 Meredith Way Carmichael 95608

MURRAY, EDWIN RENE, air traffic controller; b. Apr. 7, 1922, Oakland; s. Edwin Rene and Helen Mar (Rine) M.; m. Patricia Ruth Snow, June 11, 1949; children: Gary b. 1950, Alex b. 1952, Eugene b. 1954, Lauren b. 1958; edn: AA, Coll. of Marin, 1943, UC Berkeley 1946-48. Career: carpentry and cabinet bus., 1949-58; air traffic controller Fed. Aviation Adminstrn. Lake Minchumina, Ak. 1958-60, Anchorage 1961, Tonopah, Nev. 1961-64, Reno 1964-65, Ukiah, Calif. 1965-85, ret.; mil: 2d lt. USAAF 1943-46, pilot B-24, B-29; rec: fly fishing, mountaineering. Res: 9600 E Side Rd Ukiah 95482-9616

MURRAY, LOUANN WILSON, biochemist; b. Jan. 20, 1943, Indianapolis, Ind.; d. Donald E. and Lucile (Williams) Wilson; m. G. Victor Leipzig, Dec. 20, 1983; children: Robert L. b. 1962, Scott A. b. 1965; edn: BS, Univ. Colo. 1972, PhD, Univ. Conn. Health Center 1981. Career: research biologist Wesleyan Univ., Middletown, Conn. 1972-76, postdoctoral fellow 1981; res. assoc. Harbor

UCLA, Torrance 1981-83, asst. res. genetist 1983-84, asst. prof. Med. Center 1984-; cons. CIB Devel. Corp., Irvine 1987; scientific advy. bd. Applied Biomed. Scis., Long Beach 1987-89; honors: Alpha Lambda Delta; research grants 1983-89; mem: Am. Soc. Cell Biologists, Electron Microscopy Soc. of Am., Am. Soc. Human Genetics, We. Connective Tissue Soc. (past chair), Soc. Wetland Scientists, Huntington Beach Tomorrow (bylaws com. 1986), Amigos de Bolsa Chica (photo contest chmn. 1987), Friends of Huntington Beach Wetlands (bd. dirs. 1989), Huntington Beach Wetlands Conservancy (interpretive com. chair 1989); 43 articles and abstracts pub. on biomed. res. (1967-), photographer Images of Rural New England (1975); Democrat; Cath.; rec: photog., gardening, bird watching. Ofc: Harbor Univ. of Calif. Los Angeles Medical Center 1124 Carson Bldg E-4 Torrance 90502

MURRAY, WILLIAM EDWARD, electrical engineer; b. March 14, 1924, Chickasha, Okla.; s. William Clifford and Blanche Winifred (McIntyre) M.; m. Jeannie Morris, April 27, 1946; children: Robert b. 1947, Richard b. 1948, Daniel b. 1953, John b. 1955, Alan b. 1962; edn: BS, UC Berkeley 1947; MSEE, USC 1954; postgrad. stu., UC Irvine 1978-80. reg. prof.elec. engr (CA E2830), Life Cert. in Voc. Engr Educ (CA 3536 VPL). Career: br. chief McDonnell Douglas Astronautics Co., Huntington Beach 1969-74; senior engr., scientist Douglas Aircraft Co., Long Beach 1974-78, prin. engr., scientist 1978-84, senior staff engr.1984-85, prin. staff engr. 1985-90, prin. specialist -design 1990-; instr. engring. UC Irvine 1978-84, UCLA 1960-66, 1985-, Golden West Coll. 1972-76, CSU Northridge 1974, Los Angeles Dept. of Edn. 1960-84; honors: IEEE Centennial Medal 1984, elected eminent member, Eta Kappa Nu, 1987, elected WESCON dir. 1987-92, chmn. exec. com. 1990, chmn. bd. dirs. 1992, 6 NASA citations, 6 McDonnell Doug. cits. elected fellow, Inst. for the Adv. of Engring. 1982; IEEE-AES Internat. Tech. Paper Award, Wash. DC 1963; mem: Eta Kappa Nu (nat. pres. 1973-74, Western Rep. Award Orgn. Comm. 1983-, Vladymer Karapetoff Eminent Member Award 1990-, nat. v.p. 1972-73, nat. dir. 1970-72, pres. L.A. Alumni chpt. 1965-66), IEEE (Region 6 dir.-elect 1993-94,Los Angeles Council, chmn. 1985-86, v.chmn., secty. 1984-85, treas. 1983-84, chmn. Sects. Com. 1982-83; Orange Co. sect., chmn. 1981-82, v.chmn. 1979-81, secty. 1978-79; gen. chmn. 1982 Reg. 6 Conf., awards chmn. Power Electronics Splsts. Conf. 1977-85, secty. Elec. Power/ Energy Sys. Panel 1977-, mem. 1948-60, sr. mem. 1960-90, Life sr. mem. 1990-), Tau Beta Pi, Pi Tau Pi Sigma, Pi Kappa Alpha, Aerospace Electrical Soc., Am. Inst. Aero. & Astro.; author, 8 engring. papers presented and publ. at confs.; mil: 1st lt. US Army Signal Corps 1943-45, 1950-52; Republican; Methodist; rec: literature, technology, travel. Res: 1531 Wyndham Court Rd Santa Ana 92705 Ofc: Douglas Aircraft Co., 3855 Lakewood Blvd Long Beach 90846

MUSKET, RONALD GEORGE, scientist; b. Feb. 4, 1940, St. Louis, Mo.; s. George Henry and Geraldine (Morris) M.; m. Yvona Marie Hoehne, Aug. 19, 1961; children: Kevin b. 1966, Brian b. 1968, Daren b. 1970; edn: BS engring. physics, Univ. Colorado, Boulder 1962; PhD engring. sci., UC Berkeley, 1967. Career: physicist NASA Lewis Research Ctr., Cleveland, Oh. 1967-69; lectr. Cleveland State Univ., p.t. 1968-69; physicist Sandia Lab., Livermore, Calif. 1969-77; mgr. surface instrumentation Kevex Corp., Foster City 1977-80; physicist Lawrence Livermore Nat. Lab., Livermore 1980-; awards: AEC nuclear sci. & engring. fellow UCB 1962-65, NASA predoctoral fellow UCB 1965-67; mem. Am. Physical Soc., Am. Vacuum Soc., Materials Research Soc.; publs: 70+ sci. papers; mil: capt. US Army 1967-69; rec: reading, tennis, travel, jogging. Res: 9452 Thunderbird Pl San Ramon 94583 Ofc: LLNL, Livermore 94550

MUTSCHLER, LAWRENCE HOWARD, real estate investment; b. Oct. 9, 1934, St. Cloud, Minn.; s. Lawrence V. and Leah Mildred (Luther); edn: Claremont McKenna Coll. 1953-54, USC 1959, BS; Art Center Coll. 1960; UCLA 1980-84.; mem. Bel Air Navy League, Presidents Councils CMC; clubs: Palm Valley CC (Palm Desert), Riviera CC, L.A. Athletic, Calif. Yacht, Fredricksburg CC,Virginia; R.Cath.; rec: collecting antiques & art, travel. Res: 7172 Hawthorn Ave Los Angeles 90046, and Southbrook Farm, Port Royal District,Caroline Cty, VA.

MYERS, MILES A., teacher association executive director; b. Feb. 4, 1931; s. Alvin Frank and Katheryn Pauline M; m. Celest, three children; edn: AB rhetoric, UC Berkeley, 1953; MA tchg., 1979; MA English, 1982; PhD edn., language and literacy div., 1982; cand. in philosophy, UCB, 1981; Calif. tchg. credentials: secondary 1957, vocat. 1964, adminstrv. 1979, Calif. Comm. Colls. cred. (in process). Career: secty., bd. dirs. Alpha Plus Corp., non-profit corp. operating 2 pre-schs. and one infant sch., 1968-; English Tchr. Splst. selected by Calif. State Dept. of Edn., cons. 12+ sch. dists. and ednl. agys., 1969-73; English tchr. Oakland Dist., Eng. dept. chair Oakland High Sch. 1969-71, 72-74, Castlemont High Sch., 1975-76; one yr. leave to direct and estab. f.t. legislative pgm. for Calif. Fedn. of Tchrs., AFT, 1971-2; assoc. dir. Bay Area Writing Project (also lectr. 300+ areas nat.), Language and Literacy Div. UCB Sch. of Edn., Berkeley 1976-85, supr. UCB Sch. of Edn., Secondary English Cred. Candidates, 1976, supr. Tchr. Edn., Lang. & Literacy Div., 1984-85; mem. exec. bd. Berkeley Tchrs. Ctr., UCB, 1982-85; vis. lectr. UCSB 1983; pres. Calif. Fedn. of Tchrs., AFT, Oakland 1985-, ed. (contract pos.) California Teacher, 1981-, earlier contract period 1966-75; exec. dir. Nat. Council of Tchrs. of English, Champaign, Ill., 1991-; recipient gen. excellence awards from AFT's Union Tchr. Press Assn. (1969, 70, 72, 74, 75), UTPA award for best column (1986), OFT-AFT Service Award (pres. 1964-65); mem. Nat. Bd. of Consultants, Nat. Endowment for the Humanities 1978-; author books, book chapters, numerous monographs and articles in ednl. jours.; mem: Am. Fedn. of Tchrs., Am. Edn. Res. Assn., Calif. Assn. of Tchrs. of English (Cent. Calif. Council, disting. svc. award 1986), English 300 Soc., Phi Delta Kappa/UCB, UCB Alumni Assn., Internat. Reading Assn., Calif. Reading Assn., Secondary Tchrs. Assn. of Reading of East Bay, Nat. Conf. on Research in English, Assn. for Childhood Edn.; mil: sgt. AUS 1953-56. Res: 6308 Heather Ridge Way Oakland 94611 Ofc: 5236 Claremont Ave Oakland 94618

MYERS, WALLACE JAMES, marine engineer, ret.; b. Nov. 25, 1920, San Francisco; s. James Ira and Gertrude (Phillips) M.; m. Betty, June 25, 1960; 1 dau, Debra b. 1954; edn: BA, UC Berkeley, 1951; Calhoon MEBA Engineering Sch., Baltimore; Career: engring. ofcr. U.S. merchant and naval vessels, 1942-85, ret.; mem: Masons, Scottish Rite, Elks, Moose, UC Berkeley Alumni Assn., Calif. Alumni Club of Long Beach, Sierra Club, ARRL, BMW CCA, South Coast BMW Riders, Am. Legion, VFW, Palm Springs Desert Mus., China Coaster Chapt. American Merchant Marine Veterans; mil: Lt.(s.g.) USNR, WWII veteran; Republican; rec: amateur radio (call N6QM), investing and portfolio mgmt. Res: 1635 E Ocean Blvd Long Beach 90802 Ofc: 1 World Trade Center PO Box 32126 Long Beach 90832-2126

NADLER, RICHARD LEE, certified public accountant; b. Nov. 27, 1932, San Francisco; s. Max and Leona G. (Urbanus) N.; m. Joan Chrisman, June 24, 1950 (div. 1958); m. Barbara Beaver, June 17, 1960; children: Deborah b. 1951, Rhonda b. 1954, Jeffrey b. 1955, Daniel b. 1963, David b. 1965; edn: C.P.A. Calif. (1961). Career: pub. acct. trainee Arthur M. Haddock, Redwood City 1950-54; govt. contract splst. Hiller Helicopters, Palo Alto 1955-57; chief acct. Pulse Engring. Inc. 1957-58; govt. contract splst. Aerojet Gen. Corp., Sacto. 1958-62; owner Nadler Accountancy Corp., Orangevale 1962-; bd. dir. Christian Estate Planners 1973-; adult edn. tchr. Folsom Cordova Unified Sch. Dist., Rancho Cordova 1965-73; mem: Am. Inst. C.P.A., Calif. Soc. C.P.A., Soc. Calif. Accts., Nat. Soc. Accts., Sacto. Estate Planning Council, Linc Soc. of C.P.A. Fin. Planners, Orangevale Rotary (pres. 1977-78), Orangevale C.of C. (bd. dirs. 1962-64); article pub. in profl. jour. 1981, contbr. Simplified Bookkeeping for Churches 1990; Republican; Conservative Baptist; rec: sports, music. Res: 9400 Shumway Dr Orangevale 95662 Ofc: Nadler Accountancy Corp. 9276 Greenback Ln Ste C Orangevale 95662

NAKAGAWA, ALLEN DONALD, radiologic technologist; b. Mar. 14, 1955, N.Y.C.; s. Walter Tsunehiko and Alyce Tsuneko (Kinoshita) N.; edn: BS in environmental studies, St. John's Univ., Jamaica, N.Y. 1977; MS in marine biol., C.W. Post Coll., 1980; Cert. radiologic technologist, 1986, Cert. in fluoroscopy, 1987. Career: research asst. environ. studies St. John's Univ., 1976-78; lab. asst. Bur. of Water Surveillance, Nassau County Health Dept., Wantaugh, N.Y. 1978; clin. endocrinology asst. Univ. Calif. VA Hosp., San Francisco 1981-83; student technologist St. Mary's Hosp., S.F. 1985-86; radiologic technologist Mt. Zion Hosp., S.F. 1986-88; Univ. Calif. San Francisco 1988-, senior rad. technologist UCSF 1989-; awards: UCSF Medical Ctr. Director's Commendn. letter for 1989 earthquake preparedness, biog. listings in Who's Who in West, cross-ref. in Who's Who in Am., Internat. Directory of Disting. Leadership (2d edit.); mem: Sigma Xi, Calif. Soc. Radiologic Technologists, AAAS, Am. Registry RTs (Cert.), Calif. Acad. Scis., Planetree Resource Ctr., ACLU, Japanese-Am. Nat. Mus. (charter mem. 1991), Marine Mammal Ctr. (formerly Calif. MMC); recruiting chmn. hunger project C.W. Post Coll. 1979; att. radiology, biotech. and computer related confs.; co-author chpts. in books, contbr. articles to profl. jours.; Democrat; Methodist; rec: computer illustration, reading, bowling, vol. activities, studying advanced technologies, photog. Ofc: Univ. Calif. Dept. Radiology Box 0628 Rm C324 Third Ave at Parnassus San Francisco 94143

NAKANO, HIROYUKI, company executive; b. Sept. 20, 1935, Matsumoto, Japan; s. Homare and Kogane N.; m. Yuki, Apr. 14, 1964; children: Tomoyo b. 1965, Takayo b. 1967; edn: BA, Tokyo Univ. 1959. Career: engr. Hitachi Ltd., Tokyo, Japan 1967-; devel. of Tel. Exchange System 1967-68, chief design engr. Real Time Computer Sys. 1978-82, dept. mgr. Microprocessor devel. 1983-85, dept. mgr. product plnng. of small computer sys. 1986-90, current: gen. mgr. Hitachi Computer Products, Santa Clara, Calif.; mem. IEEE (sr. v.p.); Buddhist; rec: classical music, golf. Res: 288 Casitas Bulevar Los Gatos 95030 Ofc: Hitachi Computer Products 3101 Tasman Dr Santa Clara 95054

NAKANO-MATSUMOTO, NAOMI NAMIKO, social worker; b. May 3, 1960, Salt Lake City, Utah; d. Rokuro "George" and Miyuki (Tashima) Nakano; m. Robert Hideo Matsumoto, Aug. 10, 1991; edn: BS sociology, soc. work, Weber State Coll., Ogden, UT 1982; MSW, Univ. Denver, 1986; Lic. clin. soc. wkr. Colo. 1991, Calif. 1992-. Career: caseworker Children's Aid Soc. of Utah, Ogden 1982-85; social worker Asian/Pacific Ctr. for Human Devel., Denver 1985-87; soc. worker II, Santa Clara County Dept. Soc. Svs., San Jose 1988; school soc. worker Denver Public Schs., Denver 1986-91, mem. Asian Edn. Advy. Coun. Denver Pub. Schs. 1988-91; soc. worker/supr. Asian Americans for

Comm. Involvement, San Jose, Calif. 1991-; awards: Outstanding Young Women of Am. 1988, Outstanding Volunteer Denver Girls Inc. 1990, listed Who's Who in West 1992; mem: Nat. Assn. Soc. Workers 1987-, Coalition for Asian/Pacific Islander Youth 1992-, Nat. Assn. Asian & Pacific Am. Educators 1986-, Asian Am. Psychol. Assn. 1986-, Asian Human Svs. Assn. 1985-91, Coalition for Multi-Ethnic Svc. Providers 1988-91, Japanese Am. Citizens League San Jose, Asian Women Advocating for Rights & Empowerment 1992-, Asian Pacific Islanders for Reproductive Health 1993-; Democrat; Jodo Shinshu Buddhist; rec: jogging, biking. Ofc: Asian Americans for Community Involvement 232 E Gish Rd Ste 200 San Jose 95112

NALBANDIAN, A. EUGENE, company president; b. Mar. 7, 1937, Fresno; s. Arnold Stephan and Elizabeth (Kalunian) N.; m. Fern Perrin, Oct. 14, 1952; children: Michelle b. 1963, Stephan b. 1966, Jon David b. 1971, Jeanne b. 1979, Derek b. 1980; edn: BS, Fresno State Univ. 1960; MBA, UCLA 1964. Career: merchandise mgr. Bullocks, Los Angeles 1964-68; sr. cons. Peat Marwick Mitchell 1969-70; pres. Blums of San Francisco 1970-72; exec. v.p. Swensens Ice Cream 1972-76; pres. Tweezer Lite, Inc., L.A. 1976-85; pres., dir. Jardinier Planter Systems Inc., Fullerton 1985-; patentee: Tweezer Lite 1980, Screwdriver Lite 1981, Sub-irrigation container 1990; Republican; Prot.; rec: tennis. Res: 1741 Brookdale La Habra 90631 Ofc: Jardinier Planter Systems, Inc. Fullerton 92635

NAPLES, CAESAR J., university administrator; b. Sept. 4, 1938, Buffalo, N.Y.; s. Caesar M. and Fannie (Occhipinti) N.; children: Jennifer b. 1965, Caesar b. 1967; m. Sandra L. Harrison, 1983; edn: AB, Yale Univ., 1960; JD, SUNY at Buffalo, 1963; admitted bar: N.Y. 1963, Fla. 1977, Calif. 1987, U.S. Supreme Ct. 1969. Career: counsel and staff dir. Select Jt. Legislative Com. on employee rels. New York Legislature, Albany 1969; asst. dir. Gov.'s Office on Employee Rels., N.Y. 1969-70; assoc. v.chancellor State Univ. New York, 1970-74; gen. counsel State Univ. Sys. of Florida, 1974-83; prof. CSU Long Beach, 1983-; v.chancellor The Calif. State Univ., 1983-92, vice chancellor emeritus and Trustee Professor, 1992-; cons. Curtin Univ., Perth, Austr. 1992, CUNY, N.Y.C. 1992, Minn. State Univ. System, Mpls. 1987-, Canadian Public Univs., Can. 1971-; bd. chair Metlife Higher Edn. Bd., N.Y.C. 1987-; mem. Acad. for Academic Personnel Adminstrn. (co-founder 1972-), Ctr. for the Study of Collective Bargaining in Higher Adminstrn. (dir. 1973-); coauthor w/Victor Baldridge (novel) Romanoff Succession 1988; mil: capt. US Army, Armor, 1963-72; rec: writing, tennis, opera. Res: 816-B N Juanita Ave Redondo Beach 90277

NATHANSON, THEODORE HERZL, aerospace engineer; b. Apr. 20, 1923, Montreal, Quebec, Canada, naturalized U.S., 1984; s. Henry and Minnie (Goldberg) N.; edn: SB aero. engring., M.I.T., 1944; M Arch., Harvard Univ., 1955; reg. engr. Quebec, 1946, reg. arch., Quebec, 1956. Career: res. engr. Noorduyn Aviation Ltd., Montreal 1944-45; stress engr. Canadair Ltd., 1945-46; struct. engr. A.V. Roe (Canada) Ltd., Malton, Ont. 1946-47; mem. tech. staff Rockwell Internat., Downey, Calif. 1979-92, space transp. syst. div. 1979-86, space station syst. div., 1986-87, space station elec. power syst., Canoga Park, 1987-92; L. Mies van der Rohe Arch., Chgo. summer 1949, R.Buckminster Fuller designer, Forest Hills, N.Y. summer 1951; cons. Montreal, Boston, L.A., 1956-; lectr. in arch. McGill Univ., Montreal 1967-68; awards: sustained superior performance award for outstanding achiev.- NASA Space Station Cupola design, Rockwell Intl. Space Station Systems Div., Downey 1987; mem: Royal Arch. Inst. of Canada 1956-, Am. Inst. of Aero. and Astro. 1960-, British Interplanetary Soc. (Fellow 1981), Nat. Mgmt. Assn. 1980-, Harvard Club of Boston 1955-; exhibitions: projects and models included in group shows: Mus. of Fine Arts, Springfield, Mass. 1961, N.Y. World's Fair 1965, Winterfest, Boston 1966, Boston Artists' Project '70; publs: author: Proceedings AIAA/ ASME/ ASCE/ AHS/ ASC 21st Structures, Structural Dynamics and Materials Conf., Long Beach, Calif. 1990; Jewish; rec: travel, photog. Res/Ofc: 225 S Olive St #1004 Los Angeles 90012

NAVARRE, GERALD LEO, obstetrician-gynecologist, educator; b. April 10, 1931, Ecorse, Mich.; s. Leo Curtis and Harriet Celina (Raupp) N.; m. Rita, June 11, 1960; children: Mark b. 1961, Mary b. 1963, Matt b. 1965, Michael b. 1966, Martin b. 1970; edn: BS chem., Mich. St. Univ. E. Lansing 1953; MD, Univ. Mich. Ann Arbor 1957; cert. Am. Coll. Ob-Gyn. 1968. Career: intern San Bernardino Co. Hosp. 1957-58; resident ob-gyn. Fresno Co. Hosp. 1962-65; physician ob-gyn. Kaiser Found. Hosps. in Bellflower 1965-83, in Anaheim 1983-; asst. clin. prof. Harbor UCLA Med. Center, Torrance 1970-84; clinical prof. UC Irvine 1981-; mem: Am. Soc. Colposcopy & Cervical Pathology 1972-, Internat. Fedn. Colposcopy, Am. Assn. Pro-Life Obstetricians & Gynecologists (Fla.), Pro-Life Med. Assn.; 4+ pub. articles in med. jours. (1975-84); mil: capt. USAF 1956-62; Republican; R.Cath.; rec: golf, scuba diving. Res: 4965 Westfield Ct Anaheim Hills 92807 Ofc: So. California Permanente Medical Group 441 Lakeview Anaheim 92807-3089

NAVARRO, ARTEMIO EDWARD, educator, city elected official; b. Nov. 12, 1950, East Los Angeles; s. Artemio G. and Maria Bertha (Bustamante) N.; m. Sally J., Aug. 7, 1983; children: Natalie b. 1984, Julie b. 1986, Laura b. 1987; edn: AA, East L.A. Coll., 1972; BA, CSU Los Angeles, 1974, MA, 1982; Calif. Std. tchg. cred. Career: tchr. Sura Intermediate School, Montebello 1974—;

elected City Council City of Commerce, 1988-92, mayor 1991-92, reelected, 1992-96; del. League of Calif. Cities 1988-89; honors: Outstanding Young Man Am., U.S. Jaycees, Tulsa 1983, Outstanding local pres. Calif. Jaycees 1986-87; mem: Assn. for the Advance. of MexAmer. Students (1976-, past bd.), Calif. Assn. for Bilingual Edn., Montebello Tchrs. Assn., Calif. Tchrs. Assn.; civic: E.L.A. Jaycees (pres. 1986-87, chmn. bd. 1987-88), Commerce Lions Club; mil: quartermaster USCG 1969-71; Democrat; R.Cath.; rec: photography, travel, carpentry. Res: 5514 E Village Dr Commerce 90040 Ofc: City Hall, 3535 Commerce Way Commerce 90040

NAY, SAMUEL W., JR., consulting engineer; b. May 29, 1914, Steamboat Springs, Colo.; s. Samuel W. and Josephine L. (Bartz) N.; m. Edythe L. Winberg, May 31, 1942; 1 son, Samuel W. III b. 1943 (decd.); edn: BS engrg., CSU Los Angeles; Reg. Mech. Engr. Calif., Fire Protection Engr. Calif. Career: tooling Lockheed Aircraft Burbank 1940-47; mech. engr. assoc. Dept. of Water & Power L.A. 1947-78; tchr. UCLA Extn. 1978-81; cons. engr. S.W. Nay Assoc., owner/ptnr. in cons. engr. & parliamentary law firm 1978-; mem: Soc. Fire Protection Engrs. (past chpt. pres.), L.A. Council of Engineers & Scientists (pres. 1990-91), Am. Soc. Mech. Engrs., Inst. for Advancement of Engrs. (past treas.), Toastmasters Internat. (past area gov., ATM), Brookside Men's Golf Club; editor: The Flame (tech. soc. publ. 1978-81); mil: sgt. USAAF 1942-45, Meritorious Svc.; Republican; Prot.; rec: golf, photog. Ofc: POB 4663 Glendale 91202

NAZZARO, DAVID ALFRED, sales executive; b. Sept. 15, 1940, Malden, Mass.; s. Alfred Anthony and Louise (Cunningham) N.; m. Jane Valentine, June 26, 1971; 1 son, David Thomas; edn: BME, US Merchant Marine Acad., 1962; MS, Columbia Univ., 1965; MBA, Pepperdine Univ., 1975. Career: regional mgr. Turbo Power and Marine Systems div. United Technologies, Hartford, Conn. 1965-74; mgr. bus. devel. S & Q Corp., San Francisco 1974-78; v.p. and gen. mgr. Con-Val, Oakland 1978-85; pres. and c.e.o. Dasa Controls, Belmont 1985-87; mgr. bus. devel. Johnson Yokogawa Corp., San Francisco 1987-; mem: Instrument Soc. Am. (Sr. Mem., pres. No. Calif. sect. 1987-88), ASME, Am. Water Works Assn., Elks, Jaycees, Clearview HOA (bd. 1976); mil: lt. USNR 1963-69; St. Bartholomew's Ch. San Mateo (Parish Council pres. 1986, Mens Club pres. 1977); rec: skiing, tennis, racquetball, handball, bridge. Res: 30 Tollridge Ct San Mateo 94402 Ofc: Johnson Controls, Inc. 50 Park Lane Brisbane 94005

NEBELKOPF, ETHAN, psychologist; b. June 14, 1946, NY, NY; s. Jacob Aloysius and Fega (Carver) N.; m. Ellen Rozek, Nov. 15, 1966 (div. 1971); m. Karen Horrocks, July 25, 1974; children: Demian b. 1967, Sarah b. 1974; edn: BA, City Coll. N.Y., 1966; MA, Univ. Mich., 1969; PhD, Summit Univ., 1989; lic. Marriage Family and Child Counselor, Calif. 1979. Career: social worker Proj. Headstart, N.Y.C. 1965; coord. Proj. Outreach, Ann Arbor, Mich. 1968-69; dir. White Bird Clinic, Eugene, Oreg. 1970-75; tng. dir. Walden House Inc., San Francisco 1979-; cons. Berkeley Holistic Health Ctr., 1979-84; herbalist Medcine Wheel, San Diego 1977-80; adj. prof. S.F. State Univ. 1982-87; lectr. Laney Coll., Oakland 1990-91; awards: Silver Key, House Plan Assn. 1966, Phi Beta Kappa 1966; mem: Calif. Assn. of Drug Pgms. (pres. 1988-92), Calif. Assn. of Family Therapists, Calif. Assn. of Drug Educators 1990-; appt. S.F. Mayor's Task Force on Drugs 1988-92, Gov's. Policy Council on Drugs, Treatment Com., Sacto. 1989-92; author: White Bird Flies to Phoenix (1973), The Herbal Connection (1981); rec: baseball cards, rocks, yoga, herbs. Res/Ofc: 6641 Simson St Oakland 94605

NEEDLER, MARTIN CYRIL, university administrator; b. Mar. 23, 1933, Manchester, England, naturalized U.S., 1954; s. Thomas Anthony and Beatrice (Rosenberg) N.; m. E. Lore Heyman, Mar. 16, 1955 (div. Mar. 1976); children: Stephen b. 1956, Daniel b. 1970; m. Jan Knippers Black, July 23, 1976; edn: AB, Harvard Univ., 1954, PhD, 1960. Career: tchg. fellow Harvard 1957-59; instr. Dartmouth, 1959-60; instr., asst. prof. Univ. Mich., Ann Arbor 1960-65; research assoc. Harvard 1965-66; assoc. prof., prof., dir. Univ. of New Mexico, Albuquerque 1966-90; dean Sch. of Internat. Studies, Univ. of the Pacific, Stockton 1990-; lectr. Foreign Service Inst., Rosslyn, Va. 1967, 80, 81; cons. NSF, NEH, Smithsonian, W.D.C., 1970-, Dept. of State, W.D.C., 1976-77, various members U.S. Congress, 1962-86; vis. prof. Univ. Pitts., Inst. for Shipboard Edn. at Sea, 1988; awards: postdoctoral fellow UCLA 1962, senior assoc. mem. St. Antony's Coll., Oxford 1971, senior research fellow Univ. Southampton, Eng. 1974, Bishop Miller Lectr. Covell Coll. U.O.P. 1977, Phi Beta Kappa (Alpha of N.Mex. pres. 1987-88); mem. Consortium of Latin Am. Studies Pgms. (chmn. steering com. 1970), Latin Am. Studies Assn. (pgm. chmn. 1972-73), "Armed Forces & Society" (assoc. editor 1983-); author: Political Devel. in Latin Am. 1968, Politics & Society in Mexico 1971, The Problem of Democracy in L.A. 1987, The Concepts of Comparative Politics 1991 and 10 other books; mil: pfc US Army 1954-56; Democrat; Jewish; rec: cooking, acting, singing, swimming, languages. Res: 4 La Playa Monterey 93940 Ofc: Sch. of Internat. Studies, Univ. of the Pacific, Stockton 95211

NEFF, LESTER LEROY, clergyman, church executive; b. Nov. 20, 1923, Medford, Ore.; s. James Asher and Ruth (Turnbow) N.; m. Avon Maxine Bostwick, Aug. 15, 1942; children: Lawrence b. 1944, Carol b. 1948, Donald b.

1950; edn: BA, Ambassador Coll., 1959; MA theol., 1962. Career: dept. mgr. Ambassador Coll., Worldwide Ch. of God, Pasadena 1955-81, ch. pastor, faculty, treas., chief fin. ofcr. 1981-90; pub. articles in religious jours., 1957, 1990; mil: sgt. USAAF 1943-46. Ofc: Worldwide Church of God Pasadena 91129

NEIL-WILSON, JOYCE, caterer; b. Dec. 3, 1926, Chgo.; d. Floyd Barkley and Irene Emma (Serville) Parker; m. Douglas Stoddard Neil, Oct. 2, 1982; children Leslie Floyd Wilson b. 1946, James Harrison Wilson b. 1947, Deborah L. Wilson b. 1949. Career: U.S. Post Office, Richmond, Calif. 1942-44; Veteran's Admin., San Francisco 1944-46; Party Time Caterer, San Pablo 1956—; bd. dirs. Scholarship Found., Contra Costa Coll., 1991-; honors: recipient personal letter of commendn. from US President, woman of Year City of San Pablo (1974), feature subject in natl. mag. Entrepreneur (11/87), honoree Exchangite of Year and Exchangite of Sierra Pacific Dist. (1990), Goodwill Amb. to Japan (1975), Indonesia (1977), to Mexico; civic: Richmond Soroptimist Cor. Sect., Exchange Club (dir. 1987-89), Bus. & Profl. Women (3-time pres.), Salesian Boys Club (2-time pres., dir. 1965-), Soroptomist (1965-, Woman of Achiev. 1987), Beautification Commn. (2-time pres.), Museum and Historical Soc. (2-time pres.), Portuguese-LUSO (2-time pres.), San Pablo-Manzanilla, Mexico Sister City Bd., Vice Pres.; lodges: Richmond Moose, San Pablo Eagles, Rod & Gun Club; author cookbook: From Caterer's Kitchen To You (1978); restored (15 yr. project) the garden estate that once belonged to John Rockefeller for partytime catering.

NELSON, CAROLYN MARIE, artist; b. Jan. 4, 1945, Oak Park, Ill.; d. Carl Lewis and Mary Wilma (Clark) Eilers; m. Michael Woodrick, June 5, 1970 (div. Sept. 1977); children: Katrina, Matthew; m. Stephen Paul Nelson, Aug. 31, 1985; edn: student, Palm Beach Art Inst., West Palm Beach, Fla. 1962-65, Palm Beach Jr. Coll., Lake Worth, Fla. 1964-65, Maude King. Sch. Art, West Palm Beach, Fla. 1959-69, Cerritos Coll. 1987. Career: owner, instr. art school and gallery, Lake Park, Fla. 1972-80; art. dir. Studio 3, 1974-80; artist, instr. Scottsdale Ctr. of Arts, Ariz. 1982; artist Contracting Agys., Los Angeles 1983-85; asst. dir. fine art Adamson-Duvannes Galleries, L.A. 1985-86; artist, v.p., dir. Gateways to History, L.A. 1986-; artistic dir. Steve's Stitchery, L.A. 1988-; asst. engrs. on MD-11 Flt. Manual - comml. aircraft; v. chmn. Amer. Heritage Bicentennial Commn., City of Norwalk 1991-; major exhibit in Laguna Beach 1990; Fellow L.A. Co. Mus., Gallery One Guild (v.p. 1977-78); works: artist cartoons AMA, 1976, typography Christmas in Dixie parade float (trophy 1978), painting NASA, 1977, graphics Kenyatia Univ., Nairobi, 1979, Getty Oil Co., 1984, Medical Illustrating, 1989; res. in environmental engring. in S. Am. 1991; Lutheran. Res: 10912 E. Hopland St Norwalk 90650

NELSON, CHARLES ROBERT, financial planner; b. Jan. 14, 1930, Philippines; m. Beverly Ann Nelson, May 17, 1980. Career: v.p., mgr. Paine Webber Jackson and Curtis, Newport Beach, Calif. 1972-73, Bache Halsey Stuart, Tucson, Az., 1973-77; owner, mgr. King of the North, Irvine, Calif. 1978-84; owner, mgr. Nelson Fin., Laguna Hills, 1983-84; gen. mgr. First Liberty Securities, Carlsbad 1984-86; sr. ptnr. Nelson Financial Assocs., Dana Point 1986-; advy. bd. Monarch Bank, Laguna Niguel; mem. Internat. Assn. Fin. Planners, Alpha Delta Phi, Rotary Internat.; civic bds: Orange County Hosp. Planning Advy. Com. 1979, Palm Desert Resort Country HOA (bd., v.p. 1982-83), South Coast YMCA (bd. mgrs. 1988-), vol. bus. editor Dana Point News; club: Marbella CC (San Juan Capistrano). Res: 33945 Primavera Dana Point 92629 Ofc: Nelson Financial Associates 24671 La Plaza Ste 2 Dana Point 92629

NELSON, LINDA ANN, bank examiner; b. May 22, 1959, Sioux City, Iowa; d. Charles Howard and Mary Joyce (Forney) N.; edn: BA bus., Univ. Wash., Seattle 1981; MBA fin., Boston Coll., 1987. Career: ins. cons. Washington Mutual Ins., Seattle 1982-85; cons. Manassa Systems Inc., Boston 1986; budget analyst Kendall Corp., 1986; bank examiner Fed. Reserve Bank of Boston, 1987-89; cons. Welling & Woodard, San Francisco 1990; bank examiner Fed. Reserve Bank of San Francisco 1990-; mem. Nat. Assn. Bus. Economists (v.p. S.F. chpt. 1993-94); rec: skiing, scuba. Ofc: FRB of S.F. 101 Market St San Francisco 94105

NEMIR, DONALD PHILIP, lawyer; b. Oct. 31, 1931, Oakland; s. Frank and Mary Madelyn (Shavor) N.; edn: BA, UC Berkeley, 1957, JD, Boalt Hall, Sch. of Law, 1960; admitted bar: Calif. 1961. Career: pvt. law practice, San Francisco 1961-; mdm. Am. Bar Assn., Calif. State Bar, S.F. Bar Assn., Phi Delta Phi; rec: chess, hiking. Res: PO Box 1089 Mill Valley 94942 Law Offices of Donald Nemir, APC, One Bush St. Ste 200 San Francisco 94104

NEMIROW, LAWRENCE HARVEY, risk manager/financial services co. president; b. Dec. 4, 1948, Bklyn.; s. Hyman Wolf and Irma Carver (Schnitzer) N.; m. Rochelle, Oct. 12, 1969 (div.); m. Shari, June 5, 1983; children: Jennifer b. 1971, Adam b. 1976, Aaron b. 1977, Jaime b. 1980; edn: BBA, Univ. Detroit, 1978, MBA, 1980; Western State Univ. Coll. of Law (JD anticipated 1993); desig: ARM (Risk Mgmt.) 1991. Career: subrogations supr. Royal Globe Ins. Co., NY, NY 1971-73; insurance splst. Ford Motor Co., Dearborn, Mich. 1973-80; dir. insurance and benefits John Morrell & Co., Chgo. 1980-84; risk mgr. Honda North America, Torrance 1985-88; prin. risk mgmt. consulting div. Windes & McClaughry Acctncy. Corp., Long Beach 1988-89; pres. The

Nemirow Group, 1989-; mem: Soc. of Risk Mgmt. Consultants, Risk & Ins. Mgmt. Soc., Nat. Risk Mgmt. Panel (1986-); Democrat; Jewish; rec: racquetball. Res: 3690 Daisy St Seal Beach 90740

NESS, OLIVER ROSCOE, JR., physician, ophthalmologist; b. Jan. 15, 1927, Long Beach; s. Oliver R. and Clara (McCullough) N.; m. Margaret Huefner, Oct. 31, 1928; children: Daryl Lynn b. 1953, Robert Oliver b. 1956, Kelly Jean b. 1958, Paige Ann b. 1961; edn: AB, UCLA 1948; MD, UCSF 1952. Career: physician, Long Beach 1956-; clin. prof. UC Irvine 1986-; cons. Long Beach VA Hosp. 1957-; mem: AMA, CMA, L.A. Co. Med. Assn.; mil: USNR 1944-46; Republican; rec: flying. Res: 6481 Montova St Long Beach 90815

NETZEL, PAUL ARTHUR, management and fund raising consultant; b. Sept. 11, 1941, Tacoma; s. Marden Arthur and Audrey Rose (Jones) N.; m. Diane Viscount, Mar. 21, 1963; children: Paul M., Shari Ann; edn: BS in group work edn., Geo. Williams Coll., 1963. Career: program dir. YMCA South Pasadena-San Marina, 1963-66; exec. dir. Culver-Palms Family YMCA, 1967-73; v.p. metropolitan fin. devel. YMCA Met. Los Angeles, 1973-78, exec. v.p. devel. 1979-85; pres. bd. dirs. YMCA Employees Credit Union, 1977-80; chmn. N.Am. Fellowship of YMCA Devel. Officers, 1980-83; adj. faculty USC Coll. Continuing Edn., 1983-86, Loyola Marymount Univ., CSU Los Angeles, 1986-; chmn. bd./c.e.o. Netzel Associates Inc., 1985-; indep. cons., fund raiser; mem. Nat. Soc. Fund Raising Execs. (chpt. pres. Greater L.A. chpt. 1989-90, nat. bd. 1989-92, award Profl. of Year 1983); civic: elected Culver City Bd. of Edn. 1975-79, pres. 1977-78; elected Culver City City Council 1980-88(mayor 1982-83, 86-87, v.mayor 1980-82, 85-86), bd. L.A. Co. Sanitation Dists. (1982-83, 85-87), bd. Culver City Redevel. Agy. (1980-88, chmn. 83-84, 87-88); mem. civic bds: Calif. Youth Model Legislature Bd. Dirs. (chmn. 1987-92), Culver-Palms Family YMCA (bd. of mgrs. 1985-, chmn. bd. 1991-93), Culver City Guidance Clinic (pres. 1971-74), Culver City Edn. Found. 1982-, Los Angeles Psychiat. Service, United Way/W. Reg. (1986-, v.chmn. bd. 1991-), World Affairs Council L.A. 1989-, Town Hall 1991-, Rotary Intl. L.A.#5 (bd. 1989-, pres. 1992-93), Goodwill Industries of So. Calif. (bd. dirs. 1993-); clubs: Los Angeles Athletic, Mountaingate CC; R.Cath. Res: 12336 Ridge Circle Los Angeles 90049 Ofc: 9696 Culver Blvd Ste 204 Culver City 90232

NEWACHECK, DAVID JOHN, lawyer; b. Dec. 8, 1953, San Francisco; s. John Elmer and Estere Ruth Sybil (Nelson) N.; m. Dorothea Quandt, June 2, 1990; edn: AB in English, UC Berkeley, 1976; JD, Pepperdine Univ. Sch of Law, 1979; MBA, CSU Hayward, 1982; LLM (tax) Golden Gate Univ., 1987; admitted bar: Calif. 1979, US Supreme Ct. 1984, Dist. of Col. 1985. Career: tax consultant Pannell Kerr Forster, San Francisco 1982-83; atty. at law, legal writer, Matthew Bender & Co., Oakland 1983-; lectr. in law, Oakland Coll. of Law 1993-; dir. Aztec Custom Cos. 1982-; mem. ABA, Calif. Bar, Alameda County Bar Assn., Mensa, Calif. Alumni Assn., Pepperdine Law Alumni; staff author & consultant: California Taxation, California Closely-Held Corporations, Illinois Tax Service, New Jersey Tax Service, Pennsylvania Tax Service, Bender's Federal Tax Service (pub. Matthew Bender) 1983-; Republican (life mem. Repub. Nat. Com.); Lutheran (deacon); rec: music, competitive running, youth work. Res: 21 Tappan Ln Orinda 94563-1310 Ofc: Matthew Bender & Co. (POB 2077 Oakland 94604-2077) 2101 Webster St Oakland 94612

NEWBERRY, CONRAD FLOYDE, professor of aeronautics and astronautics; b. Nov. 10, 1931, Neodesha, Kans.; s. Ragan McGregor and Audra Anitia (Newmaster) N.; m. Sarah Louise Thonn, Jan. 26, 1958; children: Conrad, Jr., b. 1958, Thomas b. 1962, Susan b. 1965; edn: AA, Independence Jr. Coll. 1951; BEME (Aeronautical Sequence), USC 1957; MSME, Calif. St. Univ. L.A. 1971; M.Ed., 1974; D.Env., UCLA 1985; profl. engr. Calif. 1970, Kans. 1978, Tx. 1979, N.C. 1978; cert. air pollution control engr. Am. Acad. Environmental Engrs. 1988. Career: mathematician L.A. div. N. Am. Aviation 1951-53; jr. engr. 1953-54, engr. 1954-57, sr. engr. 1957-64; asst. prof. aerospace engring. dept., Calif. St. Polytech. Univ., Pomona 1964-70, assoc. prof. 1970-75, prof. 1975-90, professor emeritus 1990-; staff engr. EPA, Res. Triangle Park, N.C. 1980-82; engring. specialist Rockwell Internat. Space Div., 1984-90; prof. aeronautics and astronautics (and academic assoc. for space systems engring.) 1992-, Naval Postgraduate Sch., Monterey 1990-; awards: John Leland Atwood Outstanding Aerospace Engring. Educator award 1986-87, Tau Beta Pi, Sigma Gamma Tau, Kappa Delta Pi; mem: Fellow AIAA (dir. tech.-aircraft systems 1990-93), Fellow Inst. Advancement Engring., Fellow British Interplanetary Soc., ASEE (chmn. Aerospace Div. 1979-80; pgm. chmn. Ocean and Marine Engring. Div. 1991-93), AHS, EAA, ASME, SNAME, AWMA, AMS, SAE, CSPE, CWPCA, AAEE, NAEP, AAAS, IEEE, NSPE, IES, ASPA, Planetary Soc., Am. Soc. of Naval Engrs., U.S. Naval Inst., Soc. of Allied Weights Engrs., Assn. for Unmanned Vehicle Systems, Royal Aeronautical Soc.; Democrat; Disciples of Christ. Res: 9463 Willow Oak Rd Salinas 93907-1037 Ofc: Naval Postgraduate Sch., Monterey 93943-5000

NEWBURN, REX D., police polygraphist; b. Dec. 2, 1934, Malta, Ohio; s. Clancy E. and Ida Christine (Dougan) N.; edn: BS, State Coll. of Wash. 1958; MA, Wash. St. Univ. 1961; designated Expert Polygraphist, Nat. Tng. Ctr. of Lie Detection, NY 1968; lic. Calif. Polygraph Examiner 1985-90. Career: police ofcr. San Jose Police Dept., 1964-70, police sgt. Bur. of Field Ops., 1970-; bd. dirs. San Jose Police Union, Local 170, 1983-87; mem: Am. Polygraph Assn., Calif. Assn. of Polygraph Examiners, Am. Assn. of Police Polygraphists, Acad. of Certified Polygraphists Inc., Calif. Peace Officers Assn., San Jose Police Benevolent Assn., Monterey Bay Aquarium, American Air Museum (founding mem.), U.S. Senatorial Club 1981-, U.S. Com. for The Battle of Normandy Mus.; Republican (Presdl. Task Force); Christian Ch.; rec: reading. Ofc: San Jose Police Dept POB 270 San Jose 95103-0270

NEWHOFF, STANLEY NEAL, advertising executive; b. Jan. 31, 1944, Bronx, N.Y.; s. Norman and Daisy (Weiss) N.; m. Hayde Mathilde Stekkinger, June 16, 1969 (dec. Nov., 1984) children: Michelle Hayde, Angela Robin; edn: BA engring. UCLA 1967. Career: columnist UCLA Daily Bruin 1963-64; tabulator, asst. supr., asst. dir. corp. comms. Audience Studies Inc., L.A. 1964-65; engring. tchr. Beit Safer Tichon Makief H.S., Qiryat Gat, Israel 1969-70; advt. copywriter Doyle Dane Bernbach, Foote Cone & Belding, and others, L.A. 1970-74; v.p., creative dir. Basso Boatman Inc., Newport Beach 1976-79; prin., pres. Lerner Newhoff Advt., L.A. 1974-76, Stanley Newhoff & Prochnow Inc., Costa Mesa 1981-85; prin., chmn. Newhoff & Russakow Inc., Newport Beach 1985-87; pres. Stanley Newhoff Advt. Services, Irvine 1987-; contbr. articles on advt. to pubs.; mem: Med. Mktg. Assn., Irvine Edn. Found. (founding pres.), Nat. Energy Research & Info. Inst. (founding task force), Mensa; Republican; Jewish; rec: writing, golf, racquetball, biking, hiking. Res: 21 Silkberry Irvine 92714 Ofc: Stanley Newhoff Advertising Services 17780 Fitch Ste 165 Irvine 92714

NEWMAN, ANNETTE GOERLICH, shopping center manager; b. Jan. 19, 1940, Fresno; d. David August and Mary Eloise (Simpson) Goerlich; children: Anne Kristen b. 1963, Mark David b. 1965, Gregory Hartley b. 1966; edn: PharmD, UC San Francisco Sch. of Pharmacy 1963, lic. pharm. Calif. 1963; cert. shopping center mgr., CSM 1977. Career: pharmacist Village Drug, 1963-69; pharmaceutical cons. 1962-72; store mgr. The Drug Store of Fig Garden Village, 1972-77, gen. mgr. Fig Garden Village Shopping Center, Fresno 1977-; corp. secty. Fig Garden Village Inc.; bd. dirs. Fig Garden Village Mchts. Assn.; mem. Calif. Club Hon. Soc. UCSF, Blue Gold Club UC Sch. of Pharm., UC Pharmacy Alumni Assn., Nat. Assn. of Female Execs.; civic: Fresno Arts Center (exec. bd. dirs.), Fresno Arts Center and Museum Council of 100, Junior League of Frresno, CSUF Arts & Humanities Advy. Bd., Sen. Ken Maddy's Central Calif. Conf. on Women Advy. Com., St. Agnes Med. Center Found. (bd. dirs.), Childhelp USA, Fig Garden Village Inc. (sec. treas.); rec: ski, equestrian, metaphysics, phys. fitness. Res: 3909 W Fir Fresno 93711 Ofc: Fig Garden Village Shop Ctr. 5082 N Palm Ste A Fresno 93704

NEWMAN, JEFFREY RICHARD, electronic engineer; b. Nov. 6, 1955, New York, N.Y.; s. Leo and Ellen Ruth (Groer) N.; m. Marushka Ann Wohl, May 29, 1988; edn: BA in physics, CSU Fullerton 1978; MS in physics, CSU Fresno 1982. Career: teaching asst. CSU Fresno, physics dept., 1978-82; research asst. Univ. Colo., Boulder, Colo. 1983-85; technical staff TRW, Redondo Beach 1985-; cons. Los Angeles Educational Ptnrship., L.A. 1987-88; cons. Los Angeles Aerospace Task Force 1992; listed Who's Who in Am. Universities, Who's Who Young Am. Profls.; mem: L.A. Organizational Devel. Network 1990-, CPSR 1992-, ASTD 1992-, Beyond War, Sigma Pi Sigma, Beach Cities Democratic Club, Redondo Bch. (v.ch. 1989-), IEEE-MTT, So. Bay chapt. (v.ch. 1986); author articles pub. profl. jours. 1987, 92; Democrat (elected L.A. Co. Dem. Cent. Com. 1991-); rec: organizing, reading. Res: 2000 Mathews Ave #5 Redondo Beach 90278 Ofc: TRW, One Space Park Redondo Beach 90278

NEWMAN, JOHN JOSEPH, electrical engineer; b. Jan. 15, 1936, Wolf Point, Mont.; s. Leon Vincent and Anna Agusta (Muller) N.; m. Linda Carol Hawthorne, July 11, 1964; children: Vincent b. 1965, Penelope b. 1966, Michael b. 1970, Jennifer b. 1975; edn: BSEE, Mont. St. Univ. 1958; MSEE, Univ. N.M. 1961; PhD, Univ. Santa Clara 1968. Career: staff Sandia Corp., Albuquerque, N.M. 1958-61; sr. engr. Lockheed Missiles & Space, Sunnyvale 1961-66; engr. Fairchild Semiconductor, Palo Alto 1967; prin. scientist Memorex Corp., Santa Clara 1967-82; Burroughs Corp. 1982-87; prin. engr. Unisys Corp. 1987-89; cons. in Magnetics and Magnetic Recording, 1989-; tchg. asst. Univ. Santa Clara 1965-67; honors: BSA dist. award of merit 1981, Silver Beaver 1983; mem: IEEE, Santa Clara Valley Magnetics Soc. (secty. 1969, treas. 1970, v.p. 1971, pres. 1972), BSA (scoutmaster 1976-80, dist. membership chair 1980-84, dist. commr. 1984-86, SME chmn. 1987); 14 articles pub. in tech. jours. (1962-), patent held for thermomagnetic copying of mag. rec. (1968); Republican; R.Cath.; rec: photog., auto mechanics, woodworking. Res: POB 24624 San Jose 95154

NEWMAN, NANCY MARILYN, ophthalmologist, educator, consultant, inventor, entrepreneur; b. Mar. 16, 1941, San Francisco; edn: BA psychology (magna cum laude), Stanford Univ., 1962, MD, Stanford Univ. Sch. Medicine, 1967; diplomate Am. Bd. Ophthalmology. Career: NIH trainee neurophysiology, Inst. of Visual Scis., S.F. 1964-65; clin. clk. Nat. Hosp. for Nervous and Mental Disease, Queen Sq., London, Eng. 1966-67; internship Mount Auburn Hosp., Cambridge, Mass. 1967-68; NIH trainee in neuro-ophthalmology, jr., sr. asst. resident, assoc. resident dept. ophthal. Washington Univ. Sch. of Med., St. Louis, 1968-71; Internat. Eye Found. fellow with Dr. Humberto Escapini, San

Salvador, El Salvador, 1971; NIH spl. fellow neuro-ophthal. with William F. Hoyt, M.D., Univ. Calif. Sch. of Medicine, S.F. 1971-72; fellow Smith-Kettlewell Inst. of Visual Scis., 1971-72; clin. asst. prof. ophthal. UCSF Sch. Med., 1972, cons. neuro-ophthal. VA Hosp. S.F. 1972-74, cons. nerve fiber contract, Nat. Eye Inst., NIH, DHEW, at UC Sch. Med. S.F. 1973-75, physician/cons. dept. neurology UC Sch. Med./VA Med. Ctr. Martinez, 1978-; asst., assoc. prof. and chief div. neuro-ophthal. Pacific Med. Ctr., S.F. 1972-88; prof. dept. spl. edn. CSU San Francisco 1974-79; vis. prof. Centre Nat. D'Ophtalmologie des Quinze-Vingts, Paris, France 2-5/80; clin. assoc. prof. Sch. Optometry UC Berkeley, 1990-, cons. VDT and Occupational Health Clinic, Sch. Opt. UCB, 1990-; pres. and c.e.o. Minerva Medica, Inc.; cons. num. med. device and biomed. cos.; recipient merit awards: Internat. Eye Found., NSPI Award for outstanding instrnl. materials in ophthal. SIMO; dir., advy. bds: Fifer Street Fitness, Larkspur 1990-92, Rose Resnick Ctr. for the Blind and Handicapped 1988-92, N.African Ctr. for Sight Tunis, Tunisia (internat. advy. com. 1988-), Internat. Soc. for Orbital Disorders 1983-, Frank B. Walsh Soc. 1974-91, No. Calif. Soc. for Prevention of Blindness 1978-88; mem: AMA (ldr. Calif. delegation cont. med. edn. 1982, 83), S.F. Med. Soc., Calif. Med. Assn. (subcom med. policy coms. 1984-, chair com. on accred. cont. med. edn. 1981-88, chair quality care rev. commn. 1984), Assn. for Res. in Vision and Ophthal., Pan Am. Assn. Ophthal., Soc. of Heed Fellows, Pacific Coast Oto-Ophthal. Soc., Lane Med. Soc. (v.p. 1975-76), Internat. Soc. Neuro-Ophthal. (founding), Cordes Soc., Am. Soc. Ophthalmic Ultrasound (charter), Orbital Soc. (founding), West Bay Health Systems Agy., Oxford Ophthalmol. Soc., Pacific Physicians Assocs., Soc. Fr. d'Ophtalmologie; author: Eye Movement Disorders; Neuro-ophthalmology: A Practical Text (1992); mem. Opthalmology Practice 1993-; editorial bd. J. Clin. Neuro-ophthalmology, Am. J. Ophthalmology 1980-92; contbr. num. articles in profl. jours. Res: 819 Spring Dr Mill Valley 94941

NEWTON, RICHARD HOWARD, engineering executive/program manager; b. Oct. 12, 1932, Milw.; s. Howard Leslie and Evelyn Jennie (Shove) N.; m. Martha Jane Dinsmore, Sept. 11, 1954 (dec.); children: Scott b. 1955, Gayle b. 1957, Jeffrey b. 1958, Mark b. 1962; m. Dorothea Elaine Gregloit, Feb. 19, 1966; edn: BSME, Purdue Univ., 1954; MBA, Claremont Grad. Sch., 1984. Career: engr. Robbius & Myers, Springfield, Oh. 1954; project engr. Aerojet Avionics, Azusa, Calif. 1956-63, dept. mgr. Aerojet Meas. Dept. 1963-67, asst. to div. mgr. Aerojet Microelectronics 1967-68, special projects mgr. Aerojet Astrionics 1968-82, mgr. central program Aerojet Electro Systems 1982-; bd. dirs. Citrus College Found., Glendora 1988-, Recording for the Blind, Pomona 1987-91, L.A. Sanitation Dist. 1978-89, L.A. County Private Ind. Council 1980-84; recipient Awards of Honor: L.A. County Board Suprs. 1980, L.A. County 1st Dist. 1990; mem. ASME 1954-, Air Force Assn. 1988-, Nat. Space Club 1991-, Masonic Lodge (W.Lafayette, Ind.); mil: capt. USAF 1954-56; Republican; Presbyterian; rec: bicycling, golf, skiing. Res: 2270 Tulsa Ave Claremont 91711 Ofc: Aerojet Electronic Systems Div. PO Box 296 Azusa 91702

NG, JAMES T., college counselor; b. Jan. 28, 1951, Singapore; nat. 1982; s. Yaw-Cheng and Sai-Pek (Yeo) Ng; edn: BS econ. & psych., Univ. Wis. 1976; MS psychology, 1977; MSE counseling, 1978; PhD admin. & psych., Univ. No. Colo., 1981; Calif. Community Coll. credentials: psych. instr. (life), counselor (life). Career: tchr. Labrador Sch., Singapore 1969-70, 1973; soldier 2d Inf. Regt., Singapore Armed Forces, 1971-73; assoc. psychologist Counseling Center Univ. No. Colo., Greeley 1979-81; employee rels. ofcr. Exxon Chemical, Singapore 1981-82; cons. PSI Assocs., Monterey Park, Calif. 1983-88; hd., student program Foreign Student Office, East L.A. Coll., Monterey Park 1988-; instr., res. asst. Univ. Wis., Superior 1976-78; awards: doctoral scholar Univ. No. Colo. 1979-81, Univ. No. Colo. Study Award at Harvard Univ. Grad. Sch. of Edn.'s Moral Edn. Workshop (Summer 1980), grad. assistantship Univ. Wis. 1976-78, recogn. for doubling internat. student enrollment from 300 to 600 in 3 mos. at East L.A. Coll., Los Angeles Community Coll. Dist. 1989; listed Internat. Who's Who, Who's Who Among Human Svs. Professionals; mem: Am. Psychol. Assn. (Ethnic Minority Psychologist, Gen. Psychology, Counseling Psychologist), We. Psychol. Assn., Nat. Assn. Fgn. Student Affairs (presentation award NAFSA Region XII 1989 Annual Conf. on Community Coll. Advising), Asian Am. Psychol. Assn.; PhD diss. pub. (1981); Republican; Prot.; rec: swimming, travel, speaking. Res: PO Box 1472 Monterey Park 91754 Ofc: Foreign Student Pgm. East Los Angeles College, Monterey Park 91754

NGUYEN, HUGH DAN, business executive; b. Jan. 8, 1944, Saigon, Vietnam; s. Austin Dang and Thong Thi (Le) N.; m. Kimberly Chau, Jan. 1, 1974; children: Esther b. 1976, David Dan b. 1980; edn: BA, Saigon Law Sch., 1970. Career: high sch. tchr. Dong-Tien H.S., Vietnam, 1965-70, Nhan-Chu H.S., also An-Lac H.S., Saigon, 1967-70; lawyer, mem. Vietnamese Lawyer Assn., Saigon; job developer Gov.'s Task Force for Indochinese Resettlement, Des Moines, Ia., 1976-77; eligibility worker Dept. Social Svs., Santa Clara County, Calif., 1978-81; real estate agt. West Realty, San Jose, 1980-85; real estate broker West Realty H-1, San Jose, 1985-; owner opr. Monterey AM/PM Mini Mart, San Jose; club: Nautilus; Republican; R.Cath.; rec: tennis, wt. lifting. Ofc: 5498 Monterey Rd San Jose 95111

NGUYEN, THINH VAN, physician; b. April 16, 1948, Vietnam; nat. 1983; s. Thao Van and Phuong Thi (Tran) N.; m. Phi Thi Ho, Jan. 2, 1973; children: Anh-Quan b. 1974, Andrew Anh-Tuan b. 1982; edn: BS, Univ. Saigon Vietnam 1970; MS, Univ. Mo. 1974; MD, Univ. Tx. Houston 1982; diplomate Am. Bd. Internal Medicine 1988, Am. Acad. of Pain Mgmt. 1989. Career: research asst. Univ. Tx. SW Med. Sch., Dallas 1974-78; resident physician rep., Texas Med. Assn. Com. on Cardiovascular Diseases 1982-84, Council of Scientific Affairs 1984-85; internist, area chief FHP Inc., Long Beach, Calif. 1985-89; pvt. practice in San Jose, 1989-; chmn. interdisciplinary practice com. Charter Comm. Hosp., Hawaiian Gardens 1989-; listed Who's Who in Texas 1985; mem: A.C.P., Calif. Assn. Med. Dirs. (bd. dirs.), So. Med. Assn.; articles pub. in med. jours. 1975, 77; rec: photog., tennis, dancing. Address: 2470 Alvin Ave Ste 5 San Jose 95121

NICE, CARTER, symphony conductor; b. Apr. 5, 1940, Jacksonville, Fla.; s. Clarence Carter, Jr. and Elizabeth Jane (Hintermister) N.; m. Jennifer Smith, Apr. 4, 1983; children: Danielle b. 1968, Christian b. 1972; edn: BMus., Eastman Sch. of Music, 1962; MMus., Manhattan Sch. of Music, 1964. Career: asst. conductor, concertmaster Florida Symphony, Orlando 1965-66; asst. prof. Univ. of Oklahoma, Norman 1966-67; asst. conductor, concertmaster New Orleans Philharmonic, La. 1967-79; music director Sacramento Symphony, Calif. 1979-92; music director Bear Valley Music Festival, Bear Valley, Calif. 1985-. Res: 200 P St #B-36 Sacramento 95814

NICHOLAS, P.K., public accountant; b. May 31, 1917, Orange, N.J.; s. Fred Q. and Edith (Stevens) N.; m. Betty Jane McClure, Pittsburgh, Pa., Dec. 31, 1941; children: Barbara Ann b. 1947, David King b. 1949, Becky Jane b. 1951; edn: BS in bus. adm., Lehigh Univ., 1939. Career: staff acct. U.S. Steel Corp., Pittsburgh, Pa. 1939-41; Beckwith Mach. Co., Pittsburgh 1946-47; pub. acct. practice, Bakersfield, Calif. 1948-89; mem. Soc. of Calif. Accts. (state pres. 1962-63); civic: Little League Baseball Bakersfield (coach 1951-65), Kiwanis Club Kern of Kern (Bakersfield pres. 1958); mil: capt. US Army 1942-45; Presbyterian; rec: golf. Res: 1301 New Stine Rd #601 Bakersfield 93309 Tel: 805/831-4722

NICHOLS, DAVID NORTON, elementary school principal; b. Mar. 26, 1954, Lancaster, Calif.; s. Norton, Jr. and Sarah Jane (Jones) N.; edn: AA, Antelope Valley Coll., 1974; BA, UCLA, 1977; MA, San Diego St. Univ., 1986; CSU Long Beach, 1977-79. Career: tchr., 5, 6, 7, 8 gr., Carlsbad Unified Sch. Dist., Carlsbad 1979-90, summer sch. prin. 1987, 88, adminstrv. intern 1985-87; principal Lakeside Union Sch., Lakeside 1990-; sci. staff devel. Calif. Sci. Implementation Network; honors: Mentor tchr. Carlsbad USD 1988-89, Internat. Man of Achiev. 1989, Outstanding Young Man of Yr. 1986, outstanding ranking NASSP Assessment Ctr. #60 (1986), Who's Who in Am. Edn. 1987-88; mem. NEA 1979-, ASCD 1984-, CASCD 1989-, ACSA 1990-, NAESP 1990-, Heartland Sch. Adminstr. Assn.; Democrat; Christian; rec: gourmet cooking, gardening, travel, theatre. Res: 6860-B Caminito Montanoso, 8, San Diego 92119

NIGRO, DENNIS MICHAEL, plastic surgeon; b. July 29, 1947, San Francisco; edn: art, UCLA, 1967-68; BS chem., Univ. Notre Dame, 1969; MD, Creighton Med. Sch., 1974; cert. Am. Bd. of Plastic Surgery, 1987, Fellow Internat. Coll. Surgeons (FICS) 1989, Fellow Am. Coll. Surgeons (FACS) 1990. Career: extern Shriner's Nat. Burn Unit Galveston, Tex., Ben Taub Hosp. Emerg. Svc., Parkland Hosp. Trauma Svc. 1973; surgical resident Creighton affil. hosps. Omaha, Neb. 1974-75; resident gen. surg. UC San Francisco 1975-77; chief resident extremity svc., burn unit San Francisco Gen. Hosp. 1977; plastic surg. resident UC San Diego 1977-79, chief res. 1979; emerg. room phys. Scripps Encinitas Hosp. 1978; attg. phys. COAD Internat. Plastic Surg., UCSD/Interface servicing Latin Am., 1979-; pvt. practice Encinitas 1979-; chief plastic surg. Scripps Hosp. Encinitas 1980-86, 90-; clin. prof. plastic surg. UC-San Diego 1988-; dir. and founder Project Fresh Start - Reconstrv. Procedures for Underprivileged (recipient Pres. Bush "Thousand Points of Light" award); pub. lectr. on plastic surgery; awards: Outstanding Young Men in Am. 1982, AMA Award for Postgrad. Med. Edn. 1985-91; mem. Am. Cancer Soc. (advy. bd. 1984-), Notre Dame Univ. Alumni Assn. S.D. (Monogram Club rep.); plastic surgery advisor to SHAPE Mag.; La Costa Spa; Family Fitness; advy. bd. to IDEA, ACE; publs: research papers, presentations, newspaper article. Res: 304 La Costa Ave Leucadia 92024 Ofc: 351 Santa Fe Dr Ste 1 Encinitas 92024

NILSSON, KAREN BRAUCHT, publisher; b. Aug. 13, 1936, Oakland; d. Frank E. and Bernice (Sherwin) Braucht; m. Nils J. Nilsson, July 19, 1958; children: Kristen b. 1962, Lars b. 1964; edn: Stanford Univ. 1958; Syracuse Univ. 1960. Career: mgr. Ladera Recreation, Portola Valley 1968-71; founder, exec. dir. Environmental Volunteers, Palo Alto 1972-77; exec. dir. Trust for Hidden Villa, Los Altos 1979-83; publisher Tioga Publishing, Palo Alto 1974-; mem: Theatre Works (dir. 1987-90), League to Save Lake Tahoe 1985-88; Democrat; rec: hiking, tennis. Res: 150 Coquito Way Portola Valley 94028

NISICH, ANTHONY JOSEPH, city engineer; b. Apr. 19, 1951, San Jose; s. Louis Marco and Lena D. (Passantino) N.; m. Patricia Massi, Aug. 30, 1975; children: Kelli Lyn b. 1968; edn: BS in C.E., Univ. of Santa Clara 1973; MS in C.E., CSU San Jose 1978; Reg. Profl. Civil Engr., Calif. Career: civil engr. Calif. State Office of Archit. & Constrn., 1973-74; land devel. engr.

Environmental Mgmt./ Gen. Services Agy., Santa Clara Co. 1974-78, asst. mgr. Building Insp. Div., 1978-79; chief Bldg. Insp. and Land Use Enforcement Div., Dept. Pub. Works, County of Sacto. 1979-82; dir. Bldg. & Safety, City of Beverly Hills 1982-86; dir. Developmental Services, City of San Marcos 1986-90; div. mgr. Willdan Assoc. 1990-91; city engr. City of Santa Clarita, 1992-; vice pres. Lou Nisich Constrn. Co. Inc., San Jose 1975-; mem. DOE, HUD, and Nat. Assn. of Counties task force on Bldg. Energy Perf. Stds., W.D.C. 1978-81; tech. advy. com. Sacto. Co. Overall Econ. Devel. Pgm. 1979-82; Calif. Energy Commn. advy. com. on Insulation Stds. 1978-84, Bldg. Ofcls. Advy. Com. 1979-82; mem: Am. Planning Assn., Nat. Inst. of Bldg. Scis. (Consultative Council), Calif. Bldg. Ofcls. Assn. (pres. 1985), Internat. Conf. of Bldg. Ofcls. (v.p. L.A. Basin chpt. 1985), Internat. Conf. of Bldg. Ofcls. (code change moderator 1985, 87), Am. Concrete Inst., Nat. Soc. Profl. Engrs., Calif. Soc. Profl. Engrs., ASCE (past chair Nat. Engrs. Week, Santa Clara Co.), Constrn. Spec. Inst., Am. Pub. Wks. Assn., ASHRAE, Santa Clara Co. Engrs. and Archs. Assn. (pres. 1977-79). Ofc: City of Santa Clarita.

NISSELSON, JANET, educational psychologist, family child counselor, certified hypnotherapist; b. Jan. 15, 1918, NYC; d. Max and Clara (Albert) Watnik; m. Cyril Barnert Jr., Mar. 1, 1940, dec. 1947; m. 2d. Michael M. Nisselson, July 1, 1954 (dec. Sept. 10, 1984); children: Cyril Barnert III, b. 1942; Anthony L. Barnert, b. 1943; edn: BA, Hunter Coll. 1938; MS, City Coll. of NY 1956; PhD, Pacific Western 1977; attended, Columbia Univ., NYC & Yeshiva Univ. NYC; Edn. Psych.; Cert. Hypnotherapist; Family Child Counselor. Career: intern child psychology Mt. Sinai Med. Ctr., NYC 1957-58; psychological cons. NYC Childrens Svcs. 1958-69; staff psychol. Psychiat. Clinic for Children, Stamford, Conn. 1961-64; supvg. clin. psychol. Comm. Mental Health, Delaware Co. Mental Health Clinic, Walton, NY 1970-74; sr. psychologist, NY Prisons 1975-76; pvt. practice, Granada Hills, Calif. 1976-; tchr. Coll. of the Canyons, Valencia; volunteer work, Battered Women; mem: Am. & Calif. Psychological Assns.; dir. Granada Hills Comm. Hosp. Widowed Person Support Program. Address: 17163 Courbet St Granada Hills 91344

NITZ, FREDERIC WILLIAM, electronics co. executive; b. June 22, 1943, St. Louis; s. Arthur Carl Paul and Dorothy Louise (Kahm) N. m. Kathleen Sue Rapp, June 8, 1968; children: Frederic Theodore, Anna Louise; edn: AS, Coll. of Marin, 1970; BS in electronics, Calif. Poly. State Univ., S.L.O., 1972. Career: electronic engr. Sierra Electronics, Menlo Park 1973-77; RCA, Somerville, N.J. 1977-79; engring. mgr. EGG-Geometrics, Sunnyvale 1979-83 v.p. engring. Basic Measuring Insts., Foster City 1983-; cons. in field, Boulder Creek 1978-; patentee in field; civic bds: San Lorenzo Valley Water Dist., Boulder Creek (dir. 1983-), Water Policy Task Force, Santa Cruz County (1983-84); mil: AUS 1965-67; Democrat. Res: 12711 East St Boulder Creek 95006 Ofc: BMI 335 Lakeside Dr Foster City 94404

NIXON, GEORGE, tax accountant; b. July 3, 1942, North Belfast, No. Ireland, came to U.S.A. 1971; s. George and Ethel Florence (Cunningham) N.; edn: grad. Instn. of Electronic & Radio Engrs., London 1966; chartered engr., U.K.; tchg. cert. Victoria Univ. of Manchester, Eng. 1969; BS in acctg., Univ. San Francisco 1976. Career: product devel. engr., England 1965-70; instr. Bolton Tech. Coll., England, 1969; acct., owner tax acctg. and bookkeeping bus., San Francisco 1972-, pres. Shamrock Tax & Bookkeeping Corp., 1975-; mem: Nat. Soc. Pub. Accts., Instn. of Elec. Engrs., London; rec: ham radio, writing, civil rights/pol. causes, fitness, programming. Ofc: Shamrock Tax & Bookkeeping Corp. 6033 Geary Blvd San Francisco 94121-1907

NOAH, ERIC LINNAEUS, conservationist, consultant, writer; b. June 20, 1955, Long Beach; accredited tax advisor Accreditation Council for Acctncy. & Taxation, 1991. Career: tax advisor/prin., Fountain Valley, 1978-83; ops. mgr. Long Beach Zoo, 1982-84; cons. prin., Fountain Valley 1982-86; cons., hypnotherapist, prin. Alpha Integrated Services, Bayside, 1986-; founder Biocultural Inst., Arcata, 1988-; appraiser, numismatist, owner ZooArt Tangible Assets, Bayside, 1990-; publisher (periodical) The Herpetofile, 1975-78; author 3 books: Inner Vision (1980), Zoocide (1980), Zoocentric Art (1981); frequent speaker bus., vocational, and hobbyist organizations 1975-; mem: Nat. Wildlife Fedn. (life), Soc. for Conservation Biology, Internat. Soc. for Ecological Economics, Am. Numismatic Assn., Am. Soc. of Tax Profls. (fellow); rec: wildlife art & book collecting, bicycling, target archery, drumming.

NOBLE, JOHN ROBERT, retired mutual fund president, investment adviser; b. June 4, 1921, Manila, Philippines; s. Frederick Handy and Suzanne Maude (Ely) N.; m. Georgia Eleanor Faith, Nov. 21, 1942; children: David b. 1944, Bonnie b. 1947, Cynthia b. 1953; edn: BA, Colgate Univ. 1942. Career: chemist Monsanto Chem. Co., St. Louis, Mo. 1942-43; research chemist, Springfield, Mass. 1943-44; chemist Manhattan Dist., Oak Ridge, Tenn. 1944-46; mktg. asst. Standard Vacuum & Oil, Iloilo and Manila, Philippines 1946-51, area mgr., N.Y.C. 1951, mktg. asst., Bombay, India 1951-54; gen. ptnr. Investors Research Co., Santa Barbara 1955-92; pres. Investors Research Fund Inc. 1959-92; honors: Phi Beta Kappa, Alpha Chi Sigma, Mu Pi Delta; U.S. Treasury Silver Life Saving Medal, Boy Scout Life Saving Medal (1938); mem: Fifty Families, Santa Barbara Museum of Art, Pres. Club Colgate Univ., Santa Barbara Symphony (pres., dir. 1962-82); author: How to Start a Mutual Fund (1966), Mgmt. of Money (1962); mil: T-4 Spl. Det. Engrs. 1944-46; Episcopalian; rec: yacht racing, model building.

NOCAS, ANDREW JAMES, lawyer; b. Feb. 4, 1941, Los Angeles; s. John R. and Muriel P. (Harvey) N.; m. Beverly De La Mare, June 20, 1964; 1 son, Scott b. 1972; edn: BS physics, Stanford Univ. 1962; JD, 1964. Career: ptnr. Thelen Marrin Johnson & Bridges, Los Angeles 1964-71; Law Offices of David M. Harney 1972-; arbitrator Am. Arbitration Assn., L.A. 1979-; speaker legal programs 1970-; mem: Am. Bar Assn. (antitrust sect., tort & ins. practice sect., litigation sect., Fellow Am. Bar Found. 1990-), Calif. State Bar Conf. (del.), Los Angeles Bar Assn. (trustee 1990-92, chair litigation sect. 1989-90), San Marino City Club; articles pub. in profl. jours.; mil: capt. USAR 1966-72; Republican; Episcopalian. Law Ofcs. of David M. Harney, 201 N Figueroa St Ste 1300 Los Angeles 90012

NOGUCHI, THOMAS TSUNETOMI, professor of forensic pathology; b. Jan. 4, 1927, Fukuoka, Japan, naturalized U.S. citizen 1960; s. Dr. Wataru and Tomika (Narahashi) N.; m. Dr. Hisako Nishihara, Dec. 31, 1960 (div. 1982); edn: pre-med. Nippon Medical Sch., Tokyo 1944-47, MD, 1951; MD (nat. lic.) Japan 1951, Calif. 1955; cert. Am. Bd. of Pathology: Pathologic Anatomy 1960, Clin. Path. 1962, Forensic Path. 1963. Career: asst. prof. path. Loma Linda Univ., L.A. 1960-61; dep. med. examiner, 1961-67, chief med. examiner - coroner County of Los Angeles, 1967-82; prof. forensic pathology USC Sch. of Medicine, also chief of autopsy and forensic pathologist L.A. Co.-USC Med. Ctr. and dep. med. examiner & dep. coroner County of L.A. in LAC-USC Med. Ctr., 1987-; awards: JD (hon.) Univ. of Braz Cubas, Sao Paulo, Brazil 1980, D.Sc. (hon.) Worcester State Coll. 1985, Dutton Prof. of Legal Medicine USC Sch. of Med. 1987, numerous honors from various orgs. incl. Outstanding Svc. Nat. Assn. of Med. Examiners 1991; mem: Nat. Assn. of Med. Examiners (pres. 1982-83, chmn. past pres.'s com. 1985-91), World Assn. of Med. Law (v.p. 1980-), L.A. County Med. & Bar Assns. Jt. Com. on Bio-Med. Ethics Com. 1980-91, Calif. State Coroners Assn. (pres. 1974-75), Am. Acad. Forensic Scis. (Council, sect. chair 1968-69); author (fiction, mystery): Physical Evidence 1990, Unnatural Causes 1988, (non-fiction): Coroner 1983, Coroner At Large 1985, 80+ sci. articles in forensic field; Republican; Christian; rec: fine arts, painting, still & landscape, photography, travel. Ofc: LAC-USC Medical Ctr. 1200 N State St Rm 2520 Los Angeles 90033-1084 Tel:213/226-7126

NORDEN, ROBERT AUGUST, insurance claim litigation consultant; b. Aug. 28, 1935, San Jose; s. August Friedrich and Marie Katherine (Mauer) N.; m. Theresa McGuire, July 30, 1960; children: John b. 1961, Maryanne b. 1963, Stephen b. 1964; edn: BS, Santa Clara Univ., 1957; Santa Clara Law Sch. 1958-59, Penn State Univ. 1970-71, Allen Mgmt. Pgm. 1973. Career: trainee INA 1959-60, claim rep., San Jose and Santa Rosa 1960-62, resident rep., Santa Rosa 1962-66, claim supr. 1966-70, San Francisco, home office supr., Phila., Pa. 1970-72, asst. claim mgr. N.Y.C. 1972-74, claim mgr. 1972-76, Chgo. 1976; claim mgr., v.p., asst. secty. Sequoia Ins. Co., Menlo Park, Calif. 1976-90; indep. cons. ins. claim litigation, 1990-; mem. Fedn. of Ins. and Corp. Counsel 1988-, Internat. Assn. of Defense Counsel 1989-, Def. Research Inst. 1988-, past mem. Pacific Claim Exec. Assn. (Calif. Arson Prevention Com. 1978-90); mil: sgt. USMCR 1954-60; Democrat; R.Cath.; rec: sports, travel. Address: 504 Charles Cali Dr San Jose 95117

NORDSTROM, RICHARD DEAN, educator; b. Feb. 7, 1933, Topeka, Kans.; s. Albert Edwin and Wanda Lyle (Officer) N.; m. Margaret Anne Throm, Oct. 25, 1958; children: Neal b. 1960, Pam b. 1962; edn: BS, Univ. Kans. 1954; MBA, Wichita St. Univ. 1969; PhD, Univ. Ark. 1974. Career: dealer Nordstrom Ford, Newton, Kans. 1958-70; asst. prof. Wichita St. Univ., Kans. 1970-71; Univ. Ark., Fayetteville 1971-74; prof. Western Ill. Univ., Macomb, Ill. 1974-81; prof. CSU Fresno, 1981-; awards: Arkansas Purchasing Assn. fellow 1972, Fresno Sch. of Bus. Duncan award 1983; mem: Am. Mktg. Assn., Assn. Forensic Economists, Western Mktg. Educators; lodge: Masonic; author: Introduction to Selling (1981), 41+ articles pub. in profl. jours.; mil: lt.j.g. USN 1954-56; Republican; Lutheran; rec: golf. Address: 93711.

NORMAN, DONALD ARTHUR, cognitive scientist, educator; b. Dec. 25, 1935, N.Y.C.; s. Noah N. and Miriam F. N.; m. Martha Karpati (div.); children: Cynthia, Michael; m. Julie Jacobsen; children: Eric; edn: BSEE, M.I.T., 1957; MSEE, Univ. Pa., 1959, PhD in psychology, 1962. Career: prof. dept. psychology UC San Diego, La Jolla 1966-, dept. chair 1974-78, dir. cognitive sci. pgm. 1977-88, dir. Inst. for Cognitive Sci. 1981-89, prof. and chair dept. cognitive sci. UCSD, 1988-93 (retired); sr. fellow Apple Computer, Inc., Cupertino 1993; lectr. Harvard Univ. 1982-86; mem. Sci. Advy. Bd., Naval Personnel Res. Ctr., San Diego 1982-86; cons. to industry on human computer interaction and user-centered design; awards: Excellence in Res., UCSD; fellow: AAAS (Fellow), Am. Psychol. Soc. (Fellow), Assn. for Computational Machinery, Cognitive Sci. Soc. (chmn. and founding mem.), Am. Assn. for Artificial Intelligence; author: Learning and Memory (1982), Human Information Processing, 2d edit. (1977), User Centered System Design (1986), The Psychology of Everyday Things (1988), Turn Signals Are the Facial Expressions of Automobiles (1992); ed:

Perspectives on Cognitive Science (1981), series editor: Explorations in Cognition (1975), Cognitive Science Series Lawrence Earlbaum Assocs. (1979-), Cognitive Science Jour. (1981-85). Res: 111 Eleventh St Del Mar 92014 Ofc: APPLE Computer Inc 1 Infinity Loop Cupertino 95014

NORRIS, ERIC ALEXANDER, urban planning consultant; b. July 5, 1959, Frankfurt, Germany; s. Arthur F. and Jutta M. (Kropf) N.; m. Cynthia Pauleen Abell, Aug. 2, 1986; children: Gregory b. 1991; edn: BA communication, Cal Poly. St. Univ., Pomona 1982, M. Urban & Reg. Planning, 1992; A.I.C.P., Am. Planning Assn., 1989. Career: planner Planning Network, Ontario, Calif. 1985-88; planner EDAW, San Bernardino 1988; dir. plng. RHA Inc., Riverside 1988-92; planner City of Chino Hills 1992-; mem. Regional Trails Com. 1991-, Am. Planning Assn. (1985-, awards for disting. svc. Inland Empire chpt. 1988, 89), State Outstanding Planning Award 1992, Am. Inst. Cert. Planners 1989-; civic: Water Bottle Transit Co., Redlands; publs: num. articles on bicycling & planning (1983-); rec: ultramarathon cycling. Ofc: City of Chino Hills 2001 Grand Ave Chino Hills 91709

NORSELL, PAUL ERNEST, executive recruiter; b. Jan. 28, 1933, Salt Lake City, Utah; s. Alf Raae and Florence Emily (Freer) N.; m. M. Rynda, Sept. 2, 1958; children: Stuart b. 1961, Daryl b. 1964, Paula b. 1967; edn: BSEE, Purdue Univ. 1954; MS engring., UCLA 1956. Career: program mgr. applcn. tech. satellite Hughes Space Systems, El Segundo 1954-64; dir. advanced programs devel. Litton Industries (data systems div.) 1964-67, v.p. engring. and ops. 1967-69, pres. LITCOM div., Melville, N.Y. 1969-73, v.p. Profl. Services & Equipment Group, Beverly Hills 1973; pres. Paul Norsell & Assocs., Inc., Woodland Hills 1974-92, Auburn 1993-; awards: St. Johns Univ. businessman of year 1969, GM-Hughes Electronics masters fellow 1954-56, Purdue Alumni Assn. engring. scholar 1952-54; mem: IEEE, Eta Kappa Nu, Valley Industry & Commerce Assn. (bd. dir., govt. rels. com., exec. com.), Woodland Hills C.of C. (devel. pgms. com.), Calif. Exec. Recruiters Assn., Entrepreneurs of Am., U.S. C.of C., Los Angeles Area C.of C. (econ. devel. council), L.I. Assn. Commerce & Industry (dir., exec. com. 1970-73); clubs: Transpacific Yacht, Long Beach Yacht, Braemar CC; publs: trade jour. articles re sales and comms. (1963-); rec: transoceanic & local yacht racing. Ofc: POB 6686 Auburn 95604-6686

NUGENT, JOHN WILLIAM, company president; b. July 21, 1945; Sharon, Pa.; s. John William and Lillian Elizabeth (Rigby) N.; m. Nancy, Dec. 25, 1967; children: Derric James b. 1968, Shane Elden b. 1972; edn: Univ. Cincinnati 1963-64; BS, Youngstown State 1968. Career: corp. sales N/S Corp. Sharon, Pa. 1968-70, nat. sales mgr. 1970-73, mktg. mgr. 1973-75, v.p. mktg. Inglewood 1975-82, exec. v.p. 1982-90; pres. Nugent International Corp., 1990-; dir.: N/S Corp. 1975-90, Nugent Convalescent Home Inc. 1979-, Nat. Car Wash Council 1981-82; honors: disting. service, NCC 1982, Paul Harris Fellow, Rotary 1985; mem: Advt. Frat. 1967-68, Am. Pub. Works Assn. 1983-85, Assn. School Business Ofcls. 1981-83, Internat. Car Wash Assn. 1970-; civic bds.: Westchester C.of C. (bd. 1990), Rotary Internat. (Westchester Club pres. 1988-89, dir. 1986-90, Dist. #5280 long range planning com. 1990-93, Dist. gov. elect 1993-94), Westchester YMCA (bd. 1988-, bd. chmn. 1991-92, chmn. major gifts com. 1990); patentee: vehicle washing machine; Republican; Lutheran; rec: horticulture, art, ski. Res: 7335 Vista Del Mar Playa Del Rey 90293

NUNEZ, RAUL RODRIGUEZ, county employees union president; b. Aug. 1, 1931, Ontario; s. Ynez Resendez and Maria (Rodriguez) N.; m. Celia Gomez, June 18, 1960; children: David b. 1961, Raul Devin b. 1962, Steven b. 1966, Caroline b. 1968; edn: AA, East L.A. Coll., 1956; BA, CSU Los Angeles, 1958. Career: social worker Bur. of Public Assistance, L.A., 1958-60; sr. probation ofcr. Dept. Probation, L.A., 1960-66; human rels. cons. L.A. Co. Commn. on Human Relations, 1966-70; personnel analyst Comm. Devel. Dept., L.A., 1970-80; spl. asst. assessor Office of Assessor, L.A., 1980-87; spl. asst. Co. Hosp., L.A. Co. Dept. of Health, 1987-88; elected pres. L.A. Co. Chicano Employees Assn., 1982-, pres./c.e.o. L.A. Co. Employees Assn., L.A., 1988-; dir: United Hispanic Scholarship Found. 1985-, United Hispanic Latino Fund 1989-, N.E.W.S. For America 1990-; awards for service: Calif. St. Senate 1980, L.A. Co. Bd. Suprs. (1983, 1988), Congressman 30th Dist. 1985, Los Angeles Mayor and City Council 1988, Calif. St. Assembly 1988; mem. Lions Internat.; civic: Amer. GI Forum, Montebello; mil: s/sgt. USAF 1950-53; Democrat; R.Cath.; rec: golf, public speaking. Res: 1319 W Victoria Ave Montebello 90640

NUNN, ERNEST EUGENE, company executive; b. Feb. 16, 1935, Parma, Mo.; s. Ernest F. and Rosa Lee (Pope) N.; m. Jo Ellen Neely, Jan. 25, 1957; children: Julie, b. 1959; Jeffrey, b. 1966; edn: BS, Indiana Univ. 1961. Career: v.p. to chmn. Lazarus Dept. Store (div. of fed. dept. store), Columbus, Oh. 1961-75; pres. Drapery Mfg. Inc., Columbus, Oh. 1975-77; pres. New Ideal Dept. Store, Birmingham, Ala. 1977-80; regl. mgr. Nat. Revenue Corp., Columbus, Oh. 1980-82; pres. Jani-King of Calif. Inc. also owner, c.e.o. and pres. Related Service Inc., Phoenix, Az., dba Jani-King of Phoenix, 1982-, v.p. Jani-King, Inc., J & N Service Inc. dba Jani-King of Tuscon; bd. dirs. Better Bus. Bur. Indpls., Ind. 1973-75; dir. Birmingham C.of C. 1977-79; mil: sgt. US Army 1956-58; rec: woodworking, golf. Res: 5981 E Cowboy Circle Anaheim Hills 92807 Ofc: Jani-King of California, Inc. One Centerpointe Dr Ste 330 La Palma 90623

NUNN, ROBERT HARRY, engineer, educator; b. Nov. 9, 1933, Tacoma, Wash.; s. Harry and Muriel Day (Paul) N.; m. Caroline Lee Stahl, Sept. 13, 1955; children: Michael b. 1957, Theodore b. 1958, William b. 1961; edn: BS engring., UCLA 1955; MSME, 1964; PhD, UC Davis 1967; lic. profl. engr. Career: research aerospace engr. Naval Weapons Center, China Lake 1960-68; prof. mech. engring. Naval Postgrad. Sch., Monterey 1968-89, emeritus prof., 1989-, dept. chmn. 1971-75; dept. sci. dir. Office of Naval Research, London 1975-77; Pacific Grove City Council 1986-92; dir. Assn. Monterey Bay Area Govts. 1986-92; awards: NWC fellow 1964-67, Royal Naval Engring. Coll. vis. research fellow 1982-83; mem: Am. Inst. Aeronautics & Astronautics (assoc. fellow), ASME, Sierra Club; patentee in field, 100+ articles pub. in tech. jours., author Intermediate Fluid Mechanics 1989, ed. Power Condenser Heat Transfer Tech. 1981; mil: lt. USN 1955-60; rec: leaded glass, bicycling, tennis.

NUTT, NAN, retired church administrator; b. Dec. 15, 1925, Pasadena; d. Paul Geltmacher and Estelle Boggs (Love) White; m. David Ballard Norris, Jan. 8, 1944 (div. 1966); children: Teresa b. 1945, Anita b. 1947, Carol b. 1947, Steven b. 1951; m. Evan Burchell Nutt, July 12, 1969; edn: AA, Chaffey Coll., 1967; BA, Pomona Coll., 1969; grad. work UC Riverside 1969-70. Career: adminstrv. asst. to dept. hd. E.E., Univ. of Tenn., Knoxville 1951-53; organizer, adminstr. troop camping San Gabriel Valley (Calif.) Girl Scouts Am., summers 1953-57; adminstrv. asst. Church Sch. Claremont UCC, Claremont 1957-64; asst. to personnel dir. Pomona Coll., Claremont 1964, 1964; bus. mgr. First Congregational Ch. of Long Beach, UCC, Long Bech 1982-86, adminstr. 1986-90, ret. 1990, , bd. pres. 1993; mem: Plymouth West, Long Beach 1988-89; listed Who's Who of Am. Women 1989-90; civic bds: Nat. Womens Polit. Caucus of Calif. (state advy. bd. 1988-, mem. NWPC nat. bd. 1981-89, nat. bd. steering com. 1972-79, 82-), OASIS/Older Adult Service & Info. Svc. L.B. (advy. com. 1986-), Cultural Heritage Commn. L.B. (mem. 1984-, chair 1987-89), Toastmistress Internat. Knoxville, Tenn. (founding pres. 1951-52), bd.dir. Public Corp. for the Arts, Long Beach; Democrat; Congregational, UCC; rec: politics. Res: 2867 Lomina Ave Long Beach 90815

NUTTER, BEN EARL, port development and planning consultant; b. May 17, 1911, Baldwin, Kans.; s. John Alva and Lillian Capitola (Boggs) N.; m. Leone Rockhold, Nov. 26, 1936; edn: Glendale City Coll. 1929-31; BSCE Oregon State Univ. 1936; reg. civil engr. Calif. 1938, Hawaii 1946. Career: asst. engr. materials to Chief of Engrg. Div. Honolulu Dist. US Army Corps of Engrs., mil. constrn. to harbor and flood control 1941-52; asst. mgr., asst. chief engr. Hawaii Harbor Bd. 1952-53; chmn. Hawaii Irrigation Authority and planning and constrn. for Hawaii Aeronautics Commn. 1953-57; supt. of public works Terr. of Hawaii, chmn. Hawaii Harbor Bd., hwy. engr., mem. Honolulu Bd. of Water Supply 1953-57; chief engr., asst. exec. dir. Port of Oakland 1957-62, exec. director 1962-77; cons. port devel. & mgmt. to ports and steamship cos. 1977-; honors: ASCE Civil Govt. Award 1971, Public Works Man of Yr. Kiwanis Internat./Am. Public Works Assn. 1967 Meritorious Civilian Service Overseas US War Dept. 1943, Sigma Xi Sigma, Tau Beta Pi; mem: Am. Soc. Civil Engrs. (past sect. pres.), Am. Assn. Port Authorities (pres. 1974-75), Regional Export Expansion Council, Nat. Defense Exec. Reserve, Internat. Assn. Ports & Harbors (chmn. containers com.), Internat. Cargo Handling Coord. Assn. (hon. mem.), Nat. Defense Trans. Assn., Rotary Internat., Masons, Scottish Rite, Beta Theta Pi, Propellor Club; Republican; Christian. Res: Santa Rosa.

NYBERG, LINDLEY VINCENT, electronics industry consultant; b. Oct. 19, 1931, Madison, Wis.; s. Alvar F. and Ellen A. (Lund) N.; m. MaryLou Benedict, Apr. 5, 1952; edn: electronics, RCA Inst. Inc., N.Y. 1953-55. Career: display system specialist in research and devel. 1955-70; sales and mktg. 1970-74; mfg. engr. specializing in printed board assembly 1974-92; Surface Mount Technology (SMT) consultant 1992-; awards: Archery State Champion, N.H. 1968; mem. SMTA (No. Cal. chapt. pres. 1986-89), past mem. Soc. Info. Display, Inst. of Radio Engrs., IEEE, Internat. Soc. of Hybrid Mfrs.; clubs: Masonic, Driftwood Yacht; 2 patent disclosures re cathode ray tube displays, classified, 1965-67; mil: US Coast Guard 1949-51; Republican; Prot.; rec: yachting, photog. Res/Ofc: 4368 Strawberry Park Dr San Jose 95129

NYBO, L. BRUCE, consulting civil engineer; b. Mar. 6, 1944, Glendale; s. Luverne Bernard and Elise; m. Jean W., May 29, 1965; children: Elisabeth b. 1967, David b. 1969, John b. 1970, Joy b. 1972; edn: Bakersfield Coll. 1961-63; Christian lib. arts Highland Coll. 1965; BSCE UC Los Angeles 1966; Reg. Profl. Engr. Miss. 1977, Reg. Civil Engr. Calif. 1978. Career: transp. ofcr. US Naval Base Adak, Alaska 1966-67; asst. resident ofcr. in charge of constrn. USMCAS Cherry Point, N.C. 1967-69; constrn. engr. The Kroger Co. Houston, Tex. 1969-71; dir. of engrg. Jitney Jungle Stores of Am. Jackson, Miss. 1971-75; corp. dir. engrg. Peter J. Schmidt Co. Buffalo, NY, Erie, Pa. 1975-78; gen. mgr., dir. engrg. and surveying services Smith & Assoc. Bakersfield 1978-79; pres. L. Bruce Nybo Inc., Civil Engineering, Planning & Land Surveying, Bakersfield 1979-; mem: Calif. Council Civil Engrs. and Land Surveyors (past chpt. pres.), Am. Soc. Civil Engrs., Nat., Soc. Profl. Engrs., Profl. Engrg. Assn. of Antelope Valley, Am. Planning Assn., Bakersfield C.of C.; mil: lt. USNR Civil Engineer Corps, active duty 1966-69; Republican. Ofc: L. Bruce Nybo Inc. 4200 Easton Dr Ste 10 Bakersfield 93309 also: 2635 Diamond St Rosamond 93560

NYDAM, WILLIAM JOSEPH, healthcare executive; b. Apr. 11, 1950, Lynwood; s. Bernard John and Marian (Polich) N.; m. Dorothy I. Kowalczewski, Jan. 21, 1984; son, Barron b. 1989; edn: BS acctg. (honors), UC Berkeley, 1972, MBA, 1973; C.P.A., Calif., 1975. Career: staff acct., sr. acct., mgr. Audit Staff, Deloitte, Haskins and Sells, 1973-79; treas./c.f.o. and bd. dirs. Centinela Hosp. Medical Ctr., 1979-84; exec. v.p./c.o.o. Memorial Health Technologies (for-profit subs. co.), also v.p. corp. devel. for parent co. (of regional healthcare network with 3 hosps. incl. Memorial Med. Ctr. of Long Beach) 1984-86; sr. v.p./c.f.o./treas. American Healthcare Sys. (AmHS), San Diego, 1986-; tchg. asst. UCB Sch. of Bus. 1972-73; lectr. in fin. Ambassador Coll. Sch. of Bus. (Pasadena) 1975-78; lectr. fin. acctg. and auditing USC Sch. of Bus. 1978-80; mem. bd. dirs. Vista Hill Found., 1988-; awards: "An Emerging Leader in Healthcare" The Healthcare Forum and Korn/Ferry Internat. 1988, "Up and Comer in Healthcare" Modern Healthcare/ Am. Coll. of Healthcare Execs. 1989; mem: Am. Inst. CPAs, Calif. Soc. Public Accts., Hosp. Financial Mgmt. Assn., Financial Execs. Inst., Am. Coll. of Healthcare Execs.; nat. speaker and panelist on topics incl. Medical Liability, Future of Healthcare, Working Capital Loans, Proactive Strategies for Reduction in Malpractice Liability Costs, The Value of a Healthcare Alliance; Republican; R.Cath.; rec: skiing, jogging. Ofc: American Healthcare Systems 12730 High Bluff Dr 3d Flr San Diego 92130

OAKESHOTT, GORDON BLAISDELL, geologist; b. Dec. 24, 1904, Oakland; s. Philip Sidney and Edith May (Blaisdell) O.; m. Beatrice Darrow, Sept. 1929 (dec. 1982); children: Paul b. 1931, Phyliss Joy b. 1933, Glenn Raymond b. 1947; m. Lucile Spangler Burks, Feb. 1986; edn: BS, Univ. Calif., 1928, MS, 1929; PhD, USC, 1936. Career: field geologist Shell Oil Co., Santa Maria 1929; instr. Compton Community Coll., 1930-48; supr. mining geologist State Div. Mines, San Francisco 1948-56; deputy chief State Div. Mines, San Francisco 1956-57, chief 1958, dep. chief, 1959-72, San Francisco and Sacramento; instr. state univs.; geol. consultant, Oakland 1973-80; honors: Phi Beta Kappa 1936, Webb award Nat. Assn. Geology Tchrs., Human Needs Award 1993; mem. Assn. Petroleum Geologists (Hon.), Assn. Engring. Geologists (Hon.), AAAS (Fellow), Geol. Soc. Am. (Sr. Fellow), Calif. Acad. Sci. (Sr. Fellow); mem. Commonwealth Club (S.F.), Byron Park Residents; author: Calif. Changing Landscapes- A Geology of the State (1973-), Geologic Violence (1975), 100+ technical papers (1935-80); Democrat; Methodist. Res: Byron Park #443 1700 Tice Valley Blvd Walnut Creek 94595

OBERSTEIN, MARYDALE, geriatric specialist, nursing home administrator; b. Dec. 30, Red Wing, Minn.; d. Dale Robert and Jean Ebba-Marie (Holmquist) Johnson; children: Mary Jean, Brennon, (from previous marriage): Kirk Robert, Mark Paul; edn: Univ. Oreg. 1961-62, Portland State Univ. 1962-64, Long Beach State Univ. 1974-76; Cert. geriatric specialist, lic. florist. Career: florist, owner Sunshine Flowers, Santa Ana 1982-; pvt. duty nursing aide Aides in Action, Costa Mesa 1985-87; activity dir. Bristol Care Nsg. Home, Santa Ana 1985-88; owner, adminstr. Lovelight Christian Home for the Elderly, Santa Ana 1987-; founder, tchr. hugging classes/healing therapy 1987-; activist for nursing home reform, discussion leader, speaker, 1984-; authored Assembly Bill AB180 changing Calif. nsg. home laws, 1985; awards: Carnation silver bow Carnation Service Co. 1984-85, Kiwanis Woman of Year 1985, honored on AM L.A.-TV by Calif. Lt. Gov. McCarthy 1984, biog. listings in 12 books incl. Who's Who in West, Who's Who in Am.; mem: Calif. Assn. Residential Care Homes, Calif. Assn. Long Term Care Facilities; civic bds: Orange Cty. Council on Aging (bd. 1984-), Orange Cty. Epilepsy Soc. (bd. 1986-), Helping Hands (chair 1985-), O.C. Women Aglow - Huntington Beach (v.p., Evangelist, spokesperson, actress), Pat Robertson Com. 1988; Joy Christian Fellowship Ch. (Praise and Worship leader). Res: 2722 S. Diamond Santa Ana 92704

OBERTI, SYLVIA MARIE ANTOINETTE, vocational and rehabilitation counselor and consultant; b. Dec. 29, 1952, Fresno; d. Silvio Lawrence and Sarah Carmen (Policarpo) O.; edn: BA in communicative disorders, CSU Fresno, 1976, MA in rehabilitative counseling, 1977; Calif. Comm. Colls. life instr. cred.; Calif. lic. vocat. cons., Nat. Certified Counselor, Cert. Rehab. Counselor. Career: intern Calif. Dept. Rehabilitation, Fresno 1977; vol. counselor Fresno Commn. on Aging, 1976-77; senior rehab. cons. Crawford Rehabilitation Svs. Inc., Emeryville 1978-80; vocat. rehab. counselor Rehabilitation Associates Inc., San Leandro 1980-81; textile cons., owner Rugs and Carpets of the Orient, Oakland 1979-; adminstr., counselor The Oberti Co., Oakland, 1981-, vocat. tng. for disabled, disability cons. to individuals, industry and ins. cos.; honors: HEW grantee 1976-77; first woman to race the Mille Miglia (Italy) solo and finish, May 1992; in 1951 SIATA 300 BC 750 Spyder; 3rd place of USA in Mille Miglia, 1993, racing vintage car solo; former dir. Pacific Basin Sch. of Textile Arts, 1982-86; mem: Calif. Assn. Physically Handicapped Inc., Am. Personnel and Guidance Assn., Am. Rehab. Counseling Assn., Calif. Assn. Rehab. Professionals (dir. 1990 CARP Conf., Monterey), Industrial Claims Assn., Internat. Round Table Advancement of Counseling, Nat. Rehab. Assn., Nat. Rehab. Counseling Assn., Nat. Vocat. Guidance Assn., Women Entrepreneurs. Ofc: 3629 Grand Ave Ste 101 Oakland 94610

O'BRIEN, PHILIP MICHAEL, college librarian; b. Jan. 5, 1940, Albion, Nebr.; s. Lawrence Joseph and Mary Helen (Ruplinger) O'B.; m. Christina Bartling, Feb. 1968; children: Tara Jennine b. 1973, Kirsten Ann b. 1977; m. Ann Johnson Topjon, Mar. 10, 1990; edn: BA, Whittier Coll., 1961; MSLS, USC, 1962; PhD, USC, 1974. Career: asst. librarian Whittier Coll., 1962-66, Special Collections librarian 1970-74, coll. librarian, 1974-; librarian soc. sci. dept. Chico State Coll. 1966-67; librarian US Army Europe, Germany 1967-70; awards: Whittier Coll. Athletic Hall of Fame 1988, Besterman Medal, Library Assn. (GB) London 1989; mem: Am. Library Assn. 1974-, Ronce & Coffin Club 1977-, Los Compadres con Libros 1975-, Am. Coll. & Res. Libraries 1974-, 1195 Club (bd. dirs. 1979-); author: T.E. Lawrence & Fine Printing (1980), T.E. Lawrence: a Bibliography (1988), contbr. articles in The T.E. Lawrence Puzzle (1984), Explorations in Doughty's Arabia Deserta (1987), Sweetbriar Gazette (Spring 88); rec: book collecting, bicycling. Ofc: Wardman Library Whittier College, Whittier 90608

O'CONNOR, GREGORY MICHAEL, optometrist; b. April 8, 1952, South Bend, Ind.; s. Joseph Bernard and Irene Ellen (Kearney) O'C.; m. Patricia Ranville, Dec. 30, 1977, div. Dec. 1991; edn: BS, Univ. of Mich. 1973; BS, Ill. Coll. of Optometry 1975, OD, 1978; Reg. Optometrist, Calif. 1979. Career: staff optometrist Chicago Eye, Ear, Nose & Throat Hosp., Chicago, Ill. 1977-78; chief of optometry svc., Naval Reg. Med. Ctr., Barstow 1978-81; pvt. practice, Malibu 1981-; tchg. asst. Ill. Coll. of Optometry 1977-78; awards: State of Mich. Undergrad. Scholarship, Univ. of Mich. Honors Convocation, Armed Forces Health Professions Scholarship, Tomb & Key, Beta Sigma Kappa; mem: Am. and Calif. Optometric Assns., Mojave Desert and L.A. Co. Optometric Socs., Malibu C.of C. (bd. 1988-, pres. 1992); clubs: Optimist (Malibu dir. 1982, pres.-elect), Rotary Intl. (Barstow dir. 1979-80), Big Ten Club; works: Cataractogenesis and Exposure to Non-ionizing Radiation Sources, Dept. of Defense Study 1979; mil: lt. USN 1976-81, Letter of Commendation.; Republican; Roman Cath.; rec: running (finished Los Angeles Marathon 1988, 89, 90, 91, 92, 93), writing, hiking, woodworking. Res: 5785 Oak Bank Trail, # 101 Agoura Hills 91301 Ofc: 3840 Cross Creek Rd. Malibu 90265

O'DOWD, DONALD DAVY, higher education consultant; b. Jan. 23, 1927, Manchester, N.H.; s. Hugh Davy and Laura (Morin) O'D.; m. Janet Louise Fithian, Aug. 23, 1953; children: Daniel b. 1955, Diane b. 1957, James b. 1959, John b. 1962; edn: BA, Dartmouth Coll., 1951; MA, Harvard Univ., 1955, PhD, 1957. Career: asst. prof. Wesleyan Univ., Middletown, Ct. 1955-60; provost and prof. Oakland Univ., Rochester, Mich. 1960-70, pres. 1970-79; exec. v.chancellor State Univ. of N.Y., Albany 1980-84; pres. Univ. of Alaska, Fairbanks 1984-90; chmn. U.S. Arctic Research Commn., W.D.C. 1991-; sr. cons. Assn. of Governing Bds. Univs. and Colls., W.D.C., 1992; mem. New York State Regents Com. on Higher Educ. 1992-; cons. Greenhills Software Inc., Santa Barbara 1991-; honors: D.Litt. (Hon.) Oakland Univ. 1980, Presdl. medal Dartmouth Coll. 1991; mem. AAAS 1955-, Am. Psychol. Assn. 1955-, Phi Beta Kappa 1950-, Sigma Xi 1957-; mil: t5 US Army 1945-47. Res: 1550 La Vista Del Oceano Santa Barbara 93109

OEI, KOK-TIN, investor; b. Jan. 10, 1924, Indramayu, Java, Indonesia; came to U.S. 1971; s. Han Siong and Ie Boen (Tjan) O.; m. Christina Khoe, June 21, 1952; children: John b. 1955, Tony b. 1957; edn: degree, textile engr. Hogere Textile Sch., Netherlands 1952. Career: weigher to asst. mgr. in fathers rice mills, Indonesia; agent, textile dyes, Indonesian import-export firm in Amsterdam, Holland 10 yrs., Hamburg, Germany 4 yrs., Bangkok, Thailand 4 yrs.; investor in apartment bldgs., No. Calif. 1971-; clerk, Metropolitan Life 1971-80; linguist: Indonesian, Dutch, English German, French; rec: art, antiques, philately, coins. Res: 2054 Sloat Blvd San Francisco 94116

OFFENHAUSER, BOB RAY, architect; b. Feb. 8, 1927, Los Angeles; s. O.D. and Laura (Putney) O.; m. Katherine, Apr. 17, 1958; 1 son, Madison b. 1960; edn: B.Arch., USC, 1952; Calif. reg. architect, AIA, Am. Inst. Arch. Career: architect prin. Bob Ray Offenhauser & Assocs., archtl. and interior design co., 1982-, incorporated, now pres. Offenhauser Associates Inc., also Offenhauser Decorating Corp.; mem. Architl. Guild USC, mem./founder L.A. Music Center, New Mus. of Contemporary Art, L.A. County Art Museum, Fellows of Contemporary Art, Frat. of Friends L.A. Music Center; clubs: Valley Hunt (Pasadena), Men's Garden (L.A.); mil: USCG; Republican; rec: gardening. Res: 445 Columbia St South Pasadena 91030 Ofc: Offenhauser Associates Inc., 3800 W Alameda Ave Ste 1190 Burbank 91505

OGAWA, PATRICK LEE, government drug abuse executive; b. Sept. 17, 1952, Kyoto, Japan; nat. 1959; s. Haruji and Teresa (Kurisu) O.; m. Gail M. Hatanaka, Nov. 19, 1977; children: Kristin M. b. 1981, Justin H. b. 1985, Erin M. b. 1990; edn: BA in sociology, Loyola Univ., L.A. 1974; MS in criminal justice, CSU Long Beach 1977. Career: exec. dir. Asian Am. Drug Abuse Program Inc., L.A., 1976-82; dir. of adminstr. Japanese Am. Cultural & Comm. Center Inc. 1982-85; chief planning program devel., tech. asst. L.A. Cty. Dept. Health Services Drug Abuse Program Office 1985-; apptd. bd. Office for Substance Abuse Prevention (OSAP) Advy. Bd., 1991-; mem & past chair State Advy. Bd. of Drug Programs 1981-; mem. review coms. ADAMHA, NIAAA, OSAP, 1980,

88, 89; mem: Am. Public Health Assn. 1990-, Calif. Assn. Alcohol & Drug Program Execs. 1985-, Korean Youth Center Inc. (bd.), Asian Pacific Planning Council, Nat. Assn. Prevention Profl. & Advocates, Nat. Assn. Pacific Am. Families Against Substance Abuse, United Way, White House Conf. on Families; Democrat; R. Cath. Res: 2705 S Cold Plains Dr Hacienda Heights 91745

OGG, WILSON REID, poet, graphic artist, publisher, curator, lawyer, ret. administrv. law judge, educator; b. Feb. 26, 1928, Alhambra; s. James Brooks and Mary Newton (Wilson) O.; edn: BA, UC Berkeley 1949; JD, UCB Boalt Hall Sch. of Law 1952; admitted Calif. State Bar 1955, lic. R.E. Broker 1974, Calif. Comm. Colls. tchg. creds., law, real estate and social scis. 1976. Career: psychology instr. 25th Station Hosp., Taequ, Korea, also English instr. Taequ English Language Inst. 1953; pvt. practice of law 1955-78; arbitrator Am. Arb. Assn. 1963-; sr. editor Continuing Edn. of the Bar, Univ. of Calif. 1958-63; secty., bd. trustees First Unitarian Ch. of Berkeley 1957-58; pres. Calif. Soc. of Psychical Study 1963-65; treas. The World Univ. 1977-79; dir. admissions The Internat. Soc. for Philosophical Enquiry 1981-84; pub. Pinebrook Press, 1988-; poet, curator-in-residence Pinebrook, 1964-; honors: Cultural Doctorate in Philosophy of Law, The World Univ. Roundtable 1984; Life patron Internat. Biographical Assn. and dep. dir. Internat. Biographical Centre, dep. gov. Am. Biographical Inst. Research Assn.- awarded Grand Amb. of Achievement. (ABIRA), Golden Acad. for lifetime achievement. (ABI 1991), Most Admired Man of Decade (ABI 1992), The Internat. Honors Cup (ABI 1992), 20th Century Award for Achievement (IBC 1992); mem.: State Bar of Calif., Am. Arb. Assn., Am. Assn. of Fin. Profls., World Future Soc. (profl. mem.), Bar Assn. of S.F., City Commons Club of Berkeley, Am. Soc. for Psychical Research, Inst. of Poetic Scis., The Wisdom Soc., AAAS, Parapsychol. Assn., Berkeley Archtl. Heritage Assn., Artists Embassy Internat., World Acad. of Arts And Culture, The World Literary Acad., The Ina Coolbreth Circle, Commonwealth Club, Town Hall of Calif., Faculty Club (UCB), Elks, Masonic Orders, Am. Legion, VFW, Amvets, Mensa, Triple Nine Soc.; sr. ed. var. law handbooks (UC Regents, 1958-63), articles in Internat. Soc. of Philosophical Enquiry Jour. 1981-84, poems pub. in The Best Poems of the '90's (Nat. Lib. of Poetry, 1992), Disting. Poets of Am. (The Nat. Lib. of Poets 1993) other poetry anthologies, Am. Poetry Assn. 1987; mil: cpl. AUS 1952-54, commendation.; Libertarian; Unitarian; rec: theater, horticulture, archtl. design. Address: Pinebrook at Bret Harte Way, 1104 Keith Ave Berkeley 94708-1607

OH, JANG OK, microbiologist-virologist; b. Jan. 15, 1927, Seoul, South Korea; s. Ki Yang and Moo-Duk (Lee) Oh; m. Won Yung Hyun, PhD, June 18, 1955; children: Dennis, MD, PhD b. 1963; edn: MD, Yonsei Univ. Med. Sch., Seoul 1948; PhD, Univ. Washington, Seattle 1960. Career: pathologist Carle Clinic Hosp., Urbana, Ill. 1956-57; res. instr. Univ. Wash., Seattle 1957-61; asst. prof. Univ. Brit. Col. Med. Sch., B.C., Can. 1961-66; res. microbiologist Univ. Calif., San Francisco 1966-, assoc. dir. Proctor Found., UCSF, 1985-; cons. NIH, USPHS, Bethesda, Md. 1979-83, 90-92; awards: NIH res. grantee 1970-, grantee Nat. Soc. Prevention of Blindness, USA 1974, medical exhibit award Am. Med. Assn. 1977, Lederle Med. Faculty Award, Lederle Pharmaceuticals USA 1963; mem: Am. Assn. of Pathologists 1965-, Am. Soc. of Microbiology 1958-, Assn. for Rsrch. in Vision & Ophthalmology (1970-, com. chair 82-85); author articles in med. books and jours.; editor monographs: Herpetic Eye Infections (1976), Intl. Conf. on Herpetic Eye Diseases (1987); Christian; rec: reading, gardening, carpentry. Ofc: Univ. Calif., San Francisco 94143-0412

O'HANLON, GEORGE ALAN, advertising agency executive, author; b. Mar. 29, 1955, San Jose, Calif.; s. Charles Adelbert and Dolores (Palacios) O'H.; m. Laura Colin, Aug. 9, 1974; children: Michele b. 1974, Bianca b. 1977, Sahara b. 1979, Vanesa b. 1981, Shante b. 1984; edn: BS internat. mktg., Univ. Mexico, 1976; BA advt., San Jose St. Univ., 1980. Career: mktg. mgr. Backgammon, S.A., Mexico, D.F. 1976-79; v.p. Advt/Mktg Systems, Santa Clara, Calif. 1980-87; pres., dir. and chief ops. ofcr. AD&MS (subs. of Shin-Etsu, Tokyo, Japan), Union City, Calif. 1987-92; cons. dir. On Target, San Jose 1992-; mem: Business/Profl. Advtg. Assn. (award for excellence B/PAA, L.A. 1988), Western Art Directors Club (show award, S.F. 1988), San Jose Met. C.of C.; author 4 books: How to Get Full Value from Advertising Sales Leads 1988, Effective Sales Literature for Business Marketers 1989, How to Increase Profits with Business Direct Mail 1990, Visual Communication 1991; Jehovah's Witness. Ofc: 1430 Truly Rd San Jose 95122

O'HARE, FRANCIS, consulting engineer, project adminstrator, owner's representative; b. Oct. 15, 1930, Millom, Cumbria, U.K.; s. Francis and Margaret Mary (Orr); m. Louise, Nov. 23, 1957; edn: dipl. land surveying, Newbury Coll., Hampshire, U.K. 3 yrs.; field engring./land mgmt., Newton Rigg Coll., Penrith, U.K. 2 yrs.; civil field engr. Corps Engrs., Worcestshire, U.K. 2 yrs. Career: field civil engr., sci. and tech. ofcr. govt. land devel. and mineral exploration projects in Central and So. Africa: Kenya, Rhodesia, Botswana, 1957-65, opened tech. coll. for Botswana Govt. for tng. of topo. survey technicians; proj. engr. new sugar plantations and mills in Malawi and Somalia, Muir Wilson Assocs.; large indsl. facilities constrn. in Central Africa of Aluminum smelter plant, cooling, refrigeration and meat packing plants, National Roads, 1965-79; came to U.S. 1979; internat. constrn. consultant, 1979-, splst. in proj. mgmt. of high tech fabrication facilities, computer facilities and hosp. rehab.; cons./assoc. Kellor and Gannon, Consultants, 1979-84; owner, pres. Field Services Management, constrn. consultants, 1984-87; resident cons. engr. U.S. Govt. State Dept. "Voice of America" Carribean area, 1987-90; constrn. mgr. Jacobs Internat., Intel Micro Electronic Wafer Facility, Ireland, 1990-93; mem: Constrn. Mgmt. Assn. Am. (L.A. chpt. v.p.), Constrn. Spec. Inst., Nat. Soc. of Profl. Engrs.; Republican; R.Cath. Res: 1207 S Buena Vista Hemet 92343

O'KEEFE, MICHAEL ADRIAN, physicist; b. Sept. 8, 1942, Melbourne, Australia; s. Peter Francis and Nadezhda (Mineekeena) O'K.; m. Dianne Patricia Fletcher, June 15, 1976; children: Eleanor b. 1988, Carlene b. 1990; edn: dipl. in physics, RMIT, Melbourne, Aust. 1965; BS physics (First Class hons.), Univ. Melbourne, 1970, PhD physics, 1975. Career: tech. asst. CSIRO, Melbourne 1961-69, exptl. ofcr. 1969-75; res. assoc. Ariz. State Univ., Tempe 1976-79; sr. res. assoc. Cambridge Univ., U.K. 1979-83; staff scientist Univ. Calif./ Lawrence Berkeley Lab., 1983-; cons. Xerox, Palo Alto 1984-, Shell, Houston 1985-87; recipient cert. of merit Univ. Calif./LBL, Berkeley 1991; Fellow Royal Microscopical Soc. 1983-, mem. Australian Inst. of Physics 1970-, Microscopy Soc. of Am. 1976-; inventor: EREM (pat. 1992); publs: 80+ sci. papers (1972-), editor conf. proceedings: TMS (1990), 10th Pfefferkorn (1991). Ofc: Univ. Calif. LBL 1 Cyclotron Rd Berkeley 94720

OKIMOTO, DANIEL IWAO, college professor; b. Aug. 14, 1942, Santa Anita; s. Tameichi and Kirie (Kumagai) O.; m. Nancy Elizabeth Miller, Jan. 27, 1970; children: Saya b. 1971, Kevin b. 1977; edn: BA, Princeton Univ. 1965; MA, Harvard Univ. 1967; PhD, Mich. Univ. 1977. Career: asst. prof. Stanford Univ. 1977-84, assoc. prof. 1984-; advy. council Dept. Politics, Princeton Univ. 1988-; overseas bd. Research Inst. Ministry of Internat. Trade & Industry, Tokyo, Japan 1988-; cons. Aspen Inst., Colo. 1978-82; awards: Harvard Univ. Nat. Language fellow 1965-67, Aspen Inst. Mellon fellow 1976-77, Hoover Inst. nat. fellow 1979-80; mem: NE Asia U.S. Forum on Internat. Policy (co-dir. 1980-), Council on Fgn. Rels., Palo Alto Little League (coach, mgr. 1988-89); author Between MITI & Market (1989), co-ed. The Political Econ. of Japan (1988), Inside Japanese System (1988), Semiconductor Competition & Nat. Security (1988); Democrat; Prot.; rec: bicycling, sports. Ofc: Northeast Asia Forum Stanford University Stanford 94305-6055

OLARTE, DENNIS, company president; b. May 16, 1957, Bogata, Colombia; nat. 1976; s. Jaime Calderon and Rina Cathy (Baroni) O.; Career: sales engr. Strasmann Machinery, Long Beach 1976-80; sales mgr. Associated Machinery, Sunnyvale 1980-82; v.p. Acu-tec Manufacturing Inc., Milpitas 1982-90; pres. Acu-Tec Industries Inc., San Jose 1990-; v.p. Internat. Mgmt. Council, San Jose 1984-85; Republican; Christian. Res: 35122 Lido Blvd #F Newark 94560 Ofc: Acu-Tec Industries, Inc. 761 E Brokaw Rd San Jose 95112

OLDFIELD, A. BARNEY, writer, radio commentator, specialist in international relations; b. Dec. 18, 1909, Tecumseh, Nebr.; s. Adam William and Anna Ota (Fink) O.; m. Vada Margaret Kinman, May 6, 1935; edn: AB, Univ. Nebraska, Lincoln 1933. Career: columnist, feature writer Journal, Lincoln, Nebr. 1932-40; publicist Warner Bros. Studio, Burbank, Calif. 1946-47; corporate dir. internat. relations (77 countries) Litton Inds., Beverly Hills 1963-89; adj. prof. Pepperdine Univ., Malibu 1975-81; mil: ROTC commission, June 6, 1932, Univ. of Nebr.; served thru ranks to lt. col. US Army WW II, ETO 1940-45, Col. Reg., USAF, US Air Force 1947-62: worldwide, Korea, first newspaperman to become a paratrooper in early Class 23; decorated Legion of Merit USAF No. Am. Aerospace Def. Command 1962; founder/treas. Radio & TV News Dirs. Found., WDC 1967-; founder/sec.treas. Found. of the Americas for the Handicapped, WDC; founder Aviation/Space Writers Found., WDC 1977-84; bd. mem., trustee Triple L Youth Ranch, Center, Colo. 1978-88; trustee USAF Museum and mem. bd. of nom. Aviation Hall of Fame, Dayton, Oh.; honors: humanitarian award Am. Res. & Med. Svs. Anaheim 1978, disting. svc. Radio & TV News Dirs. Assn. 1973, disting. svc. Aviation/Space Writers Assn., inducted Hall of Champions, Invent America (US Patent Model Found.) Alexandria, Va. 1989, disting. Nebraskalander of year, Lincoln, Nebr. 1983, HDL (Hon.) Univ. Nebr. (5/9/92), Veterans of Fgn. Wars "VFW Distinguished Citizen" 1992; mem: Overseas Press Club of Am. 1962-, Gr. LA Press Club 1963-, Radio & TV News Dirs. Assn. 1949-, Radio & TV News Assn. So. Calif. 1964-, Writers Guild Am./West 1964-, Armed Forces Bdcstrs. Assn. 1970-, AF Assn. (life), Navy League (life); author: Never a Shot in Anger (now in 3d printing); (novel) Operation Narcissus (repub. 1991); Those Wonderful Men in the Cactus Starfighter Squadron (2-vol. set); contbr. to collections: Yanks Meet Reds; Sale I Made Which Did Most For Me; (script) Road to Berlin, for Walter Cronkite's 20th Century. Republican; Prot.; avocation: philanthropy, has estab. 250+ scholarships. Ofc: PO Box 1855 Beverly Hills 90213

OLDHAM, MAXINE JERNIGAN, realtor; b. Oct. 13, 1923, Whittier; d. John K. and Lela H. (Mears) Jernigan; m. Laurance Oldham, Oct. 28, 1941; children: John Laurence, b. 1942; edn: UC San Diego 1951-80; Western State Univ. 1976-77; LaSalle Ext. 1977-78; AA, San Diego City Coll. 1974. Desig: GRI, Grad. Realtors Inst., CAR 1978. Career: Pacific Telephone, S.D. 1952-57; US Civil Svc. Commn., US Naval Aux., Air Sta., Brown Field, Chula Vista 1957-

58; San Diego Bd. of Edn., 1958-59; real estate sales 1966-; realtor Shelter Island Realty, S.D. 1977-; awards: Outstanding achiev. public speaking Dale Carnegie 1988; mem: Nat., Calif. Assns. Realtors, San Diego Bd. Realtors, Calif. Assn. GRI, Apartment Owners Assn., FIABCI Internat. Real Estate Fedn., Internat. Platform Assn. (Speakers), S.D. Geneal. Soc., Internat. Fedn. Univ. Women, Native Daus. of Am. Rev., Native Daus. of Golden West, Colonial Dames 17th Century; author: Jernigan Hist. 1982, Mears Genealogy 1985; Republican; R.Cath.; rec: painting, music, theater. Res: 3348 Lowell St San Diego 9106 Ofc: Shelter Island Realty, 2810 Lytton St San Diego 92106

O'LEAR, HAROLD DWIGHT, aerospace co. engineer; b. July 8, 1926, Warren, Ohio; s. Micheal Jame and Eva May (Shilling) O'L.; m. Carol Langmaid, Feb. 6, 1956 (div.); son, Dennis Harold b. 1957; edn: Univ. Mich., 2 yrs.; engring. and metallurgy courses; desig: Quality Assurance Engr. (1986). Career: insp. Chrysler Corp., Trenton, Mich. 1952-55; chief insp. Bathey's Mfg. Co., Plymouth, Mich. 1955-61; inventory control Ford Motor Co., Rawsonville,Mich. 1961-62; lab tech. Cyclop's Corp., Sharon, Pa. 1962-63; pub. rels. U.S. Steel Corp., Pittsburgh, Pa. 1963-68; carpenter, self empl., Los Angeles 1968-70; quality control mgr. Advantec, Inglewood 1970-72; sr. asst. qual. control mgr. Sun Weld Fitting Co., Los Angeles 1972-77; calibrated tool insp. Gultons Inc., Costa Mesa 1977-79; qual. control Advanced Control, Irvine 1979-86; qual. assur. engr. McDonnell Douglas, Long Beach 1986-; mem. Am. Soc. of Quality Control; club: Holiday Spa (Anaheim); publs: tech. articles on Q.C. (1964, 68, 70); mil: seaman 1/c USN 1944-46; Democrat; Prot.; rec: build model airplanes. Res: 3333 Pacific Pl. Apt. 405 Long Beach 90806 Ofc: McDonnell Douglas, 3855 Lakewood Blvd 106-11 Long Beach 90846

OLIPHANT, CHARLES ROMIG, physician; b. Sept. 10, 1917, Waukegan, Ill.; s. Charles L. and Mary (Goss) R.; m. Claire E. Canavan, Nov. 7, 1942; children: James R., Cathy Rose, Mary G., William D.; edn: student St. Louis Univ., 1936-40, MD, 1943; postgrad. Naval Med. Sch., 1946. Career: physician Med Corps US Navy 1943-47; pvt. practice medicine and surgery, San Diego 1947-; pres., chief exec. ofcr. Midway Med. Enterprises; former chief staff Balboa Hosp., Doctors Hosp., Cabrillo Med. Ctr.; chief staff emeritus Sharp Cabrillo Hosp.; awarded Golden Staff Award Sharp Cabrillo Hosp. 1990; mem. staff Mercy Hosp., Children's Hosp., Paradise Valley Hosp., Sharp Memorial Hosp., secty. Sharp Senior Health Care, San Diego; charter mem. Am. Bd. Family Practice; Fellow Emeritus Am. Geriatrics Soc., Fellow Am. Acad. Family Practice, Fellow Am. Assn. Abdominal Surgeons, mem. AMA, Calif. Med. Assn., Am. Acad. Family Physicians (past pres. San Diego chpt., del. Calif. chpt.), San Diego Med. Soc., Pub. Health League, Navy League, San Diego Power Squadron (past comdr), SAR; clubs: San Diego Yacht, Cameron Highlanders. Res: 4310 Trias St San Diego 92103

OLIVEIRA, ROBERT GEORGE, music professor, conductor; b. Mar. 8, 1923, Fortuna, Calif.; s. John Antone and Henrietta (Bittencourt) O.; edn: undergrad., USC, 1942-46; AB music edn., Humboldt State, Arcata 1948; MA music, Columbia Univ., 1951; Cert. d'Etudes, Conservatoire Nationale de Musique, Paris, Fr. 1951-52, student of Nadia Boulanger, Paris 1952. Career: music tchr. 4 pub. schs. So. Humboldt, 1948-50; pvt. music instr. D.E.G. Schs., Paris 1953-55; music instr. Paris American High Schs., France 1956-67; conductor for the A Coeur Joie movement, France 1959-65; founder, condr. Musique Vivant en Guyenne Internat. Festival, St. Cere, Fr. 1960-71; prof. of music Los Angeles City Schs., San Pedro, Calif. 1967-69; Kern Comm. Coll. Dist., Bakersfield 1969-86, music dept. chair 1980-86; pvt. music coach, Bakersfield 1986-, conductor Symphony Singers, 1990-; awarded French Recording Industry's Prix de Disque for recording: Schoenberg - Gurre Lieder 1957; mem: ACDA 1975-, SCDA 1967-75, Arts Council of Kern 1980-, ACLU 1985-; condr. recordings: Pergolese - Stabat Mater (1962), Stravinsky - Symphony of Psalms (1963), Verdi - Four Sacred Works (1964), Schonberg - Peace on Earth (1965), Britten Misericordium (1966), Brahms Requiem (1968), Schoenberg - Gurre Lieder (1957); mil: t5 AUS 1942-46; Democrat; R.Cath.; rec: gardening, travel. Res: 653 Magnolia Ave Bakersfield 93305

OLIVER, JOYCE ANNE, international columnist, high technology editorial consultant; b. Sept. 19, 1958, Coral Gables, Fla.; d. John Joseph and Rosalie Cecile (Mack) Oliver; edn: Mathematics scholarship, Miami-Dade Coll. (Fla.) 1972-73; BA, CSU Fullerton 1980, MBA, 1990. Career: corporate editor Norris Industries Inc., Huntington Beach 1979-82; pres. J.A. Oliver Assocs., La Habra Hts. 1982-, editorial clients include Norris Inds., Hunt. Bch. 1982; Better Methods Consultants, Hunt. Harbour 1982-83; The Summit Group, Orange 1982-83; UDS, Encinitas 1983-84; ALS Corp., Anaheim 1984-85; General Power Systems, Anaheim 1984-85; MacroMarketing Corp., Costa Mesa 1985-86; PM Software, Huntington Beach 1985-86; Compu-Quote, Canoga Park 1985-86; Nat. Semiconductor Canada Ltd., Mississauga, Ont. 1986; Maclean Hunter Ltd., Toronto, Ont. 1986-90; Frame Inc., Fullerton 1987; The Johnson-Layton Co., L.A. 1988-89; Corporate Research Inc., Chgo. 1988; Axon Group 1990-91; American Mktg. Assn., Chgo. 1990-92; Schnell Publ. Co., NY 1992-; contbg. ed. Chemical Bus. 1992; bus. columnist, Marketing News 1990-92; contbg. editor Canadian Electronics Engineering mag., 1986-89; West Coast editor CEE, 1990; spl. feature editor The Electron (Cleveland Inst. of Electronics)

1988-89; contbg. editor Reseller Mgmt. Mag. 1987-89, Computer Mdsg. Mag. 1982-85; contbg. writer to Business, NOMDA Spokesman, PC Week, Administrative Mgmt., Leadership and Organization Development Journal, Service Mgmt., Entrepreneur, High-Tech Selling, Video Systems, Technical Photography, Computing Canada, Research & Development, Portable Office, American Demogaphics, ID Systems, Materials Engineering, Visual Merchandising and Store Design, H.R. Executive, H.R. Mag. and Stores Mag.; mem: Soc. of Profl. Journalists, Nat. Writers Club, Internat. Platform Assn., IEEE, L.A. World Affairs Council, Internat. Mktg. Assn., Soc. for Photo-Optical Instrumentation Engrs., Inst. Mgmt. Scis., Assn. Computing Machinery, Research Council of Scripps Clinic and Research Found. (biomed. res.), Internat. Assn. of Bus. Communicators (IABC award for outstanding dedication 1979, pres. Fullerton chpt. 1979-80, treas. Orange Co. chpt. 1982), Communications Advy. Council (pres. Fullerton chpt. 1979-80); Republican; R.Cath.; rec: sailing, water ski. Ofc: J.A. Oliver Associates 2045 Fullerton Rd La Habra Heights 90631-8213

OLP, ANITA LOUISE, lawyer; b. May 7, 1962, Culver City; d. Robert Olp and Amalia Irene (Williams) Fraker; edn: BS in crim. justice, CSU Long Beach, 1985; JD, Southwestern Univ., 1990; admitted bar Calif. 1991. Career: res. extern Los Angeles Superior Ct., Torrance 1991; atty., assoc. Cone, Chairez & Kassel, Irvine 1992-; honors: Am. Jurisprudence Award in legal professions 1989, Wall Street Journal award for acad. achiev. 1990, listed Outstanding Young Women of Am. 1988, Who's Who Among Students in Am. Colls. and Univs. 1989-90, Who's Who Among Am. Law Students (8th, 9th, 10th edits.), Who's Who in West 1992-93; mem. ABA, Calif. State Bar Assn., L.A. Co. Bar Assn., Women Lawyers L.A., Phi Alpha Delta law frat. intl. (L.A. Alumni Bd. 1990-), Nat. Charity League (O.C. South Coast chpt.), Town Hall of Calif.; Republican; Christian; rec: political campaigns, theatre, singing, Special Olympics. Res: 26829 Basswood Ave Palos Verdes 90274 Ofc: Cone, Chairez & Kassel, 2603 Main St Ste 1000 Irvine 92714

OLSEN, CLIFFORD WAYNE, physical chemist; b. Jan. 15. 1936, Placerville; s. Christian William and Elsie May (Bishop) O.; m. Margaret Clara Gobel, June 16, 1962 (div. Dec. 1985); children: Anne Olsen Cordes, PhD b. 1964, Charlotte Olsen b. 1966; m. Nancy Mayhew Kruger, July 21, 1990; edn: AA, Grant Technical Coll., Sacto. 1955; BA, UC Davis, 1957, PhD, 1962. Career: physicist, project leader, task leader, actg. program ldr. Univ. Calif., Lawrence Livermore Nat. Lab., Livermore 1962-; cons. Aerojet Gen. Nucleonics, San Ramon 1969; organizer 2d Symposium on the Containment of Underground Nuclear Explosions, 1983, also 3rd, 4th, 5th, 6th, 7th (1985, 87, 89, 91, 93), editor symposium proceedings (2d-6th); appt. US Dept. Energy Containment Evaluation Panel, Las Vegas, Nev. 1984-; mem. Cadre for Jt. Verification of Underground Nuclear Testing 1988-; awards: Eagle Scout 1952, Life mem. Alpha Gamma Sigma, Calif. 1955, Chevalier Order of DeMolay 1953; mem. AAAS 1970-, Seismological Soc. Am. 1969-, Am. Radio Relay League 1988-; civic bds: Foothill H.S. Band Boosters, Pleasanton (sec. 1991, parade chmn. 1991-92), Calif. Lutheran Univ. (bd. convocators 1976-78); contbr. profl. papers J. Geophysical Res., Bull. of Seismol. Soc. of Am., J. Am. Chem. Soc., Physics of Fluids (1960-); Democrat; Lutheran; rec: amateur radio, cooking, gardening. Res: 997 Sherman Way Pleasanton 94566 Ofc: Lawrence Livermore National Lab. PO Box 808 Livermore 94551

OLSEN, STEVEN KENT, dentist; b. Nov. 20, 1944, Spanish Fork, Utah; s. Earl Clarence and Adela (Faux) O.; m. Karin Hurst, Oct. 5, 1984; children: Christopher Steven b. 1984, Sara Kate b. 1988, Vanessa Leigh b. 1992; edn: L.A. Valley Coll. 1969-70, Univ. of Utah 1967-68; BS, Brigham Young Univ. 1969; DDS, Univ. of Pacific 1974. Career: ptnr., practice dentistry spec. in surg. and endodontic procedures Brooks & Olsen, Salt Lake City, 1974; gen. practice dentistry San Francisco 1974-, solo 1977-76, Steven K. Olsen, D.D.S., Profl. Corp., 1977-83, ptnr. Olsen & Bergloff, 1984-; med. staff Latter-day Saints Hosp.; chmn. bd. Am. Dentists Ins. Corp., Grand Cayman, W.I., 1978-81; dir. Wilks & Topper, Inc., S.F.; instr. Univ. of Pacific, 1978-, instr. Stanford Inst., Palo Alto 1979-82; cons., dir., editor corr. course, Calif. Inst. for Continuing Edn., S.F., 1981-; cons. Pacific Coast Soc. of Marine Explorers, 1990-; honors: Alpha Epsilon Delta (life), Good Citizenship medal SAR (1963), biog. listings in Who's Who in West, Who's Who in World, Who's Who Emerging Leaders Am., Men of Achievement Vol. 1, Internat. Register of Profiles; polio pioneer 1954 initial group; mem: Assn. Coll. of Physicians and Surgeons, Am. Dental Assn., Calif. Dental Assn., Utah Dental Assn.; club: Physicians and Surgeons (SF). Res: 385 Old La Honda Rd Woodside 94062 Ofc: Two Embarcadero Ctr Podium Level San Francisco 94111

OLSHEN, ABRAHAM CHARLES, actuarial consultant; b. Apr. 20, 1913, Portland, Oreg.; m. Dorothy Olds, June 21, 1934; children: Richard Allen (PhD), Beverly Ann (Jacobs) (PhD); edn: AB, Reed Coll., 1933; MS, Univ. Iowa, 1935, PhD, 1937. Career: chief statistician City Plnng. Commn., Portland, Oreg. 1933-34; resrch asst. math. dept. Univ. Iowa 1934-37, biometrics asst. Med. Ctr., 1936-37; actuary and chief examiner Oreg. Ins. Dept. 1937-42, 1945-46; actuary West Coast Life Ins. Co., San Francisco 1946-, chief actuary 1953-63, v.p. 1947-, 1st v.p. 1963-67, senior v.p. 1967-68, bd. dirs. 1955-68, ret.;

cons. actuarial & ins. mgmt./pres. Olshen & Assocs., San Francisco 1979-; dir. Home Federal Sav. & Loan Assn., S.F. 1972-85, v. chmn. bd. 1979-85, bd. chmn. 1985-86, ret.; guest lectr. var. univs.; mem. Calif. com. Health Insurance Council, Univ. Calif. Med. Care Adminstrn. com., San Mateo County Retirement Bd. 1975-77; awards: Sigma Xi (Fellow), AAAS (Fellow), USN Ordnance Devel. Award 1945, disting. service US Office of Sci. Res. & Devel. 1945, Presdl. Cert. Merit 1947; mem: Health Ins. Assn. Am. (mem., past chmn. Blanks Com., actuarial & stat. com.), Actuarial Club of Pacific States (past pres.), Actuarial Club of S.F. (past pres.), Am. Acad. of Actuaries (charter), Am. Math. Soc., Am. Risk and Ins. Assn., Calif. Math. Council, Commonwealth Club (life), Fellow Conf. of Actuaries in Public Practice, Inst. Mgmt. Scis., Inst. Math. Stats., Internat. Actuarial Assn., Internat. Assn. Consulting Actuaries, Internat. Cong. Actuaries, Ops. Resrch. Soc., Stock Exchange Club S.F., Press Club S.F. (life), San Francisco C.of C. (edn. com.); contbg. writer Ency. Britannica, Underwriters' Report, The Nat. Underwriter, Life Underws. Mag., Annals of Math. Stats., other publs.; mil: resrch. assoc. Div. of War Resrch. 1942-44, Ops. Resrch. Gp., H/Q Comdr.-in-Chief, US Fleet 1944-45. Res: 2800 Hillside Dr Burlingame 94010 Ofc: 760 Market St Ste 739 San Francisco 94102

OLSON, KIM L., insurance executive; b. June 27, 1956, Gary, Ind.; s. Melvin L. and Sylvia A. (Parker) O.; m. Robin Lynn Zabrek, Jan. 18, 1981; children: David Michael b. 1983, Stephanie Lynn b. 1985, Sean Thomas b. 1992; edn: AA, Santa Barbara Comm. Coll., 1976; BA, UC Santa Barbara, 1980. Career: t.v. reporter, talk show host, teleprompter Cable TV, 1972; profl. tennis instr., 1975-81; ins. broker MONY Inc., 1982-83; chmn. bd., pres., c.e.o. Alamar Financial Services Inc. (ins., fin. products), Santa Barbara 1984-88; founder/owner The Olson Group (ins. & fin. products), 1988-; awards: Agent of the Yr. (nat. top prod.) General American Ins. 1992, Million Dollar Round Table Top of the Table 1992, Intv. Gen. Am. magazine 1992, MDRT Court of the Table 1990, Leading Producers' Round Table `Eagles Club' award Nat. Assn. Health Underws. (top award of health ins. ind.), disting. sales awards from Aetna Life, Combined Insurance, Congress Life, Kentucky Central, UNUM, Transamerica-Occidental, Am. Bankers Life, Blue Cross of Calif., Blue Cross/Blue Shield of Ohio, Old Line Life; listed Who's Who in Fin. & Ind. 1992-93; mem: Nat. Assn. Health Underws. (Santa Barbara Co. chpt. bd., past pres. 1987-8), Nat. Assn. Life Underws., Internat. Platform Assn., Nat. Fedn. of Indep. Business (charter mem. nat. Council of 100, moderator Nat. Pub. Policy Forum, Hot Springs, Va. conf. on health ins. crisis in Am., 1990), Santa Barbara C.of C., Easter Seal Soc. (S.B. Co. bd. 1982-83), Young Life Internat. (bd. 1984-86); publs: Life Ins. Selling (11/90), interviewee Transamerica Mag. 1987, Blue Cross Mag. 1989; rec: tennis, basketball. Ofc: The Olson Group, 4141 State St Ste C-4 Santa Barbara 93100

OLSON, THOMAS PETER, building contractor; b. June 6, 1947,Elmhurst, Ill.; s. George Wm. and Ima-Jean Louise (Stenberg) O.; m. Terry Fahrenracher, July 30, 1983; children: Thomas Michael, Katherine Louise, Terissa Lynn; edn: BS aerospace engring., Texas A&M, 1969; Calif. lic. contr. 1976, lic. real estate broker. Career: engr. Douglas Aircraft, 1969-70; real estate sales agt. Forest E. Olson 1970-72; contr./prin. Olson Constrn. Co., home remodel projects (150+), build apt. and condominium projects, custom homes, real estate devel. projects, 1972-; mem. Calif. Taxpayers Union, Nat. Tax Reduction Movement, Nat. Rifle Assn., Aircraft Owners & Pilots Assn., Heritage Found., B.P.O.E., Century Club, Smithsonian Instn., Nat. Geog. Soc., Loyal Order of Moose, L.A. Dep. Sheriffs Assn. (sponsor); Republican (Senatorial Club, Nat. Rep. Congl. Com.); Lutheran; rec: pvt. pilot, fishing. Res: 18486 Barroso Rowland Hts 91748

OLVERA, CARLOS NELSON, engineering executive, research consultant; b. Aug. 16, 1942, Antioch, Calif.; s. Manuel Carlos and Faye Sibyl (Ames) O.; m. Pamela Lords, Oct. 20, 1966 (div. 1979); children: Jason b. 1969, Jared b. 1970, Jamie b. 1973, Janel b. 1974; m. Georgelean Nielsen, Mar. 19, 1983; edn: BSME, Brigham Young Univ., 1972; reg. profl. engr. Ida., Calif. Career: engring. mgr. Westinghouse Elec. Corp., Idaho Falls, Ida. 1972-82; maintenance cons. Philippine Nuclear Plant, Manila, Philippines 1982-83; senior engr. So. Calif. Edison, San Clemente, Calif. 1983-; owner, prin. Olvera Research, 1991-; honors: BYU Dean's Honors list 6 of 7 semesters, listed Who's Who in West 1978, 79, Who's Who in Technology Today 1981, Who's Who Calif. 1992, 93, 94; mem. Am. Nuclear Soc., Am. Soc. Mech. Engrs., Naval Reserve Assn., Am. Legion, Mercer County, Pa. Hist. Soc., Polk County, Mo. Hist. Soc., Calif. Preservation Soc., Calif. Hist. Soc.; civic bds: Dana Point Planning Commn. (chmn. 1990-91, v. chmn. 1993-94, commnr. 1989-), Dana Point Underground Utilities Com. (chmn. 1990-), Dana Point Hist. Soc. (bd. 1990-, pres. 1993-, chmn. Museum Proj. 1991-93, newsletter editor 1991-, membership chmn. 1991-92), Danawoods HOA (bd. 1989-90), Dana Point C.of C. (10K run com. 1990-92, historian 1992), Capistrano Valley Symphony's Treble Clef Guild (charter mem., bd. 1990-93, parliamentarian 1990-92); author: "Los Olveras, Journey to America" a family history, 400 pp. 1991, profl. article 1988; mil: nuclear opr. MM1 (SS) US Navy 1963-69, comdr. USNR (Ret.) 1974-91, decorated Merit. unit Commendation, Good Conduct, Nat. Def., Vietnam Service w/star, Armed Forces Res., Navy Expert Pistol, Navy Expert Rifle medal, Navy and Marine Corps Overseas Svc. rib., Naval Reserve Assn. rib., Qualified in

Submarines; Republican; Ch. of Jesus Christ of Latter Day Saints; rec: antique auto restoration, geneal. research. Res: 24901 Danafir Dana Point 92629 Ofc: So. Calif. Edison POB 128 San Clemente 92672

OMHOLT, BRUCE DONALD, design and manufacturing co. president; b. Mar. 27, 1943, Salem, Oreg.; s. Donald Carl and Violet Mae (Buck) O.; m. Darla Faber, Oct. 27, 1972; children: Madison, b. 1964; Natalie, b. 1969; Cassidy, b. 1975; edn; BSME, Heald Coll. of Eng. 1964. Career: real estate salesman R. Lea Ward & Assoc., San Francisco 1962-64; sales engr. Repco Engring., Montebello 1964; var. mfg. eng. & mgmt. pos. Ford Motor Co., Rawsonville, Saline, Owosso & Ypsilanti, Mi. 1964-75; chief engr. E.F. Hauserman Co., Cleveland, Oh. 1975-77; dir. of design & eng. Am. Seating Co., Grand Rapids, Mi. 1977-80; principal Trinity Engring., Grand Rapids, Mi. 1980-81, Rohnert Park, Calif. 1981-84; pres. Trinity Engrg., Rohnert Park 1984-; inventor, patentee: U.S. (6), Japan (3); Res: 1034 Holly Ave Rohnert Park 94928 Ofc: Trinity Engineering, 583 Martin Ave Rohnert Park 94928

ONIK, FRANK JOSEPH, JR., engineering executive; b. June 12, 1949, Omaha, Nebr.; s. Frank Joseph, Sr. and Irene Rose (Mruk) O.; m. Diane Grace, July 14, 1984; children: Stephanie b. 1985; edn: BS in E.E.T., Univ. Nebr., 1976. Career: project engr. Reach Electronics, Lexington, Nebr. 1977-84; product engr., TCXO Crystal Filter, Dale Electronics, Tempe, Az. 1985-86; engring. mgr. Standard Crystal Corp., El Monte 1986-; mem: American Legion (post cmdr. 1982-83, Lexington, Nebr.), VFW (All State post comdr. 1983-84), K.C. (grand kt. Temple City, Ca. 1987-89); mil: sgt. U.S. Army 1969-72; Democrat; R.Cath.; rec: philately. Ofc: Standard Crystal Corp., 9940 E Baldwin Pl El Monte 91731

OPFELL, HARRIET MONSON, physician, hospital medical director; b. Aug. 20, 1924, Shenandoah, Ia.; d. Harry Nelson and Mary Frances (Poulsom) Monson; m. Richard William Opfell, Aug. 21, 1948 (div. 1977); children: Alexander b. 1953, Andrew b. 1955, Amy b. 1958, August b. 1959; edn: AA, Columbia Coll., Mo. 1943; BS, State Univ. of Iowa, 1945, MD, 1949; cert. Am. Bd. Pediatrics 1967, Fellow Am. Acad. of Pediatrics 1968. Career: med. intern Methodist Hosp., Indianapolis, Ind. 1949-50; fellowship Mayo Clinic, Rochester, Minn. 1953-56; pvt. practice pediatrics, San Antonio, Tx. 1951-53, Orange, Calif. 1958-82; med. dir. Childrens Hosp. Orange County, Orange 1982-, chief of staff 1981-83; clin. prof. pediatrics UC Irvine Coll. of Med., 1983-; dir: So. Calif. Physicians Insurance Exchange 1981-, Blue Shield of Calif. 1983-; advy. bd. Orange Nat. Bank 1981-; awards: distinguished alumnae Columbia Coll. 1973, physician of year Orange County Med. Assn. 1988; mem: Orange County Pediatric Soc. (pres. 1969), Orange Co. Med. Assn. (1959-, pres. 1979-80, del. CMA 1974-), Calif. Med. Assn. (del. AMA 1985); Republican; Christian; rec: music, gardening, orchidist. Res: 118 Calle Alta Orange 92669 Ofc: Childrens Hospital Orange Co. 455 S Main St Orange 92668

OPPENHEIM, SAMUEL AARON, history educator; b. Nov. 11, 1940, N.Y.C.; s. Harold and Dorothy (Sobel) O.; m. Alyne Faye Bernstein, Aug. 15, 1965; children: Michael b. 1968, Andrew b. 1969, Dorothy b. 1973, Sarah b. 1982; edn: BA, Univ. Ariz., Tucson 1962; AM, Harvard Univ., 1964; PhD, Indiana Univ., 1972. Career: instr. in Russian lang. & hist. Bishop Coll., Dallas, Tx. 1964-67; Austin Coll., Sherman, Tx. p.t. 1965-67; asst., assoc., full prof. history CSU Stanislaus, Turlock, Calif. 1972-74, 1974-79, 1979-; honors: Phi Beta Kappa 1962, Phi Kappa Phi 1962, Phi Alpha Theta 1959, Phi Eta Sigma 1961, w/wife jt. community service award Univ. of Judaism, L.A. 1976; mem: Am. Asssn. for Adv. of Slavic Studies 1965-, Am. Historical Assn. 1970-, Calif. Faculty Assn.; author: The Practical Bolshevik: A.I. Rykov, 1881-1938, 1979, textbook, Soviet Russia: A History 1991, 70+ articles in Slavic Rev., Soviet Studies, The History Teacher, Australian Slavonic & E. European Studies, Modern Ency. of Russian & Soviet History; mil: A2c Ariz. USAF Reserve 1958-65; Democrat; Jewish (pres. Cong. Beth Shalom, Modesto 1973-75); rec: jogging, classical music, reading.

ORENSTEIN, MICHAEL, philatelic dealer, columnist; b. Jan. 6, 1939, Bklyn.; s. Harry and Myra (Klein) O.; m. Linda Turer, June 28, 1964; son, Paul David b. 1970; edn: BS, Clemson Univ. 1960; grad. studies UC Berkeley 1960-61. Career: regional mgr., So. Calif., Minkus Stamp & Pub. Co., 1964-70; mgr. stamp div. Superior Stamp & Coin Co. Inc., Beverly Hills 1970-91;Superior Galleries, director stamp div. 1991, dir. space memorabilia 1992-; stamp columnist Los Angeles Times 1965-; tech. advisor "The Video Guide to Stamp Collecting" narrated by Gary Burghoff (of M.A.S.H. fame) 1988; author: The Fun of Stamp Collecting (award winning lighthearted basic guide); bd. govs. Adelphi Univ. N.Y. Inst. of Philatelic & Numismatic Studies 1978-81; mem: Am. Stamp Dealers Assn., C.Z. study group, German Philatelic Soc., Confederate Stamp Alliance, Am. Philatelic Soc. (Writers Unit 1975-80), Internat. Fedn. of Stamp Dealers; listed in 1977 World Book Ency. yearbook as purchaser (agt. Superior Stamp & Coin Co.) of most valuable US stamp (Sc#85A) for $90,000, subsequently handled the resale (Dr. Jerry Buss Auction 1987) for $418,000, highest price ever paid for a single US stamp and 2d highest for any stamp in world (at the time); mil: pfc AUS 1962-64; Republican; rec: fishing. Ofc: Superior Stamp & Coin Co. Inc. 9478 W Olympic Blvd Beverly Hills 91326

ORLAND, JEROME I., county government construction project executive; b. Dec. 1, 1937, Los Angeles; s. Alex and Betty (Kooba) O.; m. Cindy Goldstein, May 7, 1978; children: Lori b. 1960, Karen b. 1963, Tali b. 1990; edn: AA, L.A. City Coll., 1960; cert. constrn. specifier, Calif. 1978. Career: chief of specifications, Los Angeles County, 1969-77, hd. contracts adminstrn. 1977-83, hd. project mgmt. 1983-; instr. Woodbury Univ., L.A. 1978-89; mem. Am. Arbitration Assn. Nat. Panel Arb., 1985-, constrn. advy. com. 1989-; awards: Constrn. Specs. Inst. J. Norman Hunter Award, Cert. of Merit, appreciation A.I.A. 1978; Fellow Constrn. Specifications Inst.; civic: Friends of Children's Pavilion LAC-USC Med. Ctr. (bd. 1988-), San Fernando Valley Adminstrn. Ctr. Advy. Com., B'nai B'rith (pres. 1970), PTA (hon. life mem. 1975); contbr. articles to trade and profl. jours.; Democrat; Jewish; rec: tennis. Ofc: L.A. County Project Management Div., 550 S Vermont Ave Los Angeles 90020

ORLANDO, ROBERT ANTHONY, pathologist, educator, musician; b. Mar. 5, 1938, NYC, NY; s. Lawrence E. and Ida Ernst (Karnikofsky) O.; m. Joan Crofut Weibel, Nov. 29, 1981; children: William, b. 1959; Robert, b. 1969; Vivian, b. 1971; edn: BA, NY Univ. 1960; MD, NJ Coll. of Med., 1965; PhD, Univ. of Chgo. 1971. Career: faculty, Univ. of Chicago 1966-71; UC Irvine 1971-81; So. Calif. Coll. of Optometry 1972-; chief of pathology Mercy Gen. Hosp. 1972-74; Canyon Gen. Hosp., 1974-1981; Whittier Hosp. Med. Ctr., 1981-, also chief of staff 1989-90; chief pathology and dir. of labs. Beverly Hills Hosp., Montebello 1990-; Pathology and Laboratory Med. Group, Inc.; dir. sci. affairs Biomerica, Inc.; med. dir. UNIMED Labs Inc., Salick Health Ctr. Lab, Humana Hosp. West Anaheim, Coast Plaza Med. Ctr.; bd. dirs: Lancer Corp., Biomerica, Allergy Immunotechnologies, Whittier Hosp. Med. Ctr.; prof. path. So. Calif. Coll. Optometry, 1972-, Univ. Calif. Sch. of Medicine, 1971-73; Fellow Coll. of Am. Pathologists, Am. Soc. Clin. Pathologists, Internat. Acad. Pathologists, Royal Soc. Medicine (London); mem. Orange County Soc. of Pathologists (sec. 1973-), AMA, Calif. Med. Assn., Orange Co. Med. Assn., Am. Fertility Soc., Am. Assn. for Study of Liver Disease, Reticuloendothelial Soc.; mem. Trumpet Guild of Am., L.A. Doctors Symphony Orch. co-prin. trumpet (pres. 1990-92). Mail: PO Box 9949 Newport Beach 92658-1949

ORLEBEKE, WILLIAM RONALD, lawyer; b. Jan. 5, 1934, El Paso, Tx.; s. William Ronald Orlebeke and Frances Claire (Cook) Hammon; m. Barbara Pike, Aug. 29, 1954 (div. June 1989); children: Michelle b. 1955, Julene b. 1957, David b. 1959; m. Kathie Menlove Waterson, June 19, 1989; edn: BA, Willamette Univ., 1956; MA, Univ. Kansas, 1957; MA, Oxford Univ., U.K. 1958; JD, Willamette Univ., 1966. Career: senior scholar history Willamette Univ. 1955-56; instr. Univ. Kansas, Lawrence 1956-57; claim supr. Travelers Ins., Sacramento 1958-61; claim mgr. New York Life, San Francisco 1961-62; claim mgr. Transam., S.F. 1962-63; law clk. Oregon Supreme Ct., Salem 1964-65, investigator Ore. State Police, Salem, Ore. 1964-66; atty. law firm Coll, Levy & Orlebeke, Concord, Calif. 1967-77; W. Ronald Orlebeke Law Office, 1977-; judge pro tem Mt. Diablo Jud. Dist., Concord 1973-77; awards: Phi Beta Kappa 1956, Pi Gamma Mu 1956, Woodrow Wilson Fellow 1956-57, Rhodes Scholar, Oxford, Eng. 1957-58, Rotarian of Yr. Dist. 5160 Rotary Intl. 1989-90; clubs: Rotary Club of Clayton Valley-Concord (pres. 1987-88, dist. mem. 1989-90, chair, dist. conf. chmn. 91-92, gov. liaison 90-92), S.A.R. 1980-, Sons of Union Veterans of Civil War 1984-, Sons of Confederate Veterans 1984-, Masonic 1956-, Shrine 1977-, Elks 1972-; coauthor: Orlebeke Family in Europe & America (1987); mil: 1st lt. USMCR 1952-59; Republican; Prot.; rec: mil. and legal hist. of England. Ofc: 3330-B Clayton Rd Concord 94519

ORNELLAS, DONALD LOUIS, explosives chemist; b. July 7, 1932, San Leandro; s. Louis Donald and Anna (Gerro) O.; m. Linda Vee, Mar. 24, 1972 (div. 1982); children: Timothy b. 1961, Kathy b. 1964, Melinda b. 1975; edn: BS chem., Santa Clara Univ., 1954. Career: chemist Kaiser Gypsum Co., Redwood City 1954-55; Kaiser Aluminum & Chem., Permanente, Calif. 1957-58; Lawrence Livermore Nat. Lab., Livermore 1958-; recipient Annual Medal Award, Am. Inst. of Chemists, Santa Clara 1954; civic: Parents Without Partners (Hayward pres. 1970-72, Livermore bd. 1983-92); inventor, 2 patents on explosives (1973, 76); publs: 15+ jour. articles on detonation chem. (1962-); mil: capt. US Army 1955-57; Democrat; R.Cath.; rec: hunting, fishing, boating, gardening. Res: 559 South N St Livermore 94550 Ofc: LLNL PO Box 808, L-282, Livermore 94550

ORR, LEONARD, rebirthing movement founder, author, resort owner; b. Nov. 15, 1937, Walton, N.Y.; s. William and Eva O.; m. Magdalena Katarzyna, April 3, 1984; 1 child, Spirit b. 1985; edn: BA, L.A. Pacific Coll. 1962. Career: founder Rebirthing, San Francisco 1974-; Money Seminar 1974-; author: Money (book, video, audio tape 1978), Prosperity Consciousness 1979, How to be a Successful Profl. in the Self-Improvement Bus. 1988, Physical Immortality 1980, Physical Immortality for Christians 1986, Bhartriji - Immortal Yogi 2000 Years in the Same Body 1986, Common Sense of Physical Immortality 1985, How to Make Democracy Work 1987, Breath Awareness 1985, Rebirthing in the New Age 1977, Turning Senility Misery into Victory 1991, About Your Femininity 1991, Fire, Babaji - Angel of the Lord 1992, Government Without Taxes 1992, and numerous audio tapes; clubs: 1000 Friends, Sierra; mil: Nat. Guard 1955-56; rec: farming. Res: Box 5320 Chico 95927 Ofc: Consciousness Village 1 Campbell Hot Springs Rd Sierraville 96126-0234

ORTIZ-FRANCO, LUIS, mathematics educator; b. June 11, 1946, Teocaltiche, Mexico; nat. 1973; s. Luis and Antonia O.-F.; m. Judy Weissberg, Nov. 26, 1983; children: Rebeca Xochitl b. 1986, David Tizoc b. 1989; edn: BA, UCLA 1969; MAT, Reed Coll. 1970; PhD, Stanford Univ. 1977. Career: lectr. UCLA Ext., 1971; math. instr. UCLA Spl. Edn. pgm. 1970-72; dir. San Diego St. Univ. Student Support Pgm. 1972-73; math. instr. De Anza Coll., Cupertino 1976-77; Foothill Coll., Los Altos 1974-77; assoc. dir. NSF grant Univ. N.M., Albuquerque 1977-78; ednl. researcher SW Reg. Lab., Los Alamitos 1978-79; res. assoc. NIE U.S. Dept. Edn., WDC 1979-82; res. coord. UCLA Chicano Res. Ctr., L.A. 1983-86; math. instr. East Los Angeles Coll. 1984-87; assoc. prof. math. dept. Chapman Coll., Orange 1986-; awards: Chapman Coll. Summer Res. fellowship 1987, Ford Found. dissertation 1976-77, fellowship 1975-77, U.S. Dept. Edn. fellowship 1973-75, UCLA scholarship 1965-66; mem: Internat. Study Group on Ethnomath. (3d.v.p. 1988-), Nat. Council Tchrs. of Math., Math. Assn. Am., Soc. Advancement Chincanos & Native Am. in Sci., Am. for Democratic Action (bd. dirs. 1982); co-author: Ethnic Groups in Los Angeles (1987), Bibliography on Civil Rights Lit., articles pub. in profl. jours. (1982, 89); Democrat; rec: soccer. Ofc: Chapman College Math. Dept. Orange 92666

O'SULLIVAN, SHEVAUN EILEEN, antiques and arts dealer; b. Dec. 28, 1937, Albuquerque, N.Mex.; d. William Twiss and Sofia Ann (Fedison) O'Sullivan; edn: Univ. of N. Mex. Career: antiques and arts dealer, Los Angeles 1967-; past pres. So. Calif. Orgn. of Antique Dealers; secty./co-coordinator first and second annual Downtown Los Angeles St. Patrick's Day Parade 1984, 85, chief organizer third annual parade 1986, parade pres. 1987, 88, 89; co-prod. seventh annual "Avenue of the Stars St. Patrick's Day Parade" Century City 1990; producer eighth Annual Parade, Century City 1991; founder am.-Irish Heritage Week Com., L.A. 1987; mem: Magic Castle, Variety Arts Center, So. Calif. Orgn. of Antique Dealers, Harp & Shamrock Club, Am.-Irish Hist. Soc., Irish Network, Los Angelenas (secty. to bd. 1990), Califlower Alley Club, Golden State Boxers & Wrestlers Assn. (secty.); contbg. writer Bradbury Building Mag. 1977-78; Republican; R. Cath.; rec: preserving arts and antiques. Res: 2623 Kent St Los Angeles 90026

OVERTON, LEWIS MARVIN, JR., management/turnaround consultant; b. July 2, 1937, Des Moines, Iowa; s. Lewis Marvin and Helen Jane (Thomas) O.; m. Helen Virginia Hawthorne, Sept. 9, 1961 (div. Feb. 1984); children: Thomas William b. 1966, Anne Hawthorne b. 1971; m. Priscilla Craig Franklin, Dec. 28, 1985; edn: BS chemistry, Stanford Univ., 1961; MBA (honors) Pace Univ., 1967. Career: assoc. A.T. Kearny Consult., N.Y.C., 1967-72; Alan Patricof Assocs., 1972-75; v.p. finance Jon-T Chemicals Inc., Houston, Tx. 1975-79; pres. Lewis Overton Jr. Consultants, Houston 1979-; pres. D-CEMCO Inc., Burbank 1984-87; sr. v.p. The Belet Group Inc., Newport Beach 1987-89; ptnr. Belet Partners, N.B. 1989-92; pres. and c.e.o. Microwave Products of Am., Memphis, Tenn. 1989-91; mng. dir. Menumaster Inc., Sioux Falls, S.D. 1991-93; receiver District Ct. State of Texas 1981-93; acting exec. dir. Am. Lung Assn. of Los Angeles Co. 1993-; mem. Nat. Assn. Bankruptcy Trustees, Am. Bankruptcy Inst., Turnaround Mgmt. Assn.; club: California Yacht; pub. jour. article (1968); Episcopalian; rec: sailing. Res: 180 W State St Pasadena 91105 Ofc: 1021 W Mountain Rd Glendale 91202

PACE, DENNY, writer, retired law enforcement official, educator; b. Aug. 27, 1926, Clemenceau, Ariz.; s. Leroy and Mauretta (Eager) P.; m. Eleanore Ruth, June 19, 1946; children: Cynthia Ann b. 1947, Susan Carole b. 1948, Taina Marie b. 1949; edn: BS pub. adminstrn., USC, 1955, MSPA, 1964; EdD, Texas A & M, 1975. Career: sgt. Los Angeles Police Dept., 1946-64, decorated Purple Heart LAPD 1948; state crim. justice planner Gov. Office, Austin, Tx. 1972-73; dep. regional adminstr. U.S. Justice Dept., Dallas, Tx. 1972-73; faculty CSU Long Beach, Calif. 1965-67, Kent State Univ., Oh. 1968-70, Tarrant Co. Comm. Coll., Fort Worth, Tx. 1967-68, Univ. Texas, Arlington, 1973-74; dept. head Long Beach City Coll., Calif. 1975-88; researcher, writer in pub. adminstrn., edn. and human relations; author, coauthor 4 textbooks incl. Concept of Vice, Narc. & Org. Crime (1975-92), chpts. in 8 books; mem. Calif. Assn. Crim. Justice Educators (1970s-), V.F.W. (life), Marine Corps Raiders Assn. (life). Res: 3842 Montego Huntington Beach 92649

PACELLI, JOSEPH GERARD, JR., designer, author; b. May 10, 1934, Bklyn.; s. Joseph Gerard and Ann Dorothea (Rescigno) P.; m. Lydia Colon, Aug. 4, 1956; m. 2d. Alesta Ericsson, Sept. 9, 1967; children: Mia Lynn b. 1962, Blayne Joseph b. 1965; edn: BFA, Univ. Conn., 1955, grad. pgm. MFA, 1955-56. Career: archtl. designer, assoc. major architects, Los Angeles 1956-65; commercial interior designer- hotels, restaurants and amusement parks, nat., 1965-78; motion picture set designer, feature film and t.v., 1978-; art production designer/director, feature film, 1983-; exec. v.p. K/P Services, Inc., hospitality management, 1991-; guest lectr. Santa Monica City Coll., 1976; mem. Internat. Alliance of Theatrical and Stage Employees 1965-, Am. Football Coaches Assn. 1990-, Big Bear Lake Film Comm. 1988-, mem. Nat. Trust for Hist. Preservation 1992-, Smithsonian Assoc. 1993-; civic: H.S. football coach; author: Building Your High School Football Program: In Pursuit of Excellence 1987; coauthor: George Allen's Guide to Special Teams 1989; Republican; R.Cath. Res: 42689 Constellation Dr Big Bear Lake 92315 Ofc: Inter/Plan Limited PO Box 3752 Big Bear Lake 92315

PACKARD, BETTY J., marketing consultant, writer; b. Oct. 1, 1937, Idpls.; d. Raymond Roy and Juanita Doris (Copeland) Reed; m. James R. Packard Jr., Nov. 28, 1958 (dec. Oct. 1, 1960); children: Lisa Lynn Packard Beaudry b. 1959, James R. Packard III b. 1961; m. Stephen Milton Voris, Sept. 26, 1975; edn: BA, Franklin Coll., 1967. Career: English tchr. and hd. dept. journalism Ben Davis High Sch., Indianapolis 1967-69; tchr. In H.S. Journalism Assn., Ball State Univ., 1968; ed. Res. & Review Svc. of Am., 1969-75; owner, pres. Packard Consulting, 1975-; co-owner Hoosier Hospitality, 1985-89; dir. Indiana Mutual Fire Ins. Co., 1974-; seminar instr. financial svs. ind. world-wide, 1973-; ed. WLUC News, Women Life Underwriters, Clinton, Md. 1988-90; awards: 11 nat. writing awards Nat. Fedn. of Press Women, Mo. 1971-75, 74 state writing awards Ind. and Calif. Press Women 1971-89, Woman Writer of Yr. Indiana Women's Press Club 1975, 1989 Sweepstakes Winner annual writing contest Calif. Press Women 1989; mem: Calif. Press Women (exec. bd. 1985-), Nat. Fedn. of Press Women (1967-, nat. bd. 1971-79), Am. Auto Racing Writers & Bdcstrs. Assn. (annual dinner com. 1990), Championship Auto Race Aux. 1987-, Calif. Abortion Rights Action League (bd. 1985-89); S.F. Symphony Store (vol. 1985-); clubs: Pi Beta Phi Alumnae S.F. (ways & means com. 1984-), Presidio of S.F. Officers' Wives (Xmas Project chair 1982-), Republican Fed. Womens; author: (book) When Someone Is Crying (1976), (brochure) I Love You (1976); Republican; Disciples of Christ; rec: family, classical music. Res: 1419 DeHaro St San Francisco 94107 Ofc: Packard Consulting 20 Edgewater Ct Brownsburg IN 46112

PADVE, MARTHA BERTONNEAU, urban planning and arts consultant, fundraiser; b. Feb. 22, Scobey, Mont.; d. Henry Francis and Marie (Vaccaro) Bertonneau; m. Jacob Padve, May 9, 1954 (div. 1980); edn: student, Pasadena Jr. Coll., 1938-40; cert., SW Univ. Bus. Coll., L.A., 1940-41, Pasadena Inst. for Radio, 1946-47; student, Claremont Colls., 1972-74, Univ. So. Calif., 1983-84, Com. Coll., Pasadena, 1987-88. Career: juvenile roles Pasadena Comm. Playhouse 1935-37; ptnr., bus. mgr. restaurant devel. ventures, Pasadena 1940-50; club dir. Red Cross, Nfld., Can. 1944-45; leading roles Penthouse Theatre, Altadena, Calif. 1946-48; club dir. armed forces spl. svs. Red Cross, Austria 1949-52; head dept. publs. Henry E. Huntington Lib., San Marino, Calif. 1953-57; cons. art planning Model Cities program, Omaha 1975; founding instr. contemporary art collecting class 1979-80; dir. devel. Bella Lewitzky Dance Found., L.A. 1980-81; instr. Art Ctr. Coll. Design, Pasadena 1981-82, assoc. dir. devel. 1981-83; instr. Coll. Continuing Edn. Univ. So. Calif., L.A. 1983-84; urban planning and arts cons. The Arroyo Group, Pasadena 1979-; cons. in field, 1984-; developer edn. program Mus. Contemporary Art, L.A. 1984-86; curator, Vroman's Exhibition Program 1992-; trustee, v.p., Pasadena Art Mus. 1967-74; co-chmn. bldg. fund Norton Simon Mus. Art, Pasadena 1968-70; chmn. Pasadena Planning Commn. 1973-81, Pasadena Street Tree Plan 1975-76, High Rise Task Force, San Gabriel Valley Planning Council 1977-78; mem. Pasadena Downtown Urban Design Plan 1980-83; founding mem. Arts, Parks. & Recreation Task Force 1978-80; vice-chmn. Pasadena Design Review Commn. 1974-78; founding chmn. So. Calif. Fellows of Contemporary Art 1976-78; mem. advy. com. Univ. So. Calif. art galleries 1976-82, UCLA oral history program contemporary art 1983-; chmn. audit com. L.A. Co. Grand Jury 1986-87; founder, Robinson Mem. Fund, Inc. 1990-92, acting exec. dir., 1990-92, adv., 1992-; mem. City Cultural Arts Div. Peer Panels, Grants Program 1989-92; awards: named Woman of the Yr., Pasadena Women's Civic League 1980; recipient Gold Crown award Tenth Muse, Pasadena Arts Council 1983; Commendation awards: Pasadena City Dirs. 1975, 80, 82, 83, L.A. County Bd. Supervisors 1987; Graphic Arts award So. Calif. Fellows Contemporary Art 1978; listed Who's Who in the West 1990; mem: Metropolitan Assoc., Pasadena Heritage, Calif. Inst. Tech. Assoc.; civic: Am. Heart Assn. (regional chair); United Way (committees), Rosemary Cottage, Foothill Family Svc., Pasadena Urban Coalition; author: arts segment Pasadena Gen. Plan 1980-83. Republican. Roman Catholic; rec: theater, music, wine, food. Res: 80 N. Euclid Ave. Pasadena. Ofc: 80 N. Euclid Ave. Pasadena 91101

PAHL, STEPHEN DONALD, lawyer; b. July 23, 1956, Los Angeles; s. Donald Alfred and Verlene Virginia (Dunaway) P.; m. Louise A. Dodd, Feb. 18, 1978; edn: BA, UC Santa Barbara 1977; JD, Univ. Santa Clara 1980. Career: research atty. Santa Clara County Superior Ct., San Jose 1980-81; atty., assoc. Littler Mendelsohn 1981-82; ptnr. Tarkington et al 1983-89; mng. ptnr. Pahl & Gosselin, San Jose and San Francisco 1989-; dir. St. Johns Restaurant, Sunnyvale 1984-; Nat. Intercity Bank, Santa Clara 1983-86; awards: UC regent scholar 1977, St. of Calif. fellow 1977-80; mem: ABA, FBA, Calif. Bankers Assn., Calif. St. Bar Assn. (com. on fed. cts., resolutions com.), Los Altos Hills Planning Commn. (commr. 1989-); author A Ct. Divided: An Analysis of Polarization on U.S. Supreme Ct.; Republican; Baptist; rec: racquetball, golf, flying. Res: 27431 Black Mountain Rd Los Altos Hills 94022 Ofc: 160 W Santa Clara St 14th Fl San Jose 95113 Ph: 408/286-5100

PAI, KIHO, pharmacist, educator; b. July 13, 1944, Taegu, Korea; s. Yuwee and Sodeuk (Kim) P.; m Susie Kim, Apr. 30, 1971; children: David; James; edn: BS, Sung Kyun Kwan Univ. Pharmacy Sch., 1965; MS, Seoul Nat. Univ. Pub. Health, 1971; PharmD, Butler Univ. Pharmacy Sch., 1975. Career: pharmacist Indiana Retired Persons Pharmacy, Idpls., Ind. 1975-77; asst. mgr. Calif. Retired Persons Pharmacy, Lakewood, Calif. 1977-90; prof. Samra University, Los Angeles 1990-; staff cons. Kaiser Hosp. Pharmacy, 1982-; owner The

Pharmacy, Anaheim; awards: 15-yr. service AARP Pharmacy 1990, Korean Soc. of Indiana 1977, Sung Kyun Univ. Alumni 1978; mem: Indiana Pharmacist Assn. 1975, Calif. Employee Pharmacist Assn. 1977-90, Korean Pharmacist Assn. of Calif. (Prof. tchg. instr. 1983-), Calif. Pharmacists Assn. 1990-; civic: Orange Co. Central Y's Mens Club 1983-, Internat. Soc. of Friendship & Goodwill (hon. 1983-), Universala Esperanto Assn.; Democrat (secty. Asian-Pac. Caucus of O.C.); Christian. Res: 1598 W Tedmar Ave Anaheim 92802 Ofc: 3055 W Orange Ave Anaheim 92804 Tel:714/995-4161

PAINTER, AMELIA ANN, marketing professional, writer; b. Oct. 26, 1946, Hot Springs, Ark.; d. Jack H. and Emily C. (Hosmer) Chapman; m. Douglas M. Painter, June 12, 1988; children: Katrina b. 1967, Bruce b. 1969, Emily Grace b. 1973; lic. R.E. sales agt. Calif. 1978, Texas 1985. Career: salesmgr. Commercial Systems, Houston 1984-85; mktg. dir. Southmark Mgmt., Dallas 1985-86; sales dir. Noble Design & Set Construction, San Diego 1986-89; mktg. dir. Scenic Drive Set Design & Constrn., Los Angeles 1990-91; freelance writer 1992-; editorial asst. and mem. Houston Motion Picture Council, Tx. ("Newsreel Publication"), Nat. Assn. of Women in Commercial Real Estate, Houston ("Shoptalk Newsletter"), 1984-85; contbg. author: Consumers Form Letter Collection (1991), Cleaning-Up Your Credit (1991); rec: writing, gardening. Ofc: PO Box 154 San Luis Rey 92068-0154

PAINTER, JOEL HAROLD, clinical psychologist; b. July 3, 1936, Ashland, Ohio; s. Harold Dennis and Margaret Ruth (Stone) P.; m. Saundra Sue Brunn, Nov. 28, 1958; children: Daniel b. 1968, Jeremy b. 1973; edn: Westmont Coll. 1954-57; BS hons., Old Dominion Univ. 1967; PhD, Ariz. St. Univ. 1972; lic. clin. psychologist Calif. Career: psychologist VA Hosp. Atlanta 1971-74; coord. DDTP VA Med. Ctr., Long Beach 1974-80; corp. secty., treas. Emily K. Sports Wear Inc., Santa Barbara 1984-; cons. psychologist Schick Shadel Hosp. 1982-; chief psychologist Dept. Vet. Affairs 1980-; pvt. practice, Goleta 1981-; honors: Who's Who West; mem: Pres. Assn., S.B. Psychologists in Clin. Practise (secty., treas.), S.B. Psychol. Assn., Calif. St. Psychol. Assn., Am. Psychol. Assn., Christian Bus. Mens. Com., Gideons Internat., Am. Legion, Am. Cancer Soc.; author: Modification of Smoking Behavior Controlled Pub. Clinic (1972), 3 articles pub. in profl. jours. (1974-83); mil: sgt. E-5 AUS 1961-64, Army Commend. Medal 1964; Republican; United Methodist; rec: bicycling, music. Res: 6590 Camino Venturoso Goleta 93117

PALADINI, ACHILLE GEORGE, seafood company president; b. June 8, 1936, San Francisco; s. Walter Louis and Jennie Marie (De Vincenzi) P.; m. Joan Ernestine, May 14, 1960; children: Laura b. 1962, Gina b. 1963, Diana b. 1965; edn: Univ. San Francisco Career: production mgr. Paladini Seafoods Co., Los Angeles 1958-60; salesman A. Paladini Inc., San Francisco 1960-66; sales mgr. Calif. Shellfish Co. 1966-68; gen. mgr. Cal East Foods Co., Oakland 1968-73; pres. A. Paladini Inc., San Francisco 1973-74; owner A. Paladini 1975-; real estate investor; awards: Lung Assn. (1987, 88); mem: Nat. Fisheries Inst., Calif. Seafoods Inst., World Trade Club; publs: family hist. articles in Pioneers of West, and S.F. History; Republican; R.Cath.; rec: boating. Ofc: A. Paladini Seafoods Corp. 500 Mendell St San Francisco 94124

PALAFOX, BRIAN A., general thoracic and cardiovascular surgeon; b. Feb. 9, 1951, Honolulu, Hawaii; s. Anastacio L. (PhD) and Jesusa A. P.; edn: BS biol., Univ. of Hawaii 1972; MD, UC Irvine 1975. Diplomate Am. Bd. Surgery, Am. Bd. Thoracic Surgery, Fellow Am. Coll. Surgeons (FACS). Career: extern in obstets., intern in pathol. Orange Co. Medical Center, resident, chief resident gen. surgery UCI Med. Ctr., Orange 1977-81, fellowship thoracic and cardiovascular surgery UCI Med. Ctr. and Long Beach VA Hosp., 1981-83; ER physician Kaiser Permanente Hosp., Bellflower, Glendora Comm. Hosp., Circle City Hosp., Corona; surgeon pvt. practice, Santa Ana 1983-; instr. US Army Health Sci. Command, asst. clin. prof. UCI Med. Ctr.; awards: Comm. Scholarship pgm. Honolulu, Eagle Scout, Resident of the Year UCI Med. Ctr. 1980-81; Fellow Internat. Coll. of Surgeons (FICS), Fellow Coll. of Chest Physicians (FCCP), mem. AMA, AMSUS, Calif. Med. Assn., Orange Co. Med. Assn., Orange Co. Surgical Soc.; mil: LtCol Calif. Army Nat. Guard 143D Evacuation Hosp.; R.Cath. Ofc: 1310 West Stewart Dr Ste 502 Orange 92668

PALFREYMAN, RICHARD WARWICK, financial executive; b. Aug. 14, 1942, Springville, Utah; s. Warwick Charles and Ione (Averett) P.; m. Lindy Olson, June 9, 1966; children: Mandi b. 1968, Scott b. 1968, Michael b. 1972, Matthew b. 1975, Timothy b. 1980; edn: BS, Univ. Utah 1966; MBA, 1967. Career: treasury analyst Kaiser Aluminum & Chemical Corp., Oakland 1967-72; asst. treas. Natomas Co., San Francisco 1972-80; CFO Simmons Oil Corp., Phoenix, Ariz. 1980-83; sr.v.p. fin. Computerland Corp., Hayward 1983-88; CFO Photo & Sound Co., San Francisco 1989-, pres. and c.e.o. 1992-; mem: BSA (exec. bd. 1984-), Cerebral Palsy Center (bd. mem.); mil: SP-4 Army Nat. Guard 1959-66; Republican; Mormon; rec: racquetball. Res: 320 LasSalle Ave Piedmont 94610 Ofc: Photo & Sound Co. 140 Hubbell St San Francisco 94107

PALMER, PATRICIA TEXTER, educator, administrator; b. June 10, 1932, Detroit, Mich.; d. Elmer Clinton and Helen (Rotchford) Texter; m. David Jean Palmer, June 4, 1955; edn: BA, Univ. Mich. 1953; MEd, Nat. Coll. of Edn.

(now National-Louis Univ.) 1958; MA, CSU San Francisco 1966; postgrad. work Stanford Univ. 1968, CSU Hayward 1968-69; Calif. Life Tchg. Creds. (gen. elem., gen. secondary, spl. Speech Arts). Career: chair Speech Dept. Grosse Pointe Univ. Sch., Mich. 1953-55; tchr. South Margerita Sch., Panama 1955-56; tchr. Kipling Sch. Deerfield, Ill. 1955-56; Rio San Gabriel Sch., Downey, Calif. 1957-59; Roosevelt High Sch., Honolulu 1959-62; El Camino High Sch., South San Francisco 1962-68, chair ESL Dept. South S.F. Unified Dist. 1968-81; dir. English as Second Lang. Inst., Millbrae 1978-, Calif. master tchr. ESL, Calif. Council Adult Edn. 1979-82; adj. faculty New Coll. of Calif., 1982-, Skyline Community Coll., San Bruno 1990-; mem. Calif. State Adult Basic Edn. Advy. Com. on vocational ESL; awards: Concours de Francais Prix 1947, Jeanette M. Liggett Meml. award for excellence in hist. 1949, Cum Laude Soc. 1949, Zeta Phi Eta Speech Hon. 1953, Scroll Hon. Soc. 1953, outstanding alumna Univ. of Mich. Sesquicentennial Awards 1968, commendation. for achieve. in journalism Hawaii State Legislature 1962; mem: Tchrs. of English to Speakers of Other Languages, Calif. affiliation, Faculty Assn. of Calif. Comm. Colls., Assn. for Supvn. and Curriculum Devel., Speech Communication Assn., AAUW, Internat. Platform Assn., Univ. Mich. Alumnae Assn., National-Louis Univ. Assn., Ninety Nines, Chi Omega, Nat. Assn. of Female Execs., Computer Using Educators (CUE), Faculty Assn. of Calif. Comm. Colls., Nat. Assn. for Foreign Student Affairs (NAFSA), Peninsula Lioness Club, Soroptimist Intl.; Republican; R.Cath.; rec: flying. Res: 2917 Franciscan Court San Carlos 94070 Ofc: New College of California 450 Chadbourne Ave Millbrae 94030

PAN, WILLIAM JIAWEI, trading company president; b. July 24, 1935, Shanghai, China; s. You-Yuan Pan and Ruth (Li) Tien; m. Fengqiu Liu, Dec. 26, 1965; 1 child, Song b. 1967; edn: BS, Peking Univ. 1958; Ching Hwa Univ., Beijing 1961-63. Career: engr. Beijing Radio Factory, Beijing 1958-78; Dong Feng TV Factory, 1978-80; asst. gen. mgr. China National Electronics Imp./Exp. Corp., Beijing br. 1980-91; mgr. electronics dept. China Resource Products, NY, NY 1985-91; pres. and c.e.o. King Trading Inc., San Francisco 1987-91; pres. and c.e.o. Kings International, Inc., San Jose 1990-91; rec: photog., tennis, swimming, badminton. Res: 175 Calvert Dr Cupertino 95014

PANETTA, LEON EDWARD, government official; b. June 28, 1938, Monterey; m. Sylvia Marie Varni, 1962; 3 sons: Christopher, Carmelo, James; edn: BA, magna cum laude, Univ. of Santa Clara 1960, JD, 1963; admitted to Calif. Bar 1965. Career: individual law practice, Monterey; legis. asst. to U.S. Senator Thomas H. Kuchel of Calif. 1966-69; spl. asst. to secty. HEW, WDC. 1969; dir. U.S. Ofc. for Civil Rights, Wash. 1969-70; exec. asst. to mayor, NYC 1970-71; ptr. firm Panetta, Thompson & Panetta, Monterey 1971-76; elected to U.S. House of Reps. from 16th Congl. Dist., Calif. 1976, reelected 1978, 80, 82, 84, 86, 88, 90, 92; chmn. 95th Congress New Members Caucus 1977-78; No. Calif. Majority Regional Whip 1981-84; Dep. Majority Whip for budget issues 1985-93; House Budget Com. mem. 1979-93, chmn. 1989-93, appt. Director Office of Mangement and Budget by Pres. Clinton 1993-; mem. House Agric. Com., House Adminstrn. Com., House Select Com. on Hunger; founder Monterey Coll. of Law; trustee, Univ. Santa Clara Law Sch.; awards: NEA Lincoln Award 1969, Lawyer of the Year 1970, Bread for the World Award (1978, 80, 82), Nat. Hospice Orgn. Award 1984, Am. Farm Bur. Fedn. Golden Plow Award 1988; mem: Carmel Valley Little League; Parish Council of Our Lady of Mt. Carmel Ch.; mil: 1st lt. US Army 1963-65, Army Commdn.; author: Bring Us Together, 1971; Democrat (Monterey Co. Dem. Central Com. 1972-75); Cath. Ofc: 339 Cannon House Office Bldg Washington DC 20515

PAPAGEORGE, ANDREW JACKSON, professor of management; b. Mar. 6, 1922, Ironton, Ohio; s. Harry X. Papageorge and Cora (Gauze) Stiles; m. Nan A. Taylor, 1947 (div. 1984); m. Elizabeth Anne Jackson, Sept. 15, 1984; edn: BS, U.S. Naval Acad. 1943; MBA, Stanford Univ. 1954; PhD, UCLA 1967. Career: officer, U.S. Navy 1943-64; asst. dean, Dean U.S. Int. Univ., San Diego 1966-77; prof., dept. chair Whittier Coll. 1977-79; acad. v.p. Hawaii Pacific Coll. 1979-81; prof., dept. chair Christopher Newport Coll., Va. 1982-84; prof. CSU Turlock 1984-; awarded: Air Medal, U.S. Navy 1944; mem. Acad. of Mgmt., Masonic Lodges (San Diego); mil: cmdr. U.S. Navy 1943-64; Republican; Protestant; rec: flying, fishing. Ofc: Calif State Univ Stanislaus 801 W Monte Vista Ave Turlock 95380

PAPPAS, NICHOLAS, psychiatrist, physician; b. June 30, 1937, Brooklyn, N.Y.; s. Michael George and Chrisanthy Ann (Nicholakakis) P.; m. Margaret Carol Murphy, Nov. 24, 1963; children: Katina b. 1964, Christy b. 1966; edn: BA, Indiana Univ. 1959, MD 1962; lic. psychiatrist, 1970. Career: rotating internship Detroit Receiving Hosp. 1962-63; psychiatric resident Indiana Univ. Med. Ctr. 1963-65; psychiatrist, staff Central State Hosp, Indpls. 1965-66; psychiatric resident Napa St. Hosp., Imola 1968-70, staff psychiatrist 1970-73; priv. psychiatric practice, Novato 1971-; med. dir. Canyon Manor Drug Rehab. Hosp., Novato 1972-73; preceptor, supvr.: Napa St. Hosp. (psych. resident) 1970-73, Sonoma Univ. (nursing stu.) 1974-; Calif. Sch. of Profl. Psychol. 1975-; mil: capt. U.S. Army, chief Mental Hygiene Consultation Service, Ft. McClellan, Ala. 1966-68; Republican; Greek Orthodox; rec: golf, racquetball, woodworking, carpentry, computers. Ofc: Dr. Nicholas Pappas 1025 5th St Novato 94945

PARADY, JOHN EDWARD, information systems executive; b. Sept. 26, 1939, Inglewood; s. Raymond Oliver and Ella Louise (Timm) P.; m. Barbara Louise Pettit, Aug. 13, 1966; children: John b. 1968, Renee b. 1970, Stacy b. 1975; edn: BS, CSU 1966; MS, USC 1969. Career: computer operator Systems Devel. Corp., Santa Monica 1962-64; systems ofcr. Security Pacific Bank, Los Angeles 1964-66; industry analyst IBM Corp. 1966-69; mgmt. cons. Norris & Gottfried Inc. 1969-71; Arthur Young, Santa Ana 1971; Mordy & Co., Los Angeles 1972-75; dir. info. systems Weyerhaeuser Corp., Tacoma, Wash. 1975-82; exec. dir. McKenna Conner & Cuneo, Los Angeles 1983; sr.v.p. techn. Bank of Am., S.F. 1984-85; mgmt. cons., Los Angeles 1986; exec. v.p. tech., Pacific Stock Exchange 1987-; mil: 2d. lt. AUS 1959-63; Republican; Mormon; rec: fishing, hiking, horseriding. Res: 1004 Vista del Valle La Canada 91011 Ofc: The Pacific Stock Exchange 233 S Beavory Ave Los Angeles 90012

PARBURY, CHARLES ALAN, sales executive; b. Aug. 13, 1947, Palo Alto; s. Charles B. and Ethel (Noakes) P.; m. Sandra Wanderer; children: Cynthia Jane, Holly Rogers; edn: BSC, Univ. Santa Clara 1970; Coll. San Mateo 1972; BA, Univ. of Pacific, 1991. Career: sales & ops. mgr. GranTree Corp, Portland, Ore. 1970-74; gen. mgr. BWA Dairy Products Ltd. 1975-78; Alameda Joe's Inc. 1978-81; funding dir. Womens Profl. Golf Tour 1982-86; sr. mgmt. cons. Gustafson Williams Cons., Walnut Creek 1981-82; v.p. TWA Mgmt. Corp., Walnut Creek 1982-89; v.p. Cypress Capital Corp. 1983-89; Fortune Planning Systems Inc. 1984-88; sales mgr. Metromedia Paging /Southwestern Bell Corp., 1989-; award for Outstanding Sales, Southwestern Bell Corp. 1991; mem. Internat. Assn. of Financial Planning (bd. dirs. East Bay chpt. 1987-), Kiwanis (pres.), San Jose Elks, Walnut Creek C.of C.; civic: Contra Costa Devel. Assn., Special Olympics (vol.), Big Brothers Assn., Little League of Am.; author: Sales Management Techniques; Republican; R.Cath.; rec: golf, baseball, volleyball. Ofc: 353 Vintage Prk Ste B Foster City 94404

PARDO, SHERRI LORRAINE, holistic medical doctor; b. Feb. 23, 1953, NY, NY; d. Albert Solomon and Susan (Alhanti) P.; edn: Masters T.C.M., Emperor's Coll., Santa Monica, 1984-89; Homeopathic Medical Doctor (HMD), British Inst. of Homeopathy, Santa Monica, 1990-92; NMD, Amer. Naturopathic Med. Assn., Santa Monica, 1991-93; NCCA Lic. #6245; Lic. Acupuncturist, Calif. Lic. #3905. Career: goodwill publicist, AHFOL, L.A., 1987-93; med. adv., EBNO Enterprises, L.A., 1989-93; lectr. alternative medicine, Bnai Brith, Beverly Hills, 1990-; traditions of Tao, Union of Tao & Man, Santa Monica, 1991-92; lectr. Aida Grey Salon, Beverly Hills, 1992; ISAIS 5 step prog. to better health; mem. Bnai Brith, Beverly Hills; public relations for Goodwill (Hope Boxes), 1987-93; fundraiser for LIFE (feeding the homeless); rec: reading, astrology, music appreciation. Res: 3067 B Via Serena N. Laguna Hills 92653

PARER, JULIAN THOMAS, physician, maternal-fetal medicine educator, administrator; b. Sept. 2, 1934, Melbourne, Australia; m. Robin M.W. Fletcher, Apr. 23, 1962; children: William John; edn: B.Agr.Sc., Univ. Melbourne, 1959; M.Rur.Sc., bioclimatology, Univ. of New England, Aus. 1962; PhD, Oregon State Univ., Corvallis 1965; MD, Univ. Washington, Seattle 1971; dipl. Am. Bd. Ob-Gyn, 1976, splty. dipl. maternal-fetal medicine, 1977. Career: rsch. asst. rural sci. Univ. New England, Aus. 1958-61; grad. fellow dept. animal sci. Oregon State Univ. 1961-63; grad. asst., summer fellow, res. fellow Heart Res. Lab. Univ. Oregon Med. Sch., 1961-66; vis. scientist Oregon Reg. Primate Res. Ctr. 1964-66; instr. dept. ob.-gyn. Univ. Wash., 1966-68, sr. fellow 1969-71, also mem. med. res. unit Child Devel. and Med. Retardation Ctr., mem. Anesthesia Res. Ctr.; res. affiliate Reg. Primate Ctr., Seattle 1969-71; resident ob-gyn. L.A. Co.-USC Sch. of Med., 1971-74; asst. prof., assoc. prof., prof. dept. obstets., gyn. and reproductive scis. UC San Francisco, 1974-, dept. assoc. v.chmn. 1987-, assoc. staff Cardiovascular Res. Inst. 1976-, dir. obstets. 1980-87, dir. maternal-fetal med. fellowship tng. pgm. 1983-, codir. North Coast Perinatal Access System, UCSF, 1984-89; vis. scientist Nuffield Inst. for Med. Res., Univ. Oxford, Eng. 1981-82, Univ. de Chile, Santiago, Chile 1985, 86, 87, 88, 89, 91, Univ. of Auckland, N.Z. 1988, 89, 90; mem: Am. Coll. OB-Gyn (Fellow), Am. Physiol. Soc., Aus. Perinatal Soc., La Sociedad Chilena de Obstetricia y Ginecologia (hon.), Pac. Coast Obstet. Gynecol. Soc. (pgm. com. 1992), Perinatal Rsch. Soc., S.F. Gynecol. Soc. (pgm. chmn. 1989-90), Soc. for Gynecol. Investigation, Soc. Perinatal Obstets. (bd. 1988-91, pgm. chmn. 1991), Soc. for the Study of Fetal Physiology (org. com. 1990); spl. interests: Fetal responses to asphyxia; the circulation and oxygen transport in pregnancy; clin. fetal monitoring; Rh disease; High risk pregnancy; author: Handbook of Fetal Heart Rate Monitoring 1983; editor: Res. in Perinatal Medicine (w. P.W. Nathanielsz), Antepartum and Intrapartum Mgmt. 1989, contbr. numerous med. jour. articles and abstracts. Ofc: Univ. Calif. 505 Parnassus Ave San Francisco 94143-0550

PARK, KATHY LEE, data processing company president; b. June 18, 1949, Seoul, Korea; d. Chan Keun and Whaksil (Kim) Lee; m. Jon H. Park, Sept. 7, 1974; children: Christina b. 1979, Eugene b. 1981; edn: BS, Univ. Mich. 1972; MS, Ore. St. Univ. 1974. Career: sys. programmer Computer Sci. Corp., Los Angeles 1975-77; comml. program Times Mirror 1977-78; tech. rep. Gen. Electric 1978-80; ops. mgr. United Compudata 1980-85; pres. CDS Info. Service

1985-; prof. Computer Coll. Los Angeles 1985-; mem: Korean Am. Computer Profl. Assn. (dir.); rec: music, travel. Res: 611 S Kingsley Dr 4th Flr Los Angeles 90005 Ofc: CSD Information Services Inc. 7975 Oceanus Dr Los Angeles 90046

PARKER, QUENTIN DART, architect; b. Dec. 1, 1953, Miami, Fla.; s. Alfred Browning and Martha (Gifford) P.; m. Anne Trueblood, Nov. 15, 1985; edn: Baccalaureate/ Abitur, Padagogium Otto Kuhne Schule West Germany 1972; B.Environmental Design, No. Carolina State Univ. Sch. of Design 1977; Master in Arch., Harvard Univ. 1979; reg. architect Fla. 1981, Calif. 1984; mem. Am. Inst. of Architects, Nat. Council of Arch. Reg. Boards. Career: architect, Alfred Browning Parker Arch. 1979-83; project mgr. Arch. Dept. Cannell & Chaffin Commercial Interiors 1983-84; architect prin. and ptnr. Art Function Inc. (arch. corp.); consultant Terry George Hoffman & Assoc.; dir. Alfred B. Parker 79-83; awards: "Dreamhouse 1990" Architect L.A. West Magazine, judge Soc. of Illumination Engrs. 1983, EPROM 1977; mem. AIA nat., state & L.A. chapt.; works: residences, office bldgs., renovations, remodels, churches, banks, hospitals & profl. offices, residential development. Project locations Ca., Fl., N.Y., S.C., Ut., Vt.; Furniture, Product Graphic Design; Republican; Episcopalian. Address: Quentin Dart Parker Architect, 15412 Albright St Pacific Palisades 90272

PARKER, THEODORE CLIFFORD, manufacturing co. president; b. Sept. 25, 1929, Dallas, Ore.; s. Theodore C. and Virginia Bernice (Rumsey) P.; m. Jannet Barnes, Nov. 28, 1970; 2 daus: Sally, Peggy; edn: BSEE, magna cum laude, USC 1960. Career: v.p. engring. Telemetrics Inc. 1963-65; chief engr. Information Systems, Northrop-Nortronics 1966-70; pres. Avtel Corp. 1971-74; pres. Aragon Inc. 1975-77; v.p. engring. Teledyne McCormick Selph 1978-82; mgr. electronic systems FMC Corp., Ordnance Div. 1983-85; pres. Power One Switching Products (engring. & mfg.) 1985-86; pres. Condor Inc., D.C. Power Supplies, 1987; pres. Intelligence Power Inc., Camarillo 1988-; chmn. Autotestcon 87; honors: Tau Beta Pi, Eta Kappa Nu; mem: IEEE, Am. Prodn. & Inventory Control Soc., Electronics Assn. of Calif. (founding dir.), Am. Def. Preparedness Assn. Res: 1290 Saturn Ave Camarillo 93010 Ofc: Intelligence Power, Inc. 829 Flynn Rd Camarillo 93010

PARKS, RICHARD DEE, theater director; b. Aug. 29, 1938, Omaha; s. Charles and Josephine Marie-Rose P.; edn: BA, San Jose St. Univ., 1961; MA, Univ. Wash., 1963; postgrad. Stanford Univ. Career: faculty San Jose St. Univ., 1964-65, 1966-71, dir. theater SJSU, 1972-79, coordinator performance area, 1979-92, coord. auditions, 1975-92, chmn. performance area, coordinator M.F.A. performance degree program, 1983-92; instr. oral interpretation Stanford Univ., 1965-66, B.F.A. program Univ. Wash., 1971-72; exchange prof. Ventura Coll., spring 1982; actor, dir., prod.; exec. dir. Actors Symposium of Hollywood; sr. prod. Star Weekend projects NBC, 1978-91; cons. profl. and community theater orgns.; interim coordinator theater arts grad. program, 1977-78; dialects coach, voice and diction tutor; research cons. Ednl. Films of Hollywood; cons. Fourth Street Playhouse, Monterey Peninsula; cons. dir. Gen. Electric Sales Conf., Pajaro Dunes, 1983; awards: for new play directing Am. Coll. Theater Festival Reg. I 1975; mem: Calif. Ednl. Theater Assn. (exec. sec. treas. 1978-80), Am. Theater Assn., AAUP, Calif. Assn. Am. Conservatory Theater, Am. Coll. Theater Fest., Am. Film Inst., Dramatists Guild, Authors League Am.; clubs: Brit. Am., San Jose Players; author: plays: Charley Parkhurst Rides Again! 1978, Wild West Women 1980, Ken Kesey's Further Inquiry 1980, stage adaptation of Tamden Prodns. Facts of Life 1982; books: How to Overcome Stage Fright 1978, American Drama Anthology 1979, The Role of Myth in Understanding Amber in the Ancient World 1983, textbooks: Oral Expression 1985 (2d rev. edit. 1986, 3d rev. edit. 1988-89, 4th rev. ed. 1994), Voice and Diction 1990, tchg. supplement: Calendar of Am. Theater Hist. 1982, Principles of Rhetoric 1993. Ofc: 37428 Centralmont Place Fremont 94536

PARLETTE, CAROL HOLLAND, association executive; b. Feb. 21, 1944, Springfield, Mo.; d. Marvin Benjamin and Georgia Genevieve (Hagar) Holland; m. G. Nicholas Parlette, May 23, 1975; edn: BS in edn., Southwest Mo. State Univ., Springfield, Mo. 1966; MPH in health adminstrn./ plng., UC Berkeley, 1976; CAE/cert. assn. exec., ASAE, 1978. Career: coord. Am. Pub. Health Assn., West San Francisco 1968-72; exec. dir. Calif. Soc. Internal Medicine, San Francisco 1972-85; owner/pres. Holland-Parlette Associates, S.F. 1985-, exec. dir. Kite Trade Assn. Internat., 1988-, Western Occupational Med. Assn., 1990-; adminstr. Western Office, Am. Soc. of Assn. Execs. 1985-, newsletter columnist "Making the Rounds" We. Assn. News, 1984-; awards: No. Calif. Soc. Assn. Execs. exec. of year 1989; mem. Am. Soc. Assn. Execs. 1972-, Am. Assn. Med. Soc. Execs. 1990-, Bay Area Exec. Women's Forum (founder, charter sec.), Commonwealth Club 1985-. Ofc: Holland-Parlette Assocs 50 First St Ste 310 San Francisco 94105-2411

PARROTT, JAMES EDWARD, chiropractor, acupuncturist, hypnotherapist; b. Aug. 7, 1924, El Paso, Tex.; s. John N. and Marie (Boudreaux) P.; m. Marilyn Fowler, Mar. 5, 1985; children: Joseph, Brynda Monique, Heidi Jacqueline; edn: DC, L.A. Coll. of Chiro. 1957; CBS Cert., basic sci., Ariz. State Univ., 1958; MA, Baptist Comm. Coll.; Oriental preceptorship in acupuncture, herbal med., Hong Kong Inst., 1960; grad. Hynotism Tng. Inst., 1979; bd. cert. Acad. of Am.

Pain Mgmt., 1990; Calif. lic. radiographer 1979, cert. instr. Hunter Safety. Career: lectr. and tchr. basic scis., Oriental Med.; chiropractor, acupuncturist, hypnotherapist, Acutherapy pioneer in U.S. 1960-; bd. chmn. Karmel Kookies Inc.; founder/ pres. San Pedro Prebuilt Homes; honors: Delta Sigma Hon. Scholastic Soc. of the Healing Arts (elected 1957); mem: NY Acad. of Sci., AAAS, Elks, Nat. Rifle Assn. (life), Calif. Rifle & Pistol Club (life), Sigma Chi Omega; mil: pharmacist 2c USN, USMC, WWII, Korean War, decorated Presdl. Unit Citations Korea & USA, Philippine medal, Am. Campaign medal w/ 1 Star, Asia-Pac. w/ 4 Stars, Nat. Def., Victory, UN, Korean Svc. w/ 2 Stars; Democrat (State Central Com.); Cath. (Brother, student priesthood W. Orthodox Cath.); rec: music, art, sculpture. Address: 812 W 5th St Oxnard 93030

PARSONS, STUART OVERTON, JR., industrial psychologist, human factors consultant, educator; b. Aug. 11, 1926, Denver; s. Stuart O. Sr. and Gladys (East) P.; m. Harriet Jaggard, July 11, 1955; children: Carol, Cynthia, Pamela; edn: BA psych., Colorado Univ., 1948; MA psych., USC, 1950, PhD indsl. psychology, 1958; lic. psychologist, reg. profl. engr., Calif. Career: aviation electronics technician USN 1944-46, WWII, served to col. (ret. 1983) Navy and Air Force reserve, assignments in human factors in AF Systems Command, was mobilization asst. to dir. maint. Sacto. Air Logistics Ctr., decorated USAF Total Force Award and Meritorious Service Medal 1983; psychometrician Colo. Merit System, Denver 1947-48; personnel technician City of Denver 1950-51; res. assoc. Psychological Svs. Inc., Los Angeles 1951-53; industrial relations splst. Lockheed Corp. Offices, Burbank 1954-57, engring. mgr. Lockheed Missile & Space Co., Sunnyvale 1958-87; pres. Parsons and Assocs., Saratoga 1987-, cons./splst. human factors/ergonomics, mgmt., organizational and forensic psychology, energy systems, maint. and safety tng.; condr. mgmt. seminars for execs. of Commonwealth of Independent States (CIS) 1990-91; lectr. Coll. of Notre Dame 1993-; lectr. San Jose State Univ. 1964-92, adj. assoc. prof. USC 1969-91, adj. prof. Univ. Denver 1987-, res. faculty Waseda Univ., Tokyo 1988089; past instr. mgmt. courses Lockheed and McClellan AFB; mem. Human Factors Soc. (fellow), AIAA (assoc. fellow), Bay Area Human Factors Soc. (charter, dir.), Internat. Ergonomics Soc. (1991 U.S. del., chmn. Power Sys. Tech. Group 1992-), Soc. Logistics Engrs., Reserve Ofcrs. Assn.; author 40+ books and jour. articles (1960-92); Episcopalian; rec: skiing, golf, tennis, travel. Address: 19740 Via Escuela Dr Saratoga 95070 Ph./Fax: 408/865-0987

PASAROW, REINEE ELIZABETH, food brokerage company executive; b. Sept. 30, 1950, Glendale; d. Homer Armand Beaulieu and Lou Fay (Card) Beaulieu Fender; m. 2d Michael Robert Pasarow, Nov. 30, 1975; 1 son, Torin Michael Wade b. 1970; edn: BA, UCLA, 1982. Career: free-lance writer, 1982-85; v.p./owner Velling Pasarow Corbett, 1986-, chief op. ofcr. 1990-; v.p./owner Pasarow Foods Inc., Monterey Park 1986-; pub. poetry in World Order Mag. (1986), contbr. TV pgm. ABC-TV 20/20 (1985), contbr. to books: The Human Animal, Heading Towards Omega (1986, 87); Baha'i (dir. Valley Inter Faith Council 1984-86, exec. rep. Interreligious Council So. Calif. 1984-90, v.p. 1990). Ofc: Pasarow Foods 9 Cupania Circle Monterey Park 91754

PASTEN, LAURA JEAN, veterinarian; b. May 25, 1952, Tacoma, Wash.; edn: Stanford Univ. 1970; BA physiol., UC Davis 1970, DVM, 1974; postgrad., Cornell Univ. 1975; Career: vet. Nevada Co. Vet. Hosp. Grass Valley 1975-80; pvt. practice vet., owner Mother Lode Vet. Hosp. Grass Valley (certified wildlife rehab. ctr.) 1980-; veterinarian for Morris, the 9-lives cat (of t.v. comml. fame) 1985-; lectr. in field, spokesperson for Nat. Cat Health Month; affil. staff Sierra Nevada Meml. Hosp.; bd. dirs. Sierra Svcs. for the Blind; syndicated TV show on vet. medicine, guest on Today Show re wildlife; honors: Regent's Scholar, Woman of Yr. Am. Biog. Inst. 1991, Woman of Decade Who's Who Soc.; mem: Am. Vet. Med. Assn. (ethics com.), Sacto. Valley Vet. Med. Assn. (exec. com., CVMA del.), Mother Lode Vet. Assn., Am. Animal Hosp. Assn., Nat. Ophthalmic Soc., Nat. Pygmy Goat Assn., Nat. Llama Assn., Internat. Assn. of Arabians, Denver Area Med. Soc., Internat. Vet. Assn., Mensa, Nat. Soc. Underwater Instrs., Am. Endurance Riding Soc.; civic: Nevada Co. CofC (bd. dirs.), Grass Valley Bus. Women, affiliate staff mem. Sierra Nevada Meml. Hosp., bd. dirs. Sierra Services for the Blind, adv. bd. Veterinary Forum; publ: Canine Dermatology (w. Dr. Muller 1970), contbr. articles to profl. jours.; Republican; Lutheran. Address: 11509 La Barr Meadows Rd Grass Valley 95949

PATE, CHRISTINE VETTER, superior court judge; b. Sept. 27, 1943, San Diego; d. William Paul and Ethel Marguerite (Waters) Vetter; m. William Craig Pate, Oct. 30, 1966; children: William C., Bryan L., David G., Douglas F.; edn: BA, Univ. Calif., 1965; JD, Univ. San Diego, 1969; admitted bar: Calif., U.S. Dist. Ct. so. dist. Calif. 1970. Career: atty., shareholder law firm Jennings, Engstrand & Henrikson, San Diego, 1970-88; judge Superior Ct., San Diego 1988-; bd. dirs. San Diego Law Center; mem: Calif. Bar Assn. (dist. rep. 1983-86), Calif. Judges Assn., San Diego Co. Bar Assn. (past dir., v.p., sec.), Lawyers Club of San Diego (past pres.), San Diego Vol. Lawyers (bd. 1984-87), Rotary Internat.; Republican; R.Cath. Ofc: Superior Court 220 W Broadway San Diego 92101

PATERSON, THOMAS GLYNN, management consultant, inventor, author and speaker; b. Mar. 12, 1925, Kearny, N.J.; s. Robert Burns and Marion (Glynn) P.; m. Virginia Katherine White, Sept. 30, 1944; children: Thomas b.

1945 (dec.), James b. 1948, Jay b. 1951, Deborah b. 1954 (dec.), Kathleen b. 1959, Carol b. 1961, William b. 1963; edn: BS, Boston Univ., 1947; MBA, Pepperdine Univ., 1978. Career: staff mem. Air Transport Plng. Team, McDonnell Douglas Corp., Santa Monica 1952-55; dir. market plng. Northrop Corp. Electronics Div., Hawthorne 1955-60; dir. bus. plng. IBM Corp. Fed. Systems Div., Wash. DC 1960-62; dir. corporate plng. pgms. RCA Corp., Camden, N.J. 1963-70; pres. Paterson and Company, Acton, Ca. 1970-, recognized internat. for devel. of the "Tom Paterson Process" a form of participation mgmt. enabling instns. to achieve higher levels of performance through enterprise system mgmt. and cross-functional teamwork; founded Thomas G. Paterson Ctr. for cross-functional tng. 1993; dir: Process Equipment Co., Anaheim 1987-90; mem: bd. govs. City of Hope Nat. Med. Ctr., Duarte 1975-, Research Advy. Council, The Planning Forum; honors: Nat. Mktg. Assn. marketing man of yr., NYC 1968, hon. overseas cons. to The Peoples Rep. of China and the Chinese Acad. of Scis., Beijing 1987; listed and 10th Ed. dedication in Who's Who of Intellectuals, Cambridge, Eng. 1992, 5000 Personalities of World for outstanding contbn. to mgmt. scis. (3d. ed.), Human Resources Hall of Fame Ingersoll-Rand Co. 1993; Order of Merit, Internat. Biographical Ctr., Cambridge, England 1993; invention: Automatic Cash Dispensing System (pat. 1969); publs: 200+ articles and essays 1950-; mil: pfc USMC 1943-44; Republican (Pres.'s Club of Rep. Nat. Com., Senatorial Commn. award Rep. Senatl. Inner Circle); Prot.; rec: organist, swimming, garden. Address: Paterson and Company, PO Box 6676 Big Bear Lake 92315

PATRICK, CAROL SUE, real estate executive; b. June 6, 1944, Bakersfield; d. Lester Lewis and Freda Evelyn (Headlee) Williams; m. Charles Patrick, Jan. 13, 1961; children: Kelley b. 1962, LeAnne b. 1966; edn: Bakersfield Coll. 1977; USC 1980; limited svc. cred. Calif. Bd. Edn. (1978). Career: realtor 1971-; gen. bldg. contractor 1979-1983; owner Mid-Valley Real Estate 1976-; secty CMC Corp. 1986-; mem: Bakersfield Bd. of Realtors Calif. Nat. Assn.; civic: First Baptist Ch.; Bakersfield Coll. Alumni Assn.; Republican; Baptist; rec: crafts, sewing, cooking. Res: 12632 Kern Canyon Rd Bakersfield 93306 Ofc: Mid-Valley Real Estate 4664 American Ave Bakersfield 93309

PATRICK, CHARLES LEON, real estate broker/ building contractor; b. Feb. 3, 1938; s. Elby Leon and Dorothy Aline (Hicks) P.; m. Carol Sue, Jan. 13, 1961; children: Kelley, b. 1962; LeAnne, b.1966; edn: Bakersfield Coll. 1968-69; Lumbleau Real Estate Sch. 172, 73, 75; UC Santa Barbara 1977; USC 1982; Limited Svc. Cred., Calif. State Dept. of Edn. 1977; Cert. Real Estate Appraiser 1986. Career: draftsman, surveyor, instrument-man, engr. Southern Pacific Transp. Co., Bakersfield 1961-75; gen. building contr., real estate broker, Bakersfield 1976-; owner Mid-Valley Real Estate, and C.L. Patrick Construction; mem: Bakersfield Board of Realtors, Calif., Nat. Assns. of Realtors, Independent Contractors Assn. 1971-; clubs: Bakersfield Trade, Meudell Lodge Freemasons, Bakersfield Christian Life Schools Booster, Bakersfield College Alumni Assn., UCSB Alumni Assn., Bakersfield Racquet; Republican; Baptist; rec: antique cars. Res: Star Route 4 Box 705, Bakersfield 93306 Ofc: Mid-Valley Real Estate/C.L. Patrick Construction, 4664 American Ave Bakersfield 93309

PATRICK, KELLEY DENISE, lawyer; b. Feb. 13, 1962, Wasco, Calif.; d. Charles Leon and Carol Sue (Williams) Patrick; m. Larry Dean Smith, June 15, 1983 (div. Dec. 1988); children: Jordan b. 1988; edn: AA, Bakersfield Coll., 1985; CSU Bakersfield, 1986; JD, Calif. Pacific Sch. of Law, 1991; admitted bar: Calif. 1991. Career: Kern County Counsel's Office, 1989-; mem. Calif. Bar Assn., Kern Co.Bar Assn., Kern Co. Women Lawyers Assn., Small Claims Advisors Assn.; Republican (Kern Co. YR); Calvary Bible Ch.; rec: snow and jet skiing, scuba, crafts. Res: 6008 Auburn St #D Bakersfield 93306 Ofc: 1115 Truxtun Ave 4th Fl Bakersfield 93301

PATRICK, LEANNE KAY, teacher; b. Aug. 16, 1966, Bakersfield, Calif.; d. Charles Leon and Carol Sue (Williams) Patrick; edn: AA, Bakersfield Coll., 1986; BA, CSU Bakersfield, 1990; Cert. Attorney Asst. Tng. Pgm. (hons.), UC Los Angeles, 1988-89; Calif. tchg. credential (sec., social studies), Calif. Lutheran Univ., 1992. Mem. Nat. Assn. of Legal Assts., CSU Bakersfield Alumni; Republican; Prot.; rec: golf, crafts, roller blading, youth work. Res: 12632 Hwy 178 Bakersfield 93306

PATSKY, JOAN MARIE, fine arts businesswoman; b. Oct. 20, 1938, Glen Ridge, N.J.; d. John Philip and Florence Marie (Gromas) Sulzer; m. Robert W. Patsky (dist. sales mgr. Allstate Ins. Co.); children: Jamie b. 1957, Robert b. 1959, Tracy Lenore b. 1970; edn: AA (honors), Crafton Jr. Coll., 1986; paralegal/ communications courses, CSU San Bernardino. Career: staff Manpower Service Agency, San Bernardino 1981-85; legal secty. 1985-87; mktg. secty 1987; exec. secty. and editor San Bernardino Valley Board of Realtors, 1988; entrepreneur mktg. Very Fine Arts, 1992; awards: Omicron Delta Epsilon, Hon. cert. East Valley Mental Health Tng. Pgm., title Mrs. Cherry Valley, Mrs. Calif. Pageant 1987, Secty. of Year Manpower Service Agy. 1988, appreciation Edward-Dean Mus. of Decorative Arts; mem: Cherry Valley C.of C., Friends of EDMDA, Pass Artists, Humane Soc. San Bernardino, East Valley Mental Health, 459th Bomb Group Assn. WWII Veterans; designer: New Conceptions, (c.1984); theme: Communications; art works include charcoal lithographs, oils, prose and tchg. materials (photo-realism to op art), Wildlife Conservation art series, periodic exhibs. var. public instns.; publs. in newspaper op-ed. sects. The Record Gazette, Press Enterprise, Sun News; Republican; Trinity Episcopal Ch.; rec: art, singing, writing. Mail: PO Box 528 Beaumont 92223

PATTEN, BEBE HARRISON, clergywoman, educator; b. Sept. 3, 1913, Waverly, Tenn.; d. Newton Felix and Mattie Priscilla (Whitson) Harrison; m. Carl Thomas Patten, Oct. 23, 1935; children: (twins) Priscilla Carla and Bebe Rebecca, Carl Thomas; edn: DD, McKinley- Roosevelt Coll. 1941; D.Litt., Temple Hall Coll. & Sem. 1943. Career: ordained to ministry, Ministerial Assn. of Evangelism 1935; evangelist in various cities of US 1933-50; founder/pres. Christian Evangelical Churches of Am. Inc. 1944-; founder/pres. Patten Acad. Christian Edn., Oakland 1944-; Patten Bible Coll., Oakland 1944-83; pres.-emeritus/chancellor, Patten Coll. 1983-; founder/pastor Christian Cathedral of Oakland 1950-; condr. pgm., The Shepherd Hour, 1934-, weekly telecast 1976-, nat. telecast 1979-, KUSW world-wide radio ministry heard in 70 countries, 1989-90; WHRI (2 million watts), WWCR (3.5 million watts) world coverage short wave, 1990-; mem. Global bd. trustees 1991, exec. bd. and Hon. Fellow, Bar-Ilan Univ., Israel; Dr. Bebe Patten Chair in Social Action established, Bar-Ilan Univ. 1982; ldr. 20 pilgrimages to Israel in interest of Christian-Judaic relationship since 1962; private interview w/Israeli Prime Ministers: David Ben-Gurion 1972, Menachim Begin 1977, Yitzhak Shamir 1991; awards: medallion, Ministry of Religious Affairs, Israel 1969; medal, Govt. Press Ofc., Jerusalem 1971; Christian honoree of Year, Jewish Nat. Fund of No. Calif. 1975; Hidden Heroine award, S.F. Bay Council, Girl Scouts USA 1976; Ben-Gurion medallion, Ben-Gurion Research Inst. 1977; mem: Am. Assn. for Higher Edn.; Religious Edn. Assn.; Am. Acad. Religion & Soc. Bibl. Lit.; Zionist Orgn. of Am.; Am. Jewish Hist. Soc.; Am. Israel Pub. Affairs Comm. 1983; works: author, Give Me Back My Soul, 1973; editor, Trumpet Call, 1953-; composer 20 gospel & religious. songs 1948-; listed in num. biographical publs.; rec: swimming, tennis. Ofc: 2433 Coolidge Ave Oakland 94601

PATTEN, BEBE REBECCA, academic dean, Patten College; b. Jan. 30, 1950, Berkeley, Calif.; d. Carl Thomas and Bebe (Harrison) Patten; edn: BS (summa cum laude), Bible, Patten Bible Coll., Oakland, Calif., 1969; BA, Philosophy, Coll. of the Holy Names, Oakland, Calif., 1971; MA (with honors), New Testament, Wheaton Coll., Chgo., Ill., 1972; PhD (with honors), New Testament, Drew Univ., Madison, N.J., 1976; MA, Philosophy, Dominican Coll., Berkeley, Calif., 1990; 6 units, Higher Edn. Adminstrn., UC Berkeley 1991-92. Career: co-pastor, Christian Cathedral of the Christian Evangelical Churches of Am., Inc., Oakland 1964-; tchg. fellow prof., Drew Univ. 1974-75; assoc. prof., Patten Bible Coll., Oakland 1975-82; prof. of New Testament, Patten Bible Coll., 1982-; academic dean, Patten Coll. 1977-; mem., bd. of dir., Christian Evangelical Churches of Am., Inc. 1964-; fellowship, Kierkegaard Lib., St. Olaf's Coll. 1990, 91; awards: Patten Bible Coll.: Honor Student 1966, Gold "P" 1969, Most Beloved Student award 1968, Heart award 1971; listed in: Outstanding Young Women of Am. 1976, 77, 80-81, 82, Notable Americans 1976-77, 78-79, The World Who's Who of Women 1977, 79, 81-82, Personalities of the West and Midwest 1977-78, 80, Book of Honor (A.B.I.) 1979, Dictionary of Internat. Biography 1979-80, Men and Women of Distinction 1979-80, Personalities of Am. 1979, Who's Who in Calif. 1979-80, 81-82, Comm. Leaders and Noteworthy Americans 1980, Who's Who of American Women 1981-82, 83-84, 85-86, 93-94, Who's Who in the West 1985, 92, 93-94, Who's Who in Religion 1985, 92-93, Who's Who in the Humanities 1992, Who's Who in Am. Edn. 1991, 92-93, Who's Who of Emerging Leaders in Am. 1991; mem: Am. Acad. of Religion 1975-, Soc. of Biblical Lit. 1975-, Am. Assn. of Univ. Professors 1975-, Christian Assn. for Student Affairs 1980, Phi Delta Kappa 1980, Inst. for Biblical Res. 1981, Assn. for Christians in Student Devel. 1981; civic: founder, 45-mem. youth orchestra, Christian Cathedral 1969-71; founder/conductor, 45-mem. intermediate orch., Patten Christian Schools 1975-82; violinist, harpist, Christian Cathedral; symphony mem.: Holy Names Coll. 1966-71, Berkeley Symphony Youth Orch. 1968, Wheaton Coll. Symphony 1971-75, Young Artists Symphony (N.J.) 1972-75, Somerset Hill Symphony (N.J.) 1973-74, Peninsula Symphony (Calif.) 1977-81, Madison Chamber Trio (N.J.) 1973-75, Redwood Symphony (Calif.) 1990-; author: Before the Times, 1980; The World of the Early Church, 1990; The Role of Reason in Faith in Kierkegaard and St. Thomas (in process); 7 publ. articles in Internat. Standard Biblical Encyclopedia, Rev. Edit., 1983-; 2 book reviews publ in the Nacada Jour. 1990, 93. Res: 190 Alderwood Lane Walnut Creek 94598. Ofc. 2433 Coolidge Ave Oakland 94601

PATTERSON, DAVID ANDREW, computer science educator; b. Nov. 16, 1947, Evergreen Park, Ill.; s. David Dwight and Lucie Jeanette (Ekstrom) P.; m. Linda Ann Crandall, Sept. 4, 1967; children: David Adam b. 1969, Michael Andrew b. 1971; edn: BS math., UCLA, 1969, MS computer sci., 1970, PhD computer sci., 1976. Career: mem. tech. staff Hughes Aircraft Co., Los Angeles 1972-76; Thinking Machines Corp., Cambridge, Mass. 1979; prof. UC Berkeley 1977-, chair div. computer sci. 1990-93; UC Berkeley campus- wide endowed Pardee Chair 1992-97; cons. Sun Microsystems Inc., Mtn. View 1984-; Thinking Machines Corp., Cambridge 1988-; awards: Karl V. Karlstrom out-

standing educator, Assn. of Computing Machinery, W.D.C. 1991, Corporate fellow Thinking Machines Corp., Cambridge 1989, mem. sci. advy. bd. Data General Corp., Westborough, MA 1982, Disting. tchg. Berkeley Div. of UC Academic Berkeley 1982; mem. com. to study scope and role of computer sci. (SCOPE) NAS, W.D.C. 1990-92; program com. chair Hot Chips Symp. IV, Santa Clara 1992; mem: IEEE (Fellow 1989), Computing Res. Assn., W.D.C. (bd. dirs. 1991-94), elected Nat. Assn. Engring. 1993; coauthor: Computer Architecture: A Quantitative Approach (1990), Computer Organization & Design: The Hardware/ Software Interface (1993); rec: biking, football, soccer. Ofc: Computer Science Div. UC Berkeley 571 Evans Hall TE01 94720

PATTERSON, DAVID STEPHAN, artist, art professor; b. May 24, 1942, Hartford, Conn.; s. James Albert Patterson and Francis Ann (Wheeler) Gibbs; m. Patricia Faye Hetzel, Aug. 18, 1962 (div. 1985); m. Monica Irene Possner, Nov. 21, 1987; children: David b. 1967, Camille Marie b. 1968; edn: BA, CSU Long Beach 1965; MA, Claremont Grad. Sch. 1974; MFA, 1970. Career: acting curator Lang Art Gallery, Scripps Coll., Claremont 1973-77; prof. art Fullerton Coll. 1970-72; El Camino Coll., Torrance 1972-80; dir. Laguna Beach Sch. of Art 1980-81; curator El Camino Coll. Art Gallery 1981-; chmn. Creative Arts Liaison Com. 1978-81; 10 one man shows 1970-; vis. artist Claremont Grad. Sch. 1973; mem: Am. Fedn. of Arts, Am. Assn. Museums; 100+ paintings in pub. and pvt. collections; mil: E-5 AUS 1965-67. Res: 1425 W Santa Cruz St San Pedro 90732 Ofc: El Camino College Via Torrance 90506

PATTERSON, J. MICHAEL, certified public accountant; b. Mar. 6, 1946, Washington, Ia.; s. J. Kenneth and Jo Ann P.; m. Marci Feiock, Aug. 28, 1979; children: Lori b. 1964, Lisa b. 1966, Todd b. 1970, Staci b. 1972; edn: BBA, Univ. of Iowa 1968; JD, Univ. of Chgo. 1973; CPA, Iowa 1970, Ill. 1971, Calif. 1973; Realtor, Calif. 1978. Career: acct. Price Waterhouse, Chgo., then San Jose, Calif., ptnr. in charge, San Jose br.; frequent pub. spkr.; honors: Beta Alpha Psi (v.p. 1968), Phi Delta Phi; mem. Am. Inst. CPA, Calif. Inst. CPA, ABA, Calif. St. Bar Assn., Santa Clara Bar Assn. (Tax Sect. exec. com.), Estate Planning Council, Am. Electronics Assn. (tax subcom., No. Calif. exec. com.); civic bds: Kiwanis San Jose (dir.), Southwest YMCA (dir.), Santa Clara Co. Trunk & Tusk Club, Childrens Discovery Mus. (dir.), Villa Montalvo Assn. (pres.); mil: spec. E5 US Army 1968-70; Republican (Fin. Com. for Morgan for Senate 1983-93); Methodist; rec: sports. Res: 17286 Clearview Dr Los Gatos 95030 Ofc: Price Waterhouse, 150 Almaden Ave San Jose 95113

PATTERSON, MARION L., college photography instructor; b. Apr. 24, 1933, San Francisco; d. Morrie Leslie and Esther Elizabeth (Parker) P.; edn: BA (cum laude) philosophy w. art minor, Stanford Univ., 1955; MA, San Francisco St. Univ., 1970; adv. studies Calif. Sch. of Fine Arts 1956-58, Univ. Fla. 1969, studies in photography under Ansel Adams, Dorothea Lange, Minor White, Jerry Uelsmann, Don Worth, Beaumont and Nancy Newhall. Career: clk. Best's Studio, Yosemite (Ansel & Virginia Adams owners) 1958-61; asst. to photog. editor Sunset Mag., Menlo Park 1961-64; freelance photog., Ozxaca, Mexico 1964-66; comms. cons. Projects to Advance Creativity in Edn., San Mateo 1966-68; instr. photography Foothill Coll., Los Altos Hills 1968-, photog. dept. chair 86-; instr. DeAnza Coll., Coll. of Marin, Coll. of San Mateo, West Valley Coll., Merced Coll., UC Santa Cruz, S.F. St. Univ.; workshops: Calif. Acad. of Scis., Oakland Mus., The Ansel Adams Workshop, The Friends of Photography Workshop, Nature Expeditions Internat. (NEI), and pvt. workshops; mem. Am. Soc. of Magazine Photographers; rep. by Photo Researchers, NY, NY; rep. in permanent collections: M.I.T., George Eastman House, Univ. Ariz., Oakland Mus., Ansel Adams, Dorothea Lange, Minor White, others; photographic exhibits: one-woman: S.F. Mus. of Modern Art, Focus Gal. Oakland, Oakland Mus., Gallery 115, Montery County Mus. of Art, Oaxaca Mus., Stanford Univ., Kasteel Hoensbroeck Holland, Ansel Adams Gal. Yosemite, Univ. of Bayreuth W.Ger.; group: M.I.T., George Eastman House, Polaroid Corp., Art Embassies, Indiana Univ., Univ. Fla., Critics Choice Traveling Exh., CSU Humboldt Arcata, New Light L.A., New Directions Palo Alto; photographic expeditions in East Africa, Cent. Am., Mexico, Nepal, Pakistan, P.R.O.China, India, Sikkim, Bhutan, Tibet, Japan, Thailand, we. U.S.; TV interviews on KQED, KRON, local cable stations, subject 1/2 hr. documentary by First Generation (NEA grant), recipient Point Found. "Most Creative and Extraordinary" award, biog. listed Who's Who of Am. Women, Who's Who in West, Internat. Biography of Women. Res: Box 842 Menlo Park 94026 Ofc: Foothill College 12345 El Monte Rd Los Altos Hills 94022

PAULING, LINUS CARL, chemist, educator; b. Feb. 28, 1901, Portland, Ore.; s. Herman Henry William and Lucy Isabelle (Darling) P.; m. Ava Helen Miller, June 17, 1923; children: Linus Carl, Peter Jeffress, Linda Helen, Edward Crellin; edn: BS, Ore. State Coll. 1922, ScD, hon., 1933; PhD, Calif. Inst. Tech. 1925; ScD, hon., Univ. Chicago 1931; Princeton Univ. 1946; Univ. Cambridge; Univ. London; Yale Univ. 1947; Oxford 1948; Brooklyn Polytechnic Inst. 1955; Humboldt Univ. 1959; Univ. Melbourne 1964; Univ. Delhi, Adelphi Univ. 1967; Marquette Univ. Sch. Med. 1969; LHD, Tampa 1950; UJD, Univ. N.B. 1950; LLD, Reed Coll. 1959; edn. in France: Dr. H.C., Paris 1948, Toulouse, 1949, Montpellier, 1958; Jagiellonian Univ. 1964; DFA, Chouinard Art Inst. 1958. Career: with. Calif. Inst. of Tech. 1922-64; tchg. fellow 1922-25; research fellow 1935-37; asst. prof. 1927-29; assoc. prof. 1929-31; prof. chem. 1931-64; chmn. div. chem. and chem. engring.; dir. Gates & Crellin labs. 1936-58; mem. exec. com.; bd. trustee 1945-48; res. prof. Ctr. for Study of Dem. Instns. 1963-67; prof. chem. UC San Diego 1967-69; prof. chem. Stanford 1969-74; pres. Linus Pauling Inst. Sci. & Med. 1973-75, res. prof. 1973-; George Eastman prof. Oxford Univ. 1948; lectr. chem. sev. univs.; honors: Fellow Balliol Coll. 1948, NRC 1925-26, Jon S. Guggenheim Meml. found. 1926-27; num. awards in field of chem. incl. US Presdl. Medal for Merit 1948, Nobel Prize in chem. 1954, Nobel Peace Prize 1962, Internat. Lenin Peace Prize 1972, US Nat. Medal of Sci. 1974, Fermat Medal, Paul Sabatier Medal, Pasteur Medal, medal with laurel wreath of Internat Grotius Found. 1957, Lomonosov Medal 1977, Chem. Scis. award Nat. Acad. Scis. 1979; author: sev. books 1930-; contbr. articles to profl. journs. Ofc: Linus Pauling Institute of Science & Medicine 440 Page Mill Rd Palo Alto 94306

PAULSEN, PATRICK LAYTON, entertainer/comedian; b. July 6, 1927, South Bend, Wa.; s. Norman Inge and Beulah Inez (Fadden) P.; m. Betty Jane Cox, div.; children: Terri b. 1959, Monty b. 1962, Justin b. 1964; edn: att. San Francisco City Coll. Career: comedian, entertainer "Smothers Brothers Comedy Hour" 1967-69, 1975, 1987-88, 1989, "Pat Paulsen's Half a Comedy Hour" 1970; film appearances: "Harper Valley PTA", "Elly", "Night Patrol", "They Still Call Me Bruce"; owner Pat Paulsen Vineyards, Cloverdale, Calif. 1980-; owner Cherry Co. Playhouse, Traverse City, Mich. 1975-; awards: Emmy Award 1968, Smile Award Calif. Travel Industry 1990; mem: Actor's Equity Assn., Comedy Hall of Fame (bd. dirs.), Screen Actors Guild, Am. Federation of Television & Radio Artists; presdl. candidate 1968, 72, 76, 84, 88, 92; mil: USMC 1945-46; rec: tennis, golf, reading. Ofc: Entertainment Alliance PO Box 5734 Santa Rosa 95402-5734

PAULSON, RAYMOND ARNOLD, engineering executive, law college founder; b. Dec. 29, 1921, Eagle Rock, Calif.; s. Arnold Edwin and Clara (Martin) P.; m. Beverly Doris, Sept. 21, 1941; children: Larry b. 1949, Jerry b. 1952, Celeste b. 1953; edn: JD, Calif. Coll. of Law; grad. studies Citrus Coll., Nat. Inst., USC. Career: radar navigator USAAF, WWII, crewman on a diversionary aircraft during A-bombing of Heroshiima and Nagasaki, Aug. 1946; law instr. U.S. Armed Forces Inst.; dir., mgr. for nat. major mfr., prod. 1st tactical Army Missile, The Corporal, 1959; sales mgr., asst. dir. So. Calif. Credit Bureau; engr., designer radiation and chem. eval. test laboratories for USAF; dir., mgr. electro-mechanical bus.; founder Calif. Coll. of Law; pres., chmn. bd. Paulson Internat. Corp., 1971-90, ret., hon. chmn. 1990-; pres. World Trust Agency (an agy. of fin. engring. of country and bank fin. re-structuring by the Paulson Private Trust, a Denmark Heritage since 1900), div. Paulson Devel. Corp.; founder Paulson Products Co.; sole prop. Paulson Co.; devel. and taught exec. leadership tng. pgm. Baldwin Park Schs. Adult Edn. Dept.; talent locator for "I Love Lucy Show" (Lucille Ball & Desi Arnaz); w/ Harry Lubke started TV Acad. of Arts and Science (originator, Life Assoc. Member); estab. Paulson Trust (a pvt. trust), Guatemala Private Sector Country Trust Fund (1st country trust fund for mng. and mktg., A country bridge to free trade of S.Am. and the world); designer; assoc. dir. World Internat. Air & Space Show 1993, Las Vegas, Nev., Sky Harbor and McCarron Airports, Hqs. for World Air & Space Tours; assoc. designer of thermal battery and developer of 1st semi-perpetual electric vehicle (1980); pioneered color telecasting as assoc. dir. w/Carlton Winckler of CBS Color TV "Union Pacific - Ed Wynn" (1st full color 2-hr. TV show) Hollywood (1940); recipient merit award L.A. Co. Supt. of Schools div. Research & Sci. Guidance; leadership tng. dir. Boy Scouts Am. Monte Vista dist.; jt. originator of the Toys for Tots (US Marine Corps Christmas Pgm. for underprivileged kids); works: surveyed and designed the U.S. Canal, 1400 hundred mile waterway National City-Brownsville, Tx., feasibility approved by US Congress 1982; designed the Fly by Wire Flight Control System 1983 and mfr. first all composite single eng. two place jet spacecraft in world; Paulson Trust developed the 1st all composite semi perpetual electric jet small passenger train; designed and devel. "VAC-PAC All Purpose Shipping Container" ship, rail & truck (12/91), designed and produced semi-perpetual self-contained charging system for elect. vehicle battery sources. Ofc: World Trust Agency POB 4369 Covina 91723

PAULSON, TERRY LEE, lecturer, author, psychologist; b. Oct. 23, 1945, Panama City, Fla.; s. Homer Frederick and Ann Marie (Carlson) P.; m. Kathleen Wynn Hiebert, Mar. 16, 1968 (div. 1976); m. 2d. Valorie Ann Leland, June 19, 1976; 1 son, Sean Douglas b. 1971; edn: BA psychology, UCLA 1968; MA theology, Fuller Theological Seminary 1975; PhD psychology, Fuller Grad. Sch. Psychology 1974. Career: staff psychologist Orange Co. Mental Health, Anaheim 1974-76; pres., trainer, speaker, author Paulson & Assoc. Inc., Agoura Hills 1974-; ext. lectr. UCLA 1976-91; UC Berkeley 1982-90; awards: Nat. Speakers Assn. CSP Cert. Spkg. Profl. 1988, CPAE Council of Peers Award of Excellence 1991, Am. Soc. Tng. & Devel. Top Presenter 1981; mem: Nat. Speakers Assn., Am. Soc. Tng. & Devel., Westlake Lutheran Ch., Wellness Comm. (advy. bd.); author: Teacher Training on Discipline, 1975, Making Human Work, 1989, They Shoot Managers Don't They?, 1989, Secrets of Life Every Teen Needs to Know, 1990; author, ed. Management Dialogue, 1980-; Republican; Lutheran; rec: backpacking, running, travel. Ofc: Paulson & Associates Inc 28717 Colina Vista Agoura Hills 91301

PAYNE, LOUIS DONALD, writer, poet, ret. electrical engineer; b. Nov. 29, 1905, Alturas; s. Ernest Drury and Blanche Mar (Wallace) P.; m. Jeannette Abbot, Aug. 30, 1931 (dec. Oct. 16, 1981); children: Donald Wallace b. 1935, Grace Abbott b. 1938; edn: BSEE, UC Berkeley, two years grad. work in physics, UCB 1931-33; past Reg. Profl. Engr. (Elec.). Career: surveyor Calif. Forest Exptl. Sta. 1933-35; engr. Shell Oil Co., Martinez 1935-37; Shell Devel. Co., Emeryville 1937-39; Pacific Elec. Mfg. Corp. (and successor Federal-Pacific Elec. Co.), San Francisco and Santa Clara 1941-61, ret.; independent sci. researcher/ writer on topics relating to earth scis., physics, earthquake and weather forecasting, health; author/pub.: Earthquake Patterns of the San Francisco Bay Area, 1978, 79; Ballads of Outer Space and Other Poems, 1985; physics research: On the Mass of a Photon, 1985, The Velocity of Light as Changed by the Doppler Shift, 1989; contbg. poet 2 anthologies: The World of Poetry, In a Nutshell; mem: Calif. Writers Club, Calif. Fedn. of Chaparral Poets, The Alameda (CA) Poets, El Camino Poets (Sacto.), The Ina Coolbrith Circle (Berkeley), Nat. Rifle Assn., Commonwealth Club of S.F.; volunteer work for East Bay Municipal Utility Dist.; Republican; rec: sawing wood, camping, vol. work Tilden Nature Area. Address: 1543 Beverly Pl Berkeley 94706

PAYNE, MAX BIEHL, petroleum geologist, ret.; b. Jan. 23, 1910, Glenns Ferry, Idaho; s. Fred C. and Alice Amanda (Biehl) P.; m. Karen Amundson (div.); m. Charlotte Louise Annin, Dec. 8, 1946; children: Anne b. 1947, Fred b. 1949, Martha b. 1955, Robert b. 1963; edn: undergrad. Univ. Puget Sound, Tacoma, Wa. 1932-34; BS geology, Univ. Wash., Seattle 1936. Career: paleontol. lab. and field geologist Union Oil Co. of Calif., Bakersfield 1936-37; oil field mapping and resrch. Richfield Oil Corp. in Rio Bravo and Coles Levee Oil Fields, Cuyama Valley, and Wheeler Ridge, western U.S. 1937-42; served to lt. cmdr. US Navy 1942-46, So. Pacific during WWII with PB4Y Bomber Sq. VB109, later in chg. field party geologic field mapping for USN Petroleum Reserve #4 Umiat, Alaska on the north slope, decorated 5 campaigns, Bronze Star, Am. Theatre, Presdl. Unit cit. w. bronze star; engring. dept. Union Oil Co., Bakersfield, 1946-47; dist. geologist Signal Oil & Gas Corp., Bkfld. 1947-52; v.p./gen. mgr. Natural Gas Corp. of Calif. (sold to PG&E) 1952-53; oil & mineral cons. Stansbury-Del Webb, 1953-54; res. Eocene/ Cretaceous on west side of San Joaquin Valley, 1936-76; chief geologist Norris Oil Co., Bkfld. 1955-65;Chairman, Am. Assn. of Petroleum Geologists; Texfel Pet. Corp., Westwood 1965-68; indep. exploration cons. 1968-69; mgr. oil concessions for Weaver Pet. of Pa., P.R. and Jamaica, 1969; exploration cons. for oil and gas, hard minerals, geothermal in western U.S., 1970-87; honors: Sigma Alpha Epsilon 1934, guest of Chinese Govt. geol. dept. via People-to-People 1983; mem: Am. Assn. Pet. Geologists (cert. 1938), Soc. Econ. Paleontology and Mineralogy 1960-, Am. Inst. Profl. Geologists (cert. 1962), Am. Assn. for the Advancement of Sci. (elected Fellow 1962), Paleontol. Research Inst., Fellow Geol. Soc. Am., Retired Oilmen Long Beach; publs: guidebooks on geology of Calif. for geol. assns., tech. reports for Calif. Div. Mines; speaker AAPG annual nat. meeting, S.F. on K/T Cretaceous/Late Paleocene Boundary We. San Joaquin Valley, Ca. (1990); Republican; Presbyterian; rec: photog., geology, music, art. Res: 300 Deer Valley Rd #2S San Rafael 94903-5514

PAYTON, PHILLIP W., college and university administrator, educator; b. Dec. 26, 1929, Santa Barbara; s. Curtis Charles and Dorothy (Godfrey) P.; m. Gertrude Payton, Mar. 4, 1961 (div. 1976); children: Paul b. 1961; edn: BA, Reed Coll. 1951; MA, Stanford Univ. 1954; Ed.D, 1960; postdoctoral, UC Berkeley 1969-70; CSU Hayward 1970-71. Career: assoc. prof., dept. chmn. Golden Gate Univ., San Francisco 1966-70; sr. adminstrv. analyst City of Oakland 1969-73; asst. dir. Univ. San Francisco 1980-82; mgr. mgmt. devel. MCI Telecomms. 1985; bus. program coord. Nat. Univ., North Las Vegas, Nev. 1987; coord., dir. bus. and econ. Lincoln Univ., San Francisco 1987-; p.t. acct. Heath Zenith Electronics, Redwood City 1989-; BSA, Palo Alto 1987-88; personnel and fin. adminstr. GTE Govt. Systems, Mountain View 1982-85; corp. manuals coordinator McKesson Corp., San Francisco 1973-78; personnel cons. R.J. Carroll Assoc., San Mateo and Phila., Pa. 1969; awards: Reed Coll. scholarships 1947-49, Portland Ore. Jour. All A award 1947; mem: Western Mktg. Educators Assn., Western Econ. Assn., Am. Econ. Assn., City of Millbrae Personnel Bd., City of Oakland (sr. adminstr. 1970-73), City of Mountain View (acct.); 2 monographs and 2 articles pub. in profl. jours. (1961-86); mil: staff sgt. USAF, U.S. Air Nat. Guard 1948-55; Democrat; Prot.; rec: hist. newspaper collecting, old time music record collecting. Ofc: Lincoln University 281 Masonic Ave San Francisco 94118

PEARSON, JAMES EDWARD, physician; b. Aug. 3, 1956, Grand Junction, Colo.; s. Thomas Harris and June Elizabeth (Cook) P.; edn: BA, Univ. Colo. Boulder 1978; MD, Univ. Colo. Denver 1982. Career: anesthesia resident Stanford Univ. 1986; pvt. practice anesthesiology, San Francisco 1986-; honors: Phi Beta Kappa; mem: Am. Soc. Anesthesiologists, Calif. Soc. Anesthesiologists, No. Calif. Anesthesia Soc., Soc. Anesthesia in Developing Countries, Peninsula Sportmans Club, Mortar Bd. (pres. 1977-78); articles pub. in med. jours. (1986, 87); Republican; rec: hunting, shooting, theatre. Ofc: 1259 El Camino Ste 330 Menlo Park 94025

PEASLAND, BRUCE RANDALL, financial executive; b. Mar. 24, 1945, Buffalo, N.Y.; s. Kenneth Arthur and Edith Grace (Bristow) P.; m. Debra Myers, June 13, 1981; children: Michael John, Timothy Scott, Amanda Jean; edn: BS, USC, 1971, MBA in fin. 1978; JD, Western State Univ., 1983. Career: price and cost analyst McDonnell Douglas, Long Beach 1966-70; mgr. cost acctg. The Gillette Co., Santa Monica 1971-78; controller Lear Siegler Inc., Santa Ana 1978-85; British Petro. - Hitco, Newport Beach 1986-87; v.p. fin. & adminstrn. Control Components Inc., Rancho Santa Margarita 1987-90; chief fin. ofcr. MacGillivray Freeman Films Inc., Laguna Beach 1990-91; exec. v.p./cfo Prevue Systems Corp. 1992-; mem: Nat. Mgmt. Assn. (mgr. of yr. Santa Ana chapt. 1984), USC MBA Assn., USC Trojan Club, USC Alumni Assn.; mil: USMC 1963-69; Republican; Episcopalian; rec: sailing, skiing. Res: 25211 Yacht Dr Dana Point 92629 Ofc: Prevue Systems Corp. 2102 Business Center Dr. Irvine 92705

PECHTER, STEVEN J., retail sporting goods company executive; b. May 26, 1958, Brooklyn, N.Y.; s. Lawrence Stanley and Harriet Shirley (Silverman) P.; edn: BS biological scis., UC Irvine 1980; MBA, 1983. Career: lectr. UC Irvine 1980-83; ops. mgr. United Merchandising Corp., El Segundo 1975-87, asst.v.p. information systems 1987-89, v.p. MIS & Ops., 1990-91, senior v.p. 1992-; mem: BSA (asst. scoutmaster 1979-83), Nat. Eagle Scout Assn.; rec: skiing, computers, sail boarding. Res: 2513 Voorhees Ave #2 Redondo Beach 90278

PEELER, JOSEPH DAVID, lawyer; b. Sept. 29, 1895, Nashville; s. Joseph David and Virginia (McCue) P.; m. Elizabeth F. Boggess, Apr. 27, 1927; children: Stuart Thorne, Joyce Woodson; edn: AB, Univ. Ala., 1915; LLB cum laude, Harvard, 1920; admitted bar: Ky. 1920, Calif. 1929. Career: lawyer pvt. practice, Louisville 1920-29, Los Angeles 1928-87, ret.; mem. firm Musick, Peeler & Garrett; bd. fellow Claremont Univ. Center; honors: Phi Beta Kappa, Delta Kappa Epsilon, mem. U.S. team Internat. Tuna Tournament (1939, 47, 48, 55); mem: ABA, Calif. Bar Assn., L.A. Co. Bar Assn.; clubs: California, Univ. (past pres.), Los Angeles (past pres.), Wilshire CC; mil: capt. US Army Air Corps WWI, lt. col. USAAF WWII; Republican; Congregationalist. Res: 131 N June St Los Angeles 90004 Ofc: One Wilshire Bldg Los Angeles 90017

PEHL, RICHARD HENRY, physicist; b. Nov. 27, 1936, Raymond, Wash.; s. Henry Leopold and Annabelle (Moyer) P.; m. Paula Bhatia, July 1, 1980; edn: BS chem. eng., Wash. State Univ., Pullman 1958, MS nuclear eng., 1959; PhD nuclear chemistry, UC Berkeley, 1963. Career: grad. asst. Lawrence Berkeley Lab., Berkeley 1960-63, res. assoc. 1963-65, staff mem. 1965-78, senior scientist 1978-; mem. Instrument devel. sci. team NASA, 1984-; adj. staff physicist Indiana Univ. Cyclotron Facility, Bloomington, Ind. 1987-; mem. Am. Physical Soc., IEEE; author chapt. in book Nuclear Spectroscopy and Reactions 1974, 150+ tech. articles 1960-92; rec: sports. Res: 2550 Dana St, 6D, Berkeley 94704 Ofc: LBL Bldg 29 Berkeley 94720

PEISER, RICHARD B., educator; b. Aug. 12, 1948, Houston, Tx.; s. Maurice Bondy and Patricia (Levy) P.; m. Beverly Gail Siegal M.D., May 23, 1976; children: Allison b. 1981, Michael b. 1985; edn: BA, Yale Univ., 1970; MBA, Harvard Univ., 1973; PhD, Cambridge Univ., Eng. 1980. Career: builder, real estate developer, owner Peiser Corp., Dallas and Los Angeles, 1978-; asst. prof. So. Methodist Univ., Dallas 1978-85; assoc. prof. Stanford Univ., 1981; dir. Lusk Center for Real Estate Devel., Univ. So. Calif., L.A. 1986-; Fellow, Urban Land Inst.; civic: South Coast Botanical Garden (trustee), YMCA Camp Grady Spruce, Dallas (trustee); author: Professional Real Estate Development, The ULI Guide to the Business 1992. Ofc: 351 VKC, USC, Los Angeles 90089-0042

PELLEGRINI, ROBERT JEROME, professor of psychology; b. Oct. 21, 1941, Worcester, Mass.; s. Felix and Teresa (DiMuro) P.; m. Susan Jean Myers, June 8, 1986; children: Robert J., Jr. b. 1971; edn: BA psychology, Clark Univ. 1963; MA, Univ. Denver 1966; PhD, 1968. Career: assoc. dean research, dir. office of sponsored programs San Jose St. Univ. 1983-85, prof. psychology 1967-; pres. Western Inst. Human Devel. 1985-; dir. Criminal Justice Res. Assn.; honors: prof. of year Psi Chi 1981-82, Phi Beta Kappa 1963, merit performance San Jose St. Univ. (1987, 89); mem: We. Psychol. Assn., Am. Psychol. Assn., Sigma Xi, Psychonomic Soc.; author: 2 books, book chpt., study guides and manuals (1969-), 59+ articles in profl. jours. (1967-), rec: tennis, wilderness exploration, conservation. Res: 4816 Rue Nice Ct San Jose 95136 Ofc: San Jose State University Dept. of Psychology San Jose 95192

PENN, CHARLES JAMES, writer, editor, publisher; b. May 30, 1914, Perth, W. Australia; s. James Albert and Kate Sarah (Leckie) P.; m. Verle Rowles, 1940, div. 1960; children: Russell b. 1945, Wayne b. 1948, Gary b. 1954; m. 2d Mary Faith Taylor, June 1, 1970; edn: lib. arts, Univ. of W. Australia, Perth Tech. Coll. 1929-36; Santa Monica Coll., UCLA, 1963-64; stu. of Bhagavan Sri Sathya Sai Baba, India 1966-. Career: copy boy, cub reporter Daily News newspaper, Perth 1929-36; ed. West Australian Mining Review and West Australian Mining Annual 1936-39; ed./pub. Canadian Oil & Gas Jour., Toronto 1940-42; dir. Australian War Supplies Mission, W.D.C. 1942-43; ed. Internat. Petroleum Register, Los Angeles 1946-49; mng. dir. Russell Publs. Ltd., London 1950-52; ed./pub. Nat. Indsl. Publs., Los Angeles 1953-60, Western Oil & Gas Jour., L.A.

1961-63; exec. Trade Service Corp., San Diego 1966-92; chmn., ceo The Found. of Higher Learning 1987-89; dir. London Court Ltd., Piccadilly Arcade Ltd., Perth W.A. 1936-39; charter pres., gov. Sertoma Internat. L.A. 1955-59; lectr. in US, Canada, S.Am., guest speaker 4, World Confs., delegate 5th World Conf. Sri Sathya Sai Service Orgn., Bombay and Prasanthi Nilayam, India; author: "My Beloved" The Love and Tchgs. of Bhagavan Sri Sathya Sai Baba (1981, pub. in Hindi, Spanish, Italian, and Chinese edits.), "Finding God" My Journey to Bhagavan Sri Sathya Sai Baba (1990), "Lord Sai and I in Vaikunta," coauthor (w/ Mary Faith Penn) Am. edit. Part I "Sathyam - Sivam - Sundaram" - "Sai Baba" (1969), "Sai Ram" Experiencing the Love and Teachings of Bhagavan Sri Sathya Sai Baba (1985), contbr. "Sanatha Sarathi," "The Divine Master," "Golden Age," "Sai Chandana" (1965), "The Sri Sathya Sai Inst. of Higher Learning (Deemed Univ.) Homage Volume," "Sai Vandana," (1990), India; "The Sri Prasanthi Soc. Homage Volume," "Sathya Sai -The Eternal Charioteer" (1990), India; Sri Sathya Sai Seva Orgns. Golden Jubilee Homage Volume (1990), "Soham," Canadian Jours. (1986), prin. speaker 1st Annual Symp. Sri Sathya Sai Service orgns. of W. Canada (1984); mem: Boy Scouts of Australia, King Scout, Rover (1921-30); Scarborough Surf Life Saving Assn. West Australia 1931-35, Masonic Grand Lodge of Western Australia 1937-39, Sathya Sai Soc. of Am. (charter v.p. 1968-75); inventor: Letters ejectable help summoning device (pat. 1966); mil: capt. Brit. Army staff, W.D.C. 1944-45, Def., War medals; capt. USAF Civil Air Patrol 1963-66; Republican; rec: lectr. on humanities, travel, biking. Address: San Diego 92054

PENN, MARY FAITH, lecturer, writer, editor; b. Oct. 22, Vancouver, B.C., Canada; d. Henry Boardman and Althea (Marston) Taylor; m. Charles Penn, June 1, 1970; edn: liberal arts major Tower Coll., San Antonio, Tx. 1944-46, Long Beach Coll. 1951-52; Yoga student of Paramahansa Yogananda (Yogas Raja, Bhakti, Karma, Hatha, Selfless Service), Self-Realization Fellowship Internat. Hqtrs., L.A. 1949-52; adv. Yoga studies in India: Sri Aurobindo Inst. 1968, Sri Sathya Sai Inst. of Higher Learning 1968, 72, 75, 80, student of Bhagavan Sri Sathya Sai Baba 1965-. Career: meditation counselor, Yoga instr., West and Southwest U.S. 1953-; pvt. estate mgr. 1954-; exec. secty. Charles Luckman Assocs., Los Angeles 1962-68; pres./cfo The Found. of Higher Learning, 1987-89; lectr. on humanities, E. and W. philosophy and meditation, retreats/confs. and seminars in U.S., Canada, S.Am., Hong Kong, 1961-; author, writer, editor, 1969-; coauthor (w/C.J. Penn) Am. edition Part I "Sathyam - Sivam - Sundaram" "Sai Baba" (1969), "Sai Ram" Experiencing the Love and Teachings of Bhagavan Sri Sathya Sai Baba (1985), contbr. "Soham," Canadian Jours. (1986); prin. speaker 1st Annual Symp. Sri Sathya Sai Service Orgns. of W. Canada 1984, guest speaker 4th World Conf. Sri Sathya Sai Service Orgns., Prasanthi Nilayam, India 1985, delegate 5th World Conf. 1990; guest speaker Sri Sathya Sai Foreign Devotees Programs, Prasanthi Nilayam, India 1990; pres. bd. trustees San Antonio Gospel Tabernacle 1985-; First woman recipient Award of Forensic Excellence, S.W. Texas Univ. 1943; Republican; rec: travel, cymbidiums and bromeliads, music, biking. Address: San Diego 92054

PENNISE, SEBASTIAN (SAM), engineer; b. Jan. 20, 1934, Easton, Pa.; s. Salvatore and Julia (Francavillese) P.; m. Lorraine Stewart, Sept. 19, 1954; children: Michael b. 1955, Gerald b. 1956, Randall b. 1958, Diana b. 1961, Jeffrey b. 1962; edn: BS in E.E., Lafayette Coll., 1956; MS systems engring., West Coast Univ. 1965. Career: res. engr. Rocketdyne Div. Rockwell Internat., Canoga Park 1956-57; res. engr. U.S. Army ordnance fire control div. Aberdeen Proving Grounds, Md. 1957; lead engr. Rockwell Internat. Rocketdyne Div. 1958-76, instr. elec. systems for Saturn Rocket Engine and Space Shuttle Main Engine, Energy Systems Group, Clinch River Breeder Reactor Control System 1976-84, sr. staff engr. Rocketdyne Div. 1985-, recipient Rocketdyne Achievement Award 1976; mem: Nat. Mgmt. Assn., Rockwell Valley Chpt. (mgr. Speakers Bur. 1987), Rocketdyne Div. Bowling League (past pres.); tech. research: Equipment Monitoring Systems (1981); mil: capt. AUS Ord. Corps 1956-64, Reserves; Republican; R.Cath.; rec: camping, hunting, ski, auto mechs. Res: 6001 Sadring Ave Woodland Hills 91367

PENROSE, JOHN MORGAN, educator; b. June 16, 1942, Tulsa, Okla.; s. John Morgan and Garnet (Haston) P.; m. Margaret Iwanaga, June 15, 1983; edn: BSJ, and MS, Ohio Univ. 1964, 1966; PhD, Univ. Texas, Austin 1978. Career: dir. of annual giving Ohio Univ., Athens 1966-69; lectr., asst. to dean So. Ill. Univ., Edwardsville 1969-72; lectr., sr. lectr. Univ. Texas, Austin 1972-88; prof. San Diego St. Univ. 1988-; cons. Sohio/Standard Oil, British Petroleum, 1980-; honors: disting. member and best paper awards Assn. for Bus. Comm. 1985; mem. editl. rev. bd. Mgmt. Comm. Qtr. USC 1985-, J. of Bus. Comms., Abilene Christian Univ. 1984-, Iowa State J. of BTC 1985-; mem: Assn. for Bus. Comm. (1968-, pres. 1988-89), Internat. Comm. Assn. 1969-, Acad. of Mgmt. 1985-, Nat. Bus. Edn. Assn. 1989-, S.W. Fedn. of Adminstrv. Disciplines 1980-, Delta Sigma Pi (chpt. adv. 1970-88), Phi Kappa Phi 1974-, Sigma Delta Chi 1965-; sr. author (text) Advanced Bus. Comm. (1989), coauthor Bus. Comm. Strategies & Skills (1991 4th edit.), Readings & Applications in Bus. Comm. (1985), contbr. articles in numerous scholarly jours. (1975-); rec: sailing. Res: 1522 Berenda Pl El Cajon 92020 Ofc: San Diego State University IDS Dept. San Diego 92182

PERELSON, GLENN H., healthcare executive; b. Oct. 10, 1954, N.Y.C.; s. Bruce I. and Shirley M. P.; m. Sofia, Feb. 21, 1992; children: Adriana b. 1985, Alexander b. 1990, Brandon b. 1992; edn: AB, Hamilton Coll., 1975; MD, Boston Univ.,1979; MBA, Univ. of Phoenix, Fountain Valley 1991; bd. cert. Internist and Cardiologist 1983, bd. cert. Medical Mgmt. 1992. Career: founder, pres. Zero-G Industries, Boston 1985-; med. dir. Physician Med. Ctr., Boston 1985-88; medical director FHP Inc., Fountain Valley, Calif. 1988-; dir: Buckingham Properties, Buckingham, Pa. 1986-; mem. corporate speakers bur. Am. Heart Assn., San Diego 1992-; bd. dir. Am. Heart Assn., Chula Vista; awards: Golden Heart, Cardiovascular Res. in Space Soc., Houston 1990, Winning Idea award FHP Inc. 1991; mem. Am. Coll. of Physician Execs. 1989-, Am. Heart Assn. 1983-, Cardiovascular Res. in Space Soc. (1985-, past pres.), Zero-G Found. (chmn. bd. dirs. 1987-); author (text): Zero-G Medicine (1989), articles in sci. publs. (1981-); rec: underwater photog., composing music. Ofc: FHP, Inc. 2333 Camino del Rio South Ste 250 San Diego 92108

PEREZ, HERMAN, administrator; b. Mar. 8, 1950, Hanford; s. Merced R. and Trinidad (Aspeitia) P. Career: regional dir. Proteus Adult Training Inc., Hanford 1974-80; sr. operations analyst King County E&T Office, Hanford 1980-82; director Madera County Private Industry Council, Madera 1982-; mem bds: Madera EDC (1984-, past pres.), Madera Co. IDC (1985-, past pres.), Madera Linkage Found. (1985-, past pres.), State Center Community Vocat. Advy. Com. 1986-, Madera Co. Film Commn. 1986-, Madera Drug & Alcohol Master Plan 1990-; mem. Madera Hispanic C.of C., Elks; mil: sgt. USAF 1970-74; Democrat; R.Cath.; rec: golf. Ofc: Madera County Private Industry Council 114 S "C" St Madera 93638

PEREZ, KATHERINE DIANA, educator; b. Nov. 15, 1949, Elyria, Ohio; d. Timothy James and Donna Dale (Dickason) Donovan; m. Robert Henry Perez, Aug. 24, 1974; children: Hart b. 1985, Devon b. 1987; edn: BA hons., english, Holy Names Coll. 1971; MS ednl. psychology, CSU Hayward 1977; Ed.D, Brigham Young Univ. 1983. Career: asst. dean and dir. spl. edn. and reading leadership Saint Marys Coll., Moraga 1984-; tchr. Richmond Unified Sch. Dist., Richmond 1973-77, reading splst. 1976-77, spl. edn. tchr. 1977-78, coord. project STEP 1978-81, curriculum and staff devel. splst. 1981-84; lectr. CSU Hayward, UC Berkeley Ext., Contra Costa Coll., 1981-84; cons. Project HATCH, Oakland 1979-84; spl. activities dir. Santa Barbara Recreation Dept. 1971-75; awards: Rotary Internat. Fellow 1979-80; mem: Learning Disabilities Assn. Intl. (ednl. chair, conf. spkr. 1990), Council for Exceptional Children (com. chair), Calif. Council Edn. of Tchrs. (program com.), Internat. Reading Assn., Calif. Reading Assn., Calif. Assn. Prof. of Spl. Edn., Assn. Supervision & Curriculum Devel. (nat. staff Devel. Coun.), Glide Found. (chair), Delta Kappa Gamma (past pres.), Center for Adaptive Learning (advy. bd.), Clausen House (advy. bd.); author: Teachers Guide (Janus Pub. Co. 1985), Resource Specialist Handbook 1983, 5+ articles pub. in profl. jours. 1983-; Democrat; R.Cath.; rec: swimming, aerobics. Res: 286 Vernon St Oakland 94610 Ofc: Saint Marys College School of Education PO Box 4350 Moraga 94575

PEREZ, RICHARD LEE, lawyer; b. Nov. 17, 1946, Los Angeles; s. Salvador Navarro and Shirley Mae (Leyerle) P.; children: Kristina, Kevin, Ryan; edn: BA, UCLA 1968; JD, UC Berkeley 1971; admitted Calif. U.S. Dist. Ct. (no. dist.) 1974, U.S. Ct. Appeals (9th Cir.) 1974, U.S. Dist. Ct. (ea. dist.) 1982, Tex. U.S. Dist. Ct. (no. dist.) 1984. Career: associate McCutchen, Doyle, Brown & Enersen, San Francisco 1972-74; John R. Hetland, Orinda 1974-75; ptnr. Lempres & Wulsferg, Oakland 1975-82, Perez & McNabb, Orinda 1982-; spkr. real estate brokerage and computer groups and seminars; mem. adv. bd. Computer Litigation Reporter, Wash. 1982-85, Boalt Hall High Tech. Law Jour. 1984-90; mem: ABA, Alameda Co. Bar Assn., Contra Costa Co. Bar Assn.; assoc. ed. Univ. Calif. Law Review 1970-71; mil: capt. U.S. Army, 1968-79. Ofc: Perez & McNabb 140 Brookwood Orinda 94563

PERILLOUX, BRUCE EDGAR, optics manufacturing product line manager; b. Mar. 24, 1961, New Orleans, La.; s. Louis Francis, Jr. and Edna Eloise (Zirkle) P.; m. Anne Mary Jeansonne, Jan. 19, 1985; edn: BS in E.E., Univ. New Orleans, 1983, MSE, 1984. Career: grad. tchg. asst. Univ. New Orleans, 1983-84, grad. res. asst. 1984-85; Thin Film res. & devel. engr. Coherent Inc., Auburn, Calif. 1985-87, sr. Thin Film engr. 1988-89, product line mgr. 1989-; awards: Phi Kappa Phi 1984, Sigma Xi 1984, outstanding res. award 1985, employee of yr. nom. Coherent Inc. 1985; mem. Optical Soc. of Am. 1983-, Soc. of Photo Optical and Instrumentation Engrs. 1983-92; inventor in optical engring. (5 Patents 1988, 88, 90, 91, 92); publs: 11+ tech. articles (1984-91); rec: reading, physics, philosophy, music. Ofc: Coherent, Inc. 2301 Lindbergh St Auburn 95602-9595

PERLOFF, JEFFREY MARK, professor of agricultural economics; b. Jan. 28, 1950, Chgo.; s. Harvey S. and Miriam (Seligman) P.; m. Jacqueline B. Persons, Aug. 15, 1976; children: Lisa b. 1986; edn: BA, Univ. Chgo., 1972; PhD, M.I.T., 1976. Career: asst. prof. econ. Univ. of Pa., Phila. 1976-80; asst. prof., assoc. prof., prof. agric. econ. Univ. Calif., Berkeley 1980-82, 82-89, 89-; coauthor: Modern Industrial Organization (1990); numerous articles in profl. jours. Ofc: Dept. Agricultural & Resource Economics 207 Giannini Hall Univ. Calif. Berkeley 94720

PERNICIARO, GIANVITTORIO, writer, entrepreneur; b. Dec. 5, 1940, Bari, Italy, nat. 1975; s. Antonino (Div. General Italian Army), and Anita (Russo); m. Liliana Peripoli, Nov. 24, 1970; 2 daus.: Patrizia b. 1964, Elena b. 1972; edn: spl. courses English Inst. of Languages, Palermo, Italy 1962, Univ. of Palermo, 1963, Am. Mgmt. Assn., L.A. 1973. Career: interpreter/polyglot, US Govt., Dept. of State, US Consulate General, Palermo, Italy to 1968; shipping co. exec. AGIP USA, N.Y to 1969, U.S. Lines, Oakland to 1974, and Zim Lines, Los Angeles to 1985; owner Bike Tours Unlimited, 1985-; founder The Heritage of Italy in America, 1988; free lance writer Long Beach Press Telegram, Los Angeles Times, and Orange County Register, 1979-; shipping industry cons. and lectr. Transp. Tng. Ctr., 1984; principal on stage "Dream Gold Wings" TV commercial for Calif. State Lottery, 1989; author: My Baja Story 1981; Container Terminal Operations Textbook 1984; One Wing for the Road 1986; Dictionary of the Italian-American Immigrant 1988; The Adventure of a Lifetime 1988; awards: Press Telegram outstanding achiev. award 1983, conferee U.S. Flag in U.S. Capitol Rotunda 1984, hon. mention on Vol. 131, No. 58 Congl. Record, 99th Congress for personal views on Amendment XVI to U.S. Constn., U.S. Library of Congress hon. mention for contbns. to study of Italian-Am. culture 1989, honoree Calif. State Senate 1991, honoree Calif. State Assembly 1991, recipient George Washington Medal of Honor for excellence in public svc. and constrv. participation in the nat. political life 1991, also recipient awards from Am. Mgmt. Assn. 1974, Employment Devel. Dept. (E.U.) Oakland 1976, Republican Presdl. Task Force 1986; mem: The Britannica Soc. 1972, The Propeller Club Port of L.A.-Long Beach 1977, US Senatl. Club 1984, Ellis Island Centennial Commn. 1986, Order of Sons of Italy in America 1991, Freedoms Found. at Valley Forge 1991, Trabuco Highlands HOA (dir. 1990-); supporter Orange Co. Diocese charitable activities 1991-; R.Cath.; rec: piano, classical music, motorcycle touring abroad. Res: PO Box 384, Trabuco Canyon 92678-0384 Ofc: The Heritage of Italy in America PO Box 1965 San Pedro 90733

PERRISH, ALBERT, steel co. executive; b. Nov. 18, 1914, Vancouver, B.C., Can., Am. citizen by parentage; s. Sam and Nettie (Prezant) P.; m. Helen, June 11, 1985; children: Peggy b. 1953, James b. 1953, Kathleen b. 1956, Jeffrey b. 1948, Larry b. 1955; edn: BS bus. adminstrn., UC Los Angeles 1938. Career: asst. to the pres. Southwest Steel Rolling Mills, 1946-50; chmn./CEO Ferro Union Inc. (fmr. Winter, Wolff & Co., then Triangle Steel & Supply Co.), Torrance 1950-; apptd. L.A. Board of Harbor Commissioners (1962-66, pres. 1965); awards: Star of Solidarity (Italy), Chevalier Order of Commerce and Industry (France), Order of Leopold (Belgium), Bronze Plaque, Los Angeles C.of C. 1963; mem: Fgn. Trade of So. Calif. (pres. 1963), West Coast Metal Importers Assn. (pres. 1986), Assn. of Steel Distbrs., Steel Service Center Inst., American Inst. of Imported Steel (dir.); mil: capt. US Air Force 1942-46. Address: Torrance 90502

PERSCHBACHER, REX ROBERT, law professor; b. Aug. 31, 1946, Chgo., Ill.; s. Robert Ray and Nancy Ellen (Beach) P.; m. Debbie Bassett Hamilton; children: Julie b. 1977, Nancy b. 1981; edn: BA, Stanford Univ. 1968; Oxford Univ. 1969; JD, UC Berkeley 1972; admitted St. Bar Calif. 1972. Career: legal writing instr. UC Berkeley 1972-73; law clerk to federal district court judge Alfonso J. Zirpoli 1973-74; asst. prof. Univ. Tx., Austin 1974-75; atty., assoc. Heller Ehrman White & McAuliffe, San Francisco 1975-78; assoc. prof. Univ. San Diego 1978-81; prof. law, dir. clin. edn. UC Davis 1981-; instr. Inst. Internat. & Comparative Law, Kings Coll., London, England 1984, 88; instr. Nat. Inst. Trial Advocacy 1988; honors: Phi Beta Kappa, Order of Coif, Distinguished tchg. award 1992; mem: Am. Bar Assn., Am. Assn. Law Schs.; co-author: Civil Procedure (1987, 2d edit. 1992), California Legal Ethics (1992), California Trial Practice (1991), 5 revs. in law jours. (1982-); Democrat; rec: travel, hiking. Res: 1438 41st St Sacramento 95819 Ofc: Univ. California Davis 95616

PERSHADSINGH, HARRIHAR AJODHYA, physician scientist; b. Mar. 29, 1946, Kingston, Jamaica, naturalized Am. citizen, K.C., Mo., 1983; s. Harrihar Jang-Bahador and Bishun Devi (Tewari) P.; m. Deborah Lyn Montgomery, July 12, 1975; edn: BA, San Jose State Univ.,, 1969; PhD, UC Santa Barbara, 1975; MD, Univ. of Mo., Columbia, 1984. Career: postdoctoral fellow biochemistry McGill Univ., Montreal, 1976-78; postdoc. fellow 1978-80 and clin. pathology resident 1984-86, Washington Univ. Sch. of Med., St. Louis, Mo.; asst. prof. of lab. medicine UC San Francisco, 1986-90; pres. and research dir. Hap-Tek Biomed, Inc., Bakersfield, 1990-; ad hoc referee sci. journals: Diabetes 1986-, Cytometry 1987-, Canadian J. Biochemistry & Cell Biology 1988-; awards: Research Fellow Max and Victoria Dreyfus Found. 1989-90, res. & devel. Am. Diabetes Assn. 1987-89, Young Investigator award Acad. of Clin. Lab. Physicians & Scientists 1985, Fellow Sigma Xi 1981, Fellow Nat. Acad. of Clin. Biochem. 1980, res. fellow Juvenile Diabetes Found. 1979-80; mem: Am. Soc. Biochem. & Molecular Biol., Am. Diabetes Assn., NY Acad. Sci., Am. Assn. of Clin. Chemistry; author 8 sci. book chapters and 40+ sci. jour. articles; Indep.; rec: gardening, hiking, cosmology. Ofc: Dept. Family Practice, Kern Medical Center, 1830 Flower St Bakersfield CA.

PERSINGER, JOE MADDEN, psychologist, consultant; b. Feb. 3, 1944, Wash., DC; s. David and Mary Esther (Madden) P.; m. Susan Harriet Katz, Mar. 28, 1952; edn: BA, Univ. Va. Charlottesville 1966; MA, Calif. Sch. Profl.

Psychology 1974; PhD, 1977; lic. psychologist, lic. marriage and family counselor. Career: mental health counselor Sonoma Co. Health Dept., Santa Rosa 1979-82; pvt. practice clin. psychology 1983-; dir. Milton Erickson Inst. 1985-; Oral Examination Commn., Calif. State Psychology Examining Com. 1986-; mem: Am. Psychological Assn., Calif. State Psychological Assn., Redwood Psychological Assn. (pres. 1987), Democratic Club, Mensa; rec: tennis, gardening, meditation. Ofc: Erickson Institute 1180 Montgomery Dr Santa Rosa 95405

PESCAN, TODD LINE, stockbroker; b. Feb. 13, 1959, Columbus, Ohio; s. Alexander and Faith Lee (Line) P.; m. Lisa Hix, May 3, 1986; edn: BA in econs./psychol., UCLA 1981; MBA in corp./internat. fin., USC 1983. Career: stockbroker, fin. cons., v.p. Shearson Lehman Brothers, Beverly Hills; mem: Am. Mktg. Assn., Am. Fin. Assn., Phi Kappa Sigma, Alpha Phi, Sonance; Republican; Presbyterian; rec: coin collecting, tennis. Res: 9802 Ludwig St Villa Park 92667 Ofc: Shearson Lehman Brothers 9665 Wilshire Blvd Ste 700 Beverly Hills 90212

PETER, CHRISTOPHER RAYMOND, microbiologist; b. Nov. 27, 1948, Sacramento; s. Raymond Vincent and Cynthia Grace (Roberts) P.; m. Dolores Mary Rupprecht, June 23, 1989; children: Brendan b. 1979, Rachel b. 1982; edn: BS, Sacto. St. Coll. 1970; MA, UC Davis 1975; PhD, 1975. Career: clin. lab. tech. trainee UC Davis Med. Center 1970-71; clin. lab. tech. Am. River Hosp., Carmichael 1971-75; postgrad res. microbiologist UC Davis 1972-75; postdoctoral res. fellow Oreg. Regional Primate Res. Ctr., Beaverton, Oreg. 1975-76; adj. faculty biology dept. San Diego St. Univ., 1982-; asst. chief, San Diego Co. Pub. Health Lab. 1976-89, chief 1989-; awards: Landgraf Found. Christine Landgraf Meml. 1974; mem: AAAS, Calif. Assn. Pub. Health Lab. Dirs. (chmn. res. and devel.), Am. Soc. Microbiology, So. Calif. Assn. Pub. Health Microbiologists, BSA (cubmaster 1988-90); 3 articles pub. in profl. jours. (1984-89); Democrat; R.Cath.; rec: gardening, hiking, bicycling. Res: 2450 Grafton St El Cajon 92020 Ofc: San Diego County Public Health Laboratory POB 85222 San Diego 92138-5222

PETERS, BARBARA STRATTON, career counselor; b. Apr. 18, 1949, Pocatello, Idaho; d. Richard Wendell and Margaret (Harris) S.; m. Thomas H. Peters, Aug. 7, 1984; edn: BA in govt. Idaho State Univ., 1971, MA edn. student personnel, 1976. Career: asst. dir. Career Planning & Placement, Idaho State Univ., Pocatello 1974-77; assoc. dir. Career Devel. Ctr., Humboldt State Univ., Arcata, Calif. 1977-90, career counselor 1990-, asst. to v.p. for student affairs 1988; honors: Phi Kappa Phi 1970; appt. Coll. of the Redwoods counseling svs. advy. com., Eureka 1987-, Redwoods Occup. Educ. Council, Eureka (pres. 1985-86); Democrat; R.Cath.; rec: singing, baseball, camping. Res: 221 Dollison Eureka 95501 Ofc: Career Development Center, Humboldt State Univ., Arcata 95521

PETERS, DONALD LOUIS, lawyer, b. Sept. 28, 1932, Jacksonville, FL; edn: BSC, Univ. Notre Dame, 1955, JD, Southwestern Univ., 1964; adm. State Bar of Calif. 1965. Career: Exec. Asst. to the Exec. Ofcr., 1962-65; Judge Pro Tem, Los Angeles Cty. Superior Ct., 1976-77; mem: bd. of dir., Beverly Hosp., Montebello 1966-, treas. 1967-74, second vice pres. 1991-, chmn. Med Malpractice Review Com. 1993-; awards: listed in Who's Who in Amer. Law, 4th and 5th ed.; mem: Orange Cty. Bar Assn.; mil: lt.jg. USNR active duty 1955-57; Democrat; R. Cath.; rec: aviation, tennis, golf. Ofc: Donald Peters, 1300 Dove St. #200, Newport Beach 92660

PETTERSEN, THOMAS M., financial executive; b. Nov. 9, 1950, Poughkeepsie, N.Y.; s. Olsen T. and Reva (Palmer) P.; edn: BS, SUNY, Albany 1973; lic. CPA, N.Y. 1976. Career: senior acct. Arthur Andersen & Co., N.Y., N.Y. 1973-77; financial analyst Paramount Communications, N.Y., N.Y. 1977-78; dir. acctg. systems, dir. auditing Nat. Broadcasting Co. Inc., Burbank 1979-90; v.p. fin. & adminstrn. Data Dimensions Inc., Culver City 1991-92; cons. Westwood One, Inc., Culver City 1992-; mem. Am. Inst. CPAs 1976-, Financial Execs. Inst. 1992-; Republican; rec: sports, travel. Res: 217 First Place Manhattan Beach 90266 Ofc: Westwood One Inc 9540 Washington Blvd Culver City 90232

PETTIGREW, THOMAS FRASER, social psychologist, educator; b. March 14, 1931, Richmond, Va.; s. Joseph Crane and Janette (Gibb) P.; mm. Ann Hallman, Feb. 25, 1956; 1 son, Mark b. 1966; edn: BA psych., Univ. Va., 1952; MA and PhD in social psychology, Harvard Univ., 1955, 56. Career: asst. prof. Univ. North Carolina, Chapel Hill, 1956-57; Harvard Univ., Cambridge, Mass. 1957-62, lectr., assoc. prof. 1962-68, prof. 1968-80; prof. UC Santa Cruz 1980-; Univ. Amsterdam, Netherlands 1986-; mem. White House Task Force on Edn., WDC 1967; Phi Beta Kappa Emerson Book Award Com. 1971-73; trustee Ella Lyman Cabot Trust, Boston, Mass. 1978-80; adj. fellow Joint Center for Political Studies, WDC 1982-; cons. U.S. Office of Edn. 1966-68; U.S. Commn. on Civil Rights 1966-71; awards: Guggenheim Found. Fellow 1967-68, (hon.) HDL, Gov. St. Univ. 1979, Am. Sociol. Assn. Spivack Award 1978, UC Santa Cruz Faculty Res. Award 1984, Soc. Psychol. Study of Social Issues Kurt Lewin Memorial 1987, Gordon Allport Intergroup Relations Res. Award 1988; mem: Am. Psychol. Assn. (fellow), Am. Sociol. Assn., Soc. Psychol. Study of Social

Issues (past pres.), European Assn. Exptl. Social Psychology, Soc. Exptl. Social Psychology; author; A Profile of Negro Am. (1964), Racially Separate or Together (1971), Sociology of Race Rels. (1980), coauthor: Prejudice (1982), Tom Bradley's Campaigns for Governor; 200+ articles pub. in profl. jours.; mil: 2d. lt. AUS 1952; Democrat; Episcopalian; rec: chess. Ofc: Stevenson College Univ. Calif., Santa Cruz 95064

PETTUS, JOSEPH HODSON, energy co. executive; b. Aug. 1, 1947, Louisville, Ky.; s. Thomas N. and Nancye B. (Trimble) P.; m. Judith C. Nenno, Aug. 26, 1969; children: Jeffrey W. b. 1976, Jeremy H. b. 1979, Jenna C. b. 1989. edn: BS civil engrg., bus. adminstrn., Univ. Colo. 1970. Career: engr. Exxon Co. USA Houston 1970-75; proj. mgr. Fluor E&C Houston 1976-77; v.p. ops. United Energy Resources Houston 1978-81; senior v.p. supply & transp. Cal Gas Corp., Sacto. 1981-88; dir. Propane Transport Inc. Milford, Ohio, Minden Pipeline Co. Minden, La., Norco Transp. Co. L.A., Beacon Petroleum Co. Shreveport. La.; pres. Sun Valley Energy Inc., Sacto. 1988-; honors: Chi Epsilon, listed Who's Who in Am.; Gov.'s Internat. Host Com. of Calif.; mem. bd. dirs. KVIE-TV Ch. 6 (PBS); Republican; Protestant. Res: 8800 Triple Crown Ct Fair Oaks 95628

PEZZUTI, THOMAS ALEXANDER, architect; b. Dec. 29, Harrisburg, Pa.; s. Hamil Ralph and Dorothea Marie (Graham) P.; m. Diane Marie Paplham; 1 son, Graham Alexander; edn: BArch, Univ. of Notre Dame; reg. arch. Pa. 1964, Calif. 1968. Career: div. dir. Maxwell Starkman AIA & Assocs., Beverly Hills 1977-83; mgr. of design and constrn. (acting) US Postal Svc., Santa Monica 1983-87; project mgr. Daniel, Mann, Johnson and Mendenhall, 1986-; instr. design workshop Univ. of Notre Dame, 1963; candidate U.S. Congress, 27th C.D. Calif. 1976; honors: 2d prize Beaux Arts, Paris, France 1963, listed Who's Who in the West 1975, Contemporary Authors 1976; mem. Am. Inst. Architects 1973-, Internat. Mensa Soc. 1962-, Command Performance Telecable (pres. 1982-84); author: You Can Fight City Hall and Win 1974, EZ Golf 1985, invention: Hammerhead Putter (pat. 1989); mil: USAR Corps of Engrs.; Indep.; Cath.; rec: writing, computers, simulation gaming. res: PO Box 2901 Beverly Hills 90213-2901 Ofc: Daniel, Mann, Johnson & Mendenhall, 3250 Wilshire Blvd Los Angeles 90010

PFUHL, JOHN WESLEY, accountant; b. June 26, 1938, Lansing, Mich.; s. Edward Carl, Sr. and Gladys Dorothy (Williams) P.; m. Maren C. Thoresen, June 22, 1965; children: Scott, Shari; edn: BA acctg., Mich. State Univ. 1960; Certified Public Acct., Calif. 1969. Career: staff acct. Arthur Young & Co., Santa Ana office; staff acct. Jones, Elliott & Assocs., Fullerton; ptnr. Sherlock, Soule & Pfuhl, La Jolla; pres. John W. Pfuhl Acctncy. Corp.; pres. Pfuhl & Knight Acctncy. Corp., El Cajon currently; mem: Am. Inst. CPAs, Calif. Soc. CPAs; civic: past pres. Torrey Pines Kiwanis Club (Kiwanian of Year 1975), mem. El Cajon Valley Lions Club, past treas. La Jolla Town Council; mil: Lt. US Navy; Republican; Lutheran; rec: softball, skiing, woodworking. Ofc: 237 Avocado Ave Ste 210 El Cajon 92020

PFUND, EDWARD T., JR., aerospace co. engineer, executive; b. Dec. 10, 1923, Methuen, Mass.; s. Edward Theodore Sr. and Mary Elizabeth (Banning) P.; m. Marga Andre, Nov. 10, 1954 (div. 1978); children: Angela b. 1954, Gloria b. 1956, Edward III b. 1961; m. 2d. Ann Lauren Dillie, Jan. 10, 1988; edn: BS, magna cum laude, Tufts Coll. 1950; grad. studies, USC 1950, Boston Univ. 1950, Columbia Univ. 1953, UCLA 1956, 58. Career: radio engr. WLAW, Lawrence-Boston 1942-50; foreign svc. staff ofcr. US Dept. of State Voice of Am., Tangier, Munich, 1950-54; proj. engr. Crusade for Freedom, Radio Free Europe, Munich, Ger. 1955; proj. mgr./ material splst. United Electrodynamics Inc., Pasadena 1956-59; dir. eng./ chief engr. Electronics Specialty Co., Los Angeles & Thomaston, Conn. 1959-61; with Hughes Aircraft, var. locations 1955, 1961-89: chmn. subcom. on communications Space Flt. Ops. Gp. 1963, chief Johannesburg Ops. 1961-63, dir. Spacecraft Performance Analysis and Command 1964-68 (directed the command control & perf. of all USA unmanned soft lunar landings and the world's first lunar liftoff and translation 1966-68), pgm. mgr. Lunar Rover Ground Data Sys. Design 1969-70, mgr. new bus. devel. Middle & Far East Africa and So. America 1971-84, tech. chmn. Internat. Consortium 1974-78, dir. internat. pgms. devel. Hughes Communications Internat., Inc. 1984-89; dir. pgms. development Asia-Pacific, TRW Space & Technology Group, Redondo Beach, Calif. 1990-; cons., mng. dir. E.T. Satellite Assocs. Internat. 1989-; cons. H.I. Thompson Co., L.A. 1958-60, Andrew Corp., Chgo. 1959, Satellite Bdcst. Assocs., L.A. 1982; faculty, Pasadena City Coll. 1958-60; honors: Phi Beta Kappa, Sigma Pi Sigma, award of merit Materials in Design Engring. for design devel. 2 unique kinds of coaxial cable having low losses at over 1000 degrees F. for Mach 3 vehicles 1958-59, Surveyor Test Pilot, Surveyor's Hon. Roll, Aviation Week & Space Technology 1966; mem: Am. Inst. of Aero. & Astro. 1973-(tech. com. Commun. Sys. 1973-76); publs: num. articles. in fields of communications satellites, real- time control and data processing, distributed amplifiers, transmission lines, transistorized telemetering devel. and elect. insulation; mil: 2nd lt. US Army Air Corps 1942-46; rec: amateur radio K6OUW (1939-). Res: 25 Silver Saddle Ln Rolling Hills Estates 90274

PHAM, PHO VAN, lawyer; b. Feb. 23, 1939, Ninh Binh, Vietnam; s. Tan Van and Che Thi P.; edn: Saigon Univ. Faculty of Law 1974; JD w. honors, Western St. Univ. 1986. Career: journalist, ed. Tu Do Daily News, Saigon, Vietnam 1959-71; press attaché Vietnamese Conf. of Labor 1971-73; tchg. asst. Univ. Hue 1973-75; health plan rep. Calif. Health Plan, Los Angeles 1978-81; ins. agent and broker Pho Van Pham Ins. Agency, Westminster 1981-; real estate broker First Home 1986-; atty. 1987-; mem: Vietnamese Cath. Comm. in Orange Diocese (v.p. 1992-), Vietnam Human Rights Watch Inc. (v.p. 1991-), Vietnamese Cath. Overseas Movement (v.p. 1991-), Saigon Students Assn., L.A. Vietnamese Catholics Assn. (gen. secty. 1978-79), Little Saigon Comm. Devel. Orgn.; ed., writer articles and editorials 1964-75; ed. Hiep Nhat (Solidarity) Mag. 1992-; Catholic; rec: tennis, fishing, travel. Ofc: Pho Van Pham 9361 Bolsa Ave Ste 202 Westminster 92683

PHAM, THIEN XUAN, aka **PHAM, DAVID**, real estate broker, accountant, notary public; b. June 13, 1948, Vietnam; nat. U.S. 1984; s. Lai Xuan and Tuyen Thi (Vu) P.; nephew of Mr. Thai Xuan Pham, former Minister of Information of South Vietnam under Pres. Ngo Dinh Diem; m. Linda, July 7, 1984; children: Elizabeth b. 1986, Paul Xuan b. 1990; edn: BS, CSU L.A.; BA, Saigon Univ. Career: library student supr. CSU, L.A. 1980-85; accountant Pham's Income Tax, N. Hollywood 1985-; accountant, real estate broker Pham's Income Tax, My Home Realty, Van Nuys 1986-; mem. Nat. Soc. of Public Accts., Nat. Soc. of Tax Professionals, Am. Inst. of Profl. Bookkeepers, Nat. Notary Assn., San Fernando Board of Realtors; composed 30 pieces of music and lyrics, 1977-80; mil: 1st lt. S. Vietnam Psychological Warfare Dept. 1968-75; Republican; Prot., Vietnamese Evangelical Ch., North Hollywood; rec: music. Res: 22212 Oxford Ln Saugus CA 91350 Ofc: My Home Realty 6900 Van Nuys Blvd Ste 6A Van Nuys CA 91405

PHELPS, DONALD G., college district chancellor; b. July 22, 1929, Seattle; s. Donald G. Phelps and Louise (Gayton) Adams; m. Pamela McGee, July 4, 1981; children: Richard, Michael K., Dawn S.; edn: music major Cornish Sch. of Allied Arts, Seattle, 1948-51; BEd, Seattle Univ., 1959, MEd, 1963; EdD, Univ. Wash., 1983; Harvard Grad. Sch. of Edn. Inst. for Mgmt. of Lifelong Edn., 1987. Career: exec. asst. to Pres. Bellevue (Wash.) Comm. Coll., 1969-72; dir. Nat. Inst. on Alcohol Abuse & Alcoholism, 1972-76; interim supt. Lake Washington Sch. Dist., Seattle 1976-77; dir. exec. adminstrn. King County, Seattle, 1977-80; pres. Seattle Central Comm. Coll., 1980-84; chancellor Seattle Comm. Coll. Dist. VI, 1984-88; chancellor Los Angeles Comm. Colleges, L.A. 1988-; dir: Federal Reserve Bank S.F., L.A. 1991-94; advy. bd. Inst. for Mgmt. of Lifelong Edn. Harvard; awards: Univ. Wash. Alumni Legend 1987, Seattle Post Intelligencer Jefferson Award nom. 1987, pres.'s award Nat. Bus. League Wash. 1988, L.A. Harbor Coll. Faculty award Amicus Collegii, Wilmington, Calif. 1989, Frederick Douglass award Black Fac. Staff Assn. 1989; mem: Comm. Coll. League of Calif., Sacto. (dir.), Am. Assn. of Jr. & Comm. Colls., WDC (Nat. Council on Black Am. Affairs, Commn. on Minorities in Higher Edn.); civic: YMCA (bd.), L.A. Area C.of C. (dir.); contbr. articles in scholarly jours.; mil: s/sgt. US Army 1951-53; Prot.; rec: vocal music, tennis. Ofc: Office of the Chancellor Los Angeles Community Colleges 617 W Seventh St Los Angeles 90017

PHILLIPS, ANITA JUNE, journalist-writer; b. June 9, 1928, Butte, Mont.; d. Louis and Regina (Rubin) Phillips; m. Dec. 18, 1960; 1 son, Lew S. Murez b. 1961; edn: BA, Univ. Mont. 1950. Career: reporter/society ed. Lewistown Daily News, Mont. 1949; copywriter Wm. E. Phillips Co., Los Angeles 1950; asst. ed. New Outlook Mag. 1951; pub. rels. Anita Phillips 1952; asst. ed., ed. Linley Pub. Co. 1953-58; travel writer Eur. and Middle East, L.A. Times 1958-59; Hollywood ed. Vance Pub. Co., (Chgo., Ill.) So. Calif. 1959-76; pub. rels. rep. Gift-Pax Co. Inc. (W. Hempstead, N.Y.) So. Calif. 1970-75; free lance journalist writer 1975-; also owner Darcy Splties. Co. (mail order co.), Manhattan Beach; awards: Quill and Scroll 1945, Theta Sigma Phi 1950, assoc. ed. Mont. Kaimin 1949-50 and The Mountaineer, lit. mag. (1948-50) UM; mem: Western Soc. Bus. Pub., L.A. Press Club, L.A. Pub. Club (employ. Comm. Chmn. 1956-57), Am. Film Inst., Acad. TV Arts and Scis., Univ. Mont. Alumni Assn. (life mem.); Democrat; Jewish; rec: photography, travel. Ofc: 1134 20th St Manhattan Beach 90266

PHILLIPS, GENEVA FICKER, academic editor; b. Aug. 1, 1920, Staunton, Ill.; d. Arthur Edwin and Lillian Agnes (Woods) Ficker; m. James Emerson Phillips, Jr., June 6, 1955 (dec. 1979); edn: BS in journalism, Univ. Ill., 1942; MA in English lit., UCLA, 1953. Career: copy desk Chicago Journal of Commerce, 1942-43; editorial asst. patents Radio Research Lab., Harvard Univ., 1943-45; asst. editor adminstrv. publs. Univ. Ill., Urbana, 1946-47; teaching fellow UCLA, 1950-53, grad. fellow 1954-55, editorial asst. Quarterly of Film, Radio and TV, UCLA, 1952-53; mng. editor The Works of John Dryden, Dept. English, UCLA, 1964-; bd. dirs. Univ. Religious Conf., Los Angeles 1979-; mem: Assn. Acad. Women UCLA, Friends of Huntington Library, Friends of UCLA Library, Renaissance Soc. of Calif., Samuel Johnson Soc. of So. Calif., Associates of Univ. Calif. Press, Conf. Christianity and Literature, Soc. Mayflower Descs.; Lutheran. Res: 213 First Anita Dr Los Angeles 90049 Ofc: UCLA Dept. English 2225 Rolfe Hall Los Angeles 90024

PHILLIPS, GEORGE SCOTT, land developer, home builder, real estate consultant; b. Feb. 28, 1939, Charleroi, Penn.; s. George Francis and Gaynell Pauline (Milliken) P.; m. Rena Louise, Apr. 20, 1985; 1 child Kim b. 1961; edn: BA in geol., UC Berkeley 1961; Cert. in Land Devel. Adminstrn., Golden Gate Univ. 1973; MA bus. adminstrn., Kensington Univ., Glendale 1979, PhD bus. adminstrn., 1980; Calif. State lic. Gen. Building Contractor 1978, Real Estate Broker 1968; SR/WA (Reg. Senior Mem.), Internat. Right of Way Assn. 1970. Career: asst. mgr. Donald D. Davis Constrn. Co., Greenbrae 1960-63; right-of-way agent Calif. Div. Hwys., San Francisco 1963-66; Acquisition and Appraisal Assocs., S.F. 1966-67; dir. R.E. mktg. and bus. devel. San Francisco Redevelopment Agy., 1967-73; v.p., forward planning mgr. Kaufman & Broad, No. Calif., Burlingame 1973-76; dir. planning and devel. Ponderosa Homes, Santa Clara 1976-77; v.p./div. mgr. M.J. Brock & Sons Inc., Dublin 1977-82; pres. Barratt Northern California, Inc., Sacramento 1982-84; pres. Warmington Homes-No. Calif., San Ramon 1985-86; frequent spkr. var. service and profl. groups, 1969-; qualified expert witness on valuation, mktg. and disposition of real estate, Superior Ct. City and County of San Francisco 1970; appt. mem. qualification appraisal panel for selection of Deputy Real Estate Commr. trainees; awards: Housing design award City of Novato 1974, Special appreciation Capitol Area Devel. Auth. 1983; mem. Internat. Right of Way Assn. (exec. com. 1968-71), Theta Tau (Epsilon Chap. Regent 1960) Land Execs. Assn. (pres. No. Calif. 1971); contbr. articles and interviews in New Homes Mag. 1980, Homes for Sale 1981, 82, Homebuyers Guide 1978; mil: seaman USCGR 1961-69, Calif. Wrestling & Track Teams 1961; Republican; Prot.; rec: fitness, collect Egyptian, Asian and Pre-Columbian artifacts, weapons and coins. Res: 3343 Marsh Hawk Ct Pleasanton 94588 Ofc: Davidon Homes 1600 S Main St Ste 150 Walnut Creek 94596

PHILLIPS, JAMES LAWRENCE, financial consultant; b. Aug. 26, 1931, Fresno; s. Sidney Frank and Dorothy Maxine (Puccini) P.; m. Maureen Sullivan, May 11, 1962; children: Daniel, b. 1952; Karen, b. 1957; Kathleen, b. 1959; Denise, b. 1960; Cynthia, b 1960; James, . 1969; edn: AS, Memphis Tech. 1951; BS, CSU Fresno 1957; PhD, in progress, Southwestern Univ. 1984; Life, Disability, NASD 1968; CLU, Mass. Mutual 1958. Career: supvr./brokerage mgr. Mass. Mutual Life Ins. Co. 1957; v.p. G.M. Mazz-Zee Chemical Corp., Fresno ; v.p. Vista Inc. (Mining Op.), Mariposa, 1980; cons. Physicians Funding Svcs. Ltd., Fresno; pres. Digital Concepts Inc.; owner Phillips & Assocs., Fresno; v.p. International Resort Concepts Inc., Phoenix, Az.; pres. Seton Financial Services Inc., Scottsdale, Az.; v.p. Renaisance Pictures Inc., Scottsdale; dir: Mazz-Zee Corp., Maz-Zee S.A., Mex., Anaconda Mining S.A. Mex., Traditional Industries Inc.; honors: Man of Year Mass Mutual Life Ins. Co. 1958, Nat. Top Ten award VAMCO, Detroit; mem: Life Underwriters Assn., Am. Chem. Soc., Downtown Exchange Club (bd.), Sub 20-30 (pres. 1960-61); civic: Prevention of Child Abuse (chmn.), Heart Assn., Boys Club (bd. dirs.), Fresno Nutritional Hour (bd. dirs.), No. Spartan Baseball League (pres.), Gr. Fresno Spartan League (dir.); inventions: Zeron (pat. 1978), Universal Rescue Aid Device (1975); co-pub.: The Pucca Plant - desert magic (1978); rec: Republican; Prot; rec: sports car racing & restoration, coaching youth sports. Res: 13022 N 50th St Scottsdale AZ 85254 Ofc: Phillips & Associates 1025 San Pablo Fresno 93703

PHILLIPS, JOHN RICHARD, engineering professor; b. Jan. 30, 1934, Albany, Calif.; s. Eric Lester and Adele Catherine (Rengel) P.; m. Joan Elizabeth Soyster Mar. 23, 1957; children: Elizabeth b. 1962, Sarah b. 1963, Kate b. 1966; edn: BS, UC Berkeley, 1956; M.Eng., Yale Univ., 1958, D.Eng., 1960; reg. profl. engr. Calif. Career: chemical engr. SRI, Menlo Park 1960; res. engr. Chevron Research Co., Richmond 1962-66; asst., assoc., prof. engring. Harvey Mudd Coll., Claremont 1966-, dir. Engring. Clinic 1977-, James Howard Kindleberger Prof. of Engring. 1991-; founder Claremont Engring. Co., Claremont 1973-; vis. prof. Univ. Edinburgh, Scotland 1975, Cambridge Univ., Eng. 1981, ESIEE, Paris 1981, Naval Postgrad. Sch., Monterey, Calif. 1984-85; Calif. Polytechnic Univ., San Luis Obispo 1992; cons. various cos. and govt. 1966-; mem. Am. Inst. Chem. Engrs.; author 3 US patents, 25+ profl. publs.; mil: 1st lt. US Army 1960-62. Ofc: Harvey Mudd College Dept. Engineering, Claremont 91711

PHILLIPS, LACY DARRYL, creative and performing artist; b. Feb. 24, 1963 Brooklyn, NY; s. William Lacy and Sandra Ann (Reaves) P.; edn: diploma (Regents), Springfield Gardens H.S., Queens, NY, 1980; Herbert H. Lehman Coll., Bronx, NY, 1980-81. Career: tchr./choreographer Queens Coll., Queens, NY, 1980; choreographer Bway Dance Ctr., Tokyo, Japan, 1985-90; asst. to dir Red Bird Productions, L.A., 1988-92; choreographer, Ruthless Records, L.A., 1991; co-dir. Painted Black Productions, L.A., 1991-92; mem: Actors Equity Assn. 1973-, Screen Actors Guild 1978-, AFTRA 1980-, Dancers Alliance 1990-, Soc. of Stage Directors & Choreographers 1991-; song writer/lyricist, Compilation, 1989-; Democrat; Christian; rec: music, writing, singing.

PHILPOTT, DELBERT EUGENE, biologist; b. Sept. 24, 1923, Loyal, Wis.; s. Lacey D. and Nettie A. (Goering) P.; m. Donna A. Naylor, Dec., 1985; edn: BA, Ind. Univ., 1948, MS, 1949; PhD, Boston Univ., 1963. Career: res. assoc. Univ. Ill. Med. Sch., Chgo. 1949-52; hd.electron microscope lab. Inst. Muscle Research, Woods Hole, Mass. 1952-63; asst. prof. biochem. Univ. Colo. Med.

Sch., Denver 1963-66; hd., co-dir. Inst. Biomed. Research, Mercy Hosp. 1966; hd. Electron Microscope Lab., NASA Ames Research Center, Moffett Field 1966-90, sci. coord. Student Space Biology 1974-, chmn. Radiation Safety 1987-; sci. coord. Historically Black Colls. 1989; faculty advisor Delta Coll., Stockton 1982-; awards: PhT (hon.) Coll. Optometry 1976, NASA Apollo Biocore Achievement 1974, Joint U.S./USSR Mission 1976, Cosmos 936 Group Achievement 1978; mem: Nat. Bd. Cert. Electron Microscopists, No. Soc. Electron Microscopists (past. pres., v.p.), Electron Microscope Soc. Am., N.Y. Acad. Scis., Sigma Xi, Exptl. Aircraft Assn. (v.p. 1978); 200+ papers pub. in sci. jours. (1949-), sci. pictures pub. on cover of Jour. Applied Physics, Sci., A.I.B.S. (1951-62); mil: pvt. 1c AUS 1942-45, Bronze Star, Purple Heart; rec: flying, photog. Ofc: NASA Ames Research Center Moffett Field 94035

PIASECKI, JACK O., physician-orthopedic surgeon; b. June 7, 1950, Ontario, Canada, naturalized U.S. cit. 1956; s. Andrew Leon and Christine Anna (Pozniak) P.; m. Tracy Holtzman, May 31, 1980 (div. 1988); edn: BS in biology (magna cum laude), Univ. of Pittsburgh, 1972, MD, 1976; MBA, UC Irvine, 1989. Career: orthopedic surgeon Fronk Clinic, Honolulu 1982-84; chmn. dept. orthopedic surg. Family Health Program, Fountain Valley 1984-88; orthopedic surgeon pvt. practice Jefferson Med. Group, Santa Ana 1988-, staff cons. Charter Hosp. 1986-; supr. of P.A. St. of Calif., Sacto. 1988-; tchg. cons. UC Irvine Grad. Sch. of Mgmt. 1988-; honors: Phi Beta Kappa 1972; mem: New York Co. Med. Soc., Orange Co. Med. Assn., Calif. Med. Soc., Calif. Orthopedic Assn., Calif. Soc. of Indsl. Medicine & Surgery; clubs: Laguna Niguel Racquet, Caribou (Aspen); publs: 3 sci. papers re scoliosis, spinal fusion 1982, 83, 86; Republican; R.Cath.; rec: oil painting, skiing, tennis. Res: 25511 Rue Terrase Laguna Niguel 92677

PICK, GEOFFREY GORDON, printing company president; b. July 23, 1950, Los Angeles; s. Richard O. and Marjrie (Gerrard) P.; m. Janet Rae Lamontagne, June 21, 1970 (div. 1977); m. Helen Colleen Petersen, Oct. 4, 1980; children: Jason b. 1971, Vanessa b. 1982, Denise b. 1984, Brandon b. 1987; edn: BS, CSU Northridge 1973. Career: asst. mgr. Westchester Music Inc., Los Angeles 1967-73; store mgr. Pacific Stereo, Emeryville 1973-76; gen. sales mgr. University Stereo, Culver City 1976-79; v.p. Union Nat. Investment, Beverly Hills 1979-80; pres. Commercial Clear Print, Chatsworth 1981-; dir. sales inst. PIA SC, Commerce 1986-88; recipient outstanding achievement award Printing Industries of Am. 1988; mem: PIA SC (dir 1991-), Chatsworth C.of C., Woodland Hills C.of C.; Ch. of Scientology; rec: fine woodworking, skiing. Ofc: Clear Print 9025 Fullbright Ave Chatsworth 91311

PICKETT, DAVID FRANKLIN, JR., aerospace executive; b. May 3, 1936, Littlefield, Tx.; s. David Franklin and Dottie Ardel (Britton) P.; m. B. Christine Klop, Aug. 21, 1971; edn: BS in chemistry, Univ. Texas, Austin 1962, MA, 1965, PhD, 1970. Career: res. chemist, consulting chemist Am. Magnesium Co., Snyder, Tx. 1969-70, 70-71; chemist USAF Wright Labs., Dayton, Ohio 1970-74, chem. engr. 1975-78; senior staff engr. Hughes Aircraft Co., El Segundo 1978-79, battery sect. hd. 1979-84, asst. dept. mgr. 1984-86, dept. mgr. 1986-90, product line mgr. Hughes Aircraft Co., Torrance 1990-92, program mgr. 1992-; awards: Phi Lambda Upsilon 1965, USAF inventions, Wright Labs. 1972-73, S.D. Heron Award 1975, nom. Fed. employee of yr. Wright Labs. 1975, various awards Hughes Aircraft 1978-92; mem: Electrochemical Soc. 1970-, (councilor So.Cal/Nev sect. 1990-92), am. Chem. Soc. 1962-, AIAA 1977-, Jr. Chamber Snyder, Tx. 1969-70; inventor: Preparation of Nickel Electrodes 1974, Prodn. of Cadmium Electrodes 1975; editor: Proc. of 2d Ann. Battery Conf. on Applications and Advances 1985, author 40+ sci. papers on batteries 1970-91; mil: aviation storekeeper 3c USN 1955-57; Democrat; Baptist; rec: fishing, travel, golf. Res: 4 Hilltop Circle Rancho Palos Verdes 90274-3432 Ofc: Hughes Aircraft Co. 3100 Lomita Blvd, 231/1040, Torrance 90505

PIEROSE, PERRY NICHOLAS, physician; b. Aug. 15, 1910, Butte, Mont.; s. Nicholas Peter and Mary (Brant) P.; m. Elizabeth Bissel Van Wormer, 1938 (dec. Feb. 1990); m. Dorothy Jane Stout, July 14, 1990; children: Anne, b. 1943; Susan, b. 1945; Gale, b. 1954; edn: AB, Stanford Univ. 1933; Asstship., biochem. research, USC Sch. of Med. 1934, faculty mem. USC Sch. of Med. 1939. Career: pvt. practice internal medicine; senior staff St. Vincent Medical Centre, Los Angeles, Pasadena; med. dir. Calif. Portland Cement Co., J.G. Boswell Co.; Doctor of Year honoree St. Vincent Medical Centre, L.A. (10/86); honors: Nu Sigma Nu, Delta Tau Delta Hall of Fame Stanford Univ.; clubs: Stanford, Valley Hunt, (past) Bohemian, S.F. (courtesy mem. WWII), Balboa Bay Club, Newport Beach, Big Canyon Country Club, Newport Beach; mil: capt. USMC WWII 5th armored div. chief surgery, Ft. McDowell Sta. Hosp., S.F. WWII, four med. commendns.; Republican; Prot.; rec: hunting, fly-fishing, gardening, art. Res: 698 La Loma Rd Pasadena 91105 also: 3622 Blue Key Corona del Mar 92625 Ofc: 201 S Alvarado St Los Angeles 90057

PILATO, JOHN J., real estate broker; b. May, 1933, Island of Ischia, Italy, came to U.S. in 1935; s. John J. and Vincenza (Icono) P.; edn: BA, grad. Penna. Military Coll.; children: John J., Jr., Vivian, Theodore, Vincent; m. Diane Louise Stewart, Feb. 18, 1983. Career: worked in family bakery bus. 1959-61; insurance sales agt. Metropolitan Life, 1961-68, field trainer Los Angeles Area, Million

Dollar Round Table; real estate agt. Walker and Lee Real Estate, 4 years, set-up and managed new div. for land sales; reg. v.p. in charge 18 offices Red Carpet Realty, 1974-79; auto salesman to gen. sales mgr. Porsche, Audi, Peugeot Dealership, San Diego Co., 1979-85; gen. sales mgr., Timeshares broker, representing Lawrence Welk Resort Villas (in 3 years built volume to one of ten top U.S. selling Resorts), Escondido 1985-90; internat. consultant dir., Timeshare sales/mktg., Baja, Mexico, 1990-91; v.p. sales/mktg. San Felipe Marina Resort & Spa, Baja, CA. Norte, first resort of its kind in Baja, with R.V. Park, Timeshares, Villas. Mail: c/o Vivian Morfin, 5842 Abbey Dr Westminster 92683

PINES, BURT, lawyer, former city attorney; b. May 16, 1939, Burbank; s. Charles and Ruth (Pines) Landeau; m. Karen, Apr. 9, 1966; children: Adam b. 1969, Ethan b. 1971, Alissa b. 1974; edn: BA, USC, 1960; JD, N.Y. Univ., 1963. Career: asst. U.S. atty. U.S. Dept. of Justice, Los Angeles, 1964-66; atty., assoc. law firm Kadison & Quinn, 1966-67; Schwartzman, Greenberg & Fimberg, 1968-69; ptnr. Pines & Dunn, Beverly Hills, 1970-73; city atty. City of Los Angeles, 1973-81; sr. ptnr. Alschuler, Grossman & Pines, Los Angeles, 1981-; mem. bd. trustees NIMLO, Wash. D.C., 1973-81; appt. Calif. Commn. on Personal Privacy (chmn. 1981-82), L.A. Dept. of Airports Citizens Advy. Com. (chmn. 1985-87), Calif. Coun. on Criminal Justice, L.A. (mem. 1974-81); honors: Phi Beta Kappa 1960, Root-Tilden Scholar, N.Y.U. 1960-63, Order of the Coif 1963, recipient num. civic awards; mem: State Bar of Calif. 1964, Am., L.A. County, Fed. bar assns., Public Counsel/L.A. (dir. 1985-86), Constnl. Rights Found./L.A. (dir. 1975-82); civic: Town Hall, World Affairs Council, L.A. C.of C. Ofc: Alschuler, Grossman & Pines, 1880 Century Park East 12th Flr Los Angeles 90067

PINKERTON, CLAYTON DAVID, artist, professor of fine arts; b. Mar. 6, 1931, San Francisco; s. David B. and Kathryn Irene (Davies) P.; edn: BA edn., Calif. Coll. Arts & Crafts, 1952, MFA, 1953; postgrad. Univ. of N.Mex. (Harwood Found. fellow), Taos, N.M. 1955; Univ. of Paris, Fr. 1958. Career: instr. Richmond Art Center, Richmond, Calif. 1952-62, asst. director and curator 1955-60; prof. fine arts Calif. Coll. Arts & Crafts, Oakland 1958-, dir. grad. div. 1969-72, dir. grad. internship pgm. 1968-78; one-person exhibitions: San Francisco Mus. of Art (1957, 66), Calif. Palace of Legion of Honor, S.F. (1960), M.H. De Young Memorial Mus., S.F. (1961), Univ. of Pacific, Stockton (1989), Am. Cultural Ctr. American Emb., Brussels, Belgium (1991), Michael Himovitz Gallery, Sacto. 1993,; group exh: Mus. of Modern Art, N.Y., Whitney Mus. Am. Art, N.Y., Mus. of Contemp. Art, Chgo., Virginia Mus. Art, Richmond, Va., Boston Mus. of Fine Arts, Triton Mus., San Jose, others; collections: Ill. Bell Tel., Chgo., Macdonald Corp., Calif., Crocker Art Mus., Sacto., M.H. De Young Mem. Mus., S.F., Dennis Hopper, L.A.; awards: James D. Phelan award in painting (1958, 62), Fulbright scholar to France 1958, award in painting Monterey Mus. of Art 1987. Res: PO Box 77 Amador City 95601 Ofc: Calif. College of Arts & Crafts, 5212 Broadway Oakland 94618

PINKHAM, CLARKSON WILFRED, structural engineer; b. Nov. 25, 1919, Los Angeles; s. Walter Hampden and Dorothy Rebecca (Burdorf) P.; m. EmmaLu Hull, May 8, 1942; children: Nancy b. 1942, Timothy b. 1949, Anthony b. 1955; edn: BAS in C.E., UC Berkeley, 1943, BS, 1947; reg. civil and structural engr., Calif., Wash.; reg. struc. engr. Ill., Ariz.; reg. profl. engr. Fla., Ga., Ind., Iowa, Ks., Md., Ore., Tx., Wis. Career: active duty USN 1941-46, retired lt. cmdr. USNR 1954; engr., exec. pres. S.B. Barnes Associates (structural engring. consulting firm), Los Angeles 1947-; mem. Struc. Engrs. Assn. of So. Calif. (pres. 1971, 75, hon. mem. 1984, Stephenson B. Barnes Award for Research 1985, 90), Am. Soc. Civil Engrs. (life, Fellow), Internat. Assn. Bridge and Struc. Engring., Earthquake Engring. Res. Inst., Building Seismic Safety Commn., Am. Concrete Inst. (Fellow, bd. dirs. 1975-78, bldg. code subcom. chmn. on seismic provisions 1983-, Henry L. Kennedy Award 1986), Am. Soc. Testing and Materials, Am. Welding Soc., The Masonry Soc. (charter, bd. 1986-87), Struc. Stability Research Council, Am. Arbitration Assn., Seismol. Soc. Am., Internat. Conf. Building Ofcls., Am. Inst. Steel Constrn. (specs. com.), Inst. for Adv. Engring., Nat. Inst. of Bldg. Scis. (charter mem. consultative council), L.A. Tall Bldg. Struc. Design Council (Pres.'s Award 1989), Am. Iron and Steel Inst. (spec. com. design of cold formed steel struc. members); civic: L.A. Co. Earthquake Commn. 1971-74, Town Hall of Calif., L.A. C.of C. 1957-85; author tech. reports and articles, book chapter "Design Philosophies" in Building Structural Design Handbook (1987); rec: philately, family genealogy. Ofc: S.B. Barnes Associates 2236 Beverly Blvd Los Angeles 90057

PINOLI, BURT ARTHUR, international airlines management executive; b. Nov. 23, 1954, Santa Rosa, Calif.; s. Norris L. and Grace (Williams) P.; m. So Yen, May 9, 1987; 1 son, Lucas b. 1991; edn: BS agri-bus., CSU Fresno; MIM, Am. Grad. Sch. of Internat. Mgmt., Thunderbird, Glendale, Az.; proficient in Mandarin Chinese. Career: loan ofcr., mgmt. trainee Lloyds Bank Calif., Sanger 1979-81; mgr. sales and bus. devel. Transamerica Airlines, Oakland 1981-86; credit analyst, comml. loan ofcr. Farm Credit Bank System, Ukiah 1986-87; city mgr. Northwest Airlines, Shanghai, China; honors: Nat. 4-H Council, nat. winner health proj. 1974, BSA Life award 1973, Blue Key 1978, Alpha Gamma Rho (pres. 1978-79), Alpha Zeta, Internat. Farm Youth Exchange del. to India, AGSIM Asia and China Clubs; Ch. of Jesus Christ of Latter Day Saints. Res: 1551 Boonville Rd Ukiah 95482

PINTAR, JOE, consulting engineer; b. June 5, 1915, McGill, Nev.; s. John M. and Helen Yeka (Bakarich) P.; m. Dorris Berta Driggs, Feb. 23, 1942 (dec. 1985); edn: St. Mary's Coll., Moraga 1936; AA, Pasadena City Coll., 1938; BS, UC Berkeley, 1940; grad. work Cal Tech. Career: mech. engr. So. Western Eng. Co., Los Angeles 1940-41; U.S. Army Ordnance Corp., 1942-45; US Corps of Engrs., Okinawa Dist. 1946-48; marine engr. US Navy, Long Beach 1949-51; dep. dir. facility engring. US Army, Fort Ord 1951-81; consulting engr. prin., Pacific Grove 1981-; awards: gold medal, 40 year service Dept. Army 1981, soc. service ASME, Pacific Grove, Calif. 1980, outstanding service Calif. Soc. Profl. Engrs., Pacific Grove 1981; mem: Fellow Soc. Am. Mil. Engrs. (past pres.), Calif. Soc. Profl. Engrs. (past pres.), ASME (life), Calif. Board Reg. Profl. Engrs. 1948-, Assn. of U.S. Army 1960-, Ft. Ord Fed. Credit Union (pres. 1965-80); civic: Monterey Co. Air Pollution Advy. Com. (chmn. 1970-78), Monterey Regional Water Pollution Control Agcy. 1970-81, Assn. Monterey Bay Area Govts. Tech. Advy. Com. 1970-81; invention: Central Electronics Control System for Heating (1958); 3 tech. articles (1956, 60, 62); Democrat; rec: golf. Address: Pacific Grove 93950

PITCHESS, JOHN PAUL, insurance broker; b. March 21, 1942, Kansas City, Mo.; s. Peter J. and Athena (Takis) P.; m. Wendy M. Marquand, Aug. 28, 1965; children: Peter b. 1967, Julie b. 1969, Kathleen b. 1975; edn: BS, USC 1965; MBA, USC 1967. Career: pres. Pitchess & Perricone Ins., Newport Beach 1973-83; pres. Pitchess Ins. Assoc. 1983-; mem. Western Assn. Ins. Brokers, S.F. and L.A. 1980-88; bd. mem., rep. Profl. Ins. Agents of Calif. 1983-88; civic: Newport Harbor C.of C. (dir. 1976-83), Vikings of Orange Co.; club: Balboa Bay; Republican; rec: golf, tennis, soccer coaching. Res: 4 Corona Irvine 92715 Ofc: Pitchess Insurance Associates 1601 Dove St #220 Newport Beach 92660

PLATZKER, ARNOLD C.G., physician, professor of pediatrics; b. Aug. 26, 1936, N.Y.C.; s. Irving Golembe and Faye (Cassin) P.; m. Marjorie A. Sanek, June 9, 1963; children: David I. b. 1965, Elizabeth F.; edn: AB (honors in biology), Brown Univ., 1958; MD, Tufts Univ., 1962; med. lic. Mass. 1963, Calif. 1964. Career: asst. prof. pediatrics Univ. Calif. San Francisco 1971-73; asst. prof. pediatrics USC Sch. of Medicine, L.A. 1973-78, assoc. prof. 1979-85, prof. 1986-; head div. neonatology/ pulmonology Childrens, L.A. 1973-; bd. dir. University Childrens Med. Group, 1982-; exec. com. 1982-86, pres. 1982-86; steering com. and exec. com. NHLBI Study of Pediatric Pulmonary and Cardiac Complications of Vertically Transmitted HIV Infection (chair Pulmonary Subcom. 1989-); cons. state agys. and hosps.; awards: life mem. Clare Hall, Cambridge Univ., U.K. 1986; mem: We. Soc. for Pediatric Res. 1973-, Calif. Thoracic Soc. 1972-, L.A. Pediatric Soc., Calif. Perinatal Assn. (1977-, pres. 1978-79), Am. Lung Assn. of L.A. Co. (bd. 1988-93, exec. com. 1992-93), Am. Lung Assn. of Calif. (bd. 1990-), Am. Acad. of Pediatrics (Fellow 1973-, fetus and newborn com. 1973-, chmn. 75-78), Am. Coll. Chest Physicians (Fellow 1974-), Am. Thoracic Soc. (1971-93, com. health care policy and tech.1987-92, long range plng. com. 85-89, com. ped. pulmonology manpower 85-89), AAAS, NY Acad. Scis., Soc. for Critical Care Medicine, AAUP, Royal Soc. of Medicine, UK 1986-, European Respiratory Soc. 1991-; author 70+ peer reviewed articles, book chapters; mil: lcdr USNR 1966-68; Democrat; Jewish; rec: swimming, photography. Ofc: Childrens Hospital 4650 Sunset Blvd Box 83 Los Angeles 90027

PLESTED, WILLIAM GORDON, III, thoracic and cardiovascular surgeon, state medical association president; b. June 1, 1936, Wichita, Kans.; s. Wm. Gordon, II and Flora Estella (Lonergan) P.; m. Carolyn Martin, 1980; children: Tamara Lynn, Stephanie Pamela, Wm. G. IV, Andrea MacKenzie, Scott Lonergan; edn: BA, Univ. Colo., 1958; MD, Univ. Kans. Med. Sch., 1962; cert. Am. Bd. Surgery 1969, Am. Bd. Thoracic Surgery 1970. Career: surgical intern, resident UC Los Angeles, 1962-63, 63-67, instr. in residence 1967-68, adj. asst. prof. 1968-74, asst. clin. prof. 1974-; sect. chief gen. surgery Wadsworth V.A. Hosp., Los Angeles 1968-71, asst. chief thoracic surgery 1968-74, attdg. cons. 1974-; sr. staff surgeon Santa Monica Hosp. Med. Ctr. 1971-, St. John's Hosp. & Hlth. Ctr. 1971-; gubnat. appt. Med. Quality Assur. Bd. Calif. 1978-80; honors: Nat. Honor Soc. 1953, Alpha Epsilon Delta 1957, Phi Sigma 1958; mem. bd. trustees Calif. Assn. of Hosps. and Health Systems 1988-89; ex-officio bd. trustees Audio-Digest Found., Glendale 1986-89; corp. mem. Blue Shield of Calif. 1986-87, bd. trustees 1987-; mem: Longmire Soc., Bay Surgical Soc., W. Thoracic Surgical Assn., Soc. Clin. Vascular Surgery, Soc. of Thoracic Surgeons, Am. Coll. Surgeons (fellow, mem. So. Calif. com. on applicants), Am. Coll. Chest Physicians (fellow), AMA (del.), CMA (pres. 1988-89), LA Co. Med. Assn. (pres. 1984-85, bd. trustees 1981-, chmn. 1987-88, PAC), Flying Physicians Assn., Aesculapian Soc.; contbr. num. articles to med. jours.; frequent speaker med. assns. and writer med. assn. mag. editorials; rec: fishing, hunting, flying. Ofc: Thoracic and Cardiovascular Specialists Medical Group AMC 1260 15th St Ste 913 Santa Monica 90404

PLUSKAT, THOMAS J., real estate property manager; b. Aug. 17, 1951, Sheboygan, Wis.; s. Edwin C. and Virginia P.; m. Rosemary T., Apr. 8, 1978; children: David b. 1981, Suzanne b. 1984; edn: BS nuclear engring., Univ. Wis. Madison 1973; DBA, Pacific Western Univ. 1987; real estate cert. Fullerton Coll.; reg. profl. engr. Calif., lic. gen. contractor Calif., lic. real estate salesman

Calif. Career: cons. Bechtel Corp., Norwalk 1973-79; prin., CEO Innovative Dynamics, Lakewood 1975-; mem: Tau Beta Pi, Phi Eta Sigma; author: Real Estate To a Better Future & Fin. Independence, 1986; Republican; rec: woodworking, hiking, bicycling. Ofc: Innovative Dynamics Co PO Box 4474 Lakewood 90711

PLUTCHAK, NOEL BERNARD, consulting co. executive/scientist; b. Dec. 14, 1932, Green Bay, Wisc.; s. Bernard Edward and Violet Marie (Sherman) P.; m. Sandra Kolvig (div.); 1 child, Channin P. b. 1969; edn: BS geology, Univ. Wisc., 1960; MS meteorology, Fla. State Univ., 1964. Career: research asst. Columbia Univ., Lamont Inst., 1963-65; hd. theortical studies Bendix - Marine Advisers, La Jolla 1965-69; research assoc. Univ. So. Calif., 1972-75; chief scientist Interstate Electronics Ocean Eng. Div., Anaheim 1975-83; chief scientist Raytheon Services Corp. Ocean Engring. Div., Ventura 1984-87; pres./c.e.o./chief scientist Active Leak Testing, Inc. San Pedro 1985-; mem: Am. Geophysical Union 1960-, Marine Technology Soc. 1968-, Am. Chem. Soc. 1990-, Am. Mgmt. Assn. 1972-, Exptl. Aircraft Assn. 1985-; patentee (2, 1960s); contbr. 40+ jour. articles, reports and papers; mil: sgt. USAF 1952-56; Republican; Prot.; rec: soaring, wind surfing. Res: 1120 W 27th St Los Angeles 90007

PLUTSCHOW, HERBERT EUGEN, cultural historian, educator, author; b. Sept. 8, 1939, Zurich, Switzerland; s. Eugen Franz and Martha (Geiger) P.; m. Yoshiko Kogure, Apr. 5, 1966; children: Patrick b. 1968, Nickolas b. 1971; edn: dipl. Univ. of Paris, Fr. 1962; MA, Waseda Univ., Tokyo 1966; PhD, Columbia Univ., 1973. Career: asst. prof. Univ. of Ill., Urbana, Ill. 1971-73; asst., assoc., prof. of Japanese literature and cultural history, UCLA, Los Angeles 1973-78, 78-86, 86-; dept. chair East Asian Studies, 1983-; named hon. citizen of Hakodate, Japan 1991; mem. Internat. House of Japan 1988-; author: Historical Kyoto 1986, Historical Nagasaki 1988, Four Japanese Travel Diaries of the Middle Ages 1986, Chaos and Cosmos 1990, others. Ofc: UCLA, 405 Hilgard Ave Los Angeles 90024

POER, EDGAR CALVIN, real estate agent; b. Dec. 15, 1923, Denver, Colo.; s. Edgar C., Sr. and Augusta Frances (Brock) P.; m. Mildred Irene, Sept. 11, 1989; edn: AA, City Coll. of San Francisco 1956; stu. San Franciso St. Univ. 1956, Sonoma St. Univ. 1966; Calif. lic. real estate salesman 1957. Career: real estate salesman Bill Greer Realty, San Francisco 1957-59, Coronet Realty, S.F. 1961-64, Strout Realty, Santa Rosa 1964-65, Gehrke Realty, Santa Rosa 1965-67, self empl. in real estate field, 1967-; mem: S.F. Bd. of Realtors 1963, Sonoma Co. Bd. Realtors (past mem. Legislative Com.); past mem. Sonoma County Planning. and Zoning Commn.; mem. Rose Soc. of Sonoma Co.; Democrat; Mormon; rec: stockmarket, swim, rosarian. Res: 1634 Ronne Dr Santa Rosa 95404

POGGIONE, WILLIAM JOSEPH, law professor; b. May 7, 1935, Glendale; s. Joseph Frank and Una Etta Lee (Marshall) P.; m. Joan Ireland; children: Pamela b. 1955, Lorraine b. 1960, William M. b. 1962; edn: JD, Southwestern Univ., 1970; BA, Univ. Redlands, 1977; MPA, Univ. La Verne, 1980; PhD pub. adminstrn., Pacific Western, 1986. Career: legal advisor and Capt. of Detectives Los Angeles Co. Sheriff, 1957-88; commr. Inmate Welfare Commn., Los Angeles 1988-91; prof. of law Mt. San Antonio Coll., Walnut 1972-80, Kensington Univ., Glendale 1987-, Univ. of La Verne 1977-, Univ. of Redlands 1983-; honors: Red Cross Medal Govt. of Japan, Tokyo 1972, diploma of honor Phi Kappa Phi 1981, diploma of honor Pepperdine Univ. 1984, diploma of honor Pi Epsilon Tau 1985, Hon. PhD in polit. sci. & Hon. PhD pub. adminstrn. Clayton Univ., Clayton, Mo. 1986, disting. service US Air Force 1986, Hon. Dr. Pub. Adminstrn. Kensington Univ., Glendale, Calif. 1986, Hon. LLD Pacific States Univ., L.A. 1986, Royal Pouch Medal Kingdom of Thailand 1987, elected Internat. Hall of Fame, L.A. 1987, disting. service Govt. of Honduras 1988, Order of the White Elephant Kingdom of Thailand 1989; mem. FBI Acad. Assocs.; lodge: Al Malaikah Temple, Peace Ofcrs. Shrine; 1st lt. USAR 1954-62; Republican; rec: golf, Western history, British mil. history.

POHL, JOHN HENNING, engineering consultant; b. May 29, 1944, Fort Riley, Kans.; s. Herbert Otto and Ellen Irene (Henning) P.; m/ Judith Lynn Sykes, Aug. 10, 1968; children: J. Otto b. 1970, Clint b. 1975; edn: AA, Sacto. City Coll., 1964; BS, UC Berkeley, 1966; SM, M.I.T., 1973, ScD, 1976. Career: inspr. dam constrn. C.O. Henning Const. Engrs., Sacramento 1965; engr. E.I. du Pont Nemours, Wilmington, Dela. 1966-71; res. asst. M.I.T., Cambridge 1971-75; lectr. 1975-76; mem. tech. staff Sandia Nat. Labs., Livermore, Calif. 1976-81; dir. fossil fuels Energy & Environmental Res., Irvine 1981-86; dir. res. & devel. Energy Systems Assocs., Tustin 1986-89; sr. scientist energy W.T. Schafer Assocs., Irvine 1989-91; pres. Green Burner Co., Laguna Hills 1991; prin. Energy Internat., Laguna Hills 1988-; awards: technology achievement US EPA, Raleigh, N.C. 1987, best energy project Energy Com. Taiwan, R.O.C. 1989, 92; mem: Combustion Inst. (pgm. subcom. 1978-, exec. com. Western States sect. 1986-), ASME (advisor corrosion and deposits combust. gasses 1989-), Am. Inst. Chem. Engrs. (combustion advisor 1988-), Engring. Found. (steering com. ash deposition 1989-); civic: Headstart, Cambridge, Mass. (treas. 1975-76); author 65+ tech. publs. 1972-, inventor (num. pats. 1987-). Res: 26632 Cortina Mission Viejo 92691 Ofc: Energy International 27075 Cabot Rd Ste 114 Laguna Hills 92653

POINDEXTER, WILLIAM MERSEREAU, lawyer; b. June 16, 1925, Los Angeles; s. Robert Wade and Irene (Mersereau) P.; m. Cynthia Converse Pastushin, Nov. 10, 1979; children: James Wade b. 1952, David Graham b. 1954; edn: BA, Yale Univ., 1946; postgrad. Univ. Chicago, 1946-47; LLB, Boalt Hall UC Berkeley, 1949; admitted bar: Calif. 1952. Career: pres. Consolidated Brazing, Riverside 1949-52; atty. Bledsoe, Smith, et al, San Francisco 1952-54; Robertson & Poindexter, L.A. 1954; atty., ptnr. Poindexter & Doutre', Inc., Los Angeles 1964-; dir. Trio Metal Stampings, 1965-80; secty. Production Aids, Inc. 1969-78; secty. MOB, EPD Industries, 1969-72; mem: American Coll. Trust & Estate Counsel (Fellow), Calif. Bar Assn., L.A. Co. Bar Assn., Conf. of Insurance Counsel (pres. 1975); civic: San Marino School Board (1965-69, pres. 67), S.Pasadena-San Marino YMCA (1960-65, pres. 63); publs: Tax Notes, L.A. Bar Jour.; Calif. Cont. Edn. Practice Book Calif.: Non-Profit Corporations; mil: USMCR 1943; Republican; Presbyterian; rec: fishing. Res: 1825 Braemar Rd Pasadena 91103 Ofc: Poindexter & Doutre', Inc. 624 S Grand Ave Ste 2420 Los Angeles 90017

POLLACK, ALAN MYRON, physician; b. Feb. 16, 1958, N.Y.C.; s. Samuel and Jean Anna (Friedman) P.; edn: BS in biochemistry, UCLA, 1979; MD, Univ. Texas, Southwestern, Dallas 1983. Career: resident physician Cedars-Sinai Med. Ctr., L.A. 1983-86; staff physician Kaiser Permanente, Panorama City 1986-; honors: Phi Beta Kappa 1979, Alpha Omega Alpha 1982; civic: Concern II, L.A., Lincoln County (N.M.) Heritage Trust; Jewish; rec: collect rare books & documents from Old West, guitar. Ofc: Kaiser Permanente 13652 Cantara St, NS3, Module 4, Panorama City 91402

POLLAK, NORMAN L., certified public accountant; b. Aug. 16, 1931, Chgo.; s. Emery and Helen (Solomon) P.; m. Barbara Zeff, Aug. 21, 1955 (div. 1980); m. Jean Lambert, Sept. 21, 1986 (div. 1991); children: Martin Joel, Elise Susan McNeal, Rhonda Louise; edn: Valedictorian: Hyde Park H.S., Chgo., 1949; BS (Delta Mu Delta), Sch. of Commerce, Northwestern Univ., 1955; C.P.A., R.E. lic., Calif. Career: sr. acct. two C.P.A. firms, 1951-58; public acctg. practice 1958-86, semi-ret.; C.P.A./ fin. and mgmt. cons., pres. Norman L. Pollak Acctncy. Corp., Westlake Village; expert witness on dissolution matters; frequent lectr. profl. orgns.; dir. AmeriVox (div. World Telecom Group); mem: Am. Inst. CPAs, Calif. Soc. CPAs (S.F.V. Tech. Discussions Group chmn. 1960-61), Nat. Assn. Accts., Am. Acctg. Assn., Valley Estate Planning Council (charter, pres. 1964-65), Northwestern Univ. Alumni Club, Westlake Village C.of C., Optimist Club (chmn. Comm. Contest for Hearing Impaired), Conejo Future Found., Oak Forest HOA; past mem. Ventura Co. Estate Planning Council (pres. 1975-78, 78-79), Conejo C.of C., Internat. Assn. Fin. Planners, Com. to elect Sybil Nisenholz City Council Westlake Village (treas.), coach Braille Olympics for Blind, chmn. Emergency Com. for Disaster Preparedness Oak Forest Mobile Estates Assn., dir. Honokowai Palms Homeowners Assn., Kailua -Kona, HI; Guardians of L.A., Westlake Cultural Found. (trustee), Sponsor Code 3 for Homeless Children 1993; publs: article in Conejo Mag. (Nov-Dec 82), biog. listings Who's Who in West, Who's Who in World, Who's Who in Fin. & Ind., Community Leaders of Am., Men of Achiev., Two Thousand Men of Achiev., Dict. of Internat. Biography; Address: 143 Sherwood Dr Westlake Village 91361

POLLOCK, RICHARD EDWIN, real estate investor, retired county official; b. Aug. 27, 1928, Phila.; s. Ernest Edwin and Evelyn Marie (Scarlett) P.; m. Yvonne May Graves, Oct. 11, 1952 (div. Aug. 1989); children: Colleen May, Karen Marie, Richard Irvin, Annette Yvonne, Mary Ann; edn: Armstrong Coll., 1947; UC Berkeley, 1949-51, 55; BA (Recreation), San Jose State Univ., 1961; postgrad. San Fernando Valley State Univ., 1969-70, UC Davis, 1963-77, UCLA, 1964, UC Santa Barbara, 1970, Univ. Redlands, 1979; Calif. Comm. Colls. instr. cred., Calif. Std. tchg. creds. elem., sec.; reg. recreator and park mgr.; lic. comml. aircraft pilot 1974-. Career: swim pool mgr./instr. Berkeley Tennis Club, 1955-56; police ofcr. City of Berkeley, 1956; recreation and aquatic supr. Pleasant Hills Rec. & Park Dist., 1956-62; gen. mgr. Pleasant Valley Rec. & Park Dist., Camarillo 1962-68; bldg. insp. Ventura Co. 1969-71; adminstr. Sacramento Co.-Carmichael Rec. & Park Dist., 1971-73; dir. parks and recreation Imperial Co. 1973-81, ret.; faculty Imperial Valley Jr. Coll. 1974-; aquatic cons., 1957-; real estate investor, 1984-; magician, 1944-; hypnotherapist, 1988-; chmn. S.F. Bay Area Conf. for Cooperation in Aquatics, 1958-59; honors: Am. Red Cross recognition for 50 years volunteer svs. (1989); civic: Boy Scouts Am. Desert Trails Council (advr., scoutmaster), Am. Red Cross (bd., instr.), work with devel. disabled and handicapped children and adults; mem: Calif. Nat. Rec. and Park Assn., AAHPER, Calif. Park and Rec. Soc., Calif. Co. Dirs. Parks and Rec. Assn., Calif. Boating Safety Officers Assn., Aircraft Owners and Pilots Assn., Nat. Assn. Emergency Med. Technicians; publs: Bibliography: A Pool of Aquatic Sources, 1960; mil: lt. US Army, Korea 1951-55; Democrat. Address: PO Box 3011 El Centro 92244

POLLYEA, CHARLES JAMES, shopping center developer; b. Dec. 11, 1942, Chgo.; s. Samuel S. and Miriam (Oiring) P.; edn: JD, Chicago-Kent Coll. of Law, 1965; admitted bar: Ill., Calif. Career: pvt. practice law until 1967; proj. mgr., treas., gen. counsel, dir. mgmt., v.p., COO Irmco Corp. (mid-western comml. real estate firm), 1967-73; pres. Arthur Rubloff & Co. of Calif. (comml.

and indsl. real estate brokerage & mgmt.) 1973-74; prin. Charles J. Pollyea & Assocs. (mgmt., leasing, brokerage and counselling org.); bd. chmn. Crossroads Devel. Corp. (r.e. devel., acquisition, leasing, mgmt. shopping ctrs. in Calif.); rec: bicycling, contemporary art. Res: 1427 Summitridge Dr Beverly Hills 90210 Ofc: Crossroads Development Corp. 445 S Beverly Dr Beverly Hills 90212

POLYAKOV, OLEG PAUL, company president; b. July 20, 1958, Kiev, USSR; nat. 1978; s. Granit Victor and Maria (Kenigsberg) P.; m. Angela, Aug. 19, 1979; children: Stephanie b. 1983, Daniel b. 1988; edn: BS, Grossmont Coll.; BS, CSU Los Angeles Career: photog. Custom Picture, S.D. 1979-81; customer rels. Sumitomo Bank, Los Angeles 1981-82; mgr. Standard Shoes 1982; v.p. Transam. Stamps Ltd. 1982-84; gen. mgr. MLK Inc. 1984-86; owner, pres., Pals Inc., Van Nuys 1986-; tchr. Grossmont Coll., S.D. 1979-81; honors: L.A. Olympics translator 1983-84; mem: ASDA, CTBA, Van Nuys C.of C.; articles pub., contbr. jours. and newspapers, poster designer; Republican; rec: philately, oceanography, mountaineering. Ofc: Pals 14915 Oxnard St Van Nuys 91411

POONAWALA, ISMAIL KURBANHUSEIN, educator, author; b. Jan. 7, 1937, Godhra, Gujarat, India, naturalized U.S. 1981; s. Kurbanhusein Fidahusein and Sakina (Sakina) P.; m. Oumayma H. Ali-Ahmad, Jan. 6, 1981; children: Qays b. 1989. edn: BA, Bombay Univ., 1959; MA, Cairo Univ., 1964; PhD, UCLA, 1968. Career: asst. prof. McGill Univ., Montreal, Can. 1968-71; research assoc. Harvard Univ., 1971-74; prof. of Arabic, UCLA, 1974-; author: Al-Sultan al-Khattab (1967), Al-Urjuza al-Mukhtara (1971), Bibliography of Ismaili Literature (1977), History of al-Tabari, vol. ix (1990); Muslim. Res: 28749 Covecrest Dr Rancho Palos Verdes 90274 Ofc: Dept. Near Eastern Languages and Cultures UCLA, 405 Hilgard Ave Los Angeles 90024

POPKOFF, BURTON R., lawyer; b. Nov. 14, 1942, Chicago, Ill.; s. Paul and Lillian P.; m. Janet S. Sires, Oct. 28, 1962; children: Lisa b. 1963, Hillary b. 1966; edn: BS, UCLA 1963; JD cum laude, Southwestern Univ. 1970; C.P.A. Calif. 1965; admitted Bar: Calif. 1971, U.S. Supreme Ct. 1988. Career: C.P.A. Miller & Co., Los Angeles 1963-65; controller Markab Mgmt. Assn., Beverly Hills 1965-69; ptnr. Miller Handzel & Co., Encino 1969-71; atty. sole practice, Los Angeles 1971-86; sr. ptnr., atty. Popkoff & Stern 1986-; prof. of law Golden West Univ., Los Angeles 1979-81; referee hearing dept. St. Bar Ct. 1981-89; dir. Miller Fluid Heads USA 1986-, Urethane Service Inc., Torrance 1974-, Tele-Talent Inc., Hollywood 1981-; awards: Southwestern Univ. Am. Jurisprudence 1966-69; mem: Childrens World (life), Am. Assn. Atty-C.P.A., Calif. Soc. Atty.-C.P.A., L.A. Co. Bar Assn., Am. Bar Assn., So. Calif. Council of Elder Attys. (charter mem., dir. 1992-), Wilshire Bar Assn., Desert Bar Assn., No. Hills Jaycees (secty. 1976-78), Police Aux. League (dir. 1981-82), Buhai Ctr. for Family Law (dir. 1992-). Ofc: Popkoff & Stern 3550 Wilshire Blvd Ste 1518 Los Angeles 90010 and 225 So. Civic Dr. Ste 212 Palm Springs 92262

PORTER, BARRY ALAN, investment banker; b. July 30, 1957, New York, N.Y.; s. Jerome and Barbara (Wescourt) P.; edn: BS in econ.(summa cum laude), Wharton School of Bus., Univ. Penn. 1979; JD, Boalt Hall School of Law, UC Berkeley 1983; MBA, UC Berkeley 1983. Career: atty. Wyman Bautzer Kuchel & Silbert, Los Angeles 1983-86; managing dir. Bear, Stearns & Co. Inc., Los Angeles 1986-; mem: State Bar of Calif., Am. Bar Assn., Beverly Hills Bar Assn. Ofc: Bear, Stearns & Co. Inc. 1999 Avenue of the Stars Los Angeles 90067

PORTER, EDWIN CLOYD, retired military officer; b. Oct. 8, 1917, Logansport, Ind.; s. Cloyd and Lena Mae (Hinkle) P.; m. Dorothy Ross, Dec. 28, 1940; children: Frederick b. 1941, Timothy b. 1943, Edwin, Jr. b. 1953, Susan b. 1954, Kathleen b. 1959, Deborah b. 1960; edn: diploma, Loganport H.S., 1935; BS, Univ. Minn., 1941; MS, DePaul Univ., 1960; USAF Command Staff Coll., 1967, USAF Air Univ., Montgomery, Ala. 1968, Air War Coll., 1969. Career: served to Col. (Ret.) US Air Force 1942-78; organized and activated 1st Nat. Guard Unit in Logansport, Ind., 38th Inf. Div., Hq. Bn. 293rd Inf. Regt. 1948; dir. USAF Reserve, State of Ill., 1970-79; field rep. Social Security Adminstrn., Kokomo, Ind. 1945-56, dist. mgr., Muncie, Ind. 1952-66, East St. Louis, Ill. 1966-67, Chgo., Ill. 1967-79; high school tchr. and substitute coach, Muncie, 1956-66, Downers Grove, 1964-78; honors: mem. Logansport, Ind. High Sch. State Basketball Champions 1934, Univ. Minnesota Nat. Champion Football Team 1940, 1941; mem: Nat. Assn. Ret. Fed. (pres. 1982-86), Reserve Ofcrs. Assn. (life mem.), The Retired Ofcrs. Assn. (chpt. pres. 1991-92, life mem.); civic: Masons, Rotary, Scottish Rite, Shrine, Elks, Kiwanis, 40/8, Am. Legion; white paper Social Security "Why" 1980; mil. decorations: Unit Citation, Explosive Ordnance Disposal Comdr. Combat Inf. badge, Army commendation AF commendation US Def. medal, Asiatic Theater, ETO, Am. Theater, Victory medal, Reserve medal Army and AF, Good Conduct w/3 clusters, AF Good Conduct w/2 clusters; Presbyterian; rec: swimming, sports. Res: 20397 Eyota Ln Apple Valley 92308

POSSNACK, JUDITH ANNE, psychotherapist; b. Aug. 26, 1939, Albion, Nebr.; d. Bruce Arnold and Helen Lavonne Kunkel; m. David Possnack, Aug. 16, 1987; children by prev. marriage (nee Vanderpool): Jeffrey Scott b. 1958, Douglas Brent b. 1960, Kimberly Joy Adair b. 1961; 9 grandchildren; edn: AA, Cypress Comm. Coll., 1979; BA in bus. mgmt., Univ. Redlands, 1986; MA marriage, family therapy, Azusa Pacific Univ., 1988; Calif. lic. Marriage Family Therapist 1988. Career: dep., sgt. L.A. County Sheriff's Dept., 1963-80; internal investigator Safeway Markets, 1981-84; ins. fraud investigator Insurance Crime Prevention Inst., 1984-86; instr. Long Beach City Coll., 1986-88; marriage, family, individual therapist in pvt. pract. 1988-; instr. Leadership Training Inst., Crystal Cathedral; profl. speaker var. coll., community and church groups on: Communicating & Relating, Self-Esteem, Healing of Memories, Self Defense for Women, others; awards: numerous media appearances radio, TV, and print, honors relating to law enforcement 1967-79, Speakers awards various civic and comm. groups, L.A. Co. Bar Assn., Youth Forum 1971; mem: Am. Assn. for Counseling & Devel., Assn. for Psychological Type (bd. 1986-), Assistance League for Bus. & Profl. Women, Executive Women's Club, Alumni Assn. Univ. Redlands, Rep. Women's Club; Republican; Crystal Cathedral Garden Grove; rec: travel, camping, weekends in Baja, Calif., volunteer work. Res: 6022 Marilyn Dr Cypress 90630 Ofc: 3532 Katella Ste 210 Los Alamitos 90720 Tel 714/ 952-7883

POWERS, DIANE ELIZABETH, artist, designer, owner international shops and restaurants complex; b. July 8, 1942, Los Angeles; d. Jack and Virginia Gruss; m. Robert Sibley Powers, Oct. 10, 1964; edn: BA fine arts (honors), San Diego State Univ., 1964. Career: interior designer, owner/opr. Design Center Inc. (int. design bus. and showroom), San Diego 1968-; owner/opr. Bazaar del Mundo (16 retail internat. shops, 4 restaurants), S.D. 1971-; instr. craft and clothing classes at Bazaar del Mundo; guest lectr. on int. design and color San Diego St. Univ., UCSD, Cal Western Univ., Grossmont Union H.S., other schs. and ladies clubs; collect and exhibit crafts of China, India, Morocco, Mexico, Guatamala, and Peru; exhibits of personal art works as well as internat. collection: Fine Arts Gal. S.D., Southwestern Coll., Cal Western Internat. Univ., SDSU Gal., Spanish Village Gal., Mingei Internat. Mus. World Folk Art; awards: Disting. Alumna Coll. of Profl. Studies & Fine Arts SDSU 1982, orchid award A.I.A. for creation of one of most beautiful San Diego environments - Bazaar del Mundo 1979, outstanding San Diegan Pacific Tel. Co. 1983, San Diego Woman of Achiev. L.W.V. 1988; civic: Festival of the Arts (past pres.), S.D. Conv. & Vis. Bur., S.D./ Calif./ Nat. Restaurant Assn., San Diego C.of C., S.D. Old Town C.of C., SDSU Art Council Advy. Bd., S.D. Parking & Plng. Commn., Design Counsel SDSU, Nat. Wildlife Fedn., Mingei Internat. Mus. of World Folk Art, Crafts & Folk Art Mus., S.D. Mus. of Art, S.D. Mus. of Man, Am. Crafts Council, SDSU Alumni & Assoc. Univ. Club, S.D. Hist. Soc., The Fashion Group Inc., Old Town Task Force, Pub. Arts Advy. Council; rec: fashion and craft design, collect folk art and fine crafts, travel, landscaping, equestrian. Ofc: 2754 Calhoun St 92110

PRADA, ALFREDO, computer systems consultant; b. July 20, 1933, Bogota, Colombia, nat. 1985; s. Alfredo and Mercedes (Pulido) P.; m. Maria Elena Pulido, June 30, 1973; children: Constanza, b. 1961, Claudia, b. 1961, Alfredo M., b. 1963, Estella, b. 1966; edn: BSEE, Univ. of Tex. 1958; BSIE, Univ. of Mich. 1961; lic. Indsl. Engr. 1964, Elec. Engr. 1964, Colombia. Career: systems analyst and pgmr. Exxon, Colombia 1959-62; univ. program coordinator, IBM, Colombia 1962-64; systems and pgmg. mgr. Ecopetrol, Colombia 1962-68; systems gen. mgr. Colgate Palmolive, Central Am. 1968-71; ops. res. dept. head Ecopetrol, Colombia 1971-75; ops. res. staff splst. A.G. McKee, Cleveland, Oh. 1975-78; systems cons. Computer Scis. Corp., El Segundo 1978-82; prin./pres. Omni Systems Consultants, Lomita 1982-; coll. lectr. sev. univs. in Bogota, Col. 1961-74; awards: Good Neighbour Scholar, Univ. of Tex. 1956-58, Orgn. of Am. States (OAS) Scholar, Univ. of Mich. 1960-1; past mem. AIEE, ACM; publs: profl. conf. proceedings 1967, 69, 72; series of articles in Software News, 5/11/83; rec: x-country, swimming. Address: Omni Systems Consultants, 1981 Mt. Shasta Dr. San Pedro 90732

PRAG, ARTHUR BARRY, physicist; b. Apr. 14, 1938, Portland, Oregon; s. Arthur Edwin and Margaret (Twombly) P.; m. Mary Ann Tomaschko, Aug. 14, 1986; 1 son, Patrick b. 1961; edn: BS physics (maxima cum laude), Univ. Portland, 1959; MS physics, Univ. Wash., Seattle 1962, PhD, 1964. Career: mem. tech. staff The Aerospace Corp., L.A. 1964-69; staff scientist 1969-75, res. scientist 1975-; awards: Sigma Xi 1960-, NSF co-op fellowshop 1960-61; mem: Am. Physical Soc. 1961-, Am. Geophysical Union 1965-, AAAS 1965-, NY Acad. Scis. 1978-; publs: sci. res. papers in profl. jours. 1961-; R.Cath.; rec: computer pgmg. Res: 17357 Hartland St Van Nuys 91406-4416 Ofc: The Aerospace Corp. PO Box 92957 MS M2/256 Los Angeles 90009-2957

PRATT, JANEEN ROMINE, marketing, community, public relations, graphics publications executive; b. Jan. 22, 1948, San Francisco; d. Sidney Abbott and Miriam Georgia (Morgan) Smith; m. James Homer Pratt, III, Sept. 22, 1984; children: Bruce b. 1967, Raymon b. 1969, Michelle b. 1971, Sarah b. 1973; edn: San Jose St. Univ. 1970. Career: drafter Pacific Bell, San Jose 1966-69; secty., sales 1970-75; secty., drafter Microwave Assoc., Sunnyvale 1975-76; tech. illustrator Aydin Energy, Palo Alto and Sunnyvale 1976-78; tech. sales, advtg., word processing, editing, supr. Litton Applied Tech., San Jose and Sunnyvale 1978-90; adminstr. Berg Senior Services, Concord 1990; marketing/comm. relations dir. "The Family Affair" 1990-; honors: West Valley Dean's List 1969, Campbell H.S. Hon. Soc. 1964-66, U.S. Savings Bonds patri-

otism award 1987-89, ATD Suggestion Award 1988; mem: NCGA, NAFE, ATDFCU (publicity chair 1987-); Prot.; rec: painting, computer graphics, fitness. Ofc: "The Family Affair", 1081 Mohr Ln Concord 94518

PREMO, EUGENE MILTON, appellate court justice; b. Aug. 28, 1936, San Jose; s. Milton A. and Mary Teresa (Fatjo) P.; m. Georgine Drees, Jan. 24, 1959; children: Nicole, b. 1961, Michelle, b. 1965, Patrick, b. 1967, Richard, b. 1968; edn: BS, Santa Clara Univ. 1957, JD, 1962. Career: research atty. Court of Appeal, San Francisco 1962; practicing atty. Santa Clara Co. 1963-69; apptd. judge Municipal Ct, Santa Clara Judicial Dist. 1969-75, judge Superior Ct. 1975-88; associate justice Ct. of Appeal, Sixth Dist., 1988-; lectr. Santa Clara Univ. Sch. of Law; lectr. Rutter Group mem: Alpha Sigma Nu, Calif. Judges Assn. (v.p. 1984-85); civic: West Valley Kiwanis, Bronco Bench, Santa Clara Univ. Athletic Bd., Salvation Army Advy. Bd., Sisters of Notre Dame De Namur Advy. Bd.; mil: 1st lt US Army C.I.C.; Republican; R.Cath.; rec: golf, travel, photography. Res: 19161 Portos Dr Saratoga 95070

PRESS, BARRY HARRIS JAY, plastic surgeon, educator; b. Apr. 10, 1951, Marshalltown, Iowa; s. Robert Alfred and Phyllis Elaine (Rovner) P.; m. Cynthia Jane Witz, Aug. 11, 1973; children: Sarah Jane, Rachel Ann; edn: BS (hons. microbiology), Univ. Iowa, 1973, MD, 1977; Diplomate Am. Bd. Med. Examiners 1979, Am. Bd. Surgery 1989, Am. Bd. Plastic Surgery 1989, cert. surgery of hand 1990. Career: intern, resident gen. surgery Univ. of Minnesota Hosps., Mpls. 1977-78, 78-79, 80-85, chief res. 1984-85, resident otol. 1979-80; resident plastic surgery NY Univ. Med. Ctr., 1985-87, chief res. 1986-87; asst. prof. plastic surgery Stanford Univ. Coll. Med., 1987-; dir. Burn Ctr. and assoc. chief div. plastic surg. Santa Clara Valley Med. Ctr., San Jose 1987-; awards: Old Gold Scholar Univ. Iowa 1969, summer res. fellow Univ. Iowa Coll. Med. 1974, 1st pl. Resident Trauma Essay competition ACS, Minn. 1981, 1st pl. Resident Res. competition Minn. Surgical Soc. 1983, PSEF res. grantee 1986, NIH biomed. res. grantee 1988; Fellow ACS, mem. Am. Soc. Plastic and Reconstrv. Surgeons, Am. Soc. Surgery of the Hand, Am. Burn Assn., Santa Clara County Med. Soc., Calif. Med. Assn., AMA; author 19+ med. jour. articles and book chapters, 8+ sci. presentations. Ofc: Santa Clara Valley Medical Ctr. 751 S Bascom Ave San Jose 95128 Tel: 408/299-5452

PRESS, SKIP (LLOYD DOUGLAS), writer; b. July 26, 1950, Commerce, Texas; s. Lloyd Douglas Press, Sr. and Bettie Eleanor (Jacobs) Davidson; m. Debra Ann Hartsog, July 30, 1989; children: Haley Alexander b. 1990, Holly Olive b. 1992. Career: mng. editor Today's Professionals mag., L.A. 1979-80; editor Entertainment Monthly, L.A. 1984; writer, producer How-to-Videos, 1986-; freelance writer, 1978-; instr. writers pgm. UCLA Ext., 1992-; author: young adult novels: Cliffhanger (1992), Knucklehead (1993), non-fiction: The Devil's Forest Fire (1993), A Rave of Snakes (1993), The Importance of Mark Twain (1993); writer, tech. manuals Franchise Cons. Group, L.A.; writer, cons. First Interstate Bank, L.A.; co-writer Fair Game feature, Braunstein-Hamady Prodns., 1991, Allure feature Chessler Prodn., 1991; writer TV Zoobilee Zoo, 1986; writer, packager video Jan Stephenson's How to Golf, 1986; writer, co-producer video A Woman's Guide to Firearms, 1987; writer, cons. video Wedding Helper, 1989; writer radio show Alien Worlds, 1978; playwright, producer, director several stage plays; awarded Silver Medal for video "A Woman's Guide to Firearma" New York Internat. Film Fest. (1987); mem: Independent Writers of So. Calif. (dir. at lg. 1989-90, v.p. 1990-91, dir. Script-a-thon, Century City 1990), Dramatists Guild 1984-, PEN, Poets and Writers 1986-; rec: golf, music. Address: 710 E Palm Ave Burbank 91501 Ph:818/954-8900

PRESTON, ROBERT ARTHUR, astronomer; b. June 29, 1944, N.Y.C.; s. Arthur Lloyd and Dorothy Elizabeth (Smith) P.; m. Ann Lee Archer, July 18, 1970; children: Karen b. 1973; edn: BS, Cornell Univ., 1966, M.Aerospace Eng., 1967; PhD, M.I.T., 1972. Career: project scientist Lockheed Research Lab., Palo Alto 1972-73; Jet Propulsion Laba., Pasadena, 1973-, group supr. 1975-, mgr. astrophysics res. pgm. 1979-92, project scientist, 1991-; vis. prof. Calif. Inst. of Tech., 1989-90; prin. investigator Vega Venus Balloon Experiment, Phobos Lander Mission, Hipparcos Mission, Extragalactic Radio Astronomy Grant (NASA); awarded NASA Special Svc. Medal (1986); discoverer of 20 archeoastronomy sites in American Southwest; author 150+ pub. sci. papers; mem. Am. Astronomical Soc. 1973-, Internat. Astronomical Union 1976-; rec: piano, running. Res: 24618 Golf View Dr Valencia 91355 Ofc: Jet Propulsion Lab. 238-600, 4800 Oak Grove Dr Pasadena 91109

PRICE, FREDERICK KENNETH CERCIE, clergyman; b. Jan. 3, 1932, Santa Monica; s. Fred Cercie and Winnifred Bernice (Ammons) P.; m. Betty Ruth Scott, Mar. 29, 1953; children: Angela Marie P. Evans, Cheryl Ann P. Crabbe, Stephanie Pauline P. Buchanan, Frederick Kenneth; edn: Dipl. (hon.) Rhema Bible Tng. Ctr., Tulsa 1976; DD (hon.), Oral Roberts Univ., 1982; Hon. student Pepperdine Univ., Malibu, Ca., 1/21/90; Ordained to ministry Baptist Ch., 1955, African Methodist Episcopal Ch., 1957, Kenneth Hagin Ministries, 1975; Friends Internat. Christian Univ., Fresno, B. Biblical Stu. 1978, M. Div. 1982, D. Ministry 1988, D. Humane Letters 1991, PhD religious studies 1992, Career: asst. pastor Mount Sinai Baptist Ch., Los Angeles 1955-57; pastor AME Ch., Val Verde, Calif. 1957-59; Christiam Missionary Alliance West

Washington Community Ch., Los Angeles 1965-73; Crenshaw Christian Ctr., L.A. 1973-; founding mem. bd. trustees Internat. Convention Faith Ministers Inc., Tulsa 1979-; founder, chmn. bd., pres. Fellowship of Inner City Word of Faith Ministries (FICWFM), L.A., 1990; author: How Faith Works 1976, Explanation to Receiving Your Healing by the Laying On of Hands 1980, High Finance, God's Financial Plan, Tithes and Offerings 1984, How to Believe God for a Mate 1987, Marriage and the Family, Practical Insight for Family Living 1988, The Origin of Satan 1988, Living in the Spiritual Realm 1989, Concerning Them Which are Asleep 1989, Homosexuality, State of Birth or State of Mind 1989, Prosperity on God's Terms 1990, other books; Democrat; Ofc: Crenshaw Christian Center 7901 S Vermont Ave POB 90000 Los Angeles 90009

PRICE, GEORGE WENDELL, financial and investment advisor; b. May 26, 1930, Rockville Centre, N.Y.; s. Arthur and Hilda May (Gooch) P.; m. Joan Natasha Kerekach (div.); children: Laura, Debra, Gary, Gregory. Career: quality engr. IBM, San Jose 1965-68; stockbroker Sutro & Co., San Jose 1968-81; Bateman Eichler, Santa Clara 1981-84; pres. Price Financial Inc., 1984-, nat. ranked No. 1 by Hulbert Financial Digest for stock market performance (1990); mil: pfc USAF 1949-50; Republican. Ofc: The Price Trend, Price Financial, Inc. Apt. 2 Stony Creek Apartments 150 Stony Point Rd Santa Rosa 95401

PRICE, JOE (A.), artist, educator; b. Feb. 6, 1935, Ferriday, La.; s. Edward Neill and Margaret (Hester) P.; edn: BS, Northwestern Univ., 1957; postgrad. Art Center Coll., L.A. 1967-68; MA, Stanford Univ., 1970. Career: actor and freelance artist, illustrator in N.Y.C. 1957-60, in L.A. 1960-68, commercial artist, San Carlos 1968-69; package designer Container Corp. Am., Santa Clara 1969; prof. studio art and filmmaking and chair dept. art Coll. of San Mateo, 1970-; One-man shows incl. Richard Sumner Gal., Palo Alto 1975, San Mateo County Cultural Ctr. 1976, 82, Tahir Gals., New Orleans 1977, 82, Kerwin Gals., Burlingame 1977, Editions Gal., Melbourne, Australia 1977, Ankrum Gal., L.A. 1978, 84, Editions Ltd. West Gal., S.F. 1981, Miriam Perlman Gal., Chgo. 1982, San Mateo County Arts Council Gal. 1982, Candy Stick Gal., Ferndale 1984, Assoc. Am. Artists, N.Y.C. and Phila. 1984, Gallery 30, Burlingame 1991, San Mateo 1984, Triton Mus. Art, Santa Clara 1986, Huntsville Mus. Art, Ala. 1987, Gallery 30, San Mateo 1988-91, Concept Art Gal., Pitts. 1991; num. group shows nat. incl. 15th Ann. Nat. Invitational Drawing Exhbn. Emporia State Univ., Kansas 1991, internat. group shows incl. Nat. Gal. Australia 1978, Editions Galleries, Melbourne 1988, 6th Internat. Exhbn. Carnegie-Mellon Univ., Pa. 1988, 5th Internat. Biennale Petite Format de Papier, Belgium 1989, 4th Internat. Biennial Print Exh., Taipei Fine Arts Mus. P.R.China 1990, Interprint, Lviv '90, USSR 1990, Internat. Print Triennale, Cracow, Poland 1991, "Directions in Bay Area Printmaking: Three Decades" Palo Alto Cultural Ctr. 1992-93, Am. Printmaking, Halem Gallery W.D.C. 1993; represented in permanent collections San Francisco Mus. Modern Art, Achenbach Found. Graphic Arts, S.F., Phila. Mus. Art, New Orleans Mus. Art, Portland Mus. Art, Me., The Library of Congress, W.D.C., Huntsville Mus. Art, Midwest Mus. Am. Art, Ind., Cracow Nat. Mus., Poland, Cabo Frio Mus., Brazil, Nat. Mus. Am. Art, Smithsonian Instn., W.D.C.; awards: Kempshall Clark award Peoria Art Guild 1981, Paul Lindsay Sample Meml. award 25th Chautauqua Nat. Exhbn. of Am. Art 1982, 1st Ann. Creative Achiev. award Calif. State Legislature /Arts Coun. San Mateo Co. 1989; mem: Am. Color Print Soc., Audubon Artists (Louis Lozowick Meml. award 1978, Silver medal of honor 1991), Boston Printmakers (Ture Bengtz Meml. award 1987), Calif. Soc. Printmakers council 1979-81), L.A. Printmaking Soc., Phila. Print Club (Lessing J. Rosenwald prize 1979), Arts Council of San Mateo Co., Theta Chi; Democrat; Rel. Sci. Res: PO Box 3305 Sonora 95370 Ofc: College of San Mateo Art Dept 1700 W Hillsdale Blvd San Mateo 94402

PRIMACK, MARVIN HERBERT, physician, anesthesiologist; b. Mar. 20, 1931, Detroit, Mich.; s. Abraham and Florence (Zeman) P.; m. Bune Rothbart, Dec. 26, 1934; children: Todd b. 1957, Teri b. 1959, Daren b. 1962, Heidi b. 1964; edn: BS, Wayne St. Univ. 1953; MD, Univ. Mich. Ann Arbor 1957. Career: staff Harper & Hutzel Hosp., Detroit, Mich. 1960-66; St. Josephs Med. Center, Stockton 1966-; bd. chmn., pres. Found. Med. Care 1981-83; M.H. Primack MD Inc. 1979-88; v.p. Stockton Anesthesia 1969-79, 1989-; asst. prof. Wayne Univ. Med. Sch., Detroit, Mich. 1963-66; mem: Calif. Soc. Anesthesiologists, Am. Soc. Anesthesiologists, AMA, CMA, San Joaquin Med. Soc.; rec: computers, photography. Ofc: Stockton Anesthesia Medical Group Inc. 2626 N California Suite G Stockton 95204

PRINCE, LAUREE SIMONNE, company owner, creative consultant; b. Dec. 2, 1952, Council Bluffs, Iowa; d. Homer Lawrence and Lillian Mae (Franklin) Prince; m. Robert Nicolini, July 25, 1974 (div.); edn: BS edn., Univ. Nebr., Lincoln 1974; grad. studies UC Irvine, 1978. Career: coordinator Youth Program City of Council Bluffs 1970-74; tchr. City of Council Bluffs, Iowa 1974-77; cataloger Anaheim Pub. Library, Anaheim 1977-82; student liaison, alumni affairs, Calif. Coast Univ., Santa Ana 1983-84; owner Luckie Louie, Orange 1985-; mem. Pi Lambda Theta (pres. 1972-74), Pi Beta Phi (scholarship chair 1973-74), Co-Op America; sponsor Chabad Charity Telethon (ann. 1989-); Republican; Roman Catholic; rec: cookery Address: Orange 92665½

PRITCHARD, ARTHUR OSBORN, retired church business administrator; b. Oct. 7, 1910, Scarsdale, N.Y.; s. Arthur Osborn and Emeline Augusta (Gunning) P.; m. Dorothy Eleanor White, March 24, 1945 (dec. 1982); m. 2d., 1984 (div. 1987); edn: BA, Pomona Coll., 1932; MA, Columbia Univ., 1934. Career: computer clk. supr. Agi. Adj. Adminstrn., U.S. Dept. Agri., Wash. D.C. 1934-36; auditor Gen. Acctg. Office, Berkeley 1936-41; acct., office mgr. Talbot Bird & Co., San Francisco 1946-60; church bus. adminstr. No. Calif. Conf. United Church of Christ, 1960-76, ret.; bd. dirs. No. Pacific Council Nat. Peace Inst. Found. 1986-91; honors: citation UN Assn. 1966, plaque Berkeley City Club 1982, plaque City Commons Club 1989, listed Who's Who in West; civic: City Commons Club Berkeley (pgm. dir. 1985-86, pres. 1989, bd. 1990-), Berkeley City Club (pres. 1978-82), UN Assn.-USA (No. Calif. Council pres. 1959-65, East Bay Chapt. UNA-USA hon. bd. life mem.), Am. Assn. for UN/Alameda Co. (pres. 1956-59), Outlook Club Calif. (secty. 1967-93), World Affairs Council (charter mem. 1947), Commonwealth Club Calif. (life mem.); mil: s.sgt. Med. Corps AUS 1941-45, Bronze star; Democrat; Congregational (United Ch. of Christ); rec: world travel, photography, adult edn. Res: 989 Tulare Ave Berkeley 94707

PRITZ, MICHAEL BURTON, academic physician, neurological surgeon; b. Oct. 8, 1947, New Brunswick, N.J.; s. John Ernest and Helen Violet (Rockoff) P.; m. Edmay Marie Gregorcy, Feb. 18, 1973; children: Edmond b. 1976, Benjamin b. 1979; edn: BS (high honors, highest distinction psychology), Univ. Ill., 1969; PhD, Case Western Reserve Univ., 1973, MD, Case Western Reserve Univ. Sch. of Medicine, 1975; Diplomate Am. Bd. Neurol. Surgery (1984). Career: asst. prof. div. neurosurg. UC Irvine, Calif. Coll. of Medicine, Orange 1981-85, assoc. prof. 1985-; awards: Edmund J. James scholar Univ. Ill., Champaign-Urbana 1968, 69, NSF fellow 1968, Psi Chi Award - psychology 1969, Herbert S. Steuer award Case Western Reserve Univ. 1975; mem: Am. Coll. of Surgeons (Fellow 1986-), Soc. Neurol. Surgeons of Orange County (sec. treas. 1983-84, pres. 1985-86), Am. Assn. Neurol. Surgeons 1985-, Soc. for Neuroscience 1972; publs: peer rev. jour. articles on cerebrovascular disease 1978-, on comparative neurobiology 1974-; rec: tennis, biking. Ofc: Univ. California Irvine Medical Ctr. 101 City Dr South Rm 205 Orange 92668

PRIX, WOLF D., architect; b. Dec. 13, 1942, Vienna, Austria; s. Josef and Erika (Urban) P.; m. Roswitha Gottschlich, Aug. 8, 1968; 1 child, Florian b. 1972. Career: co-founder, prin. architect, COOP HIMMELBLAU, Vienna, 1968-, prin. arch. COOP HIMMELBLAU, Los Angeles, Calif. 1987-; COOP HIMMELBLAU teaches at SCI-Arc, L.A.; honors: COOP HIMMELBLAU was selected for a solo exhibition at the Centre Pompidou in Paris, France 1992-93, and was included in the MOMA Deconstructivist exhib. 1988; creative works: the Reiss-Bar, Vienna 1977, the Red Angel, Vienna 1980-81, the Passage Wahliss 1986, ISO-Holding Ag exec. offices 1986, the Studio Bauman, Vienna 1985, the Rooftop Remodeling, Vienna 1987-88, the Funder Factory, St. Veit/Glan 1988-89; works in progress: Rehak House (Malibu), part of the Groninger Mus. of Art (Holland), addition to the Munich Academy of Art (Germany), remodelin of Dresden Hygiene Mus. (Germany), Anselm Kiefer Studio (France), design for LACMA German Expressionism exhib (L.A.). Ofc: 8561 Higuera Street Culver City 90232

PROUD, JOHN FREDERICK, manufacturing consultant, educator, speaker; b. Apr. 11, 1942, New Prague, Minn.; s. John Cranston and Avis Kathryn (Kamish) P.; m. Marsha Anne Ross, Feb. 29, 1964 (div. Feb. 1979); m. Darlene Elizabeth Sundal, July 4, 1980; children: Karen Lynn b. 1964, Michael James b. 1967; edn: BS math., Calif. Polytech. State Univ., S.L.O., 1964; MS mgmt. scis., West Coast Univ., 1973; desig: CFPIM, Am. Prodn. & Inventory Control Soc. 1978. Career: MIS mgr. Century Data Systems, Anaheim 1971-74; mfg. proj. leader Burroughs Corp., City of Industry, 1968-71; project team mrpII Xerox Corp., El Segundo 1974-76; mfg. cons. Xerox Computer Svs., L.A. 1976-79, Arista Mfg. (Xerox) Winston-Salem, N.C. 1979-81; mgr. nat. customer edn. Xerox Computer Svs., L.A. 1981-86; mgr. JIT mfg. Xerox Corp., L.A. 1986-87; prin. Oliver Wight Cos., Newbury, N.H. 1988-, instr. 1987-, internat. educator- U.K., Australia, N.Z., 1988-; pres. Proud Ents. Corp., Palm Desert 1987-; asst. prof. CSU Fullerton; speaker World Congress, Vienna, Austria 1985, annual speaker APICS Internat. Conf. various U.S. cities, also Toronto and Montreal, Can. 1980-92; awards: cert. P&IM Fellow APICS (Falls Ch., Va. 1978), listed Who's Who in West 1992; mem. APICS (mem. 1976-, internat. conf. com. 1987, 92, Orange Co. chapt. pres. 1985-86); club: Palm Desert Golf; publs: 20+ articles in field (1980-), tech. editor book series: Computers in Mfg. (1980-81), devel. mfg. courses: Master Scheduling (1987), Materials Mgmt. (1987), Capacity Mgmt. (1987); mil: lt.jg USN 1965-68, decorated Vietnam campaign, Vietnam svc., Nat. Def.; Republican; rec: golf, travel, outdoors. Res: 260 Desert Holly Dr Palm Desert 92260 Ofc: Proud Enterprises Corp. 76849 New York Ave Palm Desert 92260

PROUTY, KENNETH BLAKE, insurance co. executive; b. Apr. 21, 1928, Oakland; s. Chester Harbour and Edith Florence (Blake) P.; m. Martha Lee Pitts, July 4, 1952; children: William b. 1954, John b. 1957, Anne b. 1957, Laura b. 1959, Andrew b. 1960; edn: BS, UC Berkeley 1950; MBA, Univ. San Francisco 1968; MS fin. services, American Coll., Bryn Mawr, Pa. 1982; desig: CLU (chartered life underwriter), American Coll. 1960, ChFC (ch. finl. cons.) 1982; CPCU (ch. property and casualty underwriter) Am. Inst. of Prop. and Liability Underws. 1980; FLMI (Fellow Life Mgmt. Inst.) Life Office Mgmt. Assn. 1958. Career: vineyardist, rancher self-empl. Geyserville 1950-51; underwriter State Farm Life Ins. Co., Western Office, Berkeley 1953-57, chief underwriter NW ofc. Salem, Ore. 1957-61, dir. of adminstrn. W. ofc. 1961-62, reg. life mgr. No. Calif. ofc., Santa Rosa 1963-86, reg. life and health mgr. State Farm Ins. Cos., Rohnert Park 1986-; occasional lectr. in ins. Santa Rosa Jr. Coll.; mem: Redwood Empire Life Underws. Assn., Am. Soc. of CLU (Redwood Empire chpt. pres. 1969-70); civic: Family Service Agcy. of Sonoma County (pres. 1974-76), Rotary Internat. (W. Santa Rosa Club pres. 1976-77, Paul Harris Fellow), Empire Breakfast Club; mil: major US Army Arty. 1951-53; Republican; Episcopal; rec: ski, flying, fishing. Res: 2222 Sunrise Ave Santa Rosa 95409 Ofc: State Farm Insurance Cos. 6400 State Farm Dr Rohnert Park 94928

PUCKETT, RICHARD EDWARD, artist, consultant, recreation executive, ret.; b. Sept. 9, 1932, Klamath Falls, Ore.; s. Vernon Elijah and Leona Bell (Clevenger) P.; m. Velma Faye Hamrick, Apr. 14, 1957 (dec. 1985); children: Katherine Michelle b. 1958, Deborah Alison b. 1960, Susan Lin b. 1961, Gregory Richard b. 1962; edn: stu. Monterey Peninsula Jr. Coll., Hartnell Jr. Coll., CSUSJ, Lake Forest Coll., Ill., So. Ore. Coll. of Edn.; BA in public service, Univ. San Francisco 1978; desig: profl. recreator Am. Recreation Soc. 1964, Armed Forces Rec. Soc. 1970, Nat. Park & Rec. Soc. 1976. Career: asst. arts and crafts dir. Ft. Leonard Wood, Mo. 1956-57; arts & crafts dir./ asst. spl. services ofcr./museum dir. Fort Sheridan, Ill. 1957-59, designed and opened 1st Fort Sheridan Army Museum; arts & crafts dir. Fort Irwin, Calif. 1959-60; arts & crafts br. dir. Fort Ord, 1960-86, opened first Presidio of Monterey Army Museum 1961; ret. 1986; artist in oils, watercolor, blownglass sculpture, graphics; one-man shows: Seaside, City Hall (1975), Fort Ord Arts & Crafts Center Gal. (67-85), Presidio of Monterey Art Gal. (1979), exhibits in Mo., Ill., Calif., work in pvt. collections in U.S., Canada and Europe; contrib. author for book to be pub. on Army arts & crafts and Army combat artist prgm; awards: 1st pl. programming Dept. of Army (6 awards 1975-85), 1st pl. programming and publicity Armed Forces Command (5 consec. awards 1979-84), Commanders' Award for Civilian Service 1986, 1st & 3d pl. modern sculpture Monterey Fair Fine Arts Exh. 1978, 19 awards for outstanding performance, 2 sustained superior performance awards (1978, 84), numerous ribbons for arts and crafts; Life mem. Am. Biographical Soc., FABA and Golden Acad. Award for lifetime achiev. (1991), Life mem. Internat. Biog. Soc. "FIBA Internat. Man of Yr." (1991-2); past mem. Am. Park & Rec. Soc., cur. mem. Salinas Valley Fine Arts Assn., Am. Craftsman Assn., Glass Arts Soc., Monterey Mus. Assn.; Democrat; Prot.; rec: walking, antiques. Res: 1152 Jean Ave Salinas 93905 also summer Res: PO Box 7 Keno OR 97627

PUGACH, ROBERT GLENN, physician-urologist; b. June 16, 1952, Englewood, N.J.; s. Louis and Beatrice (Safane) P.; m. Judy, Oct. 3, 1982; children: Brian b. 1987, Jason b. 1989; edn: BA, N.Y. Univ. 1974; MD, Univ. Guadalajara 1978. Career: head dept. urology CIGNA Healthplan, Long Beach 1985-88; pvt. practice urology, Long Beach 1988-; staff Long Beach Comm. Hosp. 1985- (coms: chmn. Utilization Rev., 1987-, mem. Quality Assur., Operating Rm. Policy, Bioethics, Cancer Activities, Anesthesia Search, Medical Exec.), Long Beach Memorial Med. Ctr. 1987-, Doctors Hosp. Lakewood 1988-, Woodruff Comm. Hosp.; awards: N.Y. Acad. Medicine F.C. Valentine Urology Essay Contest 1983; mem: Am. Cancer Soc. (bd.), Am. Heart Assn. (bd.), L.A. Urological Soc., AMA, L.A. Co. Med. Assn. (physician advy. com.), Steamship Hist. Soc. Am., Richter Club (founding mem., v.chmn.); res. articles and papers pub. in med. jours. (1983-86). Ofc: 1760 Termino Ave Ste 207 Long Beach 90804

PUJOL, JOHN JEROME, customs broker; b. July 18, 1954, Landstuhl, Germany; s. Jerome Paul and Gertrud Vera (Lindhorst) P.; m. Karen Jean, Sept. 5, 1976; children: Tyler b. 1989, Griffin b. 1991. Career: plant mgr. Process Control Corp., Atlanta, Ga. 1978-79; account rep. EFI, N.Y.C. 1979-83, v.p. 1983-87, pres. and c.e.o. Valley Stream, N.Y. 1987-; dir: Pier Container Corp., EF Warehousing Inc., E.O.L. Inc., AP Holding Corp.; mem: Young Pres. Orgn., Am. Motorcyclists Assn.; rec: outdoor sports. Ofc: EFI 6033 W Century Blvd Ste 720 Los Angeles 90045

PULLEY, DOUGLAS BOYD, physician, ophthalmologist; b. Apr. 1, 1942, San Francisco; s. Boyd H. and Beth (Paxman) P.; m. Katherine Anne Bennion, June 25, 1966; children: Anne b. 1970, Matthew b. 1972, David b. 1975, Susan b. 1977, Stephen b. 1981; edn: BS zoology, Brigham Young Univ. 1966; MD, UCLA 1970. Career: pres. Douglas B. Pulley MD Inc., San Jose 1976-; mem: Am. Acad. Ophthalmology (fellow), AMA, CMA, SCCMS, Santa Clara Valley Orchid Soc.; mil: capt. AUS 1971-73; Republican; Mormon; rec: orchids, woodturning. Ofc: 275 Hospital Parkway Ste 510 San Jose 95119

PULLIAM, PAUL EDISON, electrical engineer; b. June 6, 1912, Nickerson, Kans.; s. George Washington and Hattie Lucy (Vandeventer) P.; m. Ila M. Catrett, Feb. 3, 1945; children: Carol Ann b. 1946, Paula Ann b. 1953; edn: ROTC to 2nd lt., FA-Res., Univ. of Mo. 1937; var. spl. courses incl. radar- electronics completed as a reserve ofcr.; BSEE, Univ. of Mo., Feb. 1951; Reg. Profl.

Elec. Engr., Mo., Nev., Calif. Career: elec. engr. Ozark Dam Constructors, bldg. hydroelec. powerhouse at Bull Shoals Dam in Baxter Cty., Ark. 1951-52; mech. plan checker Clark Co. Bldg. & Safety Dept., Las Vegas, New.; constrn. insp. Regional Waste Water Treatment Plant, Sacramento Cty. Dept. of Pub. Works, Sacto.; qualified as Guided Missile Ofcr., Ft. Bliss, Tex. 1949; provided two concepts used in devel. of thermonuclear hydrogen bombs, 1949; initiated weatherization of Fort Irwin, Calif., 1985 and provided two concepts for redesign of Sergeant York weapon system, caused USAF personnel to devel. VHF Balun antenna arrays; initiated re-develop. of torpedoes for USN and USCG, 1986; initiated changes in afterburner use w/devel. by others in modification of B-52H and B-52G aircraft, 1986, 88; honors: Army Commendn. for suggesting WWII F.A. use of Radar Set SCR-584 and formation of Radar Set SCR-784; named the Polaris Weapon System 1952, named the Pershing Weapon System at Redstone Arsenal, Ala.; provided definition and coined term 'afterburner' for jet aircraft thrust reaction, Ft. Bliss 1949; initiated dynamic guidance modification of submarines, 1990; mem: Reserve Ofcrs. Assn. of the USA (life, 50-yr. mem 5/29/87), IEEE (life), Am. Soc. of Mil. Engrs., VFW (life), Calif. Soc. of SAR, The Retired Officers Assn. (life); mil: served pvt. to cpl., Field Arty. 1930-34, 2nd lt. to maj. FA Reserve and US Army, ret. 1972, provided concept for ammunition used in A-10 aircraft in 1990-91; Democrat; Baptist. Res: 7916 Grandstaff Dr Sacramento 95823

PURCELL, STUART MCLEOD, III, financial planner; b. Feb. 16, 1944, Santa Monica; s. Stuart M., Jr. and Carol (Howe) P.; edn: AA, Santa Monica City Coll., 1964; BS, CSU Northridge, 1967; grad. CPA Adv. Personal Fin. Plnng., 1985; CPA 1976, reg. prin. NASD 1984, Registry of Fin. Plnng. Practitioners 1987. Career: sr. acct. Pannell, Kerr, Forster CPA, San Francisco 1970-73; fin. cons./prin. Purcell Fin. Services, 1973-74; controller Decimus Corp., S.F. 1974-76; Grubb & Ellis Co., Oakland 1976-78; Marwais Steel Co., Richmond 1979-80; fin. cons./prin. San Rafael 1980-, fin. counselor/owner Purcell Wealth Mgmt., 1981-; guest lectr. Master's Pgm. in fin. plnng. Golden Gate Univ. 1985-, lectr. comm. workshops, Larkspur 1984; awards: Eagle Scout BSA 1959, dean's list CSUN 1967, best fin. advisor and fin. newsletter Marin Indep. Jour., Novato 1987, top prod. Unimarc 1986, achiev. United Way Marin Co. 1984; mem: Am. Inst. CPAs, Calif. Soc. CPAs, Marin Estate Planning Council, Nat. Speakers Assn., Internat. Assn. for Fin. Plnng. North Bay Chpt. (exec.dir. 1984), Soc. of CPA Financial Planners (S.F. dist. mem. chair 1986), Internat. Soc. of PreRetired Planners, Sigma Alpha Epsilon; civic: United Way Marin Co. (div. chair 1984), San Rafael C.of C. 1983-, Salvation Army San Rafael, San Anselmo, Fairfax Chpt. (treas. 1987-), March of Dimes Marin Co. (funding com. 1987-), Arthritis Found. (funding com. 1988-); publs: contbr. articles in newspapers and bus., fin. profl. jours.; mil: lt. j.g. USNR 1968-76; Presbyterian; rec: travel, auto racing, skiing, gardening. Res: 45 Vineyard Dr San Rafael 94901

PURDY, RUTH MELISSA SANDERS, family therapist, professor; b. Nov. 5, 1910, Rocky, Okla.; d. Henry Allen and Ada Selena (Payton) Sanders; m. Allen B. Purdy, Sept. 14, 1935; children: Joseph D. b. 1937, John b. 1941; edn: BA, CSU Long Beach, 1951, MA, 1952; PhD, Univ. of Okla., 1966; extensive post doctoral studies. Career: faculty Long Beach City Coll., estab. & devel. 1st college reading lab, 1952-68; Cypress Coll., estab. & devel. 1st individualized instrn. adult edn. lab, 1968-76; marriage, family & child therapist Pacific Counseling Ctr., Fullerton 1976-81; dir. Christian Counseling Ctr., Huntington Beach 1981-; former adj. prof. Sch. of Psych., Azusa Pacific Univ., former faculty Pepperdine Univ.; mem: Internat. Reading Assn. (past pres. Long Beach chpt.), Western Coll. Reading Assn. (treas. 1974-75, archivist 1979-86), Am., Calif. Assn. Marriage & Family Therapists (Orange Co. chpt. pres. 1991-92, sec. 1979-80), Calif. Soc. for Hypnosis in Family Therapy (sec. 1982-84, treas. 1985-), Council for Exceptional Children, Nat. Alliance for Family Life Inc. (founding clin. mem.), Mothers and others Against Child Abuse (co-founder/co-dir.), named Californian of Community for outstanding volunteer contbns. 1988; author textbook: English Basics for Clerical Workers (1981); Republican; Christian; rec: book and stamp collections, travel. Res: 9400 Larkspur Dr Westminster 92683 Ofc: Christian Counseling Center of Huntington Beach, 1207 Main St Huntington Beach 92648

PURSELL, PAUL DENNIS, hospital rehabilitation director; b. Jan. 26, 1950, Altadena; s. Robert Ralph and Thelma Winifred P.; edn: BS, CSU Long Beach 1972; reg. physical therapist Calif. Career: asst. athletic trainer CSU Long Beach 1968-71; chief physical therapist Tustin Comm. Hosp., Tustin 1972-78; disaster planning coordinator St. Josephs Hosp., Orange 1984-90, dir. human devel. 1987-91, dir. rehab. 1978-; instr. CSU Long Beach 1989-; chmn. bd. Health Assn. Fed. Credit Union, Orange 1985-86; Orange/Long Beach Area Health Edn. Center 1984-85; chmn. Pres.'s Advy. Council on Phys. Therapy, CSU Long Beach, 1987-; awards: St. Joseph Hosp. spirit of St. Joseph 1987, Carnation Found. commend. for vol. 1984; mem: Orange C.of C. (pres. 1990-91), Am. Physical Therapy Assn. (pres. Calif. chpt. 1983-84), Am. Coll. Sports Medicine, Inst. Profl. Health Services Adminstrn., Nat. Fire Protection Assn. 1990-; civic bds: Orange Citizen of Yr. Selection Com. 1988-89, Mgmt. Audit Com. City of Orange 1991-, Leadership Orange (exec. com. 1991-, chmn. 1992-94), Finance Com. City of Orange 1993; Democrat; R.Cath.; rec: fishing. Ofc: St. Josephs Hospital 1100 W Stewart Orange 92668

PUTRIMAS, DONALD J., entertainment company financial executive; b. Feb. 11, 1952, Bridgeport, Conn.; s. Peter P. and Sophie S. (Stumbris) P.; m. Diane J. Elias, May 7, 1982; edn: BS, Univ. Bridgeport 1975. Career: acct. Peace Corps, Ceara, Brazil 1976-78; sr. acct. Louis Marx & Co., Stamford, Conn. 1978-80; controller Atco Industries, Stratford, Conn. 1980-82; v.p. fin. reporting Lorimar Telepictures, Culver City 1982-89; v.p., controller Warner Hollywood Studios, West Hollywood 1989-; mem: Fin. & Adminstrv. Mgmt. in Entertainment, Motion Picture & T.V. Credit Assn., Hollywood C.of C. (treas., dir.), Univ. Bridgeport Alumni Assn.; Democrat; R.Cath. Ofc: Warner Hollywood Studios 1041 N Formosa Ave West Hollywood 90046

PYROS, GREGORY GEORGE, architect, computer software author, consultant; b. Jan. 10, 1957, Kingston, Pa.; s. Nicholas Jonathan and Artemis (Veras) P.; m. Susan Stachowiak Gubala; edn: BS Bldg. Sci., Rensselaer Polytech. Inst. 1978, MBA 1979, BArch 1980; Reg. Arch. Calif. 1983, Pa. 1987; cert. Nat. Council of Architl. Registration Bds. (NCARB). Career: owner The Pyros Partnership, Newport Beach 1982-; pres. and chief exec. ofcr. Sno-Tek Inc., Newport Beach 1988-; instr. archtl. design course Orange Coast Coll., 1988; pvt. consulting and seminars on computer applications to bldg. industry; honors: Who's Who Am. Colls. and Univs. 1978; corp. mem. Am. Inst. of Architects (CAD chmn. in arch. com.), Archtl. Telecommunications Network/So. Calif. (chmn. 1986), So. Orange Co. AutoCAD User's Gp. (charter); coauthor computer pgm: Architect's Office Mgr. (nat. distbn.), author digitizer menu for AutoCAD for Architecture/ Facilities Mgmt.; 3D Multimedia and Film Animations; Republican; Greek Orthodox; rec: sailing, skiing, tennis. Res: 274 Cecil Pl Costa Mesa 92627 Ofc: The Pyros Partnership, 1201 Dove St Ste 550 Newport Beach 92660

QAQUNDAH, PAUL YOUSEF, pediatrician, allergist, educator; b. Feb. 26, 1933, Ramleh; s. Yousef Ibrahim and Soraya Salim (Qare) Q.; m. Susan Salib, Oct. 20, 1966; children: John b. 1967, Joyce b. 1968, Jennifer b. 1970, Michelle b. 1974, James b. 1979; edn: MD, Ein Shams Univ., Cairo 1960; DCH, dipl. child health, Univ. of London 1964; diplomate Am. Bd. of Pediatrics 1969, cert. subsplty. Allergy & Immunology 1975. Career: physician, pres. Pediatric Care Medical Group Inc., Huntington Beach 1971-; asst. assoc. prof. ped. UC Irvine 1971-, clinical prof. ped. UC Irvine, 1987-; vol. tchg. UCI- Childrens Hosp. Orange County; mem: Am. Acad. Pediatrics (charter pres. Orange Co. chpt. 1986), Orange Co. Ped. Soc. (pres. 1982-), Orange Co. Med. Soc. (pres.), Am. Lung Assn. O.C. (ped. com. 1975-, bd. dirs. 1974-85); contbr. num. articles and abstracts in med. jours.; Repub.; Greek Orthodox; rec: deep sea fishing, hunting, tennis. Ofc: Pediatric Care Medical Group 17822 Beach Blvd. Huntington Beach 92647

QUACKENBUSH, CHARLES W., legislator, business executive; b. Apr. 20, 1954, McChord Air Force Base; m. Rita "Chris" Christiansen, Dec. 14, 1978; children: Carrey b. 1979, Joseph b. 1985, Charles b. 1989; edn: BA, Notre Dame Univ., 1976; career: Captain, US Army 1976-82; v.p., Q-Tech 1982-86; state assemblyman, Twenty-Fourth Dist. 1986-; mem: vice chmn, Com. on Revenue and Taxation; Governmental Orgn.; Ways & Means; former vice chmn: Banking, Finance and Bonded Indebtedness, Econ. Devel. and New Technologies, Select Com. on the Census; delegate, Nat. Conf. of State Legislatures; former mem. appointed by Pres. Bush, U. S. Dept. of Defense Environmental CFC Advy. Com.; vice chmn., Assembly Com. on Revenue and Taxation 1993-; Assembly Com. on Governmental Orgn. 1993-; Assembly Com. on Ways & Means 1993-; awards: Almaden Valley Homeowner's Assn. Appreciation Award 1989, Am. Electronics Assn. High-Tech Legislator of the Year 1991-92, CA Abortion Rights Action League Legislator of the Year 1990, CA Bus. Properties Assn. Appreciation Award 1990, CA Instr. Video Consortium Appreciation Award, CA Sch. Bd. Assn. Hispanic Caucus Award 1989, Cert. Appreciation Jr. League of Palo Alto 1989, Cert. Appreciation San Jose Lions Club, City of Cupertino Proclamation for Resolving Trial Court Funding 1988, City of Saratoga Resolution for Resolving Trial Court Funding 1988, Comm. Svc. Award for Caltrain Track Attack Steering Com. 1991, Computer Using Educators Golden Disk Award 1991, Gann Spending Limit Watchdog Coalition's Taxpayer's Hang Tough Award 1987, L. A. Jr. C. of C. Award, Reg. Educational TV Advy. Council Award, Sr. Citizens Escort & Outreach Paratransit Assn. Cutting Gov. Red Tape Award, U. S. Army Commendation Medal; mem: Calif. Republican Assn., Calif. Cong. of Republicans, Santa Clara Chpt.; delegate, Republican Nat. Conv. 1988; Calif. Republican League; Peninsula Republican Assn.; Republicans for Choice; Santa Clara Cty. Republican Central Com.; mil: capt., US Army, 1976-82. Res: Cupertino Ofc: State Capitol, Rm. 4130 Sacramento 95814

QUE HEE, SHANE STEPHEN, environmental health scientist, educator; b. Oct. 11, 1946, Sydney, New South Wales, Australia; s. Robert and Jean (Byers) Q.H.; edn: BSc (hons.) Univ. Queensland, Brisbane, Aus. 1968, MSc, 1971; PhD, Univ. Saskatchewan, Can. 1976; postdoctoral McMaster Univ., Hamilton, Ont., Can. 1975-78; Fellow Am. Inst. of Chemists 1986. Career: asst., assoc. prof. Univ. Cincinnati, Oh. 1978-84, 1984-89; assoc. prof. dept. environmental health scis. UCLA, Los Angeles 1989-; reviewer US EPA, ATSDR, Wash. DC 1978-; mem. TOXNET, Nat. Library Medicine, Bethesda, Md. 1985-89; mem.

editorial bd. CRC Press, Boca Raton, Fl. 1988-, advy. bd. lab. methodology 1987-; awards: noteworthy contbn. US EPA 1981; mem: AAAS 1971-, Am. Chem. Soc. 1971-, Am. Coll. Toxicology 1981-, Am. Conf. Govt. Industrial Hygienists 1987-, Am. Ind. Hygiene Assn. 1978-; civic: Univ. Saskatchewan Squash Club (founder, pres. 1971-72), Saskatoon Cricket Assn. (sec. treas. 1974-75), Saskatchewan Cricket Assn. (sec. treas. 1974), Cincinnati Coal. Against Apartheid (facilitator 1985), Cinti. Gay/Lesbian March Activists (facilitator 1987-89); author: The Phenoxyalkanoic Herbicides 1981, contbg. editor: Fundamentals of Biological Monitoring 1992; rec: writing, civil rights, music. Res: 923 Levering Ave, Unit 102, Los Angeles 90024 Ofc: Dept. Env. Hlth. Sciences, UCLA School Public Health, 10833 Le Conte Ave Los Angeles 90024-1772

QUINN, JOHN JOSEPH, bank executive; b. Apr. 8, 1939, New Haven, Ct.; citizen USA and Rep. of Ireland; s. Frank X. and Celia A. (Kelley) Q.; first cousin, George M. Conway, Chief Justice Conn. Supreme Ct.; m. Nancy Deick, 1968; children: Cara b. 1975 (Australian cit.); Marc, b. 1978; edn: BA, and BS, UC Berkeley 1963, MBA, 1968. Career: sr. v.p./gen. mgr. We. Canada, First Interstate Bank of Canada, 1990-; exec. First Interstate Bank 1976-90: v.p./ corres. Bank and Trade Finance, S.F. Intl. Div. 1976-78, v.p./mgr. S.F. Internat. Div. 1978-80, v.p./gen. mgr. and mgr. Continental Europe, 1980-90; UCB rep. Sydney, Australia, 1973-76; mgr., dir. Euro Pacific Finance Corp., Melbourne, Aust., 1970-73; asst. v.p. UCB, L.A. Internat. Reg.mgr., SEA, 1970; mng. dir. Multinatl. Bus. Corp., London, U.K. 1968-70; First Nat. City Bank, N.Y. and Repub. of Philippines; honors: Beta Gamma Sigma, Bus. Sch. Hon. Soc.; mem: World Trade Club, Bankers Club (SF), Canadian Am. Assn. (dir.), British Am. C.of C. (dir.), Naval and Mil. Club (Melbourne), Naval Ofcrs. Assn. of Brit. Columbia, Vancouver Board of Trade, British Trade Assn. (Canada), Phi Kappa Sigma frat.; mil: lt.cdr. USN 1963-67, also Royal Australian Naval Reserve 5 yrs.; Republican (contbg.); Episcopalian; rec: boating, skiing, gardening. Res: Orinda, Calif. and Vancouver BC Canada Ofc: #790 - 999 W Hastings St Vancouver BC V6C 2W2 Canada

QUINN, JOHN R., archbishop; b. March 28, 1929, Riverside, Calif.; s. Ralph J. and Elizabeth (Carroll) Quinn; 3 siblings: Anthony G., Mrs. William Bash, Mrs. Noel deJarnette (dec.); edn: priesthood studies, St. Francis Sem. and Immaculate Heart Sem., San Diego, 1947-48, philosophy and theology, North American Coll., and Gregorian Univ., Rome, Licentiate in Sacred Theology, 1954; ordained priest in Rome at Ch. of San Marcello, by Archbishop Hector Cunial for the Diocese of San Diego, 1953; Hon. degrees Jesuit Sch. of Theology, Berkeley, Univ. of San Francisco, Santa Clara Univ., Univ. of Notre Dame. Career: apptd. assoc. pastor St. George`s Parish, Ontario, Calif. 1954; mem. theology faculty Immaculate Heart Seminary, San Diego 1955-, apptd. pres. St. Francis Coll. Seminary, 1962, rector Immaculate Heart Sem. Sch. of Theology, 1964; ordained Bishop, San Diego, 1967; apptd. first provost of the Univ. of San Diego, 1968, also mem. bd. trustees; apptd. pastor St. Therese Parish, San Diego, 1969; apptd. by Pope Paul VI as a consultor to the Congregation for the Clergy, Rome, 1971; installed Bishop, Oklahoma City and Tulsa, Okla., 1972, by the Apostolic Del. to the U.S., The Most Rev. Luigi Raimondi; installed as first Archbishop of Oklahoma City, Cathedral of Our Lady of Perpetual Help, 1973; appt. by Pope Paul VI as rep. Fourth Synod of Bishops, Vatican City, 1974; elected pres. Okla Conf. of Churches, 1976-78; Archbishop of San Francisco, 1977-; apptd. by Pope John Paul II Pontifical Del. for Religious in the U.S., 1983; mem: Nat. Conf. of Catholic Bishops (pres. 1977-80, past chmn. com. of the liturgy, elected to att. Synod on the Family in Rome, 10/80, past chmn. com. on doctrine, mem. com. for pro-life activities 1989-), Canon Law Soc. of Am., Cath. Theol. Soc. Am., U.S. Cath. Conf. (past chmn. com. on family life), Calif. Cath. Conf. (pres. 1985-88), Inst. of Living, Hartford, Ct. (bd. govs.); contbr. articles in L'Osservatore Romano, America, The Priest, The Catholic Ency., Catholic Hospital, and in various newspapers. Address: Office of the Archbishop, 445 Church St San Francisco 94114

QUINN, TOM, communications media executive; b. Mar. 14, 1944, Los Angeles; s. Joseph M. and Grace (Cooper) Q.; m. Amy Lynn, Nov. 25, 1982; children: Douglas b. 1967, Lori b. 1969, Shelby b. 1991; edn: BS, Northwestern Univ. 1965. Career: reporter City News Bureau of Chicago, 1964; reporter WLS Radio, Chgo. 1965; reporter, newswriter ABC Radio, Los Angeles 1965; reporter KXTV Ch. 10, Sacramento 1966; city editor City News Service of Los Angeles, 1966-68; pres. Radio News West, L.A. 1968-70; campaign mgr. Jerry Brown for Secty. of State, L.A. 1970; dep. Secty. of State Calif., Sacto. 1971-74; campaign mgr. Jerry Brown for Gov., 1974; chmn. Calif. Air Resources Board and Secty. of Environmental Quality, State of Calif., Sacto. 1974-79; mem. Calif. Governor's Cabinet, 1975-79; chmn./pres. City News Service, L.A. 1980-85; pres. Americom, L.A. 1985-; pres. KODS-FM, Reno, Nev. 1982-, pres. sta. KFBI, Las Vegas 1989-, pres. KFSO Radio, Fresno 1985-, pres. December Group, L.A. 1981-; Democrat (chmn. Mayor Tom Bradley Reelection Campaign 1985); rec: skiing. Ofc: Americom, 6255 Sunset Blvd Ste 1901 Los Angeles 90028

RABINOWITZ, MARIO, physicist; b. Oct. 24, 1936, Mexico City, Mex.; U.S. citizen by parentage; s. Laib and Rachel (Loschak) R.; m. Laverne Marcotte; children: Daniel, Benjamin, Lisa; edn: BS in physics, Univ. Wash., Seattle, 1959,

MS physics, 1960; PhD physics, Wash. St. Univ., Pullman 1963. Career: res. engr. Boeing Co., Seattle 1958-61; res. asst. Wash. St. Univ., Pullman 1961-63; sr. physicist Westinghouse Res. Ctr., Pittsburg, Pa. 1963-66; mgr. gas discharges and vacuum physics Varian Assocs., Palo Alto, Calif. 1966-67; res. physicist Stanford Linear Accel. Ctr., 1967-74; sr. scientist and mgr. Electric Power Res. Inst., Palo Alto 1974-; adj. prof. Case Western Reserve Univ. 1975-77, Boston Univ. 1975-77, Ga. Inst. Tech., Atlanta 1987-, Virginia Commonwealth Univ., Richmond 1990-, Univ. Houston, Tx. 1990-; awards: del. and counselor Boys State, Am. Legion 1953-55, Vancouver (Wa.) High Sch. Boy of the Yr. 1954, George F. Baker Scholar, Baker Found. 1955-58, Boeing Co. Grad. Study Pgm. 1958-60, Wash. St. Univ. Alumni Achiev. Award, Pullman, Wa. 1992; inventor 30 U.S. patents, plus many fgn. (1968-), author 106 sci. papers (1962-), 6 ency. articles incl. 3 feature articles (1981, 82, 86, 87, 89, 92); rec: philosophy, mathematics. Res: 715 Lakemead Way Redwood City 94062

RABOVSKY, JEAN, staff toxicologist; b. Aug. 18, 1937, Baltimore, Md.; edn: BS, Univ. of Maryland, College Park, Md., 1959; PhD, Brandeis Univ., 1964. Career: research chemist, NIOSH, Morgantown, W. Va., 1978-89; staff toxicologist, State of Calif., Sacto., Calif., 1989-; mem. Sigma Xi, N.Y. Academy of Sciences, Amer. Chemical Society, Amer. Assn. for the Advancement of Science; author of peer-reviewed journal articles on xenobiotic metabolism and occupational and environmental health issues. Ofc: Office of Environmental Health Hazard Assessment, 601 North 7th St., P.O. Box 942732 Sacramento 94234

RACHMELER, MARTIN, university research administrator, technology transfer director; b. Nov. 21, 1928, Bklyn.; s. Jack and Sophie (Rosenbloom) R.; m. Betty Karkalis, June 9, 1956; children: Susan b. 1966, Ann b. 1970, Helen b. 1970; edn: AB, Indiana Univ., 1950, PhD, Case Western Reserve, 1960. Career: asst. res. geneticist UC Berkeley, 1961-62; asst. prof., assoc. prof. microbiology Northwestern Univ., Evanston, Ill. 1962-67, 67-89, dir. Res. Svs. Adminstrn. 1977-89; dir. technology transfer UC San Diego, La Jolla, Calif. 1989-; awards: USPHS postdoctoral fellow 1959-61, USPHS career dev. award 1967-72; mem: Nat. Council of Univ. Res. Adminstrs. 1978-, (reg. chair 1988), Sigma Xi 1960-, Am. Soc. for Microbiology 1957-, AAAS 1962-, Licensing Exec. Soc. 1979-, Assn. of Univ. Technology Mgrs. (pres. 1991); author: med. book chapt. 1966, 22+ articles in microbial genetics 1959-77; mil: cpl. US Army Chem. Corps 1952-54; rec: tennis, plays, movies, jogging. Ofc: UCSD, Technology Transfer Office, 0093, La Jolla 92093

RADADIA, VRAJLAL MANJI, chiropractor; b. June 2, 1944, Devkigalol, Gujarat, India; s. Manji Gangdas and Raliat Manji (Ratanpura) R.; m. Bhanuben, Aug. 17, 1980; children: Nilkanth b. 1984; Anil b. 1985; edn: BSc, Saurashtra Univ., India 1968; BS, Los Angeles Coll. of Chiropractic 1979, DC 1979. Career: draftsman Curt G. Joa Inc., Ft. Worth, Fla. 1973-74, Sensor Techonology Inc., Chatsworth 1974-75; draftsman, machinist, Back Industries, Chatsworth 1975-76; machinist Stainless Steel Prods., Burbank 1976-80; chiropractor Wilshire Center Chiropractic Group, Los Angeles 1981-, also Family Chiropractic Healing Ctr., San Gabriel 1983-; Who's Who Worldwide, Oxford's Who's Who, Doctor of the Year 1987; mem: Am., Calif. Chiropractic Assn., San Gabriel Chiro. Soc., San Gabriel C.of C., Lions Club Internat.; rec: painting, photography, reading. Ofc: Family Chiropractic Healing Center, 915-1/2 E Las Tunas Dr San Gabriel 91776

RAE, MATTHEW SANDERSON, JR., lawyer; b. Sept. 12, 1922, Pittsburgh, Pa.; s. Matthew S. and Olive (Waite) R.; m. Janet Hettman, May 2, 1953; children: Mary-Anna b. 1959, Margaret Rae Mallory b. 1961, Janet Rae Dupree b. 1962; edn: AB, Duke Univ. 1946, LLB, 1947; postgrad. Stanford Univ. 1951. Career: asst. to dean, Duke Law Sch. 1947-48; admitted to Md. bar 1948, Calif. bar, 1951, Supreme Ct. of US 1967; assoc. Karl F. Steinmann law firm, Baltimore, Md. 1948-49; nat. field rep. Phi Alpha Delta Law Frat. 1949-51; research atty. Calif. Supreme Ct. 1951-52; partner Darling, Hall & Rae and predecessor firms, 1953-; mem. Calif. Commn. on Uniform State Laws 1985-; chmn. drafting com. for rev. Uniform Principal and Income Act of Nat. Conf. of Commrs. on Uniform State laws, 1991-, mem. Probate Law Consulting Group, Calif. Bd. of Legal Specialization 1977-88; active Republican Party: mem. L.A. County Repub. Assembly (v.p. 1959-64), L.A. County Repub. Central Com. (1960-64, 1977-90, exec. com. 1977-90), 29th Senatorial Dist. (chmn. 1977-90), 17th Congl. Dist. (v. chmn. 1960-62), 28th Congl. Dist. (v. chmn. 1962-64), 46th Assem. Dist. (chmn. 1962-64), Repub. State Central Com. of Calif. (1966-, exec. com. 1966-67), Calif. Repub. League (pres. 1966-67), Repub. Associates (pres. 1983-85); mem. Air Force Assn., Aircraft Owners and Pilots Assn., Allied Post Am. Legion (comdr. 1969-70), South Bay Bar Assn., Fellow Am. Coll. of Trust and Estate Counsel, Internat. Acad. Estate and Trust Law (exec. council 1974-78), L.A. County Bar Assn. (chmn. probate and trust law com. 1964-66, chmn. Legislation Com. 1980-86, chmn. Program com. 1981-82, bd. trustees 1983-85, L.A. County Bar Found. bd. dirs. 1987-, recipient Shattuck-Price Award 1990), Am. Bar Assn. (sect. probate, trust, and real prop. law and taxation), Calif. State Bar (bulletin chmn. 1970-72, chmn. Probate Com. 1974-5, exec. com. 1977-83, Legis. chmn. 1978-89, Legis. co-chmn. 1991-92, Estate Planning. Trust and Probate Law Sect.; Conf. of Dels. exec. com. 1987-90), Breakfast Club (pres. 1989-91), Lawyers Club of L.A. (first v.p. 1983), Phi

Alpha Delta (supreme justice 1972-74, elected. to Distinguished Service Chpt. 1978), Legion Lex (pres. 1969-71), Chancery Club, World Affairs Council, IPA, Rotary Intl., Commonwealth Club, St. Andrews Soc., Town Hall (pres. 1975), L.A. Com. on Fgn. Relations, Lincoln Club, Phi Beta Kappa (v.p. Alpha Assn. So. Calif. 1984-86), Omicron Delta Kappa; mil: 2d lt. USAAF, WWII; United Presbyterian; rec: theater, volleyball, swimming. Res: 600 John St Manhattan Beach 90266 Ofc: 777 S Figueroa St 34th Flr Los Angeles 90017

RAINES, FRANCES ELIZABETH, real estate broker; b. Aug. 14, 1928, Norfolk, Va.; d. Ernest Chapman and Lula Elizabeth (Bibb) Clark; m. Horace Franklin Raines, Aug. 19, 1950; children: Sandra b. 1952, John b. 1955, Elizabeth b. 1960, Rebecca b. 1960, Joan b. 1962; edn: stu. William and Mary, 1946-47, Converse Coll. 1947-48; BA, fgn. affairs, George Washington (D.C.) Univ. 1950; San Francisco St. Coll. 1955-57; Calif. Secondary Tchg. Cred. 1957. Career: res. clk. typist, Dept. Navy, Pentagon, Wash. 1950, Dept. Army, Pentagon 1951-53, Dept. Army, Presidio, San Francisco 1954-55; high sch. tchr./counselor Hayward Union High Sch. Dist., San Lorenzo H. Sch., 1957-60; bus. owner, Sacramento 1970-73; real estate sales spec. in resales, San Jose 1974-76, Orange Co. 1976-82; broker assoc., New Home Sales, The Ryness Co., Danville 1982-87; Tri Development, San Francisco 1987-88; The Ryness Co., 1988-; awards: Ford Found. III Fellow 1956-57, Highest producer Forest E. Olson Co. (11/77) Million$ Sales (1979, 80, 81), Multi-million$ Sales (1983, 85, 86, 87, 88, 89); mem: Nat. Assn. of Realtors 1974-82, Calif. Assn. Realtors 1974-82, San Jose Bd. Realtors 1974-76, West Orange Co. Bd. Realtors 1976-77, Huntington Bch. Fountain Valley Bd. Realtors 1977-82, Sales & Mktg. Council of BIA 1983-87; Republican; Prot.; rec: needlepoint, profl. seminars, travel. Res: 8120 Maid Marion Ct Sacramento 95828 The Ryness Company 801 San Ramon Valley Blvd Danville 94526

RAJ, PRITHVI, chemical engineer, business owner; b. Nov. 22, 1939, Hyderabad, India; s. Bhavani Singh and Gulab Bai; m. Padma; children: Praveen b. 1971, Poonam b. 1978; edn: BSChE, Osmania Univ. India 1964; MSChE, Indian Inst. of Tech. Kharagpur 1970. Career: chem. engr. Black Sivalls & Bryson Inc., Houston, Tx. 1971-77; project engr. Gulf Interstate, Houston, Tx. 1977-79; sr. engr. Fluor Engring. 1979-84; chief process engr. Saudi Cons., Saudi Arabia 1984-86; owner Avalon Plating (tech. svs.), South El Monte 1986-; mem: Chemical Engrs. Club, Indian Profls. Houston; chem. engring. articles pub. in tech. jours., speaker safety seminars; Hindu; rec: travel, photog., music. Res: 22613 Ironbark Dr Diamond Bar 91765 Ofc: Avalon Plating 1934 Cogswell Rd South El Monte 91733

RAM SAMUJ, DOUGLAS SHELTON, internationally acclaimed fabric artist, lecturer, teacher; b. Suva Fiji, naturalized Australian 1967; s. Ratu and Stella (Dudley) Ram Samuj; edn: univ. entrance, Scots Coll., Wellington, N.Z. 1944-52; Royal Melbourne Tech. Coll., Australia 1955; DA (Dip. of Associateship), Manchester Coll. of Art, England 1957-59; NDD (Nat. Dip.in Design) 1957-59; ATD (Art Tchrs. Dip.) Sydney Tchrs. Coll., Australia 1960. Career: designer David Whitehead Ltd., Lancashire, Eng. 1956; art tchr. New South Wales Edn. Dept., Sydney, Australia 1961-65; freelance designer, fabric artist, guest lectr., Los Angeles 1968-, sponsored in U.S. by Edith Head, Academy Award winning Hollywood costume designer; exhbns: The Macquarie Galleries, Sydney, 1965, Argus Gal., Melbourne, 1965, Von Bertouch Gal., Newcastle, 1965, The Johnstone Gal., Brisbane, 1966, White Studio Gal., Adelaide, 1966, Coombe Down Gals., Geelong, 1966, Gal. De Tours, S.F., 1967, Richard Brooks, Dallas, 1975, 83, The Egg and Eye, L.A., 1968, Johnstone Gal., Brisbane, 1972, Garlicks, Capetown S.A., 1973, Robinson's Stores, 1973, Bullocks, 1973, 74, Denver Petroleum Club 1986; Am. Craft Council Registry (New York 1992), num. others; work rep. in textile collections: Brigham Young Univ., Colo. State Univ., Bauder Fashion Coll. (Tx.), Oreg. State Univ., vis. lectr. num. univs. and colls. nat., 1974-; awards: The Heywood Prize Royal Manchester Instn., England, 1959, Scots Coll. prefect, house capt. and capt. 1st XI at cricket, 1951-52, Duncan Bat, best batting average cricket, 1951, 52, music prize Scots Coll., 1949; clubs: Summerhill Cricket Club, Melbourne, Austr. 1955- (Silver Cup and Ball for best Bowler 1955-56), Didsbury Cricket Club, Manchester, Eng. 1957-59 (Championship winners 1957); newspaper feature stories on art in L.A. Times, S.F. Chronicle, Women's Wear Daily, Kansas City Star, L.A. Herald Examiner, Chgo. Sun-Times, St. Louis Globe-Democrat, Sew News, AFTA (the Australian Forum for Textile Arts), Surface Design J., Australian Expatriate, Pacificway (Air N.Z.), Ornament, Oz Arts (Austr.), Am. Quilter, Filter Arts, others; Methodist; rec: films, jazz, cricket. Address: 2618-1/2 W Marathon St Los Angeles 90026

RAMER, BRUCE M., lawyer; b. Aug. 2, 1933, Teaneck, NJ; s. Sidney and Anne (Strassman) R.; m. Ann Greenberg, Feb. 15, 1965; children: Gregg B. b. 1967, Marc K. b. 1969, Neal I. b. 1972; edn: AB, Princeton Univ. 1955; JD, Harvard Law Sch. 1958. Career: assoc. law firm of Morrison, Lloyd and Griggs, Hackensack, NJ 1959-60; partner law firm Gang, Tyre, Ramer & Brown, Inc., Los Angeles, Ca. 1963-; exec. dir. Entertainment Law Inst., bd. of councilors USC Law Center, 1973-; awards: community service Am. Jewish Com. 1987, Bev. Hills Bar Assn. Exec. Dir.'s Award 1988, NCCJ annual brotherhood award 1990; mem. Am. Bar Assn., Calif. Bar Assn., L.A. County Bar Assn., Beverly Hills Bar Assn., Calif. Copyright Conf. (pres. 1973-74), L.A. Copyright Soc.

(pres. 1974-75), The Fellows of the Am. Bar Found., Princeton Club (So. Calif. pres. 1975-78); civic bds: United Way (v.chair 1991-, corporate bd. dirs. 1981-, exec. com., chair Coun. of Presidents 1989-, mem. Comm. Issues Coun.), Loyola Marymount Univ. L.A. (trustee 1987-), Am. Jewish Com. (chair nat. bd. trustees, chair Nat. Exec. Council, chair Pacific Rim Inst., mem. nat. bd. govs., nat. v.p. AJC 1982-88, pres. L.A. chapt. AJC 1980-83, chair AJC We. Region 1984-86), Jewish Fedn. Council of Gr. L.A. (bd., mem. comm. relations com.), Jewish TV Network (bd.), L.A. Urban League (bd.), Frat. of Friends of L.A. Music Ctr. (v.p.), Calif. Community Found. (v.chmn. bd. govs.); mil: pvt. U.S. Army 1958-59, 2d lt. 1961-62. Res: 622 Alta Dr Beverly Hills 90210 Ofc: Gang, Tyre, Ramer & Brown, Inc., 6400 Sunset Blvd Los Angeles 90028

RAMSTEIN, WILLIAM L., financial executive; b. July 9, 1950, Los Angeles; s. Robert J. and Norma E. (Knapp) R.; edn: BS, CSU Northridge 1975; MBA, USC 1984; CPA, Calif. 1980, Cert. Internal Auditor 1980. Career: senior internal auditor Los Angeles County 1975-78; audit senior, mgmt. cons. Alexander Grant & Co., Van Nuys 1978-80; hd. fin. Missile Sys. Gp. Hughes Aircraft Co., Canoga Park 1980-89; mgr. financial reporting Space & Electronics Group TRW, Redondo Beach 1989-; indep. financial cons., advisor 1980-; awards: Haskins & Sells Award for Outstanding Achiev. in Acctg. 1974, Beta Gamma Sigma 1984; mem. Calif. Soc. of CPAs; rec: investments, softball, bodybuilding, running. Res: 4310 Torreon Dr Woodland Hills 91364 Ofc: TRW, Inc. One Space Park Redondo Beach 90278 Tel:310/812-8839

RANCE, QUENTIN E., interior designer; b. Mar. 22, 1935, St. Albans, Hertfordshire, England; s. Herbert Leonard and Irene Anne (Haynes) R.; m. India Perlin, May 17, 1974; children: Brian b. 1954, Zane b. 1959, Steven b. 1960; edn: Beaumont Sch., St. Albans, Hert., U.K. 1946-53; Eastbourne Sch. of Art, Eastbourne, Sussex, U.K. 1955-60; NCIDQ, pvt. study programs, N.Y.C., 1983. Career: buyer, sales mgr. Dickeson & French Ltd., Eastbourne, Sussex, U.K. 1955-62; head designer/dir. Laszlo Hoenig Ltd., London 1962-73; mng. dir. Quentin Rance Interiors Ltd., London 1973-81; pres. Quentin Rance Enterprises Inc., Encino, Calif. 1981-; awards: chapter presdl. citation ASID, L.A. (1984, 85, 86, 87, 91), hon. mention Nat. Assn. of Mirror Mfrs. 1987, First pl., Nat. Pub. Service award Designer Specifier /ASID 1990; mem. Chartered Soc. of Designers, U.K. (Fellow 1982-), ASID (profl. mem. 1983-, admissions chmn. L.A. chpt. 1985-, avanti chmn. 1983-85); publs: pictorials in Designers West Mag. (1983), Design House Preview (1983), Profiles (1987), Designer Specifier (1990); mil: sr. airman Royal Air Force, U.K. 1953-55; rec: antiques, world travel, cycling. Ofc: Quentin Rance Enterprises Inc. 18005 Rancho St Encino 91316 Ph: 818/705-8111 Fax: 818/705-2213

RANDALL, JAMES GRAFTON, trial lawyer; b. Dec. 2, 1951, Great Lakes, Ill.; s. Cmdr. John A. (USN, ret.) and Barbara Blanche (Coen) R.; m. Valerie Sue, Oct. 18, 1980; children: Wm. Douglas, Michael Coen (twins) b. 1981; edn: AA, Chaffey Jr. Coll. 1972, BS, Univ. N.Y. 1978, J.D., Western St. Coll. of Law 1981; admitted bar: Mont. 1985, Mont. Fed. Dist. Ct. 1986, Calif. 1986, Ct. of Appeals 9th dist. 1987, U.S. Dist. Ct. Cent. dist. Calif. 1987. Career: personal injury trial lawyer, instr. (evidence/labor law) Am. Coll. of Law 1985; author: California Personal Injury Form Book (Bancroft-Whitney, 1987), num. law jour. articles; contbg. editor L.A. Trial Lawyers Assn. "Advocate" mag., 1990; awards: Speaker of year Chaffey Jr. Coll. 1972, So. Calif. Coll. Debate Champion 1973, Am. Jurisprudence Awards in crim. law 1978 and constnl. law 1979; mem: ABA, Calif. Bar Assn., Los Angeles Trial Lawyers Assn., Calif. Trial Lawyers Assn., Am. Trial Lawyers Assn. (speaker Melvin Belli Seminar, ATLA Conv. 1991, 1992), San Diego Trial Lawyers Assn. (Tort editor S.D. Trial Bar News); mil: sp4c AUS (1969-71, 1973-76, Vietnam Svc., Vietnam Campaign, Vietnam Cross of Gal. w/palm); rec: writing, local politics Res: Anaheim Hills.

RANKIN, HELEN CROSS, cattle ranch/guest ranch owner; b. Kern County, d. John Whisman and Cleo Rebecca (Tilley) Cross; m. Leroy Rankin (dec. 1954), Jan. 4, 1936; children: Julia (Sharr) b. 1939, Patricia (Denvir) b. 1940, William John b. 1945; edn: AB, CSU Fresno 1935. Career: owner/opr. Leroy Rankin Cattle Ranch (founded 1863 by Walker Rankin Sr.) with husband 1936-1954, 1954-, founder, pres. and gen. mgr. Rankin Ranch, Inc., guest ranch with internat. clientele, 1965-; frequent lectr. various groups on Calif. and Rankin family history; mem. US Bur. of Land Mgmt., Sect. 15; honors: mem. US Food and Agri. Leaders Tour China 1983, Tour Australia and N.Z. 1985, Calif. Hist. Soc. award 1983, Kern River Valley Hist. Soc. award 1983, named Kern County Cattlewoman of the Year 1987; mem: Nat. Cattlemens Assn./Kern Co. chpt., Am. Nat. Cowbelles Assn. (pres. Kern Co. Cowbelles 1949); civic: Camp Ronald McDonald for Children (advy. bd.), Childrens Home Soc. of Calif. (pres. Central Sect. 1945), Lori Brock Jr. Mus. (patron), Calif. Hist. Assn., Kern River Valley Hist. Assn.; publs: advt. for Rankin Ranch Inc., hist. research on Calif. and Rankin Family hist.; Republican; Baptist; rec: painting, gardening. Address: Rankin Ranch Box 36 Caliente 93518

RANNEY, HELEN MARGARET, physician/educator; b. Apr. 12, 1920, Summer Hill, N.Y.; d. Arthur Clark and Alesia Cecilia (Toolan) Ranney; edn: AB (Cum Laude), Barnard Coll., Columbia Univ., 1941; MD, Coll. of Physicians and Surgeons, Columbia Univ., 1947. Career: technician Babies

Hosp., New York, 1941-43; med. intern Presbyterian Hosp., 1947-48, asst. med. resident, 1948-50; clin. fellow in medicine Am. Cancer Soc., Dept. Med., Coll. Physicians and Surgeons, Columbia Univ., 1951-53; instr. in medicine 1954-45, assoc. 1956-58, asst. prof. clin. med. 1958-60, Columbia Univ.; assoc. prof. 1960-65, prof. med. Albert Einstein Coll. of Med., New York, 1965-70; prof. med. S.U.N.Y. at Buffalo, 1970-73; prof. med. Dept. Med., UC San Diego, 1973-90, dept. chair 1973-86, prof. emeritus of med. 1990-; distinguished physician Dept. Veterans Affairs, VAMC San Diego, 1986-91; dir: Squibb Corp. 1975-89; trustee Population Council 1976-88; bd. sci. cons. Memorial Sloan-Kettering Cancer Ctr. 1986-88; awards: Phi Beta Kappa, Alpha Omega Alpha, Sigma Xi (Faculty), Joseph Mather Smith Prize, Columbia Univ. 1955, Dr. M.L.King, Jr. Med. Achiev. Award for outstanding contbn. in field of sickle cell anemia 1972, Gold Medal, Coll. Physicians and Surgeons Alumni Assn. Columbia Univ. 1978, Disting. Alumni Award Barnard Coll. 1980, Mayo H. Soley Award for excellence in res. We. Soc. for Clin. Investigation 1987; mem: Nat. Acad. of Scis. (1973-,council 1977-80, chair Sect. 41 1986-89, class IV sec. 1989-92), Inst. of Med. NAS (1973-, council 1980-83), Assn. of Am. Physicians (1968-, council 1978-85, pres. 1984-85), Am. Coll. Physicians (1968-, Master 1980), Am. Acad. of Arts and Scis. (1975-, Fellow), AAAS (Fellow 1979), We. Assn. of Physicians (1974-, pres. 1976-77), Am. Physiol. Soc. 1973-, Am. Soc. Biol. Chemists, Am. Soc. for Clin. Investigation, Am. Soc. Hematology (pres. 1973-74), Am. Soc. Biochemistry and Molecular Biology 1972-, Central Soc. for Clin. Res.; author 2 books, 77 original sci. articles, 40 invited articles. Res: 6229 La Jolla Mesa Dr La Jolla 92037

RAPHAEL, MARY D., teacher, church real estate appraiser/broker, author; b. May 28, 1950, Marysville; d. Lloyd Cass and Margaret Marie (Nisonger) Dovell; m. David A. Raphael, Aug. 29, 1971; children: Tammy b. 1978, Doug b. 1979; edn: AA, Yuba Coll., Marysville 1969; BA, CSU Long Beach 1971; MA, USC 1976; Calif. std. tchg. cred.; R.E. broker lic.; cand. MAI (Mem. Appraisal Inst.), CREA (Cert. R.E. Appraiser). Career: tchr. Bellflower Unified Sch. Dist. 1970-71, Bonita U.S.D., San Dimas 1971-; real estate sales agt. American Realtors, Bellflower 1978-80; owner/broker Raphael Realty Church Specialists, Bellflower 1980-, appraiser churches, 1985-; bd. dirs. Mitchell Camp; honors: Phi Kappa Phi; author: Punt, Pass & Kick for NFL, 1977; Democrat; Presbyterian; rec: pvt. pilot, skiing, motorcycling. Res: 10356 Park St Bellflower 90706 Ofc: Raphael Realty Church Specialists, PO Box 57 Bellflower 90706

RASCO, CORNELIA NELLIE, architect; b. Dec. 24, 1932, Sarata Nova, Romania; nat. 1982; d. Stefan and Ecaterina (Agafonov) Ivanov; edn: BS, Univ. Bucharest Sch. Arch. 1959; Orange Coast Coll 1978-79; Coastline Comm. Coll. 1978; UC Irvine 1984. Career: arch., bldg. safety dept. City of Turda, Romania 1958-59; arch. field rep., Constrn. Co. #1, Bucharest 1959-61; prin. arch. Bucharest Inst. of Plan & Archs. 1961-69; draftperson C.F. Murphy Assoc., Chgo. 1970-75; arch., staff II, EMA/recreation facility design Co. of Orange 1975-77; arch. designer, Co. GSA/A&E Div. 1977-89; asst. proj. mgr. 1989-92; awards: CSCAS 1st prize for design Motel in Mountain Resort, 1st prize Museum of Archeol.; mem: Romanian Archs. Assn. 1963-69, AIA (assoc. mem. 1978-91); civic: Orange Co. Employees Assn. 1977-; rec: travel, classical music, opera.

RASMUSSEN, MIKE JOSEPH, community college financial aid officer; b. Aug. 1, 1947, Avalon, Calif.; s. Herman Joseph and Nina (Walker) R.; m. Phyllis Ann Freedman, Aug. 4, 1968 (div.); children: Dawn Michelle b. 1970, Stephen Michael b. 1973; edn: AA in liberal arts, 1967, bilingual studies, 1980, bus. edn., 1983, BA soc. sci., 1969, MA edn., 1976; stu. West Valley Coll. 1965-67, San Jose State Coll. 1967-69, CSU San Jose 1974-77, Butte Coll. 1977-83; Calif. Comm. Coll. life credentials: counseling 1976, basic pupil personnel svs. 1977, supr. 1980, instr. psych., personnel wkr., and chief adminstrv. ofcr., 1982. Career: Veterans Pgms. coord./counselor Butte Community Coll. Dist., 1977-80, interim dir. fin. aid 1980-81, dir. financial aid and veterans affairs, 1981-92, dir. special pgms. & svs. 1992-; appt. Butte Coll. EOP/S Advy. Com. 1983-, Chancellor's Fin. Aid advy. group 1985-87, 88-91, VA reg. office advy. bd. 1978-79; bd. dirs. Chico Comm. Hosp. Found. 1985-; awards: appreciation Community Companions Inc. (1976, 77), Butte-Glenn Co. Vet. Employment Com. 1979, BSA Troop 770 (1985), Paradise Pride Lioness Club 1986, Butte Coll. EOP/S (1986, 87), pub. service award Calif. Health & Welfare Agy. 1980; mem: Calif. Comm. Coll. Student Fin. Aid Adminstrs. Assn. (1980-, pres. 1989-90, chair Fed. Issues com. 1991-92, state awards: 3 for outstanding service, 7+ appreciation), Calif. Assn. SFAA, Western Assn. SFAA, Nat. Assn. SFAA, Vet. Pgm. Adminstrs. of Calif.; mil: p.o. 2c USN 1970-74, Merit. Unit Cit., Vietnam Svc. Medal, Vietnam Cpgn. Medal, Combat Action Rib.; rec: motorcycling, sports cars, golf, fishing, bicycling. Ofc: Butte College Financial Aid Office, 3536 Butte Campus Dr Oroville 95965

RATALAHTI, HEIKKI, graphics designer; b. June 28, 1937, Kauhajoki, Finland; nat. 1974; s. Eino and Sanni R.; edn: Univ. of Helsinki, Finland, 1962-63; Acad. of Art Coll., S.F., Calif., 1969-70. Career: exec. trainee, Doubleday & Co., NY (US State Dept. student exchange program) 1960-62; operated family-owned book bus. in Finland 1963-67; design staff, Am. Conservatory Theater, S.F. 1967-69; graphics designer, Nagase Advt., S.F. 1970-71; co-founder, v.p., design dir., Jayme, Ratalahti, Inc., Sonoma, Calif. 1971-; mem. guest faculty, Stanford Univ. and Radcliffe Coll. pub. courses; designed graphics for Japan Ctr. complex, S.F. 1970-71; designed promotion materials that launched Smithsonian, Bon Appetit, Air & Space, Food & Wine, Mother Jones, Cooking Light, Worth, Paris Hebdo (France), and other publs. 1971-; awards: numerous profl. awards from art directors' clubs, Folio Magazine, Direct Mktg. Assn.; profiled, NY Times Sunday Magazine, Aug., 1990; mil.: 2nd lt., Signal Corps, Finnish Army, 1958-59. Ofc: Jayme, Ratalahti, Inc. 1033 Bart Road Sonoma 95476

RATCLIFF, BRUCE EPHLIN, hoist company executive; b. Oct. 3, 1941, Canton, Ill.; s. Ralph A. and Margaret H. (Buck) R.; edn: BA econ., San Francisco State Univ., 1967. Career: v.p. sales Ratcliff Hoist Co., San Carlos, 1967-79, exec. v.p. 1969-75, pres. 1975-, pres. and c.e.o. Ratcliff Co. Inc. 1976-. Res: 1308 Sunnyslope Ave Belmont 94002 Ofc: 1655 Old Country Rd San Carlos 94070

RATEAVER, BARGYLA, organic/conservation gardening and farming educator, writer, international consultant; b. Aug. 13, 1916, Ft. Dauphin, Madagascar; came to U.S. 1935; d. Eugene Alaric and Margaret (Schaffnit) Rateaver; children: Gylver; edn: grad. (Valedictorian) American Sch., Ft. Dauphin, 1934; San Francisco Jr. Botany, 1951; MSLS, lib. sci., UC Berkeley, 1959; Calif. std. jr. coll. Adult Edn. credential, 1966, Eminence cred. for elem. and sec. schs., 1969; Calif. R.E. lic., 1968. Career: plant collecting in Madagascar, 1930-34; plant intro. for USDA, UCB Genetics Dept., 1935; plant collection in U.S. for European collections, 1936; herbarium and bot. dept. res. asst. UC Berkeley, 1938-43; organized herbarium Palm Springs Desert Mus., 1944; res. asst. bot. dept. Univ. Mich. 1945-51; bot. res. UCD, 1951-52, UCLA Hort. Dept. 1953-54, San Diego County, 1954-55; organized biology library, Kaiser Labs., 1958-59; org. sci. libraries in Calif., histology lab. Univ. Alberta, Calgary, 1959-64; lectr. on organic gardening, radio and TV, 1965-67; re-org. sci. collection Santa Rosa City-Co. Library, 1968-69; lectr. on organic gardening radio, TV, univs., demonstrations and expo. booths, pvt. classes, author/pub. books in field, columnist nat. mags., 1968-, promote internat. liaison and maintain internat. corr. service in field, 1972-; initiated and intro. into U.S. ednl. system the first course in organic gardening and farming, intro. first coll. and univ. level course (TM) "Conservation Gardening and Farming" at: San Jose Sch. Sys., 1965, Coll. of Marin, 1966, UC San Diego Ext., Marin County Adult Edn., and private classes San Francisco, 1968; instr. courses Univ. Calif. Extension, Calif. State Univ., jr. colls., campuses statewide, 1970-77, garden plots UC Berkeley, UC Irvine, Santa Rosa Jr. Coll., and Palomar Jr. Coll., 1970, CSU Sacto., 1972; mem. Internat. Fedn. of Organic Agriculture Movements (IFOAM) 1978-: editl. bd. 1988, coord. com. 1978-82, and mem. working Groups: Information, Edn.; exh. of Organic Method Primer in IARC Book Exh., Beijing (1982), multiple exhibits Del Mar Fair, Del Mar, Ca. (1984, 91), lectr. World Food Expo, L.A. 1986, exhibits IFOAM Internat. Conf., Santa Cruz 1988 and Burkina Faso 1989, lectr. 1988 and exh. Eco Farm Conf., Asilomar, Monterey 1989-92 author: Organic Method Primer (1973), condensation of: Bio Dynamic Farming and Gardening by E.E. Pfeiffer, M.D. (1973); monthly columns in- Clear Creek, 1972, Let's Live, 1972-, Mother Earth News, 1972, Acres USA, 1973-, bimonthly column- Natural Life Styles, 1972-73, Health Quarterly, 1977, Calif. Organic Jour., 1977-, articles: Natural Life, Harrowsmith, Natural Gardening, Health Food Age, Answer mag., others; weekly bdcast. TV, Ch. 6, Healdsburg, 1969, guest num. talk shows and interviews San Francisco, Los Angeles, San Diego, 1970-; awards: pres.'s scholar DePauw Univ. 1935, award for plant introduction of 1935 for USDA and Joel Spingarn Clematic Collection 1935, honors stu. UCB 1938, 1st prize Della Sizler Graphic Arts Collection, UCB, for collection "Preparation for bot. res. in Madagascar" 1959; grantee Longwood Gardens 1955, award Chgo. Mus. Natural Hist. 1955, Am. Acad. Arts and Scis. 1955; Bible student. Res/Ofc: 9049 Covina St San Diego 92126

RATLIFF, WILLIAM ELMORE, historian, academic senior research fellow and curator, journalist, arts critic; b. Feb. 11, 1937, Evanston, Ill.; s. Harold Shugart and Marjorie (Elmore) R.; m. Lynn Robbins, June 9, 1959; children: Sharon, Paul, Susan, David, John; edn: BA in English, Oberlin Coll., 1959; MA Chinese history, Univ. Washington, Seattle 1968, PhD Latin Am. history, 1974. Career: res. fellow Hoover Instn., Stanford Univ., 1968-79, sr. res. fellow, 1986-; chief editorial writer, arts critic Times Tribune, Palo Alto 1979-86; cons. risk analysis Res. Internat., San Francisco 1972-79, indep. cons., 1979-; writer on classical music, music stringer Los Angeles Times, 1975-, Opera News, Met. Opera, N.Y. 1977-; instr. courses, seminars Stanford Univ., UC Berkeley, 1983-86, San Francisco St. Univ., Univ. of S.F., Univ. Wash., Monterey Naval Postgrad. Sch., Austrian Defense Acad. (Vienna), and Inst. of Internat. Relations (E.Berlin); lectr. for Am. Bar Assn., Amnesty Internat., Wash. Ctr. Strategic and Internat. Studies, US Nat. Def. Univ., US DoD, other agys.; US Govt. cons. and journalist (40 trips to 20 Latin Am. countries 1958-), USIA lecture tours in We. and Ea. Europe and Canada; splst. in politics of Latin Am. and Caribbean and US reg. policy, monitored elections El Salvador, Costa Rica and Chile, talked with Latin Am. presidents incl. Fidel Castro; author: Castroism and Communism in Latin America (1976), author/editor: The Selling of Fidel Castro: The Media and the Cuban Revolution (1987), co-editor (w. S. Amaral) Juan Peron: Cartas del exilio (1991), coauthor (w. R. Fontaine) Changing Course: The Capitalist

Revolution in Argentina (1990), (w. Roger Miranda) Civil War in Nicaragua: Inside the Sandinistas (1993); Latin Am. area ed. of Hoover Instn.'s Yearbook on Internat. Communist Affairs, 24 yrs.; num. articles and revs. in scholarly jours., book anthologies, mags.; awards: Oberlin Shansi Memorial 1959-62, Nat. Def. Edn. Act 1963-68, Hoover Instn. Nat. fellow 1971-72; rec: classical music, hiking. Ofc: Hoover Institution, Stanford CA 94305

RAUFMAN, WILLIAM LEONARD, lawyer, lease company executive; b. Dec. 27, 1946, Los Angeles; s. Zale and Minnia Judith (Davis) R.; m. Mary Costley, July 4, 1973; son, Jason b. 1980; edn: AA, L.A. Valley Coll., 1967; BA, CSU Northridge, 1970; UCLA Grad. Sch., 1971; JD, Southwestern Univ., 1978; adv. law studies USC, 1984; admitted Calif. St. Bar 1981, Fed. Dist. Ct. Central Dist. 1981. Career: personnel/advt. mgr. Environmental Quality Magazine, Los Angeles 1970-71; area mktg. mgr. Swimrite, Inc. Van Nuys 1972-74, lectr. service & sales tng. seminars througout U.S., atty. pvt. practice, Encino 1981-83, Van Nuys 1983-; Lease co. exec. KMI Leasing, Van Nuys 1983-87; leasing mgr. Westside Investments, Marina Del Rey 1987-90; area mgr. GE Capital, 1990-, also lectr. and Showroom Lease Tng. Seminars; honors: CSUN Associated Students outstanding service award 1969, 2 years yell leader (1969, 70), apptd. atty. general 1970; mem: Calif. Trial Lawyers Assn., Los Angeles Trial Lawyers Assn., Lawyers Club of L.A., Calif. Bar Assn., Nat. Vehicle Leasing Assn., Delta Theta Phi, Zeta Beta Tau (Northridge chpt. v.p.), Chi Sigma Chi (Van Nuys chpt. v.p.), UCLA Alumni Assn., CSUN Alumni Assn.; civic: counseling Boys Club Am. 1967-68, Valley Cities Jewish Community Ctr. 1968-70; co-founder mag., Environmental Quality (1970); Jewish; rec: golf, tennis, music publishing, photog. Res: 2116 Kasten Simi Valley 93065 Law Offices of Wm. L. Raufman, 6454 Van Nuys Blvd Ste 150 Van Nuys 91401 also: GE Capital Auto Leasing 333 City Blvd W. #1800 Orange 92668

RAVEN, BERTRAM H(ERBERT), psychology educator; b. Sept. 26, 1926, Youngstown, Ohio; s. Morris and Lillian (Greenfeld) R.; m. Celia Cutler, Jan. 21, 1961; children: Michelle G., Jonathan H.; edn: BA, Ohio State Univ., 1948, MA, 1949; PhD, Univ. Mich., 1953. Career: res. assoc. Res. Ctr. for Group Dynamics, Ann Arbor, Mich. 1952-54; lectr. psychology Univ. Mich., 1953-54; vis. prof. Univ. Nijmegen, Univ. Utrecht, Netherlands, 1954-55; psychologist RAND Corp., Santa Monica, Calif. 1955-56; prof. and chmn. dept. psychology UCLA 1956-, co-dir. Tng. Pgm. in Health Psychology, UCLA, 1979-88; vis. prof. Hebrew Univ., Jerusalem 1962-63, Univ. Wash., Seattle, Univ. Hawaii, Honolulu, 1968, London Sch. of Economics and Polit. Sci., England, 1969-70; external examiner Univ. of the West Indies, Trinidad and Jamaica, 1980-; participant Internat. Expert Conf. on Health Psychology, Tilburg, Netherlands, 1986; cons. in field, expert witness Calif. cts., 1978-, cons. World Health Orgn., Manila 1985-86; author: (with others) People in Groups (1976), Discovering Psychology (1977), Social Psychology (1983); editor: (with others) Contemporary Health Services (1982), Policy Studies Rev. Annual (1980); contbr. articles to profl. jours., editor J. of Social Issues (1969-74); awards: Guggenheim fellow, Israel (1962-63), Fulbright scholar, Britain 1969-70, Netherlands 1954-55, Israel 1962-63, citation L.A. City Council 1966, NATO sr. fellow, Italy 1989, citation for res. on social power Calif. Sch. Profl. Psychology, L.A. 1991; mem: Am. Psychol. Assn. (Fellow, chair bd. social and ethical responsibility 1978-82), Soc. for Psychol. Study of Social Issues (Fellow, pres. 1973-74), AAAS, Am. Sociol. Assn., Internat. Assn. Applied Psychology, Soc. Experimental Social Psychology, Assn. Advance. of Psychology (founding, bd. 1974-81), Am. Psychol. Soc., Internat. Soc. Polit. Psychology, Interam. Psychol. Soc., Am. Psychology/Law Soc.; rec: guitar, travel, internat. studies. Res: 2212 Camden Ave Los Angeles 90064-1906 Ofc: UCLA Dept. Psychology Los Angeles 90024-1563 Ph: 310/825-2296

RAWLINGS-MERCER, BETTE, investment manager; b. June 18, 1921, Fullerton, Nebr.; d. Floyd Perry and Verda Mae (Hood) Rawlings; m. Clair Eugene Mercer, June 4, 1939 (dec. 1981); children: Linda L. b. 1941, D. Scott b. 1951; edn: San Bernardino Valley Coll. 1965-69. Career: coordinator, campaign monitor, advocate Common Cause, 37th Congressional Dist. 1973-80, St. bd. of dirs. 1974-77; active Democratic Party: pres. Democratic Club, Redlands 1974-76, exec. bd. 1970-82; dep. registrar of voters County of San Bernardino; Democratic State Central Committeewoman 1975-91; mem: Smithsonian Instn., Nat. Acad. Political & Social Sci.; Presbyterian; rec: political and medical research. Address: Redlands 92374

RAWSON, MICHAEL JAMES, machine company president; b. Sept. 28, 1957, Santa Monica; s. Charles Edward and Marie Jean (Thiroux) R.; m. Dona Marie Bunzel, July 31, 1982; children: Christopher b. 1984, Matthew b. 1986; edn: BS, Santa Clara Univ., 1979; grad. work, UCLA. Career: asst. controller Kingsley Machines, Hollywood 1979-82, sec.treas. 1982-86, exec. v.p. and c.f.o. 1986-90, pres. and c.e.o. 1990-; cons., guest lectr. UCLA Sch. Grad. Mgmt., 1984-85; listed Who's Who in Am. Colls. & Univs. 1979, Who's Who in Finance 1986, Who's Who in West 1991, Who's Who Among Young Execs. 1991; civic bds.: Boys & Girls Club Hollywood (pres. 1986-, c.f.o. 1985-86), St. Jerome Sch., L.A. (advy. bd. 1989-); club: Wilshire Country; Republican; R.Cath.; rec: coaching, running, fishing, sports. Ofc: Kingsley Machine Co. 850 Cahuenga Blvd Hollywood 90038

RAY, DAVID LEWIN, lawyer; b. June 17, 1929, Los Angeles; s. Herbert and Beatrice (Lewin) R.; m. Arlene Opas, July 15, 1951; children: Stephan b. 1954, Robyn b. 1957; edn: BS, UCLA, 1954; JD, Univ. of La Verne, 1970. Career: ptnr. Ray and Ray, Los Angeles 1957-71; Zigmond, Ray & Co., Beverly Hills 1971-73; Ray & Murray, B.H. 1973-75; Ray, Rolston & Ress, B.H. 1975-80; Saltzburg, Ray & Bergman, L.A. 1980-; v.p. Management Affiliates, L.A. 1975-; v.p. Things From All Over, L.A. 1972-; lectr. symp. UCLA, Citicorp Nat. Exec. Sem.; mem: Am. Inst. of CPAs, Am. Bar Assn., L.A. County Bar Assn. (chair exec. com. Prejudgment Remedies Sect.), L.A. Bankruptcy Forum, Fin. Lawyers Conf.; club: Brentwood CC; contbr. articles to ABA Jour., Lawyer/Manager, Law Office Econs. and Mgmt., The Compleat Lawyer; mil: pfc US Army 1951-53; rec: sailing, diving, golf, tennis. Ofc: 10960 Wilshire Blvd 10th Fl Los Angeles 90024

RAYNER, ARNO ALFRED, investment executive; b. Sept. 23, 1928, San Francisco; s. Kurt Hugo and Angela (Flasch) R.; m. Kenyon Lee Reid, June 14, 1951; children: Eric b. 1957, Jill b. 1959, Neal b. 1967; edn: BS, UC Berkeley, 1950, MBA, 1954; Chartered Fin. Analyst (C.F.A.) 1967. Career: investment analyst Bank of California, San Francisco 1950-54; sr. v.p. Industrial Indemnity, 1954-74; v.p. Bechtel Corp., 1975-76; pres. Rayner Associates, Mill Valley 1977-; vis. lectr. UC Berkeley, Santa Clara Univ.; mem. bd. dirs. num. corps., and non-profit orgs.; clubs: Bohemian 1979-, World Trade 1962-, San Francisco Bond (1957-, dir.), Tiburon Peninsula (1954-, past pres.), Harbor Pt. Tennis 1991-, S.F.Kiwanis (v.p., dir.), Am. Philatelic Soc. 1988-; mil: chief cashier Army Strawberry Dr Mill Valley 94941 Ofc: Rayner Associates, Inc. 655 Redwood Hwy Ste 370 Mill Valley 94941

REA, JAMES EDMOND, wholesale distribution co. president; b. Nov. 11, 1935, Tallahassee, Fla.; s. Russel E. Rea and Muriel (Pair) Edwards; m. Zhita Nash, March 19, 1983; children: Darbi b. 1964, Kirsten b. 1966; edn: BA, San Diego St. Coll. 1962; MA, UCLA 1967. Career: asst. prof. philosophy No. Ariz. Univ., Flagstaff 1966-72; Tx. Tech. Univ., Lubbock 1973-74; marine electrician Duthie Electric, Wilmington 1974-85; owner, pres. Beach Electric Supply (formerly Beacon Internat. Electric Supply), Long Beach 1985-91; mgr. Walters Wholesale Electric 1991-; mil: USN 1954-57; Democrat. Res: 3736 Cedar Ave Long Beach 90807 Ofc: Walters Wholesale Electric 1687 W 9th St Long Beach 90813

REA, RICHARD LEONARD, corporate executive; b. June 17, 1942, Alameda; s. Samuel Leonard and Margaret Mary (Kenney) R.; edn: AA, Foothill Coll. 1963; BS, San Jose State Univ. 1966. Career: acctg., Fairchild Semiconductor, Mtn. View 1967-70; Smith Kline Instruments, Palo Alto 1970-72; Arcata National, Menlo Park 1972-75; Hyatt Corp., Burlingame 1975-76; Medical Life Systems, Mountain View 1976-81; Automatic Data Processing, Santa Clara 1981-83; Ready Systems, Sunnyvale 1984-90; c.f.o., sec.treas. Human Affairs Internat. of Calif. (healthcare svs. co.) 1990-; fin. cons., tax return preparer; mem. Inst. of Mgmt. Accts. (nat. dir. and chapt. past pres.), Kiwanis Club of Palo Alto (past v.p.); mil: p.o. USNR 1966-70; Republican; R.Cath.; rec: golf, tennis. Res: 23038 Cricket Hill Rd Cupertino 95014 Ofc: Human Affairs International of Calif., 2105 S Bascom Ave Ste 295 Campbell 95008

REAGAN, JOSEPH BERNARD, aerospace scientist, research & development executive; b. Nov. 26, 1934, Somerville, Mass.; s. Joseph Bernard, Sr. and Helen (Lowry) R.; m. Dorothy Marie Hughes, March 2, 1957; children: Patrick b. 1958, Michael b. 1959, Kevin b. 1961, Kathleen b. 1962, Brian b. 1964, John b. 1968, Maureen b. 1975; edn: BS, Boston Coll. 1956. MS, 1959; PhD space scis., Stanford Univ. 1975; tchr. and res. asst. Boston Coll. 1956-58; scientist Lockheed Missile & Space Co. 1959-: sr. scientist 1961-63, res. scientist 1963-68, staff scientist 1968-74, program mgr. space payloads 1974, mgr. Space Scis. Lab. 1975-84, dir. Electronic Scis. Lab. 1984, dir. Physical & Electronic Sci. Lab. 1985-86, Lockheed Res. & Devel. Div. dep. gen. mgr. 1986-88, v.p./asst. gen. mgr. 1988-91, v.p./gen. mgr. 1991-; dir: Southwall Tech. Inc. 1987-92, Planning Systems Inc. 1989-91; dir. Technology Ctr. of San Jose 1992-; advy. council Schs. of Engring. at Stanford Univ. and UC Berkeley; awards: Disting. service Pioneer Venus Pgm. NASA, AIAA/ S.F. Chpt. Outstanding Engr. 1988; Fellow AIAA 1990, mem. Am. Geophysical Union, Sigma Pi Sigma, IEEE; patent: Transistorized Amplifier (1963); publs: 130+ papers in tech. jours.; invited lectr. 12 nat. & internat. tech. soc. meetings; mil: capt. AUS 1956-63; Republican; R.Cath.; rec: computers, woodworking. Res: 13554 Mandarin Way Saratoga 95070 Ofc: Lockheed R&DD (0/90-01 B/201) 3251 Hanover St Palo Alto 94304

REAGAN, NANCY, First Lady during 40th U.S. Presidency; b. July 9, 1923, NYC, raised in Chgo.; d. Dr. Loyal and Edith (Luckett) Davis; father, prof. surgery emeritus, Northwestern Univ. (dec. 1981); bro. Dr. Richard Davis, neurosurgeon, Phila.; m. Ronald Reagan, March 4, 1952; children: Patricia Ann, b. 1952, Ronald Prescott, b. 1958; Pres. Reagan's children by 1st marriage: Maureen, b. 1941, Michael, b. 1946; two grandchildren; edn: grad. Girls' Latin Sch., Chgo.; drama major Smith Coll., 1943. Career: actress, stage (road tours to Broadway and Radio City Music Hall; film (11 films include: The Next Voice You Hear; East Side, West Side; Hellcats of the Navy), TV prodns., 1949-56;

First Lady of Calif., 1966-74; First Lady of U.S., 1980-88; ldr. Foster Grandparent Program, 1967-, coauthor (w/Jane Wilkie) To Love A Child, with song by same title written and dedicated to her by Hal David and Joe Raposo, recorded by Frank Sinatra (all book and record sales benefit pgm.); activist for POWs and MIAs, hon. sponsor Vietnam Vets Mem. Fund; spl. project fighting substance abuse among youth, 1980-, traveled 170,000+ miles vis. rehab. centers and schs., held briefing for 30 First Ladies and internat. drug conf. 1985; hon. chair Nat. Fedn. of Parents for Drug-Free Youth, "Just Say No" Found., Nat. Child Watch Campaign, Pres.'s Com. on the Arts and Humanities, Wolf Trap Found. Bd. Trustees, Nat. Trust for Historic Preservation, Cystic Fibrosis Found., Nat. Republican Women's Club, hon. pres. Girl Scouts of Am.; awards: Hon. DHL, Georgetown Univ. 1987, Hon. LLD, Pepperdine Univ. 1983, num. humanitarian awards U.S. C. of C., USO, Salvation Army, Entertainment Inds. Council, Rotary Clubs Intl., Lions Club Intl., var. drug treatment programs, Am. Camping Assn., Nat. Council on Alcoholism, United Cerebral Palsy, Intl. Ctr. for the Disabled, Boys Town Father Flanagan Award, Kiwanis Intl. World Service Medal 1986, Variety Clubs Intl. lifeline award, Gallup Poll list of 10 most admired women in world (1981-, most admired 81, 85, 87), Good Housekeeping mag. survey of 10 most admired women in world (1981-, ranked number one 1984, 85, 86), LA Times Woman of the Year 1968, Permanent Hall of Fame of Ten Best Dressed Women in Am. Res: Bel Air

REAGAN, RONALD WILSON, 40th President of the United States; b. Feb. 6, 1911, Tampico, Ill.; s. John and Nellie (Wilson) R.; m. Jane Wyman, 1940, div. 1948; children: Maureen, Michael; m. 2d. Nancy Davis, Mar. 4, 1952; children: Patricia, Ronald; edn: BA in econ. and sociol., Eureka Coll. 1932. Career: radio sports broadcaster and editor, 1932-37; film actor, over 50 feature-length motion pictures, 1937-50s; prodn./host General Electric Theatre TV series 1950s, host, Death Valley Days TV series 1964-65; elected Gov. of Calif. 1966-70, re-elected 1970-74; syndicated radio commentary pgm., newspaper column, extensive speaking schedule to civic, bus., polit. groups nat., 1974-; mem. Presidential Commn. investigate the CIA, 1974-75; candidate for Repub. presidential nom. 1976, campaigner for 86 candidates in 1978 elections; elected US President (by electoral vote 489-40), Nov. 4, 1980, sworn in as 40th US President Jan. 20, 1981, elected 2d term 1984-88; founder Citizens for the Republic; past bd. dirs. Com. on the Present Danger; past pres. Screen Actors Guild 6 terms; past pres. Motion Picture Indus. Council 2 terms; awards include Nat. Humanitarian, NCCJ; Torch of Life, City of Hope; Horatio Alger; Am. Newspaper Guild; Freedoms Found. awards; Distinguished Am., Nat. Football Found. Hall of Fame; Am. Patriots Hall of Fame; Medal of Valor, State of Israel; mil: capt. USAAF 1942-45, WWII; Tau Kappa Epsilon. Address: Bel Air

RECORD, CLAYTON ARCHIE, corporate relations executive; b. Aug. 19, 1927, Hemet; s. Clayton Austin and Georgia Mae (O'Loan) R.; m. Ella Mae Quandt, Aug. 21, 1948; children: Clayton b. 1950, Michael b. 1951, Randolph b. 1952, Keith b. 1953, Nanciana b. 1955; edn: AA, Riverside Comm. Coll., 1947; BS, Cal Poly S.L.O., 1952. Career: mgr. Record Rancho, San Jacinto 1952-72; elected 3d dist. Riverside County Bd. Supervisors, 1973-80, chmn. 1974-75, v.p. So. Calif. Assn. of Govts. (SCAG) 1979-80; sr. v.p./relations NBS/Lowry, Hemet 1981-; dir. Bank of Hemet 1975-; awards: Book of Golden Deeds, Hemet/San Jacinto Exchange Club 1985, Disting. citizen Inland Empire Boy Scout Council San Bdo. 1987, honoree Inland Empire Am. Cancer Soc. 1989, Leadership award The Valley Group 1990, Lifetime Svc. Award So. Calif. Bldg. Ind. Assn. 1992; mem: So. Calif. Building Industry/Riv. Chpt. (past pres.), League of Calif. Milk Producers /Sacto. (pres. 1970-71), Calif. Assn. Co. Suprs./Sacto. (pres. 1979), SCAG Regional Advy. Council (chmn. 1982-85), Calif. Desert Conservation Area Advy. Council (chmn. 1978, 80, 81-83), Calif. Sch. Board Assn. (pres. 1966), Hemet Hospital Found. (pres. 1991-92), Riverside Monday Morning Group (1981-, pres. 1988-89), Hemet/San Jacinto Exchange Club (pres. 1956, dist. gov. 1957); mil: Naval Aviation V-5 Pgm. 1945-47; Republican; rec: photog., hiking, fishing. Res: 890 N Lyon Ave San Jacinto 92583 Ofc: NBS/Lowry 1545 W Florida Ave Hemet 92343

RECSEI, ANDREW ANDOR, research chemist; b. July 22, 1902, Kula, Yugoslavia; s. Maximilian and Ernestine (Vogl) R.; m. Mila Ivanovich, Nov. 2, 1942; children: Eric J. b. 1943, Paul A. b. 1945, Claire R. Hirsch b. 1945; edn: BA, Univ. Vienna, Austria 1920; MA, Univ. Kiel, Ger. 1922; PhD, Univ. Brno, Czech. 1925. Career: chemist Dr. Honsig Lab., Brno, Czech. 1925-27; chief chemist Pharmador Lab., East London, S.Africa 1928-38; research assoc. UCLA 1939-41; Cal Tech Pasadena 1941-42; owner Research Lab., Santa Barbara 1944-88; instr. UC Santa Barbara 1943-53; cons. Recsei Labs., Goleta 1988-; awards: Toastmasters Internat. dist. trophy 1950; mem: Am. Chemical Soc., Sierra Club, UCSB Univ. Affiliates, Santa Barbara Museum of Art, Music Acad. of West, Lions, Toastmasters Internat. (pres. 1947), Sigma Xi (pres. 1948), Montecito Union Sch. Bd. (pres. 1955); research articles pub. in sci. jours. 1924-86, patent in field of alcoholic beverages 1971; Unitarian; rec: writing, gardening, tennis. Res: 633 Tabor Ln Santa Barbara 93108

REECE, MONTE MEREDITH, lawyer; b. May 29, 1945, Jackson, Tenn.; s. Jerrel Rexford and Marjorie (Ricks) R.; m. Melanie; children: Hugh b. 1970, Bryan b. 1973, Andrew b. 1974, Jerrel b. 1985, Rebecca b. 1986; edn: Louisiana

State Univ. 1963-64, 66; Louisiana Coll. 1964-65; LLB, Western State Univ. Coll. of Law 1974; admitted Calif. State Bar 1974. Career: assoc. atty. English & Marotta APC 1974-78; atty. pvt. practice 1978-; US magistrate US Dist. Ct. Eastern Dist of Calif. 1983-; judge pro tem Lake Valley Jud. Dist. El Dorado Co. 1983-85; comm. coll. instr. 1983-85; mem. Lions Club (bd. 1986-); civic: Sudden Infant Death Syndrome S.Lake Tahoe (bd. 1988-, pres. 89-90), Tahoe Human Svs. (legal advisor 1986-), Eldorado County Sheriff Search and Rescue (legal advisor 1988-), AYSO Reg. 82 (bd. 1982-, commr. 1985); mil: SK2 USNR 1967-72, Navy Achievement medal w. combat V, Navy Unit comendn., Vietnam Svc., Viet. Campaign (3), Nat. Def. medals, Viet. Cross of Gallantry w/palm; Republican; Prot.; rec: antique furniture restoration, photography. Address: 3330 Lake Tahoe Blvd Ste 10 S Lake Tahoe 96150

REED, DALE D., executive; b. July 22, 1931, Veedersburg, Ind.; s. Clyde and Aline (Jones) R.; m. Donna Ellen Bartley, April 16, 1955; children: Katherine b. 1956, Richard b. 1957, Ann b. 1960; edn: BS engring., Purdue Univ. 1953. Career: pres. Blakemore Equipment, Oakland 1962-66; Bay Area Kenworth, San Leandro 1966-84; chmn. and c.e.o. Buran & Reed Inc. 1984-; dir: Civic Bank of Commerce 1984- civic bds.: San Leandro Planning Commn. (chmn. 1990), San Leandro Scholarship Found. (trustee 1986-), Goodwill Industries of E. Bay (trustee 1988-), San Leandro C.of C. (pres. 1985-86); mil: 1st. lt. AUS 1954-56; Republican; Prot. Res: 1560 Daily Ct San Leandro 94577 Ofc: Buran & Reed, Inc. 1801 Adams Ave San Leandro 94577

REED, DWIGHT THOMAS, III, lawyer, chief executive; b. Feb. 25, 1955, Rep. of Singapore; s. Marvin C. Reed; 1 son, Josh Simmons b. 1980; edn: BA and BS, UC Berkeley, 1977, JD, Boalt Law Sch. UCB, 1981. Career: asst. export trade ofcr. US State Dept. Fgn. Service, Am. Embassies in Singapore, China, Japan, 1981-90; litigation dir. law firm Horowitz and Reed, Berkeley 1990-92; c.e.o. Dwight Inc., Richmond 1992-; awards: Man of Yr. Nat. League of Black Lawyers Berkeley 1991, Law firm of Yr. ACLU Berkeley 1991; mem: Nat. Assn. Crim. Def. Lawyers, Nat. League Black Lawyers, Calif. Trial Lawyers Assn.; author: The Growth of Cocaine 1981, The State Dept. for Blacks (1992); Democrat; rec: sky diving, scuba diving. Ofc: Dwight, Inc. 2224 Ohio Ave Richmond 94804

REED, GERARD ALEXANDER, educator; b. Jan. 19, 1941, Colorado Springs, Colo.; s. Paul Alexander and Lula (Taylor) R.; m. Roberta Kay Steininger, May 26, 1963; edn: BA, So. Nazarene Univ., 1963; MA, Univ. Oklahoma, 1964, PhD, 1967. Career: asst. prof. So. Nazarene Univ., Bethany, Okla. 1966-68; assoc. full prof. MidAmerica Nazarene Coll., Olathe, Kans. 1968-82; prof. Point Loma Nazarene Coll., San Diego 1982-; awards: Parriot Found. fellow, Norman, Okla. 1966, "B" Award So. Nazarene, Bethany, Okla. 1980, merit cit. Gen. Assembly Ch. of Nazarene, K.C., Mo. 1980; mem: Am. Soc. Environmental History, Am. Maritain Soc., Conf. Faith and History, Wesleyan Theol. Soc., Western History Assn., Sierra Club; publs: 12+ articles; Ch. of the Nazarene; rec: running. Res: 4217 Loma Riviera Ln San Diego 92110 Ofc: Point Loma Nazarene College, 3900 Lomaland San Diego 92106

REED, ROBERT DANIEL, publisher, entrepreneur; b. May 24, 1941, Pottsville, Pa.; s. Robert Daniel and Thelma June (Weiss) R.; m. Sonja Kathy, Dec. 15, 1963; children: Robert b. 1966, Alan b. 1968, Tanya b. 1969. Career: buyer Viking Labs, Sunnyvale 1962-69; mktg. mgr. Plaza Press 1969-70; pres. R&E Research Assoc., Palo Alto 1971-85, pres., pub. 1986-; pres., CEO Edgecombe Corp., Saratoga 1986-; pres. The Other Money Inc, Saratoga 1986-; awards: incentive award U.S. Armyu Intelligence Group 1960, 61, 62; mem: Amnesty Internat., Nat. Geographic Soc., Cent. for Democratic Institutions, Friends of the San Jose Library; author and co-author of 60 books 1976-, pub. 1100+ books in edn., sociology, self-help 1966-, 10 copyrights var. products 1980-, var. electro-mech. inventions in works 1970-; mil: U.S. Army, 1959-62; Republican; rec: idea creation, generalist, oil painter, inventions, gardner. Ofc: R&E Publishers POB 2008 Saratoga 95074

REEDS, ROBERT TERRILL, construction consultant; b. Nov. 24, 1932, Montebello; s. John Wm. and Maxine (Keifer) R.; m. Elizabeth Isaacs, June 26, 1960; children: Judy b. 1963, Leonard b. 1967; edn: BSME, Calif. Berkeley 1960; grad. studies Ind. Univ. Sch. of Bus. 1960-62, UCLA Sch. of Bus. 1962-64; reg. profl. engr. Calif. 1976. Career: design engr. RCA Corp., Indpls. 1960-63; quality control supr. Endevco Corp., Pasadena 1963-67; Raytheon Co., Santa Ana 1963-73; indep. constrn. cons./prin. American Home Inspection, Mission Viejo 1974-; guest lectr. UC Irvine 1980-82, Santa Ana Coll. 1978-82, Saddleback Coll. 1978-81, Irvine Valley Coll. 1988; writer, newspaper column "Around The House" 1979-86; editor: Calif. Real Estate Insp. Assn. Newsletter 1977-84, 91-, Real Estate Winners Circle 1988-, Home Buyer's Manual 1988; co-editor, Consumer Reports; honors: "Top 50" Orange Co. Register 1985, CREIA John Daly award 1989, ASHI Phillip Monahon award 1990; mem: Calif. Real Estate Insp. Assn. (bd. 1977-), Am. Soc. of Home Inspectors (sr.), Nat. Soc. of Profl. Engrs.; mil: s/sgt. USAF 1949-53; rec: computers, motorcycling. Ofc: American Home Inspection 26916 Pueblonuevo Dr Mission Viejo 92691

REESE, ALBERT M., public relations consultant; b. Apr. 5, 1933, Morgantown, W.Va.; s. Albert Moore and Nelle (Summers) R.; m. Susan Gail Holt, Apr. 3, 1971; edn: BA, W.Va. Univ., 1954; MS, Boston Univ., 1959; Accredited (APR) Pub. Relations Soc. of Am. Career: pub. relations dir. United Community Services of Met. Boston, Mass. 1960-68; United Way of San Diego County, Calif. 1968-75; v.p. pub. affairs San Diego Convention & Visitors Bureau, 1975-92; mem. bd. dirs. San Diego County Unit, Am. Cancer Soc., 1985-; chmn. San Diego County Quincentenniel Commn., 1992-93; mem. tourism sect. Mexico-U.S. Border Governors' Conf.; mil: capt. USAF 1954-56; Democrat; Episcopalian. Res: 5317 E Palisades Rd San Diego 92116

REICHENBACH, THOMAS, veterinarian; b. Jan. 6, 1947, NYC; s. Harry J. and Helen M. (Kelly) R.; m. Cleda L. Houmes, Nov. 23, 1984; edn: BS in chem., Univ. of Notre Dame, 1968; MS in chem., UC Davis, 1973; AA in prodn. agri., Shasta Jr. Coll., 1975; DVM, UC Davis 1981; Diplomate Am. Board Vet. Practitioners, 1991-. Career: staff veterinarian Marina Pet Hosp., San Francisco 1981-82; relief veterinarian Vet. Mgmt. Services, Salinas 1983-; guest lectr. UC Davis 1986; bd. dirs. Vet. Post-Graduate Inst., Santa Cruz 1989-; mem: Santa Barbara Vet. Emergency Group (pres. 1991-), Am. Vet. Med. Assn. 1977-, Calif. Vet. Med. Assn. 1977-, Santa Barbara-Ventura Vet. Med. Assn. 1992-, Nat. Notre Dame Monogram Club 1965-; author software pgms: Clinical Simulator 1990, Wedding Planner 1988; profl. jour. articles re vet. medicine, computers in vet. medicine; mil: E4 US Army 1970-72; Republican; R.Cath.; rec: computer pgmg. Ofc: Vet. Management Services 1887 #1 Cherokee Dr Salinas 93906

REILLY, TERRENCE WELDON O., electron microscopist; b. Jan. 21, 1962, Stockton; s. Terrence Lester and Diane Michelle (Black) R.; m. Cecille T. Leveriza, May 29, 1988; children: Terrence Lester II b. 1990; edn: electron microscopist, San Joaquin Delta Coll., 1982. Career: scanning electron microscope/apps. engr. engr. Nanometrics Inc., Sunnyvale 1983-85; asst. mgr. electron microscope group, Nissei Sangyo America - Hitachi Sci. Instruments, Mtn. View 1985-; EM lectr., Lincoln Sch. 1981-82; mem: Electron Microscopy Soc. of Am., San Joaquin Delta Coll. Electron Microscopy Soc. (pres. 1982), E. Clampus Vitus, Stockton Art League; awarded Best of Show: Unitarian Ch. Art Show 1982, CSU Stanislaus Art Show 1980; contbr. tech. articles in J. Electron Microscopy Techniques, Electron Microscopy Soc. of Am. (Proc. 45, 46, 49), IEEE Conf. on Micrometer and Submicrometer Lithography (1987), XII Internat. Cong. of Electron Microscopy (1990), Internat. Soc. for Optical Engring. (1992); article in Modern Photography (1980); Republican; R.Cath.; rec: windsurfing, art, astronomy, astro-physics, rose hybredizing. Res: 1375 Emory St San Jose 95126 Ofc: NSA-Hitachi 460 E Middlefield Rd Mountain View 94043

REINER, THOMAS KARL, manufacturing company president; b. Dec. 29, 1931, Budapest, Hungary; nat. U.S. citizen, 1961; s. Pal and Josefa (Keller) R.; m. Joyce Ann, Feb. 10, 1960 (div.); m.2d. Eleanore Ruth; children: Paul b. 1960, Renee b. 1962; edn: diploma optics trade sch., Budapest, 1952; MSME, Tech. Univ., Budapest 1955; MSEE courses, London Coll. 1958; var. courses Univ. Pittsburgh , Royal McBee, UCLA, 1952-71. Career: engr. Central Power Generating Sta., Hungary 1954-56; cons. engr.; test engr. Blaw-Knox Co., London 1956-57; sr. engr. Eubank & Ptnrs., London 1957-58; research engr. Pittsburgh Plate Glass Co., Pa. 1959-60, product mgr. Copes-Vulcan div. 1960-62; chief engr. J.W. Fecker div. of Am. Optical Co., 1962-66; product mgr. Carco Electronics, Menlo Park 1966-68; chief engr. Fairchild Camera, El Segundo 1968-70; dir. engring. Templeton, Kenly & Co., Los Angeles and Chgo. 1970-72; general mgr. Foremark Corp., Gardena 1972-74; pres. Kinetron, Inc., Long Beach 1974-76; pres. GRW Inc., Hawthorne 1977-; adj. prof. Tech. Univ., Budapest 1951-54; mem. Internat. Soc. of Weighing and Measurements 1973-, mem. ASME 1960-79; bd. pres. Peacock Ridge Homeowners Assn., Palos Verdes; patents: post tensioning device for concrete, spherical air bearing and gimballed slave connector, synchronization of hydraulic jacking systems, bending of automotive side windows; inventions: tug/barge latching system, membrane type loadcell, ultra low profile platform and truckscales; mil: lt. armored div. Hungarian Army, 1951-57; Republican. Res: 121 Cottonwood Circle Rolling Hills Estates 90274-3430

REINJOHN, RICHARD G., lawyer; b. Mar. 24, 1939, Los Angeles; s. George R. and Lorine Reinjohn; m. Ann Thomas (div. Jan. 1988); children: Laura b. 1963, Andrew b. 1966; edn: att. UC Berkeley; BA, UCLA, 1960; LLB, USC Law School, 1964; admitted Calif. St. Bar 1965; nat. import-export mgr. Watson Bros. Transportation Co. 1960-61; assoc. Von Herzen & Hutton 1966-67; ptnr. Von Herzen, Catlin, Reinjohn, & Clements 1967-77; mng. ptnr. Reinjohn, Catlin, Clements & Burgess, 1977-80; ptnr. Reinjohn, Clements, Burgess & Holston 1986-87; managing ptnr. law offices of Richard G. Reinjohn 1988-; lectr. num. organizations; advisor pgms. for paraprofessionals and legal assts. at num. univ. and colleges; instr. USC Law Sch. 1971-72, Pasadena Comm. Coll. 1972-74; mem: Am. Bar Assn., LA Co. Bar Assn. (past chmn., exec. bd. Law Ofc. Mgmt. Sect., del. to St. Bar), Lawyers Assistance Com. (exec. bd. mem.), Orange Co. Trial Lawyers Assn., Assn. of So. Calif. Defense Counsel, Am. Trial Lawyers' Assn., special com. on Paraprofessionals and Legal Assts. (1971-), Trial Lawyers Club (bd. govs. 1968-, treas. 1969-70, pres.-elect 1973, pres. 1973-

74), Calif. Trial Lawyers Assn., Assn. of Bus. Trial Lawyers, Spkrs. Bureau (1969-); weekly radio host: "Let's Talk About The Law" KBRT Radio, 1984-85. Ofc: Law Office of Richard G. Reinjohn 606 S Olive St Ste 1700 Los Angeles 90014

REISS, JERRY MILBOURNE, municipal official, construction consultant; b. Sept. 15, 1937, Torrance; b. James Milbourne and Emma Helen R.; m. Collette Martin, Aug. 17, 1973; children: Jonathan b. 1968, Devin L. b. 1975; edn: AA, El Camino Coll. 1957; psychol., Univ. Ariz. 1958-61; arch., Calif. Polytech. St. Univ. 1962-64. Career: owner Wildbird Properties 1964-69; pres. and c.e.o. Bunnell Construction Inc. 1968-91; prin., constrn. cons. in area of constrn. defect and contract litigation J.M. Reiss & Assocs., 1991-; honors: Calif. Scholarship Soc. (life); mem. San Luis Obispo Contractors Assn. (bd. dirs., past pres. 1979-82); civic bds: Calif. Consortium for the Prevention of Child Abuse (bd. 1990-), Mission Coll. Prep. Sch. (regent 1985-87), San Luis Obispo Architectural Review Commn. 1976-81, City Planning Commnr. 1981-87, Economic Opportunity Commn. (bd. 1988-) City Council San Luis Obispo (elected 1987-, v. mayor 1989-); Republican (congl. nominee 16th C.D. Calif. 6/90); mil: Calif. Air Nat. Guard; Christian. Res: 1364 San Marcos San Luis Obispo 93401

REMIGIO, SAL J., accountant; b. July 19, 1910, Cavite, Philippines; nat. 1984; s. Emiterio T. and Paciencia (Kalambakal) R.; m. Felicia L. Yrigan, Sept. 14, 1944; children: Remy b. 1945, Rita b. 1947, Ruben b. 1949, Ruby b. 1953, Redentor b. 1961; edn: elem. tchr. cert. (scholarship honors), Philippine Normal Sch., Manila 1931; BS in commerce (Valedictorian), National Univ., Manila 1941; first MBA grad. Univ. of San Jose, Cebu City 1965; computer sci. courses Rancho Santiago Coll., 1985, cert. in real estate, 1990; CPA, 1941; lic. ins. broker, Ill., 1978, ins. agt., Calif., 1986, R.E. agt., Calif., 1989. Career: pub. sch. tchr. Philippine Bur. of Edn., 1931-35; mcpl. treas. Bay, Laguna, Phil. 1936-37; asst. paymaster Met. Water Dist., Manila 1938-45, also auditor MWD Employees Coop. Credit Union; 1st Lt. (G-2) 34th Guerrilla Div., USAFFE, 1942-45; asst. navy auditor USN Contract NOY 13531, Guam 1946-47; CPA pvt. practice, Cebu City, 1948-71; p.t. office mgr. Southeast Med. Center, Chgo., Ill. 1972-83; pres. and gen. mgr. Underwriters Engineering Service, Chgo. 1975-78; ins. broker p.t., Chgo. 1978-83; asst. auditor Chase Bank Intl. of Chicago, 1978-79; claims adjuster Creators, Inc. 1979-80; acct. and p.t. ins. agent M.G. Internat. Ins. Center, Chgo. 1981-83; acct. Rancho Santiago Coll. Found., Santa Ana, Calif. 1984-; p.t. acct. Lourdes Church, Santa Ana, 1981-; p.t. ins. agt. 1986-, p.t. real estate rep. 1989-; founder and mgr. 5R2 Associates, Santa Ana 1991-; awards: pres. National Univ. Supreme Student Council 1940-41, mem. Coll. Editors Guild of Phil. 1940-41; mem: AARP, Am. Legion Post 131 (Santa Ana), Am. Assn. of Individual Investors, Am. Philatelic Soc., Calbayog City Assn. of So. Calif., Rosary Group of Orange Co., St. Jude League (Chgo.), March of Dimes, Arthritis Found., Century 21 Four Sons Realty, H.B.-F.V. Bd. Realtors, Financial Independence Club, Repub. Presdl. Task Force; writer 3 short stories (1934, 35, 40); R.Cath.; rec: coins & stamps, movies, dancing, classical music, reading. Ofc: Rancho Santiago College Foundation 17th & Bristol St Ste 217 Santa Ana 92706

REMINGTON, DAVID ASTAIRE, computer and electrical engineer, mathematician; b. Feb. 16, 1948, Colorado Springs, Colo.; s. Vernon Ivor and Mary Jane (Miller) R.; m. Susanna, Nov. 3, 1972; children: David b. 1976, Robert b. 1978, Melanie b. 1981, Timothy b. 1990; edn: BSEE (honors), Univ. Colo. 1971, MSEE, 1974, MA in Math., 1976. Career: staff mem. Los Alamos Sci. Lab., 1976-80: electrical engr. Electronics Div. LASL, control systems programmer for Eight Beam HELIOS Laser Fusion Res. Facility (3 yrs), in chg. E div. Computer Aided Design (1 yr); senior engring. cons. (systems analysis, modeling and simulation) Los Alamos Tech. Assocs. 1980-81, did control systems models for a liquid metal fast breeder reactor, and a complete plant transient model for Tritium Systems Test Assembly of LASL; guest scientist, cons. for Los Alamos Sci. Lab, 1980-81; power prodn. engr. Pacific Gas and Electric, Diablo Canyon Plant 1981-, in chg. plant security computer system, 2 plant turbine control computer sys. and turbine network data servers; awards: 2 NSF scholarships, Tau Beta Pi 1970, Eta Kappa Nu 1970, Sigma Tau 1970, 5 performance recognition awards PG&E 1984-90; mem. IEEE 1969-, Computer Sci. Book Club, Electronic Engring. Book Club; 6 tech. publs. in field; Republican; bicycle road racing, running. Res: 1821 Royal Way San Luis Obispo 93405 Ofc: PG&E Diablo Canyon PO Box 56 Avila Beach 93424

RENNICK, SYDELLE, speech pathologist; b. Mar. 6, 1941, Bklyn.; d. Alexander Simon and Ethel (Yarvis) Shatkin; m. Harley Rennick, Aug. 6, 1970; dau. Gwen b. 1962; edn: BA, and MA communicative disorders, CSU Long Beach, 1983, 86; lic. speech/lang. pathologist 1987. Career: pathologist Acute Care, La Habra Rehab. Assn. Inc. 1986-89, also Rehabilitation Unit 1987-, covering affil. hosps. Memorial Hosp. of Gardena 1986-, Midway Med. Ctr., L.A. 1986-90; area supr. Alta Therapies, L.A. 1991-; stroke support group United Stroke Found., Hawthorne 1987-; pvt. practice Speech and Hearing Services, Torrance 1987-; honors: Golden Key, Kappa Delta Pi; mem: Acad. Neurologic Communication Disorders and Scis. 1990-, Am. Speech Language Hearing Assn. (PAC), Calif. Speech Language Hearing Assn., So. Calif. Sp.-Lang.

Pathology & Audiology Dirs. Council, Soroptimist Internat., Redondo Bch.-P.V. Chpt. (1974-, v.p. 1975-77); rec: breed thoroughbred horses and Shar-Pei dogs, travel. Res: 32706 Via Palacio Rancho Palos Verdes 90274

RESSA, AMES DANIEL, physician, surgeon; b. Jan. 18, 1954, Rockville Centre, N.Y.; s. Ames Daniel and Roselyn (Maguire) R.; m. Mona Lisa Ascoli, Aug. 12, 1979; children: Ames Edward b. 1985, Thomas Michael b. 1988, Francesca Elyse b. 1991; edn: BA, Brown Univ., R.I. 1976; MD, Columbia Coll. Physicians & Surgeons, N.Y. 1980; cert. Am. Bd. Surgeons 1988. Career: gen. surgical resident St. Vincent's Hosp. & Med. Center, N.Y.C. 1980-85; attdg. surgeon So. Calif. Permanente Med. Group, San Diego 1985-; mem: A.C.S., S.D. Soc. Surgeons. Res: 6898 Bluefield Ct San Diego 92120 Ofc: 4647 Zion Ave San Diego 92120

RESTER, GEORGE G., architect, master planner, designer, showman, artist, painter, sculptor; b. Oct. 5, 1923, Panchatoula, La.; s. Kelly C. and Myra V. (Adams) R.; m. Virginia Nacario, June 25, 1955; children: Gina b. 1956, Taira b. 1959, Licia b. 1963; edn: spl. engring. tng., US Combat Engrs. WWII; law, bus. actg. Soule Coll. 1945-48; stu. arch. and engring. Delgado Tech. Inst. 1949-50; Art Center Coll. of Design 1961-62; reg. arch. La. 1960, Calif. 1963, Fla. 1984, Ariz., Colo., N.J., Mich., Minn., N.Y., Tx. 1985, Wash. 1986, N.M. 1988; cert. NCARB 1985. Career: cabinet work, carpentry, constrn. foreman, gen. supt., gen. contr. 1945-53; gen. architectural practice in pvt. practice and with var. firms incl. project arch./designer Welton Becket 1961-64, sr. prin. engr. Ralph M. Parson Co. 1973-76; chief architect, dir. archtl. design and prodn. Walt Disney Imagineers, Glendale 1965-71, 1976-87, retired; recipient profl. accolades internat. for work incl. Disneyland, Calif., Disneyworld and Epcot, Orlando, Fla., and Tokyo Disneyland 1987; founding pres. and c.e.o. New Visions Resorts Inc., retired; George G. Rester Architect A.I.A. and Associates, internat. projects: master plan design, overview constrn. entertainment ctrs., destination resorts, hotels, shopping centers, and entire new communities; mem: AIA 1973, New Orleans Amateur Artists Soc. (founding pres., host of weekly radio bdcstg. pgm. 1940-42); mil: pfc AUS Combat Engrs. Corps WWII, European, African, Middle Eastern, Purple Heart; Republican; R.Cath.; rec: painting, sculpting, metal work, crafts. Address: 26337 Dunwood Rolling Hills Estates CA 90274

REUBEN, LEEDELL, neonatologist-pediatrician; b. Camden, Ala.; s. Willie Frank and Mary (Freeman) R.; m. Sylvia Staton, Dec. 23, 1972; children: Adrienne b. 1976, Annita b. 1980; edn: M.T., Coll. of Med. Technology, Mpls. 1962; undergrad. work, 1967-70, MD, 1974, Univ. Wash., Seattle. Career: rotating intern Letterman Army Med. Ctr., San Francisco 1974-75; pediatric resident Letterman Army Med. Ctr., 1975-77; gen. pediatric practice, chief dept. ped. Darnell Army Hosp., Ft. Hood, Tx. 1977-79; neonatology fellow Tripler Army Med. Ctr., Honolulu 1979-81; staff neonatologist Frankfurt Army Regional Med. Ctr., Frankfurt, W.Ger.; asst. neonatologist Kadlec Med. Ctr., Richland, Wash. 1983-84, med. advr. Benton-Franklin Headstart, Tri-Cities March of Dimes, 1984; senior neonatologist, San Joaquin Gen. Hosp., Stockton, Calif. 1984-, dir. neonatal intensive care unit 1984-88, asst. dir. ped. 1986-91, dir. pediatrics 1991-; San Joaquin Cty. Fetal - Infant Death Review Team 1992-, San Joaquin Cty. Child Death Review Team 1992; mem. bd. Black Women Initiative Perinatal Bd., med. advisor Black Women Initiative Pgm., 1990-; mem. Maternal, Child and Adolescent Health Bd.; mem. San Joaquin County Drug Abuse and Prevention Council; mem. Calif. Med. Assn., Calif. Perinatal Assn., San Joaquin Co. Med. Soc. Triplet Connection (bd. dirs. and sci. advy. bd. 1985-) ; clin. research articles in med. jours.; mil: maj. AUS 1978-83, GCM, Nat. Defense, Commendn. medals, Overseas, Am. Svc. rib.; AME; rec: fitness, family activities.

REVEAL, ARLENE HADFIELD, county librarian; b. May 21, 1916, Riverside, Boxelder Co., Utah; d. Job Oliver and Mabel Olive (Smith) Hadfield; children: James L. b. 1941, Jon A. b. 1944; edn: BS (valedictorian), Utah State Univ. 1938; tchg. cred., CSU San Diego 1970; MLS, Brigham Young Univ. 1976. Career: tchr. Logan High Sch., Logan, Utah 1937-38; social case worker Boxelder Co., Utah 1938-39; branch librarian Tuolumne Co. Library, Calif. 1948-54; acct. Strawberry (Calif.) Inn 1954-66, asst. mgr. Dodge Ridge Ski Area, Long Barn 1949-66, office mgr. Pinecrest (Calif.) Permittees Assn. 1955-66; Library Asst., Mono Co. Office of Edn. 1961-64; asst. to co. supt. of Mono Co. Office of Edn. 1964-67; librarian LaMesa-Spring Valley Sch. Dist., LaMesa 1968-71; county librarian Mono Co. Library, Bridgeport 1971-; honors: John Cotton Dana Award 1974, Woman of Year, Beta Sigma Phi 1980, Bridgeport Citizen of the Yr. 1993; mem: Am. Library Assn., Calif. Library Assn., Calif. Media and Library Educators Assn. (historian 1970), Mountain Valley Library System (chair 1988-90), Delta Kappa Gamma (chpt. pres. 1984-88), Beta Sigma Phi, Xi Omicron Upsilon (treas. 1981, 83, 1990-, chpt. pres. 1982, 85); civic: Aurelia Rebekah Assembly (treas. 1973-90), Pinecrest Vol. Fire Dept. (pres. 1953-54), Mono County Friends of the Library 1976-, Mono Co. Hist. Soc. (secty. 1982-), Developmentally Disabled Area Bd. #12 (chair 1990-92); jt. author: Mono County Courthouse; Pinecrest School History; (ERIC document) Team Teaching in the Library; Ch. of Jesus Christ of Latter Day Saints; rec: archaeol., knitting, Native Am. basketry. Res: Kingsley St Bridgeport 93517 Ofc: Mono County Free Library POB 398 Bridgeport 93517

REY, JUAN CARLOS, academic science and engineering researcher; b. Feb. 25, 1957, Obera, Argentina; s. Juan Carlos Rey and Dolly Beatriz (Prytz) Nilsson; m. Emma Beatriz Rocchi, Apr. 25, 1981; children: Diego b. 1982, Javier b. 1983; edn: nuclear engr., Balseiro Inst., Bariloche, Arg. 1981. Career: senior researcher INVAP, Bariloche, Arg. 1981-89; sci. and engring. assoc. Stanford Univ., Stanford, Calif. 1989-; pub. articles in profl. jours. and conf. proc. 1989-. Ofc: Stanford University AEL#206 Stanford 94305

REYBURN, STANLEY SHORTRIDGE, real estate consultant, expert witness, writer, educator; b. May 28, 1930, Los Angeles; s. Wilbur Wm. and Margaret (Leslie) R.; m. Jeanette Smith, May 29, 1982; children: Valerie, b. 1953; Stephen, b. 1955; Stuart, b. 1959; Paul, b. 1971; edn: AA, El Camino Coll. 1956; BS, CSU Los Angeles, 1959; MBA, USC, 1961; grad. Sch. of Mortgage Banking, Northwestern Univ., 1964; postgrad. work, USC 1965-66; DBA, Kensington Univ., 1988; A.I.B. std. certs. 1967; life jr. coll. tchr. cred. (bus. ad., econ.) 1968; cert. Sr. Loan Escrow Ofcr., Calif. Escrow Assn. 1970; desig: CRA, RMU, Nat. Assn. R.E. Appraisers, CREA. Career: asst. secty./asst. treas. Western Mortgage Corp. 1961-66; v.p./mgr. Security Pacific Nat. Bank 1967-77; pres. Commonwealth Escrow Co. and Commonwealth Svc. Co., 1977-79; 1st v.p.; sr. v.p.-admin. Century Bank, Los Angeles 1979-82; exec. vice pres., corp. secty., loan adminstr. and dir. Wilshire State Bank, 1982-86; sr. v.p., mgr. real estate industries div. Sterling Bank, 1986-90; real estate consultant, expert witness and writer, 1990-; instr. Calif. Cont. Edn. of the Bar; faculty Pacific States Univ. 1991-, College of the Desert 1990-, UCLA Ext. 1964-68, L.A. Valley Coll. 1968-, CSU Long Beach. 1966-67; mem. Calif. Escrow Assn. (dir. 1970-82, 89, contbr. monthly column in CEA News), L.A. Escrow Assn. (pres. 1968), Desert Escrow Assn., Am. Escrow Assn., Calif. R.E. Educators Assn. (awarded 1992 Norman Woest Award as Most outstanding real estate teacher), Nat. Assn. Mtg. Underwriters & Appraisers, Toastmasters Intl. (pres. 1990, ATM Bronze), Palm Springs Writers Guild (pres. 1991-92), Desert Press Women (treas. 1992); author: Careers in Escrow (Calif. Escrow Assn. 1976); Calif. Escrow Procedures: A Blueprint for the Nation (c. 1986, Stanley S. Reyburn); co-author Calif. R. E. Finance (coll. text, Scott, Foresman & Co., 1988); Escrow Procedures and Title Ins. (2 separate 8 hr. and 45 hr. courses, Anthony Schools, 1988); How To Get Better Performance and Profitability from Your Escrow Operation (Fulkerson & Assocs., 1988); What A Wonderful World This Could Be (World of Poetry Press, 1990); Appraisal Performance and Standards (Anthony Schools, 1991); Environmental Hazards Disclosure Requirements (3 hr. course, Calif. Comm. Colls. Real Estate Depository, 1991); technical ed. Calif. R.E. Practice (3d. ed. Scott, Foresman & Co., 1988); co-author One Up on Trump (Am. Capital Found., 1993); pub. poetry, radio plays prod. KCSN, 88.5 FM, numerous mag. & newsletter articles; Republican; Presbyterian; rec: numismatics, preservation of radio hist., writing. Res/Ofc: 73-702 Desert Greens Dr N, Palm Desert 92260-1206

REYES, ELOISE GOMEZ, lawyer; b. Jan. 27, San Bernardino.; d. Isaias R. and Jessie (Reynoso) Gomez; m. Frank G. Reyes, Jan. 24, 1981; children: Kristofer David b. 1985; edn: AA, S.B.V.C., 1976; BS, USC, 1978; JD, Loyola Law Sch., 1981; admitted bar Calif., 1982. Career: atty. Schwartz, Steinsapir, Dohrmann, et al, Los Angeles, 1982-84; Garza, Jure & King, San Bdo., 1984-88; pvt. practice law, San Bernardino, 1988-; vol. atty. Legal Aid, 1984-; v.chair Comm. Health Ctr., Bloomington, 1988-; awards: Citizen of Achievement League of Women Voters 1982, Nat. Hispanic Democrats 1988, Pro-Bono award State Bar of Calif. 1988; mem: Am. Bar Assn., San Bdo. County Bar Assn., Calif. Applicant's Attys. Assn., Calif. Trial Lawyers Assn., Latino Lawyers Assn. (bd.); R.Cath. Res: 25547 Nicks Ave Loma Linda 92354

REYNOLDS, ALBERT GORDON, ret. medical director, spa director; b. Jan. 25, 1926, Vashon Isl., Wash.; s. Albert Hargrave and Claire Louise (Stowell) R.; m. Polly Staples, Aug. 29, 1948 (div. Jan. 1989); children: Scott b. 1949, Debra b. 1952, Lori b. 1956; edn: MD, Univ. of Michigan 1949; Diplomate Am. Bd. of OB-Gyn. 1958. Career: intern, res. OB-Gyn. Univ. of Mich. Ann Arbor; pvt. practice OB-Gyn. Redlands, Calif. 1955-82; asst. clin. prof. UC Los Angeles and Loma Linda Med. Ctr.; past chief of OB-Gyn. dept., chief of staff Redlands Comm. Hosp.; currently med. and spa dir. La Costa Spa preventive med. and fitness; Fellow Am. Coll. of Surgeons 1960-, Am. Coll. of Preventive Med. 1984-, Am. Coll. Sports Med., Am. Geriatric Soc.; coauthor: The La Costa Book of Nutrition (Pharos Publ); mil: corpsman Navy Hosp. WWII 1943-45; capt. MC US Army Korean War 1950-51, Med. Combat Medal, Purple Heart, Meritorious Award from Crown Prince Thailand; Republican; Prot. Res: 1942 Swallow Ln Carlsbad 92009

REYNOLDS, MARGARET ANN, cleric, teacher; b. Dec. 9, 1920, York, Nebr.; d. Emmett and Nora Estelle (Jacobs) Osborn; m. John M. Reynolds, June 27, 1948; children: Matthew b. 1951, Jonathan b. 1955; edn: Hartford Sch. Religious Edn. 1940-41; BA, Univ. Nebr. 1938-42; MA, Columbia Univ. 1946-47; M.Div., Union Theol. Sem. N.Y.C. 1948; ordained minister Disciples of Christ (1948), Congregational Christian (1950), United Ch. of Christ (1961). Career: dir. Christian Edn. First Congregational Ch., Ft. Wayne, Ind. 1942-43; nat. secty. Forerunners, N.Y.C. 1943-45; dir. youth campaign Japan Internat. Christian Uni. 1949-50; moderator N.J. Assn. Congregational Christian Ch.

1954-56; moderator Kern Assn. United Ch. of Christ 1963-64; county dir. Retarded and Handicapped Center, San Bernardino 1966-67; tchr. McKinley Sch., Colton 1967-78; assoc. minister Neighborhood Congregational Ch. U.C.C., Laguna Beach 1979-83, minister emerita 1983-; mem. bd. Pacific Southwest Conf. on World Christian Mission, Asilomar, Pac. Grove 1989-96; secty. Friends of Oak Park Cemetery, Claremont 1986-90; mem. Centennial Com. United Ch. of Christ So. Calif. Council 1985-87; mem. Exec. Planning Com. for Annual Conf. So. Calif. (4 years); resrch. advy. bd. Am. Biog. Inst. Inc., 1989; awards: Cert. Merit Colton Unified Sch. Dist (1978), Vestals of Lamp Univ. Nebr. 1939, del. Oslo World Christian Youth Conf. 1947; mem: So. Calif. Campanology Club (pres. 1987-89), Nat. Egg Art Guild, Retired Tchrs. Assn. of Calif., Ch. Women United (chmn. World Day of Prayer 1988), Foothill Assn. of United Ch. Christ (nom. com. 1989-90), McKinley P.T.A. (life mem. 1978), The Nat. Museum of Women in the Arts (charter); author w. John M. Reynolds Smiles for Miles (1967) handbook for retarded and handicapped; Democrat; Prot.; rec: painting, swim. Res: 729 Plymouth Rd Claremont 91711

REZA, JACQUELYN VALERIE, college counselor, educator, therapist; b. Sept. 12, 1953, San Francisco; d. Armando Rosalio and Jacquelyn Joan (Jordan) Reza; children: 1 son; edn: BA, La Raza studies, San Francisco State Univ., 1979; BS in Zoology (honors), Ahmadu Bello Univ., Zaria, Nigeria, W. Africa 1978; MS in Rehab. Counseling, San Francisco State Univ., 1981; lic. Marriage Family Child Counselor (MFCC) 1982; Nat. Cert. Counselor 1981-, Cert. Hypnotherapist 1988-. Career: counselor SF State Univ. 1980-82, CSU Stanislaus, Turlock 1982-84, Gavilan Community Coll., Gilroy 1984-85, De Anza Community Coll., Cupertino 1985-, exec. bd. De Anza Faculty Assn. 1987-89, pres. De Anza Faculty Senate 1989-91; v.p. Latina Leadership Network of the Calif. Comm. Colls. 1991-93, pres. 1993-94; exec. bd. mem. Academic Senate Calif. Comm. Colls., 1990-92; MFCC therapist and workshop cons., pvt. practice therapist, San Francisco, Sacramento, San Jose, 1982-; cons. examiner Bd. of Beh. Scis., Sacto. 1986-92; cons. Driver Performance Inst., S.F. 1984-91; cons. EOPS Student Leadership 1987-; awards: honored graduate SFSU 1979, Outstanding Young Woman Am. 1987, special recogn. as Faculty Senate pres. DeAnza Coll. 1991, Women Leaders in Education Award 1990, SFSU Alumni Golden Torch Award 1993; mem. Minority Staff Assn., Third World Counselors Assn., La Raza Faculty Assn., Am. Assn. of Women in Comm. & Jr. Colls., Calif. Assn. for Counseling & Devel.; publs: (booklet) A Guide for I.D. and Referral of Students in Stress 1985, (articles) "Faculty Hiring Excellence Affirmatively" (1991) in Rostrum Newsletter, "17 Points of Latina Leadership" (1992), "What is Latina Leadership?", "On Being Latina" (1993) in Esperanza Newsletter; rec: equestrienne, travel. Res: 6262 Thomas Ave Newark 94560 Ofc: De Anza College 21250 Stevens Creek Blvd Cupertino 95014

RHEA, WILLIAM EDWARD, III, physician, pediatrician; b. July 30, 1933, St. Louis, Mo.; s. William Edward and Helen Dorothy (Kelly) R.; m. Rhoda Mary Myers, Dec. 20, 1958; children: William b. 1960, Vincent b. 1960, Siobhan b. 1961, Regan b. 1963, Fiona b. 1965; edn: BS, Georgetown Univ. 1955; MD, Univ. Md. Sch. Medicine 1959; dipl. Am. Bd. Pediatrics 1966. Career: intern Providence Hosp., Wash. D.C. 1959-60; resident Children's Hosp., Oakland 1962-63, chief resident 1963-64; pvt. practice, Berkeley 1964-; tchr. Children's Hosp., Oakland 1965-, chief medicine 1974-80, pres. med. staff 1985-86; awards: Children's Hosp. Bronze Bambino 1980, Am. Acad. Pediatrics Spl.Cert. Appreciation 1973; mem: E. Bay Pediatric Soc. (pres. 1969-71), Am. Acad. Pediatrics (fellow), CMA, Alameda-Contra Costa Med. Assn., Cath. Physicians Guild (pres. 1976-80); mil: capt. USAF 1960-62; Democrat; R.Cath. Res: 1190 Shattuck Ave Berkeley 94707 Ofc: 2999 Regent St Ste 325 Berkeley 94705

RHEINSCHILD, GARY WAYNE, surgeon; b. Aug. 30, 1934, Los Angeles; s. Rudolph Waldo and Hazel (Allard) R.; m. M. Sue Haukenberry, Aug. 7, 1955; children: Linda Diane b. 1968, Gary Steven b. 1971; edn: BA, Occidental Coll., 1956; MD, Loma Linda Univ., 1966; Dipl. Am. Bd. Urology; Fellow Am. Coll. Surgeons (FACS) 1990. Career: urology intern L.A. Co.-USC Med Ctr. 1966-67, urology resident UC Irvine 1967-71; surgeon, urologist pvt. practice; chief of surgery Anaheim Memorial Hosp., Anaheim 1987-89; bd. dirs. Anaheim Mem. Hosp. Found., 1987-; mem: Am. Urol. Assn., Western Sect. AUA, Orange Co. Urol. Soc., Los Angeles Urol. Assn., Internat. Coll. Surgeons; mil: sp4 US Army Reserve 1957-63; Republican; Presbyterian; rec: golf. Ofc: Gary W. Rheinschild, M.D., Inc. 1211 W La Palma Ave Ste 303 Anaheim 92801

RIACH, DOUGLAS ALEXANDER, sales and marketing executive, retired military officer; b. Oct. 8, 1919, Victoria, B.C., Can.; s. Alex and Gladys (Provis) R.; came to U.S., 1925, naturalized, 1942; m. Eleanor Montague, Mar. 28, 1942; dau., Sandra Jean; edn: BA, UCLA, 1948; Fenn Coll. 1959, Grad. Sch. Sales Mgmt. and Mktg. 1960, US Army Command and Gen. Staff Coll. 1966, Armed Forces Staff Coll. 1968, Ind. Coll. Armed Forces 1970-71. Career: field rep. GM Acceptance Corp. 1940-41, 46-47; with Ridings Motors 1947-48; Gen. Foods Corp. 1948-80, territory. sales mgr. San Francisco 1962-80; with Mel-Williams Co., Elgaaen-Booth Co., 1980-86, Summit mktg. 1986-87; exec. v.p. Visual Market Plans Inc., Novato, Calif. 1984-87; account exec. Thunderbird Mktg. 1987-89; territory. mgr. RBT Assoc., 1989-90; Ibbotson,

Berri & De Nola & Assoc., 1990-; served to capt. Inf. US Army 1941-46, to col. Inf. USAR 1968, ret. 1973, decorated Bronze Star w. "v" and o.l.c., Legion of Merit, Purple Heart, Combat Inf. Badge, inducted US Army Infantry Hall of Fame 1982; served as col. to brig. gen. 1990, Calif. State Mil. Reserve, dep. comdr. 1980-84, comdr. 1984-87, 2d Inf. BDE, decorated Calif. Medal of Merit (2), and Commendation. Medal w. pendant; 10 fgn. WWII awards- Croix de Guerre Avec Palm, Medaille de la France Liberee, Commemorative War Medal, and Croix du Combattant Voluntaire, France, Commemorative War Cross, Yugoslavia, Medaille de la Reconnaisance, and Commemorative War Medal, Belgium, Cross of Freedom, Poland, Medaille Commemorative de la Campaign d'Italia, Italy, Grand Cross of Homage, Mil. Order of the Ardennes (Intl.), Knight Royal Order of Compassionate Heart (Intl.), Knight Sovereign Mil. Order of the Temple of Jerusalem (Knights Templar) (to Comdr 1989) Comdr., Commandery of Calif. (MOJ) 1992, Knight Comdr, Sovereign Order of St. John of Jerusalem (Knights Hospitaller), Comdr, Commandery of St. Francis (OSJ) 1990-, Knight Comdr, Order of Polonia Restituta (Polish State Order); mem: Long Beach Food Sales Assn. (pres. 1950), Assoc. Grocers Mfrs. Reps. (dir. 1955), Am. Security Council (nat. advy. bd. 1975-), Reserve Officers Assn. (S.F. Presidio pres. 1974-6, v.p. 1977-82, v.p. dept. Calif. 1979, exec. v.p. 1980, pres. 1981, nat. councilman 1981-2), Assn. U.S. Army (gov. East Bay chpt. 1974-82, S.F. chpt. 1982-); civic: Boy Scouts Am. L.A.: asst. scoutmaster 1936-9, asst. dist. commr. 1940-1, Eagle Scout w/ 2 silver palms award; Long Beach Tournament Roses (co-chmn. 1947); clubs: Exchange (v.p. Long Beach 1955), Mdsg. Execs. S.F. (dir. 1970-5, 1981-6, sec. 1976-7, v.p. 1978-9, pres. 1980), Commonwealth Club of Calif. (nat. def. sect. v. chmn. 1964-6, chmn. 1967-72), Elks. Res: 2609 Trousdale Dr Burlingame CA 94010-5706 Ofc: 5677 Landregan St Emeryville CA 94608

RICARDO-CAMPBELL, RITA, economist; b. Mar. 16, 1920, Boston, Mass.; d. David A. and Elizabeth (Jones) Ricardo; m. W. Glenn Campbell, Sept. 15, 1946; children: Barbara b. 1954, Diane b. 1956, Nancy b. 1960; edn: BS, Simmons Coll. 1941; MA, Harvard Univ. 1945, PhD, 1946. Career: tchg. fellow, tutor, instr. Harvard Univ. 1946-48; asst. prof. Tufts Coll. 1948-51; economist, Nat. Wage Stab. Bd., 1951-53, Ways & Means Com., US House of Reps., 1953; cons. econ., 1957-61; archivist and research assoc., Hoover Instn. 1961-68, senior fellow, 1968-; mem. bd. dirs., chmn. finance com. The Gillete Co., Boston; bd. Watkins-Johnson, Inc., Palo Alto 1974-; mgmt. bd. Samaritan Med. Ctr., San Jose; Pres. appt. Health Services Industry Com., 1971-74; Pres. appt. Nat. Council on Humanities, NEH, 1982-88, Pres.'s Nat. Economic Policy Advy. Bd. 1981-89; mem. advy. council SRI Internat., mem. Pres.'s Medal of Science Com. 1988-; dir. Mont Pelerin Soc. 1988-, V.P. 1992-; awards: senior fellow Nat. Endowment for the Humanities 1975, Alumnae achiev. Simmons Coll., Boston 1972, Phi Beta Kappa, Radcliffe Coll., Harvard Univ., Cambridge 1946; recognized authority on the health care sector, Soc. Sec. policy, and drug ind. regulations; lectr. internat. on med. care in U.S.; author: The Economics and Politics of Health (1982, paperback ed. 1985); Social Security: Promise and Reality; Drug Lag: Federal Government Decision Making; Food Safety Regulations; The Economics of Health and Public Policy; coauthor (w/Glenn Campbell) Economics of Mobilization and War (1952); coeditor (w/Edward Lazear) Issues in Contemporary Retirement (1988), coeditor (w/ Kingsley Davis, Mikail S. Bernstam) Below-Replacement Fertility in Industrial Societies (1987). Ofc: The Hoover Instn., HHMB Stanford 94305-6010

RICE, ASHLEY WESTON-XAVIER, manufacturing company executive, scientist; b. Samuel Daniel and Della Mae (Bell) R.; m. Rose Anne Doyle, Feb. 24, 1949; edn: BS, Univ. Mont. 1940; MS, Univ. Wash. Seattle 1943. Career: 1st trumpet Anaconda Band, Mont. 1924-33; Pollack Bros. Band and Traveling Circus 1933-36; survey, crest design Olsen & Sons, West Yellowstone 1936-39; 1st trumpet Cole Orchestra, Seattle, Wash. 1939-46; aircraft tools Boeing Aircraft 1940-41; engr. Alaska shipment U.S. Army Engrs. 1941-44; ship design, Piper in Foundry 1944-46; design engr. Bechtel Cone Engring., Los Angeles 1946-47; Shell Oil Co. 1947-48; owner, engring. mgr. Rice Mfg. Co., Van Nuys 1949-; awards: Soc. Plastics Engrs. pioneer in plastics 1967, Tennis Club Seattle and Los Angeles tennis cups 1941-46; mem: Soc. Plastics Engrs., Los Angeles Tennis Club, ASCAP; inventor dip-molding process (1949), dip-molding vinyl gloves (1950), dip-molding caps (1953), dip-molding vinyl traffic cones (1959), dip-molding disposable vinyl products (1966); Republican; Unitarian; rec: tennis, golf. Ofc: The Rice Manufacturing Co. 14941 Oxnard St POB 8422 Van Nuys 91409

RICH, MICHAEL DAVID, research corporation executive; b. Jan. 23, 1953, Los Angeles; s. Ben R. and Faye (Mayer) R.; m. Debra Paige Granfield, Jan. 12, 1980; children: Matthew b. 1980, William b. 1985; edn: AB, UC Berkeley, 1973; JD, UCLA, 1976; admitted bar Calif., 1976. Career: research exec. RAND, Santa Monica, 1985-; assoc. hd. Political Sci. Dept. 1981-85, dir. Resource Mgmt. Pgm. 1980-86, v.p. Nat. Security Res. and dir. Nat. Defense Res. Inst. 1986-; mem. bd. editors Jour. of Defense Res.; trustee WISE Senior Services, Santa Monica; awards: Wilson Scholar UCLA Law Sch. 1973-74; mem. Coun. on Fgn. Rels., Internat. Inst. of Strategic Studies; publs: num. unclassified and classified articles, reports. Ofc: RAND 1700 Main St Santa Monica 90407

RICHARDS, ALFONSO, physician, surgeon-urologist; b. Jan. 28, 1923, Princeton, N.J.; s. Angelo and Louise (Suth) R.; m. Gillian Montford, Sept. 16, 1956; children: Christopher b. 1958, Elizabeth b. 1960, Katherine b. 1962, Robert b. 1964; edn: BS, Univ. Ala. 1950; MS pharmacology, Okla. Sch. Medicine 1952; MD, N.Y. Med. Coll. 1956. Career: pvt. practice urology, Petaluma 1961-; mem: AMA, CMA, No. Calif. Urological Assn., Sonoma Co. Med. Assn., A.C.S., Am. Urological Assn. (and Western section), Am. Bd. of Urology, Rotary Club Petaluma, Sigma Xi; mil: AUS 1943-46; Republican; Episcopalian; rec: ranching, running, bicycling. Res: 200 8th St Petaluma 94952 Ofc: 30 W El Rose Dr Petaluma 94952

RICHARDS, MORRIS DICK, psychotherapist, county agency administrative analyst, educator; b. Aug. 20, 1939, Los Angeles; parents: Morris Dick Richards, Lynn Rich Briggs, Annette (Fox) Briggs; m. Leslie Sondra Lefkowitz, Mar. 22, 1975; edn: BA (cum laude) Claremont Men's Coll., 1962; MA, Univ. Chgo., 1964; MBA, Chapman Coll., 1985; LLB, La Salle Ext. Univ., Chgo. 1971; MS Hygiene, Univ. of Pittsburgh, 1973, PhD, 1973; MPA, USC, 1965; Calif. lic. Marriage Family Child Counselor (MFCC), Clinical Social Worker (LCSW), Psychotherapist, Adminstr.; diplomate, Acad. Cert. Soc. Workers, NASW, 1962. Career: settlement house worker Benton House, Chgo. 1963-64; psychiatric soc. worker Jewish Big Brothers of Gr. L.A., 1964-67; L.A. Co.: Dept. Soc. Svs. supvy. child welfare worker 1967-68, pgm. analyst 1968-69, hd. child welfare wkr. 1970-71, exec. asst. 1971-72; group therapist Spl. Svs. for Groups, Watts, 1967-68; psychiatric soc. worker Calif. State Dept. Soc. Welfare, L.A. 1969-71 p.t.; asst. dep. dir. Mental Health Dept., Santa Ana 1973-77; soc. wkr. Jewish Fam. Svs., Garden Grove 1973-75 p.t.; pvt. practice, Santa Ana 1975-77; gen. mgr. and industrial therapist Paragon West, Anaheim 1977-83; sr. psychiatric counselor and actg. pgm. dir. Horizon Health, Newport Beach 1983-84; Co. of Orange: sr. social worker O.C. Social Svs., Santa Ana 1983-85, adminstrv. analyst O.C Environmental Mgmt. Agy. 1985-88, staff analyst 1988-90, exec. asst. to Env. Mgmt. Dir. of Planning, 1990-92; ed. dept. newsletter 1991-; adminstrv. cons. various cos., Calif.; instr. Calif. Graduate Inst., Orange 1988-; instr. Univ. of Phoenix 1992; mem. O.C. Mental Health Advy. Bd. 1981-87, Alliance for the Mentally Ill O.C., Anaheim Affirmative Action ad hoc com., cons. Head Start Agy., Child Abuse Policy Com., Sch. Attendance Rev. Bd., Foster Home Coord. Task Force, Inter-Dept. Cont. Care Task Force, Juv. Delinquence Com., Diversion Comm. Based Alternatives Task Force, Calif. Curriculum Framework Com., coord. United Way; awards: Haynes scholar Claremont Men's Coll. 1959-60, Univ. Chgo. fellow 1962-64, NIMH fellow 1963-64, USC Alumni fellow 1964-65, adj. prof. teaching excellence award Chapman Coll. 1982; mem. Nat. Assn. Soc. Workers (NASW Social Worker of Yr., O.C., 1987), O.C. Mental Health Assn. (1988-91, past sec.), Am. Jewish Com. (1964-, past dir.), Broadmore Northridge Assn. (sec., newsletter ed. 1991-), ACLU; mil: sp4 Army, active 1957, Reserve 1958-64; Indep.; Jewish; rec: tennis, wt.lifting, karate, reading.

RICHARDSON, GERALD CLEMEN, marriage family and child therapist, corporate executive; b. Jan. 8, 1937, Glendale; s. Gerald O. and Kathleen E. R.; m. Jo Ann Cox, Sept. 21, 1963; children: Jo Ann b. 1964, Gerald b. 1967, Charles b. 1970, John b. 1972; edn: BA, L.A. Baptist Coll. 1979; MA, Calif. Grad. Sch. Theology 1981; MA, Azusa Pacific Univ. 1982; D.Min., Calif. Grad. Sch. Theology 1983; cert. Nat. Bd. Cert. Counselors 1988, Internat. Bd. Standards & Practice for Cert. Fin. Planners 1988. Career: assoc. pastor First Baptist Ch., Van Nuys 1977-79; pastor Foothill Baptist Ch., Sylmar 1979-86; owner, Gerald Richardson Ins. & Fin. Services, Northridge 1976-; pres. Brittain Co., Covina 1987-88; v.p. Speare & Co., Santa Monica 1988-89; pres. Growing Edge Counseling, Granada Hills 1983-; prof. Calif. Grad. Sch. Theology, Rosemead 1985-; moderator SW Baptist Conf., W. Covina 1988-89; bd. mem., trustee SW Baptist Conf. 1984-89; lectr. L.A. Baptist Coll., Newhall 1983-86; mayor City of Manhattan Beach 1972-73, city councilman 1970-74 and Planning Comm. chair 1968-69; awards: City Manhattan Beach Commend. 1974, Co. Bd. Suprs. Commend. 1972, Jr. C.of C. Outstanding Young Men Am. 1970; mem: Christian Assn. Psychological Studies, Am. Assn. Counseling & Devel., Internat. Assn. Fin. Planners, Inst. Bus. Appraisers, French Am. C.of C.; co-author Counseling in Time of Crisis (1987); mil: sgt. 1c Army Nat. Guard 1955-63; Republican; Baptist; rec: fishing, travel, hiking. Ofc: 9420 Reseda Blvd Ste 513 Northridge 91324

RICHARDSON, JOHN FRANCIS, business executive, educator; b. Nov. 22, 1938, Newark, NJ; s. John Stanley and Helen Ana (Rathburn) R.; m. Monika Gatzweiler, Mar. 14, 1966; son, Christopher J. b. Dec. 15, 1966; edn: BA, Montclair St. Coll., 1960; IBM computer sys. schs., 1962-67; MS, Polytech. Univ. of New York, 1968; BSL, Calif. Coll. of Law, 1978, JD, 1980; MBA, summa cum laude, Pepperdine Univ., 1982; doctoral pgm. strategic mgmt. U.S. Internat. Univ., 1991-; grad. studies Purdue Univ., Rutgers Univ., Seton Hall Univ., Fairleigh Dickinson Univ. Career: high sch. math tchr., NJ 1960-62; mktg. rep. IBM Corp., NYC 1962-68; pres Universal Learning Corp., NYC 1968-70; acct. mgr. Realtronics, Inc., NYC 1970; acct. exec. Merrill Lynch, NYC 1970-71; Bache rep. Bache & Co., NYC 1971; v.p. John S. Studwell Assoc., NYC 1972-73; sales rep. Control Data Corp., NYC 1973; asst. prof. Purdue Univ., Fort Wayne, Indiana 1973-74; physics tchr. Kearney (NJ) High Sch. 1975; biochem.

tchr. Sparta (NJ) H.S. 1975-76; acct. exec. Dean Witter, Santa Monica 1976; lectr. USC, Los Angeles 1977-78; mktg. rep. National CSS, Inc., Newport Bch. 1977-80; realtor assoc. Coldwell Banker, Santa Ana 1980-81; mktg. rep. Informatics, Inc., L.A. 1981-82; exec. v.p. Computique, Santa Ana 1982-83; pres. ILAR Systems, Inc., Newport Bch. 1983-; past mem. New York C.of C., NYAC, Pepperdine Univ. Assocs.; computer systems cons. numerous cos. internat.; author numerous computer applications pgms. incl. Bottomline-V (corporate fin. planning system w/ 15,000+ installations worldwide), 12 academic study courses w/ tapes, numerous tape lectures, 6 travel books w/ tapes; honors: Kappa Delta Pi 1958, Am. Jurisprudence award 1978; mem: Internat. Platform Assn., Pepperdine Univ. Mgmt. Partners, U.S. Tennis Assn., U.S. Chess Fedn.; club: John Wayne Tennis (team capt. 1989-91 OCTA Champions); Republican; Presbyterian; rec: travel, writing, tennis, computers, math & sci., chess, fgn. languages. Address: 334 Baywood Dr Newport Beach 92660

RICHARDSON, JOHN VINSON, JR., educator; b. Dec. 27, 1949, Columbus, Ohio; s. John Vinson and Hope Irene (Smith) R.; m. Nancy Lee Brown, Aug. 22, 1971; edn: BA, Ohio State, 1971; MLS, Vanderbilt, Peabody Coll., 1972; PhD, Indiana Univ., 1978. Career: asst. prof. UCLA, Los Angeles 1978-83, assoc. prof. 1983-; pres. Information Transfer Associates (consulting bus.); pres. Wesley Found., L.A.; awards: Newberry Fellow, Newberry Library, Chgo. 1982, NEH grantee, W.D.C. 1984, Lancour Scholar, ALISE, Research Tri, N.C. 1986, Justin Winsor Prize, Am. Library Assn., Chgo. 1990; mem: Am. Library Assn. 1972-, Assn. of Lib. and Info. Sci. Edn. 1975-, Beta Phi Mu 1972-, Sigma Xi 1987-, ACM, SIGAI 1990-, Grad. Council UCLA 1992-, Grad. Council UC Statewide 1993-; author: Calligraphy (1982), Spirit of Inquiry (1982), Knowledge-Based Systems (1994), Gospel of Scholarship (1992); mil: conscientious objector, alt. svc. 1972-75; Green; United Methodist; rec: travel internat., reading, oenology. Ofc: UCLA GSLIS, GSLIS Bldg Ste 204 Los Angeles 90024-1520 Ph: 310/206-9369

RICHARDSON, MARTIN NATHANIEL, office automation executive, educator; b. Oct. 12, 1951, New Orleans; s. Cardosia, Jr. and Elizabeth Louise (Martin) R.; m. Gwendolyn Donald, June 26, 1982; edn: bus. edn. major, USC 1969-74; Cert. Office Automation Profl. (COAP) OASI, 1987. Career: office systems supr. Fluor Corp., Irvine 1975-86; regional office sys. mgr. Norrell Corp., Newport Beach 1986-89; exec. v.p. OA Training Systems 1989-; pres. G and M Enterprises 1990-; office automation instr. Cypress Coll. 1979-, Golden West Coll. 1985-89, Irvine Valley Coll., Saddleback Comm. Coll. 1979-81, Coastline Comm. Coll. 1983, Fullerton Coll. 1981-86; honors: Silver Seal bearer Manual Arts H.S., L.A. 1966-69, hon. soc. AISP 1983-90; mem: Assn. Info. Systems Profls. (internat. dir. 1988-90), AISP Orange Co. (pres. 1982-84, exec. adv. 1984-86, regional liaison 1982-90, editor mo. newsletter 1985-91); apptd. bds.: Calif. Comm. Colls. Bus. Edn Advy. Commn. 1990, NOCCD Edn. Advy. Com. Fullerton 1978-, OIS advy. com. Saddleback Coll. 1990-, L.A. Cty. R.O.P. Pgm. Advy. Com., Downey 1986-90, bus. adv. Golden West Coll. 1981-90, CRC Trade Advy. Com. City of Norco 1983-; mem: Newport Harbor Area C.of C.; Democrat; Baptist (minister of music, choir dir.); rec: pianist, organist, song writer. Ofc: Office Automation Training Systems, 1550 Bayside Dr Ste 1 Corona Del Mar.

RICHARDSON, MARY ELIZABETH, motion picture film librarian; b. Nov. 27, 1916, Los Angeles; d. Ford Ingalsbe and Frances Caroline (Willey) Beebe; m. Lloyd Leland Richardson, June 6, 1936 (div. 1948); children: Lloyd L. III b. 1939, Mary Elizabeth b. 1943; edn: grad. Benjamin Franklin H.S., L.A. 1932; AA, L.A. Jr. Coll., 1935; undergrad. UC Berkeley, 1935, BA, UCLA, 1937. Career: continuity clk. Republic Studios, Studio City 1945-55, film librarian 1955-57; film librarian Warner Brothers, Burbank 1957-63, Universal Studios, Universal City 1972; head film librarian Banner Prodns., Studio City 1964-65, Columbia Bdcstg., Studio City 1965-67, Desilu (later Paramount/ Gulf Western), Hollywood 1967-71, Columbia Pictures TV, Burbank 1973-82, ret.; also owner/prin. dba The Winged Cap, 1946-: continuity clk. Walter Lantz Prodns. 1946-83, free lance continuity Alperson Prodns. and others 1946-83, office svs. Zahler Prodns. 1971-73; bd. dirs. Valley Water Assn. 29 Palms 1985-87; honors: Calif. Scholarship Soc. (life); mem: Motion Picture Film Eds. Guild (1955-, Gold Card Life), Office & Profl. Employees Internat. Union (founding 1946-), Desert Writers' Guild of 29 Palms (past chmn., treas. 1989-, editor/printer Annual 1991, 92, 93); civic: Morongo Basin Coalition for Adult Literacy (1987-, bd. 1989-); contbr. poetry, fiction Desert Writers' Guild Annual (1991, 92); Republican; Rosicrucian faith; rec: writing, music, sci., rel., health & nutrition. Res: HC02, Box 324L, 29 Palms 92277 Ofc: The Winged Cap PO Box 1896, 29 Palms 92277-1260

RICHARDSON, WALLACE G., airline pilot, real estate executive; b. Oct. 19, 1923, Inglewood; s. Frank Wallace and Alvina Louise (Younge) R.; m. Jenny Montandon, Mar. 14, 1958; children: Linda b. 1950, Deborah b. 1954, Stanley b. 1959, Susan b. 1961; edn: US Naval Aviation Cadet Pgm. 1943-45, Sawyers Univ. of Commerce 1947-48. Career: lt. cmdr. US Navy (1941-47, 50-53), decorated Air medal w/5 stars; office mgr. Burroughs Adding Machine Co., 1949-50; capt. United Air Lines 1950s, ret.; gen. ptnr., mgr. Real Estate Syndicator, 1956-; dir: Ocean Science Services 1970-72, Ceric Corp. 1971-73; chmn.

Bonsai exh. San Mateo Co. Fair (1984-88); mem. Sei Boku Bonsai Kai (Green Tree Bonsai Club, pres. 1988); coauthor: Path to Illumination; Spiritual Value of Gemstones (1980); Republican; Prot. (deacon); rec: writing, stained glass, bonsai. Res: 35 Buckeye Portola Valley 94028 Ofc: United Air Lines SFO Flt Ops., San Francisco.

RICHENS, MURIEL WHITTAKER, counselor, educator; b. Prineville, Oreg.; d. John Reginald and Victoria Cecilia (Pascale) Whittaker; children: Karen, John, Candice, Stephanie, Rebecca; edn: BS, Oregon State Univ.; MA, San Francisco State Univ., 1962; postgrad. UC Berkeley 1967-69, Univ. Birmingham, Eng. 1973, Univ. Soria, Spain, 1981; spl. postgrad. studies Ctr. for Human Comms., Los Gatos 1974, Univ. P.R. 1977, Univ. Guadalajara, Mex. 1978, Univ. Durango, Mex. 1980, Univ. Guanajuato, Mex. 1982; Lic. marriage, child and family counselor (MFCC), Calif.; Calif. tchg. and sch. administrn. credentials, 7-12, pupil personnel specialist. Career: instr. Springfield H.S., Springfield, Oreg.; San Francisco St. Univ.; instr., counselor Coll. of San Mateo, San Mateo H.S. Dist., 1963-86; therapist AIDS health project Univ. Calif., San Francisco 1988-; pvt. practice MFCC, San Mateo; mem: UC Berkeley Alumni Assn., Am. Contract Bridge League (life master, cert. instr., tournament dir.), Women in Comms., Computer-Using Educators, Pi Lambda Theta, Delta Pi Epsilon, Commonwealth Club; civic: Am. Red Cross (lifeguard); R.Cath. Res/Ofc: 847 N Humboldt St #309 San Mateo 94401-1451

RICHEY, EVERETT ELDON, religious educator; b. Nov. 1, 1923, Claremont, Ill.; s. Hugh Arthur and Elosia Emma (Longnecker) R.; m. Mary Elizabeth Reynolds, Apr. 9, 1944; children: Eldon b. 1947, Clive b. 1950, Loretta b. 1953, Charles b. 1956; edn: ThB, Anderson Univ., 1946; MDiv, Sch. of Theology, Anderson, Ind. 1956; ThD, Iliff Sch. Theology, Denver 1960; ordained minister Ch. of God, 1948. Career: pastor Church of God, Bremen, Ind. 1946-47, Laurel, Miss. 1947-48, First Ch. of God, Fordyce, Ark. 1948-52, Cherry Ave. Ch. of God, Long Beach, Calif. 1964-68; prof. Arlington Coll., Long Beach 1961-68; Azusa Pacific Univ., 1968-; mem. Commn. on Christian Higher Edn. of Ch. of God, Fullerton, Calif. 1982-; pres. Church Growth Investors, Glendora 1981-; mem: Gr. L.A. Sunday Sch. Assn. 1968-, Assn. of Profs. and Researchers of Rel. Edn. 1976-, Rel. Edn. Assn. 1956-, General Assembly Ministers of Ch. of God 1946-; publs: curriculum, ednl. manuals, contbr. ch. periodical 1971-83; Republican; rec: gardening. Res: 413 N Valencia Glendora 91740 Ofc: Azusa Pacific University 901 E Alosta Azusa 91702

RICHTAREK, JOHN GREGORY, sales executive; b. May 31, 1952, Hartford, Conn.; s. Wm. John and Patricia Blake (O'Meara) R.; m. Laura Ness, Mar. 7, 1987; edn: BA, Randolph Macon Coll., 1974; MA, Northeastern Univ., 1977. Career: project coordinator C.S.I., Elmsford, NY 1977-79; sales engr. Mergenthaler-Linotype, Hayward, Calif. 1979-80; dir. edn. Shast General Sys., Sunnyvale 1980-82; mgr. systems engring. Fortune Systems, Belmont 1982-84; sales services mgr. Micro Focus Inc., Palo Alto 1984-86; internat. sales mgr., dir. of sales, pres. Presentation Technologies, Sunnyvale 1986-91; v.p. sales Mirus Industries, Milpitas 1991-; honors: outstanding youth leader C.of C. Westfield, N.J. 1970, key employee Fortune Systems, Belmont, Calif. 1983; mem. Am. Motorcyclist Assn., Motorcycle Safety Found. (cert. instr. 1984-), Cousteau Soc.; Episcopalian; rec: motorcycling, sailing, hiking, running. Ofc: Milpitas.

RICHTER, BURTON, physicist/linear accelerator center director; b. Mar. 22, 1931, Bklyn.; s. Abraham and Fannie (Pollack) R.; m. Laurose Becker, July 1, 1960; children: Elizabeth b. 1961, Matthew b. 1963; edn: grad. The Mercersberg Acad., 1948; BS, M.I.T., 1952, 1956. Career: research assoc. Brookhaven Nat. Lab., Upton, N.Y. 1954; res. assoc. high energy physics, Stanford Univ. 1956-59, asst. prof. dept. physics 1960-63; assoc. prof. Stanford Linear Accelerator Center, 1963-67, prof. 1967-, tech. dir. 1982-84, dir. 1984-; Paul Piggot Prof. in the Physical Scis., Stanford Univ.; mem. bd. dirs. Varian Corp., Palo Alto 1974; awards: Loeb lectr. Harvard Univ. 1974, DeShalit lectr. Weizmann Inst. 1975, E.O. Lawrence Medal 1976, Nat. Acad. of Sci. 1976, Nobel Prize in Physics 1976; Fellow Am. Acad. of Arts & Scis., Am. Physical Soc. (v.p.), AAAS; mem. European Physical Soc.; rec: skiing, squash, music. Ofc: Stanford Linear Accelerator Center POB 4349 Stanford 94309

RIDDELL, ROBERT JAMES (JR.), physicist, ret.; b. June 25, 1923, Peoria, Ill.; s. Robert James and Hazel Marion (Gwathmey) R.; m. Kathryn Jane Gamble, Aug. 12, 1950; children: Cynthia b. 1953, Stephen b. 1955, James b. 1957; edn: BS, Carnegie Inst. of Tech., 1944; MS, Univ. Mich., 1947, PhD, 1951. Career: asst. prof. physics Univ. Calif., Berkeley 1951-55; sr. physicist Lawrence Berkeley Lab., Berkeley 1951-81; physicist AEC, Germantown, Md. 1958-60; Pacific Sch. of Religion 1971- (trustee 1971-, bd. chair 1979-84), Graduate Theological Union 1983- (trustee 1983-, bd. chair 1990-); advy. bd. Coll. Natural Resources, Univ. Calif. 1990-; mem: Friends of Univ. Calif. Botanical Garden (pres. 1985-), Calif. Horticultural Soc. (council 1988-); mil: lt.jg USN 1944-46; United Ch. of Christ, First Congl. Ch., Berkeley (moderator 1973-74, treas. 1989-92); rec: gardening, model making, photography. Res: 1095 Arlington Blvd El Cerrito 94530

RIDGWAY, DAVID WENZEL, academic film producer; b. Dec. 12, 1904, Los Angeles; s. David Nelson and Marie (Wenzel) R.; m. Rochelle Mary Devine, June 22, 1955; edn: AB, UCLA, 1926; MBA, Harvard Univ., 1928. Career: sound engr. RKO Studios, Hollywood 1928-42; producer Ency. Britannica, Wilmette, Ill. 1946-60; film producer/ exec. dir./ dir. Chemical Edn. Material (CHEM) Study, Lawrence Hall of Sci., UC Berkeley, 1960-89, dir. 1989-; advisor CalTech, Pasadena 1982-85; awards: Chris award Film Council Greater Columbus, Ohio 1962, Best film, Brussels 1965, Gold Camera, Chgo. 1971, Golden Eagle (5 awards) CINE, W.D.C. 1973, Diploma of Honor ISFA, Cairo 1978; mem: Soc. Motion Picture & TV Engrs. 1929-, Alpha Kappa Psi 1928-, Delta Upsilon 1928-; clubs: UC Faculty 1963-, Bohemian 1967-, Berkeley City; author: w. R.J.Merrill, The CHEM Study Story (1969), articles in SMPTE J., J. Chem. Edn., Canadian Chem. Edn., Sci. Activities, Ednl. Screen and Audio Visual Guide; mil: lt. cdr. USN 1943-46; Republican; rec: dancing, bridge, travel. Res: 1735 Highland Pl Berkeley 94709 Ofc: University of California, Lawrence Hall of Science, Berkeley 94720

RIEDER, RONALD FREDERICK, public relations/advertising consultant; b. Nov. 10, 1932, Oshawa, Ontario, Can., naturalized 1962; s. Joseph Samuel and Minnie (Collis) R.; m. Pauline Feldman, Sept. 22, 1957; children: Mitchell b. 1961, Stephen b. 1962, Robert b. 1964; edn: BA, Sir Geo. Williams Univ. (now Concordia U.), Montreal, 1955; B.Journalism, Carleton Univ., Ottawa, 1956. Career: reporter Montreal Star, Montreal, Canada 1956-58; night city editor Valley News, Van Nuys, Calif. 1958-66; v.p. Hal Phillips & Assocs., Beverly Hills 1966-72; dir. communications Daylin, Inc. 1972-80; ptnr. The Phillips Group, 1980-89; dir. pub. affairs Jewish Fedn. Council of Greater L.A., 1989-92; pres. Ron Rieder & Assocs., Sherman Oaks 1992-; mem: Valley Press Club (1960-, past pres.), Soc. of Profl. Journalists 1962-, Pub. Relations Soc. Am. 1972-. Res: 5420 Sylmar Ave #322 Sherman Oaks 91401 Ofc: Ron Rieder & Associates 5420 Sylmar Ave #322 Sherman Oaks 91401

RIGGS, HENRY E., college president; b. Feb. 25, 1935, Chgo.; s. Joseph Agnew and Gretchen (Walser) R.; m. Gayle Carson, May 17, 1958; children: Elizabeth, Peter, Catharine; edn: BS indsl. engring. (with distinction), Stanford Univ., 1957; MBA (high distinction) Grad. Sch. Bus. Adminstrn., Harvard Univ., 1960. Career: process engr. Ampex Corp., Redwood City 1957-58; industrial economist, techno-economic res. and cons., Stanford Res.Inst., 1960-63; Icore Industries, Sunnyvale 1963-70; treas. controller 1963-64, v.p. ops. 1964-65, exec. v.p. 1965-67, pres. and c.e.o. 1967-70; v.p. fin. Measurex Corp., Cupertino 1970-74; academic splst. in fields of technology mgmt., technical strategy, new venture mgmt., fin. analysis and control; instr. Foothill Coll., Los Altos 1961-66; faculty Stanford Univ. 1967-88: instr. 1967-70, cons. prof. 1970-76, adj. prof. 1976-80, prof. engring. 1980-88, Thomas W. and Joan B. Ford Professor of Engring. 1986-88, Ford Professor of Engring., Emeritus 1990-, chmn. dept. indsl. engring. and engring. mgmt. 1978-82, v.p. devel. Stanford Univ. 1983-88, founder, dir. Stanford-AEA Exec. Inst. for Mgmt. of High Technology Cos. 1975-83, dir. Industrial Affiliates Pgm. 1979-82; pres. and prof. of engring. Harvey Mudd Coll., Claremont 1988-; dir: Income Fund of Am., Growth Fund of Am., Am. Balanced Fund, Fundamental Investors Inc., AMCAP, Sera Solar Corp.; mem. AIIE (editorial rev. com. Transactions J.); civic bds: Bay Area Com. advy. to SEC, Phillips Acad. (trustee), Stanford Alumni Assn. (dir., chmn, 1993), United Way Cpgn. Mt. Baldy Region (chmn. univ. and coll. div.), YMCA Palo Alto (dir.), BSA Stanford Area Council (ofcr., dir.); author: Accounting: A Survey (McGraw-Hill, 1981), Managing High-Technology Companies (Van Norstrand Reinhold, 1983), 11+ profl. jour. articles and tech. reports (1962-). Res: 495 E 12th St Claremont 91711 Ofc: Harvey Mudd College Kingston Hall 301 E 12th St Claremont 91711

RILES, WILSON CAMANZA, educational consultant; b. June 27, 1917, Alexandria, La.; s. Wilson Roy and Susie Anna (Jefferson) R.; m. Mary Louise Phillips, Nov. 13, 1941; children: Michael b. 1943, Narvia b. 1945, Wilson Jr. b. 1946 Phillip b. 1947; edn: BA, No. Ariz. Univ., 1940, MA, 1947; awarded Hon. Dr. of Laws degree, Pepperdine Coll., 1965, Claremont Grad. Sch., 1972, USC, 1975, No. Ariz. Univ., 1976, Univ. of Akron, 1976, Golden Gate Univ., 1981, Hon. Dr. Humane Letters degree, St. Mary's Coll., Moraga 1971, Univ. of Pacific, Stockton 1971, Univ. of Judaism, L.A. 1972. Career: elementary sch. tchr., adminstr. Arizona Public Schs., 1940-54; exec. secty. Pacific Coast reg. Fellowship of Reconciliation, L.A. 1954-58; cons., dir. compensatory edn. Calif. Dept. Edn., Sacto. 1958-70; supt. of pub. instrn. Calif. Dept. of Edn., Sacto. 1971-83; pres. Wilson Riles & Associates Inc., Sacto. 1983-; dir. (emeritus) Wells Fargo Bank; awards: Berkeley Citation UCB 1973, Spingarn Medal NAACP 1973, Disting. service Harvard Club S.F. 1978, Robert Maynard Hutchins award Ency. Britannica 1978, Medal for disting. service Teachers Coll. Columbia Univ. 1979, Disting. Alumnus Am. Assn. of State Colls. and Univs. 1979; mem: The Cleveland Conf., NAACP, Phi Beta Kappa, Nat. Advy. Coun. Nat. Schs. Volunteer Pgm., Assn. of Calif. Sch. Adminstrs., Am. Assn. Sch. Adminstrs., Save the Redwoods League Council; editl. advy. bd. Early Years Mag.; mem. nat. com. on U.S.-China Relations Inc.; mil: vet. WWII, US Army Air Corps. Ofc: 400 Capitol Mall Ste 1540 Sacramento 95814

RILEY, JAMES D(ANIEL), mathematician; b. June 25, 1920, Tuscola, Ill.; s. Fred Thomas and Ruth Elizabeth (Dearduff) R.; m. Elaine Kutschinski, June 2, 1952; children: Dane b. 1953, Gregory b. 1957; edn: AB, Park Coll., 1942; MA, Univ. Kans. 1948, PhD, 1952. Career: mathematician Naval Ordnance Lab. 1952-54; asst. prof. Univ. Ky., 1954-55, Iowa State Univ., 1955-58; staff mem. Space Technology Labs, 1958-61, Aerospace Corp., 1961-66, sr. staff MDAC, 1967-74; lectr. National Univ. of Malaysia, 1975-77; staff mem. Honeywell, 1977-85; sr. staff Lockheed Calif., Burbank 1985-90; instr. Moorpark Coll., 1990-; lectr. USC, UCLA, 1958-68; honors: Phi Beta Kappa 1948, Sigma Xi 1948, Pi Mu Epsilon 1948; mem. var. math. socs., U.S. Power Squadron; contbr. tech. articles in sci. jours.; mil: sgt. AUS 1941-46; Lutheran; rec: nature study, ornithology. Res: 6195 Sylvan Dr Simi Valley 93063

RILEY, REX (CHARLES LOGAN), health administrator; b. Jan. 20, 1946, Toledo, Ohio; s. Charles Allen and Phyllis Mary (Logan) R.; m. Rosemarie Jeanette Webster, Apr. 10, 1971; children: Paul b. 1977, Ross b. 1980; edn: BA, Univ. Mich., 1968; MHA, Univ. of New South Wales, Sydney, Australia 1976; health exec. devel. pgm. Cornell Univ., 1988. Career: prodn. planner Internat. Harvester, Melbourne, Australia 1972-74; adminstrv. staff Royal Women's Community Hosp., 1974-79; chief ops. Preston Northcote, 1979-84; c.e.o. Geelong, Victoria, Australia 1984-89; chief ops. Valley Children's Hosp., Fresno, Calif. 1989-; Fellow Australian Coll. of Healthcare Adminstrs. (1976, ofcr. 1982-88, pres. 1987-88), mem. Am. Coll. of Healthcare Execs. 1989-; civic: Rotary Fresno, Leadership Fresno, Ronald McDonald House, Combined Health Appeal Fresno; pub. article "Two Avenues to Improve Comm. in an Org. 1988; mil: capt. USMC 1968-72, Vietnam 70-71, Navy commendn. 1971; Lincoln Republican; Lincoln Presbyterian; rec: family, A. Lincoln, Sir Donald Bradman, Civil War, gardening, walking. Res: 2287 W Pinedale Ave Fresno 93711 Ofc: Valley Children's Hospital 3151 N Millbrook Fresno 93703

RIORDAN, CAROL CAMPBELL, university television producer, entertainment and media consultant; b. May 15, 1946, Fresno; d. Alexander Boyle and Jeanne Carol (Yarnell) Campbell; m. Samuel Gresham Riordan, May 27, 1966; children: Loren Jeremy, Rachel Elisabeth; edn: AA, San Diego City Coll., 1976; BA, The Union Inst., 1976; grad. studies San Diego State Univ. Career: instr., dir. San Diego Jr. Theatre, 1963-66, Actor's Lab., San Francisco, 1966-68; costume designer Playhouse/Interplayers Theatres, San Francisco 1966-68, Stage 7 Dance Theater, San Diego 1981-83; producer TV edn. San Diego Co. Edn. Office, 1974-76; producer, dir. Comm. Video Ctr., San Diego 1976-78, program mgr. 1978-79; designer-in-residence Three's Co. and Dancers, San Diego 1976-89, bd. dirs., 1981; media producer TV San Diego State Univ., 1982-; consultant in field; awards: North County Comm. TV Found. grantee 1985, Calif. Council Humanities grantee 1988; producer, director TV: Poems of Wonder and Magic, 1986 (Emmy award 1987, Best of Western Ednl. Soc. Telecommunications 1986, ITVA Excellence award 1986), The Fearless Vampire Dressers, 1984 (Best of Western Ednl. Soc. Telecommunications 1985); coauthor w/others: Framework & Instructional Units for Teaching CCTV, 1980; mem: Women in Film, Nat. Acad. TV Arts and Scis. (bd. govs. San Diego chpt. 1989-), Internat. TV Assn. (S.D. chpt. merit award 1986); civic: Sierra Club (com. 1982), Environmental Defense Fund, Greenpeace Internat.; Zen Buddhist. Ofc: San Diego State Univ. Media Tech Svcs San Diego 92182-0524

RISELEY, JERRY BURR, JR., lawyer; b. Mar. 17, 1920, Stockton, Kans.; s. Jerry B. and Esta Ella (Scott) R.; m. Eunice Olive Smith, July 31, 1943; children: Valrie b. 1944, Stephanie b. 1947, Gheri-Lynn b. 1958 (dec. 1988), Melanie b. 1961, Christopher b. 1965; edn: BS, Univ. Kans., 1941; JD, USC, 1948; MS, Fort Hays State Univ., Ks. 1969, Fellow Sch. of Edn. FHSU 1971-72; MS library sci., USC, 1972; admitted Calif. State Bar 1948, life tchg. credential Calif. 1969, Pub. Acct. Calif. 1954. Career: atty. pvt. practice, Los Angeles 1948-, trial atty. Maryland Casualty, L.A. 1972-80; arbitrator Los Angeles Superior Court, 1974-; sr. trial atty. Continental Ins. Co., L.A. 1980-88; publisher Authentic Res. Press, Sepulveda 1969-; author 5 books: When Sex Is Illegal (1966), Henry Miller's Tropic Trial (1967), Academic Freedom (1969), Sex and Doctors (1970), Sex and Teachers (1971); writer, contbr. UCLA Archive Special Collections, 1970-, incl. "The Adjutant's Journal" (the adjutant's account of the parachute attack on Lae, New Guinea 9/43); contbr. Airborne Quarterly, Summer 1992, "The Great Fire Fight between the Rear Base Det., 503d Prcht Inf., and the 11th Airborne Div.;" mem: 158th Inf. Bushmasters 1942-, 503d Parachute Inf. Assn. 1945-, Disabled Emergency Ofcrs. of WWII (dir. 1952-60), Disabled Ofcrs. Assn. (dir. 1960-64), UCLA PC Users Gp., Kiwanis Studio City (ed. 1954-64); mil: 1st lt. AUS Inf. 1941-45, Combat Inf. Badge; Prot.; rec: computers. Res: 8856 Lemona Ave North Hills 91343 Ofc: Authentic Research Press PO Box 2512 Van Nuys 91404

RISKAS, MIKE, coach, physical education instructor; b. June 22, 1934, Ely, Nev.; s. Nicholas Vasiliou and Helen (Massouris) Riskas; m. Barbara Lou Watson, July 16, 1960; children: Michelle b. 1962, Steven b. 1966; edn: BS, UCLA, 1958, MS, 1967. Career: coach, baseball and football, UCLA, 1958-59; journeyman plumber Reese Plumbing Co., Alhambra 1960-61; coach, football, Alhambra High Sch., 1961; actor, extra/Actor Guilds, Hollywood 1958-; physical edn. instr./coach Pomona Coll., Claremont 1961-; baseball clinician US

Baseball Fedn./Olympics, Columbia, S.A. 1984, Gt. Brit. 1987, Am. Baseball Coaches Assn., Europe 1970; editor P.E. courses, Azusa Pacific Coll., 1970-73, P.E. curric. advisor Univ. of Laverne, 1973-76; awards: Coach of Year NCAA Div. III Bsb., San Diego 1986, Coach of Quarter Century Am. Bsb. Coaches Assn., San Diego 1986, French Nat. Coach, French Bsb. Fedn., Paris 1988; mem: Am. Football Coaches Assn. 1961-, Am. Baseball Coaches Assn. 1963-, U.S. Baseball Fedn. 1980-, NCAA Baseball Com. (chmn. div. III 1985-86), Internat. Baseball Assn. 1986-, Screen Extras Guild/SAG 1958-86; civic: Inland Hospice Assn. (life), UCLA 10th Player; author: Baseball Course 1972; mil: seaman USNR 1951-55, sp3c US Army 1955-57; Democrat; Greek Orthodox; rec: sports, gardening. Res: 1655 Clemson Claremont 91711 Ofc: Pomona College 220 E Sixth St Claremont 91711

RITCHIE, ROBERT OLIVER, engineering educator, researcher, administrator; b. Jan. 2, 1948, Plymouth, U.K., nat. U.S., 1989; s. Kenneth Ian and Kathleen Joyce (Sims) R.; m. Connie Olesen, 1969 (div. 1978); children: James b. 1972; edn: BA, Cambridge Univ., 1969, MA, 1973, PhD, 1973, ScD, 1990; C.Eng. (cert. engr.) U.K. Career: Goldsmith's Res. Fellow, Churchill Coll., Cambridge Univ., U.K. 1972-74; Miller Res. Fellow, lectr. UC Berkeley, Calif. 1974-76; assoc. prof. mech. engring. M.I.T., 1977-81; prof. materials sci. UC Berkeley, 1981-, dir. Ctr. for Advanced Mats., Lawrence Berkeley Lab. 1987-, dep. dir. Mats. Scis. Div. Lawrence Berkeley Lab. 1990-; cons. on topics of engring. and bio-prosthetic implant (medical) devices: Westinghouse, Rockwell, GE, Garrett Turbine, Exxon, Alcan, Northrop, Chevron, Grumman, St. Jude Med., Shiley Inc., Carbomedics Inc., Baxter Healthcare, USCI/BARD, Carbon Implants, other cos.; awards: Marcus A. Grossmann award Am. Soc. for Metals 1980, Champion H. Mathewson gold medal, Minerals Metals Mats. Soc. 1985, George R. Irwin medal ASTM 1985, Curtis W. McGraw research award Am. Soc. Engring. Educators 1987, Rosenhain medal Inst. of Materials, London 1992, Science Digest mag. list of Am. Top 100 Young Scientists (12/84); Fellow Am. Soc. for Metals 1980-, Inst. of Materials, U.K. 1972-, Internat. Congress on Fracture (hon. fellow, 1989), mem. Minerals Metals & Materials Soc. 1975-; publs: 200+ tech. papers and editor 6 books on fatigue, fracture mechanics and materials sci. of structural mats.- metals, intermetallics, ceramics & composites (1971-); Republican; rec: orchidist, gardening, x-c skiing. Ofc: Dept. Mats. Sci. & Mineral Engring. Univ. Calif., Berkeley 94720

RITZ, SUZANNE C., public accountant, tax consultant; b. Sept. 26, 1931, Detroit, Mich.; d. Harvey McCoullough and Edna (McNeeley) Milford; children: Thomas b. 1951, Edward b. 1955, Paul b. 1956, Arthur b. 1958, Suzanne b. 1960, Wayne b. 1962; edn: BSBA, CSU Sacramento, 1979; Calif. lic. pub. acct., 1971, lic. building contractor, 1989. Career: bookkeeper clk., 1945-; US Postal Service 1966-72; tax preparation, public acct., credit cons., pres. Financial Tax Consultant, Sacto. 1971-; pres. Money Concepts of Fair Oaks, Calif. 1982-86; instr. adult edn., Sacto. 1986-; honors: Student Body Senate CSUS, 1977-79; mem. Nat. Assn. of Female Execs., 1989-, Am. Assn. of Business Building Accts., 1991-, Nat. Speakers Assn. Sacto., 1986-, Sunrise Toastmasters (CTM); civic: Miss Sacramento County Scholarship Assn. (fin. chair 1991-), Eastern Star (Cavitey, Philippines 1953-55); author: Tips for Small Businesses, 1991, booklet "Tax Tips", 1973-; Unitarian; rec: travel, swimming, speaking. Ofc: Financial Tax Consultant, 5800 Antelope Rd. Suite 3 Sacramento 95842

RIZZO, RONALD STEPHEN, lawyer; b. July 15, 1941, Kenosha, Wis.; s. Frank E. and Rosalie (LoCicero) R.; m. Mary Catherine, Sept. 10, 1963; children: Ronald S., Jr. b. 1965, Michael R. b. 1967; edn: BS, St. Norbert Coll. 1963; LLB, Georgetown Univ. Law Sch., 1965, LLM in taxation, 1966. Career: atty., assoc. Kindel & Anderson, Los Angeles 1966-71, ptnr./chmn. Employee Benefits Dept., 1972-86; ptnr. Jones, Day, Reavis & Pogue, Los Angeles 1986-; faculty UCLA Engring. and Mgmt. Pgm. 1981-85; dir: Reid Plastics Inc., Monrovia, Calif., Amante Internat., Palm Desert, Calif., Guy Lo Cicero & Son Inc., Kenosha, Wis.; awards: Georgetown Law Journal 1965, Schulte zur Hausen Fellow Inst. of Internat. and Fgn. Trade Law, Georgetown Univ. Law Sch. 1965-66, Fellow Am. Coll. of Tax Counsel; mem. Am. Bar Assn. (Sect. on Taxation, Com. on Empl. Benefits, chmn. 1988-89), Calif. Bar Assn. (Sect. on Taxation, co-chair Com. on Empl. Benefits 1980), Wis. Bar Assn., Los Angeles Co. Bar Assn. (Sect. on Taxation, chmn. Employee Benefits Com. 1977, mem. Tax Sect. Exec. Com. 1977-79, 89-91), Western Pension Conf. (LA chpt. Steering Com. 1980-83); club: Indian Wells CC; publs: contbr. taxation and law jours.; speaker annual profl. confs., lectr. ALI-ABA, PLI, Law & Bus., Calif. CEB, t.v. and video: Am. Law Inst. (ABA, 1984), Window on Wall Street; rec: reading, golf, travel. Res: 1101 Singingwood Dr Arcadia 91106 Ofc: Jones, Day, Reavis & Pogue, 555 W Fifth St Ste 4600 Los Angeles 90013-1025

ROBBINS, JACK HOWARD, lawyer; b. May 16, 1957, Los Angeles; s. Albert M. and Helen (Karabenick) R.; m. Cindy L. Cannon, Jan. 7, 1990; edn: BA polit. sci. (cum laude) CSU Northridge, 1979; JD, Loyola Law Sch., 1982; admitted bar: Calif. 1982, U.S. Dist. Ct. 1982. Career: atty., assoc. Wilson, Kenna & Borys, L.A. 1985-88; Bottum & Feliton, L.A. 1988-90; sole law practice, Sacramento 1991-; mem: Arbitration Panel Sacto. Co. Superior Ct. 1992-, Am. Bar Assn., Calif. State Bar Assn., Sacto. Co. Bar Assn. (Atty. Client Relations Com.), Assn. of Def. Council of No. Calif.; civic: Citrus Hts. C.of C. 1991-, Fair

Oaks Comm. Planning Advy. Council (1991-, chmn.); Democrat (Sacto. Co. Dem. cent. com. 1991-), Culver City Dem. Club (1987-89, past pres.); Jewish; rec: skiing, tennis. Res: 8605 Jaytee Way Fair Oaks 95628-2976 Law Office of Jack Robbins 1900 Point West Way Ste 248 Sacramento 95815-4704

ROBBOY, MERLE S., physician; b. Feb. 9, 1941, Cleveland, Ohio; s. George M. and Mary Rose (Frankel) R.; m. Christine E. Stevens; children: Susan b. 1961, Meade b. 1964; edn: AA, Western Reserve Univ. 1961; MD, Ohio St. Univ. 1965. Career: rotating intern USPHS, Seattle, Wash. 1965-66, surgeon, San Francisco 1966-68; resident UCLA Med. Center, Los Angeles 1968-71; gen. and surgery oncology City of Hope Med. Center, Duarte 1972; pvt. practice ob-gyn., Newport Beach 1972-93; assoc. clin. prof. UC Irvine Med. Center 1974-93; chmn. dept. ob-gyn. Hoag Meml. Hosp., Newport Beach 1982-84; awards: Roessleer Research scholarship 1964; mem: Orange Co. Ob-Gyn. Soc. (pres. 1983-84), Pacific Coast Fertility Soc., Am. Fertility Soc., Am. Coll. Ob-Gyn. (fellow), Pacific Coast Ob-Gyn. Soc., Southwest Ob-Gyn. Soc., Am. Assn. Gynecology Laparoscopists, Newport Harbor Orchid Soc., Am. Dahlia Soc.; 3 articles pub. in med. jours. 1971-87; mil: surgeon major USPHS 1966-68; Republican; Jewish; rec: orchids, dahlias, gardening. Ofc: 1401 Avocado Ave Ste 801 Newport Beach 92660

ROBERCK, CECIL MELVIN, JR., clergyman, church history educator; b. Mar. 16, 1945, San Jose, Calif.; s. Cecil Melvin and Berdetta Mae (Manley) R.; m. Patsy Jolene Gibbs, June 14, 1969; children: Jason Lloyd b. 1972, John Mark b. 1974, Peter Scott b. 1977, Nathan Eric b. 1979; edn: AA, San Jose City Coll., 1967; BS, Bethany Bible Coll., Santa Cruz 1970; MDiv, Fuller Theol. Sem., 1973, PhD, 1985; ordained minister Assemblies of God, 1973. Career: grad. tchg. asst. Fuller Theol. Sem., Pasadena 1973-78, adj. instr. 1981-85, asst. prof., assoc. prof. church history 1985-88, 88-92, assoc. prof. church history and ecumenics, 1992-, adminstrv. staff 1974-, dir. admissions 1977-79, dir. student svs. 1979-83, dir. acad. svs. 1983-85, asst. dean, assoc. dean acad. pgms. Sch. of Theology 1985-92; awards: Joseph L. Gerhart scholar 1969, staff devel. grantee Assn. Theol. Schs. in U.S. and Canada 1977; mem. World Council of Churches Plenary Commn. on Faith and Order 1991-; mem. Nat. Council of Churches working gp. on faith and order 1985-, NCC Pentecostal Dialogue (co-chair St. Louis, Mo. 1988, Fresno, Ca. 1989, Louisville, Ky. 1990, Lakeland, Fla. 1991), Internat. R.Cath./Pentecostal Dialogue, Vatican City (internat. steering com., treas. 1985-, co-chair 1992-), Local Evangelical/ R.Cath. Dialogue, L.A. (1987-, co-chair 1992-), N.Am. Acad. of Ecumenists (bd. 1989-); trustee Bethany Bible Coll. (1985-88, exec. com. 1986-88); fellow Wesleyan/ Holiness Studies Ctr. Asbury Theol. Sem. 1987-90; mem: Soc. for Pentecostal Studies (1977-, pres. 1982-83), Am. Acad. of Religion 1984-, Pacific and Am. Assns. of Collegiate Registrars and Admissions Ofcrs. 1975-85, Nat. Assn. Student Personnel Adminstrs. 1980-85; author: Prophecy At Carthage (1992), editor (books) Charismatic Experiences in History (1985), Witness To Pentecost (1985), (journal) Pneuma: The J. of the Society for Pentecostal Studies (1984-), num. jour., book and dict. articles (1974-); Republican; rec: writing, camping, travel. Ofc: Fuller Theological Seminary Pasadena 91182

ROBERTS, CHARLES MORGAN, optometrist; b. June 13, 1932, Roswell, N.M.; s. Clarence A. and Annie Lorene (Perkins) R.; m. Gloria Vivian Lasagna, Feb. 24, 1962; children: Michael b. 1963, Janis b. 1965; edn: AA engring., Mt. San Antonio Coll., 1958; BS organic chem., Univ. La Verne, 1961, MA organic chem., 1970; BS physiol. optics, So. Calif. Coll. Optometry, Fullerton 1972, OD, 1974; Diplomate of Cornea & Contact Lenses Am. Acad. of Opt. 1977, bd. cert. contact lenses N.E.R.F. 1981. Career: electronic engr. Aerojet General, Covina 1955-65; research chemist Sunkist Orange Prod. Div., Ontario 1965-70; cons. physician U.S. Pub. Health Service, San Pedro 1974-77; asst. prof. So. Calif. Coll. Optometry, Fullerton 1974-; dr. optometry pvt. practice, San Juan Capistrano, 1975-; awards: research fellow, outstanding achieve. award Bausch & Lomb 1974, instr. of yr. SCCO 1975; mem: Am. Acad. Opt. (fellow 1976-), Am. Opt. Assn. 1970-, Calif. Opt. Assn. 1970-, Orange County Opt. Soc. (bd. dirs. 1981-83); clubs: Rotary Intl. (San Juan Cap. pres., bd. dirs. 1975-82), Elks (San Clemente); author: Contact Lens Modification 1980, Math of Contact Lens 1985, editor: Dict. of Visual Science 1990; mil: RM2 USN 1951-55; Republican; Lutheran; rec: computers, aviation. Ofc: Charles M. Roberts, O.D., Inc. 32282 Camino Capistrano "B" San Juan Capistrano 92675

ROBERTS, ERIC STENIUS, computer science educator; b. June 8, 1952, Durham, N.C.; s. James Stenius and Anne Hall (Estep) R.; edn: AB (cum laude), Harvard Coll. 1973, SM, Harvard Univ., 1974, PhD, 1980. Career: asst. prof. Wellesley Coll., 1980-85; research scientist DEC Systems Res. Ctr., Palo Alto 1985-90; assoc. prof. Stanford Univ., 1990-; vis. prof. Harvard Univ., 1984-85; awards: NSF grad. fellow, Harvard 1973-76; pres. Computer Profls. for Social Responsibility 1990-; mem: Assn. for Computing Machinery, IEEE, Democratic Socialists of Am.; author: Thinking Recursively (1986); Democrat; Soc. of Friends. Res: 2256 Bowdoin St Palo Alto 94306 Ofc: Dept. Computer Sci. Stanford University, Stanford 94305

ROBERTS, LEE MACK, JR., president private investigation, security and alarm co.; b. Sept 14, 1948, Gastonia, NC; s. Lee Mack Sr. and Bonnie Estelle

(Smallwood) R.; m. Vernon Wooten, Nov 11, 1972; children: Paula b. 1963, Paul b. 1965; edn: AA, Golden West Coll. 1974; BA, Univ. of Redlands 1977; Licenses: pvt. investigator/ pvt. patrol/alarm co. Career: detective Newport Beach Police Dept. 1970-81 (med. ret.); pres. Roberts Protection & Investigations, 1982-; instr. Newport Beach Police & Fire Depts.; instr. Golden West Coll., Criminal Justice Tng. Ctr.; awards: named Outstanding Police Ofcr. of the Yr. 1973, 3 time recipient Police Award of Merit (1976, 77, 79) Newport Beach Police Dept., Am. Law Enforc. Ofcrs. Assn. Legion of Honor, Honored citizen Orange Co. Bd. Supvrs. 1979, listed Who's Who in Am. Law Enforcement; mem: Calif. Conf. & Internat. Assn. of Arson Investigators, Internat. Police Assn., Calif. & Western US Confs. of Safe & Burglary Investigators, Internat. Assn. for Identification, Am. Fedn. of Police, BSA Police Explorer Sect.; works: Procedural Crime Scene Investigators Handbook, Newport Bch. PD; proposal for creation of multi- jurisdictional burglary impact team; plan to create Orange Co. Police Mus.; contracted, placed first pvt. security team into Kuwait, 20 days after cease-fire with Iraq to protect Am. owned businesses; mil: cpl. USMC 1965-68; Republican; Baptist; rec: police memorabilia collector. Ofc: Roberts Protection & Investigations, 838 N Van Ness Ave Santa Ana 92701

ROBERTS, LESLIE ANN, certified public accountant; b. July 23, 1960, Palo Alto; d. N. Neil and Ann (DeLaney) Berger; m. Mark Andrew Roberts, Sept. 10, 1983; children: Christopher b. 1987, twins, Ryan and Kate b. 1990; edn: BS in commerce, Santa Clara Univ., 1982; MS in Taxation,Golden Gate Univ. 1992; lic.C.P.A., Calif. 1985. Career: staff acct. Price Waterhouse, San Jose 1981; staff acct., tax sr., tax mgr. Deloitte Haskins & Sells (now Deloitte & Touche), San Jose 1982-88; owner Leslie A. Roberts CPA firm, Fremont 1988-; tax coordinator So. Alameda Co. CPA Discussion Group 1989-90; honors: Beta Gamma Sigma nat. seminar attendee, Soc. Distinguished Am. H.S. Students; mem: Am. Inst. CPAs, Calif. Soc. CPAs, Bus. Owners Network (v.p. 1989-90), Fremont C.of C., Tri-City Mothers of Multiples Club (treas. 1991); Republican; rec: skiing, tennis, bicycling. Ofc: Fremont

ROBERTS, WALTER HERBERT BEATTY, physician, medical educator; b. Jan. 24, 1915, Field, Canada; nat. 1965; s. Walter McWilliam and Sarah Caroline (Orr) R.; m. Olive Louise O'Neal, Sept. 1, 1937; children: Gayle b. 1939, Sharon b. 1942, David b. 1949; edn: MD, Coll. Med. Evangelists Loma Linda Univ. 1939. Career: med. dir. Rest Haven Hosp. & Sanitarium, Sidney, B.C. 1940-53; instr., prof. anatomy, Loma Linda Univ. 1955-; chmn. anatomy dept. 1974-81; honors: Alpha Omega Alpha, Sigma Xi; mem: San Bernardino Co. Med. Assn., CMA Am. Assn. Anatomy; articles pub. in med. jours., 1959-84; Republican; SDA; rec: nature. Res: 11366 Campus Loma Linda 92354 Ofc: Department of Anatomy Loma Linda University Stewart St Loma Linda 92350

ROBINSON, GILL, professor; b. March 28, 1948, Balt.; d. Lowman G. Daniels and Beatrice (Muse) Price; m. Garrison Michael Hickman, Apr. 21, 1990; 1dau. by previous marriage, Kimberly b. 1973; edn: BA, Univ. Denver 1970; MPA, UCLA, 1973; PhD, USC, 1978. Career: dir. class personnel Montclair Sch. Dist., Ontario 1976-77; dir. staff personnel CSU Dominguez Hills, Carson 1977-79, prof. pub. adminstrn. 1979-, MPA program coord. 1983-84, interim dean faculty affairs 1987-88, interim dean Sch. of Health 1988-90; cons. Sierra Univ., L.A. 1986-87, Arthur Young & Co. 1986-87, City of Inglewood 1985-87, Dobbs Assoc. 1980; awards: D.R. Gerth service award CSU-DH 1989, campus nominee Womens' Council "Woman of Achiev." 1989, Pi Alpha Alpha, Pi Gamma Mu, UCLA grad. advancement pgm. fellow 1973, Who's Who Among Black Americans, recogn. Soroptimist Club 1974; mem: Nat. Assn. Sch. of Pub. Affairs & Adminstrn., Womens Council of St. Univ., Am. Soc. Pub. Adminstrn., Calif. Black Faculty & Staff Assn.; author: Person Centered Management; Democrat; Rel. Sci. Ofc: Calif. State Univ. Dominguez Hills 1000 Victoria St Carson 90747

ROBINSON, JOHNNIE DELL, photographer; b. Jan. 26, 1915, Greensboro, Ala.; d. Johnnie Morse and Della (Cain) Miranda; m. Willie Pope, July 29, 1934 (div. 1959); m. James Asa Robinson, July 12, 1966; children: Pamela Jean b. 1950, Rebecca Sue b. 1952; Career: window trimmer Pausons Clothing Store, San Francisco 1951-60; Hinks Dept. Store, Berkeley 1969-85; ret.; photographer Womens C.of C., Berkeley 1984-89; awards: Nat. Council Negro Women Cert. Merit 1976, Internat. Finishing Sch. scholarship 1948; mem: Acorn Camera Club (life), Berkeley Hist. Soc. (bd. mem. 1982-85), Negro Hist. Soc., Berkeley Arch. Heritage Assn., Landmarks Commn., Eastern Star Lodge; 4 photo documentaries (1959-64); Democrat; African Methodist; rec: architectural photography. Res: 1428 67th St Berkeley 94702

ROBINSON, MURIEL F. COX, physician, psychiatrist; b. Nov. 6, 1927, Columbus, Ohio; d. Henry Willard and Veola Garry (Isbell) Cox; m. Julius Ceasar Robinson MD, June 2, 1950 (div. 1976); edn: Ohio St. Univ. 1945-48; MD, Meharry Med. Coll. 1952. Career: psychiatry resident Homer G. Phillips Hosp., St. Louis 1953-56; staff psychiatrist St. Louis Child Guidance Clinic, Mo. 1956-57; Napa St. Hosp., Imola 1958; Richmond Health Center, Richmond 1958-75; gen. psychiatry pvt. practice, Richmond and Oakland 1960-79; staff psychiatrist E. Oakland Mental Health Center, Oakland 1976-79; Dept. Youth

Authority, Sacto. 1979-92; Locum Tenens Physician Group, 1992-; biog. listed Who's Who Among Black Am.; mem: Am. Psychiatric Assn. (Life), Black Psychiatrists of Am., Nat. Med. Assn., AMA, AAAS, Sacto. NAACP; Prot.; rec: flute (recorder). Res: PO Box 292148 Sacramento 95829

ROBINSON, WILLIAM JAMES, computer engineering scientist, manager; b. June 26, 1953, La Jolla; s. Clarence Barss and Irene Florence (MacDonald) R.; m. Catherine Easterly, Sept. 22, 1979; edn: engring. tech., elec., Grossmont Coll. 1974; engring., electronics, CSU San Diego 1975-77; BSCS Nat. Univ. 1985. Career: electronics design engr./instr. Dyn-Aura Engring. Labs., 1975-77; electronics test engr. Doric Scientific, 1978-82, also in-house tchg., cons.; engr., engring. mgr. Metrox Inc., San Diego 1985-; honors: 1st pl. Engring./Electronics, Sr. Div. 1971, ASME 1971, Inst. of Elec. and Electronic Engrs. 1971, Pickett Slide Rule Award 1971; works: 3-D animated characters, FMC Unit 4-80, Linear Displacement Transducer 7-82; Republican; Christian; rec: 3-D animated characters controlled by personally designed electronics. Res: 1127 Dawnridge Ave El Cajon 92021 Ofc: Metrox Inc. 7165 Construction Ct San Diego 92121

ROBISON, WILLIAM ROBERT, lawyer; b. May 5, 1947, Memphis, Tenn.; s. Andrew Cliffe, Sr. and Elfrieda (Barnes) R.; m. Hye Sook Park, Dec. 17, 1982 (div. Apr. 1992); edn: AB, Boston Univ. 1970; JD, Northeastern Univ. 1974; admitted bar: Mass. 1974, Dist. Col. 1975, Calif. 1978. Career: atty., assoc. Meyers, Goldstein & Crossland, Boston 1975-76; assoc. Cooley, Shrair, et al Springfield, Mass. 1976-78; assoc. Hertzberg, Koslow & Franzen, Los Angeles 1978-79; assoc. Marcus & Lewi, 1980-81; atty. solo practice, Santa Monica 1981-; judge pro tem L.A. Mncpl. Ct. 1984-, L.A. Superior Ct. 1987-; instr. Northeastern Univ. 1975-76; bd. dirs. Action for Boston Comm. Devel. 1972-76, Boston Legal Assistance Project 1972-76; mem: Am., Mass. 1974-78, Calif., Los Angeles Co., Santa Monica bar assns.; coauthor: Commercial Transactions Desk Book, Inst. for Bus. Planning (1977); Democrat; Unitarian; rec: econs. Res: 2546 Amherst Ave Los Angeles 90064 Ofc: William R. Robison 2546 Amherst Ave Los Angeles 90064

ROBLEDO, GILBERTO, college counselor, professor; b. Sept. 1, 1940, Santa Paula; s. Felix and Virginia (Reyes) R.; m. Joy Moody, Sept. 24, 1966; children: Maya b. 1971, Alma b. 1975; edn: Santa Barbara Comm. Coll. 1960-62; BA sociology, UC Santa Barbara 1964; MA sociology, San Diego St. Univ. 1968; PhD, edn., adminstrn., UC Santa Barbara 1978. Career: probation ofcr. Santa Barbara and San Diego Co. Probation Depts., Santa Maria and San Diego 1966-69; prof. Chicano studies San Diego Comm. Coll. and San Diego St. Univ. 1969-72; assoc. dir. Chicano Fedn. San Diego Co. 1972-73; coord. grad. minority program UCSD, La Jolla 1973; extended opportunities dir., counselor Santa Barbara Comm. Coll. 1973-83, coord. student operations/admissions and records 1983-84, coord. disabled student svs. 1984-88, counselor/ prof. 1988-; pres. Chicano Research & Resources Inc. 1987-; cons. migrant edn. Santa Barbara County Sch. Dist. 1989; awards: UCSB post doctoral fellowship 1987, City of San Diego mayoral cand. 1971, Santa Barbara City Schs. bd. of edn. cand. 1979; mem: UCSB Alumni Assn. (bd. dirs. 1985-, exec. com. 1988-89), Fund for Santa Barbara, Raza Advocates/Calif. Higher Edn., CCC EOPS Assn. (v.p. 1974-75), La Casa de la Raza Inc. (pres. 1980-85), Santa Barbara Chicano Scholarship Found. (secty. 1985-86), Calif. 19th Dist. Agri. Assn. (bd. dirs. 1983-86); contbr. Ghosts in the Barrio 1973, publs: Job Shadowing in Bus. & Industry & Employees with Disabilities 1986; MA thesis 1968, doc. diss. 1978; mil: sp4 USAR 1959-65; Democrat; Prot.; rec: hiking, latin jazz percussion. Res: 1422 W Valerio St Santa Barbara 93101 Ofc: 721 Cliff Dr Santa Barbara 93109

ROCHE, JOHN FRANCIS, III, aerospace museum executive director; b. Aug. 11, 1930, Albany, N.Y.; s. John Francis, Jr. and Marion (Spayne) R.; children: Kathryn b. 1953, Jennifer b. 1957, John b. 1959, William b. 1961, Constance b. 1963, Ian b. 1983; edn: Baccalaureate, English, Virginia Mil. Inst., 1952; MS Internat. Rels., George Washington Univ., WDC 1966. Career: served to Colonel USMC, 1952-77; writer, free lance, 1979-85; exec. dir. Internat. Aerospace Hall of Fame, San Diego, 1985-; rec: flying, writing, building model aircraft. Ofc: Internat. Aerospace Hall of Fame Balboa Park San Diego.

ROCHE, ROBERT BRUCE, communications company executive; b. Oct. 31, 1932, San Francisco; s. Theodore Hollis and Kathryn Margaret (O'Brien) R.; m. Sally Jean Floyd, June 26, 1954; children: Robert b. 1955, Teri b. 1957, David b. 1961; edn: BSEE, UC Berkeley 1954; USC, L.A. 1977; Bell System Advanced Mgmt. Program 1982; lic. electrical engr. Calif. 1961, N.J. 1980, lic. contractor Calif. 1986. Career: div. mgr. Pacific Telephone, San Francisco 1957-79; AT&T, Piscataway, N.J. 1979-80; v.p. Pacific Bell, San Ramon 1980-85; pres. Roche Construction, Lafayette 1985-; councilman City Govt. Lafayette 1976-80, mayor 1979-80; mem: Olympic Club (dir. 1977-79, treas. 1979), Lafayette Comm. Center Found. (founder, chair 1985-88), Sigma Nu (pres. 1954); contbr. Am. Mgmt. Assn. Handbook, 1981; mil: AUS 1954-56; Republican; Catholic; rec: running, tennis, handball. Res: 3162 Condit Rd Lafayette 94549

ROCHLIS, JEFFREY AARON, entertainment company executive; b. May 11, 1945, Phila.; s. James Joseph R.; m. Ellen M. Dondorf (div.); children: Jennifer b. 1973; edn: BA, Bard Coll., Annandale- on- Hudson, N.Y. 1967.

Career: acct. exec. Benton & Bowles, N.Y.C. 1970-72; acct. supr. McCann-Erickson, 1972-73; v.p. mktg. Aurora Products Corp., W.Hempstead, N.Y. 1973-76; pres. Mattel Electronics, Hawthorne, Calif. 1976-80; pres. and c.e.o. IXO Inc., Culver City 1980-83; pres. and c.o.o. Sega Ents. Inc. and director Paramount Pictures Corp., L.A. 1983-85; exec. v.p. Walt Disney Studios, Burbank 1985-87; exec. v.p. Walt Disney Imagineering, Glendale 1987-89; pres. King World Ents., L.A. 1990; bd. chmn. and c.e.o. Rockann Ents. Inc., Beverly Hills 1990-; mem. Acad. TV Arts & Scis. 1986-; mil: 1st lt. US Army Security Agy. 1967-70. Ofc: Rockann Enterprises, Inc. 301 N Canon Dr Ste 315 Beverly Hills 90210

RODGERSON, ELEANOR BURGESS, physician; b. Aug. 8, 1909, Sacramento; d. Robert and Nellie Jane (Chisholm) Rodgerson; m. Donald Aloysius McKinnon, Jan. 17, 1942 (dec. 1978); children: John b. 1943, Donald b. 1944, Jane b. 1947, William b. 1948; edn: AB, Stanford Univ. 1931; MD, 1935; lic. ob-gyn. 1945. Career: splty. tng. Stanford Univ. 1930-31; Children's Hosp., San Francisco 1931-32; Chgo. Lying-In, Ill. 1932-37; Chgo. Maternity Center 1938; pvt. practice ob-gyn., Sacto. 1939-49, 1960-85; gynecologist CSU, Sacto. 1965-80; asst. clin. prof. UC Davis Med. Sch. 1975-85; ret.; mem: AMA, CMA, Sacto. Co. Med. Soc., Med. Soc. Editorial Com., Am. Coll. Ob-Gyn., Comstock Club; articles pub. in med. and non-med. jours., column Questions Women Ask; Republican; Presbyterian; rec: writing. Res: 1401 38th St Sacramento 95816

ROE, BENSON BERTHEAU, retired academic cardiothoracic surgeon; b. July 7, 1918, Los Angeles; s. Hall and Helene (Bertheau) R.; m. Jane F. St. John, Jan. 20, 1945; children: David b. 1948, Virginia b. 1950; edn: AB, UC Berkeley, 1939; MD (cum laude) Harvard Med. Sch., 1943; Bd. cert. Am. Bd. Surgery, 1950, Am. Bd. Thoracic Surgery, 1953. Career: intern and jr. resident in surgery Mass. General Hosp. 1943-44, asst. res. 1947-49, chief resident in surgery 1950; Nat. Research Fellow physiology dept. Harvard Med. Sch. 1948-49; Moseley Travelling Fellow of Harvard Med. sch., Univ. of Edinburgh & Royal Infirmary Edinburgh, 1950-51; instr. surgery Harvard Med. Sch. 1950-51; chief of thoracic surgery St. Lukes Hosp., San Francisco 1953-58, also St. Joseph's Hosp., S.F., 1954-58; asst. clin. prof. surgery UC San Francisco 1952-57, prof. of surgery 1965-89, emeritus prof. 1989-, chief of cardiothoracic surgery UCSF 1958-76, co-chief 1976-87, senior mem. Cardiovascular Research Inst., UCSF, 1958-86; cons. in thoracic surgery VA Hosp., S.F. 1958-87, S.F. Gen. Hosp. 1952-87, Letterman Army Hosp. 1979-91; vis. prof. Univ. Utah 1973, Univ. Ky. 1974, Univ. Gdansk, Poland 1977, 1985, Centro Medico Nacional, Santander, Spain 1977, Univ. Ibadan, Nigeria 1979, Nat. Heart Hosp., London 1979, The Sanger Clinic, Charlotte, N.C. 1980, Rush-Presbyn. Hosp., Chgo. 1981, Penrose Hosp., Colo. Springs, Colo. 1981; dir: Control Laser Corp. 1986-88; cons. Laser Surgery Software Inc. 1989-; cons. Appleton-Davies Pubs., 1981-; editl. bd. Pharos, 1986-; honors: UCB Varsity Crew (NRA Champions), Golden Bear, Winged Helmet, Scabbard and Blade, Psi Upsilon Frat. 1939, Harvard- Alpha Omega Alpha, Aesculapian Club, Boylston Med. Soc., Nu Sigma Nu Frat. 1943; mem: Am. Surgical Assn., Am. Assn. for Thoracic Surgery, Am. Coll. Cardiology, Am. Coll. Surgeons (chmn. advy. coun. thoracic surg. 1975-78, cardiovasc. com. 1978-87), Am. Heart Assn. (nat. coms. 1971-75, pres. S.F. 1964-65), AMA, Am. Soc. for Artificial Internal Organs, Calif. Acad. of Medicine (pres. 1970), Chilean Soc. Cardiology (hon.), Dallas Clin. Soc. (hon.), Internat. Cardiovasc. Soc., Howard C. Naffziger Surg. Soc., Pacific Coast Surg. Assn., S.F. Surg. Soc., Soc. Polish Surgeons (hon.), Soc. Thoracic Surgeons, Soc. Univ. Surgeons, Soc. Vascular Surg., We. Soc. for Clin. Research, We. Thoracic Surgical Assn.; civic bds: Am. Cancer Soc. (chmn. exec. com. S.F. 1964-66), Am. Medico-Legal Found. (cons. 1988-), Avery Fuller Found. (trustee 1979-), Miranda Lux Found. (trustee, pres. 1982-), Internat. Bioethics Found. (dir. 1988-), United Bay Area Crusade (bd., exec. com. 1965-70, spl. gifts com. 1977-81), Planned Parenthood Alameda-S.F. (trustee 1986-90), Point Reyes Bird Observatory (trustee 1989-); clubs: Calif. Tennis, Cruising Club of Am., Pacific Union, St. Francis Yacht, Joyce Island Gun; mil: med. ofcr. USNR, USS Philadelphia 1944-46; author 172+ sci. publs. incl. 2 textbooks, 20 textbook chapters, 1 Presdl. Address; mil: lt. US Naval Reserve 1939-46. Res: 1070 Green St San Francisco 94133 Ofc: Univ. California M593, San Francisco 94143-0118

ROEMMELE, BRIAN KARL, electronics, publishing, financial and real estate executive; b. Oct. 4, 1961, Newark, N.J.; s. Bernard Joseph and Paula M. Roemmele; grad. high sch., Flemington, N.J.; reg. profl. engr., N.J. Career: design engr. BKR Techs., Flemington, N.J. 1980-81; electronic design and software consultant, 1980-; acoustical engr. Open Reel Studios, 1980-82; pres. Ariel Corp., 1983-84, Ariel Computer Corp., 1984-89; pres. and c.e.o. Ariel Financial Devel. Corp., N.Y.C. 1987-91, Avalon America Corp., Temecula, Calif. 1990-; pres. Coupon Book Ltd., 1987-89, Value Hunter Magazines Ltd., AEON Consulting Group, Beverly Hills, Calif.; bd. dirs. Waterman Internat., Whitehouse Station, N.J.; editor and pub. Computer Importer News, 1987-; lectr. Trenton State Mus., N.J. 1983; organizer Internat. Space Week or Day, 1978-83; chmn. bd. Safe Water Internat., Paris; mem: AAAS, AIAA, IEEE, Boston Computer Soc., Ford/Hall Forum, Am. Soc. Notaries, Planetary Soc.; rec: musician, surfing, cycling, reading, numismatics. Ofc: Avalon America Corp. PO Box 1615 Temecula 92593-1615

ROESCHKE, DONALD FREDERICK, lawyer; b. Mar. 20, 1938, Pago Pago, Samoa; s. Charles Edward and Madeline (McCarty) R.; m. Suzann Hogue, July 12, 1969; 1 son: David, b. 1976; edn: BS, CSU Northridge 1961; JD, Southwestern Univ. Sch. of Law 1965; admitted bar: Calif., US Supreme Ct., US Dist. Cts., 9th Cir. Ct. Appeals. Career: self- empl. atty. 1966-72; dep. atty. gen. (IV), Calif. Dept. of Justice, Ofc. of Atty. Gen. 1972-, writs coord. for L.A. Ofc. of State Atty. Gen.; lectr. on writs, write deputy tng. manuals on state & fed. writ & state appellate procedures; prosecutor, Daniel Caudillo case (described by Preble Stolz in Judging Judges); defender for people when Sirhan Sirhan filed for release in Fed. Ct., various cases in Appellate and Supreme Cts. (state & fed.); civic: L.A. Opera League, Sacto. Opera League, State R.R. Mus. (Sacto.), L.A. Co. Nat. History Mus.; publs: Mastering the Art of the Great Writ, Los Angeles Lawyer (2/81); Contg. Role of the Peace Ofcr. After a Crim. Conviction, Police Ofcr. Law Report (6/81); Hist. Aspects and Procedural Limitations of Fed. Habeas Corpus, Am. Jur. Trials (vol. 39 Lawyers Co-operative, 1989, Bancroft-Whitney Co.); Habeas Corpus: Pretrial Rulings, Am. Jur. Trials (vol. 41, 1990, Bancroft-Whitney Co.); Withdrawal of Guilty Plea, Am. Jur. Trials (vol. 42, 1991 Bancroft-Whitney Co.); Republican (Presdl. Task Force); R.Cath.; rec: model R.R., wt. lifting. Office of State Atty. Gen., 3580 Wilshire Blvd Rm 703 Los Angeles 90010

ROGAWAY, BETTY JANE, school system administrator, social worker; b. Sept. 8, 1921, San Francisco; d. Irvine and Dorothy (Nathan) Hyman; m. Roderick Matthew Rogaway, Jan. 16, 1945 (dec. Aug. 1964); children: Stephen, Kathryn Rogaway Farrell; edn: BA, U. Calif., Berkeley, 1942; MA, Calif. State U., San Jose, 1968. Career: Lic. social worker, Calif. Social worker Travelers Aid 1942, Child Welfare Svs. Sutter County, Calif. 1945, ARC, 1942-45; juvenile welfare ofcr. Palo Alto (Calif.) Police Dept. 1945-49; tchr., cons. coord. Palo Alto Unified Sch. Dist. 1958-82, ret., 1982; cons. HeadStart, San Francisco 1966, Calif. State Dept. of Edn., Sacramento 1982. mem: City of Palo Alto Task Force on Child Care 1973, County Task Force on Reasonable Efforts for Child Abuse Prevention, San Jose 1988-90; pres., Palo Alto Hist. Assn. 1989-; v.p., Calif. Child Devel. Adminstrs. Assn., Sacramento 1981-82; pres., mem. Children's Shelter Assn. of Santa Clara Cty., San Jose 1983-. Rec: reading, gardening, bird watching. Res: 1302 Greenwood Palo Alto 94301-3414

ROGGERO, MIGUEL LEONARDO, consumer product company executive; b. May 17, 1962, San Diego, Calif.; s. Roland Victor and Dinorah S. (Lopez) R.; edn: BS, Univ. of So. Calif., L.A., 1984; MBA, The Wharton Sch., Univ. of Penn., Phila., 1989; lic. real estate broker, Calif. 1992. Career: project analyst, Stephen J. Cannell Productions, Hollywood 1984-85; sr. analyst, Paramount Pictures Corp., L.A. 1985-87; pres. & co-founder, Prolube, Inc., L.A. 1989-90; finance mgr./region controller, Pepsico/Pizza Hut, Irvine 1990-; cons., Oto-Telick, Inc., Sherman Oaks 1987-88; cons., Mgmt. Info. Network, L.A. 1987-88; awards: scholarship, Calif. Masonic Found., L.A. 1982; life mem. Beta Gamma Sigma, L.A. 1983; life mem., Sigma Alpha Mu Frat.; mem: USC Sch. of Bus. Alumni Assn. 1984-, Wharton Club of So. Calif. 1989-, USC Associates, 1992-; Republican; Catholic; rec: skiing, cycling, jogging, exotic travel, photography. Res: 4338 N. Oakglen St. Calabasas 91302

ROHRBERG, RODERICK GEORGE, company president, manufacturing equipment design consultant; b. Sept. 25, 1926, Minneola, Iowa; s. Charles H. and Emma (Minsen) R.; m. Genevieve Mary Sogard, June 19, 1949; children: Karla b. 1950, Roderick K. b. 1952, Cheries b. 1957, Timothy b. 1959, Christopher b. 1964; edn: B. Naval Scis., Marquette Univ. 1946; BSCE, Iowa State Univ. 1949; Reg. Profl. Engr., Calif. Career: bridge design engr. Alaska Rd. Commn., US Dept. Int. 1949-51; sr. tech. spec. res.engr. No. Am. Rockwell, Los Angeles 1951-69; currently, pres. Creative Pathways Inc.; pvt. cons. on advanced welding process, micropro mgmt. controls for SPF/DB semi cond fab. equipment design & devel., Torrance 1972-; honors: NASA Commdn. 1965; 1st Nat. Airco welding award 1966; Profl. Achiev. Citation, Iowa State Univ. 1973; 3rd pl., Von Karman Memorial Grand Award, 1974; listed Who's Who in Aviation and Aerospace 1983; mem: Am. Welding Soc., Am. Mfg. Engrs.; mil: USNR 1944-46; rec: flying. Res: 2742 W 234th Torrance 90505 Ofc: Creative Pathways Inc., 3121 Fujita St Torrance 90505

ROIZ, MYRIAM, foreign trade executive; b. Jan. 21, 1938, Managua; came to U.S., 1949; d. Francisco Octavio and Maria Herminia (Briones) R.; m. Nicholas M. Orphanopoulos, Jan. 21, 1957 (div.); children: Jacqueline (Doggwiler), Gene, George; edn: BA interdisciplinary soc. sci. (cum laude), San Francisco St. Univ., 1980; lic. ins. agt. Career: sales rep. Met. Life Ins. Co., San Francisco 1977-79; mktg. dir. Europe/Latin Am., Allied Canners & Packers, S.F., 1979-83, M-C Internat., S.F., 1983-88; v.p. mktg. Atlantic Brokers Inc., Kinard Foods Inc., Bayamon, P.R., 1988-92; pres./owner Aquarius Enterprises Internat. 1992-; awards: Outstanding employee of yr. Hillsborough City Sch. Dist. 1973, sales award Met. Life Ins. Co. (1977, mem. Am. Soc. Profl. and Exec. Women; civic: coord. Robert F. Kennedy Presdl. campaign, Millbrae, San Mateo Co., local Mayoral campaign, Millbrae, 1975; bd. dir., organizer fundraising cpgns. Nicaragua (following earthquake devastation); mem: World Hunger Program, ChildHelp, World Vision, Covenant House, Common Cause, Commonwealth Club of Calif., World Affairs Council,

Club Latino de Foster City. Ofc: PO Box 372 San Mateo 94401 Ph: 415/341-1023 Fax: 415/341-4602

ROKEACH, LUIS ALBERTO, molecular cell biologist; b. Nov. 1, 1951, Buenos Aires, Argentina; s. Salomon and Ines (Fridman) R.; m. Batia Maslaton Tarrab, Sept. 21, 1973; children: Gaby b. 1975, Alan b. 1980; edn: BS, Hebrew Univ. of Jerusalem, 1974; predoc. student Univ. Libre de Bruxelles, Belgium and Odense Univ., Denmark, 1980-84; MS, PhD, Univ. Libre de Bruxelles, Belgium 1981, 1984. Career: research asst. Clinica Olivos, Buenos Aires, 1977-80; postdoc. res. assoc. San Diego State Univ., Calif. 1984-86; res. scientist The Agouron Inst., La Jolla, 1986-; awards: fellowships CGER, EMBO, Danish Ministry of Edn. and FEBS, Odense, Denmark 1981-83, NIH first award, San Diego 1989-94, Phi Beta Delta (founding mem. 1987), Sigma Xi 1990; mem: Am. Soc. Microbiology 1986-, AAAS 1986-, Am. Soc. of Biochem. and Molecular Biology 1990-; publs: 30+ (1981-); rec: photography. Ofc: The Agouron Institute 505 Coast Blvd S La Jolla 92037

ROLL, DOROTHY (INN YUNG) D(UNG), scientist/federal agency regional data base administrator; b. Feb. 26, 1927, Honolulu; d. William Ah Lien and Agnes Kam Lin (Goo) Dung; m. Frederick M. Stewart, July 30, 1954; 1 son, Lorin D.M. b. 1959; m. 2d. Milton Roll, May 15, 1971; edn: att. Tacoma Catholic Coll., Tacoma, Wash. 1945; BS in zoology, Univ. of Wash., 1949; grad. work Univ. of Hawaii, 1950-51. Career: fishery aide U.S. Bureau of Commercial Fisheries, Pacific Oceanic Fisheries Investigations, Honolulu 1949-57; tech. computer Lockheed Corp. Missiles Div., Sunnyvale 1957; fisheries biologist U.S. Bur. of Comml. Fisheries, Ocean Research Lab. Stanford 1957-70; fisheries biologist U.S. Nat Marine Fisheries Service, Southwest Fisheries Center, La Jolla 1970-74, computer systems analyst 1974-75, chief ADP Ops. 1975-86, chief Information Technology Services, 1987-, mem. (chair 1991-92) Nat. Data Mgmt. Com. 1987-, regional data base adminstr. 1988-; awards: U.S. Fed. Service superior meritorious performance, 1953, 62, 70, 74, 81, 84, 90, 91, 92; mem: Fed. ADP Council of So. Calif. & Ariz. (treas. 1981-82); clubs: Univ. Wash. Newman 1945-49, Chinese Students 1945-49, Orchesis Modern Dance 1946-48, Pi Alpha 1946-49; publs: spl. sci. reports, U.S. Fish & Wildlife Service, 1953, 58, 67; Democrat; Episcopal; rec: gardening, flower arranging, cooking, needlework. Res: 13886 Mira Montana Dr Del Mar 92014 Ofc: Southwest Fisheries Center 8604 La Jolla Shores Dr La Jolla 92037

ROLLIN, GRANT ERICK, financial executive; b. April 5, 1947, Detroit, Mich.; s. Emil Raymond and Esther Evelyn (Engel) R.; m. Suzanne Finocchio, June 23, 1984; children: Garth b. 1975, Gray b. 1975, Alex b. 1985, Erik b. 1987; edn: BBA, Western Mich. Univ. 1968; MBA, Mich. St. Univ. 1969. Career: staff Deloitte & Touche, San Francisco 1969-75, mgr. 1975-79, ptnr. 1979-87; chief fin. ops. Velobind Inc., Fremont 1987-91; exec. v.p. and chief fin. ops. San Jose Sharks, San Jose 1991-; prof. St. Marys Coll., Moraga 1980-87; chmn. internat. com. U.S. Chamber, Wash. D.C. 1979-81; mem: Commonwealth Club of Calif. (Santa Clara Valley chpt. bd.), Fin. Execs. Inst. (Santa Clara Valley chpt. bd.), Assn. Corp. Growth, Am. Heart Assn. (chmn. 1978), Bus. Vols. for Arts (chmn. 1986), Easter Seals (treas. 1985), S.F. Symphony, Am. Conservatory Theatre (co-chair 1981-82); author: Expanding Your Business Overseas (1985), Exporting (1982), articles pub. in profl. jours. (1986, 87); rec: tennis. Ofc: San Jose Sharks 525 W Santa Clara St San Jose 95113

ROMERO, RICHARD D., auto dealer; b. Sept. 4, 1935, Socorro, N.M.; s. James D. and Clara (McCullough) Romero; m. Valerie A., June 20, 1962; children: Valerie b. 1964, Richard b. 1967, Christine b. 1973; edn: BA in bus. adminstrn., Univ. Mex. Career: jr. auditor 20th Century Fox, Hollywood 1956-57; asst. state auditor State of N.M., Santa Fe. 1957-59; gen. mgr. Bob Wickett Chrysler Plymouth Inc., San Bernardino 1960-70; pres. Pomona Valley Nissan 1970-; J. McCullough Corp., Upland 1973-; B.R.A.S. Internat., Reno, Nev. 1975-; Romero Corp., (Romero Buick), Ontario, Calif. 1976-; Romero AMC/Jeep Renault Inc. 1976-; chmn. bd., CEO Collateral Control Systems, Norwalk 1979-; Norwalk Auto Auction 1979-; chmn. bd. Empire Bank N.A., Rancho Cucamonga 1982-; commr. Calif. Transp. Commn., Sacto. 1983-; awards: Time Mag. Dealer Quality award 1972, Datsun Quality Dealer 1971-, Mr. Hispanic Businessman of Yr., Hispanic Youth Task Force 1985; mem: So. Calif. Nissan Dealers Assn. (options com.), Pomona Valley Auto Dealers Assn., So. Calif. Datsun Dealers Assn., Outstanding Business Achievement award, Alliance of Latino Business Associates, 1987; Imported Automobile Dealer of Distinction, Am. Internat. Auto Dealers Assn. and Sports Illustrated, 1987; trustee Univ. of LaVerne, counsel of Rose Inst. Claremont McKenna Coll.; active Cath. Social Services So. Calif. (dir), Pomona C. of C., Kiwanis; mil: AUS Tank Reserve Corp 1956-62; Republican; R.Cath. Res: 257 W Clark St Upland 91786 Ofc: Empire Nissan, 1377 Kettering Loop Ontario 91761

ROSEN, DAVID ALAN, marketing executive; b. April 1, 1951, Chicago, Ill.; s. Irving L. and Lorraine (Levine) R.; edn: BS speech and theatre arts, Bradley Univ. 1973. Career: sales rep. I Rosen & Assoc., Skokie, Ill. 1973-82; Arena USA, Huntington Beach 1984-85, nat. sales mgr., 1984-85, v.p. sales 1985-86; v.p. sales & mktg. TYR Sport, Long Beach 1986-; Jewish; rec: windsurfing. Ofc: TYR Sport POB 1930 Huntington Beach 92649

ROSEN, SANFORD JAY, lawyer; b. Dec. 19, 1937, N.Y.C.; s. Alexander Charles and Viola S. (Grad) R.; m. Catherine Picard, June 22, 1958; children: Caren E. Andrews b. 1961, R. Durelle Schacter b. 1963, Ian D. b. 1965, Melissa S. b. 1969; edn: AB, Cornell Univ., 1969; LLB, Yale Univ., 1962. Career: law clk. Chief Judge Simon E. Sobeloff, U.S. Ct. Appeals, 4th Cir. Balt., Md. 1962-63; prof. Univ. Md. Sch. of Law, Balt. 1963-71; assoc. dir. Council on Legal Edn. Opportunity, Atlanta, Ga. 1969-70; vis. prof. law Univ. Texas, Austin 1970-71; asst. legal dir. ACLU, N.Y.C. 1971-73; legal dir. Mex. Am. Legal Defense & Edn. Fund, San Francisco 1973-76; ptnr. Rosen, Remcho & Henderson, S.F. 1976-80; ptnr. Rosen & Remcho 1980-82; prin. Law Ofcs. Sanford Jay Rosen 1982-86; sr. ptnr. Rosen & Phillips 1986-89; prin. Rosen & Assocs. 1990; sr. ptnr. Rosen, Bien & Asaro 1991-; judge pro tem S.F. Superior Ct. 1990-; interim monitor U.S. Dist. Ct., no. dist. Calif., 1989, early neutral evaluator 1987-; ad hoc adminstrv. law judge Calif. Agric. Rels. Bd., S.F. 1975-80; awards: Bouton law lectr. Princeton Univ. 1971, Legal svs. honoree Mex. Am. Legal Def. & Edn. Fund Inc. S.F. 1987; appt. nat. advy. com. US HEW, W.D.C. 1974-75, Com. on Adminstrn. Crim. Justice, Balt. 1968, commr. Balt. Human Rels. Commn. 1966-69, commr. Patuxent Instn., Balt. 1967-69; mem: ABA, Am. Trial Lawyers Assn., Calif. Attys. for Crim. Justice, Calif. Bar Assn., Bar Assn. S.F., D.C. Bar Assn.; publs: articles in law jours., public press, and cont. legal edn. books; rec: reading, travel, movies.

ROSENBAUM, MICHAEL FRANCIS, fixed income securities specialist/co. executive; b. Feb. 9, 1959, New York; s. Francis Fels, Jr. and Joyce (Keefer) R.; m. Elika Sosnick, March 8, 1986; children: Erin Sosnick b. 1989, Sarah Greer b. 1991; edn: BA, Princeton Univ. 1981; lic. NASD series 3, 7, 8, 24, USALE series 63. Career: summer intern Salomon Brothers, N.Y.C. 1979; specialist clk. Spear Leeds & Kellogg, N.Y.C. summer 1980; mgr. special products, fixed income dept. Sutro & Co. Inc. 1981-85; instnl. salesman fixed income securities/v.p. Pacific Securities Inc., San Francisco 1985-89; br. office mgr. instnl. sales/v.p. Rauscher Pierce Resfnes Inc., S.F. 1989-92; v.p. inst. sales Smith Mitchell Investment Group Inc., San Francisco 1992-; dir. S.G. Rosenbaum Found. 1977-; clubs: Princeton Univ. Rowing, University Cottage, Princeton (N.Y.), Power Ten (N.Y.), Olympic (S.F.); mem. East Bay Ski Patrol, S.F. Zoological Soc.; publs: The Role of Political Cartoonists post-1940 (1981); Democrat; Jewish; rec: sailing, scuba diving, skiing. Res: PO Box 1035, 14 Madrona Ave Ross 94957 Ofc: Smith Mitchell Investment Group, Inc. One Montgomery St. Ste 1030 San Francisco 94104

ROSENBERG, CLAUDE N., JR., investment advisor, author; b. April 10, 1928, San Francisco; s. Claude N. and Elza (Wolff) R.; m. Marjorie Kay Feder (div. 1966); m. Louise Jankelson, Dec. 19, 1968; children: Linda R. b. 1954, Douglas R. b. 1957; edn: BA, Stanford Univ. 1950; MBA, Stanford Grad. Sch. Bus. 1952. Career: ptnr. J. Barth & Co., San Francisco 1955-70; sr. ptnr. RCM Capital Mgmt. 1970-; awards: Stanford Bus. Sch. Ernest C. Arbuckle 1984, Maccabiah Games bronze medal 1989; mem: San Francisco Ballet Assn. (trustee 1975-), Jewish Comm. Fedn. (dir. 1978-), The Family, Calif. Tennis Club (pres. 1968); author 4 books incl. Stock Market Primer (1962), Investing with the Best (1987); Republican; Jewish; rec: music writing, tennis, fly fishing. Address: San Francisco 94115

ROSENBERG, HOWARD ALAN, manufacturing company executive; b. Nov. 2, 1927, N.Y.C.; s. Nathan A. and Anna (Bernstein) R.; m. Carol H., Feb. 21, 1951; children: Ellen Sue b. 1957, Robin Jill b. 1958, Ira Scott b. 1960; edn: BS, Long Island Univ., 1949; MA, New York Univ., 1951; engring. scis. Peter Cooper Union, 1953-55; reg. profl. quality engr. ASQC, 1958, Calif. cred. univ. instr. 1957, 75. Career: jr. engr. Wright Aeronautics, Woodbridge, N.J. 1950-52; engr. Fairchild Engine, Farmingdale, N.Y. 1952-56; quality control mgr. Burndy Corp., Norwalk, Conn. 1956-61; mgr. quality assurance Lab for Electronics, Boston, Mass. 1961-64; mgr. q.a. AirBorne Inst. Lab., Deer Park, N.Y. 1964-70; pres. Western Technology, Anaheim 1970-85, c.e.o. 1985-; instr. New Haven (Conn.) Coll. 1956-68, Univ. at Bridgeport, Conn. 1957-61, Northeastern Univ., Boston 1962-64, cons./instr. Irvine (Calif.) Valley Coll. 1980-; awards: Eagle Scout BSA, NYC 1941, Sagian service award Long Island Univ. 1951, civic committment ADL, Orange City, Ca. 1991; mem: Phi Epsilon Pi Frat. 1950-, Alpha Phi Omega BSA (pres. 1946), Screen Printers Assn. 1975-, Inst. of Printed Circuits 1980-, Am. Soc. for Quality Control 1951, Anti-Defamation League (chapt. chair 1986-88, commr. 86-), B'nai B'rith (chapt. v.p. 1985-87), Masons; tech. papers: Quality Control and The Small Businessman 1958, Metal Etching Techniques 1975, Precision Circuit Etching 1982; mil: 1st lt. Army Nat. Guard 1948-62; Republican; Jewish; rec: stamps, coins, exercise, travel. Res: 133592 Carroll Way Tustin 92680 Ofc: 2897 E La Cresta Ave Anaheim 92806

ROSENBLUM, STEVEN ZVI, physician; b. Feb. 9, 1951, Tel-Aviv, Israel, nat. 1962; s. Dr. David and Dr. Basia (Smolar) R. (both parents MDs); edn: BS chem., UCLA, 1972; MD, Univ. Autonoma Guadalajara, 1976; Fifth Pathway, S. Baltimore Gen. Hosp., Univ. Md., 1976-77; MD lic. Md. 1978; Calif. 1978; cert. Am. Bd. Internal Med. Career: resident surgery Cedars-Sinai Med. Ctr., Los Angeles 1977-80; resident int. med. San Joaquin Gen. Hosp., Stockton, and Stanford Univ. Med. Ctr., Palo Alto, 1980-83; internist pvt. practice, Northridge 1983-85; Hawthorne Comm. Med. Group, Torrance 1985-88; Community Med.

Group of the West Valley, Simi Valley 1988-; cons. internal medicine Simi Valley Hosp., Westlake Hosp., Numed Regional Med. Ctr., Humana West Hills Hosp., 1988-, Torrance Mem. Med. Ctr., South Bay Hosp., Redondo Bch., Bay Harbor Hosp., Harbor City, 1986-88; honors: 1st pl. Calif. Fedn. of Chapparal Poets Conv. (1961), life mem. Calif. Scholarship Fedn., B.of A. award english lit., honors at entrance UCLA (1968), AMA phys. recognition (1980, 83, 86, 90, 92); mem: Am. Coll. Physicians, A.C.S. (assoc. 1977-80), AMA, CMA, Calif. House Ofcr. med. Soc. (1980-83), Nat. Assn. Res. & Interns (1980-83), Univ. Autonoma Guadalajara Alumni Assn., Alpha Chi Sigma (UCLA treas. 1971-72), B'nai Brith Youth Orgn. Northridge (v.p. 1969-71); Jewish; rec: swimming, diving, painting, play piano, guitar.

ROSENFELD, DORRIN BETH, chiropractor; b. April 19, 1963, Bellefonte, Pa.; d. Herbert Bernard and Roberta P. (Weiss) Rosenfeld; m. Robert Marlin Woolery, Sept. 21, 1992; edn: BA in philosophy/women's studies, Amherst Coll., Amherst, Mass. 1985; DC, Life Chiropractic Coll.-West, San Lorenzo, Calif. 1992. Career: secondary school tchr., Peace Corps, Belize, Central Am., 1985, 1987-88; postceptor, DC, Central Valley Health Care, Sherman Oaks, Calif. 1992; prin., DC, Miracle Chiropractic, Riverside, Calif. 1993-; awards: partial scholarship L.A. College Chiropractic, 1988; mem: Returned Peace Corps Volunteer (RPCV) 1988-, Toastmasters Internat. 1991-92, Utne (Reader Group) 1992-; Conservative-Jewish. Res: 2324 2nd Ave San Bernardino 92405 Ofc: Miracle Chiropractic 3824-12th St Riverside 92501

ROSENFELD, MARTIN, accounting firm executive; b. May 27, 1932, Chgo.; s. Meyer and Bessie (Kite) R.; m. Beatrice Premazon, Mar. 21 1953; children: Elysa b. 1955, Sherri b. 1958, David b. 1961; edn: AA, L.A. City Coll., 1950; BS, CSU Los Angeles, 1956; grad. studies UCLA; C.P.A., Calif. Bd. Career: supr. Lefkowitz & Berk, Beverly Hills 1957-63; c.f.o. KRHM Bdcstg. Co., L.A. 1963-69; mng. ptnr. Rosenfeld & Bueno, L.A. 1969-; pres. Automated Bookeeping, L.A. 1980-; dir. Connector Distbn., L.A. 1984-; award: distinguished service US Air Force, L.A. 1983; mem. Am. Inst. CPA 1979-, Inst. Mgmt. Accts., Soc. Calif. Accts. (past pres.), Nat. Soc. Pub. Accts.; lodges: Kiwanis, F&AM; pub. articles in field (1979 84, 87, 91, 92); mil: cpl. US Army 1954-56; Democrat; Jewish; rec: investing. Ofc: Rosenfeld & Bueno, 642 Larchmont Blvd Los Angeles 90004

ROSENFIELD, STANLEY WILLIAM, public relations executive; b. Jan. 1, 1939, Okla. City, Okla.; s. Stanley W., Sr. and Bertha (Angelman) R.; m. Casey Zekley, 1971 (div. 1989); children: Chase b. 1973, Zachary b. 1976; edn: BBA, Univ. of Okla. 1962. Career: exec. v.p. Jay Bernstein Public Relations, Beverly Hills 1965-75; owner, pres. Stan Rosenfield Public Relations, Beverly Hills 1975-; instr. public rels. Univ. of Southern Calif., 1984-90; mem: Acad. of Motion Picture Arts & Sci., Acad. of Television Arts & Sci., Italian-Am. Lawyers Assn. of Los Angeles, Variety Club of So. Calif. (bd. dirs. 1975-85); Democrat; Jewish. Ofc: Stan Rosenfield Public Relations 9595 Wilshire Blvd Ste 511 Beverly Hills 90212

ROSOFF, ELAYNE, clinical psychologist; edn: BA psychology, UCLA, 1977; MA comm./clin. psychology, Pepperdine Univ., 1979; PhD, Calif. Sch. Profl. Psychology, 1984. Career: faculty res. asst. UCLA, 1975-76, 77-78; psychology intern: cancer res., Center for Healing Arts, L.A. 1978, halfway house, Beverlywood After Care Ctr., L.A. 1978-79, Santa Monica Bay Area Drug Abuse Council "New Start," Santa Monica 1979-80 (chmn. bd. dirs. 1980-82), Brentwood VA Hosp., L.A. 1980-82; pvt. practice psychologist in West Los Angeles and Las Vegas, 1982-; clin. therapist chem. dependency pgm. Beverly Glen Hosp., L.A. 1983-84; vol. facilitator victim support groups for MADD (Mothers Against Drunk Driving) 1983-90, mem. bd. advisors 1986-90; num. lectures and seminars in field, 1984-; awards: Tak Yoshino Scholar Calif. Sch. Profl. Psychology 1980, "Angel of Yr." MADD 1986, "Caring Californian" May Co. Stores 1987; mem: Psi Chi, Mensa, Calif. State Psychol. Assn. (reg. legislative coord. 1985-89), L.A. Co. Psychol. Assn. (dir. 1985-, chair pub. affairs com. 1985-89), Am. Psychol. Assn. Mail: PO Box 1346 Santa Monica 90406-1346

ROSS, HUGH COURTNEY, manufacturing company executive; b. Dec. 31, 1923, Turlock, Calif.; s. Clare William and Jeanne Frances (Pierson) R.; m. Sarah A. Gordon, Dec. 16, 1950 (dec. Sept. 1983); children: John b. 1953, James b. 1955, Robert b. 1957; m. Patricia A. Malloy, Apr. 1, 1984; edn: Caltech, 1942, San Jose State Univ., 1946-47, BSEE, Stanford Univ., 1950, postgrad. Stanford Univ. 1954. Career: instr. San Benito H.S. and Jr. Coll., 1950-51; chief engr. ITT Jennings Radio Mfg., San Jose 1951-62; owner, chief engr. HV Consultants, Saratoga 1964-; owner, pres. and gen. mgr. Ross Engineering Corp., Campbell 1964-; mem: IEEE (Fellow, life mem. 1947-, Santa Clara Valley chapt. chmn. 1960-61), Am. Vacuum Soc. 1955-, Am. Soc. for Metals 1955-; author, inventor, patentee high voltage devices, major devel. in high power vacuum relays, vacuum switches, vacuum circuit breakers, high voltage voltmeters, digital and analog, fiber optics; contbr. articles to IEEE Transactions and other tech. jours.; mil: s/sgt. US Air Corps 1943-46; Prot.; rec: electronics, electric auto, camping, ranching. Ofc: Ross Engineering Corp., 540 Westchester Dr Campbell CA 95008

ROSS, JEAN MARJORIE, educator; b. Mar. 11, 1926, Revere, Mass.; d. James William and Edith May (Beyer) West; m. Clayton Garner Ross, June 26, 1948; children: Janet b. 1950, David b. 1953, Betsy b. 1957; edn: BS, Simmons Coll., Boston, 1948; grad. work UC Berkeley, 1968, Western Baptist Coll., 1968; MA, San Francisco St. Univ., 1969. Career: home economics tchr. high sch., Revere, Mass., 1950-51; spl. edn. tchr. U.S. DOD, Heidelberg, Ger., 1964-65; spl. edn. tchr. Mt. Diablo Unified Sch. Dist., Concord, Calif., 1969-82, sch. dist. home economics tchr. and coord. for dist. high schs., 1978-81; home economics tchr. Walnut Creek Christian Acad., 1982-; home economics tchr.-trainer of Headstart tchrs., Merritt Coll., Oakland, 1989-; area rep. and fund raiser Western Baptist Coll., Salem, Oreg., 1980-; hostess for husband's Certified Fin. Planner (CFP) bus., 1982-; awards: Exemplary Program Mt. Diablo USD, Concord 1980, Sky Club, Simmons Coll., Boston 1987; mem: Calif. Tchrs. Assn. (life), Diablo Valley Home Economists, Pleasant Hill 1963-, AAUW, Christian Educators Assn. Internat. (life), Women's Ministry First Baptist Ch. Walnut Creek 1952-, Alumni Club Simmons E.Bay Chpt. 1986-; civic: Presdl. Found. (sustaining sponsor 1987), Assemblyman Bill Baker's Victory Team 1988, Bible Study Fellowship 1959-64; Republican; First Baptist Ch. Walnut Creek (jt. bd. 1978, Missions team, Flower chair, 1982-, wrote hist. for 50th anniversary 1989); rec: grandchildren (11), flower arranging, travel (China, Japan, Korea, Caribbean, Europe), Scrabble. Res: 3 Dale Ct Walnut Creek 94595

ROSS, JOHN, professor of physical chemistry; b. Oct. 2, 1926, Vienna, Austria; came to U.S. 1940; s. Mark and Anna (Krecmar) R.; m. Virginia Franklin (div.); children: Elizabeth A., Robert K.; m. Eva Madarasz; edn: BS, Queens Coll., 1948; PhD, MIT, 1951; Hon. Dr., Weizmann Inst. Sci., Rehovot, Israel, 1984, Queens Coll. SUNY, 1987, Univ. Bordeaux, France 1987. Career: prof. chemistry Brown Univ., 1953 66; MIT, 1966-80, dept. chmn. 1966-71, chmn. of Faculty 1975-77; prof. physical chemistry Stanford Univ., 1980-, dept. chmn. 1983-89; industrial cons. 1979-; mem. bd. govs. Weizmann Inst. Sci. 1971-; awards: medal Coll. de France, Paris 1987, 1992 Irving Langmuir Award in chem. physics Am. Chem. Soc. 1992; mem: AAAS (Fellow), Am. Phys. Soc. (Fellow), NAS, Am. Acad. Arts and Scis., Am. Chem. Soc.; author: Physical Chemistry, 1980, editor: Molecular Beams, 1966, contbr. articles in profl. jours.; mil: 2d lt. US Army 1944-46. Res: 738 Mayfield Ave Palo Alto 94305-1044 Ofc: Keck Bldg Dept Chemistry Stanford University, Stanford 94305

ROSTVOLD, GERHARD NORMAN, economist, author, lectrurer, and financial counselor; b. Oct. 15, 1919, Nashwauk, Minn.; s. Arndt A. and Olive W. (Ness) R.; m. Virginia Faubon, Feb. 3, 1945; children: Roger b. 1949; Laura b. 1950, Christine b. 1951, Ellen b. 1957; edn.: BA., Econ. - Accountancy (with great distinction), Stanford Univ. 1948; MA., Econ., Stanford 1949;BA., Ph.D., Econ., Stanford 1955. Career: accounting instr., Stanford 1949-51; prof. of econ. and accounting, Pomona Coll. 1952-66; vis. prof., Stanford 1974; econ. newscaster, KHJ, Channel 9's "Ten O'clock News" 1978-82; adjunct prof. of econ., Pepperdine Univ., Presidential/Key Exec. MBA Program; awards: Wig Disting. Professorship Award, Pomona Coll. 1962; NSF Fellow, Stanford 1965-66; Secty. of the Interior's Conservation Award 1975; Am. Men of Sci., Contemporary Authors, Who's Who in Am., Dictionary of Internat. Biography, Men of Achievement and others; mem.: Am. Econ. Assn.; We. Econ. Assn. (pres., 1966-67); Natl. Advy. Bd. on Public Lands (1962-75), chmn. 1971-74; Bd. of Trustees, Mortgage and Realty Trust 1962-; Lambda Alpha Hon. Frat. (Land Econ.), pres., L.A. Chpt. 1976-77; author: textbook, Financing Calif. Govt., 1967; The Econ. of Energy, 1975, Econ. and the Environment, 1975, The Econ. of the Public Utility Enterprise, 1975, Understanding How The Econ. System Works, 1976, Charting Your Path to Econ. and Fin. Survival in the 1980's, 1979, How to Stretch Your Dollars to Cope with the Inflation of the 1980's, 1981, Fin. Planning for Retirement in the 1980's, 1983; numerous articles, book reviews, and monographs; mil: t/sgt., Army Air Force 1942-45; Lutheran. Res: #4 Montpellier, Laguna Niguel 92677 Ofc: Urbanomics, 23276 South Pointe Dr. Laguna Hills 92653

ROTBART, HEIDI LEE, entertainment personal manager; b. Oct. 10, 1957, Cleveland, Oh..; d. Alan Jerome and Yetta (Ringer) Rotbart; edn: BS, Bradley Univ., Peoria, Ill., 1979; career: p.r. dir. Carousel Theatre, Ravenna, Ohio, 1979-80; tour mgr., Phyllis Diller, Los Angeles, 1981-86; pres. Rotbart Mgmt., Los Angeles, 1987-; lectr. Berkeley Alum. Orgn., Los Angeles, 1991; awards: listed in Who's Who in the West 1991-92, Dictionary of Internat. Biography 1992, Men & Women of Distinction 1991, Who's Who Rising Young Americans 1992; author: book, Hollywood Gophers, 1990; Democrat; Jewish; rec: traveling, theatre. Ofc: Rotbart Mgmt. 1810 Malcolm Ave. Los Angeles 90025

ROTHROCK, STEVEN LEROY, lawyer; b. Aug. 9, 1943, Pomona; s. E. Spurgeon and E. Vernice R.; children: Darren b. 1969, Heather b. 1972; edn: AA, Pasadena City Coll. 1966; BS, Cal State Polytechnic Coll. 1966; JD, UC Davis 1969; admitted Calif. St. Bar (1970), U.S. Central Dist. Ct., U.S. 9th Cir. Ct. Appeals. Career: atty., ptnr. Launer, Chaffee, Rothrock & Schulman, Fullerton 1970-; referee State Bar Ct. 1972-; mem: Am. Bar Assn., Calif. Bar Assn., Orange Co. Bar Assn.; civic: Fullerton C.of C., Boys' Club of Fullerton (past pres., bd. 1971-); publs: res. contbr. Republican; Prot.; rec: tennis, golf, horticulture, music, Street Rods, owner of a comml. recording studio. Res: PO Box 7155 Fullerton 92632 Ofc: Launer, Chaffee, Rothrock & Schulman, Attys. 2600 E Nutwood Fullerton 92631

ROY, ROBERT PHILIP, lawyer; b. Aug. 27, 1950, Columbus, Ga.; s. Frank Thomas and Constance (Mitsopoulos) R.; m. Marianne Davis, July 25, 1987; children: Michael Philip b. 1988, Jenna Elizabeth b. 1990; edn: AA, Orange Coast Jr. Coll.; BA, UC Irvine; JD, Calif. Western Univ. Sch. of Law; admitted bar: Calif. 1977, U.S. Supreme Ct. 1980, U.S. Ct. Appeals 9th Cir. 1980, U.S. Dist. Ct.- Cent., Ea., So., No. Dist. Career: atty., assoc. Dressler, Stoll & Jacobs, Newport Beach 1977; gen. counsel Ventura County Agricultural Assn., Oxnard 1977-, pres. 1983-; mem: Am. Bar Assn. (chmn. subcom. on St. Agri. Labor Law Devel. 1987-), Calif. Bar Assn. (Labor and Employ. Law Sect. 1982-), Ventura Co. Bar Assn., Phi Delta Phi Legal Frat.; coauthor: Employer's Handbook on Farm Labor Law (1977), ABA sub-com. report on State Agricultural Labor Law (1989-); Republican; R.Cath.; rec: golf, ski (water, snow), tennis. Ofc: Ventura County Agricultural Assn. 916 W. Ventura Blvd. Camarillo 93010

ROYAN, C. WILLIAM, real estate executive; b. July 3, 1933, Pontiac, Mich.; s. Charles William and Carmetta M. (McCullough) R.; m. Donna M., May 7, 1977; 5 children; edn: BA actg., Univ. Detroit 1955. Career: controller The Taubman Co. Inc., Hayward 1965-80; pres. Concord Sun Valley Inc. 1970-74; v.p., property mgr. Nasher Co., Dallas, Tx. 1980-82; senior v.p. Franklin Property Co., Chevy Chase 1983-86; Duffel Fin. & Constrn. Co., Lafayette 1986-91; owner C. William Royan Co. 1991-; occasional lectr. Hayward St. Univ.; Internat. Council of Shopping Centers; honors: Beta Alpha Psi; mem: Contra Costa Taxpayers Assn. (dir., pres. 1972-73, 1991-92), Internat. Council Shopping Centers; civic: Newark TSM Advsy. Com.; mil: SP-2 AUS 1956-57; Republican; R.Cath. Ofc: C. William Royan Co., 3128 Shire Lane Walnut Creek 94598

ROZANSKI, THOMAS JAMES, missile test center supervisory mathematician; b. Jan. 12, 1945, Brooklyn, N.Y.; s. John and Valeria (Bojalski) R.; m. Jane Marie McAndrew, July 1, 1967; children: Roderick b. 1970, Danielle b. 1971; edn: AA, Ventura Coll. 1965; BA, CSU Long Bch., 1967. Career: jr. mathematician Pacific Missile Test Ctr., Pt. Mugu 1967-68, F-14 mathematician 1968-75, F-14 lead mathematician 1975-76, electronic warfare mathematician 1976-81, EW task mgr. 1981-86, head of missile s/w support branch 1986-; Keynote speaker Optimist Club (Camarillo, 1980, 84), Camarillo C.of C. 1985, Rotary Club 1990, Master of ceremonies Toastmasters, Ventura Co. 1987; civic bds: Ventura Co. Symphony Ball 1989, Pleasant Valley Rec. & Parks Dist. (adv. 1982-89), Am. Youth Soccer Orgn. (commnr. 1981-84), Toastmasters (pres. 1980-81), AYSO Cultural Exchange (chmn. 1984), Comm. Cong. (team leader 1986), Comm. Awards Argn. Com. (chmn. 1989-91); author manuals: Alternative Strategies Re Missile Software Support (1991), Software Development (1985), Radar Warning Trainer Plan (1983), DTS Load Tape Generation (1978), Maintenance Diagnostics (1973), Sample/Delay Analysis (1969); Republican; rec: tennis, comm. service. Ofc: Pacific Missile Test Center, Code 1057, Point Mugu 93042

RUBIN, ALAN LEE, physician; b. Sept. 17, 1940, New York; s. Julius Nathan and Edith (Horowitz) R.; m. Enid Jane Feinsilber, Aug. 15, 1965; children: Renee b. 1969, Larry b. 1971; edn: BA, Brandeis Univ. 1962; MD, N.Y. Univ. Sch. Medicine 1966; lic. State Calif. Bd. Med. Examiners 1968. Career: intern Bellevue Hosp., N.Y.C. 1966-67, resident 1967-68; Mt. Zion Hosp., San Francisco 1970-71; fellow in endocrinology UCSF 1971-73; pvt. practice endocrinology, San Francisco 1973-; asst. clin. prof. UCSF 1978-; chmn. cont. edn. St. Francis Hosp. 1983-; mem: Am. Diabetes Assn. (profl. sect.); author: Self-Monitoring Blood Sugar in Diabetes, 1983; mil: major AUS 1968-70; Democrat; Jewish; rec: gardening, backpacking, singing. Res: 25 Via Capistrano Tiburon 94920 Ofc: 490 Post St San Francisco 94102

RUBIN, GARY ANDREW, computer software engineer; b. June 26, 1956, Pleasanton, Calif.; s. Budd and Joanne Lee Rubin; edn: BA, UC Berkeley 1978; MS, Stanford 1982. Career: software engineer IBM/Rolm, Santa Clara 1978-91, technical trainer computer networks 1991-93; mem: Chai Soc. Jewish Singles (pres. 1987-88), Toastmasters (treas. 1987-89); editor, functional specification "Common Application Service Elements" 1985. Address: POB A-M, Stanford 94309

RUBIN, GERALD M., molecular biologist, genetics educator, administrator; b. Mar. 31, 1950, Boston; s. Benjamin H. and Edith (Weisberg) R.; m. Lynne S. Mastalir, May 7, 1978; 1 son, Alan; edn: BS biology, M.I.T., 1971; PhD molecular biology, Univ. Cambridge, England 1974. Career: tech. asst. lab. of Dr. Boris Magasanik, M.I.T., 1971; Helen Hay Whitney Found. fellow Stanford Univ. Sch. of Med. 1974-76; asst. prof. Harvard Univ. 1977-80; staff dept. embryology Carnegie Instn. of Wash., Balt. 1980-83; John D. MacArthur Prof. Genetics dept. molecular & cell biology UC Berkeley, 1983-, hd. div. genetics, 1987-, assoc. faculty cell & molecular biol. div. Lawrence Berkeley Lab.; investigator Howard Hughes Med. Inst. 1987-; adj. prof. biochem. & biophysics UC Sch. of Med., S.F. 1987-; honors: Phi Beta Kappa 1971, Phi Lambda Epsilon 1971, NSF predoc. fellow 1971-74, US Churchill Found. Fellow 1971-73, Helen

Hay Whitney Found. Fellow 1974-76, co-winner Passano Found. Young Scientist Award 1983, co-winner AAAS Newcomb Cleveland Prize 1984, Am. Chem. Soc. Eli Lilly Award in biol. chem. 1985, co-winner NAS-US Steel Found. Award molecular biol. 1985, Genetics Soc. Am. Medal 1986, NAS 1987, AAAS Fellow 1992, Am. Acad. Arts & Scis. Fellow 1992. Ofc:Univ. Calif. Dept. MCB 539 LSA Bldg Berkeley 94720

RUBY, CHARLES LEROY, educator, lawyer, civic leader; b. Carthage, Ind., Dec. 28, 1900; s. Edgar Valentine and Mary Emma (Butler) R.; m. Rachael Elizabeth Martindale, Aug. 30, 1925; children: Phyllis Arline (Mrs. Norman Braskat), Charles L., Martin Dale; edn: certif. Ball State Univ., 1921-22; AB, Central Normal Coll., 1924, LLB, 1926, BS, 1931; BPE, 1932; MA, Stanford Univ., 1929; JD, Pacific Coll. of Law, 1931; PhD, Olympic Univ., 1933; admitted bar: Ind. 1926, U.S. Supreme Ct. 1970. Career: principal Pine Village (Ind.) High Sch., 1923-25; Glenwood (Ind.) Pub. Schs. 1925-26; tchr. El Centro Pub. Sch., Calif. 1926-27, Central Union High Sch., Fresno 1927-29; prof. law Fullerton Coll., 1929-66; life trustee Cont. Learning Experiences pgm. CSUF mem. CSUF Pres.'s Com., hon. chmn. fund com. Gerontology Bldg., Charles L. and Rachael E. Ruby Gerontology Center named in his and late wife's honor; prof. edn. Armstrong Coll., summer 1935, Cent. Normal Coll., summers 1929-33; civic: Ret. Service Vol. Program, North Orange Co. (pres. 1973-76, 83-84), North Orange Co. Vol. Bur. (dir.), Fullerton Sr. Citizens Task Force (dir.), Fullerton Public Forum (founder, dir. 1929-39), Rotary/Fullerton (pres. 1939-40, hon. life mem. 1983-), U.S. Assay Commn. 1968-, Fullerton Sr. Multi-purpose Ctr. (bd. 1981-), O.C. Senior Citizens Advy. Council (bd.), benefactor CSUF Gerontology Ctr.; awards: medal of merit Am. Numismatic Assn. 1954, Special commendn. Calif. State Assembly (1966, 88) and State Senate (1978, 86), recipient commns. from Indiana Sec. of State 1984, Gov. of Calif. 1989, Orange Co. Bd. Suprs. (1985, 86), Exec. Com. Pres. CSUF 1986; mem: Pres.'s Assocs. CSUF, Fullerton Coll. Associates (Spl. Retiree of Yr. 1986), Calif. Tchrs. Assn. (life, pres. So. Sect. 1962-63, treas. 1964-65, dir. 1956-65), O.C. Tchrs. Assn. (pres. 1953-55), Fullerton Coll. Tchrs. Assn. (pres. 1958-60, NEA (life), Stanford Univ. Law Soc. (pres.'s exec. com.), Calif. State Council Edn., Calif. Bus. Educators Assn. (hon. life), Calif. Assn. Univ. Profs., Ind. Bar Found. (fellow), Ind. Bar Assn. (hon. life), Pacific S.W. Bus. Law Assn. (pres. 1959-70, life), Am. Numismatic Assn. (gov. 1951-53, life advy. bd.), Numis. Assn. So. Calif. (life, pres. 1961), Calif. Numis. Assn., Indpls. Coin Club (hon. life), L.A. Coin Club (hon. life), U.S. Supreme Ct. Hist. Soc., Town Hall Calif., North O.C. Mus. Assn. (life, dir., benefactor), Stanford Univ. Alumni Assn. (life), Old Timers Assay Commn., Elks (life), Fullerton Jr. Coll. Vets. (hon. life); contbr. articles to profl. jours.; Democrat (O.C. Dem. Cent. Com. 1962-78). Res: 308 N Marwood Ave Fullerton 92632

RUDIN, ANNE, mayor; b. Jan. 27, 1924, Passaic, N.J.; d. Philip and Angela (Macri) Noto; m. Edward Rudin, June 6, 1948; children: Nancy b. 1949, Barbara b. 1950, Carol b. 1950, Jay b. 1953; edn: BS edn., RN, Temple Univ., 1946; MPA, USC, 1983; Reg. Nurse, Pa. 1946, Calif. 1948. Career: nursing instr. Temple Hosp., Phila. 1946-48, Mt. Zion Hosp., San Francisco 1948-49; elected Sacramento City Council, 1971-83, mayor of Sacramento, 1983-; awards: Girl Scouts Am. Role Model Award 1989, Sacto. History Ctr. Woman of Courage 1989, League Women Voters Civic Contbn. Award 1989; mem: Calif. Elected Women's Assn. 1973-, US Conf. of Mayors 1983-, World Conf. of Mayors for Peace (v.p. 1985-), Nat. Commn. on Distressed Public Housing, Japan/Am. Conf. of Mayors, Chamber of Commerce Presidents. Ofc: City Hall 915 I St Ste 205 Sacramento 95822

RUDOF, MEREDITH ANN, chiropractor; b. Sept. 17, 1951, Los Angeles; d. Joel and Lucille (Swonetz) Rudof; edn: DC (magna cum laude), Cleveland Chiropractic Coll. 1986. Career: chiropractor assoc. Thie Chiropractic, Pasadena 1983-84, Westside Chiropractic Center 1986-89; prin. Meredith Ann Rudof, D.C., Los Angeles 1989-; faculty Cleveland Chiropractic Coll. 1986-; honors: Delta Tau Alpha 1983, dean's list C.C.Coll. 1984-86, misc. student body awards; mem: Calif. Chiropractic Assn., Am. Chiropractic Assn., Profl. Women's Breakfast Group, Women in Mgmt., The Network; ed. articles pub. in profl. jours. (1987-), ed. seminar brochures (1987-); rec: theatre, film, tennis. Address: 2001 S Barrington Ave Ste 220 Los Angeles 90025

RUDOLPH, ELAINE TAYLOR, accounting & financial personnel specialist, former mayor; b. Nov. 25, 1926, Milw.; d. Harry A. and Florence Ann (Randall) Taylor; m. Gordon E. Rudolph, Aug. 9, 1947; dau. Nancy Jean b. 1954; edn: BA, Univ. Wis., 1950; grad. studies USC 1961; reg. employment cons. 1979. Career: personnel A.O. Smith, Milwaukee Wis. 1950-52; hosp. personnel Red Cross, San Antonio, Tx. 1952-54; tchr. USAF Dependents, Denver, Colo. 1954, Yuma, Ariz. 1955-56; substitute tchr. Duarte Azusa 1963-64; mem. Presidential Electoral Coll., WDC 1960; political coord. A.D. Bramble Assembly 1964; program rep. Red Cross, Los Angeles 1965; personnel cons./v.p. Casco 1972-79; elected Sierra Madre Council, 1978-82, mayor 1981-82; del. White House Conf. on Small Bus., WDC 1986; mem. bd. dirs. Sierra Madre Hosp. 1982-, pres. 1987-; recipient Small Business Accounting Advocate dist. and reg. awards 1987; mem: Nat. Assn. Accts. (nat. com., bd., pres. L.A. chpt. 1987-88), AAUW (past pres.), Sierra Madre Crime Prevention Bd. (chair); articles pub. in profl. jours.

(1981-86); Republican (State Central Com., chair state job and econ. devel. com. Burbank 1989-93, local pres. Sierra Madre Republicans 1987); Presbyterian; rec: swimming, politics. Ofc: Accountants Bookkeepers Plus 1100 Glendon Ave Ste 1417 Los Angeles 90024 also: 10061 Talbert Ste 200 Fountain Valley

RUEBNER, BORIS HENRY, academic pathologist; b. Aug. 30, 1923, Germany, nat. U.S. cit. 1964; s. Alfred and Marta (Klein) R.; m. Susan Mautner, Sept. 26, 1957; children: Sally b. 1962, Anthony b. 1964; edn: MB, and MD, Edinburgh Univ., Scotland. Career: prof. pathology Univ. Calif., Davis 1968-, pathologist UCD Medical Ctr., Sacto. 1968-; mem. Assn. of Pathologists, Calif. Med. Assn.; author: Pathology of the Liver 1992, The Gastrointestinal System 1982. Ofc: Dept. Medical Pathology University of California, Davis 95616

RUIZ, FREDERICK R., food products company president; b. Aug. 26, 1943, Los Angeles; s. Louis F. and Rosie R.; m. Lesta Travis; m.2d. Mitzie Haller, Jan. 10, 1986; children: Kim b. 1966, Kelly b. 1970, Frederick Bryce b. 1976, Matthew b. 1985; edn: AA, Coll. of Sequoias 1964. Career: pres., CEO Ruiz Food Products Inc., Tulare 1964-; awards: U.S. No. 1 Small Bus. Person of Yr. 1983; mem: Am. Mgmt. Assn. (pres. assn. 1979-89), Nat. Fedn. Indep. Bus., Valley Bus. Coll. (chmn. advy. bd.), UC Fresno (bus. advy. council), Coll. of Sequoias (bd. mem.), U.S. C.of C., Calif. C.of C., Tulare C.of C., Tulare Rotary, Tulare Dist. Hosp. Found., Hispanic Bus. Top 100; Republican; R.Cath.; rec: numismatics, philately. Res: 150 Woodward Dr Tulare 93274 Ofc: Ruiz Food Products 1025 E Bardsley Ave Tulare 93274

RUMBAUGH, CHARLES EARL, electronics company executive, lawyer; b. Mar. 11, 1943, San Bernardino; s. Max E. and Gertrude M. (Gulker) R.; m. Christine, Mar. 2, 1968; children: Heather, Aaron, Cindy, Eckwood; edn: BS, UCLA 1966; JD, Cal Western Sch. Law 1971; adv. legal studies, USC; Cert. in Advanced Mgmt., USC Sch. of Bus. Admn.; admitted Calif. State Bar 1972, US Dist. Ct. (cent. dist. Calif.), US Ct. of Appeals (9th cir.); Certified Profl. Contracts Mgr., 1987. Career: engr. Westinghouse Electric Corp. 1966-68; corporate counsel Calif. Dept. of Corporations 1971-77; legal counsel Hughes Aircraft Co. 1977-84, asst. to Corporate Contracts Dir. 1984-89, asst. to Corporate Contracts V.P. 1990-; honors: ed.-in-chief Cal Western Internat. Law Jour. and Appellate Moot Ct. Board, 1970-71; mem: Nat. Contract Mgmt. Assn. (Fellow, South Bay Chpt. pres. 1991, nat. dir. 1992, nat. v.p.-elect Southwestern Region 1993), Fed. Bar Assn. (pres. Beverly Hills Chpt. 1992-93), Calif. Bar Assn. (real prop. sect., bus. law sect., franchise law com. 1992-), L.A. Cty. Bar Assn., South Bay Bar Assn., Christian Legal Soc., IEEE, Phi Alpha Delta, Phi Kappa Psi, Nat. Security Industrial Assn. (legal & spl. tasks West Coast Gp.), Aerospace Industries Assn. (chmn. procurement techniques com. 1987-88, 1993-94), Am. Defense Preparedness Assn.; civic: Judge Pro Tem L.A. Superior Court; Arbitrator, Am. Arbitration Assn.; City of Palos Verdes Estates Citizen Advy. Com. 1986-90; Boy Scouts Am. 1976-; publs. in profl./legal jours.; Christian; rec: jogging, skiing, camping, equestrian. Res: PO Box 2636 Rolling Hills 90274 Ofc: Hughes Aircraft Co. PO Box 80028 Los Angeles 90080-0028

RUMMEL, H. GEORGE, hydroelectric engineer; b. Aug. 4, 1939, Riverton, Wyo.; s. Elmer George and Mary Elizabeth (Sinner) R.; m. Arleen B. Strasheim, June 14, 1987; children: Andrew George b. 1969, Amron Suzanne b. 1974; edn: BSCE, Valparaiso Univ. 1962; MSCE, CSU Sacramento 1972; Reg. Civil Engr. Calif. 1966. Career: asst. civil engr. Calif. Dept. Water Resources Sacto. 1962-72; civil engr. (hydroelectric) Fed. Power Commn. Wash. DC 1972-75; dept. head Harza Engring. Co. Chgo. 1975-80, supr. design of world's largest storage proj.; proj. mgr. (hydroelectric) Sacto. Municipal Utility Dist. 1980-, supr. planning, licensing, design, and initial constrn. for 2 new hydro projects; civic: Little League (team mgr.); Republican; Lutheran (Stephen minister, Evangelism chmn.); rec: baseball, skiing, outdoors, fishing. Ofc: SMUD Sacramento 95817

RUMP, MARJORIE ELLEN, librarian; b. Jan. 19, 1919, St. Joseph, Mo.; d. Edward August and Adeline (Boller) Gummig; m. John S. Rump, July 25, 1943; children: Jack b. 1946, Susan b. 1950, Marilyn b. 1953; edn: BA, Univ. Redlands 1941; MS lib. sci., USC 1957; Calif. sec. tchg. cred. (1941). Career: sales, book buyer Sierra Book Store 1953-66; librarian Kern County Lib. Adult Extension 1961-66, East Bakersfield High Sch. 1966-68; Kern County Lib. Shafter Br. 1968-69, KCL Young Adult Ext. and audio-visual supr. 1969-71, KCL Adult & Young Adult Ext. supr. 1972-73, KCL -Beale coord. 1973-79, KCL asst. to County Librarian 1979-82, KCL Adult Ext. supr. 1982-84, KCL acquisitions librn. 1984, KCL Bakersfield Area br. supr. 1985-87, KCL Beale hd. librn., 1987-88, Dep. dir. 1988-; mem. Bakersfield Coll. Pres.'s Advy. Council; dir. Taft Comm. Theater 1949-52; honors: Beta Phi Mu, Theta Alpha Phi, Doubenmeir Award for pub. adminstrn. Am. Soc. for Pub. Adminstrn. 1979, Citizen recogn. City of Bakersfield 1983, Jubilee Medallion Univ. Redlands 1984, Soroptimist Woman of Distinction 1990; mem: Calif. Lib. Assn., Am. Soc. for Pub. Adminstrn. (chpt. pres. 1978), Soc. of Archivists, Conf. of Calif. Hist. Socs. (reg. v.p. 1984-90, CCHS Trust treas. 1986-), Kern Co. Hist. Soc. (pres. 1981), Libraria Sodalitas USC; civic: AAUW (pres. Taft Br. 1948, Bksfld. Br. 1958-9), Women's Assn. First Presbyn. Ch. (pres.), Child Guidance Guild, Assistance League of Bksfld. PEO-MB, Soroptimist Internat. of Bksfld. (pres. 1978-9), Univ. Redlands Alumni Bd., Kern Co. Mus. Alliance,

Dorian Soc. CSUB, Wakayama Sister City (bd. 1981-), Calif Living Mus., Gr. Bksfld. C.of C. Womens' Div., Beta Lambda Mu Sor.; author: Inside Historic Kern; Presbyterian; rec: travel. Res: 3000 Elmwood Bakersfield 93305 Ofc: Kern County Library 701 Truxtun Ave Bakersfield 93301

RUPERT, DAVID ANDREW, clergyman, administrator; b. Aug. 16, 1940, Oil City, Pa.; s. John Reuben and Wealtha Audrey (Smoyer) R.; m. Lois Martha Annable, June 30, 1962; children: Glenn David b. 1967, Martha Jean b. 1970; edn: BA, Roberts Wesleyan Coll., 1962; BDiv, Western Evangelical Sem., Portland, Or. 1967, MDiv, 1972; DMin, Fuller Theological Sem., Pasadena 1980; ordained deacon, 1965, elder, 1967, Free Methodist Ch. of N.A. Career: Free Methodist Ch. asst. pastor, Herkimer, N.Y. 1962-63, Portland, Or. 1963-64, Salem, Or. 1964-67, pastor, Redmond, Or. 1967-71, sr. pastor (Free Meth.) Willow Vale Community Ch., San Jose, 1971-79, Sacramento, Ca. 1979-84; conf. supt. Calif. Conference Free Methodist Ch., Sacto. 1984-, mem. secty. Gen. Bd. of Adminstrn., Idpls. 1989-, del. Gen. Conf. FM Ch. Winona Lake, Ind. 1985, Seattle, Wa. 1989; mem., secty. Gen. FM Youth Conf., Winona Lake, Ind. 1969; trustee Western Evangelical Sem., Portland 1984-, trustee Seattle Pacific Univ., Wa. 1987; LIFO cons./trainer Stuart Atkins Inc. Beverly Hills 1981-; exec. com. Gr. Sacto. Bill Graham Crusade, 1983; awards: 2d Pres.'s Award for service above self Redmond (Oreg.) Rotary 1971, listed Who's Who in Am. Christian Leadership, Who's Who in Religion, Who's Who in West; mem. Nat. Assn. Evangelicals Nor Cal (1972-, pres. 1988-91), Calif. Council on Alcohol Problems 1985-; editor: Celebrating One Hundred Years (1983); Republican (nat. com.); rec: travel, photography, swimming, sports. Res: 9241 Linda Rio Dr Sacramento 95826-2209 Ofc: California Conference Free Methodist Church, 9750 Business Park Dr Ste 212 Sacramento 95827-1716

RUSH, HERMAN E., television executive; b. June 20, 1929, Phila.; s. Eugene and Bella (Sacks) R.; m. Joan Silberman, Mar. 18, 1951; children: James Harrison, Mandie Susan; edn: BBA, Temple Univ., 1950. Career: with Official Films, 1951-57; owner Flamingo Films, 1957-60; with Creative Management Assocs., N.Y.C., 1960-71, pres. TV div. Creative Mgmt. Assocs., 1964-71, exec. v.p. parent co., dir., 1964-71; indep. producer 1971-75; producer Wolper Orgn., 1975-76; pres. Herman Rush Assocs., Inc. (Rush-Flaherty Agy. subs.) 1977-78, Marble Arch TV, Los Angeles 1979-80, pres. Columbia Pictures TV, Burbank 1980-87; chmn. bd. and c.e.o. Coca-Cola Telecomms. 1987-88, Rush Assocs. Inc., Burbank 1988-91; ptnr. Katz Rush Entertainment 1992-; chmn. Entertainment Industries Council; mem. Acad. TV Arts and Scis., Hollywood Radio and TV Soc., Producers Caucus; civic bds: trustee Sugar Ray Robinson Youth Found. 1967-75, pres. Retarded Infant Svs., N.Y.C. 1957-63, bd. dirs. U.S. Marshall's Service Found., STET 1986-93, conferee White House Conf. for a Drug Free America (1987, 88); clubs: Friars, Filmex. Ofc: Katz Rush Entertainment 345 N Maple Dr Beverly Hills 90210

RUSH, JOHN A., insurance agent; b. Oct. 6, 1928, Toledo, Ohio; s. Arnold E. and Bessie A. Rush; m. Patricia Bush, Oct. 1977; children: Leslie b. 1954, Kurt b. 1957, Linda b. 1958, Karl b. 1960, (step) Sana Peterson b. 1956, Eric Peterson b. 1958; edn: AA, Univ. of Toledo 1951. Career: mgr. Ventura Calif. Retail Credit Co. 1951-58; asst. mgr. customer svc. Sears-Roebuck 1958-59; ins. agent State Farm Ins. Co. 1960-; owner/ptnr. New Horizons Travel, Camarillo; appt. Ventura Co. Planning Commn. (commr., chmn. 1963-76), Pleasant Valley Rec. & Parks Dist. (chmn., dir. 1970-86), Calif. Assn. Rec. & Parks Dists. (v.p. 1975-76), elected Camarillo City Council 1976-80 (mayor 1979-80), Camarillo Sanitation Dist. (dir. 1976-80), Ventura Regional Co. Sanitation Dist. 1978-80, Regional Coastal Commn.-Ventura, Santa Barbara, San Luis Obispo (commr., chmn. 1976-79), Calif. State Coastal Commn. (v. chmn. 1979-81); awards: Dunlap Fellow Kiwanis Fund 1988, Hospice Gold Benefactor Award 1990, Hospice Benefactor Award 1990, 91, 92, Camarillo Chamber of Commerce businessman of yr. 1986 C.of C. volunteer of year 1992; mem.: Lima Bean Soc., Bean Hive No. 1 (pres. 1983), Calif. Macadamia Soc., Calif. Rare Fruit Growers, Internat. Palm Soc.; civic bds: Mayor's Blue Ribbon Com. City of Camarillo 1987, Camarillo Hospice (bd. 1983-89, chmn. 1986-88, pres. Hon. Bd. Dirs. 1988, Hospice Endowment Bd. 1991), Kiwanis Intl. (life fellow, Camarillo Club charter pres. 1966, pres. 1967-68, 1982-83, 1989-90, hon. life mem. 1985, div. 42 lt. gov. 1985-6), Las Posas Prop. Owners Assn. (bd. 1986, pres. 1987-94), Camarillo Boys & Girls Club (bd. 1986-, pres. 1991-92), Boy Scouts Exec. Com. for Fundraising 1992, Pleasant Valley Rec. & Park Dist. Citizens Com. for Park Devel. & Funding 1992, Camarillo Health Care Dist. (pres. 1992) Camarillo C.of C.; mil: sgt. AUS 24th Inf. Div. Japan, 1946-47; Indep.; rec: garden. Res: 1404 Calle Aurora Camarillo 93010 Ofc: John A. Rush, POB 156 Camarillo 93011

RUSSELL, BRUCE ROBERT, electrical engineer; b. July 29, 1949, Red Bluff; s. Norman Earl and Bobbie Jean Foord (Dorvall) R.; m. Mary Ellen Inserra, July 30, 1977; children: Jennifer b. 1980, Ryan b. 1984; edn: UC Davis 1967-70; BSEE magna cum laude, CSU Chico 1972; reg. electrical engr. Calif. 1976, Ore. 1979. Career: engring. trainee Pacific Gas & Light, San Mateo 1972-73, asst. electrical distbn. engr. 1973-75, substation engr., San Francisco 1975-79; proj. electrical engr. CH2M Hill Cons., Corvallis, Ore. 1979-83; electrical engr. City of Redding Electric Dept., Redding 1983-84, engring. mgr. 1984-;

awards: CSU Chico Outstanding Electrical Engring. Grad. 1972; mem: IEEE, Phi Kappa Phi; Republican; Protestant; rec: hunting, fishing, camping. Res: 7333 Terra Linda Redding 96003 Ofc: City of Redding Electric Department 760 Parkview Ave Redding 96001

RUSSELL, CAROL (ANN), personnel services company president; b. Dec. 14, 1943, Detroit, Mich.; d. Billy Koud and Ann (Withers) Salerno; m. Victor Rojas; edn: Hunter Coll. 1961-64; Univ. of Phoenix, S.F. 1991-; reg. employment consultant Calif. Assn. Personnel Consultants, 1974. Career: v.p. Wollborg Michelson, San Francisco, 1974-82; pres., co-owner Russell Personnel, S.F. 1983-; firm listed in "Inc. 500" Inc. Mag., Boston (1989, 1990); mem: No. Calif. H.R. Council (com. chair, mem. 1983-), Calif. Assn. of Temp. Services (pres. Golden Gate chpt. 1983-84), Internat. Assn. for Personnel Women (pres. Bay Area chpt. 1984), Internat. Platform Assn.; contbr. articles in trade jours., media guest and seminar leader; Indep.; D.N.D.; rec: reading, collect Bible commentaries. Ofc: 120 Montgomery St 3d Fl San Francisco 94104 and San Raphael 94903

RUSSELL, GARY DOUGLAS, director hospital information systems; b. May 31, 1954, Klamath Falls, Ore.; s. Bill David and Ann Amelia (Adams) R.; m. Marja Martina Keyner, Aug. 20, 1977; children: Robyn b. 1981, Kristine b. 1982; edn: BS chemistry, Univ. Santa Clara 1977; PharmD, USC 1981. Career: clin. pharmacist San Gabriel Valley Med. Center, San Gabriel 1981-86, ancillary and p.c. systems mgr. 1986-87, dir. hosp. info. systems 1987-; pres. Pharmasoft Inc., Pomona 1985-89; awards: USC Person & Covey Outstanding Achievement 1981; mem: Hosp. Information Mgmt. Systems Soc.; developer computer software 1985; Baptist; Address: 2316 Monteverde Dr Chino Hills 91709

RUSSELL, MARY, clinical social worker; b. Feb. 21, 1910, Madison Co., Ark.; d. John Riley and Lillie (Carter) Russell; edn: BA, Coll. of Ozarks 1932; MA, Univ. Chgo. Sch. Social Service Adminstrn. 1940; bd. cert. diplomate and clinical social worker 1988. Career: case worker Cook Co. Pub. Welfare, Chgo., Ill. 1934-35; child welfare worker Ill. Div. Child Welfare, Ill. 1935-41; exec. dir. Family Service, Richmond, Ind., Pasadena, and Bakersfield 1941-55; clin. social worker, Bakersfield 1955-; tchr. Madison Co., Ark. 1928; vol. lectr. schs. and colls., Ind., Ill., Calif. 1934-; awards: Dictionary Internat. Biography Cert. Hon. 1971, Who's Who of Women 1973, Comm. Leaders of Am. 1971, Nat. Registry Health Care Profs. 1980, Phi Kappa Delta (distinc. pub. speaking and debate 1932); mem: Nat. Assn. Social Workers (charter mem., conf. advancement social work in pvt. practice 1964, bd. mem., ofcr. 1968-71), Soc. Clin. Social Workers (charter fellow mem. 1967-89), Conf. Advancement Social Work in Pvt. Practice (bd. ofcr. 1964-71), Altrusa Internat.; author: A Father's Role in Care & Custody of His Children, 1969; Protestant; rec: knitting, music, philately. Res: 1928 17th Bakersfield 93301

RUSSELL, THOMAS ARTHUR, lawyer; b. Aug. 2, 1953, Corona; s. Larry Arthur Russell and Patricia Helena (Collins) Heath; m. Mary Ellen Leach, June 20, 1992; edn: BS, UC Berkeley, 1976; JD, USC, 1982; admitted bar: Calif. 1983. Career: atty. Graham & James, Long Beach 1982-88; ptnr. Williams, Woolley, Cogswell, Nakazawa & Russell, Long Beach 1988-; mem. bd. dirs. Ctr. for Internat. Commercial Arbitration, L.A. 1990-; awards: Bronze key ABA, Chgo. 1982; mem: Am. Bar Assn. (v.ch. subcom. on yacht fin. 1992-), Nat. Marine Bankers Assn. (speaker, panelist 1987-), Maritime Law Assn. of U.S. (subcom. on recreational boating edn. chmn. 1991-), Legion Lex Am. Inn of Ct. (Barrister 1985-), Harbor Assn. of Ind. & Commerce 1989-, Internat. Bus. Assn. of So. Calif. (bd. 1989-); coauthor: Recreational Boating Law 1992, contbr. J. of Maritime Law & Commerce 1987; Republican; R.Cath.; rec: skiing, sailing. Ofc: Williams Woolley et al, 200 Oceangate Ste 700 Long Beach 90802 Tel: 310/495-6000

RUTAN, RICHARD GLENN, test pilot, company president; b. July 1, 1938, Loma Linda; s. George A. and Irene (Goforth) R.; children: Holly Lynn b. 1965, Jill Lynn b. 1970; edn: BS, Am. Technological Univ. 1972. Career: served to lt. col. (Ret.) US Air Force 1958-78, awarded the Silver Star, 5 D.F.C., 16 Air Medals and the Purple Heart; prodn. mgr. and chief test pilot of Rutan Aircraft Factory (bro. Burt's co.) 1978-81: test flight devel. pilot of the Defiant, the Beech Starship proof of concept prototype, the European Micro Light, the T-46 scaled demo. for Fairchild Aircraft and the Long-EZ (set num. individual world speed and distance records in 1982); founder, pres. Voyager Aircraft Inc., 1981-, with ptnr. Jeana Yeager completed the first around the world, non-stop, non-refueled flight in Voyager, Dec. 14-23, 1986 (more than double prev. absolute world distance record held by a USAF B-52 bomber); awarded Presdl. Citizen's Medal of Honor by Pres. Ronald Reagan (12/27/86) at a spl. ceremony for the Voyager Team; other awards include: Hon. Doctorate Sci. & Technology Central New England Coll. 1987, Hon. Doctorate Humanities Lewis Univ., Ill. 1989, The Collier Trophy Nat. Aviation Club & Nat. Aeronautic Assn. 1986, Iven C. Kincheloe Award Soc. Exptl. Test Pilots 1987, Louis Bleriot Medal 1982, Gold Medal 1986 and The Absolute World Records 1987, Fedn. of Aeronautique Internationale, Nat. Air & Space Mus. Trophy for outstanding achiev. in aerospace tech. 1987, Royal Aero Club of the U.K. gold medal presented by H.R.H. Prince Andrew, Duke of York, with H.R.H., the Duchess of York and Prince Phillip, Royal Consort (May 21, 1987), Paris Aero Club's Grande Medallion & Medalle de Ville Paris, VFW Aviation & Space Award Gold Medal & Citation

1987, Guinness Book of Records Hall of Fame 1988, Nat. Aviation Hall of Fame Spirit of Flight Award 1987, Golden Plate Awrd Am. Acad. of Achiev. 1987, Person of Wk. Peter Jennings ABC World News Tonight 1986, World Record Awards Aero Club of So. Calif., Diamond Wings Award Internat. Order of Characters, Disting. Alumni Dinuba C.of C. 1987, Flying Tiger Pilot Award 1989, Breathe Easy Award Am. Lung Assn. 1989, Eagles of Aviation Embry-Riddle Aero. Univ. 1987, Edward Longstreth Medal of Merit Franklin Inst. 1988, The Hist. of Aviation Award Hawthorne C.of C. 1988, Royal Aero. Soc. Award 1987, The Lindbergh Eagle Chas. A. Lindbergh Fund 1987, Greater LA Citizen of Yr. Boys' Clubs 1988, Internat. Aviation Achiev. Intl. Varieze & Composites Hospitality Club 1989, Ft. Worth Hall of Fame 1987, Meridian Award Children's Mus. 1987; mem: Soc. of Exptl. Test Pilots, Nat. Aeronautic Assn., Exptl. Aircraft Assn., Order of Daedalians (prior Flight Capt. Flt 56 Test Flight Edwards AFB); Republican; rec: aviation. Ofc: Hanger 77 Airport Mojave 93501

RYAN, EDWARD JOHN, JR., private investigation co. president; b. May 25,1936; s. Edward and Thelma E. R.; m. Dorothy C., Oct., 1970; edn: BS, Northeastern Univ. 1963, MBA, 1965; Calif. R.E. lic., Calif. Private Investigator lic. Career: purchasing agent Fenwal, Farmingham, Mass. 1960-63; var. pos. DuPont Co., mfg. supvr. to corp. personnel 1963-70; corp. employment mgr. Appalacian Reg. Hosps. Inc. 1970-72; v.p. med. relations Hospital Corp. of Am., Nashville, Tenn. 1972-79; dir. internat. recruitment Whittaker Corp., Los Angeles 1979-80; sr. v.p. Nat. Medical Enterprises, Los Angeles 1980-82; chmn., CEO, pres. EJR Enterprises Inc., Chatsworth 1982-90; pres. Windham Associates, 1990-; mem: Counsel of Investigative Services, Ohio Detective Assn., Delaware Pvt. Detective Agys., Am. Med. Assn., Calif. Assn. of Licensed Investigators, Conejo Bd. Realtors; lodges: Masons, Scottish Rite; clubs: Peace Officers Shrine, Los Angeles CC, North Ranch CC; mil: airman 1/c USAF 1954-58; Republican; Prot.; rec: auto racing, motorcycles, mechanics. Ofc: Windham Assoc. 6318 Vesper Ave Van Nuys 91411

RYAN, KEVIN DURWOOD, retail executive; b. Jan. 9, 1961, Syracuse, N.Y.; s. William D. and Sally Ann (Foelker) R.; edn: AA bus., Allan Hancock, 1983, AS mgt., AS acctg., 1986; CalPoly S.L.O., 1985. Career: municipal recreation dept. supr. Santa Maria Rec. Dept., 1975-80; sales mgr. Builders Emporium, 1979-84; mgr. Los Padres Theatres, 1980-89; mgr. GNW Partners, Novato 1987-; recipient Wickes Corp. achiev. awards home improvement splst. (1980, 81, 82) and nursery splst. (1983, 84); civic: Vallejo Police & Fireman Benefit Assn. 1991-92, Dept. Spl. Svs. for Handicapped (youth ldr. 1978-82, wkly. newsletter editor: Volunteer Vine, Santa Maria 1979-80), Founders Soc. KTEH 1990-92; mem. Kts. of Columbus 1980-; Republican; R.Cath.; rec: photography, travel. Res: 530 Fairgrounds Dr #29 Vallejo 94589

RYDER, OLIVER ALLISON, geneticist, educator; b. Dec. 27, 1946, Alexandria, Va.; s. Oliver A. Ryder and Elizabeth Rose (Semans) Paine; m. Cynthia Lou Ryan, Dec. 5, 1970; children: Kerry b. 1978, Ryan b. 1982; edn: BA biology (high honors) UC Riverside, 1968; PhD biology, UC San Diego, 1975. Career: postdoctoral fellow dept. reproductive med. UC San Diego, La Jolla 1975-77, dept. pathology 1977-79, res. assoc. dept. biology 1979-87, adj. prof. 1988-; res. fellow Res. Dept. Zoological Soc. of San Diego, San Diego 1975-79, geneticist 1979-85, Kleberg Chair in Genetics Ctr. for Reproduction of Endangered Species, 1986-; cons. UN, US Congress, San Diego Unified Sch. Dist., Nat. Geographic Soc., Nat. Commn Wildlife & Conservation Kingdom S.A., Sierra Club, County of Orange Dist. Atty., County of San Diego Dist. Atty., others; awards: USPHS trainee genetics 1968-75, Bank Am. Giannini Found. Med. Rsch. Fellow 1975-76, NIH Nat. Res. Svc. Award 1976-78, San Diego Soc. Natural Hist. fellow, Sci. Fellow of N.Y. Zool. Soc. 1990, San Diego Mag. list of 91 San Diegans to Watch in '91 (1991), grantee, prin. investigator NIH (1979-82, 82-85, 85-88), Inst. Mus. Svs. conserv. proj. 1987-88, Calif. Dept. Fish & Game Calif. Condor 1987-89, Marine Mammal Commn. Fla. Manatees 1988-89, John and Beverly Stauffer Trust mgmt. genetic resources 1989-92, J.N. Pew Jr. Memorial Trust 1989-92, Morris Animal Found. mtn. gorillas 1990-92, John and Beverly Stauffer Found. global mgmt. Przewalski's Horse 1992-94; mem: Am. Soc. Mammalogists, Am. Genetics Assn. (assoc. ed. Jour. of Heredity 1990-), Am. Soc. for Cell Biology, Soc. for Systematic Zoology, Am. Soc. for Microbiology, Am. Assn. Zool. Parks and Aquariums (Profl. Fellow), Internat. Soc. for Animal Blood Group Res., Soc. for Conservation Biology, Am. Soc. Human Genetics, Soc. for Study of Evolution; author 120+ books, book chapters, popular and sci. jour. articles and monographs in field; Ofc: Zoological Society of San Diego PO Box 551 San Diego 92112

RYU, EDWIN K. S., financial advisor/planner; b. Nov. 24, 1951, Monterey, Calif.; s. Henry and Helen (Lee) R.; m. Julie Satake; children: Nicole b. 1989, Danielle b. 1991; edn: H.S. diploma, York Sch., Monterey, Calif.; BA in economics, Stanford Univ. 1976; Certified Public Accountant (CPA). Career: supr./mgr. Touche Ross & Co. (now Deloitte & Touche), S.F. 1979-84; v.p. finance Van Kasper & Co., S.F. 1984-85; pres. Ryu and Company, S.F. 1985-; tchr. Golden Gate Univ., S.F. 1986-89; bd. dirs. Willow Tree Invest., S.F. 1991-; mem. Stanford Alumni Assn. 1989-; civic: bd. dirs. Stonestown YMCA, S.F. 1989-92; author: International Investments & Taxation (grad. level, Golden Gate Univ.) 1987-89; rec: basketball, traveling. Res: 716 Ulloa St San Francisco 94127

SABHARWAL, RANJIT SINGH, mathematician, educator; b. Dec. 11, 1925, Dhudial, India, nat. US cit. 1981; s. Krishan Chand and Devti (Anand) S.; m. Pritam Chadha, 1948; children: Rajinderpal b. 1949, Armarjit b. 1951, Jasbir b. 1955; edn: BA, honors, Punjab Univ. 1944, MA, 1948; MA, UC Berkeley 1962; Phd, Wash. State Univ. 1966. Career: lectr. in math. Khalsa Coll., Bombay, India 1951-58; tchg. asst. UC Berkeley 1958-62; instr. in math. Portland State Univ. 1962-63; instr. in math. Washington State Univ. 1963-66; asst. prof. Kansas State Univ. 1966-68; assoc. prof. CSU Hayward 1968-74, prof. math. 1974-; mem: Am. Mathematical Soc., Mathematical Assn. of Am., Sigma Xi; research: non-desarguesian geometries. Res: 27892 Adobe Ct Hayward 94542 Ofc: California State University Hayward 94542

SACA, RICARDO EDUARDO, physician; b. May 19, 1956, Usubetan, El Salvador; nat. Nov. 1990; s. Ricardo Jacobo and Maria Luisa (Gonzalez) S.; m. Nidia Maria Colomer, Mar. 22, 1986; children: (twins) Cristina Maria b. 1990, Nidia Maria b. 1990; edn: MD, UC Irvine, Calif., 1987. Career: physician, private practice, 1987-; dir. Diabetes Ctr., Chino Comm. Hosp. 1993-; bd. mem. Am. Diabetes Assn., 1993-; rec: traveling. Ofc: 12598 Central Ave. #D Chino 91710

SACKETT, DALE MILTON, investor, contractor, engineer, executive; b. May 14, 1923, Long Beach; s. Leonard Frank and Corinne Thelma (Beggs) S.; m. Connie Bawden, Mar. 15, 1987; children: Linda b. 1953, Daniel b. 1957; edn: AA, Pasadena City Coll. 1948; BE mech. engring. (cum laude), USC, 1950. Career: chief air condtg. engr. C.F. Braun & Co., Alhambra 1950-54, designed systems for petroleum and chem. plants; air condtg. contr./engring. cons. D. M. Sackett & Assocs., Los Angeles 1954-60; cons. Chemet Engrs. Inc., Pasadena 1958-60; designed unique process & storage air-condtg. systems using steam refrigeration and utilizing waste coffee bean husks for fuel, for MJB Co., Nicaragua 1959; investor, property devel. & mgmt., 1960-; specialist comml. & indsl. air-condtg. systems, pres./ceo Authorized Service Corp. (contract and service engring.), Los Angeles 1960-; honors: Pi Tau Sigma 1949; mem. ASHRAE 1957-; Rotary Internat. (pres. East L.A. Club 1965-66, Rotarian of Yr. 1967, Dist. 530 Best Club award 1966); mil: non-commd. ofcr. US Army 1943-46, ETO, anti-aircraft unit under Gen. Patton, 3 campaign medals; Republican; Prot.; rec: art collector, photography. Ofc: 1256 S Atlantic Blvd Los Angeles 90022

SADLER, WILLIAM ALAN, JR., professor of sociology; b. Mar. 2, 1931, Evanston, Ill.; s. William A. and Marjorie (Eason) S.; m. Sallie I. Off, Apr. 23, 1977; children: William, Lisa, Kirsten; edn: BA, Univ. Mich., 1953; ThM, General Theol. Sem., 1956, Harvard Univ., 1957; PhD, Harvard Univ., 1962. Career: clergyman Episcopal Church, Diocese of New York, 1959-64; asst. prof. Bishops Univ., Lennoxville, Quebec 1964-68; assoc. prof. Bates Coll., Lewiston, Me. 1968-72; prof. sociology and hd. div. interdisciplinary studies Bloomfield (N.J.) Coll., 1972-85; dean and exec. dir. planning Lock Haven (Pa.) Univ., 1985-89; chief academic ofcr. and prof. sociology Holy Names Coll., Oakland 1990-; vis. prof. Univ. Victoria, B.C. Canada, 1977, Pacific Sch. Religion, Berkeley 1974, Chapman Coll., Orange 1981; awards: Frederick Sheldon fellow Harvard 1958-59, postdoc. fellow Soc. for Values in Edn., New Haven, Ct. 1973, Danforth Assoc., St. Louis, Mo. 1976, Distinguished Scholar Chapman Coll. 1981, 15 grants from NEH, FIPSE, Kittredge Found., Ford Found., Pa., others; mem. Am. Sociol. Assn. 1971-, Am. Assn. for Higher Edn. 1975-, Columbia Univ. Education Seminar, N.Y. (mem., dir. 1978-89), Outward Bound (advy. bd. 1990-); author: More Life To Live (1993), Existence & Love (1970), Personality & Religion (1970), 25+ jour. articles, editor: Master Sermons Through Ages (1962); Democrat; Episcopalian; rec: aquatic sports, running, skiing, camping, hiking. Res: 34 Turtle Creek Oakland 94605 Ofc: Holy Names College 3500 Mountain Blvd Oakland 94619

SAHLEIN, DON, manufacturing co. executive; b. March 7, 1924, Jackson, Mich.; s. David A. and Pauline (Byoir) S.; m. Lee Silver, March 28, 1952; children: Gail b. 1952, Stacey b. 1955; edn: BS, UCLA 1948. Career: v.p. Leoff & Rose Publicist, Hollywood 1948-52; sales mgr. Los Angeles Wholesale Elec. Co., 1952-56; pres. Hollywood Camera Co., Hollywood 1956-71; corp. exec. Alan Gordon Enterprises, North Hollywood 1971-; mem: Am. Soc. Photogrammetry, Soc. Photo Instrumentation Engrs., Soc. Motion Picture & TV Engrs., Masons, Founders Guild, Vikings, Wine & Food Soc. Holleywood (chmn.), Les Gastronomes, HOME (v.chmn.); mil: 1st lt. USAAF 1942-45, USAAFR 1945-59, Disting. Flying Cross, Air Medal w. 3 Clusters; Republican; Jewish; rec: photog., water skiing, flying. Res: POB 6038 North Hollywood 91603 Ofc: 1430 Cahuenga Blvd Hollywood 90028

SAIKI, LOREL KEIKO, art director, photographer; b. May 8, 1954, Chgo.; d. Hiroshi and Jessie Keiko (Kawasuna) S.; edn: Univ. Colo. 1972-73, Art Center Coll. of Design, L.A. 1973-76. Career: art director Robertson Co., L.A. 1975-76; art dir. Bozell & Jacobs, Inc., L.A. 1976-82; sr. art dir. Evans/Weinberg Advt. Inc., L.A. 1982-84; freelance art dir., advertising consultant 1984-86, 1989-, freelance photographer 1987-, writer/producer 1989-; dir. advt. La Salsa Franchise, Inc. (gourmet Mexican restaurant chain) 1987-88; awards: Art Dirs. Club of L.A. Advt. Show 1978, Cert. of Merit Am. Advt. Fedn. Show 1978, Gold Medal Indsl. TV Assn. 1982, Graphics gallery award Strathmore Paper Co. 1988; mem: L.A. Advt. Industry Emergency Fund, U.S. Polo Assn., Independent Feature Project/West.

SALAMATI, FARSHID, environmental engineer company president; b. May 31, 1949, Tehran, Iran; nat. 1980; s. Plato and Kharman (Yezeshmi) S.; m. Fariba Azari, June 19, 1958; 1 child, Behan b. 1988; edn: BSEE, Univ. Tehran 1974; MS energy, UC Berkeley 1984. Career: field engr. Shahin Factory, Tehran, Iran 1968-72; supr. Irom Engring. Co. 1972-75; project mgr., pres. Techno Band 1975-80; field engr. Eal Corp., Richmond 1980-85; CFO, v.p. Inov Corp., Oakland 1985-87; pres., CFO EIC 1987-; mem: Nat. Asbestos Council (tech. co-chair Calif. chpt. 1988-), Nat. Assn. Environ. Profls., BOMA, Persian Zoroastrian Orgn. (cofounder, secty. 1983-88), Fedn. of Zoroastrian Assns. of No. Am. (v.p. & chair of planning, bus. devel. 1990-), World Safety Orgn. (co-founder No. Calif. chpt. 1993-);mil: lt. col. Tehran 1975-77; rec: swimming, surfing, snorkeling. Res: 6160 Mt Diablo Castro Valley 94552 Ofc: EIC 675 Hegenberger Rd Ste 110 Oakland 94621

SALAZAR, KATHLEEN VIRGINIA, budget analyst; b. Oct. 10, 1947, Oakland; d. Lee Monroe and Sarah Catherine (Clement) Harp; m. Michael Robert Carroll, Aug. 8, 1970 (div. 1974); m. Ernest Montellano Salazar, April 21, 1979; stepchildren: Ernie b. 1954, Sonny b. 1956, George b. 1957, Candy b. 1965; edn: BS indsl. engring., Calif. Polytech. St. Univ. 1969; MBA, 1974. Career: mfg. mgmt. program Gen. Electric Co., Louisville, Ky. 1969-71, quality control engr. 1971-73, purchasing splst. 1973-74, cons., Bridgeport, Conn. 1975-76, purchasing mgr., San Jose 1976-79, inventory and production control mgr. 1979-80, material support mgr. 1980-81; buyer Co. of San Luis Obispo 1982-83, central services mgr. 1983-91; budget analyst SUN Technical Services 1992-; lectr. Calif. Polytech. St. Univ., bus. dept. 1981-82; awards: GE At Your Service 1980; mem: Calif. Assn. Pub. Purchasing Ofcrs (dir. S. 1987-89, chair audit com. 1987), Central Coast Purchasing Assn., Soroptimist Internat. (dir. 1988-90, pres. 1987-88, v.p. 1986-87, recording secty. 1985-86), Santa Maria Kennel Club; Democrat; rec: obedience train & show dogs, walking, horseback riding. Res: 1231 Newport Ave Arroyo Grande 93420 Ofc: SUN Technical Services c/o PG&E PO Box S6 Avila Beach 93456

SALKIN, DAVID, research physician, administrator, educator; b. Aug. 8, 1906, Ukraine; s. Samuel Salkin and Eva Sturman; m. Bess Marguerite Adelman, Sept. 12, 1934; children: Barbara Ruth b. 1938, Robert David b. 1941 (dec. 1947); edn: MD, Univ. of Toronto, Ont., Can. 1929. Career: medical director Hopemont (W.Va.) Sanitarium, 1934-41, medical/hospital dir. 1941-48; med. dir. San Fernando (Calif.) VA Hosp., 1949-67, med./hosp. dir. 1967-71; dir. research La Vina Hosp., Altadena 1972-83; sr. researcher, pulmonary/cancer, Huntington Med. Res. Insts., Pasadena 1984-; asst. prof. medicine Univ. West Va., Morgantown 1934-48; assoc. prof. medicine UCLA, Los Angeles 1949-58; clin. prof. medicine USC, L.A. 1958-, Loma Linda Univ., L.A. 1958-; awards: Veterans Adminstrn. American Acad. TB Physicians 1958, 1962, Gold medal Calif. Thoracic Soc. 1972, Am. Coll. Chest Physicians 1973, Internat. Coccidioides Symp. 1976, Am. Lung Assn. of LA County 1980; staff Huntington Med. Research Insts., Huntington Memorial Hosp., Cedars Sinai Hosp., Barlow Hosp.; mem. Sigma Xi; publs. in med. jours. and texts; Jewish; rec: the Arts. Res: 1820 Linda Vista Ave Pasadena 91103 Ofc: Huntington Medical Research Insts. 660 S Fair Oaks Pasadena 91105

SALMASSI, SADEGH, surgeon; b. Aug. 14, 1946, Baghdad, Iraq; s. Jafar and Kobra (Alavi) S.; m. Tahereh, Jan. 17, 1970; children: Ali b. 1971, Nahal b. 1975; edn: premed., Pahlavi Univ., Shiraz, Iran 1964-66, MD, 1973; bd. certified Am. Bd. Pathol. 1981; lic. Ill. 1978, Mo. 1980, Kans. 1980, Calif. 1983. CC rotating intern Pahlavi Univ. affil. hosps. 1972-73; resident anatomy & clin. pathol. Univ. Ill. 1975-78, chief res. pathol. 1978-79, fellow blood banking and immunohematology 1979-80; emerg. rm. phys. Louise Burg Hosp. Chgo. 1979-80; instr. pathol. Univ. Ill. 1976-80; asst. prof. pathol. Univ. Mo. Kansas City, assoc. dir. anatomic pathol., asst. dir. blood bank Truman Med. Ctr. UMKC 1980-84; dir. Delano Med. Clin. & Lab. Delano, Calif. 1984-; chmn. dept. family practice Delano Regl. Med. Ctr. 1985-87; staff Delano Reg. Med. Center, v.chief staff, chmn. utilization rev. 1988-89, chief of staff 1989-90, pres. Delano Med. Group IPA 1989-; chmn. credential com. 1990-91, chmn pharmacy & therapeutic com. 1990-91; recipient AMA physician recogn. awards; Fellow Am. Coll. Pathologists 1981, Fellow ACIP 1988, mem. AAFP 1988, AMA, AAAS, NY Acad. Scis., Ill. Med. Soc., Chgo. Med. Soc., Iranian Med. Assn., Am. Assn. Blood Banks, Kansas City Soc. Pathols., Pahlavi Univ. Med. Sch. Alumni Assn.; publs: 20+ articles in med. jours., papers presented Univ. Ct., K.C. Soc. Pathols.; mil: 1st lt., physician Rezayeh Mil. Hosp., Iran 1973-75; Muslim; rec: videotaping. Res: 1121 Sussex Circle Bakersfield 93311 Ofc: Delano Med. Clin. 1005 11th Ave Delano 93215

SALMON, NATHAN, philosopher, educator; b. Jan. 2, 1951, Los Angeles; s. Mair and Rebecca (Sene) Ucuzoglu; m. Eileen Mary Conrad, Aug. 28, 1980; edn: AA, El Camino Coll. 1971; BA, UCLA 1973; MA, 1974; PhD, 1979. Career: instr. UCLA, CSU Northridge, CSU Long Beach, 1976-77; lectr. CSU Northridge 1977-78; asst. prof. Princeton Univ. 1978-82, vis. senior research philosopher 1982; assoc. prof. UC Riverside 1982-84; UC Santa Barbara 1984-85, prof. 1985-; awards: Council of Grad. Schs. in U.S. Gustave O Arlt award 1984, Council Internat. Exchange of Scholars Fulbright Disting. Prof. lecturing grant 1986; mem: Am. Philosophical Assn., Bertrand Russell Soc., Royal Inst. Philosophy Gt.

Britain (lifetime hon.); author: Reference & Essence (1981), Frege's Puzzle (1986), co-editor: Propositions & Attitudes (1988). Res: 1105 Orchid Dr Santa Barbara 93111 Ofc: UCSB Dept. Philosophy, Santa Barbara 93106

SALVAGNO, ROB, investment broker; b. Aug. 28, 1947, Corning, Calif.; s. William R. and Annie Sue (Hopkins) S.; m. Ana Maria Salinas, July 5, 1975; children: Robert b. 1976, Lita b. 1980, Alexa b. 1982; edn: BA, Chico State Coll., 1969, MS, Univ. Texas, 1975; reg. rep. SEC, 1981. Career: reg. sanitarian Calif. St. Health Dept., L.A. 1969-71; E-5, environmental splst. US Army, San Antonio, Tx. 1971-74; rsch. assoc. Texas A&M Univ., College Sta. 1974-75; systems mgr. Alamo Area Council of Govts., San Antonio, Tx. 1975-77; pres. Allied Energy Systems Inc., Chico, Calif. 1977-81; senior v.p. investments Paine Webber, Chico 1981-, branch mgr. 1992-; recipient Paine Webber Pacesetter award 1982-88, Pres.'s Council 1989-, Direct Inv. advy. bd. 1982-87, reg. inv. advr. 1991-; civic bds: Chico Youth Football (dir. 1987-88), Chico Youth Soccer (coach 1985-86), Chico Econ. Planning Corp. (dir. 1990-); mem. Rotary 1987-, Elks 1988-, Am. Legion 1990-; publs: book, tech. reports 1975, 2 TV films 1972, 73; Republican; R.Cath.; rec: skiing, travel, tennis, barbershop singing, Arabian horses. Res: 3585 Keefer Rd Chico 95926 Ofc: Paine Webber, 1051 Mangrove Ave Chico 95926

SAMET, MARC KRANE, pharmacologist; b. Apr. 30, 1950, Chgo.; s. Herman and Nora (Krane) S.; edn: BS biochem., No. Ill. Univ., 1973; MS devel. biology, Northwestern Univ., 1975; MS anat. Northwestern Univ. Med. Sch., 1978; MS, PhD pharmacology and toxicology, Kansas Univ., 1983. Career: NIH postdoc. fellowships Univ. Calif. at Berkeley and San Francisco, 1983-85; founding scientist immunology pgm. Applied Immunesciences Inc., Menlo Park 1985-87; assoc. Glenwood Ventures, Menlo Park 1987-88; coord. new technology appls. Vitaphore Corp., 1988-90; dir. new bus. Plan AConsulting Partners, 1991-92; Merck & Co., 1992-; mem: AAAS, Soc. for Neurosci., Am. Assn. Immunologists, N.Y. Acad. Scis., Controlled Release Soc., Internat. Fedn. for Adv. of Genetic Engring. and Biotechnology; publs: 16+ books, chapters, sci. jour. articles re pharm. emerging technology & mktg. strategy Jewish; rec: biking, tennis, photography, hiking. Res: 923 Menlo Ave #1 Menlo Park 94025 Ofc: PO Box 1428 Menlo Park 94026

SAMOFF, JOEL, political scientist, educator, consultant; b. Nov. 27, 1943, Phila.; s. Bernard Leon and Zelda (Semser) S.; m. Rachel, Mar. 31, 1967; children: Erika b. 1971, Kara b. 1972; edn: BA history, Antioch Coll., 1965, stu. Univ. de Neuchatel, Switz. 1963-64; MA political sci., Univ. Wis., 1967, PhD, 1972; languages: French, Swahili. Career: asst. prof. Univ. Mich., Ann Arbor, 1970-80; lectr. Univ. Zambia, Lusaka, 1973-75; assoc. prof. internat. development edn., Stanford Univ., 1980-88, dir. African Studies Ctr. 1984-85, vis. scholar African Studies, 1988-; res. assoc. dept. edn. Univ. of Dar es Salaam, 1983-85; vis. assoc. prof. UC Santa Barbara 1989-90; vis. prof. UCLA 1993; prin. cons. UNESCO-ILO interagy. task force on austerity, adjustment and human resources, 1990-; cons. Swedish Internat. Devel. Authority 1987-; awards: Antioch Coll. scholar 1961-65, Wis. Ford Area fellow 1965-66, fellow Nat. Def. Edn. Act Fgn. Language Pgm. 1966-68, fellow Fgn. Area Fellowship Pgm. 1968-70, H.H. Rackham Grad. Sch. Faculty fellow 1973-74, Univ. Mich. disting. svc. 1978, Spencer Found. grantee 1980-81, Stanford Sch. of edn. excellence in tchg. 1983, grantee: Soc. Sci. Rsch. Council 1983, Fulbright Sr. res. in Africa 1984, Rockefeller Found. 1984-86, Spencer Found. 1986-88, William and Flora Hewlett Endowment Fund 1988; mem: African Assn. Polit. Sci., African Studies Assn. (bd. 1982-85), Am. Ednl. Res. Assn., Am. Polit. Sci. Assn., Assn. Concerned Africa Scholars (bd. 1979-), Comparative and Internat. Edn. Assn., Internat. Polit. Sci. Assn., Pacific Coast Africanist Assn., So. Africa Res. Assn., Tanzania Hist. Soc., We. Assn. of Africanists. Res: 3527 South Court Palo Alto 94306 Ofc: African Studies Ctr 200 Encina Hall Stanford Univ. Stanford 94305-6055 Tel/Fax: 415/856-2326

SAMPSON, RICHARD ARNIM, security executive; b. June 9, 1927, New Haven, Conn.; s. Richard Arnim Sampson and Ora Viola (Reese) Sampson-Jackson; m. Marilyn Jo Gardner, June 10, 1950 (div. Mar. 1962); children: Gary b. 1951, Susan b. 1955; m. Janet Margaret Battaglia, Jan. 26, 1963 (div. July 1987); children: Cynthia b. 1964, David b. 1965; m. Alice Annette Whitfield, July 23, 1988; children: Shareasa b. 1970, Anthony b. 1972, Erika b. 1976; edn: BS, Mich. State Univ., 1951; MPA, Auburn Univ., 1972; grad. Air War Coll., Montgomery, Ala. 1972. Career: exec. Central Intelligence Agy., W.D.C., 1951-76; mgr. spl. projects Hughes Aircraft Co., El Segundo, Calif. 1976-80; mgr. security Northrop Aircraft Adv. Systems Div., Pico Rivera 1980-83; security mgr. General Dynamics Electronics Div., San Diego 1983-92; security mgr. GDE Systems Inc. 1992-; faculty Southwest L.A. Coll. 1978-79, Webster Univ., San Diego 1991-, mem. advy. group leadership & mgmt. program in security Mich. St. Univ. 1990-, guest lectr. 1991-, adv. security mgmt. curriculum Calif. State Univ. San Marcos 1992-; awards: Order of the Moon Rep. of China, Taiwan 1961, outstanding unit award USAF, Las Vegas 1971, C.I.A. Intel. Medal of Merit, Career Intel. Medal, W.D.C. (1975, 76); mem: Security Affairs Support Assn. 1989-, Mich. State Univ. Alumni Assn., Am. Soc. for Indsl. Security (1957-, acad., placement coms.), CIA Retirees Assn. 1976-, Signa Soc. 1976-, Nat. Mgmt. Assn. 1976-, Indsl. Security Working Group 1980-,

Contractor SAP/SAR Working Group 1988-, Aerospace Inds. Assn. Security Com. 1987-92, Research Security Assocs. (1987-); publs: mag. article "The Police of Taiwan" 1960, manual, Special Projects Security 1965, thesis: Excessive Bureaucracy: Causes and Cures 1972; mil: capt. USAR 1949-66; Republican; Congregationalist (trustee, personnel com.); reading, tchg., writing. Res: 1408 Westwood Pl Escondido 92026 Ofc: GDE Systems, Inc. PO Box 1198 Poway 92074

SAMUDIO, JEFFREY BRYAN, architect, planner, educator; b. Oct. 3, 1966, San Gabriel; s. Lazaro and Grace (Alvarez) S.; edn: B Architecture, minor in Urban & Regional Planning, USC, 1989, grad. student, cand. M Arch/MURP, 1993; AIA intern. Career: asst. slide curator USC Arch. & Fine Arts Library, Los Angeles 1985-88; v.p. Northeast Design & Devel. Group, Glendale 1989-90; instr. L.A. Trade Tech. Coll., 1989-; ptnr. Design A.I.D., Architects & Planners, L.A. 1987-; awards: appreciation City of L.A. 1984, 1989, award of service A.I.A., Pasadena 1991, Phi Beta Phi 1992; mem: Hist. Soc. So. Calif. (life), Soc. of Arch. Historians (life), AIA (intern), Am. Planning Assn. (assoc.); civic: The Eagle Rock Assn. (bd. 1988-, chair preservation advocacy 1988-), Town Hall of Calif., Los Angeles Conservancy, Neutra Centennial Com. (advisor 1991-), Colorado Blvd. Specific Plan (bd. 1987-90); coauthor: Frank Lloyd Wright's Freeman House 1992; Republican; rec: preservation advocacy, flying, travel. Ofc: Design AID, Architects & Planners 2320 Langdale Ave Los Angeles 90041-2912

SANCHEZ, RUBEN DARIO, clergyman, psychotherapist, writer, educator; b. Feb. 12, 1943, Buenos Aires, Argentina, naturalized U.S. citizen 1989; s. Ramon Jose and Maria Concepcion (Pardino) S.; m. Lina Alcira Tabuenca, Feb. 7, 1966; children: Adrian b. 1971, Vivian b. 1973; edn: BA in edn. and theology, River Plate Coll., Entre Rios, Argentina 1968; MA rel. edn., Andrews Univ., Berrien Springs, Mich. 1976; PhD rel. edn., Calif. Graduate Sch. Theology, L.A. 1979; MA clin. psychology, National Univ., L.A. 1992; ordained minister Seventh Day Adventist Ch. Career: minister Calif. Conf., Glendale 1970-71, Ill. Conf., Brookfield, Ill. 1972-77, Oregon Conf., Portland 1977-80; dir. development Adventist Media Ctr., Newbury Park, Calif. 1980-92; leader seminars nat., 1980-92; pres. Advi Internat., Newbury Park 1989-92; clin. counselor pvt. practice, San Fernando, Calif. 1992-; founder, chancellor Pacific Northwest Christian Sch., Woodburn, Oreg. 1979-80; founder, dir. Christian Bible Inst., Woodburn, Oreg. 1980; dir. Voice of Prophecy Bible Sch., Newbury Park, Calif. 1980-84; awards: Outstanding svs. to the Spanish community radio sta. KROW (1460 AM), Independence, Oreg. 1980, listed Who's Who in Religion 1986, 92, Who's Who in West 1992; mem: Calif. Assn. Marriage and Family Therapists, United Assn. Christian Counselors 1989-, Nat. Fund Raisers Assn. 1991-, Christian Mgmt. Assn. 1980-92; author: Fascinating Bible Inspiration, 1977; Intro. to the Old Testament, 1979; Hungry Heart, 1984; Aceptame Asi (Spanish), 1992; rec: sculpture. Res: 2983 Elinor Ct Newbury Park 91320 Ofc: 1100 Rancho Conejo Blvd Newbury Park 91320

SANDELL, JAN RUNE, financial services executive; b. May 26, 1954, Kristianstad, Sweden; s. Hugo Leonard and Anna Beata Matilda (Andersson) S.; m. Kathleen Maria Burgi, May 13, 1984; edn: BSEE, Tech. Inst. Hassleholm Sweden 1974; MBA strategic planning, Univ. Lund Sweden 1979; MBA finance, UC Riverside 1980. Career: com. Mornstam AB, Malmo, Sweden 1978-79; financial analyst, senior fin. anal., mgr. budget & planning Fox & Carskadon Fin. Corp. San Mateo, Calif. 1981-84; dir. fin. planning Homestead Financial Corp. Burlingame 1984; senior dir., senior home office mgr., v.p. Industrial Indemnity Fin. Corp., a Xerox Fin. Services Corp., San Francisco 1984-92; founder and mng. ptnr. Sandell and Assoc., a fin. and mgmt. cons. firm 1992-; honors: Cementa Co. Honorary Award (Malmo, Sweden), Calif. Edn. Abroad Scholar (Univ. Lund); mem. Am. Mgmt. Assn. 1985; mil: Swedish Army 1977-78, commendations for computer efficiency improvements (Kristianstad, Sweden); Lutheran; rec: computers, golf, philately, travel, swim, abstract art. Ofc: Industrial Indemnity Financial Corp., San Francisco CA 94111

SANDERS, AUGUSTA, nurse, county mental health services administrator; b. July 22, 1932, Alexandria, La.; d. James and Elizabeth (Thompson) Swann; m. James Robert Sanders, Jan. 12, 1962 (div. 1969); edn: RN, Morgan State Univ., Provident Hosp. Sch. of Nursing, Balt. 1956; RN, Md. 1956. Career: head nse. VA Hosp., Downey, Ill. 1956-57; staff nse. Huntington Hosp., Pasadena 1957-58; head nse., evening supr. VA Hosp., Los Angeles 1958-60; head nse. NPI-UCLA, 1960-61; staff nse. Am. Red Cross, 1960-64; public health nse. Fed. Govt., W.D.C., 1964-66; staff nse. L.A. County Sheriff's Dept., 1967-72; RN, asst., mental health counselor L.A. County Dept. Mental Health Svs., 1972-89, senior mental health counselor and mental health svc. coordinator, 1989-92; Calif. Gov. appt. mem. 11th Dist. Bd. Med. Quality, 1981-87; awards: Woman of Year Crenshaw/La Tijera B.P.W., L.A. 1987, Wilshire B.P.W., L.A. 1989, elected pres. Md. State Student Nurses Assn. 1955-56; mem. Internat. Assn. Bus. & Profl. Women (1978-, past chapt. pres., pres. L.A. Sunset Dist. 1988-89); mem. steering com. State Sen. Diane Watson, Calif. Assembly Rep. CarolAnn Peterson; rec: writing, movies, travel. Res: 13338 Appleblossom Ln Apple Valley 92308-5415

SANDERS, LES, trade association executive; b. June 10, 1936, Santa Barbara; s. Emery L. and Betty B. (Leiser) S.; edn: Am. River Jr. Coll., CSU Sacto., Inst. of Orgn. Mgmt. at Santa Clara/San Jose St. Univs., 6 yr. pgm. and 2 yrs. post-grad. work; CAE cert. Am. Soc. Assn. Execs. 1981. Career: met. devel. mgr. Sacramento C.of C. 1967-69; dir. of transp./lobbyist Calif. C.of C., Sacto. 1969-72; exec. dir. Transp. Council of Calif., Sacto. 1972-74; exec. dir. Sacto. Sports Complex Com. (jt. city/co. proj.) Sacto. 1974-75; dir. Calif. Nevada Soft Drink Assn., Sacto. 1975-86; pres. Les Sanders & Associates, Sacto. 1986-89; exec. v.p. Lumber Merchants Assn. of No. Calif., 1989-; mil: A/2c USAF 1955-59; Republican; Lutheran; rec: golf, photography. Res: 8959 Cliffside Ln Fair Oaks 95628

SANDISON, ERNEST FORTE, real estate agent, columnist; b. Sept. 5, 1938, Olney, Md.; s. Forte Holliday and Rosabell (May) S.; edn: BA English, Washington Coll., Chestertown, Md. 1960; desig: Realtor, NAR 1977. Career: Realtor Landes Realty, Riverside; instr. Calif. Assn. Realtors, L.A., 1979-, newspaper columnist Riverside Press-Enterprise, 1984-, TV host/prod. CenCom TV, Riv. 1990-; newsletter editor Riverside Realtor Rev., 1985-89; awards: Malana Trophy 1985 and Clanton Awards (1984, 86) Riverside Board of Realtors, Good Neighbor Award City of Riverside 1990; mem: Riverside Bd. of Realtors (pres. 1984, legislative advocate R.E. Council, 1985-86), Calif. Assn. Realtors (dist. RVP, Riv., 1987, chmn. comms., L.A., 1988), BIA (Riv. dir. govt. affairs 1986-87); civic: Shared Housing Inc. (pres. 1990-91), SAR (Riv. chpt. pres. 1991), Old Riverside Found. 1980-, Nat. Trust for Hist. Preservation 1978-, Mission Inn Found. 1987-, Riverside Mcpl. Mus. (mem., pres. 1986-87), Riverside Cultural Heritage Bd. 1990; contbg. writer California Real Estate Mag. 1984-87; mil: Lt. USNR 1960-72; Democrat; Episcopal; avocation: owner The Vintage Shop Antiques and Collectibles, and city landmark home. Res: 4539 Rubidoux Ave Riverside 92506

SANDS, RUSSELL BERTRAM, insurance executive; b. Feb. 14, 1940, Santa Cruz; s. Clarence Russell and Betty Ellyn (Weeks) S.; m. Jacquelyn Hall, Sept. 9, 1960; children: Douglas b. 1962, Gwendolyn b. 1970; edn: undergrad. Wheaton Coll. 1957-59, UCB 1959-61; BA, Western Ill. Univ., 1984. Career: mgr. Insurance Co. of No. Am., San Francisco 1961-69; v.p. Bayly, Martin & Fay, S.F. 1969-76; chmn. bd. and CEO Frank B. Hall & Co., S.F. 1976-92; pres. Rollins Hudig Hall of No. Calif. 1992-; dir. Hammerwell, Inc.; ptnr. San Bro Holdings I; gen. ptnr. Wendy Petroleum; prin. Sands Properties; ptnr. Dixon Oaks MHP; mem.: Nat. Assn. of Ins. Brokers, Western Mobilehome Assn. (ins. com.), World Trade Club, Churchill Club; civic bds.: City Team (dir.), Fellowship Acad. (dir.), Young Life San Francisco (dir.), Mt. Hermon Assn. (advy. council.); Republican; Presbyterian; rec: tennis, golf, travel. Ofc: Frank B. Hall & Co., One Market Plaza San Francisco 94105

SANFORD, RON, travel and wildlife photographer; b. June 13, 1939, Gridley, Calif.; s. Dr. Keith D., DDS, and Ailene (McIntyre) S.; m. Nancy K. Wallace, June 17, 1961; children: Michael b. 1962, Daniel b. 1964; edn: BS, UC Berkeley, 1961. Career: corp. pres. Gridley Growers Inc., Gridley 1965-78; travel and wildlife photographer, internat., 1978-: represented in New York (Black Star), Seattle (Allstock), Tokyo (Imperial Press), Milan (Grazia Neri), Springfield, Vt. (f/STOP); selected credits 1992: N.Y. Times, Washington Post - Insight, U.S.A. Today, Newsweek Mag., Sunset Books, Nat. Geographic WORLD, Nat. Geo. books, Ducks Unlimited Publs., Petersen's Photographic, European Travel & Life, Bon Appetite, Outside, Gourmet, Aloha, Sierra, Glamour, Islands, Stern, Travel- Holiday, Motorland, Harrowsmith, Field & Stream, National Parks, Nat. Wildlife, Backpacker, Buzzworm, Backpacker, Time, Life, Outdoor Photographer, Woman's World, Stock & Commodities, Architectural Digest, Calif. Parklands, Audubon, Vogue, Birder's World, Reader's Digest, Alaska Mag., Popular Photog., Natural History Mag., Airone mag. (Italy), Inflight mags: TWA, US Air, Northwest Orient, American, Calendars: Audubon, Nat. Geographic, Sierra Club, Falcon Press, Nikon, Argus Silver Creek, Nature Conservancy, World Wildlife Fund, Eastman Kodak & others; awards: Wildlife Photographer of Year Calif. Dept. Fish & Game 1984, World Press Photo"Nature Series" Holland Found., Amsterdam (1988, 1990); mem. Am. Soc. of Magazine Photographers, Rotary Internat., Gridley (pres. 1973-74, Paul Harris Fellow 1989); mil: capt. US Army 1962-65; rec: religion, philosophy, mythology. Ofc: Ron Sanford PO Box 248 Gridley 95948 Tel/Fax: 916/846-4687

SANTEE, DALE WILLIAM, lawyer; b. Mar. 28, 1953, Washington, Pa.; s. Robert Erwin and Elsbeth Emma (Bantleon) S.; m. Junko (Mori) S.; children: s. Enri b. 1983; edn: BA, Washington & Jefferson Coll., Pa. 1975; JD, Univ. Pittsburgh Sch. of Law, 1978; MA, No. Arizona Univ., Flagstaff 1982; admitted bar: Pa., 1978, Ct. of Military Appeals, 1979, Calif., 1989. Career: served to major US Air Force, 1979-; asst. staff judge advocate 832CSG/JA, Luke AFB, Ariz. 1979, area def. counsel Det. ULQD5S 1979-81; claims ofcr. 343GSG/JA, Eilson AFB, Ak. 1981-83; staff legal advisor Bd. of Veterans Appeals, W.D.C. 1983-89; asst. staff judge advocate HQ USAF/JAJM, Bolling AFB, D.C. 1986-89; 63CSG/JA, Norton AFB, Calif. 1989-91, 445AW/JA, 1991-; awarded AF Commendation Medal (1981, 89), Meritorious Svc. 1991, Outstanding unit (1979, 91); dep. pub. defender San Diego County, 1990-; v.p. Neuer Enterprises,

Huntington, Ind. 1984-; honors: Washington & Jefferson Coll. academic scholar 1971-75, Dean's List (1973, 74), Beta scholar 1974, Mathew Brown Ringland Polit. Sci. Award 1975, Pa. Senate law sch. scholar 1975-78, No. Ariz. Univ. Dean's List (1980, 81), Outstanding Young Man in Am. 1981, VA performance award 1988; mem: San Diego Co. Bar Assn. 1989-, Reserve Officer Assn. 1992-, Internat. Platform Assn.; civic: San Diego Comm. Child Abuse Coord. Com. 1990-, Zamorano Elem. Sch. (site com. chmn. 1990-92, PTA pres. 1991-92); Republican; Methodist; rec: sports, coins & stamps. Res: 1110 Manzana Way San Diego 92139 Ofc: Public Defender of San Diego, 8525 Gibbs Dr Ste 300 San Diego 92123

SANTILLAN, ANTONIO, banker, motion picture finance executive; b. May 8, 1936, Buenos Aires; naturalized, 1966; s. Guillermo Spika and Raphaella C. (Abaladejo) S.; children: Andrea, Miguel, Marcos; edn: grad. Morgan Park Mil. Acad., Chgo. 1954; Coll. of William and Mary, 1958; Calif. lic. real estate broker. Career: asst. in charge of prodn. Wilding Studios, Chgo. 1964; pres. Adams Financial Services, Los Angeles 1965-; writer, producer, dir. (motion pictures) The Glass Cage, co-writer Dirty Mary/ Crazy Larry, Viva Knievel; contbg. writer Once Upon a Time in America; TV panelist Window on Wall Street; contbr. articles to profl. fin. and real estate jours.; recipient Am. Rep. award San Francisco Film Festival, Cork Ireland Film Fest. 1961; mem. Writer's Guild Am., Los Angeles Bd. Realtors, Beverly Hills Bd. Realtors (income, inv. div. steering com.), Westside Realty Bd. (dir.), Los Angeles Ventures Assn. (dir.), Rotary Internat.; Jonathan Club, Round Table, Toastmasters Internat.; mil: USNR 1959. Ofc: Winning Visions, Inc. 425 N Alfred St Los Angeles 90048

SANTOS, AQUILINO BOCOBO, realty co. owner; b. Dec. 26, San Nicolas, Ilocos Norte, Phil.; s. Valeriano S. and Margarita (Bocobo) S.; m. Juanita Peralta Cortina, Sept. 8, 1946; child: Michael A., b. 1959; edn: AA, San Diego St. Coll. (now SDSU) 1930s; law stu. Cosmopolitan Coll. of Law, Manila 1948-51; BA, Calif. Western Univ. (now US Internat. Univ.) 1955, MA, 1957. Career: counselor, contact rep., US Vets. Adm., 1946-52; real estate, life & disability ins. broker/owner, San Diego 1952-66, 1975-; empl. counselor, State of Calif. Employment Devel. Dept., S.D. 1965-74; civic bds: Phil.- Am. Bus. & Profl. Soc. of San Diego County (founder, Achievement Award 1977), The Phil.-Am. Community of San Diego County, Inc. (cofounder, permanent adviser), San Diego County Affirmative Action Advy Bd., Am. Legion (state tech. adviser Commn. on Americanism 1990-91, past comdr. Post 625 22d dist. Calif.), mem. U.S.Internat. Univ. Alumni Assn. & Pres.'s Club; mil: sgt. US Army 1943-45; R.Cath.; rec: tennis, horticulture. Res: 827 26th St San Diego 92102 Ofc: A.B.Santos Realty, PO Box 8217 San Diego 92102

SAPAN, YISROEL PINCHAS, obstetrician, gynecologist; b. Feb. 15, 1942, Brooklyn, N.Y.; s. Michel and Basha (Hordes) S.; m. Pnina, Apr. 2, 1967; children: Shaindyl Pia b. 1968, Faivel Yaakov b. 1969, Yonason Yosef b. 1981; edn: BS cum laude, Bklyn Coll. 1961; MD, St. Univ. N.Y. 1965; lic. Am. Bd. Ob-Gyn. Career: intern Long Island Jewish Hosp., New Hyde Park, N.Y. 1965-66; resident North Shore Hosp., Manhasset, N.Y. 1966-69; ob-gyn. USAF Richards-Gebaur AFB, Mo. 1969-70, chief of ob-gyn. 1970-71; staff ob-gyn. Kaiser Permanente Med. Group, San Francisco 1971-; vol. physician Hospice of Marin, San Rafael 1977-; awards: Kaiser Hosp. Tchr. of Year 1984, Chabad of Marin Honoree 1988; mem: S.F. Med. Soc., Am. Coll. Ob-Gyn., Calif. Perinatal Assn., CMA, Chabad of Marin (co-founder 1984-); article pub. in profl. jour. 1973; mil: capt. USAF 1969-71; Jewish; rec: Torah study. Address: 2200 O'Farrell St San Francisco 94115

SAPIANO, JOSEPH M., association executive, marine explorer; b. June 7, 1962, Central Falls, R.I.; s. James A. Sap and Angela Zobina Page; steps. Jack L. Page; edn: BS, So. Oregon St. Coll., 1982. Career: pres. Tech. Support Svs. Walnut Creek, 1985-87; cons. U.S. Army, S.F. Presidio; systems mgr. Photo & Sound, San Francisco 1987-88; MIS splst. Syva Corp., Mountain View, 1988-89; mem., pres., chmn. bd., dir. Pacific Coast Soc. of Marine Explorers, Mountain View, 1989-, co-ed quarterly log: Pacific Explorer (1990, 91), coauthor annual marine art book: Oceanic Explorer (1991); faculty World College West, Petaluma, 1988-89; mem: AOPA, Calif. Acad. Scis., Cousteau Soc.; L.D.S. Ch.; rec: photog., scuba, pvt. pilot, hiking. Res: 385 Old La Honda Rd Woodside 94062 Ofc: PCSME 334 State St Ste 106 Los Altos 94022

SARTINI, RICHARD LEE, physician; b. June 23, 1946, Meriden, Conn.; s. Silvio Joseph and Lena Josephine (Cacioli) S.; edn: BA, Holy Cross Coll. 1968; MD, Tufts Univ. Med. Sch. 1972. Career: intern, med. resident Univ. Cincinnati 1975; pulmonary fellow UC Irvine 1980; internist Alexian Bro. Hosp., San Jose 1976-78; pulmonologist San Clemente Hosp., San Clemente 1981-88; med. dir. respiratory therapy San Clemente Hosp. 1981-88; mem: Am. Coll. Chest Physicians (fellow), A.C.P., AMA, CMA, Am. Soc. of Int. Medicine, Nat. Assn. Med. Directors Respiratory Care, Calif. Thoracic Soc., Orange Co. Med. Assn.; R.Cath.; rec: French, skiing. Res: 169 High Dr Laguna Beach 92651

SASS, JAMES ROBERTUS, international commodities trader, investment manager; b. Mar. 6, 1945, Bartlesville, Okla.; s. Andrew Michael and Norma Bea (Hegwer) S.; m. Diane Marie Quandt, July 12, 1979 (div. 1991); children:

Charlene, John, Carridad; edn: AA in Behavioral Sci., Coll. of Marin, 1974; BA, San Francisco State Univ., 1976. Career: devel. fin. mgr. Calif. Equity Investment Group, San Rafael, Calif. 1974-76; v.p. fin. Group 80, Inc., S.F. 1976-80; pres. Mass. Plan, Inc., Pittsfield, Mass. 1980-82, Republic Mortgage & Investment Corp., Cocoa Beach, Fla. 1982-86, InterAmerican Fin. & Trade Group, Miami, Fla. 1986-88, Ocean Star Internat. Corp., San Rafael 1988-90; ptnr. Orchid Internat., San Rafael 1990-; mng. ptnr. J.R. Sass and Assocs., San Rafael,1988-; pres. InterAmerican Food Products, San Rafael 1990-93; ptnr. Four C's Internat. Corp., San Rafael 1991-93; gen. ptnr Equity Ptnrs. IV, San Rafael 1991-; gen. ptnr. Cencal Devel. Fund, San Rafael 1991-92; dir. Firebird Internat. Inc., Petaluma 1991-; gen. ptnr. Cencal Devel. Fund II, San Rafael 1993; bd. dirs. Zelinsky Ctr. and Mus., Moscow, Russian Federation; Cybertech Joint Venture, Minsk, Republic of Belarus; Land and Timber Holdings, Ltd., Belize City, Belize; Internat. Peninsular S.A. de C.V., Mex.; cons. Mitsui Trading Co., Georgetown, Grand Cayman 1986-; awards: recipient grant and scholarship NSF, Okla. State Univ. 1962, Tex. Chem. Coun. award 1963; decorated two Bronze Stars, Purple Heart and others, US Army for service in Vietnam 1967-68; appt. chmn. of the US Trade Advy. Bd., WDC 1993; mem. MENSA, US Coun. for Internat. Bus., Am. Assn. Exporters and Importers, World Trade Ctr. Club, US C. of C., Am. Legion, Union Entrepreneurs Republic Belarus; state v.p. Young Rep., Bishop, Tex. 1963-64; past chpt. pres. US Jaycees, Vacaville, Calif. 1978; mem: Am. Vets, Alliance, San Rafael 1990, Commonwealth Club of Calif., S.F. 1993, San Francisco Internat. Program, S.F. 1993; author: (pamphlet) Investing in Mexican Real Estate, 1988; (booklet) Business In Kazakhstan, A Handbook for the Commercial Traveler, 1993; mil: sgt., US Army, 1966-72; rec: sailing, travel, martial arts, archaeology, international law study. Res: 325 Fairhills Dr San Rafael 94901-1110

SAUERS, LAWRENCE BARBER, fundraising executive; b. April 19, 1946, Bethlehem, Pa.; s. William Francis and Joyce Ruth (Barber) S.; m. Janine Laura Baldewicz, June 4, 1983; 1 dau. Tess; edn: BA, UC Santa Barbara, 1972; JD, George Mason Coll. Law St. Univ., Va. 1979; Internat. cert. in fundraising Loyola Marymount Univ., 1987. Career: legal intern U.S. Commn. Civil Rights, congressional primary coordinator 1976-79; exec. dir. Sportsmen's Club, City of Hope, L.A. 1979-81; Pacific reg. dir. St. Jude Childrens Research Hosp., Memphis, Tenn. 1982-84; Foundation pres. and development counsel Mount Diablo Med. Center, Concord 1984-; honors: Phi Delta Phi (pres.), Phillip C. Jessup Internat. Moot Ct. Best Oralist 1977, v.p. Internat. Law Soc. 1976-77; mem: Contra Costa Century Club (program chair), Internat. Platform Assn., Concord C.of C., Rotary Internat. (Paul Harris Fellow); civic bds: Concord Pavilion Devel. Board, No. Calif. Songwriters' Assn.; mil: capt. AUS Spl. Forces 1966-70; Combat Infantryman Badge, Parachutist Badge, Jungle Expert Badge, Bronze Star, Air Medal w. Clusters, Vietnamese Honor Medal, Aircraft Crew Chief Wings; rec: reading, music, skiing, walking. Res: 309 Mountaire Pkwy Clayton CA 94517

SAUNDERS, FRANK HENRY, private investigator, police court expert witness; b. Dec. 6, 1934, Rochester, NY; s. Wm. H., Sr. and Frances E. (Lovejoy) S.; m. Michelle Anne Lamar, July 18, 1981; edn: Univ. of Ariz. (Tucson) 1954-6, 1958-9, UC Santa Cruz 1982; Calif. lic. Pvt. Investigator 1982; Qual. Police Ct. Expert, State Ct. 1981, Federal Ct. 1983. Career: investigator Continental Casualty Ins., 1964; ofcr. Santa Monica Police Dept. 1965-80; expert police ct. witness, prin. Frank Saunders Investigations, Santa Cruz, 1981-; recipient medal of valor City of Santa Monica 1978, citations Santa Monica City Council, State Sen. Paul Priolo 1967, commendn. S.M. Chief of Police (1967, 78), listed Who's Who Am. Law Enforcement, Intl. Directory of Disting. Leadership, Who's Who in West, Who's Who in World; mem: Nat. Assn. Chiefs of Police, Nat. Forensic Center, Santa Monica Police Assn. (founder/ed. newsmag. Soundoff 1970-79), Santa Monica Retired Police Assn., Monterey Co. Peace Ofcrs Assn. Peace Ofcrs Research Assn. of Calif., Americans for Effective Law Enforcement, Intl. Platform Assn.; club: Imperial Courts Tennis (soquel); mil: A/2c USAF 1956-58; Republican; Prot.; rec: tennis, bicycling, creative writing. Ofc: Frank Saunders & Assocs., POB 1730 Capitola 95010

SAUNDERS, SALLY L., writer, poet, poetry therapist; b. Jan. 15, 1940, Bryn Mawr, Pa.; d. Lawrence W. and Dorothy (Love) Saunders; edn: att. Temple Univ., 1962-63, summer stu. Sophia Univ. (in Tokyo) 1963, We. Ill. Univ. (in Africa) 1964; BS, George Williams Coll., 1965; coursework in tchg., The New Sch. of Soc. Res., N.Y.C. 1968-69. Career: poet; pub. poems in 2 hardback books of poetry: Pauses (1978), Fresh Bread (1982), Golden Quill Press; The Times Literary Supplement (London), The New York Times, N.Y. Times Internat. Edit., Empire of The Denver Post, Wormwood Rev., Quaker Life, Mark Twain Jour., New Athenaeum, Villager, The Cristian Sci. Monitor, Univ. Penn. Literary Rev., The Hartford Courant, others; tchr., lectr., num. readings at poetry workshops, bookstores, frequent guest on radio and tv talk shows; group worker Dorchester (Mass.) Settlement House, summer 59, Margaret Fuller House, Cambridge, Mass., summer 51/61; asst. Ten Acre Sch., Wellsley, Mass. 1960-61; group wkr. Univ. House, Phila., 1961-63; vol. Good Shepherd Mission, Fort Defiance, Az., 1963; group wkr. Young Mens Jewish Ctr., Chgo., 1965-66; wkr. Office of Econ. Opp., King Ferry (NY) Migrant Camp, summer 1965; poetry therapist/grant recipient (2) The Inst. of The Penn. Hosp. of Phila.; grantee City

of Phila. to tch. poetry writing to children in pub. libraries, U.S. State Dept. to tch. poetry writing schs. in We. Penn., San Francisco YWCA to tch. poetry writing workshops; lectr./tchr. The Miquon (Pa.) Sch., The Montgomery Country Day Sch., Wynnewood, Pa., The Agnes Irwin Sch., Rosemont, Pa., The Shipley Sch., Bryn Mawr, Pa., The Phelps Sch., Malvern, Pa., The Ballard Sch., N.Y., Chestern County (Pa.) Adult Night Sch.; poetry awards include: Pa. Poetry Soc. prize poem 1963, Nat. League of Am. Pen Women best poet 1965, Poetry Soc. of Ga. hon. mention, The Poetry Day Book Award -Spearman Pubs. 1966, The Nutmegger Book Award 1967, Phila. Writers' Conf. 3d prize 1968, Wilory Farm Poetry Contest finalist 1981; mem: Assn. of Am. Poetry Therapy, Internat. Women's Writing Guild, Poets' and Writers' Guild (NYC), Poetry Soc. Am., Pen and Pencil Club, Assn. for Humanistic Psychology, Nat. Writers Club, Press Club S.F., Assn. for Poetry Therapy, Ina Coolbrith Cir., Acad. of Am. Poets; biog. listings in: Who's Who of Am. Women, Who's Who in Am., Ency. of Am. Biography, others. Res: Apt #501 2030 Vallejo St San Francisco 94123 Ofc: 617 Williamson Rd Bryn Mawr PA 19010

SAVAGE, GRETCHEN SUSAN, information services company president; b. Jan. 15, 1934, Seattle, Wash.; m. Terry R. Savage, Sept. 26, 1964; children: Terry C., Christopher W., Richard T.; edn: BA, UCLA 1955. Career: head librarian Douglas Missiles & Space Systems, Santa Monica 1957-63; div. dir. NASA Scientific & Tech. Info. Facility, Bethesda, Md. 1963-64; cons. in library automation, WDC and Calif. 1964-67; pres. Savage Info. Services, Torrance 1977-; honors: Phi Beta Kappa, Motorboard, Delta Phi Upsilon, Pi Lambda Theta; mem: Spl. Libraries Assn. (chair info. tech. div. 1985-86, secty. 1980-82, chair cons. sect. library mgmt. div. 1982-83, profl. devel. com. 1988-90), Am. Soc. Info. Sci. (profl. devel. com. 1989-), Assn. Records Mgrs. & Adminstrs., Soroptimists Internat. (bd. mem.), Alpha Phi, Chorusliners (pres. 1989-90), S. Bay Infant Center (bd. mem.), New Place Theatre Co. (bd. mem.); num. papers presented to profl. orgns. and confs.; rec: gardening, cooking. Res: 30000 Cachan Pl Rancho Palos Verdes 90274 Ofc: Savage Information Services 2510 W 237th St Ste 200 Torrance 90505

SAXENA, AMOL, podiatrist; b. June 5, 1962, Stanford, Calif.; s. Arjun N. and Veera (Saxena) S.; m. Karen Palermo, Aug. 11, 1985; children: Vijay b. 1988, Tara b. 1991; edn: DPM (cum laude), BS biol. scis., William M. Scholl Coll. of Podiatric Medicine, 1988. assoc. (bd. eligible pod. surg.) Am. Coll. of Foot Surgeons, 1990. Career: podiat. surgical resident VA Med. Ctr. Westside, Chgo. 1988-89; pvt. pod. practice specializing in sports medicine, pediatric foot problems, podiatric surgery, 1989-, hosp. affils. El Camino and Stanford Univ. Hosps.; team podiatrist Stanford Univ., Univ. of Notre Dame Football, and local high sch. athletic teams, 1989-; podiatrist, med. staff 1992 U.S. Olympic Track & Field Trials; Fellow Am. Acad. Podiat. Sports Medicine 1990; athletic footwear cons. Puma-Etonic-Tretorn, 1986-; guest lectr. podiat. surg. and sports medicine Am. Coll. Foot Surgeons, Calif. and Scholl Colls. of Podiat. Medicine, various orgs.; listed Who's Who in the World 1993; contbr. articles and columns for RunCal mag., others; Republican; rec: running. Res: 840 Ames Ave Palo Alto 94303 Ofc: 2204 Grant Rd Ste 203 Mountain View 94040

SCANNELL, WILLIAM EDWARD, management consultant, aerospace company executive; b. Nov. 11, 1934, Muscatine Iowa; s. Mark Edward and Catharine Pearson (Fowler) S.; m. Barbara Hoemann, 1957; children: Cynthia b. 1958, Mark b. 1959, David b. 1961, Terri b. 1962, Stephen b. 1966; edn: BS, Univ. Nebr., Omaha 1961; BS indsl. engring., Ariz. St. Univ. 1966; MSE systems engring., So. Methodist Univ. 1969; Western St. Univ. Coll. Law 1981-82; PhD psychology, U.S. Internat. Univ., 1991. Career: master navigator, lt. col. USAF (Ret.) 1954-75: aviation cadet, navigator bombardier B-47 Strategic Air Command; chief mgmt. engring. team hdqtrs. USAF Europe; 182 combat missions, forward air controller O-2A DaNang, Vietnam; pgm. mgr. USAF Hq., Air Staff, mem. AF Operating Budget Review Com., asst. to the Dir. Orgn. & Mgmt. Planning Office, US Secty. of Defense, decorated D.F.C. (4), Air Medal (12), Meritorious Service Medal; acct. exec. Merrill Lynch, Pierce, Fenner and Smith; sr. res. engr., econ. analysis, prog. engring. chief ILS Engring., engr. chief, logistic planning/analysis, prog. mgr. CX Aircraft, mgr. sys. support Ground Launched Cruise Missile, mktg. mgr. advanced space pgms., pgm. mgr. MX composite deployment module, General Dynamics 1977-84; mgr. Integrated Logistics Support, Northrop/Electronics, Hawthorne, mgr. pgm. planning & scheduling Northrop B-2 Division, 1984-91; pres. Scannell and Associates, Borrego Springs 1991-; adj. faculty U.S. Internat. Univ., San Diego 1991-; cons. Imperial Co. Mental Health Dept., El Centro 1992-; honors: Psi Chi (psych. hon. soc.), 1st. in class Merrill Lynch Acct. Exec. Tng. Sch.; mem: Am. Inst. Industrial Engrs. (sr. mem.), Nat. Mgmt. Assn., Am. Psychol. Assn. 1992-, Calif. Psychol. Assn. 1992-, Soc. for Indsl. and Organizational Psychology; author: The Nature of Motivation in Aerospace Executives (1991); club: Coronado Cays Yacht; Republican; R.Cath. Res: 692 Horseshoe Rd Borrego Springs 92004 Ofc: P.O. Box 2392 Borrego Springs 92004 Tel:619/767-3077

SCEMONS, DONNA J., executive public health nurse; b. April 20, 1947, Chicago, Ill.; d. Harold M. and June Elaine (Sellers) Strange; edn: cert. enterostomal therapy, USC; AA, Trade Tech. Coll. Los Angeles; BS nursing, CSU; MA health. Career: patient care coordinator Visiting Nse. Assn. L.A. 1979-80; therapy dir. home health Med. Center Tarzana 1980-81; dir. home care and infusion, Shield Healthcare, Van Nuys 1981-83; corp. dir. home health NSI, Beverly Hills 1983-87; exec. dir. home health and hospice St. Joseph Med. Ctr., Burbank 1987-90; cons., lectr. Healthcare Devel. System, Panorama City 1989; exec. pub. health nse. St. Joseph Med. Center, Burbank 1989-90; pres. Healthcare Systems, 1989; v.p. Advanced Nursing Svs., 1990; lectr., faculty Azuza Pacific Univ. 1988-; faculty Learning Tree Univ., Chatsworth 1986-; lectr. UCLA 1986-88; honors: Who's Who in Am.; mem: Calif. Assn. Health Scis. at Home (bd. mem. 1989), Mt. St. Marys Coll. (advy. bd.), So. Calif. Pub. Health Assn., Internat. Assn. Enterostomial Therapist, Am. Heart Assn.; articles and article reviews pub. in profl. jours. (1984-); rec: photog., computers. Res: 13314 Winfield Panorama City 91402 Ofc: Advanced Nursing Services 1800 N Highland St #306 Los Angeles 90028

SCHAELCHLIN, PATRICIA ANN, historian, writer; b. July 7, 1924, Flint, Mich.; d. Norbert Louis and Minnie Ida (Klein) McKeown; m. Juerg W. (Bob), April 20, 1946; children: Anne b. 1947, Margaret b. 1951, Kenneth b. 1958; edn: BA Anthropol., S.D. St. Univ. 1970; MA, 1979. Career: hist. res. pvt. individuals & co.; preparation nomination forms for city & nat. hist. site desig. 1974-86; supr. Office Hist. Preservation Sacto., "La Jolla, A Historical Inventory" 1977; hist. res. S.D. Assoc. Govt., "Carlsbad Survey" 1978; cons. City of S.D. "Barrio Logan & Logan Heights Survey" 1979; mem. La Jolla Town Council Coms. Centennial 1985-87; Cultural & Arts Com. 1985-88; honors: Appreciation Placque S.D. Rowing Club 1978, Save Our Heritage Orgn. Predl. Award 1981, City of S.D. Commendation 1983, Co. of S.D. Proclamation (declaring Sept. 23, 1983, as "Patricia A. Schaelchlin Day In San Diego", Who's Who in S.D.; mem: Save Our Heritage Ogn. (bd. mem. 1975-84, pres. 1978-79), San Diegans for the Rowing Clubhouse Inc. (bd., pres. 1981-83), Save the Coaster Com. 1981-84, Save Our Heritage Orgn. (Ad Hoc Com. Chmn. 1981-84), Nat. League of Am. Pen Women (La Jolla Br. pres. 1989-90), La Jolla Womans Club 1978-; civic: S.D. Hist. Site Bd. (v.chair 1978-80), La Jollans Inc. (v.chair 1981-83), Comm. Planners Com. (bd. 1982-83), La Jolla Hist. Soc. Bd. (life mem., bd. 1988-, v.p. 1990-), Friends of the Library (bd. 1986-7, pres. 1987-8); publs: contbr. Heritage, S.D. Home/Garden Mag. (1979-81), Schaelchlin's Olde La Jolla, La Jolla Report (1982-83), Centennial, La Jolla Light Newspaper (1986-87), Rest Haven, S.D. Hist. Jour. (1983), The Little Clubhouse on Steamship Wharf: S.D. Rowing Club 1888-1983 (1984), La Jolla The Story Of A Community 1887-1987 (Friends of La Jolla Library, 1988); R.Cath.; rec: San Diego hist. research. Adress: 1257 Virginia Way La Jolla 92037

SCHAFF, ALFRED, microelectronics consultant, research & development lecturer; b. June 8, 1920, Panama; s. Alfred and Juanita (Krogstadt) S.; m. Flavia Olingi, Oct. 3, 1949; children: Edward b. 1950, (by prev. marriage) Anita b. 1943, Thomas b. 1944; edn: BSME, Calif. Inst. of Tech. 1941; PhD, Kensington Univ. 1986; FAA Lic. Airline Transport Pilot, Aircraft & Eng. Mech. Career: maint. supt. Pan Am.-Grace Airways, 1941-44, capt. 1946-51; large liquid rocket test engr. Aerojet General, Azusa Plant 1951-57, mgr. Test & Field Service Div., Solid Rocket Plant 1957-60, mgr. Spl. Solid Rocket Projects 1960-65, engring. mgr. Nuclear Rocket Test Facility 1965-69; v.p./gen. mgr. (dir. R&D) Ametek/Micro Electronics, El Segundo 1969-87; mem. Am. Rocket Soc. 1951-, ISHM 1976-, IEEE 1975-, SME 1986-, ASTM 1986-, Associate Calif. Inst. of Technology; 2 US patents; publs: An Analysis of Evaporative Rate Analysis (Am. Chem. Soc. 1971), Test Facility for 5000 MW Nuclear Rocket Propulsion Service (AIAA 1967), A Look At Amateur Rocket Experimentation 1958, Understanding Solid Propellant Rocket Safety (Am. Ordinance Soc. 1959), Some Observations Relative to ERA Data Reduction (ACS 1970), Mechanical Considerations for Solid State Pressure Transducers (ISATA, Florence, Italy 1981); Republican; Fundamentalist; rec: flying. Res: 8143 Billowvista Dr Playa Del Rey 90293

SCHAMBER, GARY ALLAN, entrepreneur, management consultant, author, and self made multi-millionaire; b. Sept. 13, 1944, Maywood, Calif.; s. son Jean W. Schamber; m. Dianne L., May 27, 1968; children: Tammy b. 1969, John b. 1970, Robert b. 1972; edn: BA, CSU Los Angeles, 1966; Citrus Belt Law Sch., 1981. Career: former top mgmt. exec. with 6 nat. and internat. cos.: Schick Safety Razor Co., Milford, Ct., Kitchens of Sara Lee, Deerfield, Ill., Cadbury Schweppes Inc., Stamford, Conn., Loctite Permatex Inc., Cleveland, Oh., Demets Inc., Chgo., Ill., Manco Tape Inc., Cleveland, Oh.; founder and owner eleven various cos.; author mgmt. cassette tape program and book: Anyone Can Be A Millionaire (c. 1990); owner two Del Taco fast food franchises, parent co. Schamber & Assocs.; mem. bd. dirs. of sev. orgs. and cos., 1970s-; mil: USMC 1962; Republican; rec: sports, reading; hobby: Rolls Royce autos. Address: 1021 Coronet Dr Riverside 92506

SCHECHTER, FREDERICK GARY, cardiac-thoracic-vascular surgeon; b. April 13, 1941, New York; s. Victor and Gertrude Elaine (Silinsky) S.; m. Roberta Rubin, Oct. 3, 1964; children: Naomi b. 1966, Danielle b. 1969, Damon b. 1972; edn: BS cum laude, Queens Coll. City Univ. N.Y. 1961; MD, SUNY Downstate Med. Ctr. 1965; bd. cert. Am. Bd. Surgery 1972, Am. Bd. Thoracic Surgery 1974. Career: surg. res. fellow St. Univ. N.Y. Downstate Med. Center 1967-68, surg. intern and resident 1965-71; cardiac surg. fellow N.Y. Univ. 1971-73; asst. instr. surg. SUNY Downstate Med. Center 1966-71, clin. instr. surg.

N.Y.U. Med. Center 1973, instr. surg. 1974; asst. prof. surg. Louisiana St. Univ. Med. Center, New Orleans 1974-79, assoc. prof. surg. 1979-84, actg. head thoracic and cadiovascular surg. 1977-81; pvt. practice cardiac, thoracic and vascular surgery, Whittier 1984-; med. dir. Advanced Cardiovascular Surgical Care -A Med. Group, also Advanced Thoracic Surgical Care, A Med. Group; assoc. clin. prof. UC Irvine Coll. Med. 1984-; chmn. thoracic and cardiovascular surgery Presbyterian Intercommunity Hosp., Whittier 1988-89; apptd. clove cigarette sci. advy. bd. Calif. Dept. Hlth. Svs. 1986; research in thoracic trauma, staging of bronchogenic cancer, coronary artery surg.; discovered index case of pulmonary damage associated w. smoking clove cigarettes; awards: Upjohn Achievement award for outstanding surgical res. 1968, Am. Heart Assn. res. award, E.G. Schlieder Found. grantee (1976-79); mem: A.C.S. (fellow), Am. Coll. Cardiol. (fellow), Am. Coll. Chest Physicians (fellow), Am. Coll. Preventative Med. (fellow), Am. Assn. Surgeons of Trauma (fellow), N.Y. Acad. Scis., The Harvey Soc., So. Thoracic Surgical Assn., Soc. Thoracic Surgeons, Assn. Mil. Surgeons of US, New Orleans Surgical Soc., Assn. for Academic Surgery, Whittier Acad. of Medicine, Am. Diabetes Assn. (profl. sect.); civic: Boys Scouts Am., Boys and Girls Club Whittier; mil: capt. USAR; rec: orchidist, photog., sailing, woodworking. Ofc: 7630 S Painter Ave Ste B Whittier 90602

SCHIELE, PAUL ELLSWORTH, JR., science writer, educator, consultant; b. Nov. 20, 1924, Phila.; s. Paul Ellsworth Sr. and Maud (Barclay) S.; m. Sarah Irene Knauss, Aug. 20, 1946; children: Patricia S. Tiemann, Sandra S. Kicklighter, Deborah S. Hartigan; edn: AT, Temple Univ., 1949; BA, LaVerne Univ., 1955; MA, Claremont Graduate Sch., 1961; PhD, U.S. Internat. Univ., San Diego 1970; Calif. secondary tchg. creds., 1961. Career: tchr. sci. and math. Lincoln High Sch., Phila. 1956-57; tchr., coordinator Ontario School Dist., Ontario, Calif. 1957-65; cons. mathematics and sci., Hacienda La Puente Unified Sch. Dist., 1965-75; asst. prof. CSU Fullerton, 1975-83; owner/pres. Creative Learning Environments and Resources (CLEAR), Glendora 1983-, Sci. Curriculum cons., 1983-; author and writer: Model units for 21 Sci. Activity books-Title III, ESEA project; numerous articles for profl. mags. incl. Teaching Tools, Science Teacher, Nat. Aeronautics, The Instructor, 1960-82; 9+ sound film strips in sci., incl. Western Birds, Processes of Science; 2 sci. educational games; editor 21 Science Activity books ESEA Title III project; writer & co-director TV series (SCI-TV) Los Angeles; author: Primary Science (science text, tchr.'s manual, 4 film strips) 1972-1976; editor Living World (sci. text, games) 1974-; appt. advy. com. Sci. and Humanities Symposium, Calif. Mus. Sci. and Industry, 1974; mem: Calif. Music Theater, Calif. Elem. Edn. Assn. (hon.), Nat. PTA (hon.), Calif. Inter-Science Council (pres., chmn. 1971), Elem. Sch. Scis. Assn. (pres. advy. bd. 1967), Phi Delta Kappa (charter mem., project dir.), Internat. Platform Assn., ABIRA; Republican; Lutheran; Res: 231 N Catherine Park Dr Glendora 91740

SCHIRMER, JOHN RAYMOND, printer, investor; b. June 28, 1910, Miles City, Mont.; s. John Valentine and Mary Ellen (Danaher) S.; m. Lois Steverson, Dec. 21, 1961; edn: BA, Univ. Wash. Seattle 1941; tchg. cert., Univ. Montana Billings 1936; FCC lic., US Maritime Commn., Boston, Mass. 1943; printing cert., Calif. Comm. Coll., 1953; Hon. degree E. Mont. State Coll. Career: factory sales rep., Liggett & Myers Tobacco Co., Billings, Mont. 1932-34; public sch. educator, Mont. Dept. of Edn. Klein & Big Horn Counties 1936-41; welder Seattle-Tacoma Shipbuilders, Seattle 1942-43; chief radio ofcr. US Maritime Commn., Pacific Ocean Theater 1942-46; equip. engr. Western Elec. Co., Cicero, Ill. 1946-51; journeyman printer Los Angeles Times 1953-75; officer L.A. Superior Ct. 1968; indep. fin. investor assoc. Property Mortgage Co., L.A. area 1975-; mil: pvt. US Army 76th Field Arty. Citizens Mil. Tng. Corps, Ft. Russell, Cheyenne, Wyo. 1928; pvt. Montana Nat. Guard 1936-37; chief radio USN 1942; US Maritime Commn., Gallups Island, Mass., PTO 1942-47; Republican (Presdl. Task Force); Prot.; rec: wildlife, volunteer work, landscaping, reading. Res: 8501 E Drayer Ln South San·Gabriel 91770-4209 Ofc: Los Angeles Times Mirror Los Angeles 90053

SCHMID, RUDI (RUDOLF), professor of medicine and medical school dean emeritus; b. May 2, 1922, Glarus, Switzerland, naturalized Apr. 7, 1954; s. Rudolf and Bertha (Schiesser) S.; m. Sonja D. Wild, Sept. 17, 1949; children: Isabelle b. 1952, Peter R. b. 1955; edn: BA, Gymnasium, Zurich 1941; MD, Univ. of Zurich 1947; PhD, Univ. of Minn., 1954. Career: asst. prof. medicine Harvard Med. Sch., Boston 1959-62; prof. medicine Univ. Chicago, Ill. 1962-66; Univ. Calif., San Francisco 1966-91, dean Sch. of Medicine UCSF, 1983-89, assoc. dean for internat. relations UCSF, 1989-, prof. emeritus on recall 1991-; awards: Friedenwald Award, Am. Gastroent. Assn. 1990, Disting. achiev. award Am. Gastroent. Assn. 1980, Am. Assn. Study of Liver Disease 1990, Rudolf Aschoff Medal, Univ. of Freiburg, Germany 1979, Canad. Liver Found. gold medal 1985, Disting. Lectr. Assn. Am. Physicians 1976; mem. Nat. Acad. Scis. USA 1974-, Am. Acad. Arts and Scis. (fellow 1982-), Internat. Assn. Study of Liver (1968-, pres. 1980-82), Am. Assn. Study of Liver Disease (1955-, pres. 1965), Assn. Am. Physician (1963-, pres. 1986); clubs: Bohemian (S.F.), mem. Swiss, British, Am. Alpine Clubs; publs: 200+ articles in peer rev. jours. 1950-; mil: senior investigator USPHS 1955-57; rec: reading, internat. travel, history, skiing, mtn. climbing. Res: 211 Woodland Rd Kentfield 94904 Ofc: Univ. of Calif. San Francisco S-224 San Francisco 94143-0410

SCHMIDT, CYRIL JAMES, research library network director; b. June 27, 1939, Flint, Mich.; s. Cyril August and Elizabeth Josephine (Smith) S.; m. Martha Meadows, May 22, 1965; children: Susan, Emily; edn: BA, Catholic Univ. of Am., 1962; MSLS, Columbia Univ., 1963; grad. study Univ. Tx., Ohio State, 1966-70, PhD, Fla. State Univ., 1974. Career: hd. ref. librarian General Motors Inst., Flint, Mich. 1962-65; assoc. librarian SW Texas State Univ., San Marcos, Tx. 1965-67; head, UG & Reg. Campus Libraries, Ohio State Univ., 1967-70; dir. of libraries SUNY at Albany, NY 1972-79; univ. librarian Brown Univ., Providence, R.I. 1979-81; exec. v.p. Res. Libraries Group, Inc. Stanford 1981-83, v.p./dir. RLIN (res. libraries info. network) 1983-; vis. scholar Univ. Nebr. 1983, Univ. Center of Ga., 1986; awards: fellow Mich. St. Library 1962-63, Pi Sigma Alpha, Title II-B fellow 1970-72, Beta Phi Mu; mem: ALA, Am. Mgmt. Assn. Ofc: Research Libraries Group, Inc., 1200 Villa St Mountain View 94041

SCHMIDT, TERRY LANE, health care executive; b. Nov. 28, 1943, Chgo.; s. LeRoy C. and Eunice P.S.; m. Nancy Lee Anthony; children: Christie Anne, Terry Lane II; edn: BS, Bowling Green State Univ., 1965; MBA health care adminstrn., George Washington Univ., 1971. Career: resident in hosp. adminstrn. Univ. Pittsburgh Med. Ctr., VA Hosp., Pitts. 1968-69; adminstrv. asst. Mt. Sinai Med. Ctr., N.Y.C., 1969-70; asst. dir. Health Facilities Planning Council of Met. Washington, 1970-71; asst. dir. dept. govtl. relations Am. Medical Assn., W.D.C., 1971-74; prin. Physician Svs. Group, pres. Terry L. Schmidt Inc., San Diego 1974-; pres. Physicians Services Group, La Jolla 1987-; exec. director and c.o.o. Emergency Health Assocs., P.C., Phoenix, Az. 1989-91, Charleston Emergency Physicians, S.C., 1990-, Joplin Emergency Physician Assocs. 1991-92, Big Valley Med. Group 1991-92, Blue Ridge Emergency Physicians, P.C. 1992-93, Berkeley Emergency Physicians, P.C. 1992-; pres. Med. Cons. Inc., 1983-84; v.p. Crisis Comms. Corp. Ltd. 1982-90; pres. Washington Actions on Health 1975-78; ptnr. Washington counsel Medicine and Health 1979-81; pres. Ambulance Corp. Am., La Jolla 1984-87; chmn. Univ. Inst. 1992; lectr., p.t. faculty dept. health care adminstrn. George Washington Univ., 1969-84, preceptor 1971-84; asst. prof. Nat. Naval Sch. Health Care Adminstrn. 1971-73; mem. faculty CSC Legislation Insts. 1972-76, Am. Assn. State Colls. and Univs. Health Tng. Insts.; mem. bd. dirs. Nat. Eye Found. 1976-78; author: Congress and Health: An Intro. to the Legislative Process and the Key Participants (1976), A Directory of Fed. Health Resources and Svs. for the Disadvantaged (1976), Health Care Reimbursement: A Glossary (1983), num. articles in profl. jours.; mem. Am. Hosp. Assn., Med. Group Mgmt. Assn., Hosp. Fin. Mgmt. Assn., Med. Group Mgrs., Assn. Venture Capital Groups (bd. 1984-89), Med. Adminstrs. of Calif., San Diego Venture Group (chair 1984-87), UCSD Faculty Club, Alpha Phi Omega (Bowling Green alumni chpt. pres. 1967-70, sec. treas. alumni assn. 1968-71); clubs: George Washington Univ., Nat. Democratic (life), Nat. Republican (life), Capitol Hill. Ofc: 9191 Towne Centre Dr Ste 360 San Diego 92122

SCHMITT, CAROLYN SUE, educator, vocational counselor; b. Dec. 19, 1940, Charleston, W.V.; d. Charles Lee and Louise Mary (DeHainaut) Jarrett; m. Carveth J. R. Schmitt, May 14, 1965; edn: BS in bus. adm., Univ. Charleston, Morris Harvey Coll. 1962; dip. human svcs. UC Riverside Ext. 1971; BS, liberal studies, Univ. NY, Albany 1978; BA, soc. sci., Thomas A. Edison State Coll., Trenton, NJ 1979; MA, edn./manpower adm., Univ. Redlands 1974; tchg. creds: Calif. Comm. Coll. instr. 1979, psychol. 1979, counseling 1979, supv. 1979, Calif. Comm. Personnel Wkr. cred. 1979. Career: adminstrv. asst. TRW Inc., Def. & Space Sys., San Berdo. 1962-63; ins. dept. So. Calif. Mortgage & Loan Corp., San Berdo. 1963-66; empl. counselor Calif. State Empl. Devel. Dept., 1966-78; instr. Pacific Am. Inst./Whitehead Coll., Redlands 1979; sr. voc. supv. rehab.counselor Westside Counseling Center, San Berdo. 1979-80; voc. counselor pvt. practice, Rialto 1980-84; placement splst. Goodwill Ind. of Inland Counties Inc., San Berdo. 1984-85; voc. rehab. counselor/placement splst. Voc-Aid, Inc., Encino 1985-86; employment splst. Lutheran Soc. Services of So. Calif., San Berdo. 1986-87; job search coordinator GE Government Services/Edn. Services/Gen. Electric, San Bernardino 1987-88; tchr. Advocate Schs., Grand Terrace 1989-; honors: recogn. Westside Counseling Ctr. 1980, listed num. biographical dictionaries; mem: Calif. Personnel & Guidance Assn., Calif. Career Guidance Assn., Calif. Rehab. Counselor Assn., Internat. Assn. of Personnel Empls. (chpt. vp 1970); Univ. of Redlands Fellows; Valley Prospectors (Life), Rosicrucian Order AMORC, Phi Kappa Kappa Sor., Modern Woodmen of Am., Nat. Travel Club, Fontana Tour Club, Am. Philatelic Soc., Arrowhead Stamp Club, Am. Topical Assn. (life), Regents Coll. Alumni Assn., Thomas A. Edison St. Coll. Alumni Assn., Univ. of Charleston Alumni Assn., Univ. of Redlands Alumni Assn.; Republican; rec: philately, badminton, hiking. Res: 538 N Pampas Ave Rialto 92376-5258 Ofc: 11980 S Mount Vernon Ave Grand Terrace 92324

SCHMITT, CARVETH JOSEPH RODNEY, corporate credit manager; b. Sept. 10, 1934, Manitowoc, Wisc.; s. Clarence Charles and Thelma June (White) S.; m. Carolyn Sue Jarrett, May 14, 1965; edn: dipl. in bus. adm. & acctg., Skadron Coll. of Bus., San Bernardino 1959; AA in bus. mgmt., San Bernardino Valley Coll. 1962; BS in bus. adm., Univ. Riverside 1970; BS, liberal studies, Univ. of NY, Albany 1977; BA, soc. sci., Thomas A. Edison State Coll., Trenton, NJ 1978; MA, edn./manpower adm., Univ. Redlands 1975; dipl. human

svcs., UC Riverside ext. 1977; Calif. Comm. Coll. instr. cred., counselor, and personnel worker. Career: reg. rep. Ernest F. Boruski Jr., N.Y.C. p.t. 1956-61; acct. Barnum & Flagg Co., San Bernardino, 1959-70; credit mgr. Stationers Corp., 1970-77, office mgr./credit mgr. 1977-83; registered rep., ins. agt. (part-time), Inland Amer. Securities, Inc., 1966-70, reg. rep. Parker-Jackson & Co., 1970-73, LeBarron Securities, Inc., 1974; internal auditor Stockwell & Binney Office Products Centers, 1983-85, corp. credit mgr. 1985-; listed Marquis-Who's Who in West (18, 19, 20, 21, 22 editions), Who's Who in World (9, 10 eds.), Who's Who in Finance and Industry, others; mem: Nevada Mining Assn., (past) North West Mining Assn., (past) Colo. Mining Assn., Gold Prospectors Assn. of Am. (life), Valley Prospectors (life), Nat. Travel Club, Fontana Tour Club, (past) Univ. Redlands Fellows, Am. Philatelic Soc., Arrowhead Stamp Club, Nat. Rifle Assn. (life), Nat. Geog. Soc., Am. Legion, Am. Assn. Retired Persons, Modern Woodmen of Am., Rosicrucian Order AMORC, Masons, Regents Coll. Alumni Assn., Thomas A. Edison State Coll. Alumni Assn., Univ. Redlands Alumni Assn.; mil: Personnel splst. USAF 1954-58, GCM, Nat. Def. medal; Republican; rec: collector first editions, rock collector. Res: 538 N Pampas Ave Rialto 92376-5258 Ofc: Stockwell & Binney Office Products Centers, 420 South E St (POB 5129) San Bernardino 92412

SCHNAPP, ROGER HERBERT, lawyer; b. Mar. 17, 1946, NY, NY; s. Michael Jay and Beatrice Joan (Becker) S.; m. Candice, Sept. 15, 1979; children: Monica Alexis b. 1992; edn: BS, Cornell Univ. 1966; JD, Harvard Sch. of Law 1969; Univ. Mich. 1978; admitted bar: N.Y. 1970, Calif. 1982, US Dist. Cts. (N.Y., Calif.), US Cts. Appeals, US Supreme Ct. 1974. Career: atty. Civil Aeronautics Bd., Wash. DC 1969-70; labor atty. Western Electric, N.Y.C. 1970-71; mgr. employee relations American Airlines, 1971-74; labor counsel Am. Electric Power Service Corp., N.Y.C. 1974-78, senior labor counsel 1978-80; counsel indsl. rels. Trans World Airlines, 1980-81; sr. assoc. Parker, Milliken, Clark & O'Hara, L.A. 1981-82; ptnr. Rutan & Tucker, Costa Mesa 1983-85; ptnr. Memel, Jacobs, Pierno, Gersh & Ellsworth (later Memel, Jacobs & Ellsworth), Newport Beach 1985-87; sole practice, Newport Beach 1987-; trustee Chapman Univ., Orange 1992-; dir. Dynamic Constrn. Co., Laguna Hills 1986-; mem. US Sec. of Labor's Bus. Research Advy. Council 1989-; mem. Orange County Advy. Council and cons. American Arbitration Assn., 1981-; commentator Financial News Network, Santa Monica, 1982-91; political commentator KOCM, Newport Beach, 1990-91; lectr. Cal. Western Law Sch., San Diego, 1981-; mem: Conf. of Railroad and Airline Labor Lawyers; civic: O.C. Sheriffs Advy. Council 1983-; clubs: Center, Balboa Bay; author: Arbitration Issues for the 1980s (1981); govt. rels. columnist Orange County Business J. 1989-91, chief editor Industrial & Labor Relations Forum J. 1964-66; Republican; Jewish. Res: 20 Vienna Newport Beach 92660 Ofc: 4675 MacArthur Ct Ste 430 Newport Beach 92660

SCHNEIDER, EDWARD LEWIS, physician, university dean, gerontology center administrator; b. June 22, 1940, N.Y.C.; s. Samuel and Ann (Soskin) S.; m. Leah Buturain, June 6, 1987; children: Samuel b. 1989, Isaac b. 1993; edn: BS, Rensselaer Polytech., 1961; MD, Boston Univ., 1966. Career: intern and resident N.Y. Hosp., Cornell Univ., 1966-68; staff fellow Nat. Inst. Allergy & Infectious Diseases, Bethesda, Md. 1968-70; res. fellow Univ. Calif., San Francisco 1970-73; chief sect. on cellular aging Nat. Inst. on Aging, Balt., Md. 1973-79; prof. of med. and dir. Davis Inst. on Aging, Univ. Colorado, Denver 1979-80; assoc. dir. Nat. Inst. on Aging, Bethesda 1980-84, deputy dir. 1984-87; dean and exec. dir. Leonard Davis Sch. of Gerontology, USC, Los Angeles 1986-, prof. med. USC Sch. of Medicine 1987-, William and Sylvia Kugel Prof. Andrus Gerontology Ctr., USC, 1989-; scientific dir. Buck Ctr. for Res. in Aging, Novato, Ca. 1989-; awards: Roche Award, Alpha Omega Alpha, Boston Univ. Alumni Award, Disting. lectr. Sigma Xi, Jacobson lectr. Faculty of Med. Univ. of Newcastle upon Tyne, England; mem. Gerontology Soc. of Am. (Fellow), Am. Soc. of Clinical Investigation, AARP; civic: US Naval Acad. sailing squadron coach 1980-86; editor 4 books: The Genetics of Aging (1978), Biological Markers of Aging (1982) Handbooks of the Biology of Aging (1985, 90), Eldercare and the Work Force (1990); rec: sailing, skiing. Ofc: Andrus Gerontology Ctr. 3715 McClintock St Ste 103 Los Angeles 90089-0191

SCHNEIDER, HAROLD NORMAN, actuary; b. Nov. 17, 1950, Los Angeles; s. George Herman and Rosa (Fuller) S.; m. Marsha Carol Shapiro, Apr. 7, 1991; edn: BA, UCLA, 1972; MA, SUNY, Stony Brook, 1973. Career: actuarial analyst Farmers Group Inc., Los Angeles 1973-76, asst. actuary 1976-78, actuary 1978-84, vice pres. 1985-; honors: Phi Beta Kappa; Fellow Casualty Actuarial Soc., mem. Am. Acad. of Actuaries, So. Calif. Cas. Actuarial Club (pres. 1988-89). Ofc: Farmers Insurance Group, Inc. 4680 Wilshire Blvd Los Angeles 90010

SCHNEIDER, MEIER, industrial hygienist/environmental specialist; b. Worcester, Mass.; m. Theresa Bell Gershman; children: Alan L., Leah S. Bergman, Diane F.; edn: BA chem./biol., Univ. Rochester; MS occupatonal and environmental health and safety, CSU Northridge; nat. scis. and soc. studies, CSU Los Angeles; Calif. reg. profl. engr. (PE)- chem., safety; cert. safety profl. (CSP), cert. indsl. hygienist (CIH, Ret.), cert. hazard control mgr. (CHCM) Master Level cert. hazardous mats. mgr. (CHMM) Master Level. Career: sr. chemist L.A. Co. Air Pollution Control Dist., 1948-52; res. splst. Rockwell

Internat., L.A. Div. 1955-68; safety and industrial hygiene coord. Lockheed-California Co., Burbank 1968-70; sr. industrial hygiene engr. Calif. State Dept. Health, 1970-73; industrial hygiene engr. City of Los Angeles dept. personnel, med. svs. div. 1974-81; chief occup. safety and health Met. Water Dist. So. Calif., 1981-87, ret.; assoc. and full prof. p.t. CSU Northridge 1974-88, USC 1976-86, CSU Los Angeles 1981; apptd. State Calif. Advy. Coms.: Noise Control, Cal/OSHA Haz. Chem. Labeling, and Revision exposure limits for airborne toxic substances; lectr. in field USC, UCLA Sch. of Pub. Health, Pomona Coll., L.A. City Coll., CalPoly Pomona, UC Irvine Sch. of Med., CSU L.A., CSU Fullerton, Nat. Safety Council Gr. L.A.; cons. McGraw-Hill Book Co., 1958-68; cons. indsl. hygiene to ind. and govt., contbr. to Nat. Acad. of Scis., W.D.C. study of vapor phase organic air pollutants; honors: Sigma Xi; mem. Am. Indsl. Hygiene Assn. (past pres. So. Calif.), Am. Conf. Govtl. Indsl. Hygienists (chemical agents TLV com.); author book chapt. in An Atty.'s Guide to Engring. (Matthew Bender & Co., 1989), articles in sci. jours., contbr. to Calif. Building Stds. (1971, 72); mil: Ltc. (Ret.) US Army Chem. Corps. Res: 1208 Point View St Los Angeles 90035-2621

SCHNEIDER, RICHARD C., humanities educator; b. Sept. 20, 1927, Jefferson, Wis.; s. Carl F. and Adele (Gau) S.; edn: BA, Carthage Coll., 1948; MDiv, Luther Northwestern Sem., St. Paul, Minn. 1951; MEd, Univ. Texas, Austin 1955; Calif. lic. psychotherapist, 1956-. Career: organizer, administrator Lutheran Church, Dallas, Austin, Corpus Christi, Tx. 1951-55; faculty, adminstr. Carthage Coll., Ill. 1955-56; assoc. prof. psychology and humanities Riverside Community Coll., Riv., Calif. 1956-; awards: NSF psych. seminars, Beloit Coll. 1964, Faculty lectr. Riverside Comm. Coll. 1970, humanities study grantee US Dept. Edn. in India, Egypt, Nigeria 1980, 81, 82; civic: Sierra Club 1979-, Nature Conservancy 1985-, Earthwatch 1985-; publ: (pamphlet) Freedom and Lawful Behavior 1964; Indep.; Unitarian; rec: backpacking, hiking, biking. Res: 24117 Fir Ave Moreno Valley 92553 Ofc: Riverside Community College 4800 Magnolia Ave Riverside 92506

SCHNEIDER, SANFORD, academic physician, administrator; b. Feb. 4, 1938, Tappan, N.Y.; s. Jacob and Ann S.; m. Joan Helene; edn: BA, Univ. Rochester, 1959; MD, New York Univ., 1963. Career: child neurologist; prof. neurology and pediatrics Loma Linda Univ. Sch. of Medicine, 1971-, head div. of child neurology; Fellow Am. Acad. Neurology, Fellow Am. Acad. Pediatrics; mil: capt. USAF 1966-68. Ofc: LLU School of Medicine Div. Child Neurology Rm 150 West Hall 11262 Campus St Loma Linda 92354

SCHNEIDER, WILFRED JOHN, JR., lawyer; b. April 17, 1951, Whittier; s. Wilfred John and Elizabeth (Clay) S.; edn: AA, Rio Hondo Coll. 1972; BA, UCLA 1974; JD, Southwestern Univ. 1978; admitted bar: Calif. 1979, U.S. Dist. Ct. and U.S. Ct. Appeals, 1982. Career: atty., assoc. Chase Rotchford Drukker & Bogust, San Bernardino 1979-87, dir. 1987-; judge pro tem San Bernadino Superior Court, judicial arbitrator San Bernadino, Riverside Counties, Am. Arbitration Assn.; honors: Rio Hondo Coll. student body pres. 1971-72; mem: ABA, San Bernadino Cty. Bar Assn., Los Angeles Cty. Bar Assn., Assn. of So. Calif. Defense Counsel; Republican; Episcopalian. Ofc: Chase Rotchford et al 600 N Arrowhead Ste 201 San Bernardino 92401

SCHNITZER, GARY ALLEN, company executive; b. Jan. 29, 1942, Portland, Oreg.; s. Gilbert and Thelma S.; children: Andrea b. 1968, Greg b. 1973; edn: BS, USC, 1964. Career: exec. v.p. Schnitzer Steel, Oakland 1964-; West Coast rep. No. Calif. chpt. Scrap Iron & Steel Assn. (pres. 1972-73, nat. dir. 1976, 84-86); v.chmn. ISRI fgn. trade comm., No. Calif. chpt. (1974-77, 83-84); awards: Small bus. Oakland C.of C. 1989, innovative recycling Calif. State Waste Mgmt. Bd., Sacto. 1991; civic: Bay Area Tumor Inst. (bd. 1989), Oakland Mus., Alameda Co. Hon. Deputy Sheriff, Oakland C.of C., Soc. Prevention of Child Abuse (bd. 1990-); civic: mem. Oakland Mayor's Emergency Economic Task Force 1993; clubs: Lake Meritt Breakfast (Oakland), Berkeley Tennis, Calif. Tennis, Multhomah Athletic (Portland, Oreg.); Republican; Jewish; rec: reading, tennis, golf, travel. Ofc: Schnitzer Steel Products PO Box 747 Oakland 94604

SCHOETTGER, THEODORE LEO, city official; b. Sept. 2, 1920, Burton, Nebr.; s. Frederick and Louise Cecelia (Gierau) S.; m. Kathlyn Marguerite Hughey, June 3, 1943; children: Gregory Paul, Julie Anne; edn: BSBA (w. distinction), Univ. Nebr., 1948; C.P.A., Calif. Career: sr. acct. Haskins & Sells, Los Angeles 1948-55; controller Beckman Instruments Inc., Fullerton 1955-58, corp. chief acct., 1958-60; treas. Docummun Inc., L.A. 1960-77; fin. director City of Orange, 1977-; fin. com., treas., bd. dirs. Childrens Hosp.; mem: Calif. Soc. CPAs (nat. dir., v.p., past pres. L.A. chpt.), Fin. Execs. Inst., Mcpl. Fin. Ofcrs. Assn., Town Hall of Calif., Beta Gamma Sigma, Alpha Kappa Psi; club: Jonathan; mil: lt. USNR1942-45. Res: 9626 Shellyfield Rd Downey 90240-3418 Ofc: 300 E Chapman Ave Orange 92666-1591

SCHOIJ, SUZANNE CAROL, petroleum engineer; b. July 7, 1951, Chicago, Ill.; d. Edgar and Gladys Rosalie (Rampick) Schoij; edn: BS cum laude, chem. engring., CSU Long Beach 1979; MBA finance, 1992; reg. petroleum engr. Calif. 1986. Career: engr. Amoco Oil, Chgo., Ill. 1977-78; reservoir engr. Exxon USA, Los Angeles 1979-81; sr. process engr. Exxon Research & Engring.,

Florham Park, N.J. 1981-83; sr. petroleum engr. City of Long Beach Oil Properties 1984-; honors: Tau Beta Pi. Ofc: City of Long Beach Oil Properties 333 W Ocean Blvd Long Beach 90802

SCHOONHOVEN, CLAUDIA BIRD, professor; b. Oct. 7, 1943, Highland Park, Mich.; d. Claude Marsh and Glenna Jean (May) Bird; m. Gerald R. Schoonhoven, Dec. 27, 1965; son, Scott G. b. 1971; edn: BA (honors history), Univ. Ill.; MA and PhD, sociol., Stanford Univ. Career: asst. traffic operating mgr., service advisor, cons. Bell System Operating Cos.: Mich. Bell, New England T&T, and Pacific Tel., 1965-68; instr. sociology Chabot Coll. 1969-71; fellow orgns. res. tng. pgm., Stanford Univ. 1972-75, postdoc. fellow decision making in orgns., 1975-77, asst. prof. sociol. dept. Stanford Univ. 1976-77, vis. scholar Stanford Grad. Sch. of Bus. 1984-85; vis. prof. Univ. Santa Clara, Leavey Sch. of Bus. 1986; prof. of organization and mgmt. San Jose State Univ., 1977-; honors: Univ. of Ill. Phi Alpha Theta scholar, L. Noyes scholar, and E.M. Cartier scholar 1965, PHS pre-doctoral fellow 1971, outstanding prof. SJSU Sch. of Bus. (1981, 1982), Phi Kappa Phi (mem. 1981, disting. acad. achiev. award 1984), NASA Faculty Fellow 1983, prin. investigator US Dept. Commerce grants (1985-87, 86-88), Nat. Sci. Found. grantee 1989; mem: Acad. of Mgmt., Am. Sociol. Assn., We. Acad. of Mgmt. (pres.), Strategic Mgmt. Soc., NOW; author: The Innovation Marathon (1989), and num. res. publs.; rec: skiing, sailing. Ofc: Dept. Orgn. and Mgmt. School of Business San Jose State Univ. San Jose 95192

SCHORR, MARTIN M., forensic psychologist; m. Dolores G. Tyson, 1952; edn: AB cum laude, Adelphi Univ., 1949; MS, Purdue Univ., 1953 (pub. Alumni Publications, Purdue Univ. 1952-53); PhD, Denver Univ., 1960; Rhodes Scholarship Balliol Coll., Oxford Univ., England; lic. sch. psychologist 1955, clin. psychologist 1962, forensic splty. 1962; diplomate Am. Bd. of Professional Psychology 1990. Career: chief of clin. psych. services San Diego County Mental Hosp. 1963-67; pvt. practice, specialist forensic examinations, Dektor counterintel. and political violence, 1962-; forensic examiner Superior, Fed. and Mil. Cts., 1962-; assoc. director Timberline Productions, Inc. 1990-; guest prof., abnormal psych., San Diego St. Univ. 1965-68; chief dept. psych. Centre City Hosp. 1976-79; cons. St. Dept. Corrections, Minnewawa 1970-73, Dept. Health, Disability Eval. 1972-75, St. Indsl. Accident Commn. 1972-78, Crim. Justice Adminstrn. 1975-77; cons. Vista Hill Found. (17 yrs), Mercy Hosp. Psychiatric (18 yrs), Foodmaker Corp. (6 yrs), Convent of the Sacred Heart, El Cajon (4 yrs); FAA Examiner, assoc. film dir.; awards: Resolution, Calif. St. Assembly for assistance in formulating Whistleblower Protection Act of 1986; mem: Am. Psychol. Assn., Am. Acad. Forensic Scis., AAAS, Fellow Internat. Assn. of Soc. Psychiat., Internat. Platform Assn., World Mental Health Assn., Mystery Writers Am., PEN Internat., Nat. Writers Club, Mensa Soc. Mail: University City San Diego 92122

SCHRAMBLING, WILLIAM EMMETT, accountancy firm executive; b. June 12, 1947, Phoenix, Ariz.; s. William Leon and Patricia (Collins) S.; m. Alaine Carter; children: Derrik b. 1969, William b. 1972; edn: AA, El Camino Coll. 1967; BS, USC 1970; C.P.A., Calif. 1973. Career: staff acct. Arthur Andersen & Co. 1970-73; ptnr. in charge of predecessor firms 1973-88; owner Schrambling and Assocs., San Francisco 1988-; mem: Am. Inst. CPAs, Calif. Soc. CPAs, Nat. Assn. of Accts.; Democrat; R.Cath.; rec: fishing, old cars. Ofc: Schrambling and Associates One Market Plaza 1770 Steuart Tower San Francisco 94105

SCHROEDER, CORRINE FLORENCE, school psychologist; b. March 3, 1936, Watertown, So.Dak.; d. Leo and Florence Helen (Maher) O'Connor; m. Martin Henry Schroeder, Jr., Aug. 10, 1957; children: Susan b. 1971; edn: BA, San Diego St. Univ. 1958; MA, 1963; Lic. Ednl. Psychologist (LEP), Nat. Cert. Sch. Psychologist (NCSP), Calif. pupil personnel cred. 1965. Career: tchr. San Diego City Schs. 1958-63; Brawley Elem. Sch. Dist. 1963-64; San Diego City Schs. 1964-65, sch. psychologist 1965-; awards: Girl Scouts Silver Service 1982, Green Angel 1983-86, recogn. cert. San Diego City Sch. 1985-86, Bell Jr. H.S. staff person of week / Psychologist Appreciation Day 1989, attendance awards San Diego City Schs. 1987-92; mem: Delta Zeta Sor., CTA, NEA, SDTA, CASP, SAN CASP, San Diego Imperial Council Girl Scouts, AAUW, Heartland Youth Symphony (treas. 1983-84), San Diego Jr. Womens Club (edn. chmn. 1966-69), St. Martins Ch.; rec: travel, crafts, bridge, theater. Ofc: San Diego City Schools.

SCHUCK, LAWRENCE ANDREW, manufacturing co. executive, pharmacist; b. Aug. 23, 1915, Oxnard; s. John Frank and Anna Francis (Bryant) S.; m. Doris H. Altland, July 26, 1941; children: Lawrence B., b. 1943; Thomas B., b. 1946; Michael R., b. 1959; edn: AA, Ventura Coll. 1935; BS in pharm., UC Berkeley 1938; Ensign USNR, Cornell Univ. 1943. Career: pharmacist, Owl Drug Co., 1939-, mgr. 1942; pharmacist Parke-Davis & Co., 1946-, dist. mgr. 1951-, gov. sales supr. Parke-Davis Div. Warner Lambert 1965, ret. 1975, devel. corp. clerk training pgm.; honors: Phi Delta Chi (treas. 1938), treas. UCB Coll. of Pharm. (1938), recipient nat. sales award (new Pontiac) 1947, nat. sales dist. mgr. award 1954, 58; Fellow Am. College Pharmacists 1955; mem. Bay Area Pharmacy Assn., BSA (past councilor), Elks, UC Berkeley Blue & Gold Assn. (life mem. & donor UC Coll. of Pharmacy), American Legion Post 339 (Ventura), V.F.W.

Post 1679 Ventura (life); mil: lt. USNR, decorated 2 combat awards, Presdl. Unit citation for Solomon Island Op., then assigned to Staff of Com Ten, San Jose, P.R. as personnel ofcr. under Adm. Griffin; "Plank Owner" U.S. Navy Memorial; Republican (charter mem. Presdl. Task Force, Charter issue Who's Who in Republican Party); R.Cath.; rec: workshop, keeping current with pharmaceutical devels. Res: 15711 W Telegraph Rd F-125 Santa Paula 93060

SCHUETZ, JOHN MICHAEL, automotive sales executive; b. Apr. 16, 1947, Chgo.; s. Henry Albert and Ann Delores (Kunst) S.; m. Jacqueline Claire Furneaux, Apr. 22, 1972; children: Michael Richard, Sean David; edn: BS in advt., Marquette Univ., 1969. Career: gen. field mgr. Ford Motor Co., San Jose 1972-85; v.p. western region IVECO Trucks of North America, Huntington Beach 1985-91; Nat. Dealer Devel. mgr. Wynn Oil Co. 1992-; dir. Forsyte Research Group, Santa Rosa 1988-; civic: Boy Scouts Am., El Toro (ldr. 1988-), Am. Youth Soccer Orgn., Saddleback Valley (coach 1988); mem. Phi Theta Psi; club: Sun and Sail; mil: lt. US Navy 1969-72; Republican; R.Cath. Res: 21821 Ticonderoga Ln El Toro 92630 Ofc: IVECO Trucks of North America 5500 Bolsa Ave Ste 125 Huntington Beach 92649

SCHULZ, JOHN CHRISTIAN, manufacturing co. executive; b. July 12, 1936, Bklyn.; s. John Valentine and Betty (Dauelsberg) S.; m. Kathleen Brower; children: Alison b. 1963, Christian b. 1968, Amanda b. 1987; edn: BME Rensselaer Polytechnic Inst. 1958; cert. profl. engr., Calif.; cert. mgr. NMA. Career: mgr. quality engring. Bourns Inc., Riverside 1962-64, dir. quality control 1964-68; chief supplier control Gen. Dynamics, Pomona 1969-70, mgr. procurement quality 1970-74, mgr. quality engring. 1974-77, mgr. quality control 1977-80; mgr. quality assur. service Loral Aeronutronic, Newport Beach 1980-; instr. Mt. San Antonio Coll.; current bd. chmn., past pres. Measurement Science Conf. Inc.; mem: ASQC (past chmn., mem. exec. bd.), ASME, Nat. Mgmt. Assn., Riverside Rifle & Pistol Club, Am. Legion; mil: lt. USN, chief engr. USS Pursuit (AGS 17) 1958-62; Rep.; Prot.; rec: photog., shooting. Res: 4492 11th St Riverside 92501 Ofc: Loral Aeronutronic 1000 Ford Rd Newport Beach 92660

SCHUTZ, JOHN ADOLPH, historian, educator; b. Apr. 10, 1919, Los Angeles; s. Adolph John and Augusta K. (Glicker) S.; edn: AB, UCLA 1942, MA, 1943, PhD, 1945. Career: asst. prof. Calif. Inst. of Tech., 1945-53; assoc. prof./prof. Whittier College, 1953-65; prof. of history USC, 1965-91, dean 1976-82; vis. prof. (summers) Univ. of Brit. Columbia 1960, Univ. of Waterloo, Ont. 1966, Boston Coll. 1969, CSCLA 1953-65; trustee Citizens Res. Council; awards: grantee Nat. Endowment for Humanities 1971-74, Danforth Fellow 1959; mem. Am. Hist. Assn. (Pacific Coast Br. pres. 1973, sec.treas. 1951-87), New England Historic Geneal. Soc. (trustee 1988-), Historic Geneal. Soc., Orgn. of Am. Historians, So. Calif. Hist. Soc.; author: The American Republic (1978), The Dawning of America (1981), William Shirley: King's governor of Massachusetts (1961), Spain's Colonial Outpost: California (Boyd & Fraser 1985), chpt. in Generations and Changes: Genealogical Perspectives in Social Hist. (Mercer Univ. Press 1986); jt. editor Golden State Series (Boyd & Fraser, 1979-); chpt. in Making of America (US Ofc. Info. 1988, Univ. N.C. 1992); Democrat; R.Cath.; rec: philately, travel. Res: 1100 White Knoll Dr Los Angeles 90012 Ofc: USC, College Park, Los Angeles 90089-0034

SCHUTZ, WILL, psychologist, educator, consultant; b. Dec. 19. 1925, Chicago, Ill.; s. Carl Milton and Ruth Helen Tausig (Burns) S.; m. Ailish Patricia Mellard, Aug. 24, 1985; children: Laurie b. 1953, Caleb b. 1956, Ethan b. 1966, Dana b. 1971, Ari b. 1976; edn: BA, UCLA 1947; MA, 1950; PhD, 1951. Career: tchg. asst. UCLA 1948-50; lectr., exec. secty. Univ. Chgo. 1950-51; research assoc. prof. Tufts Univ., Medford, Mass. 1953-54; lectr., research assoc. Harvard Univ., Cambridge 1954-58; research educator UC Berkeley 1958-62; assoc. prof. Einstein Med., Bronx, N.Y. 1963-67; sr. assoc. Esalen, Big Sur 1967-75; prof., dept. chmn. Antioch Univ., San Francisco 1978-84; pres. Will Schutz Assoc., Muir Beach 1980-; author: The Truth Option, 1984, Profound Simplicity, 1979, Joy, 1967, FIRO, 1958; mil: lt. USN 1943-45, 1951-53; Jewish; rec: sports, handball. Address: Box 259 Muir Beach 94965

SCHUYLER, ROB R., lawyer; b. Aug. 13, 1932, Larchmont, N.Y.; s. William and Margaret (Sternbergh) S.; widowed 1990; children: Marc Philip b. 1964, Clifford Robert b. 1968, Paul Frederic b. 1969; edn: certificate, Univ. of Paris, Sorbonne Ecole de Scis. Politques, 1950-52; BA, USC, 1955; JD, Univ. Mich., 1958; admitted bar Calif., 1958. Career: atty. pvt. practice in Los Angeles, 1958-73; ptnr. Mihaly, Schuyler & Mitchell, Los Angeles, 1973-; mem: Am. Bar Assn., Calif. State Bar Assn., L.A. Co. Bar Assn. (past chmn. Internat. Law Sect.), Wilshire Bar Assn. (past pres.), Am. Immigration Lawyers Assn. 1973-, Century City Rotary Club 1973-; mil: major US Nat. Guard, USAR, 1959-73; Republican; Episcopalian; rec: skiing, tennis. Ofc: Mihaly, Schuyler & Mitchell, 1801 Century Park East Ste 1201 Los Angeles 90067

SCHWAB, ALICE GWILLIAM, nursing education consultant; b. Feb. 10, 1938 Park City, Utah; d. James Llewellyn and Alice (Lefler) Gwilliam; m. Harry Loren Holbrook, Aug. 19, 1961 (dec. May 22, 1985); children: Jimmy Edward b. 1961, William Loren b. 1963, Mary Alice b. 1963, Daniel Raymond b. 1964; m. Donald Eugene Schwab, June 26, 1988; edn: Nsg. Diploma, R.N., L.A.

County Sch. of Nursing, Gen. Hosp., L.A. 1959; BA, Univ. Redlands, 1974, MA, 1978. Career: staff nse., supvg. nse. University Med. Ctr., Irvine 1963-72; supvg. nse. Fountain Valley Hosp., F.V., 1972-76; Hoag Memorial Hosp., Newport Beach 1976-78; dir. of nurses Los Banos Community Hosp., 1978-80; Sonoma Valley Hosp., Sonoma 1981-83; dir. of edn. Rancho Arroyo Vocat. Inst., Sacto. 1986-88; nsg. edn. cons. Calif. St. Bd. of Registered Nursing, Sacto. 1989-; instr. North Orange Co. Comm. Coll., Merced Comm. Coll.; rec: handicrafts. Res: 620 Jones Way Sacramento 95818

SCHWAB, CHARLES R., executive, discount broker; b. Woodland, Calif.; m. Helen O'Neil; 5 children; edn: BS Stanford Univ.; Grad. Bus. Sch., Stanford Univ.; Career: mutual fund mgr.; founder, chmn. Charles R. Schwab & Co., San Francisco 1971-; author: How To Be Your Own Stockbroker (1984); Republican. Res: Woodside Ofc: Charles R. Schwab & Co 101 Montgomery St 28th fl San Francisco 94104

SCHWARTZ, JEFFREY SCOTT, lawyer; b. Aug. 2, 1959, NY, NY; s. Philip Harold and Carolyn (Stern) S.; m. Lynette Pam Vigdor, Dec. 23, 1984; edn: BA SUNY Oneonta, 1981; JD, Western St. Univ. Coll. of Law, San Diego 1984; admitted bar: Calif., 1987. Career: law clk., 1983-87, atty., 1987-88, Law Office of William O'Connell, San Diego; prin. Law Office of Jeffrey S. Schwartz, San Diego 1988-; awards: Percy J. Power Outstanding Alumnus Delta Theta Phi Law Frat. 1987, Outstanding Young Men of Am. 1989, Wiley W. Manuel Legal Services Award 1991, listed Who's Who Among Practicing Attorneys 1989, Who's Who in Am. Law 1989; mem: Delta Theta Phi Law Frat. Internat. (Supreme Ct. Justice 1987-), Am. Bar Assn., Am. Trial Lawyers Assn., Calif. Bar Assn. (advisor gen. practice sect. 1989-), Calif. Trial Lawyers Assn., L.A. Co. Bar Assn., San Diego Co. Bar Assn., Call for Action (chair 1989, 91), PIRC (v.chair 1991), San Diego Trial Lawyers Assn., San Diego Inns of Court; contbr. articles in Crim. Justice Jour. (1983), Metal Trades People (1990); Democrat; Jewish. Law Office of Jeffrey S. Schwartz 1200 Third Ave Ste 1200 San Diego 92101

SCHWARTZ, STEVEN NORMAN, lawyer; b. Nov. 27, 1945, Wash. DC.; s. George and Sylvia (Ritzenberg) S.; m. Deborah Slobin, April 6, 1972; children: Adam b. 1978, Jennifer b. 1982; edn: AB magna cum laude, Dartmouth Coll. 1967; LL.B, Yale Law Sch. 1970; admitted U.S. Supreme Ct. 1976. Career: atty. Defenders Inc., San Diego 1970-73; Brav & Schwartz 1973-; bd. dirs. Defender's Organizations San Diego Inc. 1974-78; honors: Phi Beta Kappa; mem: Calif. Bar Assn., Coronado Men's Golf Club; Democratic; Jewish; rec: golf, fitness. Res: 1228 Churchill Pl Coronado 92118 Ofc: Brav & Schwartz 4026 Dave St San Diego 92103

SCHWARZ, FREDERICK CHARLES, physician, lecturer, writer; b. Jan. 15, 1913, Queensland, Australia; s. Paulus Friedrich Charles and Phoebe (Smith) S.; m. Lillian May Morton, Dec. 26, 1939; children: John Charles Morton, David Frederick, Rosemary Gai Esler; edn: BS, Univ. of Queensland, Australia 1933, BA, 1938, U.O.Q. (MD equiv.), MB-BS, 1944. Career: high sch. tchr., Queensland, Australia 1934-38; lectr. Queensland Teachers Coll., 1939-44; med. practitioner, Sydney, 1946-55; founder, pres., exec. dir. Christian Anti-Communism Crusade, Long Beach, Calif. 1953-; lectr. extensively on Communism in U.S., Australia, and internat., instr. numerous week-long schools; recipient Thomas Jefferson award The Council for Nat. Policy USA 1988; author 2 books: You Can Trust Communists (To Be Communists) (1960, Prentice Hall, 13 printings hard cover, num. printings paper back Chantico Pub. Co.), The Three Faces of Revolution (1972, Capitol Hill Press), var. booklets. Ofc: Christian Anti-Communism Crusade 227 E 6th St Long Beach 90802

SCHWEITZER, DON ALAN, university dean; b. Feb. 2, 1941, Los Angeles; s. Floyd Arthur and Dorothy Madge (Marcell) S.; m. Julie Jordan, Aug. 18, 1963; children: David Jordan b. 1967, Lisa Dyann b. 1970; edn: BA, UC Riverside 1962; MA, Univ. Nev. Reno 1965; PhD, 1967. Career: asst. prof. Okla. St. Univ., Stillwater 1967-69; CSU Fullerton 1969-73, assoc. dean 1973-79, dean 1979-; dir. Ruby Gerontology Center, Fullerton 1988-; gov. appointee Calif. Council for Humanities 1987-; honors: Psi Chi, Golden Key, Edn. Policy Fellowship Pgm. fellow 1985-86, Danforth Assn. Program fellow 1973; mem: Literacy Vols. of Am. (nat. secty. 1988-), Literacy Vols. of Am.-Calif. (founding pres. 1985-), Council of Colls. of Arts & Scis.; author 15+ book chpts. and articles in profl. jours.; Republican; Presbyterian; rec: magic, golf. Res: 431 Rospaw Way Placentia 92670 Ofc: California State University Fullerton 92634

SCIARRA, JOHN DOMENIC, real estate broker; b. Nov. 22, 1914, San Francisco; s. Domenico and Pasqua (DiPietro) S.; m. Ida Rose Cattani, Aug. 15, 1942; son, John b. 1944; edn: 275 units, I.C.S., NY, NY (USN); ACMMI, Univ. Chgo., 1944 (USN); attended Veronica Sch. Real Estate, S.F., 1960; Coll. San Mateo, 1960; lic. real estate broker, Calif. Career: prop. Sciarra Market, San Francisco 1946-50; owner/pres. Fitch Mt. Water Co., Healdsburg 1950-55; owner/pres. Sciarra Water Co., Inc. Healdsburg 1955-62; owner/broker Safeway Investments Co., South S.F. 1960-; sec.-treas. Pyramid Investments, an assn. 1965-, Galway Investments Inc. 1965-, Linda Mar Land Co. Inc. 1964-; clubs: Presidio Golf, Sharp Park Golf, San Mateo Golf; invention: Flip Top Cigarette

Pack (pat. pend. 1950); mil: aviation chief mach. mate USN 1940-46, served aboard battleship USS Washington invasion of Guadalcanal 1942 Naval Air Unit, decorated Euro.-Asia.-Pac. medal, African-Am. Def. medal, 7 Bronze Stars, served in Coast Guard Air Reserve 1955-75, ret.; Democrat; R.Cath.; rec: golf, antiques. Res: 2475 Galway Pl South San Francisco 94080 Ofc: Safeway Investments Co. 214A Miller Ave South San Francisco 94080

SCIOLARO, CHARLES MICHAEL, surgeon; b. July 5, 1958, Kansas City, Kans.; s. Gerald Michael and Charleen Gwen (Walter) S.; m. Vicki Lynn Mizell, Sept. 29, 1984; children: Rachel Diane, Lynsey Michelle, Ryan Michael; edn: BA biol./chem., Mid-Am. Nazarene Coll., 1980; MD (magna cum laude) Univ. Kansas Sch. of Med., 1984; bd. cert. Am. Bd. Gen. Surgery, 1991; bd. cert. A.C.S., adv. cardiac life support, 1984-, adv. trauma life support, 1987-, adv. cardiac life support instr., 1991-. Career: postgrad. tng. Univ. Ariz., gen. surgical resident Tucson Hosps. 1984-86, 87-89, cardiothoracic res. assoc. fellow 1986-87, gen. surgery chief res. 1989-90; physician, gen. surgeon Cigna Urgent Care, Tucson 1985-89 (p.t.), Navapache Comm. Hosp., Show Low, Az. 1985-87, VA Med. Ctr., Tucson 1985-89, Kaiser Permanente Med. Ctr., Fontana 1990-92, Loma Linda Univ. Med. Ctr., Loma Linda 1992-; honors: Categories Quiz Team State Champion, Nat. Hon. Soc. 1976, campus govt. rep., academic top ten scholarship, Phi Delta Lambda, undergrad. res. fellow biochem. Univ. Kansas, Nat. Dean's List 1976-80, Gen. Surgery Resident Teaching Award 1986, listed Dir. of Disting. Americans, Internat. Youth in Achiev., Personalities in Am. 1980-84, Who's Who Am., Who's Who in Med. Specialist 1991; mem: AAAS, AMA, Ariz. Med. Soc. 1984-90, A.C.S. (cand. gp. 1985-), Am. Coll. Cardiologist (affil. 1990-), Am. Coll. Chest Physicians (affil. 1990-), Calif. Med. Soc. 1990-, Internat. Coll. Surgeons 1990-, San Bdo. Med. Soc. 1990-; publs: contbr. articles in J. Thoracic and Cardiovasc. Surg. (1991), abstracts (1987, 88), nat. presentations Internat. Soc. Heart Transplantation Conf., Ft. Lauderdale, Fla. (4/90), We. Thoracic Surgical Assn., Colo. Springs, Colo. (6/87, Resident Prize finalist), Am. Soc. Anesth., Atlanta, Ga. (10/87), Am. Coll. Chest Physicians, Atlanta, Ga. (10/87); Ch. of Nazarene (youth pgm. supporter). Res: 11464 Via Norte Loma Linda 92354-3839 Ofc: LLU Medical Ctr. 11234 Anderson St Rm 2562B Loma Linda 92354

SCOLLARD, JEANNETTE REDDISH, entrepreneur, lecturer, author; b. July 26, 1947, Nashville, Tenn.; d. Andrew Jackson and Ruby Jewel (Wheeler) Mabry; m. Gary Scollard, July 4, 1979; div. 1987; edn: BA, Vanderbilt Univ., Nashville, Tenn. 1968; career: ed., Wall St. Transcript, NY NY 1972-74; sr. ed., Financial World, NY, NY 1974-79; v.p., Chesebrough Pond's, Greenwich, Conn. 1978-79; vice chmn., MMT Sales, NY, NY 1980-87; chmn., Costa Resort Properties, Carlsbad, Calif. 1989-; chmn., SCS Marketing, Carlsbad, Calif. 1987-; tchg. fellow, Woodrow Wilson Found. 1987-88; awards: Small Biz. Advocate of San Diego, SBA 1992; mem: steering com. Mentor Program/SBA 1989-; advy. com., Entrepreneurial Ctr., Manhattanville Coll. 1986-; trustee, Am. Women in Radio & TV 1986-91; trustee, Internat. Radio & TV Found. 1988-90; bd. mem., Milestone House 1992-; gov., NY Financial Writers, NY, NY 1978-79; author: 3 books: No-Nonsense Mgmt. Tips, 1984; The Self-Employed Woman, 1987; Risk to Win, 1990; columnist, Sounding Off, Entrepreneur Magazine, 1990-; Protestant; rec: piano, Himalayan art.

SCOTT, A. GORDON, engineer; b. Oct. 25, 1937, Manchester, U.K.; naturalized U.S. citizen, 1965; s. Rex Yarrington and Alice (Tilson) S.; m. Marilyn Elliot, July 2, 1960, Belleville, Ont., Canada; (div. 1992); children: Heather b. 1961, Robert b. 1962; edn: BS in electronics, indsl. tech., CSU Long Beach 1982. Career: techn. TRW Semiconductors, Lawndale 1959-64, techn. TRW, Inc., Redondo Beach 1964-66, I.C. Lab. supr. 1966-79, microelectronics process engr. 1979-82, product engr. 1982-85; reliability project engr. Northrop Electronics, Hawthorne 1985-87; hybrid mfg. sub-project mgr. TRW, Inc., Redondo Bch. 1987-88; owner Uniglobe In-World Travel agency, Lawndale 1988-; Episcopal; rec: photog., travel. Res: 3757 W 182nd St Torrance 90504 Ofc: Uniglobe In-World Travel 15901 Hawthorne Blvd Ste 120 Lawndale 90260

SCOTT, DOLORES H., psychiatrist; b. Newark, N.J.; d. Albert E. and Rosetta Louise (Hill) S.; div. David Bridgeford III, MD; children: Denise Bridgeford b. 1964; edn: BA, Fisk Univ., 1953; MD, Mehary Med. Sch., 1960; psychiat. residency King/Drew-UCLA, 1981. Career: med. intern, psychiatry resident Co. Med. Ctr. St. Louis, Mo. 1960-62, 61-62; physician pvt. practice, Los Angeles 1962-78; psychiatrist L.A. Co. Dept. Mental Health, Los Angeles 1981-; cons. Midland Med. Clinic 1979-, Angelica Bd. & Care 1988-; honors: Beta Kappa Chi 1952, Phi Beta Kappa 1953, disting. women YWCA San Gabriel Valley 1986; mem. Black Psychiatrists of Am., Nat. Med. Assn., Fisk Alumni Assn. (v.ch. We. Region), Alpha Kappa Alpha Sor.; civic: NAACP 1960-; Republican; Episcopalian; rec: travel. Ofc: West Central Mental Health Clinic, 3751 Stocker L.A. 90008

SCOTT, RICHARD THOMAS, corporate trainer, technical writer; b. Oct. 17, 1939, Ogden, Utah; s. Thomas Bradshaw and Reah (Child) S.; m. Connie Greenwood, May 15, 1959; children: Richard T., Jr. b. 1960, Paul S. b. 1961, Stephen B. b. 1962, Aaron D. b. 1965; edn: Univ. Utah 1958-59, Weber State Univ. 1959-60, Syracuse Univ. 1969-70. Career: customer engr., system maint.

IBM Corp., Salt Lake City 1960-64, advisory instr. IBM Corp., Kingston, NY 1964-71, St. Louis, Mo. 1971-77, San Jose, Calif. 1977-78, senior instr. IBM Corp., Los Angeles 1978-91; owner Conejo SkunkWorks, Thousand Oaks 1991-, tchr., consultant, and tech. writer, 1964-; mem. Trainers Assn. of So. Calif. (1985-, bd. 1987-91, exec. secty. 1992-); civic: Boy Scouts of Am., St. Louis, San Jose, Thousand Oaks (merit badge counselor: computers, pub. speaking, communications); author and support methodology: Course Devel. System (IBM internal product) 1985-91; mil: E5 USAF Reserves 1957-65; Republican; Latter Day Saints; rec: golf, music DIY puttering. Res/Ofc: Conejo Skunk Works 79 E Avenida de los Arboles Thousand Oaks 91360

SCOTT, ROBERT MILES, conservationist, systems evaluator, science/ engineering writer; b. Aug. 24, 1922, Columbus, Ohio; s. Roy Milton and Icy Pearl (Rogers) S.; m. Mildred Gladstone (dec.), Apr. 20, 1963; children: Elizabeth b. 1947, Roberta b. 1953; edn: BS conservation, natural resources, Ohio St. Univ., 1951 (an OSO first); honor grad. Indsl. Coll. of Armed Forces 1974, Command and Gen. Staff Coll. 1972, Air War Coll. 1976, Air Defense Sch. (3) 1953, 65, 69. Career: timber-cruiser Payette Nat. Forest, Idaho 1947-48; ranger-naturalist Big Bend Nat. Park, Texas and Glacier Nat. Park, Mont. 1951-53; publs. splst. Aerojet-Gen., Sacto. 1957; engr.-writer Convair-Astronautics, San Diego 1959, initiated concept of hands-on verification of opl. manuals; sr. missile specification engr. Lockheed-Sunnyvale 1961; design engr. and documentation mgr. Northrop-Ventura, Newbury Park 1963; mem. tech. staff Hughes Aircraft Co., Culver City 1965; staff writer Douglas Aircraft Co., Long Beach 1967; systems/ specs. consultant, 1973-90, cons. Rohr Industries, Aerojet, Teledyne, ARAM-CO, Rockwell, Hughes, RCA; judge (rep. US Army R&D) Jr. Sci. Fairs, Fullerton Coll.; mem: AF Assn., Assn. of US Army, Exptl. Aircraft Assn., Assn. of Civilian Conserv. Corps, Ohio St. Univ. Alumni Assn. (life) mem. San Diego Aerospace Mus., "Battle of Normandy Mus." (charter mem.), EAA Mus. (charter contbr.); works: "Takeoff Visual Data" Patent Contract to USN (1969), "Bright Light Identifier" concept to EAA (1984); R&D (civilian): Titan propulsion systems, Triplex Satellite facility, Atlas propellant transfer system, Apollo Earth Landing Sys., Athena & Sparta Re-entry Veh., Samos and MIDAS telemetry, MX Stage IV Missile, F-14/-18 digital radar; R&D (mil.): Nike-X Data Sys., Sentinel/Safeguard and Patriot ADA Systems; mil: s/sgt. tail gunner Army Air Corps 1941-45, 1st sgt., btn. cmdr., staff ARADCOM, R&D Div. cmdr. DA, col. ADA 1950-82, combat svc. Africa, Sicily, Italy, France, decorated 7 battle stars, Air Medal, Meritorious Service; Indep.; Christian; rec: flying, exptl. aircraft, biking, classic autos, writing (humor, haiku and tanka poetry). Address: 22829 Nadine Circle Torrance 90505

SCOULAR, ROBERT FRANK, lawyer; b. July 9, 1942, Del Norte, Colo.; s. Duane Wm. and Marie Josephine (Moloney) S.; m. Donna Votruba, June 3, 1967; children: Bryan, b. 1971; Sean, b. 1975; Bradley, b. 1980; edn: Carroll Coll. 1960-61; BS, Aero. Engring., St. Louis Univ. 1964; JD, St. Louis Univ. Sch. of Law 1968; admitted to Calif., Mo., Colo., N.Dak. and US Supreme Court Bars. Career: aerodynamics engr., contract adminstr. Emerson Electric Co., St. Louis, Mo. 1964-66; law clk. Chief Judge Charles J. Vogel, US Ct. of Appeals for the Eighth Circuit, St. Louis 1968-69; ptnr. Bryan, Cave, McPheeters & McRoberts, St. Louis, 1969-89; mng. ptnr., Los Angeles office, 1979-84, sect. leader Tech., Computer and Intellectual Property Law Sect., 1984-89; ptnr. Sonnenschein Nath & Rosenthal, Chicago, mng. ptnr. L.A. office, co-leader Intellectual Property Sect., 1990-; dir. Corley Printing Co., St. Louis 1973-82; honors: disting. svc Mo. Bar Young Lawyers Sect. 1978, outstanding senior St. Louis Univ. 1964, nat. outstanding cadet and Internat. Air Cadet Exchange Civil Air Patrol 1960; mem: Am. Bar Assn. (nat. dir. Young Lawyers Div. 1977-78, chmn. Young Lawyers Div. Corp. Law Comm. 1973-74), Missouri Bar (dir. Mo. Lawyers Credit Union 1978-79, chmn. Credit Union Task Force 1977-78, chmn. Young Lawyers Sect. 1976-77), Bar Assn. Met. St. Louis (v.p. 1978-79, chmn. Young Lawyers Sect. 1975-76), St. Louis Bar Found. (dir. 1975-76, 79), Calif. Bar Assn., Am. Judicature Soc., Conf. on Personal Fin. Law, Assn. of Bus. Trial Lawyers, Computer Law Assn., St. Louis Univ. Law Sch. Alumni Assn. (secty. 1970-72), St. Louis Univ. Alumni Council, Town Hall of Calif., L.A. C.of C.; contbr. articles in law journals; Republican; R.Cath.; rec: golf, tennis, running. Res: 1505 Lower Paseo La Cresta Palos Verdes Estates 90274 Ofc: Sonnenschein Nath & Rosenthal 601 S Figueroa St Ste 1500 Los Angeles 90017

SEAGREN, DANIEL ROBERT, chaplain, clergyman; b. Oct. 31, 1927, Chgo.; s. Elmer Frederich and Selma (Hill) S.; m. Barbara Anne Johnson, Mar. 21, 1959; children: Laurie b. 1960, Scott b. 1964; edn: BA, Univ. Minnesota, 1950; MA, USC, 1959; dipl. North Park Seminary, Ill. 1953; ordained Evangelical Covenant Ch. 1956.; cert. in counseling Univ. of Calif., Santa Barbara 1987. Career: faculty Azusa Coll. 1959-62; admin. No. Park Coll. 1962-66; pastor Evangelical Covenant Ch., Berkeley 1970-74; internat. pastor Immanuel Ch., Sweden 1974-77; pastor Evangelical Covenant Ch., Mich. 1977-82, internat. pastor, Mexico 1982-84; chaplain Samarkand Retirement Community, Santa Barbara 1985-; exec. dir. Conference Ctr. 1957-62; minister of youth/music First Covenant Ch., L.A. 1955-59, minister of youth (Minn.) 1966-69; secty. Morning Song, 1985-; mem: Rotary (Berkeley), Kiwanis (Muskegon, Mich.); author numerous articles, plays, booklets, papers, radio talks, TV scripts, columnist; anchor man The Living Word (weekly TV pgm.) 1977-82; columnist The City Parson (daily newspaper) 1971-74; author 9 books for youth and adult 1969-; mil: U.S. Navy, 1946; Independent ; Protestant Evangelical Covenant; rec: music, writing, sports, travel. Res: 2843 Miradero Dr #B Santa Barbara 93105 Ofc: 2550 Treasure Dr Santa Barbara 93105

SEAMOUNT, DANIEL TAYLOR, land surveyor, forester; b. May 26, 1923, Newton, Kans.; s. Dan and Flossie Mabel (Taylor) S.; m. Janet Underwood, Sept. 9, 1950; children: Daniel, Jr. b. 1951, Ann Marie b. 1953, Nancy b. 1955, forestry, UC Berkeley 1950, MBA, 1951; Reg. Profl. Forester, Calif. 1974, lic. Land Surveyor in Wash., Calif. 1964, Calif. Std. tchg. cred.- surveying, math., lic. Agricultural Pest Control Advr. 1990, Calif. Peace Officer. Career: forester Union Lumber Co., Fort Bragg 1951-52; tchr. South Fork Union High Sch., Miranda 1952-55; logging engr. Crown Zellerbach Corp., Cathlamet, Wash. 1955-57; jr. coll. instr. Olympic Coll., Bremerton, Wash. 1957-60; wage-hour investigator US Dept. of Labor, Riverside, Calif. 1960-62; researcher Tree Crop Harvesting Systems and Farm Labor Efficiency, UC Riverside, 1962-73; timber mgmt. Golden State Building Prods., Redlands 1973-74; forester and land surveyor Calif. Dept. Forestry, 1974-; honors: Lettered in track (3 yrs.) and cross-country (4 yrs.) UC Berkeley, Zi Sigma Phi, Order of the Golden Bear; mem. Soc. of Am. Foresters (chpt. chmn. 1986), Calif. Land Surveyors Assn.; patentee: swing seat used in picking fruit; contbr. 14 research publs. in harvesting efficiency of agricultural tree crops (1965-74); mil: s/sgt. US Army Air Corps 1943-46; Democrat; R.Cath.; rec: road racing, backpacking, x-c skiing. Res: 6655 N Anna St Fresno 93710 Ofc: Calif. Dept. Forestry 366 Hwy 49 North Mariposa 95338

SEARS, BRIAN FRANCIS, company president; b. Jan. 17, 1936, San Francisco; s. Frank James and Rosemary D. S.; m. Elizabeth Bailey, Feb. 14, 1970; children: Brian Patrick b. 1970, Rosemarie A. b. 1962, Constance E. b. 1960; edn: AA, Coll. of San Mateo, 1960; BA in bus. adminstrn., San Jose State Univ., 1962. Career: sales engr., food proc. and pkg. equip., FMC Corp., San Jose 1959-63; we. reg. mgr. Icore Div., Acurex Corp., 1963-70; pres. West-Link Corp., 1970-; chmn. bd. Necor Corp., Menlo Park, 1977-; dir: Trax Ind. Prod., Burlingame 1978-87, Tonko Corp., Campbell (1981-82); awards: sales mgmt. achiev., Mfrs. Rep. Assn. 1980; mem: Western Packaging Assn. (dir. 1981, chmn. bd. sponsors WPA Exhib. 1982, WestPak 1977, 79, 81, 83, 85, 87, 89, 91); Elks Club; publs: articles in trade mags., advt. and mktg. brochures; devel. internat. sales pgm. for Icore/Acurex for eletonic sorting machine product line; mil: cpl. AUS 1956-57; Republican; R.Cath.; rec: skiing, racquetball, sports. Res: 857 Viewridge Dr San Mateo 94403 Ofc: 1650 Borel Pl Ste 225 San Mateo 94402

SEAWRIGHT, MARY SILAN, teacher, promoter of fine arts in education, philanthropist; b. Aug. 17, 1916, Rankin, Pa.; d. Kliment and Bozana (Jovan) Silan; m. Delmar Seawright, Sept. 11, 1943 (dec.); edn: cert. Music Inst., Pgh. 1937-43; BA, CSU Sacto., 1954; MA, and PhD, Century Univ., 1986, 1987. Career: pvt. piano tchr., Pittsburgh, Pa. 1937-43, 46-48; tchr. Trenton (N.Dak.) Sch., 1943-45; Marysville (Ca.) Jt. Unified Schs. 1948-52, (travel Europe 1952-53), 1953-, mem. curriculum com. 1987, 88, 89; advy. bd. Animal Health Technology Pgm., Yuba Coll.; honors: pres's award Am. Lung Assn. No. Calif., Chico 1979-80, outstanding tchr. Feather River Service Ctr., Marysville 1986; mem: Marysville Unif. Tchrs. Assn., Calif. Tchrs. Assn., NEA, PTA, Delta Kappa Gamma, Century Univ. Alumni Assn. (bd.); civic: Arts Council Marysville, Western Soc. of Naturalists (donor 1978-), Trenton Sch. N. Dak. (scholarship donor 1986-), Veterinary Sch. of Med. UC Davis (scholarship donor 1987-), Endowment Circle Sacramento Opera Assn. (donor), Am. Lung Assn. No. Calif. (bd. 1972-87), Fund for Animals 1976-, Met. Opera Guild (NY), Endowment Instrumental Music Dept. of Sacramento Country Sch., charter supporter U.S. Holocaust Mus., W.D.C.; Dissertation: Fine Arts in Primary Grades 1987; Democrat; rec: opera, painting, travels. Res: 229 E 12th St Marysville 95901

SEDLAK, BONNIE JOY, biologist, biotechnology consultant; b. Jan. 30, 1943, Oak Park, Ill.; d. Raymond and Eleanore Mildred (Rada) Sedlak; edn: BA, Northwestern Univ., 1965; MA, Case Western Reserve, 1968; PhD, Northwestern Univ., 1974. Career: res. asst. Case Western, Cleveland, Oh. 1965-68, res. assoc. Northwestern, Evanston, Ill. 1965-74, post-doc. Rush Med. Coll., Chgo. 1974-75; asst. prof. Smith Coll., Northampton, Mass. 1975-77; asst., assoc., tenured prof. State Univ. New York, Purchase, N.Y. 1977-81; assoc. res. scientist Univ. Calif., Irvine, 1981-85; biomed. field sales cons. N. Am. Sci. Assocs., 1986-87; pgm. mgr. Microbics Corp., 1987-88; sr. analyst Fritzsche, Pambianchi and Assocs. Inc., internat. cons. firm in health care bus., 1988-90; cons. prin., San Diego 1990-91; new bus. devel. and licensing mgr. Becton Dickinson Adv. Cellular Biology, San Jose 1991-92; listed Who's Who of Am. Men & Women of Sci. (1979, 86); publs: 17 peer rev. sci. papers (1975-86), 9 pub. abstracts (1974-88), 22+ bus. articles (1987-92); rec: painting. Address: PO Box 3021 Half Moon Bay 94019

SEEGALL, MANFRED ISMAR LUDWIG, contract research engineer, technical writer, real estate executive, retired physicist; b. Dec. 23, 1929, Berlin, Germany, came to U.S., 1952, naturalized, 1957; s. Leonhard and Vera Antonie (Vodackova) S.; m. Alma R. Sterner Clarke; 2 stepchildren: James, Mark; edn:

BS (magna cum laude), Loyola Coll., 1957; MS, Brown Univ., 1960; PhD, Stuttgart Tech. Univ., Ger. 1965. Career: res. engr. Autonetics Corp. div. of North Am. Aviation, Downey, 1959-61; physicist Astronautics div. Gen. Dynamics, Inc., San Diego 1961-62; res. scientist Max Planck Inst., Stuttgart, 1962-65; instr. statistics and algebra San Diego City Coll., 1966; sr. res. engr. Solar div. Internat. Harvester, San Diego 1967-73; res. cons. in energy and pollution, San Diego 1974-83; sr. scientist Evaluation Res. Corp., San Diego 1981-82; RCS analyst Teledyne Micronetics, 1983-84; sr. design specialist Alcoa Defense Systems, 1984-87; cons. physical scis., 1987-89; independent contr. engring. res., tech. writing, and real estate 1990-; instr. Mesa Coll. 1980-81, Grossmont Coll. 1981; mem.: IEEE (senior), Internat. Platform Assn., Calif. Parapsychology Found. (secty. resch. com.), Cottage of Czechoslovakia of House of Pacific Relations, Rosicrucian Order, Loyola Coll., Brown Univ. alumni assns.; inventions: Catalyst for reducing NOx (1975), App. for Indicating Gas Temp. (1975), Temp. Meas. Apparatus & Method (1974); publ: Parametric Design Study of Comp. (1987); Republican; R.Cath.; rec: history, philosophy, parapsychology, chess, travel. Res: 8735 Blue Lake Dr San Diego 92119

SEFTON, WILLIAM LEE, certified public accountant; b. Dec. 7, 1943, San Francisco; s. Seibert Lee and Mimi (Stone) S.; m. Wilann Jean, Feb. 14, 1970; children: Robin; edn: BA, Willamette Univ. 1965; M.Acctg., USC 1966; CPA, Calif. Career: controller Dataquest Inc., Cupertino 1979-80; pvt. practice public acctg., San Ramon 1980-; mem: Am. Inst. CPAs, Calif. Soc. CPAs, Crow Canyon HOA (past pres.); mil: US Coast Guard 1977; Republican; Mormon. Res: 2011 Saint George Rd Danville 94526 Ofc: 12901 Alcosta Blvd. Ste A San Ramon 94583

SEGEL, KAREN LYNN JOSEPH, attorney, certified tax professional; b. Jan. 15, 1947, Youngstown, Ohio; d. Samuel Dennis and Helen Anita Joseph; grandfather, James Michael Joseph; m. Alvin Gerald Segel, June 9, 1968, div. 1977; 1 son, Adam James b. 1975; edn: BA in Soviet & E. Euro. Studies, Boston Univ., 1968; JD, Southwestern Univ. Sch. Law, 1975. Career: High Sch. tchr. People-To-People Org., 1963; adminstrv. asst. Olds Brunel & Co., NYC 1968-69; U.S. Banknote Corp., NYC 1969-70; tax acct. S.N. Chilkov & Co., CPAs, Beverly Hills 1971-74; intern Calif. Corporations Commr., L.A. 1974-75; tax sr. Oppenheim, Appel & Dixon, L.A. 1977-78; Fox, Westheimer & Co., L.A. 1978; Zebrak, Levine & Mepos, L.A. 1978-79; indep. cons. acct., tax splst., Beverly Hills 1980-; dir. World Wide Motion Picture Corp.; honors: Boston Univ. Dean's List, honors dorm Raleigh House, Disting. Lecture Series 1965-68, listed Who's Who in West 1978; mem. editl. advy. bd. Am. Biog. Inst. (ABI), advy. bd. Women's Inner Cir. of Achiev., named ABI woman of yr. 1991, listed with issue dedication: 2000 Notable Am. Women (3d), World Who's Who of Women (11th), Internat. Dir. Disting. Leadership 1991, Intl. Who's Who of Intellectuals (9th), listed Comm. Leaders Am.; mem. Nat. Soc. of Tax Profls.; civic: Center Theater Group, Young Symphonians L.A., Nat. Trust for Hist. Preserv., Winterthur Guild, Am. Mus. Natural Hist.; Jewish; rec: travel, collect seashells, raise Lhasa Apso dogs.

SEIFF, GLORIA LOUISE, education and civic activist; b. Apr. 3, 1929, Denver, Colo.; d. Edward Hyatt and Lillian Pearl (Blend) Holtzman of Fort Worth, Tx.; m. Stephen Seiff, M.D. Apr. 16, 1950; children: Dr. Stuart b. 1954, Sherri b. 1957, Karen b. 1960; edn: att. Washington Univ., St. Louis, Mo. 1947-48. Civic bds: Beverly Hills Public Works Commn. (commr. 1990-98), Los Angeles Co. West Mosquito Abatement Dist. (bd. trustees 1988-92, pres. 1988-89), L.W.V. (L.A. Co. bd. dirs. 1988-90, Bev. Hills pres. 1985-87), The Associates of Vista Del Mar (bd. dirs. 1978-91), Assistance League of So. Calif. (bd. dirs., exec. com. 1989-92), Southwest HOA of Beverly Hills (bd. 1985-), Beverly Vista Sch. PTA (pres. 1970-71), PTA Council of Beverly Hills (pres. 1972-73), Beverly Hills Edn. Found. (founding trustee 1975-79); awards: hon. service Beverly Hills PTA 1972, appreciation outstanding comm. service City Council Beverly Hills (1986, 87), resolution Beverly Hills Unified Sch. Dist. 1986; club: California Yacht; rec: sailing. Res: Beverly Hills 90212

SEIPLE, WILLARD RAY, engineering geologist; b. July 29, 1924, Gibsonburg, Ohio; s. George Harrison and Ella Oberst (Bissell) S.; m. Shirley Maxine Perry, Aug. 5, 1951; 1 son, Eric Von; edn: BS, USC 1960; MS, 1968; reg. geologist Calif., Me.; cert. engring. geologist, Calif. 1989. Career: project engr. Firestone Tire & Rubber Co., Los Angeles 1964-65; sr. engring. geologist Dames & Moore, L.A. 1965-74, mng. principal in charge, Santa Barbara 1974-77, resident geotechnical engr. Dames & Moore, Burlington, Kans. 1977-80; indep. cons., Santa Barbara 1980-82; supervising. geologist Calif. St. Div. of Mines & Geology, Sacto. 1982-89; cons. Abu Dhabi Nat. Oil Co., Middle East 1980; cons. Quatar Ministry of Pub. Works, Middle East 1981; cons. Getty Minerals, Toelle, Utah 1982; honors: W.A. Tarr award Sigma Gamma Epsilon 1960; mem: ASCE, Assn. of Engring. Geologists (v. chair L.A. Sect. 1974-75, chair Sacto. Sect. 1992-94), Soc. of Mining Engrs. (chair Sierra Nev. Sect. 1985-86), Geol. Soc. of Am., Assn. of Environmental Profls (charter mem. 1975-76); sci. jour. article 19783; mil: t/sgt. US Army 1943-45; Democrat; Prot.; rec: photography, chess, hunting, fishing. Res/Ofc: 6233 Cassady Way Carmichael 95608

SEITZ, WALTER STANLEY, cardiologist; b. May 10, 1937, L.A., Calif.; s. Walter and Frances Janette (Schleef) S.; edn: BS, physics & math, UC Berkeley, 1959; Plasma Physics Inst., Princeton, N.J., 1964; PhD, biophysics, Univ. of Vienna, Austria, 1981; MD, Univ. of Vienna Faculty of Medicine, 1982; E.C.F.M.G. Cert. 1982; Med. License, State of Ill., 1983. Career: health physicist, UC Radiation Lab., 1959-61; res. assoc., NIH at Pacific Union Coll., res. physicist at Lockheed Res. Labs., Angwin and Palo Alto, Calif., 1961-63; staff scientist, Xerox Corp., Pasadena, Calif., 1963-66; sr. scientist, Applied Physics Consultants, Palo Alto, 1966-75; grad. student in medicine and biophysics, resident in internal medicine, Univ. of Vienna, Stanford Univ. Hosp. and res. assoc. at the Inst. for Med. Analysis, Vienna, 1975-82; instr., clinical sci., Univ. of Ill. Coll. of Medicine, Urbana, 1983-84; post-doctoral res. scholar, Cardiovascular Res. Inst., UC Sch. of Medicine, S.F., 1984-87; cons. in cardiology, Cardiovascular Res. Inst., UC Sch. of Medicine, S.F., and sr. scientist , Inst. for Med. Analysis and Res., Berkeley, 1987-; honors: Post-Doctoral Res. Fellowship, UC, S.F., 1984; Fellow, Am. Coll. of Angiography, NY, 1987; mem: AAAS, 1983-; NY Acad. of Sciences, 1984-; Physicians for Social Responsibility, 1985-; The Royal Soc. of Medicine, London, 1985-; publs.: over 25 res. and profl. papers pub. in scientific journals, 1964-; patent application: instrument to measure mitral valve pressure gradient and capillary wedge pressure from standard electrocardiogram, 1980; rec: reading, music, painting.

SELL, EVELYN, civic activist, medical assistant, clinic executive volunteer; b. Feb. 8, 1936, Binger, Okla.; d. Raymond Avril and Minnie Oneida (Jay) Skelton; m. Glenn Eugene Sell, May 28, 1959; children: Lisa Renee b. 1959, Jeffrey Eugene b. 1961; edn: grad. Chowchilla High Sch. 1955; lic., grad. Esquire Beauty Coll. Neosho, Mo. 1973; AS med. asst., Modesto Jr. Coll., 1983; cert. photog., Merced Jr. Coll., 1988. Career: linework F & P Cannery, Merced, 1952-54; waitress Red Dot Cafe, Chowchilla 1956-57; cosmetics sales Avon 1964-66; bkkpr./clk. p.t. Copeland Lumber, Patterson 1979-80; med. receptionist Del Puerto Hosp., Patterson 1981-83; civic bds: Anna Belle Bertrand Clinic, sponsored by Lioness and Soroptimist, Chowchilla (v.p. 1989-92, sec. 1992-93, receptionist 1989-93), DAR (Dist. V Calif. secty. 1989-91, charter org. Madera Chapt. El Portal De Las Sierras Charter 1985, registrar 1991-93, Regent 1992-94; past: historian, Svs. for Veteran Patients, Flag Of USA, Nat. Def., PR, Insignia chair, Constn. chair, DAR Local Scholarship, Tel. com., secty.), Nat. Soc. of Colonial Dames (Stanislaus Co. v.p. 1988-91; Ceres Chpt. XVII charter org. mem. 1988, 1st v.p. 1988-, past chair: Program, Scholarship, Heraldry & Coats of Arms), Lioness Club Chowchilla (past 2d v.p. 1991-92, 1st v.p. 1992-93, rec'd Pres.'s award 1992), Chowchilla Hist. Soc. (curator 1989-92 and History Book chair for another to be published in future; assisted chmn. on Res. & Family Histories and helped organize "Yesterdays of Chowchilla" 1987), Am. Legion Aux. Le Grand Unit 660 (exec. com. Americanism 1990-91, chair for Girls State 1991-92, 2d v.p. 1992-93, audit com. ofcr. 1992-93), Friends of Library Chowchilla (secty. 1991-2, 92-3); mem. Madera Geneal. Soc., Chowchilla Dist. Hist. Soc., Nat. Geneal. Soc. (Arlington, Va.), N.Caro. Friends Hist. Soc. (Greensboro), Forsyth Geneal. Soc. (Winston-Salem), Schuyler Co. Geneal. Soc. (Rushville, Ill.), Phillips Co. Geneal. Soc. (Phillipsburg, Ks.), Crawford Co. Geneal. Soc. (Pittsburg, Ks.), Daus. of Union Veterans 1861-1865 Julia Dent Grant Tent 16 (St. Louis, Mo.); author: Sell & Allied Families (1991), Jay & Allied Families (1992), biog. articles "Reuben Sell & Wife" (1991), "John Franklin Skelton, Civil War Vet. from Ind. 1961-65" in St. Louis-Our Civil War Heritage, Julia Dent Grant Tent 16 (1992), 4 biog. articles "Thomas Jay and Wife, Lillian," "Thomas Oscar Jay and Wife, Minnie," "Abraham Martin and Wife, Mourning," "Hezekiah and Wife, Eliza" in Newton Co. Families in Neosho, Mo. by Genealogy Friends of the Libr. (1992); Republican; Prot.; rec: genealogy, travel, photog., cake decorating. Res: Chowchilla.

SELLECK, ROBERT DEAN, real estate investor; b. Dec. 27, 1921, Lapeer, Mich.; s. George Samuel and Nellie Louise (Fife) S.; m. Martha Jagger, Apr. 11, 1942; children: Robert II, Thomas, Martha, Daniel; edn: Ohio Wesleyan Univ.; Calif. lic. real estate broker (1948). Career: ptnr. George S. Selleck & Sons, gen. contrs., Detroit, Mich. 1946-48; Coldwell, Banker & Co., Los Angeles 1948-63, v.p./ mgr. 1963-84, sr.v.p./dir. corp. communications Coldwell Banker Commercial Group, 1984-87; owner The Selleck Company, 1987-; honors: recipient w/wife, First Annual Premier Parents Award, March of Dimes Birth Defects Found. 1984, San Fernando Valley Humanitarian Award, Project Heavy 1982 and the Fernando Award 1982; apptd. civic bds: Los Angeles Memorial Coliseum and Sports Arena Commn. (1977-84, pres. 1980), L.A. Olympic Organizing Com. (dir. 1979-86), L.A. Rec. & Parks Commn. (1977-84, pres. 1979 and 1984), Health Dynamics, Inc. (dir., v.chmn.), Valley Presbyterian Hosp. (bd. dirs.); mem: Valley Industry and Commerce Assn. (dir, pres. 1973), L.A. Bd. of Realtors 1948-; clubs: Lakeside Golf (pres. 1976-77), Desert Horizons CC; mil: Army Air Corps 1943-45; Republican; Congregational; rec: golf, gardening. Ofc: The Selleck Company, 21600 Oxnard St Ste 350 Woodland Hills 91367

SELZ, PETER HOWARD, educator; b. Munich, Germany, Mar. 22, 1919; came to US 1936, nat. 1942; s. Eugene and Edith S.; m. Thalia Cheronis, June 10, 1948; div. 1965; children: Tanya Nicole Eugenia, Diana Gabrielle Hamlin; m. Carole Schemmerling, Dec. 14, 1983; edn: student, Columbia Univ., Univ.

Paris; MA, Univ. of Chgo., 1949; PhD 1954; DFA, Calif. Coll. Arts and Crafts, 1967. Career: instr, Univ. of Chgo. 1951-56; asst. prof. art history, head art edn. dept. Inst. Design, Ill. Inst. Tech., Chgo. 1949-55; chmn art dept., dir. art gallery Pomona Coll. 1955-58; curator dept. painting and sculpture exhbns. Mus. Modern Art 1958-65; dir. univ. art mus. UC Berkeley 1965-73, prof. history of art, 1965-; Zaks prof. Hebrew Univ., Jerusalem 1976; vis. prof. CUNY 1987; mem. president's council on art and architecture Yale Univ. 1971-76; trustee Am. Crafts Council 1983-88; pres. Berkeley Art Project 1988-; mem. advy. council archives Am. Art 1971-; project dir. Christo's Running Fence 1973-76; awards: decorated Order of Merit Fed. Republic Germany, Fulbright grantee Paris 1949-50, fellow Belgian-Am. Ednl. Found., sr. fellow Nat. Endowment for Humanities 1972; mem: Coll. Art Assn. (dir. 1959-64, 67-71), AAUP, Internat. Art Critics Assn.; author: German Expressionist Painting, 1957, New Images of Man, 1959, Art Nouveau, 1960, Mark Rothko, 1961, Fifteen Polish Painters, 1961, The Art of Jean Dubuffet, 1962, Emil Nolde, 1963, Max Beckmann, 1964, Alberto Giacometti, 1965, Directions in Kinetic Sculpture, 1966, Funk, 1967, Harold Paris, 1972, Ferdinand Hodler, 1972, Sam Francis, 1975, The American Presidency in Political Cartoons, 1976, Art in Our Times, 1981, Art in a Turbulent France, 1985, Chillida, 1986, Max Beckmann: The Self Portraits, 1992; editor, Art in Am., 1967-; Art Quarterly., 1969-75, Arts, 1981-; contbr articles to art publs.; with OSS AUS 1941-46. Ofc: Dept. Art History Univ. of California, Berkeley 94720

SEMAS, LEONARD A., real estate appraiser, b. Feb. 2, 1947, Taunton, Mass.; s. Leonard and Mary (Lopes) S.; 1 son, Michael b. 1979; edn: BS biology, Santa Clara Univ. 1968; MBA fin., 1975. Career: ops. mgr. Am. Hosp. Supply Corp., Ocala, Fla. 1972-76; owner Len Semas Co., San Jose 1976-82; v.p. mktg. and ops. Connolly Devel., Oakland 1982-83; owner Attkisson & Semas, San Jose 1983-; instr. Central Fla. Comm. Coll., Ocala 1975-76; awards: Ft. Belvoir Disting. Mil. Grad. 1969; moderator Real Estate Forum 1987, 88, 89; mem: Santa Clara Univ. Bd. Fellows, MBA Alumni Bd. (pres. 1988-89), Silicon Valley Capital Club (founding mem.) Kiwanis (dir. 1987-88, pres. 1988-89), BSA (bd. dirs., past mem., v.p.); articles pub. in profl. jours. 1983, 88; mil: 1st lt. AUS 1969-72; Republican; Protestant; rec: tennis, golf, computers. Ofc: Attkisson & Semas 40 S Market St Ste 430 San Jose 95113

SEPPI, EDWARD JOSEPH, physicist; b. Dec. 16, 1930, Price, Utah; s. Joseph and Fortunata (Seppi) S.; m. Betty Stowell, Aug. 25, 1953; children: Duane b. 1955, Kevin b. 1959, Cynthia b. 1968; edn: BS, Brigham Young Univ., Provo 1952; MS, Univ. Idaho, 1956; PhD, Calif. Inst. of Tech., 1962, Research fellow 1962. Career: staff physicist Inst. for Def. Analysis, W.D.C., 1962-64; cons. 1964-72; head exptl. fac. dept. SLAC, Stanford 1966-68; mgr. medical diagnosis Varian Assocs., Palo Alto 1974-76, senior scientist 1980-90, 1991-; senior scientist Superconducting Super Collider, Dallas 1990-91; honors: Phi Eta Sigma 1952, Phi Kappa Phi 1962; mem.: Am. Physical Soc. 1952-; civic: BSA, Menlo Park (asst. scoutmaster 1969-75), Ladera Comm. Assn., Portola Valley (bd. 1988-90); inventor 18 sci. patents (med. instrumentation), author 82+ sci. publs. and abstracts; Ch. of Jesus Christ of LDS; rec: photography, gardening, computers. Res: 320 Dedalera Dr Portola Valley 94028

SERRANTINO, SALVATORE, research company president; b. Aug. 30, 1932, Hartford, Conn.; s. Sebastian and Vencenza (Felichia) S.; m. Margaret Multz, May 14, 1966; dau., Sabrina b. 1973; edn: AA, State Tech. Inst., 1955; BS, Univ. Conn., 1960. Career: asst. v.p., v.p. American Savings Bank, Whittier 1960-64; v.p. Home Savings of Am., Beverly Hills 1964-66; v.p. Ray Burn Inc., L.A. 1966; advt. adminstr. Petersen Pub. Co., L.A. 1966-69; v.p. First Charter Fin. Corp., Beverly Hills 1969-75; exec. v.p. Market Insight Corp., San Francisco 1975-77; CFO, dir. California Site Finders, Santa Monica 1977-; pres., dir. California Research Corp., 1977-, publisher, mng. editor CRC Report, 1984-; dir. Columbia Nat. Bank 1983-85; chmn. bd., dir. Nat. Lenders Network 1986; chmn. bd., dir. CRC Mortgage Corp., 1987; seminar lectr. UC Berkeley 1981-82, UCLA 1980-84, UC Irvine 1983-84, American Banker 1990; conf. lectr. Grad. Sch. of Mgmt., UC Irvine, 1986; awards: Gold Medal Long Beach Senior Olympics (racquetball, singles) 1992, 2 Silver Medals 1993; mem. Consultants Roundtable (chmn., pres., dir., 1980-); mil: M.I. AUS 1955-57. Res: 1134 Coldwater Canyon Dr Beverly Hills 90210 Ofc: California Research Corp. 2719 Wilshire Blvd Santa Monica 90403

SESSLER, ANDREW MARIENHOFF, physicist; b. Dec. 11, 1928, Brooklyn; s. David and Mary (Baron) S.; m. Gladys Lerner, Sept. 23, 1951; children: Daniel Ira, Jonathan Lawrence, Ruth; edn: BA in math. (cum laude), Harvard Univ., 1949, MA in theoretical physics, 1953. Career: NSF Fellow, Cornell Univ., N.Y. 1953-54; asst. prof. Ohio State Univ., Columbus 1954, assoc. prof. 1960, on lv. Midwestern Univs. Res. 1955-56, vis. physicist Lawrence Radiation Lab. 1959-60, Niels Bohr Inst., Copenhagen summer 1961; res. scientist Univ. Calif. Lawrence Berkeley Lab., Berkeley, 1961-: in theoretical physics 1961-73, energy and environment 1971-73, dir. 1973-80, sr. scientist plasma physics 1980-, sci. policy bd. Stanford Synchrotron Radiation Lab. 1991-92, sci. policy com. Superconducting Super Collider 1992-94; L.J. Haworth dist. scientist Brookhaven Nat. Lab. 1991-92; chmn. sci. policy bd. Stanford Synchrotron Radiation Project 1974-77, mem. advy. com. Lawrence Hall of Sci. 1974-78,

EPRI Advanced Fuels Adv. Com. 1978-81, BNL external advy. com. on Isabelle 1980-82; appt. U.S. advisor Punjab Univ. Physics Inst., Chandigarh, India; mem. U.S.-India cooperative pgm. for improvement of sci. edn. in India 1966, high energy physics advy. panel to U.S. AEC 1969-72; mem. hon. advy. bd. Inst. for Adv. Physics Studies, La Jolla Internat. Sch. of Physics 1991-; awards: E.O. Lawrence award U.S. AEC 1970, U.S. Particle Accelerator Sch. prize 1988, fellow Japan Soc. for Promotion of Sci. at KEK 1985; mem: AAAS (fellow, nom. com. 1984-87), Am. Physical Soc. (fellow, chmn. com. internat. freedom scientist 1982, study of directed energy weapons panel 1985-87, chmn. panel public affairs 1988, chmn. div. physics of beams 1990, com. on appls. of physics 1991-), NAS, IEEE (sr. mem.), Fedn. Am. Scientists Council (v.chmn. 1987, chmn. 88-), N.Y. Acad. Sci., Assoc. Univ. Inc. (bd. 1991-); publs: editl. bd. Nuclear Instruments and Methods 1969-, corr. Comments on Modern Physics 1969-71, articles in profl. jours. Res: 225 Clifton St Apt 201 Oakland 94618 Ofc: Univ. California Lawrence Berkeley Lab. 1 Cyclotron Rd MS 71-259 Berkeley 94720 Tel: 415/486-4992

SEVERO, ORLANDO CHARLES, JR., air force officer, space & missile center commander; b. Dec. 22, 1940, Greenwich, Ct.; s. Orlando C., Sr. and Filomena (Ferraro) S.; m. Joan Elza Skogstrom, June 16, 1962; children: Lori b. 1964, Michael b. 1965, Karen b. 1968; edn: BSEE, Va. Mil. Inst., Lexington, Va. 1962; MSEE, AF Inst. Tech., Wright-Patterson AFB, Oh. 1968. Career: served to Col. (0-6) U.S. Air Force, 1962-; spacecraft proj. mgr. Los Angeles AFB 1972-76; dir. STS computer systems Vandenberg AFB 1977-81, dir. STS engring. 1981-84; dep. pgm. mgr. STS, NASA, Houston, Tx. 1984-85; cmdr. Shuttle Test Group, USAF, Vandenberg AFB 1985-86;cmdr. Western Space & Missile Center, Vandenberg AFB 1986-, first Air Force Space Command installation comdr., Vandenberg AFB; awards: num. mil. decorations, NASA Exceptional Service Medal, Houston 1985, Manned Flight Awareness Honoree, NASA, WDC 1991, Air Force Assn. meritorious service award 1991, Hon. PhD-Humane Letters Nat. Christian Univ., Mo. 1986; mem. bd. trustees Western Spaceport Mus., Lompoc 1988-; Kts. Columbus, Odenton, Md. (charter, fin. sec. 1963-66); Republican; R.Cath.; rec: golf, bicycling, backpacking, camping, hunting, fishing. Res: 129 Hercules Ave Lompoc 93436 Ofc: WSMC/CC Vandenberg AFB CA 93437-6021

SEYFERTH, HAROLD HOMER, lecturer, real estate appraiser, retired city planner; b. Jan. 22, 1922, Stockton; s. Lester L. and Bernice (Perkins) S.; m. Betty Jean Stanley, Apr. 12, 1943; children: Mary B., Laurence P.; edn: BA, San Jose State Univ., 1948; MBA, and PhD, Pacific Western Univ., 1981. Career: locomotive engr. Western Pacific R.R., 1939-50; asst. planner City of San Jose, 1950-54; city mgr. Hollister, 1959-63; property mgr. City of Salinas, 1963-68; redevel. chief land officer City of Seaside, 1968-69; pres. H. Seyferth Assocs., Monterey 1969-92, ret.; teacher, lectr. in field; awards: Coro fellow 1950; mem: Am. Assn. Cert. Appraisers (cert.), Am. Planning Assn., Calif. Assn. R.E. Tchrs., Internat. Coll. R.E. Cons. Profls., Internat. Inst. Valuers, Internat. Orgn. R.E. Appraisers, Internat. Right of Way Assn., Nat. Assn. Cert. Real Property Appraisers, Nat. Assn. Review Appraisers, R.E. Educators Assn., Urban Land Inst.; civic bds: Enterprise Sch. Dist., Hollister (trustee), Carmel Riviera Mutual Water Co. (chmn.), Boy's City Boy's Club San Jose, Am. Cancer Soc. San Jose; mil: USN 1942-45. Res: 50 Yankee Point Carmel 93923

SHAFFER, JOHN ORDIE, physician, surgeon; b. Aug. 29, 1920, Mpls., Minn.; s. John Ordie and Della Helen (Stewart) S.; m. Dorothea L. Lidberg, May 17, 1947; children: Ann Helen b. 1950, John Ordie IV b. 1953; edn: BS, Univ. Minn. 1941; MD, Univ. Minn. Med. Sch. 1944; MS surgery, 1950; dipl. Am. Bd. Surgery (1952). Career: intern Phila. Gen. Hosp., Pa. 1943-44; surgery resident Univ. Minn. Hosp., Mpls. 1944-46, 48-50; chief surgery U.S. Hosp. Ship Comford 1946-48; chief surgery resident Univ. Minn. Hosp. 1949-50; instr. surgery Univ. Utah, Salt Lake City 1951-52; pvt. practice surgery, Hayward 1952-; lectr. Am. Cancer Soc., Alameda 1952-; awards: S.F. Surgical Soc. spl. award 1955; mem: A.C.S. (fellow), Hayward C.of C., AMA, CMA, Alameda Contra Costa Med. Assn., So. Alameda Surgical Soc. (founder, charter pres. 1961-63), Am. Cancer Soc. (bd. dirs.); articles pub. in med. jours., internat. med. lectr.; mil: capt. AUS 1946-48; Republican; rec: tennis, golf, gardening. Res: 4584 Ewing Rd Castro Valley 94546 Ofc: 1375 B St Hayward 94541

SHAH, KIRTI JAYANTILAL, electrical engineer; b. Dec. 10, Patan, North Gujorat, India; s. Jayantilal Khemchand and Bhagwatiben Jayantilal Shah; m. Sudha, Dec. 9, 1980; children: Binal Kirti Shah b. Feb. 11, Kruti Kirti Shah b. Aug. 23; edn: BE, VJTI, Univ. Bombay, India 1968; MS, Univ. Pittsburgh, Pa. 1971. Career: field and electrical engr. Westinghouse Electric Corp., Siemens Corp.; consulting application engr., computer support systems Teledyne Corp., Inet Div. (now Magnetek), Torrance, 1988-; awards: Patan Jain Mandal 1st, 1968-69; mem: Eta Kappa Nu, Sigma Xi, ISA, IEEE; rec: travel, debating, photography. Res: 23015 Madison St. Torrance 90505 Ofc: Magnetek 2750 W Lomita Blvd Torrance 90505

SHALLAT, RONALD FREDERICK, physician, neurological surgeon; b. May 22, 1941, Chicago, Ill.; s. Charles O. and Minnie A. (Kort) S.; m. Judith Mary McHugh, Aug. 24, 1968; children: Ryan b. 1971, Erin b. 1972, Kevin b.

1976; edn: MS w. honors, Univ. Ill. Sch. Medicine 1966; cert. Am. Bd. Neurosurgery 1976. Career: neurosurgical resident Univ. Ill., Chgo. 1966-73; pvt. practice neurological surgery, Berkeley 1973-; assoc. clin. prof. UCSF Sch. Medicine 1976-; chief div. neurological surgery Children's Hosp., Oakland 1980-86; mem: Am. Assn. Neurological Surgeons, Calif. Assn. Neurological Surgeons, S.F. Neurological Assn., A.C.S. (fellow); num. articles pub. in profl. jours.; mil: capt. USAF 1968-70; rec: golf, jogging. Res: 33 Evergreen Dr Orinda 94563 Ofc: East Bay Medical Group Inc 3000 Colby St Berkeley 94705

SHAMES, RICHARD LEIGH, physician; b. June 21, 1945, Norfolk, Va.; s. George Joseph and Rosalie (Weisman) S.; m. Karilee Feibus, Apr. 29, 1979; children: Shauna b. 1979, Georjana b. 1981, Gabriel b. 1986; edn: BA, Harvard Univ. 1967; MD, Univ. Pa. 1971; hypnotherapist, San Francisco Acad. of Hypnosis 1973; Diplomate Nat. Bd. Med. Examiners 1971. Career: researcher Nat. Insts. of Health 1970, intern USPHS, San Francisco 1971; chief clin. physician Marin Co. Health Dept. San Rafael 1972-75; chief med. svcs. The Assn. for Res. and Enlightenment, Edgar Cayce Clin. Phoenix 1979; pvt. practice fam. med., preventive and holistic health Mill Valley 1979-; researcher Nat. Inst. Health 1970; med. dir., founder Wholistic Health & Nutrition Inst. Mill Valley 1975-78; fam. practice residency instr. UCSF Med. Sch. family practice dept. 1976; bd. dirs. Children's Circle Center Private Sch. 1984; honors: Rose Meadow Levinson Meml. Prize for Cancer Res. 1970; mem: Phys. for Social Responsibility; publ: books: Healing with Mind Power (Rodale Press 1978), The Gift of Health (Bantam Books 1981); contr. ed. and author of Ask the Family Doctor column for Internat. Jour. of Holistic Health and Med. 1984-85; mil: lt. USPHS 1971; rec: gardening, skiing, sailing. Res: 77 Lomita Mill Valley 94941 Ofc: 10 Willow Ste 4 Mill Valley 94941

SHAPERO, HARRIS JOEL, pediatrician; b. Nov. 22, 1930, Winona, Minn.; s. Charles and Minnie Sara (Ehrlichman) S.; m. Byong Soon Yu, Nov. 6, 1983; children: Bradley b. 1965, Charles b. 1969, Laura b. 1959, James b. 1966; edn: AA, UCLA, 1953; BS, Northwestern Univ. 1954, MD, 1957; diplomate and certified splst. occupational medicine Am. Bd. Preventive Med. 1977, cert. aviation medicine FAA 1976, indep. med. examiner WCAB 1989, indep. med. examiner in preventive and occupational medicine, Calif. Dept. Indsl. Rels., Div. Indsl. Accidents 1989. Career: intern L.A. Co.-Harbor Gen. Hosp. 1957-58, resident in pediatrics, 1958-60, staff physician Harbor-UCLA 1960-64; attdg. physician perceptually Handicapped Children's Clinic, 1960-63; disease control ofcr. for tuberculosis, L.A. Co. Health Dept., 1962-64; pvt. practice splst. in pediatrics and occupational medicine, Cypress, Calif. 1965-85; pediatric cons. L.A. Health Dept., 1963-85, disease control ofcr. sexually transmitted diseases, 1984-85; pediatric cons. Bellflower Clinic, 1962-85; emergency room dir. AMI, Anaheim 1968-78; mem. med. staff Anaheim Gen. Hosp., pediatric staff Hosp. de General, Ensenada, Mex. 1978-; primary care clinician Sacramento Co. Health and a private practice of Medico-Legal Evaluation, 1987-88; founder Calif. Legal Evaluation Med. Group; health care provider/advisor to cities of Anaheim, Buena Park, Cypress, Garden Grove, Cypress Sch. Dist., Magnolia Sch. Dist., Savanna Sch. Dist., Anaheim Unified Sch. Dist., Orange Co. Dept. Edn.; pediatric and tuberculosis cons. var. orgns.; founder Pan American Childrens Mission; named Headliner of year Orange Co. Press Club 1978; mem: Fellow Coll. Preventative Medicine, L.A. Co. Med. Assn., L.A. Co. Indsl. Med. Assn., Am. Coll. Emergency Physicians, L.A. Co. Pediatric Soc., Orange Co. Pediatric Soc., Am. Public Health Assn., Mex.-Am. Border Health Assn., Toastmasters; author: The Silent Epidemic (1979); Republican; Jewish; rec: antique books and manuscripts, photog., graphics, beekeeper. Res: Rural Box 228 Wilton 95693 Ph: (213) 658-6765 Ofc: PO Box 10874 Beverly Hills 90213 also: 5266 E Pomona, East L.A. Ph: 213/721-0763

SHAPIRO, EVERETT HALE, lawyer; b. Oct. 9, 1927, Stockton; s. Abraham Louis and Sophie (Todresic) S.; m. Phyllis Sylvia Malk, Nov. 15, 1953; children: Tad Steven b. 1955, David Jay b. 1958; edn: BA, UC Berkeley 1950; JD, San Francisco Law Sch. 1966. Career: pvt. law practice; advy. bd. Nat. Bank of the Redwoods; comml. law instr. Empire Coll., Santa Rosa 1968-69; guest lectr. Santa Rosa Jr. Coll. Bus. Edn. Dept. 1978-; apptd. Sonoma Co. Film & Video Commn. 1991-, Sonoma Co. Library Bd. 1970-75; City of Santa Rosa Parks & Rec. Com. bd. 1975-76, Luther Burbank Com. 1977-84; mem: Sonoma Co. Bar Assn., Am. Bar Assn., Assn. Trial Lawyers of Am., Calif. Trial Lawyers Assn., Redwood Empire Trial Lawyers Assn. (pres. 1972), Am. Judicature Soc.; civic bds: Commonwealth Club of Calif. (Sonoma Co. steering com.), Special Olympics 1990, Social Advocates for Youth (1990), Am.-Israeli Pub. Affairs Com. (nat. advy. bd. 1985-89), B'nai B'rith (past pres.), past bd. dirs. United Crusade, Red Cross, Kiwanis, and YMCA; mil: AUS 1945-47; Democrat; Jewish; rec: swimming, walking, tennis. Res: 2030 Eleanor Dr Santa Rosa 95404 Ofc: 717 College Ave 2d Fl Santa Rosa 95404

SHAPIRO, ISADORE, chemical consultant, engineer; b. April 25, 1916, Mpls.; s. Jacob and Bessie (Goldman) S.; m. Mae Hirsch, Sept. 4, 1938; children: Stanley Harris b. 1941, Jerald Steven b. 1943; edn: BChE (w. high distinction), Univ. Minn. 1938, PhD 1944, postdoctoral res. fellow 1944-45; Career: asst. instr. chem. Univ. of Minn. 1938-41; res. fellow 1944-45; research chemist E.I. duPont de Nemours & Co., Philadelphia, Penn. 1946; head chem. lab. USN

Ordnance Test Sta., Pasadena 1947-52; rater US Civil Svc. Bd. Examiners 1948-52; dir. res. lab. Olin Mathieson Chem. Corp., Pasadena 1952-59; head chem. dept. Hughes Tool Co. Aircraft div., Culver City 1959-62; pres. Universal Chemical Systems, Inc. 1962-; pres. Aerospace Chemical Systems, Inc. 1964-66; dir. contract res. HITCO, 1966-67; prin. scientist McDonnell Douglas Astronautics Co., Santa Monica 1967-70; cons. Garrett AiResearch Mfg. Co., Torrance 1971-82; indep. cons. 1982-; dep. gov. Am. Biographical Inst. Research Assn. 1988, dep. dir. gen. Internat. Biog. Ctr. Eng. 1989; mem: Fellow Am. Inst. of Chemists, Am. Chemical Soc., Am. Physical Soc., Nat. Inst. of Ceramic Engrs., Soc. for Adv. of Materials & Process Engring., Am. Ceramic Soc., AAAS, Am. Ordnance Assn., Am. Inst. Aero. & Astro., Internat. Plansee Soc. for Powder Metal., Am. Assn. Contamination Control, Am. Inst. of Physics, Soc. of Rheology, Am. Powder Metallurgy Inst., Sigma Xi, Tau Beta Pi, Phi Lambda Upsilon; works: 50+ presentations tech. soc. confs. including XVI (Paris), XVII (Munich) and XIX (London) Internat. Congs. for Pure and Appl. Chem.; 5th CIMTEC Italy 1982; XV Latin Am. Chem. Congress, Puerto Rico; Engring. Ceramics, Jerusalem 1984; 6th CIMTEC, Milan 1986; PM '86 in Europe, Dusseldorf (1986); Pittsburgh Conf., Atlantic City 1987; IUPAC Internat. Symp. on Polymers, Jerusalem 1987; First Internat. Conf. on Ceramic Powder Processing, Orlando, Fla. 1987; 3rd Internat. Symp. on Ceramic Materials, Las Vegas 1988; 198th Am. Chem. Soc. Nat. Meeting, Miami Beach (1989); Advances in PM, Chgo. 1991; 1992 Powder Metallurgy World Cong., San Francisco 1992; contbr. 100+ papers in sci. journs. incl. J. of Inorganic and Nuclear Chem., Review Sci. Instr., others; holder 20 patents, others pend.; research: discovered and named Carborane Series of compounds; contbr. cataly-sis, mass spectrometry, infrared spectroscopy, nuclear magnetic resonance spec-trometry, propellant and missile chemistry, boron hydrides, organoboranes, reac-tion kinetics, surface chemistry, fiber and composites technology incl. Boron Carbide and carbon filaments, compaction of powders; mil: 1st lt. US Army Anti-Aircraft Artillery 1941-44, WWII; rec: European travel. Res: 5624 W 62nd St Los Angeles 90056

SHAPIRO, JERALD STEVEN, aerospace co. scientist, mortgage banker, executive; b. Dec. 3, 1943, Mnpls.; s. Isadore and Mae (Hirsch) S.; edn: BS, UC Los Angeles 1964, cert. small bus. mgmt., 1970, real estate mgmt. courses, 1969-76; Calif. lic. real estate broker 1970; desig: Cert. Investment Broker 1977, Investment Splst. 1981, Cert. Escrow Ofcr. 1983, CRA (cert. review appraiser, 1986), RMU (reg. mortgage underwriter, 1986). Career: mgr. process engring. and quality control Aerospace Chem. Systems Inc., Gardena 1963-66; chem. engr. HITCO, Gardena 1966-67; mats. & process engr., product reliability engr. McDonnell Douglas Corp., Long Beach 1967-70; chemist Los Angeles Co. Sanitation Dist., 1971-74; staff scientist TRW Def. and Space Systems Gp., Redondo Beach 1974-, team mem. VLBI, Signature appears on MARS via Viking Orbiter (Viking Lander Biol. Instrument); cons. Century 21 Beverlywood Realty Inc., L.A.; pres. Nationwide Mortgage Corp., L.A.; pres. Heritage Realty Group, L.A., exec. v.p. Wilshire Doheny Investments Corp., Beverly Hills, exec. v.p. JSK Capital Group Inc., Beverly Hills; bd. trustees and prof. Internat. Coll. of California, Irvine; bd. dirs. Internat. Wellness Inst., Beverly Hills; advy. bd. First Women's Bank of Calif. 1977-78, bd. dirs: Western Advanced Technology Systems Inc. 1980-, Environmental Protection Polymers Inc. 1980-; mem: Am. Chem. Soc., Nat. Assn. of Mortgage Brokers, Mortgage Bankers Assn. of Am., L.A. Bd. Realtors, Calif. Assn. Realtors, Calif. Escrow Assn., Nat. Assn. Realtors, Nat. Assn. Review Appraisers and Mortgage Underws., Am. Def. Preparedness Assn.; author: Aware and Beware, Guide to Intelligent Home Buying. Ofc: Nationwide Mortgage Corp. 2800 S Robertson Blvd Los Angeles 90034

SHAPIRO, MARTIN AARON, financial planner; b. Aug. 30, 1956, Santa Monica; s. Raymond and Lois Yvonne (Malcolm) S.; m. Joann Janine Goodman, Nov. 14, 1987; children: Natalie b. 1989; edn: BA econ. UCSD 1981; Chartered Fin. Cons. 1989, Chartered Life Underwriter 1989, Cert. Fin. Planner 1991. Career: comm. systems cons. AT&T, L.A. 1981-85; reg. rep. The Equitable, San Diego 1985-88; assoc. Capital Analysts 1988-91; owner Wealth and Tax Specialists 1991-; honors: UCSD Provosts Hons. List (1978-81); mem: Nat. Assn. Accts. (dir. 1991-), UCSD Alumni Assn. (v.p. 1989-), Lead San Diego, Southern Caregiver Resource Ctr. (dir. 1991-); articles pub. in Cabrillo Chronicle (1989), La Jolla Light (1992); Republican; Jewish; rec: sports. Res: 11541 Camino Playa Catalina San Diego 92124 Ofc: 9360 Towne Centre Dr Ste 200 San Diego 92121

SHARMA, ARJUN DUTTA, cardiologist, educator; b. June 2, 1953, Bombay, India; s. Hari D. and Gudrun (Axelsson) S.; m. Carolyn D. Burleigh, May 9, 1981; children: Allira b. 1982, Eric b. 1985, Harrison b. 1991; edn: BSc, Univ. Waterloo, Canada 1972, MD, Univ. Toronto, 1976; desig: FRCPC (1981), FACC (1985), FACP (1989). Career: research assoc. Barnes Hosp., Washington Univ., St. Louis, Mo. 1981-83; asst. prof. medicine Univ. of Western Ontario, London, Can. 1983-88, asst. prof. pharmacol. tox. 1983-89, assoc. prof. medi-cine 1988-89; assoc. clin. prof. medicine UC Davis, 1989-; dir. interventional electrophysiol. Sutter Memorial Hosp., Sacramento 1990-, mem. research com. 1991-, exec. com. Sutter Heart Inst. 1992-; awards: Dr. C.S. Wainwright Award, Univ. Toronto, 1973, 74, 75; John Melady Award, Univ. Toronto, 1972; 1st

Prize resrch. Toronto Gen. Hosp., 1980; career scientist award Ontario Ministry of Heart, 1983-89; med. research grantee MRC, Canada, Ottawa, 1983-89; Fellow Am. Coll. of Cardiology, 1981-, Canadian Cardiovascular Soc., 1981-; mem: Am. Fedn. for Clinical Research, 1981-, NY Acad. of Scis.; civic: Sierra Club, 1991-, Crocker Art Mus., 1989-; publs: 130+ sci. articles; rec: tennis, ski-ing, philately. Ofc: Diagnostic and Interventional Cardiology Consultants, 3941 J St Ste 260 Sacramento 95864

SHARMA, SURENDRA P., scientist; b. Feb. 3, 1943, Gorakhpur, India; s. Suresh Dutt and Dhan Pati (Devi) S.; m. Prabha Durgapal, May 12, 1983; chil-dren: Seema b. 1985; edn: BSc, Univ. Gorakhpur, India 1962; MS engring., P.F.U., Moscow 1968; DSc, M.I.T., 1978. Career: scientist C.S.I.R., Govt. India, New Delhi 1968-70; lectr. aero. and astro. I.I.T. Bombay, 1970-71; adj. prof. Naval Postgrad. Sch., Monterey, Calif. 1979-80; res. engr. U.T.S.I., Tullahoma, Tenn. 1980-81; sr. engr. Brown & Root, Houston 1981-82; Smith Internat. 1982-86; research scientist NASA Ames, Moffett Field, Calif. 1986-; recipient of num. NASA awards; mem: Sigma Xi 1975-, AIAA (assoc. fellow 1975-); civic: PTA, Cupertino Schs. 1991-; publs: 20+ sci. jour. articles; Democrat; Hindu; rec: gar-dening. Ofc: NASA Ames 230-2 PO Box 1000 Moffett Field 94035

SHARMAN, WILLIAM, professional basketball player, coach, executive, ret.; b. May 25, 1926, Abilene, Tex.; m. Joyce; children by previous marriage: Jerry, Nancy, Janice, Tom; edn: Univ. So. Calif. Career: basketball player Washington Capitols, 1950-51, Boston Celtics, 1951-61; coach Los Angeles/Utah Stars, 1968-71; coach Los Angeles Lakers, 1971-76, gen. mgr., 1976-82, pres., 1982-88; named to Nat. Basketball Assn. All Star First Team (1956-59), 2d Team (1953, 55, 70), All League Team (7t), named Coach of Year NBA (1972), inducted Naismith Basketball Hall of Fame (1976); author: Sharman on Basketball Shooting (1965). Ofc: 4511 Roma Ct Marina Del Rey 90292

SHARP, ULYSSES S. GRANT, retired naval officer; b. Apr. 2, 1906, Chinook, Mont.; s. Ulysses S. G. and Cora (Krauss) S.; m. Patricia O'Connor, Aug. 2, 1930 (dec. 1986); children: Patricia (Mrs. Russell F. Milham) b. 1931, Grant Alexander (Rear Admiral USN-Ret.) b. 1938; m. Nina B. Blake, Feb. 4, 1987; edn: BS, US Naval Acad., 1927; engring. Annapolis Postgrad. Sch., 1934-36; Naval War Coll., 1949-50; Hon. Dr. of Sci. Mont. St. Univ. 1972. Career: served to Admiral U.S. Navy 1923-68: sea assignments abd. USS New Mexico (battle-ship), USS Henderson (transport), USS Sumner, USS Buchanan (destroyers), USS Saratoga (aircraft carrier), 1927-34; abd. USS Richmond (cruiser), USS Winslow (destroyer) 1936-39; Bur. of Ships, 1940-42; Comdg. ofcr. USS Hogan (destroyer-minesweeper) Atlantic 1942-43, USS Boyd (destroyer) PTO, award-ed 2 Silver Star medals, 1943-44; staff, Comdr. Destroyer Force, U.S. Pacific Fleet 1944-48; comdg. ofcr. Fleet Sonar Sch., San Diego 1948-49; Comdr. Destroyer Sq. Five Korean War 1950-51, and staff of Comdr. U.S. Seventh Fleet/ fleet planning ofcr. for Inchon invasion; staff of Comdr. U.S. Second Fleet 1951-53; Comdg. Ofcr. USS Macon (cruiser) 1953-54; staff, Comdr.-in-Chief U.S. Pac. Fleet 1954-55; first Flag assignment as Comdr. Cruiser Div. Three 1956-57; dir. strat. plans div. Office of the Chief Naval Ops., Wash. DC 1957-58; Comdr. Cruiser-Destroyer Force, Pacific Fleet, based in San Diego 1959-60, Comdr. U.S. First Fleet 1960; promoted to Vice-Adm., Dep. Chief Naval Ops. Plans and Policy, 1960-63, awarded Navy Distinguished Service Medal; promot-ed to Adm., Comdr.-in-Chief U.S. Pacific Fleet, 1963-64; apptd. by Pres. Comdr.-in-Chief Pacific (unified command of 1 mil. Army, Navy, Marine Corps and Air Force personnel in 85-mil. sq. mi. area) supr. combat ops. in Vietnam and Pacific, 1964-68; decorated Navy Disting. Service (2d.), Army Disting. Service, decorated by govts. of Thailand, Rep. of China, Rep. of Korea, Rep. of Philippines, Rep. of Vietnam and Brazil; mem. U.S. Navy League; club: La Jolla CC; author: Strategy for Defeat - Vietnam in Retrospect 1978; Republican; Episcopalian; rec: golf. Res: 876 San Antonio Pl San Diego 92106

SHARPE, ROLAND LEONARD, consulting earthquake engineer; b. Dec. 18, 1923, Shakopee, Minn.; s. Alfred Leonard and Ruth Helen (Carter) S.; m. Jane Esther Steele, Dec. 28, 1946; children: Douglas b. 1954, Deborah b. 1957, Sheryl b. 1965; edn: BSECE, Univ. Mich., Ann Arbor 1947, MSE, 1949; Calif. reg. profl. civil engr., 1952, structural engr., 1954. Career: v.p. 1950-65, exec. v.p. and gen. mgr. J.A. Blume Engineers, San Francisco 1965-73, also technical dir. Aetron-Blume-Atkinson, Palo Alto 1961-66, exec. v.p. J. Blume Engrs.-Iran, Tehran, Iran 1970-73; mng. director Applied Technology Council, Palo Alto 1973-84; pres. Calif. Engring. &.Devel. Co., Las Vegas, Nev. 1976-84; chmn. and c.e.o. Engring. Decision Analysis Co. Inc., Palo Alto 1974-87; pres. R. Sharpe Consulting Structural Engrs., Cupertino 1987-; mng. dir. EDAC, GmbH, Frankfurt, Ger. 1974-82; chair U.S. Jt. Com. on Earthquake Engring. 1983-88, U.S. nat. advy. com. Nat. Earthquake Hazard Reduction Pgm. 1990-; honors: Tau Beta Pi 1949, cit. for contbns. to constrn. industry Engring. News Record, NY, NY (1978-79, 86-87), cit. for devel. of improvements in structural design Applied Technology Council 1990)and Japan Struct. Consultants Assn., Tokyo 1990; mem: Am. Soc. Civil Engrs. (1947-, fellow, life), Am. Concrete Inst. (1947-, life), Struct. Engrs. Assn. of No. Calif. and Calif. (1955-, life), Japan Structural Cons. Assn. (hon. mem.- only non-Japanese, 1992-); civic: Jr. C.of C. Palo Alto (pres. 1954-56); publs: 50+ tech. articles and papers (1961-), coauthor 3 books: Earthquake Engrg. for Nuclear Power Plants (1969),

Earthquake Mitigation Guidelines for Data Processing Ctrs. (1989), Seismic Safety Guidelines (1982); mil: sgt. USMC 1942-46; Prot.; rec: skiing, gardening, music. Res: 10320 Rolly Rd Los Altos 94024 Ofc: Sharpe Struct. Engrs. 10051 Pasadena Ave Cupertino 95014

SHATNEY, CLAYTON HENRY, general surgeon, educator; b. Nov. 4, 1943, Bangor, Me.; s. Clayton Lewis and Regina (Cossette) S.; m. Deborah Gaye Hansen, Apr. 1977; children: Anthony, Andrew; edn: grad. (valedictorian) Orono (Me.) H.S., 1961; BA (cum laude, State of Maine Scholar) Bowdoin Coll., 1965; MD, Tufts Univ. Sch. Med., 1969; PhD Cand. Univ. Minn. Grad. Sch., 1974-82; MD lic. Minn. 1970, Calif. 1975, D.C. 1977, Md. 1979, Fla. 1983; bd. cert. Am. Bd. Gen. Surgery 1978, cert. adv. cardiac life support 1979, adv. trauma life support instr. 1981. Career: med. intern Mayo Clinic, Rochester 1969-70, surg. resident Univ. Minn. Hosps., Mpls. 1970-77; served to major US Army Med. Corps, Walter Reed Army Med. Ctr., W.D.C., 1977-79; cons. VA Coop. Studies Pgm., W.D.C. 1980-; asst. prof. surgery Univ. Md. Hosp., Balt. 1979-82; assoc. prof. Univ. Fla. Sch. Med., Jacksonville 1982-87, dir. trauma Univ. Hosp. 1982-85; clin. assoc. prof. surgery Stanford Univ. Sch. of Medicine 1987-; surg. practice Santa Clara Valley Med. Ctr., San Jose; vis. prof. surgery The Upjohn Co., 1974-, Hoechst-Roussel Pharm., 1983-, instr. VALTRAC Anastomosis, Davis & Geck, 1990-91; awards: Garcelon Merit Med. Scholar 1965-69, clin. fellow Am. Cancer Soc. 1971-73, Phi Kappa Phi 1976-, Am. Acad. Fam. Physicians tchg. award 1980, tchg. cit. dept. preventive med. Ohio State Univ. 1981, pres. Fla. Soc. of Critical Care Med. 1987-88, investigator 23+ funded research projects; mem. Assn. for Acad. Surgery, The Shock Soc. (charter), Soc. Critical Care Med., AAAS, Kans. City Surg. Soc. (hon.), So. Med. Assn., SE Surg. Cong., Surg. Infection Soc., A.C.S. (Fellow), Fla. Soc. Critical Care Med., Am. Acad. Surg. Research (charter), Lillehei Surg. Soc., Internat. Platform Assn., Soc. for Surgery of Alimentary Tract, Panamerican Trauma Soc. (charter), Internat. Coll. Surgeons, Am. Assn. for Surgery of Trauma, Santa Clara Co. Med. Assn., Calif. Med. Assn., SW Surg. Cong., Internat. Soc. Surgery; publs: 83+ med. jour. articles, 29+ abstracts, 23+ texts & symposia, 3 films, numerous nat., internat. meeting presentations. Ofc: Dept. Surgery Santa Clara Valley Medical Center, 751 S Bascom Ave San Jose 95128 Tel: 408/299-5142

SHAW, DONALD J., lawyer; b. Rochester, N.Y.; s. Clarence and Anna (Reichel) S.; m. Peggy Jean; children: Mark, James (Sgt. USMC); edn: stu. acctg./fin. L.A. City Coll., S.F.V. Jr. Coll., CSC Northridge; JD, Southwestern Univ.; admitted bar: Calif., U.S. Dist. Ct. (cent. dist.), U.S. Supreme Ct.; lic. real estate sales agt. Calif. Career: acctg. pos. various cos. including GM, Litton, American Safety and TRW; full charge controller Western Amusement Co. Film Ventures (exhibitor & distbr. of motion pictures), 6 yrs.; Chapman and Olson Film Co. (prodn. t.v. commercials); solo law practice, Beverly Hills; corporate counsel USA Video Corp., Micron Mining Co., Micron Minerals Corp., APH Recycling Inc., Hi-Tech Metal Refiners Inc.; honors: letter of commendn. the White House, resolution Calif. St. Senate (Sen. Alan Robbins) and Assembly (Rep. Richard Katz), commendn. Calif. St. Assembly (Rep. Marion La Follette), L.A. City Mayor Bradley and L.A. Co. Bd. Suprs. (Supr. Michael D. Antonovich); mem: ABA, L.A. Trial Lawyers Assn., Beverly Hills Bar Assn., Century City Bar Assn., Motion Picture and TV Controller's Assn. (1st v.p.), Forum Com. on Entertainment and Sports Industries, Actor's Fund (life), Am. Film Inst., Variety Club (Tent 25), Internat. Footprinters, British United Svs. Club, Kiwanis (pres. 1985-86). Ofc: 9744 Wilshire Blvd Ste 310 Beverly Hills 90212

SHAW, WILLIAM JAY, business banking officer; b. Jan. 14, 1962, San Francisco; s. William Cooper and Mary Elizabeth (Wolfe) S.; m. Kimberly Ann Kocman, Aug. 24, 1991; son, William Henry b. 1992; edn: BS, Univ. of Pacific, 1984; MPA, USC, 1989. Career: market analyst Am. Savings, Stockton 1984-85; builder account mgr. Bank of Am., San Francisco 1985-88; development specialist L.A. County C.D.C., Monterey Park 1990-93; bus. banking ofcr., Wells Fargo Bank 1993-; honors: award of merit USC Graduate Sch. 1989, Outstanding Young Men of Am. 1988, Eagle Scout BSA 1976, listed Who's Who in West 1992, founder pres. Delta Sigma Pi Univ. Of Pacific Lambda Mu (1984, #00001); mem. Soc. of Mayflower Descendants (life), Soc. Calif. Pioneers (life), Soc. Colonial Wars 1990-; Republican; Methodist; rec: golf, tennis, bicycles.

SHEA, THEODORE WILLIAM, obstetrician-gynecologist; b. Feb. 14, 1960, Los Angeles; s. William Henry and Karen Ruth (Olsen) S.; edn: BS, Andrews Univ., Berrien Springs, Mich. 1982; MD, Loma Linda Univ. Sch. of Med., 1987; bd. eligible Am. Bd. Ob-Gyn, 1991. Career: staff physician Sutter Solano Med. Ctr., Vallejo 1991-; cons. Great Beginnings Prenatal Clinic, Vallejo 1991-92;mem: Am. Assn. Gynecologic Laparoscopists (Resident award for laparoscopy, Glendale 1990), Am. Coll. Ob-Gyn. (jr. fellow), Calif. Med. Assn., Solano County Med. Soc.; Republican; Prot.; rec: golf, tennis, running. Ofc: 127 Hospital Dr Ste 102 Vallejo 94589

SHEEHAN, LAWRENCE JAMES, lawyer; b. July 23, 1932, San Francisco; s. Lawrence Victor and Mary (Fallon) S.; edn: AB, Stanford Univ., 1957, LLB, 1959. Career: law clk. Chief Judge U.S. Ct. Appeals, N.Y.C. 1959-60; atty., assoc. O'Melveny & Myers, Los Angeles 1960-68, ptnr. 1969-; dir: TCW

Convertible Securities Fund, L.A. 1987-, Source Capital Inc., L.A. 1991-, 15 American Capital Mutual Funds, Houston 1991-; honors: Order of Coif Stanford Law Sch. 1959. Ofc: O'Melveny & Myers Ste 700 1999 Avenue of Stars Los Angeles 90067

SHEFRIN, HAROLD MARVIN, economist; b. July 27, 1948, Winnipeg, Canada; s. Samuel and Clara (Danzker) S.; m. Arna P., June 28, 1970; edn: BS hons., Univ. Manitoba Canada 1970; MS math., Univ. Waterloo 1971; PhD, London Sch. of Economics England 1974. Career: asst. prof. Univ. Rochester, N.Y. 1974-79; asst. prof., assoc. prof., prof. Santa Clara Univ. 1979-; cons. Dept. of Energy 1979-82; Syntex Corp. 1983-88. Address: Menlo Park 94025

SHELDON, KENNY, orchestra leader; b. May 1, Berlin; s. Benjamin and Hilda (Erreich) Scheflan; m. Rita Levy, Feb. 21, 1961; edn: student, NYU; student, Columbia Univ., Juillard, Manhattan Sch. of Music. Career: entertainer, orchestra leader Kenny Sheldon and his 'Swing and String' Orch., N.Y. Hilton Hotel, Hotel Plaza, Hotel Pierre, Waldorf Astoria Hotel, N.Y.C., 1947-72; entertainer nightclubs, resorts, country clubs, colleges, award dinners; performer hotels, So. Calif. since 1972-, incl. Hotel Bel Air, Beverly Hilton, Century Plaza, Bonaventure, L.A. Ambassador, Sheraton Miramar; country clubs incl. Bel Air CC, Brentwood CC, 1972-, Beverly Hills CC, 1985-, also Marina City Club, Sportsmen's Lodge, Santa Monica Civic Auditorium; 1989 TV appearances in NBC series "Quantum Leap" and CBS series "Peaceable Kingdom"; mem. Am. Fedn. of Musicians (Fellow). Consummate in field. Address: 1420 N Fuller Ave Ste 304 Los Angeles 90046

SHEN, MASON MING-SUN, acupuncturist; b. March 30, 1945, Shanghai, China, nat. US cit. 1975; s. John Kaung-Hao and Mae Chu (Sun) S.; m. Nancy, Aug. 7, 1976; children: Teresa b. 1978, Darren b. 1980; edn: BS, Taiwan Normal Univ. 1968; MS, So. Dakota State Univ. 1971; PhD, Cornell Univ. Med. Coll. 1977; OMD, San Francisco Coll. of Acup. 1984. Cert. Acupuncturist, Calif. (1979). Career: Chinese medicine apprenticeship, Taiwan 1962; acupuncturist Acupuncture Inst. of New York, 3 yrs.; pvt. practice Chinese medicine, dir. Pain and Stress Management Center, Pleasanton, 1982-; appt. commr. Acupuncture Com., Medical Bd. of Calif., 1988-92; honors: Nat. Svc. Award for heart research, 1977, Hon. Doctorate, Asian-American Univ., 1985, Hon. Life Pres., Hong-Kong and Kowloon Chinese Medical Assn., 1985, Hon. Pres. S.F. Sch. of Chinese Medicine (1986), Modern Who's Who in Chinese Medicine, 1991, The Internat. Who's Who of Intellectuals, 1989, Disting. Leadership Award, 1988; mem: Acupuncture Assn. of Am. (v.p. 1986-89), Am. Assn. Acup. and Oriental Medicine (pres. 1989-90), Calif. Cert. Acup. Assn. (pres. 1984-85), Calif. Acup. Alliance (pres. 1986-87, N. regional chmn. 1985-86), AAAS, NY Acad. of Sci., Am. Found. of Traditional Chinese Med., Rotary Club of Livermore Valley (charter), Contra Costa Chinese Republican Com. (pres. 1988-), Ronald Reagan Trust Fund (charter); publs: 40+ med. papers; cancer res. Cornell Univ. Med. Coll. (5 yrs), heart resrch. UCB (2 yrs), Lawrence Livermore Lab. (1 yr); mil: 2nd lt. Chemical Corps Army R.O.C.; Republican; rec: travel, equestrian. Res: 3240 Touriga Dr. Pleasanton 94566 Ofc: Pain and Stress Management Center, 1393 Santa Rita Rd Ste F Pleasanton 94566 also:185 Frond St #207 Danville 94526

SHENEMAN, JACK M., food and drug scientist; b. March 26, 1927, Grand Rapids, Mich.; s. Ralph M. and Henrietta (Eichhorn) S.; m. Hielke Brugman, Dec. 22, 1957; 1 dau., Elisa b. 1966; edn: BS, Mich. St. Univ. 1952; MS, 1954; PhD, 1957. Career: research asst. Mich. St. Univ., East Lansing 1954-57; research assoc. Wis. Malting Co., Manitowoc 1957-63, asst. dir. research 1957-63; sr. mocrobiologist Eli Lilly & Co., Indpls., Ind. 1963-69; Basic Vegetable Co., Vacaville 1969-74; food and drug scientist Calif. Dept. Health Food & Drug Branch, Sacto. 1975-92, expert consultant (food) 1992-; articles pub. in profl. jours. 1957-75; mil: sgt. AUS 1945-47; Presbyterian; rec: piano. Res: POB 2476 El Macero 95618 Ofc: California Food & Drug Branch 714 P St Sacramento 05618

SHEPARD, KATHRYN I., public relations counselor; b. Jan. 6, 1956, Tooele, Utah; d. James Lewis and Glenda Verleen (Slaughter) Clark; m. Mark L. Shepard, June 5, 1976; edn: BA history, comm., Boise State Univ., 1980; pub. relations, UCLA, summer 1992. Career: creative svs. KTTV Channel 11, Hollywood, 1982-86; public relations Hollywood Chamber of Commerce, 1986-87; prin. Kathy Shepard Public Relations, Burbank 1987-; instr. UCLA Ext., 1991-92; mem. Publicity Club of Los Angeles (bd. 1987-, pres. 1991-92); rec: genealogy, travel.

SHEPHERD, ROBIN, educator; b. June 28, 1933; s. Maurice Sidney and Ruby Stevens (Orr) S.; children: Mark b. 1962, Paul b. 1963; m. 2d. Maureen Shackel, Jan. 3, 1986; edn: BS in C.E., Univ. of Leeds, Eng. 1955, MS, 1965, DSc, 1973; PhD, Univ. Canterbury, N.Z. 1971; reg. profl. civil engr., Calif. 1981. Career: asst. engr. De Havilland Aircraft Co., Hatfield, Eng. 1955-57; Ministry of Works, Auckland, N.Z. 1958; faculty Univ. Canterbury, Christchurch, N.Z. 1959-71; assoc. prof. Univ. of Auckland, 1972-79; dir. N.Z. Heavy Engineering Research Assn., 1979-80; prof. UC Irvine, 1980-; cons. Seismic Resistant Design, N.Z. 1962-80; expert advisor Attorneys & Insurance Assessors, Calif.

1981-; pres. Forensic Expert Advisers Inc., 1990-; awards: E. R. Cooper medal and prize Royal Soc. N.Z. 1972, Erskine Fellow Univ. Canterbury (1969, 87), Fulbright travel grantee, vis. prof. Caltech 1977, vis. res. fellow Imperial Coll. Sci. & Tech., London 1984, vis. overseas fellow St. John's Coll., Cambridge, Eng. 1984; mem: Fellow Am. Soc. of Civil Engrs., Fellow Instn. of Civil Engrs. (U.K.), Nat. Acad. of Forensic Engrs., Earthquake Engring. Res. Ins., Seismol. Soc. of Am., N.Z. Nat. Soc. for Earthquake Engring.; Rotary Club (Auckland 1976-80, Newport/Irvine 1980-89, South Coast Met. 1990-); publs: 100+ tech. jour. papers re earthquake resistant design 1963-; rec: sailboarding, racquetball, golf, opera. Ofc: Dept. Civil Engg University California Irvine 92717

SHERIFF, GARTH IRVING, architect; b. Feb. 7, 1946, Los Angeles; s. David Henry and Yvonne Marie (Smith) S.; m. Ruth Yvette Prins, Nov. 27, 1980 (div. 1989); m. Lauren Anne Perreault, June 24, 1989; edn: B.Arch., USC 1969; reg. architect Calif. (1973). Career: draftsman Leach Cleveland & Assoc., Los Angeles 1969-71; project mgr. Ebbe Videriksen & Assoc., Sherman Oaks 1971-73; assoc. Les Lippich & Assoc., Encino 1973-74; project architect PSDA Inc., Sherman Oaks 1974-75; prin. Garth Sheriff & Assoc., Santa Monica 1974-75; ptnr. Allen & Sheriff, Los Angeles 1977-84; prin. Sheriff & Assoc. 1984-; instr. USC Exptl. Coll. 1969; cons., instr. City Building Edn. Program 1977-79; awards: Soc. Art Center cert. merit 1978, City of Beverly Hills cert. commendation 1982, City Alhambra beautiful award 1986, Calif. Legislative Assembly cert. recognition 1986, Gen. Electric Edison award 1986; mem: Architects Designers & Planners for Social Responsibility/L.A. (pres., nat. bd. dirs., exec. com.), AIA, Amnesty Internat., Nat. Trust for Historic Preservation, Watts Urban Workshop (fellow 1973-75), Self Realization Fellowship (cons. 1975-); author, city initiative, Santa Monica Pier Preservation Ordinance (1974), monograph on wind pub. (1969); Democrat. Ofc: 3440 Motor Ave 2d Flr Los Angeles 90034

SHERMAN, A. ROBERT, psychologist, educator; b. Nov. 18, 1942, N.Y.C.; s. David R. and Goldie (Wax) S.; m. Llana Sherman, Aug. 14, 1966 (div.); children: J. Colbert b. 1970, Relissa A. b. 1972; edn: BA (w/hons.), Columbia Univ. 1964; MS, Yale Univ. 1966, PhD, 1969; Calif. lic. psych. 1981. Career: faculty dept. of psychology UC Santa Barbara 1969-, clin. psychologist practice, 1981-; res. evaluation cons. Santa Barbara County Schs. 1974-77, cons. and guest lectr. var. orgns.; honors: Phi Beta Kappa 1963, predoctoral res. fellow Nat. Inst. of Mental Health (1964-67, 1968-69), Sigma Xi 1967, Samuel Miller Res. award 1967, Psi Chi Nat. Hon. Soc. in Psychology 1979, vol. of the yr. award Santa Barbara Mental Health Assn. 1979; mem: AAUP (chapter pres. 1978-79), Santa Barbara Co. Psychol. Assn. (pres. 1985), Am. Psychol. Assn., Phi Beta Kappa (chap. pres, 1977-78), Assn. for Advancement of Behavior Therapy, Behavior Therapy and Research Soc., Calif. State Psychol. Assn.; Santa Barbara Mental Health Assn. (pres. 1978, 85, 91), Santa Barbara Contg. Edn. Advy. Council, Mountain View Sch. Site Council (pres. 1978-84); publs. include 1 book, sev. book chpts., num. articles in profl. jours. Res: 545 Barling Terr Goleta 93117 Ofc: Dept. Psych. UCSB 93106 also: 5290 Overpass Rd. Ste 232 Santa Barbara 93111

SHERMAN, ERIC, filmmaker, educator; b. June 29, 1947, Santa Monica; s. Vincent and Hedda (Comorau) S.; m. Eugenia Blackiston Dillard, Apr. 1, 1978; children: Cosimo b. 1978, Rocky b. 1982; edn: BA, Yale Univ., 1968. Career: owner/opr. Film Transform, Inc., Los Angeles 1982-; film faculty Art Center Coll. of Design, Pasadena 1976-, Pepperdine Univ., Malibu 1976-86, Mellon lectr. Cal Tech, Pasadena 1978; awards: Peabody Bdcstg., Ga. 1990, Cine Gold Eagle, W.D.C. 1990, CINDY, L.A. 1990, numerous other film festivals; mem.: Film Forum (bd. dirs. 1988-), American Cinematheque (trustee 1986-); author: The Director's Event (1968), Directing the Film (1976), Frame by Frame (1987), Selling Your Film (1989). Ofc: Film Transform, Inc. 2427 Park Oak Dr Los Angeles 90068

SHERWOOD, ARTHUR LAWRENCE, lawyer; b. Jan. 25, 1943, Los Angeles; s. Allen J. and Edith S.; m. Frances M., May 1, 1970; children: David b. 1971, Chet b. 1973; edn: BA, UC Berkeley, 1964; MS, Univ. Chicago, 1965; JD, Harvard Law Sch., 1968; admitted bar: Calif. 1968. Career: atty., ptnr. Gibson, Dunn & Crutcher, Los Angeles 1968-; instr. UCLA Law Sch., 1968-69; judge pro tem Municipal and Small Claims Cts., L.A.; arbitrator N.Y. Stock Exchange, Nat. Futures Assn.; honors: Phi Beta Kappa; mem. Am. Bar Assn., L.A. Co. Bar Assn.; club: Brentwood CC; author 2 CEB textbooks: Civil Procedure Before Trial, Civil Procedure During Trial; Republican; Jewish. Ofc: Gibson, Dunn & Crutcher, 333 S Grand Ave Los Angeles 90071

SHERWOOD, ROBERT PETERSEN, educator; b. May 17, 1932, Black Diamond, Wash.; s. James Brazier and Zina (Petersen) S.; m. Merlene Burningham, Nov. 21, 1951; children: Robert Lawrence b. 1953, Richard W. b. 1954, Rolene b. 1956, RaNae b. 1961; edn: BS, and MS, Univ. Utah, 1956, 57; EdD, UC Berkeley, 1965. Career: tchr. Arden-Carmichael Sch. Dist., Carmichael 1957-60; vice prin., principal San Juan Unified Sch. Dist., Sacto. 1960-62, 62-65; assoc. prof. CSU Sacramento, 1965-70; prof. American River Coll., Sacto. 1970-, chair Sac./Anthro. Dept. 1980-86, pres. Academic Senate 1990-91; honors: report to nation Boy Scouts Am., Morgan, Ut., 1950, nat. spirit medal USN, San Diego, 1954, hon. life mem. Calif. P.T.A., Sacto., 1965, merit svc. West Assn. S. & C., Burlingame, 1981, profl. svc. Phi Delta Kappa, 1987;

mem: Calif. Tchrs. Assn., Nat. Edn. Assn. (life), Phi Delta Kappa (life), Calif. Fedn. of Coll. Profs., Faculty Assn. of Calif. Comm. Colls., Toastmasters Club Carmichael (pres. 1966-68); civic: Arden Park Rec. Dist., Sacto. (dir. 1966-72, bd. pres. 69-72); mil: CT2 USN 1953-55; Republican; Latter Day Saints; rec: reading, woodworking, travel. Res: 4053 Esperanza Dr Sacramento 95864 Ofc: American River College 4700 College Oak Dr Sacramento 95841

SHEVOCK, JAMES R., botanist; b. June 7, 1950, Spangler, Pa.; s. Simon Joseph S. and Betty Mae (Elchin) Washington; edn: BS botany, CSU Long Beach 1976; MA biology, 1978. Career: forest botanist Forest Service Sequoia NF, Porterville 1978-82, forest ecologist 1982-84; data base botanist Calif. Dept. Fish & Game, Sacto. 1984-86; regional botanist Forest Service Regional Office, San Francisco 1986-; lectr. botanical groups 1978-; awards: Calif. Acad. Sci. research assoc., Rancho Santa Ana Botanic Garden research assoc., USDA Forest Service cert. of merit 1980, 82, 86, 88, 90, 92; mem: Calif. Native Plant Soc. (field trip leader 1978-), Am. Soc. Plant Taxonomists, Calif. Botanical Soc., So. Calif. Botanists, Nature Conservancy; num. articles pub. in botanical jours. 1979-; Democrat; Prot.; rec: classical music, opera, camping. Res: Opera Plaza #811 601 Van Ness Ave San Francisco 94102 Ofc: U.S. Dept. of Agriculture Forest Service 630 Sansome St Room 823 San Francisco 94111

SHIELDS, CYNTHIA ROSE, educator, small business owner; b. June 1, Monterey; d. William Lawrence and Rose (Virdell) Jackson; m. Franklin Shields, Sept. 19, 1981; child: Brett b. 1983; edn: AA, City Coll. S.F., BS, Univ. San Francisco, MPA, Golden Gate Univ.; Calif. Comm. Colls. tchg. and supvy. life credentials. Career: account exec. KFSN-TV, Fresno, 1982-85; recruiter, instr. Merced County Schs., 1985-89; gen. mgr./owner AdLine Advertising, Merced, 1986-; Merced Coll. instr., 1989-90, cons. 1989-91, Youth Outreach coordinator, 1990-; senior assoc. San Joaquin Administrators Training Ctr., Madera, 1989-92; awards: Leadership Merced (grad. 1989); civic bds.: Merced Community Medical Ctr. Found. (dir. 1990-91), Merced Union High Sch. Dist. Ednl. Found. (dir. 1992), Merced County Community Housing Resource Bd. (coord. 1987-89), Merced Conv. & Visitors Bur. (chair 1991), Merced City C.of C. (dir. 1990-94, fin. com. 1991-94), Castle Joint Powers Auth. (minority issues v.chair 1991-93), Merced County Bus. and Edn. Roundtable (1992-94); mem: AAUW, Phi Delta Kappa; author: Maturity Skills for Successful Employment (1986), curriculum: Pre-Employment/Work Maturity (1989); Democrat; Prot.; rec: community volunteer, golf, cycling, reading. Ofc: PO Box 3346 Merced 95344

SHIMER, DONALD ALBERT, foundation administrator; b. Dec. 5, 1929, Easton, Pa.; s. Arthur Charles and Dora Alice (Uhler) S.; m. Virginia Ries (div.); m. Patricia Nan Worthington, Apr. 12, 1970; children: W. Ralph Lammers b. 1958, Donald A., Jr. b. 1958, Peter A. b. 1962; edn: BA in history, Lafayette Coll., 1951. Career: exec. YMCA, Worcester, Mass., Asbury Park, N.J., Livingston, N.J., Portland, Oreg. 1951-69, mem. San Francisco YMCA planning & ops. com. 1975-, v.p. YMCA Model Legislature/Court Bd. 1985- sr. v.p. J. Panas & Ptnrs., Chgo. 1969-74; pres. Shimer & Sons Ltd., Chgo., Ill., Walnut Creek, Calif., 1974-; v.p. devel. Childrens Hosp., San Francisco 1975-77; exec. dir. Childrens Hosp. Found., Fresno 1978-82; exec. dir. Marin General Hosp. Found., Greenbrae, Calif. 1982-87; exec. v.p. Gandhi Found., Orinda 1987-; pres. Dollbergen & Worthington, Inc. 1992-; Rotarian; mil: sgt. US Army 1951-53; Republican; Episcopalian; rec: running, golf, travel, reading, computer. Res: 1510 Arkell Rd Walnut Creek 94598-1207

SHIMKHADA, DEEPAK, art history educator; edn: BFA 1968, MFA 1971, Univ. of Baroda, India; MA, USC, 1974; PhD, Ohio State Univ., (ABD) 1979; Languages: Nepali, Sanskrit, English, Hindi, Gujarati, Newari, French. Career: teaching assoc. Ohio State Univ. 1977-81; instr. Scripps Coll. 1981-82; instr. CSU Long Beach 1989; curator "Exhibition of Napali Art" Montgomery Art Gallery 1973; contbr. Woven Jewels: Tibetan Rugs from So. Calif. Collections (exhibn. cat.) 1992; Tibet: The Contented Heart (book) 1992; coord., contbr. "USC Collects: A Sampling of Taste" (exhib.) USC 1974; organizer, cochair "Himalayan Art & Culture" Univ. Wisc. 1980; organizer, cochair "Innovation Without Loss of Tradition" art history panel, Univ. Mo. 1981; curator "God, Man, Woman and Nature in Asian Art" Scripps Coll. (exhib.), Claremont 1985; curator "Indian Miniatures from the Hariette Von Breton Collection" (exhib.) Pacific Asia Museum, Pasadena, 1986; organizer "Himalayas at the Crossroads" (symposium), Pacific Asia Museum, Pasadena 1987; editor 2 books: Popular Buddhist Mantras in Sanskrit, 1984, Himalayas at the Crossroads: Portrait of a Changing World, 1987; organizer, contbr. "Himalayan Art: Patrons and Public" art history panel CSU-LB 1989; curator "Eye of India: Art of the People" (exhib.) Palos Verdes Art Center, Palos Verdes, 1991; head librarian Buckeye Village Library, Columbus, Ohio 1980-81; pgm. coord. Claremont Grad. Sch. 1987-; editor newsletter: Himalaya, 1987-; lectr. various institutions 1977-; mem: College Art Assn. of Am., Art Historians of So. Calif., Am.-Nepal Soc. of Calif., Assn. for Asian Studies, Assn. for Asian Studies on the West Coast, Nepal Studies Assn., Pacific Asia Museum, Nepal Assn. of Fine Arts, Assn. of Nepalis in the Americas (exec. bd.); awards: Jr. then Sr. Cultural Fellow govt. of India (1962-71), Fulbright fellow U.S. State Dept. (1972-74), tuition fellowship Univ. Chicago 1974-76, Jr. Research Fellow Am. Inst. of Indian Studies for Smithsonian Instn. 1979-80, Ohio State Univ. Grad. Students Alumni Res. Award

1980, Council of South Asia Grant, Assn. for Asian Studies 1989, Honorable Mention in painting Triennale of World Contemporary Art, India 1970, certificate awards, juried exhibs. of Nepal Assn. of Fine Arts, Nepal 1966-69, Dean's List, USC 1973; exhibits: Chicago Public Library 1977, Expo-70 Osaka, Japan, Triennale of World Contemporary Art, India (1967, 70), 1-man show Max Gallery, Kathmandu 1968; publs: numerous articles and papers in profl. jours. Ofc: Claremont Graduate School 165 E 10th St Claremont CA 91711

SHIRASAWA, RICHARD MASAO, systems coordinator; b. Jan. 18, 1948, Cleveland, Ohio; s. Thomas S. and Mae (Yokota) S.; edn: BS psychology, Mich. St. Univ., 1970; biochem., George Washington Univ., 1992. Career: vol. U.S. Peace Corps, W.D.C. 1970-71; NIH 1972-73; lab. tech. Litton Industries, Bethesda, Md. 1973-74; biologist Nat. Inst. Mental Health 1973-81; mgmt. intern Dept. Health Human Sci. 1981-83; system coordinator Health Care Fin. Adminstrn., San Francisco 1984-; trainer/computer systems analyst Health Care Fin. Adminstrn. 1986-; profl. awards: Health Care Fin. Adminstr. (1988, 89, 90), Shopsmith Inc. 1981; mem: Asian Pacific Personnel Assn. (secty.), Asian Bus. League, Toastmasters Internat. (newsletter editor Toastmasters S.F. 1986-, awarded Competent TM 1987), 4-H Club (group leader 1985-); 3 article pub. in profl. jours. (1974, 75, 78); rec: Masters' swimming, woodworking. Ofc: Health Care Financing Adminstration 75 Hawthorne St San Francisco 94105

SHIRE, HAROLD RAYMOND, professor, author, inventor; b. Nov. 23, 1910, Denver, Colo.; s. Samuel and Rose Betty (Herman) S.; m. Cecilia; children: David, Esti, Darcy; edn: Cert. in Bus., UCLA; MBA, Pepperdine Univ.; MLA, USC; JD, Southwestern Univ.; PhD, US Internat. Univ.; admitted bar: Calif., US Supreme Ct. Career: deputy dist. atty. Los Angeles County 1937-39; asst. U.S. atty. 1939-42; pvt. practice law, Los Angeles & Beverly Hills 1946-56; pres. General Connectors Corp., Certified Spotwelding Corp., Quality Aircraft Corp., Quality Trading Corp. 1956-70; chmn. bd. General Connectors Corp., also Bestobel Aircraft Ltd., U.K., 1970-73; prof. structural orgn. & law Pepperdine Univ. 1973-78; investor, builder 1973-; prof. mgmt. & law U.S. Internat. Univ., San Diego 1981-85; served in U.S. Army Infantry 1942-46; honors: Companion Royal Aero. Soc. U.K., Chevalier du Vieux Moulin Fr., Service Ofcr. and Adj. Gen.'s Ward & Chenault Post, Am. Legion, Shanghai, China; awards: recipient commendations from U.S. Atty. Gen., Pres. J.F. Kennedy and Pres. L.B. Johnson, Hon. LLD Pepperdine Univ. 1981, Jewish Nat. Fund medal of honor and elected comdr. JNF Legion of Honor 1992; mem. univ. bd. Pepperdine Univ.; mem: Fed., Calif. and Beverly Hills Bar Assns., Am. Soc. Internat. Law, Am. Welding Soc., Material & Process Engrs., Am. Legion, AAUP, AF Assn., alumni assns., Lambda Delta Beta, Psi Chi, Japan-Am. Soc., Japanese Com. of San Diego (hon. pres.), Urasenke Cha No Yu, The Founders/ L.A. Music Ctr., Union of Orthodox Jewish Congregations of Am. (exec. com., bd. govs.), Masons, Scottish Rite, and Shrine; publisher (art): Symbolic Interactionism and Cha No Yu: A Method of Analyzing Japanese Behavior (pub. in Japanese 1982); inventor, high-pressure high-temperature flexible pneumatic, anti-icing, compression & air conditioning sys. used in jet aircraft; research, Japanese behavior, the Way of Tea; Republican; rec: big-game fishing, Chinese ceramics, Japanese bronzes. Ofc: PO Box 1352 Beverly Hills 90213

SHIRILLA, ROBERT MICHAEL, consulting company executive; b. Mar. 21, 1949, Youngstown, Oh.; s. Michael and Jayne (O'Shea) Shirilla; edn: BA in Economics (magna cum laude), UCLA, 1967-71; MBA (with honors), Harvard Bus. Sch., 1973-75. Career: cons., Boston Cons. Group, 1974; asst. prod. mgr., General Foods Corp., 1975-76; prod. mgr., Hunt-Wesson Foods, 1977, marketing mgr., 1978, sr. marketing mgr., 1979, group marketing mgr., 1980; dir. of strategic planning, Citicorp, NY, NY, 1981; v.p. strategic planning, Citicorp, 1981-83; v.p., Crocker Bank, S.F., Calif., 1983-84; senior v.p. marketing, Amer. Savings, L.A., Calif., 1984-85; pres., Computerized Vehicle Registration, L.A., 1985-91; managing dir./general mgr., Inst. of Mgmt. Resources, West Lake Village, Calif., 1991-92; prin./partner, FBS Internat., West Lake Village, Calif., 1993-; cons., So. Calif. Republican US Congl., State Senate and State Assembly races; awards: elected to the following nat. honor societies while at UCLA: Pi Mu Epsilon (math.), Beta Alpha Psi (accounting), Psi Chi (psychology), Pi Gamma Mu (social sci.), Phi Eta Sigma (freshman scholastic excellence), Omicron Delta Epsilon (econ.), Pi Sigma Alpha (political sci.), Beta Gamma Sigma (bus.) Alpha Kappa Psi (econ. and bus.); recipient of scholarship awards for scholastic excellence from Alpha Kappa Psi (econ) and USA ROTC; capt., USA ROTC Brigade (UCLA); pres. of mil. honor soc., Pershing Rifles; received Outstanding Achievement award, USA Reserve Officers Assn., 1980; listed in Directory of Disting. Americans, Personalities of Am., Comm. Leaders of Am., Who's Who in the West, Book of Honor, Internat. Registry of Profiles, Internat. Who's Who, Personalities of the West, Internat. Men of Achievement, Who's Who in Finance & Industry, Personalities of the Mid-West, Two Thousand Notable Americans, Internat. Platform Assn., Internat. Biographical Assn., Am. Biographical Inst.; mem: President's Commn. on White House Fellowships, L.A. Rotary, World Affairs Council, Acad. of Political Sci.; past dir., March of Dimes, L.A. Jr. C.of C., Am. Mgmt. Assn.; past chmn., Hugh O'Brian Youth Found. Calif. Leadership Seminar, March of Dimes Advy. Com.; vol., 1984 Reagan/Bush campaign, 1988 Bush/Quayle, 1988 Wilson for US Senate, 1990 Wilson for Gov.; author: numer-

ous pub. articles on econ., banking, marketing and foreign policy. Mil: col., US Army Reserves, mil. intelligence 1973-; Republican; Roman Catholic; rec: golf, skiing, running; Res: 5540 Owensmouth #223 Woodland Hills 91367

SHIRLEY, ROBERT BRYCE, corporate lawyer; b. Feb. 5, 1951, Morehead City, N.C.; s. Robert Wayne Shirley and JoAnn Elaine (Shook) Myers; m. Marilyn Jeanette Roy, June 30, 1973; children: Robert b. 1983, James b. 1986, Emma b. 1991; edn: Ba, Stanford Univ., 1973, JD, 1977, MBA, 1977. Career: atty., assoc. McKenna & Fitting, L.A. 1977-79; general counsel The Way International, New Knoxville, 1979-87; ptnr. Morrison & Shirley, Irvine 1987-88; sr. atty. Taco Bell Corp., Irvine 1988-92; corp. counsel Pepsico, Inc. 1993-; mem. ABA 1977-, Calif. Bar Assn. 1977-, Orange County Bar Assn. 1987-; Republican; Christian; rec: skiing, fishing, tennis. Res: 13692 Andele Irvine 92720 Ofc: Taco Bell Corp. 17901 Von Karman Irvine 92714

SHISHIDO, FUMITAKE, company executive; b. Mar. 3, 1960, Tokyo, Japan; s. Osamu and Miyoko (Sugiue) S.; m. Kayoko Matsubara, June 21, 1986; edn: BA polit. sci., Waseda Univ., Tokyo 1982; MBA, Columbia Univ., N.Y. 1987. Career: line mgr. Nippon Yusen Kaisha, Tokyo 1982-84, inv. analyst 1984-85, project team member 1987-88; dir. fin. and asst. secty. Crystal Cruises Inc., Los Angeles 1988-92; v.p. treas. and asst. secty. Crystal Cruises, Inc. 1993; honors: Columbia Univ. Dean's List 1986, Beta Gamma Sigma 1986; mem. Columbia Bus. Sch. Club, Beta Gamma Sigma Alumni Orgn.; rec: travel, skiing, tennis, music. Ofc: 2121 Avenue of the Stars Ste 200 Los Angeles 9006

SHONK, ALBERT D., JR., publishers representative; b. May 23, 1932, Los Angeles; s. Albert D., Sr. and Jean (Stannard) S.; edn: BS in bus. adminstrn., USC 1954. Career: field rep., mktg. div. Los Angeles Examiner, 1954-55, asst. mgr. 1955-56, mktg. div. mgr. 1956-57, account exec. Hearst Advt. Svc., 1957-59; acct. exec. Keith H. Evans & Assoc., 1959-63, San Francisco mgr. 1963-65; owner/pres. Albert D. Shonk Co., 1965-; gen. ptnr. Shonk Land Co., Ltd., Charleston, W.V. 1989-; mem: Nat. Assn. of Publishers Reps. (West Coast v.p. 1981-83), Magazine Reps. Assn. of So. Calif., Bus./Profl. Advt. Assn., Town Hall of Calif., Phi Sigma Kappa (dist. gov. 1960-62, nat. v.p. 1962-70, PSK Medallion of Merit 1976, Grand Council 1977-83, Grand Pres. 1979-83, Chancellor 1983-87, 1990-91, Court of Honor -life), Phi Sigma Kappa Found. Inc. (pres., trustee 1984-), Alpha Kappa Psi, Skull and Dagger USC, Interfrat. Alumni Assn. So. Calif. (v.p., pres. 1957-61), recipient Nat. Inter-Fraternity Conf. Interfraternal Award 1989, Inter-Greek Soc., USC (founder, v.p., life dir. 1976-, pres. 1984-86), USC Commerce Associates (nat. bd. 1991-), USC Assocs., Signet Circle Corp. (hon. life dir., pres. 1977-81, treas. 1989-), Florence Crittenton Services (exec. v.p. 1979-81, pres. 1981-83, bd. chmn. 1983-85, hon. life dir.), Crittenton Assocs. (founding chmn. 1978-80), Junior Advt. Club of L.A. (hon. life mem., past dir., treas., v.p.); Presbyterian. Res: Wilshire Towers 3460 West 7th St Los Angeles 90005 Ofc: 3156 Wilshire Blvd Los Angeles

SHORT, JAMES HARVEY, military officer and educator; b. June 26, 1919, Berkeley; s. James Vernon and Ethel Grace (MacFadyen) S.; m. Margaret Lewis Duncan, Oct. 5, 1943; children: James b. 1951, Ellen b. 1954, Scott b. 1959; edn: BS, US Mil. Acad., West Point, 1943; MA, CSU Hayward, 1977. Career: served to col. US Army 1938-73; plat. ldr. and co. comdr. 382d Inf., 96th Div., Leyte and Okinawa, 1943-45; staff ofcr. G-3 Sec, X Corps, Korea 1950-51; Secty. to the Gen. Staff and op. ofcr. HQ Sixth USA, San Francisco 1951-53; plans ofcr. & EXO JUSMAG, Philippines 1954-56; instr., staff secty. USACGSC, Ft. Leavenworth, Kans. 1956-60; instr. Brit. Army Staff Coll., Camberley, Surrey, Eng. 1960-63; Bde. cmdr., Post G-1, Personnel Center cmdr. Ft. Dix, N.J. 1963-66; sr. liaison ofcr. with Capitol ROK Infantry Div. and Korean Corps in Vietnam 1967-68; director US Military Strategy Studies, and coord. Military Strategy Seminar, Dept. of Strategy, US Army War Coll., Carlisle Barracks, Pa. 1968-71; Dept. of Strategy Chmn. and Elihu Root Chair of Strategy, 1971-73; battle campaigns WWII Asia Pac. 2, Korea 5, Vietnam 3; decorated Legion of Merit w/ o.l.c., Bronze Star Medal for valor w/2 o.l.c., Air Medal w/o.l.c., Army Commendn. Medal w/2 o.l.c., Purple Heart, Philippine Presdl. Unit Cit. for 96th Inf. Div. Leyte Cpgn., Rep. of Korea Order of Chung Mu and Presdl. Unit Cit., Rep. Vietnam Honor Medal 1c, Combat Inf. Badge, others; mem. V.F.W., Disabled Am. Vets, Am. Security Council (spkrs. bur.), Internat. Inst. for Strategic Studies London (1969-), Assn. of the U.S. Army, Retired Ofcrs. Assn., Rotary, Masons; pub. articles in Mil. Rev. (10/69), Ejercito (2/70), and Assegai (2/70); Republican; Episcopalian; rec: study of nat. and mil. strategy. Res: 2565 Rose St Berkeley 94708

SHUKLA, PRADIP KANTILAL, educator, management consultant; b. Sept. 7, 1956, Ahmedabad, India, nat. U.S.A. 1978; s. Kantilal T. and Manju K. S.; m. Yatri P. (Thaker), Jan. 6, 1983; children: Monica b. 1985, Amy b. 1989; edn: AA in math., Compton Comm. Coll., 1976; BS in bus. admin./BA econ., CSU Long Beach, 1978, MBA in human resources mgmt., 1979; MS in bus. admin., USC, 1983; MEd, UCLA, 1983; PhD, UCLA, 1989; Calif. Std. secondary tchg. cred., Calif. Comm. Colls. instr., supr., chief adminstr. credentials; cert. in prodn. & inventory mgmt. (CPIM) APICS, 1985. Career: lectr. in mgmt. and mktg., Calif. State Univs., Long Beach, L.A., Northridge, Fullerton, 1978-91; assoc. prof. mktg. and mgmt. Chapman Univ., 1985-; dir. instnl. res. Compton

Coll., 1986-88; mgmt. cons. prin., 1980-; honors: Alpha Gamma Sigma, Beta Gamma Sigma, Omicron Delta Epsilon, Phi Delta Kappa, Phi Kappa Phi (past chapt. v.p.), Bank of Am. scholar, So. Calif. Edison scholarship finalist, TRW project achiev. scholar, UCLA Grad. Sch. of mgmt. doctoral stipend, CSULB Alumni Assn. Award, 49er gold life pass CSULB, Who's Who Among Students in Am. Univs., UCLA Outstanding Doctoral Graduate Alumni Award; mem: Acad. of Mgmt., We. Mktg. Educators Assn., Am. Mktg. Assn., Am. Ednl. Research Assn., APICS (1983-88); author software pgms.; Republican; Hindu; rec: poetry, photog. Res: 3148 N Hartman St Orange 92665

SHULTZ, FRED TOWNSEND, consulting geneticist; b. Mar. 5, 1923, Grinnell, Iowa; s. J. Gordon and Katharine (Townsend) S.; m. Carolyn Covell, June 24, 1961; children: Trina Michele b. 1962, Rebecca Lynn b. 1963, Daniel Kenyon b. 1964, Brian Gregory b. 1965; edn: AB, Stanford Univ., 1947; PhD, UC Berkeley, 1952. Career: pres. Animal Breeding Consultants, Sonoma 1952-; director Biological Frontiers Inst., Sonoma 1962-; pres. Avian Allure, Sonoma 1990-; recipient Poultry Sci. Res. Award 1953; mem.: Poultry Sci. Assn., World Poultry Sci. Assn., World Aquaculture Soc., Am. Genetics Assn., others; inventor: Artificial seeds & nuts (1992), co-inventor Abalone culture (patents); publs: num. research articles (1950-); mil: 2d lt. USAF 1942-45; Republican; rec: sailing. Res: 1944 Marna Ln Sonoma 95476

SHULTZ, GEORGE PRATT, former secretary of state, economics educator; b. Dec. 13, 1920, NYC; s. Birl E. and Margaret Lennox (Pratt) S.; m. Helena M. O'Brien, Feb. 16, 1946; children: Margaret Ann S. Tilsworth, Kathleen Pratt S. Jorgensen, Peter Milton, Barbara Lennox S. White, Alexander George; edn: BA Econs., Princeton Univ., 1942; PhD Indsl. Econs., MIT, 1949; Hon. doctorates Univ. Notre Dame, Loyola Univ., Univ. Pa., Univ. Rochester, Princeton Univ., Carnegie-Mellon Univ., Baruch Coll., NYC, Northwestern Univ. Career: faculty Mass. Inst. Technology 1949-57, assoc. prof. industrial relations 1955-57; prof. indsl. relations Grad. Sch. Bus., Univ. Chicago, 1957-68, dean sch., 1962-68; fellow Ctr. for Advanced Studies in Behavioral Scis., 1968-69; appt. U.S. Sec. Labor, 1969-70; dir. Office of Mgmt. and Budget, 1970-72; U.S. Sec. Treasury, and asst. to the Pres., 1972-74; chmn. Council on Econ. Policy, East-West Trade Policy com.; exec. v.p. Bechtel Corp., San Francisco 1974-75, pres. 1975-77, v.chmn. 1977-81; also dir.; pres. Bechtel Group Inc. 1981-82; prof. mgmt. and public policy Stanford Univ. 1974-82; chmn. Pres. Reagan's Economic Policy Advy. Bd.; U.S. Sec. of State 1982-89; prof. internat. economics Grad. Sch. Bus., Stanford Univ. 1989-, distinguished fellow Hoover Instn., Stanford 1989-; dir: GM, Bechtel Group Inc., Tandem Computers Inc., Boeing Corp., Chevron Corp.; chmn. J.P. Morgan Internat. Council, chmn. advy. council Inst. Internat. Studies; mem. Am. Econ. Assn., Indsl. Relations Res. Assn. (pres. 1968), Nat. Acad. Arbitrators; Author: Pressures on Wage Decisions (1950), The Dynamics of a Labor Market (1951), Labor Problems: Cases and Readings (1953), w/T.A. Whisler, Managment Organization and the Computer (1960), w/Arnold R. Weber, Strategies for the Displaced Worker (1966), Guidelines, Informal Controls and the Market Place (1966), w/A. Rees, Workers and Wages in the Urban Labor Market (1970), w/Kenneth W. Dam, Economic Policy Beyond the Headlines (1977), contbr. chpts. in books, articles; mil: capt. USMCR 1942-45. Ofc: Hoover Institution Stanford University Stanford 94305-6010

SICILIANO, A. VINCENT, bank president; b. July 19, 1959, Washington, D.C.; s. Rocco Carmine and Marian (Stiebel) S.; m. Susan Campbell, May 25, 1974; children: Michael Carmine b. 1983; edn: BS environ. engring., BA human biol., Stanford Univ. 1972; MS environ. planning, UC Berkeley 1976. Career: coord. for coastal zone mgmt. Nat. Oceanic Atmospheric Adminstrn., WD. 1972-73; spl. asst. energy planning Calif. Coastal Commn., San Francisco 1974; planning cons. Calif. Coastal Commn. and Govs. Office, Sacto. 1975-79; internat. credit office Bank of Am., Taipei, Taiwan 1976-79, head planning and analysis group, Manila, Philippines 1979-82, v.p., section head, Singapore 1982-83; pres. Internat. Savings Bank, San Diego 1986-; MOPA 1984-; commr., chmn. Internat. Trade Com.; chmn. Calif. League S&L Smaller Assn.; advy. com. San Diego Comm. Found.; honors: Tau Beta Pi, F.E.Terman engring. scholastic achievement 1972, Beatrix Found. UD Regents, UC Berkeley fellowship 1974-76; mem: Museum of Photo. Arts, Univ. Club, Internat. Trade Commn., Bldg. Inst. Am., Calif. Bankers Assn., Inst. Real Estate Mgmt., World Affairs Council; Republican; Christian; rec: amateur radio, skiing. Ofc: International Savings Bank 1455 Frazee Rd Ste 204 San Diego 92108

SIDHU, GURMEL SINGH, academic research scientist, geneticist; b. May 23, 1943, Jullundur, India, naturalized U.S. 1991; s. Naranjan Singh and Kartar (Hoti) K.; m. Baljit Kaur, Mar. 23, 1979; children: Vikram b. 1980, Roop b. 1981; edn: BSc, 1960, MSc, 1962; PhD, Univ. British Col., Vancouver 1973. Career: postdoc. fellow S.F. Univ., Burnaby 1973-75, res. scientist, 1975-80; asst. prof. UN, Lincoln 1980-86; res. scientist, prof. CSU Fresno, 1986-; research pathologist Germain's, Fresno 1987-; awards: res. fellow UBC, Vancouver 1972, SFU, Burnaby 1973-75, Univ. Wis., Madison 1985; mem.: AAAS 1987-, Phytopath Soc. USA (assoc. editor 1980-86), Crop Improvement Soc. India (assoc. editor 1984-); editor: Genetics of Plant Pathogenic Fungi (1989); rec: sports, poetry writing. Res: 1637 Gettysburg Clovis 93612 Ofc: Calif. State Univ. Fresno, Cedar and Shaw Fresno 93740

SIEGEL, BROCK MARTIN, chemist; b. Aug. 25, 1947, Binghamton, N.Y.; s. Samuel Joseph and Louise (Davenport) S.; m. Catherine Sandra Bloomfield, Dec. 18, 1978; children: Justin, Aaron, Rachael; edn: BS, Syracuse Univ., 1969, PhD, Univ. Ill., 1974. Career: postdoc. fellow Columbia Univ., 1974-76; asst. prof. Univ. Minnesota 1976-78; scientist Henkel Corp., Mpls. 1978-86; dir. Henkel Research Corp., Santa Rosa, Calif. 1986-89; mgr. Millipore Corp., Novato 1989-91; mgr. Applied BioSystems, Foster City 1991-. Ofc: Applied BioSystems, Inc. 850 Lincoln Center Dr Foster City 94404

SIEGEL, GILBERT BYRON, educator; b. April 19, 1930, Los Angeles; s. Morris DeSagar and Rose (Vancott) S.; m. Darby Day Smith, Oct. 16, 1954; children: Clark Byron b. 1958, Holly May b. 1960; edn: BS pub. adminstrn., USC 1952; MS, 1957; PhD political sci., Univ. Pittsburgh 1964. Career: adminstrv. analyst and mgr. County of Los Angeles, 1954-57; vis. asst. prof. USC in Tehran, Iran 1957-59; instr. Univ. Pittsburgh, 1959-61; asst., assoc. prof. and assoc. dean Univ. So. Calif., Los Angeles 1965-, dir. USC Productivity Network 1985-; vis. assoc. prof. in Rio de Janeiro, 1961-63, cons. Brazilian govt. 1961, 76, 77, 79; evaluator USN Demonstration Project, China Lake and San Diego 1979-81; cons. UN in Bangkok 1981, USAID in Panama 1986; awards: Olson award So. Calif. Personnel Mgmt. Assn. 1984, Vargas Found. medal of merit 1975, Mosher award Pub. Adminstrn. Rev., W.D.C. 1967; mem: So. Calif. Personnel Mgmt. Assn. (bd.), Internat. Personnel Mgmt. Assn., Am. Soc. Pub. Adminstrn., Pi Sigma ALpha, Pi Alpha Alpha; author: Pub. Employee Compensation and its role in Pub. Sector Strategic Management 1992; co-author Pub. Personnel Adminstrn. 1985, 89; ed. Breaking w. Orthodoxy in Pub. Adminstrn. 1980; coauthor: Mgmt. in Pub. Systems 1986; editor Human Resource Mgmt. in Pub. Orgns. 1974; mil: sgt. AUS 1952-54; rec: classical music, travel. Res: 208 N Poinsettia Ave Manhattan Beach 90266 Ofc: Univ. So. Calif. School of Public Administration Los Angeles 90089-0041

SIEGFRIED, WILLIAM, chemist; b. July 4, 1925, Phila.; s. Howard and Sadie Lavinia (Wolverton) S.; m. Brenda Mary Bowen, Jan. 2, 1947 (div. 1964); children: Patricia b. 1948, Michael b. 1952; m. Katherine Ann Delia, Feb. 29, 1964; dau. (step), Patricia b. 1949; edn: BS in chem., Bucknell Univ., 1950. Career: chemist Ohio-Apex div. F.M.C. Corp., Nitro, W.Va. 1950-52; chief chemist The Kindt-Collins Co., Cleveland, Ohio 1952-62; chief chemist Freeman Mfg. Co., Cleve. 1962-66, 70-79; tech. director Victrylite Candle Co., Oshkosh, Wis. 1966-70; mng. dir. res. & devel. Blended Waxes Inc., Oshkosh 1979-85; chief chemist J.F. McCaughin Co., Rosemead, Calif. 1985-; inventor: Adhesive coated wax (Pat. 1954), Transparent candle (pat. 1969); mil: USN 1943-46, PTO; Indep.; Prot.; rec: building exact scale ship models. Res: 1409 Tamar Dr Valinda 91746 Ofc: J.F. McCaughin Co. 2628 River Ave Rosemead 91770

SIGAL, SANFORD DAVID, commercial developer; b. Jan. 28, 1964, Los Angeles; s. Martin Irving and Gloria Kuth (Blatter) S.; m. Cindy Sisino, Mar. 12, 1988; children: Hayden b. 1991; edn: BA, UCLA, 1987. Career: owner Am. Computer Software, Marina del Rey 1982-85; dir. commercial devel. West Venture Devel., Encino 1985-; mem. Internat. Council of Shopping Centers 1985-; civic: Mar Vista President's Club 1985-, City of Azusa Econ. Devel. Com. 1992-; pub. article (1991); Republican; Jewish; rec: skiing, computers. Ofc: West Venture Development 6345 Balboa Blvd Ste 225 Encino 91316

SIIPOLA, JOHN ERNEST, business executive, manager; b. Milford, Mass., Dec. 22, 1943; s. George Ernest and Doris (Seymour) S.; m. Edna L. Barrett, Apr. 19, 1965; children: Nikki Leigh b. 1976, Jacqueline Danielle b. 1988; edn: Univ. of Texas, Austin; BA (honors) bus. Northeastern Univ., Boston 1972; BS (honors) computer sci. Northeastern Univ. 1976. Career: software engr. to cons. mgr. Keane, Inc., Wellesley, Mass., Boston, Detroit, Mich. 1965-70; dir. info. systems Dept. Public Health, Boston, Mass. 1970-72; cons. mgr. Arthur D. Little, Inc., 1972-74; br. mgr, dir. Source Services, Inc., Hartford, Conn., San Francisco, Calif. 1975-84; founder, pres. Computer Alternatives, Inc., San Francisco 1984-87; pres. The Barrett Group, San Francisco 1988-92; chmn., c.e.o. Barrett Publishing, Inc. 1992-; dir Big O Tires, Inc. (1988-, chmn. 1991-); mgmt. cons. restructurings 1988-; author: prof. articles in the mgmt. and info. proc. (1970-); mem: Am. Mgmt. Assn., ASM, DPMA, Bay Area LUG, Nat. Rifle Assn. (life); civic: Hartford C. of C. , BPOE 1264; mil: USNR 1962-68; Republican; Methodist; rec: golf, hunting, skiing.

SILLS, DAVID GEORGE, jurist; b. Mar. 21, 1938, Peoria, Ill.; s. George Daniel and Mildred Mina (Luthy) S.; m. Susan Mildred La Croix, Dec. 12, 1989; edn: BS, Bradley Univ., 1959; LLB, Univ. of Ill., 1961. Career: pvt. law practice Orange County, Calif. 1965-85; elected Irvine City Council, 1976-85, mayor City of Irvine, 1976-77, 79-82, 84-85; judge Superior Ct., Orange County 1985-90; presiding justice Calif. Court of Appeal, 4th Dist. Div. 3, Santa Ana 1990-; chmn. Irvine Health Found. 1985-; mem: Orange County Bar Assn. 1965-, Banyard Inn 1990-; mil: capt. USMC 1960-62-65; Republican; rec: golf, jogging, history, travel. Ofc: Court of Appeal, 925 Spurgeon Santa Ana 9270

SILVERA, JOHN STEVEN, doctor of chiropractic; b. June 8, 1954, Burbank, Calif.; s. Errol Karl and Mildred Emma (Berry) S.; m. Deborah Ann, Aug. 26, 1979; children: Jordan John b. 1990, Braighlee b. 1993; edn: AA, L.A. Pierce,

Woodland Hills, Calif. 1974; BS, UCLA 1977; DC (magna cum laude, Dean's List), L.A. Coll. of Chiropractic, Whittier, Calif. 1982. Career: beach lifeguard (summers), L.A. County 1975-83; chiropractor, private practice, Northridge, Calif. 1983-; mem: Le-Tip Woodland Hills (v.p. 1988-90, 1992-93; pres. 1990-91); Creston Club (Help Youth Found.), Burbank, Calif. 1991-92; author: Life Reflections (in process); rec: exercise, outdoors, gardening, writing, reading. Ofc: Silvera Chiropractic 8555 Reseda Blvd. Northridge 91324

SILVERMAN, KENNETH PHILIP, media executive/strategist; b. Nov. 25, 1945, NYC; s. Harry T. and Roberta (Neuhoff) S.; m. Ginger, Dec. 26, 1966 (div. 1972); m. Margot, June 20, 1980; children: Matthew b. 1967, Lauren b. 1981, Andrew b. 1987; edn: BS in film, Boston Univ., 1967. Career: asst. advt. mgr. Columbia Pictures, N.Y., N.Y., 1967-69; dir. advt. & publicity Cinema 5/Rugoff Theatres, 1969-72; dir. Pay-Television Programming & Sales, Warner Comms., 1972-74; pres. Cinemerica Inc., Beverly Hills, Ca. 1974-82; pres. Cinemerica Premium Network Inc., Irvine, Ca. 1976-81; pres. Cinemerica Satellite Network Inc., Beverly Hills, Ca. 1978-82; pres. Silverman Associates, Monrovia 1982-, pres. Silverman Found. Inc., 1987-; cons.: L.A. Co. Office of Edn., L.A., 1985-88; L.A. Cath. Archbishop Roger Mahoney, 1987; KLCS-TV, L.A., 1987; Reg. Ednl. TV Advy. Council, L.A., 1985-88; Santa Fe Comms., Burbank, 1989-90; Russ Reid Co., Pasadena, 1990-91; awards: Academy Award nomination (co-producer) Best Live Action Short Film 1972; mem: Nat. Cable TV Assn. 1974-, Am. Advt. Fedn. 1988-, Am. Film Inst. 1987-, Hollywood Radio & TV Soc. 1988-, Tierra Del Sol Found. (v.p., dir. 1988-), The Friars Club (NY); author num. articles on film, cable tv and pay-tv (1974-84). Ofc: Silverman Foundation 183 N Madison Ave Monrovia 91016

SILVERMAN, RONALD I., lawyer, real estate law specialist; b. Aug. 30, 1939, Big Spring, Tx.; s. Herbert and Tillie S.; m. Patricia Lynn Whalen, July 3, 1981; children: Adam b. 1963, Jordan b. 1969; edn: BA, UCLA, 1961, JD (Top 15%), UCLA Law Sch., 1966. Career: corporate atty. O'Melveny & Myers, L.A. 1966-69; real estate atty. Aaronson, Weil & Friedman, L.A. 1969-71; dir. No. Am. Ops. Pacific Hotels & Development, Ltd. 1971-73; atty. Cox, Castle & Nicholson, L.A. 1972-75, real estate ptnr. 1975-; instr. Nat. Mtg. Bankers confs., N.Y., Seattle (1985, 86), Nat. Soc. for R.E. Finance, Palm Beach, Fla. 1986, Nat. Assn. Homebuilders 1990, L.A. County Bar Assn. 1990, Urban Land Inst., W.D.C. (1988, 91); mem: ABA 1967-, Calif. Bar Assn., L.A. County Bar Assn. (sec. treas., co-chair real prop. sect. 1989-93, chair 93-), Urban Land Inst. 1989-; civic: Central City Assn. 1988-, Govt. Affairs Council, an alliance of Calif. Builders 1990-, Westside Fam. YMCA, L.A. (1987-, v. chmn. 1994); author book chpts. in R.E. Finance (1988), profl. jour. articles in field; mil: lt. US Army 1961-63; Jewish; rec: travel, reading, films, golf, scuba, country inns, magic, theatre. Res: 10777 Weyburn Los Angeles 90024 Ofc: Cox, Castle & Nicholson 2049 Century Park East 28th Fl Los Angeles 90067-3284

SIMMONS, PAULA JOAN, marketing consultant; b. Dec. 1, 1961 Long Beach, Calif.; d. Elton Newman and Joan Marilyn (Perrin) Rockwell; m. Christopher Laird Simmons, July 25, 1992; 1 child: Abby b. 1981; edn: Calif. State Univ. Honors Program, Long Beach, Calif., 1979-81. Career: photographic supr., Olan Mills, Inc., Scottsdale, Ariz. 1982-84; asst. mdsg. mgr., Max Factor & Co., Hollywood, Calif. 1984-87; sr. account exec., Transworld Systems, Inc., Long Beach 1987-89; marketing cons., Sebastian Internat., Woodland Hills 1989-91; marketing cons., Paris Ace, Commerce 1992-93; mem. NAFE, Wash., DC 1986-; awards: Top Regional Sales award, Pacific Div. Transworld Systems, Long Beach 1988; Outstanding Line Devel. award, Sebastian Internat., Woodland Hills 1990, 91; mem: PTA 1986-, Amnesty Internat 1986-90, Parent advy. council 1986-90, Lakewood Artists Guild, Lakewood, Calif. 1976-80; creative works: artist, poet; Democrat; rec: voice studies.

SIMMS, RONALD JAMES, doctor of chiropractic; b. Jan. 5, 1965, Sacramento, Calif.; s. Ronald Bernard and Linda Catherine (Shelboe) S.; m. Carie Lynn Humphries, Jan. 2, 1989; children: Tyler James b. 1993; edn: under grad. study, UC Santa Barbara, Goleta, 1983-85; BA in physical edn. & exercise physiology, Calif. State Univ., Long Beach, 1988; DC, L.A. Coll. of Chiropractic, Whittier, 1991; Calif. State Bd. Cert. #22467. Career: sales mgr. Rossmoor Athletic Club, Seal Beach 1985-90; assoc. doctor of chiropractic, Back Pain Center, Long Beach 1991-; instr./doctor of General Health & Spinal Health (weekly class) 1991-; work injury com. Topko, Long Beach 1991-; cons. lectr. on work safety Long Beach State 1992, P.A.C.T.O.W., Long Beach 1992; honors: Scholar Athlete of Year, County Sch., El Dorado County 1983; Dean's List, L.A. Chiropractic Coll., Whittier 1991; mem: Calif. Chiropractic Assn. (CCA) 1991-, Am. Chiropractic Assn. (ACA) 1991-; ACA-Sports Counsel 1993-, Long Beach C. of C.; Republican; Christian; rec: mountain biking, waterskiing, weightlifting. Res: 5172 Marion Ave. Cypress 90630 Ofc: Back Pain Center 532 Redondo Ave Long Beach 90814

SIMONS, ROBERT WALTER, geneticist, educator; b. Jan. 28, 1945, Rockford, Ill.; s. DeWayne Kimble and Helen Lucille (Bush) S.; m. Elizabeth Lindsay; children: Sarah Christina, Rebecca Ann; edn: BS, Univ. of Ill., 1972; PhD, UC Irvine, 1980; career: staff res. biochemist Univ. N. Mex., Albuquerque 1972-75; lectr., dept. biology 1973-74; tutor, lectr., molecular biology Bd.

Tutors Biochem. Scis./Harvard Univ. 1981-84; postdoctoral fellow dept. molecular biology Harvard Univ. 1980-85; mem. Jonsson Comprehensive Cancer Ctr./UCLA 1985-; asst. prof. microbiology and molecular genetics UCLA 1985-90; assoc. prof. 1990-; awards: Steinhaus award for Outstanding Grad. Tchr., UC Irvine 1978; Nat. Res. Svc. award in Molecular Biology and Biochemistry 1977-80; Postdoctoral Fellowship, Damon Runyon-Walter Winchell Cancer Fund 1980-82, NIH 1982-83, Leukemia Soc. of Am. 1983-85; Jr. Faculty Res. award Am. Cancer Soc. 1986-89; numerous grants in field; mem: Am. Soc. Microbiology, AAAS, Genetics Soc. Am., Sigma Xi; editor: Molecular Biology Jour., 1990-; contbr. articles to profl. jours.; mil: USN, 1965-69, Vietnam; Democrat; rec: backpacking, camping, history of Am. Civil War. Ofc: Dept. Microbiology and Molecular Genetics/UCLA 5304 Life Science Los Angeles 90024

SIMPSON, BARCLAY, manufacturing company executive; b. May 25, 1921, Oakland; s. Walter Chapin and Jessie B. (Smith) S.; m. Joan Devine, Oct. 10, 1945; children: John b. 1946, Anne b. 1948, Jean b. 1951, Julie b. 1964, Amy b. 1967, Elizabeth b. 1967; m. 2d. Sharon Hanley, June 8, 1974; edn: BS in bus. admin., UC Berkeley, 1966. Career: chmn./CEO Simpson Mfg. Co., Inc. San Leandro 1956-; dir. Barclay Simpson Fine Arts, Lafayette 1982-; dir: McFarland Energy, Santa Fe Springs 1976-, Civic Bank Corp., Oakland 1985-, Calendar-Robinson Ins., S.F. 1980-; elected dir. Bay Area Rapid Transit 1977-88; bd. trustees: John Muir Hosp. 1962-76, Calif. Coll. of Arts & Crafts 1986-, University Art Museum, Berkeley; mil: lt. cmdr. USN 1942-46, USNR 1946-60; art collector.

SIMPSON, MILTON CRAWFORD, artist, management consultant; b. Aug. 26, 1963, Los Angeles; s. Milton C. Simpson and Dana Gail (Flynn) Rucker; edn: BA, The Johns Hopkins Univ., 1985. Career: sr. devel. asst. The Johns Hopkins Univ., Balt. 1982-84; parochial sch. dir. devel. Junipero Serra High Sch., Gardena, Calif. 1985-87; dir. devel. Crossroads Sch. for Arts and Scis., Santa Monica 1987-88; exec. dir. Social and Public Art Resource Ctr., Venice 1990-91; mgr. grant awards pgm. to profl. artists to work with neighborhood youth to create comm. murals throughout City of Los Angeles; management cons., 1988-, clients include Highways Performance Space, High Performance Mag., E.F. Hilton & Company, KCET-TV, 5th Intl. Black Dance Cos. Conf. and L.A. Contemp. Dance Theatre, Media Images Inc., Installations Two Gal., Rainbow TV Workshop, Internat. Artists Mgmt., Golden Gate Minority Found., Eisenhower Med. Ctr., The Johns Hopkins Univ. we. reg. office; affil. Broadcast Music Inc. (BMI), 1991-; mem. bd. dirs./trustees: Beyond Baroque Found. 1990-, Crime Victims Ctr. 1988-90, The Johns Hopkins Univ. (exec. com. L.A. Alumni chpt. 1985-); frequent lectr., panelist in arts funding field; solo exhibit: Installations Two Gallery, Santa Monica (1990); Lead singer ECO (1991), dir. "Hair" JHU Prodn., Balt. 1984. Ofc: Box 5142 Santa Monica 90409

SIMPSON, TIMOTHY WINSTON, teacher; b. Oct. 4, 1957, Los Angeles; s. Walter Lowell and Bessie (Jones) S.; edn: BA sociology, UCLA 1980. Career: physical dir. 28th Street YMCA, Los Angeles 1979-83; asst. mgr. Thrifty Drugs, Santa Monica 1983-85; fitness gym mgr. Jack La Lanne, Inglewood 1985-87; admissions rep. and coll. outreach coord. Watterson Coll., West Covina 1987-88; child care worker Childrens Baptist Home, Inglewood 1988-; teacher, 1988-; math teacher Washington Prep High 1992-; awards: Bank of Am. vocat. arts, 1975, Calif. St. scholar, 1975, Phi Beta Sigma; Democrat; Seventh Day Adventist (SDA peer counselor Univ. Ch. 1988-); rec: singing, sailing, marathon (Los Angeles Marathon finishing times: 1991- 5:46, 1992- 5:19, 1993- 5.21). Res: 3801 Fernwood Street Rosamond 93560

SIMPSON, WILLIAM BRAND, economist, educator; b. Nov. 30, 1919, Portland, Ore.; s. John Alexander and Janet Christie (Brand) S.; m. Ruth Decker, June 12, 1957; edn: BA, Reed Coll. 1942; MA, Columbia Univ. 1943; PhD, Claremont Grad. Sch. 1971. Career: consultant Nat. Defense Mediation Bd., Portland 1941-42, US Dept. of Interior, Portland 1942, head Economic Sect. Counter-Intelligence Office, Manila, 1945; spl. representative Supreme Cmdr. of Allied Powers, Japan, 1945-46; cons. U.S. War Dept. Tokyo, 1947; asst. research dir./exec. dir. Cowles Commn. for Resrch in Econ., Chgo. 1948-53; co-founder and bd. mem. Inst. of Soc. and Personal Relations, Oakland 1955-61; prof. economics, CSU Los Angeles 1958-; mng. editor and co-ed. Econometrica, 1948-53; cons. to var. univs. and higher education agcs., 1954-; honors: Phi Beta Kappa 1942; Fellow Nat. Soc. Sci. Research Council, 1946-48; mem: Econometric Soc. (internat. secty 1948-52); AAUP (state pres. 1975-76, chmn. Com. on Issues and Policy 1981-, Nat. Com. on Econ. Status of Acad. Prof. 1976-79, Nat. Council 1978-81, Com. on Govt. Rels. 1982-88); Am. Economic Assn. (ch. panel on polit. discrimination 1978-81); Am. Assn. for Higher Edn.; ACLU; Cong. of Faculty Assn.; author: Cost Containment in Higher Education (Praeger) 1991, profl. jour. articles in Socio-Economic Planning Scis. (Oxford) 1975, Jour. of Higher Edn. (Amsterdam) 1985, 86, Academe 1987, others; mil: spl. agt. counter-intell. US Army 1943-46; Democrat; Unitarian; rec: travel, Scottish postal history, pre-Columbian sculpture. Res: POB 41526 Los Angeles 90041 Ofc: California State University 5151 State University Dr Los Angeles 90032

SINGH, RAMESHWAR, professor of civil engineering; b. July 2, 1937, Bihar, India; s. Har Nandan and Dhan Dai Singh; m. Shanti Devi Singh, May 18, 1955; children: Usha b. 1956, Sheila b. 1959, Veena b. 1965, Vinod b. 1967; edn: BS, and MS, Auburn Univ., Ala., 1962, 1963; PhD, Stanford Univ., 1965; Reg. Profl. Engr., Calif. Career: supvg. engr. State of Bihar, Patna, India, 1956-60; asst. prof. Univ. of British Col., Vancouver, Can., 1965-67; researcher B.C. Hydro, 1965-67; prof. San Jose State Univ., San Jose, Calif., 1967-; cons. num. corps., USA, 1967-, cons. Lockheed, Sunnyvale 1977-85; researcher NSF, WDC, 1970-74, NASA - Ames, Moffet Field, Calif. 1984-85; cons. Santa Clara Water Dist., San Jose, 1970-90; honors: Sr. Mentor San Jose St. Univ. 1987-90; mem: Calif. Soc. Profl. Engrs., Sacto. (pres. 1984-85), Indo-Am. Fedn. No. Calif. (founding pres. 1986-90), ASCE (Fellow, mem. 1964-); civic: City Commnr. City of San Jose 1990-, Intergroup Commn. Calif. 1975-77, Century Club San Jose 1985-90; publs: 60+ engring. reports (1970-), 15+ res. papers in sci. jours. (1970-); Democrat; Hindu; rec: walking, computer, spa. Res: 631 Rocking Horse Ct San Jose 95123-5522

SINHA, DIPENDRA KUMAR, mechanical engineer; b. Feb. 18, 1945, Patna, Bihar, India; s. Jogendra Prasad and Saraswati (Varma) S.; m. Basanti Srivastawa, July 30, 1971; children: Priyamvada b. 1972, Udayan b. 1986; edn: BSME, Patna Univ., India 1967; Postgrad. Diploma in bus. mgmt. Xavier Labor Relations Inst., India 1976; MSME, Univ. Manchester, U.K. 1978, PhD M.E., 1981. Career: asst. design engr. Tata Steel, Jamshedpur, Bihar, 1970-75, devel. engr. 1975-76; asst. prof. Univ. Manitoba, 1981-84; assoc. prof. Univ. Wis., Platteville 1985-87; assoc. prof., prof. mech. engring. dept. San Francisco State Univ., 1987-; mem: ASEE 1987-, ASME (assoc. 1986-); author: Engineering Graphics With Autocad (1990), Fortran77 for Engrs. (1993) coauthor: FEM By Microcomputers (1988), Advanced Machine Design by MicroComputer (1989), Computer Aided Design - An Integrated Approach (1992); Hinduism; rec: numismatics, photography, Shakespeare. Ofc: San Francisco State University 1600 Holloway Ave San Francisco 94132

SIRI, JEAN BRANDENBURG, community activist; b. Mar. 11, 1920, Lakota, N.Dak.; d. Tunis Orville and Edith Marion (Molloy) Brandenburg; m. William Emil Brandenburg Siri, Dec. 3, 1949; children: Lynn Kimsey b. 1953, Ann Siri b. 1955; edn: BS, Jamestown Coll., 1942; RN, UC San Francisco, 1945; pre-med. UC Berkeley 1945-47. Career: biologist Donner Lab., Lawrence Lab., Berkeley 1947-54; appt. Contra Costa County Grand Jury, Martinez 1967; advy. council Calif. Solid Waste Mgmt./Resource Recovery 1973-75; pub. rep. BA SWM Plan, Oakland 1976, advy. com. EMTF-ABAG 208 Plan, Oakland 1977, mem. EB MUD land use com., wastewater treatment com., Oakland 1977-79; bd. mem., chair Stege Sanitary Dist., 1975-79, com. on aging 1985-92; elected El Cerrito City Council 1980-84, 1987-91, mayor 1982-83, 1988-89, chair West County Mayors 1989; Contra Costa Co. bds: Disaster Council 1983, Hazardous Waste Task Force 1984-85, Haz. Mat. Commn. 1986-93, Envir. Health Coord. Council 1985-87, cochair Pub. and Envir. Health Advy. Bd. 1987-, homeless advoc. Wild Women (W. Contra Costa) 1987-, cochair Homeless Advy. Council 1989-93; JPA mem. Solid Waste, West Co. 1988-89, Transp. 1990-91; awards: Sol Feinstone Nat. Environ. Award, Syracuse Univ. 1976-77, Clean Air award Am. Lung Assn. Santa Clara/San Benito Ctys 1976, Pott Award for Individual Achiev. in toxics 1986; mem: LWV West Contra Conserv. League (pres., 1968-), LWV-BA Haz. Mats. Com. 1986, Pol. Act. Coal. for Envir. (co-ch.1974-76), People for Open Space (Contra Costa rep. 1967-), Sierra Club 1965-, Audubon Soc., Contra Costa Shoreline Parks Com., Richmond 1965-, NAACP 1980-, Gray Panthers of W.Contra Costa Co. (co-chair, v.p. 1992), Bay Area League of Conserv. Voters (bd. 1979), El Cerrito Hist. Soc. (v.p. 1984), Elmwood Inst. (peer 1989-91), Women's Therapy Ctr. (bd. 1986), Women's Forum (charter 1985-), elected dir. ward 1 E. Bay Reg. Park Bd. 1992-; mil: lt. USNR WVS 1942-45; Democrat; avocation: advocacy. Res: 1015 Leneve Pl El Cerrito 94530

SKIBBEN, BERNARD DAVID, estate homebuilder, executive; b. Jan. 13, 1928, Leeds, England; s. Florrie and Louise S.; m. Ann, Sept. 10, 1954 (dec.); children: Beverley b. 1955, Gail b. 1960; m. Betty, July 26, 1988; edn: grad. in arch. & constrn., Leeds Coll. of Tech. 1942. Career: formed constrn. co. in England, 1950-75, building new homes in authentic designs of bye-gone eras (bldr. 8 period-homes in Ripon, near Yorkshire Moors in 17th century designs); came to Calif. 1975, pres. Skibben Construction, builder custom homes re-creating 18th century manor houses and French Normandy period homes in Bel-Air and Beverly Hills, also Mediterranean and modern styles in various locations; lectr. & film presentations on "New Homes 200 Years Old"; mem: Nat. Assn. of Estate Agents, England (founder/ 1st nat. chmn.), Fellow Inst. of Directors, Exec. Assn. of San Fernando Valley (past pres.), British Am. C.of C., Am. Historical Soc.; works: due to period authenticity his houses have been used by var. film studios, appear in newspaper feature articles; mil: sgt. British Army, JAG, 1946-49; rec: video filming (Fellow Inst. of Amateur Cinemaphotogs.). Res: 2025 Beverly Glen Blvd Los Angeles 90025

SKOTHEIM, ROBERT ALLEN, educator, museum president; b. Jan. 31, 1933, Seattle; s. Sivert Olaus and Marjorie (Allen) S.; m. Nadine Esther Vail, June 14, 1953; children: Marjorie b. 1956, Kris b. 1957, Julia b. 1961; edn: BA, Univ. Washington, Seattle, 1955, MA, 1958, PhD, 1962. Career: asst. prof.

Wayne State Univ., Detroit 1963-66; assoc. prof. UC Los Angeles, 1966-67; prof. Univ. Colorado, Boulder 1967-72; provost, hobart, Wm. Smith Colls., Geneva, N.Y. 1972-75; pres. Whitman Coll., Walla Walla, Wash. 1975-88; pres. Huntington Library, Art Collections, Botanical Gardens, San Marino 1988-; dir: Pacificorp, Portland 1985-88; awards: John Simon Guggenheim fellow, N.Y. 1967-68); mem. Am. Hist. Assn. 1962-, Org. of Am. Historians 1962-, Am. Antiquarian Soc. 1989-; clubs: Princeton (N.Y.), Rainier (Seattle), Washington Athletic (Seattle), Twilight (Pasadena), Calif. (Los Angeles); author: American Intellectual Histories and Historians (Princeton Press, 1966). Res: 1650 Orlando Rd San Marino 91108 Ofc: Huntington Library 1151 Oxford San Marino 91108

SLAUGHTER, JOHN BROOKS, college president; b. Mar. 16, 1934, Topeka, Kans.; m. Ida Bernice Johnson, Aug. 31, 1956; children: John Brooks, Jr. b. 1959, Jacqueline Michelle b. 1964; edn: undergrad. Washburn Univ. 1951-53, BSEE, Kansas St. Univ., 1956, MS engring., UCLA, 1961, PhD engring. sci., UC San Diego, 1971; reg. profl. engr., Wash. Career: physical sci. adminstr. and hd. Naval Electronics Lab. Ctr., 1960-75; dir. and prof. elec. engring. Applied Physics Lab., Univ. Wash., 1975-77; asst. dir. for Astronomical, Atmospheric, Earth and Ocean Scis., Nat. Sci. Found. 1977-79, dir. 1980-82; acad. v.p. & provost Wash. State Univ. 1979-80; chancellor Univ. of Maryland, Coll. Park 1982-88; pres. Occidental Coll., Los Angeles 1988-; dir: ARCO, Avery Dennison Corp., IBM, Monsanto Co., Union Bank; awards: Whiting scholar 1951-53, Republic Aviation award best speech on airpower 1955, Sigma Tau 1954, Eta Kappa Nu 1954, NELC scientist of yr. 1965, NELC fellow 1969, UCLA engring. alumnus of yr. 1978, disting. svc. NSF 1979, Tau Beta Pi 1980, disting. svc. in engring. Kans. St. Univ. 1981, alumnus of yr. UCSD 1982, Nat. Acad. Engring. 1982, Unity Media Award Lincoln Univ. 1985, disting. alumnus Washburn Univ. 1985, U.S. Black engr. of yr. 1987, Phi Beta Kappa 1988, UCLA Medal 1989, Roger Revelle Award UCSD 1991, rec'd. Hon. Doctorates-Washburn Univ. of Topeka 1992, Calif. Lutheran Univ. 1991, Alfred Univ. 1991, Pomona Coll. 1989, Univ. of the Pacific 1989, Kansas State Univ. 1988, HDL, Morehouse Coll. 1988, Bowie St. Coll. 1987, Univ. Miami 1983, Rensselaer Polytech. Inst. 1981, Univ. Ill. 1986, SUNY 1986, Univ. Toledo 1985, Texas Southern Univ. 1984, Univ. Mass. 1983, Wayne State Univ. 1983, Ea. Mich. Univ. 1983, Notre Dame 1982, Univ. Md. 1982, Tuskegee Inst. 1981, USC 1981; mem: IEEE (fellow 1977), AAAS (fellow 1978), NAACP (life 1985), Town Hall of Calif. (bd. govs. 1990), LA World Affairs Council (bd. govs. 1990); co-editor Computers and Electrical Engring. internat. jour. (Pergamon Press), contbr. num. articles to sci. and higher edn. jours.; Presbyterian; rec: model R.R., tennis. Office of the President, Occidental College 1600 Campus Rd Los Angeles 90041

SLAWSON, CHARLES JAMES, engineer; b. Feb. 14, 1923, Simpson, Kans.; s. Charles Milton and Esther Ruby (Copas) Decker; m. Beverly Busenbark, Dec. 29, 1943 (dec. 1985); children: James Jean b. 1946, Melody Jan Oconnor-Allen, MD b. 1949; m. Reece Foster, 1986; edn: US Naval Acad. 1942-45; BSEE, Kans. St. Univ. 1948, MSEE, 1953; grad. sgu. CSU Long Beach 1973-80; FAA desig. engring. rep. 1975. Career: instr. Kans. State Univ. elec. engring. dept., 1946-50; proj. engr./res. engr. North Am. Rockwell, Los Angeles 1950-82; FAA desig. engring. rep. Aerospatiale Corp., Grand Prairie, Tx. 1982; sr. proj. engr., Bradley Fighting Vehicle Pgm., Hughes Aircraft Corp., El Segundo 1982-88; avionic engring. cons. Falcon Jet Corp., Little Rock, Ark. 1982; honors: Eta Kappa Nu, Phi Kappa Phi, Sigma Tau, named Seal Beach Man of Year 1986-87; civic: Elks L.B. (chmn. ranger's com.), Interval House, O.C. home for battered women (selected for volunteers Hall of Fame 1987); mil: ensign U.S. Maritime Service 1945-46; Republican; Presbyterian; rec: antique auto restoration, radio controlled model aircraft, golf. Res: 1340 La Mirada Ave Escondido 92026

SLOVER, ARCHY F., chemist; b. July 8, 1920, Oshkosh, Wisc.; s. Archie F. and Josephine Petronella (Zindler) S.; m. Mary Beatrice Corkill, May 25, 1946 (dec. June 17, 1987); 1 dau. Mary Kay b. 1947; edn: BA, UCLA 1947. Career: chemist Kelite Products Co., Los Angeles 1946-49; gen. mgr. Delco Chemicals Inc., Los Angeles 1949-57; mgr., Ind. Spec. Pennwalt Corp., Los Angeles and Phila. 1957-75; chemist Custom Chemical Mfg. Co., Cudahy 1976; gen. mgr. Cherokee Chem. Co. Inc., Compton 1977-89; mem: Fellow Am. Inst. of Chemists, Fellow AAAS, Am. Chemical Soc. (senior), Nat. Assn. of Corrosion Engrs. (corrosion splst.), Reserve Ofcrs. Assn., Am. Ordnance Assn., Am. Eletroplaters Soc., Air Force Assn., Kentucky Colonel, Sigma Alpha Epsilon; mil: capt. CAC, 1941, 1942-46; R.Cath.. Res: 21 Hacienda Dr Arcadia 91006

SMALL, MARILYN ANNAVIEVE, healthcare executive; b. Nov. 3, 1934, Robinson,Ill.; d. Frederick Charles and Anna Mary (Conrad) Schroeder; m. Richard F. Small, Jan.14, 1984; children: L. Scott b. 1957, Mark D. b. 1959, J. Blair b. 1962; edn: AA mgmt., Saddleback Coll., 1975; BA English, theatre, Indiana St. Coll. 1956. Career: reg. adminstr. Combustion Engring. Corp., Irvine 1972-75; internat. adminstr. VTN Corp., Irvine 1975-79; reg. bus. ofcr. Phoenix House Found., Santa Ana 1979-84; mgmt. cons. Western Pacific Assoc., Irvine 1979-; dir. fiscal svs. CareUnit Hosp., Orange 1984-85; mgr. patient relations, admissions St. Joseph Hosp., Orange 1986-88; mgr. Anescor Corp., Orange 1988-; profl. actress and dancer, 1944-51; television show anchor WPGO, Pittsburgh, Pa. 1963-66; drug rehabilitation counselor Phoenix House, Santa

Ana 1979-84, Half Way House cons. Yorba House, Tustin 1984-87; honors: star thespian Indiana St. Univ. 1953, mayor Girls' State, Ill. 1950, mgmt. achievement award Phoenix House 1984, student tng. commendn. Kingdom of Saudi Arabia 1979; mem: Oil & Gas Processing Assn. 1954-, Crawford County Drama Soc. 1949-, Orange County Mental Health Soc. 1979-, Orange County Health Care Assn., Pittsburgh, Pa. Symph. Soc. (co-chair 1963-66); works: Children's Plays (1950-62), Symphony in C Minor (1953), artist in oils, acrylics, charcoal (1963-); Republican; rec: the Arts. Res: 26534 Monteil Mission Viejo 92691 Ofc: Anescor Corp. 1310 W Stewart Dr Orange 92668

SMALL, RICHARD F., county official, mechanical engineer, consultant; b. July 2, 1936, Buffalo, NY; s. Frank and Rose (Cohn) S.; m. Marilyn A. Schroeder, Jan. 14, 1984; children: Scott, Mark, James; edn: AS Mech. Engring. Tech., SUNY, Buffalo, 1957; BSME, Tri-State Univ., 1968; MBA, UCLA, 1973; JD, UC Irvine, 1974; STD; Registered profl. engr., Calif., Ill., Fla., Eng., Italy. Career: engring mgr. Worthington Corp., Buffalo, 1959-68; div. mgr. Pulsation Controls Corp., Santa Paula, Calif., 1968-70; project mgr. Pioneer Svc. & Engring. Corp., Chgo., 1970-72; mgr. internat. projects Bechtel Power Corp., Norwalk, Calif., 1972-74; v.p. VTN Corp., Irvine, 1974-76, STD Res. Corp., Arcadia, Calif., 1977-78; dir. U.S. Dept. of Energy, Oakland, Calif., 1976-77; sr. ptnr. Western Pacific Assocs., Costa Mesa, Calif., 1978-88; dir. architecture and engring. Orange County Gen. Svs. Agy., Santa Ana, Calif., 1988-; sr. cons. Airesearch Mfg. Co., Torrance, Calif., 1980-85; contract cons. Rockwell Space Systems, Downey, Calif., 1980-81; mem. Res. ret.; mem: Nat. Soc. Profl. Engrs., ASME, Am. Nuclear Soc., Am. Mgmt. Assn., Orange Co. Mgmt. Forum; counselor, advisor, Phoenix House Found., Santa Ana, 1982; author: Energy Alternatives, 1976; contbr. numerous articles on energy to profl. jours.; patentee equipment for energy conversion. Mil: sgt., U.S. Army, 1951-54, Korea. Res: 26534 Monteil, Mission Viejo 92691-5932. Ofc: Orange County Gen. Svs. Agy. 14 Civic Ctr. Santa Ana 92701

SMATHERS, JAMES BURTON, medical physicist; b. Aug. 26, 1935, Prairie du Chien, Wis.; s. James Levi and Irma (Stindt) S.; m. Sylvia Lee Rath, Apr. 20, 1957; children: Kristine b. 1958, Kathryn b. 1959, James b. 1961, Ernest b. 1964; edn: BNE, N.C. State Coll., Raleigh 1957, MS, 1959, PhD, Univ. Md., College Park 1967; profl. desig: CHP, PE, DABR, DABMP. Career: res. engr. Atomics Internat., Canoga Park, Calif. 1959; 1st lt. US Army, W.D.C., 1959-61; research scientist U.S. Govt., W.D.C. 1961-67; prof. nuclear engring. Texas A&M Univ., College Station 1967-80; prof. med. physics Univ. Calif. Los Angeles, 1980-; mem.: Am. Assn. Physicists Medicine (treas. 1992-94), Health Physics Soc., Am. Coll. of Med. Physics Am. Coll. of Radiology, Nat. Soc. Profl. Engrs.; publs: 50+ sci. articles; Lutheran. Res: 18229 Minnehaha St Northridge 91326

SMILEY, ROBERT WILLIAM, industrial engineer; b. Oct. 18, 1919, Phila.; s. Albert James and Laura Emma (Hoiler) S.; m. Gloria Morais, June 30, 1990; children: (by previous marriage) Robert, James, Lauralee, Mary, (step) Deborah, Sheila, Vicki, James, Sonja, Michelle; edn: cert. in I.E., Gen. Motors Inst., 1942; stu. Univ. Rochester 1948, Univ. Pitts. grad. Sch. Bus. 1968, CSU San Jose 1969; BSBA, Coll. Notre Dame, Belmont 1972, MBA, 1974; Reg. profl. engr. Calif. Career: with A.S. Hamilton consulting engrs., Rochester, N.Y. 1946-48; Capt. USNR-Ret., active 1942-46, 51-52, LCDR USN 1952, CDR 1960, resigned 1966: tech. contract mgmt. Poseidon/Polaris and Terrier Missile Pgms. 1952-64, ofcr. in charge Polaris Missile Facility Pacific, Bremerton, Wash. 1964-66, chmn. Polaris/ Minuteman/ Pershing Missile Nondestruct Test Com. 1958-64; mgr. product assurance Missile Systems div. Lockheed Missiles and Space Co., Sunnyvale 1966-72, mgr. materiel Missile Systems div. 1972-77; quality control cons. Dragon Missile Pgm., US Army, 1971; mgr. product assurance McDonnell Douglas Astronautics, 1977-78; dir. product assur. Aerojet Tactical Systems, Sacto. 1978-83; dir. quality assurance Aerojet Solid Propulsion Co., Sacto. 1984-92; dir. q.a. Tahoe Surgical Instruments, 1992-; Fellow ASQC (chmn. S.F. sect. 1969-70, exec. bd. 1966-, chmn. reliability div. 1971, 81, nat. v.p. 1984-85), mem. Aircraft Inds. Assn. (chmn. q.a. com.), Navy League, AAAS, Am. Mgmt. Assn. author: Reliability Engineering and Management (1988), chapters and articles in field. Res/Ofc: 9144 Green Ravine Ln Fair Oaks 95628-4110

SMISEK, THOMAS MILO, marketing executive; b. Dec. 15, 1938, Cleveland, Ohio; s. Milo and Adele (Ejze) S.; m. Angela, Aug. 7, 1982; children: Cassandra b. 1963, Brandon b. 1964, Kahana b. 1983; edn: Cleveland Inst. of Art. Career: pres. Tom Smisek Advtg. 1967-80, Tom Smisek Advtg./ Mktg. Cons. 1980-; instr. advtg. copywriting Orange Coast Coll.; honors: Scholastic Keys 1957, num. advtg. awards for creativity including 4 Golden Orange Awards from Orange Co. Ad Club; mem: Orange Co. Sheriff's Adv. Council, Orange Co. Ad Fedn., Am. Ad Fedn., Am. Soc. Profl. Cons.; mil: E-3 USAF (SAC); Republican. Res: Smisek Ranch POB 374 Silverado 92676 Ofc: Tom Smisek Cons. 4000 MacArthur Blvd Ste 3000 Newport Beach 92660

SMITH, CHESTER, broadcasting executive; b. March 29, 1930, Wade, Okla.; s. Louis L. and Effie S. (Brown) S.; m. Naomi L. Crenshaw, July 19, 1959; children: Lauri, Lorna, Roxanne; Career: recording artist Capitol Records, Los

Angeles 1947-61; owner, mgr. KLOC-AM, Modesto 1963-81; owner, ptnr. KCSO-TV, Modesto 1966-, KCBA-TV, Salinas 1981-86, KREN-TV, Reno, Nev. 1986-, KTA-TV, Santa Maria 1986-, KCVU-TV, Paradise 1989-, KVMG-TV, Merced 1992-, and KBVU-TV, Eureka 1992-; mem. Calif. Broadcasters Assn.; elected Hall of Fame, Western Swing Soc.; Republican; Christian. Res: 31110 E Lee Rd Escalon 95320 Ofc: Sainte Limited, 100 Sycamore Ave Ste 3 Modesto 95354

SMITH, DONALD RICHARD, editor, publisher; b. Aug. 20, 1932, Stockton; s. Robert Gordon and Gertrude (Schweitzer) S.; m. Darlene Ruth Thomas, May 7, 1961; children: Douglas Robert b. 1972, Deboreah Renae b. 1974; edn: Delta Coll., 1948-50, Coll. of the Pacific 1950. Career: ed., pub. Calif. Odd Fellow & Rebekah, Linden, Calif. 1950-; ed. Elk Grove Citizen 1953-55; asst. dir. Un Pilgrimage, New York, N.Y. 1956, 59; ed., pub. Linden Herald 1959-86; ed., pub. Internat. Rebekah News 1963-86; ed., pub. Internat. Odd Fellow & Rebekah 1986-; pres. IOOF Internat. Press Assn. (Md.) 1962-63, v.p. 1960-61, nominating chmn. (NC) 1986-89; bd. dirs. Three Links Youth Camp 1959-61; pres. Linden Municipal Council 1983, council mem. 1981-90; bd. trustees San Jose Co. Historical Soc. 1986-91; honors: Legion of Honor, Order of DeMolay 1961, John R. Williams Award, S.J. Co. Teachers Assn. 1963, 87, Golden Key Award Stockton Tchrs. Assn. 1971, Achievement Award Stockton Bd. of Supervisors 1970, Citizen of Yr. Lions Internat. 1982; mem: Desktop Pub. Assn., Linden-Peters C.of C. (pres. 1968-69); civic: Odd Fellows of Calif. (Grand Master 1958-59), Charity Odd Fellows Lodge #6, Stockton 1950-, Internat. Odd Fellowship (Sovereign Grand Master 1969-70), Lions Internat. (Linden chapt. 1960-); author/pub. books "From Statestop to Friendly Comm." 1976, "Three Link Fraternity" 1993; author book "Leadership Manual Internat. Order Odd Fellows" 1980; Republican; Methodist; rec: Lionel trains, modeling railroad, stamps, coins, history. Ofc: Linden Publications POB 129 Linden 95236

SMITH, ELIZABETH MARTINEZ, county librarian; b. Apr. 14, 1943, Upland; d. Miguel Serrato and Venus (Espinoza) Martinez; m. Michael W. Smith, June 29, 1968; children: Nicolas Miguel, b. 1973, Maya Maria, b. 1977; edn: BA, UCLA 1965, MLS, USC, 1966. Career: intern Pomona Public Library, 1965; children's librarian Rosemead Regional Library, 1966; coordinator Way Out Project, Los Angeles County Public Lib., 1968; regional adminstr. Instns., L.A. County Public Lib., 1972, regl. adminstr., 1976-79; county librarian Orange County, 1979-; lectr. Sch. of Library Sci. CSU Fullerton 1973-76; Gov.'s appointee Cal. State Summer Sch. for the Arts Bd. of Trustees, 1988; honors: George I. Sanchez Award 1976, Hispanic Women's Recognition Award League of United Latin Am. Citizens 1982, Orange County Woman of Achiev. 1986; mem: Calif. Library Assn. 1966-, Am. Library Assn. 1968-, Reforma, Nat. Assn. of Spanish Speaking Librarians, Mexican Am. Polit. Assn., AAUW; contbr. var. library jours. 1972-80; Prot. Res: Upland Ofc: Orange County Public Library, 431 City Dr South, Orange 92668

SMITH, GEORGE IRVING, geologist; b. May 20, 1927, Waterville Me.; s. Joseph Coburn and Ervena (Goodale) S.; m. Patsy Jean Beckstead, Oct. 31, 1953 (div. May 1970); children: Randall b. 1958, Laura b. 1964; m. Teruko Kuwada, Aug. 2, 1974; stepchildren: Michele b. 1963, Marla b. 1967, Mireya b. 1969; edn: AB, Colby Coll., 1949; MS, Calif. Inst. of Tech., 1951, PhD, 1956. Career: instr. Occidental Coll., Eagle Rock 1951-52; geologist, proj. chief US Geol. Survey, Claremont 1952-58, Menlo Park 1958-66, branch chief USGS, Menlo Park 1966-69, project chief 1969-; Fullbright scholar, Australian Nat. Univ., Canberra, 6 mos. 1981; awards: Meritorious svc. US Dept. of Interior, W.D.C. 1983; mem: Geol. Soc. of Am. (1954-, fellow), Mineral. Soc. of Am. (1952-, fellow), Geochemical Soc. 1958-, Am. Quaternary Assn. 1969-, Sigma Xi 1955-; publs: 81+ articles and 24+ abstracts (1953-); mil: p.o.3c USN 1945-46; Indep.; rec: photography, travel. Ofc: U.S. Geological Survey 345 Middlefield Rd Menlo Park 94025

SMITH, GILBERT SHERMAN, JR., chiropractor; b. Feb. 2, 1938, East Prairie, Mo.; s. Gilbert Sherman, Sr. and Bessie Marie (Laxton) S.; m. Yvonne Irene Crane, May 2, 1959; children: Keith b. 1960, Gilbert, III b. 1963, Gwendolyn b. 1964, Sheila b. 1965, Dorothy b. 1966; edn: DC, Palmer Chiropractic Coll., 1960, Upper Iowa Univ. off-campus pgm. Career: instrument tech. Bendix Aviation, Davenport, Iowa 1959; Litton Indus., Hollywood 1961; chiropractor assoc. in Orangevale, Ca. 1962; prin. Smith Chiropractic Office, Auburn 1963-; off-campus instr. intern program Palmer Coll. of Chiropractic, 1987-; mem. state and local chiropractic assns. (past pres., coms.); Toastmasters Intl. (dir., ofcr. 1958-60); Christian (deacon 1966-70, elder 1971-); Republican; rec: hunting, fishing, pvt. pilot. Res: 2120 Andregg Rd Auburn 95603; Smith Chiropractic Office, 13136 Lincoln Way Auburn 95603

SMITH, GORDON EUGENE, airline pilot, b. Nov. 22, 1953, Corpus Christi, Tx.; s. Orvis Alvin and Helen Lucille (Lockhart) S.; m. Crisanta Lacson Oqueriza, Jan. 5, 1979; children: Pia b. 1974, Helena b. 1980; edn: AAS, electronic tech., Riverside City Coll. 1983-85; BS, electronic engring., Cal Poly, Pomona, Calif. 1985-89. Career: corporate pilot, Varco Oil Tools, Orange, Calif. 1980-83; motor home insp., Fleetwood Motor Homes, Riverside, Calif. 1983-85; B-1B electrician, Rockwell Internat., Palmdale, Calif. 1985-87; B-727 first ofcr.,

Orion Air, Raleigh, N. C. 1987-90; asst. chief pilot, National Air, Riverside, Calif. 1990-92, dir. of maintenance, 1990-92; honors: Men of Achievement, 1992; listed Who's Who in Calif. 1981-91; Who's Who Among Rising Young Americans 1991-92; Who's Who In The West 1991-92; mem: AOPA 1978-92, Team One (v.p. 1980-92); mil: t/sgt., USAF 1972-92; Republican; Dunkard Brethren; rec: flying, golf, hiking.

SMITH, JAMES THOMAS, mathematics educator, author; b. Nov. 8, 1939, Springfield, Oh.; s. Earl Gearhart and Betty Mae (McCartney) S.; m. Helen Marie Patteson, Jan. 26, 1963; 1 son, Jedediah b. 1968; edn: AB, Harvard, 1961, MA, San Francisco State Univ., 1964, MS, Stanford Univ., 1966, PhD, Saskatchewan Univ., 1970. Career: mathematician US Navy, San Francisco 1962-67; lectr. San Francisco St. Univ., 1965-67, prof. math. 1969-; vis. prof. Mills Coll., Oakland 1982-83; software engr. Blaise Computing, Berkeley 1984-85; vis. prof. Inst. Teknologi MARA, Subang Jaya, Malaysia 1988-89; mem. Math. Assn. Am. (1967-, chair No. Calif.), Am. Math. Soc. 1987-, Deutsche Mathematiker Vereinigung (1970-), Harvard Club (SF, v.p. 1989-); author: C++ for Scientists & Engineers (1991), Advanced Turbo C (1989), Getting the most from Turbo Pascal (1987), 9+ rsch. papers in math. (1970-85). Res: 1363 27th Ave San Francisco 94122 Ofc: Math. Dept. San Francisco State Univ. 1600 Holloway San Francisco 94132

SMITH, JAMES WILLIAM THOMAS, chiropractor; b. Apr. 15, 1925, Alvey, Tenn.; s. Gilbert Sherman, Sr. and Bessie Melissa (Laxton) S.; m. Kathleen Ellis, Nov. 17, 1944; children: James b. 1947, William b. 1948; edn: stu. Okla. A&M Coll. 1943-44, Sacramento City Coll. 1949-50, CSU Sacto. 1950; DC (valedictorian), Palmer Chiropractic Coll., 1956. Career: airplane comdr., engring. test pilot US Army Air Force, 1943-46, crew chief, flt. engr. USAF, 1946-51, ret. 2d. lt.; pvt. practice Smith Chiropractic, Orangevale 1957-; bd. dirs. IVAC Investors Inc., 1964-; mem. Internat. Chiropractic Assn. of Calif. (pres. 1957, editor Chiropractic Inst. of Calif. 1958); Masonic Lodge, Scottish Rites; publs: Nat. Health Edn. Soc. (1970, 72, 80); Republican; Methodist. Res: 7627 Mountain Ave Orangevale 95662 Ofc: Smith Chiropractic 6487 Main Ave Orangevale 95662

SMITH, JEFFRY ALAN, public health administrator, physician, consultant; b. Dec. 8, 1943, Los Angeles; s. Stanley W. and Marjorie E. S.; m. Jo Anne Hague; edn: BA (philosophy), UCLA 1967, MPH, 1972; BA (biology), CSU Northridge 1971; MD, UACJ, 1977; diplomate am. Bd. Family Practice. Career: resident in family practice WAH, Takoma Park, Md., NIH, Bethesda, Md., Walter Reed Army Hosp., Wash., Children's Hosp. nat. Med. Ctr., Wash.; occupational physician U.S. Dept. of Energy Nevada Test Site, Las Vegas, NV 1980-82; dir. occupational medicine and environ. health Pacific Missile Test Ctr., Point Mugu 1982-84; dist. health ofcr. State Hawaii Dept. Health, Kauai 1984-86; asst. dir. health Co. of Riverside Dept. Health 1986-87; med. dir. Comm. Human Servises, Monterey 1987-; regional med. dir. Calif. Forensic Med. Group, Salinas 1987-; fellow Am. Acad. Family Physicians; mem: AMA, Am. Occupational Medicine Assn., Flying Physicians, Am. Pub. Health Assn. Res: 27575 Via Sereno Carmel 93923 Ofc: POB 10009 Salinas 93912

SMITH, KERRY CLARK, lawyer; b. July 12, 1935, Phoenix, Ariz.; d. Clark and Fay (Jackson) Smith; m. Michael Waterman, 1958; children: Kevin b. 1964, Ian b. 1966; edn: BA, Stanford Univ. 1957; JD, 1962; admitted U.S. Supreme Ct., St. Bar Calif. Career: atty., assoc. Chickering & Gregory, San Francisco 1962-70, ptnr. 1970-81; ptnr. Pettit & Martin 1981-; dir. Allied Properties 1974-77; ofcr. Pebble Beach Corp. 1974-79; bd. editors Stanford Law Review 1961-62; mem: St. Bar Calif. (bus. law sect., fin. institutions com. 1984-87), San Francisco Bar Assn., Am. Bar Assn. (bus. law sect. banking and savings and loan com.); clubs: University (S.F.), Orinda CC, La Quinta Golf; mil: lt. USN. Ofc: Pettit & Martin 101 California St San Francisco 94111

SMITH, LOUIS, equestrian; b. Nov. 2, 1934, Shreveport, La.; s. Louis and Savannah (Durham) S.; m. Velma, Jan. 1, 1962; 1 son, Gerald b. 1962; edn: grad. Freemont H.S., Los Angeles, 1955. Career: maint. engr. L.A. Dept. Water & Power, Pasadena 1968-92; chauffeur Cowboy Limosine Service, 1988-92; civic: mem. Tournament of Roses, equestrian Old Fashioned Day Parades, Pasadena; Altadena Town Council 1982; mem.: Golden West Parade Assn., San Bernardino. Co. 1990-, Internat. Platform Assoc.; awards: Fancy Western Rider, 1st Place, Barstow 1987, 1st, 2d Place, San Bernardino 1990, 92, Leading Rider, Monty Police, Palm Springs 1991, 92, 1st Pl. Western Singleman Rider, Lancaster 1991, featured rider in Palm Springs Feb. 1992, 93; mil: US Army 1957-58; Democrat; Baptist; rec: Tournament of Dominoes, deer hunting, fresh water fishing, country western guitarist. Res: 1980 Santa Rosa Pasadena 91104

SMITH, MARSHALL SAVIDGE, educator, college dean; b. Sept. 16, 1937, East Orange, N.J.; s. Marshall Parsons and Ann Eileen (Zulauf) S.; m. Carol Goodspeed, June 25, 1960 (div. Aug. 1962); m. Louise Nixon Claiborn, Aug. 22, 1964; children: Adam b. 1968, Jennifer b. 1969, Matthew b. 1971, Megan b. 1973; edn: AB, Harvard Univ., 1960, EdM, 1963, EdD, 1970. Career: computer analyst and programmer Raytheon Corp., Andover, Mass. 1959-62; instr., assoc. prof. Harvard Univ., Cambridge 1966-76; asst., assoc. dir. Nat. Inst. of Edn.,

W.D.C. 1973-76; asst. commr. edn. HEW, 1976-79; chief of staff to Dept. of Edn. Secty., 1980; prof. Univ. Wis., Madison 1980-86; prof. and dean Sch. of Edn. Stanford Univ. 1986-; dir: Holmes Group, E.Lansing, Mich.; chmn. bd. Am. Insts. for Res., 1990-, mem. Nat. Council on Stds. and Testing, 1991-; cons. US Dept. Edn.; awards: Commnr.'s award and Secty.'s award US Dept. Edn. (1978, 80), 1st vis. scholar Nat. Inst. Edn. 1973; mem: Am. Ednl. Res. Assn. (chair orgn. instl. affiliates 1985-86), Cleve. Conf., Nat. Acad. Edn., NAACP, Amnesty Internat., Madison West Hockey Assn. (pres. 1982-84); author: The General Inquirer (1967), (w/Jencks) Inequality: A Reassessment of the Effect of Family and Schooling in America (1972), 50+ publs. incl. book chapters, profl. jour. articles; Democrat; rec: coaching youth soccer and hockey. Res: 1256 Forest Ave Palo Alto 94301 Ofc: School of Education Stanford University, Stanford 94305-3096

SMITH, MICHAEL STEVEN, computer services executive; b. May 7, 1956, San Antonio, Tx.; s. Columbus and Mary Patricia (Leahy) S.; m. Lynda M. Gillen, July 1992; edn: City Coll. Chgo. London England 1979-80; Univ. Md. London 1979-80; corresp. stu. L.A. Comm. Coll. in Agana Guam 1977-78; San Bernardino Valley Coll. 1973-76, 1981-83. Career: computer support splst. Smith Comms., London, England and Highland 1979-84; engring. computer splst. Aerojet Electro Systems, Azusa 1983-85; data processing mgr. Bonita Unified Sch. Dist., San Dimas 1985-89, dir. computer info. services 1989-, tchr. 1982-83; computer system cons. Smith Comms., Guam, London and San Bernardino 1974-84; mem: Calif. Assn. of Sch. Business Officials, Calif. Ednl. Data Processing Assn., Digital Equipment Computer Users Soc., Consortium of Ednl. Digital Systems, Pentamation Users Soc.; mil: PO-2 USN 1976-82; rec: sports, system design. Ofc: Bonita Unified School District 115 W Allen Ave San Dimas 91773

SMITH, NORMA GUEST, occupational health nurse; b. June 2, 1925, Lancaster, N.Y.; d. Joseph Whitehouse and Norma Ethel (Montgomery) Guest; m. Gerald Francis Smith, Feb. 11, 1950 (dec. Apr. 1981); children: Gerald, Kathleen, Gordon, Mary, Dan, Ann, Joseph, Elizabeth, Chris, and Teresa; edn: AA, West Los Angeles Coll., 1977; BS, and MA, Chapman Coll., 1981, 1985; R.N., cert. occupational health nurse, Calif. Comm. Colls. instr. credential. Career: psychiatric nurse, Los Angeles, 1947-48; clinic nurse L.A. City Health Dept., 1952-54; staff nurse Daniel Freeman Hosp., Inglewood 1954-77; occupational health nurse Flying Tiger Air Lines, L.A., 1977-86, Chevron Corp., El Segundo, 1986-; vol. nurse Am. Red Cross 1964-, recipient Clara Barton Medallion ARC 1972; mem. Harbor Area Occupational Health Nurse Assn., St. Luke's Hosp. Alumnae Assn., L.A. World Affairs Council; Republican; St. Anastasia Cath. Ch., L.A. (Parish Council 1983-88, Eucharistic Minister 1988-). Res: 8120 Fordham Rd Los Angeles 90045 Ofc: Chevron Corp. 324 El Segundo Blvd El Segundo 90245

SMITH, NORMAN HENRY, insurance executive; b. Jan. 26, 1937, St. Louis, Mo.; s. Norman Joseph and Helen Ann (Wiedey) S.; m. Susan Sommerfeld, Oct. 5, 1968; children: Carson b. 1977, William b. 1979; edn: BS in Engring., Univ. of Ill. 1960, MBA, honors, 1965; lic. Surplus Lines Broker & Agent Calif. State Dept. of Ins. Career: owner, chmn. bd. Capital Workshop Financial Ins. Services, San Francisco, 1974-; chmn./owner Capital Workshop Internat. Ins. Services Ltd., Grand Turk, B.W.I., 1986-; chmn./owner Capital Workshop Gen. Ins. Agy., S.F., 1986-; pres./owner Professionals Prototype Ins. Cos. Ltd., Grand Turk, B.W.I., 1986-; S.F.; instr. engring. and mgmt. depts. Univ. Ill. 1963-65; honors: valedictorian Monticello (Ill.) H.S. 1955, Univ. of Ill. Ma-Wan-Da and Sachem activity honors 1957, 59, listed Who's Who in U.S. Executives; clubs: San Francisco Yacht, Olympic (S.F.), Snowmobilers (Bear Valley); mem. HOA (Bear Valley); several pub. articles on legal malpractice; mil: lt. jg USN 1960-63; Republican. rec.: skiing, diving, sailing, art. Res: 2400 Paradise Dr Tiburon 94920 Ofc: Capital Workshop General Insurance Agency, 550 California St, Sacramento Tower 5th Flr San Francisco 94104 also: Capital Workshop International Insurance Serv. Ltd., Hibiscus Sq, Cockburntown, Grand Turk B.W.I.

SMITH, STANLEY THEODORE, physicist; b. Nov. 5, 1927, Rochester, N.Y.; s. Stanley Robin and Beatrice Marie (McDonald) S.; edn: AB, Univ. Rochester 1951; MS, Utah State Univ. 1981. Career: physicist Naval Weapons Center, China Lake 1953-, missile data analyst 1953, flt. test engr. 1957, infrared systems analyst 1962, dep. program mgr. Optical Signatures Pgm. 1975, ednl. fellowship 1979-81, prin. investigator, performance of electro-optical seekers in global environments 1981, prin. investigator devel. of the spiralling toroidal spectro-interfer, 1982-; prin. investigator hypersonic infrared seeker pgm., 1987-; recipient 3 Sustained Superior Performance awards (1974, 76, 79), Superior Achievement 1978, Spl. Act 1982, Technical Director's award 1988, Patent award 1979, Fellow in sci. and engring. 1990; author 25+ res. papers (1974-), numerous tech. presentations; rec: travel, philately, folkdance, study dolphins. Res: 612 Weiman Ave Ridgecrest 93555 Ofc: Naval Weapons Center China Lake 93555

SMITH, STEVEN ALAN, Oriental medical doctor, psychologist, minister, physiotherapist; b. June 3, 1947, L.A., Calif.; s. Arthur G. and Minnie (Cohen) S.; edn: physiotherapist, Strong-Berg Inst., L.A., Calif., 1969; Certified Acupuncturist, Calif. Acupuncture Coll., L.A., 1980, Dr. Oriental medicine,

1983; BS in Psychology, Ryo Kan Coll., L.A., 1993; Univ. of Santa Monica (masters cand., psychology, 1994); Religious Sci. Theol. Sem. of So. Calif., Thousand Oaks. (religious sci. practitioner/minister cand. 1994). Career: body bldg. instr. Palms Jr. High, L.A., 1963; camp counselor Beverly Hills YMCA, 1964; football team strength coach Santa Monica City Coll., 1966; physical conditioning instr. US Navy, 1967-69; body bldg. instr. Riveria CC, L.A. 1970; massage therapist El Cabillero CC, Tarzana, 1971; owner/operator The Gym Club, L.A. 1972-75; physiotherapist, Dr. Joseph Walters, MD, Sherman Oaks, 1975-78; pvt. practice physiotherapist, L.A., 1978-80; pvt. practice trad. Chinese medicine, homeopathic medicine, metabolic nutrition, 1980-; awards: listed Who's Who In Calif. 1983-86; Religious Sci. Service award, Torrance, Calif. 1993; mem. Amer. Acupuncture Com., 1990-91; mil: seaman, USN, 1966-69; Jewish, Buddhist, Christian; rec: Chinese and Indian cooking. Res: 3147 Durango Ave Los Angeles 90034

SMITH, STEVEN SIDNEY, molecular biologist; b. Feb. 11, 1946, Idaho Falls, Idaho; s. Sidney Ervin and Hermie Phyllis (Robertson) S.; m. Nancy Louise Turner, Dec. 20, 1974; BS, Univ. Idaho, 1968; PhD, UCLA, 1974. Career: asst. res. scientist Beckman Research Inst., City of Hope Nat. Med. Ctr., Duarte 1982-84, staff Cancer Center, 1983-, asst. res. scientist depts. thoracic surgery and molecular biology, 1985-87, assoc. res. scientist div. surgery 1987-90, dir. dept. of Cell & Tumor Biology, 1990-; cons. Molecular Biosystems Inc., San Diego 1981-84; awards: Phi Beta Kappa, Swiss Nat. Sci. Found. fellow Univ. Bern 1974-77, Scripps Clinic and Research Found., La Jolla 1978-82, NIH fellow Scripps Clinic 1979-81, NIH grantee 1983-, Council for Tobacco Research grantee 1983-92, Smokeless Tobacco Res. Council grantee 1992-, March of Dimes grantee 1988-91; mem: Amer. Crystallographic Assn., Am. Soc. Cellular Biology, Am. Assn. for Cancer Research, Am. Weightlifting Assn.; rec: backpacking. Ofc: City of Hope National Medical Center, 1500 E Duarte Rd Duarte 91010

SMITH, WILLIAM CLARKE, clergyman; b. Jan. 22, 1926, Bend, Oreg.; s. Jay Harvey Smith and Amelia Grace (Starr) Poor; m. Veta Maxine Davidson of Warren, Ark.; children: Carolyn Jean Aldama, Virginia Ann Bennett, Barbara Lynn Farstad, Rebecca Ruth Sickler, Donald Allen, Patricia Bea Weinbrenner, Dwight David; edn: A.B. Cum laude, Ouachita Baptist U., 1949; postgrad. Golden Gate Baptist Theol. Sem., 1951-53; ordained to ministry So. Baptist Ch., 1948. Career: pastor Owensville Baptist Ch., Ark., 1949-50, Grace Bapt. Ch., Corning, Calif., 1951; assoc. pastor 1st So. Bapt. Ch., Richmond, 1951-53; pastor Montalvin Bapt. Ch., San Pablo, 1953-60, First So. Bapt. Ch., Clovis, 1961-85, Hillside Bapt. Ch., La Puente, 1985, Trinity Bapt. Ch. Modesto, 1986-89, ret.; mem. So. Bapt. Gen. Conv. of Calif. (exec. bd. 1981-85, cons. stewardship dept., 1976-89, parliamentarian, 1964, 69, 74, 78), Calif. So. Bapt. Ministers Conf. (pres. 1979), Clovis Ministerial Fellowship (pres. 1963-65, 67-70, 75-77), So. Bapt. Bd. Child Care (1964-67, chmn. 1966-67), Mid-Valley So. Bapt. Assn. (moderator 1965-66, clk. 1969-78), Fresno Bapt. Assn. (moderator 1962-64); civic: Clovis Civic Improvement Bond Com. (chmn. fin. com. 1976), Clovis Bicentennial Com. (chair religion 1975-76), Clovis Parks Advy. Com. (1977-78); listed Who's Who in Religion, Who's Who in the West, Who's Who in Fresno; mil: US Army, 1944-46; Republican; Res: 2644 Crescent Ave Clovis 93612

SMITH, WILLIAM HUGH, municipal internal audit manager; b. Feb. 12, 1920, Peoria, Ill.; s. Hugh Norman (C.P.A.) and Catherine Litta (O'Brien) S.; m. Betty Lou, June 4, 1941; children: Beverly Ann Clark b. 1944, William H., Jr. b. 1948, Mildred Judkins b. 1950, Hugh N. b. 1953, Patrick J. b. 1958; edn: BSBA (hons.), Univ. of Dayton, Ohio 1946; Univ. Ill. Grad. Law Sch. 1940-41; desig: CFE, Cert. Fraud Examiner, Nat. Assn. Cert. Fraud Examiners, 1989. Career: resident mgr. Hugh N. Smith CPAs, Chgo. 1947-75; v.p. and chief auditor United of America Bank, Chgo. 1975-78; audit mgr. internal audit City of Anaheim, Ca. 1979-; chmn. audit com. Hoover Dam Uprate Project; mem. Inst. of Internal Auditors, Inc. Orange Co. (speaker com., bd. govs. 1990-93, Internat. Com. on Govt. Affairs), Nat. Assn. of Cert. Fraud Examiners (bd. regents candidate), V.F.W.; mil: capt. Inf. US Army 1941-46, chief counter intell. SE Procurement Dist., provost marshal Tinian Is. Marianas Islands; Republican (life charter mem. Repub. Presdl. Task Force, Who's Who in Republican Party); R.Cath.; rec: sports. Res: 14415 Baker St Westminster 92683 Ofc: City of Anaheim 200 S Anaheim Blvd Ste 710 Anaheim 92805

SMITH, WILLIAM RAY, engineer; b. June 26, 1925, Lyman, Okla.; s. Harry Wait and Daisy Bell (Hull) S.; edn: BA, Bethany Nazarene Coll. 1948; MA, Wichita State Univ. 1950; Univ. of Kans. 1950-51; PhD, UCLA 1967. Career: structures engr. Beach Aircraft Corp., Wichita, KS 1951-53; sr. gp. engr. McDonnell Aircraft, St. Louis, MO 1953-60; sr. engr. Lockheed Aircraft, Burbank 1961-63; sr. engr. sci. McDonnell Douglas Corp., Long Beach 1966-71; mem. tech. staff Rockwell Internat., Los Angeles 1973-86; CDI Corp., Costa Mesa 1986-88; McDonnell Douglas Corp., Long Beach 1988-; tchr. Pasadena Coll. (now Point Loma Nazarene Coll.), San Diego 1960-62; Glendale Jr. Coll. 1972; Mt. St. Mary's Coll. 1972-73; honors: Citation for Profl. Achievement, McDonnell Douglas Corp. 1968; Tech. Utilization Award, Rockwell Internat. 1981; NASA Cert. of Recogn. 1982; mem: NY Acad. of Scis., AAAS, Inst. of Aero. and Astro., Yosemite Nat. Hist. Assn. (life), L.A. World Affairs Council, Town Hall of Calif., UCLA Chancellor's Assocs.,

Internat. Visitors Council of L.A., Sigma Xi, Pi Mu Epsilon, Delta Epsilon; tech. publs. 1969, 1981; Republican; Presbyterian (deacon); rec: sailing. Res: 2405 Roscomare Rd Los Angeles 90077 Ofc: McDonnell Douglas Corp. 3855 Lakewood Blvd Long Beach 90846

SMITHAM, H. BRUCE, real estate broker; b. July 22, 1934, Los Angeles; s. Thomas and Emilie W. (Mac Kinnon) S.; m. Sandra Burke, Sept. 14, 1957; children: Hugh, b. 1961, Andrew, b. 1963, Jane, b. 1965, Bruce, b. 1967, Sarah, b. 1970; BA, UCLA 1961. Career: chmn., Aid to Families w/ Dependent Children, State of Calif. Welfare Dir.'s Assn. 1975-76; asst. dir. Kings Co. & Mendocino Co. 1969-77; owner/ opr. Stage Coach Realty, Ukiah, and Redwood Valley, Ca. 1977-83; currently realtor/owner Smitham Real Estate, Del Mar; mem: Realtors Active in Politics (past chmn.), San Dieguito Assn. Realtors, Mendocino County Bd. Realtors (past chmn. profl. stds. & ethics com.), Nat. Assn. Realtors, past mem. Farm & Land Inst.; clubs: Downtown Ukiah Kiwanis (past pres.), Optimists Del Mar-Solana Beach (pres.); Republican; Episcopal; rec: aviation, computers, real estate. Ofc: Smitham Real Estate, PO Box 2804 Del Mar 92014

SMOLENSKY, EUGENE, economist, professor and graduate school dean; b. Mar. 4, 1932, Bklyn.; s. Abraham and Jennie (Miller) S.; m. Natalie Joan Rabinowitz, Aug. 16, 1952; children: Paul b. 1955, Beth b. 1958; edn: BA econ., Brooklyn Coll., 1952; MA econ., American Univ., W.D.C. 1956; PhD econ., Univ. Pa., 1961. Career: prof. economics Univ. Wisconsin, Madison 1968-88, chair dept. econ. 1978-80, 86-88, director Inst. for Research on Poverty, 1980-83; prof., dean Grad. Sch. of Public Policy, UC Berkeley, 1988-; mem. Nat. Acad. Scis./Nat. Rsch. Council Panel on Child Care Policy, and NAS Commn. on Women's Employment & Related Issues, 1985-91; editor J. of Human Resources, 1985-88; mem.: Assn. for Pub. Policy Analysis & Mgmt. 1988-, Internat. Inst. for Pub. Finance 1980-; coauthor: Public Expenditures, Taxes and the Distbn. of Income: The U.S., 1950, 1961, 1970 (1977), American Economic Growth (1972), Aggregate Supply and Demand Analysis (1964); mil: USN 1952-56; Democrat; Jewish; rec: collect old master etchings and lithographs. Res: 669 Woodmont Ave Berkeley 94708 Ofc: Graduate School of Public Policy UC Berkeley 2607 Hearst Ave Berkeley 94720

SNELL, DAVID MOFFETT, manufacturing company executive; b. Nov. 22, 1949, Boston, Mass.; s. John Raymond and Florence (Crawford) S.; m. Janice Marie, June 7, 1974; children: Dustin Moffett b. 1976, Joshua Raymond; edn: BFA, Mich. St. Univ. 1972; MFA, Cranbrook Acad. Art 1974. Career: asst. dir. Gallery 555 Ltd., Birmingham, Mich. 1975-76; mgr. Norman Thomas Co. 1976-77; sales mgr. SWest Inc., Glendale 1977-79; sales mgr. Western Brass Works, Los Angeles 1980-85, gen. mgr. 1985-; gen. mgr. and v.p. Western Brass Works, Western Raintrol Proven Pump 1991-; mem: Non Ferous Founders Soc.; sculptor, 1969-75; mil: Reserve USMC 1969-72; Republican; Prot.; rec: fishing. Ofc: Western Brass Works 1440 N Spring Los Angeles 90012

SNOW, ALAN ALBERT, humanist ministry administrator, insurance agent, author, publisher; b. July 20, 1946, Van Nuys; s. Perry William and Virginia (Show) S.; edn: BA, Pepperdine Univ., 1969; MA, Sch. of Theology, Claremont 1974; Magister Operae Onerosae (hon.) Inst. Antiquity Christianity, Claremont 1972; Calif. Lic. fire, cas., life and disability ins. agt. Career: dir. Independent Humanist Ministries Newport Beach; agt. Farmers Ins. Group of Cos., Fountain Valley; appt. Mayor's advy. com. L.A.; mem. bd. dirs. Inst. for Judeo-Christian Origins Studies, CSU Long Beach; listed Who's Who in Religion 1993; mem: Nat. Notary Assn. (ethics com., Cert. Accomplishment), Am. Soc. Notaries, Am. Humanist Assn., Ethical Cultural Soc. L.A., N.Y., Inst. for Dead Sea Scrolls Studies W.D.C., Biblical Archaeology Soc. W.D.C. (charter mem. Dead Sea Scroll Research Council); Libertarian. Res: 518 S Bay Front Balboa Island 92662-1040

SNOW, BECKY (REBECCA) H., real estate broker; b. Nov. 20, Donalsonville, GA; d. John R. and Frances Jenelle (Lindsay) Hornsby (dec.); m. Gordon E. Snow, Aug. 29, 1958; children: Jenelle b. 1959, Misty b. 1964, Gordon, Jr. b. 1968; edn: Coll. of the Redwoods 1965, Ventura Coll. 1972, Oxnard Coll. 1981; GRI, Grad. Realtors Inst. 1976. Career: govt. civil service 1960-70; broker/pres. Snow Real Estate 1973-, real estate exchanger, consultant; sponsor tax/R.E. seminars 1978; guest speaker salesmanship in local colls.; awards: Beneficial suggestion US Civil Service 1967, excellence Client Follow-up Pgm. 1987; mem: Nat. Bd. Realtors, Calif. Bd. Realtors, Oxnard Harbor Bd. of Realtors (past pres. Women's Council of Realtors), Oxnard Harbor & Camarillo MLS, Central Coast Exchangers (past secty.), Nat. Council of Exchangers Temp. Gold Card holder, Channel Is. Toastmistress Club (past); contbr. articles in Real Estate Today; writer/prod. The Golden Rule, a R.E. play (1977); Independent; Foursquare; rec: travel. Ofc: Snow Real Estate, 1392 Thousand Oaks Blvd Ste 385 Thousand Oaks 913362

SNYDER, JOHN JOSEPH, ret. optometrist; b. June 30, 1908, Wonewoc, Wisc.; s. Burt Frederick and Alta Lavinia (Hearn) S.; edn: AB, honors, UCLA 1931, post grad. 1931-32; post grad. Univ. of Colo. 1936, 1938, 1940, 1941; post grad., USC, p.t. 1945-47; BS, Los Angeles Coll. of Optometry 1948, OD, 1949. Career: tchr. Rockvale Jr. Sch. and Mayday Sch., La Plata Co., Colo. 1927-28;

supt. pub. schs., h.s. tchr. Marvel, Colo. 1932-33; tchr. biology, physics, chemistry, Durango, Colo. 1933-41; optometrist self-empl., Los Angeles 1952-72, Torrance 1972-78; vacation and relief optometrist 1979-; mem: AAAS, Am. Inst. of Biol. Scis., Am. Optometric Assn., Calif. Opt. Assn., L.A. County Opt. Soc., Intl. Biographical Assn. (Fellow), Exchange Club of So. L.A. (pres. 1957, secty. 1962), Francia Boys Club, L.A. (bd. dirs. 1956-64); Republican; rec: fishing, limnology. Address: 25937 Reynolds St Loma Linda 92354

SNYDER, NORMAN GENE, physician; b. Apr. 28, 1923, Adel, Iowa; s. Milo Myran and Phoebe Dillworth (Crouse) S.; m. Delphia Norman, Aug. 13, 1950; children: Michael b. 1951, David b. 1953, Catherine b. 1956, Jonathan Scott b. 1957; edn: undergrad. Drake Univ. 1940-42, Iowa State Univ., Ames 1946-47; MD, Univ. of Iowa 1951; lic. Calif. Career: intern Los Angeles County Harbor Gen. Hosp., Torrance 1951-52; gen. & family medicine practice, West Covina 1953-76; emergency phys. Covina Intercommunity Hosp., 1976-81; gen. & family practice phys. Cigna Health Plans, West Covina 1981-; pres./organizer San Gabriel Valley Hot Line 1969-71; dir. Chase-King Devel. Ctr., Upland 1974-76; elected councilman (mayor 1964-65) City of West Covina 1960-68; named Man of the Year for contbn. to human rights, Covina - W. Covina - La Puente Human Rights Council; mem. Am. Med. Assn.; Rotarian; mil: US Navy 1943-46, lt.jg. Reserve 1947-55; Republican (Rep. Central Com. 49th Assem. Dist. 1962-66); rec: bridge, hiking, boating. Ofc: Cigna Health Plans 1500 S Sunset Ave West Covina 91790

SOKARI, HASS, international management and finance consultant; b. Oct. 7, 1930, Cairo, Egypt; nat. 1975; s. Hanafi M. and Fatima H. Ali (Dakhakhni) Sokari; m. Farida, Feb. 28, 1963; children: Halah b. 1964, Angie b. 1968; edn: BS, Cairo Univ., Egypt 1957; MBA, Univ. Santa Clara 1975; EdD, Univ. San Francisco 1980. Career: chartered acct. Hass Sokari Chartered Acct. Offices, Cairo, Egypt 1960-69; dir. Egyco-Nasr Co. 1964-69; hd. dir. (dean) Kroitor Instn., Cairo 1965-69; acctg. supr. City Hall, San Francisco 1969-71; instr. San Jose St. Univ. 1972-81; cons. Consultco Internat. Ltd., Mountain View 1975-, advisor edn. to fgn. govts. and insts. 1980-; fin. advisor to bd. dirs. and trustee NE Air Services, Inc., Del. 1987-; v.p. finance TPI Marketing, Inc., Canada 1990-; awards: Egypt Nat. Award for Outstanding Achievement 1952, 62, Nat. Award for best athlete 1954, Nat. Award for outstanding directorship 1968; mem: Accts. & Auditors Assn., MBA Assn., Commerce Club, Egyptian Cultural Club, Am.-Philippines Cultural Club, Am.-Arab Ednl. Center, Nat. Club (Gizera), Automobile Club (Cairo); author, text: Human Asset, 1975; dissertation: Predictors of College Success, 1980; mil: capt. Nat. Def. 1954-57; rec: golf, fencing, travel. Ofc: Consultco International Ltd. 211 Hope St Box #9 Mountain View 94042

SOKOLOFF, ALEXANDER, professor emeritus (biology), b. May 16, 1920, Tokyo; nat. Oct. 8, 1943; s. Dimitri Fyodorovitch and Sofia Alexandrovna Solovieff S.; m. Barbara Bryant, June 24, 1956; children: Alexandra 1961; Elaine 1963; Michael 1964; edn: PhD, U. of Chgo., 1954; AB, UCLA, 1948; AA, UCLA, 1942; career: res. assoc. and instr., U. of Chgo. 1954-55; instr. and asst. prof., Hofstra Coll., Hempstead, NY 1955-58; guest investig., Biology Lab., Cold Spring Harbor, NY 1955-58 and 1961; geneticist, W.H. Miner Agri. Res. Inst., Chazy, NY 1958-60; assoc. res. botanist, UCLA 1960; assoc. res. geneticist, UC, Berkeley 1961-66; geneticist, UC, Berkeley 1966-68; assoc. prof., Calif. State Univ., San Bernardino 1965-1990; cons., UC, Berkeley 1967-68; editor, Tribolium Inf. Bull. 1960-; edit.bd., J. Stored Prod. Res. 1965; assoc. ed. and advy. bd., J. Advanced Zool. 1980-92; assoc. ed., Evolution 1972-74; mem. com. maintenance genetic stocks, Genetics Soc. of Am., 1973-86; chmn., subcom. Insect Stocks, 1973-76; awards: fellow, Royal Entomol. Soc., London 1988-; res. grants NSF, W.D.C. 1957-59 and 1967-73; res. grant, USPHS, W.D.C. 1961; res. grants, U. S. Army Res. Ofc., Triangle Park, SC, 1973-76 and 1976-79; mem: Sigma Xi; Soc. For The Study Of Evolution; Genetics Soc. Am.; Am. Genetic Assn.; Am. Soc. Naturalists; Am. Soc. Zool.; Genetics Soc. Can.; Japanese Soc. Population Ecol.; Soc. Western Naturalists; Pacific Coast Entomol. Soc.; civic: Elks, San Bernardino; author: The Genetics of Tribolium and Related Species, 1966; The Biology of Tribolium vol. 1, 1972; The Biology of Tribolium vol. 2, 1975; The Biology of Tribolium vol. 3, 1977; over 200 papers and research notes; mil: sgt., USAAF, 1942-46; Democrat; Protestant; rec: travel; res: 3324 Sepulveda Ave San Bernardino 92404; ofc: Biology Dept. Calif. State U., 5500 N. University Pkwy. San Bernardino 92407

SOKOLOV, JACQUE J., utility company vice president and medical director, physician; b. Sept. 13, 1954, Los Angeles; s. Albert I. and Frances B. (Burgess) S.; edn: BA in medicine (magna cum laude), USC, 1974, MD (honors), USC Sch. of Med., 1978. Career: intern, resident in internal medicine, Mayo Clinic, Rochester, Minn. 1978-81; cardiologist/ nuclear cardiologist Univ. of Texas Health Sci. Ctr., Dallas 1981-84; healthcare strategic planning cons. 1985-87:Texas Instruments; Southwestern Bell; AT&T; Wang; Rosewood Corp.; chief med. ofcr. Baylor Ctr. for Health Promotion, also Wellness & Lifestyle Corp., Dallas 1985-87; v.p./med. dir. So. Calif. Edison Co., Rosemead 1987-; awards: NIH tng. grantee; civic: Los Angeles Coalition, Los Angeles C.of C.; coauthor 8+ abstracts and med. jour. articles (1983-91); Ofc: So. California Edison Co. 8631 Rush St Rosemead 91770

SOLBERG, RONALD LOUIS, consultant, banker, international economist, author; b. May 15, 1953, Madison, Wis.; s. Carl Louis and Gladys Irene (Oen) S.; m. Anna Maria Gorgol (div. Aug. 1992), May 16, 1983; edn: BA in econs. (honors), Univ. Wisc. 1975; MA and PhD in econs., UC Berkeley, 1977, 1984. Career: country risk analyst Wells Fargo Bank, N.A., San Francisco 1978-79, asst. v.p./country risk analyst Wells Fargo Bank Ltd., London, Eng. 1979-81; tchg. assoc., actg. instr. econ. UC Berkeley 1981-83; cons. The RAND Corp., 1982-84; adj. asst. prof., econ. devel. and country risk analysis, Grad. Sch. Pub. Adminstrn. USC, 1985-92 v.p./sr. internat. economist Security Pacific Nat. Bank, Los Angeles 1984-87, 1st v.p./ chief internat. economist 1988-90, 1st v.p./portfolio risk mgr. 1991-92; internat. finl. cons. 1992-; del. Inst. of Internat. Fin., W.D.C. mission to Malaysia, 1986; advy. com. Cross-Rates, Business Int'l, N.Y. 1988-; advisor on LDC debt swap issues to Sen. Alan J. Dixon; awards: Phi Eta Sigma 1971-72, Newton Booth Fellow in Economics UCB 1975-76, Internat. Res.Fellow Inst. of Internat. Studies UCB 1982-84; mem: Am. Economic Assn., Asia Soc. (Corporate Council So. Calif. chapt. 1989-), Nat. Assn. of Bus. Economists, Soc. for Internat. Devel., Town Hall of Calif., L.A. Athletic Club; author: Country Risk Analysis: A Handbook (London: Routledge, 1992), Sovereign Rescheduling: Risk and Portfolio Management (London: Unwin Hyman Ltd., 1988); pub. res. papers: RAND (4/83), Shipping Economist (Lloyd's of London Press 12/87), Economic Devel. and World Debt (London: Macmillan Press 9/89), numerous profl. presentations; rec: fishing, x-c skiing, squash, billiards. Res: 1411 Elkgrove Circle Apt. 2 Venice 90291 Ph: 310/399-4792

SOLOW, LEE HOWARD, clinical psychologist; b. Jan. 16, 1953, Fairfield; s. Robert Avrom and Marilyn Cynthia (Anes) S.; m. Toni Eileen Gingold, Apr. 5, 1987; children: Max b. 1988, Hannah b. 1990, Sophie b. 1992; edn: BA, UC Irvine, 1974; MA, Calif. Sch. Profl. Psychology, San Diego 1976, PhD, 1978. Career: faculty Coastline Comm. Coll., Fountain Valley 1974-; director Wellness Resources, consultants, 1974-; pvt. practice psychologist, Newport Beach 1978-; dir. stress mgmt. Univ. Athletic Club, N.B.; mem. Am. Psy. Assn. 1985-, CSPA 1985-; author: Wellness Resource Guide (1984); Democrat; Jewish; rec: numismatics, gardening, sports. Res: 702 Heliotrope Corona Del Mar 92625

SOMERSET, HAROLD RICHARD, sugar company president; b. Sept. 25, 1935, Woodbury, Conn.; s. Harold Kitchener and Margaret Mary (Roche) S.; m. Marjory Deborah Ghiselin, June 22, 1957; (dec. 1984); m. Jean MacAlpine DesMarais, Jan 2, 1985; children: Timothy Craig, Paul Alexander; stepchildren: Cheryl Lyn, James Fenelon; edn: BS, U.S. Naval Acad. 1957; BCE, Renesselaer Poly. Inst. 1959; LL.B, Harvard Law Sch. 1967; admitted St. Bars Mass. 1967, Hawaii 1973. Career: atty. Goodwin Procter & Hoar, Boston, Mass. 1967-72; counsel, sr. counsel Alexander & Baldwin, Honolulu, Hawaii 1972-74, v.p., gen. counsel 1974-77, group v.p., exec. v.p. 1978-84; exec. v.p., c.o.o. Calif. & Hawaiian Sugar Co., Concord 1984-88, pres., CEO 1988-; bd. dirs. World Sugar Res. Organization, London, England 1989-; Bay Area Council, San Francisco 1988-; mem. Sugar Assn. (bd. dirs. 1989-), Bankers Club S.F.; civic bds: San Francisco Nat. Maritime Mus. (trustee 1990-), Mt. Diablo Council (exec. com.), BSA; mil: lt. USN 1953-64. Res: 19 Donald Dr Orinda 94563 Ofc: C&H Sugar Co. 1390 Willow Pass Rd Concord 94520

SOMORJAI, GABOR A., professor of chemistry; b. May 4, 1935, Budapest, Hungary (nat. US, 1962); s. Charles and Livia (Ormos) S.; m. Judith Kaldor, Sept. 2, 1957; children: Nicole b. 1964, John b. 1966; edn: PhD, UC Berkeley, 1960. Career: res. staff, IBM, Yorktown Heights, NY 1960-64; asst. prof. of Chem., UC Berkeley 1967-72; prof. of chem., UC Berkeley 1972-; faculty sr. scientist, Materials Sciences Div., Lawrence Berkeley Lab. 1964-; prog. leader, Catalysis Prog., Ctr. for Adv. Materials, Lawrence Berkeley Lab. 1988-; honors: Guggenheim Fellowship 1969, vis. fellow Emmanuel Coll., Cambridge, Eng. 1969, Unilever vis. prof. Univ. of Bristol, Eng. 1972, chmn Div. of Colloid and Surface Chem., Am. Chemical Soc. 1975; recipient Kokes Award, Johns Hopkins Univ., Baltimore, Md. 1976, Emmett Award, Am. Catalysis Soc. 1977; Fellow, Am. Physical Soc. 1976; Baker resident lectr., Cornell Univ. 1977; Miller Professorship, UC Berkeley 1978; recipient, Colloid and Surface Chem. Award, Am. Chemical Soc. 1981, Henry Albert Palladium Award 1986; fellow, Am. Assn. for Advancement of Sci. 1982; Centenary Lectr., Royal Soc. of Chem. 1983; chmn, Gordon Conf. on Catalysis 1983; recipient, Peter Debye Award, Am. Chemical Soc. 1989, Sr. Dist. Scientist Award, Alexander von Humboldt Found. 1989, E.W. Mueller Award, Univ. of Wis. 1989, hon. doctorate Technical Univ., Budapest 1989, Universite Pierre et Marie Curie, Paris, France 1990; hon. mem., Hungarian Acad. of Sciences 1990; mem: Nat. Acad. of Sciences 1979-, Am. Acad. of Arts & Sciences 1983-, Cosmos Club, Wash., DC; author: textbooks, Principles of Surface Chem., 1972, Chemistry in Two Dimensions: Surfaces, 1981; monograph, Adsorbed Monolayers on Solid Surfaces, 1979; over 500 scientific papers. Res: 665 San Luis Rd. Berkeley 94707

SOOR-MELKA, MARIANNE, physician; b. Jan. 4, 1930, Budapest, Hungary; d. Emery I. and Suzanne (Csanyi) Soor; m. John B. Melka, July 19, 1958; children: John C. b. 1964, Bryan A. b. 1967; edn: MD, Univ. Montreal 1956; cert. physician Calif. 1961. Career: pvt. practice psychiatry, Covina; mem: Am. Psychiatric Assn., So. Calif. Psychiatric Soc., AMWA, Altrusa Club. Ofc: 246 W College Ste 204 Covina 91723

SORCSEK, JEROME PAUL, composer; b. Sept. 22, 1949, Lebanon, Pa.; s. Martin Raymond and Agnes Geraldine (Ondrusek) S.; m. Joan Marie Kissinger, Nov. 20, 1976; edn: MusB, Temple Univ., 1974; MusM, Univ. Miami, 1975. Career: composer Symphony #1, 1980, Symphony #2, 1981, Music of the Pearl, 1985, Orchestral Variations, 1989; guest composer Festliche Musiktage, Uster, Switzerland, 1981, 85; recipient composition awards: Nat. Band Assn., Chgo. 1978, New Music for Young Ensembles, NY, NY 1986; mem.: ASCAP 1976-; mil: E5 US Army 1967-70. Res: 11018 Swinton Ave Granada Hills 91344

SORSTOKKE, SUSAN EILEEN, systems engineer; b. May 2, 1955, Seattle; d. Harold William and Carrol Jean (Russ) Sorstokke; edn: BS in sys. engring., Univ. Ariz., 1976; MBA, Univ. Wash., 1983. Career: whse. team mgr. Procter & Gamble Paper Products, Modesto 1976-78; quality assurance engr. Westinghouse Hanford Co., Richland, Wa. 1978-80, supv. engring. document ctr. 1980-81; mgr. data control & adminstrn. Westinghouse Electric, Madison, Pa. 1981-82, mgr. data control & records mgmt., 1982-84; prin. engr. Westinghouse Elevator, Morristown, N.J. 1984-87, reg. adminstrn. mgr. Westinghouse Elevator, Arleta, Calif. 1987-90; ops. res. analyst American Honda Motor Co., Torrance 1990-; adj. prof. Univ. LaVerne, 1991; c.f.o. Optimist Charities Inc., Acton 1991-; instr. Excell, L.A. 1991-92; mem. Soc. of Women Engrs. (1975-, past pres. Ea. Wash. sect.), Am. Inst. Industrial Engrs.; civic: Optimist Intl. Santa Clarita 1991-, Am. Edn. Connection, Santa Clarita (1988-89, 91), Junior Achievement, Greensburg, Pa. 1982-83, Westmoreland Literacy Council 1983-84, EF Found., Santa Clarita 1987-88; Republican; Methodist. Res: 21647 Spice Ct Saugus 91350 Ofc: American Honda Motor Co. Inc. 1919 Torrance Blvd 100-4E-8D Torrance 90501

SOSA-RIDDELL, ADALJIZA, educator; b. Dec. 12, 1937, Colton; d. Luz Paz and Gregoria (Lopez) Sosa; m. William A. Riddell, Aug. 24, 1957; 1 child, Citlali b. 1985; edn: BA, UC Berkeley 1960; MA, 1964; PhD, UC Riverside 1974. Career: tchr. Colton Union H.S., Colton 1961-68; asst. prof. UC Davis 1971-78, prof. of Chicano studies 1978-, coord. Chicano/Latina research project; awards: Nat. Assn. Chicano Studies 1989, Sacto. Area YWCA Woman of Year award in edn. 1992; mem: Comision Femenil, Mujeres Activas en Letras y Cambio Social (past chair), Nat. Assn. for Chicano Studies, Mexican-Am. Political Assn.; writer poetry 1974, 75; 5 research articles pub. in profl. jours. 1975-84; Democrat; rec: writing, community service. Ofc: Chicano Studies Program University of California Davis 95616

SOUDERS, STUART ALLEN, physician, radiologist; b. Feb. 24, 1941, Nebraska City, Neb.; s. Allen E. and Jeannette (Campbell) S.; m. Ursula Kachel, May 11, 1977; children: Alexander b. 1979, Natasha b. 1984; edn: BA, Univ. Neb. 1963; MD, Univ. Neb. Coll. Medicine 1968; residency diagnostic radiology Duke Univ. Med. Ctr. 1975-78; fellow neuroradiology USC, L.A. 1981-83; fellow CT-US 1984. Career: instr. USC/L.A. Co. Coll. Medicine, Los Angeles 1981-84; locum tenens coverage, currently; mem: AMA, RSNA, ASNR, ACR, Orange Co. Neuroradiological Soc., Orange Co. Radiological Soc., L.A. Radiological Soc.; mil: active duty US Army, Ger. 1969-74, Col. Calif. Army Nat. Guard 1983-, sr. flt. surgeon and chief of profl. svs. 143d EVAC Hosp.; Republican; Prot.; rec: flying, sailing, skiing. Address: 5901 Warner Ste. 151 Huntington Beach 92649

SPALLA, RICK (a.k.a. Joseph S. Spalla), film producer, director, cameraman; b. May 22, 1923, Sandusky, Ohio; s. Anthony and Vincenzina (Catania) S.; m. Shirley Egland, Dec. 17, 1955; children: Jeffrey b. 1957, Michael b. 1959, Maralee b. 1962, Richard b. 1967; edn: BA, Univ. of So. Calif. Cinema 1953. Career: cameraman Open Road Prodns., Hollywood 1953-56; CEO, producer/gen. mgr. Jet TV, Hollywood 1956; exec. producer/owner Rick Spalla Video Prodns., Hollywood 1957-; producer/dir. Hollywood Newsreel Syndicate, Inc., Hollywood 1957-; mem: IATSE, Acad. of TV Arts & Scis., Friars Club; prod./dir. TV series: Hollywood Backstage, 39 half hours (1967), Hollywood Star Newsreel, 26 half hours (1964), Portrait of a Star, 12 hours (1968); prod./dir. TV spl.: Miss Calif. Internat. Beauty Pageant, 8 yrs.; prod./dir. hundreds of TV pgms. & specials; mil: pfc., U.S. Army Air Force, 1943-46 (WWII); rec: stock footage library w/millions of feet Hollywood & newsreel. Ofc: Rick Spalla Video Prodns 1622 N Gower St Hollywood 90028

SPANGLER, CHARLES BISHOP, company president, b. Jan. 7, 1932, Meadows of Dan, Va.; s. Charles Langhorne and Kittie Clyde (Cockram) S.; m. Bettie Smith, Sept. 12, 1954; children: Peggy b. 1955, Charles b. 1957, Thomas b. 1959; edn: AB, Berea Coll. 1953, MS, Univ. of Pittsburgh 1955, PhD, 1963. Career: sr. res. engr. Gen. Dynamics, San Diego 1956-60; asst. prof. math. San Diego St. Univ. 1960-62; mgr. ops. research Litton Data Systems, Van Nuys 1962-69; dir. systems engring. Teledyne Ryan, San Diego 1969-71, dir. advanced sys. 1971-75; pres. Quest Equities Corp. 1976-89; founder and pres. C.B. Spangler Inc. 1989-; dir: Topaz Div. Intermark Corp. 1962-68, Cosumark Corp. 1976-78; awards: Clark Prize in Physics, Berea Coll. 1953, outstanding citizen award Patrick Co., Va. 1975; mem. Am. Math. Soc.; Torrey Pines Christian Ch. (bd. chmn.). Res: 335 Fern Glen La Jolla 92037

SPANIER, JEROME, mathematician, educator, administrator; b. June 3, 1930, St. Paul, Minn.; s. David Howard and Anne (Goldman) S.; m. Bernice Hoffman, Aug. 31, 1952; children: Stephen b. 1956, Ruth b. 1959, Adrienne b. 1959; edn: BA, Univ. Minn., 1951; MS, Univ. Chicago, 1952, PhD, 1955. Career: senior mathematician Bettis Atomic Power Lab., West Mifflin, Pa. 1955-59, Westinghouse fellow 1959-66, advy mathematician 1966-67; mem. tech. staff Science Ctr. No. American Rockwell, Thousand Oaks, Calif. 1967-70, group ldr./math. 1970-71; prof. math. The Claremont Graduate Sch., Claremont 1971-, dean of faculty 1982-87, also v.p. academic affairs 1985-87, v.p. and dean Claremont Grad. Sch., 1987-90; awards: Westinghouse Distinguished svc. 1963, US ERDA and NSF grants, Claremont 1976-80, govt. Siam vis. consultant 1979- and vis. lectr. Siam 1981-, Pres.'s medal CGS, Claremont 1990, Fulbright senior scholar Massey Univ., Palmerston North N.Z. 1990; mem.: editl. bd. J. Statistical Physics 1971-, Mathematical & Computer Modelling 1979-; author: An Atlas of Functions (1987), The Fractional Calculus (1974), Monte Carlo Principles & Neutron Transport Problems (1969); rec: brush painting, music, swimming. Ofc: The Claremont Graduate School 143 E Tenth St Claremont 91711

SPARER, MALCOLM MARTIN, rabbi; b. New York City; m. Erna "Kitty" Reichl (dec. 1990) (fought with the resistance WWII, interpreter at the Nuremburg Trials); children: Ruth, Arthur (dec. 1993), Jennifer, Shoshana; edn: AB, MHL, ordained rabbi, Yeshiva Univ.; MA sociology, City Coll. N.Y., cert. pastoral counselling Des Moines Coll. of Osteopathic Med.; PhD sociology, New York Univ. Career: exec. dir. Rabbinical Council of Calif., Los Angeles 1957-66, adminstr. Torah Univ. (later Yeshiva Univ.) Teacher's Coll. of West Coast, liaison for Union of Orthodox Jewish Congs. of Am., 1957-66, moderator radio series "Lest We Forget" 1962, moderator TV specials on Jewish religion and holiday observances, KNXT Los Angeles, 1964-65; rabbi Beth El Jacob, Des Moines, Iowa 1966-69, TV moderator Des Moines, 1967-69; rabbi, Chevra Thilim, San Francisco, 1969-72; co-chmn. Jerusalem Fair, 25th Ann. of State of Israel, 1973; current: cons. internat. leaders, founder Menorah Inst. (inter-faith activities and communications, devel. econ. interdependence; cons. Commn. on Christian-Jewish and Moslem Relations to European Parliament Nations; fgn. rels. and econ. cons. various govt. and non-govt. orgns.; writer and frequent lectr. on coll. campuses, ch. groups on Judaica and World Affairs; pres. No. Calif. Board of Rabbis; Rabbi, Jewish Home for Aged, S.F.; chmn. dept. world affairs/internat. politics Community Coll. of S.F.; chaplain Letterman Army VA Hosp., S.F. Presidio; co-founder Black & Jewish Clergy; mem. S.F. Council of Churches (bd. Food Bank Pgm.), Coalition of S.F. (food basket pgm.), Mayor's Commn. on Holocaust Memorial (hon. chmn.), Mayor's Task Force for the Homeless, Gov.'s Fam. Task Force (co-chair), United Jewish Appeal (Rabbinic Cabinet we. reg.); Ofc: 121 Steuart Ste 403 San Francisco 94105 Mail: POB 15055 San Francisco 94115 Tel:415/788-3630

SPEED, RICHARD BERRY, historian; b. Sept. 27, 1948, Pasadena; s. Richard Berry and Harriet (Caltis) S.; m. Lillian Castillo, Aug. 18, 1976; children: Nathan Richard b. 1977; edn: BA, UC Riverside 1971; MA, CSU Long Beach 1975; PhD, UC Santa Barbara 1987. Career: lectr. dept. of history CSU Hayward 1988-; mem: Am. Hist. Soc., Orgn. of Am. Historians, Soc. Historians of Am. Fgn. Rels., Acad. Political Sci., Center for Study of Presidency; author: Prisoners, Diplomats and the Great War; Republican. Res: 1807 Pheasant Dr Hercules 94547 Ofc: California State University Dept. of History Hayward 94542-3045

SPEER, RICHARD, consultant; b. July 31, 1942, Upland; s. Donald Walter and Alleta Faye (Ganoung) S.; edn: BS, Lewis and Clark Coll. 1964; MA, Bowling Green State Univ. 1965; PhD, Univ. Iowa 1971; postgrad., USC, CSU Los Angeles, Southwest Tx. State Univ., Austin Presbyterian, Theol. Sem., Episcopal Theol. Sem. SW. Career: prof. communication Univ. Tx. 1968-70; Univ. Ark. 1970-71; political cons. 1971-78; fundraiser Synod of Mid-Am., Presbyterian Ch. 1978-79; realtor 1979-80; assoc. Interpretation and Stewardship, Synod So. Calif. and Hawaii, Presbyterian Ch. 1980-82; cons. politics and real estate investments, West Covina, Calif. 1982-88; funds counsel Presbyterian Church (USA) 1988-; honors: Pi Kappa Delta, Delta Sigma Rho, Tau Kappa Alpha, Alpha Psi Omega; mem: Nat. Assn. Realtors, Calif. Assn. Realtors; 100+ publs. acad., creative, and political; Democrat; Presbyterian; rec: railroad travel. Res: 4331 Jerry Ave Baldwin Park 91706 Ofc: PO Box 2152 West Covina 91793

SPEIZER, MARK ADLER, executive; b. July 30, 1943, Youngstown, Ohio; s. Alfred T. and Maxine Ruthe (Adler) S.; m. Linda S. Beasley, Aug. 23, 1979; children: Stephanie Loren b. 1980, Stacey Michelle b. 1982; edn: H.S. dipl., att. Santa Monica City Coll.; lic. fire & cas. ins. agt. & broker, Calif. Career: ins. solicitor fire & cas. Southland Corp. (merged into Lytton Fin. Corp.), Hollywood 1962-64; f & c ins. agent, broker Pacific Growth Corp., Concord 1964-66; Bay Cos. Ins. Agency Inc., San Mateo 1966-70, pres. 1970-74; chmn. bd. and pres. Fastrac Systems, Inc. Insurance Agent & Broker, South San Francisco 1972-; chmn. bd. Great Pacific Ins. Co., So. S.F. 1977-; chmn. bd. and ceo National Ins. Group (holding co. GPIC, both Fastracs, PDC), So. S.F. 1986-; Pinnacle Data Corp., So. S.F. 1988-; San Mateo Fin. Corp., San Mateo 1989-; Great Pacific

Bank, s.s.b., San Mateo 1989-91, chmn. bd. and sr. exec. ofcr. 1991-; Fastrac Systems, Inc., So. S.F. 1991-; mil: cpl. US Army; Republican; rec: water skiing, boating, swimming. Res: Hillsborough Ofc: National Insurance Group, 395 Oyster Point Blvd Suite 500 South San Francisco 94080-1933

SPELLMAN, JAMES, JR., television producer/aerospace educator/military officer; b. Oct. 14, 1958, White Plains, N.Y.; s. James, Sr. and Virginiann (Futia) S.; edn: AA, Moorpark Coll., Ca. 1978; BA and MA, Loyola Marymount Univ., L.A., 1981, 1983; desig: Audiovisual Officer (TV Prod./Dir.) USAF 1983. Career: Capt. U.S. Air Force, 1983-: t.v. prod./dir. 1369th Audiovisual Sq. Vandenberg AFB, 1983-88, interim chief of ops. 1988-89, senior television producer/director 1989-; exec. dir. Nat. Space Soc., Vandenberg AFB, 1988-, recipient NSS Space Pioneer awards- for Publicity 1989, Membership 1989, Recruitment (1990, 91); mem: Nat. Space Soc. (1984-, exec. dir. 1988-), Challenger Ctr. for Space Science Education (charter mem. 1987-), U.S. Space Found. 1987-, The Planetary Soc. 1984-, British Interplanetary Soc. 1988-; civic: Young Astronaut Council VAFB 1988-, Civil Air Patrol VAFB 1988-; contbr. op-ed pages var. periodicals (1983-); Democrat; R.Cath.; avocation: aerospace edn. Ofc: National Space Society 4617 Oak Lane Mountain Mesa 93240-9713

SPENCER, ROBERT ALLEN, business administration educator; b. Oct. 14, 1946, Aberdeen, Wash.; s. Harold Leroy and Florence Irene (Rutherford) S.; m. Diane A. Allen, Feb. 2, 1968; children: Michele b. 1969, James b. 1972; edn: BA social sci., Chapman Coll. 1981; MPA, Auburn Univ. 1984; BS, Calif. Baptist Coll. 1987. Career: chief curriculum and evaluation USAF, March AFB 1977-81, chief student evaluation div., Gunter AFS 1981-84, chief curriculum and evaluation, March AFB 1984-86; admnstrv. dir. Linda Drake Assoc., Riverside 1989; asst. prof. bus. adminstrn. Calif. Baptist Coll. 1986-; honors: Phi Sigma Alpha, Who's Who Among Students, Outstanding Coll. Students, Faculty Mem. of Yr. Calif. Baptist Coll.; mem: Nat. Assn. Ch. Bus. Adminstrs.; mil: s.m.sgt. USAF 1966-86; Republican; So. Baptist; rec: jogging, swimming. Res: 5935 Maybrook Circle Riverside 92506 Ofc: California Baptist College 8432 Magnolia Ave Riverside 92504

SPENCER, ROBERT LEO, merger and acquisition co. principal; b. Nov. 12, 1917, NY, NY; s. Leo and Carolyn (Saxe) Sternfeld; m. Grace Seidman, Aug. 27, 1941; children: Kathy S. Freeman b. 1944, Barbara L. Spencer b. 1950; edn: BS comml. sci. (summa cum laude), N.Y. Univ., 1937; LLB, Golden Gate Coll., 1945; C.P.A., Calif.; admitted Calif. State Bar 1945. Career: senior ptnr. Seidman & Seidman, CPAs, N.Y. 1937-41, Beverly Hills 1941-79; ptnr. Spencer-Wittenberg, 1979-83; ptnr. Spencer Niemiec, 1983-86; prin. Spencer Assocs., 1986-; frequent speaker and numerous tax articles; honors: highest g.p.a. in history of coll., class pres., and frat. chancellor, NYU 1937; mem: Am. Inst. CPAs (past governing Council, com. chmn.), Calif. Soc. CPAs (past pres. L.A. Chpt.); civic: Cedars-Sinai Med. Ctr. Bd. Dirs. (exec. com., past bd. chmn.), Jewish Comm. Found. (trustee, past pres.), Jewish Fedn. Council of Gr. L.A. (active 1949-, past dir., v.p.), Hebrew Union Coll. Bd. of Overseers, Pitzer Coll. Bd. Dirs., L.A. United Way (past bd. govs.); club: Hillcrest CC (past pres.); mil: lt.s.g. USNR 1942-46; Democrat; Wilshire Blvd. Temple (past bd. mem., v.p.); rec: golf. Res: 10350 Wilshire Blvd #904 Los Angeles 90024 Ofc: Spencer Associates, 9911 W Pico Blvd Ste 670 Los Angeles 90035

SPERBER, NORMAN DONALD, forensic dentist; b. Nov. 18, 1928, NY, NY; s. Irving J. and Ada (Miller) S.; m. Janet; children: James Irving b. 1956, Jill Anne b. 1958; edn: BA, Carleton Coll. 1950; DDS, NY Univ. 1954. Career: dentist, chief dental cons. Calif. Dept. of Justice (missing persons/ unidentified persons unit); chief dental cons. (devel. Dental Div.) FBI Nat. Crime Info. Center (NCIC); chief forensic dentist for San Diego and Imperial Counties; recipient Gov. Deukmejian's svc. award in recogn. of outstanding service in field of victim svc., State Atty. Gen.'s commendn. for significant contbns. to law enforcement agencies; mem: Am. Dental Assn., Calif. Dental Assn. (chmn. Council on Dental Health 1984-85), San Diego Dental Soc. (pres. 1974-75), Acad. of Gen. Dentistry, Fellow Am. Soc. of Forensic Odontology (pres. 1984-85); publs: 5 articles in FBI Law Enforcement Bulletin (1977-83), chpt. on bitemark evidence in Calif. Dept. of Justice manual on child abuse, Coll. of Am. Pathologists chpt. on forensic dental examination and identification (1986); mil: lt. US Navy Dental Corps; rec: tennis, photog. Ofc: 3737-A Moraga Ave San Diego 92117

SPIEGEL, MARILYN HARRIET, real estate broker; b. April 3, 1935, Brooklyn, N.Y.; d. Harry and Sadie (Oscher) Unger; m. Murray Spiegel, June 12, 1954; children: Eric Lawrence b. 1959, Dana Cheryl b. 1961, Jay Barry b. 1965; edn: grad. Erasmus H.S. 1953; lic. real estate broker (1980). Career: exec. secty. S&W Paper Co., N.Y.C. 1953-54; Japan Paper Co. 1954-59; decorator Royal Decorators, Kans. City, Mo. 1965-70; real estate agent C.P. Relators, Los Alamitos 1975-79; broker, owner S&S Properties, Garden Grove 1979-; named Realtor of the Yr. CAR (1989); mem: West Orange Bd. of Realtors (dir. 1983-), Calif. Assn. Realtors (dir. 1985-), Summit Orgn., Nat. Council Jewish Women, Toastmasters Intl. (#550, pres.); Democrat; Jewish; rec: decorating. Res: 4765 Candleberry Seal Beach 90740 Ofc: S&S Properties 3502 Katella Ave Ste 208 Los Alamitos 90720

SPILMAN, JAMES BRUCE, science teacher; b. July 27, 1947, Marysville, Calif.; s. James M. and Mary E. (Stafford) S.; edn: BA, CSU Chico, 1969, Calif. std. sec. tchg. credential, 1970. Career: biology tchr. Lompoc Valley Middle Sch., Lompoc 1970-85, sci. dept. hd. 1974-82, activities dir. 1976-78; tchr. biology, chemistry, adv. placement biology, Lompoc High Sch., 1985-, sci. dept. hd. 1989-93; awards: Hon. service PTA, Lompoc 1974, listed Who's Who Among Am. Tchrs., Who's Who in West; mem. Am. Chem. Soc., Nat. Rifle Assn., Lompoc Valley Club; Republican; Ch. of Jesus Christ of Latterday Saints; rec: trap shooting, scuba, hunting, computers. Res: 920 W Hickory Ave Lompoc 93436 Ofc: Lompoc High School 515 West College Ave Lompoc 93436

SPINDLER, STEPHEN RICHARD, university professor; b. Apr. 22, 1948, Salt Lake City, Utah; s. Thornton Fred S.; m. Patricia L. Mote-Spindler; children: Jeremiah b. 1974, Jared b. 1976, Joseph b. 1978; edn: BA, UC San Diego, La Jolla, 1971; PhD, Univ. of Texas, Houston, 1976. Career: postdoctoral fellow, Colo. State Univ., Ft. Collins, Colo. 1976-78; postdoctoral fellow, UC San Francisco 1978-81; asst. prof., UC Riverside 1981-87; assoc. prof., UC Riverside 1987-; awards: research grantee, NIH, Bethesda, Md. 1984-87, 1988-91, 1992-; mem. Physiol. Sciences Study Section, NIH, Bethesda, Md. 1992-97; mem: AAAS 1981-, Am. Soc. Biochemistry and Molecular Biology 1988-; author: numerous profl. articles publ. in scientific journals 1978-, numerous book chapters 1980-; rec: surfing, running, body-building, skiing. Ofc: University of California, Riverside, Dept. of Biochemistry, Riverside 92521

SPINELLA, CHRISTOPHER DAMIAN, health care company executive; b. Apr. 20, 1960, Fallbrook; s. Anthony and Jeanne B. S.; edn: BS, Arizona St. Univ., Tempe 1983; MBA, Harvard Bus. Sch., 1990. Career: mktg. asst. I.B.M., Phoenix, Az. 1982-83; sales rep. American Hospital Supply Corp., Spokane, Wash. 1983-84; devel. cons. CIGNA, Dallas 1984-86, dir. of devel. CIGNA, Hartford, Ct. 1986-88; asst. v.p. Salick Health Care, Los Angeles 1990-92, v.p. 1992-; honoree: Man of Yr. Ariz. State Univ. 1983; civic: mem.: Glendale, Az. Parks & Rec. Bd. and Juvenile Concerns Task Force 1977-78. Ofc: Salick Health Care, 8201 Beverly Blvd Los Angeles 90048

SPOLTER, PARI DOKHT, author, publisher; b. Jan. 30, 1930, Tehran, Iran; nat. Nov. 18, 1964; m. Herbert Spolter, MD, Aug. 16, 1958; children: David b. 1966, Deborah b. 1967; edn: Licence chimie biologique, Univ. of Geneva, Switzerland 1952; PhD in biochemistry, Univ. of Wisconsin, Madison, Wis. 1961. Career: postdoctoral fellow Temple Univ., Phila. 1961-62; instr. Temple Univ. 1962-66; researcher U.S. Public Health Svc. Hosp., S.F., Calif. 1966-68; writer and publisher of scientific books Orb Publishing Co., Granada Hills, Calif. 1988-; mem: AAAS 1989-, Am. Math. Soc. 1989-; author: num. jour. articles, 1961-68; books: Gravitational Force of the Sun, 1994, Gravitational Force of the Proton (to be publ.); rec: classical music, opera. Ofc: Orb Publishing Co. 11862 Balboa Bl. #182 Granada Hills 91344-2753

SPRING, DEE, psychotherapist; b. Sept. 22, 1934, Clayton, Ga.; d. James Rusk and Maxie Marie (Thompson) Grant; m. John B. Spring, Mar. 15, 1957 (div. 1981); children: Jay b. 1958, Angela b. 1960, David b. 1965; edn: BA, CSU Fullerton 1976; MA, Vt. Coll. Plainfield 1977; MA clin. psychology, Fielding Inst. S.B. 1985; PhD, 1988. Career: dir. Women's Crisis Center, Placentia 1974-81; asst. prof., Calif., Mont., Vt. and Ore. 1976-; psychologist, Mont. 1981-83; dir. Earthwood Center, Ventura 1983-; pvt. practice, Calif. and Mont. 1976-; cons. Fullerton Coll. 1977-80; awards: City of Ventura Nat. Cons. Vols. 1984, Am. Mental Health Counselors Assn. Doctoral fellowship 1984, Am. Art Therapy Assn. Nat. Research 1978, Fullerton Coll. Lena & Fay Reynolds scholarships 1974-77, listed: Who's Who Mental Health, Who's Who Among Human Services Profls., Who's Who in West, Who's Who of Am. Women; mem: Am. Art Therapy Assn. (treas. 1984-89), So. Calif. Soc. Clin. Hypnosis, Internat. Soc. MPD & Dissociation; author pub. book: Shattered Images, 1993; articles, book chpts., and presentations pub. 1980-; rec: art. Ofc: 2021 Sperry Ave Ste 23 Ventura 93003

SPRINGER, PAUL D., film studio executive, lawyer; b. April 27, 1942, New York; s. William W. and Alma (Markowitz) S.; m. Mariann Frankfurt, Aug. 16, 1964; children: Robert b. 1968, William b. 1972; edn: BA, Univ. Bridgeport 1964; JD, Bklyn. Law Sch. 1967; admitted bar: N.Y. 1968, Calif. 1989. Career: atty., assoc. Johnson & Tannenbaum, NYC 1967-70; assoc. counsel Columbia Pictures 1970; sr. v.p. and asst. gen. counsel Paramount Pictures Corp., Los Angeles 1970-; mem: Am. Bar Assn., Acad. Motion Picture Arts and Scis., Los Angeles Copyright Soc., W. Cunningham Park Civic Assn. (trustee 1975-); Jewish. Res: 15915 High Knoll Rd Encino 91436 Ofc: Paramount Pictures Corp. 5555 Melrose Ave Los Angeles 90038

SPRINKEL, RITA L., diplomat, retired executive; b. Aug. 6, 1935, Bergen, Norway; U.S. citizen, 1965; d. Sverre Johannesen Indrebo and Ingeborg N. (Kongsvik) I.; m. Warren Reed Sprinkel, Aug. 12, 1978. Career: former bd. dir. Pritikin Research Found.; former dir. public/employee relations Fontana Paving Inc.; former owner Rita's Tennis Affair, Newport Beach; former v.p. Cort Fox Ford Leasing Inc., Hollywood; representative Royal Norwegian Embassy; clubs:

Jonathan (L.A.), Balboa Bay (Newport Beach), Newport Beach Country, Harbor Yacht (Newport Beach), Center (Costa Mesa), Kona Kai Yacht (San Diego), Royal Danish Yacht (Denmark); rec: tennis, sailing. Res: 1026 Santiago Dr Newport Beach 92660

SPRINKEL, WARREN REED, retired engineering contractor, asphalt paving exec.; b. June 30, 1922, Los Angeles; s. Walter and Florence Louise (Werdin) S.; m. Rita L., Aug. 12, 1978; 3 children by previous marriage: Steve, Annette and Susan; edn: BS indsl. mgmt., USC 1946. Career: var. pos. family owned asphalt constrn. cos.- L.A. Paving Co. (founded by grandfather E.R. Werdin, 1912), Vernon Paving Co. (founded by father 1936); gen. engring. contr., pres. and chmn. bd. Fontana Paving, Inc. (opr. three rock and asphalt plants, mfr. asphalt paving mats., construct highways, airports, indsl. and residential subdivs.) 1956-88, sold co. to Boral Industries (Australian co.) 1988; mem., chmn. Contractors' State License Bd. (12 years); honors: Blue Key, Skull and Dagger, Kappa Alpha frat. (pres.), Kt. Sovereign Order of the Oak 1990, named Contractor of Year 1974; mem: Am. Road and Transp. Builders Assn./Contractors Div. (sr. v. chmn. 1987-88, ARTBA Award 1989), Fontana C.of C. (past pres.), (current) Assoc. Gen. Contrs. of Calif., Rotary Club (past pres.); mil: command pilot B-24, 15th AF in Italy, WWII, decorated D.F.C., major USAF Korean War, flew B-26 and in chg. Base Ops. and Flying Safety, 60 combat missions in both wars; Republican; cty. campaign chmn. for Gov. Reagan 1965 and 1969, city chmn. Reagan for Pres. 1980; del. Nat. Repub. Conv. (1972, 76), cpgn. chmn. San Bernardino Co. for Pete Wilson for US Senate 1984; Prot. (deacon); rec: tennis, sailing: yacht "Viking Princess" (flagship for Challenger Races for the America's Cup Races, San Diego Apr.-May 1992). Res: 1026 Santiago Dr Newport Beach 92660

SPROULE, BETTY ANN, computer industry market researcher; b. Dec. 30, 1948, Evanston, Ill.; d. Harold Fletcher and Lois (Reno) Mathis; m. J. Michael Sproule, Mar. 3, 1973; children: John Harold b. 1981, Kevin William b. 1982; edn: BS, Ohio State Univ., 1969, MS, 1970, PhD, 1972; Cert. Data Processing, Inst. for Certification of Computer Profls., 1979. Career: mem. tech. staff Bell Tel. Labs., Columbus, Ohio 1973-74; asst. prof. Univ. Texas, Odessa 1974-77; analyst bus. systems GE major appliance bus. div., Louisville, Ky. 1977-78; dir. forecasting and analysis Brown & Williamson Tobacco Corp., Louisville, Ky. 1978-86; mgr. market res. Hewlett Packard Corp., Palo Alto, Calif. 1986-; speaker, presentations numerous profl. convs., 1970-, contbr. articles in profl. jours., 1970-; invention (1975, U.S. Pat. 3,982,229); mem: IEEE (senior mem. 1974-), Soc. of Women Engrs. (senior mem. 1974-), Assn. for Computing Machinery 1969-, Am. Mktg. Assn. Res: 4135 Briarwood Way Palo Alto 94306 Ofc: Hewlett Packard 19483 Pruneridge Ave Cupertino 95014

STACEY, KENNETH ERMES, contractor; b. Oct. 28, 1946, Los Angeles; s. George T. and Erminia R. (Rota) S.; m. Marie Estes, 1989; children: Christine b. 1967; edn: BS, Cal. Poly. Pomona 1969; UCLA 1970. Career: tchr. Moreno Valley High Sch. 1970-72; owner The Stacey Co., cabinet and gen. contractor 1972-; ptnr. D.K. Development 1981-, Miken Co. 1985-, Cost Enterprises 1987-, Stockdale Greens Associates 1988-; mem. City of Riverside Cultural Heritage Bd. 1981-89; mem. Arabian Horse Assn. of So. Calif. (bd. dirs. 1982-89, chmn. 1984-86, pres. 1988), meMission Inn Found. 1984-86, Inland Empire Nat. Bank Advisory Bd. 1987-92, Ronald McDonald House (bldg. com. 1991-), CCF-CHOA (pres. 1991-), Nat. Trust for Historic Preservation, Old Riverside Found. (bd.), Riverside Ballet Theater (bd.); rec: skiing, racquetball, horse shows. Ofc: The Stacey Co. 2675 3rd St Ste K Riverside 92507-3368

STAMOS, JAMES WILLIAM, computer scientist; b. Aug. 17, 1959, Salem, Mass.; s. William James and Jenny James (Pappas) S.; m. Mary Ellen Muldoon, Oct. 27, 1990; edn: BS, M.I.T., 1982, MS, 1982, PhD, 1986. Career: research staff IBM Almaden Research Ctr., San Jose 1986-; awards: IBM Grad. Fellow, M.I.T. 1983-85, Tau Beta Pi 1980, Sigma Xi 1983, Eta Kappa Nu (recording sec. 1980-81); mem.: Assn. for Computing Machinery 1978-; pub. articles in field (1984, 90, 91); rec: wt.lifting, running, hiking, reading. Res: 1515 Constanso Ct San Jose 95129 Ofc: IBM Almaden Research Center 650 Harry Rd San Jose 95120-6099

STANBRIDGE, ERIC J., educator; b. May 28, 1942, London, England; s. John William and Helen Margaret (Lichfield) S.; m. Polly Nancy Sarah Ellen Raffel, May 29, 1971; children: Helena b. 1974, Andrew b. 1978; edn: PhD, Stanford Univ 1971, postdoctoral work, 1972-73. Career: research asst. Wistar Inst., Phila., Pa. 1965-67; scientific staff Nat. Inst. Med. Research, Stanford, Pa. 1968-69; research assoc. Stanford Univ. 1972-73, instr. 1973-75; asst. prof. UC Irvine 1975-78, prof. 1982-; assoc. ed.: Cancer Research (Phila., Pa.) 1985-, J. Cell. Physiology, 1989-; awards: Eleanor Roosevelt Int. Fellowship UICC 1983, 84, merit Award Nat. Inst. of Health 1987, Disting. Faculty Research Award UCI Alumni Assn. 1988; mem: Am. Soc. for Microbiology, Internat. Orgn. of Mycoplasmologists, Am. Assn. for Cancer Research, Sigma Xi, Tissue Culture Assn.; author 100+ articles on cancer research and mycoplasmology. Res: 501 Seaward Corona del Mar 92625 Ofc: Univ of Calif, Calif College of Medicine, Irvine 92717

STANLEY, JOHN LANGLEY, professor of political science; b. Nov. 16, 1937, Boston; s. John Willis and Marion (Langley) S.; m. Charlotte Whitcomb Colony, Nov. 28, 1963; children: John C. b. 1967, Andrea Page b. 1969, Marjorie Page b. 1973; edn: AB, Kenyon Coll., 1960; Selwyn Coll., Cambridge, 1960-61; PhD, Cornell Univ., 1966. Career: asst. prof. dept. polit. sci. Univ. Calif., Riverside 1965-71, assoc. prof. 1971-79, prof. 1979-; vis. assoc. prof. UC San Diego, 1974; vis. lectr. Hertford Coll., Oxford 1986; awards: Woodrow Wilson Fellow 1961, John L. Senior Fellow 1965, Haynes Found. Summer Fellow 1967, NEH Fellow 1969-70; author: The Sociology of Virtue: The Political and Social Theories of Georges Sorel (Univ. Calif. Press, 1981), 4 books in progress; editor, translator Georges Sorel essays and works (4 books); author chapters in books, book reviews (13+), articles in scholarly jours. and ency. articles (3); numerous profl. papers and presentations, panels; editl. bd. Transaction Books, 1980-, Cahiers Georges Sorel (Paris) 1983-, The Political Sci. Reviewer, 1990-; Democrat; Episcopalian; rec: amateur radio. Ofc: Dept. of Political Science Univ. California Riverside 92521

STANNARD, RALPH ELY, scientist/engineer/optoelectronics executive; b. Chicago, Ill.; s. Ely Martin and Ina Maude (Perego) S.; edn: BA, San Jose State Univ.; pres. R. Stannard & Assocs., Irvine 1978-86; founder/pres. ODASER Technologies, Newport Beach 1986-; mem: Soc. of Automotive Engrs., IEEE, Optical Soc. Am., Optical Soc. So. Calif., Navy League (dir. Bel Air chpt. 1988); civic: Beverly Hills Pops (bd. 1987-), Opera Pacific, Irvine (founder 1985-), Wagner Soc., Woodland Hills 1987; jour. article "Duane, Prince of Faultland" (1985); aviation cadet Navy Air Corps; Episcopalian; rec: audiophile, opera buff. Ofc: ODASER Technologies PO Box 7458 Newport Beach 92658

STAPLES, ROBERT EUGENE, university professor; b. June 28, 1942, Roanoke, Va.; s. John Ambrose and Anna Theresa (Anthony) S.; edn: AA, L.A. Valley Coll., 1960; AB, Calif. State Univ., Northridge, 1964; MA, San Jose State Univ., 1965; PhD, Univ. of Minn., 1970. Career: asst. prof., Bethune-Cookman Coll., Daytona Beach, Fla. 1967-68; asst. prof., Calif. State Univ., Hayward 1968-69; asst. prof., Fisk Univ., Nashville, Tenn. 1969-70; lectr., UC Irvine 1970-71; assoc. prof., Howard Univ., Wash., DC 1971-73; prof., UC S.F. 1973-;awards: Disting. Achievement Award, Howard Univ. 1979; Simon Bolivar Lectr., Universidad Del Zulia, Venezuela 1979; Disting. Achievement Award, Nat. Council on Family Relations, Mpls., Minn. 1982; Matie Peters Award, Nat. Council on Family Relations, Mpls. 1986; author: World of Black Singles, 1981; Black Family Essays & Studies, 1991; ed., Urban Plantation, 1987; co-author, Black Families at Crossroads, 1992; Independent; rec: tennis reading, travel. Ofc: Univ. of Calif., Box 0612, San Francisco 94143-0612

STARK, MARLENE S., business owner, real estate broker, airline stewardess; b. Sept. 19, 1944, New York; d. Henry and Greta Stark; m. Thomas W. Haney, June 5, 1976 (div.); children: Joshua b. 1979, Jason b. 1982; edn: BA psych., San Francisco St. Coll. Career: language tchr. and translator (Eng., Sp., Ger.) Berlitz Sch. of Languages, Mexico and Nassau, Bahamas 1968-69; teacher, v.p. Stardust Temporaries, MIT Temps., Gateway Temps, N.Y. 1969-71; stewardess Pan Am. World Airways 1971-86, internat. div. United Airlines 1986-; coord. and founder of tutorial schs. for disadvantaged children, San Francisco 1965-68, volunteer counselor Napa State Mental Hosp., S.F. Youth Guidance Ctr., Homeward Terrace Sch. for Autistic Children S.F., 1962-68; founder, owner Mini Luggage Carriers Co. 1972-, popularized the luggage carrier worldwide and mfr. of the first luggage carriers made in USA; mem: Calif. Bd. Real Estate; rec: travel, swimming. Res: 13080 Mindanao Way Ste 85 Marina del Rey 90292

STARR, DAVID, makeup artist, photographer, fashion consultant, fine artist; b. Oct. 4, 1950, Los Angeles; edn: biol. sci. and pre-med., Stanford Univ., 1966; BFA, UCLA 1972. Career: makeup artist/owner David Starr Enterprises, San Francisco and Los Angeles, 1971-80; dir. mktg., makeup artist Chanel Beauty- West Coast, S.F. 1980-81; owner, mgr. David Starr Makeup, S.F. 1984-; cons. Motown Records-Artist Advancement, L.A., 1974, Sta. KGO-TV, 1987-88, Sta. KCRA-TV, Sacto. 1988; beauty judge Miss Gilroy Pageant, 1986, Miss Oakland Pageant, 1988; awards: named Best Makeup Artist, Harper's Bazaar 1987, San Francisco mag. 1987, 88, Best Makeup Artist in S.F. Nob Hill Gazette 1990, Best eyebrows "Image" Vogue 1990, Cable Car Award 1990, outstanding fundraiser Connie Francis Look-A-Like Contest, achievement Doer's Scotch 1988; mem. San Francisco C.of C.; civic: Pacific Presbyn. Hosp. Project Open Hand, S.F. (fundraiser 1987-), S.F. Zool. Soc. (fundraiser), S.F. Opera Guild, Mus. of Modern Art, Shanti Project. Ofc: 990 Jones St San Francisco 94109

STAUFFACHER, CHARLES FENTON, JR., manufacturing co. executive; b. July 25, 1921, San Francisco; s. Charles Fenton, Sr. and Margaret (Popert) S.; edn: BA, UC Berkeley 1942; M.Arch., 1947. Career: architectural draftsman & designer Ambrose & Spencer, S.F, 1947-51; v.p. Fink & Schinder Co. 1951-69; pres. 1969-83; chmn. bd. & CEO 1983-; former mem. Trade Advsy. Com. Calif. St. Dept. of Corrections; Calif. St. Ednl. Advsy. Com. for Cabinet Making & Millwork Trade; mem. Am. Arbitration Assn.; mem: Woodwork Inst. Calif. (past pres.), Cabinet & Fixture Mfrs. Guild (past pres.), Assoc. Cabinet Mfrs., Rotary, Univ. Calif. Alumni Assn., Kappa Alpha Alumni Assn.; mil: lt. j.g. USN

1942-46; Republican; rec: amateur chef, gardening, interior design. Res: 66 Brushwood San Rafael 94901 Ofc: The Fink & Schindler Co. 560 Brannan St San Francisco 94107

STEBBINS, ELIZABETH J., university administrator, educator; b. Sept. 14, 1923, Los Angeles; d. James Tee and Evangeline M. (Russell) Hinton; children: James Wyatt (dec.), John Russell; 2 granddaus., Jessica and Jennifer; edn: BA, USC, 1945; MA, Chapman Coll., 1964; adv. studies in edn. adminstrn., learning theories and sociology USC; PhD, U.S. Internat. Univ., 1989; Calif. tchg. credentials: Elementary, Secondary, Gen. Adminstr., Pupil Personnel Supr., Jr. Coll. (all Life creds.). Career: (past): dir. special pgms. Brea-Olinda Unified Sch. Dist.; dir. res. and eval. Norwalk-La Mirada Unif. Sch. Dist.; benefits adminstr., personnel mgr. Calif. Credit Union League; v.p. The Bradford Group, exec. recruiters; curriculum & evaluation cons. L.A. Co. Supt. of Schs.; dir. Career Devel. Ctr. National Univ., Irvine, Academic Senate mem. and newsletter editor; adj. instr. and subject splst. for mgt. & supvn. Coastline Comm. Coll. 8 yrs.; pres. Hinton and Assocs.; prof. statistics & res. Univ. of Phoenix, Orange Co.; awards: Ford Adminstrv. Leadership Award 1963, NISOC Award for Excellence in tchg. Nat. Inst. for Staff and Orgnl. Devel. 1991; mem: Assn. Calif. Sch. Adminstrs. Reg. XVII (chair R&D com., cons. to State Elem. Principals for in-service series), Calif. Assn. Psychologists and Psychometrists, Calif. Personnel and Guidance Assn., Orange Co. Test Com., Calif. Com. for Measurement in Guidance, Calif. Com. for Measurement in Edn. (conf. com.), Calif. Assn. for Curriculum Devel., Chapman Coll. Faculty, CSUF Faculty; active: Soroptimist (1st v.p. Brea), AAUW, Ebell, Junior Women's Club, Sorority Alumnae Pres., Trojan Jr. Aux., USC Alumnae, L.A. C.of C. (hist. docent, edn. legis. com.), Hon. Assn. of Women in Edn., Women in Edn. Leadership; publs: (diss.) A Study of Career Change in Sr. Aged Leaders, Calif. Edn. Environmental Handbook, 2 articles in Assn. Calif. Sch. Adminstrs. Reg. XVII Res. Reports, author 4 Bi-Lingual Projects (fed. funding), 5 Sch. Dist. Pgms. (jt. funding Calif. Dept. Edn./Fed. Govt.). Ofc: 550 N Coast Hwy Laguna Beach 92657

STECHMAN, JOHN VANCE, professor of rangeland management; b. Aug. 1, 1934, Peoria, Ill.; s. John Henry and Helen Jean (Vance) S.; m. Dorothy Jean McKowan, Aug. 18, 1956; children: John Carl b. 1960, Jennifer Jean b. 1963; edn: grad. Herbert Hoover H.S., Glendale, Calif. 1952; BS, UC Davis, 1957, MS in rangeland mgmt., 1960; cert. consultant Soc. for Range Mgmt., Denver, Co. 1989-. Career: forest aide US Forest Svc., El Dorado Nat. Forest 1956; range tech. US Agricultural Res. Svc., Davis 1956-57, 59-60; food tech. US Army, QMC Chicago, Ill. 1957-59; prof. Calif. Polytechnic St. Univ., San Luis Obispo, 1960-; rancher La Cuesta Ranch, San Luis Obispo, 1971-91; cons. La Cuesta Consulting, 1964-; honors: Alpha Zeta hon. agric. frat. 1955, suggestion awards US Army 1958, Hon. chpt. farmer Future Farmers of Am. S.L.O. 1978, Range mgr. of yr. 1991 Calif. sect. Soc. for Range Mgmt. 1992; mem: Soc. for Range Mgmt. (Calif. sect. dir. 1988-90, historian 1990-), S.L.O. Brush Range Improve. Assn. 1972-, Range Sci. Edn. Council 1965-, Watershed Council of Calif. 1988-, League to Save Lake Tahoe 1988-; civic: Pelican Point Homeowners Assn. Avila Bch. (water bd. 1991-) Montana de Oro State Park Advy. Com. Morro Bay (chmn. 1965-74); author: Common Western Range Plants (1986), Illustrated History Cal Poly Agriculture (1985), jour. articles and manuals in field; mil: sp4c USA Quartermaster Corps 1957-59; Republican; Lutheran; rec: reading, art. Res: PO Box 2211 Avila Beach 93424

STEEL, DAWN, motion picture studio executive; b. Aug. 19, New York, NY; d. Nat and Lillian (Tarlow) Steel; m. Charles Roven, May 30, 1988; children: Rebecca b. 1987; edn: mktg. Boston Univ. 1964-65, N.Y.U. 1966-67. Career: sportswriter Major League Baseball Digest and NFL/N.Y.C., 1968-69; editor Penthouse, N.Y.C. 1969-75; pres. Oh Dawn!, N.Y.C. 1975-78; mdsg. cons. Playboy, N.Y.C. 1978-79; v.p. mdsg. Paramount, N.Y.C. 1979-80, v.p. prodn. Paramount, L.A. 1980-83, sr. v.p. prodn. 1983-85, pres. of prodn. 1985-87; pres. Columbia Pictures, 1987-90; formed Steel Pictures, 1990-; awards: Crystal award Women in Film, L.A. 1989; mem. Acad. of Motion Picture Arts & Scis., Am. Film Inst. (bd. 1988-90), NOW Legal Def. Fund (NYC), UCLA Sch. of Theater, Film and Television (dean's advy. bd. 1993-); Democrat; Jewish; rec: skiing, tennis, gardening. Ofc: Steel Pictures 345 N. Maple Dr Beverly Hills 90210

STEFFEY, EUGENE PAUL, educator, veterinarian; b. Oct. 27, 1942, Reading, Pa.; s. Paul E. and Mary (Balthaser) S.; m. Marcia Matzelle, June 10, 1967; children: Michele A. b. 1972, Bret E. b. 1975, Michael R. b. 1978, Brian T. b. 1985; edn: Muhlenberg Coll. 1960-63; VMD, Univ. Pa., Phila. 1967; PhD, UC Davis, 1973. Career: NIH spl. fellowship 1972-73; anesthesia res. fellow UCSF Med. Center 1973; asst. prof. UC Davis 1974-77, assoc. prof. 1977-80, prof. 1980-, chmn. dept. vet. surgery 1980-; bd. scientific reviewers Am. Jour. Vet. Res. 1984-87; awards: UC Davis Outstanding Intern 1968; mem: num. profl. mems. incl. AAAS, AVMA, Am. Coll. Vet. Anesthesiologists, Am. Physiolgy Soc., Am. Soc. Pharm. Exptl. Therapeutics, Am. Soc. Anesthesiologists, Calif. Soc. Anesthesiologists; author 75+ articles in profl. jours., 12 textbook chpts.; rec: fishing, outdoor photog., sports. Ofc: Univ. California Dept. of Surgery School of Veterinary Medicine Davis 95616

STEINER, PIERRE GERALD, physician, clinician, dietician; b. Sept. 14, 1912, Gland, Vd, Switzerland; Calif. resident 1981-; s. Paul and Gertrude (Piotrowski) S.; children: Jacques b. 1939, Catherine b. 1941, Claire-Marie b. 1945, Dominique b. 1946, Pierre b. 1951, Marc b. 1969; edn: Latin "Baccalaureate" at State Coll. of Geneva, Switz, 1931; Swiss Fed. Med. lic. 1938; MD Doctorate 1941; 5 years internship: Internal Med., Dietetic; 1 yr. Gyn./Ob. St. Univ. Hosp. of Geneva, and 1 semester Emergency Dept., Frankfurt St. Univ. Hosp.; Swiss govt. res. grantee on tobacco toxicity, 1942-43; asst. prof. for lectures in dietetics, State Univ. of Geneva 1950-51. Career: founder/dir. world's first "walk-in clinic," open 24 hrs./day, Geneva, Switz. 1946-80; indep. researcher La Jolla 1982-89, resulting in total suppression of the tars in tobacco smoke, and cure of nicotinic addiction; pres. SDICC corp. (dietetics, cons.) 1987; mem. Am., Internat., and San Diego Soc. of Clinical Hypnosis; Am. Coll. of Advance. in Medicine; U.S. Senatorial Club; works: was first to find and explain the existence of intracellular vitamin and mineral deficiencies and imbalances hidden by normal blood levels (1940); devised in vivo test of cellular vulnerability toward heavy metals and tobacco smoke; discovered Vit. B3 in tobacco could suppress approx. 80% of its acute toxicity (1943); devel. an easy 2 steps method to quit for heavy smokers (1983-84); 2 U.S. & internat. patents- suppression of 100% of tars generated by direct & indirect cig. smoke; author new concept re mechanism of Addiction, and a new wide definition of "Life," with insights into direction mankind is taking (in progress), numerous pub. articles in European med. jours.; mil: capt. Swiss Army 1939-43; Republican; R.Cath. Address: 417 Sea Ridge Dr La Jolla CA 92037

STEINER, WILFRED WARREN, association director, real estate executive; b. Feb. 12, 1907, Berkeley; s. Antone Karl and Anna (Dickelt) S.; m. Ruby Grace Kulchar, May 23, 1930; son, Wilfred Jr.; edn: BA, Armstrong Coll., 1927; R.E. cert., UCLA, 1960. Career: land agent So. Pacific Co., San Francisco 1927-53; pres. W.W. Steiner Co. (indsl. and comml. R.E.), Oakland 1953-55; mgr. real estate So. Pacific Co., Los Angeles (purch. land for indsl. parks and R.R. in Orange, San Bdo. and L.A. Counties and in Ariz., disposed of rights of way Pacific Electric Railway, acquired land for freight yards in Industry, and Colton and the entire right of way for new rail line between Colton and Palmdale) 1955-72; R.E. cons. to pres. So. Pacific Land Co., indsl. coord. Nat. Engring. Co.; exec. dir. Industry Mfrs. Council, City of Industry 1973-; pres., dir. El Encanto Sanitorium, Industry 1981-; honors: disting. alumni and commencement speaker Armstrong Univ. 1982, man of yr. City of Industry 1984; civic: Methodist Hosp. Found. (pres.'s circle), United Way Campaign (div. chmn. 1983-84), Mt. San Antonio Coll. Found. (dir.), Colo. River Assn. (dir.), Armstrong Alumni Assn. (pres. 1982), Masons (32 deg., past master), Shrine; Republican; Methodist; rec: gardening. Res: 521 N Alta Vista Ave Monrovia 91016 Ofc: Industry Manufacturers Council 255 N Hacienda Blvd Industry 91744

STELLA, SALVATORE LUCIA, pediatric ophthalmologist; b. May 21, 1932, Omaha, Nebr.; s. Frank L. and Lucia (Turco) S.; m. Donna Lee Carney, Dec. 22, 1963; children: Francis b. 1965, Lisa b. 1967, Salvatore b. 1969, Maureen b. 1971, Lucinda b. 1973; edn: BS, San Diego St. Coll. 1954; Univ. N.M. 1954-55; O.D. (honors), Los Angeles Coll. of Optometry 1958; MD, Calif. Coll. Medicine 1962. Career: research chemist Ryan Aero., San Diego 1954; fellow pediatric ophthalmology and strabismus Inst. Visual Scis., San Francisco 1966-69; ophthalmologist Pediatric Adolescent Ophthalmology Med. Surgical Group, San Diego 1969-; resident Univ. Mo. Med. Ctr., Columbia, Kans. City 1963-66; med. intern Mt. Sinai Hosp., LA 1962-63; dir. pediatric ophthalmology service UCSD Med. Ctr. 1984-; awards: Calif. Coll. Medicine Hon. scholastic 1962; mem: Am. Assn. Pediatric Ophthalmology & Strabisbus, San Diego Co. Med. Soc., CMA, Resthaven Preventorium for Children (bd. dirs. 1973); Republican; R.Cath.; rec: investments, gardening. Ofc: 207 Walnut Ave San Diego 92103

STEPHENS, WILLIAM LEONARD, university administrator; b. Apr. 19, 1929, Covington, Ky.; s. Leonard Edwin and Mary Blanche (Wright) S.; m. Claire Neall Matsinger, Apr. 12, 1957; edn: AA, New Mexico Military Inst., 1949; BA in biology (hons.), CSU Sacramento, 1957; PhD microbiology, UC Davis, 1963. Career: res. asst. UC Davis, 1957-63; asst. prof. Chico State Coll., 1963-67, assoc. prof. 1967-70, chair dept. biol. scis. 1968-74; prof. CSU Chico, 1970-, dean Coll. of Natural Scis., 1977-91, provost and v.p. acad. affairs, 1991-; honors: CSAA/EOP Award 1985-86, Phi Kappa Phi 1988; mem. Am. Soc. for Microbiol. 1957-, Sigma Xi 1962-, Am. Assn. Univ. Adminstrs.; civic: Science Fair judge, Chico 1963-88, Corning 1973, 74, host numerous elem. and high sch. classes to introduce use of microscope and world of microorganisms, guest lectr. comm. orgs., biol. scis. rep. to Willows H.S. Career Day 1974, 75, 76, mem.: Stansbury Home Preserv. Assn. 1981-, Century Club 1975-89, 91, Univ. Club 1975-89, 91, comm. blood donor 1963-; publs: articles in field (4); mil: HM2 US Navy 1950-54. Res: 1661 Oak Vista Chico 95926 Ofc: Calif. State Univ., Chico 95929

STEPHENSON, IRENE HAMLEN, biorhythm analyst, columnist and author; b. Oct. 7, 1923, Chgo.; d. Charles Martin and Carolyn Hilda (Hilgers) Hamlin; m. Edgar B. Stephenson, Sr. Aug. 16, 1941 (div. 1946); 1 son, Edgar B. Career: author biorhythm compatibilites column National Singles Register, Norwalk, Calif. 1979-81; instr. biorhythm Learning Tree Open Univ., Canoga Park 1982-

83, instr. biorhythm character analysis 1980-, instr. biorhythm compatibility 1982-; owner and pres. matchmaking service Pen Pals Using Biorhythm, Chatsworth 1979-; editor newsletter The Truth, 1979-85, Mini Examiner, Chatsworth 1985-; researcher biorhythm character and compatibility, 1974-, selecting a mate, 1985-, biorhythm column True Psychic Inquirer, 1989-, True Astrology Forecast, 1989-; writer numerous mag. articles, frequent guest radio and TV, clubs; author: Learn Biorhythm Character Analysis 1980, Do-It-Yourself Biorhythm Compatibilities 1982. Ofc: PO Box 3893 WW Chatsworth 91313

STERN, ARTHUR PAUL, business executive, engineer; b. July 20, 1925, Budapest, Hungary, nat. US cit. 1956; s. Leon and Bertha (Frankfurter) S.; m. Edith Samuel, 1952; children: Daniel b. 1954, Claude b. 1955, Jacqueline b. 1958; edn: BS, Univ. Lausanne 1946; MS (Dipl. Ing.), Swiss Fed. Inst. of Technol. Zurich 1948; MEE, Syracuse Univ. 1955. Career: research engineer Jaeger Inc. Basel, Switzerland 1948-50; instr. Swiss Fed. Inst. of Technol. 1950-51; mgr. Electronic Devices & Applications Lab., Gen. Electric Co. 1951-61; dir. engrg. Electronic Systems and Products Div., Martin Marietta Corp. 1961-64; dir. ops. Defense Sys. Div., The Bunker- Ramo Corp. 1964-66; v.p., gen. mgr. Magnavox Research Labs. 1966-75; senior v.p., gen. mgr. Magnavox Govt. and Indsl. Electronics Co., Advanced Products Div. 1975-80; pres. Magnavox Advanced Products and Systems Co. 1980-90; pres. Eastern Beverly Hills Corp. 1991-; hon. res. staff mem. M.I.T. 1956-59, course leader G.E. Profl. Bus. Mgmt. Tng. course; advy. bd. elec. and computer engrg. dept. UC Santa Barbara 1980-92; advy. and devel. council CSU Long Beach Sch. of Engrg. 1985-91; guest speaker Club of Rome mtg. Phila. 1976; awards: IEEE Centennial Medalist 1984; mem: IEEE (fellow 1962, guest editor spl. issue of Proceedings of IEEE on Integrated Electronics 1964, gen. chmn. Internat. Solid-State Circuits Conf. 1960, dir. 1970-77, treas. 1973, v.p. regl. activities 1974, pres. 1975), AAAS (fellow 1982), Am. Astronautical Soc. 1976-90, United Jewish Appeal (chmn. engrg. div. 1955-57); publs: 20+ tech. and sci. articles, coauthor 2 tech. books; 12 U.S. & several fgn. patents; Jewish. Res/Ofc: 606 N Oakhurst Dr Beverly Hills 90210

STERN, LOUIS, art dealer; b. Jan. 7, 1945, Casablanca, Morocco, naturalized U.S. cit. 1962; s. Frederic and Sultana (Ifergan) S.; m. K.A. Honeman, Oct. 12, 1969 (div. 1992); children: Deborah b. 1978, Daniel b. 1981; edn: BA, CSU Northridge, 1968. Career: dir. Wally Findlay Galleries, Beverly Hills 1975-80, pres. 1980-82; pres. Louis Stern Galleries, 1982-; expert witness Superior Ct., Police Dept., Dist. Atty., L.A., 1980-; mem.: Art Dealers Assn. of Calif. 1990-91 L.A. County Mus. of Art Pres.'s Circle, Internat. Found. for Art Research (N.Y.), Friends of French Art, Am. Friends of Blerancourt (Paris); mil: E5 US Army 1968-71, DoD Jt. commendn. medal 1971; rec: art, music, wine.

STERNBERG, LARRY FREDERICK, accounting executive; b. July 11, 1927, Chicago, Ill.; s. Herman J. and Kitty F. (Gordon) S.; m. Eleanor, July 17, 1948; children: Kathleen b. 1959, James b. 1961; edn: BS in acctg., UC Los Angeles 1949; C.P.A. Calif. (1959). Career: auditor Bd. Equalization, St. Calif. 1949-51; lt. USN 1951-55; Guill Blankenbaker & Co. C.P.A.s 1955-59; sr. auditor Glasspar Boat Co. 1959-62; controller Runglin Co. 1962-85, treas., pres. 1981-85, dir. 1973-85; sr. v.p. ICEE-USA 1985-87, dir., 1973-85; sr. v.p. BIS Computer Solutions, 1988-; mem: Am. Inst. CPAs 1957-, Calif. Soc. CPAs 1957-, Toastmasters; mil: lt. USNR 1951-55; Republican (cand. for Rep. nomination for Congress 40th dist. 1988, mem. Calif. Rep. Assembly, Tustin chpt.); Jewish; rec: inv. stocks, sailing. Res: 1865 Cockscrow Ln Santa Ana 92705 Ofc: BIS Computer Solutions, Inc. 2428 Foothill Blvd La Crescenta 91214

STERNITZKE, VINCENT LEO, psychologist; b. July 7, 1925, Boonville, Mo.; s. William Leo and Maurene A. (Knapp) S.; m. Mary Margaret Jones, July 8, 1947; children: David b. 1952, Carol b. 1953; edn: Ed.D, Univ. Kans. Lawrence 1957; BS, Pittsburg St. Univ. 1948; MS, 1953; lic. psychologist Med. Bd. of Calif. 1969. Career: newspaper printer-opr. Southwestern Pub. Co., Joplin, Mo. 1948-49; advtg. sales Corpus Christi Caller-Times, Tx. 1949; instr. graphic arts No. Okla. Coll., Tonkawa 1949-55; asst. reading clinic Univ. Kans., Lawrence 1955-57; asst. prof., assoc. prof. Sam Houston St. Univ., Huntsville 1957-66; test ofcr. CSU Chico 1966-68; sr. psychologist Fairview St. Hosp., Costa Mesa 1968-70, program dir. habilitation 1970-77; counseling psychologist VA Reg. Office, San Francisco 1977-79; staff psychologist Napa St. Hosp. 1979-88; pvt. practice, Vallejo 1988-; mem: Am. Psychol. Assn., Calif. Psychol. Assn., Vallejo React Team (treas. 1986-), State Mil. Reserve (adj. 1988-); 2 articles pub. in profl. jours. (1959, 70), booklet pub. (1964), ed. periodical (1967-68); mil: comdr. USNR 1945; Republican; R.Cath.; rec: Citizens' radio, rubber stamp making. Res: 1424 Granada St Vallejo CA 94591-7633 Ofc: 1516 Napa St Vallejo CA 94590-4493

STETLER, CHARLES EDWARD, professor; b. Sept. 12, 1927, Pitts., Pa.; s. Charles Edward and Katherine (Seidel) S.; m. Ellen Donovan, June 25, 1955 (div. Nov., 1981); m. Kristin Jill Brown July 17, 1984 (div. Apr., 1993); children: Peter b. 1959, Paul b. 1963, Casey b. 1966; edn: BA, Duquesne Univ., Pitts., Pa., 1950; MA, Duquesne Univ., 1961; PhD, Tulane Univ., New Orleans, La., 1967. Career: reporter, Pitts. Sun-Telegraph 1951-61; instr., Rollins Coll., Winter Park, Fla. 1961-62; asst. prof., Loyola Univ., New Orleans, La. 1962-67;

prof., Calif. State Univ., Long Beach 1967-; exchange prof., Hull Univ., Hull, England, fall term 1984; prof. for Calif. State Univ., Long Beach Students in London, London, England, spring semester, 1991; author: (poetry) Roger, Rick, Karl & Shane Are Friends Of Mine, 1972; approx. 30 essays publ. in profl. journals; approx. 300 poems publ. in magazines and anthologies; book reviews; ed., anthology, New Geography of Poets, 1992. Mil: QM3, USN, 1945-45, 1950-52; Democrat; rec: bridge, golf, tennis. Res: 5905 E. Pacific Coast Hwy. Long Beach 90803. Ofc: Calif. State Univ. 1250 Bellflower Blvd. Long Beach 90840

STEVENS, ROBERT BOCKING, university administrator, lawyer; b. June 8, 1933, Leicester, England, nat. 1971; s. John Skevington and Enid Dorothy (Bocking) S.; m. Rosemary Wallace, Jan. 28, 1961; m. Katherine Booth, Dec. 23, 1985; children: Carey b. 1963, Richard b. 1966, Robin Elizabeth b. 1988; edn: BA, Oxford Univ., Eng. 1955, B.C.L. 1956, D.C.L. 1984; LLM, Yale Univ., 1958; Barrister at Law, Gray's Inn, London 1956. Career: prof. of law Yale Univ., 1959-76; provost Tulane Univ., 1976-78; pres. Haverford Coll., Pa. 1978-87; chancellor Univ. Calif., Santa Cruz 1987-91; mem. Nat. Council on Humanities, WDC 1985-; honors: LL.D. (hon.) New York Sch. of Law 1984, Villanova Univ. 1985, Univ. Penna. 1987, D.Litt (hon.) Haverford Coll. 1991; author: Law School (1984), Law & Politics (1979), coauthor: Welfare Medicine (1975), In Search of Justice (1969), Lawyers and the Courts (1967), The Restrictive Practice Court (1965). Ofc: Covington and Burling, 46 Hertford St WIY 7TF, London, England.

STEVENS, WILBUR HUNT, certified public accountant; b. June 20, 1918, Spencer, Ind.; s. John Vosburgh, MD, and Isabelle Jane (Strawser) S.; m. Maxine Dodge, Sept. 28, 1941; children: Linda b. 1950, Deborah b. 1952; edn: Milton (Wis.) Coll. 1935-37, BS, UC Berkeley, 1949, MBA, 1949; C.P.A., Calif. 1951. Career: staff acct. McLaren, Goode, West & Co., San Francisco 1949-52; mng. ptnr. Wilbur H. Stevens & Co., Salinas 1952-70; regional ptnr. (Calif.) Fox & Co., Salinas 1970-73; nat. dir. of banking practice Fox & co., Denver, Colo. 1973-80; owner Wilbur H. Stevens, CPA, Salinas 1980-; chmn. bd./pres. Valley Nat. Bank, Salinas 1963-71; faculty mem. and advy. com. Nat. Banking Sch., Charlottesville, Va. 1976-86; adj. prof. acctg. Univ. Denver 1975-78; instr. bank auditing, Am. Inst. CPAs, NYC 1969-80, v.p. dir. 1971-75; honors: Frank G. Drum Fellow UCB 1949, Phi Beta Kappa 1949, Paul Harris Fellow, Rotary Internat. 1977, disting. service Calif. Soc. CPAs 1988; mem: Calif. Soc. CPAs (pres. 1968), Accounting Research Assn. (pres. 1973), Nat. Assn. of State Boards of Acctncy. (pres. 1976), Salinas C.of C. (pres. 1960), Burma Star Assn. (London), CBI Veterans Assn., Commonwealth Club of Calif., Masons (master 1992), Rotary (dist. gov. 1983); publs: articles on auditing 1956-71, banking 1976-79; mil: capt. AUS, Fin. Dept., 1942-53, Bronze star, China War medal, China Victory medal; Republican; Methodist; rec: travel, Am. hist., profl. and service org. activities. Res/Ofc: 38 Santa Ana Dr Salinas 93901-4136

STEVENSON, IVAN KELLY, lawyer, consultant; b. Oct. 4, 1949, Quonset Point Naval Air Sta., Wickford Co., R.I.; s. Ivan Julius and Mary Theresa (Schaefer) S.; edn: BA, UC Los Angeles 1971; JD, Southwestern Univ. Sch. of Law 1974; admitted bar Calif (1974), Third Party Adminstr., Dept. Ins. (1983). Career: asst. supr., tech. writer Occidental Life Ins. Co. 1969-72; law clerk, atty. assoc. Martin & Stamp, Long Beach 1972-74, 78-81; Judge Advocate Gen. Corps USN, 1974-79; mng. atty./ptnr. Martin & Stamp, Long Beach, Santa Ana 1981-83; atty. Law Offices of Ivan K. Stevenson, 1983-; ptnr. Benefits Counseling Svc. 1983-; ptnr./ Third Party Administrator, Tayson Ins. Administrators, 1983-; ptnr. Ski Pak, 1990; v.p. Woodson R.R. Devel. Co., 1989-; judge pro tem Orange County Superior Ct.; guest lectr. re med. malpractice: L.A. Co. Med. Assn., Met. Hosp.; lectr. re govt. tort liability: City of Seal Beach, Am. Public Works Assn.; lectr. re client relations: Dispute Resolution Services; cons. on claims administn.; awards: Humanitarian Svc., USN (1975, 76), Outstanding Young Man Am. 1983, listed Who's Who in Calif. (1988, 89, 90, 91); mem: Am. Bar Assn., L.A. Co. Bar Assn. (state bar del. 1989, v. chair atty./client rels. com. 1985-91), Orange Co. Bar Assn., Am. Arbitration Assn., Am. Soc. Law and Med., U.S. Naval Reserves, U.S. Naval Inst., Judge Advocate Assn., U.S. Navy Memorial Found.; civic: Townhall of Calif., Seahill Townhomes HOA, Torrance Windemere HOA, L.A. Co. Judicial Arbitration Panel, L.A. Co./ Orange Co. Fee Mediation Com., Orange County Forum; mil: lt. cdr. USNR 1971-, active duty lt. JAGC USN 1974-78; R.Cath.; rec: triathlete, racquetball, volleyball, marathoner, slalom water skier. Ofc: 959 South Coast Dr Ste 490 Costa Mesa 92626 also: 3868 W Carson St Ste 300-6 Torrance 90503

STEVENSON, MARILYN ESTHER, company executive, community volunteer; b. June 9, 1933, Chicago, Ill.; d. John Michael and Mary Ann (Dusanic) Marchok; m. James Harold Stevenson, Aug. 13, 1955; children: J. Mark b. 1957, Mary b. 1959, J. Scott b. 1962, David b. 1963; edn: DePaul Univ. 1951-52, BA English, Univ. Ill., 1955, grad. studies Purdue Univ. 1956-58. Career: library asst. Purdue Univ., Lafayette, Ind. 1955-56; tchr. Ind. Schs., Battle Ground, Ind. 1956-57; comm. vol., tchr. Multi, Calif. and Mex. 1971-; v.p., secty., treas. James H. Stevenson Inc., Palos Verdes 1978-; v.p. Calif. Library Services Bd., Sacto. 1988-; pres., v.p. Palos Verdes Library Dist. Bd. Trustees 1979-84; awards: ALA Alta nat. trustee 1989, YWCA woman of year, Palos Verdes PTA hon. service 1970, cont. hon. service 1972; mem: Calif. Assn. Library Trustees (pres., v.p.),

Calif. Library Assn., Am. Library Assn., Am. Assn. Individual Investors, Am. Assn. Univ. Women, LWV,, Slovak Cath. Sokol; co-author: Trustee Tool Kit for Library Trustees (1987); Republican; R.Cath.; rec: bonsai, tennis, travel. Address: James H. Stevenson Inc. 2640 Via Carrillo Palos Verdes Estates 90274

STEWART, DAVID WAYNE, professor of marketing; b. Oct. 23, 1951, Baton Rouge, La.; s. Wesley A. Stewart, Jr. and Edith L. (Richhart) Moore; m. Lenora Francois, June 6, 1975; children: Sarah b. 1979, Rachel b. 1983; edn: BA, Northeast La. Univ., 1972; MA, PhD, Baylor Univ., 1973, 1974. Career: res. psychologist St. of Louisiana, Pineville 1974-76; res. mgr. Needham, Harper & Steers Advt., Chgo. 1976-78; assoc. prof. Jacksonville State Univ. 1978-80; assoc. prof. Owen Grad. Sch. of Mgmt. Vanderbilt Univ., Nashville, Tenn. 1980-86, assoc. dean 1984-86; prof. mktg. Univ. So. Calif., Los Angeles 1986-, The Robert E. Brooker Prof. of Marketing, 1991-, The Ernest W. Hahn Prof. of Marketing, 1990-91; vis. scholar Gen. Motors, Detroit 1988-90; cons. FTC, Wash. D.C. 1986-88, Hewlett Packard, Palo Alto 1986-, Ford Motor Co., Louisville, Ky. 1986, Weyerhauser, Seattle 1986-89; Coca-Cola, Atlanta 1990; awards: Phi Kappa Phi, Alpha Iota Delta, Beta Gamma Sigma, innovation in tchg. Decision Scis. Inst. 1983, Outstanding Young Men of Am. 1985, N.Y. Acad. Sci. 1988, sr. res. fellow Am. Acad. of Advertising 1988; mem: Soc. for Consumer Psychology (pres. 1985-86), Am. Mktg. Assn., Am. Psychol. Assn. (Fellow 1986, Council of Reps.), Am. Psychol. Soc. (Charter Fellow 1988), Assn. for Consumer Res., Inst. for Mgmt. Scis., Town Hall of Calif.; author 6 books: Secondary Research: Sources and Methods 1984, Effective TV Advertising 1986, Consumer Behavior and The Practice of Mktg. 1987, Nonverbal Communication in Advertising 1988, Focus Groups: Theory and Method 1990, Advertising and Consumer Psychology 1991; mem. editorial bds.: J. of Marketing Research, J. of Marketing, J. of Advertising, Current Issues and Research in Advertising, J. of Promotion Managment, Management Issues; Republican; Am. Baptist. Res: 9340 La Alba Dr Whittier 90603

STEWART, LELAND PERRY, minister, coordinating council executive, writer; b. Mar. 4, 1928, Detroit, Mich.; s. Hoyt Clifford and Gladys (Woodward) S.; m. Elizabeth Elliot, June 13, 1953; children: Deanna b. 1954, Dana b. 1956, Lynn b. 1958; edn: BSE, Mech. Engring., Univ. of Mich., Ann Arbor, 1949; BSE, Math, Univ. of Mich., 1949; STB, Harvard Div. Sch., 1953; Secondary Life cred., Calif. State Univ., L.A. & Northridge, 1962. Career: founding minister, Unity-and-Diversity Spiritual Group, L.A. 1958-; sec. tchr., L.A. Unified Sch. Dist. 1960-72, 1993-; tchr., Santa Monica/Malibu Unified Sch. Dist. 1993-; central coord., Unity-and-Diversity World Council, L.A, 1965-; trumpet player, dance band & Harvard orch. 1945-53; instr., Univ. of Oriental Studies, L.A. 1975-78; ministry trainer, Unity-and-Diversity Spiritual Group, L.A. 1973-; tchr., World Univ., L.A. 1988-90; bd. mem. Interfaith Council for UN., L.A. 1988-; life bd. mem. Unity-and-Diversity World Council 1965-; mem: Unitarian Universalist Assn., Boston, Mass.; author: From Industrial Power to Lasting Peace, 1951; author/compiler, Central Scriptures, 1952 and World Scripture, 1953; ed./musician, Creative Music, 1950; ed., Marriage & Other Services, 1953; Democrat and Independent; Universalist; rec: trumpet playing, meditating, swimming, walking, being in nature. Ofc: 1010 S. Flower St. Ste. 401 Los Angeles 90015-1428

STIEB, WILMA BEVERCOMBE, community worker; b. Oct. 28, Orient, Iowa; d. Alvin Lester and Ella Elmira (Reed) Bevercombe (both dec.); brother, Gale Reed Bevercombe (dec.); m. Clyde William Stieb, 1944 (dec.); 1 son, Jackson Wm. (dec.); edn: stu. Gregg Bus. Coll.; Univ. of Oreg.; Univ. of Nebr.; BS in edn., Univ. Idaho, 1931; MS psychol. (fellowship), Univ. Idaho 1933. Career: spl. tchr. Bus. Adminstrn. Dept., Univ. of Idaho; secty. Standard Oil Co. of Calif.; secty. PEO Sisterhood, Chpt. NK; biographical listings in Who's Who of Calif. Exec. Women, The Idaho Digest and Blue Book, The Calif. Register, Who's Who in the World, Am. Women, Five Hundred First Families of Am.; Family archives record 21 ancestral Coats of Arms; mem: Nat. Soc. Daus. of the Am. Colonists, Sons and Daughters First Settlers of Newbury (Newburyport, Mass.), DAR Achois Comihavit Chpt., Nat. Soc. of Magna Charta Dames, PEO Sisterhood (NK Chpt.); author: Occupations in the State of Idaho (1934); Democrat; Christian Ch.; rec: lectures, travel, collect old Bibles, poetry, and thoughts for special occasions. Res: 15652 Woodvale Rd Encino 91436

STILES, CASSANDRA DANE, international banker; b. Nov. 1, 1953, West Palm Beach, Fla.; d. Philip Henry and Cassandra (Quickel) Stiles; edn: BA econ., Rollins Coll. 1975; MA internat. mgmt., Thunderbird, 1976. Career: fin. analyst F.C.I.A., N.Y.C. 1976; credit analyst Ariz. Bank, Phoenix 1976-78, internat. ofcr., v.p. 1978-84; v.p. trade fin. First Interstate Bank, San Diego 1984-; instr. Grossmont Coll., El Cajon 1986-; apptd. bd. Calif. Export Finance Office L.A. 1988-, commr. Internat. Trade Commn. S.D. 1988-90; mem. San Diego C.of C. (internat. advy. council 1984-), World Trade Assn. S.D. (pres. 1988-90), Dist. Export Council. Ofc: First Interstate Bank 401 B St Ste 2201 San Diego 92101

STILLER-COMBS, ALICE MARIE, company president; b. March 19, 1942, Tulsa, Okla.; d. George R. and Charlotte C. (Coogan) Dickinson; m. Hans J. Stiller, 1962 (div. 1982); children: Jeanette b. 1966, Debbie b. 1968; m.2d.

Michael Bruce Combs, Aug. 5, 1989; edn: BA, CSU Hayward 1974. Career: salesperson Vulcan Inc., Dublin, Calif. 1974-75, ptnr. 1975-77, owner 1977-78, pres. Vulcan Inc. Pleasanton, Calif. 1978-93; mem. Royal Order of Calif. Can Carriers 1978-89; mem. Snowflakes Ski Club; Republican; Prot.; rec: swimming, skiing, bicycling. Res: 5860 Victoria Ln Livermore 94550 Ofc: Vulcan, Inc. 21066 Cabot Blvd Hayward 94545

STOCKING, GERARDA, real estate broker; b. Oct. 30, 1947, Utrecht, Netherlands, nat. U.S. citizen 1960; d. Heiko Tjark and Gladys Elizabeth (Yardley) de Man; m. Bosco Barney Stocking, June 2, 1966; children: Damian, Rachel, Emily, Charlie, Veronica; edn: Am. Coll. Paris 1965-66; Chabot Coll. 1976-78; Chabot Coll. Livermore 1982-83; lic. real estate broker Calif., 1978; cert. real estate appraiser 1987; GRI, Grad. Realtors Land Inst., 1989; CRB, cert. R.E. Brokerage mgr. 1990; Accred. Land Cons., cand. 1992. Career: owner Stocking Bakery, Livermore and Dublin 1972-78; real estate agent Better Homes Realty, Dublin 1977-78; Estate Realtors 1978-81; real estate broker Stocking Realty & Investment, Livermore 1981-; mktg. dir. FIABCI, Paris, France 1987-88; awards: So. Alameda Bd. of Realtors Dist. Grand Master (highest vol. of sales 1988), Chabot Coll. Walter Ng scholarship 1981, SACBOR Million Dollar Club 1979, SACAR Grand Masters Club (1989, 90, 91); mem: Internat. Real Estate Fedn., Realtors Land Inst. (Calif. chapt. v.p. 1989-91, pres. 1991-92), So. Alameda Co. Bd. Realtors, Contra Costa Bd. Realtors, Tracy Bd. Realtors; civic: St. Michael's Sch. Bd. of Edn. (1990-94, v.p. elect), mem. PTA Group; painting: "Under The Bridge" (!980); Republican; R.Cath.; rec: scuba diving, painting. Ofc: 392 S Livermore Ave Livermore 94550

STOKER, WILLIAM ROBERT, JR., insurance broker; b. Oct. 2, 1950, San Bernardino; s. Wm. Robert and Bonnie Clair (Lindsey) S.; edn: BS in edn., summa cum laude, Univ. of N.Y. 1971; tchg. credentials, N.Y., Calif. Career: underwriting/mktg. mgr. EBI Co., 1977-79; Div. mgr., asst. secty. ICW Co., 1979-81; v.p. underwriting Mission Ins. Cos., 1982-87; prin. Davis-Stoker and Assocs., Thousand Oaks 1987-; mem: NCCI (underw. com. 1982-), WCIRB (exec. com. 1983-84), ACIC, CWCI; mil: enlisted NCO US Army Airborne; Republican. Res: 32105 Harborview Ln Westlake Village 91361 Ofc: Davis Stoker and Associates, 187 E Wilbur Rd Ste 6 Thousand Oaks 91360

STOKES, GORDON ARTHUR, educator, consultant; b. Aug. 28, 1929, Salt Lake City; s. Lovell Arthur and Viola (Condi) S.; m. Geraldine Lillie, June 21, 1952; children: Michael b. 1963. Career: pres. Three In One Concepts, Burbank; splst. in stress mgmt., commns., and alt. health procedures using acupressure and kinesiology, author videotape tng. series: Three Methods of Relieving Pain, Intro. to Body Circuits, Reactive Muscles, Bach Flower Testing, Basic One Brain Examination, others; created spl. stress reduction pgms. for extended edn. courses Trumbull Nurses Coll., CSU Long Beach Ext., Pepperdine Univ.; devel. tng. & sales pgms. for Touch for Health Found., Pasadena, Parent Effectiveness Training (P.E.T.) Solano Beach, The PACE Orgn. North Hollywood, Coll. of Personology Sacto.; tchr., developer (W. Daniel Whiteside) One Brain pgm. defusing stress related learning difficulties, 1986-, taught nat. in Russia, India, Japan, N.Z., Australia, Brazil, England and Europe; author: Belling The Cat, and (with Daniel Whiteside): Five Elements Balancing, Under The Code, One Brain, Advanced One Brain, Structural Neurology, New Options For Decision Makers. Ofc: 2001 W Magnolia Blvd Ste B and C Burbank 91506

STOLTZFUS, BEN F., university professor emeritus; b. Sept. 15, 1927, Sofia Bulgaria; s. B. Frank and Esther Alfrida (Johnson) S.; m. Elizabeth Burton, Aug. 20, 1955 (div. Oct. 20, 1975); m. Judith Palmer Nov. 8, 1975; children: Jan b. 1957, Celia b. 1962, Andrew b. 1966; edn: BA, Amherst Coll., Amherst, Mass., 1949; MA, Middlebury Coll., Middlebury, Vt., 1954; Univ. of Paris, Paris, France, 1955-56; PhD, Univ. of Wis., Madison, Wis., 1959. Career: tchg. asst., Univ. of Wis., Madison 1956-58; French instr., Smith College, Northampton, Mass. 1958-60; prof. of French, comparative lit. & creative writing, Univ. of Calif., Riverside 1960-93; awards: Fulbright -Hays Res. Grants to Paris, France 1955-56, 1963-64; Univ. of Calif. Creative Arts Inst. awards 1967, 75; Univ. of Calif. Humanities Inst. awards 1969-72; LittD, Amherst Coll. 1974; Camargo Found. Grants 1983, 85; fellow, Ctr. for Ideas & Society, Univ. of Calif. 1991; listed, Contemporary Authors, The World Who's Who of Authors, The Writer's Directory, Who's Who In The West, and others; mem: Modern Lang. Assn. 1960-, Am. Comparative Lit. Assn. 1980- So. Comparative Lit. Assn., 1980-, Hemingway Soc. 1987-, Camus Soc. 1988-, PEN 1989-, Amer. Lit. Assn. 1990; author: (novels) The Eye Of The Needle, 1967; Black Lazarus, 1972; Red White And Blue, 1989; monographs of literary criticism: Alain Robbe-Grillet and the New French Novel, 1964, Georges Chenneviere Et L'Unanimisme, 1965, Gide's Eagles, 1969, Gide and Hemingway: Rebels Against God, 1978, Alain Robbe-Grillet: The Body of the Text, 1985, Alain Robbe-Grillet: Life, Work and Criticism, 1987, Postmodern Poetics: Nouveau Roman and Innovative Fiction, 1987, La Belle Captive: Magritte and Robbe-Grillet (trans. of novel with critical essay), 1994; short fiction and poetry; numerous literary criticisms, articles and essays publ. in profl. literary journals and reviews; Democrat; rec: skiing, tennis, scuba diving. Res: 2040 Arroyo Dr. Riverside 92506

STONE, RICHARD ALAN, physician; b. Nov. 21, 1942, Cambridge, Mass.; s. Jack David and Gail (Polak) S.; m. Suzanne Poteet, Dec. 5, 1982; children: Lisa b. 1970, Caroline b. 1973, Chelsea b. 1985, Jordan b. 1990; edn: AB, Brown Univ. 1964; MD, Tufts Univ. 1970. Career: physician, nephrologist; asst./assoc. prof. of medicine UC San Diego, 1977-79; dir. Hemodialysis & Hypertension, VA Hosp., San Diego 1977-79; chmn. Nephrology Eisenhower Med. Ctr., Rancho Mirage 1979-, chmn. Medicine 1981-; sr. attg. phys. Eisenhower Med. Ctr. 1985; honors: Alpha Omega Alpha 1969; Tufts Med. Alumni Prize Physiology, Anatomy, Pathology, Microbiology; mem. Am. Soc. of Nephrology, Am. Heart Assn., Am. Found. Clin. Res., Nat. Kidney Found.; publs: over 100 med. arts. on high blood pressure and kidney disease; mil: capt. USAR 1970-76; rec: tennis. Res: 40563 Desert Creek Ln Rancho Mirage 92270

STONE, WESTCOT BELL, III, airline pilot; b. Aug. 23, 1920, Los Angeles; s. Earle Reynolds and Casandra (Bell) S.; m. Bette Werner, Apr. 25, 1956; children: Elizabeth b. 1957, Kimberley b. 1958, Westcot, IV, b. 1962, granddaughter Ashley Elizabeth Bateman, b. 1982; edn: USC. Career: pilot Trans World Airlines Inc. 1946, airline capt. Western Airlines, 1946-80, ret.; mem. Silver Chiefs, Cabrillo Yacht Club, Kaneohe Yacht club (Hawaii), Sigma Alpha Epsilon, Sigma Delta Psi; mil: capt. USAAF 1941-46, decorated Air Medal w/3 o.l.c., D.F.C.; Republican; United Ch. of Christ; rec: pvt. pilot, sailing, travel. Res: 2820 Via de la Guerra Palos Verdes Estates 90274

STONE, WILLIAM THOMAS, church organist, music teacher; b. Mar. 24, 1921, Sacramento; s. Wm. T. and Henrietta Dorothy (Jurgens) S.; m. Ruth Danielsen, July 25, 1954; children: Michael b. 1955, Peter b. 1957; edn: BS, UC Berkeley 1942. Career: owner Wm. T. Stone Music Studio; organist/choir dir. St. Paul's Episcopal Ch., Salinas 1951-54, Temple Sinai, Oakland 1948-77; organist St. Mark's Episcopal Ch., Berkeley 1947-51; USCG Tng. Center Chapel, Alameda 1963-79; St. Bonaventure's Catholic Ch., Concord 1979-90; St. Timothy's Episcopal Ch., Danville 1990-; mem. Am. Guild of Organists (dean Contra Costa County chpt. 1966-68), Rotary; mil: sgt. USAF 1943-45; Republican; Episcopal. Res: 2645 San Carlos Dr Walnut Creek 94598

STOOB, JOHN CHARLES, educator; b. May 23, 1934, San Francisco; s. Johann Christoff and Clara Mary (Humann) S.; m. Idella McCurdy Hill, Aug. 31, 1956; children: Sandra b. 1958, Susan b. 1960, Michael b. 1962; edn: BSBA, UC Berkeley 1956; MS computer scis., Tx. A&M Univ. 1965; PhD indsl. engring., 1972. Career: Dept. of Air Force 1956-78, chief supply mgmt., W. Germany 1978-80, dir. of supply for USAF in Europe 1980-81; assoc. prof. Humboldt St. Univ., Arcata 1981-84, dept. chair CIS 1984-87, prof. computer info. systems 1987-, v.chair acad. senate 1988-, faculty personnel com. mem. 1986, 88-; awards: Humboldt St. Univ. Merit. Performance (1984, 87), Am. Bus. Womens Assn. Bus. Assoc. of Year 1987, Dept. of Air Force Bronze Star Medal 1968, Legion of Merit Medal 1983; mem: Assn. Computing Machinery, Ops. Res. Soc. Am., Phi Kappa Phi, Upsilon Pi Epsilon, Alpha Pi Mu; articles pub. in profl. jours. (1984-87), conf. presentation (1984); mil: col. USAF 1957-81; Republican; Unitarian; rec: hiking. Res: 799 Crestwood Dr Arcata 95521 Ofc: Humboldt State Univ. CIS Dept. Arcata 95521

STOTLER, ALICEMARIE HUBER, federal judge; b. May 29, 1942, Alhambra; d. James Russell and Loretta (Montoya) H.; m. James Allen Stotler, Sept. 11, 1971; edn: BA, USC, 1964, JD, 1967; admitted bar: Calif. 1967, Fed. Ct. no. dist. Calif. 1967, cent. dist. Calif. 1973, US Supreme Ct. 1976; cert. Crim. Law Specialist, 1973. Career: Orange County dep. dist. atty. (first woman hired f.t. O.C.) 1967-73; pvt. practice law, 1973-76, 83-84; appt. municipal ct. judge, Harbor Judicial Dist., Newport Beach 1976-78; appt. judge Superior Ct., Orange Co. 1978-83; appt. judge U.S. Dist. Ct., Central Dist. of Calif., 1984-; instr. Orange Co. Sheriff's Dept. Acad., 1982; instr. CEB State Bar Conf. course in courtroom conduct, 9/83; honors: winner Hale Moot Ct. Competition, statewide Appellate argument compet. 1967, named Judge of yr. O.C. Trial Lawyers & Trial Lawyers Sectys. 1978, Franklin G. West Award for contbns. to advance and elevate justice and law Orange Co. Bar Assn. 1985; mem. U.S. Judicial Conf.Coms.: Standing Com. on Rules of Practice and Procedure 1991-94; mem. Ninth Circuit Coms.: Jury Com. 1990-92, Exec. Com., 9th Cir. Jud. Conf. 1989-92, Fed.-State Jud. Council 1989-93; mem: Fed. Judges Assn. (bd. 1989-), Ninth Circuit Dist. Judges Assn., Am. Law Inst., ABA (jud. admin. div. and litigation sect.), Nat. Assn. Women Judges, Calif. Judges' Found. (pres. 1981-82); mem. Orange Co. Bar Assn. (1968-, dir. 1976, sec. 1984), O.C. Trial Lawyers' Assn. (1973-, dir. 1975); civic: Legion Lex USC (bd. 1981-83), Arthritis Found. O.C. (planned giving com. 1976-81), Geo. A. Parker Law Found. (trustee 1979-82); Republican; Prot.; rec: walking, dog shows. Ofc: U.S. District Court 751 W Santa Ana Blvd Ste 403 Santa Ana 92701

STRAND, CARL LUDVIG, earthquake consultant; b. Nov. 6, 1950, Memphis, Tenn.; s. Sylvester Eugene and Barbara Harris (Maier) S.; edn: BA math. with specialization in earth scis., Revelle Coll., UC San Diego, 1973; MS geology, San Diego St. Univ., 1980; wilderness trip leadership adminstrn. certificate, Coll. of Extended Studies, SDSU, 1980; UCLA, 1982-. Career: pres. Strand Earthquake Cons., Los Angeles, 1987-; honors: La Frontera Award, San Diego Inst. Hist. 1980, NCCEM Region IX Executive Citation 1990, BSA Eagle Scout;

mem: Earthquake Engrg. Research Inst., Earthquake Investigations Com. (secty.), Earthquake Actuated Automatic Gas Shutoff Sys. Standards Com. (secty.), Internat. Assn. of Plumbing and Mech. Officials' Earthquake Valve Ad Hoc Com., Nat. Coordinating Council on Emergency Mgmt. (chair Earthquake Subcom.), So. Calif. Emergency Services Assn.; author: Pre-1900 Earthquakes of Baja Calif. and San Diego County 1980, articles pub. in profl. jours. 1979-93; Democrat; rec: backpacking, scuba diving, genealogy. Ofc: Strand Earthquake Consultants, 1436 S Bentley Ave Ste 6 Los Angeles 90025

STRAUBEL, JOHN FREDERICK, advertising and public relations agency executive; b. May 19, 1928, Greenbay, Wis.; s. Clarence Weise and Ethel (Puchner) S.; edn: BS in English, Northwestern Univ., 1950. Career: comms. dir. Hiller Aircraft Corp., Palo Alto 1956-63, Fairchild Hiller Corp., W.D.C. 1963-66; owner/pres. Straubel Communications, Portola Valley 1966-; pub. rels. mgr. Volunteers for Nixon-Lodge, W.D.C., 1960 Campaign; mem.: Pub. Rels. Soc. Am. 1960-; civic: The New Forum, Palo Alto (dir., v.p. 1985-89), Boys & Girls Club Am., Palo Alto (chapt. dir. 1992-); author, editor: One Way Up (1963), Pacific Diary I (1952), Pacific Diary II (1953); mil: lt.j.g. USN 1950-53; Indep.; Presbyterian; rec: comic book artist/writer. Ofc: Straubel Communications, 4370 Alpine Rd Ste 206 Portola Valley 94028

STRAUSS, VICKI LYNN, graphic designer, public relations, marketing consultant; b. Mar. 30, 1942, Salt Lake City; d. Wm. Joseph Selman and Verna Mayne (Arnold) Allem; m. Dennis J. Strauss, Oct. 15, 1961 (div. 1975); children: Richard Scott, Sean Eric; m. Wm. McKinney, May 19, 1989; edn: AA, Cypress Coll., 1973 BA with honors, CSU Fullerton, 1984. Career: instrnl. aide, coordinator Centralia Sch. Dist., Buena Park 1973-76, secty., fed. project dir., 1976-80, pub. info. ofcr. 1980-85; ptnr./owner The Graphics Haus, Tustin 1985-88; cons. Calif. Assn. Pgm. Splts., Anaheim 1985-88; documentation mgr. Toshiba America, CSD Div., 1987-; mem. Assn. Calif. Adminstrs. (O.C. PAC 1982-85), presenter st. conf. Calif. Sch. Bd. Assn., Anaheim 1985; recipient outstanding service award Centralia Adminstrs. Assn. 1985, hon. silver svc. award Buena Park PTA Council 1985, outstanding employee Buena Park Classified Sch. Employees Assn. 1979; mem: Soc. Technical Communicators, So. Counties Women in Ednl. Mgmt. (exec. com., pub. info. ofcr. 1984-), Am. Bus. Womens Assn., Nat. Sch. Pub. Relations Assn.; civic: Am. Cancer Soc. Buena Park chpt. (1983-85), vol. tnr. of witnesses for Police Victim Assistance and Crisis Pgms. of Huntington Beach, Irvine, Costa Mesa, and Westminster (1985-); Democrat; rec: photog. Res: 12872 Alonzo Cook St Garden Grove 92645 Ofc: Toshiba America Information Systems, Inc. 9740 Irvine Blvd Irvine 92718

STROBL, DONALD LOUIS, physician, psychiatrist; b. May 18, 1947, Cleveland, Ohio; s. Charles John and Rose Helen (Sourek) S.; m. Sally Joanne Derrick, June 27, 1970; children: Staci Elizabeth b. 1973, Kerry Allison b. 1976; edn: BS, Cornell Univ. 1969; MD, Ohio State Univ. Coll. Medicine 1973; cert. psychiatrist Am. Bd. Psychiatry & Neurology 1980. Career: staff psychiatrist Tri-City Mental Health, Mesa, Ariz. 1977-80, interim dir. 1980-81; pvt. practice, Tempe, Ariz. 1981-82; La Mesa 1982-; asst. prof. UCSD Med. Sch. 1983-. Res: 1485 Hillsmont Dr El Cajon 92020 Ofc: 5565 Grossmont Center Dr #540 La Mesa 92042

STROMME, GARY L., law librarian; b. July 8, 1939, Willmar, Minn.; m. Suzanne Readman, July 21, 1990; edn: BA, philo., Pacific Lutheran Univ. 1965; BLS, Univ. of Brit. Columbia Sch. of Librarianship, 1967; JD, Hastings Coll. of the Law 1973; admitted State Bar of Calif. 1973, US Supreme Ct. Bar, 1977. Career: serials librarian, Univ. of Minn., St. Paul Campus Librarian 1967-69; asst. librarian law firm McCutchen, Doyle, Brown, Enersen, San Francisco 1970-71; asst. librarian Graham & James, S.F. 1971-73; ind. contracting atty., 1973-74; law librarian Pacific Gas & Electric Co., S.F. 1974-; mem: Internat. Soc. Gen. Semantics (S.F. chpt. pres. 1978-80, bd. dir. 1980-81), Am. Assn. Law Libraries (chmn. AALL Com. on indexing of legal periodicals 1986-88), Am. Bar Assn. (chmn. lib. com. Sect. Economics of Law Practice 1978-82); author: An Intro. to the Use of the Law Library (1974); Basic Legal Research Tech. (rev. 4th ed. 1979); mil: elect. tech. USAF 1959-63. Res: 6106 Ocean View Dr Oakland 94618 Ofc: PG&E, 77 Beale St 31st Flr San Francisco 94106

STRONG, GARY E., state librarian; b. June 26, 1944, Moscow, Idaho; s. Arthur Dwight and Cleora Anna (Nirk) S.; m. Carolyn Jean Roetker, March 14, 1970; children: Christopher Eric b. 1971, Jennifer Rebecca b. 1974; edn: BS, Univ. of Ida. 1966; MA lib. sci., Univ. of Mich. 1967. Career: instr. in public lib. adminstrn. Div. of Cont. Edn., State of Ore. 1972; ref., adminstrv. asst. Univ. of Ida. Library 1963-66; extension librarian Latah Co. (Ida.) Free Lib. 1966; hd. librarian Markley Residence Lib., Univ. Mich., 1966-67; library dir. Lake Oswego (Ore.) Pub. Lib. 1967-73, Everett (Wa.) Public Lib. 1976-79; assoc. dir. for svs. Washington State Lib. 1976-79, dep. state librarian 1979-80; Calif. State Librarian, 1980-; mem./CEO Calif. Library Svs. Bd.; exec. dir./ex-officio mem. bd. dirs. Calif. State Lib. Found.; mem. bd. dirs. Coop. Lib. Agcy. for Systems and Svs. (v.p. 1981-84); mem. Lib. Adminstrn. and Mgmt. Assn. (pres. 1984-85), Chief Officers of State Lib. Agencies (pres. 1984-86), Calif. Historic Capitol Commn., W. Council of State Libs., No. Reg. Lib. Facility (bd.), Calif., Am. and Spl. Libs. Assn., Calif. State PTA (advsy. bd.), Advsy. Com. to the Lib. of Cong.

on Laser Disc Technol.; mem. Book Club of Calif., S.F./Sacto. Book Collectors Club, Book Collectors Club of L.A., Press Club of S.F., Roxborghe Club; past activities: Ore. Lib. Assn. (pres. 1970-71, hon. life mem. 1981), Pacific Northwest Lib. Assn. (pres. 1978-79, hon. life mem. 1981), Pacific Northwest Bibliographic Center (bd. 1977-80), Everett, WA Library Access (prod., host weekly cablevision pgm. 1974-76), Am. Lib. Assn. Commn. on Freedom and Equality of Access to Info. 1984-86, Alpha Phi Omega nat. svc. frat. (sect. chmn. W. Reg. 1967-71); awards: Ore. State Lib. scholarship for grad. study 1966, disting. alumnus Univ. Mich. Sch. of Lib. Sci. 1984, disting. svc. Calif. Literacy Inc. 1985, spl. commendn. Calif. Assn. of Lib. Trustees and Commnrs. 1985; publs: compiler, On Reading - In the Year of the Reader (1987); num. profl. and gen. interest articles, media interviews, frequent keynote speaker. Ofc: State Librarian of California POB 942837 Sacramento 94237-0001

STRONG, PAMELA KAY, material and process engineer; b. Oct. 17, 1950, Mesa, AZ; d. Wayland Thorton and Adele (Gaumer) S.; edn: MS, Bryn Mawr Coll., 1974; BS, Phila. Coll. of Pharmacy and Science, 1972; career: res. chemist, W. Industrial Enterprises, Phoenix 1974-75; analytical chemist, Henkel Corp., Hawthorne 1975-80; process engr., Hughes Aircraft, Radar Div., El Segundo 1980-83; sr. process engr., Irvine Sensors Corp., Costa Mesa 1983; sr. adv. composite engr./sr. adv. quality (material) engr., General Electric, Aircraft Engine Business Group, Albuquerque 1983-85; mantech engr. splst./sr. quality assurance process engr. splst., Northrup Corp., Pico Rivera 1985-87; material & process engring. tech. splst./adv. material & process lead engr., McDonnell Douglas Missile and Space Systems Co., Huntington Beach 1987-; awards: General Electric Manufacturing Technology Excellence Award 1984, Am. Chemical Soc. Scholastic Award, Am. Chemical Soc. Petroleum Res. Fellow, Nat. Science Found. Undergrad. Res. Fellow; listed Who's Who In Science and Engring., Who's Who in the West, Who's Who of Am. Women, Who's Who in U.S. Exec.; mem: Am. Chemical Soc., Am. Inst. of Chemists, Am. Assn. for the Advancement of Science, Soc. of Applied Spectroscopy (chmn 1977-79, sec. 1979-81), Soc. of Automotive Engineers (Engring. Soc. for Advancing Mobility Land Sea Air Space), Soc. for Women Chemists, Iota Sigma Pi, Soc. of Women Engineers, Soc. for the Advancement of Materials and Process Engineers (treas. 1984-85), Nat. Assn. for Female Exec. Res: 4912 Hilo Circle Huntington Beach 92649 Ofc: McDonnell Douglas Space Systems, 5301 Bolsa Ave. Huntington Beach 92647

STROUD, SHARRON PATRICIA, minister; b. July 29, 1944, Okemah, Okla.; d. Raymond Dean and Zora Margaret (Woods) Jacobs; widow, Neil Stroud; children: Tricia Lorraine b. 1969. edn: CSU Northridge 1963-64, Pierce City Coll. 1964-65; Ministerial Degree, Un. Ch. Rel. Sci. Sch. of Ministry 1973-75; Master Degree, Motivational Sci. Humanetic Inst. 1976; PhD cand. in behav. psych., La Jolla Univ. Career: religious sci. minister and motivational instr. Self Image Inst., Santa Ana Coll. of Para Medical Arts and Sci. 1972-73; num. self-image seminars, 1972-; founding minister Sci. of Mind Ch. of Positive Thinking 1975-78; minister Rel. Sci. Ch. Ctr., San Diego 1978; minister S.D. Comm. Ch. of Rel. Sci. 1978-; founding minister San Diego Church for the Celebration of Life, Jan. 1, 1989; num. tv and radio appearances, prod. radio show "The Choice is Yours," host local tv ministry "Passport To Life " (1986-); torch carrier First Earth Run, participant Human Unity Conf., and The March for Peace and Hands Across Am., lectr. U.N. Univ. for Peace, Costa Rica, chaired Planetary Commn., World Peace Event (S.D.); mem. United Clergy of Rel. Sci. (v.p. 1986-87); mem. Rel. Advy. Council, U.S. 42nd Congl. Dist.; recipient speaking awards Nat. Forensic League 1961, United Ch. Rel. Sci. Sch. of Ministry, Resolution San Diego City Council (2/14/75), svc. award Nat. Mgmt. Assn. 1979-80; Beta Sigma Phi Humanitarian sor. (v.p. 1968-72); hon. PhD Heritage Inst. Santa Barbara; Woman of Religion award, Soroptimists Internat.; Hollywood's Salute to Beautiful Women (1972); 1st woman pres. of Sch. of Ministry 1974-75; listed: Outstanding Young Women of Am. (1970, 80), Who's Who in Calif., Who's Who of the New Thought Movement 1975, Who's Who San Diego Women 1982, Who's Who in Metaphysics; mem: Beta Sigma Pi (v.p. 1968-72), Nat. League of Am. Pen Women, Soroptimist Internat.; publs: The Spiritual Side of Success; The Power of Knowing Who You Are (Herself Mag. 1979); published poet; author: book in progress, Living On The Edge; featured in Time, Newsweek, US News & World Report; Apolitical; Religious Sci.; rec: bicycling, yoga, swimming. Res: Mt. Helix Ofc: 4201 Avenida Gregory Spring Valley 92077

STRUBLE, GORDON LEE, nuclear chemist; b. Mar. 7, 1937, Cleveland, Oh.; s. Fred Clarence and Elizabete Frances S.; m. Jean Louise Wells, June 14, 1961; children: Elizabeth b. 1962, Andrea b. 1964, Stephanie b. 1967, Gretchen b. 1968; edn: BS chem., Rollins Coll., 1960; PhD chem., Fla. St. Univ., 1964. Career: instr. chemistry dept. UC Berkeley 1964-65, asst. prof. 1966-71; post-doc. fellow Lawrence Berkeley Lab. 1964-65; staff Lawrence Livermore Nat. Lab. (LLNL) Nuclear Chemistry Div., 1971-73; group ldr. nuclear structure gp. 1973-75, sect. ldr. nuclear properties sect. 1976-79, assoc. div. ldr. for res. 1979-84, group ldr. nuclear properties gp. 1984-, sci. editor Research Monthly, and Energy and Technology Rev., LLNL, 1984-85; instr. dept. applied sci. UC Davis, 1979-; vis. prof. physics dept. Univ. Munich 1975; awards: Omicron Delta Kappa 1958, Phi Soc. 1958, Sigma Xi 1959, Woodrow Wilson Fellow 1960, State of Fla. nuclear sci. fellow 1960, AEC fellow 1961, NSF fellow 1962,

NATO fellow Advanced Studies Inst., Fr. 1969, res. fellow German Fed. Republic 1970, excellence Soc. for Tech. Comm. (1983, 84, 85); mem: Am. Chem. Soc., am. Physical Soc., AAAS; rec: music, sailing, backpacking. Res: 2 Deodar Ln Alamo 94507 Ofc: LLNL POB 808 L-233 Livermore 94551

STRUNK, HAROLD KENNETH, medical plan executive; b. June 23, 1933, McCreary County, Ky.; s. Obal Edmund and Matilda Luverne (New) S.; m. Nancy Lou Patton, June 12, 1954; children: Nancy Karen b. 1955, Melanie Ann b. 1958, Kenneth Wayne b. 1959; edn: BA psychology, CSU Fullerton 1967; MSW, UCLA 1969; MPH, 1970; DPH, 1972. Career: proj. dir. PSRO Support Center for Calif. 1974-78; exec. dir. TakeCare HMO Blue Cross of No. Calif., Oakland 1978-80; sr. health planner Arabian Bechtel Co. Ltd., Jubail, Saudi Arabia 1980-82; hosp. adminstr. Saudi Arabian Mil. Hosp., Dhahran, Saudi Arabia 1982-83; Const. Nat. Med. Enterprises, Al Hada Hosp., Taif, Saudi Arabia 1983-85; physician recruiter Hosp. Staffing System, Pleasanton 1985-87; reg. mgr. Blue Shield of Calif., San Francisco 1987-; awards: British Sub-Aqua Club Per Holmquist 1983; mem: Assn. Mil. Surgeons of U.S., Healthcare Execs. No. Calif., World Affairs Council S.F., British Sub-Aqua Club, Am. Legion, Naval Reserve Assn., Am. Pub. Health Assn., Middle East Inst., Balloon Platoon (chmn. 1985-); publs: proceedings, Diving Hazards in Persian Gulf; mil: Cdr. USNR 1977-; Republican; Presbyterian; rec: scuba diving, competition rifle shooting, photog. Res: 4365 Clovewood Ln Pleasanton 94566 Ofc: Blue Shield of California 2 Northpoint San Francisco 94133

STUART, DOROTHY MAE, artist; b. Jan. 8, 1933, Fresno; d. Robert Wesley Williams and Maria Theresa (Gad) Tressler; m. Reginald Ross Stuart, May 18, 1952; children: Doris b. 1954 Darlene b. 1957, Sue b. 1962; edn: grad. Fresno H.S., 1951, student CSU Fresno 1951-52, Fresno City Coll. 1962-64, pvt. courses 1965-68. Career: artist, prin., Fresno 1962-, 1160+ oils, graphics, watercolors, drawings, paintings (1966-); art demonstrations and judging for schools, fairs and orgns., San Joaquin Valley, 1962-; awards: 53 Fine Art awards art shows Calif. (1966-), Spl. award Soc. of Western Artists- DeYoung Mus., S.F. and Frye Mus., Seattle 1971, invitation 1st Contemporary Western Art Tour to P.R.O.China (1974), degree of honor Soc. of Western Artists, S.F. (1975); mem. Soc. Western Artists, Fresno (bd. 1968-74, v.p. 1968-70), Fresno County Womens Trade Club (1982-, bd. 1986-92, pres. 1988-90), Fresno Art Mus. (1970-), Patrons for Cultural Arts Fresno (adviser 1987-, bd. 1991-92), Fresno H.S. Centennial (bd. 1988-90); appt. advy. com. State Sen. Ken Maddy's Cent. Calif. Conf. on Women 1989-; publs: art adviser: (book) "A Portrait of Fresno" (1985), artist: (book) "Heritage Fresno" (1975), editor and artist (book) "Fresno High Sch. Centennial 1889-1989" (1989); Republican; christian; rec: travel (40+ countries), collect art and dolls internat. Res/Studio: 326 S Linda Ln Fresno 93727

STUDEMEISTER, PAUL ALEXANDER, geologist; b. Mar. 20, 1954, Caracas, Venez., naturalized U.S. 1966; s. Alexander Ernst and Marguerite (Preobrajensky) S.; edn: BA, UC Berkeley, 1977; PhD, Univ. of Western Ontario, London, Ont., Can. 1982; reg. geologist Calif. (RG4635, 1988), Ariz. (RG26152, 1992), lic. engring. geologist Calif. (CEG1746, 1993), OSHA Supvy. Cert. (29CF12 1910.120). Career: geology prof. Univ. of Ottawa, 1982-83; proj. geologist Dunraine Mines, Toronto, Ont. 1983-84; geology prof. Laurentian Univ., Sudbury, Ont. 1984-85; proj. geologist Agassie Resources, Toronto 1985; res. petrographer Construction Tech. Labs., Skokie, Ill. 1985-90; project geologist, pvt. consultant, Menlo Park 1990; proj. geologist Applied GeoSystems, Fremont, Calif. 1990; sr. geologist EVAX Technologies, Scotts Valley, Calif. 1990-93; proj, geologist AGS, Inc. San Francisco 1993-; mem. Assn. engring. Geologists, Groundwater Resources Assn. of Calif., Sierra Club; publs: 14+ articles, thesis: Distbn. of Gold and Copper Occurrences Around an Archean Granitic Stock Near Wawa, Ont. (1982); Conservative Republican; Lutheran; rec: swimming, travel, geol. mapping, exploration. Res: D-105, 2140 Santa Cruz Ave Menlo Park 94025 Ofc: AGS Inc. 160 Howard St Ste 600 San Francisco 94105

STUTMAN, HARRIS RONALD, pediatrician, educator; b. May 7, 1947, Phila.; s. Sydney and Sally (Press) S.; m. Eileen E. Letson, Apr. 18, 1971; children: Jessica b. 1974, Timothy b. 1978; edn: BA in polit. sci., Univ. Pa., 1968; MD, Penn. State Univ., 1972; MD lic. Pa. 1973, N.J. 1976, Okla. 1982, Calif. 1986; bd. certified Am. Bd. Pediatrics 1977, recert. 1987). Career: pediatric resident Univ. Pittsburgh, 1972-75; infectious disease fellow Univ. Okla., 1982-84; chief resident pediatrics, Childrens Hosp., Pittsburgh 1975-76; pvt. practice, coord. perinatal edn. Kimball Med. Ctr., Lakewood, N.J. 1976-82; attdg. physician Univ. Okla. and Okla. Childrens Hosp. 1984-86; pediatric faculty Univ. of Okla., 1984-86, Univ. Calif. Irvine, 1986-; assoc. dir. res. Miller Childrens Hosp., Long Beach 1986-87; dir. ped. inf. dis./assoc. dir. Cystic Fibrosis Ctr., 1987-; mem. UC Irvine Academic Senate 1986-, Human Subjects Review Com. 1987-90; awards: Mosby Award 1972, Central Okla. Pediatric Soc. Award 1983, So. Med. Assn. Found. Award 1984, Okla. Health Scis. Ctr. pediatrics award 1984, res. grants Nat. Inst. Allergy Inf. Disease, NIH 1987-93, res. grants Cystic Fibrosis Found. 1986-; Fellow Am. Acad. Pediatrics; mem. Am. Soc. for Microbiology, Infectious Disease Soc. of Am., Internat. Soc. for Human Mycology, W. Soc. for Ped. Res., Ped. Infectious Disease Soc., European Soc. for Clin. Microbiology, Mensa (exec. bd. 1985-86); publs: 19+ med. book chpts.

(1986-), 27+ jour. articles (1984-), 48+ res. papers (1983-); Democrat; Jewish; rec: photog., computer pgmg. Res: 5952 Langport Circle Huntington Beach 92649 Miller Childrens Hospital 2801 Atlantic Ave Long Beach 90801

STYLES, BEVERLY, musician/entertainer, non-profit organization executive; b. June 6, 1923, Richmond, Va.; d. John Harry Kenealy and Juanita Russell (Robins) Carpenter; m. Wilbur Cox, Mar. 14, 1942 (div.); m. Robert Marascia, Oct. 5, 1951 (div. 1964); edn: studies w/ Ike Carpenter, Hollywood 1965-, Am. Nat. Theatre Acad. 1968-69, w/ Paula Raymond, Hollywood 1969-70. Career: freelance performer, musician, 1947-81; owner Beverly Styles Music, Joshua Tree, Calif. 1971-; composer songs: Joshua Tree, 1975, I'm Thankful, 1978, Wow, Wow, Wow, 1986, records include: The Perpetual Styles of Beverly, 1978. Albums include: The Primitive Styles of Beverly, 1977, Colour Chords (And Moods), piano arrangement, 1990; mem: Internat. Platform Assn. 1993-94, ASCAP (Gold pin award), Am. Fedn. Musicians; civic: v.p. special programs "Lawrence Program" of Calif. (public benefit, non-profit corp. to assist in recovery from alc. and drug addiction thru a structured pgm.), Yucca Valley (1992-); Republican; rec: abstract artist. Ofc: PO Box 615 Joshua Tree CA 92252-0615 Tel:619/365-7473

SUD, HARJIT J., physician; b. Feb. 23, 1946, Punjab, India, nat. 1980; d. Jodh Singh and Gian Kour Sud; m. Thomas Streeter, Jan. 9, 1974; children: Monica b. 1975, Jody b. 1980, Ashley b. 1984; edn: MBBS, B.J. Med. Sch., India 1969. Career: intern, resident Ob-Gyn, Michael Reese Hosp., Chgo. 1970-74; staff physician Kaiser Permanente, Vallejo 1976-78; pvt. practice, Ob-Gyn., fertility, 1978-; bd. dirs. Alan Short Gallery Sunflower; mem: San Joaquin Med. Soc., Calif. Med. Assn., Planned Parenthood (dir.), Women's Centre (dir.); civic: Stockton Symphony (dir.); rec: skiing, cooking, sewing. Res: 7125 Uyeda Rd Stockton 95205 Ofc: 2509 W March Ln Stockton 95207

SULLIVAN, JEREMIAH SAWYER, company president, photographer, inventor; b. June 2, 1954, San Antonio, Tx.; s. Jeremiah Jack and Peggy Jean (Sawyer) S.; edn: AS, Grossmont Coll. 1975; BS marine biology, UCSD Ext. Scripps Instn. of Oceanography, 1979. Career: marine and natural history lectr. 1973-, internat. published photographer, 1974-; divemaster, lectr. M/V Lindblad Explorer 1973-79; pres. Neptunic Inc. 1983-; owner Sullivan Studio, San Diego 1984-; expedition leader, lectr., divemaster Raymond & Whitcomb N.Y.C. 1984-87; co-host Mutual of Omaha's TV show, Wild Kingdom, 1982-87; frequent guest on radio talk shows, TV documentaries; recipient numerous photography awards (1983-); mem: ASMP, East African Wildlife Soc. (life), Leakey Soc. (fellow), CAG, Screen Actors Guild; inventor shark suit (1981), patentee Neptunic shark suits; publs: numerous articles on shark behavior (1980-), test results and theories on anti-shark remedies (1980-); rec: outdoors. Address: San Diego 92107

SULLIVAN, PATRICK ALLEN, strategic management educator; b. Oct. 31, 1932, Peoria, Ill.; s. Francis Richard and Carmela Marie (Smith) S.; m. Gwendolyn Jo Herndon, Aug. 25, 1958; children: Richard b. 1953, Sharon b. 1957, Patrick b. 1960, Cecelia b. 1963, Catherine b. 1967; edn: BCE, Marquette Univ., 1955; MBA, CSU San Diego, 1975; DBA, U.S. Internat. Univ., 1987. Career: civil, gen. engr. (GS-12) US Marine Corps, Twentynine Palms, 1958-63; US Navy, San Diego, 1963-67, mgmt. analyst (GM-15), 1967-88; asst. prof., asso. prof. U.S. Internat. Univ., San Diego 1988-; honors: Chi Epsilon 1954, Tau Beta Pi 1955, Sigma Iota Epsilon 1975, Beta Gamma Sigma 1975; mem.: ASCE, Strategic Mgmt. Soc., Acad. of Mgmt., Planning Forum; mil: 1st lt. USMC 1955-58; Republican; R.Cath. Res: 98 E Emerson St Chula Vista 91911 Ofc: U.S.I.U., 10455 Pomerado Rd San Diego 92131

SUMMERS, FRANK GILBERT, JR., certified public accountant; b. June 4, 1928, Fresno; s. Frank G. and Vesta Marie (Straley) S.; m. Shirley Turner, Dec. 16, 1956; children: Janelle b. 1959, James b. 1962; edn: AA, Chaffey Coll., 1948; BS, UC Berkeley, 1950, MBA, 1954; C.P.A., Calif. 1954. Career: staff acct. Gerald R. Case, CPA, Pomona 1952-54; senior acct., then ptnr. Will A. Bowen, CPA, 1953-56, ptnr. Bowen, McBeth & Summers, CPAs, 1956-58; prin. Frank G. Summers, Jr., CPA, 1958-67; ptnr. Case, Summers & Hardy, CPAs, 1967-69; pres. Summers Acctncy. Corp. CPAs, 1970-; dir. Hank's Freight Svc. Inc., Fontana 1984-; gen. ptnr. Phicen Ltd. (shopping ctr.), Chino 1970-88; mem. Cal Poly Pomona acctg. curriculum advy. council (1976-); mem: Nat. Assn. of Accts. 1956-66, Calif. Soc. CPAs (mem. 1954-, dir. 1962-63, Citrus Belt Chpt. (mem. 1962-63), Am. Inst. CPAs 1954-; civic: Toastmasters Club #12 Pomona (pres. 1954-56), Pomona Jaycees (pres. 1958-59), Pomona C.of C. (dir. 1959-60, 86-88), Central Business Dist. Pomona Inc. (pres. 1986-88), commr. Pomona Budget Advy. Commn. 1972-74, chmn. Pomona Veh. Parking Dists. #1 and #3 (1978-89), spearhd. downtown Pomona revitalization, redesign of Pomona Pedestrian Mall and expanded parking 1977-; mil: midshipman USN (UCB) 1948-52; Republican; Baptist; rec: real estate, travel, golf, photog. Ofc: Summers Accountancy Corp., CPAs 10737 Laurel Ave Ste 110 Rancho Cucamonga 91730

SUN, HUGO SUI-HWAN, mathematics professor; b. Oct. 19, 1940, Hong Kong, naturalized U.S. cit. 1975. Career: Jun Tao and Sarah H.K. (Hu) S.; m. Nancy L. Feng, July 10, 1967 (div. Nov. 1988); children: Ester E. b. 1970, H. Isaac J. b. 1972, Hugette A. b. 1979; m. Ixin Wen, June 6, 1989; edn: att. Pui Ching Middle Sch. H.K. 1953-56; BA, UC Berkeley, 1963; MA, Univ. of Md., College Park 1966; PhD, Univ. New Brunswick, Fredericton, Can. 1969. Career: asst. prof. math. Univ. of New Brunswick, 1969-70; asst. prof. CSU Fresno, Calif. 1970-74, asso. prof. 1974-78, prof. math. 1978-; research prof. Academia Sinica, Taipei, China 1980, vis. prof. Peking Univ., Beijing 1987; awards: First award in anthology Fifth World Cong. of Poetry, S.F. 1981, Hon. consultant Academia Sinica, Hefei, China 1990-, Hon. prof. in Chinese Litt. Fuyang Normal Univ., Fuyang, China 1987-, Hon. prof. math. & computer sci. Anhui Univ., Hefei, China 1990-; mem.: Am. Math. Soc. 1970-, Internat. Platform Assn. 1992-; Republican; Prot.; rec: antique numismatics, philatelics. Res: 4949 N Winery Cr #106 Fresno 93726 Ofc: Dept. Mathematics, Calif. State University, Fresno 93740

SUND, MICHAEL WARREN, public relations practioner; b. Sept. 2, 1943, San Diego; s. Warren LeRoy and Patricia (Connors) S.; m. Maureen Ellin Murphy, Apr. 7, 1973; children: Gretchen b. 1980, Gregory b. 1983; edn: AB journ., San Diego State Univ., 1966; MS journ., Northwestern Univ., 1967; Accredited pub. relations practitioner (APR) Pub. Relations Soc. Am., 1984. Career: reporter San Diego Tribune, 1967-69; dist. staff mgr Pacific Bell, San Diego, San Francisco, 1969-80; exec. v.p./prin. The Gable Agency, San Diego 1980-84; dir. pub. rels. Joan B. Kroc Found., San Diego 1984-86; pres./owner Mike Sund Pub. Relations, Rancho Santa Fe 1986-92; dir. corp. comms. Mycogen Corp, 1993-; lectr. UC San Diego Ext., 1984-87; clubs: Century S.D. (assoc.), Rancho Santa Fe Golf; civic bds: Comb. Health Agys. Drive San Diego (dir. 1991-), Pub. Interest Commn. Rancho Santa Fe (commr. 1991-), Roads & Traffic Commn. Rancho Santa Fe (commr. 1990-); mil: capt. USMCR 1968-72; Republican; R.Cath.; rec: golf, gardening. Ofc: Mycogen Corp 4980 Carroll Canyon Rd San Diego 92121

SUSMAN, ALLEN E., lawyer; b. Feb. 12, 1919, Chelsea, Mass.; s. Hyman Susman and Frances Heifetz; m. Dorothea; (div.); m. Tracy; (div.); children: Kenneth b. 1948, Laura b. 1949, Teresa b. 1952, Priscilla b. 1956; edn: BA, Harvard Coll., Cambridge, Mass., 1940; JD, Harvard Law Sch., Cambridge, Mass., 1943-46. Career: capt., USAF, 1942-46; assoc., Loeb & Loeb, L.A. Calif. 1947-50; partner, Loeb & Loeb, L.A. 1950-57; partner, Rosenfeld, Meyer & Susman, Beverly Hills 1957-; adj. prof. of law, Southwestern Univ., L.A. 1947-50; awards: named One of Best Lawyers in America 1988-, Lawyer of the Year, Beverly Hills Bar Assn. 1989; mem: ABA 1947-, Am. Bar Found. (fellow 1986-), Am. Judicature Soc. (20 yrs.), L.A. Bar Assn., Beverly Hills Bar Assn., numerous civic organizations; mil: capt., USAF, 1942-46; Independent. Res: 115 Ketch Mall Marina Del Rey 90292. Ofc: Rosenfeld, Meyer & Susman 9601 Wilshire Blvd. Beverly Hills 90210

SUTTERBY, LARRY QUENTIN, physician; b. Sept. 11, 1950, North Kansas City, Mo.; s. John Albert and Wilma Elizabeth (Henry) S.; m. Luciana Risos Magpuri, July 5, 1980; children: Leah b. 1981, Liza b. 1983; edn: BA, William Jewell Coll., Liberty, Mo. 1972; MD, Univ. Missouri, K.C., Mo. 1976; certified (ABIM) Am. Bd. Internal Medicine, 1991. Career: internal medicine resident Mt. Sinai Hosp., Chgo. 1979; physician Mojave Desert Health Service, Barstow, Calif. 1979-86; physician-internist solo practice, 1986-; medical director Hospice of Mojave Valley, 1984-, Rimrock Conv. Hosp., 1986-89; staff Barstow Comm. Hosp. (chief of staff 1983); recipient Loving Care award Visiting Nurse Assn., San Bdo. Co. 1988; mem: Soc. Gen. Internal Medicine 1990-, AMA 1980-, Calif. Med. Assn. 1980-, San Bdo. County Med. Assn. 1980-, Am. Soc. Internal Medicine 1989-, Nat. Assn. of Physicians Who Care, Acad. of Hospice Physicians (founding), Am. Geriatrics Soc. 1990-, Am. Numismatic Assn.; Democrat; R.Cath.; rec: astronomy, Error Lincoln cents. Ofc: 209 N 2nd Ave Barstow 92311

SVEC, RICHARD S., insurance and surety broker; b. Oct. 16, 1942, Los Angeles; s. Stanley F. and Dorothy (Whaley) S.; m. Barbara Ann Gerzin, Sept. 24, 1966; 1 son, David b. 1971; edn: BA, St. Mary's Coll., Moraga 1964. Career: underwriting trainee Fireman's Fund Ins., San Francisco 1965-67, sales rep. L.A. office, 1967-69, surety mgr., San Jose office, 1969-77; v.p. Alexander & Alexander, San Jose 1977-85, senior v.p. 1987-; awards: Summit Club Alexander & Alexander 1987-92; mem.: Assoc. General Contractors (1977-, Sacto. chpt. bd. 1991, chmn. constrn. awareness pgm. 1984-86, mktg. com. 1989-90), Nat. Assn. Surety Bond Producers 1985-, Constrn. Fin. Mgrs. Assn. 1988-; civic: Almaden Valley Youth Sports Assn., S.J. (bd. 1969-75); contbr. articles in constrn. trade jours. (1984-); mil: USCG Res. 1964-70; Republican; R.Cath.; rec: tennis, golf, water skiing. Res: 7007 Quail Cliff Way San Jose 95120

SWARD, ROBERT STUART, author, poet, academic writer-in-residence; b. June 23, 1933, Chgo.; s. Dr. Irving Michael and Gertrude (Huebsch) S.;m. Sonnie Cox, Jan. 31,1956 (div. 1958); children: Cheryl b. 1957. m. Diane Kaldes, Feb. 26, 1960 (div. 1967); children: Barbara b. 1960, Michael b. 1963; m. Judith Essenson, Mar. 21, 1969 (div. 1972); children: Hannah b. 1970; m. Irina Schestakowich, Aug. 28, 1975 (div. 1987); children: Nicholas b. 1978; edn: BA (hons.), Univ. Ill., Urbana 1956; MA, Univ. Iowa, 1958; postgrad. Univ. of Bristol, Eng. 1960-61, Middlebury Coll., Vt. 1958-62. Career: writer-in-residence Connecticut Coll., New London, Conn. 1958-60, Cornell Univ., Ithaca, N.Y. 1962-64, Univ. of Iowa, Iowa City 1967-68, Univ. of Victoria,

B.C., Canada 1969-73, Cabrillo Coll., Aptos, Calif. 1987-, Univ. Calif. Ext., Santa Cruz 1987-; poet-in-residence Univ. Calif. Santa Cruz 1991-; radio bdcstr. Canad. Bdcstg. Corp., Toronto 1982-84; editor, pub. Soft Press, Victoria, Can. 1970-79; assoc. fellow York Univ., Toronto 1984-; awards: Guggenheim Found. fellow, N.Y. 1964-66, D.H. Lawrence fellow, Univ. N.M. 1966-67, Fulbright fellow, W.D.C. 1960-61, Canada Council grantee 1981-82, Villa Montalvo Award, Saratoga, Calif. 1990; mem: Nat. Writers Union 1985-, Modern Poetry Assn. 1992-, Phi Beta Kappa 1956-, League of Canadian Poets 1970-, Calif. St. Teachers Assn. 1987-; civic: creative writing instr. Oak Bay Sr. Citizens, Victoria, B.C., Can. (1970s), Poet In the Schools Pgm., Cultural Council of Santa Cruz Co. 1985-; author fiction, poetry, 16 books incl: Four Incarnations, Poems (1991), Poet Santa Cruz (1985), Half A Life's History (1983), Kissing The Dancer (1964); mil: Y3c US Navy 1951-54; Democrat; rec: photog. Res: 435 Meder St Santa Cruz Ofc: PO Box 7062 Santa Cruz 95061

SWARTZ, ALLAN JOEL, pharmacist, hospital administrator, educator; b. July 2, 1935, Phila.; s. Milton and Rosalie S.; m. Roslyn Thelma Holt, June 2, 1963; edn: PharmD, USC, 1958; Loyola Univ. Sch. of Law, L.A. 1964-66; MA edn. Pepperdine Univ., 1976. Career: asst. dir. pharmacy City of Hope Nat. Medical Ctr., Duarte 1966-69, dir. pharm. svs. 1969-78; dir. pharmacy svs. Encino Hosp., 1978-, quality assurance coord. 1986-, hazardous materials officer 1986-, risk and safety mgr. 1987-, dir. of quality mgmt., 1991-; chmn. bd. Visiting Nurse Home Services Inc., L.A. 1986-; asst. clin. prof. pharmacy USC, 1971-82, 87-; asst. clin. prof. Univ. of Pacific, 1978-86, reg. coord. externship pgm. 1982-86; chmn. pharm. group purch. com. Hosp. Council So. Calif. 1978-82, mem. profl. edn. com. Am. Cancer Soc. 1970-78, bd. dirs. H.O.P.E. Unit Found. 1980-83, bd. dirs. Vis. Nurse Assn., L.A. 1983-; Founder L.A. Co. Music Ctr.; awards: Order of Golden Sword Calif. div. Am. Cancer Soc. 1974, recogn. awards USC Comprehensive Cancer Ctr. (1978, 83); mem: AAAS, Am. Med. Writers Assn., Am. Soc. Hosp. Pharmacists (commendn. 1976), Calif. Soc. Hosp. Pharmacists (pres. 1976), QSAD Centurions, Rho Pi Phi; mil: Med. Corps AUS 1958-59; publs: editorial bd. Cancer Nursing (1983-, feature ed. pharmaceutics 1977-81), cons. ed. Am. Jour. Hosp. Pharmacy 1978-83. Res: 1353 Comstock Ave Los Angeles 90024 Ofc: 16237 Ventura Blvd Encino 91436

SWARTZLANDER, EARL EUGENE, JR., engineering educator; b. Feb. 1, 1945, San Antonio, TX; s. Earl Eugene and Jane (Nicholas) S.; m. Joan Vickery, June 9, 1968; edn: BS, Purdue Univ., 1967; MS, Univ. of Colo., 1969; PhD, USC, 1972; reg. profl. engr. in Ala., Calif., Colo. and Texas. Career: devel. engr. Ball Bros. Research Corp., Boulder, CO 1967-69; Howard Hughes doctoral fellow Hughes Aircraft Co., Culver City, CA 1969-73; mem. research staff Technology Svc. Corp., Santa Monica 1973-74; chief engr. Geophysical Sys. Corp., Pasadena 1974-75; sr. staff engr. TRW Defense & Space Sys. Gp., Redondo Beach 1975-79; asst. mgr. TRW Huntsville Lab., Huntsville, AL 1980-81; mgr. advanced devel. TRW Defense Systems Group, Redondo Bch. 1982-85; mgr. digital processing lab. TRW Electronic Systems Gp., Redondo Beach 1985-87, dir. IR&D TRW Defense Systems Group, 1987-90; prof. electrical and computer engring. Univ. of Texas, Austin 1990-; speaker univ. seminars at UCLA, Univ. Md., American Univ., Univ. Mich., Auburn Univ., Univ. Minn., George Mason Univ., others 1978-; awards: Howard Hughes doctoral fellow 1969-72, Best Paper award Hawaii conf. on sys. sci. 1983, Tech. Paper award Internat. Systolic Arrays Workshop, Oxford 1986, Purdue Univ. disting. engring. alumnus 1989, Schlumberger Centennial Chair in Engring. 1990-, Louisiana Disting. Lectr. 1991, Purdue Univ. outstanding electrical engr. 1992; Fellow IEEE 1988, mem. IEEE Computer Soc. (bd. of govs. 1987-91), IEEE Signal Proc. Soc. (ADCOM 1992-94); civic: Casiano Estates (dir. 1976-79, pres. 1979-80), Benedict Hills Homeowners Assn. (dir. 1984-, pres. 1991-); author: VLSI Signal Processing Systems (Kluwer Academic Pub. 1985); 100+ papers on signal processing, computer architecture and VLSI; editor-in-chief: J. of VLSI Signal Processing 1989-, IEEE Transactions on Computers 1991-, ed. IEEE Transactions on Computers 1982-86, IEEE Transactions on Parallel and Distributed Systems 1989-90, assoc. ed. IEEE J. of Solid-State Circuits 1984-88, area ed. ACM Computing Reviews 1982-; book editor: Computer Design Development, (Hayden Book Co. 1976), Computer Arithmetic (Hutchinson Ross Pub. Co. 1980), Systolic Signal Processing Systems (Marcel Dekker Inc. 1987), Wafer Scale Integration (Kluwer Academic Pub. 1989), Computer Arithmetic Vol. 1 and Vol. 2 (IEEE Computer Soc. Press, 1990). Ofc: Univ. Texas Dept. Electrical & Computer Engineering, Austin TX 78712

SWEENEY, W(ILLIAM) ALAN, research scientist; b. Sept. 12, 1926, Ocean Falls, B.C., Canada, naturalized U.S. cit., 1958; s. William Patrick and Florence Harriet (Lewthwaite) S.; m. Sally Grant, Apr. 11, 1953; children: Michael A. b. 1954, Peter G. b. 1955, Alison E. b. 1959; edn: B.A.Sc. chem. eng., Univ. British Columbia, Vancouver B.C., 1949; PhD. org. chem., Univ. Washington, Seattle, 1954; 5 ext. courses UC Berkeley 1967-71, also 30+ short courses - human rels., mgmt., personal skills. Career: devel. chemist Canadian Industries Ltd., Toronto, Ontario, Can., 1949-50; res. chemist to res. scientist Chevron Research & Technology Co., Richmond, Calif. 1954-90, mgmt. positions 1964, 75, 84, 86; cons. (internal) Chevron Res. & Tech. Co., 1976-90; cons. Teltech Inc., Mpls., Mn. 1990; cons. D.O.E., Idaho Falls, Id. 1990; awards: scholar Univ. of Brit. Col. (1944, 45), Procter & Gamble fellow Univ. Wash. 1952, Phi Lambda Upsilon

1953, Sigma Xi 1954; mem: Am. Chemical Soc. 1951-, N.Y. Acad. of Scis. 1970-, Chevron Employee Clubs; civic: HOA, Larkspur (pres., bd. 1979-82), United Way - Chevron (chmn., dept. ldr. 72, 73, 86), Marin Co. Canoe Club, PTA; inventor, 100+ Patents in petrochemical area (1961-90); publs: 5 tech. papers on biodegradability (1964-89), Kirk-Othmer Review article on BTX (1991), 9 papers on academic & petrochem. resrch. (1954-69), newsletter articles on technology & org. behavior (1989-90); mil: Canadian OTC 1944-45; Republican; rec: tennis, bridge, travel, boating, hiking. Res: 27 Corte Del Bayo, Larkspur 94939

SWENSON, BARBARA JOAN, tax preparer; b. Nov. 14, 1931, Huntington Park, Calif.; d. Daniel Carlton Storrs and Dorothy Elizabeth (Cryan) Verrett; m. Darrell Leroy Swenson (div.); children: Christine b. 1948, Carol b. 1950, Billie b. 1955, Delilah b. 1958, Lincoln b. 1961; edn: Highlands Univ. 1958; Coll. of Desert 1962-63. Career: tax preparer, bookkeeper, Cathedral City 1969-93; enrolled agent I.R.S., 1985-; dance instr., 1979-93; mem: Inland Soc. Tax Cons. (pres. 1984-85); Republican; Religious Scientist; rec: round dancing, square dancing. Ofc: Barbara Swenson E.A. 36770 Cathedral Canyon Dr Ste 17 Cathedral City 92234

SZEGO, CLARA MARIAN, cell biologist, educator; b. Mar. 23, 1916, Budapest, Hungary, naturalized U.S. 1927; d. Paul S. and Helen (Elek) S.; m. Sidney Roberts, Sept. 14, 1943; edn: AB, Hunter Coll., 1937; MS (Garvan fellow) Univ. Minn., 1939, PhD, 1942. Career: instr. physiology Univ. Minn. 1942-43; Minn. Cancer Rsch. Inst. fellow 1943-44; rsch. assoc. OSRD, Nat. Bur. Stds. 1944-45, Worcester Found. Exptl. Biology 1945-47; res. instr. physiol. chemistry Yale Univ. Sch. Medicine 1947-48; faculty UC Los Angeles, 1948-, prof. biology, 1960-, res. on steroid protein interactions, mechanisms of hormone action and lysosome participation in normal cell function; awards: Woman of Year in Sci. Los Angeles Times 1957-58, Guggenheim fellow 1956-57, inducted Hunter Coll. Hall of Fame 1987, CIBA award Endocrine Soc. 1953, Phi Beta Kappa (pres. UCLA chpt. 1973-74), Sigma Xi (pres. UCLA chpt. 1976-77); mem.: AAAS (Fellow), Am. Physiol. Soc., Am. Soc. Cell Biology, Endocrine Soc., Am. Soc. for Endocrinology (G.B.), Biochem. Soc. (G.B.), Internat. Soc. Research Reprodn.; numerous sci. publs. in field. Res: 1371 Marinette Rd Pacific Palisades 90272 Ofc: UCLA Dept. Biology, Los Angeles 90024-1606

TAAM, BRENDA JOY, promotion manager, b. May 8, 1965, San Francisco; d. Calvin and Valerie (Ng) Taam; edn.: BS, bus. adminstrn., UC Berkeley, 1987; career: res. asst., Geer DuBois Advt., NY, 1987-88; assoc. proj. mgr., BASES, San Ramon, 1988-90; asst. prod. mgr. Nestle Beverage Co., S.F., 1990-91; asst. marketing inf. mgr., Nestle Beverage Co., S.F., 1991-92; promotion mgr., Nestle Beverage Co., S.F., 1993-; Presbyterian; rec.: cycling, teaching children, jazz dancing; ofc: Nestle Beverage Co. 345 Spear St. San Francisco 94105

TAFT, BRADFORD HOWE, outplacement company executive; b. May 17, 1952, Columbus, Ohio; s. Jackson Howe and Marcelle (Perkins) T.; m. Pamela Ann Haney, Dec. 3, 1988; edn: BA, USC 1974; MBA, 1976. Career: assoc. Korn Ferry Internat., LA 1976-78; treasury assoc. Global Marine Inc. 1978-79; pres. Taft & Assoc. 1979-80; sr. assoc. N.W. Gibson Internat. 1980-81; v.p. Univance 1981-85; pres. Career Transition Group 1985-90; v.p. Lee Hecht Harrison Inc. 1990-; guest lectr. UCLA 1987-; mem: Employment Mgmt. Assn. (bd. dirs.), Employment Mgmt. Assn. (outplacement affiliate group chmn.), Personnel & Industrial Relations Assn. (profl. devel. com.), USC Commerce Associates (bd.); Republican. Ofc: 3415 S Sepulveda Blvd Ste 1100 Los Angeles 90034

TAGGART, SONDRA, certified financial planner; b. July 22, 1934, N.Y.C.; d. Louis and Rose (Birnbaum) Hamov; children: Eric Hofer b. 1961, Karen Hofer b. 1965; edn: BA, Hunter Coll., 1955; C.F.P.; reg. prin. NASD. Career: cert. fin. planner The Taggart Group, Beverly Hills, pres. The Taggart Co. Ltd., 1981-. Ofc: The Taggart Group 9720 Wilshire Blvd Ste 205 Beverly Hills 90212

TAIMUTY, SAMUEL ISAAC, physicist; b. Dec. 20, 1917, West Newton, Pa.; s. Elias and Samia (Hawatt) T.; m. Betty Jo Travis, Sept. 12, 1953 (dec.); children: Matthew, Martha; m. Rosalie Richards, Apr. 3, 1976; edn: BS, Carnegie Mellon Univ., 1940; PhD, USC, 1951. Career: sr. physicist U.S. Naval Shipyards, Philadelphia, Pa. and Long Beach, Calif. 1942-46; research asst. USC, 1947-51; sr. physicist U.S. Naval Radiological Defense Lab., 1950-52, SRI Internat., Menlo Park 1952-72; sr. staff engr. Lockheed Missiles & Space Co., Sunnyvale 1972-89; cons. physicist 1971-; mem. Am. Physical Soc., Sigma Xi; patentee, sci. publs. in field; Episcopalian. Res: 3346 Kenneth Dr Palo Alto 94303

TAKAHASHI, BEN KIYOSHI, lawyer; b. Oct. 17, 1921, Tokyo, Japan; s. Naosaku and Yukino (Mizushina) T.; m. Tomiko Arai; children: Robert b. 1947, Eugene b. 1952, Sophie Fung b. 1955; edn: B.Law, Tokyo Imperial Univ. Law Sch. 1944; JD, Southwestern Univ. Law Sch. 1965; admitted bar: Calif., U.S. Supreme Ct. Career: Foreign Ofc. of Japan, Tokyo 1945; dir. Airinkai Meguro Wakabaryu (Orphanage) 1947; law practice, Calif. 1967-; pres. Assn. of Immigration & Nationality Lawyers, L.A. chpt. 1973-74; legal cousel Consulate General of Japan, Los Angeles 1976-; mem. Calif. Bar Assn.; Democrat; rec: golf, photography. Res: 14976 El Soneto Dr Whittier 90605 Ofc: 420 E Third St Ste 1012 Los Angeles 90013

TALLEY, WILSON K., foundation executive, professor emeritus; b. Jan. 27, 1935, St. Louis, Mo.; s. Samuel K. and Isabella G. (McCurtain) T.; m. Helen, July 1, 1981; children: Steve b. 1962, Elaine b. 1964, Edward b. 1965, (stepdau.) Donna b. 1959; edn: BA, UC Berkeley, 1956; MS, Univ. Chgo., 1957; PhD, UC Berkeley, 1963. Career: asst. prof, prof. Dept. Applied Sci. UC Davis 1963-91, prof. emeritus 1991-; White House Fellow 1969-70; hd. theoretical physics div. Lawrence Livermore Nat. Lab. 1971; asst. v.p. Univ. of Calif. statewide, 1971-74; dir., pres. Fannie and John Hertz Found. 1972-; study dir. Commn. on Critical Choices for Americans, N.Y.C. 1974; asst. adminstr. for resrch. USEPA, Wash. D.C. 1974-77; dir. Helionetics Inc. 1982-86; tech. advy. bds.: Johnson Controls 1981-, Phoenix Laser Systems Inc. 1989-; awards: disting. pub. adminstr. Denver Univ. 1976, outstanding civilian svc. medal AUS 1986; mem: Army Sci. Bd. (chmn. 1983-86), Army Medical Research Advy. Bd. 1989-; clubs: Commonwealth, Capitol Hill, Castlewood Country Club; patentee; author 2 books, 36+ research papers; Republican. Ofc: Hertz Foundation, Box 5032 Livermore 94551-5032

TALLMAN, JOHANNA E., university library director, ret.; b. Aug. 18, 1914, Lubeck, Germany; d. Friedrich Franz and Johanna (Voget) Allerding; m. Lloyd Anthony Tallman, May 8, 1954; edn: AB, Univ. of Calif. 1936, cert. in Librarianship, 1937. Career: San Marino Pub. Library, 1937-38; L.A. County Pub. Library, 1938-42; Pacific Aeronautical Library, 1942-44; hd. Engineering and Math. Scis. Library, UCLA, 1945-73; lib. dir. Calif. Inst. of Tech., 1973-81; lectr. UCLA Sch. of Library Service, 1961-73; Fullbright lectr., Brazil 1966-67; mem: Librarians Assn. Univ. Calif. (pres. 1970-71), Spl. Libraries Assn. (chair Sci.-Tech. Div. 1969-70, pres. So. Calif. chpt. 1965-66), L.A. Regional Group of Catalogers (chair 1946-47), Pasadena Hist. Soc. (trustee), Zonta Internat. (pres. Pasadena chpt. 1976-77), Fine Arts Club of Pasadena (pres. 1982-84); author: Check Out a Librarian, Scarecrow Press, 1985; contbr. 61+ profl. jours. Res: 4731 Daleridge Rd La Canada Flintridge 91011

TAMAROFF, MARC ALLEN, physician; b. May 22, 1948, Phoenix, Ariz.; s. Sam Al and June Ann T.; m. Sybil Abelsky, Nov. 26, 1978; children: David, b. 1980; Rachael, b. 1986; edn: BS, Univ. of Ariz. 1970, MD, 1974. Career: intern St. Mary Med. Ctr., Long Beach 1974; resident internal med. 1975-7; post-doc. fellow Div. of Clin. Immunology & Allergy, UCLA Med. Ctr. 1977-79; pvt. practice, Allergy 1979-; assoc. dir. for Pgm. Developments, Ctr. for Interdisciplinary Research in Immunologic Diseases (CIRID) UCLA 1979-86; assoc. dir. of Skin Test Svc. and spl. cons. Div. of Clin. Immunol. & Allergy UCLA Med. Ctr. 1979-80; chmn. med. edn. com.Los Altos Hosp., Long Beach 1980-84; chmn. pharmacy & therapeutics com. St. Mary Med. Ctr., Long Beach 1988-91; asst. clin. prof. medicine UC Irvine 1982-85, UCLA 1985-; awards: Phi Kappa Phi 1970, AMA Physician Recognition 1977, Calif. Med. Assn. 1979; Nat. Research Svc. Award, NIH-PHS 1977-79; mem: Am. Coll. of Chest Physicians, Am. Coll. of Allergists, Los Angeles Soc. of Allergy and Clin. Immunology (exec. Council 1990-, pres. 1993), Long Beach Soc. of Internal Medicine (pres. 1990-92), Immunology Research Group. UCLA Sch. Med., Am. Lung Assn., Asthma & Allergy Found. of Am., Am. Acad. of Allergy, Am. Assn. of Clin. Immunol. & Allergy; pub. med. research; Democrat; Jewish; rec: tennis, softball. Res: 18171 Ivorycrest Ln Huntington Beach 92648 Ofc: Allergy & Asthma Care Center, 3325 Palo Verde Ste 107 Long Beach 90808

TANAKA, JEANNIE E., lawyer; b. Jan. 21, 1942; d. Togo W. and Jean M. Tanaka; edn: BA, Internat. Christian Univ., Tokyo 1966; MSW, UCLA, 1968; JD, Washington Coll. of Law, American Univ., W.D.C., 1984. Career: atty., assoc. Seki & Jarvis, Los Angeles 1984-86; Jones, Day et al 1986-87; Reavis & McGrath 1987-89; asst. counsel Union Oil Co., L.A. 1989-91; legal counsel pvt. practice, 1992-; instr. Aoyama Gakuin; Meiji Gakuin; Sophia Univ.; Tokyo, Japan 1968-75; instr. Honda, Mitsubishi, Ricoh Corps., Tokyo 1975-80; mem: L.A. County Bar Assn., Japanese Am. Bar Assn., Women Lawyers Assn. L.A., ABA, Calif. Bar Assn., D.C. Bar Assn.; civic: Japan America Soc.; Methodist. Ofc: 100 S Doheny Dr Ste 322 Los Angeles 90048

TANAKA, TOGO WILLIAM, financial executive; b. Jan 7, 1916, Portland, Oreg.; s. Masaharu and Katsu T.; m. Jean Wada, Nov. 14, 1940; children: Jeannine b. 1942, Christine b. 1944, Wesley b. 1950; edn: BA in pol. sci., UC Los Angeles 1936; grad. studies Univ. Chgo. 1944; Career: editor Calif. Daily News 1935-36; L.A. Japanese Daily News 1936-42; Manzanar Relocation Center, Apr.-Dec. 1942; staff Am. Friends Service Com., Chgo. 1943-45; ed./hd. publs. Am. Tech. Soc. (Chgo.) 1945-50; pub. Chicago Publishing Corp. 1950-55; editor American School News, 1949-68; publisher School-Industrial Press, Los Angeles 1955-68; pres./CEO Gramercy Ents., Los Angeles 1960-80, bd. chmn. 1980-; chmn. T.W. Tanaka Co. 1980-; dir: Fed. Reserve Bank of S.F. 1979-88, Los Angeles Wholesale Produce Market Devel. Corp.; advy. council Calif. World Trade Commn. 1985-87; former commnr. Los Angeles Community Redevel. Agy.; honors: Phi Beta Kappa, Pi Gamma Mu, Pi Sigma Alpha, merit award Soc. for Advancement of Mgmt. 1950, 1st award Internat. Council Indsl. Editors 1955, UNESCO Literacy Award 1974, L.A. Catholic Archbishop ecumenical award 1986; civic: Los Angeles Area C.of C. (past dir.), Methodist Hosp. of So. Calif. (bd. dirs.1978-93), L.A. chpt. Nat. Safety Council, Am. Red Cross, Goodwill Industries of So. Calif. (past dir.), L.A. Visitors and Conv. Bur.,

Wellness Community -Nat., Nat. Strategy Information Ctr. (N.Y.); trustee Whittier Coll.; Commn. on Innovation, Calif. Community Colls., Western Justice Ctr. Found.; clubs: Los Angeles Rotary No. 5 (past pres., dir.), Lincoln, Shriners, Beverly Hills Lodge, Masons; co-author w/ Frank Kern Levin, English Composition & Rhetoric 1948, w/ Dr. Jean Bordeaux, How To Talk More Effectively 1948, w/ Alma Meland, Easy Pathways in English 1950; Republican; United Methodist; rec: gardening, world travel; Res: 949 Malcolm Ave Los Angeles 90024 Ofc: 1912 S Benecia Los Angeles 90025

TANIS, NORMAN EARL, dean of university libraries; b. Aug. 15, 1929, Grand Rapids, Mich.; s. Aaron Orrie and Gertrude (Medendorp) T.; m. Terese Tiernan, Dec. 27, 1981; children: Kathy, b. 1962; Laura, b. 1964; edn: AB, Calvin Coll. 1951; AMLS, Univ. of Mich. 1951; MA, 1956. Career: library coord. Henry Ford Comm. Coll., Dearborn, Mich. 1956-66; library dir. Kans. State Univ., Pittsburg 1966-9; dir. univ. libs. CSU Northridge 1969-88, dean of university libraries 1988-91; editor/mgr. The Santa Susana Press 1973-; secty. and mem. bd. trustees Univ. San Fernando Coll. of Law 1978-80; v.p./bd. mem. Univ. Club 1988-89; honors: Phi Kappa Phi, Beta Phi Mu, and DHL (hon.) Univ. San Fernando 1975, LLD (hon.) Mid-Valley Coll. Law 1979, Kts. of Col. 1991, Knight Cmdr. Order of the Templars 1989, Ordo Sancti Constantini Magni 1991, dist. alumnus Univ. Mich. Sch. of Information & Libr. Sci. (3/28/89), Nat. Libr. Assn. (pres. 1980), Assn. of Calif. & Res. Libraries (pres. 1973-74); mem: Book Club of Calif., Publishers Mktg. Assn., Pacific Ctr. for the Book Arts, COSMEP, Am. Film Inst., Nat. Trust for Preservation, Marine Memorial Club of San Francisco 1976-, Rounce & Coffin Club 1978-, China Inst. (Northridge) 1988-; ed. of the series: People of Achievement in So. Calif.; author books: Cost Analysis of Libr. Functions (Jai Press 1978), Fiscal & Acquisition (Santa Susana Press 1977), Implications of the Tax Reform Act of 1969 (Santa Susana Press 1969), The Faculty Speaks (Kansas State College 1968), Three Hundred Million Books (Tamalpais Press 1974), Libr. Svcs. for Kansas State Coll. (Kansas State Coll. 1968), Lynton R. Kistler: Printer-Lithographer (Santa Susana Press 1976), The Twilight of Orthodoxy in New England (Santa Susana Press 1987); coauthor: Native Americans of North America (Scarecrow Press 1975), Problems in Developing Academic Library Functions (Jai Press 1978), China in Books (Jai Press 1979); mil: cpl. US Army 1952-4, Nat. Defense Medal.; Democrat; Cath.; rec: theatre, travel, swap meets, horsemanship, art collector. Res: 10009 Jovita Chatsworth 91311 Ofc: Calif. State University 18111 Nordhoff Northridge 91330

TANNER, LYNN, actress; b. Mar. 22, 1953, N.Y.C.; d. Harry J. and Barbara Sylvia (Hirschman) Maurer; m. Allen Barry Witz, Aug. 31, 1975; edn: BS, New York Univ., 1975; JD, DePaul Univ., 1980; admitted bar: Ill., 1980. Career: actress, 1975-, appeared in (film) Human Error, 1987, Another Time, Another Place, 1988, (theatre) Pack of Lies, Back at the Blue Dolphin Saloon; mem. Screen Actors Guild, AFTRA, Actors Equity Assn., Women in Film, Women in Theater, Friends and Artists Theatre Ensemble.

TAPPAN, JANICE VOGEL, animal behavior researcher, traditional fiddler; b. Mar. 13, 1948, Pasadena; d. Robert Samuel and Etta Lillian (Berry) Vogel; m. David Stanton Tappan IV, Dec. 20, 1970; children: Stacey b. 1973, Christina b. 1975, Daniel b. 1978; edn: Oberlin Coll. 1966-68, BA in anthropology, UC Berkeley, 1970. Career: research asst. Los Angeles Zoo, 1982-; owner Fiddlers Crossing, Pasadena 1989-; judge Scottish Fiddling Revival, Virginia Beach, Va. 1989-; awards: folklore grantee Calif. Arts Council 1989-90, Phi Beta Kappa 1970; mem: Scottish Fiddling Revival (v.p. 1986-), Scottish Fiddlers of Calif. (v.p. 1986-), Calif. Traditional Music Soc. (devel. dir. 1990-), Scottish Fiddlers of Los Angeles (music dir. 1990-), Am. Assn. Zoological Parks & Aquariums 1978-; Democrat; Quaker; rec: Scottish traditional fiddling. Res: 1938 Rose Villa St Pasadena 91107 Ofc: L.A. Zoo 5333 Zoo Dr Los Angeles 90027

TARADASH, ROSLYN, electrical supplies distributor; b. Feb. 18, 1927, Chgo.; d. Maurice Charles and Florence (Blumenthal) T.; m. Elmer Finkel, Dec. 4, 1949 (div.); children: Cathy (Beth) b. 1952; edn: BA, Univ. Miami, 1948; lic. R.E. sales, Calif. 1958. Career: R.E. sales agt., Beverly Hills 1958-, assoc. Mike Silverman, 1960, Mary Robertson & Assocs. 1970; v.p. Hyland Elec. Supply Co., 1965-80, pres./bd. chmn. 1980-81; pres. Tara Electric, Chgo. 1981-; initiated successful annexation by City of Beverly Hills (2d largest in B.H.) of so. boundary homesites divided between the Cities of L.A. and B.H. (1975-79), enabling homes to be solely within B.H.; estab. trust fund for diagnostic test and res. in genetically acquired affective illness (1986); involved in affective illness res., nat.; subject of feature article Chicago Tribune Bus. Section (1980); civic: Affective Illness Research, funds res. for manic-depression (founder, pres. 1989), Waif; club: Indian Wells Country, Carlton Club (Chgo.); mem. Internat. Platform Com., Intl. Biog. Ctr., listed: 2,000 Am. Notable Women, and World Who's Who of Women; Jewish; rec: golf, swimming.

TARI, MEL, religious organization executive, evangelist, author; b. March 18, 1946, Indonesia; nat. 1979; s. Jacob and Theresia (Bees) T.; m. Joyce Purdy, June 21, 1986; children: David Joseph b. 1987, Michael Jacob b. 1990, Joshua John b. 1993; edn: Sekolah Dasar #1, SOE Timor, Indonesia 1952-58; SMP Negeri, 1958-61; SMA Negeri, Kupang Timor Indonesia 1961-64. Career: minister, evangelist, missionary, travel internat. 500,000+ miles yearly for var. Christian orgns.; participate num. confs. incl. World Council of Chs. World Conf. Nairobi (1975), Internat. Conf. for Itinerant Evangelist, sponsored by Dr. Billy Graham, Amsterdam (1986); corp. secty./exec. v.p./dir. All Seasons Resort Inc. 1986-; pres. Christ Ambassadors Fellowship of Indonesia 1965-, founder/pres. Mel Tari Evangelistic Assn., 1976-; mem. Full Gospel Businessmens Fellowship Internat.; author 4 books: Like A Mighty Wind, The Gentle Breeze of Jesus, Am., Jesus is Here, and The Kingdom; Republican (Presdl. Task Force); Christian; rec: collect Bibles in var. languages. Ofc: All Seasons Resort PO Box 3355 Dana Point 92629

TARTER, BLODWEN, brokerage marketing, strategic planning and information technology executive; b. Dec. 2, 1954, Sacto.; d. Bill and Blodwen Edwards (Coburn) T.; m. Alan May; edn: BA, MA, Stanford Univ., 1976; MBA, Univ. Chicago, 1978; PhD, Golden Gate Univ., 1991; lic NASD Series 7, Series 63. Career: mktg. various divs. Mead Corp., Dayton, Oh., N.Y.C., 1978-82; v.p. mktg., v.p. online Info. Access Co., Belmont, Calif. 1982-86; dir. mktg. Channelmark Corp., San Mateo 1986-87; v.p. mktg. Insurance Equities Corp., Palo Alto 1987-89; dir., v.p. Charles Schwab & Co., San Francisco 1989-; mem: Commonwealth Club of Calif. 1990-, Stanford Univ. Alumni (fundraiser 1988-), AIDS Memorial Grove S.F. (vol. 1992-); pub. articles in profl. jours. (1986), The Computer Law Jour. (1992). Res: 1956 Bush St San Francisco 94115 Ofc: Charles Schwab & Co. Inc. 101 Montgomery San Francisco 94104

TATE, L. KENNETH, company president; b. July 18, 1923, Hamilton Co., Ill.; s. Loran Kent and Hattie Wilma (Vantrease) T.; m. Wanda M. (div.); children: Ronald Leroy b. 1946, Kenneth Dean b. 1949, Paulette Nadine b. 1949; m. Dorothy M., Dec. 8, 1960; edn: Aeronautical Engr., Curtis-Wright Tech. Inst., 1948; LLB, Am. Sch. of Law, 1952; spl. courses Univ. Ill., CalTech, Valley Jr. Coll., Contra Costa Jr. Coll., Weaver Coll. Law, USN; reg. Profl. Engr. (#5615) Calif. 1978. Career: quality supr. American Car & Foundry, St. Charles, Mo. 1952-54; insp. and test foreman Bendix Corp., No. Hollywood, Calif. 1955-60; technical sect. mgr. Calif. Inst. of Technology, Pasadena 1960-78; mgr. reliability & quality engring. Fairchild/Xincom Systems, Canoga Park 1978-82; dir. quality assurance JBL Inc., Northridge 1982-86; owner, pres. Ken Tate Enterprises (wholesale sports orgn., sales worldwide), Reseda 1986-; mem. Am. Soc. for Quality Control (Sr. mem., past sect. chmn. S.F.V. Sect. 0706) 1962-, Am. Numismatic Soc. 1954-, West Valley Coin Club 1978-; lodges: AF&AM, Galatia, Ill. #684 1944-, Masonic, Reseda #666 1982-; publs: articles on statical controls 1978, regression analysis 1982, scrap reduction 1983, spacecraft quality 1986; mil: 1c p.o. USN 1943-46; Democrat; Prot.; rec: bowling, sports cards. Address: 7725 Wilbur Ave Reseda 91335

TATOMER, WILLIAM REEVES, psychiatrist; b. Apr. 29, 1945, Niagara Falls, N.Y.; s. Harry Nicholas and Norma Ethyl (Reeves) T.; m. Mary Catherine Hourican, Sept. 9, 1978; children: Deirdre b. 1980, Meghan b. 1982, Andrew b. 1985; edn: BA, Univ. Va. 1967; MD, 1971; cert. Am. Bd. Psychiatry & Neurology 1983. Career: resident San Mateo Co. Mental Health Services 1974; pvt. practice, San Mateo 1974-; pres. Healthcare Found. San Mateo Co. 1989-91; bd. dirs. Calif. Found. for Med. Care 1990-; councilor No. Calif. Psychiatric Soc. 1988-; staff Peninsula Hosp., Burlingame 1974-; Mills Meml. Hosp., San Mateo 1980-; co-host The Celtic Connection radio show 1987-89; mem: Am. Psychiatric Assn. (fellow), San Mateo Psychiatric Soc. (pres. 1985), Calif. Psychiatric Soc., CMA, AMA, Suicide Prevention San Mateo Co. (v.p. 1985-87); Christian; rec: tennis, wine collecting. Ofc: 101 S San Mateo Dr Ste 300 San Mateo 94401

TATUM, THOMAS DESKINS, film and television producer, director; b. Feb. 16, 1946, Pineville, Ky.; s. Clinton Turner and Gaynelle (Deskins) T.; m. Laura Ann Smith, Aug. 15, 1968 (div. 1974); m. Suzanne Pettit, Sept. 29, 1983; children: Rhett Cowden, Walker Edwin; edn: BA, Vanderbilt Univ., 1968; JD, Emory Univ., 1974; admitted bar: Ga. 1974, D.C. 1980. Career: special asst. City of Atlanta, 1974-76; dep. dir. fed. relations National League of Cities, W.D.C., 1977-78; dir. communications Office of Conservation and Solar Energy, 1979-80; chmn. and exec. producer Tatum Communications of Colorado Inc., Telluride and Burbank, Calif. 1981-; chmn., pres. Western Film & Video Inc., Telluride 1987-; appt. mem. advy. bd. Solar Electric Light Fund, W.D.C. 1990-91; producer feature film: Winners Take All (1987), prod./director documentaries: Double High (1982, award), Maui Windsurf (1983); home videos: Greenpeace in Action (1988), Girls of Winter/Skiing mag., Am. Ultra Sports Series with prime network (1989-91); various TV, cable, home video sports pgms. (1982-90); dep. campaign mgr. Maynard Jackson 1973; staff conf. Dem. Mayors 1974-75; nat. urban affairs coord. Carter Mondale campaign 1976 and mem. transition team 1976-77, media cons. Greenpeace 1988; bd. dirs. Atlanta Ballet (v.p. 1975); mem.: Ga. Bar Assn., Washington Bar Assn., Hollywood Film and TV Soc.; club: Los Angeles Tennis; Presbyterian; rec: skiing, sailing, Yoga, tennis, travel. Res: 103 S Davis St Telluride CO 81435 Ofc: Tatum Communications Inc. 2920 W Olive Ave #102 Burbank 91505

TAUSCH, JOSEPH HENRY, real estate broker co. president; b. May 1, 1928, Norfolk, Va.; s. Henry Joseph and Marguerite (Scherrer) T.; m. Patricia Agnes Cullen, July 4, 1952; children: Kathleen, Cynthia, Julia, Valerie; edn: BA, San

Diego St. Univ. 1950; MA, 1958. Career: adminstv. asst. San Diego Unified Sch. Dist. 1953-59; engr. planning and estimating Astronautics G.D. 1960-61; pres. Fund Raising Assoc. 1962-72; Bus. Opportunities Unlimited 1973-; mil: capt. AUS 1951-53; Democrat; R.Cath. Res: 8622 Pinecrest Ave San Diego 92123

TAWFIK, HUSSEIN H., food service company president; b. Jan. 1, 1938, Mansoura, Egypt; s. Hussein and Monira (Rashid) T.; m. Heidi, Aug. 3, 1963; child: Tarik b. 1964; edn: BA, Alexandria Univ. 1961; MA, Vanderbilt Univ. 1963; CPA review courses, Golden Gate Univ. 1970. Career: v.p. fin. & adminstrn. Nutritional Foods Inc., S.San Francisco, 1973-82; fin. controller Beta Co., Riyadh, S.A. 1982-84; v.p. fin. & adminstrn. MCM Financial Inc., Santa Clara, 1984; pres. Rhodes Enterprises Inc., Santa Clara, 1985-86; pres. Isis Food Co., San Jose, 1986-; awarded Hon. Citizen State of Tennessee by Gov. Buford Ellington 1962; chartered mem. Nat. Accts. Assn., San Mateo chpt. 1973-; Republican; rec: gourmet cook. Ofc: Isis Food Company 1040 Commercial St Ste 102 San Jose 95112

TAYLOR, CLIVE ROY, academic physician; b. July 24, 1944, Cambridge, Eng.; s. Roy and Mildred (Harrison) T.; m. Susan Hoyland, July 29, 1967; children: Matthew b. 1969, Jeremy b. 1970, Ben b. 1974, Emma b. 1978; edn: BA, MA, Cambridge, Eng. 1966, 1970, MB, BS (MD equiv.) 1969; PhD philos., Oxford 1974. Career: lectr. Univ. Oxford, England 1971-75; fellow Medical Res. Council, 1975-76; assoc. prof. USC, L.A. 1976-81, prof. 1981-84, chmn. pathology dept. 1984-; mem. sci. advy. bds.: Techniclone Internat. 1984, Impath 1989, Biogenex 1991; awards: Karger Research Award, Karger, Switz. 1976, Phi Beta publishing award USC 1987, Bachelor scholar Univ. Cambridge 1966, Hobson scholar Univ. Oxford 1969; mem: Royal Coll. Pathologists, Am. Soc. Clin. Pathologists, Planetary Soc.; active AYSO, So. Pasa. (founding commr. 1977); author: Lymph Node Pathology (1979), Immuno Microscopy (1986), Concise Pathology (1992), 10 other books, 200+ sci. papers; rec: soccer coach, tennis, skiing. Res: 1601 Marengo Ave South Pasadena 91030 Ofc: USC Dept. Pathology 2011 Zonal Ave Los Angeles 90033

TAYLOR, EDNA JANE, state employment program counselor; b. May 16, 1934, Flint, Mich.; d. Leonard Lee Harvey and Wynona Ruth (Davis) Belders; m. Bill Frank Taylor, Mar. 17, 1951 (div. 1955); children: Wynona Jane MacDonald b. 1952, Cynthia Lee Zellmer b. 1954; edn: BS, No. Ariz. Univ., 1963; MEd, Univ. Ariz., Tucson 1967. Career: high sch. tchr. Sunnyside School Dist., Tucson 1963-68; employment counselor Calif. State Employment Devel. Dept., Canoga Park, Calif. 1968-; mem. advy. council Pierce Community Coll., Woodland Hills 1979-81; advy. council Van Nuys Community Adult Sch., 1983-93, elected steering com. 1989-90, 90-91; mem. local leadership council Van Nuys Adult Sch., 1991-92; mem: Internat. Assn. Personnel in Employment Security 1968-, Calif. Employment Counselors Assn. (state treas. 1978, 79, state sec. 1980), Delta Psi Kappa (life 1960); rec: writing, tennis, health & fitness. Ofc: State Calif. Employment Development Dept. Canoga Park 91303

TAYLOR, IRVING, consulting engineer, turbomachinery; b. Oct. 25, 1912, Schenectady, N.Y.; s. John Bellamy and Marcia Estabrook (Jones) T.; m. Shirley Milker, Dec. 22, 1943; children: Bronwen b. 1945, Marcia b. 1946, John b. 1947, Jerome b. 1949; edn: BSME, Cornell Univ. 1934; reg. profl. engr., N.Y., Mass., Calif. Career: test engr. Gen. Electric Co., Lynn, Mass. 1934-37; asst. mech. engr. M.W. Kellogg Co., N.Y.C., 1937-39; head turbomachinery applications sect. The Lummus Co., N.Y.C. 1939-57; devel. engr. Gilbert & Barker Mfg., West Springfield, Mass. 1957-58; wind-tunnel project engr. Marquardt Corp., Ogden, Utah 1958-60; engring. splst. Bechtel Inc., San Francisco 1960-77; indep. cons. P.E. on indsl. pump applications, Berkeley 1977-; adj. prof. Columbia Univ., New York Univ. (1950s); awards: Henry R. Worthington medal for eminent achiev. in the field of pumping machinery ASME (1990); mem: ASME (life Fellow), Sigma Xi (assoc.), Pacific Energy Assn., Soaring Soc. of Am. (life); publs: 24+ papers and articles to engring. soc. meetings and petroleum ind. jours.; Unitarian-Universalist; rec: skiing (1935-), sailplane-soaring (1958-), Biased-bowl Lawn Bowling (1987-). Address: Irving Taylor P.E., 300 Deer Valley Rd #2P San Rafael 94903-5514

TAYLOR, KENDRICK JAY, microbiologist, civic volunteer; b. Mar. 17, 1914, Manhattan, Mont.; s. Wm. Henry and Rose Ann (Carney) T.; m. Hazel Griffith, July 28, 1945; children: Stanley b. 1947, Paul b. 1949, Richard b. 1951; edn: BS, Mont. St. Coll. 1938; postgrad. fellow Univ. Wash. 1938-41, postgrad. work Univ. Calif. 1952; cert. Drama Studio of London. Career: microbiol. research Cutter Labs., Berkeley 1945-74; microbiologist Berkeley Biologicals 1974-84; ret.; mem. Am. Soc. for Microbiol. (chmn. 1953, No. Calif. br. v.p. 1963-65, pres. 1965-67); awards: Boy Scouts Am. Wood Badge 1962; mem. Am. Legion; civic bds: Calif. PTA (life), Mount Diablo Council BSA (cub pack com. 1955, dist. v.chair 1960-61, dist. chmn. 1962-65, cubmaster 1957, scoutmaster 1966), Contact Ministries 1977-80, Santa Clara Community Players (bd. 1980-85), English as a Second Language (ESL instr. 1979-80), Sons & Daus. of Montana Pioneers 1976-; mil: lt. col. AUS 1941-46, Reserve -1965; Presbyterian (Elder 1954-).; rec: vol. VA Hosp. and Am. Red Cross. Res: 550 South 13th St San Jose 95112

TAYLOR, KENNETH WILLIAM, physician; b. May 7, 1938, Chicago, Ill.; s. Kenneth Robert and Ruth J. (Summers) T.; m. Carolyn Conley, June 16, 1961; children: Andrew, Matthew; edn: BA, Northwest Univ. Evanston 1960; MA, So. Ill. Univ. Carbondale 1961; MD, Duke Univ. Med. Sch. 1965; diplomate Am. Bd. Family Practice. Career: physician, pvt. practice, San Diego 1968-88; chmn. family practice dept. Mission Bay Hosp., San Diego 1989; mem: San Diego Co. Med. Soc., CMA; mil: lt. comdr. USNR; Republican; Presbyterian; rec: computers. Ofc: 2185 Garnet St San Diego 92109

TAYLOR, RICHARD EDWARD, physicist; b. Nov. 2, 1929, Medicine Hat, Alberta, Canada; s. Clarence Richard and Delia Alena (Brunsdale) T.; m. Rita Jean Bonneau, Aug. 25, 1951; children: Norman Edward b. 1960; edn: BSc, Univ. Alberta, Edmonton, Can. 1950, MSc, 1952; PhD, Stanford Univ., 1962. Career: boursier Lab de l'Accelerateur, Orsay, France 1958-61; physicist Lawrence Berkeley Lab, Berkeley 1961-62; staff mem. Stanford Linear Accelerator Ctr., 1962-68, prof. (SLAC) Stanford Univ., 1968-, assoc. dir. SLAC, 1982-86; awards: fellow J.S. Guggenheim Found. 1971-72, sr. scientist von Humboldt Found., Bonn, Ger. 1982, W.K.H. Panofsky Prize div. of particles & fields Am. Phys. Soc. 1989, Nobel Prize in Physics, Stockholm, Sweden 1990; mem. Canadian Assn. of Physicists; Fellow: Am. Physical Soc., Royal Soc. of Canada, Am. Acad. Arts and Scis., AAAS; publs: num. articles in sci. jours. Ofc: SLAC, PO Box 4349 MS-96 Stanford 94309

TAYLOR, VIVIAN LUCILLE, registered nurse; b. May 5, 1951, Oceanside; d. Howard Eugene and Frances Alice (Brunner) Phelps (one of triplets, 3 girls not identical); m. Kenneth Thomas Taylor, Jr., June 26, 1971; children: Kristine Patricia b. 1977, Thomas Howard b. 1979; edn: AA in nsg., Sacramento City Coll., 1973; RN, 1976; CNOR (cert. nurse in operating rm.) AORN, 1984. Career: graduate nurse to RN, Mercy Hosp., Sacto. 1973-76; operating room nse. Kaiser Found. Hosp., Sacto. 1976-84; Kaiser So. Sacto., 1984-; mem: Assn. of Operating Room Nurses 1976-, Calif. Nurses Assn. 1973-, Am. Nurse Assn. 1973-, Calif. Student Nurse Assn. 1971-73, NCUA (supvy. bd. 1989-); Republican; Lutheran (Luth. Ch. Women Sacto. circle chair, ofcr., mem. 1977-); rec: needlework, raising Texas Longhorn cattle.

TAYLOR MC CURRY, MARGUERITE FAYE, academic administrator; b. Feb. 23, 1935, Roswell, N.M.; d. John Robert and Alice Marguerite (Gordon) Wilhite; m. O.L. Ted Taylor, Feb. 18, 1954 (dec. 1969); m. Liam R.A. McCurry III, Dec. 18, 1971; children: Lois b. 1959, M. Lee b. 1962, Michael b. 1963; edn: BA, Univ. N.M. 1974; MAPA, 1976; PhD, 1980; cert. fund raising exec. 1988. Career: pub. info. staff Univ. New Mexico, Albuquerque 1967-76, dir. med. center pub. info. 1976-80, dir. devel. pub. affairs 1981-85; res. splst. NIH, Bethesda, Md. 1980-81; exec. dir. coll. advancement Stephens Coll., Columbia, Mo. 1985-86; exec. dir. univ. advancement CSU, Sacto. 1986-; mem. bd. dirs. Sacto. Opera Assn., Med. Alert Fedn. N.M. (chmn. 1982-85), Lovelace Med. Ctr., Albuquerque (dir. 1982-85), Nat. Health Agys. N.M. (pres. 1985); awards: John McGovern scholarship 1979; mem: Planned Giving Forum of Sacto. (pres. 1989-90); 50+ articles pub. in profl. jours. and newspapers 1985; Episcopalian. Res: 8366 Mediterranean Way Sacramento 95826 Ofc: California State University Sacramento 95819

TEALL, RALPH CROMWELL, physician; b. Oct. 26, 1907, Gardena; s. Robert James and Alice Louise (Olds) T.; m. Mary Louise Gregson, Dec. 1949 (div. 1963); m. 2d. Grace Marianne Boye, Oct. 26, 1972; children: Sharon b. 1943, Heather b. 1945, Hana b. 1950; edn: BS, UC Berkeley 1928; MD, UCSF 1932. Mem: Sacto. Co. Med. Soc. (pres. 1949), CMA (pres. 1965), AMA (v.p. 1970), Del Paso Co. Club; mil: col. ret. USAF 1972-; Republican; Prot.; rec: music, photography. Res: 3343 Lynne Way Sacramento 95421

TEASLEY, LARKIN, insurance company president; b. Sept. 23, 1936, Cleveland, Ohio; s. Gordon and Ruth (Wright) T.; m. Violet Williams, Nov. 26, 1959; children: Lisa b. 1962, Erica b. 1967, Laura b. 1972; edn: BA, Fisk Univ., Nashville 1957; grad. work in Actuarial Sci., Occidental Coll., L.A. 1957; grad. sch. of bus. admin. Ex. Prog., UCLA, 1971-72; cert. FSA, Society of Actuaries 1966. Career: res. engr. General Motors, assoc. engr. Douglas Aircraft, actuarial trainee Golden State Mutual Life Ins. Co., Los Angeles 1957-62; actuary No. Carolina Mutual LIfe Ins. Co., Durham, NC 1963-69; v.p. actuary & investment ofcr. Golden State Mutual 1970, bd. dirs., exec. com. 1971-72, sr. v.p. actuary & investment ofcr. 1973-77, exec. v.p. 1977-80, pres., c.o.o. 1980-90, pres. and chief exec. 1991-; dir: Broadway Fed. Savings & Loan Assn., Calif. State C.of C., Calif. Life & Health Ins. Guarantee Assn., Golden State Minority Found.; honors: Phi Beta Kappa, Beta Kappa Chi (Sci.), Fellow Soc. of Actuaries; mem: Am. Acad. of Actuaries, L.A. Actuarial Club, Actuarial Club of the Pacific States, Nat. Assn. of Bus. Economists, Alpha Phi Alpha, Fisk Univ. Alumni Club; civic: L.A. World Affairs Council, Town Hall of Calif., L.A. Area Council Boy Scouts of Am. (bd.); Democrat; Christian Science; rec: music, sports, reading. Ofc: Mutual Life Insurance Co 1999 W Adams Blvd Los Angeles 90018

TEMKO, ALLEN BERNARD, writer; b. Feb. 4, 1924, NY, NY; s. Emanuel and Betty (Alderman) T.; m. Elizabeth Ostroff, July 1, 1950; children: Susannah b. 1955, Alexander Max b. 1957; edn: AB, Columbia Univ., NY, NY, 1947;

postgrad. UC Berkeley, 1949-51; Sorbonne, 1948-49, 51-52. Career: lectr., Sorbonne, 1953-54, Ecole des Arts et Metiers, Paris, 1954-55; asst. prof. journalism UC Berkeley, 1956-62; lectr. in city planning and social scis. UC, 1966-70; prof. art, Calif. State Univ., Hayward, 1971-80; lectr. art Stanford Univ., 1981, 82; lectr., Grad. Sch. of Journalism, UC Berkeley, 1991; architecture critic , S.F. Chronicle, 1961-; West Coast ed., Archtl. Forum, 1959-62; art ed., S.F. Chronicle, 1979-82; archtl. planning cons.; referee in architecture, Guggenheim Found.; awards: recipient, Gold Medal Commonwealth Club Calif. 1956, Guggenheim fellow 1956-57, journalism award AIA 1961, Rockefeller Found. grantee 1962-63, Twentieth Century Fund grantee 1963-66, Silver Spur award 1985, 1st prize in archtl. criticism Mfrs. Hanover/Art World 1986, Critic's award Mfrs. Hanover/Art World 1987, Profl. Achievement award Soc. Profl. Journalists 1988, Nat. Endowment for the Arts grantee 1988, Pulitzer Prize for Criticism 1990, Inst. Honor award, AIA 1991, appt. Pulitzer Prize juries 1991, 92; author: Notre Dame of Paris, 1955, Eero Saarinen, 1961, No Way to Build a Ballpark, other essays on architecture, 1993; contbr. articles to US and fgn. magazines and newspapers; civic: environmental adv. to former Pres. John F. Kennedy and former Calif. Gov. Edmund G. Brown; organized the Governor's Design Awards Prog.; chair, Yosemite Falls Design Workshop 1992. Mil: served with USNR 1943-46. Ofc: S.F. Chronicle S.F. 94103

TENNEY, JOSEPH RICKS, security executive; b. Sept. 29, 1936, New Orleans, La.; s. Joseph Fosdick and Cecile Clara (Ricks) T.; m. Jean Sherrill Wilcox, Dec. 28, 1963; children: Joseph Wilcox, Laurie Sherrill, Karl Ricks; edn: BS in engring., U.S. Naval Acad. 1960; student USMC Command and Staff Coll. 1970-71; M. in human behavior, USIU, San Diego 1974; JD, Western State Univ. 1984. Career: officer US Marine Corps 1960-80: num. command/staff billets, jt. and naval staff, in combat, recruiting, and recruit training; 8 personal decorations include Silver Star, Vietnamese Cross of Gal. w/Gold Palm, Purple Heart, Joint Svc. Commendation Medal, Navy Commendation w/Gold Star & Combat V, N.O.V. 4th CL, DSO 1st CL, Navy Achiev. Medal; (his family military history in Am. predates colonial period (1650) forbears fought in Fr. and Indian War, Am. Revolution, War of 1812, Civil War, WWII, Korea and Vietnam, eldest son Marine ofcr. Persian Gulf War); currently dir. security Hyatt Regency Irvine; mem: Army/Navy Co. Club; civic: Collie Club Am. (show rules com. 1978-80, trophy com. 1978-80), Fullerton Booster Club (pres. 1985-87), Fullerton Quarterback Club (v.p. 1981-86), San Diego Collie Club (pres. 1977-80); contbr. article for CCA annual pub., Valley of the Shadow Autobiography (1974), poem Fame, Am. Poetry Anthol. (1986); Republican; Episcopalian; rec: showing dogs. Res: 601 E Glenwood Fullerton 92631 Ofc: Hyatt Regency Irvine 17900 Jamboree Irvine 92714

TERESI, JOSEPH, publisher; b. Mar. 13, 1941, Mpls.; s. Cliff I.A. and Helen Ione (Leslie) T.; m. Ruby (div.); 1 son, Nicholas. Career: chief exec. ofcr. Jammer Cycle Products Inc., Burbank 1968-80; pres./c.e.o. Paisano Publications Inc., Agoura Hills 1970-, pub. magazines: Easyriders, 1971-, In the Wind, 1974-, Biker Lifestyle, 1986-, Tattoo, 1986-, American Rodder, 1987-, Womens Enterprise, 1987-; holder World Speed Record S-AF Motorcycle 1978-1989, new record set in 1990 at 322.150 m.p.h. - world's fastest motorcycle; rec: motorcycles, race cars, boats, marlin fishing, skiing. Ofc: Paisano Publications, Inc. Box 3000 Agoura Hills 91301

TERHUNE, CHARLES HOUSTON, III, engineering company business manager; b. July 25, 1950, Wash., D.C.; s. Charles Houston and Beatrice (Holcombe) T.; m. Kathryn, May 17, 1975; 1 son, Charles b. 1981; edn: BSME, Purdue Univ. 1972; MS, UCLA 1981; lic. mechanical engr. Calif. Career: heat transfer engr. The Ralph M. Parsons Co., Pasadena 1973-75, mechanical process engr. 1976-78, project engr. 1978-79; Parsons Overseas Co., Ahwaz, Iran 1980; project mgr. The Ralph M. Parsons Co., Pasadena 1981-82, bus. devel. mgr. systems div. 1983-, v.p. 1992-; mem: Am. Inst. Aeronautics & Astronautics, Soc. Am. Mil. Engrs., Soc. Mfg. Engrs., Rotary Internat., Am. Cancer Soc. (chair Tournament for Life 1986-88); Republican; Methodist; rec: guitar, skiing, painting. Ofc: The Ralph M. Parsons Co 100 W Walnut St Pasadena 91124

TERRA, DALE EDWARD, industrial psychologist, personnel selection consultant; b. July 16, 1948, Berkeley; s. Albert Lewis Terra and Norma Mae (Angeles) Bernardi; m. Robin Davison, Aug. 24, 1976 (div. 1978); m. Diane Mae Sankari, July 3, 1983; edn: att. Coll. of Redwoods 1968-70, Solano St. Coll. 1970-72, BA, CSU Sacto. 1977, MA industrial psychology, 1977. Career: mgr. Burns Internat. Security Svs., Martinez 1976-77; staff svs. analyst Calif. State Personnel Bd., Sacto. 1977-80, test validation and devel. specialist, 1980-84, personnel selection cons., 1989; mgr. Calif. Dept. of Corrections, Sacto. 1989-; personnel selection cons. Orange County Dept. Corrections, Orlando, Fla. 1988-92; guest lectr. UC Davis 1985-86, Calif. Assn. Affirmative Actions Ofcrs., Sacto. 1986, key speaker Med-Tox, L.A. 1988, Presley Inst. of Corrections, Napa 1989; expert witness jt. legis. com. on pub. retirement, Sacto. 1981, 82; awards: Phi Kappa Phi 1977, Psi Chi 1977, recipient superior accomplishment award State Pers. Bd., Sacto. 1983; mem: Intl. Personnel Mgmt. Assn., Am. Correctional Assn. 1991-, Am. Acad. Scis. 1991-, NOW, Sacto. Zool. Soc. 1991-, Disabled in State Service 1981-90; pub. 4 profl. reports (1981, 83, 90, 91); mil: sgt. USAF 1966-70; Democrat; Prot.; rec: astronomy, photog. Res: 336 Chisum Ave Rio Linda 95673

TERRANELLA, CHARLES ARTHUR, investment banker; b. May 23, 1944, NY, NY; s. Charles John and Ann (Westuba) T.; m. Mary Ellen, Dec. 24, 1985; children: Sarah b. 1986, Charles F. b. 1989; edn: BBA, City Coll. N.Y., 1967; MBA, Columbia Univ., 1971. Career: fin. exec. Time, Inc. NY, NY 1971-76; fin. officer Calif. Housing Fin. Agy., Sacto. 1977-78; v.p. Lehman Bros. Kuhn Loeb, NY, NY 1979-80; v.p. Dean Witter Reynolds, San Francisco 1981-87; senior v.p. First Calif. Capital Markets Group, S.F. 1988-90; prin. McCarty, Terranella & Carlson, S.F. 1991-93; managing dir. Westhoff-Martin & Associates, Lafayette 1993-; mem. Mensa, Commonwealth Club Calif., World Affairs Council No. Calif. Res: 767 Oak Hollow Ave Vacaville 95687 Ofc: Westhoff-Martin & Associates 3675 Mt. Diablo Blvd Lafayette 94549

TERRELL, JOAN RICHARDSON, nurse anesthetist; b. Feb. 5, 1942, Durham, N.C.; d. Henry and Bartavia Eleanor (Ellis) Richardson; m. Clodas George Terrell, Apr. 9, 1965 (dec. Jan. 16, 1983); children: Brian V. b. 1966, Jonal D. b. 1970; edn: RN, BS, Winston-Salem State Univ., 1963; Masters Pgm., CSU Los Angeles, 1967-68; Cert. Reg. Nse. Anesthesist (CRNA) Kaiser Sch. of Anesthesia, 1976; Reg. Electrologist (RE) Calif. Inst. Electrology, 1983. Career: hd. nse. Metropolitan Hosp., NYC 1963-65, Dominguez Valley Hosp., Compton, Calif. 1965-67; dir. of nurses Cardinal Med. Ents., L.A. 1969-73; patient care educator Central Med. Group, L.A. 1973-76; anesthetist Kaiser Permanente, Panorama City, Calif. 1976-78; indep. anesthetist F.P.A. (Family Planning Associates), Long Beach 1978-88; tchr. Lynwood H.S. 1967-68, Compton Adult Sch. 1968-70; appt. coordinator Bereavement Com., L.A., 1988-91; mem., secty. Human Relations Commn., City of Carson; honors: Career Day speaker Wash. Prep. H.S., L.A. 1991, appreciation for contbns. as bereavement coord. West Angeles Ch. of God in Christ, L.A. 1988; mem: Calif. Nurses Assn. 1965-, Am. Assn. Nurse Anesthestist 1974-, So. Poverty Law Ctr. 1989-, Nat. Assn. Negro Women, Delta Sigma Theta; class mother 4th gr. West Angeles Acad.; Democrat; Pentecostal Holiness; rec: designing, sewing, travel. Res: 19613 Enslow Dr Carson 90746 Ofc: Terrell Anesthesia POB 4864 Carson 90749

TESTA, STEPHEN MICHAEL, geologist, environmental services co. president; b. July 17, 1951, Fitchburg, Mass.; s. Guiseppe Alfredo and Angelina Mary (Petitto) T.; m. Lydia Mae Payne, July 26, 1986; son, Brant Ethan Gage; edn: AA, L.A. Valley Jr. Coll., 1971; BS geol., CSU Northridge, 1976, MS geol., 1978; reg. geologist, 1983; reg. environmental assessor, 1989; Cert. profl. geological scientist, 1983; cert. engring. geologist, 1990; cert. environmental insp., 1991. Career: engring. geologist R.T. Frankian & Assocs., Burbank 1976-78; Bechtel, Norwalk 1978-80; Converse Consultants, Seattle 1980-82; senior hydrogeologist Ecology & Environment, Seattle 1982-83; senior geologist Dames & Moore, Seattle 1983-86; v.p. Engineering Enterprises., Long Beach 1986-90; pres. Applied Environmental Services, 1990-; instr. geology and environmental sci. CSU Fullerton 1989-90, instr. environmental sci. USC, 1991; mem: Am. Inst. of Profl. Geologist (profl. dev. com. 1986, cont. edn. com. 1988, annual meeting com. 1989, program chmn. 1990, presdl. merit award 1987), Geological Soc. of Am., L.A. Basin Geol. Soc. (pres. 1990-91), Am. Assn. of Petroleum Geologists (AAPG), AAAS, Assn. of Engring. Geologist, Mineral. Soc. of Amer., Mineral. Soc. of Canada, Hazardous Mats. Control Research Inst., Assn. of Ground Water Scientist and Engrs., Calif. Water Pollution Control Assn., Calif. Groundwater Assn., Sigma Xi, Soc. of Am. Military Engrs.; author: Restoration of Petroleum-Contaminated Aquifers; Principles of Technical Consulting and Project Management; Geologic Aspects of Hazardous Waste Management; editor (book) Environmental Concerns in the Petroleum Industry (pub. AAPG Pacific Sect., 1989); 60+ tech. res. papers 1978-; rec: water color artist, collector natural hist. books, minerals. Res: 31232 Belford Dr San Juan Capistrano 92675 Ofc: Applied Environmental Services, 27282 Calle Arroyo San Juan Capistrano 92675

THAL, MICHAEL LEWIS, teacher specialist; b. Feb. 28, 1949, Oceanside, N.Y.; s. Herman Leon and Vivian (Friedman) T.; m. Daphna Oded, Dec. 23, 1980 (div. Dec. 1991); children: Channie b. 1983, Koren b. 1988; edn: BA history, SUNY at Buffalo, 1971; MA in elem. edn., Washington Univ., St. Louis 1973; MA sec. edn./reading specialist, CSU Northridge, 1978, sch. adminstrn. cred., 1991; Calif. std. tch. credentials, reading specialist, sch. adminstn. Career: tchr. substitute Los Angeles Unified Sch. Dist., 1973-77; dir. of edn. Readwrite Educational Pgms., Newport Beach 1977-79; tchr. Montebello Unified Sch. Dist., 1980-85; tchr. Glendale Unified Sch. Dist. 1985-, tchr. specialist 1991-, Roosevelt Jr. High Sch. reading dept. chmn. 1985-91, mentor tchr. 1989-91, sch. site council chmn. 1990-91; awards: $1500 cash grantee Glendale USD, Roosevelt Jr. High 1988; mem. Glendale Tchrs. Assn. 1985-; publs: articles "Learning to Love Books" Early Years-K-8 (1984), "Fathers on Fathering" LA Parent Mag. (1986); Republican; Jewish; rec: writing. Res: 5811 Woodman Ave #18 Van Nuys 91403 Ofc: Marshall Elementary School 1201 E Broadway Glendale 91205

THATCHER, DICKINSON, lawyer; b. May 26, 1919, Huntington Beach; s. Charles Harold and Gladys T. (Dickinson) T.; m. Dale Nadine Mortensen, Feb. 2, 1952; children: Kirk Randolph, b. 1962; Jeffrey Lawrence, b. 1963; edn: BS, UCLA 1941; postgrad., New York Univ. 1943-4; Univ. of Paris 1945-46; JD, Stanford Univ. 1948; LL.M. in Taxation, USC 1962. Career: admitted to Calif. State Bar 1948; Los Angeles Deputy City Atty. 1948-51; credit atty. Union Oil

Co. of Calif. 1951-54; trial atty. Tax Div., Dept. Justice, Wash. DC 1954-56; asst. US Atty. Los Angeles 1956-57; practicing lawyer in North Hollywood, Van Nuys, Ojai, 1957-; mem: St. Bar of Calif. (Disciplinary Bd. 1970-72, Client Security Fund Com. 1973-75), San Fernando Valley Bar Assn. (pres. 1966), Am. Bar Assn, Los Angeles Co. Bar Assn. (Commn. on Arbitration 1963-71, chmn. Council Affiliated Bar Pres. 1968-70, exec. com. Probate and Trust Law Sect. 1985-87), Kiwanis (pres Van Nuys Club 1975-76); mil: US Army 1942-46. Address: 211 Bristol Rd Ojai 93023-2409

THIBAULT, DARRYL ROBERT, lawyer; b. June 16, 1938, Eureka; s. Edgar Exave and Cecilia Marie (Roberts) T.; m. Lori Williams, Apr. 12, 1982; children: Adam b. 1983, Stacey b. 1985; edn: BA in psychology, UC Riverside 1963; Soviet studies, UCLA, 1963-64; internat. law, Univ. Vienna, Austria 1970; JD, George Washington Sch. Law 1979; admitted bar: Dist. Col. 1980, Federal Cts. 1987. Career: intelligence ofcr. Central Intelligence Agency, Washington, D.C. 1970-91, with service in Asia, Europe, and U.S.; v.p. Nationwide Executive Security Services, San Diego 1991-92; pres. PrivIntel, Inc., San Diego 1992-; mem: Am. Bar Assn., D.C. Bar Assn., Fed. Bar Assn., Cal. Assn. Lic. Investigators, Am. Soc. Indus. Security (pres., San Diego Chapt.), Assn. Former Intel. Ofcrs.; mil: U.S. Army 101st Airborne Div. 1957-59; Republican; R. Cath. Res: 2360 Palo Danzante Alpine 91901

TIIIROUX, JACQUES PAUL, professor of philosophy; b. Aug. 7, 1928, Santa Monica, Calif.; s. Jacques and Mary Helen (Garrotto) T.; m. Angelita Solis, July 26, 1952 (div. 1975); m. Emily Louise Lofton Apr. 8, 1984; children: Mark b. 1954, Stephen b. 1956, Paul b. 1959, Jason Ragle b. 1971, Abigale Ragle b. 1972; edn: BA, Pomona Coll., Claremont, Calif., 1949; MA, S.F. State Univ., 1961; AM, Univ. of So. Calif., L.A., 1971. Career: apr. publicist, MGM Studios, Culver City, Calif. 1949-50; T/Sgt., USAF, 1950-61; prof. of Eng., Bakersfield Coll., Bakersfield, Calif. 1961-69; prof. of Philosophy & chair, Bakersfield Coll., 1969-90; lectr. in Philosophy, Calif. State Univ., Bakersfield 1990-; bioethics cons., Delano Reg. Med. Ctr., Delano, Calif. 1988-; bioethics cons., Pacific Regency, Bakersfield, 1989-; mem., bioethics com., Kern Med. Ctr., Bakersfield 1988-; awards: fellowship, NEH, Wash., DC, 1973; mem: (life) Calif. Tchrs. Assn. & NEA 1961-, Calif. Faculty Assn. 1990-, VFW 1984-, AAUW 1990-; author: Practical Eng., 1977, Philosophy: Theory & Practice, 1985, Ethics: Theory & Practice (4th ed.), 1990; Living Fully Through Facing Dying, 1991. Mil: T/Sgt., USAF, 1950-61; rec: acting, singing, dancing. Ofc: Calif. State Univ. 9001 Stockdale Hwy. Bakersfield 93311

THISSELL, JAMES DENNIS, physicist; b. June 1, 1935, Lincoln County, S.Dak.; s. Oscar H. and Bernice Grace Janet (Olbertson) T.; edn: BA (cum laude) Augustana Coll., 1957; MS in space physics, Univ. of Iowa, 1963. Career: research physicist Univ. Iowa, 1956-64; engr. McDonnell Douglas, St. Louis, Mo. 1965-66; scientist E.G. & G., Las Vegas, Nev. 1967-68; engr. Bendix Field Engring., Ames Research Ctr., Moffett Field, Calif. 1970-77; engr. Lockheed Missiles & Space Corp., Sunnyvale, 1978-; mem: AIAA, IEEE, Am. Physical Soc., Am. Geophysical Soc., Sigma Xi, Nat. Rifle Assn., Safari Club Internat.; Republican; Lutheran; rec: hunting, fishing, pvt. pilot. Res: 38475 Jacaranda Dr Newark 94560-47227 Ofc: LTOC Dept 21-70, Fac.1, PO Box 61687 Sunnyvale 94088-1687

THODE, JEROME PAUL, information systems management consultant; b. July 26, 1947, Chicago, Ill.; s. Howard Jacob and Lilla Maria (Wojceiowska) T.; m. Kathleen Anne Ferris; children: Christopher b. 1984, Andrew b. 1988; edn: BS math., Ill. Inst. Tech. 1969; MS computer sci., 1972; M.Mgmt., fin. & mktg., Northwestern Grad. Sch. Mgmt. 1979. Career: tech., mgr. Motorola, Chgo., Ill. 1969-76; project mgr. FMC 1976-78; mgr. MIS Morton Norwich 1978-81; prin. Deloitte & Touche, Los Angeles 1981-; guest lectr. UCLA GSM 1988-; mem: Soc. Info. Mgmt. (bd. mem.), Info. Assoc. UCLA Grad. Sch. Mgmt. (exec. bd.), L.A. Athletic Club; articles pub. in profl. jours.; rec: jogging, theatre. Ofc: 1000 Wilshire Blvd Ste 1500 Los Angeles 90017

THOMAS, ESTHER MERLENE, educator; b. Oct. 16, 1945, San Diego; d. Merton Alfred and Nellie Lida (Von Pilz) T.; edn: AA, Grossmont Coll., 1966; BA, San Diego St. Univ., 1969; MA, Univ. Redlands, 1977; Calif. elem. and adult edn. tchg. creds., Career: tchr. Cajon Valley Union Sch. Dist., El Cajon 1969-tchr. native Amer.(AZ and UT); mem. Nat. Tchrs. Assn., Calif. Tchrs. Assn., Cajon Valley Educators Assn., Christian Bus. & Profl. Women, Lakeside Hist. Soc.; civic: Lakeside Centennial Com. (1985-86), Intl. Christian Women's Club (Seoul 1974), Dir. Bible sch., Sunday Sch. Supt., Cajon Valley Union Sch. Dist. Project AIDS (health articulation com. 1988), Marine Corps Mus. San Diego (charter), Lakeside Hist. Soc. Mus. (curator 1992-1993), contrib. author; Republican (U.S. Senatl. Club 1984-, Medal of Merit Ronald Reagan Presdl. Task Force 1986, Presdl. Citizen's Advy. Commn. 1989-92, at large del. Repub. Platform Planning Com. 1988, 92). Res: 13594 Hwy 8 Apt 3 Lakeside 92040 Ofc: Flying Hills Elementary School 1251 Finch St El Cajon 92020

THOMAS, JULIA DESSERY, planner; b. Dec. 4, 1938, Riverside; d. Floyd Gordon and Myrtle (Thomas) Dessery; m. David B. Thomas, Nov. 30, 1963 (div.), children: Leslie; m. Michael Lawrence Bobrow, Mar. 24, 1980, 3 stepchildren, Elizabeth, Erica, David; edn: BA, CSU San Francisco, 1963; MA, Sch. Architecture and Urban Planning UCLA, 1974. Career: dir. communications William L. Pereira Assocs., L.A. 1972-73; sr. assoc. Bobrow/Thomas and Assocs., L.A. 1973-78, pres. 1978-84, chmn. bd. 1984-; guest lectr. USC, Columbia Univ., UCLA, Scripps Coll., Calif. Polytechnic Univ. Pomona, Pepperdine Univ.; prin. works include: San Bernardino Co. Replacement Medical Center, Stanford Univ., Palo Alto, Shriners Hosps. for Crippled Children, L.A., Shreveport; Santa Monica Hosp. Med. Ctr.; UCLA Arroyo Bridge; Motion Picture and Television Hosp. and Country Home, Woodland Hills, Calif.; Kings Road Housing for the Elderly, Hollywood; awards include: UCLA Alumni award for excellence in profl. achiev. 1988, AIA/NAVFAC award of merit for US Navy Med. Clinics, Kaneohe, Hawaii 1988 and Port Hueneme, Calif. 1986, Am. Planning Assn./Calif. Chpt. outstanding leadership 1986, DOD design excellence for US Navy Med. Clinic, Port Hueneme, Calif. 1986, L.A. Conservancy award for Parsons-Gates Hall of Adminstrn. Caltech 1984, AIA award for Kings Road Housing for Elderly 1981; mem: Am. Inst. Certified Planners, Am. Planning Assn., L.A. Area C.of C. (bd.); civic: UCLA Grad. Sch. of Arch. and Urban Plng. Dean's Council (exec. com. 1975-), UCLA Found. (bd. trustees 1984-), UCLA John E. Anderson Grad. Sch. of Mgmt. Bd. of Visitors (exec. com. 1986-), UCLA Sch. of Med. The Aesculapians (exec. com. 1988-), Calif. Council for Humanities (v.chair), Mt. St. Mary's Coll. Bd. Regents 1984-, Com. of 200 (pres. 1984-85); club: Regency (L.A.); contbr. articles to num. profl. publs. Ofc: Bobrow/Thomas and Associates 1001 Westwood Blvd Los Angeles 90024 Ph: 213/208-7017

THOMAS, ROGER HARRY, physician; b. July 24, 1944, Waco, Tx.; s. Ray B. and Dorothy (Barland) T.; m. Jolane Oberle, Aug. 6, 1966; children: Allyson b. 1969, Julie b. 1971, Suzanne b. 1975; edn: BA, Georgetown Univ. Wash. DC 1966; MD, St. Louis Univ. 1970; reg. Am. Coll. Radiology 1975. Career: intern Harbor Gen. Hosp., Torrance 1970-71; resident UCSD 1971-75; staff radiologist Hoag Hosp., Newport Beach 1975-; mem: CMA, Calif. Radiological Soc., Orange Co. Med. Assn., Orange Co. Radiological Soc., Am. Coll. Radiology, Radiological Soc. N. Am., Am. Inst. Ultrasound in Medicine; Republican; Catholic; rec: golf. Res: 1636 Anita Ln Newport Beach 92660 Ofc: Newport Harbor Radiology 355 Placentia Ste 207 Newport Beach 92660

THOMAS, TENA S., real estate broker, civic volunteer; b. May 28, Jackson, La.; d. Toney and Lucy (Barnes) Scott; edn: BS, Southern Univ., Baton Rouge; MS, postgrad. studies, USC, Los Angeles. Career: real estate broker/prin., Los Angeles; former supr. Morehouse Parish Sch. Dist., Bastrop, La.; tchr. L.A. Unif. Sch. Dist.; postgrad. student and researcher at USC (sch. dist. sabbatical lv.); trainee Hampton (Va.) Inst.; bd. dirs. Teen Challenge, L.A. and counselor Teen Post; honors: commendn. L.A. Police Dept. (1975, 86), citation City of Los Angeles 1971, citizen of year Wilshire Comm. Police Council 1973, resolution L.A. City Council and L.A. Police Dept. and plaque from Lt. Gov. and State Dept. Calif. awarded at Volunteers for Love & Cheer 20th Annual Luncheon 1989, Realtor of Year award Westside R.E. Assn. 1990; mem. Westside R.E. Assn. (pres.-elect, recipient Pres.'s award 1987); civic: Town Hall Calif., L.A. World Affairs Council, Volunteers for Love & Cheer (founder, dir. 1970-), Wilshire Comm. Police Council (a founder, dir. 1971-75); Prot.; avocation: helping people thru prayer, counseling and love; rec: football. Ofc: Tena S. Thomas Real Estate 5225 Wilshire Blvd Ste 411 Los Angeles 90036

THOMAS, TIMOTHY WARREN, pest control co. executive, federal census supervisor; b. July 6, 1953, Los Angeles; s. Frank Harry and Dorothea Albertine (Kieffner) T.; edn: AA, El Camino Coll. 1976; lic. opr. Calif. Structural Pest Control Bd. (1977). Career: book store clerk El Camino Coll., Gardena 1973; termite control techn./gen. mgr. Lincoln Termite & Pest Control, Santa Monica 1974-6; mgr. termite div. Hydrex Pest Control, W. L.A., and subs. cos. Calif. Exterminator, and Lincoln Termite and Pest Control, 1977-86; urban entomology cons., service system adviser and struct. specialist, Queen Termite and Pest Control, Inglewood 1986; T&D Co., Lancaster 1989-; instr. cert. courses Pest Control Oprs. of Calif., L.A. Dist. (1980, 81), Calif. Dept. Agri. 1982, Struct. Pest Control Bd. 1982; winner 1st pl. trophy Rosamond, Calif. Chili Cook-off 1981, finalist Nevada State Chili Cook-off 1980; mem: Nat. Pest Control Assn., Pest Control Oprs. of Calif. (L.A. Dist. chmn. 1985-86, bd. dirs.), Delta Phi Sigma Frat., Internat. Chili Soc., Harley Davidson Owners Group, Profl. plus Network Group; field supr. for U.S. Census, Antelope Valley; Democrat; Lutheran; rec: computer pgmmg., painting, cooking, gunsmith, silversmith. Address: 3753 East Ave I Sp 122 Lancaster 93535

THOMAS, VIOLETA MARIA DE LOS ANGELES, real estate broker; b. Dec. 21, 1949, Buenos Aires, came to U.S. 1968; d. Angel and Lola (Andino) de Rios; m. Jess Thomas, Dec. 23, 1974; son, Victor Justin; edn: BA, Pine Manor Coll., 1970; BBA, Univ. Bus. Adminstrn., Buenos Aires 1971. Career: mgr. book div. Time-Life, N.Y.C., 1970-74; real estate broker First Marin Realty Inc., Mill Valley, Calif. 1985-; named Woman of Year City of Buenos Aires 1977, R.E. Agent of Year Marin County & S.F. 1987, 88, 89, 90, 91, 92; civic commr. City of Tiburon Art & Heritage Commn. 1987-. Res: PO Box 662, Ten Owlswood Rd Tiburon 94920

THOMAS, WILLIAM BOWEN, manufacturing company executive; b. May 29, 1920, Castleford, Idaho; s. William Warner Thomas and Laura Vivian Taylor; m. Wave Young, Jan. 22, 1951 (div. 1981); m. Miraijana Cvijanovich, Jan. 18, 1983; children: Gail Ann Westwood; edn: Burley H.S., Burley, Idaho. Career: co-founder, Big O Tires, Inc., 1962-92; v.p., Big O Tires, Inc., 1962-85, pres., 1985; bd. of dirs, Big O Tires, Inc., 1962-92; dir., Am. Retreaders Assn., Louisville, Ky. 1968-78, pres. 1978-82; awards: AMF Industry Leadership award, Am. Machine Foundry, 1980; Hall of Fame, Big O Tires, Inc., Englewood, Colo., 1993; President's Club (life), Brigham Young Univ., Provo, Utah; mem: Nat. Tire Dealer & Retreader Assn. (NTDRA), 1950-92; patents: first retractable seat belt, stitcher for laying rubber on tires being retreaded, windshield wiper, ejector impact socket; avocation: rancher, study of history (Winston Churchill). Res: P.O. Box 2468 Portola 96122

THOMAS, WILLIAM HENRY, manufacturing co. executive; b. Nov. 23, 1935, Pasadena; s. Daniel Waylette and Mary Elizabeth (Evans) T.; m. Eunice McAlear, Dec. 20, 1959; 1 son: Kirk Henry, b. 1960; edn: BS, Univ. of Montana 1962. Career: adminstr. Dinklespiel, Pelavin, Steefel & Levitt, San Francisco; financial mgr. Vinnel Steel Corp., Oakland; acct./ ofc. mgr. Smyth Van & Storage, San Francisco and Redwood City; secty./ treas. Utility Body Co., Berkeley; dir. Utility Body Co., Podllok Co., Pac Masher Co.; mil: E-5 USN 1954-9, Nat. Def. Medal; Republican; Disciples of Christ ; rec: antiques. Res 1209 Lafayette St Alameda 94501 Ofc: Utility Body Co. 1727 16th St Oakland 94607

THOMASON, DOUGLAS NAAMAN, lawyer; b. Oct. 29, 1949, San Bernardino; s. Ryland Marston and Evelyn Anna (McCutcheon) T.; edn: BA, UC Berkeley, 1979; JD, Santa Clara Univ., 1985; admitted bar: Calif. 1988. Career: atty., assoc. Ericksen, Arbuthnot, Brown, Kilduff & Day, Oakland 1989-90; Law Offices of John C. Shaffer Jr., Menlo Park 1991-; Pres.'s research grantee Santa Clara Coll. 1986; mem. San Mateo County Bar Assn. 1991-, ACLU; publ: law rev. article (1990); Democrat. Res: 3653 20th St San Francisco 94110 Law Offices of John C. Shaffer Jr. 750 Menlo Ave Ste 250 Menlo Park 94025

THOMASON, PHILLIP BRIAN, linguist, educator; b. dec. 12, 1949, Shawmut, Ala.; s. Marchel Earl and Margaret Evelyn (Wall) T.; m. Cathy Lea Ray, Aug. 19, 1972; 1 son, Brian b. 1977; edn: AB (highest hons.), Univ. of Montevallo, Ala. 1972; MHS in Hispanic studies, Auburn Univ., 1975; PhD, Univ. Ky., Lexington 1987. Career: tchr. of Spanish Kendrick High Sch., Columbus, Ga. 1972-74; Marion (Ala.) Military Inst., 1975-81; grad. asst. Univ. of Ky., 1981-85; instr. Asbury Coll., Ky. 1986; assoc. prof. Pepperdine Univ., Malibu, Calif. 1986-, Language Ctr. director 1990-91; awards: Innovative tchg. ideas Ga. Dept. Edn., Atlanta 1976, fellow Ministry of Culture of Spain, Madrid 1985, Outstanding Young Men of Am. (1977, 88), Who's Who in West 1992-93, Who's Who in Am. Educ. 1993; mem: Fgn. Lang. Alliance of So. Calif. (com. 1991-92), Am. Assn. of Tchrs. of Spanish & Port. 1985-, S.W. Conf. on Lang. Teaching (advy. coun. 1987-), Soc. of the Seven Sages 1983-, Sigma Delta Pi 1972-; publs: diss: El Coliseo de la Cruz Madrid's First Permanent Theatre (1987); article in Bull. of Hispanic Studies (1993), translator various religious articles; Ch. of Christ; rec: jogging, gardening. Res: 76 W Avenida de las Flores Thousand Oaks 91360 Ofc: Pepperdine Univ. Modern Language Dept. Malibu 90263-4212

THOMFORD, WILLIAM EMIL, mechanical engineer, railway equipment technical consultant; b. March 15, 1927, San Francisco; s. Emil George and Anna Marie (Robohm) T.; m. Irene Shapoff, March 21, 1948; children: Elaine Margaret b. 1951; John William b. 1955; edn: AA, City Coll. of San Francisco 1949; BA, UC Berkeley 1951; transp. mgmt., Stanford Grad. Sch. of Bus. 1967; Reg. Profl. Engr. Calif. 1978. Career: with So. Pacific Transp. Co., San Francisco 1951-: locomotive and car draftsman 1951, asst. chief draftsman 1958, asst. mgr. mech. engring. & res. 1964, mgr. design engring. 1966, mgr. car engring. 1972, asst. chief mech. ofcr. 1978, mgr. research & test 1980, ret. 1983; currently, tech. cons. railway equip. and transp.; mem. Assn. of Am. Railroads Car Constrn. Com. 1965- (subcom. chmn., 10 yrs., com. chmn. 1981-83); honors: Henderson Medal, The Franklin Inst., Phila. 1964, Best Design In Steel-Transp. Equip., Am. Iron & Steel Inst. 1971, Arnold Stucki Award, ASME, Rail Transp. Div. 1991; mem: Am. Soc. of Mech. Engrs. (Fellow 1986), Nat. Soc. of Profl. Engrs., Car Dept. Ofcrs. Assn., Engrs. Club of San Francisco, Pacific Railway Club; inventor: "Hydra-Cushion" (1st hydraulic impact cushioning device for freight cars), "Vert-A-Pac" (for shipment of 30 autos), Double-Stack Container Car; mil: USN, WWII 1944-46; Lutheran; rec: fishing, golf. Address: Transportation Consulting Services, 1176 Glenwood Dr Millbrae 94030

THOMPSON, CHRISTOPHER ALAN, real estate developer; b. Jan. 21, 1957, San Rafael; s. Robert Edward Thompson and Connie Francis (Egbert) Pope; edn: BBA, Harding Univ. 1983; Calif. lic.: R.E. Broker, Gen. Bldg. Contr., Gen. Engring. Contr., Securities Dealer. Career: apprentice painter W.G. Thompson Inc., San Francisco 1971-73; ski techn. Seasons Ski & Sport, San Anselmo 1973-75; foreman painter Barbara Cross Inc., San Rafael 1974-78; shopping mall mgr. Walnut Woods Ctr., Oakdale 1978-80; painter self-empl., San Anselmo 1980-83; project mgr. Jay & T. Development Inc., Petaluma 1983-

84; exec. v.p. Thompson Devco Inc., San Rafael 1984-; pres. TDI/St. Helena Home Corp., 1990-; mem: Soc. of Collegiate Journalists, C.of C., US Jaycees (charter); Republican; Ch. of Christ. Res: 851 Irwin St San Rafael 94901 Ofc: Thompson Devco, Inc. PO Box 829 Larkspur 94939

THOMPSON, CLAYTON HOWARD, software engineer, aerospace co. technical director; b. Aug. 29, 1939, Albert Lea, Minn.; s. Howard Truman and Bernice Neisina (Munson) T.; m. George Ann DeVault, Mar. 5, 1961 (div. 1979); children: Clayton b. 1961, David b. 1964; m. Kari Joan Dahlinger, Apr. 6, 1985; edn: BS, Colo. State Univ., 1973, MBA, 1974. Career: served to lt. col. US Air Force 1959-80; software engr. Hughes Aircraft, L.A. 1980-81; software mgr. Contel Info Systems, Dayton, Oh. 1981-82; software mgr. Ford Aerospace, Colorado Springs, CO 1982-86; tech. dir. Northrop, L.A. 1986-; mem: Assn. of Computing Machinery 1983-, Soc. of Concurrent Engring., Retired Ofcrs. Assn.; civic: Conejo Futures Found., Thousand Oaks; rec: jogging, mtn. biking. Ofc: Northrop 1 Northrop Ave Hawthorne.

THOMPSON, DAVID JOHN, association executive, consultant; b. June 2, 1942, Blackpool, England; nat. 1976; s. Herbert and Edith Una (Clayton) T.; m. Ann Mary Evans, Sept. 6, 1980; edn: AA, Santa Monica 1970; BA, UCLA 1973; MA, 1977. Career: dir. western region Norman Hilton 1965-68; salesman Carroll & Co., Beverly Hills 1969-79; dir. western region Nat. Cooperative Bank, Wash. D.C. 1979-84; v.p. Nat. Cooperative Bus. Assn. 1984-91; pres. Thompson Consulting, 1991-; pres. Twin Pines. Cooperative Found., Berkeley 1985-; v.p. Associated Cooperatives, Richmond 1985-; advy. bd. Working Assets, San Francisco 1986-; advy. com. Calif. Assembly Select Com. on Small Bus., Sacto. 1984-; consumer advy. com. Calif. Dept. Food & Agri. 1977-79; honors: Grad. Sch. of Arch. & Urban Planning Dean's comm. service award 1977, Dean Ruenitz award Santa Monica Coll. 1969; mem: Nat. Museum of Labor History (Manchester, Eng.), Fairtrade Found. (bd. 1989-), Center for Cooperatives Univ. Calif. (advy. bd. 1988-); publs: 100+ articles on cooperatives; editor: Cooperative Bus. in U.S.A. 1985, Where Credit Was Due 1985, A Rainbow on the Mountain 1980; mil: pvt. U.K. Territorial Army 1958-59; Democrat; rec: co-ops, arch. & urban plng., bibliophile. Ofc: 516 Rutgers Dr Ste 2 Davis 95616

THOMPSON, EVON LEE, mortgage broker; b. Dec. 1, 1946, Baltimore; d. Edward W. and Altia (Nixon) Lee; m. Nathan Beams, Nov. 1, 1981 (div. 1987); children: Christopher M.; edn: BS, Morgan State Coll., Balt., 1968; MBA, Atlanta Univ., 1969. Career: pub. service employment coordinator City of Oakland, Calif. 1971-75; dep. dir. recreation, parks and community svsc. City of Berkeley, 1975-79; sales agt. Fox and Carskadon Realtors, Oakland 1979-83; mortgage broker Canty & Assocs., Oakland 1984-90; mortgage broker/prin. Mortgage Loan Professionals, 1990-; awards: Ford Found. fellow 1968, Morgan State Coll. grantee (1962-64); mem: Am. Mktg. Assn. (sec. 1965-68), Soc. for Advancement of Mgmt. (chartered), Morgan State Coll. Alumni Assn. (v.p. 1985-), Alpha Kappa, Chi Psi Sigma; civic: Bay Area Big Sisters (1975-80), Hope Acad. Parents Assn. 1982-89, Fairview Home Club 1990-; Republican; Methodist. Res: 333 Hegenberger Rd #215 Oakland 94621

THOMPSON, JACK COATS, meterologist, educator, ret.; b. Oct. 5, 1909, Donner Summit; s. William and Elizabeth Bruce (Coats) T.; m. Violette Rausch, Oct. 6, 1934 (dec. Mar. 1992); edn: AB, UCLA 1948; grad. Scripps Inst. Oceanography 1949; Am. Univ. 1951; Ind. Univ. 1959; Meteorologist US Nat. Weather Service (1929-65). Career: aerologist Sacto. Airport Comm. 1928-29; observer US Weather Bureau, S.F. 1930-36; meteorologist, Pomona 1937-47; meteorologist in charge L.A. 1948-56; dir. systems devel. Wash. D.C. 1957-65; prof. meteorology San Jose St. Univ. 1966-75; cons. World Meterorol. Orgn., Geneva, Switz., 1965-72, USAF, 1974, Stanford Res. Inst., 1974; awards: US Dept. Commerce silver medal, 1955, Sigma Xi, 1959; mem: Am. Meteorol. Soc. (nat. councilor 1965), Wash. Acad. Sci., 1956; author (w. Albert Miller): Elements of Meteorol. (Charles E. Merrill Pub. Co., 1970, 2d ed. 1975, 3d ed. 1979), 40+ sci. papers; rec: lawn bowling. Address: c/o The Samarkand, 2550 Treasure Drive Santa Barbara CA 93105

THOMPSON, JOSIAH, investigator, author; b. Jan. 17, 1935, Ohio; s. Donald and Marion P.; m. Nancy W., Dec. 27, 1958; edn: BA, Yale Univ. 1957; MA, 1962; PhD, 1964. Career: instr. Yale Univ., New Haven, Conn. 1964-65; asst. prof. Haverford Coll., Pa. 1965-70, assoc. prof. 1970-75, prof. 1975-78; owner Josiah Thompson Investigations, San Francisco 1980 ; awards: Guggenhcim Found. Fellowship 1969-70; mem: Am. Assn. Univ. Profs., World Assn. Detectives, Calif. Assn. Legal Investigators; author: Six Seconds in Dallas, 1967, The Lonely Labyrinth, 1967, Kierkegaard, 1973, Gumshoe, 1988; mil: lt. j.g. USN 1951-57. Ofc: 2176 Union St #4 San Francisco 94123

THOMPSON, LARRY ANGELO, lawyer, film producer, personal manager; b. Aug. 1, 1944, Clarksdale, Miss.; s. Angelo and Ann (Tuminello) T.; edn: BBA, Univ. Miss., 1966, JD, 1968; admitted bar: Miss. 1968, Calif. 1970. Career: in-house counsel Capitol Records, Hollywood 1969-71; sr. ptnr. in entertainment law, Thompson, Shankman and Bond, Beverly Hills 1971-77; pres. Larry A. Thompson Orgn., Inc. 1977-; co-owner New World Pictures, 1983-85; lectr. entertainment bu. UCLA, USC, SW Univ. of Law Sch., co-chmn.

Repub. Nat. Entertainment Com.; apptd. by Gov. to Calif. Entertainment Commn.; recipient Show Bus. Atty. of Yr. award Capitol Records 1971; mem: ABA, Miss. Bar Assn., Calif. Bar Assn., Inter-Am. Bar Assn., Hon. Order Ky. Colonels, Am. Film Inst., Nat. Acad. Recording Arts and Scis., Acad. of TV Arts and Scis., Hollywood Radio and TV Soc.; author: How to Make a Record Deal & Have Your Songs Recorded (1975); Prime Time Crime (1982); producer motion pictures: Crimes of Passion (1984), My Demon Lover (1987), Quiet Cool (1987), Breaking the Rules (1992); prod. t.v. shows: Jim Nabors Show (1977, Emmy nominee), Mickey Spillane's Mike Hammer (1981), Bring 'Em Back Alive, CBS series (1984), The Other Lover, CBS Movie (1985), Convicted, ABC Movie (1986), Intimate Encounters, NBC Movie (1986), The Woman He Loved, CBS Movie on Duke & Duchess of Windsor (1988), Original Sin, NBC Movie (1989), Class Cruise, NBC Movie (1989), Little White Lies, NBC Movie (1989), Lucy & Desi: Before The Laughter (1990); served w/ JAGC, AUS 1966-72; Republican; R.Cath. Res: 9451 Hidden Valley Pl Beverly Hills 90210 Ofc: Larry A. Thompson Organization 345 N Maple Dr Ste 183 Beverly Hills 90210

THOMPSON, LARRY EDWARD, massage therapist; b. May 2, 1943, San Jose; s. James E. and Lowie B. (Thompson) T.; edn: Calif. Polytech. Univ. 1961-62; Foothill Coll. 1975-78; Harbin Hot Springs Sch. of Shiatsu and Massage, 1989-90; Sports Massage Therapy Inst., 1990; adv. course participant USSR Therapeutic and Sports Massage, Moscow, 1990. Career: conf. coord. Syntex USA Inc., Palo Alto 1967-77; mgr. corp. office svs. Cooper Cos. Inc. 1977-89; owner Life Energy Therapies, Los Altos 1990-; mem: Am. Massage Therapy Assn. (v.p. Silicon Valley Unit, 1991-92), Adminstrv. Mgmt. Soc. (past pres.), U.S. Figure Skating Assn., Community Skating Inc. (bd. dirs.); mil: SP-4 AUS 1964-66; rec: ice skating, skiing, sailing. Res: 638 Homer Palo Alto 94301 Ofc: Life Energy Therapies, 960 N San Antonio Rd 131-B Los Altos 94022

THOMPSON, THOMAS MICHAEL, naval logistics management executive; b. Dec. 3, 1943, Eureka; s. Henry Clay and Margaret Marion (Lee) T.; edn: BA, Seattle Univ. 1965; MA, Univ. San Francisco, 1989. Career: gen. supply splst. US Army Weapons Command, Rock Island, Ill. 1966-67; inventory mgmt. splst. Sharpe Army Depot, Lathrop 1967-69; inventory mgmt. splst. Naval Ship Weapon Systems Engineering Sta., Port Hueneme 1969-73, logistics mgmt. splst. 1973-83, asst. for logistics tech. ops. 1983-86, div. mgr., 1986-91, dept. mgr., 1991-92, dept. mgr. Port Hueneme Div., Naval Surface Warfare Center, 1992-; recipient Sustained Superior Performance awards; Republican; R.Cath.; rec: teach religious edn. Res: 2507 Grapevine Dr Oxnard 93030 Ofc: PHD, NSWC Code 5B00 Port Hueneme 93043-5007

THOMSEN, ELEANOR A., retired municipal real property manager; b. July 26, 1925, Omaha, Neb.; d. Tony and Rose M. (Pesek) Dimitroff; m. John W. Thomsen, Sept. 11, 1948; children: Gary L. b. 1949, Ronnie K. b. 1952; grandsons, Michael C. b. 1987, Brian M. b. 1991; edn: AA, Chabot Jr. Coll. 1976; BS, Univ. San Francisco 1979; MPA, CSU Hayward 1983; Calif. lic. real estate broker, 1965. Career: clk. Alameda County Public Works Agy. 1964-65, steno., secty. 1965-73, asst. right of way agent 1973-76, assoc. right of way agent 1976-87; real property mgr. City of Hayward, 1987-90; honors: Right of Way Profl. of the Yr. (1982), cert. of achievement in real estate, prop. mgmt. (1974, 77); mem: South Bay Engrs., East Bay Engrs., Am. Public Works Assn., Internat. Right of Way Assn. (pres. 1985); contbr. num. animal rights orgns.; Republican; R.Cath.; rec: crocheting, travel. Res: 909 Regency Court San Ramon 94583-5626

THOMSON, JAMES ALAN, research organization president and chief executive; b. Jan. 21, 1945, Boston, Mass.; s. James Alan and Mary Elizabeth (Pluff) T.; m. Linda Jayne Eggert, June 10, 1967 (div. Dec. 1988); children: Kristen b. 1970, David b. 1972; m. Darlene Marie Weaver, Jan. 5, 1990; edn: BS, Univ. New Hampshire, Durham 1967; MS, Purdue Univ., 1970, PhD, 1972. Career: res. fellow Univ. Wisconsin, Madison 1972-74; systems analyst U.S. Dept. Def., W.D.C. 1974-77; staff Nat. Security Council, 1977-81; v.p. RAND, Santa Monica, Calif. 1981-89, pres. and CEO 1989-; awarded Hon. Doctorate in Sci., Purdue Univ. 1992; mem.: Internat. Inst. of Strategic Studies, London (1982-, Council mem., trustee 1985-), Council on Foreign Relations; author: Conventional Arms Control and the Security of Europe (1988), chapters in books and pub. articles. Ofc: RAND 1700 Main Street PO Box 2138 Santa Monica 90407-2138

THOMSON, ROBERTA NELSON, genealogical researcher/historian; b. Dec. 11, 1909, San Francisco; d. Robert Elwood and Florence Corle (Rubicam) Nelson; m. John Burnside Thomson, Jr., July 19, 1930 (dec. Aug. 10, 1981); children: Phyllis Lea Sykes b. 1937, Joyce Beth Crowell b. 1941, Victoria Rose Broadhurst b. 1948; edn: grad. Madison Grammar Sch., S.F., Girls' High Sch., S.F., Miss Barclay's Business Sch., S.F., 1926. Career: author: (Suppl.) genealogical book: Patterson-Andrews Register, 1963-73; (family hist.) Roberta Remembers, 2 vols., 1983; (family hist.) Ancestral Anthology, 2 vols., 1984; author, compiler: Sequoia Chapter DAR 100 Year History 1891-1991, 4 vols., 1991; researcher Andrews/ Clapp/ Stokes/ Wright/ Van Cleve Genealogy Book, 1975; active Nat. Soc. Daughters of Am. Revolution, Sequoia Chpt. (first DAR chpt. Calif., organized 1891; regent 1975-77, chaplain 1983-85, 88-90, historian/speaker 1980-82, 89-93), Colonial Dames XVII Century, Anne Bradstreet Chpt. (active mem. as chaplain/speaker 1981-93), Chester County Hist. Soc., Pa. (donor/ writer/ manuscripts), Montgomery Clan of N.Am., Calif. (researcher), Calif. Genealogical Soc. (S.F.), Rittenhouse Family Assn. (Pa.), Mechanics Inst. Library, S.F. (life); recipient nat. and Calif. state NSDAR Awards as Sequoia Chpt. regent, chmn. and speaker: Bicentennial Planting and Marking of 5 trees in Golden Gate Park and Parade Grounds of The Presidio of San Francisco; Marking of 4 Revolutionary War Ancestors' Graves in Pa. (1979); Yorktown Com. "World Turned Upside Down" (1981); Two-Volume Ancestral Anthologies (1984); Restoration, Statue of Liberty (1984); Remembrances of old San Francisco (1987); Rittenhouse Tricentennial Reunion (1988); Coit Tower (Lillie Hitchcock Coit: A Pioneer DAR Member) (1989); 100 Year History of Sequoia Chapter DAR (1991); recipient Martha Washington Medal, Nat. Soc. Sons of the Am. Revolution (1993); Republican; Presbyterian; rec: researching & collecting Old San Francisco memorabilia.

THORP., CHARLES PHILIP, clergyman; b. Nov. 27, 1949, San Francisco; s. Robert Jay and Natalie Ann (Lotti) T.; edn: Diablo Valley Jr. Coll., San Francisco St. Univ. Career: cons. est, San Francisco 1973-75; counselor S.D.S.I., 1976-78; ordained minister and founder The Church For Unity And Service, San Francisco 1978-, lectr. seminars and retreats; radio show host "Radio Free Religion" KWUN, 1985; cons. Rivendell Sch., S.F. Francisco 1976-78; counselor Am. Humanist Assn. 1974-83; honors: Hon. PhD, USSR (1979); mem. Nat. Caption Inst., COAST User Group, Berkeley/Oakland (1st pres. 1986-88, 90), E.B.M.U.G., D.V.A.U.G. and B.M.U.G. user groups; civic: Child Abuse Prevention Council Contra Costa Co.; author pub. poetry, 1965-70, (inspirational books) Quotes From The Inner Door, 3 vols., 1980-88; Democrat; rec: watercolorist (exhibs.), computers, desktop publishing, acting, writing, dance. Res: 1015 Esther Dr Pleasant Hill 94523-4301

THUESON, DAVID OREL, medical scientist; b. May 9, 1947, Twin Falls, Idaho; s. Orel Grover and Shirley Jean (Archer) T.; m. Sherrie Linn Lowe, June 14, 1969; children: Sean, Kirsten, Eric, Ryan, Todd; edn: BS, Brigham Young Univ., 1971; PhD, Univ. of Utah, 1976. Career: research scientist Univ. of Texas, Galveston 1976-77, asst. prof. Univ. Texas Med. Br., 1977-82; sr. res. assoc. Parke-Davis Pharm., Ann Arbor, Mich. 1982-88; dir. Immunetech Pharm., San Diego, Calif. 1988-90; dir. Tanabe Research Labs., San Diego 1990-93; v.p. Cosmederm Technologies, La Jolla 1993-; awards: Doyle scholar Santa Rosa Jr. Coll. 1965-66, NIH pre-doctoral fellow, W.D.C. 1971-75, McLaughlin post-doc. fellow Univ. Texas Med. Br. 1975-77, NIAID Young Investigator, NIH-Allergy, Galveston, Tx. 1978-81; mem: Am. Acad. Allergy & Clin. Immunol. 1978-, Am. Assn. of Immunologists 1981-, Am. Thoracic Soc. 1991-; author: 4 U.S. patents, Fgn. filed (1990-), 38+ sci. jour. articles (1974-), 1 book (1992). Res: 12740 Boxwood Ct Poway 92064 Ofc: Cosmederm Technologies La Jolla Corp Ctr La Jolla 92037

TIEN, CHANG-LIN, university chancellor; b. July 24, 1935, Wuhan, China, naturalized U.S. cit. 1969; s. Yun Chien and Yun Di (Lee) T.; m. Di-Hwa Liu, July 25, 1959; children: Norman Chihnan, Phyllis Chihping, Christine Chihyih; edn: BS, Nat. Taiwan Univ., 1955; MME, Univ. Louisville, 1957; MA, PhD, Princeton Univ., 1959. Career: actg. asst. prof. dept. mech. engring. UC Berkeley, 1959-60, asst. prof. 1960-64, assoc. prof. 1964-68, prof. mech. engring. 1968-89, 1990-, A. Martin Berlin Prof. 1987-88, 1990-, dept. chmn. 1974-81; vice chancellor research UC Berkeley, 1983-85;exec. v. chancellor and UC Irvine distinguished prof. 1988-90; chancellor UC Berkeley, 1990-; tech. cons. Lockheed Missiles & Space, GE Corp.; trustee Princeton Univ. 1991-; dir: Wells Fargo Bank 1991-; awards: Guggenheim fellow 1965, Heat Transfer Memorial Award 1974, ASME Gustus L. Larson Memorial Award 1975; Fellow: AAAS, ASME (Max Jakob Memorial Award), AIAA (Thermophysics Award 1977), mem. NAE; contbr. articles in profl. jours.; rec: sports. Ofc: Chancellor's Office University of California Berkeley 94720

TILL, FRANKLIN LEROY, JR., school district administrator; b. Jan. 20, 1947, San Diego; s. Franklin L., Sr. and Luella Till; m. Barbara, May 1, 1971; children: Marlo b. 1970, Jeffrey b. 1974; edn: BA, San Diego St. Univ. 1969, MA, 1973; EdD, USC, 1981. Career: tchr. San Diego Unified Sch. Dist., 1970-76, edn. coordinator 1976-78, vice prin. 1978-83, principal 1978-83, dist. ops. mgr. 1985-87, asst. supt. ednl. and services div. 1986-93, deputy superintendent 1993-; instr. SDSU 1975-86; recipient 3 hon. service awards PTA 1983, 84, 85, appreciation YMCA 1984, 85, 86, golden award ACSA 1980; mem: Assn. Calif. Sch. Adminstrs. (dir. 1976-85), ASCD, Nat. Assn. Secondary Principals; civic: YMCA (bd. 1983-), United Way, Optimist (chmn. 1983-87); editor Networker Mag. 1976-77; author (math curr.) Individualized Approach 1973-76, Thaust Mag. 1988-, Technology in Classroom; Democrat; Methodist; rec: running, reading. Res: 5851 Torca Ct San Diego 92124-1020 Ofc: San Diego City Schools 4100 Normal St Rm 2011 San Diego 92103

TILLMAN, DONNA, educator, marketing consultant; b. Dec. 23, 1940, Linn, Mo.; d. Clarence A. and Josephine G. (Bakenbush) Tillman; m. Dr. Mahmood A. Qureshi, July 1974 (div. 1983); 2 children by previous marriage Monica Iven b. 1964, Greg Iven b. 1965; edn: BS in edn., Lincoln Univ., Jefferson City, Mo.

1966; MA research sociology, PhD sociology (dept. fellow 2 yrs.), St. Louis Univ., 1967, 70; MBA, DePaul Univ. Grad. Sch. of Bus., 1980. Career: tenured prof. mktg. Calif. State Polytechnic Univ., Pomona; p.t. faculty Claremont Grad. Sch. and UC Riverside; former prof. sociol. and dept. chair Northeastern Ill. Univ., Chgo. 10 yrs., also vis. prof. and chair bus. dept. Barat Coll., Lake Forest, Ill.; past asst. prof. We. Ill. Univ., Macomb; hon. res. fellow dept. soc. adminstrn. Univ. Birmingham, U.K.; cons. industry and govt. mktg. agys. (incl. Gen. Motors, Calif. Avocado Commn., Calif. Grape Growers Assn.); frequent speaker profl. confs.; pub. res. and case studies, book reviews; awards: profl. promise Coll. Bus. Adminstrn. CalPoly for excellence in tchg., res. and univ. & comm. svc. 1989, Lottery grant to provide mktg. mgmt. assistance to Women and Minority owned bus. 1988, presdl. merit Northeastern Ill. Univ. 1979-80; mem: Am. Mktg. Assn., So. Calif. AMA, We. Mktg. Educators Assn.; rec: sailing, flying, dancing. Res: 1024 S Tait Oceanside 92054

TILTON, ROGER, video and motion picture producer/director; b. Jan. 14, 1924, E. St. Louis, Ill.; s. Leon Deming and Leila Olive (White) T.; m. Patricia Diane Badham, Jan. 29, 1960; children: Wendi Tilton Dvorak b. 1961, Sharon Tilton Montgomery b. 1962, Cynthia Tilton Sartain b. 1962, Kimberly Tilton Riley b. 1964; edn: BA, Stanford Univ., 1947; MA, Columbia Univ., 1948; MFA, Univ. Iowa, 1950. Career: pres. Roger Tilton Films, Inc., San Diego, 1954-; dir. documentary film: "Jazz Dance" 1954, producer feature film: "Spiker" 1984, prod./dir. 300+ films and TV commercials, 1960-; instr. motion pictures City Coll. N.Y., 1954-60, Columbia Univ., 1952-60; awards: Cannes Gold Medal, Cannes, Fr. 1963, Edinburgh Award of Merit, Edinburgh Festival, Scot. 1954, various cinematic awards, USA 1960-85; mem. Nat. Acad. TV Arts & Scis. (1980-); mil: lt.jg USNR 1943-46; Republican; Prot.; rec: sailing. Ofc: Roger Tilton Films, Inc. 1715 Soledad Way San Diego 92109

TIMBOE, RICHARD RAY, university administrator; b. Jan. 22, 1949, Long Beach; s. Floyd Robert and Bobbie Sue (Gates) T.; m. Verna Lee Stricklin, June 8, 1972; children: Scot Richard b. 1973, Branden Lee b. 1976; edn: BS, Mil. Acad. West Point, 1972; MS engring., Boston Univ., 1977; JD, Western States Univ., 1982. Career: cons. Price Waterhouse & Co., Los Angeles 1977-78; asst. v.p. CSU Long Beach 1978-; mil: capt. US Army 1972-77; Republican; Presbyterian; rec: sports. Ofc: California State University 1250 Bellflower Blvd Long Beach 90840-0101

TIMM, ROBERT MERLE, university administrator and extension wildlife specialist; b. Oct. 7, 1949, Pomona; s. Herbert Merle and Mary Elsie (Beasley) T.; m. Janice Howard Hawthorne, May 31, 1986; children: Anna Elizabeth b. 1989, Sarah Beatrice b. 1990; edn: BS biology, Univ. Redlands, 1971; MS ecology, UC Davis, 1973, PhD, 1977; cert. wildlife biologist The Wildlife Soc. 1981. Career: Ext. vertebrate pest specialist and assoc. prof. Univ. Nebraska, Lincoln 1978-87; supt. and Ext. wildlife specialist Hopland Res. and Extension Ctr., Univ. Calif., Hopland, Calif. 1987-; cons. rodent control, USAID and USDA, to Bangladesh 1989; invited speaker 2nd Symposium on Rodent Control, Kuwait City, Kuwait 1985; awards: outstanding book Natural Resource Council of Am., W.D.C. 1983, Rotary Internat. group study exchange fellow to Rep. South Africa 1982, outstanding new specialist Nebr. Coop. Extension Assoc., Lincoln 1982, excellence in pgmg. Nebr. Coop Ext. 1983; mem: Vertebrate Pest Council (chair elect 1992), The Wildlife Soc. 1974-, Am. Soc. of Mammalogists 1985-, Soc. for Range Mgmt. 1987-, Nat. Animal Damage Control Assn. (co-editor newsletter 1991-); publs: 90+ pub. articles on wildlife mgmt. and animal damage control, co-editor proceedings: Predator Mgmt. in North Coastal Calif. (1990), editor (book) Prevention & Control of Wildlife Damage (1983); United Ch. of Christ, Congregational (ch. pres. First Evangelical Covenant Ch., Lincoln, Nebr. 1983-85, Grace Luth. Ch., Ukiah, Ca. 1991-92). Res: 968 Riverside Dr Ukiah 95482 Ofc: UC Hopland Res. and Extension Ctr., 4070 University Rd Hopland 95449

TIMMINS, JAMES DONALD, venture capitalist; b. Oct. 3, 1955, Hamilton, Ontario, Can.; s/ Donald Gardiner and Myrna Letitia (Seymour) T.; edn: BA, Univ. of Toronto, Ontario, Can., 1978; law study, Queen's Univ., Kingston, Ontario, Can., 1979; business study, Stanford Univ., Stanford, Calif., 1981. Career: assoc. Salomon Brothers, S.F., Calif., 1981-84; managing dir. McKewon & Timmins, S.D., Calif., 1984-87; ptnr.Hambrecht & Quist, S.F., Calif., 1987-90; ptnr. Glenwood Capital, Menlo Park, Calif., 1991-; chmn. bd. dir. Paradigm Technology, Inc., San Jose, 1991-; bd. dir.: Iwerks Entertainment, Inc., Burbank 1991-, Magellan Systems, Inc., W. Covina,1991-, Visualization Technologies, Inc., Fremont 1991-; mem. Olympic Club, S.F., Calif.; Presbyn. Res: 735 Laurelwood Dr. San Mateo 94403 Ofc: Glenwood Capital 3000 Sand Hill Rd. Bldg. 4, Ste. 230, Menlo Park 94025

TINTAREV, KYRIL, mathematician; b. Aug. 9, 1956, St. Petersburg, Russia, naturalized U.S. 1985; s. Alexei P. Sokolov and Samuella A. Tintareva; m. Sonia Pratt, Sept. 1, 1981; children:, Nava b. 1982; edn: MSc, Univ. Leningrad, 1978; PhD, Weizmann Inst., Israel 1986. Career: vis. asst. prof. Purdue Univ., 1985-86; Univ. Minn., 1986-87; asst. prof. UC Irvine, 1987-; mil: Israel Defence Forces 1980-81; Jewish; rec: ancient Hebrew manuscripts. Ofc: Dept. Math. Univ. California Irvine 92717

TOBIN, HAROLD WILLIAM, lawyer; b. Apr. 7, 1922, San Francisco; s. Robert Douglass and Rita Mary (Lannon) T.; m. Julie de Laveaga, Apr. 6, 1946; m. 2d. Shirley Traynor, Jan. 5, 1965; children: Douglass b. 1947, Kathleen b. 1949, Harold, Jr. b. 1951, Suzanne b. 1956, Neil b. 1970; edn: undergrad. Univ. San Francisco 1940-42, U.S. Air Corps Aviation Cadet Sch. 1942-43, JD, U.S.F. Sch. of Law; admitted Calif. State Bar 1949, U.S. Dist. Ct. No. Dist. Calif. 1949, U.S. Ct. Appeals 1949. Career: aviation cadet U.S. Air Corps 1942-43, 1st lt. U.S. Army/ instr. Calif. State Guard, 1943-46; U.S. atty. Dept. of Army War Crims Trials, Manila, P.I. 1946-48; atty., assoc. Hone & Lobree; assoc. Benjamin I. McKinley 1951-53; ptnr. Jacobsen & Tobin 1953-57, Tobin and Ransom 1957-67; sole practice San Francisco 1970-71, Antioch 1971-, v.p. and gen. counsel 120 Fellowship, Pasadena 1973-; honors: 2nd Hearst Nat. Oratorical Contest, Hearst Newspapers, S.F. 1943; mem: Am. Bar Assn., Calif. Bar Assn., Am. Trial Lawyers Assn.; civic: Smithsonian Instn. (sustaining 1970-), Nat. Audubon Soc. (sustaining 1970-), Native Sons Golden West, Am. Legion S.F. Post @1 (post adjutant 1949-51), S.F. Press Club 1950-70, Commonwealth Club of Calif. 1949-57; works: play, Snap Back (1943); Republican (S.F. Repub. Co.Com. 1949-51, 68-70); R.Cath.; rec: books, poetry, ornithology. Res: 2100 Reseda Way Mira Vista Hills Antioch 94509 Ofc: 3240 Lone Tree Way Ste 103 Antioch 94509

TODD, BLAKE T., financial consultant; b. Aug. 20, 1955, San Diego; s. Roger Grey and Mary Martha (Tramill) T.; m. Darcena Lee Shears, May 24, 1986 (div. Apr. 1, 1989); edn: undergrad. Pepperdine Univ. 1973-75, study abd. in Heidelberg, Germany 1974-5; BA in hist., UC Santa Cruz, 1977. Career: asst. mgr. Pacific Stereo, Glendale 1977-79; account exec. Dean Witter Reynolds, Pasadena 1979-81; assoc. v.p. Kidder Peabody & Co., Los Angeles 1981-88; portfolio mgr., v.p. Shearson Lehman Brothers and v.p. reg. inst. sales group Lehman Bros, Glendale 1988-; mem. Pasadena Bond Club (dir. 1982-, pres. 1991-92), Rotary (past), Tripod Directors Circle, Newcommen Soc., Los Angeles Bond Club 1992-; Republican. Res: 3009 San Gabriel Ave Glendale 91208 Ofc: Shearson Lehman Brothers, 550 N Brand Blvd Ste 1100 Glendale 91203

TOFTNESS, CECIL GILMAN, lawyer; b. Sept. 13, 1920, Glasgow, Mont.; s. Anton Bernard and Nettie (Pederson) T.; m. Chloe Vincent, 1951; edn: AA, San Diego Evening Jr. Coll. 1943; BS, UCLA, 1947; JD, Southwestern Univ. 1953. Career: pvt. practice of civil law, 1954-, legal splty. Estate Planning; active duty US Navy 1938-46, naval ofcr. USNR 1946-; honors: Class rep. Class 1953 Southwestern Law Sch., listed Who's Who in Am. Law 1985, Who's Who in Am. Fin. and Ind.; mem: Kiwanis (P.V.), Masons (Manhattan Beach-Redondo Beach #742 Blue Lodge, Royal Arch Mason, Knight Templar, LA Commander #9), Phi Delta Legal Frat.; Democrat; Lutheran; rec: travel (partipant in Society Expedition thru the Northwest Passage), gardening, golf. Ofc: 2516 Via Tejon Palos Verdes Estates 90274

TOLLENAERE, LAWRENCE R., company chairman and chief executive; b. Nov. 19, 1922, Berwyn, Ill.; s. Cyrille and Modesta (Van Damme) T.; m. Mary Elizabeth Hansen, Aug. 14, 1948; children: Elizabeth b. 1951, Homer b. 1952, Stephanie b. 1953, Caswell b. 1956, Mary Jennifer b. 1964; edn: BS and MS in engring., Iowa State Univ., 1944, 1949; MBA, USC, 1969; LLD. (hon.), Claremont Grad. Sch., 1977. Career: engr. Aluminum Co. of Am., Huntington Park 1946-47; asst. prof. indsl. engring. Iowa State Univ. Ames 1947-50; sales rep. Am. Pipe and Constrn. Co. (name changed to Ameron, Inc., 1970), South Gate, Calif. 1950-53, specialist rep. to S.Am. 1953-54, 2d v.p./ div. mgr. Colombian Div., Bogota 1955-57, v.p./div. mgr. So. Calif. 1957-63, v.p. concrete pipe ops., Monterey Park, 1963-64, pres. corp. hq. 1965-67, dir., pres. and c.e.o. Ameron Inc. 1967-89, chrmn. bd. and c.e.o. 1989-; dir: Avery Dennison, Pasadena; Newhall Land and Farming Co., Valencia; Pacific Mutual Life Ins. Co., Newport Beach, The Parsons Corp., Pasadena, bd. chmn. Gifford-Hill-American, Inc., Dallas; mem: Merchants and Mfrs. Assn./L.A. (fmr. bd. chmn., dir.), The Beavers (hon. dir., past pres.), Calif. C.of C. (dir. 1977-92), Nat. Assn. of Mfrs., Soc. for Advancement of Mgmt., AMA Presidents Assn., Newcomen Soc. in N.Am., Alpha Tau Omega; civic bds: The Huntington Library, Art Gal. and Botanical Gardens (bd. trustees), Soc. of Fellows, The Huntington Library (life mem.), Claremont Univ. Ctr. Bd. of Fellows (emeritus 1991), Iowa State Univ. Found. (bd. of govs., Order of Knoll.); clubs: California (dir., pres.), Jonathan, Pauma Valley Country, San Gabriel Country, Bohemian (S.F.), Commanderie de Bordeaux (L.A.), Los Angeles Confrerie des Chevaliers du Tastevin, Twilight, Lincoln; mil: ensign to lt.jg USNR 1944-46, WWII; rec: philately, hunting, fishing, equestrian. Res: 1400 Milan Ave South Pasadena 91030 Ofc: 245 S. Los Robles Ave. Pasadena 91101

TOLMACH, JANE LOUISE, civic activist; b. Nov. 12, 1921, Havre, Mont., raised in Ventura, Calif.; d. Robert Francis and Veronica A. (Tracy) McCormick; m. Daniel Michael Tolmach, MD (pediatrician), Sept. 9, 1946; children: James, Richard, Eve Alice, Adam, Jonathan; two grandchildren; edn: AB, UCLA, 1943; MS soc. sci., Smith Coll., 1945; JD, Southwestern Univ. Sch. of Law, 1981. Career: volunteer community service orgns., Oxnard 1948-; mem. Ventura County Grand Jury 1958; Oxnard City Planning Commn. 1957-62; bd. trustees Camarillo State Hosp. 1959-68 (chmn. 1966-68); bd. trustees Oxnard Union H.S. Dist. 1965-72; elected Oxnard City Council 1970-78; bd. dirs. South Coast Area Transit (mem., chmn. 1973-78), So. Calif. Assn. of Govts. (comprehensive transp. steering com. 1974-75, SCAG exec. bd. 1975-76, v.ch. utilities and transp. com. 1977-78), Ventura County Energy Com. (1973-74), Ventura Co. Flood Zone II Advy. Com. (1972-77); mem. bds: St. John's Regional Med. Ctr. (dir. 1986-89), Calif. Comm. Colls. (bd. govs. 1982-87), State Reclamation Bd. (1981-82); Democrat: active local, state and nat. campaigns (mem., chair Ventura Co. Dem. central com. 1953-70, Calif. State central com. 1958-76, 89, Women's Chair South 66-70; del. nat. conv. 1960, 68, 76, 88, alt. del. 1956, 64; nominee State Assembly, 36th Dist. 1976); R.Cath: Res: 656 Douglas Ave Oxnard 93030

TOMEI, JOEL ALAN, architect; b. May 11, 1941, San Mateo; s. Joseph Ambrose and Grace Leona (Nunes) T.; m. Patricia Hayden Brown, July 12, 1964; children: Amanda H. b. 1978, Elizabeth Y. b. 1983; edn: AA, Santa Rosa Jr. Coll. 1961; BArch, MArch, UC Berkeley, 1966, 1967; Master City Plnng. in Urban Design, Harvard Univ., 1973; reg. arch. Calif. (1970), Ill., Mass.; cert. NCARB. Career: arch. Skidmore, Owings & Merrill, Archs./ Engrs., 1967-78: designer, job captain, Chgo. 1967-70, urban designer Boston 1971-74, San Francisco, also Tehran 1974-80, mem.steering com. chmn. Skidmore, Owings & Merrill 1976; project mgr. Hope Consulting Group, Archs./ Engrs., San Francisco 1979- v.p. 1980-, prin. architect 1983-; design team: Sears Tower, Chgo. 1968, U.S. Embassy, Moscow 1977, Bandar Shapour, New Town, Iran 1975, Yanbu, New Town, Saudi Arabia 1976, Saudi Naval Acad., Jeddah, S.A. 1981, project mgr. Moscone Conv. Ctr. Expansion, San Francisco 1987, project mgr. Hall of Justice Expansion, S.F. 1990; design jury critic UC Berkeley 1975; awards: Mellon Scholar Harvard Univ. 1972, 28th annual Progressive Architecture design awd. 1981, AIA award Republic Newspaper Plant, Columbus, Ind. 1980, AIA award Hall of Justice Expansion 1992; mem. Am. Inst. of Planners (AIP), Harvard Club (S.F.), S.F. Planning and Urban Research, S.F. Market Street Proj.; Democrat; Episcopalian; rec: photog., film making, gardening. Res: 167 20th Ave San Francisco 94121 Ofc: Williams & Tanaka 340 Pine St San Francisco 94104

TOMPKINS, DWIGHT EDWARD, lawyer; b. June 29, 1952, Toledo, Ohio; s. Leonard Charles and Amanda Virginia (Bunce) T.; m. Marilyn Vergara, June 15, 1974; children: Jason b. 1978, Kristin b. 1981; edn: BA anthropology, San Diego St. Univ., 1974; MPA, CSU Long Beach, 1982; JD, Loyola Law Sch., L.A. 1990; admitted bar: Calif. 1990, US Dist. Cts., Cent. Dist. Calif. 1990 and So. Dist. Calif. 1991. Career: mgr. City of South Gate 1976-81; supr. City of Long Beach 1981-85, budget analyst, 1985-89; law clk. Ching, Kurtz & Blix, 1989-90; atty., assoc. Ching & Associates, 1990-91; solo practice Law Offices of Dwight Edward Tompkins, 1991-; lectr. CSU Long Beach 1986; honors: Am. Jurisprudence Award for Trial Advocacy, Pi Alpha Alpha, Phi Kappa Phi, Phi Delta Phi; mem: Orange Co. Bar Assn., Order of DeMolay (master councilor 1969-70); publs: article, J. of Law & Edn. (Summer 1991). Address: PO Box 2817 Seal Beach 90740

TOOLEY, WILLIAM LANDER, real estate development company executive; b. Apr. 23, 1934, El Paso, Tx.; s. William Lander and Virginia Mary (Ryan) T.; m. Reva Berger, Mar. 5, 1966; children: William b. 1968, Patrick b. 1969, James b. 1972; edn: BA, Stanford Univ. 1956; MBA, Harvard Grad. Sch. 1960. Career: treas., mgr. Pickwick Hotel Co., San Diego 1960-63; David H. Murdock Devel. Co., Phoenix, Ariz. 1963-66; ptnr. Ketchum Peck & Tooley, Los Angeles 1967-74; chmn. Tooley & Co. 1974-; dir. Nat. Realty Com., Wash. D.C. 1975-; bd. dirs. Federal Reserve Bank San Francisco 1988-; mem: Urban Land Inst., Lambda Alpha, Loyola Marymount Univ. Bd. Regents 1982-, Bd. Trustees 1975-82, Calif. Club, Calif. Yacht Club; mil: lt. j.g. USNR 1956-58; Catholic. Ofc: 3303 Wilshire Blvd 12 Floor Los Angeles 90010

TOPP, ALPHONSO AXEL, JR., radiation protection consultant, retired army officer, environmental scientist; b. Oct. 15, 1920, Idpls.; s. Alphonso Axel and Emilia Kristina (Karlssen) T.; m. Mary Catherine Virtue, July 7, 1942; children: Karen b. 1943, Susan b. 1944, Linda b. 1946 Sylvia b. 1948, Peter b. 1950, Astrid b. 1953, Heidi b. 1956, Eric b. 1958, Megan b. 1960, Katrina b. 1962; edn: BSChE, Purdue Univ., 1942; MS applied physics, UCLA, 1948; atomic energy splst. US Army, 1957; reg. health physicist, N.Mex. 1982. Career: served 2d lt. to col. US Army, USA, Europe, and Asia, 1942-70, decorated Legion of Merit 1971, Bronze star medal w/2 o.l.c. (1945, 50, 51), Jt. Svs. commendn. medal DoD 1970; health scientist supr. radiation sect. Environmental Improvement Agy., State of N.Mex., Santa Fe 1970, environ. scientist 3, 1970-78, environmental program mgr. Env. Improvement Div. (EID), Radiation Protection Bur. 1978-81, health program mgr./chief Radiation Protection Bur EID., 1981-83; mem: Sigma Xi 1948-, Triangle Frat. 1939-, Health Physics Soc. 1981-, Council of Radiation Control Program Directors (1981-83, emeritus mem. 1983-87), Rotary Internat. (1971-, Paul Harris Fellow), Eagle Scout BSA 1936; Republican; Presbyterian; rec: GMC motorhome, photography. Res: 872 Highland Dr Los Osos 93402

TORRES, LEONARD, university professor; b. Oct. 12, 1926, Anaheim; s. Sylvester Torres and Cecelia Mae (Miranda) Johnson; m. Gerene Arletta Verheyden, June 14, 1954 (dec. 1972); m. Marian Florence MacColl, May 7, 1987; edn: BA, UC Santa Barbara 1951; M.Ed, Ore. St. Univ. 1956; Ed.D, Univ.

No. Colo. 1963. Career: tchr. Excelsior H.S. Dist., Norwalk 1951-56; prof. CSU Long Beach 1956-88; curriculum Ednl. Planning Service, Greeley, Colo. 1962-63; Calif. St. Dept. Edn., Sacto. 1965-; honors: Kappa Delta Phi, Phi Delta Kappa, Who's Who West, Dictionary of Internat. Biographies, hon. Internat. Tech. Edn. Assn.; mem: Internat. Tech. Edn. Assn., Calif. Indsl. & Tech. Edn. Assn., Am. Vocational Assn., Energy Resources Commn.; num. articles pub. in profl. jours.; mil: cpl. USAAF 1944-46; Republican; Prot.; rec: sailing, gardening. Res: 9892 Oma Pl Garden Grove 92641 Ofc: California State University Occupational Studies Dept. Long Beach 90840

TORRES, MICHAEL ALFONSO, state workman's compensation underwriter; b. Dec. 10, 1956, San Diego; s. Alfonso and Adele Marie (Mazzeo) T.; m. Teresa Elaine Ortiz, June 20, 1975 (div. 1977); m. 2d Virginia Shirley Teas, July 6, 1985; children: Elaine Marie b. 1975, Michael Alfonso II b. 1988, John Miles b. 1992; edn: BA in music edn., San Diego St. Univ. 1988; currently attending Western State Univ. Sch. of Law. Career: auditor State Compensation Ins. Fund, San Diego 1988-92, underwriter 1992-; honors: auditor of mo. SCIF (Oct. & Nov. 1988), SDSU Fencing Club (pres. 1979-81); mem. AOPA, Skyliters (past sec.), NRA, Calif. Reserve Peace Officers Assn., San Diego Police Dept. Reserve Officers 1989-; mil: E4 US Army 1975-78; rec: pvt. pilot. Res: 3765 Utah St San Diego 92104 Ofc: State Compensation Insurance Fund 9444 Waples San Diego 92121

TOTTEN, GEORGE OAKLEY, III, political science professor emeritus, author; b. July 21, 1922, W.D.C.; s. George O. Totten Jr. and Vicken (von Post) Totten Barrois; m. Astrid Maria Anderson, June 26 1948 (dec. Apr. 26, 1975); children: Vicken Yuriko, Linnea Catherine; m. Lilia Huiying Li, July 1, 1976; 1 child Blanche Lemes; edn: cert. Univ. Mich., 1943; AB, Columbia Univ., 1946, AM, 1949; MA, Yale Univ., 1950, PhD, 1954; docentur i Japanologi, Univ. Stockholm, 1977. Career: lectr. Columbia Univ., N.Y.C., 1954-55; asst. prof. MIT, Cambridge 1958-59, Boston Univ. 1959-61; assoc. prof. Univ. Rhode Island Kingston 1961-64; assoc. prof. polit. sci. USC, Los Angeles 1965-68, prof. 1968-92, emeritus 1992-, dept. chmn. 1980-86, dir. East Asian Studies Ctr. 1974-77; affil. scholar Ctr. for Multi-ethnic and Transnat. Studies, USC 1993-; founder/dir. Calif. Pvt. Univs. and Colls. year-in-Japan pgm. Waseda Univ., 1967-73, So. Calif.-UCLA Jt. East Asian Studies Ctr., 1976-77; vis. prof. Univ. Stockholm, 1977-79; first dir. Ctr. for Pacific Asia Studies, 1985-89, sr. counsellor, bd. dirs., 1989-; mem: U.S.-China People's Friendship Assn., W.D.C. 1974-, Com. on U.S.-China Relations, N.Y.C. 1975-, L.A.-Pusan Sister City Assn., L.A. (chmn. 1976-77), L.A.-Guangzhou Sister City Assn. (bd. 1982-), Japan-Am. Soc. L.A. 1981-, nat. advy. com. of the Japan-Am. Student Conf. 1986-; awards: Social Sci. Res. Council fellow 1952-53, grantee Ford Found. 1955-58, grantee NSF 1979-81, grantee Korea Found. 1993, commendn. award for pgm. on Korean studies Consulate Gen. of Republic of Korea 1975; mem: founding mem. USC Beta Kappa chpt. Phi Beta Delta nat. honor soc. 1993-, Assn. for Asian Studies, Am. Polit. Sci. Assn., Internat. Polit. Sci. Assn., Internat. Studies Assn., Japanese Polit. Sci. Assn., European Assn. Japanese Studies; club: Faculty (USC); author: Social Democratic Movement in Prewar Japan (1966, Chinese edit. 1987), coauthor: Socialist Parties in Postwar Japan (1966), Japan and the New Ocean Regime (1984), co-editor, author: Developing Nations: Quest for a Model (1970, Japanese edit. 1975), China's Economic Reform: Administering the Introduction of the Market Mechanism (1992), co-translator: Traditional Government in Imperial China (1982), contbg. author: The Politics of Divided Nations (1991); mil: 1st lt. US Army 1942-46, PTO; Episcopalian; rec: learning languages, jogging, aerobics, dancing. Res: 5129 Village Green Los Angeles 90016-5205 Ofc: Ctr for Multiethnic and Traansnational Studies (CMTS) Kerckhoff Hall 734 W Adams Univ. of Southern California, Los Angeles 90089-7724

TOWNES, CHARLES HARD, astrophysicist; b. July 28, 1915, Greenville, SC; s. Henry Keith and Ellen Sumter (Hard) T.; m. Frances H. Brown, May 4, 1941; children: Linda Lewis b. 1943, Ellen Scriven b. 1946, Carla Keith b. 1949, Holly Robinson b. 1952; edn: BA, BS, Furman Univ. 1935, MA, Duke Univ. 1937, PhD, Calif. Inst. Technol. 1939. Career: mem. tech. staff Bell Telephone Lab. 1939-47; assoc. prof. physics Columbia Univ. 1948-50, prof. 1950-61; exec. dir. Columbia Radiation Lab. 1950-52, chmn. physics dept. 1952-55; provost, prof. physics M.I.T. 1961-66, Inst. Prof. 1966-67; v.p., dir. res. Inst. Def. Analyses Wash. DC 1959-61; univ. prof. physics UC Berkeley 1967-, now emeritus; bd. dirs: Gen. Motor (1973-86), Perkin- Elmer, Carnegie Inst., Pacific Sch. of Religion, Calif. Inst. of Tech.; honors: Comstock Prize 1959, Rumford Premium 1961, Thomas Young Medal 1963, Nobel Prize for Physics 1964, Medal of Honor, I.E.E.E. 1966, Earle K. Plyler Prize 1977, Nat. Inventors Hall of Fame 1976, Niels Bohr Internat. Gold Medal 1979, Nat. Medal of Sci. 1982, Engring. & Sci. Hall of Fame 1983, Berkeley Citation 1986, mem. Legion of Honor (Ofcr. 1991-); mem: Am. Physical Soc., Nat. Acad. Arts & Scis., Am. Phil. Soc., Am. Astron. Soc., The Royal Soc. of London, Max Planck Soc., W. Ger. (1986), Pontifical Acad. of Scis. (Rome), President's Sci. Advis. Com. 1966-69 (vice chmn. 1967-69); chmn. Sci. & Tech. Advy. Com. for Manned Space Flight NASA 1964-69; inventor MASER, co-inventor LASER; research on nuclear and molecular structure, microwave and infrared astronomy; co-author Microwave Spectroscopy; Prot.; rec: natural history. Res: 1988 San Antonio Ave Berkeley 94707 Ofc: UC Berkeley Dept. of Physics Berkeley 94720

TRAILL, DAVID ANGUS, classicist, educator; b. Jan. 28, 1942, Helensburgh, Scotland; s. Angus Nicolson and Elizabeth Blyth (Wilson) Traill; edn: MA, classics, Univ. St. Andrews, Scotland, 1964; PhD, classics, UC Berkeley, 1971. Career: lectr. McGill Univ., Montreal, Can. 1964-65; tchg. asst. UC Berkeley 1965-68; asst. prof. UC Davis 1970-78, assoc. prof. 1978-85, prof. 1985-, program dir. Classics, 1985-; prodn. cons. documentaries on Schliemann and Troy, BBC, London 1980-81, 85; mem.: Am. Philol. Assn. 1968-, Archaeol. Inst. Am. 1980-, Medieval Assn. of the Pacific 1972-; author: Walahfrid Strabo's Visio Wettini (1978); Myth, Scandal and History: The Heinrich Schliemann Controversy (1986). Res: 1351 Monarch Ln Davis 95616 Ofc: Classics Dept. Univ. California, Davis 95616

TRAN, DOUGLAS A., physician; b. Jan. 12, 1950, Saigon, Vietnam, nat. USA 1981; s. Khoe Van and Tram Thi (Nguyen) T.; m. Trang Truong, June 21, 1980; children: Derek b. 1982, Duke b. 1987, Dustin b. 1992, Dylan b. 1993; edn: pre-med. and 5 yrs. medicine, Saigon Univ. 1969-75; MD, Univ. of Calif., Irvine 1979; certified Am. Board of Otolaryngology 1985. Career: intern and resident USC Medical Center 1979-84; pvt. practice otolaryngology in Orange County 1985-; awards: Am. Field Service Scholarship, senior yr. H.Sch. in US, 1967-68; mem. AMA, Orange County Med. Assn., Calif. Med. Assn., Am. Assn. of Otolaryngology, Head & Neck Surgery, USC Alumni Assn.; Republican; Buddhist; rec: fgn. language and cultures, painting, piano, tennis, skiing. Res: 23 Bayporte Irvine 92714

TRAUTMAN, LORETTA AMARYLLIS, physician-pathologist; b. Nov. 13, 1933, St. Francis, Kans.; d. Max F. and Emma (Rueb) Lengner; m. Arnold H. Trautman, Sept. 13, 1956; edn: BA, Univ. Wash. Seattle 1957; MA, 1960; MD, Howard Univ. 1968; Diplomate Am. Bd. Pathology, anat. path. 1973, clin. path. 1976. Career: intern internal medicine French Hosp., San Francisco 1968-69; resident in pathology Stanford Univ. 1969-72, Kaiser Hosp., S.F. 1972-74, UCSF, 1974-76; pathologist Alexian Brothers Hosp., San Jose 1976-77, Watsonville Hosp., Watsonville 1978-82, Kaiser Hosp., South S.F. 1983-85; dir. anatomical pathology Laboratory Services Inc., San Jose 1985-89; lab. dir. Spectra Laboratories Inc., Fremont 1990-; honors: Nat. Honor Soc. 1950, Swedish Govt. Scholar Univ. Stockholm 1957-58, Nat. Premed. Honor Soc. 1963, fellow Am. Soc. Clin. Pathologists; mem: South Bay Path. Soc., Am. Soc. Cytology, Calif. Soc. of Pathologists; rec: travel (70 countries), pvt. pilot, the arts, golf. Res: 7530 Sunset Way Aptos 95003 Ofc: Spectra Laboratories Inc 48818 Kato Rd Fremont 94538

TRAVIS, PAUL NICHOLAS, banker; b. Jan. 11, 1949, N.Y.C.; s. Nicholas and Mary T.; m. Carol Ann Rush, Aug. 31, 1971; children: Tanya Ann b. 1976, Paul John b. 1980; edn: BA, Rutgers Univ., 1971; M. Sch. Advanced Internat. Studies, W.D.C. 1973. Career: asst. agent Bank of Montreal, N.Y.C., 1974-76, asst. representative Bank of Montreal, Tokyo, Japan 1976-77; dep. v.p. ABN Bank, N.Y.C., 1977-79; gen. mgr. Banco Real S.A., N.Y.C., 1979-80, gen. mgr. Banco Real Internat. Inc., Houston, Tx. 1980-88; v.p. corporate finance Sumitomo Trust and Banking Co., Ltd., Los Angeles 1988-; mem.: Assn. of Energy Engrs. 1988-91, Houston C.of C. 1980-87, Houston Inter-Am. C.of C. (dir. 1987-88); Alumni assn. Boys Club of New York; Republican. Res: 3280 Paloma St Pasadena CA 91107 Ofc: The Sumitomo Trust & Banking Co. 333 S Grand Los Angeles CA 90071

TRAYLOR, WILLIAM ROBERT, author, publisher, printing industry consultant; b. May 21, 1921, Texarkana, Ark.; s. Clarence Edington and Seba Ann (Talley) T.; m. Elvirez Traylor, Oct. 9, 1945; children: Kenneth Warren, Gary Robert, Mark Daniel, Timothy Ryan; edn: student Univ. Houston, 1945-46, Univ. Omaha, 1947-48. Career: Div. mgr. Lily Tulip Cup Corp., N.Y.C., 1948-61; asst. to pres. Johnson & Johnson, New Brunswick, N.J. 1961-63; mgr. we. region Rexall Drug & Chem. subs. Dart Industries, L.A. 1963-67; pres. Prudential Pub. Co., Diamonds Springs, Calif. 1967-; cons. to printing ind., 1976-; syndicated writer "Bill Friday's Bus. Bull." 1989-; pub. Profl. Estimate and Mgmt. Software for printing ind. (1992); author: Instant Printing (1976, Japanese transl.), Successful Mgmt. (1979), Quick Printing Ency. (1982, 7th edit. 1988), How to Sell Your Product Through (Not to) Wholesalers (1980); honors: Man of Year Quick Printing Mag. 1987, Who's Who in the World 1993-94; mem. Nat. Assn. Quick Printers (hon. life), C.of C., Kiwanis, Toastmasters; Democrat; rec: skiing, boating. Res: PO Box 852 El Dorado 95623 Ofc: 7089 Crystal Blvd Diamond Springs 95619 Ph: 916/622-8928

TRENT, RICHARD JAMES, newspaper owner/publisher; b. Jan. 16, 1946, Logan, W. Va.; s. Herman Clarence and Lita (Mounts) T.; edn: BA, George Washington Univ. 1969; postgrad., Am. Univ. 1973-6. Career: advtg. mgr. The Washington Post, W.D.C. 1968-77; Seattle Post 1977-82; ad. dir. 1977-78; mktg. dir. 1978-79; gen. mgr. 1979-82; pres. Harte-Hanks Calif. Newspapers 1982-84; pub. California Magazine, 1985-87; pres. and c.e.o. Community Media Enterprises 1987-; chmn. California Free Press Assn., 1991-; instr. Am. Press Inst.; vis. com. Univ. of Wash. 1979-81; awards: Eagle Scout BSA, Newsmaker of the Future, Time Mag. 1978, silver medal Am. Advt. Fedn. 1980; mem: Am. Advtg. Fedn. (govt. relations com., chmn. 1983-84; past gov. Wash., Oreg., Ida., Mont. and Ak.; We. Reg. chmn. Western 13 States 1986-87), Am. Newspaper

Publishers Assn., Calif. Newspaper Publishers Assn.; civic: Downey Community Hosp. Emergency Room Com. (chmn. 1991-), YMCA Downey (bd. dirs. 1989-); contbr. articles in nat. trade mags.; inventor tng. device: Time and Territory Management for the Newspaper Industry; rec: flying, music, sailing. Ofc: 8800 National Ave South Gate 90280

TRICOLES, GUS PETER, engineer, b. Oct. 18, 1931, San Francisco, Calif.; s. Peter Constantine and Eugenia (Elias) T.; m. Dec. 20, 1953; widowed Dec. 4, 1974; m. Aileen, Apr. 1, 1980; div. Sept., 1980; children: Rosanne b. 1958, Robin b. 1961; edn: BA, physics, UCLA, 1955; MS, applied math, San Diego St. Coll., 1958; MS, physics, UC San Diego, 1962; PhD, applied physics, UC San Diego, 1971; career: design splst. Convair Div., Gen. Dynamics, San Diego, 1955-59; physicist Smyth Res. Assocs., San Diego, 1959-61; res. asst. Scripps Institution, San Diego, 1961-62; sr. engring. staff splst. Gen. Dynamics Electronics, San Diego, 1962-92; sr. engring. staff splst. GDE Systems, Inc., San Diego, 1992-;cons. to: Aero Geo Industries, San Antonio 1979-80, Transco Industries, L.A. 1972-73, Ministry of Defense, Haifa, Israel 1981, Synergistic Comms., Columbus, Oh. 1989, 1992, Georgia Inst. of Tech., Atlanta 1982, 1984; mem: IEEE (fellow 1956-), Optical Soc. of Am. (fellow 1957-), Am. Geophysical Union 1965-, NY Academy of Sciences 1970, US Comms., Internat. Scientific Radio Union 1972; civic: San Diego St. Univ. Found.; author: book chpt., Radome Engring. Handbook, 1970; book chpt., Antenna Handbook, 1987; author/inventor: patent, Microwave Holograms, 1965; patent, Anistropic Radomes, 1985; mil: midshipman USN, 1952-54; rec: woodworking. Res: 4633 Euclid Ave. San Diego 92115. Ofc: GDE Systems, Inc. P.O. Box 85227 San Diego 92138-5227

TRIPP, R(USSELL) MAURICE, product development and manufacturing co. president; b. July 12, 1916, Holten, Kans.; s. Maurice Hall and Alma Bell (Cottrell) T.; m. Catherine Graham Burr, Aug. 12, 1937; children: Tinka b. 1938, Wendy b. 1940, Betsy b. 1941, Maurice b. 1943, David b. 1944, Tim b. 1946, Molly b. 49; edn: Geo. Eng., Colo. Sch. Mines 1939; MS geophysical engring., 1943; ScD, MIT 1948. Career: seismic observer/computor Geotechnical Corp., Dallas, Tx. 1936-37; faculty mem. Colo. Sch. of Mines, Golden, Colo. 1941-44; asst. to pres. Geotechnical Corp., Cambridge, Mass. 1944-46; sr. scientist USN Bureau of Ships, Bikini, Marshall Isl. 1946; mineral exploration cons., Lincoln, Mass. 1946-48; dir. geochem. res. lab. Boston, Univ. 1948; v.p., dir. of res. Research Inc., Coffeyville, Kans. 1949-55; pres., chmn. bd. Tripp Research Corp., Dallas, Tx. 1955-; pres., bd. chmn. SKIA Corp., Saratoga 1972-; pres./chmn. bd. Aktina Corp., Santa Clara 1984-; dir. Torginol of Am., Las Vegas, Nev. 1960-63; Sherwin Instrument Co., N.Y.C. 1955-58; Sonic Research Corp., Boston, Mass. 1948-57; awards: Corbett Found., YMCA comm. service 1982, BSA Silver Beaver 1976, Calif. PTA hon. mem., MIT George B. Morgan 1986; mem: Am. Assn. Petroleum Geologists (chmn. standing com.), Am. Inst. Mining Engrs. (sr.), Soc. Exploration Geophysics, El Camino Trust (pres.), Los Gatos Youth Park (pres. 1985-90), Golden C.of C. (v.p. 1942-44), Nat. Council BSA; patentee - mineral benefication, bldg. materials, depth perception, radiography, 3-dimensional TV, ophthalmic instruments; pub. tech. jour. articles (1942-60); Republican; Christian Scientist; rec: camping, gardening, Indian woodcraft and lore. Ofc: Aktina Corp. 5181 Lafayette Santa Clara 95054

TROUT, MONROE E., healthcare executive; b. April 5, 1931, Harrisburg, Pa.; s. David Michael and Florence Margaret (Kashner) T.; m. Sandra Lemke, June 11, 1960; children: Monroe E. b. 1962, Timothy William b. 1966; edn: BA, Univ. Pa. 1953; MD, 1957; LL.B, Dickinson Sch. Law 1964; JD, 1969. Career: dir. drug regulatory affairs Pfizer, NYC; v.p., med. dir. Winthrop Lab.; sr. v.p. med. and sci. affairs Sterling Drug Inc.; chmn. bd., pres., c.e.o. Am. Healthcare Systems, San Diego; elected New Canaan Town Council, Conn. 1978-86, v.chmn. 1984-86; appt. secty. HEW Commn. on Medical Malpractice 1970-72, jt. commn. Prescription Drug Use 1976-80; awards: recogn. AMA, pres.'s award Am. Coll. Legal Medicine, Dickinson Sch. of Law disting. alumni, Univ. Pa. alumni of merit, Who's Who in Bus. & Fin.; mem: Am. Arbitration Assn. (nat. health advy. bd. 1972-), AMA, Nat. Council Patient Info. & Edn. (advy. bd. 1983-), Am. Coll. Legal Medicine Found. (trustee 1983-), Am. Soc. Med. Adminstrs., Fairbanks Ranch Country Club; 142+ articles pub. in profl. jours.; mil: lt. cmdr. USN; Republican; Lutheran; rec: golf, tennis. Ofc: American Healthcare Systems 12730 High Bluff Dr Ste 300 San Diego 92130-2099

TROVER, DENIS WILLIAM, computer consultant; b. Feb. 1, 1945, Columbus, Ohio; s. Kenneth Harold and Virginia June (Denis) T.; m. Ellen Lloyd, June 12, 1971; 1 dau: Florence Emma, b. 1977; edn: BS, physics, Mich. State Univ. 1967; MBA, Coll. of William and Mary 1972; MS, Vassar Coll. 1973. Career: optical physicist Internat. Business Machines, Fishkill, NY 1967-71; staff assoc. & sys. prgmr. Rockwell Int. Sci. Ctr., Thousand Oaks 1974-8; pres./ dir. Sonix Systems, Inc., Thousand Oaks 1978-83; computer cons. 1983-; mem: Conejo Future Found. 1975- (chmn. Energy Task Force 1980-1); bd. dirs. Vassar Club of So. Calif.; Democrat; Presbyterian; rec: astronomy, photog. Res: 11355 Presilla Rd Camarillo 93012 Ofc: 1107 East Thousand Oaks Blvd Thousand Oaks 91362

TROVER, ELLEN LLOYD, lawyer; b. Nov. 23, 1947, Richmond, Va.;d. Robert VanBuren and Hazel Pauline (Urban) Lloyd; m. Denis W. Trover, 1971; children: Florence, b. 1977; edn: AB, Vassar Coll. 1969; JD, Coll. of William and Mary 1972. Career: assoc. ed. Bancroft- Whitney 1973-74; sole practioner Ellen Lloyd Trover, Atty. at Law 1974-82, 89-; partner Trover & Fisher 1982-89; mem: Com. Law Ofc. Lawout Design of Economics of Law Practice Section 1978-79, Word Processing Applications Com. 1981-84; Conejo Future Found. (trustee 1979-91, chair 1984-88, trustee emeritus 1992-), Hydro Help for the Handicapped (trustee/exec. com. 1980-85), World Affairs Council of Ventura Co. (spl. mem.), Phi Alpha Delta Legal Frat., Am. Bar Assn., Calif. State Bar, Va. Bar Assn., Ventura Co. Bar Assn., former mem. Conejo Valley Bar Assn. (pres. 1979-80, dir. 1983-85); editor Handbooks of State Chronologies (1972-73); Democrat; Presbyterian. Res: 11355 Presilla Rd Camarillo 93012 Ofc: 1107 E Thousand Oaks Blvd 91362

TRUMAN, EDWARD CRANE, property mgr., investor, composer; b. Dec. 28, 1921, Des Moines, IA; s. Wright Edward and Annie Louise (Cate) T.; m. Maxine H., Jun. 28, 1947, dec. Apr. 25, 1983; children: Robert Edward b. 1949; edn: BA English, Immaculate Heart Coll., L.A. 1978; MA psych., Univ. Redlands, Redlands 1980; real est. ctf. & labor studies, Univ. Calif., L.A. 1965-66; fine arts, Drake Univ., Des Moines 1936-39; career: musician/leader., KSO & KRNT, Des Moines, IA 1938-44; music dir. (small groups), ABC-TV, L.A. 1952-55; music dir., NBC-TV, Burbank 1955-59; freelance musician, ASCAP, L.A. 1956-; owner, Truman R.E., L.A. 1965-; owner, Truman Bus. Assoc., L.A. 1975-; co-chair scholarship com., Univ. Calif. Santa Barbara 1992-; dir., General Affiliates of Univ. Calif. Santa Barbara 1987-; chmn., Coldwater Counseling Ctr., Studio City 1992-93; emmy panelist, Academy of TV Arts & Sci., N. Hollywood 1984-; bd. mem., Episcopal Campus Overnight Com., L.A. 1993-96 (3 yr. term); awards: Career Educ. Citation, U.S. Dept. Educ., Washington 1978; City Atty. Citation, L.A. 1993; R.E. Svc. Citation, Univ. Calif. L.A. 1976; Diamond Circle Award Radio & TV Industry, Pacific Pioneer Broadcasters, Studio City 1992; past pres., Indep. Living Ctr., Van Nuys 1988; mem: TV Academy 1984-; Am. Soc. Composers Authors & Publ. 1956-; Pacific Pioneer Broadcasters 1943-; author: many music recordings 1950-60; television main titles & backgrounds (Ellery Queen, Untouchables) 1955-58; mil: s/sgt Signal Corps/AFRS HQ 1944-46; Democrat; Episcopal; rec: coin collecting. res: 1826 Jewett Dr Los Angeles 90046-7702

TRUMBULL, TERRY ALAN, environmental lawyer; b. Nov. 5, 1945, Berkeley; s. Larry Edward and Emily Josephine (Grote) T.; m. Patricia Vogel (Hon. Magistrate Judge), Aug. 24, 1968; children: Eryn Jennifer b. 1977, Morgann Vogel b. 1985; edn: BA, UC Davis, 1967; JD, Georgetown Univ., 1971; LLM, George Washington Univ., 1973; admitted bar: D.C. 1971, Calif. 1973, U.S. Supreme Ct. 1975. Career: land use atty. Atkinson, Farasyn & Trumbull, Mountain View, Ca. 1978-79; chmn. Calif. Waste Mgmt. Bd., Sacto. 1979-84; environmental atty. The Trumbull Law Firm, Palo Alto 1984-88, San Jose 1992-; Low, Ball & Lynch, Menlo Park 1988-89; Richards, Watson & Gershon, San Francisco 1989-92; appt. chmn., commr. Santa Clara County Planning Commn. 1976-79, dir. Calif. Hazardous Waste Mgmt. Council 1982-84, commr. Nat. Commn. on Resource Conservation and Recovery, W.D.C. 1981-; mem. Peninsula Industrial & Bus. Assn. (chmn. govt. affairs com. 1987-), No. Calif. Resource Recovery Assn. 1979-; author mo. legal column, Refuse News 1985-, 3 chapters on Calif. Solid Waste Law in Calif. Environ. Law and Land Use Practice 1989-; mil: Nat. Guard Army Reserve 1979-85; Democrat; rec: computer games, birdwatching. Ofc: The Trumbull Law Firm, 55 S Market St Ste 1080 San Jose 95113

TRUNK, GARY, physician/medical consultant; b. July 12, 1941, Detroit, Mich.; edn: BA, UC Los Angeles, 1963; MD, UC Irvine, 1967; MBA, Health Care Mgmt., 1991. Career: med. cons. Dept. of Social Svs., Disability Evaluation Br.; Diplomate Am. Bd. Qual. Assur. and Util. Rev. Physicians, Fellow Am. Coll. of Medical Quality; mem: AMA, Am. Coll. Physicians, Am. Acad. of Disability Evaluation Physicians. Res: 7533 Clear Sky Rd San Diego 92120

TSAI, WILMAN, chemical engineer; b. Nov. 2, 1960, Hong Kong; s. John Man-Ma and Kathy (Kwei) T.; m. Wen Lee Wen-Hsing, July 1984; children: Jonathan Michael b. 1988, Betsy Rachael b. 1991; edn: BSc chem. engring., BSc environmental engring., Syracuse Univ., 1982; MS chem. engring., Calif. Inst. Tech., 1985, PhD chem. engring., 1987; reg. profl. engr. Calif. Career: research engr. Air Products & Chemicals, Allentown, Pa. 1987-89; research scientist Varian, Palo Alto, Calif. 1989-; awards: Tau Beta Pi, King fellow; mem.: AIChE; rec: astrophotography. Ofc: 611 Hansen Way, K224, Palo Alto 94303

TSENG, ANDREW E., acupuncturist, artist; b. Nov. 24, 1917, Shanghai, China, nat. 1984; s. Rev. Shao-yin and Shien-yun Ngi; m. Alice Ma, Sept. 6, 1956; 1 child; edn: BA, Univ. of Shanghai 1939; OMD, Dr. Oriental Medicine, 1983. Career: Chinese medical doctor, acupuncturist, Shanghai, China 1956-78, San Francisco, Calif. 1979-: Haight Ashbury Free Clinic 1980-81, S.F. Coll. of Acupuncture and Oriental Med. 1981-; profl. Chinese landscape painter 1950-, tchr. and cons. in field; contbr. articles on acupuncture techniques; mil: lt. col. Chinese Army 1945; rec: classical music, lit., fine arts. Res: 5095-312 Valley Crest Dr Concord 94521

TSUEI, WEI, college president, educator; b. April 14, 1926, Chekiang, China; nat. 1979; s. Shi-Chen and Lin-Chen (Chang) T.; children: Jack b. 1964, David b. 1966; edn: Taiji Quan Assn. 1954-64; Sun's Acupuncture Inst. Taiwan 1968; OMD, San Francisco Coll. Acupuncture & Oriental Medicine 1984; lic. acupuncturist Calif. 1979. Career: cons. Taipei Nat. Martial Arts Assn., Taiwan 1970-72; dir. China Assn. of Taiji Quan 1971-72; instr., Chinese med. dr. Kwang Hwa Chinese Medicine & Acupuncture 1975-76; master of martial arts Taoist Center, Oakland 1976-, exec. dir. and chief acupuncturist 1980-; pres., prof., chmn. of bd. Acad. Chinese Culture & Health Scis. 1982-; instr. Chinese Martial Arts Soc., Nat. Univ. Taiwan 1969-72; Taiji Quan Assn. of China 1954-64; mem: Grand Lodge of China; author Theory of Chinese Medicine: Cultural & Philosophical Roots 1986, Roots of Chinese Culture and Medicine 1989; rec: Chinese calligraphy, Chinese brush painting. Res: Academy of Chinese Culture and Health Sciences 1601 Clay St Oakland 94612

TUCHMAN, GLORIA MATTA, teacher; b. Dec. 18, 1941, Pecos, Tx.; d. Manuel Natividad Matta and Mary Lydia (Lerma) Garza; m. Terry Franklin Tuchman, Jan. 26, 1964; children: Michael Allen b. 1969, Bret Allen b. 1974; edn: BA, Ariz. St. Univ. 1963; CSU Fullerton 1966-68; UC Irvine, La Verne Coll. Career: sch. bd. mem. Tustin Sch. Bd., 1985-94; Nat. Advy. and Coordinating Council for Bilingual Edn., Wash. D.C. 1986-88; Nat. Advy. Council Child Nutrition 1988-89; Nat. Advy. Council Fund for Improvement & Reform of Schs. & Tchg. 1988-93; awards: League United Latin Am. Citizen woman of year 1987, Taft Elem. Sch. tchr. of year 1988, Santa Ana Educators Assn. We Honor Ours Award 1988; mem: Hispanic Caucus Calif. Sch. Bd. Assn. (treas. 1987-), Calif. Elected Womens Assn. for Edn. & Research (secty. 1987-89), Am. Assn. of Univ. Women, Santa Ana Educators Assn. (chair bilingual com.), Tustin C.of C., City of Tustin Ad Hoc Com. for Child Care Svs., ednl. chair for Drop-out Prevention Program-Santiago Club, co-chair Tustin Child Care Coalition Com. sch. bd. liaison to Tustin City Council; Independent; R.Cath.; rec: skiing. Res: 1742 Lerner Ln Santa Ana 92705

TUCKER, LINDA BARNES, fashion industry business consultant; b. June 1, 1948, Mesa, Ariz.; d. Alfred C., Jr. and Leona C. (Walters) B.; div. 1986; children: Julie Simon b. 1971; edn: AA, Stephens Coll. 1968, BFA, 1970; MS San Diego State 1980. Career: exec. trainee The Broadway, Los Angeles 1970; owner, Simon Sez, San Diego 1971-73; v.p. mktg. Arlin, Inc., San Diego 1979-86; owner L.A.X. (fashion accessories design co.), San Diego 1986-90, Linda Tucker & Associates (Consultants) 1990-; pgm. coord. Southwestern Coll, Chula Vista 1974-83; instr: San Diego State 1985-87, Fashion Institute 1989-, Mesa Coll. 1989-; mem: The Fashion Group of San Diego (bd. 1986-); Republican; Christian. Ofc: Linda Tucker & Associates, PO Box 85152 MB 283 San Diego 92186

TUCKER, MARCUS OTHELLO, judge; b. Nov. 12, 1934, Santa Monica; s. Dr. Marcus Othello, Sr. and Essie Louo (McLendon) T.; m. Indira Hale, May 29, 1965; dau., Angelique b. 1977; edn: BA, USC 1956; JD, Howard Univ. Sch. of Law 1960. Career: pvt. practice of law, Santa Monica 1962-63 and 1967-74; dep. city atty. City of Santa Monica 1963-65; asst. U.S. Attorney, Los Angeles 1965-67; Superior Ct. commr. L.A. Co. 1974-76; judge Long Beach Mcpl. Ct. 1976-85; judge Superior Ct., L.A. Co. 1985-; asst. prof. of law Pacific Coast Univ. Law Sch. (1984, 86); awards: Blackstonian Soc. USC 1956, editl. staff Howard Law Jour. 1958-60, judge of the yr. Juvenile Ct. Dependency Dept. 1986; mem: Juvenile Ct. Lawyers Assn., Santa Monica Bay Dist. Bar Assn. (mem. 1963-74, treas. 1969), Calif. Judges Assn. (chmn. Juvenile Ct. com. 1987), John Langston Bar Assn. (pres. 1972, 73), Lawyers Ref. Svc. (bd. dirs. 1968-72), Legal Aid Found. of L.A. (pres. 1977-78); civic: BSA (advy. bd., 1977-), Vols. of Am. (bd. dirs.), Capitol Classroom (bd. dirs.), Long Beach Comm. Hosp. Found. (bd. dirs., 1977-), Comm. Rehabilitation Industries Found. (pres. 1985-86); mil: sp5 USAR 1960-66; Democrat; Baptist; rec: legal hist. and philosophy of law, travel. Ofc: Superior Court Dept 233 210 W Temple St Los Angeles 90012

TUCKER, MARTIN S., manufacturing & distributing co. president; b. Oct. 4, 1939, St. Louis, Mo.; s. Irwin and Gigi (Schwartz) T.; grandparents: Max and Minnie Schwartz, (noted Russian entrepreneur and famous Russian chef), Dave and Charlotte Tucker (shoe designer and noted organizer of the Am. Red Cross, St. Louis area); children: Scott b. 1964, Tracy b. 1967; grandchildren: Dabid b. 1990, Megan b. 1992; edn: BS, Wash. Univ., 1961; MS, UCLA, 1965; Reg. Profl. Engr., Calif. 1967. Career: research scientist McDonald Douglass Aircraft, 1961-73; adj. faculty UCLA and Long Beach Community Coll., 1965-68, faculty 1966-67; instr. Metals Engring. Inst., 1969-71; pres. Topco Sales (main products include electronic light/water decorative gifts, novelty gifts, radio-controlled cars, Bugs Bunny Toys and cosmetic/bath products), offices in Taiwan, Hong Kong, and Los Angeles, 1973-; awards: fellowship Hughes Aircraft 1962-63, fellowship Am. Welding Soc. 1960, profl. achiev. Douglas Aircraft 1967; mem. Am. Welding Soc. for Metals 1959-, Am. Soc. for Technion 1990-; lodge: Elks 1979-; author 2 books: Secret Joys, Crystal Energy; Jewish; rec: tennis, volleyball, basketball. Ofc: Topco Sales 11960 Borden Ave, PO Box 9010 San Fernando 91341-9010

TUPIN, JOE PAUL, academic physician-psychiatrist, medical administrator; b. Feb. 17, 1934, Comanche, Texas; s. Joe Henry and Florence Fern (Cauley) T.; m. Betty Ann Thompson, June 19, 1955; children: Paul b. 1957, Rebecca b. 1969, John b. 1968; edn: BS, Univ. of Texas, Austin 1955, MD, Univ. Texas Med. Sch., Galveston 1959. Career: sr. asst. surgeon, lt. comdr. U.S. Pub. Health Service, 1962-64; asst. prof. Univ. of Texas, Galveston 1964-67, assoc. prof. and assoc. dean, 1967-69; assoc. prof. Univ. Calif., Davis 1969-71, prof. 1971-, chair psychiatry 1978-84, medical director UC Davis Med. Ctr., Sacramento 1984-93; vis. prof. King's Coll. Med. Sch., London 1974; awards: Friars Soc. Univ. Tex. 1954, Alpha Omega Alpha 1958, Sigma Xi, Rho Chi, Mosby scholar, Ginsberg fellow Group for Adv. of Psychiatry 1960-62, NIMH career tchg. award 1964-66, Nat. Found. Infantile Paralysis fellow 1957, res. grantee Univ. Tex. Med. br. 1964-69, NIMH (1965-58, 59-77), UC Davis (1969-77, 73-), UCD and Sacto. Med. Ctr. 1973-77; mem: Yolo County Med. Soc. (bd. 1989-93), Calif. Med. Assn. (bd. HMSS 1991-), Calif. Assn. of Hosps. and Health (bd. 1992-), AMA, Am. Psychiatric Assn. (1962-, Fellow 1969-), Am. Coll Psychiatrists (1969-, Fellow 1978-), AAAS, AAUP; author books, numerous sci. papers and jour. articles; mem. editl. bd. Am. J. Forensic Psychiatry (1985-88), J. Clin. Psychopharmacology (1981-), Psychiatry (1985), Texas,Reports and Biology and Medicine (1965-67, 68-69), Western J. Medicine (1979-89); mil: lt. comdr. USPHS 1962-64, Reserve 1964-80; rec: fishing. Res: 1108 Kent Dr Davis 95616 Ofc: Univ. Calif. Davis Medical Ctr 231 Stockton Blvd Sacramento 95817

TURCHI, PATRICE E.A., physicist; b. June 23, 1952, Lorient, France, naturalized U.S. 1992; s. Pietrino and Solange B.A. (Dubois) T.; m. Michele E. Boyle, Mar. 20, 1986; children: Elodie b. 1987; edn: Dipl. Eng., Nat. Superieure Sch. of Chemistry, Paris 1975; These de Docteur Ingenieur, Univ. Paris VI, 1982, These de Doctorat d'Etat es Scis. Physiques, 1984. Career: asst. prof. Univ. of Paris VI, France 1975-85; vis. res. asst. UC Berkeley 1985-86; sr. vis. scientist Lawrence Livermore Nat. Lab., 1986-89, sr. scientist 1989-; cons. AGARD-NATO, Chatillon, Fr. 1989; dir. NATO-ASI, Rhodes, Greece 1992; awards: medal for highest ranking Alumni of Nat. Sup. Sch. of Chemistry, Paris, Fr. 1975), DOE award for outstanding research accomplishment DOE-OBES, W.D.C. (1987; mem: Am. Physical Soc. 1986-, Materials Research Soc. 1989-, The Minerals Metals & Mats. Soc. 1989-, The Alloy Phases Com. (elected 1991), Societe des Ingenieurs & Scientifiqes de France 1986-; civic: Amnesty Internat., Am. Orchid Soc.; publs: 100+ sci. papers in refereed jours.; mil: Sci. of the Contingent Air Force, Fr. 1977-78; Republican; R.Cath.; rec: history of sci., skiing, tennis, orchidist, painting. Ofc: LLNL Condensed Matter Div. (L-268) PO Box 808 Livermore 94550

TURNER, BURNETT COBURN, architect and planning consultant; b. Dec. 3, 1902, Los Angeles; s. Harry Coburn and Marie Ada (Burnett) T.; m. Miriam Fechimer, Jan. 23, 1932; children: Peter b. 1949; edn: BS engrg., Princeton Univ. 1925, CE, 1926; BS arch., M.I.T. 1928; Am. Inst. Arch. NY 1932, Am. Inst. Cert. Planners 1952. Career: assoc. arch. Horace W. Peaslee, WDC 1928-30; lic. arch. 1932, staff Alfred Hopkins & Assocs., NY 1930-35; leader WPA Housing Survey, upper eastside NYC 1932-38; dir. Pub. Housing Exhib., arch.-engr., cons. arch. US Housing Authority, Wash. DC 1935-38; regl. tech. adv. USHA West Coast, S.F. 1939-40; asst. dir. West Coast Ofc., Housing Div., Fed. Works Adminstrn. 1940-42; arch. and planning cons. pvt. practice, L.A. 1946-; pres., trustee Turner Oil Trust L.A. 1946-; arbitrator Am. Arbitration Assn. Soc. 1958-; dir. Calif. Heritage Council 1965-; recipient Resolution of recogn. and appreciation by Mayor and L.A. City Council for many yrs. of distinguished service to Pueblo de Los Angeles Historic Park 1987; mem: Am. Inst. Archs. (Fellow), AIA/L.A. chpt. (dir. 1967-70, chmn. pub. works, zoning, hist. bldgs.), So. Calif. Historical Soc. 1946- (dir. -v.p. 1966), Econ. Round Table 1941-86 (pres. 1970), Sierra Club Urban Land Use Commn. 1980-, L.A. City Bicentennial Com. 1968-69, Town Hall 1946-, Univ. Club. 1946-, Nat. Trust Hist. Preservation, Soc. Archtl. Historians, Southern Skis (pres. 1953-54); works: devel. master site plan for largest public housing project in USA 1937; preliminary designs and cost estimates for 60 military posts, camps & stations in Philippines & Ryukos. 1946; Master Plan for Civic Ctr. of L.A. 1947; 30+ tech. papers for ERT (1942-84); mil: served to major US Army Corps of Engrs. 1942-46, lt.col. USAR 1947-54, decorated Medal for Military Merit 1946; Democrat; R.Cath.; rec: tennis, skiing, volunteer for public svc.; Res: 3730 Amesbury Rd Los Angeles 90027

TURNER, MICHAEL S., public relations/marketing executive; b. July 28, 1948, San Diego; s. Charles I. and Lee (Yomin) T.; m. Marlene Meyer, Sept. 7, 1981; edn: BA, San Diego State Univ., 1970; MA, Iowa State Univ., 1971. Career: instr. Univ. Nebr. at Omaha, 1971-72; news dir. and assoc. station mgr. KFJM/KFJM-FM, Grand Forks, N.D. 1972-78; station mgr. KUOP-FM, Stockton 1978-79; dir. of pgmmg. and promotions KCSN-FM, Northridge 1980-, host/prod. KCSN-FM Radio pgm. "L.A. Connections" weekly lifestyle, entertainment and travel pgm. 1980-; prin. Turnery-Meyer Communications, 1989-; panelist Annual Public Svc. Workshop, So. Calif. Bdcstrs. Assn.; honors: Rotary Internat. Group Study Participant for Young Bus. Profls. 1978, listed Who's Who in the Midwest 1979, Outstanding Young Men of Am. 1982-84; mem: Public Interest Radio and TV Ednl. Soc. (pres. 1984-87), Publicity Club of L.A. (pres. 1988-89, dir. 1984-88), Profl. Development Seminars(1982-83; civic: North Hills Jaycees (dir.), Calif. Jaycees (chmn. Project Awards Judging Conf.),

Northridge Park Arts Fest. (com.), Great Western Boy Scout Council (pub. rels. com.); coauthor Nat. Telecommunications Information Adminstrn. Grant 1986; rec: gourmet cooking. Res: 10341 Canoga Ave #29 Chatsworth 91311 Ofc: KCSN-FM 18111 Nordhoff St Northridge 91330

TURNER, NANCY KAY, teacher, artist, critic; b. Feb. 26, 1947, Bronx, NY; d. Murray Aaron and Florence (Drimer) T.; children: Michael Garrett Hilsman; edn: MA, Univ. Calif., Berkeley, 1969; BA, Queens Coll., Queens, NY, 1967; Skowhegan Sch. of Painting/Sculpture, Skowhegan, ME; Calif. State Univ., post baccalaureate Calif. State Univ., San Diego and L.A.; career: instr., Thomas Knowlton High Sch., South Bronx, NY, 1970-72; instr, San Diegito High Sch., San Diego, 1975-77; instr, San Diego City Coll., 1973-79; instr, Mira Costa Coll., Mira Costa, 1978-79; instr., Rhode Island Sch. of Design, 1985; asst. prof., Glendale Comm. Coll., 1979-; instr., Loyola High Sch., L.A., 1979-; dir., Glendale Comm. Coll. Art Gallery, 1990; bd. dirs. Woman's Building; awards: finalist Kennedy Ctr. Teaching Fellowship, 1990; Douc Langur Award, Calif. Edn. Assn., 1988; Art Honors Seminar, Rhode Island Sch. of Design, 1984; Youth Ctr. for the Arts Award, Queens Coll., 1967; Juror's First Award "In Celebration of Women", Sculpture Gallery, San Diego, 1977; First Award "All Media-Juried Exhibition", Escondido Regional Arts Gallery, 1976; First Award "Small Images", Gallery 8, La Jolla and San Diego City/Co. Art, 1975; mem: Am. section of Assn. for Internat. Art Critics, Gallery Com. Arroyo Arts Collective, So. Calif. Women's Caucus for the Arts, Affirmative Action Com.; creative works: many solo and group exhibitions, selected private and public collections, numerous publs.,art writer/contbr. ed.: Artweek 1984-92, Artscene 1989-, Visions mag. (12/93); Democrat; Jewish. Res: 682 South Mentor Ave Pasadena 91106

TURPIN, PEARL JOYCE, speaker, consultant; b. Oct. 26, 1937, Denison, Tx.; d. Hansel and Laura Elizabeth (Hardy) Fritts; m. Denzel James Cook, Nov. 7, 1954 (div. 1960); m. Peterfield Burleigh Turpin, May 7, 1966; 1 dau., Isabelle b. 1968; edn: Riverside City Coll. 1958-63; Glendale City Coll. 1963-65. Career: collector Med. Bureau, Riverside 1955-60; collection mgr. Riverside Bus. Mens. Assn. 1960-63; Med. Coll. Service, Glendale 1963-68; Imperial Collection, Sherman Oaks 1968-71; mgr. Gen. Fin., Los Angeles 1971-81; pres., owner Creditors Services of L.A. 1981-91; owner Pearl Turpin SPEAKS, Glendale 1991-; bd. chmn. Consumer Credit Counseling Service 1988-90, bd. mem., ofcr. 1976-; spl. cons. Atty. Gen. Task Force Subcomm. Consumer Edn. 1979-81; dir. Consumer Edn. Resource Found. 1993-; commr. Senate Advy. Com. of Debt Collection Industry 1984-92; awards: Credit Women Internat. "Credit Woman of Year" 1975-76, 89-90, Consumer Credit Counselors achievement award 1984, Glendale Credit Women Internat. "Boss of Year" 1982-83, Calif. Bur. of Collections recognition award 1991, Calif. Assn. of Collectors "Star" awards 1990, 91, 92), Richard Bullock Award 1992, Chapter 8 Calif. Assn. of Collectors "Cohen-Ferber" outstanding achiev. award 1989-90, Calif. Credit Union Collectors Coun. "Star" award 1991, Nat. Finance Adj. "Special Service" 1991, Nat. Leadership Council "Capitol Award Recipient" 1991, Internat. Credit Conf. Quebec "Internat. Credit Professional of Year" (May 1990); mem: Calif. Assn. Collectors (pres. 1990), Internat. Credit Assn. (bd. mem. 1979-80), Credit Profls. Glendale/L.A. (past pres. & parliamentarian); Republican; Prot.; rec: reading & teaching. Ofc: 3608 Rosemary Ave Glendale 91208

TUTTLE, LEON E., financial executive; b. July 24, 1934, Chicago; s. Leon E. Tuttle and Matilda Teresa Perona; m. Roberta Mae Norton, July 20, 1957; children: Katherine b. 1958, Karen b. 1959, John b. 1961, Joe b. 1965; edn: BS, Univ. Wyoming, Laramie 1956; MBA, Mich. State Univ., 1966; M in Bus. Taxation, USC, 1977; C.P.A., Calif. Career: served to Col. US Air Force 1956-80; exec. v.p. Resource Systems Inc., Englewood, Co. 1980-87; mgr. investor relations Tri-Ex Oil & Gas, Denver 1981-82; assoc. director Colorado Lottery, Denver 1983-85; senior cons. Scientific Games Inc., Sacto., Calif. 1985-88, senior plant controller Sci. Games Inc., Gilroy 1988-; honors: Beta Alpha Psi 1966, Beta Gama Sigma 1966; civic: Gilroy C.of C. 1988-, Rotary Club; Republican; R.Cath.; rec: golf. Res: 3825 Clover Valley Rd Rocklin 95677 Ofc: Scientific Games, Inc. 8100 Camino Arroyo Gilroy 95020

TWIST, MELVIN L., construction co. president; b. Dec. 21, 1938, Ponca City, Okla.; s. Fred G. and Myrtile M. T.; m. Glenda L. Van Alstyne, Feb. 25, 1961; children: Tanja b. 1964, Tisja b. 1969; edn: Bakersfield Coll. 1957-59; Long Beach Coll. 1961-62; Riverside City Coll. 1968-69. Career: field engr. Macco Corp., Paramount 1960-64; project mgr. Allied Webb Corp., South Gate 1964-67; constrn. mgr. J. Putman Henck Corp., San Bernardino 1967-76; pres. TeePee Engring. Inc., Riverside 1976-; cons., tchr. Jr. Achievement, Riverside 1987-89; constrn. cons. United Indian Devel. Assn. 1985-89; dir. Nat. Center UIDA 1987-89; awards: United Indian Devel. Assn. Owner of Yr. 1978, CAMAS Outstanding Indian Contractor 1985, Award of Excellence 1986, Am. Illustrated Mag. feature story 1988, KTLA tv spl. article 1988, Channel 4 news spl. 1978; mem: Assn. Gen. Contractors (dir. 1988-89), Nat. Center Am. Indian Devel. (bd. dirs. 1987-), Assn. Gen. Contractors (bd. dirs. 1988-), Jr. Achievement Program Sherman Indian H.S. (cons., tchr.), Cherokees of Calif., Industry Hills CC, Quail Ranch CC Nat. Contractors Assn., March of Dimes, APA, POA; Democrat; Methodist; rec: golf, skiing, hunting. Res: 10450 Mull Ave Riverside 92505 Ofc: 3011 E La Cadena Riverside 92507

TWITCHELL, KENT, artist; b. Aug. 17, 1942, Lansing, Mich.; s. Robert Edward and Wilma Doris (Berry) T.; m. Susan Catherine Fessler, Dec. 27, 1975 (div. 1986); m. Pandora Seaton, Feb. 23, 1990; children: Rory b. 1986, Art b. 1992; edn: AA, East L.A. Coll., 1969; BA, CSU Los Angeles, 1972; MFA, Otis Art Inst., 1977. Career: illustrator, E4, US Air Force, Hutchinson, Kans. 1960-62, London, England 1962-65: display artist JC Penney Co., Atlanta, Ga. 1965-66; free lance artist, Los Angeles 1968-: abstract espressionist 1968-70, fine artist, muralist, 1971-, portrait artist 1977-; drawing instr. L.A. City Coll. 1979-80, Otis/Parsons Art Inst. 1980-83, painting instr. L.A. County High Sch. for the Arts 1987-90; cons. artist Olympic Murals Pgm., L.A. 1983-84; awards: Outstanding Alumnus CSU L.A. 1987, Hon. Doctor of Arts, Biola Univ. 1989, Artist of year L.A. Co. H.S. for the Arts Found. 1991; mem. advy. bds: Mural Conservancy of L.A. 1988-, Artist Equity Assn. of L.A. 1980-, Hollywood Arts Council 1991-; works incl. design and paintings: 10 story mural Michael Jackson monument, Hollywood (1991-93), 8 story mural L.A. Chamber Orch., dwntwn. L.A. (1991-93), 3 story mural Julius Erving monument, Phila. (1989), 2 story mural Steve McQueen monument, L.A. (1971); avocation: theology. Ofc: 2160 Sunset Blvd Los Angeles 90026

TWOREK, MICHAEL LYNN, corporate business manager; b. Aug. 8, 1948, Bremerton, Wash.; s. John Joseph Tworek and Doris Virginia (Bowne) Corcoran; m. Jaunita Marie Walle, Mar. 21, 1970 (div.); children: Cheryl b. 1970, Philip b. 1973; edn: BSE, Arizona State Univ., Tempe 1973; MSEE, Air Force Inst. of Tech., Wright-Patterson AFB, Oh. 1976; MBA, Golden Gate Univ., 1988. Career: served to major USAF 1966-87: program mgr. microcomputer systems USAF Sch. of Aerospace Medicine, Brooks AFB, Tx. 1976-80; asst. prof. Air Force Acad., Colo. 1980-83; project engr. NASA, Kennedy Space Ctr., Fla. 1983-85; chief shuttle fluids div. 6595 Shuttle Test Gp., Vandenberg AFB, Calif. 1985-87, ret. USAF; business devel. mgr. Bechtel Nat. Inc., San Francisco 1987-90; mgr. M&BD Info. Sys., Bechtel Corp., San Francisco 1990-; honors: Eta Kappa Nu 1971, Tau Beta Pi 1972, Phi Kappa Phi 1972, Outstanding Young Man in Am. 1982, listed Who's Who in the West 1992; mem: Inst. of Electrical & Electronic Engrs. 1971-, Air Force Assn. 1980-, Internat. Platform Assn. 1992-; Republican (spons. Nat. Rep. Congl. Commn. 1983-); rec: running, tennis, backpacking. Res: 160 Bay St. #222 San Francisco 94133 Ofc: Bechtel Corp. PO Box 193965 San Francisco 94119

UCHIDA, PRENTISS S., entrepreneur, management executive; b. Nov. 30, 1940, San Jose; s. Fred Toshio and Elise Chiyoe (Kurasaki) U.; m. Patricia A. White, Oct. 17, 1981; children: S. Akemi b. 1971, T. Christopher b. 1973, K. Kansai b. 1982; edn: BA, CSU San Jose 1963. Career: programmer Lockheed Missile & Space Co., 1963-66; Adage Inc., 1966-69; founder, pres. and chmn. bd. Vector General, Inc. 1969-79; pres. Inner Game Corp., 1979-83; pres. and chmn. bd. Secom General Corp., 1984-86; mgmt. cons., venture capitalist 1986-; dir: Instar Informatique (Paris, Fr. 1981-), Potter Electronics, Nickel Equipment Co., Secom Comms. Co. 1984-86, R.E. Development 1987-88, Commodity Trader 1989-, Internat. Distbr. Environmental Products 1990-; civic: United Way (dir. 1977-79). Res: 2504 Sierra Creek Rd Agoura 91301 Ofc: 5010 N Parkway Calabasa Calabasas 91302

UDALL, DON ALLEN, urological surgeon and vasectomy reversal specialist; b. Jan. 10, 1938, St. Johns, Ariz.; s. Gilbert Douglas and Sarah (Brown) U.; children: Lanette b. 1962, John b. 1965, Brook b. 1966, Don b. 1972, Sara b. 1974; edn: Brigham Young Univ. 1960; MD, Baylor Univ. 1965; cert. Am. Bd. Urology 1973. Career: surgical resident UCLA; urology resident Univ. Oreg. Hosp., Portland; pvt. practice physician, 1973-; asst. clin. prof. UC Irvine 1970-82; mem. Am. Urological Assn.; club: Balboa Bay; mil: major USAR 1967-73; rec: tennis, flying, skiing, travel. Res: 1000 White Sails Way Corona Del Mar 92625 Ofc: 1401 Avocado Ste 602 Newport Beach 92660

UDE, CHEMA, urban planner; b. Dec. 13, 1947, Ibadan, Nigeria; s. Azutoru Alfred and Oyema (Lydia) U.; m. Arrinita Holloway, May 9, 1984 (div. May 1989); children: Justin b. 1978, Dane b. 1984; edn: BS in bus./pub. adminstrn., Calif. Baptist Coll., Riverside 1975; MPPA, plng. & pub. adminstrn., Pepperdine Univ., 1978; Calif. life tchg. credential. Career: youth group counselor Good Samaritan Home, Corona, Calif. 1975-76; group counselor Riverside County Juvenile Probation Dept., Riv. 1976-77; assoc. planner County of Riverside, 1978-84; code enforcer City of Riverside, 1984-85; environmentalist splst. Co. of San Bernardino, 1985-86; sr. planner City of Moreno Valley, 1986-89, City of Fontana, 1989-; awards: creative planner cash award County of San Bdo. 1986, gold award (Class B) Photographic Soc. of Am., Riv. (1985), So. Calif. Poetry Assn. award 1985; mem: Am. Black Writers Assn. 1986-, Internat. Writers Orgn. of So. Calif. (bd., fiction rev. 1987-), VCC Victoria Camera Club, Riv. (newsprint ed.), NAACP, Amnesty Internat., Greenpeace, Sierra Club, YMCA; inventor: Extend-a-sill (pat. appl. 1985); contbg. writer Rand McNally Weekend Escapes Southern Calif. Travel Guide (1986-87), newspaper photo-articles in The Sentinel (AUS, Nurenberg, Ger. 1983-84), Sunday Concord, Lagos, Nigeria (1985), pub. poems in Essence Mag. (1987), fiction and poetry in Mosaic, UC Riverside (1986, 87, 88, 89); New Jerusalem Four Square Ch.; rec: photog., tennis, writing. Ofc: POB 4111 Riverside 92514

UEBERROTH, PETER VICTOR, travel industry executive, former baseball commisioner b. Sept. 2, 1937, Chicago, Ill.; s. Victor C. and Laura (Larson) U.; m. Virginia Nicolaus; four children; edn: CSU, San Jose. Career: founder Transportation Consultants International 1963-, co. went public 1967; chmn. bd./chief exec. First Travel Corp. 1967-; pres. Los Angeles Olympic Organizing Com. 1979-84; commissioner of baseball 1984-89; head, cons. Contrarian Group, Newport Beach 1992; co-chmn. Rebuild Los Angeles. 1992-93, bd.dirs. 1992-; dir. Transamerica Corp.; mem: Delta Upsilon, Bel Air CC; Christian; rec: water sports, golf, tennis. Ofc: Los Angeles 90084

UNGER, ARLENE KLEIN, employee assistance program consultant; b. May 12, 1952, Brooklyn, N.Y.; d. Eli N. and Harriet Barbara (Shapiro) K.; m. Stefan Howard Unger, Aug. 19, 1979; children: Max b. 1981, Elana b. 1989; edn: MS (equivalency), CSU Hayward 1983; BS, Emerson Coll. 1974; MS, So. Conn. State Coll. 1976; PhD, W. Grad. Sch. of Psych. 1991; lic. MFCC (1985). Career: site admin., tchr. splst. Santa Clara Severly Delayed Language Pgm., Santa Clara 1976-81; language & movement splst. Peninsula Children's Center, Palo Alto 1981-84; dir. tng. and sales Human Resources Services, EAP, Sunnyvale 1984-86; employee assistance program mgr. Occupational Health Services, Inc., Sunnyvale 1986-91; pvt. practice employee assistance program cons., prin. Counseling & Consulting Resources, Palo Alto 1991-; mental health trainer, cons. Decathlon Club, Santa Clara 1986-; leader, splst. Sunnyvale Recreation, Sunnyvale 1976-78; counselor, cons. Pinewood School, Palo Alto 1981-83; therapist Woodside Psychological Services, Redwood City 1981-85; awards: CEAP cert. Almaca 1988, Am. Dance Therapy Registry 1986, appointed ch. Almaca "Conf. on AIDS in the Workplace" (1987); mem: Employee Assistance Pgm. Assns., Am. Assn. of Marriage and Family Therapists, Am. Dance Therapy Assn., Am. Speech and Hearing Assn., Am. Assn. of Counseling and Devel., Albert Shultz Jewish Community Ctr. (vol.), Decathlon Club, Palo Alto Run Club, EAP Almaca com.; contbr. articles in profl. jours. (1986, 88); founder, creator multicultural nightclub, Cafe Matek, 1976-81; founder, pres. retail jewelry, Boutique Supply, 1983-; creator and dir. Children's Creative Movement & Art Pgm., Sunnyvale 1976-78; rec: consulting, jogging, swimming, guitar playing, painting. Res: 2250 Webster Palo Alto 94301 Ofc: Counseling & Consulting Resources 4151 Middlefield Rd Ste 110 Palo Alto 94303

UNTERMAN, THOMAS EDWARD, lawyer; b. Oct. 23, 1944, Newport, R.I.; s. Dr. Martin D. and Ruth Rose (Marcus) U.; m. Patricia Fogel, June 24, 1969; m. Janet M. Mead, Sept. 27, 1980; children: Rebecca b. 1981, Amy b. 1985; edn: AB, Princeton Univ., 1966, JD, Univ. Chicago Law Sch., 1969; admitted bar: Calif. 1970. Career: atty., assoc. Orrick, Herrington & Sutcliffe, San Francisco 1969-75, ptnr. 1975-86; ptnr. Morrison & Foerster, S.F. 1986-89, v.p. gen. counsel The Times Mirror Co. L.A. 1989-; appt. Calif. State Senate Commn. on Corporate Governance, 1986-; civic: Public Counsel (dir. 1992-); Democrat; Jewish. Ofc: The Times Mirror Co. Times Mirror Sq Los Angeles 90053

UNWIN, STEPHEN FORMAN, advertising educator; b. Aug. 7, 1927, Higham, Leicestershire, England; s. Phillip Henry and Decima (Forman) U.; m. Pamela Susan Brett, June 6, 1953; children: Phillip b. 1954, Tessa b. 1955, Sam b. 1963; edn: BA, and MA with honors in modern history, Oxford Univ., Eng. 1952, 1968; desig: MIPA, Inst. of Practitioners in Advt., London, 1960. Career: account exec. The London Press Exchange Ltd., London, Eng. 1951-66, dir. The London Press Ex. Org. 1966-67, assoc. dir. LPE Ltd. 1967-69; advt. cons. Illinois Bell, Chgo., Ill. 1974-75; dir. Forest Industries Communications Inst., Atlanta, Ga. 1975-76; publicist British Tourist Auth., London, Eng. 1978-81; advt. cons. J. Walter Thompson Co., San Francisco 1983; sr. analyst Business Dynamics, Carmel, Calif. 1985-; vis. lectr. 1969-70, asst. prof. Univ. Ill., Urbana 1970-74; assoc. prof. Univ. Alabama, Tuscaloosa 1974-79, Washington State Univ., Pullman 1979-81, Univ. Oregon, Eugene 1981-85; mem. Internat. Advt. Edn. Com. Chgo. 1982, Nat. Com. for Advt. Edn. N.Y.C. 1983-84; awards: key to the city of Lubbock, Tx. 1969, vis. prof. Am. Assn. of Advt. Agys., Chgo. 1971, bicentennial judge Advertising Age, Chgo. 1976, vis. prof. Am. Ad Fedn., S.F. 1983; mem: Worcester Coll., Oxford 1952-, Am. Acad. of Advt. 1970-, Kappa Tau Alpha nat. soc. journ. (1973-, Future of Journ. Edn. Com., Eugene, Oreg. 1982-84); Canterbury Cathedral (friend 1985-); author: How Nations Grow Rich (1992), 2 book chapters in The New World of Advertising (1975), contbr. book revs. and articles in jours. and trade mags. 1970-; mil: 2d lt. British Army 1945-48; Episcopalian; rec: travel, genealogy. Ofc: Business Dynamics, 8th & San Carlos, Box S-3197 Carmel 93921

UPTON, HENRY YEOMANS, physician, ophthalmologist; b. Feb. 17, 1936, Seattle, Wash.; s. Leland Bickford and Charlotte (Hamblen) U.; m. Virginia Nielson, Feb. 12, 1972 (div. 1980); edn: BS, Stanford Univ. 1959; MD, Univ. Wash. Seattle 1966; diplomate Am. Bd. Ophthalmology. Career: pvt. practice, Auburn, Wash. 1971-72; San Carlos 1972-; assoc. clin. prof., dept. ophthalmology Stanford Univ. 1974-; mem. Am. Acad. Ophthalmology (fellow), Peninsula Eye Soc. (pres. 1986); mil: lt. USN 1959-61, 1966-67; Protestant; rec: skiing. Ofc: 1178 Brittan Ave San Carlos 94070

UYEDA, LANCE D., environmental health specialist, city project manager; b. July 24 1943, Denver; s. John N. and Etsu T. (Kawata) U.; m. Yoshie Susie Takahashi, Jan. 30, 1970; children: Craig b. 1970, Shelley b. 1972, Lauren b. 1974, Scott b. 1975; edn: MBA cand. San Jose State Univ.; Reg. Environ. Health Splst., Calif. Career: prev. med. splst., E5, SP/5, US Army, Fort McArthur, 1967-69; environmental health sanitarian County Health Dept., San Jose 1969-79; envir. health sanitarian City of San Jose, 1979-86, code enforcement supr. 1986-89, 90-, code enforcement div. actg. chief 1989-90, Project Blossom mgr. 1990-92; instr. Health 21, Los Altos Hills; mem.: Calif. Envir. Health Assn. (p.r. chmn. 1974), SCCO Envir. Health Assn. San Jose (pres. 1975); civic: Am. Youth Soccer Orgn. (commr. region 45 1988); Democrat; rec: photography. Ofc: City of San Jose 801 N First St San Jose 95110

UYEHARA, OTTO ARTHUR, professor emeritus; b. Sept. 9, 1916, Hanford, Calif.; s. Rikichi and Umi (Nakayama) U.; m. Chisako Suda, Aug. 12, 1945; children: Otto Kenneth; edn: BS, Univ. Wisconsin, Madison, 1942, MS, 1943; PhD chemical engr., 1946. Career: post doctoral fellow, Univ. Wisconsin, Madison, 1945-46, res. assoc., 1946-47; asst. prof. (mech. engr.), 1947-51, assoc. prof., 1951-57; prof., 1957-81; prof. emeritus, 1982-; awards: Benjamin Smith Reynolds Teaching. Award, Univ. Wisconsin, Madison; SAE Fellow, Soc. of Automotive Engrs., 1985; hon. mem. Japan Soc. of Mechanical Engring., 1986; Scientific Award, Japan Soc. of Automotive Engrs., 1987; mem: Soc. of Automotive Engrs. (fellow) 1945-, Am. Soc. of Mechanical Engrs. 1945-, Sigma Xi 1947-; civic: Kiwanis Club of Anaheim (pres. 1987-88); author: three inventions for special valves for IC engines, 1960; low voltage bed wetting sensor, 1975; rec: golf; res: 544 S. Bond St. Anaheim 92805

VALDEZ, ARNOLD, dentist; b. June 27, 1954, Mojave; s. Stephen Monarez and Mary Lou (Esparza) V.; edn: BS biol. sci., CSU Hayward 1976; BS dental sci., and DDS, UC San Francisco, 1982; MBA, Calif. St. Polytech. Univ. 1985; law student Pacific West Coll. of Law; Calif. State Indep. Med. Examiner and Qualified Med. Examiner. Career: past assoc. dentist Jack E. Bamesberger, Pomona; Robert C. Borland, Claremont; pvt. practice splst. in temporomandibular joint and myofascial pain dysfunction disorders, 1982-; staff Pomona Valley Hosp. Med. Ctr. 1989-; vol. dentist San Antonio Hosp. Dental Clinic, Rancho Cucamonga 1984-, Pomona Valley Assistance League Dental Clinic 1986-; advy. council Chaffee Comm. Coll. 1982-; bd. dir. Pacific West Coll. of Law 1993-; honors: Who's Who Am. H.S. Students 1972, Who's Who Am. Student Leaders 1972, Outstanding Teenagers of Am. 1972, Calif. State scholar 1972-76 and fellow 1978-82; Fellow Acad. of General Dentistry 1991, Master Acad. of Gen. Dentistry 1994, mem. ADA, Calif. Dental Assn., Tri Co. Dental Soc. (chmn. School Screening Com. 1985-87), The Acad. of Gen. Dentistry, Am. Equilibration Soc., USC Sch. of Dentistry Golden Century Club, Psi Omega, Delta Theta Phi, UCSF Alumni Assn., Toastmasters; R.Cath.; rec: Kenpo Karate, racquetsports, gymnastics, volleyball, skiing. Res: 1320 Malaga Upland 91786 Ofc: 410 W Baseline Rd Claremont 91711

VALENTINE, DE WAIN A., artist; b. Aug. 27, 1936, Fort Collins, Colo.; s. Glenn Valentine and Rouine (Lass) Pope; m. Jeanne C. Clayman, Feb. 14, 1985; children: Christopher b. 1958, Sean b. 1959, Nelsen b. 1960; edn: BFA, Univ. Colo., Boulder 1958, MFA, 1960; fellowship Yale Univ., 1958. Career: instr. Univ. Colo., Boulder 1958-61, 1964; Univ. Calif. Los Angeles, 1965-67; awards: artist in residence Aspen Inst. 1967, 68, Guggenheim fellow 1980, NEA grantee 1981. Res/Studio: 4223 Glencoe Ave Ste B-127 Marina del Rey 90292

VALENTINE, JAMES WILLIAM, professor integrative biology, paleontologist; b. Nov. 10, 1926, Los Angeles; s. Adelbert Cuthbert and Isabel (Davis) V.; m. Diane Mondragon, Mar. 16, 1987; edn: BA, Phillips Univ., Enid, Ok. 1951; MA, UCLA, 1954, PhD, 1958. Career: asst. prof., assoc. prof. Univ. Missouri, Columbia 1958-62, 62-64; assoc. prof., prof. UC Davis, 1964-78; prof. geol. scis. UC Santa Barbara, 1978-90; prof. integrative biology UC Berkeley, 1990-; author: Evolutionary Paleoecology (1973), Evolution (1977), Evolving (1979), Phanerozoic Diversity Patterns (1985); mem: Nat. Acad. of Scis. 1984-, Am. Acad. Arts & Scis. (1984-, Fellow), AAAS (Fellow), Geological Soc. of Am. (Fellow), Paleontological Soc. (pres. 1974-75); mil: QM2/c USNR 1944-46; rec: collect works of Charles Darwin.

VAN BENSCHOTEN, MARK MATHEW, acupuncturist, doctor of oriental medicine; b. Aug. 13, 1956, Los Angeles; s. Peter and Judith (Greenrock) V.; m. Celeste Tina Katz, Feb. 7, 1983; children: Noah Alexander b. 1983, Gabriel Peter b. 1988; edn: UCLA, 1973-77; MA, Goddard Coll. 1980; grad. Calif. Acupuncture Coll. 1980, OMD, 1983; Cert. Acupuncturist, Calif. Career: pvt. practice in acupuncture, herbal medicine, Reseda, Ca. 1980-; clinical dir. Acupuncture Treatment and Research Center, Los Angeles 1982; res. assoc. instr. Oriental Healing Arts Inst., L.A. 1980-84; prof./ chmn. dept. of herbal med., Calif. Acupuncture Coll. 1983-84, prin. instr. oriental med. pgm.; appt. hon. advy. bd. Internat. Acad. Scientific Acupuncture 1990; awards: Academic scholar Bunker-Ramo Corp. 1973, Fellow Pharmacognosy, Oriental Healing Arts Inst. 1979 and Hon. Life Mem. 1983), PhD (hon.) Medicina Alternativa 1988; mem. Calif. Acupuncture Alliance (bd. dirs. 1987); research: Epstein Barr Virus syndrome 1987, HIV/AIDS 1988-91, Qi Gong 1989, Biophoton Diagnostics 1990; contbr. articles in Am. J. of Acupuncture, 1985-91, CAA Phoenix J., 1987-88, Bull. of Oriental Healing Arts Inst., 1981-85, Am. Inst. of

Homeopathy, American Dowser, Qi Gong Universal, 1989, The Tester, J. of Functional Medicine, 1989-90, Biological Therapy, 1989-90, Int. J. Or. Med. 1990; rec: music, painting, martial arts. Res: 8009 McNulty Canoga Park 91306 Ofc: Victory-Tampa Medical Sq 19231 Victory Blvd Ste 151 Reseda 91335

VAN BISE, WILLIAM LLOYD LAFITTE, biomedical engineer; b. June 3, 1937, Slidell, La.; s. Lloyd Wm. and Alice Lorena (Gardner) van Lafitte Bise; edn: ASEE, Tulane Univ., Delgado Tech. Inst., 1962; Hon. MD, Oregon Health Scis. Univ. Sch. of Med., Portland, 1975-77; doctoral studies Oreg. Grad. Ctr., Beaverton 1977-79; E.E. biomedical instrumentation. Career: electroacoustic engr. Pendulum Club, New Orleans, La. 1954-57; photographer Van Bise Studios, 1957-60; instrumentation cons. Rad. Sect. Oreg. State Health Div., Portland 1972-78, clin. instr. Sch. of Med. 1975-79; cons. engr., 1976-80, dir. chief res. scientist, founder Pacific Northwest Center, Portland 1980-84, treas. 1988-; chief biomedical res. Tecnic Res. Labs., San Leandro, Calif. 1984-, pres. Tecnic Med. Labs. Inc. 1988-; pres. Electromagnetic Signal Labs., Inc. 1992-; res. cons. Pomona Coll. 1970-71; honors: invited paper and comments U.S. Senate radiation health & safety hearing & com. 1977, guest lectr. Learned Socs. Conf., Ottawa 1980, guest lectr. Kaiser Permanente Hosp., Portland 1981; mem: IEEE, ICWA, AAAS; co-inventor w. Dr. E.A. Rauscher: cardiac (pat. 1988) and pain control (pat. 1989) devices, ELF detection system (pat. 1988), author 56+ tech. papers - ELF, Microwave, Biological effects, Instrumentation measurement techniques (1970-). Ofc: Electromagnetic Signal Laboratories, Inc. 7685 Hughes Dr Golden Valley NV 89506

VAN CLEEF, ROBERT EDWARD, computer specialist; b. May 20, 1946, Fall River, Mass.; s. Jacque Edward and Ellen D. (Fagan) Van C.; m. Mary Bradley, June 5, 1971; children: James, b. 1975, Anna-Marie, b. 1976; edn: AS, Santa Barbara City Coll.; BBA, magna cum laude, National Univ., 1982, MBA, w/distinction 1984. Career: enlisted man US Navy, 1964-76; field engr. Honeywell Corp., Santa Barbara 1976-79; senior tech. support engr. Computer Sciences Corp., San Diego 1979-84; sys. analyst Gateway Computer Sys. Inc., 1984-85; information sys. analyst Gen. Electric Corp. 1985-89; computer specialist NASA, 1989-; awards: NASA appreciation cert. 1989, group achiev. NAS projects office 1986, GE profl. recogn. pgm. (4/87), GE recogn. for contbn. NAS/ISC 1986; mem: IEEE, USENIX, Assn. for Computing Machinery (reviewer "ACM Computing Reviews" 1984-90), San Diego Computer Soc. (pres. 1984, ed. journal "Personal Systems" 1984-85), S.D. Osborne Users Gp. (past pres.), Internat. Assn. of Computer Using Gps. (bd. 1984-86), Charismatic Pastoral Service Team (ed. newsletter 1993-) Diocese of San Jose; mil. decorations incl. Vietnam Cpgn. w/8 stars, RVN Armed Forces Meritorious (2), Nat. Def., GCM (2), Unit Commendn. (2), Combat Action Ribbon; Republican; R.Cath.; rec: PC, church choir, camping. Res: 192 Warwick Dr Campbell 95008 Ofc: NASA Ames Research Center Moffett Field 94035

VANDENBERGHE, RONALD GUSTAVE, accountant; b. Oakland; s. Anselm Henri and Margaret B. (Bygum) V.; m. Patricia W. Dufour, Aug. 18, 1957; children: Camille, Mark, Matthew; edn: BA, honors, San Jose State Coll. 1959; postgrad., UC Berkeley Extension 1959-60; Golden Gate Coll. 1961-63; CPA Calif. State. Career: real estate developer/investor, Pleasanton 1964-; instr. accounting UC Berkeley, 1963-70; CPA, Pleasanton 1963-; mem. Calif. Soc. CPA's, Masons, Shriners; mil: USAF; Republican; Presbyterian. Res: PO Box 803 Danville 94526 Ofc: POB 728 Pleasanton 94566

VANDERBILT, KERMIT, professor of English (Emeritus); b. Sept. 1, 1925, Decorah, Iowa; s. Lester and Ella (Qualley) V.; m. Vivian Osmundson, Nov. 15, 1947; 1 child: Karen b. 1951; edn: BA, Luther Coll., Decorah, Iowa, 1947; MA, Univ. of Minn., Mpls., Minn., 1949; PhD, Univ. of Minn., 1956; Career: Instr. of Eng., Univ. of Minn., 1954-57; asst. prof. of Eng., Univ. of Wash., Seattle, Wash., 1958-62; asst. prof. of Eng. to prof. of Eng., San Diego State Univ., San Diego, Calif., 1962-91; awards: Outstanding Prof., San Diego State Univ., San Diego, 1976; LittD, Luther Coll., Decorah, Iowa, 1977; Guggenheim Fellow, 1978; Huntington Lib. Fellow, San Marino, Calif. 1980; Outstanding Academic Book (CHOICE), 1988; author: biography, Charles Eliot Norton, 1959; The Achievement of Howells, 1968; American Literature and the Academy, 1986; ed., La Litterature Americaine, 1991; mil: comms. ofcr., USN, 1943-46. Res: 6937 Coleshill Dr. San Diego 92119

VAN DER MEULEN, JOSEPH PIERRE, physician, educator, university hospital administrator; b. Aug. 22, 1929, Boston, Mass.; s. Edward Lawrence and Sarah Jane (Robertson) V.; m. Ann Yadeno, June 18, 1960; children: Elisabeth, Suzanne, Janet; edn: AB, Boston Coll. 1950; MD, Boston Univ., 1954. Career: instr. neurol. Harvard Med. Sch. 1964-65, assoc. 1966-67; asst. prof. neurol. dept. of med. Case Western Reserve Univ. 1967-69, assoc. prof. 1969-71; asst. in neurol. Univ. Hosp., Cleveland 1967-71; asst. nerol. Highland View Hosp.; prof., chmn. dept. neurol. USC 1971-79, chief physician L.A. County-USC Med. Center 1971-79, physician specialist neurology 1979-; prof. neurol. USC 1971-, VPHA USC 1977-, dean sch. of med. 1985-86, director Allied Health Services 1991-; chmn. bd. USC University Hosp. 1990-; appt. Calif. Gov.'s Task Force on Toxics, Waste, and Tech. 1985-; pres. and c.e.o. Kenneth Norris Cancer Hosp. and Research Inst.; bd. dirs: Childrens Hosp., Calif. Hosp., Good

Samaritan, Good Hope Med. Found., Doheny Eye Hosp., House Ear Inst., Barlow Respiratory Hosp., Assn. of Academic Health Centers (chmn. elect 1991, bd. 1987-), Thomas Aquinas Coll. (bd. govs. 1987-); awards: clin. tchg. excellence USC 1976, USN Rear Adm. Campbell Chambliss Navy Award 1978, Founders' humanitarian award Myasthenia Gravis Found. 1982, disting. alumnus Boston Univ. 1984, outstanding tchr. USC Dept. Family Medicine 1984, outstanding vol. City of L.A., Alpha Omega Alpha, Phi Kappa Phi 1982; civic: United Way (co-chmn. 1982), Music Center Unified Fund (chmn. med. div.); res. programs: Medical Ethics, Cerebral Death, Computer Assisted Image Analysis of Muscle Biopsies, Hypertension and the CNS, Epidemiological Studies of ALS, Cortical Evoked Potentials, Neurological and Psychological Evaluation in Perinatal Injury; mil: lt. USN med. corps. 1956-58; rec: golf, skier. Res: 39 Club View Ln Rolling Hills Estates 90274 Ofc: USC, 1985 Zonal Ave Ste 100 Los Angeles 90033

VAN DER VEEN, GEORGE OLIVER, management consultant; b. July 4, 1945, Boise, Idaho; s. George and Martha (Avery) Da Prone; m. Dagmar Krueger, Sept. 10, 1966; children: Eric b. 1968, Lars b. 1972; edn: AA, Pasadena City Coll. 1970; BS math., CSU Los Angeles 1973, MS math., 1979. Career: computer opr. Bendix Field Engring. Corp., Pasadena 1967-70; computer ops. supr. Inventory Mgmt. Systems, Los Angeles 1970-71; comp. opr. Office of the Chancellor Calif. St. Univs. and Colls., 1971-72; pgmmr./analyst CSU Los Angeles 1972-76; pgmmg. supr. Ralph M. Parsons Co., Pasadena 1976-79; founder/pres./bd. chmn. GOV Systems Inc., Pasadena 1979-; lectr. UCLA Ext. 1980-81, Pasadena City Coll. 1981-; mem: Pasadena C.of C., CSULA Alumni Assn., Rotary Alhambra (dir. 1987-88, Paul Harris Fellow 1988); club: Woodhaven Country (Palm Desert); mil: sp4c E4 AUS 1963-66; Democrat; San Marino Congregational Ch. (moderator 1987-88); rec: golf, tennis, jogging. Address: GOV Systems Inc. 3025 Millicent Way Pasadena 91107

VANE, SYLVIA BRAKKE, anthropologist, author, publisher, cultural resource management executive; b. Feb. 28, 1918, Fillmore County, Minn.; d. John T. and Hulda Christina (Marburger) Brakke; m. Arthur Bayard Vane, May 17, 1942; children: Ronald Arthur, Linda, Laura V. Ames; edn: AA, Rochester Jr. Coll., 1937; BS (w/distinction), Univ. Minn., 1939; student Radcliffe Coll., 1944; MA, CSU Hayward, 1975. Career: med. tech. Dr. Frost and Hodapp, Willmar, Minn. 1939-41; head labs. Corvallis Gen. Hosp., Oreg. 1941-42; lab. dir. Cambridge Gen. Hosp., Mass. 1942-43, Peninsula Clinic, Redwood City, Calif. 1947-49; v.p. Cultural Systems Res. Inc., Palm Springs and Menlo Park, 1978-; pres. Ballena Press, Menlo Park 1981-; cons. cultural resource mgmt. So. Calif. Edison Co., Rosemead 1978-81, San Diego Gas and Elec. Co., 1980-83, Pacific Gas and Elec. Co., S.F. 1982-83, Wender, Murase & White, W.D.C. 1983-86, Yosemite Indians, Mariposa, Calif. 1982-84, San Luis Rey Band of Mission Indians, Escondido 1986-, U.S. Ecology, Newport Beach 1986-, Riverside Co. Flood Control and Water Conservation Dist. 1985-, Met. Water Dist. 1989-; author: (w. L.J. Bean) California Indians, Primary Resources (1977, 1990), The Cahuilla and the Santa Rosa Mountains (1981), The Cahuilla Landscape (1991), chapters in several books; mem: Soc. Applied Anthropology (fellow), Southwestern Anthropology Assn. (pgm. chair 1976-78, newsletter editor 1976-79), Am. Anthropology Assn. (fellow), Soc. for Am. Archaeology; civic: Girl Scouts U.S. Sequoia Area Council (bd. 1954-61, cons. S.F. Coun. 1962-69), L.W.V. S.San Mateo Co. (bd., v.p., pres. 1960-65); United Ch. of Christ. Ofc: Ballena Pres 823 Valparaiso Ave Menlo Park 94025

VAN GUNDY, SEYMOUR DEAN, nematologist, university dean and professor; b. Feb. 24, 1931, Toledo, Ohio; m. Wilma C., June 12, 1954; children: Sue Ann b. 1956, Richard b. 1959; edn: BA, Bowling Green S.U., Ohio, 1953; Ph.D., Univ. Wisconsin, 1957. Career: asst. nematologist UC Riverside 1957-63, assoc. nematologist 1963-68, prof. nematology 1968-73, prof. nematology and plant pathology 1973-, chmn. dept. nematology UCR, 1972-84; assoc. dean of res. Graduate Div. UCR 1968-70, asst. v. chancellor res. 1970-72; assoc. dean res. Coll. of Natural & Agricultural Scis., 1985-88, actg. dean 1986, interim dean 1988-90, dean 1990-; lectr., invited spkr. num. campuses and past consultant to various companies; Fellow AAAS 1964-, Am. Phytopathological Soc. 1978-, Soc. of Nematologists 1984-; Rockefeller Found. res. grantee: Cancer Res., Nat. Sci. Found. Res., USDA Competitive Res.; past mem. ed. bd. Revue de Nematologie, Journ. of Nematology and Plant Disease; publs: num. res. papers and articles in profl. jours. Res: 1188 Pastern Rd Riverside 92506 Ofc: UCR College of Natural & Agricultural Sciences Riverside 92521

VAN HOOSER, DAVID BARTON, real estate broker, litigation consultant, arbitrator; b. July 13, 1939, Oakland; s. Cornelius Barton and Ruth David (Harrison) Van Hooser; m. JoAnn Southwick, July 2, 1979; children: David b. 1960, Lance b. 1963, Aaron b. 1971; edn: BBA, Calif. State Coll. 1970; spl. courses in indsl. suprvn., purchasing, personnel & labor rels., 1957-69; La Salle Ext. Univ. of Law, 1966-9; Northwood Inst. of Mdsg. 1969; cert. specialist: IS, RS, and MS (investment, residential, mgmt. splst.), Century 21, 1985. Career: adminstrv. asst. to the pres. Kaiser Jeep Corp., Oakland 1966-68, dist. sales mgr., So. San Francisco 1968-69; dist. mgr. Winnebago Industries, Concord, Ca. 1970, nat. bus. mgr. in Forrest City, Iowa 1970-71, nat. dealer devel. mgr., 1970-71; we. reg. mgr. Apollo Motor Homes, Reno, Nev. 1979, nat. sales mgr.

hdqtrs. Downey, Calif. 1980, v.p. sales 1981, v.p. mktg. & sales, Carson, 1981-84; v.p./mgr. Century 21 Tri Cities Realty, Hesperia 1985-, pres. Foster Financial Funding, Foster and Associates, Foster Group-Tri Cities Realty, 1992-; pres. and gen. mgr. Carl J. Molino Ents. Inc., George Foster Ents. Inc.; prin. broker Utah-Nev.-Calif. Land Exchange (Utah & Calif. co.) 1991; mem: Am. Arbitration Assn. (Panel of Arbitrators), Am. Mgmt. Assn., Calif. Assn. Realtors, Nat. Assn. Realtors, Victor Valley Bd. of Realtors (chmn. profl. & stds. com. 1990-02, past chmn. grievance com.), Century 21 Investment Soc., La Salle Univ. Alumni Assn. (charter); Republican; Ch. of Jesus Christ of Latter Day Saints. Rec: guns/desert survival. Res: 9889 Tradepost Rd Lucerne Valley 92356 Ofc: Century 21 Tri Cities Realty 14465 Main St Hesperia 92345

VAN KIRK, JOHN ELLSWORTH, physician; b. Jan. 13, 1942, Dayton, Ohio; s. Herman Corwin and Dorothy Louise (Shafer) V.K.; children: Linnea b. 1979; edn: BA, cum laude, De Pauw Univ. 1963; BS, Northwestern Univ. 1964; MD, distn., Northwestern Univ. Sch. of Med. 1967; bd. cert. Am. Bd. Internal Med., Cardiovascular Disease. Career: med. internship Evanston Hosp., Northwestern Univ. 1967-68; USPHS staff assoc., NIAID, senior asst. surgeon NIH 1968-70; resident in medicine, fellow in cardiology, Univ. Mich., 1970-74, instr. in internal med. 1973-74; staff cardiologist Mills Memorial Hosp., San Mateo 1974-, dir. critical care and dir. pacemaker clinic; awards: Alpha Omega Alpha, 1st Prize Landscaping, Calif. 1977, Physician's Recogn. Awards (1969, 72, 75, 77, 80, 82, 85, 88, 92); mem: Am. Coll. Cardiology (fellow), Am. Heart Assn., San Mateo Co. Hearth Assn. (pres. 1977-79), Am., Calif. and San Mateo Co. Med. Assns.; works: research in devel. of live viral respiratory vaccines for human use; publd. articles in med. journs.; mil: USPHS 1968-70; Republican; United Brethren; rec: gardening, amateur radio, computer science. Res: 235 Amherst Ave San Mateo 94402 Ofc: 50 S San Mateo Dr Ste 270 San Mateo 94402

VAN MAERSSEN, OTTO L., aerospace engineer, consultant; b. Mar. 2, 1919, Amsterdam, North Holland, The Netherlands, came to U.S. 1946; s. Adolph L. and Maria Wilhelmina (Edelman) Van M.; m. Hortensia Maria Velasquez, Jan. 7, 1956; children: Maria, Patricia, Veronica, Otto, Robert; edn: BSChE, Univ. Mo., Rolla 1949; reg. profl. engr. Tex., Mo. Career: petroleum engr. Mobil Oil, Caracas, Venezuela 1949-51; senior reservoir engr. Gulf Oil, Ft. Worth, Tx. and San Tome, Venezuela, 1952-59; acting dept. mgr. Sedco of Argentina, Comodoro Rivadavia, 1960-61; export planning engr. LTV Aerospace and Defence, Dallas, 1962-69, adminstr. ground transp. div., 1970-74, engr. specialist new bus. programs, 1975-80; mgr. cost and estimating San Francisco/Alaska, 1981-84; owner OLVM Consulting Engrs., Walnut Creek, Calif. 1984-, cons. LTV Aerospace and Def., 1984-; mem. SPE (sr.), Toastmasters Internat., Dallas (sec. treas. 1963-64), Pennywise Club, Dallas (treas. 1964-67); Democrat; R.Cath. Address: 1649 Arbutus Dr Walnut Creek 94595

VAN NORDSTRAND, ROBERT ALEXANDER, research chemist, educator; b. Feb. 17, 1917, Schenectady, N.Y.; s. Robert Daniel and Amelia Gertrude (Pierson) Van N.; m. Wanda Zentera, Feb. 22, 1941 (dec. Dec. 30, 1989); children: Carol b. 1942, Nancy b. 1944, Peggy b. 1947; edn: undergrad. Union Coll., 1934-35; BS chem., Univ. Mich., Ann Arbor 1938, MS chem., 1939. Career: res. chemist Sherwin-Williams Co., Chgo. 1940-42; Sinclair Oil Co., East Chicago, Ind. 1942-47, Harvey, Ill. 1947-62, Tulsa, Okla. 1962-69; research chemist Filtrol Corp., Los Angeles 1972-77; Chevron Res. Co., Richmond, Calif. 1977-, ret. 1992; faculty: physics instr. Indiana Univ. Ext., E.Chgo., Ind. 1945-47, Gary, Ind. 1961, catalysis instr. Roosevelt Univ., Chgo. 1959-61, Mexican Inst. of Petroleum, Mexico City, Mex. 1969, assoc. prof. physics Univ. of Tulsa, 1969-72; mem: Am. Chemical Soc. 1945-, Am. Crystallographic Assn. 1950-, Royal Soc. of Chemistry 1955-, British Zeolite Assn. 1978-, Internat. Zeolite Assn. 1978-, Graphic Arts Council S.F. Museum 1978-; inventor, 6 patents (1950-80), discoverer: new crystalline material "Nordstrandite" (1955), new crystalline Zeolites (1980-92); publs: 30+ sci. articles; rec: tennis, print collecting, poetry, Russian language. Res: 520 Montecillo Rd San Rafael 94903

VAN NOY, TERRY WILLARD, insurance company executive; b. Aug. 31, 1947, Alhambra; s. Barney Willard and Cora Ellen (Simms) V.; m. Betsy Helen Pothen, Dec. 27, 1968; children: Bryan, Mark; edn: BS in bus. mgmt., Calif. State Polytechnic Univ., 1970; MBA, Pepperdine Univ., 1991, CLU, Am. Coll. Career: life underwriter Mutual of Omaha, 1970-: group sales rep. Atlanta 1970-74, dist. mgr. 1974-77, regional mgr. Dallas 1977-82, nat. sales mgr. Hq., Omaha, Nebr. 1982-83, v.p. group mktg. 1983-87, regional v.p. and dir. Mutual of Omaha, Orange, Calif. 1987-; speaker Health Ins. Assn. of Am., Chgo. 1984, Life Ins. Mktg. & Research Assn., S.F. 1987; advy. bd. Chapman Univ. Sch. of Business; mem. Am. Soc. CLUs, Orange County Employee Benefit Council, Western Pension & Benefits Conference, Adaptive Business Leaders; Republican; Lutheran (ch. bd. 1987). Res: 381 S Smokeridge Terrace Anaheim 92807 Ofc: Mutual of Omaha 333 S Anita Dr Ste 650 Orange 92668

VAN STRALEN, ERIC, title insurance executive; b. Dec. 4, 1952, Montebello; s. Albert Phillip and Evelyn Ruth (Murray) Van S.; m. Linda Kozan Hunt, June 19, 1972 (div. 1979); m. Diane Alene Laizure, May 18, 1980; children: Katrina b. 1974, Rebecca b. 1981, Candice b. 1981; edn: grad.

Lakewood H.S., 1971, course work Long Beach City Coll., Solano Comm. Coll., UC Davis. Career: mgr. Title-Tax, Inc., L.A. 1976-79; customer svc. First American Title Co., Fairfield 1980-83; title dept. mgr. Transam. Title Ins. Co., Walnut Creek 1983-87; title ops. mgr. Stewart Title Co., Santa Ana 1987; br. mgr. North Am. Title Co., Glendale 1987-90; title ops. mgr. World Title Co., Burbank 1990-92, county mgr. World Title Co., Pleasanton 1992-; mem. Calif. Land Title Assn. (Speaker's Bur. 1983-85), Calif. Trustees Assn. 1983-; mil: E4 USN 1972-75; Republican; Episcopalian; rec: camping, fishing, hunting. Res: 4409 Valley Ave. #F Pleasanton 94566 Ofc: World Title Co. 7031 Koll Center Pkwy Ste 120 Pleasanton 94566 Tel: 510/462-5353

VAN VLIET, STEPHANIE DIANA, numismatist; b. July 20, 1947, Los Angeles; d. Lawrence Joel and Selma Marcia (Kaplan) Misrach; children: Jennifer b. 1969, Adam b. 1970, Jason b. 1974, Jill b. 1976; edn: Fgn. langs., James Monroe H.S., Sepulveda, 1965; AA, L.A. Valley Coll., 1967; cert. CSU Northridge cont. edn. div. bus. and ind. svs., 1989; reg. hypnotherapist, 1991. Career: summer camp counselor Doubs, Fr. 1965; nursery sch. asst., elem. sch. tchr. aide, playground dir., Van Nuys 1966-68; v.p. American Coin Co., Studio City 1968-83; pres. Rubio Medical Center, 1980-; pres. Internat. Gold & Silver, Encino 1983-; honors: capt. of the Saftys, Brentwood Elem. Sch. Playground 1958, ed.-in-chief Sepulveda Jr. H.S. newspaper 1962, student body senator/rep. Fgn. Language Dept., LA Pierce Coll. 1989-90; mem: Am. Numismatic Assn. (life), Am. Numismatic Soc., Nat. Assn. of Watch and Clock Collectors, Israel Numismatic Soc., Casino Chips and Gaming Tokens Collectors Club, Fla. United Numismatics (FUN), ACLU, Older Womens League, N.O.W., NAACP (life), Womens Am. ORT (life), Nat. Council of Senior Citizens (life), ASPCA, Encino C.of C., Lambda Legal Defense and Edn. Fund, Native Am. Rights Fund, Human Rights Campaign Fund, The Acad. of Polit. Sci., L.A. World Affairs Council, Sierra Club, L.A. Co. Mus. of Art, The Nature Conservancy, NRA (life), ICTA, Parents & Friends of Gays & Lesbians, Act-Up, Women Only, So. Calif. Women for Understanding, Women For, Win PAC, B'nai Brith Women, New Jewish Agenda, ARZA, Am. Soc. for Yad Vashem, Jewish Geneal. Soc. L.A., Hillel, Dignity, Longhunter Soc., YWCA, Gene Autry We. Heritage Mus. (founding mem.), Nat. Audubon Soc., Inst. of Noetic Scis., Theta Sigma Tau, Sigma Kappa; Stonewall Democratic Club; Calif. Republican Party (sustaining 1991); publs: her 1st article written in elem. sch., 1957, for Brentwood Sch. newspaper, pub. by LA Times, 2/26/83; volunteer: VA Med. Ctr. (Sepulveda), Childrens Hosp. (L.A.), Gay & Lesbian Comm. Svs. Ctr. (L.A.), Am. Red Cross; Stephen S. Wise Temple; rec: baseball, theater, comedy. Res: 15615 Meadowgate Rd Encino 91436

VARELA, GEORGE G., management consulting and government relations; b. May 25, 1947, Los Angeles; s. Jorge E. and Bessie P. (Barber) V.; m. Terryl Ann Field, May 31, 1966; children: Cynthia Kathleen b. 1967, Eric Jason b. 1970; edn: BA, Whittier Coll., 1970; MPA, CSU Fullerton, 1975; postgrad. studies Dartmouth Bus. Sch., UC Riverside, and Caltech; Calif. Comm. Colls. instr. credential. Career: recreation supr. City of Santa Fe Springs, 1966-70; admin. asst. City of Montebello, 1970-73; asst. to city mgr. City of Chino, 1973-78; personnel dir. City of West Covina, 1978-81; asst. city mgr. City of Covina, 1981-88; asst. city mgr. City of Mission Viejo 1989-; owner/pres. mgmt. cons. and govt. relations 1989-; past pres. San Gabriel Valley Labor Relations Assn. 1973; past dir. So. Calif. Personel Mgmt. Assn. 1977; award: Outstanding Svc. in Local Govt. from Calif. State Assembly 1977; mem: Internat. City Mgmt. Assn., League of Calif. Cities Task Forces 1972, 74, Whittier Coll. Hispanic Alumni Assn., U.S. Hispanic C.of C.; civic: past pres. Don Lugo High Sch. Booster Club, past coach Chino Little League/Pony Baseball and Chino Am. Youth Soccer Orgn.; author: pub. technical articles on affirmative action; spkr. various trade groups; Democrat; R.Cath.; rec: baseball, fishing, hunting, camping, skiing. Res: 7203 Manzanita St Carlsbad 92009-5127

VASA, HARK MANILAL, software & consulting firm executive; b. Feb. 8, 1944, Bombay, India; nat. U.S. citizen, 1976; s. Manilal Panachand and Prabha (Dholakia) V.; m. Kusum B. Doshi, Nov. 8, 1970; children: Anita b. 1972, Sarita b. 1975; edn: BS in elec. engring., V.J.T.I., Bombay, India, 1966; MS, West Va. Univ., 1968. Career: engr. Union Carbide, W.Va. 1968-70; v.p. DSC, Pa. 1970-82; pres. Pac Decision Science Co., Santa Ana 1982-; cons. PDSC, 1982-89; lectr. conferences, 1988; author: articles, 1983, 85, 86, 87; Republican; Jain; rec: social activities, traveling.

VASCONCELLOS, JOHN, legislator, atty.; b. May 11, 1932, San Jose, Calif.; s. John and Teresa (Jacobs) V.; edn: BS, Santa Clara Univ., 1954; LLB, Santa Clara Univ., 1959; admitted Calif. State Bar, 1959. Career: atty., Ruffo & Chadwick, San Jose, 1959; travel sec., Gov. Pat Brown, Sacto., 1960; assemblyman, Calif. State Legislature, Sacto., 1966-; chair, Assembly Ways & Means Com., Calif. State Legislature, 1980-; founder, Calif. Task Force to Promote Self-Esteem and Personal and Social Responsibility, 1987; chmn., Assembly Democratic Econ. Prosperity Team (ADEPT), 1992-; awards: Legislator of the Decade (1980's), Faculty Assn. of Calif. Comm. Colleges; over 100 other awards during tenure as assemblyman; mem: State Bar of Calif., 1959-; bd. of dir., Calif. Leadership, 1987-; author: A Liberating Vision, 1979; Toward a Healthier State, a 7-yr. comprehensive prog. incl. Human Corps, Sr. Partners,

Edn. Reform, Legislative Ethics. Mil: first lt., US Army, 1954-56; Democrat; rec: racquetball. Res: 1915 Bellomy #5 Santa Clara 95050. Ofc: 100 Paseo de San Antonio #106 San Jose 95113

VASQUEZ, GADDI HOLGUIN, county supervisor; b. Jan. 22, 1955, Carrizo Springs, Tex.; s. Guadalupe Garcia Vasquez and Eva V.; m. Elaine Gutierrez, Oct. 14, 1978; children: Jason b. 1979; edn: AA, Rancho Santiago Comm. Coll., Santa Ana 1972; BA, Univ. Redlands, 1980. Career: police ofcr. Orange Police Dept., 1975-79; comm. relations coord. City Mgr.'s Office, Riverside 1979-81; exec. asst. Orange Co. Bd. Suprs., Santa Ana 1981-85; Hispanic liaison Gov.'s Office, Sacto. 1985, dep. appts. sec. 1985-87; apptd. supr. Orange Co. Bd. Suprs. 1987, elected supr. 1988-: mem. Orange Co. Transp. Auth. 1991-, Transp. Corridor Agys. 1987-, Local Agy. Formation Commn. 1988-, Nat. Assn. Latino Elected Officials 1989-, Calif. Council on Crim. Justice 1989; honors: list of 100 most influential Hispanics Hispanic Bus. Mag. 1986-91, Humanitarian award NCCJ 1989, Govt. Hispanic Business Advocate 1991, U.S. Hispanic Chamber 1991, Tree of Life award Jewish Nat. Fund 1991, State Child Devel. Advy. Com. Award 1990; civic bds: Orange County Salvation Army 1991-, Pediatric Cancer Res.Found. 1990-, Orange Co. Boy Scout Council 1988-, Calif. First Amendment Coalition 1991-; Republican; Prot.; rec: reading. Ofc: Orange County Bd. of Supervisors 10 Civic Ctr Plaza Santa Ana 92701

VASU, BANGALORE SESHACHALAM, bioscience and technology educator, administrator; b. Bangalore, India, naturalized U.S., 1982; edn: MA, Univ. of Madras, India 1959, MSc, 1962; PhD, Stanford Univ., 1965. Career: UNESCO specialist in biology, Paris, France and Univ. of Zambia, Lusaka, 1968-73; vis. prof. biology CSU Chico, Calif. 1974-77; professor biology and chair Biosci./Biotech. Mgmt. Menlo Coll., Atherton 1978-; award: Fullbright fellow US Edn. Founds., U.S. and India 1962. Ofc: Menlo College 1000 El Camino Real Atherton 94027

VAUGHAN, DANIEL G., physician-surgeon; b. Mar. 15, 1921, Montana; s. Daniel G. and Katherine (Browne) V.; m. Courtney Sprague, Dec. 3, 1949; children: Laurie b. 1950, Cecilia b. 1952, James b. 1954, Matthew b. 1956, Mary b. 1959, Daniel b. 1960, Katherine b. 1960, Elizabeth b. 1963; edn: BS, Univ. of Wash., Seattle 1942; MD, Univ. of Oregon Med. Sch., Portland 1945; Diplomate Am. Board Ophthalmology 1953. Career: postdoctoral intern King County Hosp., Seattle 1945-46; resident in ophthalmology Univ. of Calif., San Francisco 1948-51; pvt. practice ophthal., San Jose 1951-; staff O'Connor Hosp. (pres. 1964; bd. mem. O'Connor Hosp. Found.); founder/pres. Sight Conservation Res. Center, 1960-; clin. prof. UCSF Dept. Ophthal. San Francisco; mem. bd. govs. Francis I. Proctor Found. for Res.in Ophthalmology 1990-; awards: Oregon State Junior Golf Championship 1938, disting. service Francis I. Proctor Found. for Res. in Ophthalmology 1984, outstanding contbn. in med. edn. Santa Clara Co. Med. Soc. 1988; mem: AMA, Assn. for Res. in Ophthal. (exec. sec. We. Sect. 1961-66), Fellow Am. Coll. of Surgeons (Western US rep. to Advy. Council for Ophthalmic Surgery 1971-74 and chmn. 1974-76), Frederick C. Cordes Eye Soc. (pres. 1965), No. Calif. Soc. for Prevention of Blindness (pres. 1971-73), Pacific Coast Oto-Ophthalmological Soc. (pres. 1980-81), Santa Clara Co. Med. Assn., Santa Clara Univ. (bd. fellows); author eye chapters in 2 med. texts, coauthor: General Ophthalmology, 12th edit. (Lange Med. Pub., transl. 6 langs.), contbr. 25+ sci. articles in ophthalmic jours.; mil: First Marine Div. Med. Corps, China 1946-47. Ofc: 220 Meridian Ave San Jose 95126

VAUGHAN, MICHAEL J., trust company president; b. Jan. 26, 1942, N.Y.; s. Michael J. and Florence R.; m. Sherree R. Vaughan, June 26, 1965; children: Gary R., Andrew M.; edn: AA, Santa Ana Coll. 1962; BA, psychol., CSU Fullerton 1964; postgrad., USC 1966-67; M. in bank trust, Univ. Wash. 1973; lic. real estate Calif. Career: v.p. Union Bank, L.A. 1965-74; Lloyds Bank, Santa Ana 1974-79; pres. M.J. Vaughan & Co. Inc. 1979-83; sr. v.p. Valencia Bank, Newport Beach 1983-85; pres./CEO Imperial Trust Co., L.A. 1985-; thesis rev. Pacific Coast Banking Sch., Seattle, Wash. 1973-77; mem: Orange Co. Planned Giving Council, So. Calif. Trust Officers. Assn., Internat. Assn. Fin. Planners, Internat. Found. Employee Benefit Plans, Western Pension Conf., Am. Soc. Pension Actuaries, L.A. World Affairs Council, USC Gen. Alumni (life mem.), USC Trojan Club (pres. 1982-83), USC Cardinal & Gold, USC Scholarship Club, USC Commerce Assocs. USC Cancer Assocs. (bd. dirs.); active Hoag Hosp. 552, St. Joseph Hosp. Todo's, bd. dirs. St. Joseph Hosp. Found.; clubs: Pacific, City, Tustin Ranch Golf; MS thesis: The Devel. of Bus. in Orange Co., hons. recognition 1973; contbr. article, Calif. Planner Mag. (1986); Republican; Lutheran; rec: golf (course record Mission Viejo C.C.; Res: 11581 Ranch Hill Santa Ana 92705 Ofc: Imperial Trust Co. 201 N Figueroa St Ste 610 Los Angeles 90012

VAUGHN, JAMES ENGLISH, JR., neuroscientist; b. Sept. 17, 1939, Kansas City, Mo.; s. James English and Sue Katherine V.; m. Christine Singleton, June 18, 1961; children: Stephanie b. 1965, Stacey b. 1968; edn: BA, Westminster Coll., 1961; PhD, UCLA, 1965. Career: postdoctoral fellow Univ. of Edinburgh, Scotland 1965-66; asst. prof. Boston Univ. Sch. of Med., Mass. 1966-70; assoc. prof. Beckman Research Inst. of City of Hope, Duarte, Calif. 1970-73, prof.

1973-, chmn. div. neuroscis. 1987-; awards: res. grantee NIH 1969-, United Cerebral Palsy Found. 1965-66, NSF 1983-87, Huntington's Disease Found. 1987-88, Sadie & Norman Lee Found. 1990-91; mem.: Soc. for Neurosci., Internat. Brain Research Orgn., N.Y. Acad. of Scis., Am. Soc. for Cell Biology, AAAS; publs: book chapters, research articles in profl. jours. (1965-); editl. bd. Synapse (1986-), reviewer J. of Comparative Neurology, Brain Research (1974-), asso. editor J. of Neurocytology (1978-86). Ofc: Beckman Research Inst. City of Hope 1450 E Duarte Rd Duarte 91010

VAUGHN, MARY, convalescent hospital administrator, community activist; b. April 20, 1930, Trafford, Ala.; d. Grover Webster and Vivian Lenore (Dorman) V.; m. James T. Lovvorn, July 4, 1951, dec.; edn: Cert., Birmingham Bus. Coll. 1949; modeling, Howard Coll. 1962; Thearapeutic Activities Cert., Grossmont Adult Sch. 1975; Cert., Mgmt. Success Inst. 1977; Lic. Adminstr., Calif.; Cert. Notary Public, Calif. Career: pres./ treas. Balboa Manor Health Facility, San Diego; owner/adminstr. Balboa Manor Intermediate Care Ctr., San Diego; awards: Women's Internat. Center honoree and Living Legacy Award 1988, Congl. distinguished service award and citizen of month presented by Cong. Jim Bates (11/87), Women's Internat. Center vol. of year award (3/7/92), City Beautiful campus beautiful vol. award (5/90), So. Dist. BPW woman of achiev. (1987, 90, 91) and nominee to Calif. State BPW Hall of Fam (3/92); mem. Am. Assn. of Health Facilities, Calif. Assn. of Health Facilities; civic bds: Girls Club of San Diego, Southland Bus. & Profl. Women (past pres.), Women's Internat. Center (treas.), Mary Vaughn Scholarship Fund for Aging Res. (treas.); author: Exploring Mental Therapy, 1978; Democrat; Methodist; rec: volleyball, volunteer. Res: 2804 C Street San Diego 92102 Ofc: Balboa Manor Inc., 1119 28th St San Diego 92102

VEERAPPA, CHANDIAH, retired consulting physician; b. July 10, 1925, Chikmagalur, India, nat. 1971; s. M. P. and R. (Rudramma) Chandiah; m. N. Suvarna, Apr. 21, 1957; children: Vinitha b. 1958, Uma b. 1964, Vishwanath b. 1965; edn: L.M.P. (lic. med. practitioner), Univ. Med. Sch., Bangalore 1948; MB, BS, Andhra Med. Coll. Andhra Univ., Vizag, India 1955; dipl. tropical medicine, Univ. Liverpool, U.K. 1958; MD lic. Calif., Me. Career: cardiology fellow The Jewish Hosp. 1969, Gen. Hosp., Univ. Cinti. 1970; gen. medicine residency (tchg. fellow) Cleveland (Ohio) Clinic, 1972-73; cardiology fellow Wadsworth VA Hosp., UCLA, Los Angeles 1974-75; staff physician, cardiology/int. med., Long Beach VA Hosp. 1975-78; solo med. practice, consultant non-invasive cardiology and internal med., Whittier 1978-1992; med. and social community consultative service, USA and India, 1992-; honors: AMA phys. recognition award (1989, 92-95), appreciation Jewish War Veterans USA 1977, disting. service Amvets 1977; pres., Karnataka Cultural Assn of So. Cal., 1987; Rep. Presidl. Task Force Am. ceremonial flag award 1986; mem: Am. Heart Assn., Am. Coll. of Chest Physicians, Am. Echocardiographic Soc., Whittier Acad. of Medicine, Rotary Internat.; Republican (Rep. Presidl. Task Force Honor Roll 1991, Wall of Honor 1992, recogn. in "Who's Who"); rec: flying, tennis, philosophy.

VEGA, BENJAMIN URBIZO, jurist; b. Jan. 18, 1916, La Ceiba, Honduras; s. Benjamin Urbizo (former Honduras Consul General in Mobile, Ala. and Los Angeles, Ca.) and Catalina (Tablas) V.; m. Janie L. Smith, Oct. 12, 1989; edn: BA, USC, 1938, postgrad. 1939-40; LLB, Pacific Coast Univ. Law, 1941; admitted Calif. St. Bar 1947, US Dist. Ct., So. Dist. 1947, Bd. Immigration Appeals 1948, US Supreme Ct. 1958. Career: atty., assoc. Anderson, McPharlin & Connors, Los Angeles 1947-48, Newman & Newman, 1948-51; deputy dist. atty. County of Los Angeles, 1951-66; judge L.A. Co. Municipal Ct., East L.A. Judicial Dist., 1966-86, retired 1986; awards: distinguished public service L.A. Mayor Sam Yorty 1973, commendation for svs. as Dep. Dist. Atty. Los Angeles County Bd. of Suprs., commendation Municipal Judges Assn., proclamation for svs. Montebello City Council, City of Commerce, Resolution of commendation 55th Assembly Dist. Calif., honored for svc. as judge US Congressman Matthew Martinez 30th Dist. Calif.; mem. Beverly Hills Bar Assn., past mem. ABA, Inter-Amer. Bar Assn., Inglewood, East L.A., Montebello bar assns., Am. Judicature Soc., L.A. Lawyers Club, Conf. of Calif. Judges, Municipal Ct. Judges Assn.; civic: Las Campanitas, League of the Americas, Youth Opportunities Found. (past dir.); Internat. Com. L.A. Philharmonic, Navy League of Beverly Hills. mil: cpl. USAF 1942-46; Democrat; R.Cath.; rec: world travel, collect video cassettes, books. Res: Apt 1207 101 California Ave Santa Monica 90403

VEGA, FRANK, distribution executive, softball association area director; b. July 30, 1954, Havana, Cuba; s. Antonio and Luisa Rosa (Santos Cisneros) V.; m. Cecelia Selayandia, Oct. 7, 1989; children: Liza M. Gallant b. 1969, Mark Asa b. 1980; edn: H.S. dipl. Don Bosco Technical Inst., S. San Gabriel, Calif. 1972; stu. East L.A. Jr. Coll., 1973. Career: documentation draftsman Apollo Motorhomes, Downey 1972-74; design draftsman Robinhood Motorhomes, Carson 1974-75; customer service rep. General Bearings, Vernon 1976-81; br. ops. mgr. Bearings Inc., Pico Rivera 1981-85, sales rep. Bearings Inc., Ontario 1985-86; ADC mgr. Hub City Inc., Santa Fe Springs 1986-; softball player awards: 1985 All Tournament selection Memorial Day NIT, All State selection 1984 Hispanic State\Championship, others; area dir. United States Slo-Pitch

Softball Assn., San Gabriel Valley, 1978-; rec: softball, reading, sports. Res: 2896 Buckhaven Rd Chino Hills 91709 Ofc: Hub City 11801 E Smith St PO Box 4187 Santa Fe Springs 90670

VELASQUEZ, RUTH LIND, teacher; b. May 8, 1926, San Francisco; d. Axel and Edith Viola (Carlson) Lind; m. Thomas Aquinas Velasquez, Aug. 14, 1957; children: Laura b. 1959, Donna b. 1962; edn: BA in elem. edn., San Francisco State Univ., 1947, MA, 1953. Calif. std. tchg. credentials: elem. 1947, adminstrv., 1953. Career: tchr. San Francisco Unified Sch. Dist., 1947-90, kindergarten tchr. 1965-70, 1985-90, staff devel. specialist 1970-85; early childhood edn. consultant San Francisco USD 1990-93; honoree, named Outstanding Teacher Delta Phi Upsilon S.F. 1991; mem: Calif. Kindergarten Assn. (profl. devel. leader 1989-92, editor "Take 5" 1989-92, grant com. chair 1989-92, bd. 1993-), Delta Kappa Gamma (co-pres. 1992-93), Delta Phi Upsilon (Grand Council pres. 1989-90); clubs: Margrethe Lodge Danish Sisterhood (S.F.), Epson Salts Computer (Redwood City); author (book, workshop) Recycle for Learning 1990, coauthor (reading pgm.) First Stage Reading Program. Res: 703 Higate Dr Daly City 94015

VERBICA, PETER COE, trustee, real estate principal, developer, financial executive; b. Jan. 31, 1961, San Jose; s. Robert George and Winnifred (Coe) V.; gr. grandson of Henry Willard Coe b. 1820, N.H., opr. cotton textile plant, came overland to Oregon 1847, discovered and worked a gold mine in Amador Co., Calif. 1848-58, married Hannah Smith of N.Y., 1858, settled in 'The Willows' San Jose, Calif., H.W. Coe was first in the region to grow hops, fruit trees, tobacco, and first to produce silk for mfr. (the silk Am. flag he presented US Congress is displayed in the Smithsonian), he ret. to San Felipe Valley where sons Henry Jr. and Charles raised cattle and enlarged Rancho Los Huecos (The Hollows) to include "Pine Ridge Country" (13,000 acres & original Coe ranch bldgs. of 1860s) of the present day Henry Coe State Park, donated in memory of Henry Willard Coe (now the 2d largest state park in Calif. with 63,000 acres, 14 mi. E. of Morgan Hill); m. Karen Kennedy Toole, Sept. 16, 1988; children: d. Vanessa Coe; edn: Bellarmine Coll. Prep.; BA, Univ. Santa Clara 1983; MS, M.I.T 1992. Career: area mgr. Pacific Bus. Products, Santa Clara 1978; account exec., assoc. v.p. Dean Witter Reynolds, Inc. San Jose 1983-88; fin. cons./2d v.p. Shearson Lehman Hutton, Inc. 1988-89; current: sole trustee fam. bus. holdings and real estate; advisor New England holdings, rancher; chief exec./dir. Coe Corp. (real estate holdings; gen. ptnr. CV Equity Partners I, a Calif. Ltd. Ptnrship, gen. ptnr. CV Income Partners I, a Calif. Ltd. Ptnrship); founder, former pres. AMS+ (Advanced Maintenance Services+, a Commercial Bldg. Maint. Co.); lectr., investments, Calif. Comm. Colls., Cupertino 1987; awards: Dean Witter Director's Club 1987, Fox & Carskadon Century Club 1985; mem. Calif. Cattleman's Assn., Santa Clara Cattleman's Assn., (past) Bldg. Ind. Assn., Nat. Assn. Real Estate Inv. Trusts (acad. assoc.), Nat. Assn. Corp. Dir.; civic bds: (past and current): Santa Clara Univ. (Pres.'s Club, Bd. of Fellows, Kenna Club, Class agt., Internship Pgm. sponsor, writer contbr. Santa Clara Mag., guest lectr.), Bellarmine Coll. Prep. Sch. (St. Robert Cardinal Bellarmine Bd. of Fellows, Pres.'s Club, Reunion Orgnzr.), DeAnza Comm. Coll. (instr.), KTEH-TV (bd. trustees), The Technology Ctr. of Silicon Valley (mem.), NCCJ (patron), Lucille Salter Packard Children's Hosp. at Stanford (patron), O'Connor Hosp. Found. (patron), Pub. Affairs Council (founding mem.), S.J. Downtown Kiwanis (coms.), Boy Scouts Am. (chmn. Century Club), Am. Heart Assn. (chmn. Planned Giving), KBAY Bus. & Fin. Update (reporter), Junior Achievement (advisor), Music and Arts Found. S.C.V. (patron), San Jose Repertory Theatre (bd. trustees), YMCA (campaign com.); clubs: Silicon Valley Capital, Commonwealth (S.F.), Rotary, Ducks Unltd., Courtside (Los Gatos), St. Claire; Republican (YR); Episcopal. Ofc: PO Box 7933 San Jose 95150-7933

VERRONE, PATRIC MILLER, writer; b. Sept. 29, 1959, Glendale, N.Y.; s. Pat and Edna (Miller) V.; m. Margaret Williams, July 1, 1989; edn: BA (magna cum laude) Harvard Coll., 1981; JD, Boston Coll. Law Sch., 1984; admitted bar: Fla. 1984, Calif. 1987. Career: atty. Allen, Knudsen, Swartz, DeBoest, Rhodes & Edwards, P.A., Ft. Myers, Fla. 1984-86; writer "Tonight Show Starring Johnny Carson" Burbank, 1987-90; filmmaker Calloo Callay Inc., Hollywood 1990-; producer, director, writer (film) The Civil War - The Lost Episode, 1992; writer "The Larry Sanders Show Starring Garry Shandling" Hollywood, 1992-; awards: Emmy nom. Acad. TV Arts & Scis., Hollywood 1989, Blue rib. Am. Film & Video Assn., Chgo. 1992, Hon. mention IMAGE Film Fest., Atlanta 1992; mem: Writers Guild West 1986-, California Bar Assn. 1987-, Fla. Bar Assn. 1984-, ABA 1984-, L.A. County Bar Assn. (homeless shelter com. 1991-, chmn. artists and the law com. 1992-, Appelate Judicial Eval. Com 1992-, Barrisaters Secty., Exec. Com. 1993-), Harvard Club of So. Calif. (interviewer 1991-); publs: contbr. articles in Nova Law Review (1993), Los Angeles Lawyer (1992), ABA J. (1990), Boston Coll. Law Rev. (1982-84), Fla. Bar J. (1987-89), author, illustrator articles in Harvard Lampoon (1978-84); Republican; R.Cath.; rec: baseball, movies. Ofc: Calloo Callay Inc. 6466 Odin St Hollywood 90068

VICE, CHARLES LOREN, consulting mechanical engineer; b. Jan. 2, 1921, LaVerne, Okla.; s. Cyrus Christopher and Ethel Segwitch (Hoy) V.; m. Katherine Maxwell, July 16, 1949; children: Katherine Lorene b. 1950, Charles Clark b. 1952, Ann Marie b. 1955; edn: ASTP Cert., Ore. State Univ. 1944, BSME, 1947; grad. wk. USC, 1948-55; Reg. Profl. Engr. (mech.), Calif. Career: mgr. Magnetic Head Div., General Instrument Corp., Hawthorne 1959-62; sr. staff engr. Magnetic Head Div., Ampex Corp., Redwood City 1962-66; chief mech. engr. Collins Radio Corp., Newport Beach 1967-69; pres./bd. chmn. FerraFlux Corp., Santa Ana 1970-78; component engr. & engring. buyer McDonnell Douglas Computer Systems Co., Irvine 1979-90; prin. Precision Consultants Inc., Orange 1990-; cons. Sabor Corp. of Japan 1982-, Teac Corp. of Japan 1974-78, Crown Radio Corp. of Japan 1979-80, Otari Corp. of Japan 1975-77, Univac Corp., Salt Lake City 1975-76, Digital Peripherals Corp. of Taiwan 1989-, Puritan Bennett, El Segundo 1989-; patentee (14) in fields of magnetic recording and profl. sound reproduction, internat. recognized authority on magnetic recording techniques; mem. Nat. Soc. of Profl. Engrs., Toastmasters Internat.; mil: tech. 4/c US Army Engrs. 1943-46, GCM, Victory, Asiatic Pacific Service, Philippine Service with Bronze Star medals; Republican; Christian; rec: piano, singing. Ofc: Precision Consultants, Inc. 5902 E Bryce Ave Orange 92667 Tel: 714/998-5979

VIGILIA, LARRY P., physician; b. Feb. 2, 1952, Philippines; s. Eleuterio G. and Consuelo (Pobre) V.; edn: BA chem., Loma Linda Univ.; MD, Montemorelos Univ., Nuevo Leon, Mex.; lic. physician and surgeon BMQA 1982. Career: med. intern White Mem. Med. Ctr., Los Angeles 1980-81; resident Loma Linda Univ. Med. Ctr. 1981-82; attdg. physician San Gabriel Valley Med. Gp., Temple City 1982-84; med. dir./prin. Colorado Family Health Ctr., Glendale 1983-, pres. Urgent Health Clinic Med. Gp Inc., 1983-; med. dir. Broadway Sports Medicine Rehabilitation Ctr., Glendale 1988-; coll. physician Glendale Comm. Coll. 1985-90; med. staff ER dept. Olive View Med. Ctr., Sylmar 1982-89, med. staff Glendale Adventist Med. Ctr. 1983-, Century Comm. Hosp., L.A., 1984, Linda Vista Comm. Hosp., L.A., 1987; mem: Am. Coll. Physicians, Acad. Neuromuscular Thermography, Am. Occupational Med. Assn.; civic: Glendale Sunrise Rotary Club Glendale C.of C. 1983-, Hollyview HOA (dir. 1989-); inventions: Cardio Pressaide 1984, Autovest 1987, A-R Insert, CPR mouthpiece 1988; Seventh-day Adventist; rec: photog, bicycling, backpacking. Ofc: Colorado Family Health Center, 1141 E Colorado St Glendale 91205

VIJAYAN, NAZHIYATH, physician, neurologist; b. Feb. 27, 1941, Kerala, India; nat. 1988; s. Gopalan and Parukutty Amma V.; children: Sushmita b. 1968, Shalini b. 1973; edn: MBBS, Trivandrum Med. Coll. India 1964; MD, 1967. Career: asst. prof. UC Davis Sch. Medicine, dept. neurology 1971-81, assoc. clin. prof. 1981-; dir. Headache Clinic, Sacto. 1981-; mem: Am. Acad. Neurology, Am. Assn. Study of Headache, Internat. Cluster Research Group; num. articles pub. in sci. jours., contbr. med. books; Democrat; rec: computers, electronics. Address: Sacramento 95816

VILLEGAS, RICHARD JUNIPERO, artist; b. Apr. 19, 1938, Santa Monica; s. Robert Narciso and Jessie V. (Rodrigues) V.; edn: stu. Art Students League, N.Y.C. 1965-66. Career: artist Joseph Sarosi Inc., N.Y.C. 1961-62; Vozzo & Binetti, 1962-64; Siegman-Ambro, 1964-77; chief artist Greenbaum Bros., Paterson, N.J. 1978-89; owner The Villegas Art Studio, Thousand Oaks 1989-; mem.: C.G. Jung Found. 1960-, Am. Mus. of Natural History 1964-, Nat. Trust for Hist. Preservation 1975-, Westlake Village C.of C. 1989-, Gold Coast Bus. & Profl. Alliance 1991-; rec: Jeffersonian studies, photography, collecting Indian relics, classical music. Res/Studio: The Villegas Art Studio 980 Camino Flores Thousand Oaks 91360-2367

VINSON, THOMAS EUGENE, trust banker; b. Mar. 10, 1945, Oakland; s. Eugene Mullaly and Virginia Phare (Pearson) V.; m. Margaret Kelly, Aug. 16, 1969; edn: BA in pol. sci., CSU Hayward, 1969; cert. trusts, Pacific Coast Banking Sch., Univ. Wash. 1978, num. special courses. Career: Trust/ Investment Advisors Wells Fargo Bank, 1969-82; mgr. trust systems analysis, private capital banking, The Crocker Bank, 1982-85; Trust Global Custody and v.p./mgr. No. Calif. Instnl. Trust Services Adminstrn., Bank of America NT&SA, San Francisco 1985-87; v.p. State Street Bank-Calif., Alameda 1988-89; v.p. Bank of America and reg. mgr. Custody Svs. Adminstrn, 1989-; mem: No. Calif. Trust Cos. Assn., Western Pension and Benefits Conf., Securities Indus. Assn., Internat. Ops. Assn.; civic: Commonwealth Club of Calif., Lincoln Child Ctr. Found. (pres. 1981-83, bd., treas., fin. chair), Oakland Mus. Assn. (dir., asst. treas. 1980-86, 1988-89), Calif. Hist. Soc., Soc. of Calif. Pioneers, Nev. Hist. Soc.; clubs: Dolphin Swimming and Boating, St. Francis Yacht, Lakeview; Republican; R.Cath.; rec: Calif. hist., art, yachting, railroading. Ofc: San Francisco.

VITALE, DONALD EUGENE, publisher; b. Feb. 16, 1930, Oak Park, Ill.; s. Sylvester and Anne (Potenza) V.; m. Sarah Alice Brengle (dec. 1993), June 9, 1956; children: Mark Francis b. 1957 (dec. 1986), John Vincent b. 1958, Valerie Anne (Mrs. Kurt Bergquam) b. 1959, Paul Keigwin b. 1962; edn: Loyola Univ. 1948-51, Northwestern Univ. 1952, UCLA 1956-57. Career: copy-boy, reporter, re-write City News Bur., Chgo. 1951-52; editor Los Angeles Daily Journal, legal newspaper, 1954-59; asst. dir., dir. pub. rels. LA Area Chamber of Commerce 1959-65, and ed. So. California Bus. (weekly) 1959-61; assoc. dir.

corp. commns. Dart-Kraft (then Rexall Drug & Chem.) 1965-67; Postal Instant Press franchisee, 1969-79; publisher Who's Who In California 1978-93; sr. lectr. USC Sch. of Journalism 1966-71; prod. radio show Big Problems in Small Business, LA 1966-67; appt. LA Mayor Sam Yorty's Small Bus. Council (exec. secty. 1967); playwright: The Aquarium (New Playwrights Found., Hollywood 1973), Bidding and Other Fables (3 one-act plays, Evergreen Stage Co. Hollywood 1976, 78), The Volunteer (one-act play, Northeastern Coll. 1990), Twister (screenplay, 1990); mem: Am. Library Assn., Gr. LA Press Club, Pub. Rels. Soc. of Am. 1961-65, Cath. Press Council of So. Calif. (pres. 1966-67), Town Hall of Calif., Seattle Tilth; radio host weekly travel interview pgm. for B.I. Bdcstg. 1988; past chmn. Info. Com. to Save Descanso Gardens; advy. bd. Mount St. Mary's Coll. 1963-65; mil: sgt. AUS 1951-53, Reserve 1954-56, Korea w/ 3 bronze stars, UN Svc., Korean Svc.; rec: theatre, historical newspapers, breadbaking. Address: PO Box 11410 Bainbridge Island WA 98110

VITALE, PAUL KEIGWIN, musician; b. July 18, 1962, Inglewood; s. Donald E. and Sarah (Brengle) V.; m. Dorothy Pettit, 1983 (div. 1992); 1 son, Peter K. b. 1995; edn: San Clemente H.S., Saddleback Jr. Coll. Career: photog. darkroom, Gallant Charger Pubs., 1983-85; mail carrier USPS, 1985-; songwriter, founder The Mongers, mus. group, perform local clubs Orange County area; rec: numismatics, reading, songwriting. Res: PO Box 5161 San Clemente 92674

VOGEL, ERWIN ROYALE, real estate developer; b. May 22, 1922, Alliance, Nebr.; s. Fred John and Aline Sarah (Farquet) V.; m. Georgia Ilene Dilbeck, Sept. 13, 1952; edn: att. L.A. City Coll. 1940-42; B.Arch., USC, 1950; lic. real estate broker, gen. contr., Calif. Career: pres. E. R. Vogel Co., Torrance 1952-; ptnr. Vogel-Kolleck, Vista 1958-; ptnr. Vogel-Singer 1991-; secty. Airtels Inc., Torrance 1959-; recipient 4 merit awards for outstanding buildings Manhattan Beach C.of C.; mem: Realty Boards: Torrance-Lomita-Carson-Greater South Bay 1978-, Aircraft Owners & Pilots Assn., USC Alumni Assn., USC Architl. Guild, Scarab hon. architl. frat. 1950, Am. Bonanza Soc.; civic: BPOE/Redondo Beach, US C.of C., Torrance Airport Boosters Assn.; club: Los Verdes Mens Golf; mil: 1st lt., pilot USAAF 1942-47, AF Reserve 1947-52; Republican (Presdl. Task Force); Prot.; rec: pilot (multi-engine, instrument), golf, gardening. Res: 909 Via Del Monte Palos Verdes Estates 90274 Ofc: E.R. Vogel Co. PO Box 1067 Torrance 90505

VOGT, PAUL DALE, marketing executive; b. May 17, 1958, National City; s. Leo Dale and Mary Alice (Roman) Vogt; m. Rhonda Joanne Burgess (b. Oct. 20, 1959, d. Paul Franklin Burgess Jr. and Daisylee (Barnes) Burgess Hagen), June 18, 1978; edn: religion major Loma Linda Univ., 3 yrs. Career: mgr. Cal Stereo Inc. Riverside 1978-81; pres. Sound-Tech Speaker Systems, San Diego 1981-83; CEO Vogt-Audio Inc., El Cajon 1983-85; pres. Digital Designs Inc., La Mesa 1985-87; gen. mgr. La Jolla Marketing Inc., Chula Vista 1987-88; sales exec. Volutone Distbg., Tarzana, 1990-; founder and loudspeaker engr. Nova Sound Labs, Tarzana, 1990-; mem. Am. Loudspeaker Mfrs. Assn. 1991-; Republican; Seventh Day Aventist; rec: golf, scuba, audio engring. Res: 4271 Panorama Dr La Mesa 91944 Ofc: Volutone Dist. 6025 Yolanda Ave Tarzana 91357

VOGT, ROCHUS EUGEN KAMILL, physicist; b. Dec. 21, 1929, Neckarelz, Germany; s. Heinrich and Paula (Schaefer) V.; m. Micheline Alice Yvonne Bauduin, Sept. 6, 1958; children: Michele b. 1963, Nicole b. 1967; edn: cand. phys. Univ. of Karlsruhe, Ger. 1950-52, Univ. Heidelberg, 1952-53; SM, Univ. Chgo., Ill. 1957, PhD, 1961. Career: asst. prof. Calif. Inst. of Technology, Pasadena 1962-65, assoc. prof. 1965-70, prof. physics 1970-, R. Stanton Avery Distinguished Service Prof. 1982-, chmn. of Faculty 1975-77, chief scientist Jet Propulsion Lab. 1977-78, chmn. div. physics, math. and astronomy 1978-83, actg. dir. Owens Valley Radio Observatory 1980-81, v.p. and provost 1983-87, dir. Caltech/MIT Laser Interferometer Gravitational Wave Observatory (LIGO) Project 1987-; vis. prof. physics M.I.T., Cambridge, Mass. 1988-; awards: mem. Studienstiftung des deutschen Volkes 1950-53, Fulbright Fellow 1953-54, profl. achiev. award Univ. Chgo. Alumni Assn. 1981, NASA exceptional scientific achiev. medal (1981); mem. Am. Physical Soc. (1961-, fellow), AAAS (1965-, fellow); author: (with R.B. Leighton) Exercises in Intro. Physics (Addison Wesley Pub., 1969), "Cosmic Rays," World Book Ency. (1978), sci. papers in High Energy Astrophysics and Gravitation pub. profl. jours. Ofc: Caltech 102-33, Pasadena 91125

VOLCKMANN, DAVID BOYD, professor of psychology; b. Jan. 19, 1942, Kingston, N.Y.; s. Frederick W. and Norma (Hill) V.; m. Jean Pierce, Aug. 27, 1967 (div. 1986); m. Barbara Currier Green, June 6, 1987; children: Matthew; edn: BA, Hamilton Coll. 1964; PhD, Ind. Univ. 1970. Career: tchg. asst. Hamilton Coll., Clinton, N.Y. 1963-64; Ind. Univ., Bloomington, Ind. 1964-65, res. asst. 1965-68, tchg. assoc. 1967-70; tchg. faculty Whittier Coll. 1970-, coord. institutional res. 1983-, chmn. psychology 1973-74, 80-83, 89-, dir. CAPHE grant 1988-; awards: NSF scientific equipment grant 1972, Dept. Health Edn. & Welfare grantee 1975, Lilly Found. vis. scholar 1975, Whittier Coll. tchg. award 1976; mem: Western Psychological Assn., Am. Psychological Assn., Am. Assn. Univ. Profs., Calif. Assn. Institutional Res., Chorale Bel Canto, BSA; author Instructors Resource Book in Psych. (1980, 83, 84). Ofc: Whittier College 13406 E Philadelphia Whittier 90608

VON BEHREN, RUTH LECHNER, adult day health care specialist; b. April 10, 1933, Dubuque, Iowa; d. Adolph John and Elva Mae (Fedeler) Lechner; m. Donald Dean Von Behren, Dec. 16, 1952 (div. 1965); children: Debi b. 1954, Jerry b. 1956, LuAnn b. 1958; edn: BS, Ill. St. Univ. 1965; MA, 1968; PhD, UC Davis 1972. Career: asst. prof. CSU, Sacto. 1978-79; research asst. Calif. Health & Welfare Agency 1972-74; analyst Calif. Dept. Health Services 1974-75, sect. chief ADHC branch 1975-80; project dir. LTC st. plan Calif. Health Welfare Agency 1980-82; ADHC specialist On Lok Senior Health Services, S.F. 1982-; cons. UCSF, NCOA 1982-; honors: Alpha Phi Gamma, Alpha Psi Omega, Kappa Delta Phi, Phi Alpha Delta, Phi Kappa Phi, Rural Adult Day Health Models award Sierra Found. 1988-89, Kaiser Found. Adult Day Health Tech. award 1983-86, first recipient Nat. Inst. on Adult Daycare Ruth Von Behren Award for outstanding dedication to the growth and devel. of adult day care 1992; mem: Nat. Council on Aging (bd. mem. chmn. Nat. Inst. Adult Day Care 1988-90), Yolo Co. Hist. Soc., Yolo Co. Museum Soc. (dir. 1980-82); author: Adult Day Care in Am. 1986, Adult Day Care: A Program for Functionally Impaired 1989, book chpt. pub. 1989, num. articles pub. in profl. jours. 1985-; rec: antiques, opera, bird watching. Ofc: On Lok Senior Health Services 1455 Bush St San Francisco 94109

VON BEROLDINGEN, DOROTHY, judge; b. Feb. 12, 1915, Chgo.; d. Alex R. and Anna (Stastny) Gundelfingen; (div.); son, Paul b. 1944; edn: AA, UC Berkeley, 1934; Northwestern Univ.; LLB, JD, Univ. San Francisco Sch. of Law and S.F. Law Sch., 1954. Career: atty., tax specialist, solo practice, San Francisco 1955-77; judge San Francisco Municipal Ct., 1977-; prof. taxation Lincoln Univ. Sch. of Law, S.F. 1959-69, prof. legal acctg. 1964-69; adj. prof. legal acctg. Hastings Coll. of Law, 1973-74; appt. commr. S.F. Civil Service Commn. 1964-66, v.p./exec. mem. Economic Opportunity Council 1964-66; elected San Francisco Bd. Suprs. 1966-77: chair fin. com. 1968-77, chair plng. & devel. com. 1966-68; honors: Order of the Woolsack, Equity Jurisprudence, Univ. S.F. 1952, Am. Jurisprudence awards in contracts, corps., constnl. law, equity, labor law, evidence 1950, 51, 52, 53, Woman of Achiev. Bus. & Profl. Women 1973, Comm. Leadership SF Fellowship 1979, Women Helping Women Soroptomists 1980, Diligence in Crim. Justice Women in Crim. Justice 1984; mem: ABA, SF Lawyers Club, St. Thomas More Soc., Queen's Bench (bd. 1981-87). Ofc: Hall of Justice, 850 Bryant St San Francisco 94103

VON HOELSCHER, RUSSEL, author, marketeer, consultant; b. Aug. 10, 1942, St. Paul, Minn.; s. Clarence and Francis von Hoelscher; m. Ginger June Julian, Dec. 5, 1980 (div. Oct. 1987); edn: Grossmont Coll., San Diego. Career: bestselling business, investment and motivational writer 1970s-; author: How To Achieve Total Success (1983), 40+ books and manuals on business, marketing and motivation, also newsletters, reports and articles; copywriter and direct mktg. consultant; seminar/workshop leader; advr. Pres. Carter's Com. on Small Bus. in Am., 1978; honors: Sales & Mktg. Exec. of the Yr. 1986; mem: San Diego Sales & Mktg. Execs., Internat. Writers Guild, Direct Mktg. Assn., Toastmasters Internat.; Libertarian; Metaphysics; rec: chess. Res: 6685 Archwood Ave San Diego 92120

VON MOOS, MARLA MARIE, bank executive; b. March 25, 1937, Glen Rose, Tx.; d. Harlan Glen and Rosa Velma (Smith) Shackelford; m. Louie Joseph von Moos, Feb. 5, 1956; children: Tom b. 1957, Jerry b. 1960, Rick b. 1965; edn: grad. Patterson H.S. 1954. Career: clk. Drug Store, Patterson 1956-57, 70-77; self-employed Marlas Gift & Jewelry 1977-80; teller Lloyds Bank 1980-83; asst. mgr. Westside Bank 1983-84, mgr. 1984-; speech class Dale Carnegie, Modesto 1988-89; german classes Modesto Jr. Coll. 1975-76, banking 1981; leadership Westside Bank, Tracy 1988; awards: Westside Bank employee of qtr. (1986), United Way vol. of month 1989); mem: Patterson Bus. Assn. (sec. 1983-85), Soroptimist Patterson (sec. 1985-86, v.p. 1989-90, pres. 1990-91, Woman of Distinction 1991-92), Chamber of Commerce (pres. 1987-89), United Way (chair 1989); author: Country Cooking (1991-92); Democrat; R.Cath.; rec: painting, travel, decorating. Res: 455 Poppy Ave Patterson 95363 Ofc: Westside Bank PO Box 1328 Patterson 95363

VON STUDNITZ, GILBERT, state official; b. Nov. 24, 1950, Hamburg, Germany; s. Helfrid and Rosemarie Sofie (Kreiten) von S.; m. Erica Lynn Hoot, May 26, 1990; edn: AA, East L.A. Coll., 1971; BA, CSU Los Angeles, 1978. Career: licensing registration examiner Calif. Dept. Motor Veh., L.A. 1982-84, supvg. motor veh. rep., 1984-85, mgr. I, 1985-87, D.M.V. admnstrv. hearing ofcr., Montebello, 1987-91, mgr. III, Sacramento, 1991-93; ops. mgr, Driver Safety Review 1993-; recipient Calif. D.M.V. cert. of quality 1988, appreciation 1989; mem: Calif. State Mgrs. Assn., Sacto. 1986-, Driver Improvement Assn. of Calif., Sacto. (v.p. 1991-), Intertel 1981-, Phi Sigma Kappa 1973-, Mensa 1981-, Assn. of German Nobility in N.Am. (pres. 1985-), West Adams Heritage Assn., L.A. (dir. 1989-91), Benicia Hist. Soc. 1992-; publs: articles in The Blumenbaum mag. (4/92, 6/92); rec: genealogy rsch. Res: 1101 W Second Benicia 94510

VON WIESENBERGER, ARTHUR, beverage industry executive, author, publisher; b. Sept. 13, 1953, N.Y.C.; s. Arthur and Frances Louise (Bayes) V.W.; m. Leslie Sinclair, May 13, 1988; children: Alexander Robert b. 1990, Christopher William b. 1992; edn: grad. Brooks Inst., Motion Picture Div. 1977; art and language studies in Switz. and England, 1968-73. Career: assoc. prod. Swissair, Switz., 1972; prod. Comorian govt./ Air Comores Africa 1973; prod./dir. Aurora Films Worldwide, Switz. 1974; assoc. prod. FMS Prodns., Hollywood 1977; assoc. prod. Warrior's of the Wind, Japan 1978; beverage industry cons. to Anheuser-Busch Inc., Arrowhead Water Co., Ionics Inc., Irons & Sears, Manitou Corp., Perrier Group of Am., Poland Spring Water, Stanford Wine Co., Valgos Consiel Inc., Vittel (USA) Inc., Wheeler Inc.; bd. chmn. Internat. Source Management, Inc., 1982-87; publisher Best Cellar Books, 1990-; dir. American Inst. of Wine and Food; dir. Internat. Festival Du Film De Villars 1975, 76, spkr. Whole Life Expo, Pasadena 1984, 85, 86; contbg. writer Celebrity Society Mag. (travel editor 1988-89), Entree 1984-89, San Francisco Mag., Epicurean Rendezvous, Private Clubs; awards: Photog. Soc. of Am., Ten Best 1975, MPD travel film award 1975, best menu, NRA 1984, 85; mem: So. Calif. Restaurant Writers Assn. (pres.), Internat. Food, Wine and Travel Writers Assn.; civic: Westside Boys Club (bd.); clubs: Coral Casino/ Santa Barbara (dir.); publs: Oasis - The Complete Guide to Bottled Water Throughout the World, Capra Press 1978, Charting the Waters, Runner's World 1981, A Guide to Bottled Water, Fit 1982, Shape's Guide to Bottled Water 1984, Delights of Sushi, Centervoice 1982, Mystique of Caviar, In Mag. 1983, Bottled Water 1001 Varieties, Market Watch 1987, H2O The Guide to Quality Bottled Water, Woodbridge Press 1988, Pocket Guide to Bottled Water, Contemporary Books 1990, Shaping Up in Santa Barbara, Valley Mag. 1990, Bed & Breakfasts of Santa Barbara, Valley Mag. 1991, Champagne & Caviar 1992, Capra Press; Republican; Ch. of England; rec: swim, ski, tennis, mountaineering, enology. Res: POB 5658 Santa Barbara 93150

VOORHEES, LORRAINE ISOBEL, college administrator; b. Sept. 23, 1947, Pittsburgh, Pa.; d. Glenn Alvin Jr. and Helen Laverne (Urban) Voorhees; edn: OD, So. Calif. Coll. of Optometry, Fullerton 1971; MS, CSU Fullerton, 1986. Career: faculty So. Calif. Coll. Optometry, Fullerton 1972-80, director admissions & records 1980-86, dir. student affairs 1986-90, dean of student affairs 1990-; mem: Am. Opt. Assn. 1967-, Calif. Opt. Assn. 1967-, Am. Acad. Optometry (Fellow 1974-). Ofc: Southern Calif. College of Optometry, 2575 Yorba Linda Blvd Fullerton 92631

WACHTELL, ESTHER, music center president; b. June 30, New York; m. Thomas Wachtell, Jan. 27, 1957; children: Roger Bruce, Wendy Anne, Peter James; edn: BA, Conn. Coll. 1956; MA, Cornell Univ. 1957. Career: pres. The Music Center, Los Angeles 1988-, mem. bd. of govs. and bd. dirs. Music Center Operating Co., bd. dirs. edn. div.; mem. civic bds: Coalition 100 Hugh O'Brien Youth Found. (dir.), Trusteeship for the Betterment of Women, L.A. Vis. & Conv. Bureau, L.A. Central City Assn., Merchant & Mfrs. Assn., L.A. Partnership, Calif. Comm. Found., Am. Council for Arts, Japan American Soc., Town Hall of Calif.; club: Regency (bd.). Ofc: The Music Center 135 N Grand Ave Los Angeles 90012-3013

WADIA, MANECK SORABJI, management consultant, author; b. Oct. 22, 1931, Bombay, India, came to U.S., 1953; s. Sorabji Rattanji and Manijeh Sorabji (Pocha) W.; m. Harriet Fern Schilit, Nov. 21, 1962; children: Sara b. 1968, Mark b. 1970; edn: BA (Hons.) St. Xaviers, Bombay 1952; MA, Indiana Univ., Bloomington, Ind. 1954, PhD, 1957, MBA, 1958. Career: faculty Indiana Univ. 1958-60; Ford Found. Fellow Univ. of Pittsburgh, Pa. 1960-61; faculty Grad. Sch. Bus. Stanford Univ., 1961-65; pres. Wadia Assocs., Inc., Del Mar, Calif. 1965-, cons. 100+ orgs. (100,000+ execs. have attended his seminars); awards: grad. asst., scholar Indiana Univ., Bloomington 1953-58, Ford Found. fellow 1959, 1st prize invited papers Acad. of Mgmt., Stanford Univ. 1961; mem.: Kts. of the Round Table 1982-, Mothers & Fathers of Indian Ancestry 1985-; author 4 books in bus., mgmt. and mktg.; Indp.; Zoastrian; rec: cooking, gardening, humor. Res: 1660 Lunetta Dr Del Mar CA 92014

WADSWORTH, KEVIN WARREN, retired political consultant, rancher; b. May 22, 1948, Fairmont, W.Va.; s. Warren Wade and Gloria Jean (McClung) W.; edn: AA, Valencia Comm. Coll., Orlando, Fla. 1969; BA comm., Univ. of Central Fla., 1971; grad. studies Fla. A&M Univ., 1975-76. Career: exec. asst. U.S. Senator Ed Gurney, W.D.C., 1972-74; adminstrv. asst. Mayor and City Council, Orlando, Fla. 1976-77; dir. of govt. affairs San Francisco Chamber of Commerce, 1980; a.v.p. purch. Crocker Bank, S.F. 1981-85; v.p. and c.f.o. Pinnacle Courseware Inc., San Jose 1985-86, bd. dir. 1983-86; v.p. corporate adminstrv. svs. First Nationwide Bank, S.F. 1986-90; polit. cons. various candidates and issues, 1971-; honoree for Outstanding vol. svc. Nat. Volunteers Service, S.F. 1983; civic bds: El Dorado AIDS Task Force (treas., bd. 1991-), Grassy Run Community Svs. Dist. Placerville (dir., pres. 1991-92); mem: Disabled Am. Veterans 1967-, Am. Legion 1981-, Tau Kappa Epsilon Frat. (Kt. of Apollo 1971-); author books: Circuit Breakers (1975), Thoughts and Other Transgressions (1984), song: I Want (by The Lettermen, 1977), editor: White Paper on the Gay Community (1983); mil: E3 USMC 1966-67; Republican; Met. Community Ch.; rec: politics, non-profit fundraising, vineyard & sheep.

WAETJEN, HERMAN CHARLES, professor of New Testament; b. June 16, 1929, Bremen, Germany; s. Henry and Anna (Ruschmeyer) W.; m. Mary Suzanne Struyk, July 15, 1960; children: Thomas b. 1961 (dec.), Thembisa b. 1963, Elaine b. 1965, David b. 1970; edn: Concordia Jr. Coll., Bronxville, NY;

BA, Concordia Sem., St. Louis, Mo., 1950; BD, Concordia Sem., 1953; Dr. Theol., Univ. of Tuebingen, Germany, 1958. Career: instr. Concordia Sem., St. Louis, 1957; asst. prof. Univ. of So. Calif., L.A., 1959-62; assoc. prof. S.F. Sem., San Anselmo, 1962-72; prof. S.F. Sem., 1972-; vis. prof.: Univ. of Nairobi, Kenya, 1973-74, Federal Sem., Pietermaritzburg, So. Africa, 1979-80, Univ. of Zimbabwe, Harare, Zimbabwe, 1986-87; awards: scholarships, Hebrew Univ., Jerusalem, Israel, 1954-55, and Lutheran Found., Geneva, Switzerland, 1955-56; fellowships, Assn. of Theol. Schools, 1965-66, 1979-80; mem: Soc. of Biblical Lit. 1959-, Pacific Coast Theol. Soc. 1962-; author: The Origin & Destiny of Humanness, 1976-78, A Reordering of Power, 1989; Democrat; Presbyn.; rec: backpacking, photography, travel. Res: 83 Jordan Ave. San Anselmo 94960. Ofc: S.F. Theol. Sem. San Anselmo 94960

WAGEMAKER, DAVID ISAAC, management consultant, professional seminar leader and speaker; b. Feb. 10, 1949, Grand Rapids, Mich.; s. Raymond Ogden and Inez Loraine W.; edn: BA philos., Grand Valley St. Univ., 1971. Career: owner Education Ctr., and apiarist Bee Haven Honey, Grand Rapids, Mich. 1970-72; speaker and tnr. productivity seminars since 1971-, lead nat. and internat. seminars in time mgmt. and leadership tng., for Fortune 500 cos., small orgns., profit & nonprofit orgns., profl. assns.; cons. American Leadership Coll., WDC 1972-78, Wagemaker Co., Honolulu, 1978-80; ednl. cons. Batten, Batten, Hudson and Swab Inc. (consulting firm), San Diego 1980-81, mgr. 1981; mgmt. cons. The National Mgmt. Inst., and The Podium Inc., San Diego State Univ., 1980-, seminarist Penton Learning Inc., NYC 1982-; securities broker, ins. agt. The Equitable Assurance Co., San Diego 1982; assoc. cons. Pacific Southwest Airlines (now USAir), San Diego 1982-83; organizational devel. adminstr. Hughes Aircraft Co., Westchester, 1983; speaker 100+ presentations yearly for co.; v.p. Wagemaker, Inc., Grand Rapids 1984-; sr. cons. Nat. Mgmt. Inst., Flower Mound, Tx. 1985-; pres. Par Golf Co., Redondo Beach 1984-; publs: (self-help book) Building A Better You, (6-hr. cassette tape series) How To Organize Yourself to Win, (res. paper) Total Quality Mgmt., and num. tng. workbooks; Fellow Acad. Mgmt., mem. Sigma Chi, Zeta Nu (pres. 1968-70), Hughes Golf Club (El Segundo); Republican; Congregationalist. Res: 2226 Bataan Rd Redondo Beach 90278

WAGNER, C. PETER, seminary professor; b. Aug. 15, 1930, NY, NY; s. C. Graham and Mary (Lewis) W.; m. Doris Mueller, Oct. 15, 1950; children: Karen b. 1954, Ruth b. 1960, Rebecca b. 1964; edn: BS, Rutgers Univ., New Brunswick, N.J., 1952; M. Div., MA, Fuller Theol. Sem., Pasadena, 1955, 1968; Th.M., Princeton Theol. Sem., Princeton, N.J., 1962; PhD, Univ. of So. Calif., L.A., 1977. Career: missionary, S.I.M. Internat., Bolivia, So. Am., 1956-71; prof., Fuller Theol. Sem., Pasadena, 1971-; pres., Global Harvest Ministries, Pasadena, 1991-; awards: Phi Beta Kappa, Rutgers Univ., 1951; author: over 30 books publ. on missions and ch. growth incl.: Your Church Can Grow, 1976, Your Spiritual Gifts, 1979 and Warfare Prayer, 1992; Congregational. Ofc. Fuller Seminary Pasadena 91182

WAGNER, CHRISTIAN JOERGEN, business educator; b. Apr. 2, 1960, Hamburg, Germany, came to U.S., 1988; s. Helmuth Ludwig Hugo and Iris Karin (Schalcher) W.; m. Rano Jacqueline Sihota, Mar. 21, 1990; edn: BS, Tech. Univ., Berlin 1981, MS, 1984; PhD, Univ. British Columbia, 1989. Career: res. assoc. Daimler-Benz AG, Berlin, 1981; lectr. Univ. British Columbia, Vancouver 1985-88; asst. prof. bus. USC, Los Angeles, Calif. 1989-; dir. VCS Res., Inc., Vancouver, B.C.; panelist Aspen Inst. Berlin, 1983; speaker VWI Congress, Berlin 1983; keynote speaker confs., 1988-, Acad. for Management Information Conf., Tokyo, 1991; awards: fellow Deutscher Akad. Austauschdienst 1984, World Univ. Service Canada (1986, 87), NSF res. grantee 1991-; mem: Arbeitsgruppe Wirtschaftsingenieure (bd. 1983-84), Verband Deutscher Wirtschaftsingenieure, Inst. Mgmt. Sci., Decision Scis. Inst., Internat. Circle L.A. (advy. bd. 1991-); rec: windsurfing, writing short stories. Res: 15641 Hortense Dr Westminster 92683 Ofc: USC School of Business, Bridge Hall 401S, L.A. 90089-1421 Tel: 213/740-0178

WAGNER, RAY DAVID, aerospace museum historian/archivist; b. Feb. 29, 1924 Phila.; s. James D. and Ethel S. (Shreiber) W.; m. Beatrice Walsh, Apr. 1952 (div. Nov. 1965); m. Mary Davidson, Nov. 17, 1967; children: Roger b. 1952, Wendy b. 1968, David b. 1971; edn: BS, Univ. Pa., 1953, MS Edn., 1955; postgrad. San Diego State Univ., 1958-65. Career: tchr. Crawford High Sch., San Diego 1957-84; instr. USN/Pace, San Diego 1985; archivist San Diego Aerospace Mus., 1985-; awards: research grantee Air Force Hist. Ctr. 1988; mem. Am. Aviation Hist. Soc. 1957-, Air Force Hist. Found. 1980-; author: American Combat Planes (1960, 1968, 1982), North American Sabre (1963), German Combat Planes (1970), Mustang Designer (1990), editor: Soviet Air Force in WWII (1973); rec: travel, airplane history. Res: 5865 Estelle St San Diego 92115 Ofc: San Diego Aerospace Museum 2001 Pan American Plaza San Diego 92101

WAHDAN, JOSEPHINE BARRIOS, librarian; b. Jan. 11, 1937, Firebaugh; d. Jose and Vera (Balderama) Barrios; div.; children: Dean Burni b. 1959, Laila b. 1975, Nadia b. 1978; edn: BA in foreign langs.(w/distinction), San Diego State Univ. 1970; MLS, Univ. Wis.-Milwaukee 1975. Career: comm. librarian intern Milwaukee Pub. Library 1972-74, comm. librarian 1975-78; acting co. librarian

San Benito Co. Library, Hollister 1979, co. librarian 1980-; founder Friends of San Benito Co. Libraries 1979; pres. Libraries Plus 1983-84; chairwoman S. Bay Cooperative Library System 1984-85; mem. World Congress of Poets 1989-, mem. Calif. Library Assn. 1980-, County Librarians Assn. 1980-, REFORMA, Nat. Assn. to Promote Library Svs. to Spanish Speaking 1985-, awards: Library Bookfellow of Yr. Friends Milwaukee Pub. Library, 1974; cert. of appreciation United Comm. Center and Milw. Library Bd. Trustees, 1978; Mex. Am. Com. on Edn. Citizen of Year, 1987; Calif. State Library Award of Merit, 1990; Gavilan College Puente Program, Cert. of Appreciation, 1988, 89; Calif. State Library Recognition of Excellence in Community Partnerships, 1993; poems pub. in American Poetry Anthology, 1986; Hearts On Fire: A Treasury of Poems On Love, 1986; Brisas Poeticas Modernas, 1991 (1st & 2nd edit.); Carta Internacional de Poesia, 1993; Moslem; rec: Folkloric dancing, tennis, camping. Ofc: San Benito Co Library 470 Fifth St Hollister 95023

WAHLEN, BRUCE EDWARD, mathematician; b. Dec. 5, 1947, Chgo.; s. Ralph Edward and Jeanne Elizabeth (Buchanan) W.; m. Margaret Ruth Craig, July 18, 1975; children: Sarah b. 1979, Rebekah b. 1982; edn: BA math. (hons.), UC San Diego, 1969; MS statistics, San Diego St. Univ., 1978; PhD math., UC San Diego, 1991. Career: statistician Southwest Fisheries Scis. Ctr., La Jolla 1976-91; mathematician Naval Command, Control and Ocean Surveillance Ctr., San Diego 1991-; awards: Am. Soc. for Engring. Edn. postdoctoral fellow Nat. Inst. of Stds. & Technology, 1991; mem: Inst. of Math. Stats. 1987-, Soc. for Industrial & Applied Math. 1989-; publs: diss: A Nonparametric Measure of Independence 1991, jour. articles in Marine Fisheries Rev. (1975), Fishery Bull. U.S. (1982, 85, 86), Report of Internat. Whaling Commn. (1986, 87, 88), Statistics & Probability Letters (1992); mil: sp5 US Army 1970-72. Res: 5118 Constitution Rd San Diego 92117-1230 Ofc: Naval Command, Control & Ocean Surveillance Center, San Diego 92152-5000

WALD, JEFF SOMMERS, communications executive; b. Jan. 27, 1944, N.Y.C.; s. Sidney Sommers and Shirley Waldstein; m. Helen Reddy, Nov. 1, 1966 (div. 1982); children: Traci, Jordan; m. Candy June Clark, Jan. 1, 1987 (div. 1988); m. Deborah Benson, Nov. 17, 1990. Career: pres. Jeff Wald Assocs., Beverly Hills 1963-87; senior v.p. Barris Industries Inc., Los Angeles 1987-89; pres. Guber-Peters Television, Beverly Hills 1987-91; chmn. Jeff Wald Entertainment., 1991-; Betty Ford Bd. Dirs., Exec. Com.; civic: Education 1st (bd. dirs.), USO, Wash. DC (nat. bd. 1977-81), Calif. Bd. Econ. Devel., L.A., 1980-84, Cedars Sinai Hosp. (bd. govs. 1976-87), L.A. Olympic Orgn. Com. (bd. 1979-84); recipient City of Hope spirit of life award, 1977; Jewish; rec: equestrian, tennis. Ofc: Jeff Wald Entertainment 1990 S Bundy Dr Penthouse Ste Los Angeles 90025

WALKER, CAROLYN LOUISE, nursing professor; b. Apr. 4, 1947, Ft. George Wright, Wash.; d. Marvin John and Louise Olive (Billings) W.; m. Simon Zemel, Apr. 6, 1968 (div. 1981); children: Michelle b. 1971, Brent b. 1971; edn: AA nsg., Fullerton Coll., 1968; BSN, CSU Fullerton, 1976; MSN, CSU Los Angeles, 1979; PhD Nursing, Univ. Utah, 1986. Career: staff nse. CCU, ICU, Burn Unit, Orange County Med. Ctr., 1968-69; staff nse. Children's Hosp. Orange County, 1969-71, summer 1973, ped. oncology hematology unit, 1980-81; office nse. and mgr. Simon I. Zemel MD 1971-77; nsg. instr. Cypress Coll., Cypress 1978-79, instr. obstets. and geriatrics Saddleback Coll., Mission Viejo 1979-80, instr. pediatrics and adv. med.-surg. nsg. Cypress Coll. 1981-82; asst. prof. peds. and obstets. Univ. of Utah, 1984-85; asst. prof. pediatrics San Diego State Univ., 1986-90, assoc. prof. and grad. advisor pediatrics 1990-, co-dir. Ctr. for the Applied Study of the Child, SDSU, 1991-; awards: outstanding student nurse Student Nurse Assn. of Calif. 1967, CSU Fullerton Dean's List 1976, Nat. Deans List 1984, excellence in research Davol Inc. 1986, Outstanding Faculty 1988, research grantee (5, 1988-); mem: Soc. Pediatric Nurses 1991-, Oncology Nsg. Soc. (1988-, ped. spl. interest gp. 1990-), Sigma Theta Tau (faculty advr. 1987-89), Assn. Ped. Oncology Nurses (1983-, chair 1987-91), Am. Nses. Assn., Calif. Nses. Assn. (1978-, alt. nsg. edn. commnr. CNA regn II 1990-92), Am. Cancer Soc. (San Diego Children's com. 1989-, psychosocial care cons. 1991-, med. com. 1990-, Camp Reach for the Sky Nse. 1990-, Family Camp com. 1989-, chair 1990); author, editor books and jour. articles in field, sci. presentations at nat. confs. (15+); mem. editl. rev. bds: Am. J. of Cont. Edn. in Nsg. (1987-89), Oncology Nsg. Forum (1988-91), J. of Pediatric Oncology Nsg. (1992-, assoc. res. editor 87-91), Professional Update (1990-); Democrat; Episcopalian; rec: skiing, swimming, golf. Ofc: San Diego State University Sch. of Nursing, San Diego 92182-0254

WALKER, DAVID ALLEN, high technology co. executive; b. Aug. 19, 1956, Los Angeles; s. Steve and Florence (Rothman) W.; edn: BS in engring., UC Los Angeles 1978; MBA fin./mktg., Univ. Chgo. 1982. Career: team mgr. Procter and Gamble Paper Prods. Co., Oxnard 1978-80; sr. fin. analyst Dataproducts Corp., Woodland Hills 1982-83; mgr. bus. plnng. and fin. Burroughs Corp., Camarillo 1983-85; dir. fin. plnng. MICOM Systems Inc., Simi Valley 1985-89; corp. controller TeleTech, Inc., Sherman Oaks 1989; dir. corp. devel. Infonet, El Segundo 1990-; ptnr. DeHart Walker Ents. 1986-91; honors: Gov.'s Scholar 1974, Dean's List (UCLA 1974-77, U.Chgo. 1981), Phi Eta Sigma 1975, Tau Beta Pi 1977; assoc. mem. ASME 1978-; Republican; Jewish; rec: computer modeling, historical simulations. Res: 2100 E Grand Ave B279 El Segundo 90245-1022

WALKER, GRANT SCOTT, engineer; b. March 7, 1953, Los Angeles; s. Lee Grant and Edwina Mae (Steele) W.; edn: dipl. Russian lang., Defense Lang. Inst. West Coast 1973; dipl. var. mil. sch. USAF 1972-74; BS mech. engring., UC Berkeley 1981; reg. prof. engr. Calif. 1986. Career: Russian linguist USAF, Fairbanks and Anchorage, Alaska 1972-75; asst. engr. Hughes Aircraft Co., Culver City 1978; prin. engr. EDS Nuclear Inc., S.F. 1979-81; sr. engr. Johnson Engring. Corp., Orinda 1981-84; nuclear contracts supr. Pacific Gas & Electric Co., S.F. 1984-85; project engr. Johnson Engring. Corp., Orinda 1985-87; sr. engr. ERIN Engineering & Res., Inc., Walnut Creek 1987-88; proj. mgmt. engr. PG&E Co., San Francisco 1988-90, contract engineer 1990-; awards: scholastic achiev. USAF (1973, 75); mem: Am. Soc. Mech. Engrs. 1980-, Nat. Soc. Profl. Engrs. 1986-, Calif. Soc. Profl. Engrs. 1986-; civic: The Library Assoc. UC Berkeley, UC Alumni Assn. (life mem.); designer Calif. 1st high pressure, large diameter polyethylene natural gas line (1983); mil: sgt. USAF 1972-76; Republican; R.Cath.; rec: skiing, gourmet cooking, jazz guitar, photog. Res: 3155 Plymouth Rd Lafayette 94549 Ofc: Pacific Gas & Electric Co. 333 Market St A1058 San Francisco 94106

WALKER, RENEE CHRISTINA, writer; b. Dec. 14, 1949, Lynwood, Calif.; d. James Bruce and Kitty Annabelle (Clock) Walker; m. Burton Steven Pritzker, Nov. 22, 1969; edn: H.S. diploma, Magnolia H.S., Anaheim, Calif., 1968; gen. edn., Coll. of the Redwoods, Eureka, Calif., 1974-75; Spanish study, Santa Rosa Jr. Coll., Santa Rosa, Calif., 1984; BA (cum laude), Eng., Sonoma State Univ., Rohnert Park, Calif., 1990. Career: writer; awards: Poetry Prize, UC Santa Barbara, 1979; Sally L. Ewen Mem. Scholarship, Sonoma State Univ., Rohnert Park, Calif., 1986-90; Fellowship Residency, Dorland Art Colony, Temecula, Calif., 1988; Presidential Scholar, Sonoma State Univ., 1988-90; Runner-Up, Fiction '89, S.F. Bay Guardian, S.F., Calif., 1989; First Place award, Sonoma County Playwrights Festival, Santa Rosa, Calif., 1990; author: poetry, Contemporary Women Poets: An Anthology of Calif. Poets, 1974; publ. articles, essays, interviews, 1980-93; one-act play, The Hope Chest, 1990; screenplay, Along the Gulf, 1992-93; full-length play, Wake Up, It's Wednesday, Jane Du Preez, 1992; rec: travel, reading, gardening, bird watching, watercolor painting. Ofc: R. C. Walker 558 Rose Ave. #2 Venice 90291

WALKER, ROBERT LAMAR, JR., political party executive director; b. April 26, 1942, Pasadena; s. Robert L. and Denise Elizabeth (Fildew) W.; edn: BA history, Claremont McKenna Coll. 1964; MA history, Stanford Univ. 1966. Career: exec. dir. Republican Party S.C. Co. 1968-; v.p. Walker Mfg., Los Angeles 1970-; owner Valhalla Miniatures 1976-; fin. chmn. Republican Party S.C. Co. 1988-; mem. Calif. Republican Party 1988-; awards: Republican Party of S.C. Co. hon. 1978, Calif. Republican Party disting. vol. service 1988, Calif. St. Assembly commend. and service 1980; mem: World Affairs Council, Pres. Circle of Republican Party of S.C. Co., Fgn. Affairs Forum, Bay Area Mil. Miniatures Soc., Toy Soldiers Collectors of Am., Sunnyvale Alliance Soccer (coach 1976-89); guest columnist San Francisco Chronicle, sculptor wall sculpture Stanford Art Gallery (1967); collecting, travel, bicycling. Ofc: Republican Party 522 N Monroe St San Jose 95128

WALKER, SALLY C., fund raising executive; b. Wash. D.C.; d. William S. and Ellen (Oswald) Walker; edn: BA (cum laude with honors), Stetson Univ., Deland, Fla., 1971; grad. Grantsmanship Ctr. Training Pgm. 1980, Mgmt. Fund Raisers Pgm. 1987. Career: devel. consultant, dir. Direct Relief Found., Santa Barbara 1977-82; prin., cons. Walker & Assocs., Santa Barbara 1982-; devel. cons., endowment dir. planned giving United Way Santa Barbara, 1982-; devel. cons. and trainer United Way of Am., Alexandria, Va. 1984, 87; devel. cons. Santa Barbara Sym., 1984-85, Child Abuse Listening Meditation, Santa Barbara 1987-88, Easy Lift Transport Inc., Goleta 1988; steering com., del. Nat. Conf. Planned Giving, 1987-88, Nat. Editorial Bur. chief, 1989; faculty mem. Nat. Acad. for Voluntarism, W.D.C.; contbg. editor: The Endowment Builder; mem.: Nat. Soc. of Fund-Raising Execs. (1984-), Planned Giving Roundtable Santa Barbara County (co-founder, pres. 1986-88, v.p. 1984-86), Santa Barbara Audubon Soc. (pres. 1992-, bd. 1989-). Ofc: 1423 W Valerio St Santa Barbara 93101

WALL, GLENNIE MURRAY, historic preservation professional; b. Oct. 8, 1931, Roseburg, Ore.; d. James Matheny Corbin and Emily L. Aten; m. Louis Wall, Jan. 3, 1975; 2 daughters; edn: BS, History, Portland State Univ. 1965; Environmental Ed., Univ. of Missouri 1969; Bus. Admin., Univ. of Michigan 1978; Practicing Law Institute 1981-82. Career: historian/park ranger National Park Service, Pipestone, N.M. 1966-68; historian/park supt. Herbert Hoover NHS, West Branch, Iowa 1968-69; historian, Western Regional Ofc., San Francisco 1969-72; historian, Advy. Council on Historic Preservation, Denver, Colo. 1972-74; div. chief National Park Service, Denver Service Ctr. 1974-83; mus. mgr (Maritime) Golden Gate Nat. Recreation Area, San Francisco 1983-89; cultural resources splst./curator, Presidio Project, San Francisco 1989-90; Principal, Historic Preservation Planning., 1991-; dir: Council of Am. Maritime Museums, Phila. 1987-88; Nat. Maritime Museum Assn., San Francisco 1983-88; chair Equal Opportunity Com., Nat. Park Service, Denver, Colo. 1979-81; instr., lectr. Nat. Park Service preservation law & policy (nationwide) 1972-84; lectr. Nat. Trust for Historic Preservation, Wash., D.C. 1971-88; awards: Hoover Scholar 1992, Nat. Preservation Award, President's Advy. Council 1988, commendation from Nat. Park Service 1987, Citation for Excellence, U.S. Dept. of Interior 1976, spl. achievement awards from Nat. Park Service (1969, 72); mem: Am. Assn. of Museums, Internat. Council of Museums, Internat. Cong. of Maritime Museums, Amer. Assoc. For State and Local History, Amer. Decorative Atrs Forum, Colorado Corral of the Westerners, Nat. Orgn. of Women; author, ed.:agency standards & guidelines "Cultural Resources Mgmt." (1983); short course, book "Maritime Preservation" (1987); author "Interpretive Plan, Herbert Hoover NHS" (1968); editor, photographer book, "Pipes on the Plains" (1967); author, photographer "Pictographs & Petroglyphs of Lava Beds National Monument" (1965); Democrat; Prot.; rec: travel, photography, needlework, orchids, writing. Ofc: P.O. Box 370634, Montara CA 94037-0634

WALL, MICHAEL L., hospital administrator, president and chief executive; edn: BS edn., Eastern Mich. Univ., 1970; M.Hospital Adminstrn., Univ. Minn., 1976. Career: varsity football & basketball coach Saint Thomas High Sch., Ann Arbor, Mich. 1968-70; 1st lt. US Army 1970-74: c.o. 62nd Med. Group, Ft. Lewis, Wash. 1970-71, asst. batt. surgeon, exec. ofcr. med. co. 23rd Inf. Div., Da Nang, Vietnam 1971-72, asst. adminstr. Ireland Army Gen. Hosp. (400 bed), Ft. Knox, Ky. 1972-74; adminstrv. resident Comm. Mental Health Ctr. at Yale Univ., New Haven, Ct. 1975-76; adminstr. Walnut Creek Hosp., Walnut Creek, Calif. 1976-77; asst. adminstr. Mt. Diablo Med. Ctr., Concord 1977-81; asst. adminstr. Alexian Brothers (200 bed gen. acute care hosp.), San Jose 1981-82; assoc. adminstr. Mt. Diablo Med. Ctr. (303 bed hosp., Reg. Cancer Ctr. and Health & Fitness Inst.), Concord 1982-86, pres. and c.e.o., 1986-; mem. Am. Coll. Healthcare Execs., Hosp. Fin. Mgmt. Assn. (adv. mem.), Health Care Execs. of No. Calif., Univ. Mich. Alumni Assn. Res: 1302 Easley Dr Clayton 94517 Tel: 510/674-2002

WALL, SONJA ELOISE, nurse, nursing registry owner; b. Mar. 28, 1938, Santa Cruz; d. Ray Theothornton and Reva Mattie (Wingo) Wall; m. Edward Gleason Holmes, Aug. 1959 (div. 1968); children: Deborah Lynn, Lance Edward; m. John Aspesi, Sept. 1969 (div. 1977); children: Sabrina Jean, Daniel John; m. Kenneth Talbot LaBoube, Nov. 1, 1977 (div. 1987); 1 dau., Tiffany Amber; edn: bA, San Jose City Coll., 1959, BS, Madonna Coll., 1967, att. Univ. Mich. 1968-70; RN Calif., Mich., Colo. Career: staff nse. Santa Clara Valley Med. Ctr., San Jose 1959-67, Univ. Mich. Hosp., Ann Arbor 1967-73, Porter and Swedish Med. Hosp., Denver 1973-77, Laurel Grove Hosp., Castro Valley, Calif. 1977-79, Advent Hosp., Ukiah 1984-86; motel owner LaBoube Enterprises, Fairfield, Point Arena, Willits 1979-; staff nse. Northridge Hosp., Los Angeles 1986-87, Folsom State Prison, 1987; mng. ptnr. nursing registry Around the Clock Nursing Service, Ukiah 1985-, staff RN Kaiser Permanente Hosp., Sacto. 1986-89; Hospice RN, 1989-93; HSSI-Carepoint Nsg. Reg., 1993 ; owner Royal Plantation petites miniature Horse Farm; mem. Am. Heart Assn. (CPR trainer, recipient awards), Am. Assn. Critical Care Nurses, Calif. Critical Care Nurses Assn., Soc. of Critical Care Medicine, Hospice Nurses Assn., Am. Motel Assn. (beautification and remodeling award 1985), Am. Miniature Horse Assn. (winner nat. grand championship 1981, 82, 83), Internat. Biog. Ctr. England (1990); club: Cameron Park CC; civic: Coloma 4-H (ldr. 1990, asst. 1987-92); contbr. articles to various publs.; Republican; Episcopalian; rec: horses (1/4, pinto-paints, miniatures, thoroughbreds, racing), real estate devel., hiking, golf, swimming. Address: Around the Clock Nursing Service PO Box 559 Coloma 95613 Ph: 916/626-5815

WALLER, BRADLEY ALLAN, systems engineer; b. Nov. 17, 1963, Panorama City, Calif.; s. Paul Siegfried and Joan Ruth (Coshever) W.; m. Charlotte Louise (Burger); edn: BS physics, M.I.T., 1986. Career: engring. assoc. IBM Instruments, Danbury, Ct. 1985; research asst. M.I.T. Frances Bitter Nat. Mgmt. Lab., Cambridge 1985-86; systems engr. Hughes, EDSG, El Segundo, Calif. 1986-; awards: Wunsch Award M.I.T. mech. eng. dept. 1985, Hughes-EDSG personal achiev. award 1991 and team achiev. awards (4); mem. The Nature Friends 1986-; Democrat; Jewish; rec: skiing, classic autos. Res: 720 Ave D Redondo Beach 90277 Ofc: Hughes EDSG PO Box 902 E51/A290 El Segundo 90245

WALLER, LARRY GENE, mortgage banker; b. Nov. 18, 1948, Corpus Christi, Tex.; s. Paul Hobson and Marie (Armellini) W.; m. Mary Sandra Cupp, Dec. 27, 1969 (div. 1987); children: Stacey Ann, Jaime Lynn; m. Sharon Elizabeth Falls, Jan. 28, 1988; 1 child, Lisa Suzanne Cantello; edn: AA, Bakersfield Jr. Coll., 1970; lic. R.E. broker Calif. Career: asst. v.p. Bank of Am., Stockton 1970-78, Wells Fargo Realty Fin. Co., Sacto. 1978-81; regional v.p. Weyerhaeuser Mortgage Co., Sacto. 1981-89; sr. v.p. Koll Realty Advisors, Sacto. 1989-91; pres. Waller, Kaufman & Sutter, Sacto. 1991-; civic: Com. to Help Attract Major Profl. Sports to Sacto.; mem. Nat. Assn. of Industrial & Office Parks (bd. Sacto.), Mortgage Bankers Assn. (income property com.), Calif. Mortgage Bankers Assn.; clubs: The Capitol Club. Res: 453 S. Lexington Dr Folsom 95630 Ofc: Waller, Kaufman & Sutter, 2277 fair Oaks Blvd #400 Sacramento 95825

WALSER, CAROL BEEBE, clinical psychologist; b. Natick, Mass.; d. H. Ward and Margaret (Pardee) Beebe; children: Wendi Michelle b. 1969; edn: BA, Cedar Crest Coll. 1962; MA, Univ. Houston Clear Lake City 1980; PhD,

Calif. Sch. Profl. Psychology, Berkeley 1984; lic. clin. psychologist Calif. 1986. Career: dir. comm. services Univ. Tx. Mental Scis. Inst., Tx. Med. Center, Houston 1973-81; family therapist Pathways Agency, San Leandro 1981-82; chief psychology intern Pacific Presbyterian Med. Center, San Francisco 1982-84; NIMH postdoctoral clin. psychology fellow Univ. Tx. Mental Scis. Inst. 1984-85; psychologist John Muir Memorial Hosp., Walnut Creek 1985-86; chief psychologist Davies Med. Center, San Francisco 1986-; adj. faculty Calif. Sch. of Professional Psychology, Berkeley-Alameda 1989-; honors: Who's Who Human Service Profls. (1986-87, 1987-88); mem: Am. Psychol. Assn., San Francisco Psychol. Assn. (pres. 1993), Alameda Co. Psychol. Assn. (pres. 1994), No. Calif. Soc. Psychoanalytic Psychology, No. Calif. Neuropsychology Forum. Ofc: 2180 Greenwich St San Francisco 94123 also: 19 Gleneden Ave Ste 4 Oakland 94611 Tel:510.339-3155

WALSH, WILLIAM DESMOND, private investor; b. Aug. 4, 1930, New York; s. William J. and Catherine Grace (Desmond) W.; m. Mary Jane Gordon, April 5, 1951; children: Deborah, Caroline, Michael, Suzanne, Tara Jane, Peter; edn: BA, Fordham Univ. 1951; LL.B, Harvard Univ. 1955; admitted St. Bar N.Y. (1955). Career: asst. U.S. Atty. So. Dist. N.Y., N.Y.C. 1955-58; counsel N.Y. Commn. Investigation 1960-61; mgmt. cons. McKinsey & Co. 1961-67; sr. v.p. Arcata Corp., Menlo park 1967-82; gen. ptnr. Sequoia Assocs. 1982-; pres., c.e.o. Atacra Liquidating Trust 1982-89; chmn. bd.: Newell Indsl. Corp., Lowell, Mich.; Champion Rd. Machinery Ltd., Goderich, Ontario; URS Corp., San Francisco; Nat. Edn. Corp., Irvine; Basic Vegetable Products, King City; mem. bd. of overseers com. on univ. resources Harvard Univ.; bd. vis. USC Bus. Sch.; bd. trustees Fordham Univ.; mem. Am. Bar Assn., N.Y. St. Bar Assn.; club: Harvard (N.Y.C., S.F.). Res: 279 Park Ln Atherton 94027 Ofc: 3000 Sand Hill Rd Bldg 2 Ste 140 Menlo Park 94025

WALSH, WILLIAM FRANK, construction engineering executive; b. Aug. 13, 1947, Chgo.; s. Gerald Joseph and Bernice Katherine (Dugan) W.; m. Linda Crossley, Jan. 30, 1976; edn: Metallurgical Engring., Ill. Inst. of Tech., 1970; reg. profl. engr. Tenn. Career: shop welding engr., project welding engr. Chicago Bridge and Iron Co. (CBI) in Memphis, Tn., Cordova, Al., Secunda, S.Africa, Yanbu, Saudi Arabia, marine yard mgr. Pascagoula, Miss., and currently dist. mgr. CBI Services Inc., Fremont, Calif.; mem. Am. Welding Soc. 1974-; rec: tennis. Res: 6923 Corte Barcelona Pleasanton 94566 Ofc: CBI Services Inc., PO Box 5005 Fremont 94537

WALSON, R. BARRY, accountant; b. April 30, 1942, Milford, Del.; s. Ralph L. and Betty (James) W.; m. Joanna Grimmer, June 5, 1965; children: Forrest b. 1966, Coreen b. 1969; edn: BSME, UC Berkeley 1964; MS, MIT 1966. Career: bus. economist Humble Oil & Refining, Santa Monica 1966-69; stock broker Dean Witter & Co., Hayward 1969-71; fin. planner, Rossmoor 1971-76; tax preparation and acctg., Anaheim 1976-; dir. Precision Mechanism, City of Industry 1982-; tchr. Long Beach St. Univ. 1974-76; honors: Pi Tau Sigma merit award, 1964; mem: Securities Exchange Commn. (investment advisor), Nat. Assn. Enrolled Agents, Calif. Enrolled Agents, Nat. Soc. Pub. Accts., MIT Club So. Calif., Calif. Berkeley Engrs. Soc., Calif. Alumni Assn.; Republican; Christian Scientist; rec: golf, fishing, skiing. Res: 2941 La Travesia Dr Fullerton 92635 Ofc: Year Round Tax Service 300 S Harbor Blvd Ste 914 Anaheim 92805

WALTER, BERT MATHEW, federal labor commissioner; b. July 11, 1915, Devils Lake, N.Dak.; s. Alois and Margaret (Bauer) W.; m. Phyllis Ann Traynor, July 3, 1950; edn: AA, Univ. Minn., 1936, BBA, Univ. Baltimore, 1938. Career: shop employee Gen. Electric Co., Pittsfield, Mass. 1938-41; dir. industrial relations Consol. Vultee Aircraft Co., Tucson, 1941-49, Bendix Aviation Corp., Kansas City, Mo. 1949-55; v.p. indsl. relations Clark Equipment Co., Buchanan, Mich. 1955-64; dir. indsl. relations Chesebrough Pond's, N.Y.C. 1964-66; pres. Leasing Internat. Corp., Madrid, Spain 1966-68; commr. Fed. Mediation and Conciliation Service, L.A. 1968-; pres. Buchanan United Funds, Mich. 1956-57; mem.: Industrial Relations Research Assn. (founder, pres. Inland Empire chpt. 1984-92), Council Internat. Progress Mgmt. (New York dir. 1967), Conseil Internat. Orgn. Scientifique (dir. 1967), Nat. Metal Trades Assn. (Chgo. - N.Y. pres. 1962-63), Am. Soc. Personnel Adminstrn. (founder, v.pres. 1958-59), Soc. Profls. in Dispute Resolution (v.p. 1972-73), Soc. Human Resource Mgmt. (founder, pres. 1958-59), Rotary Intl. (Niles, Mich. pres. 1959-60); numerous articles in profl. publs.; Republican; R.Cath.; rec: gardening, travel. Res: 2598 N Ayala Dr Unit 92 Rialto 92376-8819 Ofc: 420 Tishman Executive Towers, 1100 Town & Country Rd Orange 92668 Tel: 714/836-2622

WALTERS, STACEY ANN, television reporter; b. Nov. 11, 1957, Spokane, Wa.; d. Robert James and Roberta Joyce (Woods) W.; edn: BA, Wash. State Univ. 1980; various courses, Univ. College, Cardiff, U.K. 1978-79. Career: intern, BBC 1978-79; anchor, writer, reporter KWSU-TV, Pullman, Wa. 1979-80; floor dir. KING-TV Prodn., Seattle, Wa. 1980-81, assoc. prod. KING-TV News 1981-83; anchor public affairs KCPQ-TV 1983-84, news cut-in anchor, prod. KCPQ-TV News, Tacoma/Seattle, Wa. 1983-84, reporter 1984-86; reporter KCRA-TV Entertainment, Sacramento 1986-87; reporter KXTV-TV News, Sacramento 1988-; awards: Rotary Foundation Journalism Award 1980, honors pgm. exchange scholar 1978, Viola V. Coulter scholarship 1977, Mrs. Saul Haas (Haas Found.) grant 1978, Internat. Pgms. scholarship 1978, Phi Beta Kappa 1980. Ofc: KXTV 400 Broadway Sacramento 95818

WANCHOW, SUSAN BETH, target marketing professional; b. Aug. 28, 1965, East Orange, N.J.; d. John Joseph and Trudie (Haddon) W.; edn: BBA, Univ. Notre Dame, 1986; MBA, USC, 1989. Career: tech. cons. TRW Target Mktg., Orange 1987-89; account exec., mktg. rsch., Nat. Decision Systems, Encinitas 1989-; awards: GSBA fellow USC 1986-87; mem. Am. Mktg. Assn. 1987-. Ofc: National Decision Systems 539 Encinitas Blvd Encinitas 92024

WANG, CHEN CHI, executive - electronics, real estate, and financial corporations; b. Aug. 10, 1932, Taiwan, China, came to U.S. 1959, naturalized 1970; s. Chin-Ting and Chen Kim (Chen) W.; m. Victoria Rebisoff, Mar. 5, 1965; children: Katherine Kim, Gregory Chen, John Christopher, Michael Edward; edn: BA in econ., Nat. Taiwan Univ., 1955; BSEE, San Jose State Coll., 1965; MBA, UC Berkeley, 1961. Career: with IBM Corp., San Jose 1965-72; founder/CEO Electronics Internat. Co., Santa Clara 1968-72, owner, gen. mgr., 1972-81, reorganized as EIC Group, 1982, now chmn. bd./pres.; dir. Systek Electronics Corp., Santa Clara 1970-73; founder/senior ptnr. Wang Enterprises, Santa Clara 1974-80, founder/sr. ptnr. Hanson & Wang Devel. Co., Woodside 1977-85; chmn. bd. Golden Alpha Enterprises, San Mateo 1979-; mng. ptnr. Woodside Acres-Las Pulgas Estates, Woodside 1980-85; founder/sr. ptnr. DeVine & Wang, Oakland 1977-83; Van Heal & Wang, West Village 1981-82; founder/chmn. bd. EIC Fin. Corp., Redwood City 1985-; chmn. bd. Maritek Corp., Corpus Christi, Tx. 1988-89; mem. Internat. Platform Assn., Tau Beta Pi; author: Monetary and Banking System of Taiwan 1955, The Small Car Market in the U.S. 1961; mil: 2d lt. Nationalist Chinese Army 1955-56; Christian Ch. Res: 195 Brookwood Rd Woodside 94062 Ofc: 2075 Woodside Rd Redwood City 94061

WANG, ROBERT TUNG-HSING, physician; b. Jan. 29, 1949, Taipei, Formosa, citizen USA; s. Shih Yi and Chun Lien (Chi) W.; m. Eva Maria Dohrn, Sept. 10, 1976; edn: BS in physics, M.I.T., 1969; PhD physics, Caltech, 1976; MD, PhD - MD Pgm., Med. Sch. Univ. of Miami 1976-78; dipl. Am. Bd. Internal Med. 1981, cert. in geriatrics ABIM 1988. Career: instr. computer pgmg. dept. physics Johns Hopkins Univ. 1967, Caltech, 1969-70; postdoc. asst. res. scientist physics dept. N.Y. Univ. 1975-76; internal med. resident Wadsworth VA Med. Ctr., 1978-81, staff physician 1983-85; geriatric fellowship UCLA, 1981-83; pvt. practice internal medicine and geriatrics, 1983-; adj. asst. prof., 1983-85, clin. asst. prof. UCLA Sch. of Med., 1985-; med. staff Century City Hosp. 1983-, Los Alamitos Med. Ctr. 1987-; med. dir. Nat. Med. Home Health Care, 1985-87, Leisure World Med. Clinic, 1987-, Comm. Nsg. Home Proj. UCLA Div. Geriatrics, 1987-; med. cons. Beverly Ents. 1984-87; awards: Cum Laude Soc. 1965, Nat. Merit Scholarship Finalist 1965, Sigma Xi 1969, NSF trainee 1969, Woodrow Wilson Spl. Summer Fellow 1974, Robert A. Millikan Fellow 1975; Fellow, UCLA/USC Long Term Care Gerontology Ctr.; mem: AMA, Am. Geriatrics Soc., Am. Soc. Internal Med., Am. Med. Directors Assn.; pub. res. and jour. articles in field. Ofc: 2080 Century Park East Ste 1410 Los Angeles 90067

WANGBERG, ELAINE GREGORY, university administrator; b. Aug. 4, 1942, Huntington, W.Va.; d. Bradford W. and Freda (Smith) Gregory; children: Brigitte M. b. 1966, Leslie G. b. 1971; edn: BS summa cum laude, Univ. Minn. 1964; MA, Univ. Mich. 1970; PhD, 1979. Career: language arts cons. Ann Arbor Pub. Schs., Mich. 1975-78; interim dir. language arts dept. 1977-78; asst. prof. Univ. New Orleans, La. 1979-81, assoc. prof., dir. literacy project 1981-85, dir. res. and devel. 1983-86; v.provost, dean, prof. CSU Chico 1986-; cons. univs. and sch. dists. 1975-; awards: Univ. Mich. Outstanding Dissertation 1979, La. St. Univ. Outstanding Tchr. 1983, U.S. Dept. Edn. Cert. Recog. 1984, Phi Delta Kappa, La. Ednl. Adminstr. of Yr. 1985; mem: Am. Assn. Univ. Adminstrs., Am. Assn. Univ. Research Parks, Council of Grad. Sch., Western Assn. Grad. Schs., Nat. Assn.Women Deans Adminstrs. & Counselors, Phi Delta Kappa, Metro. Leadership Forum, Rotary Internat., Eskaton Steering Bd., Chico C.of C.; num. articles pub. California State University 114 Kendall Hall First and Normal Sts Chico 95929-0875

WARBRITTON, JOHN D., III, orthopaedic surgeon; s. John David and Nancy Ann (Payne) W.; m. Martha Lucia Icaza, Dec. 8, 1985; edn: BA, UCSD 1975; MD, Harvard Univ. 1980. Career: resident dept. surgery UCSF 1980-82, resident orthopaedic surgery 1982-84, chief resident St. Mary's Hosp. 1984-86; staff surgeon Oak Hill Med. Group, Oakland 1986-89; pvt. practice orthopaedic surgery 1989-; orthopaedic cons. Fairmont Hosp., San Leandro 1988-; assoc. staff Summit Medical Ctr. 1986-; dir. orthopaedics Oak Hill Med. Group 1986-89; awards: Harvard Univ. Shipley Prize 1980, Western Orthopaedic Assn. Thompson Prize 1986, Nat. Merit Finalist 1971; mem: Moraga Country Club, Harvard Club S.F., Lloyd Taylor Alumni, Alameda Contra Costa Med. Assn., AMA, Nicaragua Relief Fund. (med. dir. 1987-89); research articles pub. in med. jours. 1979-80, thesis pub. in Harvard Med. Jour. 1980; Republican; R.Cath.; rec: skiing, golf, tennis. Res: 172 Alice Ln Orinda 94653 Ofc: 350 30th St Ste 530 Oakland 94609

WARBURTON, AUSTEN DEN, lawyer; b. Nov. 12, 1917, Santa Clara; s. Henry Luke and Mary A. (Den) W.; edn: AB, San Jose St. Univ. 1938; JD, Univ. Santa Clara 1941. Career: secty. St. Bar Calif. 1941-42; prof. law Univ. Santa Clara 1946-66; pvt. practice Campbell Warburton Britton Fitzsimmons & Smith, San Jose 1946-; mem. Coll. of Probate Attys.; lectr. San Jose Adult Edn. 1950-60; chmn. Santa Clara Youth Advy. Com., mem. and past chmn. Santa Clara Co. Juvenile Justice Commn., and S.C. Co. Delinquency Prevention Commn.; honors: attorney of year Univ. Santa Clara, Edward Owens award, Silver Beaver BSA; civic: Santa Clara Co. Pioneer Soc. (bd. mem., past pres.), Valley Village Retirement Com. (bd.), United Way Santa Clara Co. (chmn. allocation com.), Santa Clara Scout Found (bd.), City of Santa Clara (vice mayor, mem. plng. commn.), Historical & Landmark Com., Civil Service Com., Freeholders (chmn. of bd.); author Indian Lore of North Calif. Coast 1966, newspaper series Santa Clara Saga 1986-, articles on hist. and legal topics; AUS 1942-46; Republican; Episcopalian; rec: history. Res: 790 Locust St Santa Clara 95052 Ofc: Campbell Warburton Britton Fitzsimmons & Smith, 12th Flr Bank America Bldg 101 Park Center Plaza San Jose 95113

WARD, JAMES DAVID, lawyer; b. Sept. 8, 1935, Sioux Falls, S.D.; s. Charles David, Jr. and Juanita Marion (Senecal) W.; m. Carole J. Sander, Aug. 4, 1956; children: Kelly, Bruce, Mark; edn: BA, Univ. S.Dak., 1957; JD, Univ. San Francisco, 1959; admitted bar: Calif. Career: deputy dist. atty., Riverside 1960-61; atty., ptnr. Badger, Schulte & Ward, Riverside 1961-64; ptnr. Thompson & Colegate, 1964-; adj. prof. UC Riverside, 1983-89, Univ. of LaVerne, 1988-89; mem. Lawyer Representative- Ninth Circuit Judicial Conf. 1992-; editl. bd. Calif. Lawyer Mag. 1989-; honors: argued and won 2 cases before U.S. Supreme Ct. Press Enterprise v. Superior Ct., W.D.C. 1984-86, merit. service award Riverside County Bar Assn. 1986, Resolution and appreciation cert. Calif. Legislature, Sacto. 1987; mem.: Calif. State Bar Assn. (1960-, bd. govs. 1981-84, v.p. 1984), Am. Judicature Soc. (1965-, bd. dirs. 1984-87), Am. Board of Trial Advocates 1989-, Riv. County Bar Assn. (1960-, pres. 1973-74), So. Calif. Defense Counsel 1975-; civic: Monday Morning Group Riv., Citizens Univ. Com. (secty. 1992), UCR Found., Riverside Comm. Hosp. Found., Riverside Art Assn., Frank Miller Club (Mission Inn); publs: articles Civil Discovery Practice, CEB (1988), contbr. Calif. Lawyer, Calif. Legal Secretaries Mag., other jours.; mil: sgt. Army Reserve 1957-63; Republican; Prot.; rec: skiing. Res: 2649 Anna Riverside 92506 Ofc: 3610 14th St Riverside 92502

WARD, ROBERT STACY, real estate broker; b. Dec. 15, 1959, Anderson, Ind.; s. Edgar Elmer and Nedra (Smallwood) W.; m. Deborah, May 8, 1982; children: Stacie Ann b. 1984, Robert Jacob b. 1987; edn: BS bus. Indiana Univ. Career: mgr. Cal-Tahoe Realtors, South Lake Tahoe, 1982, owner/broker Century 21 Cal-Tahoe Realtors, 1982-88; mgr. Tahoe Sands Realty, 1988; gen. mgr. for mktg. and sales NaKoro Resorts, Fiji Islands, 1988; owner/broker South Lake Tahoe Realtors, 1988-; mem: Nat. Assn. Realtors, Calif. Assn. Realtors, South Lake Tahoe Bd. of Realtors, Kiwanis Club (sec. 1982-3, treas. 1983-4, 2d v.p. 1991-2); Republican; Presbyterian. Res: 1688 Hekpa (POB 6020) South Lake Tahoe 95729 Ofc: South Lake Tahoe Realtors, 2634 Hwy 50 South Lake Tahoe 96150

WARE, DAVID JOSEPH, expert witness, financial planner; b. Dec. 1, 1928, Oberlin, Ohio; s. Elmer Edwin and Jessie Vanstone (Potter) W.; m. Diane Adams, Sept. 12, 1958 (dec.); children: Stacey b. 1961, Joel b. 1964; m. Mary Spadafora, Aug. 15, 1981; edn: Univ. of Mexico, 1949; BA, DePauw Univ., 1950; bus. sch. Miami Univ., 1950-51, 54-55; grad. course Univ. of Granada, Spain 1957; C.F.P. Coll. Fin. Planning 1984. Career: grain trader Chemurgy Div., Glidden Co., Chgo. 1955-57; commodity dept. mgr. Merrill Lynch, San Francisco 1958-69; br. and regional mgmt., investment sales Dean Witter Reynolds, S.F. 1969-92; mem. bd. dirs. Pacific Commodities Exchange 1972; panelist, research UC Berkeley Bus. Sch., 1970, guest lectr. UCB Grad. Seminar, 1971; instr. grad. sch. Golden Gate Univ., 1987-89; adj. prof. Coll. for Fin. Planning, Denver 1986-87; honors: Alpha Delta Sigma 1949, Phi Beta Kappa 1950, achiev. Chgo. Board of Trade 1956, nat. recognition Junior Achievement, S.F. 1963, regional recognition Jaycees Mill Valley 1964; mem: NASD (arbitrator W.Coast 1985-), Nat. Futures Assn. (arbitrator 1985-), NYSE Disciplinary Com. W. Coast 1975-92, Am. Arbitration Assn. (arb. 1988-), Internat. Assn. Fin. Planners, Registry of Cert. Fin. Planners (CFP), San Francisco C.of C. (chmn. mem. com. 1975-78); clubs: Olympic (chmn. house com. 1987), S.F. Commodity (pres. 1971); contbr. articles Money Mag. 1987-; mil: lt. AUS Signal Corps 1951-53; Republican; Congregational; rec: bridge, tennis, handball, sailing. Res/Ofc: 248 E Strawberry Dr Mill Valley 94941

WARNE, WILLIAM ELMO, water resources consultant; b. Sept. 2, 1905, Seafield, IN; s. William R. and Nettie Jane (Williams) W.; m. Edith M. Peterson, 1929; children: Jane Ingrid (Beeder), b. 1934; William Robert, b. 1937; Margaret Edith (Monroe), b. 1944; edn: AB, Univ. of Calif. 1927; hon. LLD, Seoul Nat. Univ. 1959; hon. Dr. of Econ., Yonsie Univ., Korea 1959. Career: reporter S.F. Bulletin and Oakland Post-Inquirer 1925-27; news ed. Brawley News, Calif. 1927; news ed. Calexico Chronicle 1928; ed./staff writer Assoc. Press., L.A., San Diego, Wash DC 1928-35; ed. Bur. of Reclamation, US Dept. of Interior 1935-42; asst. commr. 1943-47; asst. secty. Dept. of Interior

1947-51; chief of staff War Prodn. Drive, War Prodn. Bd. 1942; dir. AID, Iran 1951-55; Brazil 1956; Korea 1956-59; dir. Calif. Dept. of Fish & Game 1959-60; Agri. Dept. 1960-61; adminstr. Calif. Resources Agy. 1961-63; dir. Calif. Dept. of Water Resources 1961-66; v.p. Devel. and Resources Corp. 1967-69; adj. prof. USC Sch. of Public Adminstrn., Sacto. 1976-79; independent water resources cons. 1969-; appt: Pres.'s Com. on San Diego Water Supply (chmn. 1944-46), Fed. Inter-Agy. River Basin Com. (chmn. 1948), Fed. Com. on Alaskan Devel. 1948, Group Health Assn. Inc., Wash DC (pres. 1945-52), chmn. US delegation 2nd Inter-Am. Conf. on Indian Life, Cuzco, Peru 1949, US del. 4th World Power Conf., London 1950, Near East Found. (dir. 1956-8, 1959-64), Calif. Water Pollution Control Bd. 1959-66, advy. bd. Fed. Water Pollution Control 1962-65, Gov.'s Cabinet 1961, US com. Internat. Commn. on Large Dams; mem. Nat. Water Supply Improvement Assn. (1971-88, pres. 1978-80), CAREW (assoc. dir. 1973-90); pres. Warne & Blanton Publishers 1985-90, editor Geothermal Report, 1985-90; awards: Distinguished public service Foreign Ops. Adminstrn. 1955, Shah of Iran Order of the Crown 1955, Outstanding service citation UN Command 1959, Distinguished service Dept. of Interior 1951, Merit Award Lambda Chi Alpha 1963, Lifetime achievement award NWSIA 1981, lifetime distinguished service award Internat. Desalination Assn. 1991, Order of Industrial Service Merit Bronze Tower, Rep. of Korea 1991; mem: Soc. of Profl. Journalists, Lambda Chi Alpha, Nat. Press Club (Wash. DC), Sutter Club (Sacto.), Fellow Nat. Acad. of Pub. Adminstrn.; author: Mission for Peace, Bobbs- Merrill 1956; the Bureau of Reclamations, Praeger Publs. 1973; How the Colorado River was Spent, NWSIA Jour. 1975; Mass Transfer of Water Over Long Distances, The California Experience, proceedings spl. session, Internat. Commn. on Irrigation and Drainage, Athens 1978; mil: 2nd lt. ORC 1927-37. Res: 1570 Madrono Ave. Palo Alto 94306

WARNER, CHARLES SAMPSON, metal distribution and fabrication executive; b. June 26, 1927, Sharon, Pa.; s. John Theodore, Sr. and Jennie Mae (Lucas) W.; m. Jane M., Aug. 16, 1952; children: Kathleen Jane b. 1954, Lori Ann (Ward) b. 1959; edn: BA chem., DePauw Univ., 1950; Indiana Univ. 1950-51; counselor alcohol and drug addiction, UC Berkeley (1983); Calif. lic. real estate broker 1985. Career: sales mgr. Kasle Steel Corp., Chgo. 1959-, gen. mgr. 1963-, v.p. sales and mktg. Kasle Steel, Dearborn, Mich. 1966-71; gen. mgr. Ducommun Metals Co., Berkeley 1971-74; pres. and c.e.o. Rich Steel Co., div. Azcon, Los Angeles 1975; exec. v.p. Azcon Corp., NY, NY 1976; pres. and c.e.o. Bayshore Metals Inc., San Francisco 1977-; mem. corporate bds. of six nat. corporations; mem. Nat. Assn. of Corporate Directors, pres. S.F. chapter; vis. lectr. UC Berkeley Grad. Sch. of Bus. 1973-; appt. to US Pres.'s Drug Advy. Commn. 1992-; civic fundraiser for Nat. Urban League, Navy League of U.S., and the Homeport issue City and Co. of San Francisco; nat. chmn. for Fleet Adm. Nimitz Lectureship, UCB; awards: Rector Scholar, DePauw Univ. 1946-50, Small Bus. Advocacy Award for No. Calif. 1982, Secty. of Navy meritorious service award 1984, Vernon E.Jordan Humanitarian Award 1984, Mayor's Proclamation of Charles S. Warner Day in S.F. for efforts on behalf of US Navy 1985, UCB Regents Award 1985, US Navy League scroll of honor 1985 and Top Recruiter for past 7 yrs. 1981-, Presdl. Citation for Excellence 1987, USCG top award for service 1985, KRON-TV bus. comm. service award 1982, KABL-Radio outstanding citizen 1983; mem: Steel Service Center Inst., No. Calif. (pres. 1972-74), Nat. Assn. Aluminum Distbrs. (pres. 1973-75), Foundation Ctr. of S.F., Chief Execs. Club N.Y. (pres.), Presidents Assn. 1984-, Sales Mktg. Exec. Clubs (Chgo., Detroit, S.F.), Nat. Urban League (exec. bd. 1983-86), San Francisco C.of C. (bd. dirs., exec. bd.), Propeller Club, Navy League of U.S. (nat. v.p. 1987); civic: 2 Percent Club of S.F., S.F. Econ. Devel. Commn., Small Bus. Advy. Commn. S.F., S.F. Leadership Sch. 1985 (appt. by Mayor Feinstein), S.F. C.of C. (chmn. Homeporting -Navy Com., S.F. 1984-, v.chmn. USS Missouri Homeporting Com.); mil: capt. USNR (Ret.); R.Cath.; rec: fishing, garden, sailing. Res: 991 DeSoto Ln Foster City 94404 Ofc: Bayshore Metals, Inc. 244 Napoleon St San Francisco 94124

WARNER, ROLLIN MILES, JR., educator; b. Dec. 25, 1930, Evanston, Ill.; s. Rollin Miles and Julia Herndon (Polk) W.; edn: English-Speaking Union Schoolboy Exchange to Oundle Sch., Eng.; BA, Yale Univ., 1953; cert. Harvard Law Sch., 1955-56; MBA, Stanford Univ., 1960; supv. cred., Univ. San Francisco, 1974; lic. R.E. broker; Realtor; Cert. Fin. Planner (CFP) Coll. Fin. Plnng., 1977; Registered Investment Adviser. Career: buyer Matson Navigation Co., 1956-58; asst. dir. devel./asst. to VP Fin., Stanford Univ. 1960-63; dean student activities and tchr. Town School, San Francisco 1963-70, 1975-; school prin. and dir. devel. and plant, Katharine Branson Sch., Mt. Tamalpais Sch., 1970-75; ednl. cons. Educators' Collaborative, Nat. Center for Fin. Edn.; dep. dir. gen. Internat. Biographical Centre; dep. gov. Am. Biog. Inst. Research Assn.; honors: World Decoration of Excellence, Cum Laude Soc., Silver Beaver Award BSA, Scouter's Key, All-America Prep Sch. Swimming, Mt. Tamalpais Sch. Cup, SAR Award (NROTC), Fisher Body Craftsman's Guild 2d prize Ill.; mem: Am. Econ. Assn., Inst. of CFPs, Calif. R.E. Edn. Assn., Manteca Bd. of Realtors, R.E. Certificate Inst., Marines Meml. Assn., Chi Psi frat., Lincoln's Inn at Harvard Law Sch., Am. Mgmt. Assn., Nautical Research Guild; civic: Boy Scouts Am. (Troop 14); clubs: University (SF), Grolier (NY), SF Yacht, Old Oundelian (London), Mory's, Book Club of Calif.; author: Free Enterprise at Work 1989, Africa, Asia, Russia 1986, America 1986, Europe 1986, Greece,

Rome 1981; mil: lt. USNR 1953-55, Korean, UN, Nat. Service ribbons; Republican; R.Cath.; rec: ship models, computers, bibliophile. Res: 1164 Marion Street Manteca 95337 Ofc: Town School 2750 Jackson St San Francisco 94115

WARNER, WALTER D., executive; b. Feb. 26, 1952, Davenport, Iowa; s. Robert Martin and Opal Louise (Gibbons) W.; edn: BS in Finance, Drake Univ., Des Moines, Iowa, 1975. Career: operations ofcr. Iowa-Des Moines Nat. Bank, Des Moines, 1975-78; v.p. Central Savings & Loan Assn., San Diego, Calif., 1978-85; pres. The Lomas Santa Fe Companies, Solana Beach, Calif., 1985-91; pres. Ebert Composites Corp., Nat. City, Calif., 1991-; dir.: Inst. of the Americas, La Jolla, 1985-90, Lomas Group, Del Mar, 1985-90, Nature Preserved of Am., San Clemente, 1988-90, Torrey Pines Bank, Solana Beach, 1986-90, The Lomas Santa Fe Companies, Solana Beach, 1985-91, Ebert Companies Corp., Nat. City, 1991-; mem: The Exec. Comm. 1987-90, Internat. Forum for Corporate directors 1991-; civic: founding dir. & treas. Golden Triangle Arts Found., La Jolla, 1989-90; chmn. of the bd. Arthritis Found., San Diego, 1985-87; pres. Gildred Found., Solana Beach, 1986-91; Republican; rec: tennis, piano.

WARREN, KAREN M., national medical and research cancer center executive; b. May 12, 1943, Boulder, Co.; edn: BS (bus. admin.), Univ. of Redlands; children: Mark b. 1963, Kimberly b. 1965, Shay Kristine b. 1970; p.t. offce mgr. Kellogg-Voorhis Credit Union, Cal Poly, Pomona 1961-62; corp. secty.-treas., exec. secty. to the pres. Luxrite Products Co., Inc. 1962-70; acct. Bernard V. Ousley and James S. Baker, attys. at law 1975-77; corp. secty.-treas. and co-owner Warren Automotive, Inc. 1970-78; office mgr., acct. Armstrong Enterprises, Inc. 1973-79; mgr. corporate gen. acctg. City of Hope National Medical Center and the Beckman Res. Inst., 1979-80, dir. revenue acctg. 1980-83, asst. nat. controller 1983-85, nat. controller 1985-86, chief operating ofcr. 1986-, exec. v.p. and chief operating ofcr. 1987-; mem. Am. Mgmt. Assn., Healthcare Financial Mgmt. Assn., Nat. Assn. of Female Execs., Healthcare Execs., Hosp. Council of So. Calif. (AIDS com.). Ofc: City of Hope 1500 E Duarte Rd Duarte 91010-0269

WARREN, THOMAS SPENCER, manufacturing executive; b. July 26, 1903, Anaheim; s. Henry E. and Emily T. (Thomas) W.; m. Barbara Blaisdell, Oct. 28, 1928; children: Paul b. 1933, Bethany b. 1935, Virginia b. 1945; edn: BA, Pomona Coll. 1926. Career: pres. Ultra Violet Products, Los Angeles 1932-71; chmn. UVP Inc., San Gabriel 1971-83; pres. Black Light Corp. of Am., Los Angeles 1955-; dir., chmn. Ulta Violet Products Ltd., Cambridge, England 1969-83; mem: Pomona Coll. Alumni Assn. (Council 1977-81), East Bay Mineral Soc. (hon.), L.A. Lapidary Soc. (hon.), Fluorescent Mineral Soc. (hon.), San Diego Mineral Soc. (hon.), Am. Gem & Mineral Suppliers Assn. (pres. 1952-54, dir. 1954-58), Rotary Intl. (Hollywood Club 1942-50, dir. 1948, L.A. Club 1950-); coauthor, editor (revised): Ultra-Violet Guide to Minerals (1992), contbr., Identification & Qualitative Chemical Analysis of Minerals (O.C. Smith), Collectors Book Fluorescent Minerals (Manuel Robbins); Republican; Prot.; rec: fluorescent minerals. Ofc: PO Box 1501 San Gabriel 91776

WASSERMAN, BRUCE ARLEN, dentist, newsletter editor; b. June 7, 1954, San Mateo; s. Albert and Dunia (Frydman) W.; m. Pamela Carole Ward, June 8, 1972; children: Rachael b. 1972, Rebecca b. 1975, Meir b. 1977, Keren b. 1977; edn: BA mass communications, Winona St. Univ., Minn. 1981; DDS, Univ. of Pacific Sch. of Dentistry, S.F. 1985. Career: apprentice blacksmith Reuben Syhre, Blacksmith, Pine River, Minn. 1973-74; blacksmith Walden Forge, Pine River, Minn. 1974-79; founding dir. and ed. Team Redeemed, 1984-; dentist/prin. pvt. practice, San Mateo, Calif. 1985-; pres. Manx USA, 1987-; honors: Mosby scholar 1985, Tau Kappa Omega 1985, Pierre Fauchard Acad. 1987, disting. alumni Winona State Univ. 1988, disting. svc. Calif. Dental Assn. Sacto. 1987, recogn. Am. Dental Assn. (1987, 89, 90), Order of Kentucky Colonels 1989; mem: ADA, Acad. of Gen. Dentistry, Acad. of Dentistry Internat. (fellow 1987, assoc. ed. 1988-90, ed. 1990, by-laws com. 1990), Am. Coll. of Dentists (fellow 1990), Royal Soc. of Health London (fellow 1988), Calif. Dental Assn., San Mateo Co Dental Soc. (ed. 1986-89, Dir.'s award 1987, Pres.'s award 1989); clubs: Christian Classic Bikers Assn. Eugene, OR (Calif. rep. 1983-), BSA San Mateo (cubmaster 1986), Am. Lung Assn. S.M. (bd. 1989-, bike trek com. 1989-90, fund devel. com. 1989-90, mem. com. 1991, bike tour com. 1992), Pacific Road Riders S.F. (pres./ ed. 1983-85), Son Riders Castro Valley (v.p./chaplain 1984), 78th Fraser's Highlanders Regt. (v.sgt. 1989, lt. and No. Calif. recruiting ofcr. 1990-); publs: A Manual of Uniforming (78th Fraser's Highlanders Regt.); newsletter ed: (quarterly) Good News, 1984-; No. Cal. Reporter, 1987-90; Cycle Lines, 1983-85; (monthly) The Mouthpiece, 1986-89; International Communicator assoc. ed. 1988-89, ed. 1990; rec: bicycling, motorcycling, writing, metalworking. Ofc: 410 N San Mateo Dr San Mateo 94401

WASTE, WILLIAM TEN EYCK, insurance executive; b. Aug. 10, 1925, Oakland; s. Wm. Ewing and Elizabeth (Ten Eyck) W.; m. Laura Piccirillo, Aug. 6, 1949; children: William H. b. 1951, Ann Elizabeth (Woodbridge) b. 1953, Carlin (McCarthy) b. 1955, Mary Lou (Ashford) b. 1959, Katherine Margaret (Spurlock) b. 1959; edn: Univ. Mich. 1943; BA, Univ. Calif. 1949. Career: various pos. Industrial Indemnity Co., West Coast 1950-74, retired 1974; pres. Beaver Insurance Co., San Francisco, 1974-85, v. chmn./c.e.o. 1985-87, bd. dir.

1974-89; appt. commr. Calif. State Seismic Commn. 1987-91, v.chmn. 1990-91; Oreg. Gov.'s Accident Advy. Com. 1969-72; mem. Oregon Western Ins. Info. Service Bd. 1963-72; recipient pres.'s citation Oregon Ins. Agts. Assn. 1965; mem. Assn. Calif. Ins. Cos. (pres. 1983-85), Workers Compensation Rating Bur. (govng. com.), Calif. Workers Compensation Inst. (pres. 1985-87, dir. 1979-89); mem. bds: The Claremont Colls. (bd. overseers 1981-), Scripps Coll. (v.chmn., chmn. investment com. 1981-91), St. Luke's Hosp. (dir. 1988-), Salvation Army (San Francisco advy. bd. chmn. 1977-78, Nat. Advy. Bd. 1980-, v.chmn. 1990-93), USO (S.F. bd. dirs. 1973-82), Episcopal Homes Found. (chmn. fin. com. 1977), Church Divinity Sch. of the Pacific (trustee 1988-), Pacific Rim Soc. (bd. 1990-); mem. Royal Photographic Soc. (Licentiate), SAR, Sigma Phi; clubs: Pacific Union, Bohemian, The California, St. Francis Yacht, Claremont CC, The Club, Kiwanis (pres. S.F. club 1979-80), Masons, K.T.; publs: articles on insurance subjects, and on travels to USSR and China; mil: 1st lt. CIC, US Army 1944-47, 51; Republican (v.chmn. Kern Co. Central Com. 1960-63); Episcopalian (sr. warden 1968); rec: photography, skiing, hiking, numismatics. Ofc: 2288 Broadway San Francisco 94115

WATANABE, RICHARD MEGUMI, research fellow, exercise physiologist; b. Sept. 7, 1962, San Fernando, Calif.; s. Takashi and Toshiko (Yamane) W.; edn: BS biol. scis., USC, 1986, MS applied biometry, 1989, postgrad. studies in exercise physiology (in progress). Career: res. asst. dept. physiology & biophysics USC Sch. of Medicine, 1985-87, res. assoc. 1987-89, dir. Kinetic Core, Metabolic Resrch. Unit, 1991-; stats. analyst and computer pgmr. L.A. Co.-USC Med. Ctr. Women's Hosp., 1985-89; honors: Outstanding Young Men of Am. 1983, Outstanding Senior USC 1985, Serono Symposia in-tng. award, 1st prize, Pacific Coast Fertility Soc. 1990, student award for meritorious resrch. Am. Fedn. for Clin. Resrch., Western Soc. 1990, NIH predoctoral tng. fellow 1990-; student mem: Am. Diabetes Assn., AAAS, Am. Physiol. Soc.; publs: MS thesis: Mathematical Modeling of Insulin Secretion: Issues of Mode Complexity, 1989, peer reviewed sci. papers and abstracts (20+), med. jour. revs. for Diabetes Care, Diabetologia, Internat. J. of Obesity, others; rec: woodworking, music. Ofc: USC School of Medicine Dept. Physiology & Biophysics, Metabolic Research Unit, 1333 San Pablo St MMR-128 Los Angeles 90033 Tel: 213/342-1939

WATKINS, JUDITH A., nurse; b. Mar. 11, 1942; Chicago; d. Russell G. and Louise B. (Aloy) Keim; m. Thomas H. Watkins, Dec. 24, 1961; children: Tamara, b. 1965; Randall, b. 1967; edn: BSN, Pacific Union Coll., Angwin, Calif., 1991; nursing diploma, Knapp Coll. of Nursing, Santa Barbara, 1963; career: ob/gyn supr. Bowling Green, Warren Co. Hosp., Bowling Green, KY 1963-67; clinical staff nurse Chula Vista Med. Clinic, Chula Vista 1967-69; instr. Sawyer's Coll., Ventura 1972; ob/gyn supr. Westlake Comm. Hosp., Westlake 1972-77; acute patient care Bakersfield Med. Pool, Bakersfield 1984; dir. of allied health San Joaquin Valley Coll., Bakersfield 1984-88; dir. of nurses Bakersfield Family Med. Ctr., 1988-92; client svs. rep. Bakersfield Family Med. Ctr., 1992-; awards: Mother of the Yr. Frazier Park Comm. Ch., Frazier Park, Calif., 1979; Lady of the Yr., Pine Mt. Club, Pine Mt., Calif., 1983; Instr. of the Yr., San Joaquin Valley Coll., Bakersfield, 1986; mem: Pine Mt. Country Club 1977-, Sundale Country Club 1986-, Calif. R.N. Soc. 1991-, Toastmasters 1990-, Kern Co. Perinatal Comm. 1992-; founder, Lilac Festival, Pine Mt. Club, 1982; dir., Kern Co. Sr. Expo, 1991; Republican; Christian; rec: swimming; golf; ofc: Bakersfield Family Medical Center 5700 Stockdale Hwy #300 Bakersfield 93309

WATSON, JEANETTE MARIE, municipal elected official, historian; b. Mar. 12, 1931, San Josep d. Joseph Vincent and Jennie Isabel (Yerkovich) Gomes; m. Courtland Leroy Watson, May 29, 1954 (dec. Sept. 30, 1991); children: Kathleen b. 1955, Teresa b. 1957, Courtland Joseph b. 1959; edn: BA, San Jose State Univ., 1953. Career: historical researcher, author: Campbell, the Orchard City (1990); elected City Council, City of Campbell, 1985-, mayor 1988-89, chair Redevel. Agy. 1988-89, 2d v.p. Santa Clara Co. Cities Assn. 1990-92, chair Santa Clara Valley Water Commn. 1992-93; chair Civic Improvement Commn., Campbell 1972-78; awards: Citizen of Year Campbell C.of C. 1968, Historic Preserv. Resources award Santa Clara Co. Bd. of Suprs. 1979; civic bds: West Valley/Mission College Foundation Inc. (bd. 1987-), Campbell Hist. Mus. Assn. (pres.), Campbell Citizens for Beautification (chair 1989-), Campbell C.of C. (pres. 1978-79); club: Country Woman's Club (bd. 1960-, pres. 1964-65); Republican; R.Cath.; rec: hist. res. Ofc: City of Campbell, 70 N First St Campbell 95008

WATTS, JAMES LAWRENCE, investment banker; b. June 3, 1949, Minot, N.Dak.; s. Lawrence Robert and Deloris Marie (Anderson) W.; edn: BA, econs., Univ. Wisc., 1972; MA, internat. econs., American Univ., W.D.C. 1975, JD, Washington Coll. of Law Am. Univ., 1981; admitted bar: Dist. Col., U.S. Supreme Ct.; lic. NASD Series 7, Series 63. Career: legislative asst. US House of Representatives, W.D.C. 1975-76; assoc. dir. Nat. Assn. of Small Bus. Invesment Cos., W.D.C. 1976-81; of counsel Buchanan Ingersoll, W.D.C. 1981-85; atty. cons. Venture Internat. Inc., Alexandria Va. 1985-86; v.p. corp. fin. FAS/Bekhor Internat., San Diego 1986-87; senior v.p. corp. fin. Cruttenden & Co. (venture fin., mergers & acquisitions, pub. offerings), Newport Beach 1987-; dir: Candys Tortilla Factory, Pueblo, Colo. 1991-, IRSC Inc., Anaheim

1988-, Gores Systems Inc., Studio City 1992-; awards: merit cert. Pres. Jimmy Carter 1980, career achiev. Nat. Assn. Small Bus. Inv. Cos. 1981; mem. Am. Bar Assn.; Republican. Res: 3150 Manistee Dr Costa Mesa 92626

WATTS, VAN, naval philosopher and sea power advocate; b. Aug. 26, 1920, Mooers, N.Y.; s. Bert and Margaret (Baker) W.; m. Lilie Remoreras, 1971; children: Michelle Remie b. 1978, (by previous marriage): Philip b. 1942, Charlotte b. 1946, Britt b. 1947, Lance b. 1948, Douglas b. 1950; Career: U.S. Navy 1937-62, retired 1962-: USN travels to 6 continents and pub. author on 2 of them; sailed with Byrd and Michener 1942; his "Our Expanding Language" was read before the Sydney chpt. British Empire Soc., 1944; intro. on return to Norfolk as "a Navy instn." 1952; his televised & broadcasted pgms. used by Mayor of Norfolk to promote goodwill drive; subject of full-page editorial in OUR NAVY, 1953, ideas extolled in Navy Dept. press release to 2,562 ships, stations and overseas commands 1953; producer t.v. and radio navy-slanted shows from Norfolk, Va., 1952-54, and originated the Navy's Sailor of the Week, Month and Year programs, also assisted other svs. in starting pgms.; prod. shows: Norfolk's Sailor of the Week's Big Welcome to Town WTAR-TV 1952-53, WTOV-TV 1954; Sailor of the Week's Bon Voyage WCAV 1952-53, WGH 1954; Navy Guide Cover Girls WLOW 1952-54; Marine of the Month WTAR 1954; Oceana Navy Band WBOF 1954; Portsmouth Sailor of the Week WSAP 1953-54; Sailor of the Year WTOV-TV 1954, WGH 1954; enrollment of all t.v. and radio media in area to promote Norfolk-Navy goodwill drive inspired the formation of the Navy League's Hollywood Council, 1954; created Norfolk's famed Big Ship Welcoming Ceremonies, described by Navy Dept. a "centerpiece of Norfolk-Navy rels." 1958; ofcr. courier to NATO Paris Hq. during 1st Lebanon crisis, 1958; LIFE Mag. paid tribute to value of his pgms. in feature "Mighty New Navy" pub. on 10th anniv. of his Sailor of Week, Month and Year pgm., 1962; Nat. Planning Assn. endorsement of Atlantic Union entered by Rep. Paul Findley in Congl. Record June 23, 1966; editorialized in Navy Supply Corps OAK LEAF as "Father of an important part of today's people-oriented Navy," 1972; tribute in Congl. Record by Rep. Thomas Rees 1973; sponsor Mich.'s USS Mackinac/Byrd Memorial Navy Bicentennial, 1975; recipient ltr. of commendn. Nat. Trust for Hist. Preservation, 1975; decorated Nat. Def. Serv., Am. Def. Serv., Am. Campaign, Asiatic-Pac. Campaign, WWII Victory, Navy Occup. Serv. (Europe), Armed Forces Exped. (Lebanon), Guadalcanal and New Guinea battle stars, others; recipient num. honors incl. City of Norfolk official thanks 1954 and Royal Mace Pin 1988, Hollywood Council Navy League's gold plaque for the founder of pgms. that spread around the globe, with 3 of his "nautical celebrities" returned from Persian Gulf duty for the ceremonies at Bob Hope Hollywood USO 1988, tribute from ship assn. of USS Enterprise 1988, Navy League Pacific SW Regl. Award 1989, called "Sailor of the Century" by Navy League Hollywood Council Pres. Charles Cabot 1991, advy. bd. WWII Nat. Commemorative Assn. 1992, biographied in The History of Warrant Ofcrs. in the US Navy and Chiefs in the US Navy 1993, achievements noted in Official History of the USN Supply Corps in celebration of Corps Bicentennial 1995; mem: USS Albany CA123 Assn., USS Enterprise CV6 Assn., USS Fremont APA44 Assn., USS Sierra AD18 Assn., NCPO Assn., Tin Can Sailors Assn., Surface Navy Assn. (San Diego Ch.), VFW, Am. Legion (John Philips Sousa Post), Guadalcanal Campaign Vets Assn., US Naval Inst., Naval Hist. Found., Navy Supply Corps Assn., Fleet Reserve Assn., Botsford Family Hist. Assn., New Hampshire Hist. Soc., Brattleboro (Vt.) Hist. Soc., Chesterfield (NH) Hist. Soc., Burbank (CA) Hist. Soc., Hollywood Council Navy League (life mem.). Res: 13561 Sherman Way #216 Van Nuys 91405-2874

WAY, TSUNG-TO, bank executive; b. Sept. 20, 1912, Fu Ch'in, Fukien Province, China; s. Kuang-Yen and S.P. (Yang) W.; m. Shun-Hwa Chiang, Oct. 16, 1938; children: Helen K.L., Suzanne I.L., Raymond T.Y.; edn: St. John's Sch., Shanghai, Yenching Univ., Peiping. Career: Bank of China 1936-, staff mem. Shanghai Branch 1936-38, hd. Foreign Dept., Kunming Br. 1938-39, hd. Loiwing Agy., Yunnan 1939-40, asst. mgr., sub-mgr. Tientsin 1941-43, sub-mgr. Peiping 1943-44, Tientsin 1944-45, Saigon 1946-51, mgr. Saigon 1951-65, Tokyo 1965-70, asst. gen. mgr. in charge, Bank of China, Tokyo 1970, gen. mgr. Bank of China, Taipei, ROC 1970-71; pres./CEO The Internat. Commercial Bank of China (fmr. Bank of China), Taipei 1971-75, bd. chmn. 1975-, branches throughout E. and S.E. Asia, Panama, USA, Saudi Arabia; mng. dir: China Devel. Corp., China Ins. Co., United World Chinese Comml. Bank (all, Taipei, ROC); apptd. dir. Euro-Asia Trade Orgn., ROC-USA Econ. Council, Assn. of East Asia Rels., China-Netherlands Cultural and Econ. Assn., mem. Chinese Nat. Assn. of Indus. and Commerce/Taipei; clubs: Taipei Internat. Businessmen's, The Yuan Shan (Taipei), Kuo Hwa Golf and CC (Taipei), American (Tokyo), Korean (Taipei); rec: golf, travel, music. Res: 1411 Laguna Ave Burlingame 94010 Ofc: Director, Bank of Canton of California, 555 Montgomery San Francisco 94111

WAYMAN, TONY RUSSELL, author; b. March 3, 1929, Poole, England; s. Russell James and Amy Ivy (Whiteman) W.; m. Norah Lena Norman (div. 1973); edn: Poole Grammar Sch. England. Career: gen. mgr. Progress Advertising Ltd., Singapore 1954-57; dep., secty. gen. Singapore Exposition, Chinese C.of C., Singapore 1958-59; mgr. Ace Advt. 1961; dir. Advt. Aids Malaya Ltd., Kuala Lumpur, Malaya 1962-63; novelist, columnist, pub. rels., radio bdcstr., film writer 1957-, author sci. fiction and fantasy novels, 1967-, biography of William Holden (1990), numerous pub. articles, columns and opinion pieces; cons. in edn. and tng. devel. Oakland Econ. Devel. Corp. 1968-69, El Dorado Co. Library 1988-; mem: Friends of Library El Dorado, Internat. Press. Assn., El Dorado Arts Council (bd. dirs. 1984-87), Marshall Hosp. Aux. (bd. dirs. 1984), Downtown Assn. 1987-88; mil: Leading Writer Royal Navy 1946-54; Conservisionist. Res: Apt. A 442 Main St Placerville 95667

WAYNE, KYRA PETROVSKAYA, actress, author, lecturer; b. Dec. 31, 1918, Crimea, USSR, naturalized U.S. cit. 1952, W.D.C.; d. Vasilly and Zinaida (von Haffenberg) Obolensky; m. George J. Wayne, M.D., Apr. 21, 1961; children: Ronald G. Wayne, M.D. b. 1953; edn: BA, Inst. of Theatre Arts, Leningrad 1939, MA, 1941. Career: actress Leningrad Drama Theatre, Leningrad Theatre of Miniatures, Moscow Satire Theatre, 1939-46; enrichment lectr. Royal Viking Lines cruises, 1978-88; free lance author, 1948-: books: (autobiography) Kyra, 1959, (cookbook) Kyra's Secrets of Russian Cooking, 1960, (juvenile) Quest For The Golden Fleece, 1962, (autobiography) Shurik, 1970, (novel) The Awakening (1972), The Witches of Barguzin (1975), (juv.) Max, the Dog that Refused to Die, 1980, (hist. novel) Quest for Empire, 1989, (juv.) Lil' Ol' Charlie, 1990; awards: Red Star For the def. of Leningrad, Red Army USSR 1943, excellence recogn. City Council Leningrad 1945, City Council Moscow 1945, exceptional svc. Crusade for Freedom, W.D.C. 1955, sev. awards of merit Am. Lung Assn., L.A. County Lung Assn. 1963-88, Best Fiction Book, Dog Writers Assn. of Am. 1980; pres. Med. Faculty Wives UCLA 1970-71; civic bds: Carmel Music Soc. (dir. 1992-), L.A. Co. Lung Assn. (founder, pres. Clean Air Pgm. 1973-75); mil: lt. Red Army Inf. WWII; Republican/Indep.; Russian Orthodox; rec: orchidist, Fgn. languages (6), needlepoint.

WEATHERUP, ROY GARFIELD, lawyer; b. April 20, 1947, Annapolis, Md.; s. Robert Alexander and Kathryn Crites (Hesser) W.; m. Wendy Gaines, Sept. 10, 1977; children: Jennifer Ruth b. 1980, Christine Ann b. 1983; edn: JD, Stanford Law Sch. 1972; AB, Stanford Univ. 1968. Career: atty., asso. Haight, Brown & Bonesteel, Los Angeles 1972-78, ptnr. 1979-; Moot Ct. judge UCLA Law Sch.; mem: Calif. Acad. of Appellate Lawyers, Los Angeles Co. Bar Assn. (Superior Cts. Com., Economical Litigation Com., Judicial Evaluation Com.), Am. Bar Assn., Town Hall of Calif.; author: Standing Armies and Armed Citizens: An Historical Analysis of the Second Amendment, Hastings Constl. Law Quarterly Vol. 2, 1975, reprint U.S. Senate Document, 94th Cong. 2d Session; Republican; Methodist; rec: bridge, chess, backpacking. Res: 17260 Rayen St Northridge 91325 Ofc: 1620 26th St, Ste 4000 North, Santa Monica 90404

WEBB, LELAND FREDERICK, professor of mathematics; b. July 27, 1941, Hollywood; s. Robert Wallace and Evelyn Elaine (Gourley) W.; m. Janie Rae Yoder, Jan. 26, 1963; children: Robert Leland, Tamara Lynn Elaine; edn: BA (with high hon.), UC Santa Barbara, 1963; MA, Calif. Polytech. State Univ., 1968; PhD, Univ. Texas, Austin 1971. Career: lectr. dept. edn. Calif. Polytech. State Univ., S.L.O., 1967-68; tchg. asst. dept. math. Univ. Texas, Austin 1970-71; res. assoc. IV Res. and Devel. Ctr. for Tchr. Edn., 1971; asst. prof. CSU Bakersfield 1971-73, assoc. prof. 1973-78, prof. mathematics edn., 1978-, chmn. dept. math. & computer sci., 1982-85, chmn. dept. mathematics 1990-; mem: Calif. State Dept. Edn. math. assessment advy. com. 1985-88, math. framework com. 1983-85, math. test 12th grade writing com. Calif. Assessment Program 1986-87, nat. Mathcounts Question writing com. 1987-90; cons. NSF workshops 1972-76, Tokyo, 1975, sch. dists. and county offices of edn. statewide; on sabbatical lv., vis. prof. Agder Regional Coll., Kristiansand, Norway 1980; author K-8 math. texts, Houghton Mifflin Co., 1985-; awards: grantee NSF 1972-76, fellow U.S. Office Edn. 1968-71, outstanding prof. award CSU Bakersfield 1980, Calif. State Univ. Chancellor's Office 1981-83; mem: Math. Assn. Am., Nat. Council Tchrs. of Math., Calif. Math. Council (central sect. v.p. 1982-84, nat. counc. rep. central sect. 1982-90, nat. coun. state rep. 1986-90), Bakersfield Math. Council (pres. 1976-78), Sch. Sci. and Math. Assn., Sigma Xi, Phi Kappa Phi; mil: capt. US Army 1963-67; Unitarian. Res: 7300 Dos Rios Way Bakersfield 93309 Ofc: Math. Dept., California State University, Bakersfield 93311-1099

WEBBER, CARL ENDICOTT EDWARDS, federal administrator; b. Sept. 9, 1908, Salem, Mass.; s. Harry Endicott and Alice Bates (Edwards) W.; m. Catharine Marple (dec.), Dec. 3, 1932; m. 2d Madeline Oliver, Jan. 21, 1984; children: Martha b. 1935, Sandra b. 1937, Carl Jr. b. 1940; edn: B.Journ. Boston Univ. 1930; Yale Univ. Grad. Sch. 1944-45; grad. Sr. Ofcrs. Mil. Mgmt. Sch., Air Univ. 1949; grad. Indsl. Coll. of the Armed Forces 1958. Career: mgr. Social Security Ofc., Santa Monica 1946; asst. regional rep., area dir. Soc. Sec. Regional Ofc., San Francisco 1947; supervised Fed. Soc. Sec. Ofc. Networks Wash., Oreg., Alaska, Calif., Ariz., Nev., Hawaii, and Pacific Territories; ret.; appt. Solano County Grand Jury, 1990-92; awards: Commissioner's Citation Dept. Health Edn. Welfare SSA; mem: Reserve Ofcrs. Assn. (Dept. v.p.), Am. Legion (comdr.), Leisure Town Home Assn. (pres.), Redwood Empire Wally Byam Caravan Club Internat. (pres.), Phi Sigma Kappa, Commonwealth Club, Knights Templar, Internat. Caravan Club, Retired Ofcrs. Assn.; mil: reserve ofcr. AUS and USAF 1930-69: maj./insp. gen. Army Inf. WWII, lt. col. air insp., dir. materiel Korean War, decorated combat inf., purple heart, bronze star; Republican; rec: trailering. Res: 430 Yellowstone Dr Vacaville 95687-3360

WEEKS, MARGARET LORRAINE, nurse/educator; b. Nov. 15, 1925, Baltimore, Md.; d. Dr. Edgar Tilton and Lucille Margaret (Barens) Moseley; m. Theodore Robert Weeks, May 10, 1945 (div. 1988); children: Kathleen b. 1946, Theodore b. 1947, Kevin b. 1950 (dec.); edn: AAS hons., Lorain Co. Comm. Coll. 1970; cert., Mt. San Antonio Coll. 1979-82; CSU Ext. 1984. Career: patient care coordinator Santa Teresita Hosp., Duarte 1978; head nurse, med. surgical Baldwin Park Comm. Hosp., Baldwin Park 1978-79; emergency room charge nurse Monterey Park Hosp., Monterey Park 1982-83; R.N., critical care Profl. Nurses Bureau, W. Covina 1979-92; tchr. Baldwin Park Adult Sch., Baldwin Park 1982-; substitute nursing clinical instr. Citrus Coll., Glendora 1989; dir. nurse asst. program Baldwin Park Adult Sch. 1983-90, instr. health edn. 1982-; CNA clinical instr., Adult Careers Training Ctr., Baldwin Park, 1991-; instr. Med. Asst. Core Prog., Baldwin Park, 1993-; affil. faculty Am. Heart Assn., Covina 1986-; awards: County of Los Angeles award of merit 1991, Women of Achievement Award San Gabriel Valley YWCA 1991, service award Am. Heart Assn. 1982-91, Student Nurse Assn. Ohio 1969, 70, biog. listings in Who's Who in Am. Nursing 1990-91; mem: Inland Area Health Edn. Council, Calif. Council Adult Edn., Am. Assn. Critical Care Nurses, Sci. Council Cardiovascular Nursing, Internat. Toastmistres (2d. v.p.y 1980-82), Lorain Co. Comm. Coll. Nurses Alumni Assn. (pres. 1974, 75), Ohio Nurses Assn. (com. nursing practice 1970-77), Order of Eastern Star, San Gabriel Valley Civic Light Opera Guild 1988-; mil: cpl. AUS Womens Corps 1944; Republican; Lutheran; rec: watercolors. Res: 2717 Arrow Hwy #67 La Verne 91750 Ofc: Baldwin Park Adult School 4640 N Maine Ave Baldwin Park 91706

WEICHSEL, MORTON E., JR., physician; b. June 17, 1933, Pueblo, Colo.; s. Morton E. and Beatrice Clara (Weintraub) W.; children: Kelly b. 1965, Kimberly b. 1966, Courtney b. 1968; edn: BA, Univ. Colo. Boulder 1955; MD, Univ. Buffalo 1962. Career: clin. instr. pediatric neurology Stanford Univ. Med. Center 1968-69; asst. prof. human devel. medicine and psychiatry Mich. State Univ. Coll. Human Medicine, E. Lansing 1971-74; assoc. prof., prof. pediatrics and neurology Harbor-UCLA Med. Center, UCLA Sch. of Medicine, Torrance 1974-; dir. quality assurance, prof. pediatric neurology King-Drew Med. Center, Los Angeles 1989-; chief profl. services Calif. Children's Services, L.A. 1993-; awards: NIH-Stanford Med. Center fellowship neurology 1965-68, NIH-USPHS fellowship devel. neurochemistry 1969-71; mem: Soc. Neuroscis., Soc. Pediatric Research, Am. Coll. Physician Execs., Western Soc. Pediatric Research, Calif. Neurology Soc., Am. Acad. Pediatrics (fellow); 40+ articles pub. in sci. jours. 1974-; mil: lt. j.g. USN 1955-58; rec: interior design, sports, computer technology, financial and estate planning. Res: 650 Avery Long Beach 90807 Ofc: 19720 East Arrow Hwy Covina 91724

WEIL, STEVEN MARK, educator; b. Feb. 28. 1949, Chicago; s. Ronald Leo and Leona Ann (Fein) W.; children: Meredith b. 1974; Nethaniel b. 1982; Rachael b. 1984; edn: BS psychology and physical sci. edn., Roosevelt Univ., Chgo. 1980; MS, Univ. Nebraska, Omaha 1982; career: educ., Chgo. Public Sch. 1980; educ., Fremont Public Sch., Fremont, NE 1981-86; educ., Stockton Unified Sch. District., Stockton 1986-; cons., Stockton 1991-; dir. edn. and exhibits, Children's Museum of Stockton 1992; NSF Grant Proposal Reader, 1987-89; San Joaquin Cty. Sci. Olympiad Judge 1990-92; San Joaquin Cty Sci. Fair Judge 1988-92, Univ. of Pacific, At-Risk Youth Conf. Advy. Com. 1988-92; Nat. Edn. Assn., Jewish Affairs Caucus, vice-chmn. 1991-93; awards: NSF Honors Workshop for Superior Sci. Tchrs. 1985; Who's Who of Emerging Leaders in Am. 1992; Who's Who in the West 1991-92; mem: Nat. Science Tchrs. Assn. (life, spl. edn. advy. bd. 1983-86, spl. edn. advy. bd. chmn. 1986-87, The Sci. Tchr. advy. & manuscript review bds. 1988-91, NSTA Reports! advy bd. 1991-94); Nat. Edn. Assn. 1989-92; Phi Delta Kappa; author: A Modified Coop Procedure in Gardening, 1984; numerous presentations and publ. articles; Jewish. Res: 7100 Shoreline Dr #113 Stockton 95219 Ofc: Stockton Unified School District Discovery School 300 N Gertrude Stockton 95215

WEINBERG, WILLIAM HENRY, professor of chemical and nuclear engineering, and chemistry; b. Dec. 5, 1944, Columbia, S.C.; s. Vivian Ulric and Ruth W.; m. Ann Elizabeth, Mar. 25, 1989; edn: BS, Univ. South Carolina, 1966; PhD, UC Berkeley, 1970; NATO postdoctoral fellowship Univ. of Cambridge 1971. Career: asst. prof. chem. engring. Calif. Inst. of Technology, Pasadena 1972-74, assoc. prof. 1974-77, prof. chem. engring. and chem. physics, 1977-89, Chevron prof. 1981-86; prof. chem. and nuclear engring. and chem., UC Santa Barbara, 1989-, assoc. dean Coll. of Engring. 1992-; vis. prof. chem. Harvard Univ., 1980, Univ. Pittsburgh, 1987-88; Materials Dept., Univ. of Oxford 1991; Alexander von Humboldt Found. fellow Univ. Munich, 1982; cons. E.I. DuPont Co.; awards: Phi Beta Kappa, Sigma Xi, fellow NSF 1966-69, Alfred P. Sloan Found. 1976-78, Camille and Henry Dreyfus Found. fellow 1976-81, Wayne B. Nottingham Prize Am. Phys. Soc. 1972, Victor K. LaMer Award Am. Chem. Soc. 1973, Allen P. Colburn Award AIChE 1981, Giuseppe Parravano Award Mich. Catalysis Soc. 1989, Kendell Award Am. Chem. Soc. 1991; mem: Am. Physical Soc. (Fellow), Am. Chem. Soc., AIChE, AAAS, Am. Vacuum Soc.; author: Low-Energy Electron Diffraction 1986, 380+ journal articles (1970-), editor 4 books in field, editl. bd. J. Applications Surface Sci. (1977-85), Handbook Surfaces and Interfaces (1978-80), Surface Sci. Reports

(1980-, general editor 1992-), Applied Surface Sci. (1985-), Langmuir (1990-), Surface Sci. (1991-). Ofc: Dept. of Chemical & Nuclear Engineering, Univ. California, Santa Barbara 93106

WEINER, JEFFREY CHARLES, design engineering and construction co. president; b. Oct. 13, 1958, Phila.; s. Raphael David and Shirley Faye (Litwin) W.; edn: BA, pol. sci., USC 1980. Career: pres. Gotech Builders, Inc.; guest lectr. USC, UCLA, CSU Fullerton; guest speaker various real estate orgns.; speaker Orange Co. Communication Task Force; freelance writer newspaper articles, mag. cover & feature stories: Los Angeles Times, Orange County Register, Automation in Housing (internat. factory blt. housing mag.), Zinc (nat. steel ind. mag.), others; mem: Am. Arbitration Assn. (AAA Arbitrators' Panel), Building Industry Assn., Am. Building Contrs. Assn., Nat. Assn. of Home Mfrs., Nat./Calif. Assn. of Realtors, U.S. Congl. Advy. Bd., Delta Sigma Phi Gen. Alumni Assn.; Republican (Nat. Com., U.S. Congl. Advy. Bd.); rec: architectural design, music. Address: 701 S Parker St Ste 2000 Orange CA 92668

WEINY, GEORGE AZEM, educator, aquatics consultant; b. July 24, 1933, Keokuk, Iowa; s. George Dunn and Emma Vivian (Kraushaar) W.; m. Jane Louise Eland, Sept. 29, 1956 (div. 1985); children: Tami L., Tomas A., Aaron A., Arden G.; m. Lori Arlene Rowe, Aug. 1985; children: Austin George, Breck Philip; edn: BA, Iowa Wesleyan Coll., 1957; MA, State Univ. Iowa, 1962; PhD, Univ. Beverly Hills, 1980. Career: phys. dir. YMCA, Keokuk, 1956-57; asst. dir. pub. relations Iowa Wesleyan Coll., Mt. Pleasant, Iowa 1957-58; prin., tchr., coach Hillsboro (Iowa) High Sch. 1958-59; tchr., coach Burlington (Iowa) High Sch. and Jr. Coll., 1959-62, Pacific High Sch., San Bernardino 1962-67; prof. phys. edn. CSU San Bernardino 1967-; ednl. cons. Belau Modekngei Sch., West Caroline Islands 1984-85; swim meet dir. Nat. Collegiate Athletic Assn., 1982-84, 86-92; tng. dir. for ofcls. So. Calif. Aquatics Fedn., 1967-78; scuba tour guide Dive Maui Resort, Hawaii 1982-83; salvage diver U.S. Trust Territories, 1973; coach YMCA swim team, San Bernardino 1962-77, 84-93; awards: Who's Who Among Students in Univs. & Colls. 1953, outstanding service So. Calif. Aquatics Fedn. 1978, 25-yr. service NISCA, 1985, 25-yr. service Coll. Swim Coaches Assn. 1987, 40-Yr. Outstanding svc. Commodore Longfellow Award Am. Red Cross, 1991; listed Who's Who in Am. Edn. 1992; mem: Profl. Assn. Diving Instrs. (cert.), Nat. Assn. Underwater Instrs. (cert.), Am. Assn. Health Phys. Edn. Recreation and Dance, Coll. Swim Coaches Assn., Am. Swim Coaches Assn. (cert.), Nat. Interscholastic Swim Coaches Assn. (NISCA); civic: Am. Red Cross (county water safety com. San Bdo. 1968-80), YMCA (bd. 1970-77), Bicentennial Commn. San Bdo. 1975-76; club: Sea Sons Dive, Rialto (pres. 1982-83, sec. 1983-93); ed. Swimming Rules and Case Studies, 1970-73, author Snorkeling Fun for Everyone, 1982, contbr. articles various publs.; mil: sgt. U.S. Army 1953-55, named outstanding trainee US Army 1954, Iowa Nat. Guard (SFC) 1955-58; rec: scuba. Res: PO Box 30393 San Bernardino 92413 Ofc: California State University 5500 University Pkwy San Bernardino 92407

WEIR, ALEXANDER, JR., utility consultant; b. Dec. 19, 1922, Crossett, Ark.; s. Alexander and Mary Eloise (Feild) W.; m. Florence Anna Florschner, Dec. 28, 1946; children: Alexander III, b. 1950; Carol Jean, b. 1952; Bruce Richard, b. 1955; edn: BSChE, Univ. Arkansas, 1943; MChE, Polytechnic Inst. of Brooklyn, 1946; PhD, Univ. Michigan, 1954. Career: analytical chemist Am. Cyanamid & Chemical Corp., W. Bauxite, Ark, 1941-42; chem. engr. Am. Cyanamid Stamford Res. Lab., Stamford, CT, 1943-47; res. assoc./prin. investigator Univ. Mich. Engring. Res. Inst., 1948-57; lectr./asst. prof. Univ. Mich., Dept. of Chemical and Metallurgical Engring., 1954-57; head Atlas Missile Captive Test Prog., Ramo-Woolridge Corp., L.A., 1956-60; tech. adv. to pres. Northrup Corp., Beverly Hills, 1960-70; prin. scientist for air quality/mgr. systems R&D/chief res. scientist Southern Calif. Edison Co., Rosemead, 1970-88; pres. Weir Cons., Playa del Rey, 1988-; awards: session chmn. First Nuclear Science and Engring. Cong., Cleveland, 1955; U.S. Delegate, NATO(AGARD) Combustion Colloquium, Belgium, 1955; Nat. Academy of Science, 1975; Nat. Academy of Engring., 1975; Environ. Protection Award (Power), 1980; EPA "Excellence in Sulfur Dioxide Control", 1985; mem: Am. Inst. of Chem. Engr.(emeritus) 1943-, Am. Chem. Soc. 1943-, Sigma Xi 1946-, Am. Assn. for the Adv. of Science (fellow) 1963-90, N.Y. Academy of Science (emeritus) 1966-, Am. Geophysical Union (life) 1970-; civic: Civic Union of Playa del Rey.(com. chmn., gov., pres., 1955-65), Boy Scouts of Am., L.A. (merit badge team, Sea Scout Leader., 1965-70), U.S. Power Squadron, Greenwich, CT and Redondo Beach, 1946-, Santa Monica Yacht Club (fleet capt., scctty., canoneer), Phi Lambda Upsilon, Phi Eta Sigma (hon.), Alpha Chi Sigma (prof.), Lambda Chi Alpha (social); inventor of the Weir Scrubber (4 U.S. patents, German, Japanese, and Canadian patents); author, books: Two and Three Dimension Flow of Air Through Square Edged Sonicoyes, 1954; Notes on Combustion with R.B. Morrison and T.C. Adamson, Univ. Mich. Press, 1955, 2nd ed. 1956; over 50 papers pub. and numerous presentations, rec: sailing; res: 8229 Billowvista Dr. Playa del Rey 90293

WEITZENHOFFER, MARVIN NOAH, company executive; b. March 19, 1930, Philadelphia, Pa.; s. Harry and Ida (Schectman) W.; m. Marilyn Joyce Boyer, Feb. 19, 1955 (div. 1972); m. Elizabeth Agnes Davis, April 30, 1978 (div. 1992); children: Howard b. 1958, Scott b. 1959, Sondra b. 1961, Warren b.

1962, Keith b. 1966; edn: BSEE, Drexel Univ. 1959; MBA, Temple Univ. 1963; lic. landscape contractor Calif. Career: applications engr. Fischer & Porter, Hatboro, Pa. 1955-58; field sales Ampex Corp., Phila., Pa. and Culver City 1959-65; exec. Comp Serv Co., Los Angeles 1965-71; Systems Furniture 1972-75; pres. Plantique, Inglewood 1976-; indep. mktg. cons., 1971-79; guest lectr. UCLA Ext. 1980-; Mt. San Antonio 1980-; mem: Profl. Interior Plantscape Assn. (founding mem. 1987), Assn. Landscape Contractors Am., Sitzmark Condo. Assn. (pres. bd. dirs.); Republican. Ofc: Plantique 224 West Florence Inglewood 90301

WELLING, CONRAD GERHART, ocean minerals company executive; b. June 21, 1919, St. Louis, Mo.; s. Conrad Arthur and Otilla (Brefeld) W.; m. Mary Katherine Henderson, Aug. 26, 1944; children: Bonnie Lynn b. 1947, Conrad Gerhart b. 1950, Patricia b. 1953; edn: MS, U.S. Naval Postgrad. 1948. Career: staff sci. Lockheed, Sunnyvale 1959-61, mgr. operations research 1961-65, mgr. ocean mining 1965-79, v.p. ocean minerals 1979-85, sr. v.p. ocean minerals, Santa Clara 1985-; bd. dirs. Offshore Tech. Conf., Dallas 1982-; mem: Am. Assn. for Advancement of Sci., Maine Tech. Soc., Am. Soc. of Mining Engrs.; inventor Deep Ocean Miner, 1980; mil: cmdr. U.S. Navy, awarded Bronze Star 1943; Republican; R.Cath.; rec: woodworking, photography. Res: 102 Catalpa Dr Atherton 94027 Ofc: Ocean Minerals Co POB 2227 Menlo Park 94026

WELLS, CAROL, corporate education consultant, academic intervention consultant; b. July 3, 1942, N.Y.C.; m. Roger Wells; edn: BS (cum laude), Univ. Bridgeport 1963; MA, Rutgers Univ., 1964; PhD synaesthesia-multisensory perceptual devel. edn. and psychology in edn., Univ. of Conn., 1984, DpEd in ednl. admin., 1981. Career: instr., adminstr. all levels of edn. including 5 colleges and a major mus.; devel. educ. programming for Top Fortune 10 cos.; v.p. Am. Mgmt. Inst., Hartford, Ct. 1984-85; principles of learning instructional specialist Ariz. State Dept. Edn., 1985-86; dir. Academic Intervention/Academic Assocs., Beverly Hills and Orange County, 1986-, consultant sch. systems and pvt. acad. interventions for families and hosps., related orgns.; awards: Dana scholar (undergrad.); mem: Phi Delta Kappa, various orgns. rel. to disabilities; pub. articles on acad. intervention, creativity, corp. publs. on program mgmt., curric., administrn. Ofc: Academic Associates PO Box 3854 Fullerton 92634 Ph: 714/692-5555, 310/246-9995

WELLS, JOHN S., physician; b. June 15, 1934, San Francisco; s. Phillip H. and Marguerite (Brown) W.; m. Retha, 1962 (div. 1971); m. 2d. Judith A. Martois, July 7, 1973; children: Phillip b. 1963, Charles b. 1964, Martin b. 1977, Matthew b. 1979; edn: BA, Stanford Univ. 1956; MD, Univ. Iowa 1965. Career: physician, Arcadia 1969-; deputy dir. Los Angeles Co. Dept Mental Health 1970-93 (ret.); chief of psychiatry Riverside Co. Gen. Hosp. Dept. of Mental Health 1993-; asst. prof. psychiatry USC, L.A. 1977-; mem: Am. Psychiatric Assn. (fellow), So. Calif. Psychiatric Soc. (Councilor 1991-94), Arcadia Police Dept. (res. ofcr. 1980-), BSA (asst. scoutmaster 1988-); mil: lt. USNR 1958-61; Presbyterian; rec: skiing, computers, hiking. Ofc: 735 Duarte Rd #406 Arcadia 91007

WELLS, ROGER F., engineering manager, mechanical engineer; b. Jan. 6, 1945, Portsmouth, England; m. Carol (Maiden Name) W.; children: Nicholas, b. 1971; Lance b. 1971; Darrel, b. 1971; Simon, b. 1973; Geoffrey, b. 1974; edn: C.Eng. MI Mech.E., Inst. of Mechanical Engineers, London, England, 1971; Industrial Adminstrn., Farnborough Technical Coll., 1968; HND Mech., Portsmouth Coll. of Tech., Portsmouth, Eng., 1966; ONC Mech. Engr./Aero, S. Hampton Tech. Coll., Southampton, Eng., 1962; career: managing engr. in charge of vehicle test labs Ministry of Defence, Military Vehicles and Engring. Establishment, Chobham, Eng., 1971-76; programs mgr. UTC, Bicester, Eng., 1976-81; chief engr of preliminary design UTC, Tucson, Ariz., 1981-86; sensor devel. mgr. UTC, Mansfield, Oh., 1986-87; sensor devel. mgr. UTC, City of Industry, Calif., 1987-90; sr. prog. mgr. TRW, Irwindale, Calif., 1990-; mem: Soc. of Automotive Engineers, Inst. of Mechanical Engineers, Inst. of Diagnostic Engineers; author: numerous tech. papers for the Ministry of Defense, England, S.A.E. papers; U.S. patent; rec: gardening; inventing; res: P.O. Box 3854 Fullerton 92634

WELSH, JULI WITTENBERG, building design consultant - computer assisted drafting and design; b. June 11, 1946,New Ulm, Minn.; d. Delmer Henry and Elizabeth Elsie Wittenberg; m. Gregg Welsh, Nov. 13, 1976 (div.); children: Suzanne b. 1978, James b. 1980; edn: BA, Univ. Minn. 1968; BS, City Coll. S.F. 1973; Calif. lic. real estate broker 1980. Career: real estate sales Battino Real Estate, Berkeley 1973-75; designer cons. for residential property remodel, restorations, and revitalization of investment properties; mem. AAUW (chpt. v.p.), League Women Voters (ed. Berkeley L.W.V. mo. newsletter), PTA (Unit pres., Council v.p.); rec: gardening. Res: 95 Depot Rd Montecito 93108

WELSH, WILLIAM DANIEL, physician; b. May 18, 1950, Baltimore, Md.; s. Joseph Leo and Bessie Mary (Tangires) W.; m. Lorraine Lynn Bark-Haus; children: Sean William, Ryan Daniel; edn: BS in biol., cum laude, Fairleigh Dickinson Univ. 1972; Russian lang. stu. Johns Hopkins Univ. 1971; D.O. Coll. of Osteopathic Med. and Surg. 1975; lic. Calif., Mich.; bd. cert. Am. Coll. of Osteo. Gen. Practitioners; Diplomate Nat. Bds. 1976. Career: tng. clerkships,

Mercy Hosp., Baltimore, COMS Coll. Clinics, Des Moines, Haight Ashbury (S.F.) Free Clinic; resident internal medicine Martin Place Hosp., Madison Hts., Mich. 1975-77; physician/ptnr. Family Practice Associates, Whittier 1979-; mem. Friendly Hills Health Network; med. dir. alcohol treatment pgm. Whittier Hosp. Medical Ctr., mem. bd. dirs. 1983- (past: exec. com., v.chief staff, dir. emergency dept., chmn. EG and transfusion com.); med. dir. Mirada Hills Rehab. Hosp. 1980-86; admissions com. Coll. of Osteopathic Med. of the Pacific, clin. assoc. prof. 1980-89; A.C.L.S. instr., past med. dir. Family Asthma Forum 1978-85; honors: Phi Zeta Kappa (FDU), Recognition Awards Pathology 1973, 74; mem. Am. Osteopathic Assn., Calif. Osteo. Assn., Los Angeles Co. Osteo. Assn.; patron Coll. of Osteo. Med. & Surg. Alumni, UCLA Alumni, Loyola H.S., Coll. of Osteo. Med. of the Pacific; pubs: op-ed NY Times; Christian; rec: ocean boating, skiing. Res: 15705 E Gun Tree Dr Hacienda Heights 91745-6346 Ofc: 14350 E Whittier Blvd Ste 100 Whittier 90603

WELSHANS, GARY KEITH, consulting engineer; b. June 3, 1945, Jersey Shore, Pa.; s. Merrill LeRoy and Janet Rae (Dieffenbacher) W.; m. Carolyn Victoria Goudsmit, Jan. 3, 1986; edn: BS engring., UCLA 1968; MS, CSU Los Angeles 1971; DS, N.J. Inst. Tech. 1978; lic. civil engr. Calif. Bd. Profl. Engrs. 1971. Career: civil/hydraulic engr. AUS Corps Engrs., L.A. 1968-71; project engr. Ray Cons. Co., Highland Park, N.J. 1973-74; environ. engr. Stone & Webster Engring. Corp., N.Y.C. 1977-78; assoc. Fred C. Hart Assocs. 1978-80; sr. environ. engr. Stone & Webster Engring Corp. 1980-85; Dames & Moore, San Francisco 1985-; expert witness; mem: ASCE, Nat. Soc. Profl. Engrs., Sigma Xi, West Side YMCA (squash club pres. 1980-85), Jewish Comm. Center (handball club dir. 1986-88); author: Paper Recycling: Recovery of Secondary Fibers by Selective Wettability, 1978; num. papers pub. in tech. jours.; Democrat; Protestant; rec: handball, squash, ballet. Res: 1319 Ortega St San Francisco 94122

WELTON, MICHAEL PETER, dentist; b. Apr. 19, 1957, Milw.; s. Lloyd Peter and Allegra Irene (Nimmer) W.; m. Etsuko Suehiro, Nov. 21, 1986; edn: BS biology, Carroll Coll., 1979; DDS, Univ. of Minn. Sch. of Dentistry, Mpls. 1983. Career: served to lt. USN 1983-90; gen. practice resident in dentistry Naval Hosp., Camp Pendleton, Oceanside, Calif. 1983-84, periodontics dept. Naval Dental Clinic, Yokosuka, Japan 1984-85, clinic director Negishi Dental Annex, Yokohama, Japan 1985-87, general dentist Br. Dental Clinic Mare Island, Vallejo, Calif. 1987-90, div. officer 1988-90; general practice Gateway Dental Office, Rohnert Park, Calif. 1990-91, Napa Valley Comm. Dental Clinic, Napa 1991-; awards: legislative extern Am. Student Dental Assn., W.D.C. 1982, outstanding achiev. Delta Sigma Delta 1983; mem.: Am. Dental Assn. 1979-, Calif. Dental Assn. 1987-, Napa Solano Dent. Soc. (com. chmn. 1988-), Commonwealth Club Calif. (S.F.), World Affairs Council No. Calif. (S.F.), Art Deco Soc. Calif. (S.F.), No. Calif. Golf Assn. (Pebble Beach); Republican; rec: golf, skiing. Res: 480 Evelyn Circle Vallejo 94589 Ofc: Napa Valley Community Dental Clinic 935 Trancas St Ste 4B Napa 94558

WENDELL, PETER C., venture capitalist, educator; b. May 16, 1950, Englewood, NJ; s. Eugene O. and Virginia M. (Robiolio) W.; m. Lynn Mellen, June 14, 1980; children: Christopher b. 1981, Brian b. 1982, Jennifer b. 1984, Carolyn b. 1985, Patrick b. 1988, Emily b. 1990; edn: AB, magna cum laude, Princeton Univ. 1972, MBA, w/high distinction, Harvard Univ. 1976. Career: asst. to Dr. Geo. Gallup Poll, Inc., Princeton, NJ 1971-72; corporate exec. IBM Corp., held 5 positions Data Processing Div., N.Y.C., White Plains and Chgo., 1972-81; pres., gen. ptnr. Sierra Ventures Mgmt. Co., $160 million venture capital fund, Menlo Park, Calif.; dir.: Resna Industries Inc., S.F., Centex Telecommunications Inc., S.F., Providential Corp., S.F.; prof. of entrepreneurship Stanford Univ. Grad. Sch. of Business 1990-; civic bds: Exploratorium (S.F.); clubs: Pacific Union Club, NY Athletic, Harvard (NYC), Princeton (NYC), Univ. Cottage (Princeton); contbr. Journal of Higher Edn. (1980, Ohio St. Univ. Press); R.Cath.; rec: squash, running, lacrosse. Res: 3550 Washington St San Francisco 94118 Ofc: Sierra Ventures, 3000 Sand Hill Rd Menlo Park 94025

WENNERBERG, GUNNAR, electrical engineer, scientist; b. Stockholm, June 3, 1918; s. Gustoaf Alfred and Elin Ida Kristina (Wennerberg) Gustafsson; m. Elsie Christina Forzelius, July 9, 1949 (dec. 1991); children: Leif, Kim, Ingrid, Stefan, Monica; edn: MSEE, Royal Inst. Tech. Stockholm 1942; cert. profl. engr. Calif. Career: tchr., research asst. Royal Inst. Tech. 1941-42; devel. engr. ITT, Stockholm 1942-47; project engr. Lear Inc., Santa Monica 1947-59; devel. engr., mgr. Lockheed, Los Angeles and Sunnyvale 1959-69; sr. staff scientist Measurex Corp., Cupertino 1970-92; cons. in field 1992-; awards: Measurex Corp. 20th Anniversary Technical Achievement. award 1987; mem: IEEE (sr.), Instrument Soc. Am. (past pres. Santa Clara Valley sect.), AAAS; patentee in field. Res: 8129 Park Villa Circle Cupertino 95014

WENTWORTH, THEODORE SUMNER, personal injury lawyer; b. July 18, 1938, Brooklyn, NY; s. Theodore S., Sr., and Alice Ruth (Wortman) W.; m. Sharon Arkush, Mar. 26, 1965 (dec. 1987); children: Christina Linn b. 1968, Kathryn Allison b. 1969; m. Diana von Welanetz, Dec. 9, 1989; stepdau. Lexi b. 1968; edn: JD, UC Hastings Coll. of Law 1962. Career: atty., assoc. Adams, Hunt & Martin, Santa Ana 1963-66; ptnr. Hunt Liljestrom & Wentworth 1967-

77; prin. Law Offices of Theodore S. Wentworth, 1978-; pres. InterProfessional Leasing Inc. 1970-78; dir. Don Burns Inc. and Don Burns Prestige Porsche Audi, Garden Grove, 1970-76; owner Rancho Oro Verde, Pauma Valley 1970-78; owner, developer Eagles Ridge, Temecula 1985-; diplomate Nat. Bd. of Trial Advocates; mem: Calif. Bar Assn., Orange Co. Bar Assn. (bd. dirs. 1972-6), Amer. Trial Lawyers Assn., Calif. Trial Lawyers Assn. (bd. govs. 1968-70), O.C. Trial Lawyers Assn. (pres. 1967-8, Judge pro tem, Attys. Panel 1968-),Lawyer Pilot Bar Assn., Aircraft Owners & Pilots Assn.; civic: Santa Ana - Tustin Comm. Chest (pres. 1972), So. Orange Co. United Way (v.p., dir. 1973-74), Orange Co. Fedn. of Funds (pres. 1972-3), Orange Co. Mental Health Assn. (dir. 1971-74); clubs: Center (Costa Mesa), Pacific (Newport Bch), Balboa Bay (Newport Bch), Bahia Corinthian Yacht (Newport Bch), Corsair Yacht (Emerald Bay, Catalina Is.),Fourth of July Yacht Club (Catalina Is.), Club 33 (Anaheim); works: Vedic researcher & lectr. synthesizing Eastern & Western laws of living in conjunction with num. Vedic scholars in India; Republican; Christian - Vedic; rec: 51 ft. motor yacht "Salute". Res: Corona del Mar Ofc: 2112 Business Center Dr Irvine 92715

WERNER, ROGER H., archaeologist; b. Nov. 11, 1950, N.Y.C.; s. Harry Emile Werner and Rena (Roode) Warren; m. Kathleen Diane Engdahl, Feb. 20, 1982; children: Amber F. Parker (stepdau.) b. 1975, Merly L. b. 1982, Sarah M. b. 1985, Jeremy M. b. 1988; edn: BA, Belkap Coll., 1973; MA, CSU Sonoma, Rohnert Park 1982. Career: curatorial asst. Sonoma State Univ., Rohnert Park 1975-77, staff archaeologist 1977-81; staff archaeologist Lake County Planning Dept., Lakeport 1977; Western Archaeological Ctr., Tucson, Az. 1978; pres. Archaeological Services Inc., Stockton 1979-; instr. CSU Fresno, 1992, San Joaquin Delta Coll. 1991-; mem.: Soc. Profl. Archaeologists 1982-, Soc. of Am. Archaeology 1977-, Soc. of Calif. Archaeology 1977-, Soc. of Historic Archaeology 1991-, Great Basin Anthropol. Conf. 1982-; civic: Kiwanis Club (Stockton), Valley Mountain Regional Ctr. (pres. 1991-92), Stockton Corral (trustee), Colonial Hts. PTSA, Stockton (sec., v.p., 1985-88); contbr. articles in profl. jours. (1979, 91, 92); Democrat; rec: reading, computers, home improve. Res: 1117 Aberdeen Ave Stockton 95209 Ofc: Archaeological Services, Inc. 8110 Lorraine Ave Ste 408 Stockton 95210

WESSLUND, RICHARD ERIK, consulting company president; b. Oct. 18, 1955, Elmhurst, Ill.; s. Richard H. and Erika (Seyboth) W.; m. Magda L. Gutierrez, July 15, 1978; children: Sean Erik b. 1986, Marissa Lynn b. 1987; edn: BS, Elmhurst Coll. 1978; MM fin. and acctg., Kellogg Grad. Sch. of Mgmt. Northwestern Univ., 1980; CPA, Ill., 1981. Career: acct., cons. Coopers & Lybrand, Chgo., Ill. 1980-81; sr. assoc. Booz Allen & Hamilton, S.F. 1981-84; dir. review div. Mission Services Corp., Daly City 1984-85; sr. v.p. Mercy Healthcare, San Diego 1985-90; pres. and c.e.o. BDC Advisors, San Francisco 1990-; dir: J.D.A. Inc., 1988-, Mercy Medical Services Inc. 1989-; pres., The Leadership Inst., 1991-; mem. bd. Ronald McDonald House; honors: Beta Gamma Sigma, Delta Mu Delta, Disting. Scholar Northwestern Univ. (1980); mem: Calif. CPA Soc. 1984-, Am. Hosp. Assn. 1981-, Healthcare Fin. Mgmt. Assn. 1981-, Calif. Assn. of Hosps. & Health System 1989-; Democrat; United Ch. of Christ; rec: sailing, skiing, bicycling. Ofc: BDC Advisors Four Embarcadero Ctr Ste 1570 San Francisco 94111

WEST, JOHN BURNARD, professor of medicine; b. Dec. 27, 1928, Adelaide, Australia (US citizen); s. Esmond Frank and Meta Pauline (Spehr)W.; m. Penelope Hall Banks, Oct. 28, 1967; children: Robert b. 1968, Joanna b. 1971; edn: MBBS, Adelaide Univ. Adelaide, Australia, 1952; MD, Adelaide Univ. 1958; PhD, London Univ., London, Eng., 1960; DSc, Adelaide Univ. 1980. Career: resident Royal Adelaide Hosp., Adelaide, Australia, 1952; resident Hammersmith Hosp., London, Eng., 1953-55; physiologist Sir Edmund Hillary's Himalayan Expedition, 1960-61; dir. Postgraduate Med. Sch., Resp. Res. Group, London, Eng., 1962-67; reader in medicine Postgraduate Med. Sch., London, Eng., 1968; prof. of medicine, physiology, UC San Diego, Calif., 1969-; leader Am. Med. Res. Expedition to Mt. Everest, 1981; US organizer China-US Conf. on Respiratory Failure, Nanjing, 1986; awards: Josiah H. Macy Jr. Found. Faculty Scholar 1974 Ernst Jung Prize for Medicine, Hamburg, W. Germany, 1977, Presidential Citation, Am. Coll. of Chest Physicians 1977, Kaiser Award for Excellence in Tchg. 1980, Orr Reynolds Prize for History, Am. Physiological Soc. 1987, Doctor Honoris Causa, Univ. of Barcelona, Spain 1987, Cosmos Biosatellite award, NASA 1990, Jeffries Med. Res. award, Am. Inst. of Aeronautics and Astronautics 1992, fellow, AAAS 1987-, founding fellow, Am. Inst. for Med. and Biological Engring. 1992-, disting. lectr. at colleges, universities and profl. assns. in US, Canada, England, Russia, the Philippines, So. Africa, Australia and New Zealand 1971-; mem: Am. Physiological Soc., Am. Soc. for Clinical Investigation, Am. Soc. for Gravitation and Space Biology, Am. Thoracic Soc., Assn. of Am. Physicians, Assn. of Chmn. of Depts. of Physiology, Explorers Club, The Fleischner Soc., Harveian Soc. of London, Internat. Soc. for Mountain Medicine, Physiological Soc. (of Great Britain), We. Assn. of Physicians; fellow, Royal Institution of Great Britain, Royal Geographical Soc.(UK); mem. Hurlingham Club, London, Eng., La Jolla Beach & Tennis Club, S.D.; author, books: Ventilation/Bloodflow and Gas Exchange, 1965, 70, 77, 85, 90 (2 fgn. lang. transl. 1980); Respiratory Physiology-The Essentials, 1974, 80, 85, 90 (11 fgn. lang. transl. 1975-90); ed.,

Translations in Respiratory Physiology, 1975; ed., Regional Differences in the Lung, 1977; ed., Bioengineering Aspects of the Lung, 1977; Pulmonary Pathophysiology-The Essentials, 1977, 82, 87, 91 (7 fgn. lang. transl. 1978-89); Everest-The Testing Place, 1985; ed., Pulmonary Gas Exchange. I. Ventilation, Bloodflow and Diffusion. II. Organism and Environment, 1980; ed., High Altitude Physiology, 1981; co-editor, High Altitude and Man, 1984; Everest-The Testing Place, 1985; ed., Best & Taylor's Physiological Basis of Medical Practice, 1985, 91, study guide & self-examination review 1985; co-ed., High Altitude Medicine and Physiology, 1989; chief ed. with R.G. Crystal, The Lung: Scientific Foundations (2 vols.) 1991, Lung Injury 1992. Ofc: UCSD Dept. of Medicine 0623, 9500 Gilman Drive La Jolla 92093-0623

WEST, JULIAN RALPH, photographer; b. Dec. 12, 1915, Hot Springs, S.Dak.; s. Joseph C. and Helen E. (Nason) W.; m. Marvel E. Knorr, May 1, 1937, Alliance, Nebr.; children: Stuart J. b. 1938 (dec. Apr. 28, 1988), R. Bruce b. 1940, Judy (Mrs. Donald L. McDermott) b. 1943; edn: BA, Univ. Okla. 1969; Cert. Profl. Contracts Mgr., CPA (Calif., inactive), Cert. Internal Auditor (inactive). Career: public acct. 1946-49; acct. Office of Auditor General, USAF, 1949-62; audit policy div. Ofc. of Secty. of Defense, Pentagon, 1962-67, chief Procurement Review Div. 1967-73; instr. UCLA Ext. Univ. 1977-81; freelance photography and audio/visual presentations, 1979-; pres. Julmik Enterprises, 1980-; mem: Am. Inst. of CPAs, Nat. Contract Mgmt. Assn. (fellow, past nat. dir.), Internat. Freelance Photogs. Orgn., Assoc. Photographers Internat., Photographic Soc. Internat.; civic: Gr. L.A. Zoo Assn., Christian Businessmen's Com. of USA, Hollywood YMCA (bd. govs.); sev. travel clubs; Presbyterian (elder). Res: 1955 No Tamarind Ave, No. 14, Hollywood 90068

WEST, SANDI JEAN, real estate loan agent, marketer of trust deeds, and telecommunications reseller; b. Sept. 12, 1945, San Francisco; d. Lyle Hazen and Georgia Arlene (West) Reiswig; edn: AA (bus. administration), San Joaquin Delta Jr. Coll. 1977. Career: eligibility worker San Joaquin County Welfare Dept., Stockton 1968-75; child support collections supr. San Joaquin County Dist. Atty.'s Ofc., Stockton 1975-79; credit mgr. E.D. Wilkinson Grain Co., Stockton 1979-80; agent, estates mgr. Calif. Dept. Devel. Svcs., Sacramento 1980-85; trust ofcr. Sonoma Devel. Ctr., Eldridge 1985-88; pres. West and Associates, Sonoma 1989-; dist. dir. Communications Group of Am. (CGA), Vacaville 1992-; fund raising coord. Sonoma County NOW 1993-; loaned executive alumni United Way for North Bay 1990-, loaned executive United Way for North Bay 1989; volunteer police ofcr. Stockton Police Dept. 1968-74; Nonpartisan. Res: POB 1488 Eldridge 95431 Ofc: West and Associates 164 Vista Dr Sonoma 95476 Tel:707/935-0486; Ofc: CGA 479 Mason St #213 Vacaville 95688 Tel: 707/448-1071

WESTERDAHL, JOHN BRIAN, nutritionist, health educator; b. Dec. 3, 1954, Tucson, Ariz.; s. Jay Emanuel and Margaret Camille (Meyer) W.; m. Doris Mui Lian Tan, Nov. 18, 1989; edn: AA, Orange Coast Coll., Costa Mesa, Calif. 1977; BS, Pacific Union Coll., Angwin, Calif. 1979; MPH, Loma Linda Univ., Loma Linda, Calif. 1981; reg. dietitian Am. Dietetic Assn., 1983. Career: nutritionist, health educator Castle Medical Ctr., Kailua, Hawaii, 1981-84, health promotion coord. 1984-87, asst. dir., dir. of health promotion 1987-89; dir. nutrition and health research Health Science, Santa Barbara, Calif. 1989-90; senior nutritionist Shaklee Corp., San Francisco 1990-; talk show host "Nutrition and You" KGU Radio, Honolulu 1983-89; apptd. mem. nutrition study gp. Gov.'s Conf. on Health Promotion and Disease Prevention for Hawaii, 1985; nutrition com. mem. Am. Heart Assn. Hawaii Div. 1984-87; awards: Outstanding Young Men of Am. US Jaycees 1984, One of 10 Outstanding Young Persons in Hawaii, Hawaii Jaycees 1988; mem: AAAS, Am. Coll. of Sports Medicine, Am. Dietetic Assn., Calif. Dietetic Assn., Am. Soc. of Nutrition, Am. Soc. Pharmacognosy, NY Acad. Scis., Hawaii Nutrition Council (v.p. 1983-86, pres. 1989), Seventh-Day Adventist Dietetic Assn.; Republican; Seventh-Day Adventist; rec: swimming, scuba. Ofc: Shaklee Corp. 444 Market St San Francisco 94111

WESTHEM, ANDREW DAVID, financial service co. president; b. May 5, 1933, N.Y. state; s. David Sigmond and Nancy (Addington) W.; m. Emily Wigchert, Aug. 6, 1955; children: David Andrew, Lisa Ann; edn: USC 1955, Wharton Sch. of Exec. Mgmt. 1979; Chartered Life Underwriter. Career: gen. mgr. Mutual of New York, Beverly Hills 1962-83; pres. Nat. Employment Leasing Corp., 1983-85; chmn./pres. Western Capital Group 1985-, consulting and design co. (design tax-advantage investment pgms. for major insurance cos.), reg. securities broker/dealer, insurance agency w/clients in 46 states; Western Capital sponsors Westhem Racing, Inc. (profl. off-road racing team); civic: YMCA Beverly Hills (dir. 1977-80), Cystic Fibrosis Found. (chmn. 1968-70), Hemophiliac Found. (chmn. 1973-80); Episcopal; rec: tennis, auto racing. Res: 2187 Century Woods Way Los Angeles 90067 Ofc: Western Capital Financial Group 1925 Century Park East, Suite 2350 Los Angeles 90067

WESTON, J. FRED, economist, professor emeritus; b. Feb. 6, 1916, Ft. Wayne, Ind.; s. David Thomas and Bertha (Schwartz) W.; m. June Sherman, May 16, 1942 (dec. 1986); children: Kenneth F. b. 1945, Byron L. b. 1948, Ellen F. b. 1949; m. Eva Dixon, Jan. 3, 1987; edn: AB, MBA, PhD, Univ. of Chicago, 1937, 43, 48. Career: instr. Univ. Chgo. 1940-42; economic cons. to the pres. American Bankers Assn. 1945-46; asst. prof. Univ. Chgo. 1947-48; prof. emeritus UCLA, Los Angeles 1949-; res. pgm. in competition and bus. policy Anderson Grad. Sch. of Mgmt. UCLA 1969-, dir. Res. Ctr. for Managerial Economics and Pub. Policy, AGSM-UCLA 1983-; awards: Cardinal O'Hara Memorial lectr. Notre Dame Univ. 1965, Disting. Lecture Series- Univ. Okla. 1967, Miss. St. Univ., Univ. Utah 1972, Wright St. Univ., Miami St. Univ. 1975, disting. tchg. UCLA 1978, Cordner Chair, UCLA 1983; mem: Western Economic Assn. (pres. 1960), Am. Finance Assn. (pres. 1966), Western Finance Assn. (honoree for contbns. to fin., S.F., 6/79), Am. Econ. Assn., Econometric Soc., Am. Statistical Assn., Royal Econ. Soc., Financial Analysts Soc., Financial Mgmt. Assn. (pres. 1979-80, exec. bd. 81-83); editl. bds: Business Economics, J. of Financial Res., Managerial and Decision Economics, Southern Business Review; coauthor 5 texts, contbr. articles to profl. jours.; mil: chief warrant ofcr. Ord. D., US Army 1943-45; Indep.; rec: music, walking, tennis, dancing. Res: 500 Bonhill Rd Los Angeles 90049 Ofc: UCLA 405 Hilgard Los Angeles 90024-1481

WESTOVER, SAMUEL LEE, medical insurance financial executive; b. May 30, 1955, Soap Lake, Wash.; s. Gordon Kent W. and Janice Lelia (Matlock) Jensen; m. Susan Kern, July 13, 1977; children: Michael b. 1980, S. Fielding b. 1981, Austin b. 1983, Clinton b. 1986, Cassandra b. 1989; edn: BS acctg., Brigham Young Univ., 1978; C.P.A., Calif. 1981. Career: acct. Price Waterhouse, L.A. 1978-80; c.f.o. and senior v.p. Maxicare Health Plans, L.A. 1981-88; c.e.o. and chief ops. Western Health Plans, San Diego 1988-90; c.f.o. and senior v.p. Blue Cross of Calif., Woodland Hills 1990-93; c.f.o. and sr. v.p. Wellpoint Health Networks, Woodland Hills 1993-; LDS Ch. Ofc: Wellpoint Health Networks Woodland Hills 91367

WETTACH, GEORGE EDWARD, physician; b. June 11, 1940, San Jose; s. George Angevine and Glodine Lillian (Wilks) W.; m. Rose Ann Nemeth, Nov. 24, 1966 (div. Mar. 1988); children: George Randolphe b. 1971, Shannon Elizabeth b. 1977, Robin Scot b. 1978; m. Linda Kay Ridgley, June 10, 1989; edn: pre-med., San Jose State Coll., 1962; MD, St. Louis Univ., 1966. Career: chief medical resident St. Louis Univ., Mo. 1973-74; emergency physician St. Louis (Mo.) City Hosp., 1974-75, St. John's Mercy Med. Ctr., Creve Coeur, Mo. 1975-77; med. dir. St. Louis EMS, 1977-85; emergency physician Nat. Emergency Services Inc., Tiburon, Calif. 1985-90; attdg. physician San Francisco Gen. Hosp., 1988-; clin. instr. Univ. Calif., San Francisco 1989-; sr. flight surgeon Naval Air Reserve, NAS Alameda 1990-, Capt. Med. Corps USNR, 1968-; pres. Health Edn. Foundation for Television Inc., Menlo Park 1978-; awards: Tau Delta Phi 1959, Nat. Polaroid Photo Contest Award 1985, US Naval Inst. Maritime Photo Contest 1989, Stock car racing award Allied Auto Racing Assn., St. Louis, Mo. 1980; mem: Aerospace Med. Assn. (assoc. fellow 1973-), Assn. of Military Surgeons of U.S., U.S. Naval Inst., Naval Reserve Assn., Reserve Ofcrs. Assn., Tailhook Assn.; civic: Pasadena Community Symphonic Orch. (mem. 1971-72), Menlo Park Art Commn. (chair 1987-); publs: 20+ med. jour. articles (1973-86); Republican; Prot.; rec: stock car racing, music, photog., art. Res: 193 Willow Rd Menlo Park 94025 Ofc: Naval Air Reserve, Medical, Bldg 16, NAS Alameda 94501

WETZEL, SANDRA KAYE, actress, sales & marketing executive; b. Feb. 10, 1954, Greenville, Tx.; d. Royce Monroe and Connie Faye (Chesshier) Collins; m. Stephen Robert Wetzel, Feb. 4, 1984; edn: H.S. grad., 1972; cert., corporate sales & mgmt. tng. courses Holiday Inn Corp., Tenn. Univ., 1986, Cornell Univ., 1989. Career: sales mgr. Holiday Inn Anaheim 1986-87; dir. of tour & travel Ibis Hotel, Anaheim 1987; dir. sales Holiday Inn Fullerton 1987-89; dir. sales & mktg. Ramada Inn Norwalk 1989-, sales mgr. Embassy Suites, Mandalay Beach, 1990-; actress, appeared on Twin Peaks (TV series), Johnny Mathis Christmas Video, Working Trash (TV movie), Kaiser Permanente industrial film; mem: Performing Arts Conservatory, Screen Actors Guild, Hotel Sales & Mktg. Assn. (Anaheim chpt. bd. 1989), Anaheim C.of C., Fullerton C.of C.; civic: St. Jude's Hosp., Boys Ranch of Edmonton, Okla., Make a Wish Found.; pub: poems: A Time To Be Free (Quill Books, 1989), Days of our Future Past, Vol. II; rec: sing, write poetry, model (New Model Pageant 1989, Calif. Gold Coast Pageant 1987). Res: 3658 Barham Blvd #P203 Los Angeles 90068-1121

WEXLER, JUDIE GAFFIN, dean of academic affairs; b. Apr. 15, 1945, New York; d. Isaac Pearlman and Sara (Widensky) P.; m. Howard M. Wexler, Mar. 11, 1973; children: Robyn b. 1975, Matthew b. 1978; edn: BA, Sociology, Russell Sage Coll., Troy, NY, 1965; MA, Demography, Univ. of Pa., Phila., 1966; PhD, Sociology, UC Berkeley, 1965; career: dir., NY State Dept. of Mental Hygiene, Albany, NY, 1966-67; demographer and urban sociologist, S.F. Dept. of City Planning, S.F., Calif., 1967-68; prof. of sociology, Holy Names Coll., Oakland, Calif., 1974-91; dean of academic affairs, Holy Names Coll., 1992-; mem: grant proposal review bd., Sociology Prog., NSF, 1990; Am. Sociological Assn.; Am. Psychological Assn., Div. on Women; Calif. Sociological Assn.; Sociologists for Women in Soc.; awards: S.F. Police Dept. Recognition Award, 1984; Pi Gamma Mu, Nat. Social Sci. Honor Soc.; Population Council Fellowship, Univ. of Calif., 1968-69 and 1970-71; NDEA

Fellowship, Univ. of Pa., 1965-66; Milhouse Award in Sociology, 1965; listed in Who's Who in the West (1991), Dictionary of Internat. Biography (1990), Internat. Who's Who of Prof. and Bus. Women (1989-); Two Thousand Notable Amer. Women (1988); Personalities of the Americas (1987), Who's Who of Emerging Leaders in Amer. (1987-), Who's Who of Amer. Women (1982-); editor: Berkeley Jour. of Sociology, 1973-74; author: numerous publs. in prof. jours.; papers and lectures presented to prof. assns. and colleges. Ofc: Holy Names College 3500 Mountain Blvd. Oakland 94619

WEYGAND, LEROY CHARLES, security consultant; b. May 17, 1926, Webster Park, Ill.; s. Xaver William and Marie Caroline (Hoffert) W.; m. Helen V. Bishop, Aug. 28, 1977; children: Linda M. Weygand Vance (dec.), Leroy Charles, Cynthia R., Janine P.; edn: BA in sociology (cum laude), Univ. Md., 1964. Career: enlisted U.S. Army, 1944, commd. 2d lt., 1950, advanced through grades to lt. col., 1966, service in Korea, 1950, chief phys. security U.S. Army, 1965-70, ret. 1970, decorated Legion of Merit; pres. Weygand Security Cons. Services, Anaheim 1970-, W & W Devel. Corp., 1979-; security dir. Jefferies Banknote Co., 1972-78; pres. Kern County Taxpayers Assn., 1986-; dir. Mind Psi-Biotics, Inc.; mem. Nat. Assn. Control Narcotics and Dangerous Drugs (bd.); patentee Office Equipment Locking Device; contbr. articles profl. jours. Address: 1415 - 18th St Ste 407 Bakersfield 93301

WHALEY, CHARLES EDWARD, health organization executive director; b. Feb. 29, 1928, Williamstown, Ky.; s. Charles Fred and Mary Kathleen (Neal) W.; m. Carol Sutton, Nov. 23, 1957 (dec. 1985); children: Carrie Elizabeth (Orman), Kate Wallace; edn: AB in journ., Univ. Ky., Lexington 1949; MS, Columbia Univ. Grad. Sch. of Journ., 1950; MA arts & scis. (Marshall scholar), Univ. of Manchester, Eng. 1957; grad. study in edn. Univ. Louisville, Ky. 1965; Accred. in Pub. Rels. (APR) Public Relations Soc. Am. Career: asst. to research dir. School Executive Magazine, N.Y.C. summer 1949; reporter The Courier-Journal, Louisville, Ky. 1950-60, edn. editor 1960-64; dir. of res. and info. Kentucky Edn. Assn., 1964-72, dir. pub. relations and res., 1972-82, dir. communications, 1982-85; exec. dir. American Lung Assn. of San Francisco, 1985-; author: Beyond the Minimum: A New Dimension for Kentucky's Foundation Program for Edn. (1967); columnist, reviewer STAGES mag., N.Y.C. 1986-; awards: Sullivan Medallion for outstanding senior Univ. Ky. 1949, British govt. Marshall scholar 1954-56, Phi Beta Kappa, Sigma Phi Epsilon frat. pres., Yearbook editor The Kentuckian 1948-49, winner top nat. award Education Writers Assn. 1962, named outstanding P.R. profl. in Ky. and Tenn. We. Ky. Univ. 1982; mem: Pub. Rels. Soc. Am. (pres. S.F. Bay Area chapt. 1991, pres. Bluegrass chapt. Louisville 1978), Bay Area Theatre Critics Circle (sec. treas. 1990-); past mem. civic bds., Louisville, Ky.: L. Theatrical Assn., L. Art Gallery, Louisville and Jefferson County Youth Orch., Sister Cities of Louisville Inc. (chmn. Quito Com. 1982-84), First Unitarian Ch., L. (pres. bd. trustees 1980); rec: music, theatre, reading, travel. Res: 443 Prentiss St San Francisco 94110 Ofc: American Lung Assn. of San Francisco 562 Mission St Ste 203 San Francisco 94105 Tel: 415/543-4410

WHANG, SUKOO JACK, clinical pathologist; b. Feb. 3, 1934, Korea; nat. 1963; s. Seung Il and Young Sook (Kim) W.; m. Chung A. Park, Nov. 30 1963; children: Selena b. 1964, Stephanie b. 1970, John b. 1972; edn: BS, Ore. St. Univ. 1957; MS, UCLA 1960; PhD, UCLA 1963; MD, Korea Univ. 1972; diplomate Am. Bd. Pathology, Am. Bd. Tropical Medicine. Career: asst. prof. CSU, Pomona 1963-64; chief microbiologist Providence Hosp., Southfield, Mich. 1964-65; dir. microbiol. Immunol. Div. Reference Lab., Newbury Park 1965-69; adj. prof. Pacific Union Coll., 1977-87; currently clin. pathologist/dir. microbiology-serology div., White Meml. Med. Ctr., Los Angeles, also chmn. Infection Control Com.; honors: Sigma Xi., Am. Men & Women of Sci., Who's Who in West; mem: AMA, Calif. Med. Assn., Coll. of Am. Pathologists (Fellow), Am. Coll. Physicians (Fellow), N.Y. Acad. Scis., Soc. of Hosp. Epidemiologists of Am.; res. in clin. microbiol., syphilis, serology & diagnostic tests for detection of inborn errors of metabolism; Republican; Seventh Day Adventist; rec: tennis, swimming, music. Res: 1325 Via Del Rey South Pasadena 91030 Ofc: White Memorial Medical Center 1920 Brooklyn Ave Los Angeles 90033

WHIPPLE, ELEANOR BLANCHE, educational and social work administrator; b. June 7, 1916, Bellingham, Wash.; d. Charles Wm. and Blanche (Campbell) W.; m. Robert Auld Fowler, Oct. 1, 1938 (div. 1947); children: Lawrence b. 1942, Jeanice Marie Roosevelt b. 1946; edn: BA sociology, Univ. Wash., 1938; MSW, 1949; PhD ednl. psych., Univ. Santa Barbara 1983; Lic. Clin. Social Worker, Calif. 1969. Career: founder/dir. Camp Cloud's End for Disadvantaged Children, Deception Pass, Wash. 1939-42; caseworker Family Counseling Service, Seattle 1949-58; social service dir. Hollygrove Children's Residential Ctr., Hollywood 1960-66, exec. dir. 1966-81; adj. lectr. Biola Univ., La Mirada 1972-80; prof. and dean Calif. Christian Inst., Orange 1981-85; pres. Trinity Coll. of Grad. Studies 1985-; exec. dir. Hotline Crisis Help Ctr., Orange 1989-; honors: gold card Nat. Assn. Social Workers 1975; mem: No. Am. Assn. Christians in Social Work (past pres. disting. service award 1986), Assn. of Christian Therapists, Christian Fellowship for the Blind Internat. (v.p. 1984-89); publs.: jour. articles in Social Work and Christianity 1980, 84; Democrat;

Christian Ch.; rec: camping, watercolor. Res: 1105 Mound Ave #9 South Pasadena 91030 Ofc: Trinity College of Graduate Studies 1744 W Katella Ste 26 Orange 92667

WHITAKER, JULIAN MC KEY, president, founder medical treatment center; b. Aug. 7, 1944, San Antonio, Tx.; s. William George and Elise (McKey) W.; children: Julian McKey b. 1972; edn: AB, Dartmouth Coll. 1966; MD, Emory Univ. Medical Sch. 1970. Career: med. surgery intern Emory Univ. 1970-71, res. surg. sub-splty., Univ. of Calif. Med. Center, San Francisco 1971-73; pvt. practice medicine, Van Nuys 1973-76; staff physician Longevity Center (dir. Nathan Pritikin) 1976-77; originator of LEAN, system of disease prevention, 1977-78, founder/pres. Calif. Heart Medical Clinic, Inc. 1978-; instr. Adv. Life Support Systems, The Am. Heart Assn.; frequent lectr. profl. groups, univs., colls.; mem: Orthomolecular Med. Soc. (v.p. 1976-78), Calif. Orthomolecular Med. Soc. (founder, v.p. 1974), Internat. Acad. of Metabology, Am. Holistic Med. Soc. (founder), past mem. Acad. of Orthomolecular Psychiatrists; author: Reversing Heart Disease (hardback, Warner Books, 1985, paperback ed. in press), Reversing Diabetes (hardback, Warner Books, 1987); Methodist; rec: distance runner, tennis, golf. Ofc: The Whitaker Wellness Institute 4400 MacArthur Blvd Newport Beach 92660

WHITAKER, THOMAS W., biologist, plant geneticist; b. Aug. 13, 1904, Monrovia; s. Walter Raymond and Mamie (Dunn) W.; m. Mary Beverley Somerville, Aug. 15, 1931 (dec. 1971); children: Thomas W., Jr. b. 1934, Beverly W. Rodgers b. 1936; m. Dixie Long, July 7, 1978; edn: BS, UC Davis, 1927; MS, Univ. Va., 1929, PhD, 1931. Career: DuPont fellow Univ. Va., 1927-31; fellow Arnold Arboretum Harvard Univ., 1931-34; assoc. prof. biol. Agnes Scott Coll., 1934-36; assoc. geneticist, sr. geneticist and investigation ldr. U.S. Dept. Agric., 1936-73, La Jolla 1936-73, collaborator USDA 1973-86, ret.; res. assoc. marine biol. UC San Diego, 1964-73; awards: Alpha Zeta, Sigma Xi, Andrew Flemming prize in biol. Univ. Va. 1931, Guggenheim Found. Fellow (1946-47, 59-60), guest lectr. horticulture Purdue Univ. 1964, disting. lectr. biol. Tulane Univ. 1967, guest lectr. genetics Univ. Ariz. 1967, guest lectr. genetics Univ. Rajistan & Indian Agric. Res. Inst. 1972, mem. Whitaker-Knight plant expedition to Mexico 1980, Whitaker-Providenti plant expdn. to Turkey and Greece 1983, del. Hortic. People to People, Peoples Republic of China 1985, Explorers Club, Man of Yr. Calif. Garden Clubs Inc.; mem: Am. Soc. Hortic. Sci. (pres. 1974-75, jour. editor 1970-75), Soc. Econ. Botany (pres. 1969, Econ. Bot. Award 1980), Zool. Soc. San Diego (advisor), Bot. Soc. Am., Am. Plant Life Soc. (exec. secty., jour. editor 1959-87, rec'd Herbert Medal 1989), Am. Soc. Naturalists, N.Y. Acad. Sci., AAAS (fellow), Can. Hort. Soc. (hon. life), Am. Soc. Archeology, Torrey Pines Bot. Club (pres.), Explorers Club 1986; author: The Cucurbits; introduced 6 new varieties of lettuce and melons, developed for disease resistance; contbr. 150+ res. papers in sci. jours.; Democrat; rec: plant breeding - Amaryllids. Res: 2534 Ellentown Rd La Jolla 92037

WHITE, BRIAN WILLIAM, stockbroker; b. Sept. 5, 1934, Seattle; s. George Carlos and Mae Mary (McCann) W.; m. Christine Catherine Nelson, June 2, 1955 (div. 1970); m. Barbara Maureen Scott, May 21, 1974; children: Catherine b. 1956, Teresa b. 1958, Patrick b. 1959, Melissa b. 1962, Christopher b. 1964, Meghan b. 1980, Erin b. 1982; edn: BS, UC Berkeley, 1958, MBA, 1959. Career: acctg. mgr. Pacific NW Bell Tel. Co., Seattle, Wash. 1959-68; reg. rep. Dominick & Dominick, Sea. 1968-74; dir. Western Search Assocs., San Diego 1974-82; investment exec. Bateman Eichler, San Diego 1982-90; pres. White Securities Inc., La Mesa 1990-; Republican; R.Cath.; rec: golf. Res: 1038 Vista Sierra Dr El Cajon 92019 Ofc: 8363 Center Dr Ste 600 La Mesa 91942

WHITE, JAN, business consultant; b. July 14, 1949, Yonkers, N.Y.; d. Max E. and Shirley D. (Hamburger) Feinberg; children: Shawn b. 1972; edn: BA acctg., Columbia Pacific Univ. 1984. Career: asst. gen. mgr. Greyhound Food Mgmt. Corp.; asst. chief cost acct. United Bank Denver, Colo.; acctg. supr. Payless Stores Corp., corp. offices, Oakland; acctg. mgr. Equitec Fin. Group, Lafayette; controller, cost acctg. mgr. I T Corp., Martinez; cost acctg. mgr. and mgr.- systems design, data processing and budget/forecasting, Membrana Inc., Pleasanton; business consultant, pres. J W Business Solutions; past co-owner/c.f.o. Gamma Graphics, Inc.; appt: comml. arbitrator on behalf of the Am. Arbitration Assn., assoc. ed. of the "Update" (bus. mag.), advsy. bd. of the "Diablo Business" mag.; listed Internat. Who's Who of Profl., Bus. Women, Who's Who in West, 2000 Notable Women in Am., The World Who's Who of Women, Standard & Poor's Register of Corps., Dirs. and Execs.; mem: Nat. Assn. Accts. (dir. 1982-85, 2 tech. manuscript awards), Assoc. Builders & Contractors (referral bus. cons. 1987-), Bay Area Soc. Info. Centers, Entrepreneurs Assn. Diablo Valley, Walnut Creek C.of C., Contra Costa Council, Internat. Trade Assn.; author: Cost Acctg. Principles and Applications for Layman Use (1984); The Break Even Relationship for Cost Conscious Managers; articles: Power of the Word (philosophical), When It's Time To Take The Band-Aids Off, When It's Time To Find The Right Consultant, Paper Flow Problems May Be Costing You More Than You Realize, Purchasing The Perfect Computer & Software Isn't Enough, Handling Substance Abuse In The Workplace, Pricing Your Services For Long Term Survival; media interviews, lectr. seminars; rec: equestrienne, x-c skiing, walking. Ofc: 103 Crosby Ct Ste 1 Walnut Creek 94598

WHITE, KATHERINE E., physician, pediatrician; b. Mar. 23, 1920, Syracuse, N.Y.; d. Rufus M. and Marguerite Mary (Eselin) White; m. Nicholas V. Oddo, Feb. 12, 1947 (dec. 1966); edn: BA, Syracuse Univ. 1941; MD, 1943. Career: intern Syracuse Univ. Med. Center, Syracuse, N.Y. 1944-45; asst. resident, chief resident Buffalo Children's Hosp. 1945-47; resident, outpatient dept. Los Angeles Children's Hosp. 1947; pediatrician, Long Beach 1947-90; asst. clin. prof. pediatrics UC Irvine Sch. Medicine 1967-; bd. trustees Miller Children's Hosp., Long Beach 1970-; bd. dirs. Children's Clin. 1974-88; bd. med. edn. Meml. Med. Center & Univ. 1987-; honors: Phi Beta Kappa, Citizen of Year Rotary 1967, recogn. Children's Clinic Long Beach 1981, Meml. Med. Center Found. Commend. 1984, Found. Children's Health Care Humanitarian 1987, Soroptimist Woman of Distinction 1987, Soroptimist Hall of Fame 1990, 1st Annual Katherine White MD Humanitarian 1990, Long Beach Rotary Outstanding Philanthropist Award Meml. Med. Ctr. Found. 1990; mem: Am. Acad. Pediatrics, CMA, L.A. Co. Med. Assn., Long Beach Med. Assn., Am. Women's Med. Assn., L.A. Co. Pediatric Soc., Soroptimist Internat., Found. Children's Health Care, Kappa Delta Alumni Assn.; Republican; Catholic; rec: numismatics, philately. Res: 6354 Riviera Circle Long Beach 90815

WHITE, ROBERT LEE, university professor; b. Feb. 14, 1927, Plainfield, N.J.; s. Claude and Ruby H. E. (Levick) W.; m. Phyllis Arlt, June 14, 1952; children: Lauren A. b. 1954, Kimberly A. b. 1956, Christopher L. b. 1952, Matthew P. b. 1967; edn: BA, Columbia Coll., NY, 1949; MA, Physics, Columbia Univ., NY, 1951; PhD, Physics, Columbia Univ., 1954. Career: sci. staff Hughes Res. Labs, Malibu, 1954-61; dept. head General Tel. & El. Labs, Palo Alto, 1961-63; assoc. prof EE, Stanford Univ., 1963-67; prof., EE & MS & E, Stanford Univ., 1967-87; dir. The Exploratorium, S.F., 1987-90; prof. EE & MS & E, Stanford Univ., 1990-; dir.: Stanford Ctr. for Res. on Information Storage Materials, 1991-, Spectrotherm Corp., Santa Clara, 1965-70; initial limited ptnr. Mayfield Funds I & II, Menlo Park, 1969-73; dir.: Biostim Corp., Princeton, N.J., 1975-81, Analog Design Tools, Menlo Park, 1981-86; gen. ptnr. Halo Partners, Ft. Lauderdale, Fla., 1985-; awards: Fellow, Amer. Physical Soc., NYC 1962; Fellow, Inst. Elect. & Electronic Engring. NYC. 1975; Guggenheim Fellow, Guggenheim Found., Oxford 1969-70, Zurich 1978; vis. prof. Japan Soc. for Promotion of Sci., Tokyo, 1975; Christensen Fellow, Oxford Univ., Oxford, Eng., 1986; mem: Phi Beta Kappa 1949, Sigma Xi (hon. sci. soc.), 1952; author: 120 tech. articles publ. in profl. journals, 1952-; Basic Quantum Mechanics, 1967; ed., Magnetism & Magnetic Materials, 1965. Mil: ETM 3/C, USN, 1945-46; Independent; Prot.; rec: reading, gardening, travel. Res: 450 El Escarpado Way Stanford 94305

WHITE, ROBERT STEPHEN, physicist, emeritus prof. of physics; b. Dec. 28, 1920, Ellsworth, Kans.; s. Byron F. and Sebina Ethyl (Leighty) White; m. Freda Marie Bridgewater, Aug. 30, 1942; children: Nancy b. 1945; Margaret b. 1949; John b. 1950; David b. 1953; edn: AB, Southwestern Coll., Winfield, Kans., 1942; MS, Univ. of Ill., 1943; PhD, UC Berkeley, 1951; career: physicist, Lawrence Radiation Lab., Berkeley and Livermore, 1948-61; head, particles and fields dept., Aerospace Corp., El Segundo, 1962-67; prof. of physics, UC Riverside, 1967-92; dir., inst. of geophysics and planetary physics, UC Riverside, 1967-92; chair, physics dept., UC Riverside, 1970-73; awards: NSF Sr. Postdoctoral Fellow, Munich, Germany, 1961-62; Honorary DSc, Southwestern Coll., 1971; grantee numerous grants and contracts, NASA, NSF, ONR, OAR, DOE, others, 1967-92; mem: fellow, mem., Am. Physical Soc., 1951-; Am. Geophysical Union, 1959-; Am. Astronomical Soc., 1970-; AAAS, 1975-; AAUP, 1967-; author: Space Physics, 1970; 125 pub. articles in scientific journals, 1949-; mil: lt. j.g. USN, 1944-46; Republican; Methodist. Res: 5225 Austin Rd. Santa Barbara 93111. Ofc: Inst. of Geophysics and Planetary Physics, Univ. of Calif. Riverside 92521

WHITE, STANLEY ARCHIBALD, research electrical engineer; B. Sept. 25, 1931, Providence, R.I.; s. Clarence Archibald White and Lou Ella (Givens) Arford; m. Edda Maria Castano-Benitez, June 6, 1956; children: Dianne, Stanley Jr., Paul, John; edn: BSEE, Purdue Univ., 1957, MSEE, 1959, PhD, 1965; reg. profl. engr. Ind., Calif. Career: engr. Rockwell Internat. Corp., Anaheim 1959-68, mgr. 1968-84, senior scientist 1984-90; pres. Signal Processing and Controls Engineering Corp., 1990-; adj. prof. elec. and computer engring. Univ. Calif. 1984-; cons. and lectr. in field; dir: Asilomar Signals Systems, Computer Corp.; bd. dirs., mem. exec. com. SSC Conf. Corp., Dayle McIntosh Ctr. for Independent Living; awards: N.Am. Aviation Sci. Engring. Fellow 1963-65, Eta Kappa Nu (internat. dir. emeritus), Tau Beta Pi, Sigma Xi (pres. Autonetics club), Disting. lectr. Nat. Electronics Conf., Chgo. 1973, Engr. of Yr. award Orange Co. Engring. Council (1984), Engr. of Yr. award Rockwell Internat. 1985, Leonardo Da Vinci Medallion 1986, Sci. Achiev. award 1987, Disting. Engring. Alumnus Purdue Univ. 1988, Meritorious Inventor Rockwell Internat. 1989; Fellow AAAS, Inst. Advancement Engring., N.Y. Acad. Scis., IEEE, IEEE/Acoustics, Speech and Signal Processing Soc. (founding chmn. Orange County chpt., gen. chmn. Asilomar Conf. on circuits, systems and computers, 1982, v.chmn. internat. 1983 symposium on circuits and systems, gen. chmn. 1984 internat. conf. on acoustics, speech and signal process, gen. chmn. 1992 internat. symposium on circuits and systems), mem. Audio Engring. Soc., Internat. Neural Network Soc., Nat. Mgmt. Assn., Am. Inst. of Physics, Am. Assn. of Physics Teachers. Res: 433 E Ave Cordoba San Clemente 92672 Ofc: Signal Processing and Controls Engineering Corp., PO Box 337 San Clemente 92674

WHITE, THOMAS F., stock and bond broker; b. Feb. 14, 1936, Chicago, Ill.; s. Frank H. White and Margaret Norman; 1 son, Shane b. July 25, 1984 edn: BA econ., Beloit Coll. 1960. Career: reg. rep. Merrill Lynch, Cleveland, Ohio 1963-70; First Calif. Co., San Francisco 1970-75; Birr Wilson 1975-78; chmn. Thomas F. White & Co. Inc. 1978-; editor/pub. The White Paper on Municipal Bonds, 1985-, chmn. Lombard Instl. Brokerage Inc. 1992-, chmn. Chouteau, Gilmore, & Sheriff Inc. 1992-; mem: Calif. Assn. of Independent Brokers Inc. (v.p. and dir. 1991-), City Club, S.F. Bond Club; civic bds: Chanticleer (dir. 1991-92), S.F. Chamber Orch. (dir. 1985-89), S.F. Chamber Symphony. (dir. 1989-90), S.F. Genealogy Soc., Fine Arts Museums; mil: cpl. USMC 1956-58; rec: model yacht racing, travel, camping, Spanish. Ofc: One Second St San Francisco 94105

WHITESCARVER, OLIN DRAVO, oil company executive; b. Jan. 4, 1936, Pasadena; s. Loren and Hannah Olivia (Beatty) W.; m. Jacqueline George, June 24, 1961; children: Laura Lea (Mohun) b. 1963, William Loren b. 1964; edn: Petroleum Engr., Colo. Sch. of Mines, 1958. Career: petroleum engr. Pure Oil Co., Van, Tx. 1959-60, Midland, Tx. 1960-63, area prodn. engr., Lafayette, La. 1963-65; area prodn. engr. Unocal, Houma, La. 1965-73, sr. prodn. engr., Lafayette, La. 1973, dist. prodn. supt., Santa Rosa, Calif. 1973-79, dist. ops. mgr., Indio, 1979-92; v.p. gem. mgr. Unocal Geothermal of Indonesia, Ltd., Jakarta, Indonesia 1992-; mem: Am. Pet. Inst. 1959-, Soc. of Petroleum Engrs. of AIME (1959-, 25 Year Club), Geothermal Resource Council, Geothermal Assn. of Imperial County, Colo. Sch. of Mines Alumni Assn.; civic: Dulac Mission, Dulac, La. (pres. bd. dirs. 1972), Boy Scouts Am., Santa Rosa (troop com. chair 1978); inventor, 5 patents in geothermal; mil: 1st lt. US Army Reserve, C.E. 1958-59; Republican, First United Methodist Ch. (chmn. bd. trustees 1988). Res: Park Royale Apt. No. 1612 Jalan Gatot Subroto Jakarta 10210, Indonesia Ofc: Rata Plaza Office Tower PO Box 1264/JKT Jakarta 10012, Indonesia.

WHITESIDE, CAROL GORDON, stage agency executive; b. Dec. 15, 1942, Chgo.; d. Paul George and Helen Louise (Barre) Gordon; m. John Gregory Whiteside, Aug. 15, 1964; children: Brian b. 1970, Derek b. 1973; edn: BA, UC Davis, 1960. Career: personnel mgr. Emporium, Santa Rosa 1965-67; personnel asst. Levi Strauss & Co., San Francisco 1967-69; education counselor Army Edn. Ctr., Landstuhl Germany 1970-72; school trustee Modesto City Schs., Modesto, Ca. 1979-83; elected councilmem. City of Modesto, 1983-87, mayor 1987-91, advy. bd. U.S. Conf. of Mayors, W.D.C. 1990-91, dir. Calif. League of Cities, Sacto. 1990-91, pres. Nat. Republican Mayors & Councilmembers, W.D.C. 1991; gubnatl. exec. appt., asst. secty. Calif. State Resources Agy., Sacto., 1991-; dir. Lincoln Inst., Cambridge, Mass. 1990-; honors: County outstanding woman Commn. for Women Stanislaus Co. 1988, Woman of Yr. 27th Assem. Dist. Modesto 1991, Soroptimists Modesto 1988; civic bds: United Way Stanislaus Co. 1986-90, Muir Trail Girl Scouts 1983-88; Republican; Lutheran. Res: 1319 Highland Dr Modesto 95354 Ofc: State Resources Agency 1416 9th St Sacramento 95814

WHITING, JAMES VINCENT, cartoonist; b. May 19, 1926, Canton, Pa.; s. George Edward and Grace Electa (Dann) W.; m. Bernita Mae Blanchard, Nov. 20, 1945; children: James, Donna, John, Andrea, David; edn: Chicago Acad. of Fine Arts, Chgo. 1948, Sch. of Visual Arts, N.Y.C. 1949-51. Career: radio sales and air work, Sta. WFLR AM & FM, Dundee, N.Y. 1956-84; free lance cartoonist, Solana Beach, Calif. 1984-; mem. team producing "Ad Libs" Gen. Features Syndicate, Los Angeles Times Syndicate, 1956-72, also produced "Li'l Ones" and "Wee Women" for same two syndicates, 1957-76;mem: So. Calif. Cartoonists Soc. (pres., co-founder 1986-), Upstate Cartoonists League of Am. (co-founder 1953-), Assn. of Home-Based Businesses (pres. San Diego AHB 1990-92); mil: p.o.2c USN 1944-46; Republican; Presbyterian; rec: magic, tennis, reading. Res: 773 S Nardo M-10 Solana Beach 92075

WHITNEY, DAN, anthropologist; b. July 25, 1937, Alma, Mich.; s. Frank J. Whitney and Ethel Irene (Duffy) Morey; m. Hiroko Saito, Jan. 7, 1958 (div. Feb. 7, 1982); m. Phyllis A. Tubbs, May 7, 1983; children: Teresa b. 1962, Wendi b. 1965; edn: BA journ., Mich. State Univ., E. Lansing 1962, MA sociology/anthropology, 1963, PhD anthropology, 1968; JD (Valedictorian), Western State Univ., San Diego 1976; admitted bar: Calif. 1976. Career: asst. dir. Ctr. for Asian Studies, Mich. State Univ. 1965-66; prof. anthropology and dept. chair San Diego State Univ., 1966-, assoc. dean Arts & Letters, 1969-72, dir. Ctr. for Asian Studies SDSU, 1987-89; ptnr. law firm Gallatin & Whitney, San Diego 1976-83; awards: editor Law Rev. Western State Univ. 1975, Fulbright Prof., Japan 1985-87, Merit. performance San Diego St. Univ. 1989; mem.: Am. Anthropol. Assn. (1966-, newsletter editor 1974-77), Southwestern Anthropol. Assn. 1966-, Calif. Faculty Assn. 1980-, State Bar Calif. (inactive); author: Cultural Context (1980), monograph, Rhade of South Vietnam (1962), contbr. articles in anthropol. and law jours.; mil: A/1c USAF 1955-59; Democrat; Prot.; rec: golf, music, reading, fishing, backpacking, camping. Res: 5352 W Falls View Dr San Diego 92115 Ofc: Anthropology, California State Univ., San Diego 92182

WHITTINGTON, JEREMIAH, physician; b. Jan. 25, 1946, Eagle Mills, Ark.; s. George Washington Jr. and Lula (Brooks) W.; m. Mary Ellen Branch, July 1, 1972 (div. July 1976); dau., Carrie Kenyatta; m. Kaye Francis Atkinson, June 18, 1977; son, Christopher Jerome; edn: Calvin Coll., 1969; MA, Univ.

Mich., 1970, postgrad. work 1971-72; MD, Mich. State Univ., 1979; Diplomate Am. Bd. Ob. Gyn. Career: intern, resident ob-gyn, Youngstown, Ohio 1979-83; physician Planned Parenthood of Mahoning Co., Youngstown 1980-83, Ashtabula (Ohio) Co. Commn. Action Agy., 1981-83; ob-gyn practice, Grand Rapids, Mich. 1984-89; attdg. physician City of Faith Med. and Research Ctr., Tulsa 1985-89; asst. prof. dept. ob-gyn Oral Roberts Univ. Sch. Medicine, Tulsa 1985-89; clin. asst. prof. UCLA, Sylmar; physician splst. dept. ob-gyn Los Angeles Co. Hosp., Olive Med. Ctr., Sylmar 1989-90; ob-gyn physician So. Calif. Permanente Med. Group, Panorama City 1990-93, Providence Hosp. Med. Ctrs., Southfield, Mich. 1993-; physician Ambulatory Gyn., Infertility and Ob., Claremore, Okla., staff physician USPHS and Claremore Indian Hosp., also cons. physician Rogers Co. Health Dept., Claremore, 1983-86; lectr. in Stockholm, Sweden, 1987, People to People Citizens Amb. Pgm. delegation to Finland, 1987, speaker Sch. Medicine Univ. Zambia, Lusaka, Africa 1990, Victory Celebrations, Zambia, 1988, 90, 91; awards: fellow Univ. Mich. 1969-70, 71-73, tuition grants Kalamazoo Coll. 1973-74, Mich. St. Univ. 1974-76, Univ. N.M. Sch. of Medicine basic sci. enrichment pgm. 1974, Nat. Med. Fellow 1974-75, USPHS pub. health svc. scholar 1976-79, Overseas Scholar in surgery, New Delhi, India 1979; Fellow Am. Coll. Ob.-Gyn.; mem.: AMA, CMA, L.A. Co. Med. Assn., L.A. Ob-Gyn. Soc, Okla. Med. PAC 1986; Democrat; Ch. of God in Christ (minister 1992-); rec: art, poetry, basketball, jogging, music. Res: PO Box 25 Novi MI 48376-0025 Ofc: 2575 North Woodward Ave #120 Panorama City 91402 and Providence Hosp. Med. Ctrs. 16001 West 9 Mile Rd Southfield MI 48037

WHITTLE, SCOTT HAROLD, mortgage banking executive; b. Dec. 25, 1951, Los Angeles; s. Hal Glenny and Jeanne Jacques W.; m. Terry A. Tegnazian, Jan. 4, 1986; edn: BA, Pomona Coll. 1974; MA, Christ's Coll., Cambridge 1977. Career: asst. v.p. Ralph C. Sutro Co., Los Angeles 1978-84; v.p./secty. CrossLand Capital Corp., L.A. 1985-86; first v.p. Metmor Financial, Inc. 1987-89; pres. Incal Assocs. Ltd., 1989-; v.p. legal affairs ARCS Mortgage, Inc. 1991-; mem: So. Calif. Mortgage Bankers Assn. (legislative chmn.), Calif. Mortgage Bankers Assn. (legislative chmn.), Mortgage Bankers Assn. of Am. (legislative, and state & local liaison coms.); clubs: The California, L.A. Tennis, St. James (London); rec: tennis. Ofc: Incal Associates, Ltd. 1145 Gayley Ave Ste 309 Los Angeles 90024

WIBBELSMAN, NANCY CASTO BENSON, b. Feb. 19, 1949, Lancaster, Ohio; d. Frank S. and Nancy Ann (Casto) Benson Jr.; m. Patrick Nesbitt 1975, div. 1981; m. 2d. Robert John Wibbelsman (stockbroker), Sept. 2, 1984; children: (nee Nesbitt): Elizabeth Paige b. 1977, Patrick Michael Jr. b. 1978; (by spouse's prev. marriage): Robert John Jr. b. 1968, Warren Mahlon b. 1969; edn: Bradford Jr. Coll. 1967-69; Ohio State Univ. 1972, KK7 sorority. Career: campaign chmn. for Reagan, Republican primary, Marina Del Rey, 1976; (postprimary) chmn. People for Ford, in chg of vol. groups, orgns., subcoms. in Calif., 1976; civic: Los Angeles Junior League, DAR; Republican; Episcopal. Res: Los Angeles.

WICHMANN, MARY LYNNE, association public relations director; b. May 2, 1955, Gainesville, Fla.; d. Joseph Anthony Lopez and Betty Jean (Wood) Van Doorninck; m. Jeffrey Thomas Wichmann, July 14, 1979; children: Tyler b. 1987; edn: BA, CSU Sacto., 1984. Career: assoc. editor Calif. Optometric Assn., Sacto. 1982-84; public info. asst. City of Sacramento Parks & Comm. Svs., 1984-86; pub. relations dir. Tierra del Oro Girl Scout Council, Rancho Cordova 1986-; mem: Sacto. Pub. Relations Assn. (1986-, sec., pgm. chair 1991-92), Calif. Nature Conservancy, The Nature Conservancy, Yolo Basin Found., Sacto. Zool. Assn.; rec: gardening, scuba, backpacking, skiing. Res: 1700 37th St Sacramento 95816 Ofc: Tierra del Oro GS Council 3005 Gold Canal Dr Rancho Cordova 95670

WICKWIRE, PATRICIA JOANNE NELLOR, psychologist, consultant; b. Sioux City, Iowa; d. William McKinley and Clara Rose (Pautsch) N.; m. Robert Wickwire, Sept. 7, 1957; 1 son, William b. 1958; edn: BA, Univ. of Northern Iowa 1951; MA, Univ. of Iowa 1959; PhD, Univ. of Texas Austin 1971; postgrad., USC, UCLA, CSU Long Beach 1951-66. Career: tchr., sch. psychologist, administr. South Bay Union H.S. Dist. 1962-; indep. cons. in mgmt. & edn. 1981; pres. The Nellor Wickwire Group, 1982-; univ. lectr.; honors: Psi Chi, Sigma Alpha Iota, Pi Lambda Theta, Alpha Phi Gamma, Kappa Delta Pi; Journalism and English awards; South Bay Woman of the Year; mem: Calif. Interagency Mental Health Council, Am. Assn. of Univ. Women (pres. 1962-72), Beach Cities Symphony Assn., CSU Dominguez Hills, L.A. Co. Dir. of Pupil Svs. (pres. 1974-79), L.A. Co. Directors Spl. Edn., Calif. Personnel & Guidance Assn., L.A. Co. Personnel & Guidance Assn. (pres. 1977-80), Assn. of Calif. Sch. Adminstrs., Calif. Assn. for Measurement & Evaluation in Guidance (exec. bd. pres. 1981-), Calif. Assn. of Sch. Psychologists (exec. bd. 1981-), Internat. Career Assn. Network (dir. 1985-), Am. Assn. Career Edn. (pres. 1990-92, bd. 1988-), Assn. Measurement and Evaluation in Counseling & Devel. (exec. bd. 1987-91), Calif. Assn. for Counseling and Devel. (pres. 1988-89); contbr. articles to profl. jours. Res: 2900 Amby Pl Hermosa Beach 90254

WIDAMAN, GREGORY ALAN, financial advisor; b. Oct. 4, 1955, St. Louis, Mo.; s. Raymond Paul, Sr. and Louise Agnes (Urschler) W.; edn: BS in bus. & econ., Trinity Univ., 1978; C.P.A., 1985. Career: senior auditor Arthur

Andersen & Co., Houston 1978-82, audits of Fortune 500 cos.; sr. cons., mgmt. & litigation, Price Waterhouse, Houston 1983-85; mgr. corp. fin. planning Teledyne Inc., Los Angeles 1985-, fin. advisor to segment pres., Teledyne Inc.; honors: outstanding student of finance Fin. Executives Inst., San Antonio, Tx. 1978, Blue Key nat. hon. frat. 1978, biog. listings in Marquis Who's Who In The West, Who's Who In Fin. & Ind., Who's Who In The World; mem: Am. Inst. CPAs, Calif. Soc. CPAs, Christian Business Men's Com. of USA, World Affairs Council, MIT/Cal-Tech Ent. Forum; Republican; Christian; rec: white water rafting, skiing, camping, asst. in small bus. startups. Res: 1416 S Barrington #4 Los Angeles 90025 Ofc: Teledyne, Inc. 1901 Avenue of the Stars Ste 1800 Los Angeles 90067

WIEMER, ROBERT ERNEST, film and television writer, producer, director; b. Jan. 30, 1938, Highland Park, Mich.; s. Carl Ernest and Marion (Israelian) W.; m. Rhea Dale McGeath, June 14, 1958; children: Robert Marshall, Rhea Whitney; edn: BA, Ohio Wesleyan Univ., 1959. Career: child actor Jam Handy Orgn., Detroit 1946-48; indep. producer 1956-60; dir. documentary ops. WCBS-TV, N.Y.C. 1964-67; indep. producer of t.v., theatrical and bus. films, N.Y.C. 1967-72; exec. prod. motion pictures and t.v. ITT Corp., N.Y.C. 1973-84, also pres. ITT subs. cos: Blue Marble Co. Inc., Telemontage Inc., Alphaventure Music Inc., Betaventure Music Inc.; founder, pres. and CEO Tigerfilm Inc. 1984-, chmn. bd. Golden Tiger Pictures, Hollywood 1988-; dir. Princeton-American Communications, Inc. 1986-88; exec. producer children's t.v. show "Big Blue Marble" (winner Emmy and Peabody awards); writer, producer, director feature films: My Seventeenth Summer, Witch's Sister, Do Me a Favor, Anna to the Infinite Power, Somewhere, Tomorrow, Night Train to Kathmandu; director TV series "Superboy," "Star Trek: The Next Generation;" recipient CINE award (1974, 76, 77, 79, 81); mem: Directors Guild of Am., Nat. Acad. T.V. Arts and Scis., Information Film Producers Assn. (outstanding prod. award), Nat. Assn. T.V. Programming Execs., Am. Women in Radio and T.V., New Jersey Broadcasters Assn.; mil: capt. USAF 1960-64; Dutch Reform Ch. in Am. (deacon). Ofc: Golden Tiger Pictures 205 S Beverly Dr Ste 200 Beverly Hills 90212 Tel: 213/271-5213 FAX: 213/271-5935

WIENER, HOWARD B., state appellate judge; b. Feb. 1, 1931, Providence, R.I.; s. Henry and Mildred (Woolf) W.; m. Joan, May 23, 1954; children: Daniel b. 1954, Anne b. 1956, Carol b. 1958; edn: AB, cum laude, Brown Univ. 1952; LLB, Harvard 1955; LLM, Univ. Virginia 1982; admitted Calif. State Bar 1956. Career: clerk Hon. Ben Harrison, U.S. Dist. Ct. L.A. 1955-56; gen. practice atty. Egly & Wiener, L.A. Co. 1956-75; judge San Bernardino Co. Superior Ct., 1975-78; assoc. justice Ct. of Appeal 4th Appellate Dist., Div. 1, 1978-; adj. prof. Univ. San Diego Law Sch., 1979-85, Cal Western Law Sch., 1988-; co-author Rutter Group, Civil Appeals & Writs, lectr. The Rutter Group, Calif. Judges Assn. 1985, Ctr. for Jud. Edn. and Res., Claremont Grad. Sch. Exec. Mgmt. Pgm. 1977-78; mem. bd. overseers UC San Diego, and chmn. bd. vis. USD Law Sch.; honors: Phi Beta Kappa 1952, past pres. Pomona Valley Bar Assn. 1968, bd. trustees L.A. Co. Bar Assn. 1969-71, bd. govs., v.p. Calif. State Bar 1972-75, appellate judge of yr. L.A. Trial Lawyers 1981 and San Diego Trial Lawyers 1984; mem. Calif. Judges Assn.; (exec. bd. 1987-90, v.p. 1989-90, past chair appellate cts. com.); Pres. William B. Enright Am. Inn of Court 1991-; civic: Inter-Comm. Hosp. Covina (bd. trustees 1967-75), Law in a Free Soc. (exec. com. 1975-79), San Diego Univ. Hosp. (comm. advy. bd. 1979-84); Res: 7755 Ludington Pl La Jolla 92037 Ofc: 750 B St Ste 5000 San Diego 92101

WILCOX, WINTON WILFRED, JR., small business consultant, educator; b. Aug. 24, 1945, Independence, Mo.; s. Winton Wilfred Wilcox and LaPreal (Adams) Craig; m. Janette Moss, Oct. 9, 1965 (div. 1990); m. Kathy L. Postell, July 4, 1990; children: Steven M. b. 1975, Jake A. b. 1991; edn: cert. Carolina Sch. of Bdcst., Charlotte, N.C. 1966; BS, Univ. Nev., Reno 1973. Career: nat. pdt. dir. Amer. Photo Corp., N.Y.C., 1974-77; gen. mgr. Golden Valley Coffee, Minn. 1977-80; div. mgr. Cable Data, Sacto., Calif. 1982-85; c.f.o. Cultch Ent. Inc., Sacto. 1980-89; v.p. mktg. Parallex, Winston Salem N.C. 1985-88; owner IK & Consultants, Sacto. 1988-; instr. Heald Bus. Coll., Hayward 1989-90, Sacto. 1990-; author (text) Professional Selling System (1979), contbg. author: Apple Fun & Games (1986); listed Who's Who in West 1990, bd. govs. Am. Biog. Inst. 1991-; mil: E5 USAF 1966-70; Republican; rec: model R.R. Ofc: IK & Consultants 3009 1/2 C St Sacramento 95816

WILDEY, JAMES ALLEN, county computer services manager, real estate broker, general contractor; b. Feb. 13, 1943, Binghamton, N.Y.; s. Leon Earl and Constance Evelyn (Springer) W.; m. Barbara Ann Marold, Sept. 10, 1966; children: J. Dane b. 1968, Eric E. b. 1970; edn: AA, Rochester Inst. Tech. 1964; BS, 1965; MS, Pa. St. Univ. 1967; Calif. lic.: gen. contr., R.E. broker, care facility provider. Career: sr. systems and procedures analyst IBM Corp., Pt. Chester, N.Y. 1967-72; owner Guide Farms, Lebanon, Pa. 1972-77; sr. project mgr. Gen. Public Utilities Service Corp., Reading, Pa. 1977-80; mgr. MIS Quaker Alloy Casting (div. of Harsco), Myerstown, Pa. 1980-83; corp. dir. MIS/EDP Vendo Co., Fresno, Calif. 1983-84; div. mgr. computer services Fresno County, 1984-; owner Fresno Home Services, Clovis 1984-; co-owner Comm. Home Providers - Alzheimers Elderly Care Facility; Fresno Surf 'N Turf, Fresno 1984-; co-owner Affordable Pool Service, Clovis 1988-; honors: Who's Who East, Who's

Who Fin. & Industry; mem: Assn. Systems Mgmt., Data Processing Mfg. Assn., Fresno Evangelical Free Ch. (bd. mem. 1989-91), Family Life Ctr. (bd. dirs., secty. 1987-89), Lebanon Youth for Christ (bd. dirs. 1979-80); Republican; Prot.; rec: home constrn. & remodeling, sailing. Res: 2390 Alluvial Ave Clovis 93612 Ofc: Fresno County 1020 S 10th St Fresno 93702

WILEY, JAMES GUYTON, SR., customs broker, international freight forwarder; b. Mar. 28, 1915, Sidney, Ohio; s. Harley M. and Marvel (Smith) W.; m. Mary Kathryn Lindner, 1945; children: James b. 1946, Melissa b. 1950, Thomas b. 1953, Susanne b. 1958, Melanie b. 1959; edn: grad. Van Nuys H.S., 1933, stu. USC, 1938; lic. customs broker, internat. freight forwarder, gen. insurance broker. Career: chmn. bd. James G. Wiley Co. Inc., Los Angeles; mem: Los Angeles C.of C. 1946-, Foreign Trade Assn. 1946-, U.S. Customs Brokerage Assn. 1948-; mil: 1st lt. Army Transp. Corps 1942-46; Democrat; Prot.; rec: equestrian, motorcycling. Res: 28951 Palos Verdes Dr E Rancho Palos Verdes 90274 Ofc: 5305 W 102nd St Los Angeles 90045

WILHELM, ROBERT OSCAR, lawyer, civil engineer; b. July 7, 1918, Baltimore; s. Clarence Oscar and Agnes Virginia (Grimm) W.; m. Grace Sanborn Luckie, Apr. 4, 1959; edn: BS in C.E., Georgia Inst. of Tech., 1947, MS in Indsl. Mgmt., 1948; JD, Stanford Univ., 1951; admitted bar: Calif. 1952, U.S. Supreme Ct. Career: lawyer, sr. ptnr. law firm Wilhelm, Thompson, Wentholt & Gibbs, Redwood City 1952-, civil engr. and land surveyor in pvt. practice, 1952-; land developer and bldg. contr.; gen. counsel and pres. Bay Counties Builders Escrow Inc., 1972-; mem: Calif. Bar Assn., San Mateo Co. Bar Assn., Calif. Builder's Exchange (past treas.), Peninsula Builder's Exchange (bd. 1956, pres. 1958, 1971), Bay Counties Civil Engrs. and Land Surveyors Assn. (gen. counsel, pres. 1957), Assn. of Gen. Contrs. S.F. (past dir.), Engring. and Grading Contrs. Assn. (bd., gen. counsel); lodges: Masons, Odd Fellows, Eagles, Elks; author: Constrn. Law for Contractors, Architects and Engineers, (constrn. handbook) Manual of Procedures for the Constrn. Ind. (8th Edit.), columnnist "Law and You" Daily Pacific Builder (1954-); mil: 1st lt. Army Corps of Engrs. 1942-46. Res: 134 Del Mesa Carmel 93923 Ofc: 600 Allerton Redwood City 94063

WILKES, PENNY F., writer, educator, consultant; b. Aug. 8, 1946, Pasadena; d. Wesley Innis and Margaret (Lewis) Dumm; m. Michael B. Wilkes, June 29, 1968; edn: BA, USC, 1968. Career: dir. of publications and assoc. in devel. The Bishop's Sch., La Jolla 1973-78; mng. editor Am. Jour. of La Jolla Orthodontics, 1978-85; writer, instr., cons. prin. Creative Communications, La Jolla 1985-; dir. Creative Collaborative, La Jolla 1991-; awards: most creative LEAD, San Diego Inc. 1990; mem.: Nat. League of Am. Penwomen (chapt. v.p. 1986-87), Toastmasters La Jolla (pres., TM of Yr., 1991), Laughmasters (v.p. 1992); author (col. short stories): Seven Smooth Stones (1991); rec: Carousel art collection. Res/Ofc: Creative Communications PO Box 2201 La Jolla 92038-2201

WILKINSON, LAURA, radio personality/radio station owner; b. Dec. 11, 1957, Auburn, NY; d. Burton Francis Wilkinson, Jr. and Mary (Casten) W.; m. Gary Don Herron, July 25, 1981; div., June 25, 1991; children: Matheson Charles Herron b. 1984, Cameron James Herron b. 1986; edn: under grad. studies, UCLA, 1975-77; BA, San Diego State Univ., 1985. Career: radio personality, WLUP radio, Chgo., Ill., 1979-80, KPRI FM radio, San Diego, 1980-82; on-air personality/radio, KCBQ AM/FM radio, San Diego, 1982-87; TV personality, KGTV-10 Eye on San Diego, 1985-87; vice chmn. and exec. v.p., McNulty Broadcasting Corp., Chico, Calif., 1987-; dir., AFTRA, San Diego, 1985-87; dir., Tehama County United Way, Red Bluff, Calif., 1989-90; dir., Chico Advt. Club, Chico, 1990-91; dir., KIXE TV, Redding, Calif., 1991-; dir., CEPCO, Chico, 1991-; awards: 3 "Beam" awards, Chico Advt. Club, 1990, 91; nominee, Businessperson of Year, Chico C.of C., 1992; mem: Chico Sports Club, Chico; Democrat; rec: scuba diving, whitewater rafting, snow skiing and windsurfing. Ofc: KALF-FM P.O. Box 7950 Chico 95928

WILKINSON, ROSEMARY REGINA, poet, author, lecturer; b. Feb. 21, 1924, New Orleans, La.; d. William Lindsay, Jr. and Julia Regina (Sellen) Challoner; m. Henry B. Wilkinson, Oct. 15, 1949; children: Denis James b. 1952, Marian Regina b. 1954, Paul Francis b. 1959, Richard Challoner b. 1967; edn: tchg. cert. San Francisco St. Univ., 1978, Lifetime tchg. credential, poetry. Career: ten yrs. in hosp. adminstrn., 1939-47, 1957-61; poet and author, Burlingame, Calif. 1965-; secty. gen. World Acad. of Arts and Culture/ World Congress of Poets (WAAC/WCP), Burlingame 1985-, and Placerville 1988-; author 18 poetry books (translations in 33 languages now): A Girl's Will (1973), California Poet (1976), Earth's Compromise (1977), It Happened To Me (1978), I Am Earth Woman (1979), The Poet & The Painter (1981), Gems Within (1984), In The Pines (1985), Longing For You (1986), Purify The Earth (1988), Sacred In Nature (1988), Earth's Children (1990), New Seed (1990); Prose work: An Historical Epic (trans. into Mandarin 1974); lectures, poetry readings internat.; awards: Dame of Malta (1981- Dame of Grace, Dame of Merit 1985), Dame of St. George (Vt. 1991, Algarve Portugal 1992), Dame of Order of Polonia Restituta, Poland 1989, Dame of St. Sepulcre, Australia 1990, Dame of Knights-St. John of Jerusalem-Portugal 1993, Gold medal, India 1986, Bronze medal World Poetry Soc. Conf. India 1987, Silver medal Accad. Internaz. Di

Pontzen Italy 1988, Schilla Dynasty "Kaya" Crown (gold/jade) Korea 1988, disting. service Nat. League Am. Pen Women USA 1990, Yunus Emre award World Acad. Arts & Culture Taiwan 1991, Acad. Michael Madhusdan- Italy 1991, Acad. Roma- Italy 1991, Unione Della Mondiale Culture- Italy 1991, All India Writers award 1992, HDL (hon.) L'Universita Libre, Pakistan 1975, World Acad. Arts & Culture, Taiwan 1981, merit Am. Poets Fellowship Soc. 1973, Poet Laureate Int'l '74 Int'l Woman of 1975, Fellow Internat. Biog. Ctr., Cambridge, Eng. 1981-, Chancellor Internat. Poets Acad., India 1988-, mem: WAAC/WCP (1973-, secty. gen. 1985-), Nat. League Am. Pen Women (mem. 1977-, nat. bd. 1986-90, Berkeley Br. pres. 1988-90), Authors Guild League of Am. N.Y. 1980-, Ina Coolbrith Circle (1966-, dir. emeritus), WPSI-POET India (v.p. 1986-); civic: founder poetry San Mateo County Fair 1977-, Fine Arts Fair Poetry Workshop (Dr. Williams) Burlingame H.S. (founder 1981-85), Soroptimist (hon. 1981), Avalon Library Assn., Glastonbury, England 1989-; Democrat; R.Cath.; rec: reading, brush painting, gardening. Res: 3146 Buckeye Ct Placerville 95667

WILLARD, ROBERT EDGAR, lawyer; b. Dec. 13, 1929, Bronxville, N.Y.; s. Wm. Edgar and Ethel Marie (Van Ness) W.; m. Shirley Fay Cooper, May 29, 1954; children: Laura Marie, Linda Ann, John Judson; edn: BA in econs., Wash. State Univ., 1954; JD, Harvard Univ., 1958; admitted bar: Calif. 1959. Career: law clk. to U.S. dist. judge 1958-59; atty., assoc. law firm Flint & Mackay, Los Angeles 1959- 61; sole practice, L.A. 1962-64; mem. firm Willard & Baltaxe, L.A. 1964-65, Baird, Holley, Baird & Galen, L.A. 1966-69, Baird, Holley, Galen & Willard, L.A. 1970- 74, Holley, Galen & Willard, L.A. 1975-82, Galvin & Willard, Newport Beach 1982-88; Davis, Punelli, Keathley & Willard, Newport Beach 1989-; mem: ABA, Calif. Bar Assn., L.A. Co. Bar Assn., Assn. Trial Lawyers Am., Am. Judicature Soc., Acacia Frat.; club: Calcutta Saddle and Cycle; mil: AUS 1946-48, 50-51; Congregationalist. Res: 1840 Oriole Costa Mesa 92626 Ofc: Davis, Punelli, Keathley & Willard, 610 Newport Ctr Dr Ste 1000 Newport Beach 92660

WILLIAMS, DIANE MARIE, manufacturing company president; b. Dec. 9, 1946, Albany, NY; d. William Edward and Margaret (McEvoy) Mayo; m. Richard L. Williams, Dec. 11, 1971; edn: BA, Whittier Coll., 1968. Career: work measurement analyst, auditor Aetna Life & Casualty, Los Angeles 1968-71; purchasing agent Precision Tube Bending, Santa Fe Springs, 1971-82, also: sales, estimating, production mgr. to general mgr. 1982-; mem. C.of C. Santa Fe Springs, Rotary, Los Angeles; Republican; R.Cath.

WILLIAMS, DONALD SPENCER, scientist; b. May 28, 1939, Pasadena; s. Charles G. and Delia S. W.; edn: BS engring. sci., Harvey Mudd Coll., 1961; MS in E.E., Carnegie Mellon Univ., 1962, PhD computer sci., 1969. Career: mgr. computer ctr. Univ. of Pittsburgh, Pa. 1965-67; senior engr. RCA Corp., Palo Alto, Ca. 1969-71; principal investigator JPL, Pasadena 1972-80; chief engr. ops. TRW, Redondo Beach 1980-; cons. prin., 1975-; awards: study grantee Japan Economic Found., Tokyo 1983; mem: AAAS, Assn. for Computing Machinery, Audio Engring. Soc., Nat. Fire Protection Assn., IEEE, Soc. of Motion Picture and TV Engrs.; civic: Town Hall of Calif., Community Assn. Inst., Am. Theatre Organ Soc.; Republican; Presbyterian; rec: theater preservation. Res: PO Box 607 Lawndale 90260-0607 Ofc: TRW Inc., One Space Park Dr, R3-2089, Redondo Beach 90278-1071

WILLIAMS, LORNA MARIAN, osteopathic physician; b. March 6, 1912, Watford, Ontario, Canada; d. Lorne Joseph and Marian Lillian (Templeton) Williams; edn: DO, Kirksville Coll. Osteopathy & Surgery, 1934; reg. osteopathic physician Bd. Reg. for Healing Arts (1934). Career: pvt. practice physician, Ontario, Canada 1934-39, Berkeley, Calif. 1939-92, ret.; awards: appreciation Am. Osteopathic Assn. 1984; mem: Am. Osteopathic Assn., Osteopathic Physicians & Surgeons of Calif., Bus. & Profl. Womens Club; Republican; Presbyterian. Res: 2041 Francisco St Berkeley 94709

WILLIAMS, PATRICIA L., president of a national training corporation; b. Oct. 12, 1941, Slidell, La.; d. Adam A. and Lena M. (Pichon) Faciane; m. John T. Graves (comml. R.E. developer), June 28, 1986; dau. Nikki Renee Williams b. 1973; edn: AA in pol. sci., Los Angeles City Coll. 1970; pol. sci. courses UCLA UCLA Labor Inst.; lic. life & disability ins. agt. Calif. Career: treas. Rosey Grier's Giant Step Inc., cons. Robert Farrell's Recall Campaign 1975-78, We. States staff dir. of Lexington Group of DNC, 1981-83; adminstrv. asst. UAW Local 887, 1962-77; dir. UAW youth Project, 1979-83; dir. UAW Program Planning R&D, 1983-84; comptroller UAW-LETC (Labor Employment and Tng. Corp.) 1984-85, job tng. cons. 1985-88 (only woman on 6-mem. US team during formulation of UAW/ GM-Toyota jt. venture creation of New United Motors Mfg. Inc.), v.p. mktg. resrch. & devel. 1988-89, senior v. p. UAW-LETC, 1989-92, pres. 1993-; established Career Ctr. at World Trade Ctr. N.Y.C. (opened 1/93); owner/pres. Faciane and Assocs. (pub. relations, program plng., mktg.), Los Angeles; co-owner J.T. Graves Commercial R.E. Inc.; apptd. by Spkr. Willie Brown mem. Calif. State Employment Tng. Panel; apptd. by Senate Rules Com. to Calif. State Public Procurement Advy. Com.; apptd. by Supr. Ed Edelmann commr. L.A. Co. Hwy. Safety Commn. (chair 1985); apptd. by Mayor Tom Bradley mem. L.A. Private Industry Council (dir.), mem. L.A.

Co. Employment Tng. Action Council, mem. advy. bd. Calif. St. Youth Auth.; honors: appreciation for community interface Rockwell Internat., mother of year Notre Dame Acad. 1987, listed Who's Who in Business & Exec. Women, 5000 Personalities of the World, 2000 Notable Am. Women; mem. UAW Local 509; civic: Coro Found. (bd.), L.A. Urban League (bd.), Democratic Lexington Gp. (charter), Nat. Museum of Women in the Arts (charter), Am. Film Inst. (assoc.), Women Aware, Lullaby Guild of Childrens' Home Soc. (chair Ebony Fashion Fair fundraiser 1990, 91), Jack and Jill of Am., L.A. Co. Public Guardian's Office (vol.); Democrat; R.Cath.; rec: writing. Res: 6605 Bedford Ave Los Angeles 90056 Ofc: Faciane & Associates 5150 E Gage Bell 90201

WILLIAMS, RALPH B., services company executive; b. May 30, 1947, Boston, Mass.; s. Ralph B. and Florence (Porter) W.; m. Karen Denise Belville, Jan. 1, 1980; children: Krista B. b. 1981, Lindsay B. b. 1984; edn: BA, Coll. of the Holy Cross, Worchester, Mass. 1969; MBA, Suffolk Univ., Boston 1970; DBA, USC, L.A. 1981; Cert. Mgmt. Acct.; lic. CPA, Mass., Calif. Career: in charge acct. Ernst & Whinney, Boston, Mass. 1970-73; v.p. fin. and ops. Coollight Co., Inc., North Hollywood 1976-79; exec. v.p. and chief operating ofcr. K-COMP, Inc., Glendale 1980-82; pres./CEO Technology Solutions Corp., L.A. 1982-84; pres./CEO Omnar Corp., Los Angeles 1984; indep. consultant fin., acctg., systems, and planning, 1985-89; asst. prof. acctg. CSU Bakersfield 1973-74; lectr. in acctg. USC Sch. of Bus. Adminstrn., 1974-78; assoc. prof. acctg. CSU Los Angeles, 1978-89; dir.: Coollight Co. Inc., K-COMP Inc., Tech. Solutions Corp., Omnar Corp.; awards: outstanding professor Iota chapt. Beta Alpha Psi (USC), doctoral fellow Price Waterhouse Found., consortium fellow Am. Acctg. Assn., doctoral fellow Deloitte, Haskins & Sells Found., teaching fellow Suffolk Univ., advisor award Suffolk Univ.; mem: Am. Inst. of CPA's, Calif. Soc. of CPA's, Inst. of Mgmt. Acctg., Alpha Kapa Psi; contbr. articles to profl. jours. Res: 4215 Clubhouse Dr Lakewood 90712

WILLIAMS, ROGER A., pathologist; b. Jan. 29, 1939, Dayton, Ohio; s. Harry Roger and D'Esta Marjorie (Humberger) W.; m. Barbara Twist, July 1, 1961; children: Andrew b. 1964, Jason b. 1967; edn: BA, Cornell Univ. 1961; MD, Baylor Univ. 1965; cert. in anatomical and clin. path. Am. Bd. Pathology 1970, blood banking 1973, pediatric pathology 1990. Career: intern, resident in pathology, Harvard Univ., Mass. Gen. Hosp., 1965-66, 1966-69; tchg. fellow Harvard 1967-69; instr. Tufts, 1967-69; pathologist San Diego Inst. of Path. 1971-80; Coroner's pathologist San Diego Co., 1970-84; lab. dir. El Centro Comm. Hosp., 1971-74; clin. asst. prof. UC San Diego 1972-83; chief pathology Childrens Hosp., San Diego 1974-84, Childrens Hosp., Oakland 1984-; clin. assoc. prof. UCSD 1983-84, UC San Francisco 1985-93; clin, prof. UCD 1993-; honors: Alpha Omega Alpha 1964; mem: AMA, Calif. Med. Assn. (CMA Task Force on Child Abuse 1983), Study Gp. for complications of perinatal care 1983, Children's cancer study gp. 1984, Fellow Coll. of Am. Pathologists (1970, Task Force for Missing and Abused Children 1984), Fellow Am. Soc. of Clin. Path. 1971, Calif. Soc. Path. (bd. dirs. 1978-80), Am. Assn. of Blood Banks, U.S./Canadian Acad. Path., Soc. for Pediatric Path.; civic: Children's Home Soc. (bd. dirs. 1980-81), Rotary Intl.; clubs: San Diego Yacht, Claremont CC; num. publs. in medical literature; mil: lcdr USNR 1969-71; Prot.; rec: trout fishing, tennis, gardening. Res: 95 Inverleith Terrace Piedmont 94611 Ofc: Childrens' Hospital 747 Fifty Second St Oakland 94609

WILLIAMS, RUTH H., management consultant, civic activist; b. Mar. 15, 1938, Bklyn.; d. Oscar and Lillian (Steinberg) Forster; div.; children: Steven b. 1960, Richard b. 1963, Michael b. 1970; edn: Fairfax H.S. 1952-55. Career: asst. studio mgr. Columbia Records, L.A. 1966-71; West Coast Adm. Custom Div., RCA Records, L.A. 1972-75; studio mgr. Motown Records, L.A. 1975-80; central scheduling supr. Golden West TV-KTLA, 1980-85; ops. mgr. West Hollywood Paper, L.A. 1985-86; personnel dir. LFP, Inc. 1988-; indep. mgmt. cons., 1986-; appt. City of West Hollywood public safety commr., 1990-, past commr. Rent Stabilization Commn., 1988-90; mem. West Hollywood Neighborhood Council, Citizens for Seniors (founder, chair), Nat. Womens Political Caucus; fmr. cand. West Hollywood City Council; Democrat (past pres. and v.p. W. Hollywood Dem. Club, del. Co. Central Com., exec. bd. Stonewall Dem. Club, mem. W.H.I.S.E.); avocation: community involvement. Res: 7548 Lexington Ave West Hollywood 90046

WILLIAMS, STEVE REX, physician; b. Aug. 3, 1953, Henderson, Tx.; s. James Marion and Ruth May (Harrison) W.; m. Toby Barto Richards, 1988; edn: BA cum laude, Southern Methodist, 1973; MD, Univ. Texas Med. Branch, 1977; Fellow Am. Acad. Family Phys. 1982; phys. surgeon lic. Calif. BMQA. Career: intern in gen. surgery L.A. County-USC Med. Center 1977-78; resident in family med. Baylor Coll. of Med. 1979-82; pvt. practice of medicine, Santa Maria 1982-87; dir. Family Practice and Emergency Med. Svs., Valley Hosp. 1983; founder Family Practice Div. at two hosps. in Santa Maria, 1984; pvt. practice, McCloud 1987-91, Valley E.R. Physicians Group, 1991-; awards: full academic scholarship So. Methodist Univ. 1970, Locum Tenens study award at Middlesex Hosp., London 1976; biog. listings in Men of Achievement, 5,000 Personalities of Am., Personalities of World 1989, Internat. Who's Who of Intellectuals; mem: AMA, Am. Acad. Family Practice, Am. Coll. Emergency Phys., Am. Mensa Assn.; civic: Am. Hydrogen Assn., Citizens for Alternative

Tax Structure, Presdl. Repub. Task Force 1986-, Civic Group against Landfill Dumping of Toxic Chems., Keepers of the Flame Frat., Rosecrucian Order; Thebetan Buddhist; rec: equestrian, ski, travel, hiking, camping. Res: Box 269 McCloud 96057 Ofc: 1032 Cedar Ct McCloud 96057

WILLIAMS, THEODORE EARLE, company president; b. May 9, 1920, Cleveland, Ohio; s. Stanley and Blanche (Albaum) W.; m. Mae Schiner, Aug. 16, 1942 (dec. Apr. 15, 1952); m. Rita Cohen, Aug. 28, 1952; children: Lezlie b. 1944, Shelley b. 1948, Wayne b. 1953, Patti b. 1962; edn: BSE in mech. engring., Univ. Mich., 1942, BSE in M.E., 1942. Career: ptnr. and gen. mgr. M&W Mfg., Detroit, Mich. 1942-43; pres. Wayne Products, L.A. 1947-50; pres. Williams Metal Prod., L.A. 1950-68; pres., chmn. bd., and CEO Bell Industries, L.A. 1968-; instr. Univ. Mich., Ann Arbor 1942; recipient Humanitarian Award City of Los Angeles 1977; civic bds.: Early Childhood Devel. Ctr., L.A. (pres. 1975-80), OPIC-A Day Care Ctr., L.A. (pres. 1980-91); inventor: Air Collet closers (Pat. 1955), Machine Tool Device (Pat. 1957); mil: 1st lt. U.S. Army, Saipan 1943-46; Democrat; Jewish; rec: photography, tennis. Res: 435 N Layton Way Los Angeles 90049 Ofc: Bell Industries 11812 San Vicente Blvd Ste 300 Los Angeles 90049

WILLIAMS, ZENEO BERNARD, real estate broker/appraiser, financial planner; b. Feb. 27, 1954, Jacksonville, Ala.; s. Clarence Robert and Eunice Christene (Porter) W.; m. Tamyra, Dec. 28, 1985; children: Cameron Vaughn b. 1988, Zachary Bernard b. 1990; edn: BS, Grambling St. Univ. 1976; MBA, So. Ill. Univ. 1979; MS, USC 1985; Calif. lic. R.E. Broker 1985; cert. cost/budget analyst 1984, cert. R.E. appraiser 1985. Career: cost acct. Marathon Oil Co., Houston, Tx. 1976-77; staff auditor USAF, San Bernardino 1978-80; cost/budget analyst Defense Meteorological Satellite Program Office, El Segundo 1981-83; mem., CEO Nat. Inst. Real Estate Investing & Fin. Planning, Inc., 1986-; asst. prof. USAF Acad., Colorado Springs, Colo. 1984-88, Univ. Phoenix, Denver, Colo. 1985-86; honors: Outstanding Your Men Am. 1984, 86, Pres. Bush's 384th Point of Light Award for prin. participation in the Wright-Stepp Sci. & Engring. Pgm.; mem: Inst. Cert. Cost Analysts, Nat. Assn. Real Estate Appraisers, Nat. Assn. Accountants, Assn. Govt. Accountants; author: Real Estate Investment Strategies for the 90's, Money Growth Strategies for the 90's; mil: major USAF 1976-, Commendation Medal 1984; Democrat; Methodist; rec: golf, skydiving. Res: 17317 Morningrain Ave Cerritos 90701 Ofc: National Association of Real Estate Investing & Financial Planning Inc. 2306 E Distinctive Dr Colorado Springs CO 80918

WILLIAMSON, NEIL SEYMOUR, III, aerospace company executive; b. Jan. 5, 1935, Dumont, N.J.; s. Neil Seymour, Jr. and Mary Louise (Bittenbender) W.; m. Sue Carrole Cooper, Dec. 15, 1959; children: Deborah D. b. 1959, Leisa L. b. 1961, Neil S., IV b. 1966, Dirk A. b. 1968, Wendy L. b. 1970; edn: BS, U.S. Mil. Acad., West Point 1958; MSME, Univ. Mich., 1963. Career: commd. 2d lt., served to col. US Army 1958-81: assoc. prof. dept. earth, space and graphic scis. U.S. Mil. Acad., West Point, 1965-68; chief edn. sect. Fort McNair, D.C., 1970-71; analyst armor infantry systems group Army, Pentagon, W.D.C., 1972-73; systems analyst, program analyst requirements office Pentagon, 1974-76; chief adv. systems concept office Redstone Arsenal, Ala. 1976-77; comdr., dir. fire control and small caliber weapon systems lab., Dover, N.J. 1977-78; project mgr. TOW, Redstone Arsenal, 1978-81, retired U.S. Army 1981, decorated Bronze Star with o.l.c., Legion of Merit with o.l.c., Air medal with 7 o.l.c., Purple Heart; mem. Soc. Automotive Engrs., Am. Defense Preparedness Assn., Army Aviation Assn. (pres. Tenn. Valley chpt. 1980), Am. Helicopter Soc., U.S. Armor Assn., Disabled Am. Vets. Ofc: Hughes Aircraft PO Box 902 Bldg E1 M/S F120 El Segundo 90245

WILLIAMSON, RICHARD ARTHUR, English and film educator; b. Oct. 16, 1930, S.F., Calif.; s. Arthur Louis and Edith Lillian (Partridge) W.; edn: AA, City Coll. of S.F., 1950; BA, S.F. State Univ., 1953; MA, S.F. State Univ., 1958; Ctr. for Adv. Film Studies, L.A., 1971; Dirs. Guild of Am. internships: UCLA 1978, Brooklyn Coll., City Univ. of NY 1979-82; career: tchg. asst. S.F. State Univ., 1957; instr. language arts, S.F. State Univ., 1957-58; instr.,Eng., Santa Barbara City Coll., 1958-63; chmn. Eng., Santa Barbara City Coll., 1961-63; lectr. edn., S.F. State Univ., 1966; coord. Film & Composition, Univ. of Calif. Extension, S.F., 1971; instr./prof. of Eng. and film Coll. of San Mateo, 1963-;cons. Coll. Entrance Exam Bd., S.F. 1966-67; juror, Nat. Endowment for the Humanities, S.F. 1973-74, S.F. Internat. Film Festival, 1979-80; judge, Calif. State Student Film Festival, Los Angeles, 1974-75, 1979; writer/cons. Aspen Inst. for Humanistic Studies, Palo Alto, 1974-79; mem: Conf. on Coll. Composition and Comm. 1963- (exec. com. 1969-76, chair coll. comm. 1972-74), Nat. Council of Tchrs. of Eng. 1963-, Bay Area Film/Tape Council 1985-, Film Arts Foundn. 1985; coauthor of 3 books: Anatomy of Reading, 1965, Design For A Composition, 1966, Anatomy of Reading, 2nd. Ed. 1970; author: numerous articles and fiction for newsletters/magazines, 1971-92; The Archaeologist and the Handyman's Wife, (pub. review of The Mother Tongue by Bill Bryson) 1992; mil: PNT3, USN, 1953-55; Democrat; Buddhist; rec: writing. Ofc: Film Department (17-149), College of San Mateo 1700 W. Hillsdale Blvd. San Mateo 94402

WILMORE, H. SYLVIA, broadcaster, theologian, association president; b. June 15, 1938, Indpls., Ind.; d. Archie Case and Gladys Mae (Beckleiheimer) Wilson; m. James Austin, June 14, 1970; edn: MDiv, Fuller Theol. Sem., 1989; Jerusalem Ctr. for Biblical Studies, Jerusalem, Israel 1987; The Episcopal Theol. Sch. at Claremont 1990. Career: founder, pres. Christian Businesswomen Internat., Pasadena 1980-; radio bdcstr. internat. Messages of Hope, 1990-; asst. to sr. v.p. Atlantic Richfield Co., L.A. 1974-84; grade sch. tchg. asst. Los Angeles Unified Sch. Dist. 1979-80; dir. evangelism St. Stephens Ch., Fullerton 1976-80. secty., ofcr. 1980-84; mem. Big Sisters, Orange; biography pub. Victor L. Liotta, 1973; Episcopalian; rec: music, art, bicycling. Ofc: Christian Businesswomen Intl. 16 N Marengo Ste 300 Pasadena 91101

WILSON, DOUGLAS EDWIN, lawyer, b. Apr. 23, 1917, Sacramento; s. Richard Matthew and Ethel Ruth (O'Brien) W.; m. Helen Marie Lewis, Apr. 5, 1942; children: Sandra (Olds) b. 1943, Kent b. 1948, Jay b. 1950; edn: BA, Univ. of Pacific 1939; JD, UC Hastings Law Sch. 1948; admitted Calif. State Bar 1949. Career: atty. ptnr. Forslund & Wilson, Stockton, 1949-83, Wilson & Wilson, 1983-; US magistrate Stockton, Eastern Dist. of Calif., 1962-76; mem. San Joaquin County Retirement Bd. 1952-72; honors: Silver Beaver award Boy Scouts 1966, Disting. Eagle Scout award 1971; mem. Calif. Bar Assn., San Joaquin County Bar Assn., Am. Legion, Commonwealth Club (SF); Mason (Shriner, K.T.), Elk, Rotarian; mil: capt. Arty., US Army 1941-46; Rep.; Methodist; rec: golf, gardening. Res: 2134 Gardena Ave Stockton 95204 Ofc: Wilson & Wilson, Attys. 11 S San Joaquin St Stockton 95202

WILSON, JEANETTE KURTZ, educator; b. July 15, 1929, Albion, Mich.; d. Ivory Lee and Nora (Coates) Kurtz; m. Lucius Wilson, Nov. 21, 1953 (div.); children: Michael b. 1954, Debra b. 1955, Karen b. 1961; edn: medical steno cert. Cleary Coll., Ypsilanti, Mich. 1949; BS in bus., W.Va. State Coll. Inst., 1952; MA adminstrn. Newark State Tchrs. Coll., 1966; EdD (4.0 g.p.a.), Calif. Coast Univ., 1992. Career: sec. to Asst. Pres., W.Virginia St. Coll. Inst., 1950-52; guidance counselor McManus Jr. High Sch., Linden, N.J. 1970-72; personnel dept. Anaconda Telecom., Anaheim, Calif. 1980-75; middle sch. tchr., lit. & soc. studies, Moreno Valley (Calif.) Sch. Dist., 1980-; mem. bd. Sch. Site Coun. Allessandro Middle Sch., Moreno Valley, 1992; recipient Hon. Dr. Degree for dedication to students, Prin., Alessandro Middle Sch. 1992; mem: Assoc. Tchrs. of Met. Riverside 1987-91, Nat. Edn. Assn. 1980-, Calif. Tchrs. Assn. 1980-, Nat. Assn. Female Execs., Delta Sigma Theta Sor. (mem. 1950-, soc. action chair, co-chair 1986-90, v.p. DST Human Svs. Corp. 1990-91, v.p. Human Rels. Corp. 1991-), Nat. Coun. Negro Women (pres. 1979-82); author (autobio.) Every Knock A Boost (1980), contbr. poetry anthology: New Voices in Am. Poetry (1972, 75, 82); Republican; Prot.; rec: travel, writing, reciting poetry, modeling. Res: 8374 Magnolia Ave #37 Riverside 92504 Ofc: 1110 N Eaton St Albion MI 49224

WILSON, JOHN MURRAY, JR., manufacturing company president; b. May 22, 1933, Los Angeles; s. J. Murray and Elizabeth E. (Reese) W.; m. Marily Anne Purkiss, July 14, 1955 (div. 1971); children: J. Murray b. 1957, Craig A. b. 1959, Kimberley R. b. 1961, Durinda C. b. 1969; edn: BSME, UC Berkeley 1955; MBA, Harvard Bus. Sch. 1960. Career: prodn engr. Hewlett Packard, Palo Alto 1960-61; stock broker Shuman Agnew & Co., San Francisco 1961-63; fin. planning mgr. Ford Motor Co. (aero. div.), Newport Beach 1963-65; gen. mgr. Disc Instruments Inc., Santa Ana 1965-69; pres. Telcor Instruments Inc., Irvine 1969-; founder Biotronic GmbH, W. Germany 1970-; chmn. Cortron Corp., Irvine 1969-; dir. Electro Mechanical Systems, Stuart, Fla. 1975-; mem: Harvard Bus. Sch. Assn., So. Calif. Marine Assn., Nat. Marine Mfrs. Assn., Bohemian Club, S.F.; mil: lt.j.g. USN 1956-58; Republican; Presbyterian; rec: yachting, flyfishing. Ofc: Telcor Instruments, Inc. 17785 Sky Park Circle Irvine 92714

WILSON, JOHN RICHARD MEREDITH, college professor; b. Feb. 16, 1944, Vancouver, B.C.; nat. 1958; s. John Abraham Ross and Nora Margaret (Mains) W.; m. Mary Ann Ahlberg, Aug. 5, 1967; children: Amy b. 1969, Christine b. 1972; edn: diploma, Santa Barbara H.S., 1961; BA, UC Santa Barbara, 1964; PhD, Northwestern Univ., 1971. Career: instr. to assoc. prof. Minot State Coll., Minot, N.D., 1966-74; contract historia FAA, Wash., DC, 1974-76; assoc. prof. to prof., Mid Am. Nazarene Coll., Olathe, Kans., 1976-89; prof. So. Calif. Coll., Costa Mesa, 1989-; Fellow, Summer Inst., N.E.H., Princeton, N.J., 1980; Fellow, Summer Inst., N.E.H./Christian Coll. Coalition, Boston, Mass., 1984; Malone Fellow, Nat. Assn. of US-Arab Relations, Cairo, Egypt, 1986; delegate, Witness For Peace, Nicaragua, 1986; adv. placement reader, Ednl. Testing Svc., Princeton, N.J., 1987-; awards: Univ. of Calif. Abroad Pioneer, Bordeaux, France, 1962-63; Hearst Fellowship, Northwestern Univ., Evanston, Ill., 1964-65; Danforth Assoc., Danforth Found., St. Louis, 1980-86; mem: Orgn. of Am. Historians 1976-, Am. Historical Assn. 1976-, Conf. on Faith and History 1976-, Phi Delta Lambda Honor Soc. 1981-; civic: cand. for House of Representatives, N.D. Democratic party, 1972; Cultural Arts Comm., Costa Mesa, 1990; author: Turbulence Aloft, 1979, A New Res. Guide in History, 1986, Herbert Hoover and the Armed Forces 1993; ed., Forging The American Character, 1991; Democrat; Assemblies of God; rec: baseball fan, softball, mountain hiking, reading. Res: 924 Tanana Place Costa Mesa 92626. Ofc: So. Calif. Coll. 55 Fair Dr. Costa Mesa 92626

WILSON, JON STEPHEN, consultant; b. June 10, 1935, Chickasha, Okla.; s. Marion Alfred and Zella Mae (Eisfelder) W.; m. Nancy Lee, May 31, 1958; children: M. Howard b. 1959, Stephenie b. 1961; edn: BSME, Oklahoma Univ., 1958; M.Automotive E., Chrysler Inst., Detroit 1960; MSE in I.E., Ariz. St. Univ., Tempe 1969. Career: engr. trainee Chrysler Corp., Detroit 1958-60, test engr. 1960-61; test engr. ITT Cannon Elect., Phoenix, Az. 1961-65; environmental lab. mgr. Motorola, S.P.D., Phoenix 1965-74; applications engring. mgr. Endevco div. Allied Signal, San Juan Capistrano, Ca. 1974-78, mktg. mgr. 1978-85; cons. prin. The Dynamic Consultant, 1985-; mem: Am. Consultants League (certified cons. 1986-), Assn. of Profl. Consultants and Advisors (cert. profl. cons. 1991-), Soc. Automotive Engrs. 1958-, Instrument Soc. Am. 1974-, Inst. Environmental Scis. 1965-, Am. Soc. for Tng. & Devel. 1990-, Toastmasters Intl. Dana Point 1984-; author: Climatic Testing Procedures 1990, Instrumentation for Test & Measurement 1991, editor (books): Dynamic Pressure Measurement Technology 1991, Shock & Vibration Measurement Technology 1986; Indep.; Methodist; rec: photography, computers, philately. Res/Ofc: The Dynamic Consultant 32871 Via Del Amo San Juan Capistrano 92675

WILSON, LINDA LOU, librarian; b. Nov. 17, 1945, Rochester, Minn.; d. Eunice Wilson; edn: BA grad. with distinction, Univ. Minn., Mpls. 1967, MA, 1968. Career: hd. physical scis. catalog dept. UC Riverside 1968-71; city librarian Belle Glade Municipal Library, Belle Glade, Fla. 1972-74; childrens lit. instr. Palm Beach Jr. Coll. Glades Center 1973; adult /YA extension hd. Kern County Library, Bakersfield 1974-80; dist. dir. Lake Agassiz Regional Library System, Crookston Minn. 1980-85; supvg. librarian San Diego Co. Library, San Diego 1985-87; county librarian Merced Co. Library, Merced 1987-; awards: fellowship to library sch., valedictorian h.s.; mem: Am. Library Assn., Calif. Library Assn. 1969-; past pres. pub. library div. Minn. Library Assn. 1985; active Chamber of Commerce, Bus. and Profl. Womens Clubs; helped write ref. study of San Diego Co. Library; Lutheran; rec: swimming, walking, travel. Ofc: Merced Co Library 2100 O St Merced 95340

WILSON, PETE, governor; b. Aug. 23, 1933, Lake Forest, Ill.; s. James Boone and Margaret (Callaghan) W.; m. Betty Robertson (div.); m. Gayle Graham Edlund, May 29, 1983; edn: BA in English lit., Yale Univ., 1955; JD, Boalt Hall UC Berkeley, 1962; Hon. LLD, Grove City Coll., 1983, UC San Diego, 1983, Univ. San Diego, 1984; admitted bar: Calif., 1962. Career: atty. pvt. practice, San Diego 1965-66; elected representative California State Assembly, 1966-71; mayor City of San Diego, 1971-83; U.S. Senator from Calif., 1983-91; Governor, California, 1991-; trustee Conservation Found.; mem. exec. bd. BSA San Diego County Council; hon. trustee So. Calif. Council Soviet Jews; advy. mem. Urban Land Inst., 1985-86; founding dir. Retinitis Pigmentosa Internat.; hon. dir. Alzheimer's Family Ctr. Inc., 1985; hon. bd. dirs. Shakespeare-San Francisco, 1985; awards: Golden Bulldog award (1984, 85, 86), Guardian of Small Bus. 1984, ROTC scholar Yale Univ. 1951-55, Legislator of Year League of Calif. Cities 1985, Man of Yr. Nat. Guard Assn. Calif. 1986, Man of Yr. citation UC Boalt Hall 1986; advy. bd. Nat. Mil. Family Assn.; mem. Phi Delta Phi, Zeta Psi; Republican; Episcopalian. Ofc: State Capitol Office of Governor Sacramento 95814

WILSON, RONALD L., banking executive; b. Oct. 12, 1953, Hyden, Ky.; s. Calvert Clen Clay and Elaine Rose (Anderson) W.; m. Valarie Gay Metsopolos, Oct. 20, 1971 (div. Nov. 1981); m. Deanna Jo Darlington, Dec. 11, 1982; children: Stephanie b. 1981, Colin b. 1984, Holly b. 1987, Emily b. 1990; edn: BA, Grand Canyon Coll. Phoenix, Az. 1975. Career: asst. cashier Thunderbird Bank, Phoenix, Az. 1971-77; v.p. Rainier Nat. Bank, Seattle, Wa. 1977-83; sr. v.p. Desert Comm. Bank, Victorville, Ca. 1983; exec. v.p. Cuyamaca Bank, Santee 1984-89; pres. and c.e.o. Desert Comm. Bank, Victorville, 1989-; faculty Olympic Comm. Coll., Olympia, Wa. 1978-81; chmn. bd. Inland Empire Comm. Devel. Corp., Ontario, Ca. 1991; awards: Santee Exchange Club Exchangite of Yr. (1986, 1988); civic: Victor Valley Child Abuse Task Force (v.p., dir. 1990-), Victorville C.of C. (dir. 1991), St. Mary's Desert Valley Hosp. (exec. dir. 1990-), Santee C.of C. (v.p., dir. 1985-89), San Diego Child Abuse Prevention Ctr. (treas., dir. 1985-89); clubs: Victorville Rotary, Santee Exchange (treas., dir. 1985-89); Republican; Baptist; rec: bicycling, running, gardening, hiking, writing. Res: 18805 Mingo Rd Apple Valley 92307 Ofc: Desert Community Bank 14800 La Paz Dr Victorville 92392

WILSON, SONJA MARY, business educator, school board official, speaker, consultant, poet; b. Mar. 28, 1938, Lake Charles, La.; d. Albert Ronald and Annelia (DeVille) Molless; m. Willie McKinley Williams, Apr. 28, 1956 (div. 1969); m. 2d Howard Brooks Wilson, Nov. 12, 1982; children: William, Dwayne, Rachelle Smith, Devon, Lisa Lewis, Ricardo, stepchildren (by 2d marriage): Howard, Yvonne; 21 grandchildren; edn: grad. Manual Arts High Sch. of L.A., 1956; AA soc. & behav. scis., Mt. San Jacinto Jr. Coll., 1976-92; bus. edn. tchg. cred., UC San Bernardino, 1982; LaVerne Univ., 1984-5, CalPoly 1986; So. Ill. Univ., 1985-92; Calif. tchg. creds.- adult edn., bus. and vocat. edn. Career: sales clerk, National Dollar Stores-1 yr.; sales clk., receptionist Royal Fruit & Produce, L.A. Terminal Annex-4 yrs.; PBX operator, payroll acct., secty., clk. Lake Elsinore Mil. Acad2 yrs.; steno-typist, telegraph clk., typist Co. of L.A.-5 yrs.; secty., purchasing clk., mgr. General Electric Supply Co.-7 yrs.;

with Lake Elsinore Unified Sch. Dist. 31+ yrs.: sec. to prin. Elsinore H.S. 1974-83, tchr. adult vocat. edn. 1979-84, notary pub. 1981-85, coord. vocat. edn. 1983-84, tchr. bus. and vocat. edn., class adviser, 1983-88; elected mem. Lake Elsinore Unified Sch Dist. Board, 1988-, bd. pres. 1988-89, clerk 1991-; Lake Elsinore Sch. Dist. mem. 1979-, clk., pres., 1982-84, v.p. 1988-89; mem. Calif. Sch. Bds. Assn. (dir. region 18, Golden Bell Award com., audit com., nominations com., conf. planning com., legis. com., media com.); mem. Riverside County Sch. Bds. Assn. (1979-, pres. 1989-90, legislative facilitator planner 1988-90); mem. Calif. Coalition of Black School Bd. Members (pres. 1990; presiding ofcr./ speaker Fresno Conf., Bakersfield Conf. 1989, Sacto. City Unified 1990); advisor Black Student Union/Future Leaders of Am. (1983-, appreciation tribute 1989); speaker, panelist and facilitator num. workshops and profl. meetings; mem. St. Dept. Edn. Hoenig's Tri Council/African-Am. Com. 1990-92; honors: PTA Golden Oak Award for svc. to community and youth 1992, Proclamation City of Lake Elsinore 1989, Proclamation Co. of Riverside 1984, appreciation for comm. service Lake Elsinore C.of C. 1989, 90, Leukemia Soc. of Am. 1989, United Way 1988-89, Lions Club 1976-77, NAACP Outstanding contbns. to comm. services & academic devel. of youth & edn. (4/8/89, 90), Sojourner Truth in Media Network, Hilltop Community Center dedication for excellence in field of edn. 1989, Eta Phi Beta Sor. Inc. for dedication & leadership 1989, Black Art & Social Club for leadership & sensitivity to individual needs of children 1989, Calif. Bus. Edn. Assn., Calif. Elected Women Ofcls. Assn., Calif. Sch. Employees Assn. (pres., treas., regional rep. asst., state negotiation com., conf. del.), Eta Phi Beta (Gamma Alpha chpt. pres., treas., v.p., reg. ofcr.); civic bds: Girl Scouts (ldr.& camp dir.-2 yrs.), Boy Scouts Am. (leader & den mother); publs: CSEA President's Column, 1974-78; Valley News local news writer under pen name "Sunshine" 1974; article "Riverside County Schools" in Vision Mag., 1990; poem "Oh To Be Looked In The Eye" Betty Ford Ctr. at Eisenhower "Professional In Residence" Jour.; World of Poetry hon. mention: Double Image-Blackchild; Little Girl, Pain, others; Democrat (Ctr. comm. rep. & del.); rec: travel, gardening, sewing, reading, vintner. Res: 21330 Waite St Lake Elsinore 92530

WILSON, SUSANNE BOOTHE, county supervisor; b. Sept. 30, 1928, Gonzales, Tx.; d. Wm. Henry, Jr. and Maurine (Ingraham) Boothe; m. Robert Wilson, 1947; children: William Munsey b. 1949, Robert Howell b. 1952, David Richard b. 1957; 3 grandchildren; edn: Univ. Tx. 1946-48, Coll. of William and Mary 1948-49; BA in polit. sci. (honors), CSU San Jose 1976. Career: politician, splst. in land use, toxics, transp., and health; elected 2 terms City Council of San Jose 1973-78, v. mayor 1977; elected 3 terms Santa Clara Co. Bd. of Suprs. 1979-90; chair: Women's Concerns Task Force 1984-, Housing & Comm. Devel. Council, Transp. 2000 (1984-), Safe Water Council 1984-; honors: woman of distinction The Woman's Alliance 1984, disting. alumni San Jose St. Univ. 1982, citizen of year Youth Sci. Inst. 1984, named Pub. Health Defender, Silicon Valley Toxics Coalition 1985, Juliette Gordon Low award Girl Scouts Santa Clara Co. 1988; mem: Calif. Elected Women for Edn. and Res. (founding mem., past pres.), Calif. Women in Agri., Nat. Women's Polit. Caucus (founding mem. 1973-), LWV; civic: City Ctr. Ballet (trustee), Women's Alliance Advy. Bd., Big Brothers/Big Sisters, BSA Advy. Council, Youth Sci. Inst., Valley Med. Ctr. Prenatal Task Force; contbr. articles to YWCA Mag. (1972), Women & Crime (1976), Westplan (Am. Planning Assn., 1982); Democrat; Methodist; rec: garden, philately, sewing. Res: 1743 Valpico Dr San Jose 95124 Ofc: County of Santa Clara 70 W Hedding St San Jose 95110

WILSON, THEODORE HENRY, electronics company executive, aerospace engineer; b. Apr. 23, 1940, Eufaula, Okla.; s. Theodore V. and Maggie E. (Buie) W.; m. Barbara Ann Tassara, May 16, 1958 (div. 1982); children: Debbie Marie, Nita Leigh Wilson Axten, Pamela Ann, Brenda Louise, Theodore Henry II, Thomas John; m. Colleen Fagan, Jan. 1, 1983 (div. 1987); m. Karen L. Lerohl, Sept. 26, 1987; edn: BSME, UC Berkeley 1962; MSME, USC 1964, MBA, 1970, MSBA, 1971. Career: sr. res. engr. No. Am. Aviation Co. div. Rockwell Internat., Downey 1962-65; propulsion analyst, supr. div. applied tech. TRW, Redondo Beach 1965-67, mem. devel. staff systems group 1967-71; sr. fin. analyst worldwide automotive dept. TRW, Cleve. 1971-72; contr. systems and energy group TRW, Redondo Beach 1972-79; dir. fin. control equipment group TRW, Cleve. 1979-82, v.p. fin. control indsl. and energy group 1982-85; v.p. fin. space and def. group TRW, Redondo Beach 1985-; lectr., mem. com. acctg. curriculum UCLA Ext. 1974-79; mem: Fin. Execs. Inst. (com. govt. bus.), Machinery and Allied Products Inst. (govt. contracts coun.), Nat. Contract Mgmt. Assn. (bd. advisors), Aerospace Industries Assn. (procurement and fin. coun.), UCLA Chancellors Assocs., Tau Beta Pi, Beta Gamma Sigma, Pi Tau Sigma; Republican. Res: 3617 Via La Selva Palos Verdes Estates 90274

WINCHELL, ROBERT ALLEN, government auditor; b. Oct. 28, 1945, Ft. Monmouth, N.J.; s. Robert Winslow and Mary M. (Allen) W.; edn: BA, UC Santa Barbara, 1967; MBA, Wharton Grad. Div. Univ. Pa., 1969; C.P.A., Calif. Career: fin. analyst, treas. div. S.C. Gas Co., Los Angeles 1975-76; with Defense Contract Audit Agency, 1976-, senior auditor and resident ofcr. Rockwell Internat. B-1 div., El Segundo 1976-79; Hughes Aircraft Co., El Segundo 1979-84; senior auditor Defense Contract Audit Agency regional office, L.A. 1984-86; supvy. auditor, resident office Litton Systems, Woodland

Hills 1986-87; Litton Inds. Inc., suboffice, Beverly Hills 1987-89; supvy. auditor AiResearch, Torrance 1989-92; supvy. auditor San Fernando Valley branch AiResearch 1993-; mem: Am. Inst. CPAs, Assn. of Govt. Accts.; club: Los Angeles CC; mil: 1st lt. US Army 1969-71, Bronze Star; Republican; Presbyterian; rec: golf, hiking, travel. Res: 2008 California Ave Santa Monica 90403 Ofc: Defense Contract Audit Agency, San Fernando Valley Branch Office, Van Nuys

WINCOR, MICHAEL Z., psychopharmacology educator, clinician, researcher; b. Feb. 9, 1946, Chgo.; s. Emanuel and Rose (Kershner) W.; m. Emily E.M. Smythe; children: Meghan Heather, Katherine Rose; edn: SB in zoology, Univ. Chgo., 1966; PharmD, USC, 1978. Career: research project specialist Univ. Chgo. Sleep Lab, 1968-75; psychiatric pharmacist Brotman Med. Center, Culver City 1979-83; asst. prof. USC, 1983-; cons. Federal Bur. of Prisons Drug Abuse Pgm., Terminal Is., 1978-81, Nat. Inst. Drug Abuse, Bethesda, Md. 1981, The Upjohn Co., Kalamazoo, Mich. (1982-87, 91-), Area 24 Profl. Stds. Rev. Orgn., L.A. 1983, Brotman Med. Ctr., Culver City 1983-88, SmithKline Beecham Pharms. Phila. 1990-, Tokyo Coll. of Pharm., Tokyo 1991; mem. bd. dirs. USC Sch. of Pharm. Alumni Assn. 1979-; awards: cert. appreciation Mayor of Los Angeles 1981, Bristol Labs Award 1978, USC Faculty scholar 1978, Rho Chi; mem: AAAS, Am. Assn. of Colls. of Pharmacy (mem. focus group on liberalization of the profl. curric.), Am. Coll. Clinical Pharmacy (chmn. constn. and bylaws com. 1983-84), Am. Soc. Hosp. Pharmacists (chmn. edn. and tng. advy. working group 1985-88), Am. Pharm. Assn. (del. annual meeting Ho. of Dels. 1989), Sleep Research Soc., Am. Sleep Disorders Assn.; civic: Franklin Avenue School Advy. Council 1986-89, K.I. Children's Ctr. Bd. Dirs. 1988-89, The Sequoyah Sch. Bd. Trustees 1992-; author 30+ jour. articles, book chapters, and papers presented nat. and internat. meetings and reviewer; rec: photography. Ofc: Univ. So. Calif. 1985 Zonal Ave Los Angeles 90033

WINEMAN, PAUL RAYMOND, JR., marketing consultant, contract negotiator; b. Oct. 22, 1936, Hollywood, Calif.; s. Paul Raymond and Frances Neale (Dienst) W.; edn: BA communs., Univ. Wash. 1958, MA Arabic studies, Am. Univ. Beirut, Lebanon 1967. Career: gen. mgr. Television of Iran 1967; contract supv. US Corps of Engrs. Saudi Arabia 1968; regl. dir. Avco Internat. Svcs., Avco Corp. Beirut, Lebanon 1969-73; regl. dir. United Technols. Internat. Beirut 1973-77; pres. Paul R. Wineman & Assoc. Inc. Marina del Rey, Calif. 1977-; seminar leader on negotiating domestic & internat. 1981-; honors: Phi Kappa Psi 1958, recipient Dick Laybourne Memorial award Avco Corp. 1971; mem. Rotary; mil: capt. US Army Signal Corps 1958-65; rec: tennis, travel. Res: 4267 Marina City Dr Apt 1108WTS Marina del Rey 90292

WINKLER, DELAINE LAUREN, environmental consultant; b. Aug. 17, 1953, Los Angeles; parents: Earl Theodore and Sara (Landman) Winkler; edn: BS, USC 1975, MS, 1979. Career: tchg. asst. USC 1976-79; marine scientist, lab. supvr. Ichthyoplankton Coastal and Harbor Studies, USC and L.A. Co. Natural Hist. Mus., 1979-81; res. asst. Getty Synthetic Fuels 1981; asst. environmental scientist Port of Los Angeles, San Pedro 1981-86; assoc. environmental planner So. Calif. Assn. of Govts., L.A. 1986-89; indep. cons. Winkler Environmental Planning, 1989-; taxonomic cons. Taxon 1979; academic advr. USC Biology dept. 1978; honors: Bank Am. Music Award 1971, Calif. State Scholar 1971-75, Calif. State Fellow 1975-78; mem: Assn. of Environmental Profls., Am. Planning Assn., Phi Sigma (Alpha Alpha chpt.), Nat. Trust for Hist. Preservation, Los Angeles Library Assn., Jewish Geneal. Soc. L.A.; profl. presentations incl. Pacific Slope Biochem. Conf., Santa Barbara 1978, pub. res. article in Fishery Bulletin (1983); Democrat; Jewish; rec: genealogy, tennis, hiking. Res: PO Box 24633 Los Angeles 90024 Ofc: Winkler Environmental Planning POB 24622 Los Angeles 90024

WINKLER, HOWARD LESLIE, investment banker, business consultant; b. Aug. 16, 1950, NY, NY; s. Martin and Magda (Stark) W.; m. Robin Lynn Richards, Sept. 12, 1976; son, David Menachem; edn: AA in mktg., bus. data proc., and bus. mgmt. degrees, Los Angeles City Coll., 1973, 77, 81; NASD securities lic. 1981-. Career: senior cons. Financial Consultants Inc., Los Angeles 1972-81; asst. v.p. Merrill Lynch Inc., L.A. 1981-83; v.p. Drexel, Burnham, Lambert Inc., Beverly Hills 1983-84; pres. Howard Winkler, Investments 1984-; ptnr. N.W.B. Assocs., L.A. 1988-90; nat. political editor B'nai B'rith Messenger, 1986-; chmn. bd. Community Adult Care Ctrs. of America, 1990-91; dir. Federal Home Loan Bank of S.F., 1991-; chmn. bd. dirs. United Community and Housing Devel. Corp., L.A. 1986-; apptd. L.A. Co. Narcotics & Dangerous Drugs Commn. 1987-; Gov. Deukmejian apptd. trustee Minority Health Professions Edn. Found., 1989-, sec.-treas. 1990-; recipient awards for community service & leadership- Agudath Israel of Calif., Pres. Reagan, US Sen. Pete Wilson, Gov. G. Deukmejian, US Cong. Bobbi Fiedler 1986, resolution of commendn. Calif. State Assembly 1986, L.A. County Bd. of Suprs. and City of L.A. 1986, 1990, community leadership Iranian-Jewish Comm. of L.A. 1990, Calif. State Senate Resolution of commendn. spons. Sen. Edward Royce 1992, listed Who's Who in World 1986-, Who's Who in America 1993-, charter issue Who's Who in Republican Party; civic: Calif. Lincoln Clubs PAC (pgm. chair 1987-91), Agudath Israel of Calif. (commr. legis. and civic action 1985-), V.F.W., Jewish War Vets; Republican: Calif. Rep. Party Platform Com. 1988, 90, Calif. YR 1975-, Calif. Rep. Assembly 1982-, full mem. Calif. State Central Com. 1985-, Los Angeles Co. Rep. Central Com. 1985-93, chmn. 45th A.D. 1988-90, Nat. Rep. Senatl. Com. nat. fin. bd. 1986-90, state co-chair Pete Wilson for Gov. '90, 1989, state chmn. Kemp for Pres. '88, 1987, mem. Nat. Steering Com. Bush-Quayle '88, 1987, mem. Nat. Exec. Com. Bush-Quayle '92, 1991, fin. com. John Seymour for Senate '92, 1991, mem. Rep. Presdl. Task Force 1985- (Legion of Merit Award 1992), Senatl. Inner Circle 1986-, Golden Circle of Calif. 1986-, GOP platform planning com. at large del. 1992, appt. del. by Gov. Pete Wilson to GOP nat. conv. Houston 1992; mil: adminstrv. supr. CID US Army 1969-72, SE Asia; Jewish (Orthodox); rec: philanthropies, family time, eating. Ofc: PO Box 480454 Los Angeles 90048

WINN, DYANNA MICHELE, pharmaceutical company executive; b. Mar. 26, 1943, Chicago, Ill.; d. Donald Orin and Barbara Jeanne (Ewbank) Brazeal; m. Dennis Derr, Mar. 23, 1960; m. 2d. Thomas Winn, Sept. 18, 1977; children: Kevin b. 1960, Jacquelynn b. 1966, Kristynn b. 1968, Maureen b. 1970, Melissa b. 1983; edn: Fresno City Coll. 1979-80; West Valley Coll. 1972-78; MBA, Pepperdine Univ. 1990. Career: dental asst. Howard G. Melze, Chgo. 1961-63; secty., correspondent Motorola, Franklin Park, Ill. 1963-65; gen. mgr. Sheraton Labs. Inc., Santa Clara 1973-79; corp. staff analyst Drug Service Inc., Fresno 1979-81; dir. adminstrn. Synergex Corp. 1981-85, corp. secty. 1982-85; dir. telecomms. Bergen Brunswig, Orange 1985-91; v.p. supplier relations America's Pharmacy Inc., Laguna Hills 1991-; speaker IBM 1983-85; awards: 1st woman mgr. of profit center Sheraton Labs. Inc. 1977, 1st woman corporate ofcr. Synergex Corp. 1982; mem: TCA, ICA, IOWIT, active in Am. Legion Aux.; Republican; Prot. Res: 25191 Darlington Mission Viejo 92692 Ofc: America's Pharmacy, Inc. 140 Columbia Laguna Hills 92656

WINNING, ETHAN A., management and human resources consulting executive; b. Dec. 26, 1939, New Bedford, Mass.; s. Edward A. and Ruth W.; m. Sharon Carol Fogel, Jan. 26, 1964; children: Jennifer b. 1967, Amy b. 1969; edn: BA sociology, CSU Northridge, 1963; MS soc. psychology, Univ. Oregon, Eugene 1965, MA edn. and psychology, 1966. Career: psychologist and rehab. counselor State of Calif. and County of L.A., Rancho Los Amigos Hosp., Downey 1966-68; v.p. personnel and tng. Wells Fargo Bank, L.A., Wellsco Data Corp., San Francsco, and Wells Fargo and Co., San Francisco, 1968-73; nat. dir. and v.p. human resources Komatsu America Corp., San Francisco 1974-77; founder, pres. and c.e.o. Ethan A. Winning Associates Inc., Walnut Creek 1977-, estab. Personnel Mediation Services subs. co., 1990-; expert witness in labor, mgmt. disputes, and unemployment claims issues; assoc. ed. for nat. paper, The Personnel News, and monthly columnist for Calif. Job Journal; past secty. Calif. Small Financial Instns. Group; instr. Diablo Valley Coll., 1975-86; past v.p. Contra Costa Execs. Assn.; invited guest radio and TV shows; author: Common Sense Employer-Employee Relations (pub. Merchants and Mfrs. Assn., L.A., 1991); rec: racquetball, biking, writing, tennis, photography, amateur radio (adv. lic. WD6GKF). Ofc: Ethan A. Winning Associates, Inc. 3050 Citrus Cir Ste 104 Walnut Creek 94598 Tel: 510/944-1034 Fax: 510/944-1667

WINSLOW, DAVID ALLEN, naval officer and chaplain, writer; b. July 12, 1944, Dexter, Iowa; s. Franklin Earl and Inez Maude (McPherson) W.; m. Frances Lavinia Edwards, June 6, 1970; children: Frances b. 1975, David b. 1979; edn: BA, Bethany Nazarene Univ., 1968; MDiv, Drew Univ., 1971, STM, 1974; postgrad. N.Y. Univ. 1974-75; ordained United Methodist Ch., 1973. Career: minister of visitation Marble Collegiate Ch., N.Y.C. 1970-71; pastor Trinity United Methodist Ch., Jersey City, N.J. 1971-73; Westside United Methodist Ch., Paterson, N.J. 1973-75; lt. cdr./chaplain US Navy, 1975-; treas. Santa Clara Valley Council of Churches 1993-; listed Who's Who in Religion, Who's Who In West; mem: Am. Assn. for Counseling and Devel., Am. Mental Health Counselors Assn., The Acad. of Political Sci., Internat. Soc. for Traumatic Stress Studies, The Military Chaplains Assn. of USA; clubs: Dick Richards Breakfast Club 1988-91, Nat. Exchange Club, Navy League (hon.), F&A Masons, Scottish Rite, Salaam Temple; civic bds: Am. Red Cross Orange Cty. (disaster service, family service coms. 1989-91), Exchange Club Child Abuse Prevention Ctr. 1990-91; columnist Jersey Jour. 1971-73, The Chaplain 1978, mil. newpapers 1975-; Republican (Greater Irvine Rep. Assembly, Republican Assocs. Orange Co., Assembly Club 69th dist. 1988-92); United Methodist; rec: sailing, swimming, golf. Res: 757 Inverness Way Sunnyvale 94087

WINSLOW, FRANCES EDWARDS, public administrator; b. Sept. 12, 1948, Phila.; d. Harry Donaldson and Anna Louise (McColgan) Edwards; m. David A. Winslow, June 6, 1970; children: Frances b. 1975, David b. 1979; edn: BA, Drew Univ., 1969, MA polit. sci., 1971; M Urban Planning New York Univ., 1974, PhD pub. adminstrn., 1978; cert. hazardous mats. mgmt., UCI Ext., 1991. Career: asst. to city mgr. City of Florham Park, N.J. 1970-73; instr. Kean Coll. N.J., Union 1973-75; public safety asst. Irvine Police Dept. 1984-85, mgmt. analyst 1985-86, senior mgmt. analyst and dir. emergency mgmt. City of Irvine 1986-91; dir. Office of Emergency Svs., City of San Jose, 1991-; adj. prof. National Univ., L.A. campus 1984-86, Orange County 1986-89; cons. Nat. Ctr. for Earthquake Engring. Research; gubnat. appt. mem. Seismic Safety Commn., Calif.; mem. Nat. Coordinating Com. on Emergency Mgmt.; Calif. Emergency

Svcs. Assn.; awards: Loula D. Lasker Found. fellow 1973-74, Navy League Volunteer Svc. Award 1984, Fire Marshal's Commendn. 1988, outstanding svc. So. Calif. Emergency Svs. Assn. 1991, Soroptimist Intl. Woman of Distinction - Environment 1991, listed Who's Who Among Students in Am. Colls. & Univs., Who's Who in Fin. & Ind., Who's Who Among Women, Who's Who in World, Who's Who Among Emerging Leaders; mem: Orange Cty. Cities Emergency Mgmt. Org. (pres. 1991), Am. Soc. Pub. Adminstrn. (charter bd. mem.,com. chair), Am. Planning Assn. (com. mem.), Acad. Criminal Justice Scis. (fellow), Internat. City Mgmt. Assn., San Jose Mgmt. Assn. Bd.; civic: Boy Scouts Am. (P.R. com.), Santa Clara Valley Am. Red Cross Disaster Preparedness Com.; editor Urban Resources J. 1989, contbg. writer, Emergency Mgmt. 1990; produce and write videos 1986-; Republican; Methodist; rec: church activities, politics, reading, handcrafts. Ofc: City of San Jose 855 M. San Pedro St Ste 404 San Jose 95110

WINSLOW, NORMAN ELDON, business consulting executive; b. Apr. 4, 1938, Oakland; s. Merton Conrad and Roberta Eileen (Drennen) W.; m. Betty June Cady, Jan. 20, 1962 (div. Aug. 1971); children: Todd K. b. 1966; m. Ilene Ruth Jackson, Feb. 3, 1979; edn: BS, CSU Fresno, 1959. Career: retail asst. mgr. Proctor's Jewelry, Fresno 1959-62; ins. sales, dist. mgr. Allstate Ins. Co., Fresno 1962-69; ins. agt. Fidelity Union Life, Dallas, Tx. 1969-71; field rep., dist. mgr., zone mgr. The Southland Corp., Dallas 1971-78; owner Ser-Vis-Etc, bus. consultants, Goleta, Calif. 1978-; bd. dir. United Retailers, Inc. 1993-; ed./publ. Franchisservice News; author: Hands in Your Pockets (1992); affil. mem. Nat. Coalition of Assn. of 7-Eleven Franchise Assn. 1984-90, Sigma Chi; mil: A1/c Calif. Air Nat. Guard 1961-67; Republican; Methodist; rec: gardening, photography. Res: 1179 N Patterson Santa Barbara 93117 Ofc: Ser-Vis-Etc PO Box 2276 Goleta 93118

WINSLOW, PHILIP CHARLES, manufacturing company executive, marketing professional; b. Jan. 13, 1924, Carthage, Ind.; s. William Howard and Ione (Morris) W.; m. Arlis Brown, Oct. 6, 1951; children: Mark b. 1952, Jay b. 1955, Julie b. 1963; edn: BS, Purdue Univ., 1948. Career: dist. mgr. Ralston Purina Co., San Luis Obispo 1950-52, reg. product mgr., Palo Alto, 1953-58, asst. div. sales mgr., Charlotte, N.C., 1959-60, div. sales mgr., Bloomington, Ill. 1960-66, nat. mktg. mgr., St. Louis, Mo. 1967-71; v.p. Namolco Inc., Willow Grove, Pa. 1971-84; dir. mktg. Cargill Inc., Willow Grove, Pa. 1984-86, mktg. cons. Cargill Inc., Mpls. 1986-88; v.p., cons. Walt Montgomery Associates, Huntingdon, Tenn. 1989-; pres., bd. mem. Winslow Farms Inc., Carthage, Ind. 1981-; mem., com. chair American Feed Ind. Assn. 1971-88; clubs: Purdue (Phila., pres. 1981-86), Big Ten (Phila., pres. 1981-82), Purdue (San Diego, mem. 1986-), Big Ten So. Calif. (mem. 1986-), Shadowridge Golf (1986-, sec. treas. 1991-93, bd. of gov. 1993), Masonic Lodge (Carthage, Ind.); mil: s/sgt. US Army 1948-50; Republican; Lutheran; rec: golf. Res: 1305 La Salle Ct Vista 92083

WINTER, DENNIS WAYNE, treasurer; b. June 6, 1937, Milwaukee, Wis.; s. Jerome J. and Emma (Shaffer) W.; m. Susan Carole Gerathy, Sept. 19, 1964 (div. 1984); children: Anette b. 1968, James b. 1970; edn: BA, Univ. Wis. 1962; MBA, 1964. Career: internat. fin. rep. Allis Chalmers, Milwaukee, Wis. 1962-66; vice dir. Internat. Harvester Fin. AG, Zurich, Switzerland 1966-70; treas. Planning Research Corp., Los Angeles 1970-78; treas. Hydril Co. 1978-; mem: Tax Execs. Inst., Risk & Ins. Mgmt. Soc.; clubs: Treasurers (pres. 1987), Braemar CC, L.A. Athletic; mil: airman 2c. USAF SS 1955-59; Republican; R.Cath.; rec: golf, skiing. Res: 5112 Dumont Pl Woodland Hills 91364 Ofc: Hydril Co. 714 W Olympic Blvd Los Angeles 91364

WINTERS, KAREN COLE, writer, producer, computer graphics designer; b. Dec. 28, 1948, Long Beach; d. Homer Gray and Kathryne Lenore (Levenstein) Cole; m. Glenn Stuart Winters, Mar. 3, 1974; children: Kelly b. 1981, Michael b. 1985; edn: BA (Phi Beta Kappa), UCLA, 1970, MA journ., UCLA, 1971. Career: asso. creative dir. Honig-Cooper & Harrington, Los Angeles 1971-78; asso. creative dir. Rogers Weiss & Partners, Los Angeles, 1978-79; v.p., creative dir. Winters Productions, La Canada, 1979-, co-prod., interviewer and writer num. shows for ABC-TV news mag. "20/20", 1980-; prod./writer w/Walter Cronkite, documentary on marine pollution, 1990; awards include a Clio (1987, 1st award, outdoor, Sea World of Ohio), an Emmy (1981, Nat. Acad. of TV Arts and Scis., News & Documentary Producers for outstanding individual achievt. ABC-TV news pgm. 20/20), 3 Addy Awards 1988, So. Calif. Newspaper Execs. First Award 1988, Internat. Assn. of Bus. Communicators, Gold Quill Award (1988, for spl. video pgmmg.), PBS "Superfest" selected show (1988, "Changing Roles"), Chgo. Internat. Film Fest. silver plaque (1987, 1/2 hr. PBS show "Changing Roles"), N.Y. Internat. Film Fest. finalist 1987, numerous other creative awards; mem: Women in Design 1988-, Writers Guild 1977-, Verdugo Hills Art Assn. 1989-, Women in Communications, Crescenta-Canada YMCA 1985-; author: Your Career in Advertising, Nat. Textbook Co., 1980-90; rec: watercolor painting, skiing. Ofc: Winters Productions 1855 Foothill Blvd La Canada 91011

WINTON, ANNE BUSH, real estate brokerage president; b. Sept. 10, 1934, Oxford, Miss.; d. Wm. Darling and Annie Louise (Wooton) Bush; m. Fred B. Winton, Feb. 26, 1956 (div. 1979); children: Steven b. 1957, Mark b. 1960, Fred

III b. 1967; edn: BA edn., Univ. Miss., Oxford 1956; lic. speech therapist. Career: speech therapist U.C.P. Clinic, Pensacola, Fla. 1956-57; spl. edn. tchr. Warwick (R.I.) and Middletown (R.I.) Schs., 1964-65; speech therapist pvt. casework, Fla., Miss., R.I. and Calif., 1965-74; real estate agt., 1974-, founder, owner Anne Winton & Assocs. (with 100+ sales associates), offices in Poway, Rancho Bernardo, and Penasquitos, Calif. 1981-; advy. bd. The Bank of Rancho Bernardo, Rancho Bernardo Savings Bank; awards: Soroptomists Internat. Woman of Distinction 1989, Kiwanis Honoree 1991; current civic bds: Palomar Pomerado Hosp. Health Found. (bd.), CSUSM North Co. Advy. Council, Leadership 2000 (bd.), Golden Eagle Club (bd.), Clean Found. (bd.), Profl. and Exec. Women of the Ranch (founding mem., v.p.), Soroptomists; past bds: Am. Cancer Soc. North Co. Chpt. (past v.p.), Ranchos Del Norte Corral of the Westerners (sheriff 1983), Green Valley Civic Assn. (19+ yr. mem.), C.of C.-Rancho Bernardo (bd. 2 yrs.), Poway, Penasquitos, Escondido and San Diego; Republican; Episcopalian. Ofc: 16476 Bernardo Center Dr San Diego 92128

WITHERSPOON, GREGORY JAY, financial company executive; b. Sept. 30, 1946, Quantico, Va.; s. Thomas S. and Dorothy (Jordan) W.; m. Judith Ann Klein, Feb. 12, 1966 (div.); children: Lisa b. 1966, Michelle b. 1975; edn: BS, CSU Long Beach, 1970; C.P.A., Calif. Career: acctg. senior KMG Peat Marwick, Los Angeles 1969-72; senior mgr. Deloitte & Touche, L.A. 1972-79; c.f.o. Nanco Ents., Santa Barbara 1979-84; ptnr. BWV&P, Santa Barbara 1984-87; pres. Pea Soup Andersens, Buellton 1984-86; senior v.p. and c.f.o. Aames Financial, L.A. 1987-; mem. Am. Inst. CPA 1970-, Calif. Soc. CPAs 1970-; Republican; Presbyterian; rec: all sports.

WITT, HERBERT, federal health and human services executive; b. May 9, 1923, Stockton, Calif.; s. Arnold and Sarah (Peletz) W.; m. Hiala Einhorn, Nov. 17, 1957; children: Heidi b. 1959, Julie b. 1962, Amy b. 1967; edn: AB, Coll. Pacific, Stockton, 1943; MBA, UC Berkeley, 1949; C.P.A., 1955. Career: staff auditor, Price Waterhouse, S.F., Calif. 1953-55; asst. dist. mgr., U.S. Army Audit Agy., 1951-53, 55-65; chief, spl. projects, Defense Contract Audit Agy., 1965-66; reg. inspector gen. audit, Dept. Health & Human Svs., 1966-; instr. auditing, UC Berkeley, 1960-; adj. faculty, Univ. of S.F., 1983-; awards: Assn. Govt. Accountants Presdl. award, 1975; Office Inspector Gen. Profl. Devel. award, 1987; Office Inspector Gen. Thomas D. Morris Leadership award, 1988; Exceptional Achievement award, 1990; We. Intergovtl. Audit Forum Jack Birkholtz Leadership award, 1989; Inst. of Internal Auditors S.F. Area Chpt. Disting. Svc. award, 1992; mem: Inst. Internal Auditors (past pres., S.F. chpt.); Am. Inst. C.P.A.; Calif. Soc. C.P.A.; Am. Acctg. Assn.; We. Intergovtl. Audit Forum; author w. Brink, Modern Internal Auditing, 1982; with R. Atkisson and V. Brink, Modern Internal Auditing, 1986; mil: lt., USNR 1943-48; Democrat; Jewish; rec: hiking, swimming. Res: LaVerne Ave. Mill Valley 94941. Ofc: Dept. of Health and Human Services 50 United Nations Plaza San Francisco.

WITTBERGER, RUSSELL GLENN, broadcast executive; b. July 7, 1933, Milwaukee, Wis.; s. Anton George and Libbie Elizabeth (Kresnicka) W.; m. Patricia Elizabeth Bradley, June 26, 1971; children: Steven, Robert, Elizabeth, Gary, Scott, Jennifer; edn: BS journ., Marquette Univ., 1955. Career: gen. sales mgr. WEMP, Milw., Wis. 1968-69; gen. mgr. WNUW-FM, 1970; pres. Rand Broadcasting Corp., Miami, Fla. 1970-73; v.p., gen. mgr. KCBQ Inc., San Diego 1973-78; pres. Downe Communications, 1978; exec. v.p., pres. Charter Broadcasting Co., San Diego, 1978-82; exec. v.p. Cantor Advertising Corp., San Diego 1982-85; v.p. and gen. mgr. Boyd and Farmer Advt., San Diego 1985-86; v.p., gen. mgr., prin. KLZZ-FM, San Luis Obispo, 1987-90; dir. mktg. Metro Traffic Control, prin. Video Passport, San Diego, 1990-; mem: Milwaukee Ad Club (v.p., bd. 1970), Building Industry Assn., San Diego Broadcasters (pres. 1973-75); civic bds: Project Concern Internat. (dir. 1975-78), Radio Advt. Bur. (bd. dirs. 1978), COMBO San Diego (bd. trustees 1981), Food Bank S.L.O. Co. (v.chmn. 1989-90); Republican. Res: 1152 Hanover Place Alpine 91901 Ofc: Metro Traffic Control 591 Camino De La Reina Ste 525 San Diego 92108

WITTROCK, MERLIN CARL, educational psychologist; b. Jan. 3, 1931, Twin Falls, Idaho; s. Herman C. and Mary Ellen (Baumann) W.; m. Nancy McNulty, Apr. 3, 1953; children: Steven, Catherine, Rebecca; edn: BS biology, Univ. Mo., 1953, MS ednl. psych., 1956; PhD ednl. psych., Univ. Ill., Urbana 1960. Career: prof. grad. sch. edn. UC Los Angeles, 1960-, chmn. div. Educational Psychology, founder Ctr. Study Evaluation 1966, chmn. of the Faculty, 1991-93; fellow Ctr. for Advanced Study in Beh. Scis., 1967-68; vis. prof. Univ. Wis., Univ. Ill., Ind. Univ., Monash Univ., Australia; bd. dirs. Far West Labs., S.F. 1989-; chair com. on evaluation and assessment L.A. Unified Sch. Dist., 1988-; nat. advy. panel for math. scis. Nat. Research Council of Nat. Acad. Sci., 1988-89; chair nat. bd. Nat. Ctr. for Res. in Math. Scis. Edn., 1991; awards: Thorndike award for outstanding psychol. res. 1987, UCLA Distinguished Tchr. of the Univ. award Acad. Senate & Alumni Assn. 1990, grantee Ford Found.; Fellow AAAS, Charter Fellow Am. Psychol. Soc. (pres. div. ednl. psych. 1984-85, APA award for outstanding svc. to ednl. psych. 1991, assn. council 1987-), Fellow Am. Psych. Assn., mem. Am. Ednl. Res. Assn. (chmn. ann. conv., chmn. publs. 1980-83, AERA Council 1986-89, bd. dirs. 1987-89, chmn. com. on ednl.-TV 1989-, awards for outstanding contbns. 1986,

outstanding service 1989), Phi Delta Kappa; mil: capt. USAF; author, editor: The Evaluation of Instruction (1970), Changing Education (1973), Learning and Instruction (1977), The Human Brain (1977, Danish transl. 1980, Spanish 1982), The Brain and Psychology (1980), Instrnl. Psychology: Education and Cognitive Processes of the Brain, Neuropsychol. and Cognitive Processes of Reading (1981), Handbook of Research on Teaching (3d edit. 1986), The Future of Ednl. Psychology (1989), Research in Learning and Teaching (Macmillan, 1990), Testing and Cognition (1991). Ofc: UCLA 321 Moore Hall L.A. 90024 Ph:310/825-8329

WITZMAN, JOSEPH E., land developer, educator, publisher; b. Oct. 5, 1929, Minneapolis; s. Melvin King and Anita (Shepherd) W.; m. Joyce Wolfson, Jan. 25, 1953; children: Cindy b. 1955, Scott b. 1958; edn: BA pre-law, Univ. Minn., 1951, BS edn., 1953. Career: hotel mgr., gen. prop. Midland Hotel Chain, Mpls. 1958-63; motel owner/opr. Travelodges, San Diego 1964-68; tchr. San Diego City Schools, 1964-68; R.E. investor, 1968-; pres. Hiway Host Motor Inns, chain, Hiway Host Motels, 1969-; prof./coordinator San Diego Comm. Coll. Dist., 1970-, dir. Sch. of Hotel Adminstrn. Mesa College; dir. San Diego Golf Academy; publisher Apartment Guide of San Diego, 1974-, pub./c.e.o. Educators' Publications, 1984-; pres. All-Suites International; financial advisor, 1978-; awards: Travelodge Corp. Golden Egg award for most outstanding Travelodge opr. (1966); mem: Council on Hotel, Restaurant and Institutional Edn., San Diego C.of C., San Diego Comm. Coll. Dist. Advy. Bd.; developed first travel trailer co-op. park in USA in Yuma, Az.; publs: Front (hotel mgmt. manual), college text, hospitality and ednl. texts; mil: cpl. US Army 1953-55; Republican; rec: stamps, rosarian. Res: 5946 Soledad Mountain Rd La Jolla 92037 Ofc: Educators' Publications, 1585 Rosecrans San Diego 92106

WIZARD, BRIAN RUSSELL, author, publisher, entertainer, video producer; b. June 24, 1949, Newburyport, Mass.; s. Russell and Ruth (Hidden) Willard; edn: BA, CSU Sonoma, 1976. Career: jeweler, sculptor, artisan prin., Sebastopol, 1974-79; prin. The Starquill Publishing, Port Douglas, Queensland, Australia 1981-, publisher, movie producer, dir. "Thunderhawks" Starquill Internat., Santa Rosa, Calif. 1986-; author: "Permission to Kill" 1985, "Tropical Pair" 1986, "Shindara" 1987, "Metempsychosis" 1988, "Heaven On Earth" 1989, "Coming of Age" 1990; singer, songwriter, 1988-, producer cassette: Brian Wizard Sings for His Supper, 1989; Space Arc contbr. 1991; mil: US Army 1967-70, decorated 26 Air medals; mem. Vietnam Helicopter Crewmember Assn. 145th Combat Aviation Bn. Assn., Vietnam Combat Vets. Assn., Vietnam Vets. Asm., Vietnam Vets. Australia Assn.

WOELFEL, ROBERT WILLIAM, broadcasting executive; b. Nov. 5, 1944, Los Angeles; s. William Herman and Mary Jane (Hiatt) W.; edn: AA, Mt. San Antonio Coll., 1965; BS in bus., CSU Los Angeles, 1969; MBA, USC, 1972. Career: salesman Burroughs Corp., El Monte 1969-71; sales mgr., announcer radio station KMFB/KPMO, Mendocino 1973-81; gen. mgr. Sta. KOZT, Fort Bragg, 1981-85, Sta. KBLC, Lakeport, 1984-85; v.p., sales mgr. Sta. KZOZ/KKAL, San Luis Obispo, 1985-86; corp. gen. mgr. Visionary Radio Euphonics, Santa Rosa, 1986-87; dir. mktg., gen. sales mgr. Sta. KUBA/KXEZ, Yuba City 1987-88; gen. mgr. Sta. KMRJ, Ukiah 1988-; princ. ptnr. Electoral Target Advertising, 1988-; instr. advt. comm. colls.; elected councilman City of Ft. Bragg, 1979-85, mayor 1984-85; civic bds: Mendocino Coast Ednl. TV Assn. (dir. 1983-85), Ukiah C.of C. (dir. 1990-); mil: USN 1966-68; Presbyterian; rec: basketball, reading. Res: 835 Waugh Ln Apt 16 Ukiah 95482 Ofc: 110 W Standley Ukiah 95482

WOHL, ARMAND JEFFREY, cardiologist, educator; b. Dec. 11, 1946, Phila.; s. Herman L. and Selma (Paul) W.; m. Marylou Giangrossi, Sept. 4, 1977; children: Michael b. 1979, Todd b. 1981; edn: undergrad. Temple Univ. 1964-67; MD, Hahnemann Univ. 1971. Career: intern Bexar County Hosp., San Antonio, Tx. 1971-72; resident in med. Parkland Meml. Hosp., Dallas 1972-74; fellow in cardiol. Univ. of Tx. (Southwestern) Med. Sch. of Dallas 1974-76; chief cardiology USAF Hosp. Elmendorf, Anchorage, Alaska 1976-78; chief of cardiology Riverside Med. Clinic, Riverside, Calif. 1978-79; cardiologist, Grossmont Cardiology Med. Group, La Mesa 1980-84; pvt. practice, La Mesa 1985-; chief of cardiology Grossmont Hosp., La Mesa 1988-90; asst. clin. prof. of med. Univ. Calif., San Diego 1990-; mem: Am. Coll. of Cardiology (Fellow 1979, mem. Health Care Issues Com., Calif. chpt. 1990-), Am. Coll. of Physicians (Fellow 1979), Council on Clin. Cardiology (Fellow 1981), Am. Heart Assn. (San Diego chapt. bd. 1981-87); publs: 5 abstracts, contbr. 8 articles in med. journals; mil: major USAF 1976-78. Ofc: 5565 Grossmont Center Dr Ste 126, La Mesa 91942

WOLD, ROBERT MILES, optometrist; b. Dec. 5, 1942, Devils Lake, N.D.; s. Anton Miles and Florence (Strommen) W.; m. Margery Wilson, June 13, 1964; children: Peter b. 1968, Dawn b. 1971; edn: AA, Devil's Lake Jr. Coll. 1961; BS, Pacific Univ. Ore. 1963; OD, 1964; MS, 1966. Career: pvt. practice optometry, Los Altos 1965-69; Chula Vista 1969-; awards: Calif. Optometric Assn. Young Optometrist 1970, Best Editorial 1973, S.D. Optometric Soc. Optometrist of Year 1978, Coll. Optometrists A.M. Keffington award 1974; mem: Am. Acad. Optometry (fellow), Coll. Optometrists in Vision Devel. (fellow, secty. 1970),

Am. Optometric Assn., Calif. Optometric Assn., Am. Optometric Found. (pres. 1991-92), San Diego Co. Optometric Soc. (pres. 1975, 81), Rotary (past dir.), Chula Vista C.of C. (past dir.), BSA (scoutmaster 1982-); 120+ articles pub. in profl. jours; rec: camping, swimming. Res: 627 Mission Ct Chula Vista 92010 Ofc: Drs. Wold and Mason 353 H St Suite C Chula Vista 91910

WOLF, BRIAN DAVID, lawyer; b. Nov. 4, 1959, Los Angeles; s. France B. and Mildred J. W.; edn: att. USC 1977-79, AA in police sci. Fullerton Coll. 1983, BSL and JD, Western St. Univ. Coll. of Law, 1984, 85; admitted bar: Calif., US Dist. Ct. cent. dist. Calif. 1986, US Ct. Appeals 9th cir. 1988. Career: atty., assoc. Anderson & Ross, El Toro 1986-87; DiLiberti & Goldsman, Santa Ana 1987; Liebman, Reiner & McNiel, 1987-88; res. atty. Orange County Superior Ct., Santa Ana 1988-89; sr. atty. Calif. Ct. of Appeals 4th Dist., Santa Ana 1989-; honors: Nat. Dean's List 1985-86, Am. Jurisprudence Awards- torts, bus. orgn., crim. law, wills (1983, 84), top 10 percent of class WSU Coll. of Law 1985, bd. editors law rev. (1984, 85); mem: ABA, Calif. St. Bar, Civil Air Patrol USAF Aux. (lt. col. 1973-), Orange Co. Sheriff Santa Ana (reserve dep. 1987-89); Democrat. Ofc: Court of Appeal, Fourth District, 925 N Spurgeon Santa Ana 92701

WOLFF, NELS CHRISTIAN, government contracting officer; b. March 26, 1936, Cedar Falls, Iowa; s. Jens Christian Wolff and Anna Marie Sorensen; edn: AA, Long Beach City Coll., 1981; JD, Pacific Coast Univ. Sch. Law, 1985; studies in progress: Cert. Profl. Contracts Mgr. (CPCM); att. govt. contract law course, AF Inst. of Tech., 1989, mgmt. of def. acquisition contracts Army Logistics Mgmt. Sch., Cont. Edn. of Bar courses Univ. Calif.; Career: acct. Bethlehem Steel, Terminal Island, San Pedro, Calif. 1977-80; supply techn. US Army 1980-81; contracting ofcr. US Coast Guard, Long Beach 1981-84, supvy. contracting ofcr., chief procurement, 1984-; bar review instr. Pacific Coast Univ. Sch. of Law 1984, 85; honors: Sigma Delta Kappa (chancellor Alpha Xi chpt. 1982/3, 1984/5, grand chancellor SDK 1984/5, editor Si-De-Ka for SDK Grand Chapter 1985-87, SDK Service Key 1988, plaque as nat. conv. chair 1987); mem: Am. Soc. Mil. Comptrollers (v.p. Coast Guard LA chpt. 1986/7, 1987/8), Nat. Contract Mgrs. Assn., Am. Trial Lawyers Assn., CTLA, LATLA, Sigma Delta Kappa law frat., Am. Legion, Air Force Assn., Navy League, Ethics Comm. NCMA 1993-; civic: vol. probation monitor State Bar of Calif., Long Beach 1992-; vol. tchr. aide Long Beach Pub. Schs. VIPS/ Volunteers in Pub. Schs. 1976, 77; USCG Aux. (1973-: flotilla staff ofcr. 73, 74, 75, 87, Div. staff ofcr. 76, 77, served on boat crews as comms. ofcr., as pub. instr. safe boating courses, and as courtesy motorboat examiner); mil: USMC 1953-59, USAF 1959-60, lt.(jg) USCG 1971-75; Democrat; E. Orthodox; rec: boating, amateur radio. Ofc: Eleventh Coast Guard Dist. 501 W Ocean Blvd Ste 7170 Long Beach 90822-5399

WOLFINGER, BARBARA KAYE, research specialist, film-maker; b. Sept. 3, 1929, NY, NY; d. Louis and Margaret (Goodman) Kaye; m. Raymond E. Wolfinger, Aug. 7, 1960; 1 child: Nicholas b. 1966; edn: AB, Univ. of Mich. (year); grad. study, City Coll. of NY (year), Mass. Inst. of Tech. (year). Career: dir. design res., McCann-Erickson, Inc., NY, 1954-58; res. cons., Stanford Univ. Inst. for Res. in Political Studies, Langley Porter Inst., Market Planning Corp., Calif. Dept. of Public Health, 1960-70; res. assoc., Inst. for Res. in Social Behavior, Oakland, Calif., 1971-76; res. assoc., Survey Res. Ctr., UC Berkeley, 1976-77; pres., Berkeley Productions, Inc., 1978-; ptnr., Qualitative Res. Assoc., 1978-; awards: CINE Golden Eagle Award, US Indsl. Film Festival, First Prize for film Catch a Falling Star, 1979; Best Film, LEARNING Award, Best in Category, Family Life Video Award for film Black Girl, 1982-83; Red Ribbon, Am. Film Festival, for film Sister of the Bride; author: profl. papers, 1973, 87; pub. articles in Ideology and Discontent 1964, Design Research 1957; films: Catch a Falling Star, Black Girl, Chile Penguin, Sister of the Bride, Your Move, Almost Home; video, Nine Months. Res: 715 The Alameda, Berkeley 94707

WOLLMER, RICHARD DIETRICH, professor of operations research and statistics; b. July 27, 1938, Los Angeles; s. Herman Dietrich and Alice Myrtle (Roberts) W.; edn: BA in math., Pomona Coll., Claremont 1960; MA, app. math., Columbia Univ., 1963; PhD, engring. sci., UC Berkeley, 1965. Career: operations research scientist RAND Corp., Santa Monica 1965-70; prof. ops. res. and statistics, CSU Long Beach, 1970-; lectr. UCLA 1970, 74, vis. assoc. prof. Stanford Univ. 1976, vis. prof. CSU Northridge 1981-82; cons. McDonnell Douglas, Long Beach 1978-80, 82, 1985-91, Logicon, San Pedro 1979-81; awards: NSF fellow Columbia Univ. 1960-61, best paper mil. appls. Operations Res. Soc. Am., Balt. 1969; mem: Ops. Res. Soc. Am. 1965-, The Inst. of Mgmt. Sci. 1965-, So. Calif. TIMS-ORSA (1968-, past chair); pub. jour. articles in Operations Res. J. 1992, 70, 64, Mgmt. Sci. J. 1968, Mathematical Prog. 1985, 80, Mathematics of Ops. Res. 1977, Networks 1990, 80, 72; Republican; Presbyn. (deacon Bel Air Presbyn. 1982-84); rec: sports, music. Res: 6132 Fernwood Dr Huntington Beach 92648 Ofc: Dept. Info. Systems, School of Business CSU Long Beach 1250 Bellflower Blvd Long Beach 90840

WOMACK, THOMAS HOUSTON, manufacturing company executive; b. June 22, 1940, Gallatin, Tenn.; s. Thomas Houston and Jessie (Eckel) W.; m. Linda D. Walker, July 20, 1963 (div. Dec. 1989); children: Britton b. 1969,

Kelley b. 1971; m. Pamela Ann Reed, Apr. 20, 1991; edn: BSME, Tenn. Tech. Univ., 1963. Career: project engr. U.S. Gypsum Co., Jacksonville, Fla. 1963-65; project mgr. Maxwell House Div., Gen. Foods Corp., Jacksonville, 1965-68; mfg. mgr., Hoboken, N.J., 1968-71, div. ops. planning mgr., White Plains, N.Y., 1971-73; sales mgr. J.R. Schneider Co., Tiburon, Calif. 1973-79; pres. Womack Internat., Inc. Novato 1979-; mem.: Soc. Tribologists and Lubrication Engrs., Am. Filtration Soc., Soc. of Mfg. Engrs., Am. Soc. of Chemical Engrs.; Republican; Prot. Ofc: Womack International, Inc. One Digital Dr Novato 94949

WONG, DOUGLAS LIM, martial arts teacher, trainer and author; b. Dec. 7, 1948, Los Angeles; son Bing and Mary W.; married Carrie Jean Ogawa, Oct. 24, 1981; children: Travis Todd b. 1985, Tia Alese b. 1988; edn: Aeronautical Engring., Northrop Inst. of Tech., 1967-69, Mktg. Mgmt., Woodbury Bus. Coll., 1969-71. Career: assistance medical record supr. Occupational Health and Safety Div. City of Los Angeles, 1980-; founder White Lotus System of Kung Fu, Master, hd. instr. Sil Lum Kung Fu Studio, Northridge; world lectr., seminars, tng. camps, appearances in movies, tv shows, radio interviews, magazines, newspapers; promoted over 20 tournaments; author: Kung Fu the Way of Life; Shaolin Fighting Theories and Concepts; The Deceptive Hands of Wing Chun; Kung Fu the Endless Journey; Martial Arts editor for nat. physical fitness mag., Exercise for Men Only, 1991-; appt. by AAU Chinese Martial Arts Div. as the Association Chinese Martial Arts Chairperson for So. Pacific area (includes So. Calif.) 1991-; reg. chmn. Pacific Assn. (CA, NV,AZ 1991-); nat. v. chmn. AAU-CMAD elected Sept. 1992; Nat. AAU (life mem. July 1992); Sullivan Nomination Bd.; video series Shaolin Fighting Theories & Concepts, Chinese Martial Arts Fighting Skills, Chinese In-Fighting, 1992; awards: Inside Kung Fu Mag. list of 100 Most Influential Martial Arts Personalities of All Time (2/91), recipient Commendations and Resolutions - Calif. State Senate and Assembly, Gov. of Calif., L.A. City Council, L.A. Mayor Bradley, San Diego Mayor, City Council and County Bd. Suprs., U.S. Marine Corps, Am. Red Cross, Lion Internat., Save the Children Found., Ethiopian Famine Relief Project, Kiwanis, Rotary Internat., others; listed in Who's Who in Karate and the Other Martial Arts, Who's Who in Am. Martial Arts; Leaders of the Chinese Martial Arts; Masters, Founders and Leaders of Am. Martial Arts; Res: 18215 Chase St Northridge 91325-3731 Ofc: Sil Lum Kung Fu Studio 19641 Parthenia St Ste A1 Northridge 91324 Tel:818/993-9664

WONG, HING CHUNG, physician; b. Sept. 29, 1941, Hong Kong; nat. US citizen 1978; parents: Chui Y. and Shui Man (Tang) Wong (dec.); m. King Y. Wong; 1 son, Kin Wong; edn: B.Med., Nat. Taiwan Univ. 1969; MD, USA, 1976. Career: Family Practice (solo), Chinatown, Los Angeles 1978-; expanded May 1984 Hing C. Wong Med. Clinic, San Gabriel; chief cons. Chaus Jou Assn. in USA, pres. So. Calif. 1986; med. advisor Am. Vietnam Chinese Friendship Assn., Eng Family Ben Assn., Chinese Garment Assn., Elderly Indochinese Assn.; staff French Hosp., chief of staff 1984-85; bd. dirs. Chinatown Service Center 1983-86, mem. Chinatown Comm. Advy. Com. 1988-90; judge Miss L.A. Chinatown Beauty Pageant, 1987, Miss Indochinese Beauty Pageant, 1988; awards: good citizenship City of L.A., service Paralyzed Veterans Assn. 1977; mem. AMA, L.A. Co. Med. Assn.; rec: golf, pool, tennis, karaoke. Ofc: H.C. Wong, MD, 709 N Hill St Ste 19 Los Angeles 90012; also 808 E Valley Blvd San Gabriel 91776

WONG, JAMES BOK, management consultant, economist, engineer; b. Dec. 9, 1922, Canton, China, nat. US cit. 1962; s. Gen Ham and Chen (Yee) W.; m. Wai Ping Lim, Aug. 3, 1946; children: John b. 1948, Jane b. 1955, Julia b. 1956; edn: BS in agric., Univ. Md. 1949, BS in chem. eng. 1950; MS chem. eng., Univ. Ill. 1951, PhD, 1954. Career: research asst. Univ. Ill., Urbana 1950-53; chem. engr. Standard Oil Indiana at Whiting 1953-55; process design & research engr. Shell Devel. Co., Emeryville, Calif. 1955-61; senior plnng. engr., mgr. long range plnng. & econs., chief economist Rexall Drug & Chem. Co., Los Angeles 1961-70; dir. econs. & ops. analysis, dir. internat. technologies Dart Industries (fmrly. Rexall), 1970-81; pres. James B. Wong Associates, Los Angeles 1981-; dir., chmn. exec. com. United Pacific Bank, L.A. 1982-, chmn. bd. dirs. 1988-89; honors: Outstanding Volunteer Svc. award City of Los Angeles 1977, named to Exec. Order of Ohio Commodores, Gov. Ohio 1982, Sigma Xi, Tau Beta Pi, Phi Kappa Phi, Pi Mu Epsilon, Phi Lambda Upsilon, Phi Eta Sigma; mem: Am. Inst. Chem. Engrs., Am. Chem. Soc.; civic: Chinese Am. Citizens Alliance Found. (dir., pres., 1971-), Asian Am. Edn. Commn./L.A. 1971-81; contbr. articles in A.M.A. Archives of Indsl. Hygiene and Occupational Medicine, Indsl. and Engring. Chemistry, and J. Applied Physics; mil: enlisted US Army 14th Air Force Flying Tigers, 1943-46. Res: 2460 Venus Dr Los Angeles 90046

WONG, KIN-PING, educator, biotechnology researcher, science administrator; b. Aug. 14, 1941, Guangzhou, Guangdong, China; s. Kwok-Keung and Yuan-Kwan (Loo) W.; m. Anna S. K. Koo, Sept. 16, 1968; children: Voon-Chung, 1971; Ming-Chung, 1974; edn: postdoctoral, Duke Univ., Durham, NC, 1968-70; PhD, Purdue Univ., Lafayette, IN, 1968; BS, Univ. Calif., Berkeley, 1964; teachers diploma, Grantham Teachers Coll., Hong Kong, 1958-59; career: asst./assoc. prof., Univ. South Florida, Tampa, 1970-75; visiting scientist, Max Planck Inst. Molecular Genetics, Berlin, Germany, 1972; visiting prof., Univ.

Uppsala, Uppsala, Sweden, 1975; assoc. prof./prof., Univ. Kansas, Kansas City, KS, 1975-83; visiting prof., Univ. Tokyo, Tokyo, Japan, 1979; dean, grad. studies, Univ. Kansas, Kansas City, KS, 1980-83; program dir. biophysics, Nat. Science Found., Washington, 1981-83; science dean/prof., Calif. State Univ., Fresno, 1983-; visiting prof., Stanford Univ. Medical Ctr., Stanford, 1985; adjunct prof. medicine, Univ. Calif. Medical Sch., San Francisco, 1986-; adjunct prof. biochemistry and biophysics, Univ. Calif. Medical Sch., San Francisco, 1987-; trustee, Univ. Calif. San Francisco, Fresno, 1987-; hon. prof., Shantou Univ. Medical, Shantou, People's Republic of China, 1987-; consultant, Dept. Health & Human Resources, Washington, 1985-; awards: res. professorship, Nat. Science Found., Stanford Univ., 1985; sr. res. fellow, European Molecular Biology Orgn., Uppsala, Sweden, 1975; Res. Career Development Award, NIH, Bethesda, 1972-75; Grant on Ribosome, Nat. Inst. General Medical Sciences, Bethesda, 1972-80; Grant on Protein Folding, Nat. Inst. Heart, Lung, and Blood, Bethesda, 1972-87; Health Career Opportunity Grant, Dept. Health & Human Resources, Rockville, MD, 1986-89; Laval Res. Award, Calif. State Univ., Fresno, 1985; hon. mem., Golden Key Hon. Soc., Atlanta, 1986; Pres./Key Executive MBA Prog., Pepperdine Univ., L.A., 1986-88; Calif. Sea Grant, Dept. Commerce, Washington, 1987-90; fellow, Am. Inst. of Chemists, Washington, 1987-; fellow, Royal Soc. of Chemistry, London, England, 1988-; numerous cancer res. grants and awards; mem: Am. Soc. of Biological Chemists, 1976-; Am. Assn. for Advancement of Science, 1975-; Am. Chemical Soc., 1978-; Biophysical Soc., 1970-; Soc. of Sigma Xi, 1969; author: more 50 res. articles in biology, chemistry biochemistry, biophysics, endocrinology; 3 review articles in educational journals, 32 pub. research abstracts; keynote speaker, convocation lecture, symposium, and colloquium lectures; rec: travel; downhill skiing; mountain climbing; res: Fresno; ofc: Calif. State Univ. Sch. Natural Sciences Fresno 93740-0090

WONG, LAURA KWAN JEUNG, jewelry retailer, designer, real estate investor; b. Aug. 18, 1932, Guaymas, Sonora, Mexico, nat. US cit. 1957; d. Zee Nang and Felicitas Lai Fong (Chang) Kwan; m. Albert Wong, July 16, 1970; children: Sharon Lee Jeung b. 1954, Craig Lee Jeung b. 1959, Curtis Lee Jeung b. 1960; 2 grandchildren: Kacey Cameron b. 1980, Jameson Tuck Parvizad b. 1984; edn: courses in apparel design, cosmetology, oil painting, real estate: Lux Coll. S.F. 1953, Marinello Sch. of Beauty 1969, Univ. Hawaii, Hilo 1970, Coll. of San Mateo 1975; languages: English, Spanish and Chinese. Career: tutored children in Mexico; past pos. with Pacific Tel. Co., Safeco Ins. Co., Bechtel Corp., Ultronix Electronic; owner House of Kwan Yin (retail jewelry, gift & beauty salon), San Mateo; pres. Orchid Floral & Interior Design, San Mateo; awards: hon. life Calif. Scholarship Fedn. 1952; mem. Hair Dressers Assn.; civic: Foster City Chinese Club, YWCA, Tri G Club, High Sch. of Commerce Alumni Assn., San Mateo Downtown Assn., Orgn. of Chinese Americans Inc. Peninsula Chpt. of San Mateo Co., Peninsula Orchid Soc.; rec: needlepoint, oil painting, sewing, tennis, jewelry & floral design, collecting & growing orchids, cruise travel worldwide. Res: 35 Verbalee Ln Hillsborough 94010 Ofc: House of Kwan Yin 55 E 4th Ave San Mateo 94401 also: Orchid Floral & Interior Design 61 E 4th Ave San Mateo 94401

WONG, NATHAN DOON, dental surgeon; b. Mar. 21, 1934, Kwongtung, China; s. Bing Toy and Yue Hone (Lew) W.; edn: AA, S.F. City Coll., 1957; undergrad. UC Berkeley, 1962; DDS, Howard Univ., 1967; postgrad. UCLA, 1971. Career: dental ofcr. NIH, HEW, Wash. D.C. 1967-68; staff mem. Group Health Assocs., W.D.C. 1968-71; chief of dentistry Petersburg (Va.) Tng. Sch. & Hosp., 1971-72; staff North-East Medical Service, San Francisco 1973-76; staff S.F. City Pub. Health, 1974-76; sr. staff West Oakland Health Ctr., Oakland 1973-; pvt. dental practice, S.F. 1973-; listed Who's Who in South & Southwest 1976, Who's Who in West 1980; mem: Acad. of Gen. Dentistry (Fellow, Master), Pierre Fauchard Acad. (hon. dental org.), ADA, Calif. Dental Assn., S.F. Dental Soc., AAAS, Chinese Am. Citizens Alliance, The Commonwealth Club of Calif.; mil: Army 1958-60; Democrat; Prot.; rec: tennis, classical music. Ofc: Nathan D. Wong, DDS, 2000 Van Ness Ave Ste 612 San Francisco 94109

WONG, ROBERTA JEAN, pharmacist, educator; b. Nov. 23, 1957, Cleveland, Ohio; d. Robert Young and Ellen Jean (Woo) Wong; m. Michael Wool; edn: UC Davis 1976-79; PharmD, UC San Francisco, 1983. Career: res. pharmacist AIDS Clinic, San Francisco General Hosp., 1984-89; asst. clin. prof. UCSF Sch. of Pharmacy 1985-89; instr. UCLA Sch. of Medicine, Los Angeles 1989-91, drug info. pharmacist UCLA Med. Ctr. 1989-90, investigational drug pharmacist, 1990-; awards: fellow ASHP 1991, US Pub. Health Svc. asst. sec. health award, W.D.C. 1991; mem. ASHP (practice advy. panel 1990-92), Am. Pharm. Assn. 1987-, CSHP 1983-; author book chapt. in Pharmacologic Treatment of HIV Infection (1988), med. jour. articles; rec: skiing, tennis, golf. Ofc: UCLA Medical Ctr. 16-131 CHS 10833 Le Conte Ave Los Angeles 90024

WOO, WILBERT YUK CHEONG, government contracting officer; b. Feb. 7, 1942, Honolulu; s. Jacob Yue Tak and Beatrice Yuet Laan (Wong) W.; edn: BS, CSU Los Angeles, 1970, MBA, 1977; CPA, Calif. 1980; cert. cost analyst, 1985; Calif. Comm. Coll. instr. cred. Career: acct. So. Calif. Gas Co., L.A. 1971-73; auditor Defense Contract Audit, Pasadena 1973-74; Dept. Health & Human Services, Beverly Hills 1974-86; Defense Contract Audit, Gardena

1986-88; price analyst U.S. Air Force Space and Missile Systems Ctr., Los Angeles 1988-92, contracting officer, 1992-; instr. Southwest Coll. 1980-, El Camino Coll. 1984-87; mem: Am. Inst. CPAs, Calif. Soc. CPAs (govt. contracts com.), Assn. of Govt. Accountants, Soc. of Cost Estimating and Analysis, Chinese Am. Assn. of So. Calif. (bd.); mil: sp4 AUS 1965-67. Ofc: U.S. Air Force, Los Angeles AFB.

WOOD, FERGUS JAMES, geophysicist, consultant; b. May 13, 1917, London, Ont., Canada, came to U.S. 1924, naturalized 1932; s. Louis Aubrey and Dora Isabel (Elson) W.; m. Doris M. Hack, Sept. 14, 1946; children: Kathryn Celeste W. Madden, Bonnie Patricia W. Ward; edn: Univ. Oreg. 1934-36; AB, UC Berkeley, 1938, postgrad. 1938-39; postgrad. Univ. Chgo. 1939-40, Univ. Mich. 1940-42, Calif. Inst. Tech. 1946. Career: tchg. asst. Univ. Mich. 1940-42; instr. in physics and astronomy Pasadena City Coll. 1946-48, John Muir Coll. 1948-49; asst. prof. physics Univ. Md. 1949-50; assoc. physicist Johns Hopkins Univ. Applied Physics Lab. 1950-55; sci. editor Ency. Americana, N.Y.C., 1955-60; aeronautical and space res. scientist, sci. asst. to the director Office Space Flight Programs, Hqtrs., NASA, W.D.C., 1960-61; program dir. fgn. sci. info. Nat. Sci. Found., W.D.C., 1961-62; physical scientist, chief sci. and tech. info. staff U.S. Coast and Geodetic Survey (now Nat. Ocean Service), Rockville, Md. 1962-66; phys. scientist Office of Dir., 1967-73, res. assoc. 1973-77; cons. tidal dynamics, Bonita, Calif. 1978-; awards: special achievement Dept. Commerce, NOAA (1970, 74, 76, 77); mem: Sigma Pi Sigma, Pi Mu Epsilon, Delta Phi Alpha, Am. Geophysical Union; writer, tech. dir. documentary film: Pathfinders from the Stars (1967); contbr. numerous articles to encys., reference sources, profl. jours.; author: The Strategic Role of Perigean Spring Tides in Nautical History and North American Coastal Flooding 1635-1976 (1978), Tidal Dynamics: Coastal Flooding and Cycles of Gravitational Force (1986); editor-in-chief: The Prince William Sound, Alaska, Earthquake of 1964 and Aftershocks, vols. 1-2A and sci. coordinator vols. 2B, 2C and 3 (1966-69); mil: capt. USAAF 1942-46; Democrat; Presbyterian. Res: 3103 Casa Bonita Dr Bonita 91902-1735

WOOD, LARRY (MARY LAIRD), journalist, university educator, environmental consultant; b. Sandpoint, Idaho; d. Edward Hayes and Alice (McNeel) Small; children: Mary, Marcia, Barry; edn: BA, summa cum laude (pres. Assoc. Women Students; recipient many campus honors incl. Pasadena Rose Bowl Princess), Univ. Wash., 1938, MA with highest honors, 1940; postgrad. Stanford Univ. 1941-42, postgrad. teaching fellowship 1940-43; postgrad. UC Berkeley 1946-47, cert. in photog. 1971; postgrad. journalism Univ. Wis. 1971-72, Univ. Minn. 1971-72, Univ. Ga. 1972-73; postgrad. in art, arch. and marine biol. UC Santa Cruz, 1974-76, Stanford Hopkins Marine Sta. 1977-80. Career: campus corresp. Seattle Times 1941-42, nat. model for Wonder Bread and store model for I. Magnin, Frederick & Nelson, The Bon Marche; P.R. cons. Seattle and S.F. Bay Area YMCA & YWCA, Eastbay Hosp. Assn., Forestry Res., 1946-; by-line columnist Oakland Tribune, S.F. Chronicle, 1946-62; Parents' Mag. far west contbg. ed. (mo. travel, community and fam. features, arch., home and garden articles) 1946-65; disting. expert witness Nat. Forensic Ctr., N.J. 1965-; feature writer W. reg. Christian Sci. Monitor, CSM Radio Syn. and Internat. News, 1973-, CSM/Los Angeles Times News Syn., Register and Tribune Syn., Des Moines, 1975-, Times-Mirror Syn., San Jose Mercury News (Nat. Headliner Award), Seattle Times, Chevron USA, Calif. Today mag.; contbg. ed. Travelday mag., also Travelin' Mag., 1976-, Calif. Travel Guides, Fodor (NY and London, David McKay Pubs.) 1981-, Random House 1987-; coauthor Travelguide to Calif. (jt. pub. Fodor/State of Calif.) 1986-, Focus on Science Series, 3 vol. high sch./univ. texts (Bell & Howell) 1987; 1990-91 feature stories include: Calif.'s Water Wars, Calif.'s New Wilder Ranch State Park, Marvel of Tugs, Nat. Counter-Narcotics Inst. (San Luis Obispo), Calif. Youth Auth. Problems, Sch. Crime in Calif., Calif.'s `Hip' Teens, Jumping Frogs Contest (Calaveras County), Features on Calif. writers Jack London, Mark Twain and Robert Louis Stevenson and their homes in Calif., Mystique of the Migrating Monarch Butterflies, New Nipomo Dunes State Preserve, Elkhorn Slough Nat. Estuarine Reserve at Moss Landing, Ferndale's Victorians (lead, cover article Westways Mag. 6/91); author 22 books including: Wonderful USA! A State by State Guide to Natural Am. (Crown Books, NY, 1989); coauthor: West Winds, anthology of Calif. writers 1989; 2000+ bylined articles in Sunday Mag. sections and newspapers (syndicates: USIA, Knight Ridder, Times Mirror, Hearst), mags: Journalism Quarterly, Parents, Popular Mechanics, Mechanix Illustrated, Country Roads (Donnelley Pubs. for Goodyear Co.), House and Garden, House Beautiful, Oceans, Sea Frontiers, Motorland and Westways (AAA), Scholastic Publs., Nat. Geographic World, others; feature writer Linguapress, Paris; book reviewer texts for Bell & Howell, journalism book reviews for Profl. Communicator; prof. journalism (tenure) CSU San Diego 1975-, distinguished vis. prof. CSU San Jose 1976, CSU Hayward, UC Ext. 1979, Univ. Pacific (1979, 82); frequent speaker profl. and ednl. confs.; mem. advy. bd. KRON-TV, NBC, 1987-; invited to attend and report major confs. including: Internat. Geographers' Union & Assembly 1992, Internat. Soc. Ecol. Econs., Costa Rica 1992, Internat. Ocean Disposal Symp., Asilomar, Ca. 1986, USN and coop. univs. Marine Medicine: Diving & Health Hazards of Marine and Aquatic Environments, Monterey 1985, IEEE ann. meetings (1985 Ocean Engring. and the Environment), AMA Athletic Assn., HI 1985, Oceans Conf. and Expo.

1985; selected by Am. & Brit. govts. to cover 1983 visit of Queen Elizabeth II and Prince Philip to Calif., also 1986 visit of Prince Charles and Princess Diana to EXPO '86, Vancouver B.C.; work with state and fed. agys. in wildlife mgmt. pgms.; profl. del. EPA del. to Soviet Union and Ea. Europe 1991; VIP press invitee to: Earth Summit, Brazil 1992, Ecol. Soc. Am./Inst. Biol. Scis. ann. conf. Honolulu 1992, Intl. Soc. Ecol. Econs. 1991, Am. Geophys. Union conf. (1982-, press del. AGU annual convs. 1987-, Disting. press del. 1990 nat. conv.), Internat. Conv. Mapping Global Chang 1992, Rockefeller Found. Media Seminar "Feeding the World, Protecting the Earth," Commonwealth Awards Banquet (4/92, Wilmington), Gorbachev's visit to Stanford Univ., Calif. Gov.'s Conf. on Tourism, trip to Hong Kong by LA Times and Cathay Pacific; press del. AAAS annual convs. 1987-; press del. to Russia, Ukraine and Czech. for Communications Consortium, 1992; trustee Calif. State Parks Found., 1976-; 6 works selected by Wolters Noordhoff and Longman, pub. English language texts in Europe; 1989-90 works include: Earthquake '89, Restoration of San Francisco's Chinatown, So. Calif.'s Teens-Trend setters for world fashions, Beverly Hill's High Fund Raising Project; award winning features include Sea Frontiers (1983), B.C. Totem Pole series (1982), "Ebey's Landing" Nat. Hist. Reserve series (1982); one of 40 top Calif. authors pub. in anthology, West Winds Four, Strawberry Hill Press, 1989; "Columbia: Glacier in Retreat" one of 350 top sci. articles of 1987 and reprinted in Soc. Issues Resources series 1988; honors: recogn. US Forest Svc. 1975, US Nat. Park Svc. List of nation's top environmental writers, Oakland Mus. Assn. (1979, 81), Port Directors' Assn. 1979, UW Hall of Fame and Mortar Board honoree (1984, 87, 88, 89), Seattle City Ctr. Hall of Fame 1984, Calif. Woman of Achievement (3t), award for article and photographs on California's Underwater Parks, Calif. Writers' Club list of California's Top 40 Writers 1989; Dict. of Intl. Biography of Cambridge, Eng. (12), Am. Biographical Inst. (15); mem: Nat. Soc. of Environmental Journalists (charter mem.1990-), Calif. Writers' Club (del. 1989, bd. 1987-88, keynote speaker All-West Writers Conf. Asilomar 1987, statewide banquet honoree 1990), Public Rels. Soc. Am. (Consultants Acad. 1983-), Women in Communications, Inc. (past sect. v.p., nat. bd. 1968-73, nat. resolutions com. 1983-), Nat. Acad. TV Arts and Scis., World Internat. Environ. Consultants, Environ. Consultants No. Am., Am. Mgmt. Assn., Am. Med. Writers Assn., Seattle Advt. & Sales Club (past pres.), Seattle Junior Ad Club (past pres.), AD/Mark Bay Area (past ofcr.), East Bay Advt. & Mktg. Assn., Oceanic Soc., Internat. Oceanographic Soc., Nat. Parks Assn., World Wildlife Fund, Am. Assn. Edn. in Journ. (exec. bd. nat. mag. div. 1978), Investigative Reporters and Editors, Soc. Am. Travel Writers (exec. bd. 1980-82), Soc. Profl. Journalists, Council for Advance. of Sci. Writing, Calif. Acad. Environ. News Writers, Nat. Press Photogs. Assn., Nat. Assn. Environmental Journalists USA (elected, charter mem. 1990-), Nat. Assn. of Sci. Writers, Calif. Acad. of Scis., Calif. Fine Arts Museums, Nat. Audubon Soc., Smithsonian, UCB Alumni Assn. (life), UW Alumni Assn. (life), UW Oceanscis. Alumni Assn. (charter), UW Sch. of Communications Alumni, Nat. Sch. PR Assn., Stanford Alumni Assn. (life), Phi Beta Kappa Alumni (scholarship ch. and PR dir. No. Calif. 1969-), Sigma Delta Chi, Theta Sigma Phi, Mortar Board, Totem Club, Pi Lambda Theta; clubs: Nat. Press (W.D.C.), S.F. Press, Eastbay Womens' Press; Ofcs: San Francisco, San Diego, Pebble Beach/Monterey, Seattle and 6161 Castle Dr Oakland 94611

WOOD, MICHAEL NEALL, cardiovascular/thoracic surgeon; b. Feb. 15, 1956, Temple, Texas; s. Harold Lee and Betty Jane (Bottomley) W.; m. Sandra Jean Quinn, Aug. 6, 1988; edn: BA chem., Southern Coll., Tenn. 1977; MD, Loma Linda Univ. Sch. of Med., 1981. Career: attdg. surgeon LLU Med. Ctr., Loma Linda 1989-; co-med. dir. cardiovascular surgery San Antonio Comm. Hosp., Upland 1990-93, med. dir. cardiovascular surgery 1993-; mem: Soc. Critical Care Medicine 1989-, Calif. Thoracic Soc., Soc. Thoracic Surgeons, San Bdo. Co. Med. Soc., Am. Coll. Surgeons (assoc. 1986, assoc. fellow 1989), Internat. Coll. Surgeons (fellow 1989), Am. Coll. Chest Phys. (assoc. 1986), Assn. for Academic Surgery 1990, AMA 1983, Calif. Med. Assn. 1982. Ofc: 1060 E Foothill Blvd Ste 201 Upland 91786

WOOD, RAYMUND FRANCIS, emeritus professor of library science; b. Nov. 9, 1911, London, England, naturalized U.S., 1931; s. George Stephen and Ida Agnes (Lawes) W.; m. Margaret Ann Peed, Feb. 26, 1943; children: Paul George b. 1947, Gregory Leo b. 1952, David Joseph b. 1955; edn: AB, St. Mary's Univ., 1931; MA, Gonzaga Univ., 1939; PhD, UCLA, 1949; MS Libr. Sci., USC, 1950. Career: instr. English, Univ. Santa Clara, 1939-41; tchg asst. history dept. UCLA, 1941-42; registration ofcr. VA Rehab. Pgm., L.A. 1946-48; prin. reference librarian Fresno State Coll., 1950-66; prof. libr. sci. UCLA Grad. Sch. of Library and Info. Sci., Los Angeles 1966-77, asst. dean 1967-70, asso. dean 1975-77, prof. emeritus 1977-; awards: Del Amo Found. Scholar, travel grantee 1974, merit award Alliance Francaise de Fresno 1966, travel grantee Nat. Book Found., N.Y. 1964, L.A. Mayor's merit award 1983; mem.: Jedediah Smith Soc., Stockton (pres. 1987-90, Eager Beaver award 1989), Calif. Libr. Assn., Sacto. 1950-, Fresno County Hist. Soc. (1952-, hon. life, newsletter editor 1959-66), Mariposa Co. Hist. Soc. (1957-, hon. life), So. Calif. Hist. Soc. 1959-, Friends of Encino/Tarzana Br. Libr. (treas. 1989-, pres. 1977-80, 87-90, newsletter editor 1981-), E Clampus Vitus (Fresno & Bakersfield chapters 1954-), The Westerners (L.A. Corral 1969-), Am. Red Cross (S.F.V. 1977-), Boy Scouts Am. (Encino 1970-75); author: California's Agua Fria (1954), Life and

Death of Peter Lebec (1956), History of Mission San Jose (1958), joint author: Ina Coolbrith: Librarian & Laureate (1973); mil: WOJG US Army 1942-46, ETO; Democrat; Byzantine Catholic; rec: travel, photography, writing. Res: 18052 Rosita St Encino 91316

WOOD, ROGER HOLMES, educator, financial planner; b. Apr. 26, 1920, Corning, N.Y.; s. James Orville and Helen Lucille (Winemiller) W.; m. Phyllis Elizabeth Anderson, Dec. 26, 1947; children: Stephen b. 1951, David b. 1955, Elizabeth b. 1958; edn: cadet US Mil. Acad. West Point 1941-42; AB, Univ. Pitts., 1944; MS, Columbia Univ., 1945; MA, San Francisco State Univ., 1951; PhD, Internat. Coll., L.A. 1978; profl. desig: CLU, ChFC, CFP. Career: tchr. San Francisco pub. schools, 1949-54; agent, reg. rep. New York Life, San Francisco 1954-; instr. Coll. San Mateo, 1960-70; tchr. Jefferson Union High Sch., Daly City 1965-; nat. faculty American Coll., Bryn Mawr, Pa. 1960-70; lectr. Golden Gate Univ., S.F. 1983-84; contbg. editor, Western Underwriter, S.F. 1959-63; mem.: Phi Gamma Delta 1943-, Phi Delta Kappa 1950-, West Point Soc. 1945-, Internat. Transactional Analysis Assn. 1970-, SAR 1960-, Am. Risk and Ins. Assn. 1983-, Internat. Assn. Fin. Planning 1983-, Soc. of Genealogists London 1985-, Am. Soc. of CLU and ChFC (v.p. S.F. chapt. 1960-62), S.F. Estate Planning Council 1960-, Peninsula Estate Planning Council 1960-, Leading Life Ins. Producers (S.F. pres. 1960-62); S.F. Council of Churches (dir. 1954-60); author: Family (1992), Life Is A Four Letter Word Game (1992); mil: pvt. med. dept. US Army 1940-41; 1st Presbyterian Ch. Burlingame (ruling elder); rec: genealogy, photography, travel. Res: 65 Capay Circle South San Francisco 94080

WOOD, WAYNE BARRY, freelance photojournalist; b. June 23, 1958, Oakland; s. Byron and Marylaird (Small) W.; edn: cert. photography, UC Berkeley, 1974-79; BS in transp. w. high honors, CSU Hayward and San Francisco, 1980; MBA w. high honors, CSU Hayward, 1982. Career: bylined photojournalist 1971-, with CSM News Syndicate since 1973, with 25+ million readers worldwide and 200 synd. radio stations in U.S. & Can.; coauthor: Fodor's San Francisco, and Fodor's California (guidebooks) 1981-88; photojournalist, specialist in travel, sci., transp., urban renewal, people profiles, and edn.; photos appear in Sea Frontiers (Internat. Oceanographic Found., Popular Mechanics, Focus On Science textbook series (Charles Merrill Co.), Linguapress, Off Duty, Model Railroader, Fashion Showcase, others; awards: Close scholar and outstanding jr. in econ. and bus., photography awards Railroad Assn., exhib. juried art show CSU Hayward; mem: Soc. of Profl. Journalists, Nat. Press Photogs. Assn.; Presbyterian; rec: magic, natural science. Res: 6161 Castle Dr Oakland 94611

WOODS, ARLEIGH MADDOX, presiding justice State Court of Appeal; b. Aug. 31, 1929, Los Angeles; d. Benjamin Harris and Ida Lota (Evans) Maddox; m. William T. Woods, Aug. 3, 1952; edn: BA, Chapman Coll., 1949; LLB, Southwestern Univ. Sch. of Law, 1953; LLM, Univ. Va., 1984; Hon. LLD, Univ. West L.A. (1984); admitted Calif. St. Bar (1953). Career: general practice of law, 1953-57; atty., prtnr., Levy, Koszdin & Woods, 1957-76; judge Los Angeles Superior Ct., 1976-80; assoc. justice Calif. Ct. of Appeal, 1980-82, presiding justice, 1982-, adminstrv. presiding justice, 1984-87; mem. Judicial Council of Calif. 1985-87, Commn. on Judicial Performance 1986-; honors: Westside Bus. & Profl. Woman of Year 1982, CTLA Apellate Justice of Year 1983, YWCA Silver Medal of Achiev., Profl. Woman of Yr. 1984, honored Black Women Lawyers Assn. 1984, L.A. Basin Equal Opp. League life commitment award for judicial excellence 1985, Alumni Assn. bd. dirs outstanding judicial ofcr. 1987; mem. num. judicial and bar assns., Constl. Rights Found. (v.p., bd. dirs. 1982-), Am. Cancer Res. Found. (bd. dirs. 1981); mem. bd. trustees Southwestern Univ. 1986-; rec: painting, needlepoint, youth civic edn. Ofc: Calif. Court of Appeal 3580 Wilshire Blvd Ste 433 Los Angeles 90010

WOODS, ROBERT DOUGLAS MURRAY, lawyer; b. July 31, 1946, London, England, naturalized U.S., 1966; s. Eric Robert and Dorothea Elizabeth (Armstrong) W.; m. Joan Francis Shoop, 1971 (div. 1973); m. Alexis Jean Perry, May 23, 1975; children: Heidi b. 1964, James b. 1967, Yvette b. 1971 (nee Kone), David Woods b. 1977; edn: BA, Univ. San Diego, 1968, JD, 1973; Grad. Seminary Dipl. Claremont Coll. Episcopal Theol. Sch., 1984; postgrad. studies Kennedy Inst. of Ethics, Georgetown Univ. 1987, 88, 90; admitted bar: Calif. 1973, Fed. Cts. 1973, U.S. Supreme Ct. 1978; ordained Episcopal Priest, 1986, Deacon 1984-86. Career: law clk., civil litigation atty., assoc. Higgs, Fletcher & Mack, San Diego 1973-77; Schall, Boudreau & Gore, 1978-81, ptnr. 1982-86; chief deputy litigation Kern Co. Counsel, Bakersfield 1986-92; chief deputy special litigation 1992-; adj. lectr. Univ. San Diego Law Sch. 1978-81; adj. prof. dept. philosophy & religious studies CSU Bakersfield, 1989-, assoc. Kennedy Inst. of Ethics Georgetown Univ. 1991-. Fellow, Kegley Inst. of Ethics, CSUB, 1988-, lectr. and pub. discussions in areas of legal, med. and govt. ethics, 1989-; instr. Calif. Pacific Sch. of Law, 1990-; judge pro tem. and jud. arbitrator, 1978-86; Am. Arbitration Assn. Nat. Panel, 1980-87; honors: Sigma Psi, Book awards in Constnl. law, evidence and crim. procedure, Varsity swimming, sailing and golf, Outstanding trial lawyer San Diego Trial Lawyers Assn. 1980, State Bar merit certs. (1983, 86), pres.'s award for outstanding Pro Bono Svc. 1985, arbitration service awards (1978, 80); contbg. author: Marine

P&I Policy Annotations, ABA Practicing Law Inst. (1980), Effective Direct and Cross-Examination, Calif. CEB (1984), numerous cont. edn. lectures in trial techniques and splties. (1981-); mil: E4 personnel splst. Adj. Gen. Corps US Army 1969-70; Democrat; Episcopalian (asst. priest St. Luke's, Bksfld. 1988-); rec: mountaineering, backpacking, musician, bicycling, skiing, canoeing. Ofc: Kern County Counsel 1115 Truxtun Ave 4th Fl Bakersfield 93301

WOODWARD, DANIEL HOLT, librarian; b. Oct. 17, 1931, Ft. Worth, Tex.; s. Enos Paul and Jessie Grider (Butts) W.; m. Mary Jane Gerra, Aug. 27, 1954; children: Jeffrey b. 1958, Peter b. 1960; edn: BA, Univ. of Colo. 1951, MA, 1955; PhD, Yale Univ. 1958; MS in L.S., Cath. Univ. of Am. 1969. Career: faculty Mary Washington Coll. Univ. of Va., 1957-72, librarian, 1969-72; librarian Huntington Library, Art Gallery and Botanical Gardens, San Marino 1972-; honors: Phi Beta Kappa, Beta Phi Mu; mem. Renaissance Soc. Am., Bibliog. Soc. Am., Golier Club, Zamorano Club (gov.); editor: The Poems and Translations of Robert Fletcher (1970). mil: AUS 1952-54. Res: 1540 San Pasqual St Pasadena 91106 Ofc: Huntington Library 1151 Oxford Rd San Marino 91108

WOODWORTH, STEPHEN DAVIS, business consultant, investment banker; b. Nov. 4, 1945, Stillwater, Okla.; s. Stanley Davis and Elizabeth (Webb) W.; m. Robin Lee, 1992; children: Lisa b. 1968, Ashley b. 1974; edn: BA, Claremont McKenna Coll. 1967; MBA, Calif. Lutheran Univ. 1975; USC Managerial Policy Inst. 1981. Career: div. mgr. Security Pacific Bank, Los Angeles 1970-87; prin. Woodworth Assoc., Westlake Village 1987-88; pres. Channel Islands Equities, Oxnard 1988-; instr. fin. Grad. Bus. Program Calif. Lutheran Univ. 1978-80; adj. faculty Command & Gen. Staff Coll. Ft. Leavenworth 1985; dir.: Hanson Lab. Furniture Inc., Newbury Park; Hetherington Inc., Ventura; bd. trustees Calif. Lutheran Edn. Found., Thousand Oaks 1983-; So. Calif. bd. dirs. U.S. Olympic Com., L.A. 1982-84; mem: Calif. Lutheran Univ. Alumni Assn. (pres. 1980-82, Outstanding Alumnus honoree 1986), Tower Club, Reserve Ofcr. Assn. (life), Ventura Co. Econ. Devel. Assn., Conejo Future Found., Am. Mgmt. Assn., MIT Enterprise Forum/ Central Coast (dir. 1988-), Conejo Sym. Orch. (former dir.), Alliance for Arts (dir., chmn. 1984-); contbr. numerous articles to bus. jours.; mil: lt. col. USAR 1967-; Republican; R.Cath.; rec: tennis, jogging, travel. Res: 2384 McCrea Road Thousand Oaks 91362 Ofc: Channel Islands Equities 300 Esplanade Ste 900 Oxnard 93030

WOOLARD, HENRY WALDO, aerospace engineer; b. June 2, 1917, Clarksburg, W.Va.; s. Herbert William and Elsie Marie (Byers) W.; m. Helen Stone Waldron, Aug. 16, 1941; children: Shirley b. 1945, Robert b. 1949; edn: BS aero. engrng., Univ. Mich., Ann Arbor 1941; MSME, Univ. Buffalo, 1954. Career: aeronautical engr. NACA (now NASA), Hampton, Va., and Moffett Field, Calif., 1941-46; assoc. prof. aero. engring. West Virginia Univ., Morgantown, 1946-48; res. aero dynamicist Cornell Aero. Lab., Buffalo, N.Y. 1948-57; sr. staff engr. applied physics lab. The Johns Hopkins Univ., Silver Spring, Md. 1957-63; sr. res. specialist Lockheed Calif. Co., Burbank 1963-67; mem. tech. staff TRW Systems Group, Redondo Beach 1967-70; owner, prin. investigator Beta Technology Co., Palos Verdes 1970-71; aerospace engr. Air Force Flight Dynamics Lab., WPAFB, Oh. 1971-85; aerospace engr., cons. Dayton, Oh. 1985-87, Fresno, Calif. 1987-; recipient award for scientific achiev. Air Force Systems Command, W.D.C. 1982; mem. Am. Inst. Aero. & Astro. (assoc. fellow 1946-), Sigma Xi 1954-, Sigma Pi Sigma 1948-, ASME; author numerous pub. tech. reports and tech. jour. papers; rec: personal computers, gadgeteering, Dixieland jazz. Res/Ofc: 1249 W Magill Ave Fresno 93711

WOOLEY, CHRISTOPHER JOHN, commercial banking sales; b. Jan. 24, 1959, England; s. Norman John and Patricia Marie (Lockwood) W.; m. Jackie Ellen Soble, Sept. 16, 1984; children: Amanda b. 1989, Alexander b. 1992; edn: BA summa cum laude, UCSB 1981; reg. CPA Calif. 1984. Career: accountant Arthur Andersen & Co., Los Angeles 1981-84; controller, CFO Daum/Johnstown Am. 1984-86; fin. cons. Shearson Lehman Hutton, La Jolla 1987-89, Wells Fargo Bank 1990-; lectr. UCSB 1980-81; bus. columnist Calif. Press Bureau, L.A. 1987-89; Republican; rec: running, tennis, skiing. Res: San Diego Ofc: Wells Fargo Bank 101 West Broadway #300 San Diego 92130

WOOLSEY, ROY BLAKENEY, electronics company executive; b. June 12, 1945, Norfolk, Va.; s. Roy Blakeney and Louise Stookey (Jones) W.; m. Patricia Bernadine Elkins, Apr. 17, 1988; edn: undergrad. Calif. Inst. Tech., 1962-64; BS (w.distinction), Stanford Univ., 1966, MS, 1967, PhD, 1970. Career: senior physicist Technology for Communications Internat. (TCI), Mountain View 1970-75, mgr. radio direction finding systems 1975-80, program mgr. 1980-83, dir. strategic systems 1983-88, dir. rsch. & devel. 1988-91, v.p. engring. 1991-; dir: Merit Software Corp., Menlo Park 1990-; awards: grad. fellow NSF 1966-70, Phi Beta Kappa 1966, Sigma Xi 1966; clubs: Stanford, Palo Alto; Sequoia Yacht, Redwood City; YMCA Fitness Ctr., Palo Alto; contbg. author (books): Appls. of Artificial Intelligence to Command and Control Systems (1988), Antenna Engineering Handbook (1992), profl. jour. articles (1968-74); Republican; Presbyterian; rec: sailing, racquetball, tennis, skiing, contract bridge, travel. Res: 26649 Snell Ln Los Altos Hills 94022 Ofc: Technology for Communications Intl. 222 Caspian Dr Sunnyvale 94089

WRIGHT, FREDERICK HERMAN GREENE, II, computer systems designer, consultant; b. Feb. 23, 1952, Quincy, Mass.; s. Frederick Herman Greene and Dorothy Louise (Harrold) W.; edn: M.I.T., 1968-69. Career: test and measurement technician The Foxboro Co., Foxboro, Mass. 1968; hardware and software designer M.I.T. Project MAC, Cambridge, 1969; Information Internat., Brookline, Mass. 1969; Stanford Artificial Intelligence Lab, Palo Alto 1971-73; Systems Concepts, San Francisco (1970, 73-74, 76-90); hardware and software designer, then pres. Resource One, San Francisco 1974-76; computer cons. Langley-Porter Neuropsychiatric Inst., S.F. 1976; private cons. 1991-; mem. Digital Equipment Corp. Users Soc.; mem. Bay Area Soaring Assn., Pacific Soaring Council S.F. (bd. 1984-85); recipient gold soaring badge Fed. Aeronautique Internat. 1983; Republican. Res: 251 C St San Rafael 94901-4916

WRIGHT, HELENE SEGAL, managing editor; b. Jan. 31, 1955, L.A., Calif.; d. Alan and Lila Esther (Hambro) Segal; m. David Scott Wright, May 6, 1979; edn:. Calif. State Univ., Fullerton, Calif., 1973-75; BA, Eng., UC Santa Barbara, 1978. Career: lib. asst., ABC-CLIO, Santa Barbara, 1979-80; editorial asst., ABC-CLIO, Santa Barbara, 1980-81; asst. ed., ABC-CLIO, Santa Barbara, 1981-83; managing ed., ABC-CLIO, Santa Barbara, 1983-; advy. bd. mem., Current World Leaders, Santa Barbara, 1989-; mem: Am. Political Sci. Assn.; Democrat; Jewish; rec: swimming, collecting, art, theatre, literature. Ofc: ABC-CLIO 130 Cremona Santa Barbara 93117

WRIGHT, KENNETH LYLE, psychologist; b. American Falls, Ida.; s. Jesse Joshua and Martha Sophia (Dickenson) W.; children: Anne Collins, Corrella Carmelette Brown (AA), Sandra Lynne Sutherland (PhD); edn: BA, Univ. Wash. 1941; MA, USC, 1957; PhD, San Gabriel Coll. 1958. Career: coach State Tng. Sch. for Boys, Chehalis, Wash. 1941; dep. probation ofcr., L.A. Co., 1945-56; vis. lectr. Whittier (Calif.) Coll. 1956; dist. sch. psychologist Anaheim Union H.S. Dist.; edn. splst. Dept. Army, Orleans (France) Am. H.S., psychol. svs. and spl. edn. coordinator Dependent Edn. Group Hdqrs., Karlsruhe, Germany 1959-62; edn. splst. USN, San Diego 1962-63; pvt. practice psychologist, San Diego 1963-64, 1969-; founder Niagara Inst. of Human Devel.; chmn. Instl. Res. Board, Harborview Hosp., San Diego 1984- (5 year award Dec. 1989); psychol. cons. Clin. Bd. Speech Therapy, Children's Hosp., San Diego 1962-63; vis. prof. Univ. Western Ontario and lectr., sch. psychologist London (Ontario, Can.) Bd. of Edn., 1964-66, lectr. Toronto Bd. of Edn., 1964-69; lectr. Brock Univ. 1969-70; dir. psychol. svs Niagara Falls, NY, Dist. Bd. Edn. 1966-69; lectr. Syracuse Univ., NY, 1966-69; honors: recipient 3 awards Instl. Res. Bd., Biomedical Res. Inst. of Am., inducted into Hall of Fame for Contributions to Psychology 1984, award and fellowship Biomedical Res. Inst. Am./San Diego chapt. Dec. 1989, outstanding svc. San Diego Co. Assn. for Retarded Children, 5 awards for judging at Sci. Fair 1987-92; mem: Agoraphobic Soc. (founder N. Co. S.D. chapt. 1990), Assn. Children with Learning Disabilities, Council Exceptional Children, Royal Soc. Medicine Eng., Am., San Diego Co. Psych. Assn., San Diego Assn. Clin. Psychologists (pres. 1991), San Diego Forensic Soc. (founder 1988), Forensic Cons., Mensa; civic: Coord. Council City of Whittier (past pres.); clubs: Kona Kai, Masons; mil: USNR 1942-62. Res: 751 Amiford Dr San Diego 92107 Ofc: 3314 Fourth Ave San Diego also: 1865 Valley Pkwy Escondido.

WRIGHT, LLOYD GORDON, licensed acupuncturist; b. Sept. 28, 1954, Chgo., Ill.; s. Paul Allen and Frances Aileen (Pollard) W.; m. Jie Min Lin, July 23, 1988; edn: H.S. diploma, Wooster H.S., Reno, Nev., 1972; certified massage therapist, Sonoma Sch. of Holistic Massage, Santa Rosa, Calif., 1979; BA in Psychology, S.F. State Univ., 1981; lic. acupuncturist, Am. Coll. of Trad. Chinese Medicine, S.F., Calif., 1985, State of Calif., 1985. Career: mental health worker, Nevada Mental Health Inst., Reno, 1973-76; Peninsula Hosp. & Med. Ctr., Burlingame, Calif., 1978-87; lic. acupuncturist, private practice, Los Altos & Palo Alto, Calif., 1985-; guest lectr. Xian Yang Sch. of Trad. Chinese Medicine, Xian, China, 1986; Stanford Univ., Palo Alto, 1989; Foothill Coll., Los Altos, 1990; examiner, Calif. Acupuncture Lic. Exam, State of Calif., 1991; qualified med. examiner in acupuncture, Ind. Med. Council, State of Calif., 1992; mem. Acupuncture Com., Consumer Affairs, State of Calif., 1993; awards: Outstanding Svc. and Leadership, Calif. Acupuncture Assn., 1991, 92; mem. Calif. Certified Acupuncture Assn. 1987-; advy. bd. mem. Am. Found. of Trad. Chinese Medicine, 1987-; mem. Calif. Acupuncture Assn. 1987-, bd. of dirs. 1991-; bd. of dirs., Res. Inst. of Chinese Medicine 1993; author: contbg. writer, CAA News Bulletin, 1992-93; Republican; rec: fencing, Chi-Kung. Ofc: 4161 El Camino Way Ste. A-2 Palo Alto 94306

WU, FRANCIS YING WAI, physician; b. June 25, 1936, Shanghai, China; s. Chow Han and Yik Tsee (Wong) W.; m. Amy C.M. Hu, Aug. 24, 1965; children: Rose b. 1966, Justin b. 1967, Andrew b. 1980; edn: MB, BS, Univ. Hong Kong 1963; diplomate Am. Bd. Ob-Gyn. 1974. Career: staff So. Calif. Permanente Med. Group, Bellflower 1970-; asst. clin. prof. ob-gyn. UCLA Sch. Medicine, L.A. 1984-; profl. staff Harbor/UCLA Med. Center 1980-; article pub. in med. jour. 1972; Catholic; rec: swimming, travel, philately. Res: 837 Rivera Pl Palos Verdes Estates 90274 Ofc: Southern California Permanente Medical Group 9449 Imperial Hwy Downey 90242

WU, LI-PEI, banker; b. Sept. 9, 1934, Taiwan; s. Yin-Su and Chiaw-Mei (Hsiao) Wu; m. Jenny S. Lai, March 24, 1964; children: George T. b. 1964, Eugene Y. b. 1967; edn: BA, Nat. Taiwan Univ. 1957; MS bus. admin. Fort Hays State Univ., Hays, KS, 1969; commercial banking exec. pgm., Grad. Sch. of Bus., Columbia Univ., 1974. Career: asst. v.p., v.p. Nat. Bank of Alaska, Anchorage 1969-73, v.p./controller 1973-76, sr. v.p./chief fin. ofcr. 1976-78; chmn. exec. com. Alaska Nat. Bank of the North, Anchorage 1978-79, chief adminstrv. ofcr. 1979-80, pres. 1980-81; pres. & CEO, dir. General Bank & GBC Bankcorp, Los Angeles 1982-84, chmn., pres. & CEO, dir. 1984-; pres. Taiwanese United Fund (1991-92); recipient Outstanding Entrepreneur Award Nat. Assn. of Investment Cos.; mem: Taiwanese Am. Citizens League (founder, past pres.), Nat. Taiwanese Am. Citizens League (pres.), Taiwanese Am. Political Action Com. (pres. 1992-93). Ofc: General Bank 201 So Figueroa St Los Angeles 90012

WU, SHU-YAU, scientist in ferroelectric materials and related devices; b. Nov. 6, 1936, Taiwan; s. Tang-Chao Wu; m. Chih-Ing Lee, Feb. 8, 1969; children: Lillian b. 1969, Benjamin b. 1971; edn: PhD, Univ. Ill., Urbana 1966. Career: fellow scientist Westinghouse Electric Corp., Pittsburgh, PA 1967-89; sr. tech., prin. scientist McDonnell Douglas Aerospace Corp., Huntington Beach, Calif. 1989-; mem. editl. bd. in integrated ferroelectrics, Gordon and Breach Sci. Pubs., N.Y., N.Y. 1992-; awards: engring. achiev. Westinghouse Research Ctr., Pitts. (1985, 86), recognition award ISIF, Colo. Springs 1991; mem: IEEE 1970-, Sigma Xi 1970-; author 8 U.S. patents, 50+ sci. papers; Republican; rec: fishing, bridge, tennis. Ofc: McDonnell Douglas Space Systems Co. 5301 Bolsa Ave Huntington Beach 92647

WYCKOFF, ROBERT LEWIS, psychiatrist, attorney; b. Oct. 17, Los Angeles; s. Spofford Frank and Lenora Maxine Tenesch (Helsom); m. Hazel June Tarter, Sept. 10, 1947; children: Jenna Patrice, Karla Kaye; edn: BA, Loma Linda Univ. 1949; LL.B, Univ. Colo. Boulder 1952; MD, Loma Linda Univ. 1958; grad. Yale Univ. Law Sch. 1960; admitted St. Bar Calif. Career: dep. co. counsel Kern Co., Bakersfield 1952-54; med. intern 1958-59; med. practice 1960-67; tchr. legal medicine Loma Linda Sch. Medicine 1960-66; psychiatry resident Patton St. Hosp. 1966-71; staff psychiatrist Napa St. Hosp. 1977-91; asst. clin. prof. psychiatry Loma Linda Univ. 1968-72; cons. Superior Ct., Solano, Napa and Marin counties; N. Bay Suicide Prevention 1985-; med. dir. Anchor Pharmaceuticals Inc., Nev. 1988-; awards: Prohibition Party Nom. and Candidate for Gov. 1962; patentee; SDA; rec: writing, inventing. Res: 2099 W Lincoln Napa 94558

WYCOFF, CHARLES COLEMAN, retired physician, anesthesiologist; b. Sept. 2, 1918, Glazier, Texas; s. James Garfield and Ada Sharpe (Braden) W.; m. Gene Marie Henry, May 16, 1942; children: Michelle, Geoffrey, Brian, Roger, Daniel, Norman, Irene, Teresa; edn: AB, UC Berkeley, 1941; MD, UC San Francisco, 1943; Diplomate Am. Bd. Anesthesiology. Career: founder The Wycoff Group of Anesthesiology, San Francisco 1947-53; chief of anesthesia St. Joseph's Hosp., S.F. 1947-52, San Francisco County Hosp., 1953-54; asst. prof. anesth. Columbia Univ., N.Y.C. 1955-63; creator residency tng. pgm. in anesthesiology St. Joseph's Hosp., S.F., 1950, S.F. County Hosp., 1954; practice anesthesiology, instr. Presbyterian Med. Ctr., N.Y.C., 1955-63; clin. practice anesthesiology St. Francis Memorial Hosp., 1963-84; mil: served to capt. Med. Corps US Army 1945-47; producer, dir. films on regional anesthesia; contbr. articles to med. jours.; councilor at lg. Alumni Faculty Assn. Sch. Medicine UCSF 1979-80; scoutmaster Boy Scouts Am., S.F. 1953-55; Democrat. Res: 394 Cross St Napa 94559

WYLIE, JUDITH BABCOCK, author, travel writer, journalist; b. Oct. 7, 1943, Balt.; d. Joseph Brooks and Louise Boynton; m. Frank Winston Wylie, Feb. 19, 1984; edn: BA in biology & English, Univ. of Akron, 1966; MEd, Univ. Kentucky, 1967. Career: pgm. advisor Student Union, Ohio Univ., Athens 1968-71; pgm. dir. Student Union, Univ. Arizona, Tucson 1971-77; program dir. Student Union, CSU Los Angeles, 1977-78, dir. student devel. CSU Los Angeles, 1978-80, asst. to v.p./adminstrn. 1980-83; radio travel commentator Sta. KPCC-FM, Pasadena 1991-92; radio travel commentator KUSP-FM, Santa Cruz 1993-; chief travel writer Pasadena Star News, 1987-, San Gabriel Valley Tribune Newspapers Inc. 1991-; instr. writing seminars Pasadena City Coll. 1985-88, New York Univ., N.Y.C. 1989-; mem. PEN 1989-, Kappa Kappa Gamma (Pasa. Alumnae), Pasadena Humane Soc. (vol. 1991-); publs: travel and gen. lifestyle articles (100+) in newspapers and mags. incl. Travel & Leisure, New Woman, Westways, Diversion; coauthor: The Spa Book (1983), The Romance Emporium (1986). Ofc: 1900 Smith Grade Santa Cruz 95060

WYLLIE, LORING A., JR., structural engineer; b. Aug. 21, 1938, Oakland; s. Loring A. and Ruth Helen (Adelman) W.; m. Beverly Jane Middleton, Oct. 20, 1962; children: Blair b. 1966, Kelly b. 1968; edn: BS, UC Berkeley 1960, MS, 1962; reg. profl. engr., struct., Calif. 1970. Career: structural designer to chmn. bd. H.J. Degenkolb Associates, San Francisco 1960-; awards: Henry L. Kennedy Award, Am. Concrete Inst., Detroit 1985, H.J. Brunnier Award, Am. Soc.Civil Engrs., San Francisco sect. 1985; mem: Nat. Acad. Engring.1990-, Structural Engrs. Assn. of Calif. (pres. 1987-88), ASCE (pres. S.F. sect. 1980),

Am. Concrete Inst. (1968-, dir. 1985-88), Earthquake Engring. Research Inst. (1973-, dir. 1986-89), Engineers Club (S.F.); publs: various tech. papers, editor earthquake reports: Armenian 1988, Chile 1985; mil: 1st lt. USArmy 1962-64; Republican; Episcopalian; rec: travel, golf. Ofc: H.J. Degenkolb Associates, 350 Sansome St Ste 900 San Francisco 94104

WYMAN, PHILLIP DAVID, state legislator, rancher, lawyer; b. Feb. 21, 1945, Hollywood; s. Elliott Sherwood and Rosalie Jane (Mauzy) W.; m. Lynn Dee Larson, May 21, 1977; children: Andrea Dee b. 1978, Elizabeth Frances b. 1982, David Elliott b. 1987; edn: BA, UC Davis 1967; JD, McGeorge Sch. of Law 1973; grad. studies, Ateneo de Manila Univ. Philippines. Career: former exec. v.p. Antelope Valley Board of Trade; elected Calif. Legislature, Assembly coms: Higher Education, Water Parks and Wildlife, Agriculture and Ins.; mem. Little Hoover Commn.; mem: Am. Legion, Native Sons of the Golden West, Rotary, Greater Bakersfield, Lancaster, Palmdale, Ridgecrest Chambers of Commerce, Kern Co. Farm Bureau, Desert Tortoise Preserve Com., China Lake Astronomical Soc.; was founder Philippine Astronomical Soc.; Mountain Bible Ch.; mil: sgt. USAF; Republican; rec: astronomy. Ofc: California Legislature State Capitol Sacramento 95814

WYNNE, (LESLIE) BERNARD, artist; b. May 13, 1920, Indianapolis; s. Leslie Bernard, Sr. and Catherine Marie (Basso) W.; m. Lorena Gouaux, Oct. 15, 1949; children: Leslie b. 1950, Mary b. 1952, Leontine b. 1954, Laura b. 1956, Leonard b. 1964; edn: student, Pasadena City Coll. 1938-40; Claremont Coll. 1941-42; Pasadena Art Inst. 1945-47; spl. course L.A. County Art Museum 1948. Career: illustrator/commercial artist Lockheed Aircraft, North Am. Aviation, Aerojet Gen. Corp., 1952-59; Stanford Res. Inst., 1959-69; tchr. classes in landscape, still life, portrait work, Lafayette, La., 1962-64; self employed artist 1970-, represented Simic Galleries, Carmel, La Jolla, Beverly Hills; awards: Ventura Forum of Arts First Award, Bryan Waller Award Long Beach Museum of Art, Home Savings and Loan Purchase Prize L.A. All-City Outdoor Festival, Artists of Southwest Award, Hoosier Salon Prize of Distinction, Ind.; mem: Calif. Watercolor Soc., Laguna Beach Art Assn., Artists of Southwest; mil: cpl. AUS 1942-45; Republican; R.Cath. Res: 465 N Baldwin Ave Sierra Madre 91024

YAGJIAN, MICHAEL ARTHUR, company president; b. May 10, 1949, Lynn, Mass.; s. John Peter and Cora (Mekalian) Y.; m. Anita Paleologos, May 25, 1987; edn: BA in polit. sci., USC, 1970, JD, USC Sch. of Law, 1973; admitted Calif. bar: 1973. Career: founder, pres. and CEO Gourmet's Fresh Pasta, Los Angeles 1971-, Sub Station Ltd., L.A. 1987-; mem.: Calif. Bar Assn. 1973-, Inst. of Food Technologists 1989-, Calif. Restaurant Assn. 1985-, Mensa 1970-; civic: Community Counseling Svs., L.A. (dir. 1986-90); Republican. Ofc: Gourmets Fresh Pasta 2200 S Figueroa St Los Angeles 90007

YAMAHATA, WAYNE ICHIRO, plastic surgeon, educator; b. Sept. 27, 1947, Los Angeles; s. Kyu and May (Suehiro) Y.; m. Pamela, Jan. 26, 1985; children: Jeffery b. 1968, Ashley b. 1987; edn: AB, USC, 1971; MD, UC Davis, 1978; diplomate Am. Bd. Surgery 1987, Am. Bd. Plastic Surgery 1989. Career: intern, resident in surgery, fellow in nutrition, resident in surgery, resident in plastic surgery, Univ. Calif. Davis 1978-86, asst. clin. prof. UC Davis, 1986-; plastic surgeon pvt. practice, Sacto. 1986-; named resident of year UCD 1984; mem: Sacto. El Dorado Med. Soc., Am. Med. Assn., Calif. Med. Assn., Calif. Soc. of Plastic Surgeons, Earl J. Wolfman Surgical Soc., Am. Soc. of Plastic and Reconstrv. Surgeons; author: Clinical Nutrition 1984, contbr. articles in med. jours. 1974, 81. Ofc: 95 Scripps Dr Sacramento 95825

YARIV, AMNON, physicist, educator; b. Apr. 13, 1930, Tel Aviv, Israel; s. Shraga and Henya (Davidson) Y.; m. Frances; children: Danielle b. 1959, Dana b. 1964, Gabriela b. 1974; edn: BS, UC Berkeley, 1954, MS, 1958, PhD, 1960. Career: staff Bell Labs, Murray Hill, N.J. 1960-64; faculty Calif. Inst. of Tech., Pasadena 1964-; chmn. bd. ORTEL Corp., Alhambra, 1980-, Accuwave, Santa Monica, 1991-; awards: Ives Medal Opt. Soc. Am. 1986, Pender award Univ. Pa. 1985, Quantum Electronics Award IEEE 1980, Nat. Acad. of Engring., Nat. Acad. Scis. 1991, fellow Am. Acad. Arts and Scis. 1982, Harvey Prize 1992; mem.: Opt. Soc. Am., Am. Phys. Soc., IEEE, Am. Acad. Arts & Scis.; mil: sgt. arty. Israel 1948-50; Jewish; rec: hiking, body surfing. Res: 2257 Homet San Marino Ofc: Caltech 1201 California Ave Pasadena 91125

YASNYI, ALLAN DAVID, media communications executive; b. June 22, 1942, New Orleans; s. Ben Z. and Bertha R. (Michalove) Y.; m. Susan K. Manders, artist; children: Benjamin Charles, Judith Evelyn; edn: BBA, Tulane Univ., 1964. Career: indep. film producer, writer, actor, designer for TV, feature films, and stage prodns., performer and producer The Second City, 1961-73; dir. fin. and adminstrn. Quinn Martin Prodns., Hollywood 1973-76, v.p. fin. 1976-77, exec. v.p. fin. and corp. planning 1977; vice chmn., CEO QM Productions, Beverly Hills 1977-78, bd. chmn./CEO 1978-80; pres./CEO The Synapse Communications Group, Inc. 1981-; exec. producer first live TV & radio broadcast to 120+ nations combining INTELSAT, INTERSPUTNIK, Voice of Am. and Moscow World Radio Svc., 1990; bd. chmn. Found. for Global Bdcstg., Wash. D.C., 1987-; bd. dirs. Internat. Ctr. for Integrative Studies, NY, NY 1988-92, Assn. of Transpersonal Psychology 1986- (keynote address publ. 1988), bd. trustees Hollywood Arts Council, exec. v.p., trustee Hollywood Hist. Trust 1981-91; publ. participant, ICIS Forum, 1990-; honors: Citizen's State Audience with the Dali Lama, Daramsala, India 1988; Aspen Inst. Exec. Seminars Resource Guest, Global Comms., 1990; inducted Tulane Univ. Hall of Fame 1992; mem: Am. Acad. TV Arts and Scis., Hollywood Radio and TV Soc., Screen Actors Guild, Hollywood C.of C. (dir., exec. com. 1978-), Asthma & Allergy Found. of Am. (bd. dirs. 1981-85), Inst. of Noetic Scis. 1986-; mil: logistical combat ofcr. US Army 1964-66, Vietnam. Ofc: 4413 Babcock Ave Studio City 91604

YAW, ELBERT M., public speaker, counselor, trainer; b. May 5, 1940, Kansas City, Mo.; s. Elbert F. and Juanita F. (Black) Y.; m. Holly H. Chilson, May 16, 1982; children: Kimberly M. b. 1962, Sandi M. b. 1969; edn: pol. sci., Fullerton Coll. 1958-60; L.A. Trade Tech. Coll. 1962-3; BSME, Northrop Univ. 1966; Grad. Sch. Bus., CSU Los Angeles 1968; wholesale mgmt., Stanford Univ. 1980. Career: engr. So. Calif. Gas Co., Los Angeles 1966-67; systems and territory sales Paul-Munroe Co., Pico Rivera 1967-69; western reg. mgr. Fluid Power Systems Div., Ambac Inc., Burlingame 1969-74; area mgr. Paul-Munroe Co., Santa Clara 1974-79, v.p. mktg. and ops./dir. sales, Whittier 1979-85, v.p. No. Calif. area, 1985-87, v.p. distbn., sales and service, 1987-89; speaker, counselor, trainer dba Bert Yaw & Assocs., 1989-; consultant, engr. and bus. 1969-74; honor soc. Northrop Univ. 1965; mem. Auburn C.of C., Grass Valley and Nevada Co. C.of C.; Republican; Christian; rec: hunting, fishing, writing. Res: 24712 Scooterbug Ln Auburn 95603

YEAGER, JEANA LEE, aircraft manufacturer, flight test pilot/engineer; b. May 18, 1952, Fort Worth, Tx.; d. Royal Leland and Alice Evaree (Snyder) Y.; grad. Commerce H.S., 1970. Career: var. pos. in engring. design drafting, mech., struct., architl., aeronautical and comml. illustr., 1967-, design drafting engr. for retired USN capt. Bob Truax, rocket expert (his co. Project Private Enterprise, Inc. is devel. manned-reusable space shuttle rocket), 1981; founder/owner with ptnr. Dick Rutan, Voyager Aircraft Inc., 1981-, flight test pilot/engr. and crew mem. for the Voyager, Around the World Non-stop Non-refueled Project (1,000+ hours total flying time and holder FAA single/multi engine and instrument pilot ratings, has flown 66 of the 69 Voyager flt. test missions); part owner/builder (w/ Dick Rutan) of the Long EZ aircraft; holder 13 World Records (FAI): 5 in Long EZ (1982, 3 Female and 1 Open), 1 in Vari Eze (1984, Open), 8 in Voyager (1986, 5 Open Absolute, unrefueled endurance 117 hrs, previous 84.5 hrs set in 1931); recipient Collier Award, Pres. Trophy, Royal Aero Club gold medal, Newsmaker of Yr., patriot of yr. Am. Acad. of Achievement; mem: Nat. Aeronautic Assn., Exptl. Aircraft Assn., Aircraft Owners and Pilots Assn.; rec: flying airplanes and ultralights, horses. Ofc: Voyager Aircraft Hangar 77 Airport Mojave 93501

YEAGER, KURT ERIC, research and development executive; b. Sept. 11, 1939, Cleveland, Ohio; s. Joseph Ellsworth and Karolyn Kristine (Pedersen) Y.; m. Rosalie Ann McMillan, Feb. 5, 1960 (div. 1968); m. Regina Ursula Querfurt, May 12, 1970; children: Geoffrey b. 1961, Phillip b. 1963, Victoria b. 1975; edn: BA chemistry, Kenyon Coll. 1961; MS physics, UC Davis 1964. Career: ofcr., program mgr. Air Force Tech. Applications Ctr., Alexandria, Va. 1962-68; assoc. dept. dir. Mitre Corp., McLean, Va. 1968-72; dir. energy res. and devel. planning U.S. E.P.A., WDC 1972-74; dir. fossil power plants dept. Electric Power Res. Inst., Palo Alto 1974-79, dir. coal combustion systems div. 1979-83, v.p. generation and storage 1983-91, sr. v.p. EPRI Technical Operations, 1991-; bd. mem. Nat. Coal Council, Arlington, Va. 1988-90; mem. Commerce Tech. Advy. Bd., WDC 1974-75; bd. chmn. Coal Quality Inc., Homer City,, Pa. 1989-; tchg. asst. Ohio St. Univ., Columbus 1961-62; mem. bd. ASME Res. Policy Bd., N.Y.C. 1982-84; awards: E.P.A. outstanding service 1974, British Coal Utilization Res. Assn. Robens medal 1989, Fellow ASME 1991; mem. AAAS; Nat. Republican Party, Calif. Republican Party; 146 articles and chpts. pub. on energy and environ. (1968-); mil: capt. USAF 1962-68, 2 AF commendation medals 1966; Republican; Episcopalian. Res: 687 Erie Dr Sunnyvale 94087

YEAGER, PHILIP J., real estate executive; b. Mar. 1, 1930, Columbus, Ohio; s. William P. and Anna C. (Meidl) Y.; m. Peggy Wetzler, Nov. 1, 1952; children: Melissa b. 1954, Susan b. 1955, Kurt b. 1956 (dec.), Stephen b. 1959, Christine b. 1961, Jennifer b. 1966; edn: Claremont Men's Coll. 1951; grad. study Ohio State Univ. 1956; Calif. lic. real estate broker (third generation Calif. Realtor); Calif. Comm. Colls. life tchg. credential, real estate; FAA lic. instrument rated pilot (2700 hours). Career: realtor; bd. chmn./CEO Century 21 Region 105 (135 realty offices, adminstrv. hq. Ontario, Calif.), Century 21 Region 113 (175 realty offices, adminstrv. hq. Seattle, Wash.); cons. ptnr. Century 21 Mexico (70 realty offices in 36 cities adminstrv. hq. Mexico City); Founding Dir. of Mex. Tech. Exchange, Inc. (MXT) a US corp. providing goods and svs. relating to the real estate industry in Mex.; honors: Eagle Scout; mem: Covina Valley Bd. of Realtors (past pres.), Nat. Assn. of Realtors (past dir.); civic: Boy Scouts Am. (former scoutmaster and dist. chmn.), Toastmasters (past pres. 2 clubs); contbr. num. real estate articles in nat. publs.; mil: 1st lt./pilot USAF Korean Campaign 1952-56; Republican; rec: flying, power boating, golf, tennis. Res: 2808 Monte Verde Covina 91724 Ofc: Century 21, Region 105, 3400 Inland Empire Blvd Ontario 91764-5510; Century 21, Region 113, 18000

Pacific Hwy S, Seattle WA 98188; Century 21 Mexico, Monte Libano #245, Lomas de Chapultepec, 11000 Mexico, D.F.

YEEND, WARREN ERNEST, geologist; b. May 14, 1936, Colfax, Wash.; s. Kenneth Edward and Frances Leone (Lynch) Y.; m. Nancy Eloise Neal, June 6, 1965 (div. Dec. 1980); 1 dau., Erica b. 1972; m. Elissa Hirsh, Sept. 29, 1985; edn: BS geology, Wash. State Univ., 1958; MS, Univ. Colo., 1961; PhD geology, Univ. Wis., 1965. Career: geologist US Geological Survey, Menlo Park, Calif. 1965-; honors: Phi Beta Kappa 1958, Outstanding tchg. asst. Univ. Wis. 1965, USGS special achiev. award 1975, 1980; mem. History of Earth Scis. Soc. 1982-, Geol. Soc. Am. 1976-85, Am. Quaternary Assn. 1974-81; publs: profl. papers (1969, 74), bull., Gold Placers of the Circle Dist., Alaska (1991); rec: books, gardening. Ofc: USGS, 345 Middlefield Rd Menlo Park 94025

YEN, TIEN-SZE BENEDICT, virologist, educator; b. Oct. 15, 1953, Taipei, Taiwan, naturalized U.S. cit. 1972; s. Yen-Chen and Er-Ying Chi Y.; m. Maria He, Mar. 26, 1983; children: Cecilia b. 1984, Brian b. 1987; edn: BS, Stanford Univ., 1973; MD, Duke Univ. Sch. of Med., 1982, PhD, 1982. Career: asst. prof. Univ. Calif., San Francisco 1985-91, assoc. prof. 1991-; publs: 50+ jour. articles. Ofc: PO Box 0506 University California, San Francisco 94143

YEN, WEN-HSIUNG, association president, ethnomusicologist, composer, educator, writer; b. June 26, 1934, Tainan, Taiwan, R.O.C.; nat. citizen U.S.A. 1986; m. Yuan-yuan Yen, Jan. 6, 1961; 3 sons; edn: BA, Nat. Taiwan Norman Univ. 1960; MA, Chinese Cluture Univ. 1964; Univ. of Calif. 1971; PhD cand., Chinese Culture Univ., Univ. of Maryland. Career: instr. Taiwan Provincial Taichung Teacher Coll., 1961-62; prof. Chinese Culture Univ. 1964-69; lectr. West Los Angeles Community Coll., 1978-82; grad. teaching asst. Univ. of Md. 1982-83; instr. L.A. City Coll. 1983-, CSU Los Angeles 1984-, Pasadena City Coll. 1989-; prof. of Chinese, Santa Monica Coll. 1986-, CSU Northridge 1986-; founder Wen Yen Piano Studio, 1972-, founder Chinese Culture Sch. of L.A., 1976-; founder, dir. Chinese Music Orch. of So. Calif., 1974-, TV appearance 1979, and conductor Yue You Chorus of So. Calif.; honors: recognition award Calif. Mus. Found. Bd. of Trustees 1976, recogn. award Chinese Amer. PTA 1980, outstanding tchr. Confucius Commemorative Day Ceremony, L.A. 1984, service award Nat. Taiwan Normal Univ. Alumni Assn. of So. Calif. 1985, recipient Commendations from Pres. George Bush and Pres. Lee Teng-hui (Rep. of China), Calif. Gov. Deukmejian and Lt. Gov. Leo McCarthy on occasion of 10th anniversary of Taiwan Benevolent Assn. of Calif. 1989; musical compositions include: Collection of Works by Mr. Yen, 1969; recordings: Art Songs and Chinese Folk Songs (13 pieces) 1982; Instrumental Ensemble for Chinese Traditional Orch. incl. A Hope of New Spring and San Yang Kai Tai; publs: Taiwan Folk Songs, Vol. 1 (1967), Vol. 2 (1969); A Dictionary of Chinese Music and Musicians (coauthor, 1967), A Collection of Wen-hsiung Yen's Songs (1968, vol. 2 1987); Achievement and Methodology for Comparative Musicology (1968), transl.; Chinese Musical Culture and Folk Songs (Zhong Wen Book Co., Taipei, 1989); organizer concerts in So. Calif. incl. Chinese Musical Culture Concert at CSU Los Angeles (1989, 91), Chinese Art Festival of So. Calif., Evening of Performing Arts at Pasadena City Coll. (6/92), conductor new composition for mixed chorus sung by Yue You Chorus and So. Calif. Catholic Choir; mem: Chinese-Amer. Musicians Assn. of So. Calif. (pres.), Chinese Culture Sch. of L.A. (pres.), Chinese Choral Soc. of So. Calif. (music dir.), Soc. of Ethnomusicol., The College Music Soc., Internat. Council for Traditional Music, Alumni Assn. for Chinese Culture Univ. in USA (pres.), Taiwan Benevolent Assn. of Amer. (bd. 1987-), Taiwan Benevolent Assn. of Calif. (bd. 1985-, v.p. 1986, pres. 1987-89), Chinese Amer. P.T.A. of So. Calif. (supr. 1985-); res. presentations China and Confucianism Internat. Conf., CSU L.A. (6/90), 4th Internat - Archaeology Symposium, Paris, Fr., Internat. Council for Traditional Music (10/90), Chinese Am.: Origins and Destinations (8/92); rec: walking, Tai Chi Chuan, table tennis. Address: 1116 Drake Rd Arcadia 91007

YESKE, DAVID BRENT, financial planner; b. May 21, 1957, Albany, Calif.; s. Ronald A. and JoAnn R. (Huntsman) Y.; m. Virginia Folwell, Jan. 10, 1987; edn: BS applied econs., Univ. San Francisco, 1989; cert. fin. planner (CFP). Career: gen. ptnr. PCM, Ltd., Napa, Calif. 1977-84; wire trader Goldberg Securities, San Francisco 1984-85; brokerage cons. Paul Revere Group, S.F. 1985-90; pres. Yeske & Co., Inc. S.F. 1990-; mem. Inst. of CFP 1990-, Commonwealth Club of Calif., Hermetic Order of the G.D.; rec: Hermeneutics, opera, history. Ofc: Yeske & Company, Inc. 220 Bush St Ste 1109 San Francisco 94104

YEUNG, CATHERINE SUET-KWUN, real estate broker, appraiser, tax preparer, environmental inspector; b. Nov. 13, 1947, Hong Kong, nat. 1984; d. Hung-Chiu and Yuet-Ping (Lee) Poon; children: Bernice Millie b. 1977, Melissa Michelle b. 1979; edn: AA home econ., Northcote Coll. of Edn., H.K. 1968; mgmt. major, St. Mary's Coll. 1988-; Hong Kong tchg. credentials: Jr. H.S., domestic sci., home econs., spl. edn. for the visually handicapped, 1971; Calif. lic. Notary Public 1985, R.E. Broker 1989; Grad. Realtor Inst. (GRI) 1988, Cert. Residential Specialist (CRS) 1990, Cert. R.E. Appraiser (CREA) 1989, Cert. Environmental Insp. (CEI) 1991; lic. appraiser Calif. 1992. Career: tchr., hd. domestic sci. dept. Rosaryhill Sch., Hong Kong 1968-70, Ebenezer Sch. and

Home for the Blind 1970-71; English tchr. (1-6) Gold & Silver Exchange Sch., H.K., and pvt. tutor to children of Amb. of Vietnam, H.K. 1971-72; adminstrv. asst. to mgr. fusion power, Elec. Power Research Inst., Palo Alto 1974-77; prop. Cathie & Jenny Imports & Exports, San Jose 1981-83; realtor and VIP relocation dir., Century 21 Blossom Hill Realty, San Jose 1984-87; real estate broker Contempo Realty, Almaden Office 1988-, also free lance appraiser 1989-, cert. tax preparer 1990-, cert. environmental insp. 1991-; sales awards: C21 Blossom Hill Realty top prod. mo., 1st quarter (11/86, 1987), Contempo Realty million dollar club (1988) and salespsn. of mo. (7/89); mem. Nat. Assn. Realtors, Calif. Assn. Realtors, San Jose Bd. of Realtors, Womens Council of Realtors NAR, Resdl. Splst. Council, Am. Appraiser Assn., Environmental Assessment Assn., Nat. Notary Assn., Nat. Assn. Female Execs. Inc., Chinese-Am. R.E. Assn., Chinese Am. C.of C.; rec: music, sports, arts and crafts, cooking. Ofc: Contempo Realty 1096 Blossom Hill Rd San Jose 95123 also: Bethel, Griffin and Co., Appraisers 12333 S Saratoga-Sunnyvale Rd Saratoga 95070

YOCAM, DELBERT WAYNE, computer manufacturing co. executive; b. Dec. 24, 1943, Long Beach, Calif.; s. Royal Delbert and Mary Rose (Gross) Y.; m. Janet McVeigh, June 13, 1965; children: Eric Wayne, Christian Jeremy, Elizabeth Janelle; edn: BA bus. adminstrn., CSU Fullerton 1966; MBA, CSU Long Beach 1971. Career: mktg./ supply changeover coord. automotive assembly div. Ford Motor Co. Dearborn, Mich. 1966-72; prodn. control mgr. Control Data Corp. Hawthorne, Calif. 1972-74; prodn. and material control mgr. Bourns Inc. Riverside 1974-76; corp. material mgr. Computer Automation Inc. Irvine 1976-78; prodn. planning mgr. central staff ITT Cannon Electric div. world hdqs. Santa Ana 1978-79; exec. v.p. and c.o.o. Apple Computer Inc., Cupertino 1979-91; dir: AST Research Inc. 1992-, Oracle Corp. 1992-, Adobe Systems Inc. 1991-, Technology Center of Silicon Valley 1987-, v.chmn. 1988-89; mem. Am. Electronic Assn. (nat. bd. 1989); appt. special advy. council Office of Technology Assessment U.S. Congress 1987-89; faculty Cypress Coll. 1972-79; Republican; Methodist. Ofc: Woodside.

YOKLEY, RICHARD CLARENCE, firefighter, operations chief; b. Dec. 29, 1942, San Diego; s. Clarence Ralph and Dorothy Junese (Sackman) Y.; m. Jean Elizabeth Liddle, July 25, 1964; children: Richard Clarence II, Karin Denise; edn: San Diego City Coll., 1967, AS in fire sci., Miramar Coll., 1975; Calif. St. certified fire officer, fire investigator, fire instr. Career: disc jockey Sta. KSDS-FM, San Diego 1966-67; building engr. Consol. Systems Inc., San Diego 1968-72; firefighter Bonita-Sunnyside Fire Dept., 1972-, ops. chief 1991-; med. techn. Hartson Ambulance, San Diego 1978-80, Bay Gen. Hosp. (now Scripps Chula Vista Hosp.) 1980-83; chmn. bd. South Bay Emergency Med. Svc. 1988; awards: exemplary svc. award Fire Dept. Directors (1984), Heroism and community svc. Firehouse Mag., N.Y.C. (1987), Chula Vista `Star News Salutes' (1987), Golden svc. San Diego Co. Credit Union (1988); mem: San Diego County Fire Prevention Ofcrs. (pres. 1985), S.D. Co. Fire and Arson Investigators, Calif. Conf. Arson Investigators, Soc. Fire Prevention Engrs., Bonita Bus. and Profl. Assn. (dir. 1991-93, historian award 1987), South Bay Communications 1988, Masons; civic bds: Firehouse Mus., San Diego (asst. curator 1972-88), Boy Scouts Am. Tr. #874 Bonita (scoutmaster 1978-79), Bonita Hist. Mus. (co-founder 1986); mil: USAF 1962-66, Peshawar, West Pakistan; Republican; Methodist; rec: scuba diving, Sport Chalet Diveclub (v.p. 1990-91), collect firefighting memorabilia (co-owner Dick-Jeans Antiques), visit fire depts. worldwide (Moscow, Leningrad, Paris, Helsinki, London, others). Res: Box 718 Bonita 91908-0718 Ofc: Bonita-Sunnyside Fire Dept. 4900 Bonita Rd Bonita 91902-1327

YONG, DAVID C., clinical microbiologist, director public health laboratory b. Feb. 9, 1943, Lipis, Pahang, Malaysia; s. Ban Yien and Shin Yin (Ngaw) Y.; m. Lily Lian Loh, Dec. 21, 1968; children: Celina Mei b. 1979, Charles Tat b. 1985; edn: BSc (hons.), Univ. Manitoba, 1968, MSc virology, 1970, PhD med. microbiology, 1973, postdoctoral studies, 1974; Cert. pub. health and clin. microbiologist, Calif. Career: microbiologist, scientist Public Health Lab. Ontario Ministry of Health, Windsor, Ont., Canada 1975-85; instr. St. Clair Coll., Windsor 1976-84; adj. asst. prof. Univ. Windsor, Ont. 1983-84; pub. health lab. dir. Sonoma Co. Health Dept., Santa Rosa, Calif. 1986-; lectr. Sonoma State Univ., Rohnert Park 1986-87, adj. prof. 1991-92; awards: Dr. Stanley Reitman Memorial award for outstanding achiev. in teaching Internat. Soc. Clin. Lab. Technicians and Am. Assn. Bioanalysts 1988, Craftsman and Master of Photographic Arts awards (1984, 1986), Profl. Photog. of Canada; mem: Am. Soc. Microbiology, Calif. Assn. Pub. Health Lab. Dir. (exec. com. 1988-89); Chinese United Methodist Ch.; rec: profl. photog., classical guitarist. Ofc: Sonoma County Public Health Laboratory, 3313 Chanate Rd Santa Rosa 95404

YOUNG, BRYANT LLEWELLYN, lawyer; b. Mar. 9, 1948, Rockford, Ill.; s. Llewellyn Anker and Florence Y.; m. Elizabeth MacMillan, Apr. 16, 1983; children: Kendra, Megan, Lauren; edn: AB, Cornell Univ., 1970; JD, Stanford Univ., 1974. Career: law clk. US Dist. Ct. no. dist. Calif., San Francisco 1974-75; atty., assoc. Dinkelspiel, Pelavin, Steefel & Levitt, S.F. 1975-77; White House fellow, 1977-78, spl. asst. to Secty. of HUD, WDC 1977-79, actg. dep. exec. asst. for ops. 1979; dep. gen. mgr. New Comm. Devel. Corp., 1979, actg. gen. mgr. 1979-80; mgmt. cons. AVCO Corp., 1980; spl. asst. to the c.e.o. and

chmn. U.S. Synthetic Fuels Corp., WDC 1980-81, project dir. 1981; pres. Trident Mgmt. Corp., San Francisco 1981-87; counsel Pelavin, Norberg, Harlick & Beck, S.F. 1981-82, ptnr. 1982-87; mng. ptnr. bus. and R.E. sect., Carroll, Burdick & McDonough, S.F. 1987-90; founding ptnr. Young, Vogl & Harlick, S.F. 1990-; advy. com. Nat. Multi Housing Council; prin. The Council for Excellence in Govt., WDC 1986-; honors: Stanford Law Rev., Student Body pres., Hilmer Oehlmann Award for excellence in legal writing, Lawrence Fletcher Award for outstanding contbn. 1974, del. P.R.O.China 1980; mem: White House Fellows Alumni Assn. (chmn. annual meeting 1979, treas., bd. White House Fellows Found. 1980-84), State Bar Calif. (R.E. sect.), State Bar Nev., Dist. Col. Bar Assn., S.F. Bar Assn.; civic: Netherlands-Am. C.of C., Canadian-Am. C.of C. (bd. dirs. 1990-), S.F. Aid Retarded Citizens Inc. (pub. affairs com. 1977), US-USSR Housing Agreement /New Towns Working Group (US co-chair 1979-80), Am. Field Service Returnees Assn. 1967-, Holland-Am. Soc., Netherlands Am. Univ. League, Commonwealth Club. Ofc: Young, Vogl & Harlick, 425 California St San Francisco 94104

YOUNG, BURT CARL, controller; b. April 27, 1945, Lindsay; s. Carl William and Alyce Esther (Waldron) Y.; m. Margaret Ann Peterson, June 10, 1967; children: Careen b. 1968, Timothy b. 1973; edn: BS, Cal Poly SLO 1973; MBA, Golden Gate Univ. 1985. Career: acct. Guy F. Atkinson Co., South San Francisco 1973-75, project acct. 1975-78, div. acct. 1978-83, fin. analyst 1983-85; controller Atkinson Systems, Sacto. 1986-88; Vellutini Corp. 1988-; bd.mem. GFACO Fed. Credit Union 1980-81, secty., treas. 1981-82, v.p. 1982-84, pres. 1984-86; mem: Nat. Corp. Cash Mgmt. Assn., Constrn. Fin. Mgmt. Assn.; mil: staff sgt. USAF 1965-70, commendation 1967; rec: fishing, swimming, photog. Ofc: Vellutini Corp. POB 9907 Sacramento 95823-0907

YOUNG, DOUGLAS REA, lawyer; b. July 21, 1948, Los Angeles; s. James Douglas and Dorothy Belle (Rea) Y.; m. Terry Forrest, Jan. 19, 1974; 1 dau: Megann Forrest, b. 1979; edn: BA, cum laude, Yale Univ. 1970/71; JD, UC Berkeley 1976; admitted Calif. State Bar, 1976, US Supreme Ct., 6th and 9th Circuit Cts. of Appeal, Fed. Dist. Cts. (no. and central dists. Calif.) Career: law clerk to US Dist. Judge Alfonso J. Zirpoli 1976-77; assoc. atty. Farella, Braun & Martel 1977-82, partner 1982-; apptd. spl. master in federal litigation (4t), judge pro tem S.F. Municipal Ct. 1984-, S.F. Superior Ct. 1990-; faculty Nat. Inst. for Trial Advocacy 1983-, Hastings Coll. of Advocacy 1985-, Calif. Contg. Edn. of the Bar, Practising Law Inst.; author: (w/ Purver & Davis) California Trial Handbook 2d ed. (Bancroft-Whitney 1987), (w/ Purver, Davis & Kerper) The Trial Lawyer's Book: Preparing and Winning Cases (Lawyers Cooperative 1990), (w/Lynch, Taylor, Purver & Davis) California Negotiation and Settlement Handbook (Lawyers Cooperative 1991), (w/Lynch, Taylor, Purver & Davis) Negotiation and Settlement (Lawyers Cooperative 1992), contbr. articles in legal jours.; lawyer representative from the No. Dist. of Calif. to the Ninth Cir. Judicial Conf., 1992-94; co-founder Berkeley Law Foundation; bd. dir. Legal Aid Soc. of San Francisco 1981-, Public Interest Clearinghouse 1981-; awards: ABA Pro Bono Publico Award 1992, appreciation Berkeley Law Found., appreciation Public Interest Clearinghouse, Award of Merit S.F. Bar Assn., exec. editor Calif. Law Rev. 1975-76; mem: Calif. St. Bar, Calif. Acad. of Appellate Lawyers (bd.), Berkeley Law Found., ACLU, Bar Assn. of San Francisco, Crim. Justice Act Defense Panel No. Dist. Calif., Environmental Defense Fund, Litigation and Criminal Law Sects. of Am. Bar Assn., Lawyers Club of S.F., Bar Assn. of S.F. (bd. 1990-91, chair litigation sect. 1989), ABA, Calif. Bar Assn.; publs: Cal. L. Rev. 1975; mil: Sgt., USMC 1971-73; Democrat; Prot.; rec: skiing, mountaineering, running. Res: 67 Weybridge Ct Oakland 94611 Ofc: Farella, Braun & Martel, 235 Montgomery St Ste 3000 San Francisco 94104

YOUNG, GORDON ALLEN, retired naval officer, computer systems specialist; b. March 10, 1945, N.Y.; s. Dick and Minnie (Pang) Y.; m. Yuko Koga, Aug. 24, 1973; children: Gregory, Jessica; edn: AAS, N.Y. Inst. Tech. 1965; BS, Purdue Univ., 1972; MS, Naval Postgrad. Sch., 1976. Career: served to comdr. US Navy 1965-90; instr. Chapman Coll., San Diego 1989-; training specialist Southeastern Computer Consultants 1990-92; prin. analyst/facility security ofcr./AIS security ofcr. Integrated Systems Control, Inc. 1992-; mem. TROA. Res: San Diego

YOUNG, JEFFREY WILLIAM, mechanical aerospace engineer, consultant; b. Jan. 13, 1947, Pittsburgh, Pa.; s. William Norman and Wilma (Myers) Y.; m. Karen Lynn Young, Nov. 23, 1973; children: Scott N., Witney R.; edn: BS mech. engring., UC Davis, 1969; MS in M.E., M.I.T., 1970; PhD in M.E. (spec. in dynamic systems and controls), UC Davis, 1974; Reg. profl. engr. Calif. Career: lectr. and devel. engr. UC Davis, 1974-75; asst. prof. mech. and aero. engring. Univ. Missouri, Kansas City 1975-79; dir. engring. Structural Dynamics Research Corp., San Diego 1979-, cons. engr. on analysis and design of mech. and aerospace products using computer-aided engring. i.e. Space Shuttle, MX Missile, Space Station, high performance computer Disk Drives, Mobile Cmd. Control & Comm. Sys., Radar Def. Unit Veh.; awards: NSF fellow MIT 1964-70, NASA cash award for creative devel. of technical innovation 1983, Tau Beta Pi, Phi Kappa Phi; mem. Am. Soc. Mech. Engrs.; author: (video prodn.) Dynamic Analysis of Space Station Freedom (1990), 20+ tech. publs.; rec: tennis, bicycling. Res: 1482 Sanford Ln Leucadia 92024 Ofc: SDRC 11995 El Camino Real Ste 200 San Diego 92130

YOUNG, KENNETH ROGER, art educator; b. Aug. 25, 1936, Los Angeles; s. John Richardson and Jency Florence (Leman) Y.; m. LaVonne Bonita Kurowski, Mar. 17, 1963 (div. June 1970); m. Suzanne Cecelia Murray, June 20, 1970; children: Christina b. 1971, Steven b. 1974, Joseph b. 1974; edn: AA, Sacto. City Coll., 1956; BA, CSU Sacto., 1958, MA, 1968; Calif. gen. sec. tchg. credential, 1959. Career: art tchr. Roseville High Sch. Dist., 1960-70, Sequoia High Sch. Dist., 1970-82; art resource splst. San Carlos H.S. 1970-73, Morgan Hill Unified Sch. Dist. 1982-, Britton Middle Sch. 1982-85, Live Oak H.S. 1985-; performer- Artists' Theater: San Jose Mus. of Fine Art, Fresno Art Mus., Kingsley Art Club (Crocker Art Mus., Sacto.), Placer and Nevada Counties Art Docent luncheons, Calif. Art Edn. Assn. confs. and various schs. and orgs. in No. Calif.; awards: tchr. of year San Carlos H.S. 1972, Golden Bell Award (1st) Calif. Sch. Boards Assn. 1987; mem.: Am. Fedn. Tchrs. 1982-, Calif. Tchrs. Assn. 1960-82, Nat. Edn. Assn. 1960-82, Calif. Art Edn. Assn. (1970-, no. area sec. rep. 1988-90); civic: Young Audiences of San Jose (bd. 1985-88); mil: sp5 Calif. Army Nat. Guard 1954-65; Democrat; R.Cath.; rec: travel, film study, drawing & painting. Res: 1137-A Reed Ave Sunnyvale 94086

YOUNG, ROBYN GAIL, neurologist; b. Dec. 24, 1950, Danville, Ill.; d. Martin and Selma Lee (Mervis) Young; m. David Richard Cox, MD., PhD., June 12, 1977 (div. Nov. 1985); 1 child, Ian Richard Cox b. 1984; edn: BS, Stanford Univ., Stanford, Calif., 1973; MD, Yale Univ. Sch. of Medicine, New Haven, Conn., 1977. Career: internship, Pacific Presbyn. Hosp., S.F., 1977-78; residency, internal medicine, Pacific Med. Ctr., S.F., 1978-80; residency, neurology, UC S.F., 1980-83; neurologist, private practice, Oakland, Calif., 1984-; clinical instr., UC S.F. Dept. of Neurology, 1983-; active staff: Summit Med. Ctr., Oakland, Calif. 1983-; courtesy staff: Alta Bates-Herrick Hosp., Berkeley, Calif. 1984-; Alameda Hosp., Alameda, Calif. 1988-; Pacific Med. Ctr., S.F.; board certification: Diplomate of the Nat. Bd. of Med. Examiners 1978; Am. Bd. of Internal Medicine 1980; Am. Bd. of Psychiatry & Neurology 1986; awards: Nat. Merit Scholarship; Honors in Chem., Stanford, 1973; Nicholas J. Giarman award for outstanding theses, Yale, 1977; mem.: Am. Acad. of Neurology 1983-, Alameda-Contra Costa County Med. Assn. 1983-, CMA 1983-, AMA 1991-, Profl. Advy. Bd. of the M.S. Soc. 1987-, Bd. Dir. & Chair Profl. Advy. Bd. Easter Seal Soc. of Alameda County 1990-; med. dir. Easter Seal Soc., Oakland Ctr. 1993-; publs.: The Interactions of Cholinergic and Anticholinergic Drugs with Nigro-neostriatal Dopaminergic Neurons (Yale thesis) 1977; co-author, Early CT Findings of Global CNS Hypoperfusion, 1983. Ofc: Robyn G. Young, MD, APC 2832 Summit St. Oakland 94609

YOUNG, RONALD DUANE, engineer; b. June 21, 1960, Los Angeles; s. Larry and Doris Mae (Gong) Y.; m. Nerisa Marie Lim, Sept. 20, 1986; children: Brittany Mae; edn: BS engring., UCLA, 1983; reg. Profl. Engr., Calif. Career: project mgr. TRW Space & Defense, Los Angeles 1982-; pres. Young Engineering Co., 1985-; honors: Eagle Scout BSA, L.A. 1984; mem. Soc. of Profl. Engrs.; civic: Found. for the Junior Blind. Res: 1810 Pavas Ct Rowland Hts 91748 Ofc: TRW, One Space Park Redondo Beach 90278

YOUNG, STEPHEN DEAN, disability technology specialist; b. Apr. 11, 1942, Pasadena; s. Robert Thornton and Asenath (Kinnear) Y.; m. Sylvia Tannhauser, June 1, 1963; children: Michael Andrew b. 1974, Melissa Kim b. 1975; edn: BA, Reed Coll., Portland 1964; MA, UCLA, 1966, PhD, 1969. Career: postdoc. fellow Univ. North Carolina, Chapel Hill 1969-71; asst. prof. Indiana Univ. N.W., Gary 1971-73; res. assoc. Univ. Calif., San Diego 1973-75; asst. prof. St. John's Univ., Jamaica, N.Y. 1975-80; pgmr./developer prin., Santa Monica, Calif. 1980-88; asst. technologist CSU Northridge, 1988-; lectr. Mount St. Mary's Coll., L.A. 1981-82, L.A. Southwest Coll., 1987-88, CSU Northridge, 1988-89; bd. mem. Computer Access Ctr., Santa Monica 1986-; mem: We. Soc. of Naturalists 1967-, N.Y. Acad. Scis. 1978-, Sigma Xi 1976-, AAAS 1990-; civic: Boy Scouts Am., Santa Monica (cubmaster 1984-86, asst. scoutmaster 1987-); Democrat; Unitarian; rec: camping, hiking, natural history. Ofc: Calif. State Univ. DVSS, 18111 Nordhoff St Northridge 91330-0001

YOUNGBLOOD, RONALD F., seminary professor; b. Aug. 10, 1931, Chgo., Ill.; s. William C. and Ethel V. (Arenz) Y.; m. Carolyn J. Johnson, Aug. 16, 1952; children: Glenn b. 1960, Wendy S. Morrissey b. 1962; edn: BA, Valparaiso Univ., Valparaiso, Ind., 1952; BD, Fuller Theol. Sem., Pasadena, 1955; PhD, Dropsie Coll. for Hebrew & Cognate Learning, Phila., 1961; career: prof. of Old Testament, Bethel Theol. Sem., St. Paul, Minn., 1961-78; lectr. in Hebrew, Luther Theol. Sem., St. Paul, Minn., 1975-77; dean and prof. of Old Testament, Wheaton Grad. Sch., Wheaton, Ill., 1978-81; prof. of Old Testament, Trinity Evangelical Div. Sch., Deerfield, Ill., 1981-82; adjunct prof. of Old Testament, No. Baptist Theol. Sem., Lombard, Ill., 1981; prof. of Old Testament, Bethel Sem. W., S.D., 1982-; transl., ed., New Internat. Version of the Bible, Wayne, N.J., 1970-78; exec. com., Evangelical Theol. Soc., Jackson, Miss., 1975-; ed., Evangelical Theol. Journal, Lynchburg, Va., 1975-; sec. and bd. mem., Near East Archaeological Soc., St. Louis, Mo., 1979-; mem., Inst. for Biblical Res., Wheaton, Ill., 1985-; awards: Owen D. Young fellowships in religion, Gen. Electric Found., 1959-61; travel and workshop fellowship, NYU, Israel, 1966; Archaeological fellowship, Hebrew Union Coll., Jerusalem, Israel, 1967-68; mem: exec. com. on bible transl., New

Internat. Version of the Bible, 1981-; mem, Coll. Ave. Baptist Church, San Diego, 1982-; moderator, SW Baptist Conf., W. Covina, 1992-93; bd. dir., Internat. Bible Soc., 1992-; author: four books: The Heart of the Old Testament (1971), Exodus (1983), Genesis: An Introductory Commentary (1991), 1 and 2 Samuel (1992); Republican; Baptist Gen. Conf. Ofc: Bethel Seminary West 6116 Arosa St. San Diego 92115

YOUNGER, CLARA THERESA, physician; b. Sept. 28, 1917, Minneapolis; d. Constant James and Sophia Clara (Dolney) Younger; m. Gardner B. Archer June 7, 1949 (div. 1952); 1 dau. Diane b. 1950; edn: BA, UCLA, 1940, tchr. cred.- Gen. Secondary, 1941, MA Zool., 1945; MD, UC San Francisco, 1949; charter mem. 1952, diplomate Am. Acad. of Family Practice (1978, recert. 1993); diplomate Am. Soc. of Bariatric Physicians 1974, bd. cert. (applicant) Am. Med. Bd. of Hypnosis 1993-94. Career: pvt. med. practice, Family Practice in South Gate & Lynwood, 1951-74; pediatric practice Mullikin Med. Center, Artesia 1974-83; ret. (temp. disabled) 1983; mem: AMA, Calif. Med. Assn., L.A. County Med. Assn., Am. Med. Women's Assn. (br. #38 pres. 1973-75), Am. Soc. Bariatric Physicians, L.A. Pediatric Soc. (life), Am. Soc. Clin. Hypnosis, Soc. of Clin. and Exptl. Hypnosis, Internat. Soc. Clin. Hypnosis, So. Calif. Soc. Clin. Hypnosis (bd. 1970-, pres. 1973, program v.p. 1990-91, annual workshop ch. 1975, 77), Orange County Soc. Clin. Hypnosis (pres. 1990-92), Am. Cancer Soc. (lectr.; 15 Yr. pin for service), Am. Heart Assn., L.A. Gen. Practice Assn. (sec. 1971-73); vol YMCA South Gate 1970-73; publs: Internat. J. Clin. Hypnosis, 1973; Democrat; Prot.; rec: swim, nature study, collector limited ed. plates. Address: Cypress.

YOUNGS, JACK MARVIN, cost engineer; b. May 2, 1941, Bklyn.; s. Jack Wm. and Virginia May (Clark) Y.; m. Alexandra Marie Robertson, Oct. 31, 1964; dau., Christine Marie; edn: BE engring., CCNY, 1964; MBA, San Diego State Univ., 1973. Career: mass properties engr. Gen. Dynamics Corp., San Diego 1964-68, res. engr. 1968-69, senior res. engr. 1969-80, senior cost devel. engr. 1980-81, cost devel. engring. specialist 1981-; res.in life cycle costing and econ. analysis; awards: 5th pl. World Body Surfing Championships 1987, 6th pl. award 1988, Beta Gamma Sigma, Chi Epsilon, Sigma Iota Epsilon; mem: N.Y. Acad. of Scis., AIAA, Soc. of Cost Estimating and Analysis (pres. San Diego Chpt. 1990-91), Inst. Cost Analysis (cert., charter mem., chapt. treas. 1986-90), Internat. Soc. Parametric Analysts (chapt. bd. 1987-90), Nat. Mgmt. Assn. (space systems div. charter mem. 1985, chapt. award of honor 1975), Assn. MBA Execs., SDSU Business Alumni Assn. (charter 1986); civic bds: Scripps Ranch Civic Assn. (dist. dir. 1976-79), Scripps Ranch Swim Team (pres. 1980-82, dir. 1986-87), Greater San Diego Sci. and Engring. Fair (judge 1981-92), mem. Princeton Univ. Parents Club; club: Scripps Ranch Swim and Racquet (dir. 1977-80, treas. 78-79, pres. 79-80); Lutheran. Res: 11461 Tribuna Ave San Diego 92131 Ofc: PO Box 85990 San Diego 92138

YURIST, SVETLAN JOSEPH, mechanical engineer; b. Nov. 20, 1931, Kharkov, Ukraine, naturalized U.S. cit. 1985; s. Joseph Abram and Rosalia Samoilovna (Zoilman) Y.; m. Imma Lea Erlikh, Oct. 11, 1960; children: Eugene b. 1964; edn: MS mech. engring. (hons.) Polytechnic Inst., Odessa, Ukraine 1954. Career: engr. designer Welding Equipt. Plant, Novaya Utka, Russia 1954-56; sr. engr. Heavy Duty Automotive Crane Plant, Odessa, Ukraine 1956-60, asst. chief metallurgist 1971-78; supr. res. lab. Inst. Special Methods, Odessa 1960-66; project engr. in foundry industry, 1966-71; designer Teledyne Cast Product, Pomona, Calif. 1979-81; sr. mech. engr. Walt Elliot Disney Prodn., Glendale 1981-83; foundry liaison engr. Pacific Pumps, Dresser Industries, Huntington Park 1984-86; casting engr. Superior Industries Intl., Van Nuys 1986-89; mech. engr. Tamco Steel, Rancho Cucamonga 1989-; recipient design awards USSR Ministry of Machine, Moscow 1966, nat. econ. achiev. All Union Exhibition, 1966-70, Moscow: automatic lines for building & handtools, casting electric motorparts, permanent mold casting (pat. 1966-70); mem. Am. Foundrymen Soc. 1984-. Res: 184 W Armstrong Dr Claremont 91711 Ofc: Tamco 12459 Arrow Hwy Rancho Cucamonga 91739

ZACHMAN, JOHN A., information management consultant; b. Dec. 16, 1934, Toledo, Ohio; s. Arthur S. and Margaret E. (Morrow) Z.; m. Constance L. DeVito, May 14, 1972; children: Sherri b. 1960, John P. b. 1973; edn: BA in chem., Northwestern Univ., 1957; Tufts Univ. 1960-62. Career: comdr. USNR-Ret., 1957-71, instr. Tufts Univ., USN, 1960-62, exec. ofcr., Long Beach, Calif. 1962-64; with IBM, 1965-91: sales, Chgo. 1965-70, internat. account mgr. in N.Y. and L.A., 1970-74, cons., Los Angeles 1974-91; pres. Zachman Internat., La Canada, 1991-; bd. counsellors USC Sch. of Libr. & Info. Mgmt., 1980-87, bd. advisors Rosary Coll. Sch. of Libr. & Info. Mgmt., River Forest, Ill. 1991-, Emporia State Univ. Sch. Libr. & Info. Mgmt., Kans. 1991-, bd. advisors for info. resource mgmt. Smithsonian Instn., W.D.C. 1992-, bd. dirs. Repository/AD Cycle Users Gp., Chgo. 1991-, bd. advisors DAMA Internat. 1980-; awards: data resource mgmt. DAMA, N.Y. 1988, ann. excellence award R/AD Cycle Users Gp., Chgo. 1991; mem: Elder Coun. Ch. on the Way, Van Nuys 1978-, Living Way Ministries 1978-, bd. dirs. Marriage Plus Ministries 1980-, Worship Seminars Internat. 1990-; pub. articles "BSP and BICS: A Comparison" (1982), "Framework for Information Systems Architecture"

(1987), "Extending and Formalizing the Framework for Information Systems Architecture" (1992); Republican; Prot. Ofc: Zachman International 2222 Foothill Blvd Ste 337 La Canada 91011

ZACK, TERESA ISON, civil engineer; b. Aug. 30, 1950, Ft. Campbell, Ky.; d. Venon Harrison and Frances Lorene (Jarvis) Ison; m. Richard Zack, July 7, 1973; edn: BS edn., Univ. Ga. Athens 1972; BSCE, CSU Fresno 1982; reg. civil engr. 1987. Career: asst. engr. Conlan Engring., Tulare 1983-85; asst. civil engr. City of Hanford 1985-87, asst. city engr. 1987, acting city engr. 1987-88, city engr. 1988-; awards: City of Hanford Employee of Year (1986); mem: ASCE, Inst. of Transportation Engrs., Am. Pub. Works Assn., Kiwanis, Beta Sigma Phi; Republican; Methodist; rec: cross stitch. Ofc: City of Hanford 900 S 10th Ave Hanford 93230

ZACKRISON, EDWIN HARRY, university professor; b. Oct. 15, 1941, Hinsdale, Ill.; s. Harry Albin and Esther Virginia (Thorp) Z.; m. Jolene Ann Martinson, June 11, 1963; children: Jill b. 1968, Mark b. 1971; edn: BA, La Sierra Univ., Riverside, Calif., 1959-63; MA, Andrews Univ., Berrien Springs, Mo., 1963-64; BD, Andrews Univ., 1964-66; PhD, Andrews Univ., 1975-84. Career: pastor, Seventh-day Adventist Ch., Alhambra, Calif., 1966-67, Camarillo, Calif., 1967-72; religion prof., Southern Coll., Collegedale, Tenn., 1972-84; chmn., religion dept. La Sierra Acad., Riverside, Calif., 1984-88; religion prof., La Sierra Univ., 1988-; dir., LSA Performing Arts Soc., Riverside, 1984-; pres., La Sierra Comm. Performing Arts Soc., Riverside, 1989-; pres., LSU Alumni Assn., Riverside, 1989-92; dir., Destination Players, Riverside, 1989-92; awards: LSA Faculty Creativity Award, La Sierra Acad. Alumni Assn., 1989; LSA Performing Arts Soc. Comm. Support Award, LSA, 1988; mem: Assn. of Adventist Forums, 1974-; Religious Edn. Assn., 1977-; Amer. Acad. of Religion, 1978-; Evangelical Theol. Soc., 1978-; Ednl. Theatre Assn. 1988-; book ed., La Sierra Univ. Press, 1988-; author: numerous articles and periodicals, 1975-91; book, In The Loins of Adam, 1993; Republican; Seventh-day Adventist; rec: producing/directing high sch. plays. Res: 5651 Peacock Ln. Riverside 92505. Ofc: La Sierra Univ. 4700 Pierce St. Riverside 92515

ZAJAC, JOHN, research scientist; b. July 21, 1946 NY, NY; s. John A. and Cathy (Canepa) Z.; m. Vera Barbagallo, Jan. 13, 1973; children: Jennifer b. 1984, Michelle b. 1985; edn: A.A.S., Univ. of NY, Farmingdale, NY, 1966; E.E., Univ. of Ky., Lexington, Ky., 1968. Career: engr., B.C.D. Computing, Deer Park, NY, 1967-68; v.p. engring., Con Labs., N. Babylon, NY, 1968-69; v.p. engring., Beacon Systems, Deer Park, NY, 1969-73; v.p., gen. mgr., Electrotec, Santa Clara, Calif., 1973-77; v.p. res., Eaton Corp., Sunnyvale, 1977-82; v.p., res., General Signal, Los Gatos, 1982-83; adv. prod. devel. mgr., TEGAL/Motorola, Novato, 1983-86; v.p., res., Results Corp., San Jose, 1986-; awards: 20 patents, US Patent Office, Wash., DC, 1978-92; author: The Delicate Balance, 1989; numerous journals in Plasma Physics, 1978-83; TV and radio speaker, The Future of America, 1989-; rec: white water rafting, trains, computers, raising koi. Ofc: P.O. Box 21237 San Jose 95151

ZALTA, EDWARD, otorhinolaryngologist, utilization review physician; b. Mar.2, 1930, Houston, Tx.; s. Nouri Louis and Marie Zahde (Lizmi) Z.; m. Carolyn M. Gordon, Oct. 8, 1971; children: Nouri Allan, Lori Ann, Barry Thomas, Ryan David; edn: BS, Tulane Univ., 1952, MD, 1956; Diplomate Am. Bd. of Quality Assurance & Utilization Review Physicians 1986. Career: served to capt. Med. Corps US Army 1957-60, intern Brooke Army Hosp., San Antonio 1956-57, resident in otolaryngology U.S. Army Hosp., Ft. Campbell, 1957-60; practiced medicine spec. in otolaryngology in Glendora, W.Covina and San Dimas, Calif. 1960-82; ENT cons. City of Hope Med. Ctr., 1961-76; current: med. staff Foothill Presbyterian Hosp.; co-founder/CEO/chmn. bd. CAPP CARE INC., Newport Beach; founder/bd. chmn. Medical Data Management; honors: Kappa Nu, Phi Delta Epsilon, award of merit Order St. Lazarus 1981; mem: AMA, Calif. Med. Assn., L.A. Co. Med. Assn. (past pres.), Am. Coll. Medical Quality, Am. Acad. Otolaryngology, Am. Council Otolaryngology, Am. Assn. Preferred Provider Orgns. (past pres.), Los Angeles Found. Community Service (past pres.), L.A. Poison Info. Ctr., So. Calif. Physicians Council, Inc. (founder Inter-Hosp. Council Continuing Med. Edn.); Republican; Jewish; clubs: Center, Pacific Golf, Glendora Country, Centurion, Sea Bluff Beach and Racquet. Res: 3 Morning Dove Laguna Niguel 92677 Ofc: CAPP CARE, West Tower, 4000 MacArthur Blvd, 10,000, Newport Beach 92660-2526

ZAX, ADAM, glazing company president, real estate developer; b. June 2, 1962, Houston, Tx.; s. Robert Barney and Elaine Francis (Cohn) Z.; edn: BS bus., Univ. Colo. 1984; Glass Mgmt. Inst., George Mason Univ., 1990. Career: pres. Capistrano Valley Glass, San Juan Capistrano 1979-; pres. Gemini Shower Door 1987-; pres. C.V. Industries, 1991-; mem. Delta Chi (founder Univ. Colo. chapt.); author computer software for glass industry; Republican; Jewish; rec: drumming, horses, dogs, magic, Shaolin Kempo martial arts. Ofc: Capistrano Valley Glass 33012 Calle Perfecto San Juan Capistrano 92675

ZEIDMAN, HEYWOOD WILLIAM, psychiatrist, educator; b. Jan. 30, 1941, Brooklyn, N.Y.; s. Irving and Henrietta (Hertz) Z.; m. Ronni Kay Reider, Nov. 27, 1982; children: Jared b. 1985; edn: BA, Bard Coll., 1963; MS, N.Y. Med.

Coll., 1969, MD, 1973; Diplomate Am. Bd. Psychiatry & Neurology, 1978, Diplomate Am. Bd. of Adolescent Psychiatry, 1992. Career: ptnr. Psychiatric Centers, San Diego 1976-; med. dir. Broad Horizons, Ramona, Calif. 1986-89; Villa View Hosp., San Diego 1983-90; Adolescent Drug Diagnosis Pgm., San Diego 1988-90, Adol. Day Pgm. 1991-92; New Life Treatment Ctr., 1990-92; asst. clin. prof. UC San Diego, 1988-; dir. Hosp. Adolescent Svcs. Southwood Hosp., Chula Vista 1992-; cons. Adult Protective Svs., San Diego 1986-; honoree, tchr. of yr. UCSD 1987; mem: AMA 1976-, Calif. Med. Assn. 1976-, San Diego Co. Med. Soc. (del. 1991-), Am. Psychiat. Assn. 1976-, Calif. Psychiat. Assn., San Diego Soc. Psych. Physicians, Am. Soc. Adol. Psychiatry (Fellow), San Diego Soc. Adol. Psychiatry (exec. com. 1976-), ASAM, CSAM 1988-; publs: articles, Am. J. Physiology (1970), We. J. of Medicine (1975), Fedn. Proceedings (1968); mil: sp4 US Army Nat. Guard 1963-69; Democrat; Jewish; rec: skiing. Res: 62618 Via Regla San Diego 92122 Ofc: Psychiatric Centers 6475 Alvarado Rd Ste 233 San Diego 92120

ZEIGER, STEPHEN ALLEN, executive recruiter; b. Mar. 29, 1951, Joliet, Ill.; s. Jack and Doris (Barkin) Z.; m. Robin Sellin, Oct. 21, 1979; children: Alexis b. 1982, Joshua E. b. 1988; edn: BS in edn. psych., Loyola Univ., Chgo. 1972; MS in edn. vocat. counseling, No. Ill. Univ., 1973; Ill. tchg. cert., 1972; Calif. lic. employment agy., 1980. Career: vocational counselor Greater Jewish Fedn., Los Angeles 1973-75; employment recruiter Mainstream Eng., Encino 1975-76; exec. tech. recruiter Purcell Employment Service, L.A. 1976-79; mgr. exec. recruiting Creative Employment Service, Tarzana 1979-80; pres. and CEO Zeiger Technical Careers (exec. recruitment), Woodland Hills 1980-; mem. Nat. Assn. of Personnel Consultants, 1979-; Jewish; rec: computers, racquetball, reading. Res: 6021 Lindley Ave Tarzana 91356 Ofc: 20969 Ventura Blvd Ste 217 Woodland Hills 91364

ZEITLIN, HERBERT ZAKARY, management consultant, real estate executive, retired college president; b. N.Y.C.; s. Leonard and Martha Josephine (Soff) Z.; m. Eugenia F. Pawlik, July 3, 1949; children: Mark Clyde, Joyce Therese Harris, Ann Victoria, Clare Katherine; edn: BS, New York Univ., 1947, MA, 1949; EdD, Stanford Univ., 1956. Career: tchr., counselor, dir. testing Phoenix Union High Sch. and Coll. Dist., 1949-57; dean evening coll., prin. high sch. Antelope Valley Union H.S. and Coll. Dist., Lancaster 1957-62; dean instrn. Southwestern Coll., Chula Vista 1962-64; founder, pres., chancellor Triton Coll., River Grove, Ill. 1964-76; pres. and dean West Los Angeles Coll., 1976-80; mgmt. cons., pres. Trident Consultants, Los Angeles 1976-; adj. faculty Ariz. State Univ., Flagstaff 1953-55, No. Ill. Univ., DeKalb, 1971-74, UC Santa Barbara, 1979; elected mayor Upper Woodland Hills, Calif.; past pres. Rotary, Maywood, Ill., 1974; awards: recipient spl. commendations Chicago Tribune, Illinois Gov. Richard Ogilvie, named adminstr. of year Ill. Adminstrs. Assn., Triton Coll. Faculty Assn. award, 1974, medal of achiev. Triton Coll. Trustees, 1973; mem: NEA (life), Am. Assn. Community and Jr. Colls., Assn. Calif. Community Coll. Adminstrs., Am. Vocat. Assn.; author, editor in field. Ofc: 21731 Ventura Blvd Woodland Hills 91364

ZELLMER, ARLENE, teacher/learning handicapped specialist; b. Aug. 21, 1920, Audubon, Iowa; d. Clyde Lewis and Susan (Law) Hogueisson; m. Neale A. Zellmer, June 21, 1953; children: Alan b. 1957, Scott b. 1960; edn: BA psychology, San Diego State Univ., 1948; Calif. Std. elem. tchg. credential, 1951, Life cred. 1954, Learning Handicapped cred. 1978. Career: elementary sch. tchr., La Jolla 1949-51, Valencia Park Sch., San Diego 1951-53, San Carlos Sch. Dist. 1953-57; home tchr. special edn. San Carlos Sch. Dist. 1967-86, also Belmont Sch. Dist. 1968-86; prin., pvt. tutoring service for learning handicapped children, Belmont, 1980-; mem: Calif. Tchrs. Assn. 1949-51, AAUW 1986-, Daughters of Norway 1992-, Indep. Order of Foresters 1966-, Presbyn. Womens Assn. (hon. life mem., San Mateo 1985), AARP 1986-, Commonwealth Club San Francisco 1993-, Daughters of Norway 1992-93; civic: Peninsula Sym. Aux., Belmont 1962-70, 4H Club Belmont (vol. 1965-75), Cub Scouts (vol. 1966-70); contbr. poetry, World of Poetry Anthology (1991); Republican; Presbyterian Ch. San Mateo (1960-, deacon 1968-71, 81-84); rec: reading, theatre, symphony, travel. Res: 1588 Harbor Blvd Belmont 94002

ZIEGENBUSCH, TED WAYNE, radio-television personality; b. Mar. 10, 1951, Lima, Ohio; s. Charles Paul and Esther C. (Newman) Z.; m. Ann Pearl Cordell, Aug. 21, 1971 (div. Sept. 1977); m. April Ann Lorenz, Dec. 10, 1977; children: Seth b. 1972, Jeffrey b. 1974, Ryan b. 1980; edn: AA, San Bernardino Valley Coll., 1971. Career: announcer KMEN Radio, San Bdo. 1967-73; KCAL-FM Radio, 1973-80; program director KLAV Radio, Las Vegas, Nev. 1980-81; The Mighty 690, San Diego 1981; announcer KGB Radio, San Diego 1981-82; KOST Radio, Los Angeles 1982-; cons. KIFM Radio, San Diego 1982-83, KOLA Radio, San Bdo. 1980-87; awards: Best actor Nat. Thespians Soc. 1969, Outstanding graduate San Bernardino City Schs. 1984; mem.: Screen Actors Guild 1983-, Am. Fedn. of TV-Radio Artists 1981-; Republican; Prot.; rec: screenwriting, travel, music. Ofc: KOST Radio 610 S Ardmore Los Angeles 90005

ZIEL, DONNA RAE, university administrator; b. Sept. 12, 1943, Santa Barbara; d. Raymond Joseph and Emma Josephine (Osner) Gilbreth; m. T. Brian Ziel, Sept. 8, 1962 (div. Jan. 1976); children: Laura b. 1965, Brian b. 1967; edn:

BA (w/distinction), San Jose State Univ., 1973, MA Asian hist., 1979. Career: dept. secty. San Jose State Univ., 1973-76, liberal studies advisor 1976-, dir. Student Advisement Ctr. SJSU, 1979-89; assoc. dir. San Jose State Univ. Monterey County Campus, 1989-92; assoc. dir. Student Outreach 1992-; honors: invited participant Humanities Honors SJSU 1961-, Sourisseau Soc. grantee SJSU 1975, CSU Administrv. Fellows Pgm. fellow 1980-81, Phi Kappa Phi Nat. Hon. Soc. (1992, disting. service award SJSU chapt. 1992); mem: Calif. Women in Higher Edn. (pres. 1980-81), CSU Women's Council (standing com. on student affairs 1988), Center for Innovative Programs (expert com. 1988), Calif. Advocates for Re-entry Edn. 1980-, Calif. Council of Academic Advisors 1978-, Nat. Assn. Student Personnel Adminstrn. 1978-, Nat. academic Advisors Assn. 1984-; civic bds: Industry Edn. Council of Monterey County (pres. 1990-91), Sierra Club 1978-, Santa Cruz County Women's Commn. (co-chair 1986-87), Valley Women's Club Boulder Creek, Santa Cruz Women's Network (scholarship com.), Monterey Bay Aquarium (docent 1984-); Democrat. Res: 8121 Fremont Ave Ben Lomond 95005 Ofc: San Jose State Univ. Monterey County Campus PO Box 1758 Salinas 93902

ZIEMER, ROBERT RUHL, research hydrologist; b. Oct. 25, 1937, Oklahoma City, Okla.; s. Herman Vernon and Floranna (Ruhl) Z.; m. Ruth Puckett, June 24, 1965 (div. 1975); m. Marian Denise Westwick, Jan. 1, 1977; children: Tanya b. 1969, Amy b. 1973, Karen b. 1979, Ryan b. 1982; edn: AA, Fullerton Jr. Coll. 1957; BS, UC Berkeley 1959; MS, 1963; PhD, Colo. St. Univ. 1978; lic. profl. forester Calif. 1973. Career: research and tchg. asst. UC Berkeley 1959-60; res. forester U.S. Dept. Agriculture Forest Service 1960-77; photo-radar intelligence ofcr. Nev. Air Nat. Guard, Reno 1961-67; res. hydrologist U.S. Dept. Agriculture Forest Service, Arcata 1977-; adj. prof. Humboldt St. Univ. 1977-; mem: Am. Geophysical Union (nat. chmn. erosion and sedimentation 1982-88, nat. chmn. evaporation), Internat. Union of Forestry Research Organizations (internat. chmn. 1987-); 65+ research papers pub. in sci. jours.; mil: 1st lt. Nev. Air Nat. Guard 1961-67; rec: carnivorous plant cultivation. Res: 2220 Elizabeth Rd McKinleyville 95521 Ofc: Pacific Southwest Research Station 1700 Bayview Dr Arcata 95521

ZIFFREN, LESTER, lawyer; b. Apr. 13, 1925, Davenport, IA; s. Jacob and Belle (Rothenberg) Z.; m. Paulette C. Rolando; 1 dau. Mimi b. 1959; edn: BA, UCLA 1949; JD, UCLA Law Sch 1952. Career: dep. atty. gen. Calif. Dept. Justice, Atty. Gen. Office 1953-59; partner Greenberg, Ziffren & Shafton 1959-61; partner Ziffren & Ziffren 1961-79; retired partner/advy. council Gibson, Dunn & Crutcher 1979-; bd. dir. Westminster Capital Inc. (NYSE) 1979-; mem: State Bar Calif., Los Angeles Co. Bar Assn., Beverly Hills Bar Assn.; trustee UCLA Found., bd. vis. UCLA Sch. of Med., UCLA bd. advisors Center on Aging, Chadbourne Fellow Sch. of Law, legal com. Sch. of Law; mem. Brandeis Univ. Pres.'s Council; Hebrew Union Coll.-JIR (nat. v.chmn., bd. govs. L.A. Campus, v. ch. bd. overseers, chair nomination com., exec. com.); L.A. Music Center Opera (bd.), State of Israel Bonds-L.A. (v.chmn. bd., exec. com., past pres. Prime Minister's Club), Cedars Sinai Med. Ctr. (bd. govs.); rec: tennis. Ofc: Gibson, Dunn & Crutcher, 2029 Century Park East 41st Flr Los Angeles 90067

ZIL, JOHN STEPHEN, psychiatrist-physiologist; b. Oct. 8, 1947, Chgo.; s. Stephen Vincent and Marillyn Charlotte (Jackson) Zilius; dau. Charlene-Elena b. 1984; edn: BS (magna cum laude) Univ. Redlands, 1969; MD, UC San Diego, 1973; MPH in pub. health law (honors), Yale Univ., 1977; JD (w. distinction), Jefferson Coll., 1985. Career: intern, resident in psychiatry and neurology Univ. Ariz. 1973-75; fellow in psychiatry, advanced fellow in social and community psychiatry, Yale Univ. 1975-77; instr., psychiatry and physiology, Yale Univ., Univ. of Mass. 1976-77; Yale Community cons. to Connecticut State Dept. of Corrections 1975-77; chief Inpatient and Day Hosp. Unit, Conn. Mental Health Ctr., Yale-New Haven Hosp. Inc. 1976-77, actg. chief 1975-76; asst. prof. psychiatry UC San Francisco 1977-82, assoc. prof. psychiatry and medicine 1982-86, v. chmn. dept. psychiatry 1983-86; adj. prof. Calif. St. Univ. 1985-87; chief psychiatry and neurology VA Med. Ctr., Fresno 1977-86, prin. investigator Sleep Res. & Physiology Lab 1979-86; chief psychiatrist Calif. Dept. of Corrections, State Capitol 1986-, and clinical faculty UC Davis Sch. of Med. and affil. hosps. 1986-; councillor federally mandated council for Calif. St. Mental Health Plan 1988-; invited faculty contbg. editor Am. Coll. of Psychiat. resident-in-tng. exam. 1981-; assoc. ed. Corrective & Social Psychiatry Jour. 1978-; referee, reviewer Corrections Today, J. of Am. Correctional Assn. 1980-; nat. cons. on Mental Health Svs. in Jails & Prisons, Am. Psychiatric Assn., W.D.C. 1993-; awards: Nat. Merit Scholar 1965, Bank Am. nat. award in Lab. Scis. 1965, Julian Lee Roberts chemistry award, Univ. Redlands 1969, Delta Alpha 1969, Alpha Epsilon Delta nat. medical freshman of yr. 1969, Kendall res. paper award Internat. Symp. in Biochem. Res. 1970, UCSD Pres.'s Scholar in Medicine 1970-71, thesis res. honors Yale 1977, Univ. Calif. Pres.'s Commend. 1978, Univ. Calif. Alumni Assn. profl. achiev. award 1992; mem: Am. Assn. of Mental Health Profls. in Corrections (nat. pres. 1978-82, 1990-94), Fellow Royal Soc. of Health, London 1979, Fellow Am. Assn. for Soc. Psychiat. 1977, Am. Pub. Health Assn., Calif. Scholarship Fedn. (past pres.), life mem., charter pres. UC Sch. of Medicine), Ephebians, AAUP, Am. Psychiat. Assn., Nat. Council on Crime & Delinquency; author: The Case of the Sleep-

Walking Rapist (Forensic Monographs, 1992), first author, Mentally Disordered Criminal Offenders, 5 vols. 1989; num. res. publ. and presentations 1970-. Res: PO Box 163359 Sacramento 95816-9359

ZILVAR, KEVIN JOSEPH, chemist; b. Nov. 6, 1954, Timmins, Ontario, Canada; s. Joseph and Rita Margarette (LeBrasseur) Z.; edn: AA, East Los Angeles Coll. 1974; CSU Long Beach 1974-77; Azusa Pacific Univ. 1993-. Career: res. and devel. tech. Hysol Div. Dexter Corp., Industry 1975-79; process engr. McDonnell Douglas Corp., Long Beach 1979-81; chemist W.W. Henry Co. Huntington Park 1981; PTM & W Industries Inc., Santa Fe Springs 1981-83; material application chemist Keene Tech. Corp., Rancho Cucamonga 1983-85; sr. chemist, cons. Sweco Inc., Commerce 1985-86; lab. supr. Composite Structures Div., Alcoa Composites, Monrovia 1986-; chemist, cons. Sweco Inc. 1983-86; Seam Masters, Southgate 1982-83; sr. application chemist, cons. G.S. Polymers, Riverside 1987-; publicity chmn SAMPE, Arcadia 1988; awards: McDonnell Douglas Composite cert. 1980, Sweco Inc. Hazardous Waste cert. 1985, Composite Structures Supr./Mgmt. 1988; mem: A.C.S., SAMPE, Am. Standard Test Method, Am. Soc. for Testing & Materials, Am. Karate Fedn.; U.S. Judo Assn.; Independent; Catholic; rec: karate, judo. Res: 9429 Friant St. Rancho Cucamonga 91730-4025 Ofc: Composite Structures Div., Alcoa Composites 801 Royal Oaks Dr Monrovia 91016-3630

ZIMMERMAN, LINDA, cookbook author, writer, editor; b. Sept. 30, 1946, Chgo.; d. Louis Joseph and Jean (Lakovitz) Zimmerman; edn: photography, Santa Monica Coll., 1981-83. Career: TV and film prodn., L.A., 1970-84; writer, author, editor 1985-: clients incl. Warner Bros. Pictures, Cannon Films, L.A. Celebrations, Epicurean Cooking Sch., Ma Cuisine Cooking Sch. contbr. articles in numerous magazines and newspapers; books: Grills & Greens (1993), Cobblers, Buckles & Other Old-Fashioned, Fruit Desserts (1991), Puddings, Custards & Flans (1990); editor/pub. source directory, The Food Yellow Pages (1988, 91); editor "The Food Paper," editorial writer, recipe devel. & editing (books): Make-Over Miracles by Michael Maron (1993), Gault Millau-The Best of Los Angeles (1992), Entertaining with Robin Leach by Diane Rozas (1992), Calif. Bistro by Tony DiLembo (1991), Chicken Breasts II by Diane Rozas (1990), Fresh from the Freezer by Michael Roberts (1990), Beauty & Cancer by Peggy Mellody (1988), Catalon Cuisine by Colman Andrews (1988); mem. AFTRA, Ciao Italia (ednl. bd. 1992), Los Angeles Culinary Alliance (founding bd. 1988-89), So. Calif. Culinary Guild (bd. 1989-90). Res/Ofc: 9171 Hazen Drive Beverly Hills 90210

ZIMPFER, VINCENT, retired executive; b. Oct. 17, 1915, Anna, Ohio; s. Albert and Ethel (Hensel) Z.; m. Kathryn R. Royer, July 26, 1941; children: Patrick R. b. 1946; edn: BA, Ohio No. Univ. 1941; Univ. Mich. 1941, 42, 55; Univ. Ill. 1956. Career: professional baseball, basketball player 1935-39; owner, mgr., engr. Zimpfer Tool Col., Sidney, Ohio 1946-48; staff indsl. engr. Purdue Univ., W. Lafayette, Ind. 1948-52; engring. asst., pres. Standard Screw Co., Chgo., Ill. 1952-57; Harvey Aluminum, Torrance 1957-60; project engr., adminstr. Aerojet, Fullerton 1960-62; project and mfg. engring. specialist Allied Signal, Los Angeles 1962-78; staff instr. Purdue Univ., W. Lafayette, Ind. 1948-52; adminstrv. Chgo. Standard Screw, Chgo., Ill. 1952-57; Harvey & Aerojet, Torrance and Fullerton 1957-62; Allied Signal, Torrance 1962-78; mem: ASM, ASME, CSM, ASTME, Camera Club; mil: engr. splst. (P-39, P-63, P-51) US Air Force 1942-45, classified res. publs. (1954-72); Republican; Lutheran; rec: photog., electronics, athletics. Res: 2960 Deer Trail Circle Solvang 93463

ZIONY, JOSEPH ISRAEL, consulting geologist; b. Apr. 6, 1935, Los Angeles; s. Aaron and Annie (Mondlin) Z.; m. Denise Pourroy, Sept. 9, 1961; children: David b. 1962, Daniel b. 1967, Sarah b. 1972; edn: undergrad. Univ. Wis. 1951-53; AB, UC Los Angeles 1956, MA, 1959, PhD, 1966; reg. geologist, cert. engring. geologist, Calif. (1970). Career: geologist U.S. Geological Survey 1957-86: Mil. Geology Br., Wash. DC, 1957-59; Fuels Br., Menlo Park, Calif. 1959-60; S.W. States Br., 1960-69; Engring. Geology Br., 1969-73; dep. chief Office of Earthquake Studies USGS, Reston, Va. 1973-76; Earthquake Hazards Br., Menlo Park 1976-77; asst. chief geologist for Western Region, 1977-81; Engring. Seismology and Geology Br., 1981-86, ret. USGS; gubnat. apptd. asst. director for Mining and Geology, Calif. Dept. of Conservation, Sacto. 1988-91; U.S. rep. Central Treaty Orgn. (CENTO) conf. on earthquake hazard mitigation, Tehran, Iran (11/76); awards: Burwell Awd. from Geological Soc. of Am. for USGS Profl. Paper 1360, "Evaluating Earthquake Hazards in the Los Angeles Region"; mem: Geol. Soc. of Am., Assn. of Engring. Geologists, Seismol. Soc. of Am.; publs: 57 reports and maps on earthquake hazards of Western US and on geology and mineral resources of Calif., Nev., and Utah; mil: pfc AUS 1960, USAR 1960-68; Jewish (pres. Cong. Beth Am, Los Altos Hills 1972-73); rec: hiking, fishing, hunting. Res: Palo Alto 94306 Ofc: San Francisco.

ZIRSCHKY, STEPHEN LEE, corporate counsel, law professor; b. Dec. 11, 1949, Stockton; s. Carl W. and Josephine C. (Whitehead) Z.; m. Susan K. Simons, Aug. 21, 1976; children: Stephen Lee, II b. 1989; edn: Loma Linda Univ., 1968-70; BA, Chapman Coll., 1972; JD, Western St. Law Sch., 1976; LLM, McGeorge Sch. of Law, 1990; internat., corp. law studies UCLA 1979-

81, USC 1986, Harvard Law Sch. 1983, Univ. of Salzburg Faculty of Law 1989; lang. studies: Japanese, Arabic, Spanish; admitted bar: Ind. 1983, Fed. Dist. Cts. Ind. (No., So. 1983), Fed. Dist. Ct. Calif. (No. 1984), US Fed. Ct. Appeals 1986, US Claims Ct. 1986, US Supreme Ct. 1991, US Internat. Ct. of Trade 1991. Career: contracts adminstr. Hughes Aircraft Co., Fullerton 1977-79; sr. contracts adminstr./mktg. pgm. mgr. Aerojet Ordinance Co., Downey 1979-81; corporate counsel, mgr. of contracts Cartwright Electronics, Fullerton 1981-; corporate counsel (Internat. Legal Exchange Program) Pharmacia Euro Centre, Brussels, Belgium; atty. cons. law practice, Ind. and Yorba Linda, Calif. 1983-; adj. prof. of law and contracts Naval Postgrad. Sch., Monterey 1991-; awards: Eagle Scout 1966, Order of Arrow 1968, Eastern Star scholar 1968, Chapman Coll. speaker of yr. and debater of yr. awards 1972 Varsity Debate Team, Nat. Forensics League; mem: Am. Bar Assn., Fed. Bar Assn., Internat. Ba Assn., Nat. Contract Mgmt. Assn.; polit. cand. for Orange Co. Supr. 1972, campaign mgr. for City Council candidates 1970-76, area rep. for a cand. for US Congress 1972, fin. chmn./campaign mgr. for Calif. St. Assembly cands. 1974-76; civic bds: Orange Co. Human Rels. Commn. 1972, O.C. Manpower Plng. Commn. 1972-76, Calif. Water Resources Commn. 1976, Calif. Consumer Fedn., Yorba Linda Parks & Rec. Commn. (1968-72, Y.L. Environ. Com. 1970-76, O.C. Housing Coalition 1976, Council on Employment, Environ., Econs. and Devel. of O.C. 1976, O.C. Welfare Coalition (co-dir. 1976), Calif. Council of Youth 1966; Republican; Baptist; rec: helicopter flt., hunting, fishing. Res: 18062 Avolinda Yorba Linda 92686

ZOLBER, KATHLEEN KEEN, nutrition educator, management consultant; b. Dec. 9, 1916, Walla Walla, Wash.; d. Wildie H. and Alice (Johnson) Keen; m. Melvin L. Zolber, Sept. 19, 1937; edn: BS foods and nutrition, Walla Walla Coll., 1941; MA, Wash. State Univ., 1961; PhD, Univ. Wis., 1968; Registered Dietitian. Career: dir. food service Walla Walla Coll., 1941-50, mgr. coll. store, 1951-59, asst. prof. food and nutrition, 1959-62, assoc. prof., 1962-64; assoc. prof. nutrition Loma Linda Univ., 1964-72, prof. nutrition, 1973-, dir. dietetic edn., 1967-84, dir. dietetics Med. Ctr., 1972-84, dir. nutrition program Sch. of Pub. Health 1984-; awards: Mead Johnson grantee 1965-67, Alumna of Yr. Walla Walla Coll. 1977, Delores Nyhus award Calif. Dietetic Assn. 1978, Am. Dietetic Assn. Copher Award 1992; mem: Am. Dietetic Assn. (pres. 1982-), Am. Public Health Assn., Am. Home Econs. Assn., Am. Mgmt. Assn., AAUP, Soc. Food Service Res., Soc. Personnel Adminstrn., Omicron Nu, Delta Omega. Res: PO Box 981 Loma Linda 92354 Ofc: Nutrition Dept LLU School of Public Health, Loma Linda 93354

ZSCHAU, ED, former congressman, company executive; b. Jan. 6, 1940, Omaha, Nebr.; s. Ernest and Alice (Fay) Z.; m. Jo Ann Wiedmann; children: Ed, Elizabeth, Cameron; edn: AB philosophy (cum laude), Princeton Univ., 1961; MBA, Stanford Univ., 1963, MS statistics 1964, PhD bus. adminstrn. 1967. Career: vis. asst. prof. Harvard Bus. Sch., Cambridge, Mass. 1967-68; asst. prof. GSB Stanford Univ., Palo Alto 1965-69, lectr. bus. policy 1969-81; founder, c.e.o. System Industries Inc., Milpitas 1968-82; U.S. congressman, WDC 1983-87; gen. ptnr. Brentwood Assocs., Menlo Park 1987-88; chmn. bd. and c.e.o. Censtor Corp., San Jose 1988-; founding chmn. The Technology Ctr. of Silicon Valley, San Jose; dir. Am. Council Capital Formation, WDC; dir. Bay Area Council, S.F.; mem. Calif. Council on Sci. & Technology, Sacto.; awards: Electronics Engring. Times list of Top 5 most influential legislators (1984, 85), rookie of yr./best freshman congressman Wash. Monthly 1984, congl. friend of sci. Nat. Coalition for Sci. & Tech. 1984, Wm. A Steiger award Nat. Venture Capital Assn. 1986, Hon. LLD Univ. of San Francisco 1989; Republican; Congregational; rec: jogging. Ofc: Censtor Corp. 530 Race St San Jose 95126

ZUCKER, ROBERT STEPHEN, professor of neurobiology; b. Apr. 18, 1945, Phila.; s. Irving Aaron and Dorothy Ruth (Pittenturf) Z.; m. Glenda Anita Teal, Sept. 1, 1968 (div. Apr. 1982); m. Susan Henrietta Schwartz, Jan. 3, 1983; children: David b. 1975, Mark b. 1985, Ariel b. 1986; edn: SB physics, M.I.T., 1966; PhD neurological sci., Stanford Univ., 1971. Career: vis. investigator University College London, London, Eng. 1971-73; Ctr. Nat. de la Recherche Sci., Gif-sur-Yvette, France 1973-74; asst., assoc., prof. physiol. UC Berkeley 1974-80, 80-85, 85-90, prof. neurobiology, 1990-; appt. bd. sci. counselors N.I.N.C.D.S., N.I.H., Bethesda, Md. 1982; mem: study sections NIH, Bethesda (1983-84, 1990-91); corp. Marine Biological Lab., Woods Hole, Mass. 1981-; editl. bds. J. of Neurobiology 1982-86, J. Neurosci. 1988-; awards: nat. winner Westinghouse Nat. Science Talent Search (1962, predoctoral fellowships NSF, NIH, Woodrow Wilson 1966-71; postdoc. fellowships Helen Hay Whitney Found., NATO, NIH, NSF 1971-74, res. fellow Alfred P. Sloan Found. 1976-80, Javits Award NIH 1987-94; AAAS 1968-, Sigma Xi 1966-, Soc. for Neurosci. 1977-, Biophysical Soc. 1982-, Union of Concerned Scientists 1981-, Amnesty Internat., People for the Am. Way, ACLU, Sierra Club, Common Cause; author 60+ book chpts. and res. articles in Science, Nature, J. of Physiol., J. of Gen. Physiol., Biophysical J., J. Neurophysiol., J. of Neurosci., J. of Neurobiol., Neuron, Proc. Nat. Acad. of Science USA, Annals N.Y. Acad. Sci., Brain Res., J. of Theoretical Biol., J. of Comparative Physiology, Annual Rev. of Neuroscience, Developmental Biol., others; Democrat; Jewish; rec: hiking, sailing, canoeing, skiing. Res: 1236 Oxford St Berkeley 94709 Ofc: University of California MCB Dept 111LSA, Berkeley 94720

ZUNICH, BARBARA JANE, writer, research specialist; b. Dec. 13, 1930, Springfield, Ill.; d. Samuel and Mable Scott Best; children: LeAnn b. 1953 (BA journ. Redlands Univ. and JD Loyola Univ., L.A.), Jana b. 1955 (BA sociol./psychol. Linfield Coll.), Lark b. 1959 (BA communication Azusa Univ. and MA divinity Princeton Univ.), Jay b. 1961 (BSBA CSU-San Diego); edn: AA, Long Beach City Coll., 1948; BA, CSU Long Beach, 1952; MA, CSU Los Angeles, 1970; Calif. Tchg. credentials in Admin. Adult Ed., Elem., Sec. Voc., Community Coll. Career: tchg. elem. ed. 1952-69; coord./owner Country Club Sch. (pvt. elem.) 1967; adminstr. Comm. Life Sch.- Adult Sch. 1969-73; asst. supt. La Puente Valley Reg. Occupation Ctr. 1973-75; freelance writer, owner, workshop facilitator The Writing Place, facilitator "Marketing Training" classes, 1975-; awards: San Gabriel Valley Homemaker of Yr., LBACC Bus. Person of Month; civic bds: CSULB Alumni Assn. and Sr. Care Action Network (SCAN) Found., LBCC Alumni, LBACC Womens Council, American Cancer Soc. Volunteer Bd., Tippers Business Club; publs: reading instrn. books; Morovian; rec: thimble collecting. Res: 110 Termino #304, Long Beach 90803

ZWAAF, DAVID, restaurant executive; b. Sept. 28, 1951, NYC; s. Emanuel and Paulette Rose (Groensteen) Z.; m. Rosa Maria Lopez, July 27, 1974; children: David Emanuel, Christopher Robin; edn: Washington Univ., St. Louis 1970-71; New York Univ. 1971-73. Career: supr. The Saloon, Beverly Hills 1973-74; comptroller Mr. Chow, Beverly Hills 1974; pres. Rangoon Racquet Club, Beverly Hills 1974-; mem: Beverly Hills Restaurant Assn. (v.p. 1986-), Calif. Restaurant Assn., Beverly Hills C. of C.; Republican; Jewish. Ofc: Rangoon Racquet Club 9474 Santa Monica Blvd Beverly Hills 90210

ZWICK, BARRY STANLEY, newspaper editor, speechwriter; b. July 21, 1942, Cleveland, OH; s. Alvin Albert and Selma Davidovna (Makofsky) Z.; m. Roberta Joan Yaffe, Mar. 11, 1972; children: Natasha Yvette, Alexander Anatol; edn: BA journalism Ohio State Univ. 1963; MS journalism Columbia Univ. 1965. Career: copy ed. Phila. Inquirer 1964; night news ed. Detroit Free Press 1965-67; west coast ed. L.A. Times/ Washington Post News Svc. 1967-77; makeup ed. L.A. Times 1978-; adj. instr. USC 1975-77; awards: NEH profl. journalism fellow Stanford Univ. 1977-78; author: Hollywood Tanning Secrets (1980); Jewish. Ofc: L.A. Times, Times Mirror Sq Los Angeles 90053

ZWILLINGER, MICHELE B., marketing consultant; b. Jan. 16, 1945, Los Angeles; m. Morton G. Rosen, Feb. 14, 1982; children by previous marriage: Zachary b. 1972, Zeff b. 1974; edn: BS sociology (honors), UC Berkeley, 1966; MS in criminology, 1967. Career: coding supr. Audience Studies Internat., summer 1965; statistician San Francisco Unified Sch. Dist., 1967-69; res. assoc. Erwin Wasey Inc. 1969-70; proj. supr. Haug Assocs., 1970-72; proj. dir. Grey Advtg., 1974-75; consumer res. mgr. Vivitar Corp., 1975-78; v.p./res. dir. Wells, Rich, Greene/West, 1978-81; res. dir. New Products Network, 1981-82; cons. consumer mktg., owner Zwillinger Research, 1982-; honors: Dean's List, Honor Students' Soc., NIMH intern fellow for indep. res. 1966-67; mem: Am. Mktg. Assn./So. Calif. (bd.), Qualitative Res. Consultants Assn. (co-founder L.A. chpt.), Product Devel. & Mgmt. Assn., Women in Business (bd., WIB Found.); civic bds: Young Leadership Forum, S.F.V. Jewish Fedn. Council, Jewish Bus. & Profl. Women (bd. 1990-92), PTA Stephen S. Wise Elem. and Middle Schs. 1977-87, PTSA Birmingham High Sch. Leadership Council 1989-92, Arthritis Found. (bd. govs.). Ofc: 4414 Petit Ave Encino 91436

ZYROFF, ELLEN SLOTOROFF, educator, librarian; b. Aug. 1, 1946, Atlantic City, N.J.; d. Joseph George and Sylvia Beverly (Roth) Slotoroff; m. Jack Zyroff, June 21, 1970; children: Dena b. 1973, David b. 1976; edn: AB (cum laude), Barnard Coll., 1968; MA, Johns Hopkins, Balt. 1969, PhD, 1971; MS (hons.), Columbia Univ., 1973. Career: instr. Johns Hopkins., 1970-71; Brooklyn Coll., 1971-72; Yeshiva Univ., N.Y. 1971-72; librarian and instr. UC San Diego, La Jolla 1979, 81, 91; librarian and instr. San Diego State Univ. 1981-85; instr. San Diego Mesa Coll. 1981-; prin. librarian San Diego Co. Library, 1985-; dir. The Reference Desk Search Services, La Jolla 1983-; mem: Calif. Statewide Task Force for Library User Edn. 1989-; honors: life mem. Beta Phi Mu, internat. library sci. hon. soc. 1973; mem: Am. Library Assn. (com. chair, 1981-), Calif. Libr. Assn. 1985-, San Diego Online Users' Group (exec. bd. 1989-94), Am. Philological Assn. 1970-, World Future Soc. 1991-, Toastmasters Internat. (chapt. v.p. 1991-92), Women's Am. ORT (S.D. pres. 1979-81), L.W.V., Friends of the Libr. for Children's Svs. S.D. Pub. Libr. (first pres. 1979-80); publs: diss: The Author's Apostrophe in Epic from Homer through Lucan (1971), curriculum: Project CLIMB: Cooperative Libr. Instrn. for Maximum Benefit (1987); rec: bicycling, jogging, writing. Ofc: 5555 Overland Ave Bldg 15 San Diego 92123